THE OXFORD COMPANION TO
MILITARY HISTORY

THE OXFORD COMPANION TO MILITARY HISTORY

Edited by Richard Holmes

Consultant editor: Hew Strachan

Associate editors: Christopher Bellamy and Hugh Bicheno

OXFORD

UNIVERSITY PRESS

OXFORD

UNIVERSITY PRESS

Great Clarendon Street, Oxford OX2 6DP

Oxford University Press is a department of the University of Oxford.
It furthers the University's objective of excellence in research, scholarship,
and education by publishing worldwide in

Oxford New York

Athens Auckland Bangkok Bogotá Buenos Aires Calcutta
Cape Town Chennai Dar es Salaam Delhi Florence Hong Kong Istanbul
Karachi Kuala Lumpur Madrid Melbourne Mexico City Mumbai
Nairobi Paris São Paulo Shanghai Singapore Taipei Tokyo Toronto Warsaw

with associated companies in Berlin Ibadan

Oxford is a registered trade mark of Oxford University Press
in the UK and in certain other countries

Published in the United States
by Oxford University Press Inc., New York

© Oxford University Press 2001

Database right Oxford University Press (maker)

First published 2001

British Library Cataloguing in Publication Data

Data available

Library of Congress Cataloging in Publication Data

Data available

ISBN 0-19-866209-2

1 3 5 7 9 10 8 6 4 2

Typeset by Alliance Phototypesetters
Printed by Giunti Industrie Grafiche
Prato, Italy

CONTENTS

INTRODUCTION

I T is almost obligatory for authors to declare that their works fill gaps in the existing literature, but in this case I do so with unusual confidence. There are dictionaries of battles, of military leaders, and even of military history. This is none of those things, although, in its way, it subsumes them all. It provides a source of dependable information and thoughtful assessment for intelligent general readers of many kinds, but also serves as a reliable and quick reference for scholars in this particular field and its related disciplines. It goes further, by cross-referencing so that readers are led from individual entries to others on associated topics. A reader can manoeuvre his way round this companion like a parrot using claws and beak to circumnavigate his cage, swinging from one entry to another, from macro to micro and back again.

No companion can claim to be comprehensive. This does not list all battles and all military leaders, only those that seemed to the editors to be the most important. However, many lesser engagements and individuals that do not merit an entry of their own often feature in other entries: thus a reader who fails to find his target amongst the headwords should consult the index, which lists people and places that do not constitute headwords in their own right. Although its main concern is with land warfare, war in the air (which, almost by definition, impacts upon the land battle) and at sea are not excluded.

Because this is a companion and not simply a dictionary, its net is cast deliberately wide. Thus alongside battles and individuals come wars and campaigns; military concepts like manoeuvre warfare or the caracole; weapons, uniforms, and equipment; wider issues like casualties, the military in politics, and gender in war; and points of detail like the duties of a sentry or the limitations of the Martini rifle. Although our main concern has been with events in Europe and North America in the past three centuries, there are few parts of the world or periods in history not considered.

The process of creating this book involved the formulation of the headword list, which embodied lengthy consultation with many scholars in the field. That there is an element of subjectivity is beyond dispute, and it will always be possible for a reader to speculate that if x is included, then so too should be y. The authors of individual entries, often authorities with established reputations in that area, were encouraged to combine fact with interpretation, and have done so in a variety of ways. I have not sought to use the editorial red pen to impose consistency of opinion or style, and where an author has a marked view—like that of Gerard de Groot on Haig or Hugh Bicheno on Braxton Bragg—I have not sought to tone it down. That said, I have made editorial interventions in many cases. This was usually because individual entries either overlapped others, and so had to be gently pruned to fit, or left gaps (invisible to individual authors) which had to be filled by editorial additions. Thus although entries are signed, there are times when the eventual form of the entry embodies some editorial changes. Where these changes are notable, the fact is indicated by the inclusion of an editor's initials alongside the author's. It must be said that this level of intervention implies no criticism, simply the fact that the final shape of the Companion emerged only during the last six months of editing, and the result differed, properly and inevitably, from the plans sketched out over five years before. However, where, in the process of editing, I have inserted errors or blurred sense the fault is unquestionably my own. There are some decisions which proved difficult and will remain contentious, most notably the question of transliteration, where adherence to the best modern practice might give a battle or individual a name which few would recognize: again, *mea culpa*.

The editorial team deserves my thanks for meeting a series of difficult deadlines and dealing with a variety of structural issues not always eased by the vagaries of computers. Without Chris Bellamy's assistance the project might have foundered in mid-voyage, and but for Hugh Bicheno it would have sunk in sight of harbour. In addition to the individuals formally acknowledged in the list of contributors, I offer special thanks to Heather Taylor, who took time off from her doctoral research on contemporary Russia to knock the first printed draft into shape and then dealt with the index. Any academic reading these lines will know, all too well, just how much any department relies upon its secretary. It remains a mystery how Steph Muir has not only coped with the demands of a busy office and a new degree, but has acted as Berthier to the general editor's Napoleon. Indeed, without her I would unquestionably have met the Waterloo I deserved. Lizzie, my long-suffering wife, joins my neglected daughters Jessie and Corinna in deserving my gratitude and your commiseration.

Any military historian worth his or her salt will be aware that the subject is laced with light and shade, and that enthusiasm for the dramatic and heroic needs to be tempered with a recognition of what war means for those who participate, so often unwillingly, in it. As I end six years' work I cannot but agree with the poet William Cowper, who reminded us that

> . . . war's a game, which, were their subjects wise
> Kings would not play at.

RICHARD HOLMES

Ropley
October 1999

LIST OF EDITORS AND CONTRIBUTORS

AA1	Adrian Ailes	DES	D. E. Showalter
AA2	Alex Alexandrou	DF	David Fletcher
AB1	Anthony Babington	DG	David Gates
AB2	Antony Beevor	DJD	David Dutton
AB3	Arden Bucholz	DJJ	David Jordan
AC	Anne Curry	DM	Daniel Moran
AD	Alex Danchev	DMJ	Danny M. Johnson
AF-H	Anthony Farrar-Hockley	DMM	David Moore
AG1	Azar Gat	DOM	David Morgan
AG2	Adrian Gregory	DW	David Whitehead
AH	Andrew Haughton	DWM	David Morray
AJP	A. J. Pollard	ECK	Eugenia C. Kiesling
AKG	Adrian K. Goldsworthy	EK	Efraim Karsh
AL	Andrew D. Lambert	EM	Evan Mawdsley
AM	Alan Millett	EMS	Edward M. Spiers
APC-A	Peter Caddick-Adams	FBS	Barry Smith
AR	Adam Roberts	FGAN	Geoffrey Noon
AS	Anthony Short	FW	Fiona Watson
BB	Bob Bushaway	GDS	Gary Sheffield
BC	Bruce W. Collins	GDWW	Geoffrey D. W. Wawro
BH	Brian J. Hilton	GJDG	Gerard J. DeGroot
BHR	Brian Holden Reid	GT	Geoffrey Till
BJB	Brian Bond	HA	Holger Afflerbach
BR1	Brian Robson	HEB	Hugh Bicheno
BR2	N. Boris Rankov	HFAS	Hew Strachan
CA	Catherine C. L. Andreyev	HHH	Holger H. Herwig
CD	Christopher Dandeker	HK	Hugh Kennedy
CDB	Christopher Bellamy	HMPDH	Peter Harclerode
CEB	C. E. Bosworth	HS	Hamish Scott
CG	Colin S. Gray	IB	Ian Beckett
CH	Carole Hillenbrand	IG	Ian Gentles
CJE	Charles Esdaile	JAL	John A. Lynn
CJT	Christopher Tuplin	JB	Jamie Belich
CK-P	Caroline Kennedy-Pipe	JBAB	Jonathan B. A. Bailey
CT	Charles Townshend	JDB	John Buckley
CTA	Christopher Allmand	JDF	Julian Freeman
CW	Craig Wilcox	JF1	Jürgen Förster
DA	Donald Abenheim	JF2	John France
DD	Dominick Donald	JFL	John Lazenby

JFVK	J. F. V. Keiger	PJF	Peter J. Francis
JG1	Jeffrey Grey	PMacD	Peter MacDonald
JG2	James Gow	PMT	Philip M. Taylor
JH	John Hussey	PO'B	Patrick K. O'Brien
JJW	James J. Wirtz	RAMSM	Mungo Melvin
JL	John Lonsdale	RH	Richard Holmes
JMB	John M. Bourne	RKPP	Richard Pankhurst
JPC	John P. Campbell	RO	Richard Overy
JR-W	Jon Robb-Webb	RO'N	Robert O'Neill
JW	Jay M. Winter	RRJ$_1$	Richard Rhodes James
KDeV	Kelly DeVries	RRJ$_2$	Robert Rhodes-James
KvonH	Karin von Hippel	RSOT	Roger S. O. Tomlin
LMW	L. Michael Whitby	RT	Robert Tombs
LS	Leonard V. Smith	RTF	Robert Foley
MB	Matthew Bennett	RW	Richard Woodward
MC	Marios Costambeys	SA	Simon Adams
MCB	Malcolm Barber	SCW	Stephen Wood
MCM	Chris Mann	SDB	Stephen Badsey
MCP	Michael Prestwich	SJLR	Sebastian Roberts
MCW	Matthew C. Ward	SJP	Stephen Pollington
MEY	Malcolm E. Yapp	SMcC	Stephen McCotter
MGT	Marcus Tanner	SPMacK	S. Paul MacKenzie
MH	Matthew Hughes	SRT	Stephen Turnbull
MI	Matthew Innes	ST	Shaun Tougher
MJ	Michael C. E. Jones	SWL	Scott W. Lackey
MJO	Michael J. Orr.	SWN	Stephen Nutt
MJS	Matthew Strickland	TAH	Tony Heathcote
MK	Maurice H. Keen	TGF	Tom Fraser
NAMR	N. A. M. Rodger	TJB	Tim Bean
NB	Niall Barr	TM	Toby McLeod
NF	N. Fields	TR	Trevor Royle
PC	Paul Cornish	VDH	Victor D. Hanson
PDA	Peter D. Antill	VHA	Virginia H. Aksan
PGM	Piers G. Mackesy	VRB	V. R. Berghahn
PJ	Peter Jarvis	WS	William A. Speck

EDITORS

General Editor: HOLMES, PROFESSOR RICHARD, CBE, TD, is Professor of Military and Security Studies at Cranfield University and the Royal Military College of Science. His publications include *The Little Field Marshal: Sir John French* (1984); *Firing Line* (1985) (US title *Acts of War*); and *Riding the Retreat* (1995). In 1996–9 he presented the two BBC TV series *War Walks* and a series on *The Western Front* and wrote the accompanying books. A reserve infantry officer for over thirty years, his last military appointment was as Director of Reserve Forces and Cadets in MOD. [**RH**]

Consultant Editor: STRACHAN, PROFESSOR HEW, is Professor of Modern History and Director of the Scottish Centre for War Studies, University of Glasgow. He is joint editor of *War in History* and was Lees Knowles Lecturer, Trinity College, Cambridge, in 1995. His books include *European Armies and the Conduct of War* (1983); *Wellington's Legacy: The Reform of the British Army 1830–1854* (1984); *From Waterloo to Balaclava: Tactics, Technology and the British Army 1815–1854* (1985)—awarded the Templer medal; *The Politics of the British Army* (1997)—awarded the Royal United Services Institute's Westminster medal; (as editor) *The Oxford Illustrated History of the First World War* (1998). [**HFAS**]

Associate Editors: BELLAMY, PROFESSOR CHRISTOPHER, is Professor of Military Science and Doctrine and Co-director of the Security Studies Institute, Cranfield University. For seven years before joining Cranfield in 1997 he was Defence Correspondent of the *Independent* newspaper and saw armed conflict in the 1991 Gulf war, Bosnia, and Chechnya. His doctorate is on the Russian view of future war. He is the author of five major books and is writing a new history of the 1941–5 Soviet-German war. [**CDB**]

BICHENO, HUGH, after several years during which every country he lived in plunged into chaos, became an expert in the field and abandoned an academic career to become an intelligence officer and later a private security consultant. He lived and worked in Chile, Argentina, Guatemala, Peru, Colombia, moved to Miami and then to Texas, and recently retired to Cambridge to write about it. He has completed a book on the battle of Gettysburg. [**HEB**]

Advisory Editors: BOSWORTH, PROFESSOR C. E., FBA (Islamic World), is Emeritus Professor of Arabic at Manchester University. He is the author of several books on Arabic culture and on the history of the Islamic East. He is the British editor of the *Encyclopaedia of Islam*, new edn. [**CEB**]

LAZENBY, PROFESSOR JOHN (**Classical World**), is Professor of Ancient History in the Department of Classics at the University of Newcastle. [**JFL**]

PORCH, PROFESSOR DOUGLAS (**USA**), has recently retired after 40 years teaching ancient history at the University of Newcastle upon Tyne. Among other works, he is author of *Hannibal's War* (1978), *The Spartan Army* (1985), *The Defence of Greece* (1993), and *The First Punic War* (1996).

PRESTWICH, PROFESSOR MICHAEL (**Medieval Period**), is Professor of History at the University of Durham. He is the author of several books on medieval English history, including *Armies and Warfare in the Middle Ages: The English Experience* (1996). [**MCP**]

TURNBULL, DR STEPHEN (**Far East**), specializes in the religious and military history of Japan, on which he has produced fifteen books. He has also lectured at Leeds University and the Royal Armouries. [**SRT**]

CONTRIBUTORS

Abenheim, Dr Donald, is at the Naval Postgraduate School, Monterey. [**DA**]

Adams, Dr Simon, is a Senior Lecturer in History, University of Strathclyde. Editor, *England, Spain and the Gran Armada* and *Armada Correspondence* (1998). [**SA**]

Afflerbach, Dr Holger, was recently in Klagenfurt, Austria, with a scholarship of the Humboldt Foundation, and is Falkenhayn's most recent biographer. [**HA**]

Ailes, Adrian, is a Reader Adviser at the Public Record Office, Kew. He has written and lectured on medieval heraldry, and his publications include *The Origins of the Royal Arms of England*. [**AA1**]

Aksan, Professor Virginia H., is an Associate Professor in the Department of History, McMaster University, Hamilton, Ontario, Canada. Her field of research is the Ottoman Empire. [**VHA**]

Alexandrou, Alex, graduated in History from the University of London in 1986 and gained a Master's degree in Industrial Relations from the University of Warwick in 1988. He currently lectures in Human Resource Management at Cranfield University. [**AA2**]

Allmand, Professor Christopher, is Emeritus Professor of Medieval History at the University of Liverpool. He has written extensively on late medieval war, and is the author of the standard biography of King Henry V. [**CTA**]

Andreyev, Dr Catherine C. L., is a Student (that is, Fellow) of Christ Church College Oxford and a University Lecturer in Modern European History at the University of Oxford. She is currently writing a book about the Russian emigration between the two world wars for Yale University Press. [**CA**]

Antill, Peter D., is a graduate of Staffordshire University and UCW, Aberystwyth, and holds degrees in International Relations and Strategic Studies. He is currently a Research Assistant at Cranfield University. [**PDA**]

Babington, His Honour Anthony, is a retired Circuit Judge. He served in the army during WW II, receiving the Croix de Guerre with Gold Star. [**AB1**]

Badsey, Dr Stephen, is a Senior Lecturer with special responsibilities in the Department of War Studies at the Royal Military Academy Sandhurst. [**SDB**]

Bailey, Brigadier Jonathan B. A., MBE, is a British army brigadier and is currently Director of the Royal Artillery. He served in Rhodesia 1979–80, the Falklands war 1982, and was head of Army Defence Studies. While serving in NATO's Rapid Reaction Corps, he took part in operations in Kosovo in 1999. [**JBAB**]

Barber, Professor Malcolm, is Professor of Medieval History at the University of Reading. Among his publications are two books on the Templars and a history of medieval Europe. [**MCB**]

Barr, Dr Niall, is at the Department of War Studies, Royal Military Academy Sandhurst. [**NB**]

Bean, Tim, is a Senior Lecturer at the Royal Military Academy Sandhurst. He specializes in 18th-century warfare and naval history, and has contributed to several books. [**TJB**]

Beckett, Professor Ian F. W., is Professor of Modern History at the University of Luton. His publications include *The Amateur Military Tradition, 1558–1945* (1991). [**IB**]

Beevor, Antony, FRSL, is the author of *The Spanish Civil War* (1982), *Inside the British Army* (1990), *Crete: The Battle and the Resistance* (1991), *Paris After the Liberation* (1994), and *Stalingrad* (1998). [**AB2**]

Belich, Professor Jamie, is a Professor of History at the University of Auckland, New Zealand. [**JB**]

Bennett, Matthew, is a Senior Lecturer at the Royal Military Academy Sandhurst, specializing in ancient and medieval warfare, but with a general interest in the Mediterranean and Near East. [**MB**]

Berghahn, Professor V. R., is in the Department of History at Brown University, Rhode Island. [**VRB**]

Bond, Professor Brian, is Professor of Military History at King's College London and specializes in the pursuit of victory since Napoleon, WW I, and military thought. [**BJB**]

Bourne, Dr John M., is Senior Lecturer in Modern History at the University of Birmingham. He is currently working on a revisionist history of the British Army during the Great war. [**JMB**]

Bucholz, Professor Arden, is Professor of History at the State University of New York College, Brockport, New York. His most recent work is *Delbruck's Modern Military History* (Nebraska, 1997). *Moltke and the German Wars, 1864–1871*, will appear in 2001. [**AB3**]

Buckley, Dr John, is a Lecturer in the Department of History and War Studies, University of Wolverhampton, UK. He has written widely on many aspects of air power history. His latest book is *Air Power in the Age of Total War*. [**JDB**]

Bushaway, Dr Bob, lectures at the University of Birmingham. [**BB**]

Caddick-Adams, Peter, TD, lectures in Military and Security Studies at Cranfield University. He has written one book and several papers on a variety of military topics including the Great War and psychological warfare. [**APC-A**]

Campbell, Dr John P., has published *Dieppe Revisited: A Documentary Investigation* (London, 1993) and, more recently, articles in *Intelligence and National Security*, *Journal of Military History*, and *War in History*. [**JPC**]

Collins, Professor Bruce W., is Dean at the School of Humanities, Language, and Law, University of Derby. [**BC**]

Cornish, Dr Paul, is at the Centre of International Studies at the University of Cambridge and a Fellow of Wolfson College, Cambridge. [**PC**]

Costambeys, Dr Marios, is currently Leverhulme Special Research Fellow at the University of Manchester, where he was previously Lecturer in Medieval History. He has also been a Scholar at The British School at Rome and a Research Editor on the *New Dictionary of National Biography*. [**MC**]

Curry, Dr Anne, is Senior Lecturer in History at the University of Reading. She is the author of *The Hundred Years War* (1993) and of several articles on English military organization in the 15th century. [**AC**]

Danchev, Professor Alex, is Professor of International Relations at Keele University. He is the author of a number of histories and biographies, including widely acclaimed studies of John Dill, Oliver Franks, and, most recently, Basil Liddell Hart. [**AD**]

Dandeker, Professor Christopher, is Professor of Military Sociology and Head of the Department of War Studies at King's College London. He is joint founder and Secretariat member of the British Military Studies Group. [**CD**]

DeGroot, Dr Gerard J., is a Senior Lecturer in the Department of Modern History, University of St Andrews. He is the author of numerous books and articles on the history of war, including *Blighty: British Society in the Era of the Great War* (1996). [**GJDeG**]

DeVries, Prof Kelly, is in the Department of History at Loyola College, Baltimore. [**KDeV**]

Donald, Dr Dominick, read modern history at Magdalen College Oxford, served in the British army, and worked as a scriptwriter and teacher before completing a PhD in War Studies at King's College London. [**DD**]

Dutton, Dr David, is Reader in History at the University of Liverpool and Visiting Professor in the School of Arts and Sciences at Bolton Institute. [**DJD**]

Esdaile, Dr Charles, is a Lecturer in History at the University of Liverpool, and has written numerous works on the Napoleonic period. Primarily a Hispanist, he is author of *Spain in the Liberal Age* (1999). [**CJE**]

Farrar-Hockley, General Sir Anthony, GBE KCB DSO MC, was a professional soldier in the British army for 42 years, and saw active service during WW II, in Korea, and many other campaigns. His twelve books of biography and military history include the two-volume history of the British part in the Korean war published by the Cabinet Office. [**AF-H**]

Fields, Dr N., is now in Edinburgh, having spent some time at the British School of Archaeology in Athens. [**NF**]

Fletcher, David, is Librarian at the Tank Museum. He is author of a series of books on the mechanization of the British army. [**DF**]

Foley, Dr Robert, has recently completed his PhD in German WW I strategy at King's College London and his annotated translation of Alfred von Schlieffen's writings is being published by Frank Cass Publishers. [**RTF**]

Förster, Professor Jürgen, is at the Military Historical Research Office, Potsdam (Militärgeschichtliches Forschungsamt). [**JF1**]

France, Dr John, is a Reader at the University of Wales, Swansea. He specializes in the history of medieval warfare and crusading. [**JF2**]

Francis, Peter J., is the Media and Public Relations Manager for the Commonwealth War Graves Commission. [**PJF**]

Fraser, Professor T. G., was Head of the School of History, Philosophy, and Politics at the University of Ulster. His area of research includes ethnic conflict in the Middle East, parading in Ireland, and US foreign policy. [**TGF**]

Freeman, Julian, is a Critic, Curator, Co-ordinator of Complementary Studies at Eastbourne College of Arts and Technology, and an acknowledged expert on British art of WW I and WW II. [**JDF**]

Gat, Professor Azar, is Chair of the Department of Political Sciences at Tel Aviv University. [**AG1**]

Gates, Dr David, is Deputy Director at the Centre for Defence and International Security Studies, Lancaster University. [**DG**]

Gentles, Professor Ian, is with the Department of History at Glendon College, York University, Toronto. [**IG**]

Goldsworthy, Dr Adrian K., was a member of the Ancient History Section at University of Wales, Cardiff. His main research interests are aspects of warfare in the Greek and Roman world. [**AKG**]

Gow, Dr James, is a Reader in the Department of War Studies, King's College London. [**JG2**]

Gray, Dr Colin S., is Professor of International Politics and Director of the Centre for Security Studies at the University of Hull. His recent books include *The Leverage of Sea Power* (1992) and *Explorations in Strategy* (1996), and *Modern Strategy* (1999). [**CG**]

Gregory, Dr Adrian, is at Pembroke College Oxford. [**AG2**]

Grey, Dr Jeffrey, is Professor of History at the University College, Australian Defence Force Academy. He is the author or editor of 14 books, including *The Oxford Companion to Australian Military History* (with Peter Dennis). [**JG1**]

Hanson, Professor Victor D., is the author of many books and some 40 articles and reviews on Greek military and agrarian history. He is currently Professor of Greek at California State University, Fresno, where he directs the Classical Studies Program. [**VDH**]

Harclerode, Peter, is an author with seven books published to date, including *Go To It! The History of the 6th Airborne Division, PARA! Fifty Years of The Parachute Regiment, Arnhem: A Tragedy of Errors, The Lost Masters: The Looting of Europe's Treasurehouses,* and *Secret Soldiers: Special Forces in the War Against Terrorism.* [**HMPDH**]

Haughton, Dr Andrew, received his PhD from the Department of War Studies, King's College London, and is the author of *Training Tactics and Leadership in the Confederate Army of Tennessee* (2000). [**AH**]

Heathcote, Dr Tony, has published widely on military subjects. He was Curator of the RMA Sandhurst Collection and, until retiring in 1997, the Senior Curatorial Officer in the Ministry of Defence. [**TAH**]

Herwig, Professor Holger H., is Professor of History at the University of Calgary. He has written extensively on German naval and military history. [**HHH**]

Hillenbrand, Professor Carole, is Professor of Arabic and Islamic Studies at the University of Edinburgh. [**CH**]

Hilton, Dr Brian J., is an economist at Cranfield University and Associate Fellow of Templeton College Oxford. He is an adviser to the UK delegation to NATO and publishes regularly on issues to do with defence

financial management and industrial policy. [**BH**]

Hughes, Dr Matthew, is Lecturer in Modern History in the Department of History, School of Social Sciences at University College Northampton. [**MH**]

Hussey, John, OBE, served British Petroleum for 30 years in various parts of the world. He has a lifelong interest in British naval and military history and has contributed many articles to specialist journals. [**JH**]

Innes, Dr Matthew, is currently lecturing at Birkbeck College, University of London. He is author of *State and Society in the Early Middle Ages* and has written numerous essays in academic journals. [**MI**]

Jarvis, Dr Peter, has a long-standing interest in industrial archaeology and is a trustee of Bletchley Park Trust. [**PJ**]

Johnson, Danny M., is employed by the 5th Signal Command in Germany. The former Command Historian, US Army Signal Command, he is pursuing a doctorate. [**DMJ**]

Jones, Professor Michael C. E., is Professor of Medieval French History at the University of Nottingham. [**MJ**]

Jordan, Dr David, specializes in 20th-century British military history and air power history. He is a Lecturer in the Department of Defence Studies, King's College London and the Joint Services Command and Staff College, and author of *Tactical Air Power in the First World War.* [**DJJ**]

Karsh, Professor Efraim, is Head of the Mediterranean Studies Programme in the School of Humanities at King's College London [**EK**]

Keen, Dr Maurice H., is a former Fellow and Tutor at Balliol College Oxford, specializing in 14th- and 15th-century history. His research interest is mainly late medieval heraldry. [**MK**]

Keiger, Professor J. F. V., is Professor of International History at Salford University Manchester and is the author of *France and the Origins of the First World War* (1983) and *Raymond Poincaré* (1997). [**JFVK**]

Kennedy, Professor Hugh, is Professor of Medieval History at the University of St Andrews. His research interests are early Islamic history and military fortifications. [**HK**]

Kennedy-Pipe, Dr Caroline, is Reader in Politics at the University of Durham. She has a first-class degree in history, an MSc in strategic studies, and a DPhil in international relations. [**CK-P**]

Kiesling, Professor Eugenia C., is Associate Professor at the United States Military Academy, author of *Arming Against Hitler: France and the Limits of Military Planning,* and editor of Raoul Castex, *Strategic Theories*. [ECK]

Lackey, Dr Scott W., is Chief, Research and Development Branch, US Army Center for Lessons Learned at Fort Leavenworth, Kansas. He is the author of numerous publications. [SWL]

Lambert, Professor Andrew D., Professor of Naval History in the Department of War Studies, King's College London, specializing in naval and strategic history. His books include *The Crimean War: British Grand Strategy against Russia 1853–1856* and *The Foundations of Naval History: Sir John Laughton, the Royal Navy and the Historical Profession*. [AL]

Lonsdale, Dr John, is Reader in African History at the University of Cambridge and Fellow of Trinity College and co-author, with Bruce Berman, of *Unhappy Valley: Conflict in Kenya and Africa*. [JL]

Lynn, Professor John A., is Professor of History at the University of Illinois and Adjunct Professor at Ohio State University. His main research interest is the French army 1610–1815. [JAL]

MacDonald, Peter, is an author, Visiting Lecturer, and Tutor in War Studies at the Universities of Birmingham and Wolverhampton and specializes in military psychology and unconventional warfare. [PMacD]

MacKenzie, Professor S. Paul, is currently Associate Professor of History at the University of South Carolina. He is the author of *The Home Guard* and several other books on military affairs. [SPMacK]

Mackesy, Piers G., is Emeritus Fellow of Pembroke College Oxford and Fellow of the British Academy. His books include *The War for America, 1775–1783*. [PGM]

Mann, Dr Chris, is a Lecturer at the University of Surrey and University College London in Scandinavian history. He completed his PhD at King's College London on Britain and Norway in WW II. [MCM]

Mawdsley, Professor Evan, is a member of the Department of History and the Scottish Centre for War Studies at the University of Glasgow. He has written on Russia in WW I and on the Russian civil war of 1917–20, and is currently working on a history of WW II on the eastern front. [EM]

McCotter, Dr Stephen, teaches in Byzantine Studies at The Queen's University, Belfast. His PhD was on late antique siege warfare and he is currently researching the military history of Constantinople. [SMcC]

McLeod, Toby, is Programme Co-ordinator in War Studies in the School of Continuing Studies at the University of Birmingham. [TM]

Melvin, Brigadier Mungo, OBE, formerly Deputy Director of the Higher Command and Staff Course at the United Kingdom Joint Services Command and Staff College, he has contributed to a wide range of military doctrine, training and historical studies. He is currently serving in an NCO appointment in Germany. [RAMSM]

Millett, Dr Allan, is Raymond E. Mason, Jr. Professor of Military History at Ohio State University. A specialist in the history of American military policy and institutions, he is the author or co-author of six books. [AM]

Moore, David, is Co-director of Cranfield University's Acquisitions and Logistics Unit where he has designed and implemented a Masters programme in Logistics. [DMM]

Moran, Professor Daniel, teaches international history and strategic theory at the Naval Postgraduate School. His recent work focuses on wars of national liberation. [DM]

Morgan, Dr David, is Reader in the History of the Middle East in the University of London. He is the author of *The Mongols* (1986) and *Medieval Persia 1040–1797* (1988), and is editor of the *Journal of the Royal Asiatic Society*. [DOM]

Morray, Dr David, lectures in Arabic and Islamic History at University College Dublin. Published works include a book on 13th-century Ayyubid Aleppo and articles on medieval military sites in the Levant. [DWM]

Noon, Dr Geoffrey, did National Service in the Royal Navy as a medical officer, and was in general practice for 34 years with part-time appointments in anaesthesia and trauma. Now retired, he is Chairman of the Wolverhampton branch of the Western Front Association. [FGAN]

Nutt, Dr Stephen, holds a PhD from the University of Newcastle upon Tyne in Hellenistic military history. He lives in Colchester where he teaches history. [SWN]

O'Brien, Dr Patrick K., FBA, is Centennial Professor of Economic History at the University of London and Senior Research Fellow at the Institute of Historical Research. [PO'B]

O'Neill, Professor Robert, is the Chichele Professor of the History of War, All Souls College Oxford. He is also Chairman of Trustees of the Imperial War Museum, Chairman of the Council of the International Institute for Strategic Studies, and has published widely. [RO'N]

Orr, Michael J., is a Senior Lecturer at the Conflict Studies Research Centre, Camberley. [MJO]

Overy, Professor Richard, is Professor of History at King's College London. His interests include 20th-century

German economic and military history. He is the author of *Why the Allies Won* (1995) and *Russia's War* (1998). [**RO**]

Pankhurst, Professor Richard, was the founder of the Institute of Ethiopian Studies, Addis Ababa University (formerly Haile Selassie I University). He is the author of *An Introduction to the History of the Ethiopian Army* (Addis Ababa, 1967). [**RKPP**]

Pollard, Professor A. J., is Professor of History at the University of Teesside. Among his many publications are *North-Eastern England during the Wars of the Roses* and *Richard III and the Princes in the Tower.* [**AJP**]

Pollington, Stephen, has written widely on early English subjects. His *The English Warrior: From Earliest Times to 1066* is a comprehensive account of early medieval warfare in Britain. [**SJP**]

Rankov, Dr N. Boris, is Senior Lecturer in Ancient History at Royal Holloway, University of London. Among his publications are works on Roman military staffs, Roman military intelligence, and the Greek trireme reconstruction. [**BR2**]

Rhodes James, Richard, was commissioned into 3rd Gurkha Rifles 1942. He served in the second Chindit operation 1944 and was mentioned in dispatches. Author of *Chindit*, he assisted in the BBC documentary on the Burma Campaign 1995. [**RRJ₁**]

Rhodes-James, the late Sir Robert, published widely, was Chairman of the History of Parliament Trust and a Fellow of Wolfson College Cambridge. [**RRJ₂**]

Reid, Professor Brian Holden, is in the Department of War Studies at King's College London. His publications include works on the American civil war and J. F. C. Fuller. [**BHR**]

Robb-Webb, Jon, is a Lecturer in Defence Studies at the Joint Services Command and Staff College. He has also taught in the Department of War Studies, King's College London, and published on the Royal Navy in the Pacific, the Cold War, and sea power. [**JR-W**]

Roberts, Professor Adam, is Montague Burton Professor of International Relations at Oxford University, and a Fellow of Balliol College. He has written extensively in the fields of strategic studies, international organization, and international law. [**AR**]

Roberts, Brigadier Sebastian, OBE, has been Military Assistant to the Chief of the General Staff and Colonel Land Warfare 2 (Doctrine). He is now Director of Corporate Communication Army in the Ministry of Defence. [**SJLR**]

Robson, Brian, CB, FSA FRHists, entered the civil service in 1950, becoming Deputy Under-Secretary of State in MOD in 1984–6. His publications include *Swords of the British Army* (2nd edn., 1996), *The Road to Kabul: the Second Afghan War 1878–1880* (1986), *Roberts in India: The Military Papers of Lord Roberts* (1993), *Fuzzy Wuzzy: The Campaigns in the Eastern Sudan* (1993), and *Sir Hugh Rose and the Central Indian Campaign 1858* (2000). [**BR₁**]

Rodger, Dr N. A. M., is Anderson Fellow of the National Maritime Museum. The first volume of his *Naval History of Britain, The Safeguard of the Sea, 660–1649* was published in 1997. [**NAMR**]

Royle, Dr Trevor, is the author of *The Kitchener Enigma* (1985), *Glubb Pasha* (1992) *and Orde Wingate: Irregular Soldier* (1995). He is a Fellow of the Institute for Advanced Studies in the Humanities at the University of Edinburgh. [**TR**]

Scott, Professor Hamish, is Professor in International History at the University of St Andrews. His research area is government and international relations in 17th- and 18th-century Europe. [**HS**]

Sheffield, Dr Gary, taught in the Department of War Studies, Royal Military Academy Sandhurst, before becoming Senior Lecturer at the Joint Service Command and Staff College. He is a past secretary of the British Commission for Military History. [**GDS**]

Short, Anthony, is a former Reader in International Relations, Aberdeen University. He has written *The Communist Insurrection in Malaya, 1948–1960* and *The Origins of the Vietnam War.* [**AS**]

Showalter, Professor D. E., is in the Department of History at Colorado College and has also been a visiting professor at the United States Military Academy and the United States Air Force Academy. [**DES**]

Smith, Professor Barry, is Emeritus Professor of History at the Australian National University. His books include *Florence Nightingale* (1982) and a section of *Medicine at War* (1994). [**FBS**]

Smith, Professor Leonard V., is with the Department of History at Oberlin College, Ohio. [**LS**]

Speck, Professor William A., retired from the University of Leeds in 1997 as Emeritus Professor of Modern History. His publications include *The Butcher: the Duke of Cumberland and the Suppression of the Forty-Five.* [**WS**]

Spiers, Professor Edward M., is the Professor of Strategic Studies at Leeds University. The author of eight books on military history and chemical warfare, he has also edited *Sudan: The Reconquest Reappraised.* [**EMS**]

Strickland, Dr Matthew, is Senior Lecturer in Medieval History at the University of Glasgow. His main research interests are chivalry and conduct in medieval warfare. [**MJS**]

Tanner, Marcus, MBE, worked for six years as the *Independent*'s correspondent in Belgrade from 1988 to 1994. His book, *Croatia: A Nation Forged in War* was published in 1997. He was appointed MBE for services to journalism in 1994. [**MGT**]

Taylor, Dr Philip M., is Professor of International Communications at the University of Leeds. He is the author of numerous books and articles on propaganda and communications. [**PMT**]

Till, Professor Geoffrey, is the Dean of Academic Studies at the Joint Services Command and Staff College, Shrivenham, and is the Head of the Defence Studies Department. He is also Visiting Professor in Maritime Studies in the Department of War Studies at King's College London. [**GT**]

Tombs, Dr Robert, is a Fellow of St John's College Cambridge and University Reader in French History. His research areas are French nationalism, and ideas and politics in the 19th century. [**RT**]

Tomlin, Dr Roger S. O., is a Fellow of Wolfson College Oxford. His research area is Roman epigraphy and the late Roman empire. [**RSOT**]

Tougher, Dr Shaun, is Lecturer in Ancient History at the University of Cardiff. He has written on Leo VI, Julian 'the Apostate' and Byzantine eunuchs. [**ST**]

Townshend, Professor Charles, is Professor of International History at the University of Keele and specializes in political violence in the modern world and Irish history. [**CT**]

Tuplin, Dr Christopher, is the author of *The Failings of Empire* (1993), *Achaemenid Studies* (1996), and of over 50 papers and book contributions on Achaemenid, Greek, and Roman studies. [**CJT**]

von Hippel, Dr Karin, is a Political Adviser to the Representative for the United Nations Secretary-General for Somalia. She has also been a Research Fellow and Project Manager at the Centre for Defence Studies, University of London. [**KvonH**]

Ward, Dr Matthew C., is a Lecturer in the Department of History at the University of Dundee. His major research interests are in colonial American history and the history of Indian–White relations. [**MCW**]

Watson, Dr Fiona, is a Senior Lecturer in History at the University of Stirling. She has recently completed a book on the English occupation of Scotland. [**FW**]

Wawro, is Professor Geoffrey D. W., is Professor of Strategic Studies at the US Naval War College in Newport, Rhode Island. He is the author of *The Austro-Prussian War* (1996), and *Warfare and Society in Europe 1792–1914,* (2000). [**GDWW**]

Whitby, Professor L. Michael, is with the Department of Classics and Ancient History at the University of Warwick. His major research interests are the late Roman army and ecclesiastical historiography. [**LMW**]

Whitehead, Professor David, is Professor of Classics at the Queen's University Belfast. His major area of research is Classical Greece. [**DW**]

Wilcox, Dr Craig, is a military historian who lives and writes in Sydney, New South Wales. [**CW**]

Winter, Dr Jay M., is Reader in Modern History in the University of Cambridge. [**JW**]

Wirtz, Professor James J., is an Associate Professor of National Security Affairs at the Naval Postgraduate School, Monterey, California. [**JJW**]

Wood, Stephen, was Keeper of the National War Museum of Scotland and is the author of books and articles on military history and artefacts and on the role and function of military museums. [**SCW**]

Woodward, Richard, has worked for both the Royal Collection and the British Museum. His book on George IV is to be published soon, and will be followed by the story of his grandfather's experiences as a WW I armoured car officer. [**RW**]

Yapp, Professor Malcolm E., is Emeritus Professor of the Modern History of Western Asia, School of Oriental and African Studies, University of London. He is the author of books and articles on Central Asian, Indian, and Middle Eastern history. [**MEY**]

ABBREVIATIONS

AC2	Aircraftsman 2nd Class	Fl Sgt	Flight Sergeant
ACM	Air Chief Marshal	FM	Field Marshal
ADC	Aide-de-camp	FO	Flying Officer
Adjt	Adjutant	Fr.	French
Adm	Admiral	Gen	General
AF	Admiral of the Fleet	Ger.	German
AG	Adjutant General	GHQ	General Headquarters
Air Cdre	Air Commodore	Gnr	Gunner
AM	Air Marshal	GOC	General Officer Commanding
APC	armoured personnel carrier	Gov-Gen	Governor-General
AVM	Air Vice Marshal	Gp Capt	Group Captain
Brig	Brigadier	Gr.	Greek
Brig Gen	Bridgadier General	HMS	Her/His Majesty's Ship
Capt	Captain	hp	horsepower
CB	Companion (of the Order) of the Bath	IDF	Israeli Defence Force
		IFF	identification of friend or foe
Cdr	Commander	IRA	Irish Republican Army
Cdre	Commodore	It.	Italian
CGS	Chief of General Staff	Jap.	Japanese
CIA	Central Intelligence Agency	KGB	Committee of State Security of
CIGS	Chief of the Imperial General Staff		the former USSR (Komitet Gosudarstvennoi Bezopasnosti)
C-in-C	Commander-in-Chief	km	kilometres
CO	Commanding Officer	km/ph	kilometres per hour
Col	Colonel	km/sec	kilometres per second
Col Gen	Colonel General	LAC	Leading Aircraftsman
COS	Chief of Staff (of Field Formation)	Lat.	Latin
		LCpl	Lance Corporal
Cpl	Corporal	LS	Leading Seaman
CPO	Chief Petty Officer	Lt	Lieutenant
CQMS	Company Quartermaster Sergeant	Lt Cdr	Lieutenant Commander
		Lt Col	Lieutenant Colonel
CSgt	Colour Sergeant	Lt Gen	Lieutenant General
CSM	Company Sergeant Major	Maj	Major
DCGS	Deputy Chief of General Staff (at	Maj Gen	Major General
		MC	Military Cross
National Level)		MIA	missing in action
DCOS	Deputy Chief of Staff (of Field Formation)	MICV	mechanized infantry combat vehicle
DSO	(Companion of the) Distinguished Service Order	Mid	Midshipman
		mph	miles per hour
FBI	Federal Bureau of Investigation	MRAF	Marshal of the Royal Air Force
Fl Lt	Flight Lieutenant	NAAFI	Navy, Army, and Air Force

Abbreviations

	Institutes	SDI	Strategic Defense Initiative
NATO	North Atlantic Treaty	sec	second
	Organization	Sgt	Sergeant
NCO	non-commissioned officer	SIGINT	signals intelligence
OS	Ordinary Seaman	SOE	Special Operations Executive
OSS	Office of Strategic Services	Sp.	Spanish
pl.	plural	Spr	Sapper
PLO	Palestine Liberation Organization	sq	square
PO	Petty Officer	Sqn Ldr	Squadron Leader
P O	Pilot Officer	SS	Shutzstaffeln
POW	prisoner of war	SSgt	Staff Sergeant
PM	Prime Minister	Sub-Lt	Sub-Lieutenant
Pres	President	UN	United Nations
Pte	Private	USAAF	United States Army Air Force
QM	Quartermaster		(1941–7)
QMG	Quartermaster General	USAF	United States Air Force (1947–)
R Adm	Rear Admiral	VAD	Voluntary Aid Detachment
RAF	Royal Air Force	V Adm	Vice Admiral
Revd	Reverend	VC	Victoria Cross
RMS	Royal Mail Steamer	Wg Cdr	Wing Commander
RN	Royal Navy	WO	Warrant Officer
RQMS	Regimental Quartermaster	WO1	Warrant Officer Class 1
	Sergeant	WO2	Warrant Officer Class 2
RSM	Regimental Sergeant Major	WW I	World War I
Russ.	Russian	WW II	World War II
SAS	Special Air Service	2Lt	Second Lieutenant

KEY TO MAPS

⊠	infantry
◹	cavalry/light armour/armoured reconnaissance
⬭	'armored cavalry' (US)/cavalry mechanized (Soviet)
⊠	armoured/mechanized infantry
◯	armour
⊷	artillery
⊓	engineers
✈	air
〰	amphibious/marine forces
▽	airborne forces, also airborne units/formations, even if otherwise delivered (e.g. heliborne in Gulf war)
⇐	advances/raids
⚔	battle
✕	battle (medieval/Roman/pre-Roman)
✈←	air attacks
✈ or ▯	airfield
▽	airborne troop landings
⛴	naval forces

⌂ AAAAA	army group/front
⌂ XXXX	army
⌂ XXX	corps
⌂ XX	division
⌂ X	brigade
⌂ III	regiment (typically three battalions)
⌂ II	battalion (sometimes called a regiment)
⌂	company/squadron/battery
—— XXXX ——	army operations boundary
✸	fortress/siege
◈	fort
••••	mines
✕	battle lost
✕	battle lost (medieval/Roman/pre-Roman)
⚜	bombardment
┼┼┼┼	railway
▨ or ⛰ or ☀	high ground of military significance

Abbas I, Shah (1587–1629). Abbas I reversed the trend of Persia's defeat by the Ottoman *Turks and regained much territory lost in the 16th century. His achievement was chiefly based on his reorganization of the Persian army. By 1600 he had established a 12,000-strong modern artillery arm, whose gunners were known as the *topchis*. Over 500 brass cannon were cast in Persia during his reign. He imported Europeans such as the Englishman Sir Robert Sherley to train a body of 6,000 disciplined Armenian and Georgian *musketeers or *tufangchis*.

Moreover, he strengthened the Persian cavalry by cutting down the vast horde of unreliable and ill-disciplined *feudal *quizilbashes*, replacing them with a corps of *janissary-style infantry, and a regular *ghulam* or military *slave cavalry corps of 10,000 *qullar*, raised from Christians of the Caucasus. His personal bodyguard was made up of an élite 'King's Friends' regiment. The army was paid in cash from the royal treasury, which assured its loyalty, particularly when the *ghulams* were appointed military governors in the provinces.

In 1598 he defeated the marauding Uzbeks and Turcomans, recapturing Herat. He took Tabriz from the Turks in 1603, and Erivan in 1604. In 1605 he defeated an Ottoman army at Sufiyan, and in 1606 repulsed the Turks with heavy losses at Sis. However, despite a temporary peace settlement, Turco-Persian rivalry was intense, and war grumbled on throughout his reign, flaring up in 1616–18 and 1623–38. In 1623 Abbas drove the Ottomans from the siege of Baghdad. He also took the rich prize of Kandahar in the north from the Moghul empire in 1622, but it was captured by the Uzbeks in 1630, after his death. He left the legacy of a modern, efficient force that was to preserve his domains for his successors, including *Nadir Shah.

TM

Abd al-Qadir (1807–83), Algerian emir and staunch opponent of French colonization. In 1832, two years after French capture of Algiers, he opposed an advance into the interior, raising the tribes around his capital Mascara and proclaiming holy war. Beaten at Oran, he concluded a treaty with the French which enabled him to gain ascendancy over the western tribes. A second bout saw him defeat Trezel on the Macta only to lose his capital and make terms with Bugeaud in 1837. This left him virtual king of the unconquered portion of *Algeria, and in 1839 he again attacked the French, this time with Moroccan support. His household was captured in 1843, and the following year his allies were defeated by Bugeaud at Isly. He did not surrender until 1847. Interned in France until 1853, he ended his days in honourable exile in Damascus.

Abd al-Qadir's prospects for success were small, for many tribes were as resistant to his control as they were hostile to the French. However, he was a resolute *guerrilla leader who not only inspired future Algerians, but helped persuade Frenchmen that Arabs were a warlike race whose qualities could be used in the French interest. It was typical of his magnanimity that he saved many Christians during the Damascus massacre of 1860, and ironic that, as one of France's most successful opponents, he was decorated with the Légion d'Honneur.

RH

Abrams, Gen Creighton Williams (1914–74). Commissioned into the cavalry from *West Point in 1936, Abrams served with 1st Cavalry Division before joining the newly formed 1st Armoured Division in 1940. He transferred to 4th Armoured Division in 1942 and was given command of 37th Tank Battalion in September 1943. Landing in Normandy in July 1944, he was in action for the remainder of the war, spearheading the relief of Bastogne that

December. He earned a public commendation from *Patton and was a temporary colonel by the war's end.

After the war Abrams held a variety of important staff and command appointments, and in 1968 succeeded *Westmoreland as commander of the US Military Command, *Vietnam. He worked with US ambassador Ellsworth Bunker to develop the 'Vietnamization' programme, which included the raising of a new People's Self Defence Force and the improvement of rural security. Abrams reduced emphasis on big battles and ordered more small-scale raids supported by artillery and air strikes, inflicting serious damage on the North Vietnamese. He recommended the Cambodian incursion of May 1970, though political reaction outweighed military results. Appointed COS of the army in July 1972, Abrams began to grasp the problems confronting it, notably the legacy of Vietnam and the ending of conscription, but died in office. He was the most distinguished American tank officer of his generation: the M-1A1 main battle tank bears his name.   RH

Abwehr (Ger.: *Abwehr*, defence), the German intelligence and counter-intelligence service, 1920–45. The Abwehr served several political masters, being founded, against the spirit of the Versailles Treaty, in 1920. After 1933 it took on foreign espionage/sabotage assignments, and became the equivalent of the FBI, *CIA, and *OSS combined. The Abwehr was subdivided into five departments (*Abteilungen*), covering overt intelligence collection abroad; espionage; sabotage and subversion; counter-intelligence; and finally, administration, archives, and personnel. Abt II (sabotage and subversion) was extremely successful at engineering the pro-Nazi uprisings which were the essential prerequisites to the invasions and annexations of Austria, Czechoslovakia, and Poland, and raising pro-Nazi contingents of soldiers from *POWs. Abt III (counter-intelligence) achieved the penetration of a Soviet espionage ring known as the Red Orchestra, and turned *SOE agents. These successes were not matched by Abt I (espionage), which failed to control any worthwhile agents in Great Britain or the USA, and really only achieved useful intelligence gathering in Spain. From 1935, the Abwehr was directed by Adm Wilhelm *Canaris, assisted by Maj Gen Hans Oster, who headed the personnel department (Abt Z). Both Canaris and Oster were early members of the Widerstand (German anti-Hitler Resistance movement), and the Abwehr paradoxically served as a useful centre for them and their colleagues. Throughout the Third Reich, the Abwehr fought a turf war with the Sicherheitsdienst (SD) and Gestapo over responsibilities. Although Canaris maintained an unofficial *truce with his opposite number, Heydrich, head of the SD, rivalries hindered their operational efficiency, particularly under Walter Schellenberg (Heydrich's successor from 1942). The SD and Gestapo—effectively the Nazi state's security services—spent as much

time and effort monitoring the Abwehr—the state's intelligence service—whom they (correctly) considered politically suspect, as they spent on all their other activities against the Reich's enemies. After Canaris had expressed his doubts about victory in 1944, he left office and the Abwehr was put under SD control. In the wake of the failed July bomb plot against Hitler, Canaris and Oster were arrested and eventually executed by their adversaries in the Gestapo.

APC-A

Abyssinia (Ethiopia), **British expedition to** (1867–8). This expedition ended years of negotiation between Emperor Tewodros (Theodore) II and the British. The Ethiopian ruler, a modernizer, wanted close relations, but Britain was reluctant to involve itself in his conflict with Egypt, then invading his country. Tewodros wrote to Queen Victoria in 1862, but his letter was left unanswered. He responded by imprisoning a British consul and several other Europeans. The British despatched 13,000 well-equipped United Kingdom and Indian troops from Bombay, led by Sir Robert *Napier. The advance force landed at Annesley Bay, on 21 October 1867, and the main force on 2 January 1868. With the co-operation of the local ruler of Tegray, it proceeded inland, across 250 miles (402 km) of mountainous country, toward the emperor's fortress of Maqdala (Magdala). At the decisive battle of Aroge (Arogee), on 10 April, the British, using cannon, *breech-loading rifles, and *rockets, inflicted immense casualties on Tewodros's poorly equipped forces. Their dead included the emperor's childhood friend Fitawrari Gabreye'. Tewodros then released his European prisoners, and sued, unsuccessfully, for peace. British forces thereupon stormed Maqdala on 13 April and Tewodros committed suicide. British troops looted his capital, before leaving the country, in accordance with earlier promises. Ethiopian defeat owed much to a striking inferiority in weapons: in 1896 a much better-equipped Ethiopian army beat the Italians at *Adowa.   RKPP

Arnold, Percy, *Prelude to Magdala* (London, 1992).

Beyene, Taddese, Pankhurst, Richard, and Bekele, Shiferaw, *Kasa and Kasa* (Addis Ababa, 1990).

Markham, Clements, *A History of the Abyssinian Expedition* (London, 1869).

Myatt, Frederick, *The March to Magdala* (London, 1970).

Abyssinia (Ethiopia), **Italian invasion of** (1935–6). This invasion, which was condemned futilely by the League of Nations, was effected with poison *gas, and created great popular indignation, in Britain, Africa, and elsewhere. The conflict had its roots in the rise of fascism in Italy, and in *Mussolini's ambition to avenge *Adowa, and win Italy 'a place in the sun'. He and his aide Emilio De Bono decided, in 1933, to invade Abyssinia 'no later than 1936'. The pretext was the Wal Wal incident of December 1934, when Ethiopian forces clashed with Italian colonial troops, which had infiltrated 62 miles (100 km) into Ethiopian territory. Mussolini used the ensuing period of negotiations to build up his armies in Italian Eritrea and Somalia. They eventually numbered 200,000 men. Britain and France, which together controlled the remainder of the coastline around Abyssinia, imposed an arms embargo on both parties. This fell heavier on Abyssinia, which imported arms, than on Italy, which manufactured them.

Mussolini's armies finally attacked, from the north and south, without any declaration of war, on 3 October 1935. They enjoyed vast superiority in weapons, and total control of the air. The League of Nations declared Italy guilty of aggression, but imposed only ineffective economic sanctions. The Italian advance, from Eritrea under De Bono, was initially slow, and that from Somalia under Gen Rodolfo Graziani (the subsequent Italian viceroy) relatively unimportant. Mussolini accordingly dismissed De Bono, in November, and replaced him by Gen Pietro Badoglio, a career soldier, whom he authorized to use *chemical weapons. The Italians, who employed heavy aerial bombardments and used mustard gas extensively, then advanced rapidly. They defeated Emperor Haile Selassie's chiefs early in 1936, and the monarch's own army at Mai Chew, at the end of March 1936, and entered Addis Ababa on 5 May. The emperor had left for Europe three days earlier. He appealed to the League in vain, on 30 June. The Italian conquest was soon recognized by most of the world. Ethiopian patriotic resistance nevertheless continued throughout the Italian five-year occupation. RKPP

Del Boca, Angelo, *I gas di Mussolini* (Rome, 1996).
Mockler, Anthony, *Haile Selassie's War* (London, 1984).
Pankhurst, Richard, 'The Ethiopian Patriots', *Ethiopia Observer*, 8 (1970).
Steer, George, *Caesar in Abyssinia* (London, 1936).

Abyssinia (Ethiopia), WW II campaign in (1941). This led incidentally to Ethiopia's liberation after five years of Italian fascist occupation, and was a direct consequence of *Mussolini's declaration of war on Britain and France on 10 June 1940. The British, fearing that the enemy in Libya and Italian East Africa might jointly threaten Britain's position in Egypt, Sudan, and the Middle East, and realizing the potential military value of the Ethiopian 'Patriots', who had never surrendered to the invaders, flew Emperor Haile Selassie from Britain to Sudan in July. They later despatched two British officers, Brig Dan Sandford and Col Orde *Wingate, into Gojjam to make contact with the Patriots, in August and November respectively. Meanwhile the Italians overran British Somaliland in August.

The Allied campaign against Italian East Africa opened on 19 January 1941, when British and Indian forces under Gen Sir William Platt advanced from Sudan into Italian Eritrea. On the following day, and almost 200 miles (320 km) to the south, the emperor, with Wingate as his prin-

cipal adviser, entered Gojjam, also from Sudan. Four days later, and almost 1,000 miles (1,600 km) to the south-east, British, East African, and South African forces under Gen Sir Alan Cunningham struck from Kenya into Italian Somalia. The Italian forces, which had been isolated from metropolitan Italy for half a year and were demoralized by four years of Ethiopian Patriot activity, put up weaker resistance than initially anticipated. British Commonwealth forces from the south captured Mogadishu, capital of Somalia, on 25 February, and swept northwards to Jigjiga, on 17 March, and Harar, ten days later. Allied forces from the west meanwhile captured Keren, after fierce fighting, on 26 March, and Asmara, capital of Eritrea, on 1 April. The emperor's army, though poorly armed and often lacking *air support, captured Debra Marqos, capital of Gojjam, on 10 April. The Patriots under Ras Abeba Aregai meanwhile consolidated themselves around Addis Ababa. The capital itself fell shortly afterwards, on 6 April, to South African troops. The emperor returned on 5 May, exactly five years after its capture by Gen Badoglio. The next few months were spent in 'mopping up'. This ended with the fall of Gondar to the British and the Patriots on 27 November. Ethiopia thus became the first country to be freed from Axis conquest. RKPP

Glover, Michael, *An Improvised War* (London, 1987).
Pankhurst, Richard, 'The Ethiopian Patriots and the Collapse of Italian Rule in East Africa', *Ethiopia Observer*, 10 (1966).
Shirreff, David, *Bare Feet and Bandoliers* (London, 1995).
Steer, George, *Sealed and Delivered* (London, 1941).

academies, military The emergence of military academies is closely associated with the development of the concept of a professional officer corps. The claim of career officers to be regarded as members of a distinct profession rests largely on their having received a formal *education in their own specialization, while at the same time being indoctrinated with the social attitudes expected of those in their chosen way of life.

The first military academy in Asia, and probably the world, was established in Vietnam in the 14th century. The term 'military academy' is generally used in western countries to refer to an establishment training young men, and now *women, to become junior officers. In eastern Europe and the former USSR it usually refers to a 'staff' or 'war college' training more senior officers; junior officer training establishments are called 'higher military command schools'.

Until the middle of the 18th century, European military officers learnt their duties mostly through following the advice, instructions, and example of senior colleagues, who had every personal interest in ensuring the efficiency of their subalterns. The conventional heroic qualities expected of leaders in war were assumed to have been developed by their position in the social order of their times. Specifically military skills were acquired by actual practice and performance under supervision. Companies of cadets (a term originally meaning the younger scions of noble houses) were first formed in France in 1682, to teach young noblemen the duties of an officer. The scheme was soon abandoned, but was revived in 1751, with the formation of the École Militaire Royale, which offered a general military education, primarily to the sons of aristocrats. *Ritterakademien* and 'Cadet Houses' existed in Germany and the Habsburg dominions from the late 16th century onwards, though these were really preparatory schools with a military ethos rather than colleges producing trained officers.

The first European military academies came into existence in the 18th century to provide future officers of the highly specialized scientific branches, the artillery and engineers. This aim was fused with the realization that the nobility and gentry could only justify their monopoly on officership if they could demonstrate superior professional skill and education. Among the earliest institutions was the British army's Royal Military Academy, formed in 1741 at Woolwich, where it remained as a separate establishment, training gentlemen cadets for the Royal Artillery and Royal Engineers, until it closed on the outbreak of WW II in 1939. The Royal Military College, which trained gentlemen cadets for the cavalry and infantry, originally at Marlow, Buckinghamshire, and later at Sandhurst, Berkshire, was not founded until 1799. This too closed in 1939 and a combined establishment reopened in 1947 as the Royal Military Academy Sandhurst. The English East India Company maintained its own Military Seminary (patterned on the Royal Military Academy) at Addiscombe, near London from 1809 to 1861. In Austria, the first military college, known by the name of its foundress, the Empress Maria Theresa, was formed at Wiener Neustadt in 1748. In France, a school of military *engineering was opened at Mézières in 1748, followed by a school of artillery in 1756. Swept away by the Revolution as relics of the *ancien régime*, their role was assumed in 1795 by the new *École Polytechnique. This soon became, and remains, the most prestigious scientific academy in France, producing not only officers for artillery and engineers, but also for the technical branches of the navy, and other government departments. The corresponding school for future officers of the line, the École Spéciale Militaire, was established at *Saint-Cyr in 1802. In Prussia, the *Scharnhorst reconstruction of its military system after being humiliated by Napoleon at *Jena/Auerstädt in 1806, converted the Ritterakadamie at Berlin into the Kriegsakademie, a military academy of the modern type. Even so minor a power as Portugal set up an Academia Real de Fortifiçao e Defesso in 1790 and formed an all-arms cadet college in 1837.

The possession of a military academy became one of the symbols of independent nationhood. The first to be formed outside Europe was the US Military Academy (USMA) at *West Point, New York, originally projected at the time of the foundation of the Republic, but not actually opened

(from Congressional reluctance to encourage the development of a professional army) until 1812. At first combined with the Corps of Engineers (at that time, as in all armies, composed only of officers) the USMA became an all-arms academy. Its graduates were intended not only to play a part in the development of their nation and the garrisoning of its frontiers, but also to act as a cadre for the untrained militia or volunteers on whom its defence rested in time of major war. A similar role, with many making their careers in civil life, was performed by the graduates of the Virginia Military Institute, Lexington, founded in 1839, and the Military College of South Carolina (the Citadel), established in 1842. The Royal Military Colleges of Canada and Australia, opened respectively at Kingston, Ontario, in 1874 and Duntroon, Canberra, in 1911, also had a nation-building role, signalling the emergence of their countries as self-governing dominions with their own armed forces. In British India, the formation of the Indian Military Academy at Dehra Dun in 1932 was a long-awaited step on the road to self-government. The Heroic Military College of Mexico was formed in 1823, two years after independence. The National Military College of Argentina traces its descent from the Academia Militar de Matematicas, founded by General Belgrano in 1812 and an academy for infantry and cavalry cadets, established by the provisional government of the United Provinces of the River Plate in 1817.

Military academies are not combat units and their cadets are of infinitely more value as potential officers than as fighting soldiers. In extreme circumstances some have undertaken active service, with the military instructors and professors at the head of their students in the ultimate practical demonstration of what they taught. Among the most famous examples are the École Polytechnique, which manned a battery at the Barrière du Trône, defending Paris against the Allies (30 March 1814); the Heroic Military College of Mexico, whose title commemorates its cadets (*niños heróicos*), who fought in the battle of Chapultepec, defending Mexico City against the Americans in the *Mexican war, and the Virginia Military Institute, at the battle of New Market, Virginia, on 15 May 1864, where its cadets captured a Union battery and gained a Confederate victory. Officer cadets fought as military units in the 1917–20 Russian civil war. In 1940, in a similar emergency, the French military academy at *Saumur was also mobilized to fight as a military unit.   TAH

Barnard, Henry, *Military Schools etc of France, Prussia, Austria, Russia, Sweden, Switzerland, Sardinia, England and the United States* (repr. West Point, 1969).
Stephens, Michael D., *The Educating of Armies* (London, 1989).

ace, air combat The concept of the air ace was born in WW I, a product of propaganda and the long-held human desire to highlight individual excellence. Once true aerial combat emerged in 1915 the hero concept began to develop.

The fighter ace suited the need of the public for heroes in a war that had degenerated into bloody *attrition, and despite the discomfort of the military, the chivalrous 'Knights of the Air' image was created. Tallies of kills were reported and the individual deeds of famous aces could be welcomed by a public craving good news.

The French and the Germans were first to develop the notion of the ace for propaganda purposes and the British eventually followed suit. Initially there was much difference of opinion as to what precisely constituted an ace: the French called for five confirmed victories; the Germans ten, although they did not permit shared victories to count; while the British never officially recognized the concept of the ace at all. By the end of the war the Allies were counting half- or quarter-kills towards tallies and in WW II, the USAAF allowed pilots to count enemy aircraft destroyed on the ground, though as this became much more commonplace in 1944, new terms were adopted such as 'strafing ace'. What did become commonly accepted was the figure of five kills for a pilot to gain the title of ace, and in WW II some 4,500 western Allied and Soviet pilots achieved this, along with at least 4,000 Germans.

However, the image of the air ace as a chivalrous knight of the skies is decidedly ill-founded and has obscured the nature of air warfare, particularly in WW I. Air combat was little different to other areas of war: battles and campaigns were won by collective action, operational effectiveness, and resources. There was a short period at the very beginning of aerial combat in 1915–16 when the actions of a few individuals shaped the war in the skies, but this was soon replaced by the larger scale actions such as the air superiority campaign over *Verdun. By WW II the relevance of the air ace in anything but a propagandist sense was low indeed.   JB

Paris, Michael, *Winged Warfare: The Literature and Theory of Aerial Warfare in Britain 1859–1917* (Manchester, 1991).
Philpott, Bryan, *Famous Fighter Aces* (London, 1989).

ACE reaction forces NATO's Allied Commander Europe (ACE) has immediate reaction forces—the ACE Mobile Force (AMF)—and rapid reaction forces, of which the ACE Rapid Reaction Corps (ARRC) is the land component.

The AMF was formed in 1960; it provides a quick conventional response with land and *air forces to demonstrate NATO's will to reinforce and defend the territory of any member nation. It can be deployed by Supreme Allied Commander Europe (SACEUR) at short notice at the request of a nation(s) and upon the approval of NATO's Defence Planning Committee. NATO could subsequently deploy the ARRC. The AMF is about 5,000 strong, comprising infantry, artillery, and supporting units. In 1991 it undertook its first operational deployment to Turkey during the *Gulf war. Thirteen nations (all NATO nations

except France, Portugal, and Iceland) currently contribute to the AMF which is now being adapted to undertake peace support operations (PSO). Its headquarters is at Heidelberg in Germany.

The ARRC comprises staff and assigned military formations from fourteen nations and is also ready to undertake combined, joint operations ranging from PSO to high-intensity warfare. It was established following NATO's Rome summit meeting in 1991. It supports ACE's crisis management through *deterrence, reinforcement, and operations. On 20 December 1995, following the Dayton Peace Accord, the ARRC deployed to Bosnia-Herzegovina to assume command of the NATO-led Peace Implementation Force (IFOR), NATO's first full operation. In 1999 it deployed to the Former Yugoslav Republic of Macedonia, and entered *Kosovo following Serb withdrawal. It has a permanent headquarters in Rheindahlen, Germany.   JBAB

ARRC Home Page: www.arrcmedia.com
Cordesman, A. H., *NATO's Central Region Forces* (London, 1988).
Gander, T., *Encyclopaedia of the Modern British Army* (Cambridge, 1982).
NATO Handbook (Brussels, 1992).
Palin, R. H, *Multinational Military Forces: Problems and Prospects* (London, 1995).

Actium, battle of (31 BC). Fought on 2 September during the War of the Second Triumvirate, the battle took its name from the promontory south of the entrance to the Gulf of Arabracia, and effectively decided the civil war between Octavian, the future Augustus, and Mark *Antony. The latter, his forces eroded by enemy action and the *desertion of some of his principal Roman supporters because of his relationship with Cleopatra, decided to break out by sea. He had about 230 ships of various sizes, Octavian 400, many of them smaller. Octavian's admiral Agrippa probably tried to draw Antony's fleet out to sea, where his more numerous and manoeuvrable ships would have had an advantage, while Antony, bent chiefly on escape, had to wait for the sea breeze to veer north so that he could clear Leucas. When battle was joined, Agrippa's left tried to outflank Antony's right, which, in covering the enemy's move, parted company from its centre. Cleopatra and about 60 ships which had remained behind the line of battle then managed to escape through the gap, possibly as planned, and Antony joined her with about twenty more. His left either refused to fight or was forced back into the gulf, where it surrendered or was burnt by incendiary missiles.
                                                                JFL

Carter, John, *The Battle of Actium* (London, 1970).

Aden, counter-insurgency campaign in (1964–7). In 1964 the British government announced that independence was to be granted to the Federation of South Arabia

(FSA) by 1968, but British forces would remain in Aden. Arab nationalists resented the continuation of government by traditional rulers and the British military presence. Encouraged by *Nasser, they formed the National Liberation Front (NLF) in Yemen and in late 1964 began a campaign in the Radfan border region, stirring up the local tribes. Between January and June 1964 Federal and British forces campaigned in the Radfan, and succeeded in largely suppressing the revolt. From November 1964 the NLF began to focus on an urban terrorist campaign in Aden, targeting British troops and their families in addition to members of the local security forces, and others associated with the FSA government. The campaign of intimidation made it difficult for the security forces to gather intelligence, as the local population was reluctant to co-operate. This problem was exacerbated after the British government announced in February 1966 that the British forces would be withdrawn on independence. Attempts to carry out a 'hearts and minds' policy were undermined, as many locals did not believe that the FSA would survive without British support. The NLF escalated their attacks and a second group of nationalist insurgents, the Front for the Liberation of Occupied South Yemen (FLOSY) began a terrorist campaign in December 1966. Two mutinies by local police led to 1st Battalion Argyll and Sutherland Highlanders under Lt Col Colin 'Mad Mitch' Mitchell reoccupying the Crater area of Aden in July 1967. As the date for the British withdrawal in November 1967 approached, the NLF and FLOSY turned on each other and fought for control of Aden. Aden was Britain's last colonial *counter-insurgency campaign: its conduct was marred by even poorer military-political co-ordination than had been achieved during the *Malayan emergency or *Cyprus insurgency.   GDS

Pimlott, J. (ed.), *British Military Operations 1945–1984* (London, 1984).

Adowa, battle of

Adowa, battle of (1896). This was one of the greatest victories of an African over a European army. The Italians, who had seized Massawa port in 1885, had been steadily penetrating inland, when they signed a Friendship Treaty, at Wechalue in 1889, with Menilek, King of Shewa. By it they recognized him as emperor, while he recognized their presence in the north, where they established their colony of Eritrea in 1890. The treaty had two texts, one in Amharic and the other in Italian. The former stated that Menilek *could* use Italian good offices in his correspondence with other powers; the latter, that he *must*. This the Italians used to claim a protectorate. After long negotiations, during which he imported many firearms, largely from France, Menilek denounced the treaty in February 1893.

The Italians then advanced into Tegray, but were defeated by Menilek at the mountain of Amba Alagi in December 1895 and fell back on Adowa. There the two armies confronted each other, reluctant to attack first. On 25 February 1896 the Italian premier, Francesco Crispi, telegraphed the Italian commander, Gen Oreste Baratieri, that Italy was ready for any sacrifice. The Italians had 17,000 soldiers (1,650 Italians, the remainder Eritreans). Menilek had about 100,000 men, mostly with modern weapons. Baratieri attempted a surprise attack, on 1 March, but his plans were disclosed by double agents, and his *maps faulty. The Ethiopians, in one day, crushed the three Italian contingents separately. Italy lost 43 per cent of its fighting force. Three out of five commanders were killed, a fourth was captured. Menilek's victory, despite heavy losses, was so complete that Italy recognized Ethiopia's full independence—but Menilek felt unable to expel the Italians from Eritrea.   RKPP

Ahmad, Abdussamad H., and Pankhurst, R. (eds.), *Adowa: Centenary of the Victory* (Addis Ababa, 1998).

Berkeley, George, *The Campaign of Adowa and the Rise of Menelik* (London, 1835).

Del Boca, Angelo (ed.), *Adua: Le ragioni di una sconfitta* (Rome, 1997).

Work, Ernest, *Ethiopia: A Pawn in European Diplomacy* (New York, 1936).

Adrianople, battle of

Adrianople, battle of (378). In the afternoon of 9 August 378, Gothic warriors shattered the élite infantry of the eastern Roman empire, a defeat which crippled the imperial army and is often regarded as one of history's most decisive battles. The role played by cavalry was decisive, but there was no innovation in tactics or armament. In 376 the *Goths had been a German people living north-west of the Black Sea who were dislodged by nomad *Huns. Two groups, the Tervingi and the Greuthungi, asked for permission to cross the Danube and settle in Thrace. The Tervingi were duly admitted, but the Greuthungi crossed illicitly and joined them when they rebelled against Roman coercion. These rampaging Goths could not be penned north of the Balkan mountains, despite heavy fighting, so in 378 the western Emperor Gratian left the Rhine frontier for the Danube, while the eastern Emperor Valens brought up his own field army from the Euphrates. That summer, advanced elements of both armies were in action, but Valens fatally decided to risk a decisive battle before Gratian could arrive, perhaps because faulty *reconnaissance misled him that only half the Goths were actually present. Eight miles (12.9 km) north of Adrianople (modern Edirne, west of Istanbul) he advanced in column of march against the Gothic encampment, a wagon circle, which hindered the deployment of infantry in line of battle with cavalry on both wings. The Roman army was also suffering from heat, thirst, and hunger, and in the absence of the Gothic cavalry a *truce was being negotiated, when a disorderly assault by Roman cavalry units provoked a general engagement. This assault failed, and suddenly the Gothic cavalry returned and charged the exposed left flank of the Roman infantry, whose ranks were crushed together by fighting on two fronts until they broke entirely. Two-thirds of the Roman army died in the rout, including Valens, whose body was never found. RSOT

> Ammianus Marcellinus: Roman History Book 31, trans. W. Hamilton (Harmondsworth, 1986).
>
> Heather, Peter, Goths and Romans 332–489 (Oxford, 1991).

Aegates Islands (Isole Egadi), battle of (241 BC).

This was the last battle of the first *Punic war, fought on 10 March 241 BC between a Carthaginian fleet of about 250 quinqueremes commanded by Hanno, and 200 Roman quinqueremes commanded by the Consul Caius Lutatius Catulus and the *praetor urbanus* Quintus Valerius Falto. Although it had more warships, the Carthaginian fleet had been hastily raised, may have been undermanned, and was hampered by the supplies for the army in Sicily it was either escorting or carrying. Its intention was to land these supplies and only to fight when it had taken on board some of the veteran soldiers from that army. The Roman ships, on the other hand, had been modelled on a particularly fast captured vessel, and were manned by the best crews available. The stormy conditions thus favoured the Romans, and they won decisively, disabling or capturing about 120 Carthaginian vessels, for the loss of perhaps only about 30. Only the fact that the wind shifted to the east, enabling the remnant of the Carthaginian fleet to hoist sails and flee, saved it from complete destruction. JFL

> Lazenby, J. F., *The First Punic War* (London, 1996).
>
> Polybius, 1. 59–61.

Aegospotami (Aigospotamoi), battle of (405 BC).

The name means 'Goat's Rivers' (probably the modern Büyükdere), and it was the scene of the final battle of the *Peloponnesian war. The Spartan fleet of perhaps 200 triremes under Lysander had a secure base in Lampsakos (Lampsacus, Lapseki) opposite, but the 180 Athenian ships under various commanders had to make do with an open beach, probably adequately watered but with food having to be brought from Sestos, 12 miles (19 km) to the southwest. The latter had to recover control of the sea lanes to the Black Sea, whence came Athens' essential grain supplies, and dared not risk the tiring row against the current from Sestos. What actually happened is controversial. *Xenophon has Lysander ignore the Athenian challenge for four days, carefully noting how they dispersed after delivering it, and on the fifth, at a signal from his scout-ships, fall upon a scattered enemy. Diodoros has him attack 30 ships apparently sailing off to Sestos for supplies and pursue them back to Aegospotami. However, both are agreed that he achieved complete surprise, with many Athenian ships being only partially manned or completely unmanned, and that very few escaped. JFL

> Kagan, Donald, *The Fall of the Athenian Empire* (Ithaca, NY, & London, 1987).

Afghanistan, Soviet campaign in (1979–89). The Soviet military intervention in Afghanistan was a conspicuous element in the long civil war in Afghanistan which began about 1974 and grew in intensity after the Saur (April) revolution of 1978. The military coup of 27 April 1978 brought to power the People's Democratic Party of Afghanistan (PDPA), a small group of left-wing intellectuals and military officers who embarked upon a programme of radical reform. Of this, the central feature was a comprehensive land reform intended to break the power of the notables and enlist peasants for the revolution, but which instead unleashed a series of rural disturbances which the PDPA found it difficult to contain. Moreover the PDPA was divided and a struggle for power led in September 1979 to the victory of the leader of the radical Khalq (People) faction, Hafizallah Amin.

The USSR had sympathized with the aims of the revolution and given help, including the services of military and civilian advisers, but had become convinced that the PDPA was too radical and called for the adoption of a more conciliatory programme and the formation of a broader based government. Sometime between September and December 1979 the decision was taken to intervene with military force, overthrow Amin, and establish a broad-based government under Amin's rival, Babrak Karmal, leader of the Parchami faction of the PDPA. This operation was carried out on 27 December 1979: *airborne troops seized control in Kabul, killing Amin, and four weak motor rifle divisions, assembled mainly from reservists in central Asia, entered Afghanistan across the land frontier.

It seems likely that the USSR hoped that the new government would shortly stabilize the situation and Soviet troops could be quickly withdrawn. In fact Karmal proved unable to form a broad-based government or to offer a sufficiently conciliatory programme, the Afghan army (which had mainly Khalqi officers) disintegrated, and the resistance, supported by overwhelming international condemnation of the Soviet action, gained in strength. A massive flight of refugees took place: eventually c.3.5 million to Pakistan and c.2 million to Iran. Although the Soviet aim seems to have been to confine the use of Soviet troops to garrisoning main cities and safeguarding communications, particularly the supply line from the Soviet border to Kabul via the Salang Pass, 'the limited contingent', as the Soviet Fortieth Army in Afghanistan was termed, was obliged to take a larger part in military operations until the PDPA could recruit and train a sufficient force to keep order and also, by political means, win over some of its opponents.

The resistance (known as the mujahedin by themselves and as *dushmans* by Soviet writers) consisted of two elements: local units who fought in different areas more or less independently of each other; and a group of seven Islamic parties based in Peshawar in Pakistan who claimed (not always with much justice) authority over the local groups and acted as channels for foreign aid to them. In 1980 there was very little attempt by the Soviet and PDPA forces to do more than try to protect the main cities and lines of communication and the resistance had a free run in much of Afghanistan. In many areas they fought little but conducted their own affairs; when they did fight they usually fought from ambush. Only gradually did the Soviet forces reorganize to deal with the problem, in particular by introducing more *air power, especially *helicopters—the Mil-24 armoured helicopter became one of the major weapons of the war. New tactics were developed involving the use of helicopter-borne troops to seize commanding heights and to cut off the retreat of the mujahedin. In the meantime the PDPA improved its intelligence and gradually rebuilt its forces, training new officers; extending conscription; and developing new forces such as the Sarandoy, a heavily armed militia, Revolutionary Defence Forces to guard installations, commando brigades for strike action, and much later irregular militias recruited from ex-resistance fighters. In the late 1980s these last units undertook an increasing amount of the fighting and they became dominant in certain localities. Also, with Soviet aid, the air force and air defence forces were greatly improved. By 1983 the improved capacity of the reformed PDPA forces was demonstrated as in the siege of Khost. Most larger operations against the mujahedin were conducted as joint operations, for example the series of attacks on the Panjshir valley, the refuge of one of the most renowned of the mujahedin commanders, Ahmad Shah Mas'ud.

Although the PDPA-Soviet operations were far from subduing the resistance they were enjoying some success by 1985 in extending government control over the country and hampering the passage of supplies from Pakistan and Iran. Concerned that resistance might flag, the USA decided to supply improved weapons to the mujahedin, in particular British Blowpipe and US Stinger anti-aircraft missiles. Many commentators have seen this decision as the turning point in the war: the new missiles diminished the PDPA-Soviet ability to deploy air power and, it was argued, inclined the USSR to seek peace. Undoubtedly the new missiles helped to restore the military balance which had been tilting the Soviet way in 1985 but the mujahedin's Chinese 12.7 mm machine gun claimed far more successes against helicopters; moreover, the USSR, which had been seeking a basis for withdrawal since May 1980, had already decided in 1985 to press more urgently for a way out of Afghanistan. In October 1986 Gorbachev told the new Afghan leader, Najiballah, that the Soviet forces would be withdrawn and that he should put his house in order quickly. The national reconciliation programme in Afghanistan was speeded up, nearly all the radical reforms abandoned including land reform, and peace was actively sought through the *UN. Negotiations, which had begun in 1981, had stalled on the question of a timetable for Soviet withdrawal. Agreement was reached at Geneva on 14 April 1988 that half the 100,000 or so Soviet troops would be withdrawn on 15 August 1988 and the remainder within nine months; the last Soviet troops left on 15 February 1989, having suffered some 64,000 casualties in ten years. The PDPA regime survived until April 1992 when it was overthrown not by the mujahedin but by the defection of its own irregular militias.

The war left Afghanistan unstable and prey to continuing civil war. Its effect on the Soviet army was in some respects analogous to that of the *Vietnam war on the US army: mistrust between military and political leaders, together with feelings of waste, betrayal, and diminished self-confidence.   MEY

Cordovez, Diego, and Harrison, Selig, *Out of Afghanistan* (Oxford, 1995).

Roy, Olivier, *Islam and Resistance in Afghanistan* (2nd edn., Cambridge, 1990).

Sarin, Maj Gen Oleg, and Dvoretsky, Col Lev, *The Afghan Syndrome* (Novato, Calif., 1993).

Urban, Mark, *War in Afghanistan* (2nd edn., New York, 1990).

African-American troops Variously called negro, coloured, and black, the history of African-American soldiers is that of US race relations in general. Even after the abolition of formal discrimination by colour, advancement within the military has corresponded rather closely to skin shade.

During the *American independence war both sides employed negroes mainly in a support capacity. In 1775, Lord Dunmore issued an emancipation decree similar to the one by *Lincoln in 1862, declaring the freedom of only the *rebels'* slaves and indentured servants. In the *War of 1812 a 'Battalion of Free Men of Colour' fought under Jackson at the battle of New Orleans and coloureds served under him in the first war against the Seminole, which was fought to recover escaped slaves. But in general the self-fulfilling argument that they made poor soldiers prevailed.

During the *American civil war, African-Americans were mainly regarded as an economic asset to be denied to the South. Abolitionists struggled to get free northern coloureds into the war, the subject of the 1989 film *Glory*, but not in time to defuse the resentment that exploded in the bloody anti-negro 1863 draft riots. US Coloured Troops distinguished themselves in 1864–5, notably at Chapin's Farm where they won thirteen Congressional Medals of Honor. But attempts by African-Americans to become officers were cruelly discouraged in the armed forces until the mid-20th century, providing a further self-fulfilling rationale that they were unfit to lead.

During the latter *Plains Indians wars and the *Spanish-American war, two cavalry and two infantry regiments of 'Buffalo Soldiers' served with distinction in the regular army, but that was the limit set on African-American participation against a background of segregationist 'Jim Crow' laws, although some states still permitted them to join the National Guard. During WW I, 140,000 were sent to France and 40,000 served in combat, most under French command, winning over three hundred Croix de Guerre and seven Légions d'Honneur. During WW II, segregationists sought to keep over 500,000 uniformed African-Americans in secondary roles, and denigrated those who did manage to engage in combat, notably the pilots of the 332nd fighter group, the subject of the 1995 film *Tuskegee Airmen*. In the 1990s, after an investigation documented contemporary discrimination, Congressional Medals of Honor were posthumously awarded to one African-American in WW I and seven in WW II.

The *de jure* abolition of American apartheid began in the armed forces in 1948 but continued de facto, the two Medals of Honor won by blacks in *Korea being in the 'Buffalo Soldier' 24th Infantry. *Vietnam was the first war fought with fully integrated units, as the middle class generally sought to exempt itself and leave the fighting to the underclass, black and white. There were repeated complaints that blacks, constituting a substantial part of this underclass and less able to avoid conscription than the well-to-do, were disproportionately represented in Vietnam and many were radicalized by their experiences there.

Yet there was another side to the story: with desegregation a growing number of blacks saw the armed forces as offering social mobility, and by the 1960s were about twice as likely to re-enlist as their comrades of other races. There is also evidence that military service improved race relations. A WW II white sergeant from South Carolina admitted that he had been reluctant to serve with black soldiers, but 'after that first day when we saw how they fought, I changed my mind'. A black soldier in Korea commented: 'if all white people were like the white boys in this company it wouldn't take long before everybody would get along swell.' Gen Colin *Powell's role in the *Gulf war as chairman of the Joint Chiefs of Staff was the final milestone in a 200-year struggle for recognition. Although only 12 per cent of today's US population, African-Americans constitute 28 per cent of the army, 19 per cent of the Marines, and 15 per cent of the air force and navy.   HEB/RH

Afrika Korps (Deutsches Afrika Korps, or DAK) evolved from 'Reconnaissance Detachment *Rommel', sent to Tunisia in early 1941. It was expected to have a blocking role, following British defeat of the Italians and the westward advance by *O'Connor, and so was strong in machine gun and *anti-armour units. Although *Hitler gave it the title Afrika Korps on 19 February, it remained small, with 5th Light (later renamed 21st Panzer) and 15th Panzer Divisions. On 15 August 1941, after heavy fighting which had shown that it was the principal Axis combat force in Africa, the Afrika Korps became part of Panzer Group Africa, a title changed on 30 January 1942 to Panzer Army Africa and later to First Italian Army, which became part of Army Group Africa in February 1943.

The Allies tended to call all German troops in theatre, whether part of the DAK or not, the Afrika Korps. And whatever the terminology of the military organization of which it formed part, the Afrika Korps played a consistently distinguished role. At *Gazala it hooked round the Eighth Army's desert flank, and although it suffered heavy losses at *Alamein that autumn, it fought on resolutely until the surrender in *North Africa in May 1943.

There was something about the DAK which commended it to its opponents. It fought hard and skilfully, developed a sartorial style which mingled the utilitarian with the flamboyant, and behaved with magnanimity in victory and dignity in defeat. The distinguished military historian Ronald Lewin, who witnessed the end in Africa, felt his own pride in victory mingled with 'a sense of compassion, too: this had been a good enemy'.   RH
Lewin, Ronald, *The Life and Death of the Afrika Korps* (London, 1977).
Lucas, James, *Panzer Army Africa* (London, 1977).

Agincourt, battle of (1415). Fought between the forces of France and England near Agincourt in northern France on 25 October 1415 (the feast of Sts Crispin and Crispinian), this battle ranks high on any list of English victories. Having invaded France in August and captured Harfleur by the end of September, and now intent upon returning to England, *Henry V was marching to Calais when his force was challenged by a large French army blocking his advance. The king had little choice but to fight. Under his command he had some 6,000 fighting men; the enemy army may have been three times the size. Following a night of rain, the English drew up their thin battle line, with several large groups of *archers, to await the French attack. After some manoeuvring, this eventually came, the French, many of them mounted, advancing over the land rendered soft by the recent rain. As they approached, probably in close formation, they were met by a hail of arrows which killed or wounded large numbers of mounts and horsemen, as well as heavily armed knights fighting on foot, so lessening the force of the attack, impeding those wishing to retire, and obstructing those advancing from the rear. Having thus sown confusion in the French lines, the English, mostly fighting on foot, moved in to the kill. While the English dead may have numbered some 300–400, the French lost several thousand men, including many nobles, either killed or taken captive. The battle is an excellent example of a small, well-disciplined, well-led, and highly motivated force with little to lose overcoming a much larger one lacking discipline and proper leadership, and overconfident of victory.   CTA
Allmand, Christopher, *Henry V* (London, 1998).

AIF See AUSTRALIAN IMPERIAL FORCE.

airborne forces comprise specialist troops landed by parachute, *gliders, or *helicopter. Their development involved three major issues. First, were they special forces, best suited for *coups de main* and the like, or a major arm in their own right? Secondly, what balance should be struck between parachute delivery, which might leave men scattered over a wide area, or glider landing, where men arrived in small groups but were vulnerable as they did so? Finally, how should they compensate for the fact that they usually lacked firepower and heavy equipment, and were hard to support logistically?

The first unit of airborne troops was established during the 1920s by Italy which formed a company of parachutists. By the end of that decade the USSR had formed and trained a battalion of paratroops and during the early 1930s conducted a number of *exercises culminating in 1934 in a drop of a complete regiment of 1,500 men. France followed in 1938 with the formation of two companies of Infanterie de l'Air.

It was the Germans who saw the opportunities offered by airborne units operating in conjunction with armoured formations. In 1938 7th Flieger Division, commanded by Maj Gen Kurt *Student, was formed by the Luftwaffe, comprising parachute and airlanding units with their own integrated air assets which included a number of gliders. Elements saw action for the first time in May 1940 during the invasion of the Low Countries, featuring in the attack on the fortress at Eben Emael when parachute engineers landed by glider on top of the casemates. In May 1941 7th Flieger Division, by then part of XI Air Corps, was subsequently used in the invasion of *Crete which was the first battle won by airborne troops alone. However, together with XI Corps' Assault Regiment, it suffered very heavy losses and *Hitler decreed that German airborne forces were thereafter to be used solely in the ground role.

The Allies followed the Germans' lead. In October 1941, Britain formed the 1st Airborne Division and in May 1943 the 6th Airborne Division, each comprising two parachute brigades, a gliderborne air-landing brigade, and divisional troops. *Air transport was provided by the RAF which converted bombers for dropping parachutists; from the latter part of 1944 onwards these were replaced by *Dakota (Douglas C-47) transports. Air-landing units and the majority of divisional troops travelled in Horsa and Hamilcar gliders crewed by members of The Glider Pilot Regiment and towed by RAF bombers. The Americans formed five airborne divisions: 11th, 13th, 17th, 82nd, and 101st. Larger than their British counterparts, each comprised three parachute and one glider infantry regiments (each of three battalions) with supporting arms. Parachutists were carried in C-47 Dakotas which were also used as tugs for the Waco and Horsa gliders of the gliderborne units. British airborne forces first saw action when 1st Parachute Brigade, part of 1st Airborne Division, was deployed to *North Africa during the period 1942 to 1943. Subsequently the complete

division, commanded by Maj Gen G. F. 'Hoppy' Hopkinson, took part in operations in *Sicily and *Italy during 1943. Airborne units were also used in two *coup de main* operations in 1942. In February, a company of 2nd Parachute Battalion was dropped at Bruneval, on the French coast, in a successful operation to capture a new type of German *radar. In November, a force of sappers from 1st Airborne Division was flown in two gliders to Norway in an unsuccessful attempt to sabotage a factory producing heavy water for the German atomic weapon development programme. In November 1943, 2nd Independent Parachute Brigade Group under Brig C. H. V. Pritchard was deployed to Italy and was subsequently employed on operations in southern France, as part of 1st Airborne Task Force, and Greece during the following two years. In June 1944 6th Airborne Division, commanded by Maj Gen Richard Gale, took part in the invasion of Normandy, along with the 82nd 'All American' and 101st 'Screaming Eagles' US Airborne Divisions under Maj Gens Matthew *Ridgway and Maxwell Taylor respectively. The division remained on operations in France until withdrawn three months later.

In September 1944 Lt Gen 'Boy' Browning's I Airborne Corps, part of First Allied Airborne Army under Lt Gen Louis Brereton, was deployed on MARKET GARDEN. It comprised 1st Airborne Division under Maj Gen Roy Urquhart, 82nd and 101st US Airborne Divisions commanded respectively by Brig Gen James Gavin and Maj Gen Maxwell Taylor, and 52nd Lowland Division. The two American divisions achieved their objectives but 1st Airborne Division, dropped and landed too far from its objectives, was decimated in the ensuing battle of *Arnhem and Oosterbeek against elements of two *SS panzer divisions. In late March 1945 the XVIII US Airborne Corps under Ridgway, comprising 6th Airborne Division under Maj Gen Eric Bols and 17th US Airborne Division commanded by Maj Gen William 'Bud' Miley, took part in VARSITY, the highly successful crossing of the Rhine. Avoiding the mistakes made at Arnhem, both divisions were dropped and landed directly on to their objectives which were taken by the end of the first day after hard fighting.

The *Indian Army had in 1941 formed 50th Indian Parachute Brigade which subsequently saw extensive action in the infantry role in the *Burma campaign. In 1944, 44th Indian Airborne Division (later redesignated 2nd Indian Airborne Division) was formed under Maj Gen Eric Down, comprising two parachute brigades and an airlanding brigade. Only one airborne operation was carried out, a composite battalion group being dropped at Elephant Point in May 1945. Airborne operations in Burma otherwise consisted of landings behind Japanese lines in 1944 by *Chindits of Maj Gen Orde Wingate's Special Force which comprised 14th Long Range Penetration Brigade; 16th, 23rd, 77th, and 111th Infantry Brigades; and 3rd West African Brigade. Pathfinders and airstrip construction teams of a USAAF airborne engineer squadron were landed in gliders of the USAAF's No.1 Air Commando. Troops were subsequently landed by RAF and USAAF C-47 transports, with fire support and casualty evacuation being provided by P-51 fighters and L-5 light aircraft of No.1 Air Commando.

The principal American airborne formation deployed in the *Pacific theatre was the 11th US Airborne Division, commanded by Maj Gen Joe Swing. At the beginning of February 1945, two battalions dropped at Tagaytay Ridge and later that month the 503rd Parachute Infantry Regiment dropped on to the Japanese-held fortress on Corregidor, an island off Manila Bay in the Philippines. Six days later, the 1st Battalion 511th Parachute Infantry Regiment dropped north-east of Tagaytay Ridge, 20 miles (32 km) behind Japanese lines, to release POWs from a Japanese prison camp. In June, elements of 11th Airborne Division carried out an airlanding operation to intercept the Japanese withdrawal from Luzon.

The Italians, having led the way at the outset, expanded their airborne forces to two under-strength parachute divisions but never used them in the airborne role, though they fought with distinction on the ground. Similarly the Soviets increased their airborne forces but made little use of them, carrying out a small number of brigade-sized parachute operations in 1943 and 1944. The Japanese also made little use of their airborne forces during their invasion of South-East Asia. Two successful operations, at Menado and Palembang in the Dutch East Indies, were carried out in 1942 but thereafter no further use was made of airborne units until December 1944 when two parachute regiments took part with limited success in an attack on three American airfields in the area of Burauen in the Philippines.

The aftermath of WW II saw drastic reductions in western airborne forces, Britain eventually reducing hers to two parachute brigade groups (one a Territorial Army formation) and America retaining only one of its airborne divisions. Five years later elements of the 187th Parachute Infantry Regiment carried out two operations during the *Korean war in October 1950 and March 1951. France was the exception, forming the 10th and 25th Airborne Divisions and subsequently using them in the first of the postwar colonial wars in *Indochina where they fought heroically at *Dien Bien Phu. In 1956 French paratroops of the 2ème Régiment Parachutiste Colonial and 11ème Demi-Brigade Parachutiste de Choc, together with the British 3rd Battalion The Parachute Regiment Group, took part in MUSKETEER, the airborne operation conducted during the initial stage of the disastrous invasion of *Suez. In 1957, the Soviets revealed they had been developing a complete airborne army comprising six divisions. Indeed, they had surpassed the West in development of equipment designed for airborne operations, including light armoured vehicles and *self-propelled (SP) guns capable of being dropped by parachute.

During the last thirty years, the delivery of large numbers of troops by parachute to their objectives has been made more difficult by a number of factors such as the development of sophisticated air defence systems, which has increased the risk of interception of transport aircraft, and modern battlefield *surveillance and target acquisition systems which render dropping zones vulnerable. Furthermore, light scales of equipment and limited organic logistical support inevitably limit the ability of parachute formations to conduct extended operations, particularly against a heavily armoured enemy. There has thus been a shift of emphasis in airborne deployment away from the parachute to a method of tactical air transport which overcomes many such problems and offers greater flexibility: the helicopter.

It was in the 1950s that helicopters first saw real operational employment. During the Korean war, US forces employed them for liaison, supply, casualty evacuation, and troop transportation. Four years later, French forces used them for deployment of airborne units on *counter-insurgency operations during the *Algerian independence war. Some were armed with missiles and employed successfully in the attack role. The *Vietnam war saw the helicopter come into its own as a method of large-scale transportation of troops and equipment. During the early 1960s the 11th Air Assault Division, commanded by Maj Gen Harry Kinnard, was formed as the US Army's first dedicated airmobile formation. Subsequently redesignated 1st Cavalry Division (Air Mobile), it saw extensive service in Vietnam and developed the role to a fine art. Today the 101st Airborne Division (Air Assault) is the US army's major helicopter-borne formation, equipped with its own light, medium, and heavy lift transport as well as attack helicopter assets.

Helicopters were also extensively used during the war in *Afghanistan, during the period 1979 to 1989, where the Soviet army used them on operations against mujahedin *guerrillas. Airborne and air-assault units mounted tactical air-assault operations against guerrilla-held areas, being landed under supporting fire from artillery, multi-launch rocket launchers, and ground-attack (see *fighter) aircraft. Heavily armed attack helicopters preceded landings, laying down suppressive fire if necessary.

The parachute does still have a role to play in operations where delivery is beyond the range of helicopters. An example of this occurred in 1978 when the French Foreign Legions's 2ème Régiment Étranger de Parachutistes and the Belgian Régiment Para-Commando were flown from Corsica and Belgium, subsequently being dropped on to an airfield at Kolwezi in Zaire, in an operation to rescue Europeans under threat from rebel forces. Moreover, the use of free-fall parachuting, developed for military use since the 1960s, continues to be a viable method of long-range airborne delivery of small groups for pathfinding and reconnaissance tasks.

Airborne forces still form part of many armies. The US army features two major regular formations: the 82nd Airborne Division and 101st Airborne Division (Air Assault).

France has its 11ème Division Parachutiste and 4ème Division Aéroportée, both of which form part of its Force d'Action Rapide. Germany's airborne forces currently comprise the Airborne Forces Command, incorporating the 26th and 31st Airborne Brigades which have parachute and airmobile capabilities, while the Italian army has the Folgore Parachute Brigade and a *carabinieri* parachute battalion. Since the collapse of the USSR, Russia's airborne forces currently comprise five airborne divisions, an independent brigade, three regiments, an independent battalion, and a Spetsnaz regiment.

The year 2000 will see 16th Air Assault Brigade as the British Army's newly formed airborne formation, possessing its own attack and light helicopter assets which will include three Army Air Corps regiments equipped with the GKN Westland Apache WAH 64 attack helicopter. Light- and medium-support helicopters of the RAF will be provided as required by the newly formed tri-service Joint Helicopter Command. Two of the three regular army battalions of The Parachute Regiment will form the infantry component, together with an airlanding battalion. These two units will retain their parachute capability for long-range airborne operations or those requiring the insertion of a leading parachute battalion group.

Coming as they do at the air–land interface, airborne forces do not always fit comfortably into structures which have tended to separate air from land. Germany's WW II parachute arm was part of the air force, and it was only with the 1998 Strategic Defence Review that Britain established a unified command structure for its helicopters. The *doctrine governing their use is still developing, and in the West is increasingly linked to manoeuvre warfare. Airborne forces offer the opportunity of creating room for manoeuvre by using the third dimension, achieving 'vertical envelopment', in addition to—or instead of—envelopment achieved by ground manoeuvre, and helping shape deep, non-linear, battlefields. The traditional functions of their component arms are likely to become blurred, with a growing emphasis on linking troops who move by air to battle with fires delivered by artillery and aircraft against targets identified or designated from the ground. Their mobility gives them a particular utility in intervention operations, and the qualities engendered in their training supply an important combat edge. HMPDH

Allen, Patrick, *Screaming Eagles: In Action with the 101st Airborne Division (Air Assault)* (London, 1990).

Edwards, Roger, *German Airborne Troops* (London, 1974).

Grau, Lester W., *The Bear Went Over The Mountain: Soviet Combat Tactics in Afghanistan* (Washington, 1996).

Harclerode, Peter, *PARA! Fifty Years of the Parachute Regiment* (London, 1992).

Tugwell, Maurice. *Airborne to Battle* (London, 1971).

air forces are the instrument by which *air power is applied. During the 20th century there have been many inno-

vations in warfare but perhaps the most significant has been the emergence of air power, and, with it, of independent air forces. The expansion of military activity into the third dimension revolutionized the conduct of war and resulted in the development of a new arm, demanding resources and technical and financial investment on a whole new scale. Such have become the costs of maintaining large and technologically advanced air forces that, by the end of the 20th century, only the USAF can be counted as first rate.

Moreover, the emergence of strategic air forces fundamentally changed the nature of war. Civilian populations became involved in industrial war on an increasing scale as they were often mobilized and deployed to support the war effort, but they became even more directly involved when nations began to target enemy workers. The use of strategic bombers, particularly in the closing stages of WW II, helped to make war as *total as it was ever to become.

Concepts on the use of air forces date back long before powered flight became a reality. Many fictional accounts of how large air fleets might be used to destroy enemy states and populations were widely read, even before the most famous, H. G. Wells's *The War in the Air*, was published in 1908. In the years leading up to WW I and following the innovations of the Wright brothers, the great powers began investigating the military use of aircraft. Contrary to popular belief armies and *navies did explore the possibilities of the aerial dimension, if only to ensure that opponents did not gain an advantage, but the realities of pre-1914 aero-technology precluded great progress. Nevertheless, on the outbreak of war in 1914 all major powers had some form of nascent air force, though these were firmly tied to the coat-tails of the existing armed services. Britain had made the first move towards a unified air service. Her Royal Flying Corps (RFC) was formed in 1912. It had a Military Wing, a Naval Wing, a Central Flying School, the Royal Aircraft Factory, and a reserve. In 1914 the naval wing was detached from the RFC to form the Royal Naval Air Service, clear evidence of the assertion of control along traditional lines.

In 1914 Russia and Germany had the most aircraft, but France, the leading light of European aviation at this time, had the best developed aero-industry. For the most part it was considered that air forces would be used primarily for scouting and *reconnaissance missions, both overland and at sea. Only limited consideration had been given to aerial bombing, using naval airships (see BALLOONS). WW I saw major innovation and expansion of air arms, and by 1918 in each major power they numbered tens of thousands of personnel and thousands of operational aircraft. To support this expansion increasing demands were made on economies, adding a further drain on resources. Only the most sophisticated states could meet the challenge of air war. Still, the most important activity undertaken by aircraft between 1914 and 1918 was reconnaissance. Once the war had settled into the trench stalemate, aerial observation of enemy forces became critical to intelligence gathering and artillery direction. Artillery was the biggest killer on the battlefield and aircraft were responsible for making it more deadly. In many ways air forces reinforced the stalemate by reducing the likelihood of surprise attacks, and by aiding the defensive capability of artillery. In order to deny the use of the air to the enemy, fighters and air superiority campaigns were born, the first being the air battle over *Verdun in 1916. Control of the skies also allowed the employment of aircraft on ground support operations and bombing raids as well as reconnaissance and by 1918 air forces were participating in co-ordinated ground offensives helping to break the stalemate.

Both the Central Powers and the Allies used aircraft on strategic bombing raids, targeting enemy industries and to a lesser extent enemy civilians. These produced more panic than destruction, but they resulted in April 1918 in the creation of the world's first independent air force, the Royal Air Force (RAF), to defeat the aerial threat posed by German Zeppelins and heavy bombers. Its birth was not easy. An Air Ministry was formed in late 1917 in an effort to assert greater centralized control, and *Trenchard, the first chief of the air staff, was convinced that air units would be returned to their parent services once the war was over. However, the new service, its independence symbolized by its distinctive light-blue uniform, new titles, and badges of rank (and even short-lived full-dress headgear intriguingly based on a flying helmet), was to prove remarkably durable. The Americans took a step in the same direction, removing aircraft from the control of the Signal Corps and creating an Army Air Service. However, subsequent progression to an independent air force was slow, and was accompanied by the bitter personal and institutional feuding which generally surrounded the creation of these forces. Although a Committee of the House of Representatives recommended the creation of an independent air force in 1925, it took more than twenty years for the United States Air Force to emerge. France, the USSR, and Germany all formed independent air forces in the inter-war period.

However, the creation of new institutionalized air forces had little direct impact on the formulation of air warfare theory. The manner in which air forces would be used was shaped more profoundly by the strategic environment. The USA and Japan developed maritime air forces to a higher level than other powers in the 1930s because a war in the Pacific against each other appeared a likely scenario. New notions of carrier-based aircraft delivering 'shells' beyond the range of even the largest guns developed and by the early 1940s the fast carrier task force had been born, eventually relegating the surface battleship to a supporting role. Aircraft carrier battlegroups were to decide the outcome of the war in the *Pacific, and as the US Navy acknowledged the supremacy of the air dimension in maritime operations to a degree that the imperial Japanese navy never did, they held a significant advantage throughout the war.

Other nations recognized differing strategic needs for their air forces and thus pursued alternative lines of development. The land-based European powers required air forces to support ground operations, either directly or at an *operational level. Although studies of and investment in strategic air power took place in France's Armée de l'Air, Germany's Luftwaffe, and in particular the USSR's VVS (Voyenno-Vozdushnye sily), the priority for these air forces remained the support of land-based operations. The VVS's broadly based thinking, which included a major role for strategic bombing, was jettisoned in Stalin's purge of the armed forces in the late 1930s. By 1941 the VVS was deployed in a dispersed manner to support the army, and was thus swamped and overwhelmed by the Luftwaffe during *BARBAROSSA. The French Armée de l'Air was created in July 1934 but suffered from political and inter-service wrangling from the start. Some wanted the air force tied directly to localized support of ground forces, others argued it should be deployed at a divisional level, while the disastrous BCR (Bombardement Combat Reconnaissance) programme drew the French up a blind alley. How the Armée de l'Air was to be used remained open to speculation until it was far too late. The Luftwaffe's development was tied very much to Germany's strategic needs, initially being a deterrent force, and then an operational level support arm for land campaigns. Despite being prohibited from building an air force, Germany studied the lessons of WW I in great detail in the 1920s and concluded that the aircraft should be used to aid ground offensives. However, it should be noted that the Luftwaffe was never conceived and designed to be a close *air support force for the army. It was a hotchpotch of a force broadly capable of many tasks but not particularly proficient at any one, although at the beginning of WW II it benefited from the flexibility conferred by broadly undefined *doctrine.

The inter-war period also saw the development of strategic bombing theory, most notably in the USA and Britain. Since the end of WW I the RAF had been studying the concept of using massed heavy bombers to bombard enemy nations into submission, and in the 1930s such thinking became central to RAF philosophy (for strategic bombing was a function of air power which argued strongly for the independence of the force that performed it) and briefly to British defence policy. In the USA, theoretical work in the 1930s, especially at the Air Corps Tactical School at Maxwell airbase, laid the foundation for the daylight bombing formations that were to be deployed in WW II. In both Britain and the USA a far too sanguine view of the unescorted heavy bomber's ability to survive and be able to find and bomb targets prevailed, leading to bloody early failures in WW II.

From the mid-1930s onwards aircraft had reached a high level of technical capability, but had not become so advanced that they could be mass-produced without crippling a nation's economy, as has occurred since the 1950s.

Thus WW II was to witness the largest expansion and employment of air forces to date, on a scale almost certainly never to be repeated. The demands of maintaining a first-rate mass air force were huge and only thoroughly developed and organized economies could meet the challenge. Notably, militaristic nations such as Nazi Germany and imperial Japan were unable or unwilling to mobilize the industrial and technological resources required, and their air forces declined markedly as the war progressed. Conversely, those of the West and the USSR expanded considerably, overwhelming the Axis powers in the last two years of the war.

Tactical air power was employed with spectacular success to spearhead the German *blitzkrieg campaigns of 1939–41, and their opponents returned the favour massively during the ground offensives in 1944–5. The strategic bombing campaigns prosecuted by the RAF and the USAAF eventually overcame many operational difficulties, wore down and broke the German air defences, and inflicted enormous damage on Germany and Japan in 1944–5. Such strategic air forces alone were never able to bring those states to the point of capitulation, but they contributed significantly to Allied victory. By 1945 air forces were considered an essential part of the mix of military forces necessary for success in war, but the degree of destruction they could visit upon cities had reached unacceptable levels. In the post-war years air forces, most notably the independent USAF created in 1947, were predominantly concerned with strategic nuclear war, certainly until the emergence of long-range ballistic missiles. Indeed, some of the arguments over ownership (and importance) of nuclear weapons reflected earlier debates over strategic bombing, and both the USAF and the RAF took a keen interest in grand-strategic bombers like the ill-starred B-36 and much more successful B-52 in America and the V-bombers (Valiant, Victor, and Vulcan) in Britain.

Non-strategic air forces rather stagnated in the *Cold War era with much greater emphasis being placed on the delivery of missiles and stand-off bombs. Innovations occurred, notably the introduction of *helicopters and the growing input of high level technology, but it was not until the 1970s that major investment in air forces grew again. The Soviet VVS expanded considerably from the late 1960s onwards, but it was the US interest in the 'air–land battle' concept and 'follow-on forces attack' that brought tactical air forces back to the forefront of military thought. Of note throughout the post-war years has been the growing reliance on technology missiles, *radar, fly-by-wire, ECMs (Electronic Counter Measures), stealth, to name but a few. This has resulted in smaller numbers of aircraft than the WW II era, but much more sophisticated and with extravagant unit costs. Stealth technology has escalated costs still further, to such a degree that middle powers such as France and Britain can no longer compete and even the USSR fell behind, after bankrupting itself to maintain parity with the USA in this and other areas of military technology.

The future use of air forces in the wake of the end of the Cold War is crystallizing into two particular roles. First, they may be used in large scale multinational operations such as the *Gulf war, or on occasion in 'surgical' strikes or what are in effect policing duties. In both cases qualitative and quantitative superiority is almost certainly assured, and the likelihood in the near future of massive air-superiority campaigns is low. Secondly, they may be deployed in peace-keeping or peace implementation roles, again almost certainly in conjunction with allied powers, or under the aegis of the UN or NATO. In both cases the need for precision to limit collateral damage is vital to meet the requirements of public opinion, if not military necessity. There is little doubt that air forces in the 21st century will offer a sophisticated global reach to the USA in particular, but they cannot be considered a panacea. Limitations will continue to exist and in complicated low-intensity operations the ability of air forces to intervene decisively continues to remain open to question. JB/RH

Buckley, John, *Air Power in the Age of Total War* (London, 1999).
Gooch, John, *Airpower: Theory and Practice* (London, 1995).
Mason, Tony, *Airpower: A Centennial Appraisal* (London, 1995).
Overy, Richard, *The Air War 1939–1945* (London, 1980).
air power (feature)

air power (*see opposite page*)

air support, close (CAS). Close air support is one facet of battlefield air attack, the role played by *air power in supporting ground operations. It is a term often used rather loosely and imprecisely to cover all aspects of battlefield air support (BAS). Technically, CAS is defined as actions against enemy forces which are in close proximity to friendly units, thus requiring close integration and careful planning to avoid errors. Battlefield air *interdiction (BAI) is the use of air power to attack enemy forces before they can be deployed effectively against friendly units, or to degrade enemy capability by disrupting and destroying rear zone units and logistical support. BAI operations take place within the battle area but not close enough to the front line to require detailed and careful integration of actions with friendly ground forces.

The earliest examples of BAS date back to WW I. Aircraft, as smaller and more manoeuvrable targets, proved to be more suited to BAS than the airships (see BALLOONS) which had been used in the early stages of the war. Aircraft initially played an important role in *reconnaissance and artillery-spotting duties, and fighter aircraft were developed to drive off or protect such aircraft. Once this had been achieved, the opportunity arose for friendly aircraft to intervene on the ground, and thus CAS was born. By 1917

(*cont. on page 22*)

air power

IR power is the application of air force, more expansively defined by Billy *Mitchell as 'the ability to do something in the air'. Its history, as a means of war and as an element of strategic theory, has been defined by competing visions of what that 'something' should be. Mitchell's imprecision was an effort to gloss over what had, within a few years of the aircraft's invention, become a divisive issue among air enthusiasts: were aircraft new elements of modern combined-arms warfare, whose significance depended upon successful integration with other, more familiar means of fighting, or were they harbingers of a new kind of war, capable of achieving decisive strategic results by direct attack on the social, political, and psychological resources of the enemy?

No definitive answer to these questions has emerged, if for no other reason than because air power's assimilation to warfare has necessarily been shaped less by theoretical inferences than by the concrete interests, strategic predilections, and the institutional dynamics of individual states. The fact that independent *air forces have become the norm among advanced societies testifies to the strength of the claim that air power has unique characteristics, which can only be mastered by those professionally committed to it. Yet the conduct of major military operations by air forces alone remains deeply suspect, and not just by those ignorant of air power's undoubted potential.

War in and from the air was imagined long before it became a realistic possibility. Fantasies of flight are as old as western civilization, and have often included elements of violence and dark premonition: the wings of Icarus melting in the sun is among the earliest and most enduring metaphors for technological hubris. *Leonardo da Vinci's fanciful drawings of flying machines would contribute to his fame as a universal genius; but he kept them secret while he was alive, because he feared they would appeal to the evil in mankind. Eighteenth-century Frenchmen who witnessed the Montgolfier brothers' early experiments with hot-air *balloons had no difficulty picturing soldiers dropping out of the sky; while Tennyson, a half-century later, imagined 'a ghastly dew' descending from 'the nations' airy navies, grappling in the central blue' (*Locksley Hall*, 1842). By the turn of the 20th century, the English novelist H. G. Wells was able to present a fully fleshed-out vision of strategic bombardment directed against cities, in which the bridges and public buildings of New York were suddenly destroyed by airships launched from Germany, half a world away (*War in the Air*, 1908). It is no exaggeration to say, in cultural terms, that when air power became a reality it was almost literally a dream come true.

Almost indeed, for as a practical matter air power has frequently fallen short of the hopes it has inspired. At the time Wells wrote, there were perhaps 100 military aircraft in the world, plus a larger number of lighter-than-air craft. The prospective military value of such 'airships' had been increased by the development, in the 1880s, of steering mechanisms (hence the French-derived word dirigible), which might allow such vessels to be used for tactical observation, and even as weapons. The Hague Conference of 1899 was persuaded by the Russian delegate to ban airships as platforms for guns or explosives, although the American representative successfully argued that the ban should last only five years on the grounds that military aircraft, once perfected, would prove a boon to mankind, by making war shorter and less destructive.

The hope that this promise should somehow be fulfilled was only heightened by WW I, in which air power played a considerable, but not a pre-eminent, part. Throughout the war, the most important air mission was scouting. In this role aircraft were aided by two other new technologies: photographic film (developed by the Kodak company as a replacement for coated glass plates) and wireless telegraphy. Film exposed by aerial photographers could be dropped directly to relevant headquarters, developed, interpreted, and put to immediate operational use; while aircraft (including balloons) equipped with wireless sets were regularly employed as observers for artillery. In practice, the problems of understanding and applying such intelligence proved formidable, and the confidence of commanders on the ground that they possessed what a later age would call 'information dominance' over their opponents was often misplaced. Nevertheless, by the end of the war it was essential to conceal one's forces as far as possible from the airborne eyes of the enemy and another French-derived word, *camouflage, had long since become known to all combatants.

The value of aerial reconnaissance was certainly sufficient to make it worth denying to the other side. It was the need to shoot down the enemy's scouts and spotters while protecting one's own that gave rise to air-to-air combat, initially by pilots and back-seat observers using ordinary firearms or machine guns mounted on the fuselage, then by aeroplanes that had themselves become weapons. The main obstacle to the creation of an effective fighter plane was the propeller, which made it difficult to mount a centre-line gun the pilot could aim himself. The solution, a synchronizing gear that allowed the engine to control the gun, was devised at the end of 1915 by Anton Fokker, a Dutch engineer working in Germany. In early 1916 his redesigned machines acquired a fearsome reputation, and gave the Germans, for a time, true air superiority over the western front—which was lost almost immediately after one of the new planes accidentally landed at a French airfield, giving the secret away. Although the Germans were usually a step ahead of their opponents technologically at most stages of the war, superiority in the air ultimately rested with the western Allies for the same reasons that applied on the ground: they possessed significantly greater economic and industrial resources, which allowed them to out-build their opponents.

The men who flew the fighters became popular figures of mythic proportions, partly because of the sheer, romantic improbability of flight, but also because they seemed to have restored an element of single combat to the anonymous slaughter of modern war. Victory in the air was thought to be a matter of personal skill, heroism, and the luck of the brave—an image that survived long after air tactics had begun to acquire the characteristics of deadly routine. The lone *ace was largely a figure of the war's first two years. Thereafter, air combat was increasingly dominated by squadrons or 'wings' comprising dozens of planes, which flew in prescribed formations, and engaged in mass combats that were normally decided by speed, numbers, and an opportunistic approach from behind. At the end of the war, some of the most talented German pilots were opting to fly observation planes, which allowed some scope for individual initiative. As America's most famous aviator, Eddie Rickenbacker, would later admit, fighting in the air had quickly lost the qualities of a 'sport', and had become instead 'scientific murder' (*Fighting the Flying Circus*, 1919).

Over the course of the war, the major belligerents in Europe produced tens of thousands of military aircraft of all types, only a tiny fraction of which were committed to offensive operations. Airmen, needless to say, showed themselves eager, hurling *grenades and firing their weapons at targets on the ground from the earliest days of the war. In time, their ability to strafe troops and destroy selected transportation, command, and storage facilities would inspire a justified measure of fear among those below (including, it must be admitted, those on their own side). Technically the problems of delivering genuinely significant fire from the air took time to solve. The vessels that H. G. Wells had imagined devastating New York had been Zeppelins—immense, rigid, motorized airships named after their German inventor—and such craft were the only ones capable of lifting more than a few hundred pounds when the war began. Their vulnerability to artillery fire and fixed-wing aircraft soon became apparent, and their value against defended targets was severely limited.

True bombers emerge during the middle years of the war, in the form of large, multi-engine mono-planes capable of lifting up to a ton of explosives—German Gothas and Handley-Page 0/100s and 0/400s. London and Paris were both attacked repeatedly from the air during the war, and sustained several thousand civilian casualties. Berlin was too remote to suffer retribution, though one intrepid French pilot did manage to drop a load of leaflets there, and German cities in the Ruhr and Rhineland were struck by British and French aviators. In October 1917 Britain created an independent air wing (41 Wing) for strategic bombing, the precursor of the RAF, which was created on 1 April 1918—the world's first independent air force. Had the war lasted longer it is certain that the scale of such efforts would have increased, despite reservations on all sides about the moral and political consequences of attacks upon civilians. Although the absence of effective bomb sights (and in some cases effective navigation) made strategic air attacks decidedly indiscriminate, this did not lessen their psycho-logical impact, which exceeded the physical destruction involved. A week of Zeppelin and bomber raids directed against London in September 1917 caused 300,000 people to seek shelter in under-ground rail stations (not for the last time); and by the end of the war an equal number were manning the vast network of anti-aircraft artillery and so-called barrage balloons with which the world's largest city, and now its greatest target, sought to defend itself.

Air-power theory, strictly understood, arose by way of reflection upon these experiences. Among the most incisive (if little read at the time) early interpreters was the Italian *Douhet, whose *Command of the Air* (1921) first set down a number of basic propositions that, however contestable, have proven central to all subsequent discussions of its subject. He believed that, if nothing else, recent events had demonstrated the futility of offensive ground operations under modern conditions. In the air, in contrast, everything seemed to favour offensive action, a conclusion that was justified less by the actual accomplishments of aeroplanes so far than by the apparent difficulty of shooting them down. Aeroplanes had also made conventional distinctions between combatants and non-combatants irrelevant. While some might conceive scruples about deliberate attacks upon civilians (a war crime under the same Hague Convention (see GENEVA AND HAGUE CONVENTIONS) that tried to outlaw war in the air), it was certain that others would not, and they would impose an inexorable strategic logic upon all alike. Wars in the future would begin with massive air offensives, directed not against the enemy's armed forces (whose role had been reduced to that of holding a defensive line) but against his cities. Such attacks would achieve their effects by psychological shock so profound as to leave the government no alternative but surrender—perhaps within hours. Logically, the only de-fence against such a disabling blow would be the ability to deliver one in reply, for which a standing air force in a state of perpetual alert would be indispensable.

Less baleful interpretations were possible. Many who favoured strategic bombing doubted that its impact on public *morale would suffice to end a war. It was not obvious exactly how such psycho-logical effects as Douhet imagined, even should they occur, would make themselves felt upon a gov-ernment, nor whether a government thus delegitimized would still be capable of coming to terms. The air war envisioned by Wells had not been short and decisive. While strategic bombing as he had imagined it was sufficient to destroy public order, the result was not peace, but 'universal guerrilla war'. Air enthusiasts in maritime countries especially—*Trenchard in Britain and Mitchell in the USA—were less inclined to conceive of air power as a stand-in for Armageddon—though Mitchell's prophetic description of Japan's 'paper cities' in flames stand out, even by the apocalyptic standards of the time. Air power might best be understood as a form of economic warfare, which worked like a particularly brutal naval *blockade, by destroying the enemy's war industries and productive capacity over time. In this context, victory through air power required only conventional strategic rationality on the part of an opponent: the losing side would be the one that first judged the price of continued bombardment to outweigh whatever prospects of success remained. For Mitchell and Trenchard, what mattered in any case was not the precise theory that governed the conduct of air war, but the establishment of independent air forces that would be free to explore their unique environment, without being held hostage to the obsolete conceptions of those condemned to fight on the ground.

Those thus condemned were nevertheless prepared to press their own claims. In continental countries with strong traditions of land warfare, air power was seen less as an alternative to tactical stalemate than as a solution to it. Although no major power was prepared to dismiss strategic bombing out of hand, those like Germany that were least equipped to sustain a protracted war of *attrition were more inclined to view aeroplanes as akin to flying artillery. The *Ludendorff offensive of March 1918 had employed squadrons of aircraft in direct support of infantry, and it was not entirely fanciful to wonder whether such a potent combination of fire and movement, had it been available in quantity a few years earlier, might not have changed the outcome of the war. Aircraft in this role, it was considered, might confound those higher in the sky, by assisting in the achievement of a decisive breakthrough on the ground, before the effects of strategic air bombardment could begin to bite. In these terms, 'command of the air' did not make effective ground operations unnecessary; it simply made them possible.

A narrower range of choices confronted those who fought on the sea. Sailors were no less ready than soldiers to employ aircraft to solve traditional problems—above all fleet reconnaissance, for which specialized planes and tenders were already in action in 1914. But few imagined that aircraft launched from ships could transform naval operations. Most regarded *naval power and air power as rival conceptions: both were promoted, by their most committed advocates, as means of rendering the clash of land armies ancillary to strategic success. The spectacle of the German dreadnought *Ostfriesland* being sunk from the air—arranged by Billy Mitchell in July 1921 as a demonstration of the aircraft's value for coastal defence—was superficially unnerving, but in the end unconvincing: the ship had been undefended and tethered when it was sunk. It was only the advent of effective *radar and *radio in the late 1930s that made aircraft carriers effective all-weather warships.

Thereafter the prospect that battleships might lose their pre-eminence was foreseeable—though it was only the actual experience of war that made it clear to everyone. The nature of the change should not be overestimated: aircraft carriers revolutionized naval tactics, but not naval strategy. Carriers replaced battleships only because aircraft could perform the functions of naval guns more effectively. They also proved helpful in controlling another, even more profound menace to the future of surface navies: submarines. In the absence of escort carriers and long-range land-based observation aircraft, the battle of the *Atlantic might easily have lasted another year—though the outcome would almost certainly have been the same. Still, the simple fact that the idea of the 'capital ship' survived the aircraft's ascendancy illustrates how little had changed. Navies now fought each other at vastly greater ranges, but for a familiar purpose: to command the sea, while denying its use to the adversary. Air power proved an essential means to this end, but not more than that.

The aircraft's most profound impact on naval operations in WW II involved the interaction between maritime forces and the land. The threat of attack by land-based aircraft exerted a continuous influence on all surface navies, most decisively so in the Mediterranean, while the need to establish forward-deployed island airbases controlled the basic rhythm of the island-hopping offensive in the *Pacific. Conversely, the strategic bombardment of Japan, conducted by land-based aircraft launched from islands seized and sustained by naval forces, was less a vindication of air power per se than a demonstration of the lethality of naval power, ruthlessly applied. The atomic bombs that devastated *Hiroshima and Nagasaki were immediately hailed by air enthusiasts as the technical embodiment of the old Douhet prophetic vision. They were in reality projectiles ultimately fired by the US navy.

The war in Europe presented a similarly variegated picture of air power in action. It demonstrated the centrality of 'doing something in the air' to all aspects of modern combat; but in ways that were difficult to analyse independently. The promise that aircraft would restore the power of manoeuvre to armies on the ground was fulfilled from the start, as German forces supported by a purpose-built fleet of ground-attack aircraft swept across Europe. Yet the war did not end as a result, and as it dragged on air power emerged less as an alternative to attrition than as one of its many instruments. Those who might still have imagined that the air was a realm of personal daring and bold expedients were destined for disappointment. Command of the air in WW II was an industrial process, in which numbers and sheer weight of metal ultimately proved decisive.

This is not to suggest that success was in any sense automatic once the necessary investment had been made. On the contrary, the expectations that attached to air power before the war had depended on a false assumption: that, as Stanley Baldwin told the House of Commons, 'the bomber will always get through'. In fact, rapid advances in the speed, range, and firepower of fighter aircraft, combined with the development of ground-based radar capable of guiding them to their targets, made aerial bombing a decidedly haphazard and risky enterprise. Even planes that managed to avoid being shot down could be driven off their aim by a vigorous defence, with the result that only about half the bombs dropped in the early years of the war fell within 5 miles (8 km) of their targets. Casualties among air crews were also alarming. When the war ended, losses in the RAF exceeded those of the Royal Navy, a possibility that few would have credited at the outset.

These problems had broader implications. If the goal of strategic bombardment was to erode 'the enemy's will'—which is to say, civilian *morale—the accuracy of individual air strikes made little difference. The natural targets were cities—the only thing large enough to be struck with real confidence in any case; and they could be hit more safely and no less well at night. This was a conclusion to which both the Luftwaffe and the RAF were drawn as a consequence of severe early losses. The USAAF, in contrast, remained committed to what it liked to call 'precision' daylight bombing—though it may be noted that only the lead aircraft actually tried to aim its bombs, while the rest simply dropped theirs as close to simultaneously as possible. In time, a kind of archetypal target list emerged, whose underlying logic continues to influence the conduct of air campaigns to this day. At the top were air defence assets—it had quickly been concluded that the Luftwaffe's failure to concentrate on the RAF's airfields and radar stations had hurt its chances during the battle of *Britain. Next came transportation targets, especially rail junctions and fuel storage facilities, upon which the movement of large ground forces depended. Bombing of this kind played a critical role in preparing for the Normandy invasion, and appears in retrospect to bridge the conceptual gap between direct support of forces in contact with the enemy, and the more remote effects of strategic bombing as originally conceived. Daylight raids were also carried out against factories producing war *matériel*, against hardened military targets like submarine pens, and against targets of special political importance, like the launching sites for the V-weapons in 1944—an unnerving premonition of what air power would soon become.

The relative risks and rewards of 'area' versus 'precision' bombing were contested throughout the war, without yielding any firm conclusions about their relative merits. Efforts to draw a moral distinction, at any rate, are misplaced: all forms of strategic bombing in WW II entailed deliberate attacks upon civilians. Certainly the losses incurred in daylight raids could be daunting. In its famous attack on the Schweinfurt ball-bearing works in June 1943, the US Eighth Air Force lost 147 out of 376 planes, to little purpose other than to induce the enemy to move some of his factories to more remote locations. The odds were improved the following year with the appearance of a long-range fighter, the P-51 'Mustang', that could escort attacking planes all the way to their target. By then, the lifting capacity of the average front-line bomber had also improved five- or even tenfold from what it had been early in the war. Most of the bombs that fell on Germany, by day or night, did so during the last year; which was also the year in which German aircraft production—overwhelmingly fighters—reached its peak. Whether this testified to the ultimate futility of the strategic air campaign, or to the disproportionate fear it inspired, would be hotly disputed once the smoke had cleared.

Such quibbling aside WW II effectively decided the question whether 'air power' was real or not. It remained to discover what kinds of institutional arrangements were best suited to make use of it. At first glance there was much in recent experience that argued against a firm distinction between air warfare and other kinds. The fact that people could no longer conceive of any major military operation that did not involve an air component seemed to many sufficient to justify the decentralized integration of air forces within armies and *navies. Against this temporizing view stood the previously unimaginable devastation of the strategic air campaigns, whose stunning climax in the skies over Japan seemed to have drawn a line under the military experiences of the past. The world had finally been made new, and air power had done it. When the USA, the only country to possess *nuclear weapons, decided in 1947 to place them in the hands of an independent air force (along with most military aircraft), a half-century of speculation about what air power would look like in its maturity seemed to have been settled.

Although nuclear weapons became the ultimate expression of aerial bombardment as an independent strategic force, it was the advent of intercontinental bombers and ballistic missiles that truly freed air power from its residual dependence upon the enabling actions of other services. They did so, however, at the cost of ensnaring it in the atavistic logic of the wonderfully apposite acronym MAD (mutually assured destruction), whose only rational purpose was to ensure that such weapons would never actually be used. By the middle of the 1950s, few doubted that air power could bring an end to civilization—which, in a sense, placed it in a category so special that it barely qualified as warfare at all.

Air advocates, even those most deeply committed to nuclear *deterrence as the air mission of the future, were not disposed to accept relegation to the remotest corner of the strategic universe. On the contrary, it seemed obvious that the warrant to wreak unlimited havoc from the air implied a claim upon less cataclysmic military missions as well. Curtis LeMay, COS of the USAF, did not hesitate to present strategic air power as the universal solvent of modern war, based upon doctrinal principles that, as he testified before Congress in 1961, had not changed since the formation of America's first Air General Headquarters in 1935. A few years later, when the call came to devise a bombing plan that would compel North Vietnam to cease undermining the independence of the South, it was a simple matter to devise a list of military, logistical, and industrial targets whose systematic destruction would rapidly bring the enemy to terms.

The strategic air campaign conducted by the USA in Indochina between 1964 and 1972 was the largest such effort in history and testified, if nothing else, to the exaggerated confidence that air power now inspired. Over half of all the money spent on the war by the USA was expended to conduct air operations, only about 20 per cent of which were linked to operations on the ground. The remainder were strategic strikes as traditionally defined, intended to coerce the enemy by degrading his military and economic infrastructure, demoralizing the population, and persuading the political leadership that it had more to gain by settling than by continued resistance. These efforts failed. Post-war analysis revealed that the material cost of conducting the air war far exceeded the value of the things it destroyed (human life excepted), without ever coming close to breaking the North's will to continue, or to denying it the physical means of supporting its forces in the South.

Airmen were quick to blame political considerations that limited their choice of targets, and prevented their attacks from developing sufficient intensity early in the war, before the enemy could take steps to disperse his population and build up his air defences. Critics responded that restrictions intended to avoid provoking Soviet or Chinese intervention were scarcely unreasonable in military terms; and that the political leadership of a democratic country, engaged in a war that did not threaten its existence, could not be indifferent to the stigma of having inflicted massive civilian casualties. Strategic air power, moreover, was by definition supposed to achieve not merely military, but political, results. Its purpose was to coerce political choices, and it was entirely logical that operational control should be shared by political experts.

Vietnam exposed the limits of air power theory as it emerged from WW II, without entirely discrediting it. Operationally, the much-admired capacity of air forces to attack logistical and economic targets became subject to more severe discounting. Demolishing the industrial infrastructure of a pre-industrial society accomplished less than had been imagined; while the logistical base of a revolutionary insurgency proved too attenuated to be struck by so blunt an instrument as an aerial bomb. Strategically, the vaguely speculative social psychology embedded within phrases like 'breaking the enemy's will' came in for closer scrutiny. In a totalitarian state like North Vietnam, where political decision-making was sustained by ideological passion, and insulated from public opinion, it was hard to know what level of suffering might be necessary to convince the government to call it quits—a consideration that had been obviated in WW II by the intention to compel unconditional surrender in any case. In Vietnam, by contrast, strategic bombardment was employed as a form of negotiation, and was regularly halted and restructured to support more conventional diplomatic efforts. Such a practice, although strictly reasonable in theoretical terms, proved profoundly demoralizing. Having escaped from the labyrinth of deterrence theory, American airmen found themselves trapped in a semiotic hall of mirrors.

From which, it may be added, they have not yet escaped. Despite the disillusionment of Vietnam, air power has remained the instrument of choice for the conduct of limited war by advanced democracies, if for no other reason than because it holds out some prospect of achieving useful military results with minimal own casualties. Whether the pulverizing Gulf war air campaign conducted by the USA and its allies against Iraq, following its invasion of Kuwait in 1990, would have counted as 'strategic' bombardment in the eyes of Curtis LeMay is difficult to say. Air operations in the Gulf were designedly part of an integrated, joint military campaign, rather than a free-standing enterprise. Yet normal tactical considerations dictated a protracted period of aerial bombardment at the start; and while it was underway it proved impossible, even for those most knowledgeable of military realities, to suppress the hope that the bitter cup of ground combat might somehow pass from them.

In such circumstances, the commitment of ground forces ceases to be a normal military act, implicit in the original decision to go to war, and becomes a discrete political moment with its own logic and consequences. This pattern has been strengthened by the development of *stealth aircraft and *precision-guided munitions, including highly accurate, pilotless cruise missiles, which have further reduced the risk of casualties to the side that employs them (and often to the other side as well). Such weapons have proven remarkably easy to use, to the point where they have become an almost predictable expedient of crisis diplomacy. Yet there is no evidence to suggest that the remarkable precision of modern aerial weapons extends to their political effects. On the contrary, weapons that are easy and painless to use are poor instruments for communicating resolve—though they may be effective in inspiring it in those on the receiving end. Although one should not be too quick to underestimate the coercive power of such methods, they remain subject to all the friction, uncertainty, and escalatory pressure that afflict war in any environment—a proposition that no serious student of air power would wish to dispute. DM

Boog, Horst (ed.), *The Conduct of the Air War in WW II: An International Comparison* (New York, 1992).
Clodfelter, Mark, *The Limits of Air Power: The American Bombing of North Vietnam* (New York, 1989).
Higham, Robert, *Air Power: A Concise History* (New York, 1972).
Kennett, Lee, *The First Air War, 1914–1918* (New York, 1991).
Mitchell, William, *Winged Defense: The Development and Possibilities of Modern Air Power* (New York, 1925).
Pape, Robert A., *Bombing to Win: Air Power and Coercion in War* (Ithaca, NY, 1996).
Sherry, Michael S., *The Rise of American Air Power: The Creation of Armageddon* (New Haven, 1987).

ground strafing and the use of bombs to attack enemy lines was widespread on all sides.

Aircraft types split into two distinct groups during this developmental period and this split effectively remains today. The Allies who had invested heavily in air-superiority fighters began using them in a dual role, as fighter-bombers. They were designated to attack enemy ground forces, but if necessary they could handle themselves effectively in aerial combat as well. Conversely, the Germans developed their BAS aircraft from their reconnaissance and escort models, essentially larger designs capable of carrying greater payloads of bombs, and often more rugged and better able to absorb anti-aircraft gunnery, but quite vulnerable to enemy fighters. Loss rates on CAS operations were always high, usually around 30 per cent.

In the inter-war period, the US army air service introduced a new range of aircraft, the 'attack' series, culminating in WW II in the Douglas A-20 Havoc. The Germans worked hard at integrating aircraft into ground operations, but co-operation was limited and despite success in 1939–42, only some 15 per cent of the Luftwaffe was designated for CAS. Only the Henschel Hs 123 biplane and the infamous Junkers Ju 87 Stuka proved adept at CAS, and they operated under a blanket of fighter protection, suffering heavily if they left it. The Soviets used ground-support aircraft in vast numbers, particularly the Ilyushin Il-2 Shturmovik. This was a rugged two-seater design, but although successful it was vulnerable to enemy fighters. It could only survive on the *eastern front because air strength was never widespread enough to preclude the use of dedicated CAS aircraft.

On the western front, the Allies took a different route, concentrating mostly on the use of fighter-bombers. The West relied heavily on air power to defeat the qualitatively superior German ground forces, employing fighter-bombers, dedicated CAS designs such as the A-20, and even heavy four-engined bombers to support their ground forces in the 1944–5 campaign. For the most part they were highly successful, despite having to learn a good deal as they progressed.

Post-war development rather stagnated as air forces concentrated on strategic roles. It was only in the 1980s that BAS in the so-called 'air–land battle' theory came back into vogue. Air units were to be co-ordinated by new high technology to stall enemy attacks and to disrupt and destroy the enemy's follow-on forces. Most CAS aircraft in the post-war world have been fighter-bombers, though they are in reality ground-attack (see FIGHTER) aircraft, and many do not maintain effective air-to-air combat capability. A few dedicated CAS types have persisted, such as the Sukhoi Su 25 Frogfoot, the Fairchild-Republic A-10 Thunderbolt (known as the Warthog), and of course helicopters such as the AH-64 Apache.

It should always be noted that for CAS aircraft to operate effectively they require friendly air superiority, especially if they are dedicated ground-attack aircraft or helicopters. Without such air cover they remain as vulnerable now as ever, perhaps more so with the advent of efficient and cheap surface-to-air *missiles. JB

Cooling, B. (ed.), *Case Studies in the Development of Close Air Support* (Washington, 1990).
Hallion, Richard, *Strike from the Sky* (Washington, 1989).

air transport The ability to move large amounts of military equipment and personnel around the globe by air offers many strategic and operational advantages, especially to those powers which consider themselves to have a world role. However, the potential has only slowly been realized and the development of true military transport aircraft with appropriate features only came to fruition in the 1950s.

Before 1918, aircraft were only used as transports in rare and exceptional circumstances, with improvised efforts having only limited success. However, after the cessation of hostilities, the major colonial powers began to recognize the potential of transport aircraft to link their enlarged empires together in an efficient and cost-effective manner. Aircraft facilitated the rapid deployment of troops and equipment to areas of unrest and maintained communications and links with largely inaccessible regions. Arguably the first purpose-built transport aircraft was the British Vickers Vernon which entered service in 1922, and replaced the Vickers Vimy bomber which had been used hitherto in a limited air transport role. The Vernon, and its successor the Vickers Victoria, were involved around the globe in policing, leafleting of civilians, and evacuation duties to name but a few. The French mirrored the British and used aircraft to forge links with North Africa in particular. In the early 1920s the USA purchased its first military transport aircraft, the T-2 from Fokker, a design which could carry 10,850 lb (4,925 kg).

However, the norm in the inter-war period was for large aircraft to be capable of fulfilling the role of both bomber and transport aircraft. In addition, many large aircraft of the period were either water-based aircraft such as flying boats, or were based on civil designs. This led to constraints being placed on the inclusion of transport aircraft features, such as large front or rear hatches, lowering doors, and a low-level cargo floor to facilitate loading and unloading of large pieces of equipment. The most famous of these inter-war types was the Junkers Ju 52 which performed a number of different tasks from bombing to the deployment of parachute troops. It was not particularly proficient at any task, but illustrated what could be done, most notably during the dropping of *airborne forces in 1940 and in MERCURY, the capture of *Crete in 1941. As a general workhorse the Ju 52 was invaluable, but it left a good deal to be desired as a transport aircraft.

The first aircraft to include many key transport features was the German designed Messerschmitt Me 321 Gigant introduced in 1941, which although a glider could boast a cavernous interior and large swinging doors in the nose. Up to 48,500 lb (22,000 kg) could be carried (three times the lift capacity of the Ju 52) including half-track vehicles, and 88 mm guns. The glider was superseded by a powered version, the Me 323, as well as a number of new designs, such as the Junkers Ju 352 and the Arado Ar 232. All developed the true transport aircraft still further.

The Allies produced large numbers of transport aircraft in WW II, most famously the *Dakota (Douglas C-47), but in essence this was a similar, although superior, aircraft to the Ju 52. Other transports developed the type more effectively, such as the Curtiss C-46 Commando and the Lockheed C-69 Constellation, though both still owed much to civil aircraft development. The use of *gliders in WW II should also be noted for these aircraft allowed the deploy-ment of troops and equipment in support of other airborne forces. As the war progressed the Allies in particular developed the role of airborne forces and the British introduced gliders such as the Airspeed Horsa and General Aircraft Hamilcar, both of which were used in Normandy and in the closing stages of the war. The Horsa could carry 25 fully equipped troops and the Hamilcar a 6.9 ton (7 tonne) *armoured car. The Americans developed the Waco CG-4a as their principal glider of which almost 14,000 were built.

However, the first fully fledged military transport aircraft was the Lockheed C-130 Hercules which appeared in 1954. This revolutionary design included all the major features of a transport aircraft, for example, a clear low-level cargo deck, large rear doors for loading/unloading and air-dropping of equipment, powerful engines, all-weather capability, and rough-field landing gear. The Hercules became the most widely adopted military transport aircraft and was used by 32 nations and was still in production a quarter of a century after it first appeared, with close on 2,000 having been built.

The most significant developments since have surrounded the introduction of much larger transport aircraft, most notably the Lockheed C-5A Galaxy and the Soviet Antonov An-22 Antei. Both of these designs are capable of very long range and are able to carry over 60 tons (62.8 tonnes) of equipment, including tanks. Such aircraft provided 'global reach' for the superpowers and allowed the Soviets in particular to ferry equipment and supplies to allies such as Ethiopia and *Angola, something which would have proved inordinately difficult with smaller and shorter ranged transports. In the post-*Cold War world, the Galaxy allows the Americans to move troops and equipment around the world to support the USA's global role in a manner with which no other power can compete. Global reach was enhanced in the post-war world by the development of airborne tanker aircraft and mid-air refuelling techniques, which have allowed much longer range and reach to smaller combat aircraft. The US initially reworked the B-29 bomber into the KC-97 of which some 888 were built, but then moved on to a jet-propelled tanker, the KC-135—a design based on the Boeing 707 airliner.

From the early colonial communications and policing roles, through the development of airborne forces, into the Cold War links with allies, and now into the 21st century, air transport has had and continues to have a significant place in the development of modern warfare.   JB

Chapman, Keith, *Military Air Transport Operations* (London, 1989).

Aisne, battle of the (1914). This marked the end of the brief *pursuit following German defeat on the *Marne, high water mark of their advance into France in 1914. The British Expeditionary Force (BEF), placed between the French Fifth and Sixth Armies on the Allied left, endeavoured to force its way across the Aisne, from south to north, on 13 September. That day set the pattern for what was to follow. The Germans, dug in on spurs looking down on the river, enjoyed artillery superiority, and the British infantry, attacking repeatedly with a bravery worthy of more realistic plans, could make little headway. The seizure of crossings was in itself a remarkable feat, but it soon became evident that both terrain and balance of forces made it impossible to dislodge the Germans. On 15 September *French recognized that 'it is no longer a question of pursuit, but of a methodical attack, using every means at our disposal and consolidating each position in turn as it is gained'.

Although French hoped to continue the advance when circumstances permitted, it was clear that the BEF lacked the strength to break the German position. The fighting settled down into *trench warfare, with the Germans now on the attack, but unable to dislodge the BEF. The weather was appalling, and German artillery made life unpleasant for the British. Meanwhile, both belligerents began to shift troops to the north-west (the 'Race to the Sea') in the hope of turning the enemy flank. French informed *Joffre, the French C-in-C, that a move to the north-west flank would shorten the BEF's line of communications and in early October the BEF left the Aisne for Flanders.   RH

Brown, Malcolm, *The Imperial War Museum Book of the Western Front* (London, 1993).

Edmonds, Sir James, *Military Operations, France and Belgium 1914*, vol. 1 (London, 1933).

Ajnadain, battle of (634), probably the first major engagement between the Byzantine forces defending Syria and Palestine, and the Arabs expanding northwards from the peninsula at the start of the Islamic conquests. Accounts differ on details of the battle, which took place on ?30 July between Jerusalem and Gaza, including the identity of the Arabs' leader. As many as 20,000 Arabs defeated a similar number of Byzantines. Ajnadain marked the start of a confrontation which ended in the battle of the *Yarmuk and the replacement of Byzantine with Arab hegemony in the region.   DWM

Donner, Fred M., *The Early Islamic Conquests* (Princeton, 1981).

Akbar 'the Great' (reigned 1556–1605), the greatest Mughal emperor of India. The foothold gained by Akbar's grandfather *Babur was lost by the latter's son Humayun, and the work of constituting Mughal authority in northern India fell to the 13-year-old Akbar. This he achieved by a prolonged series of military campaigns which unified all northern India under his rule. Firearms were now in general use throughout India, but notable was Akbar's use of individual, mobile gun carriages for his field guns instead of transporting them on carts to the battlefield and unloading them for static use.

A great centralizer, he was concerned to bring into the governmental structure both able Hindus, especially the *Rajputs, and the Muslim Turco-Afghan nobility. The *mansabdari* system provided civil and military officers with ranks in a hierarchy, involving the requirement to maintain a specified number of heavy cavalrymen. The holders of such ranks were supported by land grants, something like the *feudal system, and the whole system linked the *mansabdars* to the throne as the focus of loyalty and advancement. It made the Mughal army supremely powerful and effective for close on 150 years. Akbar was further a great patron of culture and a keen student of the various religious faiths in the subcontinent, while himself remaining a firm Muslim.   CEB

Irvine, William, *The Army of the Great Moguls* (London, 1903).

Richards, John F., *The New Cambridge History*, vol. 1.5. *The Mughal Empire* (Cambridge, 1993).

Smith, V. A., *Akbar, the Great Mughal* (2nd edn. Oxford, 1919).

Akkadian warfare The city of Akkad (Agade) became the centre of a great Mesopotamian empire for over a century (2300–2200 BC) as a result of the military energy of its greatest ruler Sargon (c.2334–2279). Although the site has not been identified with certainty, and no excavations have taken place, it was probably Akkad on the Tigris, lying just to the north of Lagash and Sumer, and came firmly in the orbit of *Sumerian warfare. This meant the employment of *phalanxes of infantry spearmen supported by ass-drawn *chariots. Sargon came to the region as the leader of a Semitic people, and had a major impact on a style of warfare that had grown up at the beginning of the third millennium BC. He subjugated the Sumerian peoples, as had former rulers, but he also expanded his frontiers along the Euphrates to conquer desert tribes on the edge of the Fertile Crescent. These peoples used the bow for hunting, and part of Sargon's genius was to adopt it for use in warfare. The only contemporary representation of a bow is seen on a stela depicting his grandson Naram-Sin. In addition to the traditional Sumerian city levies, Sargon created a 'professional' force of 5,400 men with which to pursue his warfare. This he did relentlessly, calling himself 'He Who Keeps Travelling the Four Lands' (meaning the known world), and claimed to have fought 34 wars in his half-century reign. In one year, he boasted of campaigning in what is now the Lebanon, Syria, and southern Turkey. As a result he created an empire that ran from the 'Lower Sea' (Persian Gulf) to the 'Upper Sea' (Mediterranean). He also led his forces across the Taurus and Amanus range into central Anatolia. In his empire building Sargon set the pattern for the kind of military state that endured for over a millennium. He created a professional force, trained and well equipped with the bow in addition to the usual Sumerian weapons. Such armies were flexible enough to operate in all kinds of terrain and against many different opponents. His own empire was conquered *c.*2000 BC by people known as the Ammurru or Amorites (a term meaning westerner) who came from northern Syria and established their power at Babylon.   MB

Hackett, Gen Sir John (ed.), *Warfare in the Ancient World* (London, 1989).

Yadin, Yigael, *The Art of Warfare in Biblical Lands* (London, 1963).

Alamein, battles of (1942), part of the *Western Desert campaigns in WW II. Alamein (or al-Alamayn) lies on the Egyptian coast some 60 miles (96 km) west of Alexandria. With the extremely inhospitable—if not impassable—Qattarah Depression lying just 40 miles (64 km) to the south, in summer 1942 Alamein took on vital strategic significance. The British Eighth Army, outperformed and pursued by Axis troops, sorely needed a defensive position, which could not be turned by the manoeuvrist *Rommel. The survival of the Eighth Army would depend on their defence of the Alamein Line, as would Allied hopes of halting Rommel's rapid advance to the Suez Canal.

In June 1942, having been defeated at *Gazala by Rommel's German-Italian army, and with the loss of *Tobruk on 21 June, *Auchinleck withdrew the Eighth Army to the Egyptian border. After the disastrous battle of Mersah Matruh, which it had been hoped would buy time to consolidate the defence of the Alamein Line, Auchinleck finally reached Alamein in early July. Rommel pursued Eighth Army throughout its withdrawal. However, his lines of communication were overextended and vulnerable to air attack. German fuel supplies could only be sent by sea, where they were also vulnerable to *interdiction. As a result, German formations arrived at the Alamein Line too weak to break through it.

Rommel conducted a series of attacks against the Alamein Line, but with no success. Auchinleck responded with attacks of his own. The first, the battle of Tell el Eisa (10 July 1942), was an attempt by XXX Corps (Ramsden) to turn the German position from the northern end of the Alamein Line. Ramsden deployed two divisions (1st South African and 9th Australian), both of which secured their immediate objectives. But Rommel prevented further penetration and disrupted the overall plan. The second Eighth Army attack—the first battle of Ruweisat (14–16 July 1942)—was orchestrated by XIII Corps (Gott). The New Zealand and 5th Indian Divisions took on two Italian divisions—Brescia and Pavia. The Germans counter-attacked successfully in support of the Italians and retook lost positions. The second battle of Ruweisat (21–3 July 1942) was a night attack which, although initially successful, was at once sealed off by a German counter-attack. In both the Ruweisat battles, co-ordination and co-operation between infantry and armour was ad hoc and inadequate to the task. Unwilling to contemplate further failures and losses, Auchinleck opted to regroup and rebuild his force.

In August 1942, at Churchill's insistence, Auchinleck was replaced by *Montgomery as commander of the Eighth Army, by now a somewhat demoralized force. The new commander set about turning Eighth Army into a confident, capable, aggressive, and successful force. The turning point for Eighth Army was undoubtedly the battle of Alam Halfa (30 August–7 September 1942), sometimes hailed as the first battle of Alamein. Montgomery's operational competence was displayed, as was his sense of caution and his reluctance to commit his forces unless conditions were overwhelmingly in his favour. Its attack blunted, the *Afrika Korps withdrew to regroup; but Montgomery refused to counter-attack and pursue. Instead, firmly in command of a confident force, which had tasted victory, he waited for his moment.

After much deliberation and disagreement among the Allies, it had finally been agreed that the 'Germany first' strategy should begin in autumn 1942 with an attack against Axis forces in the Mediterranean. The outcome would be TORCH, the Anglo-American landings in the western Mediterranean. Against this strategic background, Montgomery's moment arrived on 23 October 1942, when he launched the Eighth Army's 230,000 men and 1,030 tanks against Rommel's 100,000 men and 500 tanks. By 4 November 1942, the Afrika Korps had been routed. Days later, the TORCH landings took place in Morocco and Algeria, and, with the counter-offensive at *Stalingrad on 19 November, WW II changed its course.

Montgomery executed his attack on Rommel (who was on sick leave in Germany when the battle began) in three phases. In the first, the 'Break-In', XXX Corps (Leese) attacked the Axis defence in its centre, heavily fortified and defended by minefields; XIII Corps (Horrocks) attacked in the south. Neither XXX nor XIII Corps were able to break through to exploit the more open country to the rear of the Axis position. Montgomery's second phase—the 'Dog-fight'—therefore took place in the midst of the Axis position. Between 26 and 31 October Axis fortifications were steadily, and characteristically for Montgomery, reduced by *attrition. Axis counter-attacks were repulsed with the use of *air power. The final phase—the 'Break-Out'—took place between 1 and 4 November. The reinforced New Zealand Division drilled through the weakened Axis defensive position, making it possible for X Corps, which had been in reserve, to break out into the Axis rear. Counter-attacking constantly, the Afrika Korps was nevertheless unable to wrong-foot Montgomery and resist the torrent. Those German and Italian divisions which were mobile fell into a headlong withdrawal, leaving infantry divisions to surrender. On 23 January 1943, Eighth Army reached Tripoli.   PC

Alamo, siege of the (1836), the most celebrated episode in the Texas war of independence. The name 'cottonwood tree' was given to the walled compound of the secularized Franciscan frontier mission of San Antonio de Valero outside San Antonio de Bexar, the principal centre for Spanish settlement in Texas. In 1813, Spanish Governor Saucedo and his officers were killed after they had surrendered by Mexican rebels and Anglo adventurers, who were treated likewise by a Spanish expedition including then-Lt Santa Anna. In 1835, Gen Cos, the brother-in-law of Santa Anna, now president, surrendered the Alamo after a siege of 56 days. The scattered, mostly Anglo rebel forces were destroyed in detail when Santa Anna counter-attacked the following year, giving no quarter. A garrison of less than 200 with eighteen pieces of artillery under the command of Jim *Bowie and William Travis and including the legendary David *Crockett held the Alamo from 23 February to 6 March. All were killed during and after the final assault in which they inflicted more than twice their number of casualties. 'Remember the Alamo' was the battle-cry of the Texans at San Jacinto on 26 April, where Santa Anna was captured and the independence of Texas won.   HEB

Alanbrooke, FM Alan Francis, 1st Viscount (1883–1963).
Born and educated in France, Alan Brooke came, like so many other distinguished British soldiers, from an Ulster family. He was commissioned into the Royal Field Artillery in 1902, and during WW I became an artillery staff officer. His command of French enabled him to adapt French *barrage techniques to English practice, and he was instrumental in developing the 'creeping barrage' first used on the *Somme. Between the wars he held a series of key appointments, notably commandant of the School of Artillery at Larkhill on Salisbury Plain and director of military training.

He commanded II Corps of the British Expeditionary Force (BEF) in 1939–40, and distinguished himself in the retreat to *Dunkirk. C-in-C Home Forces in 1940–1, when invasion was expected, he replaced Dill as CIGS in Dec 1941 and held the post for the remainder of the war. It is hard to overestimate Alanbrooke's impact on British strategic policy. He was Churchill's principal military adviser, and it speaks volumes for his tact, willpower, and consummate professionalism that he was able to turn many of the PM's schemes into military reality, and to deter him from some—but by no means all—of the less realistic. He was scarcely less important in his dealings with other British and Allied commanders. Although he got on badly with Gen George *Marshall, his evident clarity of thought gained him grudging American respect. He was a good judge of men, and championed his protégés like *Montgomery and *Slim against Churchill. He remained one of the few senior officers for whom Montgomery, never an easy subordinate, had genuine regard.

He turned down the appointment of C-in-C Middle East in August 1942, feeling that he ought to serve on as CIGS.

But it was a personal disappointment that the post of supreme commander for the invasion of Europe went to *Eisenhower and not to him. He was a keen ornithologist, a passion which helped him cope with his ferocious workload. Promoted field marshal in 1944, and created baron in 1945 and viscount in 1946, Alanbrooke deserves to be regarded as one of the most significant figures in British military history. His diaries formed the basis for Arthur Bryant's books *Turn of the Tide* (1957) and *Triumph in the West* (1959), which were critical of both Churchill and Eisenhower.   RH

Fraser, David, *Alanbrooke* (London, 1982).

Alba, Fernando Alvarez de Toledo, Duke of
(1507–82), Spanish general, military innovator, and overseer of brutal repression in the Netherlands from 1567 to 1573. Alba began military service under Emperor *Charles V, aged 16, was made a general at 25, and commanded an army at 30. Although a fanatical Catholic, he fought against Pope Paul IV for Spain in 1556–7, as well as against German Protestants in 1546–8. He already enjoyed a distinguished military reputation when in 1566 he was ordered to put down the revolt in the Spanish Netherlands, now predominantly Protestant, following a wave of iconoclasm. Alba's careful study of military affairs had been as much theoretical as practical. He conducted more sieges than any general since Roman times, and avoided battle whenever the outcome looked uncertain. But, as Motley, the fiercely Protestant historian of the Dutch republic, observed, his 'thrift of human (his own troops') life was not derived from any love of his kind'.

In summer 1567 he arrived in the Netherlands at the head of a small but perfectly balanced army, comprising 10,000 picked veterans, each accoutred like a captain, 1,200 cavalry, and, to maintain the force's physical, rather than spiritual, health, 2,000 'courtezanes à cheval, belles et braves comme princesses' (courtesans on horseback, beautiful and courageous like princesses). On 22 August he was met by Count Egmont, a distinguished soldier and national champion of the Dutch Protestants. Alba began a scheme to entrap Egmont and his colleague Horn, who were tried and executed in June 1568. They need not have been a threat to Alba: their execution made them martyrs. Meanwhile, the papacy had passed the first judicial act of *genocide of modern times. On 16 February 1568 the entire population of the Netherlands—three million—was condemned to death as heretics apart from a few named exceptions. Ten days later, the Spanish King Philip II ordered Alba to carry out the sentence. In the terror which followed, the wealth of the prosperous merchants made them a particular target, and axe, rope, and fire consumed the natural leaders of Dutch society. Alba wrote to Philip coolly estimating the number to be executed after Holy Week 1568 'at eight hundred heads'. Alba is said to have admitted to personal responsibility for

18,600 executions during his six-year tenure—a plausible figure, but the additional number massacred with increasing barbarity by his troops is incalculable.

Faced with this reign of terror, the population had nothing to lose by armed resistance. In 1572 there was a general revolt in the northern provinces, the beginnings of the *Netherlands revolt, led by *William 'the Silent', Alba's great adversary. Alba was recalled to Spain in 1573 following a letter from William to King Philip outlining his crimes against humanity and demanding his removal. The bitter fighting in the Netherlands led to military changes which helped shape the appearance of modern professional armies in the next centuries. Alba replaced the hand-held firearm of the time, the arquebus, which still faced competition from the crossbow and longbow, with a bigger, heavier, longer-barrelled firearm which needed a supporting rest but which fired a massive ball of around an inch in calibre and would smash through body *armour, flesh, and bone as never before. It was the Spanish *mosquete*—the original *musket. The greater power and range of this weapon enabled infantry to deploy more thinly, beginning a process which would lead to the adoption of linear tactics in the next century.

On 18 December 1573 Alba left the Netherlands, never to return. On his return to Spain he was disgraced and imprisoned and only released, still under sentence, when an experienced general was needed to conquer Portugal in 1580. He died on 12 December 1582, not regretting his harshness in the Netherlands, but complaining of his royal master's ingratitude.   CDB

Albert I, King of the Belgians (1875–1934), C-in-C during WW I. Albert became king in 1909 and in 1914 most of Belgium was occupied by the army of his Hohenzollern relatives. He became the symbol of Belgian resistance to Germany. After the initial battles of 1914 the Belgians stayed on the defensive and Albert held the tiny strip of Belgium left to him, aloof from his French and British allies. However, in the final months of the war he commanded the Allied army group that broke out of the *Ypres salient.
                    GDS

Albigensian Crusades A series of military expeditions directed against the Cathar heretics of Languedoc between 1209 and 1226, and an example of a military conflict fuelled by both *religion and politics. In about 1172 the Cathars had been converted to absolute dualism by a mission of Bogomils from Constantinople. Unlike the mitigated dualists who explained the origin of evil as a fall from grace by the Devil, the absolute dualists accepted the existence of two co-eternal deities, one good, who presided over the spiritual realm, and one evil, who had created the material world. Predictably, papal efforts to find a solution to what it per-

ceived as a dangerous heresy were unsuccessful and, in 1208, when Peter of Castelnau, the papal legate, was murdered by a vassal of Raymond VI, Count of Toulouse, Pope Innocent III called a crusade. For this he could rely on the Augustinian argument that the use of force against religious deviation was justified both to protect orthodoxy and to compel heretics to abjure their errors for their own good. A largely northern army, led by Arnold Aimery, abbot of Cîteaux, the papal legate, captured Béziers and Carcassonne in July and August 1209, and imprisoned Raymond Roger Trencavel, the viscount. Most of the crusaders then returned home, leaving only a small force under *Simon de Montfort, Lord of Montfort l'Aumary. Montfort, nevertheless, overcame most of the opposition, and his campaign culminated in the defeat and death of Peter II, King of Aragon, at the battle of Muret (1213).

By this time the conflict had become largely a political struggle, for Peter of Aragon was no defender of heresy. When Raymond VI and his son were condemned as *fautors* of heresy in 1215, they began a new offensive. Montfort was killed while besieging Toulouse in 1218, so undermining the Crusade that by 1225 the count's lands had been regained. It took the intervention of the French King Louis VIII in 1226 finally to overcome southern resistance. In the Treaty of Pans, 1229, Raymond VII gave up approximately two-thirds of his lands and agreed to the marriage of his daughter, Jeanne, to one of the brothers of the king. The real victor therefore was the French crown, now able to extend its authority into Languedoc. Catharism remained influential, at least until the 1240s, when a combination of royal military intervention, northern settlement, and papal inquisitorial tribunals, slowly eroded its social base.   MCB

Wakefield, Walter, *Heresy, Crusade and Inquisition in Southern France, 1100–1250* (London, 1974).

---

alcazar (Sp.: *alcázar*, from Arabic: *al-Qaflr*, a palace or fortress). From the Umayyad period (661–750) there was a tradition of building fortified palaces in the Middle East, in both town and country. After the establishment of Umayyad family rule in Spain in 756, they began to develop the alcazar of Cordoba, immediately to the west of the great mosque, which served as the centre of administration until the 10th century when it was replaced by the palace-city of Madinat al-Zahra, some 9.3 miles (15 km) to the west of the old city. With the fall of the caliphate in the early 11th century, power shifted to provincial centres and alcazars were built for local rulers, notably the Aljafería of Saragossa which dates from the 11th century. Alcazars were also built in towns along the northern frontiers of Muslim Spain, notably at Mérida, where the 9th-century structure still survives, and at Toledo.

The alcazar at Toledo was founded in the 9th century by the Umayyads and became the palace of the Taifa kings of Toledo in the 11th century. After the Christian conquest of

1085, it became one of the main residences of the kings of Castile. Nothing remains of these early structures and the present massive, four-square castle-palace dates back to the reign of *Charles V. In 1936 the alcazar was held by nationalist rebels including military cadets under Col José Moscardó against government forces and, during an epic siege, most of the old structure was reduced to rubble. The massive replica of the 16th-century alcazar which now dominates the Toledo skyline has been reconstructed since the *Spanish civil war.   HK

---

alcohol The Cavalier poet Richard Lovelace testifies to the connection between military life and alcohol.

> Let others glory follow
> In their false riches wallow
> And in their grief be merry,
> Leave me but love and sherry.

In peacetime alcohol helped blur the boredom of *barracks life. British soldiers often drank themselves into insensibility in the 'wet *canteen'. As the 19th century went on reformers helped institute libraries and day rooms where tea and lemonade presented less risk, and the Army Temperance Society encouraged total abstinence. Officers and men on lonely garrison duty were especially vulnerable. The future Union general, *Grant, fell victim to drink in the Pacific Northwest, while in the Caucasus Lermontov's character Capt Maxim Maximich, drawn from life, warned: 'I've gone a whole year without seeing a soul, and if you once take to drinking vodka, you're done.'

Drink also played its part in the bonding process. Anglo-Saxon warriors boasted over their drinking-horns about the deeds they would perform in battle; Capt Stuart Mawson noted 'a subtle parade of manhood, an unconscious swagger in the manner of drinking' the night before his battalion dropped on *Arnhem in 1944, and Samuel Janney recalled how a night's drinking with his new platoon in *Vietnam 'definitely initiated me'.

But alcohol has played a more spectacular part on the battlefield. British soldiers campaigning in the Low Countries in the 16th century were so impressed by the effects of a nip of *genever* as to coin the expression 'Dutch courage'. *British civil war armies were well aware of it. In 1643 the parliamentarian governor of Gloucester was reported to give raiding parties 'as much wine and strong waters as they desired', and at Preston in 1648 Capt John Hodgson's men had martial zeal revived by 'a pint of strong waters among several of us'. The two French divisions which attacked the Pratzen plateau at *Austerlitz in 1805 had received a triple ration of brandy—nearly half a pint—per man: small wonder that they were reported to 'burst with eagerness and enthusiasm'.

Drinking helped calm pre-battle nerves. While the *forlorn hope waited to assault Badajoz in 1812, Maj O'Hare of the 95th Regiment confided to Capt Jones of the 52nd that he felt depressed. 'Tut, tut man!' replied Jones. 'I have the same sort of feeling, but keep it down with a drop of the cratur', and passed his calabash. As they endured filthy weather the night before *Waterloo, the British drank what they could. A footguards officer reported that with plenty of gin he was 'wet and comfortable', while the formidable prize-fighter Cpl John Shaw of the Life Guards rather overdid things and was killed the following day, fighting drunk, after hewing down several Frenchmen. Jack Vahey, regimental butcher of the 17th Lancers, spent the night before Balaclava in 1854 under guard because of over-indulging in commissariat rum, but the next morning he took part in the Charge of the Light Brigade in his bloody overalls, wielding an axe.

The British army issued rum in both world wars. Brig Gen James Jack argued that it was 'in no sense a battle dope'. It helped men endure the misery of the trenches: an officer told the 1922 War Office *Shell Shock Committee that he did not think the war could have been won without it. Col W. N. Nicholson agreed that rum made life more bearable, but thought that it also blunted the impact of battle and aided recovery from its shock. 'It is an urgent devil to the Highlander before action,' he wrote, '[and] a solace to the East Anglian countryman after the fight.' Rudolf Binding guessed that 50,000 Germans were the worse for captured drink during the offensive of March 1918, and Stephen Westmann complained that the attack was delayed 'not for lack of German fighting spirit, but on account of the abundance of Scottish drinking spirit'.

There was a similar pattern in WW II. John Horsfall, an officer in an Irish regiment, acknowledges that 'We simply kept going on rum. Eventually it became unthinkable to go into action without it.' Maj Martin Lindsay of the Gordon Highlanders saw some of his comrades get 'well rummed-up' and leave for an attack 'in a state bordering on hilarity'. A German infantryman said that 'There's as much vodka, schnapps and Terek liquor on the [Eastern] front as there are Paks [anti-tank guns] . . . Vodka purges the brain and expands the strength.' Alcohol was often home-made. Aqua-Velva aftershave could be mixed with orange juice to make a Tom Collins, and in both Italy and the Pacific copper piping from crashed aircraft was used by American soldiers to make stills for 'raisin jack' or 'swipe'.

Alcohol has played its part in promoting fighting spirit, but it is far from risk-free. It can inhibit clear thought. The royalist Capt 'Wicked Will' Hodgkins launched a successful raid on the parliamentarians but 'was so loaded with drink that he fell off by the way', and a parliamentarian gunner in the Lostwithiel campaign of 1644 was too drunk to reload his piece. It may provoke fighting frenzy, but is incompatible with the use of the sophisticated equipment: it was for this reason that the Royal Navy discontinued its rum ration. Lastly, exultation is followed by drop-off, and the combination of exhaustion and hangover is an unenviable one.

Yet alcohol is not without merits. Lt Col Alan Hanbury-Sparrow, an infantry officer on the western front, admitted: 'Certainly strong drink saved you. For the whole of your moral forces were exhausted. Sleep alone could restore them, and sleep, thanks to this blessed alcohol, you got.' Cdr Rick Jolly, a medical officer in the *Falklands war, noted that 'the traditional use of alcohol' helped stressed men sleep.

There seems no sign that armed forces' thirst for alcohol has disappeared. If there was little of it in the *Gulf war it was because of a rigid Saudi Arabian policy of prohibition, while in the (former) *Yugoslavia there have been many painful confrontations between tender constitutions and local slivovitz.   RH

Alesia, siege of (52 BC), the final defeat of the great *Gallic rebellion led by *Vercingetorix. The rebels (as always, in Julius Caesar's memoirs, outnumbering him) had fortified themselves in the hilltop stronghold of Alesia (modern Alise-Sainte-Reine). Caesar, with perhaps 45,000 troops, judged assault impractical, so decided to *blockade his enemy, constructing a massive series of fortifications to fence the Gauls in. The line of circumvallation was strengthened by 23 redoubts and 8 larger camps. The remains of this elaborate system have been traced by archaeologists. Before it was complete, Vercingetorix despatched his cavalry to return to their home tribes and muster a relief force, which Caesar absurdly claimed numbered 258,000. To guard against this threat the Romans constructed another line of fortifications facing outwards. A series of desperate combats developed as the defenders and the relief force attacked the Roman lines from both sides. The fighting became focused on a Roman camp positioned in a vulnerable spot and occupied by two legions. Caesar managed to hold the rest of his line while still concentrating enough reserves to hold this vital position. After the failure of this last assault the relieving army dispersed and Vercingetorix surrendered. He was led through the streets in chains when Caesar staged his formal triumph in Rome in 46 BC and then strangled, the customary fate of a captured enemy leader at the end of a Roman triumph.   AKG

Alexander, FM Harold, 1st Earl Alexander of Tunis (1891–1961), considered by *Churchill, his stalwart patron, to be the personification of the British officer and gentleman. *Liddell Hart said of him: 'he might have been a greater commander if he had not been so nice a man'.

The younger son of an earl, he was commissioned into the Irish Guards in 1911, won an MC and DSO in WW I, commanding a battalion in 1915 and was acting brigadier, aged 27, by 1918. In 1939, he led 1st Division to France and commanded I Corps during *Dunkirk. He narrowly avoided capture in *Burma in early 1942 and was appointed C-in-C Middle East that August, with *Montgomery under him. Later commanding the Eighteenth Army Group, he oversaw the destruction of the Axis forces in Tunisia and worked extremely well with *Eisenhower, the overall commander and another genuinely nice man.

Appointed Commander of Fifteenth Army Group, he directed the invasions of *Sicily and *Italy and the bloody battles at *Salerno, *Anzio, and *Cassino. Perhaps nobody could have done much better, but his conduct of the long slog up the Italian peninsula was illuminated by few signs of inspiration, while his failure to control Gen Mark *Clark, who rode into Rome in unopposed triumph rather than execute the encircling manoeuvre he was ordered to perform, stands as a clear example of the disadvantages of 'niceness' in command.

Promoted field marshal and appointed C-in-C Mediterranean in November 1944, he received the surrender of German forces in *Italy the following year and a viscountcy in 1946. Churchill appointed him governor general of Canada in 1946–52 and awarded him an earldom. He was also minister of defence in 1952–4.   APC-A

Nicolson, Nigel, *Alex: A Life of Field Marshal Earl Alexander of Tunis* (London, 1973).

Reid, Brian Holden (chapter) in John Keegan (ed.), *Churchill's Generals* (London, 1991).

Alexander 'the Great' (336–323 BC), son of Philip II and king of Macedon, was the greatest military commander of the ancient world; his achievements inspired envy and imitation from Roman generals such as *Pompey, *Caesar, and Trajan, and achieved legendary status in the Christian and Islamic worlds through the *Romance of Alexander*. The main surviving sources were written between 300 and 500 years after Alexander's death by the Greek authors Plutarch, who wrote a biography and also wrote two encomiastic essays; Arrian, whose history focuses on military action; and Diodorus and Curtius (Roman), whose interconnected accounts merit attention for preserving some darker aspects of Alexander's reign.

Aristotle was among his teachers and imparted a love for Homer as well as general intellectual curiosity. In 340 Alexander briefly served as royal regent, in 338 he led the decisive cavalry charge at *Chaeronea and, in spite of dynastic tensions in 337–336, he was the only serious candidate to succeed when Philip was assassinated in 336. Alexander at once consolidated his hold with characteristic energy: an important Macedonian enemy, the nobleman Attalus, was murdered, the Thessalians elected him as leader, and the Greek states in the League of Corinth recognized his hegemony. In 335 Alexander marched north to impose his authority over Balkan neighbours, demonstrating strategic skill, tactical resourcefulness in response to sudden challenges, and a desire to surpass all previous achievements. *Thebes rebelled during his absence, but his speed of movement disconcerted his Greek opponents; the Macedonians captured the city after fierce resistance and everything, except for temples and the house of the poet Pindar, was razed; survivors were sold into slavery. This severe treatment, which Alexander had his Greek allies confirm, cowed potential opponents such as Athens.

Alexander was now ready for the campaign against Persia which Philip had planned; Antipater remained in Macedon as regent and supervisor of Greek affairs. In 334 Alexander crossed the Hellespont with somewhat over 40,000 infantry and 5,000 cavalry; the crack troops were Macedonian, though there were also important units of Thessalian cavalry, and archers and javelin men from Crete and Thrace. His first undertaking was a pilgrimage to *Troy, part of his heroic image building: Alexander was the new Achilles (a maternal ancestor), to whom his companion Hephaestion played Patroclus. Military matters then impinged, and the local Persians were overwhelmed at the *Granicus. This allowed Alexander to dominate western Asia Minor, where the Greek cities welcomed their self-proclaimed liberator with mixed enthusiasm; Miletus attempted to remain neutral and was besieged, while the Persian garrison at Halicarnassus defended the citadel even after the loss of the lower town. As Alexander secured territory he ensured that Persian administrative arrangements were maintained, under Macedonian supervision, for financial and logistical reasons.

Alexander was now embarrassed by Persian supremacy at sea: his own naval forces were limited, since he could not rely on Athenian help; he focused on securing coastal cities but could do little to contain a Persian offensive in the Aegean during 333. The balance only shifted when the dynamic Memnon of Rhodes died and Darius recalled the Greek mercenaries to bolster his land army. In 333 Alexander rapidly traversed central Asia Minor, without imposing effective control on a marginal area, but was then detained in Cilicia by serious illness. The rout of Darius at *Issus in November left the whole of the Levant open to Alexander, and 332 was spent securing the cities of Phoenicia: Tyre, apparently safe on its island, only succumbed after a six-month siege which demonstrated all Alexander's considerable determination and skill; Gaza too held out bravely, and the black side to Alexander's heroic character was revealed in the mutilation of the gallant enemy commander. Control of the Levant brought with it the submission of the last Persian naval contingents. Alexander's final action before leaving the Mediterranean world was to visit Egypt, where he was recognized as pharaoh; more important for his image was the trip to the oracle of Ammon, located in the desert at the Siwah Oasis—stories about miracles during the desert crossing and the welcome and responses he received at the shrine were all intended to elevate him above the normal run of humanity.

In 331 Alexander turned east for the decisive confrontation with Darius at *Arbela. Victory opened up the Persian heartland: the capitals and treasuries of Babylon and Susa were occupied, and before winter Alexander forced his way across the Zagros range to reach the upland capital of Persepolis. In Caria and Egypt Alexander had already appointed locals as provincial governors, and this policy was now extended to his former Iranian enemies, though usually with Macedonian garrison commanders as overseers. In spring 330 Alexander left Persepolis, after burning the palace—symbolic revenge for the Persian destruction of the Athenian Acropolis in 480, but also a product of the excessive consumption of alcohol in which Macedonians frequently indulged. Alexander closely pursued the fleeing Darius, who was deserted and killed by his entourage; Alexander honoured the corpse, and set about establishing his succession to Darius as Lord of Asia by securing the northeastern satrapies: here Bessus, murderer of Darius, had proclaimed himself king and a protracted rebellion ensured tough campaigning in harsh conditions. Alexander was reasserting royal authority, but also exceeding the boundaries of predecessors' achievements, including those of his divine ancestor Heracles.

Alexander now encountered a series of challenges at court. In 330 Philotas succumbed to intrigue, and was adjudged guilty of treason for failing to report a conspiracy; his execution entailed the death also of his father Parmenio, loyal lieutenant of Philip and Alexander's second-in-command. Philotas may have been innocent, but his family had become disenchanted with the self-glorification of Alexander at the expense of other Macedonians; it also had jealous rivals at court. Macedonian resentment was increasingly fuelled by Alexander's progressive acceptance of oriental customs and dress. Tensions exploded in another drunken banquet after the 328 campaign season: Clitus the Black articulated the opposition of traditionalists to Alexander's innovations, and his increasing tendency to disparage Philip as his father in favour of divine parentage from Ammon. In drunken rage Alexander himself speared Clitus, but then collapsed in remorse. In 327 a further plot, this time involving the royal pages, was uncovered; the extension of oriental customs to include prostration was a key factor. The culprits were stoned to death and Callisthenes, the court historian, who was alleged to have encouraged them, was also killed.

In 326 Alexander advanced into India, again with a tenuous claim to reassert Persian control, with support from the ruler of Taxila. King Porus failed to prevent the crossing of the *Hydaspes, and victory appeared to open the route eastwards towards the Ganges, but at the Hyphasis (Beas) the long-suffering troops eventually mutinied: monsoon rains and rumours of powerful kingdoms demoralized them, and Alexander was forced to abandon plans to reach the ocean via the Ganges. Reluctantly instead he turned south down the Indus and, in some of the most bloodthirsty campaigning of a gory career, overwhelmed various tribes. Among the Malli he received a serious chest wound, and the danger to his life produced an outpouring of loyalty from his troops.

From the mouth of the Indus Alexander returned west; part of the army was dispatched by a northern route, and Nearchus was appointed to sail the fleet up the Persian Gulf, while Alexander himself marched directly across the Gedrosian Desert (Makran)—rivalry with predecessors was again the spur: in a rare lapse Alexander's *commissariat failed to respond to the enormous challenge, and there were severe losses, particularly among the camp followers. Back in the Persian heartland, Alexander turned to administrative matters neglected during his long absence, but also prepared for future campaigns: geographical discovery on the Caspian, conquest of Arabia because the inhabitants refused to worship him, and probably an attack on Carthage. His army was remodelled with the honorific discharge of numerous veterans and the incorporation of Persians trained in Macedonian ways: these developments provoked a fresh *mutiny by the Macedonians, who felt they were being abandoned. Death anticipated full implementation of these developments. Hephaestion had already died in Iran in autumn 324, and Alexander succumbed at Babylon in June 323; circumstances prompted rumours of poisoning, but apart from repeated wounds his constitution had also been undermined by heavy drinking. There was no obvious successor, though his Bactrian wife Roxanne was pregnant and soon produced a son. Within two years the empire was rent by conflicts between the powerful successor generals, whose ambitions had only been repressed by their devotion to the authority of Alexander. The *Macedonian army was the key to Alexander's success; his courage, endurance, and sharing of sufferings merited its loyalty. There were few breaks in the hard fighting, but the Macedonians enjoyed their profession and responded to their leader's talent and charisma.   LMW

Bosworth, A. B., *Conquest and Empire* (Cambridge, 1988).
Fuller, J. F. C., *The Generalship of Alexander the Great* (London, 1958).
Lane Fox, R., *Alexander the Great* (London, 1973).

Alexander's successors (Diadochi) were a group of generals who fought for control of his empire after his premature death in 323 BC. They were, with the exception of Eumenes, drawn from the Macedonian military aristocracy. All had fought under Alexander; they were ruthless and veteran military leaders. Prominent among them were Antigonus 'the One-Eyed' and his son Demetrius Poliorcetes—whose descendants would become kings of Macedon—Lysimachus, Antipater, Cassander, Polyperchon, Ptolemy—later king of Egypt—and Seleucus—founder of the Seleucid dynasty which came to control the Syrian and Iranian parts of the Alexandrian empire.

The wars these men fought fell into four main phases. First, in the immediate aftermath of Alexander's death a series of confused campaigns were fought as numerous generals jockeyed for position. Secondly, Antigonus and Demetrius fought an extensive and successful campaign for control of Syria and Mesopotamia against Eumenes which culminated in the battles of Paraitakene (317 BC) and Gabiene (316 BC). Thirdly, Greece and western Asia Minor were the scene of interminable conflicts dominated by small actions and sieges, in which Cassander and Polyperchon were eliminated from the contest. Finally, Seleucus and Ptolemy put paid to Antigonus' dreams of reuniting the empire under his leadership at Gaza (312 BC) and the decisive *Ipsos (301 BC). These wars set the political scene in the Hellenistic east until the conquest of the region by Rome, Greece divided between competing city states and leagues and three large Macedonian-dominated monarchies, Macedon, Egypt, and the Seleucid empire.

Militarily developments saw the Macedonian style of war based on the long-spear-armed *phalanx and aristocratic lance-armed charging cavalry reaffirmed as the dominant tactical system of the eastern Mediterranean and Near East. Added to it were certain native traditions—such as missile armed infantry and cavalry—and the widespread use of the elephant. The size of armies grew rapidly in response to the military needs of the combatants; they were, however, unreliable and battles were often decided by cavalry actions on the flanks, as at Gaza and Ipsos, where infantry centres surrendered once outflanked. There were also major developments in fortification with the rapid evolution of larger and more complex defences for cities and fortresses. In response siege technology leapt forward with the development of ever larger and more effective equipment, such as mobile towers and catapults.   SWN

Algeria, French conquest of (1830–57). In 1827 the dey of Algiers struck the French consul round the face with a fly-whisk. The dey ruled a small unstable state: half of his 28 predecessors were said to have met violent ends. He, like the neighbouring rulers of Constantine, Oran, and Medea, were nominally subject to Turkey, but the activities of pirates on the North African coast had already provoked European and American intervention. Inland, the deys had no authority over the proud and warlike Berber tribesmen. Not only were French merchants heavily involved in trade with Algiers, but the government of Charles X scented an opportunity to gain domestic popularity by foreign adventure, and in June 1830 a French expeditionary force landed at Sidi Ferruch, marched on Algiers, and took it a week later. This success did little for Charles X, who abdicated on 2 August.

As the French moved inland they were fiercely opposed by the tribes, and *Abd al-Qadir, emir of Mascara, led three major risings. In 1836 Gen Thomas Bugeaud was sent to command in Algeria, and the success of the French campaign owed much to his efforts. In 1844 he defeated Abd al-Qadir's Moroccan allies at Isly, though the emir himself did not *capitulate until 1847. Bugeaud lightened the equipment of his troops, forming 'flying columns' which pushed deep into the hinterland under able subordinates like Cavaignac, Changarnier, and Lamoricière.

If resistance to invasion was weakened by factionalism, it was nonetheless determined. In 1836 a French assault on Constantine was beaten off, and the following year the city fell only after a week of bitter house-to-house fighting and the death of Gen Damrémont, the French commander. It was a vicious war, and French methods could be brutal. *Razzia* (raids) and pillage were standard tactics, and Pélissier, one of the heroes of the conquest, asphyxiated some 600 civilians who had taken refuge in a cave. Yet Bugeaud was as much pacifier as conqueror. He used public works to help reconcile the tribes he had beaten, and the raising of local units, forerunners of French African troops like *spahis and *zouaves, who were to distinguish themselves on many battlefields, helped provide warlike men with a martial outlet. White colonists, many of them ex-soldiers, moved in behind the fighting: there were 109,000 of them by 1847. The whole of Algeria was not physically occupied until 1857, and complete pacification was not achieved before 1881.   RH

Algerian independence war (1954–62), one of the most bitter post-war conflicts fought between former colonizers and nationalists. From 1945 onwards there was growing tension between the *colons* or *pieds noirs*, as the settlers were known, and the longer-established Muslim majority, many of whom hoped that their support for France during WW II would bring political concessions. In March 1954 Ahmad Ben Bella, a former NCO in the French army, together with another eight Algerian exiles, formed the revolutionary committee which later became the National Liberation Front (Front de Libération Nationale, FLN) in Egypt. From November 1954 the FLN, using bases in neighbouring Tunisia, launched co-ordinated strikes on public buildings, communications installations, police, and military posts, in its first real bid for Algerian independence. *Guerrilla attacks escalated over the following two years, compelling the French to reinforce. Ultimately, although Algeria was considered to be constitutionally part of France, 400,000 French troops were stationed there to support French rule.

The FLN strategy, which combined the guerrilla warfare of *Abd al-Qadir with provocative acts of *terrorism, was met by the French *doctrine of *guerre revolutionnaire, developed following experience against the Vietminh in *Indochina. Indiscriminate kidnapping and killing of Europeans, Muslim supporters, and non-activists by the FLN elicited brutal 'counter-terrorist' measures from the French military. Remote villages in pro-FLN areas were raided and their inhabitants butchered. By 1956 warfare had spread to Algiers, where FLN targets included schools, shops, and cafés, striking at the heart of *colon* society. Again, French suppression was ruthless and effective. Gen Jacques Massu's 10th Colonial Parachute Division won 'the battle of Algiers', effectively wiping out the FLN infrastructure there albeit at the price of resorting to torture which diminished France's standing in the world and the army's in French society. Outside the cities, suspect or vulnerable groups were relocated to 'model villages' and electrified fencing and fortified posts were strung along Algeria's borders with Tunisia and Morocco to stop infiltration. While largely conscript garrison units held down the countryside—their action was likened to that of a wet blanket over a fire—élite units of the general reserve, making increasing use of *helicopters, mounted specific actions against insurgent forces.

Although effective in the short term, French military action was unable to provide a satisfactory political solution. France was under growing pressure from the international community and the war was generally unpopular at home. The war was more complex than a simple struggle between nationalists and colonialists. There was a political struggle for the middle ground in Algeria; a civil war among Muslim Algerians themselves (many of whom fought bravely for the French); a dispute within the FLN's leadership; and a battle, in the wider world, for international support. The conflict also induced elements of the French army, influenced by settler opinion, to oppose their own government. On 13 May 1958 French officers in Algeria rose against their government, an action which brought *de Gaulle to power. However, once in power he offered self-determination by referendum, a move which forced dissenting officers underground and the creation of the Organisation Armée Secrète (OAS).

Unsuccessful military revolts against de Gaulle were mounted in 1960 and again in 1961. However, the bulk of the army remained loyal to the government, with the notable exception of some parachute and legion units, though France was perilously close to civil war. The OAS continued attacks against both the FLN and French authorities. In March 1962 a ceasefire was agreed between the FLN and the government at Evian in France. This resulted in a mass exodus to France by the *colons* and by the year's end the majority had departed to the mainland.

Independence was achieved on 3 July 1962 with Ahmad Ben Bella as premier. The FLN offered full civil rights and protection to the *colons* who chose to remain. France in turn ceded the commercially developed oil-rich Sahara and established an aid programme to counter the damage of the eight-year war. The devastation to Algeria was immense. In human terms the cost was high: French casualties were around 100,000 to 1 million Algerian, with a further 1.8 million displaced. Things were particularly bad for the Harkis, Muslims who had supported the French, and about 150,000 of them were killed in post-ceasefire revenge attacks.

The war in Algeria marked the *French army, which was to take many years to recover from the strains of the fighting and, even more significantly, the internal divisions it produced. Many of the returning *pieds noirs* felt betrayed, while Muslims who had supported France and were fortunate enough to escape there found their loyalty ignored, and eked out a poverty-stricken existence: their children, often alienated and without hope, constitute the last casualties of this bitter war.   PMacD

Horne, Alistair, *A Savage War of Peace: Algeria 1954–1962* (London, 1977).

Allenby, FM Edmund Henry Hynman, 1st Viscount of Megiddo and Felixstowe (1881–1936),

British cavalry general plucked from the inconclusive battles on the western front in April 1917 and who, given his head, achieved brilliant success against Turkish forces in Palestine in 1917–18. An imposing and intimidating figure, Edmund Allenby (nicknamed the 'Bull') was commissioned into the Inniskilling Dragoons in 1882, and saw action in several minor colonial wars of the 1880s. As with so many British Great War commanders, it was his performance in the Second *Boer War that established his military reputation and destined him for higher things. From column commander in South Africa he graduated to command the 5th Lancers, 4th Cavalry Brigade, and then became inspector general of Cavalry in 1910. He commanded the Cavalry Division in August 1914 with mixed success, and on the arrival of a second cavalry division, was given command of the Cavalry Corps, whose defence of Messines Ridge during the first battle of *Ypres did much for his reputation. He was promoted to lead Third Army in October 1915, and survived the *Somme (only two of his divisions attacked at Gommecourt on the battle's first day), but shared the inability of his colleagues to grasp offensive operations on the western front at *Arras/Vimy Ridge in April 1917. After a promising start Third Army made relatively little progress, and, much to his irritation, he was sent to command British and Commonwealth forces in Palestine, following the sacking of Gen Murray for failing to take Gaza in March and April 1917.

Arriving on 28 June, Allenby immediately reorganized his command with energy and flair—perhaps there was never the opportunity or incentive to do so in France—and soon showed skill denied him by *trench warfare. While he feinted a frontal attack on *Gaza at the end of October, his Desert Mounted Corps of horsed and camel units mounted a surprise right-flanking attack on *Beersheba. Attacking out of the desert, they began to roll up the enemy flank and forced the general retreat of the Turkish forces. From Gaza, Allenby moved north and entered Jerusalem on 11 December. Lack of reserves robbed Allenby of the ability to take the offensive again until 19 September 1918, when he attacked at *Megiddo. In an almost modern battle, using a combination of surprise, artillery bombardment, and air attack, he paralysed the *Turks and blasted a 5 mile (8 km)

gap in their lines, through which his XXI Corps poured to roll up the coast. His personal drive was echoed by his troops. By 1 October Damascus had fallen, and during a relentless *pursuit over 360 miles (579 km), his men took 76,000 prisoners for 5,000 casualties, and forced Turkey to sue for peace on 30 October.

Though he had failed to shine in France, Allenby's tactical skill was demonstrated by his success after the failure of Dobell and Murray at Gaza, and at Megiddo. He was lucky to be moved to Palestine, where his cavalryman's feel for manoeuvre could be rewarded, and exploited the opportunity offered to the fullest degree. Fortunate to be able to operate without *Haig or *Lloyd George breathing down his neck at every turn, this relative freedom may have inspired his operational skill. His hard-won successes in Palestine won him his field marshal's baton and a peerage in 1919, but he never ceased to mourn the loss of his only son Michael, an artillery officer, on the western front.

APC-A

Almansour, Muhammad (952–1002). Abi ëmir, correctly known as Al-Manßür ('the Victorious'), was the last ruler of Muslim Spain to pose a threat to the survival of the Christian kingdoms. Born into an ancient but not powerful Arab family from Algeciras, he began his political career in the household of the wife of the Umayyad Caliph al-akam II (961–76). When the caliph died, his son and heir Hisham was only 8 years old and within three years of ruthless manoeuvring, Almansour had disposed of his rivals and made himself effectively military dictator.

He used his position to launch attacks on the Christian north almost every year until his death in 1002. These attacks were certainly damaging and they culminated in the sack of Santiago de Compostela in 999, but no attempt seems to have been made at systematic conquest or occupation of new territory. Their purpose was partly propaganda, to establish his reputation as a leader of the *jihad and so justify his effective usurpation of power. When he died, the Christians had survived the onslaught and within a decade were on the offensive in the beginnings of the *Reconquista. Almansour, on the other hand, by undermining the prestige of the Umayyad dynasty, had paved the way for the long-term fragmentation and defeat of Muslim Spain. Even his enemies acknowledged that he was a fine natural warrior. It was said that on returning from campaign each year he would have his mail shirt shaken out over a chest, so that he could eventually be buried in the dust of all his campaigns. A lofty peak overlooking the Tagus bears his name.

HK/RH

Almanza (Almansa), battle of (1707), best remembered for the fact that the British-Allied army was commanded by a Frenchman, the Huguenot Henri de Massue

de Ruivigny, Earl of Galway, and the Franco-Spanish army by an Englishman, James FitzJames, Duke of Berwick, illegitimate son of *James II and Arabella Churchill—and thus the Duke of Marlborough's nephew. But it was a decisive battle in its own right. There was extensive campaigning in Spain during the War of the *Spanish Succession, and it proved as detrimental to the Allied war effort as it was to Napoleon's a century later. In 1705 the Earl of Peterborough captured Barcelona, the following year Galway took Madrid. He was outmanoeuvred by the capable Berwick, gave up Madrid, and fell back to the coast to retain the support of the fleet. On 25 April 1707 Galway, with a British, Dutch, and Portuguese force, advanced on Berwick at Almanza, between Albacete and Alicante. Although things went well at first, the Portuguese on Galway's right broke, and Berwick seized the opportunity to outflank and encircle the survivors. Despite the valour of Galway's British contingent—the 6th and 9th Foot bore themselves especially well—almost all Galway's 15,000 men were killed or captured. The battle led to the Allied claimant to Spain, the Archduke Charles, losing all except Catalonia, and left the French claimant, Philip V, secure on his throne.   RH

Alpini Italian *mountain troops. There were eight regiments in 1914, and their members wore a jaunty hat with a feather.

Alvarado, Pedro de (1485–1541), ruthless right-hand man to *Cortés in Mexico and conqueror of Central America. Left in charge of Tenochtitlán in 1520, his brutality sparked a temporarily successful Aztec revolt. He led an expedition into Maya country, allying with the Cakchiquel against the Quiché and then turning on them in campaigns whose savagery even fellow *conquistadores found remarkable. He founded the first Guatemala City (now Antigua) in 1524 and in 1527 returned to Spain to be confirmed as governor (*adelantado*). In 1534–5 he led a 'poaching' expedition to Quito (now Ecuador), but when confronted by Pizarro's lieutenant Almagro he sold his ships and equipment and returned to Guatemala. Although his rule was marked by desperate revolts and illegal slave trading, the Spanish crown again confirmed him as governor during a 1537 visit and authorized him to explore the Pacific. He built a fleet and prepared an expedition but was persuaded instead to pursue the chimera of the 'Seven Cities of Cibola' in northern Mexico. He became involved in the suppression of an Indian revolt and was crushed to death by a horse near modern Guadalajara. A year later his widow and successor died in an earthquake that destroyed Antigua.   HEB

Alvinczy, FM Josef Freiherr von (1735–1810). The Transylvanian-born Alvinczy had first seen action in the

*Seven Years War, and by the time of his service in the *French Revolutionary wars he was an experienced field commander who had performed sterling service against the *Turks. He was present at the Austrian victory of Neerwinden in 1793 with Prince Friederich of Saxe-Coburg. In Italy he faced the young Gen Bonaparte, but despite a courageous defence he proved unable to adapt to the new way of war and was decisively defeated at *Arcola on 15–17 November 1796 and Rivoli on 14 January 1797, where he lost half his army and left the French in possession of northern Italy. He was then replaced by Archduke *Charles, the Austrian emperor's brother.   TM

ambulances The transport of sick or wounded forms an important element of the organization of military *medicine, and its efficiency directly affects survival rates. An ambulance is effectively any vehicle designed for the transport of the ill or the injured. However, in the military context the term can also be used to encompass vehicles primarily designed for another purpose and either adapted, or pressed into service, to transport casualties. Such movement might either be from the field of combat to a local treatment centre, for example a Regimental Aid Post (RAP) or from a RAP to a Field Hospital. The transportation of the wounded between one hospital and another, or from a hospital to the safety of a rear area facility, is largely dependent on available resources and the distance to be covered. During the *American civil war, rail transport became available for this type of movement, and *railways continued to remain an important means of casualty evacuation at this level throughout 20th-century wars in Europe and elsewhere.

Prior to the advent of motor vehicles, casualty evacuation and transportation was largely reliant on horse- or oxen-drawn vehicles. Litters, pack animals, and handcarts were also used to remove wounded from the battlefield, in fact generally anything that increased a man's chances of survival was considered, occasionally leading to the unusual, such as the French use of dogcarts during WW I. During the *Napoleonic wars the French surgeon *Larrey played an important part in developing military ambulances.

The use of straw as a means of preventing further injury and providing a modicum of comfort for the injured soldier, was widely utilized before suspension was introduced to wagons. Straw had the additional advantage of soaking up fluids that would otherwise be circulating either around the bodies or on the floor of the vehicle, in the days before the nature of contamination and cross-infection were understood.

In addition to stretcher mountings secured to a resilient base, in order to prevent jarring the wounded, modern military ambulances are equipped with many of the up-to-date devices of their civilian counterparts. Such gear would normally include blood-transfusion apparatus and oxygen-inhalation sets. While civilian ambulances in the main are built for speed and a smooth ride along metalled roads, their military equivalents more often have a cross-country ability and a larger carrying capacity. The most commonly used military 4 × 4 and 6 × 6 vehicles have ambulance variants and these may carry from three stretcher-cases or five 'walking wounded' casualties upwards. The nature of *armoured warfare has led to tracked ambulances, based on the *APCs of their respective army, which offer protection against *small arms and support weapons fire, as well as blast or *chemical and biological attack. The use of this type of vehicle allows ambulances to deploy with tanks and other armour, when wheeled transport would be unsuitable.

The most effective means of casualty evacuation in current use is the *helicopter. In recent years civilian 'air ambulances' have played an important role in the emergency treatment and transportation of injured patients, a method first exploited on any scale by US armed forces during the *Vietnam war. Today purpose-equipped 'medevac/casevac' helicopters are employed by all modern western armies enabling, where the tactical situation allows, casualties to be moved quickly from combat directly to secure areas where surgeons and other treatment specialists await them.

PMacD

American civil war (1861–5), the most important event in the history of the USA. It resulted from a fundamental disagreement between two sections, North and South, about the place of chattel slavery in the Union. Without the slavery question there would have been no war. The southern emphasis on 'states rights' was essentially a coded phrase for the defence of slavery. By the 1840s a pro-slavery ideology had grown up in the Deep South which argued that slavery was a positive good and by 1860 this had become popular throughout the entire South and imbued it with a strong feeling that the slave states enjoyed a unique culture. Increasing numbers of secessionists claimed that this culture could only be protected by gaining independence. The war itself was detonated by the refusal of the slave states to accept the decision of the 1860 presidential election, which had seen the first Republican candidate, Abraham *Lincoln, sweep the northern states but did not gain a single electoral vote in the South. From December 1860–February 1861 seven states in the Deep South passed ordinances of secession, occupied federal installations, and called out their militias. These states set up their own Confederacy with a pro-slavery constitution headed by a Confederate president, Jefferson *Davis, and this new government located its capital initially at Montgomery, Alabama. The rebel government was eager to remove the two remaining federal outposts on their territory, at Pensacola in Florida and at Fort Sumter in Charleston harbour. After a stand-off

lasting four months, the Confederacy bombarded the latter on 12–13 April 1861.

President Lincoln responded by issuing a proclamation calling for 75,000 volunteers for three months to suppress a rebellion against federal authority. Virtually all participants believed that the conflict would be short. Perhaps it would have been if the seceded states had remained only seven in number; however, four important states of the Upper South, Virginia, Tennessee, North Carolina, and Arkansas, seceded rather than co-operate in the 'coercion' of their sister slave states. They added not only to the Confederacy's population and territory but also to its sparse industrial resources. However, geography placed Virginia and Tennessee especially in the very front line should military operations escalate. So large was the Confederacy that a number of influential figures doubted whether it could be physically occupied and placed their hopes in the naval *blockade which was announced on 19 April. Certainly, the South's geographical advantages added to a prevailing sense of overconfidence that independence could be achieved easily.

A widespread belief in a short war was buttressed in the North by an awareness of a great disparity in resources. The total population of the USA in 1860 was 31,443,321. Of these the population of the southern states was 8,726,644 (of whom 3,953,760 were slaves). The Border States (Kentucky, Maryland, and Missouri) had a population of 3,588,729. Throughout 1861–2 ensuring the loyalty of the Border States remained a top priority for the Lincoln administration. Should secession be limited to eleven states then the northern states could mobilize 4 million fighting men to the Confederacy's 1,100,000. The industrial disparity was even greater. The states of Massachusetts and Pennsylvania alone produced more manufactured goods than the entire Confederacy. The South could produce sufficient food to feed itself but lacked the means to transport it. In 1860 only 9,000 miles (14,481 km) of the American total of 31,000 miles (49,879 km) of railway track could be found in the South, and southern engineers had completed only nine of the 470 locomotives built before 1860. Yet a material disparity in itself does not guarantee victory and Lincoln's main problem was in mobilizing and organizing the great resources available to him for waging war.

The secession crisis had generated the largest arms race yet seen in North America. In the North the 75,000 volunteers were soon supplemented, and by 1 July 1861 300,000 men had been raised, the majority for three years. Jefferson Davis had succeeded in raising 200,000 Confederate volunteers by August 1861. These hosts on both sides were difficult to command. The men believed that they were civilians in uniform and enjoyed all their previous rights; they were not deferential to their officers, who were often elected. Many incompetents had to be weeded out by commissions boards over the next year. Important politicians, such as John C. Frémont, Benjamin F. Butler, and Nathaniel P. Banks, were awarded generals' commissions. Consequently, armies on both sides were subject to political influences, but especially those Union forces that were encamped near Washington, known by the summer as the Army of the Potomac, because the process of congressional and presidential elections continued unabated despite the war.

Political pressure helped shape the first campaign. The elderly general-in-chief, Winfield *Scott preferred to launch a well-prepared campaign in the Mississippi basin relying on the economic strangulation of the South. This concept was strategically sensible but was unacceptable to public opinion because it would work slowly. The press dubbed it the 'Anaconda Plan'. The power of the press and propaganda was potent throughout the conflict. In the spring of 1861 the Confederacy decided to move its capital to Richmond, Virginia, a mere 100 miles (161 km) from Washington. A clamour developed that the federal army should move 'on to Richmond'. The result was an advance towards Centreville and a Confederate defensive victory at first *Bull Run. However, Confederate forces were disorganized by their success and could not exploit it. *McClellan was appointed to command the Army of the Potomac and began an energetic programme of consolidation, reorganization, and training. In November he replaced Scott as general-in-chief and became overburdened by his dual

role. The first lull in the eastern theatre ensued, but this brought immense political dissatisfaction with the war's conduct and culminated in the creation of the Congressional Joint Committee on the Conduct of the War on 20 December 1861. This body was highly critical of McClellan's conciliatory policy, which stressed that the war aimed at the restoration of the Union and not the destruction of slavery.

Despite rising discontent with 'champagne and oysters on the Potomac'—a sarcastic reference to McClellan's penchant for elaborate reviews of his troops, the federal government made rapid progress in suppressing the Confederacy by the spring of 1862. Indeed by March of that year it looked as if the optimistic view that the civil war would be short was the right one. A series of successful *amphibious operations on the coastal littoral of the Carolinas was followed by the seizure of New Orleans (the greatest city in the Confederacy) on 24–5 April 1862. An early Confederate victory at Wilson's Creek, Missouri, in August 1861 was followed by crushing Union victory at Pea Ridge, Arkansas, 6–8 March 1862 which made incursions into the south-west possible. In Tennessee, *Grant seized Forts Henry and Donelson, which led to the fall of Nashville on 25 February 1862. The Confederate forces, commanded by Albert Sidney Johnston, launched a counterstroke and took

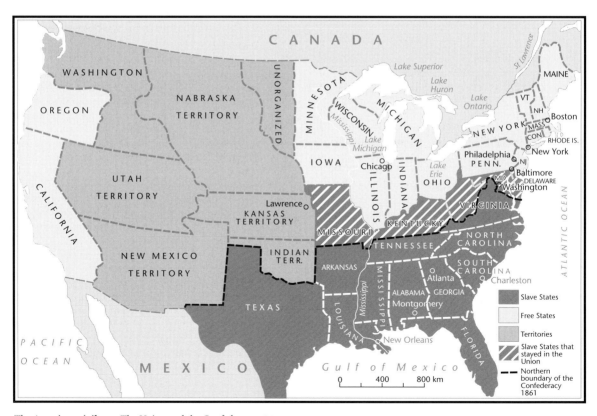

The **American civil war**: The Union and the Confederacy, 1861.

Union troops by surprise at *Shiloh on 6 April, Grant recovered, parried the Confederate blows, and then threw in a counter-attack in co-operation with Don Carlos Buell's Army of the Ohio. This success enabled the overall commander in the west, *Halleck, to concentrate 130,000 men and occupy Memphis.

But appearances were deceptive and the war was actually taking the form that would prevail for a further three years. Although military operations took place in the areas west of the Mississippi, and in Arkansas, there were three central theatres of operations: first, the west centred in western Tennessee and Mississippi, where the Union attempted to complete its stranglehold of the Mississippi basin; second, eastern Tennessee and Kentucky, focused around the railway junction of Chattanooga; and third, northern Virginia between the Rappahannock and Potomac rivers. As strategic movement over such huge distances was dependent on the railway, railway junctions assumed an enormous importance in all three theatres. The eastern theatre was the most sensitive politically and also bore more on the atten-

tion of the great European powers. Great Britain and France sympathized with the Confederacy, the former having awarded the Confederacy belligerent rights in 1861; France was supporting a puppet government in Mexico; but neither would enter the war, thus transforming its character, until the Confederacy could demonstrate that it could win its independence by its own exertions; and that meant winning a battle on northern soil. By the spring of 1862 Confederate armies had given scant evidence that they were capable of such efforts.

In April 1862 McClellan set out on his 'grand campaign' designed to seal the Confederacy's doom by an amphibious operation up the peninsula between the James and York rivers, occupying Yorktown and the Confederate capital at Richmond. He was relieved of his duties as general-in-chief and replaced by Halleck. Lincoln had disliked McClellan's plan, preferring a direct advance towards Manassas Junction and thence on Richmond from the north. He ordered that a corps be retained at Fredericksburg to cover Washington. But McClellan advanced so cautiously that he

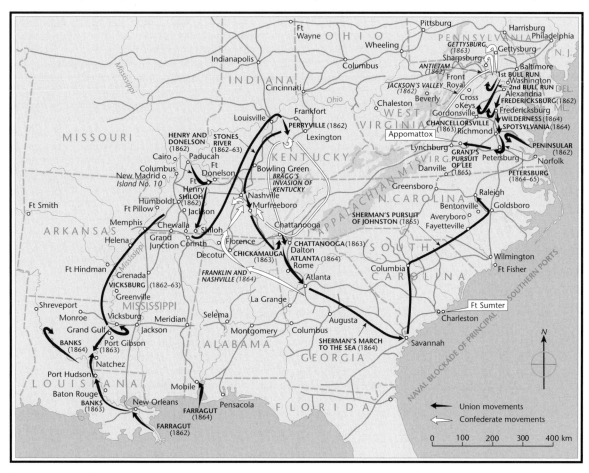

The **American civil war**: principal campaigns, 1861–5.

permitted a Confederate concentration before the city. An initial Confederate counterstroke at Seven Pines (31 May–1 June) was bungled and the Confederate commander *Johnston was severely wounded. In a fateful decision Davis replaced him with *Lee, who had meanwhile encouraged *Jackson to carry out his campaign in the *Shenandoah which distracted Lincoln's attention; he was then ordered to join Lee's forces before Richmond and help turn McClellan's right. In a brilliantly conceived operation (and despite several tactical repulses) Lee's Army of Northern Virginia in the *Seven Days battles succeeded in driving McClellan back to Harrison's Landing, shattering his nerves and political prestige. However, Lee failed to secure his ultimate objective, the destruction of the Army of the Potomac.

Thereupon Lee moved to tighten his hold on the initiative, defeated the Army of Virginia at second Bull Run and then crossed over into Maryland, determined to seek an outright Confederate victory at the earliest opportunity. McClellan's army had been evacuated from the peninsula and covered Washington. One of Lee's orders detailing the dispersal of his army was found by Union troops and enabled McClellan to attack him at *Antietam before his concentration was complete. Yet McClellan's attack was clumsy and poorly co-ordinated; Lee was able to parry his blows. Nonetheless, he was forced to evacuate Maryland, and this meagre strategic success enabled Lincoln to issue the Preliminary Emancipation Proclamation on 22 September. His move widened the social dimension of the war and freed all slaves currently held in Confederate territory; the war was no longer solely for the Union as it was. The Maryland adventure, in any case, was only one wing of a Confederate counter-offensive. *Bragg, the Confederate commander in Tennessee, moved into Kentucky, but on 8 October Don Carlos Buell caught up with him at Perryville, and repulsed his attacks; only one-third of the Union army was engaged but Bragg escaped through the Cumberland Gap. A fleeting opportunity to gain foreign intervention was allowed to slip through Confederate fingers.

The civil war now entered a period of stalemate, and increasingly the Union resorted to an *attritional strategy to bring the Confederacy down. McClellan, the chief spokesman for limited war, was removed on 8 November. But Lincoln's chief problem was in finding a general who could match Lee's operational skills and put into practice a grim strategy that would wear away the Confederacy's lighter, more mobile armies which excelled at manoeuvre. Union defeats at *Fredericksburg and *Chancellorsville almost brought Lincoln's administration to its knees. A defensive success at Murfreesboro (Stone's River, 31 December 1862–2 January 1863) in central Tennessee seemed a greater triumph than it actually was. It was also becoming clear that battles could no longer be won in a single day and demanded nerve and stamina not only from the fighting troops but from the commanders as well.

The spring of 1863 placed the Confederacy uncomfortably on the horns of a strategic dilemma. Grant was inching closer to the crucial Mississippi communications centre at *Vicksburg. Yet the brilliant victory at Chancellorsville offered an opportunity to renew the campaign north of the Potomac. Davis had already sent a recuperated Johnston to take charge of the west, but he was cautious and acted without confidence. Lee's view prevailed and he invaded Pennsylvania. Lacking cavalry while *Stuart indulged in a cavalry raid that skirted Washington, Lee allowed himself to be drawn into the battle of *Gettysburg (1–3 July 1863), where he was defeated. As for operations in the west, Grant slipped south of Vicksburg and crossed to the east bank of the Mississippi river. In an object lesson in calculated audacity, he advanced towards Jackson, Mississippi, and then turned west, defeating the Confederates at Champion's Hill before investing Vicksburg on 19 May. The city surrendered on 4 July 1863 thus cutting off the Confederate Trans-Mississippi from Richmond and permitting untrammelled Union passage of the Mississippi river. A third success for Union arms was recorded when William S. Rosecrans occupied most of east Tennessee in August 1863 in a series of sweeping turning movements that drove Bragg back into Georgia with his army intact.

The Union needed to deliver a knockout blow. Despite its successes, Confederate armies still remained in the field, Richmond was inviolate, and the secessionist heartland in the Deep South remained untouched. The capacity of the Confederacy to strike back was revealed in the autumn of 1863 when Bragg defeated Rosecrans's Army of the Cumberland at Chickamauga (19–20 September) and moved to besiege Chattanooga. His opportunity was thrown away by what amounted to a virtual *mutiny of the general officers of the Confederate Army of Tennessee, most of whom called for Bragg to be dismissed. This unseemly fracas required the presence of Jefferson Davis to sort out. In the meantime, Grant was given command at Chattanooga, and first concentrated overwhelming Union forces before defeating the Confederates who occupied the high ground south and east of the town. This success led to his promotion (as lieutenant general) to general-in-chief of the Union armies, and he moved to Washington to take command in March 1864.

Although it had been tried before, Grant was determined to unleash a simultaneous concentric advance on all fronts that would prevent a Confederate concentration at key points. However, he would be frustrated because the terrain favoured the tactical defence in the two major theatres, Virginia and Georgia, and the war had demonstrated that the defensive was growing in potency. The civil war was an infantryman's war. Soldiers were equipped with rifled muskets which fired the *Minié bullet to a range of about 1,000 yards (914 metres); this was a significant improvement on the Napoleonic musket. Consequently, soldiers of both sides increasingly resorted to entrenchments by 1863; but as the rifle-musket still had to be fired standing up in volleys, these consisted of shallow rifle pits, perhaps 3–4 feet (0.9–1.2 metres) deep with a breastwork several feet high placed on top of this. The role of cavalry was reduced to that of intelligence gathering and screening, and as a result, often fought its own separate, mounted engagements away from the main battlefield. Artillery was experiencing a transitional period; it still had to be 'pointed' by direct fire at the enemy. Although devastating against attacking infantry, it as yet lacked explosive power to destroy even shallow entrenchments. In short, Grant's dynamic strategy faced severe tactical obstacles, but he was remorseless in pursuit of his objective.

The 1864 campaign consisted of two attritional thrusts on geographical objectives, Atlanta and Richmond. The two overall Union commanders, Grant and *Sherman, sought to destroy the two Confederate armies in front of them before either could fall back into Richmond or Atlanta's defences. The main difference between them was that Lee fought Grant for the initiative whereas Joseph E. Johnston did not contest this with Sherman. The result in Virginia, where two well-matched adversaries were determined to fight it out, was a ferocious series of great attritional battles, Wilderness (4–6 May), Spotsylvania (8–21 May), followed by the shattering Union repulse at Cold Harbor on 3 June. The Confederates inflicted casualties equal to their own strength, but Grant recovered from this setback to cross the James river and on 15 June advance on Petersburg, Richmond's communications centre on the Appomattox river. Lee arrived in the nick of time but only ensured that the siege that he had always feared was the result of his tenacious defence. Sherman, who now commanded the Military Division of the West, was determined to apply pressure on Johnston so that he could not send reinforcements to aid Lee. The strategic co-ordination of Union armies over such great distances was facilitated by the use of the *telegraph. Outflanking his opponent's position on the Rocky Face Ridge, Sherman almost cut the Army of Tennessee off from its communications. Johnston considered launching a counter-attack at Cassville but refrained, and withdrew back through the Allatoona Pass behind the Etowah river. Sherman moved into the woods around his left, and was blocked at New Hope Church. Sherman tried to force the Confederate lines at Kennesaw Mountain but was repulsed on 27 June with 3,000 casualties. Yet Sherman inched towards Atlanta and by 9 July was only 4 miles (6.4 km) from its centre. Johnston was replaced by the impulsive *Hood. He launched a series of disastrous counter-attacks, which failed to prevent Sherman from extending his tentacles south of Atlanta, and the city was finally evacuated on 1 September 1864. This tremendous success guaranteed Lincoln's re-election in the presidential contest in November, and offered Sherman the chance to cut the Confederacy in two by marching towards the Atlantic coast.

The event which made this possible was the rash decision by *Hood to attack towards Chattanooga, thus evacuating the critical theatre of operations. Sherman was eventually able to advance towards Savannah with impunity. Neither Grant nor Lincoln was keen on this alternative, but Sherman reassured them by sending George H. Thomas and the Army of the Cumberland to Nashville to defend his rear. There on 15–16 December 1864 Thomas crushed Hood's army. Sherman's prime targets in his famous marches were Confederate war-making resources and *morale. Property rather than the people themselves were the victims of his depredations but his attacks were aimed just as much at the civil will as the morale of Confederate soldiers. He set about demonstrating that the Confederacy was an 'empty shell'. In January 1865 he moved through South Carolina and thence into North Carolina, determined to link up with Grant.

The final Confederate collapse was precipitate. A much enfeebled Army of Northern Virginia was besieged in Richmond. Lee's efforts the previous summer to distract attention by sending a small force under Jubal A. Early up the Shenandoah valley towards Washington brought an awful retribution on this beautiful rural area. Confederate troops were driven back and the new Union commander *Sheridan, was ordered by Grant to destroy all provisions and crops, a duty which he executed with great zeal. Denied the foodstuffs of the Shenandoah, the fall of Richmond was just a matter of time. Sheridan rejoined Grant and shattered Lee's right flank at Five Forks (31 March 1865), causing the evacuation of Richmond on 1–2 April. Grant pursued the remnants of the Confederate army and forced their capitulation at Appomattox Court House on 9 April 1865. Remaining Confederate troops in North Carolina surrendered to Sherman at Durham Station on 26 April, although small detachments in the Trans-Mississippi did not surrender until May.

The civil war had cost 620,000 American soldiers' lives (360,000 Union and 260,000 Confederate), although two-thirds of these were victims of disease not bullets. The economic damage inflicted on the South was enormous. Total southern capital, heavily invested in now-demonetized slaves, shrank by 46 per cent, whereas northern capital grew by 50 per cent. In 1860 the slave states contained 30 per cent of the total wealth of the USA, by 1870 this figure had slumped to 12 per cent. The war's political significance was enormous: the issue of secession was dealt with once and for all; slavery was abolished; and the power of the federal government was greatly increased. Its military significance was no less momentous. The civil war pointed to the great importance in modern war of organization, especially in the related spheres of logistics, communications, and transportation. Further, as the North was dragged into an attritional conflict due to early disappointments, so the deployment of numbers and quantities of equipment became more important than operational skill. Consequently, victory in the civil war (as in the two world wars of the twentieth century) went to the side with the largest population, the most durable financial system, and the greatest industrial capacity. But if Lincoln had been less able to unite the North, and Davis more successful in rallying the South, it could have been otherwise. BHR

Grant, Susan-Mary, and Reid, Brian Holden (eds.), *The American Civil War* (London, 2000).

Hattaway, Herman, and Jones, Archer, *How the North Won* (Urbana, Ill., 1983).

McPherson, James M., *The Battle Cry of Freedom* (New York, 1998).

Parish, Peter J., *The American Civil War* (London, 1975).

Reid, Brian Holden, *The Origins of the American Civil War* (London, 1996).

American independence war (1775–83). By the Treaty of Paris in 1763, British fortunes in North America had reached their zenith. All threat of French intervention had been removed from the American colonies, which enjoyed considerable wealth and freedom from external interference in local affairs. Yet within fifteen years bloody revolution would shatter the calm of this prosperous land.

The American population grew rapidly, from about 500,000 in 1713 to 4 million in 1775. This new people, many of them of non-Anglo-Saxon origin, felt stronger ties to their local area than to the distant authority of the crown. Increasingly, the restrictions and controls imposed from London were seen as irrelevant and onerous. Furthermore, the *Seven Years War had cost huge sums of money, and it was felt by London that the colonists themselves should bear the brunt of the cost of the American garrison of 8,000 British soldiers. In 1764 Chancellor Greville levied a Sugar Tax on molasses brought into the thirteen colonies from outside the British empire, in order to pay for American defence. However, this duty proved inadequate, and in 1764 the additional Stamp Act was passed, which levied a duty on all legal transactions and newspapers. In 1766, nine colonies sent representatives to debate the measure. They resolved not to accept any tax imposed without prior consultation. Riots soon flared up and tax-collectors were attacked. These measures were repealed, but soon financial pressure led to a tax on the import of paper, paint, glass, and tea, all of which was bound to be unacceptable to the colonists, who now found themselves put in the position of rejecting British sovereignty outright. Thus it was that in 1770, the unpopularity of British methods led to violent street disturbances, and troops fired on a rioting mob, killing five—the 'Boston Massacre'. In 1772, the revenue cutter *Gaspée* was wrecked by Rhode Islanders, and in 1773 the 'Boston Tea Party' saw British-monopolized tea thrown into the harbour in a gesture of contempt for the taxation system. As a result, Boston was closed to shipping, and generous trade concessions were given to the newly integrated French Canadians in Quebec.

In April 1775 the British C-in-C, Gen Thomas Gage, mounted a sortie to seize a stockpile of arms and powder at Concord, promptly became involved in a running fight, and, in retreating to Boston, suffered severe losses at *Lexington. The affair quickly escalated and colonial militia began to entrench themselves enthusiastically around Boston Harbour, overlooking the British garrison. In June Gage's newly arrived replacement, Sir William Howe, launched a successful frontal assault against the American earthworks on Breed's Hill and Bunker Hill, which cost the British over 1,000 casualties, 40 per cent of the attacking force, and was a serious blow to their pride, *morale, and capability for offensive operations.

In June 1775, the Continental Congress appointed *Washington, a wealthy Virginian planter with experience in the colonial militia, as its C-in-C. In autumn 1775, the British found themselves under pressure on all fronts. The Boston garrison was hemmed in, and American patriots had also seized the forts at Crown Point and Ticonderoga, threatening the Canadian urban centres of Montreal and Quebec. In the southern colonies Sir Henry Clinton attempted a *coup de main* in May at Charleston, but was bloodily repulsed, losing a ship and many men in an abortive artillery duel with shore batteries at Fort Moultrie. Meanwhile, Howe had brought 9,000 reinforcements from England to Boston, but his supply ships failed to arrive, and by early spring of 1776, his situation began to look desperate. The British had no choice now but to evacuate Boston, and this they did, making for Halifax, Nova Scotia, in March.

British strategy now came to centre on the Hudson river and the Canada–New York axis, in an effort to advance from Canada to capture New York, thus splitting Pennsylvania and the southern colonies from New England and New York. It was hoped that many Loyalists would rally to the crown in upstate New York, and that the riverine transport system would ease supply and communication.

But the British proceeded at a snail's pace and lacked any unifying direction, confused as they were by contradictory instructions, arriving at a time lag of three months from London. Meanwhile Howe's army was rapidly starving in Nova Scotia, where it was delayed until June 1776 waiting for provisions. Once victualled, the fleet set out for Staten Island, where it deposited the army. In August the Brigade of Guards arrived, accompanied by a Hessian force and Clinton's sorry refugees from Charleston. Howe felt ready to launch his offensive. He was ably supported by his brother, Richard, commanding the fleet, and had a force of 25,000 mainly crack troops.

After a token resistance, American forces abandoned New York, retreating northwards. Howe took the city, but had failed to deal a knockout blow to the rebels. A month later he mounted another amphibious assault against the American positions north of New York, on the Harlem Heights. The patriots were beaten, and Fort Washington

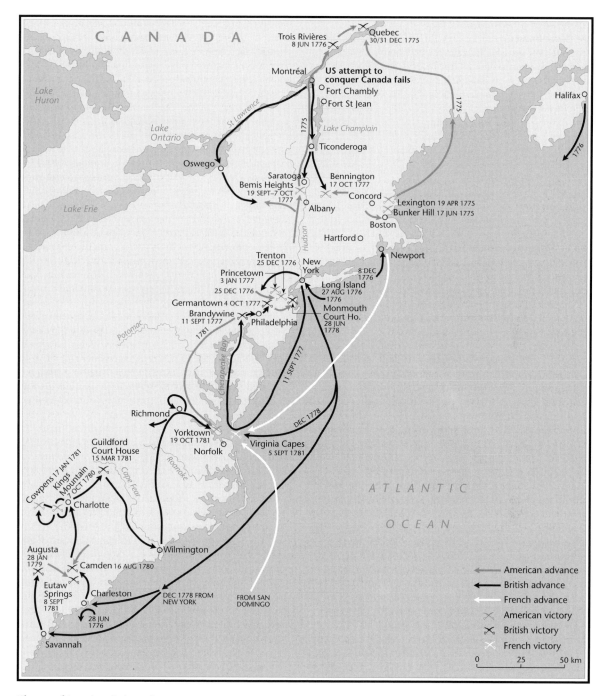

The war of **American Independence**.

captured, but the Americans were not cowed by these set-backs, and scurried back to White Plains. The American cause now seemed to be in serious decline. However, Washington advanced across the Delaware, surprising a Hessian detachment at Trenton on Boxing Day 1776. This developed into a general engagement between the forces of Cornwallis and Washington on New Year's Eve, and the Americans were bundled back to Princeton where the British were checked, and in consequence abandoned New Jersey.

Lt Gen John Burgoyne was appointed to command the Canadian offensive. He was a flamboyant and charismatic leader, but he was also ambitious and headstrong, and this proved to be his undoing. Howe, meanwhile, was concentrating on a push towards Philadelphia, the congressional capital, and it was unclear how the two commanders would be able to co-ordinate their operations effectively. In the event Howe did not land at the mouth of the Delaware, but sailed instead to the head of Chesapeake Bay, ending up no nearer to Philadelphia than where he had started from. After a month at sea, his army was in bad shape, whereas Washington was ready and waiting. Nevertheless at Brandywine Creek, the Americans proved unable to resist a *bayonet charge, combined with a subtle flanking manoeuvre. However, the British were worn out by their march from the sea, and a hard fight, and could only look on as the Americans recoiled in abject panic. By 25 September, Howe had occupied Philadelphia. On 4 October Washington launched another surprise attack, at Germantown, but a confused, running battle proved inconclusive. The year 1777 ended with Howe penned in at Philadelphia, while further away to the north, events of far greater import had taken place.

In late June 1777, Burgoyne, with a force of 9,500, captured Ticonderoga, pressing southwards to Hubbardton and Fort Edward on the Hudson. Lost in the back country and after a string of reverses, the British came under mounting American pressure at Freeman's Farm, on 7 October, losing 700 casualties. They withdrew under punishing American assaults until on 14 October Burgoyne surrendered to Horatio Gates at *Saratoga: only 1,500 of his remaining force were to survive a captivity that lasted until 1782. Burgoyne was released on *parole, and returned to London to attempt to vindicate himself.

Despite this signal victory, the congressional forces remained in disarray. Gates and Washington feuded constantly with Congress, and the Continental Army endured great hardship during a severe winter at Valley Forge outside British-occupied Philadelphia. But hungry eyes in Europe looked on intently. France now resolved to enter the war on the side of the colonists. The war had changed from civil insurrection to a world war which would engulf the West Indies, Europe, and India. To prevent a separate peace treaty, France recognized the nationhood of the USA in December 1777. Spain joined the war as France's ally in June 1779. The French and Spanish fleets were poorly co-

ordinated and much Spanish attention was diverted by the siege of *Gibraltar, and even the 1780–1 campaigns in Florida failed to divert any substantial British forces away from the main theatre of operations. As the war dragged on, the Dutch took up arms on behalf of the Americans, although distracted by their own problems, and eventually in 1780 Denmark, Sweden, Russia, Prussia, Austria, Portugal, and the Two Sicilies formed the League of Armed Neutrality against British attempts to seize and search shipping suspected of supplying the American war effort. By the spring of 1778, Lord North, the British premier, found himself embroiled in a world war, and had to contend with a domestic opposition which regarded American war aims as eminently reasonable.

In the winter of 1777–8, Howe remained supine in Philadelphia until replaced by Sir Henry Clinton in May. Clinton promptly withdrew from Philadelphia to New York, where he planned to disperse his forces to the West Indies, Florida, and Halifax, retaining New York itself as a base for naval and *amphibious operations. In contrast, the French alliance had strengthened patriot morale, and Washington felt confident enough to launch an assault on Clinton's rearguard at Monmouth, as the British retreated overland to New York. The Americans under Charles Lee launched an attack with 4,000 disciplined regulars, but were repulsed, as Clinton executed a masterly withdrawal. Washington himself had to intervene to prevent the flight of his army in the face of determined British counter-attacks.

During the winter of 1778–9, the French fleet regrouped in the West Indies and the war continued in raids and skirmishes. The Americans had entertained high hopes from French intervention, but initially these had proved to be misplaced, as little had been achieved by the alliance in 1778. Furthermore, a force of 3,000 British, aided by the Florida garrison, recaptured Georgia in February. In August 1779, in response to a request from the governor of South Carolina, the French Adm d'Estaing reappeared, having successfully completed his operations in the West Indies. He immediately laid siege to Savannah, and launched an abortive storming, in which he was wounded, and at once departed for France. It was a discouraging move. Washington was still hampered by lack of *war finance, and so far the French intervention had proved indecisive. Runaway inflation was crippling the American war effort, and morale among the population had reached a low ebb: there seemed to be no way forward.

In February 1780 Clinton landed 8,000 troops in the southern theatre, with the objective of capturing Charleston as a base of operations. From the outset, the Americans were heavily outnumbered, and surrendered 5,000 men there in May. Opposition in South Carolina crumbled, and the way was open for a strike to the north, where Rochambeau, with a sizeable French force was threatening New York. Clinton duly returned north, nominating Lord

Cornwallis as his successor in the south. Cornwallis hoped that many Loyalists would rally to the British cause, but in the event this support proved unreliable. Congress, for its part, renewed the effort against the British in the south. Horatio Gates, the victor of Saratoga, was sent to the army and set about engaging the British without delay. At Camden, on 16 August 1780, the Americans suffered one of the worst defeats of the war: Gates himself fled. As Cornwallis moved into North Carolina in September 1780, his capable subordinate *Ferguson, inventor of an early *breech-loading rifle which bears his name, was ambushed and killed at King's Mountain, losing 1,000 men. This provided a major boost to American morale, and the British retired to Winnsborough under continuous attack.

Cornwallis was reinforced in January 1781, and he could draw on a force of 4,000 tough and disciplined local supporters—'Tories'—and regulars. For their part, the Americans were invigorated by the appointment of Nathanael Greene as overall commander in the south, assisted by 'Light Horse Harry' Lee and the veteran Pennsylvania commander Daniel Morgan. Cornwallis was forced to protect his extended posts from Greene's pinprick attacks. Tarleton's detached corps was caught at Cowpens on 17 January and almost annihilated. Cornwallis swiftly turned on the Americans, but Greene retired into the marshes and waterways of North Carolina, followed by the British who were plagued by sickness, *desertion, lack of supplies, and harassing attacks. By the time it had reached Virginia, Cornwallis's army was in such poor condition that he was obliged to withdraw towards Hillsboro, pausing at Guilford Courthouse to regroup. Seeing Greene close at hand with a substantial force, Cornwallis seized the opportunity to attack. Despite a magnificent and hard-fought victory, Cornwallis could not exploit his advantage, and was forced to march down the Cape Fear river to Wilmington for much-needed rest.

In 1781 Clinton prepared an expedition to the Chesapeake in support of Cornwallis, to be commanded by *Arnold. The British landed, occupied Portsmouth, and resisted all attempts to dislodge them. The patriot cause seemed all but lost, and the French were horrified by the apparent weakness of their allies. Inflation and profiteering were turning the population against the patriot cause, and continued inaction only served to advance British interests. In May 1781 Cornwallis and Arnold united their forces near Richmond. Clinton wished to establish a safe anchorage, and instructed Cornwallis to fortify Yorktown on Chesapeake Bay to command the sea approaches. Rochambeau appealed to Adm de Grasse to bring his fleet to the Chesapeake, while Washington moved 7,000 French and American regulars to Yorktown, soon to be reinforced by de Grasse with 28 ships of the line and 4,000 more troops. In September Hood attempted to drive off the French fleet with 19 ships of the line, but his force was badly mauled in the battle of Chesapeake Bay and pulled back to New York,

leaving 6,000 British facing 16,000 French and continental troops when the siege of *Yorktown began on 28 September 1781. The following day Cornwallis withdrew from his outer works, and by 9 October he was under heavy and continuous fire, and attempted an evacuation across the river to Gloucester Point, but this was foiled by bad weather. By then, with only 3,000 men fit for duty and artillery ammunition exhausted, Cornwallis surrendered on 19 October, four years after Saratoga.

The British command had failed to prevent Washington's move to Virginia or to intercept the French fleet as it left its base at Rhode Island. De Grasse, Washington, and Rochambeau had co-ordinated their efforts in a way hitherto unimaginable. The campaign was a masterpiece that only served to highlight the weakness of the British command. It was a shattering blow, well described by Jeremy Black as 'the biggest humiliation of British military power until the surrender of *Singapore in 1942'. The British participants were aware that something momentous had taken place. As they marched out with the *honours of war, their bands played a popular tune called 'The World turned Upside Down'. When news reached London of the surrender, Lord North cried out 'Oh God! It is all over', and the way was clear for the Treaty of Versailles (1783).

The treaty recognized the independence of the USA, and though it left Britain defeated it sacrificed none of her essential interests, and in the years that followed she was able to extend her global reach. On the other hand, the few gains that France had made, like Tobago, could not compensate for the enormous cost of the war to the French exchequer, and this proved to be a decisive factor in the crisis of 1789. The war had old and new aspects. It was an early and important instance of a successful popular revolt, an example not lost on many Frenchmen. Yet its conduct was anything but revolutionary. Although both sides made wide use of *light troops, the Americans, like the British, placed heavy reliance on regular infantry fighting in line, and the contribution of the Continental Army—itself shaped by European drillmasters like Steuben—was at least as important as that of Morgan's riflemen or the 'over the mountain men' who beat Ferguson at King's Mountain. Conversely, there were times when the British and their Hessian allies were actually more flexible than the Americans, and Cornwallis's victory at Camden deserves to be better remembered. British commanders wrestled with significant disadvantages. Although they enjoyed some popular support (and like so many wars of independence, this contained elements of civil war) it was rarely strong enough for them to be able to glean supplies within America. They remained dependent on sea transport to bring supplies from Britain, and the strength of their field army was constantly eroded by the need to garrison bases threatened by a hostile population. Only by decisive defeat of the Continental Army, followed by the large-scale occupation of territory, could the British hope to win. Before France's entry into the war such a task was difficult, not least because Washington recognized that he could not afford to risk major defeat. After it, it was all but impossible, and the British lost their colonies as much in the waters off the American coast as in the hamlets or backwoods of the hinterland.　　　TM/RH

Black, Jeremy, *War for America: The Fight for Independence 1775–1783* (Stroud, 1991).

Conway, Stephen, *The War of American Independence 1775–1783* (London, 1995).

Hibbert, Christopher, *Redcoats and Rebels* (London, 1991).

American Indian wars (1587–1890). North American Indian population densities never approached those of Mexico and Peru, but their greatest concentrations were around the Chesapeake Bay area, in the south-east, the Pueblo/Navajo in the south-west, and along the Pacific coast. Their fate reflects how early they were exposed to Anglo-American contact. Today California has the largest population, followed by Oklahoma (the old 'Indian Territory' dumping ground) and the south-west.

The 300-year intermittent war began with the extermination of Drake's Virginia colony by the Croatan, while only the influence of Chief Wahunsenacock of the Powhatan confederation saved the Jamestown settlement from a similar fate. Modern perception is conditioned by Hollywood's emphasis on the *Plains Indians wars, but by the time the whites crossed the Allegheny mountains most serious resistance was over, with eight or nine named 'wars' leading up to the *French and Indian war and *Pontiac's rebellion. Once the Anglo-American population achieved critical mass and their use as allies against the French ended, Indians were regarded either as an inconvenience to be 'concentrated' on marginal lands or as vermin to be exterminated.

Combat was far less significant than the near-genocidal effect of introduced bacteria and distilled liquor. A decimated population resistant to European diseases eventually emerged, but over time the abiding Indian predisposition to alcoholism has been even more devastating. Once defeated, North American Indians became the objects of the world's longest-running social engineering programme, successfully designed to reduce the target population to a state of hopeless dependency. When one considers the arbitrary expropriation of the 'civilized' tribes of the south-east, the way the tenuous authority of accommodationist Indian leaders was invariably undermined by Anglo-American bad faith, and the fact that the Indian government's agents were usually either profiteers or else missionaries hostile to

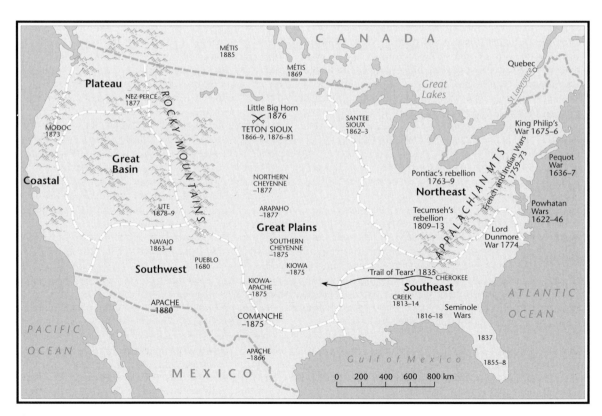

The **American Indian wars**.

Indian culture, it is impossible not to sympathize with the braves who preferred honourable death in battle.

This said, 'noble savage' romanticism cannot survive clear-eyed examination. Warrior tribes, who required no lessons in the arts of treachery and massacre, predominated. White rapacity, hypocrisy, and cant are hard to stomach, but so are cannibalism, headhunting (and its symbolic extension, scalping), and the refined torture of captives. Nor was there any solidarity among the Indians. With a few fleeting exceptions such as Tecumseh's confederation of 1805–13, they never united against the whites in significant numbers. By contrast, their willingness to ally with them against rival tribes was a permanent feature of the conflict.

From a pre-contact population in the millions, by 1900 they were reduced to a culturally destroyed remnant of 250,000. No less brutal than the Anglo-Americans, to the south the Spanish *conquistadores placed a market value on Indians to work the lands they conquered. No such consideration palliated the treatment they received in the north. Regardless of its inevitability, the dispossession of the American Indians makes melancholy reading, and illustrates the grim truth that when two peoples compete for the same land, the stronger will prevail and the weaker must accept whatever terms it can get.   HEB

Amiens/Montdidier, battle of (1918), one of the most significant battles of WW I, its first day what *Ludendorff called 'the black day of the German army in the history of the war'. For the British army, having shouldered the main burden of combat after the French mutinies and the Russian Revolution of November 1917, and before American strength could make itself felt on the battlefield at *Saint-Mihiel the following month, Amiens is a distinguished, if poorly remembered, *battle honour. And for the Australian and Canadian troops who played a leading part in the battle, Amiens was yet more proof of New World valour on the battlefields of the old (see ANZAC, AUSTRALIAN IMPERIAL FORCE, CANADIAN EXPEDITIONARY FORCE).

By August 1918 the Allied artillery had established dominance over the German but the Germans still held a salient bulging out towards the main railway from Paris to Amiens. The Allied command planned to clear the salient of Germans along a 20 mile (32 km) front. The British Fourth Army, under Gen Sir Henry Rawlinson, comprising the British III Corps, the Australian Corps, and the Canadian Corps, plus XXXI Corps of the French First Army, concentrated for the attack: a total force of 18 infantry and 3 cavalry divisions, with 3,532 guns (2,070 of them British), 534 tanks—the largest number in any battle of the war—and about 1,000 aircraft of which 800 were British, from the newly formed RAF. The opposition in this area was the German Second Army with 7 weak infantry divisions, 840 guns, and 106 aircraft. On 8 August the British and French at-

tacked without the customary long preliminary bombardment, achieving surprise. For some days the sound-ranging sections and flash-spotting observation posts and the RAF had been engaged in plotting the positions of the German artillery. The moment the assault began, as Maj Gen Sir Archibald Montgomery said, the German artillery was 'deluged by a hurricane bombardment and neutralised to such an extent that hostile artillery retaliation was almost negligible'. Using tanks in co-ordination with the well-adjusted artillery fire and aircraft the British penetrated 7 miles (11 km) on the first day, killing or capturing 28,000 Germans and taking 400 guns. On the second day the full strength of the French First Army was brought in to the south, and on 10 August part of the French Third Army was engaged even further to the south. However, heavy losses of Allied tanks slowed the advance, and the Germans fought ferociously and well in the air, downing 45 aircraft and irreparably damaging 52 on the first day—a tenth of the total force engaged and a fifth of the bombers. By the end of 13 August the British and French had penetrated up to 18 km (11 miles) on a 47 mile (75 km) front, killed or wounded 18,000 Germans, and captured 30,000.

The operation succeeded, in part because the German defences were too shallow and insufficiently prepared, in part because of surprise and the use of tanks and aircraft en masse. However, the tanks were designed and used only for breakthrough, and were unsuitable for deep exploitation which was still the task of cavalry. After Amiens the strategic initiative now passed irretrievably back to the Allies. And the kind of war they were fighting was looking increasingly like aspects of WW II. In terms of its careful emphasis on surprise, artillery concentration, and methodical planning, Amiens pointed the way ahead to *Alamein.   CDB

Blaxland, Gregory, *Amiens 1918* (London, 1968).
Terraine, John, *White Heat* (London, 1982).

---

ammunition, artillery The NATO tactical symbol for artillery is a box with a black dot in it: a cannon ball. Yet the first artillery projectile ever recorded, in the de Milemete manuscript of 1327, is not a cannon ball but an arrow or, as we would call it today, an armour-piercing, fin-stabilized projectile. There is no evidence of the discarding 'sabot', from the French for 'boot', which would enable such a projectile to be fired from a gun with any efficiency. Without a sabot, sufficient pressure from the gun's explosive charge would not be applied to the arrow, suggesting the medieval artist may have heard of guns but not seen one.

The gun itself is not a weapon: it is a delivery system. The projectile or shell is the weapon. Whatever the reason for de Milemete's enigmatic arrow, within a few years, cannon balls were the norm. They were often of stone, which was far cheaper and, from a technical point of view, lighter than metal. Incendiary rounds were also used right from the start. Cannon balls remained the principal form of ammunition for 500 years, their kinetic energy providing the means both for breaching fortifications and for slicing through successive lines of men and horses at great range. In the 16th century, grapeshot—a package of smaller balls which separated after leaving the gun muzzle—and case-shot—still smaller balls—were introduced as efficient close-range killers, making field artillery a practical proposition.

Specialized ammunition was developed for naval warfare, most famously 'chain shot'—two cannon balls joined by a chain which would orbit murderously and cut through rigging, masts, or people. Exploding shells—initially hollow metal spheres filled with *gunpowder—were first introduced in the second half of the 16th century. In 1803 the British Gen Henry Shrapnel devised the shell which still bears his name, containing numerous musket-ball sized projectiles, which were blown from the shell by a 'burster charge'. Nevertheless, round shot remained the most devastating long-range projectile and at *Waterloo Wellington regarded the French shells which landed near him, with their fuses fizzing, with disdain.

In the mid-19th century the cylindro-conical projectile—the familiar *bullet or shell-shape—replaced the cannon ball. Ammunition for rifled muzzle-loading guns required ingenious methods to enable it to engage with the rifling, often projections or 'blisters' on the projectile, which slotted into the grooves of the rifling. Rifled ordnance and breech-loading, from the 1860s, gave rise to the modern design of artillery shell, with a copper (now often plastic) driving band into which the rifling bites when the shell is rammed into the breech and then fired, imparting the spin to the projectile. The outer diameter of the driving band is greater than the inner diameter of the bore (the top of the ridges of the rifling) by 0.2 to 0.5 mm. As the shell is propelled, spinning, up the barrel, the driving band fills the entire space ensuring obturation—a gas-proof block.

By the start of WW I most armies were equipped with High Explosive (HE) shell—pyroxilin, melinite, and trotyl—and shrapnel, now designed to fire its bullets forward and sideways as it burst before or over the target. The Germans also had HE fragmentation shells, designed for use against troops in the open. Shrapnel, intended for fast-moving battle in the open, was of little use against troops in trenches, however. The British 'battle bowler' (steel helmet), also adopted by the USA, was designed to protect against shrapnel bursting directly above.

Artillery's rate of fire, and therefore shell expenditure, increased exponentially. In the 1870–1 *Franco-Prussian war an estimated 650,000 rounds were fired. In the *Russo-Japanese war 900,000 were fired and in 1914–18 about 1 billion. All the combatants in WW I were unprepared for the consumption of artillery shell. By mid-September 1914 all the combatants on the western front were short of ammunition and in 1915 the 'shell shortage' became a universal phenomenon. During the war Germany fired 275 million shells; France 200 million; Britain 170 million; Austria-Hungary 70 million; Russia 50 million. On one day—28–9 September 1918—the British army fired nearly a million rounds in their attack on the *Hindenburg Line.

Chlorine gas shells were first used by the Germans against the Russians at Bolimov on 31 January 1915. They may have used some at Neuve Chapelle on 10–12 March but the first large scale use of gas was at Langemarck, near *Ypres, on 22 April. Much of the poison *gas used in the war was released from static cylinders, but this depended on the wind and gas shells, which put the gas exactly where it was wanted, proved far more effective.

An important, related innovation during WW I was the *smoke shell. Smoke pots were used to obscure attacking forces on their start lines from 1915, but smoke shell, which could be fired ahead of them, was not available until 1917 and only widely used in 1918. Smoke shell, in combination with high explosive, helped the infantry see where the artillery *barrage had got to, and it also hid them from machine guns and rifle fire. A second important innovation was *illuminating shell.

In the inter-war period more artillery ammunition was developed including: rockets, notably the Soviet 132 mm M-13 'Katyusha' and M-30 'Ivan the Terrible'; concrete-busting rounds for use against fortifications; and even propaganda rounds, containing leaflets. Explosive artillery rounds were big enough to deal with most tanks of the time, but during WW II specialist armour-piercing *anti-armour rounds were developed for tank guns and artillery. There are three main types of anti-armour round: a simple high explosive round, in which the explosive is flattened against the outside of the tank and then explodes, blasting fragments off the inside; a shaped charge round, in which the explosive is moulded round the outside of a cone, funnelling the explosive power into a jet of gas which burns a hole through the armour; and solid shot, which mimics the action of the medieval arrow. By applying the great power of an artillery propellent charge to a projectile smaller than the calibre of the gun, a 'sub-calibre' device, its effect can be multiplied—like a hammer hitting a nail. In order to transmit the energy from the charge to the sub-calibre projectile a sabot is needed, which acts as a 'sling' either to drive an armour-piercing core harder, or to throw a sub-calibre projectile further.

During the 1950s nuclear rounds for artillery were developed, beginning with the giant US 280 mm atomic cannon. Later, they were reduced in size to fit 155 mm NATO and 152 mm Soviet artillery. It is doubtful whether their use would have been a practical proposition (see NUCLEAR WEAPONS).

In the 1980s, there were further developments to conventional ammunition: extended range sub-calibre projectiles (ERSC), using sabots and extended range full-bore (ERFB) projectiles, more streamlined in design than traditional shells, tapered all the way from the driving band. An ERSC

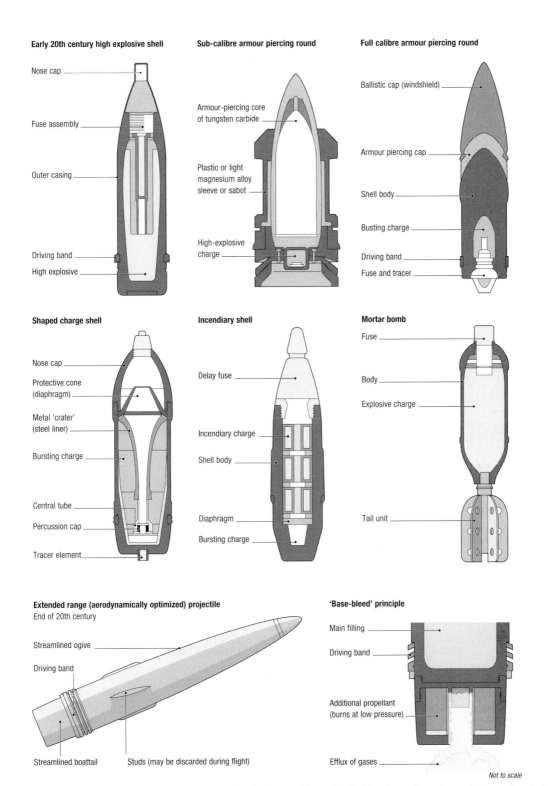

Early 20th century high explosive shell

- Nose cap
- Fuse assembly
- Outer casing
- Driving band
- High explosive

Sub-calibre armour piercing round

- Armour-piercing core of tungsten carbide
- Plastic or light magnesium alloy sleeve or sabot
- High-explosive charge

Full calibre armour piercing round

- Ballistic cap (windshield)
- Armour piercing cap
- Shell body
- Busting charge
- Driving band
- Fuse and tracer

Shaped charge shell

- Nose cap
- Protective cone (diaphragm)
- Metal 'crater' (steel liner)
- Bursting charge
- Central tube
- Percussion cap
- Tracer element

Incendiary shell

- Delay fuse
- Incendiary charge
- Shell body
- Diaphragm
- Bursting charge

Mortar bomb

- Fuse
- Body
- Explosive charge
- Tail unit

Extended range (aerodynamically optimized) projectile
End of 20th century

- Streamlined ogive
- Driving band
- Streamlined boattail
- Studs (may be discarded during flight)

'Base-bleed' principle

- Main filling
- Driving band
- Additional propellant (burns at low pressure)
- Efflux of gases

Not to scale

The artillery shell has been used to carry a wide variety of loads, from smaller projectiles like shrapnel or sub-munitions to chemicals, and even propaganda leaflets. Improvements in ammunition design, exemplified by the extended-range projectiles at the foot of the illustration, have recently enabled artillery to double its range without any major technological innovations.

round fired from a US 155 mm M-109 howitzer has a range of over 14 miles (22 km) instead of the normal 9 miles (14.6 km). A final new development is 'base bleed' technology. This uses a combustible material at the base of the shell which burns, generating gases which fill the vacuum which normally forms behind a shell in flight. It is not a form of rocket assistance, as in a rocket-assisted projectile (RAP), but it does increase the pressure at the base of the shell, largely eliminating base drag, one of three types of drag which act on a shell in flight. Base bleed can increase the range of a round by 13 to 30 per cent. The Austrian GHN-45 155 mm *howitzer will fire a non-base bleed ERFB shell to 19 miles (30 km). It will fire a base bleed shell to 24 miles (39 km) and, in the rarefied air in the Middle East, 27 miles (43 km). Comparable artillery systems in use in the 1970s had ranges of 9–11 miles (14–17 km). Thus, in the last twenty years, incremental improvements to artillery ammunition have more than doubled the range of artillery systems without loss of accuracy.

The lethality of ammunition has also increased exponentially, at first due to more efficient fragmentation creating more but smaller fragments. The most unpleasant are flechettes—tiny sharp needles. Flechette rounds enable artillery to fire right onto friendly armoured vehicles, without damaging them, but killing enemy troops all around. Improved Conventional Munitions (ICMs) distribute sub-munitions over a wide area. Finally, there are Fuel Air Explosive (FAE) devices, which spread a cloud of vapour over the target area and then explode it, in just the same way as the fuel-air mixture in a car engine, creating a more even pressure over the target. The USA used these in *Vietnam and the Russians in Afghanistan and Chechnya. These can neutralize a vastly greater area than a conventional round, and are also particularly useful for clearing mines.   CDB

Bellamy, Christopher, *Red God of War* (London, 1986).

Lee, R. G., *Introduction to Battlefield Weapons Systems and Technology* (London, 1985).

---

amphibious operations (*see opposite page*)

---

amphibious ships and landing craft

Amphibious operations, which are so much a feature of modern war, came fully of age only when suitable craft from which to launch seaborne assaults had been built. In 1899, a French staff officer designed an armoured landing craft fitted with a detachable landing ramp, of about 80 tons displacement. As he had designed it for an invasion of England (Anglo-French relations were appalling due to the Fashoda incident), no notice was taken of his sensible proposal. Adm *Fisher, the British First Sea Lord, had also foreseen the importance of amphibious operations in modern war, but no appropriate craft were developed. On the *Gallipoli peninsula, seaborne landings were made in 1915, despite the fact that no specially designed craft were available, troops transferring from seagoing vessels to lighters to be ferried ashore. In 1917, specialist landing craft had been designed to land British troops engaged in an amphibious operation on the Flanders coast, intended to form part of the third battle of *Ypres but never actually mounted.

The Japanese first used a purpose-designed landing craft with a hinged bow ramp in 1938, in landings along the Yangtse river. Their success sent a ripple of interest around the world, and the British designed two similar craft. A total of ten plywood Landing Craft, Assault (LCA), capable of landing infantry, and Landing Craft, Motor (LCM), for vehicles and material, were first used at Narvik in late April 1940 in the *Norwegian campaign. This was the first use of landing craft in European war and before their arrival in Norway troops had to be landed from destroyers or merchantmen in ports, without any heavy equipment or tanks. Britain's lack of landing craft was underlined at *Dunkirk, where the British Expeditionary Force (BEF) had to abandon most of the 63,400 vehicles, 20,500 motorcycles, and 2,500 heavy guns it took to France, because there was no way of quickly re-embarking them. The *Wehrmacht belatedly started to convert some of its River Rhine barges for the invasion of England in July 1940, but the failure to win the battle of *Britain brought such designs to a premature halt.

Modern landing craft were really developed in the USA, where the Marine Corps experimented with the several designs of assault craft throughout the 1930s. A private contract marine engineer, Andrew Higgins, produced the best of these. By combining his 36 foot Eureka boat with the Japanese hinged bow-ramp, the basic landing craft of today was born. Able to carry an infantry platoon (36 men), 8,000 lb (3,600 kg) of cargo, or a 3 ton truck, his plywood design was known as the Landing Craft Vehicle, Personnel (LCVP) or 'Higgins Boat'. The ramp and sometimes the sides were armoured, and the British used many, which were superior to their own LCAs. From 1941, some 23,400 LCVPs were manufactured in the US. There was also a less satisfactory wooden Landing Craft Personnel, Large (LCP-L) which likewise carried a platoon, but had no ramp, the assault force jumping from the prow.

Higgins was also commissioned to design a larger craft capable of carrying a single 30 ton *Sherman tank. He responded in 1942 with the 50 foot (15 metre) Landing Craft, Mechanised (LCM) of which 11,400 were produced, replacing the earlier British LCM. A larger tank landing craft was designed separately in Britain in 1940. The Landing Craft Tank (LCT) could carry six tanks, or thirteen trucks, and nearly 1,500 were mass-produced in the USA for Britain. These were flat-bottomed craft with a shallow draft, and were lowered from the davits of larger troop-carrying merchantmen, like lifeboats. With a cross-Channel invasion always in mind, the British also needed larger assault vessels

(cont. on page 53)

amphibious operations

AMPHIBIOUS operations are operations launched from the sea onto the land by naval and landing forces. The threat or execution of such operations can serve a wide range of purposes, extending from a demonstration of capability for coercive intent, all the way to the opening of a new campaign by means of the conduct of expeditionary warfare from the sea.

Amphibious operations need to be approached as just one of the ways in which power can be projected from the sea against the land. Naval suasion via what long has been known as gunboat diplomacy, bombardment of the shore by guns, sea-based aviation, and missile, and maritime *blockade, comprise other regions of action along the full spectrum of power projection from the sea to the land.

The persisting attractiveness of amphibious operations in particular, and of power projection from the sea in general, reposes in the fact that the importance of maritime (including major riverine) communications, civil and military, has been a constant in human history. Not only does physical geography impose an essential unity, a continuity of the potential for human passage, upon all the oceans, seas, bays, and rivers of the world, but the 70 per cent of the Earth's surface that is water, on its littorals, grants ready access to 70 per cent of the Earth's population.

Amphibious operations require the integrated, certainly the well co-ordinated, conduct of sea and land (and, today, air) warfare. To launch a military operation from the sea requires an expertise that is more than simply the sum of military and naval skills. All too often, as British Maj Gen Sir Charles *Callwell observed in 1905, 'soldiers and sailors in the past in this and other countries, knowing little of each other's duties and objects, often failed to appreciate them at times of crisis'. There are huge and persisting differences between land warfare and sea warfare, yet of necessity amphibious operations comprise warfare where the land and the sea meet. Professionally excellent generals and admirals are almost doomed by their genuine, if geographically limited, expertise, to be less than thoroughly empathetic to the operational imperatives of 'the other culture'.

Insular powers are obliged by geography to wage war both overseas and, ultimately, from the sea, since wars against continental adversaries cannot be won at sea. Victorious wars at sea have to be 'cashed' strategically in effect for success on land. More to the point perhaps, in the words of *Liddell Hart, 'amphibious flexibility is the greatest strategic asset that a sea-based power possesses'. Given the strategic significance of the land–sea interface, the littoral region where land power meets sea power, it follows that the ability to dominate that region translates as the ability to project power either from the shore to the sea, or from the sea to the shore. Understandably, perhaps, even in this newly 'joint' era, military minds—professionally trained principally for land, sea, or air duties—are not always readily adaptable to the needs of amphibious, let alone triphibious (with air), operations. When sea forces bring land forces to combat on the enemy's littoral for amphibious operations, distinctively geographically based service cultures and *doctrines are apt to make unusually challenging demands upon each other.

At least seven strategically significant purposes lend themselves to support by amphibious operations. First, the advertisement of possibility of such operations, supported by physical demonstration of capability (though short of actual use), may have coercive effect. To know, for certain, that there is an amphibiously competent foe on or just over the horizon, can concentrate the mind and encourage political co-operation. Second, the credible menace of amphibious operations can be intended not so much to persuade for co-operation, but rather militarily to deceive and distract. Modern means of land communication by road and rail certainly have tilted the playing field in favour of the (land) power with interior lines of communication, but still the lurking menace of amphibious power on or over the horizon is apt to promote uncertainty as to where the blow will fall.

Third, amphibious operations, taking advantage of the vastness of the sea that facilitates operational surprise, has been a classic way to raid. In the words of Adm Sir Philip H. Colomb, 'ravage and destruction', as contrasted with 'conquest and occupation', can be wrought by seaborne raiders. Given, frequently, the length of enemy coastline, it is not difficult to appreciate the attractiveness of the raiding option. Fourth, noted immediately above, the objective of an amphibious operation may be conquest and occupation.

Fifth, an amphibious operation itself may be designed to open a campaign. D-Day, 6 June 1944, was just such an operation. When there is a strategic stand-off between insular and continental prowess, each side has to use its environmentally based superiority to seek decisive advantage in the geography preferred by the foe. In June 1944 the western Allies translated their maritime superiority into the capacity to put ashore in Normandy a capability for land-air warfare good enough to sustain itself in continental campaigning. Alternatively, when one of two continental belligerents uniquely enjoys the ability to manoeuvre from the sea, an amphibious thrust for operational advantage may be attempted. A classic example of an endeavour to outflank an enemy's army by means of maritime manoeuvre, was Gen McClellan's amphibious expedition (March–August 1862) with the Union's Army of the Potomac to threaten Richmond from the peninsula between the York and James rivers.

Sixth, amphibious menace, or actual assault, can expedite the conduct of a continental campaign that is already underway. The classic example of an amphibious operation intended to achieve such an effect was the *Anzio operation of 22 January 1944. Whether or not an amphibious operation can function as a force multiplier for a great continental campaign depends, all too obviously, upon the quality of the commander (*inter alia*), not to mention the enemy. Seventh, amphibious operations can extract an army from a position of more or less dire continental peril. The evacuation of the British Expeditionary Force (BEF) from *Dunkirk has to be the exemplar of amphibious rescue on the grand scale under fire. Nonetheless, maritime powers have had occasion to exercise their capabilities for amphibious extraction at least as often as they have practised amphibious insertion. Gen Douglas MacArthur's amphibious 'left-hook' around the Korean peninsula to *Inchon, thereby threatening both to recapture Seoul and, especially, to cut off the North Korean army that was locked in battle deep in South Korea, is far better known than is the no less amphibious manoeuvre that enabled Allied (UN) naval forces to extract the X Corps from the ports of Hungnam and Wonsan (5–15 December 1950).

The importance of the sea and of rivers for transportation—communications—in human history, has guaranteed their strategic importance. Because we use, rather than occupy, the sea, and because the sea—and inland waters—frequently, indeed generally, have been the only practicable geographical medium for strategic exploitation, amphibious operations have been a hardy perennial of strategic history. The technical and tactical details will vary from Julius *Caesar's invasion of Britain in 55 and 54 BC, to Byzantine Emperor Nicephorus Phocas' invasion of Arab-held Crete in 960, to the 1066 invasion of England by *William 'the Conqueror', right up to the extraordinarily amphibious dimension to WW II both in Europe and the *Pacific, to Korea, to the present day.

Amphibious operations have fluctuated in political and military popularity, and in apparent technical-tactical, *operational, and therefore strategic feasibility. But, to date, amphibious operations as a form of war generically have survived every assault by technology and doctrine that, for a while, has seemed to menace their military practicability. Although amphibious operations have a strategic history as old as warfare itself, it was really only in the 20th century that their conduct truly was professionalized by means of systematic study, the preparation of formal doctrine, dedicated planning and training, the acquisition of specialized equipment, and the designation of some forces to be specifically amphibious in their tactical and operational focus.

Britain approached a truly 'strategic moment' for amphibious operations, *Gallipoli 1915, with good, if not excellent, understanding of the general character and particular needs of such operations. Unfortunately, first-rate British ideas about how to conduct amphibious operations—expressed in books and in official doctrine—found next-to-no reflection in the actual preparation of forces and acquisition of specialized equipment, not to mention the all-too-specific problems of 1915.

The fiasco of Gallipoli demonstrated nothing of particular importance about amphibious operations, other than the obvious points that they need to be well, rather than poorly, conducted, according to the general *principles of war, and that the often extraordinarily stressful contexts for such operations are apt to be uniquely unforgiving of error. Some people believed that the failure of the Gallipoli campaign demonstrated that amphibious operations, specifically amphibious assault operations, had been overtaken by modern technology. *Railways and the several uses of the internal combustion engine—neither of which were factors at Gallipoli—allegedly meant that a continental power could transfer forces more rapidly than could the amphibious power, to win 'the battle of the build-up' between continental defenders and maritime attackers. Similarly, it was believed that modern firepower rendered the beach, shallow water, and the littoral approach, impractically lethal for amphibious assault.

American and British amphibious doctrine developed between the world wars challenged this popularly negative view. Looking for a new role in a harsh post-war context, the US Marine Corps reinvented themselves in the 1920s as the specialized force uniquely prepared to seize insular bases for the prosecution of a great maritime campaign across the western Pacific. The central strategic idea found enabling doctrinal support in *The Tentative Manual of Landing Operations* of 1934, subsequently elevated to the status of Landing Operations Doctrine, US Navy 1937. The British, whose understanding of amphibious operations—resting upon three and a half centuries of distinctly mixed experience—tended to be better than their practice, produced *The Manual of Combined Operations* (1938), which was congruent in all essentials with its contemporary American counterpart.

Argument in the 1930s about the obsolescence or otherwise of amphibious operations, was simply rendered irrelevant by the events of 1940–1. Germany's defeat of France and expulsion of the BEF from continental Europe in June 1940 meant that any restoration of a western front could be effected only by a grand scale of amphibious manoeuvre. Whether one liked it or not, aside from the (post-22 June 1941) land combat in the east and the none-too-promising bomber offensive, the war against Hitler's *Festung Europa* had to be amphibious in basic character. There was even less scope for argument over the character of the war in the Asia-Pacific region. For reasons of geography, the war against Japan had to take the form of a maritime siege of an overextended maritime empire. Landing by landing, even extraction by extraction British and American amphibious power learnt by painful practice how to apply the doctrine that in its basics was sound enough.

There can be no doubt that D-Day in *Normandy and the assaults upon *Iwo Jima and Okinawa comprise the finest, most complete, historical examples of successful amphibious operations. Justly celebrated though those extraordinary cases certainly are, and deserve to be, the more important fact remains that amphibious operations—for all of the purposes suggested earlier—great but more usually small, are prospectively a permanent feature of strategic history.

The leading difficulty with amphibious operations lies not in grasping the rather obvious 'principles' that should guide and shape them, but rather in learning how, let alone being able, to apply them in historically unique strategic situations. Nonetheless, principles are important: eight such especially command attention.

First, it is essential that each geographically specialized fighting force should comprehend, in general terms at least, the limitations, advantages, and conditions that govern the operational characteristics of the others. For example, soldiers do not need to master tide tables, but they do need to know that tides exist, and matter. Second, there is no magic formula for successful command of an amphibious operation—it may be unified, or it may be co-ordinated but sequential—what matters is that the key principles of essential unity of command should be followed.

Third, although the furtive amphibious insertion of a small raiding party—for example by a solitary submarine—is always likely to be feasible, if not reliably so, amphibious operations on a scale suitable to effect either a major raid or the seizing and holding of substantial real estate, require as a prerequisite the securing of (possibly temporary) command of the sea and of the air. Fourth, a decisive combination of common sense and bitter historical experience (Tarawa) obliges the would-be amphibious warrior to pay the most careful attention to minute details of local hydrography, as well as to the much less reliable detail likely to be available on the weather.

The fifth principle of amphibious warfare is that except for the benign conditions that permit 'administrative' landings, specialist doctrine, training, and equipment are required for the successful conduct of such warfare. A particularly notable feature of the Anglo-American conduct of amphibious assault in WW II was the invention of well-armed amphibious tractors for the transport of troops from the offshore 'line of departure' to points inland, the development of amphibious tanks, and indeed the proliferation of dedicated amphibious shipping on all scales.

Sixth, amphibious operations frequently require *tactical* surprise if they are to succeed. Any amphibious insertion of forces across an enemy's littoral is most likely to translate as an initial military inferiority for the amphibious power. It follows, necessarily, that the success of amphibious operations, on any scale, almost requires that the foe should be deceived as to the points of attack, though it is not the case that amphibious operations require *absolute* surprise.

Seventh, where feasible, amphibious forces should land where the enemy is not present, prepared, and in strength. For example, in the *Falklands campaign the British in May 1982 landed at San Carlos on the west coast of East Falkland island, rather than close to the strong Argentine garrison around Port Stanley.

Eighth and finally, amphibious operations, even when conducted on a large scale, typically can have only an enabling effect upon the course of a war. The tactical, technical, and operational difficulties that attend efforts to land on a hostile shore not infrequently are so great in anticipation that too little thought is given to post-beachhead campaigning. CG

Bartlett, Merrill L. (ed.), *Assault from the Sea: Essays on the History of Amphibious Warfare* (Annapolis, Md., 1983).
Evans, M. H. H., *Amphibious Operations: The Projection of Sea Power Ashore* (London, 1990).
Liddell Hart, B. H., 'Marines and Strategy', *Marine Corps Gazette*, 64 (1980).
Till, G., Farrell, T., and Grove, M., 'Amphibious Operations', *Occasional*, 31 (1997).

that could travel from port direct to the invasion beach. As a result, the seagoing 158 foot (55 metre) Landing Craft Infantry, Large (LCI-L) was produced, capable of carrying up to 200 soldiers (over a company); three of these could land a whole battalion. Just over 1,000 of these craft were constructed, being used mainly by the Canadians and British. Of a different design to the smaller craft, the LCI-L carried two gangways either side of the bow, instead of a front ramp.

To complement the LCI-L, the British and Americans designed a small ship capable of carrying twenty Shermans on a lower deck and lighter vehicles on an upper, an elevator connecting the two. The Landing Ship Tank (LST), of which 1,050 were eventually built, was 328 feet (100 metres) long, 50 feet (15 metres) wide, and had a displacement of 2,100 tons. As a seagoing vessel, it had a ballast system that enabled it to take on seawater and sail with a deep draft, for stability; on approaching land, it pumped out the water, becoming a shallow-draft vessel, and beached directly onto the shore. Several cross-Channel ferries had earlier been converted to a similar design, by way of experiment, and there were several Landing Ship, Hospital, Anti-Aircraft, and Headquarters variants.

This range of landing craft were first employed in the TORCH landings in French North Africa, November 1942. A few LCAs had been used before in minor commando raids, for example on the Lofoten Islands, at Spitzbergen and Vaagso in 1941, and LCP-Ls in the unsuccessful *Dieppe raid of August 1942, when a few Churchill tanks were landed from LCMs. Thereafter, these craft were used at *Salerno, *Anzio, in southern France, and in the *Normandy invasion, where 4,126 of all types were used. LSTs, particularly, were in short supply, the European and Pacific theatres vying for the same vessels, as they were a vital ingredient in MacArthur's island hopping *Pacific campaign. As the smaller craft could only do 2–3 knots in heavy seas, the effect on the assault troops usually resulted in seasickness. Landing craft were converted to a wide range of support functions, being equipped with rockets, artillery, anti-aircraft guns, and there was even a Landing Craft, Kitchen (LCK).

Equally important came to be amphibious craft, capable of driving ashore with troops or supplies, such as the Landing Vehicle, Tracked (LVT). It was 8 feet (2.4 metres) tall, weighed 12 tons when empty, and could travel at 20 mph (32 km/hr) on land and 7 mph (11.2 km/hr) in water. First used at *Guadalcanal as an armoured ship-shore ferry, it was subsequently used in a direct assault role. Some of the 18,620 variants produced carried a turret that converted it into an amphibious tank. It was known to the British as Buffalo, who used it to clear the *Scheldt and to cross into the *Rhineland. Also relevant was the six-wheeled amphibious truck, DUKW. Developed in 1942, some 21,000 were built, and could carry 25 troops or 5,000 lb (2,200 kg) of supplies, and there was also an amphibious jeep.

Various river assault craft were used in *Vietnam, as were hovercraft, which may be included in this category. Landing craft were used also at the *Inchon landing in the *Korean war, to unload troops at *Suez and in the *Falklands, and remain a vital item in the inventory of modern armies, while roll-on-roll-off (RoRo) ferries have replaced the concept of the LST.   APC-A

Chandler, David G., and Collins, James Lawton (eds.), *The D-Day Encyclopaedia* (London, 1994).

Amritsar massacre   On 10 April 1919 in Amritsar, the holy city of the Sikhs (see SIKH WARS), rioting broke out following the arrest of nationalist leaders by British authorities. Some Europeans were killed, British women attacked, and British commercial interests burned. On 13 April, 20,000 protesters crammed into the Jallianwala Bagh, an enclosed square. The local British commander, Brig Gen Reginald Dyer, arrived with a company of troops. He gave the order to open fire. In a matter of minutes, 1,650 bullets were fired into the crowd, killing 397, including women and children, and wounding 1,500. In 1920, an official inquiry condemned the massacre and Dyer was forced to retire. He nevertheless enjoyed some public support in Britain and remained convinced that he had carried out his duty, arguing that he had neither panicked nor overreacted, but taken deliberately firm action to suppress a potentially explosive situation.   PC

ancient naval warfare   Ancient warships of the Mediterranean were distinguished from merchant ships, partly by having a ram, partly by being oar-powered, at least in battle, though they carried masts and sails for cruising with the wind astern. The simplest arrangement of oarsmen was a single file, bow to stern, at the same level, but this led to single file of oarsmen at more than one level (for example, as is now generally accepted, three in a trireme), and to more than one file of oarsmen at one or more levels (probably true of all the polyremes from the quadrireme onwards). The later developments were clearly designed to increase oar-power, whether for speed and manoeuvrability, or for sheer size and ability to carry numbers of Marines. Such ships could make relatively long sea voyages, but they were designed primarily for combat, and had little room for supplies, particularly of water.

This imposed limitations on both tactics and strategy. In battle, ramming and boarding, or a combination of the two, were the only ways of eliminating enemy vessels, and both literally involved contact. Catapults were sometimes mounted on warships from the 4th century BC onwards—for example in the battle off *Salamis in Cyprus in 306 BC—but they were man-killers, not ship-smashers, and there seems to be no example of an ancient warship being sunk by ship-borne artillery, though Carthaginian ships were once driven off by land-based mangonels in the first *Punic war. Thus it was impossible to lay off and cripple or sink an enemy at long range, and both ramming and boarding were likely to be effective only once. After a successful ram, ships could back water and go after another enemy, but one wonders how many such shocks a ship could take; boarding involved leaving at least some of one's Marines on the captured vessel.

To get round some of these problems tactics were developed at least to avoid ramming prow to prow. Because the ram was the only ship-smashing weapon available, fleets fought in line abeam so as to present as many rams to the enemy as possible. Sometimes, in retreat, they even backed away from the enemy to avoid presenting their vulnerable sterns to his rams. But by steering for the gaps between opposing vessels one could try to cut right through their line (the *diekplous*), then turn to ram their sterns (the *anastrophe*), or, if that was not possible, could ram their sides or, by at least shipping one's own bow oars, shatter the enemy's by steering a converging course. An alternative, particularly if one had a larger fleet, was to try to turn an enemy's flank (the *periplous*). Such tactics were a speciality of the 5th-century BC Athenian navy in particular, but also of the Carthaginian in the 3rd.

However, it was too easy for a fleet which knew its limitations to nullify such tactics by either fighting in a confined space, as the Syracusans and their allies, for example, did during the siege of *Syracuse in 413 BC, or by forming a circle as Peloponnesian ships did both in the Gulf of Corinth in 429 BC, or off Corfu in 426 BC, or by deploying in a double line abeam as the Athenians did at *Arginusae. The ultimate counter to superior ships was, perhaps, the *corvus*, the boarding-gangway invented by the Romans in the first Punic war. Thus the *diekplous*, like 'crossing the T', remained more of an ideal than a practical possibility, and was rarely used, it seems, in large-scale battles.

But it was in the realm of strategy that ancient warships were most limited. Naval power is a concept that appeared at least as early as Herodotus (see GREEK HISTORIANS), who credited both Greeks and Persians with recognizing its importance. There is no doubt that it enabled the Persians, for example, to strike at Athens directly in the *Marathon campaign, in 490 BC, and later enabled the Athenians twice to create and maintain empires in the Aegean; in the western Mediterranean, similarly, sea power held together the far-flung Carthaginian empire.

But naval power can never, by itself, win wars except where either island states, or ones dependent on sea power for survival, are the belligerents, or the conflict itself is for control of an island. Mahan's 'far distant, storm beaten ships' may have stood between Napoleon and the dominion of the world, but they could not defeat the Grande Armée by themselves precisely because it never looked upon them. Similarly, in the ancient world, Athens could not defeat *Sparta by sea power alone, nor Carthage Rome, whereas Sparta could defeat Athens by sea power, as she did in the *Peloponnesian wars, because Athens was dependent on seaborne supplies, and, similarly, Rome could defeat Carthage in the first Punic war because the conflict was basically for control of Sicily.

In particular, *blockade of even single seaports, let alone whole coastlines, was virtually impossible for ancient warships, simply because they could not remain permanently on station. The most they could do was to establish a nearby base and hope to be able to set to sea in time to intercept enemy vessels, either on their way out or their way in. Thus ancient naval warfare is full of incidents in which either single ships or even whole squadrons break in or out in the face of overwhelming enemy superiority. The exploits of Hannibal the Rhodian at the siege of Lilybaeum, in the first Punic war, are a classic case, but earlier, for example, a squadron of twelve ships managed to get into Syracuse, in 413 BC, even though the Athenian commander, Nicias, had sent out twenty ships to watch for them.

The limitations of sea power were something ancient states forgot at their peril, and it is significant that both the classic encounters between land powers and sea powers—the Peloponnesian wars and the first Punic war—ended in victory for the land power. JFL

Gardiner, Robert (ed.), *The Age of the Galley* (London, 1995).
Starr, Chester G., *The Influence of Seapower on Ancient History* (Oxford, 1989).

Anglo-Afghan wars (1838–1919). The steady advance southwards of the Russian empire into central Asia and the equally relentless advance north-westwards of the British dominion in India in the first half of the 19th century forced Afghanistan—the kingdom of Kabul—into the uneasy position of a buffer state between the two. The possibility of a Russian invasion of India via Kabul and the *Khyber Pass or via Herat, Kandahar, and the Bolan Pass obsessed the authorities in Calcutta and London. The attitude of the emir at Kabul was thus of paramount importance and in 1837 a British envoy, Alexander Burnes, was despatched to Kabul to enlist Emir Dost Muhammad's firm support. The latter was anxious to obtain a British alliance but the price he required was assistance in the return of the former Afghan possession of Peshawar, seized by the Sikhs in 1834 (see SIKH WARS). It was a price the British would not pay because, forced to choose between the Afghans and the Sikhs, they preferred to stay with the powerful kingdom of the Punjab, under its able ruler, Ranjit Singh. Dost Muhammad, despairing of British support, therefore prepared to listen to the Russians and a Russian envoy, Vitkevich, arrived in Kabul on 19 December 1837 while Burnes was still there.

Convinced that the emir was now pro-Russian, the governor-general of India, Lord Auckland, decided to cut the Gordian knot by replacing Dost Muhammad with a former ruler, Shah Shuja. The Sikhs were persuaded to enter a Tripartite Treaty for this purpose and in December 1838 the British army of the Indus assembled at Ferozepore in the Punjab to escort Shah Shuja to Kabul. It made its way slowly down the Indus and then up the Bolan Pass to Kadahar. There, in May 1839, it was joined by another force from Bombay, and the combined force reached Kabul on 7 August 1839, having stormed the immensely powerful fortress of Ghazni en route. Shah Shuja was installed as emir and Dost Muhammad fled, eventually surrendering in November 1840 and being exiled to Calcutta.

It soon became clear that Shah Shuja lacked popular support. A British army could not be maintained in Afghanistan indefinitely and by October 1841 there were ominous signs of Afghan insurrection. Elphinstone, who had succeeded Keane, was an infirm, vacillating man, and his political advisers, Macnaghten and Burnes, faced with the potential ruin of their Afghan policy, were reluctant to accept the evidence of a growing revolt. The storm burst in November 1841 when Burnes was murdered by a mob. Feeble attempts to retrieve the situation strengthened Afghan opposition. At the end of December Macnaghten attempted to negotiate a peaceful withdrawal with Muhammad Akbar Khan, Dost Muhammad's son and leader of the insurgents round Kabul. At a conference on 23 December 1841 Macnaghten was treacherously murdered but Akbar offered to allow the British force at Kabul to retire in peace. It was a trap and when the British began their retreat on 6 January 1842 they came under immediate attack from Akbar's tribesmen. Under constant attack and enfeebled by the bitterly cold weather, the army and its followers were gradually destroyed in the passes leading to India and only a handful escaped. At Jalalabad a garrison under Brig Sale hung on under constant siege and in the south Maj Gen Nott maintained his position at Kandahar.

When news of the outbreak reached India preparations were made to assemble a relief force under Maj Gen George Pollock at Peshawar. Pollock took his time in cementing *morale among his troops and in careful preparation. He began his advance on Kabul on 5 April 1842, and, picketing the heights as he went, relieved Jalalabad a few days later. There 'the Army of Retribution' remained for some months while the new governor-general, Lord Ellenborough, tried to decide what to do. Finally, Nott at Kandahar was given permission to retire via Kabul if he wished. Pollock seized the opportunity to advance to Kabul to meet Nott and the two armies were united there on 17 September 1842. Pollock succeeded in rescuing the British captives still in Afghan hands and after blowing up the Kabul bazaar as an act of retribution the combined forces reached Peshawar on 6 November. A grand review was held at Ferozepore and the first Anglo-Afghan War was at an end. Shah Shuja having been murdered the preceding March, Dost Muhammad was released from captivity and reassumed his throne.

The British annexation of the Punjab in 1849 after two bloody wars brought the boundaries of Afghanistan and British India into contact. But Dost Muhammad was absorbed in consolidating his kingdom and the British, shocked by their defeat in 1841–2, were averse to risking further meddling in Afghanistan and followed a policy of 'masterly inactivity' until 1876. In that year a new Conservative administration under Disraeli decided that the expansion and consolidation of Russia in central Asia, which had also brought its southern border into direct contact with Afghanistan, constituted a real threat to India. Attempts to persuade the emir, Sher Ali, to enter into an alliance and to accept a resident British envoy failed and Viceroy Lytton became convinced that Sher Ali had become pro-Russian rather than simply neutral.

In the summer of 1878, at the height of the Near Eastern crisis, Sher Ali was pressured into receiving a Russian mission but refused to receive a parallel British embassy. That gave Lytton the excuse he needed and three British columns invaded Afghanistan in November 1878, defeating the Afghans in the Khyber Pass at Ali Masjid and in the Kurram valley at Peiwar Kotal; in the south, Kandahar was occupied virtually without a fight. Sher Ali fled, dying in February 1879, and his successor, his eldest son Yakub Khan, sued for peace, which was signed at Gandamak in May 1879. It provided *inter alia* for a British envoy to reside at Kabul. In September 1879 the envoy, Cavagnari, was murdered in Kabul with his escort. The only readily available striking force was the column under *Roberts at Kurram and in October he occupied Kabul after a decisive victory at Charasia. Yakub Khan was deposed and exiled to India on suspicion of involvement in Cavagnari's death and Roberts proceeded to execute some scores of Afghans suspected of being involved in the envoy's murder. Two months after seizing Kabul a popular uprising forced Roberts to abandon Kabul and retire into his base at Sherpur where he was besieged for three weeks. On 23 December 1879 he defeated a major attack, routing his besiegers and reoccupying Kabul.

In May 1880 Sir Donald Stewart marched from Kandahar to Kabul, defeating an Afghan attack at Ahmed Khel en route, and took over the overall command from Roberts. The British still had no political solution and could see no option but to break up the country while retaining Kandahar. At this point in the summer of 1880 Abdurrahman Khan, a nephew of Sher Ali long exiled in Russia, decided to try his luck and entered Afghanistan. The British accepted him as emir of Kabul and of whatever he could control, except for Kandahar which was to remain in British hands. At this moment Sher Ali's younger son Ayub Khan, the governor of Herat, decided to make his own bid for the throne. He and his army were intercepted by a British brigade force at *Maiwand. The British force was utterly defeated on 27 July 1880 and the survivors besieged until the famous *Kabul to Kandahar march by Roberts at the end of August, who then defeated Ayub outside Kandahar on 1 September 1880.

Kabul had been evacuated by the British in August 1880 and the cabinet after much debate decided to give up Kandahar, finally evacuating Afghanistan in May 1881. Abdurrahman then gradually established his rule over the whole of Afghanistan, agreeing nevertheless to conduct his foreign relations in agreement with the government of India. Abdurrahman died in 1901, having successfully united Afghanistan and restored good relations with the British. His son Habibullah continued that policy but was murdered in 1919 and a period of dynastic instability followed. Habibullah's third son, Amanullah, emerged on top but his hold was shaky and in an effort to bolster his popularity he decided to invade India to seize the old Afghan frontier provinces west of the Indus and to proclaim full Afghan independence. It was a shrewd move because he could count on the support of his fellow-religionists among the Pathan transborder tribes and it caught the Indian army in the throes of post-war *demobilization.

Afghan troops crossed the frontier in April 1919, occupying the village of Bagh from which the water supply to the advanced British post at Landi Kotal at the entrance to the Khyber Pass could be cut. War was declared on 6 May 1919 and despite severe transport and communications difficulties in the Khyber, the Afghan army was quickly dislodged. The Afghan base of Dakkha was occupied and arrangements made to advance and occupy the Afghan provincial capital of Jalalabad. This advance was suspended as a result of further Afghan invasions from Khost into the Kurram and Tochi valleys further south, under the Afghan Gen Nadir Khan. By now the war had been complicated by the participation of the hostile Pathan tribes. In the Tochi valley of northern Waziristan, the advanced British posts were withdrawn and the focus of attention became the important British post of Thal at the entrance to the Kurram, where a British brigade was besieged until relieved by a column under Brig Gen Dyer, subsequently responsible for the *Amritsar massacre. The Afghan army was pushed back over the border and the hostile tribes gradually subdued.

Further south, in Baluchistan, the threat of an Afghan invasion was countered by the British attacking the strong Afghan fortress of Spin Baldak, which guarded the road to Kandahar. The fort was stormed and captured in an old-style assault on 27 May 1919, putting an end to the Afghan threat. A peace treaty was signed on 8 August 1919, bringing the third Anglo-Afghan war to a close but also formal recognition of full Afghan independence. The war had caused upheaval among the transborder tribes, leading to a major campaign in Waziristan in 1919–21, and was perhaps the most critical frontier campaign ever fought by the *Indian army. BR1

Anglo-Irish war (1916–22). This issue of Home Rule, or independence, for Ireland was a persistent factor in late 19th century British politics. Home Rule was welcomed by most of the Catholic majority in Ireland, but strongly opposed by the Protestant minority, mainly concentrated in the north (Ulster). In 1902 the 'Sinn Fein' ('Ourselves Alone') party was founded to promote Home Rule, closely linked to the militant Irish Republican Brotherhood (IRB). The frequent return of Irish nationalist candidates in elections convinced the British government in 1912 to grant Home Rule for Ireland, to come into force in 1914. The Ulster 'Unionists', politically well organized and with sympathizers among senior Army officers, armed themselves to resist Home Rule, the IRB responded, and civil war seemed likely. The outbreak of WW I led to the suspension of Home Rule, leaving the crisis unresolved, although many Irishmen (Catholic and Protestant) volunteered to fight for Britain in the war.

The '*Easter Rising' organized by the IRB in Dublin in 1916, was a farcical failure, more important as a later symbol than for its actual result. On Easter Monday, 24 April, and IRB group of about 1,600 under Padraig Pearse and James Connolly seized locations in central Dublin including the main post office, and declared a republic, expecting a popular uprising, which failed to happen. All were killed or captured by 30 April, largely by Irish troops. The British saw this rebellion as treason, and fifteen of the IRB leaders were shot, a reaction that did much to create wider sympathy for their cause. Among those who survived were Eamon de Valera, an American citizen, Michael Collins, and Constance Countess Markovitz. The British, anxious to placate the United States with its powerful Irish lobby, opened negotiations, unsuccessful at first, for an independent but partitioned Ireland. Lloyd George, British prime minister from December 1916, was also sympathetic to Irish nationalist aspirations.

In October 1917 all republican movements consolidated themselves as the Irish Volunteers under de Valera, who was also declared president of Ireland. The first Volunteer attacks on British military posts began in 1918. More support was gained when the British, who had introduced conscription for the rest of Britain in January 1916, passed legislation extending this to Ireland in April 1918 (although this was not enforced), and about 2,000 Volunteers were imprisoned without trial as suspect revolutionaries. At the war's end, in the British general election of 14 December 1918, Sinn Fein won 73 out of 105 Irish seats. Refusing to take these up in London, its members convened in Dublin on 21 January 1919 as the 'Dáil Eireann', the parliament of an independent Ireland. This amounted to a declaration of civil war.

The symbolic start of the war was the killing by Volunteers of two policemen at Soloheadbeg in Tipperary on 21 January 1919. Led by Michael Collins, about 3,000 Volunteers—increasingly known as the Irish Republican Army (IRA)—kept 80,000 troops and police at bay. IRA strategy was to attack isolated police and military barracks, sometimes by 'flying columns' in vehicles, forcing the police to abandon them and so lose control of the countryside. The IRA also used terror, intimidation and assassination, including in Dublin. The British recruited Auxiliary police from demobilized soldiers, including the notorious 'Black and Tans' (for their uniforms), who carried out brutal reprisals in return.

In December 1919 the British proposed a new form of Irish Home Rule with two separate parliaments, one of them responsible for six of the nine counties of Ulster (to be known as 'Northern Ireland'); this became the 1920 Government of Ireland Act. On 11 July 1921 a ceasefire was agreed between the British and Sinn Fein. The elections took place in August, with a separate parliament for Northern Ireland convening in Belfast, dominated by Ulster Unionists, while Sinn Fein assembled in Dublin again as Dáil Eireann. Negotiations headed by Collins led, on 6 December 1921, to the settlement of the Treaty of London, including the recognition by British of an Irish 'Free State' (an agreed form of words stopping short of an independent republic) without Northern Ireland. De Valera, leading the 'Anti-Treaty' protest against partition, resigned as president. The British withdrawal was followed by a further year of civil war between Irish government forces and 'Anti-Treaty' nationalists, in the course of which Collins was killed.   SDB

Coogan, Tim Pat, *The IRA* (London, 1971).

Smith, M. L. R., *Fighting For Ireland?* (London, 1995).

Townshend, Charles, *The British Campaign in Ireland 1919–1921* (Oxford, 1975).

Angola Former Portuguese colony in South-West Africa whose particularly unpleasant and intractable civil war has run since independence in 1975. The balance of forces has prevented either side from achieving outright military victory, yet despite a decade of UN involvement each has repeatedly turned to external actors—Cuban, Soviet, South African, Zairian, and freelance—to turn the tide. Characterized during the 1970s and 1980s by protracted high-intensity and *guerrilla confrontations, the war has since 1992 seen the emphasis shift to more indirect strategies based on control of, and denial of access to, resources and inflicting huge casualties on the civilian population.

Three organizations which had fought the 1961–75 'Liberation War' against the Portuguese and each other vied for control as independence neared. The theoretically Marxist MPLA (Movimento Popular de Libertação de Angola), led by Augustinho Neto, drew its support from the Mbundu (approx. 26 per cent of the population) in the centre of the country; Holden Roberto's FNLA (Frente de Libertação de Angola) recruited from the Bakongo (17 per cent) in the north-west and had support from, and bases in, Zaire; while Jonas Savimbi's UNITA (Uniao Naçional para Independencia de Angola) was made up mostly of Ovimbundu (38 per cent) from the south and centre. The announcement of Portugal's imminent withdrawal in September 1975

saw FNLA-Zairian and UNITA-South African offensives against the militarily weak MPLA thwarted with Cuban support. At independence (20 November 1975) two governments (UNITA-FNLA in Ambriz and MPLA in Luanda) claimed sovereignty, but the MPLA's military successes quickly broke up the FNLA and drove UNITA into the bush where, despite Zambian bases and Moroccan *matériel*, a poorly conducted guerrilla campaign posed little threat to Luanda.

During the 1980s, the conflict's apparent reflection of an intensifying *Cold War meant increasing external involvement. The USA's 'Reagan Doctrine' of unconditional support for anti-Soviet movements, and South Africa's fight to suppress SWAPO's (South West African People's Organization) Angolan bases, helped UNITA strengthen its hold over the north, centre, and south. But the battle of Cuito Canavale (August 1987–March 1988) showed increasing MPLA competence, the loss of Pretoria's military superiority, and the war's unpopularity with South Africa's white public and township-stretched soldiery alike. This led to the December 1988 Angola-Namibia Accord, with the linkage of Cuban–South African withdrawals from Angola to the independence of Namibia.

External actors were now pushing both parties to a negotiated conclusion. When UNITA swiftly broke a June 1989 ceasefire it was nearly destroyed in the MPLA's subsequent nine-month offensive, so offered a Lusophone Africa-brokered cessation of its own. This and the MPLA's renunciation of one-party rule paved the way for the Bicesse and Estoril Agreements (April–May 1991), specifying UN-conducted military integration and multi-party elections for September 1992. Despite breaches, the ceasefire generally held. But when MPLA leader Eduardo Dos Santos won the first round of the elections with 49.6 per cent, Savimbi refused to abide by the result, or conduct the obligatory run-off. Incomplete *demobilization and reintegration facilitated the resumption of full-scale civil war. UNITA captured Soyo—producer of one-third of Angola's oil—and Huambo, the latter after a 55-day siege which killed 10,000 and forced a 100,000-strong exodus to the coast; but the failure of UN-sponsored Addis Ababa and Abidjan processes led to the MPLA's recognition by Washington, Security Council condemnation, and arms and petrol embargoes. These and substantial MPLA advances (helped by South African *mercenaries) caused Savimbi to sign the Lusaka Accord in November 1994, ratified in May 1995, by which he accepted Dos Santos as president in return for a vice-president's post once UNITA had disbanded. A third UN operation was mounted. The 'Third War' had cost perhaps 300,000 lives (3 per cent of Angola's population).

But low-level conflict persisted. Mutual distrust prevented Savimbi from disarming and assuming his post, while Dos Santos moved against UNITA strongholds, particularly in the diamond-producing north-east (which provide perhaps $600 m a year). Luanda's desire to shut down UNITA's bases in Zaire and so separate it from the outside world led to its substantial support for Laurent Kabila in the latter's May 1997 ousting of UNITA-supported President Mobutu. Despite Kabila's failure to act against UNITA, Luanda had to save him from rebellion in August 1998 to guarantee a regime which would not support them. Since autumn 1998 the FAA (Forças Armadas Angolanas) and UNITA have rearmed and reorganized, but the FAA has been hampered by its ongoing commitment to the Democratic Republic of Congo (renamed in 1997); UNITA has made substantial gains, having driven out UN observers. Full-scale hostilities resumed in 1999, but with neither side able to gain a decisive advantage, or to restrict the other's access to funds, no end appears in sight.   DD

Alao, Abiodun, *Brothers at War* (London, 1994).
Brittain, Victoria, *Death of Dignity* (London, 1998).
Vines, A., 'Angola and UNAVEM III', *Brassey's Defence Yearbook* (London, 1997).

animals and the military (see also HORSES). Man has made use of the strength, speed, and stamina of his companion animals, in war as well as in peace, from the earliest recorded times. Domesticated animals have shared with their human comrades all the hardships of military service, suffering and dying from the effects of disease, thirst, hunger, the violence of the enemy, and privations stemming from military necessity or financial callousness. Even harmless farm stock or household animals have become casualties of war, killed in land or air bombardments of the fields and towns in which they lived alongside their owners, or sometimes deliberately slaughtered in acts of economic warfare or as part of a policy of terror.

Dogs, the first animals to be domesticated, and man's associate since at least the 11th century BC, served originally as auxiliaries in the hunt and protectors against other predators. These roles were easily adaptable to military purposes, and dogs were then used to detect the location of enemy patrols, to give the alarm, or to attack as the occasion arose. Large aggressive animals were used as attack dogs in the armies of Ptolomaic Egypt, the Persian empire, classical Rome, and in medieval Christendom, where they were used against armoured cavalry. A similar role was performed by dogs of the Red Army during WW II, who were trained to run under enemy tanks, where explosive charges carried on their backs would be triggered. In the 16th century, English mastiffs were famous for their courage and ferocity as war dogs, and were used in Spanish armies both in Europe and America. The best counter to the fighting dog, who usually wore a spiked collar or other protection, was found to be another dog of similar type and training. In WW I, both the French and Belgian armies used large dogs (which in the civilian society of the day were commonly used to pull milk floats) as light draught animals for wheeled machine guns. Such dogs could pull loads of up to 441 lb (200 kg), or carry backpacks of up to 33 lb (15 kg) of ammunition or emergency rations to troops pinned down by enemy fire. In both world wars of the 20th century, dogs were also used to carry messages to and from the firing line, as they could move much faster than human runners and presented a smaller target to the enemy. In static conditions, dogs were employed to lay field *telephone cable, paid out from a small drum strapped on their back. In the late 19th and early 20th centuries, German, French, and other armies used dogs, sometimes fitted with medical packs, to find casualties after a battle, and either to help them to safety or else go for help. Dogs continue to serve as patrol or guard animals, especially in extensive but lightly manned installations such as ordnance depots or airfields, and as 'sniffers', trained to detect mines, explosives, etc.

Many kinds of beast have been employed in military transportation, generally the same ones used in ordinary local transport of the period. Such animals include horses, ponies, mules, asses and donkeys, elephants, camels, reindeer, buffaloes, oxen or bullocks, yaks and zebus. The suitability of all these for pack transport makes them particularly useful for operations in wild or roadless terrain. The mule, famous for its sense of balance, was the favoured animal of the Indian Mountain Artillery, which drew most of its animals from Missouri. During WW II, mules, with their vocal cords cut to prevent them giving away concealed positions, were included in the glider-borne 'Chindit' forces, landed behind Japanese lines in *Burma.

Elephants were used not only for transport but also for a variety of military pioneer tasks, such as demolishing obstacles, acting as mobile cranes to move materials of all kinds, forming living bridges over which armies could cross shallow rivers, or pushing down the gates of besieged fortresses. They were used in combat in India from at least the 6th century BC and were taken into use by the successors of *Alexander 'the Great', who first encountered them in force at the battle of the *Hydaspes. Elephants, probably of a small North African species, were first used in European warfare by the Carthaginians at the siege of Agrigentum (262 BC). The war elephant, fitted with a formidable weapons array and capable of great speed in the charge, later became a powerful component of Roman and other armies in the Levant and Asia Minor, but was eventually displaced by the cataphract (armoured heavy cavalry) as the shock action element of the battle line. Indian generals continued to place great reliance on their elephants, despite the fact that time and again in the medieval period they were routed by invading armies from Central Asia. Despite their terrifying effect on men and horses unfamiliar with them, elephants could easily be defeated by well-trained troops, or panicked into trampling down either side indiscriminately. Elephants were finally driven from the Indian battlefield by the advent of modern musketry, though they retained their old role as mobile command posts until the *Sikh wars of the 1840s. The Royal Artillery in India used these sagacious pachyderms to pull its siege guns as late as the beginning of the 20th century.

Camels, both the one-humped Arabian or dromedary and the two-humped Bactrian variety, have been used to support campaigns in desert areas from biblical times onwards. Frequently ill-tempered and ill-used, their natural ability to survive for long periods without food or water nevertheless makes them valuable both as baggage animals and troop-carriers. The *mehari* or fast riding-camel provided a passable substitute for horses when cavalrymen had insufficient mounts and was ideal for *mounted infantry or *reconnaissance patrols operating in arid regions. Both the British and the French made full use of camel corps in their colonial campaigns in the Sahara, the Sudan, Somalia, the Levant, and Sind, in a period stretching from the 1840s until after WW II. At Sardis (547 BC), Cyrus II of Persia, faced by the predominantly cavalry and *chariot army of Croesus of Lydia, positioned his baggage camels in front of his army. Their unfamiliar appearance and smell so unsettled the enemy horses that the Lydian troopers were forced to dismount and fight on foot, where they were decisively defeated.

Domestic cats, though by their nature not amenable to military *discipline, have nevertheless played their part in war. The ever-inventive Cyrus II is said to have used cats to defeat an army of Egyptians in 500 BC. Each of his soldiers was ordered to carry a cat on his shield, thus preventing the Egyptians, to whom the cat was sacred, from striking a blow. The continuing value of cats as self-operating anti-rodent systems allows them to be tolerated, sometimes even encouraged, in military installations. 'Simon', ship's cat of the British frigate HMS *Amethyst*, despite being wounded by the fire of Chinese shore batteries, continued his part in the fight against rats which infested this ship while she was trapped in the Yangtse river from April to June 1947. He became the only British cat to be awarded a posthumous *decoration for gallantry. The Russian cat 'Murka' became a Hero Cat of the USSR for services at the battle of *Stalingrad in 1942–3. Rats are the common enemy of all soldiers, as they spoil or consume food and other military stores, scavenge on the fallen, and carry numerous diseases. In siege conditions starving garrisons have found roast or stewed rat a valuable source of protein. During WW II, the USAAF experimented with bats, who were to be fitted with incendiary devices and released over Japan, where it was hoped that they would roost under the eaves of wood and paper buildings before the incendiaries ignited.

The military have long sought to use wild animals as auxiliaries. Samson's legendary exploits included the destruction of Philistine crops by releasing 150 pairs of foxes with torches tied to their tails. The classical Hindu treatise on statecraft, the *Arthasastra*, recommends the use of monkeys or birds to set fire to the thatched roofs of enemy towns. Even the friendly and highly intelligent dolphin has been trained by the US navy to serve in roles similar to those performed on land by dogs, including planting or finding explosive devices, and patrolling to detect and attack enemy frogmen. The US army has experimented with coyotes, ferrets, skunks, and racoons as landmine detectors.

Homing or 'carrier' pigeons are known to have been used in Mesopotamia as early as *c.*1150 BC and have been employed for this purpose in various times and places ever since. During WW I, the British army alone used some 10,000 carrier pigeons, with a 95 per cent successful delivery rate, despite many birds arriving injured by enemy action or hawk attacks. The services of their French comrades are memorialized in the citadel of Lille. During WW II, the British employed 20,000 homing pigeons. Many aircrews of RAF bombers forced to come down in the sea owed their rescue to such messengers. Canaries were used by military as by civil miners to detect the presence of dangerous gases in their workings. Geese performed the duty of sentinels from the days of Ancient Rome, where a sacred flock was kept on the Capitoline Hill to commemorate their giving warning of a night attack by the Gauls during the sack of Rome (390–386 BC).

Many insects harbour diseases to which soldiers are as vulnerable as other men, but often without the acquired immunity of the native inhabitants of the countries where they are required to serve. The anopheles mosquito, carrying the scourge of malaria, was the unwitting executioner of thousands of European soldiers sent to garrisons in the West Indies, Africa, or India. The US army fighting in Cuba during the *Spanish-American war and subsequently in the *Philippines insurrection, lost far more men to malaria than to enemy action. During WW I, insects played a direct part in the battle of Tanga during the *German East Africa campaign in October 1914, when the attacking Indian troops were routed by swarms of angry wild bees. On the western front, one officer of the British Tank Corps used glow-worms to mark the way forward in the dark. Fleas carrying plague may have been used by the Japanese in China in the 1930s. In the *Vietnam war, the US army tried using parasitic bugs (creatures stimulated by the approach of humans) to detect enemy infiltrators.

Many kinds of animals have been adopted as mascots, sometimes with official approval to enhance the appearance of units on ceremonial parades or otherwise build up esprit de corps. These include goats, ponies, rams, antelopes, bears, and tigers. Smaller creatures such as piglets, rabbits, cats, and dogs are the more usual companions of sentimental soldiers. A domestic fowl, 'Myrtle the Parachick', made several landings with the British 4th Parachute Brigade and was killed at *Arnhem. Dogs remain the favoured companion of most soldiers, in legend as in history. Homer's *Odyssey* records the name of 'Argos', Odysseus' dog, the only creature to recognize him when he returned to Ithaca from the Trojan war. In the Hindu epic, the *Mahabharata*, the hero Yudhisthira refuses to enter heaven without his faithful dog (generally regarded as the only favourable mention of this animal in all Sanskrit literature). In the *British civil wars, Prince *Rupert's dog 'Boy', regarded by his Puritan enemies as his familiar spirit, was killed at *Marston Moor. In the late 1970s, during the troubles in Northern Ireland, 'Rats', a stray terrier, achieved fame by attaching himself to successive British units in their dangerous post at Crossmaglen. He was deemed a 'legitimate target' by the *IRA, but survived several wounds and eventually retired to a Kentish farm.   TAH

Cooper, Jilly, *Animals in War* (London, 1983).

Gray, Ernest A., *Dogs of War* (London, 1989).

Harfield, Alan, *Pigeon to Packhorse* (Chippenham, 1989).

anti-armour weapons The increasing importance of armoured fighting vehicles, in particular the tank, in the 20th century required the development of specialized weapons capable of countering their armoured protection. The first tanks deployed during WW I possessed relatively light armour and were vulnerable to field artillery. The Germans produced an anti-tank rifle (essentially a beefed-up heavy calibre bolt action weapon) which was unpleasant to fire but ranks as the first specialist anti-armour weapon.

The development of the tank as the main striking arm during WW II necessitated the design of specialized anti-armour weapons. At the beginning of the war, most armies deployed dedicated anti-armour guns of around 40 mm. Tanks were soon equipped with thicker armour to protect them from these weapons, which in turn forced the fielding of heavier anti-armour guns. By the end of the war, the Germans were regularly using their 88 mm anti-aircraft gun with conspicuous success in the anti-armour role and the British had fielded a 77 mm gun. A gun versus armour race had developed, which continues to this day.

WW II also saw the development of the two basic types of anti-armour rounds which still continue to be used in modified form. The first, and simplest, of these is based on kinetic energy (KE). This round depends on mass and velocity; the denser the projectile and the higher its velocity, the deeper it penetrates armour. Originally, the projectile itself was made of a very hard metal, such as tungsten, and fired down a long, tapered barrel to give it a high velocity. The German 88 mm gun is probably the best example of this type of weapon. It fired a 9.5 kg solid-shot round at 2,657 feet/sec (810 metres/sec) which was capable of penetrating 60 mm of armour at 3,936 feet (1,200 metres).

By 1944, the British had developed an improved version of the KE round. A round invariably lost velocity in flight due to wind resistance. To help overcome this problem the British invented a 'discarding sabot' round. This consisted of a small solid shot encased in a pot (the sabot) which disintegrated when leaving the gun's barrel, allowing the smaller projectile to fly to the target with the propulsion force concentrated on a smaller area. In the modern version

of this type of round, the projectile is often made of depleted uranium, an extremely heavy and dense metal.

The second type of round developed relied upon chemical energy (CE) rather than kinetic. In its simplest form, this was merely a projectile that exploded on contact with the tank—a basic high explosive round. During the war, a more sophisticated version of this was invented based upon a hollow charge. This round was made of a cone of explosive (the hollow, or shaped, charge) lined with metal. When the warhead struck its target, the explosive would detonate and its cone shape would focus the energy of the explosion driving its now molten metal lining through the armour in a tight stream. This basic idea is still utilized by 'high-explosive anti-tank' (HEAT) rounds in use today.

This shaped charge also allowed the deployment of lightweight, man-portable anti-armour rockets. The first of these was the German Panzerfaust used initially in 1942. These proved capable of penetrating up to 200 mm of armour at up to 328 yards (300 metres). Simple to operate and produce, the Germans distributed these weapons liberally to their troops. The Allies also used weapons with similar effects, like the British PIAT (Projector Infantry, Anti-Tank) and the US Bazooka.

Most nations today still use a portable anti-armour rocket similar to those produced during WW II in order to provide the infantry with a degree of organic anti-armour capability. These weapons are lightweight and have a limited range (generally under 547 yards (500 metres)). An example of this type of weapon is the Russian RPG-7. Weighing 8.5 kg fully armed, its 2.2 kg warhead is capable of penetrating 260 mm of armour at a distance of up to 383 yards (350 metres). These weapons were exported widely during the *Cold War.

By the end of WW II improvements in armour made necessary the deployment of ever larger and heavier anti-armour guns. These weapons became more and more difficult to manoeuvre on the battlefield. Two solutions emerged from this; first, the *self-propelled (SP) gun; second, the Anti-Tank Guided Missile (ATGM). The latter has the advantage of being far lighter and more accurate than the gun and has been deployed extensively by the world's armies, both on the ground and in the air.

These weapons can be broken down into two broad categories. First, there are the man-portable ATGMs. These are lightweight and have a relatively short range. In most of these weapons, the missile is guided to the target by commands from the gunner transmitted along a wire running from the launch tube to the missile. The gunner has merely to keep the target in his sights to hit it. The best example of this type is the French-designed MILAN (Missile d'Infanterie Léger Anti-char), used by over 30 nations. The current model, the MILAN 2, fires a 3 kg HEAT warhead up to 3,280 yards (3,000 metres) and can penetrate up to 1,000 mm of armour. The missile and launcher together weigh around 30 kg and the system is normally served by a two-man crew.

In addition to man-portable ATGMs, a heavier, vehicle-mounted version is also used. This type has greater penetration and range than its lighter cousin, but operates along the same principles. The US-produced TOW (Tube-launched, Optically-sighted, Wire-guided) missile is an example of a heavy ATGM. First fielded in 1972, the 100 kg TOW is normally fitted to a HMMWV ('Hummer') or a light armoured vehicle, but is also fitted to the AH-1 Cobra helicopter. The current TOW 2 fires a 10 kg HEAT warhead up to 4,100 yards (3,750 metres), which can penetrate over 1,000 mm of armour. Two other versions are in production; the TOW 2A, which fires a tandem charge designed to defeat reactive armour, and the TOW 2B, which is designed to attack the thin top armour of a target.

The next generation of ATGMs are laser- rather than wire-guided. These have the advantage of being more accurate than the traditional variety. The only example of this type currently in use is the US Hellfire missile. While the Hellfire is normally fitted to the Apache helicopter, it can also be fitted on ground vehicles. It has a 7,653 yard (7,000 metre) range and its warhead consists of a tandem-shaped charge to penetrate reactive armour.   RTF

Jane's Armour and Artillery, 1998–1999 (London, 1998).
Jane's Infantry Weapons, 1998–1999 (London, 1998).
Mellenthin, F. W., *Panzer Battles: A Study of the Employment of Armour in WW II* (London, 1955).

Antietam, battle of (1862), bloodiest single day of the *American civil war. *Lee capitalized on his crushing victory at second *Bull Run to take the war into enemy territory, hoping also to rally Maryland to the Confederate cause. Underestimating how quickly *McClellan would revitalize the Army of the Potomac, he scattered his army in drives on the Federal arsenal at Harper's Ferry and towards Harrisburg, the capital of Pennsylvania. Despite possessing a windfall copy of Lee's disposition of forces, McClellan failed fully to exploit the opportunity, permitting the Confederates to beat a fighting retreat and regroup along a ridgeline around the town of Sharpsburg, with their backs to the Potomac river, faced by more than twice their number.

Through the early morning of 17 September first *Hooker, then Mansfield's corps, and then Sedgwick's division of Sumner's corps advanced against Jackson's corps on the Confederate left flank. There were 10,000 combined casualties including Hooker and Mansfield, mostly incurred over a 20 acre (8 hectare) cornfield which changed hands fifteen times. This drew in troops from D. H. Hill's corps at the Confederate centre, where first French's and then Richardson's divisions of Sumner's corps struck at the aptly named Bloody Lane through late morning. Richardson died achieving a breakthrough, but McClellan refused to commit his reserve and Lee was able to restore the hinge of his position.

The most flagrant of all the wasted Union opportunities was the simultaneous failure of *Burnside to cross Antietam Creek against the Confederate right, threatening Lee's line of retreat and the direction from which desperately awaited reinforcements had to advance from Harper's Ferry. With a brute obstinacy which prefigured the massacre into which he was to send his army at *Fredericksburg three months later, he permitted a brigade of Georgia *sharpshooters to hold up his 12,000 men throughout the morning by persistently attacking across a narrow bridge, when the creek was easily fordable. After the opposite bank was gained, he paused for two hours before resuming an advance that drove the remains of the Confederate right under *Longstreet back around Sharpsburg, but McClellan again held back his reserve of 20,000 men. The last minute arrival of A. P. *Hill with 3,000 men after marching 17 miles (27 km) in eight hours from Harper's Ferry took Burnside in the flank and he fell back.

Stunned by the carnage, the two sides devoted the next day to dealing with their casualties: over 12,000 Unionists and nearly 11,000 Confederates, one out of every four men engaged. Despite the arrival of two fresh divisions, McClellan took no further offensive action and permitted Lee's army to retreat unhindered, an inaction which precipitated his dismissal as army commander by an exasperated *Lincoln.

Missed opportunity though it was, the defeat aborted Confederate hopes for early British recognition and gave Lincoln the opportunity to issue the Emancipation Proclamation. By introducing a moral element into a war which many believed unjustly waged against states as entitled to secede as the original 13 colonies, the proclamation made recognition by the premier abolitionist world power impossible.   HEB

Antioch (The Orontes), **battle of** (1098), an encounter of the First *Crusade with important military and political repercussions. On 3 June 1098, an alliance of Frankish leaders seized from its Turcoman occupiers the originally Byzantine city of Antioch, strategically situated within massive walls on the Orontes river in north-west Syria. Almost immediately, a large force under the Turcoman ruler of Mosul in Iraq appeared and took up position on the Orontes in order to invest the city. Preoccupied with a military threat in Anatolia, the Byzantine emperor was unable to assist his Frankish allies in protecting his possession, and their situation became desperate. But the discovery of a supposed holy relic raised the crusaders' morale, and perilous sortie from the city turned into a decisive victory over the besiegers on 28 June. With Antioch relatively secure, the main body of crusaders was able to proceed to their principal goal of recovering the Holy Land. Using the Byzantine emperor's absence from the battle as a pretext, one of the Frankish leaders claimed Antioch for himself, and established an independent principality that was to play an important part in the subsequent history of the Crusades. DWM

Runciman, Stephen, *A History of the Crusades*, vol. 1 (Cambridge, 1951).

Antony, Mark (correctly Marcus Antonius), (83–30 BC), Roman general and political leader who took part in the final destruction of the republic. Born in 83 BC, he served under Julius *Caesar in Gaul and in the *Roman civil war of 49–45 BC, and was consul when Caesar was assassinated in 44. In the following year, he formed the Second Triumvirate with Octavian and Lepidus. After his victory at *Philippi, he took control of the east to campaign against the Parthians. Having reorganized the eastern empire into three provinces and five client kingdoms, he invaded Armenia in 37, but was forced to withdraw in 36 with disastrous losses. He reinvaded successfully in 34, but the propaganda value of this was negated by the quasi-triumph he held at Alexandria and his granting of client kingdoms to his mistress Cleopatra and their children. Octavian finally declared war on Cleopatra in 31 BC, leading to Antony's defeat in the naval battle off *Actium in Greece. Antony and Cleopatra fled to Egypt where they took their own lives a year later. BR2

Cassius Dio, 41–51.
Huzar, Eleanor G., *Mark Antony, A Biography* (London, 1986).
Plutarch, *Life of Antony*.
—— *Appian Civil Wars*, ii–v.
Syme, Ronald, *The Roman Revolution* (Oxford, 1939).

Antwerp, sieges of (1814, 1832, and 1914). Antwerp's location on the Scheldt gives it commercial and strategic importance. In November 1576, when the city was part of the Spanish Netherlands, its garrison under *Alba massacred thousands of citizens in the 'Spanish fury'. Nine years later it was retaken from the Protestants by *Parma.

Part of the Austrian Netherlands for the second half of the 18th century, Antwerp fell to the French early in the *French Revolutionary wars. *Napoleon saw it as 'a pistol pointed at the heart of England' and built its first dock. Besieged by the Allies in 1814, Antwerp was stoutly defended by Lazare *Carnot, who had done much to raise French armies in the 1790s but had not been employed under the empire. In 1814 Holland and Belgium were united in a kingdom ruled by William of Orange. In 1830 fighting broke out between Dutch and Belgian elements, and in 1832 a French army under Marshal Gerard moved north to support the Belgians, besieging Antwerp, which was compelled to surrender. It became part of an independent Belgium.

In 1887 it was decided to turn the city into a 'national redoubt' protected by outlying forts designed by Henri-Alexis *Brialmont. These embodied armoured cupolas and subterranean works like those at Namur and *Liège. In 1914, as the Germans swept into Belgium, the Belgian field army fell back on Antwerp. German planners knew that Antwerp must be taken to safeguard the right rear of their armies swinging down into France, and initially allocated five reserve corps to the task. In the event Gen von Beseler had only six divisions, and was also responsible for guarding lines of communication through Belgium. He approached Antwerp from the south, covering Brussels against sorties, instead of from the east as planned, and thus had to cross the river Nethe. It was not until 29 September that, well provided with heavy guns like those which had already reduced Liège, he was ready to attack.

Beseler's guns speedily smashed the forts. The British first sent a naval and marine division, assembled from pensioners and recruits, and then on 5 October dispatched the 7th Division and 3rd Cavalry Division. The French agreed to send Marines and infantry under Adm Ronarc'h. On 9 October Beseler demanded Antwerp's *capitulation, and its governor recognized that continued resistance was impossible.

The majority of the Belgian field army escaped westwards, and most of the British naval division also got away. Beseler was ordered to move on the Flanders coast via Ghent and Bruges, following up the Allies and covering the right flank of newly formed German reserve corps which were making for *Ypres in the hope of turning the northern flank of the fast-evolving western front. He could not prevent the Belgians from taking up a position on the river Yser between Ypres and Dixmude, while Ronarc'h held the Dixmude area. The two British army divisions, which became Lt Gen Rawlinson's IV Corps, joined the British Expeditonary Force (BEF) at Ypres. RH

Anzac (see also AUSTRALIAN IMPERIAL FORCE). Anzac is by turn an acronym, a place, a day of commemoration, and a cultural force. During the preparations for the *Gallipoli landings the term was coined as 'telegraphese' to describe the Australian and New Zealand Army Corps commanded by *Birdwood. The stretch of Turkish coastline where the Australians and New Zealanders had gone ashore quickly became known as Anzac Cove, and the whole of their position as 'Anzac', while the men themselves were known as 'Anzacs'; this was underpinned with the subsequent issue of a small letter 'A', sown on the colour patch, worn by all survivors of the campaign. Anzac Day, 25 April, was first observed in Egypt, London, and Australia in 1916 and has evolved into Australia's true (though unofficial) national day. It is marked by solemn services at dawn and a march of *veterans later in the morning and continues at the end of the 20th century to draw increasingly large crowds in attendance.

The Anzac legend grew out of the Great War experience, and helped to define the national character and national symbols in a country which had only been created in 1901. Although there were many writers, artists, and public figures who had a hand in shaping the Anzac legend, foremost among them was C. E. W. *Bean, the official historian of Australia's war effort. The legend, like the control of Anzac Day observances, has been contested territory within Australian public life, and critics have argued that it militarizes the national culture and excludes those groups, especially *women, for whom war service was generally not an option. While there is some truth in this, Anzac Day itself has functioned in a more inclusive manner in recent times with veterans from the communities of post-1945 non-British migration claiming a place in the march. JG1

Anzio, battle of (1944). By winter 1943 the Allied *Italian campaign was making disappointing progress. Both *Clark and the Fifth US Army on the west coast, and *Montgomery and the Eighth British Army on the east, had been fought to a standstill on the Gustav Line, in difficult terrain and atrocious weather. German defence of *Cassino proved especially obdurate. As early as October *Eisenhower, Supreme Allied Commander, and *Alexander, commanding in Italy, discussed an amphibious operation to outflank German defences. SHINGLE, the plan for Anzio, was championed by the British premier *Churchill, but there was competition for amphibious resources between it and the coming invasion of France, and a dangerous lack of operational clarity.

The landings took place under Maj Gen John P. Lucas on 22 January 1944 and achieved complete surprise, the British 1st Division going ashore north-west of Anzio, the US 3rd Division near Nettuno, to its east, and Anzio being taken by US Rangers. Within 48 hours Lucas had secured a beachhead 7 miles (11.3 km) deep, but he was unsure what to do with it. Clark had ordered him to secure a beachhead, and then advance to the Alban hills, but had privately warned him not to stick his neck out. FM Albert Kesselring, the German C-in-C, did not react by pulling back from Cassino, as the Allies had hoped, but counter-attacked. The beachhead became the scene of vicious fighting, with ground disputed yard by yard and German guns ranging across the whole area. By early April it was clear that fighting had reached a stalemate.

On 11 May the Allies launched DIADEM, a weighty offensive which smashed the Gustav Line and eventually enabled the Anzio force to break out. Though Clark took Rome, he failed to strike through the Velletri gap to reach Valmontone, which would have cut off many of the defenders of Cassino. Anzio aroused lasting controversy. Lucas, relieved of command in February, was not an inspiring commander, but was hamstrung by lack of a clear mission: had he pushed straight for Rome he could have been engulfed. The fighting cost the Allies 7,000 killed and 36,000 wounded, as well as 44,000 sick. Kesselring estimated German losses at 40,000, including 5,000 killed and 4,500 captured. RH

d'Este, Carlo, *Fatal Decision: Anzio and the Battle for Rome* (London, 1991).

APCs (armoured personnel carriers) are, as the term suggests, vehicles designed primarily to transport troops, while at the same time affording those carried some protection against *small arms, light support weapons, blast, and nuclear, bacteriological, and chemical attack. Unlike *MICVs, they are not designed to be fought from and any offensive armament they may carry is usually an afterthought. There are three main types of APC: wheeled, tracked, and half-tracked (although the last is now largely obsolete). The *Wehrmacht led the way in the development of APCs, *blitzkrieg requiring mobile infantry to keep up with tanks. The Hanomag-designed Schutzenpanzerwagen (SPW) series was based on a three-quarter tank chassis, with its tracks bearing most of the vehicle's weight, while front wheels combined with the tracks to steer it. The SPW was capable of carrying a squad of eight to nine men plus a driver and commander. Britain's Universal or 'Bren Gun' Carrier provided her and Commonwealth forces with a fully tracked APC, while the US army's White and International half-tracks provided the Allies with an equivalent to the SPW and were employed extensively during the latter stages of the war.

Half-tracked APCs were generally difficult to steer and complicated to maintain and post-war APC manufacture has concentrated on either fully tracked or wheeled types. The most popular tracked APC must be the US army's M113. Adopted throughout NATO, with the exception of France, Britain, and Portugal, the aluminium alloy armoured M113 remains in general use in many of the world's armies. Britain also built a tracked APC, the FV 432, to meet the same operational requirements while the French opted for wheeled vehicles, such as the Panhard M3/VTT and Berliet VAB. The decision to adopt either a wheeled or tracked APC is largely dependent on the role in which it will be employed. *Armoured warfare on the plains of west and central Europe is very different from internal security operations in an urban area or patrolling across desert wastes in the sub-Sahara. Tracked APCs are generally more heavily armoured and have better cross-country capabilities than wheeled vehicles, which are lighter and faster on most surfaces, while also less expensive to manufacture and maintain. The jury is still out on whether the hybrid MICV can deliver the infantry support punch that the APCs were built to provide. PMacD

Arab–Israeli wars The first Arab–Israeli war formally began on 15 May 1948 when the League of Arab States announced its 'intervention' against the state of Israel which

David Ben-Gurion had proclaimed hours before. In fact, the final months of the British Mandate in Palestine, from the vote in the *UN General Assembly on 29 November 1947 to partition the country into Arab and Jewish states until the end of the Mandate on 14 May 1948, had seen an increasingly bitter civil war as Arabs and Jews fought to control territory. The Arabs of Palestine, supported by virtually the entire Arab world, rejected partition, while the Jews regarded it as a unique opportunity for statehood. The aim of the Arab coalition was to sustain the Palestinian Arabs. The armies which attacked Israel were those of Syria, Lebanon, Iraq, Saudi Arabia, Egypt, and Jordan; in addition, there was the 10,000-strong Arab Liberation Army, a semi-regular force led by the Syrian Fauji el-Kaukji. The military contribution of the various elements in the Arab command was mixed. Saudi Arabia, Lebanon, and Iraq made little more than token efforts, while el-Kaukji proved to be an erratic field commander. Overall military command rested, in theory at least, with Abdullah of Jordan, but he was suspected of fighting to acquire parts of Palestine for himself. In reality, there was no central command of the Arab forces. Even so, the Arabs began the war with certain advantages. Egypt, Iraq, and Syria had *air forces. Egypt and Syria had tanks, while all had some modern artillery. They had been trained for modern warfare by British and French instructors. This was particularly true of the strongest Arab formation, Jordan's Arab Legion of 10,000 men commanded by Lt Gen Sir John Glubb.

By contrast, the Israelis started the war with few modern weapons beyond *mortars, some ancient artillery, and no aircraft. They were being forced to defend a narrow coastal plain and isolated Jewish settlements, which made defence in depth impossible. Even so, they enjoyed certain assets. With some 40,000 troops organized in nine brigades, they had a coherent military force, many of whose members, unlike the Arabs, had seen service in WW II. They were fighting in defence of the first Jewish homeland since Roman times, and in the knowledge of the recent Holocaust. Moreover, in contrast to the Arabs, they had a clear overall strategy, Plan Dallet, designed to secure the area assigned to the Jewish state under the UN partition resolution and to safeguard outlying Jewish settlements.

The first phase of the war saw the Israelis repel Syrian attacks in the north, as well as serious fighting with a strong Egyptian force advancing into the Negev desert. But the decisive battle was on the Jerusalem front where the Arab Legion succeeded in capturing the historic Jewish quarter of the Old City, which held the Western Wall, sacred to Jews. The Legion also secured the strategic Latrun salient, which dominated the lines of communication from Tel Aviv to Jerusalem, although the Israelis circumvented this by cutting a new road between the two cities. On the outbreak of war, Sweden's Count Folke Bernadotte had been appointed UN mediator. He succeeded in negotiating a *truce which lasted from 11 June until 8 July, a breathing space which worked greatly to Israel's advantage. Ben-Gurion's government, which had established close links with Czechoslovakia, used the truce to bring in tanks, artillery, and, above all, modern aircraft. These enabled the Israelis to make important strategic advances once the war resumed. Extensive areas of Galilee were taken, as well as the key towns of Lydda, with its airport, and Ramle. On 12 July, the Arab inhabitants of the Lydda-Ramle area, amounting to some 70,000, were expelled in what became known as the 'Lydda Death March'. A second truce, which came into force on 18 July, found the Israelis in a much stronger position and permitted Bernadotte to work for a negotiated settlement. His proposals, submitted on 16 September, would have allowed Israel to retain Galilee in return for surrendering much of the Negev desert, and returning Lydda and Ramle to the Arabs. In addition, Jerusalem was to be an international city and Palestinian refugees were to be allowed to return. The following day, he was murdered in Jerusalem by members of the right-wing Jewish group, Leh'i.

Faced with the implications of the Bernadotte Plan, the Israeli government decided to resolve the future of the Negev, which it believed vital for the state's progress. Manufacturing an attack on a supply convoy, on 15 October the Israelis attacked the Egyptians around the strategic Faluja crossroads. By the end of 1948, they looked set to gain their final objective, the coastal strip from Rafah to Gaza. But in January 1949 their fighters shot down five British Spitfires across the Egyptian frontier. The consequent international pressure persuaded Ben-Gurion to halt operations. An armistice agreement between Egypt and Israel, signed at Rhodes on 24 January, was followed by others with Lebanon, Syria, and Jordan. The war had enabled Israel to sustain its independence within frontiers, which, if not strategically ideal, were considerably larger than those set out in the UN partition resolution. For the Palestinian Arabs it had been a disaster. Not only had their country ceased to exist, but over 750,000 were refugees. Defeat also set the scene for the Arab revolutions of the 1950s, particularly that which brought *Nasser, a veteran of the war, to power in Egypt.

Although tension between Israel and the new Egyptian regime had built up by 1956, the second war between the two countries was provoked by outside pressures. On 19 July 1956, the USA and Britain informed Egypt that they would not provide grants to assist with the building of the Aswan Dam. Nasser retaliated by announcing the nationalization of the Suez Canal Company. Choosing to see this as a threat to their security, Britain and France began to assemble military forces in the eastern Mediterranean. But with the Suez Canal operating normally and the American government hostile to military action, the excuse for intervention relentlessly slipped away. Faced with this, the French approached Ben-Gurion's government for collaboration. At a secret meeting between French, British, and Israeli ministers at Sèvres on 22–4 October 1956, Israel was

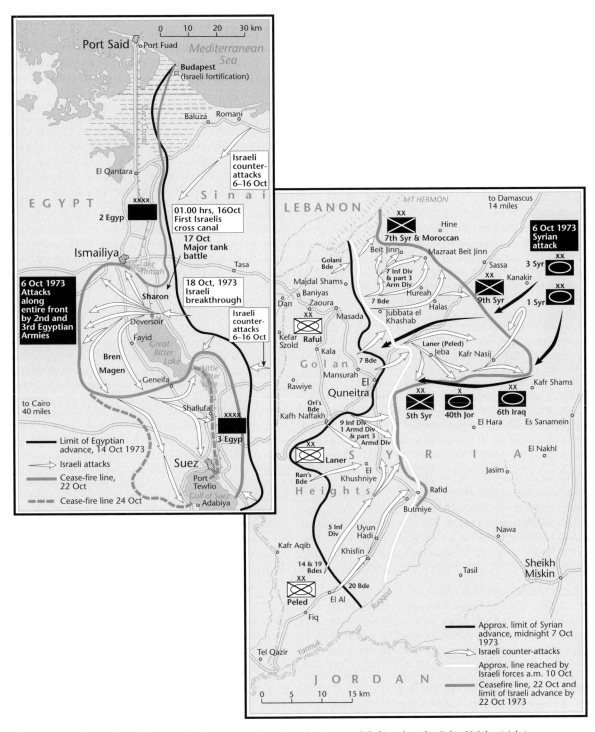

The **Arab-Israeli war** ('Yom Kippur war') of 1973: operations along the Suez canal (left) and on the Golan Heights (right).

committed to an attack on Egypt in the Sinai desert. This would allow Britain and France to issue an ultimatum for each side to withdraw its forces 10 miles (16 km) on either side of the canal. If, as anticipated, this were not done, Britain and France would intervene to 'separate the combatants'. On 29 October, Israeli military action began with a paratroop drop at the strategic Mitla Pass. Israel's offensive force, directed by COS *Dayan, consisted of ten brigades, two of which were mechanized and one armoured. To oppose them, Egypt deployed an infantry division and an armoured brigade in the Sinai, with a Palestinian division in the Gaza Strip. Despite initial setbacks at the Mitla Pass, by 2 November the Israelis had taken the central Egyptian positions around Abu Ageila. In subsequent operations, Israeli forces captured the Gaza Strip and moved down the Gulf of Aqaba and Gulf of Suez to capture Sharm al-Sheikh on the Strait of Tiran. As they did so, British and French aircraft had begun bombing Egyptian air bases in preparation for a seaborne landing. On 5 November the long-delayed Anglo-French paratroop landings took place on the Suez Canal, to be followed the next day by amphibious landings at Port Said. It proved to be a short-lived adventure since that evening financial pressure from an angry USA government forced the British government to call a ceasefire. The *Suez campaign marked the end of Britain and France as major powers in the Middle East. The Americans also forced the Israelis to withdraw from all their conquests, including Gaza and Sharm al-Shaikh. In return, Israel was guaranteed free passage through the Strait of Tiran, symbolized by the presence of the UN Emergency Force (UNEF). Pres Nasser became the hero of the Arab world, but his enhanced status masked deficiencies in his armed forces and their commander, FM Abdul Hakim Amer, which would cost him dear in the next Middle East con-flict.

The most significant development of the next decade was the revival of Palestinian activism, chiefly directed by the Movement for the Liberation of Palestine (Fatah), led by Yasser *Arafat. Its raids, which began in 1965, measurably increased Arab–Israeli tension. Israel's relations with Syria, never good at the best of times, also worsened as Israeli settlements came under intermittent bombardment from the *Golan Heights. The immediate crisis which provoked the 1967 war was a warning, incorrect as it turned out, to Nasser from the USSR that Israel was about to mount an attack on Syria. In an attempt to take the pressure off his Syrian ally, on 14 May the Egyptian leader deployed two armoured divisions in the Sinai desert. There is no evidence that at this stage he wanted war but when the Israelis countered this with a tank brigade it was clear that danger might be at hand. On 16 May, Nasser further escalated the situation by ordering UNEF to concentrate in the Gaza Strip and then on the following day demanding its total withdrawal. The presumption that this would be the signal for diplomatic moves was confounded by the decision of UN Secretary-General U Thant to accede to Nasser's demand.

Emboldened by assurances from FM Amer that his forces could match the Israelis, on 21 May Nasser announced a *blockade of the Strait of Tiran. This ran counter to assurances he had given in 1957 and was done in knowledge that Israel had insisted such a move would constitute a *casus belli*. Diplomatic efforts by the USA and the USSR having failed to resolve the crisis, on 5 June Israel launched devastating air strikes against the Egyptian and other Arab air forces. Directed by air force commander Gen Mordechai Hod, it proved to be one of the most daring, and decisive, blows in the history of *air power. In a matter of hours the Egyptian air force alone lost 309 of its 340 operational aircraft. Hod and his pilots had won the war for Israel.

Although the diplomatic crisis saw Moshe Dayan appointed as defence minister, the real genius behind the land campaign was COS Yitzhak Rabin. His plan was for a three-pronged offensive in Sinai by armoured and mechanized forces led by Gens Israel Tal, Avraham Joffe, and Ariel Sharon. Facing them the Egyptian commander Gen Abd el Mohsen Mortagui had five infantry and two armoured divisions with over 1,000 tanks, but robbed of air support he had no hope of victory. As the extent of the Egyptians' plight started to emerge, he was further confounded by contradictory orders issuing from Amer's headquarters. On 8 June, Israeli forces reached the Suez Canal, having destroyed the Egyptian forces in the Sinai for a loss of some 300 killed. By then, the focus had switched elsewhere. On 5 June, out of a sense of Arab solidarity, King Hussein of Jordan entered the war. At his disposal he had a well-trained force of eight infantry and two armoured brigades, as well as some Iraqi support, but, like the Egyptians, no air support. Israeli forces in the central sector were largely reservists of the Jerusalem brigade but once Jordan's intentions became clear these were reinforced by Col Mordechai Gur's 55th Parachute Brigade, diverted from the Sinai front. While Israeli aircraft disrupted communications between the Arab Legion in Jerusalem and its headquarters, Gur's paratroopers attacked the Old City from the north. After intense fighting, on 7 June his men entered the Old City. Their arrival at the Western Wall was, for Israelis, the emotional pinnacle of the war. With the collapse of the Jerusalem sector, the Jordanians had no hope of holding the remainder of the West Bank. The territory, with its key cities of Nablus, Ramalah, Bethlehem, and Hebron, fell to the Israelis. With the Gaza Strip captured from the Egyptians, Israel now controlled all of pre-1948 Palestine.

Having secured their southern and central fronts, the Israeli command now resolved to remove the threat from the Golan Heights. On 9 June, armoured units of Gen David Elazar's Northern Command began an assault on strongly held Syrian positions, preceded by ground-attack (see FIGHTER) aircraft. In the face of a tenacious resistance, by the next day the Israeli forces had taken the Heights and, with positions on Mount Hermon, could look towards Damascus. All that clouded Israel's victory was the attack on 8 June on the USS *Liberty*, a surveillance vessel off Gaza, with the death of 34 American sailors. The explanation that it had been a case of mistaken identity was not accepted in Washington. Otherwise, Israel had secured one of the decisive victories of recent history, but with extensive Arab territories under her control it was one which held the seeds of future conflict, should a diplomatic solution fail.

Fail it did. The period after the 1967 war saw the reorganization of the Palestine Liberation Organization (PLO) under the chairmanship of Yasser Arafat, and the beginning of armed Palestinian actions against Israel and Israelis at home and overseas. Palestinian activism also threatened the stability of other Arab states. In September 1970 there was bitter fighting in Jordan between King Hussein's troops and *PLO *guerrillas. While negotiating a ceasefire, Pres Nasser died. His successor, Anwar al-Sadat, was determined to restore Egypt's lost territories in the Sinai. By 1972, having failed to achieve diplomatic momentum, he began planning a military campaign, together with the Syrian president, Hafiz al-Assad. Their training and planning were intense. In contrast, the edge had gone off the *IDF (Israeli Defence Force).

In the early hours of 6 October 1973, 700 Syrian tanks attacked on the Golan, their *commandos seizing key positions on Mount Hermon. Only tenacious fighting and the sacrifice of some 40 aircraft allowed the Israelis to stabilize the front by 9 October. Meanwhile, the Egyptian Second and Third Armies crossed the Suez Canal with textbook precision and broke through the poorly held *Bar-Lev Line. Heavy fighting on 8 and 9 October, in which the Egyptians operated from behind concentrated missile batteries, resulted in the virtual destruction of the Israeli 190th Armoured Brigade. The 9th proved pivotal. An Egyptian armoured assault was broken up, and the Israelis persuaded US Pres Nixon to send replacements, allowing Israel to commit her reserves. On 16 October, with the American resupply operation in full swing, an Israeli force under Gen Sharon crossed the canal just north of the Great Bitter Lake, opening a gap between the Second and Third Armies. The Israeli counter-attack on the northern front began on 11 October. As in the Sinai, fighting was intense, with the Syrians supported by Jordanian and Iraqi units. But by 22 October, the Israelis had recaptured Mount Hermon and had Damascus potentially within their grasp. By the time a ceasefire, largely brokered by US Secretary of State *Kissinger, took effect on 27 October, the Egyptian Third Army and the city of Suez had been encircled.

Despite Israeli successes in the second phase of the conflict, the war had revealed new potential on the part of the Egyptian and Syrian armed forces and dented the myth of Israeli invincibility. The war also saw the effective use of the Arab 'oil weapon' by oil-exporting states. In subsequent negotiations, Sadat and Assad succeeded in recovering territory, and the war helped create the conditions for the Camp David Agreements of 1978 and the subsequent

Egyptian–Israeli peace treaty. But the basic quarrel between Israel and the Palestinians was far from resolved. By 1981 there was serious tension between Israel and PLO guerrilla forces in southern Lebanon. An attempted assassination of the Israeli ambassador in London by dissident Palestinians gave the Israeli government of Menahem Begin the occasion for an invasion of *Lebanon on 6 June 1982, titled PEACE FOR GALILEE, to create a 25 mile (40 km) security zone in southern Lebanon; it was soon apparent that Begin's government was in pursuit of a wider agenda. By 13 June, despite determined PLO resistance, Israeli forces were on the outskirts of Beirut, opening up the prospect of street fighting in which there would be heavy Lebanese casualties. By then, there was widespread opposition to the war in Israel and the US administration of Pres Ronald Reagan was deeply unhappy. On 12 August, after heavy bombardment of west Beirut, Reagan demanded a ceasefire. A multinational force of American, French, and Italian troops supervised the evacuation of PLO guerrillas. Tragedy then followed. The assassination of Israel's Christian ally Bashir Gemayel led to an Israeli occupation of west Beirut. On 16 September, Lebanese Christian forces entered the Palestinian refugee camps of Sabra and Shatila where they massacred hundreds of elderly men, women, and children. Such was the outcry at this in an area under Israeli military control that Israeli forces withdrew from west Beirut. They were replaced by a reconstituted multinational force but this, too, ended in tragedy. On 23 October 1983, suicide car bombers attacked the French and American bases, killing 78 French troops and 241 American marines. In 1985, Israeli troops evacuated most of Lebanon, leaving a security zone in the south of the country, finally withdrawing in 2000.

In December 1987, a new phase of the Arab–Israeli conflict started with the outbreak of the Palestinian intifada in the Occupied Territories. Despite widespread Palestinian casualties, there were moves towards a diplomatic settlement. In September 1993, after secret contacts in Norway, PLO Chairman Yasser Arafat and Israeli PM Yitzhak Rabin concluded an agreement which seemed to open up the prospect of a more peaceful resolution of one of the world's most intractable conflicts, even though Rabin, Israel's most distinguished soldier, was later murdered by a fellow Israeli opposed to what he had done.   TGF

Bickerton, I. J., and Pearson, M. N., *The Arab-Israeli Conflict* (London, 1993).
Cordesman, A. H., and Wagner, A. R., *Lessons of Modern War: The Arab-Israeli Conflict 1973–1989* (New York, 1991).
Dupuy, T. N., *Elusive Victory* (London, 1978).
Fraser, T. G., *The Arab–Israeli Conflict* (London, 1995).
Herzog, C., *The Arab-Israeli Wars* (London, 1984).

Arab revolt (1916–18). During *WW I, Britain and her Allies found allies against the Ottoman *Turks from among Arab nationalists. The most famous of the many revolts against the Turks was that headed by Sharif Hussayn, ruler of the Holy Cities of the Hijaz, and his son Faisal. They received military support from the French as well as the British and had several advisers, the most famous of whom, Capt (later Col) *Lawrence, became known as 'Lawrence of Arabia'. Although criticized then and now for headline grabbing, Lawrence is still regarded as an excellent *guerrilla leader. He worked closely with Faisal, enabling Arab forces to maximize their military potential in support of the Allies and of their own aspirations.

Lawrence knew the region as a result of pre-war archaeological and spying activities, and also formed a crucial link to British higher command when supplies were needed. He helped plan the capture of Wejh on the Red Sea coast in January 1917, inspired and led the attacks on the Hijaz railway which cut off the Turkish troops in the southern part of the Arabian peninsula, and encouraged the attack on the vital port of Aqaba from the undefended landward side in July. This last achievement enabled the port to be used to supply *Allenby during the Palestine campaign, not least by transporting the Sharifian Regular Army to the front. This force of some 8,000 men was composed of ex-Ottoman Arab regulars, under the command of Ja'afar al Askari, who had formerly led *Senussi troops against the Italians in Libya. Many other Ottoman soldiers, including Syrians and Armenians, defected to join the Arabs, retaining their old uniform and equipment but adding a *khaki *keffiyeh* (headcloth). By the summer of 1917, this army was strong enough to convince the Ottoman's German Gen *Liman von Sanders that the Turks ought to abandon the Hijaz as indefensible, although giving up the Holy Cities proved politically unacceptable.

Lawrence and the Northern Army played a crucial role on Allenby's desert (right) flank. Generally lightly armed, its only heavy weapons were provided by the French contingent, comprising a six-gun artillery battery, another six mule-transported mountain guns, eight machine gun sections, and an engineer company; but these fought with the Arabs almost everywhere. In December 1917, Faisal's Northern Army took part in Allenby's victory parade in Jerusalem. In early 1918, it also seized Tafila after a hard fight lasting several days (21–7 January). This was the Arabs' most famous victory over regular troops, which assured their military reputation. Their extreme mobility became legendary. It is calculated that they fought over 994 rail miles (1,600 km) and 2,983 camel miles (4,800 km) from Medina to Muslimyia Junction (the final engagement when they again defeated the Turks) in the course of the campaigns. During the final operation they seized Der'aa (27 September) and then dashed the last 120 km (75 miles) (much of it desert) to reach Damascus (1 October), two days before Allenby's column.   MB

Nicolle, D., *Lawrence and the Arab Revolts* (London, 1989).
Wavell, A. P., *The Palestine Campaigns* (London, 1928).

Arafat, Yasser (b. 1929), Palestinian resistance leader and Arab statesman. Born in Cairo, Arafat moved with his family to Gaza in 1939. After becoming involved in anti-Israeli activities in the late 1940s, he entered the University of Cairo to study civil engineering and there became involved in student activist groups.

Arafat came to prominence with his election to the chairmanship of the Executive Committee of the *PLO in 1969. Under his leadership, the PLO began its terror campaign against Israel designed to gain independence for Palestine, and Arafat was branded a ruthless terrorist. This campaign culminated with the forming of the intifada in 1987, aimed at undermining the Israeli administration in the occupied West Bank and Gaza.

Under his direction the PLO was transformed from a terrorist organization to a civil administration. In 1988, the PLO officially renounced the use of terrorism and recognized the state of Israel. Then in 1993, Arafat signed the Oslo Peace Accords with the Israeli PM Yitzhak Rabin, which ended the intifada and gave the occupied territories limited self-rule. For this, both Arafat and Rabin were awarded the *Nobel Peace Prize. In January 1996, Arafat was elected by an overwhelming majority president of the Palestinian National Authority, the body set up to govern the West Bank and the Gaza Strip. However, the slow progress of the peace process has made it extremely difficult for him to keep Palestinian extremists in check. Late in 1998 he admitted that he was seriously ill, an unhappy development at a time when peace seems as elusive as ever.   RTF

Arbela (Gaugamela), battle of (331 BC). Located west of the Tigris about 50 miles (80 km) from modern Erbil (Arbela), Gaugamela was the site of Alexander's third and decisive victory over the Persians in September 331 BC. Following defeat at *Issus, King Darius had assembled a massive army from his eastern provinces, especially heavy cavalry: 200,000 infantry and 45,000 cavalry are the lowest of various grossly exaggerated figures. Alexander disposed his 40,000 infantry and 7,000 cavalry to offset this numerical difference: his strike troops, primarily Macedonians, occupied the front line (*phalanx in the centre, cavalry on the wings), while his Greek allies and mercenaries constituted a second line which could face-about to form a square if the Persians threatened to encircle. *Alexander advanced obliquely, threatening to drag the Persians off the terrain prepared for an attack by scythe-*chariots; a Persian outflanking move on the right failed, their chariots were neutralized by Thracian javelin men, and Alexander then charged with the cavalry on the right wing, broke the Persian centre, and forced Darius to flee. On the Macedonian left Parmenio endured a fierce assault, which was only terminated when Alexander was recalled from pursuing Darius.   LMW

Marsden, E., *The Campaign of Gaugamela* (Liverpool, 1964).

archers formed a significant element of many medieval armies, though their numbers, tactical deployment and thus their effectiveness varied widely. As medieval European warrior elites generally preferred close-combat weapons and eschewed the bow except for hunting, archers were drawn from non-noble classes. English victories in the Hundred Years War served to increase the social status of the archer, although in late medieval France fear of peasant insurrection and the availability of mercenary crossbowmen restricted the development of an efficient archer corps until the reforms of Charles VII.

At the battle of *Hastings, *William 'the Conqueror' demonstrated the great tactical potential of combining a significant body of archers with cavalry against a strong infantry formation, while Harold's deficiency in archers proved a grave weakness. Archers also played an important role in the battles of Bourgthéroulde (1124) and the Standard (1138), operating on the defensive with dismounted knights, though these successful tactics were not to be repeated until the 14th century. For obvious reasons, archers were particularly useful to both sides in *siege warfare, a prominent victim being *Richard 'the Lionheart'. Welsh archers supported knights during the Anglo-Norman conquests in Ireland from 1169, and were employed during the *Crusades to combat the relentless Turkic horse archers who harried crusader armies on the march and tried to shoot down the knights' vulnerable chargers.

From at least the 11th century, crossbowmen appear as an elite, with their bolts capable of penetrating mail armour, so much so that in 1139 Pope Innocent II prohibited the use of 'the deadly art, hated by God, of crossbowmen and archers' against fellow Christians. This was of course ignored and in the Franco-Angevin wars crossbowmen formed the mainstay of castle garrisons, drawing higher wages than other bowmen. Civic militias, particularly the ferociously independent Swiss, favoured the use of the crossbow, but even aristocratic armies employed *mercenary crossbowmen, most famously the Genoese.

The growing importance of longbowmen in English armies stemmed from their deployment in very large numbers during the reign of Edward I (1272–1307), who levied thousands for his Welsh and Scottish wars. The serious problem of very variable quality was addressed by commissions of array, in which royal officials selected the best men from those mustered in the shires. This improved standards, but it was the growing reliance from the 14th century on contract armies, whereby the king contracted for a certain number of knights and archers with his nobles, that ensured the necessary standardization.

The second major development was tactical. Whereas in his defeat of William *Wallace at Falkirk in 1298, Edward I had used archers offensively in support of his cavalry against the bristling Scottish *schiltroms, the great victories of Dupplin Moor (1332) and Halidon Hill (1333) against the

Scots were won by adopting a strong defensive position in which the archers were protected by dismounted knights, who only charged after the former had winnowed the enemy. This system was then used to great effect against the French throughout the *Hundred Years War, from the battles of Morlaix (1342) and *Crécy (1346), to Poitiers (1359), *Agincourt (1415), and Verneuil (1424). The proportion of archers in English armies grew steadily until longbowmen constituted almost the entire infantry force, and, by the early 15th century, the normal ratio of archers to knights was at least three to one. *Henry V is estimated to have had around 900 men-at-arms and about 5,000 archers at Agincourt.

The exact nature of these English formations has been much debated. The traditional view, held by Sir Charles *Oman, Alfred Burne, and others, was that wings of archers were placed on either flank of each unit (known as a 'battle') of knights, thrown forward to give enfilade fire, and forming an apex or 'wedge' when they adjoined the archers on the wing of a neighbouring 'battle'. This view was contested by Jim Bradbury, who argued that archers were only placed on the extreme wings of English armies, and not in wedges between 'battles'. While in some engagements archers do seem to have been posted on the wings of each battle (definitely the case at Halidon Hill and possibly so at Agincourt), a consensus has now been reached that the position of archers did not conform to a rigid blueprint and they were deployed in a variety of formations, including forming a screen in front of the knights, which could change during the course of an engagement.

Where possible, archers defended themselves against cavalry attack by the use of pits (Crécy and Aljubarotta), broken ground and hedges (Poitiers), and subsequently by sharpened stakes (Agincourt), planted not as a solid palisade but like a chequerboard, allowing the archers freedom of manoeuvre while hampering mounted knights. This flexibility was vital, for archers not only fought with the bow but were highly adaptable as universal light infantrymen. At Agincourt, for example, the archers put down their bows after their initial volleys and attacked the French knights, now hopelessly crushed together by their weight of numbers, with axes, daggers, mauls, and other close-combat weapons, wreaking terrible slaughter.

Little is known of the archers' command structure, though there were officers in charge of 100 men (*centenars*) and deputies in charge of 20 (*vintenars*), while overall command might be given to a veteran captain such as Sir Thomas Erpingham at Agincourt, who threw up his baton as a signal to shoot. It is likely that their leadership style was quite modern, in the style of Shakespeare's *Henry V*. Some archers wore virtually no defensive equipment and were even barefoot, carrying perhaps a small buckler as well as a sword, dagger, or lead maul. Others, such as those depicted on the famous *Beauchamp Pageant* (c.1485–90), wore a helmet and a short mail coat under a jack or brigandine, a form of doublet lined with small, overlapping metal plates. Whatever they wore would be useless against a carelessly released shaft at close range.

As an individual infantry weapon, the longbow was superior to most firearms until the advent of the rifle, but it had serious disadvantages. It required great physical strength and skill, acquired through constant practice (skeletons of archers found aboard the *Mary Rose* revealed significant distortions to vertebrae, arm, and shoulder bones), and it was with increasing desperation that royal statutes prohibited football and other pastimes in favour of archery practice at the butts. Nostalgic Tudor commentators regarded the decline of the longbow as synonymous with the decline of England's military might, but men whose forefathers had despised the crossbow took readily to the 'fiery weapon' as both powerful and simple to learn. By the later 16th century few professional soldiers doubted that the arquebus, musket, and effective field artillery were now the real arbiters of the European battlefield.

MJS

Bennett, Matthew, 'The Development of Battle Tactics in the Hundred Years War', in Anne Curry and Michael Hughes (eds.), *Armies and Fortifications in the Hundred Years War* (Woodbridge, 1994).

Bradbury, Jim, *The Medieval Archer* (Woodbridge, 1985).

Hardy, Robert, *The Longbow: A Social and Military History* (Cambridge, 1992).

Oman, Sir Charles, *A History of the Art of War in the Middle Ages*, 2 vols. (London 1898, rev. 1924, repr. 1991).

Prestwich, Michael, *Armies and Warfare in the Middle Ages: The English Experience* (London, 1996).

Arcola, battle of (1796). In November 1796 Austrian armies under *Alvinczy (28,000) and Davidovich (18,000) advanced on Bassano and Trent to attack the French Army of Italy under *Napoleon besieging Mantua with well under 40,000. A deception plan masked Davidovich's advance, and although Napoleon saw through it, his northern wing was beaten by Davidovich, and he found himself facing two enemy armies.

Napoleon determined to deal with the southernmost threat first, by cutting Alvinczy's communications at Villanova and forcing the Austrians to turn and fight him in difficult ground between the rivers Alpone and Adige. To reach Villanova he had to cross the Alpone at Arcola. On 15 November *Augereau was checked at the bridge, and all Napoleon's personal energy could not help him. There were no major gains the following day, but Alvinczy's nerve was shaken and his force was split to cover the river line in marshy countryside. On 17 November *Masséna outmanoeuvred the Austrians in Arcola, while Augereau crossed the Alpone further south. Alvinczy fell back with the loss of 7,000 men. Napoleon jabbed northwards, but just missed Davidovich. Arcola is a graphic illustration of the ability of a weaker army to use interior lines to defeat stronger opponents in detail, and shows Napoleon at the peak of his form.

RH

arctic and mountain warfare (see also MOUNTAIN TROOPS) makes the most extreme demands on a soldier, who must at all times combat a lethal environment while only sporadically engaging his human enemy. The polar regions have not, of course, been fought over, and 'arctic' refers to conditions of extreme cold. A combination of the two factors creates almost unimaginably demanding conditions, yet there are peoples with a long tradition of arctic and mountain warfare and the major powers have developed highly specialized troops for that purpose. The more extreme possible or actual areas of deployment are in northern Scandinavia, the Alps, the Pyrenees, the Andes, southern Arabia, and the northernmost parts of the Indian subcontinent.

Mountainous regions of military significance are generally characterized by rugged, often compartmentalized terrain, with steep slopes and few if any natural or man-made lines of communication. Weather is usually seasonal varying from extreme cold to temperate. Dramatic and sudden weather changes are not uncommon and wind, where accelerated over ridges or when converged under pressure through passes and narrow valleys, can quickly reach gale force. In cold weather, the wind-chill factor significantly increases the chance of frostbite and other disabling injuries. Troops operating in such terrain need to be exceptionally fit, experienced, and equipped.

At altitudes in excess of 8,202 feet (2,500 metres), a period of acclimatization is required. As with professional mountaineers, this acclimatization phase is only complete when personnel fully understand the limitations imposed on both them and their equipment. For example it is only after months spent at high altitude that 70 per cent of sea-level work-capacity standards can be achieved. This is a fact understood by the trainers of world class athletes and taken for granted by indigenous populations, and an important factor to be considered in planning operations. The effects of high altitude on unacclimatized troops include increased errors in performing simple mental operations; decreased ability for sustained concentration, memory deterioration, decreasing awareness, increased irritability, and self-evaluation impairment.

In addition there are several health hazards that exist in mountainous climates. Due to the thinner atmosphere at higher altitudes, more direct sunlight reaches the earth than at lower levels and in snowy conditions common in such areas, 'snow blindness' becomes a risk, because about 75 per cent of the sun's rays are reflected and can quickly overload the eyes. Although snow blindness is normally temporary, troops affected may be completely disabled for several days. Other health conditions associated with mountainous climates include sunburn and potentially fatal dehydration and hypothermia, while heat transference may bond naked flesh to weapons or vehicles. These, in turn, require special oils and an elevated amount of maintenance, while the greater demand for heating and transport fuel (motors must be kept running or at least 'turned over' regularly), as well as spare parts, imposes greater demands on logistics that may already be dangerously stretched over extremely limited and vulnerable lines of communication.

Command of the heights is crucial for successful mountain operations, as seen most recently (1999) in the *India-Pakistan clash in Kashmir, because it means controlling the valleys. Soviet forces rediscovered to their cost in *Afghanistan that even main arterial routes through broad valleys cannot be kept open when nearby mountainous terrain harbours a determined enemy, especially when he is equipped with man-portable artillery. At higher altitudes, narrow mountain roads are often restricted to single-line traffic, especially for wide-bodied military vehicles, with little room for passing. One disabled vehicle may stop an entire column. It then becomes a matter of boxing in the target and destroying it piece by piece. This consideration is central to Swiss defence planning and may be the reason why Chile and Argentina have never gone to war. Mountain chains make excellent borders.

Prior to this century mountains were often seen as an almost impenetrable defence against invading armies. However, the advent of modern skis and skiing techniques has changed this assumption and almost all modern armies whose existing or possible theatre of operations includes such areas, have some ski-warfare capability. Such theatres include NATO's northern flank, where its forces have conducted extensive annual or biennial manoeuvres over recent years; and the alpine regions of Europe. The origins and development of skiing lie both in Scandinavia and the Alps. Scandinavian or 'Nordic' skiing originated in what are now Finland and Sweden some 4,000 years ago on skis made from wood and leather, curved bow-like front and rear, designed to support and spread the wearer's weight and allowing him to glide along the surface of the snow aided by hand-held poles. The equipment remained little changed until the 1880s, when the introduction of flat skis in Austria first caught the attention of British sportsmen, who explored and chartered alpine regions with a view to winter recreation. The concept spread to Germany and later France and by the turn of the century both countries had established national ski clubs. Alpine or downhill skiing was born.

The military spin-off was most dramatically revealed during the Finno-Soviet war of 1939–40), where well-trained and equipped Finnish ski troops initially trounced a Soviet force which outnumbered them five to one. Following their own revealed deficiencies in Norway early in WW II, the British began to train specialist mountain troops, and the Americans and Canadians were to combine their training to produce the famous 'Devil's Brigade'.

Following WW II recreational skiing became even more popular and widespread. This has had the effect of introducing a 'normality' to the concept of skiing and increasing facilities associated with it. Lest the military connection should be forgotten, the Biathlon was introduced in the winter Olympics of 1960, in which competitors cross-country ski for 12 miles (20 km), stopping to engage targets with single-shot rifles at combat range (110–273 yards (100–250 metres)) every 2.5 miles (4 km). The event illustrates how skiing ability alone does not make a ski-soldier. Fitness, stamina, and care of equipment are vital, as are the qualities and knowledge that enable him to survive and fight in a bitterly hostile environment. Arctic and mountain warfare, although a relatively recent variant in armed conflict, remains one of the most challenging.   PMacD

Ardant du Picq, Col Charles-Jean-Jacques-Joseph (1821–70), French officer and military thinker. Du Picq was the author of two original and insightful studies, *Ancient Battle* and *Modern Battle*, compiled as the classic Battle Studies (*Études sur le combat*). The question that motivated his work was how soldiers would fight in the age of mass firepower and mass armies. He set out to discover the essence of battle performance in individual and group psychology. He completed his study of ancient battle in 1868. Then, inspired by mid-19th-century French scientism, he adopted stricter methods in studying modern battle. He compiled a highly detailed questionnaire, soliciting first-hand experience among his fellow officers for every aspect of troops' behaviour under fire. Du Picq believed that face-to-face fighting was unnatural to man and only made possible from ancient times by the combination of *discipline, cohesive organization, and thoughtful tactics. How could these be maintained in the age of the rifled breach-loader which enforced troops' dispersal? In the debate in France following the crushing success of the Prussian mass armies in 1866, du Picq sided with the conservatives in contending that only highly trained professionals could cope. Du Picq was killed in the *Franco-Prussian war. His work was published posthumously (1880), but remained virtually unknown until the second edition (1903) which achieved great popularity. Although du Picq believed that the defence had the advantage under modern conditions, his stress on moral quality without his balancing regard for 'destructive action' was adopted by the young officers in the French army who advocated Bergsonian vitalism and the spirit of *l'offensive à l'outrance* (the all-out attack).   AGI

Ardant du Picq, C. J. J. J., *Battle Studies* (Harrisburg, Pa., 1947).
Gat, Azar, *The Development of Military Thought: The 19th Century* (Oxford, 1992).

Arginusae, battle of (406 BC), fought near the end of the *Peloponnesian war. The battle was named after small islands (now Garipadasi and Kalemadasi) between Lesbos and the mainland. The Spartan commander, Kallikratidas, had to leave 50 triremes to cover Athenian ships blockaded in Mytilene, and so had only 120 to face about 155, but had the advantage of trained crews, whereas the Athenians, commanded by eight of their generals, had only a scratch fleet. This explains their unusual double line abeam, intended to prevent the enemy from breaking the line; possibly, too, to prevent their being outflanked by the enemy's single line abeam, the Athenians also kept wider gaps than usual between the ships of their front line, with the ships of their second line covering the gaps. Few details of the actual fighting survive, but Kallikratidas was killed, and the Spartans lost over 70 ships as against 25. The Athenian victory was marred by the failure to rescue survivors from their wrecked ships, allegedly owing to bad weather. This resulted in the subsequent trial and execution of six of the eight commanders who had won what was then the greatest naval battle between Greeks. JFL

Kagan, Donald, *The Fall of the Athenian Empire* (London, 1987).

Armageddon, battle of (date unknown), where, according to the Revelation of St John the Divine (Rev. 16: 16), the Kings of the Earth under the leadership of the Evil One will confront the Army of God, thus signalling the end of history, military or otherwise. The name comes from the Hebrew *Har* (hill) and the place is *Megiddo. Also hyperbole commonly employed to describe the hypothetical all-out use of *nuclear weapons. HEB

Armistice, 1918 The eleventh hour of the eleventh day of the eleventh month will always be '*the* Armistice', a moment when we try to imagine the silence falling over the western front as the guns fell silent after four years and three months of hellish slaughter. Less remembered is that the word implies only a temporary cessation of war, and although the Allies treated it as a surrender, a 21-year *truce was all it turned out to be.

In October the Austro-Hungarian and German governments separately proposed an armistice to US Pres Wilson, preliminary to a peace conference based on his 'Fourteen Points'. There was some delay occasioned by the fact that the Allies were emphatically not in agreement with Wilson's vision of a New World Order, Clemenceau fairly commenting that the good Lord himself had only ten points. Armistice with Austria-Hungary was signed in Vienna on 3 November and with Germany eight days later, in a railway carriage near Compiègne, hostilities ceasing six hours later. The terms were those of a surrender: German evacuation of all occupied territory; evacuation of the west bank of the Rhine; acknowledgement of the Allies' right to claim damages; surrender of submarines and internment of the German fleet; abrogation of the Treaties of Bucharest and Brest-Litovsk; destruction of German aircraft, tanks, and artillery; return of *POWs and deported civilians; 150,000 railway cars, 5,000 locomotives, and 5,000 trucks to be given to the Allies. The Allied *blockade was to be maintained until the signing of the peace treaty at the Versailles conference.

The German government hid behind the fig leaf that surrender had not been unconditional, an important component of the 'stab in the back' myth that was to help *Hitler to power. In fact its armies were spontaneously disbanding and its population starving and beginning to die of influenza in numbers soon to rival those of the war. The Allies were to insist on 'unconditional surrender' in WW II, giving Hitler's opponents no prospect of a better deal if they got rid of him. PC/HEB

armour, body Warriors have protected their bodies against the weapons of their opponents since the dawn of warfare. Generally, the type of armour worn has been appropriate to the nature of the weapon and as the technology of the latter has changed so has the protective value of the former—although the change has not always been immediate. The concept of body armour has crossed cultural frontiers and been present in any culture in which warfare has existed. A variety of materials have been used to protect the warrior's body and these materials themselves have reflected the level of technological competence attained by that warrior's society. Body armour has also transcended the purely military role, being worn by civilians in fear of assassination and by policemen and -women on certain duties. It has also developed a ceremonial function, as part of the military uniform of the mounted bodyguards of heads of state in western countries. Body armour is one of the few consistently continuing threads which link the modern warrior not only with his primeval ancestor but also with warriors throughout the history of mankind.

Body armour can best be studied by separating it into its principal components as they relate to the body itself: protection for the head; for the body, arms, and legs; and, finally, the versatile protection provided by the shield. The Ancient world was familiar with all these types and areas of protection, just as it was with the differing kinds of armour itself. Broadly, armour falls into three categories: plate, mail, and soft. Plate armour can, itself, be subdivided into three: very large sections of plate, such as the breast- and backplate of a cuirass; smaller plates laced together; small plates sewn or riveted to a fabric background, itself often padded, to produce the garment generally known as a coat of plates.

The manufacture of metal plate armour involves a similar process and range of skills as that involved in the making of helmets. Since metal helmets have survived from the Assyrian civilization (9th–7th centuries BC), it has been assumed that metal plate armour—in some form—was in use in that culture too. However, plate armour was produced in lighter, more organic, materials than just metal: leather, horn, and whalebone are all known to have been used, the leather hardened and shaped to fit by soaking in hot beeswax to create a material later known as *cuir-bouilli*. Armour made in leather, *cuir* in French, has given us the name of the long-lived protection for the human torso: cuirass. Leather was also used as a covering for *shields. Covering a light wood or wickerwork frame and suitably hardened, it not only made this most versatile defence easier to manoeuvre, but also it facilitated the shield's decoration—leather providing a welcoming canvas for paint, gold and silver leaf, and embellishment with studs.

Since there has been little survival of examples of body armour from the classical period, other than helmets, evidence for the types and styles of such armour is largely based upon depictions of warriors from surviving contemporary illustrations, such as bas-relief sculpture. From these sources it is known that light armour was worn by the Assyrian cavalryman and aided his independence in battle since it meant that he could dispense with a cumbersome shield. Illustrations, together with the texts of epic *poetry, provide evidence for the body armour of the hoplite, the foot soldier of Ancient Greece from the 7th century BC to the decline of that civilization. The hoplite was protected by a helmet, a shield, and a breastplate, with leg protection in the form of greaves. This style of body armour was a developed form of that existing in earlier eastern Mediterranean civilizations. In Egypt the foot soldier's body armour—helmet and breastplate—were of leather, sometimes strengthened with metal; he carried a leather-covered shield too. His equivalents in Minos and Mycenae from 3,000 BC to 1,000 BC wore helmets and carried oxhide shields around their necks; later the shield became smaller and was carried on the arm. In India, in the 3rd century BC, the soldiers of the army of the Maurya empire were similarly protected: shields of rattan reinforced with leather and light armour of leather or metal or both.

The body armour of Rome has, of all the armour of the classical period, probably been the most intensively studied and copied, the latter form of admiration not being confined to just 20th-century re-enactment societies. By increasing the size of the shield, which was wooden, covered in leather, and reinforced with metal strips, Rome was able to protect its legionaries' bodies with comparatively light armour. Each of the categories of armour and types of plate armour were utilized by the Roman armies, from the republic to the collapse of the empire: metal or hardened leather helmets and greaves, cuirasses, and other body protection fashioned from leather and reinforced with differing styles and patterns of sewn or laced plates. Enhancement of armour's decorative possibilities was also practised and a hierarchy of ornament established, particularly in relation to the helmet and the cuirass. Roman cavalry, bereft of the infantry's shields, tended to be more heavily armoured, beginning a western tradition continued until the

present day. The decline of Rome and its eventual collapse in the face of the Germanic migrations in the 5th and 6th centuries AD resulted in the armour of its soldiers being both adopted and adapted by those of the tribes who supplanted Roman influence with their own. Originally little armoured, these invaders swiftly took over Roman armour, which had—itself—evolved into the beginnings of new styles, and the conversion of late Roman armour into fashions more historically associated with the beginnings of western chivalry is one profoundly affected by the period of invasions and the concomitant decline of Rome.

In the first millennium AD the most widely owned, and commonly depicted, form of body armour was the coat of mail. Mail was in use in the classical period from, apparently, the 3rd century BC and may have had an eastern derivation—although there is equally convincing evidence of a Celtic origin. With the mail coat or shirt, the western warrior wore a helmet derived from late Roman styles and known to scholars as a Spangenhelm. Spangenhelms were made in differing styles but their common design feature was a conical form made of separate plates riveted together, sometimes embellished by cheek pieces, a separate neck guard, and a nasal protection strip. The helmet from the Sutton Hoo ship burial in England is of embellished Spangenhelm form, as is the York Coppergate *Viking helmet, worn 200 years later in the 9th century AD. Viking warriors are known to have worn mail shirts, as well as ones made from sewn plates—the style known as lamellar armour, but perhaps the most famous depiction of the mail shirt and Spangenhelm combination is the *Bayeux Tapestry*, in which the armour of *William 'the Conqueror' and his knights is so depicted. By 1066, the Spangenhelm had generally lost its neck guard and cheek pieces and in its reduced form of a simple cone with nasal protector it remained a common style of helmet until the 13th century. By the 11th century the armourer's techniques had advanced sufficiently for the helmet to be forged from a single piece of iron, thus preparing the way for the armours of the late medieval period.

Mail has a long history and was worn in varying forms across a wide diversity of cultures. Although it exists today as the decorative shoulder chains worn on the blue patrol jacket by officers of some British cavalry regiments, its greatest age as a form of body armour was in the six centuries after the 7th century AD. In this period, and especially during its second half, mail was most widely worn in the form of a coat or shirt, worn over a cloth undershirt, reaching to the knees and often split at the fork either at the back or at both front and back. This garment, known as the hauberk or birnie, often incorporated a coif or hood, of mail too, from which—in turn—developed a ventail or lower face protection. Mail chausses were worn to protect the legs, initially laced at the back and not incorporating an integral foot, but later developed as full mail stockings, gartered at the knee. The arms were protected, initially, by long mail sleeves which later incorporated mail mittens to

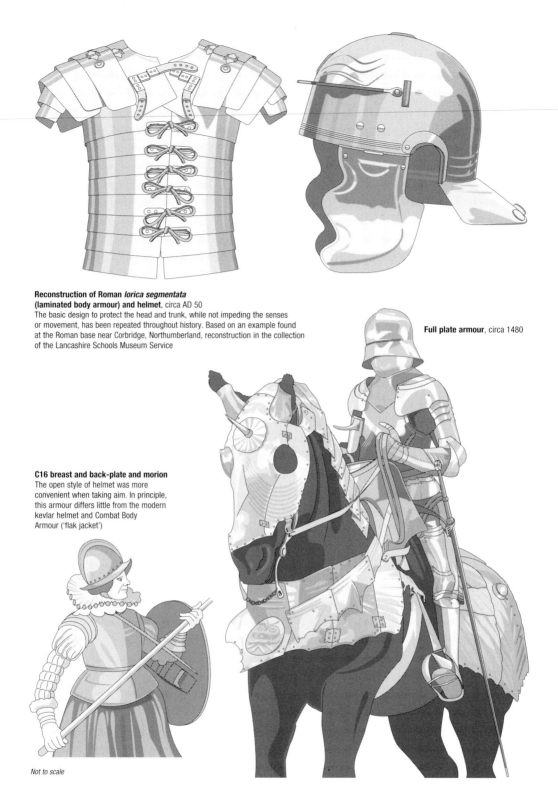

**Reconstruction of Roman *lorica segmentata*
(laminated body armour) and helmet**, circa AD 50
The basic design to protect the head and trunk, while not impeding the senses
or movement, has been repeated throughout history. Based on an example found
at the Roman base near Corbridge, Northumberland, reconstruction in the collection
of the Lancashire Schools Museum Service

Full plate armour, circa 1480

C16 breast and back-plate and morion
The open style of helmet was more
convenient when taking aim. In principle,
this armour differs little from the modern
kevlar helmet and Combat Body
Armour ('flak jacket')

Not to scale

Throughout military history, from the Roman *lorica* to the modern flak jacket, armour has been used to protect the most vital parts of the body: the head and trunk. The appearance of full-plate armour in Europe in the late Middle Ages was an aberration.

cover the backs of the hands, leaving the palms and finger-tips covered in leather to provide a non-slip surface for wielding weapons. When not at combat readiness, the mailed knight would unfasten his ventail, throw back his coif, and turn back his mittens but, for combat, he would be wholly covered in mail except at the groin and upper face. Mail itself came in a variety of sizes and types but was principally constructed of riveted rings interlinked with each other to lie flat. In some cases, lines of riveted rings alternated with solid rings. In the Orient mail rings were made (until well into the 19th century and even today as re-productions of ancient mail) with butt joints. By the mid-12th century the surcoat was in use, a long flowing garment worn over the mail coat. Possibly derived from Crusade ex-perience as being efficacious in reducing the effects of the sun on a body encased in metal, the surcoat later—by the 14th century—partnered the shield in becoming a canvas for the wearer's personal heraldry or for that of his master, the latter case providing one of the origins of military uni-form.

The retention of the shield by the mailed knights is one of the many indicators of the limitations of mail. Able to deflect some cuts, it was not proof against a thrust and the wearer's head—rigid in the skull, vulnerable in the brain tissue, and essential for the body's function—was particu-larly at risk. The helmet remained essential. Knights con-tinued to wear conical helmets into the 12th century, at which period other forms with round and flat tops began to appear. Foot soldiers, less élite, more numerous—and thus more cheaply armed—were helmeted with kettle hats, a form of low, broad-brimmed Spangenhelm, by the 13th century. The round- or flat-topped helmet, or helm, en-cased the head completely by *c*.1300; it was worn over the mail coif and padded inside either with a separate quilted arming cap or integral padding. Eventually, the anonymity provided by the helm resulted in it being crested with the wearer's personal device; these crests and the personal dec-oration of shield and surcoat had fully developed by the 15th century into the art and science of heraldry. As an add-itional head protection, but occasionally worn alone be-neath the mail coif, a metal skullcap called a basinet was developed. Additional body protection, another indicator of mail's limitations, was provided by quilted under-garments called aketons and padded surcoats called gam-besons; neither were wholly effective and so plate body armour began to develop during the 13th century.

Plate body armour seems to have begun as defences for the arms and legs, which were vulnerable in their mail sheaths, less well defended by the shield, and essential for the warrior's function. Elbows and kneecaps were the first to be protected, respectively, by couters and poleyns—known by the end of the 13th century. Shoulder protection, by espaulers, arrived soon after, as did gauntlets for the hands. During the 14th century the lower leg became pro-tected first by schynbalds—a metal shin-guard protecting

from the front only—and then by greaves, which encased the lower leg. The thighs, which had been protected be-neath the mail hauberk by padded, or gambossed, cuisses in the 13th century, received plate cuisses early in the next cen-tury. Sabatons for the feet arrived contemporaneously. Vambraces were provided for the arms during the 14th cen-tury and by the end of that century, the western knight was fully covered for combat in plate armour. In the West, the age of mail had been supplanted by that of plate.

From *c*.1400 until the end of plate armour in the 17th century the story of body armour in the West is one of gradually increasing sophistication of style, of decoration, and of diversification followed by a sharp and rapid decline as the increase in the power and use of firearms contributed strongly to the rendering of armour anachronistic and obsolete. It would be oversimplistic to ascribe the decline of armour solely to the invention of *gunpowder and the port-able personal weapon. Heavily armoured French knights at *Agincourt were toppled in quantity by the penetrative power of the English arrow tipped with an armour-piercing bodkin point and 400 years later, at *Waterloo, British infantrymen recorded hearing the sound of their musket balls bouncing off the cuirasses of the French *cuirassiers and carabiniers. Armour and gunpowder coexisted un-easily for some time before the latter triumphed and, even then, tactics on the battlefield and changing attitudes in post-Renaissance Europe were factors in the decline of armour almost as significant as the great chemical leveller.

Once the body had been finally encased in an armour composed of its different component parts, the concept of the garniture began to appear. This reached its apogee dur-ing the 15th century and was paralleled by a growth in the quality and quantity of decoration of armour and in the establishment of national design and decorative styles: once technology could advance no further, aesthetics took over. Principal among the centres of armour design and manu-facture in the 15th century were northern Italy, centred upon Milan, and southern Germany, centred upon Augs-burg. Burgos and Seville in Spain, Bordeaux in France, and both Lombardy and the Low Countries all contributed to the making of armour and each centre had its own charac-teristics. The 15th century also saw significant developments in the *tournament and those led to the concept of the armour garniture, whereby different types or components of an armour would be used in differing combinations for the various types of combat practised in the tournament: foot combat with *pole arms would require a different style of dress from the joust in the tiltyard. Since the tourna-ment, and especially the differing types of joust, were popular—and codified—in Germany and the Holy Roman Empire, it was from German manufacturers that the func-tion-specific components of the armour garniture sprang. The most popular forms of joust, developed in Germanic areas, were the Gestech and the Rennen. Both involved mounted combat with lances; the former was a peaceful joust, using blunted lances and seeking to score points by splintering lances, the latter was a warlike joust, using pointed lances with unhorsing the principal aim. Specialized armour was developed for both. For the Gestech the knight was bolted into a very heavy and largely inflexible armour equipped with a lance rest; jousting almost standing in his *stirrups he was virtually impregnable—which was the idea. For the Rennen the armour was lighter above the waist and flexible—more like the armour worn in combat, for which the Rennen was practice. In decorative terms the period was marked by a growth in engraving and etching and a decline in the painting and cloth-covering of armour; cut designs were usually heightened with gold and would frequently have a linking theme or style throughout the components of an armour. At the same time as the rich were commissioning decorated garnitures for both the field and the tournament, they were buying, in bulk and ready-made, rudimentary armour for their retainers. The ordinary soldier, fighting on foot, was armoured in accordance with his battlefield role: all wore helmets, increasingly of the sweeping aerodynamic shape called sallets; the hand-gunner wore a breastplate over his mail shirt; the pikeman a padded, metal-reinforced coat called a jack, a small shield, and some form of protection for his right arm; the archer wore two layers of quilted body defence and protection for his arms and throat.

By the beginning of the 16th century, the power of the *musketeers, protected from their mounted armoured victims by the pikemen's 18 foot (6.3 metre) pikes, was significantly changing the nature of warfare. After the battle of Pavia in 1525 it was clear that armour had, at best, a parade use and, although it would be worn in combat for the next century and a half, the art of the armourer turned increasingly to decoration and away from function. It is ironic that not until the early 16th century did England have its own centre for the manufacture of armour—that established by Henry VIII in Greenwich in c.1511 and utilizing the skills of imported Italian and German armourers. Greenwich remained an important centre for much of the 16th century, while the importance of armour gradually declined in battlefield terms and was focused increasingly on the forms required for the stylized combat of the tournament. By the end of the 16th century few soldiers in the West went into battle fully armoured and the trend continued during the wars of the early 17th century.

Battlefield role after 1600 continued to determine the type and degree of armour worn. The pikeman's head was protected by a high combed morion in the Spanish style, rather than the earlier sallet; he wore a breastplate with attached tassets over his thighs and—if an officer—a gorget to protect his throat. The musketeer wore a thick coat of buff leather and a morion but, by c.1630, would exchange his helmet for a broad-brimmed hat, sometimes with an iron skull cap or 'secret' beneath. Three-quarter armours, reaching only to the knee, were worn by heavy cavalry—known increasingly as *cuirassiers—who also wore heavy knee-length boots; arquebusiers, or light cavalry armed with firearms, wore breast- and back-plates over buff coats and protected their left forearms, or bridle-arms, with long metal or buff leather gauntlets. Cuirassiers retained the closed or 'close' helmet; arquebusiers adopted the continental Zischägge or 'lobster-tail' helmet with its triple-barred visor. Once the decline of armour was complete, by the end of the 17th century, the cavalryman's cuirass and the infantry officer's gorget were all that remained: both were retained into the 20th century as symbols of their wearer's status. Cuirasses are still worn by mounted bodyguards, such as the British Household Cavalry, and the gorget remained in some western countries, worn by both officers and, especially, *military police.

From the 1680s, functional body armour disappeared from the European battlefield, although it was retained in extra-European cultures, such as in India and in Japan—where it continued to have both a functional and formal role. Not until the 20th century did it reappear, first with the readoption of the steel helmet on the battlefields of WW I in 1915 and then with the use of the heavy steel breastplate, especially in the German army, by machine-gunners, *snipers, sentries, and other troops in exposed positions. Body shields of differing types were sold by private manufacturers, the greatest variety and use being, apparently, found in the British army; some officers had their uniform tunics reinforced in front with metal plates. Britain led the way with army body armour in WW II too, an initiative copied and developed by the USA, first, for the crews of its bombers and then for other branches of its Armed Forces. Having taken up the initiative, the USA then promoted the development of the 'flak' jacket through the *Korean and *Vietnam wars, in which variations were worn by the US Marine Corps, the army, and helicopter aircrew. The combat role of the latter arm militated against too much weight being carried and this was a major factor in the development of flak jackets utilizing non-metal protection such as ceramics or glass-reinforced plastics. Floating flak jackets were developed for the crews of the US Navy's inshore patrol craft. Terrorism has inspired its own body armour reaction in the last quarter of the 20th century as new materials, such as the aramid fibre developed by DuPont under the name Kevlar, became utilized for flak jackets and vests. Development is progressive in this area and so soldiers and other members of the security forces worldwide have new types of better, lighter body armour made available to them, in their roles as troops, policemen, or as bomb-disposal personnel. Consistently, as through history, each new missile provokes a new protection as the twin technologies of attack and defence keep pace with each other.   SCW

Blackmore, David, *Arms and Armour of the English Civil Wars* (London, 1990).

Blair, Claude, *European Armour* (London, 1958).

Dunstan, Simon, *Flak Jackets: 20th Century Military Body Armour* (London, 1984).

Edge, David, and Paddock, John M., *Arms and Armour of the Medieval Knight* (London, 1988).

armoured car The first cousin to the tank: an armed and armoured, wheeled military vehicle, with a good road and limited cross-country ability. Its origins stem from 1898, when a Maj Davidson of the US army bolted a machine gun to a 3-cylinder car. Although the idea was taken no further in the USA, it caused a ripple of interest in Europe. In 1902, British and French manufacturers separately exhibited their vehicles armed with Maxim machine guns within an armoured cab, and in 1903 Daimler demonstrated the world's first purpose-built armoured car to Austrian Emperor Franz Josef. It caused horses to bolt and a celebrated general was thrown from his mount, sufficient reason for no further interest to be shown until 1914.

Armoured cars are first recorded in combat just before WW I, used by the Italians in 1913 to subdue Tripoli and Cyrenaica. During 1914–18 all the major combatant nations developed four-wheeled armour-plated cars, usually equipped with fully revolving turrets, armed with one or two machine guns. Belgium employed various models of improvised armoured cars and these, together with the crude designs of France and Britain, were used as weapons of opportunity, relying on their mobility to hit and run. By the time the Royal Navy, at Churchill's behest, had designed a really effective, turreted armoured car—the Rolls-Royce—the barbed wire and trenches of the western front had rendered them impotent. Armoured cars found their way to the Middle East, where *Allenby and *Lawrence used them to great effect against the *Turks, while at *Amiens in August 1918, twelve Austin armoured cars got behind deep German lines for several hours, caused mayhem, and returned without loss.

Germany went to war in 1939 using her wheeled armour for *reconnaissance and scouting. They moved at high speed, often with motorcycle combinations, ahead of the panzer divisions, to reconnoitre routes and maintain the momentum of the assault. They included an impressive range of four-, six- and eight-wheeled turreted vehicles, usually armed with 20 mm guns, and were able to travel great distances between refuelling. France, too, used armoured cars for reconnaissance and communications work, but much of her fleet dated from 1918. Britain's fleet was largely of 1920 vintage, mostly Rolls-Royces, and used for colonial policing. In 1941, Daimler and Humber all-wheel drive armoured cars were introduced, armed with 2 pounder guns, and Britain also introduced the Dingo, a turretless scout car.

In the *Western Desert, armoured cars engaged in much traditional raiding, as their cavalry forebears had done, but in Europe the passive role of reconnaissance foretold that the era of wheeled armour as an aggressive weapon was over. The USA developed a series of armoured cars, of which the six-wheeled M8 ('Greyhound' to the British) was the most numerous, but their main purpose, too, was reconnaissance. Armoured cars remain in service with many armies today, often redesignated as scout cars, although *MICVs are better armed and can travel faster. The comparatively poor cross-country performance of armoured cars has always limited their usefulness.   APC-A

Harris, J. P., and Toase, F. N. (eds.), *Armoured Warfare* (London, 1990).

armoured personnel carriers See APCS.

armoured warfare The trade-off between survivability and mobility on the battlefield has been a feature of warfare since the beginning of recorded history: indeed, one can imagine primitive man pondering the merits of a heavy garment over fleetness of foot before conducting a raid on his neighbours. From the Celtic warriors dressed only in warpaint to the *hoplites who could only bear to don their panoply immediately before battle, the answers were as varied as the cultures in question. The military advent of the *horse merely added a new dimension to the age-old question, with horsemen facing the immensity of the great plains favouring speed and endurance, while others gravitated towards the greater protection of ever more elaborate *armour, thus defining the two main types of *cavalry. The protection versus mobility argument transferred itself to sea with the advent of the ironclad, adding a third dimension of hitting power, an equation famously miscalculated by *Fisher with his 'battlecruisers'. But what we mean by 'armoured warfare' today is combat among *tanks, *self-propelled (SP) guns, *MICVs, *APCs, and *armoured cars, in an environment in which *air power plays a crucial role.

As a dream, the concept can be dated back at least to *Leonardo da Vinci, who doodled a round, wheeled, armoured vehicle with cannon firing out of ports. Although armour and steam power were joined successfully in warships and less so in armoured trains (the latter's rails being fatally vulnerable, as *Churchill was to discover in South Africa), the weight to strength ratios of engines and steel plate for cross-country applications did not intersect until the early 20th century. Despite attempts to portray its subsequent development as a revolution in warfare piloted by far-seeing visionaries like *Fuller, *Liddell Hart, and *Guderian, armoured warfare went through a long and painful gestation, dependent at every stage on incremental improvements in engineering and electronic technology and, above all, in the understanding necessary to evolve the necessary *doctrine. The latter process was conditioned especially by the human and material catastrophe of WW I and an urgent desire not to repeat it.

Armoured cars rattling about and frightening horses and camels in Italian and British imperial ventures before WW I were little more than an extension of traditional cavalry applications. Serious business began at Flers-Courcelette on the *Somme in September 1916, when a handful of tracked British 'tanks' (their cover name to preserve security) were committed and achieved some local success before breaking or bogging down. Only 32 actually reached the start line; their crews were inexperienced and tactics undeveloped. Although *Haig was to be criticized for premature use of a new weapon, it was not unreasonable to derive practical operational experience before, as was the case, ordering tanks on a large scale, and the costly stalemate on the Somme that summer demanded radical solutions. Early tanks were intended to crush a path through the wire and suppress or destroy machine gun nests and troops in trenches. What was lost by their 'premature' use was the element of surprise and a reduction in their subsequent ability to strike terror into the heart of an unprepared but otherwise resolute enemy.

Tanks were used the following spring as part of the *Arras/Vimy Ridge battle, their attack wrecked by a ponderous approach march. At *Cambrai in November they were altogether more successful when used en masse with a devastating short artillery barrage. By 1918 there were not merely heavy tanks like the relatively reliable British Mk V and the cumbersome German A7V, but light tanks like the French two-man Renault FT-17 and the British Whippet. That April saw the first tank versus tank action, when 2Lt Frank Mitchell's Mk IV stopped an A7V, and British tanks were used successfully at Hamel in July and on a larger scale at *Amiens in August. The war ended before Fuller's scheme for a large-scale fast-moving tank attack—Plan 1919—could be fully developed, and in any event it is unlikely that the fast tanks it demanded could have been developed in time.

Not surprisingly, the inter-war years were dominated by a 'never again' mentality. Advocates of armoured warfare in Britain and France found themselves contending with what Liddell Hart portrayed as hidebound military officialdom, but the political and economic climate of the 1920s militated against radical reform, and the issue is far more complex than the simple opposition of conservatives to radicals. As J. P. Harris has pointed out, there was no unified 'theory of armoured warfare' at the time, but rather a number of ideas (some brilliantly if futuristically sketched out in Fuller's *Lectures on FSR III*) which were often unsupported by technology, funding, or strategic requirements. The relationship of armoured to unarmoured forces remained a matter of debate, not least in armies like the French and German, where complete *mechanization would never be possible, and the proportion of tank to other units even within armoured formations exercised theorists and practical soldiers alike. In Germany, the development of what became known by the shorthand *blitzkrieg sprang from a desire to use interior lines to check numerically superior enemies, a process which put a premium on rapid manoeuvre, giving the development of armoured warfare in Germany a strategic mainspring missing elsewhere. Yet even there the process was not simple, and Hitler's accession to power in 1933 accelerated developments which had been proceeding without the single-minded determination which post-war critics of British and French performance were eager to detect.

Given the legacy of WW I and the lack of a perceived need to mount offensive operations (which in the French case would have meshed uncomfortably with the logic of the *Maginot Line) it is not surprising that in Britain and France there was an emphasis (and even there it was not an exclusive concentration) on slow but sure armoured vehicles supporting and protecting the infantry and advancing at a pace that permitted the artillery to keep up. It was this type of tank that Guderian specifically rejected in his 1938 book *Achtung Panzer!* as being 'a weapon adjusted to the foot soldier's scale of time and space values', a phrase which lies at the very core of the development of armoured warfare doctrine. He also advocated the concentration of tanks in panzer divisions and the application of these divisions to the decisive point. Useful lessons were learnt in the *Spanish civil war and in the *Polish campaign of 1939. Although an intrinsic superiority in their engineering culture may explain the Germans' ability to produce 'open-ended' armoured vehicle designs in the run up to WW II, basic platforms like the Panzer Mk III and IV that lent themselves to endless modification and improvement, in the campaign which led to the fall of *France and Belgium in 1940 German tanks were neither numerically nor (markedly) technically superior. Emphasis on radio communications did give them an important edge, especially over the French, but it was in tactical doctrine—and, more fundamentally, in the mindset that both informed and sprang from it—that German competence was decisive.

Armoured warfare was the clearest expression of that competence and found its fullest expression on the *eastern front. There, in numbers and across distances that make the western European theatres look like sideshows by comparison, two peoples and their respective totalitarian systems clawed for supremacy and by the end had evolved all the components of modern armoured doctrine, complete with close *air support, SP guns, powerful main battle tanks, APCs, and even MICVs. The *Russian army's development of armoured warfare, which reflected its doctrinal commitment to the offensive, had been badly disrupted by the purges of the 1930s, and in 1941–2 the Germans enjoyed a clear lead. They lost it thereafter, in part because of twice squandering armour in attritional fighting at *Stalingrad and *Kursk and by a series of other flawed decisions, by no means all of them *Hitler's. But the war on the eastern front, for too long marginalized by western historians, was at least as much won by the Russians as lost by the Germans. In their development of the *operational level of war the Russians honed the ability to achieve decisive force ratios where it mattered by massing, usually covertly, on the vital axis, and minting operational victory from tactical success.

Charles Dick is right to point out, in his chapter of Harris and Toase (eds.), *Armoured Warfare*, that 'Soviet armoured forces developed a capacity for the conduct of *manoeuvre warfare which . . . was as great as that of the Wehrmacht at any stage in the war.'

After the war *NATO—heavily influenced by German generals in person and in print—was encouraged to emphasize German tactical achievements in the face of a worsening force ratio, and did so at the price of neglecting the Russian army's real achievement in the field of armoured warfare. It was probably the US *nuclear umbrella that ensured that the long-planned armoured battle in Europe's central region never took place, and after the fall of the Warsaw Pact many commentators belittled its military potential. However, the degree to which western armies would have been able to compensate for inferior numbers by superior ability must remain doubtful.

For the *IDF, faced with defending a state which lacked defensible frontiers and strategic depth, armoured warfare was attractive. Its devastating attack at the opening of the Six-Day War of 1967 had much in common with German blitzkrieg and Soviet doctrine, and success led to an overemphasis on the role of the tank which was to cause difficulties in the War of Atonement in 1973. The war suggested not, as several commentators immediately opined, that the day of the tank was over, but that armoured warfare was the business of combined arms teams.

With the end of the Cold War, reductions in defence expenditure, and the widespread shrinkage of armies, armoured warfare on the scale of WW II seems unlikely to recur. Nevertheless, armies which seek to remain in the first rank strive to retain a capability to fight it. In future, however, it is likely to be influenced by the wish—at least in the West—to minimize casualties, and to capitalize on a less dense battlefield by emphasizing manoeuvre rather than attrition. The oft-heralded demise of the tank, notably in the face of the armed *helicopter, has yet to occur, and recent evidence suggests that the troop protection accorded by equipment designed for armoured warfare gives it a particular merit in areas like the former Yugoslavia, emphasizing, yet again, the relationship between survivability and mobility.   RH

Harris, J. P., and Toase, F. N. (eds.), *Armoured Warfare* (London, 1990).

arms control and disarmament The idea that war can be abolished, or its effects mitigated, by agreed measures of arms control and disarmament among states has a long history. Arms control involves measures of internationally agreed restraint in arms policy. It may involve two, more than two, or all countries. It may set limits on the level of arms, research and development, testing, manner of deployment, and use. Some arms control measures may not require any reduction or abolition of arms at all: rather they

may involve opening them up to inspection, relocating them away from particular areas, or prohibiting certain forms of testing or use. Disarmament is the generic term for reduction or abolition of arms. It may be unilateral, bilateral, or multilateral; imposed or agreed; general or local; comprehensive or partial; formally verified or unverified. It encompasses much international practice, as well as proposals for ambitious and as yet unrealized schemes. It encompasses most of what is included in the category of 'arms control', but obviously does not encompass such measures as involve no reduction or abolition of arms.

Arms control and disarmament are distinct from the *laws of war. Whereas the laws of war are concerned in part with limitations on use of weapons in the actual conduct of armed conflict, the arms control and disarmament approach is mainly concerned with the limitations on possession and deployment of weapons in peacetime (though the terms of any agreements may remain applicable in wartime as well). In practice there has been some natural degree of overlap between the two approaches.

Before the 19th century, most schemes for ambitious measures of disarmament had been the work, not of political leaders, but of philosophers: Jean Bodin in *Six Livres de la République* (1577), William Penn in *An Essay toward the Present and Future Peace of Europe* (1693–4), and Immanuel Kant in *On Perpetual Peace* (1795). However, throughout history there have been cases of limited measures of arms control and disarmament, whether agreed or imposed, formal or informal. For example, under the Treaty of Utrecht (1713) France agreed to demolish a fort at Dunkirk; and the Russo-Turkish Treaty of Kuchuk Kainarji (1774) prevented Turkey from fortifying the Crimean peninsula.

Ambitious political schemes for general limitations on arms by all states date from the 19th century. In 1816, directly after the final defeat of the Napoleonic empire, Tsar Alexander I of Russia proposed 'a simultaneous reduction of armed forces of all kinds which the powers have brought into being to preserve the safety and independence of their peoples'. In reply the British foreign minister, Lord Castlereagh, expressed the realist critique of such ambitious schemes: 'It is impossible not to perceive that the settlement of a scale of force for so many powers, under such different circumstances as to their relative means, frontiers, positions and faculties for rearming, presents a very complicated question for negotiation.'

When he convened the 1899 Hague Peace Conference, Tsar Nicholas II was concerned about the cost and dangers of arms competition, and also about Russia's technical inferiority. He wanted to bring about major reductions in arms, but actually this conference and its successor in 1907, while reaching agreement on some other matters, failed to achieve any significant arms reductions.

After WW I, the Covenant of the League of Nations called for 'the reduction of national armaments to the lowest point consistent with national safety and the enforcement by common action of international obligations'. Some measures of arms restraint were achieved in the inter-war years, including the 1922 Washington Naval Treaty and the 1930 London Naval Treaty. However, the ambitious disarmament aims of the League were not translated into reality. In November 1927 Maxim Litvinov, head of the Soviet delegation to a League disarmament commission in Geneva, made the first-ever formal diplomatic proposal for 'complete and general disarmament'—the 'complete' referring to all armaments, the 'general' to all countries. This proposal gained little support. Subsequently the League convened the much-heralded Conference for the Reduction and Limitation of Armaments: held in Geneva in 1932– 4, at the very time of increasing challenge from Japan and Germany, this failed to achieve any significant results. Overall, the League's combination of high aspiration in the disarmament field and poor performance contributed to the perception of the organization as a failure.

On disarmament as on other matters, the UN was based on more realistic assumptions than the League. Articles 11 and 26 of the Charter make only cautious references to disarmament and the regulation of armaments. As the *Cold War developed and East–West arms competition intensified, there were increasing calls for disarmament, especially from the non-aligned countries which came to form a majority of UN membership. Both the USSR and the USA put forward schemes for general and complete disarmament in 1959–60. The UN General Assembly held Special Sessions on Disarmament in 1978, 1982, and 1988, which were long on rhetoric but short on achievement.

In the UN era, a sharp distinction came increasingly to be drawn between general and complete disarmament on the one hand, and arms limitation (largely synonymous with arms control) on the other. The former was widely criticized as unattainable. Some argued that the idea of all countries agreeing to disarm at the same time was not credible; that arms still had a function within societies, and in their defence against external enemies; and that inspection of disarmament would be very difficult, especially as *nuclear weapons, so large in their effects, were relatively easy to conceal. Against a background of such pessimistic arguments, advocacy of more modest measures of arms limitation gained much ground from about 1960 onwards. Considerable emphasis was placed on the possibilities of effective verification of such measures, especially on account of the rapid development of satellite monitoring technology from the 1960s onwards.

The main international arms control and disarmament agreements concluded since 1945 are as follows.

- 1963 Partial Nuclear Test Ban Treaty (PTBT).
- 1968 Treaty on the Non-Proliferation of Nuclear Weapons (NPT).
- 1972 Biological Weapons Convention (BW Convention).

- 1972 US–Soviet Accords resulting from the *Strategic Arms Limitation Talks, placing limits on long-range nuclear weapons delivery vehicles and on anti-ballistic missile systems (SALT-I Accords).
- 1987 US–Soviet Treaty eliminating intermediate-range nuclear forces (INF Treaty).
- 1990 Treaty on Conventional Armed Forces in Europe (CFE Treaty).
- 1991 US–USSR Strategic Arms Reduction Treaty (START I Treaty).
- 1993 US–Russia Strategic Arms Reduction Treaty (START II Treaty).
- 1993 Convention on the Prohibition of the Development, Production, and Use of Chemical Weapons and on Their Destruction (CW Convention).
- 1996 Comprehensive Nuclear Test Ban Treaty (CTBT).
- 1997 Ottawa Convention Prohibiting the Use, Stockpiling, Production, and Transfer of Anti-personnel Mines (APM Convention).

There are also treaties concluded by states in the following regions establishing nuclear-weapon-free zones: Latin America (Treaty of Tlatelolco, 1967); South Pacific (Treaty of Rarotonga, 1985); Africa (Treaty of Pelindaba, 1985); South-East Asia (Treaty of Bangkok, 1995). The purposes of these and other agreements concluded since 1945 were not the reduction of armaments as an end in itself, but were more limited, specific, and also varied. Specialists in the field have identified the possible purposes of arms control and disarmament negotiations as, in general, encompassing the following:

- To reduce the risk of war breaking out, for example by limiting weapons systems, manoeuvres, or deployments seen as particularly destabilizing.
- To reduce the severity and extent of war if it does break out, for example by limiting possession and use of nuclear and *chemical and biological weapons.
- To reduce the economic costs of armed confrontation, for example by placing limits on numbers of expensive items of military hardware such as large naval vessels and nuclear-armed ballistic missiles.
- To introduce an element of predictability into the strategic plans of states.
- To reduce certain undesirable side effects of arms competition, such as the radioactive pollution caused by nuclear weapons tests in the atmosphere and in the sea.
- To reduce or eliminate the use of certain weapons that are indiscriminate in character, such as anti-personnel landmines.
- To prevent the extension of great power military confrontation to new areas (treaties limiting military activities in Antarctica and in outer *space are among the many examples).

- To facilitate peaceful and co-operative relations between adversaries in particular geographical areas or on particular subjects.
- To facilitate a dialogue between military powers, to enable them to understand each other's security concerns, and to assist them in seeing security in multilateral terms.

In short, arms control and disarmament are widely seen as instrumental, the underlying goal being security. Any agreement, and any given set of negotiations, might involve tension or even conflict between some of the purposes outlined above. Multilateral arms negotiations have not provided an escape from moral complexity and political controversy.

There have been many criticisms of arms control and disarmament negotiations and agreements. Although an underlying purpose of diplomacy in this area has been to build up a degree of mutual understanding between adversaries, this has not always worked: conferences on armaments have often been the scene of polemical statements, including complaints about the adversary's allegedly poor record of implementation. Even when states have not openly violated an agreement's provisions, they have sometimes evaded its purposes in their development and deployment of weapons. Some agreements, whether on naval matters in the 1930s or on nuclear non-proliferation since 1945, have been criticized as inherently discriminatory. There has been a natural tendency for arms control negotiations to focus on matters (such as numbers of missiles) that are relatively easy to count and control, but to be slower in addressing matters (such as the development of multiple independently targeted missile warheads) that are potentially more destabilizing. Sometimes arms limitation negotiations have been criticized as failing to tackle qualitative aspects of arms competition, or more generally for being too mildly reformist when more fundamental change was needed. Local wars with an East–West dimension, including in *Vietnam and *Afghanistan, continued despite the simultaneous conclusion of arms control agreements between the USA and USSR. Laboriously negotiated and highly detailed agreements have sometimes been of reduced relevance by the time they were actually concluded, because political and military circumstances had changed.

Despite such criticisms, arms control and disarmament negotiations and agreements respond to perennial problems of the international system, and remain an important part of statecraft. In the period of the Cold War, the habit of mutual consultation, and the emergence of some elements of common understanding of strategic problems, may have contributed something to the larger process of change in the USSR that resulted, in 1989–91, in the end of the Cold War and the collapse of the USSR itself.   AR

Bull, Hedley, *The Control of the Arms Race* (London, 1961).
Goldblat, Jozef, *Arms Control: A Guide to Negotiations and Agreements* (London, 1994).
Sims, Jennifer E., *Icarus Restrained: An Intellectual History of Nuclear Arms Control* (Boulder, Colo., 1990).
Stockholm International Peace Research Institute, *SIPRI Yearbook* (Oxford annual).
Talbott, Strobe, *Deadly Gambits: The Reagan Administration and the Stalemate in Nuclear Arms Control* (London, 1984).

arms trade The arms trade has always been in the forefront of technology transfer between more and less developed societies, usually just behind the advance of imperialist designs but occasionally, to the discomfiture of those desirous of picking up Kipling's 'white man's burden', in advance of it. Without the culture or the *doctrine to employ modern arms effectively, as in the case of the *Dahomey expedition, or without the numbers necessary, as in the case of the American *Plains Indians, the trade never tipped the balance in favour of the soon-to-be downtrodden. But this may change once modern weapons of mass destruction spread, hence the western world's intense interest in arms control. In general the term refers to the transfer (by sale, exchange, or gift) of 'conventional' weapons—such as armoured fighting vehicles, combat aircraft, and warships—together with associated military equipment and technology. The proliferation of nuclear and *chemical and biological weapons is the concern of a separate series of control regimes.

Formal arms transfers generally take place between governments, although other agencies such as arms manufacturers, banks, 'off-set' brokers, and some law-abiding individuals can be closely involved in the process. There are also informal arms transfers, where the identity of the participants may be more difficult to discern, and where the legality of the transaction is more questionable. Measuring the size of the international arms market is technically difficult and politically controversial. Market analysis is provided by a number of government and non-government agencies whose statistics must be treated with a great deal of caution. All such agencies have a vested interest in exaggerating the trade, because it justifies their own budgets. As a result, the size of even the formal international arms market is more a matter of debate than fact. The Stockholm International Peace Research Institute (SIPRI) estimates the value of the trade in 1997 to have been approximately $25 billion, using a unique trend-indicator system, rather than attempt to measure the real value of transfers. The US government's *Arms Control and Disarmament Agency takes a broader sample, including small-calibre weapons, other military equipment, and some 'dual-use' equipment (with both civilian and military applications), and they value the market several billion dollars higher.

Most agencies agree that the market has contracted dramatically since the late 1980s. This is explained by the end of the *Cold War and the resulting downturn in defence spending around the world; the economic collapse of the USSR; and economic uncertainty in the Asia-Pacific region and beyond. If the formal arms market is difficult to measure, informal or 'grey market' transactions, as well as wholly 'black' supplies to terrorist and criminal organizations, are impossible to gauge with any confidence. Estimates of the size of the covert arms market range between $1 and $10 billion annually. As well as being extremely difficult to measure and control, the covert arms trade funnels arms into areas of tension placed under a formal embargo.

For much of the 1990s the main arms importing regions of the world have been Europe, the Middle East, and the Asia-Pacific region. On the supply side, the five permanent members of the UN Security Council (the USA, Russia, China, France, and Great Britain) are responsible for between 80 and 90 per cent of arms exports around the world. The principal arms manufacturers and exporters are to be found in western Europe and North America, with the USA in an unassailable position at the top of the league. The predominance of these western suppliers is an important indication that the international arms market has changed fundamentally since the end of the Cold War. The collapse of the USSR saw the collapse of a major source of new weapons systems (military surplus being another matter). But the end of the Cold War also meant the end of the adversarial logic which had underpinned much arms export activity and was often not governed by straightforward commercial considerations. The notion of the world divided into spheres of influence no longer provides an adequate explanation for the dynamics of arms supply and demand, and commercial and industrial considerations are increasingly shaping debate and policy-making.

The post-Cold War international arms market is being shaped by three forces. The first is the sharp reduction in military spending around the world, expressing the widespread reluctance of public opinion to support expensive military establishments. With manufacturing potential exceeding any likely demand, the only recourse for many arms manufacturers, and for governments wishing to sustain a defence industrial base, has been to secure and expand international market share, albeit in a much-diminished global market. This increasing pressure to export is partly responsible for the second force; changing patterns in the production of arms and military equipment. Arms manufacturers are increasingly relying upon joint manufacturing and marketing ventures, in order to share costs and reduce risks, gain access to foreign innovation, achieve economies of scale, and penetrate foreign markets. In many cases, manufacturers have shifted whole sectors of their production cycle to developing regions in order to take advantage of cheaper labour and production costs, and have outsourced the supply of certain key sub-components. The internationalization of manufacturing not only makes the control of manufacturing and export more difficult, it also results in the spread of indigenous arms manufacturing capability. Arms sales are often coupled with the transfer of key military and dual-use technologies through 'off-set'

arrangements; rather than buy complex weapon systems straight from the production line, importers increasingly expect a phased transfer of the relevant design and manufacturing technology in order that they, too, may in time become manufacturers and exporters in their own right or make use of leading-edge technology for other, non-military sectors of their domestic industry. Furthermore, since much of the relevant technology is often non-military in origin, or has clear non-military applications, the acquisition of some sort of a weapons manufacturing capability is becoming increasingly straightforward. Added to these commercial, industrial, and technological considerations is a third force; increasing political and cultural self-confidence on the part of the importer. Freed from the constraints of the Cold War, and aware of their status in international politics and law, arms importers increasingly see the ownership of modern conventional weapons, as well as the ability to manufacture them, to be normal, inalienable, and even essential attributes of a modern nation state, and are able to exploit the international market to that end.

Taken together, these three forces have created a market in which the initiative lies increasingly with the importer. With huge excesses in supply combined with declining demand, and with changing patterns of military production, the post-Cold War world has an arms market which, although considerably reduced, is in many respects more diverse, vigorous, and competitive than its predecessor. As well as these commercial and industrial considerations, the new buyer's market has important strategic implications: even the most sophisticated equipment and technologies are finding their way onto the market place, such as satellite surveillance systems, missile countermeasures, stealth technologies and cryptographic equipment. Furthermore, as the market and the manufacturing sector become more diffuse, so the prospects for timely and effective control of arms and technology exports diminish. Effective control of arms transfers requires multilateral action, including recipients as well as suppliers of arms.

Throughout history there have been attempts to control the manufacture and flow of arms and military technology thought to be strategically crucial. An early example was in 455, when the eastern Roman emperor, Marcian, banned the export of weapons and manufacturing materials to the barbarians. In other cases, the use and effect of certain weapons was thought especially repugnant, hence the Greek ban on the Roman short sword, the prohibition on crossbows ordered by the Second Lateran Council in 1139, French condemnation of the longbow in the 14th century, unease about the introduction of the machine gun in the 19th century, the banning of poison *gas and bio-weapons in the 20th, and so on.

The most recent example of this impulse came after the defeat of Iraqi forces in 1991. Information about the ease with which Saddam *Hussein had acquired the means to develop weapons of mass destruction and the embarrassing provenance of much of Iraq's military capability led to demands for better regulation of the arms trade. While most manufacturing states have developed elaborate (albeit often porous) arms and technology export control systems, after 1991 attention turned to the prospects for effective multilateral control. The early 1990s saw a series of initiatives from such bodies as the Conference on (now Organization for) Security and Co-operation in Europe, the Group of Seven industrialized nations, the European Community/Union, the permanent five members of the UN Security Council, and the UN General Assembly. The most recent formal initiative is the 'Wassenaar Arrangement on Export Controls for Conventional Arms and Dual-Use Goods and Technologies', established in 1996 by 33 states. Replacing the Co-ordinating Committee for Multilateral Export Controls (CoCom), which had been known during the Cold War as 'the economic arm of NATO', the Wassenaar Arrangement sought to be more inclusive and to complement other dual-use technology export control regimes.

Several new arms embargoes have also been put in place during the 1990s. In short, as conventional weapons have proliferated after the Cold War, so have initiatives to control or supervise the market. In most cases the expectation surrounding these initiatives far outstripped their performance. The initiatives face a number of obstacles, not least the fact that the relationship between the arms trade and the incidence and severity of war has been more assumed than proven, and remains open to question. There is also something of a political presumption of access for states to the international arms market; since all states have the right to self-defence, under Article 51 of the UN Charter, it could reasonably be argued that states without a domestic arms manufacturing sector must have access to an arms market if their security and self-defence are not to be imperilled. For these reasons, if the international arms market of the late 1990s is considerably smaller than ten years previously, this seems more likely to have been the result of market forces than multilateral control arrangements.

There is nevertheless one area where more tangible results have been forthcoming, and where scepticism may be less justifiable. On 3 December 1997, some 121 states signed the Ottawa Convention on the Prohibition of the Use, Stockpiling, Production, and Transfer of Anti-Personnel Mines and on their Destruction. The Convention was the result of a long-running, Nobel prize-winning, non-governmental campaign against anti-personnel mines. It remains to be seen whether the Convention will be observed and honoured sufficiently, and whether it achieves its goal, but it does stand in stark contrast to the failure by governments to agree a ban in 1997 during negotiations at the Conference on Disarmament in Geneva. But then again, as in the celebrated case of the ban on poison gas being respected during WW II, it may also be that some weapons are simply so 'two-edged' that their continued use becomes unattractive.

Most analyses of the international arms market suggest that the dramatic decline may have halted, and that the arms market may have reached equilibrium; the market will neither contract dramatically in the future, nor expand vigorously. That said, there will continue to be fluctuations in demand, particularly as tensions and conflicts arise, and as the effect of the global economic uncertainty of the late 1990s is felt. But even in its reduced state, the international arms market is likely to remain controversial. A series of arms export scandals in supplier states have led to demands for a more 'ethical' approach to arms trading, where closer account is taken of human rights violations and the quality of governance in the importing country. Sophisticated lobbying campaigns have as their goal the implementation of 'codes of conduct' for arms export decision-makers, nationally, regionally, and globally.   PC/HEB

Arnhem, battle of (1944), part of MARKET GARDEN, *Montgomery's ambitious two-part operation involving three *airborne divisions to secure key bridges in Holland, cross the Rhine, and advance into Germany before the winter of 1944. MARKET involved dropping 101st (US) Airborne Division to capture two canal bridges at Zon and Veghel, 82nd (US) Airborne to take bridges over the Maas at Grave and the Rhine at Nijmegen, and 1st (British) Airborne to capture the Arnhem bridge over the Rhine. While MARKET was taking place, GARDEN called for British XXX Corps to advance 64 miles over the bridges and secure the airborne corridor. There remains a highly charged doubt whether Lt Gen Browning, commanding the Allied airborne corps, was unaware that 9th and 10th *SS Panzer Divisions were refitting in the vicinity of Arnhem, or whether he mentally suppressed *ULTRA indications as being inconvenient to the grandiose plan. The same unbalanced (and deeply uncharacteristic) precipitation can be seen in Montgomery's pointed failure even to consult Dutch staff officers, who could have told him that running armour along easily defended causeways was not the manner to advance into Holland.

The choice of the Guards Armoured Division to spearhead the 64 mile (103 km) dash was also misconceived, as dash was something it was known to lack. Although it managed to advance and link up with the two US divisions, it failed to reach Arnhem. Last in a far from exhaustive list of appalling failures of planning and preparation, 1st Airborne landed at Arnhem on 17 September 1944 by parachute and glider, on landing zones 7 miles (11.3 km) distant from their objective, and their radio communications promptly broke down. One battalion (2nd Parachute Battalion) managed to reach the bridge, but was isolated and reduced by German armour. A Polish Parachute Brigade landed on 21 September on the far bank of the Rhine, but was unable to help. Faced with dwindling supplies, heavy casualties, and no prospect of relief from XXX Corps, Maj Gen Urquhart and

2,700 troops withdrew across the Rhine on the night of 25–6 September, leaving behind nearly 7,600 killed or captured. Cornelius Ryan's book of the battle, *A Bridge Too Far* (1974), was made into a celebrated *film of the same name in 1977.   APC-A

Arnold, Gen Benedict (1741–1801). Remembered mainly as a mercenary traitor during the *American independence war, Arnold was also one of the ablest commanders on either side. He led from the front and was twice seriously wounded doing so. He preferred deeds to words and, in the end, cash in hand from the British over promises from people he had reason to believe would renege.

He served in the militia during the *French and Indian war and afterwards went into business in New Haven, Connecticut, in which he attempted to compensate for his lack of ability by dishonesty. At the outbreak of rebellion in 1775, Arnold immediately joined the militia and along with Ethan Allen took Fort Ticonderoga. He then led one prong of an expedition against Quebec through the Maine wilderness, a remarkable feat, but the assault failed and he was wounded. Promoted brigadier general, he built a fleet of boats and fought a successful rearguard action against a greatly superior force at Valcour Island.

When he was not among five major generals created in February 1777 he threatened to resign, but was persuaded to stay by *Washington. Promoted after repelling the British invasion of Connecticut later in the year, he continued to resent loss of seniority. He played an important part in the defeat of Burgoyne at *Saratoga, where he was crippled. Appointed commander of Philadelphia in June 1778, he socialized with Loyalists and married one of them. Charges of financial impropriety also hung over him when, in May 1779, he made a secret approach to the British and sold them details of a proposed invasion of Canada. His intention of betraying *West Point in exchange for £20,000 went astray when Maj John André, his contact, was captured with incriminating documents. Arnold fled on a British ship and his last act was to lead a raid against his native Connecticut in September 1781. It is said he died a broken man; broke, certainly, but probably unrepentant.   HEB

Arras, battle of (1940). On 21 May 1940, 7th Panzer Division under *Rommel, leading the inner flank of the thrust from the Meuse, was temporarily checked south of Arras by an improvised British formation, 'Frankforce'. Due to hurried assembly the counter-attack was initiated by only two columns of tanks (4th and 7th Royal Tank Regiments), followed closely by two battalions of the Durham Light Infantry, but with little artillery and no *air support. That morning the columns moved from Vimy to the west of Arras and then swung eastward across the Arras–Baumetz railway, striking 6th and 7th Rifle Regiments and the *SS

Totenkopf regiment just as they were beginning a disorderly advance through the villages of Wailly, Ficheux, and Agny. Impervious to much German *anti-armour fire the British tanks wrought havoc among the chaos of troops, guns, and transport.

Although anticipating a counter-attack, Rommel was so shaken that he thought five British divisions were defending Arras. To stem the retreat Rommel himself took command of the German guns at Wailly: his ADC was killed at his side. Only on the arrival of 25th Panzer Regiment at dusk, and after twelve hours' fighting, did the few surviving British tanks and infantrymen withdraw north of Arras. The town was finally abandoned on the night of 23 May. The results of the British attack were ephemeral, but it served to instil caution in the German high command and thus contributed to the 'halt order' (24–7 May) which assisted the evacuation from *Dunkirk.   BJB

Arras/Vimy Ridge, battle of (1917). The British offensive at Arras, of which the Canadian capture of Vimy Ridge formed a notable part (see CANADIAN EXPEDITIONARY FORCE), was the result of Allied discussions in early 1917 which placed the British army, controversially, under French command for the spring offensive. Nivelle, the French C-in-C, championed what he saw as a war-winning offensive on the Aisne and in the Soissonais (see NIVELLE OFFENSIVE), and *Haig was directed to attack at Arras on 9 April to draw in German reserves.

The battle, launched at 05.30 on a sleety morning, began very well. In the north Byng's Canadian Corps, attacking with its four divisions side by side, took Vimy Ridge in a well-prepared operation which left it dominating the Douai plain. This success had wide implications, and to Canadian troops in France and their families and friends at home it was a proud demonstration of Canada's nationhood. When *Byng was promoted shortly afterwards, Maj Gen Currie of 1st Canadian Division took over, becoming the first Canadian lieutenant general.

To the south, Third Army under *Allenby attacked from the suburbs of Arras towards Monchy-le-Preux and Fampoux. German defences, laid out in three main lines, were strong, but a well-orchestrated counter-battery programme crippled artillery support. Heavy and accurate bombardment smashed defences, but tanks were a disappointment on the churned-up ground. North of the Scarpe, XVII Corps took Fampoux and the Point du Jour Ridge. Things went slightly less well for VI Corps to its south, but the long Observation Ridge was captured—together with 60 guns in Battery Valley behind it. Orange Hill also fell, and though progress at the southern end of the battlefield was poor, both Neuville Vitasse and Telegraph Hill were taken. The day ended with some attackers up on the German third line, leading *Ludendorff to write: 'The battle of Arras . . . was a bad beginning for the decisive struggle of this year . . . The consequences of a break-through 12 to 15 kilometres [7.5–9.5 miles] wide and 6 or more kilometres [3.75 miles] deep are not easy to meet.'

Allenby was in a position to do even more serious damage to the Germans, possibly compelling them to withdraw to the Drocourt-Quéant switch-line behind their front position. But he misread the battle, sending cavalry forward into the snow-flurries around Monchy on the 10th, and it proved difficult to co-ordinate fire support for fresh attacks with guns stalled behind captured trenches and communications cut. Monchy fell, though the Germans came within an ace of retaking it in a deft counter-attack on the 14th. At Bullecourt, south of the main attack sector, a promising Australian attack broke down when its tank support failed, leading to long-lasting recriminations between Australians and the Tank Corps.

By this stage some of Allenby's commanders were horrified by the losses suffered in what had become a grim attritional battle in filthy weather, and three divisional commanders took the unusual step of protesting directly to Haig. The operation was called off on 15 April having cost the Allies 150,000 men—a heavier daily loss rate than the *Somme or *Passchendaele—and the Germans some 20,000 fewer. While it succeeded in drawing in their reserves as intended, and demonstrated growing tactical skill especially as far as artillery was concerned, the losses incurred in the later stages were unconscionable.   RH

---

arsenals are places for the manufacturing and stockpiling of arms and ammunition specifically, as opposed to the general stores that all branches of the armed forces require. The need for centralized control over arms saw arsenals concentrated within royal palaces or other places of importance in the ancient world. Excavations at Heraklion in Crete have revealed evidence of rooms containing stocks of arrowheads and swords etc. in large earthenware jars. The locating of such equipment under what appears to be large state rooms is a clear indication of how politically important such control was.

Arsenals were originally designed for the storage of weapons for relatively small armies and were increasingly deployed at strategic locations within a country. Their existence and purpose gradually developed to include manufacture as well as simple stockpiling. Indeed the word arsenal probably derives from the Arabic for workshop, before passing into French and subsequently English.

Although possibly one of the most famous arsenals in the world, the Venice Arsenal was quite distinct from those maintained for land armies. In essence a huge naval dockyard, the Venice Arsenal was begun in 1104 and was used to arm and maintain the large fleet of Venetian war galleys. There is some evidence to suggest that its design was based upon the circular dockyard built by the Phoenicians at Carthage. The arsenal was a huge undertaking, being continually expanded until the later part of the 17th century, and, employing over 4,000 workers, it was probably the largest industrial undertaking in medieval Europe. As an example of Venetian state power important foreign visitors were treated to the spectacle of the arsenal rigging and arming a war galley in less than twenty minutes.

During the early modern period arsenals served as repositories for artillery and engineering equipment but gradually became more varied. By the middle of the 16th century French arsenals and the Ordnance Office in England were responsible for the issuing of cannon and equipment to field armies. The Ordnance Office subsequently developed control over all professional gunners and the artillery pieces located in fixed fortifications and garrisons. With the increasing number of firearms as a proportion of an army, arsenals took charge of infantry weapons as well. The rise in the diversity of types of firearm and calibre had produced a haphazard system of equipping which resulted in some serious operational inefficiencies. The English Ordnance Office attempts at standardization led to the issuing of its first standard patterns in 1631. When the manufacture of *gunpowder became a matter of state concern as well, it too was stored in arsenals.

Most arms during the 16th, 17th, and 18th centuries were of private manufacture so as well as ensuring adequate numbers were stored, arsenals became responsible for their quality. Standard patents and guidelines were issued. In England Henry VIII standardized artillery calibres as did Maximilian I in Germany and Henri II in France. Inspectors checked the quality of the metal used in manufacture in addition to calibres, inflicting penalties for sub-standard pieces. Powder also became part of the inspectors' remit during the 17th century in France, while in England the following century saw the Ordnance Office extend its role as more work was put out to private contract.

The siting of arsenals was also of enormous strategic importance. On continental Europe, arsenals were located in frontier fortresses. Metz and Strasbourg oversaw France's eastern border while arsenals at La Fère and Douai looked to threats from the north and Grenoble in the Alps covered the border with Savoy. Prussia's strategic situation during the 18th century necessitated the siting of arsenals to respond to threats in the east, west, and south. These were supported by a central arsenal located in Berlin. In contrast England located her arsenals at places from which the army could be despatched overseas, Plymouth, Portsmouth, Hull, as well as Woolwich on the Thames. These were augmented by smaller establishments in every county for the use of the *militia. The infant United States chose the site of its first national arsenal at Harper's Ferry, in its Virginia heartland. A 1794 act 'for the erecting and repairing of arsenals and armories' authorized its construction, and work began in 1799. Although, at the confluence of the Potomac and the Shenandoah, close to abundant water supply and well sited from the point of view of national defence,

Harper's Ferry proved vulnerable to civil strife. In 1859 the abolitionist John Brown attacked it in an effort to seize the 100,000 weapons stored there. During the *American Civil War it was often in the front line, changing hands eight times and being almost totally destroyed by the war's end.

The effects of industrialization in England and on the continent witnessed arsenals becoming greater centres of manufacturing as well as storage. The centralization of a state's military activities during this period initially saw a reduction in the amount of contracts to private industry. Locations also moved to take advantage of labour availability and better communications leaving the confines of fortification and moving to towns and cities.

Woolwich Arsenal (the area in south London from which Arsenal football team took its name before moving north of the river) was probably the largest covered factory structure in the world at the time of the industrial revolution. At its peak the largest of its four blast furnaces could process 16 tons of metal at a time for the highest quality castings. Woolwich had begun life as the Royal Laboratory Carriage Department and Powder House of Tudor times, being re-named the Royal Arsenal by George III in 1805.

As centralized arsenals became more concerned with the manufacture of arms and ammunition so the creation of divisional and corps districts exploiting conscription on the continent dispersed stores to regional arsenals. This was mirrored in England by the establishment of regimental depots after the *Cardwell army reforms.

But as the demand for arms and munitions grew, the old arsenal system gave way to an increasing reliance on private arms manufacturers, initially for parts to be assembled in the arsenals, but soon for whole weapons systems. Enormous private industrial concerns were able to 'spin off' their steel-making for commercial use into weapons and, even though in collusion with one another, could beat the state-run enterprises on price not merely for warships but for minor items like buttons. In Britain, the Second *Boer War revealed serious, structural deficiencies in the state-run production of ammunition, and these were to be magnified by the enormous demands of WW I.

The arsenals never recovered their dominant position, even though there were serious problems of quality control when manufacturers with no background in arms production were pressed to enter the field. France lost over 600 field guns in 1915 through premature explosion, and on the Somme in 1916 some 30 per cent of British shells proved to be duds. This was resolved by appointing new co-ordinating ministries or agencies rather than by reviving the arsenals' old monopoly, because only manufacturers who could turn their efforts post-war to civilian applications provided the flexibility to cope with the wildly excessive overcapacity that must afflict any specialist arms manufacturer as soon as peace is declared.   JR-W

Arsuf, battle of (1191). After the capture of Acre in July 1191 the Third *Crusade needed a base at Jaffa for its attack on Jerusalem. *Richard 'the Lionheart' of England had never commanded a great army in battle, but his military reputation ensured that he was the commander when the army left Acre on 22 August. He faced a march down the coast road in the face of a powerful army under *Saladin. This necessitated a fighting march, familiar to the Latins in the Middle East but novel for a western commander. Richard revealed his military genius by marshalling his heterogeneous army very skilfully. The cavalry were in three squadrons, the Templars at the front and the Hospitallers at the rear. Foot and *archers on their left kept the Turkish mounted bowmen out of range of the cavalry and guarded the baggage on the seaward right. The army thus resembled a mobile fortress. Saladin's attacks reached a crescendo on 7 September but Richard kept tight order, hoping to lure the enemy into a position where they could be destroyed by a single cavalry charge. In the end the pressure on his rearguard led to a premature charge which defeated but did not destroy Saladin's army. The victory had inconclusive results: Christian prestige was restored and Jaffa seized but Saladin's army remained in being.   JF2

Hooper, N., and Bennett, M., *Cambridge Illustrated Atlas of Warfare: The Middle Ages 768–1487* (Cambridge, 1996).
Smail, R. C. *Crusading Warfare 1097–1193* (Cambridge, 1956).

art, the military (*see opposite page*)

artillery (*see page 92*)

artillery fire control During the period when smooth-bore artillery ruled the battlefield, fire control was very simple. A commander of all the artillery of the force was appointed. Sometimes he was the commander of one of the units, extracted for the purpose, leaving his second in command in charge of the particular battery, company, or battalion. At *Minden in 1759 Capt Phillips was put in command of the British artillery leaving his 'second captain' in charge of the company. In large armies during the *Napoleonic wars command became more complicated. The French put the artillery commander of the Corps d'Armée in charge, and he had authority to take any divisional artillery under his command whenever necessary. At *Waterloo the British placed Col George Wood in command of all the British and King's German Legion artillery, with subordinate commanders in charge of field artillery and *horse artillery—the latter the mobile reserve. The next level down was the commander of the fire unit—the horse artillery troop or foot artillery company—equivalent to modern batteries. The battery commander, usually commanding six

(*cont. on page 98*)

art, the military

MERELY to use the term 'the military art' is to enter directly into the debate as to whether warfare is indeed an art, thus the province of unquantifiable qualities such as given ability and inspiration (not to mention the luck about which *Napoleon enquired when considering an officer for senior rank), or a science in which every military situation can be reduced to a number of variables which, if the correct formula is identified and applied, must inevitably lead to victory. *Moltke 'the Elder' was in no doubt:

> Strategy is the application of sound human sense to the conduct of war; its teachings go little beyond the first requirement of common sense. Its value lies entirely in concrete application. The main point is correctly to estimate the situation and then to do the simplest and most natural things with firmness and caution. Thus war becomes an art—an art, of course, which is served by many sciences. In war, as in art, we find no universal forms; in neither can a rule take the place of talent.

This is an area where there has been little agreement amongst military thinkers over the centuries. Some, like *Jomini, have tended towards the prescriptive, arguing that war has rules whose application brings success and whose breach courts failure. Others, like *Clausewitz, have been more descriptive, emphasizing that war is the realm of chance and uncertainty, and the pure light of reason glows darkly through its fog. Azar Gat argues that 'New ideas emerge during periods of revolutionary change or at times of crisis', and that these ideas remain dominant until they themselves are rendered inadequate by new paradigmatic changes. Jomini and Clausewitz wrote under the cultural stimulus of the Enlightenment and the Romantic movement. Gat asserts that 'The two fundamental positions which grew out of this intellectual process underlie the modern outlook and still vie for supremacy today in the humanities and social sciences.'

Even the most descriptive have recognized that even if war has no rules, it certainly possesses broad principles, and a proper grasp of its purpose, function, and scale is crucial to understanding it. The former tsarist officer Aleksandr Svechin (1878–1938), subsequently murdered on Stalin's orders, neatly linked the levels of conflict as follows: 'Tactics make the steps from which operational leaps are assembled: strategy points out the path' (*Strategy*, 1926). An understanding of these levels and what is required to be achieved by each lies at the heart of the military art. For example, any successful defensive strategy will need to embrace counter-offensive operations; often an offensive strategy will need to include defensive operations in order to guard flanks, rear areas, and borders with countries not involved in any given conflict. Various fighting techniques, or tactics, are required for each type of operation. Achieving the right balance of effort between offensive and defensive operations; determining where to seek a decision in battle and how much of the force to retain uncommitted in the form of reserves are some of the most important considerations a commander must face in developing his tactical or higher level campaign plan. In answering such questions a commander must rest on his knowledge of the military art tempered by his operational experience and the advice offered by his staff. The capability to make keenly judged and timely decisions, combined with the ability to motivate the troops under his command and the resolution to overcome the frictions and inevitable setbacks of war, constitute that rare and elusive quality of generalship.

Yet the management and conduct of war requires more than the adoption of tactical or operational schemes of manoeuvre in order to meet some strategic design. While the amount of resources allocated to conflict remains critical, much is also determined by the society, culture, and history of the armed groups or states concerned. Further, the structure, arms and equipment, *doctrine, level of training, and not least efficiency and *morale of the forces involved, all contribute to military effectiveness. Non-military influences as well as organizational and technological matters help shape the military art. While an analysis of the practice by an army of the military art will not necessarily reveal its detailed equipment list, it should indicate that force's view of conflict and suggest what military strategies, operational methods and tactics it might employ. The fate of all civilizations has been linked to their military means. The ancient Egyptians, Greeks, Persians, Carthaginians, and Romans developed well-organized standing armies and fleets to wage war against their foes in pursuit of policy ends. The Roman way of war, for example, capitalized on tough, highly disciplined, and well-trained units of manpower that could be committed flexibly over a wide geographical area and for long duration. Few nations could resist Rome's power in the long term as long as she possessed the necessary economic and social means to maintain her military forces and to sustain the will to fight. Yet ultimately, less well organized but more numerous, brutal, and committed peoples overwhelmed the Roman empire. In view of the economic effort (treasure), social commitment (blood), and political stakes (survival) involved, writers began to record the lessons from past conflict and to investigate the enduring dynamics of war. Early military historians such as Herodotus (see GREEK HISTORIANS) and *Xenophon give us detailed insights into how man fought in ancient times, giving us rich descriptions of battles, tactics, and weapons. Thucydides (see GREEK HISTORIANS) not only tells us why Athens and *Sparta waged the *Peloponnesian wars, but also explains why he wrote his famous history: 'My work is not a piece of writing designed to meet that taste of an immediate public, but was done to last for ever.'

Military literature expanded in the Roman period, reflecting a fascination in the art of war and its impact on political and social development. Polybius (see GREEK HISTORIANS) composed his *Histories* in order to inform his Greek compatriots about the way in which Rome had sought and achieved power. In their treatment of the Punic wars, there is little doubt that Polybius wrote as much to explain as to narrate the rise of Rome's military prowess while Livy (see ROMAN MILITARY HISTORIANS) stood to glorify it. *Caesar and Tacitus (see ROMAN MILITARY HISTORIANS give us full, if not entirely accurate, accounts of Roman military endeavours. But of all the Greek or Roman works on war, perhaps *Vegetius' *De Re Militari* (On Military Institutions) was the most influential in the longer term. Although largely neglected at the time of writing—a misfortune of many military philosophers down the ages—Vegetius was well read during the Renaissance. While *Machiavelli in his *Arte della Guerra* (The Art of War) based much of his work on Vegetius, he provided more than a mere historical study. Although based on classical thought, Machiavelli's 'general rules' for commanders were of considerable contemporary significance. Yet well before *Machiavelli had begun to study classical military history, Europe in the 13th century had been surprised by the sudden rise of Asian military might. *Genghis Khan had spread fear and terror through the western world. Pope Gregory IX (1227–41) prayed, 'From the fury of the Tartars, O Lord, deliver us.' *Mongol military power rested on thorough preparation, organization, training, and harsh *discipline. Its advantage in battle largely depended on the shock action delivered by its body of fierce and highly skilled horsemen. More subtle methods were employed in achieving operational and strategic success. Genghis Khan used a combination of surprise, deception, and psychological operations to put his opponents off balance, both mentally and physically. These techniques remain very much relevant today. Above all, the Mongols—a nomadic race of some three to four millions only—developed various methods to convince their enemies that they were more numerous than was the case. Frugal methods of supply (what we might now term 'lean logistics') improved the Mongols' strategic mobility as did their ruthless rape of subjugated peoples and their territory. By the mid-13th century the Mongols had attacked successfully Russia, Poland, and Hungary and dominated most of Asia. Perhaps one of the most formidable armies in history, the Mongols presented a unified force who exploited their opponents' military weaknesses and political differences. The Mongol art of war that successfully synchronized time, space, and forces was essentially one of manoeuvre, and not without lasting influence on imperial Russian and Soviet military thought. The significance of Genghis Khan's achievements was not lost on modern military thinkers. In *Great Captains Unveiled* (1927), *Liddell Hart declared that 'the tank and the airplane were natural heirs and successors to the Mongol horsemen'. Meanwhile, the earliest known treatise on the conduct of war—*The Art of War*, written by *Sun-tzu in 400–320 BC—was not accessible in Europe until a translation into French appeared in the late 18th century. By this time a series of European writers already had begun to codify the nature and *principles of war in an attempt to provide the keys to military success. Among the most prominent military commanders and writers of the period were *Saxe and *Frederick 'the Great'. Other contributors to the military art included the French Duc de Rohan and Marquis de Feuquières and the Welsh officer Henry Lloyd. In about 1644, Henri de Rohan produced a list of seven simple 'Guides for the general who wishes to engage in war' in *Le Parfait Capitaine* (The Perfect Captain), an adaptation of Caesar's account of the *Gallic wars. At the beginning of the 18th century, the Marquis de Feuquières listed maxims or rules that generals need to know in *Mémoires sur la guerre* (Memoirs on War). This work drew heavily on practical lessons he learned on campaign in the service of France. Likewise, the famous Maurice de Saxe whose work *Mes rêveries* (My musings) was published posthumously in 1757, attracted wide interest. Henry Lloyd's contribution was arguably greater and more enduring. In 1766 he wrote, 'This art, like all others, is founded on certain and fixed principles, which are by their nature invariable.' In 1781 he set out 'Rules concerning firepower' and 'Axioms on the Line of Operations' that would provide the stimulus and basis of much of what Baron Antoine Henri Jomini wrote twenty years later.

The birth of the modern military art is usually attributed to the *French Revolutionary and *Napoleonic wars. The period's pre-eminent writers, *Clausewitz and *Jomini, remain the subject of detailed study and scrutiny today. If early 19th-century tactics have become overtaken by modern technology, strategy, logistics, and command remain highly relevant elements of the military art. In this respect the enigmatic Clausewitz has more to tell us of contemporary significance in *Vom Kriege* (On War) (published posthumously in 1832) than the prolific Jomini whose *General Principles* (1816) and *Principal Maxims* (1830) now seem outdated. That said, his influence in Europe and notably in America and Russia was far greater than that of Clausewitz during the 19th century.

The work of Helmuth von Moltke 'the Elder', chief of the Prussian, and later the German, *general staff from 1858 to 1888, adds greatly to our general understanding of the military art. Moltke rejected the study of abstract Jominian principles, preferring the 'practical application' of method on a case by case basis.

If Great Britain produced no great Clausewitz, Jomini, or Helmuth von Moltke, a school of influential military writers emerged in the latter half of the 19th century. Its leading stars were Patrick Leonard MacDougall (*The Theory of War*, 1856), Edward Bruce *Hamley (*Operations of War*, 1866), J. F. Maurice (*Military History of the Campaign of 1882 in Egypt*, 1887), Charles E. *Callwell (*Small Wars*, 1896), and G. F. R. Henderson (*Stonewall Jackson*, 1899). Significantly, all were associated, whether as commandants, staff, or students, with the British army Staff College at Camberley; both J. F. Maurice and Henderson were professors of 'the military art and history'. In the USA, the military art as practised in the civil war was influenced by the works of Jomini and MacDougall, often under the guise of popular summaries. For example, the Confederate Gen *Beauregard published in 1863 a brief guide titled *Principles and Maxims of the Art of War* that borrowed much from Napoleon, Jomini, and MacDougall, including from the latter the statement: 'The whole science of war may be briefly defined as the art of placing in the right position, at the right time, a mass of troops greater than your enemy can there oppose you.' But faith in such simple truisms was not universal; nor could they always be applied readily. There are few short-cuts in the military art as a series of long and bloody conflicts since ancient times indicates. For example, success in the *American civil war had as much to do with the North's superior strategic position with her richer industrial and manpower resources as with any dominant weaponry or battlefield tactics. After the war, studies into the military art in the US Military Academy, *West Point, included military science and history. Instructional notes of the 1870s advised:

> The general principles of war are deduced from the rules and methods used by those generals who are known as great and eminent in the practice of the profession. In the 'art of war', as in all the experimental sciences, observations made upon the actual occurrences precede the theories. It is therefore evident that an intimate connection exists between the history of military operations and the 'art of war', and that a course of military history is indispensable as an introduction to the teaching of the 'science of war'.

The strong connection between the military art and science has not been lost on doctrine writers. Based on the Moltkean tradition, the *Reichswehr operations manual *Truppenführung* began with the succinct statement 'The conduct of war is an art, a free creative activity based on a scientific (disciplined) foundation.' Fuller would have agreed: in his preface to *The Foundation of the Science of War* (1925) he observed: 'I hope that military students will examine [the book], not only for its own worth, but in order to think of war scientifically, for until we do so we shall never become true artists of war.'

Traditionally, Russian and Soviet theorists have taken a broader view of military science and art, and the term 'military doctrine' has a meaning and emphasis unparalleled in the West. While at first sight it might appear to resemble Anglo-American concepts of 'policy' and 'grand strategy', in practice it was far more embracing. For the Soviets, military doctrine represented a politico-military framework and instrument for formulating the state's 'views on war, its preparations, conduct and prevention'. Ideologically influenced military science formed the theoretical basis for military doctrine, which was politically endorsed. In turn, the most important component of military science was the study and practice of the military art which encompassed strategy, operational art, and tactics. All this study was underpinned by research and development into weapons technology and the establishment of mathematical norms for the employment of forces to achieve decisive results. The Soviets were particularly impressed by the results of technology after the 'Great Patriotic War' of 1941–5 and spent much effort investigating the nature of military-technical revolutions.

Meanwhile, while science and technology have continued to drive weaponry and tactics at an accelerating rate, particularly over the last two centuries, the military art has developed on more enduring lines. If tactics belong in drill books or doctrine manuals, strategy better lends itself to study through historical example. In illustration, if descriptions of ancient or medieval weapons are irrelevant in the conduct of war today, the works of Sun-tzu, Clausewitz, and Jomini on strategy are certainly not. Likewise, it is highly likely that 20th-century writings on the military art—whether by Svechin, Fuller, or Liddell Hart—will remain topical for many more decades and the subject of detailed investigation. For example, Liddell Hart's strategy of the 'indirect approach', which defines a particular way of warfare (not solely driven by technology), underwrites the 'manoeuvrist approach' found in contemporary British *manoeuvre warfare.

Success in war demands hard training and continual practice. For centuries commanders have recognized that military proficiency requires prior study and exercise. In *The History of the Decline and Fall of the Roman Empire*, Edward Gibbon remarks:

> In the midst of peace, the Roman troops familiarised themselves with the practice of war; and it is prettily remarked by an ancient historian who had fought against them, that the effusion of blood was the only circumstance which distinguished a field of battle from a field of exercise. It was the policy of the ablest generals, and even of the emperors themselves, to encourage these military studies by their presence and example.

If the art of generalship has developed since Roman times from direct leadership to more indirect methods of command, then the responsibility of those in command to train their subordinates in the military art remains. In sum, while it is relatively easy to gain a superficial picture of the art of war, perhaps through the media of popular fiction and *film, such are the complexities of its dynamics and subtleties of its texture that war demands serious study. Like a language, the military art has its own lexicon, grammar, and syntax. Any picture of war must be viewed in relation to its constituent parts: strategy, operations, tactics, logistics, personnel, and command. As with *religion, the conduct of war requires a doctrine to ensure coherence and consistency of teaching. In most cases training, judgement, confidence, and an element of intuition are fundamental prerequisites of success in the application of force. It requires balancing theory with practice, and a flexibility of mind to learn from past experience. But for those military commanders who ignore war's unforgiving realities and who are overconfident, unwarranted risk-taking may lead to deadly gambles. For, unlike any other human activity, the costs of failure in war can be catastrophic for individuals, teams, tribes, societies, and whole nations alike. Therefore it is often wise to take a wide perspective—and here military history must play its part—in order to learn about war, to view it from a number of angles, and, above all, to stand sufficiently well back in order to place any given conflict or particular operation into proper focus. For the future, a study of the military art may point out the path ahead. If neglected, a strategic overview, a balanced analysis of a plan of campaign together with its likely consequences, may be lost in a mass of tactical and technical detail.   RAMSM

Alger, John I., *The Quest for Victory* (Westport, 1982).

Frank, Willard C., and Gillette, Philip S. (eds.), *Soviet Military Doctrine from Lenin to Gorbachev, 1915–1991* (Westport, 1992).

Gat, Azar, *The Development of Military Thought: The Nineteenth Century* (Oxford, 1992).

Handel, Michael I., *Masters of War: Classical Military Thought* (London, 1996).

Jones, Archer, *The Art of War in the Western World* (New York, 1997).

Keegan, John, *A History of Warfare* (London, 1993).

Liddell Hart, B. H., *Strategy: The Indirect Approach* (London, 1967).

Moltke, Helmuth Graf von, *Moltke on the Art of War: Selected Writings*, ed. Daniel J. Hughes and Harry Bell (Novato, Calif., 1993).

Paret, Peter (ed.), *Makers of Modern Strategy* (London, 1986).

artillery

THE word artillery (probably from Old Fr.: *atillier*, to load or charge) can refer to a type of weapon; to an arm of service, alongside infantry, cavalry and engineers; or to the art and science of utilizing these weapons. The artillery arm has produced many great generals, most notably *Napoleon.

As a weapon, artillery is the most lethal form of land-based armament. It now includes guns, *howitzers, *mortars, and *rockets, primarily designed for *indirect fire, and also anti-aircraft guns, surface-to-air, and surface-to-surface missiles. In the *Napoleonic wars and WW I and II most fatalities—over 60 per cent on the western front in WW I—were caused by artillery. In the desert in WW II, where the hard rocky landscape enhanced the effect of the shells, the percentage rose to 75 per cent. Not for nothing did *Stalin, whose artillery arm had a tradition of excellence, call it 'the God of War' in a 1944 speech. Furthermore, it is not a clean way to die. The injuries and mutilation caused by artillery, its capricious effects, its operators unseen, make it a hated and feared instrument of war. Artillery's effects are impossible to simulate in peacetime *exercises. Troops can manoeuvre and simulate direct fire, but indirect fire, when explosive power descends, unexpected, unseen until the explosions, paralysing, mutilating, and above all deafening, is impossible to mimic. Artillery therefore tends to be underestimated in peacetime. In war the artillery arm is always reinforced. In WW II a quarter of the British army was in the Royal Artillery.

From ancient times until the 14th century, all 'artillery' used mechanical principles: either the spring of a bow, as in the Roman *ballista*—a giant crossbow—or the principle of the counterweight, as in the trebuchet (see SIEGE ENGINES). The first trebuchets appear to have been operated by men pulling on one end of a lever, to propel a rock—or plague-ridden corpse, whether human or animal—in the desired direction, usually at or over a castle or city wall. Later the more familiar counterweight was introduced. By the 14th century counterweighted trebuchets with slings to multiply the force with which the projectile was hurled had reached a high degree of sophistication.

The origins of modern gun artillery are obscure. The Chinese invented *gunpowder as a propellant in about AD 1000 but used it only for pyrotechnics. *Engels thought guns were invented by the Arabs and came to Europe via the Nasrid kingdom of Granada in Spain. There are references to *cannae* (from the Latin *canna*, a hollow reed, the origin of 'cannon') in Florence in 1326. However, the first undeniable evidence of artillery in the modern sense—guns—is a picture, and comes from England. In early 1327 Walter de Milemete compiled his tract *De Regis Misericordia* (*On the Duties of Kings*) for the young King *Edward III of England. The manuscript, now in Christ Church, Oxford, has detailed and expert drawings of *ballistae* and trebuchets. On the last vellum page, however, the greatest military-technical revolution until the present era is recorded. Mechanical energy is suddenly supplemented by the chemical energy of gunpowder. There is a picture of a curvaceous gun, firing, oddly enough, an arrow (see AMMUNITION, ARTILLERY). No recoil control system is shown, suggesting, perhaps, that the artist had heard about guns but had not seen one. It is widely believed the English used some form of guns at *Crécy in 1346, and this may have begun the panic of the Genoese crossbowmen.

The gun in the de Milemete manuscript is being fired at a city or castle gate. For another 300 years, at least, this was artillery's principal function: the attack and defence of fortified positions. In common with many new technologies—such as *nuclear weapons—artillery was initially deployed as a strategic weapon—against, or in defence of, centres of power and population. It was too clumsy and immobile for anything else. Torsion and counterpoise engines of war—*ballistae* and trebuchets—could be made *in situ* with local materials—timber and fibre. Guns, made of rare and expensive metal, required the concentration of resources. The technology was closely linked to the casting of church bells. They were probably beyond the resources of local warlords. Therefore, artillery had a significant impact on centralization and the growth in the power of the nation state. It was very much the weapon of the settled community, and unsuited to the ways of war of the great nomadic Asiatic conquerors like *Timur.

In the 15th century artillery emerged as a strategic weapons system. The fall of *Constantinople in 1453 and Charles VIII of France's rapid *demolition of north Italian fortresses in 1494 showed that artillery was the preserve of—and the decisive advantage enjoyed by—well-organized, powerful national rulers with well-organized military systems. Writing at the beginning of the 16th century, *Machiavelli correctly surmised that the introduction of gunpowder was probably the greatest military revolution since the Romans. However, artillery was still relatively ineffective in the field. Had Machiavelli been able to wait a few more years, he might have thought differently. In 1537 the Italian mathematician Nicolo Tartaglia set out the ratio of calibre to the mass of shot in his *La Nova Scientia*, beginning a process of standardization of calibres which enhanced the efficiency and availability of artillery.

The *Hussites used light artillery in concert with crossbows in their *wagenburg mobile forts. In the 15th century many guns were breech-loaders, the charge being packed in a chamber which was then slotted into the breech of the gun and held in place with wooden wedges. It was impossible at this time to make a tight seal and by the late 16th century muzzle-loaders were preferred, and they dominated battlefields for another 300 years. The introduction of trunnions, the pivots in the middle of the barrel permitting it to move independently of the carriage, was a simple but important development.

In the early 16th century, the first professional bodies of artillerymen appeared across Europe: the Honourable Artillery Company (HAC), founded in 1537, in London and the Russian *pushkary*, at the about the same time. The word 'artillery' at this time still referred to any mechanical contrivances and members of the HAC were primarily *archers at first. Artillery was seen as a 'black art'. It made a horrible noise, covered its operators with black residue—probably the reason why gunners adopted a very dark blue or black uniform—and sometimes blew up.

The use of artillery as a mobile weapon in the field began in the *Thirty Years War. *Gustavus Adolphus of Sweden equipped his armies with 6- and 12-pounder guns, grouped in batteries of ten. However, he also developed a light gun—the 4-pounder 'leather gun', two of which were assigned to each infantry battalion. These were feeble little weapons, but marked the first permanent allotment of artillery to infantry units. Artillery could still not be considered a battle-winning arm, and still appears to have been used for psychological preparation rather than military effect. However, by the beginning of the 18th century light artillery was being used in concert with infantry movements. At *Blenheim, *Marlborough ordered Col Blood, his light artillery commander, to bring a battery forward to support his final move to break into the French centre. At *Malplaquet about a third of Marlborough's artillery was detailed for close support from the start, and several times it was used to provide flanking fire in support of infantry attacks.

The appearance of modern artillery regiments, organized on the same lines as the rest of the army, mirrored its integration into the general scheme of battle. The formation of the Royal Artillery, in 1716, coincides pretty well with artillery's tardy appearance as an essential part of the combined arms team on the battlefield. *Frederick 'the Great' departed from the tradition of using all the heavy artillery for a preliminary bombardment. He kept it concentrated and moved into action in support of his plan to blast an opening at the point chosen for the decisive attack. The creation of *horse artillery, to provide a mobile reserve, assisted this process. Only now, in the *Seven Years War, did artillery begin to come of age.

Technical developments in the late 18th century, led by the French designer *Gribeauval, made artillery more mobile and enabled it to become the decisive weapon of the Napoleonic wars. A round shot, *ricocheting in successive bounces, would slice through any man or horse in its path. Against densely packed formations, round shot was devastating. Closer in, guns fired grapeshot—bunches of shot about the size of snooker balls—and then case-shot—a tin container filled with musket balls. A 12-pounder case shot contained 63–170 balls, so an artillery battery could fire far more than an infantry battalion, and at much greater range. In a twenty-minute engagement, with each gun firing 20 to 30 rounds, a battery of ten guns might discharge 40,000 balls.

Napoleon knew that 'artillery, like the other arms, must be collected in mass if one wishes to achieve the decisive result'. He also placed great reliance on converging fire. During the Napoleonic wars there were increasing attempts to form huge batteries of 100 guns and more, but these were difficult to control. Individual guns and gunners, shrouded in their own *smoke, became isolated. Because most artillery fire was direct, the guns had to be placed amongst or in front of the infantry. When the latter formed squares—if attacked by cavalry, for example—the gunners would leave their guns and retire to the protection of the square.

The 19th-century industrial revolution produced bigger guns, for use in sieges, but initially no advance in their employment in the field. The numbers used in the *Crimean war, and especially at the siege of *Sevastopol where 800 Allied guns fired one-and-a-quarter million rounds, marked a revolution in scale, if not in quality or concept. The general introduction of the rifle and the cylindro-conical *bullet gave every infantryman a weapon, which could, initially, strike at the same range as artillery. Because of its greater technological complexity and problems of scale, it took longer for the advantages of rifling, then *breech-loading, and then rapid firing to be applied to artillery. Even when they were, artillery's ability to use its long range was hampered by the folds of the ground. The more numerous and less conspicuous infantry could often pick off the gunners, as happened in the *American civil and *Franco-Prussian wars. American civil war artillery was handled much as it had been in the Napoleonic wars. After the Franco-Prussian war of 1870–1 the Prussians began to explore the possibilities of using indirect fire, fire at targets invisible from the guns themselves, which revolutionized warfare and enabled targets to be engaged by all guns within range. Artillery was hardly used in the 1877–8 Russo-Turkish war and the lethal effect of artillery relative to other arms reached its nadir: 2.5 per cent, as against 94.5 per cent from *small arms. In the *Russo-Japanese war, where indirect fire was widely used, artillery's share of the carnage increased to 22.9 per cent in sieges and 13.7 in the open field. In WW I the British suffered 58.5 per cent of battlefield *casualties from hostile artillery.

The 19th century also saw developments in rocketry. The Briton Sir Samuel Congreve introduced successful rockets in the early 19th century, and the Russians became particularly interested in them during their fighting in the Caucasus because they could be carried over terrain unsuitable for guns. The Russian Konstantin Konstantinov (1817–71) realized that the problem of 'throwing a very large projectile with a very high velocity' would be solved using rockets, not guns. However, it would be another century before his prophecy was fulfilled.

In the Crimean war French and British rifled muzzle-loaders showed clear advantages over the Russian smooth-bores, and European powers began their general adoption in the 1850s. The American civil war was fought with a mixture of smooth-bores and rifled muzzle-loaders. Rifled Parrot guns were used in the defences of Washington, and by 1863 about half the Union's artillery was rifled,

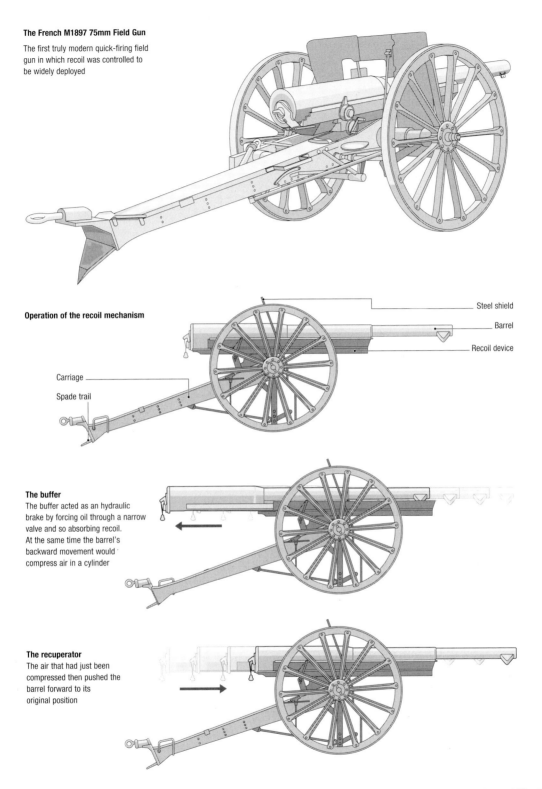

The French M1897 75mm Field Gun

The first truly modern quick-firing field gun in which recoil was controlled to be widely deployed

Operation of the recoil mechanism

Steel shield

Barrel

Recoil device

Carriage

Spade trail

The buffer

The buffer acted as an hydraulic brake by forcing oil through a narrow valve and so absorbing recoil. At the same time the barrel's backward movement would compress air in a cylinder

The recuperator

The air that had just been compressed then pushed the barrel forward to its original position

The French 'Seventy-Five' was the first widely produced gun offering the combination of 'fixed' ammunition, permitting rapid loading, and a recoil mechanism permitting the gun carriage to remain in the same place while firing. When these developments were combined with indirect fire, improved communications and survey methods, a revolution in warfare took place and artillery returned to dominate the battlefield.

but the mainstay of the Confederate artillery remained the smooth-bored 'Napoleon'. However, scarcely had rifled muzzle-loaders become commonplace than a new generation of guns appeared. The second component of this revolution was the reintroduction of breech-loading, made possible by improved technology and especially obturation—the sealing of the breech. Rifled guns loaded from the breech were brought in by the British in 1859 (although unhappy experiences caused them to return briefly to muzzle-loaders), Prussia in 1861, Russia in 1867, and the USA in 1870.

Another disadvantage of smooth-bore artillery had been that the entire gun and carriage recoiled, about 13 feet (4 metres). The piece therefore had to be re-aimed after each shot. Recoil systems, which enabled the barrel, sliding in a trough, to recoil independently of the carriage and then return to its original position using springs or hydraulics, were the next component of the artillery revolution. Between 1872 and 1875 the Russian inventor Vladimir Baranovskiy (1846–79) designed a remarkable 2.5 inch calibre gun incorporating all the features of a modern quick-firing field gun, which the Russians accepted in 1877. In 1879, Baranovskiy was killed while experimenting with ammunition designs.

Even these changes might not have brought artillery back as the greatest battlefield killer if it had only been able to fire solid shot. Explosive shells had been around for centuries, but from the mid-19th century scientifically designed explosive shells multiplied artillery's effect. In a fast-moving battle, shrapnel shells, which carried a case-shot effect right to the enemy, were ideal. However, as all the combatants discovered in the Great War, shrapnel was little use against trenches and high-explosive shell was required to dig enemy troops out of them.

The last component of the artillery revolution was the metal cartridge case and 'fixed ammunition'. Instead of loading the shell (projectile) and charge separately, quick-firing guns sometimes had the two together. However, even a relatively small calibre gun like the British 25-pounder requires the shell to be loaded first and rammed home, so that the copper 'driving band' engages with the rifling, and the brass shell-case, which can be filled with varying charges, is inserted afterwards. Larger guns still used 'bag charges'.

The first widely used field gun to incorporate all these features was the superb French 75 mm M-1897, which was still regarded as the best field gun in the world twenty years later. The Germans had 77 mm, the Russians the excellent 76.2 mm (3 inch—the origin of what may appear to be slightly odd Russian calibres), and the British the 18-pounder. However, the onset of *trench warfare altered the balance of artillery. By the end of the war the proportion of howitzers—firing their shells at up to a 70 degree angle—had increased to 40 or 50 per cent. At the beginning of the war the principal European combatants had 26,000 pieces of artillery: by the end (not counting Austria) 62,800. The total British artillery strength had increased from 1,352 to 11,000 guns, although only 6,000 were on the western front; the German from 9,400 to 19,800; and the French from 4,300 to 11,600. Artillery was a major reason for the development of *air forces (see SURVEILLANCE AND TARGET ACQUISITION).

WW I was an 'artillery war' par excellence, witnessing the dramatic development of indirect fire and *artillery fire control. It also saw the first 'super-guns,' particularly the 210 mm Pariskanone, which, in a return to artillery's original role, began a strategic bombardment of Paris on 23 March 1918 at a range of 79 miles (128 km). Known as 'Long Max', because of its 130 foot (40 metre) barrel, supported by a suspension cable to stop it bending, it fired 203 shells in all. It killed 256 people and injured 620, but did not disrupt Parisian life seriously. WW I also saw the appearance of anti-aircraft artillery (AAA or 'triple-A') and by its end 4,200 pieces were in use, often field guns remounted on special carriages.

During the inter-war period specially designed anti-aircraft guns were built and 'artillery' expanded to include *anti-armour guns. Initially, anti-armour guns were of small calibre—typically 37 or 45 mm, often the same designs as those mounted in tanks. However, the experience of the

*Spanish civil war was an object lesson in flexibility. The German 88 mm FLAK (anti-aircraft) gun proved ideal for destroying tanks, and was later modified with a carriage for the latter role, and field guns, as the future Red Army chief of artillery, Nikolai Voronov (1899–1968) realized, could kill tanks just as effectively, if more messily, than specialized anti-armour guns. Modern *mortars, relatively light and easy to move and quite different from the massive, plant-pot-like devices of the Crimean and American civil wars, had been introduced for high-angle fire from the trenches in WW I and now assumed their modern role as the infantry's own artillery. However, in the USSR, heavy mortars of 120 mm calibre and above were regarded as artillery weapons.

Artillery was an important part of the 'deep battle' thinking of the 1920s and 1930s but its role was perhaps underrated, especially by the Germans who parcelled it out in penny packets rather than retaining a structure for centralized control. The Soviets did so, and their use of artillery on the *eastern front in WW II is the principal repository of knowledge for the operational deployment of artillery. In addition to guns, howitzers, and mortars, all sides, most notably the Soviets, introduced multiple rocket launchers—the German Nebelwerfer, the Soviet 132 mm BM-13 or Katyusha, the latter known as 'guards mortars'. The need to provide fire support for tanks also meant guns that could keep up with them. There were two broad philosophies. The Germans and Soviets tended to go for *assault guns or 'tank destroyers', which were direct fire weapons but had bigger guns than the tanks. The British and Americans preferred *self-propelled (SP) guns: indirect-fire artillery pieces but mounted on tracked chassis so they could keep up with the tanks. By 1943–5 the density of artillery concentrated on 0.62 mile (1 km) of front had reached 200–300 pieces, and in the assault on Berlin the Red Army used 45,000 guns, mortars, and multiple rocket launchers.

After WW II gun artillery experienced a relative decline, as ever-scarcer resources were concentrated on aircraft and missiles. The first surface-to-surface missiles were operated by the artillery, in all countries, and when the USSR created its new Strategic Missile Forces (RVSN) in 1959, those with a range below an arbitrary 621 miles (1,000 km) were left under control of the army's artillery. Anti-armour and anti-aircraft missiles may still be operated by the artillery, as well as by other arms and services.

The most revolutionary improvements in artillery fire control since the introduction of indirect fire have been the result of Global Positioning Systems and laser rangefinders which help a good observer put the first round on the target. The Multiple Launch Rocket System now used by US and British armies proved highly successful in the *Gulf war, eliminating entire Iraqi units at a range of 25 miles (40 km). The Iraqi 'supergun'—a giant gun designed by the Canadian Gerald Bull, probably to put satellites in orbit—also indicates that the long struggle between the rocket and the gun is not yet over. In the recent past, liquid propellants have modified the use of chemical energy which was first shown in de Milemete's manuscript 670 years ago. Electromagnetic (EM) guns, which use an electrical pulse to fire the projectile faster than is possible with a chemical propellant, may create the greatest revolution in artillery technology since then. But there are problems finding a suitably compact source of energy supply. By a strange irony, the plates of a suitably powerful battery would need to be as close together as the molecules in a conventional explosive.   CDB

Hughes, B. P., *Open Fire: Artillery Tactics in the Era from Marlborough to Wellington* (Chichester, 1983).

Terraine, John, *White Heat* (London, 1982).

guns or *howitzers, led them at all times, and, since virtually all fire was direct, was with them in action. Below him came the 'number one'—the commander of the individual gun. He personally 'layed'—aimed—the gun.

The advent of *indirect fire, with guns engaging a target invisible from the gun-line, exploded this beautifully simple system. Adjusting the fire of a group of guns requires training and experience. In some armies the battery commander, as the most experienced officer, acted as the observer; in others, he was with the supported-arm commander to provide advice and co-ordinate fire support. The former system continued in use in *Warsaw Pact and successor armies until the present. The gun position itself is commanded by the 'battery senior officer' (in the Warsaw Pact tradition) or 'gun position officer'—either the second in command or, in the British army, a very senior subaltern.

The indirect-fire techniques evolved before WW I and used during it enabled an enormous amount of fire to be concentrated on a single target or group of targets by a senior artillery commander. The fire of individual fire units—batteries—was controlled by command posts which calculated the range and bearing to the target and gave the necessary orders to the guns. But only a senior officer, in command of all the artillery, could concentrate its fire and the development of specialist artillery staffs to plan and control the *barrages which became such a marked feature of WW I was crucial to the effective use of artillery.

During WW I there were enormous advances in firing techniques. Counter-battery fire—hitting the enemy's artillery—which had never been seen as a very profitable operation in the era of direct fire—became artillery's main job. Since the enemy's guns were usually invisible from the front line, as well as from the gun positions, techniques of flash-spotting, sound-ranging, and air photography were rapidly developed. In 1916 came the first use of the registration point. Adjusting fire onto a target by corrections sent by the observer until the target was hit and the command 'fire for effect' given often gave away surprise. The guns would instead adjust onto a point whose position relative to the target was known precisely. When everything was perfect, fire was suddenly switched to the real target. This meant tight control over all the firing units, giving all the necessary data but with the holding command 'fire by order' now replaced by 'at my command'.

Between 1929 and 1941 a most important development took place in the USA. The US field Artillery School at Fort Sill developed a means of concentrating any amount of artillery available on a target of opportunity. This centred on the exploitation of the new, more reliable *radios instead of field *telephones. More importantly, procedures were developed enabling adjustments to be recorded as if seen from the observer's position, instead of the battery position. Graphical firing tables in a fire direction centre (FDC) compensated for the different locations of firing units, and a common reference point was established for all artillery

in a divisional area. This also meant that supported-arm officers—infantry and armour—who might have no idea where the artillery was—could call for fire and give corrections. As a result, the fire of an entire battalion or multiple battalions could be brought down on the direction of a single forward observer, whoever he or she was.

The French retained the pre-planned bombardments of WW I, much to their disadvantage. In 1936 it took French artillery half an hour to engage a target whose range, bearing, and altitude still had to be assessed. This was not good enough in an era where targets might be armoured and highly mobile, and could move a long way in that time.

The Red Army retained the system where a senior artillery officer personally directed the fire of all his guns throughout the war on the *eastern front, but infantry units, down to regiment, had their own artillery also. In essence, the Soviets had two artillery forces: first, 76 mm field and *anti-armour guns, 122 mm howitzers, and 122 mm *mortars with the advancing infantry for close support and direct fire, and secondly, army and corps artillery with heavier guns and howitzers and multiple rocket launchers—the latter at army level—which fired the big, pre-planned bombardments.

The next revolution was the fire control computer. By the 1970s the US and British armies were using computers—the latter the Field Artillery Computer Equipment (FACE)—to do the sums, although Graphical Control Instruments (GCIs) were retained as back up. More recently, new generations of computers, for example the British Battlefield Artillery Target Engagement System (BATES), have arrived. These computerized systems are now linked to create *surveillance and target acquisition systems, such as the US Stand-Off Target Acquisition System (SOTAS) or what the Soviets call 'reconnaissance fire and strike complexes' (ROK, RUK). In combination with the Global Positioning System, which means the observer knows exactly where he or she is, and laser rangefinders, which give the exact range from observer to the target, it is now expected that indirect fire artillery will hit the target with its first round.   CDB

Bellamy, Christopher, *Red God of War* (London, 1986).
Bragg, Sir Lawrence, Dowson, A. H., & Hemming, H. H., *Artillery Survey in World War I* (Field Survey Association, London, 1971).
Hughes, B. P., *Open Fire* (Chichester, 1983).

artillery fortification See FORTIFICATION AND SIEGECRAFT.

artists, military Artists have depicted soldiers and military encounters for centuries. They have employed a huge variety of styles and talents in illustrating warfare across the ages, and carved relief depictions of military scenes can be found in many of the ancient civilizations, including the

Egyptian, the Hittite, and the Assyrian. These works, some as early as *c.*1300 BC, show static figures in profile. The Maya of Central America were still carving stylized warriors in relief in AD 500. More sophisticated are the sculptures of classical Greece, which include, besides the mythological battle of Lapiths and Centaurs by Phidias on the Parthenon, depictions of heroes fighting as *hoplites. Such scenes, common also on vases of the 6th century BC, appear on a frieze of *c.*525 BC in the Siphnian treasury at Delphi. The 4th century BC produced the 'Alexander sarcophagus' in Sidon, showing Greek soldiers fighting Asiatics, but the most famous military scene of the classical period is of *Alexander the Great putting Darius to flight at the battle of *Issus, a Roman mosaic copy of an original painting of *c.*330 BC. Trajan's (post *c.* AD 106) and Marcus Aurelius' (AD 180–96) columns in Rome also bear depictions in relief of their Dacian and Danubian campaigns respectively. The tradition of memorial art continues to this day.

The Chinese in the 3rd century BC buried an army of life-size, incredibly detailed terracotta soldiers near their first Emperor Shihuangdi to protect him in the afterlife. The Bayeux Tapestry (*c.* 1082–92) following the Norman conquest of England shows for the first time the victims and savagery of war. Mongol illustrations on paper of the period AD 1167–1370 colourfully evoke their expertise at *horse warfare. Some near-contemporary European illuminated manuscripts capture something of the mayhem the Mongols unleashed, an English manuscript of *c.*1400 showing the fight to the death between armies of the Christian Wang Khan and *Genghis Khan.

In the 15th century, Paolo Uccello was to depict contemporary military scenes in his *Battle of San Romano* (*c.*1455), and by the beginning of the 16th century both *Leonardo da Vinci and Michelangelo executed battle scenes. The latter's *Battle of Cascina* cartoon (1504–6)—at least the part he executed—was more an excuse to depict the human body nude in various poses than a battle scene, as the soldiers emerge from bathing in order to get dressed for action. But Leonardo's *Battle of Anghiari* fresco (1503–6) was altogether more heroic in action terms. Both works (now destroyed) were hugely influential and far superior to the cluttered, undynamic, and badly proportioned battle scenes by Giorgio Vasari (1511–74) and others, which replaced them in the Sala del Cinquento in Florence.

In the north, Albrecht Altdorfer's (*c.*1480–1538) *Battle of Alexander* (1529) was part of a series of famous battle scenes from antiquity. Commissioned by Duke William IV of Bavaria, it depicts Alexander the Great's defeat of Darius at the battle of Issus, and is rendered with a miniature-like deftness, despite its size and complexity. It was the most detailed and panoramic battle picture of its day.

The Swiss etcher Urs Graf (*c.*1485–1527/8) had been a *mercenary in Italy and, being more interested in the humbler warriors, drew portraits of swaggering soldiers. Introducing a degree of brutal realism, Frenchman Jacques Callot

(1592/3–1635) did a series of etchings called *Grandes Misères de la Guerre*, based on *Richelieu's invasion of Lorraine in 1633. These show the horrible effects of war, and were not only influential on the Italian Stefano della Bella (1610–64), who engraved battle scenes, but also on Goya, who was to go to further extremes in the depiction of brutality.

The money, nonetheless, lay in exalting war and in hagiographic propaganda. During the 17th century epic and truly realistic battle scenes became more common, notable artists being the Neapolitan Aniello Falcone (1607–56) and his even more talented pupil Salvator Rosa (1615–73). In Spain Velasquez (1599–1660) painted *The Surrender at Breda* (1634–5) which, along with eleven canvases by other court artists, celebrated the military victories of Philip IV who seldom went anywhere near a battlefield. Velasquez places the scene of the surrender in the foreground, while the landscape background contains the fire and smoke of the recent battle. Depicting the battle taking place was, above all, the speciality of Jacques Courtois ('Il Borgognone') (1621–76), an artist from Burgundy who painted canvases similar to those of Salvator Rosa, but with more colour, and who worked in Rome for most of his career, sometimes in collaboration with his younger brother Guillaume (1628–79). This style of battle piece was continued into the next century by Francesco Simonini (1686–1753), the Frenchman Charles Parrocel (1688–1752) (who had a remarkable knowledge of horses and military accessories), and Franco Giuseppe Casanova (1727–1802).

In Holland Philips Wouwermans (1619–68) painted cavalry skirmishes and military halts with a consummate skill, accuracy, and panache, but worked on a less epic scale than his Italian contemporaries. In France, Adam Frans van der Meulen (1632–90), a Flemish court painter to *Louis XIV, accompanied the king on campaigns and executed paintings and tapestry designs of the battles which he witnessed. While obviously propaganda, they are perhaps the first time an eyewitness observer gave a version of events we know he saw. Both the elder and the younger Willem van de Velde (1611–93 and 1633–1707) were perhaps the marine equivalent, and worked both in Holland and in England, the latter initiating the tradition of English marine painting. The Dutch can also claim Rembrandt's famous *Night Watch* (1642), depicting a militia company, as a work of military art.

In the 17th century van Dyck painted Charles I and the Duke of Monmouth was painted by Jan van Wyck (1640–1702) set against a battle scene in the background (*c.*1673). Peter Lely (1618–80) liked portraits in armour without horses, but Godfrey Kneller (1646–1723) depicted the Duke of Marlborough in armour on horseback in an allegorical military setting (*c.*1706). De Hondt designed the magnificent tapestries at Blenheim palace depicting the duke's campaigns. The trend begun by van Dyck to display beautiful clothes and uniforms rather than military action continued through the 18th century, Joshua Reynolds's

(1723–92) dashing portrait of *Banastre Tarleton* of 1782 being an excellent example. Another fine artist in this genre was Thomas Lawrence (1769–1830), and Orest Kiprensky (1782–1836) was the Russian equivalent, working as he did in a romantic, heroic style: his *Yevgraf Davydov* (1809) is perhaps the greatest Russian military portrait.

Sir William Beechey (1753–1839) produced a handsome setting for his sitter in *George III at a Review* (c.1798), but the most interesting military scenes of the period are *The Death of Wolfe* (1770) by Benjamin West (1738–1820), and John Singleton Copley's (1738–1815) *The Death of Major Peirson* (1783), both of which have structural similarities with earlier paintings of the agony of Christ. West's painting was also the first to depict a historical event in contemporary clothes. Sir David Wilkie (1785–1841) gave an even more heroic and romantic expression of history in paintings such as the *Defence of Saragossa* (1828), which shows Spanish opposition to the French. Wilkie's vision takes military art far beyond the decorative history painting of Louis Laguerre (1663–1721) or the vast panoramas of John Wootton (c.1682–1764) and Philip James de Loutherbourg (1740–1812).

In the 19th century, France produced one of the finest military artists in Horace Vernet (1789–1863), who painted enormous canvases of Napoleonic battles: we are not spared the bloodshed and adversity which the emperor's army suffered, but equally the paintings glorify a certain ideal, seen from the hindsight of the 1820s when the artist was working for the Duc d'Orléans, later King Louis-Philippe (Vernet's father, Carle, had painted battle scenes for Napoleon himself). Jacques-Louis David (a Deputy and effectively dictator of the arts after the Revolution) became an ardent Bonapartist, and his *Napoleon Crossing the Alps* and *The Emperor Distributing the Eagles* are panoramas on a grand scale. The less glorious side of French military activity was depicted by an artist rebelling against idealization, Francisco de Goya (1746–1828), who etched *Los Desastres de la Guerra* between 1810 and 1814, 65 gruesome prints provoked by the atrocities committed on both sides when the French invaded Spain during the *Napoleonic wars. In 1814 he painted two large canvases of the uprising of the people of Madrid against the French, *The Second of May, 1808* and *The Third of May, 1808*, mainly as a sign of loyalty to Ferdinand VII, newly restored to the Spanish throne.

In 1824 Eugène Delacroix (1798–1863) painted *The Massacre of Chios*, a work imbued with romantic overtones and dramatic postures, although it treats a real incident in the *Greek independence war and is sympathetic to the victims. Delacroix's work is more subjective than the stern realism of turn-of-the-century artists like Antoine-Jean Gros (1771–1835), who painted *Napoleon Bonaparte on the Battlefield of Eylau* (1808). The 19th century saw the proliferation of realistic but romantic pictures of military life. Ernest Meissonier (1815–91), for example, was noted for his extremely detailed and lively scenes of Napoleonic campaigns. His pupil was Jean-Baptiste-Édouard Detaille (1848–

1912), and their works were often disseminated via contemporary prints, including Detaille's famous *Le Rêve* (1888), a fanciful painting, but with realistic details explained by the artist's own participation in the *Franco-Prussian war. Georges Clairin (1843–1919), like Horace Vernet before him, painted apparently realistic and stirring scenes of French colonial warfare in North Africa. Pictures of contemporary or recent military endeavour, especially prints showing Napoleonic soldiers (all with uniforms accurately reproduced), satisfied the strong market for military nostalgia at a time when France had lost its martial supremacy abroad.

In Great Britain such military subjects were equally popular, firstly because of interest in the latest British campaigns, but particularly because of victory in the Napoleonic wars. J. M. W. Turner's (1775–1851) *The Battle of Trafalgar* (1823) is a huge and splendid rendering of the famous naval victory. Though this picture is technically inaccurate, contemporary military artists generally took great pains to research their subjects, as, for example, the Swiss David Morier (1705–70) and the Frenchman Alexandre-Jean Dubois Drahonet (1791–1834) did in their series of pictures of uniforms and arms drill.

However, much of the work of 19th-century military artists—many of them *camp followers—represents the kind of propaganda which was to become so familiar in the 20th century, showing handsome soldiers striving against a bestial enemy. Actions were conflated by the artist, soldiers asked to re-enact scenes, and glory given precedence over suffering. Such works were not always done as regimental commissions, but also for private sale, so great was the public demand. Prints of these pictures were widely disseminated, as indeed prints of regimental uniform patterns continued to be into the 20th century with the work of R. Simkin (active 1900–15).

Although Germany produced artists such as Christian Sell (1831–83), who painted rather insipid cavalry advances, Britain and France remained pre-eminent in the field. The best British exponents were Elizabeth Thompson, Lady Butler (1846–1933), Richard Caton Woodville (1856–1927), and William Barnes Wollen (1857–1936), artists who conveyed a sense of empire, duty, and glory, but also—to a smaller degree—the physical suffering and endurance of the individual soldier. Their narrative was essentially heroic, cinematic, and artificial, as they sought to make military action look balletic and courageous. Even death, pain, and exhaustion are made glamorous or glorious.

War diagrams and encyclopedic illustrations of all facets of warfare accompanied illustrations of derring-do by British and allied forces in magazines such as the *Illustrated London News*, which covered both world wars. As with the work of many military artists, these pictures did not challenge artistic trends, or stress the suffering and hardship of war above the excitement. The genre continued in WW II in the work of Terrence Cuneo (1907–96) and Frank Wootton (1914–98). But this is to venture into the specific province of *war art dealt with elsewhere. Following WW I, furthermore, the glory of war had lost its allure for many independent artists.

This is merely a summary review of some of the artists who have attempted military subjects. Although the majority were acting on the wishes of patrons desirous to enshrine a particular event or themselves in a favourable light for their contemporaries and posterity, certain artists of genius reveal a natural and powerful patriotism, such as Turner, a deep horror of war, for example Picasso in *Guernica* (1937), or a personal involvement exacerbated by physical discomfort, notably Goya. Of course there is a huge gulf between those who depicted battles or uniforms on a regular basis for an eager but undiscriminating general public, and those who occasionally undertook a military subject because it was an important commission or because the subject evoked strong feelings in them. In short, military art encompasses works of individual genius, as well as just propaganda.   RW

Lloyd, Christopher, 'The Sword and the Sceptre', in *The Royal Collection* (London, 1992).

Ashanti war (1873–4). By the start of the 19th century the powerful Ashanti (Asante) kingdom, with its capital at Kumasi about 109 miles (176 km) into the interior, dominated the coastal tribes of the Gold Coast (modern Ghana). Slavery was a significant part of the Ashanti economy, trading slaves with European fortified posts along the coast; they also practised ritual human *sacrifice, and had some wealth in gold. Ashanti power over the coastal tribes waned as the British, who abolished their slave trade in 1807, gradually replaced other European powers (chiefly the Danes and the Dutch) in control of the coastal forts, establishing an informal protectorate over particularly the coastal Elima and Fanti tribes.

The occasion of the war was the attempt by the new Ashanti king (Assantehene) Kofi Karikari, who came to power in 1867, to re-establish control over these disputed coastal provinces. The Ashanti mounted two military expeditions against the Elmina in 1868 and 1872, both repulsed with British help, while negotiating with the British for return of the provinces. The Ashanti were aware of British strength, but believed that the British could not penetrate deeply into the disease-ridden African bush, and that at the short ranges of bush fighting their muskets and spears could match British breech-loading rifles and cannon. A further Ashanti attack in June 1873, in which hostages were taken including European missionaries, convinced the British (who had already made earlier plans) to mount an expedition against the Ashanti.

Command was given in August to Maj Gen Sir Garnet *Wolseley, the rising star of British army reformers. Wolseley selected for the campaign 27 officers who became famous as 'the Ashanti Ring' or 'the Wolseley Ring', dominating British campaigns for the next quarter-century. Nine 'Ring' members later reached general rank or higher, including Redvers *Buller, Evelyn Wood, Frederick Maurice, and George Colley. Arriving in October, Wolseley began to raise and train local forces, and made a small but successful attack on the Ashanti encampments at Essaman. The Ashanti managed to withdraw, fighting a series of rearguard actions that lasted until November.

The poor response to his attempts to recruit local forces convinced Wolseley that only British troops could beat the Ashanti in battle, and three battalions were sent from Britain, together with further troops from the West Indian Regiment. While waiting for these to arrive and acclimatize, Wolseley's staff tackled the transport and supply problems of sustaining such a force deep into the bush, using about 6,000 local people as porters and labourers to cut muddy roads almost like tunnels through the vegetation. By December a forward base was established at Prasu, on the river Prah (Pra) about halfway to Kumasi. With the realization that the British might well reach Kumasi, Kofi's authority started to break down. By 19 January 1874 Wolseley had established at Prasu a force of 4,000, including two British battalions, a West Indian battalion, some British sailors, and some locally raised troops, with 7-pounder guns and rocket-projectors. A further British battalion and a West Indian battalion were used as reserves and replacements, and to garrison the staging post established on 24 January at Formena, halfway from Prasu to Kumasi. Wolseley's plan was for his main advance on Kumasi to be supported by three other columns of local warriors under British officers, converging on the Ashanti capital from different directions. Of 30,000 expected, only one of the flanking columns, 750 Hausa under Capt Glover of the Royal Navy, reached Kumasi. By this time Wolseley's main column, reduced by disease and skirmishing to 2,217 (including 1,509 British troops), had fought and defeated the Ashanti at the battle of Amoafu on 31 January. Wolseley's force entered Kumasi on 3 February, and finding it unoccupied burnt it to the ground and withdrew three days later. On 13 February King Kofi's representatives agreed peace at Fomena: the chief terms were that the Ashanti would pay an indemnity in gold, renounce their claims on disputed provinces, and abjure human sacrifice. Kofi, his power broken, was deposed in 1874, and the Ashanti kingdom broke up into warring tribes and factions. In 1901, after two further British expeditions, the Ashanti kingdom was absorbed into the Gold Coast protectorate.   SDB

Callwell, C. E., *Small Wars* (London 1906, 1990).

Keegan, John, 'The Ashanti Campaign 1873–1874', in Brian Bond (ed.), *Victorian Military Campaigns* (London 1967, 1994).

Lehmann, Joseph, *All Sir Garnett* (London, 1964).

Ashingdon, battle of (1016). From 1003, the Danish King Sweyn Forkbeard began a conquest of England at the expense of the English King Æðelred II Unræd (Ethelred 'the Unready'). Sweyn's son, Knut (or Canute), continued his father's conquest, while Æðelred's son, Edmund Ironside, took over the English army on the death of his father in 1014. Edmund won a series of battles over Knut, and drove him from a siege of London in 1016, forcing the Danes into Essex. On 18 October 1016, the two armies met near Southend-on-Sea between the Crouch and Roach rivers. Owing to the treachery of Ædric and his force of Hereford men, who switched allegiance to the Danes during the battle, Edmund was heavily defeated, and many Saxon nobles were killed. Edmund died the following month, whereupon Knut was proclaimed king.   APC-A

Aspern-Essling, battle of (1809). At Aspern-Essling, 5 miles (8 km) east of Vienna, Austrian forces under the command of Archduke *Charles inflicted the first major defeat suffered by *Napoleon. The latter was unaware the Austrians were so close, on the north side of the Danube, and began pushing his forces across. The Austrians had an observation post on the Bisamberg heights, which gave them a rare advantage: perfect intelligence of the location, movements, and even intentions of the enemy. They therefore caught Napoleon at his most vulnerable, with a third of his force across the river. Between 1300 and 1800 on 21 May 1809 five Austrian corps attacked the French bridgehead established on the north side of the Danube. The villages of Aspern and Essling on the left and right of the bridgehead received the brunt of the attack. As the Austrians attacked with 95,800 men and 264 guns, the French tried to pour forces into the bridgehead. They increased their strength from 23,000 and 50 guns at the start to 31,400 and 90 guns at the end of the day, but a combination of the river current and Austrian attacks destroyed the bridge. Overnight they repaired it and managed to build their force up to 70,000 and 144 guns on the second day, 22 May.

At the end of the first day both villages were still in French hands. With the bridge repaired, fighting resumed at 05.00, by which time the French had about 50,000 troops across. At 07.00 the French, enjoying the advantage of interior lines, attacked the middle of the Austrian forces. Then the bridge was damaged again and Davout's III Corps was stuck on the south side of the Danube. Realizing his situation was untenable, Napoleon withdrew across the bridge under cover of darkness. Although the French withdrew successfully—remarkable, under the circumstances—they lost up to 30,000 (some sources say as many as 37,000) men to the Austrians' 20,000 out of a smaller total force.
                                                              CDB

Assassins An Islamic sect which, under al-Hasan ibn-as-Sabbah, seized Alamut castle near the Caspian in 1090 and began a campaign of terror against orthodox (Sunni) authorities. The name means zealot but took on its present significance of politically motivated murderers through the sect's use of targeted, sometimes suicidal murders. Assassin missionary activity established the sect in Syria where in the 1130s it profited from conflict between Islam and the crusaders in the frontier area of the Ansariyah mountains to establish themselves in an enclave guarded by castles, of which the greatest was Masyaf. Their leader in the last quarter of the 12th century was Sinan ibn-Salman, the 'Old Man of the Mountains', who died c.1194.

Assassination enabled them to safeguard their mountain enclave in a world torn between Christians and Muslims. They killed Madud of Damascus in 1113, Bori of Damascus in 1131, Raymond II of Tripoli c.1130, Conrad of Montferrat in 1192, and they twice tried to kill *Saladin. By the 13th century they were a recognized part of Syrian politics and their enclave paid tribute to the Hospitallers. In 1256 the *Mongols destroyed Alamut and by 1273 their castles in Syria had fallen to the Mameluke Baybars, extinguishing the Assassins as an independent force.

Interestingly the Spanish equivalent word, *sicarios*, refers back to the Jewish sect of assassins exterminated at *Masada 1,000 years before Hasan ibn-as-Sabbah.   JF2

Lewis, B., *The Assassins: a Radical Sect in Islam* (London, 1967).

assault gun Similar to but not identical in form or function to the *self-propelled (SP) gun, the assault gun provides very close support for attacking troops. Over the centuries, field guns have sometimes been used in the assault, but these should not be placed in the same category as pieces designed specifically for that purpose. In the *Russo-Japanese war of 1904–5, the Japanese countered the weight of Russian defensive firepower by dragging light mountain pieces forward with their infantry in the assault, and the Germans used light field guns in a similar role to support their *storm troops in WW I. The first *tanks in 1916–18 were essentially the first assault guns, intended to breach defences and direct firepower onto the enemy position itself. When German tank *doctrine embraced deep operations and exploitation, it left the infantry without close support, so in 1940 the Germans produced the most famous assault gun, the Sturmgeschuetz (StuG), to destroy enemy strong points in the path of attacking infantry and tanks. It was armed with a large calibre, low velocity gun, mounted on the chassis rather than in a turret. *Guderian was a strong advocate of the assault gun. A few StuG took part in the invasion of France, but many more were deployed on the eastern front from 1941. The Soviets made assault guns such as the ISU-152 and others based on captured Pkw IIIs. British Churchill tanks were modified to provide the same service in Normandy.

The Russians employed assault guns after WW II, notably the heavy ASU-85 and the lighter ASU-57, largely designed to provide *airborne forces with the firepower they traditionally lack. Elsewhere the assault gun has fallen out of favour, partly because lack of turret limits its flexibility, and partly because the *MICV offers firepower (albeit rarely of the same weight) plus the ability to transport troops under armour. JBAB

Bailey, J. B. A., *Field Artillery and Firepower* (Oxford, 1989).
Ellis, C., *Tanks of World War 2* (London, 1981).
Perrett, B., *Sturmartillerie and Panzerjäger* (London, 1979).

Assaye, battle of (1803), a decisive engagement during the second *Maratha war when British and East India Company forces under the command of Col Arthur Wellesley (later Duke of *Wellington) defeated the combined forces of the Maratha chiefs, Sindhia and the Bhonsla. Wellesley, who had divided his forces, was greatly outnumbered (*c*.40,000 to 7,000) and outgunned (100 to 22) and was very inferior in cavalry when on 23 September 1803 he unexpectedly came upon the Marathas encamped on the opposite side of the Kaitna river at the village of Assaye in central India (modern Maharashtra). Wellesley decided it was too dangerous to retire or to wait for the rest of his forces and that he should attack. He found a ford, crossed the river, and attacked the Marathas' left flank winning a close and bloody battle in which he incurred over 1,800 casualties, mostly from the fire of the disciplined Maratha artillery. Wellesley captured 100 guns. He was too weakened to pursue the Maratha at once but on 29 November caught and defeated them at Argaum. Many years later, in response to an enquiry as to his greatest military achievement, he answered 'Assaye'. MEY

Weller, Jac, *Wellington in India* (Harlow, 1972).

Assyrians Renowned as possessing the most ruthless and efficient military organization of all the ancient Mesopotamian empires, the Assyrians dominated the region for over 600 years before being conquered by the Medes and Babylonians. The Assyrian state grew up *c*.1300 BC around Nineveh, Nimrud, and Ashur. Tiglath-pileser I led 28 campaigns against the Aramaean tribes to establish his supremacy by 1076 BC. His troops pursued harsh methods against their enemies: the destruction of villages and crops and the massacre of the population. Once they had submitted, subjects of the Assyrians paid tribute to support the war-machine. The 9th century saw expansion under Ashurnasi-apli II and Shalmeneser III, which gave them a Mediterranean coastline from the Gulf of Alexandretta (southern Turkey) as far south as Gaza. In the second half of the 8th century, Tiglath-Pileser III pushed his frontiers south to the Persian Gulf and north into the heart of Anatolia, defeating the Hurrians and the *Hittites. In 701 BC, Sennacherib defeated an Egyptian army at Eltekeh (near modern Haifa) although he failed to take Jerusalem. Eshardon and Ashurbanipal were still pressing south-west in

conquest of Egypt in the mid-7th century. At Ashurbanipal's death in 627 BC the Assyrian empire was at its greatest extent, yet a few years later the Medes and Babylonians took Ashur (614 BC) and finally conquered Nineveh (612 BC).

The Assyrian army changed over the centuries. Originally it was a seasonal militia, raised after the crops had been sown and led by the king, but as the empire expanded it became necessary to maintain a more permanent force and to place elements of it under the command of generals. Also, there were substantial enemies to overcome. At the battle of Qarqar (853 BC) the ruler of Damascus fielded an allied army (including Israelites) of 4,000 *chariots and over 60,000 infantry, with which he defeated the Assyrians. It was not until a century later under Tiglath-pileser III (745–727 BC) that reforms brought about the kind of forces more suitable for such an extensive empire. A census department kept records of the available manpower for rural projects, allowing greater specialization and the ability to keep the army in the field for longer. Specialization within the military itself led to the employment of foreign mercenaries, large numbers of enemy prisoners, and select troops such as the charioteers, in well-co-ordinated forces led by professional generals. Already, in the 10th century BC, the numbers of such forces reached 100,000, of which a fifth were archers. The Assyrians kept records of their losses, although these were played down in propagandizing memorials of victories, and also of those enemy troops killed and captured. Prisoners were especially important as they could be re-employed in the Assyrians' own forces and used for further aggressive campaigns.

There was a defined structure of unit sizes and a system of command rising from 10, 50, 100, 200, to 1,000 men. There was also a division into different troop types. The most senior were the charioteers, who provided the mobile arm for most of Assyrian history. Ninth-century bas-reliefs show heavy vehicles drawn by four-horse teams, although developments in technology enabled the development of a lighter and handier chariot. This used a metal undercarriage with better carpentry techniques to produce a flexible and manoeuvrable fighting platform. Crews were originally a driver and warrior, but by the 7th century, four fighting men, including two shield bearers, made the chariot team a mobile squad of soldiers. Their virtue was that they were capable of extremely rapid strategic movement (on one occasion a 160 mile (100 km) march is recorded in two days), and in battle provided a shock force and mobile missile platforms.

In the 7th century, cavalry became a more significant part of the mobile arm. Armoured riders could be either lancers or archers, and bas-reliefs (such as may be seen in the British Museum) show them operating in pairs. The rider sat far back, and in early representations, the archer is stationary, while his companion holds his horse. Whether the Assyrians ever achieved the kind of horse-archer known from the steppes, where man and horse seemed as one, is uncertain; but it is known that archery played an important part in Assyrian battle tactics.

The infantry operated in the same way as the cavalry, pairs of archers and a spearman, who also carried a large pavise-style shield, seem to have formed the bulk of the main battle line. In the many representations of *siege warfare, these troops are shown with ankle-length armour and tall, wicker *shields, which curve over at the top. Whether such equipment was equally in use in the field army is uncertain, since it seems rather unwieldy. The bas-reliefs show more lightly equipped soldiers with waist-length armour and protuberant, almost conical, round shields. *Slingers also seem to have played a large role as missile troops, and they are also shown in 'field' and 'siege' equipment. The body armour was of lamellar construction (small rectangular pieces of metal sown together in rows). Apart from some lightly equipped archers, every soldier wore a helmet, initially conical and pointed, later with a curved crest.

What made the Assyrian military machine most formidable was its expertise at siege warfare. Representations of sieges feature strongly on the bas-reliefs, for example the siege of Lachish in Judah, as part of Sennacherib's campaign of 701 BC. They show teams of engineers engaged in a variety of siege techniques. Undermining is prominent, depicted as men picking away at the bottom of walls, but at least one picture seems to show a man tunnelling. Another technique was the construction of a huge ramp. This was used as the base for a large ram moved up under the protection of a wooden shed, or for siege towers designed to overtop the defenders' walls. These machines were covered in leather and had their own water supplies as a defence against fire. MB

Hackett, Gen. Sir John (ed.), *Warfare in the Ancient World* (London, 1989).

Atahualpa (c.1502–33), last Inca ruler of Peru. See PIZARRO, FRANCISCO.

Atatürk, Gen Mustafa Kemal (1881–1938), revered father of modern Turkey. He began his career as an Ottoman army cadet, entering the Harbiye military college in Istanbul in 1899 and graduating in 1905. Already disenchanted with the repression of Abd al-Hamid II, he was posted to Damascus as a captain in a cavalry regiment, and became a member of the reformist Vatan 'Fatherland' secret society. He served in Tripolitania during the *Italo-Turkish war and in the two *Balkan wars, by now on the fringes at least of the Committee of Union and Progress which had ended the Hamidian despotism and brought about the 'Young Turk' revolution, though Kemal himself was a firm believer in the separation of the military from politics.

Initially opposed to Turkey's entry into WW I, once Turkey was committed Kemal threw himself into the war wholeheartedly, with a chance to display the talents for leadership and military planning for which he was already notable. He distinguished himself in the defence of *Gallipoli and then was sent as a corps commander to the eastern Anatolian front. Here he first came into contact with Ismet (later Inönü), who was to become his right-hand man and eventually his successor as president of the Republic. When the Russian army of the Caucasus crumbled at the onset of the Russian Revolution, Kemal and Ismet were both transferred to Palestine. With the loss of Baghdad to the British, Kemal became increasingly fearful that the war was lost for Turkey and was grieved that his soldiers had such inadequate weapons and supplies; he also resented the transfer of the supreme command in the east from Turkish generals to the Germans *Falkenhayn and then *Liman von Sanders.

Personally undefeated as a field commander, Kemal ended the war at Aleppo, with Turkey now bereft of its Arab provinces as well as virtually all of the Balkans. He felt a personal mission to fight for the integrity of the Turkish heartland, Anatolia. The Mudros armistice terms seemed to herald the imminent partition of Asiatic Turkey by the western Allies and Greece. Posted in 1919 as inspector general of the Turkish army in northern Anatolia, he speedily began to act independently and to arouse nationalist feeling there, not difficult when a Greek army had landed at Smyrna (now Izmir) in May 1919. The first Great National Assembly at Ankara in central Anatolia, now a rival body to the sultan's government in the capital Istanbul, assembled in spring 1920 and later elected him president in 1921. Kemal, now sentenced to death *in absentia* by the sultan's government, embarked on the most testing and decisive phase of his military career, the war for the integrity of the Turkish homeland, at a time when foreign powers had troops in the south and west of Anatolia, the sultan's government was hostile, and the Armenians had set up a state of their own in eastern Anatolia.

In 1921 the Greek army advanced eastwards from Izmir but was held on the Sakarya river before Ankara, Kemal having by now been made C-in-C, and in 1922 the Greeks were disastrously defeated and had to evacuate western Anatolia. The peace settlement of Lausanne (July 1923) gave Kemal a Turkey in Asia free of foreign troops and with essential control of the Straits, and provided for exchanges of populations. Exasperation at the feeble and defeatist role of the sultan in Istanbul led Kemal to work for the abolition of the sultanate in 1922, the proclamation of a republic in 1923, and the abolition of the caliphate in 1924; thus the rule of the Ottoman *Turks ended for ever. Kemal's later career as 'Gazi' (Warrior Hero), a title awarded to him by a grateful Assembly in 1921, and as 'Atatürk' (Father of the Turkish Nation), assumed by him in 1934, was a pacific one, concerned with establishing for Turkey a dirigiste economy, a neutralist foreign policy, and westernizing social and educational measures, involving a reduction of Islamic influence in daily life, to which Atatürk attributed much of the backwardness of his country. CEB

Kinross, Lord, *Atatürk: The Rebirth of a Nation* (London, 1964).
Mango, Andrew, *Atatürk* (London, 1999).

Atkins, Tommy The prototypical British soldier, probably originating in a *War Office publication of 1815 showing how the Soldier's Book for the cavalry should be filled up, giving Pte Thomas Atkins, No. 6 Troop, 6th Dragoons, as its example. In an 1837 edition Atkins was a sergeant, and was able to sign his name rather than make his mark. It has been suggested that the Duke of Wellington chose the name to commemorate a soldier in his battalion of the 33rd Regiment, killed in Flanders in 1794.

The nickname was widely used in the 1880s, and in 1883 the *Illustrated London News* depicted 'Pte Tommy Atkins returning from Indian Service'. Rudyard Kipling's poem 'Tommy' summed up Britain's ambivalence about those who defended her:

> Then it's Tommy this, an' Tommy that
> An' 'Tommy, 'ow's your soul?'
> But it's 'Thin red line of 'eroes'
> When the drums begin to roll.

The term was in general use in WW I, and spawned derivatives like 'Tommy cooker', a small portable stove—or, in rare German humour, the WW II *Sherman tank, well known for its inflammable qualities. It is not now used, although British officers sometimes hark back to it when speaking of their men as 'Toms'. RH

Atlantic, battle of the (1940–3), one of the pivotal campaigns of WW II, for upon its success depended Britain's capacity to survive militarily and to join the USA in the eventual invasion of occupied Europe. The Germans realized this from the start, but placed their initial hopes in the effects of surface raiders and individual warships like the *Graf Spee* and the *Bismarck*. In fact it was the U-boat that turned out to represent the most dangerous threat, under the calculating direction of Adm *Dönitz. The campaign against the U-boat ran throughout WW II, but was at its most intense from 1940 to 1943, a period which culminated in the decisive convoy battles of March 1943. At this time, massed U-boats operating in wolf packs were defeated by a variety of Allied countermeasures.

The formation of *convoys of vulnerable merchant ships protected by a variety of escorting warships and aircraft was probably the crucial element in the Allied response. However, the help provided by *ULTRA special intelligence, the role of anti-submarine aircraft operating from carriers or from land bases, and the Allied powers' ability to build merchantmen, escorts, and aircraft faster than the Germans could sink them or build U-boats, were all vital too. Nor

should the importance of the Allied strategic bombing campaign, their ship-repair industry, and the eventual efficiency of their docking and land transportation systems be forgotten.

Statistics on this campaign are notoriously hard to agree, but in all about 83,000 Allied sailors (naval and civilian) and airmen, approximately 12 million tons of merchant shipping, about 90 allied warships, and 1,700 Coastal Command aircraft were lost during the campaign. In the whole war, the Germans lost 784 U-boats, and 28,000 out of their 41,000 submariners, two-thirds in the battle of the Atlantic. Although the campaign was won, the costs were high and the late appearance of dangerous and advanced German U-boats like the Type XXI and the Type XXIII showed that the submarine threat had been managed rather than completely defeated. GT

Haworth, Stephen, and Law, Derek, *The Battle of the Atlantic 1939–1945* (London, 1994).

attrition is a word commonly employed but rarely defined, partly perhaps because it figures infrequently in official military *doctrine. Its current use suggests a style of fighting dictated by material superiority, where the enemy is worn down rather than outmanoeuvred, and where casualty rates are more important than psychological effect. Chronologically it is a child of industrialization, relying on the fruits of mass production for firepower and assuming that economic preponderance in itself will ensure victory. Intellectually its roots are said to be Clausewitzian: *Clausewitz emphasized concentration on the decisive point and put the slaughter of climactic battle at the heart of his analysis. But Clausewitz did not elevate what we would now call attrition into an operational method, nor has any major military thinker since.

Much of Clausewitz's *On War* reflects the conditions of Napoleonic warfare which the author himself experienced. Indubitably, the wars of 1792 to 1815 can be understood through the vocabulary of attrition: cumulatively they were long and bloody and they were ultimately won by the coalition with the greater resources. But most 19th-century students of war saw them in terms of manoeuvre: *Napoleon may have lost in the end but he engaged in a succession of short campaigns leading to decisive battles which resulted in the annihilation of his opponents. The successes of *Moltke 'the Elder' in the wars of German unification endorsed the Napoleonic model; it became in the hands of the German *general staff the universal tool for the interpretation of operations. But an academic, Hans *Delbrück, took exception: there was an alternative, what he called *Ermattungsstrategie*, a wearing-out strategy. In the 18th-century generals had often achieved their objectives through manoeuvre or through sieges, and without battle.

His ideas caused uproar, not least because he saw *Frederick 'the Great', whom the general staff had appropriated for their strategy of annihilation, as an exponent of *Ermattungsstrategie.* He concluded that, because Frederick's forces had frequently been inferior in number, he had had to avoid battle, to the point where attrition in the sense of wearing out his opponent had become his preferred operational method. The contrasts between the Delbrück understanding of attrition and its contemporary meaning are instructive. His idea of attrition was based on material deprivation; today's rests on abundance. For him attrition was about avoiding battle; the contemporary emphasis on firepower implies that fighting is attrition's key purpose. To avoid battle, his strategy elevated manoeuvre. But for today's theorist manoeuvre is the alternative of attrition, not an integral part of it. Indeed, the opposite of attrition for Delbrück, the general staff's strategy of annihilation, elevates battle and is congruent with today's understanding of attrition, not divergent from it.

What changed the meaning of attrition was WW I. Between 1915 and 1917 operational possibilities became subject to the tactical realities of *trench warfare. In 1915 Henry Rawlinson advocated a method of 'bite and hold'; the aim was to seize a sector of the enemy's front line, so as to force him to attack and to incur greater losses than the defence in order to regain it. The idea rested on two presumptions: one was the strength of defensive firepower and the other was the significance of the terrain being held. Attrition was elevated from tactics to strategy, to combine with economic warfare. Thus attrition came to be about the application or acquisition of material superiority.

But attrition at the tactical level could not be applied defensively in perpetuity. The logic of attrition suggested that attacks, if any, should be broken off the moment that losses exceeded those of the enemy's. It implied that the war would end through exhaustion, and that its peace settlement would be negotiated and even indecisive. Attrition became a rationalization for long, costly, and seemingly inconclusive battles. This was neither militarily nor politically acceptable. The key issue was one of time: a wearing-out battle that became an end in itself could go on almost indefinitely. Instead attrition should be the means to an end, not an end in itself. The pay-off for exhausting the enemy was the ability to regain the freedom to manoeuvre with decisive effect.

The switch in attrition, from the preferred strategy of the economically weaker power to that of the economically stronger, made it most relevant to the USA. *Grant employed this idea of attrition—industrial superiority applied through battle—in the battles of 1864–5. The reconquest of *North-West Europe in 1944–5 was achieved by dint of dogged fighting, where armour operated in close conjunction with the infantry, where air superiority provided direct support, and where casualties on both sides were high. Context was crucial: limited fields of fire, close terrain, and large cities reinforced the defensive, created strong points, and made the application of material superiority mandatory.

Similar arguments applied to the doctrines of NATO armies during the *Cold War. Committed to the forward defence of the German border, politically they could not trade space in order to gain the power of manoeuvre and counterstroke. The advent of *precision-guided munitions, and in particular their employment by the Egyptian army in a classic 'bite and hold' operation at the outset of the 1973 *Arab--Israeli war, confirmed the validity of attrition. But the reliance on Firepower which NATO encouraged, and which was embodied in the 1976 edition of the US army's Field Manual (FM) 100–5 (*Operations*), was criticized by those who reflected on the failures of *Vietnam. In its 1982 edition Field Manual 100–5 emphasized manoeuvre, even in defence. Attrition became a loaded word, associated with high casualties, waste, protracted fighting, and indeterminate outcomes. The reality of course is that attrition and manoeuvre are not mutually exclusive, any more than are attrition and annihilation. Theoretically opposites, they meld in practice. As Christopher Bellamy has put it: 'Manoeuvre means moving one's forces in such a way as to multiply their effectiveness and ability to inflict attrition.'   HFAS

Bellamy, Christopher, *The Future of Land Warfare* (London, 1987).

Bucholz, Arden, *Hans Delbrück and the German Military Establishment: War Images in Conflict* (Iowa City, Iowa, 1985).

Simpkin, Richard, *Race to the Swift: Thoughts on Twenty-first Century Warfare* (London, 1985).

Auchinleck, FM Sir Claude John Eyre (1884–1981).

Commissioned into the Indian army in 1903, Auchinleck served in Egypt and Mesopotamia (now in Iraq) in WW I and was a major general in 1939. Unusually for an Indian army officer he was summoned to Britain in 1940 and commanded troops involved in the ill-fated Narvik expedition. He then served in England, first as a corps commander and then GOC Southern Command. Promoted general in November 1940 he was appointed C-in-C India, and his swift dispatch of troops to deal with rebellion in Iraq won him Churchill's approval.

He replaced *Wavell as C-in-C Middle East in June 1941, but resisted pressure from *Churchill for an offensive until he felt ready to launch CRUSADER in November 1941. Its success was outweighed in mid-1942 by Rommel attacking Eighth Army in the *Gazala position and, after a finely balanced battle, the British fell back, losing *Tobruk. Auchinleck's relationship with Ritchie, Eighth Army's commander, was uneasy, and Auchinleck eventually relieved him, commanding the army personally and checking Rommel in the first battle of *Alamein. There is some reason to suggest that he established the conditions for subsequent victory in the desert, but he had lost Churchill's confidence and was replaced by *Alexander.

Without employment until reappointed C-in-C India in June 1943, Auchinleck played a major role for the rest of the war in mobilizing India's resources, and deserves much credit for the contribution made by the *Indian army to the campaign in *Burma. It was a particular grief for him to see the army to which he had devoted his life dismembered by partition in 1947. 'The Auk', as he was universally known, was a fine example of the type of officer who had contributed so much to the Indian army: neither luck nor history accorded him quite the treatment that his character deserved. RH

Augereau, Marshal P. F. C., Duc de Castiglione

(1757–1816). Pierre François Charles Augereau was born in Paris, son of a domestic servant or fruit dealer. He claimed to have served in the French, Russian, and Prussian armies and made a living as a fencing-master in Dresden. Returning to France in 1790 he was promoted swiftly, becoming general in 1793 and commanding a first-rate division. After serving in Spain he came under Bonaparte's command in Italy in 1796, and distinguished himself at Castiglione. His showy and rapacious habits aroused dislike, but in 1799 he backed Bonaparte's coup, and was appointed marshal when Bonaparte became emperor in 1804.

Though public recognition and private wealth mellowed Augereau, worsening health helped limit his achievements. His corps had a secondary role in the *Austerlitz campaign of 1805, and performed poorly at *Jena/Auerstadt the following year. Wounded at *Eylau in 1807, he showed a flash of his old fire at *Leipzig in 1813. In 1814 he commanded the Army of the Rhône ineptly and applauded Louis XVIII when he heard of Napoleon's abdication. He tried to change sides in 1815, but was ignored by Napoleon and dismissed by Louis.

Augereau was fatally inconsistent: physical hero but moral coward, greedy but generous, sometimes determined but often irresolute. He rose quickly in an army which appreciated his soldierly presence and natural authority, but divisional commander was his ceiling. RH

Aurangzeb

(reigned 1658–1707), Mughal emperor in India and great-grandson of *Akbar 'the Great', under whom the empire reached its greatest extent, only to collapse after his death. The son of Shajahan, he gained power by eliminating in warfare his elder brothers. His long reign was filled with a series of military campaigns, from the north-west frontier region to Assam, but the main thrust of his efforts was through central into southern India. It was during his reign that the Hindu *Marathas became active in the north-western Deccan (modern Maharashtra state) under their dynamic leader Shivaji. Aurangzeb perceived them as both a threat to the fabric of his empire and to the domination of Islam in the subcontinent, but his expeditions against them achieved only temporary results. More successful was his incorporation of the two remaining independent Shi'ite Muslim sultanates of the Deccan, those of the 'Adilshahis of Bijapur (1686) and the Qutbshahis of Golconda (1687). Thus almost all India except the extreme southern tip was nominally under Mughal control, but in practice it proved impossible for the emperor to subdue the Marathas and to retain control of outlying parts of the empire. The imposing military system built up by Akbar 'the Great' became prey to inefficiency and corruption. The ideal of religious harmony pursued by Akbar 'the Great' was deliberately rejected by the zealot Aurangzeb, reacting against the tide of Hindu militancy, yet the Muslims were no longer strong enough—if they ever had been—to impose their dominion over the non-Muslim majority. Hence after Aurangzeb's death, the outwardly impressive Mughal empire disintegrated, prey to the Marathas and outside powers like the Persians and Afghans. CEB

Richards, John F., *The New Cambridge History of India*, 1. 5. *The Mughal Empire* (Cambridge, 1993).
Sarkar, Sir Jadunath, *History of Aurangzib*, 5 vols. (Calcutta, 1912–24).

Austerlitz, battle of (1805). Fought on 2 December 1805, Austerlitz is known as the battle of the three emperors. *Napoleon faced the combined armies of Emperor Francis II of Austria and Tsar Alexander of Russia, under the nominal command of the veteran Gen *Kutuzov. Napoleon had captured an entire Austrian army of 27,000 men under Mack at Ulm on 20 October. Hearing of this disaster, Kutuzov began to retire, leaving the French to occupy Vienna. Napoleon resolved to march north to seek out and engage the Coalition forces, and allow his scattered detachments to join him on the way. He desperately needed a swift outcome to the campaign before the Austrians could reorganize, and to forestall the threatened entry of Prussia into the war. Supplies were running out, and the weather, predictably for the month of December in Moravia, was bitterly cold, adding to the discomfort of the tired and hungry French soldiers.

The Grande Armée consisted of around 73,000, not all of whom were immediately available, facing nearly 86,000 Austrians and Russians. Napoleon carefully scouted the ground in person, noting salient features. He gave orders to improve defensive positions, such as the natural bastion of Santon Hill on his left. The crucial point though was the Pratzen Heights, a large area of high ground dominating the centre of his chosen battlefield. It was here that the violent drama of the battle would reach its climax.

Fooled by Napoleon's carefully laid deception plan, the Russian and Austrian plan called for five large columns, totalling some 59,000, to overwhelm Napoleon's right before he could react, thereby cutting the French off from Vienna. A secondary assault led by *Bagration would strike on the opposite flank, held by *Lannes and the dashing *Murat, from east to west along the Olmütz to Brünn road. A final

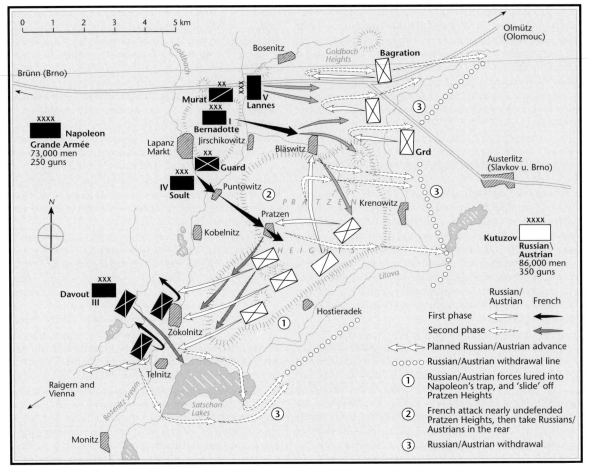

The battle of **Austerlitz**, 2 December 1805.

crushing blow would be delivered to the centre, when the French were driven back on themselves into a crocheted line, by the combined force of the Allied assault. It was a complex plan which would require excellent timing and perfect co-ordination to succeed. It was to founder in its execution.

The dawn attack on the right was soon foiled by the timely arrival by forced march of Friant's division of III Corps (see DAVOUT), whereupon the Russians and Austrians redoubled their efforts on this sector, pushing more troops through the central position of the Pratzen heights, and across the front of the French lines. The disparate Allied columns became stalled and confused as they lumbered into each other in the murk and gloom. Seeing that the Allies had, as he had hoped, exposed their flank to his attack, Napoleon ordered *Soult to lead his corps up onto the Pratzen just before 09.00, as the sun broke through the clouds and mist. Soult's men were still partially hidden by the fog lying in the low valley and the smoke of the break-

fast fires, and achieved perfect surprise as the two divisions burst on to the plateau. By 11.00, and after a stiff fight, the French had a secure hold on the vital central high ground.

Kutuzov now realized that his plan was in danger of turning to ruin, and towards 13.00 he threw in the crack Russian Imperial Guard under the Grand Duke Constantine, the tsar's brother. This attack threw the French on the Pratzen into some disarray and Napoleon's reserves were hurried forward into the fray. After a titanic clash, involving the finest horsemen in Europe, including Napoleon's Imperial Guard, the allies were pushed back off the Pratzen feature. This withdrawal soon turned to rout as Soult's troops wheeled on to the flank and rear of the enemy assaulting the right of the French position. Seeing themselves surrounded, these too fled, some across the frozen Satschan lakes behind them, where guns and teams are supposed to have fallen through the ice into the freezing water. The French *Bulletin de La Grande Armée* claimed that some 20,000 Allied soldiers were killed. However, the veracity of these claims is open to question. The true figures were probably nearer 16,000 allied troops dead and wounded and 11,000 taken prisoner, still a handsome victory.

This was Napoleon's finest hour. He had effectively smashed the Third Coalition: Austria made peace at once, and the Russians retreated to the East Prussian and Polish marches to fight again the next year. There is an interesting footnote to the battle. Rumours persist to the present day that the Russian Preobrazhenskiy Guard buried its war chest on the battlefield, and amateur treasure hunters often visit the site in search of this hoard.   TM

Australian Imperial Force (AIF) (see also ANZAC).
Australian Imperial Force was the name given to the volunteer expeditionary forces sent overseas by Australia in two world wars. The Defence Act (1903) precluded service outside Australian territory on other than a voluntary basis, and in August 1914 the government announced the despatch of a force of 20,000 men, a target met within a few weeks. A second division was raised soon after, and both served at *Gallipoli during the Dardanelles campaign between April–December 1915. After evacuation to Egypt the AIF was greatly expanded and reorganized. Five infantry divisions went to the western front in March 1916 while mounted elements comprising two more divisions remained in the Middle East to fight the Turks. Over 331,000 men served in its ranks, of whom 60,000 were killed. It was officially disbanded on 1 April 1921. The 2nd AIF was raised with the outbreak of war in September 1939, by voluntary enlistment for overseas service. Three infantry divisions served in the Middle East and a fourth was captured at Singapore in February 1942. Thereafter the AIF in Europe was withdrawn to defend the homeland and fought in the Pacific until the Japanese *capitulation. Its strength was 286,000 in September 1945, and it was disbanded on 30 June 1947.   JG1

Austrian Succession, War of the (1740–8), a loosely
related and indecisive series of struggles involving the leading European states. Though extending overseas, to the West Indies, North America, and the Indian subcontinent, it was fought mainly in central Europe, the Italian peninsula and, latterly, the southern Netherlands. Fought between two loose and frequently changing alliances, it was as much a series of manoeuvres by the diplomats as operations by the armies, and was remarkable principally for Prussia's emergence as a leading military power. It settled little, and the peace settlement in 1748 was widely seen as merely a *truce, which it soon proved to be.

The struggle took its name from the failure of Charles VI, ruler of the Habsburg monarchy and Holy Roman Emperor (1711–40), to father a male heir. A woman could not be elected to the position of emperor, which had been in

Habsburg hands since the 15th century and was now seen in Vienna as hereditary. The succession of Charles VI's elder surviving daughter Maria Theresa to the family possessions (principally the Austrian provinces, the Bohemian crown lands, and the kingdom of Hungary, together with the outlying territories of the duchy of Milan and the Austrian (southern) Netherlands) was provided for by a family agreement, the so-called Pragmatic Sanction. During the 1720s and 1730s Charles VI had secured wide-ranging domestic and international support for this arrangement. Two middle-sized German states, Bavaria and Saxony, had their own claims to the Habsburg inheritance, but when Charles VI died suddenly in October 1740 the military challenge to Maria Theresa came from the unexpected quarter of Prussia, now ruled by the young and ambitious *Frederick 'the Great'.

Until May 1740 Prussia, the lands of which consisted of three distinct, thinly populated, and economically backward blocks of territory stretched out across half of northern Europe, from the Rhineland in the west to the Niemen far to the east, had been ruled by Frederick William I. Chiefly remembered for his oddities, above all his famous regiment of tall *grenadiers (who were paraded through the king's bedchamber when he was ill, apparently making him feel much better) and for the brutal treatment of his son and successor, he had created a state to be feared on the unpromising foundations he had inherited. Frederick William I had built up the Hohenzollern army to the impressive strength of 80,000 men and created an administrative and military infrastructure to support it, yet conscious of the vulnerability of his exposed possessions he had pursued a peaceful and pro-Habsburg policy.

His son by contrast believed that Prussia's destiny required territorial expansion, to secure the resources to make it a major power, and Charles VI's death provided an ideal opportunity. Maria Theresa's inheritance was ramshackle and extremely vulnerable: she lacked competent generals and political advisers, her finances were in chaos, while the army had been defeated both in the Rhineland during the War of the Polish Succession (1733–5) and more seriously in the south in a conflict with the Ottoman empire, fought in alliance with Russia (1737–9). Within a fortnight of Maria Theresa's accession, Frederick determined to invade populous and economically advanced Silesia, part of the Bohemian lands and connected by a thin strip of territory to the central Hohenzollern province of Brandenburg.

The invasion was launched on 16 December 1740. Within six weeks the Prussian army had overrun and occupied most of Silesia. In spring 1741 an attempted Austrian counter-attack was defeated at the battle of Mollwitz (10 April), a fortuitous success for Frederick but one with enormous political repercussions. The victory gained by the Prussian infantry encouraged the formation of a European alliance against Maria Theresa. Bavaria and Saxony joined

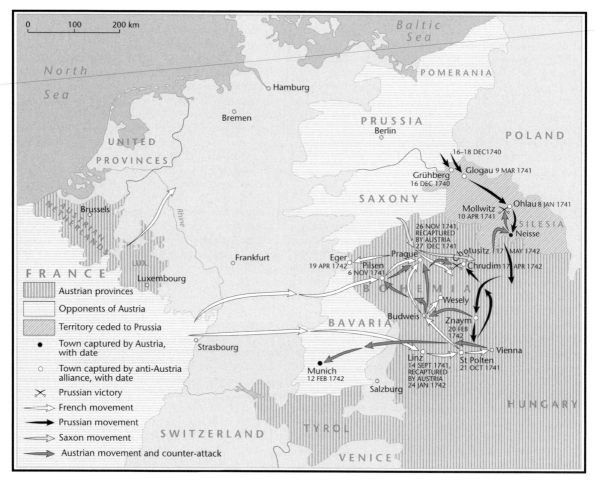

The war of the **Austrian Succession**, 1740–8: operations 1740–2.

to pursue their own claims to the Habsburg inheritance, while both the ambitious northern Italian power of Savoy-Piedmont and Spain took up the struggle against Austria in Italy. For a generation the queen of Spain, Philip V's second wife the ambitious Elizabeth Farnese, had been seeking Italian principalities for her sons by her first marriage, and the war of the 1740s was a continuation of this quest. Finally and most importantly France, the leading continental power, joined the anti-Habsburg alliance which emerged in the course of 1741.

Until that summer France had been preoccupied with her Bourbon ally Spain's struggle with Britain which had begun in 1739, the famous 'War of Jenkins's Ear'. This had its origins in the confrontation between the rising British empire and the extensive and alluring Spanish possessions, particularly in the western hemisphere. British efforts to expand trade with Spain's colonies, in defiance of trade regulations, led to a series of clashes and, in an increasingly

belligerent atmosphere, to war over the alleged cutting off of Capt Jenkins's ear by a Spanish coastguard. In 1739–41 France's octogenarian leading minister, Cardinal Fleury, was unofficially aiding Madrid and regarded full-scale war with Britain as inevitable. Franco-Spanish intervention in the continental struggle with Maria Theresa led to the colonial war becoming very much a secondary issue: particularly when Britain, in the following year, began to support her traditional ally Austria. This ensured that fighting in the Anglo-Spanish war was much reduced in intensity after 1742, when both sides came to concentrate resources on the conflict within Europe.

French intervention was championed at Louis XV's court by the Maréchal-Duc de Belle-Isle, who supplanted Fleury's pacific influence and led a French army on a dramatic but militarily unproductive invasion of the Habsburg monarchy in 1741, occupying the Bohemian capital, Prague. Frederick, conscious of his own limited resources, which

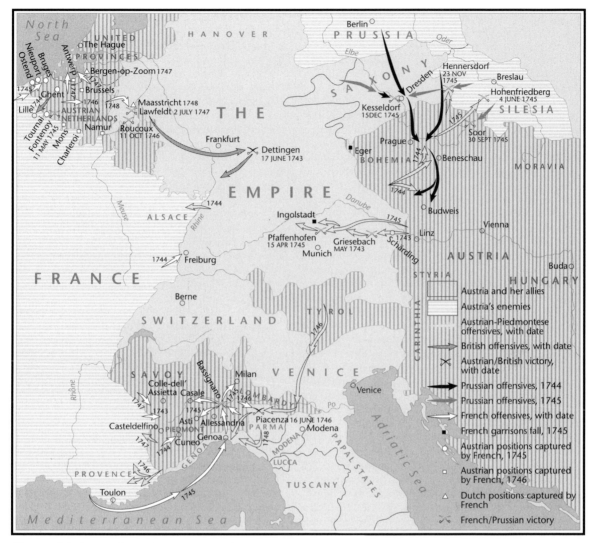

The war of the **Austrian Succession**, 1740–8: operations 1743–8.

were rapidly being exhausted and which, he believed, forced him to fight 'short and lively' wars, began increasingly to think of peace. Already in possession of large parts of Silesia, he was able to exploit Maria Theresa's vulnerability, which had been increased by the emergence of the anti-Austrian coalition and by the election of the Bavarian candidate as the Holy Roman Emperor Charles VII. In the following year Prussia abandoned her allies. By the Treaty of Berlin (July 1742) Frederick secured Habsburg acceptance of his gain of Silesia and left the war. The struggle now entered a particularly indecisive phase, with few battles, much manoeuvring by the armies which led nowhere, and futile diplomacy which accompanied and often undermined the military operations. Its middle years witnessed an Austrian recovery brought about by the leadership of

Maria Theresa, and to a lesser extent by London's financial and diplomatic support, which led to George II being the last British king to appear in person on a battlefield, at *Dettingen on 27 June 1743.

In the following year both Britain and France formally entered the conflict as principals: until then they had simply fought as auxiliaries. The war consequently became more of a purely Anglo-French struggle. During the first half of 1744 Frederick, ever watchful and anxious lest the Austrian recovery should mean that he would have to defend his gain of Silesia, moved towards re-entering the conflict, and this he duly did in August when he invaded Bohemia. The campaign which followed was notably unsuccessful: his winter retreat was little short of a disaster. In 1745 the king won notable victories at Hohenfriedberg

111

(4 June) and Soor (29 September), in the process establishing his own reputation as a commander. At the end of 1745 the veteran Prussian general *Dessau won a stunning victory over the Saxons (now the allies of Vienna) at Kesseldorf (15 December), one of the conflict's very few decisive battles, and this forced Austria to come to terms. Prussia now abandoned the war, and her allies, for a second time, securing possession of Silesia by the Peace of Dresden, signed on Christmas Day 1745. This marked the real end of the struggle over the Austrian succession, especially since Charles VII had died in the previous January and his successor had quickly concluded a settlement with Austria, by which he had secured the return of his Bavarian lands, hitherto occupied by Habsburg troops.

In 1745–6 British attention was diverted by the final *Jacobite rising, led by Charles Edward Stuart, the 'Young Pretender', who quickly proved to be an even less able leader than his father. Despite this his army reached Derby before turning back, and the Hanoverian government was forced to undertake large-scale military operations within the British Isles, involving the recall of line regiments from the continent. Only with the final defeat of the uprising at *Culloden could London's attention return to the continental war, in which it now fought in partnership with the Dutch Republic. The European struggle was very different in nature. In 1746–8 fighting only took place in the Italian peninsula, where the existing stalemate lasted for the remainder of the war, and in the Low Countries. On France's northern border the French commander Maurice de *Saxe, one of the Polish King Augustus 'the Strong''s numerous illegitimate offspring, won an impressive series of victories. His successes at *Fontenoy, Roucoux (11 October 1746), and Laufeldt (2 July 1747) led to the overrunning of the Dutch Republic during 1747, and contributed to the coming of peace. No such decisive advantage was apparent beyond Europe, where the French capture of Madras (September 1746), the sole event of importance in some small-scale fighting in the Indian subcontinent, effectively cancelled out the British success at *Louisbourg. This great fortress on Cape Breton Island in the Gulf of St Lawrence had been taken by a British combined operation in June 1745, in what was probably the most remarkable victory of the entire conflict.

Negotiations had begun among the war-weary participants at Breda in October 1746, and were subsequently continued at Aix-la-Chapelle. They were dominated, to a great extent, by Britain (now in partnership with the Dutch Republic) and France, who in the end imposed their terms on the other belligerents. The most surprising feature of the final settlement, which was not signed until October and November 1748, was that the considerable military advantage within Europe gained by Saxe for France was not reflected in the actual terms, which largely restored the territorial status quo, except in the Italian peninsula. There, Farnese's son Don Philip was given the duchies of Parma,

Piacenza, and Guastalla, while Savoy-Piedmont made some minor gains. The Peace of Aix-la-Chapelle provided an international guarantee for Prussia's possession of Silesia, to which Frederick attached considerable significance.

This was the one truly significant outcome of the war. Prussia was now clearly the equal of Austria in Germany and central Europe, and a struggle for supremacy which would not be settled until 1866, on the field of *Königgrätz, was inaugurated. In all other respects the War of the Austrian Succession was indecisive. With hindsight it marked the international eclipse of the Dutch Republic, while the failure of 'the Forty-five' marked the end of the Jacobite threat to the Hanoverian succession. Beyond Europe it was at most a pause—and in North America not even that—in the Anglo-French struggle for empire, while within Europe the Habsburgs were unreconciled to the loss of Silesia and with it their traditional dominance within Germany. Preparations for the next conflict began almost before the ink on the peace settlement was dry. When it came, it was a conflict on a wholly new scale: the *Seven Years War of 1756–63.   HS

Anderson, M. S., *The War of the Austrian Succession, 1740–1748* (London, 1995).

Browning, Reed, *The War of the Austrian Succession* (New York and Stroud, 1993).

Showalter, Dennis E., *The Wars of Frederick the Great* (London, 1996).

Austro-Prussian war (also called the Austro-Prussian-Italian war). This war was a violent solution to the 19th-century German and *Italian independence questions. The German question pitted Austria against Prussia in a struggle for control of the 39-state German Confederation established in 1815. Austria wished to uphold the loose-knit confederation; Prussia sought to meld it into a unitary German empire, whose capital would be Berlin. The Italian question ranged Austria against Italy, which claimed the Austrian province of Venetia, and allied with Prussia in April 1866 to get it.

Emperor Franz Josef I of Austria declared war in June 1866, ostensibly to punish Prussian encroachments in Schleswig-Holstein (which had been jointly administered by Austria and Prussia since 1864) and Italian troop movements near the Venetian frontier, but really to remove the Prussian and Italian threats to Austria's power and prestige. That Austria, the conservative, 'restorationist' power, was, induced to declare war on the two 'revisionist' powers was a tribute to the masterful diplomacy of Prussia's foreign minister, Count Otto von *Bismarck, who manipulated the German and Italian questions to corner Austria in 1866.

Austria fought on two fronts in the war: in Bohemia against the Prussians, in Venetia against the Italians. Although the Austrian army (400,000 men) was outnumbered by the combined armies of Prussia (300,000 men)

and Italy (200,000 men), it was highly rated, and Franz Josef entertained ambitious war aims. He aimed to partition Prussia, and refound the German Confederation by enlarging Austria's German allies (Saxony, Bavaria, Württemberg, Baden, Hessia, and Hanover) with land and treasure taken from Prussia. In Venetia, he aimed to crush the Italian army and induce a political crisis inside Italy that would set back the process of national unification.

The Austrians failed to reckon with military reforms enacted by Prussia's CGS *Moltke 'the Elder' in the years between 1858 and 1866. Moltke had streamlined the old Prus-

sian militia (Landwehr), tripled the active duty strength of the regular army, and established permanent army corps to accelerate Prussia's wartime mobilization. He had also adapted Prussia's *railways and *telegraphs for military use, a novelty at the time. Yet the most portentous Prussian reform was Moltke's adoption of the breech-loading *needle gun and small unit fire tactics in the early 1860s. This was revolutionary; the Austrian, French, and Russian armies were still using muzzle-loading rifles (to conserve ammunition) and battalion-sized *columns (to deliver 'shock') in 1866. Moltke planned to devastate Austria's massed columns

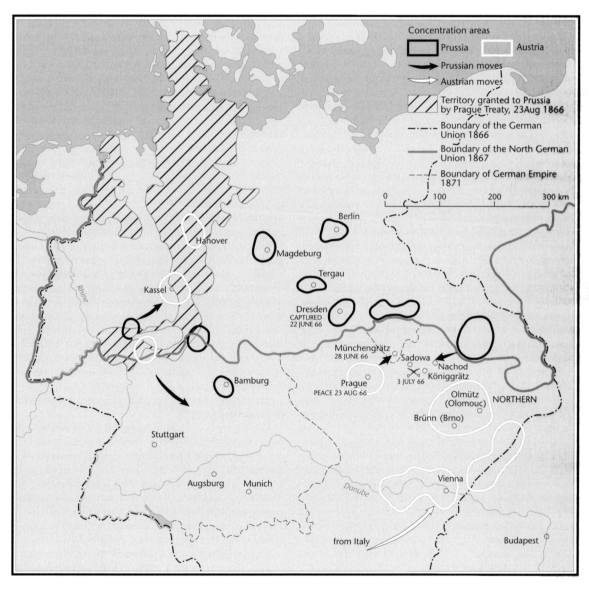

The **Austro-Prussian war**, 1866.

of infantry with rapid fire; his needle rifle could be loaded and fired four times more quickly than the Austrian rifle.

Austria's North Army of 240,000 men was commanded by *Benedek, who knew Italy well but who had no ideas for a war with Prussia, who chose Gen Alfred Henikstein, a jovial but inept boon companion, to be his COS. When both Benedek and Henikstein failed to produce plans for a war with Prussia, Emperor Franz Josef added a second COS: Gen Gideon von Krismanic. This bureaucracy stifled all initiative, and as Moltke's mobilization roared ahead, deploying 260,000 men by road and rail to the frontier of Bohemia in six weeks, Benedek's limped along so slowly that Krismanic decided to deploy the bulk of North Army at Olmütz in Moravia. This was a fateful decision. Krismanic left a single corps (and two allied Saxon divisions) in Bohemia; this 60,000-man detachment (Iser Army) was supposed to hold the Prussians long enough for Benedek to complete his mobilization in Olmütz and march westward to their rescue. It was a bad plan whose defects Moltke fully exploited.

The Prussians invaded Saxony and Bohemia on 16 June on a broad front in three armies: Elbe Army at Halle (46,000 men), First Army at Görlitz (93,000 men), and Second Army at Breslau (115,000 men). Three hundred miles (483 km) separated Elbe and Second Armies, which many considered reckless, but Moltke planned either to smash Benedek's widely separated armies in detail, or sweep them into a great, crushing 'pocket battle' (*Kesselschlacht*) in the vicinity of Königgrätz on the Elbe. Moltke's daring deployment greatly facilitated by the railway was Napoleonic in conception. The three Prussian armies would march separately to minimize logistical friction, and combine only in battle.

All went according to plan. In the last days of June, the Prussian armies passed through Saxony (obligingly vacated by the Saxon army, which was on the Iser) and into Bohemia, Austria's richest, most industrialized province. Benedek's faulty deployment at Olmütz substantiated the Moltkean aphorism that 'an error in the original concentration of an army can scarcely be corrected in the entire course of the war', for once the Prussians were through the Bohemian mountains, North Army exhausted itself marching westward to engage them. The first battles of the war demonstrated the awesome effectiveness of the Prussian needle rifle, and the obsolescence of Austrian shock tactics. At Trautenau and Vysokov on 27 June, whole Austrian corps launched repeated *bayonet attacks on isolated Prussian advance guards, with catastrophic results. At Trautenau, the Austrians lost 5,000 men, the Prussians just 1,300. The death toll among professional officers was as alarming; the Austrians lost 191, the Prussians 56. At Vysokov, a plateau that commanded a principal highway from Prussia to Austria, the Austrians spent 5,720 men in futile charges against a well-concealed Prussian division, which lost only 1,122 men. On 28 June, the Austrians attempted to hold the village of Skalice at the foot of the Vysokov plateau, but

were routed again, losing 6,000 men to Prussia's 1,300. Austrian casualties at Skalice were so dreadful that Benedek resolved never again to employ shock tactics, which partly explained his later paralysis.

On the Iser river line, where 60,000 Austro-Saxon troops awaited the approach of the 140,000 men of Elbe and first Armies, the Prussians hardly needed the advantage conferred on them by the needle rifle. They routed Iser Army in three successive battles: at Podol on 27 June, at München-grätz on the 28th, and at Jicin on the 29th. In these battles, the Prussians benefited from mass *desertion among Austria's Italian regiments, which had been shifted from Venetia to Bohemia to no good effect.

On 3 July, Benedek united the remains of Iser and North Armies on the hills between the fortress of *Königgrätz and the village of Sadowa. The position, with the Elbe river behind it, was ill-chosen; indeed it was intended only as a temporary resting place on North Army's retreat back to Olmütz. But Benedek did not reckon with the speed of Moltke's advance. The victories at Skalice and Jicin enabled Moltke to draw his three armies together to attempt a great envelopment of Benedek at Königgrätz. Moltke nearly succeeded, pinning Benedek's left and centre in the morning of 3 July with Elbe and First Armies, and turning his right in the afternoon with Second Army, which struck Benedek's flank with 110,000 men late in the day. Only rain and the distance Second Army had to cover to reach the field saved Benedek. (Paradoxically, only Benedek's excessive caution at Königgrätz saved Moltke. Because Second Army was so slow to arrive, Benedek enjoyed a considerable advantage in troop numbers until late afternoon—240,000 against 135,000—but was so intimidated by the needle gun that he dared not counter-attack.) The Austrians lost 44,000 men at Königgrätz, nearly five times Prussian losses of 9,000. With North Army ruined, Emperor Franz Josef asked for a ceasefire on 22 July, and conceded all of Bismarck's demands: Austria permitted Prussia to dissolve the German Confederation, annex Hanover, and regroup most of the remaining German states into a Prussian-run 'North German Confederation'. In this way, Prussia replaced Austria as the premier German power, and emerged as a serious rival to France in Europe.

The Austrians were more successful in Italy, where Archduke Albrecht's South Army smashed the Italian army at the second battle of *Custoza in June and defeated the Italian navy at Lissa in July. At Custoza, where 75,000 Austrians repulsed 127,000 Italians, the Austrians successfully employed the shock tactics they had used so unsuccessfully against the Prussians. This was more an indictment of the skittish Italian army than a tribute to Austrian tactics, which needlessly piled up 5,000 casualties. At Lissa, Austria's Adm Wilhelm Tegetthoff briefly revolutionized naval tactics. With just seven ironclad frigates, he routed an Italian fleet of eleven ironclads by running under their powerful broadsides and ramming them. For the new kingdom of

Italy, the war of 1866 was an unmitigated disaster. Yet Italy was a Prussian ally and a French client, and shared in the fruits of Moltke's victory in Bohemia and in Napoleon III's efforts to mediate the war's end. After Königgrätz, the Austrians tried to win France to their side by ceding Venetia to *Napoleon III and redeploying South Army to the critical northern front. The French emperor retroceded Venetia to Italy, fulfilling the promise he had made in 1859 to 'unify Italy from the Alps to the Adriatic'. GDWW

Craig, Gordon A., *The Battle of Königgrätz* (London, 1964).

Wawro, Geoffrey, *The Austro-Prussian War* (Cambridge, 1996).

Babur, Emperor (reigned 1526–30), founder of Mughal rule in India. He was a Turco-Mongol prince descended from the great military conqueror *Timur, whose ancestral princedom was Farghana in central Asia (in the modern Tadjikistan and Uzbekistan Republics); but he found himself unable to maintain himself there in face of the rising power of the Uzbeks. After several failures in central Asia, he made exploratory probes from 1519 onwards through Afghanistan into northern India, where the Lodi sultans of Delhi were racked by dissension, and in 1526 achieved a brilliant victory over them at the second battle of *Panipat, occupying Delhi and Agra and extending his authority as far as Bengal before his death.

Babur was a fine general, who valued mobility and kept strict *discipline, and on at least three occasions he defeated numerically superior forces. It was the Portuguese who first introduced artillery into India, but Babur was keen to utilize new technology, and in his *Memoirs* describes how he went to watch the casting of cannon by his Turkish master gunner.   CEB

Hasan, Mohibbul, *Babur, Founder of the Mughal Empire in India* (Delhi, 1985).

Richards, John F., *The New Cambridge History of India*, 1. 5. *The Mughal Empire* (Cambridge, 1993).

Baden-Powell, Lt Gen Robert Stephenson Smyth, 1st Baron Baden-Powell of Gilwell (1857–1941) Commissioned into the 13th Hussars in 1876, 'B-P' became a national hero as the defender of *Mafeking which was besieged by the Boers from October 1899 to May 1900. There is some controversy about his alleged use of ruthless methods during the siege. Later he took a prominent role in the South African Constabulary, and in 1903 became a mildly progressive inspector general of cavalry.

From 1907 onwards Baden-Powell became increasingly involved in the organization he founded, the Boy Scouts.

                                                                GDS

Jeal, Tim, *Baden Powell* (London, 1989).

badges and insignia are allied in military history to the art and science of *heraldry and have grown to encompass paramilitaries and civilians in uniform; in many ways, indeed, they were the earliest form of *uniform. The use of badges to differentiate friend from foe on the battlefield is thought to go back to the earliest times, and references in the Chinese Book of War of *c*.500 BC mention the decoration of banners (see COLOURS, BANNERS, AND STANDARDS) with the figures of animals and birds, real and mythological; it has been assumed that these had some significance as emblems for differing groups to fight beneath. From the classical world the most well-remembered nationally symbolic badge must be the Roman eagle, copied by *Napoleon as well as by 20th-century dictators anxious to emulate the power of Rome, but in *Thebes the figure of the Sphinx and in Greece the owl of Minerva apparently had the same symbolism. From emblems inspired by divinity to ones of a more parochial nature is a short step and the use of items of flora came, by the 7th century AD in Europe, to parallel those of fauna: the case is often cited of the British soldiers of Cadwallader wearing leeks in their *headdress in order to recognize each other at a battle with the Saxons in 640. In Highland Scotland, as well—certainly—as in other remote areas of Europe and elsewhere, tribes adopted local plants as their symbols and this practice persisted until it became linked with the families of the hereditary tribal leaders.

As heraldry developed in Europe from the 12th century, with one of its principal inducements to growth being the necessity of being identifiable on the battlefield when rendered anonymous by enveloping armour, so the badge as it is recognized today developed too. Part of the art of heraldry is to assign to individuals a unique combination of symbols which have meaning for their lives, achievements, localities, and names. While this may have begun with national symbols, it was followed very quickly by individual—and thus local—ones too. Under the *feudal system a knight was expected to be accompanied to war by retainers drawn from his estate; he was expected to arm and clothe such retainers appropriately. In order that his men might be distinguishable as such, as well as part of the larger force the knight was summoned to join, they needed insignia of both a national and a local type. In England the red cross of St George was adopted in an Article of War of 1385 as the national symbol and it developed ultimately into the national flag. As well as wearing the red cross on a white ground, English soldiers wore badges drawn from their masters' heraldry to denote their local allegiance: these developed into regimental badges in the late 17th and 18th centuries.

By the mid-18th century the development of national armies was complete in the West and each nation had its national flag, uniforms, and symbols as well as a sophisticated regimental and inter-regimental system of badges and flags. Such systems were progressions from comparatively primitive origins and, importantly, were just as easily comprehended. The fleur-de-lis of France, the eagles—single or double-headed—of Prussia, Russia, and Austria, the white horse of Hanover: all these appeared on the battlefield on the national uniforms of European soldiers. Monarchs' and emperors' ciphers and the badges and stars of national *knighthood and chivalry underlined soldiers' national allegiances. Colonels of regiments, the descendants of feudal knights with their bands of retainers, used their personal heraldry on regimental badges where and when allowed, although this was increasingly discouraged as armies became more nationally based.

Some national armies responded better to uniformity of badges than others but an area where most agreed that uniformity within a national army was of paramount importance was with badges of *rank: armies are, after all, no matter what the political system of their masters, deeply hierarchical. Once systems of rank badges were established, by the early 19th century in most western nations, attention became focused on badges for proficiency, for battlefield role and for specialization: such marks of distinction developed in the West throughout the 19th century and became codified by regulations.

At the same period, in that most regimental of armies—the British—regimental badges burgeoned, decorating and differentiating soldiers' uniforms with ancient heraldic badges and symbols—like the Sphinx for Egypt and the tiger for India—indicative of honourable past regimental service. In armies where regimental distinctions were less encouraged, like that of Germany, such distinctions were borne on the regimental colours rather than by the individual soldier; Britain bore them on the colours too.

The 20th century has seen both a reduction and a proliferation of badges and insignia. The two world wars necessitated the introduction of the formation sign as regiments became grouped together in formations, such as divisions and brigades, within their national armies. Regimental reductions and amalgamations have telescoped regimental heraldry, often rendering it complicated and contrived in the process. Ships have adopted badges and naval ratings copied soldiers in their range of proficiency and trade badges; *air forces have inevitably followed suit. Developments post-1945 have been strongly influenced by American fashions in badges and, in those countries imitative of American uniform, soldiers of all ranks now wear more badges than ever before, especially when on parade. In the military headquarters on the continent of Europe, as at the Pentagon, the pendant metal enamelled badges of officers attached to formations such as SHAPE (Supreme Headquarters, Allied Powers, Europe) accompany engraved plastic name-tags and laminated security passes hung from chains. The consistent thread of the badge's function as an identifier of friend and foe continues.   SCW

Brook-Little, John P., *Boutell's Heraldry* (London, 1973).
Cole, Howard, *Formation Badges of World War 2* (London, 1793).
Edwards, T. J., *Regimental Badges* (Aldershot, 1951).
May, William E., Carman, William Y., and Tanner, John, *Badges and Insignia of the British Armed Services* (London, 1974).

baggage Generic term covering the portable equipment of an army. In the ancient world the *logistic needs of armies were relatively straightforward compared to the complex array *matériel* needed today. Despite this any prolonged campaigning of significant size required some means of keeping supplies and equipment up with the fighting force. *Xenophon refers to twenty days of provision, mostly dried and concentrated foodstuffs being transported with the Greek army.

The *Roman army baggage train contained all the features of subsequent logistic tails—food, ammunition, and specialist equipment. When on campaign the Roman legions used pack animals to transport the ten-man tents used by the legionnaires and spare missiles for the *archers, *slingers, and catapults. It is also recorded that *Caesar used shovels from his baggage train to dig his army through snow drifts.

The *Byzantine army developed a well-equipped baggage train system. For every sixteen infantrymen there was a cart containing 'a hand-mill, a bill hook, a saw, two spades, a mallet, a large, wicker basket, a scythe, and two pick axes' (*Leo VI, 'the Wise', *Tactica, c.*900). During the Middle Ages this degree of complexity in logistics was relatively rare. The few carts that followed European armies were a disorganized affair seldom containing the amount of foodstuffs needed for the troops. This inevitably led to plundering.

French *camp followers at the battle of *Agincourt famously attacked the English baggage, causing *Henry V to order the massacre of prisoners taken in the battle.

As armies became larger so did their baggage trains. By the beginning of the 17th century *Maurice of Nassau took 3,000 wagons with him to support 24,000 men and the Spanish general *Spinola had over 2,000 for just 15,000 men. When armies consisted of fairly limited numbers of missile weapons ammunition only formed a minor part of the baggage train; with the introduction of widespread firearm use this changed. During the *British civil wars the parliamentarian *New Model Army needed over a thousand horses to move its artillery and baggage train.

Baggage trains did not just consist of the essentials for waging war such as provisions and ammunition. The personnel effects of officers often comprised a significant portion of the baggage train's total. The royalists under Charles I had a train which included 'light ladies of pleasure'. The business opportunities offered by a large army were often hard to resist.

The speed by which armies could move was usually restricted by the pace of advance that could be achieved by its baggage train. The inadequacies of the road network in Europe meant that, such as they were, they were usually only passable during the summer. Whole armies traversing the same road quickly found themselves wading through mud. Even in good weather most armies could only manage between 8 and 10 miles (13 and 16 km) per day. The limits placed on strategic mobility by the inadequacies of the baggage train system led to the development of a *magazine network though they continued in the guise of supply trains.   JR-W

Bagration, Gen Prince Pyotr Ivanovich (1765–
1812), Russian general of infantry, hero of the 1812 campaign against Napoleon, born of an old Georgian aristocratic family, and a pupil of *Suvorov and *Kutuzov. In 1799, as a major general, he commanded the advance guard in Suvorov's north Italian and Swiss campaign. At *Austerlitz in 1805 he commanded the right wing of the Allied army, successfully repulsing what *Napoleon had planned as the main French attack, and then covered the withdrawal of the main Allied force. In 1812 he lent enthusiastic support to Kutuzov's scorched earth strategy. At *Borodino, on 7 September, he commanded the left wing of the Russian army, repelling all attacks, but was mortally wounded and died two weeks later. Loved by his men, a tactical innovator, and possessing extraordinary physical courage, he was a quintessential Russian (albeit actually a Georgian) hero.   CDB

BAGRATION, Operation (1944). The Belorussian
operation by the Red Army between 23 June and 29 August 1944 was the largest of WW II, resulting in the destruction of German Army Group Centre and the reconquest of what is now Belarus. Named after the Napoleonic war hero, and timed to begin on the third anniversary of the German invasion on 22 June (in fact it was a day late), the sense of grand opera reflected its scale. Four Fronts (army groups) were involved: first Baltic (Bagramyan), Third Belorussian (Chernyakovsky), Second Belorussian (Zakharov), and first Belorussian (Rokossovsky), totalling 1.4 million men. The Germans were in deeply echeloned defensive positions 155–68 miles (250–70 km) deep, with 1.2 million. The Soviets attacked simultaneously in six places along a 683 mile (1,100 km) front, pushing west 342–73 miles (550–600 km). Minsk was recaptured on 3 July, and by 29 August the Red Army was close to Warsaw (see WARSAW UPRISING) and well into East Prussia.   CDB

Bailén (Baylen), battle of (1808). Fought in southern
Spain on 19 July, the battle of Bailén constituted a serious embarrassment to the Napoleonic imperium. Having in May overthrown the Spanish Bourbons and thus provoked a general uprising, *Napoleon ordered the forces that he had over the preceding months sent into Spain to occupy various strategic points. Among these was the port of Cadiz, the troops detailed for this purpose consisting of the first division of the army corps commanded by Gen Pierre Dupont de l'Etang. Led by Dupont himself, this division advanced as far as Cordoba which it sacked on 7 June. However, alarmed at his growing isolation, Dupont fell back on Andujar. A further two divisions were sent to assist him and by early July over 20,000 French troops were concentrated around Andujar and Bailén. By this time some 30,000 Spanish regulars under Gen Francisco Javier Castaños were attempting to envelop him from the west and south, but, though his men were poor quality second-line troops, Dupont should still have been able to escape. However, when he finally resolved on retreat a bizarre series of accidents enabled the Spaniards to occupy Bailén and cut off Dupont and a large portion of his army. On 19 July the French general tried to fight his way out of the trap, but he completely mishandled the situation and, with overwhelming numbers of enemy troops closing on all sides, was compelled to order a ceasefire. After much argument, it was eventually agreed that Dupont's entire army—not just that part of it caught in the trap—should be repatriated by sea. This agreement was never honoured: though Dupont was sent home, his troops were eventually left to die of starvation on the barren island of Cabrera. The episode was an unusual, and deeply resented, humiliation for Napoleon.   CJE

Oman, Charles, *A History of the Peninsular War* (Oxford, 1902–30).

Baker rifle Ezekiel Baker, a Whitechapel gunmaker and
protégé of the Prince of Wales (the future George IV),

designed a *flintlock muzzle-loading rifle which armed the Corps of Riflemen raised by Col Coote Manningham in 1800. Although it was not strictly speaking the first rifle in British service, for the *Ferguson breech-loader and continental *Jäger rifles had been used in North America, it was the first on general issue to rifle units. There were several versions, as well as a cavalry carbine, .62 or .70 inch in calibre with seven-groove rifling. Many were fitted with a brass-hilted sword *bayonet. It was far more accurate than the contemporary infantry musket, albeit more difficult to load: in a trial of 1803 a Baker rifle scored 9 out of 12 hits on a target 200 yards (183 metres) away. The weapon was last manufactured in 1838, but was used as late as 1851. In the 1990s it gained fame as the weapon of Richard Sharpe's men in the *Sharpe* books and television series. RH

Balkan wars (1912–13), two vicious wars in Europe's benighted south-eastern region, which ended Ottoman rule in the Balkans, leading to the a succession of ethnic and religious conflicts throughout the 20th century. The first Balkan war (9 October 1912–30 May 1913) was waged between the Balkan Alliance (Bulgaria, Greece, Serbia, and Montenegro) and the Ottoman empire. In the second (29 June–10 August 1913) the contestants changed places, with Bulgaria on one side against Greece, Turkey, Serbia, Montenegro, and Romania on the other. Although overshadowed by WW I, which after all began as a 'third Balkan war', the wars were still studied after 1918 as useful precursors of future conflict. The technology and tactics of 1914– 18 were mostly present. Armies deployed on extended fronts, and quick-firing *artillery, *machine guns, *armoured cars, and aircraft were all used, but large-scale manoeuvre was still possible. The wars are also good examples of coalition warfare and co-ordinated attacks by groups of states.

In August 1912 there was an anti-Turkish revolt in the Ottoman provinces of Albania and Macedonia. Bulgaria, Serbia, and Greece, which effectively surrounded the area, demanded Turkey grant autonomy to Macedonia and Thrace. Turkey refused and mobilized its army. On 9 October Montenegro attacked, followed by Bulgaria, Serbia, and Greece on 18 October. The Balkan Alliance mobilized 950,000 men and deployed between 600,000 and 700,000 with 1,500 guns. The Greek fleet also had 4 battleships, 3 cruisers, and 19 smaller vessels. Turkey mobilized 850,000 troops of whom 300,000 to 400,000 were deployed into the theatre of war with 1,100 guns, and a slightly smaller fleet than Greece. Although the forces appeared fairly evenly matched, the Balkan Alliance had better equipment, particularly artillery.

Three Bulgarian armies moved south-east against Istanbul, while three Serbian armies moved against the *Turks in Macedonia from the north in concert with Montenegrin forces from the west. Recognizing Bulgaria as the greatest danger, the Turks deployed the bulk of their forces (185,000

men and 750 guns) against it. Tsar Ferdinand of Bulgaria was known to covet Istanbul and the restoration of the Byzantine empire. The Bulgarian II Corps besieged Adrianople (now Edirne) and used an aircraft to drop bombs, which the Bulgarians claim was the first air bombing raid in history (see ITALO-TURKISH WAR). The Turks were beaten back in a series of encounter battles but the Bulgarian armies were unable to pursue and the Turks dug in at Catalca, about 25 miles (40 km) west of Istanbul.

The great powers watched events in the Balkans with alarm. Although Russia supported the Balkan Alliance, it did not want Bulgaria controlling access to the Black Sea, and the Central Powers, Germany and Austria-Hungary, did not want the Ottoman empire to fall apart. Under pressure from the great powers, an armistice between Bulgaria, Serbia, and Turkey was concluded in December. However, on 23 January 1913 the 'Young Turk' party seized power in Istanbul and hostilities erupted again. After more Turkish defeats, including the fall of Adrianople, peace was concluded in April although Montenegro carried on besieging Shkodra and did not sign until the London Conference the following month. In a historic peace treaty, Turkey gave up virtually all its European possessions, ending four centuries of rule in the Balkans.

No sooner was peace signed than the victors began to squabble among themselves. Serbia felt cheated of access to the Adriatic, and demanded compensation with Macedonian territory. Greece felt Bulgaria, now its neighbour, had been given too much former Ottoman territory. The second Balkan war began on 29 June when Bulgaria, egged on by Germany and Austria, attacked Serb and Greek forces in Macedonia. The Serbs stopped them and counter-attacked. On 10 July Romania, to the north, joined in, attacking Bulgaria. The Turks, smarting from the loss of their European territories, seized the chance to grab some of them back, capturing Adrianople. On 29 July, attacked from all sides and fearing complete defeat, Bulgaria surrendered. The Bucharest Peace Conference on 10 August was attended by Bulgaria, Serbia, Montenegro, Greece, and Romania. Bulgaria was deprived of most of its gains from the first Balkan war. The territories given to Serbia included Macedonia and Kosovo. At the Istanbul conference on 29 November Turkey regained a strip of land including Adrianople.

The Balkan wars were very much a dress rehearsal for WW I. The Balkan Alliance fielded 474 machine guns, the Turks 556, and entrenchments were widely used. Following the first bombing raids, ground forces began making preparations to resist air attack. CDB

balloons Two major categories of balloon have been put to military use during the last 200 years. The first, traditional balloons, are pear-shaped, carry a basket suspended underneath, but lack any means of propulsion or guidance. They float with the prevailing wind, or are tethered to the ground. Although many inventors, notably the Montgolfier brothers, had demonstrated the technique, it gained credibility in 1785 when Jean-Pierre Blanchard crossed the English Channel in two hours in a hot-air balloon. Revolutionary France began to experiment with tethered balloons for *reconnaissance, for example at the battle of *Fleurus in 1794. *Napoleon used them again at the siege of Mantua (1797) and they were more feared than considered for an invasion of Britain.

In 1849, Austrian troops unleashed unmanned balloons carrying explosives triggered by time fuses against Venice, an experiment discontinued after the vagaries of wind direction made them an embarrassment. During the *American civil war, Thadeus Lowe formed a balloon corps for the Union army and directed artillery fire from on high using a *telegraph. During the *Franco-Prussian war, balloons were used during the siege of Paris, carrying 167 people out of the city and dropping three million *psychological warfare leaflets on the Prussian siege lines. At this time, French and German balloonists first exchanged fire, though no hits were recorded. By 1900, all modern armies had established balloon corps to provide timely and accurate battlefield intelligence.

During WW I, all sides used tethered balloons for reconnaissance and artillery spotting, but they remained vulnerable to ground fire and aircraft. WW II saw the development of so-called barrage balloons, which were moored over vulnerable targets, to deny enemy aircraft the ability to make low-level attacks. Barrage balloon cables tore the wings off more than 200 V-1 flying bombs during 1944–5.

The second category of balloon is the airship, or dirigible (Fr.: *dirigible*, capable of being guided). This possessed a rigid, cigar-shaped frame in which the 'gasbags' were stored. Although the first (steam-powered) dirigible flew in 1852, it was not until 1907 that the British army acquired one, which could fly for 24 hours at up to 50 knots. The Italians first used them in action during the *Italo-Turkish war of 1912, and all sides developed airships before WW I. Airships built by Count Ferdinand von Zeppelin's company and the rival Shutte-Lantz flew 285 sorties over England, dropping 275 tons of bombs, and caused many British aircraft to be diverted from the front, but the use of highly inflammable hydrogen for lift doomed them once the fighters started using incendiary *bullets.

The British abandoned research into dirigibles between the wars after the crash of the R-101 in 1930, but interest continued elsewhere. The USA had a world monopoly of helium, so the Germans continued to use hydrogen, resulting in the fiery death of the *Hindenburg* in 1937. However, they still used their allegedly civilian dirigibles to conduct military reconnaissance of the British coast prior to WW II. The US Navy lost interest after two enormous dirigibles, equipped with unique little biplane fighters that hung on hooks below them, went down at sea with the loss of all hands.

Although some dirigible 'blimps' were used by the US Navy for coastal patrols through the 1940s and 1950s, and the Bundeswehr used them to distribute propaganda leaflets in the *Cold War, balloons and airships have all but faded from military use. Some limited trials have been conducted using blimps as platforms for airborne early warning *radar, but their slowness and vulnerability limits their application.   APC-A

Baltimore, attack on (1814), episode in the *War of 1812 that inspired Francis Scott Key to write 'The Star-Spangled Banner', belatedly the US national anthem. After sacking Washington, the British fleet bombarded the coastal works of Baltimore on 13–14 September. Hulks had been sunk to prevent the approach of larger warships, so rocket and mortar boats were employed. The 'banner' was a huge, specially made flag flying over Fort McHenry, the 'red glare' came from the ever-erratic Congreve *rockets, while the 'bombs bursting in air' were presumably the product of incorrectly cut fuses. Once it was decided not to mount a land assault, the attack was abandoned.

HEB

Bannockburn, battle of (1314), where the Scots under Robert *Bruce decisively defeated a substantial English army. An agreement had been reached in 1313 that Stirling castle would *capitulate at midsummer the following year if the English failed to relieve it. The Scots prepared a strong position near the castle to meet Edward II's relieving force. The fighting took place over two days on 23 and 24 June. On the first day the Bruce killed the English champion Bohun in single combat, after which a mounted force under Robert Clifford failed to outflank the Scots, and could not break through their *schiltroms. On the second day a dispute between the earls of Gloucester and Hereford over who should lead the van underlined the weakness of the English command structure. Gloucester died in a heroic and futile charge into the Scots schiltroms. The Scots had the upper hand in the fighting that followed; the boggy ground was unsuitable for the English cavalry, and when Edward II himself fled, the English forces disintegrated. The battle demonstrated, as in other 14th-century examples, the deficiencies of cavalry when faced with well-organized infantry in a strong defensive position.   MCP

Barrow, G. W. S., *Robert Bruce and the Community of the Realm of Scotland* (London, 1965).

Barbarossa, Adm Khair-ad-Din (c.1483–1546), North African pirate. In 1518 he paid homage to the Ottoman *Turk sultan, thereby gaining forces to conquer his home base, capturing Algiers in 1529. From here the infamous Barbary pirates terrorized Christian coasts and shipping for three centuries. In 1533, he was made admiral-in-chief of the Ottoman empire. In 1534, he conquered Tunis, although the Habsburg Emperor *Charles V recovered the city in 1535. In 1538, he defeated the Venetian fleet under *Doria at Prezeva, which preserved Ottoman naval dominance in the eastern Mediterranean until *Lepanto.

MB

Cook, M. A., *A History of the Ottoman Empire to 1730* (Cambridge, 1976).

'Barbarossa', Frederick I Hohenstauffen (c.1123–90).

Duke of Swabia from 1147, Frederick succeeded his uncle as Holy Roman Emperor in 1152. Nicknamed 'Barbarossa' from his red beard, Frederick was perhaps the dominant figure of his age. He was a bold and skilful general, an accomplished speaker, good administrator, and natural leader, although his driving ambition sometimes manifested itself in cruelty. He spent most of his reign in conflict with refractory vassals in Germany, the rebellious cities of Lombardy, and the papacy. He could not consolidate initial success in Lombardy, although he sacked Milan in 1162 and went on to take Rome. In 1176 the cities of the Lombard League, aided by Venice and the pope, defeated him at Legnano, in an unusual victory of civic infantry over feudal cavalry. Thereafter he proved conciliatory to Lombards and pope alike, converting the former into loyal subjects and in 1177 acknowledging the latter, thus paving the way for a final agreement in 1183. He bought off his strongest vassals by conferring greater titles on them, and asserted his *feudal rights over states like Poland and Burgundy.

Frederick had served with his uncle Conrad in the Second *Crusade, and in 1188, though in his 70th year, he took the Cross again, and set out for Outremer in 1189 with the largest single force ever to go on a crusade. After a difficult journey across Byzantine territory he reached Turkey, only to be drowned crossing the Calycadnus river in June 1190. *Saladin, who had feared him, regarded his death as a miracle. The emperor's body, imperfectly preserved, accompanied his army, but both disintegrated. Most of Frederick was interred in Antioch, while his army, reduced by sickness and desertion, went on to join other crusading contingents in the siege of Acre. The towering achievements of his lifetime and the strange circumstances of his death and burial helped make him the German King Arthur, the once and future king, still sleeping beneath the hills awaiting the call to arms. His name was an evocative codeword for the German invasion of Russia in 1941.

RH

BARBAROSSA, Operation (1941),

correctly 'case BARBAROSSA', was the code name for Germany's surprise attack on the USSR on 22 June 1941. It was the most ambitious campaign of WW II, planned and prepared to achieve by combat a strategic objective within a single theatre of war and a set time frame. It was also the centrepiece of a geopolitical vision clearly predicated on *genocide.

Hitler's war against the USSR had two facets, a military and an ideological one, since BARBAROSSA was meant to solve Germany's strategic dilemma and at the same time conquer *Lebensraum* (living space). Hitler succeeded in branding BARBAROSSA a war of annihilation against Bolshevism and Jewry because the army high command and other senior commanders willingly allowed the troops to 'fight the ideological war' alongside the various *SS forces. Thus the Nazi concept of extermination could also become a component of operations, rear area security, and exploitation. The brutalization of German soldiers had begun in Poland. The barbarization of warfare itself would begin on Soviet territories. Soviet atrocities and partisan activities fanned the fires of war. Hitler used them to camouflage extermination as a war necessity.

On 18 December 1940, *Hitler had issued Directive No. 21: 'to crush Soviet Russia in one rapid campaign even before the conclusion of the war with England'. The essence of the initial phase of operations was to destroy the bulk of the Red Army in a series of sweeping encirclements west of the rivers Dnieper and Dvina and to prevent the withdrawal of Soviet forces capable of combat into the expanse of Russian space. Then, by means of rapid *pursuit, the final Soviet defeat was to be accomplished and the general line Volga–Archangel to be reached within three months. Thus, no preparations were made for winter fighting. The air force's task was both *interdiction near the front and direct support of the army on the battlefield. Attacks on the Soviet arms industry in the Urals area were to be left until after the conclusion of mobile warfare. The navy's mission was to prevent Soviet forces from breaking out of the Baltic Sea.

By the end of July 1940 Hitler had decided to 'finish off' the USSR in the spring of 1941. That decision was a symbiosis of calculation and dogma, strategy and ideology, foreign policy and racial policy. The destruction of the USSR, Hitler's ultimate goal since the 1920s, would now serve as an indirect means of forcing Britain out of the war as well as opening up the acquisition of *Lebensraum*. This latter was an amalgam of notions of economy, settlement, and power politics, which also included the annihilation of 'Jewish Bolshevism'.

To defeat the Red Army, Germany massed over 3 million men and 152 divisions, including 17 panzer and 13 motorized divisions with a total of 3,350 tanks, 600,000 motor vehicles, and 625,000 horses. They were supported by 7,146 artillery pieces and 1,950 operational aircraft. The Finnish army added 17 divisions and 2 brigades, while Romania's contribution consisted of 14 divisions, 7 brigades, and 1 reinforced panzer regiment. Three army group headquarters were responsible for operations in one of the main sectors: North, led by FM von Leeb, in the direction of *Leningrad; Centre, under FM von Bock, toward Smolensk; and Army Group South, FM von Rundstedt commanding, toward Kiev. In addition, there was an Army of Norway, an expeditionary force of which was to advance toward Murmansk. These four senior field commands each had one Luftflotte (Air fleet) allocated to them, commanded by Col-Gen Keller, FM Kesselring, Gen Löhr, and Col-Gen Stumpff. The mass of the German offensive power was located north of the Pripet Marshes, with two of the four Panzergruppen assigned to Army Group Centre. Overall control lay with the army high command under FM von Brauchitsch and his operational aide Col-Gen Halder.

Drunk with the victory over France and contemptuous of the Soviets, Hitler and his advisers wrongly assessed both Soviet and German capabilities. The perception of a weak USSR, a 'colossus with feet of clay', of a Red Army without leadership, and of an inferior Russian people coincided with the belief in German superiority in experience, mobility, and staff work, as well as in racial qualities. As no aggressive *intentions* were attributed to *Stalin, Hitler and his advisers were not disturbed by the *ability* of the Red Army to fight a war. Hitler was far more worried that Stalin could upset his plans by being accommodating. It was assumed that the communist regime in the USSR would soon collapse under the German hammer blows. BARBAROSSA, with its fixation on a single summer's campaign, cannot be considered a masterpiece of military *art. It stands as a testimony to the necessity of harmonizing reach and grasp, will and means. Makeshift solutions were seen as a palliative against the truth that only 20 per cent of the German army in the east could engage in the envisaged rapid and large-scale mobile warfare: it was, as some of the critics of *blitzkrieg had warned, a two-tier structure.

The successful battles of the frontiers, especially encirclements at Bialystok and Minsk, gave the Nazi leadership the impression that BARBAROSSA had been accomplished within two weeks, whereas the struggle had only begun. The Red Army did not fall to pieces and even counter-attacked vigorously. Hitler and his advisers were forced to change their objectives. Already in August 1941, long before the offensive had come to a halt at the gates of Leningrad, *Moscow, and Rostov, it dawned on them that the blitzkrieg in the east had failed. The strategic consequences for Germany were grave: the USSR would still be fighting in 1942, Britain remained undefeated, and in December the USA entered the war. Instead of a quick victory, BARBAROSSA ushered in one of the most bitter and costly struggles of history.   JF1

Glantz, David M., and House, Jonathan, *When Titans Clashed* (Lawrence, Kan., 1995).
Militärgeschichtliches Forschungsamt (ed.), *Germany and WW II*, vol. 4 (Oxford, 1998).
Muller, Richard, *The German Air War in Russia* (Baltimore, 1992).

Bar-Lev, Gen Chaim (1924–94), Israeli general and politician. The Austrian-born Bar-Lev played a key role in the *Arab–Israeli wars. During the War of Independence (1948–9), he commanded a battalion of the Narev Brigade. By the Sinai war in 1956, Bar-Lev was the commander of the Armoured Corps, and his troops were the first to reach the canal during the *Suez campaign. During the Six Day War (June 1967), he was DCOS to Yitzhak Rabin. After studying in the USA and France, he became COS of the *IDF on 1 January 1968, a position he held until 1971.

During Bar-Lev's tenure the IDF shifted its focus from offensive to defensive operations, designed to protect the territory gained in the previous war and to reduce manpower demands. He ordered the creation of a defensive line along the eastern bank of the Suez Canal. This so-called Bar-Lev Line, completed between January and February 1969, consisted of a series of forward fortifications strong enough to withstand enemy artillery, which were supported by armoured forces in the rear. Although it had gradually become a more complex defensive position (in all more than $40 million was spent), the line was easily penetrated by the Egyptians at the beginning of the Yom Kippur war in 1973 and the armoured 'fire brigades' were ambushed and mauled by Egyptian *anti-armour forces.

Bar-Lev was later elected to the Knesset and served as a minister in various cabinets between 1972 and 1977.   RTF

Barons' war (1264–7), when the conflict between Henry III and the baronial opposition led by Simon de *Montfort, Earl of Leicester, turned into civil war. The war began with the royalist capture of Northampton in April; in May de Montfort challenged the royal army at Lewes. The battle was a disaster for Henry III and his son Edward. De Montfort, however, was not able to capitalize fully on his victory, and in May 1265 Edward escaped from custody and joined forces with Roger Mortimer and other lords of the Welsh marches. In the campaign which followed, Edward first defeated Simon's eldest son at Kenilworth by a surprise attack. Simon himself was then hemmed in by royalist forces at Evesham in a campaign skilfully managed by Edward and his allies. The defensive formation de Montfort's troops adopted could not resist the cavalry charges by the forces under Edward and the Earl of Gloucester and the battle culminated in his death. Some of de Montfort's supporters held out longer in Kenilworth, and others in the Isle of Ely, but the back of the rebellion was broken.   MCP

Maddicott, J. R., *Simon de Montfort* (Cambridge, 1994).

barracks A building or group of buildings designed to provide accommodation for military personnel. In ancient and medieval times, barracks often formed part of, or were attached to, fortifications, housing the troops that manned them. For example, barracks were incorporated at intervals along the length of Hadrian's wall in northern England, and developed into permanent settlements.

For much of European history barracks were the exception rather than the rule, and soldiers were *billeted in civilian lodgings or public houses. This was a generally unsatisfactory process, and barracks became increasingly common from the late 17th century, their construction paralleling and exemplifying the rise of standing armies. Barracks, like fortresses, were embodiments of a royal authority that their imposing interiors often reflected. *Vauban's masterpiece, the citadel of Lille, contains stately barracks designed by a local architect, Simon Vollant, while the stern Fort George, in the Scottish Highlands, contains granite barrack blocks intended almost as much to impress as to provide accommodation.

Barracks lying outside fortresses were rarely built to resist formal attack, but were usually robust enough to provide security against riot and insurrection, and the siting and construction of barracks often formed part of a government's policy on the maintenance of order. In Second Empire Paris, for example, inner-city barracks were designated as key strong points from which troops could move to secure railway stations and other vulnerable points, while outlying barracks, like that at Vincennes, to the east, could provide quick-reaction forces, notably artillery, of proven effectiveness against barricades built on Baron Haussmann's new wide boulevards. Although there was little perceived risk of large-scale civil disorder in Victorian England, the barracks built to house the county regiments created by Cardwell's reforms in the 1870s were of a uniform pattern, and embodied lofty red-brick 'keeps' which still grin out across many country towns.

Barracks were designed as much to contain as to impress. Access was generally strictly supervised, with soldiers entering and leaving past a guardroom, which housed a small detachment of men on duty 24 hours a day, as well as cells to contain petty offenders and the inebriate. A *sentry at the gate controlled access, ensuring that soldiers walking out into the town were properly dressed and those returning were fit for readmittance, as well as deterring girls—attracted by love or more pecuniary motives—hawkers, and the curious. Most barracks had a drill-square at their centre, surrounded by accommodation blocks, offices, storerooms, and, in armies like the British where officers messed in barracks rather than ate in restaurants outside, an officers' mess. The internal layout of barrack blocks was often a good deal less impressive than their imposing exteriors. Soldiers slept, often two to a bed, in large dormitories. Bucket sanitation (in the British army the vessel was neatly termed the 'sip pot') was common until at least the late 19th century. Initially dining rooms were uncommon: men messed in small groups in their rooms, with food collected from the cookhouse by one of their number. Recreation was at first limited or non-existent, but during the second half of the 19th century many armies were influenced by liberalizing officers and officials who sought to introduce canteens where men could supplement their food, and proper dining rooms were issue food could be eaten in relative comfort.

Barrack life (in some respects not wholly unlike prison life) emphasized that, as the sociologist Stanley Goffman maintains, the armies of the age were 'total institutions', in which men were subjected to a control which usually broke down social divisions and weakened (if it did not totally extinguish) external ties. A man's life was minutely supervised, by corporals who normally had a screened-off 'bunk' in the barrack room, watchful sergeants, and more remote officers. Privacy was scarce. Men were not allowed to 'walk out' until their training was well advanced, and they could dress smartly enough to 'pass the guard' on their way out. Confinement to barracks for a specified time was generally the lowest rung on the ladder of military punishments. It is small wonder that both the French and German armies offered 'one-year volunteers' (well-educated conscripts who served for a year and generally passed to the reserve as officers) the privilege of living out of barracks. It was not just soldiers who lived in barracks. Some states maintained paramilitary police (like the *gendarmerie in France) whose status was underlined by the fact that they lived in barracks. When more conventional police were forced to live in barracks or fortified police stations, it was a sure sign, like the Royal Irish Constabulary during the *Anglo-Irish war, that they were losing their grip on the civil community they needed to form part of.

Old-style barracks are inappropriate for the professional armies which are an increasing feature of the last third of the 20th century. A high level of social control is generally deemed unnecessary, certainly once basic training is complete. The retention of volunteer soldiers demands improved food and accommodation, and an increasing proportion of officers and NCOs are married, requiring married quarters or hirings outside barracks. If the barracks eventually shares the fate of the conscript army whose rise it accompanied, it will live on in memory and literature, with P. C. Wren's character Henri de Beaujolais learning the hard lessons of survival in the barracks of the Blue Hussars, and the haunting melody of Lili Marlene recalling heart-rending moments 'underneath the lamp-light, by the barrack-gate'.   AH/RH

barrage A static or rolling barrier of fire put down in front of defending troops or moving at a pre-planned rate in front of troops in the assault. The creeping barrage was first used in 1915 to protect attacking infantry who were most vulnerable from the time that the bombardment of enemy positions lifted to the moment that they reached those positions. The barrage maintained a wall of fire as close as possible in front of troops while they crossed no man's land and then moved on into the enemy's deeper defences. It would then halt to form a protective barrier against any enemy counter-attack. Planning a barrage required high level co-ordination by the newly created artillery staffs, but its control was most effective when delegated to the lower level commanders being supported. Early barrages often failed when their rigid, pre-planned timetables were overtaken by the unforeseen. If troops were held up by the enemy, the barrage would move on regardless, leaving them exposed; and rapid success often went unexploited because they could not advance through their own slower moving barrage. The ideal was to achieve tactical control over a flexible barrage, but until WW II *radios were too primitive to permit this. In the latter years of WW I, barrages became ever more sophisticated. Instead of advancing in straight lines at a constant rate, they were designed to match the shape of enemy trench lines and often dwelt on enemy strong points for longer periods before moving on to the next. The enemy would try to outwit the expected barrage by withdrawing from their front line or by placing machine-gun posts in no man's land. Sometimes a barrage would pass over sheltering enemy troops who would emerge only to find it rolling back over them.

An effective barrage required technical skills which only reached maturity in late 1917. Accuracy was all important and this required the guns to have precise survey data of their individual positions, friendly trench lines, up-to-date meteorological information, data of each gun's barrel-wear and muzzle-velocity, and measurements of propellent charge temperature and variations in shell weight. The closer the barrage could be safely placed to friendly troops, the fewer casualties they would suffer from the enemy, even if they were occasionally victims of their own guns. This principle was also held to apply in WW II. During the *Vietnam war, US army firebases such as that at Khe Sanh in early 1968 fired elaborate barrages. Long-range heavy artillery and aircraft delivered walls of fire to seal off the battlefield while lighter artillery raked up and down like a piston. The barrage survived in Soviet *Cold War armoured *doctrine with the 122 mm 2S1 designed to deliver fire directly onto enemy positions in the assault.   JBAB

Bailey, J. B. A., *Field Artillery and Firepower* (Oxford, 1989).
Griffith, P., *Battle Tactics of the Western Front* (London, 1994).
Johnson, C., *The Big Guns Go to War* (London, 1975).
Zabecki, D., *Steel Wind* (Westport, Conn., 1994).

Barry, James Miranda (1795–1865). Barry entered the British army as a hospital assistant in 1813, was appointed assistant surgeon in 1815, and rose to become inspector-general of the Army Medical Department in 1858. It was only after Dr Barry's death in 1865 that she was discovered to be a woman, having concealed her gender throughout her service.

While serving at the Cape of Good Hope, Barry was described as the most skilful of physicians and the most wayward of men: she was credited with a quarrelsome temper,

and fought a duel. She was rather feminine in appearance, with red hair, pale skin, and high cheekbones. It has been suggested that, like Polly Oliver in the popular song, she had decided to join the army to follow her love, an army surgeon, but this would hardly justify such consistent deception. She remains the most remarkable example of that numerous body of *women who served as men, sometimes pursuing a lover, but perhaps as often, as Mary Fleming Zirin puts it in her introduction to the journals of a female Russian cavalry officer, 'in rebellion against women's fate'.

RH

Rose, June, *Perfect Gentleman: The Life of Dr James Miranda Barry* (London, 1977).
Zirin, Mary Fleming (trans. and ed.), *The Cavalry Maiden* (London, 1990).

battle honours is the term applied to distinctions commemorative of battles which are placed, by order of government, on a regiment's *colours, *badges and insignia, drums, and other appropriate appointments. The origin of battle honours in the form of the names of battles is obscure but probably originated on the European continent in the early 18th century. *Heraldic augmentations for gallant individuals are recorded as far back as the battle of *Flodden in 1513, but the first British battle honour to be granted was that to the 18th Regiment of Foot for *Namur in 1695. Battle honours on colours were rare in France before 1789 and *Napoleon is credited with instituting them in 1796. Although the British practice has been widely emulated, some nations commemorate battle honours with streamers borne on the staff and some decorate their colours with medallions. Emblems have been used too, in the British army: the Sphinx signifies service in Egypt in 1801 and the tiger and elephant symbolize service in India in the 18th century. The battle honour Waterloo was shared by British and Prussian regiments, who found themselves enemies a century later.   SCW

Edwards, T. J., *Military Customs* (Aldershot, 1950).
Milne, Samuel M., *The Standards and Colours of the Army* (Leeds, 1893).

bayonet (from Bayonne, a town in south-west France noted for both its cutlery and its hams). 'Les bayonettes de Bayonne' were referred to in the late 16th century and appear to have been short daggers carried in their belts by sportsmen. They had tapering cylindrical grips, broad flat blades, and wide cross-guards so that, in an emergency—upon being charged by an enraged or wounded boar for example—the resolute sportsman could jam his bayonet into the muzzle of his musket and thus quickly convert it into a makeshift weapon not dissimilar from a boar-spear. Such bayonets would now be defined as 'plug' bayonets—since they formed a plug for the muzzle—and were retained by continental sportsmen, particularly in Spain, as part of their decorative dress until the mid-19th century.

The first military use of the plug bayonet seems, appropriately, to have been by French soldiers serving in the Netherlands *c.*1647; these were described as having both blades and hilts of 12 inches (30.5 cm) in length. In 1663 a reference was made to the refurbishment of 'Byonetts' by three London cutlers for the British government and in 1672, 900 'Byonetts' were issued to Prince Rupert's Dragoons—the earliest known issue of bayonets to the British army. The disadvantages of the plug bayonet could be painful, as the English discovered at *Killicrankie, and alternatives were experimented with in the last quarter of the 17th century, including bayonets which hinged at the muzzle and folded back beneath the stock, as some do on today's infantry weapons.

The most militarily acceptable alternative to the plug bayonet was found to be the socket bayonet. This mounted a spear-blade, usually of triangular section, on the side of a metal socket which fitted over the muzzle of the *musket, thus allowing the musket to be loaded (cautiously) and fired while the bayonet was fixed. With the socket bayonet, the soldier was thus equipped with both musket and short pike and this type of bayonet remained the standard issue for the majority of armies until the 19th century. The socket usually had a zigzag slot cut into it, which engaged on a lug on the barrel and was turned so that it locked. This lug in turn became an early foresight. This system of locking often proved faulty in action and so numerous systems of locking the bayonet more firmly to the barrel were experimented with during the long life of the socket bayonet.

Although they seriously affected the balance of the musket, given the notorious inaccuracy of the latter this was not judged to be a great loss, and the long sword bayonet became a feature in most armies. Prussian military rifles first mounted sword bayonets in 1787 and the armies of most other countries followed suit over the following 30 or 40 years. The phallic symbolism of the sword bayonet, reinforced by the rampant manner in which the rifle and bayonet were held at waist level during an advance to contact, should not be underestimated. There have been very few actions in history when the combatants actually fought each other with the bayonet; either the attackers recoiled or the defenders ran away before matters came to so-called hand-to-hand fighting. Thus the unpopularity of the short spike bayonet for the British Lee-Enfield No. 4 magazine rifle, long enough for killing, but not reassuring to the soldier. The fixing of bayonets was and remains primarily an indication of *resolve*, although as late as the *Falklands war there have been occasions when the bayonet has been used to kill the enemy as opposed to merely intimidating him.

SCW

Evans, Roger D. C., and Stephens, Frederick J., *The Bayonet: An Evolution and History* (Milton Keynes, 1985).

Stephens, Frederick J., *A Collector's Pictorial Book of Bayonets* (London, 1971).

Bazaine, Marshal F. A. (1811–88). Although François Achille Bazaine had middle-class origins, when he failed to gain admittance to military *academy he enlisted into the infantry. After transferring to the *French Foreign Legion as a sergeant, he was commissioned in 1833, and fought bravely in Algeria (see ALGERIA, FRENCH CONQUEST OF) and Spain. He commanded a brigade in the *Crimean war and a division in Italy. In 1862 he took a division on the *Mexican expedition, became C-in-C there the following year, and marshal in 1865. When *Napoleon III realized that the military commitment could not be sustained, Bazaine handled the withdrawal with skill.

On the outbreak of the *Franco-Prussian war in 1870 he commanded III Corps, and after the defeats of 6 August was given ill-defined authority over the army's left wing, and then its formal command. He was not the senior marshal, and felt uncomfortable with generals educated at military academies, but enjoyed broad political support, encouraged by his ranker background. He displayed his customary courage at Rezonville, but failed to control the battle and fell back at its conclusion. He played little part at Gravelotte/Saint-Privat (see REZONVILLE/GRAVELOTTE), and then withdrew into Metz, where he surrendered in late October. In 1873 Bazaine was *court-martialled and sentenced to death. The sentence was commuted, but he soon escaped, and died in Spain. Vilified for his failings in 1870, Bazaine was a brave soldier wholly out of his professional depth.   RH

Bean, Charles Edwin Woodrow (1879–1968), Australian official historian. A pre-war journalist, Bean served with the *Australian Imperial Force at *Gallipoli and in France for the duration of WW I as official correspondent. He was appointed official historian in 1919 and oversaw the writing of the 12-volume series *Official History of Australia in the War of 1914–1918*, of which he wrote six volumes himself. He was also the leading force behind the creation of the Australian War Memorial and in the establishment of the National Archives of Australia. His remains the major influence on Australian understanding of WW I.   JG1

Beaufre, Gen André (1902–75). One of France's leading 20th-century military intellectuals, Beaufre had a distinguished career in staff and command appointments before writing his major work. A junior staff officer at French GHQ in 1940, he wrote movingly of the moral collapse of the French high command during the German offensive. In 1945 he was chief of operations of the French First Army, and became military assistant to Gen Jean de Lattre de Tassigny when the latter was appointed C-in-C of

French forces in *Indochina. After serving in the *Algerian independence war in 1955, he commanded the French contingent sent to *Suez in 1956. He was DCOS at Supreme Headquarters Allied Powers Europe (SHAPE) in 1956, and French representative at the *NATO standing group in Washington in 1960.

Like many French officers of his generation he was marked by the experience of defeat, and in *Introduction to Strategy* (1963) he sought to find ways in which military power could be used to support policy in the nuclear age. He argued that the West must develop a 'total' strategy— political, economic, psychological, and diplomatic as well as military—to counter its run of defeats in Africa, the Middle East, and Indochina. He favoured 'indirect strategy . . . the art of making the best use of the limited area of the freedom of action' left by *nuclear weapons. It was '*total war played in the minor key', and embodied a series of responses up to and including limited nuclear use. Despite its flaws, not least of them the practical difficulty of co-ordinating such strategy within the western Alliance, Beaufre's work was important in helping define areas of military choice available to policy-makers. RH

Beauregard, Gen Pierre Gustave Toutant (1818–93).

Born in Louisiana to a wealthy Creole family, Beauregard attended the US Military Academy at *West Point and was appointed to the prestigious Corps of Engineers upon graduation in 1838. During the *Mexican war he was on the staff of Winfield *Scott and received brevets to the rank of major. In the first months of the *American civil war Beauregard commanded southern forces during the bombardment at Fort Sumter, and played a key role at first *Bull Run, sharing command with Joseph *Johnston. His limitations as a general became apparent at *Shiloh, where Gen Albert Johnston let Beauregard and *Bragg persuade him to adopt a dense formation instead of the wide, enveloping manoeuvre that might have brought victory. After Johnston was killed, Beauregard commanded the army unimaginatively until illness forced him to resign. Never one of Jefferson *Davis's favourites, he received no second chance, unlike the far less talented Bragg, and returned to his old command at Charleston. His finest hour was in bottling up a larger Union force in the Bermuda Hundred peninsula near Richmond and then, when *Grant spectacularly outflanked *Lee and would have seized Petersburg, holding out against a greatly superior force until the Army of Northern Virginia double-timed back to support him. AH

Beersheba, battle of (1918).

*Allenby took command of British forces in the Middle East in July 1917 and swiftly established that his operational alternatives were simple. He could either launch another frontal attack on Turkish positions at *Gaza, where his predecessor had failed twice, or seek a more manoeuvrist solution, as Chetwode, XX Corps commander, (and another cavalryman) had already suggested. That summer Allenby restructured his army into three corps: XX, Bulfin's XXI, and Chauvel's Desert Mounted Corps. With about 80,000 fighting men he outnumbered the 46,000-strong Turkish Eighth Army, and strengthened his hand by a deception plan which encouraged its German commander, Kress von Kressenstein, to expect a frontal assault on the Gaza position.

On 27 October he began to bombard Gaza, and then sent the Desert Mounted Corps into the open country on the Turkish left flank. After initial setbacks, on 31 October the 4th Australian Light Horse Brigade charged Beersheba, using their *bayonets as swords, and took the town and its crucial wells; XX Corps consolidated, while XXI threatened the Gaza front. On 7 November Gaza was evacuated, and, although determined rearguards delayed the *pursuit, the Turks lost heavily as they fell back. On 16 November the New Zealanders rode into Jaffa, cutting links between Jerusalem and the coast. Allenby had not merely taken the Gaza-Beersheba position, but had defeated the Turkish Eighth Army and brought Jerusalem within his grasp as well. RH

Belfort, siege of (1870).

Lying between the Vosges and the Jura in western France, Belfort was fortified by *Vauban, and its position near the Württemberg border made it important in an era of Franco-German rivalry. Attacked by the Germans in November 1870 it was vigorously defended by Col Pierre Denfert-Rochereau, its former chief engineer who had been promoted to command the fortress that year. Most of his troops were national guardsmen, but he made good use of them by holding a wide defensive perimeter and shifting his men within it. The Germans brought up siege guns in January and caused serious damage, but Belfort was the only fortress still resisting the invader when, on 15 February 1870, it surrendered on the direct orders of the French government. Its garrison was allowed to march out to French lines with the *honours of war.

Belfort and its environs were spared the annexation that befell Alsace and Lorraine, and were given the status of a *département*—Territoire de Belfort—which they retain. The gallant defence helped sustain French national *morale at a difficult time. Denfert-Rochereau had a Parisian square and metro station named after him, and the former houses a version of Bartholdi's sculpture the lion of Belfort, commemorating the siege. RH

Belgrade, battle and siege of (1717).

In August the Austrians, commanded by *Eugène of Savoy, were laying siege to the former Hungarian fortress of Belgrade. On the

16th a massive relieving force numbering some 150,000 attacked the imperial lines. The Grand Vizier, Ibrahim Pasha, opened the proceedings with a bombardment from higher ground. Eugène swiftly decided on a surprise assault with 60,000 men, covered by the early morning fog. The Turkish army was routed, losing around 15,000 men. Belgrade surrendered on 21 August, clearing the way for the Treaty of Passarowitz (21 July 1718). The Austrian Habsburgs had secured a foothold in the Banat of Temesvar, Wallachia, and northern Serbia, and Austria had emerged from her decline of the previous century. This victory, coming hard on the heels of Eugène's equally stunning success at Peterwardein, also in the Danube valley, in the previous year, seemed to offer to the Austrians the prospect of replacing the Turkish administration in Moldavia and Wallachia, and simultaneously blocked Russian access to this strategic area.   TM

Belisarius, Count (correctly Belisarios) (*c*.500–65), one of the most successful generals produced by the *Byzantine army, who played a leading part in the Emperor Justinian's reconstitution of the empire. Born in Illyria, he began his military career in the emperor's bodyguard. His first known command involved a raid on Persian-occupied Armenia in 527, and although a similar venture the following year ended in defeat, Belisarius was given command in Mesopotamia. He became supreme eastern commander in about 530, fought the Persians with much success, and was recalled to Constantinople while a 50-year truce was negotiated. He was in the capital during the Nika riots of 532, when Justinian was howled down by the mob at the Hippodrome and was then hemmed in within his palace, whose guards proved unreliable. Belisarius intervened with his *bucellarii* (private troops) who marched on the Hippodrome and slaughtered possibly 30,000 citizens.

A grateful emperor gave him command of the *Vandal expedition, the start of the western reconquest. In 533 Belisarius sailed for Africa, where the Vandal King Gelimer had subjugated the Moorish population. Landing with 15,000 regular troops and his own *bucellarii*, Belisarius surprised the Vandals, beat them at Ad Decimum, and entered Carthage, where he is reported to have eaten the feast prepared for his defeated opponent. Having refortified the city, he crushed Gelimer at Tricamerum in December. He returned to Constantinople to reply to accusations of disloyalty, but was awarded a triumph—which ended with Belisarius prostrate before the imperial box in the Hippodrome, with the captive Gelimer beside him—and the consulate for 535.

Justinian now turned his attention to Ostrogothic Italy. Belisarius arrived in Sicily in 535 with just 7,500 regulars and his indispensable *bucellarii*: only Panormus (now Palermo) resisted him. He brought his fleet close in to the walls, and had ship's boats hoisted high into the rigging, packing them with soldiers who could shoot arrows into the defenders and then jump onto the battlements. After making a brief detour to subdue a military revolt in Africa in 536 he landed on the Italian mainland and enjoyed an easy advance up to Naples, which he besieged. He was about to raise the siege and march north to winter in Rome, but discovered a water conduit through which he managed to slip some troops into the city: Naples fell, and he entered Rome on 9 December.

Although he now nominally controlled southern Italy, Belisarius had not actually beaten Vitigis's *Goths, and the war now became a prolonged struggle for the control of cities, complicated by the fact that neither side had sufficient men to garrison fully the ones they held. Rome endured a long siege, during which Belisarius deposed Pope Silverius for treason. Although its harbour was left undefended, often causing shortages, the Goths could not capture Rome. They raised the siege on hearing that the Byzantines had taken Ariminum (now Rimini) and were threatening their capital, Ravenna. Belisarius followed them north, receiving reinforcements under *Narses. Together they forced Vitigis to raise the siege of Ariminum, but co-operation ceased when Narses refused to accept Belisarius' authority. Despite this, Belisarius blockaded Vitigis in Ravenna. He secretly accepted the western emperorship, offered him by disgruntled Goths, though *Procopius, his secretary and historian, insists that it was only for military expediency. In May 540 the Goths surrendered Ravenna and Vitigis himself to him in return for guarantees of their own safety.

In the meantime, the Persians had broken the truce concluded in 532 and invaded Syria, sacking Antioch. Belisarius was sent east to meet them, and 541 saw him back on the Persian frontier, with the eastern command now divided between him and Buzes. He seemed to have lost his old touch: although he took Sisaurnon, an outbreak of dysentery amongst his troops forced him to fall back. Briefly recalled to Constantinople, in 542 he returned to face down another Persian invasion, partly, suggests Procopius, by putting on a display of nonchalant efficiency that so amazed the Persian king's ambassador that he reported that 'he had met a general who in manliness and wisdom surpassed all other men, and soldiers such as he had never seen'.

After a brief period in disfavour, largely owing to Justinian's fears that he might become the focus for a military coup, he was given the Italian command again in 544, and spent the next five years struggling against the new Gothic leader, Totila. Justinian gave him too few troops and too little authority, and although he recaptured Rome and saved Italy for the empire he was unable to complete its reconquest, a task subsequently carried out by Narses. Belisarius was recalled in 549, possibly in readiness to meet another Persian offensive, but he did not serve in supreme command again and retired in 551. He enjoyed his last moment of glory in 559 when some 2,000 Cotigur *Huns raided as far as Constantinople. With only 300 trained soldiers and a local levy he ambushed and turned back the raiders. Later he was accused of plotting against Justinian and stripped of his dignities. This episode is probably the origin of the story that Justinian had him blinded, and that he ended his days a beggar. In fact he returned to favour, and lived out his days in comfort.

Belisarius combined personal courage with tactical flair and a broader vision that was rare for his age: he was that most unusual phenomenon, a general for all seasons. The historian Edward Gibbon, paraphrasing Procopius, summed him up as 'daring without rashness, prudent without fear, slow or rapid according to the exigencies of the moment; . . . in the deepest distress he was animated by real or apparent hope, but. . . he was modest and humble in the most prosperous fortune'. His judgement failed him, however, in his choice of a wife. Antonina was older than her husband: she came, like her friend the Empress Theodora, from a theatrical background and had a murky past. At least one of her liaisons drew Belisarius ever more deeply into the (literally) cut-throat world of court politics. Ironically, she outlived him.   SMcC/RH

Browning, R., *Justinian and Theodora* (London, 1987).

Benedek, FM Ludwig Ritter von (1804–81). Best known for his disastrous leadership of the Austrian North Army in the 1866 *Austro-Prussian war, Benedek had up to that point led a distinguished military career in Habsburg service. In 1848, he distinguished himself as a regimental commander with *Radetzky in Italy, where he won the Maria Theresa Order, Austria's highest *decoration for bravery. Benedek served as COS to Radetzky in the early 1850s and commanded a corps with considerable skill during the *Italian independence war of 1859, acting as rearguard to the retreating Habsburg army at Solferino.

After the war, the Emperor Franz Josef I appointed him to act simultaneously as commander of the Habsburg army in Italy and chief of the general *QM staff (renamed the *general staff in 1864). Benedek slighted his duties as COS in favour of army command in Italy, thus Austria had no properly studied plans for prosecuting the coming war with Prussia. Given his proven record in command, Franz Josef selected Benedek to command the Habsburg North Army in early 1866 when war with Prussia threatened. Benedek did not want the post and delayed leaving Italy until the deployment of the army was well underway. Unfamiliar with the theatre of war, Benedek clung to his base at Olmütz in Moravia, fearing a Prussian advance from Silesia on Vienna, despite excellent intelligence from the Saxons to the contrary. Finally prompted to move against the enemy by Franz Josef, Benedek advanced cautiously, failing to exploit Moltke's division of forces. This caution, complicated by confused staff arrangements, led Benedek to forfeit the advantage of interior lines by failing to concentrate his forces and ultimately to funnel his forces piecemeal into the Prussian vice fashioned for him by his opponent. On 4 July 1866, Benedek was soundly defeated by the converging Prussian armies on the field of *Königgrätz. There the massive impact of breech-loading *small arms, wrought on the Austrian ranks by the Prussian *needle gun, was felt in Europe for the first time. Benedek retired with the army to Ölmütz before being relieved of command. Benedek was threatened with a court martial following the war for his mishandling of the campaign, but in December 1866, Franz Josef ordered proceedings against him and his chiefs of staff (Gideon Ritter von Krismanic and Alfred von Henickstein) to be closed. *Cashiered nonetheless, Benedek retired to Graz where he lived out his life.   SWL

Bennett, Lt Gen Henry Gordon (1887–1962). An Australian, and one of the youngest brigadier generals in the empire armies in 1918, Bennett became the senior ranking militia general by the outbreak of war in 1939. A quarrelsome nature denied him early divisional commands in the *Australian Imperial Force, but he was given the 8th Division in September 1940, which he led in the disastrous *Malaya and Singapore campaign. Unlike *MacArthur in a similar situation, he had no orders to return to Australia after empire forces collapsed, therefore by 'escaping' at the time of surrender he unquestionably abandoned his command. He then commanded III Corps in Western Australia until resigning in May 1944. He remains a controversial figure, probably beyond rehabilitation.   JG1

Beresford, Gen William Carr (1764–1854). A leading British participant in the *Peninsular war, Beresford was the illegitimate son of the Anglo-Irish Marquess of Waterford. His first independent command, an expedition in 1806 to occupy Buenos Aires, supposedly in rebellion against Spain, ended in a humiliating rout, pursued by the far from friendly natives. Oddly, this did his career no harm and in 1807 he was made governor of Madeira. Either then or previously he learned the language, so when the Portuguese government requested that a British officer be sent to take command of its ramshackle army in February 1809, he was selected. Portuguese troops were an important asset to *Wellington during the Peninsular war and Beresford deserves the credit. Unfortunately he had no talent for field command, and material not included in the published version of Wellington's correspondence suggests that he came close to a nervous breakdown on the only occasion he was forced to command in battle, at Albuera in May 1811. At the end of the war he continued as C-in-C of the Portuguese army, but the revolution of 1820 forced him to return to England. His last military appointment was Master General of the *Ordnance from 1828 to 1830. Surprisingly, he lacks a biographer.   CJE

Glover, M., 'A Very Particular Service: Beresford's Peninsular War', *History Today*, 36 (June, 1986).

Berlin airlift (1948–9). At the end of WW II, Berlin was divided into American, British, French, and Soviet sectors. Supplies for western sectors had to pass through the Soviet-controlled zone, and as friction between the USSR and the West widened so the Soviets increased interference with traffic. In March 1948 the Soviets, then chairing the Allied Control Council which governed Berlin, adjourned a meeting without setting the date for another, and the body never met again. Traffic control became more rigid, and Allied leaders considered a variety of plans from withdrawal to military action to force a route to the city.

On 5 April a British passenger aircraft crashed after being rammed by a Soviet fighter. Negotiations became more acrimonious, and on 24 June the Soviets stopped rail traffic and cut off supplies from eastern power stations. The Allies decided to take the unprecedented step of supplying West Berlin from the air, flying cargo to its three airfields, Tegel, Gatow, and Templehof. There were three narrow air corridors, airspace over Berlin was shared with the Soviets, and initially most aircraft available were *Dakotas. But soon larger C-54s appeared and the tonnage flown in increased: 1,400 tons (1,422 tonnes) arrived in June, by mid-July this quantity arrived each day, and by January 1949, with the airlift in full spate despite atrocious weather, a daily average of 5,500 tons (5,588 tonnes) arrived.

The Soviets lifted the *blockade in May, but the airlift continued until September. Its human cost had been heavy: flying conditions, often very difficult, were worsened by Soviet mock-air attacks; pilots were exhausted and dust from coal, a common cargo, worked its way into control cables. Crashes and accidents cost the lives of 70 aircrew as well as 7 Germans. The airlift was an important symbol of western resolve and a testimony to the determination of the population of West Berlin to resist Soviet pressure.   RH

Berlin, battle of (April–May 1945), the crowning, though not the last, battle of WW II in Europe. Soviet authorities have argued they might have taken Berlin as early as February, immediately after the Red Army established bridgeheads across the Oder on 3 February. However, it was only at the Yalta conference from 4 to 11 February that the wartime Allies finally agreed post-war zones of occupation. Since the demarcation line between the Soviet forces and their western Allies was the river Elbe, well west of Berlin, there was no need for *Stalin to rush. The Soviet forces which had advanced with breathtaking speed through Poland in the VISTULA-ODER operation in January were exhausted and running out of fuel. A pause was needed—especially as resistance on German soil proved even tougher. Besides, the Red Army was fully occupied moving

through Hungary, Slovakia, and Austria. It was nearly two months before Stalin assembled his Main Planning Conference, on 1 April, and asked who would take Berlin—they or the western Allies? The latter had now crossed the Rhine, and might strike for the German capital. He must have known he could have had Berlin in February, but at vastly greater cost in men and *matériel* and without consolidating the Soviet hold on south-eastern Europe. Now was the time.

The Red Army had about two million troops available for the assault, with 6,000 tanks and *self-propelled (SP) guns and 40,000 artillery pieces against 750,000 German troops with about 1,500 tanks and assault guns. Berlin lay in the path of *Zhukov and the first Belorussian Front (army group), with *Koniev and the first Ukrainian to the south. Stalin capitalized on their rivalry by scrubbing out the Front boundary line 40 miles (64 km) east of the German capital. From there on in the two commanders raced each other to the kill and many thousands of *casualties from *friendly fire resulted.

Zhukov used a huge, elaborate scale model of the city to brief his commanders, but in spite of abundant air photography, he failed to identify the main line of German resistance and his attack stalled before the Seelow heights. Impatient, he launched his two reserve tank armies (First and Second Guards Tank), in defiance of instructions from Stavka, the supreme war council. Stalin was furious but Zhukov won the race. On 23 April Stalin drew the boundary line 164 yards (150 metres) west of the Reichstag, leaving Koniev, advancing from the south, on the other side. The Red Army broke into the centre of Berlin on the 26th. By 30 April, having fought through the zoo, the Soviet 150th Division of LXXIX Rifle Corps, Eighth Guards Army, first Belorussian Front, was poised to attack the Reichstag—'target number 105'. Two sergeants raised the red flag on the second floor at 14.25 and from the roof at 22.50, although the Germans fought on. The photographer Yevgeny Khaldei later recorded a moving daylight re-enactment. That night, the Soviets learned of Hitler's suicide. Negotiations continued until the middle of 1 May when *Stalingrad veteran Gen Vassily Chuikov, commanding Eighth Guards, exasperated, ordered artillery fire to be resumed. Early on 2 May Gen Weidling, commander of the Berlin garrison, drafted an order for Berlin to give in. Germans still hiding in the Reichstag basement began to surrender. At 15.00 on 2 May, Soviet artillery finally ceased fire.   CDB

Bellamy, Chris, *Red God of War* (London, 1986).
Erickson, John, *The Road to Berlin* (London, 1982).

Bernadotte, Marshal J. B., Prince of Ponte Corvo, King Karl XIV Johann of Sweden (1763–1844). Born in Pau in 1763, Bernadotte, after a foray into the law, enlisted in the infantry in 1780, becoming regimental sergeant major in 1790. Commissioned in 1791, he was a captain at the beginning of 1794 **and a general** of division at its end. He performed well under Bonaparte in Italy in 1797, beginning his uneasy relationship with the future emperor.

In 1798 he married Desirée Clary, whose sister Julie was the wife of Napoleon's brother Joseph. Family connection and military prowess ensured his appointment as marshal, but his Gascon temperament did not make him a comfortable relative. His performance as corps commander was patchy: he made a major error in the *Jena/Auerstadt campaign and quarrelled with Napoleon after *Wagram. Courtesy to captured Swedish officers helped secure nomination as heir to the throne of Sweden in 1810. French occupation of Swedish Pomerania drove him into the alliance against Napoleon, and he fought against him at *Leipzig in 1813.

Bernadotte became king in 1818, and was largely a success, although his rhetoric never moved his subjects as it had Frenchmen. Decency underlay his flamboyant character, and he never quite threw off the bonds of his birth: 'I, who was once a Marshal of France, am now only King of Sweden.'   RH

Bernhard, Duke of Saxe-Weimar (1604–39). One of the champions of the Protestant cause during the *Thirty Years War, Bernhard of Saxe-Weimar had a disastrous start to his military career: in 1622 he was on the losing side with the mercenary Mansfeld at Wiesloch, and again suffered defeat under Prince George of Baden at Wimpfen. Joining Christian of Brunswick, he was again defeated at Stadtlohn in 1623 by *Tilly and his crack Bavarian troops.

Bernhard then distinguished himself at *Breitenfeld in 1631 where he commanded the left wing under the orders of *Gustavus Adolphus. Then at *Lützen he showed great determination after the death of the Swedish king, rallying the wavering German Protestant troops and capturing the imperialist train.

After Lützen, Bernhard was appointed commander of the army of the League of Heilbronn, but contented himself with raiding and pillaging in southern Germany. In 1634 he faced the imperialists with the Swedish general Horn at Nordlingen, but failed to co-ordinate with his allies, and was roundly defeated. Bernhard beat a hasty retreat with a tiny rearguard.

He managed to rebuild the shattered Protestant army, and resolved to co-operate with the French forces, who had entered the war against the Holy Roman Empire. In 1636 he defended the eastern border of France, counter-attacking the following year and crossing the Rhine into Germany. His success allowed him then to form an independent army and with this he attempted to establish his own principality around Breisach in Alsace. *Richelieu was disturbed by the thought of such a large independent military power right on France's border, and blocked Bernhard's plan.

He subsequently planned to work once more with his old allies the Swedes, but died before he could come to any arrangement with them. Bernhard was a tough and reliable

military commander, who had shown his mettle at Lützen, and performed solid service for the Protestant cause when competent commanders were in short supply.   TM

Berthier, Marshal L. A. (1753–1815). Amanuensis to Napoleon, Berthier has sadly received scant attention from military historians, for it was he that laid the foundations for the emperor's glory. He was the staff officer par excellence, and his meticulous attention to detail allowed his master to put his grandiose schemes into effect. He learnt his trade in the pre-revolutionary royal army, entering into the military *engineering and cartography branch in 1766. By the age of 36 he was a lieutenant colonel and had seen active service in the *American independence war in the French expeditionary force under Rochambeau.

He threw in his lot with the new republic, but in 1792 he was suspended in a wave of anti-royalist paranoia. After a period of inactivity, he was posted to the Army of Italy in 1795 as COS, where the young Bonaparte arrived the following year. He was minister of war from 1799–1807 and COS to the Grande Armée. In 1809 he took temporary command of the Armée d'Allemagne, until Napoleon arrived to take over. The two were to work intimately together until 1814, when Berthier swore loyalty to Louis XVIII on Napoleon's abdication. During the *Hundred Days, he threw himself out of a window and his emperor badly missed his excellent staff work.   TM

billeting The accommodation of soldiers in civilian lodgings or public houses. Until the advent of purpose-built *barracks, billeting was the normal method of housing troops in peacetime in European armies. It was also widely practised on campaign, when a quartermaster would normally travel ahead of his unit to arrange accommodation with the (often less than enthusiastic) civic authorities. Billets were then 'chalked up', with the names of numbers of soldiers designated for particular houses being written on the front door. Civilians who had soldiers billeted on them were required to feed them, and, at least in theory, received a set rate of repayment, sometimes in cash but, especially in wartime, in vouchers which might prove difficult to convert. 'Free quarter' was the practice, common in the 17th century, of requiring the inhabitants of hostile territory, foreign or domestic, to house troops without recompense. Sometimes it reflected shortage of funds, but was often intended to be punitive. After the Revocation of the Edict of Nantes Louis XIV sought to covert his *Huguenot subjects by billeting troops, often *dragoons, on them. Even when billeting was not deliberately punitive, it was often bitterly resented. The Quartering Act, passed by the Westminster parliament in 1765, required the American colonies to supply food and accommodation to British troops. Once the apparent need for these troops had diminished with the

end of the *French and Indian war, this arrangement became one of the leading colonial grievances in the run-up to the *American independence war.

Billeting was unsatisfactory for soldiers and civilians alike. It was difficult to preserve discipline and cohesion in a unit that might be billeted over a wide area, and in wartime a billeted unit might be surprised—a practice called 'beating up quarters' in the 17th century—by an attacker who killed or captured men as they stumbled out of their billets in the small hours. Civic fathers, fearing for the virtue of their daughters and the sobriety of their sons, lamented the corrupting presence of the 'drunken and licentious soldiery'. However, as the novels of Jane Austen testify, billeted officers might be far from unwelcome.

Even soldiers who sought to behave well in billets were not immune from gaffes. At Saalfeld, in the *Jena/Auerstadt campaign of 1806, the French Quartermaster-Sergeant Guindey killed Prince Louis Ferdinand, the Prussian commander, in an encounter in which he himself was wounded. He was comfortably billeted with a German noblewoman, but his reception changed when news of the encounter leaked out. Riding off in search of more welcoming accommodation, he discovered that his orderly had been indiscreet when one of the servants taunted him. 'I told him straight,' confessed the hussar, 'that if his prince had wounded you in the face, he would not be wounding anybody else because you had run him through with your sabre.'   AH/RH

Birdwood, FM William (1865–1951). Born in India, Birdwood served on the *North-West frontier and in the Second *Boer War on Lord Kitchener's staff. Promoted major general in 1911, he was secretary to the Army Department in India in 1914. He owed his appointment to command the forces raised by Australia and New Zealand to Kitchener, and was sent to the Dardanelles in February 1915 to report on the failure of the naval attack on the Narrows. He commanded the *Anzac Corps throughout the campaign and was responsible for planning the August offensive and, with his Australian COS Col C. B. B. White, the successful withdrawal in December. Birdwood went to France with the *Australian Imperial Force in March 1916, and commanded Anzac I Corps until November 1917 when the Australian divisions were combined into the Australian Corps. After *Gough was dismissed he received command of Fifth Army in May 1918, which then played a minor role in the defeat of the Germans in the west. He remained in administrative command of the Australian Imperial Force until the *Armistice. Birdwood toured Australia in 1920 to great popular acclaim, but his bid to become governor-general failed.   JG1

Bismarck, Prince Otto von, Duke of Lauenburg (1815–98). The 'Iron Chancellor', Prussian statesman,
architect of German unity, and eventual elder statesman of Europe, Bismarck is identified with the concept of realpolitik, which for him included a degree of enlightened liberalism (the first European 'welfare' programmes were devised by him) to keep the populace happy while he concentrated on more serious matters. Personally tough, aggressive, energetic, and with an overpowering personal presence, Bismarck wrote that 'having to go through life with principles is like walking down a forest path with a stick in one's mouth'. Nonetheless, he had some, particularly the dominance of his class, the junkers, over Prussia, and of Prussia over the fragmented Germany.

Bismarck's career has suffered from efforts during and after WW II to suggest a continuity between the modern Nazis and the Prussians of yore, ignoring the fact that the remains of the Prussian aristocracy did produce opposition to *Hitler. Some historians argue that the creation of the Nazi state was a development of the Kaiserreich, and that the 'blood and iron' ethos of nationalism, autocracy, and *militarism fostered by Bismarck led directly to National Socialism. The atheist and racist Third Reich would have been anathema to Bismarck, himself a man of dour and unbending faith, and married into a family of extremely pious Lutherans. Not that it stopped him freely breaking most of the commandments, but his success gave him the comforting assurance that he was fulfilling God's will. He was, therefore, very much more a Hegelian than the Nietzschean monster it suits some to portray him as.

Bismarck came from a family of junkers with estates in Pomerania, the heartland of Prussia. After serving in minor diplomatic posts, he had settled down to run his ancestral estate until he deputized for the local parliamentary delegate in Berlin, where he discovered his true *métier*. He was a loud and uncompromising reactionary during the revolutions and unrest of 1848, a reputation he carried with him when elected to the second chamber. Although some of his qualities were instinctive, his real schooling in realpolitik came from service as the Prussian delegate to the German Confederation at Frankfurt between 1851–8, where he saw for himself how tenuous was the authority of the Austro-Hungarian empire, and how Prussia might move into the vacuum of power.

When Wilhelm I succeeded his brother on the Prussian throne, Bismarck was posted as ambassador to St Petersburg, then to Paris, and finally he was summoned to become the chief minister of Prussia in September 1862. Unable to get the military budget he required from parliament he governed by means of royal decrees, keeping his king reassured and depending on a bureaucracy that yearned for the smack of firm government. His contempt for the elected representatives of the people was confirmed when they rallied to him two years later, when he took Prussia to war against Denmark to resolve the 'Schleswig-Holstein question', permanently. The inevitable *Austro-Prussian clash came in 1866, in which 'Prussian soldiers fought for a modern Germany; the Austrian troops battled for an age-ing empire', while Bismarck's diplomacy ensured the neutrality of Russia and France. Next on the checklist, he provoked the French into sending an insulting telegram to his king, who was opposed to a further war, and later recalled *Moltke 'the Elder' rubbing his hands in glee when the war they both wanted came about. He used the *Franco-Prussian war to bring together the scattered principalities of Germany under one banner, the Second Reich being proclaimed at Versailles in January 1871. He thus became the first chancellor of a united Germany, which had become the foremost power in Europe.

Thereafter he spent nineteen years weaving a web of alliances and intrigue to create not so much a balance of power as one of tension, believing that German security was best guaranteed by encouraging rivalries among the other powers. More for this reason than for any illusions about an overseas empire, he joined the scramble for Africa, one of the few European African ventures that was made (ruthlessly) to pay for itself.

Bismarck's tenure was ultimately cut off in 1890 by the insecure and impetuous young Kaiser Wilhelm II, and it can be argued that the 'balance of tension' he had created unravelled in the unsteady hands of his successors, leading ultimately to WW I. Perhaps, but he would not have been so foolish as to provoke the British by building a rival battle fleet, destined to spend most of its short life bottled up at Kiel, as he knew it would be. Nor is it likely that he would have entered into an alliance to prop up the ramshackle Austro-Hungarian empire, thus getting sucked into a war on two fronts. Least of all would he, who in his prime kept the far more imposing Wilhelm I firmly in his place, have permitted Wilhelm II to influence policy to the degree that he did. The unification of Germany was his life's work, in which he was greatly assisted by his opponents' inability to analyse the balance of forces realistically. He claimed in his memoirs to have been following a plan from the start, but the evidence suggests that he was a talented opportunist given some golden opportunities by feckless opponents, from which he was able to extract the maximum advantage because he was blessed with a rare ability to think matters through to a logical conclusion.

What emerges is not a power-hungry man, nor a reactionary, nor even a far-sighted liberal—and biographers have advanced all three interpretations—but a true *Machiavellian figure for whom the end indeed justified the means. But his objectives were carefully measured on a case by case basis, and his wars were mercifully swift precisely because he did calculate the balance of forces, and moved when he found them favourable. By contrast WW I and even more so WW II were wars fought with unlimited means because the instigators had unlimited ends in mind, the antithesis of realpolitik. Bismarck did not destroy the old Europe of empires; he reaffirmed it and claimed what he saw as Germany's rightful place at the head of the table.

Gargantuan appetite though he had, it would never have crossed his mind to try to make mere waiters of the other diners. APC-A/HEB

bivouac (from Fr.: *bivouac* or *bivac*). Often shortened in British army slang to 'bivvy', the word has only been used in English since about 1700 and was not in common use before the *Napoleonic wars. The French use of the word probably dates from the *Thirty Years War. Its origins can be traced into dialectal (Swiss) German and the word *beiwacht*, a term used in Aargan and Zurich to refer to a patrol of citizens (*Schaarwache*) which were added (*beigegeben*) to the ordinary town watch at night at any time of special need or danger. The marriage of the two words *beigegeben* and *Schaarwache* produced *beiwacht*. It denoted special circumstances—a night watch by a whole army kept under arms, at times when the enemy is close and contact is anticipated—what we would now call 'on alert'. Hence it came to mean a temporary encampment of troops in the field without tents and using only locally available shelter.

The experiences of the British on the eve of *Waterloo provide a vivid and grim illustration of what bivouacking entailed in the early 19th century. The 71st Regiment marched for 36 hours to reach Waterloo in time for the battle, and spent the long, cold, rainy night of 17–18 June sitting on their packs. The regiments that had fought at Quatre Bras arrived earlier and managed to set up bivouacs, such as they were, before nightfall. Sleep proved elusive. Capt Cotter of the 69th Regiment 'preferred standing and walking to and fro during the hours of darkness to lying up on mud through which we sank more than ankle deep'. Another officer kept reasonably warm after he 'smeared an old blanket with thick clayey mud' and lay down under it on some straw. The *Highlanders of the 92nd had long experience of campaigning and slept well in fours under their 'united blankets'. The cavalry had a particularly difficult time. The horses of the Scots Greys were frightened by the thunder and kept stepping on their masters, who lay at their heads. In the morning, most of the troops were petrified with cold, exhausted, and mentally numb. Some allied troops drifted away even before the battle, but the downpour contributed to the success of the British and Hanoverian troops who stood. Napoleon, whose army was somewhat better equipped, waited all morning for the ground to dry out, narrowing the time available for battle before the Prussians came up to seal his doom.

Nowadays bivouacs feature light, one- or two-man tents or specially designed 'bivvy bags', which combine the functions of a sleeping bag and a bivouac tent. MCM

'Black Prince', Edward, the (1330–76). The eldest son of *Edward III, the Black Prince took his name from the body *armour he favoured and was one of the most notable

English commanders of the *Hundred Years War. He first distinguished himself fighting under his father's command at the battle of *Crécy in 1346. His first independent command came in 1355, when he led a successful *chevauchée from English-held Gascony across to the Narbonne on the Mediterranean coast, and did much damage to French territory. In the following year he led a largely mounted force northwards, hoping to link forces with the Earl of Lancaster on the Loire. The river was too high for his troops to cross, so he turned his army southwards. The French army under King John engaged him near Poitiers, and in the subsequent battle the English tactics of fighting on foot in a defensive position, with the support of *archers, proved decisive. King John was the Black Prince's most notable captive. The prince's next notable victory came in Spain in 1367, when he and his allies defeated a Franco-Spanish force under Henry of Trastamara at *Najera. Here again the well-established tactics worked well. Archaeologists have found the defensive pits dug by the English archers, who played a major part in the victory. The reopening of the war with France in 1369 did not lead to any further spectacular successes for the prince; the sack of Limoges by his army in 1370 was an act of brutality which did him little credit. He predeceased his father in 1376. He was not responsible for any significant innovations in tactics, but he was an inspiring leader and ruthless exponent of the dubious art of the chevauchée.

MCP

Barber, R., *Edward Prince of Wales and Aquitaine* (Woodbridge, 1978).

Blake, Gen Robert (1599–1657). Blake was unusual in having a distinguished career on land and sea. An Oxford-educated West Country gentleman with Puritan leanings, Blake sat in the Short Parliament of 1640 and sided with parliament on the outbreak of the English civil war (see BRITISH CIVIL WARS). Despite his age and lack of military experience he rose to the occasion, and his defence of Taunton (1644–5) had real strategic impact, tying down substantial royalist forces which were not present at the decisive *Naseby campaign.

Appointed one of parliament's three 'generals at sea' in 1649, Blake emerged as a brilliant admiral, first defeating his old rival Prince *Rupert of the Rhine—who had also made the transition from land to sea—and then playing a leading part in the first Dutch war (1652–4). In 1655 he took a fleet into the Mediterranean, harrying the Barbary pirates and attacking Algiers, and in 1657 he captured a Spanish treasure fleet off Tenerife.

Blake was no less remarkable as a naval administrator, whose work helped lay the foundations for British sea power, and as a tactical innovator, who assisted in developing the line ahead tactics which were to dominate the age of fighting sail.

RH

Blamey, FM Thomas Albert (1884–1951). One of very few Australian officers with staff training before 1914, Blamey served as COS to *Monash in 1918. A turbulent personal and professional life between the wars did not preclude his appointment to command the 2nd *Australian Imperial Force in September 1939, and he led the Australians in the Middle East until he returned to Australia in March 1942 as C-in-C of the Australian Military Forces. He served as commander of the Allied Land Forces under *MacArthur while remaining his government's principal military adviser. He received his field marshal's baton during his final illness.

JG1

Blenheim, battle and campaign of (1704), the most important campaign of the War of the *Spanish Succession. The name itself is the Anglicized version of Blindheim, a village in Bavaria on the left bank of the river Danube. In May 1704 a possible Franco-Bavarian invasion threatened Austria, which would have triggered the collapse of the Grand Alliance against France. In a strategically decisive move *Marlborough led his army on a surprise march from the Netherlands down the Rhine valley, his aim being to crush the elector of Bavaria in his own state, along with his French allies. Only a minority of Marlborough's men were British, two-thirds being Germans and Danes.

His route was chosen to mislead the French into pursuing him, rather than marching directly to reinforce the elector. It required a miracle of planning. Such long marches in the 18th century usually resulted in mass *desertion, while those who remained were soon in poor condition. Margrave Louis of Baden and Prince *Eugène of Savoy met Marlborough briefly on 10 June at Mundelsheim, and it was agreed that Eugène should distract the French under Villeroi from intervening in Bavaria, while Baden accompanied Marlborough. On 2 July, Marlborough and Baden carried Donauworth, an important crossing point over the Danube, in the swift but costly battle of Schellenberg. They then proceeded to devastate the vicinity in an effort to draw their opponents into battle. Eugène, on discovering that the French army under Tallard had slipped away, himself marched to join Marlborough. They joined forces on 12 August at Blindheim, 10 miles (16 km) west of Donauworth. Baden having been despatched to besiege Ingolstadt, their combined strength was about 56,000.

Their Franco-Bavarian opponents, Marsin and the elector of Bavaria under the overall command of Marshal Count Camille de Tallard, slightly outnumbered the allies at 60,000. Advancing in nine columns, Marlborough and Eugène spent the morning of 13 August deploying, covered by artillery fire. Tallard, who was taken by surprise, deployed hastily to a poor position between Blindheim, on the Danube, to his right and Lutzingen on his left. In the centre was a third fortified village, Oberglau. Eugène faced Marsin and the elector between Lutzingen and Oberglau,

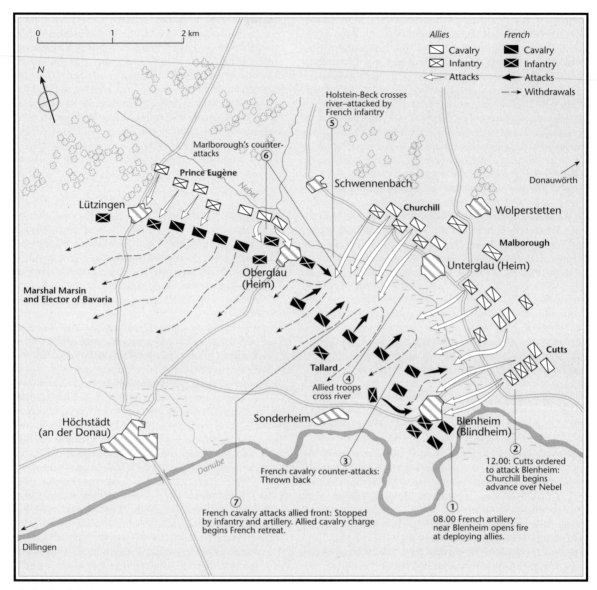

The battle of **Blenheim**, 13 August 1704.

while Marlborough stood opposite Tallard from Oberglau to Blenheim. Each Franco-Bavarian force deployed with infantry in the centre and cavalry on the wings, the two cavalry wings meeting in Oberglau. At 12.30 battle commenced when Lord John Cutts attacked Blenheim twice, which drew in French reserves, while Marlborough tried to break through at Oberglau, the hinge of Tallard's two armies. Eugène meanwhile attacked the elector and Marsin in a classic fixing operation, which presented them from supporting Tallard elsewhere. While Eugène's attack distracted Tallard's attention, Marlborough got his infantry across the

obstacle of the Nebel stream, which ran across the battlefield between the armies. Once across, his men deployed in a unique formation—two lines of infantry sandwiched between two lines of cavalry—which was able to beat off French cavalry charges. Marlborough personally led a cavalry countercharge and by 17.30 had breached Tallard's centre, his forces pouring through the gap. Blenheim surrendered, after fierce fighting, to Gen Charles Churchill, the duke's brother, at 23.00.

In a model of coalition warfare, the armies of the two great Allied commanders had acted in perfect harmony with one another to inflict a crushing defeat on the Franco-Bavarian force, whose losses totalled 38,000, the blow to their prestige being even more fundamental. Marlborough and Eugène suffered 12,000 casualties and the former's prestige and that of his army was without precedent. Significantly, he named his country house in Oxfordshire after his finest battle, but it had been a costly affair: 43 per cent of all troops engaged had been killed, wounded, or taken prisoner.   APC-A

blitzkrieg (Ger.: *Blitzkrieg*, lightning war), was probably first coined by a journalist in 1939 and has now passed into the English language as a description of a form of warfare waged by Germany at the start of WW II, and, more widely, of any violent campaign intended to achieve speedy victory. An influential subset of *armoured warfare, rather than a distinct *doctrine in its own right, it combined the use of *tanks, mechanized infantry, and *air power, often with *special forces. *Radio communications were fundamental to its success, and it is no accident that *Guderian, an influential theorist and effective practitioner of it, had spent much of WW I as a signals officer. There was neither a unifying concept of blitzkrieg, nor a body of coherent doctrine for its use prior to 1939, but German successes in 1939–40 instantly hallowed it. At its best it embodied a style of command which maximized initiative and the delegation of tactical authority within a commander's broad directive. Its origins were complex. Germany's defeat in WW I and the constraints imposed upon her army by the Treaty of Versailles encouraged military reformers, for whom 'business as usual' was not an option, to consider several new ideas. In the 1920s the army, considering the possibility of invasion, favoured people's war, which would use conventional operations, *terrorism, *guerrilla warfare, and scorched-earth policy for the defence of Germany. At the same time the doctrinal foundations were laid for the army's modernization, and a 1929 study sought to combine people's war with a new, highly mobile armoured force.

Careful attention was paid to French and, especially, British developments in armoured warfare, and an agreement with Russia allowed Germany to experiment with tanks and close-support aircraft in Russia so as to circumvent international restrictions. Developments during and experience of WW I were also influential, and *Rommel was but one of the successful practitioners of blitzkrieg who had learnt the importance of penetrating the enemy's front at a weak point, unrolling the defence by flank attack, and leading from well forward as a young *storm-troop commander.

Blitzkrieg also reflected tensions within the *Wehrmacht and political interactions between *Hitler and senior officers. Military developments gained momentum after Hitler came to power and shackles of Versailles were broken. Alongside rearmament went the development of plans, once rearmament was complete, for 'deliberate strategic attack, planned and prepared in peacetime'. During the late 1930s the *general staff came under growing political pressure to abandon its methodical approach to rearmament and doctrinal development. Just as Hitler complained that the army would never be ready for war, so too some officers scorned the general staff's quest for operational plans which formed part of a coherent strategy. In his study of German strategy in the age of machine warfare, Michael Geyer complains that 'it was these officers who now became the proponents of blitzkrieg, which was neither an outgrowth of military technology nor of the German doctrine of mobile offence, but operational management devouring professional strategy'. There is much truth in this criticism. For all its apparent success, blitzkrieg was essentially a tactical doctrine which made possible the construction of devastating operational plans like those which defeated Poland in 1939, the western Allies in 1940, and inflicted such damage on the Soviet Union in 1941. Its success encouraged Hitler to run growing strategic risk and to ignore the economic strength of his adversaries. The Wehrmacht, as many general staff officers had pointed out in the 1930s, lacked the economic base to become fully mechanized, and for a great proportion of it, marching on foot and with its horse-drawn transport, blitzkrieg had little relevance. Finally, at the tactical-operational level, blitzkrieg was increasingly vulnerable to an opponent who kept his head and avoided the panic and moral collapse which characterized so many of Germany's enemies in 1939–41, or who (as the Russians did so effectively) developed a blitzkrieg of their own. Nevertheless it was the dominant tactical doctrine in Europe and North Africa for the first three years of WW II, and there were occasions thereafter—for instance at the *Kasserine Pass in 1943—when it flared briefly into prominence again. Other nations have practised their own style of blitzkrieg: both the Red Army's *Manchurian campaign of 1945 and the Israeli army's victory in the Six Day *Arab–Israeli war of 1967 embody the main characteristics of blitzkrieg. It remains an influential tactical ideal which finds answering echoes in modern *manoeuvre warfare.   RH

Geyer, Michael, 'German Strategy in the Age of Machine Warfare', in Peter Paret (ed.), *Makers of Modern Strategy* (Oxford, 1986).

Harris, J. P., and Toase, F. H. (eds.). *Armoured Warfare* (London 1992).

blockade is an *attritional strategy using armed forces to prevent the movement of supplies into the blockaded place, be this an outpost or a continent. It has been used since the dawn of organized warfare as the passive aspect of *siege warfare. The purpose is to secure *capitulation from the lack of means to continue resistance, historically used by besieging forces that lacked either the weapons to bombard or the manpower to assault. While the classic definition relates to fortified cities or ports, the concept has a much wider application. To be successful the blockaders must also defend their own position against forces seeking to relieve the blockaded place: Caesar's siege of *Alesia consisted of two concentric lines, one facing towards the town and the other outwards.

While land blockades have altered little over time, aside from the addition of an aerial element, naval technical developments profoundly affected the scope and effectiveness of sea blockades. Before 1500 ships could invest ports, notably in Edward III's siege of Harfleur, but they could not systematically stop economic activity. After 1700, when ships could sustain blockades for long periods, they became the critical offensive instrument of British sea power. Although commercial blockades took years to produce an impact, and could never be decisive while states were essentially self-supporting in foodstuffs, they were a persuasive reason for ending limited wars. Blockades kept inferior fleets in harbour, allowing the dominant navy to exploit the sea to strategic and commercial advantage. Blockades which affected neutral shipping had to be declared to be enforced, and effective in order to be binding. Ineffective mercantile blockades were termed 'paper blockades'.

Blockade reached a new level of sophistication with Earl St Vincent's 'close' blockade of Brest 1800–14. This was the foundation of British strategy, keeping the French fleet in harbour to cover British operations from the Baltic to the East Indies. By contrast *Nelson used an 'open' blockade off Toulon, hoping to lure the enemy out for battle. After *Trafalgar Napoleon instituted a 'counter-blockade', the 'Continental System', closing all European ports to British trade, which irritated his allies and also did more economic damage to the continent than it did to Britain. Thus both the British blockade and his effort to counter it contributed to his downfall. The downside was that it provoked, *inter alia*, the *War of 1812.

During the *Crimean war the British blockade of Russia's warm water ports escalated into the land operations against Sevastopol. In the *American civil war, the North's 'Anaconda Plan' involved the economic strangulation of the South by sea and river. However, blockade-breaking by fast, British-built blockade runners meant that the blockade was only perfected by capturing the Confederate ports. Mines, submarines, and aircraft ended the close blockade of individual ports. It was replaced by the 'distant blockade' of countries, using natural choke points to intercept mercantile traffic. In the *total wars of the 20th century blockades were truly global. During WW I the British denied Germany the food and raw materials of the rest of the world. This blockade made a significant contribution to the eventual Allied victory, and the hunger it caused weakened the resistance of the Central Powers' population to the holocaust of influenza. The Germans responded with a new counter-blockade, unrestricted submarine warfare, which by April 1917 had begun to bite, leading to the belated intro-

duction of *convoys. *Churchill wrote that the U-boat campaign of WW II was the only threat that seriously disturbed him. Meanwhile US submarines sank the whole Japanese merchant fleet and more warships than their *air forces and surface navy combined. The 1948 Berlin blockade exploited the non-lethal use of force and was defeated by non-military means (see BERLIN AIRLIFT). The Americans blockaded Cuba to force out Soviet missile bases and created a large coastal and riverine navy to prevent North Vietnamese supplies from reaching the South by water.

During the 20th century pseudo-blockades known as embargoes have been used as a diplomatic fig leaf by governments unwilling or unable to resort to armed action and are completely useless unless backed up with the same. This is particularly noticeable when the target regimes are indifferent to the suffering of their people who can be exploited for propaganda purposes to undermine the necessary international consensus. A classic was the well-fed Ojukwu's use of his photogenically starving children to generate sympathy during the Biafran war, while Saddam *Hussein in Iraq provides a contemporary example.

Although hugely popular with those who profess to abjure violence, properly conducted blockades are a harsh means of applying lethal force against a whole population. They do, however, keep down the body count among the blockaders. AL/HEB

Blücher, Marshal Gerbhard von, Prince of Wahlstadt (1742–1819). Blücher came to prominence only later in a career marked by extreme dissipation during his younger days, and throughout his long life he continued to drink, gamble, and wench to excess. He was first commissioned at 16 into the Swedish army and entered Prussian service after being taken prisoner. Displeased at being passed over for promotion, he resigned in 1773 to discover he had no talent for farming. He was recommissioned in 1786 and by 1802 was a lieutenant general and governor of Münster. Prominently involved in the Prussian disaster of *Jena/Auerstadt, he had a horse shot from under him leading a charge and was later forced to surrender at Ratkau, near Lübeck. Ever troublesome to *Napoleon, he was forced into temporary retirement in 1812 at Napoleon's request. After the French were defeated in Russia, the 71-year-old Blücher was appointed to command the Prussian Army of Silesia, and at Lützen (1813) had another horse shot from under him and was wounded. He regrouped to beat the French at Katzbach in August the same year, but failed to trap Napoleon at *Leipzig in October.

Leading one wing of the Allied advance into France in the *Champagne campaign of 1814, despite two setbacks at Craonne and Rheims in March, he had the satisfaction of forcing Napoleon to abdicate, Blücher was thereupon created prince of Wahlstadt and retired. During the *Hundred Days, he emerged again to mobilize an army of 120,000, and confronted the resurgent emperor in person at Ligny while *Wellington fought *Ney at Quatre Bras. 'Marschal Vorwärts' (Marshal Forwards), as by then he was known to his adoring troops, again had a horse killed, which rolled on top of him. He was not found for two hours, but when he was rescued he reversed his subordinates' orders to retreat away from Wellington and kept his promise to join him, decisively, at Waterloo. The implacable *pursuit by the relatively fresh Prussian cavalry turned a defeat into a rout. At the end of his life he seems to have become mildly insane, confessing to Wellington that he was pregnant, with an elephant, by a French grenadier.   APC-A

Boadicea. See BOUDICCA.

Boer War, First (1880–1). The war arose from rivalry between Britain's claim to be the paramount power in southern Africa and the desire of the Boers (descendants of Dutch settlers) for autonomy. Britain recognized the independence of the two Boer republics, the Orange Free State and the Transvaal Republic, in 1852 and 1854 respectively, expecting to annex both peacefully in due course.

In June 1877, the bankrupt Transvaal was indeed peacefully annexed by Britain. In 1880 *Wolseley was succeeded as governor of Natal (also responsible for the Transvaal) by Maj Gen Sir George Colley. The Transvaal Boers under Paul Kruger petitioned London for the restoration of their independence, and when this was refused they declared a republic once more on 16 December. The Orange Free State remained neutral throughout the war. Under the 'commando' military system the Transvaal fielded about 7,000 irregular mounted riflemen with no artillery, against about half that number of British regulars plus local volunteers.

The fighting began with the wiping out of a British column on 20 December at Bronkhorstspruit, south of Pretoria, in an ambush led by Gen 'Piet' Joubert. Most of the 1,800 British troops in the Transvaal were scattered in small forts, all of which were attacked or besieged but none captured. The government in London sent reinforcements while simultaneously negotiating for a settlement, and failed to provide Colley with clear orders. He in turn, although particularly lacking regular cavalry and artillery, advanced with about 1,000 regulars and local volunteers into the pass at Laing's Nek, the frontier between Natal and the Transvaal. Colley failed to open this route with a frontal attack on twice his number of Boers on 28 January, followed by the failure of a further attack with 300 men at the battle of Ingogo river on 8 February.

On 26 February, Colley led 350 men in a night march to capture Majuba Hill, which dominated the pass below. Under heavy Boer covering fire, Joubert sent 180 men in small parties up onto the hill, where their superior marksmanship caused a British rout. Colley was killed, and al-

most his entire force was wiped out. Now London sent significant reinforcements under *Roberts, while authorizing Colley's replacement, Maj Gen Evelyn Wood, to negotiate an armistice. This was agreed on 21 March, before Roberts's force reached Cape Town. Peace was concluded by the Pretoria Convention in August, restoring independence to the Transvaal with a nod to British sovereignty. Even that was removed in the further London Convention of 1884, at which the Transvaal changed its name to the South African Republic.   SDB

Bond, Brian, 'The South African War 1880–1881', in Bond (ed.), *Victorian Military Campaigns* (London, 1967; repr. 1994).
Lehmann, Joseph, *The First Boer War* (London, 1972).

Boer War, Second (1899–1902). Fought between the British empire and the Boer republics of the Orange Free State and the Transvaal, this war made British subjects of most southern Africans for 60 years and enshrined two white tribes as South Africa's rulers for 80. That one of those tribes, the Afrikaners, included the defeated Boers was testament to the latter's hard struggle during the war and to the ideals of British imperialism in the 20th century.

During the 1880s and 1890s the autonomy, trade, and traditional way of life of the Boer republics were threatened by the prosperity of the adjoining British colonies of Cape Colony and Natal, the creation of British Rhodesia in the north, the flood of substantially British uitlander workers into Transvaal gold mines, and pressure from empire-builders in London, Cape Town, and Johannesburg who sought to overturn the settlement of the First Boer War and create a federated South Africa under the Union flag. Late in 1895 Cecil Rhodes sponsored a raid led by Jameson to stir uitlanders against Boer rule and prompt British intervention. This was suppressed by the Transvaal authorities, but it provoked the Boer republics to prepare for war, and firmed imperial resolve to eclipse Boer power.

The republics had no armies but relied on district-based mainly mounted militias called *commandos, led by elected officers and stiffened by police and modern artillery. Boer strategy was to strike swiftly before British reinforcements could arrive, rouse rebellion in the Cape, and win a negotiated peace. In October 1899 fast-moving commandos totalling perhaps 40,000 men invested British border garrisons at *Mafeking and Kimberley and invaded Natal, locking up a British force at Ladysmith early in November. A civil as well as imperial war got under way as hundreds of Cape Colonists took up arms on the Boer side, thousands of uitlanders formed volunteer regiments to fight beside British regulars, and small contingents from Canada and Australasia, arrived to join in the fighting.

Having spread their commandos thinly, the Boer offensive soon ran out of steam. But the arrival of a British army corps under *Buller did not bring the speedy victory many expected. The army had too few mounted troops to keep

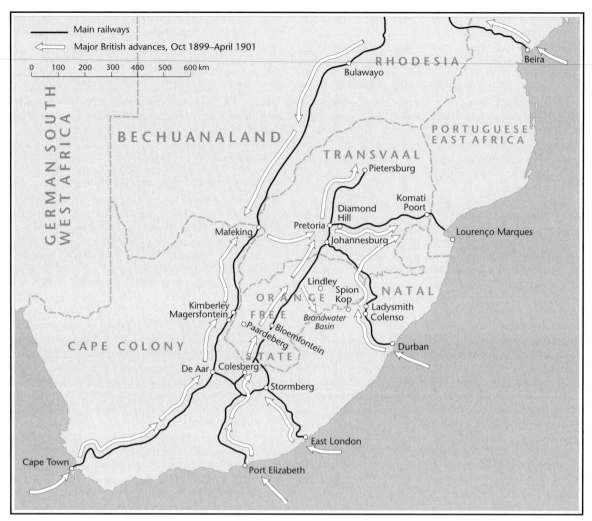

The **Second Boer War**, 1899–1902: conventional phase.

pace with their enemy, and was divided in three. During 'black week', the 'most disastrous for British arms during the century' according to Arthur Conan Doyle, the army's three components were beaten at Stormberg in eastern Cape Colony (10 December), Magersfontein south of Kimberley (11 December), and, under the personal command of Buller, at Colenso south of Ladysmith (15 December). Buller was demoted to commanding only in Natal, and in a second failed advance, 1,500 of his troops were shot down on Spion Kop (24 January 1900).

British losses could not be made good with Indian or African troops. Boers and Britons agreed that non-whites might labour and scout for them, on rare occasions fight for them, but must not be relied on as soldiers, lest white dominance of the region be unsettled. So more British regulars sailed for South Africa and white citizens around

the empire roused themselves for the first time to share in the burden of an imperial war. More local and overseas volunteer regiments, mostly *mounted infantry, were raised from the Imperial Yeomanry of Britain to the Bushman of Australia. *Roberts, Britain's senior fighting general, arrived with *Kitchener as his COS to swing a sledgehammer of over 180,000 men against the hard nut of Boer resistance.

The Boers had the sympathy of Europe and of many Americans, and fashionable Parisiennes dressed themselves *à la Boër*. But the Americans were themselves busy annexing a hostile subject people in the *Philippines, and German talk of a 'continental league' against Britain came to nothing. The trickle of foreign adventurers, idealists, and weapons that reinforced the Boers began to dry up once British diplomatic pressure on Lisbon closed off access to the Transvaal via Portuguese East Africa, and the Royal

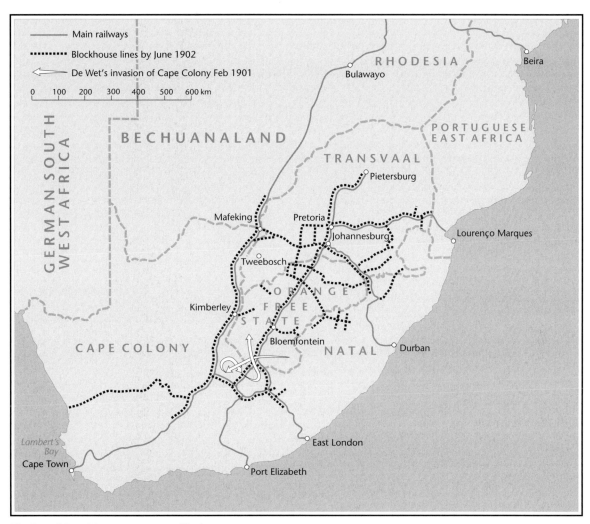

The **Second Boer War**, 1899–1902: guerrilla phase.

Navy's command of the sea allowed unhindered conveyance of men, horses, and stores to South Africa. But the disadvantages of splendid isolation were clear, and Britain would begin to make alliances with Japan, France, and Russia.

While Buller battled away in Natal, eventually relieving Ladysmith (28 February), Roberts marched 60,000 troops against the Boer capitals. After relieving Kimberley (15 February) and defeating a large Boer force at Paardeberg (18–27 February), he overcame vast distances, lack of fodder, and a typhoid epidemic to enter Bloemfontein (13 March), Johannesburg (31 May), and Pretoria (5 June). After small detachments liberated Mafeking (17 May), the ecstatic street celebrations across the white empire yielded a new name, 'mafficking', for unruly crowd behaviour. At Diamond Hill east of Pretoria (11–12 June) Roberts pushed aside a Trans-

vaal force under Louis Botha, and subsequent advances rounded up 4,000 Boers in the Brandwater basin (29 July) and rolled east to Komati Poort (25 September). Fourteen thousand Boers gave up their weapons. The British empire annexed the republics, Buller and Roberts returned to England, Kitchener assumed command of what many thought had shrunk to a police action, and Transvaal president Paul Kruger fled to Europe to plead in vain for foreign support.

Many Boers would not accept defeat. Few were the natural guerrillas of legend, some having been townsmen before the war, but those remaining 'on commando' were largely young, fit, and defiant. Hard fighting and the succession of defeats had removed old and inflexible leaders and brought to the fore enterprising and determined ones, notably Botha in eastern Transvaal, De Wet in the Free State, and De la Rey in western Transvaal. Their aim was to harass their opponent into negotiations, and their opponent was vulnerable.

The British army was overstretched, trying to guard cities, gold mines, railway lines, and *telegraph wires, escort *convoys, and send out columns to pursue an elusive enemy. Its garrisons, baggage, and depots were exposed to raids, and many of its raw volunteers proved vulnerable when cornered. Even during Roberts's advance De Wet had pounced on isolated units east of Bloemfontein (31 March 1900) taking 1,000 prisoners, and four months later his brother routed an Imperial Yeomanry battalion at Lindley (31 July 1900). Such spectacular feats grew common as the war progressed. Botha threatened Natal (7 September–2 October 1900), and De Wet broke into Cape Colony (10–28 February 1901). A few Boers even reached the sea at Lambert's Bay north of Cape Town (January 1901), exchanging shots with a British warship. Young Jan *Smuts created confusion in the north-east Cape for many months (August 1901–April 1902). They did not always evade battle: De la Rey routed a British column at Tweebosch in western Transvaal and captured a British general, Lord Methuen, on 25 February 1902.

But the Boers were hopelessly outnumbered and their movements were more often flights from pursuing columns than real offensives. Roberts had responded to Boer raids by burning farms and destroying livestock and stores to deprive commandos of supplies and shelter. Kitchener continued these old-fashioned barbarities and copied ones recently employed in Cuba, building lines of blockhouses linked by barbed wire and herding women, children, surrendered Boers, and refugee blacks into concentration camps. Life in the camps was sometimes easier than subsistence on the war-torn veld, but malnutrition, disease, and neglect killed 42,000 camp inmates. Liberal and international opinion was outraged. Patriotic opinion was unmoved.

Originally devised to protect railways, the blockhouse lines were extended from mid-1901 into the countryside, dividing it into cul-de-sacs into which columns might sweep the commandos. Mounted regulars and volunteers, led by bright young commanders such as Rimington, *Plumer, and Benson, evolved into masterful horsemen adept at night marches and dawn attacks, often guided by some of the 5,000 or more Boers, mostly poor farmers, who abandoned the cause of their often wealthy leaders. By early 1902 British columns were methodically sweeping the countryside. Armoured trains mounted with artillery and searchlights patrolled railway lines. Steam tractors began to free columns from dependence on railways and oxen. Boer leaders were faced with the choice of British rule or the destruction of their world.

The 31 May 1902 peace agreement at Vereeniging led to a federated British South Africa in which Boers and Britons shared power over non-white peoples who outnumbered them four to one. It had taken nearly 500,000 white soldiers from around the British empire, aided by the labour of 100,000 non-whites, to make British subjects of the Boers. Eight thousand blockhouses had been built and 3,728 miles (6,000 km) of barbed wire laid. Eight thousand British soldiers and 4,000 Boers had been killed. Another 13,000 Britons, 15,000 non-whites, and 30,000 Boers had died from disease or malnutrition. Thirty thousand farms had been destroyed. Also destroyed were the hopes of non-whites who had expected land and citizenship after a British victory. The war furthered military reforms throughout the British empire, allowing a rapid, united response to the German challenge in 1914. It also inspired J. A. Hobson's book *Imperialism* (1902), whose argument that the war proved that capitalism necessitated imperial expansion influenced Lenin and other communist leaders.   CW/HEB

Maurice, F., and Grant, H. M., *Official History of the War in South Africa*, 4 vols. of text, 4 vols. of maps (London, 1906–10).
Nasson, Bill, *The South African War 1899–1902* (London, 1999).
Pakenham, Thomas, *The Boer War* (London, 1979).
Smith, Iain, *Origins of the South African War* (London, 1996).
Warwick, Peter, *Black People and the South African War* (Cambridge, 1983).

Bohemond (c.1050–1111) was the nickname, meaning 'Giant', of Marc, eldest son of Robert *Guiscard who disinherited him after a second marriage. Bohemond served in Guiscard's expedition against Byzantium in 1083–5. His participation in the First *Crusade has been seen as the act of a frustrated man but he enjoyed a strong position in southern Italy. The only leader of the Crusade to have commanded a major army, he distinguished himself militarily, fighting well at Dorylaeum on 1 July 1097, ensuring the defeat of a Damascene relief army in December 1097, and commanding at the Lake battle on 2 February 1098. He entered *Antioch by treachery on 1–2 June 1098 and led the crusaders to victory over Kerbogah on 28 July 1098. Because he kept Antioch, contrary to the oath of all the leaders to return it to Byzantium, and did not go on to Jerusalem, he has been seen as a cynical exploiter of the crusade, yet he visited Jerusalem at Christmas 1099.

In 1100 he was captured by the *Turks. Released in 1103, he faced Byzantine efforts to regain Antioch, so he raised a crusade in the West which attacked Byzantium in 1107. He was defeated and forced to peace by the Treaty of Devol in September 1108, though Antioch remained under his nephew Tancred. He died in southern Italy.   JF2

Yewdale, R., *Bohemond I Prince of Antioch* (Princeton, 1917).

Bolívar, FM Simón (1783–1830), the protean figure of South American independence, a tireless general, polemicist, and lover who is unique in having a nation, Bolivia, named after him. Born in present-day Venezuela, he waged see-saw war with the Spanish there from 1811. In 1819 at the head of 2,500 men with a hard core of British and Irish adventurers, he marched over allegedly impassable terrain to surprise the Spanish in present-day Colombia, defeating them at Boyacá in August. After the proclamation of a republic that encompassed Venezuela and Ecuador, he led his army back to the former, winning the battle of *Carabobo in June 1821, then into Ecuador, where his able lieutenant Sucre defeated the Spanish at Pichincha in May 1822. Pausing only to persuade *San Martín to depart the stage, he and Sucre liberated Peru at Junín and Ayacucho in late 1824.

He tried to keep his creation together by the exercise of dictatorial authority, but his powers were sapped by tuberculosis and it broke up into warring nation states. Realizing that his position was untenable, he was on his way to exile when news that his dear friend and intended successor Sucre had been murdered broke his spirit and he died shortly afterwards.   HEB

bomb (from It.: *bomba*, in turn probably from Lat.: *bombus*, which refers to the signature booming sound). Bombs were initially fired from *mortars and engineers sought to defeat them by applying earth and masonry protection to the roofs of key fortress installations, thus giving birth to the word 'bombproof'. A conventional bomb has a casing containing explosives, a detonation or ignition system, and an initiation device or fuse. The fuse may be a simple mechanical striking mechanism, or involve the release of corrosive or volatile chemicals, or use electrical circuitry. The most complex fuses react when disturbed (physically or electrically), when atmospheric pressure changes, or when in proximity to the target area or object. The principal effect of a bomb is explosive blast, which may be combined with fragmentation or incendiary effects. It is the weapon of preference both for the very powerful, who can today drop it on those who displease them from a great height with tolerable accuracy, and of militarily negligible individuals or organizations wishing to register their lethal disapproval of something or somebody. A particularly popular sub-variant is the car or truck bomb, which lends itself to pressure, release, direct electronic (from the ignition switch), heat, remote control, tremble, and tilt initiation. The word is applied indiscriminately to everything from a nuclear device to a failed theatre production.   PC

bomb disposal The destruction of unexploded military ordnance. Live artillery shells, aerial bombs, sea and land mines, continue to be discovered many years after the conflicts in which they were used, often in a dangerously unstable state. In most cases, the device can be removed to a safe area and destroyed with a controlled explosion. Where the bomb cannot be moved, it may be appropriate to destroy it *in situ*. However, in some circumstances—for example, when a bomb has been discovered in an urban or culturally important area, but is too unstable to be removed

for destruction—the only course of action is to disarm the device. This extremely hazardous operation might require the fuse system to be disabled or the explosive material to be drained from the casing.

The work of military and civilian bomb disposal experts also involves the handling of improvised explosive devices planted by *terrorist groups. To explode such devices in place might achieve some of the terrorists' aim, hence the requirement is usually to disarm the device and in so doing ensure that important forensic evidence is not lost. But the task of disposal is made more hazardous by the likelihood of booby traps and anti-handling devices. Various disruption techniques have been developed, whereby the device is broken up by a small explosion or by a water jet, in order to prevent explosion, protect the disposal expert, and preserve evidence, but it is still an activity requiring great courage and coolness.   PC

bombardment Massive attack from the air, sea, or land by explosive munitions, particularly in sieges or against *field fortifications. Bombardment by cannon first became effective against walls in the 1450s. Famous modern artillery bombardments include those of *Port Arthur in 1904–5, *Liège by the Germans in July 1914, and Sevastopol in 1941–2. The 'preparatory bombardments' and 'counter-bombardments' of WW I sometimes made the land to be advanced over virtually impassable. Mass air and land bombardments became common during WW II and became a signature of Soviet tactics. Journalists sometimes use the word to describe merely sporadic shelling. Those who have experienced the real thing do not.   JBAB

Bonaparte, Louis-Napoleon. See NAPOLEON III, EMPEROR OF THE FRENCH.

Bonaparte, Napoleon. See NAPOLEON I, EMPEROR OF FRANCE.

boomerang A weapon usually associated with Australian Aborigines, although versions of the idea have also been observed in Africa, America, and India. Boomerangs come in various shapes and sizes, but all share certain key characteristics; they are V-shaped, with one flat and one curved side, and operate using a complex mixture of aerodynamic and gyroscopic effects. Boomerangs have recently become popular for sport and recreation, but their original use was to stun small game and to 'reload' quickly if you missed. Also used to describe any action which results in the discomfiture of its initiator, such as the Germans introducing poison *gas on the western front when the prevailing winds were against them.   PC

Borneo campaign (1962–6). When the Federation of Malaysia was created it included the old British protectorates in north Borneo and the surrounding areas. This resulted in protests from Pres Sukarno of Indonesia, who also claimed these territories. Trouble flared first in Brunei with a local revolt, and *Gurkhas arrived from Singapore on 8 December 1962. Within a fortnight they had broken the back of the rebellion.

A more serious outbreak of raids, directed by Sukarno himself, began in north Borneo on 12 April 1963. The GOC, Maj Gen Walter Walker, had only five battalions at his disposal, and applied lessons he had learned on *counter-insurgency operations in the *Malayan emergency. He set out to dominate the jungle, moving swiftly and supported by an excellent intelligence network, while at the same time trying to win the hearts and minds of the population. Light aircraft, 60 *helicopters, river boats, and hovercraft provided his mobility. Locals were recruited into a 1,500-strong force of irregulars, known as the Border Scouts, and a true tri-service HQ co-ordinated the efforts of all arms, in conjunction with the civil authority. Four nations—Britain, Malaysia, New Zealand, and Australia—contributed to the force. Rebel *guerrillas would be tracked, then intercepted before reaching their targets.

In September 1963, Sukarno started deploying Indonesian regular forces, but with little extra progress. By 1965, Sukarno's forces, numbering around 30,000 at their peak, had been forced back from the frontier, but not defeated, and the British and Allied military presence had escalated to thirteen infantry battalions, two engineer regiments, two of artillery, and the equivalent of a battalion of *SAS. Hilltop forts were also established with artillery, while SAS teams patrolled the jungle and denied the enemy any safe areas. Sukarno was overthrown in March 1966 by Suharto, landed on a crocodile-infested beach by the British intelligence service sometime earlier. Malaysia and Indonesia signed a peace agreement on 11 August 1966, and the 'confrontation' was called off. With under 100 British and Allied casualties, the Borneo campaign was one of the most efficient uses of British military force ever.   APC-A

Pimlott, John, *British Military Operations 1945–1984* (London, 1984).

Borodino, battle of (7 September 1812), the greatest battle during Napoleon's 1812 invasion of Russia, and the second bloodiest of the *Napoleonic wars, one of Jomini's three 'hecatombs', along with the 'battle of the nations' at *Leipzig and *Waterloo. At the village of Borodino, on the main road 77 miles (124 km) west of Moscow, Marshal *Kutuzov, commanding 120,000 Russian troops with 640 guns, gave battle to Napoleon's multinational Grande Armée with 130,000–135,000 men and 587 guns. More than one-third of those on each side were killed or wounded. The battle itself was indecisive, and the Russians withdrew, having lost about 44,000 killed and wounded. But they had inflicted a mortal wound on Napoleon's overextended army, which lost about 50,000.

On 3 September, after a long retreat from the frontier which included giving up Smolensk, Kutuzov dug in across a front of 5 miles (8 km) spanning the only two approaches to Moscow, the main (new) Smolensk road and the old Smolensk road to the south, with his right flank protected by the Moskva river, the left by the thick Utitsa forest, with the Kolocha stream to the front and with woods behind to conceal his reserves. In the centre was the Kurgan hill, where 'the Great (Raevsky) redoubt' was constructed. Miloradovich commanded the right near the villages of Maslovo and Gorki, strengthened with several redoubts, and *Bagration commanded the left, near the village of Semyonov where he constructed three lunettes. The strength of the wings was designed to direct any attack into the centre, commanded by Barclay de Tolly with the bulk of the artillery. Outflanking movement to the immediate north or south was impossible because of the forest and river.

There was nothing subtle or deceptive about the Russian position: it was immensely strong and any sane general would have refused to assault it under normal circumstances. But Kutuzov calculated that after a long advance over scorched earth, Napoleon would be desperate for a decisive battle, and so it proved. The French army comprised the corps of *Murat, *Davout, *Ney, and *Junot, plus the Old and Young Guard in reserve under Napoleon's own command. The first contact was at the Russian redoubt at Shevardino, to the west of the main position, where 40,000 French stumbled on 12,000 Russians on 5 September and were repulsed, giving Kutuzov confirmation of the main line of French advance and buying time to strengthen his position yet further. This included reinforcing Bagration, upon whom Napoleon's first hammer-blow was to fall.

The French attacked at 05.00 on 7 September; seven separate assaults were beaten back at enormous cost but the eighth, at about noon, succeeded. His planned turning manoeuvre already seriously dislocated, Napoleon then attacked the Great Redoubt in the centre. As he had already discovered at *Eylau, Russian infantry on the defensive fought to the death, and the battle lost any semblance of tactical refinement in an orgy of mutual slaughter. Shaken by the carnage and perhaps suddenly acutely aware of how far he was from home, Napoleon decided not to commit the Guard, whose bitterly ironic nickname of 'the immortals' may have been coined by the battered line infantry after Borodino. At about 18.00, as darkness approached, the fighting petered out through exhaustion. Not only the French were stunned. After an orderly withdrawal, six days later Kutuzov informed his subordinates of his decision to give up Moscow in order to maintain the army in being.   CDB

Bosworth, battle of (1485), the culmination of a three-week campaign by Henry Tudor in his bid for the throne of England. Having marched from Milford Haven into the heart of England, he was intercepted by Richard III near the small Leicestershire town of Market Bosworth. The armies met on the plain called Redemore on the morning of 22 August. The sparse sources make it difficult to reconstruct its course or to be sure of its precise location, but it is likely that Richard drew up his much larger army in the customary three 'battles' (large divisions of troops) across Henry's line of advance, protected by a marsh. Probably attempting to turn his enemy's flank, Tudor's vanguard under the Earl of Oxford was attacked by the Duke of Norfolk commanding Richard's right. At first Oxford's mainly French contingent gave way, but then re-forming they counter-attacked and drove Norfolk back. At this moment, seeing Tudor standing a little way off with only a small guard, Richard charged. The velocity of his attack carried him close to his enemy, but Sir William Stanley, who had held his contingent back and was in collusion with Tudor, chose this moment to show his hand. Richard was cut down and killed, having thrown away a battle he should have won. The Earl of Northumberland on the king's left was never engaged. It is possible that he deliberately held back, but it is equally possible that the course of the battle, and the king's reckless charge at Henry Tudor, left him stranded. In time, the battle came misleadingly to mark the end of the Wars of the *Roses, and to signify the establishment of the Tudor dynasty. Although its traditional location is very well commemorated, in 1990 Peter J. Foss argued convincingly in *The Field of Redemore* that the battle's actual site was further to the south.   AJP/RH

Boudicca (incorrectly Boadicea) (d. AD 61), queen of the Iceni, Celtic war leader. Abused by Roman officials after the death of her husband, Prasutagus, she revolted in AD 60–1. Together with the neighbouring Trinovantes, she destroyed part of the Ninth Legion, burnt Colchester, London, and St Albans, and caused the financial procurator of Britain to flee to Gaul. Advancing against the governor, Suetonius Paullinus, who had been away campaigning in Wales, she was utterly defeated and took poison.   BR2

Cassius Dio, 62. 1–12.
Tacitus, *Agricola* 16. 1–2.
—— *Annals* 14. 31–7.
Webster, Graham, *Boudicca: The British Revolt against Rome* AD 60 (London, 1978).

Bouillon, Godfrey de (*c*.1060–1100), venerated conqueror of *Jerusalem. The younger son of Eustace II of Boulogne, he inherited the lands of his uncle, Godfrey 'the Hunchback', Duke of Lower Lorraine *c*.1076, notably Bouillon castle. He had to fight rival claimants and then gained wider military experience in the armies of the Holy Roman Emperor Henry IV. He was the most prominent imperial vassal to join the First *Crusade and attracted a large following from Germany and Burgundy. His role was at first limited, partly because he had been injured by a bear while hunting in Pisidia, but he was always acknowledged as a major leader.

He came to prominence in spring 1099 when his will to press on to Jerusalem stilled quarrelling among other Crusader leaders. During the siege he contributed to the construction of the decisive wooden siege tower by the northern French and distinguished himself by his bravery in the assault, being recorded as sitting on its upper storey firing arrows. His fine example, coupled with the unpopularity of the rival Count of Toulouse, got him elected ruler of Jerusalem on 22 July. He led an army successfully against the Egyptians at Ascalon on 12 August, but his short reign was otherwise undistinguished.   JF2

Andressohn, J. C., *The Ancestry and Life of Godfrey de Bouillon* (Bloomington, Ind., 1947).

Bouvines, battle of (1214). On 27 July the French King Philip Augustus secured Capetian mastery in northern France by decisively defeating an enemy coalition led by Otto IV of Germany at Bouvines, 9 miles (14.5 km) west of Tournai. Philip himself narrowly escaped death when Otto's infantry broke through the French centre. The battle was won by the superior *discipline and close combat skill of the more numerous French knights who routed the cavalry of the allied right, drove Otto from the field, then annihilated the now isolated infantry on the allied left. With the capture of the counts of Boulogne and Flanders, the alliance collapsed, embroiling King John of England, who had organized and funded the coalition, in political repercussions that led directly to Magna Carta.   MJS

Duby, Georges, *The Legend of Bouvines*, trans. Catherine Tihanyi (Cambridge, 1990).
Verbruggen, J. F., *The Art of Warfare in Western Europe during the Middle Ages* (Woodbridge, 1997).

bow (see also ARCHERS). From prehistoric times until its replacement by early firearms during the 16th century, the bow remained the principal hand-held missile weapon in warfare. Bows fell into three main types: the composite bow, the crossbow, and the longbow.

Rightly regarded as one of early man's great technical developments, the composite bow was used by the armies of both classical Greece and Rome and their enemies such as the *Scythians, Persians, and Parthians. It usually consisted of a wooden core onto which thin layers of horn were glued to the belly (the inside of the bow nearest the archer) while layered strips of animal sinew were glued to the back of the bow. A protective covering of leather or parchment might then be added to prevent rain from dissolving the glue. As sinew is naturally elastic and horn compressive, their combination resulted in a bow of considerable power, yet which crucially was short enough to use with ease on horseback. The composite bow thus became the weapon par excellence of the eastern nomadic peoples such as the *Huns, Magyars, and *Mongols, whose military successes stemmed in large part from the highly effective combination of archery fire power and great manoeuvrability. The weapon was also used throughout the Levant, the Near East, and the Far East, while its predominance among the *Turks frequently led western sources to refer to this weapon as a 'Turkish bow'. Riders were trained to achieve astonishing feats of accuracy while at full gallop, often turning in the saddle to fire backwards with a 'Parthian shot'. Yet while the composite bow might achieve greater range than a longbow, the arrows it fired were lighter and its powers of penetration were much less; numerous Crusade sources speak of Frankish knights bristling like porcupines with the number of Turkish arrows lodged in their mail, yet remaining unwounded by them. The composite bow can be found as a military weapon in medieval France, appearing, for example, in manuscripts such as the Maciejowski Bible (c.1250), and was the principal form of bow in medieval and Renaissance Italy, where the longbow never supplanted it.

The most powerful hand-held missile weapon of the Middle Ages was the crossbow, constructed by securing a bow (or lath) horizontally to a stock or tiller, which contained a nut, often of bone or ivory, to hold the string when spanned, a trigger mechanism, and a groove onto which the short, thick arrows (known as bolts or quarrels) were laid for firing. The bow itself could be simply of wood or of a composite of horn or whalebone placed between two thin pieces of yew and covered in tendon, while steel bows appear from the 14th century. The crossbow was known to the Chinese as early as the 6th century BC, and their later development of the weapon included repeating crossbows of considerable sophistication. The ancient Greeks used a form of crossbow known as the *gastraphetes* or 'belly-bow', spanned by placing the stock against the stomach and pushing a sliding mechanism forward to lock with a trigger mechanism, while the Romans employed the large torsion-driven bow or *ballista* as an effective light artillery piece, particularly in *siege warfare. The hand-held crossbow seems to have had only a limited role in Roman warfare and was largely restricted to hunting.

Though considerable knowledge of classical siegecraft survived into the Dark Ages, the role of the crossbow remains obscure until the later 10th century, when mention begins to be made of its use in European warfare. Tenth- and 11th-century depictions of crossbows suggest these early weapons were spanned by placing the archer's feet against the bow stave and drawing the string upwards with his hands. By the 12th century, if not before, this cumbersome method was replaced by the use of a stirrup attached to the end of the tiller, in which the bowman placed a foot while attaching the string to a hook slung from his belt; by

straightening his back while pushing down with his foot, the bow was spanned. Stirrup and belt hook, and a variant involving a cord and pulley attached to the bowman's belt, seem to have remained the predominant method of spanning crossbows until the 15th century, when a mechanical ratchet known as a cranequin, first appearing in the second half of the 14th century, gained popularity. This allowed mounted crossbowmen, now using more compact crossbows, to reload while still in the saddle. At the same time, the windlass and pulley, hitherto restricted to large frame-mounted crossbows (sometimes called springalds) for siege work, now became widespread for spanning large, more powerful hand-held military crossbows.

Assessing the range and penetrative power of medieval crossbows is difficult because of a dearth of extant examples before the 16th century, and because it is clear that there was always a multiplicity of sizes and types of crossbow in use at any given time. Written sources leave no doubt that as early as the 11th century, crossbows could penetrate mail *armour, so much so, indeed, that in several engagements, such as the battle of Lincoln in 1217, commanders ordered their crossbowmen to shoot the enemy horses not the riders, wishing not to kill but to capture the opposing knights for rich *ransom. Nevertheless, the crossbow claimed many noble victims, most notably Richard 'the Lionheart' who died of an infected wound after being struck by a bolt at the siege of Chaluz Chabrol in 1199, and it was not unusual for captured crossbowmen to face execution or mutilation at the hands of vengeful knights. Though by the 15th century some armourers were claiming their plate armour proof against bolts, extant weapons reveal the awesome power of late medieval crossbows; a 15th-century example spanned by a cranequin had a draw weight of 400 lb—more than double that of the most powerful of longbows—while that of a large, wall-mounted crossbow spanned by a windlass was 1,200 lb or nearly half a ton, allowing it to shoot a bolt 460 yards (421 metres).

Crossbows, it seems, were generally more powerful than longbows, but their great disadvantage was their slow rate of fire, particularly with the clumsy, if reliable, windlass. A trained crossbowman might shoot one or at best two bolts to the longbowman's seventeen or more aimed arrows per minute. It was this disparity that led to the rout of the Genoese crossbowmen at *Crécy in 1346, when they were engulfed by English arrows after loosing only one volley. Crossbowmen often carried a very large shield known as a pavise to shelter behind while loading, but this restricted the speed of any tactical movement. The crossbow was at its best not in open battle but in siege, where speed of fire was less important than its power, accuracy, and ability to be used in more restricted space than could the longbow. Whereas a longbowman needed to come up to the draw before loosing, the crossbowman could span his weapon in advance. Silent in shooting, more accurate than many early firearms, and more reliable in wet weather, the crossbow remained extremely popular for hunting until modern times, and the great majority of extant examples are richly decorated hunting weapons from the 16th century and later.

The longbow was usually made from a single wooden stave of about 6 feet in length and was distinguished from other self-bows (such as the flat bow) by its deep 'D' section, with a ratio of width to depth of one to three. Several types of wood could be used; the late 12th-century writer Gerald of Wales noted the prowess of the men of Gwent with powerful longbows made from wych elm, while ash, particularly favoured for arrows, was also used for bows. Yew was best, and the finest bow-wood of all was slow-growing yew, imported from Spain and Dalmatia, which allowed a stave to possess a natural composite quality in the elastic sap wood (found nearest the outside of the tree) and the composite, more densely ringed heartwood. Few medieval longbows are extant, but excavations of Henry VIII's warship the *Mary Rose*, which sank in the Solent in 1545, revealed over 130 longbows in excellent condition. Tests revealed these weapons to have a far higher draw weight than was previous ascribed to the longbow. Whereas most modern sporting longbows have an average pull of around 60–70 lb, the majority of the *Mary Rose* bows fell into the middle or upper part of a range between 100 lb to over 170 lb. A bow of 170 lb could shoot a heavy war-arrow nearly 300 yards (274 metres) with considerable accuracy. Arrows, usually carried in quivers of 24, could have a variety of heads, ranging from wide hunting broadheads, used for game but equally effective against horses, to small, barbed anti-personnel heads, needle-like bodkin heads, and square sectioned armour-piercing heads closely resembling those of crossbow bolts. Bodkin-headed arrows could easily pierce mail, and though further ballistic tests are necessary, it seems certain that at a closer range some forms of plate armour could be penetrated. Chronicle sources amply attest to the devastating power of longbow arrows falling, as one contemporary noted of Crécy, 'so thick that it seemed snow'.

It was once thought that the longbow was developed from the late 13th century onwards from the so-called 'shortbow', a weaker weapon drawn only to the chest. But this belief, held by early military historians like Sir Charles *Oman and J. E. Morris, was based on too literal and too limited an interpretation of medieval iconography such as the Bayeux Tapestry. In fact, while a variety of types of self-bows (bows made only of wood) existed, particularly outside Europe, archaeology reveals the use of longbows (so called to distinguish them not from the 'shortbow' but the crossbow) from prehistoric times onwards. The longbow was not 'discovered' in Wales by the Angevin kings, but rather the catalyst of Edward I's Welsh and Scots wars (see WALES, CONQUEST OF and SCOTS WARS OF INDEPENDENCE) led to an existing weapon being deployed en masse, as archers were ideal infantry for operating in difficult terrain. What made the longbow so highly effective in the *Hun-

dred Years War and accounted for the victories such as Crécy, Poitiers in 1356, and *Agincourt, was less the development of any new weapon but the crucial tactical combination of archers, now numbering in their thousands, with dismounted men-at-arms. Nor was the longbow only a preserve of the English; the French knew the weapon and even had a large number of archers at Agincourt, though they were never effectively deployed; 15th-century Burgundian armies included their own longbowmen as well as English mercenary archers; and some of the finest depictions of late medieval longbows come from Germany and the Low Countries.

Cheap to produce, capable of far greater speed and accuracy than any smoothbore musket, the longbow was a formidable weapon in the hands of a seasoned archer. Its one disadvantage was that it demanded great physical strength and skill, which could only be developed through years of training. During the 14th and 15th centuries, the tactical significance of archers in English armies and a near constant war footing created a ready reservoir of expert bowmen, but by the mid-16th century, ever more desperate attempts by the government to legislate for practice with the longbow signalled an inexorable decline. While traditionalists, mindful of past glories in France, argued for the retention of longbowmen as the mainstay of English infantry, it was clear from rapid military developments on the continent that the arquebus and musket, which required far less strength or training to operate effectively, were the weapons of the future.   MJS

Brabury, Jim, *The Medieval Archer* (Woodbridge, 1985).
Hardy, Robert, *Longbow: A Social and Military History* (Cambridge, 3rd edn., 1992).
Heath, E. G., *The Grey Goose Wing: A History of Archery* (Reading, 1971).
—— *Archery. A Military History* (London, 1980).
Payne-Gallwey, Ralph, *The Crossbow* (London, 1903; repr. New York, 1996).

Bowie, Jim (*c*.1796–1836), Texas revolutionary hero whose name is associated with a large knife much used on the American frontier. Born in Kentucky, he grew up poor in Louisiana, where with his brothers John and Rezin he eventually became a slave-trader in association with Jean Lafitte, the pirate and hero of the *War of 1812. The brothers bought a sugar plantation and Jim became prominent in local society, serving in the state legislature. In 1827 he killed two men during a savage gun and knife duel in Natchez and became a GTT ('Gone To Texas', contemporary term for fugitives from justice). In San Antonio he became friendly with the vice governor and married his daughter in 1831 after acquiring Mexican citizenship and land grants. In 1835, a widower, he joined the revolution and was elected colonel of militia, in which capacity he participated in the battle of Concepción and the first siege of the *Alamo that ended with the expulsion of Mexican troops from Texas. Bowie refused to accept the authority of Travis, but by the time the Mexicans returned under Santa Anna he had been stricken with typhus. He was bayoneted to death in the sickbay, reportedly wielding his eponymous knife to the end.   HEB

Boxer rebellion (1900–1). In the late 1890s China was riddled with lawlessness, and humiliated by the loss of Korea to Japan and growing European influence. The young emperor supported reformers who wished to modernize China, but in 1898 the Dowager Empress Tzu-hsi staged a coup, suppressed the reformers, and re-established herself as regent. Resentment of foreign influence encouraged the growth of a clandestine society called 'Fists of Righteous Harmony', known to Europeans as Boxers from its Chinese name and practice of ritual shadow-boxing. The Boxers were xenophobic and anti-Christian, blamed China's ills on 'foreign devils', and used elaborate rituals to emphasize divine support and invulnerability to modern weapons. The degree to which the Boxers received official support remains unclear, but Tzu-hsi certainly sympathized with them, and little was done to prevent their attacks on foreign property and *railways.

In May 1900 the murder of two British missionaries provoked European ministers at Peking (correctly Beijing) into issuing an ultimatum demanding suppression of the Boxers, and when no action was taken the senior diplomat, the British envoy Sir Claude Macdonald, requested Adm Sir Edward Seymour, C-in-C of the China Station, stationed at Taku at the entrance to the Peiho river, to send troops. Seymour set off down the railway with a multinational force of 2,000 men on 10 June. Meanwhile, the situation in Peking worsened, with the Boxer sympathizer Prince Tuan being appointed head of the foreign office and troops of general Tung-fu-hsiang actively helping the Boxers. Europeans and Chinese Christians concentrated in the legation quarter and the Pei T'ang cathedral. A Japanese diplomat was murdered on 11 June, and on the 19th Prince Tuan warned foreigners to leave, as their safety could not be guaranteed. The German minister was murdered on his way to the foreign office on 20 June, and that afternoon the legations were attacked. They were defended by 407 troops of eight nationalities assisted by a number of volunteers. An Austro-Hungarian naval officer took command at first, but was soon replaced by Macdonald, who had been an army officer until retiring in 1896.

While Seymour was on his way the Boxers captured the Chinese quarter of Tientsin, threatening foreign legations in the town, and in response the Allied naval commanders took the Taku forts by amphibious assault. It was this that provoked the attack on the legations in Peking, and also brought Chinese troops into action against Seymour, who got to within 30 miles (48 km) of Peking before having to fall back towards Tientsin. The legations there also came under heavy attack by Boxers and regular troops, but the

garrison held out until relieved, and on 13–14 July, after Seymour's force had arrived, the Allies took the Chinese quarter, stabilizing the situation on the coast.

The Allies believed that the Peking legations had fallen and decided to assemble a substantial force under the German general Waldersee, but before he arrived news was received that they were still holding out. The British general Gaselee set off with a mixed force of 20,000 men, with large Japanese, Russian, and British-Indian contingents and smaller forces from the USA, France, Austria, Germany, and Italy. He won three major actions and entered Peking, with his contingents jostling to be first into the city, relieving the legations on 14 August. On the following day Allied troops entered the Forbidden City, and two days later Pei T'ang cathedral was relieved. After Waldersee's arrival in September the Boxer stronghold of Pao Ting Fu was captured and burned. Numerous Boxers and their sympathizers were executed or exiled to placate the Allies, the Taku forts were demolished, a substantial indemnity was paid, and the Allies acquired numerous concessions. A peace protocol was concluded on 7 September 1901, and the court returned to Peking in January 1902.

The Boxer Rebellion paved the way for the revolution of 1911, which overthrew the Manchu dynasty and resulted in the establishment of the Republic of China in 1912. The alliance which had won the war proved short-lived. The Russians and Japanese, two of its major members, shortly fought the *Russo-Japanese war, while Germany found herself opposed by the other allies during *WW I. Stung by the murder of the German minister, Kaiser Wilhelm II had told Waldersee to make his men 'feared like the Huns of old', thus coining the British WW I appellation for his troops.

RH

Bodin, L. E., *The Boxer Rebellion* (London, 1979).
Fleming, Peter, *The Siege at Peking* (London, 1959).

Boyne, battle of the (1690). Although the Boyne was not the biggest battle of the *Irish campaign of *William of Orange, the fact that the two contenders for the throne, *James II and his son-in-law, met in person gave it a lasting resonance. James landed in Ireland in 1689 to find most of the country held by his supporters. By 1690 the tide had turned against him, and he retired southwards down the east coast, making a stand on the Boyne, the last major obstacle north of Dublin.

William had 36,000 men, including Dutch and Danish contingents as well as Ulstermen, Scots, Englishmen, and *Huguenots, to James's 26,000. On 1 July he attacked across the river at Oldbridge while an outflanking force marched upstream to Rossnaree. James sent too many troops—including all his French infantry—to meet the flank attack. His centre was broken after hard fighting in which James's cavalry earned widespread admiration. William's C-in-C, the veteran Duke of Schomberg, was among the killed.

James lost about 1,000 men, William perhaps 500. James was hustled away, and left Ireland shortly afterwards. His supporters fought on with a courage worthy of a better cause.   RH

Bradley, Gen Omar Nelson (1893–1981), known as 'the soldier's general', one of the most distinguished US commanders of WW II. In 1943, during the campaign in North Africa, Bradley made his mark while in command of II Corps, which he then led into Sicily. Selected to command First Army for the *Normandy landings in June 1944, he held the initially precarious right flank of the OVER-LORD beachhead. On 1 August 1944 he was given command of the massive Twelfth Army Group which he took across France and into Germany, meeting up with Soviet forces on the Elbe. After the war, Bradley was US army COS (1948–9), and then the first chairman of the new Joint Chiefs of Staff (1949–53). In 1950 he was appointed general of the army. The M2/M3 infantry fighting vehicle, currently in service, is named after him.   PC

Bragg, Gen Braxton (1817–76). Born in North Carolina, Bragg graduated from *West Point in 1837. He earned fame as a battery commander in the *Mexican war—Gen Zachary *Taylor reportedly demanded 'a little more grape, Captain Bragg' at Buena Vista—but retired as a lieutenant colonel in 1856 to become a planter in Louisiana. In March 1861 he was commissioned brigadier general in the Confederate Army, and rose rapidly. He took over A. S. Johnston's army when its commander was killed at *Shiloh, and in June 1862 was promoted full general to command the Army of Tennessee.

Bragg invaded Kentucky, but was defeated at Perryville and Murfreesboro. Although he won at Chickamauga, he failed to grasp the fruits of victory. He went on to besiege Chattanooga, but was beaten at Missionary Ridge and replaced by *Johnston. Bragg then served as military adviser to Pres Jefferson *Davis, a personal friend. His excellent understanding of war was not matched by practical skill, and uncompromising *discipline helped make him unpopular. *Grant described him as 'naturally disputatious', while a fellow Confederate thought him indecisive and vindictive. He suffered from frequent migraines, which may partly explain his abrasive behaviour.   RH

Brasidas (d. 422 BC), Spartan commander during the *Peloponnesian wars who first came to notice in 431 BC when he saved Methone from an Athenian seaborne attack, and this may have led to his election to the ephorate that autumn. In 429 he was one of the advisers to a Spartan admiral in the Gulf of Corinth and took part in a raid on Salamis. In 427 he was again adviser to an admiral, and after

a victory off Corcyra, urged in vain an attack on its main town. In 425 he was wounded in the seaborne attack on the Athenian base at *Pylos, and in 424 was instrumental in saving Megara for the Spartan alliance. But his chief claim to fame is as commander of a force of emancipated helots and Peloponnesian mercenaries in Macedonia and Chalcidice from 424 to 422 when, by a mixture of charm and threats, he won over a number of Athens' allies, including the strategically important Amphipolis. He was finally mortally wounded outside its walls in the battle in which the Athenian Cleon also lost his life. Brasidas was a bold and charismatic commander with advanced ideas about how to use mixed forces of *hoplites and light troops.   JFL

Kagan, Donald, *The Archidamian War* (Ithaca, NY, & London, 1974).

Braun, Freiherr Dr Werner von (1912–77), scientific director of both the Nazi Vergeltungswaffen (reprisal weapon) rocket programme and of the NASA *space programme. A classic technocrat, he worked for the Ordnance Board of the German army between 1932 and 1945, becoming its director in 1937, when his project team moved to the relative secrecy of the Baltic coast at Peenemunde, where a massed RAF raid failed to kill him. His work with *rockets resulted in the second Vergeltungswaffen, the infamous V-2. Effectively the world's first ballistic missile, the first of over 1,000 was directed at London on 8 September 1944. Braun and his staff fled west to escape the advancing Soviets in March 1945 and were captured by US troops. In an operation named PAPERCLIP, he was immediately spirited across the Atlantic, where he worked on the US space programme, initially on satellites, and eventually on the Saturn V rocket and the Apollo moon landings. Decorated by *Hitler, he was honoured by the USA with citizenship, and was the director of the George C. Marshall Space Flight Center in Huntsville, Alabama, 1960–70.   APC-A

breech-loading firearms were developed in the mid-19th century by European nations for their armies but attempts to invent and produce a successful breech-loading system for firearms date back to the earliest martial use of *gunpowder in the West. First used in artillery in the 14th century, the earliest breech-loading cannons used removable chambers, individually charged with powder, which would be placed at the breech of the loaded barrel, firmly wedged in place, and then ignited through a touch-hole. Accounts of this type of artillery, which was usually quite light in weight, are found in both English and French sources during the *Hundred Years War; the cannon so referred to became known by a variety of names, of which perrier is the most common. *Leonardo da Vinci is generally credited with the earliest invention of one of the types of breech-loading system which persisted until the invention of the enclosed cartridge in the mid-19th century. In his *Codex Atlanticus* of *c.*1500–10 he illustrated a hackbutt—a type of early, heavy *matchlock musket—with an unscrewing, or 'turn-off' breech. The concept of a breech and barrel assembly separated by simply unscrewing one from the other remained popular until the 19th century because it was the most efficient breech-loading system available, with the advantage that the ball, inserted at the rear of the barrel, could be slightly oversize. This made for a tight fit, less wasted combustion power for the gunpowder and thus greater range and—in the case of rifled barrels—greater accuracy than could be provided by muzzle-loaded firearms with their necessarily looser-fitting balls. The separately charged chamber system for breech-loading firearms existed at the same time as the turn-off breech or barrel system and, although it suffered from—generally—a poorer seal between breech and barrel than had the 'turn-off' system, its concept was the one which became eventually modified in the earliest bolt-action rifles. The earliest military breech-loading firearms are thought to be the pistol shields bought by King Henry VIII of England from Giovanbattista, a Ravenna gunsmith, in the mid-1540s. These were separately chambered matchlock *pistols, the barrels of which poked through the centre of disc-shaped *shields; they are thought to have been intended to arm the king's bodyguard of the Yeomen of the Guard. Experiments into the development of breech-loaders continued for the following century and a half but were principally aimed at the civilian market for sporting firearms; not until the early 18th century did a breech-loading system suitable not only for large-scale production but also for handling by soldiers attract the attention of military authorities.

Although a French engineer is generally given credit for the development of this successful system, its origins date back to the late 16th century in Spain. The system utilized a screw-threaded plug which, by being screwed and unscrewed vertically at the rear of the barrel, sealed and unsealed the breech for loading with powder and ball. Throughout the 17th century this system was experimented with in Germany, England, and Denmark but was finally developed with success by Isaac de la Chaumette in France in 1704. The inventor was a Huguenot, however, and fled to England subsequently where, in 1721, he took out an English patent to protect his invention. For the next 50 years screw-plug breech-loading muskets and rifles were made in England as sporting guns but, in 1776, Capt Patrick *Ferguson, a Scot, took out a patent for an improved version which he intended for military use. Subsequent trials of his rifle impressed British military authorities and it was made in a small quantity to equip a Corps of Riflemen to be led by him on campaign in America. Although successful at Brandywine in 1777, Ferguson's corps was broken up after he was wounded there, and his subsequent death at King's Mountain in 1780 ended Britain's experiment with military breech-loaders for the next half-century.

By the end of the 18th century most systems of breech-loading had been tried: most were regarded as little more than curiosities by the conservative and were not seen as soldier-proof by military authorities—bodies not noted for their radicalism. Although rudimentary cartridges had been designed by Leonardo and were used in some breech-loaders, the lack of an effective gas seal bedevilled attempts to get them widely accepted. The combination of reliable cartridges and a better gas seal finally arrived in the early 19th century and was developed separately by the Parisian gunsmith Johannes Pauly and one of his staff, Johann von Dreyse. Dreyse's *needle gun utilized a bolt-action breech-locking system which sealed the chamber effectively and fired an efficient self-contained *cartridge; it was adopted by the Prussian army in 1841. In 1819, the US army had adopted a breech-loading rifle using a 'tip-up' breech-chamber developed by John Hall; Hall's system, which did not use cartridges, remained in use in the US army into the 1850s.

The development of the self-contained cartridge closely paralleled that of breech-loader in the 19th century. By 1870, brass-jacketed centre-fire and rim-fire cartridges were in use for a multiplicity of breech-loading actions, each with its own pros and cons. Bolt-action, hinging chamber, tipping chamber, tipping barrel, sliding barrel, sliding breech-bolt: all systems were tried and adopted by the armies of nations engaged in an arms race, and also in an *arms trade which benefited from regular wars in which the latest arms technology could be tried. By the end of the century, most nations had adopted some form of the action by which the breech was closed, sealed, and locked by a turning bolt; by then, too, repeating firearms had been developed and automatic firearms were in their infancy. Long before this, the very great advantage to the infantryman of being able to load and fire from a prone position, as well as the very much greater rate of fire now possible, had revolutionized battlefield tactics and the ranges at which the enemy could be engaged.   SCW

Blackmore, Howard L., *British Military Firearms 1650–1850* (London, 1961).

Blair, Claude (gen. ed.), *Pollard's History of Firearms* (London, 1983).

Peterson, Harold L. (ed.), *Encyclopaedia of Firearms* (London, 1964).

Breitenfeld, battles of (1631, 1642). At the first battle of Breitenfeld on 17 September 1631 *Gustavus Adolphus with 30,000 Swedes and John George of Saxony with 10,000 electoral troops faced 32,000 imperialists under *Tilly. Gustavus intended to capture Leipzig, but found Tilly's troops drawn up in the rolling country 5 miles (8 km) to the north. After some desultory artillery fire from both sides, the imperialists mounted a cavalry attack on both flanks. The Saxons standing on Gustavus's left were soon put to flight, but on the opposite flank *Pappenheim and his much-vaunted black *cuirassiers could make little progress against the disciplined Swedish horse. The Swedes were able to extend their line, protecting their exposed left flank, and smash their way through Pappenheim's cavalry into the side of the imperialist infantry. The Swedish centre under Horn ground forward to meet Tilly's sixteen large infantry formations or *tercios, denying them the space to manoeuvre, and eventually gaining the upper hand by dint of much hard fighting.

The imperialists lost over 7,000 killed or wounded, and a similar number of prisoners against Swedish losses of 1,500 and Saxon casualties of 3,000. Tilly pulled back westward across the Weser, leaving Gustavus a free hand in Bohemia and the valley of the Main. Military pundits often cite first Breitenfeld as demonstrating the superiority of the smaller and handier Swedish battalion system over the imperial tercio, but in truth this was a victory for combined arms: infantry, cavalry, and guns (in this case captured and turned on their former owners) working together. Moreover, tackling the massive imperial formations head-on was no easy task, whatever formation one adopted, and it was the compression of the imperial battle line from the flank that caused the eventual collapse of Tilly's army, rather than any specific tactical device.

In the spring of 1642 the ruthless Swedish commander *Tortensson was ravaging the imperial lands, coming to within 25 miles (40 km) of Vienna. Archduke Leopold and *Piccolomini forced him back through Silesia into Saxony, where Tortensson attempted to capture Leipzig. It was near here that the imperialists eventually caught up with him. The second battle near Breitenfeld on 2 November was preceded by a roaring imperial cannonade as the horse moved into position on Leopold's wings. Beset by whirring chain shot, the Swedes did not wait for the imperial army to complete its deployment, and mounted a hasty attack on the enemy's left, catching them in disarray and putting them to flight almost at once.

Meanwhile on the other flank the imperialist cavalry had repulsed the Swedish horse, and the imperial infantry was moving up in support. Tortensson was obliged to bring his victorious right-wing squadrons to the aid of the hard-pressed Swedish foot, stemming the tide of the imperial advance, and pushing the infantry back, which left their mounted colleagues surrounded. Seeing that they were alone and unsupported some fled, while others threw down their arms and surrendered. More than 5,000 imperial troops were captured, and as many again were killed. This defeat marked the nadir of imperial fortunes in the later stages of the war.   TM

Brialmont, Lt Gen H. A. (1821–1903). Brialmont was commissioned into the Belgian engineers in 1841. He travelled abroad to study fortifications, and gained royal support for his concept, much influenced by Montalambert, of defending a city by a ring of outlying forts. In the 1850s, he designed the fortifications of Antwerp, developing armoured turrets for their artillery. He went on to encircle *Liège and Namur with detached works mounting turreted guns, and his designs were influential outside Belgium. Technological advance doomed his forts in 1914, their steel and concrete being inadequate against heavy siege *howitzers, but his armoured turrets were the heart of the later *Maginot Line.   RH

Britain, battle of (1940). In the summer of 1940 the Luftwaffe attempted to win air superiority over Britain as a sine qua non for an invasion code-named SEALION. On 30 June Herman Göring issued multiple directives to draw the RAF into combat over the Channel by attacking coastal *convoys (which the Admiralty unwisely continued to run), and bombing the string of *radar stations along the south coast, the British aircraft industry, and RAF airfields. This dispersion of effort was the first of a triad of reasons why the RAF won the battle. The second was Hugh Dowding, in charge of Fighter Command since 1937. He had been involved in the procurement of the Spitfire and the Hurricane, and in the development and deployment of radar. He resisted demands by *Churchill to send his reserve of fighters to *France, and refused to commit them in strength to defending the convoys, or indeed to involve them in mass battles at all. The third was that the Luftwaffe was not well equipped for a sustained air superiority campaign. Like the RAF's Hurricanes and Spitfires, the Messerschmitt Bf 109 was a short-range aircraft, but the former were fighting over their own bases. Likewise a downed pilot who survived was lost to the Luftwaffe but returned immediately to his RAF squadron.

The battle officially began on 13 August. Fighter losses were about even, but the Luftwaffe suffered from poor operational focus and shifting priorities. Unwilling to endure such heavy losses, Göring and *Hitler switched in early September to a campaign of city bombing, allowing Fighter Command to recover. On 17 September, Hitler cancelled SEALION, although air raids continued.   JB/HEB

Hough, Richard, and Richards, Denis, *The Battle of Britain* (London, 1989).
Murray, Williamson, *Luftwaffe: Strategy for Defeat* (Washington, 1985).

British army   The British army is still composed of fiercely individualistic regiments and corps. This is a reflection of the tenacity with which it has clung to its roots in the 17th and 18th centuries, when units were raised by individual colonels. A series of reforms over the last century and a half have failed to 'nationalize' the army in a thoroughgoing fashion. Officers and men have traditionally been drawn from extremes of society. The abolition of the purchase of *commissions in the 1870s failed to end the dominance of the officer corps by the upper and middle classes, and even in the late 20th century products of fee-paying schools have been disproportionately represented in officers' messes, although the balance has been changing. With the exception of the two world wars and the period of National Service (peacetime conscription, 1947–63) the army has remained separate from mainstream British society. An inherently conservative organization, the British army has nevertheless succeeded in remaking itself at regular intervals over the last 300 years.

Since the Middle Ages, the British army and its antecedents consisted of both a part-time force and a permanent or semi-permanent component. The British have had the luxury of being able to rely on *militia-type forces and a small standing army because Britain is an island, and for much of this period had a powerful navy, so did not run the risk of sudden invasion. While the exact origins of the militia system are unclear, some historians believe that in Anglo-Saxon times there was a 'great' *fyrd (army) in which there was a general obligation for freemen to participate, and an élite 'select fyrd', perhaps of 14,000 men. Under Henry II, the Assize of Arms (1181) reaffirmed the freeman's obligation to serve in the militia. In 1558, in the reign of Mary I, county lord-lieutenants were appointed to control militia units; all adult males were, in theory, obliged to serve in them. Other preparations for home defence were put on a sensible footing, including regular training of militiamen. During the Spanish war in the 1580s the coastal county of Kent could raise perhaps 4,000 men, although under the early Stuarts the militia fell on hard times, the efficient 'trained bands' of London being a notable exception.

The militia was not the only source of troops. In the medieval period troops were raised by feudal obligation; under Henry I (1100–35) the king demanded that knights serve him for two months a year (or 40 days in time of peace). Increasingly, however, the practice of giving *scutage—a fee paid in lieu of service—became the norm, the monarch using this money to hire mercenaries, often foreigners (see MERCENARIES, MEDIEVAL). In addition there were small standing forces, usually household troops such as the *housecarls of the Saxon kings or the Yeomen of the Guard, formed by Henry VII in 1485.

Armies, above all, are instruments of foreign policy. The participation of *Richard 'the Lionheart' in the Third *Crusade, *Edward I's campaigns in Scotland, and *Henry V's French campaigns are three very different examples of medieval English kings using armies to pursue political objectives. However, in the second half of the 16th century the disadvantages of relying on 'traditional' armies became clear. Under Elizabeth I (reigned 1559–1603) England began to take her place as a major player in European affairs. In 1585 England went to war with Spain, a conflict that was to last for the rest of Elizabeth's reign. An important aspect of the war was a long-running land campaign in the Nether-

lands supporting the Dutch in the *Netherlands revolt. Ultimately, England committed about 80,000 men to this war, most of whom were militiamen. The militia was only liable for home service, but these men were, at least in theory, volunteers, although 'masterless men' could be dispatched overseas by justices of the peace. A recognizably modern, if rudimentary, administrative and command system was developed to control the army in the Netherlands. Although the 'professionalization' of the English army did not survive Elizabeth's death, it foreshadowed some important developments of the 17th and 18th centuries and demonstrated the importance of an army for an emerging great power.

The breakdown of the Elizabethan consensus under the early Stuarts brought the issue of control of armies to the fore; parliament was reluctant to grant Charles I funds to raise an army in a time of crisis in 1639–41. This unwillingness to provide the funds to deal with a Scots invasion and a rebellion in Ireland was related to parliamentary distrust of Charles's 'tyrannical' tendencies. The constitutional crisis escalated into civil war. Initially, the parliamentarian and royalist armies were drawn from the militia and volunteers, and later by conscription. In 1644 the red-coated *New Model Army was raised by parliament. Disciplined, ideologically motivated, sometimes regularly paid and commanded by effective officers—notably *Fairfax and *Cromwell—the New Model Army tipped the balance in the *British civil wars. It also became the basis of the British standing army. However, the legacy of the Army's involvement in politics and Cromwell's military rule in the 1650s was a strong distrust of standing armies that remained a factor in British politics for some 200 years.

Under the Protectorate, Cromwell used military force to conquer Scotland, subdue Ireland, and to begin to carve out an overseas empire (Jamaica was taken in 1655). Moreover, under Cromwell England had once again begun to play a role on the European stage. The advantages of a standing army, not least in terms of the survival of his regime, were clear to Charles II, and in 1660–1 he raised a tiny standing army of 5,000 men, tactfully described as the king's 'Guards and Garrisons'. A former Cromwellian unit, Monck's Regiment (now the Coldstream Guards) was technically disbanded but then remustered, and was joined by ex-royalist units such as the 1st (now Grenadier) Guards. Other units which later came into royal service such as the 1st Foot (Royal Scots) and 3rd Foot (Buffs) actually pre-dated 1660, having been raised overseas.

Charles II's army gradually increased in size, thanks to the demands of foreign wars and the requirement of a garrison for the newly acquired colony of Tangier. *James II built up the army to about 40,000 men, stoking the fears of royal, Catholic despotism that led to his overthrow by the Dutch Prince *William of Orange in the 1688 'Glorious' Revolution. The army effectively collapsed during William's coup and its aftermath. Under William who saw England as a useful source of manpower for his interminable wars with France, the army was rebuilt. Another important consequence of the 'Glorious' Revolution was the 1689 Declaration of Rights, which stated that without the consent of parliament, a standing army was illegal, and also established that parliament had the right to vote funds for the maintenance of the army. Moreover, the institution of an annual Mutiny Act effectively gave parliament a veto over the very existence of an army. Control of the army had shifted decisively from the monarch to parliament, although monarchs and other royal figures continued to have immense influence. Suspicion of a standing army did not vanish, and the militia remained, in theory if not in practice, a rival to the army. Until the establishment of civilian police forces the army had an important internal security role in Britain, which added to suspicions of a standing army.

In the first decade of the 18th century the British army (Scotland and England were politically united in 1707) once again assumed its place as a primary instrument of foreign policy. Under *Marlborough, British forces won an impressive series of victories, earning Britain a place at the top table. Like most future European conflicts, the War of the *Spanish Succession was fought as part of a multinational coalition; the outcome of the *American independence war, which became a European war in which Britain had no major continental allies, showed the wisdom of this approach. Marlborough and *Wellington both commanded armies which included large numbers of foreigners: at *Waterloo, the latter's army was barely one-third British. Similarly, at other times British forces have fought under the overall command of a foreigner: Herman von Schomberg commanded a British force in the Walcheren campaign of 1673, while in 1991 British forces in the *Gulf were under the nominal command of a Saudi Arabian prince and under the actual command of US Gen *Schwarzkopf.

Traditionally, in times of major war the British army has had the option of two strategies: committing forces to the continent or pursuing a maritime strategy of amphibious operations and peripheral campaigns. The second option—broadly what *Liddell Hart described as 'The British Way in Warfare'—sometimes worked well, as it did when Wellington defeated Napoleon's forces in the *Peninsular war. Unfortunately such successful examples are paralleled by disasters such as *Gallipoli, or the operations in the West Indies in the 1790s, which gained colonies but had little impact on the outcome of the war in Europe. The army's major roles in the 18th and 19th centuries included expansion and consolidation of empire. Wolfe's victory at *Quebec in 1759 which secured Canada and the *Wellesley brothers' campaigns in India are examples of the former, and the lot of many British soldiers into the 20th century was garrisoning India and the colonies. Colonial policing often involved small campaigns although on several occasions, such as the *Indian Mutiny and the Second *Boer War, the British became involved in major conflicts.

During the *French Revolutionary and *Napoleonic wars the British regular army remained fairly small, but home defence forces such as *yeomanry, volunteers, and *fencibles proliferated. The militia in particular formed a useful source of volunteer recruits for the regulars. Yet another species of auxiliary force emerged in 1859, when the Rifle Volunteer movement began in response to the fear of French invasion.

Between Waterloo in 1815 and *Mons in 1914, the British fought only one major war in Europe. This was the *Crimean war, the conduct of which contrasts strongly with the generally successful colonial campaigns. Following the Crimea, a series of reforms was carried out, although useful foundations had already been laid. The technical arms, the Royal Artillery and the Royal Engineers, had acquired a training institution, the Royal Military Academy Woolwich, in 1741. The infantry and cavalry had to wait until 1802 for their equivalent, the Royal Military College, which moved to Sandhurst in 1812 (the two institutions amalgamated as the Royal Military Academy Sandhurst in 1947). In 1858, military education was taken a stage further with the creation of the Staff College. In 1853 work began on Aldershot, which was to become the 'home' of the British army. Edward *Cardwell, Secretary of State for War (1868–74), and his successors, principally Edward Stanhope (1887–92) and Richard *Haldane (1905–12), carried out a number of important reforms. These included the abolition of purchase, remoulding the regimental system to create county regiments in place of the numbered regiments of the past, and the creation of a *general staff. Haldane was responsible for amalgamating the militia into the regular army (as its Special Reserve) and creating the Territorial Force (later Territorial Army) from the yeomanry and volunteers.

In 1914, the British Expeditionary Force (BEF) of six infantry and one cavalry divisions was dwarfed by the armies of its French allies and German enemies. A mass 'New Army' of volunteers was raised by Lord *Kitchener, Secretary of State for War, but was not ready to fight in strength until 1916. In 1914, the BEF fought well at the battles of Mons, *Le Cateau, and first *Ypres, although its tactical achievement—reflecting hard lessons learned in colonial warfare—was always better than the performance of its senior commanders, for whom large-scale continental operations against a first-rate opponent were unfamiliar. The British army was transformed by the war. The old Regular army was largely destroyed by the end of 1914. Reinforced by Territorials and the first divisions of the New Armies, the BEF faced the challenge of trench warfare in 1915, and began to develop the technique of launching the offensive operations demanded by the fact that the Germans were occupying a great swathe of French territory. The battle of Loos, in September 1915, the British army's biggest attack to date, proved unsuccessful, and led to replacement of the BEF's C-in-C *French by *Haig.

British army

The *Somme offensive was the debut of Britain's mass army. Despite suffering almost 60,000 casualties on the first day, the bloodiest single day in British military history, the British inflicted serious damage on the Germans and gained much experience that was applied to good effect at the battle of *Arras/Vimy Ridge in April 1917. Faced with the insatiable demands of total war, conscription was introduced in 1916. The third battle of Ypres was, in spite of its appalling reputation, a partial—if enormously costly—success that demonstrated that the BEF was now tactically highly skilled. This point was reinforced by the initial success of the battle of *Cambrai in November–December 1917, when a British invention, the *tank, was used en masse for the first time.

In the spring of 1918 the BEF weathered a series of heavy German offensives and then, at *Amiens on 8 August, went onto the attack. The subsequent 'Hundred Days' marked the greatest achievement in the history of the British army. It is the only time in history that it had taken the lead in defeating the main body of a major continental enemy in the main theatre of operations. However, this achievement remains largely forgotten by the British public, who prefer to remember the disasters of the earlier years, such as the ill-fated amphibious operation at Gallipoli and the first day on the Somme.

The British army which went to war in 1939 had forgotten many of the lessons of 1914–18. It had 'lost the lead' in tank design and *doctrine, which it had held until the early 1930s. The *Norwegian campaign in 1940 was handled as ineptly as Gallipoli in 1915, and although the major blame for the fall of *France must lay with the French, the BEF cannot escape its fair share. The British army only returned to form in late 1942 at *Alamein when *Montgomery arrived in Egypt and returned the army to the 'set-piece', attritional methods of WW I. The record of 1939–45 is decidedly mixed. British attempts to fight *manoeuvre warfare in the desert between 1940 and 1942 failed as often as they succeeded. Generalship and tactics in *Italy (1943–5) were uninspiring and the early campaigns against the Japanese were disastrous. By contrast, Montgomery was a highly effective, if cautious, general and his armies had an almost unbroken run of success in *Western Desert and *North-West Europe. Perhaps the most impressive British general of the war was *Slim, whose 1945 campaign in *Burma was a masterpiece of which the German *blitzkrieg generals would have been proud.

In 1939 Britain resorted to conscription, which was renewed in 1947 and retained until 1963. Unlike in 1914–18 there was no long-running campaign of the proportions of the western front. Indeed, many British soldiers spent the years 1940–4 in training in the UK. Specialist units increased, ranging from *airborne forces to the *Chindits and *commandos. Their military usefulness is still a matter for debate; certainly, the war in Europe and Burma was won by conventional *infantry, *armour, *artillery, and *air power.

Between 1945 and 1998 the British army fought only four conventional wars, yet between the end of WW II and 1998 there has been only one year—1968—when British soldiers were not in action somewhere over the globe. *Counter-insurgency (COIN) was the army's stock in trade in these years, as Britain disengaged from empire. The legacy of colonial policing and the experience of successful operations such as the *Malayan emergency (1948–60) and the Dhofar war (1970–5) as well as failures such the campaigns in Palestine (1945–8) and *Aden (1964–8) led to the emergence of an informal COIN doctrine. This emphasized recognition of the political nature of the insurgency, intelligence, winning the hearts and minds of the population, and political reform. While British COIN operations did not always succeed, their record of success compared very favourably with those of the US and French armies. From 1969 onwards the army was heavily involved in internal security duties in Northern Ireland. During this period the British army was engaged in UN *peacekeeping operations, such as in Cyprus (1964 onwards). A small British contingent also participated in the non-UN peacekeeping operation in Beirut (1983–4). The end of the *Cold War has seen the army gain much experience of what is now termed 'Wider Peacekeeping' in such far-flung places as Kurdistan (1991) and the former *Yugoslavia (from 1992). The British COIN experience has proved to be very useful in this new global environment.

Of the four conventional wars fought during this period by the British army the *Korean war was fought in the manner of WW II, while both *Suez and the *Falklands were species of *amphibious operation. For more than forty years, the British army trained for the war that never was: a defensive battle in northern Germany against invading Soviet forces. In the 1980s the British army underwent a series of reforms instituted by FM Sir Nigel Bagnall that transformed army doctrine from a broadly attritional approach to one of manoeuvre warfare, in line with similar developments in the US army. Ironically, as a result, in the 1991 Gulf war the British and US forces used methods that owed much to the influence of their Cold War enemy, the Soviet army.

In 1991 and 1998 governments undertook radical reorganizations of the armed forces that involved cuts in numbers but also the purchase of new sophisticated equipment. Other developments included the introduction in 1988 of a Higher Command and Staff Course dedicated to the operational level of war and, a year later, the promulgation of a formal written doctrine—the first in the army's 300-year history. Subsequently, a Permanent Joint Headquarters and a Joint Services Command and Staff College was set up to enhance co-operation between the services. Thus, at the end of the 20th century, the British army is undergoing change as radical as any in its history.   GDS

Chandler, David, and Beckett, Ian, (eds.) *The Oxford Illustrated History of the British Army* (Oxford, 1994).

Pimlott, John, *The Guinness History of the British Army* (London, 1993).

British civil wars (1638–52). In financial expense, physical devastation, and loss of life, the civil wars were the costliest conflict ever waged on British soil. Their causes were far reaching. Charles I had an exalted conception of his role as monarch, and denied that he was accountable to the people or their elected representatives. He might have been able to realize his pretensions to absolutism had it not been for a rebellion in Scotland against his attempt to impose an Anglican brand of worship on that nation. United under a 'National Covenant' in 1638, the Scots resolved to throw out the new service book and restore their native-grown Presbyterian Directory of Worship. The two 'Bishops' wars' which resulted depleted Charles's treasury and exposed the unpopularity of his regime in both kingdoms. The first conflict, in the late spring of 1639, ended in a bloodless standoff between the Scots and English armies. A year later the Covenanting army, 14,000 strong, under Alexander Leslie routed a demoralized English army of only 4,500 at Newburn and seized the nearby city of Newcastle. Forced to summon parliament, the king found it unsupportive of his war against the Scots, and determined to reform the abuses of prerogative government. Annoyance at unparliamentary taxation and absolutist pretensions was compounded by religious fear that the king and queen were bent on returning England to the Catholic fold. This fear seemed vindicated when a Catholic-led rebellion broke out in Ireland in October 1641. In England it was widely held that Charles could not be entrusted with the army that was to be sent to put down that rebellion. The struggle for control of the sword, together with Charles's refusal to countenance Puritan reform of the Church, led directly to his declaration of war against parliament in August 1642. The difficulty of governing multiple kingdoms had been a root cause of the war. Nevertheless, war would have been impossible had Charles not gained support between 1640 and 1642. The royalist party consisted of those who wished to defend the Established Church and the Book of Common Prayer, resented the Scots presence in England, and feared the disintegration of the social order.

In January 1642, having failed to arrest the ringleaders of the parliamentary opposition, Charles fled London leaving it in the hands of his enemies. Control of the capital with its population approaching 400,000, its immense financial resources, its administrative importance, its vast *arsenal, and its pre-eminence as England's largest port, was a crucial advantage to the parliamentary side throughout the war. London and its region responded quickly to parliament's call for soldiers, money, and weapons, as did the surrounding counties. Many other counties were divided, and tried to keep out of the war, but parliament quickly asserted its control over East Anglia which, with its rich agriculture, was a storehouse of provisions and money at all times. Parliament was also successful in taking control of Hull, the second greatest fortress in the kingdom. Most ports and cloth towns threw their support behind parliament. With the more prosperous and populous part of the kingdom under its control, parliament was from the beginning in a better position to conscript men and pay them. Voluntary contributions were soon replaced by loans from the merchants and financiers of the City. Initially the loans were secured on land promised in Ireland; later, on confiscated church and crown land in England. In 1643 the first ever tax on consumables—the excise—was introduced. Parliament was also able to draw on customs revenue and the income from sequestered royalist estates. By far the largest source of parliamentary revenue was the weekly (later monthly) assessment. Grounded in up-to-date appraisals of people's ability to pay, the assessment tapped the wealth of every county under parliament's control. At its height, in 1649, it generated £120,000 a month.

For his part the king drew strength from Wales, the west Midlands, Lancashire, Yorkshire, and Cornwall. With intermittent control of only one major port (Bristol) he had very little customs revenue. In the early years of the war aristocratic supporters such as the Earl of Newcastle and the Marquess of Worcester contributed handsomely to the royal coffers. Small amounts dribbled in from France, Holland, and other continental countries. There was also a royalist equivalent of the monthly assessment. But royalist finances were always more fragile than those of parliament, with the consequence that royalist armies resorted more frequently to free quarter and straightforward plunder in order to keep themselves alive.

Through a combination of bad luck and poor judgement Charles lost control of the navy several months before he fought his first battle on land. The consequences of parliament's command of the sea were momentous. The king's prestige was diminished, and European powers became wary of intervening on his behalf.

By October 1642, when the first Civil War effectively began, the king had mustered about 12,500 men, whereas the main parliamentary army under the Earl of *Essex had reached nearly 14,000. On 28 October the armies of Charles and Essex clashed on a gently sloping field below the village of *Edgehill in Warwickshire. At the end of the day Essex remained in possession of the battlefield, but strategically the victory was the king's, since the road to London was now clear. Charles's slowness in approaching the capital gave parliament the time to mobilize an army of some 24,000 men to bar his way at Turnham Green. The king wisely pulled his men back and returned to Oxford for the winter.

In 1643 Charles consolidated his position around Oxford, while Sir Ralph Hopton recruited a formidable little army in Cornwall. At Roundway Down (13 July) he and Lord Wilmot routed Sir William Waller, leader of the parliamentary forces in the west. This was the low point of the

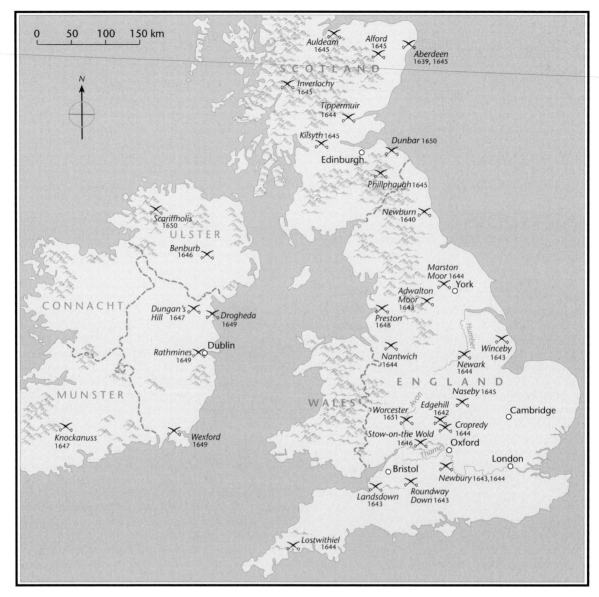

The **British Civil war** and its repercussions throughout Britain and Ireland: principal battles.

war for parliament. With its grip on the Severn Valley broken, Bristol and Gloucester were imperilled. In the south Essex's army had wasted away to 5,500, while the Earl of Newcastle dominated the north with his army of 8,000, 6,000 of whom were crack infantry. His cavalry were an élite force, led by Sir Marmaduke Langdale and George Goring. The northern parliamentary army, never more than 6,000 strong under Ferdinando Lord Fairfax and his son Sir Thomas *Fairfax, were always dangerous, but after a number of lesser engagements, Newcastle beat them decisively at Adwalton Moor near Bradford (30 June), and drove them back to Hull.

The arrival of the queen in Oxford with 3,000 troops and supplies at last gave Charles numerical superiority over Essex. This infusion of strength enabled Prince *Rupert of the Rhine with 12,000 men to overrun Bristol, the second port of the kingdom. Instead of pressing home his advantage with an immediate attack on London the king chose to protect his rear by turning and besieging Gloucester. When Essex came to the relief of the city Charles abandoned the

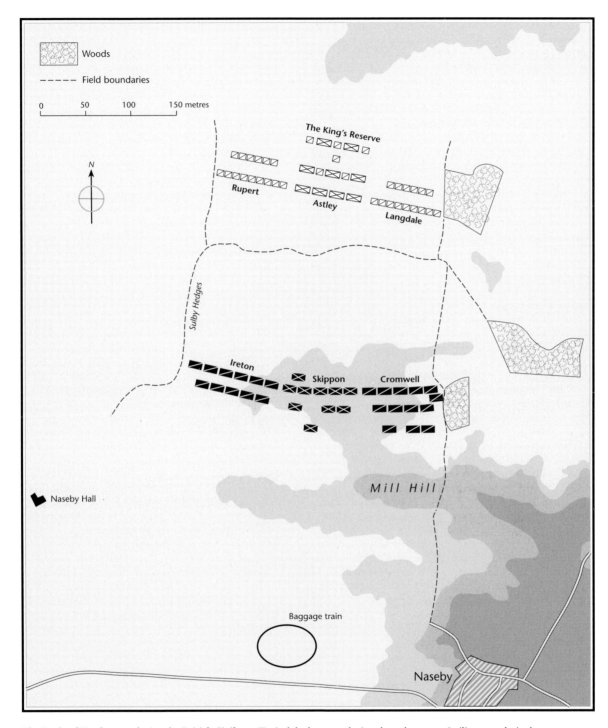

The Battle of Naseby, 1645 during the **British Civil war.** Typical deployment during the 17th-century 'military revolution'.

siege, and tried to block Essex's way back to London. The two armies, about equal at 14,000 men each, fought a pitched battle at Newbury, where many royalist cavalry were lost, and Essex's reputation was temporarily restored. Meanwhile, parliament recovered more ground in the north and south. But by the end of 1643 the armies of both sides were nearly at the end of their tether. The following year would see the arrival of outside help.

In the autumn of 1643 the parliamentary leader John Pym managed to persuade his reluctant colleagues to forge an alliance with Scotland. In December the Scots undertook to bring an army to England in exchange for a promise to establish a Presbyterian church on the Scots model. They were prompt in fulfilling their side of the bargain. In January 1644 the Earl of Leven crossed the Tweed with 21,500 troops. Six months later they would take part in the largest battle of the civil war.

Meanwhile in Ireland the Marquess of Ormonde had concluded a *truce or 'Cessation' with the Roman Catholic Confederates. This enabled Charles to bring in several thousand troops, mainly infantry, from that kingdom. Whatever military advantage he gained by this access of strength was offset by the propaganda defeat he suffered for his apparent appeasement of Roman Catholicism and Irish nationalism.

In England the next major encounter was near York. At *Marston Moor the combined royalist forces of Prince Rupert and the Marquess of Newcastle, numbering 20,000, met a combined allied force half as large again, consisting of Ferdinando Lord Fairfax's northern army, the Earl of Manchester's army of the Eastern Association, and the Scots army under Lord Leven. The result was the shattering of the royalist infantry, and the end of the war in the north.

On the other hand parliament was in danger of losing the south. While the Earl of Manchester dawdled around Lincoln, Waller failed to come to the help of Essex who was recklessly plunging deep into royalist territory in Cornwall in the hope of finishing off the royalist forces under Prince Maurice and Hopton. Charles had decided to pursue him with his main Oxford army, which at 10,000 was now equal to Essex's. The forces in the west brought the king's strength up to 16,000. All through August the royalists skilfully closed the net around the dispirited parliamentarians. At Lostwithiel Essex reached the end of the road. As defeat stared him in the face he ordered his cavalry to cut their way through the enemy lines and escape to Plymouth. The earl slipped away by boat, leaving Major-Gen Skippon to surrender the 6,000 infantry. It was the most resounding royalist victory of the war.

Discontent with the lacklustre performance of Essex, Manchester, and Waller now boiled over in London. At the beginning of December 1644 the war party in the Commons threw its support behind a Self-Denying Ordinance that excluded all Members of either House from military or civil appointments for the duration of the war. They then amalgamated the three southern armies into a new force under the command of Sir Thomas Fairfax. Oliver Cromwell's last-minute exemption from the terms of the Self-Denying Ordinance permitted him to play a leading role in the battle of *Naseby on 14 June 1645. The *New Model Army numbered nearly 17,000, while the king commanded barely 9,000 troops. Besides this crushing superiority in numbers, the victory of the New Model owed not a little to the better discipline of its cavalry. The cost of victory was relatively cheap: only perhaps 150 men lost, against nearly 1,000 for the king, in addition to 4,500 prisoners, mainly infantry, and the capture of the king's file of secret letters. The publication of these letters, with their evidence of his dealings with the Irish rebels, would do irreparable damage to Charles's reputation in England.

The events of the next year were essentially a mopping-up operation for the New Model Army. Royalist strongholds tumbled like ripe fruit into its lap: Bristol, Plymouth, Exeter, and many others. By June 1646 the west was sewn up, and Oxford had surrendered. Before this last humiliation was played out, Charles had slipped away and delivered himself into the hands of the Scots army at Newark. Obstinately rejecting the unmistakable verdict of the battlefield, he would spend the next year-and-a-half negotiating and plotting at various times with the English Presbyterians, their rivals the Independents, the Scots, and hoped-for friends in Rome, France, Holland, Denmark, and Ireland.

Thanks to the king's stubbornness the Second Civil War erupted in the spring of 1648. The New Model had little trouble annihilating the ill-co-ordinated series of uprisings in Kent, south Wales, Yorkshire, and East Anglia. A more serious threat was posed by a section of the Scots nobility, who signed an Engagement with the king, and led an invasion of England in July. Cromwell brilliantly outmanoeuvred and demolished their forces the following month at Preston. When parliament persisted in negotiating with a twice-defeated king, the army determined that he had to be destroyed. After issuing a Remonstrance calling for Charles Stuart, 'that man of blood', to be brought to justice, the army occupied London purged parliament of moderates, and oversaw the trial and execution of the king.

Once the republic had been proclaimed the grandees of the army turned to deal with the long-festering rebellion in Ireland. Cromwell was despatched with an invading force of 12,000, but before his arrival the parliamentary Col Michael Jones had crushed the royalist army under Ormonde at Rathmines, just outside Dublin. This 'astonishing mercy', as Cromwell dubbed it, meant that he did not have to fight a single field battle while he was in that country. When Drogheda refused the summons to *capitulate he stormed it, and put the entire garrison of 3,500 including civilians and clergy to the sword. Similar punishment was meted out to Wexford in October. Royalist resistance collapsed by the end of 1650, but the Catholic Confederates continued to wage a bitter guerrilla war. By 1651 it required

33,000 English parliamentary troops to occupy Ireland and cope with the continuing resistance. However, divisions within Confederate ranks brought them formally to capitulate in the autumn of 1652.

Meanwhile in the spring of 1650 Cromwell had returned to England to prepare for an apprehended invasion from Scotland, where the Kirk had recently proclaimed Charles II monarch of both kingdoms setting the scene for the Third Civil War. Rather than wait for the Scots, Cromwell decided on a pre-emptive strike. Taking an army of 16,000 across the Tweed in July, he found the Scots general David Leslie (son of Alexander) maddeningly elusive. Having stripped the counties south of Edinburgh of food and fodder, Leslie retreated behind fortified redoubts and declined Cromwell's invitation to a pitched battle. His numbers worn down to barely 10,000 by desertion and disease, Cromwell decided to return to England, but at Dunbar he found Leslie blocking his way. Thanks to excellent reconnoitring he perceived that the infantry on Leslie's left wing were wedged against a steep ravine and unable to manoeuvre quickly. Under cover of rain and darkness he therefore brought his army across the front of Leslie's regiments and launched a surprise attack on his right wing before dawn on 3 September. The reward for this masterstroke was a devastating English victory against an army twice their size. Charles II, considering it hopeless to continue the war in an impoverished and exhausted land, led a Scots royalist army into England. The royalists knew they were marching to their doom, but, as the Duke of Hamilton put it, 'we have one stout argument, despair'. Cromwell allowed them to hole up in the stronghold of Worcester, and then unleashed his overwhelming might against them on 3 September 1651.

The descent of the three kingdoms into civil war between 1638 and 1642 had released a torrent of revolutionary energy. During the decade from 1642 to 1652 armies mobilized by the Long Parliament swept away the apparatus of monarchical government and episcopacy, and subdued all opposition in England, Ireland, and Scotland. What then permitted Charles II to return to these kingdoms in 1660 without shedding a drop of blood? It was people's weariness with heavy taxation and constitutional experimentation, together with the self-destruction of the revolution by internal quarrelling. IG

Carlton, Charles, *Going to the Wars* (London, 1992).
Gentles, Ian, *The New Model Army in England, Ireland and Scotland, 1645–1653* (Oxford, 1992).
Kenyon, John, *The Civil Wars of England* (London, 1988).
Young, Peter, and Holmes, Richard, *The English Civil War: A Military History of the Three Civil Wars 1641–1651* (London, 1974).

Brodie, Bernard (1910–78), political scientist and military historian. Brodie was the pre-eminent post-war US theorist of strategic *deterrence, which he saw as the es-

sence of nuclear strategy. Brodie's argument is summarized in a much-quoted extract from his book *The Absolute Weapon: Atomic Power and World Order* (1946): 'Thus far the chief purpose of our military establishment has been to win wars. From now on its chief purpose must be to avert them. It can have almost no other useful purpose.' His theory was elaborated in *Strategy in the Missile Age* (1959), in which he demonstrated the complexity and fragility of mutual nuclear deterrence, especially where missiles are involved. PC

Brooke, Rupert (1887–1915), WW I poet, sub-lieutenant, Royal Naval Division. After Rugby and King's College Cambridge, he travelled widely, publishing his first collection of poems in 1911. A member of the Socialist Fabian Society, and considered an intellectual star of his generation, Brooke was a friend of the famous (including the Asquiths). He volunteered early, and his lines are full of patriotism and the vigour of youth. As one of them to die—of septicaemia on his way to *Gallipoli—his work lacks the brooding fatalism and despair of the later war poets. The 'corner of a foreign field that is forever England' was on the island of Scyros. APC-A

'Brown Bess' was the affectionate nickname of the British Land service *flintlock musket of *c.*1730–*c.*1815. It appears to have been in use from the first quarter of the 18th century by British soldiers and continued to be used, throughout the British empire, until well into the 19th century. The Land service musket was issued in five distinct patterns: the Long Land musket, with a 46 inch (116.8 cm) barrel, *c.*1730–97; the Short Land, with a 42 inch (106.7 cm) barrel, *c.*1745–97; the Marine and Militia pattern (a version of the Short Land), *c.*1755–63; the 'India' pattern, 1793–1815; the New Land, 1802–15. All patterns had a calibre of approximately 0.75 inch (1.9 cm). SCW

Bailey, De Witt, *British Military Longarms 1715–1865* (London, 1986).
Blackmore, Howard L., *British Military Firearms 1650–1850* (London, 1961).

Browne, Gen Sir Samuel (1824–1901), inventor of the cross-belt that bears his name (Sam Browne). Born in India, he entered the army at 16 and spent most of his life campaigning there, commanding Bengal Cavalry. In the *Indian Mutiny he was present at the capture of Lucknow, and later won a VC in August 1858 for capturing a rebel cannon at Seerporah. In the mêlée, his left arm was severed at the shoulder, after which he devised a belt, worn diagonally over the right shoulder to anchor his sword and scabbard to his left side. He later commanded troops in Afghanistan 1878–9 and was promoted general in 1888. His belt remains popular with many armies today, but its use in early WW I easily enabled *snipers to target British officers.

APC-A

Bruce, Robert (I), King of Scotland (1272–1329).

Robert Bruce, Earl of Carrick, seized the throne of Scotland from the absent King John Balliol in 1306 (becoming Robert I), assassinated his political rival, Comyn of Badenoch, and reopened the war with England. Though initially militarily inept, Bruce learned quickly from his mistakes and, after the death of Edward I in 1307, was able to attack his enemies within Scotland. There was apparently no end to the tactics he was willing to employ in order to force recognition of his independent kingship: scorched earth, the 'fiery cross', taking castles by infiltration and levelling them to prevent regarrisoning, the use of Gaelic *mercenaries, *chevauchées into the north of England, the opening of a second front in Ireland (and potentially in Wales also), the development of the offensive *schiltrom—all played their part. Blessed also with reliable commanders in his brother Edward, in James 'the Black' Douglas, and in Thomas Randolph, later Earl of Moray, the Bruce had largely gained control of his kingdom by 1309. At *Bannockburn in 1314 he successfully engaged Bohun in single combat in front of the armies and then destroyed the incompetently led English. Despite this, Edward II refused to acknowledge the Bruce's kingship and the war continued, marred by Edward Bruce's disastrous campaign in Ireland (1315–18). The Bruce finally obtained English recognition during the chaos following the deposition and murder of Edward II. He died in 1329 and had asked that his heart be buried in the Holy Land, and while on this mission the Black Douglas was killed fighting the Moors in Spain. Legend has it that he threw the casket containing his old leader's heart into the enemy ranks, bidding the Bruce to lead him into battle one last time.

FW

Barrow, Geoffrey W. S., *Robert Bruce and the Community of the Realm of Scotland* (Edinburgh, 1992).

Brusilov, Gen Aleksey (1853–1926),

Russian cavalry general and battlefield commander. Brusilov's meticulously planned offensive in summer 1916 was one of the most successful breakthrough operations of WW I. Brusilov took part in the 1877–8 Russo-Turkish war. In 1902 he became chief of the officers' cavalry school and between 1906 and 1914 commanded a cavalry division and an army corps, and was deputy commander of the Warsaw Military District. In WW I he commanded Eighth Army, and in 1916 the South-West Front (army group), where he organized his successful offensive, timed to coincide with the British offensive on the Somme. The offensive lasted from 4 June to 13 August. The Front, with 573,000 men and 1,770 guns, broke through Austro-Hungarian forces with 448,000 men and 1,300 guns

along a 342 mile (550 km) front and penetrated between 37 and 93 miles (between 60 and 150 km). The artillery preparation was meticulously organized. Although the Russians were short of guns and ammunition by western front standards, they were concentrated on very narrow breakthrough sectors and targets were carefully picked and accurately surveyed. The infantry were assembled in underground bunkers very close to the enemy trenches, to maximize surprise. Although the Austrians eventually stopped the offensive, they lost 1.5 million killed and wounded to 0.5 million Russians and had to pull 30 infantry and 3 cavalry divisions from the western and *Italian fronts. Brusilov was made supreme commander in June 1917, under the Kerensky government. After prolonged reflection, he joined the Reds in 1920, acting as president of a special commission of the Soviet Republic's armed forces and therefore advised *Trotsky and *Frunze. Thus, one of the imperial Russian army's most successful generals was influential during the formative years of the Red Army.

CDB

Bulge, battle of the (1944–5).

The German Ardennes offensive, popularly known as the battle of the Bulge, was a desperate attempt, initiated by *Hitler, to reverse the tide of the war in the west. Three German armies were engaged, Sixth SS Panzer, Fifth Panzer, and Seventh Army, under the command of *Model in Army Group B. Some experienced units had been brought back from the *eastern front, but many were newly raised *Volksgrenadier* units who were to fight surprisingly well in the attack's initial stages. The operation, deceptively code-named WATCH ON THE RHINE, sought to split the Allied armies and recapture the port of Antwerp, upon which the Allies depended for their supplies. It struck Hodges's First US Army, on the northern edge of Bradley's Twelfth US Army Group, holding the Ardennes sector thinly at a time when bad weather grounded the otherwise-dominant Allied *air forces. The attack achieved tactical surprise, for although *ULTRA indicated that the Germans were massing it was assumed that this was for defensive purposes. German *special forces, disguised in US uniforms, parachuted behind Allied lines, and achieved disproportionate results by causing US units to distrust each other.

The attack was launched early on 16 December. Some American soldiers, encircled on the snowy uplands, surrendered, and in the north Lt Col Jochen Peiper's battle group of Sixth SS Panzer Army initially made good progress. In the centre Fifth Panzer Army encircled Bastogne, containing 101st Airborne Division and part of 10th Armoured Division, but the town held out. On 19 December *Eisenhower, supreme Allied commander, cancelled offensive action elsewhere, ordering *Patton to swing his Third Army into the southern flank of the bulge. He also placed US troops in the threatened sector under *Montgomery, commander of the British Twenty-first Army Group, to the north, to ensure unity of command. With Sixth Panzer Army stuck in the north, Hitler switched the main effort to Fifth Panzer Army in the centre, but although its vanguard reached Foy-Nôtre-Dame, just 3 miles (4.8 km) from the Meuse, it was hopelessly short of its planned objectives. The weather cleared on 22 December, and German troops, jammed on poor roads and short of fuel, were mercilessly harried from the air.

On New Year's Day the Luftwaffe launched an all-out attack on Allied airfields, and although it inflicted considerable damage it did so at a cost it could not afford. The Allies attempted to cut off the German penetration, with one of Hodges's corps striking south as Patton moved northwards, but the Germans fell back before the pincers closed. Nevertheless, they lost 100,000 men, together with most of the irreplaceable tanks and aircraft they committed. Allied losses were also heavy, but they could make good their losses. The operation had no real chance of success, though it did produce a crisis in the Allied command, albeit not on the scale that Hitler had hoped for. It does emphasize the danger of complacency and the potential weakness of even the best intelligence.   RH

Macdonald, Charles B., *The Battle of the Bulge* (London, 1984).

Bull Run, battles of (1861 and 1862), Union defeats in the vicinity of Manassas Railway Junction, crucial for communications across northern Virginia to the Shenandoah valley and only 25 miles (40 km) from Washington. McDowell took the offensive in July 1861 knowing his 35,000 men were 'green'. But so were the Confederates, who were widely dispersed with 22,000 under *Beauregard close to Washington and 9,500 under *Johnston 50 miles (80 km) away in the Shenandoah. Beauregard fell back on the Bull Run river, but his left was outflanked and fell back in disorder after fierce resistance. Leading the Shenandoah reinforcements from the railhead at Manassas Junction, *Jackson formed on the reverse slope of Henry House Hill and halted the rout. Enfiladed by aggressively handled Union artillery, his position was salvaged by a spontaneous infantry charge. Union forces massed against him were outflanked in turn and dissolved in panic. Washington would almost certainly have fallen to a determined *pursuit.

Second Bull Run was where *Lincoln finally learned that he had no talent for directing armies. Having recalled McDowell when his advance on Richmond might have helped *McClellan in the *Seven Days battles, and Banks when he might have made a difference in the *Shenandoah, he put them both under the command of Pope and ordered him to advance before McClellan could return from the Jamestown peninsula. Uncannily echoing the first battle, throughout 29 August Pope battered a strong position held by Jackson's corps, which was reduced to throwing rocks. Oblivious to *Longstreet coming up on his left, he continued the attack the next day and was shattered by a Confederate counter-offensive that came very close to enveloping his whole army. Pope was sent to chase Indians in Minnesota; McClellan regained command and for once managed to act faster than *Lee expected, bringing him to battle and near-destruction at *Antietam.   HEB

Buller, Gen Sir Redvers Henry (1839–1908). Buller, scion of a notable family, joined the army in 1858 and served with the 60th Rifles in China two years later. He was one of the most dashing personalities in the 'small wars' of the era. On the Red River campaign of 1870 he encountered *Wolseley, and became part of the influential 'Ashanti Ring', serving under Wolseley on the *Ashanti expedition, in Egypt in 1882, and in the Sudan in 1884–5, where he rose to major general. Meanwhile he had distinguished himself as a leader of irregular horse in South Africa, winning the VC in a horrific battle on Hlobane Mountain in the *Zulu war (1879), and serving as Evelyn Wood's COS in the First *Boer War (1880–1).

*QMG in 1887 and adjutant general in 1890, Buller went to the army's principal command at Aldershot in 1898, and was the natural choice to head the South African Field Force the following year. However, a run of defeats—notably 'Black Week' of December 1898—led to his replacement by *Roberts. He remained commander in Natal, where defeat at Spion Kop did him more damage. In 1901, after his return to Aldershot, he defended himself in a public speech which ended his career.

Despite failure in South Africa Buller never lost popularity with the rank and file and the public: his heavy build and avuncular manner were seen as reflecting 'the best English type'. Many historians now argue that Buller was less culpable for the disasters than was once believed: he faced a well-prepared and resolute enemy in unforgiving terrain with far fewer resources than were enjoyed by his successors.   RH

bullet The word 'bullet' can be applied to any projectile fired from a firearm. The earliest bullets were made of any hard material. Early in the history of firearms lead was found to be the ideal substance for bullets and remained so until the late 19th century. Lead was readily available, cheap, with a low melting point for easy moulding and of a high density for maximum effect. In some countries, Mexico for example, a lack of domestic lead supply led to the use of copper for much the same reasons.

Until the end of the 18th century, bullets were spherical and available in differing sizes for differing calibres of weapon. They were notoriously inaccurate, chiefly as a result of 'windage', or the loose fit they had in the barrels of smooth-bore military weapons. This loose fit was necessitated by the accretion of burnt *gunpowder in the barrel after firing several rounds but was tolerated in order that a rapid rate of, albeit inaccurate, fire might be maintained. Riflemen used tightly fitting balls, forced into their rifled barrels with grease or lubricated patches of cloth, and gained resultant accuracy while sacrificing speed of loading. Various methods were investigated in the early 19th century to make musket balls fit tighter and thus be more accurate; most involved hammering the ball down the barrel, and against a projection at the breech end, in order to expand it to fit the barrel. All attempts were defeated by the burnt powder problem, together with the resultant lead residue left, and the development of conical bullets during the same period made little difference.

After many French experiments with conical bullets which expanded when hammered against pillars fixed in the breech, the solution was found in the cylindro-conoidal rifle bullet patented by Capt Claud-Etienne *Minié in 1849. The bullet named after him had an iron cup in its base which forced the lead skirts into the rifling of a barrel; it had grooves around its base to accept grease for lubricated loading. Having solved the windage problem, the next goal was the attainment of increased accuracy. This was achieved following lengthy competition between Joseph Whitworth and William Metford, whose experiments in both bullet design and rifling occupied much of the 1860s. Metford's winning bullet, three times as long as it was in diameter, bridged the period between the old short, fat bullet and that which would—when fixed in a cartridge—take ammunition into the 20th century.

Lead bullets left extensive lead fouling in barrels when fired with high-velocity *smokeless propellants and experiments with the jacketing of bullets occupied the 1890s. While most bullets have been jacketed with copper-zinc alloy, a variety of other hard metals, including tungsten, have been used. Modern warfare has necessitated differing types of bullet, for *anti-armour, for tracing the fall of shot and for setting fire to combustible targets. Rubber and plastic bullets are used for riot control by security services and police worldwide.   SCW

Blair, Claude (gen. ed.), *Pollard's History of Firearms* (London, 1983).

Peterson, Harold L. (ed.), *Encyclopaedia of Firearms* (London, 1964).

Roads, Dr Christopher H., *The British Soldier's Firearm 1850–1864* (London, 1964).

Burma campaign (1942–4). At the outbreak of WW II Burma was an agricultural country, exporting rice and teak, with an oilfield at Yenangyaung on the Irrawaddy and deposits of wolfram and rubies. It was racially and geographically diverse. The population was mainly Burman, with large Karen and Shan minorities and Chin, Kachin, and Naga hill tribes. Shut in by hills to north and east, Burma included jungle, a central plain around its second city Mandalay, alluvial deltas, and coastal swamps. It was watered by four rivers, from the east the Salween, forming the border with Thailand; the Sittang; and the mighty Irrawaddy, whose tributary, the Chindwin, marked the border with India. The British had become involved in Burma in 1824, and eventually annexed it after three wars (see BURMA WARS). They moved its capital to Rangoon, but until 1937 it was effectively controlled from India. There was a vigorous nationalist movement, some of whose members were in contact with the Japanese.

Japanese interest in Burma focused on the Burma road, which ran from Lashio in Burma to Kunming in China, and formed a source of supply to the Chinese, with whom they were at war. The British were badly overextended in the Far East, and Lt Gen Hutton, army commander in Burma, disposed of two inexperienced divisions, 17th Indian and 2nd Burma. In January 1942 the Japanese took the airfields in Tenasserim, in the far south, using them to provide air cover for their offensive. Moulmein fell, and the withdrawal of 17th Indian Division was disrupted when the Sittang bridge was blown on 23 February, with much of the division still on the far bank. Gen *Wavell, British commander in the theatre, agreed with London's suggestion that Lt Gen *Alexander should replace Hutton, and the commander of 17th Indian Division—brave, but tired and sick—was also relieved. An extra infantry brigade and 7th Armoured Brigade were shipped in.

None of this could stop the two confident and aggressive Japanese divisions. Rangoon fell, and the withdrawal of its garrison and elements of 17th Indian Division was only possible when the Japanese fortuitously removed a roadblock at Taukkyan, just north of the city. Lt Gen *Slim arrived to command the force, now called Burcorps, and Chinese forces, co-ordinated by the Anglophobe US Lt Gen *Stilwell, intervened to assist the British. Yet there was no stopping the retreat. The oil wells at Yenangyaung were blown in mid-April, and a month later Slim's survivors crossed the Chindwin after the longest retreat in British military history. It had cost them 13,000 casualties compared with only 4,000 Japanese. Tens of thousands of civilians had also made the appalling trek: some 500,000 reached safety in India, but perhaps 50,000 perished.

Some historians suggest that Burma was strategically irrelevant to the British, who could have held the borders of India with a token force as the Japanese, having cut the Burma road, had no wish to proceed further. Japanese intentions were unclear at the time, and Wavell, aware of the psychological impact of the loss of Burma—coming so soon after the fall of *Malaya and Singapore—was determined to retake it. His first attempt, launched towards Akyab in the Arakan in December 1942, was an ignominious failure which highlighted poor British and Indian tactics and the low quality of many troops.

But in February–May 1943 a weak brigade under Brig Orde *Wingate, fighting in self-contained columns, crossed the Chindwin to strike at the Japanese lines of communication. The material damage done by the *Chindits (from the

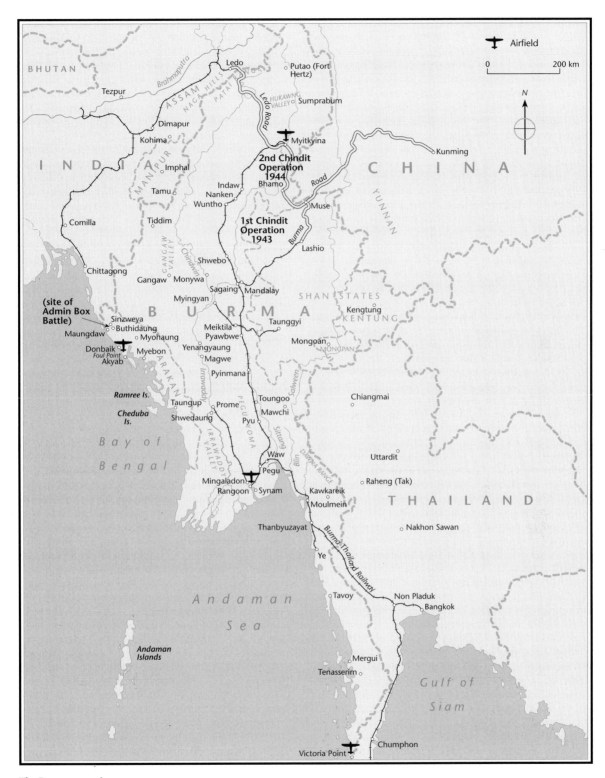

The **Burma campaign**, 1942–4.

Burmese word for the mythical beast that guards pagodas) was far less important than their moral effect. 'If ordinary family men from Manchester and Liverpool can be trained for this specialised jungle war behind the enemy's lines,' wrote a correspondent, 'then any fit man in the British army can be trained to do the same.' This first Chindit expedition gave a powerful fillip to British *morale, but it did encourage the Japanese commander in northern Burma, Lt Gen Mutaguchi, to press for authority to launch an offensive of his own. The Japanese had raised the *Indian National Army (INA) from captured Indian troops who rallied to the call of the nationalist leader Subhas Chandra Bose, and Mutaguchi hoped to use a successful attack to launch the INA into India. In the meantime, the Allies restructured their own command, with Adm Lord Louis *Mountbatten heading South-East Asia Command and Slim's force being designated Fourteenth Army. In January 1944 Mutaguchi received authority to launch his attack, U-GO. Slim knew that an offensive was coming, and decided to break it before mounting his own attack.

The Japanese began by attacking up into the Arakan to clear the left flank of their main thrust towards Imphal. This operation (HA-GO) went badly wrong. After an initial setback the British defended themselves doggedly on the ground, and quickly gained superiority in the air. The XV Corps administrative area—the 'Admin Box'—was supplied by air when the Japanese encircled it. Slim wrote that the moral effect of this victory was 'immense'. Mutaguchi's main assault, launched in March, followed the classical Japanese pattern of encirclement. Again it made initial progress, but was firmly checked at *Imphal. The little hill station of *Kohima, north of Imphal and on the road to the important railhead of Dimapur, was encircled, but held out in an epic siege. U-GO was cancelled in early July: it had cost the Japanese some 60,000 casualties.

The Japanese offensive coincided with THURSDAY, the second Chindit expedition, in which Wingate, promoted to major general, commanded a much larger force, most of which was flown in by glider. Wingate was killed when his aircraft crashed, but his columns established strongholds which became centres of fierce battles. There was some friction between Wingate's successor and Stilwell, whose men were attacking towards Myitkyina, an operation which involved 'Merrill's Marauders', the only US ground troops to serve in Burma. The operation came to an end in August. It had had less overall impact than the first expedition, but the remarkable endurance displayed by so many of those involved deserves recognition. No less remarkable were the achievements of Force 136, widely deployed across the whole theatre, working with indigenous support to carry out sabotage.

The Allied offensive began in early December 1944. It comprised a Chinese advance on the left and a thrust into the Arakan on the right while, in the centre, Slim's two corps—IV and XXXIII—pressed south. At the appropriate moment an amphibious assault would be launched against Rangoon. Slim launched XXXIII and IV Corps against *Mandalay and Meiktila respectively. Both towns were taken after hard fighting, and Slim's men advanced southwards. The Japanese abandoned Rangoon as the Allies approached, and most succeeded in escaping to the southwest. The Japanese command formally surrendered on 28 August 1945, on orders from Tokyo, though it proved difficult to notify survivors.

The war in Burma was marked by extreme difficulties caused by terrain, climate, and the prevalence of disease. The Japanese fought with extraordinary determination, and their treatment of prisoners still fuels deep resentment. The campaign has been hailed as the apotheosis of the old British-Indian army which, as Louis Allen observed, 'fought its way brilliantly and with blitzkrieg-style panache into the capital of Burma'. If its strategic function was ambiguous, the war did at least, in Raymond Callahan's words, help the British 'unlike the French, Dutch, or, later, the Americans, to leave Asia with some dignity. That, perhaps, is no small thing.'
RH

Allen, Louis, *Burma: The Longest War 1941–1945* (London, 1984).
Callahan, Raymond, *Burma 1942–1945* (London, 1978).
Slim, FM Viscount, *Defeat into Victory* (London, 1956).

Burma wars (1824, 1852, 1885–7). In the 18th century Burma was the scene of internal struggles, and her rulers fought against the Siamese and Chinese. In the 19th its proximity to British India produced minor clashes and border disputes to its north and north-west, in Assam and around Chittagong. Burmese attacks on Shahpuri island and the small British-protected state of Cachar led to the outbreak, in March 1824, of the first Burma war. Burmese forces were numerous but poorly equipped, with spearmen and swordsmen as well as *musketeers, and British-Indian forces enjoyed a consistent advantage in weaponry, *discipline, and cohesion. The British planned to defend against attacks from northern Burma and mount an expedition to Rangoon. However, a large Burmese force under Maha Bandula overran a sepoy detachment on the Chittagong front, persuading the British to send an expedition under Brig Gen J. W. Morrison along the coast. Morrison, keeping pace with a naval flotilla, made steady progress, taking Myohaung on 31 March 1825, and pushing on into the Arakan.

The main British force, meanwhile, had assembled in the Andaman islands under Brig Gen Sir Archibald Campbell, and in May 1824 it landed almost unopposed at Rangoon. Maha Bandula was ordered south to meet it and in early December British positions were heavily attacked. On 15 December Campbell counter-attacked, beating and scattering the Burmese force. He went on to kill Bandula at Danubyu, where a Burmese elephant-mounted force was routed by cavalry who rode in among the elephants and shot the men mounted on them. Campbell took Prome on 25 April 1825, checked an attack there that November, and then riposted, defeating the Burmese and killing their commander, Maha Nemyo. He then proceeded to follow the Burmese up the Irrawaddy to Malun. A treaty was negotiated, but, suspecting that the Burmese were preparing to resume fighting, Campbell captured Malun on 19 January 1826. He defeated the Burmese again at Pagan and was approaching Ava, then the capital, when peace was concluded. Burma ceded the Arakan to Britain and gave up her frontier claims.

Hostilities broke out again in 1852 after the Burmese king, Pagan, encouraged violations of the peace treaty and attacks on British shipping. Lord Dalhousie, governorgeneral of India, remonstrated, and then sent Lt Gen Henry Goodwin with an expedition which captured Rangoon in mid-April and Pegu in early June. The lower Irrawaddy valley was formally annexed in January 1853, later becoming 'British Burma' and subsequently 'Lower Burma'. Pagan was deposed by Mindon shortly afterwards, and a British Resident was accepted at court.

The third Burma war broke out in November 1885 when Thibaw, who succeeded Mindon, interfered with trade and rejected an ultimatum from Lord Dufferin demanding protection of British interests. Maj Gen Harry Prendergast swiftly invaded from Lower Burma, taking three brigades with naval support up the Irrawaddy, dispersing a Burmese force at Miha on the 17th. Thibaw surrendered on the 26th, and Mandalay was occupied two days later. Upper Burma was annexed in January 1886. Upper and Lower Burma were then administered as provinces of India. Victory did not end the fighting. Thibaw's army, disbanded with its weapons, took to *dacoitry on a large scale, and pacification operations in difficult country went on until 1892. In addition there were separate expeditions against the Chins and Lushais on the borders of Burma and Bengal in 1889–90; the Chins in 1892–3; and the Kachins in Upper Burma in 1892–3 and 1895.　　　　　　　　　　　　　　　　　RH

Bruce, G., *The Burma Wars 1824–1886* (London, 1973).
Stewart, A. T. Q., *The Pagoda War: Lord Dufferin and the Fall of the Kingdom of Ava* (London, 1972).

Burnside, Gen Ambrose Everett (1824–81).

Burnside was commissioned from *West Point in 1847 in time to serve on garrison duty in Mexico. He resigned in 1853 and set up a factory making *breech-loading rifles of his own design, but the business failed. On the outbreak of the *American civil war in 1861, he raised 1st Rhode Island Infantry and then commanded a brigade at first *Bull Run. Capture of Roanoke Island in January 1862 earned him promotion to major general and command of a corps in the Army of the Potomac. At *Antietam he launched repeated and brutally unenterprising attacks across the stone bridge which bears his name.

He succeeded *McClellan as army commander, largely because other generals preferred him to *Hooker, the alternative candidate. In December 1862 he pressed a hopeless attack at *Fredericksburg, and then embarked on the 'mud march' in fruitless search for the Confederate flank. Relieved of command, he led IX Corps for much of the rest of the war. Censured for its improper handling in the Crater battle at Petersburg, he resigned his commission and went into politics. Burnside knew that he was unfitted to command an army, but was widely liked despite his failings. His name is remembered in 'sideburns', a tribute to his muttonchop whiskers.　　　　　　　　　　　　　　　　　RH

bushido

bushido (Jap.: *bushi* + *dō*, the way of the warrior) refers to the set of concepts, traditions, and precedents that provide an overall framework for the behaviour of the *samurai, particularly regarding their relationship with the lower classes of society. Its earliest expression is 'kyūba no michi' (the way of horse and bow), referring to the most important accomplishments of the samurai when they fought as mounted *archers. Many ideas which were to become bushido were drawn from the house laws of the *feudal lords, who drew up rules of behaviour for their followers on the battlefield and in the domain, but most written accounts date from the peaceful Tokugawa Period (1603–1867). One of its most important principles was that of loyalty, an idea often honoured more in the breach than the observance, but given expression by such men as Torii Mototada, who committed suicide defending Fushimi castle for *Tokugawa Ieyasu just prior to the battle of *Sekigahara. In a letter Mototada explains how his action is motivated by his duty of loyalty to his master which is in accordance with bushido. While the samurai rendered loyalty to his master, the master responded with 'benevolence' to his followers, showing how bushido was a two-way process. Other writers stressed the need for a samurai to set an example to the lower orders of society by his conduct. A samurai had to be ready to fight as his master required, but such opportunities should not be squandered. It was not in accordance with bushido for a samurai to lose his life in a street brawl. Nor should he be ostentatious in his dress or his appearance, but self-controlled and restrained. The symbol of this restraint, as it was of the samurai status, was the possession of two swords.　　　　　　　　　　　　　　　　　SRT

Byng, FM Julian Hedworth George, Viscount Byng of Vimy (1862–1935).

Byng was the younger son of an old military family: he was related to Adm John Byng, shot on his own quarterdeck for failure to relieve Minorca in 1757, and his grandfather commanded a *guards brigade at Waterloo. He served in the 10th Hussars, where his chief distinction was playing polo, but during the Second *Boer War he raised and commanded an irregular cavalry regiment with notable success. Summoned from command in Egypt in 1914, he commanded a cavalry division in France and then succeeded *Allenby at the head of the Cavalry Corps. Sent to *Gallipoli, he oversaw the successful evacuation of Suvla, and then returned to the western front to command the Canadian Corps. The Canadian capture of Vimy Ridge in April 1917 (see ARRAS/VIMY RIDGE, BATTLE OF), one of the most remarkable set-piece attacks of the war, redounded much to his credit, and he went on to succeed Allenby in command of Third Army, having wisely if controversially recommended the Canadian militia officer Arthur Currie as his successor as corps commander.

Byng championed the *Cambrai tank attack carried out by his army in November 1917, and although its initial success brought him plaudits, he was at least in part to blame for the poor showing in the face of a well-executed German counter-attack. His army was much involved in the relentless British offensive of the last hundred days of the war. He was appointed viscount in the peace honours of 1919. In 1928–31 he served as commissioner of the Metropolitan Police, and was promoted field marshal.   RH

Byzantine army This was a continuation of the *Roman army. By the end of the 3rd century the wars of conquest were over and the army's role was to protect the imperial borders. Diocletian subdivided the old legions into smaller units, while *Constantine withdrew some units from the frontier to create strategically placed mobile reserves, the field armies. The enemy would be checked by a series of hinterland fortifications while the field army closed.

However, this system allowed damage to frontier areas and border troops' *morale dropped as they were regarded as second rate. Cities became more heavily fortified and raids and sieges became the prevalent forms of military activity. The disastrous defeat of the eastern field army at *Adrianople in 374 allowed the Visigoths to roam the empire, sacking Rome in 410. Under increasing pressure by the end of the 4th century the empire was officially split in two, east and west, with an emperor at the head of each. The western borders were irreparably breached in the early 5th century and Spain and much of Gaul passed beyond effective control.

The western army increasingly used *foederates*, foreign troops under their own commanders settled on imperial territory in return for military service, but their loyalty was often dubious. The army was also influenced by weapons and equipment copied from steppe peoples. The percentage of horse archers and heavily armoured cavalry was increased, but it was not enough to stop barbarian incursions and by the end of the 5th century the west was effectively lost.

Not until 533 was there a practical attempt at reconquest by the eastern empire. *Belisarius recaptured North Africa

and Italy. Later southern Spain was retaken but the success was short-lived. Justinian's wars exhausted imperial resources and in the late 6th century the Slavs overran Greece while the eastern frontier witnessed constant warfare. The main enemy was Persia, and the two fought a great war in the early 7th century. By 627 the Byzantines had won, but in 636 they were defeated at *Yarmuk by the newly united Arab tribes. Fighting for themselves rather than as desert forces of the two empires, they crushed the Persians and took Egypt, the Levant, and North Africa from the Byzantines. Their navy first threatened Constantinople in 654, Greek fire being one of the weapons used to defeat this and subsequent armadas.

The armies that retreated from the east were organized into *themes*, four at first. *Theme* commanders received increased control over civil matters to ensure the local supplies of the army while troops were paid from the revenues of the former imperial estates that they now occupied. This system stemmed the Arab advance, but most of the reconquered western territory was lost, the Lombards taking northern Italy. The northern frontier was overrun by the Bulgarians and the Rus (*Vikings) began to raid across the Black Sea to Constantinople (now Istanbul). While the east remained relatively secure, its borders were frequently raided. By the time the scattered troops were mustered, the enemy was already returning home and had to be ambushed in passing while laden with plunder. Increased fortification and more localized control of forces alleviated the problem and this use of fortresses and *guerrilla warfare served the empire well for centuries.

Although the *theme* system maintained the borders it led to many rebellions. *Themes* were subdivided to limit their commanders' power. Constantine V created new units, the *tagmata*, which were stationed in and around Constantinople to provide protection for the emperor but they were also crack troops. In 840 Theophilus extended their organization to the *themes* thus giving them a more effective command and control structure permitting faster mustering and better supervision for training. This system not only protected the empire better but allowed field armies to take the offensive. Reconquest began in earnest under Nicephorus Phocas and by the 11th century the Danube was re-established as the northern frontier and the empire doubled in size from Theophilus' reign.

However, the 11th century also witnessed new enemies. The Pechenegs raided across the Danube up to the walls of Constantinople. The Seljuk *Turks were a bigger threat than the Arabs and in 1071 they inflicted a humiliating defeat on the Byzantines at *Manzikert, causing the loss of much of Anatolia. The Normans captured southern Italy and Alexios I struggled to keep them from taking Greece. The army began to make increasing use of mercenaries, notably the Varangian (Viking) Guard. Alliances with western powers such as Venice proved financially ruinous and helped bring about a decline in the Byzantine navy, which in turn forced the empire to rely increasingly on such alliances. In 1094 the First *Crusade passed through Byzantium en route to the Holy Land. Although supposed to turn recaptured territory over to Alexios, the Crusaders failed to do so. Hungary began to encroach on Byzantine possessions and in 1176 another disastrous defeat was inflicted by the Seljuks at Myriokephalon. The Fourth Crusade, hijacked by the Venetians for their own purposes, sacked Constantinople in 1204 and split the empire into successor states.

Nicaea was destined to be the strongest of these successors and her army, influenced by western organization, successfully held its own. In 1261 the Nicenes recovered Constantinople and the Black Sea coast of Thrace, but it proved to be a costly gain, overstretching their resources. Despite attempts to maintain a professional 'national' army, the empire still employed many foreign contingents backed by provincial levies. The Serbs gradually took over Macedonia and then the Ottoman *Turks arrived on the scene defeating the Byzantines in 1302. Anatolia, including Nicaea, was lost and the empire, ruined financially, gradually shrank, a process aided by civil wars. In 1354 the Ottomans crossed into Europe splitting what was left of the empire into disparate elements. Constantinople was besieged in 1402 and only saved by the defeat of the Ottomans by *Timur at Ankara. The inevitable fate was merely postponed to 1453 when the city finally fell to the cannon of Mehmet II.   SMcC

Bartusis, M. C., *The Late Byzantine Army: Arms and Society 1204–1453* (Philadelphia, 1992).

Haldon, J., *State, Army and Society in Byzantium* (Aldershot, 1995).

Treadgold, W., *The Byzantine Army 284–1081* (Stanford, 1995).

Caesar, Caius Julius (100–44 BC). Probably the greatest general in Rome's history, and among the most successful of all time, Caesar was also a skilful author who wrote detailed accounts of his campaigns. His seven books of *Commentaries* on the *Gallic wars, three on the civil war, along with several books written by some of his officers to fill the gaps in the narrative, provide more information about Caesar's campaigns than those of any other ancient commander. The style of these works has had a massive influence on the writing of military history, down to the present day.

It is important to remember that Caesar was not simply a general, but also a politician. In Rome politics and war were inseparably linked. Success in war promoted a political career, which in turn led to greater opportunities for military command. Up until the year 58, Caesar's career followed the normal pattern for a Roman aristocrat, mixing military with civil posts. He served as a junior officer (tribune) in the east (80–78), being awarded Rome's highest decoration for gallantry, the *corona civica*, for saving a soldier's life at the siege of Mytilene. His first independent command came with his appointment as governor of Further Spain, where he led a small army in some successful police actions (61–60). However, after his political alliance with two of the most powerful politicians in Rome, *Pompey and Crassus, Caesar received the consulship for the year 59 and an exceptionally large provincial command including Illyria, Cisalpine, and Transalpine Gaul in 58. At first his term of office was for five years, which was later extended to ten, an unprecedentedly long period.

Caesar was massively in debt and needed the profits derived from a successful war of conquest. He may well have contemplated marching from Illyria against the Dacian kingdom on the Danube, but the migration of the Helvetii offered him a perfect excuse to intervene in Gaul, an op-portunity he accepted with alacrity (58). In eight years he conquered all of Gaul, defeated several rebellions, and advanced Rome's power to the Rhine. His victories were celebrated with public thanksgivings in Rome, and he took care to seize every chance to perform the spectacular, twice bridging the Rhine and leading expeditions to the strange and distant shores of Britain. Every winter he returned to Cisalpine Gaul to perform his judicial duties as governor, but also to keep an eye on the political climate at Rome. Vast quantities of booty and huge numbers of slaves covered Caesar's debts and made him exceptionally wealthy. He lavished much of this on his victorious soldiers, further increasing their loyalty to him.

Crassus had fallen at *Carrhae in 53 and by the end of the Gallic wars, Pompey was unwilling to accept Caesar as a political equal and rival. He sided with Caesar's ardent opponents in the Senate who were determined to prosecute him as soon as the Gallic command expired. This led to the outbreak of the civil war in 49, when Caesar led his troops across the Rubicon, the narrow stream separating his province, where he legally exercised command, with Italy, where he did not. He secured Italy in a matter of weeks, with hardly a blow being struck. Then he moved to Spain and manoeuvred a Pompeian army into a hopeless position, forcing it to surrender at Ilerda. In 48 he crossed to Macedonia and after a hard campaign defeated Pompey himself at *Pharsalus. Following Pompey to Egypt, he wintered there, making Queen Cleopatra his mistress, and fighting with small forces against a serious rebellion. In 47 he moved against Pharnaces, king of Bosphorus, who had overrun much of Asia, and defeated him in a few days at Zela. It was of this rapid victory that he made the famous comment, 'Veni, Vidi, Vici' (I came: I saw: I conquered). In 46 he smashed another Pompeian army at Thapsus in Africa, before finally crushing the last resistance at Munda in Spain in

45. Returning to Rome he was made dictator for life, but was murdered by a senatorial conspiracy on 15 March 44, a few weeks before he was to have embarked on a series of major campaigns, first against Dacia, then Parthia.

Like many great commanders Caesar did little to reform his army, but took the existing Roman army organization and raised it to the peak of efficiency. He instituted a rigorous programme of training, with regular exercises and route marches which he often led in person. As a leader he was inspirational. Conspicuous bravery was lavishly rewarded with decorations, promotions, and a larger share of the booty. In particular he rewarded his centurions, who figure prominently in his *Commentaries* for their loyalty and courage. Caesar was also skilled at fostering unit pride. When his army was reluctant to march against Ariovistus, Caesar announced that he would go on alone with the X Legion. The Tenth responded to the flattery with enthusiasm and the rest of the army was shamed into emulating their behaviour. During the civil war many of the Tenth were long overdue for discharge and mutinied at the prospect of another campaign. Caesar quelled the disturbance with a single word, addressing them as *Quirites*, civilians rather than soldiers. The legion gave the ringleaders up for execution and won the day for Caesar at Munda.

As a commander Caesar's most striking quality was his speed of action. He always tried to seize the initiative, launching counter offensives in winter with whatever troops were immediately available against the Gallic rebellions in 54 and 52. Crossing the Rubicon with a single legion, and invading Macedonia in the civil war were equally bold actions. In battle, Caesar moved around his army, ever present where there was a crisis, and willing to go into the front line himself if the situation was desperate. Modern scholars have criticized Caesar for his rashness, pointing out that his genius was all too often exercised in extricating his army from the poor position which his recklessness had placed it in. Yet this type of behaviour was typically Roman. The Romans expected a general to be very bold, ranking luck as important an attribute of a successful commander as ability.   AKG

caisson A box for carrying ammunition, mounted on two or four wheels and joined to an artillery limber. In Napoleonic times, most armies adopted the *Gribeauval system of standardized carriages with a 4 metre (13 foot) caisson divided into compartments for rounds, powder, and matches. The heavier the artillery, the more caissons were allocated. First-line caissons would be held about 55 yards (50 metres) behind the guns and second-line about 109 yards (100 metres), exchanging places when withdrawing for replenishment. Also a term describing sections of the massive prefabricated units used to make the Mulberry Harbours used in the *Normandy invasion in 1944.
                                                                                     JBAB

Haythornthwaite, P., *Weapons and Equipment of the Napoleonic Wars* (Poole, 1979).
Wise, T., *Artillery of the Napoleonic Wars* (London, 1979).

Calais, sieges of (1346–7 and 1940). As the French seaport closest to England, Calais was besieged in September 1346 by *Edward III after his victory at *Crécy. Its determined garrison under Jean de Vienne was enthusiastically supported by the citizens. Attempts at relief failed and the English land and sea *blockade starved the defenders. In July 1347 six leading citizens, led by Eustache de St Pierre, presented themselves to Edward. Wearing only shirts, they had ropes around their necks, ready for the hangman, and carried the keys to the city and the castle. Edward would have strung them up, but his wife, Philippa of Hainault, persuaded him to show mercy. Calais and a wide area round it—the Pale—remained in English hands until the Duke of Guise recaptured it in 1558. Queen Mary, shocked by its loss, declared that 'Calais' would be found written on her heart.

In May 1940, with the British Expeditionary Force (BEF) cut off from most ports, Calais was a useful base. The *War Office believed that the problem lay not in holding Calais, but in getting supplies through reportedly light German forces to the BEF. Brigadier Claude Nicholson's 30th Infantry Brigade—two motorized battalions, 1st King's Royal Rifles and 1st Rifle Brigade, with a Territorial motorcycle battalion, Queen Victoria's Rifles—was sent there, with 3rd Royal Tank Regiment added at the last moment. It became clear that the BEF could not be reached, and after order and counter-order, Nicholson was ordered to hold on for inter-Allied solidarity. He declined an invitation to *capitulate and was eventually overwhelmed on 26 May. *Churchill, who had insisted that Calais should be held, maintained that it played a key role in the evacuation from *Dunkirk; but in truth its gallant defence had little real impact on operations.   RH

Callwell, Maj Gen Sir Charles Edward (1859–1928), Anglo-Irish military writer and thinker, intelligence officer and talented linguist, author of *Small Wars* (1896) and *Military Operations and Maritime Preponderance* (1905). Interest in Callwell's work revived in the 1990s because of its relevance to *peacekeeping and its treatment of asymmetric conflict. He was commissioned into the Royal Field Artillery in 1878 and in 1886, as a captain, was awarded the Royal United Service Institute gold medal for an essay on British army operations since 1865 which became the basis for *Small Wars*, assuring his career as a military writer. It was republished in 1899 and 1906 and translated into French. In the Second *Boer War (1899–1902) Callwell served on the staff of Sir Redvers *Buller and then commanded a mobile column. He retired in 1909 to devote himself to writing but was recalled in 1914 to be Director of Military Operations and Intelligence. CDB

Cambrai, battle of (1917). Cambrai Day—20 November—is celebrated by the British Royal Tank Regiment as the first occasion when *tanks were used on a large scale and with tactics specially devised for them, after a disappointing debut on the *Somme in September 1916 and in support of infantry attacks at the third battle of *Ypres. The British attack, by Third Army under *Byng against the *Hindeburg Line west of Cambrai, had mixed parentage. The Tank Corps, under Brig Gen Hugh Elles and his chief of staff Lt Col *Fuller, saw the rolling downland as offering excellent opportunities for the use of tanks, and Fuller proposed a large-scale raid with the aim of getting tanks onto the German gun-line. Brig Gen Tudor, commanding the artillery of the 9th Division, had developed a system for marking targets by survey rather than adjusting them by

fire, so that an attack would not be heralded by artillery preparation. Surprise would be lost, however, if guns cut the belts of barbed wire in front of German trenches, and Tudor proposed that these should be crushed by tanks. These ideas were synthesized, and Third Army, recently eclipsed by operations around Ypres, supported the project. In September *Haig gave Byng outline permission to proceed with planning, but it was not until the third battle of Ypres had ended that the plan was approved. Even then it was one of limited liability: Third Army was to break the German line with tanks, push cavalry across the St Quentin Canal, and seize Bourlon Wood, Cambrai, and other objectives. If early results were not encouraging, the operation would be called off after 48 hours.

Four hundred and seventy-six tanks were assembled in the strictest security, and their crews practised battle drills with the infantry which would accompany them. There were two main types of tank, 'males', armed with a pair of 6-pounders, and 'females' with machine guns. They were to

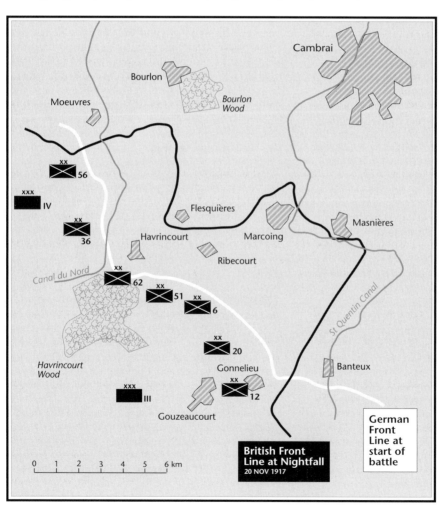

The battle of **Cambrai,** 20 November 1917.

carry fascines (bundles of sticks or pipes) to drop into trenches too broad for tanks to span. Thus equipped, they would gap the wire for the infantry following close behind, cross trenches, and then, while some tanks drove parallel with them to kill or neutralize their defenders, others were to push on to the next trench while the infantry mopped up in their wake. Over 1,000 guns supported the attack from positions which had been meticulously surveyed, opening fire at 06.10 when it was barely light enough for the horrified defenders to see the tanks and infantry bearing down upon them.

Fuller believed that, used en masse, tanks would prove a powerful psychological weapon, demoralizing the defenders and encouraging the attackers. This proved the case across much of the front, and many of the defenders were shocked into surrender by the dual impact of the stunning bombardment and the unexpected arrival of the tanks. However, at Flesquières in the centre of the attack sector, there were at least two German batteries that had recently been trained in the *anti-armour role and were not destroyed in the short but very intense bombardment that preceded the attack. While elsewhere the tanks rolled over trenches and achieved their first-day objectives by noon, at Flesquières they were checked, suffering heavy loss as they crested the ridge. Haig's dispatch later paid tribute to a German artillery officer who manned his gun single-handed until he was killed, but the episode is almost certainly a myth: in this sector well-handled guns, unfavourable ground, and a difference of tactical opinion between the tanks and the local infantry commander all contributed to the disappointing result. In all, 179 of 378 fighting tanks were lost, 65 destroyed by direct hits. Nevertheless, the day had seen the German defences penetrated at their strongest point to a depth of some 5 miles (8 km), and church bells were rung in England for the first time in the war.

The Germans rapidly recovered from their shock, and on the second day, 21 November, when the tanks rolled into villages in front of Cambrai, German infantry climbed to the first floors, above the limited elevation of the tanks' side-mounted guns, and engaged them at close range. Without infantry support, more tanks were lost and the momentum of the attack petered out. Haig, however, believed that the Germans were 'showing a disposition to retire', and decided to continue with the battle. For the next week there was a bitter struggle for Bourlon Wood, whose whaleback mass still dominates the battlefield. During it the British lost Brig Gen R. B. Bradford, at 25 their youngest general. They were tired and off-balance, with most unit commanders ordered out of the line for a well-earned rest, when the Germans counter-attacked on 30 November, jabbing in hard on both sides of the salient the British had driven into their lines. They came close to actually cutting off British troops in the centre, and though they were eventually checked, recovered about as much ground as they had lost. Both sides lost about 45,000 men, but Haig found the sudden reversal of fortune especially damaging, coming as it did after the painfully slow progress at Ypres. Cambrai suggested that, under the right circumstances, and with predicted artillery fire, the tank could indeed break through trench lines, though exploitation still lay beyond it. During their counter-attack the Germans further developed the *storm-troop tactics they had already pioneered, and the importance they allocated to surprise in artillery fire-planning, used to such effect in their offensives of spring and early summer 1918, reflected their painful experience of the British 'lightning bombardment' at Cambrai. APC-A/RH

Cooper, Bryan, *Ironclads of Cambrai* (London, 1967).
Foley, John, *The Boilerplate War* (London, 1963).
Harris, J. P., *Men, Ideas and Tanks* (London, 1995).

Camerone, battle of (1863), episode of the French *Mexican expedition. In April 1863 the 3rd Company of the Legion's 1st battalion, commanded by the one-handed Capt Danjou, was escorting a bullion convoy through the Mexican countryside when it was surrounded by a greatly superior Mexican force in a farm near the village of Camarón (Sp.: *camarón*, shrimp). Danjou refused to surrender and was killed, and his men followed his example until only a handful were left. Their ammunition gone, they made a last *bayonet charge in which all were killed or wounded. Danjou's wooden hand was recovered and takes pride of place when the Legion celebrates Camerone day on 30 April each year. RH

camouflage (from Fr.: *camoufler*, to veil). In Russian the word is *maskirovka*, meaning 'to deceive', and that is the name of the game. Considering how thoroughly it permeates the natural world, it is astonishing how long it took armies to get serious about camouflage. Whether predator or prey, or both as is usually the case, animals have evolved a bewildering range of survival strategies in which shape and colour are used to conceal, to warn, and to pretend to be something they are not. Had warfare developed simply from hunting, camouflage might have developed along with it, but with the exception of green uniforms among British *rifle regiments in North America and German *Jägers, the trend was in the opposite direction, with uniforms reaching a peak of gorgeousness shortly before *breech-loading rifles doomed the practice.

To understand why some armies persisted in making themselves conspicuous even well into WW I, one must look to the other natural use of extravagant shapes and colouring, sexual advertising, which is an almost exclusively male preserve. This becomes even more intriguing when considered in combination with, for example, the mainly symbolic *bayonet. But that is to digress. Camouflage as traditionally understood is used to veil and to deceive, and the fathers of modern military camouflage were zoologists and illustrators, Abbott Thayer in the USA and John Kerr in Britain. They applied the lessons of animal protective colouring to warfare, the former going so far as to argue that all animal markings, no matter how conspicuous, served the purpose of concealment.

Serendipitously during the period 1900–14, artists identifying themselves as Cubists and Vorticists were moving away from representational illustration towards abstraction, stressing structural form, shape, and colour as a means of interpreting an object. Their philosophy found expression in the 'dazzle' painting of ships, developed by Thayer and Kerr during WW I. US and British warships began to make a bizarre appearance with angular patterns in primary colours painted on their hulls. Kerr conceived the idea of painting a ship with a false perspective, to distort the vessel's true course and speed, making it hard for a prowling U-boat to aim a torpedo correctly. Other schemes incorporated fake bow waves or raised waterlines, designed to complicate calculation of a ship's speed or range. There is little evidence that it worked. Nonetheless, in both countries, artists were recruited to aid this work, and Cubists and Vorticists found larger canvases on which to paint. One leading Vorticist, Edward Wadsworth, supervised the camouflage of over two thousand warships, and his post-war canvases celebrated his dazzling ships. The trend continued in *WW II when the naturalist and artist Sir Peter Scott devised several dazzle colour schemes for the Royal Navy.

Personal camouflage began to be widespread with the adoption of *khaki by the British army in India, becoming standard after the First *Boer war had underlined the disadvantage of a scarlet jacket when fighting men who could shoot. The Germans replaced Prussian blue with field grey (grey-green) and the Russians replaced dark green with a greyish brown. French troops continued to wear the red trousers and blue coats, their *cuirassiers still wearing the shining breastplates of a century earlier. Casualty lists were an excellent argument for change, but it was the advent of aerial *reconnaissance that led to ever-wider applications of the art of camouflage.

The first *section de camouflage* in military history was established in 1915 by the French, under the command of a painter, and thereafter comparable units were used by all the combatants. These advised on how to break up the shape of objects and experimented with colour schemes. This coincided with several new arrivals on the battlefield, including tanks, which required deception and concealment to a high degree. By 1918, the use of military camouflage was axiomatic, and in 1939 war artists were again mobilized to advise on concealment. The colouring of aircraft cycled rapidly through the concealment-advertising-concealment process, the German fighter squadron of WW I taking personal adornment to a browbeating extreme. During WW II the pattern of irregular earth tones above and light bluegrey underneath became a standard, shelved by the USAAF once air superiority was achieved in late 1944, and its aircraft flew in bare polished metal, saving time in the manufacturing process and operational weight.

Apart from the wearing of white by *arctic and mountain troops, which began much earlier, smocks using disruptive patterns worn over normal battledress were first used by *SS troops invading the USSR in 1941. The British Denison smock, worn by paratroopers was similar. The Germans developed a wide range of camouflage suits designed for a variety of specific environments, but whether these were for concealment or as an expression of élite troops' desire to set themselves apart is open to debate. The US army attempted to introduce a camouflage suit in Normandy, but it was withdrawn because Allied troops had become used to the fact that only the Germans wore camouflage.

Nearly every army in the world now has a distinctive camouflage uniform of its own, which is worn as often in *barracks as in the field. Some designs are durable—Germany has readopted the basic pattern it used in the closing months of WW II—while most are distinctive, and it is now possible to recognize the nationality of a soldier by his camouflage. The counter-indicated use of camouflage smocks in the streets of Northern Ireland is merely the latest example of the conflict between the soldier's desire not to attract hostile attention and his wish to set himself apart as the epitome of manhood. In this respect skin camouflage also serves a dual function, both as warpaint and as a response to the practical need to disrupt tell-tale faces and hands with specialist camouflage cream made by cosmetics manufacturers.

The advent of *radar, *infra-red (IR), and satellite detection has lessened the importance of merely visual camouflage, while heightening the need to extend deception into the non-visual spectrum by heat dispersion and concealment and the use of countermeasures such as electronic jamming, spoofing, and flares to attract IR guided missiles. The latter category had its first military application in the *bold* noise-makers ejected by U-boats when the pinging of sonar indicated that those on the surface were coming too close. Stealth technology—low observability in whatever spectrum—may be considered the culmination of the art.

APC-A

Cruickshank, Charles, *Deception in WW II* (Oxford, 1979).
Reit, Seymour, *Masquerade* (London, 1979).

camp followers A term used to identify those civilians that followed in the wake of an army or served its needs while encamped or on campaign. From the start of organized warfare to the end of the 19th century and in some cases beyond, camp followers were a vital part of any army's support structure, responsible for cooking, laundry, nursing, and sexual services without which armies could not function in the field. Until *sutler services were militarized, even specifically military goods were supplied by camp followers. They accompanied the baggage trains and, during times such as the *Thirty Years War when to remain in one place was to court despoliation and death, they outnumbered the army itself, multiplying rather than solving logistical problems.

Thus, although much support was provided by camp followers, their numbers could become a liability. The problem was often exacerbated by soldiers acquiring local 'wives'. Some generals were offended by this, for example the austere *Cromwell, who banned his soldiers from marrying, under pain of expulsion from the army. But until armies expanded the services they provided to encompass most of their soldiers' needs, camp followers were an integral part of warfare. The French even had field bordellos at *Dien Bien Phu, but the prudish Anglo-American style was to ensure heightened attrition by *venereal disease, despite the efforts of such as *Montgomery to introduce some common sense.

Camp followers fulfilled a variety of roles in many armies, blurring the line between combatant and non-combatant. The Mexican *soldaderas*, for example, developed the inherited tradition of Spanish warrior women well into the 20th century. Aztec armies utilized novice soldiers as well as slaves to transport most of the army's belongings, weapons, clothing, and supplies using a primitive backpack. It has been estimated that these porters could move 15 miles (24 km) a day carrying 75 lb (34 kg). The Greeks also used young pre-warriors to carry the panoply of the *hoplite and to take care of the needs of the older men generally. Zulu soldiers were followed by young herd boys, called *Izindibi/udibi*, carrying the army's impedimenta in the rear or on the flanks of the advance. During the *Indochina and *Vietnam wars, the secret of the North Vietnamese Army's astonishingly successful logistics was a dual-purpose army of male and female soldier-porters using specially adapted bicycles.

Camp followers shared the military fortunes of the armies they accompanied. At the battle of *Lützen in 1632, *Wallenstein used camp followers as decoys and their arrival on the field at *Bannockburn was decisive. Even with the baggage train to the rear, the lives of camp followers were at risk. At *Naseby in 1645, the royalist train was assaulted and many camp followers were massacred by *New Model Army troopers, who mistook the followers of the king's Welsh infantry for 'mercenary' Irish. But this was contrary to accepted practice, as illustrated by the massacre of valuable French prisoners at *Agincourt in retaliation for an attack on the English train.

In late medieval Europe the *schutheiss* or sutler appeared from the ranks of the *landsknechts. Their job was not only to sell food and drinks to the troops, but to organize market stalls in the army encampments. By the Napoleonic period the sutler had become an almost semi-official part of the regiment. In the French army most battalions possessed prettily uniformed *vivandières* or *cantinières*, who accompanied a unit on campaign selling *alcohol, food, and other choice items to supplement the men's everyday

*rations. Often married to a senior *NCO of the regiment, they were usually adopted by the units as mascots and earned all the respect accorded them. Accompanying the unit into action they performed countless acts of kindness such as those of the 26th Léger at *Austerlitz who handed out cups of brandy against payment the following day, in full knowledge that many of their customers would die before the debt could be repaid. As national identities evolved, so military attitudes towards camp followers came to illustrate the cultures of their societies, the Germans efficient and exploitative, the British and Americans hypocritical, the Italians and French permissive and humane.

As the 19th century progressed, armies began to establish properly constituted support services and the role of the camp follower became marginalized. In the 20th century most western armies have dispensed with camp followers, but military *nurses and female entertainers in the field (see, for the use of the M-16 as an aphrodisiac by United Service Organization dancers, the *film *Apocalypse Now*), and the profiteering merchants, innkeepers, and pimps clustered around permanent military establishments, remind us of a long and sometimes honoured tradition.

JDB/HEB

Campbell, FM Sir Colin, 1st Baron Clyde (1792–1863). Campbell served in many of the great 19th-century colonial wars. Of modest origins, he was commissioned into the 8th Foot in 1808 and was bloodied in the *Peninsular war. Long stints of service in China and India were awarded with promotion to brigadier in 1844, and a knighthood in 1849. He led a brigade, then 1st Division in the *Crimea, where his fierce words at the foot of the Alma cliffs on the certainty of death for shirkers, and his command of the *Thin Red Line at Balaclava, made him famous. He returned home as a lieutenant general and was appointed to command in India after the outbreak of the *Indian Mutiny. In November he led the relief of Lucknow, which became a favourite of military *artists. By 1858 he had crushed the rebellion in fire and blood, was promoted again and created Lord Clyde. He returned home in 1860 to a popular reception akin to a Roman triumph.

APC-A

Canadian Expeditionary Force (CEF). The outbreak of war in 1914 was greeted with enthusiasm in Canada, but regular Canadian forces were minuscule—about 3,100 men—plus a poorly trained active militia of 75,000. The Minister of Militia and Defence, Col Sam Hughes, acted as a human dynamo in creating the CEF. He accepted the offer to raise a battalion of ex-regulars, Princess Patricia's Canadian Light Infantry (PPCLI), which went on to serve with the British 27th Division; he set up a major camp at Valcartier, which trained civilian volunteers; and the first contingent of the CEF left for England on 1 October. Hughes was a controversial figure, considered insane by some of his enemies. His tenure was marked by scandal, corruption, errors, and heavy-handed political interference in the CEF. Perhaps the most notorious example is Hughes's insistence on the CEF being equipped with the Canadian Ross rifle rather than the superior British Short Magazine Lee Enfield (SMLE) rifle.

The 1st Canadian Division went into the line on the western front in February 1915, under the command of Maj Gen Alderson, a British regular. The division fought heroically during the second battle of *Ypres in April 1915, when poison *gas was used on the battlefield for the first time (by the Germans). The arrival of the 2nd Canadian Division allowed the formation of a Canadian Corps in September 1915, initially commanded by Alderson. He was replaced by *Byng, another British regular, in May 1916. He proved popular with the Canadians, and the Canadian Corps became known as the 'Byng Boys' after a popular musical review. In November 1915 the PPCLI joined the Canadian Corps, and in January 1916 the Canadian Cavalry Brigade joined a British formation. The 3rd Division was formed in France in February 1916, and in August 4th Division joined the Canadian Corps in France. A 5th Division was formed in 1917 but was disbanded in 1918 to help keep the other divisions up to strength.

In 1916, with the Canadian Corps near Ypres, it fought at Saint-Eloi (May) and Mount Sorrel (June). In September it was committed to the fighting on the *Somme at Courcelette, where its record of success was mixed. However, in common with the rest of the British army, the CEF benefited from the painful lessons of the Somme. On 9 April 1917 the four-division strong Canadian Corps seized Vimy Ridge (see ARRAS/VIMY RIDGE). This marked the emergence of the Canadians as an élite force, and is seen as a formative moment in the emergence of Canada as a nation. In June 1917 Byng was promoted to command British Third Army, and was replaced by Arthur Currie, a Canadian militia officer. By this stage the corps staff was largely Canadian, and Canada had become a 'junior but sovereign ally' of the British. Under Currie's command, the Corps captured *Passchendaele Ridge in November 1917.

The CEF's finest hour came in 1918. The Canadians played a prominent role in the battle of *Amiens, and then acted as one of the spearhead formations of the Allied offensives. The Canadians broke the Drocourt-Quéant Line on 2 September, crossed the Canal du Nord in late September, and entered Mons on the morning of 11 November, the last day of the war. The Canadian Corps was considerably stronger, and had greater firepower, than equivalent British formations. Nonetheless, the tactical excellence of the Canadians and Currie's skilful generalship were major factors in the success of the Canadian Corps, which was a truly élite formation.

The reputation of the CEF for indiscipline is something of a myth, although *discipline and officer–man relations

in Canadian units were somewhat more relaxed than in some British units. Equally mythical is the notion that Canadian military effectiveness was derived from the influence of the North American frontier. Seventy per cent of the 'First Contingent' were British-born, and taking the war as a whole, under half—47 per cent—of those who went overseas were born in Canada. Of those men who enlisted by March 1916, only 6.5 per cent were farmers, while 65 per cent were manual workers. Moreover, the influence of British commanders and staff officers on the CEF was important, and the development of the expertise of the Canadian Corps should be placed in the context of the 'learning curve' experienced by the entire British army on the western front. About 418,000 served with the CEF, and 56,000 were killed.   GDS

Morton, Desmond, *When Your Number's Up: The Canadian Soldier in WW I* (Toronto, 1993).

Canaris, Adm Wilhelm (1887–1945). A highly controversial figure, Canaris was a career naval officer who directed the *Abwehr, the German foreign intelligence service, during the Third Reich. He had worked in intelligence circles during WW I and was appointed Abwehr director in 1935, reporting to the Reich War Ministry and subsequently to the Wehrmacht high command (OKW). He was not only duped by the British 'double-cross' system whereby they controlled all his agents and fed back disinformation, but was also a member of the Widerstand (German *resistance) and actively involved in treasonous contact with the Allies. On the other hand, he ran a double-cross system of his own with captured *SOE agents in Holland and broke Royal Navy codes. The tensions of his divided loyalties led to the crumbling of his façade in February 1944, when he expressed the opinion, in Hitler's presence, that Germany could not win the war. He was obliged to resign and the Abwehr was subordinated to the Sicherheitsdienst. After the failure of the July 1944 bomb plot against *Hitler he was executed in Flossenburg concentration camp.   APC-A

Cannae, battle of (now Canne della Battaglia) (216 BC), the scene of Hannibal's most famous victory and the origin of the term 'double envelopment'. It took its name from a small town on the right bank of the Aufidus (now Ofanto) and was almost certainly fought on the same side of the river and downstream from the town, with Hannibal's army facing north-east towards the sea. Hannibal deployed his 40,000 infantry with alternate companies of Celts and Spaniards in the centre and Africans on the wings; beyond the Africans he placed his cavalry, Spaniards and Celts to the left by the river and Numidians on the right, open flank. The Romans formed in their usual three lines of infantry, with citizen cavalry on the right, allied on the left. Hannibal bowed out his centre to tempt the Romans to attack it, while the cavalry on his left swept the Roman citizen cavalry from the field, then rode around the Roman infantry to help the Numidians rout the allied cavalry. Meanwhile the Roman infantry pushed back the Celts and Spaniards in Hannibal's centre, bunching inwards away from the Africans who were thus able to take them in flank. The encirclement was complete when the Spanish and Celtic cavalry, leaving the Numidians to pursue the routed allied cavalry, took the Roman infantry in the rear. The result was a massacre without parallel in the history of western warfare, with the *Roman army suffering worse casualties (48,200 killed) even than the British army on the first day of the Somme; in addition, some 19,300 were taken prisoner.

Cannae remains an ideal of all commanders, and has a resonance far beyond its own age. *Schlieffen, author of the German WW I plan which bears his name, wrote extensively about it and the Wehrmacht's vast envelopments of the Soviet armies at the start of *BARBAROSSA were called 'super-Cannaes'.   JFL

Lazenby, J. F., *Hannibal's War* (Warminster, 1978).
Livy, 22. 43–9.
Polybius, 3. 113–17.

---

cannon   The term cannon includes high-velocity, small-calibre guns mounted in aircraft and armoured vehicles as well as pieces capable of firing nuclear warheads. It is often used as a general term for any barrelled artillery piece. In the 15th century, a cannon was a specific category of gun but is now a general term for a gun that requires a mount, from long-range artillery to aircraft armament. Such ordnance was first recorded in Ghent in 1313 and was used at the siege of Metz in 1324. Cannon were probably first used on the battlefield by the English at *Crécy in 1346. The defeat of the English army by the French at Formigny on 15 April 1450 was probably the first in which field artillery played a significant role; and the eviction of the English from France was largely due to the reduction of English fortresses by French guns. The use of cannon against *Constantinople in 1453 confirmed their place in the popular imagination and pieces were often given frightening or reverential names such as the 'Lion' of 1430 and 'Mons Meg' of the 1480s.

Early pieces looked more like *mortars than the familiar 'cannon' shape of the late 14th century. They were made of wrought iron strips bound together with hoops and fired stone shot. From the mid-15th century most cannon were cast in bronze, brass, or iron and were distinct from siege mortars. Late 15th-century light pieces included the Moyen (12 oz ball), the Robinet (1 lb ball), the Aspic (2 lb ball), the Falconet (3 lb ball), the Dragon (6 lb ball), and the Culverin (18 lb ball). Heavier pieces included the Bastard Cannon (36 lb ball), the Cannon Royal (48 lb ball), and the Syren (60 lb ball). By the mid-16th century there were four basic categories of ordnance: cannon with short range and heavy hitting power; culverins with smaller shot but longer range; stone-throwing perriers, the predecessors of *howitzers; and mortars which fired in a fixed high trajectory. Stone shot had largely been replaced by cast iron shot by about 1500 and a variety of shot was developed for different targets. Canisters of balls or grapeshot increased lethality against infantry and exploding shells achieved greater range before dispensing shot over the target. The fuses to achieve this have evolved from burning cord, to time mechanisms, *radar, and modern, millimetric, terminal guidance.

Early siege cannon, or bombards, were heavy and rested in a static mount. Fortress gun carriages were soon fitted with small wheels to make loading easier, but field guns needed a lighter frame and larger wheels for cross-country mobility. The army of the French King Charles VIII that invaded Italy in 1494 had gun carriages towed by oxen with detachments on foot. In the 1620s *Gustavus Adolphus realized the need for lighter weapons with tactical battlefield mobility. His leather-bound, regimental guns were the first to fire fixed ammunition with wooden cases.

Eighteenth-century field artillery was usually dispersed with the infantry to supplement its fire. The idea of concentrating cannon in batteries for a more decisive effect was perhaps Napoleon's greatest contribution to tactics. The mainstay of the Napoleonic field artillery were the 6-pounder and the 12-pounder. By the 1860s, heavier cannon were generally reinforced with wrought iron collars to contain the higher pressures of more powerful ammunition.

August Kotter had described the greater accuracy achieved by a spinning ball as early as 1520 and the benefits of rifled barrels were explained by Benjamin Robbins in 1742, but the metallurgy of the day was inadequate for such designs. By 1858 the French had adopted rifled cannon, and rifled pieces such as the Parrot 10-pounder and the Whitworth were used in the *American civil war, alongside more numerous 12-pounder smooth-bore 'Napoleons'. Improvements in casting technology resulted in heavier smooth-bore pieces such as Rodman's 15 inch Columbiads. Breech-loaders make a tighter fit between projectile and barrel and are easier and quicker to load. They had existed since the 15th century but technology was wanting until the late 19th century. Problems were overcome by innovations such as the brass cartridge case and the De Bange 'mushroom' which sealed the breech; and mechanisms such as the sliding breech-block and interrupted screw mechanism. The British Armstrong 12-pounder was one of the first successful breech-loaders and was also used in the American civil war. Increasingly powerful ammunition destabilized the piece, reducing the rate of fire. The hydraulic buffer of 1867 provided a solution, leading to the development of 'quick firing' (QF) guns which used oil and compressed air to absorb the recoil and push the barrel back to its original position for rapid breech-loading. These were first deployed for coastal defence in the early 1890s and lighter versions for field use followed. Typical QF guns were the French M1897 75 mm or 'Soixante Quinze' and the British 13-pounder with a range of about 5,900 yards (5,395 metres). Heavier guns and howitzers proliferated during WW I, and the German 'Paris Gun', which bombarded Paris in March 1918 at a range of 120 km (75 miles), became the model for Germany's 'super-heavy' artillery of WW II. Motor vehicles began to replace the horse in the early 20th century and *self-propelled (SP) artillery became common during WW II. The most significant development in cannon between the wars was the high velocity, *anti-armour and anti-aircraft gun, the most famous being the German 88 mm flak gun. Gerald Bull was probably the greatest innovator in cannon and munitions design of the late 20th century, resulting in many long-range 155 mm towed equipments. He was also infamous for his work on the Iraqi 'super-gun' of the early 1990s which was based on the 'Paris Gun'. Field artillery today is either SP or towed. Future towed cannon are likely to be lighter to increase their air-portability, making them more strategically and tactically mobile. Accuracy will be improved by on-board navigation systems and the 'smart' terminal guidance of their munitions. JBAB

Bailey, J. B. A., *Field Artillery and Firepower* (Oxford, 1989).
Hogg, I. V., *German Artillery of World War Two* (London, 1975).
—— *British Artillery Weapons and Ammunition 1914–1918* (London, 1972).
Slattery, T. J., 'Rodman Civil War Genius of Ordnance', *Army* (Aug. 1997).
Thomas, D. S., *Cannons, an Introduction to Civil War Artillery* (Gettysburg, Pa., 1975).

Canrobert, Marshal F. C. (1809–95). François Certain Canrobert made his name as a spectacularly brave infantry officer during the French conquest of *Algeria. He commanded one of the first-formed *chasseur battalions, and, as a general, supported Louis-Napoleon's 1851 coup (see NAPOLEON III). He resigned supreme command in the Crimea in 1855, pleading inability to work with his British allies (who nicknamed him 'Robert Can't'), but showed his usual dash in Italy in 1859. In the *Franco-Prussian war he commanded VI Corps, holding the ridge at Saint-Privat on 18 August 1870 with characteristic courage. After the war he sat as a Bonapartist senator. With his wispy hair, big moustaches, and eternal cigarette, he was the archetypal Second Empire *beau sabreur*, a gallant subordinate but unwilling to take high command. RH

canteen derives from the Italian *cantina* or wine cellar, and originally meant a place on a military establishment where soldiers could get refreshments. It continues to be used in this sense to indicate places of work where food etc. is provided from a central servery. Mobile canteens also supply troops in the field when on exercise or conducting operations. Canteen more often refers to a water bottle carried by individual soldiers as part of their personal *equipment, often with a specially designed pouch or cloth cover. JR-W

cantonment (from Fr.: *cantonner*, to quarter) originally meant the housing of troops. More usually cantonment describes the place or places of encampment formed by troops for a long period during a campaign or while in winter quarters. In English cantonment is used largely in the contest of India where it was applied to permanent military stations. This is well illustrated by a description of the East India Company's Bengal Cantonments near Surat in 1783: 'a camp this singular place cannot be well termed; it more resembles a large town many miles in circumference.' MC
Forbes, James, *Oriental Memoirs* (London, 1813).

canton system of regional recruitment, introduced by Frederick William I of Brandenburg-Prussia (1620–88) in emulation of a similar system in Sweden (see CHARLES XII). During his reign (1640–88) the army doubled from 38,000 to 76,000, making it the fourth largest in Europe, and the expansion rested upon the canton system, designed to emancipate the kingdom from the need to hire undependable and expensive mercenary forces. Each regiment was assigned a geographical region, centred on a garrison town where its recruitment and administration were based. The system allowed him to apply efficiently, if selectively, the law governing military service, which obligated every subject to serve in the army. See also BARRACKS. RTF

capitulate This, in the military sense, means to make *terms* of surrender; to yield on stipulated terms. Ordinarily used in terms of a general, force, garrison, fortress, town, etc. More simply, to surrender upon terms. The stem of capitulate is capital or chapter, ultimately the same word. Both come via Old French from the Latin *capitulum* meaning small head. *Capitulum*, in the sense of 'head of a discourse or chapter' produced the derivative *capitulare*, 'draw up under separate headings'. When its past participle passed into English in the 16th century as the verb capitulate, it still held this meaning and it did not become the more specific 'make terms of surrender' until the 17th century.

Quite apart from its more widely known military meaning, capitulation, the action of the verb to capitulate, is a historical term from international law. Capitulation is any treaty whereby one state permits another to exercise extra-territorial jurisdiction over its own nationals within the former state's boundaries. There was no element of surrender in the early capitulations made between the powerful Ottoman Turk sultans and various European rulers. The sultans simply wished to avoid the expense and burden of administering justice to foreign merchants. However, later capitulations, particularly in the case of China, resulted from military pressure and came to be regarded as humiliating derogations of China's sovereignty, which indeed they were (see OPIUM WAR).

In the military sense capitulation provides a means to end conflict, either at local or a wider level. It almost uniformly involves a lesser or higher degree of negotiation although the advantage invariably rests with the party in the strongest position, usually poised on the edge of victory. Surrendering under specific terms has a long tradition in warfare. For example in 878 Alfred 'the Great' besieged a Viking camp at Edington and after fourteen days the Vikings sought terms. After Alfred had taken hostages to ensure their good behaviour the Vikings 'swore . . . that they would leave his kingdom immediately, and Guthrum, their king promised to accept Christianity'. This is a perfect example of capitulation: the Vikings, hopelessly cut off, accepted Alfred's terms and in return they were able to leave England alive. In medieval times besiegers would often dictate terms to the besieged. Although the term capitulate was not yet in use, refusal to accept these terms led to no quarter being given when the city was taken, the implicit alternative to any capitulation.

In modern warfare capitulation has often been used to refer to a country accepting defeat and disadvantageous terms, particularly territorial concession, to end a war and to secure the removal of the troops of the victorious power from its probably adjusted borders. In 1871 with Paris occupied by the Prussians, the French capitulated and under the terms of the Treaty of Frankfurt were forced to cede Alsace and three-quarters of Lorraine to Germany. In return the by-then newly renamed Germans withdrew from France.

In the era of *total war, the accepted pattern of European warfare changed. After being crushed militarily, defeated nations were usually occupied and there was little or no scope to negotiate concessions. The Allied declaration of 'unconditional surrender' in WW II was a prime example of this. There could be no Nazi capitulation in its purest form as there could be no bargaining with *Hitler and his followers, merely total surrender with no conditions. In contrast the Japanese could be said to have capitulated, in spite of the Allied declaration of 'unconditional surrender' in their case as well. They succeeded in obtaining one condition of surrender, the continued rule of Emperor Hirohito.   MCM

Asser's Life of King Alfred (London, 1983).

Caporetto, battle of (1917), Italian military debacle of WW I. Following eleven consecutive and *morale-destroying uphill offensives on the Izonzo front, the last ending on 12 September, Italian C-in-C Cadorna at last achieved some penetration against the Austrians, who appealed to Berlin for help. *Ludendorff sent six German divisions to reverse the situation. On 24 October two Austrian armies attacked the Italian salient from the south-east while

the Germans and nine Austrian divisions struck from the north-east. Italian resistance promptly collapsed amid scenes immortalized in Hemingway's *A Farewell to Arms*. There were about 700,000 casualties, mostly surrender and *desertion.

Unprepared for the magnitude of their success, the Austro-Germans gave Cadorna just enough time to reform his remaining 300,000 along the Piave river north of Venice, where they held until reinforcements were rushed to their support, including British and French units from the western front. The defeat prompted a conference of Allied political and military leaders at Rapallo in November, from which unified military command emerged. Under their new commander Díaz, the Italians beat back a further Austrian attack in June 1918 and took the offensive on the anniversary of Caporetto, winning a crushing victory at *Vittorio Veneto.   HEB

Carabobo, battle of (24 June 1821), one of the most important battles of the Latin American wars of independence, which decided the fate of the northern Spanish settlements. In 1820 a new Liberal government in Madrid had ordered royalist Gov Morillo to conclude an armistice with Simón *Bolívar, who had gained control of Colombia in 1819. Bolívar broke the agreement and marched east to Maracaibo at the head of a numerically superior army, which included a contingent of Irish and British volunteers, some of them veterans of the *Peninsular war, and Gen Páez's *llaneros*, excellent Venezuelan plains light horsemen. There does not appear to have been much tactical skill displayed and the royalist army under Gen de la Torre was overwhelmed. Bolívar proclaimed the republic of Gran Colombia, encompassing today's Venezuela (his homeland), Colombia, Panama, and Ecuador—the last of which he had not yet conquered.   HEB

caracole A manoeuvre intended to let cavalry make effective use of firearms. By 1540 German heavy cavalry, known as *reiters, were abandoning the lance for *wheel-lock pistols. They advanced in *column, and then fired either by ranks, with successive ranks firing and moving off to the rear, or by files, when the column first presented one flank to the enemy and then wheeled about for the other flank to fire. By the end of the century the tactic was widespread. The unreliability and short range of the pistol reduced its effectiveness, and from the 1630s the caracole was replaced by the shock action of horsemen charging home with the sword.   RH

Cardwell, Edward, 1st Viscount Cardwell (1813–86). A former army officer, Cardwell was responsible for a series of reforms which defined the structure, organization, and character of the British infantry until well into the 20th century. Cardwell's reforms were begun 1868–74 when he was Secretary of State for War in Gladstone's Liberal government, and were continued by his successor Hugh Childers. In the teeth of opposition from senior officers, Cardwell abolished the purchase of commissions and implemented a policy of organizing infantry regiments into two regular battalions, one in a home *barracks and the other overseas. The regiments were to be linked by name to their county recruiting area and were to have local militia and volunteer battalions affiliated to them. This involved ending the ancient system whereby the *militia had been under control of the Home Office via the county lord lieutenants. Cardwell also improved conditions of regular service, set up a new system of liability for service in a reserve capacity, and devolved their own defence requirements to Australia, Canada, and New Zealand. The Cardwell system was adapted to the needs of imperial defence and was almost wholly inappropriate for war in Europe.　　PC

Carlist wars (1834–40, 1872–6). Although the Carlist wars originated in a disputed succession to the Spanish throne, they reflected tensions between liberalism and conservatism, the Church and anticlericalism, and town and country. Female succession, recognized since the 13th century, was barred in 1713. It was re-established in 1789, but the decision was never publicized. When Ferdinand VII died in 1833 his young daughter Isabella was crowned queen, with her mother Cristina as regent. Ferdinand's brother, Don Carlos, declared himself king, and there were risings in his favour across Spain, and particularly in the Basque provinces and Navarre. Having hoped to succeed without bloodshed, in 1834 he returned to Spain to fight for his rights.

By this time Carlist forces were coalescing under Tomas Zumalacarregui, a retired colonel who proved a general of real talent. His opponents enjoyed international support, and a quadruple alliance, concluded in April 1834, bound Britain, France, and Portugal to assist Spain. However, the queen regent's relationship with a former sergeant in her guards affronted the elements in Spanish society which were likely to favour the dignified, devout, and conservative Don Carlos. A Royal Statute of 1834 produced a constitution which maintained an absolute monarchy alongside a bicameral legislature: it was a compromise which pleased few.

The first few months of fighting set the pattern for what followed. The Carlists, stronger in the countryside than the towns, dominated the north-west. They formed battalions which fought *guerrilla actions until united for major battles. Weapons were captured from government forces (Cristinos) or smuggled into northern ports. Don Carlos strengthened his position by undertaking to uphold the ancient privileges (*fueros*) of the Basques, and foreign observers praised the quality of his volunteers—known as

Requetés—with their red Basque berets. Despite their soldierly qualities, the Carlists behaved as ruthlessly as their opponents, torturing officials, shooting prisoners, and tarring and feathering women believed to sympathize with the Cristinos.

Zumalacarregui won a series of battles but, with the war going in his favour, in June 1835 he was mortally wounded in an attack on Bilbao. That month his cause suffered another blow when George de Lacy Evans, a half-pay lieutenant colonel and radical MP, was given permission to raise a British Legion of 10,000 men for service with the Cristinos. The Legion filled its ranks easily, largely from the urban unemployed, some of them veterans of the *Peninsular war. France, too, increased her support for the regency, and the *French Foreign Legion reached Spain that August.

Expectations that the war would end with the relief of Bilbao proved ill-founded. While the Cristinos had two capable generals in Espartero and Córdoba, a young volunteer called Ramon Cabrera was the rising star in the Carlist firmament. The war grew increasingly bitter. Cabrera's mother was shot, and Cabrera added to his reputation for ferocity by shooting four female hostages. In 1836 the British Legion helped raise the siege of San Sebastián, and regular Royal Marines arrived to garrison a nearby port. The Carlists might have won had they launched a single-minded advance on Madrid, but despite mounting two substantial raids through Cristino territory such strategy was beyond them. In August (another) sergeant led a coup that forced Cristina to reinstitute the liberal constitution of 1812, but the Carlists were unable to turn this to their advantage, and failed in another attempt on Bilbao.

In March 1837 the Carlists won a battle at Oriamendi, the last action of the British Legion, whose enlistment term was about to expire. That summer Don Carlos mounted the Royal Expedition to Madrid. En route the Carlists had the better of several engagements, including one at Barbastro where the French and Carlist Foreign Legions fought one another. The hesitant Don Carlos reached the outskirts of the capital but fell back, and ensuing recriminations did grave damage to his cause. Sporadic fighting went on for another year, until in August 1839 the Carlist general Maroto and his opponent Espartero shared the symbolic 'Embrace of Vergara'. Don Carlos left the country, and the last of his supporters escaped into France in July 1840.

This was not the end of Carlism. Isabella was driven from Spain in 1868, and the grandson of Don Carlos made a bid for the throne. He came close to succeeding in a vicious civil war that raged from 1872 until 1876. During the *Spanish civil war the Requetés made a valuable contribution to the Nationalist cause. After it Carlism remained a political force, but the accession of King Juan Carlos in 1975 and the modernization of Spain rendered its traditionalist *raison d'être* an anachronistic survival with declining vitality.　　RH

Holt, Edgar, *The Carlist Wars in Spain* (London, 1967).

Carnot, Lazare (1753–1823). Known as the 'Organizer of Victory', Carnot's contribution to the survival of the fledgling French Republic cannot be overestimated. A regular engineer officer in the old army, he was a member of the Legislative Assembly and the Convention, and joined the Committee of Public Safety in August 1793. He soon recognized that a new way of waging war was going to be required if France was to fight off foreign invasion, and took the first steps to creating a truly national army by bringing about the 'amalgamation', which combined the old royal army with the new revolutionary and republican troops. He reorganized the supply of weapons for the army and instituted proper *magazines and factories for the material of war.

At a time of great national emergency in the autumn of 1793, he took the field with Jourdan and beat the Austrians at Wattignies in October. Despite invaluable service to the Revolution, Carnot became ideologically suspect and was obliged to go into exile for two years. He returned in 1800, but did not at that time manage to secure employment from Napoleon. He resurfaced during the invasion of France in 1814, holding Antwerp for the Empire, and in 1815 became Napoleon's war minister. He spent his last years in German exile.   TM

Carrhae, battle of (53 BC), the first encounter between the Parthians and a *Roman army, to its misfortune led by Crassus. He was one of the triumvirate that dominated Rome and wanted to acquire military glory to balance that of the other two, *Caesar and *Pompey. The battle itself was indecisive, the Roman legionaries and Parthian horse archers and cataphracts proving unable to damage each other seriously, but a detachment led by Crassus' son Publius was lured away from the main body and annihilated. Crassus' nerve broke and he ordered a night retreat which the Parthians were swift to exploit. Crassus and 20,000 men were killed, 10,000 were captured, and the legions' eagles (see COLOURS) were taken.   AKG

cartridge is a word that may be applied to any disposable container which holds a single charge for a firearm. The earliest cartridges, in the 16th century, were cylindrical screws of paper containing a powder charge; musket balls were carried and loaded separately. Around 1600 cartridges began to incorporate the ball and by the end of the 17th century most armies had standardized the practice of wrapping the ball inside the paper containing the powder charge. Soldiers gripped the ball end in their teeth and tore it off the top of the cartridge; the charge was then poured, the paper used as a wad to pack it down, and the ball seated on top with the ramrod. This system was to contribute to the *Indian Mutiny when sepoys became convinced that the cartridges had been greased with forbidden animal fat.

This system gave way to self-contained cartridges and

bolt-action rifles in mid-century. The first military issue was the *needle gun which still used a paper cartridge, in which the detonator in the middle of the propellant was reached by a long pin. Improvement in propellent quality enabled the primer to be moved to the base and the use of sturdy firing pins to strike centre or rim fire detonators in brass cartridges. Calibres decreased as muzzle velocity increased, from 11 mm to today's fairly standard 5.56 mm (.223 inch). The need for a port to eject the cartridge case makes it impossible to keep water and dirt out of the firing mechanism, while the ejection process itself slows down the rate of fire, so weapons designed to employ caseless cartridges with electronic ignition are under development.   SCW

Blair, Claude (gen. ed.), *Pollard's History of Firearms* (London, 1983).
Peterson, Harold L. (ed.), *Encyclopaedia of Firearms* (London, 1964).
Roads, Dr Christopher H., *The British Soldier's Firearm 1850–1864* (London, 1964).

CAS. See AIR SUPPORT, CLOSE.

cashier (from Flemish: *kassern*, to disband or revoke, and Fr.: *casser*, to break). The word has come to mean the dismissal of an officer with disgrace. Once the term applied to all ranks: convicted troopers in the *New Model Army were 'cashiered the army as not worthy to ride therein', as a contemporary put it. The process sometimes involved public degradation, with the convicted officer being stripped of his *badges and insignia and having his sword broken: Capt *Dreyfus was thus degraded after conviction for espionage in 1894. Even if the offender was spared public humiliation, cashiering, with its implied loss of caste, was a painful sentence.   RH

Cassino, battles of (1944). Cassino lies south-east of Rome on Highway 6, the main road to Naples along the Liri valley. The ground rises abruptly to its north, and the abbey of Monte Cassino, founded by St Benedict in 524, dominates the town and the valleys of the Gari and Rapido. In late 1943 town and rivers were stitched into the Gustav Line, the last major obstacle between the Allies and Rome, and there were four battles there between 12 January and 5 June 1944.

In January Lt Gen *Clark, commanding Fifth Army, planned to break the Gustav Line by attacking on both sides of Cassino and then breaking out down the Liri valley. The French Expeditionary Corps under *Juin would attack into the mountains north of Cassino, then the British X Corps would attack across the Garigliano, nearer the coast, and finally the US 36th Division, in the centre, would cross the Gari (wrongly described as the Rapido in most sources) south of the town. The French attack, launched on the night of 11/12 January, gained ground in circumstances

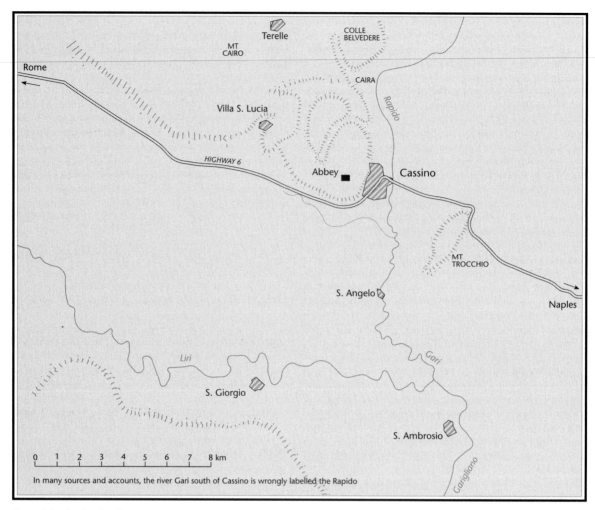

Area of the **Cassino battles**, 12 January to 18 May 1944.

which left nobody in doubt as to the qualities of Juin's men, for whom the battle was an opportunity to redeem *honour besmirched by 1940. The British seized a wide bridgehead across the Garigliano and beat off counter-attacks before running out of steam. This might have persuaded Clark that his central thrust was too weak, especially as 36th Division was already bruised. Although some Americans managed to cross the river they could not stay there, and over half the attacking riflemen and company officers were killed or wounded.

It had been hoped that there would already have been good progress on the Cassino front when the *Anzio landing began on 22 January. To distract German attention from the beachhead, Clark sent the US 34th Division into the mountains above Cassino, and launched Juin against the Colle Belvedere, further north. Although some ground was gained, the first battle ended with Lt Gen von Senger und

Etterlin, the German corps commander responsible for the sector, in firm control.

The second battle was fought by Lt Gen Freyberg's II New Zealand Corps. The monastery was levelled by heavy bombers on 15 February, despite the misgivings of those who objected on cultural grounds and feared that the Germans would fortify the ruins. Results were disappointing, both for the New Zealand Division in Cassino itself and 4th Indian Division on the high ground above it: dreadful terrain prevented the attackers from committing more than a fraction of their total force.

The third battle began on 15 March after a massive bombing raid on Cassino. This failed to destroy the *morale of the parachutists defending the town, and the New Zealanders barely picked their way into the rubble. The Indians clawed their way up the crags leading to Monastery Hill, taking and holding Castle Hill. Freyberg's men were relieved after ten days of gruelling combat which left all the vital ground in German hands.

Gen *Alexander, Allied commander in Italy, now recognized that instead of isolated attacks at Cassino he must mount an army group operation against the Gustav Line, bringing divisions from the Eighth Army, on the other side of the Apennines, into the battle. DIADEM began on the night of 11/12 May with the crossing of the Gari south of Cassino. Where one tired division had failed in the first battle, two now attacked with another on hand to exploit success. Further south, the French Corps and II US Corps pushed out of the Garigliano bridgehead in such strength and determination that the defence could not hold. The attack on the high ground around the monastery, entrusted to Lt Gen Anders's II Polish Corps, driven, like Juin's men, by the powerful mainspring of national revenge, was making the slow progress dictated by this uncompromising terrain. But FM Kesselring, the German C-in-C, recognized that Allied penetration to its south made Cassino untenable and ordered a general withdrawal: on 17 May the Poles entered the ruins of the monastery.

Cassino cost the Allies some 45,000 killed and wounded. Although the Germans also lost heavily, they succeeded in disengaging without being cut off either by the Allied southern hook or the breakout from Anzio. It is hard to disagree with John Ellis that Allied conduct of the battles was 'marred by a lack of strategic vision and slipshod staff work'. Many observers were reminded of WW I, and some Germans thought conditions at Cassino even worse than at *Stalingrad. RH

Ellis, John, *Cassino: The Hollow Victory* (London, 1984).

Castelnau, Gen Noël Marie Joseph Edouard, Vicomte de Curières de

(1851–1944). Born at Aveyron of a military, royalist, and Catholic family, Castelnau fought in the *Franco-Prussian war of 1870–1. Removed from the *general staff in 1900 for anti-Dreyfusard views (see DREYFUS), Castelnau nonetheless recovered to become deputy to *Joffre in 1911, and played an important part in formulating Plan XVII. In 1914 he commanded Second Army, whose advance into Lorraine was decisively checked at Morhange-Sarrebourg. However, he successfully defended Nancy at the battle of Le Grand Couronné, and was appointed to command Army Group Centre in 1915. In September he directed the great French offensive in Champagne, making some progress but failing to achieve a breakthrough. Reappointed as deputy to Joffre, he played a key role in shaping the defence of *Verdun. Out of favour in 1917, in 1918 he again commanded an army group, directing operations in Lorraine. From 1918 to 1924 Castelnau served in the Chamber of Deputies.

Honourable, upright, and clear-sighted, Castelnau, a lay member of a religious order, was nicknamed 'le capucin botté' (the booted friar), and represented the militant Catholic element in the French army. His background and views told against him, for despite his considerable achievements and personal sacrifice (he lost three sons in the war) he was never named marshal of France. RH

Castillon, battle of

(1453). On this field on 17 July the English lost Gascony. An Anglo-Gascon attack on a French fortified artillery park upstream from Castillon was probably launched without knowledge of the strength of its defences. For a short while, despite the hail of shot and ball, the rampart was gained. But the assault was repulsed and the attackers overrun, their legendary general John Talbot, Earl of Shrewsbury, being killed in the rout. Thus, in an action not unlike the Charge of the Light Brigade, the *Hundred Years War came to an end. AJP

castle

One of the most familiar forms of *fortification, the castle still symbolizes the entire medieval world and seems to define its military outlook. In fact, this is deceptive. The word is derived from the Latin *castellum*, a term which could mean a fortified building but had the wider sense of a walled town. Historians still write of networks of castles when they should be describing fortress strategies that continued long after the Middle Ages. Social and political changes in 10th-century Europe, many the result of invading Muslims, Magyars, and *Vikings, did emphasize local power structures. As a result, whoever controlled quite small-scale fortifications became an effective ruler. This fragmentation of authority, and its military form, is often known by its Italian name of *encastellamento*. In France, where the château became synonymous with feudal power, the main tower (called the keep in English) was known as the donjon (derived from the Latin *dominium*). The castle, as it is generally understood, was a combination of a fort, a dwelling, and a centre of authority.

An early castle was often little more than a strong house. Doue-la-Fontaine, in Anjou, was turned *c*.950 from a Carolingian residential hall into a blockhouse with thickened walls and a first floor entrance. Other stone towers, like nearby Langeais built by that pioneer of feudal government Fulk Nerra ('the Black'), Count of Anjou, were constructed from new. Not that all castles were simply stone towers. Much has been made of the introduction of castles into England at the time of the Norman conquest (1066). The English do not seem have used such private fortifications to any degree, preferring the large communal enclosures known as *burhs* (a word meaning protection) which had served them so well against the Vikings in the 9th and 10th centuries. Indeed, a rebellion in 1051–2 aimed at the destruction of the few castles constructed by Edward 'the Confessor''s Norman and French favourites. At least one of these was placed within the *burh* at Dover. The castle at Caen, *William 'the Conqueror''s 'new town' in western

Reconstruction, illustrating some key terms

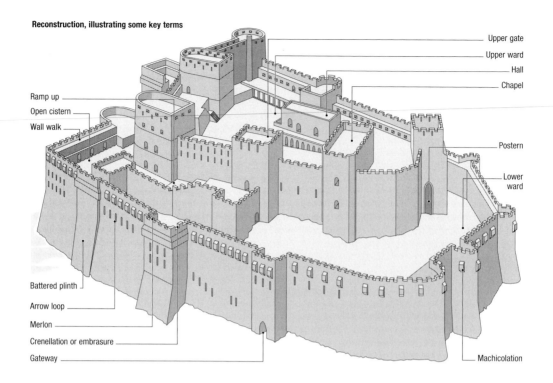

Upper gate
Upper ward
Hall
Chapel

Ramp up
Open cistern
Wall walk

Postern

Lower ward

Battered plinth
Arrow loop
Merlon
Crenellation or embrasure
Gateway

Machicolation

Plan

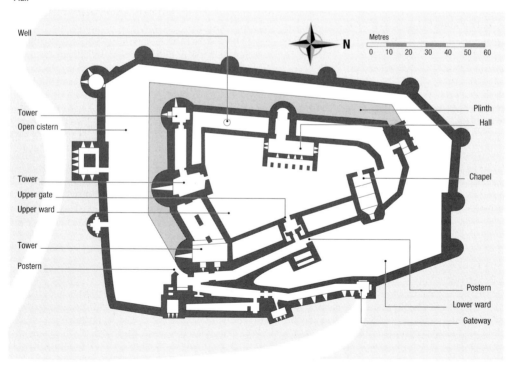

Metres
0 10 20 30 40 50 60

N

Well

Tower
Open cistern

Plinth
Hall

Tower
Upper gate
Upper ward

Chapel

Tower
Postern

Postern
Lower ward
Gateway

Krak des Chevaliers, Syria, the most powerful and imposing of the Crusader castles. The site was given to the Knights Hospitallers in 1242, who held it until it was taken by Sultan Bybars in 1271. The Hospitallers built most of it, although the Muslims added the large square tower in the middle of the south wall in 1285. Krak shows many of the typical features of a medieval castle. In less arid, flatter terrain, a water-filled moat was often added. Source: *A History of Fortification*, Sidney Toy.

Normandy, seems to have grown up in the same way. Initially this was no more than a fortified gateway to a promontory fortress on high ground, with a rock-cut ditch to isolate it further. The two castles which William had built at York after the Conquest were probably just ditch and bank enclosures inside the city's walls. His great 'White Tower' in London (built c.1072–92) was similarly placed within the eastern corner of the old Roman walls, with the river for both protection and access on the southern side.

Many Conquest castles, especially on the borders with the aggressive Welsh, were of the 'motte-and-bailey' type; that is to say, an artificially raised or heightened mound of earth surrounded by a ditch, bank, and palisade. Such constructions may have been very short-lived, perhaps never being repaired or developed, although some grew into great castles of the classical form. At Montgomery, in Shropshire, excavations have revealed a simple and small fort of this type at Hen Domen, down by the river, while a mile away there still stands the great promontory castle of Henry III, stone-built and originally plastered and whitewashed as a beacon of English royal authority.

Castles served this role, not just in England and France, of course, but all over Christendom and wherever the Latins (or Franks) extended their rule. They were especially important in the borders regions. In the Iberian peninsula, where Christian kings were 'reconquering' land from the Muslims, castles and fortified towns were crucial to strategies of conquest and consolidation. Similarly, in eastern Europe and the Baltic, crusaders constructed a range of fortresses from wooden blockhouses to the great monastery castles of the military orders. The castles of the Holy Land and the other crusader states in the Levant are best known, of course. Krak des Chevaliers and Margat (both in Syria) are perhaps the greatest achievements of castle building. The former was extensively restored under the French Mandate in the 1930s. Others have been severely damaged, as a result of the region's many wars. In Greece, briefly under the Latin empire of Constantinople (1204–61) and longer in the Peloponnese the Franks built great castles such as at Mistra (looking down on the site of ancient Sparta). On Cyprus there are wonderful examples at Buffavento and St Hilarion. The list could be added to endlessly.

There is a tendency to view castles as a specifically 'western' phenomenon, but this does not do justice to the skill in fortification of Byzantine and Arab military engineers. There was nothing in the west to match the 4th-century walls of Constantinople until possibly the 13th century; but the point does remain that crusaders often improved upon already fortified sites. Saone (Sahyun), inland from Lattakia in northern Syria, is a classic example. A huge triangular promontory site created by two deep gorges, the Latins deepened a rock-cut ditch across its base to 100 feet (30 m) and built a stone keep to guard the bridge which crossed the gap supported by needle of rock at halfway. Similar work took place at the city of Edessa (modern Urfa) a little fur-

ther north. The Muslim world was capable of huge constructions, such as the citadels of Aleppo (still largely intact) and Cairo. After the *Mameluke conquest of the Holy Land in the 13th century the Muslim rulers continued to repair and extend the great crusader castles, too. Castles also played an important role in Japan.

Although the variety of castle types has been stressed, Dover castle (Kent) is a model of castle development. Originally an Iron Age hill fort, then a Roman fort, then an English *burh*, in the 12th century Henry II had a tall, square, stone tower built in the middle of the defences. To this were added encircling 'curtain' walls. A severe French siege in 1216–17, which the castle withstood, led to further strengthening of the walls and the construction of a 'barbican' gatehouse. Called the 'key to the kingdom' by Matthew Paris, a 13th-century chronicler, Dover continued to be added to and altered, remaining of military significance for centuries. It still had a functional role in WW II, when the cliffs on which it stood were honeycombed with tunnels. Perhaps the high point of castle design was in the late 13th century, when Edward I built castles to assure his conquest of *Wales. Many of these were of a concentric design, with several lines of walls to delay an attacker. Beaumaris, on the Menai Straits, is the classic example of this form. In contrast, Conwy and Caernarfon formed part of a fortress that included town walls. Caernarfon was constructed to look like the walls of Constantinople, which Edward I had seen on crusade.

The invention of gunpowder was crucial in changing the castle into the forts and fortresses of the 16th century. Castles were built tall, often in high positions to reduce the possibility of storm. The bases of the walls were thickened with an angled 'batter' to defend against siege artillery (hurling stones), rams, and bores rolled against the walls and also undermining. But, c.1400, gunpowder artillery was becoming larger and much more powerful. Already, in Italy, new 'bastion' fortresses were under construction, with the vulnerable corners of castles protected by the first 'arrowhead' projections. A lower profile began be essential, eventually leading to the classic *trace Italienne* of the 16th century, with its elaborate geometric shapes. Rulers who did not respond quickly enough to these developments lost their territory. For example, English Normandy fell to the siege-train of Charles VII in just a few months in 1449–50.

The castle, which had always had a significant residential function, declined in military value to become a palace, château, or manor house, while forts and bastioned town walls took its place in warfare. In places where war was common in the 16th century, such as northern Italy and the Low Countries, rapid developments in fortifications soon rendered the castle redundant. In England and the British Isles generally, however, the defensive value of well-fortified castles was still apparent in the mid-17th-century civil wars. When held by royalists against the forces of parliament some proved almost invulnerable. The most famous example was Basing House, in north Hampshire, and just about the most easterly royalist possession in the south. Basing, a strong 12th-century site with modern additions, required the personal attention of *Cromwell in the last months of the first English civil war (see BRITISH CIVIL WARS) before it could be persuaded to *capitulate. Parliament's response was predictable. In order to prevent a resurgence of opposition most substantial castles were 'slighted'. That is to say, they were systematically demolished by gunpowder and pickaxe, so depriving a modern audience of the sight of some of the most impressive fortifications of the medieval world.   MB

Bradbury, J., *The Medieval Siege* (Woodbridge, 1992).
Brown, R. A., *Castles: A History and Guide* (Poole, 1980).
Thompson, M. W., *The Rise of the Castle* (Cambridge, 1984).
—— *The Decline of the Castle* (Cambridge, 1987).

Castro, Fidel (b. 1927), insurgent leader of the *Cuban Revolution and unquestioned *líder máximo* since 1959.

casualties It is sometimes said that the first casualty of war is the truth, but it is more often the language with which that truth might be expressed. The use of euphemisms to describe a ghastly reality is not new: the word casualty comes from the Latin *casualitas*, an 'unfortunate accident', and has been used to describe military losses since the 15th century. The casualties of a medieval battle were stabbed, hacked, and bludgeoned in a close-range mêlée aptly described as bloody murder. And while watching the pictures from cameras in the noses of *precision-guided munitions as they hit buildings, it is often easy to forget that there are human beings in these buildings, being torn apart or burned to death. The use of terms like 'surgical strike' blurs the fact that now, as always, the aim of combat is the destruction of the enemy's will or ability to resist, and the infliction of casualties has generally formed part of this process. There is no significant difference whether the victim is disembowelled by the latest technology released from a nuclear submarine hundreds of miles away, or by a knife in close combat. There is nothing casual about it.

The term casualty refers to any unplanned subtraction from a force's fighting strength. Its major causes are disease, *desertion, accident, and combat itself, which generates killed, wounded, captured, and missing. Of these, until recently disease was so greatly the grimmest reaper that many campaigns were decided by it outright. European microorganisms conquered the Americas, the *conquistadores, and other invaders simply mopping up the shattered Amerindian remnants. During the *Walcheren expedition of 1809, the British lost over 23,000 men to disease while suffering only a little over 200 casualties from combat. More people died in the 1918–19 influenza epidemic than in the four years of WW I, and the Allied campaign in *Italy dur-

ing WW II was the first in which combat casualties outnumbered those caused by disease, thanks to penicillin and other revolutionary advances in *medicine. Large, static encampments with poor or non-existent sanitary provisions have been a perfect culture for epidemics, from the sieges of ancient times to modern *concentration camps. During the *American civil war, the proportion of fatalities caused by disease to those in combat was almost exactly two to one, falling particularly heavily on the country boys who lacked the acquired immunities of their comrades from the cities. The *Roman army, one of the finest fighting forces in history, also paid the greatest attention to hygiene. Commanders who have not paid due attention to the health of their soldiers, like Frederick *'Barbarossa' during the Legnano campaign of 1176, have found their armies ravaged by disease before any battle was fought. If to this we add those who died of septicaemia from even light wounds, the casualty list for mankind's longest running war is billions to zero in favour of the microbes.

Next to disease, desertion has been the most common cause of casualties. Despite the draconian measures employed to discourage desertion, such is the misery of warfare that only armies enjoying the highest *discipline and *morale have ever been relatively free of it. Even invading armies campaigning in places where the likely fate of a deserter was a hideous death at the hands of vindictive inhabitants have not been spared it, as the French army found in Spain during the *Peninsular war. Sometimes desertion is internal: besieged soldiers cease to defend themselves and await the end listlessly, having become, in effect, psychiatric *casualties. Desertion is often a passive protest against a cumulatively intolerable state of affairs and can be precipitated by relatively minor grievances, the proverbial straw that breaks the camel's back. High on the list of complaints produced by French mutineers in the spring of 1917 were demands for better food and more regular leave. Some deserters have been so eager to prove that their action was not motivated by *cowardice that they have fought for the other side. Another form of protest and a persistent if unquantifiable source of casualties has been the self-inflicted wound or the murder of one's fellows, today known as *fragging.

Death and injury in combat has been the least significant source of casualties numerically, but it is the category that most captures our attention. Today we confront the paradox that weapons of mass destruction possess the potential to kill more people than even the Black Death, but a wounded soldier is far more likely to survive his injury than at any other time in history. Killing and healing *science and technology have advanced in parallel. There have been some weapons intended to exploit this fact, such as the German S-mine designed to blow off a foot, because that not only disabled one soldier but tied up stretcher-bearers, medical staff, transport, and hospital resources. Yet although the variety of injuries and the range over which casualties may be inflicted have increased steadily since chemical replaced muscle power as the principal means of weapon delivery, there has never been a single day when more men were killed in battle than at *Cannae, and it was well into the 19th century before the range, rate of fire, and lethality of the longbow was improved upon. For unmitigated horror at the point of contact, it is unlikely that the grinding crunch of the *hoplite phalanxes could be exceeded. The military greatness of *Shaka lay in the fact that he transformed normal tribal warfare, where spears might be thrown and insults exchanged, but where most of the warriors on both sides went home at the end of the day, into battles of annihilation. Successful double envelopment, every commander's beau idéal, can have no other outcome.

*POWs are also casualties, and diminish an army's strength in two ways. The POWs themselves, of course, can no longer participate in the war. But more significantly the willingness to take prisoners and treat them humanely can diminish the enemy's will to resist. Taking prisoners can thus be a pragmatic, not a humanitarian consideration. In *fortification and siegecraft, the rules were that if the garrison *capitulated after a prudent time, it might march out with all the *honours of war. If, on the other hand, resistance continued to the point where the besieger was obliged to assault the place, then it was understood that the defenders could expect no mercy. It is partly because irregular forces in general do not have the facilities to hold prisoners that they, in turn, are liable to summary execution if captured. A guerrilla leader who brilliantly turned this equation on its head was Fidel *Castro, who would scrape together a sumptuous meal for any prisoners he took, make sure they saw only his best-equipped men, and then release them back to the conscript army of the dictator Batista. Since the latter tortured and killed the rebels who fell into his hands, the result was to harden the resolve of his enemies while the morale of his own army plummeted.

Soldiers missing in action (*MIA) feature on casualty returns too. Soldiers were first reported missing on a large scale during WW I. Sometimes they had been captured, and news of this eventually filtered through. Sometimes, alas, they had been blown to tatters, mutilated beyond recognition, or simply lost in the moonscape of shell holes. Even soldiers initially accorded a known and honoured grave might be exhumed or obliterated by shellfire. Of the one and three-quarter million Commonwealth servicemen who died in two world wars, three-quarters of a million are commemorated on *memorials to the missing like the soaring arch at Thiepval on the *Somme with over 70,000 British names or the panels behind the huge cemetery at Tyne Cot near Ypres with more than 34,000. The families of soldiers reported missing in action often hope against hope that their loved one has somehow survived, or, even if they accept the worst, are denied a focus for their mourning. This explains the importance of commemorating both dead and missing, ensuring that the latter have their names engraved in stone whose endurance compensates for the transience of flesh and blood.

The calculation of casualties presents military historians with real problems. There is a general tendency for armies to understate their own and overstate the enemy's, and in ancient and medieval times casualty estimates were often wildly inaccurate. More recently, the basis on which casualty returns were made complicates matters. The *German army of WW I did not include wounded who were not evacuated; the *British army included even those wounded who were returned to duty after immediate treatment. Comparing casualties for, say, the Somme or third *Ypres thus requires an addition to published German figures, and debating the size of this addition continues to generate as much heat as light. Although the desire to limit casualties has been a marked feature of wars fought by western democracies at the close of the 20th century, wounds and death remain the currency of war. RH

Adams, G. W., *Doctors in Blue: The Medical History of the Union Army in the Civil War* (New York, 1952).

Beebe, G. W., and DeBakey, M. E., *Battle Casualties: Incidence, Mortality, and Logistic Considerations* (Springfield, 1952).

Gabriel, Richard, and Metz, Karen, *A History of Military Medicine* (London, 1992).

McLaughlin, R., *The Royal Army Medical Corps* (London, 1972).

casualties, psychiatric These are soldiers who suffer mental trauma and breakdown as a result of the experience of combat and danger on the battlefield. Although the reality of psychiatric casualties has really only been acknowledged by armies during this century, the problem is not a new one. Men in battle have been exposed to very high levels of danger and privation throughout human history and the extreme conditions on the battlefield have always resulted in mental breakdown among soldiers.

Even recognition of the damage that battle can cause to the human mind is not new. Doctors first diagnosed Swiss mercenary soldiers as suffering from 'nostalgia' in 1698. The symptoms of this illness were excessive physical fatigue, inability to concentrate, and an unwillingness to eat or drink. These are all now regarded as signs of a psychiatric breakdown but in the 17th century it was believed that these soldiers were suffering from a longing to return home.

The bloody battles of the *American civil war produced 5,213 cases of nostalgia in the first year alone and special *hospitals were established to treat soldiers suffering from the problem. Russian army doctors were the first to properly diagnose psychiatric casualties as such during the *Russo-Japanese war.

WW I, characterized by the mass use of modern weaponry and vastly destructive artillery bombardments, saw the widespread recognition of the problem in most of the combatants' armies. The increasing range and destructive power of weaponry had given rise to the 'lonely battlefield' where men were exposed to much greater danger but due to the new dispersed tactical formations could no longer draw the same level of support from their comrades. Battles often became prolonged from days into weeks and even months. The area in which a soldier was in danger was also vastly increased and infantry soldiers under artillery bombardments were literally helpless, pounded with enormous destructive power and great noise but unable to defend themselves or deal with the threat.

During the first two years of the war, British soldiers suffering from psychiatric breakdown were executed for *cowardice rather than given medical help. However, the number of cases reached such alarming levels that a new term, *shell-shock, was coined. It was believed that soldiers with shell-shock had suffered microscopic lesions of the brain from the concussion and blast of a shell explosion and that this physical cause explained their inability to function as soldiers. The fact that many cases of shell-shock had not been in close proximity to shellfire when they broke down was a difficult problem. It was still not accepted that men could suffer emotional or mental damage from combat without any physical cause, and the military authorities of all armies treated the whole matter with suspicion, as they feared that acceptance of the problem would encourage malingering.

In 1922, the British *War Office Committee of Inquiry into shell-shock arrived at important conclusions. The committee recognized that there was such a thing as a mental wound, and admitted that it was almost impossible to identify a coward who was shirking his duty from a soldier suffering from shell-shock. This finding supported the abolition of the *death penalty for cowardice in 1930.

However, WW II found armies unprepared for the problems of psychiatric breakdown in combat. It was current among civilian Freudian psychiatrists that only people with a weak character (predisposition) would break down under stress. The US army therefore instituted rigorous psychological tests for all recruits in an attempt to weed out those men with character defects who might be predisposed to breakdown. The USA screened 18 million men for military service and rejected 970,000 for psychiatric and emotional reasons but the screening did not reduce the rate of psychiatric casualties as expected. Psychiatric casualties were still the greatest single category of military disability granted by the US government in WW II. Among American GIs, 1,393,000 suffered psychiatric symptoms, and of these 504,000 had to be discharged from the army. Of the soldiers who were actually involved in combat at least 37.5 per cent suffered severe psychiatric problems.

The trend of high rates of psychiatric casualties has continued in more recent wars. In the *Korean war, a GI was twice as likely to become a psychiatric casualty as he was to be killed and during the 1973 *Arab–Israeli war, the Israelis found that 30 per cent of their casualties were due to psychiatric breakdown.

Armies suffer these high rates of psychiatric casualties due to the strain placed on soldiers in battle. Fear is the body's natural reaction to danger and virtually all soldiers can exhibit the symptoms of badly frightened human beings from uncontrollable shaking to involuntary urination or defecation. When a human being senses a threat, the autonomic nervous system begins a series of chemical changes to help the body deal with that danger. Blood pressure rises, heartbeat increases, awareness becomes heightened, and reserves of muscular strength are released. These changes, often accompanied with the well-known symptoms of fear such as sweating, dryness in the mouth, vomiting, or urination, prepare the body to fight against the threat, to run away from the danger, or to freeze as a form of *camouflage. For early man, as with all animals, this 'fight or flight' mechanism was vitally important as whenever there was danger present his nervous system prepared him to deal with the threat.

However, this natural and involuntary reaction to fight or flee in the face of danger was not designed to deal with the pressures of combat. Men in battle have always encountered extreme levels of danger and often suffered from hunger, thirst, and sleep deprivation which all adds to the stress placed on the mind and body of the soldier. Combat is also an extremely noisy, chaotic, confusing, and disorienting place which can overload the soldier's senses. This situation alone leads to intense exhaustion which can seriously affect a soldier's effectiveness, morale, and stamina.

The pressures of combat also put a great deal of strain on the human mind. Under stress, the ability to reason and make decisions declines rapidly, and the soldier is torn between his desire to remain steadfast and to fight bravely and his natural involuntary reaction to fight or to flee. Without a physical release for the stress and anxiety, such as fighting an opponent directly, eventually the mind provides 'relief' by converting the anxiety into a physical symptom. By shutting down the body's functions in one way or another, the soldier can no longer take part in the combat and is removed from the situation mentally if not physically. This mental breakdown is involuntary and caused by factors beyond the soldier's control—the natural fight-or-flight mechanism and the intensity of the danger that the soldier has experienced. American studies found that after 30 days of combat in Normandy, 98 per cent of soldiers had manifested severe psychiatric reactions. It is a plain fact that most normal men will suffer some kind of mental damage on exposure to combat.

Nostalgia, shell-shock, neuralgia, battle exhaustion, combat fatigue, battle shock, and post-traumatic stress disorder (PTSD) are all terms which have been used this century to describe the range of mental damage and trauma which soldiers can suffer through exposure to battle. It must be stressed that the human mind is an extremely complex organ and individuals can suffer similar traumatic experiences but exhibit very different symptoms. It is impossible to predict which soldiers will collapse and which will fight on bravely. Some men can cope with the stress of battle for an extended period and then suffer a total breakdown, while other men can go into shock very quickly after a particularly traumatic event. In a similar vein, some soldiers can recover from stress or shock quite quickly while others find it difficult or impossible to recover. The reaction to danger and trauma is very individual, and recovery is also individual and very difficult to predict.

After periods of great stress and activity, soldiers become physically and mentally exhausted, and eventually, if left in combat, a soldier suffering from extreme fatigue will develop deeper mental problems. Studies carried out during the Normandy campaign gave a clear idea of the effect of exhaustion and battle stress on soldiers which developed over a period of 90 to 120 days. After three weeks in combat, soldiers developed permanent fatigue which could not be cured with simple rest. Such soldiers could no longer distinguish sounds and overreacted to noises and unexpected situations. After five weeks in combat these soldiers sunk into a state of extreme exhaustion and lassitude. It was found that if the soldier was not relieved at this stage he would reach a vegetative state and be incapable of any further action. Lord Moran likened a man's courage and mental health to a bank account where every experience of combat draws on the reserve. Eventually, the bank account of courage will be exhausted and the soldier will succumb to the stress of battle.

Some soldiers suffer breakdown due to a single traumatic event which causes the soldier's mind to go into shock. Shock often manifests itself as conversion hysteria, where the mind causes the body to be incapacitated. Paralysis of the limbs, blindness, deafness, or a fugue state (coma) are all symptoms of acute battle shock.

The third main type of mental damage a soldier can suffer from battle was only properly understood after the *Vietnam war. Many Vietnam *veterans found that they suffered psychiatric problems only once they had returned home. It is believed that 500,000 to 1,500,000 Vietnam veterans suffered from PTSD. In this condition, the soldier experiences such a traumatic event that it has long-term consequences. The traumatic experience has had such an impact that the event is 'replayed' over and over again in the soldier's mind. Due to this constant reliving of traumatic events, PTSD sufferers often display severe mood swings, personality changes, and can react violently to otherwise normal situations.

Soldiers have always used various methods to cope with the stress of battle. *Alcohol, acting as it does as a relaxant, can reduce anxiety and fear for a limited period thus providing some 'Dutch courage'. Many soldiers have used other drugs. The Ghazis of Mughal India used marijuana to induce fearlessness while some Vikings used fermented deer urine to induce a berserker fury in battle. Clearly, however, use of drugs, although commonplace in Vietnam, is not helpful for the modern soldier.

However, realistic training which educates the soldier for his role in combat, and gives him confidence in his abilities and that of his comrades and leaders can help to reduce anxiety in battle significantly. During this century the importance of the small group was finally scientifically recognized, although the *Roman army had recognized the importance of soldierly comradeship with their use of five-man tents. It has been found that soldiers can derive great comfort and strength from the immediate group of three to five men around them. Just as important is good leadership from officers who can reassure their men, look after their welfare, and inspire troops in combat. However, one of the best and simplest ways of tackling the cumulative effects of battle is to ensure that soldiers are given regular rest from action, shelter from the elements, and are always kept well supplied with food and water. These elements, so often lacking from a front-line soldier's existence, can keep men going in difficult circumstances.

Measures to reduce the strain on soldiers in battle cannot eliminate the problem; there will still be psychological casualties. Lt Col Salmond of the US army first discovered the principles of treatment in 1917 which are still generally accepted today. Most armies still emphasize his three key elements to successful treatment of psychiatric casualties: proximity, immediacy, and expectancy.

Rates of recovery from mental breakdown have been found to be much higher when soldiers have been treated in close proximity to the battle zone which maintains the soldier's bonds of duty and military discipline. Soldiers also have to be treated quickly before their symptoms can deepen and become more permanent. Maintaining the expectancy that the soldier will return to his unit ensures that the bonds of comradeship are maintained and does not stigmatize the soldier as a 'patient', but rather ensures that he still sees himself as a soldier. These basic elements of treatment have been found to be effective and, with proper counselling and care, psychiatric casualties can be restored to normal health. Nevertheless, the problem of psychiatric casualties remains a major problem for modern armies and is a subject that demands serious and constant attention to ensure that armies can still function on the extremely dangerous and complex modern battlefield.   NB

Gabriel, Richard, *The Painful Field* (New York, 1988).
Holmes, Richard, *Firing Line* (London, 1985).
Keegan, John, *The Face of Battle* (London, 1976).

Cavalry (see page 186)

Cawnpore, siege of (now Kanpur, in Uttar Pradesh) (1857), an episode in the *Indian Mutiny when the sepoy (cont. on page 189)

cavalry

THE mounted arm played an important and sometimes predominant role in war from around the 8th century BC until the 20th century. Horses were first used to pull *chariots, and it was not until horses large enough to carry a man had been bred, broken, and trained that the cavalryman proper made his appearance. This was probably in the armies of Assyria, which dominated the Middle East between the 12th and 8th centuries BC. The first Assyrian horsemen formed two-man teams, one man controlling both horses while the other used a bow.

There were two major and enduring strands in the development of cavalry. Steppe horsemen formed successive waves of invaders that boiled up out of central Asia to pour into Europe, the Middle East, India, and China to produce profound and sometimes lasting effects upon regional civilizations. They burst upon the settled world without apparent reason, though often they were themselves fleeing from even more ferocious foes. These nomads, coming from peripatetic, horse-using societies, were not only masters of their steeds but of fluid tactics. Matthew Bennett has described how 'the harsh environment taught them the importance of discipline, organisation and planning, while the need to manage their flocks and herds gave them a mastery of logistics'.

The stubby composite bow was usually their chosen weapon, and they took care to avoid close combat with heavier, better-armed opponents, on horse or foot, until their mobile firepower had done its damage. Over the centuries these tactics defeated less agile opponents. In 53 BC the triumvir Crassus broke formation and was routed at *Carrhae by Parthian horse *archers; a large *Byzantine army was beaten by the classic nomad tactics of the Seljuk *Turks at *Manzikert in 1071; and in 1241 one *Mongol army smashed Henry of Silesia's knights at Liegnitz while another beat the Hungarians on the river Sajo. Underestimation of an 'uncivilized' opponent often played its part in such disasters, and it is fair to place the defeat of *Custer at the *Little Bighorn in the same category.

In contrast, heavy cavalry, wearing helmet and body *armour, sought to press home their charge and defeat their opponents in hand-to-hand combat. They could generally make little impression upon the robust infantry of the classical period, though *Alexander 'the Great' used his élite Companion cavalry to good effect. The development of the *stirrup—in use by the 9th century, although probably invented long before—made it easier for men to use sword and lance from horseback. However, its importance should not be overemphasized, for very effective heavy cavalry—notably the cataphracts of the Byzantine empire—had coped well without it. However, the stirrup did make it easier for those not bred to the saddle—like the *Franks, who were to dominate Europe in the 8th century—to adapt to mounted combat.

The mounted warrior became the dominant military instrument in early medieval Europe. In 732 the Frankish *Martel defeated an invading Moorish army at Poitiers. Although the Franks had at first fought on foot, by the time of *Charlemagne the mounted men forming the ruler's military household provided his army with its principal shock weapon. The Carolingian empire disintegrated soon after his death, and in a divided Europe at the mercy of *Viking raids responsibility for defence fell increasingly on local leaders. They relied on mounted warriors, who maintained their expensive arms, armour, and steeds through the grant of land—the fief or *feudum*.

Historians rightly shy away from the term *feudal system, for the process was never truly systematic, had wide local variations, and was usually more complex than the simple provision of 'knight service' in return for land. Nevertheless, the close relationship between economic power, social status, and military utility lay at the heart of feudalism, and the effectiveness of the knight was its *raison* *d'être* (see KNIGHTHOOD AND CHIVALRY). At *Hastings in 1066 the Normans and their French allies overwhelmed Harold's Saxons, using a classic mixture of archery and the mounted charge. The *Bayeux Tapestry* shows some knights plying their lances overarm, but others were now charging with the lance couched beneath the arm so as to focus the whole weight of horse and rider behind its thrust. Well might the Byzantine Princess Anna Comnena write that 'a mounted Frank could bore his way through the walls of Babylon'. The knight proved his superiority on scores of battlefields, and at Dorylaeum in 1097 his charge even smashed the formidable Seljuk Turk horse archers.

Yet the heavy horseman's ascendancy was not unchallenged. The light horsemen encountered by the crusaders knew that it was fatal to come within reach of charging knights, and better to hover at a distance until the knights and their steeds were tired. The longbowmen who formed the core of English armies in the *Hundred Years War gave repeated demonstrations of their prowess. At *Crécy they decisively repulsed a mounted charge by French knights. The French responded by dismounting most of their knights at *Agincourt to prevent their horses being maddened by arrows, but here too the result was the same. *Swiss pikemen had defeated a column of armoured knights at Morgarten as early as 1315 and they destroyed a powerful knightly army at Morat (1476). The *Hussite used a mobile fortification called the *wagenburg, a circle of wagons whose defenders used bows, handguns, and artillery, which also presented feudal horsemen with a serious challenge.

For some time heavy cavalry could still play a useful part in battle provided they did so as part of a combined arms team. At Marignano (1515) the disciplined charges of French cavalry broke Swiss pikemen whose ranks had first been thinned by artillery fire, leading a delighted *François I to declare that 'no one in future will be able to say that cavalry are no more use than hares in armour'. However, the proliferation of *gunpowder weapons made it increasingly difficult for cavalry to deliver shock action against the well-drilled infantry who had now come to dominate the battlefield. In the 16th century pistol-armed horsemen used a manoeuvre called the *caracole, riding up to their opponents, firing, and wheeling off to reload, but this tactic rarely succeeded against the pikemen and *musketeers now constituting the infantry.

By the *Thirty Years War cavalry was in decline, but the Swedish King *Gustavus Adolphus helped revitalize the arm by teaching his horsemen to charge home with the sword, firing pistols only in the mêlée, and using the fire of artillery and musketeers to pave the way for cavalry charges. In England *Cromwell used similar tactics, and at *Naseby his cavalry, having first beaten the royalist horse—a task made easier by the fact that the victorious horsemen on the royalist right had galloped off the field—turned in to help the infantry beat the resolute foot soldiers in the royalist centre.

The same precepts prevailed in the 18th century, when successful cavalry were trained to use shock action. *Marlborough was reported to allow his horsemen only three charges of powder and ball per campaign, and those were only for guarding the horses when they were at grass. *Frederick 'the Great' warned his cavalry commanders that they would be *cashiered if they awaited an attack. One of his generals noted: 'I have never seen a squadron depend on its fire that has not been overthrown by that which came upon it at speed without firing.' Further east firearms were more widely used. Austrian horsemen fighting the Turks preferred to disorganize their opponents by firepower rather than to take them on hand-to-hand.

In the 17th and 18th centuries cavalry became more diverse. *Dragoons, initially little more than mounted men equipped with muskets and riding cheaper, lighter horses than cavalry proper, gradually became more prestigious. Frederick 'the Great' used them both as *mounted infantry and as cavalry, and at Hohenfriedberg (1745) the Prussian Bayreuth Dragoons broke twenty Austrian battalions, capturing 66 *colours and 2,500 prisoners. Repeated contact with oriental light horsemen had encouraged the Russians, Poles, and Hungarians to maintain their own light cavalry, and in the 17th century *hussars, modelled on Magyar light horsemen, began to appear in western armies which sought cavalrymen adept at scouting and screening. They initially had a bad reputation: one French officer called them 'nothing but bandits on horseback'. The British preferred to create light cavalry by forming regiments of light dragoons, but in the 19th century these were converted to hussars or *lancers—the latter being another type of eastern European horseman widely imitated elsewhere.

In the *Napoleonic wars cavalry formed three types. Heavy cavalry, like the French *cuirassiers, were trained to deliver shock action on the battlefield; dragoons could generally fight on foot or horseback; and hussars and *chasseurs à cheval* were best at scouting and *pursuit, though they did not flinch from charging when the opportunity presented itself. *Napoleon argued that 'without cavalry, battles are without result'. At his best he orchestrated his battles so as to bring the three main combat arms together, launching heavy cavalry against an enemy already shaken by fire, and unleashing light cavalry to convert a retreat into a rout. Without such management even the best cavalry would fail, and at *Waterloo French charges made little impression on squares of Allied infantry.

The rapid improvement of firearms in the 19th century circumscribed the role of cavalry. Careful preparation and judicious handling could still make for successful charges, like von Bredow's death-ride at *Rezonville/Gravelotte, but the opportunities for shock action steadily diminished. In the *American civil war Union and Confederate cavalry alike placed increasing reliance on pistol and carbine rather than the sword. In the Second *Boer War British cavalry behaved more like mounted infantry than traditional cavalry, but there were enough examples of mounted dash (like the 'charge' by Sir John *French at Klip Drift) to persuade many observers that it was worth retaining sword and lance.

At the outbreak of WW I the British cavalry was trained to fight on foot or on horseback, while most other European cavalry placed most emphasis on shock action. The cavalry's much-advertised failure to produce a breakthrough on the western front has led to its wider role being neglected. Even on the western front there were moments when shock action worked, and as late as 1918 cavalry's inherent flexibility made it a useful reserve of mobile firepower. In other theatres of war, like the *eastern front, Mesopotamia, and especially Palestine, cavalry was literally indispensable, and at *Beersheba a charge by the Australian and New Zealand Light Horse was instrumental in securing Allenby's victory.

Cavalry survived WW I, though on a much-reduced scale, and during WW II sometimes proved useful, notably on the *eastern front, where there were occasional examples of successful shock action. In the 1960s mounted Khamba tribesmen of Tibet fought the occupying Chinese, and subsequently security forces in both *Rhodesia and South Africa used mounted infantry.

In many armies cavalry was the most prestigious arm, often recruiting its officers from exclusive backgrounds and wearing the most flamboyant uniforms. John Ellis is not alone in identifying 'a fatal contradiction within European societies' as military technology developed faster than officer corps, and 'traditional links between the military and the aristocracy' helped obstruct reform and promoted the 'stultifying tradition' that horsemen were masters of the battlefield. Yet the cavalry was not always hidebound and conservative, and among its leaders are some of the most sparkling names in military history. Napoleon's Comte de Lasalle, the *beau ideal* of the hussar general, proclaimed: 'A hussar who is not dead at thirty is a blackguard', and was duly killed leading a charge at *Wagram in 1809. When the cavalry spirit flourished, it helped produce tough, resourceful soldiers whose attitude was summed up by a British cavalry officer who declared of 1914 that 'Our motto was, "We'll do it. What is it?"'

RH

Anglesey, Marquess of, *A History of the British Cavalry* (8 vols., London, 1973–97).

Bennett, Matthew, 'Storm from the East', in Richard Holmes, *World Atlas of Warfare* (London, 1984).

Denison, G. T., *History of Cavalry* (London, 1913).

Ellis, John, *Cavalry* (Newton Abbot, 1978).

troops at Cawnpore mutinied and were persuaded by a discontented Indian prince, Nana Sahib, to besiege the small number of European troops (*c*.200) and officers, together with civilians and women and children, under the command of Sir Hugh Wheeler. After three weeks' bombardment the garrison surrendered on 27 June 1857. The men were massacred as they boarded boats on the Ganges and the women and children were murdered on 15 July in a house known as the Bibigarh and their bodies thrown into a well. About 180 were murdered, over 100 of them children. The discovery of the bodies on 17 July by troops under Maj Gen Henry *Havelock led to an outburst of feeling and cries for revenge in India and Britain. Brig James Neill ordered mutineers to lick up the blood before executing them. A *memorial, which was subsequently built over the well, became the most visited shrine of British India.   MEY

CEF. See CANADIAN EXPEDITIONARY FORCE.

---

cemeteries, military The dead are an inevitable product of war. The concept of the military cemetery dates from the 19th century, although for centuries soldiers had tried to give comrades honoured burial. The Athenians killed at *Marathon lie beneath their burial mound, and fourteen men from the city state of Plataea rest under a smaller mound nearby. But for most of history most of those killed in battle were stripped of *armour and burnt, tumbled into mass graves, or simply left where they fell, prey to weather and wild animals. Noblemen or senior officers might be repatriated for burial at home. The site of one of the grave-pits at *Agincourt is marked by a crucifix. Some French noblemen were buried in the abbey church at nearby Auchy-les-Hesdin, while the Duke of York's body was boiled to remove the flesh before the bones were sent to England.

Such treatment was increasingly regarded as unacceptable in an age when soldiers were citizens who had been conscripted or had volunteered to serve, and whose sacrifice deserved proper recognition. The *American civil war saw the institution of formal military cemeteries, authorized by Act of Congress passed on 17 July 1862. Some of the dead of the *Franco-Prussian war lie in cemeteries, and others in mass graves with the soldiers they contain commemorated on nearby regimental memorials. Sometimes the bones of the fallen were housed in ossuaries, such as the one on the battlefield of *Sedan.

At the beginning of WW I, although armies recognized the importance of the prompt and reverend disposal of the dead, the sheer mechanics of slaughter often overwhelmed them. The nature of the fighting and the destructive character of its weapons produced a large number of soldiers whose bodies were either lost altogether or recovered in unidentifiable form. The Germans repatriated some of their dead and buried others beneath dignified headstones which varied from regiment to regiment and were larger for officers than soldiers. However, they were reduced to using multiple or mass graves, and after the war embarked upon a policy of concentration, moving the dead from small cemeteries to be concentrated in fewer, larger ones. The French buried individually where they could, but they too used mass graves and ossuaries, and favoured the concentration of the dead into large *nécropoles nationaux*. The ossuary on Douaumont ridge at *Verdun contains the bones of some 130,000 men, and another 15,000 lie in the cemetery in front of it. The next of kin of American dead were given the option of selecting repatriation or burial in one of the eight overseas cemeteries: the same policy was continued for WW II, and the number of cemeteries grew to fourteen.

The British initially kept no proper record of burials, but, largely thanks to the efforts of Fabian Ware, who went to France as commander of a *Red Cross mobile unit, they developed an organization for registration and maintenance of graves. Ware's unit was retitled the Graves Registration Commission in March 1915, and became the Imperial (later Commonwealth) War Graves Commission (CWGC), today responsible for maintaining cemeteries and memorials for one and three-quarter million war dead in 140 countries and territories. Its sister organizations include the American Battle Monuments Commission and the German Volksbund Deutsche Kriegsgräberfürsorge.

The CWGC was less prone than its sister commissions to centralize burials, and although there are concentration cemeteries like Tyne Cot outside Ypres—with 12,000 graves the largest CWGC cemetery anywhere—there are other cemeteries with just a handful of graves. The smallest is probably on Ocrocoke Island, off the coast of North Carolina, which contains the graves of four sailors lost when the armed trawler HMS *Bedfordshire* was torpedoed in 1942. Repatriation was first authorized after the *Falklands war of 1982.

Allies and enemies rest alongside Commonwealth servicemen in CWGC cemeteries. Sometimes national passions militated against honouring an enemy's grave, because doing so recognized his warrior status. On the *eastern front in WW II enemy dead were disposed of without ceremony and enemy cemeteries desecrated. Such were the losses suffered by the Soviets that, even when they retained control of the battlefield, their dead were often interred in huge pits, like those on the field of *Kursk.

Military cemeteries are powerful statements of national culture. CWGC cemeteries reflect the unity of the fallen and the Christian concepts of *sacrifice and hope of resurrection, and, with their well-tended flowers and shrubs, resemble English gardens. German cemeteries are starker, and mass graves are frequent. Often their stern architecture makes them *Totenburgen* (fortresses of the dead). American cemeteries, influenced by the Park Cemetery movement in the USA, use nature to dull death's sting, and marble crosses—Stars of David for Jewish servicemen—line their manicured greensward.   RH

Edwin Gibson, T. A., and Kingsley Ward, G., *Courage Remembered* (London, 1989).

Mosse, George L., *Fallen Soldiers* (Oxford, 1990).

censorship is strictly the review by an authority of any material before publication or dissemination, with the legal right to prevent, alter, or delay its appearance. The term is often loosely used to reflect voluntary arrangements between armed forces and the media, or in criticism of any system other than complete press freedom. Historically, censorship has been habitually practised by most governments, or other political and religious authorities. Censorship in the military sense has only become an issue in modern times, with the growth of liberal or democratic governments, and new methods of press communication. Its problems arise from a collision between traditional press freedoms and the needs of military security in wartime. The USA has occupied a special place in this story, through being the world's first literate democracy, and also through the constitutional position of the press. Much censorship has been by co-operation, and it has not been unusual for the media to ask for guidance or even direct censorship from the armed forces, rather than reveal wartime secrets.

The profession of *war correspondent developed in the mid-19th century with the growth of the *telegraph and widespread newspaper readership. The first wars on which reporting probably had a direct impact were the *Crimean and the *American civil wars. In the next fifty years vague censorship regulations were established in most western countries, but only supplementing more important informal arrangements. The Second *Boer War and the *Russo-Japanese war convinced the British in particular that a more formal system was needed.

At the start of WW I all belligerents had extensive censorship legislation and practices, although military attempts to exclude the press altogether from reporting the fighting fronts proved unsuccessful. This war also saw the extension of censorship to servicemen's letters home. Comments in letters analysed by censors became a tool for commanders in judging their own side's *morale. WW II saw a revival of similar censorship practices, again with significant co-operation from the press. But this only applied chiefly to wars of national survival, and to the era of newspaper dominance. The last significant case of legally enforceable wartime censorship by the USA or Britain was the *Korean war.

The rise of radio and television to supplant newspapers in the second half of the 20th century raised a number of new issues. Controversial but highly critical claims that the unrestricted reporting of American involvement in the *Vietnam war had contributed to defeat produced concern on all sides. The result was the introduction by the USA and Britain of voluntary systems of press restraint, seen in the *Falklands and the *Gulf wars. Since then, developments in media communications technology have made censorship increasingly unfeasible.   SDB

Jowett, G. S., and O'Donnell, V., *Propaganda and Persuasion* (Newbury Park, 1992).

Taylor, Philip M., *Munitions of the Mind* (London, 1990).

Central Intelligence Agency. See CIA.

Cerignola, battle of (1503), during the early French *Italian wars, the first battle to be won by infantry firepower. Gonzalo de *Córdoba, commanding the battle-hardened Spanish army, engaged a Franco-Swiss army some 20 miles (32 km) from Barletta on the southern Adriatic. An assault led by *Swiss pikemen and French *gens d'armes* was shattered by the Spanish arquebusiers firing from the protection of pikemen behind a ditch and palisade. A deft counterattack completed the victory and the French were forced to abandon the kingdom of Naples.   TM

Cetchewayo, Chief (d. 1884). Cetchewayo was the eldest son of the longest reigning Zulu paramount chief Mpande. He came to power in the winter of 1872–3, and like *Shaka before him, was a military innovator introducing new tactics and procuring firearms. Cetchewayo did not want war against the British in 1879 (see ZULU WAR) but was left with little option, and despite a crushing success at Isandlwana, his army was destroyed at Ulundi. Captured, he was sent to England and fêted by society before being allowed to return to a divided Zululand in 1883. Grossly fat and fleeing for his life from civil war, he died at the British magistracy at Eshowe.   JDB

Chaco war (1933–5). The Chaco Boreal (or Gran Chaco) is a wilderness region of lowland swamp and jungle encompassing some 100,000 square miles (259,000 sq km) of territory between Paraguay and Bolivia. The war was caused by Bolivia's aggressive policy towards its neighbour, seeking to seize the Chaco both as a means to gaining access to the Atlantic and also because it was thought that the area contained petroleum deposits. Border clashes began in 1928 and in 1932, despite mediation efforts, full-scale war erupted, although formal declarations of war were not made until 1933. Bolivia had three times Paraguay's population and an ample supply of arms paid for by loans from American banks. However, its army was directed by a German adviser, Gen Hans von Kundt, who had trained it for the wrong kind of war. With a martial tradition second to none and led by the able Gen José Estigarribia, Paraguay attacked first and captured Bolivia's Fortín Boquerón in September 1932, followed by a wide offensive in late 1933, successfully aimed at controlling scarce sources of drinking water. The Bolivians, most of them unacclimatized highland Indians, died like flies. Even though they dismissed von Kundt and tried to fight a more flexible war, they were pushed back and by 1935, following bitter fighting around the outpost of Ballivián, the Paraguayans were in control of all the Chaco and were advancing into indisputably Bolivian territory. In June 1935, a *truce was arranged and in July 1938 a peace treaty was signed at Buenos Aires. Paraguay's sovereignty over the Chaco region was confirmed, but Bolivia gained rights to a territorial corridor to the river port of Puerto Casado on the Paraguay river. The war left 100,000 dead.   MH

Farcau, Bruce, *The Chaco War: Bolivia and Paraguay, 1932–1935* (London, 1996).

Chaeronea, battle of (338 and 86 BC). Chaeronea, a small Boeotian city located 31 miles (50 km) north of *Thebes, commanded the Cephissus valley, an important north–south route through central Greece, and provided a suitable defensive position to block forces advancing south from Thermopylae. In 338 the combined armies of Athens and Thebes, the two most powerful Greek cities, confronted Philip's Macedonians here, with the Athenians occupying the left wing, the Thebans the right. Details of the hard-fought battle are uncertain, but Philip probably enticed the Athenians out of line by a feigned retreat and then launched his cavalry, commanded by his son *Alexander ('the Great'), into the resulting gap in the Greek army. The Athenians suffered 1,000 casualties, the Thebans more; Athenian prisoners were released without payment, whereas Thebes had to *ransom its men. Victory ended Greek resistance to Philip, who now organized most Greek cities into the League of Corinth, a device to ensure Macedonian control and to promote a Greek crusade against Persia.

In 86 the army of Mithridates VI of Pontus was similarly unsuccessful in preventing *Sulla from moving south to reassert Roman control over Mithridates' Greek allies, in particular Athens.   LMW

Hammond, Nicholas, *Philip of Macedon* (London, 1994).

Châlons, battle of (451), also known as the battle of the Catalaunian Plains. Attila the Hun's first and only defeat which halted the previously unchecked advance of the *Huns into Europe. Attila, known as the 'Scourge of God', was the greatest leader of an extremely warlike people, and after he became king in 443 he led them on long, devastating raids into the declining Roman empire from their base north of the Danube. In 451 the horde rode through Gaul, sacking and burning more than a dozen cities before halting to besiege Orléans.

The Roman military commander Aetius convinced Visigoth King Theodoric of their common danger and their combined army advanced on Orléans. Attila was forced to raise the siege and retreated towards the Seine, looking for a suitable place to give battle, which he believed he had found near Châlons, where the open grasslands of the Champagne plains were suitable for his Hun cavalry. Nonetheless Attila was considerably outnumbered and a small Visigoth force under Theodoric's son Thorismond occupied the tactically important single piece of high ground overlooking the Hun left flank. Aetius and Theodoric had placed their most suspect force, a contingent of Alans, in the centre and they were promptly broken by a Hun cavalry charge. The Huns then wheeled left and fell on Theodoric's Visigoths. Theodoric was killed in the mêlée, but a ferocious counter-attack by Thorismond drove the Huns from the field. Although the battle of Châlons was not a catastrophe, it was of considerable significance as being the first time that Attila had been defeated and suffered serious casualties. Châlons dispelled the myth of invincibility that had worked so potently on both his enemies and allies.

MCM

Champagne campaign (1814). Early in 1814 the Allies invaded France, with Schwarzenberg's Austrians advancing into Alsace and *Blücher moving into Lorraine with Prussians and Russians. French detachments fell back before them. There seemed little national enthusiasm for last-ditch defence against the invader and *Napoleon decided to take the field himself, and arrived at Châlons on 26 January. He knew the area well, and hoped to use its good road system to enable him to mount a high-tempo campaign against his more numerous opponents.

Napoleon first retook Saint-Dizier and then moved against Blücher at Brienne. A crucial order was captured by a Cossack patrol, so the battle did not go as he hoped. Nevertheless, his infantry, so many of them young conscripts, fought surprisingly well, and after a hard-fought contest Blücher fell back with Napoleon behind him. The emperor halted at La Rothière for two days, redeploying his other forces in the area, and on 1 February he was attacked by Blücher and Schwarzenberg, who had met at Trannes, to the south-west. The battle was fought in a howling blizzard, and once again it was finely balanced. At its close weight of numbers told, and although both sides lost 6,000 men, 50 French guns were also lost and a retreat in appalling conditions led to a growing number of *desertions.

Schwarzenberg's caution, Blücher's confidence, and the inevitable problems of co-ordinating widely spread columns in a snowy countryside, gave Napoleon another chance. Learning that Blücher was heading for Paris via Châlons, Champaubert, and Montmirail, he detached troops to mask Schwarzenberg, and, moving much faster than Blücher, destroyed one of his corps at Champaubert and mangled another at Montmirail on 10 February. Blücher managed to break contact, blowing the bridge at Château-Thierry to delay *pursuit.

Champagne campaign

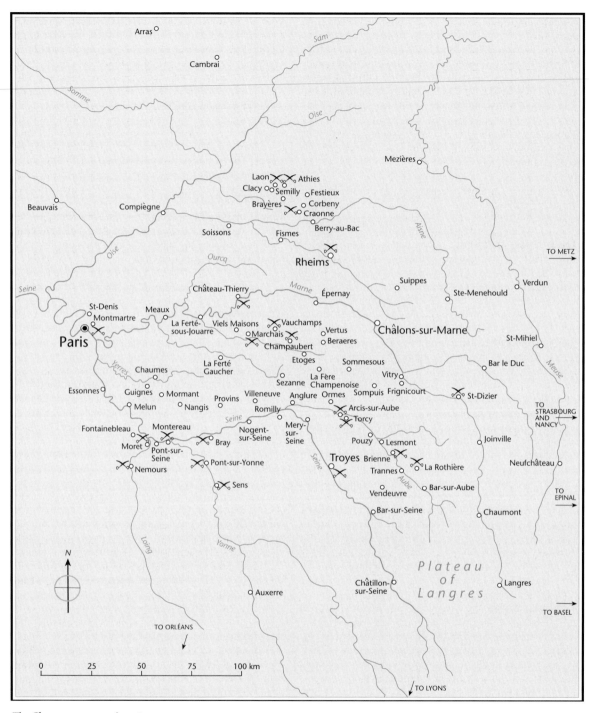

The **Champagne campaign**, 1814.

In the meantime Schwarzenberg recovered his confidence and drove French covering forces off the Seine, opening a threat from the south. Before moving down to deal with him Napoleon gave Blücher another hammering, this time at Vauchamps on the 14th. However, a Russian corps of 30,000 men joined Blücher at Châlons, making good the losses he had suffered so far. On 18 February Napoleon attacked one of Schwarzenberg's corps at Montereau, at the confluence of Seine and Yonne, beating it badly and sending Schwarzenberg reeling back to Bar-sur-Aube, where Blücher joined him on 25 February for a discussion on strategy.

Napoleon might have minted political advantage from his undoubted military success, and gained generous peace terms which would have left him secure on the throne, but he persisted in demanding 'natural frontiers'. The Bar-sur-Aube meeting provided the basis for the Treaty of Chaumont, at which the Allied leaders undertook to fight to a finish and not to conclude separate peace treaties. They offered Napoleon only the frontiers of 1791, which he scornfully rejected.

For the next phase of the campaign he sought to repeat earlier success by sending a detachment to fix Schwarzenberg while he struck at Blücher. The attempt nearly came off, but Blücher managed to cross the Aisne at Berry-au-Bac just before Napoleon caught him. There was a chaotic battle at Craonne on 7 March, and at its conclusion Blücher fell back on Laon. On the 9th Napoleon, misjudging Blücher's strength and dispositions, attacked the Allies on ground of their own choosing south of Laon. The corps commanded by *Marmont was crippled, and although Napoleon deftly warded off attacks on the 10th and slipped away to Soissons, he could ill afford the losses. However, he was dangerous even at this low ebb and, hearing that a division had been posted at Rheims to link Blücher and Schwarzenberg, duly demolished it on 13 March, yet again causing the Allies to pause for thought.

As the Allies hesitated, Napoleon lunged towards Troyes, hoping to lacerate Schwarzenberg's lines of communication. Schwarzenberg reacted in time, persuading the emperor to aim for the Marne instead, and to maul the garrison of Arcis-sur-Aube as he passed. Schwarzenberg had fortuitously concentrated nearby, and the French were roughly handled on 20 March. On the following morning Napoleon was shocked to discover that he was facing Schwarzenberg's entire army, but he was able to get his men across the Aube, blowing its bridges behind them. He then resumed his march to the Marne, hoping to do more damage to Allied communications and perhaps relieve the garrisons of Metz and Verdun.

Although Napoleon did not know it, the game was up. Most of his detachments were in full retreat, and the Allies, whose *Cossacks now dominated the countryside, regularly intercepted Napoleon's dispatches and knew his intentions. They decided to move Schwarzenberg north to join Blücher and for the combined force to press straight down the Marne to Paris. Winzingerode was sent off towards Saint-Dizier to lure Napoleon further away from the capital. He took the bait and although he beat Winzingerode on 26 March, on the following day he heard that the Allies had defeated Marmont and Mortier at La Fère Champenoise and would inevitably reach Paris before he could intervene. He assembled what troops he could at Fontainebleau, and it was there that *Ney, speaking for the other senior commanders, told him that the army would not march on Paris. Napoleon abdicated in favour of his son on 4 April but, informed that the Allies would accept only unconditional abdication, duly signed this abdication on the 6th.

The Champagne campaign saw Napoleon display skill which seemed to have deserted him over the past few years. His accomplishment is all the more remarkable in view of Allied strength, the poor weather, and the patchy quality of his own army. If he made a mistake in not treating for peace after Montereau, it was because he continued to trust in his remarkable luck, and he was never a man for half measures.

RH

Chandler, David, *The Campaigns of Napoleon* (London, 1967).

Chancellorsville, battle of (1863), *American civil war battle, and among the most daring displays of generalship in history. Between 1–4 May, faced with a well-conceived but poorly co-ordinated attack by greatly superior Union forces, *Lee divided his army twice and drove them back to their start line. Union commander *Hooker sought to fix him at Fredericksburg with Sedgwick's corps, while crossing upstream with his main force. The key element, a massed cavalry raid against Confederate communications with Richmond, was not pursued with vigour, depriving Hooker of vital *reconnaissance while utterly failing to distract Lee, who was well served by his own cavalry. Leaving a thin force under Early to contain Sedgwick, he marched against the main Union force.

The next day he kept Union attention to the front with 15,000 men, while *Jackson with 30,000 executed a flank march designed to look like a retreat, drawing Sickles's corps in pursuit. With Union forces extended towards his supposed line of retreat, Jackson enveloped their right wing and drove it for miles. Although he was mortally wounded by *friendly fire, the flank attack continued under *Stuart the next day, joining up with Lee. Concussed after Confederate artillery found the range of his command post, Hooker retreated into a tight perimeter covering his river crossing.

Sedgwick belatedly took the heights above Fredericksburg and marched towards the guns, causing Lee to turn from a third day of assault on Hooker to deal with the threat to his rear. Both Hooker and Sedgwick were well placed to defeat further attacks on them by an exhausted

Confederate army, but their will was broken and they withdrew across the river. Union casualties were 17,000, which they could afford, against the Confederates' 13,500, including the incomparable Jackson, which they could not.

HEB

Sears, Stephen, *Chancellorsville* (New York, 1996).

chaplains, military 'After being an agnostic from the age of ten, I'd started saying my prayers again—there's nothing like mortal danger for putting you in the mood; as Voltaire observed, it's no time to be making enemies.' As George MacDonald Fraser's WW II experience as a young soldier in the Fourteenth Army in *Burma indicates, the prospect of death does much to turn a man's thoughts to God. Therefore the military chaplain, responsible for the often daunting task of maintaining the spiritual welfare of the soldiery, the provision of comfort to the wounded and dying, and often the supply of welfare more generally, has long been an important part of organized armies.

As early as Anglo-Saxon times, the military chaplain was crucial to preparations of Christian armies for battle. In 871 King Ethelred 'the Unready', in the face of a *Viking army, refused to take the field before the priest had finished Mass, and would not forsake divine service for that of his men. Thankfully, his brother Alfred was able to close successfully with the Vikings without the presence of the king. Unsurprisingly the First *Crusade was accompanied by large numbers of priests. The crusaders' chaplains exerted a quite extraordinary influence on the declining *morale of the troops outside Jerusalem in 1099. A priest called Peter Desiderius had a vision that if they held a fast and then a procession around Jerusalem's walls, the city would fall. A fast was observed and on 8 July, to the astonishment of the besieged, the Crusade turned into a barefoot pilgrimage which wound its way round the walls ending at the Mount of Olives. There they listened to Robert the Hermit and other preachers. The army recovered its fighting spirit, captured the city on 15 July, and provided further proof of its devotion by indulging in a three-day orgy of bloodshed, massacring every Muslim it could find. Religious ritual remained central to preparation for battle in the high Middle Ages. *Henry V's force before the battle of *Agincourt contained a small army of priests. Henry, mirroring the behaviour of Ethelred, heard Mass three times. His soldiers also went through a religious ritual before entering the ranks that morning. They knelt, made the sign of the cross, and took earth into their mouths in symbolic gesture of death and burial.

In modern times the position of chaplain has become more formalized. From the 17th century onwards most European armies had regimental chaplains, gentlemen of officer status but wearing the cloth of their calling. Frederick 'the Great' was an atheist, but recognized the importance of chaplains, and each of his regiments had its *Feldprediger*.

He stipulated that these clergymen should be 'of good repute, learned, and if possible still wearing their own hair'. The English *New Model Army had its own senior chaplain, Edward Bowles, and several junior chaplains, who made up in zeal what they lacked in numbers. 'Mr Dell preached in the forenoon and Mr Sedgwick in the afternoon,' said a parliamentarian news-sheet of the siege of Oxford in 1645: 'many soldiers were at each sermon, divers of them climbing up trees to hear'. In the *British army, with the restoration of the monarchy in 1660 the position of chaplain became that of an officer on the establishment of regiment, his appointment in the gift of its colonel. The system was open to abuse as, although the chaplain might be paid, he did not necessarily do the work, which was more often carried out by a deputy. The failure of chaplains to attend to their duties, particularly when the regiment was abroad, was so prevalent that in 1796 a centrally controlled Army Chaplains' Department was established. Initially chaplains were solely from the Church of England, but Presbyterians were recognized in 1827, Roman Catholics in 1836, Wesleyans in 1881, and Jewish rabbis in 1892. The department received the title 'Royal' in 1919 to reflect its contribution during WW1.

Even in the British army the importance of chaplains varied with the morals and level of belief of the day. Wellington's army at *Waterloo had only one chaplain per division, and they were not particularly esteemed or influential. However, the chaplaincy became more important within army life during the reign of Queen Victoria. By the time of WW I, the British Expeditionary Force (BEF)—the army of a churchgoing nation—had a chaplain in each battalion and the place of religious ritual in preparations for battle was re-established as an important part of military life. Father Gleeson blessed his Munster Fusiliers from the back of a borrowed horse as they prepared to assault Aubers Ridge in 1915. On the eve of the battle of the Somme 2Lt John Engall wrote that 'I took communion yesterday with dozens of others who are going over . . . I placed my body in God's keeping and I am going into battle with His name on my lips.' He died the following day. In France, however, the status of priests within the army mirrored the government's relationship with the Roman Catholic Church. Napoleon's army had no chaplains—though his officers often kissed their sword-hilts, echoing an action begun when hilts were cruciform, before ordering 'Forward, in God's name'. There were military chaplains—*aumoniers militaires*—in the army of the Second Empire, when the Grande Messe Militaire became a lavish ritual, with troops parading under arms and the massed drums beating *au champs* at the elevation of the Host. The Third Republic, with its strong anticlerical streak, discouraged religious observance and even conscripted theological students to produce, in an untranslatable pun, 'le curé sac au dos'. By WW I it had not only military chaplains, but priests serving as officers and soldiers across a wide variety of combat functions, like the

Jesuit Sergeant Paul Dubrulle, whose harrowing account of *Verdun depicts a man striving desperately to cope with the dehumanizing effects of that terrible battle.

National and service approaches to the appointment and status of chaplains vary. Usually they are commissioned as officers and wear the appropriate uniform. Often, as in the US services, they are addressed as 'chaplain' ('Padre' in the British army) though they may hold a variety of commissioned ranks. Many commentators have pointed to what Waldo Smith called the 'perpetual anomaly' of a chaplain who is on the one hand an officer in a combatant force and on the other a minister of religion. Norman Dixon wrote: 'Their task is to assure their military flock that since God is on their side, the Sixth Commandment can be waived for the duration. How they reconcile this with the knowledge that enemy soldiers are in all probability receiving identical advice from their chaplains remains one of the mysteries of the ecclesiastical mind.' But the WW II soldier-cartoonist Bill Mauldin had 'a lot of respect for those chaplains who keep up the spirits of the combat guys. They often give the troops a pretty firm anchor to hang onto.' The Revd David Cooper, chaplain to 2 Para in the *Falklands, speaks movingly about men's striving after a God who might not turn a bullet, but would not turn away a soul in need.

MCM/RH

Asser, *Life of King Alfred the Great* (London, 1983).

Dixon, Norman F., *On the Psychology of Military Incompetence* (London, 1976).

Fraser, George MacDonald, *Quartered Safe Out Here* (London, 1992).

Holmes, Richard, *Firing Line* (London, 1985).

Keegan, John, *The Face of Battle* (London, 1976).

Makepeace-Warne, Antony, *Brassey's Companion to the British Army* (London, 1995).

Mauldin, Bill, *Up Front* (New York, 1945).

Mayer, Hans Eberhard, *The Crusades* (Oxford, 1988).

chariot When horses were tamed their first military use was in drawing light carts which served as shooting and fighting platforms. This happened in Bronze Age cultures the world over (except the Americas, which had no suitable animals). The earliest examples appear in Mesopotamia. The *Standard of Ur* (*c*.2500 BC) shows a clumsy vehicle with four wheels, drawn by four wild asses. *Sumerian records first describe horses some two centuries later. From around 1700 BC a much lighter chariot drawn by only two animals was developed, with which the Hyksos conquered Egypt. The technology also spread from the Caucasus into India and by 1300 BC into Shang dynasty China.

The following half-millennium was the high point of chariot warfare. Homer's Mycenaean heroes used them at *Troy. Records from Egypt and the Hittite and Hurrian states of Asia Minor show the huge resources put into the arm. Specially bred horses (all stallions no more than 14 hands high) were fed and housed in lavish stables and great forts. The sophisticated bent-wood construction technique and the complicated harness required the development of new technologies. It was also reckoned to take three years to train the teams of men and horses effectively. Unsurprisingly, the riders became a social élite. The driver carried a shield with which he covered the archer, who learnt to shoot from an unstable platform by practising on a rocking stool. Chariots were often employed in large numbers, for example at the battle of *Kadesh where Ramesses II allegedly fielded 2,500 against some 3,700 Hittite vehicles. The huge bas-relief monument at western Thebes which records his victory represents the pharaoh himself as a chariot rider driving his enemy before him. This propaganda version of events probably conceals the true tactical use of light chariots, which was to shower opposing forces with missiles, to create gaps in their battle line which could be exploited by supporting infantry.

The rise of the *Assyrians in the 9th century BC saw a return to heavier, four-horse and four-man chariots, but these were supplanted in the 7th century by the emergence of true *cavalry. Developments in China were somewhat slower, the peak of chariot use being 770–476 BC (Spring and Autumn period), and they were still employed to about 200 BC. In the Near East, chariotry became relegated to a secondary arm, often used as scythed chariots, a one-shot weapon intended to break up the enemy's battle line. They were deployed by the Persians at *Cunaxa and against Alexander 'the Great''s *phalanx at *Arbela, although without much success. Disciplined infantry had no trouble in repelling them or creating lanes in their formation through which the attacking chariots were channelled. Caesar's legionaries were able to achieve this equally well in their last recorded use at Zela (47 BC). Julius *Caesar had also encountered chariots in Britain during his invasions, although the continental Celts had abandoned them in favour of cavalry generations earlier.

MB

Yadin, Yigael, *The Art of Warfare in Biblical Lands* (1963).

Charlemagne (742–814), derived from the Latin Carolus Magnus (Charles 'the Great'), was ruler of the *Franks (whose heartland lay between the Seine and the Rhine) from 768 to 814. His family—the Carolingians—had formally replaced the Merovingian dynasty in 751 with the coronation of Charlemagne's father, Pippin. In the 8th century the Carolingians reintegrated the area which had traditionally fallen under Frankish overlordship, with the defeat of rival noble factions and the conquest of peripheral principalities which had splintered off from the Frankish empire. Although he stimulated a notable cultural revival, and initiated reform of church and society, the continuation of military success was the central fact of Charlemagne's reign.

The scope of Charlemagne's activity reflected the size of his empire: he campaigned from the Ebro to the Danube, the Elbe to the Po, against Byzantines and Muslims, Avars and Danes, Saxons and Slavs. Campaigns took place annually, contemporaries recording their surprise in those years when no army was sent forth. Before the 790s, Charlemagne as a rule led in the field in person; thereafter his sons and favoured aristocrats were given responsibility for specific campaigns. He completed the work of his predecessors in establishing direct Carolingian rule in the traditional spheres of Frankish overlordship, notably with the absorption of the Bavarian duchy—in effect an independent principality—through a series of diplomatic initiatives which reached fruition in 788. Beyond this, three new theatres of conquest emerged. First, Italy, where he followed his father's policy of intervention in defence of the papacy, defeating and annexing the Lombard kingdom which dominated the north of the peninsula in a single campaign in 774. Secondly, Saxony, where a tribal polity which had traditionally paid the Franks an annual tribute was growing increasingly assertive, and took over thirty years to conquer. The Saxons' paganism enabled Charlemagne to present his designs on a troublesome neighbour as religiously motivated. Thirdly, the Avar empire, which had dominated central Europe from its heartland in the middle Danube since the 6th century, was destroyed in a series of campaigns between 793 and 796. Here again the paganism of his opponents allowed Charlemagne to pose as the defender of Christianity, although the real motive was the securing of the south-east after the absorption of Bavaria. These conquests left Charlemagne's empire virtually conterminous with western Christendom, a fact acknowledged by the Pope at Rome on Christmas Day, 800, with the revival of the imperial title.

These military successes owed much to Charlemagne's ability as a strategist and a diplomat. The favoured tactic involved the division of Frankish troops into two forces as they entered enemy territory, enabling a pincer movement. The cream of the Frankish army was the heavy cavalry, but it is no longer believed that this élite always and inevitably carried the day due to sheer brute force or technological superiority. The heavy cavalry made up perhaps a tenth of Frankish armies, which probably numbered in tens of thousands. Charlemagne was thus far from dependent on the cavalry charge, and indeed remarkably successful at reducing enemy fortifications. The complex organization, which equipped and supplied the army, and maintaining lines of communication, was the real basis of Carolingian success. In Frankish society, an equestrian, martial lifestyle was the badge of aristocratic status. Charlemagne could thus draw on a substantial number of trained warriors as the basis of his army. He expected aristocrats, bishops, and abbots to take responsibility for the supply and maintenance of such forces; to this end he encouraged free men to enter into relationships of lordship, and granted out royal and ecclesiastical land in life-tenures. It would be a mistake to see Charlemagne as the creator of a fully fledged system of *feudal military obligation: although he made extensive use of interpersonal bonds to put armies in the field, these bonds existed within public structures of government, and did not define the obligation to serve. Armies were run by royal officials, and supplies and service were expected from all free men.

After the final defeat of the Saxons in the first years of the 9th century, the constant campaigning ended. What further expansion there was—notably in Catalonia and down the Danube—resulted from the activities of frontier commanders. Charlemagne was no fool and the end of expansion was a conscious strategic decision, not the result of war-weariness or senescence. By 800, the increased scope of Frankish power left Charlemagne facing a whole series of new challenges: securing long frontiers and newly conquered provinces; neutralizing new and potentially dangerous neighbours, notably in Denmark; putting a military machine forged by a century of aggressive expansion onto a more defensive, reactive, footing. Thus the years from 800 until Charlemagne's death in 814 see a long run of royal edicts (capitularies) attempting to regularize and define military obligations; and the creation of marches on exposed frontiers, and naval defences on exposed seaboards. The Carolingian political edifice had been built on military success, which had generated a substantial income through tribute and plunder, and had helped unite the Frankish aristocracy under Carolingian leadership; the shift from expansion to consolidation thus posed political as well as military challenges. It is now increasingly recognized that Charlemagne and his 9th-century successors responded in imaginative and original ways, attempting to move from the politics of the warband to that of the Christian empire.

MI

Bachrach, Bernard S., *Armies and Politics in Early Medieval Europe* (Aldershot, 1992).

Bowlus, Charles R., *Franks, Moravians and Magyars: The Struggle for the Middle Danube, 788–907* (Philadelphia, 1995).

Noble, Thomas (chapter), in Roger Collins and Peter Godman (eds.), *Charlemagne's Heir: New Perspectives on the Reign of Louis the Pious 814–840* (Oxford, 1989).

Reuter, Timothy (chapter), in Collins and Godman (eds.), *Charlemagne's Heir*.

—— 'Plunder and Tribute in the Carolingian Empire', *Transactions of the Royal Historical Society*, 5th ser., 35 (1985).

Verbruggen, J. F., 'L'Armée et la stratégie de Charlemagne', in Karl der Grosse, *Lebenswerk und Nachleben*, ed. W. Braunfels (4 vols., Dusseldorf 1965), vol. 1. *Personlichkeit und Geschichte*, ed. H. Beumann.

Charles V, Holy Roman Emperor

(1500–58). For a man with no military leanings, it is ironic that Charles V's life was dominated by war. Crowned by the pope in 1519, he fought his first battle in 1535 at Tunis against the *Turks, and much of his energy was devoted to preventing Turkish expansion westward into the Mediterranean and eastern

Europe, *Vienna itself coming under siege in 1529. Charles's lands were vast and bewildering in their complexity: they included the Netherlands, Burgundy, Spain, and various German fiefdoms, and his responsibilities included the nominal leadership of the Christian West. An onerous task indeed at such a time of turmoil and strife as the early 16th century.

Moreover, Charles was beset with internal and external problems: *François I of France attempted to expand his domains at the expense of the empire in Italy and the Netherlands, Pope Clement VII wished to curb the temporal power of the empire, and the rising tide of Protestantism threatened the unity of Christendom, on which the empire rested.

Remarkably, Charles managed to counter, or at least contain, all these threats. The French were destroyed at Pavia in 1525, and François was captured, Rome was sacked in 1527, and the Protestant princes put to flight at Mühlberg in 1547. Nevertheless, the inherent contradictions in a political unit that was neither holy, Roman, nor an empire, meant that Charles, exhausted, retired to a monastery in 1556. Thereafter his domains were divided between the Austrian and Spanish branches of the Habsburg family.   TM

Charles XII, King of Sweden (1682–1718), one of the most enigmatic figures in military history, about whom it is impossible to remain equivocal. Either he was a great leader and paragon of military virtue or a belligerent lunatic. Certainly, his reign saw the decline of Sweden from great power status to Baltic backwater, and this is in no small part due to the events of his dramatic and colourful career. His life invited commentary from the great writers of his age, most famously Voltaire, but Defoe, Fielding, and Dr Johnson were also moved to write about his exploits. Pope called him a Macedonian madman, comparing him to *Alexander 'the Great' in his peregrinations. Paradoxically, although the bulk of Charles's life was spent at war, he was greatly influenced by the rational ideas of the Enlightenment.

His patrimony had been assured by his father Charles XI, who had put the administration of the Swedish kingdom on a sound footing and reduced the power of the Swedish nobility, giving the king near absolute power. The army was reorganized and the *canton system (see also RECRUITMENT) of the *indelningsverket* introduced, where every province in Sweden and Finland would contribute one or more regular standing regiments named after the province itself. Every ten farmsteads were supposed to provide for a fully equipped soldier, including a horse if he was a cavalryman or *dragoon. In time of war, the other farmers would work his land, which was granted by the state. This system was also used for the navy in the coastal areas, and placed less of a burden on the taxation system.

When the young Charles came to the throne in 1697 at the age of 14, Sweden's maritime and trade supremacy in the Baltic was beginning to come under pressure from Poland, Denmark, and Russia. They formed a triple alliance against him, hoping to take advantage of his youth and inexperience to despoil the Swedish empire. The ensuing *Great Northern war lasted from 1700 until 1721, and was to dominate the rest of Charles's short life. The Swedes, led by the able Gen Rehnskjold with Charles understudying him, quickly forced King Frederick IV of Denmark to *capitulate with a swift amphibious landing. They were again victorious against the Russians in November of 1700, destroying the entire army that was besieging Narva, in Estonia.

Now 20, Charles then led his army through Courland and Poland and into Saxony. He was by now ready to take full responsibility for operations, and his 12,000 troops resoundingly beat 16,000 Saxons at Kliszow in 1702. The following year at Pultusk he crushed another Saxon force, and in 1705 they were again routed at Punitz and Wszowa. Rehnskjold scored a further convincing victory at Franstadt in 1706. Poland fell into anarchy, the Saxons were brought to the negotiating table, and the Treaty of Altranstadt was duly signed. The pro-Swedish Stanislas Leszczynski was installed as king of Poland. The western powers began to court Charles, hoping he would intervene on one side or the other in the War of the *Spanish Succession that was in full swing at the time.

Charles resolved instead to march east and deal with the Russian threat. All of Poland, Pomerania, and much of the Baltic coast lay at his feet, and he elected to pursue a war of aggression to expand into the Russian lands. On 1 January 1708, with an army of 40,000 he marched on Moscow and the Russians fell back before him, hoping that time and the vast empty spaces would swallow him up. He caught up with them at Holowczyn, and soon realized that this was not the same rabble that had thrown down their arms at Narva eight years previously. *Peter 'the Great' had reorganized his army along western lines and could boast an efficient and credible force that had retained the dogged and indomitable Russian spirit that has dismayed invaders time and again. Peter crushed a Cossack rebellion that threatened to provide Charles with much-needed allies, and the destruction of the Swedish supply column under Lewenhaupt at Ljesna in October 1708 seemed to settle matters, as it left the Swedes without resupply through an unusually bitter winter. Somehow, Charles and his army managed to hang on despite many deaths from cold and frostbite, and in the spring he marched on the Russian fortress of *Poltava, which he believed contained large amounts of food and ammunition. At 03.00 on 27 June 1709, 22,000 Swedes in four columns attacked 44,000 Russians, mostly in entrenchments and led by the tsar in person. To make matters worse, Charles had been shot in the foot during a scouting mission just before the battle. The wound had became infected, and Charles was too ill to direct the battle in person. He passed command to Rehnskjold, who was unpopular with the other officers, and they deliberately or otherwise misunderstood his orders. The attack on the Russian redoubts, at first successful due to the sheer bravery of the Swedish troops, soon degenerated into a shambles.

Seven thousand Swedes died fighting and 2,500 were captured at Poltava. The 10,000 remaining under Lewenhaupt were surrounded and surrendered at Perevolotjna on the river Dnjestr on 1 July 1709. The prisoners were marched off to the mines of the Urals, put to work building St Petersburg, or sent to Siberia. Few, if any, returned. Charles himself was spirited away on a stretcher to evade capture, and took refuge with 1,000 loyal but ragged and weary followers with Russia's ancient enemies, the Ottoman *Turks. He remained in a specially constructed camp at Bender in Bessarabia for five years, desperately trying to gather forces for a renewed invasion of Russia. He encouraged the Turks to declare war on Russia in 1710, and the more mobile Turkish army soon surrounded the Russians at Pruth. However, inexplicably the Porte made peace shortly afterwards. Tiring of their troublesome guest they besieged his camp in 1713 and he eventually negotiated his return to Sweden where, after crossing hostile territory disguised as one 'Captain Frisk', he arrived in November 1714. The war was going badly for Sweden and Charles now faced an alliance of Denmark, Saxony, and Russia, who had been joined by Hanover and Prussia. Livonia, Estonia, and the lands around the Gulf of Finland were in Russian hands, while the other allies had helped themselves to the Swedish lands in Germany. Stralsund and Vor-Pommern had fallen to the Brandenburgers.

Once back in Sweden, Charles immediately put into effect the many reforms of army and state he had thought through during his long isolation in the camp at Bender, and set about organizing the defence of Sweden. He supported the Swedish engineer Carl Cronstedt, who redesigned the Swedish artillery, making the guns more mobile and capable of rapid fire. A form of conscription was introduced, tactical formations were made more flexible, and inter-arm co-operation was developed further. Contemporaries marvelled at the skill and professionalism of the Swedish army. This new army then took the field in 1717 against Norway, where Charles was shot in the head and killed at the siege of Frederiksten. There has been some speculation that Charles was assassinated, but from forensic examination of his skull it is fairly certain that an enemy sentinel caught sight of his head peering over the parapet and managed a lucky hit. The Norwegian campaign ended in fiasco, the army collapsed, and 3,000 men were lost in a gruelling retreat over the mountains of Jämtland.

Charles's reputation as a great commander rests on his capabilities as an aggressive and courageous tactical leader, but sadly this was not enough. His utter contempt for his enemies, and almost complete lack of strategic and diplomatic subtlety was to cost Sweden dearly. The war ended with the Treaty of Nystad in 1721, where Sweden lost Estonia, Ingria, and Livonia. The Swedish economy was shattered, and Russia had gained access to the Baltic and a window on the West. TM

Englund, Peter, *Poltava* (Stockholm, 1988).

Charles, Archduke of Austria (1771–1847), dynamic military leader and reformer and a reminder of how the Habsburgs came to be great in the first place. The third son of Emperor Leopold II, his first battle was Jemappes (1792). As governor of the Austrian Netherlands he enjoyed some military success against the French at first, but then suffered defeats at Wattignies (1793) and *Fleurus. Commanding on the Rhine in 1796, he defeated Moreau and Jourdan, and again defeated the latter and *Masséna during the Second Coalition, only to see Moreau advance on Vienna after the Austrian defeat at Höhenlinden (1800).

During the *truce that followed, Charles became the president of a *council of war that began scrapping the old Habsburg military system and replacing it with one intelligently modelled on the best aspects of the French. Charles advocated an appeal to popular nationalism, previously anathema in the multinational Habsburg empire. The need for reform was brutally underlined at *Austerlitz in 1805 and Charles's efforts began to bear fruit in 1809, when he fought Napoleon twice on the Danube. He defeated him at *Aspern-Essling, but two months later lost at *Wagram, not before inflicting heavy casualties. He took no further part in the war and published his *Principles of Strategy* in 1814, based on his successful 1796 campaign. Although his own generalship was characterized by almost Napoleonic opportunism, he emphasized the importance of strategic positioning to force the enemy to give battle at a disadvantage. MB

Rothenberg, Gunter E., *Napoleon's Greatest Adversaries: The Archduke Charles and the Austrian Army 1792–1814* (London, 1982).

chassepot The Model 1866, bolt-action, single-shot, 11 mm calibre rifle in use by the French army from 1866 to 1874 was named after its inventor, Antoine Alphonse Chassepot (1833–1905), who was principal at the arsenal of Châtellerault when he invented his breech-loading rifle in 1863. Similar in form to Dreyse's *needle gun, in use for twenty years in the Prussian army, the chassepot's superior design features included a rubber obturating ring in the bolt, which sealed the chamber more efficiently, and a shorter—less fragile—firing pin which, instead of penetrating the cartridge to fire a centrally situated detonator—as Dreyse's fragile 'needle' did—pierced the propelent cartridge at its base to fire the charge. During the *Franco-Prussian war the chassepot proved so dependable and deadly that Prussian and Bavarian troops were known to have adopted captured chassepots in preference to their own Dreyse and Werder breech-loading rifles. The chassepot came equipped with a brass-hilted sword *bayonet and, in 1874, was modified to take brass centre-fire cartridges—being then renamed the Modèle 1866/74, or Gras, rifle.　　　　　　　SCW

Blair, Claude (gen. ed.), *Pollard's History of Firearms* (London, 1983).

Peterson, Harold L. (ed.), *Encyclopaedia of Firearms* (London, 1964).

---

chasseurs (Fr.: *chasseurs*, hunters) were *light troops in the French army, like their counterparts *Jägers (Ger., also 'hunters') in the German army. There were four main types, two in the cavalry and two in the infantry. *Chasseurs à cheval* (mounted chasseurs) were first raised in the 18th century as European armies responded to demands for light troops. There were twelve regiments by 1789, and 31 by 1811. Twenty-four regiments formed part of the Restoration army, but subsequent restructuring reduced this number as some were converted to *lancers. There were twelve regiments of *chasseurs à cheval* in the Second Empire, and the arm was re-established after the *Franco-Prussian war, serving on into two world wars. Chasseurs, now mechanized, are part of the French army's armoured corps. For much of their history *chasseurs à cheval* wore hussar-style uniform, often with fur hussar caps, although there was a tendency to make chasseur *uniforms more sombre than those of the showy *hussars. Green was the arm's distinctive colour, and hunting-horn insignia appeared on accoutrements.

Chasseurs d'Afrique (African light cavalry) were raised during the French conquest of *Algeria in 1831, and attracted numerous volunteers, not least those who sought to 'redeem their civil offences by heroic sabre-cuts'. There were soon four regiments, which soon gained a formidable fighting record. They formed a cavalry division in the Franco-Prussian war, and their gallant but hopeless charge at *Sedan on 1 September 1870 drew the exclamation 'Ah! Les braves gens!' (Ah! The brave fellows) from the king of Prussia, who witnessed it. The Chasseurs d'Afrique, unlike the *spahis, recruited Europeans and wore a similar uniform to *chasseurs à cheval*, though always with a *casquette d'Afrique* or képi rather than a fur cap or tall shako. But, like the spahis, they were given to non-regulation embellishments which reflected a devil-may-care style. They remained part of the French army until Algerian independence.

Although the French army had long maintained light infantry, both as regiments of *infanterie légère* and in the light companies of line regiments, by the 1820s the functional differences between light and line infantry had become thoroughly blurred. The fighting in Algeria demanded infantry who could move fast and shoot straight, and in 1838 a new experimental battalion of *tirailleurs d'Afrique* was raised. The unit was widely known, from its garrison on the eastern outskirts of Paris, as Chasseurs de Vincennes. Equipped with the new *Minié rifles from 1839, the chas-

seurs were an instant success, and ten battalions were raised in 1840. The keen interest taken in them by the monarch's brother the Duc d'Orléans earned them the title Chasseurs d'Orléans, but with the 1848 Revolution this changed to the more familiar *chasseurs à pied*.

The *chasseurs à pied* had much in common with *rifle regiments in the British army or Jägers in the German. They wore sombre uniforms, with grey-blue trousers rather than the red of the line, drilled at the quickstep, used bugles rather than drums to transmit orders, and wore the hunting-horn badge. Their training emphasized marksmanship, fieldcraft, and individual resource, and they attracted some of the best officers in the army: two of the first ten commanding officers became marshals. Although they lost some of their unique appeal when French infantry as a whole was issued with the rifle, they nevertheless managed to preserve their individuality. Their most celebrated *battle honour was Sidi-Brahim where in 1845 Major Froment-Coste's 8th Battalion defended itself against *Abd al-Qadir and was reduced to a mere fifteen survivors. A stirring bugle march, *le Sidi-Brahim*, became the chasseurs' signature tune.

Finally, the Chasseurs alpins, formed during the military renaissance following the Franco-Prussian war, were specialist mountain infantry, drawing on recruits from France's alpine *départements*. Their uniform included a huge floppy beret, a short blouse, and putties. Like their comrades the *chasseurs à pied*, they survive to this day.　　　RH

Château-Thierry/Belleau Wood, battles of (1918). In March 1918 the Germans launched the first of a series of offensives in the hope of winning the war before the Americans arrived in France in strength. The third of these offensives, BLÜCHER, was mounted along the Chemin des Dames, between Noyon and Soissons, on 27 May, and the Germans successfully crossed the river Aisne and reached the Marne. At Château-Thierry on 30 May machine-gunners of the US 3rd Division helped French troops check the German advance. Belleau Wood, taken in the offensive, was recaptured by the US 2nd Division, its attack led by the 4th Marine Brigade. It cost the USA over 9,000 casualties, in part because of tactical inexperience. However, both victories, together with a third, won by the US 1st Division at Cantigny on 28–9 May, were of enormous psychological importance. The Germans revised their hitherto low opinion of the American Expeditionary Force, and Allied *morale received a much-needed boost.　　　RH

---

chemical and biological weapons cause damage to living organisms by their physiological effects rather than by direct physical impact from blast and heat. Although they can both be dispersed in the air and can inflict damage over significant areas, there are important differences between them. Chemical warfare agents are substances, whether gaseous, liquid, or solid, which might be employed because of their direct toxic effects on man, animals, or plants. Biological warfare agents are living organisms, or infective material derived from them, which are intended to cause disease or death, and which depend for their effect on their ability to multiply in the organism attacked. Toxins, though usually produced by living (biological) organisms, are classified as chemical substances because they are inanimate and cannot multiply. Biological warfare agents act much less rapidly than their chemical counterparts, but they are much more potent on a weight-for-weight basis since, under favourable environmental conditions, they can multiply after dispersal, and so smaller and less costly amounts can inflict casualties over a much wider area. On the other hand, biological warfare agents are more susceptible than chemical warfare agents to sunlight, temperature, and other environmental factors: once disseminated, a biological warfare agent can retain its viability (ability to live and multiply) while losing its virulence (ability to produce disease and injury).

Chemical and biological weapons have a long record of historical usage. Poisonous fumes were reportedly employed by the Spartans in the *Peloponnesian war (429 BC); plague victims were thrown by *Mongols into the besieged city of Caffa (now Feodosis) in the Crimea, in 1346; and blankets infected with smallpox were given by British forces to hostile Indian tribes in Ohio in 1763. Less sophisticated techniques have also been used, including the fouling of wells or other sources of drinking water with the corpses of men or animals. However, it was only in WW I that chemical science, industry, and military technology proved sufficiently developed to facilitate the large-scale and systematic use of chemical weaponry.

After some experiments with irritant agents by the French at Neuve Chapelle (27 October 1914) and the Germans at Bolimów (31 January 1915), the first major use of *gas was by Germans at *Ypres (22 April 1915), when 177 tons (180,000 kg) of chlorine were released from cylinders over a front of 3.7 miles (6 km), causing panic amid the French Territorial and Algerian forces affected. Although the German forces captured a sizeable chunk of the Ypres salient, they chose to dig in at night allowing Allied forces the opportunity to regroup and launch a counter-offensive. Gas was never so effective again on the western front as both sides developed increasingly effective defences, employing respirators, alarms, anti-gas drills, some collective protection facilities, and rudimentary measures of decontamination.

In the hope of defeating such defences, the belligerents experimented with different gases and combinations of gases. These included numerous irritant and lethal agents, including phosgene (six times more poisonous than chlorine as a lung agent); hydrogen cyanide (a highly toxic and highly volatile blood gas); and mustard gas, an extremely persistent blister agent, soon known as 'king of the war gases' on account of its persistence, its ability to penetrate clothing, and its many-sided effects (including temporary blindness, respiratory irritation, and painful blisters). The belligerents also reduced their dependence upon unreliable cloud-gas attacks from cylinders and invested more heavily in *mortars, artillery (the preferred option for all armies other than the British), and projectors (large drums filled with highly toxic chemicals, which were fired in salvoes to deliver a massive quantity of agent over a target with the maximum of surprise). Britain introduced the Livens projector at the battle of *Arras/Vimy Ridge on 9 April 1917 and a German version was used with devastating effect at the battle of *Caporetto. Finally, the belligerents increasingly refined their chemical tactics, with Col Georg Bruchmüller developing sophisticated counter-battery tactics and co-ordinated artillery/infantry attacks on the *eastern front in 1917. Similar tactics were employed in the German spring offensive on the western front in the spring of 1918, and later, when the Germans fell back on the defensive, mustard gas was increasingly used as a defensive weapon.

Overall some 124,000 tons of toxic agents were used during the war, causing 1.3 million casualties, or 4.6 per cent of the total number, and of these casualties, 91,000 died. The relatively small numbers of gas casualties reflected the limited investment in chemical warfare, with chemical shells accounting for only 4.5 per cent of all shells and specialized chemical forces accounting for only 2 per cent of the total engineer strength. Gas, like other weapons, had failed to break the trench deadlock on the western front, but it had suffered from the further disadvantages of being new, unreliable particularly in its cloud-gas mode, and unavailable in sufficient quantities (even for the Germans in 1918). It was most easily assimilated as an artillery weapon and most effective against the poorly protected Russian soldiers and the inadequately trained American forces (accounting for 70,752 US casualties or 27.4 per cent of the American total).

After the war attempts were made to proscribe the use of chemical and biological weapons, most notably in the Geneva Protocol of 1925 (see GENEVA AND HAGUE CONVENTIONS), but some countries never ratified the agreement and others reserved the right to retaliate in kind if attacked by such weapons. Nevertheless, chemical warfare recurred with the Italians employing chemical weapons against unprotected Abyssinian forces (1935–6) and the Japanese using chemical weapons in China (1937–45). The Japanese would also experiment on a small scale with biological weapons in China. Yet chemical warfare proved a rare instance of a form of warfare, developed in one war, not being used by the principal belligerents in the next war. During WW II, most powers, other than the Japanese, developed new methods of aerial delivery (using spray tanks or bombs); many invested in *civil defence (particularly Britain); the Germans discovered new gases—the nearly odourless, extremely toxic, and rapid-acting nerve agents (tabun, sarin, and soman)—and the great powers accumulated vast stockpiles of chemical warfare agents (135,000 tons in the USA alone). The non-use of gas reflected a mix of political, military, and industrial factors, including the reservations of some political leaders (especially Franklin D. *Roosevelt); shortages of gas early in the war; intelligence misperceptions; doubts about the utility of gas in mobile warfare, amphibious landings, and in the absence of aerial superiority; the deterrent posed by threats of retaliation in kind; and the alternative, when available, of using the atomic bomb.

During the *Cold War, the superpowers and some of their allies retained and developed their arsenals of chemical and biological weapons. Although new agents were discovered (notably the V agents—the most toxic form of nerve agent), biological weapons tested, and delivery systems refined (cluster bombs, rockets, and missiles), chemical and biological weapons became increasingly controversial. China and North Korea made unfounded allegations that the USA had used biological warfare during the *Korean war, and domestic and international protests erupted over the American use of herbicides in the *Vietnam war. While many states sought to establish new international norms against chemical and biological warfare (signing the Biological and Toxin Weapons Convention in 1972 and the Chemical Weapons Convention in 1993), the weapons were still being used and developed. There were allegations that chemical weapons and toxins were used in *counter-insurgency wars in Laos, Cambodia, and Afghanistan; proven and extensive use of chemical weapons, including nerve agents for the first time, by Iraq in the *Iran–Iraq war (1980–8); and the employment of these weapons for the purposes of killing and terrorizing civilians at Halabja (March 1988) and in Japan by the Aum Shinrikyo cult (1994–5). Coalition forces had to make extensive preparations to cope with the possibility of incurring chemical and biological attacks during the *Gulf war.

By the 1980s and 1990s, several developing countries had acquired the capacity to develop, produce, and deliver chemical and biological weapons. They appreciated that these weapons, especially biological weapons, could be developed relatively cheaply (by comparison with *nuclear weapons programmes) in clandestine facilities, often using materials and technology that had legitimate civilian purposes. They realized, too, that technological advances were enhancing the utility of these weapons. Binary munitions had eased the safety problems of storing and transporting chemical weapons, while the potential application of biotechnology and/or genetic engineering held the prospect of manipulating micro-organisms to make them more virulent, more stable, or more resistant to antibiotics, and thereby complicating the tasks of identifying, detecting, and protecting forces against these weapons.   EMS

Dando, Malcolm, *Biological Warfare in the 21st Century: Biotechnology and the Proliferation of Biological Weapons* (London, 1994).

Haber, L. F., *The Poisonous Cloud: Chemical Warfare in the First World War* (Oxford, 1986).

Prentiss, Augustin M., *Chemicals in War* (New York, 1937).

Spiers, Edward M., *Chemical Weaponry: A Continuing Challenge* (London, 1989).

Stockholm International Peace Research Institute, *The Problem of Chemical and Biological Warfare*, 6 vols. (Stockholm, 1971–5).

Chetniks (from Serbo-Croat: *četnik*, armed band) were Serb *guerrilla units. Formed in 1903, they also fought in the Balkan wars in 1912–13, usually behind enemy lines. They are best known today as the royalist irregular units under Col Draza Mihailović who carried on the fight for King Peter II after Germany invaded *Yugoslavia on 6 April 1941. The Chetniks at first enjoyed the diplomatic and military support of the western Allies and Mihailović was named war minister by the royal government in exile. But from 1944, thanks partly to reports by Churchill's envoy Fitzroy Maclean, the Allies transferred their backing to the pro-Communist *Partisans of Josip Broz *Tito. The Allies' principal accusation—never accepted by the Chetniks—was that they were collaborating with the Nazis. By 1945 many Chetnik fighters had switched sides, tempted by Tito's offer of an amnesty.

After Tito entered Belgrade in November 1944, the hunt was on for Mihailović, who was captured in eastern Bosnia, put on trial, and executed for treason. The large Serb émigré community mostly revere him as a martyr. The Chetniks claimed to be fighting for a united Yugoslavia and the Karadjordgevic dynasty, and against a communist takeover. In practice their support was confined to the Serbs and among the country's non-Serbian majority, fear of communism was often outweighed by anxiety that a Chetnik victory would result in a centralized state run exclusively by the Serbs. These fears appeared vindicated by atrocities committed against the Bosnian Muslims.

As Yugoslavia dissolved into its constituent units in 1991–2, the extreme Serb nationalist leader Vojislav Seselj attempted to revive Chetnik units, along with their distinctive black flags with white skulls and crossbones, to help the Yugoslav army suppress pro-independence forces in Bosnia and Croatia.   MGT

chevauchée is a term which occurs in many chronicles relating to the period of the *Hundred Years War. It is often translated in modern works as 'raid', but more accurately means 'ride'. The reality was that a chevauchée was a campaign of destruction, pillage, and chaos perpetrated by English forces in French territories in an attempt to encourage acceptance of English hegemony. A chevauchée would typically involve a mobile English force striking deep into French territory looting, pillaging, and destroying all in its path, including towns and villages, but avoiding centres of enemy strength. Contact with enemy armies was to be avoided, unless absolutely necessary or if the English force was considerably superior.

The English employed the chevauchée many times, and the major battles of the period—*Crécy, Poitiers, and *Agincourt—all resulted from chevauchées where the English army had been run down and forced to fight. After 1415, *Henry V abandoned the chevauchée and switched to a policy of systematic conquest as the only means of bringing northern France under full English rule.   JB

Jones, A., *The Art of War in the Western World* (New York, 1987).
Oman, C., *The Art of War in the Middle Ages*, vol. ii, *1278–1485* (London, 1991).

Chiang Kai-Shek (correctly Jiang Jieshi) (1887–1975), commander of Nationalist China's armed forces and, from 1949, president of the Republic of China on Taiwan. He received most of his military training in Japan from 1906–11, and became an adherent of the revolutionary Sun Yat-sen. He returned to China to take part in the revolution of 1911, serving under Chen Qimei, which established a short-lived provisional government in Nanking. After the revolution's defeat he fled to Japan and played a low-key role during the period of WW I. In 1923, he was recalled by Sun to join the Kuomintang (KMT) or Nationalist party and given the rank of major general. In the same year he headed a military embassy to the USSR and returned to establish the KMT's Whampoa Military Academy, near Guangzhou. With Soviet help he consolidated KMT control over southern China and led the Northern Campaign (1926–7). This involved the defeat of Chinese communists and hence a break with the USSR. Making himself effective head of the KMT in 1928, he captured Beijing. There followed the extensive military operations known as the five Bandit Suppression Campaigns (December 1930–September 1934), directed against the communists in southern China. Only the last of these was reasonably successful, driving *Mao Tse-tung on the Long March. The threat of Japanese invasion, which became actual in July 1937, forced him to ally with the communists. Chiang was unable to hold the Japanese advances until after the USA entered the war in 1941. Even then, he did not co-operate well with the American commander 'Vinegar Joe' *Stilwell, and his power was so weakened that the communists were able to withstand him after 1945. Following a series of failed campaigns, he was driven into exile on Taiwan on 7 December 1949.

    MB

Chindits (corruption of the Burmese *Chinthe*, a mythical animal that sits at the entrance of Burmese pagodas to ward off evil spirits). It is a term applied to the operations carried out by Orde *Wingate in the *Burma campaign in 1943 and 1944 and the troops that took part in them. In these Wingate's novel ideas were carried out: that troops could operate in enemy territory supplied entirely from the air, and could cut enemy communications to assist offensives by regular forces.

The first expedition took place between February and April 1943 with one brigade. The tangible results were few: some bridges and railway lines blown and some Japanese bewildered; and a third of the force were casualties. But news of the adventure had a clear effect on *morale in a theatre that was still recovering from defeat.

The second expedition, which took place between March and July 1944, was much bigger. Six brigades took part, with a large US air component, four of them being flown into Burma, with an advance party in *gliders to secure and develop landing strips for the main force in *Dakotas. In a few nights 600 sorties flew in 8,000 men and about 1,400 mules, at the cost of about 30 killed in gliders.

One brigade effectively throttled the railway line and later heroically captured the town of Mogaung. The other brigades harassed to some effect, though the attempt to mount another block proved disastrous. With Wingate killed in a crash soon after the start of the operation and the American Gen *Stilwell in overall command the operation petered out in exhaustion. Argument has continued about the cost-effectiveness of the operation. Few have denied the imaginativeness of the concept.   RRJ1

Bidwell, Shelford, *The Chindit War* (London, 1979).
Thompson, Julian, *War behind Enemy Lines* (London, 1998).

Chu Teh, FM (correctly Zhu De) (1886–1976). Like many Chinese communist leaders, Chu Teh was born into a peasant family. Having entered the Yunnan Military Academy in 1911, he was caught up in Sun Yat-sen's nationalist revolution of 1911 that overthrew the Ch'ing (*Manchu) dynasty. In the 'warlord' period during and following WW I, Chu Teh served as a brigade commander but in 1922, growing disillusioned with the chaos of the period, he went to Europe to study. It was here that Chu Teh joined the Chinese Communist Party. On his return to China, Chu Teh kept secret his communist affiliations and joined *Chiang Kai-Shek and the Kuomintang (KMT) army. However, in 1927, Chu Teh took part in the communist-led Nan-ch'ang uprising, an event that marked the beginning of the Chinese Red Army, which would become the People's Liberation Army (PLA) in 1946. During the epic 6,000 mile (9,654 km) Long March of 1934–5, when *Mao Tse-tung took his communist forces north to Yenan (Yan'an) in Shensi (Shaanxi) province to escape encircling KMT armies, Chu Teh was commander of the First Front Army. Chu Teh's military career continued during the Sino-Japanese war of 1937–45 when he commanded the Eighth Route Army. During the Chinese civil war of 1945–9, Chu Teh was promoted to C-in-C of the PLA forces that defeated Chiang Kai-Shek and ejected the KMT from mainland China. In the 1950s, Chu Teh was promoted to marshal but was gradually marginalized from positions of political and military importance and his influence waned. However, his legacy in terms of PLA tactics and overall military strategy should not be underestimated. Chu Teh was responsible for emphasizing *guerrilla warfare as part of conventional operations. This presaged many of the 'small wars' of Africa and Asia after 1945. Chu Teh showed how guerrilla forces could supplement conventional armies and become strategic forces. By employing these tactics, communist soldiers were able to survive in the Chinese countryside and become indistinguishable from the mass of peasants. Under Chu Teh's command, the PLA became a highly mobile and self-sufficient force living off the land. Like the Roman general *Fabius, Chu Teh avoided set-piece battles wherever possible, preferring to pick off his enemy piecemeal using *attritional attacks. These tactics proved successful against the Japanese during the Sino-Japanese war, and were vital in the Chinese civil war when Chu Teh's PLA forces initially occupied the countryside rather than the major cities.   MH

Churchill, Sir Winston Leonard Spencer (1874–1965).

Churchill was an atavistic anachronism who found lasting glory and fulfilment as an inspirational tribal leader during WW II, but was otherwise closely associated with many of the British military, foreign, and domestic policy disasters of the first half of the 20th century. He had a nightmare childhood: his father Lord Randolph succumbed to syphilitic insanity, while his beautiful mother Jennie, an American heiress, was promiscuous even by the lax standards of her class and time. Both largely ignored him. With Randolph dead and no longer a source of embarrassment, Winston exploited his mother's well-placed connections to advance his career.

Arriving in India with the 4th Hussars, he served in the 1897 *Malakand expedition, later writing *The Story of the Malakand Field Force* (1898). His combination of serving officer and war correspondent aroused deep suspicion, particularly in the breast of *Kitchener, and only his mother's wiles enabled him to join the 21st Lancers and to take part in one of the last cavalry charges at *Omdurman, as recounted in *The River War* (1899). He resigned his commission to stand as the losing Conservative candidate at Oldham in 1899, went to cover the Second *Boer War for the *Morning Post*, was captured when the armoured train in which he was travelling was ambushed, escaped from a *POW camp, and returned to England having finally achieved the fame and (modest) fortune he sought, to win Oldham in 1900, an astonishing reversal of fortunes in just over a year.

While previously he had shamelessly used his parents' connections for self-advancement, now he was a celebrity in his own right. Not a natural public speaker, his dominance of the form emerged from hours of preparation. Later

in life, when found muttering to himself by a confidant, he explained with a grin that he was rehearsing his off-the-cuff remarks for the next day. The jury will remain out concerning whether his move from the Conservative to the Liberal party in 1904 was the product of opportunism or principle; that it was encouraged by *Lloyd George argues strongly for the former. In the 1906 general election he won a seat in Manchester for the Liberals and in 1908 finally obtained a cabinet post as President of the Board of Trade. Defeated in Manchester, he won re-election in Dundee and also wed Clementine Hozier, with whom he was to have a lifelong, happy marriage. Leaving aside his stormy tenure at the Board of Trade and his role in the curbing of the power of the House of Lords and in the matter of Home Rule for Ireland, during which time he made more enemies than most manage in a whole career, he became First Lord of the Admiralty in 1911 and oversaw the largest naval expansion programme in British history and ordered mobilization on his own authority on 2 August 1914, guaranteeing the orderly and uninterrupted passage of the British Expeditionary Force (BEF) to France. In October he went in person to Antwerp to encourage it to hold out while the Belgian army escaped and the Channel ports were secured (see ANTWERP, SIEGES OF).

Subsequently things went less well; his partnership with *Fisher foundered over Churchill's enthusiasm for a naval expedition to seize the Dardanelles. After a number of warships were sunk Adm de Robeck called it off, Fisher resigned, and Churchill was, at Conservative insistence, demoted from the Admiralty to the Duchy of Lancaster during the formation of the first coalition government. He was to be blamed for the *Gallipoli fiasco, for which he was given responsibility without any power to influence decisions. He resigned in November 1915 and served as battalion commander with the Royal Scots Fusiliers on the western front, returning to parliament in June 1916. Over intense Conservative opposition, Lloyd George gave him the non-cabinet post of Minister of Munitions in the second coalition government, a post to which he brought characteristic energy, particularly in deploying *tanks, a pet project since Admiralty days.

In January 1919 he became war minister and his name is indelibly linked with the twin debacles of the Allied *North Russia intervention and the *Anglo-Irish war. As colonial secretary from 1921, he developed an imaginative and cost-effective policy of allying with friendly local rulers and depending heavily on the independent *air force for *imperial policing, but he also confirmed an ultimately provocative and untenable policy of recognizing both Jewish and Arab rights in Palestine. Not least, he advocated confrontation with a resurgent Turkey, one of the nails in the coffin of the coalition government. He was a notable casualty of the 1922 general election.

While briefly 'without an office, without a seat, without a party', he wrote *The World Crisis* and with the proceeds bought the country house at Chartwell, which was to remain his home. He also took up painting, revealing yet another talent. The wonder is that he found time to do everything he did, usually well and always passionately. His bucolic interlude ended in 1923–4 with a return to politics as an adamant anti-socialist (although he was one of the pre-war founders of the welfare state) and a return to the Conservative fold when the Liberal party became an electoral irrelevance.

Baldwin appointed him Chancellor of the Exchequer, a post for which he was deeply unsuited and in which he received, and took, very bad advice from Treasury and Bank of England mandarins. The return to the gold standard provoked Keynes, of whom Churchill might otherwise have approved as an economist with only one hand, to follow up his insightful *The Economic Consequences of the Peace* with the equally damning *The Economic Consequences of Mister Churchill*. After 1929, after a further round of managing to offend nearly everyone of political consequence without making any compensatory friends, he began a decade in 'the wilderness' from which only the renewal of war with Germany was to retrieve him. He did not, of course, let the grass grow . . .

The most crucial relationship he developed during the 1930s was with Franklin *Roosevelt, who shared his fears of a resurgent Germany but who was unable to overcome US isolationism until the Japanese attacked *Pearl Harbor and *Hitler, not content with his titanic war against the USSR, did Churchill the enormous favour of declaring war on the USA as well. The two men established a covert liaison through the Canadian industrialist Stephenson that was clearly well within the 'high crimes and misdemeanours' for which a US president may be impeached. Their aim was to finesse the awkward fact that with a large German and Irish population, a (well-found) suspicion that British propaganda and other black arts had drawn the USA into WW I, and the strain of 'manifest destiny' that saw the British empire as the principal obstacle to US world hegemony, they were dealing with a majority public opinion that was not neutral but actively hostile to British interests. When Churchill later wrote of the New World coming to redress the balance of the Old, he knew of what he spoke, and insofar as anything today remains of the once 'special relationship', it is due as much to the abiding admiration of many Americans for Churchill as it is to more apparent than real similarities of language and culture.

Brought back to the Admiralty at the outbreak of WW II amid the panic of the civil servants and the rejoicing of the Royal Navy, the abrasiveness that ruffled so many feathers in peacetime suddenly became, even in the eyes of a class and ideological enemy like Ernest Bevin, precisely the qualities the nation needed to fight for its life. After the 1940 resignation of the unfortunate Chamberlain, there was a moment when the accommodationist Foreign Secretary Lord Halifax seemed the likely successor, but the mood of the time was for Churchill, whose maiden speech as PM promised 'blood, toil, tears and sweat'.

It has been argued that by continuing the war, Churchill not only bankrupted Britain but also precipitated the very socialism at home and retreat from empire abroad that he had fought against so strenuously. While the war undoubtedly completed the destruction of the economic underpinnings of the world in which he grew up which had begun in WW I, it is idle to pretend that the cost of any kind of deal which might have been made with Hitler would not have included at the very least national self-respect. The English Channel provided both a barrier to invasion and insurance that *force majeure* in the form of an invading army could not be adduced to compromise with what was, without doubt, absolute evil. If the old nation had to destroy itself, it could not have done so for a cause more befitting its noblest aspirations, or under a better chieftain.

Churchill's penchant for warfare on the cheap, in terms of human lives if not of treasure, led him to seek the 'soft underbelly' of the Axis and to pursue what can only be seen as strategic red herrings if one discounts the fact that his overriding aim was to avoid a repetition of the holocaust of WW I. In private he was extremely realistic about the limited achievements that the bombing campaign might bring, while assuring his impatient allies that it was tearing the heart out of Nazi Germany. Thanks to him more people died of traffic accidents than from enemy action in Britain in the five years before the *Normandy invasion, while millions of Russians and Germans were immolated on the *eastern front. He drove his CIGS *Alanbrooke to near nervous breakdown and the US *general staff to distraction, but when the invasion finally went forward it was at a time and place of his choosing, under the operational control of a British general, and even then was only just successful. The consequences of a premature invasion, as maliciously urged by *Stalin and echoed by US generals who lacked experience of what the German war machine could do, would have been the occupation of much more of Europe by the Red Army before the western Allies could regroup.

Of course numbers and industrial production counted, but at the end of the war Britain was still a great if hollowed-out power, possessed of the moral strength to conduct an orderly withdrawal from worldwide commitments she could no longer sustain. That his political heirs more than once botched the process does not diminish Churchill's legacy of the time and authority at least to try to do it right. If instead of considering him as the chief of those who led Britain through a long process where even victory concealed fundamental defeat, we instead consider him to have conducted a 50-year fighting retreat, by far the most difficult military manoeuvre, then his life's work deserves every encomium it has received. Through it all, he was the embodiment of the high Victorian ideal set out in Kipling's *If*—:

'If you can fill the unforgiving minute
With sixty seconds' worth of distance run,
Yours is the Earth and everything that's in it,
And—which is more—you'll be a Man, my son!'   HEB

Bonham Carter, Violet, *Churchill As I Knew Him* (London, 1965).

Lash, Joseph, *Roosevelt and Churchill 1939–1941: The Partnership that Saved the West* (New York, 1976).

Moran, Lord Charles, *Churchill: The Struggle for Survival* (London, 1966).

Pelling, Henry, *Winston Churchill* (New York, 1977).

CIA (Central Intelligence Agency). After its predecessor the paramilitary *OSS was abolished in 1945, the CIA was created in 1946 to co-ordinate a plethora of US military and civilian intelligence organizations. But by the following year it was fully committed to covert anti-communist operations under the *Truman Doctrine. These included working with Nazis in Germany, providing arms for the *Greek civil war and the 1952 revolution in Egypt, financing the Italian Christian Democrats, and defeating a communist insurgency in the Philippines. In 1953 it directed the overthrow of Iranian nationalist Mossadegh and in 1954 it organized the paramilitary operation that deposed Arbenz in Guatemala. Cocooned in secrecy and with limitless unaccountable funds at its disposal, it came to see itself as the president's Praetorian Guard, with no restraint on its range of action.

When a *U-2 spy plane was shot down over the USSR in 1960 and the pilot admitted he worked for the CIA, the veil began to lift. It slipped further in 1961 after an attempt to reverse the *Cuban Revolution ended in humiliating defeat at the Bay of Pigs. Despite this, Kennedy was fascinated by covert action and authorized assassination attempts against *Castro, Lumumba in the *Congo, and Trujillo in the Dominican Republic. He and his successor Johnson also involved the CIA in the Indochina labyrinth, where it ran a secret war in Laos and the mass-assassination Phoenix programme in *Vietnam. It also ran a number of *counter-insurgency operations in Latin America and contributed to the destabilization of the Allende regime in Chile.

Throughout this period Angleton, the head of counter-intelligence, was conducting a fanatic 'mole hunt' that never did uncover the moles, but did generate widespread paranoia. After his removal in 1974, counter-intelligence was given a greatly reduced priority and very real traitors were able to operate with impunity. It is possible that much of the intelligence on the Soviet bloc produced by the CIA during the 1980s and early 1990s was in fact provided by the Soviet intelligence services, which either turned existing CIA assets or provided new ones as required.

Following the 1972 Watergate scandal, its dirty laundry was washed in public with a vengeance and agents all over the world had their cover blown. A Senate Oversight Committees and other sure sources of leaks were set up, and under Carter-appointee Turner the CIA was purged of the 'old guard' and with it much of its agent-handling capability. There was a brief revival of old glories under the Reagan appointee Casey, with covert operations in Afghanistan and Nicaragua. The latter blew up in the *Iran-Contra affair and once again the CIA was attacked for following the orders of the office it is sworn to obey.

Long and unfairly accused of being the secret policeman to the world, Pres Clinton's 1995 definition of its post-*Cold War function to include industrial espionage and the fight against international crime appears to confirm that this is the direction in which it will be heading.   HEB

CID. See COMMITTEE OF IMPERIAL DEFENCE.

civil defence During and after war or natural catastrophe, civil defence involves the passive protection of civilian lives, the maintenance of communications and government, and the reconstruction of social and economic infrastructure and industry. A fully developed civil defence system would involve a programme of training, education, and preparation; a system of warning and reporting; and appropriate responses by national, regional, and local agencies (police, emergency, and medical services). Civil defence is recognized in international law, with civil defence officials having protected status. The first of the two 1977 protocols additional to the 1949 Geneva Convention (see GENEVA AND HAGUE CONVENTIONS) sets out the scope of that protection and provides a definition of civil defence: 'humanitarian tasks intended to protect the civilian population against the dangers, and to help it to recover from the immediate effects, of hostilities or disasters and also to provide the conditions necessary for its survival'.

The technological advances of the 20th century have resulted in the deliberate blurring of the distinction between soldier and civilian during war. This process began with the advent of manned, powered flight at the beginning of the century. The potential of military *air power was confirmed during WW I, and the development of the theory of strategic bombing followed during the inter-war years. Civilian populations and whole cities had now become vulnerable to systematic attack. WW II saw devastating bomb and rocket attacks on cities and towns in Britain, Germany, and Japan. Although the ability of the civilian population to endure these onslaughts undermined the more extravagant claims of the strategic bombing advocates, there was nevertheless a growing acceptance of the role of an effective civil defence system. If there was any complacency it evaporated quickly after the atomic bomb attacks on *Hiroshima and Nagasaki in 1945. The vulnerability of cities could hardly have been demonstrated more starkly, ensuring that civil defence would feature prominently in the developing *Cold War.

As the Cold War took its course during the late 1940s and 1950s, so governments on both sides of the conflict saw that civil defence could provide some means, however meagre, to warn and protect their civilian populations from the worst excesses of war. Particularly in the democratic West, public demands for such protection could not go unacknowledged. But civil defence was also attractive for other, less passive and innocent reasons. By one view, a mature civil defence system could signal to the Cold War adversary that an attack could be survived and that there would still be a society and government (however primitive) which could retaliate, thereby improving the stability of mutually assured destruction (MAD). Some critics claimed, on the other hand, that a civil defence programme could be the precursor to nuclear aggression, or might at least convey that message to the adversary and thereby undermine the delicate mutual *deterrence relationship.

Interest in civil defence peaked during the Cold War's most tense episodes, such as the disagreement over Berlin and the *Cuban missile crisis in the early 1960s. Municipal shelters were constructed and secondary communications systems established in order to ensure that government and organization would be possible after an attack. In the West, the public was deluged with advice on building and equipping family-size air raid and fallout shelters, and on the immediate action to be taken in the event of a nuclear or *chemical attack. Much of this advice—paint windows white, soak curtains in borax, wear natural fibres, curl up on the ground during an attack—now seems darkly comical when set against the likely horrors and devastation of a nuclear strike on a city. Some ideas were seen as comically naïve even at the time. In the late 1950s British government officials considered that when a nuclear attack on London became likely, mothers and children should be evacuated while their able-bodied husbands and unmarried women would remain, no doubt 'just friends' to the end. There have been plenty who have refused to see the joke; critics of civil defence have argued that such advice amounted to an attempt by government to lull the public into a false sense of security and condition them into accepting the irrationality and immorality of a nuclear strategy.

The ending of the Cold War has resulted in diminished interest in, and budgeting for, civil defence in the traditional sense as a response to military attack. Civil defence (or 'disaster relief') now covers a much broader range of contingencies, including earthquakes, eruptions, floods, forest fires, terrorist attacks, major transport disasters, crises in energy supply, and the meltdown of nuclear reactors. Some analysts argued that the inability of computers to cope with the new millennium would produce a civil defence crisis of unprecedented scope and magnitude: happily they were wrong. PC

civil power, aid to Specifically (in British usage) Military Aid to the Civil Power (MACP) means armed assistance to the police when the latter are unable to cope with riot, organized crime, or terrorism. More generally, the term can be used to embrace Military Aid to Civil Authorities (MACA) which also includes Military Aid to Civil Ministries (MACM), or (from July 1998) Military Aid to (other) Government Departments (MAGD)—strike-breaking—and Military Aid to the Civil Community (MACC) which is unarmed assistance in the event of natural or humanitarian disaster.

Military forces have long been used as an aid to enforcing civil law and order. In medieval and early modern times the distinction between keeping the peace at home and armed forces' international roles was blurred. Landowners retained their own armed retinues, which might be used for law enforcement or in civil or foreign wars. In Britain the *posse comitatus*, the armed power of the county commanded by its sheriff, could be used to meet invasion or disorder, and the concept of the 'posse' crossed the Atlantic to emerge in hot pursuit of malefactors in the Wild West. A *doctrine of that name still governs MACP by the regular armed forces in the USA.

Following the creation of modern standing armed forces in the 17th century, but before the advent of modern police forces in the 19th, law enforcement remained a primary role of armies, whether regular or militia. The *Peterloo massacre of 1819 is an infamous example of MACP going wrong. Navies were also extensively employed against smugglers and pirates—a role that differed little, except in scale, from their use against other navies. Armed forces were often unhappy with the task. Servicemen could find themselves culpable in military law for failing to act decisively, but at risk from the criminal law—perhaps represented by a hostile jury—if they were judged to have overreacted. Effective action in support of the civil power often required a level of discipline which was not easy to attain. There were fears—sometimes all too justified—that conscript soldiers would side with the rioters rather than the army, one reason for the French right's traditional mistrust of short-service conscripts.

The concept of MACA, embracing MACP, MAGD, and MACC, is peculiar to Britain and the Commonwealth because most other countries have a paramilitary 'third force' or *gendarmerie to cover these eventualities. In France the Compagnies Républicains de Securité (CRS) are specially designed to deal with riots and those circumstances which fall awkwardly between the maintenance of law and order and war. In the former USSR and other East European countries the interior ministry had its own armed troops to deal with major riots and low-level insurrection. Armed forces proper may be constitutionally prevented from taking an internal security role. Thus, when the province of Chechnya attempted to break away from Russia in 1994 after its 1991 declaration of independence, it was the interior ministry's responsibility, not that of the armed forces. The Soviet interior ministry had entire mechanized divisions with *APCs, tanks, and artillery who were better trained than the armed forces for this type of work. However, these were not sufficient and the armed forces were brought in—as 'aid to the civil power'. In the USA, the National Guard performs a similar role, which assumed an unfortunate prominence during the protests against the *Vietnam war in the 1960s: the shooting of student protesters at Kent State University was the Peterloo of its day. The US Coastguard is responsible for maritime policing tasks for which the UK would have to call on the navy.

The distinction between MACP—involving armed troops to quell riot or terrorism—and MAGD—using troops to guarantee essential services during industrial unrest and strikes—is not always clear cut. In 1911 a group of armed East European terrorists was cornered in a house in Sidney Street, east London, and killed three of the policemen who had tried to arrest them. *Churchill, the Home Secretary, ordered in a detachment of Scots Guards. The besieged house caught fire and two terrorists were later found dead. This was a classic use of MACP. Later the same year there was a dock strike in Liverpool. A serious riot occurred outside Lime Street station. The local magistrate read the riot act and 2nd Battalion the Royal Warwickshire Regiment was turned out to clear the area. On 15 August a crowd tried to rescue five police vans' worth of convicted rioters being taken to the city's Walton prison. Its cavalry escort opened fire. The following days saw several *bayonet charges and on 17 August the navy cruiser HMS *Antrim* was ordered into the river Mersey, followed by a second cruiser soon after. Again, although the root cause was a strike, armed intervention by the military was MACP, not MAGD. Churchill was quite clear about the distinction: 'It is only when a trade dispute is accompanied by riot, intimidation or other violations of law or when a serious interruption is caused . . . to the supply of necessary commodities that the military can be called upon to support the police, and then their duty is to maintain the law, not to interfere in the matter of the dispute.'

The 1920 UK Emergency Powers Act clarified the confused legal position regarding the use of troops in industrial disputes. During the 1926 General Strike the military were kept in the background as far as possible. They were mainly used to protect food *convoys and to guard power stations and other key points. The General Strike was the last occasion in Britain that troops intervened in a strike to keep the peace. The separation of military assistance to the civil power to deal with civil disorder (MACP) from assistance to other government departments to maintain essential services (MACM, MAGD) dates from this period. The British army's role in Northern Ireland since 1969 is the classic example of MACP. The army is there to assist the Royal Ulster Constabulary and is ultimately in a subordinate position to it. In practice, members of the armed forces,

the police, and the other security services work closely together.

MACC procedures are fairly similar round the world. In the event of flood, earthquake, avalanche, or volcanic eruption the military usually respond as well as they can: they may be requested, or may volunteer their services. In the more complex security environment of the 21st century the role of military forces in these areas is likely to be enhanced, as part of a formula which has been called D3: Defence, Disaster, Development.   CDB

Clark, Gen Mark Wayne (1896–1984), ambitious commander of the US Fifth Army. Clark was a first-class planner and organizer of the forces under his command, but his defining characteristics were conceit and vanity. A soldier's son and *West Point graduate, he saw service during WW I as a battalion commander. He was appointed deputy to *Eisenhower for the TORCH landing in November 1943 and was appointed commander of Fifth Army in January 1944, to plan and execute the Allied invasion of Italy. He directed his army at *Salerno in September 1944 and then through the bitter battles of *Cassino and *Anzio, entering Rome on 4 June 1944, in defiance of orders from *Alexander first to encircle the German Tenth Army. His desire to grab headlines by entering Rome (before D-Day relegated the Italian theatre to a backwater) gave the Germans time to retreat to the Gothic Line and prolong the war in Italy, but in December 1944, he succeeded Alexander as C-in-C, Fifteenth Army Group and was promoted full general in March 1945.

After the war he commanded occupying forces in Austria and in May 1952 he was called to command UN forces in the later, stalemated stage of the *Korean war, which ended with the armistice of July 1953 which is now approaching its half-century. From 1954 to 1966 he was commandant of The Citadel, a military academy in Charleston, South Carolina. Even by the standards of his profession, his memoirs are remarkably self-serving.   APC-A

Clausewitz, Carl Philip Gottlieb von (1780–1831), Prussian general and theorist of war. His posthumously published work *On War* (1832) is the most important general treatment of its subject yet produced. Clausewitz entered the Prussian army as a 12-year-old in the spring of 1792, and was soon drawn into the *French Revolutionary wars that began a few weeks before. The following year he fought in the Rhineland and the Vosges, indecisive campaigns of position and manoeuvre typical of what would soon be called 'the Old Regime', but sufficient for the moment to bring peace to northern Germany. In 1801 he was admitted to the Institute for Young Officers in Berlin. There he came into contact with the Institute superintendent, Gerhard von *Scharnhorst, the seminal intellectual influence of Clausewitz's life. Scharnhorst was among the first to recognize that the French Revolution would transform the conduct of war, and that the social and political institutions it was creating would in turn create new military possibilities which the conservative monarchies of central Europe would be hard-pressed to match. Clausewitz's earliest surviving manuscripts date from his years at the Institute. They reveal a mind already engaged by questions of the broadest military and political significance.

Scharnhorst's insights were vindicated in October 1806, when the forces of Napoleonic France crushed those of Prussia at the twin battles of *Jena/Auerstadt. Clausewitz was present as adjunct to the king's nephew. In the retreat that followed he assumed command of part of the rearguard—the only time he commanded troops in combat—and eventually spent seven months interned in France. Upon his return he became involved in the movement to reform the Prussian state and army, in which Scharnhorst, again, was a key figure. In 1812, following Prussia's acceptance of a French alliance, which Clausewitz found politically and emotionally intolerable, he resigned his commission and, along with some 30 other Prussian officers, went to serve in Russia. There he witnessed the epic campaign that would break Napoleon's hold on Europe, a process to which Clausewitz made a modest personal contribution as negotiator, on the Russian side, of the Convention of Tauroggen, by which the Prussian contingent of the Grande Armée withdrew from the war.

As the war moved back into central Europe, Clausewitz worked to raise provincial militia and other irregular forces against the French, activity that was judged treasonous by some since, like the Convention of Tauroggen, it was done without the king's consent. He regained his Prussian commission in April 1814, and was COS to a corps during the *Waterloo campaign. In 1818 he became superintendent of the Allgemeine Kriegsschule (War College) in Berlin, a purely administrative post that did not require him to teach, but did afford time for historical and theoretical work. In 1831 he set his studies aside when the outbreak of civil war in Poland caused Prussia to mobilize part of its army. Clausewitz was chosen as COS of the forces deployed to observe the conflict. He died in Breslau of cholera a few months later.

On War was published by Clausewitz's wife the following year. It has always been judged a demanding text, in part because it was never subjected to the comprehensive revision Clausewitz knew it required. The book is thus marred by inconsistencies and omissions that further work would presumably have reduced. On the other hand, anyone familiar with the first chapter of book 1, the only part that Clausewitz declared finished to his satisfaction, may wonder whether, if the entire book had been brought to a comparable state of theoretical density and analytic precision, the results would be any easier to interpret. In the end, whatever difficulty *On War* poses for the reader does not arise

from its accidental shortcomings, but from its author's intellectual ambition.

On War is only secondarily a work of strategic theory, if by that one means a work intended to improve our ability to wage war successfully. Clausewitz had his own ideas about the best way to conduct military operations, and much of *On War* is devoted to strategic and tactical analyses that were certainly intended to appeal to the practical instincts of other professional soldiers. Yet his study of the history of war had also made him aware that his insights would some day lose whatever practical value they might possess for their own time. His ultimate goal was therefore to reach beyond such instrumental concerns, in order to grasp war as a total phenomenon, and understand its relationship to the social and political world of which it is a part. The result is a work whose most essential propositions are so encompassing that they might be easily mistaken for truisms: that the essence of war is violence, which knows no natural limit; that war 'does not consist in a single blow', but involves protracted interaction between opposing wills; that every attack loses impetus as it proceeds, until it reaches a culminating point where it no longer exceeds the strength of the defence that opposes it; that war is dominated by chaos and chance, which Clausewitz characterizes metaphorically as friction; that military genius can be cultivated, but not taught; that the only means in war is combat; that war is merely a continuation of policy; and so on. Theory at this level cannot serve as a guide to action, and is not intended to. *On War* is not about how to fight. It is about how to think about war.

For Clausewitz, one requirement for clear thinking was an unflinching respect for war's physical, psychological, and historical reality. He disdained bold strategizing that took no account of how difficult the simplest action becomes in the 'resistant medium' of war. He recognized the impact of fear, danger, confusion, and fatigue on men in battle, and wrote about them with unusual candour. He also rejected the idea that contemporary military methods represented a normative standard against which past practices could be judged. If wars in the past rarely achieved the scale and violence of Napoleon's greatest campaigns, it did not mean that previous generations had somehow failed to grasp a science whose true principles had now been revealed. For Clausewitz, the goal of theory was not to transpose reality into a system of abstractions, but to illuminate it with as little intellectual distortion as possible. No theory could be adequate that did not account for the full range of military experience captured in the historical record. That record suggested that war at all times possessed what Clausewitz called a 'dual nature'. Few wars were ever intended to overthrow the enemy completely. Most sought limited goals, and were accordingly fought by limited means.

Clausewitz's recognition of the theoretical significance of limited war was both a consequence and a source of his insight into war's political and instrumental character.

Clausewitz was scarcely the first to see that wars arise from political quarrels, or that they answer to purposes beyond themselves—that they are 'about' something. But he was the first to recognize the analytic power that these perceptions possessed when rigorously applied to all aspects of war.

For Clausewitz, the 'subordination' and 'permeation' of war by politics meant that there could be no 'purely military solution' to any military problem. It also exemplified a kind of complex tension that always attracted him. War, he famously proposed, was a 'remarkable trinity', whose essential elements—primordial violence and passion, the 'free play' of chance and creativity on the battlefield, and intelligent political purpose—could never be fixed in any arbitrary relationship. War's subordination to politics was logically necessary, and the norm in practice. Yet it was never perfect or absolute. War always threatened to escape its political restraints, and often did succeed in modifying the course of policy to some extent. The violence of war and the rationality of politics were thus theoretical opposites whose real existence was nevertheless marked not by mutual repulsion or exclusion, but by intense and continuous interaction.

Similarly dynamic conceptual structures—which in Clausewitz's day would have been described as 'dialectical'—pervade *On War* at every level. Violence and reason, genius and friction, attack and defence, risk and decisiveness, ends and means, fear and courage, victory and defeat—such dualities weave their way throughout the text like musical figures, echoing and recurring in unexpected registers that may sometimes startle or disconcert us, but which finally provide the work with an intellectual integrity that transcends its superficial incongruities. In a note written towards what proved to be the end of his life, Clausewitz openly feared that his work would be liable to 'endless misinterpretation' and 'much half-baked criticism', an apprehension that has been borne out more than once. Yet his ultimate ambition—'to write a book that would not be forgotten after two or three years'—would also be amply fulfilled. Few comparably demanding works in any field have so thoroughly withstood the test of time.   DM

Carl von Clausewitz: Historical and Political Writings, ed. Peter Paret and Daniel Moran (Princeton, 1992).

Aron, Raymond, *Clausewitz: Philosopher of War* (New York, 1983), trans. from German orig. (1980).

Paret, Peter, *Clausewitz and the State* (Oxford, 1976).

Clemenceau, Georges Eugène Benjamin (1841–1929).

'War. Nothing but war': thus did Georges Clemenceau accurately summarize his policy as wartime premier in his inaugural address to the French National Assembly on 20 November 1917. His contribution to French victory ensured his place in the pantheon of French national heroes. A virulent critic of the French failure to prosecute the war successfully, he came to power in the wake of the failed *Nivelle offensive, widespread French mutinies, and the most disastrous period of the war for the Allies, to set about shoring up national *morale. Intolerant of pacifists, seekers of a compromise peace, and shirkers, in 1918 he imposed the aggressive *Foch as supreme Allied commander above the more defensive commander of the French armies, *Pétain. His attitude and determination galvanized the French war effort, ensured victory, and secured a personal prestige unrivalled among his contemporaries, allowing him to speak for France in the peace negotiations. He pursued French demands for reparations and for arrangements which would guarantee security; though he did not go far enough to please *Foch and the nationalists, he obtained the best terms he could get.

Clemenceau had never been a stranger to conflict. Born in the religious and anti-Republican Vendée region he was an anticlerical Republican. As a medical student he demonstrated in 1862 against the Second Empire and received a short prison sentence. With his medical degree he emigrated to the USA in 1865 and returned with an American wife four years later whom he divorced in 1891. Mayor of Montmartre during the *Franco-Prussian war, he helped organize the National Guard to defend Paris. Under the early Third Republic he kept to the left of the Republican movement gaining a reputation for harrying moderate governments. Temporarily tainted by financial scandal associated with construction of the Panama Canal in 1893, he turned to journalism and more than restored his reputation during the *Dreyfus affair through a passionate defence of the innocent army captain. Returning to politics in 1902 as a senator he held office for the first time in March 1906 as interior minister and by October was combining it with the premiership, where he remained until July 1909 in one of the longest uninterrupted periods of any political leader of the Third Republic. In the two years prior to WW I he vigorously campaigned for France to increase her army and stand up to Germany. Despite his wartime record, he failed to secure the presidency of the Republic in 1920 and spent his nine remaining years travelling and writing. But he remained affectionately remembered as 'Père-la-victoire' (Father Victory).   JFVK

Duroselle, J.-B., *Clemenceau* (Paris, 1988).

Watson, David R., *Georges Clemenceau: A Political Biography* (London, 1974).

Clive, Robert, 1st Baron Clive of Plassey (1725–74).

Clive conquered and organized Bengal for the East India Company (EIC). He first went to Madras as a clerk in 1743 and by 1749 had won the lucrative appointment of military commissary. In 1751 he took Arcot from Chanda Sahib, an ally of the French, with a mixed force of about 500 and then withstood a 53-day siege. He returned to England, stood unsuccessfully for parliament, and was posted back to Madras as a lieutenant colonel in charge of regular army troops in 1755. He provoked the Mughal emperor's viceroy Suraj-ud-Dowlah to attack him at *Plassey on 23 June 1757, a battle he won against great odds lessened by judicious subversion, and made himself the de facto ruler of Bengal. His first administration was marked by the virtual plundering of the province, not chiefly his doing, and he returned to Britain in 1760 to mixed reviews. On one hand he was made a peer; on the other EIC officials, stooges he had bypassed, whipped up envy against the upstart 'Nabob'. During his second administration (1764–7), he did much to reform as well as consolidate EIC government of Bengal. On return to England, powerful enemies including Pitt the Elder tried to ruin him and partisan parliamentary committees uncovered a level of corruption in the administration of the EIC that made them drool with envy. Clive defended himself (1773) with the immortal words 'I stand astonished at my own moderation' and was eventually judged to have performed 'great and meritorious service'. A lifelong sufferer from extreme mood swings, he took his own life, having laid the foundation for the second British empire just as the first was about to be lost.   HEB

clubs. See PERCUSSION WEAPONS.

coast defence has generally been the primary responsibility of navies, and fixed defence by land forces only a last resort. The debate over the merits of these two approaches has been acrimonious. The 'wooden walls' of Athens defeated the Persian fleet at *Salamis and the battles of Sluys in 1339, the defeat of the *Spanish Armada in 1588, and the battle of *Britain in 1940 were all battles to defend England's coast. The defence of coastal towns and installations has been a task for artillery for 500 years, and the characteristics of the gun have shaped the design of the fort. Geoffrey Parker has argued that such gun-forts were the foundation of the great European trading empires. Coastal defences were generally constructed to defend major cities, naval bases, shipping lanes, and vulnerable trade nodes, Gibraltar being a good example of all these. Coastal fortifications do not always face the sea. 'Palmerston's Follies', such as Fort Nelson above the British naval base of Portsmouth, face inland against a possible enemy landing further down the coast and attacking from the rear.

The advent of armoured warships at the end of the 19th century complicated the problems for coastal artillery, but the introduction of *breech-loading guns at about the same time greatly simplified coastal defence, since the detachment no longer needed access to the muzzle. A variety of complex mountings became possible. The casemate mounted a gun on a pivot which could be traversed to fire through an embrasure. In the case of *mortars, embrasures were at a high angle, permitting fire from a concealed position. The barbette mounted the gun on a pivot so that it

could fire over a parapet. In the late 1860s Alexander Moncrieff developed a 'disappearing gun' system which was adopted in varying forms around the world. This allowed the gun to be lowered for loading, rising only briefly to fire. The USA produced disappearing carriages for 16 inch guns. By the end of the 19th century, coastal forts had become increasingly invisible, with ammunition and detachments living underground along with concealed, retractable guns. Guns can also be mounted in cupolas offering the protection of an armoured dome. Many of the most impressive German fortifications of the Atlantic wall resembled armoured warship turrets set in concrete emplacements. Coastal defence artillery often pioneered developments in artillery such as survey, range-finding, breech-loading recoil systems, and the techniques of indirect fire. By the 1950s coastal fortifications had largely disappeared, being judged too vulnerable to missile attack. The Swedes still maintain formidable coastal defences and China and North Korea have developed specialized coastal defence missiles.
                                                                  JBAB

Mallory, K., and Ottar, A., *Walls of War: Military Architecture of Two World Wars* (London, 1973).
Paloczi-Horvath, G., *Coast Defence Ships and Coastal Defence since 1860* (London, 1996).
Parker, G., *The Military Revolution, Military Innovation and the Rise of the West 1500–1800* (Cambridge, 1988).
Rogers C. J. (ed.), *The Military Revolution Debate* (Oxford, 1995).
Rolf, R., and Saal, P., *Fortress Europe* (Shrewsbury, 1988).

Coehoorn, Baron Menno van (1641–1704). Born into a Dutch army family in Friesland, Coehoorn was to become one of the most influential military engineers of his age. He studied mathematics and fortification at the academy of Franeker and entered the army in 1657.

In 1674 he gave his name to a trench mortar, to be used at closer range than previous models. His great work, *The New Method of Fortification*, was printed in 1685 and advocated the simplification of *fortification design to the most geometrically elegant plan. He also made use of the high water table in the Netherlands, most of his works featuring wet ditches. Coehoorn also recommended an aggressive defence to upset the besiegers in their task. In siege operations Coehoorn advocated concentrated fire and storming rather than protracted *bombardment and this proved very successful at the sieges of Kaiserwörth and Bonn in 1689, during the *League of Augsburg war.

At *Namur in 1692, Coehoorn found himself besieged by his great contemporary and rival *Vauban. He was wounded by a bomb at the height of the siege and was forced to *capitulate. There followed a pointed exchange between the two men, where Coehoorn boasted that he had forced the Frenchman to change the sites of his batteries seven times. Coehoorn then retook the strengthened and now supposedly impregnable fortress in 1695, after a fierce bombardment and a costly storming by Cutts's English infantry; a piqued Vauban commented that the effort had been too crude by half.

Coehoorn became engineer-general of fortifications in 1695, working on the modernization of Bergen op Zoom and other fortresses to his 'new method'. During the War of the *Spanish Succession he proposed a bold bypassing drive into Brabant, but the Allies decided to winkle the French out of the Rhine and Maas forts one by one in the old style. He served as Chief Engineer to *Marlborough at the siege of Venlo in 1702, and after very careful preparations stormed the city after a short but very violent cannonade. This was a major victory for, as *Louis XIV admitted, Venlo was the key to Gelders and the Rhine fortresses, vital for the defence of France.

Coehoorn died of natural causes in 1704, at the height of the war. In Amsterdam, where he was regarded as something of a lucky charm, stock exchange prices tumbled. He was sorely missed in the field, *Eugène of Savoy saying of him, 'I know that there can be no comparison between his ability and that of the horrible little men we have with us now.'   TM

COIN. See COUNTER-INSURGENCY.

Cold War So named because vast resources were poured into a bitter 'bi-polar' ideological struggle between the West, led by the USA, and the East, led by the USSR, which never quite led to open or 'hot' hostilities between the principals. *Churchill coined or at least popularized the term 'iron curtain' in a speech at Westminster College, Fulton, Missouri, on 5 March 1946, but before that it was obvious that the two main victors of WW II were heading for confrontation. The two occasions when the war nearly got hot were both Soviet provocations, their 1948 *blockade countered by the *Berlin airlift and the *Cuban missile crisis of 1962 when a US blockade forced them to take secretly introduced IRBMs (Intermediate Range Ballistic Weapons) out of Cuba.

The Cold War might be said to have been declared in 1949, when the USSR exploded its first atomic bomb, congealing into *NATO, SEATO (South-East Asia Treaty Organisation), and other organizations, perceived as passive 'containment' by the USA and her allies and as hostile 'encirclement' by the USSR and her satellites. The latter formed the *Warsaw Pact in 1955, countering overwhelming US nuclear superiority with massive conventional forces. Although war never did break out in Europe, there were a number of 'proxy' conflicts elsewhere, in the *Korean, *Vietnam, and *Arab–Israeli wars, which both sides used to test their weaponry and each other's resolve.

The world communist threat was perceived as monolithic until Pres Nixon visited China in the early 1970s, but by that time the Soviets had achieved parity in both nuclear warheads and delivery systems, and a protracted effort to halt further attempts to achieve unilateral advantage was known as détente. Pres Reagan reversed this policy in the early 1980s and in terms of investment in military equipment, the Cold War probably peaked in about 1985, having bankrupted the Soviet system. From the mid-1980s, Mikhail Gorbachev's perestroika and glasnost tried to make the best of a bad job, but the floodgates burst and the fall of the Berlin wall in 1989 is regarded as the end of the Cold War.

The Warsaw Pact and the USSR broke up, leaving the successor state Russia to thrash about in search of a new purpose, and a triumphant NATO to develop interventionist policies it would never have dared to pursue previously. This has confirmed fears of 'encirclement' in Russia and it is not unimaginable that this could evolve into a new Cold War.   CDB

Collins, Michael (1890–1922), the outstanding leader on the republican side in the *Anglo-Irish war. The son of a west Cork farmer, his formative experience was the decade he spent in London (1906–16) as a clerical worker. It was there, paradoxically, that he discovered the Irish language, joined the Gaelic Athletic Association, and was sworn into the underground Irish Republican Brotherhood. Returning to Ireland in 1916, he joined the Irish Volunteers. He fought in the Dublin General Post Office throughout the *Easter rising, but took a dim view of its military conduct. Leading the revival of the Sinn Fein-Volunteer movement after his release from internment, he mixed political and military strategies. The Volunteers became a local *guerrilla force, and many of its officers fought elections on the Sinn Fein platform. After Sinn Fein's 1918 election victory he became Minister of Finance in the underground government, and Director of Intelligence in the Volunteers (*IRA). In partnership with Richard Mulcahy, the COS, he effectively ran the IRA, as far as an essentially local guerrilla force could be centrally controlled. He had an instinctive grasp of the strengths and limitations of this form of war. For two years Collins operated an intelligence system that neutralized British power in Dublin, though the pressure on him steadily mounted. After the Truce in July 1921 he joined the Irish delegation to negotiate the Anglo-Irish Treaty (December 1921). His argument that this was the best settlement that Eire could achieve was rejected by many republicans, whose defiance of the provisional government (of which Collins became the chairman) precipitated the Irish civil war in June 1922. Collins struggled to stop the IRA from splitting, but acted vigorously once he decided that the anti-Treaty 'irregulars' were irreconcilable. He borrowed British artillery to bombard the anti-Treaty force in the Four Courts in Dublin, and energetically built up a new army to crush the republicans. As C-in-C he continued to seek negotiations with his former comrades. It was while he was trying to make contact with the Irregular commander, Liam

Lynch, that he was ambushed and killed in west Cork on 22 August 1922. CT

....

colours, banners, and standards (including eagles) generally combine both practical and symbolic purposes. They indicate the location and *IFF of a particular indiviual or unit, and at the same time represent the prestige and spirit of the group to which they relate. Capturing an enemy standard is therefore not only a tactical but a psychological gain, and the display of such trophies is clear evidence of victory and courage. Conversely, the loss of a standard is considered a disgrace, so that standard-bearers and their escorts were regarded as men of the greatest *honour and bravery, expected to *sacrifice their lives in defence of their standards when necessary, and to set an example of valour at all times. *Caesar records the standard-bearer of X Legion in the Roman invasion of Britain (55 BC) who, seeing his comrades reluctant to disembark, jumped into the surf and obliged them to follow him or lose their standard. The earliest standards took the form of simple poles carrying representations of totemic animals, religious symbols, or similar icons, a feature that continues in military heraldry to the present day. Textile banners, emblazoned with pictorial devices, were generally carried slung from a crossbar, for ease of recognition. In the medieval period, European armies gradually adopted the practice of flying them from a staff or lance, a form more easily managed by the horsemen who had come to dominate the battlefield. Central Asian riders mostly did without such flags, and preferred to use other markers, such as horsetails, the *Mongol nine yak-tail standard being the most famous—and fearsome.

With the regimentation of western armies from the 16th century onwards, military flags were codified into various types, each with their own special name. An *ensign* was the national flag flown (technically 'worn') by a warship. The same word was also used as the rank-title of the junior subalterns, whose duty was to carry the *colours*. These, the flags of the infantry, originally measured at least 6 feet (1.8 metres) square, so that they could be seen and recognized above the *smoke of musket and cannon fire. At first allotted on a scale of one per company, their number had been reduced by the beginning of the 18th century to one or two per regiment. In the cavalry, smaller flags—rectangular standards, or swallow-tailed guidons—were used, and were in the same way reduced in numbers from one per squadron to one per regiment in response to changing tactical requirements. In the British army, standards were allotted only to household cavalry and regiments of horse (later converted to dragoon guards). *Dragoons carried guidons. Light *dragoons, *hussars, and *lancers ceased to carry guidons in 1834 and resumed their use in 1959. The Royal Tank Regiment adopted regimental standards of the heavy cavalry type in 1960. British cavalry standards and guidons are made of crimson silk embroidered with the appropriate regimental *badges and insignia and *battle honours. In the British infantry of the line, each battalion carries a royal colour (the Union flag with regimental differences) and a regimental colour (of the same colour as the regiment's full-dress facings, with the regimental badge and honours). In the US army, the regulations of 1861 ordered that each regiment of infantry or artillery should carry two colours, of which one was to be the national flag and the other the arms of the USA with the name of the regiment. For the cavalry, the same regulations prescribed one standard per regiment, and one guidon per company. By the end of the 19th century, regimental standards and colours were driven from the battlefield by the increasing range and accuracy of small-arms fire. Ornate, silken regimental colours, invested with a mystical or spiritual quality, were restricted to ceremonial and parade occasions. Their original functions were taken over by flags of various types outside formation HQs, over parade squares, on staff cars, etc. Ordinary bunting flags were also used in the symbolic role. Two of the most potent images of WW II were those of the US Marines raising the Stars and Stripes over the Japanese island of *Iwo Jima, and a Soviet soldier placing the Red Flag over the German Reichstag in Berlin. Similarly, in the *Falklands war of 1982, the image of a Royal Marine flying a Union Flag from his backpack radio antenna on the advance to recover Port Stanley received wide international coverage.

Eagles featured on the standards of Babylonian, Persian, Ptolemaic, and Seleucid armies. They were adopted by the Romans, and under the system introduced by *Marius became the characteristic standard of the legion, with different devices being used for those of cohorts and centuries. In 1804, Napoleon revived the eagle standard, copied from a Roman original, including the representation of Jove's thunderbolt held in the eagle's talons. The original scale of issue, one per infantry battalion or cavalry squadron, was later reduced to one per regiment. The spirit of the standard was deemed to lie in the eagle, not the flag carried on the same staff. Napoleonic eagles were revived in the army of the Second Empire and carried until its defeat in the *Franco-Prussian war. The German, Austrian, and Russian empires all included a double-headed eagle in their official arms. A single-headed eagle, grasping a swastika, was carried on German flags and standards between 1933 and 1945. The American eagle, part of the arms of the USA, is carried on the regimental colours of the US army. The RAF, whose badge is a soaring eagle, carries this device on its standards (awarded to all units after a continuous existence of 25 years) and colours (awarded to higher formations), with eagles carried on the finials of the latter. TAH

Davis, Brian Leigh, *Flags and Standards of the Third Reich* (London, 1975).

Ketcher, Philip, *Flags of the American Civil War* (London, 1993).

Johnson, Stanley C., *The Flags of our Fighting Army* (London, 1918).

Milne, Samuel, *The Standards and Colours of the Army* (London, 1893).

Wise, Terence, *Flags of the Napoleonic Wars* (London, 1978).

column and line One of the age-old problems of tactics and battlefield handling is the tension between the need for shock action and the requirement to deliver effective fire at a distance. This is not entirely a tactical problem: the tendency of men in combat to bunch up is something that requires rigorous training to overcome and before the advent of accurate rifle fire, it was an important factor to be weighed. Various military theorists and practitioners have wrestled with these conflicting exigencies of battle and proposed different solutions of varying effectiveness. During the Renaissance, the rediscovery of ancient military texts encouraged experimentation with different formations and this, coupled with the rise of professional troops who could be trained in various manoeuvres, meant that enterprising commanders, freed from the bonds of *feudal allegiance, could give rein to their pet tactical theories.

Initially it was the shock action of the *Swiss, and later the Spanish pike columns that was to prove decisive in battle, and although the Swiss system of an assault at a fast jogging pace in three massive columns was to come drastically unstuck at Bicocca in 1522 and at Marignano in 1515, the judicious admixture of supporting *musketeers and arquebusiers to the pike column by the Spanish was to result in the famous *tercio formation that dominated European battlefields for over a century.

It was *Maurice of Nassau and later *Gustavus Adolphus who were to find the key to defeating the tercio. Taking inspiration from ancient Roman writers, Maurice devised a smaller handier and thinner formation—the 'Dutch Brigade'—that emphasized firepower and proved far more manoeuvrable in the field. However, it is important to note that the Dutch and Swedish brigade was not universally successful against the tercio, it required a high degree of training to become fully effective, and it was not until the perfection of *flintlock firearms that were reliable, and the discontinuation of the pike in the late 17th century, that a *military revolution can really be said to have come of age.

Yet still the drill and *discipline required to defeat the enemy by firepower, and especially their cavalry, who could bowl over a thin line of troops by speed and shock alone, necessitated rigorous and extensive training. This training was possible for small militarized states like Brandenburg-Prussia, but given the large numbers required to defend a country like France, not all troops received the necessary instruction, and consequently the French infantry performed indifferently in the Wars of the *Spanish Succession and *Austrian Succession. This led a generation of French military theorists such as Maurice de *Saxe and the Chevalier de Folard to seek to recapture the offensive spirit that they felt had been lost since the glory days of *Louis XIV, by use of the infantry attack column. Although the French infantry did fare badly on the whole in the *Seven Years War, some notable successes such as Hastenbeck in 1757 were won by using the column in offence in defiance of the prevailing orthodoxy. The lesson was not lost on French military commentators and writers, and *Guibert began to formulate a theory of manoeuvre combining the offensive power of the infantry attack column with the use of close range musketry, in order to break the opposing line.

It was this system that was incorporated into the famous *règlement* of 1791 that became the standard French infantry manual until 1830. At first the ill-trained recruits of the *French Revolutionary armies found the column an expedient method of manoeuvre and attack, especially when accompanied by hordes of *tirailleurs who would snipe at enemy officers and *NCOs from cover. Several victories were won by the attack in column, but it is important to note that it was not universally successful, and against a steady enemy it could easily founder, as very few of the troops in the column could bring their muskets to bear on the enemy. In any event, the drill book of 1791 called for the approach march to be made in column of divisions, two companies wide, and for a rapid shaking out into line to deliver two or three crashing volleys before charging home with the *bayonet. Evidently, this required superb discipline and not a small amount of fancy footwork on the part of the *fantassins*. Many commanders either could not trust their troops to perform the complex evolutions required or failed to locate the enemy in time to deploy. In the *Napoleonic wars, the classic test of column versus line came at Maida in 1806, and this was to establish the pattern for the bulk of the infantry combats of the *Peninsular war, where the fire discipline of the British infantry in line was to prove decisive in many an encounter.

With the introduction of the percussion cap in 1822, and the conical *Minié rifle-bullet in 1849, the infantry attack column was doomed, as the Russians found out to their cost in the *Crimean war. By the time of the *Franco-Prussian war, infantry began to adopt an attack in an extended skirmishing line, often firing from a prone position with breech-loading rifles, and making extensive use of *field fortifications when in defence. The line had triumphed over the column for good.   TM

commando A word of Portuguese origin, first used in the 19th century to describe the military system of the two Boer republics, the Transvaal and the Orange Free State. To 'go on commando' was a legal requirement for all men to furnish themselves when required for military service, equipped with horse, rifle, ammunition, and food for eight days. Officers were elected, and the whole system was very informal. The tactics of small parties of Boers during particularly the *guerrilla phase of the Second *Boer War made the term commando synonymous in British eyes with elusive and enterprising raiders. It has become widely used in the 20th century, particularly in Africa, to describe any enterprising irregular force, sometimes with terrorist overtones.

The term commando was revived by the British army in June 1940, with the co-operation of the Royal Navy and Royal Marines, for specially selected and trained amphibious forces to conduct raids on Nazi-occupied Europe. In July the Commandos were officially designated Special Service troops, with the unfortunate initials 'SS', a designation abandoned in October 1944. They also adopted a distinctive dark green beret, which remains their symbol. A Commando (as well as meaning the individual soldier) became the equivalent of a light battalion, with about 400 men. The Commandos were particularly championed by Winston *Churchill, who had first-hand experience of the Boers.

The Royal Navy began to form its own Commandos from the Royal Marines in 1942 for the *Dieppe raid. They also inspired other raiding forces, particularly the US Rangers. By 1944 the British army had twelve Commandos, including Number 10 (Inter-Allied) Commando with troops of many European nationalities, including anti-Nazi Germans, and Number 14 (Arctic) Commando. The Royal Navy had eight Royal Marine Commandos. Of these, 1st and 4th Commando Brigades served in Europe, 2nd Commando Brigade in the Mediterranean and the Aegean, and 3rd Commando Brigade in the Far East.

After WW II the army Commandos were disbanded, and in 1946 the Royal Marines adopted the Commando role exclusively, with 3rd Royal Marine Commando Brigade (of three Commandos plus supporting troops from the army) gradually becoming Britain's sole amphibious force. Based at Hong Kong 1946–61 and at Singapore 1961–71 before returning to Britain, their specialized training and role outside Europe led to the Commandos taking part in most of the British military operations of this period, in particular the *Korean war, the *Suez campaign, and the *Falklands war.   SDB

Moulton, J. L., *The Royal Marines* (London, 1977).
Packenham, Thomas, *The Boer War* (London, 1979).
Saunders, Hilary St George, *The Green Beret* (London, 1949).

commissariat (see also SUTLER). As the name suggests, this was a military office dating from Roman times responsible for food supplies. The alternative (at least when away from home depots) is foraging, developed to a fine art form by French troops during the *French Revolutionary and *Napoleonic wars. But letting troops scatter over the countryside in search of food has a number of drawbacks, among them vulnerability to, for example, *guerrilla reprisals and increased opportunity to desert. In general, *discipline and unit cohesion require a regular and dependable supply of food by the army itself.

In some armies the commissariat is synonymous with *QM, but others have divided the duty of supplying food to the troops between the two offices. In the *American civil war, for example, Confederate commissaries were primarily responsible for the procurement of food from the agricultural regions under Southern control and arranging its transportation to the armies in the field. It was only at this point that the QM would take over and oversee the distribution process. But more typically the role of the latter has been to supply troops with all manner of goods, including weapons, munitions, clothing, footwear, tents, and a plethora of minor items. By contrast, the commissary officer has been responsible for the provision of *rations alone.

This makes the commissariat the most suspect and vilified department of any armed force, at any time and any place in history, with some justification. In the British armed forces, the commissary was also entrusted with the administration of government funds in the field (the 'chest'), far from supervision and where the opportunities for peculation could be irresistible. The fortune amassed by *Clive was already significant after a mere two years administering the commissariat in Madras, and many another has enriched himself similarly.

This said, the functions for which a commissariat is responsible are vital. The saying 'an army marches on its stomach' is attributed to Napoleon on St Helena—perhaps after having had time to consider how lack of attention to this very fact lost him armies in Spain and Russia. In Elizabethan times, the stomach was considered the fount of courage, as the phrase 'not to have the stomach' for some challenge lives on to remind us. The importance of food supplies to an army on campaign cannot be overestimated, and failure by the commissariat can imperil operations more than any other factor. To return to the Confederate example, the incompetence and suspect honesty of commissary officers was noted by many during and after the conflict as a significant contributory cause in the defeat of the rebellion.

Yet the commissary officer's lot is not a happy one. He might buy good quality food, only to have it spoil in warehouses or sent to the wrong destination, and whatever he does troops will grumble, as they always have and always will. A number of mutinies have been precipitated by grievances over food and commissaries beaten up or killed. Generally looked down on by other officers and more drably uniformed, few have had the opportunity to show their worth in combat. Assistant Commissary Dalton VC, of Rorke's Drift fame, stands like a proud lighthouse above the sea of muttering and innuendo that in general obscures the vital work done by those of his calling throughout the history of men at war.   AH

commission A document, generally signed by the head of state, denoting appointment to the *rank of officer in the armed forces. Such an appointment is usually to the lowest rank in the officer corps, for example, second lieutenant in the army, or sub-lieutenant in the navy. Commissions were once granted for each successive officer rank, and possession of his commission (which traditionally folded for ease of carriage) was a visible symbol of an officer's authority.

In modern armed forces a commission is awarded on the completion of a course of instruction at a specialist academy, but in ancient and medieval times officers were appointed from among their entourage by the rulers, absolute loyalty often being clearly more desirable than military ability. The same principle applied for a ruling class, and well into the 19th century the practice of purchasing commissions was defended on the grounds that it guaranteed an officer corps from the right social background: men with 'a stake in the country', who would not pose a threat to the state.   AH/RH

commission of array Beginning in Edward I's reign the normal method of recruiting infantry troops was to set up commissions of array, although commissioners had been used earlier to ensure that men were properly provided with military equipment. All able-bodied men were obliged under the terms of the Statute of Winchester of 1285 to possess military equipment appropriate to their status. The commissioners, normally men with military experience, were appointed to recruit specified numbers of men for individual campaigns. In practice, the task of selecting men was usually left to local communities. Those recruited were then organized into units of 20 and 100. By Edward II's reign the system was on occasion used to recruit horse as well as foot. Under *Edward III commissions of array became less important, for indentures, or contracts drawn up between the crown and the magnates, became the normal means of recruiting both *archers and cavalry. Nevertheless, commissions of array continued to be used throughout the Middle Ages and beyond. The practice was of considerable value to the crown during the Wars of the *Roses, and was revived in the 17th century under Charles I during the *British civil wars.   MCP

Powicke, M. R., *Military Obligation in Medieval England* (Oxford, 1962).

Committee of Imperial Defence The permanent establishment of the Committee of Imperial Defence (CID), a decade before the outbreak of WW I, was a turning point in the development of defence management in Britain. The creation of the CID was, in part, symptomatic of the general tendency towards closer co-ordination in a governmental system which had become increasingly complex in the late 19th century. The antecedents of the CID were the Colonial Defence Committee of 1878, the Hartington Commission of 1890, and the naval and military com-

mittee of the cabinet created by Salisbury in the same year. But the CID is best seen as a response to Britain's political, diplomatic, and military failings in the Second *Boer War. In December 1902 it was decided to revive the lapsed 1890 committee. This committee—still temporary and relatively understaffed—now comprised the PM, the Lord President, the first Lord of the Admiralty, the Secretary of State for War, the C-in-C, the First Sea Lord, and the heads of naval and military intelligence. In early 1904, soon after the publication of the damning *Report of His Majesty's Commissioners on the War in South Africa*, the *War Office (Reconstitution) Committee (the 'Esher Committee') recommended, *inter alia*, a permanent place for an expanded CID in the system of government, and that the CID should be given its own secretariat (previously it had 'borrowed' clerks from the Foreign Office). The new CID would still have little executive authority although the PM was ex officio chairman and would have an expanded membership to include foreign, colonial, and treasury ministers.

In the decade which followed, the CID developed an impressive system of subcommittees, a system which later served as a model for the organization of cabinet business and procedure. The CID also dealt with a broad range of substantive issues, including aerial navigation, the transport overseas of reinforcements in time of war, the treatment of aliens, press and postal *censorship, trading with the enemy, and the distribution of food supplies during war. Although the individual services still did the detailed planning for the movement of six divisions to northern Europe, the CID covered issues like shipping and insurance. It also prepared a Defence of the Realm Act for emergency legislation in time of war. The CID's war plans were drawn up in a War Book, which was revised periodically and put into operation in summer 1914.

Soon after the outbreak of war, Asquith permitted the CID to lapse and a War Council was formed from the cabinet, served by the CID secretariat. Thus constituted, the War Council was the CID writ large, albeit with more executive authority. In 1916 *Lloyd George established the War Cabinet, to be served by the former War Council (CID) secretariat. The secretary to the CID now served as secretary to the cabinet, responsible for forging links between the cabinet, the Service Departments, the Treasury, the Foreign Office, and other relevant departments. Full sessions of the CID were resumed in 1922. The committee turned its attention to the problem of co-ordinating supply to the three Service Departments. In 1924 the Principal Supply Officers' Committee was established, under the chairmanship of the President of the Board of Trade. The CID had thus taken the first steps towards an efficient, co-ordinated government procurement and supply system, preparing the ground for the creation of the Ministry of Supply in 1939 and its subsequent expansion.

The second major achievement of the relaunched CID was the creation, in 1924, of a Chiefs of Staff Committee as a subcommittee of the CID. The need for professional military co-ordination had been seen at several points during WW I, particularly in the Dardanelles campaign. The advent of an independent RAF underlined the case for more formal co-ordination. In 1922 the vulnerability of the British garrison at Chanak (now Cannakale) in the Dardanelles to possible Turkish aggression provided still more evidence of political and military-operational incoherence. The result was a CID review of national and imperial defence which in turn led to the creation of a committee comprising the three Chiefs of Staff, vested with 'individual and collective responsibility for advising on defence policy as a whole'. From 1927 the Chiefs of Staff were supported by a Joint Planning Committee, comprising the three Directors of Plans, and from 1936 by a Joint Intelligence Committee (the three Directors of Intelligence and a representative from the Foreign Office).

In the early 1930s the CID was preoccupied with forging cross-party policy for the World Disarmament (see ARMS CONTROL AND DISARMAMENT) Conference in Geneva. The 'Three-Party Committee' of the CID advised the British delegation until the collapse of the Conference in 1935. Thereafter, the CID began to address the problem of rapid rearmament. Responding to demands for a more co-ordinated approach to defence planning and military supply to the three Services, preferably in the form of an independent Ministry of Defence, and to claims that an overburdened PM could not chair the CID effectively, the Baldwin government announced the creation in 1936 of a new Minister for the Co-ordination of Defence. The new minister, with no department of his own, continued to work through the CID secretariat. This arrangement lasted until 1940 when the new PM *Churchill also took charge of the defence portfolio, and the functions of the CID were again taken over by the War Cabinet for the duration of the war. In 1946 the suspension of the CID was made permanent and a separate Ministry of Defence was established, initially alongside the three service ministries.   PC

Commonwealth War Graves Commission This is responsible for commemoration of those who died in the two world wars while serving with imperial, now Commonwealth, forces. Its duties are to mark and maintain the graves of the honoured dead, to build and maintain *memorials to those whose graves are unknown, and to keep records and registers. The cost is shared by the partner governments, those of Australia, Britain, Canada, India, New Zealand, and South Africa, in proportions based on the numbers of their graves.

The Commission's founder, Fabian Ware, arrived in France in September 1914 to command a British *Red Cross unit. He noted there was no organization in place to record the final resting places of casualties and became concerned that graves would be lost for ever, so his unit assumed responsibility to register and care for all the graves they could find. By 1915 Ware's unit was given official recognition by the *War Office, becoming the Graves Registration Commission. As the war progressed, Ware became convinced of the need for an official organization representing the imperial nature of the war effort, the equality of treatment due to the dead, and the permanence of graves or memorials. With the support of the Prince of Wales (the future Edward VIII), Ware submitted a memorandum to the Imperial War Conference in 1917. It was unanimously approved and the Imperial War Graves Commission was established by Royal Charter on 21 May 1917.

Since that date, the Commission has been working to sustain the commemoration of the war dead, which after WW II numbered 1.7 million, in cemeteries and on memorials in some 150 countries. The Commission's work is based upon fundamental principles established in 1920: that each of the dead should be commemorated individually by name either on the headstone on the grave or by an inscription on a memorial; that the headstones and memorials should be permanent; that the headstones should be uniform; that there should be no distinction made on account of military or civil rank, race, or creed.

In 1918 the Commission began a mammoth task of construction that would not be complete until 1938. The provision of over 587,000 headstones was perhaps the greatest challenge. Climate permitting, the headstones stand in narrow borders, where roses and small perennials grow, in a setting of lawn, trees, and shrubs. Two monuments are common to the cemeteries: the Cross of Sacrifice, representing the faith of the majority, set usually upon an octagonal base and bearing a bronze sword upon its shaft; and the Stone of Remembrance, representing those of all faiths and none, upon which are carved the words from Ecclesiastes: 'Their Name Liveth For Evermore'. Those who have no known grave were commemorated on memorials ranging from small tablets bearing a few names to great monuments bearing many thousands, such as the Menin Gate Memorial.

When war once more engulfed the world in 1939, the Commission took on the challenge of construction work to commemorate the 600,000 Commonwealth dead of the latest conflict. By 1960 the major structural work that the Commission maintains today was in place and the organization's name was changed from 'Imperial' to 'Commonwealth War Graves Commission'.

For Commission purposes, the dates between which a casualty is considered for war grave treatment are from 4 August 1914 to 31 August 1921 and 3 September 1939 to 31 December 1947. In addition, over 66,000 civilian deaths caused by enemy action during WW II are commemorated in a roll of *honour. The comprehensive records maintained by the Commission make it possible to identify precisely where any individual is commemorated. The Commission has offered this service to the public since the 1920s but the application of information technology to the records has further enhanced public access. Specialized services, such as searches on family name, regiment, or home town as criteria, are now provided, while the Commission has created truly international and immediate public access to its records on commemoration by making them available on a search by surname basis at its web site: www.cwgc.org.

Throughout the past 80 years, the Commission, in the interests of maintaining the highest standards appropriate to those commemorated, has met the challenges of construction, maintenance, and innovation, and the work continues. The Commission will continue to pay the debt of honour due to the 1.7 million Commonwealth men and women who died for their countries and for the great causes that called for their supreme sacrifice. (See also CEMETERIES, MILITARY.)   PJF

Edwin Gibson, T. A., & Kingsley Ward, G., *Courage Remembered* (London, 1989).

Commune, Paris (1871). The Commune was the revolutionary government that ruled Paris from 27 March to 28 May 1871, although the name is commonly applied to the whole revolutionary episode and the ensuing civil war. The largest of 19th-century urban revolts, it was a unique military episode too, pitching a militia, the National Guard (known as 'Fédérés'), against the French regular army. The Fédérés numbered on paper up to 80,000, armed with modern rifles, numerous artillery pieces, armoured trains, and gunboats. Their principal commanders were Gustave-Paul Cluseret, a revolutionary soldier of fortune, and Louis Rossel, a young officer; they were aided by several former Polish and French army officers, notably Jaroslav Dombrowski. Junior officers were elected by the men. The regular army, eventually numbering 130,000, was commanded by Marshal *MacMahon, veteran of the French conquest of *Algeria, the *Crimean war, and the *Italian campaign (1859) and the ill-starred commander at *Sedan.

Insurrection began on 18 March, when regular troops tried to seize artillery in the possession of the National Guard at Montmartre and other working-class districts. The government retreated to Versailles, south-west of the city—hence the name 'Versaillais' for the counter-revolutionary side. A Commune council was elected on 26 March. Skirmishes broke out in the western suburbs on 2 April, provoking a sizeable but unorganized sortie against Versailles on 3 April, which failed well short of its objective. Thereafter, the Fédérés remained on the defensive behind the city ramparts and forts built in the 1840s. The Versaillais began a formal siege on 11 April, planned by engineer general Séré de Rivière, later architect of France's eastern fortifications. On 9 May, Fort Issy, key to the south-western defences, fell. On 21 May, having sapped up to the glacis of the city ramparts, which heavy bombardment had almost made untenable, Versaillais troops entered the city. This began 'Bloody Week': fighting across the city, through the barricaded streets. Urban rebuilding during the 1850s–1860s, intended to facilitate policing, in fact hampered the attackers, for the new wide avenues were hard to pass under fire. But the defence was never effectively organized and few barricades were defended to the last: only a few thousand fought on against over 100,000 troops. The most stubborn resistance was in east-central Paris. Great material damage was done, as both sides used artillery and the Communards started fires to slow the Versaillais advance or as acts of defiance. Most notably, the Tuileries and the Hôtel de Ville were gutted. The last rebels were surrounded in working-class north-eastern Paris, and fighting ended on 28 May. The regular army lost about 1,000 killed throughout the campaign. The Communard losses were far greater: at least 10,000 were killed during 'Bloody Week' alone, many executed summarily or after drumhead *court martial. Thousands more were arrested and transported. The crushing of the Commune ended the dominance of French politics by the threat of Parisian uprisings that had begun in 1789, although the practice was revived, bloodlessly, in 1968.   RT

Horne, Alistair, *The Fall of Paris: The Siege and the Commune 1870–1871* (London, 1965).

Tombs, Robert, *The War against Paris* 1871 (Cambridge, 1981).

---

communications, military   The sine qua non of leadership, from squad level to strategic command. Gen Omar *Bradley famously declared: 'Congress makes a man a general, but communications make him a commander.' If you cannot communicate, you cannot command in any save a symbolic sense. The simplest and certainly the oldest military communications are hand signals, which have the virtue of being silent and brief and the slight disadvantage that if any conventions are employed, it is essential that both the sender and the receiver of the signal know precisely what it means. The 'out of air' signal for scuba-divers (a finger drawn vigorously across the throat) might be interpreted by the uninitiated as a statement of menacing intent, causing the receiver of the signal to flee rather than provide assistance to the sender.

Direct verbal commands are next, when the enemy is aware of your presence or the need for stealth is no longer pressing. Those amused by the characteristically shrieked orders given on the parade ground should remember that these were once given amid the roar of musketry and artillery: thus the piercing tone, usually accompanied by hand signals. To reach further than the voice can carry, distinctive commands were given by drums, or in more detail with brass instruments, ranging from the booming Roman tuba to the high-pitched hunting horn used by some British paratroopers at *Arnhem. An entire lexicon of commands developed for trumpets or bugles, many still in use.

Over slightly further range, fire by night and smoke by day was used by God to command the Israelites, and by mortal generals such as *Hannibal. This medium has the obvious disadvantage that the messages thus sent advise the enemy if not of your intentions, at least of your presence. Within sight range, the use of signal flags was not confined to the *navies of the world, although they developed it further. By the use of smaller vessels spaced out to act as repeaters, there was almost no limit to the distance a signal might be sent, given clear weather, in the *Nelson navy. The 1855 international code of signals for maritime use contained 70,000 signals using only eighteen flags. Revised in 1932 and 1969, it is still in use today. Visibility was always the main drawback to this medium, accentuated when *steam propulsion permitted ships to ignore wind direction so that flag hoists might be end-on to those supposed to read them. The failure of Vice Adm Beatty's signal staff to communicate his intentions correctly led to the failure to close on German battlecruisers at the Dogger Bank, and to near disaster at *Jutland.

Still subject to the vagaries of weather was the *semaphore, invented in 1794 by Claude Chappe and promptly adopted by both the British and the French, who built repeater towers along their respective coasts. The electrical *telegraph was invented in 1837 by the American Samuel Morse. The British first used it for military purposes during the *Crimean war, while during the *Indian Mutiny isolated British forces kept in touch with one another using the commercial telegraph system. This was dependent on a reliable source of electricity and could, of course, be interrupted very easily by cutting the wires (or, much later, 'tapped' into by the enemy). The telegraph was used extensively during the *American civil, *Austro-Prussian, and *Franco-Prussian wars, mainly for long-distance communications. The need to use it tactically was not yet pressing, since the battles of these wars were still within the limits of what a commander might hope to control with dispatch riders.

In the absence of the necessary infrastructure, the *heliograph, invented by Henry Mance in 1858, was a device for reflecting the sun with mirrors to send messages in Morse using shutters. Only the code was modern: *Alexander 'the Great' is known to have used a polished shield to send signals. Again utterly weather-dependent, it was a system more suited for wars fought where the sun could be counted upon to shine, thus of little application in northern climes. It was used extensively by the British in India, by *Kitchener in the Second *Boer War, and by the US army in the *Plains Indians wars.

Flag, semaphore, and electrical or heliographic Morse signalling were all susceptible to interception by the enemy and thus dependent on codes and ciphers. But these could only provide secure communications for the briefest of periods until the enemy captured either the code book or someone who would volunteer the information. That every cipher can be broken is a lesson hard-pressed military commanders often forget, notably the imperial Japanese forces, the *Wehrmacht, and the Royal Navy during WW II.

Albert James Myer, a US army doctor, first conceived of the idea of a separate, trained, professional military signal service. While serving as a medical officer in Texas during 1856, he proposed that the US army use his visual 'wigwag' communications system. When the army adopted his system in June 1860, the US army Signal Corps was born with Myer as the first and only signal officer. Maj Myer first used his visual signalling system while on active service in New Mexico during the 1860–1 Navajo expedition. Using flags for daytime signalling and a torch at night, wigwag was employed during the American civil war. In most European armies, communications were the responsibility of the engineers and not until 1899 did the Germans organize telegraph units which became a separate branch of their army. The Royal Corps of Signals was not organized until after WW I, more than fifty years after the creation of the US army Signal Corps.

The *telephone was patented by Alexander Graham Bell in 1876, but the first serviceable field telephone was not manufactured until the late 1880s and was not used militarily until the *Spanish-American war. Cable reels and carrying packs were developed for laying wire, and these are still in use today. The field telephone became an essential signalling system for all armies participating in WW I, which also saw extensive use of pyrotechnic signals for communications between infantry and artillery. Even the ancient standby of the carrier pigeon was resorted to by both sides.

Wireless *radio permitted commands to be given over gradually increasing ranges until today it is technically possible, using satellite communications, for someone thousands of miles away to give orders to the smallest military units. These are encrypted to a level consistent with the 'shelf life' of the orders being given; mere scrambling may be enough for a message that is to be acted upon immediately. Ease of detailed, relatively secure communication is not an unmixed blessing as it requires politicians and senior officers to respect subsidiarity and limit themselves to commands appropriate to their rank and their ability to perceive factors that may not be apparent to their juniors. Without this self-discipline, 'order, counter-order, disorder' can occur, as illustrated by the hugely resented generals in *Vietnam who attempted to micro-manage small unit engagements from observer aircraft.

During the *Gulf war, the US army, with Mobile Subscriber Equipment (MSE) for 'Corps and Below' forces and TRI-TAC signal equipment for 'Echelon Above Corps', was linked with the British Ptarmigan and French RITA systems in the largest automatic switched military communications network ever set up. Multi-channel satellite communications were the major success story in this operation due to the distances required to communicate and for command and control. Military communications during the more recent NATO intervention in the Balkans encountered extreme topographic conditions which limited the use of line of sight communications and made satellite and electronic mail indispensable. Video teleconferencing (VTC) became the key to mutual understanding among commanders from disparate nations and military traditions, and was available 24 hours a day in some key locations. We do, after all, speak with gestures and body language as well as words, and this is the first time the full panoply of human communications has been employed among officers who badly need to have a 'feel' for what each other are like as men, across the divide of mere words.

In terms of its social and political implications, very possibly the most revolutionary communications development of all time originally came of a military requirement. During 1969, the Department of Defense Advanced Research Projects Administration developed the ARPA Net to link research laboratories around the USA in the event of nuclear attack. This is the basis for the Internet system we know today.

Troops have traditionally been encouraged to roar when closing with the enemy, particularly to increase shock when springing an ambush. This is an often overlooked form of military communication: with the enemy. While it is always advantageous to know what your opponent is doing, sometimes it is important to ensure that he knows what you are doing, as for example when moving troops during a cease-fire or, most commonly, when trying to surrender. Despite pleas from his staff, Adm Togo continued to fire on Russian warships that had lowered their flags at Tsushima until they also stopped and swung their guns fore and aft, according to international convention. The sending of 'signals' by the best and the brightest in Washington to the merely battle-hardened North Vietnamese has become a paradigm of how tricky this can be: when Washington thought it was signalling restraint from a position of overwhelming military strength, it was read, correctly, as an indication of lack of resolve betraying underlying political weakness. The acronym KISS (keep it simple, stupid) is particularly applicable to communications across cultural divides.   DMJ/RH

Raines, Rebecca Robbins, *Getting the Message Through: A Branch History of the US Army Signal Corps* (Washington, 1996).

Scheips, Paul J. (ed.), *Military Signals Communications*, 2 vols. (New York, 1980).

Woods, David L., *A History of Tactical Communications Techniques* (Orlando, Fla., 1965).

concentration camp Literally a temporary or permanent encampment where people may be gathered together from a wide area to 'concentrate' them in one place. The name was first used by the Spanish in Cuba to describe the technique of withdrawing the civilian population from the countryside to deny support and 'crowd cover' to *guerrillas. Both Britain and the USA employed the same technique in the Second *Boer War and the *Philippines insurrection respectively. While not intended, the massing of people without adequate sanitation and medical services led to epidemics in these camps, giving the term an early and ominous link with *genocide. Not to be confused with internment camps such as those employed to quarantine Japanese-Americans after *Pearl Harbor, concentration camps are now associated with, at best, punishment and forced labour, as in what Solzhenitsyn called the 'Gulag archipelago' of Stalin's USSR. At worst the concentration camps of Nazi Germany were used for the systematic extermination of Jews, gypsies, homosexuals, Russian prisoners of war, and a variety of others.   HEB

Condé, Louis II de Bourbon (Duc d'Enghien)

(1621–86). Born Duc d'Enghien and later Prince de Condé, he represents the apogee of the French aristocrat's approach to war, in that he was a bold, even rash, commander whose lust for glory brought him spectacular success, as at *Rocroi in 1643, and not a few disasters. A French military historian considers him a 'military intellectual, the very pattern of the military prince of the baroque, gifted and independent'.

A prince of the blood, he was educated by Jesuits at Bourges before going to Paris in 1637 to study the military art, after which he entered the army in 1640. Both *Richelieu and Mazarin were convinced that he was a man of some considerable talent. Even at the age of 17, as governor of Burgundy, he took an interest in the training and *recruitment of troops. In 1638 he commanded the French army at the siege of Fuentarrabia, but was defeated by a relieving army. Undeterred, he joined the army of Picardy as a volunteer and took part in the siege of Arras in 1640.

At the tender age of 22 he was given command of the French army facing the Spanish in the Netherlands in April 1643. Shortly before his death, King Louis XIII told Enghien's father that he had dreamed of a great victory won by the young duke which proved prophetic. On 17 May 1643 Enghien moved to the relief of Rocroi, despite doubts in Paris over the succession of the infant *Louis XIV. The veteran Spanish army faced his force and although slightly outnumbered it was still a formidable force and disposed of the toughest infantry in Europe. Enghien led a devastating charge on the Spanish left and broke it and wheeled onto the rear of the enemy's advancing right flank, relieving pressure on the French horse on that wing, who were in some distress. This left the Spanish *tercios isolated and they were ground down by combined artillery, cavalry, and infantry attacks. Not many were able to have their surrender accepted, and many of the survivors owed their lives to the personal intervention of Enghien himself. It was a historic victory over a military formation that had dominated warfare in Europe for over a century.

The duke went on to take over command from *Turenne during the Rhineland campaign of 1644, and conducted a fine campaign in the Low Countries. By this time considered arrogant and overweening by Mazarin, he was posted to the military quicksand of Spain again, where he enjoyed only moderate success. In 1648 he was again victorious over a Habsburg army under Archduke Leopold Wilhelm at Lens.

The same year he was not only one of the leaders of the rebellion against the young king's entourage known as the Fronde (1648–53), but he also enlisted with the Spanish Habsburgs until 1659. Thus the two great contemporaries, Enghien and Turenne, fought against each other at the Dunes near Dunkirk in 1658, and the duke was roundly defeated. Although rehabilitated in 1659, he was never again fully trusted by his cousin Louis XIV, although he held military commands during the War of Devolution (1667–8) and the Dutch war of 1672–8. At Seneffe in 1674 he defeated a Dutch army of 67,000 with a much smaller force. Thereafter, in bad health, he took little part in military or civil affairs of state.

He is not generally viewed as the equal of Turenne. His style consisted of audacity, a headstrong rush, and aggressive assault full of panache, whereas Turenne was the exponent of subtle and careful manoeuvre, patient, and calculating. On the other hand, Enghien's tactical ideas are known to have been studied by Napoleon, in particular the 'pinning' of the enemy to the front while exploring for a weak point elsewhere, either for a breakthrough and encirclement by cavalry or to reposition his artillery to enfilade the pinned force. While admittedly these were tactical principles as old as *Alexander 'the Great', their application in the combined arms assault on the redoubtable tercios at Rocroi makes it one of the undisputed turning points in military history.　　　TM

---

condottiere (pl. condottieri) is a term applied specifically to commanders of *mercenaries in Italy from the 14th to the 16th centuries, taking their name from the *condotta*, or terms of service under which they agreed to fight for an employer. The large cash surpluses generated by the great merchant cities of northern Italy permitted them to hire talent wherever it was available, military skill being far more expensive than the services of the artists who produced the glories of the Renaissance. The advantage to a wealthy city like Venice was that it could hire troops only when needed, sparing itself the costs of a standing army and its citizens from the rigours of war. The disadvantage was that the condottieri did not simply go away when their contract expired and might well have negotiated a new contract with their erstwhile enemies. It was an environment which not only encouraged but demanded treachery, and the abler condottieri were in fact more cut-throat businessmen than soldiers.

As such, they appreciated that battle was a foolish gamble to take with expensively trained and equipped men, and tended to manoeuvre endlessly, plundering as they went. Although the lot of the northern Italian peasantry has never been a happy one, the era of the condottieri must

have marked a nadir. When they did feel obliged to fight each other, the condottieri showed each other professional courtesy: after capturing a sizeable force of mercenaries in the pay of Milan in 1428, Carmagnola freed them to fight again against his own patron, Venice. Perhaps unsurprisingly, the Venetians had him assassinated four years later. Over 60 years later they imprisoned the exceptionally faithless Francesco *Gonzaga after fruitlessly pouring money into his bottomless purse, and it is remarkable that Venice was able to prosper at all while depending on such men to defend and extend her interests.

The condottieri archetypes were probably Muzio Attendolo Sforza and Braccio da Montone, who were boys together and died the same year, having fought each other on behalf of a number of clients for most of their lives. Both achieved their own principalities, Braccio's Perugia lapsing upon his death, but Sforza's son Francesco going on to become the duke of Milan. Oddly, the greatest equestrian statues of all time were of condottieri: a fresco by Paolo Uccello recorded a now lost statue of Sir John *Hawkwood; Leonardo's only statue, melted down to cast cannon, was of Francesco Sforza; and Donatello immortalized Padua's Gattamelata in the mid-15th century. Not even all of Venice's condottieri came to a bad end: Verrochio's magnificent bronze of a stern Bartolomeo Colleoni on a fierce horse still stands in the Piazza dei Santi Giovanni e Paolo.　　　HEB

Confederate States Army One of the Confederate forces in the *American civil war. Because the Confederacy was besieged from birth, its army became the expression of the will of the southern American states to be free of northern domination. Regional, class, and racial fissures unquestionably became important, but any society subjected to intense pressure will crack. The struggle was not decided by inherent social and economic weakness, but by the inability of a conservative Confederate leadership to unleash the politically revolutionary power of that will.

Many arguments about the manner in which the Confederacy was suppressed, and why it took so long, arise from asking the wrong questions. Only if Lincoln's definition of the war as a police action is accepted does the duration of the conflict become remarkable; seen as an episode in American imperial expansion, it is not. In fact, it took a further century for the conquered territories to be assimilated, and fading echoes of southern nationalism continue to this day.

So much interest is concentrated on the Army of Northern Virginia that the six other military departments comprising 95 per cent of Confederate territory get correspondingly less attention. Yet outside the tiny area around the two capital cities, the Confederate States' armies had a nearly unbroken history of defeat which, particularly in the first two years, cannot be explained by the balance of forces and the river and railway systems that finally and over-whelmingly favoured the Union.

More narrowly, the argument that improvements in weapons had abolished the battlefield decision flies in the face of the rapid results achieved in the contemporary wars of Europe. Within each theatre the distances involved were not greater, and *railways between theatres rendered their wide separation less significant than mere mileage suggests. The battlefields themselves were about the same size, as were the numbers involved, at or beyond the limit of even an exceptional commander's ability to control events. By virtually any standard of measurement, if not quite what *Moltke 'the Elder' called it, a 'brawl between armed mobs', the conflict was very much more a Napoleonic war than a precursor of WW I.

With Confederate railways, industry, officers, and trained soldiers concentrated in Virginia, the correct strategy was to fight a holding action in the west while seeking a quick decision in the east. Tennessee was second in industrial development and infrastructure, and the resources of Arkansas, Alabama, Louisiana, Mississippi, and Texas were considerable. Texas also contributed a percentage of manpower second only to Virginia. A resolutely defensive posture in Tennessee would have inflicted punishing delays on the Union's 'Anaconda Plan', but instead western forces were dissipated in ill-conceived counter-invasions that became a net drain on the only theatre where the war might have been won outright.

Undue emphasis on *Lee and *Jackson tends to obscure the fact that the defining Confederate failure came from the top. As a national leader and his own de facto secretary of war, Jefferson *Davis compares most unfavourably with *Lincoln. Davis never had to use the threat of force to keep individual states in line, and if anything his great adversary's problems in maintaining political unity and with the diversion of resources by individual state governments were more debilitating. By contrast, faced with a tangible unifying threat, Davis never defined and still less rallied his nation behind realistic war aims. Above all, he was an arrogant man who refused to delegate, more concerned that talented men might usurp his authority than with harnessing their energy.

Among field officers, the fact that the South commanded the loyalty of the bulk of the pre-war officer corps worked against it. A *levée en masse in the *French Revolutionary style and Napoleon's 'career open to talent' was precluded by the extreme orthodoxy of Lee and his fellow generals. It can be argued that the spirit of the South was first crushed by its own leaders, and this can most clearly be seen in the western theatre. Only Joseph *Johnston belatedly tried to make sensible use of this much put-upon western army, but he was preceded by the rancorous *Bragg and followed by the criminally incompetent *Hood.

Neither political nor military leadership offer any explanation as to why the Confederacy survived as long as it did, nor why the Union ultimately resorted to making war on the civilian population. The answer is to be found in the casualty figures, which argue that battlefield *attrition worked very effectively—against the Union. Multiple enlistment and poor Confederate record-keeping render the figures approximate, but they appear to have fielded 1.1 million men against 2.8 million, for a military participation ratio of only 13.1 per cent versus 10.7 per cent. What is remarkable is that the Confederate armies, outnumbered over two to one, killed 110,000 and wounded 275,000 in battle, suffering only 74,500 and 137,000 themselves, even though average regimental strength declined from 500–50 in 1862 to less than 100 by 1865. *Morale had certainly eroded by the end, but although Union troops were very much better fed, shod, and clothed and received better medical attention, non-battle fatalities also favoured the Confederates by 259,000 to 124,000.

Grass-roots motivation remains the outstanding reason why an industrially underdeveloped and diplomatically isolated nation survived the onslaught of a much more powerful neighbour for four years. What made Union generals treat the Confederate States Army with extreme respect until the end was the unyielding disposition and the innate military skill of the average southern soldier. His troops might have hated Bragg less had they known what he wrote after the battle of Stones River: 'We have had to trust to the individuality and the self-reliance of the private soldier. Without the incentive which controls the officer, without the hope of reward and actuated only by a sense of duty and of patriotism, he has, in this great contest, justly judged that the cause was his own and gone into it with a determination to conquer or die.' HEB

Griffith, Paddy, *Battle Tactics of the Civil War* (London, 1987).
McMurphy, Richard, *Two Great Rebel Armies* (Chapel Hill, NC, 1989).
Vandiver, Frank, *Rebel Brass* (Baton Rouge, La., 1956).
Data bank at: *http://www.cwc.lsu.edu/other/stats/warcost.htm*

Congo, UN operations in (1960–4). The Congo (later Zaire (1971–97) and now renamed the Democratic Republic of Congo) was the scene of the most ambitious *UN military intervention in history, a unique campaign which has many lessons for present-day peace-support operations. It was the only time the UN had its own air force, and was the origin of many UN procedures used in the numerous interventions since then.

The Democratic Republic of Congo is a vast country around the river of that name, which has the second largest drainage basin in the world after the Amazon. It is a former Belgian colony, and distinct from Congo-Brazzaville, the former French colony to the north-west. At 905,568 square miles (2,345,410 sq km), it is a quarter of the size of the USA and larger than France, Germany, Britain, Spain, Italy, and the Benelux countries put together.

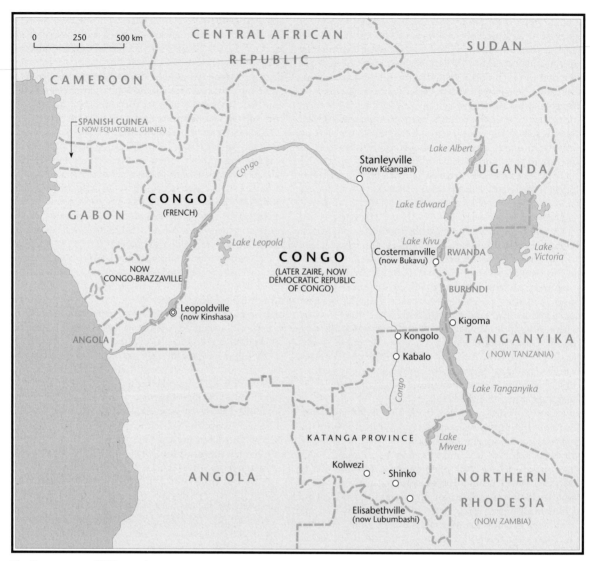

The **Congo**, scene of UN operations 1960–4.

The vast, watery maze of the Congo was the scene for Joseph Conrad's 1898 novella *Heart of Darkness*, in which the central character, Kurtz, sets off in search of ivory but also to 'civilize', and instead succumbs to the darkest aspects of the dark continent. It was adapted as the *Vietnam war *film *Apocalypse Now* and Michael Ignatieff has pointed out the similarity between the imperialist imperative and the propensity of developed countries to intervene in other people's wars a hundred years later to 'put the world to rights'.

The Congo was the scene of the first such intervention in modern times. It was totally unprepared for independence from Belgium on 30 June 1960. Chaos ensued, and Belgium sent troops back in to protect Europeans. On 11 July the leader of the mineral-rich Katanga province (later Shaba

province) in the south-east, bordering Northern Rhodesia (now Zimbabwe) and Angola, announced he was seceding. In order to maintain control of the mining industry, especially diamonds, Belgium supplied Katanga with arms and 500 *mercenaries to lead its army. Then the Congo president, Joseph Kasavubu, dismissed the PM, Patrice Lumumba, who attempted to set up a rival regime in Stanleyville (now Kisangani) in the north-east. In August, the Baluba of South Kasai proclaimed independence, so the country was split into four.

On 12 July, the Congo government requested UN assistance to repel what was simplified as Belgian aggression (the return of her troops to protect Belgian citizens). This formed the basis of the biggest and most complex civil and military operation mounted by the UN until Cambodia in 1992–3. At its peak, the UN force in the Congo (known by its French acronym of ONUC) numbered 20,000 of whom 234 died. Whereas the *Korean war had been a much bigger so-called UN operation, it had been basically a US war with UN blessing. Secretary-General Dag Hammarskjöld wanted to use the Congo as a test case of the UN as an independent international force, an ambition curtailed when he was killed in a plane crash on 17 September 1961. It has long been suspected that both he and Lumumba were assassinated at the instigation of the *CIA.

Before his death, Hammarskjöld laid down a set of principles for UN forces in civil wars which are still followed. It was a temporary deployment, until local forces were ready to take over, and had to remain impartial. It was responsible for restoring law and order, preventing civil war, training Congolese security forces, and securing the withdrawal of foreign mercenaries. In its campaign against the Katangan rebels the UN carried out air attacks, the only time it was ever to do so with its own aircraft. This air force with its own Ethiopian and Swedish jet fighters and Indian Canberra bombers was set up in October 1961. Its main role was to incapacitate the Katangan air force and provide close *air support and *reconnaissance.

The Congo saw the first use of the term 'military information' (milinfo) as a euphemism for intelligence. In 1960 Hammarskjöld refused to set up a permanent 'intelligence' agency, because to obtain access to a country for good reasons and then start gathering 'intelligence' would put countries off inviting the UN in the first place. Since the need for what could not be called intelligence was still needed, it was called milinfo instead.

In February 1961 Lumumba was murdered by the Katangan rebels and the mandate was revised, to include 'the use of force . . . as a last resort'. The *peacekeeping mandate was changed to one of peace *enforcement*, and the restitution of a democratic form of government. By February 1963, U. Thant reported to the Security Council that civil war had been quelled and that the foreign mercenaries had been removed. ONUC was then scaled down, the last small detachment being withdrawn on 30 June 1964.

Insofar as it was the one and only time the UN sponsored a military intervention independent of the wishes and control of the USA, Hammarskjöld's adventure was an act of almost foolhardy idealism. It is open to debate whether the issues left unresolved by suppressing a civil war ever go away, and after the epically corrupt dictatorship of Mobutu which ended in 1997, Zaire once again collapsed into multifactional strife. It is difficult to decide whether it was a late colonial operation or the first of the modern wars of intervention by the international community, or if indeed there ever has been any significant difference between the two.

CDB

Ignatieff, Michael, *The Warrior's Honor* (London, 1998).

conquistadores The generic name for those who won the Spanish empire in the 16th century. Not all were Spaniards. The first man to whom the term is applied was Bethencourt, a Norman who conquered some of the Canary Islands starting in 1402. The navigators who made it all possible were the Genoese Columbus, the Florentine Vespuccio, the Portuguese Magellan, and the Englishman Cabot. Among the less successful conquistadores were a group of forlorn Germans in today's Venezuela.

But most were from the frontier provinces Andalusia and Extremadura and all were in the service of Their Most Catholic Majesties Ferdinand and Isabella and successors, with the twin objectives of Christianizing the heathen and providing specie to pay for European wars against the Muslims, rival Catholic powers, and Protestant heretics. The whole phenomenon was a continuation of the centuries-long politico-religious *Reconquista of the Iberian peninsula, during which Spanish society became thoroughly militarized. The fall of the last Moorish kingdom in 1492 created a surplus of men proficient at war and very little else, and 'the Indies' provided an outlet for the boldest. Fiercely loyal to the crusading Spanish crown in the abstract, their attitude to its practical authority was captured by the phrase 'I obey but do not comply'.

Nor were all the conquistadores soldiers. Quesada was a lawyer who led a nightmarish expedition up the Magadalena river, arriving in the valley of Bogotá with fewer than 200 sick and starving men, no *gunpowder, and no horses. Using mainly diplomatic skills, he achieved dominance over much of the area today known as Colombia. The priest La Gasca prevented what is now Ecuador, Peru, and Bolivia from slipping out of his emperor's control. Starting with no more than a royal warrant, he won over the lieutenants of the fearsome Gonzalo Pizarro, while others came from as far away as Chile and the Plate river to pay homage. In Guatemala, the Dominican friar Las Casas succeeded where force had failed and pacified an area known to this day as Vera Paz ('True Peace'). The Jesuits were later to achieve the same result with the previously irreconcilable Guaraní of Paraguay, reminding us that the conquest was as much religious as political, if indeed the two can usefully be considered separately.

Conquistadores have long been tarred with the 'black legend', a device whereby the Creole élites of the independent nations of Hispanic America sought to distance themselves from the cruelty of Spanish occupation. In parallel, English-speaking historians also dwelt on the horrors of Spanish rule, charitably overlooking the fact that a much larger proportion of the Amerindian population survived south of the Rio Grande than the remnant in northern reservations. Today we appreciate that disease conquered the Americas. Battle dogs and horses, *gunpowder, steel weapons and *armour were indeed all unilateral Spanish advantages, but the Amerindians had no antibodies to the plagues that the Europeans brought with them. Not only did these exterminate whole populations, they also destroyed native faith in their rulers, culture, and gods.

It was a holocaust, but in fairness to the Spanish they placed a market value on Amerindians conspicuously absent from Anglo-American calculations. They needed a healthy population to work their mines and estates for them, so to accuse them of a deliberate policy of extermination is absurd. Nonetheless, they tortured and killed mercilessly and were brutally exploitative of the survivors. It is a multifaceted paradox that the forced immigration of African slaves was born of the saintly Las Casas's concern that the remaining natives should not be worked to death. Instead, the Africans brought new diseases that nearly finished the Amerindians off.

It is notable that the limits of Spanish conquest tended to be where they encountered tenacious resistance. Without the possibility of a population that could be reduced to docility, land alone was of no great interest to men who on many occasions proved they would rather die than work with their hands. The frontier of effective Spanish dominion throughout the colonial period was not very different to the extent of the native empires they took over, a fair indication that the areas outside were probably not worth the trouble and expense of conquest to either the Amerindian imperialists or their Hispanic successors. There were exceptions on both sides, but this and the no less significant factor of interracial breeding (*mestizaje*) provided the sharpest difference between Hispanic and much later Anglo-American settlement.

Additionally, the Amerindian peoples were constantly at war with each other, enabling the conquistadores to form tactical alliances and to divide and rule. Given the Spanish penchant for treachery and fighting among themselves, this may have been a less significant factor than is generally supposed. Overall, they prevailed because of their remorseless common will and audacity, in the face of which the Amerindians were disconcerted and inclined to believe they were battling demigods. This was crucial in the collapse of the two largest native empires, aided by the fact that the Aztec aim in battle was to take captives for ritual *sacrifice and that the Inca system was more administrative than military.

As a military adventure, the extent, speed, and permanency of the conquest bears comparison only with the Alexandrian empire. The Roman and British empires were won over centuries, while the achievements of such as *Ghengis Khan and Timur were ephemeral. The names of Columbus in the Caribbean, Magellan and Cano in the Philippines, Balboa in Panama, *Cortés in Mexico, *Alvarado from thence to Guatemala, Quesada in Colombia, the Pizarros in Peru and Ecuador, Almagro almost everywhere, and Valdivia in Chile are writ large in the pages of history. The footnotes are populated by less fortunate but no less fearless conquistadores such as Cortés's rival Narváez who died in Florida, Pizarro's lieutenant Soto who was buried in the Mississippi, Orellana of the Amazon, Mendoza of the Plate river, and many others who among them in a generation won the first truly global empire for Spain and for the militant Catholic Church with which her destiny has been so inextricably intertwined. HEB

Conrad von Hotzendorf, FM Count Franz (1852–1925). Intelligent, well-educated, and a brilliant linguist, Conrad von Hotzendorf was the Austro-Hungarian CGS from 1906 until 1917, with a brief interlude in 1911–12. He argued vigorously in favour of preventive war against Serbia or Italy, with the aim of pulling the diverse and polyglot empire together, and claimed that failure to fight sooner had been the monarchy's fatal mistake. At the beginning of the July 1914 crisis he backed political demands for action against Serbia, though he had later to admit that the army was not fully prepared for war. The politically astute Conrad ought to have predicted that the Germans would insist that Austria should throw her main weight against Russia, rather than Serbia, and that one result of German emphasis on the western front might be a long, destructive, and inconclusive struggle against Russia. Italy's entry into the war encouraged Conrad to shift his attention to the Balkans and the Adriatic, areas of his pre-war preoccupation. Dismissed by the Emperor Karl in 1917, Conrad commanded an army group on the *Italian front before being retired in the summer of 1918. He lived to see the empire he had striven to preserve destroyed by a war he had done much to promote. RH

conscientious objection is the refusal to undertake military service when legally required to do so. Although it has often been portrayed as a form of *cowardice, in fact historically it has required more courage to stand up and be counted as an individual opposed to war in general, certain wars in particular, or to military service in general, than it has to go along with the majority and submit to authority, even though secretly convinced that it is wrong. Because such objection challenges the very exercise of collective power itself, those insisting that they must and will obey the dictates of their individual conscience have generally had a very thin time of it at the hands of the governments they defy.

It should be remembered that early Christians were persecuted for reasons of state, not religion, chief among those reasons being their refusal to bear arms. The experience of the British in India with Gandhi and his followers is a more recent example of how extremely provocative *pacifists can be, although it hardly needs pointing out that non-violence as a tactic can only work against those who themselves entertain doubts about the legitimacy of using force. The early Roman emperors had no such doubts, hence the high-protein diet of the lions in the Circus Maximus.

After Christians became the oppressors rather than the oppressed, the Sixth Commandment was of course finessed and we hear little of conscientious objection through the Middle Ages. It is with the appearance of aptly named Nonconformist sects such as the Mennonites in Europe, the Quakers in England, and the anarchist Dukhobors in Russia that conscientious objection became an issue again. Of these, the last rejected all authority, including the Bible, but others could cite Scripture in support of their stand and, surprisingly, survived. Respect for the refusal to bear arms or even to serve in a non-military capacity as a statement of individual conscience caused the most institutional problems in Britain, mainly because it was one of the last countries to introduce conscription. During WW I, special tribunals granted absolute exemptions to a few, generally those whose work was deemed to be of national importance. Of the conditional exemptions, some 7,000 men agreed to undertake non-combatant military service (often as hugely respected stretcher-bearers), while a further 3,000 were placed in labour camps. Approximately 1,500 men, whose case for exemption had been rejected, continued to refuse to serve. Most of the latter were non-religious objectors for whom non-combatant military service would simply have been to support an imperialist war effort by indirect means. Many of them were transferred to military units anyway, where they would become subject to military law. For 41 of them a rather more gruesome fate was briefly contemplated, apparently the brainchild of *Kitchener, the war secretary. They were sent to France where, as well as being under military law, they would also be nominally on active service and thus could be sentenced to death by *courts martial. They were, but at the insistence of PM Asquith the sentences were not carried out. After the war, those who had refused military service of any kind were disenfranchised for five years.

During WW II the scale of the problem was greater but it was managed in a more measured way and with much less bitterness. Of the 60,000 men and women who applied to be recognized as conscientious objectors, two-thirds were given a conditional exemption and required to undertake war work. A further 3,000 were granted unconditional exemption. Of the remainder, approximately 5,000 were prosecuted, most of whom were imprisoned. Other countries, where the right to object to military service was granted, if at all, only to well-established members of pacifist religious sects, seem either to have had less problems or less publicity was given to the issue.

Since 1945, conscientious objection has been widespread, notable examples being France during the campaign in *Indochina and the *Algerian independence war and the USA during the *Vietnam war. During the last, perhaps the most celebrated case was that of heavyweight boxing champion Muhammad Ali, born Cassius Clay, who was first declared unfit to serve on the basis of subnormal intelligence, and when this failed to humiliate him reclassified and

stripped of his title. The broad discretionary range of the Draft Boards and the availability of safe billets in the National Guard meant that the children of the ruling class were often comfortably exempted from active service; it was those who lacked political connections who fled to Canada or went to prison.

Conscientious objection has become a more subtle and complex subject, no longer a relatively straightforward matter of refusing military service. Two issues have become prominent. The first concerns the problem of incompatible ethical codes, where the requirement for a soldier to obey orders might clash with other ethical obligations. In a celebrated case in the USA in the late 1960s, a US army doctor was court-martialled for refusing to provide medical training for *special forces. The second is broader still and concerns the individual moral conscience of the soldier. The defence of respect for authority and obedience to orders was specifically rejected at the Nuremberg *war crimes trials after WW II, which found individual soldiers to be morally and legally responsible for the commission of war crimes. Thus a principle far more subversive than conscientious objection was established: that the fighting soldier himself must decide what orders are morally acceptable. But decision-making in warfare cannot be a rolling referendum, and the *right* to disobey orders is one that the US military in particular is still wrestling with. Other armed forces heaved a sigh of relief after the abolition of conscription and proceed on a contractual basis. Where compulsory service still exists it is the target of international organizations such as the European Bureau for Conscientious Objection, which argues for conscription to be banned or at least for non-military alternatives to be offered, and for conscientious objection to be recognized as a fundamental human right. PC/HEB

conscription. See RECRUITMENT.

constable is a word deriving from the Latin *comes stabuli*. Under the *Franks the role of constable developed from being in charge of the royal stables to a principal officer of the Merovingian and Carolingian kings. In general, it came to mean the chief officer of a household, court, or military forces of a ruler. More specifically, by the 11th century in France, the constable had become one of the five great offices of state with powers of jurisdiction and command over the cavalry. By the mid-14th century, the constable was supreme military commander of the army. However, after the treason of the Constable Charles de Bourbon (1523), French kings viewed the office with considerable distrust and for much of the 16th century it was allowed to remain vacant, being abolished in 1627. It was briefly revived by Napoleon who appointed his brother, Louis Bonaparte, grand constable of his new empire.

In England, the position of constable with the primary duty of command of the army, was in existence by the reign of Henry I (1100–35). Together with the marshal, the constable was the chief military officer of the crown and their combined court was known as the Court of Chivalry, responsible for the enforcement of the king's statutes in times of war and with jurisdiction over disputes relating to armourial bearings. By the time of Edward I (1272–1307), the term was being used for officers with important military commands who controlled key garrisons such as Windsor, Dover, and Conwy. Under the statute of Winchester (1285), they also had responsibility for civil jurisdiction and the power to arm militias to suppress riots and violent crimes. Both the name and the powers it implied were given to civilian policemen by Peel in 1840, the royal appointment becoming an honorific. MCM

Constantine I, Byzantine Emperor (c.274–337).

Flavius Valerius Constantinus, the first Christian emperor and the only emperor to execute his own son, was a dynamic general and reformer who made Christianity the empire's religion and founded a 'New Rome' which became Constantinople. Succeeding his father in 306 as emperor of Britain and Gaul, he destroyed his two eastern colleagues in a series of civil wars. Against the Emperor Maxentius in Italy, his wife's brother, he struck with an army drawn from the Rhine garrisons, quickly conquering the north and advancing on Rome. He won the decisive battle at the Milvian Bridge (28 October 312), driving Maxentius and his troops into the Tiber. This victory by 'divine inspiration', to quote the triumphal arch erected in Rome by the still pagan aristocracy, convinced Constantine that God had chosen him to unite both the empire and the church in his name. The fact that secular considerations also favoured this course of action is, of course, beside the point. The pagan Emperor Licinius, his sister's husband and his ally against Maxentius, was now driven out of the Danubian provinces in 317 and in 324, when Constantine broke their *truce, defeated at Adrianople. Constantine then forced the Bosporus crossing and crushed Licinius near Chalcedon (modern Kadiköy) on 18 September 324.

Sole emperor at last, Constantine at once refounded Byzantium as an imperial headquarters (it was formally dedicated on 11 May 330). Licinius' ample treasury and the confiscated wealth of the pagan temples were lavished upon the imperial court, the army, and the now-established church. Immediately he found himself caught up in the fierce theological squabbles of the early church and summoned the first ecumenical council, at Nicaea in 325, which formulated the Trinitarian creed.

Throughout his reign Constantine energetically restored imperial authority on the Rhine and Danube frontiers. In the east, he was about to attack Persia when he died, leaving a costly war to his successors. The instrument of Constantine's military success was a new mobile army, the select *comitatenses* units under the emperor's immediate control, which supported the screen of frontier units (*limitanei*) and prevented any rebellion in the provinces. Officers and generals were now all professional soldiers, and the proportion of Germans and other non-Romans in the army increased. These military reforms, or rather this evolution which went back more than a century, gave new life to a tired empire.

RSOT

Barnes, Timothy D., *Constantine and Eusebius* (Cambridge, Mass., 1981).
Cameron, Averil, *The Later Roman Empire* (London, 1993).

Constantinople, siege of (1453).

Constantinople (now Istanbul) was essentially all that remained of the Byzantine empire by 1450. It had almost fallen to the Ottoman *Turks several times before, but in 1451 the new sultan, Mehmet II, made it his priority. He captured outlying centres and in 1452 built the fortresses of Rumeli Hisar on the Bosporus and Kilitbahir and Cimenlik on the Dardanelles, isolating the city. The Byzantines sought western intervention, the Emperor Constantine XI and the patriarch even agreeing to end the religious schism with Rome. Venice and others promised support but the Genoese colony opposite Constantinople remained neutral.

The siege began on 6 April with 80,000 Turks and 120 ships blockading the city. The Byzantines, commanded by a Genoese *mercenary, Giustiniani Longo, had only 7,000 troops, including western volunteers, and 26 warships, to defend 4 miles (6.4 km) of land and 10 miles (16 km) of sea walls. The inlet known as the Golden Horn was shut by a boom, so its walls were unguarded. The city was protected on its landward side by the 1,000-year-old walls, the largest ever built. The Turks had enlisted a Hungarian *cannon expert, Urban, whose services had been too expensive for the Byzantines. The latter had firearms and cannon, but their recoil was too much for the walls.

For the first fortnight the Turks assaulted the land defences, breaching the outer walls, but could still not get inside. The Ottoman navy also suffered reverses, but Mehmet turned the Golden Horn on 22 April by dragging some ships overland and launching them inside it. A Byzantine attempt to fire them failed and the walls along the inlet had to be garrisoned, stretching the defenders too thinly. The Turks kept piling on the pressure, they could take the losses, but the Byzantines refused to *capitulate, praying that help would arrive. Mehmet's grand vizier even advised withdrawal on 25 May but on the 28th the inner wall was finally broken by Urban's bombards. At 01.30 on the 29th the attack began and at dawn the *janissaries assaulted the temporary repairs. One group entered by a side gate and gained control of a section of the wall while the janissaries finally forced their way through the breach. Longo himself, the inspiration behind the defence, was wounded and, as the

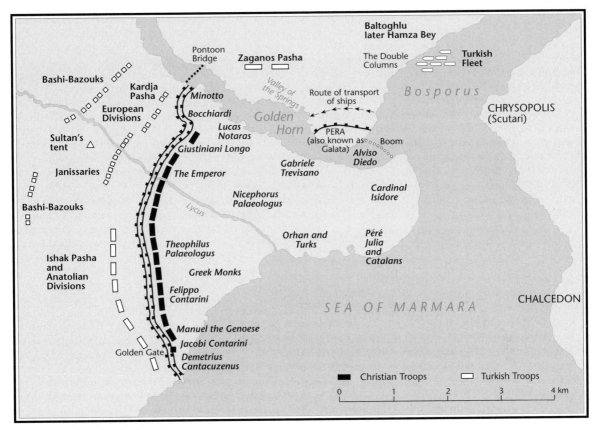

Constantinople during the siege of 1453.

defence collapsed, the emperor died fighting at the breach. Western help never arrived.   SMcC

Runciman, Steven, *The Fall of Constantinople* (Cambridge, 1965).

convoy (from Fr.: *convoyer*, to convey) is the practice of transporting men or material together for the purpose of safeguarding them. Although most famously used as a means to counter the U-boat menace in the two world wars, it has long meant the grouping together of military as well as civilian ships or vehicles for control as well as protection.

During the medieval period ships sailed in concert for mutual protection but the use of an organized convoy system as we now know it dates from the separation of ships into specialist classes and the development of a state-based navy. During the Anglo-Dutch wars of the 17th century merchantmen were regularly organized into escorted convoys along trade routes dictated by the prevailing winds. These protected them from individual raiders but not from fleet actions and in 1665 a Dutch convoy had its escort overwhelmed and 180 out of 200 merchantmen taken. In spite of events like this, insurance premiums on vessels in time of war were consistently lower for those that sailed in convoys. By the time of *Waterloo the Royal Navy had in place a sophisticated system for the protection of merchant ships.

With the coming of *steam it was argued that since ships could now move independently of the wind, they could avoid interception altogether. The 'all your eggs in one basket' argument was put forward, as were the arguments that convoys would clog up ports, delays would occur due to ships waiting for the convoy to form up, and anyway there were too many ships to convoy. Behind these arguments was a deeply felt belief that submarines could be hunted like any other warship and that convoys were somehow effeminate, a position to which the Admiralty clung despite abundant proof to the contrary until obliged by *Lloyd George to reintroduce convoys in 1917.

This same psychopathology afflicted the US Navy's Adm King in 1941–2, when he ignored bitterly won British experience and opposed the introduction of convoys in American waters, being therefore personally responsible for the loss of hundreds of merchant ships and thousands of lives. The Japanese refused to adopt the convoy system throughout WW II and lost their entire merchant navy. The British found that convoys, by enabling escort vessels to be concentrated, became the focus for hunter-killer operations with which they inflicted greater casualties on the U-boat service than suffered by any other branch of any country's armed forces. Convoys were still vulnerable to heavy German surface raiders, but with the exception of the infamous scattering of the Arctic convoy PQ 17, escort vessels self-sacrificially defended their charges against this threat also.

The 'all your eggs in one basket' argument acquired renewed vitality in the age of nuclear attack submarines and stand-off weapons that could deliver tactical *nuclear weapons. Happily the matter was never put to the test.

JR-W

Grove, E. (ed.), *The Defeat of the Enemy Attack upon Shipping* (Navy Records Society, Aldershot, 1998).

Copenhagen, battles of (1801, 1807). On 2 April 1801 a British fleet under Adm Sir Hyde Parker engaged the Danish navy under the guns of Denmark's capital city. The aim was to destroy the hostile Russian-sponsored League of Armed Neutrality that threatened to close the Baltic to British trade. The British victory knocked Denmark out of the alliance and persuaded Russia and Sweden to think again. This was the occasion when *Nelson put a *telescope to his missing eye when Hyde Parker's recall signal was drawn to his attention, saying that he had the right to be blind sometimes.

Between 2 and 5 September 1807, the British attacked the port with a surprise *amphibious landing of 25 battalions of infantry and eight squadrons of cavalry, supported by ten batteries of guns, with the intention of seizing the blockaded Danish fleet and freeing up the blockading squadron. Originally Lord Cathcart's force was to co-operate with the Swedish army, but Napoleon's victory at Friedland had put paid to this scheme. The new Congreve *rockets were employed and fourteen vessels were burned. Sixty-four warships and other vessels were taken, but 25 of these were later lost in a storm.　　TM

Córdoba, Gonzalo Fernández de (1453–1515). Justly known as 'El Gran Capitán' ('The Great Captain'), Córdoba was the right-hand man of his exact contemporary Ferdinand in the latter's stunningly successful dynastic expansion from prince of Aragon and titular king of Sicily to joint ruler of a united Spain, all of southern Italy, and the principal military power in Europe. Fernández de Córdoba's career started during the period when the successions to their respective kingdoms of both Ferdinand and his wife Isabella of Castile were threatened by rebellious nobles (1474–9). His leadership qualities emerged while serving in Christian armies during the final eight years of the centuries-long *Reconquista, taking part in the sieges of Tajara, Illora, and Monte Frío, at the last of which he was the first man over the walls. Unhorsed and saved by the self-

sacrifice of his manservant in a cavalry skirmish outside Granada, his familiarity with Arabic made him one of two crown commissioners in the secret negotiations for the surrender of that Muslim kingdom in 1492.

In 1495 he led an expedition of 5,000 veteran infantry and 600 *jinetes* (light cavalry) for Ferdinand to Sicily, in alliance with Venice, to support the Aragonese King of Naples against an invasion by French King Charles VIII. Although the latter returned rapidly to France, the forces he left behind inflicted a rare defeat on Fernández de Córdoba at Seminara. But *siege warfare and not field operations decided campaigns, and at Atella the next year his inspired use of a light cavalry screen combined with a close investment isolated and defeated the main French force, after which, and with an imaginative use of allied naval superiority, he mopped up the remaining French garrisons. The campaign ended in an armistice in 1497, after he drove French forces out of their stranglehold on Rome at the port of Ostia, at the invitation of Pope Alexander VI who earlier had bestowed the honorary title of 'The Most Catholic' on his master.

Ferdinand agreed with the new French king, Louis XII, to partition Naples between them in the Treaty of Granada in 1500, which neither intended to respect. He dispatched Fernández de Córdoba as viceroy of Sicily at the head of a large expedition to balance a similar French force, while combining with them and Venice against the Ottoman *Turks who threatened Sicily. At the head of a Spanish-Venetian expedition, he took the strongly held Turkish island of Cephalonia in December 1500. During this siege he first employed Pedro Navarro, a sometime pirate, self-taught military engineer, and later a general of distinction in his own right.

When the French tried to seize the rest of the kingdom of Naples in 1502, Fernández de Córdoba confirmed his title of 'Great Captain' by inflicting severe defeats on them at *Cerignola, where the vaunted *Swiss in French service were shattered by Spanish arquebus and light cannon fire, and at the Garigliano river (December 1503), where he outflanked and forced the surrender of a considerably larger force by a night attack, using *pontoons to bridge a flooded estuary. Ferdinand made him duke of Sessa and joined him in Italy 1506, returning with him to Spain the next year. In 1512 he was appointed grand constable of Italy to restore the situation following defeat of Pope Julius II's Holy League by the French at the battle of Ravenna, while his king took advantage of a religious schism to seize the kingdom of Navarre, a French ally.

Although Spanish military supremacy was based on the militarization of the whole society during the years of the Reconquista, Fernández de Córdoba is credited with synthesizing contemporary Moorish, French, and Swiss tactics into a potent combination of arquebusiers, gunners, and pikemen known as the *tercio, using *jinetes* to screen his movements and to report those of his less agile opponents. Heavy cavalry, difficult to transport and maintain, and often undependable because of the individualistic arrogance of the knights, had already assumed a lesser role in Spanish campaigns following several disasters during the conquest of Granada.

Above all, the Spanish under Fernández de Córdoba showed themselves masters of siege warfare at a time when *gunpowder had sounded the knell of city states and minor principalities in Europe, ushering in the era of the centralized nation state. Spanish battlefield ascendancy rested on the tercio and related formations for 150 years, until it was destroyed by combined arms tactics at *Rocroi.　　HEB

Prescott, William, *The Art of War in Spain*, ed. Albert McJoyne (London, 1995).

Cortés, Hernán (1485–1547), conquistador of Mexico. His secretary described him as ruthless, haughty, quarrelsome, and much given to women, qualities that served him well. He sailed to Hispaniola in 1504 and in 1511 joined an expedition to Cuba. As mayor of Santiago he was a magnet for dissidents and to get rid of him the governor appointed him captain general of an expedition to Yucatán, only to revoke his authority before departure. Ignoring this, in February 1519 Cortés sailed with 11 ships, 100 sailors, 500 soldiers, and 16 horses. Landing at Tabasco, among the gifts he received from local Indians was 'Malinche', who became his mistress and indispensable councillor and interpreter throughout the campaign. Sailing on, he founded Vera Cruz, declared independent authority, and in a famous episode literally burned his boats.

Thanks to Malinche he was able to exploit resentments against the Aztecs among their subject peoples, forming a military alliance with the powerful Tlaxcala. Upon arrival at the Aztec capital of Tenochtitlán at the head of a combined Spanish-Tlaxcaltec force of less than 1,500, he won over the Emperor Montezuma, already unmanned by a prophecy about the return of the god Quetzalcoatl. In mid-1520, Cortés left *Alvarado in charge while he marched to the coast to defeat and recruit to his cause a force sent from Cuba under Narváez. On return he found his lieutenant had provoked the Aztecs to revolt. Montezuma was killed when he tried to restore his people to docility and Cortés had to evacuate the city during the 'Sorrowful Night' of 30 June. Tenochtitlán was in the middle of a lake connected to the mainland by causeways and these were destroyed by Aztecs fighting from canoes, with the loss of many Spaniards and Tlaxcaltecs, much of their loot, all of their artillery and *gunpowder, and most of their horses. Despite this, six days later Cortés turned on his vastly more numerous pursuers and defeated them at Otumba.

Over the next year, Cortés won over or conquered the areas surrounding Tenochtitlán, until finally the city itself was successfully assaulted in August 1521. Cortés's authority appears to have been accepted by the peoples of Mexico, accustomed to submission to a hegemonial power and happy to be relieved of the Aztecs' 'flower wars', whose purpose was to gather captives for *sacrifice. His problems lay in Spain, where enemies sought to persuade the Emperor Charles V that he intended to establish an independent kingdom.

In 1526 he returned from a two-year expedition to Honduras to find his estates seized and Mexico in chaos. Compelled to return to Spain to plead his case in person, he was made a marquis and confirmed as captain general, but the coveted post of viceroy was withheld. He returned to Mexico in 1530 and toyed with further Pacific exploration, but eventually retreated to his estate at Cuernavaca. The rest of his life was a battle against a flood of accusations and he died in Spain after a seven-year attempt to refute them.

HEB

Corunna, battle of (correctly La Coruña) (1809). In 1808 Gen Sir John *Moore took command of British forces in Spain and Portugal following the Convention of Cintra which had allowed a defeated French army free passage home. In October he began to advance from Lisbon into Spain, but when he reached Salamanca he learnt that his Spanish allies had been scattered by Napoleon. He then heard that Madrid had fallen to the French and decided to retreat to the north-west coast, where his force could be evacuated by the navy. After a gruelling 250 mile (402 km) retreat through the snow-covered mountains of Galicia, on 16 January 1809 Moore turned to face the pursuing *Soult outside Corunna.

Although his 15,000 soldiers were outnumbered, they checked successive attacks and most were able to embark safely. Moore himself, mortally wounded by a cannon ball, was buried on the ramparts of the old town in a brief ceremony—'We buried him darkly at dead of night'—commemorated in Thomas Wolfe's poem. He was a great loss to the British army, less for his generalship than for his skill in raising and training *light troops.　　RH

Cossacks (Turkic: *kozak*, a daring or free person). Originally meaning a settler in a frontier area of the Russian empire or Ukraine who was exempt from serfdom, the Cossacks became an élite, predominantly light cavalry force within the imperial *Russian army and, from being renowned for their independent lifestyle, became identified as an instrument of repression. In the Russian civil war many Cossacks supported the Whites but there were 'Red' or 'crimson Cossacks' (*chervonnye kazaki*) also. In WW II on the *eastern front Cossacks fought on both sides. There were Cossack *Nazi auxiliary units formed to fight against the Red Army, mostly alongside the *Wehrmacht although some served in the Russian divisions of the Waffen *SS. Since the break-up of the USSR, Cossack traditions have been re-emphasized, especially by those opposed to democratic and economic reform.

From the 14th to 17th centuries the Russian frontiers were settled by frontiersmen who were exempt from taxes and serfdom in exchange for military service against the Mongols and *Turks. From the 15th century on the Dnepr, Don, Volga, Ural, and Terek rivers there were self-governing communities of so-called 'free Cossacks', mostly runaway serfs. Their military style followed that of the Mongols, and formations like the *lava* passed into the Russian army via the Cossacks. They played a major part in uprisings in Ukraine in the 16th and 17th centuries, producing a train of rebel leaders including Bogdan Khmelnitskiy and Stenka Razin, and finishing with Emelian *Pugachev. Cossack leaders were called *atamans*. Originally they were elected but were later appointed by the tsarist government. *Peter 'the Great' subordinated the Cossacks to his central authority and used them to guard his frontiers. The Cossacks became a privileged military caste, used as irregular troops. Each Cossack force had its own *ataman* and there was an *ataman* of all Cossack forces who, from 1827, was the heir to the imperial throne. The Zaporozhian Cossacks who had emerged in Ukraine in the early 16th century were abolished in 1775 after the Pugachev revolt, but new Cossack forces were founded. The Black Sea Cossacks, founded in 1787, were divided into Kuban and Tersk Cossack forces in 1860. By the beginning of the 20th century there were forces of Don, Kuban, Orenburg (founded 1855), Transbaikal (*zabaikal*) (1851), Tersk, Siberian (1808), Ural, Astrakhan (1817), Semirechensk (1867), Amur (1858), and Ussuri (1889) Cossacks. Cossack troops took part in all Russia's wars from the 18th to the 20th centuries. They were particularly adept in cavalry raids, such as that on Berlin in 1760, and in harrying the French in 1812. In the 1877–8 Russo-Turkish and the 1904–5 *Russo-Japanese wars they developed this role. In 1904 the Independent Trans-Baikal Cossack Brigade commanded by Cossack Gen P. I. Mishchenko was designated the forward detachment (*peredovoy otryad*) of the Russian Manchurian Army. The 7,500-strong detachment including Cossacks, *mounted infantry, and *horse artillery, conducted two penetrations into Korea and in January 1905 was sent to cut the *Port Arthur–Harbin railway behind Japanese lines. An Irish journalist, Francis McCullagh, was allowed to join the raid. 'I found that all the Cossack officers had changed,' he wrote. 'They had all become very studious and were taking a particularly keen interest in nitroglycerine and the blowing up of railway trains and bridges.'

By the start of WW I Cossack forces comprised 54 mounted regiments, 6 dismounted Cossack battalions (*plastun*), 23 artillery batteries, 11 independent Cossack squadrons (*sotnias*), 4 independent horse and foot battalions (*divizion*), and the specially selected Imperial Guard: 68,500 men in all. During the war their strength increased to 164 cavalry regiments, 54 batteries, 30 dismounted regiments, 179 independent *sotnias*, and other units totalling 200,000 men. Being from distant parts of the empire and in

a privileged position, they were perceived as the tsar's most loyal guards. However, in August 1917 the majority of the Cossack forces did not support Kornilov's attempted revolt against the Kerensky government, and in the November *Russian Revolution many supported the Bolshevik uprising. By contrast, in 1918–19, during the period of foreign intervention, Soviet governments in the Don, Kuban, Ural, and Orenburg Cossack areas and in Siberia were overthrown and counter-revolutionary Cossack governments headed by *atamans* were set up. The prominence of Cossacks in the White, counter-revolutionary armies did not endear them to the new Soviet regime although Red Cossack units had also played an important part in the civil war. In 1936 limitations on Cossacks serving in the Red Army were abolished and several Cossack cavalry divisions were formed. In December 1941 a Cossack cavalry corps was formed. Among the commanders of Cossack formations was Gen Issa Pliev, who commanded the Soviet-Mongolian cavalry-mechanized group in the final campaign of WW II—the August 1945 *Manchurian campaign—sweeping in across the Gobi desert to take the Japanese Kwantung army in the flank. Cossack cavalry remained effective into the nuclear age.

The passing of cavalry as a major military arm after 1945 ended the existence of separate Cossack cavalry formations. However, men from the Cossack areas including the Caucasus, Transcaucasia, and Siberia appear to have been attracted to—or sought out for *spetsnaz*—*special forces units, whether of the Soviet and Russian armies or of the interior ministry. One such unit employed in Grozny in 1995 appears to have been recruited from Brnaul, beneath the Altai mountains in Siberia. These highly trained, élite special forces units would be just the place for modern Cossacks.   CDB

McCullagh, Francis, *With the Cossacks* (London, 1906).

council of war A meeting of senior subordinates and staff called by a commander to seek their advice on a course of action, generally undertaken in extreme conditions. Their track record is generally poor, for they often encouraged irresolute commanders (like *Bazaine at Metz in 1870) to take counsel of their fears. Although councils of war were commonly called in the 17th to 19th centuries, they are infrequently employed in modern times, as more sophisticated command and staff systems are in use.

Perhaps the best-known council of war took place in December 1912, when Kaiser Wilhelm II called together his military and naval advisers in the aftermath of the German diplomatic defeat in the Agadir crisis. At this *Kriegsrat*, the kaiser discussed with his military advisers the prospects of a future war between the Triple Alliance (Germany, Austria-Hungary, and Italy), on the one hand, and the Dual Alliance (France and Russia) reinforced by Great Britain, on the other hand.

The significance of this council of war has been hotly disputed by historians. Some, such as John Röhl, believe the outcome of this meeting was a decision to undertake energetic preparations for a war which would break out within a year or two. They argue, in essence, that the council of war resulted in a decision on the course of German foreign policy, which was implemented in the year and a half before the beginning of WW I. Others, such as Wolfgang Mommsen, argue that the war council cannot be considered a policy-making body, as the civilian leadership of the German Empire were not present, and maintain that any decisions taken on this day were not carried out by the civilian government of Germany. At the heart of this dispute among historians over the significance of the *Kriegsrat* lies the larger debate over Germany's war aims, begun after the publication of Fritz Fischer's damning *Griff nach der Weltmacht* in 1961. RTF

Fischer, Fritz, *Germany's Aims in the First World War*, introd. James Joll (London, 1967), trans. from German orig. (1961).

Mommsen, Wolfgang, 'The Topos of Inevitable War in Germany in the Decade before 1914', in V. Berghahn, V. and M. Kitchen (eds.), *Germany in the Age of Total War* (London, 1981).

Röhl, John, *The Kaiser and his Court* (Cambridge, 1994).

counter-insurgency (COIN) is a relatively recent label for the measures taken by governing authorities and their armed forces to combat attempts to subvert and overthrow them. In earlier times there was no need for the term because the suppression of insurgency proceeded along the lines of 'kill them all, let God sort them out'. But once the time-honoured techniques of massacre and scorched earth ceased to be regarded as appropriate responses, 'hearts and minds' and other COIN concepts came to the fore.

It represents perhaps the key military issue of the later 20th century. As the term implies, it is an essentially reactive process, generated and shaped by the nature of insurgency. Historically the core problem in devising appropriate countermeasures has been the difficulty of clarifying or specifying the nature of the threat. The learning curve of both soldiers and politicians has been quite flat, largely because insurgency, if it is at all effective, operates beyond the margins of conventional political and military action. A number of historians have demonstrated the slowness with which even those armies, such as the British and French, with extensive experience of irregular war, developed a systematic *doctrine of counter-insurgency. In Britain, for instance, the experience of insurgency in Ireland between 1919 and 1921 was sidelined. The army held to the sensible, but almost wholly unpolitical, doctrine of imperial control codified by Gwynn in 1934 (in a book that left Ireland out), with its traditional emphasis on minimum force and subordination to the civil authorities, and ignored the more sophisticated and challenging analysis published a few years later by H. J. Simson. This argued that a new kind of conflict had emerged, requiring a new kind of strategy ignoring the traditional dichotomies between civil and military, peace and war.

In the years after WW II a recognizable idea of counter-insurgency finally began to emerge. It can be dated fairly precisely. Simson was reacting to the situation in Palestine, where from 1936 to 1939 the British authorities had great difficulty in controlling an Arab *guerrilla insurgency that was militarily quite weak. When a more formidable Jewish insurgency began in the same country after 1945, the military authorities showed no recognition of the need for different methods, or indeed any understanding of the nature of the threat they faced. But the humiliating British failure in Palestine, ending in the chaotic abandonment of a UN Mandate in 1948, was followed by a very different outcome in the *Malayan emergency, which the British authorities had effectively strangled by the early 1950s. Their method rested on bridging the gap between civil and military authorities, by means of a special commissioner, and the development of policies designed to detach the civil population from the insurgents, which became famous as 'winning hearts and minds'. The British even broke with tradition by producing a semi-theoretical handbook explaining their success. Sir Robert Thompson's immensely influential *Defeating Communist Insurgency*, published in the mid-1960s, with its 'five principles', became a bible of counter-insurgency.

The core of Thompson's analysis simply made explicit a deep-rooted British assumption about the need to maintain the government's legitimacy by operating within the law. But it departed from British experience in insisting that not only must the government have a clear political aim, it must also 'have an overall plan'. In the Malayan emergency it had been possible for the authorities to offer, in addition to political emancipation, social and economic reforms that headed off the threat of mass opposition, and exploited the ethnic difference between the mainly Chinese insurgents and the Malay majority. Where this could not be so easily done, legitimacy was harder to preserve. The French failed in *Indochina between 1945 and 1953 by attempting to secure a conventional military victory over the insurgent Vietminh. After suffering this disaster, the French army embraced a far more radical doctrine of *guerre révolutionnaire* which located the struggle for hearts and minds not so much in the material as in the ideological sphere.

The USA followed this line in a series of military interventions conceived as aspects of the Cold War struggle against international communism. On the basis of studying successful counter-insurgency campaigns like Greece, the Malayan emergency, and the Philippines, as well as unsuccessful ones, American writers argued, as in Col John McCuen's *The Art of Counter-Revolutionary War: the Strategy of Counter-insurgency* (1966), that it was possible to 'apply revolutionary strategy and principles in reverse'. This boiled down to outbidding insurgent promises and propaganda. In practice this proved to be extremely difficult to do. Michael Shafer later identified the fatal contradiction in American logic that led to the USA becoming the puppet rather than the puppet-master of its allies threatened by insurgency. If the threat was serious enough to justify American intervention (that is, a threat to US national security), the threatened government could not be effectively forced to implement the reform policies that were fundamental to the counter-insurgency strategy.

The late 1960s and early 1970s were identified by one security specialist as 'the counter-insurgency era', the heyday of belief in the possibility of preventing revolution. In broad terms, there was a common doctrine: unity of command, effective intelligence organization, and the creation of appropriate *special forces. Radical critics saw this as a threat to all political change, branding counter-insurgency experts as 'the hired prize-fighters of the bourgeois state'. The most famous British counter-insurgency text, Frank Kitson's *Low Intensity Operations* (1971), proposed an exceptionally sophisticated civil-military system to facilitate the early recognition of an insurgent threat. This concept did not transfer very easily from the British context. By the mid-1970s, after the debacle in *Vietnam, the concept seemed to be losing its charm. A decade later there was a revival of interest in the problem of low-intensity conflict (LIC) as global instability increased. In 1986 a 'Low Intensity Warfare' conference at the US Department of Defense avoided highlighting the term counter-insurgency, but indicated that the issue would remain a prime threat to 'peace and freedom' for the rest of the century at least. CT

Beckett, Ian, and Pimlott, John (eds.), *Armed Forces and Modern Counter-Insurgency* (London, 1985).

Galula, David, *Counter-Insurgency Warfare* (London, 1964).

Paget, Julian, *Counter-Insurgency Campaigning* (London, 1967).

Shafer, D. Michael, *Deadly Paradigms: The Failure of US Counterinsurgency Policy* (Princeton, 1988).

Townshend, Charles, *Britain's Civil Wars: Counterinsurgency in the 20th Century* (London, 1986).

coup d'état (Fr., stroke of state), an attempt to change a government by the threat or use of force, usually but not always associated with the military, although the willingness and ability or lack of it on the part of the armed forces to defend a government can be decisive in a *coup d'état* by others. Although the popular image is of tanks surrounding the presidential palace as in Chile in 1973, this was in fact only the second successful coup in Chilean history (there was also a civil war) and the preferred method in Hispanic countries has been the *cuartelazo*, the ominous confining of itself to barracks by the garrison of the capital, usually enough to achieve the objectives of the military leaders. The so-called *Curragh mutiny, for example, was a threatened British *cuartelazo*, and a threat of refusal to act in support of the civil power took place as recently as 1968 in France.

This is not to deny that Latin America has seen more military coups than any other continent: until the 1980s,

Bolivia had had more governments than it had years of independent life, and the record of the armed forces elsewhere in the continent has been shameful, exacerbated until relatively recently by US influence. As Franklin D. *Roosevelt said of the deplorable dictator Somoza, installed in *Nicaragua by US arms, 'he may be a son of a bitch, but he's *our* son of a bitch'. The same thought no doubt crossed the mind of *Churchill when he supported pro-British but unsavoury military leaders in the Middle East between the wars.

In general, those military coups that are not an outright grab for power and money stem from an intense dislike of the corruption and disorder of civilian politics, coupled with a belief that the armed forces represent the distillation of patriotism. The latter argument, of course, has commonly been used to justify the former and it is a rare military regime that does not promptly sink into the most appalling corruption itself. Two glowing exceptions were *Atatürk, who reached power in a coup but erected a rigid barrier between the military and politics that lasted for 50 years, and 'Pepe' Figueres in Costa Rica, who in 1948 abolished the very armed forces that originally brought him to power. Armed forces chronically involved in politics also notoriously lose sight of their primary function, as seen in the lamentable performance of the Argentine army in the *Falklands.

In most cases the coup is undertaken to displace one set of rulers, typically the civilian leadership, and establish the power of an alternative group, which is often, but not necessarily, the military. What distinguishes a coup from revolutions is that they are typically carried by relatively small groups and do not involve mass political action. The second key difference is that while those who carry out the coup are seeking to change the government or ruling group, they are not usually trying to change the regime or bring about broader social change. The coup is often an attempt to remedy a specific or immediate grievance and is very unlikely to involve any widescale change in the social order. Often the coup is undertaken to pre-empt revolutionary change from below and impose a measure of reform from above. The new government installed by the coup usually relies on some degree of civilian collaboration, particularly from the civil service, but rarely provides any useful solution to long-term social and economic problems.

Military coups occurred regularly in 19th-century Spain and the Balkans, but during the 20th century they have been largely confined to developing states in Africa, Latin America, and Asia. Coups have been less prevalent, although not unknown, in developed industrialized counties, where governments have a large degree of legitimacy and where accepted procedures for the orderly change of administration are in place. In post-WW II Europe, military intervention in civilian politics has been provoked by failures in the process of decolonization such as in France in 1958, when the revolt of the French army during the *Algerian independence war led to the return to power of *de Gaulle; the army then revolted against him in turn, which de Gaulle overcame by appealing to the troops over their officers' heads.

Other causes have been rapid economic change and political polarization as in Greece in 1967, and these factors as well as post-colonial trauma contributed to the 1974 military coup in Portugal. The farcical failure of the attempted coup of 23 February 1981 in Spain by reactionary elements within the army and Guardia Civil yearning for a return to authoritarian government demonstrated the vital role of legitimacy, in the person of King Juan Carlos if not in a brawling and intemperate parliament. Here the dreadful cost of the *Spanish civil war and the 40-year dictatorship by *Franco that followed the last *coup d'état* undoubtedly also served to render the coup a complete non-starter.

Another factor is what we might call 'trade union' disputes between the military and governments. If the military has means available to it for advancing its corporate and professional interests then the danger of direct action over differences with the government is dissipated. Furthermore many armies have a long and determined tradition of non-intervention in civil affairs. For example, despite endemic political corruption and mismanagement, as well as acute religious and regional divisions, the *Indian army has resolutely stayed out of politics, whereas in Pakistan the military appointed itself the overseer of the national interest and has on occasion seized power to 'save' the nation, seeing itself as an Atatürk-like modernizing force confronting a traditionally kleptomaniac, divisive civilian political élite.

On many occasions great powers have either intervened directly or used local surrogates to overthrow regimes that threatened their interests. The entire British conquest of India hinged on this technique, finally coming unstuck in *Afghanistan where, over a century later, the Soviets also thought they could depose rulers at will, to their ultimate sorrow. The US-sponsored overthrow of Diem in *Vietnam was likewise something akin to getting their tie caught in a mangle, as the very human tendency to reinforce error took over. A move originally intended to revitalize South Vietnam and make it better capable of defending itself ended with the commitment of a previously unimaginable level of US resources. Even the Anglo-American overthrow of Mossadegh in Iran, once considered a highly successful piece of rascality, does not today find many defenders as the West gloomily contemplates the jinnee of outraged nationalism allied with religious revivalism that emerged once their stopper the shah blew out of the Middle Eastern bottle.

HEB

courts martial Tribunals that enforce the special laws and standards of conduct expected of soldiers, once more lax but now in general more strict than the civil courts governing non-military personnel. The singular is also commonly used as a verb to describe the process, as in 'he was court-martialled for drunkenness'. The origin of this semantic awkwardness lies in the first military tribunal in Britain, the court of the *constable and the *marshal. During the 17th century the administration of military *justice was gradually taken over by ad hoc committees of army officers, at first called marshal courts and later courts martial. These evolved into general courts with a wide jurisdiction, which could try all ranks, usually sitting with a judge advocate, a civilian lawyer who advised the court on matters of law. District courts had more limited powers and could not try officers.

The right of officers to be tried by their own kind was one of the most persistent sources of friction between civil and military authorities through the 19th century and, in Spain, well into the 20th. Few countries paid a higher price than Mexico, where the issue of military and ecclesiastical *fueros* (exemptions) bloodily dominated political life for the first 50 years of independence. Military courts elsewhere developed along less stark dividing lines. General and regimental courts martial were created in the Prussian and Austrian armies, with civilian lawyers acting as procedural auditors. In France and Belgium a civilian judge sat with the military members of the court. The courts martial system in the US army was modelled on that of the British, with general courts, sitting with a civilian legal adviser, exercising the widest powers, and district or special courts dealing with lesser offences.

Military courts in the armies of most nations are still comprised entirely of officers, although in the French army *NCOs are allowed to sit as members, and if an enlisted man is being tried in the US army he can require, if he wishes, that a third of the members of the court should be enlisted men. Even during the 19th century, if an NCO or a private soldier was being court-martialled in the German army a set proportion of the members of the court had to hold the same rank as the accused. In Italy the permanent military tribunals were for the trial of non-commissioned ranks and special tribunals were appointed to try officers.

Few armies in the past permitted appeals against the decisions of their military courts. During the 20th century the pattern of military justice in *most* countries has moved closer to the procedures of the ordinary criminal courts. In Italy and the Netherlands the military courts of appeal are staffed equally by army officers and civilian lawyers, and in the USA, France, Belgium, and Germany appeals against courts martial convictions are heard by the civil appeals courts. In the British army, servicemen can now appeal against conviction or sentence to a specific court martial appeals court, which is manned by civil judges.

AB1

cowardice in a military context is the refusal to confront the hardships of combat, the possibility of injury and death, and the requirement for self-sacrifice. Cowardice is distinct from fear. In any situation, military or otherwise, fear is a natural and rational response to the prospect of extreme discomfort and pain. *Veterans of combat have often written of the fear which they and their fellows felt, and have usually been wary of if not actively hostile towards those who, professing themselves fearless, might involve them in unnecessary risks. In combat the soldier who proves unwilling to control his fear and who chooses self-preservation over duty is labelled a coward, losing the respect and loyalty of colleagues and facing punishment under military law. The concept of cowardice, therefore, incorporates both the individual's action and the reaction to it; what turns an otherwise natural, human response into something to be deplored is the context of combat.

There are two explanations for the intolerance of cowardice traditionally shown by military organizations. The first concerns general, embedded expectations of appropriate male behaviour *in extremis*; fear may be natural, but mature, dutiful, and responsible men are expected to control it. The second is that the entire purpose of military training and organization is to make sure that when the 'fight or flight' autonomic response takes place, the soldier chooses the former. A military unit must be disciplined, cohesive, and efficient if it is to withstand the pressures of combat and one individual's cowardice may undermine the whole unit's effectiveness, either by emulation or simply by opening a hole in a position that the enemy may exploit.

A distinction should be drawn between the unwillingness to confront battle, and an inability to do so. The 20th century has seen the gradual development of a more sympathetic assessment of the effects of battle on the human mind, and it is now widely accepted that some who might previously have been considered cowards may in fact be psychiatric *casualties and their behaviour the involuntary symptoms of battle stress.
PC

Crane, Stephen (1871–1900), American novelist and brilliant exponent of the short story. Best remembered for *The Red Badge of Courage* (1895), a story of a young soldier's struggle with *cowardice widely praised by *American civil war veterans as an accurate exploration of the realities of combat, although at the time the author had no personal experience to draw upon. Anxious to live what he had imagined and despite suffering from tuberculosis, Crane was a *war correspondent for New York newspapers during the *Graeco-Turkish war and the *Spanish-American war in Cuba, where he contracted malaria and fatally exacerbated his underlying condition.
HEB

Crazy Horse, Sioux Chief (1840–77) (Siouan: *Tashunca-uitco*), seer of visions and matchless exponent of light horse tactics during the last stand of the Plains Indians (see PLAINS INDIANS WARS). He was a leading participant in the successful war against the Bozeman Trail (1865–8) and led the Oglala to victory at the Rosebud and the united Lakota and Arapaho/Cheyenne against *Custer at *Little Bighorn in 1876. He was murdered after surrender at the Red Cloud Agency in Nebraska. Since 1949, at the invitation of the Lakota, the Ziolowski family has been excavating an equestrian sculpture of him in his beloved Black Hills (*Paha Sapa*) to surpass nearby Mount Rushmore in size.
HEB

Crécy, battle of (1346). The first major English victory on land in the *Hundred Years War was achieved by dismounted men-at-arms and *archers, using tactics which became classic. *Edward III had landed at La Hogue in Normandy on 12 July 1346 with *c*.15,000 men, of whom less than 3,000 were men-at-arms, *c*.4,000 mounted archers, and *c*.8,000 foot soldiers. Although he may have planned an occupation, as he marched south and east, the expedition developed as a ferocious *chevauchée, his shipping keeping abreast to carry home the enormous booty. After Caen fell (26 July), Edward announced he would seek out Philip VI of France and his army, then gathered around Paris. Ponthieu may have already been chosen for the encounter since orders were given to send supplies to the mouth of the Somme. He then marched up the Seine, reaching Poissy (13 August), whence he attacked Paris, before turning north, pursued by the enraged French.

Edward was at first unable to cross the Somme, but a ford at Blanchetacque, below Abbeville, was traversed on 24 August despite opposition. A few miles to the north-east, on a gentle slope between Crécy and Wadicourt, with a wood behind them, the English took up a position probably reconnoitred in advance. With *c*.25,000 men, Philip VI left Abbeville early on 26 August, catching the English around midday. By late afternoon his troops had formed three main divisions (battles), one behind the other, with 6,000 Genoese crossbowmen in the first rank, the main cavalry force in the second, and the king in the third. The English also formed three battles. Whether these were disposed in line abreast, with archers thrown forward on the two outer flanks; or whether the longbowmen were placed to either side of each battle (the tactics of Dupplin Moor (1332) and Halidon Hill (1333)); and whether the two battles were in the front line, with the third, commanded by Edward in the centre but to the rear as a reserve, are matters still hotly disputed: contemporary sources are ambiguous.

When the Genoese began the attack at 17.00, they were quickly repulsed, whereupon the Count of Alençon, commanding the main cavalry, rode through the retreating archers only to meet the English archers' same devastating fire while primitive cannon (this may have been their first use in the field) caused further panic. The English right wing briefly wavered, and in the centre the *'Black Prince', who was 'winning his spurs' as his father wished, was hard pressed. But the French were broken, Philip VI fleeing the field. English casualties were light but there were thousands of French dead, among them the counts of Flanders, Alençon, and Blois, the Duke of Lorraine, and blind King John of Bohemia, whose retinue, in a supremely quixotic gesture, had, at his own request, led him into battle with their bridles tied together. If the strategic gains for Edward III were slight (it needed the capture of *Calais in 1347 to consolidate Crécy), for Philip VI the battle was not only a military disaster but also a political catastrophe. MJ

Bennett, M., 'The Development of Battle Tactics in the Hundred Years War', in A. Curry and M. Hughes (eds.), *Arms, Armies and Fortifications in the Hundred Years War* (Woodbridge, 1994).

Sumption, J., *The Hundred Years War*, vol. 1. *Trial by Battle* (London, 1990).

Crete, battle of (1941), the first *airborne assault on a major island. The defenders, mainly Commonwealth forces withdrawn from the Greek mainland at the end of April, outnumbered their attackers, but of Lt Gen Freyberg's 42,460 men, barely half were properly formed and equipped. The New Zealand Division was deployed west of Canea up to Maleme airfield, the British 14th Infantry Brigade defended Heraklion airfield, and two Australian battalions covered Rethymnon airfield. The attack was no surprise. Likely dropping zones had been identified in November 1940. *ULTRA intelligence confirmed them as targets two weeks before the invasion. Freyberg's defence plan was distorted by his fixed idea that a seaborne invasion would follow rapidly behind the airborne assault. MERCURY, planned by Gen *Student, was spearheaded by 7th Airborne Division on 20 May. From well-prepared positions, the British and Commonwealth forces killed or wounded nearly two-thirds of the division. A total of over 3,000 paratroopers were killed. Student's superiors believed the battle lost. In a last-ditch attempt early on 21 May, Student sent reinforcements to the Maleme area. The New Zealand commander, still expecting a seaborne invasion, delayed sending in a counter-attack and the battalion responsible for the airfield withdrew. Student dropped his last paratroop reserves, then started to land the 5th Mountain Division. That same day, 21 May, Freyberg misread ULTRA message OL 15/389. He took it to mean that the Germans were going to land troops by sea near Canea. In fact only a small convoy of caiques, bearing a single battalion of *mountain troops, was headed for Maleme, not Canea. Freyberg concentrated his best forces close to Canea and insisted that Australian troops replace those New Zealanders earmarked for the counter-attack due that night against Maleme airfield. This delayed its start fatally. Shortly before midnight, a Royal Navy force intercepted the flotilla and destroyed much of it. Freyberg went to bed convinced that Crete had been saved. But the two understrength battalions, all that had been allocated for the counter-attack on Maleme, had started so late that they were caught in the open at daybreak on 22 May by Gen von Richthofen's fighters. Freyberg's son later claimed that his father had acted as he had only to protect the secret of ULTRA.

At Heraklion and Rethymnon the airfields had been saved through prompt and vigorous counter-attacks. But once Student had secured Maleme, he was able to fly in the rest of his mountain troops. The Commonwealth forces, exhausted from continual air attack, pulled back. Freyberg gave the order to retreat south over the White Mountains to the tiny port of Sphakia, where Royal Navy warships from Alexandria evacuated 15,000 men. Those left behind surrendered on 1 June. The Axis had conquered Crete, but at such a cost that *Hitler forbade any further airborne operations. AB2

Beevor, Antony, *Crete—The Battle and the Resistance* (London, 1991).

Davin, Dan, *Crete* (Oxford, 1953).

Freyberg, Paul, *Bernard Freyberg VC: Soldier of Two Nations* (London, 1991).

Stewart, Ian, *The Struggle for Crete* (Oxford, 1955).

Creusot, Le Burgundian town whose natural resources made it a centre of the French arms manufacturing industry. A royal foundry was established there in 1782 and produced iron and bronze cannon. In 1836 Adolphe and Eugène Schneider acquired the enterprise, and soon made cannon, locomotives, and armour plate. There were 10,000 workers by 1867, and during the *Franco-Prussian war Schneider delivered 250 cannon, with carriages and limbers. After the law was changed to permit the export of arms in 1884 the factory grew rapidly. The South African republics were among its customers, and used some Creusot guns in the Second *Boer War. New artillery workshops were opened in 1888, and a 100 tonne steam-hammer, which remains a local landmark, was built. A range was opened near Le Havre on the Normandy coast to test long-range guns, and more workshops were built nearby. There was widespread collaboration with marine engineering companies. By WW I the enterprise was enormous—60 locomotives used 168 miles (270 km) of railway within the works—and the loss of part of France's heavy industry to German invasion in 1914 increased its significance. It remained important in the inter-war years and was bombed by the Allies during WW II. Le Creusot's industry has long since diversified, and its name is now more commonly seen on cooking pots than guns. RH

Crimean war Philip Guedalla called it 'one of the bad jokes of history', and the war's immediate cause, a dispute between Orthodox and Roman Catholic monks in Jerusalem, part of the Turkish empire, certainly had an element

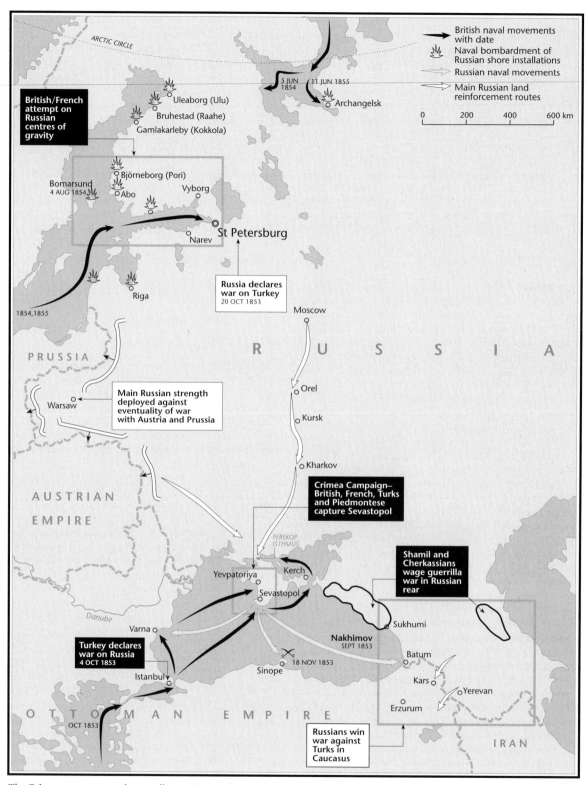

The legend in the top right corner reads:

- ➤ British naval movements with date
- ☀ Naval bombardment of Russian shore installations
- ⇨ Russian naval movements
- ⇨ Main Russian land reinforcement routes

Scale: 0 200 400 600 km

British/French attempt on Russian centres of gravity

Uleaborg (Ulu)
Bruhestad (Raahe)
Gamlakarleby (Kokkola)

5 JUN 1854 11 JUN 1855

Archangelsk

Björneborg (Pori)

Bomarsund 4 AUG 1854
Abo
Vyborg

St Petersburg
Narev

Riga

1854,1855

Russia declares war on Turkey 20 OCT 1853

Moscow

PRUSSIA

Warsaw

Main Russian strength deployed against eventuality of war with Austria and Prussia

R U S S I A

Orel

Kursk

Kharkov

AUSTRIAN EMPIRE

Crimea Campaign– British, French, Turks and Piedmontese capture Sevastopol

PEREKOP ISTHMUS

Yevpatoriya
Kerch
Sevastopol

Shamil and Cherkassians wage guerrilla war in Russian rear

Sukhumi

Danube

Varna

Nakhimov SEPT 1853

Batum

Turkey declares war on Russia 4 OCT 1853

18 NOV 1853

Istanbul
Sinope

Kars
Yerevan

Erzurum

O T T O M A N   E M P I R E

OCT 1853

Russians win war against Turks in Caucasus

IRAN

The **Crimean war**, 1853–6: the overall strategic situation.

236

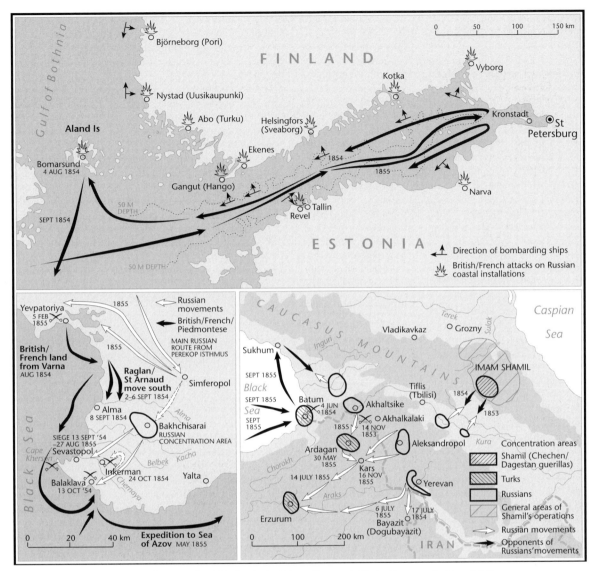

The **Crimean war**, 1853–6: main theatres. The Baltic (top); the Crimea (bottom left); the Caucasus (bottom right).

of farce. Wider causes were more serious. Turkey was in decline, and Russian ambitions alarmed both France, whose *Napoleon III favoured a forward foreign policy, and Britain, committed to preserving Turkish authority. In March 1853 the Turkish government, its resolve stiffened by the British ambassador, declined an ultimatum demanding that the Orthodox Church in Turkey should be placed under Russian protection. The Russians occupied the Danubian principalities, and when they refused to withdraw Turkey declared war. On 30 November a Turkish squadron was destroyed at Sinope in the Black Sea, and this helped push Britain and France towards war, which was declared in March 1854.

Britain and France both sent expeditionary forces to the east, the former under FM Lord *Raglan, a confidant of the late Duke of *Wellington, and the latter under Marshal St Arnaud. It was once argued that the British army had atrophied in the long peace following *Waterloo, but Hew Strachan has demonstrated that 'On many levels the British army was either being reformed or, more pertinently, reforming itself, in the period 1830 to 1854.' However, there remained areas of weakness. Raglan had some 26,000 men, many of them raw recruits, and no reserves. Transport and supply were ill-suited to a distant campaign in bleak and unproductive terrain, and army administration was chaotically decentralized. Raglan's force comprised five infantry divisions (four commanded by *Peninsular veterans aged between 60 and 70) and Lord Lucan's cavalry division, its light brigade under Lord Cardigan and its heavy brigade under Sir James Scarlett. The French had gained experience during their conquest of *Algeria, and their first contingent of four infantry divisions and two cavalry brigades (about 40,000 men) included many units from North Africa. As the war went the French were to send another seven infantry divisions: 50 of the 100 line infantry regiments served in the east. This imposed a serious strain on the French army, but the French contingent was larger, and in many respects more efficient, than the British. The Russian army loomed large in the mind of Tsar Nicholas I: in the 1820s he spend about three-quarters of his day on military matters. Its hardy but brutalized soldiers had beaten Persians, Turks, and Poles, but it was unimaginatively trained and lacked an experienced general staff. Although it had a total regular and reserve strength of perhaps 1,400,000 men, it was wholly unprepared for modern war. When Nicholas ordered it to enter the Danubian principalities on 2 July 1853 he was committing it to a task for which it was unfitted: it made heavy weather against the Turks, and laid siege to the Turkish fortress of Silistria, on the Danube.

As the Allies concentrated, first at Scutari, near Constantinople, and then at Varna, on the western coast of the Black Sea, the war seemed to be going badly for Russia. Silistria, its defence stiffened by some British officers, held out, and the Russians, their ranks thinned by cholera, withdrew from the Danubian principalities, depriving the Allies of a target. The British government believed that the Russian naval base of Sevastopol should now be attacked, and ordered Raglan to take it unless he felt the task to be impossible. Accordingly the Allies sailed for the Crimea, and landed at Calamita Bay, north of Sevastopol, on 14 September. The Russian commander, Prince Menshikov, had not believed that the Allies would invade, and when they did so he prepared to receive them inland, with more than 35,000 men in a strong position on the river Alma. The British spent two nights without tents, and when they were eventually ready to advance too few wagons had been commandeered for their baggage and the men, many of them sick, were heavily laden.

The Allies set off on 19 September, about 60,000 strong, with the British on the left and the French on the right. Some men dropped with cholera on the march, and even the fit found the advance exhausting. There was a cavalry skirmish on the little river Bulganak, and the Allies spent the night in the field, aware that Menshikov was in position on the Alma. Raglan and St Arnaud agreed that night that the French would attack the high ground on the Russian left, which St Arnaud believed to be strongly held, while the British swept round the Russian right.

The battle began at about 13.30, and it became clear that the British were facing the main Russian positions, where two redoubts—the Great and the Lesser—covered the slopes leading down to the river. Obedient to the Allied plan the French attacked first, enabling the Russians to shift some of their guns to rake them, provoking demands that the British should attack. The Russians fired the village of Bourliouk as the British advanced, causing some confusion, but the attackers were soon across the Alma and on their way up the slopes behind it. Cannon fire from the Great Redoubt caused casualties, but the guns were withdrawn prematurely, and the Light and 2nd Divisions, drawn up in line, then became involved in a firefight against Russian columns. Some British regiments gave ground against counter-attacks, but the 1st Division came up, and its Guards and *Highlanders pushed back the Russians, who withdrew in good order; Raglan declined to unleash his cavalry against them. Some Russian combatants blamed their defeat on lack of orders. One wrote that 'During the five hours of fighting we neither saw nor heard from our divisional general, our brigade or regimental commanders, nor did we receive any orders to advance or retire.' Another shrewdly observed that the rifles carried by most Allied infantry were far more effective than the muskets carried by the majority of Russians. The Allies had lost over 3,000 casualties and the Russians more than 5,000. The Allies might have mounted an immediate attack on Sevastopol, whose defences were incomplete, but St Arnaud, who was mortally ill, was not enthusiastic. Instead they marched around the city, establishing themselves on the uplands to its south, supplied through the little ports of Kamiech and Balaklava.

Raglan and *Canrobert, the new French commander, agreed to bombard Sevastopol before mounting an attack. Heavy guns were landed and batteries prepared, and on 17 October the bombardment began. British and French warships, standing inshore to take on the forts, were badly knocked about, and although the land bombardment seemed more promising, it too was strenuously opposed. The defenders, many of them sailors, were inspired by Adm Kornilov, who was mortally wounded on 17 October, and Col Todleben, an engineer officer sent down to assist Menshikov, played a leading part in repairing damaged defences and building new ones. The Allied rear, where the Woronzoff road ran eastwards, was secured by a number of Turkish-manned redoubts. Suspicions that the Menshikov's field army, which had slipped away from Sevastopol and been reinforced by fresh troops marching down from Bessarabia, might approach from this quarter led to frequent alarms. On 25 October about 25,000 Russians advanced from the east, taking the redoubts and sending a force towards Balaclava, whose capture was probably Menshikov's objective. It was checked by the *Thin Red Line of the 93rd Highlanders, and Scarlett's Heavy Brigade successfully charged Russian cavalry north of Balaclava. Raglan's order to the Light Brigade, intended to prevent the Russians from taking guns from the captured redoubts, was misunderstood. Raglan and his *QMG Airey, who drew up the loosely worded order, were on high ground with a good view of the field, but failed to appreciate that commanders in the valleys below would see less. Capt Nolan, an impetuous ADC, delivered the order to Lucan, commanding the cavalry division, and the latter sent him on to Cardigan. The personal feud between their lordships and Nolan's provocative insolence did the rest. Cardigan was presented with a formal order to attack the only guns visible to him, a battery at the end of a shallow valley with riflemen around it and cavalry in support. In the ensuing charge the Light Brigade took the battery but could not hold it, and had 247 of its 670 officers and men killed or wounded. French Chasseurs d'Afrique carried out a well-executed charge to help the survivors withdraw. The day after Balaclava the Russians mounted a sortie from Sevastopol against British lines on the complex series of ridges where the river Chernaia entered Sevastopol harbour. 'Little Inkerman' failed, but it provided the Russians with useful information, and 5 November they launched a much bigger attack, with 20,000 men advancing from Sevastopol while 16,000 from the field army crossed the Chernaia to attack the British from the east and another 22,000 men swung south to threaten the French. The battle of Inkerman was fought on difficult ground in thick fog. It was decided by the dogged determination of the British defenders, supported, as the day went on, by the French. 'The French are saving the English at Inkerman,' commented a bitter Russian officer, 'as the Prussians did at Waterloo.' Its results were terrible: the hardened Gen Bosquet described the much fought-over Sand Bag Battery as an abattoir. The British lost 2,500 men, the French 1,700, and the Russians perhaps 12,000. After Inkerman, Menshikov, deeply unpopular with his subordinates, was replaced by Prince Gorchakov, who struck many of them as scarcely an improvement. Adm Nakhimov was the soul of Sevastopol's defence: morose and fatalistic, alone among the garrison's officers he still wore his gold epaulettes.

The Allies spent an uncomfortable winter before Sevastopol, and growing concerns about the British army's inadequate administration provoked attacks on Raglan in both press and parliament, although opinion in the army was more evenly divided. Keenly sensitive to these insults, Raglan had to grapple with a French command whose sense of purpose seemed infirm. On 16 May Canrobert, exasperated by order and counter-order over the *telegraph from Paris, resigned command and was replaced by the hard-driving Pélissier. Things improved at once. Kerch, at the eastern end of the Crimea, was taken by an Allied force which did much damage and opened the way into the Sea of Azov, destroying the Russian naval squadron there: Andrew Lambert calls the episode 'amongst the finest achievements of the war'.

On land, Raglan and Pélissier agreed to attack two of Sevastopol's outwork, the Quarries, in the British sector, and the Mamelon, in the French, as a prelude to the assault on the Great Redan and the Malakoff. The Quarries and the Mamelon were duly taken on 7 June. However, ten days later the British were repulsed from the Redan with the loss of 1,500 men. The repulse greatly cheered the Russian defenders, but the gallant Nakhimov was mortally wounded. Raglan died on 28 June: his most recent biographer blames a broken heart. The Russian field army made a last attack at the Chernaia on 16 August. On 8 September Raglan's successor, Gen Simpson, attacked the Redan again, sustaining almost 2,500 casualties. But the French stormed the Malakoff that morning, and Sevastopol was untenable: the Russians withdrew on the night of 8–9 September.

Although the Crimea was the war's main theatre, the Allies also sent support to Shamyl, whose Muslim zealots were fighting the Russians in the Caucasus, and embarked upon a more ambitious strategy in the Baltic. The French first approached the Swedes, offering an alliance which was rejected, although there were suggestions that a substantial subsidy might draw Sweden into the war. It then seemed likely that Sweden would join the Allies only if Austria did, and in March 1854 the Allies launched a Baltic campaign on their own. After a succession of problems which mirrored, on a smaller scale, those in the Crimea, the Allies attacked the fortress of Bomarsund, on the Aland islands, quickly knocking it into submission. Plans for an attack on Sveaborg, on the Finnish coast, were aborted in a flurry of mutual recrimination, and the main Allied squadrons withdrew, though they maintained a blockade for the remainder of the war. The British commander, the brave but headstrong V Adm Sir Charles Napier, complained bitterly that he had been unfairly treated by Sir James Graham, first Lord of the Admiralty, and post-war bickering reflected the tensions of this ill-starred campaign.

Nicholas I had died early in 1855, leading to hopes that his successor Alexander II would agree to peace terms. The loss of Sevastopol, a renewed demonstration of Allied amphibious strength by the capture of Kinburn on the coast of mainland Russia, and Austria's threat to enter the war eventually proved decisive, and peace was concluded in Paris in 1856. The neutralization of the Black Sea was a blow to Russian expansionism, and the Danubian principalities speedily became the autonomous Romania. Troops from the Italian state of Piedmont had served with the Allies, gaining her a place at the negotiating table and marking the first step towards the Franco-Austrian war of 1859. The war underlined the British army's administrative weaknesses, and accelerated reform.   RH

Guedalla, Philip, *The Two Marshals: Bazaine, Pétain* (London, 1943).

Hibbert, Christopher, *The Destruction of Lord Raglan* (London, 1961).

Lambert, Andrew D., *The Crimean War: British Grand Strategy against Russia* (Manchester, 1990).

Seaton, Albert, *The Crimean War: A Russian Chronicle* (London, 1977).

Strachan, Hew, *Wellington's Legacy: The Reform of the British Army 1815–1854* (Manchester, 1984).

Sweetman, John, *Raglan: From the Peninsula to the Crimea* (London, 1993).

Croatian light forces were light units and storm troopers in the service of the Habsburgs, who were respected for their mobility and speed. They were known as Croatian regiments, although their commanders were rarely Croat and more usually trusted Habsburg commanders. They were recruited from the Croatian Military Border (Krajina in Croat) bordering the Ottoman empire, which the Habsburgs exempted from the control of the Croat Sabor (parliament) and ran as a *barracks. Many, perhaps most, of these troops from the frontier were Orthodox Vlach or Serb immigrants from Ottoman-ruled Bosnia.

Croat units took part in all the battles of the *Thirty Years War, the Wars of the *Spanish Succession and *Austrian Succession, and the *Seven Years Wars, and then in Austria's wars with *Napoleon. The emperor admired them, recruiting his own Croat regiments in his client state in Dalmatia, and sent Croats to military academies in Paris. The Croats' fierce reputation inspired foreign rulers to recruit them for their palace guards. The 'Royal-Cravattes' of 17th-century France gave rise to the word cravat, from their distinctive neckwear. The abolition of the frontier in the 19th century ended the special character of the Croat regiments.   MGT

Rothenberg, E., *The Austrian Military Border in Croatia* (Champaign, 1960).

Omrcanin, I., *Military History of Croatia*, (Bryn Mawr, 1984).

Crockett, Davy (1786–1836), American folk hero. The real David Crockett was a Tennessee backwoods politician who had the good fortune to be systematically promoted by the Whig party to counter the frontiersman appeal of the Democrat Andrew Jackson. The latter, under whom Crockett served in the Creek war (1813–15), made a point of ending his political career in 1835. His *Autobiography*, vigorously ghost-written by the Kentucky congressman Thomas Chilton, and several likewise imaginative almanacs ensured that the 'coonskin' image caught on during his lifetime. But his durable position in popular culture, most notably the commercial craze of the 1950s, was born of his heroic death as the best-known defender of the *Alamo. There is violent controversy whether he was among the handful killed after surrender, but the point is surely that he went to Texas to explore land investments and could easily have avoided his fate. He chose instead to share the fortunes of the volunteers and thus to symbolize uncompromising commitment to liberty.

Crockett has given his name to the M-388 'nuclear bazooka', a light vehicle-mounted recoilless rifle firing the very low-yield (10 and 20 T) Mk 54 warhead. An inherently destabilizing weapon in service with the US army 1961–71.

                                                                    HEB

Cromwell, Oliver (1599–1658), soldier and statesman, Lord Protector of the Commonwealth (1653–8). He began his career as a Member of the Long Parliament for Cambridge who returned to his native county when the English civil war broke out to raise a troop of horse against the king (see BRITISH CIVIL WARS). Until then his career had provided little clue of the greatness to come. A gentleman of modest means he had, around 1630, undergone a Calvinist conversion experience which transformed his life. His troop of horse soon swelled to two regiments, called the 'Ironsides' after the nickname that Prince *Rupert of the Rhine gave the unbending Oliver himself. His trenchant philosophy for *recruitment was: 'If you choose Godly honest men to be captains of horse, honest men will follow them, . . . I had rather have a plain russet-coated captain that knows what he fights for, and loves what he knows, than that which you call a gentleman and is nothing else.'

By contrast with the royalists, and indeed the hell-for-leather English cavalry tradition, Cromwell kept his men well in hand. At *Marston Moor he first defeated the royalist right wing under Lord Byron, then turned to attack the adjacent infantry. Obliged to leave the battlefield for treatment of a wound to the neck, he returned to lead his men to join *Fairfax in attacking and routing the remaining royalist cavalry under Goring. He served as lieutenant general to Fairfax in the *New Model Army and at *Naseby the following year Cromwell's iron control was again in evidence. After scattering the left wing of the royalist horse he again resisted the temptation of pursuit and regrouped to envelop the royalist infantry in a battle of near-annihilation.

Over a career involving many dozens of battles, sieges, and skirmishes, Cromwell was beaten once: at Clonmel in May 1650, when he walked into a trap laid by Hugh O'Neill. The blunder cost him 1,500 men. His masterpiece was Dunbar. There, in September 1650, he faced a well-equipped and trained Anglo-Scots force of 20,000 under David Leslie. His own army of 16,000 had been reduced by sickness and *desertion to 11,000 within a matter of weeks. Encamped with their back to the sea, it seemed that they were about to be rolled over by the Scots, who from their commanding position on Doon Hill controlled the road back to England. On the morning of 2 September Leslie confidently moved his army down the hill, preparatory to an attack on what he believed to be a demoralized English army.

But Cromwell had perceived a weakness in the Scots position. He saw how their left wing was crowded against the steep slope of Spott Burn Glen, thus unlikely to be able to deploy, and that the two wings of Leslie's army would not be able to support each other. He also saw a slight depression across the front of the enemy and under the cover of driving rain and darkness marched the bulk of his army along it, literally under Leslie's nose. As he launched the assault at daybreak, he shouted the words of the psalmist, 'Now let God arise, and his enemies shall be scattered.' Isolated from their comrades, the Scots right wing crumpled and the battle was over in barely an hour. Three thousand Scots were slaughtered and 10,000 taken prisoner. Cromwell lost only twenty of his own men.

He was a courageous and charismatic leader, and the only English commoner ever to seize power in a *coup d'état, which he did by expelling the unrepresentative Rump of the Long Parliament in 1653. He accepted the title of Lord Protector (some wanted him to become king) but was not able to establish a settlement which long survived his death. He was superbly successful in animating his men with his own burning conviction that they would accomplish great things as instruments of the Almighty. He was also a shrewd judge of men who chose good subordinates and trusted them to do their job well. He was a good battlefield tactician who could visualize the possibilities inherent in a piece of terrain and exploit them to devastating effect. Not least of all, he cared for his men, and was thrifty with their lives. He had the political ability to fight for and obtain the money and supplies he needed, often refusing to move forward until they were in place. Because his soldiers knew they were safe in his hands, they rewarded him with intense loyalty. He is among the greatest generals Britain has produced. IG

Crusades, the The medieval papacy frequently attempted to use its spiritual power to exhort temporal lords to perform service for it, notably during the invasion of England by *William 'the Conqueror' in 1066, an enterprise encouraged and blessed by the pope because the English Church was schismatic. But the era of what are generally regarded as *the* Crusades began in November 1095 when Pope Urban II (1088–99) proposed a military expedition to seize *Jerusalem, distant by some 2,486 miles (4,000 km) from Clermont where he preached, in a land strange to most of his hearers with an unfamiliar climate and occupied by people of an alien *religion who were implacably hostile. No king had promised to take command, no one had shown interest in conquest there, and all who went would have to fund themselves. It was ideological warfare in the purest sense—men should leave their riches, their wives, and their lands to free Jerusalem from the infidel to gain an indulgence—release from the burden of sin, and, if death should overcome them, immediate entry into the kingdom of heaven.

But the knights to whom he addressed his appeal were familiar with the notion of Holy War and the Crusade was preached to them in terms comprehensible to a landowning aristocracy, of recovery of wrongly taken land: Innocent III (1198–1216) compared the crusader's duty to that of a vassal going to aid his dispossessed lord. Moreover Urban seems always to have envisaged the founding of states in the Middle East and rightful gain was the natural consequence of righteous war. Religious enthusiasm was undoubtedly the driving force of the Crusade, but it was spiced by the hope of gain. In the end about 100,000 joined the Crusade and about 60,000 entered Asia Minor in 1097.

The Byzantine Emperor Alexius I Comnenus had planted the idea of a crusade by asking Urban II for *mercenaries because he saw in the break-up of the Seljuk *Turk empire an opportunity to reconquer Asia Minor. This was why the Crusade entered the Middle East at a moment of acute political fragmentation. This in part explains its success, but even so its achievement in liberating Jerusalem in July 1099 was remarkable, because it defeated powerful enemies—the Seljuks of Rhum, the successor states of the Seljuks in Syria, and the Fatimid caliphate of Cairo—all of which were capable of fielding great armies and outnumbering the crusaders, who had lost many men crossing Asia Minor. Moreover many of the crusaders' horses had perished on the march, so that their vital cavalry force was quite small. Able leadership—especially in the person of *Bohemond who was a fine soldier—effective unity, and an unquenchable spirit of righteousness explain their success. They also enjoyed the support of allies, notably the Byzantines and the Armenians, and sea power which was essential especially to the sieges of *Antioch and Jerusalem. It was the seizure of these cities, in which the crusaders showed a high degree of military skill, that laid the basis for Latin rule in the Holy Land. The establishment of Latin bridgeheads in the Middle East at Edessa, Antioch, Jerusalem, and later Tripoli was a remarkable achievement, however a quarrel with Byzantium meant that there was no land-bridge to Jerusalem and so the flow of pilgrims and settlers from the west was limited to those coming by sea. As a result the Latin colonies needed support in the form of further crusades—crusading became an established part of medieval life, but it was an obligation observed as much in the breach as in the performance and was episodic and dependent on other western preoccupations.

The First Crusade suffered from certain problems which were to dog many later crusades. Its leaders were only imperfectly united and while they managed to cling together for much of the journey, after the capture of Antioch in June of 1098 they quarrelled. The army, which captured Jerusalem, was deeply divided and subsequently failed to seize Ascalon because divisions in its ranks became known to the enemy. In the Crusade of 1101, the Second Crusade of 1147, the Third of 1189, the Fourth of 1204, and the Fifth of 1213 the leadership was rent by bitter divisions, while on the Crusade of Theobald of Blois and Richard of Cornwall the two leaders never met. St Louis led an almost entirely French crusade but his military judgement was defective. Moreover on a crusade all participants were in theory equal, and while in practice they took to the Middle East the social structure of the West, major leaders had to control substantial men who owed them nothing. On the Second Crusade Louis VII's army suffered severely at Mt Cadmus because of indiscipline in the vanguard while in 1204 the great barons who had contracted with the Venetians for a fleet found that many crusaders would simply not acknowledge any share in their obligation. The Fifth Crusade was bedevilled by the coming and going of whole contingents of participants.

The First Crusade received considerable help from the Byzantine empire, but after Alexius failed to come to their aid when they were threatened with destruction in Antioch in June 1098, the crusaders permitted Bohemond to keep the city and opened a breach with the Byzantines, who were cool towards the Crusades of 1101 and 1147 and downright hostile by the time of the Third Crusade, when the Germans who started out under Frederick *'Barbarossa' had to fight their way through the empire. Not the least of the aid the First Crusade received from the Byzantines was naval assistance and a base on Cyprus without which the Genoese and English fleets would have found it very difficult to operate. Estrangement from Byzantium made naval support even more vital—its lack was felt by the Second Crusade. The Third Crusade had a great fleet, and all subsequent crusades relied totally on sea power to reach the Middle East: the Fourth Crusade failed largely because its leaders lacked ships of their own. The maritime superiority of the Italian city states was the basic condition which made crusades possible: after the First Crusade the Latin footholds in the Middle East desperately needed to control the Levantine ports and by 1124 all except Ascalon had fallen with the aid of Italian fleets. The price extracted by the cities was extraterritorial rights for their citizens in the Holy Land and a virtual monopoly of the trade in luxuries.

But the most significant change affecting the Crusades was the revival of the Islamic spirit, almost dead at the time of the First Crusade, which awoke as it became apparent that Islam faced a long-term threat. This was fostered by important leaders like Zengi (d. 1146) who recaptured Edessa in 1144, Nur ad-Din (1146–74) who united Syria and Egypt, and *Saladin (1174–93) who reconquered Jerusalem and almost extinguished the Latin kingdom of Jerusalem. Under the Ayyubids, Saladin's descendants, the divisions of Islam reappeared, particularly between Syria/Palestine on the one hand and Egypt on the other, and the Crusades of the 13th century tried to profit from this. Frederick II in 1229 exploited the divisions between Damascus and Egypt to negotiate the restoration of Jerusalem and much of the kingdom, and Theobald of Champagne did the same in 1240. However after the failure of St Louis's Crusade in 1249, the rise of the *Mamelukes in Egypt and their ambitions in Syria made such exploitation impossible. The *Mongol irruption into Syria in the 1250s offered the crusader kingdom the opportunity to play them off against the Mame-

lukes, but the *Franks hesitated to ally with such terrible people and in 1260 the Mamelukes defeated the Mongols at Ain Jalut. Ultimately the Mameluke creation of a regular army and their defeat of further Mongols attacks doomed the crusader states, whose last bastion of Acre fell to the Mameluke sultan, Khalil, in 1291.

In the conflict between Middle Eastern and western warfare neither side had any technological advantage. However, warfare in the Middle East took place in a very different environment to that of the West and Islamic armies adopted tactics which were radically different. The population of the Middle East is concentrated in a few areas with large relatively empty spaces between and the close-hedged and wooded country typical of Europe is rare. In these circumstances infantry were far more vulnerable and cavalry far more vital. Availability of water, only occasionally a factor in western warfare, was always important in the dry climate. In tactical terms it was axiomatic that combat was settled by close-quarter struggle, but Islamic armies paid far more attention to the approach to this climax. There were heavy cavalry in Islamic armies, although they were rarely as heavily mounted as western knights were by the end of the 12th century, but they possessed light cavalry who could surround heavier forces, and in particular Turkish horse archers whose fire could weaken the cohesion of enemy units. The First Crusade was fortunate in that the Seljuks of Asia Minor were not numerous and were crushed at Dorylaeum by sheer numbers. The Crusade of 1101 and the Second Crusade were savaged by hit and run attacks, and although *Richard 'the Lionheart' controlled the Third well enough to combat them, these were unfamiliar tactics which placed a heavy premium on a strict *discipline rare at this time in western Europe.

It was hardly surprising that the crusading expeditions coming from the West for a short period in the Middle East clung to their own pattern of war. By the end of the first Crusade it had become clear that this could be adapted to counter Islamic methods. As the crusader army approached Ascalon in 1099 it flung its foot forward to protect the knights from light cavalry attacks and this pattern, if enforced with sharp discipline, proved very effective. Richard kept his troops in hand, notably at *Arsuf, and St Louis tried to do the same, but his knights chafed at discipline, producing defeats such as that at Gaza in 1239.

The rise of Islamic unity obliged crusaders to think seriously about strategy. During the Third Crusade Richard came to believe that it would be better to strike at Egypt, the centre of Saladin's power, and thus restore the kingdom. This was the destination of the Fourth Crusade before its diversion to Constantinople, of the Fifth Crusade in 1218–21, of St Louis in 1249, and was considered by Theobald of Champagne in 1239. Crusading in the 13th century produced markedly better organized and directed armies but they were relatively small. St Louis's army was 15,000 strong, barely adequate for the conquest of Egypt.

The Franks of the Middle East had a clear understanding of the strategic possibilities of their situation. The principality of Antioch in the north strove to seize Aleppo. The kingdom of Jerusalem at various times favoured an attack on Damascus or expansion into Egypt. The problem was that the principalities pursued their own policies independently and sometimes in rivalry with one another so that only on rare occasions was there any Frankish strategy.

To achieve their ends the Franks of the Latin kingdom had a highly effective army amenable to discipline and capable of close co-operation between horse and foot. It achieved this because its men were constantly fighting and so developed a formidable coherence. The Franks remained loyal to essentially western fighting methods with the concerted charge of the knights as their main weapon, but they recognized that this had to be timed carefully. They developed the co-operation of cavalry and infantry very highly in the fighting march which enabled their armies to travel in the presence of hostile forces This technique involved *archers backed by *pikemen forming a screen around cavalry squadrons to keep enemy horse archers out of range. If enemy cavalry formations became drawn into close-quarter battle they would then offer a target for the Frankish speciality—the mass charge, which properly delivered, was almost irresistible. In addition the crusaders used light cavalry and horse archers in large numbers to harass the enemy, to scout, and to supplement the knights.

But the great problem for the Franks was lack of numbers because of their remoteness from Europe and the lack of a land route to the Middle East. Crusades were spasmodic and tended to come in response to disaster: the zenith of crusading came in the half-century after the collapse of the kingdom in 1187. In the 12th century a Frankish population of about 120,000–150,000 could put 600 knights and 5,000 foot into the field. The *military monastic orders of the Hospital and the Temple, sworn to war with Islam, had a devotion and discipline that made them formidable. They could between them field 6,000 knights and an unknown number of foot. The army of the kingdom could also be supplemented by pilgrims and mercenaries.

It is often supposed that the numerous *castles of the Holy Land were an attempt to compensate for lack of numbers, but although castles served as useful bases most were relatively small and built as centres of lordships and only a few served any strategic purpose: Shawbak and Kerak east of the Dead Sea were established to threaten communications between Egypt and Syria. As the threat to the kingdom grew, more emphasis was placed on castle development. Belvoir, built by the Hospital c.1168, was a concentric castle and at Jacob's Ford in 1178 the Temple began a similar structure which Saladin destroyed. In the 13th century the military monastic orders constructed some massive and advanced fortifications at Crac des Chevaliers, Marqab, and Athlit. The real anchorages of the 12th-century kingdom were the fortified cities where most of the Franks

lived. The strength of the cities enabled them to adopt Fabian tactics when Saladin invaded in 1183. They raised an army but simply shadowed Saladin and refused battle, preventing any attack on the cities.

In 1187 Saladin appeared with a huge army of about 30,000 and once again Fabian tactics were suggested, but King Guy was a new and controversial king who needed a victory and many of the barons must have been anxious to punish Saladin for his constant and destructive raiding of the kingdom. The army of the kingdom marched out to battle and was overwhelmed at the battle of *Hattin on 3–4 July—partly by sheer numbers for they were less than 20,000 strong. Such was the scale of the defeat that there were almost no troops left in the kingdom which, except for Tyre, fell to Saladin.

Despite the efforts of the Third Crusade the crusading kingdom never recovered from this disaster. After the death of Amalric II (1197–1205) the kingdom sought a powerful western ruler. John of Brienne succeeded but he was replaced by the Emperor Frederick II in 1225. He restored the kingdom by treaty with Egypt in 1229, but his absolutism drove the barons into armed resistance and his return to Sicily meant that he could not win. The civil war in Jerusalem prevented the kingdom from exploiting either his success or that of Theobald of Champagne in 1240. Party strife within the kingdom meant that consistent policies could not be pursued. In 1244 a golden opportunity appeared when open war broke out between Damascus and Egypt. Under Templar influence the Franks supported Damascus and a huge allied army, including about 1,000 knights and 5,000 infantry provided by the kingdom, confronted 15,000 Egyptians on 17 October at Harbiyah north of Gaza. The crusaders, certain of victory, demanded an all-out attack and when it failed they were cut to pieces—it was a defeat on the scale of Hattin. From now on the kingdom was militarily so weak that its fate clearly lay in the hands of others. St Louis's sojourn in the Holy Land 1250–4 gave much-needed leadership but thereafter the kingdom was highly unstable with the barons ranged around the real powers of the city states and the military monastic orders who quarrelled among themselves.

The fall of Acre in 1291 was not the end of crusading and the recovery of Jerusalem continued to be a preoccupation within Christendom down to modern times, but it became less and less of a force in the politics of the Christian West. Crusading was never confined to the Holy Land: as early as 1114 a crusade was proclaimed to Spain and Innocent III launched one against the heretics of southern France. The conquest of Constantinople by the Fourth Crusade was welcomed in the West as the restoration of Orthodoxy and sustaining the Latin states of Greece who enjoyed the rewards of crusading. The conquest of the pagans of the Baltic and eastern Europe was one of the great triumphs of crusading. The Church recruited vigorously to support the tiny Christian settlements of the area. A number of military monastic orders were founded to carry the brunt of the fighting, notably the Sword-Brothers in Livonia. By the end of the 13th century the Teutonic Order moved the focus of its activities from the Holy Land to become a great political force leading the crusade and establishing a principality out of which grew Prussia. The Baltic Crusade attracted the aristocracy of Europe and succeeded in part because heavy cavalry and the crossbow were unknown to the Baltic peoples who lacked the resources and organization to sustain them. Moreover German trade, a major reason for interest in the area, provided shipping for the conquest.

The papal right to launch a crusade was undoubted, but failure in the Holy Land, manipulation of crusading for papal interests in Italy, and the problems of the papacy in the 14th century, undermined the whole movement. The Crusades ultimately failed in their primary theatre, the Middle East, but their history illustrates the remarkable durability and adaptability of European military methods.

JF2

France, J., *Victory in the East: A Military History of the First Crusade* (Cambridge, 1994).

Housley, N., *Later Crusades, 1274–1580: From Lyons to Alcázar* (Oxford, 1992).

Kennedy, H., *Crusader Castles* (Cambridge, 1994).

Marshall, C., *Warfare in the Latin East* (Cambridge, 1992).

Riley-Smith, J., *The Crusades: A Short History* (London, 1987).

Smail, R. C., *Crusading Warfare* (Cambridge, 1956).

Cuban missile crisis (1962). In May 1960, Soviet premier Nikita Khrushchev promised military assistance to the beleaguered *Castro regime in Cuba. Two years later, he saw that the USSR's relations with Cuba also represented a unique opportunity to offset the threat posed to Moscow by US nuclear missiles based in Turkey. In addition to aircraft, air defence systems, armoured vehicles, and troops, Khrushchev offered a selection of nuclear-armed medium and intermediate range ballistic missiles. Castro accepted the offer and within months the USA and the USSR were on the verge of all-out nuclear war. On 14 October 1962, following indications of increased military activity on Cuba and a growing Soviet presence, an American U-2 aircraft photographed missile sites in western Cuba. Subsequent intelligence indicated that the missiles—SS-4 and SS-5, both with 1 megaton warheads—had the ability to reach almost the entire continental USA, including every Strategic Air Command base. On 22 October 1962, after intense debate in the Executive Committee (ExComm) of the National Security Council, during which the possibilities of aerial bombardment or invasion of Cuba were discussed, US Pres John Kennedy announced a maritime *blockade to prevent further shipments of missiles and military equipment. Kennedy also demanded that Khrushchev dismantle and remove all missiles from Cuba. For six terrifying days, the two superpowers considered their options until on 28 October Khrushchev agreed to Kennedy's demands. In return, the USA agreed never to invade Cuba and (secretly) to remove its missiles from Turkey.

PC

Cuban Revolution Phenomenon of resistance to US hegemony in the western hemisphere that began with the victory of *guerrilla forces led by Fidel *Castro over the dictator Battista on 1 January 1959 and was affirmed in April 1961 with the defeat of a CIA-directed invasion of Cuban exiles at the Bay of Pigs. US Pres Kennedy subsequently ordered an undeclared war that included several attempts to assassinate Castro. Conspiracy theories about his own 1963 assassination assume either that the Cuban dictator retaliated in kind, or that the Cuban exiles betrayed at the Bay of Pigs sought revenge.

Expeditions to spread the revolution started in 1959 and ended with the 1968 death of *Guevara in Bolivia. An alternative strategy, more successful because Soviet-approved, was to support autochthonous rebellions against pro-US regimes. Successive US presidents used up considerable political capital in putting out these fires, including the invasions of the Dominican Republic (1965) and *Grenada (1983), the destabilization of the Allende regime in Chile (1973), and the *Iran-Contra affair in the 1980s.

Cuban encouragement was significant in all Latin American rural and urban guerrilla outbreaks of the 1960s and 1970s, but the principal outcome was the extermination of an entire generation of young revolutionaries by military regimes. The main appeal of the Cuban Revolution was always nationalist, and consequently it also lost attractiveness as evidence of Soviet domination grew. This was shown most clearly when Cuban regular troops acted as (highly successful) Soviet surrogates in the *Angolan and Ethiopian civil wars in the 1970s. Finally, the worldwide failure of socialism to provide answers to modern problems gradually stripped away the ideological gloss on what was clearly a dictatorship.

Latterly, Cuba played a significant role in promoting the cocaine trade, seeking as always to expose the 'contradictions' in US society, while generating independent revenues. But the extent of Cuba's economic dependency became apparent after the implosion of the Soviet empire beginning in 1989, and although Castro remains the last of the great Latin American *caudillos* and a burr under the saddle, his ability to wage war on US interests is now negligible. Nonetheless, with a large, wealthy, and vocal Cuban exile community, the USA maintains an economic embargo of the island, and the bankrupt, stagnant reality of the revolution is still able to present itself credibly as being preferable to the pre-1959 political gangsterism that is the only alternative on offer from 90 miles (145 km) across the Straits of Florida. HEB

cuirassier A type of heavy cavalryman, named for the cuirass (back- and breastplate) which he traditionally wore.

As *armour fell into decline in the late 16th century, cuirassiers retained much of it. The parliamentarian Sir Arthur Hesilrig raised a cuirassier regiment in the English civil war (see BRITISH CIVIL WARS): 'they were called by the other side the regiment of lobsters, because of their bright iron shells'. By 1670 armour on this scale had almost vanished, although back- and breastplate were often worn.

Cuirassiers never entirely disappeared, and saw a major revival under Napoleon. By 1804, twelve French heavy cavalry regiments had become cuirassiers, with cuirasses and steel helmets. They were trained to deliver shock action on the battlefield, and had a formidable reputation: the 5th Cuirassiers broke into the Great Redoubt at *Borodino in 1812. Several European armies retained cuirassiers after the *Napoleonic wars; in Britain the Royal Horse Guards and the Life Guards resembled continental cuirassiers.

In 1870 French cuirassiers charged at Reichshoffen and at *Rezonville/Gravelotte, and the spectacle of the armoured horseman, gallant but anachronistic, thundering to destruction became one of the war's enduring images. The French retained armoured cuirassiers in 1914; elsewhere the term survived simply as an honorific regimental title.

RH

Culloden, battle of

Culloden, battle of (1746). Fought on 16 April on Drummossie moor near Inverness, the battle marked the culmination of the *Jacobite uprising of 1745. It was fought by armies headed by the Duke of *Cumberland on the Hanoverian side and Charles Edward Stuart, 'Bonnie Prince Charlie', or 'the Young Pretender' on the other. The Hanoverians numbered about 9,000 and the Jacobites about 5,000. Contrary to myth the 9,000 were neither all English nor the 5,000 all Scots. There were Scots troops with Cumberland and some French soldiers in the prince's army. The rebels were not only outnumbered but outclassed in weapons, being themselves heavily dependent upon broadswords and *shields while their enemies had muskets and *bayonets and above all artillery. They also gave battle on ground totally unsuited to their most effective tactic, the *Highlander charge. Cumberland's artillery soon reduced the moor to a killing field. The Jacobites stood the fire for some time before charging, being decimated by grape and musket shot. Although their right wing reached the front line of the Hanoverian army they were forced to retreat. Charles fled the field and eventually escaped to France. Some 2,000 Jacobites were slain compared with only about 300 casualties on the Hanoverian side. It was a decisive battle, ending all prospects of a Stuart restoration.　　WS

Cumberland, William Augustus, Duke of

Cumberland, William Augustus, Duke of (1721–65). Before 1746 Cumberland, the son of George II, was called the 'martial boy' for his performance at the battles of *Dettingen, where he received a leg injury, and *Fontenoy,

where he commanded with gallantry though lack of success. In 1746 his savage suppression of the *Jacobites after the battle of *Culloden earned him the nickname 'Butcher' and there is a small ill-smelling flower in Scotland still known as 'stinking Billy'. He fought at Laffeldt in 1747, and at Hastenbeck in 1757, but was stripped of his command that year for signing the Convention of Klosterseven and retired from active service.　　WS

Speck, W. A., *The Butcher: The Duke of Cumberland and the Suppression of the 45* (Caernarfon, 1995).

Whitworth, Rex, *William Augustus, Duke of Cumberland: A Life* (London, 1993).

Cunaxa, battle of

Cunaxa, battle of (401 BC), the decisive encounter between the rebel army of Cyrus 'the Younger' (424–401 BC) and that of his brother Artaxerxes II, and the only major Achaemenid land battle between *Plataea and *Granicus about which detailed (partly eyewitness) information survives. The site lay on the Euphrates in northern Babylonia. Cyrus' Greek mercenaries chased their adversaries from the field without difficulty and so had no influence upon the crucial episode: a cavalry encounter in which Cyrus wounded the king but was killed in the ensuing mêlée. Much else (the armies' relative size, the role of Cyrus' barbarian levies, Tissaphernes' contribution) remains unclear.

CJT

Wylie, G., 'Cunaxa and Xenophon', *Antiquité classique*, 61 (1992).

Curragh

Curragh The Curragh of Kildare near Dublin became the site of a permanent camp for the British army in Ireland in 1855 and is still used by the Irish army. The Gaelic word 'Curragh' has been interpreted as 'a race course' and this is certainly another function of the modern Curragh. The camp became the scene of the Curragh mutiny in March 1914 when officers of the 3rd Cavalry Brigade, commanded by Brig Gen Hubert *Gough, and other units indicated that, if ordered to do so, they would decline to coerce Ulster into accepting Irish Home Rule. Gough secured a written guarantee from the Secretary of State for War that the army would not be used to enforce Home Rule and, although this was repudiated by the cabinet, it had the effect of paralysing government policy. The incident was not technically a *mutiny since no order was actually given or disobeyed but it poisoned civil–military relations and relationships within the officer corps on the eve of WW I. Ironically, there was a genuine mutiny at the Curragh by elements of the new Irish army in 1924.　　IB

Beckett, Ian (ed.), *The Army and the Curragh Incident, 1914* (London, 1986).

Custer, Maj Gen George

Custer, Maj Gen George (1839–76), outstanding Union cavalry commander during the *American civil war, but remembered today for his role in the *Plains Indians wars, culminating in his defeat and death at *Little Bighorn. He was a fearless and studiedly flamboyant officer, but also a highly competent and aggressive combat leader whose exploits did much to balance the moral ascendancy of Confederate cavalry under *Stuart. Promoted to the brevet rank of brigadier general when only 23, his division was prominent in the last stages of the war and he was present when *Lee surrendered.

Reverting to his regular rank of lieutenant colonel postwar, his career nearly ended when he was *court-martialled in 1867 for being absent without leave, and he was suspended for a year without pay. On return to duty with the 7th Cavalry in 1868, he implemented the winter campaign policy ordered by *Sherman at the massacre of Black Kettle's Cheyenne on the Washita. In 1874 he led an expedition that launched the gold rush into the Black Hills of South Dakota, recognized by treaty as the sacred *Paha Sapa* of the Lakota. The latter are not alone in believing it appropriate that he was the principal white casualty of the subsequent treaty revocation.   HEB

Custoza, battles of

Custoza, battles of (1848, 1866). Custoza, a tactically vital hill town in Venetia, was the site of two important battles in the struggle for *Italian independence. The first in July 1848 was a display of brilliant generalship by Austrian FM *Radetzky. After the revolt of Austrian Lombardy in March 1848, King Carlo Alberto of Piedmont drove Radetzky across the Mincio river into the *Quadrilateral forts in Venetia. There he waited until Carlo Alberto attempted to cross the Mincio and take Custoza and its surrounding heights with 22,000 men on 24 July. In a two-day battle, Radetzky concentrated 33,000 troops, took Custoza with the *bayonet, and crushed the Piedmontese army. The battle forced Piedmont out of the war and effectively ended the national revolution of 1848 in Italy.

During the 1866 *Austro-Prussian war, Piedmont was allied with Prussia and on 24 June, King Vittorio Emanuele tried to force his way across the Mincio with 127,000 men, but was roundly beaten at Custoza by 75,000 Austrians under FM Archduke Albrecht. This made no difference to the outcome, decided at *Königgrätz in Bohemia, and in the post-war settlement Austria was obliged to relinquish her Italian provinces to the new kingdom of Italy.
                                                          GDWW

Sked, Alan, *The Survival of the Habsburg Empire* (London, 1979).
Wawro, Geoffrey, *The Austro-Prussian War* (Cambridge, 1996).

Cynoscephalae, battle of

Cynoscephalae, battle of (197 BC), the Roman victory which concluded the second Macedonian war against Philip V. It demonstrated the superiority of the more flexible Roman legion over the Hellenistic pike *phalanx. The

*Macedonian army consisted of 16,000 pikemen, 5,500 other infantry, and 2,000 cavalry. The *Roman army was about the same size, but had more cavalry, including a highly effective contingent from their Aetolian allies. The battle began accidentally when the two armies encountered each other on the march at the pass of Cynoscephalae. Both Philip and the Roman commander, Titus Quinctius Flamininus, deployed their armies by wheeling their march columns to the right, the front of the column forming the right flank of the army. The Romans were formed in their normal three lines, the Macedonians in a single, deep phalanx. Both sides' right wings attacked and routed the enemy left, which had had less time to prepare for battle. A Roman tribune gathered twenty maniples from the rear lines of the Roman right wing and led them in an attack on the flank of the Macedonian right. With no reserves to counter this, Philip's army was beaten, losing 8,000 dead and 5,000 prisoners against a Roman loss of 700.   AKG

Cyprus insurgency

Cyprus insurgency (1954–9). The third largest island in the Mediterranean, lying south of Turkey and west of Syria, Cyprus has a majority population that is Greek-speaking and Greek Orthodox Christian, plus a significant minority (15–20 per cent) of Turkish-speaking Muslims. Cyprus was acquired from the Ottoman empire by Britain in 1878, and recognized as a British colony by the new Turkey in 1923.

The British, after their withdrawal from Egypt in 1954, wished to retain Cyprus as a strategic base in the Levant. The majority Greek Cypriots, under their political and spiritual leader Archbishop Makarios III, elected in 1950, saw weakening British power as the chance for a long-treasured dream of political union with Greece, known by the Greek name of Enosis. A Greek Cypriot insurgency movement formed, known as EOKA (Ethniki Organosis Kyprion Agoniston, 'National Organization of Cypriot Fighters'). Successive Greek governments found the Cypriot demands for Enosis impossible not to support, while it was strongly opposed by the Turkish Cypriots and by Turkey itself.

On 10 November 1954 Col George Grivas, a Cypriot-born Greek army officer known during the insurgency by the cover-name 'Dighenis', arrived to take command of EOKA. By April 1955 Greek Cypriot riots and demonstrations had developed into a serious insurgency. In September Sir Robert Armitage was replaced as governor of Cyprus with FM Sir John Harding. The policy of negotiating with Makarios for a political settlement while trying to split him from Grivas and EOKA continued until March 1956, when the British exiled Makarios to the Seychelles. Fighting and ambushes directed at the British alternated with atrocities by Greek Cypriots against Turkish Cypriots and vice versa. British troops unsuccessfully hunted Grivas and his men through the mountain ranges of central Cyprus, while assassinations and riots continued in the cities.

The limited value of Cyprus as a base in the 1956 *Suez campaign convinced Britain to reach a settlement based on eventual self-government for Cyprus. But any settlement was hampered internationally by the mutually incompatible positions of Greece and Turkey. In December 1957, Harding was replaced as governor by the more conciliatory Sir Hugh Foot. After further fighting and murders, a preliminary agreement was reached between the parties in Zurich and London in February 1959. Makarios, although doubtful about any political settlement, returned to Cyprus on 1 March, and a ceasefire came into force two weeks later. In return for British retention of sovereign base areas, Cyprus became independent on 16 August 1960 with Makarios as president and a power-sharing system of government between Greek and Turkish Cypriots. Britain, Greece, and Turkey became the guarantor powers of the settlement. Peace was short-lived, with fighting breaking out again by 1963, but the power-sharing arrangement lasted until the Turkish invasion of Cyprus in 1974. SDB

Crawshaw, Nancy, *The Cyprus Revolt* (London, 1978).

Holland, Robert, *Britain and the Revolt in Cyprus 1954–1959* (Oxford, 1998).

Cyrus, King of Persia (559–530 BC), who in under a quarter-century built an empire from the Mediterranean to central Asia. A four-year war (553–550) in which with modest resources and huge persistence Cyrus displaced Astyages of Media, gave him western Iran, and by 547 he had expanded into eastern Anatolia and northern Mesopotamia. Responding to Lydian aggression, Cyrus fought an indecisive battle (Pteria), then captured Sardis by siege (547–546). In an even briefer campaign (but with a pre-established bridgehead in the Diyala basin) Cyrus crossed the Tigris and captured Babylon within fifteen days (539). Some in Babylon saw his victory as desirable (for religious reasons) but their substantive contribution is unknown. Cyrus eventually died in central Asia on a frontier whose establishment involved extensive undocumented conflicts (545–540, 538–530). There is no explicit evidence for the nature of his army or the tactical/strategic details of his campaigns. He profited from treachery, could move fast, and was good at sieges, but his huge success might suggest more profound innovations. *Xenophon saw him that way, but independent confirmation is lacking. CJT

dacoit (from Hindustani: *dakait*, a term used in India and Burma for a secular rural bandit, specifically a member of an armed outlaw gang, distinct from *thāg* and the murderous cult of Kali). The word acquired a military significance when British Indian army troops used it to describe the *guerrillas who refused to surrender and fought on for a decade after Gen Prendergast's defeat of King Thibaw at the conclusion of the third *Burma war in 1887. It remains in current use as a general term for brigand in India, although today it has no specifically military application.　APC-A

Dahomey expedition (1892–4), French imperial venture typical of much of the scramble for Africa. Worsening relations between expansionist France and the warlike Fon of the West African kingdom of Dahomey came to a head in 1890 when the French seized Cotonou. Further clashes followed, culminating in a French punitive expedition in 1892. The Fon fielded a standing army of 4,000, half of whom were the fierce 'Amazons' (see GENDER), equipped with repeating rifles and artillery recently acquired from German traders, augmented by approximately 8,000 levies. France despatched 2,000 troops under Col Alfred-Amedée Dodds, an experienced Marine of Gambian paternal origin. Instead of marching overland against the Fon capital of Abomey, he sailed up the Ouémé river and struck from this unexpected quarter on 4 October.

The Fon way of war—probing for weakness and then launching a raid or an assault on a lightly held outpost— failed against Dodds's methodical advance. Their traditional tactic of a surprise dawn attack was repeatedly foiled by well-deployed sentries and by disciplined French fire power. In defence, the Fon tendency to fire high meant that many of their positions fell to the *bayonet. They could only have beaten the French if they had caught them off

guard, and Dodds did not commit the cardinal error of underestimating his enemy. The Fon army was destroyed, with perhaps 5,000 killed against French losses of only 77. With the survivors weakened by smallpox and hunger, King Behanzin sued for peace, but his failure to comply with Dodds' demands led the latter to continue his advance on Abomey, which he captured on 18 November. Behanzin fled north to reorganize his forces, and Dodds declared him deposed before outbreaks of disease forced the French back to the coast.

Further Fon overtures in spring 1893 were met by unacceptable demands for the removal of Behanzin, which would deprive the kingdom of its spiritual and political independence. Dodds re-formed his force and marched north in September, cordoning off the frontiers to block the fugitive Behanzin's escape. Meanwhile captive Fon dignitaries, hoping to secure a French withdrawal, suggested Behanzin's brother Goutchile (later renamed Agoli-Agbo) as a puppet king. He was appointed in January 1894, shortly before Behanzin's capture. The rump kingdom finally lost even its notional independence in 1900.　　　　DD

Porch, Douglas, *The French Foreign Legion* (London, 1991).
Ross, David, 'Dahomey', in *West African Resistance* (New York, 1971).

Dakota (Douglas C-47/53) Dakota is the name given by the British to the most famous transport aircraft of all time, the ubiquitous Douglas DC-3. It was a development of a line of fast, streamlined Douglas civil airliners dating back to the DC-1, which first flew in 1933. Although some of the earlier model DC-2s were acquired by the US army and navy, it was the larger and more powerful DC-3 that was adopted in large numbers by the US armed forces from 1941. The two most numerous models used by the military were the C-47 Skytrain and the C-53 Skytrooper, the latter a designated troop carrier that was introduced in 1941, while the former was used as both a troop transport and as a freighter, and followed into service in 1942. Over 10,000 were built for military use alone, 1,200 being supplied to the RAF, while approximately 2,000 were built under licence in the USSR. Although it proved almost impossible to overload, it was not purpose-built and added features such as a larger side door in the C-47 only partly alleviated basic loading and unloading limitations. It was an inferior transport aircraft to a number of contemporary German models, but it was redeemed by its mechanical reliability, ruggedness, and adaptability. It saw active service as a troop transport, *glider tug, freighter, ferry aircraft, and ambulance, and was used for dropping parachute troops. It saw action from the island-hopping *Pacific campaign to the invasion of Normandy and the crossing of the Rhine, and was the backbone of the post-war *Berlin airlift. It played a vital role in supporting the Allied war effort and the fact that it is still in use in many parts of the world today testifies to the remarkable soundness of the basic design. JDB

Darius, King of Persia (550–486 BC). Known as 'the Great', he consolidated the kingdom, transformed its administration, and founded Persepolis. After his elevation in 522, nineteen bloody battles in one year were required to suppress empire-wide secessionist disorder. Little is known of these, but they suggest a high order of political and logistical skill. His armies went on to defeat the *Scythians of central Asia, to conquer part of the Indus valley, to seize several Aegean islands, and to assert his suzerainty in eastern Thrace and Macedonia. Unsuccessful campaigns included an invasion of European Scythia and, over a decade later after the Ionian revolt (efficiently suppressed in 496–494), the large army he sent to punish Athens was defeated at *Marathon in 490. Despite this warlike record, his imperial ideology privileged co-operation over confrontation. There is no proof that he was a military innovator (relevant circumstantial evidence begins only with Darius; and royal iconography and Herodotus' account of *Xerxes gives a static picture), and the troops, strategy, and tactics of the Greek campaign may have been the same as those of earlier battles. CJT

Davis, Jefferson Finis (1808–89). Davis was commissioned from *West Point in 1828 and served in the Black Hawk war, but resigned to become a Mississippi planter in 1835. Elected to Congress as a States Rights Democrat in 1845, he resigned the following year to raise the 1st Mississippi Rifles and commanded them with distinction in the *Mexican war. He was a Senator from 1847 to 1851, and again from 1857 to 1861. Between 1853 and 1857 he served, very capably, as Secretary of War under Franklin Pierce. He an-

nounced the secession of Mississippi from the Union following the election of *Lincoln. He hoped for command of the Confederate armies, but instead he became a compromise provisional president in January 1861 and was confirmed by popular vote in December. Although his military, legislative, and administrative experience should have given him a head start for the post, he was not a success. He was faulted for refusing to delegate and for favouring incompetent friends, while his austere and overbearing manner led to clashes with state governors and military commanders. Nonetheless, his personal determination did much to keep the Confederacy in the war, and his dignity in defeat helped restore him to popular favour in the post-war South. RH

Davout, Marshal Louis Nicolas, Prince d'Eckmuhl, Duc d'Auerstadt (1770–1823). Born d'Avot, into a noble family from the Yonne, Davout was the son of an officer in the Royal Champagne Cavalry, into which he was commissioned in 1788. Soon in trouble for revolutionary views, he was imprisoned and required to resign his commission. He appealed successfully, and in 1791 was elected lieutenant colonel of a local volunteer battalion. He distinguished himself in the Low Countries and was promoted brigadier general, only to resign again when the Convention barred former aristocrats from the army.

Davout was reinstated in 1794, and his career took off in earnest when his patron Desaix introduced him to *Napoleon in 1798. He commanded a cavalry brigade in Egypt and was promoted after his return. His second marriage, to a distant relative of Napoleon's, helped confirm his position and in 1804 he was appointed marshal, at 34 the youngest of the first creation. He led III Corps with distinction at *Austerlitz in 1805, and won the more difficult part of the battle at *Jena/Auerstadt the following year. He was prominent at *Eylau, Eckmuhl, and *Wagram, and was given a series of major appointments, although never the independent command which might have allowed his talents full scope. His reputation suffered during the retreat from Moscow when he was unfairly accused of abandoning *Ney. In 1813–14 he defended Hamburg until the war ended. War minister during the *Hundred Days, he was stripped of all offices at the Second Restoration. Restored to his rank in 1816 and appointed a peer of France, he died seven years later.

Nicknamed 'the Iron Marshal', Davout was respected rather than loved, and his performance at Auerstadt induced even Napoleon to envy him slightly. Balding, short-sighted, and uncommunicative, he was driven by a powerful sense of duty and was a firm disciplinarian. His tactical skill was matched by administrative and organizational ability. Davout was one of the best of Napoleon's marshals: it was a measure of his ability that he never enjoyed his touchy master's full confidence. RH

Dayan, Gen Moshe (1915–81), Israeli general and politician. Gaoled in 1939 by the British as a member of the Haganah (Jewish underground), Dayan was released in 1941 to fight the Vichy French in the *Syria campaign, where he lost his left eye, thereafter sporting a characteristic eyepatch. A major defending the Jordan valley against a larger Syrian force at the start of the *Arab–Israeli wars (1948–9), he was GOC Southern Command by the war's end. In 1953 as its COS, he started to rebuild the *IDF, instituting rigorous training, increasing the number of infantry and armoured formations, and creating an *airborne forces élite. His reforms were vindicated in the 1956 war when his forces routed four Egyptian divisions with minimal casualties in the Sinai. Elected to the Knesset in 1959, he was minister of defence for the Six Day War (1967), destroying the Egyptian air force on the ground with a bold pre-emptive strike, and capturing the *Golan Heights from Syria. But, criticized for IDF lack of preparedness at the start of the Yom Kippur war (1973), Dayan resigned the following year. In 1977 he was appointed foreign minister but eventually resigned over policy towards the Israel–Egypt peace process. Exuding a swashbuckling, piratical air, the energetic and charismatic Dayan learned his trade the hard way, without formal military or staff training, and is considered the father of the IDF and its greatest commander.   APC-A

de Gaulle, Brig Gen Charles André Joseph Marie (1890–1970). Leader of the Free French during WW II and later president, de Gaulle graduated from the academy at *Saint-Cyr to join an infantry regiment under Col *Pétain. During WW I, he was thrice wounded, and captured at *Verdun in 1916. He made several escape attempts. A staff officer between the world wars, he wrote *Discord Among the Enemy* (1924), *The Edge of the Sword* (1932), *Towards a Professional Army* (1934), and *France and her Army* (1938), which won him the political *patronage of Paul Reynaud. Like *Fuller and *Guderian, de Gaulle advocated a fully professional army, with an armoured corps capable of swift manoeuvres. The conclusions he drew from Verdun were exactly the opposite to those of his army's high command, which advocated the *Maginot Line.

De Gaulle attracted attention during the *blitzkrieg of 1940, twice delaying Guderian with flank attacks by his 4th Armoured Division (see FRANCE, FALL OF). Promoted brigadier general (the rank he was to use thereafter), Reynaud invited him to join his government as under-secretary for national defence, an office he held for just ten days. On his way back from discussions in England, he learned of Reynaud's call for an armistice and returned to London where, on 18 June, he began his road to power with a broadcast calling for continued resistance. With no political legitimacy of any sort, he organized what became the Free French forces and set up a Committee of National Liberation, supported by *Churchill.

De Gaulle gradually rallied French overseas territories to his cause and in 1942 he linked up, via Jean Moulin, with the scattered Resistance units of what was to become the FFI (Forces Françaises de l'Intérieur). This gave him much-needed political support within France, where the left was suspicious of his Catholicism and military background and the right regarded him as a traitor for defying Pétain, the leader of Vichy France. Both thought him a pawn in Churchill's hand, whereas in fact his relations with the western Allies were remarkably tense. It was a considerable relief for all concerned when he moved his Committee of National Liberation to Algiers in 1943. There he outmanoeuvred his political rival Giraud and assumed command of all Free French military forces.

He showed considerable skill in getting the best out of the small, independently spirited Free French forces and the much larger and more conventionally minded French forces which came under his control after Allied conquest of North Africa. He landed in Normandy on 14 June, and on his return to Britain, announced that his provisional government was an established fact. He demanded that Paris be liberated by the Free French division under *Leclerc, and swiftly installed himself there as the head of the provisional government. Lacking the political skills to obtain what he wanted, he resigned in 1946 and withdrew from public life.

Recalled by popular acclaim during the *Algerian independence war, he founded the strongly presidential Fifth Republic. His immense personal authority enabled him to cut French losses and end the conflict, facing down *mutiny and surviving assassination attempts. He tried to recover lost *gloire* with a somewhat petulant foreign policy illuminated by distrust of the 'Anglo-Saxons', while asserting French leadership in the European Union. After a decade of prosperous stability, France exploded in nationwide street riots and strikes in 1968. He resigned in 1969 and died the following year, having pointedly refused burial in the Panthéon. An impossible ally in war and peace, his withdrawal of France from NATO's command structure has only recently begun to be reversed, while his exclusion of Britain from the European Union as an American 'Trojan Horse' was particularly short-sighted. But he gave France back her pride, twice, and deserves the place he occupies in the hearts of Frenchmen. It was entirely fitting that, when he died, a French newspaper headline proclaimed: 'France is a widow.'   APC-A/RH

death penalty Absolute obedience has always been regarded as the foundation of military *discipline, and disregard of orders or of duty by soldiers has incurred the severest penalties. The execution of Adm Byng in 1757 for 'failing to do his utmost' inspired Voltaire to coin the phrase *pour encourager les autres*, which neatly summarizes the ultimate reason for the practice. From the earliest times, *cowardice, *desertion, and *mutiny were considered to be the most serious military crimes and were punished with death in most armies. When large numbers were involved, the original meaning of 'decimation' refers to the custom of drawing lots and executing only one in ten, to preserve numerical strength. No army was ever more given to immediate execution for even trivial offences than the Zulu, and their discipline was legendary.

In Britain in the Middle Ages certain military offences were punished with instant execution. An ordinance issued by Edward I to his army decreed that any man who, through cowardice, abandoned his Lord or his companions should be put to death, and an ordinance of Richard II during the *Hundred Years War imposed the death penalty on a soldier who disobeyed orders, left his watch without permission, or 'spread despondency in the ranks'. During the 17th century flogging was adopted as the principal form of military *punishment by the majority of European armies, and in consequence fewer death sentences were passed by their military courts. But when flogging was abolished in the French army during the *Napoleonic wars, no fewer than 45 offences again became punishable with execution.

No death sentences were imposed by British *courts martial during the *Crimean war, and despite the fact that flogging was belatedly abolished in 1881, only one soldier in the British army was executed for desertion during the Second *Boer War. But during WW I, 3,082 officers and men were condemned to death, although the majority of these sentences were commuted to terms of imprisonment. Of the 346 executions actually carried out, 309 were for military offences, mostly desertion and cowardice. This may have been the largest number of executions carried out by any of the European armies, though records are incomplete. Despite the massive mutiny of 1917, only 133 French soldiers were shot up to the end of January 1918 partly thanks to a revival of execution by lot among those condemned. Records of executions in the German army were destroyed, but there may have been some 150 death sentences passed by courts martial and around 48 carried out. Although under US military law, almost unchanged since the *American civil war when hundreds were shot, a sentence of death could be passed on any man convicted of desertion, disobedience, sleeping on post, or 'misbehaviour in the face of the enemy', no US soldier was executed for a military offence.

Between the world wars many of the major powers reduced the number of capital offences under their military law and executions were rare in the armies of the western Allies during WW II. There were four executions in the British army and only one American soldier was shot, for repeated desertion. The Soviets executed soldiers on an infinitely greater scale, either after due process or as summary military punishment. The Germans, too, imposed the death penalty with increasing frequency, with flying courts martial imposing summary (and often totally unjustified) death penalties in the last weeks of the war. There were

probably not less than 15,000 of such executions. France and Germany have now abolished capital punishment for military offences, but in the British and US armies a death sentence may still be imposed, but only for very few offences of a military character.   AB1

Decembrists Russian revolutionaries, of whom 80 per cent were officers, responsible for the first 'bourgeois' revolution against the Russian autocracy in December 1825. Many Decembrists had fought in the *Napoleonic wars and considered themselves 'the children of 1812'. They included a number of staff officers who had written works of military history (Nikolai Muravyov, Pavel Pestel', Ivan Burtsov). Between 1816 and 1821 two societies, the 'Salvation Union' and 'Benevolent Union', were active. Soviet historians consider them to be the first revolutionary organizations of the modern era.

Tsar Alexander I died suddenly in November 1825. His brother Konstantin was the legitimate successor, but he refused the throne and passed it to his younger brother Nicholas. This was unpopular, especially among the Guards regiments, and the resulting dispute over succession was the catalyst for the Decembrist revolt. On 26 December a 'Manifesto to the Russian People' proposed the election of a temporary government and Guards units in St Petersburg led by Lt Gen Prince Trubetskoy turned out to oppose Nicholas I, assembling in the Senate Square. Gov Gen Miloradovich pleaded with them to desist, but was mortally wounded. However, most troops remained loyal to Nicholas and a force outnumbering the 3,000 rebels four to one now appeared, armed with artillery firing case-shot. The rebels had no cannon and in the ensuing battle about 80 were killed. By nightfall, the revolt was suppressed. A fortnight later, the Chernigov regiment in the Ukraine also rebelled, but was defeated after five days. Some of the leaders, including Pestel', were imprisoned in the Peter and Paul fortress, and about 120 were sent to Siberia. Some officers were reduced to the ranks and sent to the Caucasus, and the soldiers who had participated in the revolt were segregated into a ferociously controlled 1,000-strong penal battalion.

CDB

decorations and medals Rewards for merit in the form of medals have been known since the days of the Roman empire and in the last two centuries have proliferated for both soldiers and civilians. In the military context, decorations and medals fall broadly into five categories: the *badges of *orders of chivalry, decorations for gallantry, decorations for distinguished service, medals for participation in particular campaigns, and medals for long service and good conduct. Rome awarded medals according to *rank and this practice has been followed in some nations until comparatively recently, with the notable exceptions of gallantry and campaign awards. Commemorative medals have been produced by artists since before the Renaissance, but while these frequently commemorated military events, few have been conferred or worn as reward-based decorations.

The world of the warrior is one in which comradeship and the brotherhood of arms is encouraged and this, together with notions of nationhood, encouraged the growth of orders of chivalry in the medieval period. Initially military orders for knights, as the term suggests, only much later were they widened to include civilians on their merits or birth. Orders served a number of purposes initially, some of which are still maintained. Not only did their conferral reward perceived merit, but it also bound the recipient closely to the fount of *honour, his sovereign, thus creating an inner circle of reliable warriors dependent upon the monarch, while those outside the circle could be cajoled by the prospect of membership. The earliest European orders of chivalry were single-class awards distributed in very limited quantities. Some, like the British Order of the Garter founded in 1348 and the Danish Order of the Elephant (1464), have maintained this exclusivity but now have a less specifically military purpose. The now-defunct French Order of St Michael (1469) and the Habsburg Order of the Golden fleece (1429) fell into similar categories.

The establishment of a second rank of orders, often specifically to reward military service, was a product of the late 17th and 18th centuries and produced the Orders of St Louis (France 1692), the Bath (Britain, revived 1725), the Sword (Sweden 1748), and St George (Russia 1769). The Order of St Louis and the later French Order of Military Merit were replaced by the Légion d'Honneur in 1802, although the distinctive scarlet of their ribbons was retained, so associated was it with the recognition of military merit. Eighty-seven per cent of the members of the Légion d'Honneur were servicemen by 1814. Its stratified nature was copied in Britain with the reorganization of the Order of the Bath into three classes in 1814 and one division of that order became solely for award to army and navy officers. Prussia restricted her Order for Merit to military personnel in 1810. The creation of these late orders of chivalry proliferated in European nations in the 19th century and was emulated by emergent aspirant nations in their spheres of influence. Few of these newer orders recognized specifically military merit or service because, at the same time, other categories of decorations and medals were being developed for that purpose.

Warriors who had performed acts of gallantry were probably those who received the earliest types of decoration and instances of such awards are recorded from imperial Rome. After the development of *heraldry, it would not be uncommon for a knight who had performed with prominent gallantly in battle to have his arms augmented by a 'charge' celebrating the fact. During the 16th century European monarchs often awarded gold chains and medals to victorious commanders and this became particularly prevalent in the 17th century, especially for naval commanders. By the mid-18th century a distinction was being drawn between awards for individual acts of gallantry and those for distinguished service in a battle or campaign. The practice arose in Europe for gallant individuals, particularly if they were—as they often were—of low rank, to receive immediate promotions (battlefield commissions, for example, in the case of ordinary soldiers) or grants of money, or, if appropriate, suitable disability pensions. Some received unique medals or other marks of recognition of their bravery. Napoleon set great store by the award of the grade of Chevalier of the Légion d'Honneur for battlefield gallantry and Prussia's Iron Cross, founded in 1813, fulfilled the same purpose, as did the first American decoration, the Purple Heart. With the French Médaille Militaire (1852) and the British Distinguished Conduct Medal (1854) and Victoria Cross (1856), the basis of a European system of gallantry medals was established and it was copied elsewhere, the American Congressional Medal of Honor being somewhat over-awarded for lack of an alternative during the civil war of 1861–5. In some countries, notably Britain, different gallantry medals were awarded to officers and to ordinary soldiers, divisions largely abolished in the 1990s.

The concept of different degrees of bravery, suitably awarded, merges almost imperceptibly into the notion of awards for distinguished service. As mentioned above, meritorious service over a period had long been recognized and the practice of rewarding it with medals and chains, usually of gold and usually for commanders, derives from the 16th century. By the 18th century, military orders existed to reward it and, where these orders were stratified into classes, the lower classes would usually be the means by which distinguished services or leadership by mid-ranking officers would be recognized. Gold medals were instituted in Britain for Royal Naval commanders in the 1790s and, after 1806, for military officers of field rank (major) and above, who distinguished themselves in specific actions. These awards ceased in 1814 and British officers who distinguished themselves in a campaign thereafter generally received a junior grade of an Order of Chivalry, usually the Companionship of the Order of the Bath (CB). Such awards tended to be cheapened by their proliferation, particularly in the numerous colonial campaigns of the late 19th century, and so the institution of the Distinguished Service Order (DSO) in 1886 rectified the situation. Awards for distinguished or meritorious service for all ranks developed during the 19th century and, like other types of decoration, have tended to proliferate during the 20th century as qualifying definitions have loosened.

In the case of medals awarded solely for participation in a particular campaign, it is difficult to determine which were the earliest. The extent to which such awards were true campaign medals, rather than commemorative ones (purchased by the individual, for example) or minor rewards for particular service is similarly vague. Medals were worn in the 17th century by both Dutch and Swedish troops engaged in the *Thirty Years War, and British parliamentarian troops who fought at Dunbar in 1650 were awarded a medal for that event. Campaign medals became common in the 18th century, awarded by the Austrians for their campaign of 1706–7, by the Russians for the battles of Liesna (1708) and *Poltava, and by Prussia for the battle of Lissa (1757). The British East India Company awarded medals to its Indian troops for campaigns in the 1780s and 1790s and led the way in British campaign medal development with medals for the first Afghan war and the Sind Campaign of 1843. The victorious allies at *Waterloo in 1815 awarded campaign medals irrespective of rank and these, together with the East India Company's initiatives in the 1840s, paved the way for a huge surge in the growth of campaign medals during the 19th century, one which was paralleled in other nations equally engaged in wars of conquest, expansion, or imperial ambition. In the 20th century, campaign medals have continued to be a growth industry, different nations taking a variety of views on how, or indeed whether, to commemorate service in particular campaigns. Not all campaigns thus commemorated have been essentially aggressive ones, the UN awarding medals to personnel engaged on *peacekeeping operations and, by so doing, recognizing the risks thus run.

Medals for long service and good conduct were instituted as the ordinary serviceman's equivalent of the higher award which his officer might receive. Deserving old soldiers and sailors could expect to receive a pension or admission to a veterans' hospital, like those at the Hôtel des *Invalides, *Royal Hospital Chelsea, Greenwich, and Kilmainham, but the concept of a deserving *veterans medal was one introduced in Britain in the 1830s and eventually widely copied. Such medals, accompanied by a token pension, were regarded by the government, the serviceman, and—perhaps most significantly—the latter's potential employer, as a testimonial to his good character—no unimportant factor in societies which tended, almost instinctively, to regard discharged servicemen as dangerous drunken wastrels. Long service medals now exist in many branches of public services but are drawn from the military examples of the early 19th century.   SCW

Abbott, Philip E., and Tamplin, John M. A., *British Gallantry Awards* (London, 1971).
Gordon, Lawrence L., *British Battles and Medals* (London, 1971).
Mayo, John H., *Medals and Decorations of the British Army and Navy*, 2 vols. (London, 1897).

Delbrück, Hans (1848–1929), German professor, military historian, and publicist. Delbrück's scholarship on society, strategy, and tactics from antiquity to modern times transformed the history of war, influenced strategic thought and practice, and signified the rise of the independent, strategic intellectual as a feature of civil–military relations. Born into the educated middle class of mid-19th-century northern Germany, Delbrück served in the *Franco-Prussian war, tutored members of the Hohenzollern dynasty, and began a university career in Berlin, where he lectured on the history of war and world history.

His *History of the Art of War in the Framework of Political History* (1900) underscored as never before the interrelation between armies in battle and the nature of policy and society in warring states. Delbrück's method embraced a minute study of certain pivotal battles by means of the *Sachkritik*, taking previous accounts of engagements and measuring these against the limits of geography and military craft of the time.

Based on the theory of the dual nature of war in Clausewitz's *On War*, Delbrück's analysis posited strategy in two basic forms: *Niederwerfungsstrategie* (strategy of annihilation) and *Ermattungsstrategie* (strategy of *attrition). During WW I Delbrück, as editor of the influential *Preussische Jahrbücher*, dissented from what he regarded as the false pursuit of a German strategy of *Ermattungsstrategie* and argued instead for a more limited strategy of an annexationist peace, an idea that he advanced once more amid the post-1918 search for the causes of German defeat.   DA

Delhi, siege of (1857). The siege and capture of Delhi was the key operation in the *Indian Mutiny. Following the original outbreak at Meerut, mutinous sepoys from there and elsewhere marched to Delhi, rising to a peak of about 30,000. They clamoured for leadership from the aged puppet Mughal Emperor Bahadur Shah II, whose sons persuaded him to seize the moment. The British were slow to respond and the first troops did not arrive on the ridge to the north-west of the city until 8 June. For the next three months they were as much besieged as besieging, but held out until the arrival of British, Sikh (see SIKH WARS), and *Gurkha reinforcements, mainly from the Punjab, and the necessary siege-train. Under the command of Brig Archdale Wilson, the batteries opened fire on 7 September and by the 13th had made a practicable breach near the Kashmir and Water bastions. The following day Brig John Nicholson, a legendary warrior around whom a religious cult had formed, directed the assault by 4,500 men in four columns, but was killed rallying the attack at the Lahore gate. Six days of bitter street fighting followed before Delhi was in British hands.

Leasor, James, *The Red Fort* (London, 1956).

Delium, battle of (also Delion, now Dhilesi) (424 BC). This was a battle of the *Peloponnesian war, probably fought in November. An Athenian army of 7,000 *hoplites, under Hippocrates, had crossed the border into Boeotia and fortified a temple to Delian Apollo on the coast opposite

Euboea. After leaving a cavalry garrison, the retreating Athenians were caught just inside Athenian territory by a Boeotian army under Pagondas. The Boeotians also had 7,000 hoplites, 1,000 cavalry, and large numbers of light troops, although these appear to have played no part in the battle. When the hoplites closed, the Boeotian left was defeated. But on the right the Thebans, massed 25 deep, were steadily pushing back the 8-deep Athenians when two squadrons of Boeotian cavalry, sent by Pagondas to support his reeling left, suddenly appeared from behind a ridge. Thinking that their appearance heralded the approach of another army, the Athenian right broke and fled and was soon followed by their left. Although night cut short the *pursuit, the Athenian losses of nearly 1,000 hoplites killed, including Hippocrates (14 per cent of those engaged), were proportionately the worst ever suffered by a hoplite army.

JFL

Kagan, Donald, *The Archidamian War* (London, 1974).
Thucydides, 4. 90–7.

demobilization is the process of reintegrating servicemen into civilian society at the conclusion of hostilities. It has often been difficult. The disaffected ex-soldier, earning a living by plying his old trade, has long been a feature of history and literature: Macheath, the hero of John Gay's *Beggar's Opera* (1728), had been a captain in the army. However, the problem of demobilization reached an altogether new scale with the mass *recruitment of manpower and other national resources that took place during the world wars of the 20th century. Combatant nations had to make an orderly transition from a society on war-footing back to a normal peacetime society. Above all, this meant filtering several million soldiers back into normal life and shifting industrial production back to civilian goods: in other words, 'demobilizing' the nation.

This problem first arose at the conclusion of WW I and was tackled differently by each nation. Some governments tried to control the process from the beginning, while others took no steps to regulate it. At the end of the war, the British had approximately 3,750,000 men under arms. The government was afraid that releasing the bulk of these men in a short period of time would mean that most would return home and face unemployment. To avoid this, they created a detailed demobilization plan before the end of hostilities. Under this plan, the soldiers were divided into different groups, each with different priorities for release. The first and smallest group were those men who would administer the process (so-called 'demobilizers'). These men were generally civil servants. The second group came to be called 'pivotal men'. These were soldiers whom the government believed would be able to help create jobs for others. The government took advice from industrial leaders as to which personnel should be chosen for these posts. Then came the so-called 'slip men'. These were soldiers who had the promise of a job upon their return home. In order to qualify for this category, a soldier had to present a section of an employment form (the 'slip') filled out by the company which guaranteed to provide the soldier work. These men were to be 'demobbed' according to the importance of their job to the reconstruction of the civilian economy. The government created two further categories of soldiers: those who could expect to find employment rapidly upon returning to the UK and those who had little prospect of finding work. Regardless of category, the demobbed soldier would first be released on a 28-day furlough before being formally discharged. At one of the 26 'dispersal stations' he would receive a ration book, pay covering his furlough, and either a clothing allowance to buy civilian clothes or a government-issue 'demob suit'. He would also be allowed to keep his uniform and greatcoat. Further, the government would provide unemployment insurance for up to twenty weeks.

However, implementation of this seemingly logical plan revealed how unfair it was in practice. Soldiers who had served through most of the war found that men who had only recently joined the army (who consequently possessed closer contacts with potential employers) were being released before them. The result was protest from the troops. Some demonstrated in central London carrying signs which read, 'We want Civvie Suits', and 'We Won the War, Give Us Our Tickets'; others refused to board ships returning them from leave to France. After the 1918 elections, the new government quickly took steps that, in essence, scrapped the detailed plan. Instead of men with good job prospects being discharged first, priority was now given to those who had served longest. Within ten weeks of the implementation of this new system, 56 per cent of officers and 78 per cent of men eligible for release were demobbed. During the height of the procedure, up to 14,000 men were released daily and a year after the beginning of the process, the army stood at 380,000 men. Even with the changes to the plan, prior planning allowed the British to limit the adverse impact of the influx of millions of soldiers back into civilian life.

Illustrating the opposite end of the scale, whatever the problems of the British system they paled in comparison with what happened in Germany. While German historians have pointed with pride to the fact that their units marched home from the front in good order, these same units practically disintegrated upon reaching their garrisons and the army authorities found it impossible to implement any planned demobilization. The troops returned to a homeland in chaos, with their families near starvation and the central and state governments dissolving in the face of revolution. With industry in disarray, these men had little prospect of employment. Consequently, many drifted into the myriad paramilitary groups in existence, further contributing to the nation's unrest. Without a doubt, the inability to organize a progressive demobilization of the German army in 1918 exacerbated an already volatile situation and demonstrated the pitfalls of rapidly releasing millions of soldiers back into civil society unprepared.

Demobilization after WW II raised many of the same issues. Britain, with the experience of dismantling a mass army after WW I behind her, was better able to cope than the USA, whose WW I mobilization had not been on the same scale. Getting troops back from distant theatres of war caused difficulties, and there were some lapses of discipline, notably amongst US forces in the Pacific. The Soviet Union, with its command economy, simply redirected labour, and in any case did not demobilize to the same extent as the West. The situation in Germany was exacerbated by the damage caused by bombing and the gradual return of POWs.

The shrinkage of armed forces since the end of the Cold War—there were some 6 million fewer personnel under arms in 1999 than in 1987—has seen large-scale demobilization which has caused some grief in western democracies and dissatisfaction on a far larger scale in the former Soviet Union. Its successful completion has been identified as a key feature in the ending of long-running conflicts in Asia, Africa, and Central America. A high proportion of the population of countries such as South Africa, *Angola, and *Mozambique became involved in war: many soldiers—government troops, or guerrillas from various factions—had been fighting for so long that they had been thoroughly socialized into the ways of the military and knew no other skills. Failure to integrate them into peacetime society raises the risk that they will use their weapons and combat skills simply to make a living. There is now widespread recognition that it is hard to end conflicts without addressing the future of those who prosecuted them.   RTF/RH

Bessel, Richard, *Germany after the First World War* (Oxford, 1993).

DeGroot, Gerard J., *Blighty: British Society in the Era of the Great War* (London, 1996).

Graubard, S. R., 'Military Demobilization in Great Britain following the First World War', *Journal of Modern History*, 19 (1947).

demolition   There are two distinct aspects to military demolitions: those used in defensive operations and those employed by attacking forces as part of an offensive. Popular targets for both include bridges, both road and rail, especially when they comprise a main supply route (MSR). If blown up in the face of an advance they are considered defensive; if to cut off a retreating enemy or to deny him supplies, they are offensive in nature.

The success of the *blitzkrieg tactics adopted by German forces during the invasion of the Low Countries in 1940 depended on *glider and parachute units securing crossing points over the main arterial rivers and canals, in advance of the main ground attack, to prevent their demolition. The defenders' failure to destroy the bridges played a significant part in their collapse, allowing the main enemy assaults to create and exploit gaps in defences that, had the required demolition tasks been carried out, would have halted or at least slowed the German advance. The Germans found the same problem when they failed to destroy the bridge at Remagen across the Rhine in 1945, and the Americans poured across. Most armies practise the defence and appropriate destruction of 'reserved demolition', bridges which are destroyed only when friendly forces have crossed them. This is no simple task, as British and Indian defenders during the *Burma campaign discovered in 1942 when the Sittang bridge was blown with the bulk of an Indian division still on the enemy bank.

Natural barriers, such as rivers, are only effective obstacles if the man-made means of crossing them are rendered useless. The main target types for defensive demolition are bridges but may include major features such as mountain passes, or less significant ones such as houses. Demolition of buildings, for example, can block roads, clear fields of fire, and provide material for fortifications. Felling trees across roads in a herringbone pattern can be similarly effective against both cavalry and armour. Behind-the-lines strikes by *partisans or special forces can severely restrict reinforcements, as was the case during the Allied landings in *Normandy in June 1944.   PMacD

Denikin, Gen Anton Ivanovich (1872–1947), leading White Russian general, and one of the principal opponents of the communists in the 1917–20 Russian civil war along with *Kolchak and Wrangel. He graduated from the *general staff academy in 1899 and became a lieutenant general in 1916. From April 1918 he led the 'White Guard', and from January 1919 commanded all anti-Soviet forces in southern Russia. His sometimes brutal regime, known as 'Denikinshchina' in the north Caucasus and Ukraine, was supported by the WW I Allies, *Churchill directing to him much of the aid given to the Whites. Defeated in March 1920, he escaped abroad to lifelong exile.   CDB

dervishes   From the Persian *darvish* 'poor man', the semantic equivalent of Arabic *faqir* which yields the English 'fakir', but with an added sense of 'someone who is poor for religion's sake', following the feeling in all higher religions that excessive wealth is a bar to spiritual development. In medieval Islam, many dervishes became members of mystical or Sufi brotherhoods, which grew up all over the Islamic world from the 12th century onwards. These brotherhoods were headed by a spiritual leader (Arabic *shaykh*, Persian *pir*, Turkish *baba*, all with the sense 'elder', 'father'). Well-known Sufi orders were the Qadiriyya and Suhrawardiyya in the Arabic, Persian, and Indo-Muslim worlds, the Yasawiyya among the *Turks of central Asia, and the Naqshbandiyya again in central Asia and in India. Some had distinctive rituals and extravagant practices, such as the whirling dancing of the Turkish Mevlevis and the fire-walking, snake-handling, and 'howling' of the Rifa'iyya and others. There were large numbers of the orders, each with their own subdivisions.

Joined to the contemplative and ascetic aspects was frequently found a militant one, the urge to protect and spread the Islamic faith, an attitude especially strong on the peripheries of the Islamic world adjacent to the 'Lands of Unbelief', such as the Sudan and West Africa, the Balkans, the Caucasus, central Asia, and Indonesia. Such devotees often congregated in centres called *ribats, khanqahs, zawiyas*, etc., for both spiritual purposes and for missionary forays into the pagan lands. By the early 19th century, many dervish orders were in contact with European powers in Africa and Asia. Sometimes the orders came to a modus vivendi with the incoming colonial power, as happened in Senegal with the French, but more often the orders were spearheads of Islamic resistance to the infidels. Thus in the Caucasus, Shaykh *Shamyl, who had many followers among the Naqshbandiyya, opposed the advance of the Russians into Dagestan. In Black Africa, the Tijaniyya led an Islamic revival movement which was later to clash with the French and British in the Niger basin. In the central and eastern Sahara, the *Senussi engaged in the conversion of irreligious Saharan peoples, opposed the French in Chad, and from 1911 spearheaded resistance in Libya against the invading Italians. Their head, Said Muhammad Idris al-Senussi, became in 1951 the first and last king of Libya (King Idris I). In north-eastern Africa, the term 'dervish' became especially common in British usage for the followers of the Sudanese *Mahdi, Muhammad Ahmad, the originator and first leader of the Mahdiyya movement (1881–98) in what was to become the Anglo-Egyptian Sudan, and also for the followers in British Somaliland of Muhammad ibn 'Abdallah, called 'The Mad Mullah', who led local resistance to Britain and Ethiopia 1904–20. Most notable to European eyes at this time was their religious fanaticism and willingness to seek martyrdom through death in battle.   CEB

Hiskett, Mervyn, *The Course of Islam in Africa* (Edinburgh, 1994).
Trimingham, J. Spencer, *The Sufi Orders in Islam* (Oxford, 1971).

Desert Rats Nickname and emblem of the British 7th Armoured Division. In 1938, with the growing prospect of an Italian threat to Egypt and the Suez Canal, the elements of a desert 'Mobile Force' were brought together at Mersah Matruh, west of Alexandria. Gradually, the Mobile Force (Egypt) was reorganized and enlarged into something closer to an armoured division. In early 1940 the division took as its emblem the jerboa or desert rat.

From December 1940 to February 1941, as part of the Western Desert Force commanded by *O'Connor, the division took part in the audacious defeat and *pursuit of the Italian Tenth Army. Within weeks the division became involved in bitter fighting for supremacy in *North Africa

with Rommel's newly arrived *Afrika Korps. After the Eighth Army's withdrawal to *Alamein, 7th Armoured Division played a leading role in the breakout in autumn 1942 and in the pursuit to Tunis. For the remainder of the war, the division had no shortage of action, being involved in the invasion of Italy, the Normandy landings and breakout, and the advance into Germany.

The 7th Armoured Division was disbanded in 1948, revived during the *Berlin airlift, and then disbanded again in 1958. The Desert Rat emblem lives on and was seen during the 1990–1 *Gulf war, in which the British contribution to the US-led coalition included the 4th and 7th Armoured Brigades, both of which had been original elements of 7th Armoured Division.   PC

desertion is where a member of the armed forces leaves his unit without permission and with no intention of returning. Desertion is distinguished from absenteeism, often known as Absence Without Leave (AWOL), by the motives of the deserter and, consequently, there is a degree of imprecision in both its definition and measurement. This, and the fact that the penalties for desertion are often extreme—incarceration or even death—make it a highly emotional subject. It is a concept fraught with controversy, and impossible to measure with accuracy—not only because of the difficult in divining the motives of the deserter, but also because most deserters have no wish to make themselves known to the authorities who collect such statistics. Students of the subject require circumspection as much as dedication.

Desertion occurs to some degree in every military force, and can be especially prevalent during periods of conflict, or where the force is poorly trained and disciplined. It was the bane of armies across history. One Prussian regiment lost the equivalent of its entire strength during the *Seven Years War, and in 1809 there were estimated to be more than 20,000 deserters in south-western France. Most of the 287 Union soldiers executed during the *American civil war had been convicted of desertion.

Deserters, if caught, may expect to face a *court martial. The problem of divining the motives of the alleged deserter would then fall upon the officers appointed to adjudicate—no small responsibility in the light of the harsh sentences to be imposed upon the guilty. The motivations of a single soldier to fight or run are seldom simple, and to attribute the desertion of thousands of men to any one factor can be misleading. Certain factors are closely linked with faltering *morale, and may be highlighted here as the most common motives for desertion. The act of any deserter must first be set in the context. Geography, conditions, training, and experience all have a major influence on the deserter. For example, proximity to one's home and community may act as a spur to some to fight harder. Conversely, desertion can often become more prevalent in such situations because many men wish to defend their homes and family personally, or because proximity to home reminds a man of his civilian identity. In addition, during periods where an army is inactive, a soldier may wish to go home to visit the family he has not seen for some time. A short visit may all too easily slide into a longer one, as absenteeism becomes desertion.

Bad living conditions often accompanied by stress and fatigue can sometimes wear troops down to the point at which they can no longer accept their plight. Desertion could also become epidemic when confidence was lost. First, an individual may lose confidence that he will survive: he may, in short, succumb to fear. Alternatively, a soldier may desert because he no longer has confidence in the cause for which he is fighting. Some desert because they have lost confidence in the justice of the cause, but a more common cause for desertion is to avoid a senseless death when victory is manifestly impossible. In 1864–5 the experienced and unquestionably brave army under *Lee was reduced to less than half its strength during the Petersburg campaign partly due to the conditions in which the men were fighting, but in greater part thanks to an awareness in the ranks that the war could not be won.

Finally, desertion must be understood in the context of the times being studied. The wars of the early modern period, for instance, were fought by armies which contained a high proportion of *mercenaries and foreign nationals. These men were motivated by different factors from those that influenced the volunteers of 1914, or the ideologically charged soldiers of the Vietminh and Vietcong in the 1950s and 1960s. These forces were brought together for vastly different purposes, years or centuries apart, and desertion must be evaluated in the light of those purposes and times. AH/RH

Lynn, John A., *Bayonets of the Republic: Motivation and Tactics in the Army of Revolutionary France* (Chicago, 1984).
Marshall, S. L. A., *Men against Fire* (New York, 1947).

Dessau, Prince Leopold of Anhalt-Dessau (1676–1747).

'The Old Dessauer' laid the foundations for Prussia's military greatness and his life spanned both the old and new ways of war. His career started in the *League of Augsburg war, where he served at the 1695 siege of *Namur. He commanded the Prussian field army in the War of the *Spanish Succession, which distinguished itself at *Blenheim, Turin, and *Malplaquet in particular. After fighting in the *Great Northern war against Sweden, Dessau set about reforming and modernizing the Prussian infantry, concentrating on musketry. He won one last victory before his death at Kesselsdorf in 1745. TM

deterrence

To threaten a response to a given action in order that the perpetrator is convinced that the benefits of the action will be outweighed by the costs incurred and is thus persuaded not to act as planned. A number of ingredients must be in place for deterrence to function. First, the deterrer must have the capability to carry out the threat which has been made. Second, the threatened response must seem credible to the potential perpetrator. Credibility requires that the deterrer has, as well as the capability, the will to carry out the threat, and that this can be communicated to and understood by the potential perpetrator. Deterrence is therefore a relationship, and one in which both sides employ a broadly compatible rational framework and discourse.

Deterrence is common to many human relationships and situations, ranging from the upbringing of children to society's attempts to control crime: however, the term has become best known as a feature of military strategy. The basic ingredients remain: a potential aggressor's cost–benefit calculation might be influenced by the threat of a punitive response, or by the realization that the defender's preparations are so advanced and effective that the costs of carrying out the aggression would be too great. Throughout human history, when an aggressor has taken stock and decided not to proceed, it may be that deterrence played a part. The difficulty with this assumption, and with deterrence thinking generally, is that it will always be difficult to isolate the reasons for a war not taking place.

There has been no shortage of war in human history. In some cases (though by no means all), clues can be found which help explain why and how deterrence can fail. If the deterrer's military capability and his will to use it are not credible, or if the communication between adversaries is flawed, then the deterrent threat will not be convincing. Even when deterrence has none of these flaws, an aggressor may simply refuse to be deterred, calculating that, although the military balance is not in his favour, his own brilliant generalship (perhaps with the addition—in the case of such as *Cromwell, *Jackson, and *Wingate—of Divine Providence) will save the day. It is important to note that deterrence generally survived such challenges and remained a valid, respectable, and rational policy option, albeit one which could be improved next time around. But with the invention of atomic and *nuclear weapons and the onset of the *Cold War, military deterrence became extremely elaborate. In the nuclear world deterrence became not merely an element of defence and military strategy, but its defining feature. Deterrence could no longer be either challenged or ignored, no matter how brilliant the general. Rather than one among several options available to political and military leaders, deterrence became the end itself. However, deterrence could not be analysed too closely, for fear of revealing its fragility. It could not fail, but neither could it be tested. In his *Strategy in the Missile Age* (1959), Bernard *Brodie pointed to the difficulties of deterrence under the nuclear shadow: 'We expect the system to be always ready to spring while going permanently unused.'

After their use against Japan in August 1945, there was a tendency to see atomic weapons as super-bombs, and as a means to extend and amplify existing *doctrines of strategic *air power. For the first few post-war years, the USA enjoyed an atomic monopoly and could make such threats without undue reflection and with impunity. As the Cold War advanced, nuclear weapons were seen to offer other advantages. They offered more 'bang for the buck' than an expensive conventional-force posture and could offset weaknesses in conventional defences, particularly at a time when the conventional strength of the USSR was thought to have remained overwhelming while the USA and its European allies had demobilized rapidly after the war.

The communist coup in Czechoslovakia in February 1948, the Soviet *blockade of West Berlin from June 1948 to May 1949, and the outbreak of the *Korean war in June 1950 challenged any suggestion that the mere possession of a limited atomic weapon arsenal would prevent all Soviet aggression and communist adventurism. But the response of the USA and its allies was to place more, rather than less, emphasis on the deterrent value of nuclear weapons. This policy was manifested in two ways. The first, known as the policy of 'massive retaliation' was embodied in a January 1954 speech by John Foster Dulles, US Secretary of State, and in the MC (Military Committee) 48 alliance strategy adopted by *NATO in December 1954. With massive retaliation, the USA and its allies threatened an overwhelming nuclear response to any Soviet aggression. The second strand to the pro-nuclear bias was the 'New Look' policy adopted by the US National Security Council in October 1953 and thereafter by NATO. New Look placed greater reliance on nuclear forces—tactical as well as strategic—in another attempt to compensate relatively cheaply for perceived weaknesses in the West's conventional defences.

But just as the era of US atomic monopoly was short-lived, so the period when the West could enjoy atomic and nuclear superiority was to come to an end. The USSR tested its first atomic bomb in August 1949 and its first hydrogen bomb in August 1953, just nine months after the first American H-bomb test. The next step was to produce a 'deliverable' H-bomb, achieved by the USA in March 1954 and by the USSR in November 1955. In August 1957 the USSR came first in the race to test an intercontinental ballistic missile, beating the USA by almost five months, and the launch of Sputnik, the first *space satellite in October 1957 removed for ever any notion of Soviet strategic inferiority. Both sides were now on the verge of nuclear 'parity'.

Beneath the 'Missile Gap' panic which coursed through the US administration in the late 1950s, lay the realization that a major shift in Cold War politics had taken place. In the era of the *Wohlstetter 'balance of terror', nuclear weapons could no longer be seen simply as super-bombs, but would have to become instruments of stable diplomacy. The significance of the events of the late 1950s was that the equalization of capabilities brought with it the equalization

of vulnerability. Deterrence would now become increasingly more complex. At its core remained the notion of a relationship between adversaries, but the relationship would be more delicate and volatile, and the costs of breakdown higher than ever before. With each side vulnerable to a nuclear strike by the other, nuclear weapons no longer conferred a simple military advantage, and their use could not be threatened unilaterally to deter general aggression by a nuclear-capable opponent. Indeed, rather than deter action by the other side, the object of deterrence shifted to the prevention of nuclear use, with each side deterring itself as much as its adversary.

The pursuit of a stable relationship between the superpowers saw the development of a new doctrine of nuclear deterrence in the 1960s: 'mutually assured destruction' (MAD). At the heart of the new doctrine lay the ability for each side to inflict 'unacceptable damage' on the other in a retaliatory strike. This in turn required each side to possess a guaranteed second-strike capability, one which could survive the opponent's massive, and possibly unanticipated, first strike. Various devices were considered to guarantee such a capability: the 'hardening' of missile silos to protect against first strike and the use of a 'triad' system, whereby retaliatory forces would be deployed in missiles, aircraft, and submarines, with the probability that at least one element of the triad would survive. Other ideas in the same vein included the notion of 'Launch on Warning' or 'Launch under Attack', which would automate the response.

MAD had other requirements, not the least of which was the need for 'mutual vulnerability': if either side were able to defend itself against attack, then it might not be deterred against making its own first strike and any stability in the relationship would vanish. It was this realization which brought both sides to ban ballistic missile defence systems in the Anti-Ballistic Missile Treaty of 1972. MAD also emphasized the need for *arms control, to prevent an unstable arms race (the Strategic Arms Limitation Talks began in 1969), and good communications between the adversaries.

MAD had a number of credibility problems. If MAD were geared to preventing a massive strategic nuclear attack, what use could the strategic triad be in the arguably more likely event of a sub-strategic nuclear, or even conventional, aggression by the USSR and *Warsaw Pact? How could MAD compensate for the West's continuing conventional inferiority in Europe? Could MAD credibly be extended to cover US allies in Europe; would the loss of Hamburg to East German ground forces really be sufficient reason to begin an apocalyptic nuclear exchange with the USSR? These dilemmas prompted the development of two new ideas. The first was the doctrine of 'flexible response', adopted by NATO in 1967. At the heart of flexible response was the claim that aggression should be met at the appropriate level if the response (and therefore the deterrent) was to be credible. Thus, a limited conventional incursion on the central front in Europe should be met in kind, as should a limited or 'theatre' nuclear attack, and so on all the way up to a full-scale strategic assault. And as the aggressor increased the stakes, he was to be matched at every step. Deterrence, therefore, was to be 'graduated', and the fact that a 'ladder of escalation' existed from tactical up to strategic should mean that an aggressor would think twice about embarking upon any adventurism in the first place, even at the lowest level.

The second idea entailed a return to earlier thinking about the use of nuclear weapons as tools of war rather than of diplomacy. If nuclear weapons only had value in the context of MAD, then in a sense they had no practical application. In the attempt to rehabilitate nuclear weapons as weapons of defence against aggression, 'Limited Nuclear Options' were introduced into the deterrence lexicon. Among the nuclear 'war-fighting' options considered were an attack on the opponent's leadership and administration known as 'decapitation', attacks on the opponent's nuclear arsenal known as 'counterforce', and the idea of one-shot demonstration attacks against key industrial or military centres. The prospect of nuclear war-fighting attracted a great deal of criticism. In the USA, the Physicians for Social Responsibility organization described the idea thus: 'Planning on limited nuclear war is like planning to be a little bit pregnant.'

There were many other criticisms of MAD, and indeed of the whole edifice of nuclear deterrence. In the view of the USSR, deterrence was no more than rhetoric, behind which the USA had in reality not departed from its pre-parity thinking: nuclear weapons were valued not for their defensive qualities, but as a means to enhance military capability and ultimately defeat the USSR. The launch of Ronald Reagan's *SDI in 1983, whereby the USA would be made invulnerable to a Soviet attack, only fuelled the Soviet view that the USA was seeking to break out of the strategic balance and win an overwhelming advantage. There was a deeper concern about the rationality, not just of the actors in the process, but of deterrence as a whole. Deterrence relied upon bluff. But if the bluff were called and a massive first strike launched by one side against the other, how could it be said to be rational for the victim to launch a retaliatory second strike (assuming it still could), where there could be no victory and where the result might be a counter-retaliation which would only, in Churchill's words, 'make the rubble bounce'? There was also, finally, an important debate about the moral qualities of deterrence. The prevention of nuclear war could only be seen to be a moral good. But by the same token, the death of millions of non-combatants could only be seen to be morally reprehensible. If, to achieve the first, it is necessary to threaten credibly (and therefore with real intent) to carry out the second, how could deterrence be morally justifiable?

As the Cold War came to an end, the nuclear deterrence debate became less urgent, but at the same time more diffuse and challenging in other ways. Nuclear powers could not bring themselves to destroy their nuclear stockpiles, although large-scale reductions were made, with more in prospect. This begged the question: what use is even a reduced nuclear capability when there is no clear, nuclear-capable adversarial relationship? Does a nuclear arsenal constitute a 'deterrent in being', ready to be deployed against any threat, large or small, from any direction? Now that there is no massive conventional inferiority for which to compensate, should nuclear powers in NATO declare a policy of 'no first use', whereby nuclear weapons would become an insurance policy rather than a tool of diplomacy, and much less still a weapon of war? And finally, as the number of nuclear-capable states increases through proliferation of technology and expertise, is it naïve to expect the ideas and mechanisms of mutual deterrence to take hold in the same places and at the same rate?   PC

Dettingen, battle of (1743). The War of the *Austrian Succession had a slow start but in the summer of 1743 the so-called 'Pragmatic Army' (Austrian troops with British and Hanoverian auxiliaries, in all about 35,000 men) moved up the Rhine valley towards Bavaria. Their route was checked by a French force of 70,000 men under Marshal Adrien Maurice *Noailles and they were forced to push up the river Main to secure their supply line. The marshal cut that route also and, after delaying at Aschaffenburg where they were joined by King George II, the Allies decided to retreat northwards to Hanau on the night of 26–7 June. At daylight they discovered that Noailles was already blocking their retreat, putting the Allies in a 'mousetrap' between the river and the Spessart hills and exposed to the French guns west of the river.

At that point the French advantage was thrown away by Noailles's nephew, Grammont, who led the northern blocking force of 26,000 men from their position commanding the only route through the village of Dettingen, to attack the Allies. An inferior French force was thus committed to a series of uncoordinated cavalry and infantry attacks against the allied main body. The Allies' superior musketry, with artillery support, eventually broke the French infantry which retreated in considerable disorder, recrossing the Main. The Allies made no attempt to pursue but continued their withdrawal northwards. French casualties, including prisoners, were about 4,000 men; the Allies lost half that number. Dettingen was hardly a decisive battle, although it was a severe blow to French prestige. It is most often remembered as the last time a British king commanded his army in battle, but George, despite demonstrating personal courage, showed no talent as a general.   MJO

Brown, Reed, *The War of Austrian Succession* (New York, 1993).
Orr, Michael, *Dettingen 1743* (London, 1972).

dictator (Roman) In Rome the original term for the office was probably *magister populi* (Master of the People [under Arms]) and it was essentially for a special purpose, varying from military command to presiding over elections and religious ceremonies, although the first was the commonest. The holder, unlike all other officials, had no colleague, only a lieutenant known as the 'Master of the Horse' (*magister equitum*), and until the 1st century BC was limited to a six-month term, during which his authority (*imperium*) was superior to that of all others. The first dictator was appointed around 500 BC (possibly 498 or 497) and down to 368 all had military duties. But after 202 no more dictators were elected until 82, when *Sulla was appointed to 'write laws and reconstitute the state', holding the post until 78. In 49, the office was used by Julius *Caesar to give him some sort of constitutional position in the fight against his enemies, and he was reappointed in 48 after *Pharsalus and again in 46 after his African campaign, this time for ten years. About a month before his assassination he was appointed dictator for life, the last time the office was used. The term was subsequently used to describe an absolute ruler, with particular application to *Hitler and *Stalin.   JFL

Dien Bien Phu, battle of (1954), victory by 50,000 Vietminh over 15,000 French which all but ended the *Indochina war. The valley of Dien Bien Phu may have been the militarily significant route between Tonkin and Laos alleged at the time, but it was undoubtedly important in the opium trade, revenues from which were vital to the cash-starved French forces. Also, peace negotiations were underway and both sides hoped to influence them by winning a major battle. The mistaken calculation by French theatre commander Gen Henri Navarre was that at best his élite *airborne forces and *French Foreign Legionnaires could turn the valley into a killing ground, at worst they would draw in disproportionate Vietminh forces, granting him greater freedom of manoeuvre elsewhere. The French were therefore airdropped into the valley to build a series of strong points, not all within supporting distance of each other, around the 0.62 mile (1 km) airstrip upon which the fortress was to depend for supplies. In a further fatal miscalculation the hills commanding the valley were only lightly held, in the belief that French artillery could deny them to the enemy.

*Giap accepted the provocative invitation without hesitation. In a heroic *logistical feat employing mainly bicycles (the secret weapon of the Vietnam wars), he secretly surrounded the position with artillery in dugouts, some tunnelled through from the far side of the hills. From the opening *barrage the airstrip and French artillery were neutralized, while anti-aircraft fire was to force supply planes to make drops from a height that precluded accuracy. Many of the defenders, aware that they were doomed, became internal *deserters and left the fighting mostly to the Paras

under Langlais and Bigeard, who took over direction of the battle from the nominal commander de Castries. The siege proceeded in *Vauban style, with the attackers sapping towards the French strong points, all incongruously given girls' names. Following a massive bombardment, outer strong points Beatrice and Isabelle were overrun on 13–14 March, The core positions of Eliane, Dominique, Claudine, and Huguette were closely invested and finally overwhelmed on 7 May, 12,000 French officers and men surrendering. Giap later admitted that his troops suffered severe *morale problems during the protracted preparations, but the victory was to give them an aura of invincibility that carried them through the next war, against a far better equipped opponent.   CDB

Fall, Bernard B., *Hell in a Very Small Place* (London, 1967).

Dieppe raid (1942). First planned in June 1942 but cancelled on 7 July, the Dieppe raid was remounted at the urging of *Mountbatten, Chief of Combined Operations, and launched as operation JUBILEE on 19 August. The Germans were aware of the threat of cross-Channel raids and of the assembly of landing craft as early as June, but there is no evidence to support persistent rumours that security was compromised.

The plan called for a frontal assault on Dieppe at 05.20 by 2nd Canadian Infantry Division supported by 58 Churchill tanks. Unfortunately, flank landings at Puys and Pourville timed for half an hour earlier failed to neutralize defences on the two headlands dominating town and seafront. *Intelligence, moreover, had missed gun positions in the face of the east headland and *anti-armour guns wheeled out after dark at the entrance to streets leading off the esplanade; nor had the immobilizing effect of shingle on tank tracks been anticipated. Consequently, only small parties penetrated Dieppe itself and of the 27 tanks landed only 15 crossed the sea wall. Meanwhile the troops huddled on the beach were at the mercy of 302nd Infantry Division's well-directed fire. Naval and *air support was utterly inadequate to resolve this impasse: eight small destroyers and a gunboat lacked the necessary weight of shell, while the RAF's predominantly fighter force was engaged in a major battle of its own.

Of the lessons learnt by JUBILEE, at the cost of 3,367 Canadian casualties, 106 aircraft, a destroyer, and numerous landing craft, the most valuable was the urgency of providing overwhelming fire support in the initial stage of a landing. Mountbatten's apologists have implied that but for JUBILEE, the Allies would have planned the invasion in 1944 to be dependent on the prompt capture of a major port.   JPC

directive control The forerunner of what is now called mission command (also known by the German word

Auftragstaktik), in which the commander gives general instructions as to his 'intent' and what he wants done, but leaves it to his subordinates to implement his wishes. The exponent of the opposite style, known as *Befehlstaktik*, which we might translate as 'order command', supervises everything himself and imposes his view not only of what must be done, but exactly how it must be done. The latter was of particular concern to *Moltke 'the Elder', given the absence of real time communications in his day.

The difference is exemplified by that between the command styles of *Genghis Khan, the exponent of directive control (mission command), and *Timur. *Mongol generals were usually given total freedom to conduct operations in their own way, and merely had to rendezvous at a certain place at a certain time, for example a full moon. Timur, however, issued detailed orders for everything and personally took charge of jobs he could easily have delegated. Mission command is possible when subordinates are well trained and trusted; tight personal control is necessary in other circumstances. *Wellington was a particularly successful exponent of the latter. His conduct of the engagement on the huge battlefield of *Salamanca, in which he determined the exact moment at which forces should be launched against the French and personally galloped 3 miles (4.8 km) to order his brother-in-law, Maj Gen Pakenham, to attack the front of the French column, and then galloped 3 miles back again to continue to supervise the battle from the centre, was almost the antithesis of directive control. Wellington's insistence on supervising everything himself and not imparting his plans to others could have been disastrous if he had been killed or wounded in the middle of a battle, but he was also famously lucky.

In more recent times the difference between the two styles was also apparent in the methods of *Eisenhower (mission command) and *Montgomery (order command). Improvements in communications made it easier for senior military commanders to impose their methods on junior ones and for political leaders to become embroiled in tactics, starting in *Vietnam. During the *Falklands war, PM Margaret Thatcher conversed directly with the captain of the submarine *Conqueror* which sank the Argentine cruiser *Belgrano*. Military hierarchy developed in order to facilitate the transmission and dissemination of orders through a large organization: it is possible that modern communications will bypass many levels of command. On the 'digital' battlefield there is a real likelihood that brigade commanders will talk directly to sergeants or corporals commanding sections and that intermediate officers will be sidelined. In some cases this may be necessary, but with a risk of information overload at the best of times, no commander can do everything himself. A mission command structure is better able to cope both with a surfeit of information and with breakdowns in communications.

CDB

discipline is the training, indoctrination, and encouragement through reward and example of certain practices consistent with the purposes for which a soldier may be employed, such that the desired response may become self- or small unit-imposed, although ultimately failure to abide by this training and the rules laid out by the authorities will result in some form of military *punishment. This will, as in the flogging and the *drum out ceremonies, be didactic in nature, *pour encourager les autres*. Discipline has changed over time and varies according to geography and culture, so no statement on this matter may be expected to hold true for all armies or *navies. But a few initial generalizations may be permitted to form a broad picture of military discipline.

Discipline is crucial to the effectiveness of any armed force. It has, in the case of most armies, been instilled by a combination of repetition, physical and mental challenge, and punishment for failing to meet certain standards. These three primary factors work in conjunction with one another and within a contextual framework which throws a number of soldiers together, with the aim of moulding them into a team. The soldiers are encouraged to live and eat together, to form a bond which will help them overcome the obstacles placed in their path during training. Beyond this broad direction, the soldiers will be encouraged to achieve high standards in the use of their weapons and in the care of themselves and their equipment. This is done not only to improve combat effectiveness, but also to increase the command and control officers may expect on the battlefield, and to enable the troops to undertake long and difficult campaigns without becoming unnecessarily susceptible to disease, discomfort, or malnutrition. Quite simply, if the troops are able to attend to their own clothing and hygiene, their officers will be free to concentrate on other matters.

After the training period is concluded military discipline continues to have a key role in the maintenance of the cohesion and effectiveness of a unit. Individuals are held to their responsibilities by the camaraderie of the unit, but also by the self-discipline that the training period has fostered, and, in some cases, not least by the continuing threat of punishment which forms an integral part of the military system. The most obvious illustration of this factor appears in cases where a soldier deserts his unit. The harsh sentences that have traditionally been imposed for this act may be expected to deter soldiers from leaving their unit or their post in any circumstances, although statistics on *desertion in modern wars suggest that this is never quite the case. Over the centuries all manner of disciplinary measures have been used to induce such strict adherence to orders, mostly based on physical punishment or humiliation. In the *American civil war, for instance, one rather unusual military punishment was to be shot with salt. Alternatively, a transgressor might be forced to walk around in a barrel, with 'Deserter' or some such word emblazoned upon it, while his comrades looked on. This must have been physically uncomfortable, and, for men brought up in a society where *honour and dignity were paramount, excruciatingly embarrassing. This type of military punishment chastised those who had committed the transgression, warned others of the possible ramifications of similar acts, and provided an incentive for men to complete their duties.

Specific examples of the methods and uses of military discipline are not difficult to find in both fiction and fact. In the former, *films such as *Paths of Glory* and *Full Metal Jacket* highlight the importance of discipline in a military unit, and the severe consequences that may befall those who fail to comply with the rules laid out by the authorities. Books such as Stephen Crane's *The Red Badge of Courage* provide insight into the group dynamics of a military unit, and the place discipline occupies within that dynamic. *Hannibal, in particular, was known to have a strong record of discipline, and his veteran troops displayed supreme courage and cohesion in their greatest victory over a poorly disciplined and woefully led Roman force at *Cannae. The fact that Hannibal knew he could rely on his troops to maintain their cohesion and combat effectiveness even when beyond his direct view gave him the confidence and power to manoeuvre his forces without fearing loss of control over them. This advantage enabled Hannibal to execute a grand manoeuvre while his opponents remained clumsy and static.

The examples of the British *archers at *Agincourt and Frederick 'the Great''s infantry during the *Seven Years War are well-known accounts of steadiness under fire and unflinching discipline in very unpromising circumstances. This was most important in battle, where, without discipline, a commander might justifiably fear his lack of command and control, thus forcing him into simple and often costly tactics. Worse still, if put under pressure, ill-disciplined troops might easily melt away leaving the enemy to garner an easy victory. A brief example may suffice here. At *Austerlitz, Napoleon was able to overcome a larger Allied army by exploiting the comparatively poor discipline of the Austrian and Russian troops. Napoleon's own veterans maintained their discipline and cohesion, enabling Napoleon to counter-attack with devastating effect.

By contrast, ten years later at *Waterloo, a rigidly disciplined British force, abandoned by some of its allies, was able to stand under French fire for the greater part of the battle without disintegrating, until the arrival of the Prussians destroyed the belief in victory that had always sustained Napoleon's armies and the Grande Armée finally dissolved into flight.

Discipline was traditionally enforced by a mixture of formal sanction (from summary proceedings to *courts martial) and informal, sometimes brutal, coercion. The latter has been all but extinguished in most western armies, though it survives, controversially, in the *Russian army. The armed forces of modern democracies find discipline

and its legal enforcement at the very forefront of their relationship with the societies they serve. Most agree that what Gen Sir John Hackett called the 'contract of unlimited liability', which obliges servicemen to run risks unlike those accepted by most of their fellow-countrymen, continues to demand standards of discipline which must be higher than those applying to other occupations. They also admit that rigid, unthinking discipline is now neither militarily appropriate nor socially and politically feasible, and recognize that self-discipline, springing from shared values, personal *honour, moral obligation or professional pride, has particular merits. But in the last analysis discipline is a crucial part of the cement which binds armed forces together. They, and, perhaps more to the point, their political masters, forget it at their peril.   AH/RH

Crane, Stephen, *The Red Badge of Courage* (New York, 1895).
Gudmundsson, Bruce, and English, John, *On Infantry* (Westport, Conn., 1994).
Jones, Archer, *The Art of War in the Western World* (Oxford, 1987).
McPherson, James M., *For Cause and Comrades: Why Men Fought in the Civil War* (New York, 1997).

doctrine, military An approved set of principles and methods, intended to provide large military organizations with a common outlook and a uniform basis for action. Military doctrine makes explicit ideas or assumptions that in earlier times were conveyed by cultural means, or directly by commanders to their subordinates. When Sparta's *hoplites advanced slowly and in step, shield in the left hand, spear in the right, or when the English *archers at *Agincourt shot their arrows in volleys, they were acting on the basis of rules that would today be regarded as doctrinal in character, but which at the time could be adequately conveyed from one unit to another, and from one generation to the next, without benefit of official codification. As armies have grown larger, and their weapons and tactics more complex, more formal means of harmonizing their actions have become necessary. The introduction of firearms was an important impetus to the formalization of doctrine, since their use required the orchestration of complex, learned procedures by hundreds or even thousands of individuals. Seventeenth-century picture books designed to show *musketeers the many intricate steps required to load and fire their weapons, or the many 18th-century works intended to demonstrate the optimum means of besieging a fortress, organizing an encampment, or deploying infantry from *column to line and back again, are recognizably the ancestors of modern doctrinal publications.

Military doctrine is the basis of military training and, indirectly, of command and control. At the tactical level, its character is largely prescriptive. Doctrine cannot dissipate the fog of war, and but it can simplify the decisions that have to be made under the duress of combat, by limiting the range of choices that are deemed relevant to given circumstances. It also helps ensure that all the elements of an army will view similar situations in similar ways, thus conferring a degree of predictability upon the inherently chaotic actions of dispersed forces. The significance of this latter function should not be underestimated. In the absence of real-time tactical communications, the promulgation of effective common doctrine is one of the few means by which senior commanders can influence the conduct of the tactical battle. Tactical doctrine is also a foundational element of the military planning process, most especially in the case of what is sometimes called 'adaptive planning'—the improvisation of solutions to problems not foreseen at the outset of hostilities.

The value of doctrine at what is now called the *operational level of war is more complex. Doctrine achieves its clarifying effects by a judicious narrowing of the intellectual horizons of those making decisions. At more senior levels of command, where the relative value of creativity and spontaneous insight increases, the pertinacity of prescriptive doctrine declines. At the same time, senior commanders can easily become more dependent upon doctrinal solutions than their subordinates, because they have less opportunity to practise their wartime roles: commands above a division usually exist only on paper in peacetime, and actual manoeuvres employing such large formations are exceedingly rare. *Frederick 'the Great', whose approach to tactics was, broadly, that 'no one reasons, everyone executes' (*General Principles of War*, 1746), nevertheless recognized that general officers required a different kind of guidance. His *Instructions for Generals Commanding Detachments, Wings, Second Lines, and Prussian Armies* (1753) was an early attempt to formulate doctrine in a way that conveyed overall intentions and requirements, while simultaneously insisting upon the obligation of senior officers to exercise independent judgement and personal initiative. Few official publications can tread such a fine line perfectly. Contemporary American doctrine presents itself as 'authoritative but not directive', and leaves it to the reader to ponder the difference.

Modern military doctrine is markedly technocratic in character. This is a reflection of the enormous influence that technological systems exert on the conduct of war, and also of the belief that doctrine itself should have a scientific basis, which is usually summarized in terms of a small number of *principles of war. The fact that the fighting doctrines of first-class armies have tended, at any given moment, to resemble each other, provides some vindication for this point of view. Differences may, of course, remain significant. Among military victories of recent times, those by Germany over France in 1870–1 and 1940, and by Israel over its Arab neighbours in 1967, are the ones in which the doctrinal superiority of one side is conceded to have carried the greatest weight, if only because the adversaries appear otherwise to have been so evenly matched. Technological change has made military doctrine subject to constant revision, to the point where assimilating such change

to the conduct of war has become one of its core functions. At the same time, military doctrine always reflects the social conditions, cultural preferences, and historical experiences of those who promulgate it. Here again there is a fine balance to be struck between the use of doctrine to enforce innovation and its more conservative function as the bearer of professional values and institutional memories.   DM

Alger, John, *The Quest for Victory: The History of the Principles of War* (New York, 1982).

Bacevich, A. J., *The Pentomic Era: The US Army between Korea and Vietnam* (Washington, 1986).

Millet, Allan R., and Williamson, Murray (eds.), *Military Effectiveness*, 3 vols. (Boston, 1988).

Dönitz, Adm Karl (1891–1980), German commander of U-boats, later head of the Kriegsmarine, and finally führer, in succession to *Hitler. Dönitz served on surface warships during 1914–16 before transferring to submarines. His own boat was sunk in October 1918 and he remained a prisoner until July 1919, thereafter rejoining the navy. German naval officers tended towards tradition and conservative values, so Dönitz was almost unique among senior naval figures for welcoming Hitler's accession to power and joining the Nazi party. This helped his appointment to direct the U-boat fleet in 1939 and its rapid expansion, eventually totalling some 1,200 boats. Thanks to the U-boats' initial success against Allied shipping, he succeeded Erich Raeder as C-in-C on 30 January 1943, following the failure of the German capital ships to destroy Allied *convoys. This marked Hitler's loss of confidence in his surface navy and (unjustified) faith in his more ardent German submariners, whose own successes declined after 1942. Dönitz was surprised to be named as Hitler's successor on 2 May 1945, but ruled in name only until his capture on 23 May, after which he was astonished to be sentenced to ten years' imprisonment for *war crimes at Nuremberg, despite testimony by *Nimitz that he, too, had waged unrestricted submarine warfare.

APC-A

Doria, Adm Andrea (1466–1560), a naval *condottiere and developer of galley warfare in the Mediterranean. Born in Genoa, Doria began his career fighting on land for a variety of causes. Turning his attentions to the sea, he outfitted his own fleet of galleys for operations ostensibly against the *Turks and the Barbary pirates. But naval operations at this time were compelled to be self-sustaining, and Doria was never able to concentrate on the main objective. Only after the recapture of Genoa in 1528 from the French brought him recognition from the Holy Roman Emperor *Charles V, who made him admiral of the imperial fleet, was Doria able to turn his attention to attacking the Turks in the eastern Mediterranean.

In 1533 the Turkish Adm *Barbarossa began to reverse Christian advances in the Mediterranean, overturning all

Doria's conquests. Although the Turkish siege of Corfu (1537) was lifted by the arrival of Doria with a combined imperial and Venetian fleet, this success did not prevent Barbarossa waging a devastating privateering campaign. Attempts by Doria to bring the Turks to battle were unsuccessful and Venice's hold on her Greek territories was steadily weakened. By 1542 the Turks were pushing even into the western Mediterranean, forcing Doria to take refuge in Genoa. The death of Barbarossa weakened Turkish expansion, but they continued to make progress in North Africa. Doria relinquished his command to his nephew Gian Andrea Doria in 1555, who went on to win the decisive victory at *Lepanto in 1571, utilizing the fleet that his uncle had created. Doria's legacy was bringing a degree of control and systemization to naval warfare in the Mediterranean, instituting proper supply and replenishment, including the delivery of galley slaves. He was undone by a lack of sound financial resources and divided political control.   JR-W

Douhet, Gen Guilio

Douhet, Gen Guilio (1869–1930), probably the most famous of the alleged *air-power gurus, whose ideas supposedly shaped the development of military air power, particularly before and during WW II. In fact, he was little read outside Italy prior to the war and his influence on the development of air power theory was limited. His fame in this respect seems to have been the result of retrospective attribution.

Douhet was involved in the Italian air service as early as 1909 and organized the first-ever bombing raid, in Libya during the *Italo-Turkish war. Paradoxically, in his earliest writing Douhet did not consider aerial bombing on a grand scale to be acceptable, although he was of course to change his mind. It seems probable that he never learned to fly, but nonetheless became head of the Italian army air force in 1915, being removed by *court martial soon afterwards for being overly critical of his superiors. He was recalled after *Caporetto and appointed to head the Central Aeronautical Bureau. His most important contribution was his 1921 book *The Command of the Air*. In this work he put forward the notion that the enemy's cities and civilians could be targeted by massed heavy bomber aircraft, the primary aim being the crushing of the enemy's *morale. He was convinced that this brutal strategy would shorten future wars and thus avoid the long *attritional slaughter of WW I. Douhet argued that there was no defence against such an offensive and the only way to win was to bomb the enemy into *capitulation before he could do the same to you.
                                                                                      JDB

MacIsaac, David, 'Voices from the Central Blue', in Peter Paret (ed.), *Makers of Modern Strategy* (Princeton, 1986).
Segre, Claudio, 'Guilio Douhet: Strategist, Theorist, Prophet?', *Journal of Strategic Studies*, 15/3 (1992).

dragoons Although dragoons became cavalry, they originated, probably in 16th-century France, as *mounted infantry. They were originally named for their main weapon, the dragon, described in 1625 as 'a short piece with a barrel sixteen inches long of full musket bore, fitted with a *snaphaunce or firelock', but the term soon came to apply to any mounted infantry. In their early years dragoons were decidedly downmarket. Their horses were beasts of burden, not mettlesome chargers, and during the *British civil wars cost half as much as proper cavalry horses. The Duc de Rohan complained that in France 'they ruined the infantry, every man desiring to have a nag so he might be the fitter to rob and pillage'. *Louis XIV persecuted his Protestant subjects by quartering dragoons on them in the *dragonnades* that were to live on in Huguenot memory, and are remembered to our own day in the verb 'to dragoon'.

In the 18th century dragoons gradually became cavalry proper, trained and equipped to charge home on the battlefield. At Hohenfriedberg in 1745 the Prussian Bayreuth Dragoons effectively decided the battle in a charge which took 5 cannon, 67 *colours, and 2,500 prisoners. The British army, in contrast, converted its regiments of horse (heavy cavalry) to dragoons in the mid-18th century to save money on pay and mounts, but called them dragoon guards as a consolation. In 1757 the British began to introduce light dragoons, intended to take on scouting and *reconnaissance duties. In the 19th century they were converted to *hussars or *lancers, aping continental fashion. In the French army of the Napoleonic period dragoons retained something of their traditional role. Although they wore brass helmets and carried swords, they were also equipped with short muskets and *bayonets. Their ability to fight mounted and dismounted made them useful for outpost work and flank guards. After 1812 shortage of horses meant that a five-squadron French dragoon regiment might go to war with three squadrons horsed and two on foot.

As was the case with so much of the cavalry, distinctions based on traditional weapons and roles had largely disappeared by the 20th century. In the French army dragoons made a late appearance in their old guise, fighting in 1940 as *dragons portés*, using trucks rather than horses as transport to the battlefield. The title 'light dragoons' was pleasingly revived in the British army when two hussar regiments were amalgamated in the 1990s.   RH

Drepana, battle of (249 BC). This was, surprisingly, the only naval battle of the first *Punic war won by the Carthaginians. The Roman commander, the Consul Publius Claudius Pulcher, with a fleet of probably 123 warships, attempted to surprise the Carthaginians, under Adherbal, in the harbour of Drepana (now Trápani). But Adherbal, who probably had a few more ships, managed to get to sea in time and by swinging round the islands at the harbour mouth got to seaward of the enemy, where his ships had room to manoeuvre. In the ensuing battle the Roman marines still proved superior whenever it came to boarding, but lacking the *corvus* and outmatched in seamanship, their ships were unable to turn fast enough either to prevent themselves being rammed in the side or stern or do the same to the enemy. In the end, the consul, who was on the left of his line, managed to escape with the nearest 30 ships, but the remaining 93 were captured. Although on a smaller scale than other naval battles in the war, Roman losses were proportionately the highest suffered by either side.   JFL

Lazenby, J. F., *The First Punic War* (London, 1996).
Polybius, 1. 49–51.

Dresden, battle of (1813). The last great victory of *Napoleon in the German campaign of 1813, Dresden showed how near, and yet how far, he was from victory over the alliance of Prussia, Russia, and Austria. The French, initially under *Saint-Cyr, contained the allied attack on 26 August and on 27 August mounted a massive counter-attack, with three reinforcing army corps, led by Napoleon himself. The attack was spearheaded by the Imperial Guard, who stormed through the Grosse Garten, sweeping the Prussians before them. Frederick William of Prussia had insisted that the Allies stand their ground, but the disparate Allied armies found it hard to co-ordinate their defence, and their position on the left flank was split in two by vigorous French assaults. By 16.00 it was obvious that a withdrawal to the safety of Bohemia was the only option. The *pursuit was badly handled, the French lacking cavalry to harry Schwarzenburg's defeated army, which had lost 38,000 of its 158,000-strong force. Gen Vandamme rushed 30,000 men behind the retreating Allies in Bohemia, but outpaced the main army and was himself surrounded and captured at Kulm on 30 August.   TM

Dreyfus, Lt Col Alfred (1859–1935). Son of a Jewish textile manufacturer from Mulhouse in Alsace, Dreyfus was commissioned from the *École Polytechnique into the artillery. In 1894, a staff-learner in the Ministry of Defence, he was accused of betraying military secrets to Germany on the evidence of a short paper, allegedly in his handwriting. Convicted by *court martial, he was sentenced to military degradation and imprisonment for life on Devil's Island in French Guyana. A resolute but unlovable figure, Dreyfus consistently protested his innocence. When doubts arose about the conviction, the army's high command suppressed evidence and used forged documents to reinforce the case against him. In 1898 the novelist Émile Zola published *J'Accuse*, a powerful attack on the war minister, and was convicted of libel. Brought back to France for a retrial, Dreyfus was again found guilty but, ludicrously, with 'extenuating circumstances'. Pardoned, he was declared inno-

cent in 1906, restored to the army and decorated. He served in WW I, rising to the rank of lieutenant colonel.

'L'Affaire Dreyfus' split the nation, with the Dreyfusards, strong on the left and in antimilitarist circles, arguing that a morally bankrupt army had condemned an outsider to protect its own, while the anti-Dreyfusards, feeding on anti-Semitism, accused 'the Jews, the Protestants and all the enemies of France' of besmirching the army's *honour. The affair cast a long shadow over civil–military relations in France. Some aspects remain murky, although it seems clear that the real author of the incriminating paper was a Maj Esterhazy, who enjoyed powerful support and survived to die in England.   RH

Driant, Lt Col E. A. C. (1855–1916), the first hero of *Verdun. He wrecked a promising regular career by marrying the daughter of Gen Boulanger, unsteady populist war minister in the 1880s, and criticizing the keeping of dossiers on officers of clerical sympathies. Retiring as a captain, he was elected to the Chamber of Deputies, where he championed fortification of the frontier with Germany. As 'Capitaine Danrit' he wrote imaginative if Anglophobe books. Recalled in 1914, he commanded two *chasseur battalions at Verdun while condemning, in parliament, lack of defensive preparations. When the attack came he held the Bois des Caures for a day, buying valuable time, but was killed during the withdrawal.   RH

drill The peacetime exercise of soldiers, normally by constant repetition, designed to provoke a uniform and near automatic response to command. Although it is often forgotten today, the close-order drill which can be observed during recruit training in most modern armies has its roots in combat training. Until the late 19th century, the inaccuracy and short range of firearms meant that the majority of soldiers fought shoulder to shoulder in close-order formations, serving merely as a part of the basic tactical unit (since the time of *Maurice of Nassau, usually a battalion). Through the manoeuvring of these large formations on the battlefield, the commander was able to concentrate his troops at the desired point. Units required extensive training to enable their troops to move as one, and in order to perform these complex tasks of firing and moving in battle, under fire, the greatest *discipline was required. This was instilled by constant drilling during peacetime.

Drill also taught the soldier the prescribed method of loading and firing his weapon so as to increase the rapidity of fire and reduce the risk of accident. From there the training went further, teaching him how to march in step with his fellow soldiers. Once soldiers could march together, then they would be taught how to manoeuvre as a unit. Moreover, drill taught the soldiers to respond immediately to the commands of their officer, allowing a commander to move his tactical formations with ease. The advent of accurate, rapid-fire *small arms in the late 19th century put paid to the tactical usefulness of close-order formations in battle, and armies shifted to open-order tactics. These could not be taught by rote and close-order drill ceased to play a role in combat training.

However, most armed forces have retained close-order drill as part of their recruit training. Semi-affectionately called 'square-bashing' by today's British army, the drill so familiar to anyone who has served in the military still serves several important functions. First, the recruit learns to respond immediately to a superior's commands. Further, by drilling together with his fellow soldiers, the recruit learns that he is no longer an individual but part of a unit in which he is dependent upon his comrades and they upon him. It also instils alertness and helps maintain physical fitness, precision, a smart bearing, and a sense of pride. The value of drill in this context remains disputed, and certainly the highly effective *IDF is not known for its prowess on the drill square. However, Capt Robert Graves, discussing drill with fellow instructors at Etaples in 1916, concluded that 'we all agreed on the value of arms-drill as a factor in morale'.

If close-order drill has lost its battlefield function, battle drills have not. Today's armed forces employ drills known as 'standard operating procedures' to teach tasks which involve proscribed procedures, particularly those required for survival on the battlefield. For instance, 'battle drills' are designed to provoke an automatic, uniform response in the face of a particular combat situation. There is a strong case for suggesting that effective and well-understood drills are the syllables with which a successful commander constitutes the vocabulary of battle.   RTF/RH

Chandler, David, *The Art of Warfare in the Age of Marlborough* (New York, 1976).

Duffy, Christopher, *The Army of Frederick the Great* (New York, 1974).

Dyer, Gwynne, *War* (London, 1985).

drum out A dismissed soldier might be subjected to the public degradation of being drummed out of the service. In 1649 five mutinous troopers in the *New Model Army were told: 'You shall ride with your faces towards the horse tails before the heads of your several regiments, with your faults written on your breasts, and your swords broken over your heads'. In later centuries a soldier, *badges and buttons ripped off, might be marched through *barracks or garrison behind the drums and then physically kicked out of the gates. In the British and US armies the 'Rogues' March' was the traditional accompaniment to this humiliating ritual.   RH

Du Guesclin, Bertrand (*c*.1320–80), *constable of France. He first won a formidable reputation during the

Breton civil war (1341–64) fighting for Duke Charles of Blois. Ugly, short, but powerfully built, from boyhood he dominated his contemporaries. Knighted in 1354, he won wider renown defending Rennes (1356–7). In 1360 he entered French royal service. Victorious at Cocherel against the Anglo-Navarrese (May 1364), he was captured at Aurray (September 1364) when Blois was killed by John (IV) de Montfort. In 1365–6 he led a mercenary company to Spain in support of Henry of Trastamara, where in 1367 he was captured at *Najera fighting against Peter the Cruel and the *'Black Prince'. Ransomed by Charles V of France, in 1369 he helped Trastamara finally gain the Castilian crown. Named constable in October 1370, he adopted Fabian tactics by royal command and was chiefly responsible for driving the English from the lands conceded at Brétigny (1360), winning a rare field battle at Pontvallain (1370). His campaigns in Poitou and Saintonge (1372–3) were especially effective and most of Brittany was regained in 1373–4, but he failed to stop John IV returning from exile in England in 1379. He died from wounds in the Auvergne in 1380 and was buried in the royal abbey of Saint-Denis.   MJ

dugouts were roofed shelters used by troops in trenches, long used in siege operations, and were a feature of *American civil war sieges like *Vicksburg and Petersburg. They assumed major importance during WW I, when they were constructed by combatants on most of the war's fighting fronts. Dugouts were almost infinitely variable in size and construction. Front line dugouts ranged from small 'funk-holes' scooped into the sides of trenches and walled with wood, corrugated iron, or groundsheets, to larger, deeper structures with several rooms and rudimentary furniture. Further back were deep dugouts, usually built by excavating a hole, using wood, stone, or concrete to form wall and roof, and then back-filling with earth to provide over 20 feet (6.1 metres) of overhead protection. The Germans showed particular ingenuity in constructing deep dugouts, like the large *stollen* used to shelter the troops waiting to assault *Verdun in early 1916. The fact that they were generally defending ground of their choosing enabled them to make their dugouts more comfortable than those used by the Allies: panelling, wallpaper, and even running water were not unknown. Well-made deep dugouts were proof against hits by heavy shells, but their garrisons were always at risk from shells which blew in the entrances, entombing them alive. Many accounts describe life in dugouts with their characteristic musty smells, flickering lamp- or candlelight, and pervasive damp.

The term dugout was also used by the British to describe an officer 'dug out' of retirement to serve in the war.   RH

Dunant, Jean-Henri (1828–1910), Swiss merchant, humanitarian, and founder of the *Red Cross. Dunant witnessed the battle of Solferino in Lombardy in June 1859 during the *Italian campaign, an experience which turned him into a leading advocate of constraints on the conduct of war. Solferino saw particularly bitter fighting between the Austrian and Franco-Piedmontese armies, resulting in almost 40,000 casualties. Appalled by the carnage and by the sight of injured men left to die in agony, Dunant organized immediate assistance for the neglected wounded of both sides. He published his impressions of the battle in *Un souvenir de Solferino* (1862), and set about devising formal procedures for neutral mediation during conflict for the alleviation of the suffering of the wounded. He also established the important principle of immunity from attack for medical teams. Dunant's efforts resulted in a network of national Red Cross organizations, the creation of the Geneva-based International Committee of the Red Cross in 1863, and the 1864 *Geneva Convention for the Amelioration of the Condition of the Wounded in Armies in the field. After many years in obscurity, Dunant re-emerged to public acclaim at the turn of the century and was jointly awarded the first *Nobel Peace Prize in 1901.   PC

Dunkirk evacuation (1940). In the early summer of 1940, when the British Expeditionary Force (BEF) was cut off from the bulk of the French armies by the German panzer drive which broke the French front and reached the Channel coast, FM Lord *Gort began to consider a withdrawal to the coast. At the same time the *War Office envisaged the evacuation of non-combatants and key specialists from the Channel ports. Preparations were entrusted to Vice Adm Ramsay, and the fact that a room in his headquarters below Dover castle had housed electrical generators may have persuaded his staff to christen the evacuation DYNAMO.

On 21 May preparations were increased to include large-scale evacuation, and on the 25th Gort made the courageous decision—for he was acting without political authority and in the face of French pressure to counter-attack—to evacuate from Dunkirk. The evacuation began on 26 May, and over the days that followed vessels of all sorts—including warships, passenger ferries, and privately owned 'little ships'—took off troops from the east mole in Dunkirk itself and the open beaches to its north under fierce air attack.

In all 338,000 men, 120,000 of them French, were evacuated. Of the 693 British ships which took part, about 200 were sunk and as many again damaged, while RAF fighter Command, whose efforts were usually invisible to troops on the beaches, lost 106 aircraft. *Churchill warned that 'wars are not won by evacuation', but Dunkirk was both psychologically and materially vital to the British war effort. Although the BEF had lost its equipment, it formed a nucleus of trained manpower, and its almost miraculous survival, as much a consequence of unseasonably fine weather and German errors as British gallantry, reinforced popular resolve. Many Frenchmen, however, were less enthusiastic about the operation, seeing it as evidence of British self-interest.   RH

Easter Rising A nationalist rebellion launched on Easter Monday 1916 by the Irish Republican Brotherhood, together with revolutionary socialists led by James Connolly. Some 1,200 members of the Irish Volunteers and 200 of the Irish Citizen Army (ICA) seized positions in the capital and held them for a week against British artillery and infantry assaults. Patrick Pearse, the rebel commander, proclaimed the Irish Republic from the General Post Office while other units held Jacob's biscuit factory, Boland's Mill (where the commander was Eamon de Valera), the South Dublin Union, and St Stephen's Green (where the ICA ill-advisedly dug trenches, despite being overlooked by high buildings). Because of disagreements within the Irish Volunteer Executive, available rebel forces were sharply reduced and conflicting orders led most Irish Volunteers outside Dublin to stay at home. The defensive positions, although very strong, were unable to support each other and no reserves were on hand to dispute the steady penetration of the city by British forces under the command of Brig Gen Lowe and Gen Sir John Maxwell. A key part of the plan, the landing of 20,000 rifles (captured Russian weapons supplied by Germany) on the west coast, also failed. Although the German arms ship successfully ran the British coastal *blockade, it was scuttled when rebel forces failed to rendezvous with it in Tralee Bay. The most effective military action outside Dublin city was an ambush at Ashbourne in northern county Dublin, which showed the potential for an alternative strategy of *guerrilla warfare. By the time the rebels surrendered on Saturday, some 450 people (116 of them British troops) had been killed and 2,600 injured. Pearse and the other signatories of the Proclamation of the Irish Republic were tried by *court martial and executed; their deaths eventually transformed Irish public opinion from indifference to support for the Sinn Fein party.   CT

eastern front (1914–18). The German elite accepted war in 1914, in part because it feared the long-term build-up of Russian military strength. The pretext for escalating from a local war to a European one was the Russian decision to mobilize in support of Serbia. German war aims, evolved in the autumn of 1914 and realized in the spring of 1918, stressed annexations at the expense of the Russian empire. The *Schlieffen plan strategy, however, was to defeat France quickly and only then turn to the east. The calculation was disrupted when, at the urging of the hard-pressed French, the Russians advanced into East Prussia earlier than they had planned or the Germans had anticipated. While this succeeded in distracting the Germans, the price was appalling and the northern Russian armies were destroyed at the battles of *Tannenberg and the *Masurian Lakes in August–September by the team of *Hindenburg and *Ludendorff. Simultaneously, Russian arms were far more successful against the Austro-Hungarians, who were distracted by the failure of their initial offensive into Serbia and badly directed by *Conrad von Hötzendorf. The Russians occupied much of Galicia (then a region of north-east Austria-Hungary inhabited by Poles and Ukrainians, now part of western Ukraine), inflicting terrible casualties.

The western front settled down by November 1914 into *trench warfare. By contrast a war of movement continued in the east for another year, partly because of the expanse of the theatre of operations: the western front was only about 450 miles (720 km) in length, whereas the front line in the east was over twice as long. Despite the ambivalence of the new COS *Falkenhayn, Berlin temporarily reversed its grand strategy and tried to win victory in the east. After inconclusive or unsuccessful offensives elsewhere on the front Gen *Mackensen won a critical victory in May 1915 in the area of the Galician towns of Gorlice and Tarnow. The local breakthrough, achieved with the aid of operational surprise,

The **eastern front**, 1914–17.

a concentration of fresh German troops, and a heavy artillery bombardment, shattered the whole Russian line. By the end of September the Russians had abandoned most of Galicia and all of Russian Poland, retreating up to 250 miles (402 km). The defeat, did not, as Falkenhayn had hoped, force St Petersburg to the peace table, but these battles, on top of those of 1914, saw the destruction of the Russian pre-war regular army. Another fateful result of these reverses was that Emperor Nicholas II replaced Grand Duke Nikolai Nikolaevich as supreme commander of Russian forces.

A second, more static period began in 1916, with a situation superficially similar to that on the western front. Without the Polish salient the eastern front was now only 700 miles (1,126 km) long, running roughly north–south from Riga on the Baltic to the foothills of the Carpathians at the eastern tip of Galicia, along the western edge of today's Belarus and Ukraine; with Moscow over 450 miles (720 km) in the rear. Compared to what happened in 1812 or 1941, the Russian heartland was not threatened. The Germans again turned their attention to the west, with the dual pressures of *Verdun and *Somme battles, and the Austro-Hungarians had heavy commitments in the south after Italy entered the war in May 1915. The Russians achieved one successful offensive in June 1916, through a combination of surprise, innovative tactics, and Austro-Hungarian demoralization. The *Brusilov offensive, also called the battle of Lutsk, pushed the Austro-Hungarians back up to 40 miles (64 km) along a 250 mile (402 km) sector between the Pripet marshes and the Carpathians. However, the Germans were able to use a superior railway system in the race to concentrate forces, and by mid-September the Russian drive had stopped. It was nevertheless a debacle for the Austro-Hungarians, who from then were confirmed as at best the very junior partners in the Central Powers alliance. The Russian success also encouraged Romania to enter to the war, but a combination of delay and the low quality of the Romanian army meant this turned out to be of little value. Romania was overrun that autumn, and in effect the eastern front was lengthened 300 miles (483 km) from the Carpathians to the mouth of the Danube.

The onset of the March 1917 revolution in Russia (see RUSSIAN REVOLUTIONS) was influenced by the war, but the provisional government, far from being defeatist, was committed to prosecuting the fighting more effectively than the Tsar had. The revolution started among civilians and rear garrisons, and the front-line Russian army was disrupted but not disbanded. The Central Powers, for their part, adopted a passive strategy. The Russian attempt under the socialist war minister Kerensky to regenerate fighting spirit took the form of another offensive in Galicia in July 1917, but this made little progress before a German-led counter-attack pushed the Russians back beyond their starting point. The last episode was the loss in August 1917 of the Baltic port of Riga, the northern anchor of the Russian line. Although this attack featured a concentration of German artillery, a more important factor was Russian demoralization.

A strange third period of the eastern front began with the November 1917 Bolshevik Revolution. A December armistice was followed by peace negotiations, and when these failed the Central Powers attacked against Russian trenches emptied by self-demobilization. The Bolsheviks capitulated in March 1918 at the Peace of Brest-Litovsk, and the Central Powers were able to occupy vast (non-ethnic Russian) territories including the Baltic provinces, Belorussia, Ukraine, and Transcaucasia. Russia's erstwhile allies could only intervene on the periphery (at Murmansk, Arkhangelsk, Baku, and Vladivostok) to head off further German advances.

In terms of general history the eastern front was of profound importance, as it doomed the tsarist Russian and the Austro-Hungarian empires. In terms of military history the raising of huge new armies was striking, but although the Germans developed some of their concentrated artillery tactics against the Russians there was less qualitative military innovation here than on the western front. Probably the unique development was the use of political subversion as a weapon. The German 'sealed train' for Lenin achieved momentous results, although the tsarist government also played with fire with such instruments as the Czech Legion of anti-Habsburg nationalists. On the face of it the Germans achieved as decisive a victory as anyone ever has against Russia. Of the three major armies involved theirs was the most effective at an operational and tactical level. The weaknesses in the leadership, morale, equipment, and supply of the Russian and Austro-Hungarian armies were clearly displayed.

The Russians could not mobilize their economy and society to the same degree as the British, French, and Germans, but they did fight as total a war as they could, albeit of an extensive rather than an intensive kind. They could have held out had the military planners adopted a defensive strategy throughout, but they rarely refused requests to put pressure on the Central Powers with offensives. These were costly and, against the Germans, ineffective, at least in the short term. The Tsar's armies suffered, partly as a result, the heaviest combat fatalities: 2.3 million Russians, compared to 2.0 million Germans, 1.9 million French, and 0.8 million British. It is irrelevant that Russian *per capita* losses were lower. In the end the defeat of all three major eastern front combatants clouded the issue. The eastern front had a decisive impact on the course of WWI, although it was the western Allies who benefited. EM

Hergwig, Holger, *The First World War: Germany and Austria-Hungary* (London, 1997).

Lincoln, W. Bruce, *Passage through Armageddon* (New York, 1986).

Rutherford, Ward, *The Tsar's War 1914–1917* (Cambridge, 1992).

Showalter, Dennis E., *Tannenberg: Clash of Empires* (Hamden, 1991).

Stone, Norman, *The Eastern Front 1914–1917* (London, 1975).

eastern front (1941–5). The campaign on the eastern front was the largest land campaign ever fought. It was unsurpassed in the length of the front, depth of the advance and retreat, duration of continuous fighting, and the size of the armies on each side. It was unique, too, in the scale of violence and the number of casualties. It was the last great extensive war of the age of coal, steel, and *railways; weapons of mass destruction have ruled out another such massive ground war between great powers. It was very different from the campaign fought up to 1945 in the west or in the Pacific. For geographical, technological, and historical reasons neither naval forces nor strategic *air forces were much used by either the Germans or the Soviets. Although a war of machines and of movement, the eastern front was essentially a war between ground forces, albeit between armies with a large motorized component and huge tactical air forces employed as flying artillery.

The extraordinary early successes against the numerically superior Red Army achieved by the attacking German forces in *BARBAROSSA had a number of explanations: the efficiency and experience of the *Wehrmacht, the ability of Germans to concentrate the bulk of these forces in the east, the exposed position of the enemy forces along the new Soviet western frontier, and the operational (see OPERATIONAL LEVEL OF WAR) and tactical surprise achieved on 22 June 1941. In many respects the Wehrmacht succeeded in its initial objective of destroying known Soviet forces in the western frontier zones. In encirclements extraordinary in military history, the panzer formations of von Bock's Army Group Centre had by the end of the first week of the war trapped the main mass of the Pavlov's Western Army Group in the region west of Minsk. Leeb's Army Group North had meanwhile secured crossings over the river Dvina, opening the way into the Baltic region and *Leningrad. In mid-July another grand German encirclement was completed by Army Group Centre east of Smolensk. Some historians perceive a critical German mistake in Hitler's decision to secure the flanks in the Ukraine and Leningrad rather than pushing on immediately to Moscow, which was only 220 miles (354 km) to the east. In particular, when *Hitler ordered the transfer of Guderian's *Panzergruppe* from Army Group Centre to Army Group South, which had been making a relatively slow advance into the Ukraine, the result was a decisive success in the Kiev encirclement but a missed chance to take the Soviet capital.

The battle of Smolensk (July–September 1941) was thus a protracted affair, and the point when Soviet resistance in the centre began to stiffen. Only in early September did Guderian's group again become available as part of what became the final offensive of the year, TAIFUN. The attack had early successes, creating another huge pocket in the Briansk-Viazma area west and south-west of Moscow and setting off a panicky evacuation of the Soviet capital in the middle of October. At this point the weather intervened in the form of the autumn mud and then the winter snow.

*Stalin remained in Moscow, and the Soviets' ability to mobilize reserves, including formations transferred from the Far East and Siberia, proved telling. The *Zhukov counterattack before *Moscow came at the start of December. Within two weeks Hitler had himself replaced Brauchitsch as army C-in-C. The Germans now suffered their first really serious ground-war setback of WW II, as a series of successful Red Army offensives were launched along the length of the front. The Red Army did not have the operation skill it was to display in a similar situation in the following winter (at *Stalingrad) or in the winter of 1943–4, nor did it have comparable resources. The Germans were able to stabilize the situation, and indeed in the spring were to achieve some striking local successes, notably the battle of *Kharkov where an armour-led advance by *Timoshenko on the Ukrainian city was encircled, with the loss of another 250,000 Soviet troops. By the winter of 1941–2, however, the Soviets had stabilized the northern and central parts of the front.

Timoshenko's failure at Kharkov cleared the way for the main German effort in 1942. BLAU began on the anniversary of BARBAROSSA, its objectives being the destruction of Soviet reserves and capture of Soviet oil production centres in the Caucasus, sensibly avoiding the strongest part of the Soviet defences, the central sector before Moscow. The Soviets made a long retreat across the Don steppe, avoiding the encirclements of the previous summer. Hitler is often criticized for dividing his forces as a result of his initial success; Army Group A was sent south-west toward the oilfields and Army Group B west toward Stalingrad, with the result that neither could fully complete their tasks. Gen Paulus's Sixth Army did reach the outskirts of Stalingrad in early September and the famous—and pointless, in terms of overall German strategy—street-fighting epic began. It culminated in Gens Vasilevskii and Zhukov's URAN in mid-November 1942, which broke through the flanks of the Axis line and trapped Sixth Army within the ruins of Stalingrad. Hitler, on the model of his successful 'fanatical defence' directive of the previous winter, would not allow *Paulus to break out. Air supply of the pocket proved impossible, and in mid-January 1943 the newly promoted FM Paulus surrendered. The exposed southern part of the front was rolled up, Rostov was recaptured by the Red Army, and Kleist's Army Group A was only with difficulty extracted from the Caucasus.

Although the Wehrmacht had to give up all the ground captured in 1942, and even some of the positions held since the winter of 1941–2, it was able to stabilize the situation after the Stalingrad defeat. There was even a final German victory in the east, when Kharkov was recaptured in February–March 1943. But the overall outlook was poor, and not just on the eastern front. With each campaigning season the extent of the German effort had been reduced. The objective of the next, and last, major German offensive operation—ZITADELLE—was to destroy the large Soviet

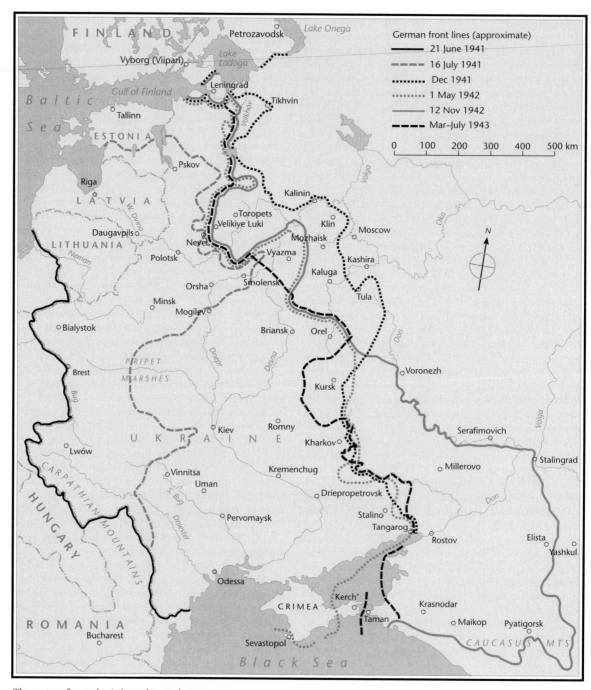

German front lines (approximate)

— 21 June 1941
- - - 16 July 1941
⋯⋯ Dec 1941
⋯⋯ 1 May 1942
— 12 Nov 1942
– – Mar–July 1943

0   100   200   300   400   500 km

The **eastern front**: the Axis on the attack, 1941–3.

Legend:

- Soviet front line, Dec 1943
- Soviet front line, mid-June 1944
- Soviet front line, Dec 1944
- Soviet front line, Apr 1945
- Soviet front line, 7 May 1945
- Western Allied front line, 7 May 1945
- Post war dividing line ('Iron curtain')
- Surrounded German Armies

Approximate areas of some principal Soviet operations
1. Battle of the Dnepr, 25 Aug–23Dec 1943
2. Winter campaign, 1943–44
3. Belorussia, 23 June–29 Aug 1944
4. Lwów–Sandomierz, 13 July–29 Aug 1944
5. Yassy–Kishinev, 20–29 Aug 1944
6. Vistula–Oder, 12 Jan–3Feb 1945
7. East Prussia, 7 Jan–25 Apr 1945
8. East Pomerania, 10Feb–4 Apr 1945
9. Berlin, 16 Apr–8 May 1945
10. Prague, 6–11 May 1945

The **eastern front**: the Soviet advance into central Europe and the defeat of Germany, 1943–5.

273

salient, halfway between Moscow and the Black Sea and centred on the town of *Kursk. The Germans built up local strength, both numerical and qualitative, and fought the largest concentrated tank battle of the war. The offensive from north and south of the bulge began early in July 1943 and was brought to a halt by the layers of the Soviet field defences. The battle of Kursk showed the Soviets could fight successfully in the summer, and after it the Germans no longer could, losing the strategic initiative irrevocably, something underlined by the simultaneous Allied landing in *Sicily. The Soviet counter-offensives that followed removed, in turn, German salients around Orel (KUTUZOV) and Belgorod-Kharkov (RUMIANTSEV). By the end of the autumn of 1943 the Red Army had reached the line of the Dnepr river and crossed it at a number of points.

The traditional Soviet view sees a third period of the war in the east from January 1944 to May 1945, and this does form a coherent period. The Soviets now combined abundant resources of *matériel* with a mature command system and military structure. Using concentrated mobile forces, especially the Guards Tank Armies, and backing them with massed artillery and tactical *air power, they finally achieved those 'deep operations' which had been the focus of Soviet strategic thought in the 1930s. Soviet propagandists spoke of the '10 Stalinist crushing blows' of 1944. The first of these was the recapture of the 'right bank' Ukraine west of the Dnepr in December 1943–April 1944, followed by the recapture of the Crimea in April–May. At about the same time, in January–March, at the other end of the front, the German stranglehold around Leningrad was finally broken. Shortly after D-Day in *Normandy came two more major offensives. The first, the Vyborg-Petrozavodsk operation north-west of Leningrad (June–August 1944), forced the Finns to sign an armistice. Much more important in the overall course of the war was *BAGRATION in Belorussia, which led to the destruction of FM Busch's Army Group Centre; in another extraordinary victory organized by Zhukov and Vasilevskii the Red Army advanced 350 miles (563 km). BAGRATION was shortly followed by breakouts further south, the Lvov-Sandomierz operation (July–August 1944), in what had been south-east Poland, and the Jassy-Kishinev operation (August 1944), which captured Moldavia (in Bessarabia), led Romania to change sides, and opened the road to the Balkans.

These striking successes, up to the autumn of 1944, were still largely being fought to recapture Soviet territory, at least taking into account the annexations of 1939–40. This process would be completed by the Baltic operation in September–November 1944, except for German units trapped in Kurland (in western Latvia). Meanwhile, in the autumn of 1944 the Red Army began the campaign for the 'liberation' of east central Europe that would indirectly have such a telling effect on post-war international relations. Having already occupied Romania the Red Army quickly invaded Bulgaria (an Axis member but not an active anti-

Soviet belligerent) in September 1944. The Belgrade operation (September–October 1944) took the Red Army into *Yugoslavia, and the Debrecen and Budapest operations (October 1944–February 1945) into Hungary.

By 1945 the Third Reich was on its last legs, under siege from east and west. The most striking Soviet success of this period was the Vistula-Oder Operation (January–February 1945) in which Zhukov and *Koniev took the Red Army from the middle of Poland to the approaches of Berlin. The flanks of this operation were secured by hard fighting in East Prussia and Lower Silesia. The final battle of *Berlin began in mid-April 1945 and ended with the German surrender.

Historians will probably not cease to see a range of explanations for the outcome of the fighting on the eastern front. Is the outcome to be explained by mistakes of Hitler and the German high command, by Soviet military skill, by geography and climate, or by the Soviet numerical advantage? It could be argued that the Soviet campaign was essential and unavoidable for the government in power in Germany, given its ultra-nationalist and ideological programme. It was also a campaign premissed from the German side on faulty 'technical' military *intelligence and an underestimation of the Soviets based on racialist theory; the invasion of the USSR was thus essentially based on political factors rather than military ones. Once the Soviet system did not collapse in the summer and autumn of 1941 the defeat of Germany in the campaign, and in the war in general, was probably inevitable. This is not to say that Hitler's defeat was not hastened by the remarkable rebirth of the Red Army's fighting qualities in the later part of the war and by a Soviet readiness to take very high losses.

Arguments will continue about the relative importance of the eastern front in the overall history of WW II. Hopefully with the end of the *Cold War these historical disagreements will become less politicized. The Soviets certainly paid the heaviest price in lives and territory, but that does not in itself make their role decisive. They did engage, in the middle part of WW II, much the greater part of mobile German ground forces, and they inflicted huge losses on those forces. On the other hand the decisive defeat of Nazi Germany would probably have been impossible without Allied naval control of the Atlantic and the Mediterranean, without American and Commonwealth ground operations (especially from mid-1943), and without the strategic bombing campaign. Although the USSR could and did survive without the 'second front', the retaking of the western borderlands and the advance into central Europe would have taken much longer and would have cost even more. At the same time the operations of the Americans and British would not have been decisive—in the framework of pre-atomic technology or barring political changes in Germany—without the immense contribution of the eastern front.   EM

Erickson, John, *The Road to Berlin* (Boulder, Colo., 1983).
—— *The Road to Stalingrad* (New York, 1975).

Glantz, David M., and House, Jonathan, *When Titans Clash: How the Red Army Stopped Hitler* (Lawrence, Kan., 1995).

Wieseczynski, Joseph L. (ed.), *Operation Barbarossa: The German Attack on the Soviet Union, June 22, 1941* (Salt Lake City, Utah, 1993).

Ziemke, Earl, and Bauer, Magna, *Moscow to Stalingrad: Decisions in the East* (Washington, 1987).

Ecnomus, battle of (256 BC). Taking its name from a hill above modern Licata, this was the greatest naval battle of the first *Punic war. Polybius (see GREEK HISTORIANS) records that the Romans had 330 warships, carrying nearly 139,000 men, the Carthaginians 350, carrying 147,000. The Roman fleet, heading west on its way to Africa, was in a triangle, with two squadrons in line ahead echeloned outwards, a third forming the base towing horse-transports, and a fourth covering the rear. The Carthaginian centre, in line abeam, feigned withdrawal to disrupt the Roman formation, while their left along the shore and their right out to sea reached around to attack the Roman rear. Thus, possibly as planned, the battle dissolved into three separate engagements. But the Carthaginian ships still had no answer to the *corvus*, and when their centre was defeated and fled, one of the two leading Roman squadrons returned to help the fourth drive off the Carthaginian right, then both went to help the third, now backed up against the shore by the Carthaginian left. Carthaginian losses were 64 ships captured and 24 sunk, the Roman 24 ships sunk.   JFL

Lazenby, J. F., *The First Punic War* (London, 1996).

Polybius, 1. 26–8.

École Polytechnique, L' This was founded in 1794 by the National Convention as the École Centrale des Travaux Publiques (Central School of Public Works) and received its current name a year later. Originally under the leadership of Lazare *Carnot and Gaspard Monge, the school was to provide *education for engineers, but it soon came to be dominated by the military. In 1802, it absorbed the state artillery school, and two years later it was transferred from the control of the Ministry of the Interior to the army. The arms requiring more scientific knowledge had been neglected under the army of the *ancien régime*, and this specialist *academy marked a change in the status of these arms. It also demonstrated the increasing importance of technology in warfare, as artillery in particular came to play a central role in Napoleon's wars.

After 1804 the École Polytechnique provided the French armed forces with scientifically educated officers. Entrance was by competitive examination, hence open to all regardless of social status. The students were normally between the ages of 16 and 20. For many years it was the main source of artillery and engineering officers for the army and gunnery officers and naval architects for the navy.

In 1976 it was relocated from Paris to Palaiseau. While in the past most graduates became officers in the armed forces, today most go on to careers in the civil service or business. The curriculum is still largely science-based; the school offers degrees in mathematics, mechanical engineering, physics, chemistry, economics, humanities, and social science.   RTF

edged weapons rival the spear and the club as man's oldest weapons and, like them, are derived from hunting tools. The earliest military edged weapons were probably stone daggers and early swords may have been made in the form of wooden paddles, their edges studded with sharp stones like the Aztecs' obsidian-edged weapons, or sharks' teeth such as those employed in Polynesia. Although edged weapons pre-date the discovery and development of metals, these permitted the creation of more lethal weapons. Metals, initially alloyed copper, then bronze, and then iron, gave greater weight with less bulk and superior penetration. Metal swords are thought to have developed in the second millennium BC, possibly as horsemen's weapons initially, and excavated examples exist from Anatolia and other areas of the eastern Mediterranean in both straight and curved forms. Crete and Mycenae were important areas of sword development in the 17th to 11th centuries BC but elsewhere in Europe similar advances were being made, principally with straight swords, in the north-west and central areas of the continent around 1500 BC. Sword design appears to have been little affected by the advent of iron and its use in sword manufacture grew between 1200 and 700 BC, the *Assyrians making great use of iron swords by both their cavalry and infantry. Perhaps the most well-known type of sword from the Bronze Age had a leaf-shaped blade, narrow near the grip and swelling towards the point, its double-curved, double-edged form ideal for thrusting but also capable of a savage cutting stroke. This type of blade shape was maintained in the iron- and steel-bladed swords of the Greek *hoplites, who tended to use their swords only when their spears had failed them. This leaf shape was modified into the *gladius* of the Roman legionary: a short, thrusting sword, said to have a Spanish ancestry like the very similarly shaped legionary's dagger. The *gladius* was to the Roman infantry what its longer brother, the *spatha*, was to the Roman cavalry. Derived from a Celtic straight-bladed slashing sword, the *spatha* had its ancestry in north-west Europe and both it and the *gladius* remained as core styles of sword long after the fall of Rome, as they were adopted and exported throughout Europe by the Germanic and Nordic occupiers who replaced the Romans north of the Mediterranean.

As the *gladius* and *spatha* gave birth to the longer *Viking sword, so it became the basis for the knightly sword of the medieval period: cross-hilted, heavy-pommelled, straight-bladed, and, increasingly, an object of veneration, of sumptuous decoration, and of bequest and inheritance. Viking swords, in their heyday from the 8th to the 12th centuries AD, had generally double-edged, pattern-welded blades, frequently signed by their skilled bladesmiths and often bearing intricately decorated cross-guards and pommels. Similar swords became used by the 9th century for ceremonial purposes too, such as coronations: the sword had become, with the mace, a symbol of majesty. The broadly triangular shape of the Vikings' sword pommels developed, in early medieval swords, into the shape of a brazil nut and that, c.1100, gradually became joined by pommels of disc or wheel shape. As the blade became longer and heavier—with an average length of 36–8 inches c.1100—so the counterbalancing pommel grew larger too. Longer sword blades, which had reached about 48–52 inches by c.1325, necessitated still larger pommels and longer grips—enabling the sword to be held and swung with two hands. Such swords, while intimidating even against a mail-clad opponent, had little other than a musical effect upon plate *armour and these great swords only persisted in cultures beyond the reach of the development or culture of the fully armoured knight, in the Highlands of Scotland, for example, where they remained in use into the 16th century. Knights began to carry shorter thrusting swords, the blades of which were reinforced with a pronounced median ridge, and similarly formed daggers, ideal for stabbing into the joints of an armour or through the slits in a visor. Men-at-arms and common soldiers carried daggers too and occasionally short, curved multi-purpose swords. These rigidly bladed thrusting swords and daggers remained) the principal edged weapons of the European soldier from the end of the 13th century to the end of the 16th century.

No survey of military edged weapons can be complete without a consideration of those from outside Europe which impinged so significantly on western warriors and affected their own cultures in a marked way. The crusading knights encountered the swords of Islam in the Near East, the soldiers of Britain and France squabbling over India in the 18th century found a tradition of swords and daggers as old as their own, and Allied servicemen in the Far East in WW II were all too aware of the potential of the *samurai sword. What all these warriors had in common, in their encounters with these extra-European cultures, was the tales that they bore and the souvenirs they brought home of their opponents' edged weapons. Few, regrettably, survive from the *Crusades—perhaps because Islam was ultimately triumphant—but it is clear that an Islamic tradition of curved swords existed side by side with one of straight swords from the 8th century to the 14th century; only after that did the curved-bladed sword of Islam become the norm, under the influence of the Ottoman *Turks. Under the Ottomans the traditional 'scimitar' form developed, with the differing blade and hilt styles known as kılıç and samsır, and remained constant, with minor sophistications to blade and hilt design, until the end of the Ottoman empire; the 'scimitar' is still a sword symbolic of the Islamic faith. Styles of Persian 'scimitar', closely resembling the Turkish samsır, were very similar to some genres of sword found in northern India since the two regions had many cultural links and similarities.

Terminological confusions abound when westerners attempt to classify non-European swords, particularly in relation to the Indian subcontinent where the Hindi word talwar simply means 'sword' (the same is true in Turkish of kılıç and samsır). Swords of a wide variety of styles can be classified as talwari but the term is generally applied, at least in the West, to a curved-bladed sword with a bulbous grip, a disc-shaped pommel, and a straight cross-guard widening at the ends; many talwari had all-metal grips, often exquisitely decorated. The warriors of the subcontinent used a wide variety of edged weapons but even the straight bladed swords, like the pata and khanda, were intended primarily for the cut rather than the thrust: the latter movement was intended solely for the dagger. Daggers existed in many blade and hilt forms and combinations in India and the Middle East and were an essential part of the dress of anyone aspiring to warrior status. Perhaps the most well-known edged weapon from this area is the Gurkha kukri from Nepal, a curved knife with a double-curved edge ideal for a drawing stroke: these are still carried by Gurkha soldiers in the British and Indian armies. The edged weapons of India paralleled those of the Near East in being considered not only the honourable weapons of the warrior but also vehicles for the display of wealth associated with warriors of high rank and status.

The same attitudes applied to edged weapons, and especially to swords, in Japan, where the craft and symbol of the sword is inextricably associated with the tenets of the Shinto religion. In Japan the art of the blademaker was equal to that of the hilt-maker; the quality of Japanese sword blades was widely recognized and had assumed almost mythological proportions by the time the West made contact with Japan in the mid-19th century. By that time the samurai warrior caste had developed the custom of owning two swords, sometimes wearing both: the long sword, or katana, and the shorter sword, or wakizashi. The wakizashi was the all-purpose sword and most Japanese military swords were of its dimensions, including those captured in such quantity towards the end of WW II and taken home as souvenirs by Allied troops. Daggers en suite with wakizashis and katanas were accorded the same care in their manufacture and decoration as their companion swords.

In the West, once the sword had declined from a major role on the battlefield, demoted by the pistol by the mid-17th century, it remained the symbol of the cavalryman and the officer. In this way it was continuing its traditional role, one which was maintained by gentlemen in civilian clothes for much of the 18th century and one which persists in the armed forces today. Swords and firearms coexisted on the battlefield from before the end of armour, since firearms had only one shot apiece before reloading and in a

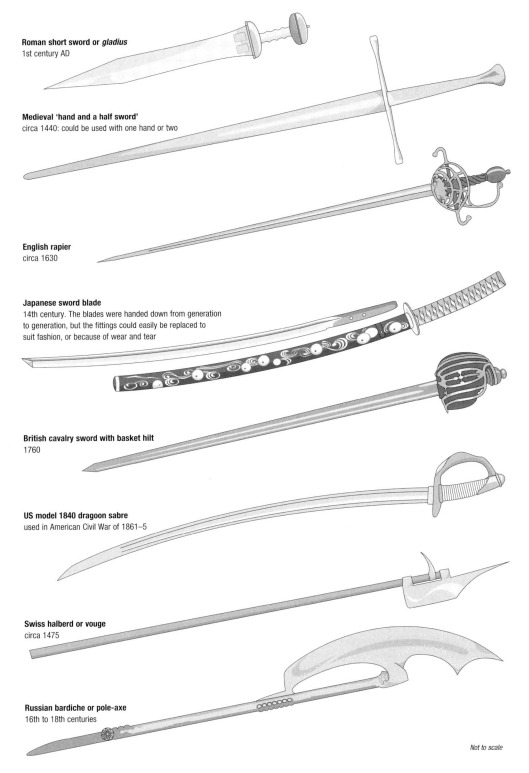

Roman short sword or *gladius*
1st century AD

Medieval 'hand and a half sword'
circa 1440: could be used with one hand or two

English rapier
circa 1630

Japanese sword blade
14th century. The blades were handed down from generation to generation, but the fittings could easily be replaced to suit fashion, or because of wear and tear

British cavalry sword with basket hilt
1760

US model 1840 dragoon sabre
used in American Civil War of 1861–5

Swiss halberd or vouge
circa 1475

Russian bardiche or pole-axe
16th to 18th centuries

Not to scale

Besides being a lethal weapon, the sword is also widely regarded as a symbol of power and aristocracy. Other weapons, such as the halberd, derived from agricultural implements, may have lacked the sword's prestige but could be more effective.

mêlée the sword remained essential. In a cavalry mêlée the hilt of the sword was almost more important than the blade since a strongly constructed hand-covering hilt could act as a very effective mailed fist on occasions when opponents were too close to each other to wield blades effectively. Swords remained in use for both infantry and cavalry soldiers during the 17th century and for the greater part of the 18th century, most infantrymen relinquishing them in the second half of the 1700s. Among the most heavily armed of 18th-century infantrymen was the Highland infantry soldier of the British army: as well as his musket and *bayonet, he carried a basket-hilted sword and a dirk, both weapons being relics of the culture from which the Highlander was drawn. Dirks were descendants of the long medieval daggers, of varying forms, had 10 to 12 inch (25 to 30 cm) blades, intricately carved bog-oak grips, and were carried from the waistbelt in tooled leather sheaths. In the late 18th century, with the romanticization of Highland Scotland, they acquired symbolic status, became much embellished, and, in the 19th century, were joined in the 'Highland' garb by the *sgian dubh*, or black knife, worn in the right stocking top by officers and civilians. At sea, cutlasses became common issue in the 18th century for most *navies and officers were equipped with swords and dirks in much the same way as their military counterparts. Although a dirk was introduced for midshipmen late in the 19th century in most navies, such efficient close-action weapons were carried by most combatant sailors during the *Napoleonic wars.

From the late 18th century until WW I, debate raged in European cavalry circles about the role of the ideal sword: was it to cut, or thrust, or to do both? Thus cavalry swords came and went in a bewildering variety of patterns for cavalry regiments of different types. Although light cavalry regiments, *hussars for example, generally carried curved swords and heavy cavalry regiments, such as *cuirassiers, generally long straight ones, the protagonists of the 'cut-or-thrust' schools continued their arguments until they were stilled for ever by the rattle of the machine gun, against which neither stroke made much sense. Although there were instances of cavalry actions with the sword during both world wars, the automatic firearm finished what its muzzle-loading ancestor had started and the sword slipped finally away into its symbolic role of today. The military dagger, whether in the form of *commando knife, *kukri*, or survival knife, has lasted longer, since it is useful as a tool as well as a weapon and so the edged weapon as tool remains, even on the highly technological battlefield of the late 20th century.   SCW

Coe, Michael D., et al., *Swords and Hilt Weapons* (London, 1989).
Edge, David, and Paddock, John M., *Arms and Armour of the Medieval Knight* (London, 1988).
Oakeshott, Ewart, *European Weapons and Armour* (London, 1980).
Robson, Brian E., *Swords of the British Army* (London, 1996).

Edgehill, battle of (1642). Edgehill was the first major battle of the *British civil wars. The main royalist army, under Charles I, was raised in Wales, Yorkshire, and the Midlands and left Shrewsbury on 12 October to march on London. Parliament's main army, commanded by the Earl of *Essex, left Worcester on 19 October and attempted to get between the king and the capital. On the morning of 23 October it became clear that the royalists had won the race, and were at the foot of Edgehill, north-west of Radway in south Warwickshire. The parliamentarians formed up south-east of Kineton. Both armies, each around 13,000 strong, were drawn up in two main lines, with infantry in the centre and cavalry on the flanks.

After an ineffective artillery duel the royalists advanced. On the flanks their cavalry drove their opponents from the field but disappeared in pursuit. The infantry battle was finely balanced, both sides fighting bravely hand-to-hand. Sir Edmund Verney, who bore the Royal Standard, was cut down: the standard was taken, and then recovered by Capt John Smith. Both sides lost perhaps 1,500 men apiece, but the royalists had a clear road to London. Charles did not exploit this, enabling Essex to reach the capital first. When the royalists approached on 13 November, they were outfaced at Turnham Green, and fell back to winter in and around Oxford.   RH

Edmonds, Brig Gen Sir James (1861–1956). Commissioned into the Royal Engineers in 1881, Edmonds served on Kitchener's staff in South Africa. He went to France in 1914 as COS of 4th Division. After wilting under the strain, he spent the rest of the war on the staff of the chief engineer in France. Edmonds was far more important after the war than during it. Director of the military branch of the historical section of the *Committee of Imperial Defence, he edited several volumes of the official history. Superficially he tended towards the view that external factors—new technologies, inexperienced commanders, staff and troops, political interference, and German fighting qualities—accounted for patchy British performance, and believed that his task was to describe rather than criticize.

In fact his approach was more complex, for he was caught up in the personalized struggle within the army, and his correspondence with other participants—so many of whom were his contemporaries—and judgements in the official history reflect this. He had been at Staff College with *Haig, and let him use some of his notes; Haig reciprocated by protecting him when he collapsed in 1914. He usually avoided criticism of senior commanders, and sometimes went as far as bending the facts so as to support the GHQ view of *Passchendaele. He had likes and dislikes, and was critical of *Gough in 1917 and *Byng in 1918. There was also a wide gap between what he wrote officially and unofficially. Supportive of Haig in the official history, privately he opined that 'he was really above the—or rather, below the average in stupidity'. He believed that Haig intended to break through, not wear down, in both 1916 and 1917, but did not dwell on the inconsistencies in the official history.

Edmonds was industrious, influential, opinionated, slippery, and disappointed. His Staff College nickname, Archimedes, sums up his comrades' view of him as a clever technician. They might have thought of an alternative had they seen—as historians now can—what he thought of so many of them.   RH

education, military This is a general term covering the full range of instruction in the art and science of war, from basic military training to higher education at master's and doctoral level. Military education embraces the instruction given to *military monastic orders, and to medieval squires aspiring to become knights, the professional training given to officers which became increasingly common in the 18th century, and the continuous process of training and education which modern professional servicemen and women undergo throughout their careers. The term also embraces many great works of military thought, which were designed as manuals for the instruction of officers, generals, and princes.

The warrior monks of ancient China, forbidden to carry weapons, were feared because of their prowess in unarmed combat. One young man joined the order, hoping to learn its secrets. For two years he was given menial duties, including carrying a heavy cauldron of water which he then had to empty each day by repeatedly striking the water with the palm of his hand. After two years, he went home on leave. His family wanted to hear all about his education, but he became angry. He could not understand why all he had to do was carry heavy weights and empty the water. In a rage, he struck the family's massive oak table with the palm of his hand. It splintered, and he realized why.

*Sun-tzu's the *Art of War* of 400–320 BC and *Vegetius' *De Re Militari* of AD 390–410 are among the first systematic treatises on military affairs which clearly had an educational purpose. After the fall of Rome, theoretical studies on military science continued in the Byzantine empire and in the Arab world. One of the first western treatises on the art and science of war was Walter de Milemete's *De Regis Misericordia*, written in 1327 for the young *Edward III of England, which includes probably the first ever picture of a cannon. Meanwhile the first military *academy in Asia was established in Vietnam in the 14th century.

Until the 18th century, most military officers were landed gentlemen whose innate skills in hunting and other rural pursuits equipped them pretty well for field command. The technical arms—the artillery and engineers—required formal training and academies were established throughout Europe. By the end of the 18th century it was clear that infantry and cavalry officers also needed some formal instruction in the increasingly complex art and science of

war. Cadets were very young—in their early teens—and general education played a large part in the syllabus. The standard, particularly in relevant modern subjects such as geography, mathematics, and science, was often higher than in the most prestigious civilian institutions. The British scientist and inventor Sir Michael Faraday, for example, taught at the Royal Military Academy Woolwich, which trained young artillery and engineer officers.

Formal military education was limited to preparing boys and young men for commissions until the 19th century, after the *Napoleonic wars, when military education expanded with the creation of staff colleges for older, serving officers, to prepare them for staff duties. During this period, officers in military command appointments also increasingly undertook professional studies. In 1831 *Wellington founded the Royal United Services Institution, for the continued professional advancement of naval and army officers, the first such institute in the world. The award of essay prizes contributed to encouraging officers to study their profession seriously. As with all education, teaching at advanced level requires continued research and development of the subject.

The emergence of mass, conscript armies helped make 'military education' more élitist. Officers who attended military schools and academies intending to pursue a military career were differentiated from the conscript soldiers and short-service officers who formed the bulk of the armies. The latter underwent military 'training'—but hardly 'education'. The majority of those who fought in both world wars were in this category. With a few exceptions, the generals and admirals on all sides were all the products of a professional military education. But one of the positive legacies of the world war experience was the introduction of first-rate education for non-officers. The increasing complexity of military technology meant that soldiers, sailors, and airmen had to do complex jobs which required quick thinking, initiative, literacy, and numeracy. Many gained an education they had missed out on in civilian life, as examinations in basic educational skills accompanied selection for promotion to senior, non-commissioned ranks.

With the end of conscription in the armies of the developed world, military education is more important than ever in attracting and retaining high-quality recruits. Increasingly, armed forces try to ensure that, besides gaining the necessary qualifications to do difficult military jobs, those skills are recognized with the award of equivalent civilian qualifications, which will help the serviceman or -woman on return to civilian life.   CDB

Edward III, King of England (1312–77), one of the most successful medieval warrior kings. He served his apprenticeship in arms by annual expeditions against the Scots in the early 1330s (see SCOTS WARS OF INDEPENDENCE), developing an army raised by contracts with magnates and gaining experience in the use of dismounted men-at-arms and *archers, tactics which later brought success against France. Claiming that kingdom's crown in 1337, he devoted the next two decades to war. An expedition to the Low Countries (1338–9) was costly and abortive, but in 1340 he won a major victory over a French fleet at Sluys. Then, fighting on several fronts, with competent lieutenants (Lancaster, Warwick, Northampton), his forces achieved notable successes in Gascony, Poitou, and Brittany where Edward campaigned personally in 1342–3. A stunning victory at *Crécy was consolidated in 1347 by the capture of *Calais after a year-long siege. In 1350 there was another naval success off Winchelsea against a Castilian fleet, colourfully described by *Froissart. But for much of the 1350s Edward directed affairs from the council chamber, although in 1359–60 he again personally led a large force to France, intent on capturing Rheims and being crowned there. But the siege failed and he was forced to accept terms at Brétigny (1360), agreeing to renounce the French crown. For nine years, war with France was suspended. By the time it recommenced in 1369, Edward was an old man, although he tried to lead his navy in 1372. His last years witnessed the loss of most of his gains before 1360. But at the height of his fame, founder of the Order of the Garter, he was recognized throughout Europe as the pre-eminent chivalric monarch of his day.   MJ

Ormrod, W. M., *The Reign of Edward III: Crown and Political Society in England* (New Haven, 1990).

Prestwich, M., *The Three Edwards* (London, 1980).

Egypt, ancient The military history of ancient Egypt spanned three millennia, spanning the Stone, Bronze, and Iron Ages. There were developments in technology, organization, *fortification, and in battle itself, although the hieratic pictures on temple walls convey a timelessness in which the pharaohs are shown seizing and dispatching their enemies. One thing that did not change was the economic and strategic situation of the Egyptian civilization: its wealth was based upon the annual inundation of the Nile flood plain. This fertile strip was only open to land invasion through narrow points of access, the Fourth Cataract in the south and the Gaza Strip in the east. There were no significant enemies to the west, but if there had been there was a similar choke point in the northern Libyan desert.

The first pharaoh to unite the 'Two Lands' of Upper and Lower Egypt (the delta and the southern Nile) is known as Menes (*c.*3100 BC). It is possible that warfare of the Archaic Period was ritualized, being based around the taking of prisoners for *sacrifice. Certainly weapons were primitive and short-ranged and no *armour appears to have been worn. These characteristics of Egyptian warfare also seem to have been long-lasting, into a period beginning with the second millennium BC when bronze weapons were already

available. Under the Old Kingdom (2686–2160 BC) there existed a system for recruiting a militia from the *nomes* (tribes) and there were officials responsible for training and for logistics, which already displayed a high level of organization. During this period the troops were entirely infantry and the hard core of warriors were mercenaries. These came from Nubia and later Libya, and towards the end of the Old Kingdom formed a great proportion of the army.

During the Middle Kingdom (2133–1786 BC), the emphasis was placed upon recruiting native Egyptians. Although still all infantry, the columns of heavy spearmen resembling the *Sumerian formations were supported by archers, perhaps split 50 : 50. By the 18th century BC it is believed that the pharaoh maintained a standing force of some 10,000 men (divided into two divisions and named after the gods Amun and Re) in addition to a more numerous militia. Soon after 1700 BC, there took place an invasion that brought about a military revolution. The Hyskos (the name means 'desert princes') brought with them a vastly superior technology, comprising bronze weapons and armour, the composite bow, and the *chariot. The domestication of horses gave the Hyskos a great advantage and they established their rule in Lower Egypt from their capital at Avaris in the Delta. The Egyptians soon adapted these innovations and made them their own and within little more than a century they had expelled the intruders and established the New Kingdom (1567–1085 BC), during which they grew to their greatest power. Chariots became heavier (with six-spoked wheels instead of four) as the crews were armoured. The composite bow was the primary weapon for charioteers, which is how the pharaoh was increasingly depicted. The navy also grew from a riverine fleet into a true maritime force, as can be seen in the reliefs at Medinet Habu (*c.*1180 BC). The ships had 50-man crews who doubled as marines, armed with bows, spears, and grappling hooks for boarding actions.

The first well-recorded battle in history took place in *c.*1485 BC. Pharaoh Tuthmosis III was then campaigning near the Sea of Galilee (some 186 miles (300 km) from Egypt proper) and we have details of the strategy and tactics he employed to attack and capture the city of *Megiddo. First he used an unexpected route to arrive before the city, then he charged with the largest chariot corps that Egypt had so far possessed and won substantial booty, including over 2,000 valuable horses. The siege of the city took another seven months, but with its fall Thutmoses was able to establish his authority as far as the Euphrates. This brought Egypt into conflict with the equally expansionist Hittite empire, and it was in exactly the same region, at *Kadesh, in 1300 BC, that Ramesses II, another great warrior pharaoh, won a victory over them. The last pharaoh to campaign in Syria was Merneptah (1236–1223 BC), after which Egypt was on the strategic defensive. Merneptah himself already had to defeat a land invasion by a group known as the Sea Peoples in the fifth year of his reign, and under his successor

Ramesses III the pressure intensified. They were defeated in a great sea battle (*c*.1180 BC) but their land migrations seem similar to those of the Germanic peoples towards the end of the Roman empire. The Sea Peoples were a mixture of tribes, possessing both a military cutting edge and the momentum of a whole people on the move. Illustrating the point exactly are the ox-carts clearly shown on temple reliefs, which they used both for transporting their families and also as battle-wagons.

Understandably, the Egyptians turned to fortification to stem this human tide, and this aspect of Egyptian war-craft became well developed. Ramesses III constructed a line of forts in the western Delta and there had been a fortified zone on the Upper Nile from the beginning of the second millennium BC. This eventually stretched some 250 miles (402 km) between the First and Fourth Cataracts, which prevented invasion from Nubia. As seen in Thutmosis III's capture of Megiddo, by the 15th century, if not earlier, they had also become adept at *siege warfare, although they did not develop the siege engines which were to make the *Assyrians such great city takers. A bas-relief depicting the capture of Ashkelon by Ramesses II shows several phases of siege. First, the defenders are driven away from outside the walls and the place is isolated, then the assault goes in, with ladders raised by the storming parties while sappers attempt to hack through the city gates with axes.   MB

Healy, M., *New Kingdom Egypt* (London, 1992).

Egyptian and Sudanese campaigns (1882–98). The chaotic state of Egypt's financial situation led the two major creditors, Britain and France, to establish joint control over Egyptian public finances in 1879 and, in effect, to control the country. A popular revolt against this foreign domination, led by an Egyptian army officer, Urabi Pasha, resulted in Europeans being murdered in Alexandria and to the bombardment of the city by a British fleet on 11 July 1882. The subsequent despatch of an army under *Wolseley resulted in the defeat of the Egyptian army at Tel-el-Kebir on 13 September 1882 and to the British occupation of the country, the French having refused to co-operate.

In occupying Egypt Britain automatically assumed responsibility for the vast Egyptian Sudan. There, a revolt led by a religious leader, Muhammad Ahmed, self-styled the *Mahdi, had started in 1881. By the end of 1882 his forces (popularly if inaccurately known as *dervishes) had occupied a major part of the Sudan. A large Egyptian army, under a retired Indian army officer, Col William Hicks, sent to smash the Mahdi was itself annihilated on 5 November 1883—the day before another Egyptian force was destroyed outside Suakin on the Red Sea and the British consul killed. To retrieve the situation at Suakin a hastily assembled force under Maj Gen Gerald Graham was despatched there and defeated the Dervish forces under Osman Digna at El Teb and Tamai after severe fighting in March 1884. Graham's

force was then withdrawn and the town remained under siege.

The British government now decided to evacuate the Sudan, with the exception of Suakin, and *Gordon was sent to superintend the evacuation of the Egyptian garrisons. Against his instructions, he elected to stay and defend the capital, *Khartoum, which came under siege from the Mahdi in May 1884. In October 1884, bowing to public pressure, the government despatched the *Gordon relief expedition under Wolseley, who advanced slowly up the Nile. In the face of increasingly desperate appeals for help from Gordon, Wolseley despatched a flying column across the desert. After a desperate fight at Abu Klea on 17 January 1885, a small party embarked at Metemmeh on two steamers and reached Khartoum on 28 January, to find that the city had fallen and Gordon been killed two days earlier. Wolseley was forced to retreat and the Sudan was abandoned to the Mahdi. To salvage something from the debacle Graham was again sent to Suakin with a large, carefully prepared force, in February 1885, with orders to smash Osman Digna and to build a railway to Berber, on the Nile, with a view to the subsequent reconquest of the Sudan. Graham defeated Osman at Hashin and Tofrek in March and succeeded in laying nearly 50 miles (80 km) of the 250 miles (402 km) of track required to reach Berber but in May 1885 the force was withdrawn, ostensibly because of the imminence of an Anglo-Russian war over Afghanistan. Suakin was retained but remained under siege.

Wolseley's withdrawal left Egypt open to a Mahdist invasion, which came in December 1885 and was defeated at Ginnis. In July 1889 a second, major invasion was launched but was decisively defeated by Grenfell at Tushki on 3 August 1889. At Suakin Osman continued to plague the garrison until he was decisively defeated at Tokar in February 1891. For ten years after Gordon's death the British and Egyptian governments concentrated on building up Egypt's prosperity and in reconstructing the Egyptian army under British officers. As each unit reached operational efficiency it was 'blooded' by being sent to Suakin or to the Sudan frontier. By 1895 the British government was concerned about Italian and French designs on the Sudan and in 1896 decided the time was ripe to start the reconquest of the Sudan, using the reorganized and retrained Egyptian army, led by its C-in-C, *Kitchener. Building a railway as he went, he moved methodically forward, inflicting severe defeats at Firket and Hafir in June and September 1896. By the end of September 1896, he had reoccupied the northernmost province of Dongola, roughly halfway to Khartoum.

The second phase of the reconquest started in January 1897. The railway was steadily pushed southwards, the dervishes outmanoeuvred and defeated at Abu Hamed on 7 August 1897, and Berbert on the Nile, only some 250 miles (402 km) from Khartoum, occupied. The dervishes seemed incapable of devising a strategic plan to halt the relentless British advance.

The final phase of the reconquest began in January 1898. For this final phase Kitchener was reinforced with two brigades of British troops. A large Dervish army under the Emir Mahmud had entrenched itself at the confluence of the Nile and Atbara rivers but it was attacked and routed on 8 June 1898. Kitchener was now only some 200 miles (322 km) from Omdurman, the Dervish capital opposite Khartoum. The final advance began at the end of August. Kitchener now had an immensely powerful force, including a cavalry brigade, four Egyptian, and two British infantry brigades, supported by a large field artillery force, 20 maxim machine guns, and some 25,000 men; 10 gunboats gave fire support from the Nile. Against this, Khalifa Abdullah, the Mahdi's successor, could muster some 60,000 men, ill-equipped by comparison and lacking in artillery.

By 1 September Kitchener was encamped on the Nile, 6 miles (9.7 km) from *Omdurman. A night attack, in which Kitchener's technological advantage would have been largely nullified, would seem to have offered the Khalifa his best chance of success but he elected to fight in daylight. Kitchener was no tactician and in the battle next day he had some moments of concern, but the Khalifa was unable to co-ordinate the actions of his various forces and in the pitiless fire of repeating rifles, machine guns, and high explosive his troops were massacred. Their losses were estimated at 11,000 killed and 16,000 wounded; British casualties were 48 killed and 382 wounded. Omdurman was occupied the same day but the Khalifa, with other leaders, escaped and was not rounded up and killed until November 1899.

Two months before the battle of Omdurman, a small French expedition from West Africa had reached Fashoda on the White Nile 470 miles (756 km) south of Omdurman and raised the French flag. Kitchener reached Fashoda on 19 September 1898 with a browbeating display of force, but an international crisis blew up and it was not until December that a face-saving formula was found for a French withdrawal.   BR1

who had narrowly missed intercepting the expedition on its outward passage, destroyed Brueys' fleet at the battle of the Nile, and severed Bonaparte's supply line to France.

Bonaparte now determined to impose a French regime, and set his scholars to work on a monumental survey of the country. In September, the *Turks, as nominal suzerains of Egypt, declared war on France, and to prevent them from using Syria as a base from which to attack him, Napoleon invaded Palestine in February 1799. At Acre his protracted siege was foiled by tenacious Turkish defenders with British naval support, and finally disease caused him to retreat to Egypt with heavy losses.

The Turks followed up with a landing in Aboukir Bay, which was repulsed. But in July, Bonaparte slipped away in a frigate to seize power in France, leaving Kléber in command. In January 1800 Kléber agreed the Convention of El Arish with R Adm Sir Sidney Smith for the repatriation of his army to France, but repudiated it after a series of misunderstandings. The assassination of Kléber in June 1800 left the command in the hands of the incompetent Menou, a convert to Islam with a passionate belief in France's colonial future in Egypt.

Although peace was imminent, Henry Dundas, the Secretary of State for War and Colonies, insisted that the French must not be left in possession of Egypt, and persuaded Pitt to send a military expedition to remove them. In March 1801, Sir Ralph Abercromby effected a brilliant assault landing in Aboukir Bay with 14,000 men and defeated Menou's counterstroke in the battle for Alexandria (21 March) where he was mortally wounded. In conjunction with the Turks his successor Hely-Hutchinson obtained the capitulation of the demoralized Cairo garrison. He then laid siege to Menou in Alexandria. Menou capitulated in September, the news reaching London a day after peace preliminaries were signed.   PGM

Chandler, David, *The Campaigns of Napoleon* (London, 1966).

Mackesy, Piers, *British Victory in Egypt, 1801: The End of Napoleon's Conquest* (London, 1995).

Egyptian expedition, French (1798–1801). This was promoted by *Napoleon, who was at a loose end during the peace that followed his first Italian campaign, but had concluded that an invasion of England was not feasible. The attractions of Egypt for France were many: to restore French trade and influence in the Levant; to undercut Britain's eastern trade round the Cape of Good Hope by opening the shorter Red Sea route; and to establish a base for a military attack on British India.

Bonaparte sailed in May 1798 with 40,000 troops and a group of administrators and academics, escorted by Adm Brueys with the Toulon fleet. Seizing Malta en route, he landed in Aboukir Bay on 1 July and occupied Alexandria, then advanced up the Nile to defeat the *Mamelukes in the battle of the Pyramids (21 July). But on 1 August *Nelson,

Eisenhower, Gen Dwight 'Ike' David (1890–1969), supreme commander of Allied forces in Europe during WW II and and later a two-term US president. The holder of the latter office is the C-in-C of the armed forces, thus the presidency is a logical final step in a military career and also the reason why so many generals have been elected president in a country with a history of unquestioned civilian control.

Eisenhower's family background is fascinating. They were originally extreme pacifist Mennonite (see CONSCIENTIOUS OBJECTION) immigrants from Germany, but his (decidedly humble) branch had briefly moved to northern Texas at the time of his birth. One might speculate about the 'Texas effect', because that state has produced a disproportionate number of famous US soldiers such as Audie

*Murphy, and during WW II the overall commanders in both Europe and the Pacific (*Nimitz) were of German descent, born in Texas. There was nothing in his early life or young manhood that hinted at future greatness and when he graduated from *West Point in the class of 1915 (famous for producing 59 generals out of 164 graduates—*Bradley was a contemporary), he was 61st academically and 125th in discipline. He was the commander of a tank training centre and just missed being posted to Europe during WW I. In 1922 he was posted to the Panama Canal Zone where Gen Conner became the first of the patrons who were to shape his career, sending him to the Command and General Staff School, from which he graduated first out of a class of 275, then to the Army War College. He did tours in France, where he wrote a guidebook to the battlefields of WW I, then in Washington before receiving the plum posting to the Philippines as aide to the army's enormously influential ex-COS *MacArthur, then organizing the new commonwealth's armed forces.

The special star that shines upon great commanders turned on the power for Ike in 1939–41, in that he was posted home before the Japanese destroyed his latest patron's forces in the Philippines, while as COS of the Third Army his planning of the largest war games ever staged in the USA, involving close to half a million men, brought him to the favourable attention of army COS *Marshall, who promoted him brigadier general. When war came to the USA, he appointed Ike to the war plans division in Washington, entrusted with the planning of the Allied invasion of Europe, and promoted him major general in March 1942 as head of the operations division of the War Department. In June, Marshall selected him over the heads of 366 senior officers to command US troops in Europe and in July he was made lieutenant general. The rank of full general followed in February 1943, following his overall command of the landings in *North Africa. He was again in overall command of the invasions of *Sicily and mainland Italy, and from the beginning of 1944 he was in London as the supreme commander of the Allied Expeditionary Forces, making the preparations for the invasion of *Normandy.

Starting with *Montgomery and at intervals ever since, critics have suggested that Eisenhower's complete lack of combat leadership made him a poor choice. To do this is to pit one's retrospective judgement against such as Marshall who chose him, Franklin D. *Roosevelt who confirmed him, and *Churchill who welcomed him. He was chosen precisely *because* he was a politician, one furthermore who had his ego sufficiently under control to be able to deal not only with the aforementioned, but also with highly competitive prima donnas like *Patton and Montgomery, not to mention the French, who had to be found a role commensurate both with their limited strength and their demand to be treated as major players.

The degree to which he continued to indulge the British need to be treated as equal partners long after American numbers and resources had become preponderant also weighs heavily in the credit balance. It may well have been one of the reasons he permitted the disastrous *Arnhem operation to go forward, although there is the slightest hint of a subconscious desire to give his aggravating British subordinate enough rope to hang himself. Few historians on either side of the Atlantic have given enough weight to his overriding concern, which was the qualitative superiority of the *Wehrmacht in most categories of equipment and at all levels of command except the very top. In the phrase later to be made famous by *Truman, the buck stopped with Ike, and when he made his fateful decision to postpone and then proceed with the invasion of Normandy, he wrote a letter assuming full responsibility if it failed. He was right to do so, and he is equally entitled to full credit for the successful outcome not merely of the invasion but for all Allied operations in *North-West Europe.

After the war, by now a five-star general of the army, he succeeded Marshall as COS and during a spell as president of Columbia university wrote *Crusade in Europe*, a bestseller that made him, at last, prosperous. Truman recalled him to be the supreme commander of the newly formed NATO, a task for which his skill at handling a multinational force made him eminently well qualified. In 1952 he resigned to run as the Republican candidate for president, although the Democrats had also courted him. He won comfortably, but it was at this climactic moment that he suffered an unforgivable failure of moral courage, in refusing to defend his old benefactor Marshall against a vicious personal attack by the anti-communist demagogue McCarthy, a lapse that caused Truman to refuse to shake his hand at his inauguration. With the world well launched into the *Cold War, it might be argued that *raison d'état* precluded him from behaving like an officer and a gentleman; unfortunately the evidence suggests strongly that his calculations were those of a politician anxious to win an election, not of a statesman concerned for the moral and physical welfare of his country.

His age and his health (he had several minor and one severe heart attack during his eight years in office) did not prevent him managing a presidency that laid down the broad outlines of US policy at home and abroad for decades to come. The key word here is 'manage'; he was not a 'hands on' president, but one who delegated authority and insisted that his staff should bring only matters of the highest political importance to his personal attention. This of course begged the question of what *were* matters of the highest importance, but the country was in the midst of the largest sustained economic boom of all time, the US had if not a nuclear monopoly, at least a great preponderance of weapons and the means to deliver them, and many of the tough decisions that faced his successors were simply not all that urgent between 1953 and 1961.

He was not a man to meet trouble halfway, but in retrospect we can see that the nation was halfway to quite a lot of troubles when he left the presidency. Among these were the implications of the 1954 Supreme Court ruling that segregation in public schools was unconstitutional, which Eisenhower affirmed by signing the 1957 Civil Rights Act and by sending federal troops to Arkansas to enforce school desegregation. Another was *Vietnam, to which he dispatched the first US advisers, and yet another was the green light he gave to a number of CIA operations to overthrow foreign rulers perceived to be hostile to US interests. He bequeathed one of the least well conceived of these, against *Castro in Cuba, to his successor John Kennedy, and it duly blew up in his face. These were not the products of cannons running loose, as future presidents were to claim, but central to the policy of containment Ike worked out with his Secretary of State John Foster Dulles, whose brother Allen ran the CIA.

At the close of his presidency, Ike came under attack for, of all things, having spent too little on the military and thus 'allowing' the Russians to catch up, as dramatized when they were the first to launch a satellite into earth orbit in 1957. They were nowhere near catching up; the 'missile gap' Kennedy made much of during the 1960 presidential election did not exist, and both he and Eisenhower knew it. But the latter, had he been given to introspection, might have concluded that the anti-communist rhetoric that served to glaze his own goose in 1952, was sauce for the Democrat gander eight years later.

During his farewell address he warned of the hidden power of the 'civil-military complex' and this remains one of the least well understood of all his often cryptic utterances. He was the last US president who believed in a decentralized state, where the powers not specifically allocated to Washington remained with the individual states, and he had an intuitive understanding of the manner in which the *political economy of war and of the 'military preparedness' that Kennedy made so much of must work against that vision. A good part of the explanation for his endorsement during his presidency of the sort of cloak and dagger operations that he had frowned upon as a general was that he thought thereby to fulfil his constitutional obligation to assure the security of the nation without involving it in the heavy expenditure that would, and has, undermined the intent of the constitution itself.

His greatness as a general will always be disputed by those who do not understand that politics and war are one and the same. Whether or not he is judged to have been a great president seems to revolve entirely around whether the person who makes the judgement believes that government is a solution, or a problem. Dwight Eisenhower, with his roots very firmly in the tradition of those who came to the USA in order to be free of state interference, was of the latter persuasion.   HEB

Ambrose, Stephen, *The Supreme Commander* (New York, 1970).
Bischof, G., and Ambrose, S. (eds.), *Eisenhower: A Centenary Assessment* (New York, 1995).

Gelb, Norman, *Ike and Monty: Generals at War* (New York, 1994).

enemy, attitudes to The soldier's attitude to his enemy is often ambivalent. On the one hand propaganda (some of it usually often founded on fact) encourages him to see an enemy as a hateful figure. This process is often exaggerated if there are radical cultural differences between combatants, and at its worst an opponent may be denied our common humanity. WW II research suggested that 44 per cent of US soldiers would 'really like to kill a Japanese soldier', while only 6 per cent expressed similar enthusiasm for killing a German. Sharp religious divides may have a similar effect. When *Cromwell stormed Drogheda in 1649 he admitted that captured priests were 'knocked on the head promiscuously', and when some of the defenders took refuge within a church it was fired. One, who jumped from the tower, survived the fall and was spared 'for the extraordinariness of the thing'. The former Israeli premier Menachem Begin once described Palestinians as 'beasts walking on two legs', a classic example of the dehumanizing epithet. *Guerrillas and irregulars may find themselves regarded not as soldiers but as murderers. Here the view is usually subjective: I am a freedom-fighter, he is a bandit.

The heat of battle may burn away a soldier's finer feelings, and opponents who try to surrender in the midst of battle are often unsuccessful. 'No soldier can claim a right to quarter', wrote a WW I British officer, 'if he fights to the extremity'. The loss of a comrade in battle or death of a relative as a result of *blockade or bombing often causes real bitterness which may be visited upon enemies who could have had no hand in the original act. During the *American civil war one Confederate soldier admitted to being so affronted by Maj Gen Butler's decree that ladies in New Orleans who jeered at Union troops would be treated as 'women of the town plying their avocation' that he refused quarter to a Union soldier. In WW I, Pte Frank Richards knew of only one occasion when prisoners were killed, by a soldier who had just lost a close friend. 'I was so pissed off when my buddy got it,' recalled a *Vietnam veteran, 'that I blew up two kids riding a water buffalo.'

The distance at which killing takes place aids the process of dehumanization, and technology may reduce an enemy soldier to a glow on a screen or a blip in a weapon sight. Sometimes soldiers have used the language of sport to describe their trade, and talk of 'making a bigger bag' can help reduce the enemy to a mere component of a body count. An Australian soldier in *Gallipoli thought shooting Turks was 'just like potting Kangaroos in the bush'. A professional soldier may feel neither hatred nor affection for the enemy. 'I simply thought about the job in hand,' recalled a British *Falklands veteran, 'and they happened to be in the way of getting the job done.'

On the other hand the abstract image of a hateful enemy is often dispelled by personal contact. In the *Peninsular war, Sgt William Wheeler found a captured French corporal 'as light hearted and merry a companion as I could wish', while his compatriot Edward Costello established 'a very amicable feeling' for the French, 'apart from duty in the field'. Shouted conversations between trenches during WW I revealed common interests. 'It is I, Fritz the bunmaker of London', shouted one German. 'What is the football news?' The hitherto most aggressive British soldier in the section opposite was nonplussed to discover that his adversary was a fellow Chelsea supporter.

It could be difficult to persuade soldiers that such men were really hostile. One British general, hearing from a *sentry that there was a bald, bearded German soldier in the trenches opposite, asked why the sentry did not shoot him. 'Shoot him,' replied the man. 'Why, Lor' bless you sir, 'e's never done me no harm.' A British soldier in Normandy was drawn closer to his enemies when searching prisoners. 'One chap of fifty empties his pockets, including his photos of wife and kiddy and his old pipe. Realise more than ever this business is crazy'.

Sometimes mutual regard grew into admiration. As French *cuirassiers thundered around his square at *Waterloo, a British officer exclaimed: 'By God! Those fellows deserve Bonaparte. They fight so nobly for him.' WW I German machine-gunners attracted the admiration of an opponent, who thought them: 'Topping fellows. Fight until they are killed. They gave us hell.' A WW II infantry company sergeant major recalled that 'when an enemy position had been taken, one tended to take the same attitude of care and welfare to the dead and wounded as if they belonged to our own side. There was an abhorrence of any maltreatment of prisoners . . . especially when they had put up a good fight.' Significantly, his enemy was German. Such comments are rarer where the Japanese were concerned, because Japanese behaviour (caused, if not excused, by cultural differences) provoked widespread bitterness. Yet one Australian sergeant admitted: 'Whatever their other qualities might be, to me they are—with envy—the brave Japanese.'

A soldier's enemy is often an image, albeit seen in a grubby and distorting mirror, of himself. As some US Marines rifled the packs of slain Vietcong they came closer to their enemies: 'In killing the grunts of North Vietnam, the grunts of America had killed part of themselves.' WW I poet Wilfred Owen wrote of a dreamlike meeting between adversaries:

> I am the enemy you killed, my friend.
> I knew you in this dark: for so you frowned
> Yesterday through me as you jabbed and killed.
> I parried; but my hands were loath and cold.
> Let us sleep now . . .   RH

Gray, Jesse Glenn, *The Warriors: Reflections on Men in Battle* (London, 1970).

Holmes, Richard, *Firing Line* (US title *Acts of War*) (London and New York, 1985–6).
Keegan, John, *The Face of Battle* (London, 1976).

Engels, Friedrich (1820–95), political economist, military writer, and theorist; friend, colleague, and adviser of Karl Marx; and founder of communism. Born at Wuppertal on 28 November 1820, he began writing political tracts in 1839. In November 1842 he visited Manchester in Britain and became a member of the Chartist movement, and first met Marx in Paris in 1844. His experiences led to writing *The Situation of the Working Class in Britain* (1844–5) and, in turn, *The Communist Manifesto* (1848). Further experience of the 1848–50 revolutions in Europe and particularly in Germany led to the writing of *Revolution and Counter-Revolution in Germany* (1851–2). In 1850 he returned to Manchester where he worked in a commercial firm, partly to subsidize Marx.

In 1870 Marx and Engels attended the Congress of the First International in London. In 1871 Engels welcomed the Paris *Commune, fitting it into his view of progress through capitalism towards a dictatorship of the proletariat. After Marx's death in 1883, Engels completed and published the unfinished second and third volumes of *Das Kapital*.

Engels was an expert analyst of military affairs and, in particular, of the mid-19th-century revolution in military affairs and the role of industry and arms manufacture. Marx considered that he had 'made the study of military questions his speciality'. Many of the articles attributed to Marx owe much to Engels. Their division of interest was fairly clear cut, Marx studying the political essence of wars and their character, Engels, the material basis of military affairs and the nature and origin of wars and armies.

Engels's detailed study of military affairs was fired by the *Crimean and *American civil wars, although much of his military analysis dates from later life. He realized that future wars between major powers would be *total war, and would depend to an unprecedented degree on technology which, in turn, depended on a nation's industrial base. In 1892 he wrote 'from the moment warfare became a branch of the *grande industries* (ironclad ships, rifled artillery, quickfiring and repeating cannon, repeating rifles, steel covered bullets, smokeless powder, etc.) *la grande industrie*, without which all these things cannot be made, became a political necessity'. In a letter of 1888 he prophesied the nature of war accurately enough. 'No war is any longer possible for Prussia-Germany except a world war, and a war of an extension and violence hitherto undreamt of.' The study of war could not be extracted from its *political economic and diplomatic context—as he wrote, 'diplomacy is higher than strategy'.

Engels's views on the *military revolution taking place at the time were sound enough, but hardly unique, and he would probably not have gone down in history as a great military thinker and analyst were it not for his friend Marx.

It is questionable whether either of them would be remembered today had their work not been taken up by *Lenin. But for the study of the 19th-century revolution in warfare his work is important.   CDB

---

engineering, military Military engineering is, in essence, civil engineering undertaken in a military environment. The duties of military engineers also include mapping and surveying, which became increasingly important as *indirect fire weapons were deployed. The constraints of time, finance, labour, and materials, which affect all civil engineering projects, weigh especially heavily on military engineers in time of war, with the added complication that engineering activities may be hampered by enemy action, sometimes in conditions of actual combat. Military engineers are required not only to construct their own works, but also to destroy those of the enemy. The engineer's role in the provision of protection against intruders may be said to have begun with the construction of simple huts and walls. These gradually developed into great positional defences of earth and stone around cities and on the frontiers of states, requiring the use of skilled engineers both to design those of their own side and to attack those of the enemy. With the advent of *gunpowder, the mathematical and scientific knowledge needed by engineers for *fortification and siegecraft became increasingly important and most modern military *academies trace their descent from schools for engineers and artillery established during the 18th century. In sieges, the engineer's duty was not merely to act as a technical expert, but also to conduct troops forward to the point of attack when a fortress was stormed. In the British army, a standard cry was 'follow the sapper', the term for those who, under engineer officers, dug the saps or shelter trenches used in the attack on fortresses. If the *demolition of an obstacle required the use of explosives, the engineers placed the charges and ignited the fuses. Among many heroic episodes of the *Indian Mutiny campaign was that of the Powder Bag party, including fourteen sepoys of the Bengal Sappers and Miners under engineer officers, who blew in the heavily defended Kashmir Gate at the British storming of *Delhi. *Field fortifications, generally made of local materials and intended to serve a temporary need, can be constructed and, in the case of enemy works, demolished by ordinary sappers and *pioneers, who are required to possess only basic field engineering skills.

The simplest form of road in field engineering consists of two parallel ditches with the excavated spoil heaped between them to produce a cambered way. An alternative type, widely used in wooded swampy areas, is the corduroy road, made by felling trees to clear a path, splitting the trunks, and laying them transversely to form a corrugated roadway. More permanent roads, built by military engineers for strategic purposes, generally assumed a wider economic role, allowing wheeled traffic to move easily where previously only less efficient pack animals could go. Examples include the straight highways of the Roman empire, the military roads built by FM Wade and his redcoats in the Scottish Highlands after the *Jacobite rebellion of 1715, and the Grand Trunk Road, 1,500 miles (2,414 km) long, in British India. In many cases, such roads continued as public highways for hundreds of years after they had served their original military purposes. Away from the combat area, military engineers assumed the role of architects, designing *barracks and camps complete with buildings for every kind of function, including housing for officers and men, kitchens and dining halls, offices, stores, workshops, stables and wagon lines, guardrooms, *hospitals, schools, churches, etc., together with roads and exercise grounds. During the 19th century, as European and American governments extended their dominions into areas of previously untamed wilderness, it was frequently the case that the only engineers available for the construction of public works were those belonging to the military. Such employment was readily sought by engineer officers, who not only had the personal satisfaction of opening up new terrain, but were also able to practise their profession in conditions similar to those of actual campaign. In the USA, the Corps of Engineers assumed, and retained, responsibility for the construction and maintenance of navigations and waterways in parts of the country long under civilized occupation. The draining of morasses, a skill in which all military engineers were trained in order to counter enemy inundations, was especially valuable in such areas.

Bridge-building, especially over rivers and watercourses across which armies have to pass, has been a vital element of military engineering from the earliest times. Bridges made of boats collected together and moored side by side, with a decking of timber planks, were used from the classical period. *Xerxes crossed the Hellespont (Dardanelles) by this method in 480 BC. *Pontoon bridges are constructed on the same principle, with the pontoons (light boats designed to be transported overland) acting as floating piers, on which the planking carried as an integral part of their bridging train is laid. In the absence of pontoons, rafts, barrels, or inflated skins could be used for flotation. 'Flying bridges', used in the campaigns of *Alexander 'the Great' and still familiar to military engineers in the early 20th century, were made by anchoring boats (usually covered by decking) to a point in mid-river. They were moved from one bank to another by angling the bows into the current. Shallow rivers and dry gullies could be bridged by lines of wagons, and with the advent of motorized transport a similar role was assumed by tracked vehicles. A standard technique for crossing ditches, moats, etc, was to build a causeway using brushwood, earth, or rocks. The application to warfare of modern industrial and scientific developments added new fields of *science and technology to military engineering. In operational areas, military engineers built and ran *railways. *Telegraph, *radio, *chemical and biological weapons, and aviation were all originally allotted by armies to their engineers, before the formation of specialist corps. TAH

Douglas, Howard, *An Essay on the Principles and Construction of Military Bridges and the Passage of Rivers in Military Operations* (London, 1853).

Kerry, A. J., *The History of the Corps of Royal Canadian Engineers* (Ottawa, 1962).

Smithers, A. J., *Honourable Conquests: An Account of the Enduring Work of the Royal Engineers throughout the Empire* (London, 1991).

English civil wars. See BRITISH CIVIL WARS.

Enigma In 1919, Hugo Koch from the Netherlands invented an electronic enciphering machine that provided 22 million different combinations. It really began to be used in 1923 as a commercial product and by this time a German named Arthur Scherbius had taken over the development of the machine, which was aimed at business needs for secure communications. The German navy became interested in the machine and it was withdrawn from the civilian market and refined for military use.

In its developed form the Enigma machine had a keyboard, plugboard, three (army, air force) or four (navy) rotors, and a lamp table. The rotors were set to a 'ground setting' (*grundstellung*), usually changed daily. Each message would be preceded by an individual 'key setting'. The message would be typed onto the keyboard, the rotors changed the cipher at each letter, and the enciphered letters would light up on the lamp table. After wireless transmission by Morse code the enciphered message would be typed by the receiver onto an Enigma machine having the same ground setting, the key setting entered, and the text deciphered automatically.

Three Polish mathematicians (Rejewski, Rozycki, and Zygalski) established the theoretical basis for breaking the output of German military Enigma machines in early 1933, through a process of combining mathematics, statistics, computational ability, and inspired guesswork. In July 1939, at a secret meeting with British representatives, the Polish government handed over their theoretical data on breaking Enigma and a replica Enigma machine, later called the Bombe (named after the ice cream, not explosive). In August the Government Code and Cypher School (GC&CS) was moved to Bletchley Park, an estate 46 miles (75 km) from London. Chess masters, mathematicians, professors, and linguists were recruited from all over Britain, many from Cambridge University. The first Bombe machine permitted the British to read some traffic during the fall of *France. This intelligence, dubbed *ULTRA, was passed on to a very limited number of recipients, among whom the most voracious reader was certainly *Churchill. ULTRA supplied advanced warning of Luftwaffe intentions during the battle of *Britain in 1940 and was instrumental in the interdiction of Axis supplies in the Mediterranean, contributing substantially to the turning point at *Alamein. Theoretical data was shared with the Americans even before they entered the war, although there were always reservations about their less stringent distribution and occasionally careless use of ULTRA.

The battle against Enigma was never completely won. Advances came from the capture of ground settings from German weather ships (taken in a 'cutting out' operation on suggestion from Bletchley Park) and a U-boat. First principle was the identification of a standard message such as 'nothing to report' and the possible key setting such as the operator's wife's name, from which it was possible to work back to the ground setting. The Bombe machine could then find the key settings for other messages in that ground setting. By 1944, over 4,000 German messages were being decrypted daily at Bletchley Park.

The flood of *SIGINT, of which the product from the attack on Enigma was only a part, crucially influenced the direction and outcome of WW II. The *North Africa, *Italian, and *North-West Europe campaigns, but above all the battles of the *Atlantic and the *Pacific (though this latter did not involve Enigma), were heavily affected by the Allies' foreknowledge of Axis intentions. Never in a major war has one combatant had his intentions betrayed so comprehensively to his opponent. It is remarkable that the secret was entirely kept for 30 years and much of it for 50 years: the story is still unfolding. DMJ/PJ

Bauer, F. L., *Decrypted Secrets: Methods and Maxims of Cryptology* (New York, 1997).

Hinsley, H., *et al.*, *British Intelligence in the Second World War* (London, 1979–88).

Hodges, Andrew, *Alan Turing: The Enigma* (London, 1992).

Kahn, David, *The Codebreakers: The Story of Secret Writing* (rev. edn., New York, 1996).

Enver Pasha (1881–1922), pro-German, pan-Turkist revolutionary. A member of the Committee of Union and Progress (CUP) ('Young Turk') military reform movement which restored the 1876 Constitution in 1908 and deposed Sultan Abdulhamid II the following year, Enver was military attaché in Berlin before leading a radical coup in 1913. One of the ruling triumvirate in the ensuing CUP dictatorship, he led the recapture of Edirne in 1913, before involving Turkey in WW I. His pan-Turkic ambitions led him to invade the Caucasus in 1914–15 and to disaster at Sarikamish. Despite considerable German support, his dispersion of resources greatly facilitated Allenby's advance through Palestine to Damascus. The defeated CUP resigned in October 1918 and Enver fled to Berlin and then Moscow. Sent by *Lenin to central Asia in 1921 to unite its Turkic peoples against British India, for which he was promised support for an eventual return to power in Turkey, Enver instead declared himself 'emir of Turkestan' and led the *basmachi* rebels against the

Bolsheviks. He was killed leading a mounted charge against machine guns in present-day Tajikistan in 1922.   DD

Hopkirk, Peter, *Setting the East Ablaze* (London, 1984).

Palmer, Alan, *The Decline and Fall of the Ottoman Empire* (London, 1992).

Epaminondas (d. 362 BC), the great Theban general who forged the Boeotian hegemony and crushed *Sparta militarily at *Leuctra and socio-economically by freeing the helots and re-establishing their state of Messenia. Little is known of his career before the battle in 371 BC other than formal philosophical schooling and his idealized friendship with his fellow commander Pelopidas. Always subject to rigid civilian control, and without great reservoirs of loyal manpower, Epaminondas nevertheless in less than a decade (371–362 BC) crafted the Theban army into the greatest infantry force in Greece. He characteristically massed his best troops to unusual depths under his own leadership on the left wing, where it was to decide the battle decisively against the enemy's crack right. His four invasions of the Peloponnese resulted in the new fortified cities of Messene, Megalopolis, and Mantineia, which robbed Sparta both of her serfs and allied *hoplites. His ultimate goals are unclear, but Epaminondas was loyal to constitutional government and may have genuinely wished similar equality and autonomy for all the *poleis* of Greece. In antiquity, his reputation for honesty and humility was legendary, and his death at the battle of *Mantineia at the moment of victory only cemented the Epaminondan legend of military genius and strategic daring.   VDH

Buckler, J., *The Theban Hegemony 371–362 BC* (Cambridge, Mass., 1980).

equipment, personal The soldier needs rapid access to his weapons and ammunition, and has scarcely less urgent need for water, food, portable shelter, the means to clean himself and his weapon, and digging tools: his personal equipment is the means by which he carries these necessaries—and too often much else besides. Equipment falls broadly into two categories: fighting order, to house the items needed in combat, and marching order, containing less immediate requirements. Although preferences have varied between nations and across history, the marching order of the legionary of the time of *Marius and thereafter will strike a chord with even 20th-century infantrymen. A forked stick across his shoulder suspended a wicker basket for carrying earth (for he was expected to make a fortified camp each night) containing enough wheat to be turned into three days' worth of the biscuits that constituted his staple diet and an assortment of tools. A pickaxe was stuck into his belt. His fighting order, carried even when heavier items had been dumped, comprised throwing spear, short sword suspended from a cross-belt and hitched up on the right hip, and a shield which might be slung when it was not held ready on his left arm. Small wonder that he was nicknamed 'Marius's mule'.

From the 17th century equipment became broadly standardized. The infantryman carried a substantial ammunition pouch, bayonet, water-bottle, and 'snapsack' for a day's rations suspended from broad cross-belts, usually made of buff leather and pipeclayed to inconvenient whiteness. On the march he had a pack on his back, often made of animal skin with the creature's face displayed: a German pack is a *dachs*, after the badger whose skin traditionally constituted it. If he was not wearing his greatcoat, it might be rolled above or below the pack. A Swiss drafted in the army of *Frederick 'the Great' complained: 'Altogether we were bound five times over by straps passing cross-wise over our chests, and to begin with we all believed we were going to suffocate under the load . . . I opened my shirt to let in a little air, and steam arose as if from a boiling kettle.' Rifleman John Harris, who endured the retreat to *Corunna in the *Peninsular war, believed that 'the soldier was half beaten before he came to the scratch . . . Many a man died, I am convinced, who would have borne up well to the end of the retreat, but for the infernal loads we carried on our backs.'

The cavalryman was luckier (though his mount was not): saddlebags alongside the pommel contained some of his necessaries, and a round valise behind him housed his cloak. A cross-belt might carry his carbine or contain an ammunition pouch. So characteristic were the double cross-belts of the infantryman and the single belt of his mounted comrade that the tactical symbol identifying the infantry on military maps is a cross, while a diagonal slash represents cavalry. Commanders needed maps and note-books, and the sabretache, hanging from the waist-belt, not only housed pen, ink, and paper but also provided a convenient writing surface.

During the 19th century the fashion changed, and fighting order generally came to comprise a waist-belt holding ammunition pouches, suspended by two leather shoulder braces. The pack soldiered on, sometimes made of skin and sometimes—like the deeply unpopular French *azor*, which has to be kept a uniform and shiny black—of polished leather. Capt Anson Miles, a US Army officer with experience of Indian fighting, went into partnership with a weaver to produce cartridge belts made of woven cotton webbing, and although the German army retained its affection for the traditional leather, the British and US armies adopted webbing equipment. The British 1908 pattern webbing consisted of waist-belt, two ammunition-pouch sets, a bayonet-frog, fitting for the entrenching tool, haversack, and large pack with supporting straps. Improved versions appeared in 1937, 1944, and 1958: the last had the considerable merit of being immune from *spit and polish. Unlike the 1937 pattern which had to be treated with blanco, it was simply scrubbed clean. The trend towards utility has continued, and most modern armed forces now use rucksack-type packs—'bergens'—and pouches made of light and robust man-made fabrics. Some use waistcoats (American 'vests'), with magazine pouches incorporated in a sleeveless jerkin.

Successive generations of soldiers have complained about the weight of their equipment. Sometimes the tough and battle-hardened, campaigning in areas where food might be scrounged or looted, stripped down to a bare minimum of rolled groundsheet worn bandolier-fashion, with a few necessities tucked into it, a water-bottle, and a spoon. However, in general the 20th-century infantryman has remained a beast of burden. The French *poilu* of WW I carried what Henri Barbusse called a 'monumental and crushing' 85 lb (38.5 kg) on the march. The *Chindits of WW II shouldered around 90 lb (41 kg), a veteran of the *Vietnam war reckoned that even his clutch-belt with fighting order 'must have weighed forty-five pounds', and a company commander in the *Falklands weighed in with 83 lb (38 kg) of weapons and equipment. The advent of the *APC and the *MICV has helped by ensuring that full marching order is less familiar than it once was. But in many tactical circumstances the infantryman is still best defined as something you hang things on.   PMacD/RH

equitation, military The *haute école* of classical equitation includes movements with direct military application, like the capriole which was originally intended to enable a horseman to use his steed to kick an attacker approaching from behind. It was believed to be relevant as late as the 18th century, and many cavalry officers learnt it as part of their formal training. The Cadre Noir (instructors) of the French cavalry school at *Saumur taught the *haute école*, and such was the reverence with which it was approached that in student slang watching the instructors perform was described as 'going to mass'.

From the 18th century most armies favoured what the British termed the 'Old German Seat'. Soldiers rode with long stirrups and almost straight legs, sitting at the trot so as to present a uniform appearance and, so it was argued, using their weapons more effectively. Prussian regulations of 1742–3 decreed that a single hand's breadth of space (two for *hussars) should emerge between a rider's backside and saddle when he stood up in the stirrups. *Frederick 'the Great' himself favoured a rather shorter style, and used a flat English hunting saddle rather than the heavily padded *Pauschensattel* preferred by most of his officers.

There were repeated complaints that riding so long produced injuries to the groin and made it harder for light cavalry, who tended to use their swords to cut rather than to thrust, to use their weapons to full advantage. In 1803 Col Thomas Pakenham ordered his men to take their stirrups up two holes before charging at Laswaree, and they cut about to good effect. His contemporary the French light cavalry theorist Brack agreed, writing that the charging

horseman should 'lean forward on his horse, so as to shield himself behind his horse's neck, to present less surface to the enemy's fire, to see danger less, and to give more spirit to his horse'. He added that before charging it was as well to tighten girths and let the men take a dram.

As a distinguished *horse artillery officer, Noel 'Curly' Birch observed, the Second *Boer War proved that riding long was 'most wearing for man and horse on the march and quite unsuitable for crossing obstacles'. It was not until the early 20th century that European cavalry generally rode with short stirrups and a bended knee, able to take rough country in their stride. The sitting trot survives, to this day, when British Household Cavalry rides on parade.   RH

Essex, Robert Devereux, Earl of (1591–1646). Retiring, taciturn, yet honest, Robert Devereux, like many of his contemporaries, gained extensive military experience on the continent before being appointed admiral in charge of operations against Cadiz, and second-in-command during the Bishops' war of 1639. During the English civil war he was appointed lord general by parliament (see BRITISH CIVIL WARS), and although not an inspired tactician he was popular with his men and gave parliament a much-needed *morale boost by relieving Gloucester in 1643. However, defeat followed at Lostwithiel in 1644 and he resigned in April 1645 with the introduction of the Self-Denying Ordinance.
JB

Eugène, Prince of Savoy (correctly Savoy-Carignan) (1663–1736). The Austrian Prinz Eugen, born in Paris, started training to be a priest but, by personal merit alone, rose to be one of the foremost military men of his age. Refused service in the army of *Louis XIV, the young Eugène was determined to become a soldier somehow. He fled France disguised as a woman and was given a commission in the imperial army in 1683. At this time the *Turks were laying siege to *Vienna, where Eugène proved his courage and as a result was appointed to the command of the Kufstein *dragoons. Campaigning in Hungary he again showed his worth as a field commander, and in 1685 was promoted to major general and then lieutenant general in 1688. By the time of the *League of Augsburg war, he had reached the rank of field marshal at the age of only 30. Although the campaign in Italy was frustrating for Eugène, he learned the art of *siege warfare and gained valuable experience in fighting the French.

In the east, the Ottoman threat was ever-present, and as the empire's most promising young commander, Eugène was despatched to counter the rising tide of Turkish expansion after the capture of *Belgrade. He utterly routed the Ottoman army at *Zenta in 1697, and retook much of Bosnia for the empire. On his return to Vienna he was hailed as a great hero. Eugène's finest hour came during the

War of the *Spanish Succession where he was in command of the Italian theatre in Lombardy. He attacked the important fortress of Cremona, by using a startling *coup de main*, but was foiled by a lack of adequate ammunition. Disgusted with the ramshackle army administration that had let him down so badly, he returned to Vienna to instigate some serious reforms. The *commissariat and cavalry arms were much improved, and Eugène paid particular attention to the conditions of service for individual soldiers.

In 1703 the empire was threatened by a war in Hungary and a large Franco-Bavarian army moving on Vienna in order to take Austria out of the war. Eugène stabilized the defence of Hungary, and linked up with *Marlborough for the *Blenheim campaign. The two brilliant commanders found an instant rapport and the result was a crushing defeat for the French and the withdrawal of Bavaria from the war entirely.

Eugène then returned to Italy, where he defeated the French at Turin in 1706 and went on to push them right out of the north Italian plain. He linked up with Marlborough again for the campaign and battle of Oudenarde in July 1708, and subsequently the Allies went on to capture Ghent and Bruges, taking Vauban's great fortress of *Lille on 9 December. The last engagement fought by the two commanders together was at *Malplaquet, a dearly bought victory that gained little for an enormous loss in life on the Allied side. In England the Tory opposition played on the feeling of disenchantment with the war, and Marlborough soon fell from favour, being recalled in 1711.

Without effective British assistance, Eugène was on his own and could rely on Vienna less and less for whole-hearted support. The French counter-attack caught him off guard and the war did not end well for him. Yet he was still able to inflict stinging defeats on the Turks when war flared up again in 1716. At Peterwardein he secured an important victory, taking Belgrade shortly thereafter. He then spent the rest of his life on his great project, the reform of the Austrian army, and lived out his days in genteel splendour in the great palace of the Belvedere in Vienna.

Eugène was a decisive and bold commander who went against the grain of the rigid and formulaic warfare of his era. From his wars against the Turks he had learned the value of scouting and *light troops, and this provided an important precedent in the development of the Austrian cavalry arm. His personal brand of leadership was an inspiration to the men under his command, and his impeccable performance in alliance warfare in co-operating with Marlborough surely ranks him among the greatest generals of the early modern world.   TM

---

exercises, military Generally involving large units, either simulated (command-post exercises, CPXs) or real (field-training exercises, FTXs), military exercises have evolved over the years as a means of training and evaluating personnel and of testing current procedures and new ideas.

Simulated combat had formed part of military training for centuries, and the *Roman army owed part of its success to its realistic training. But with the rise of professional staffs and conscript armies during the late 19th century, large-scale exercises developed in most European countries as a means of enabling commanders and staffs to gain practical experience commanding large units and as the culminating point in the annual training cycle. They were usually scheduled after the harvest, when access to land was eased and reservists, if required, could be called up with the minimum of disruption. Imperial Germany began the trend with an exercise that took place once a year in the autumn (called the *Kaisermanöver*) that pitted two army corps (each of two divisions) against one another. The *Kaisermanöver* was organized and directed by the members of the *general staff and was usually attended by the kaiser and foreign military observers. These annual manoeuvres provided the only opportunity units would have of operating together as a corps, giving valuable experience to higher commanders and troops alike. They could be gruelling affairs. For instance, during the 1912 manoeuvres, the IV Army Corps marched 65 miles (105 km) in 41 hours and fought a 'battle' at the end. At the conclusion of the exercise, the CGS would give a critique which examined the conduct of both parties, noted successes and failures, and drew lessons for distribution to the rest of the army. The manoeuvres could be crucial for an officer's career. Good performances were rewarded and poor performances could often prove detrimental to the prospect of promotion. However, there was often a tendency to stage-manage exercises so that the desired result was obtained. In the German case manoeuvres often culminated in the kaiser taking personal command and deciding the day with a cavalry charge.

The spread of enclosure and complaints from civilians encouraged many armies to procure land on which at least some of their exercises could take place, though often they combined a clash on the exercise area with cross-country movement to reach it. In 1857 the French army bought land just north of Châlons-sur-Marne (now Châlons-en-Champagne) and from 1857 to 1868 a full corps of several infantry divisions and a cavalry division spent the summer there. The British army trained on a far smaller area at Aldershot, and later bought land on Salisbury Plain. The acquisition of land for military training accelerated into the 20th century, with 'emergency' puchases during wartime tending to remain in military hands. With the end of the *Cold War western armies have come under growing pressure to divest themselves of training areas, encouraging the utilization of unproductive terrain elsewhere: the British army, for instance, makes extensive use of a vast tract of land near Suffield in Canada.

Today, military exercises are generally less formal and less regular, but serve similar functions—partly because, since the end of the Cold War, real operations are more frequent. Exercises are divided into two broad groupings. Command-post exercises involve only commanders and their staffs and simulate combat between two large-size forces. Field-training exercises, on the other hand, involve commanders and their troops training under realistic conditions and often comprise 'force-on-force' actions similar to the *Kaisermanöver* of imperial Germany. Exercises today often have the added function of serving a diplomatic role. Training involving forces from different states can work as a means of promoting contact and goodwill between nations. For instance, multinational exercises between NATO troops and former *Warsaw Pact armies serve to diffuse the tensions which had arisen between the nations during the long Cold War. Further, exercises can be used to demonstrate power in a region, either by co-operating with a particular country or by proving the capability for deployment. Occasionally, these can result in conflict. For example, in 1986, a carrier battle group of the US navy undertook exercises in the Gulf of Sirte off the coast of Libya, ostensibly to demonstrate that the USA rejected Libya's territorial claim to the entire Gulf. These operations prompted a Libyan response and resulted in the downing of several Libyan aircraft, the sinking of several Libyan missile ships, and the withdrawal of Libyan claims to the Gulf.   RTF

explosives Other than high explosives, these occur in three principal groups within the military context: propellent explosives such as *gunpowder used in firearms; atomic explosives; and explosives formed of a mixture of fuel and air, such as *napalm. Preceding all of these was Greek fire, a combustible composition utilizing naphtha and sulphur but not saltpetre; it appears to have been used first in the 7th century AD.

The discovery of saltpetre is of great significance in the history of explosives since it is a principal component of gunpowder. Believed to have been first used by the Chinese in the early 11th century, saltpetre's explosive properties were soon taken up by the Arabs and in India; its use was translated to Europe in the 14th century when both Roger Bacon and St Albertus Magnus gave written recipes for gunpowder. This was the principal propellent explosive in use for military purposes until the mid-19th century, used for both *small arms and artillery, as well as in *grenades and bursting shells, forming both the main charge and the igniting charge in *flintlock small arms. Gunpowder is a mixture of saltpetre, charcoal, and sulphur, and early gunpowder was just that: a powder. It burnt slowly, even in the confined space of a barrel's chamber, and early firearms were underpowdered as a result. The process of 'corning' gunpowder was developed during the 15th century; this allowed for the powder to be manufactured in grains of differing sizes. Large-grained or 'corned' gunpowder burnt more quickly and powerfully and increased the power of firearms and it was used as the main charge. 'Mealed', or smaller-grained, powder was used as the priming charge. Military muskets tended to use corned powder for both main and priming charges.

A fulminate of mercury composition encased in a copper cap replaced gunpowder as the igniting charge in the *percussion lock and, as breech-loading firearms began to be developed, so the search for a main charge other than gunpowder, which was both smoky and barrel-fouling, began. Gun cotton was developed and experimented with in the 1840s but proved unstable and over-powerful as a propellant. By the end of the 19th century, gunpowder had been replaced as the principal propellent explosive in small arms by the *smokeless powder known as cordite—a nitrocellulose and nitroglycerine compound with acetone as a dissolving agent. After WW I explosive propellants became refined into compounds of nitrodiglycol and nitrocellulose which caused less wear on the bores of rifle and artillery barrels. Flashless propellent explosive was achieved by adding nitroguanidine to the existing nitro-compound and this triple combination continues in use, in varying mixtures, especially for armour-piercing ammunition which requires the generation of very high muzzle velocities.

Atomic explosives were a war-led product of research into atomic fission, which was being investigated in a number of research institutes in the 1930s. Developed under the auspices of the *Manhattan Project in top secret conditions in the USA by 1945, atomic explosives were first tested in the New Mexico desert and then used at *Hiroshima and Nagasaki, claiming nearly 200,000 lives. The atomic bomb was superseded in the 1950s by the hydrogen bomb, the potential power of which was at least ten times that of its predecessor. Atomic or nuclear bombs were refined into warheads for surface, submarine, or air-launched missiles and a distinction formed between strategic *nuclear weapons and tactical ones. Strategic targets involve the use of large devices in order to create massive and condign destruction; tactical ones would be attacked by smaller devices with effects limited to an immediate and defined area.

Fuel-air explosives are a sophistication of high explosive and were developed during WW I to produce incendiary bombs and *flame-thrower fuel. Unlike true high explosive, which concentrates its destructive power at one point, fuel-air explosive produces a widespread and even blast wave, suitable for clearing minefields or destroying soft targets over a large area from point of impact. Constructed from chemical mixtures such as petrol, sodium nitrate, and powdered magnesium, the best known fuel-air explosive is probably napalm, which was first used during WW II but had widespread use during the *Vietnam war.   SCW

Bailey, A., and Murray, S. G., *Explosives, Propellants and Pyrotechnics* (London, 1989).
Freedman, Lawrence, *The Evolution of Military Strategy* (London, 1981).

Moss, Norman, *The Men who Play God: The Story of the Hydrogen Bomb* (London, 1970).

Partington, James R., *A History of Greek Fire and Gunpowder* (Cambridge, 1960).

Eylau, battle of (1807). French victory over the Prussians at *Jena/Auerstadt in 1805 left Russia in the *Napoleonic wars. *Napoleon advanced into Poland to meet Marshal Kamenskoi's armies, but failed to catch them in 'the manoeuvre of the Narew' in December 1806. The following month he was again unsuccessful in trapping them, now under Benningsen, on the river Alle, and followed them north to Preussiche-Eylau. Each army eventually totalled some 75,000 men, but was smaller for the opening moves. Napoleon awaited the corps of *Davout from his right and *Ney from his left, while Benningsen would be reinforced by Lestocq's Prussian corps.

On 8 February a bombardment began in snow which fell intermittently all day. Napoleon hoped to turn Benningsen's left flank when Davout arrived, but attempts to pin Benningsen by attacking his centre misfired: the corps under *Augereau was appallingly mauled by Russian cannon and forced back by infantry. Only a desperate massed cavalry charge by *Murat checked the Russians. Davout came up on the Russian left and pushed it steadily backwards: it was close to breaking when Lestocq appeared and checked the attack. Ney now arrived, but night had fallen.

Benningsen's generals urged him to hold his ground. But he had spent the day in the saddle, and Ney's arrival depressed him. He ordered a retreat, and Napoleon was in no condition to pursue. The French may have lost 25,000 men, the Russians and Prussians perhaps 15,000; many wounded froze to death. Ney, crossing the field on the 9th, said: 'What a massacre! And without a result!'   RH

Fabius Maximus, 'Cunctator' (*c.*280–203 BC), was Roman consul for the first time in 233/2, won a victory in Liguria, was censor in 230/29, and consul for the second time in 228/7. In 218 he was opposed to war with Carthage, but after Hannibal's victory at *Lake Trasimene he was elected *dictator. He proceeded to implement the strategy of refusing to be drawn into pitched battles, for which he earned the nickname 'Cunctator' ('Delayer') and which has become known as 'fabian' after him. The disaster at *Cannae reinforced the wisdom of this approach and led to successive consulships for himself and his son in 215/14 and 214/13. During his fifth and final consulship in 209/8 he recaptured Tarentum and was chosen *princeps senatus* ('Father of the House'). He lived on to oppose Scipio *'Africanus'' plan for the invasion of Africa and to attack him over the atrocities committed by one of his lieutenants in Locri. Renowned for his caution and conservative attitude, Fabius was rightly regarded as the man who denied Hannibal further victories in the field, at a time when even Rome's resolution might have cracked. But he arguably carried his caution too far when Rome began to recover.   JFL

Lazenby, J. F., *Hannibal's War* (Warminster, 1978).

Fairfax, Thomas, 3rd Baron Fairfax of Cameron (1612–71). Born in Denton in north Yorkshire, Fairfax served in the Low Countries under Lord Vere, whose daughter he married in 1637. He commanded a troop of *dragoons in the Bishops' war against the Scots (1639), but sided with parliament on the outbreak of the English civil war (see BRITISH CIVIL WARS) and raised troops in Yorkshire. Beaten at Seacroft Moor and Adwalton Moor in 1643, he joined *Cromwell that autumn, and at Winceby the two men checked the royalist threat to the eastern counties. He commanded part of the victorious Anglo-Scots army at

*Marston Moor, and was a natural choice for the post of captain general (C-in-C) when the *New Model Army was raised in 1645. He showed great skill as an organizer and chose his officers with care. Although the New Model had still not settled down, he led it to victory at *Naseby in June 1645, and went on to beat the royalist armies in the west.

In the second civil war he sent Cromwell, his lieutenant general (second in command), to deal with the Scots while he reduced Colchester. He had two royalist commanders shot when they surrendered as they had broken *parole given in 1646. However, he opposed the execution of the king, and although he helped put down the Leveller mutinies he laid down his command in 1650. He played a leading part in bringing about the Restoration in 1660. Fairfax possessed all the military virtues: he was brave, just, a natural leader, capable administrator, and good tactician.

RH

Falaise Gap, battle of (1944). The *Normandy campaign reached its climax in August 1944. The British operation GOODWOOD, on the eastern flank, failed to break through but attracted German reserves. After a disappointing start, the US operation COBRA, on the western flank, developed into a breakout. On 1 August Third US Army became operational under *Patton, forming part of Twelfth Army Group under *Bradley. The two commanders recognized that, instead of sweeping down into Brittany, the bulk of Third Army should be swung eastwards towards the Seine. *Montgomery, commander of Twenty-first Army Group and Allied ground forces, promptly concurred.

Patton's turn created the possibility of catching the Germans between Third Army and the Anglo-Canadian forces pressing down from Caen. The abortive Mortain counterattack, launched on 7 August, made this outcome more likely by pushing German armour deeper into the pocket. However, determined resistance slowed down the advance on Falaise, and on 13 August Bradley ordered Patton not to proceed north of Argentan, fearing accidental collision with the Canadians. Falaise did not fall until the 16th, and in the meantime thousands of Germans streamed through the Argentan-Falaise gap. On 19 August 1st Polish Armoured Division met the Americans at Chambois, in the neck of the pocket. Polish defence of Mont Ormel, north of Chambois, played an important part in closing the gap, but until the last days it remained possible for determined Germans to get away.

Perhaps 10,000 Germans died in the pocket and 50,000 were taken prisoner. Allied aircraft inflicted terrible damage: huge quantities of tanks, half-tracks, and trucks were destroyed or abandoned. It is easy to criticize the Allies for not closing the pocket more swiftly. However, envelopment on such a scale, carried out by two army groups, demanded a greater degree of operational slickness than the Allies possessed.   RH

Falkenhayn, Gen Erich von (1861–1922), one of the most criticized military leaders of WW I. He is best remembered as the author of the battle of *Verdun. Falkenhayn was a scion of a typical Prussian junker family and followed a conventional military career until 1896, when he left the army and went to China as a military adviser. In 1900 he served on the staff of the expeditionary force sent there to crush the *Boxer rebellion, thus attracting the notice of the kaiser. Returning to Germany in 1903, he reached the top of the Prussian army by merit and imperial protection, becoming Prussian war minister in July 1913.

In spite of evident success in the peacetime army, Falkenhayn disliked boring peacetime routine and desired war. During the July crisis of 1914 he did all that he could as war minister to ensure the outbreak of hostilities by putting pressure on the kaiser and the chancellor, and he applauded the outbreak of war, saying on 4 August 1914: 'Even if we perish—it was wonderful.'

In September 1914 Falkenhayn succeeded the ailing *Moltke 'the Younger' as COS. The failure of the Flanders campaign was an inauspicious beginning, but gave Falkenhayn important insights. *Trench warfare had come to stay, and major offensives were only the 'useless waste of human lives'. Falkenhayn reached his conclusions more thoroughly than many of his contemporaries. He gave up hope of a big breakthrough—and he also lost confidence in Germany's final victory. His only hope was a draw, a *parti remis*, and a separate peace with her enemies. 'If we do not lose the war,' he declared, 'we have won it.'

Both Falkenhayn's main convictions—that there could be no breakthrough in trench warfare, and that the Central Powers would lose a long war of *attrition—were correct and far-sighted. They dominated his strategy, which was very successful in 1915, when Falkenhayn won two big victories that stabilized the *eastern front and led to the conquest of Poland and Serbia. At the end of 1915 Falkenhayn thought that Russia was exhausted and unable to attack: he wished to exhaust France and Britain too by limited offensives, and make the Entente ready for peace.

In order to weaken the French he decided to attack at Verdun. His plan, launched in February 1916, to take the hills overlooking the fortress and force the French into costly counter-attacks was only partly successful. The 'blood mill' on the Meuse caused very heavy losses: French casualties of around 362,000 were only slightly superior to German losses of about 337,000.

Falkenhayn's plan to weaken Britain at the same time by unrestricted submarine warfare was not implemented because of the opposition of the kaiser and the chancellor. When the Entente managed to stage a co-ordinated series of offensives in the summer of 1916 and Romania entered the war in August, Falkenhayn was relieved of his post. He was given the chance to redeem his reputation, and defeated Romania by the end of 1916 after a brilliant campaign. Falkenhayn saw further service in Palestine in 1917 and in White Russia in 1918. He was widely criticized during and after the war. He tried to defend his strategy in his memoirs but was attacked from all sides. Even in retrospect, his support for a compromise peace and his realistic approach to the exigencies of trench warfare sit uneasily with his belief in unrestricted submarine warfare and his reputation as the butcher of Verdun.   HA

Afflerbach, Holger, *Falkenhayn: Politisches Denken und Handeln im Kaiserreich* (Munich, 1996).

Falkirk, battles of (1298, 1746). The English had been defeated in Scotland at Stirling Bridge in 1297; in the following year Edward I, determined on revenge, led an army of over 28,000 northwards. On 22 July the English engaged the Scots under *Wallace at Falkirk. The Scots formed up their army in four defensive *schiltroms on foot. These were finally broken, initially by *archers, at a cost of perhaps 2,000 English casualties. Edward's discontented Welsh infantry, numbering almost 11,000, took little part in the battle, joining in only when it became clear that the English had gained the upper hand.

After the *Jacobite army had retreated from England in December 1745 they advanced into Scotland, reaching Falkirk on 17 January 1746. There some 8,000 of them fought about 8,500 Hanoverian troops under the command of Lt Gen Henry Hawley, popularly known as the 'Hangman'. Hawley was convinced that his men were vastly superior to their opponents, and was overconfident of a victory, notoriously enjoying a leisurely lunch before engaging the enemy. He then ordered his *dragoons to attack uphill, which some of his fellow officers considered a mistake. He himself then left the field, an action for which he was much criticized, although he tried to lay the blame for the subsequent fiasco elsewhere. The Jacobite army fired on the advancing dragoons and caused them to retreat. The artillery and some infantry then beat a retreat too when heavy rain wet cartridges so that muskets failed to fire. Only the right wing of the Hanoverian army, led by Maj Gen Huske and Brig Cholmondley, held. At nightfall both armies retired from the field, the Jacobites to Falkirk and the Hanoverians to Linlithgow and then Edinburgh. The taking of Falkirk enabled the former to claim the day.   MCP/WS

Prestwich, M. C., *Edward I* (London, 1988).

Falklands war (1982). The Falkland Islands (Malvinas in Spanish) lie approximately 500 miles (805 km) east of southern Argentina. Sighted in the 16th century, they were colonized, in circumstances which remain contentious, by Britain, France, and Spain. From 1833 they were in British hands, although sovereignty was claimed by Argentina on the basis of previous Spanish occupation. In 1982 East and West Falkland had a population of only 1,800. The climate was temperate but windy, the terrain a mixture of downland, rocky hills and peat bogs. The capital, Port Stanley, had a small airport, but was not unlike a Scots fishing village. Outside Stanley people lived in sheep-farming settlements. A mutton-packing plant at Ajax Bay on the west coast of East Falkland had fallen into disuse. Further east lay the Falklands Dependencies, South Georgia, and the South Sandwich Islands.

The 150th anniversary of British occupation came when the Argentine military was looking for an external adventure to rally national support after a deeply shaming 'dirty war' in which thousands of people suspected of subversive activities had been tortured and 'disappeared'. British policy had long been one of appeasement, trying to get the islanders to accept some kind of sovereignty-sharing with the mainland, upon which they depended for contact with the outside world. The final signal may have been the announcement that the symbolically armed ice patrol vessel HMS *Endurance* was to be withdrawn. A *machista* underestimation of PM Margaret Thatcher may also have contributed to the decision to invade on 2 April 1982, when *special forces overwhelmed the 50-man garrison of Royal Marines at Port Stanley after a brisk firefight, and a detachment on South Georgia, where the defenders damaged a frigate.

On 31 March Margaret Thatcher's government received warning that invasion was imminent, and an early meeting suggested that while nothing could be done to prevent it, in the opinion of the First Sea Lord, Adm Leach, the navy could send a 'retrieval force' rapidly. The decision to mount CORPORATE was taken early and owed much to the Prime Minister's determination. The operation was controlled from the navy's headquarters at Northwood near London by Adm Fieldhouse and his staff. The idea of swift retrieval was soon replaced by one of deliberate attack, and a Task Force was assembled, incorporating the old aircraft carrier HMS *Hermes* and the new HMS *Invincible* equipped with

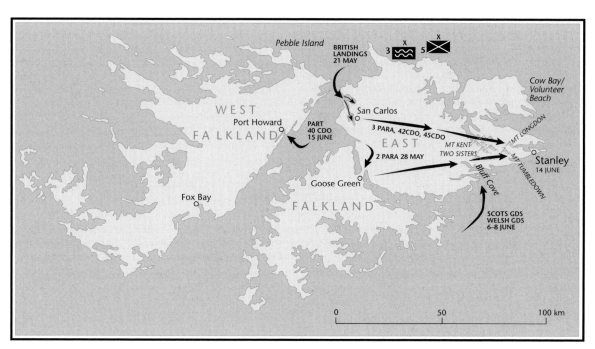

The **Falklands** (Malvinas) conflict, 1982: British recapture of the islands.

fencibles

Sea Harriers and *helicopters, other warships, Royal Fleet Auxiliaries, and chartered merchantmen. The landing forces, under Maj Gen Moore, would eventually comprise 3rd Commando Brigade (Brig Thompson), with three battalion-sized Marine Commandos and 2nd and 3rd Battalions of the Parachute Regiment under its command, and 5th Infantry Brigade (Brig Wilson), with 2nd Battalion Scots Guards, 1st Battalion Welsh Guards, and 7th Gurkha Rifles. Special forces included the Special Boat Service and 22nd SAS Regiment, and the Royal Artillery furnished both field and air defence artillery.

The Argentine garrison was reinforced to comprise two brigades under Brig Gen Menendez, the islands' military governor. The British used Ascension Island just south of the Equator as a forward base, and on 18 April the main task group (R Adm Woodward) sailed from it. On 12 April, with two nuclear submarines in the theatre, Britain announced a Maritime Exclusion Zone around the Falklands. South Georgia was recaptured by Royal Marines and Special Forces on 24–5 April, and on 1 May a Vulcan based at Ascension Island (refuelled several times en route) bombed Stanley airport, inflicting little damage but demonstrating the RAF's long reach. On the same day aircraft from Woodward's task group attacked ground targets, while his ships came under attack from Argentine aircraft. On 2 May the old Argentine cruiser *General Belgrano* was torpedoed by the submarine HMS *Conqueror* south of the Falklands, after which the Argentine navy did not venture out of coastal waters.

On 4 May the Argentine air force sunk HMS *Sheffield* with an Exocet missile, and when the British landed around San Carlos on 21 May it mounted repeated attacks on warships in Falkland Sound. HMS *Ardent* and *Antelope* were sunk and other vessels damaged. On 25 May HMS *Coventry*, on radar picket to the north of West Falkland, was also sunk. Ship casualties would have been higher if bombs had burst on impact, and British prospects would have been poor if troopships rather than warships had been lost. As it was, the sinking of *Atlantic Conveyor* on 25 May was to make land operations difficult: all but one of the heavy-lift Chinook helicopters she carried were lost.

The beachhead at San Carlos, which included the old meat plant at Ajax Bay whose buildings housed the field hospital, had been secured by 3rd Commando Brigade, and its commander had been ordered to await the arrival of Maj Gen Moore and 5th Brigade. Pressure from London in the wake of naval losses provoked a change of plan, and it was decided to send 45 Commando and 3 Para eastwards on foot, while 2 Para jabbed south to the settlement of Goose Green. On 28–9 May 2 Para took Goose Green from a superior force in a vicious battle which left its CO, Lt Col Jones, among the dead. The loss of Goose Green struck a powerful blow at Argentine confidence, for Menendez had just reinforced it.

The 45 Commando and 3 Para completed their gruelling march across East Falkland to invest Stanley and 5th Brigade

landed at San Carlos. The two guards battalions were moved by sea to Bluff Cove, on the east coast, and suffered severe casualties when the RFA (Royal Fleet Auxiliary) vessels *Sir Galahad* and *Sir Tristram* were hit by aircraft. With the bulk of his forces now investing Stanley, Moore planned attacks on the high ground around it. On the night of 11–12 June 3 Para took Mount Longdon, 45 Commando Two Sisters, and 42 Commando (flown forward by helicopter) Mount Harriet. On 13–14 June the Scots Guards took Tumbledown Mountain while 2 Para stormed Wireless Ridge. The defence began to collapse: the attackers followed crowds of demoralized men into Stanley and Menendez surrendered.

The war cost the lives of 255 British servicemen and Falklanders: well over 700 Argentines were killed (368 of them on the *Belgrano*), and the junta fell soon afterwards. It could have been averted had Britain shown clearer signs of wishing to retain the Falklands. PM Thatcher recognized that there was little choice between national humiliation (which might have proved fatal to her government) and the mounting of a complex operation at the very limit of logistic feasibility. The Argentine navy (the main mover for the invasion) was utterly outclassed and the army performed poorly, but the professionalism and fighting quality of the British armed forces was the deciding factor although luck, as always, played its part.   RH

Middlebrook, Martin, *Operation Corporate* (London, 1985).

fencibles British volunteer soldiers, with commissions commonly awarded to deserving officers on *half pay. They were a sort of early *Home Guard, dating back to the 15th century, and were open to all between 16 and 60 capable of bearing arms, with no distinction of wealth or rank. Fencibles could be either cavalry or infantry and were recruited for the duration of a war or emergency. They were strictly for home use, allowing regular troops to serve elsewhere. They were raised by lord-lieutenants of counties, and unlike the *yeomanry could be called upon to serve outside their own county in time of rebellion or invasion. The organization was abolished c.1804.   APC-A

Fenian raids into Canada (1866–71), attempts by Irish-Americans to bring about conflict between Britain and the USA during the period immediately following the *American civil war, seeking to exacerbate wartime grievances, in particular over the British-built Confederate commerce raider *Alabama*.

The term 'Fenian' was coined in the USA, and Irish-American veterans of the American civil war were also prominent in conspiracies and armed actions in Ireland and England. While Washington used their activities and attendant domestic demagoguery to remind London of the vulnerability of Canada, there is no evidence of official connivance. The setting parameter was the inability of successive British governments to deal humanely or even intelligently with the Irish question. Inept though informer-riddled Fenian operations on both sides of the Atlantic were, they did persuade Gladstone of the need for reforms.

In 1866 a combination of their electoral clout in the north-east, a slight improvement in their abysmal social and economic status, increased acceptance following their service during the war, and generalized anti-British feeling gave the Fenians a window of opportunity to raise funds and recruit soldiers, and to assemble men and weapons on the Canadian border. Rancorous internal factionalism as usual took its toll and two separate and uncoordinated invasions were attempted. An expedition to seize Campobello island was aborted when US authorities seized the ship for breach of neutrality laws. Another crossed the Niagara river near Buffalo and fought a skirmish at Ridgeway in which 12 Canadian student volunteers were killed and 40 wounded. Cut off by US authorities, the invaders withdrew, having lost 8 dead, 20 wounded, and 60 captured.

A further invasion force gathered near Detroit was dispersed by US authorities in 1870, and an attempt was made to join *Riel's rebellion the same year, but by then the window of opportunity to stir up Anglo-US trouble was closed.
HEB

Ferguson, Lt Col Patrick

(1744–80). Ferguson, an infantry officer, developed the first *breech-loading rifle used by the British army. An adaptation of Isaac de la Chaumette's design, it was loaded by rotating the trigger-guard to lower a threaded bolt, allowing access to the breech. It performed impressively in trials, and Ferguson was given a detachment of green-clad riflemen, at whose head he was wounded at Brandywine in 1777. He was killed, ironically by an American rifleman, at King's Mountain in 1780, while serving as inspector general of militia in Georgia and the Carolinas. After his death official enthusiasm for the rifle waned, reviving only during the *Napoleonic wars.　　RH

feudal service

When land was held by feudal tenure, military service was due from a tenant to his lord. This normally consisted of the provision of a knight for 40 days from each knight's fee. The practice was widespread in medieval Europe; its use in England has been the subject of detailed study. Evidence from elsewhere is less full, although a detailed survey of feudal obligations, which dates from the 1160s, survives from southern Italy.

The question of whether the system was introduced to England in fully fledged form by *William 'the Conqueror' has been much disputed. Although there were some similarities with earlier Anglo-Saxon practice, it is difficult to deny that the tenurial revolution which followed the Norman Conquest witnessed the introduction of a new system of military obligation. There is only one surviving writ

from the Conqueror's reign requesting military service. The fullest evidence for the system is provided by an inquiry made in 1166, which shows that tenants-in-chief normally owed service in multiples of ten knights. *Scutage might be paid in place of performing service; the system was as much fiscal as military. By 1166 there were over 5,000 knight's fees in England, but it is doubtful whether actual service on that scale was ever obtained. In 1157 Henry II requested one-third of the total service, and two years later took scutage from most of his tenants, rather than asking them to provide knights. In the early 13th century the service quotas were radically reduced in a piecemeal process. In 1245 Peter of Savoy, whose traditional quota stood at 140, was prepared to acknowledge that he owed a mere five knights, although he in fact provided thirteen. Despite these reductions, Edward I and Edward II continued to demand service; the largest feudal force that Edward I obtained, in 1277, consisted of 228 knights and 294 sergeants. The 400 men registered as performing feudal service in 1300 probably amounted to less than a quarter of the total cavalry force. Tradition, and the fact that the tenants-in-chief benefited from taking scutages from their own sub-tenants, explains why feudal summonses continued to be issued. The last effective English feudal summons was issued in 1327; a revival of the practice in 1385 was undertaken for financial, not military, purposes. *Henry V revived feudal service in Normandy, where many summonses were issued in the first half of the 15th century.　　MCP

field fortification

is designed to provide defence against a tactical threat expected to be of limited duration. It is commonly used by troops intending to hold a position against an advancing enemy, by rearguards covering a retreat, or by advanced parties while they wait to be reinforced. The term also covers the works constructed to defend camps and isolated posts, as well as those used for the protection of those besieging a fortress. The components are therefore basic materials that can be quickly put into place by the use of simple tools and as easily dismantled or abandoned when no longer needed. Some systems and methods have remained virtually unchanged from the beginning of organized warfare until the present day.

The most elementary field fortification is a ditch, which in itself will impede the progress of an enemy. Throwing the excavated soil behind it doubles the height of the obstacle the attacker has to cross, while at the same time providing a rampart for the protection of the defenders. Where the protection required is against missile rather than shock action, the ditch can be occupied for use as a trench, and part of the excavated material thrown in front of it, to serve as a parapet over which the defenders can shoot. The soil behind them then becomes a parados, so that the heads of entrenched defenders do not appear in silhouette against a background. An even simpler form of excavated field

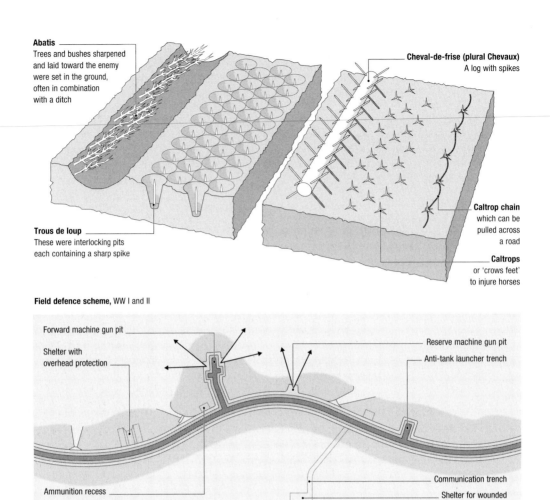

Abatis
Trees and bushes sharpened and laid toward the enemy were set in the ground, often in combination with a ditch

Cheval-de-frise (plural Chevaux)
A log with spikes

Trous de loup
These were interlocking pits each containing a sharp spike

Caltrop chain
which can be pulled across a road

Caltrops
or 'crows feet' to injure horses

Field defence scheme, WW I and II

Forward machine gun pit

Shelter with overhead protection

Reserve machine gun pit

Anti-tank launcher trench

Ammunition recess

Communication trench

Shelter for wounded

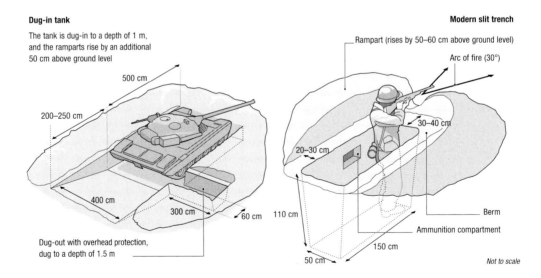

Dug-in tank

The tank is dug-in to a depth of 1 m, and the ramparts rise by an additional 50 cm above ground level

Modern slit trench

Rampart (rises by 50–60 cm above ground level)

Arc of fire (30°)

500 cm

200–250 cm

400 cm

300 cm

60 cm

110 cm

30–40 cm

20–30 cm

50 cm

150 cm

Berm

Ammunition compartment

Dug-out with overhead protection, dug to a depth of 1.5 m

Not to scale

'Digging in' is a prominent part of every soldier's life. Field fortifications can significantly slow the enemy's progress. In ancient times field fortifications were widely used in siege warfare—like Julius Caesar's fortifications at Alesia—and in the field. The appearance of rifled small arms in the mid-19th century was accompanied by a revival of digging. The future war theorist Ivan Bloch correctly noted, in 1898, that in future the spade would be as essential to the soldier as his rifle. He was not wrong.

fortification is the pit. If intended for occupation, it gives the defender cover from fire and view. An alternative purpose is to act as a *trou de loup*, with the bottom of the pit containing a sharpened stake, and the top concealed by vegetation. More sophisticated field works can be built using earth in containers such as, in modern times, sandbags or oil drums, or, in earlier periods, wicker gabions (cylindrical open baskets). In the 1990s a modern version—'bastion walling' invented by an unemployed British miner—used wire mesh and 'geo-textile' to form the basket. It was extensively used in the Gulf and Bosnia.

Revetments to keep the earth in place were generally constructed of local timber, hurdles, turf, and similar natural materials, supplemented from the late 19th century onwards by sheets of corrugated iron. Abatis are made up of trees and bushes, felled with their branches pointing away from the position to be fortified, and their trunks secured in position by ropes and stakes. In desert regions, the corresponding form of field fortification is the zariba, an enclosure protected by thorn bushes. In rocky terrain, where digging is difficult, boulders are used to build sangars, which serve the same purpose. Inundations are formed by blocking up streams and sluices so as to flood the surrounding areas. Palisades consist of stakes planted upright and fastened together to form a fence. Roman legionaries each carried a stake with which to form the palisade of the camp they constructed at the end of each day's march when on campaign. In the medieval period, *archers similarly carried a stake to protect their position against cavalry. *Fraises* are sharp stakes placed as near to the horizontal as possible in the side of steep slopes. Slopes and ditches may also be lined with flints, broken glass, agricultural harrows, and similar pointed or sharp-edged objects. *Chevaux de frise* ('horses of Friesland') are made by fastening stakes or metal spikes to a heavy beam, at right angles to each other. In modern French, the term has come to be used for portable barbed wire entanglements. Barbed wire first made its appearance on the battlefield during the *American civil war. Barricades, used to block a street or bridge, can be made of any easily assembled material, wheeled vehicles, industrial containers, furniture, rubble, etc. Caltrops or crows'-feet, made of four spikes joined so that one always points upwards, were an effective protection against cavalry in the field and were also used at fords where infantry were expected to cross. They were a precursor to modern mines, high-explosive devices that can be detonated by the completion of an electrical circuit, by pressure, or by a tripwire. The earliest explosive mines took the form of *fougasses*, buried *gunpowder charges sprung by the defenders when the need arose.

If sufficient labour, time, and materials were available, larger field fortifications such as redoubts (miniature forts open at the back, capable of holding both artillery and infantry), could be constructed and sited to support the main battle line. Domestic buildings in the right place could be fortified by having their walls pierced by loopholes, their floors either removed or strengthened, and their doors and windows blocked. Ideally, thatch roofing and other combustibles were removed. Both at the farm of Hougoumont in the battle of *Waterloo and at the mission station of Rorke's Drift in the *Zulu war, the position of the British defenders was threatened when the thatch caught fire. Fortified domestic buildings reappeared in Bosnia in the 1990s where stout timber walls filled with gravel proved effective temporary fortifications. Stockades, walls of stout timber uprights, disappeared from European battlefields with the advent of field artillery but continued in North American and colonial campaigns, where they provided protection against ill-armed native opponents. Blockhouses, isolated defence works with roofed accommodation for a small garrison, were also used most characteristically in colonial warfare. In *siege warfare, field fortifications of various types protected the besiegers against sallies by the garrison, and sheltered them as they began their approach to the walls. Although not intended as permanent features, some field fortifications remain visible long after their military purpose no longer exists. Among the oldest of these is the legionary camp built for the siege of *Masada in Roman Judaea (now Israel). The most impressive include the Lines of *Torres Vedras, constructed by Wellington's engineers in 1810 to stop the French from reaching Lisbon. In France, sections of the complicated field defences that played so important a part in the positional warfare of the western front from 1914 to 1918 are deliberately preserved. During the decades after WW I, 'in the trenches' was used as a synonym for warfare itself.   TAH

Duffy, Christopher, *Siege Warfare* (London, 1979).
Lewis, J. F. (ed.), *Text Book of Fortification and Military Engineering* (London, 1892).
Muller, John, *The Attack and Defence of Fortified Places* (London, 1791).

field manual US term for a compendium of authoritative tactical and *operational concepts intended for use especially by junior and field-grade officers. Field manuals proliferated in the era of the world wars, when, for the first time, vast armies of literate conscripts faced each other. They are the 'Book' against whose precepts soldiers proverbially rebel, but without which modern war would be impossible. Their scope and detail have lately become daunting, belying their original purpose as distillations of experience: the US army currently employs over 400 field manuals. Most are available on the World Wide Web.

Field manuals seek to represent the state of the art of war at any given moment. Their evolution is accordingly an index of intellectual and institutional change. One such bell-wether has been the US army's FM 100–5, *Operations*, which first appeared in 1939, and is now undergoing its twelfth revision. Along the way, FM 100–5 has registered and codified every perturbation in the American approach to war, including the advent of tactical *nuclear weapons in the 1950s; 'flexible response' and 'active defense' in the 1960s; and 'AirLand battle' in the 1970s, a form of aggressive, high-speed manoeuvre warfare whose influence was apparent in the conduct of the *Gulf war (1990–1). The new edition is again a reflection of changing times: its aim is to integrate the conduct of 'operations other than war' into the mainstream of army *doctrine.   DM

---

fighter, ground-attack The development of close *air support (CAS) in the latter half of WW I resulted in the beginning of the search for effective aircraft to carry out such duties. Opinion effectively split into two schools: those who argued for dedicated CAS designs and those who argued for dual-role fighter-bombers. The fighter-bomber offered a number of advantages, as the aircraft could switch between the two tasks of CAS and air-superiority combat as and when necessary. What generally happened, and was to continue to do so, was that a robust 'pure' fighter design like the Sopwith Camel could be modified for ground attack without losing air-to-air performance. However, losses were always heavy on CAS operations and efforts to improve protection against light anti-aircraft gunnery in particular were considered important. In April 1918 Sopwith introduced the first dedicated ground-attack fighter, the Salamander.

The inter-war period saw the line between 'fighter' and 'bomber' begin to widen as payloads increased, but during WW II fighter-bombers were to reappear with a vengeance. Once light bombers like the Fairey Battle and pure dive-bombers like the Stuka proved to be unable to survive in the modern air-combat environment, fighters like the Messerschmitt Bf 109 and Focke-Wulf 190 were pressed into service and proved remarkably successful. However, it was the western Allies who enthusiastically adopted the fighter-bomber from 1941 onwards. The British employed the ageing Hawker Hurricane (renamed the 'Hurribomber') on ground-support duties in the western desert with great effect. They were armed with two 250 lb bombs and four 20 mm cannon, while a later version designed to attack German armour, the II D, was armed with two 40 mm cannon. It was in 1944–5 that the most significant impact was made in Normandy and beyond. With air supremacy achieved, Allied CAS aircraft were able to play a key role. The Hawker Typhoon and the Republic P-47 Thunderbolt were employed with tremendous effect, both being rugged designs capable of absorbing considerable punishment. They were generally armed with air-to-ground rockets as well as 20 mm cannon, and the carnage in the *Falaise Gap was testament to their effectiveness. On the *eastern front the deadly Soviet Sturmovik represented a revival of the purpose-built CAS aircraft, brought to a peak of dedication when in the 1970s the USAF revived the name Thunderbolt for the armoured and systems-redundant Fairchild AH 10, built around a fuselage-length 40 mm cannon.

But *air forces do not like the low and slow approach represented by the AH 10 and post-war ground-attack aircraft have mostly been evolutions of basically sound air-superiority fighters, with the CAS function falling to attack *helicopters. Hybrid designs have been so-called fighter-bombers like the Sepecat Jaguar, Dassault Mirage 5, and the MiG-27, which do neither function well. The divergence will continue in the future with the Joint Strike fighter (JSF) filling the role of ground-attack aircraft while the F-22 will become the new air-superiority fighter. The JSF will employ stealth technology and vectored thrusters to reduce risk in CAS operations. Armies will continue to clamour for an aircraft that can loiter over the battlefield and be called in to deliver a decisive punch at 'eyeball' range, to reduce the incidence of *friendly fire incidents.   JDB

Gooderson, Ian, *Air Power at the Battlefront* (London, 1998).
Hallion, Richard, *Strike from the Sky* (Washington, 1989).

---

film, portrayal of war in Films have come to dominate or reflect popular moods and war has become one of the easiest ways to dramatize individual heroism or a love story, whether through the fictional portrayal of war, its factual representation, or contemporary newsreels and propaganda. D. W. Griffith's *The Birth of a Nation* (1915) was cinema's first epic, and follows the story of two families as the *American civil war tears them apart and forces them to take sides. Griffith started to film in July 1914, as Europe went to war. Set in the trenches, Charlie Chaplain's *Shoulder Arms* (1918) managed to inject humour into an unfunny, contemporary subject, as a young soldier in the trenches dreams of winning the war single-handedly, but it was not until three years after the *Armistice that another US film dealt seriously with WW I. Rex Ingram's *Four Horsemen of the Apocalypse* (1921) was the love story of a young Argentine who fights for his father's country, France, and was Rudolf Valentino's first important cinema role.

Mirroring literature around the world, an anti-war mood began to surface in films, initially in King Vidor's *The Big Parade* (1925). The Russian Sergei Eisenstein depicted war of a different kind in a group of three films. *Strike* (1924), *Battleship Potemkin* (1925), and *October* (1928) were all sponsored by the Soviet government to promote the theme of revolution, and were shot as if they were documentary—with shocking (for the day) battle scenes. The mammoth French epic *Napoleon* (1927), designed to be projected simultaneously onto three screens at once, preceded the talkies by three months and survived just a few showings; it was partially salvaged and rereleased in 1980. Back in America, Ronald Colman starred in a classic, silent, romanticized view of war. *Beau Geste* (1926) was P. C. Wren's tale of three brothers who join the *French Foreign Legion, suffer under a brutal sergeant, and die fighting the Arabs. America was still confused about the notion of fighting, and heading towards *pacifism was *Paramount's Wings* (1927), where two flyers who love the same girl enlist, and one accidentally shoots down the other. To compete, Warner Brothers produced *The Dawn Patrol* (1930) three years later, also about WW I flyers (which they remade in 1938, starring Errol Flynn).

In 1929 a young German, Erich Maria Remarque, penned a novel about a group of German teenagers who volunteer for action on the western front, become disillusioned and, one by one, die. *Im Westen nichts Neues* was the first book ever to sell a million copies. Within a year it had been scripted to become Lewis Milestone's highly pacifist *All Quiet on the Western Front* (1930). Another anti-war offering of this era was the British *Journey's End* (1930), based on R. C. Sheriff's play, and based around the personal tensions of a group of British officers in a dugout. In Germany, the pacifist *Westfront 1918* (1930) also stressed camaraderie in the trenches and the common suffering of both French and German soldiers. Paramount followed with an adaptation of Hemingway's emotive *A Farewell to Arms* (1932), originally written in the same year and vein as Remarque's novel. It is ironic that this wave of pacifism broke out as the dictators were coming to power throughout Europe. *Morgenrot* (1933) struck a different note, the story of German U-boat U-21 during the war, and proclaimed the merit of dying for the Fatherland. This was not a Nazi film, but promoted values the Nazis admired. However, *Hitlerjunge Quex* (1933) was an overt piece of propaganda. Goebbels understood the power of the cinema, and through this and other movies, although not strictly war films, the Nazis hoped to awaken Germany. *Quex* failed as a convincing vehicle: the *Hitler youths were too obviously clean and virtuous, and the communists excessively evil. Another solution had to be found, and Leni Riefenstahl was commissioned to make a documentary of the 1934 Nuremberg Rally. The result, *Triumph des Willens* (1935), remains a PR classic today, a chilling reminder of the power of cinema, and was as popular abroad as within Germany.

While these war drums sounded in Germany, France remained disenchanted with war, as expounded in Jean Renoir's *La Grande Illusion* (1937), set in a POW camp, where the great illusion is that the French must hate their German captors. A curiously jingoistic note was produced by Hollywood in *The Lost Patrol* (1934), featuring British soldiers trapped in the desert under Arab attack, which provided a vehicle for many remakes under different names. Alfred Hitchcock produced a steady flow of successful thrillers, prompted by the rise of Nazism. In *The Thirty-Nine Steps* (1935), he used the plot of John Buchan's pre-WW I novel of spies to warn of Germany again, while *The Lady Vanishes* (1938) deals with the disappearance of a train passenger due to sinister fascist intrigues in central Europe. In 1936, Margaret Mitchell (a pseudonym for Peggy Nash) had published a best-selling romantic novel, and within three years,

MGM had turned it into a film that caught the popular imagination in a way that no film had done, and few have done since. *Gone with the Wind* (1939) remains visually splendid, and breathtaking in its depiction of war, but is really two films, only the first half dealing with the American civil war, the rest dealing with its aftermath, and is a test of audience stamina at 220 minutes.

The outbreak of WW II prompted a new wave of films depicting war, as studios became part of the war effort. A recent study has suggested there are 608 major feature films that feature WW II, made either during 1939–45 or since. The talkies of the thirties had encouraged a cinemagoing habit, and films were used to encourage enlistment, inform, or bolster *morale. Despite earlier films, the British cinema industry came of age only during the war, although cinemas were initially closed in September 1939 for fear of air raids. Rex Harrison took the part of a British agent masquerading as a Nazi officer in *Night Train to Munich* (1940) which owed much to the plot of *The Lady Vanishes*. Leslie Howard returned from Hollywood to share in the war effort and starred in the life story of R. J. Mitchell, inventor of the Spitfire, in *The First of the Few* (1941). Continuing the flying theme, but more famous for its music (the Warsaw Concerto) than its plot, *Dangerous Moonlight* (1942) told the tale of a Polish pianist who loses his memory after flying in the battle of *Britain. The 'Boy's Own' approach to war featured heavily in *One of Our Aircraft Is Missing* (1942), about the Dutch Resistance helping the crew of a British bomber. There were a great many films honouring one or other of the wartime services. *Fires Were Started* (1943) dealt with the National Fire Service, while *Millions Like Us* (1943) told of civilian life in the blitz, and *We Dive at Dawn* (1943) was a tribute to the submarine service. They—as many wartime films—were characterized by a grin-and-bear-it philosophy that seems scarcely credible today. *The Life and Death of Colonel Blimp* (1943)—its eponymous hero originating in a David Low cartoon—was more critical, suggesting that the British army was out of touch with reality: Churchill disapproved of it.

While these were primarily for home consumption, Ealing Studios' *Went the Day Well?* (1942), where a group of Nazis take over an English chocolate-box village and eventually are defeated by alert villagers, was aimed at the USA, with a 'Britain-can-take-it' subliminal message. So too were the three outstandingly successful British films of the era, one for each armed service. *In Which We Serve* (1942), which Noel Coward wrote, produced, and starred in, was based loosely on the real life experience of *Mountbatten in a destroyer, where the crew of a torpedoed warship reflect with a classic stiff-upper-lip approach on the role of the navy in their lives. An equivalent film about army life was Carol Reed's *The Way Ahead* (1944), starring David Niven and Stanley Holloway, which takes the viewer through the sufferings of a platoon of raw recruits, from barrack room to North African battle. *The Way to the Stars* (1945), which came out just after the war's end, told a similar tale for the RAF. Written by Terrence Rattigan, with an excellent cast (Mills, Michael Redgrave, Holloway, Howard), it is a very successful, atmospheric film, even fifty years later, telling the story of the air war as seen by the guests of a small hotel near an RAF aerodrome. The last British war film was *The True Glory* (1945), a Ministry of Information production which told the story of the war through a newsreel compilation, with an excellent voice-over commentary.

Earlier wars were also invoked, notably by Laurence Olivier's portrayal of Henry V (1944), which was a clever piece of propaganda transposing the values of 1415 with 1944, and dedicated to the *commandos and *airborne troops. Kenneth Branagh's version (1989) had a good deal more mud than glory. But Eisenstein's *Alexander Nevsky* (1941) stands as the all-time classic, belatedly rallying Russian nationalism to the support of the Soviet state as war with the ancient enemy loomed.

Hollywood, conscious of its own cultural roots, went to war selling a chocolate-box England about to be invaded, Anglo-Saxon heroism, and transatlantic romance. When *Mrs Miniver* (1942) appeared, it won five Oscars, telling the story of an English housewife's view of 1940; her husband takes his boat to *Dunkirk and she captures a German flyer in her garden. James Hilton (author of *Goodbye, Mr Chips* and *Lost Horizons*) had part-scripted *Miniver*, and co-wrote *Random Harvest* (1942), really a romance between Ronald Colman and Greer Garson, but where the hero is a WW I British officer, who suffers amnesia at the 1917 battle of *Arras/Vimy Ridge. Looking back to an earlier war was Warner Brothers' *Sergeant York* (1941), the story of a US farmer (Gary Cooper) who becomes a battlefield hero. Also in the Anglophile vein was *The White Cliffs of Dover* (1944), inspired by the *Dieppe raid of 1942. The most famous Hollywood war effort remains the Bogart–Bergman partnership in Warner Brothers' *Casablanca* (1942), which gained popularity only in the 1950s for another generation reaching back to an era safe from atomic oblivion. As with *The Way to the Stars*, it is the atmosphere that lingers and convinces, even 50 years on.

As in Britain, the US studios produced many 'tribute' propaganda films: *They Were Expendable* (1945) dealt with torpedo boats; *The Cross of Lorraine* (1943) told the story of the French Resistance; while *Edge of Darkness* (1943) depicted the Norwegian underground. *Mission to Moscow* (1943) viewed the Soviets as warm-hearted allies, but was bitterly regretted during the later McCarthyite era, and *Corvette K 225* (1943) was Universal Pictures' attempt to imitate the success of *In Which We Serve*, depicting the battle of the *Atlantic via life on a Canadian corvette. Another flag-waver was *Wilson* (1944), Darryl F. Zanuck's biography of the president who had led America into an earlier war. Also in this genre, among many, are *Flying Tigers* (1942), *Bataan* (1943), which was really a remake of *The Lost Patrol*, *Guadalcanal Diary* (1943), *The Fighting Seabees* (1944), and

the swashbuckling out-of-place Errol Flynn in *Objective Burma!* (1945). Lewis Milestone announced his conversion from the pacifism of *All Quiet on the Western Front* with the patriotic *The Purple Heart* (1944) and *A Walk in the Sun* (1945), depicting flyers over Japan and GIs in Italy. William Wellman (director of *Wings*) reappeared with an anti-war movie, *The Story of GI Joe* (1945), which followed US troops in Italy, through the eyes of a war correspondent. Rossellini's *Roma Città Aperta* (Open City) (1945) included striking images showing clearly the ravages of war on the city.

After the war, it can be argued, the war movie came to rival the Western and police action/gangster movie as cinema's most-loved and profitable genre. The industry initially produced films that confirmed the public's moral certitude about the justness of the conflict, and the Germans and Japanese were all excessively nasty (as the Germans had been portrayed in the 1920s before *All Quiet on the Western Front*). There were the occasional aberrations, for example James Mason caused a sensation with his sympathetic portrayal of Rommel in *Desert Fox* (1951), and Alec Guinness's confused colonel in the *Bridge over the River Kwai* (1957) started to blur the clear-cut lines between friend and foe. There was also a continuation of celluloid homage to those who served, and their unflinching patriotism, selfless camaraderie, and stoic bravery were offered as values for another generation to aspire to, safe in the knowledge that these were qualities the enemy did not possess. In this genre were the archetypal *The Sands of Iwo Jima* (1949), and Gregory Peck's *Twelve o'Clock High* (1949). Similar productions, blending 'Boys' Own' heroism with the British stiff upper lip, include *Odette* (1950), *The Wooden Horse* (1950), Jack Hawkins' *The Cruel Sea* (1952), *The Dambusters* (1955), *Reach for the Sky* (1956), *Yangtse Incident* (1957), *Ice Cold In Alex* (1958), and *North-West Frontier* (1959), set in India. This formula lasted even into the 1960s with *The Guns of Navarone* (1961) and *The Great Escape* (1963).

As WW II and even Korea grew more distant, the human dimension was sacrificed for scale. Confidence and dollars flowed back into the military epics from throughout history 'with a cast of thousands', for example in *Ben Hur* (1959), *Spartacus* (1960), *The Longest Day* (1962), *Zulu* (1964), and *The Battle of the Bulge* (1965). *Doctor Zhivago* (1965), *War and Peace* (1967), *The Battle of Britain* (1969), and *Waterloo* (1970) are also of this genre, where war became a vast animated, historical tableau rather than an immediately personal drama.

Fear of communist invasion and nuclear war were public nightmares throughout the 1950s and 1960s. Gregory Peck led the cast in the adaptation of Nevil Shute's gloomy post-nuclear *On the Beach* (1959), while Stanley Kubrick and Peter Sellers brilliantly addressed the paranoia openly in *Dr Strangelove, or How I Learned to Stop Worrying and Love the Bomb* (1963). Also pursuing the 'what-if' theme was the amateur *It Happened Here* (1963), exploring a Nazi-occupied Britain. Returning to another generation of epics,

Tora! Tora! Tora! (1969) portrayed a subject highly emotive to the wartime generation of Americans (Pearl Harbor), but started to humanize the Japanese in a way unthinkable a generation earlier. In France, *Lacombe, Lucien* (1974) explored both sides of the occupation of France, sympathizing with a collaborator.

Perhaps the American debacle in *Vietnam was also influential in rehabilitating the Asiatic nations, for John Wayne's *The Green Berets* (1968) flopped badly, proving that the transference of WW II values to Vietnam was not appropriate. Also relevant was another generation's questioning of authority, and Richard Attenborough's shameless distortion of WW I generalship in *Oh What a Lovely War* (1969) is a good example of this. Perhaps this questioning had started with *Paths of Glory* (1957), set in the trenches of WW I, but it certainly continues with the timeless *M*A*S*H* (1970), which achieves the aim much better, with some genuinely very funny moments. Peter Weir's revisionist *Gallipoli* (1981) was a throwback to this earlier anti-authority (and anti-colonial) genre. By then, arguably, some movie-makers had lost direction in their depiction of war, the gratuitously violent and ultimately pointless *Dirty Dozen* (1967), the highly amusing spoof *Kelly's Heroes* (1970), and the black comedy *Catch-22* (1970) illustrating the point well. Biographical films escaped the worst of this trend and some excellent character studies emerged in David Lean's *Lawrence of Arabia* (1962), Francis Ford Coppola's *Patton* (1970), and Attenborough's *Young Winston* (1972).

By the time the Americans quit Saigon in 1975, the public had overdosed on war movies, and crusades against the Third Reich, Rising Sun, or Red Tide of Communism had lost their celluloid appeal. Perhaps television had a role in this, and *The Eagle Has Landed* (1976)—itself a throwback to the 1942 *Went the Day Well?*—Sam Peckinpah's *Cross of Iron* (1976), and the last great epic, Attenborough's story of *Arnhem, *A Bridge Too Far* (1977)—all with star-studded casts—failed at the box office, whereas a decade earlier they would have done well. Neither were the *veterans happy. Sir John Hackett spoke for many when observing that actors in war movies never ran out of ammunition. Yet within three years, a new genre appeared, intent on demonstrating that while individuals might be capable of heroism, war itself was corrupt and soul-destroying. *The Deer Hunter* (1978) was the first to hit back, followed by Coppola's exhausting *Apocalypse Now* (1979), Oliver Stone's *Platoon* (1986), Kubrick's *Full Metal Jacket* (1987), and *Born on the Fourth of July* (1989). Steven Spielberg has also shown the world that cinema can depict the less-than-glorious side of war, in *Empire of the Sun* (1987) and *Schindler's List* (1993). Along the way, gritty realism resurfaced in two movies of almost documentary accuracy. In Germany, Wolfgang Petersen's *Das Boot* (1981) recorded the Atlantic patrol of U-96, stressing the waste of war, while *Memphis Belle* (1990) was a loving remake of a 1944 information film. After the 1991 *Gulf war,

it seemed the Americans had finally laid to rest the ghost of Vietnam that had been haunting them for 20 years. Once done, it seemed that Hollywood had said all it could about war. Hollywood, full of surprises as ever, then unveiled *Saving Private Ryan* (1998), a saga of the *Normandy campaign. Apart from the first ever attempt to portray realistically the noise, horror, and confusion of combat during the unforgettable first half-hour, where the viewer is cast up on Omaha Beach, what does *Ryan* offer? Arguably a sobering alternative to the cardboard super-heroes of Sylvester Stallone, Bruce Willis, and Arnold Schwarzenegger. Apart from the Gulf, no Americans have been to war since Vietnam, and a whole generation is curious to know what it is like. The cinema industry has therefore given them virtual combat.   APC-A

Shipman, David, *The Story of Cinema*, 2 vols. (London, 1982–4).
Halliwell, Leslie, *Film Guide* (London, numerous edns.).

Fisher, Adm Sir John Arbuthnot, 1st Baron of Kilverstone

(1841–1920). 'Jackie' Fisher is considered the father of the modern Royal Navy. He entered the navy a midshipman in the era of cannon balls and oak hulls powered by sail, and retired as admiral of a fleet of steel, powered by *steam, that fired huge shells thousands of yards. It was during his term as First Sea Lord, 1904–10, that the Royal Navy fully entered the era of armoured warfare. Although his principal task until 1909 was to reduce the naval estimate, he commissioned the revolutionary HMS *Dreadnought* (1906) which rendered all earlier battleships obsolete. During the Anglo-German battleship construction competition, he initiated the blind alley of fast, heavy gunned, but lightly armoured battlecruisers that worked as intended against armoured cruisers at the battle of the Falklands, but not when incorrectly put in the line of battle at *Jutland. He and Adm Beresford split the navy over the need for a *general staff and war planning and in general Fisher's abrasive personality won more enemies than adherents. Nonetheless, the fleet that fought WW I was very largely his creation. Something of a visionary, he anticipated the threat of unrestricted submarine warfare, that airborne weapons would revolutionize war and that combined operations with *amphibious craft would feature in future campaigns. But when he retired in 1910, he left behind a navy torn by his reforms and with no clear *doctrine. While the 'continental' school that foresaw war in home waters with another European power was dominant, there was still a powerful 'maritime' lobby that felt that the navy should continue to spread itself around the globe, protecting imperial trade routes. First Lord *Churchill recalled him in 1914, but the appointment revived internal divisions to no good purpose. The two parted company over *Gallipoli, which saw them both resign in 1915.

APC-A

flame-throwers These particularly fearsome weapons of war were invented by the German engineer Richard Fiedler in 1900, and tested in secret by the imperial German army the following year. By 1912 a *Flammenwerfer* regiment (of three battalions) had been formed with twelve companies. Each was equipped with man-portable flame-throwers consisting of a steel cylinder tank that was worn on the back attached to a 6-foot (1.8-metre) rubber tube and nozzle. The tank was subdivided into two: an upper reservoir containing a compressed gas to provide the pressure, and a flammable liquid (usually oil) in the lower. The gas propelled the liquid down the hose, which was ignited at the end of the nozzle by a wick. Flame could be projected for 20 yards (18 metres) for about two minutes, or shorter bursts could be obtained by igniting a cartridge for each burst, as with a shotgun. This principle of design has not changed since.

The weapon was tested in action against the French in February 1915 in the Verdun sector, but was more famously used against British troops at Hooge, near *Ypres, on the night of 29–30 July the same year. The six throwers that were used formed only a small part of a larger attack, aimed at inexperienced troops of the New Army. Achieving complete surprise, the British trenches doused with flame were quickly taken, and the attack also had a great psychological effect on other defenders. Thereafter flame-throwers entered the arsenals of modern armies, usually as *pioneer weapons, but failed to achieve a spectacular success during WW I again, as troops learned to keep their trenches beyond the distance of flame, and the throwers themselves were vulnerable to conventional weapons. British, German, and American troops used flame-throwers during WW II of similar design. The American Ack-Pack design introduced in 1945 has remained in service, able to project flame for nearly 50 yards (45 metres). These later designs all tended to weigh 40–8 lb (18–22 kg), and were best used against bunkers and machine-gun nests. Several countries mounted flame-throwers on armoured vehicles, with a towed fuel supply, such as the Wasp carrier, or Churchill Crocodile tank, which could project a jet of fire for 100 yards (91 metres). APC-A

flank companies During the 18th century infantry battalions in most European armies acquired a company each of *grenadiers and light infantry. When the battalion paraded in line they took post on its flanks, grenadiers on the right and light infantry on the left, and were thus known in England as flank companies, or *compagnies d'élite* in France. The remainder were styled battalion companies in England and *compagnies du centre* in France.

The grenade emerged as a useful military weapon by the 17th century. Its effective use demanded strength and dexterity, and increasingly it was given to selected grenadiers. As they needed to sling their muskets across their shoulders to leave both hands free to light and throw the grenade, they wore rimless conical caps instead of the broad-brimmed hat worn by their comrades. Even after the grenade had fallen into disuse the grenadiers remained the tallest and most stalwart men in the battalion.

Light companies, manned with lithe, nimble soldiers, appeared later, in response to the demand for *light troops for skirmishing. They too wore distinctive dress, initially a low 'jockey' cap in the British army, where the fact that both grenadiers and light infantry wore caps led to battalion companies being known colloquially as 'hatmen'. For particular duties both grenadier and light companies could be combined with similar companies from other battalions to form grenadier or light infantry units: part of the garrison of Hougoumont, at *Waterloo in 1815, consisted of the light companies—'Light Bobs'—from Wellington's Foot Guards regiments.

Flank companies attracted increasing controversy, especially as the functional differences between them and the other companies became blurred. Their detractors complained that the need to find big men for the grenadier and good shots for the light company left the battalion companies with only the rejects, while their supporters argued that the system encouraged men to improve themselves so as to gain admission to an élite. They generally disappeared during the 19th century. Grenadier and light infantry regiments, however, survive to this day. RH

Fleurus, battles of (1690 and 1794). These two battles, fought just over a century apart, had very different results. The first, a French victory during the *League of Augsburg war, on 1 July 1690, saw Marshal Luxembourg with 35,000 troops devastate Gen Waldeck and his 38,000 Dutch and German soldiers. Taking great risks, Luxembourg divided his army in two as he approached Waldeck's position and then struck both of the enemy flanks simultaneously. In the fighting that followed, the French killed, wounded, or captured half of Waldeck's army. Luxembourg had crushed his foe with Napoleonic daring, but he did not exploit his impressive victory with the same vigour and simply imposed war taxes on the surrounding area. As a result the battle was not as decisive as it might have been, although in fairness battles of the period rarely were, and generals did not expect them to be so.

The second battle, on 26 June 1794, occurred during the *French Revolutionary wars, and it would have a more dramatic impact. The Allies who opposed the fledgling French Republic had suffered a nasty defeat at Tourcoing the previous month, and the tide of the war ran against them. After several false starts, French forces besieged Charleroi, some 6 miles (9.7 km) south-west of Fleurus. In an attempt to relieve the fortress, a dispirited prince of Saxe-Coburg marched with 52,000 Austrian and Dutch troops against the 73,000 republican soldiers led by Gen Jean-Baptiste Jourdan.

Coburg split his forces into five columns to try to surround the French, but they defeated his forces in detail. After tough resistance repelled Coburg's attacks, he withdrew across the Meuse on the following day. Although suffering fewer casualties than did his French opponents, he had spent his energy. Soon the French chased the Austrians out of the southern Netherlands, which France annexed and retained for twenty years. JAL

Lynn, John A., *The Wars of Louis XIV* (London, 1999).
Phipps, Ramsay, *The Armies of the First Republic*, 5 vols. (London, 1926–39).

flintlock Historically, writers made no distinction between this term and *snaphaunce, the former being first recorded in 1683. Not until 1939, in Dr Torsten Lenk's *Flintlåset*, was a definition of 'flintlock' proposed which firearms scholars have accepted. In Lenk's definition, a true flintlock firing mechanism is one in which the cock, in the screwed jaws of which is held the flint, can be set to both half and full cock by means of an internal vertical sear and the steel, against which the flint strikes when the cock is released from full cock by pulling the trigger, is integral with the pan cover, which covers the pan in which priming *gunpowder is placed. Striking the flint against the steel forces it back and directs a shower of sparks into the forced-open pan, which ignites the priming powder, which sends a flash through the touch-hole connecting the pan to the barrel's breech, where the main charge is ignited to fire the weapon.

The earliest flintlocks were developed from snaphaunces in the first quarter of the 17th century, by the le Bourgeoys family in Lisieux, Normandy, and the new system spread only slowly outside France. By the end of the 17th century flintlock systems were widely used in Europe and had moved from the civilian sphere to the military one. Officers were carrying flintlock *pistols by the middle of the century and flintlock military muskets were in use by the same time, albeit in limited quantities and generally only by élite or specialist troops, such as *fusiliers. The flintlock reigned supreme as a system throughout the 18th century and flintlock muskets, also referred to as 'firelocks', were the infantry's principal weapons in most European nations. The flintlock ignition system, despite the inevitable delay between the pulling of the trigger and the firing of the musket, proved far more effective militarily than the *matchlock and was much less expensive and complicated than the *wheel lock. Matched with a rifled barrel and carefully handled, it produced a military weapon of great reliability and power. Until the early 19th century, flintlock-ignited weapons systems, ranging from tiny pocket pistols to heavy naval cannon, were adopted for both civilian and military use and it was with the flintlock system that experiments were made most extensively with the earliest breechloaders. SCW

Blackmore, Howard L., *British Military Firearms* (London, 1961).
Blair, Claude (ed.), *Pollard's History of Firearms* (London, 1983).

Flodden, battle of (1513). James IV of Scotland invaded England while Henry VIII was away in France. Thomas Howard, Earl of Surrey, responsible for the north of England, gathered 20,000 men to oppose him. In medieval style, he challenged James to battle, but the battle probably owed more to the fact that the English had cut off the Scots' line of retreat northwards, and thus forced them to attack. Witnesses recalled seeing cartloads of arrows being ferried north for the English army. Late in the afternoon of 9 September 1513, the Scots attacked. The 8 foot (2.4 metre) English bill proved handier than the 15 foot (4.6 metre) Scots pike but the victory was won by the English *archers. King James and 10,000 of his soldiers and officers, including the flower of the Scots aristocracy, were killed. The lament 'Flowers of the Forest' recalls the tragedy which befell the Scots nation. CDB

Foch, Marshal Ferdinand (1851–1929). Foch is remembered for two things. Before WW I he was a prominent advocate of the *offensive à l'outrance* (all-out offensive), and as such must bear a share of the blame for the disastrous French tactics of 1914. He was also, as supreme commander of the Allied forces, one of the principal architects of the victory of 1918. Appointed a marshal in 1918, on the plinth of his statue in London are the words 'I am conscious of having served England as I served my own country.'

Foch was commissioned into the artillery but served as an infantryman in the *Franco-Prussian war. He married in 1878, and went to Staff College in 1885, returning in 1895 as an instructor. Returning to regimental duty in 1901, he became a colonel in 1903 and V Corps' COS in 1905. Promoted to brigadier general in 1907, he then became commandant of the Staff College. In 1911 Foch became commander of VIII Corps, and in 1913 of XX Corps.

At the turn of the century Foch wrote *The Principles of War* (1903) which purported to grapple with the problems posed by the increased power, accuracy, and lethality of modern fire power. To all intents and purposes, he chose to ignore it and to emphasize instead the moral qualities of the soldiers and their commander. War was a contest of wills, and both infantryman and general had to have an unquenchable will to win. 'The laurels of victory', he wrote, 'hang on the enemy's bayonets, and have to be plucked from them, by man to man struggle if need be.' Writing when artillery, machine guns, and magazine rifles were an inescapable reality of war, he declared, 'To charge, but to charge in numbers, as one mass: therein lies safety.'

In 1914 Foch's XX Corps did well in the battle of the frontiers. Promoted to command the newly formed Ninth Army, with *Weygand as his COS, at one point in September 1914 he signalled to high command, 'I am hard pressed on my right; my centre is giving way; situation excellent; I am attacking.' Foch's success led to the role of co-ordinating the armies in the northern sector, including the British Expeditionary Force; once again Foch did well and the position stabilized.

As commander of the northern group of armies from the end of 1914 to the end of 1916, Foch presided over many attacks that incurred very heavy casualties for very little gains. He enjoyed reasonably good relations with his allies, and after *Joffre and *Haig quarrelled on 3 July 1916 was responsible for co-ordinating the French efforts on the Somme with the British. Having fallen out of favour with his government, Foch was superseded and given a desk job. His fall from grace did not last long. In the aftermath of the ill-fated *Nivelle offensive, Foch was appointed army COS in May 1917, followed by (in February 1918) the post of French representative of the inter-Allied *Supreme War Council that emerged following the catastrophic Italian defeat at *Caporetto, and was also chairman of the Executive Board that was supposed to control the Allied pool of reserves.

The individual national army commanders were still extremely jealous of their prerogatives and it was not until the first *Ludendorff offensive of 21 March 1918, which threatened to divide the Allies and send them retreating on divergent axes, that the politicians were able to impose some degree of operational co-ordination upon them. *Lloyd George, who had previously been reduced to starving Haig of reinforcements in order to restrain him from expensive offensives, was delighted to avail himself of the political cover of an allied C-in-C, while *Clemenceau faced the opposite problem of shaking *Pétain out of a defensive posture. Foch was an excellent compromise choice, and although lacking the executive powers and the staff that, for example, *Eisenhower enjoyed in 1944–5, during the German spring offensives and the subsequent Allied counter-offensives of 1918, he co-ordinated not only French and British but also Belgian and American forces in a series of assaults on the German positions along virtually the entire length of the western front. The man had at last found his hour.   GDS

Liddell Hart, B. H., *Foch: Man of Orléans* (London, 1931).

Foix, Gaston de, Duc de Nemours

Foix, Gaston de, Duc de Nemours (1489–1512). In his short life, de Foix covered himself in glory in one brief campaign. French fortunes in the French *Italian wars had reached a nadir when Gaston's father was killed fighting the Spanish at *Cerignola in 1503. King Louis XII appointed his nephew the young Duc de Nemours to lead the French armies in 1511. De Foix immediately raised the siege of Bologna and force-marched on to Brescia, where he arrived in February 1512, and took the town after a brief but bloody storming. His next target was Ravenna, and the mainly Spanish army of the Holy League under Cardona and

Navarro sallied forth to do battle. The Spanish adopted their usual tactic of forming up their arquebusiers behind a stout fieldwork, and keeping their foot and cavalry in reserve behind these. The battle was unusual for the period in that it was preceded by a two-hour artillery bombardment, and the guns were expertly commanded by the leading gunner of the time, Ferrara, and therefore had the better of the long-range duel. French field artillery raking the Spanish position from behind a flank caused considerable confusion among the Spanish horse, who charged to the attack piecemeal but were cut down. At this point French-paid *landsknechts under Jacob Empser led several costly but ultimately successful assaults on the now isolated Spanish infantry, who resisted fiercely. At the height of his triumph, de Foix was killed pursuing the beaten enemy. With losses amounting to 12,000 out of a starting force of some 16,000, Spanish dominance in Italy was severely shaken.   TM

Fontenoy, battle of (1745). In the War of the *Austrian succession the French opened the 1745 campaigning season by besieging Tournai. An Allied force of 50,000 men, under George II's son the Duke of *Cumberland, approached from the east. The French commander, Maurice de *Saxe, split his 70,000 men, leaving a detachment to carry on the siege while the remainder blocked Cumberland's line of advance between Barry Wood and the river Escaut, strengthening the gently rising ground with redoubts. On 11 May, after the failure of an attack on Barry Wood, on his right, Cumberland ordered a general advance. His British infantry, advancing between Fontenoy and the wood, came close to breaking the French line—this was the occasion when the officers commanding the French and British guards invited each other to fire first—but was checked by a counter-attack in which the Irish Brigade in French service played a distinguished part. Cumberland lost 7,500 men and fell back: Tournai surrendered.   RH

forlorn hope (from Dutch: *verloren hoop*, lost troop), a party of soldiers assigned to a particularly perilous duty. In the *British civil wars the term applied both to *musketeers posted in front of an army's main body, with the task of disorganizing the enemy's advance, and to a detachment which led an attempt to storm a fortress.

During the *Peninsular war the British army regularly used forlorn hopes to lead the assault on a breach in a fortress's defences. Despite the extraordinary danger, there was no shortage of volunteers, although it was a rare stormer who had not fortified himself with *alcohol. Officers might expect (but were not guaranteed) promotion, and men regarded it as an *honour to lead the attack. Their poor prospects of survival are underlined by the fact that the term now means a desperate venture or faint hope.   RH

Forrest, Lt Gen Nathan Bedford (1821–77). A self-educated, self-made millionaire planter and slave trader, Forrest joined the Confederate Army as a private in 1861. He raised a mounted unit at his own expense and led it in the Forts Henry and Donelson campaign. Promoted brigadier general in July 1862, he showed himself a cavalry leader of genius. He ravaged *Grant's communications in the winter of 1862/3 and did such damage in *Sherman's rear during 1864 that Sherman announced that he 'must be hunted down and killed if it costs ten thousand lives and bankrupts the Federal treasury'. He ended the war as a lieutenant general commanding the cavalry of the Army of Tennessee. One of the few Confederate officers to declare unequivocally that he was fighting to maintain slavery, after the war he was the first Grand Wizard of the Ku Klux Klan.

Forest's toughness was legendary. Attacked by a disaffected officer, he held the man's pistol hand and stabbed his assailant with a clasp-knife he opened with his teeth. Credited with defining the art of tactics as to 'get there fustest with the mostest', what he actually said was the less picturesque 'get there first with the most men'.   RH

Fortescue, Sir John William (1859–1933), president of the Royal Historical Society 1921–5, and fifth son of the 3rd Earl Fortescue. Educated at Harrow and Cambridge, he worked in the Windward Islands and New Zealand before turning to writing.

In 1895 Fortescue undertook a four-volume *History of the British Army*, the first two volumes of which (to 1763) appeared in 1899. The wealth of unpublished material, the support of his publisher Macmillan, and an appointment as librarian at Windsor Castle, permitted the *History*'s expansion, the terminal date (1870) only being reached with volume xiii in 1930. It was a great literary achievement with superb *maps, parts of which may never need replacing. Indispensable for operations, it is more a history of Britain's land wars than a study of the army as an institution, and its trenchant judgements sometimes go beyond the evidence.

Fortescue wrote 25 other books, mainly military history; he also edited six volumes of George III's *Correspondence* (1927–8), but this overstretched him and damaged his reputation. In *The Story of a Red Deer* (1897) his love of Devon and hunting are movingly displayed: it was still in print in the 1980s.   JH

Fortescue's memoir, *Author and Curator* (London, 1933).
Atkinson, C. T., 'Fortescue', in *DNB 1931–1940* (Oxford, 1949).
Brereton, J. M., 'Sir John Fortescue, Historian of the British Army', *Blackwood's Magazine* (Mar. 1976).

---

fortification and siegecraft (*see page 308*)

---

fragging An American term for the ancient practice of soldiers to register lethal disapproval of members of their own side with whatever comes to hand. In *Vietnam this was the fragmentation grenade, from which the word is derived.

The historical incidence of the phenomenon cannot be known. On the one hand leadership from the front exposes the backs of officers to malcontents in their own ranks, but on the other the higher risks thereby incurred tend to strengthen the hope that the enemy may do the job. A classic illustration is the fate of a hated major at *Blenheim, whose *grenadiers punctiliously granted his request to take his chances with enemy bullets, and only shot him after the battle was over. A variant was the killing of the Anarchist Durruti during the *Spanish civil war, by men who could no longer stand to be shamed by his suicidal bravery.

There have been groups of fighting men throughout history whose religious or cultural sensibilities were ignored by officers at their peril. The largest 'fragging' incident in history was the *Indian Mutiny, provoked by just such a failure on the part of the East India Company, and while the empire lasted British officers of Arab, Sikh (see SIKH WARS), or high-caste Hindu regiments who struck their men were regularly murdered. As a general rule the more intrinsically warlike peoples are the ones most likely to avenge offences against their *honour without regard to subsequent punishment. Attempts to harness the energy of violently antisocial individuals for war have included the *French and *Spanish Foreign Legions and the Nazi and Soviet penal battalions of WW II, but the downside of this from the disciplinary point of view is self-evident.

Something more akin to vengeful despair was at work towards the end in Vietnam among those unwillingly in uniform and unwilling to be the last to die in a by-then pointless war. The system of exemptions told draftees that their society did not value them, long before this was made patent on their return home when they were spat upon by the exempt. Racial tensions in the greater society were magnified in the field, and the traditional glues of group pride and of winning honour among peers were perversely diluted by the posting of soldiers as individuals and the profligate award of medals to non-combatants. It is unremarkable that in excess of 1,000 officers and *NCOs were fragged.   HEB

France, fall of (1940). In the history of warfare few campaigns between great and approximately equal powers have been decided so swiftly and conclusively as the German conquest of western Europe in May and June 1940. Within five days of the opening of the campaign on 10 May, Holland had surrendered, the French defences on and behind the Meuse had disintegrated, and the French prime minister was already talking of defeat.

Had the original plan for a western offensive, as conceived and both ordered and postponed on numerous occasions

(*cont. on page 313*)

fortification and siegecraft

FOR as long as man has required protection and prestige he has built fortifications. Put simply, the art of fortification consists of the combination of terrain with available materials to form defences, and siegecraft concerns the attack of these fortifications. Throughout history there has been a changing balance between attack and defence as technology and tactics swing the advantage first one way and then the other. There are numerous examples of sophisticated fortifications from prehistory. Most consist of an earthwork or 'dun', which developed into the complex Celtic hill forts, the best example of which, Maiden castle in Dorset, comprises three sets of concentric banks and ditches, surrounding a wall and palisade. The gates were protected by an ingenious system of re-entrants and switchbacks, designed to lead any attacker backward and forward under a rain of missiles. We know that these were usually slingstones, as great piles of them have been found stored in convenient places.

Where the terrain was rocky, the inhabitants were forced to build upwards instead of digging into the earth. Stone forts or cashels can be found dotted all over Ireland and the Western Isles, comprising three rings of walled enclosures, in between which were to be found fiendish spiked obstacles that resembled the later *chevaux-de-frise*. Dun Aengus on the Isle of Arran is a prime example of this kind of fort. Indeed, mainland Scotland boasts some very unusual prehistoric fortifications, built like towers without mortar, and known as brochs. These refuges would be built on a peninsula, with access guarded by a series of ditches.

But it is to the ancient Near East and the lands of the Bible that we must turn to discover the origins of fortification. The walls of Jericho, the oldest city yet to be discovered, were built about 7000 BC, enclosing a permanent natural spring, valuable enough in itself to be worth defending in that arid climate. Ten different cultures subsequently inhabited the site, but the most famous monuments they left were a great tower 30 feet (9.1 metres) high, and a wall 6 feet (1.8 metres) thick, with a ditch, encircling the city, or rather a series of walls built and rebuilt over centuries, eventually forming a great mound or 'tell'. All this dates to some 6,000 years before Joshua, who must have laid siege to Jericho in about 1500 BC. A similar preoccupation with defence can be seen at Çatal Hüyük in modern Turkey dating from 6500 BC, where the houses are packed tightly together and only accessible by a narrow entry in the roof.

By 1200 BC the *Egyptians were using crenellated walls such as the ones found at Medinet Habou. We know a considerable amount about Egyptian siege techniques from surviving accounts of Tuthmosis' seven-month siege of *Megiddo, where he captured at one fell swoop all the princes from the surrounding area so 'the capture of Megiddo was the capture of a thousand towns'.

The *Assyrians were the past masters of fortification and siegecraft. They developed a startling variety of machines and equipment for assaulting enemy defences including catapults, storming towers, rams, and mines (see SIEGE ENGINES). These techniques remained largely unchanged until the introduction of *gunpowder. Assyria's expansionist policy created the need to constantly reduce fortified population centres that resisted the Assyrian yoke. An earth ramp was used to bring a metal-tipped battering ram into position. To prevent the defenders dropping rocks or burning materials onto it, the ram was often housed with an elaborate canopy, and continually doused with water. *Propaganda and the threat of fire and the sword was used to encourage *capitulation. *Blockade was a commonplace technique, and in many of the areas that the Assyrians conquered water was scarce and so fortresses usually included large underground cisterns to help them resist a siege. With their ruthless and efficient approach, the Assyrians were able to take Jerusalem in less than a year in 701 BC, but the city of Arpad held out for three years against Tiglath-Pileser, and Nebuchadnezzar took a colossal thirteen years to take Tyre, a stronghold that was destined to cause a later conqueror some inconvenience too.

The Romans were engineers par excellence and this applied to their conduct of *siege warfare. *Caesar describes in detail all the preparations for and his conduct of the siege of *Alesia against *Vercingetorix the Gaul in 20 BC. The Romans were fond of building enormous ramps to allow them to walk over the walls of an enemy's strong point. This was used to singular effect at *Masada in the winter of AD 72–3; like most Roman sieges the capture of Masada was achieved by the shovel. A gigantic earth ramp, which still remains, was constructed to bring siege engines up to the rocky plateau. The Romans also specialized in extensive frontier works such *Hadrian's wall in the north of England and the Antonine wall in Scotland. Indeed, the whole defence of the late empire was based on a series of frontier forts or limes, and coastal forts such as those found on the so-called 'Saxon Shore' in England. The best example of a fort of this type is at Pevensey. However, these forts and walls were only as good as the garrisons that served them, and relied on field armies to contain any penetration, and without reliable troops to defend the boundaries of empire the barbarians were free to pour through unmolested.

The art of fortification was lost in the West for many years after the collapse of the Roman empire, and local strongholds relied on stout stockades for defence. Settlements would grow up around these defended localities and their garrisons, and the regional war leader would offer military protection from marauders, such as the predatory Vikings and Magyars, in return for agricultural labour on the surrounding lands. This is essentially what developed into *feudal service. These wooden refuges or keeps were developed into the motte and bailey *castle, the bailey being the courtyard and the motte being a large mound of earth on which sat the inner refuge or keep. In time the wooden construction of the keep was replaced by stone or masonry, becoming bigger and more grandiose as the barons acquired wealth, fame, and influence. Experience of campaigning in the *Crusades from the 11th to the 13th centuries resulted in the import from the East of the concentric castle plan, which was the high point of medieval stone fortress design. It was found that circular towers in successive rings, linked by curtain walls, offered better defence and deflected missiles from the great stone-throwing engines or trebuchets, another import from the Middle East. Major strongholds such as Krak des Chevaliers in Syria, and the English castles in Wales—Conwy or Caerphilly, for example—were pretty much impervious to direct assault, and had to be starved into submission or undermined by the extensive digging of tunnels. These tunnels were usually beneath walls or towers in chambers which were packed with combustible material and fired. In 1215 King John's miners brought down a corner of the great keep at Rochester. 'We command you', he had written to his justiciar, 'that with all haste, by day and night, you send to us 40 bacon pigs of the fattest and less good for eating to bring fire under the tower.'

The development of siege artillery in the 15th century necessitated a complete revision of fortification, for high stone walls crumbled under the repeated impact of cannon balls. In 1494 Charles VIII of France conducted a lightning campaign in Italy, taking fortress after fortress by means of a truly modern siege-train consisting of accurate guns capable of repeated and rapid fire. Artillery fortification was born in Italy in around 1503, as a reaction to these new weapons. This new system, the *trace italienne*, was based on mathematical and geometric principles and coincided neatly with the rediscovery of *science and technology associated with the Renaissance. It developed into the geometrical fortification associated with engineers like *Vauban and *Coehoorn, and had real impact

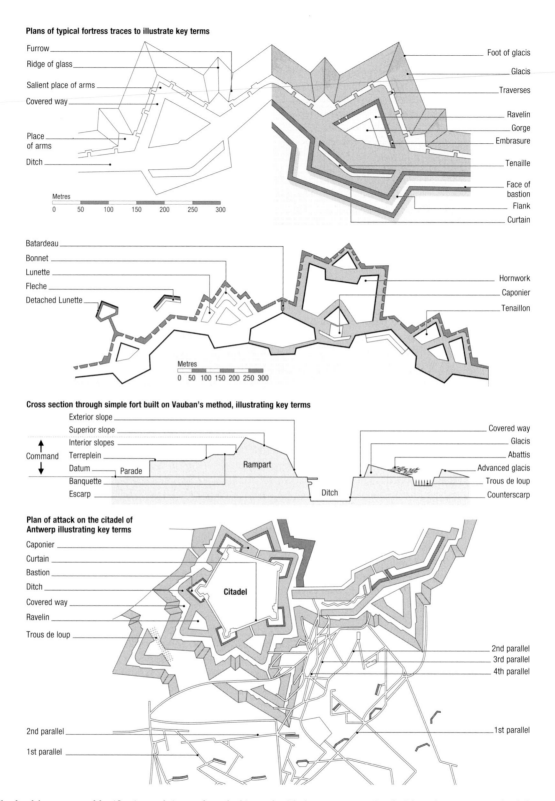

Plans of typical fortress traces to illustrate key terms

Furrow
Ridge of glass
Salient place of arms
Covered way
Place of arms
Ditch

Foot of glacis
Glacis
Traverses
Ravelin
Gorge
Embrasure
Tenaille
Face of bastion
Flank
Curtain

Metres
0 50 100 150 200 250 300

Batardeau
Bonnet
Lunette
Fleche
Detached Lunette

Hornwork
Caponier
Tenaillon

Metres
0 50 100 150 200 250 300

Cross section through simple fort built on Vauban's method, illustrating key terms

Exterior slope
Superior slope
Interior slopes
Command
Terreplein
Datum
Banquette
Escarp
Parade
Rampart
Ditch

Covered way
Glacis
Abattis
Advanced glacis
Trous de loup
Counterscarp

Plan of attack on the citadel of Antwerp illustrating key terms

Caponier
Curtain
Bastion
Ditch
Covered way
Ravelin
Trous de loup

Citadel

2nd parallel
3rd parallel
4th parallel

2nd parallel
1st parallel

1st parallel

The fearful geometry of fortification and siegecraft reached its peak with the systems associated with Vauban. However, the defensive and offensive systems actually built were often much simpler and more tailored to the terrain than the idealized examples shown in text books.

on war from the late 16th century onwards, with generations of engineers, like Montalambert and Cormontagne, making their own additions to a branch of military science which assumed the fiercely contested complexities of theology.

Quintessential to the system was the bastion, a four-sided work shaped like an arrowhead, which jutted out in front of the main line of ramparts. The guns on its two faces fired out across the glacis, a carefully sculpted open area between the fortress and the countryside beyond, and those on its two flanks swept the fronts of the ramparts with enfilade fire. Guns usually stood on a flat *terreplein*, shooting over a wide earth parapet which was intended to absorb incoming fire, although they might also fire through splayed embrasures, or be housed in vaulted casemates on a lower storey. Between the bastions ran the curtain, the main wall of the fortress. Like the bastions it had a carefully planned profile to ensure that the attacker had no vulnerable masonry to engage: from his viewpoint, the ramparts just showed above the glacis. The fortress side of the glacis ended with a palisade protecting a covered way, along which defenders could walk, and then dropped down into a deep, wide ditch which might, according to local circumstances, be wet or dry. Detached works called ravelins or (from their appearance) *demi-lunes* (half-moons) often stood out in front of the curtain between the bastions, and sometimes extra works formed an extra outer skin of fortifications. Excellently preserved examples of this type of fortress can be seen at Naarden in Holland, Le Quesnoy near Lille, Neuf-Brisach in Alsace, and Berwick-on-Tweed in Britain.

The attack of these fortifications was scarcely less methodical than their design and construction. A lucky attacker might gain admittance by a ruse or overwhelm unprepared defenders by a sudden assault. But he would usually have to mount a formal siege, first opening a trench line parallel to the defences and just out of range of their guns, and then sap forward, digging zigzag trenches to open a second parallel, and later a third. Meanwhile his gunners would concentrate on hostile pieces on the front under attack, and would also try to drop *mortar bombs into the body of the place: in 1717 a mortar bomb hit the main Turkish magazine at Belgrade, causing an explosion which killed 3,000 people. The defender might mount a sortie, but this would probably do little more than buy time. Eventually the attacker would assault the covered way, and having established a lodgement there would set up breaching batteries mounting heavy guns which would pound away at the foot of the scarp wall supporting the rampart. When this tumbled into the ditch, establishing a practicable breach, he would summon the fortress's governor to capitulate. A prudent governor usually complied, for if the attacker was compelled to mount an assault through a defended breach his maddened soldiers could not be expected to grant quarter to the garrison or to respect the property or chastity of the inhabitants. Mining, with gunpowder now replacing the pig-fat of yesteryear, might accelerate the process, but a wily defender would have prepared countermine galleries of his own, and a wet ditch presented particular problems.

With the introduction of effective rifled and *breech-loading weapons in the 19th century, and subsequently high-explosive shells, the advantage swung to the attacker who could now overwhelm most defences with devastating firepower. The Union army rapidly captured the large and complex work of Fort Pulaski in Georgia in 1862. However, this did not signal the end of masonry fortifications, for a line of forts nicknamed 'Palmerston's follies' was built in the 1860s to defend the British naval base of Portsmouth against attack from its landward side, and after the *Franco-Prussian war Sere de Rivières fortified the Franco-German border. Masonry was protected by concrete, often with a 'burster layer' of sand between the two to absorb the explosion of shells, and guns were protected in steel cupolas like those favoured by *Brialmont. As the range of artillery increased, so engineers built outlying forts to keep an attacker out of range of the body of the fortress, and key sites like *Liège, Namur, and *Verdun had rings of forts surrounding them.

Improvements in firepower enabled infantry in *field fortifications to play an increasing part in defence. The fortifications of Petersburg in the American civil war were ramshackle, but they gave the Union army pause for thought, and infantry played their own lethal part in the fighting around Plevna in the Russo-Turkish war of 1877–8 and *Port Arthur in the *Russo-Japanese war of 1904–5.

In the opening moves of WW I fortresses at Liège, Namur, and elsewhere were smashed by the fire of heavy *howitzers. Continuous lines of field fortification faced each other on the western and to a lesser extent the eastern front, and dealing with the locked front became the war's principal tactical problem. When reviewing the dreadful impact of the war, it was not unreasonable to conclude that the defensive was the stronger form of warfare, and for the French to note that Verdun forts— ludicrously under-gunned though they were—had coped far better with months of bombardment, sometimes by the heaviest guns available, than might ever have been expected. Taking these lessons to heart the French built an extensive permanent defence system, the *Maginot Line, between the wars, but the northern end of this line resting on the Belgian border was left lightly protected, and it was this gap that the Germans were able to exploit in their campaign of 1940.

Fortifications were extensively used in WW II, but the essentially fluid nature of the fighting made fixed fortresses like Singapore, the Atlantic wall, and the complex of Belgian forts around Antwerp and Maastricht, something of an anachronism. The combination of artillery, tanks, and air power co-operating with infantry and combat engineers, meant that most fortresses would eventually succumb to determined assault by well-trained troops. Indeed, in 1940 the supposedly impregnable Belgian fortress of Eben-Emael was taken by 78 German paratroops in something under half an hour of intense fighting. Examples of less ambitious fortifications abound, like the concrete *pillboxes, often hexagonal, which dot southern England. The Germans constructed huge fortifications along the French coast—the 'Atlantic wall'—using forced labour. These installations were key targets for air attack, naval bombardment, and the first troops ashore in the *Normandy campaign.

Since WW II extensive fortifications have been seen in use in the *Korean war in 1951 and the *Bar-Lev Line along the Suez Canal on the eve of the Yom Kippur war, as well as temporary fortresses such as the firebases of *Dien Bien Phu in *Indochina and Khe Sanh in *Vietnam. Moreover, permanent fortifications have been widely used for civilian and military nuclear defence. Ballistic missiles are housed in deep concrete and steel reinforced silos, which has necessitated the development of special missiles intended to burrow deep and detonate far underground in an attempt to defeat them. Hardened aircraft shelters and weapons storage bunkers are also permanent fortifications, as are deep command bunkers such as the war headquarters built at High Wycombe in England or Strategic Air Command's headquarters beneath Cheyenne Mountain in Arizona.

Fortification from its origins as a response to a need for security in an uncertain world, developed into a matter of statecraft and diplomacy, and a reflection on international circumstances. Throughout time there have consistently been misunderstandings as to the nature and purpose of fortifications, and some of the faith placed in their effectiveness has been unjustified. They still represent, as they always have, the endless duel between attack and defence, between immobility and manoeuvre. Considerations of force protection, so important in the 1990s and beyond, will encourage their construction, notably to defend logistic bases, surveillance systems, or ports of entry. Conversely, attackers will ponder technical or tactical means of attack: *plus ça change.* TM/RH

Connolly, Peter, *Greece and Rome at War* (London, 1981).

Duffy, Christopher, *Fire and Stone: The Science of Fortress Warfare 1660–1860* (Newton Abbot, 1975).

—— *Siege Warfare: The Fortress and the Early Modern World 1494–1660* (London, 1979).

—— *The Fortress in the Age of Vauban and Frederick the Great 1660–1789* (London, 1985).

between October 1939 and January 1940, been put into execution it could well have ended in stalemate. The major role was assigned to Army Group B, which was to eliminate Holland and thrust through central Belgium. Only a covering role, on its southern flank, was given to Army Group A, whose 22 divisions contained no mechanized units. Moreover, the territorial objective was limited to seizing the Low Countries and the Channel coast—presumably as bases for an attack on Britain—and there was no notion that France might also be eliminated. Hence the comparatively moderate peace terms after France's ceasefire, which permitted roughly half the country to be governed by an independent French government at Vichy.

The credit for perceiving the defects of this plan and devising an alternative to secure a decisive victory belongs chiefly to *Manstein, Army Group A's COS. It should be added that by the early weeks of 1940 the German army high command (OKH) and some senior commanders had also become dissatisfied with the original plan. Essentially, Manstein proposed to transfer the principal role and the bulk of the armoured units (initially seven out of ten panzer divisions) to Army Group A, and to stake everything on a surprise attack through the Ardennes against what was known to be the weakest sector of the French defences (the Sedan-Dinant sector of the Meuse). Manstein's bold conception was at first opposed by OKH, but in mid-February 1940 he was sympathetically received by *Hitler and his essential ideas were incorporated in the final operation order shortly afterwards. Army Group B still had the important task of drawing the Allied First Army Group into Belgium and holding it there, but the role of deep penetration—through the Ardennes, across the Meuse, and then either a sweep south behind the *Maginot Line or along the Somme valley towards the Channel Coast—now fell to Army Group A.

On 10 May 1940 Germany had 136 divisions in the west of which only 10 were armoured (panzer), 7 motorized, 1 cavalry, and 1 *airborne. The French and British together had 104 divisions (94 and 10 respectively) to which 22 Belgian divisions were added on 10 May. The French total included 3 armoured divisions, 3 light-mechanized divisions (as powerfully equipped as the panzer divisions), and 5 cavalry divisions. On the question of total comparative tank strengths on the western front, the French by themselves had more tanks than the Germans—3,254 against 2,574. As for quality, the French tanks proved inferior to the Germans in the mobile war that burst upon them because most of them were slower and had a more limited radius of action.

The only respect in which the Allies were markedly inferior was in the air, but here German superiority has sometimes been exaggerated. German air strength in May 1940 was as follows: 1,016 fighters, 248 medium bombers, 1,120 bombers, 342 Stuka dive-bombers, and 500 scout planes, a total of 3,226 aircraft. The French air force then possessed only some 1,120 modern aircraft of which 700 were fighters,

140 bombers, and 380 scout planes. To these must be added the British contribution which initially consisted of the Air Component of the British Expeditionary Force (BEF) (4 Fighter Squadrons, 4 Bomber Squadrons, and 5 Army Co-Operation Squadrons) and the Advanced Air Striking Force (10 Bomber and 2 Fighter Squadrons). Again the German air forces were better organized for their immediate purpose. The Stukas had serious defects in slow speed and vulnerability, but they played a vital part in the crucial first days.

The decisive breakthrough occurred on Army Group A's front. By the evening of 12 May, the leading German armoured divisions had reached the Meuse in two places, at least two days earlier than the defenders had thought possible. Sedan—on the east bank—had been captured by 1st and 10th Panzer Divisions (*Guderian), while 7th Panzer Division (*Rommel) had reached Dinant. It was typical of the Germans' offensive spirit that they pressed straight on with the crossings on 13 May, again to the bewilderment of the French. All the bridges had been blown and French opposition was stiff, yet by the end of the day four precarious bridgeheads had been established on the west bank. At Sedan, especially, the French artillery was almost paralysed by Stuka air attacks.

There was still an opportunity for the Allies to launch a devastating counter-attack while the Germans were confined to congested bridgeheads and makeshift bridges, but it was not taken. The Germans had deliberately struck at the junction of the two French Armies (Second and Ninth) which contained many poorly trained reserve units. On the evening of 14 May Corap, commanding Ninth Army, mistakenly ordered a general retreat to a new defensive position about 10 miles (16 km) to the west. Ninth Army's withdrawal turned into a rout, while to the south Huntziger's Second Army fared little better. By nightfall Guderian's bridgehead was already some 30 miles (48 km) wide and 15 miles (24 km) deep. That same day British and French bombers with French fighter cover made heroic but vain attempts to destroy the vital bridges at Sedan. Out of 170 bombers (the majority of them Blenheims) about 85 were shot down.

Thus by the evening of 15 May the Germans had already gained a decisive advantage. All three panzer corps had broken clean through the Meuse bridgeheads and were thrusting westward virtually unopposed in the chaotic rear areas behind French Ninth Army. Although the dynamic panzer leaders, particularly Guderian and Rommel, were full of confidence and already were thinking of driving relentlessly to the Channel Coast, which the 2nd Panzer Division reached on 20 May, some of their senior commanders, and Hitler himself, were astonished by the speed of the advance and became day by day more anxious about overextension.

With every passing day the Allies' prospects of launching an effective counter-attack diminished. Gamelin had been slow to see the need to pull back his forces from Belgium to

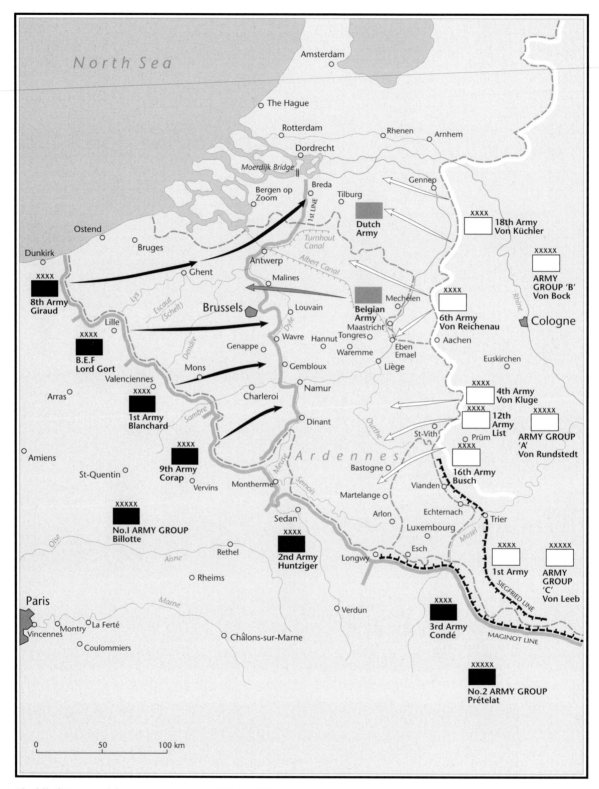

The **fall of France** and the Low Countries, 1940: Allied and German deployments.

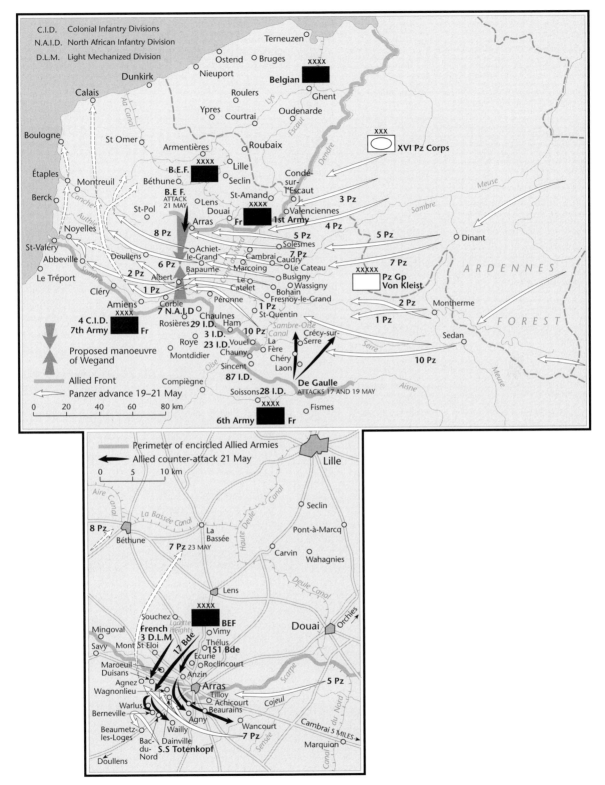

The **fall of France** and the Low Countries, the Ardennes breakthrough and attempted Allied counter-attacks.

avoid being cut off, and only on 19 May, the day of his replacement by *Weygand, did he issue a directive for a combined counter-offensive from north and south of the Somme to pinch off the German corridor and so isolate panzers from infantry. The one minor action which temporarily worried the Germans and had long-term effects on their high command, was the British counterstroke at *Arras on 21 May.

The wider significance of the Arras episode was that it reinforced the apprehension already displayed by Kluge, Kleist, and Rundstedt that the armoured spearhead was running too many risks, and helped to influence the fateful decision to halt the panzers on 24 May until the morning of the 27th. There were both political and operational reasons for the halt order: the need to let the Luftwaffe deliver the *coup de grâce*; to rest the armoured divisions before the second phase of the offensive; and to define the roles of Army Groups A and B in destroying the Allied forces in the shrinking pocket around *Dunkirk. It seems clear that it was not Hitler's intention that the BEF should escape: rather he shared the widespread German belief that escape by sea was impossible. By the time this error was realized more than 300,000 British and French troops were evacuated before Dunkirk fell on 4 June.

Although Dunkirk was treated as something of a triumph in Britain, from the continental viewpoint it marked the brilliant climax of the first phase of a whirlwind campaign. In three weeks the Germans had taken over a million prisoners at the cost to themselves of only 60,000 casualties. The Dutch and Belgian armies had been eliminated—the latter surrendering after a gallant resistance on 28 May. The French had lost 30 divisions—nearly a third of their total strength and including virtually all their armour. They had also lost the support of 12 British divisions. Weygand was left with only 66 divisions (many of them already depleted) to defend an unprepared front, longer than that originally attacked, stretching from Abbeville to the Maginot Line.

When the second phase of the German offensive (code name FALL ROT) began on 5 June, the French military situation was already hopeless. For some time the military leaders had been talking of 'saving their honour' rather than victory, and those who felt with *de Gaulle, now Under Secretary for War, that resistance must be continued even, if necessary, outside metropolitan France, found themselves in a small minority. The French cabinet had discussed the possibility of seeking an armistice independently of Britain even before Dunkirk, and thereafter PM Reynaud steadily lost ground to those, including *Pétain and Weygand, who favoured an immediate ceasefire to save France from further loss. Reynaud's resignation in favour of Pétain on 16 June signalled the end of any surviving hopes that the struggle could be continued in Brittany or in North Africa. On 22 June unconditional surrender was accepted at Compiègne.

Despite the abundant evidence of low *morale and outright defeatism in France, it still seems reasonable to find the main and sufficient causes of defeat in faulty strategic *doctrine and organization. The Allies were handicapped by an extremely complex and cumbersome chain of command in which Gamelin's role as C-in-C was uncertain. Gamelin delegated considerable power to Georges, commander of the north-east front, and beneath him, to Billotte to co-ordinate First Army Group (of French, British and Belgian divisions) between the Channel coast and the northern end of the Maginot fortifications. To make matters worse, Allied communications might just have sufficed in the slow-moving and controlled battle that Gamelin expected, but quickly collapsed once the Germans crossed the Meuse and thrust deep into France. The German triumph was not primarily due to superior numbers or equipment, but rather to superior control of the means available and ruthless efficiency in exploiting the enemy's mistakes to the full. From a military viewpoint this, then, was a victory in the classic style: the strategic conquest of a near-equal adversary achieved with economy of means and without excessive losses.   BJB

Franco Bahamonde, Gen Francisco (1892–1975),

generalissimo of Nationalist forces during the *Spanish civil war and *caudillo* (chief) of Spain thereafter. At 19 he volunteered for service with native cavalry in Spanish Morocco, becoming Spain's youngest captain. Severely wounded in 1916, in 1920 he was appointed second in command of the new *Spanish Foreign Legion, became its commander in 1923, and after brilliant service during the Rif war became the youngest brigadier general in Europe in 1926.

Although careful to avoid political activity, he was known to be a monarchist and was made inactive when the Republic was proclaimed in 1931. Restored to active duty after the centre-right took power, he directed the ruthless suppression of the Asturian miners' revolt in 1934. Appointed COS in 1935, he appealed for a state of emergency to cope with endemic violence after the election of the leftist Popular Front in 1936 and was posted to the Canary Islands' career graveyard.

From there he broadcast the signal for military rebellion and directed the crucial German airlift of the Army of Africa to the mainland. When it became apparent that the Popular Front was not going to collapse, his peers elected him C-in-C and head of the new Nationalist regime. Franco skilfully balanced all the disparate elements in the coalition, including the Germans and Italians, obtaining the maximum military benefit from them without sacrificing his own or Spanish independence. Once the increasingly Soviet-dependent Republicans were crushed, his 40-year leadership was never seriously challenged.

He was a law-and-order conservative, not a fascist. Legitimate charges against him concern his unimaginative conduct of the war and the tens of thousands of executions carried out after it, followed by a long social twilight of oppressive conformity. Against this must be set the fact that in 1936 Spain was undoubtedly tearing itself apart, that Franco seldom gave in to German and Italian pressure to wage a war of annihilation, and that he kept Spain out of WW II, despite intense pressure from *Hitler in person at Hendaye in October 1940. His legacy is a united Spain under a constitutional monarch.   HEB

François I, King of France (1494–1547). As a young prince of the Renaissance, François became caught up in the struggle between the Habsburg and Valois dynasties of Europe. On his accession to the throne in 1515 he invaded Milan, scene of many a French victory during the ongoing French *Italian wars. He met the Swiss army fighting for Milan at Marignano, and the two armies fought each other to a bloody standstill. Thereafter the Swiss concluded a permanent alliance with France, and fought and were defeated with the French at Bicocca in 1522. Milan was lost, and in 1525 François faced a large Imperial-Spanish force outside Pavia. The result was a disaster for French arms and François was taken prisoner and forced to make peace. He renewed the war as soon as he was freed but made peace again at Cambrai in 1529. The struggle with the Habsburg *Charles V continued and war flared up again in the Low Countries and Rhineland in 1535–8 and 1522–4. Although François managed to secure his borders the heartland of Habsburg and Spanish strength remained inviolate while France later slid into the *French wars of religion. François was otherwise an able ruler, but his lust for military glory overcame his good sense on many occasions.   TM

Franco-Prussian war (1870–1). In 1870–1 Prussia and her German allies defeated France in a war which helped transform Germany, changed the balance of power in Europe, and foreshadowed WW I. To contemporaries this victory seemed surprising, for the Second Empire of *Napoleon III had an impressive military reputation gained in the *Crimean, *Italian, *Mexican and *Algerian campaigns.

This success had a fragile basis. *Recruitment was based on selective long-term conscription which produced an army well suited to overseas expeditions but unable to generate numbers or inspire national commitment needed for major war. Prussian victory in the *Austro-Prussian war of 1866 showed the superiority of universal short-term conscription, but Napoleon's government, under pressure to liberalize, was too weak to implement comprehensive reform. The Loi Niel of 1868 fell short of making service universal, and attempts to create a second-line army, the Garde Nationale Mobile, were largely unsuccessful. Senior officers lacked neither courage nor experience, but the Napoleonic tradition led them to expect strong leadership which Napo-

leon III could not provide. The French had a good *breech-loading rifle, the *chassepot, also the *mitrailleuse, a primitive machine gun, but their muzzle-loading artillery was outclassed by Prussian breech-loaders.

The forces of the North German Confederation had been brought into line with the reformed Prussian army, and although the armies of the southern German states retained distinctive characteristics, Prussia set the pace. This was especially true of its *general staff, developed under *Moltke 'the Elder'. The war of 1866 had demonstrated its grasp of railway-borne deployment, and Moltke and his officers subsequently bent their energies to planning for war against France.

France was in the prickly state of a great power which feels its status slipping, and *Bismarck, chancellor of Prussia, recognized that a victorious war would help complete the unification of Germany under Prussian leadership. War broke out in July 1870 after a French attempt to persuade King William of Prussia to guarantee that the abandoned candidacy of a German prince for the throne of Spain would not be renewed. Bismarck did his best to goad France into declaring war, and she did so on 15 July, without allies, for discussions with Austria were far from fruition.

Over the next two weeks the armies mobilized and moved to concentration areas. In Germany reservists reported for duty and rattled off to the frontier by rail. Moltke deployed three armies: the first, under Steinmetz, on the lower Moselle; the stronger Second, under Prince Frederick Charles, on the Saar, and the Third, which included south German contingents, under the crown prince of Prussia, in the Bavarian Palatinate. The French attempted to save time by combining mobilization and concentration. Confusion followed, with reservists traipsing about in search of their regiments and harassed *Intendance* officials trying to feed what sometimes resembled an armed mob.

Such was the resilience of the French army that by late July it had six corps on the frontier. Douay's V was at *Belfort, MacMahon's I at Strasbourg, and Failly's V between Sarreguemines and Bitche. In or around Metz were Frossard's II, Bazaine's III, and Ladmirault's IV. Bourbaki soon joined them with the Guard, while *Canrobert prepared to move VI Corps forward from Châlons. Plans for concentrations at Strasbourg, Metz, and Châlons had been changed to enable Napoleon, who reached Metz on 28 July, to assume personal command of a quarter of a million men with a view to launching an offensive when concentration was complete. The Germans already had more than 300,000, and the balance tilted remorselessly against France in the weeks that followed.

Operations began with two minor actions. On 2 August the French took the heights above Saarbrucken, and two days later the Germans fell on one of MacMahon's divisions at Wissembourg. There were two far more significant engagements on 6 August. Moltke hoped to use Second Army to meet the expected French attack while First and Third

The theatre of the **Franco-Prussian war,** 1870, and (inset) the battles of Rezonville–Mars-la-Tour and Gravelotte–St Privat.

swung in from the flanks. However, he found it hard to keep the headstrong Steimetz under control, and in the north First Army blundered into Frossard at Spicheren. Uncertain command left Frossard unsupported, while German units marched to the sound of the guns to outflank him.

In Alsace, where the crown prince met *MacMahon at *Wörth, it was much the same story. Chassepot armed infantry easily checked their opponents, but were pounded by artillery and forced to retreat as the Germans found their flanks. Self-sacrificing cavalry charges gained glory but

little else. By nightfall the southern wing of the French army was on its way to Châlons. The northern wing fell back, in filthy weather, on Metz. *Howard points to the triple significance of the day's battles: 'the collapse of the cavalry; the transformation of the infantry; and the triumph of the gun.'

On 12 August Bazaine was given command of the force around Metz, though while Napoleon remained there was doubt as to how far his authority went. The next day his old corps held First Army at Borny, east of Metz, but Bazaine,

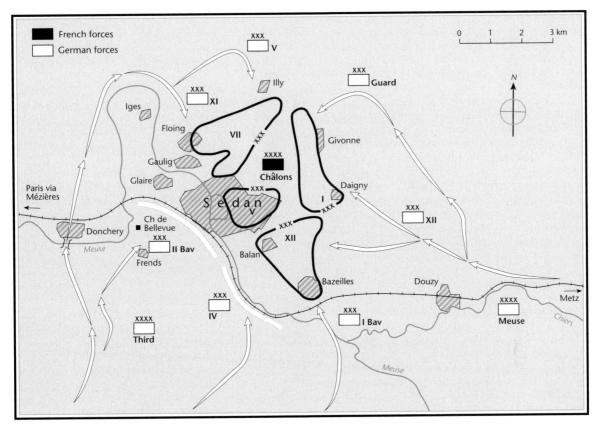

The **Franco-Prussian war,** 1870. The battle of Sedan, 1 September 1870.

intent on crossing the swollen Moselle to make for Châlons via Verdun, would not permit a counter-attack.

Squeezing through Metz would not have been easy even had French staff-work been slicker. As it was, Bazaine's army moved slower than he or his opponents expected, and the 16th found it between Gravelotte and Mars la Tour, west of the Moselle. A corps of Second Army, which had crossed the river south of Metz, swung into the French flank, unexpectedly provoking a major battle. Rezonville could have been a French victory had Bazaine shown the determination of his opponents, but he weakly retired towards Metz.

While Bazaine drew up facing westwards on the heights above the Moselle, Moltke wheeled First and Second Armies to face him. On 18 August, without grasping the extent of Bazaine's position, Moltke slid northwards along it, and a general action, the battle of Gravelotte/Saint-Privat, blazed up as German corps swung in to attack (see RE-ZONVILLE/GRAVELOTTE, BATTLES OF). Had Bazaine counterattacked he might have won a considerable victory, but towards evening the Saxon corps curled round his northern flank to take Saint-Privat, forcing him to fall back onto Metz.

Moltke left Frederick Charles with First Army and four corps of Second Army to *blockade Metz. The crown prince of Saxony was given the new Meuse Army, comprising three of First Army's corps and two cavalry divisions. On 23 August the Germans set off, looking for MacMahon's Army of Châlons, comprising the battered I, V, and VII Corps from Alsace, as well as the fresh XII Corps, a total of over 100,000 men. MacMahon was beset by contradictory instructions from Paris, encumbered by the emperor, who had left Metz just before the Germans cut the Verdun road, and was logistically dependent on the railway. Eventually ordered to relieve Bazaine, he stumbled north-eastwards and on 1 September was crushed between Third Army and the Meuse Army at *Sedan.

Napoleon was captured at Sedan and news of the battle brought down the government. In its place arose the Government of National Defence, dominated by politicians from the moderate Left: Gen Louis Trochu, who had long warned of imminent disaster, was president of the council and war minister, Jules Favre foreign minister, and Leon Gambetta minister of the interior. Favre met Bismarck at Ferrières on 18 September, but found armistice terms impossibly harsh. The new government had already set about calling the nation to arms. This was no easy task. Many of its newly appointed prefects lacked experience, old political divisions remained, and there was apathy in areas remote from the German threat.

As the Germans closed in on Paris a delegation was established at Tours to carry on the government's business. On 7 October Gambetta left in a *balloon to take charge of the delegation and unite, in his energetic person, the portfolios of the interior and war. With the assistance of Charles de Freycinet, engineer turned war administrator, he hurled himself into creating the Armies of National Defence. Civilian specialists were swept into service, arms contracts were placed abroad and domestic production was stepped up, and restrictions on promotion and appointment were swept away. It was a towering achievement, even if the armies conjured up were ultimately unsuccessful. There were never enough trained officers or *NCOs, staff-work was lamentable, standardization of weapons impossible, and for every Frenchman who fought with the armies or the irregular *francs-tireurs* there were more who stayed at home.

There were some regulars left. Garrisons, units, and individuals had escaped the destruction of the imperial armies, and there was also the rump of the Army of the Rhine at Metz. Bazaine's lacklustre performance had highlighted his limited capacity, but it would have taken extraordinary military and political skills to have enabled his force to have played a decisive role. After half-hearted attempts to break out, Bazaine surrendered on 29 October. Strasbourg, that other cornerstone of the frontier, had already capitulated.

For the remainder of the war operations focused on the siege of Paris and attempts by French provincial armies to bring succour to the capital or limit penetration. Proximity to Paris made the activities of the Army of the Loire the most important. It was reconstituted, after the fall of Orléans in October, by the veteran Gen d'Aurelle des Paladines. On 9 November he beat the Bavarians at Coulmiers and recaptured Orléans. Frederick Charles was sent down with reinforcements and, after manoeuvres which caused disquiet in royal headquarters, checked a French assault on Beaune-la-Rolande on 28 November. On 1 December Chanzy's corps won a scrambling victory near Artenay, rousing Gambetta to a fever pitch of expectation, but over the next few days the Germans beat Chanzy at Loigny, broke Aurelle's centre north of Orléans, and went on to take the city. The two divided portions of the army were reorganized under Chanzy and Bourbaki, who had escaped from Metz. Chanzy lost Le Mans on 11 January 1871, and was trying, with indomitable resolution, to rebuild his army when the armistice supervened.

Bourbaki fell back on Bourges, where he rested the three corps constituting his army. Gambetta now considered threatening German communications by thrusting up from the valley of the Saône. Local forces had caused the Germans concern around Dijon, but it was evident that they would need reinforcing to act with real effect. Freycinet de-

cided to shift two of Bourbaki's corps to the Saône by rail, and bring up another corps from Lyons, with a view to taking Dijon and moving northwards. The scheme was ruined by appalling weather, logistic difficulties, and a disunited command. On 9 January Bourbaki beat Werder at Villersexel, but a three-day French attack on well-prepared positions on the Lisaine failed. The arrival of German reinforcements under Manteuffel sealed Bourbaki's fate. With his army in hopeless retreat, he tried to kill himself. His successor, Clinchant, marched some 80,000 survivors into Switzerland.

Months before, Bourbaki had raised the Army of the North, which fought a stubborn battle at Villers-Bretonneux, near Amiens, on 24 November. His successor in Picardy was Faidherbe, a distinguished colonial administrator with a real understanding of his fragile army. On 9 December he surprised the fortress of Ham, and on the 23rd held his ground outside Amiens against a large-scale attack. In early January he fought a difficult battle at Bapaume, although he could not prevent the fall of Peronne. Finally, he was pressed to mount a limited offensive to distract German attention from Paris, and on the 19th Goeben beat him at Saint-Quentin. Faidherbe lost a third of his army, and kept the survivors in fortresses until the armistice was signed.

The Germans had encircled Paris on 20 September, with the Meuse Army to the north, Third Army to the south, and Royal Headquarters at Versailles. Its garrison totalled about 400,000 men, of varying quality, from two notionally 'regular' corps to an assortment of National Guard. German refusal to assault forced Trochu to take the initiative. On 30 September he launched a limited attack and tried another two weeks later. The latter's relative success encouraged 'Le Plan Trochu', a large-scale attack to the west. A preliminary thrust on 21 October seemed promising, but news of Aurelle's victory at Coulmiers persuaded the government to change the direction of the attack. It went in eastwards, between Champigny and Brie on 30 November, energetically led by Ducrot, once the most capable of the Army of Châlon's corps commanders. Although it bit deep into German lines and worried the crown prince of Saxony, the sortie was never close to a breakthrough. On 21 December Trochu attacked again, this time towards Le Bourget, with far worse results: the turn of the year saw the French command locked in bitter indecision as to the next steps.

At Versailles, friction between Bismarck and Moltke was sharpened by the former's demand that Paris should be bombarded. It was not until 5 January that German guns opened fire, and although the bombardment devastated outlying forts, its effect on *morale was perverse: not for the last time, citizens became bitter rather than cowed. In response to popular pressure Trochu launched 90,000 men against Buzenval, on the western edge of Paris. The venture was hopeless from the start, and its collapse was the last straw: after a flurry of civil unrest, Favre asked Bismarck for terms.

Negotiations began on 23 January, an armistice was signed five days later, and preliminaries of peace were agreed on 26 February. France lost Alsace and Lorraine (though she kept Belfort, whose successful defence had made it a national icon) and paid an indemnity of 5 milliard francs. It was no recipe for lasting peace. France could never forget the lost provinces, and the proclamation of the German empire at Versailles was but one symbol of a *militarism which was to feed on the army's achievement. France hastened to copy the institutions which had helped achieve victory, and Europe entered a dangerous era when military power rested upon universal conscription, relentless technological improvement, and general staff honing plans for a war whose likelihood entered deep into the spirit of the age.   RH

Howard, Michael, *The Franco-Prussian War* (London, 1961).

Franks were a Germanic people who invaded and conquered the prosperous central provinces of Roman Gaul during the 5th and 6th centuries. Dominating present-day northern France, Belgium, and Western Germany, they established the most powerful Barbarian kingdom in Europe after the disintegration of the Roman empire and, after their conversion to Christianity, the strongest Christian kingdom in early medieval western Europe. The name of France is derived from their name.

The Franks appear to have developed in the 3rd century from the combination of several Germanic peoples. They were divided into three groups: the Salians, established around the Ijssel river; the Ripuarians, on the right bank of the Rhine; and the Chatti, or Hessians. In the 3rd century, the Franks unsuccessfully attempted to invade Roman Gaul. They were more successful in the 4th century and in 358 Rome abandoned the area between the Meuse and Scheldt rivers to the Salian Franks. Nonetheless, during these drawn-out struggles, many of the Salian Franks had recognized Rome's authority and some Frankish leaders had become Roman allies. Indeed, many Franks served as auxiliary soldiers in the *Roman army.

When the *Vandals launched a massive invasion of Gaul in 406, decades of fighting ensued, overstretching the Roman defences. The Franks took advantage of the decline in Roman power and they began to expand their territory at the expense of the Romans, edging into north-eastern Gaul. The Franks' establishment in this area meant that the former Roman province of Germania was lost to Roman rule by 480. As the Franks colonized the territories of former Roman Gaul, they mixed and married with the current inhabitants. Therefore the small Gallo-Roman population was soon integrated with the German invaders and Latin ceased to be the everyday language. Unlike the Romans and *Goths, the Franks did not prohibit marriage between conquering and conquered peoples, hence the rapid assimilation of the populations in areas they colonized. This meant that the subjects of the Frank kings whatever their origin rapidly came to consider themselves as Franks and the Frankish kingdom soon assumed a political rather than ethnic connotation.

In 481–2, Clovis I became ruler of the Salian Franks of Tournai. Clovis subdued the other Salian and Ripuarian tribes. He then led the united Franks in a series of campaigns against the ever-weakening Roman empire and brought all of northern Gaul under Frankish rule by 497. Clovis also subdued the Burgundians and then drove southwards, defeating the Visigoths who had established themselves in southern Gaul. This meant that virtually the whole of what now is France was under Frankish control, even if Frankish settlement itself was mainly in the north and east of the territory. Clovis took a Christian wife, Clotilda, and therefore converted to Christianity. He was baptized at Rheims, probably at Easter 496, and the mass adoption of orthodox Christianity by the Franks served further to unite them as a people. It also gained them the support of the remaining Gallo-Roman elements in Gaul. Clovis was part of the Merovingian dynasty, founded by his grandfather, Merovich. As a result of Clovis's rule, a huge Merovingian empire stretched from the Pyrenees to Bavaria. By the time he died after a reign of 30 years in his new capital Paris, Clovis had founded what Lavise called 'not a nation but an historical force' which gave rise both to France and the German empire. His Merovingian successors extended Frankish powers east of the Rhine.

The Merovingian dynasty was displaced by the Carolingian family in the 8th century. *Charlemagne reigned as 'the King of the Franks' from 768 to 814. After 53 campaigns and a 'lifetime in the saddle', he extended the Frankish territories in all directions. In co-operation with the papacy, which had recently severed its links with Constantinople, he restored the western Roman empire and spread Christianity into central and northern Germany. Under Charlemagne, the powerful and extensive Frankish empire reached its zenith. Charlemagne had been the unifying force of the realm; after his death it soon disintegrated. The break-up of the Carolingian empire and the Franks' constant feuding gave opportunities that the *Vikings and other hostile peoples were quick to exploit.

In the succeeding centuries the people of the west Frankish kingdom (France) continued to call themselves Franks, although the Frankish element had long since merged into the rest of the population. In Germany the name survived as Franconia (Franken), a Duchy extending from the Rhineland to the east along the main river.   MCM

Frederick II 'the Great', King of Prussia (1713–86).
The career of Frederick 'the Great' defies a simple appreciation, despite the attempts of Wilhelmine and Nazi Germany to appropriate his memory as a national icon. He was a cultured aesthete who loved music, architecture, and

philosophy, even corresponding at length with Voltaire. Yet at the same time he was also a brutal and cynical warmonger, who dragged his kingdom through series of wars that emptied his treasury and killed a large portion of his subjects. Even his reputation as a military genius is open to question. Certainly, he won some startling victories and hung on to his conquests against the odds, but nevertheless his military system merely perfected the accepted view of the art of war, as understood by many of his contemporaries. Furthermore, when Frederick lost a battle, he tended to lose bloodily, and his record contains as many disasters as triumphs. Perhaps it is this very drama that provides the attraction that continues to fascinate military historians.

Frederick's tutelage was at the boorish armed camp of his father Frederick William's court. He inherited an efficient army and a well-organized state on his accession in 1740 and resolved to win his spurs by an unprovoked attack on Austrian-held Silesia (thus initiating the *War of the Austrian Succession), surmising that the new Empress Maria Theresa would be too weak and unsure of her position to lead a convincing resistance to his naked ambition. He met the Austrian army at Mollwitz where his infantry performed sterling service but Frederick himself fled at the head of his nervy cavalry. Thereafter his performance earned him more credit, and at Chotusitz in 1742, the chagrined Prussian cavalry restored their reputation by shattering the Austrian lines in a headlong charge. During these battles Frederick displayed little, if any, military skill and was rescued by the training and bravery of his troops and the skill of his generals.

He made peace with the Treaty of Breslau in 1742 and abandoned his allies, the French, to their own devices. By 1744 the Austrians were resurgent, and it looked as if they would invade Silesia, therefore Frederick launched the second Silesian war that was destined to last until 1745. He had rebuilt his army, which now stood at 140,000 strong, and with it he invaded Bohemia. Soon isolated and nearly surrounded by strong Austrian forces, he was obliged to undertake an arduous retreat that cost him 17,000 deserters alone. Prince Charles of Lorraine moved to invade Silesia in 1745, and was drawn down into the plains around Hohenfriedburg, where Frederick's army managed to combine infantry and cavalry in a devastating series of feints and assaults resulting in total defeat for the Austrians, and inflicting 13,000 casualties on them. Once more, Frederick swooped on Bohemia, but was forced to retire yet again, facing Charles of Lorraine in a strongly defended position at Soor. On 30 September 1745 Frederick rapidly assaulted the Austrian left and fought his way back into Silesia. The Austrians then attacked through Saxony, but were repulsed at Hennersdorf and Gorlitz. The final nail in the coffin was Dessau's rout of the Austrians and Saxons at Kesselsdorf on 15 December 1745. The Austrians were staggered by this series of defeats, and swiftly sought terms. A treaty was duly

signed at Dresden on 25 December and based on these experiences he wrote the *General Principles Of War* in 1748.

Prussia's victory seemed complete: Frederick had secured important new territories, revenue, and population by force of arms. However, his nature as a cynical pragmatist who would abandon an ally at the drop of a tricorne was exposed. His plans were to come unravelled as Austria sought a rapprochement with France, and it was soon clear that the ensuing 'Diplomatic Revolution' would leave him dangerously exposed, especially if, as seemed likely, Russia turned hostile. Frederick faced the possibility of war on every front and prepared accordingly, increasing his army to 154,000 strong. In a pre-emptive strike in August 1756 he attacked Saxony, as the weak link in the alliance against him, without warning, thus unleashing the agony of the *Seven Years War. The Saxons dug in, and Frederick was checked until the winter, even though he had beaten Browne's Austrians at Lobositz that October. An invasion of Bohemia the following spring opened with an assault outside Prague on 6 May 1757, but the Austrians had learned some important lessons from the second Silesian war, and managed to inflict some 13,000 casualties on the victorious Prussians, which Frederick could ill afford.

The formidable Austrian Gen Daun marched quickly to the relief of Prague, facing Frederick at Kolin on 18 June. Frederick opened with his traditional echelon attack, but the whitecoats stood firm and beat him off, inflicting another 12,000 casualties on Frederick's army. This wastage of manpower could not go on. Prussia was a relatively small kingdom compared to Austria, France, and Russia, and was in danger of bleeding to death. To add to his troubles, while he was in Bohemia his capital Berlin was sacked by the enemy. It was then that Frederick embarked upon the campaign that put him among the great captains. He marched west and crushed a Franco-Imperial army under *Soubise at *Rossbach in November, then promptly turned about and shattered the Austrians at *Leuthen in December 1757. This pair of stunning victories secured his borders for the time being, and established his reputation as a master at the use of internal lines.

However, his enemies were not ready to give up, and the Russians fought Frederick's army to a bloody standstill at Zorndorf on 25 August 1758. Later that year in October the Austrians under Daun surrounded Frederick's camp at Hochkirch, obliging him to fight his way out for the loss of 9,500 men and most of his artillery. True native-born Prussians, Brandenburgers, and Pomeranians were now at a premium in Prussian service, and Frederick was increasingly forced to rely on foreign recruits, often forcibly impressed and very harshly treated, who proved unequal to the ambitious tactical designs, and the desperate defensive countermarching of their draconian master.

Eventually the Russians managed to combine their forces with the Austrians, and at Kunersdorf in August 1759, Frederick had to face their combined armies, strongly entrenched with plenty of powerful artillery and commanded by the Russian general Sultykov. The Prussians were cut down almost to a man and by nightfall only 3,000 had escaped out of an army of over 50,000. It was a disaster of the first order, but Daun was still wary of the ever-aggressive Frederick, with reason. A year later at Leignitz the Prussians smashed aside the Austrians before they could once again link up with the Russians and in November Frederick beat Daun again at Torgau. But Frederick's victories were becoming ever more costly: at Torgau he lost 13,000 to the Austrians' 11,000, and was scraping the bottom of the manpower barrel when in January 1762 the Russians withdrew on the death of the Tsarina Elizabeth, which saved Frederick from almost certain ruin.

There remained the indecisive Potato War of 1778–9, so named because the soldiery spent more time scrabbling around for food than fighting. Frederick had retained Silesia, but at a cost which argues that he made war simply because he liked it. His later years were spent rebuilding his ravaged kingdom and army, and the latter became the exemplar of what ferocious drill and discipline could achieve. Its failings were to be pitilessly shown up at *Jena/Auerstadt by a very much greater commander. It has been argued that Frederick's legacy of *militarism infected first the Prussian and then the German character, but this is to overlook that Prussia had been a frontier state for centuries. The fighting power of the Prussians was nothing new; Frederick simply gave it a new focus.   TM

Duffy, Christopher, *Frederick the Great: A Military Life* (London, 1985).

Nosworthy, Brent, *The Anatomy of Victory: Battle Tactics 1689–1763* (New York, 1993).

Showalter, Denis E., *The Wars of Frederick the Great* (Harlow, 1996).

Fredericksburg, battle of (1862), defeat of the Union army under the command of *Burnside, grimly reminiscent of his performance at *Antietam three months earlier. He planned a swift crossing of the Rappahannock at Fredericksburg to outflank *Lee, but a three-week delay in the arrival of *pontoons permitted the Confederates to fortify the ridge overlooking the town. It took a further two days to establish crossings in the teeth of deadly sniping by Barksdale's Mississippians, but finally throughout 13 December Sumner's Grand Division launched nine completely unsuccessful attacks in the open against a stone wall and a sunken road held by Longstreet's corps, covered by fire from Confederate artillery on the commanding Marye's Heights.

Better progress was made on the Union left by Franklin's Grand Division where, despite galling fire from flanking *horse artillery under Pelham—a rare event in this war—Meade's division penetrated a weak spot in A. P. Hill's division of Jackson's corps. Unsupported and counter-attacked by Early's division, he was thrown back and suffered 40 per cent casualties. Union losses were 12,500 against under 5,000 for the Confederates. A satisfied Lee commented: 'It is well that war is so terrible—we should grow too fond of it.'

HEB

French and Indian war (1754–63), precursor and part of the worldwide *Seven Years War for empire. Smouldering rivalry for dominance of the Ohio valley burst into flames in May 1754, when an expedition under *Washington ambushed an alleged French 'embassy' that was stalking him. Later captured by the brother of the slain emissary, Washington was released after signing a confession to the 'murder'.

In 1755, newly arrived with regular army reinforcements, Maj Gen Braddock prepared to advance into the Ohio valley from Virginia, pausing only to alienate potential Indian allies and the colonial militia by his arrogance. With Washington as his ADC, he marched into a French-led Indian ambush at the *Monongahela, losing three-quarters of his men, his money chest, his campaign plan (written in London), and his life. Washington remained with him to the end, escaping with several bullet holes in his clothing. The defeat encouraged previously neutral and even well-disposed Indians to drive in the frontier of settlement by 150 miles, killing hundreds.

Thus long before the formal declaration of hostilities in 1756, the conflict in North America was already a full-scale war. The presence or absence of Indian allies defined the earlier engagements, in which the French generally prevailed. Defending his use of atrocity-prone Indians to do most of the fighting, the French governor boasted that thanks to them 100 British died for every Frenchman. Not counted by either side, Indian casualties are unknown.

British success during this time was limited to the capture of Nova Scotia (Fr.: Acadia) and the deportation of the French settlers, who became the 'Cajuns' of Louisiana. The New York militia with Mohawk allies won a rare victory at Lake George, and Fort William Henry was built on the spot, only to be taken (an episode depicted in *The Last of the Mohicans*) and razed after the 1756 arrival of Montcalm to command French forces. Before that, he seized New York's western outpost at Fort Oswego, and with it British hopes of controlling Lake Ontario. To forestall their move towards an overt alliance with the French, desperate colonial officials concluded treaties with the Iroquois confederation and the Delaware in 1756–8, which gave up ceded lands and promised an end to British expansion into their territory. Neither side, of course, had any intention of respecting the terms once the French were defeated.

Under the hammer of defeat and recognizing the shortcomings of the regular army, British colonial authorities encouraged the development of light infantry units and tactics better suited to frontier warfare. The outstanding practitioner was Robert *Rogers, commissioned in 1755 by the governor of Massachusetts to 'distress the French and their allies' by every means possible. But although his Rangers and a similar regiment raised by his brother were later to be incorporated into the regular army, it is fair to say that the lessons taught by this war were never accepted by the British army. Contempt for colonial militia and pound-foolish parsimony towards potentially invaluable Indian allies prevailed through the *American independence war to the *War of 1812.

The colonial militia turned the military tide in mid-1758, and this was more important than any dubious treaty in detaching Indian allies from the French. They lost *Louisbourg, Oswego, and Duquesne in quick succession, closing their St Lawrence lifeline to France and their Lake Ontario route west of the Alleghenies. Finally even the staunchly anti-British Seneca abandoned them in 1759, which contributed to the fall of Forts Niagara and Ticonderoga in July. In September *Quebec fell to a daring assault led by *Wolfe in which both he and Montcalm died. Although the French counter-attacked in May 1760, bottling up the British garrison, it was sustained by the navy until relieved when militia columns advanced from the south, combining to take Montreal in September. Some French resistance continued, but the rest of the war in North America was mainly against Indian guerrilla outbreaks.

The biggest of these was in the south where the Cherokee, in return for promises from the governor of South Carolina to defend their homelands against the pro-French Choctaw and the opportunistic Creek, sent warriors north to assist in the 1758 attack on Fort Duquesne. The forts built to 'protect' the Cherokee homeland proved to be a Trojan horse, and when a group of returning warriors clashed with scalp-hunting frontiersmen, simmering discontent erupted into an uprising which took four years and two armies to subdue. The Treaty of Paris in February 1763 formally ended French participation in the war, but within months *Pontiac's rebellion was to give renewed significance to the Indian part.   HEB

French army The French army's rise paralleled that of the state it served. Fifteenth-century kings controlled French-recruited 'bands' of infantry and *compagnies d'ordonnance* of heavy cavalry, as well as foreign *mercenaries. In 1483 the *bandes de Picardie* garrisoned the northern frontier, and were to become the Régiment de Picardie, senior regiment in the French line and, by its proud boast, the oldest in Christendom. During the 16th century a formal *rank-structure solidified and more regiments were raised. Mercenary regiments—Swiss, German, Scots, Irish, and Italian—featured prominently in infantry and cavalry alike, and in the 1630s regiments of marine infantry were formed. In 1643 the French defeated the Spaniards at *Rocroi in a battle which marked both the end of Spanish military supremacy and the French army's coming of age.

In the late 17th century the army developed to support the forward foreign policy of *Louis XIV, under the tutelage of *Louvois, his war administrator. It grew huge in wartime, at times exceeding half a million men. Captains ran their companies like commercial concerns, recruiting genuine volunteers, the duped, the dispossessed, and men pressed by the civil authorities. *Desertion was endemic: when Marshal de Vivonne inspected the infantry on the 1677 Sicilian expedition he found that 4,150 of the supposed 6,900 were missing. Provincial militia battalions, raised in 1688 for home defence and recruited by ballot, soon became recruiting pools for the regular army.

Although Louis's wars made fortunes for contractors who supplied the army, there were concerns about the cost of war and the conduct of soldiers. Shortage of recruits encouraged reliance on mercenaries: in the 18th century 12 per cent of peacetime and 20 per cent of wartime strength were foreign-recruited. There were complaints that the ranks were filled by rootless men, and officer *morale wavered because of low pay, slow promotion, and damaging defeats, notably in the 'terrible year' of 1757, when French armies were beaten in Germany and North America. Garrison life was tedious, and *barracks became 'honourable prisons' where soldiers were packed together, monotonously fed and vulnerable to epidemics like that which killed half the Régiment de la Motte in 1722. Discharged soldiers often took to brigandage: in 1718 one formed a company of footpads which raided the roads between Paris and Caen. When he was arrested, 30 guardsmen, fearing that he would implicate them, deserted.

This poorly regarded army produced some outstanding leaders and redoubtable soldiers, and several developments had long-term importance. Tactics and organization were intelligently debated. There was a long-running dispute between the proponents of shallow infantry formations, configured primarily for fire, and deeper formations, intended for shock, and *Guibert, one of the army's leading thinkers, eventually advocated a mixed order combining some of the benefits of both. *Gribeauval, inspector-general of artillery, developed a family of standardized cannon, and French military engineers set the standards by which their profession was judged. The great *Vauban had dominated engineering under Louis XIV. In the 18th century the engineers, trained in the school at Mézières, formed a professional corps whose efforts, in civil as well as military *engineering, did much to strengthen the state.

Some writers hailed peasant citizen-soldiers—'more sober, stronger, more used to work, and attached to their motherland because of the property they own there'—as the best recruits, but town-dwellers were over-represented in the army, making up about three-fifths of its strength. Many regarded the profession of arms as a career like any other, and were irritated by the poor regard in which their countrymen held them. 'Dogs, loose women and soldiers not admitted', warned signs at the entrance to public parks.

Prussian customs were copied, and the soldier of the 1780s, strangled by straps and shoulder-belts, was repeatedly drilled in close order. The Comte de Saint-Germain, Louis XV's war minister, instituted reforms which ran squarely into some of those vested interests which bedevilled the last decades of the *ancien régime*. In an effort to improve the soldier's lot he replaced a variety of punishments by beating with the flat of the sword, only to discover that men regarded this as even more degrading. 'Strike with the point,' complained one, 'and that would do less harm'.

Officer recruitment posed particular problems. In 1751 the École Militaire Royale was established to train officers. In 1776 it was replaced by twelve provincial military schools, but was resuscitated in 1777. The officer corps contained both minor nobility—some of whom, like François de Chevert a foundling from Verdun who rose to the rank of general, had gained the gentlemanly *particule* through their own efforts—who hoped to make their way by the sword, and courtiers with no real interest in their profession. As the upper aristocracy strengthened its grip first on senior appointments, and then, with the Ségur edict of 1781, on commissioned rank itself, so the army contained more and more potentially disaffected junior officers, as well as *NCOs whose hopes of promotion were blighted. Between 1781 and 1789 only 41 officers were commissioned from the ranks. One observer was to write that 'The defection of the army was not one of the causes of the Revolution. It was the Revolution itself.'

In 1789 the army consisted of household troops, which included the French and Swiss guards, regular forces—around 113,000 infantry, 32,000 cavalry, and under 10,000 gunners—and the militia of about 75,000. French regiments were unreliable when faced with disturbances in Paris, and on 14 July, the day the Bastille fell, five of the six battalions of French guards joined the insurgents. Elsewhere troops often disobeyed orders to disperse rioters. Desertion rocketed, with many deserters joining the newly formed National Guard. Yet some regiments, especially German-speaking units from the eastern frontier, remained reliable. Many NCOs—now termed *sous-officiers* (under officers) rather than *bas-officiers* (lower officers)—sought promotion, but were anxious not to see a wholesale abolition of rank in which they too would suffer.

In 1790–1 there was conflict within the army, reflecting polarization in the regiments as well as pressure from local activists. Many officers fled abroad—about 6,000 had left by the end of 1791—and soldiers continued to desert in droves, some joining national volunteer battalions, first raised in 1791, where prospects were better. All this was paralleled by political debate on the composition and role of the army, set against a background of internal unrest and, from April 1793, foreign war. Some argued that the army should simply be reformed, remaining a small, professional force. Others wished to see it transformed into a citizen army, whose members laid down the plough to take up the musket.

The Constituent Assembly recast regulations, reformed military *justice, and threw commissioned rank open to both NCOs and patriotic outsiders. By 1792 emigration and desertion meant that most soldiers had joined the army since the Revolution, and only 4 per cent were now foreigners. Regiments lost their old titles and were numbered. Yet something of the old army's spirit still remained. When the 50th Regiment attacked at Jemappes in 1792 its men, remembering it as the Régiment de Navarre, shouted the old war-cry: 'En avant, Navarre sans peur.'

In August 1793 the Convention decided that, instead of calling for volunteers and levying soldiers to meet specified targets, it would 'requisition' all fit males between 18 and 25, and decreed a *levée en masse*. This influx of citizen-soldiers, many of them active sans-culottes, intensified radicalism within the army, and many officers were expelled or guillotined. Along with sans-culotte politics came revolutionary tactics. The bayonet should be taken to the enemies of France; if bayonets were lacking, then the pike had been too long neglected. Prisoners risked being 'sacrificed to the spirits of our unfortunate brothers who also had been killed without pity'.

That year the first great amalgamation replaced infantry regiments by demi-brigades, sweeping together white-coated regulars and blue-coated volunteers as battalions of old regiments were posted to different demi-brigades. Blue became the army's uniform colour, but the distinction between regular and volunteer lived on: a recruit is still called a 'blue'. A divisional structure had already been introduced, with two brigades of infantry, a regiment of cavalry, and a detachment of artillery grouped together. This did not solve the problems faced by French generals during the *French Revolutionary wars. Frequent inexperience, constant insecurity, political pressures—often reflected through representatives with the armies—and the patchy quality of troops all combined to make their task difficult. Tactics evolved as wilder sans-culotte notions were replaced by solid training which built on pre-war theory to develop use of both *column and line, with *tirailleurs skirmishing ahead to prepare the way for assaults which were sometimes delivered with a dash that the stately warriors of old Europe could not resist. The artillery had been less damaged by emigration than other arms, and its quality often told: at *Valmy in 1792, after a sustained cannonade, the Duke of Brunswick decided not to attack the French position, a decision which probably cost him the war.

The *levée en masse* produced an army with a theoretical strength of almost 1,200,000, but its effective strength probably peaked at about 800,000. In 1795 a second amalgamation restructured the infantry again. In 1798 'requisition' was replaced by conscription, for four years in peacetime and an unlimited period in wartime. Although the proportion of old soldiers had now fallen to a mere 3.3 per cent, the army of 1798 was in general well trained, much better disciplined than in the recent past, and the young Bonaparte's stunning 1796 Italian campaign had shown what it could achieve.

Napoleon's army was built on these foundations. He maintained it through conscription, whose burden became increasingly resented, especially after 1812. In all some two million men were conscripted between 1800 and 1814. There were often more than 50,000 refractory conscripts and deserters, and more than half the conscripts from some southern *départements* declined to report for duty. Foreign troops made up about a third of French strength after 1809. The term *régiment* was revived in 1803, and Napoleon was careful to nurture martial spirit by the institution of the Légion d'Honneur, spectacular military ceremonies, and a system of emulation which established the Imperial Guard, itself eventually divided into Old, Middle, and Young, as the apogee of the army. The emperor's fierce energy enabled him to deal with much routine administration himself, and his war ministers were little more than his instruments.

At its best the imperial army had few equals, and the *Austerlitz campaign of 1806 and the *Jena/Auerstadt campaign a year later combined patriotic fervour, solid experience, and inspirational leadership. It was worn down by a long war, in which the 'Spanish ulcer' (see PENINSULAR WAR) played an enervating part. It remained dependent on its master's fragile genius, and suffered from the fact that few of Napoleon's marshals had real talents for independent command. Although Napoleon was able to return from exile to fight the campaign of the *Hundred Days that culminated in *Waterloo, by 1815 France was war-weary and convinced that military glory had been bought at too dear a price.

The restored Bourbons brought with them the military baggage of the old regime. The army was reduced to little more than 100,000 men, and many Napoleonic officers found themselves on *half pay, their places taken by returned émigrés. Infantry regiments, briefly replaced by departmental legions, were still recruited by conscription. In the 1830 Revolution the army offered little support to the Restoration monarchy, and with Louis Philippe on the throne there was the familiar scramble for promotions. The Loi Soult of 1832 decreed that at least half the army's second lieutenants should be commissioned from the ranks. The others were to come from military *academies, *Saint-Cyr for the infantry and cavalry and the *École Polytechnique for gunners and *sappers. In practice this minimum was exceeded, and although ranker officers generally rose no higher than captain they included at least one marshal, the unfortunate *Bazaine.

The same law refined conscription, dividing the annual contingent of conscripts into two parts. The first, its members selected by lot, served for seven years with the *colours: the second formed an untrained reserve. Those who could afford it paid a replacement to serve on their behalf. The law of 1855 made slight modifications, and it was not until 1868 that the Loi Niel, passed in the aftermath of

Prussian victory in the *Austro-Prussian war of 1866, attempted to introduce something approaching universal conscription.

The army created by the Loi Soult had many virtues. It was tough and, with frequent fighting in *Algeria and the *Italian, *Crimean, and *Mexican campaigns, experienced. It met the strategic requirements of France at a time when wars of national survival were perceived to be rare, and frontier fortresses were expected to buy time to raise fresh troops. It also met the political remit of the Second Empire of *Napoleon III, to which many of its officers gave their personal support, for its long-service soldiers, imbued with *esprit militaire*, would be likely to defend the regime against its internal enemies.

French defeat in the *Franco-Prussian war of 1870–1 was a reflection of these flawed assumptions. Although the army of the Second Empire had the *chassepot breech-loader and the *mitrailleuse machine gun, it was essentially an expeditionary, not a European, army, and its attempts to muddle through cost it dear in the age of the railway and national armies. The Armies of National Defence, which kept the field after the defeat of the imperial armies, pointed the way ahead.

The suppression of the Paris *Commune in 1871 reinforced the Left's suspicions of the army. As Alistair Horne was to write: 'A deep trench had been dug between the bourgeoisie and the masses, between the professional army and the Left, which would stretch on into the far distance'. Yet the years after the Franco-Prussian war were the army's Golden Age. A clear sense of national purpose, inspired by determination to expunge the stain of 1870–1 and recover the lost provinces of Alsace and Lorraine, permitted the introduction of universal conscription in 1872–5. Old military families rediscovered the profession of arms. There was a clear understanding that the army must be kept out of politics. A *general staff was created, with a Conseil Supérieure de la Guerre and, from 1890, an army CGS. The staff busied itself with perfecting a peacetime organization which meshed closely with the demands of war, so that the chaos of 1870 could never be repeated. Regiments were given fixed garrisons and grew local roots: the 39th hailed from Rouen, the 41st from Rennes, and the 110th from Dunkirk. Weapons and equipment were comprehensively transformed, and in the new 75 mm French gunners had a weapon which set the standard for field artillery.

The honeymoon did not last. The *Dreyfus affair, which broke in 1894, split the nation. The army found itself used increasingly against strikes and riots, being pilloried by the Left, and sometimes finding the strain on its loyalty too much to bear: the 100th Regiment mutinied in sympathy with rioters in 1907. In a misguided effort to nurture officers who could be relied upon 'because of their Republican sentiments', the war minister, Gen André, kept secret files which specified political and religious sympathies: the future Marshal *Foch found his promotion delayed because his brother was a Jesuit. Promotion was slow: an officer might remain a lieutenant for twelve to fifteen years and a captain for fifteen to twenty. While bureaucracy and inertia ruled in metropolitan France, service in the colonies offered challenge and responsibility, providing a shaft of light which helped illuminate the army even in its darkest days.

Yet when war came in 1914 the army rose to the challenge. Mobilization was slick and popular support for the war—despite deep reservations, especially in the countryside—was robust. There had been something of a national revival already, with the philosopher Henri Bergson expounding the concept of *l'élan vital* and the novelist Ernest Psichari demanding 'a proud and violent army'. The regulations of 1913 proclaimed: 'The French army, returning to its traditions, recognizes no law save that of the offensive.' Michael *Howard has observed that, allowing for Gallic bravura, one finds the same sentiments expressed by British and German writers of the period. Douglas Porch suggests that it was precisely because the French army was so riven by strife that it adopted such a simple-minded *doctrine: anything more complex was beyond it.

The results of Plan XVII, the all-out offensive into the lost provinces, were catastrophic. The army lost 300,000 men and almost 5,000 officers in a fortnight, and, but for the stolid imperturbability of *Joffre, its C-in-C, might easily have lost the war too. For the next eighteen months he mounted repeated offensives, with British help, which produced mounting casualties, leading a general to complain that 'The instrument of victory is being broken in our hands.' By the end of 1915 France had lost half her regular officers and her dead totalled almost what Britain and her dominions were to lose in the whole war. The fighting at *Verdun imposed its own terrible burden, and by the end of 1916 the army was worn to a thread. Its trench newspapers testify to the plight of soldiers who endured harsh conditions, monotonous food, and irregular leave. Many of the best officers had fallen, and their replacements were sometimes more conscious of privilege than duty. Hatred of the *embusqué*—the shirker with a comfortable job and another man's wife—reflected barriers which made many soldiers feel strangers in their own land.

The *Nivelle offensive of April 1917 had been oversold as a war-winning master stroke, and its failure stirred deep-seated discontent into open *mutiny. Much of the army was touched, to a greater or lesser extent, by unrest, but this was not (as military and political leaders feared) the result of a well-organized revolutionary agitation, but rather the response of citizen soldiers to an intolerable situation. Officers might be jostled—even then rarely by their own men—but they were not murdered. *Pétain, who succeeded the disgraced Nivelle, restored morale by a judicious mixture of firmness and attention to justified demands.

Although the Union Sacrée, the patriotic compact between political parties, had managed to survive, there was repeated friction among politicians, and between politi-

cians and soldiers. In November 1917 *Clemenceau became premier. His Jacobin suspicions of the military made him an uncomfortable master, but his remorseless insistence on winning the war gave Foch, appointed supreme Allied commander during the German spring offensive of 1918, the firm support he required. In November 1918 Pres Poincaré entered Metz, capital of Lorraine, with Clemenceau and Foch. He wrote in his diary: 'A day of sovereign beauty. Now I can die.'

It was the army that died. The euphoria of victory proved short-lived, and France found that the world did not recognize its balance of moral credit. French losses, proportionately heavier than German, affected the birth rate to produce 'hollow years' for recruiting in the 1930s. Inflation and unemployment seemed a poor reward for sacrifice, and with the lost provinces regained there seemed no logic in paying for defence. Some officers flirted with fascism, and the Left opposed suggestions that new weapons demanded a smaller, professional, mechanized army. *Weygand, at the head of the army until his retirement in 1935, clashed repeatedly with what he saw as an anti-military government. The *Maginot Line was built to defend much of the Franco-German border, but stopped short in the north. It was not as foolish as is sometimes suggested, but it depended on adequate mobile troops, and it brought with it a 'Maginot mentality' which helped persuade Frenchmen that invasion was impossible.

The French army which went to war in 1939 was marked by all the strains of the inter-war years. It had some good equipment, but lacked comprehensive doctrine. Morale was patchy, and tension between officers and men reflected the distrust of many officers, regular and reserve, for socialism. Defeat in 1940 reflected a failure of command, doctrine, and above all morale. There were some flickers of the old glory: French soldiers gave a much better account of themselves during the second phase of the campaign, when the Germans struck southwards, and against an opportunistic attack from Italy, than historians sometimes recognize.

Defeat split the army. *De Gaulle urged his countrymen to fight on, and Free French soldiers fought in the Middle East, *North Africa, *Italy, and eventually France itself. But the 84-year-old Marshal Pétain, head of the French state controlled from the little spa of Vichy, represented stability and continuity, and the soldiers who remained loyal to him were neither fools nor villains. The line of duty was sometimes far from clear. When the Allies invaded French North Africa in November 1942 some Frenchmen fought against them, and when the Germans moved into the Unoccupied Zone of France the same month at least one French general, de Lattre de Tassigny, disobeyed the government's orders and resisted them.

The post-war army had to cope with the tensions between soldiers who had followed different paths during the war, and did so during the long withdrawal from empire, at a time when military pay and prestige fell. Conscripts were not sent to *Indochina, and the fighting there bore down hard on regulars who felt that they were waging a dirty war without popular support. Defeat at *Dien Bien Phu and the experience of the prison camps which followed it politicized many officers, helping to crystallize the *guerre revolutionnaire* doctrine. The army then sought to apply this in Algeria, so much closer to home and, partly because of the troops it had provided since the 1830s, so close to the army's heart. The legacy of 1940 bore bitter fruit. Some officers, critical of political leadership and alienated from a society which neither understood nor appreciated their efforts, took direct action. There were military coups in Algeria in 1958 and 1961 (see ALGERIAN INDEPENDENCE WAR, and French withdrawal in 1962 was followed by a terrorist campaign in France itself.

The tensions of Algeria lingered on in an army which was incorporated in a defence policy based on the principle of 'Tous Azimuts'—enemies might come from all points of the compass, not just the east—as France withdrew from NATO's command structure. An independent nuclear deterrent, the Force de Frappe, was a prestigious symbol of this new policy. Some traditional frictions remained. On the one hand there were fears that conscripts might be infected by the revolutionary fervour of 1968, and on the other concerns about the officer corps' reaction to the Mitterrand government of 1981. Demands for the abolition of conscription were reinforced by the government's preference for using regulars for intervention operations in former colonies in Africa and, on a larger scale, in the *Gulf war.

In the 1990s France moved closer to NATO, partly because of shared experience on operations in (former) *Yugoslavia, and in 1996 took the controversial decision to abolish conscription. A restructuring programme will downscale an army of 239,000 service personnel in 1996 to 136,000 in 2015. This will involve reducing the number of professional officers and NCOs but recruiting many more professional soldiers, who will require both an attractive career and the prospect of subsequent resettlement; the civilianization of many posts; and the creation of a small volunteer reserve. The reorganization will be governed by three principles: modularity, so that forces can be packaged to meet specific circumstances; economy of force, brought about by reduction in size; and clear separation between the operational chain of command (operational headquarters and projectable units) and the organic chain of command (basic training and administrative support). Many officers who welcome the abolition of conscription on military grounds retain doubts about its wider wisdom, fearing that France and her army might grow apart. If history tells us anything, it is that armies demand popular support: the real challenge facing the French army will be to retain this beyond the millennium.   RH

Corvisier, André (ed.), *Histoire militaire de la France*, 4 vols. (Paris 1992–4).

Gorce, Paul-Marie de la, *The French Army: A Military-Political History* (New York, 1963).
Griffith, P. G., *Military Thought in the French Army 1815–1851* (Manchester, 1979).
Horne, Alistair, *The French Army and Politics 1870–1970* (London, 1984).
Howard, Michael, 'Men against Fire: The Doctrine of the Offensive in 1914', in Peter Paret (ed.), *Makers of Modern Strategy* (Oxford, 1986).
Porch, Douglas, *The March to the Marne* (Cambridge, 1981).

French Foreign Legion There is a fundamental paradox to the Legion: it a polyglot collection of refugees, roués, romantics, and rootless united to form one of history's toughest fighting units. France had long maintained *Swiss regiments, and when they were disbanded in 1830 their soldiers joined the numerous foreign refugees in the country. At the same time Algeria began to develop an appetite for French manpower (see ALGERIA, FRENCH CONQUEST OF). The connection was obvious, and on 9 March 1831 Marshal *Soult, war minister, signed a decree establishing 'A legion of foreigners to be known as the Foreign Legion for service outside France'. It comprised seven battalions, recruited in homogenous national groups, a scheme which was eventually abandoned. Sent to Algeria, the Legion was not sufficiently trusted to be given a proper role in the war against *Abd al-Qadir until it had proved itself by repulsing several raids in 1832.

After further fighting the Legion was sent to Spain to help Queen Cristina against the *Carlists, supporters of her uncle Don Carlos. Sorely tried by being ceded en bloc to Spain, the Legion fought a bitter campaign marred by atrocity and counter-atrocity, with pay and rations in short supply. In 1837 it met the Carlist Foreign Legion at Barbastro. 'Men in the conflicting ranks recognised each other,' recalled a witness, 'called out to each other by their *bruder namen*, and proceeded to disembowel each other with the bayonet.' Gen Conrad, the French commander, was killed rallying his men. The survivors found their bravery rewarded by disbandment in December 1838.

In 1835 the French had begun to raise a new Legion for service in Algeria, and in 1837 it took part in the storm of Constantine. In 1841, reinforced by survivors of the old Legion, who had volunteered to serve on, it was divided into two regiments. Thereafter its history becomes more complex, with individual regiments, and sometimes separate battalions or companies, fighting in different campaigns. In 1843 the Legion began work on what became its depot at Sidi bel Abbes, south of Oran. *Légionnaires* repeatedly proved themselves as adept with pick and shovel as with rifle and bayonet. In 1849 Gen Pelissier congratulated them: 'Out of an encampment you have made a flourishing city, from desolation a fertile township, an image of France.'

Abd al-Qadir surrendered in 1847, but fighting continued, and the 2nd Regiment took part in the capture of the oasis of Zaatcha in 1849. It went on to the *Crimean war, losing 118 killed, including its colonel, and 480 wounded in a single attack. Returning to Algeria, in 1857 it struck the decisive blow at the battle of Ischeriden, advancing without deigning to return fire. In the 1859 *Italian campaign the Legion stormed into Magenta, the battle that gave *MacMahon, its corps commander, his ducal title, and went on to take the cemetery at Solferino.

When the Legion was not sent on the *Mexican expedition its junior officers petitioned *Napoleon III. Some were disciplined, a new commanding officer was appointed, and the Legion duly went. Soon after its arrival in 1863, the 3rd Company of the 1st Battalion was destroyed at *Camerone in an engagement which lives on in Legion history. By the time of French withdrawal in 1867 the Legion had lost almost 2,000 officers and men killed or died of disease.

A Legion battalion fought in France during the *Franco-Prussian war of 1870–1. Thereafter the Legion campaigned in North Africa, playing an important part in the conquest of *Morocco by *Lyautey, facing sporadic risings in Algeria, and, with its mounted companies, pushing deep into the Sahara. It also went on overseas expeditions. In 1882 a battalion was dispatched to Tonkin, to fight against the Chinese and 'Black flag' irregulars. Another battalion formed part of the force sent in the expedition to the West African state of *Dahomey in 1892, and the Legion helped pacify Madagascar in 1895–1905.

In 1914 the Legion was restructured to prevent foreign volunteers from having to fight their countrymen. The scheme was not a success, but from 1915 the Legion maintained a first-rate composite Régiment de Marche on the western front. After the war there was an influx of recruits from Germany, Russia, Poland, and Georgia. So many had served in mounted units that the Legion raised a cavalry regiment, which was soon in action, alongside Legion infantry, in Syria and the Lebanon. There was also sporadic fighting in Morocco, where the Legion played its part in beating the Riff leader Abd-el-Krim.

In 1939 the Legion was swollen by refugees, and several regiments fought in the disastrous 1940 campaign. Thereafter its fortunes were mixed. Units in France were forced to return German refugees, and in Syria in 1941 there were *légionnaires* on both sides, some fighting for Free France and others for the Vichy regime. An outstanding contribution was made by the 13th Demi-Brigade, which fought at Narvik in the *Norwegian campaign, then in the *Abyssinian, *Syrian, *North African, and *Italian campaigns, to land in France in August 1944.

The Legion shared the anguish of withdrawal from empire. Fighting in *Indochina cost it over 10,000 dead. There were five Legion battalions in the decisive battle of *Dien Bien Phu in 1954. With its fall imminent, Col Lalande, commanding the strong point *Isabelle*, led his survivors in a *baroud d'honneur*, walking out to meet death with fixed *bayonets under the pallid light of parachute flares. The

war in Algeria touched the Legion to the heart, and it was implicated in the 1961 coup against the government. Its 1st Parachute Regiment was disbanded: the men sang Edith Piaf's 'Je ne regrette rien' on their way back to barracks for the last time.

After Algerian independence the Legion moved to France and established its depot at Aubagne near Marseilles. Its 2nd Parachute Regiment—2ème REP (Régiment Etranger de Parachutistes)—has spearheaded several intervention operations. It takes French and foreign volunteers, and attracts, as it generally has, the best French officers. If some of its recruits cannot cope with the rigorous training, others still come to find the Legion more of a homeland than a regiment.   RH

French Revolutionary wars (1792–1801). It is the deepest irony that the French Revolution, with its ideals of liberty, equality, and fraternity, led to a quarter-century of bloody war. Although the revolutionaries who formed the constitutional monarchical government of France after the fall of the Bastille in July 1789 regarded war as an aberration of tyrants, it was unlikely that Frederick William of Prussia and Leopold II of Austria would ever reach a modus vivendi with the new regime. In fact on 27 August 1791 they declared common interest in restoring an absolute monarchy in France for the 'welfare of the French nation' and threatened the use of force to bring this about. French royalist émigré forces began to gather at the frontiers and on 7 February 1792 Austria and Prussia signed the Treaty of Berlin against France. Exasperated, the French declared war on 20 April, initiating the War of the First Coalition.

Early clashes were uninspiring: French troops often fled, murdering their officers, and the American independence war veteran Rochambeau resigned in disgust. Then, on 25 July, the Duke of Brunswick, commanding an invasion force on the Rhine, issued a manifesto stating that he would invade to put down the anarchy in France and restore Louis XVI to the 'legitimate authority to which he is entitled', inviting all right-thinking Frenchmen and women to join the invaders in re-establishing the absolute monarchy of the Bourbons and warning that any action against Louis would be met with the sternest retribution. This helped promote further unrest in the already volatile Paris, and, fearing that Louis was in league with the Prussians, the mob stormed the Tuileries palace and shut the king and his family up in the grim prison of the Conciergerie.

The Prussians took the powerful fortress of Longwy with ease and went on to take Verdun. The route to Paris seemed clear, and in the capital there was panic, accompanied by the massacre of over 1,000 prisoners: priests, aristocrats, Swiss guards, and common criminals. The great revolutionary orator Danton made a stirring speech calling for 'de l'audace, et encore de l'audace, et toujours de l'audace!' (boldness, again boldness, and always boldness!), and

Europe during the **French Revolutionary wars,** 1789–1815, and (inset) naval operations in 1805.

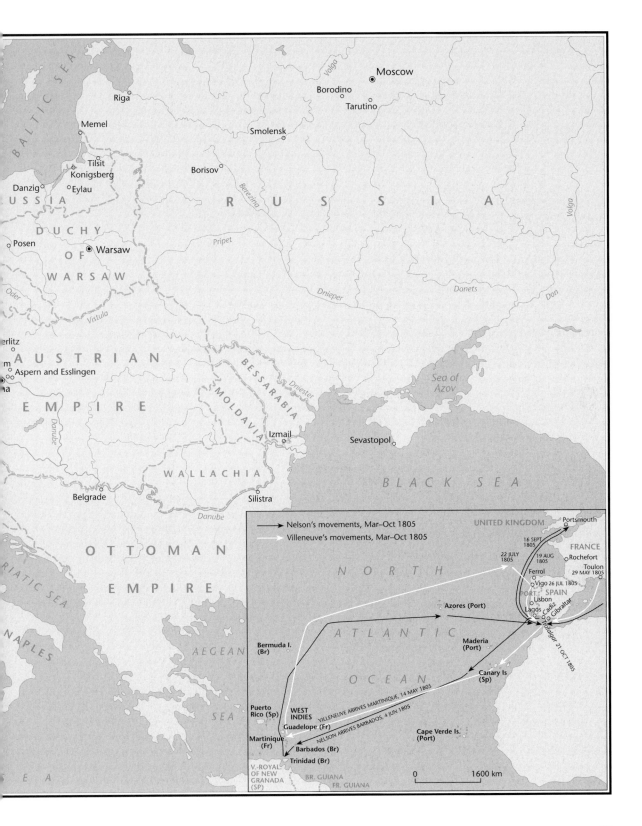

BALTIC SEA

Riga

Memel

Tilsit
Konigsberg
Danzig   Eylau

USSIA

DUCHY

OF

WARSAW

Posen

Warsaw

Oder

Vistula

erlitz

AUSTRIAN

m

Aspern and Esslingen

na

EMPIRE

Danube

Smolensk

Borisov

Berezina

R   U   S   S   I   A

Moscow

Borodino

Tarutino

Pripet

Dnieper

Donets

Don

Volga

Volga

BESSARABIA

MOLDAVIA

Dniester

Izmail

Sevastopol

Sea of
Azov

WALLACHIA

Belgrade

Silistra

Danube

BLACK   SEA

RIATIC SEA

OTTOMAN

EMPIRE

NAPLES

AEGEAN

SEA

E   A

Nelson's movements, Mar–Oct 1805
Villeneuve's movements, Mar–Oct 1805

UNITED KINGDOM   Portsmouth

16 SEPT
1805

FRANCE

Rochefort

22 JULY
1805

19 AUG
1805

Toulon
29 MAY 1805

Ferrol

N   O   R   T   H

Vigo 26 JUL 1805   SPAIN

PORT.   Lisbon

Azores (Port)

Lagos   Cadiz   Gibraltar

Trafalgar 21 OCT 1805

A   T   L   A   N   T   I   C

Maderia
(Port)

Bermuda I.
(Br)

O   C   E   A   N

Canary Is
(Sp)

Puerto
Rico (Sp)

WEST
INDIES

SEA

VILLENEUVE ARRIVES MARTINIQUE, 14 MAY 1805

Guadelope (Fr)

NELSON ARRIVES BARBADOS, 4 JUN 1805

Cape Verde Is.
(Port)

Martinique
(Fr)   Barbados (Br)

Trinidad (Br)

V. ROYAL
OF NEW
GRANADA
(SP)   BR. GUIANA
FR. GUIANA

0   1600 km

French Revolutionary wars

French soldiers rose to meet the challenge. Two French armies—Dumouriez's Army of the North and Kellermann's Army of the Centre—met Brunswick at *Valmy, a confrontation rather than a battle proper, where the steadiness of French troops in the face of artillery fire proved conclusive: Brunswick began a disastrous retreat. The day after Brunswick fell back from Valmy the monarchy was abolished and France was proclaimed a Republic. As Russell Weigley puts it, 'a series of hesitant, reluctant and misguided Allied efforts . . . had helped precipitate a seismic shift in France's internal history'.

French armies now went on the offensive in Savoy, the Rhine, and the Low Countries. Dumouriez routed the Austrians at Jemappes on 6 November, and Brussels was captured. The National Convention issued the Edict of Fraternity of 19 November 1792, calling on all oppressed peoples to rise up with the promise of French military assistance. Hitherto there had been a measure of *schadenfreude* in Berlin, London, and Vienna at the collapse of France, but revolt beyond France's borders was not to be countenanced and the Allied powers dug their heels in.

Recognizing that this was now a fight to the death, the French guillotined Louis on 21 January 1793, showing their contempt for the threats of the European monarchs, and declared war on Hanoverian Britain and Bourbon Spain for good measure. Prussia and Austria, however, became involved in partitioning Poland with Russia, which distracted them from affairs in Italy, the Low Countries, and the Rhineland. Nevertheless, the French were roundly defeated at Neerwinden on 18 March, and to add insult to injury Dumouriez, a general whose very real military ability was not matched by his political judgement, fled to the Allies. Once again the borders of France were threatened. The Prussians swiftly took Mainz, Condé, and Valenciennes and the Revolutionary Tribunal responded with an effusion of blood known as the Terror, guillotining many aristocrats and suspected counter-revolutionaries along with those whose only crime was to be unwise, unlucky, or politically exposed.

The British admiral Hood landed in Toulon in support of the Royalists, and in the west of France the royalists of the *Vendée rose in armed revolt against Paris. The combination of threats drove France to extreme measures, and decree of the *levée en masse* was issued by the Convention on 23 August 1793. All citizens were called to the defence of France: young men to the armies, women to make uniforms and muskets, children to turn rags into field dressings, and old men to give rousing speeches in the market places. Fired with new fervour, the Revolutionary armies recaptured Toulon, ejected the British from around Dunkirk, and advanced into the Alps. The organizational genius of Lazare *Carnot was brought into play to help turn a revolutionary rabble into a properly equipped fighting force. The new commander in the north, a modest ex-ranker called Jourdan, beat the Austrians in a tough contest at Wattignies on 16 October 1793, and the rebels of the Vendée and Lyons were crushed. The tough and talented *Hoche went on the offensive on the Rhine front, defeating the Allies at Frocschwiller and Kaiserslautern in December.

This success could not conceal the fact that the Revolution's real military weakness was at sea. Although the army beat the Austrians and British at Tourcoing in May 1794, it was a different matter at sea where revolutionary fervour was no substitute for professional seamanship. Most naval officers had either fled or been murdered by their mutinous crews. Small wonder, then, that a French fleet was mauled by the British Adm Lord Howe off Ushant on the Glorious First of June, 1794. Although Jourdan swept all before him at *Fleurus later that month, taking Brussels, Liège, and Antwerp, the French had no answer to Allied sea power and Corsica was lost on 10 August. French armies stormed to victory in Spain and Savoy, and by the end of 1794, tired of continual war, the Austrians signed an armistice. Prussia, Holland, and Spain made peace in April, May, and June 1795: Prussia was to remain neutral for the next ten years.

The Revolution had ensured its survival purely by force of arms, and this important lesson was not lost on observers inside and outside the Republic. The war with Austria dragged on, despite the fact that Vienna was distracted by events in Poland, which ceased to exist as an independent nation after the bloody suppression of its patriots. Further south, in Italy, the Revolutionary armies under the enterprising young Gen Bonaparte (see NAPOLEON) began to make startling progress from March 1796. By 28 April he had conquered Nice, Savoy, and Piedmont. From there he went on the offensive into the north Italian plain defeating the Austrians, taking Milan, and besieging the important communications nexus of Mantua in June. On the Rhine front Jourdan was making poorer progress against the redoubtable Archduke *Charles and was defeated at Amberg, Wurzburg, and Altenkirchen in August and September. The Austrians then moved to reinforce the Italian front, but were defeated by Bonaparte at *Arcola on 15–17 November.

Spain's entry into the war on the side of France gave planners in Paris access to a large and well-equipped navy. The British abandoned Corsica and withdrew from the Mediterranean entirely. Indeed, the British Isles themselves came under threat when Hoche attempted to land an army in Bantry Bay in Ireland, but was foiled by the weather: as the Irish nationalist Wolf Tone put it, England had not had such an escape since the *Armada. Although Bonaparte's successes in Italy continued unabated with victory at Rivoli on 14 January 1797 and the capture of Mantua, at sea the Spanish fleet was hammered by Adm Jervis off Cape St Vincent. However, it was not all plain sailing for the Coalition: there was another French landing at Fishguard in Wales (the last invasion of British soil by foreign troops) and British sailors, supposedly infected by Jacobinism but at least as much influenced by more mundane grievances, mutinied at Spithead and the Nore.

332

The Austrians now began to accept the fait accompli of French presence in Lombardy, and were alarmed by Hoche's renewed and successful offensive on the Rhine front. The French occupied Venice and the Ionian Islands, and established the Cisalpine Republic as a buffer zone. The treaty of Campo Formio, signed on 17 October 1797, gave Austria Venice, Istria, and Dalmatia in return for evacuating the Rhine. France, in a cynical move of realpolitik, recognized Austria's claim to Bavaria and Salzburg. The liberal Republic was now acting like an 18th-century absolutist state.

The British continued truculent. Adm Duncan savaged the Dutch fleet, a French ally, at Camperdown on 11 October 1797, and the French responded by trying to strike at British economic power, beginning to seize British goods on the high seas. The popular and successful Bonaparte was appointed to command an invasion army, but without control of the Channel his task was impossible, and so he cast his eyes toward the east. The British, in any event, had problems of their own: the United Irish, inspired by the ideals of the Revolution mingled with deeply held nationalist beliefs, rose in armed rebellion. Profiting from the confusion Bonaparte left Toulon for Egypt, taking Malta on the way, which only served to enrage the deluded Tsar Paul of Russia, who had appointed himself Grand Master of the Knights of St John.

Bonaparte went on to fight a glittering campaign in Egypt, capturing Alexandria on 2 July 1798, routing the *Mameluke army at the Pyramids on 21 July and entering Cairo on the 25th. However, the British Adm *Nelson caught up with the French fleet in Aboukir Bay and utterly destroyed it. Bonaparte, so successful on land, was now totally isolated from home. Furthermore, a planned invasion of Ireland had foundered: Gen Humbert landed in Killala Bay, but was surrounded and forced to surrender at Ballinamuck on 8 September.

It was obvious now that France was at a disadvantage, with her best general cut off in Egypt, and the Second Coalition was formed, consisting of Great Britain, Austria, Russia, Naples, Portugal, and Turkey. The French responded by swiftly occupying Naples but the Austrian offensive gained ground on the Rhine and in Northern Italy, and the Russians sent an expeditionary force under *Suvorov, their ablest and boldest commander. A string of French reverses followed: news of Suvorov's victory at Novi on 15 August encouraged Bonaparte to abandon his army in Egypt and return to France. Moreover, a British and Russian force had landed in Holland, beaten the French at Alkmaar on 19 September, and was now in a position to threaten the northern borders of France.

In Switzerland Masséna held Korsakov's Austro-Russians at Zurich, and the tsar, tired of the war, ordered Suvorov to withdraw over the Alps and back to Russia. Things went better for the French in Holland too: on 2 October the British and Russians had won at Bergen, but been checked at Castricum on the 6th. They agreed to evacuate Holland by the Convention of Alkmaar and Russia withdrew from the Coalition on 22 October. In France the Royalists rose again in Le Mans and Nantes. The French-sponsored Italian republics collapsed as Austria renewed the offensive, and all Bonaparte's conquests were recovered. Such an emergency needed a desperate solution, and Bonaparte led a military coup in Paris on 9 November 1799, declaring himself first Consul shortly afterwards.

Bonaparte immediately set about reversing the unpromising military situation. He descended on Italy by way of the St Gothard pass and defeated the Austrians at Marengo on 14 June 1800, recovering northern Italy and removing the danger of an Austrian invasion of France. Gen Moreau, meanwhile, advanced through Bavaria into Austria, and on 3 December beat the Archduke John at Hohenlinden, only 50 miles (80 km) from Vienna. The Austrians promptly made peace at Lunéville in February 1801, leaving the French on the left bank of the Rhine and acknowledging French satellite republics in Holland, Switzerland, and northern Italy. Bonaparte then set about isolating Britain, and a Russian-led Armed Neutrality was formed to oppose British attacks on neutral shipping. British bombardment of Copenhagen in April and the destruction of a French army in Egypt in August (see EGYPTIAN EXPEDITION, FRENCH) were setbacks, but in London the ministry led by Pitt and Greville fell and its successor negotiated peace with France, signed at Amiens in March 1802. Bonaparte was swift to grasp the fruits of victory. A plebiscite in May made him consul for life, and only two years later another plebiscite sanctioned the establishment of a hereditary empire. By this stage, however, war between France and Britain had broken out once more, and was to last for twelve long years (see NAPOLEONIC WARS).

What had started as a fight for the survival of the fledgling Republic had changed to an attempt to export liberty by 1794 and had been transformed into *total war by 1799. The whole apparatus of the state was geared to fighting a national and patriotic war. State-run arms factories multiplied, scientific research was put at the state's disposal, and many new inventions, such as the balloon and submarine, were turned to a military application. Furthermore, the size of armies had taken a quantum leap from the 50,000 or so that an 18th-century army could put into the field, to the force—briefly perhaps in excess of 1 million men in August 1794—that France mobilized to defend the republic. Although percentage casualties in individual battles were proportionate to those in the *Seven Years War, the Revolutionary wars were destructive because the French, sustained by reserves of manpower, were prepared to give battle again and again, aiming not at geographical objectives but at the destruction of enemy armies in the field.

It was not simply that the scale of war had changed. Neither the patchy performance of the Revolutionary armies, nor the harsh injustice of the political commissars who accompanied them (for so many French generals failure was a death sentence), can conceal the fact that there was something distinctive and admirable about the threadbare soldiers of the new France. They were at first less well trained than the white-coated regulars of the old regime, but their zeal and intelligence made them well suited for fluid tactics, and they were repeatedly urged to press on the close quarters with the cold steel: 'Join action with the bayonet on every occasion,' declared Carnot. The foundations of their tactics, which included the large-scale use of *skirmishers (the proportion of light infantry in the *French army rose from 4 per cent in 1789 to 23 per cent in 1795), had been laid before the Revolution. The fusion of such methods with genuine patriotic fervour produced impressive results, especially once improved training enabled the French to attack with solid shallow columns behind swarms of skirmishers. French artillery had been less damaged by emigration than other arms, and it too built on earlier work to become an arm which formed a major ingredient of Napoleon's victories.

Structural changes also reflected earlier ideas: all-arms divisions were in use by 1795 and the corps system was introduced four years later (see ORGANIZATION, MILITARY). The period produced some generals of real ability, many of whom, like Hoche and Jourdan, could not have expected to reach commissioned rank, still less command armies, under the old regime. By 1794 the average age of French generals was 33, and most of Napoleon's marshals won their spurs during this period. Although the French Revolutionary wars seem overshadowed by the Napoleonic wars, they were conflicts of lasting importance and cast their shadow not only into the next century but well beyond it. TM/RH

Blanning, T., *The French Revolutionary Wars 1787–1802* (London, 1996).

Griffith, Paddy, *The Art of War of Revolutionary France 1789–1802* (London, 1998).

Lynn, John, *The Bayonets of the Republic* (Oxford, 1996).

Strachan, Hew, *European Armies and the Conduct of War* (London, 1983).

Weigley, Russell, *The Age of Battles* (Bloomington, Ind., 1991).

French wars of religion (1562–98). The wars of religion were much more than a confessional dispute. They embodied dynastic, factional, social, and personal frictions, set against a European financial, political, and religious crisis. The Peace of Cateau-Cambrésis (1559) ended a long period of Habsburg-Valois rivalry (see ITALIAN WARS, FRENCH). France already displayed a homogeneity—summed up as 'une foi, un loi, un roi' (one faith, one law, one king)—which has encouraged André Corvisier to term it 'the model of nation-states'. However, the monarchy was not absolute, but relied on the support of a powerful and divided nobility. Its finances had been overburdened by war, causing tax increases which brought growing hardship. The nobility, though exempt from taxation, faced problems

of its own: many families had been beggared by the wars, and peace left their sons without employment. Some capitalized on patronage exercised by the crown and high nobility to enter the Church: others joined those already demanding Church reform.

Inspiring Calvinist preachers attracted growing congregations. Calvin's policy of targeting nobles for conversion bore fruit, especially in the south. Calvinism was also attractive to lesser men who saw it as an attack on the old order. The royal commander in Guienne, Blaise de Monluc, wrote that a local *Huguenot leader had claimed: 'We are the kings, and he that you speak of is a little turdy roylet; we'll whip his breech and set him to a trade, to teach him to get his living as others do.' Huguenot communities placed themselves under the protection of sympathetic noblemen, and by 1560 were organized on quasi-military lines, each church with its captain and each synod with its colonel.

Neither the crown's poverty nor the burgeoning strength of Protestantism need have proved fatal had the monarchy supported its local governors against the Huguenots. And, as N. M. Sutherland has written: 'The division of France behind religious banners, which played so dangerously into the hands of Spain, would not have been possible without . . . the old rivalry of the nobility and their new struggle for power upon the death of Henry II.' Henri II died in 1559 from a wound received in a *tournament, and his sickly son François II, 15 when he came to the throne, threw himself into the arms of his wife's relatives, the powerful Guise family. François, Duc de Guise, was a soldier who had defended Metz against Charles V and recaptured Calais from the English; his brother the Cardinal of Lorraine was an accomplished politician. Their rise affronted two other great families, the Montmorencies and the Bourbons, both divided by religion. The *constable Anne de Montmorency was Catholic, but his nephew, the admiral Gaspard de Coligny, was a devout Huguenot. Antoine de Bourbon, king of Navarre through his wife, was Protestant but infirm of purpose, while his brother, Louis, Prince de Condé, was not only a Protestant but had agreed, in 1560, to become the protector of all French Huguenots. The slide to war was gradual. In March 1560 Huguenots botched an attempt to seize the king (the Conspiracy of Amboise), and Condé was imprisoned. He was released when the king died in December, and his family claimed, as first princes of the blood, the guardianship of the young Charles IX. The Queen Mother, Catherine de Medici, refused, and strove to preserve royal authority, balancing the princes against one another and trying to achieve political and religious compromise. She also kept a watchful eye on Philip II of Spain, to whom the religious struggle in France—reflecting his own difficulties in the Netherlands—was a serious political concern. In 1561 she initiated the Colloquy of Poissy, where rival theologians failed to agree, and early in 1562 granted a measure of religious freedom to the Huguenots in the Edict of January.

The Montmorencies and the Guises had already with-drawn from court, and persuaded Antoine de Bourbon to support them. In March 1562 Guise, on his way to his estates in Lorraine, stopped to hear mass at Vassy, south-west of Saint-Dizier, and his servants became involved in a scuffle with Huguenots, about 30 of whom were killed. Open war broke out, with the Huguenots seizing control of many towns in the south and Condé taking the Loire valley to establish his headquarters at Orléans, while Guise and Mont-morency secured Paris.

This first war (1562–3) was inconclusive, and its conduct testified to the deep-seated distaste for civil war and the Queen Mother's repeated attempts to broker a negotiated settlement. The Pacification of Amboise granted the Huguenots liberty of conscience and the limited right to worship but was no basis for a lasting peace. Catherine was fortunate in that Antoine de Bourbon had been killed dur-ing the war and Guise murdered after it, increasing her room for manoeuvre. The French conflict was already part of a wider dispute, and there were growing Huguenot fears that Spanish troops, who used the 'Spanish road' through eastern France to reach the troublesome Netherlands, would be diverted to France. After Catherine met Philip's commander the Duke of Alba at Bayonne in 1565 these fears, though factually groundless, provoked a Huguenot attempt to seize the king at Meaux in September 1567. A sec-ond war (1567–8) followed. Like the first it was inconclusive, though the intervention of foreign troops—the Catholics were supported by Alba and *Swiss mercenaries, and the Huguenots by German heavy cavalry (*reiters) under John Casimir, son of the Protestant Elector Palatine—increased the conflict's ferocity and re-emphasized its international implications. The Treaty of Longjumeau re-established the Amboise terms, but proved short-lived, for the third war (1568–70) broke out almost immediately.

This time there was more serious fighting. Although the Catholics, under the king's younger brother the Duc d'Anjou (later Henri III), beat the Huguenots at Jarnac and Montcontour (1569), Coligny, who succeeded to command of the Huguenots when Condé was killed at Jarnac, kept the war alive by skilful manoeuvre. The crown's chronic short-age of money made it difficult to keep an army in the field, and peace was made at Saint-Germain in August 1570. It marked a return to the status quo, although this time the Huguenots were allowed to garrison four towns—Montauban, La Rochelle, la Charité, and Cognac—as sec-urity.

Catherine now did her best to achieve unity, agreeing to marry her daughter Margaret to the young Henri of Nav-arre (later *Henri IV) in an effort to secure a Valois–Bour-bon alliance, negotiating for the marriage of Anjou to Elizabeth I of England, and achieving a general, if short-lived, Anglo-French rapprochement. Coligny was readmit-ted to the king's council, where he urged an anti-Spanish policy and won the affection of the young king.

The odds were against Coligny. Spain's military prestige was restored by *Lepanto and Alba's successes in the Netherlands, and neither Elizabeth nor the Protestant Ger-man princes could be counted upon to provide serious mil-itary support for France. Sharp price rises promoted unease which fuelled Catholic demands to root out heresy. The Guises blamed Coligny of complicity in Duc François's murder nine years before, and Catherine now came to be-lieve that only death would lift his influence from the king, remove the prospect of a disastrous war with Spain, and enable her to maintain a balance of power. Coligny was wounded by an assassin on 22 August 1572. Some time the next day, the feast of St Bartholomew, the decision was taken to finish off Coligny and kill other Huguenot leaders, in Paris for Henri of Navarre's wedding. Early on the morn-ing of 24 August, Coligny was butchered and a massacre of Huguenots within Paris, in which the population and mili-tia played an enthusiastic part, spread, with varying inten-sity, to the provinces: thousands were killed. Henri and his cousin Henri, Prince de Condé, narrowly escaped with their lives, though both were forced to convert to Catholi-cism. Elsewhere many other Huguenots abjured their faith, but those that did not, embittered and mistrustful, armed in the expectation that war would be renewed. The fourth war (1572–3) featured the unsuccessful royal siege of La Rochelle, and ended in the peace of the same name.

Although French Protestantism had now passed its zen-ith, it remained enormously strong in the south. It also gained some support from the rise of a moderate Catholic party, the *politiques*, its members, prepared, as H. G. Koen-igsberger put it, 'to seek a way out of the horrors of religious and civil strife by sacrificing the religious rather than the political unity of the state'. Hostility to the Guises and, as always, personal ambition, played their parts. Catherine's youngest son, the Duc d'Alençon, was portrayed as an at-tractive alternative to Charles IX, while Montmorency-Damville, governor of Languedoc, was amongst those prepared to back the Huguenots against the king or vice versa to strengthen his own position.

Charles died in 1574, and his elder brother Anjou, briefly installed as king of Poland, returned to rule as Henri III. Condé escaped from court that year, and Navarre soon fol-lowed suit. Both raised troops, and John Casimir brought a large contingent to support the Huguenots. The Peace of Monsieur (Alençon) ended the fifth war (1576) on terms very favourable to both the Huguenots and to Alençon, given the dukedom of Anjou. That year saw the formation of the first Catholic League, with the declared aim of sup-porting royal authority, but with a powerful local organ-ization and strong links with Spain. It was successful in preventing Huguenots from being elected to the Estates General that met at Blois in 1576, and went on to champion the privileges of the estates and provinces against royal ab-solutism. The king, well aware of the danger, declared him-self head of the League in place of the Duc de Guise, and the

French wars of religion

Peace of Bergerac, which ended the sixth war in 1577 on terms less favourable to the Huguenots than the previous peace, abolished all leagues and associations. In 1580 a brief seventh war enabled Navarre to strengthen his hold on the south-west. Anjou, meanwhile, intrigued to obtain the sovereignty of the Netherlands in place of Philip II, but died in 1584. Henri III was childless and seemed likely to remain so, leaving Henri of Navarre as heir presumptive to the French throne.

The prospect of a heretic king induced Catholics, led by Guise and his relations, to revive the League. The Cardinal of Bourbon was persuaded to claim the succession in place of his kinsman Navarre. Leaguers replaced royalist governors and garrisons in many towns, and in December 1584 they concluded the Treaty of Joinville with Philip of Spain, who agreed to give them financial and, if need be, military support. Catherine, fearful of the growth of Spanish power, concluded the Treaty of Nemours with Guise, abolishing all previous edicts of pacification with the Huguenots, banning the practice of Protestantism.

The longest of the wars—sometimes called the War of the Three Henries, from Henri III, Henri of Navarre and Henri, Duc de Guise—raged from 1584 to 1589. In 1587 Navarre won a spectacular victory at Coutras and Guise beat John Casimir's Germans. These battles weakened Henri III's authority, which was further reduced when the volatile population of Paris rose, forcing him to flee and welcoming Guise. However, the defeat of the *Armada damaged Spanish prestige and imperilled Philip's wider strategy, encouraging Henri III to lure Guise to Blois, where he was murdered in the king's presence: his brother, the Cardinal of Guise, was killed the following day. Catherine died almost immediately, as a wave of Catholic fury saw Henri declared unfit to rule, and the League, now headed by Guise's brother the Duc de Mayenne, became an openly revolutionary party. The king moved against Paris, and was besieging it with Navarre's support when a fanatical friar stabbed him on 1 August 1589. On his deathbed, Henri nominated Navarre as successor provided he converted to Catholicism.

The last of the wars, the War of the League (1589–98), began with the League consolidating its grip on many cities. Henri IV beat Mayenne at Arques in September 1598, and even more dramatically, at Ivry in March the following year. He besieged Paris, but Philip sent his ablest commander, the Duke of *Parma, to relieve it. In the meantime, the Cardinal of Bourbon had died, and the Estates General, which met in 1593, was asked to consider the succession of the Infanta, Philip II's daughter by the late Henri III's sister. This was a deeply unpopular move, and at the crucial moment Henri IV declared that he was prepared to return to the Catholic Church. Allegedly quipping that 'Paris is well worth a Mass', he was received into the church at Saint-Denis in July 1593 and crowned at Chartres—for Rheims, where French kings were traditionally crowned, was in League hands. His con-

version removed a major obstacle to peace, and Henri exploited his position with skill. He entered Paris in March 1594, and set about winning the support of towns and commanders by lavish distribution of officers and pensions, joking that loyalty was 'vendu, pas rendu' (sold, not given). He declared war on Spain in 1595, and although this helped unite France against an external enemy, the Spaniards had the better of it. The war ended with the Treaty of Vervins in 1598, the year the last of the League's leaders made peace with Henri. The Edict of Nantes, granted that year, gave the Huguenots freedom of conscience and wide rights of worship, and the right to garrison some hundred places of security at royal expense. It was a compromise which permitted the existence of two religions in one body politic, and was to last for the best part of a century.

The wars saw little real change in the military art. Although most soldiers still wore *armour and fought with cold steel, firearms were used on a growing scale. This irritated old warriors like Monluc, who complained: 'Would to heaven that this accursed engine had never been invented, I had not received those wounds I now languish under, neither had so many valiant men been slain for the most part by the most pitiful fellows and greatest cowards'. Battles usually involved the clash of blocks of infantry, their onset prepared by arquebus and cannon fire, with cavalry—many of them pistoleers trained to use the *caracole—posted on the flanks. Armies embodied a variety of semi-feudal contingents and mercenaries: assembling 25,000 men for a major battle was no mean feat. Their cost outstripped the ability of the royal exchequer to pay them, and its attempt to do so by raising taxes further weakened social cohesion. There were some improvements in organization, though nothing the French produced could equal the Spanish *tercio. Discipline was uncertain: Condé was beaten and captured at Dreux in 1562 because his hitherto-victorious men got out of hand before the decision was secured. Much depended on brave and skilful leaders—at Ivry Henri led the crucial cavalry counter-attack in person—though they were frequently killed in battle or assassinated subsequently. As conflict became endemic in French society, many men were driven to take up soldiering, for it was better to plunder than be plundered. This helped reduce the previously high proportion of noblemen in French armies, though even at the wars' end perhaps 30 per cent of soldiers were noble. In some cases, where there were local outbursts against great men of any party, violence became democratized. Atrocities were frequent, sometimes reflecting deliberate policy inflamed by religious passions, and sometimes demonstrating the casual brutality of a society at war for too long. Civilians died in large numbers. Perhaps 12,000 of the inhabitants of Paris starved to death during the siege of 1590, and another 30,000 died of disease subsequently. In all, some two to four million perished.   RH

Corvisier, André, 'Les Guerres de religion', in Philippe Contamine, *Histoire Militaire de La France* (Paris, 1992).

Koenigsberger, H. E., 'Western Europe and the Power of Spain', in *The New Cambridge Modern History*, vol. 3 (Cambridge, 1968).

Pernot, M., *Les Guerres de religion en France* (Paris, 1987).

Roy, Ian (ed.), *Blaise de Monluc* (London, 1971).

Sutherland, N. M., *The Massacre of St Bartholomew and the European Conflict 1559–1572* (London, 1973).

French, FM Sir John Denton Pinkstone, 1st Earl of Ypres (1852–1925). Born to a family with Irish connections, French joined the navy, his late father's service, in 1866. He hankered after the army, left the navy in 1870, and slipped into the 19th Hussars by way of the Suffolk Artillery Militia. French got on well: he was a bold horseman and, with a photographic memory, an avid reader of military history. He led a detachment on the *Gordon relief-expedition of 1884, attracting the favourable notice of Sir Redvers *Buller, and commanded his regiment at the early age of 36. An amorous escapade saw him placed on half pay, but he was restored to the active list to rewrite the cavalry manual, and commanded cavalry brigades at Canterbury and Aldershot. At Aldershot Douglas *Haig, his brigade major, made him a loan when an injudicious investment failed.

In 1899 Buller asked for him to command the cavalry division in South Africa. He won a scrambling victory at Elandslaagte in Natal, and went on to clear Cape Colony. Although Buller was replaced by the less congenial *Roberts and *Kitchener, French played a prominent role in relieving Kimberley, and his 'charge' at Klip Drift gave him an international reputation. He was knighted, and after the war held several important posts and helped *Haldane reform the army. Forced to resign as CIGS over the *Curragh affair in March 1914, he was still given command of the British Expeditionary Force (BEF) on the outbreak of war.

The difficulty of working with the French on the one hand and Kitchener, now war minister, on the other, did not suit his mercurial temperament. He swung between optimism and gloom, notably during the retreat from *Mons in August–September 1914. His political touch was sometimes clumsy, especially in the spring of 1915 when the 'shells scandal' helped bring down the Liberal government. Concern for his soldiers proved a source of weakness, and in September 1915 he tinkered with Haig's conduct of *Loos in an attempt to prevent premature commitment of the reserve. Replaced by the latter in December 1915, he was given a peerage and became C-in-C Home Forces.

Appointed viceroy of a troubled Ireland in 1918, he advocated a military solution which was never politically acceptable. Recalled in 1921, he spent his retirement characteristically living beyond his means, and, again characteristically, died with remarkable courage. French was an old-fashioned general with a flair for mobile war and personal magnetism which a rather louche lifestyle could not obscure. Had he retired in 1914 he would be remembered as the most distinguished British cavalry leader since *Cromwell.   RH

Holmes, Richard, *The Little Field-Marshal: Sir John French* (London, 1981).

friendly fire Modern circumlocution for attacks on soldiers by their own side, a decidedly unfriendly act but a well-established reality of war. It even occurred in hand-to-hand combat because men were not recognized as being friendly or because, in the press of battle, a weapon drawn back to strike a foe might hit a friend instead. The sharp bronze butt of the *hoplite spear often caused casualties in the rear ranks when it was drawn back to strike: Plutarch (see GREEK HISTORIANS) describes how in a battle in the streets of Argos in 272 'many died from the accidental blows which they inflicted among each other'.

The adoption of *gunpowder weapons complicated matters. The *smoke they produced so liberally made *IFF difficult. At *Rezonville/Gravelotte in 1870 a French regiment was gently reproved by a strange brigadier who arrived to announce: 'Mes enfants, you probably do not know it, but you are firing on my brigade.' Accidents were frequent when weapons were handled in closely packed ranks, and their avoidance was one aim of *drill. Front-rank soldiers who knelt to fire and bobbed up to load were often shot by their rear-rank comrades: Marshal *Saint-Cyr attributed one-quarter of French infantry casualties in the Napoleonic era to this cause.

Carelessness and misunderstandings kill men even off the battlefield. A corporal of the British 43rd Regiment survived the storming of Badajoz in 1812, only to be killed when a soldier fired his musket while cleaning it. During the *British civil wars Lt Col Arthur Swayne 'was slain by his boy, teaching him to use his arms. He bid the boy aim at him (thinking the gun had not been charged) which he did only too well.' Lt Col Thomas Gonne of the 17th Lancers was supervising pistol practice the very day his regiment received orders to leave for the *Zulu war, and accidentally shot himself. Any army in the field will produce a steady trickle of casualties as friendly patrols are engaged: WW I poet Siegfried Sassoon was shot by one of his *NCOs when coming back from patrol. Weapon handling is worsened by tiredness, fear, and poor training. During the *Vietnam war the US army recorded 846 cases of 'accidental self-destruction' and 939 'accidental homicides', in all over 4 per cent of the total ground-action fatalities.

As engagement ranges increased so too did the propensity for friendly fire to cause casualties. Once artillery was used primarily in *indirect fire, engaging a target invisible to the gun's detachment, all sorts of errors were possible. The position of gun or target might be inaccurately located on the map; barrels might be worn or charges faulty; and the members of the detachment might load the wrong charge or set an incorrect bearing or elevation on the sight. The tactical situation might have not been grasped by the gunners: the gallant French defence of the village of Samogneux, outside *Verdun, collapsed when a newly arrived battery of French 155 mm guns engaged it. Commanders and their staff sometimes made lethal errors and engaged positions their own men held. Gen Charles Percin reckoned that 75,000 French soldiers were killed by their own artillery in WW I.

Aircraft made their own lethal contribution. Guderian's panzer corps was struck by its own supporting Stukas the day after it crossed the Meuse in 1940, and a brigade commander was among the killed. The German practice of placing the national flag on the engine-deck of tanks (and painting it on the decks of warships) arose not from patriotism but a desire to make IFF clear. Allied ground forces in *Normandy used a white star for the same reason, and in the *Gulf war in 1990–1 Allied vehicles bore a distinguishing chevron. Yet despite this there were still casualties from friendly *air power. American troops preparing for COBRA in 1944 were struck twice by strategic bombers. In one incident 111 men were killed (including Lt Gen Leslie J. McNair, the highest-ranking US army fatality of the war) and another 490 were wounded. Accidental American air attack on a British unit in the Gulf war caused both casualties and resentment.

The fact remains that casualties from friendly fire are, as John Horsfall says, 'a hazard inseparable from war'. Good training and slick procedures will help reduce them. When they occur they will be likely to generate disproportionate impact, especially if the friend producing the fire is an ally or coalition partner.   RH

Holmes, Richard, *Firing Line* (London, 1985).
Horsfall, John, *The Wild Geese are Flighting* (Kineton, 1976).

Froissart, Jean (*c*.1337–*c*.1404), prolific poet and chronicler of *knighthood and chivalry from Valenciennes, Hainault. Patronized initially by the Lord of Beaumont, uncle to Queen Philippa of England, he first gained a reputation for verse, and later wrote a long Arthurian epic, *Meliador*. He began collecting material for the *Chroniques* on which his fame justly rests even before passing into the queen's service *c*.1361. Expanded and artfully rewritten to flatter different patrons over more than thirty years, these recount in vivid detail the wars of western Europe from the 1320s onwards, especially the *Hundred Years War, for which they are an inexhaustible if unreliable source.   MJ

Froissart, Jean, *Chronicles*, ed. and trans. Geoffrey Brereton (Harmondsworth, 2nd edn., 1978).
Ainsworth, P. F., *Jean Froissart and the Fabric of History* (Oxford, 1990).
Palmer, J. J. N. *Froissart: Historian* (Woodbridge, 1981).

Frunze, Cdr Mikhail Vasilevich (1885–1925), Soviet politician, military leader, and theorist; founder and ideologue of the Red Army, Soviet military doctrine, and Soviet preparations for *total war. A student at St Petersburg Polytechnic, Frunze was active during the 1905–7 revolution and was subsequently condemned to death twice, a sentence commuted to lifelong exile in Siberia. From 1910 to 1915 he did hard labour, but then escaped and made contact with the Bolsheviks who, in an extraordinarily risky move, smuggled him into the army near Minsk under the name of Mikhaylov, to carry out political agitation. As a party activist he moved widely and thus gained an unusually comprehensive picture of the war which would stand him in good stead later, and in particular of the colossal resources consumed and the need to break through the trench stalemate.

After the March 1917 Revolution in Petrograd (formerly and now St Petersburg), Frunze established a soviet of workers and soldiers' deputies in Minsk. At the end of August he used his contacts to disrupt the movement by rail of Gen Kornilov's counter-revolutionary forces against Petrograd. He was then sent to run the Bolshevik party in Shuya, east of Moscow, and took part in the November Revolution in Moscow (see RUSSIAN REVOLUTIONS). In early 1918 he was party leader in Ivanovo-Vosnesensk province and then, in July, took part in the defeat of the Left Socialist Revolutionaries' revolt in Moscow and of the White Guards in Yaroslavl.

From August 1918 he was military commissar of the Yaroslavl Military District; from February 1919, commander of Fourth Army; from July, commander of the Eastern Front (army group) during the defeat of *Kolchak; and, from August, of the Turkestan Front. In 1920 he was appointed to the Central Committee of the Communist Party as representative for Kazakhstan and Turkestan and from September commanded the Southern Front (army group), which completed the final defeat of the main 'White' forces with the capture of Perekop, the 'White Verdun'. Frunze had begun studying military history and the science of war while commanding the Yaroslavl Military District and drew extensively on the advice of former tsarist officers including the former Gen Fedor Novitskiy. In the attack on Perekop he unearthed records of the Russian attack on the same area in 1737–8, and made sure the attacking troops practised the assault on accurate replicas of the terrain and the obstacles they would encounter.

Frunze was then commander of the armed forces of the Ukraine and Crimea. He was selected to introduce the proposal to unite Russia, Belorussia, Ukraine, and the Transcaucasian Federation in the USSR. In January 1924 he was part of a special commission set up to investigate the state of the Red Army, and in April he became its COS. In 1924–5, following the creation of the USSR, he was deputy president and then president of the Revolutionary Military Soviet of the Workers' and Peasants' Red Army (RVS RKKA), deputy people's commissar and then people's commissar for Military and Naval Affairs (Defence Minister). In this capacity he carried through the military reforms of 1924–5.

Frunze was a founder of Soviet military thinking and military *doctrine. The first issue of *Army and Revolution*, in July 1921, contained an article by Frunze, 'A Unified Military Doctrine and the Red Army', which set out the definition that remained standard until the 1980s. He also sponsored the main military journal, *Military Science and Revolution*, which became *Military Thought and the Revolution* in 1922 and, from 1925, *Military Thought*, and was editor of *War and Revolution*. He also published more than a score of books between 1919 and 1925, on civil war campaigns, national defence, the choice between a militia and a professional army, the need for command by one man as opposed to the system of commissars introduced in the civil war, and the military industrial base. He thus laid the foundations for the USSR's victory in WW II. In the documents prepared by the RKKA staff in 1925 under Frunze's direction, mobilization was viewed as the conversion not only of the army and navy, but of the whole of society to a wartime footing. Frunze's energy and genius made him many enemies, in particular *Trotsky and his supporters. By now he was suffering from a stomach ulcer and his heart was too weak for him to undergo anaesthetic for an operation. Nevertheless, he was ordered to undergo surgery in what the official enquiry subsequently decided was a 'medical murder'.   CDB

Gareev, Makhmut, *M. V. Frunze: Military Theorist* (London, 1988).

Pilnyak, Boris, 'Gibel' Narkoma M. V. Frunze', *Krasnaya zvezda*, 23 Oct. 1993.

Fuller, Maj Gen John Frederick Charles (1878–1966).

One of the most important military thinkers of the 20th century, J. F. C. 'Boney' Fuller was educated at Malvern College and the Royal Military College Sandhurst, and was commissioned into the Oxfordshire and Buckinghamshire Light Infantry in 1898. He served in the Second *Boer War, and in 1903 was posted to India, where he was able to indulge a passion for mysticism and the occult. In 1906 he married Margaretha Karnatz, known as Sonia. In the same year he befriended the occultist Aleister Crowley, and later helped him edit an occult review, the *Equinox*. They quarrelled in 1911 and the friendship was not renewed.

As he became bored with the occult, Fuller's interest in things military grew. He was promoted captain in 1905 and two years later accepted the adjutancy of the 2nd Middlesex Volunteers (10th Middlesex after 1908). Fuller began to write as a means of instruction and had completed two books before he entered the Staff College, Camberley, in January 1914. However, his student papers were condemned by the commandant, and Fuller began to demonstrate a talent for antagonizing his seniors that was to destroy his military career.

On the outbreak of WW I in August 1914, he served in various staff appointments in England before finally being transferred to the western front in July 1915. He thus escaped the decimation of the regular British Expeditionary Force (BEF) at the first battle of *Ypres. In December 1916 he transferred to the Heavy Branch Machine Gun Corps, later the Tank Corps—the most important event in his life. He wrote a series of brilliant papers on early tank tactics stressing its subordination to other arms. The major turning point in his thought was 'Plan 1919', written in the spring of 1918, a conceptual document rather than a 'plan' in the technical sense. This emphasized the importance of armour moving into the enemy's rear, co-operating with aircraft to effect psychological paralysis.

After the Armistice, Fuller sought to rationalize the lessons of the Great War. He undertook the massive task to rethink the nature of war and produce a sequence of the *principles of war. He held two colonel's posts in the Staff Duties branch at the War Office, and in 1922 he secured the permanent establishment of the Tank Corps and the prefix 'Royal'. In the following year he returned to Camberley as a chief instructor at the Staff College. During these years Fuller delivered a number of important lectures and published *The Reformation of War* (1923). In 1926 his Staff College lectures were published as *The Foundations of the Science of War* (1926), although its pretentious methodology was ridiculed. By 1925, however, he had developed an effective partnership with *Liddell Hart. In 1926 he was appointed military assistant to the CIGS, FM Sir George Milne, and his cause seemed to triumph when his appointment to command the new Experimental Brigade in 1927 was announced shortly thereafter. He wrecked this glorious opportunity to put his ideas about *armoured warfare into practice by his truculent behaviour, which resulted in his resignation and then reinstatement. He was subsequently transferred to Aldershot as General Staff Officer (GSO) 1, 2nd Division.

Thereafter his military career entered an anticlimactic phase. He commanded the 2nd Rhine Brigade at Wiesbaden and Catterick, and in 1930 was promoted major general. In February 1931 he declined command of the Second Class District of Bombay and was placed on half pay. During this period he wrote several of his most important works, including *Lectures on FSR II* (1931), *Lectures on FSR III* (1932), and *The Dragon's Teeth* (1932). Fuller was placed on the retired list in December 1933, and six months later joined Sir Oswald Mosley's British Union of Fascists (BU). Such a move complicated Fuller's re-employment in WW II, although he was not arrested (like all the other BU leaders) in June 1940. Fuller turned to journalism, and in the 1950s to the writing of military history. His most notable achievements were *The Decisive Battles of the Western World* (3 vols., 1954–6) and his studies of *Alexander 'the Great' and *Caesar. Awarded the Royal United Services Institute's Chesney Gold Medal in 1963, he died suddenly in February 1966 while in Cornwall. A controversial figure, Fuller's greatest legacy is his 45 books which have provided later generations with the tools to dissect his life's work. BHR

Reid, Brian Holden, *J. F. C. Fuller: Military Thinker* (London, 1987).
—— *Studies in British Military Thought: Debates with Fuller and Liddell Hart* (Lincoln, Nebr., 1998).

fusiliers Originally infantry soldiers armed with the *fusil*, a name used for the *snaphaunce or *flintlock musket to differentiate it from the *matchlock musket in the mid-17th century. Flintlock muskets, called *fusils* as opposed to *mousquets* (for matchlocks) in French, were expensive and more complicated to operate and so, when they were first introduced into European armies, they were intended for use by specialist troops; in the nature of things such specialists elevated themselves into élite units. In 1671 *Louis XIV raised a Régiment des Fusiliers in the French army and, as its name suggests, armed it with flintlock muskets. Flintlock muskets were also issued to *grenadiers, who required a musket that could be slung safely and quickly for *grenades to be thrown, which the matchlock, with its lighted slow match, could not; their status was already enshrined, however, in their role as assault troops. Regiments of fusiliers were assigned to guard the artillery trains, in which large quantities of gunpowder were stored and transported for the army's ordnance. Such a task was a risky one for matchlock-equipped infantry, with their glowing slow matches, and so flintlock-equipped fusiliers got the job, not only because their muskets were safer but also because they were more reliable (being faster firing and less susceptible to damp) should the artillery train require defence.

Once all infantry soldiers were equipped with flintlock muskets (by the early 18th century), and the term *fusil*—at least in English—came to mean a light flintlock musket of the sort carried by sergeants and company officers, regiments of fusiliers maintained their slightly élite status by amassing dress distinctions which made them sartorially akin to grenadiers. They adopted the badge of the flaming grenade or 'fired bomb' and the tall 'mitre' cap, originally in cloth but by the mid-18th century usually in bearskin with a metal frontal plate, and decorated their *headdress with the white plume of the grenadiers. Fusilier regiments existed in the armies of all European nations and most demonstrated essential similarities of dress. Although their élite status was recognized and authorized, and most fusilier regiments were among the senior regiments of line infantry in their armies, their battlefield role was that of line infantry once the matchlock musket had been superseded by the flintlock. However, the fusiliers' status tended, in some armies, to be further recognized, once their unique firearm was in common use, by other weapons' distinctions, such as swords of special pattern for officers and senior *NCOs. The British army, which contained six regiments of fusiliers until the 1950s, was probably at the forefront of maintaining dress and other 'traditional' distinctions for its fusiliers—the black flash worn at the back of the collar by the Royal Welch Fusiliers, a remnant of the black ribbon used to tie the *hair queue, being perhaps the most well known. SCW

Blair, Claude (gen. ed.), *Pollard's History of Firearms* (London, 1983).
Mollo, John, *Military Fashion* (London, 1972).

fyrd English kings before the invasion of 1066 were empowered to raise a fyrd or land army, consisting of *mounted infantry organized regionally through personal ties of loyalty between landholders and their leaders.

Each local leader (*dryhten*) held a retinue of chosen companions (*gesiðas*) who formed the backbone of his force. The sum of the forces of these leaders with the king's household troop constituted the fyrd.

Eligibility for service was a matter of *honour for a freeman, and carried with it a duty to protect the leader's life with his own or, if the lord fell, to die avenging him. That this is no mere literary trope was shown at *Maldon in 991, where the English 'hearthtroop' fought on to the death around their fallen leader, Ealdorman Byrhtnð. The *dryhten* had a reciprocal duty to share booty and glory with his men by publicly distributing jewellery and war-gear as badges of honour.

King Alfred 'the Great' (*c*.871–899) reorganized the pattern of individual military service from a straight 40-day stint for all men to a staggered system, leaving one group free to campaign with the king while the other was at home guarding the harvest. SJP

Gallic wars (58–51 BC), series of campaigns in which Julius *Caesar extended Roman control over all of Gaul east to the Rhine. Our main source for this conquest comes from his own *Commentaries*, which need to be treated with caution. Although the basic facts seem reliable and some have been confirmed by archaeology, these were works of propaganda intended to glorify the author and defend his actions against his political opponents at Rome. He was careful to excuse his reverses, and was highly disingenuous about the reasons for his involvement in Gaul in the first place. In 58 he needed to fight a successful war for political reasons and to recoup his massive debts. On several occasions he provoked wars with Gallic tribes when these were not threatening Roman interests.

Caesar's army was based around the legions of heavy infantry. He had six of these in 58, increasing this to ten and the equivalent of two more in independent cohorts by the last campaigns. These units included the specialists in engineering which made the army highly effective at sieges. His brilliant exploitation of unit pride turned these into exceptionally effective troops. For his cavalry and light infantry he depended on foreign allies, Numidians, Cretans, and Spanish, and large numbers of Gallic and German horse. Gallic armies, although often large, were inflexible and clumsy compared to the *Roman army. They lacked efficient logistical support and were unable to stay in the field for any length of time. Gallic warriors were furious in their first charge, but indiscipline prevented their adopting anything other than the simplest tactics in battle.

In 58 the tribe of the Helvetii migrated from what is now Switzerland, raiding a tribe allied to Rome and threatening to pass through Roman Transalpine Gaul (modern Provence). Caesar used this as a pretext to advance out of his province, brought the Helvetii to battle, and defeated them with heavy loss, forcing their return to their own lands. The tribes of central Gaul were divided between the two confederations headed by the Aedui and the Sequani. The Sequani had employed a German army, led by Ariovistus, to defeat the Aedui, who were allies of Rome. Julius claimed that Ariovistus' presence in Gaul represented a threat to Rome's interests, so led his army against the Germans and beat them in battle, driving the remnants across the Rhine. In 57 Julius marched against the Belgic tribes of the northeast, once again using the pretext of an attack on a tribe allied to Rome. His army was attacked while entrenching his camp near the river Sambre and nearly suffered defeat, being saved by the bravery and discipline of the ordinary soldiers, along with Julius' personal intervention in the fighting. The Belgians suffered heavy losses in this battle and soon capitulated when the Romans threatened their towns.

In 56 Julius divided his army to confront several of the smaller tribal groupings. After assembling a fleet and attacking them on land and sea he was able to defeat the Veneti. In 55 the Romans bridged the Rhine and mounted a punitive expedition against the German tribes. Late in the year, Julius crossed with two legions to Britain, an expedition that almost ended in disaster when much of his fleet was wrecked in a storm. The following year he returned to Britain with a much larger army and forced the powerful tribe of the Catuvellauni to surrender. These operations had no long-lasting effects, but were spectacular propaganda successes, keeping Julius in the public eye at Rome. In the winter of 54/3 the Romans, dispersed into winter quarters, were faced with a serious rebellion of the northeastern tribes of Gaul, led by Ambiorix of the Eburones. Fifteen cohorts were annihilated at Atuatuca, and another garrison commanded by Quintus Cicero only just saved by a relief column. The next year was spent in a series of punitive expeditions against the tribes involved.

The **Gallic wars**. Gaul at the time of Caesar and (insert) the native stronghold of Alesia and Roman siege works during the Gallic rebellion of 52 BC.

This proved only the prelude to an even greater rebellion in 52. Most of the tribes of Gaul, including even the traditionally pro-Roman Aedui, united under the leadership of an Arvernian noble, *Vercingetorix. Avoiding battle, but depriving the Romans of supplies, he sought to starve them into retreat. Julius pursued the main Gallic army, taking the town of Avaricum by storm, but suffering a costly repulse at Gergovia. Vercingetorix was finally defeated and captured at *Alesia. There were other rebellions, but Roman control of Gaul was never again seriously challenged.   AKG

Gallieni, Marshal Joseph Simon (1849–1916), French officer, colonial governor, and military theorist. Expert on 'small wars', of renewed relevance today. Gallieni graduated from the *Saint-Cyr academy at the outbreak of the *Franco-Prussian war in 1870, fought at *Sedan, was wounded and captured. Released in 1871, he was sent to Senegal, and in the 1880s, to Martinique, the French colony in Sudan, the Ivory Coast, and Vietnam, in French Indochina. He dealt with revolts using what became exemplary *counter-insurgency techniques, including 'hearts and minds'. He was then C-in-C of Madagascar, and understood the interrelationship between government, security, and economic development. In WW I he helped organize the 'miracle of the *Marne, was made war minister in 1915, but retired through ill health and died on 27 March 1916. CDB

Gallipoli campaign (1915–16). The attempts first by British and French warships and then troops to force the Dardanelles in 1915 constitute one of the most fascinating, and still controversial, of all the campaigns of WW I. It was the first major *amphibious operation in modern warfare, using such novelties as aircraft (and an aircraft carrier), aerial *reconnaissance and photography, steel landing craft, *radio communications, artificial harbours, and submarines. Its lessons, positive as well as negative, were studied by the British planners for Normandy and were remembered in the *Falklands conflict of 1982.

The naval assault, whose ultimate purpose was to open the warm water south to Russia, was the inspiration of the thrusting young First Lord of the Admiralty, Winston *Churchill. It foundered on 18 March, when three battleships—two British, one French—were sunk and three others badly damaged when they ran into an undetected minefield. Churchill, undeterred, wanted to persevere, but his senior naval colleagues, led by the gnarled and explosive First Sea Lord *Fisher, adamantly refused.

The British admiral at the Straits, de Robeck, shaken by the events of 18 March, agreed with Fisher. So did Gen Sir Ian *Hamilton, the newly appointed commander of the 'Mediterranean Expeditionary Force'. Thus, the two senior commanders on the spot decided on a land campaign to capture the Gallipoli peninsula.

Given the variegated troops at his disposal, which had only one Regular Division, the 29th, the shortage of time, the nature of the rugged peninsula with its few beaches, and severe logistical difficulties, Hamilton's plan for the Gallipoli landings was imaginative, indeed inspired. The Turkish commander, the German *Liman von Sanders, was totally deceived by the feint landing by the Royal Naval Division at Bulair and confused by the French one at Besika Bay and a real French landing at Kum Kale. Out of the six divisions at his disposal on 25 April, only two were on the peninsula itself.

But they turned out to be enough. Only two of the landings by the 29th Division were opposed, but that at Sedd-el-Bahr—V Beach—was definitely, and bloodily, repulsed. The commander of the 29th, Hunter-Weston, could and should have used his forces safely ashore to take Sedd-el-Bahr from the rear, but did not. It fell on the 26th, but by the time the advance began the momentum had been irretrievably lost.

The Australian and New Zealand Army Corps (*Anzac) was an unknown quantity, and had been given what had seemed to be the easier task to land further north on the western coast between the promontories of Gaba Tepe and Ari Burnu. The Anzac commander *Birdwood wanted a surprise dawn landing with no preliminary naval bombardment, which required that the warships carrying the troops had to anchor in pitch darkness. They did so 1 mile (1.6 km) to the north of the intended landing area.

This in itself need not have wrecked the plan, and after their initial surprise at the steep cliffs and tortuous gullies that faced them, the Australians, with the New Zealanders rapidly behind them, moved inland, meeting little resistance.

But von Sanders's 2nd Division, commanded by the then unknown Col Mustapha Kemal (see ATATÜRK), was based only a few miles away. Realizing that this was a serious invasion, Kemal, without higher authority, committed his entire division to driving the infidel into the sea. He very nearly succeeded. After a day of ferocious fighting, much confusion, and varying fortunes, the Anzacs were clinging to a fragment of land, and Birdwood was urging evacuation. Hamilton refused, and the epic of Anzac had begun.

Between the beginning of May and end of July, in torrid heat and plagued by dysentery and then typhoid, while the Anzacs clung on grimly to their tiny perimeter and inflicted brutal losses upon the Turks' daylight attacks, the British and French advanced with agonizing slowness and heavy losses. But a change of heart in London, despite the downfall of Churchill (removed from the Admiralty in May), now brought Hamilton almost excessive reinforcements.

The August Plan stemmed from the night reconnaissance of the New Zealander Overton that there was a feasible route from the north of the Anzac position to the key peak of the Sari Bair range, Chunuk Bair, and that it was undefended. The Anzac garrison was reinforced by 20,000

Gallipoli campaign

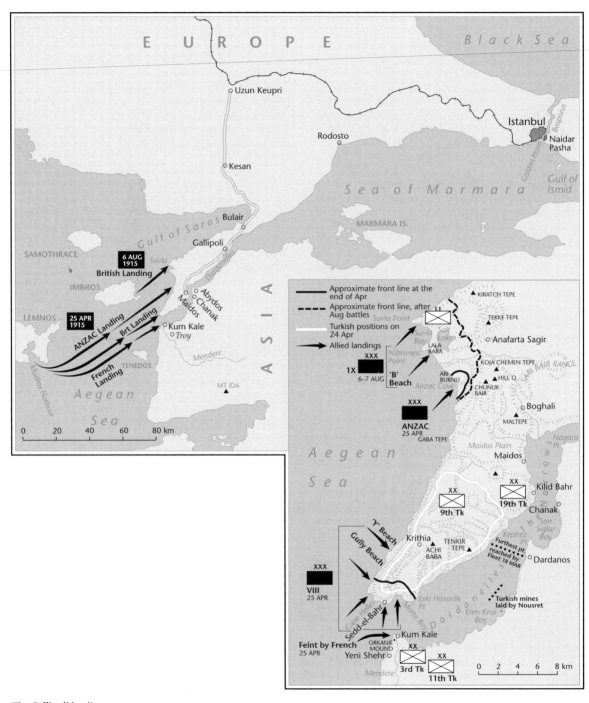

The **Gallipoli** landings, 1915.

men, primarily British and *Gurkhas, secretly over three nights and concealed in the man-made caves, in itself a remarkable coup.

The assault on the Sari Bair mountains on the night of 6–7 August was preceded by the assault of the 1st Australian Division under the command of its British Commander, Maj Gen Harold Walker on the supposedly impregnable Lone Pine position. As a result of meticulous and imaginative planning and the ardour of the Australians, Lone Pine was taken, albeit at a heavy cost.

The Right Assaulting Column, guided by Overton—who was killed in the advance—got to Chunuk Bair, but, literally within yards of spectacular success, the New Zealanders and British, admittedly exhausted, were ordered to pause, and this delay was to prove fatal.

The Left Column, consisting of Australians and Gurkhas, got hopelessly lost, but some units of British and Gurkhas got close to their objective of Hill Q, the next summit to Chunuk Bair. They were to capture it on the 8th, only to be destroyed by artillery fire, either from a British warship or an Australian battery at Anzac. At first light on the 10th, in a near-suicidal charge led by Kemal, the British reinforcements were hurled off Chunuk Bair. The great gamble, that had so nearly succeeded, had definitely failed.

The British landings at Suvla on the night of 6–7 August were an afterthought to the main August Plan, when some use had to be made of the three surplus divisions now at Hamilton's disposal. Their commanders were old and hesitant, but to be fair to them their orders were to land successfully, which they did. When it was at last realized at headquarters that they had not advanced much further Hamilton intervened furiously to demand an advance, but it was too late. The greatest battle of the campaign was fought on the Suvla plain on 21 August, but, despite grievous losses, the greatly reinforced Turks held their ground.

The rest was aftermath. Hamilton was recalled. His replacement, Monro, advised evacuation. After much anguish in London this was agreed. Churchill, who had remained in the War Cabinet, resigned, his political career apparently over, and went to the western front. It was left to the soldiers and sailors to organize the evacuations, first of Anzac-Suvla, and then of Helles. This they did with real brilliance in December and January, not a man being lost, to the stupefaction of the unsuspecting Turks and their German officers, who were lost in professional admiration.

The campaign had cost the Allies 46,000 dead, of whom 26,000 were British. The Turkish dead are unquantifiable, but an estimate of 200,000 is considered to be conservative. One is left to reflect on the many might-have-beens and the extreme narrowness between victory and a severe setback. In 1918, the Ottoman empire in ruins, the British occupied Gallipoli and Constantinople without a shot being fired. But it was three years too late.   RR-J2

Garibaldi, Giuseppe (1807–82), Italian revolutionary and irregular general. Garibaldi began his long and varied career as a revolutionary striving for the liberation and unification of Italy by joining in Giuseppe Mazzini's unsuccessful insurrection at Genoa in 1834. Forced to leave Piedmont, he fled to South America where he spent the next fourteen years, gaining experience fighting in various wars. First, he fought as a *guerrilla general and privateer for the province of Rio Grande del Sol against Brazil. He then served as a commander of an Italian legion for Uruguay against Argentina.

When Italy rose in revolt in 1848, he returned and raised 3,000 men to help the king of Piedmont, Carlo Alberto. Forced to flee the country once again after defeat at the first battle of *Custoza, Garibaldi soon returned to organize the defence of the last vestiges of the revolution—Mazzini's Roman republic. He was able to hold off the combined armies of the French, Austrians, Spanish, and Neapolitans for several weeks. However, the republic finally fell and Garibaldi escaped to America.

Although Garibaldi fought for Piedmont during the Franco-Austrian war of 1859, he is perhaps best remembered for his role in overthrowing the monarchy of the kingdom of the Two Sicilies. In May 1860, he set out to liberate southern Italy from the repressive regime of King Francis II. On 11 May, he landed with his 'Thousand Redshirts' at Marsala, Sicily, and destroyed the Neapolitan army in several battles. Garibaldi crossed the Straits of Messina on 22 August and advanced up the peninsula, being greeted enthusiastically by the people along the way. On 7 September, his forces occupied Naples.

In March 1861, Garibaldi surrendered his conquests to King Vittorio Emanuele of Piedmont in order to realize his lifelong dream, a united and independent kingdom of Italy. Although most of the Italian peninsula was under the rule of Vittorio Emanuele, the Papal States remained separate. In August 1862 and again in January 1867, he attempted to take Rome. These attempts failed due to French intervention, and the Papal States were only incorporated into the kingdom when the French withdrew their troops in 1870.

Garibaldi continued his career as a general by commanding Italian troops, with some success, during the *Austro-Prussian war of 1866, which resulted in Austria ceding Venetia to the kingdom of Italy. He again commanded an Italian volunteer force, this time in support of the new French republic during the *Franco-Prussian war of 1870–1. After the latter, Garibaldi's long career as a soldier came to an end. After serving some years as a deputy for Rome in the Italian parliament, he spent his last years on a farm in Caprera writing novels.   RTF

gas, poison The principal *chemical weapon developed and introduced during WW I and used occasionally since.

Gatling gun Perhaps the most well-known, and the most widely adopted, of early hand-cranked machine guns, the Gatling was invented by Dr Richard Joseph Gatling of Hartford County, North Carolina. An inventor's son, Gatling designed his first mechanical machine gun in 1861 as a weapon of defence, to protect bridges, buildings, and causeways against assault. Modified to fire a metal-jacketed centre-fire *cartridge, it was adopted in .50 inch calibre by the US army in 1866 and subsequently by Britain and Russia for their cartridges. Both nations' armies and *navies used the Gatling, the British with particularly devastating effect in the *Egyptian campaigns of the 1880s, and it spawned many European and American competitors in hand-cranked machine guns. Its multiple barrels fed by gravity from drum or vertical clip magazines, the Gatling progressed from being hand-cranked to having its barrels revolved by electrical motor by the late 19th century. The American M61 'Vulcan' aircraft cannon in 20 mm calibre and the helicopter-mounted 'mini-gun' in 7.62 mm calibre used in *Vietnam are both derivations of Gatling's original multi-barrelled machine gun.   SCW

Peterson, Harold L. (ed.), *Encyclopaedia of Firearms* (London, 1964).

Wahl, Paul, and Toppel, Donald, *The Gatling Gun* (New York, 1978).

Gaza, battles of (1917). At the beginning of WW I the Suez Canal, an essential link with India, was the chief cause of Britain's desire to hold Egypt. In February 1915 a small Turkish force crossed Sinai and attacked the canal but was easily repulsed, and in 1916 the British gradually moved into Sinai, defeating a Turkish attack at Rumani on 3 August.

The well-prepared Gaza position, stretching about 30 miles (48 km) from Gaza, near the coast, to *Beersheba, blocked further advance. On 26 March 1917 Gen Sir Archibald Murray, C-in-C of the Egyptian Expeditionary Force, attacked it frontally with little success, and a second battle on 17–18 April was no more fruitful. Murray was replaced by *Allenby, who conceived a more ambitious plan and made careful logistic preparations. Leaving part of his army to fix the Turks and their German allies at Gaza, he hooked round the desert flank, taking Beersheba and its all-important wells on 31 October. The Gaza position had already been penetrated by a *tank attack, and the Turks had no option but to withdraw to escape encirclement. The battle is a classic example of manoeuvre succeeding where frontal assault had failed.   RH

Gazala, battles of (1942). In January 1942 a German-Italian force under *Rommel pushed the British Eighth Army back to a line 40 miles (64 km) long from Gazala on the coast to Bir Hacheim. During a four-month lull both sides considered further offensives. Rommel hoped to take

*Tobruk and go on to Egypt. The British wished to advance into Cyrenaica to establish airfields to cover Mediterranean *convoys. *Auchinleck, the British C-in-C, had been forced to send troops to the Far East and believed that defensive strategy was more realistic, but *Churchill demanded an attack. Lt Gen Ritchie's Eighth Army held the Gazala Line in a series of 'boxes', held by infantry protected by wire and minefields, with its armour to the rear.

On 26 May Rommel led his armoured divisions around the southern end of the line and did serious damage to dispersed British armour. However, the new Grant tank was an unpleasant surprise, and German tank losses were heavy. Worse, the Free French garrison of Bir Hacheim held out. Unable to roll the line up, Rommel needed to break through it to get supplies to his armour, fighting hard to its east. He was urged to break off the battle, but penetrated the minefield in the nick of time.

The British failed to counter-attack Rommel's bridgehead until his *anti-armour screen was ready, and the Germans emerged victors from very bitter fighting in the Cauldron. Bir Hacheim had to be abandoned, and Rommel then forced the British out of the Knightsbridge box, behind the Gazala Line, making the whole position untenable. Tobruk fell on 21 June, and Rommel crossed the Egyptian frontier two days later. Auchinleck flew up to take personal command, but could not rally survivors until they reached the *Alamein position on 1 July. Gazala marked the nadir of British fortunes. Although they were numerically superior in men and tanks, hesitant command and immature tactical *doctrine led the British to lose a battle they had been within measurable distance of winning.   RH

Gempei wars (1180–5). The term 'Gempei wars' is drawn from the Chinese reading of the names of the two *samurai families whose rivalry culminated in a fierce civil war that changed the direction of samurai history. 'Gen' refers to the Minamoto family, and 'Hei' to the Taira. The Minamoto heartlands were the north-east of Japan, while the Taira were located in the west, along the coast of the Inland Sea. The Taira, in the person of Taira Kiyomori, had acquired great influence in the Japanese imperial court by marrying daughters to crown princes, and the two families had come to blows on two occasions, the Hōgen Rebellion of 1156 and the Heiji Rebellion of 1160, although it was only in the latter of these incidents that there was a direct Taira/Minamoto clash, a forerunner of the Gempei wars.

In 1180 a claimant for the imperial throne received support from Minamoto Yorimasa, who was forced to withdraw from Kyoto with his army and made a stand at Uji, using the river as a natural moat while he waited for reinforcements from the *sōhei* from Nara. The Taira attacked across the broken bridge, and Minamoto Yorimasa was forced to commit suicide in a manner that was to set the standard for future samurai to emulate. The Taira reacted

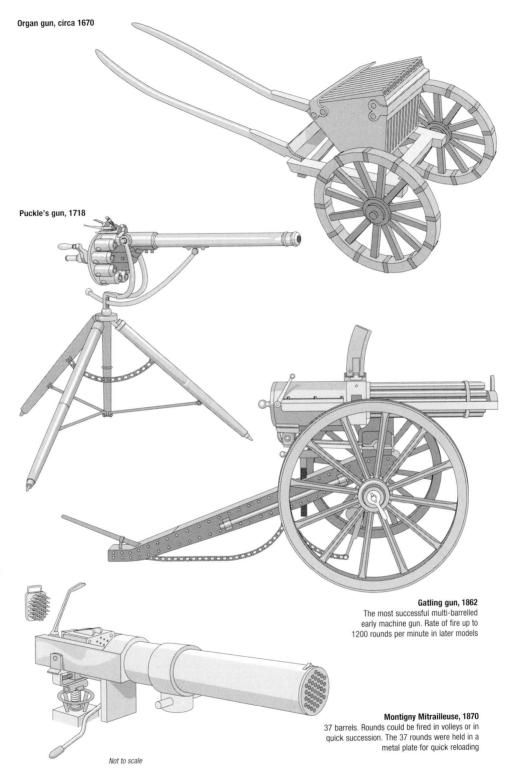

Organ gun, circa 1670

Puckle's gun, 1718

Gatling gun, 1862
The most successful multi-barrelled early machine gun. Rate of fire up to 1200 rounds per minute in later models

Montigny Mitrailleuse, 1870
37 barrels. Rounds could be fired in volleys or in quick succession. The 37 rounds were held in a metal plate for quick reloading

Not to scale

Since the earliest days of firearms, designers dreamed of firing a continuous stream of projectiles. The first attempts often involved multiple barrels. The first practical 'machine guns' appeared in the American Civil and Franco-Prussian wars but were soon supplanted by the single-barrelled machine gun, such as the Maxim introduced from the 1880s.

to the rebellion by burning the temples of Nara. Several months later another Minamoto warrior, Yoritomo, also led a disastrous rebellion against the Taira-dominated court and was heavily defeated at Ishibashiyama.

The first inkling that the Minamoto had that the Taira might be vulnerable occurred with the so-called battle of the Fujigawa, when a flock of birds made the Taira samurai think an attack was being launched against them, and they abandoned their camp. The tide finally turned for the Minamoto with the victories in 1183 of Minamoto Yoritomo's cousin Yoshinaka, who defeated a Taira army at Kurikara. At this battle Yoshinaka held a Taira army in place on a mountain pass by fighting a leisurely battle, then as night fell confused them by stampeding a herd of oxen along the path. He then forced them to retreat towards the capital with the Minamoto in *pursuit. Yoshinaka's army entered Kyoto in triumph, but their depredations caused such havoc that the court welcomed the intervention of his cousins Yoritomo and Yoshitsune, who defeated Yoshinaka at Awazu in 1184.

During 1184 *Minamoto Yoshitsune carried out a series of brilliant campaigns against the Taira. His first victory was at Ichi no tani, a fortress built on the shore near present-day Kobe. While the bulk of his army attacked from both sides along the beach, Yoshitsune led a detachment of mounted samurai in a daring rear attack down a precipitous slope. The Taira took to their ships, and Yoshitsune pursued them to Yashima on the island of Shikoku, where he again defeated them. Many of the most celebrated accounts of single combat in samurai warfare occurred at these two battles. At Ichi no tani several individual fights took place on the beach as the Taira escaped to their ships. Yashima is also remembered for the feat of Nasu Yoichi, who shot a war fan (a heavy, iron-mounted fan with a colourful emblem) from off the top of the mast of a Taira ship to demonstrate his skill.

The final battle of the Gempei wars was Dan no Ura in 1185. The Taira fleet held a strong position in the straits of Shimonoseki, the narrow gap of water that divides Honshu from Kyushu. The Minamoto attacked in a fierce sea battle, and concentrated their arrow fire on the steerers of the rival ships. A deserter informed them of the presence of the child-emperor, Antoku, on one of the ships. As the tide of battle turned against them the infant's grandmother committed suicide by jumping into the sea with the young emperor in her arms. She was followed by a mass suicide, and it was said that the seas ran red with the blood of the slain and the red dye from the Taira flags.

The end of the Gempei wars gave the samurai an ideal of behaviour that was to be cherished for centuries. It also established the Minamoto as the most powerful samurai family in Japan, and Yoshitsune's elder brother Yoritomo was proclaimed *shogun, the first military dictator of Japan. With this act the government of Japan passed decisively from the imperial court to the military class.   SRT

gendarmerie Armed *military police, from the French *gens d'armes* (men of arms), which once described heavy cavalry. The French gendarmerie was formed in 1791 when a unified Gendarmerie Nationale replaced the law-enforcement agencies of the *ancien régime*. It traces its origins to the Middle Ages: the body of provost marshal Gallois de Fougières, killed at *Agincourt in 1415, was moved to the national police cemetery in the early 20th century. The gendarmerie has not only performed military police duties but also, on occasion, fought in formed units: in 1856 the Gendarmes of the Guard lost six officers and 136 men attacking Sevastopol. Within France the gendarmerie remains responsible for law enforcement and the pursuit of criminals, and has a special interest in public order. Responsibilities for it are shared between the Ministry of National Defence and the Ministry of the Interior. Its members hold military rank, and have a wide range of firepower at their disposal.

RH

gender and war (see also WOMEN IN THE MILITARY). In the growing literature examining the issue of gender and war, the term 'gender' refers not to biological differences between men and women but to a set of culturally shaped and defined characteristics and social norms associated with masculinity and femininity. The study of gender in war involves an appraisal of the norms, characterizations, expectations, assumptions, and treatments applied differentially to men and women in the context of conflict.

States exist in what they perceive to be a competitive and dangerous international environment and, traditionally, have ranked national security as a priority. In the name of national security, large defence budgets, military conscription of male populations, foreign invasions, and the curtailment of civil liberties have been justified. The security of the state is perceived as a fundamental value that is supported by most citizens. This is especially true during wartime. The provision of national security has been and continues to be an almost exclusively male province. Most women support what are considered to be legitimate calls for state action, yet the primary task of defining and defending the security of the state has been man's work: a task that through its association with war has been rewarded in many cultures throughout history. To *sacrifice one's life for one's country in war has been regarded as the highest form of patriotism, but a failure to fight is the act of a *coward or evidence of physical or mental sub-maleness.

History records the possibly mythological Amazons of the Crimea and the blood-curdlingly real 'Amazons' of *Dahomey, also a few well-known fighting warrior queens, such as the *Indian Mutiny leader Lakshmibai of Jhansi and *Boudicca of the Iceni, plus a number of transvestite women soldiers like *Barry. There have been rather more non-combatant female war leaders such as Elizabeth I, Catherine the Great, Indira Gandhi, Golda Meir, and Margaret

Thatcher. But men have usually been the soldiers and war leaders, and women have only been peripherally involved. Some women have been engaged on the field of battle as combatants (there is a rich tradition in Hispanic military culture, ranging from Isabella of Castile to the *soldaderas* of the Mexican revolution), and as upper body strength has become less important they are increasingly doing so. But women have more typically been engaged in the 'comforting' and 'supporting' roles as mothers and carers located within the domestic sphere, or as medical staff with armies. Despite the examples cited above, women have primarily been defined as a group in need of protection.

The significance for the development of our conceptions of 'maleness' and 'femaleness' of the fact that males were expected by society as a whole and by themselves to take part in war on a regular basis is striking. Their lives and health were the proper subject of virtuous sacrifice. Jean Elshtain has argued in her work *Women and War* that women's social roles should be understood in response to the fact that war became institutionalized. This fact was not one of nature but of social construction. Thus, for both men and women, 'gender' and 'war' are inescapably bound together in the history of western thought and practice.

It is only comparatively recently that the notion that war has specific, different consequences for both men and women has been considered by scholars. This has occurred primarily in often feminist reappraisals of history and in contemporary international relations theories. Debate has focused on the specific consequences for women that war entails because during war, male and female characteristics become polarized as *militarism and masculinity permeate throughout society. This is not to argue that *pacifism per se is attributable to biological predisposition but that women are underrepresented in the decision-making processes of both civil and military society.

Berenice Carroll has suggested that the association of women with peace is one that has arisen precisely because of their disarmed condition. There are many types of feminism and a range of approaches as to how gender balances might be redressed to the benefit of both men and women; feminists agree that the gendering of social life along a male–female divide builds discrimination into accepted patterns of behaviour. During war these may resurface in an aggressive fashion and be officially sanctioned. However, the significance of area bombing during WW II as an equal-opportunity killer, oblivious of gender, race, or even species, needs to be evaluated, as does the fact that there can be no non-combatants or safe areas in the event of an all-out nuclear war.

The consequences of war for gender roles have often been ignored. It is widely accepted that WW I and WW II paved the way for the acceptance of female activity outside the private sphere of the family, and changed many attitudes towards gender, the family, and electoral rights. But key concerns such as rape, abortion, and reproductive rights have not generally been considered in the context of war, although the papal dispensation for nuns raped in the Congo bears examination (see CONGO, UN OPERATIONS IN). Recent conflicts, most notably those in the former *Yugoslavia, have reminded us that the women of an enemy are likely to be systematically raped and terrorized to rub home the totality of the conquest involved. Ilya Ehrenberg specifically exhorted the Red Army to do so in Germany in 1945. The rape of women in ethnic conflicts relates to complex male notions of the destruction of enemy culture and possession of his territory.

The reproductive rights of women may also be affected by their own state. Abortion might be outlawed or contraception restricted as leaders attempt to rebuild and restructure populations. While men fight, women quite often are perceived not just as the linchpin of families or communities but as the biological reproducers for the state. Contrary to the chivalric tradition, being female is not a guarantee of security and may in fact attract the subversion of a woman's most fundamental individual rights, and not merely by the enemy.

Gender, therefore, is an important variable in relation to war; yet so are race, ethnicity, and material well-being. Being poor and the 'wrong' colour greatly increases the chances of being abused and discriminated against, male or female, in war or peace. Much the best arguments focus on the relationship of gender and power, there being little evidence that powerful women behave very differently to powerful men, and this includes violent responses to any challenges to that power. Debate will continue over the value of specific gender viewpoints on war and whether the appreciation of such views can alter the nature of man, the state, and war. CK-P

Carroll, Berenice A., *Liberating Women's History: Theoretical and Critical Essays* (Chicago, 1976).

Elshtain, Jean Bethke, *Women and War* (Brighton, 1987).

Enloe, Cynthia, *Bananas, Beaches and Bases: Making Feminist Sense of International Politics* (London, 1989).

Tickner, J. Ann, *Gender in International Relations* (New York, 1992).

general staff The term general staff evokes a number of differing images from the bungling red tabs of the British army of WW I to the seemingly ultra-efficient red-striped German staff machine of two world wars. The first, a picture of caricature, contrasts awkwardly with a more envious perception of a Prussian military élite. In 1890 Spenser Wilkinson titled his plea for the adoption of a German style general staff in the British army the *Brain of an Army*. Nearly one hundred years later, Col T. N. Dupuy ascribed the German army's relative success to their general staff, and claimed in *A Genius for War* that he had discovered the secret of 'institutionalizing military excellence'.

The requirement for a general staff is functional. While staff officers were progressively introduced into armies from the times of *Gustavus Adolphus, the requirement for a specialist staff grew as armies increased greatly in size in the early 19th century. Generals could no longer direct personally all formations on the battlefield or attend to supporting administration. Therefore the work of the staff became essential for detailed planning, organization, supply, and the transmission of orders. In war ministries staff officers helped the C-in-C prepare campaign plans. In the field, they assisted him and his principal subordinates with operational decision-making. Development of the 'staff system' thus progressed on two related levels of war: strategic and tactical. Later, work of general staff officers underpinned the intermediate *operational level of war.

The Prussian system became the model for the rest of the world. It was based on the *QMG staff of the 17th and 18th centuries, whose functions had widened from supply to encompass military *engineering including *fortification and cartography (see MAPS). Building on the reforming work of *Scharnhorst, the Allgemeine Kriegsschule (General War Academy) was opened in Berlin in 1810; *Clausewitz became superintendent in 1818. With common instruction, *doctrine, and outlook, the graduates were dispersed throughout the Prusso-German army to provide continuity of tactical thought and practice. The office of 'COS' became increasingly important, particularly in continental armies. The period 1813–15 saw also a number of effective command and staff 'partnerships' in the Prussian army between chiefs of staff and their respective commanders, contrasting with the approach adopted by British and French commanders such as *Wellington and Napoleon who used their staffs more as a secretariat, or as 'directed telescopes'.

After the *Napoleonic wars, the Prussians began to differentiate formally between the Truppengeneralstab (general staff officers working at higher formation level) and those employed in the central, Grosser Generalstab (Great General Staff), responsible for war planning and organization, including mobilization. Under *Moltke 'the Elder' the Prussians continued to lead development. He was responsible for increasing the prestige of the CGS after he assumed this office in 1857. He selected twelve talented pupils a year from the war academy and supervised their instruction with 'ruthless efficiency'. After training, the young but highly trained general staff officers were dispatched to various parts of the Prusso-German army. The resulting cohesion and concomitant contribution to that army's fighting power played a major part in Moltke's success in wars against Denmark, Austria, and France. *Schlieffen continued this personal commitment to professional development with annual Stabsreisen (staff rides) to educate, train, and ultimately test commanders and their staffs before WW I. Meanwhile, in the staff colleges of France, Great Britain, Russia, and the USA the influence of Napoleon's practical example and of *Jomini dominated—notwithstanding the Prusso-German success in the *Franco-Prussian war of 1870. The German shift from theory towards a more practical approach in the training of officers was only partially emulated elsewhere.

Implicit in the German approach, and one which was retained throughout two world wars and survives to some extent in the present-day Bundeswehr, is that the general staff officer at any level is always regarded as a *Führergehilfe*, an aide to the commander. The commander, in turn, has a duty to consult and involve, for example, his COS in decision-making. Originally designed by Moltke to impose some order on the monarchical commanders-in-chief of the armies of the contributing German states, the general staff system was found to be so effective that it was developed further in the *Reichswehr (despite the formal abolition of the general staff at the Treaty of Versailles) and *Wehrmacht eras. Even in the dark days of 1944, general staff trainees received sufficient *education and preparation (over nine months) at both the tactical and operational levels such that they could take over the reins of command in the absence of their commander. The existence of a unified general staff system in the Prussian (and later in the German) army contributed much to German professional military competence and success, particularly at the higher tactical and operational levels of conflict. Nonetheless, no staff system can recompense for higher level failings in the grand and military strategic direction of a war, as the German defeats in two world wars demonstrate.

In contrast, the British experience has been somewhat ambivalent. After WW I *Hamilton wrote: 'the term General Staff is something of a pitfall for the unprofessional professor or amateur war correspondent. Even now, after the war G.S. remain to some extent an exotic pair of capitals in England.' In 1944, the view expressed by *Liddell Hart in *Thoughts on War* was more critical: 'The General Staff was truly . . . an all-powerful military priesthood, linked by ties of intellectual and professional comradeship. A corps of directors, a society within a society, they were to the German army what the Jesuits at their political zenith were to the church of Rome.'

Wellington's staff work was shared among a military secretary, the adjutant general, and the QMG. By the time of the *Crimean war this system had been shown to be incapable of supporting the ever more complex demands of command in war. Despite the establishment of a staff college at Camberley in 1858, reform of the regimental system, and reorganization of the *War Office under *Cardwell, progress in Britain towards the formation of a general staff remained slow. The Hartington Commission of 1890 and the writings of Spenser Wilkinson did little to improve matters as the trail of military incompetence in the Second *Boer War demonstrated. What had proved good enough for imperial control was found seriously wanting in South Africa.

The creation of a general staff followed the recommendations of the Esher Committee in 1904. After a couple of years of hard work Special Army Order 233 of 12 September 1906 set out its purpose: 'To advise on the strategical distribution of the army, to supervise the education of officers, and the training and preparation of the army for war, to study military schemes, offensive and defensive, to collect and collate military *intelligence, to direct the general policy in army matters, and to secure continuity of action in the execution of that policy.'

However, this War Office-based general staff was concerned only with intelligence, training, and military operations. The old military secretary and administrative and QMG departments branches survived at all levels. A fundamental question which split the War Office remained unresolved: was it to be the man or the job which had general staff status? Further, the opportunity, envisaged by *Haldane, to modernize the staff across the British army was eclipsed by efforts of grander design to create the post of the CGS (from 1907, CIGS) and by the army's belated attempts to impose a tactical doctrine in the *Field Service Regulations* (FSR).

Haldane envisaged a wider role for the general staff than the compilation and revision of manuals such as FSR. Its directors would also 'test ideas in Staff Rides and advise or umpire at peacetime manoeuvres', 'raise the intellectual standard of the army', and 'through Staff Rides and tests, assess the aptitudes of officers for the duties of high command'. Many of these innovations were followed through before WW I, including staff tours, as the rides were sometimes called then, and general staff conferences were held at Camberley. In the face of opposition from many vested interests, the pace of reform proved impossible to sustain and even the staff rides and conferences lacked the vigour of their German models. Sir Ian Hamilton, reporting on the German imperial manoeuvres of 1909, 'remarked upon the seriousness with which the Germans viewed their conferences with fewer speakers and lasting much longer than the British equivalents'. Ideas like accelerated promotion for Staff College graduates provoked an outcry among the more traditional elements of the British army; so did internecine arguments over the status of the past staff college (psc) qualification—were all Staff College graduates to get one, or did it depend on performance?

The British general staff, as far as it was formed, was far better than anything that existed before as its doctrine, professional standard of field training, and the smooth mobilization and deployment of the British Expeditionary Force (BEF) to France and Belgium in 1914 demonstrated. But the British adopted only a pale copy of the German system; furthermore it lacked 100 years of steady development and expert fashioning at the hands of Helmuth von Moltke and Alfred von Schlieffen. That said, Haldane had much to be pleased with in the immediate pre-war years: the efficiency of the regular army (at unit level at least) reached new heights and the Territorial Army was founded. However, much of the substantial progress made in doctrine, train-

ing, and organization before WW I was lost in the bloody afterglow of victory: the general staff was debased, its embellishments stripped, and its function undermined. *Fuller was no unthinking admirer of the German system. Looking back on WW I he declared: 'Where the German system went wrong was that it superimposed a committee of irresponsible non-fighting officers on the general, creating a staff hegemony which virtually obliterated generalship. If the general was a tiger, his staff officers were selected from the lambs; if he was lamblike, then they were chosen for their tigerishness.'

Yet Fuller also recognized the potential strengths of a general staff if it were properly controlled. He concluded in *Generalship: Its Diseases and their Cure*: 'No soldier can doubt the immense value of a general staff if it is the general's servant, and not the general's gaoler.' Despite valuable staff training conducted at Camberley, Haifa, and Quetta prior to WW II, the British army soldiered on without a fully fledged general staff. There was little opportunity to provide the doctrinal foundation and preparation for high command which all German general staff officers received. Despite the writings of Liddell Hart and Fuller, the systematic intellectual stimulus from the top downwards on the lines of the Reichswehr COS *Seeckt was missing in the British army. The difficulties in establishing an authoritative COS—the principal general staff officer in a headquarters—is instructive. Of British higher commanders of WW II, only *Montgomery created a 'true' field COS, de Guingand. Monty made his innovation of a COS under the pressures of wartime command to free him, the higher commander, from meddling in the business of the staff. It allowed him 'time to think' and sleep. After WW II, apart from the introduction of chiefs of staff into higher level headquarters against some opposition, little changed in the British staff system. Courses of instruction at Camberley stressed 'staff duties' rather than the development of strategic thinking and operational concepts on war college lines. Not until the 1970s did Camberley title its principal course as 'command and staff'. While the British army reluctantly adopted *NATO staff nomenclature in 1981, little of substance changed in either the organization or running of the staff. Yet with the establishment of an army higher command and staff course in 1988, which became fully joint (tri-service) in 1998, perhaps the foundations of a true general staff ethos have been laid.

In the 19th century other countries apart from Britain monitored Prusso-German developments and established general staffs and institutions for staff training. The French, for example, had created a high-level staff titled the Corps d'État-Major de l'Armée in 1783. The French Revolution brought no lasting improvements to either the organization or status of the staff. French military prowess during the Napoleonic wars rested rather on her impressive manpower resources and generalship. The lack of a staff system began to be felt during the Crimean war but only the defeat during the 1870 war against Prussia signalled the urgent need for reform. By the turn of the 19th century France had organized her general staff into three main bureaux, responsible for: organization, *discipline, military *justice, and supply; enemy information (the *deuxième bureau*); and orders, movement, and preparation for combat. In 1917 a fourth bureau was added and made responsible for transportation, supply, and the employment of labour units. This grouping of four principal staff divisions within a formation headquarters contrasted with the British system of a 'general' staff responsible for intelligence, operations, and training (or 'G' branch) and separate administrative and QM staffs ('A' and 'Q' branches respectively).

During the 19th century progress towards the formation of general staff in the USA was slow, as in Britain. In 1864 Pres Abraham *Lincoln had reorganized the Union army headquarters in Washington under the direction of the Secretary for War and the overall commander of the armies. But this arrangement left *Grant as a commanding general in the field and *Halleck, a former general-in-chief, as COS of the army back in Washington. Grant's own field headquarters staff was about twenty officers strong, including a COS, two military secretaries, two assistant adjutants general, and a chief QM. The *Confederate States Army notoriously paid considerably less attention to staff work.

The major impetus towards modernization of the staff came in the wake of the *Spanish-American war and the *Philippines insurrection. The father of the American general staff was Elihu Root who was Secretary of War in 1899–1904. His influence was as profound as was that of Haldane in Britain. Once a path had been set, progress in the USA was typically fast. A general order in November 1901 provided for a General Services and Staff College to be established at Fort Leavenworth, Kansas, and an Army War College Board at Washington. These two institutions later became the US Army Command and General Staff College (still at Leavenworth) and the Army War College (now at Carlisle, Pennsylvania). Equally significantly, on 14 February 1902 Root submitted a bill to Congress proposing the establishment of a central general staff.

As passed, the Dick Act of 1903 created a General Staff Corps. Its function, derived from the German Bronsart von Schellendorf's *General Staff Duties*, was 'to prepare plans for the national defence and for the mobilization of the military forces in time of war; to investigate and report upon all questions affecting the efficiency of the army and its state of preparation for military operations; to render professional aid and assistance to the Secretary of War and to general officers and other superior commanders'.

Yet these duties only dealt with the higher direction of the army in peacetime. When *Pershing sailed for France in 1917 as the commander of the American Expeditionary Forces (AEF), one of his tasks was to form a staff fit for war. After examining the British and French systems, Pershing decided on the French, meeting the need for ease of co-ordination with higher and adjacent French headquarters. The staff system adopted, which provided for a general staff organization down to divisional level, was thus an accident of history. Yet it proved its worth and was used by the USA throughout WW II and was adopted subsequently, with minor modifications, by most NATO armies. In 1918 an American staff consisted of five sections, titled G1–G5: G1 dealt with administration, including personnel; G2 was responsible for intelligence; G3 dealt with operations; G4 with supply matters; and G5 with instruction and training. In WW II, G5 became responsible for civil affairs, and is now of particular importance in humanitarian and peace support operations.

Today we see the growing importance of joint staffs in western armed forces. While there is no direct equivalent of a unified army general staff, a process of integration has been accelerated by parallel developments in naval and air staffs and by joint staff training. Navy staffs have adopted an organization of 'N' prefixed branches while their *air force counterparts have 'A' staffs. Joint staff divisions are prefaced 'J' in NATO and in many national headquarters. The joint staff organization owes its origins to the Franco-American system. Whereas J1–J4 equate to the old G1–G4 sections, J5 is responsible for plans, J6 for communications and information systems, J7 for doctrine and training, J8 for budgets and finance, and J9 for civil affairs. The role of the COS remains crucial in relieving the commander from a mass of detail and in co-ordinating the work of joint and ever more complex staff dealing in three environments: sea, land, and air. RAMSM

Dupuy, T. N., *A Genius for War: The German Army and General Staff, 1807–1945* (Fairfax, Va., 1984)

Gooch, John, *The Plans of War: The General Staff and British Military Strategy 1900–1916* (London, 1974).

Görlitz, Walter, *History of the German General Staff* (New York, 1953) (trans. from German orig.).

Holborn, Hajo, 'The Prusso-German School: Moltke and the Rise of the General Staff', in Paret, Peter (ed.), *Makers of Modern Strategy* (London, 1986).

Spiers, Edward M., *Haldane: An Army Reformer* (Edinburgh, 1980).

Wilkinson, Spenser, *The Brain of an Army* (London, 1890).

Geneva and Hague Conventions International efforts to regulate the conduct of warfare and armed conflict are often understood to consist of two main codes of legal and humanitarian thinking: Geneva and Hague. Each approach consists of a series of conventions and protocols (confusingly, the Hague approach also incorporates the Gas Protocol signed in Geneva in 1925). Although it is now widely accepted that both streams flow together, each offers a distinctive approach to the problem of regulating armed conflict. The Geneva approach, in essence, establishes the distinction between combatants on the one hand and non-combatants (civilians) or those rendered hors de combat (wounded and/or captured) on the other. The last two categories should be protected from the effects of conflict and from inhumane treatment. The Hague approach is more concerned with the rights and duties of the combatants, with setting clear restrictions on their behaviour, and with the prohibition of certain weapons and inhumane practices during war.

The starting point in the Geneva approach was the Convention for the Amelioration of the Condition of the Wounded in Armies in the Field, signed in Geneva in 1864. The Convention established that wounded enemy soldiers should receive the same care and medical attention as friendly troops. The Convention also established the legal status of medical personnel. The 1864 Convention was revised by the 1906 Convention and then, following the experience of WW I, by the 1929 Geneva Conventions for the treatment of both the wounded and *POWs. These were all superseded by the 1949 Geneva Conventions.

These have almost universal participation and are in any case regarded as being binding upon all states, whether or not participating directly. There are four conventions. The first two address the status and treatment of wounded and sick combatants on land and at sea. The third Convention is concerned with the treatment of POWs. The fourth Convention establishes rules for the protection of civilians during war. The four Conventions share a set of 'common articles' which all signatories agreed would apply 'as a minimum'. Non-combatants and those rendered hors de combat by whatever means would 'in all circumstances be treated humanely'. Certain specified practices were prohibited, including the use of 'cruel treatment and torture', the taking of hostages, degrading treatment, and summary executions.

In 1977 the 1949 Conventions were supplemented by two Additional Protocols, designed to reaffirm both the 1949 Conventions and elements of the 1907 Hague Conventions. The First Additional Protocol concerned the protection of victims of international armed conflict, and requires, *inter alia*, discrimination in target selection. The Second Additional Protocol attempts to extend the Geneva approach to include non-international armed conflict.

The Hague approach begins with the 1868 St Petersburg Declaration Renouncing the Use, in Time of War, of Explosive Projectiles Under 400 Grammes in Weight. This agreement was intended to prevent unnecessary suffering caused to troops by the use of exploding *bullets. In 1899 delegations from 26 states met in The Hague for the First Hague Peace Conference. The Conference resulted in three Conventions and three Declarations. The Conventions concerned the peaceful settlement of disputes, respect for the laws and customs of wars on land, and maritime warfare. The three Declarations banned the use of projectiles and explosives from *balloons, the use of projectiles able to dispense poisonous gases, and the use of expanding (or 'dumdum') bullets.

The Second Hague Peace Conference in 1907 was attended by delegations from 44 countries. The Conference resulted in thirteen Conventions and one Declaration. The Declaration renewed the 1899 Hague Declaration I concerning the use of balloons. The Conventions covered a wide range of subjects. The 1907 Hague Convention IV 'Respecting the Laws and Customs of War on Land' sought generally to 'diminish the evils of war, as far as military requirements permit'. Stating that 'the right of belligerents to adopt means of injuring the enemy is not unlimited', the Convention banned various weapons (such as poison weapons, and those that cause unnecessary suffering) and practices (the killing or wounding of surrendered enemy, the misuse of a flag of *truce, etc.). Other Conventions addressed the issue of neutrality in land and naval warfare, the status of enemy merchant ships, the laying of 'automatic submarine contact mines', and naval bombardment.

Although they never entered into force, the 1923 Hague (Draft) Rules of Air Warfare were an attempt systematically to apply the Hague approach, which had so far addressed mainly land and naval warfare, to war in and from the air. Thus, incendiary or explosive ammunition was not to be used by or against aircraft, aircraft were to be marked correctly and carry the correct papers, and crew escaping a crippled aircraft by parachute were not to be attacked during their descent. Article 22 of the Draft Rules overlapped the Geneva approach when it prohibited 'aerial bombardment for the purpose of terrorising the civilian population, or destroying or damaging private property not of a military character, or of injuring non-combatants'. Two years later, during a League of Nations conference on controlling the international *arms trade, the 1925 Protocol for the Prohibition of the Use of Asphyxiating or Other Gases, and of Bacteriological Methods of Warfare was signed in Geneva. The Protocol was derived from the basic Hague principle that weapons which cause unnecessary suffering should be prohibited.

The most recent illustration of the Hague approach is the 1980 Convention on Prohibitions or Restrictions on the Use of Certain Conventional Weapons Which May be Deemed to be Excessively Injurious or to Have Indiscriminate Effects. Acknowledging the general principle of restraint in warfare and the requirement to avoid unnecessary suffering, the signatories of the Convention agreed to prohibit or restrict certain weapons, listed in three Protocols to the Convention: weapons 'the primary effect of which is to injure by fragments which in the human body escape detection by X-rays'; mines, booby-traps, and 'other devices'; and incendiary weapons. In 1995 a fourth Protocol was added, prohibiting the use of blinding laser weapons, and in 1996 the existing second Protocol was revised as a result of the international campaign to ban the production and use of anti-personnel mines.   PC

Genghis (Chinggis) **Khan** (*c.*1162–1227), founder of the *Mongol empire, the largest continuous land empire in the history of the world, ultimately stretching from Korea to Hungary. He was born in the north-east of the modern Republic of Mongolia, the son of a tribal chieftain who was murdered when Genghis was a child. His early life was a hard one, but he gradually attracted followers by virtue of his increasing reputation as, in effect, a highly successful bandit. Mongolia in Genghis Khan's day was inhabited by a mosaic of nomadic tribes, some speaking Mongolian, others various forms of Turkish. The tribes' principal activities were herding (mainly horses and sheep), hunting, and raiding each other and the Chinese to the south. By a series of judiciously chosen marriage and other alliances with tribal rulers more powerful than himself, and by choosing the right moment to rid himself of such allies, as well as by military means, Genghis was able by 1206 to unify the tribes of Mongolia under his rule. This process took two-thirds of Genghis's life: only two decades remained in which he could attempt the conquest of the rest of the world.

Mongol expansion followed the tribal unification. The main target was China, divided at that time into three states: the Chin empire in the north, Hsi-Hsia in the north-west, and the Sung empire in the south. Raids into Hsi-Hsia began in 1209, and into Chin in 1211. It is probable that at this early stage there was no fully formed design for permanent conquest, but in due course raids turned into conquest, although the occupation of the Chin empire was not completed until 1234, after Genghis's death.

In the meantime Genghis's troops had ridden westwards, in 1218 conquering Qara-Khitai, in central Asia. In campaigns between 1219 and 1223 Genghis conquered and devastated the empire of the Khwārazm-shāh, the Muslim ruler of most of what is now Iran, Afghanistan, Turkmenistan, and Uzbekistan. The massacre and destruction inflicted on such great cities as Bukhārā, Samarkand, and Harāt was on a massive and previously unparalleled scale. Genghis Khan died in 1227, leading a punitive expedition against Hsi-Hsia.

Genghis's armies were composed of mounted *archers, trained from an early age in military techniques largely indistinguishable from what was required of them as hunters and herders. Hence Genghis was able to mobilize an unusually high proportion of the adult male population. As expansion continued, the Mongols secured the services of Chinese and Muslim siege engineers. The army was intensely manoeuvrable, which may partly explain the (probably misleading) impression of vast numbers. Genghis's practice of warfare has been much admired by such modern authorities as *Liddell Hart. DOM

Liddell Hart, B. H., *Great Captains Unveiled* (London, 1927).
Morgan, David, *The Mongols* (Oxford, 1986).
Ratchnevsky, Paul, *Genghis Khan: His Life and Legacy*, trans. and ed. Thomas N. Haining (Oxford, 1991).

genocide (from Gr.: *genos*, people or race, and Lat.: *caedere*, to kill) is the systematic attempt to destroy and/or eradicate an ethnic, national, racial, or religious group. The expression was first coined by the Polish writer Raphael Lemkin in 1944, in his account of the Nazi occupation of eastern Europe.

Genocidal practices have been common throughout history, from the beginning of the Christian *Crusades in the 11th century, with their brutal treatment of both Jews and Muslims, through Genghis Khan's ruthless expansion of the *Mongol empire in the early 13th century, to the exterminations practised by *Timur in Persia, India, and Syria in the late 14th century. Among many other examples, the 16th-century wars of the European Reformation saw organized massacres of religious opponents, notably by the Duke of *Alba in the Netherlands. The almost complete eradication of the *American Indians, particularly on the eastern coast of what is now the USA in the mid-17th century, was no less than genocide for the purposes of efficient colonization.

The 20th century has seen as much resort to genocidal policies and practices, and with as much alacrity, as at any time in history. The century was just a few years old when German colonial authorities destroyed the Herero people of South-West Africa (now Namibia). Hundreds of thousands of Armenians were massacred by the Turks in 1915 and in the years which followed, and many millions of kulaks (peasants) were killed during the *Stalin collectivization drive in the early 1930s. The destruction of the kulaks introduced another, characteristically 20th-century dimension: 'ideological' genocide. After WW II, the political and economic instability caused by decolonization brought about yet more acts of genocide, such as the mass killings of the Ibo that precipitated the Hausa-Ibo *Nigerian civil war in the mid-1960s, and the explosion of hatred between the Hutu and Tutsi people in central Africa in the 1960s, 1970s, and most recently in 1994. Ideological genocide reappeared in 1966, with the massacre of Indonesian communists, and in Cambodia in the late 1970s as the Khmer Rouge systematically eradicated the so-called 'bourgeoisie', killing millions. Just months before the end of the 20th century, the 'ethnic cleansing' of Kosovar Albanians in the Serbian province of Kosovo in early 1999 made it plain that the inclination to gross cruelty and inhumanity had by no means gone entirely out of fashion. The outrages committed in Kosovo may be tried under the 1948 Genocide Convention, provided sufficient evidence can be collected and the alleged miscreants captured. Indonesia's ruthless oppression of the East Timorese since 1975 also at last achieved worldwide media coverage in 1999, without it being apparent as of writing what may be done to stop it.

Improvements in communications and transport, bureaucratic organization of government, the growth of the 'police state', industrialization, and the ease of modern weapons manufacture may all have combined to make genocide the curse of the 20th century. But if this is so, it is also the case that the 20th century has seen the most concerted efforts to define, prevent, and punish genocide. The impulse to act was provided by one of the most egregious acts of genocide in history: the Holocaust. Between the late 1930s and the end of WW II, some six million people were systematically brutalized, starved, and murdered in Nazi concentration, labour, and extermination camps. The majority of them were Jews, and others included gypsies, Slavs, political opponents such as communists, religious dissidents such as Jehovah's Witnesses, and so-called 'social deviants' such as *homosexuals and the mentally disabled.

Widespread revulsion at the atrocities committed by the Nazis led to calls for an international code for the prohibition and punishment of such practices. Given the development after 1945 of legal thinking and procedure regarding *war crimes and, in particular, crimes against humanity, many argued that it was now both necessary and possible to frame international legislation directed specifically at these most outrageous of crimes. In December 1946 the UN General Assembly unequivocally described genocide as a crime against international law and invited the UN Economic and Social Council (ECOSOC) to prepare a convention. ECOSOC's deliberations resulted in the UN Convention on the Prevention and Punishment of the Crime of Genocide, adopted by the General Assembly in December 1948.

The Genocide Convention, which entered into force in January 1951, is relatively brief, with just nineteen short articles. The first Article confirms that genocide is a crime under international law, whether committed in time of peace or during war; it is this clause which provides the principal distinction between genocide and crimes against humanity—the latter are committed in connection with, or during, war. Article II defines genocide as an act 'committed with intent to destroy, in whole or in part, a national, ethnical, racial or religious group'. As well as outright killing, genocidal acts include causing 'bodily or mental harm', the infliction on the group of 'conditions of life calculated to bring about its physical destruction', the prevention of births within the group, and the forcible removal of children from the group to another group. It may well be that the atrocities in Kosovo, and in other parts of former *Yugoslavia during the wars of the 1990s, will add one more category to the list of genocidal activities: the mass rape of women in order to destroy cultures and genetic lines (see GENDER).

Genocide, as defined in the Convention, is punishable, as are conspiracy, incitement, attempts to commit, and complicity in the acts listed. Any person—whatever their position in government or society—implicated in such acts would be punished, preferably by a tribunal in the state in which the act was committed, or by an 'international penal tribunal'. From the outset, the enforcement of the Convention led to concerns about the possible violation of state sovereignty. In time these concerns gave way to a more direct and interventionist stance by the international community. As a result of the Genocide Convention and subsequent deliberations, it is now generally accepted that genocide is not an internal, domestic matter but is legitimately a question for international attention and action; a genocidal government can have no recourse to the established principles of state sovereignty and non-intervention. Neither is it possible for individuals to avoid extradition and punishment for genocidal acts through a plea of political status and asylum.   PC

German army A 'German' army did not really come into being until 1871 but the military traditions of Prussia stretched back into the 17th century. The army was instrumental in the rise of Prussia. In 1653 Frederick William, 'the Great Elector', raised a standing army. He had served during the *Thirty Years War with the Dutch, and used his experience combined with contemporary French best practice to create an effective army. With this army, Frederick William attempted with partial success to unite his scattered possessions.

In the 17th and 18th centuries Prussia's army was rivalled by those of some other German states. Saxony, alarmed by the ambitions of Prussia which became a kingdom in 1701, maintained an army of 20,000. In the 17th and 18th centuries Germany became a fertile source of mercenary troops, hired out by one German state to another, or to an outside power. The British used nearly 30,000 Hessian *mercenaries in the *American independence war.

As *Howard has written, the Prussian state 'was called into being to provide for the needs of the King of Prussia's army'. In 1740 *Frederick 'the Great' inherited an army of some 80,000 men with the bureaucratic apparatus to support it. To paraphrase a military theorist of a very different era, Mao Tse-tung, Prussian power grew from the barrels of cannons and muskets. Under Frederick I and his successor, Frederick William I (1713–40), *Dessau brought the Prussians success on the battlefield and effective training on the parade square.

Frederick 'the Great' was one of the outstanding soldiers of all time. He used his army to turn Prussia into a great power, and pose a major challenge to Habsburg domination of Germany. From 1756 to 1763 'Old Fritz' fought a powerful combination of foes that included Austria, France, and Russia. His genius lay not only in his battlefield victories, but also in holding out against superior numbers for so long. His generalship was marked by offensive action, risk taking and the use of the innovative tactics such as the 'oblique order' (see ORDER, TACTICAL). His masterpiece was probably the battle of *Leuthen in which Frederick smashed an Austrian army nearly twice as strong as his force.

The Prussian army that on 14 October 1806 faced Napoleon's armies at *Jena/Auerstadt were the inheritors of the proud traditions of 'Old Fritz's' army and had every reason to be confident. But in Clausewitz's words, 'behind the fine façade all was mildew' and by the evening of that day the Prussian forces were shattered, and so were their assumptions of Prussian military superiority. Even Frederick 'the Great''s army was not a national force. It included Saxon POWs remustered into the Prussian army, foreign deserters, and mercenaries as well as 'Prussians'. A man of his time, Frederick recoiled from the thought of a 'people's war'.

Although resistance continued after Jena/Auerstadt, most of Prussia was swiftly overrun by the French. Prussia was forced to accept humiliating terms, including limiting its army to 42,000 men. This disaster prompted the Prussian army to begin a programme of radical reform that in the short term resulted in the rebuilding of the Prussian army, and in the long term laid the foundations for Prussian military greatness.

*Scharnhorst worked with others to produce a military system that was a response to the new period of absolute war that had been unleashed by the *French Revolutionary wars. By the 1808 Treaty of Paris the Prussian army was restricted to a mere 42,000 men and forbidden to raise a militia. Scharnhorst and his colleagues circumvented these restrictions by various means. Under the *Krümper* system, soldiers were sent on leave to be replaced by new recruits, thus ensuring that a reserve of trained men was built up. By spring 1812 the Prussians had some 24,000 men available to be recalled to the colours. The military reformers also overhauled the organization of the army, introducing a system of permanent brigades, reforming officer selection, logistics, and tactical training. In December 1808 the War Ministry was founded with Scharnhorst as head of the General War Department. Perhaps of greatest significance for the future was the establishment in May 1810 of the Allgemeine Kriegsschule (General War School), an institution that allowed the training of staff officers in a methodical fashion.

While the Prussian army was undergoing humiliation and reform, the armies of other German states were sharing in British and French triumphs and disasters. The small exiled army of the Duke of Brunswick served with Wellington's army in the *Peninsular war. Hanover, having been overrun by Napoleon, provided some of Wellington's best troops in the form of the King's German Legion. In the Russian campaign of 1812, three of Napoleon's corps consisted of troops from German satellite states. Prussia unwillingly committed 21,000 troops under *Yorck but, following the French disaster, Yorck signed the Convention of Taurrogen with the Russians in December 1812. After some initial hesitation, the Prussian government backed him and entered the war against Napoleon. Reservists rejoined their units and new units were formed, including *Freikorps* (free corps) and companies of *Freiwilligen Jäger* (volunteer riflemen drawn from the well-to-do classes). Conscription was introduced, and Landwehr (militia) units were raised. These efforts produced an army of 128,000 men. While the extent of popular enthusiasm for the war should not be exagger-

ated, clearly the events of 1813 tapped into the German nationalism that Napoleon had unwittingly unleashed by his victories of 1806–7.

Prussia played a vital role in the 1813–14 campaigns. By the end of August the Prussians could field four corps and other formations, totalling about 280,000 men. The Army of Silesia was commanded by *Blücher, one of the few senior commanders in the 1806 campaign to emerge with his reputation intact. Following Napoleon's return from exile, Blücher fought a major battle at Ligny (16 June 1815) and then played a crucial role in Napoleon's defeat at *Waterloo two days later, which has fairly been described as a German victory: apart from the Prussians, Wellington's army contained a significant number of German troops from the armies of Hanover, Nassau, and Brunswick, as well as the King's German Legion.

Scharnhorst's work underpinned the Prussian 'von Boyen' conscription laws (1814), by which men in their 20s served three years with the army before going to the reserves and then progressively, as they grew older, to various types of militia unit. In 1830 the standing army consisted of 130,000 men, but by mobilizing the reserves and militia this total could be doubled. The revolutions of 1848 and the mobilization of 1859 revealed faults in the Prussian army. The next wave of reforms, which aimed to reorganize and enlarge the army and Landwehr, took place in the early 1860s under the war minister *Roon. They created a constitutional crisis that led to the appointment of *Bismarck as chancellor, who took on the parliament and prevailed.

Prussia fought and won three short wars in this period, against Denmark (1864), Austria (1866), and France (1870–1). *Moltke 'the Elder' was appointed Prussian COS in 1857. He revitalized the *general staff, which in 1870 was split into three sections, dealing with movements, *railways and logistics, and *intelligence. It was a way of 'institutionalizing excellence' and it gave the Prussian army a massive advantage over its enemies in terms of administration and command. The general staff was fairly small—in the mid-1880s it had fewer than 170 officers, rising to 625 in 1914—but they were conscious of being an élite. In the 1870s and 1880s there had been a struggle with the imperial parliament (Reichstag) over the army budget. In 1883 the general staff achieved effective independence from the war ministry, and the chief received the right of direct access to the kaiser. The Reichstag's tenuous control over the army vanished. In the process, the general staff became dangerously insulated from political control and the wider political aspects of planning and executing wars. The army had a significant impact on foreign policy. This was of particular importance in the reign of Wilhelm II, who came to the throne in 1888. Wilhelm, the 'Supreme war Leader', sacked Bismarck and entered on a bellicose policy that alienated France, Russia, and Britain and led directly to war in 1914.

Moltke proved to be highly adept as a field commander, and the army was a highly effective political tool used by

Bismarck with great skill to unite the non-Austrian German states under Prussian leadership. As a result of 1866, the other north German states were either annexed or formed into a North German Confederation; this provided Prussia with another three army corps. In 1870, this army numbered just under a million, and the additions of contingents from the southern German states of Bavaria, Baden, and Württemberg raised the total to 1.8 million.

In 1870, the Germans rapidly defeated the French army in battles at *Rezonville/Gravelotte and *Sedan and captured *Napoleon III. Unlike in 1866, which was a quintessentially limited war where the Austrians accepted the verdict of one major battle at *Königgrätz, a proportion of the French people were persuaded to fight on under a republican government. The German army became increasingly frustrated at their inability to conclude the war, and began a fairly ruthless campaign against *francs-tireurs* (*partisans); a policy of *Schrecklichkeit* (dreadfulness or frightfulness) was to characterize German *counter-insurgency down to 1945.

In 1871 the Prussian king, Wilhelm I, was proclaimed kaiser of the new German empire. The new peacetime Kaiserheer (imperial army) had about 500,000 men divided into thirteen Prussian corps, with a further one composed mainly of Prussians and two of Bavarian; Saxony, and Württemberg contributed a corps each. There were a further 370,000 reservists organized into eighteen divisions. The Bavarian kingdom maintained their own military structure. The German army saw little action in the years between the end of the Franco-German war and the outbreak of WW I. The exceptions were the brutal repression of the revolt of the Herreros in South-West Africa (1904–7), and the *Boxer rebellion when some German troops served in the multinational force in China. At home, German society became increasingly militarized. The army gained enormous respect, with the chief aspiration of the upwardly mobile being to become a reserve officer. The very conservative, even reactionary, officer corps feared the rise of the industrial working classes, represented in the Reichstag by the Social Democrats, and thus chose to take a disproportionate number of rural recruits from the annual draft—which was always selective.

In August 1914 the German army put eight armies (2.1 million out of 3.8 million men mobilized) into the field, and a further ten were raised later in the war. They initiated a plan named after Schlieffen, the CGS whose memorandum of 1905 first drew together the broad outlines and which evolved year by year thereafter. One army was left to watch the Russians, while seven were launched in a 'right hook' through northern France in an attempt to knock her out of the war in a rapid campaign, after which the Germans were to have redeployed via their strategic railways to meet the slower Russians. In the event the plan failed, albeit narrowly, and by sending German forces through neutral Belgium, it gave the British government a popular rallying cause to enter the war as an ally of France.

By the end of 1914 the war in the west had stalemated. In the east the Germans halted the Russian advance and, with their Austro-Hungarian allies, carried the war to the enemy. The Germans mostly remained on the defensive in the west in 1915, while chasing the Russians out of Poland. In April they attacked near *Ypres in Belgium, making the first use of poison *gas in history. The German army easily defeated the attempts of the British and French to break through the trench deadlock during 1916, and in February the CGS *Falkenhayn opened a battle of *attrition at *Verdun, the aim being to 'bleed the French white'. From July 1916 the Germans were attacked by a largely British force on the *Somme, and in 1917 the Germans remained on the defensive in the west. In the east they destroyed Serbia in 1915 and Romania in 1916, and in 1917 effectively knocked Russia out of the war.

Falkenhayn was replaced in August 1916 by the team of *Hindenburg and *Ludendorff, who had enjoyed success in the east. They became the effective dictators of the entire German war effort, introducing the economic programme named after the former that mobilized the state for *total war: as under the Prussian monarchs of the early 18th century, the state seemed to exist for the support of the army, rather than the other way round (see POLITICAL ECONOMY AND WAR).

At a tactical level, the German army was innovative. The Germans had suffered heavy casualties from the incessant if unsophisticated pounding of the British on the Somme, and the policy of 'Halten was zu heiten ist' (hold on to whatever can be held), which meant promptly counter-attacking Allied lodgements in the German line, was helping to bleed the defenders white. The Germans launched at least 330 counter-attacks during the 1916 battle of the Somme. A team of fairly junior officers carried out a consultation process with front-line troops and staff officers, and sifted the evidence to help develop a new *doctrine. The result was a move from linear to 'elastic' defence in depth, based on strong points and counter-attack units. In the winter of 1916–17 the Siegfried Stellung (known to the British as the *Hindenburg Line) was constructed on these principles. In February 1917 the Germans fell 15–20 miles (24–32 km) back to this new position, abandoning *inter alia* the Somme battlefield. The move shortened the German line, freeing troops to be held in reserve, and forced the Allies to occupy overlooked and otherwise inferior positions all along the line.

On the offensive side, the Germans began to organize storm-troop units in early 1915. Heavily armed and using infiltration tactics, such units were a significant step towards the creation of a more effective offensive doctrine. These developments were paralleled by those of the Allies, as were the new 'hurricane' artillery methods associated with Col. Bruchmuller. On 21 March 1918 the Germans launched MICHAEL, the first of a series of attempts to smash the British and French before the fresh American armies could arrive in large numbers. Initially successful, by the end of July the Germans had run out of steam. They committed several errors. Unlike the Allies, they had failed to develop and employ tanks in any reasonable numbers, and had most of their cavalry on the *eastern front, therefore they had no means of exploitation. Worse, German divisions insisted on driving as far as they could after they made a breakthrough, and found themselves sitting, exhausted, at the end of long lines of communication. They were thus vulnerable to the allied counter-offensive which began on the *Marne at the end of July and at *Amiens on 8 August. From then until the *Armistice on 11 November, the Germans were always on the back foot, never able to initiate.

The Allies did not repeat the German errors at the operational level, fighting a series of shallow battles that kept constant pressure on the enemy. The Germans were driven from position to position by the Allies, the Hindenburg Line falling at the end of September. With revolution breaking out in Germany and the *morale of some, but not all, German units collapsing, Ludendorff resigned on 28 October, to be replaced by Gen Groener. The German officer corps largely succeeded in shrugging off the blame for the defeat of the German army, helping to establish the stab in the back myth that it had been the fault of the politicians and elements on the home front. In reality, the German army was decisively beaten in the field by an army superior in every respect. It had suffered about 5 million casualties, including 1 million fatalities.

Most German soldiers went home when the war ended, and as Keith Simpson has observed, 'by the middle of December 1918, apart from a few scattered units there was no such thing as a German army'. Civil war seemed close as *Freikorps* units of ex-soldiers fought communists and revolutionary socialists. Early in 1919 the National Assembly at Weimar passed a provisional armed forces law, and hoped to create an army out of the *Freikorps*. However, the Treaty of Versailles imposed serious restrictions on the new army, and the Reichswehr, the German army of the twenties and early thirties, was limited to a strength of 100,000 men and was denied most modern weapons as well as a general staff. It formed an excellent basis for expansion (much as the *Krumper* system had in the Napoleonic period), and was formally abolished in 1935, when Hitler announced the reintroduction of conscription and acknowledged the existence of the Luftwaffe. The Reichswehr then became the *Wehrmacht, with the army but one element within it, alongside the navy and the Luftwaffe.

The German army expanded rapidly between 1935 and 1939, taking the lead in the development of armoured tactics (see BLITZKRIEG) but remaining essentially a two-tier organization, with a majority of old-style infantry moving behind the panzer divisions. It won an impressive (though scarcely surprising) victory over the Poles in 1939, and the following year it overran France and the Low Countries (see FRANCE, FALL OF) in a far more evenly matched campaign. Operation *BARBAROSSA, the invasion of the Soviet Union in 1941, ushered in a bitter and destructive campaign which was ultimately to wear down the German army, with *Stalingrad and *Kursk important milestones on the road to defeat, and result in the occupation of Berlin by the Russians.

It fought, always well and with at least temporary success, in Norway, Africa, Greece, Italy, and the Balkans. But for all its excellence at the tactical level, it was committed to strategic tasks which lay beyond it, and by the war's end it was utterly defeated, having suffered over 5 million casualties including 2 million killed. In the process it had become heavily politicized, its soldiers fighting not simply for their country, but also for Hitler as their führer and supreme commander, as well as for familiar motivators such as good leadership, unit loyalty, and peer-group pressure.

The German army was reborn in 1955. West Germany was then in the front line of the *Cold War. The USA desired to see West Germany, which had rapidly passed from defeated enemy to potential military ally, contribute to the defence of NATO's central front. After considerable debate in West Germany and elsewhere in *NATO the Bundeswehr (Federal Defence Force) was created. The fears of recent western victims of German aggression were somewhat allayed by the fact that the Bundeswehr would come directly under NATO command. The ethos of the Bundeswehr, which included airforce and naval elements, was consciously shaped to be very different from that of the Prussian and Nazi era: the conscript soldiers were thinking, democratic 'civilians in uniform' and the army was subject to parliamentary control. The Bundeswehr rapidly became a central pillar of NATO's defences, In the mid-1980s the army element was twelve divisions strong.

In 1956 communist East Germany raised the National People's Army (National Volksarmee, or NVA), building on a pre-existing cadre of paramilitary police. The USSR, the principal victim of German aggression in WW II, was understandably keen to keep a tight rein on the four motor-rifle and two armoured divisions of the NVA which were closely integrated into the *Warsaw Pact structure. In keeping with the Marxist-Leninist tradition, the NVA was seen as an ideological tool of the government. Its traditions were an interesting mixture of Marxism and Prussianism; its heroes included both *Engels and Clausewitz. After German unification in October 1990, when the NVA was taken over by the Bundeswehr, officers who went to inspect the East German units before takeover found them in a terrifying state of readiness. NVA officers above major were retired, with a few exceptions, and those selected for transfer to the Bundeswehr, known as 'Ossies' to distinguish them from the West German majority 'Wessies', underwent a process of retraining. The process of unification, like that of Germany, has not been easy, but the German army has since been trusted to deploy outside Germany's borders.   GDS

Craig, Gordon A., *The Politics of the Prussian Army* (London, 1964).

Howard, Michael, *War in European History* (Oxford, 1984).

Paret, Peter (ed.) *Makers of Modern Strategy* (Oxford, 1986).

Simpson, Keith, *History of the German Army* (London, 1985).

German East Africa, campaign in (1914–18). In 1914 Germany possessed four colonies in sub-Saharan Africa: Togoland, Cameroons, South-West Africa (now Namibia), and East Africa (now Tanzania). The fight for the fourth of these has most captured the public imagination. The last German troops did not surrender until two weeks after the *Armistice in Europe, on 25 November 1918. Their commander, Paul von *Lettow-Vorbeck, became a German hero, the symbol of an army that deemed itself undefeated in the field. By the 1960s he had acquired another reputation, that of *guerrilla leader. Neither interpretation can be fully sustained.

The German colonial troops, the *Schutztruppen*, were equipped and trained only for internal policing duties, but Lettow-Vorbeck, appointed through the influence of the German *general staff, aimed to contribute to the main struggle in the event of war in Europe by drawing British forces away from their principal theatres and sought battle rather than shunned it. However, his isolation from Germany meant that neither trained European soldiers nor stocks of munitions were easily replaced. After the battle of Mahiwa, which Lettow-Vorbeck began on 15 October 1917, the Germans had exhausted all their *smokeless cartridges and had to abandon German territory for Portuguese in the search for ammunition.

British strategy in Africa was much more limited. On 5 August 1914 a subcommittee of the *Committee of Imperial Defence decided that the principal objectives were to eliminate Germany's wireless stations and to deprive its navy of bases. Heinrich Schnee, the governor of German East Africa, anxious to protect the fruits of German colonialism, effectively co-operated in the achievement of both these objectives. The principal German cruiser in the region, SMS *Königsberg*, was unable to enter Dar es Salaam, and took refuge in the delta of the Rufiji river, where she was eventually located and sunk on 11 July 1915. The British colonial office lacked the troops to do much more, and it therefore called on the Indian army. Indian Expeditionary Force B, principally made up of second-line units, landed at German East Africa's second major port, Tanga, on 2 November 1914. Lettow-Vorbeck had concentrated his forces to the north, with a view to launching an attack into British East Africa, but was still able to redeploy and inflict a humiliating defeat on the British. The latter, hamstrung by overlapping administrative authorities and now deprived of any faith in the available Indian troops, did nothing in 1915. The Germans raided the Uganda railway.

The campaign was reactivated in March 1916 with the arrival of South African reinforcements under J. C. Smuts.

Like the Indians, the South Africans were not easily deployable to the western front, and to that extent Lettow-Vorbeck's strategy was not working. However, Smuts's aims were much more extensive than those of London. He wished to conquer the entire German colony and then to trade territory with Portugal, so as to extend South Africa's frontier into Mozambique at least as far as the Zambezi. He therefore invaded German East Africa from the north, cutting across the axes of the two principal railway lines and neglecting the harbours on the coast. He had earned his military reputation as the leader of a Boer *commando and conducted his campaign as though his mounted rifles could move as fast through regions infested with tsetse fly as across the veld. He accorded little recognition to the difference between rainy seasons and dry. His advance, although rapid, failed ever to grip and defeat the German forces. His troops entered Dar es Salaam on 3 September 1916, and were astride the Central railway, running from there to Tabora and Lake Tanganyika. Smuts should have paused but he did not, plunging on to the Rufiji river, and claiming that the campaign was all but over when in reality it had stalled.

Worrying for Smuts were Belgian territorial ambitions in the west. Debouching from the Congo into Ruanda and Urundi, the Belgians had reached Tabora in August 1916. Smuts's sub-imperialism was challenged even more fundamentally by the contribution of blacks to the campaign. The *Schutztruppen*, although officered by Europeans, were predominantly native Africans, and yet they had proved formidable opponents for the whites. On the British side the South Africans were particularly susceptible to malaria, and by early 1917 they were being replaced in the British order of battle by the black units of the West African Frontier Force and the King's African Rifles. Moreover, the collapse of animal transport meant that supply was largely dependent on human resources; the British ended up recruiting over a million labourers for the campaign. The long-term impact for Africa—in the development of the cash economy, in the penetration of colonial rule into areas hitherto unmapped, and in the erosion of chiefly or tribal authority—was immense.

Smuts was recalled to London in January 1917, and handed over his command to A. R. Hoskins. Hoskins set about remedying the worst of the health, transport, and supply problems, but in doing so aroused impatience in the War Cabinet in London which could not understand why a campaign which Smuts had said was over was still continuing to drain Allied shipping. (This was one area in which Lettow-Vorbeck most nearly fulfilled his overall strategy.) In April Hoskins was replaced by J. L. van Deventer, another Afrikaaner, who implemented Hoskins's plan but still failed to prevent the rump of the Germans from escaping into Portuguese East Africa in November. For the next year, Lettow-Vorbeck's columns marched through Portuguese territory, fighting largely to secure supplies and munitions.

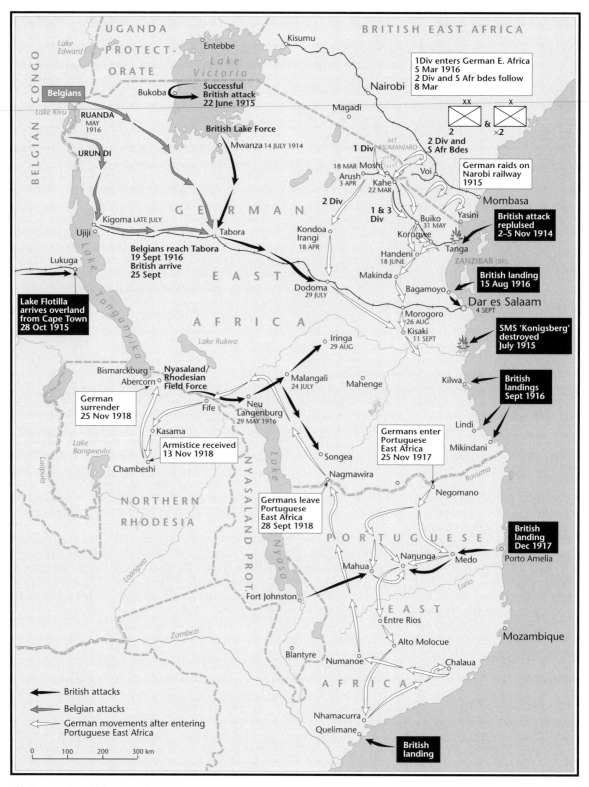

The **German East Africa campaign**, 1914–18.

The Allies still had a ration strength of 111,371 in the theatre at the war's end.

The campaign for German East Africa was effectively confined to a period of eighteen months, from March 1916 to November 1917. Its commencement had been delayed by the under-appreciated efforts of Lettow-Vorbeck's colleagues in South-West Africa (which had engaged the South Africans until 1915) and in the Cameroons (which had tied down British West African forces until 1916). The inadequacies of Portuguese military administration, rather than the failings of the British, go far to explain Lettow-Vorbeck's continued survival after all political purpose in continued fighting had been removed.   HFAS

Miller, Charles, *Battle for the Bundu: The First World War in East Africa* (London, 1974).

Page, Melvin E. (ed.), *Africa and the First World War* (London, 1987).

Geronimo (*c.*1829–1909) (Athapascan: *Goyathlay*), Chiricahua Apache and leader of resistance to the US army, although he considered his main enemy to be the Mexicans. He ruined the reputation of famed American Indian-fighter Crook, whose use of Apache scouts twice forced him into the San Carlos reservation in Arizona, only to lead raiding parties out again. Miles eventually resumed Crook's tactics, forcing Geronimo's final surrender in 1886. Promised a short gaol term and an eventual return to Arizona, he was imprisoned in Florida for eleven years and lived out his life in Oklahoma. For some reason his name became the war cry of US *airborne forces.   HEB

Gettysburg, battle of (1863), three-day engagement that marked the turning point of the *American civil war. After *Chancellorsville, there was a possibility that part of the Army of Northern Virginia would be sent to relieve *Vicksburg. *Lee argued successfully that the overall situation could best be redeemed by taking the war into the North, and for once he commanded near parity of numbers, with 75,500 men against 85,500.

After Union cavalry unexpectedly mauled *Stuart at Brandy Station on 9 June, he took half his corps on a raid around the Union army. It has been argued that by depriving himself of his 'eyes', Lee stumbled into an unwanted battle, but in fact he was eager for a decision, and Stuart's raid was an unsuccessful diversion, like Hooker's failed cavalry ploy at Chancellorsville. The battle itself began with a chance 1 July encounter between elements of the corps under A. P. *Hill and a Federal cavalry division, which sucked in both armies. The Unionists were driven through Gettysburg, falling back into a 'U' with their right curled around Culp's and Cemetery hills, and their centre and left stretching along Cemetery Ridge towards the Round Top hills. *Meade, the newly appointed Union commander, decided to hold this ground.

Corps commanders on both sides performed poorly, none more so than Sickles, who advanced the Union left into the open on 2 July, to be driven back in disorder. But at least partly because of this, *Longstreet in turn failed to perform the outflanking manoeuvre Lee entrusted to him, which could have rolled up the whole Union line. By the time the Confederates regrouped to assault the earlier unguarded Little Round Top, Union commanders had rushed just enough reinforcements to hold it. Meanwhile Ewell displayed none of his predecessor Jackson's dash and only attacked Culp's and Cemetery hills late in the day. It is likely they would have fallen earlier.

The third day has given rise to more controversy than any other in military history. Lee, who was ill, continued to show none of his customary sureness of touch and judged himself responsible for what followed, but 'Lost Cause' polemicists blame Longstreet instead. Both views discount the unexpectedly steadfast performance of the Union army. Convinced that defeats and frequent changes in commander must have shaken enemy *morale, and believing that the attacks on their flanks must have weakened their centre, Lee ordered an extremely reluctant Longstreet to launch a frontal assault against Cemetery Ridge. After a two-hour bombardment that served mainly to warn where the blow would land, Pickett's and Pettigrew's Divisions charged unsupported and with exemplary discipline over an open half-mile (0.8 km), to be beaten back by Hancock's reinforced corps.

Hindsight supports Longstreet's view that after the second day Lee should have forced Meade to attack him by getting between him and Washington. It was not a crushing defeat, because the Unionists were unable to mount a vigorous *pursuit, but the Confederates lost about 40 per cent of those engaged against only 25 per cent of their opponents, and never regained the strategic initiative.   HEB

GI Bill (GI: Government (or General) Issue, a term used of US soldiers). The GI Bill was US federal legislation which created a comprehensive package of benefits, particularly financial assistance for entering higher education, for *veterans of US military service. This has proved highly successful.

The first GI Bill was proposed during WW II in an attempt to avoid the recession that followed WW I when millions of veterans returned home to face unemployment. Pres Franklin D. *Roosevelt signed the Bill, officially known as the Serviceman's Readjustment Act, on 22 June 1944. It offered to veterans a proportion of college tuition fees and other educational costs. Other benefits included mortgage subsidies, helping veterans to buy homes with relative ease.

The programme was used by 2.2 million to enter higher education. The Bill made a college education attainable by veterans of any class, race, or religion—something that had previously been the preserve of America's upper classes.

Following the end of the *Vietnam war and the cessation of the military draft in 1973, the number of volunteers for the military declined. In 1984 Sonny Montgomery proposed a GI Bill to encourage military service even in times of peace. The Montgomery GI Bill allows servicemen and -women to contribute to a programme which allows them educational benefits after they are discharged.   MCM

Giap, Gen Vo Nguyen (b. 1912). Giap was born in the village of An Xa, Quang Binh province, just north of the 17th Parallel of Latitude. His father, an educated man who was both a mandarin and a farmer, took a close interest in his son's education, and helped to imbue the boy with the spirit of nationalism that he himself had inherited from Giap's grandfather.

Giap was caught up in nationalist agitation in the late 1920s and came to study the writings of Nguyen Ai Quoc (*Ho Chi Minh). Finding them persuasive Giap became a communist and was arrested in the course of the French suppression of the Nghe An Soviets in 1930. Spending only a few months of his sentence in prison Giap then devoted himself to study, gaining the baccalaureate in Hué before moving to Hanoi where he completed a degree in law in 1937. He then taught in a secondary school where he was able to pursue a deep interest in military history.

By this time he had become a recognized leader of the national communist movement and in 1940, with several of his contemporaries, he fled from another wave of French suppression to join Ho Chi Minh in southern China. Here he worked with Ho, Pham Van Dong, and Truong Chinh to build the core of the Vietminh (Vietnam Independence League). Returning to the far north of Vietnam in 1941, Giap's first major task was to disseminate propaganda. The (Vichy) French countered his teams, and he had to form armed bands to protect them.

From this beginning Giap began his rise as the senior military specialist in Ho's immediate entourage. As the Vietminh armed forces grew from a few hundred to many thousands, Giap's experience and confidence developed. By 1950, when Mao's armies had taken control of China and substantially equipped the Vietminh, Giap was at the head of an army of five divisions, ready to challenge the French for control of *Indochina.

Initially successful in driving the French out of northern Tonkin he attempted too much and suffered three successive defeats in 1951. Giap then decided to lure the French out of the Red River delta, rather than continue to beat his head against the firm defences of the de Lattre Line. In 1952 and 1953, in a daring series of campaigns he gained control of the highlands of Tonkin, penetrating into Laos and threatening the royal capital Luang Prabang. Major French counter-offensives achieved little and in late 1953 Gen Henri Navarre took the gamble of parachuting over 10,000 men deep into the interior. Based at *Dien Bien Phu and supplied by air,

this force was intended to force Giap to fight a pitched battle where the superiority of French conventional armament would tell. Not quite. The outcome was a smashing conventional-force victory for Giap, sufficient to destroy the remaining credibility of and public support for the French government's policies. A local engagement in a remote area broke the French will to continue the struggle. At the Geneva Conference of mid-1954 Vietnam was divided between communist and non-communist nationalist governments and the French departed.

In the late 1950s the communists in the north transformed their domain on Marxist-Leninist principles. Giap, now defence minister and deputy PM, became significant as a political counterweight to the more radical Truong Chinh in the abortive Land Reform programme. Continuing to expand, equip, and train his army, Giap did not challenge the southern government led by Ngo Dinh Diem directly, preferring to exert pressure through the Vietcong, the southern communist *guerrilla forces. In 1964, following a series of military coups in the south, Giap sent elements of his army in to press the conflict to a conclusion.

He was thwarted by the speed of USA and Allied intervention. Giap's plan to take Saigon by 1967 had to be set aside as Gen *Westmoreland built up a force of manoeuvre with strong offensive capability. Giap then focused on luring Westmoreland's forces out into the countryside, where he kept them engaged while the Vietcong prepared to rise in the cities, damaging Westmoreland's credibility and humiliating Pres Lyndon Johnson. The *Tet offensive of 1968 was a military victory for the Americans and South Vietnamese but a political triumph for the North and Vietcong, because it broke US political will. From then on the US aim was to get out and hand over responsibility for defence of the south to the South Vietnamese. Pres Richard Nixon's policy of 'Vietnamization' proved inadequate to hold Giap and his divisions, and Saigon fell in 1975.

Since the end of the war for unification, Giap's fortunes have waned in the face of new challenges such as those of the Cambodian invasion and the Chinese attack of 1979–80, and competition from younger commanders and old political rivals. He retired essentially in 1982, continuing to hold a place of honour in Hanoi. With some 30 years in the position of supreme military command of his nation's forces, Giap has had a career which few can match. He has, however, had to learn by bitter failures and costly defeats. He was fortunate in having under his command soldiers who were imbued with strong faith in their cause and ready to die because the alternatives to victory were unacceptable to them. Giap himself played a notable part in creating both this spirit and the force which it bound together in victory and defeat.   RO'N

Gibraltar, siege of (1779–83). Since its capture in 1704, many politicians had considered trading Gibraltar for peace with Spain, but public feeling kept it in the forefront of the British mind. During the *American independence war, 7,500 British and Hanoverian troops conducted a spirited defence against the Spanish and French, repulsing every assault. Indeed the Hanoverian regiments who fought bravely for King George during the siege, were to wear 'Gibraltar' as a *battle honour on their sleeves while fighting in the *German army during WW I.

The Rock held out for three years, seven months, and twelve days until its eventual relief. The high point of the siege of Gibraltar came on 13 September 1783, when ten floating batteries of 200 guns were brought to bear on the defenders. Although these batteries were stoutly built with layers of sand and cork, and fireproofed by constant dousing with sea water, the British still managed to set them alight with concentrated fire by red-hot shot, forcing the Spanish commander Moreno to order their scuttling. A raid by British gunboats rescued and captured more than 350 prisoners.

From then on the besiegers settled into a lengthy *blockade. A relief *convoy of 34 fast newly copper-bottomed ships of the line, commanded by Adm Lord Howe, evaded Córdoba's 49 French and Spanish ships, and broke through to relieve the garrison in October 1782. The commander of Gibraltar, Lt Gen George Eliott, had looked after his men very well while living a Spartan existence himself, and was rewarded with a peerage for his efforts, becoming Lord Heathfield. 　　　　　　　　　　　　　　　　TM

Gladiators' war (73–71 BC), also known as the Third Servile War. Rome had acquired vast numbers of slaves who periodically turned on their masters. The first two Servile Wars (135–132 BC, 103–99 BC) both took place on Sicily and were ruthlessly put down. The third outbreak of armed slave dissent was by far the most serious occurring as it did in Italy itself. An army of rebellious slaves, led by the Thracian gladiator Spartacus, defied the might of Rome from their base on the slopes of Mt Vesuvius. Their terrorizing of southern Italy and mere presence was a direct challenge to the fabric of the empire. Thousands of slaves flocked to this sanctuary which became an armed camp of considerable size and organization.

Spartacus' defeat of Varinius with 40,000 men gave the gladiators virtual control over most of Campania. With victory over two Roman consuls sent against him, Spartacus and his army were then able to range over all of Italy. Although defeated twice by Crassus it was only with the return of *Pompey from putting down another revolt in Spain that the uprising was finally extinguished. Spartacus himself was killed and his followers hunted down and executed. JR-W

Glendower, Owen (correctly Owain Glyn Dwr) (?1350–?1416), Welsh prince who came to prominence in the early 15th century when his actions proved to be the catalyst for a widespread rebellion against English rule. The immediate cause of the rebellion is unclear, being a dispute either over land or over Glendower's supposed unwillingness to fight in Scotland, but it occurred against a backdrop of growing Welsh discontent. In September 1400 Glendower had himself proclaimed prince of Wales and took up arms against the English. The rebellion spread across Wales and the ineffectiveness of English countermeasures alienated the cross-border Percy family, which consequently rebelled and sided with Glendower. The rebellion reached its height in 1405, but political and military setbacks resulted in the insurrection being brought to a halt in 1406, with the future *Henry V playing a prominent role. The loss of Aberystwyth and Harlech by 1409 indicated that the rebellion was effectively over and Glendower, his family incarcerated, went into hiding. From this point on he disappears into legend, although Henry V tried unsuccessfully to reconcile with him in 1415. Glendower probably died soon after and his burial place remains unknown. 　　　　　　JDB

Allmand, C., *Henry V* (London, 1992).

Davies, R. R., *Conquest, Coexistence and Change: Wales 1063–1415* (Oxford, 1987).

gliders first saw military use during WW II and were used by Axis and Allied forces for the movement of troops, heavy weapons, and equipment. The Germans were the first to use gliders operationally, having developed them during the period 1933–7. The DFS 230 entered service in 1940 as the standard cargo- and troop-carrier, accommodating ten troops including the pilot. Comprising a tubular steel frame covered with fabric and wooden wings, it was normally towed by a Junkers Ju 52, Heinkel He 111, Henschel 126, Messerschmitt Bf 110, or Junkers Ju 87, at speeds of up to 120 mph (193 km/ph). The DFS 230 was used to particularly good effect during the assault on Eben Emael in May 1940 when nine gliders carrying a handful of engineers landed on the top of the fortress whose 5 foot (1.52 metre) thick reinforced concrete casemates were then breached with hollow charge explosives.

The DFS 230 saw action again in May 1941 when 71 gliders landed elements of the 1st Battalion of XI Air Corps' Assault Regiment on *Crete. A large number of gliders were destroyed during the landings, which took place under heavy fire, while others suffered damage from the rocky terrain on which they landed.

In mid-1941 a partial replacement for the DFS 230, the Gotha 242, entered service. With a wingspan of 79 feet (24.08 metres) and payload of 8,000 lb (3,629 kg), it could carry 23 troops, a field gun, and light vehicle. Its construction comprised a nacelle of fabric-covered tubular steel with twin tail booms and wings of wood. With a maximum towing speed of 180 mph (290 km/ph), it was towed by a Junkers 52 or Heinkel 111.

In 1941 the Luftwaffe introduced the Me 321 'Gigant'. With a wingspan of 181 feet (55.2 metres), its payload was 28 tons of cargo or 200 troops. The fuselage was of fabric-covered tubular steel and the wings of tubular steel were covered with plywood and fabric. Take-off was assisted by rockets in racks under the wings. A special five-engined tug aircraft, the Heinkel 111Z, was developed to tow this glider. A powered version of the Me 321, the Me 323, entered service in 1942. Equipped with six engines and a wingspan of 181 feet (55.2 metres), it could carry up to 21,500 lb (9,752.4 kg) of cargo, an 88 mm gun, or 130 troops.

The first British glider to enter service was the Hotspur. Flown by a crew of two, it was, however, capable of carrying only eight troops or approximately 1 ton of cargo. Thus, shortly after entering service, it was relegated to use as a trainer. The workhorse of British *airborne forces was the Horsa which was also used by US airborne divisions. Constructed of plywood with a fabric skin, it had a wingspan of 88 feet (26.8 metres) and a crew of two. Towed by a Stirling or Halifax bomber, or *Dakota, it had a maximum towing speed of 160 mph (257 km/ph). With a payload of 3.5 tons, it could carry 28 troops, a jeep and trailer or 6-pounder *anti-armour gun, or a 75 mm pack howitzer and jeep.

In 1941, the Hamilcar entered service. Constructed of wood and metal, with a wingspan of 110 feet (33.5 metres) and a payload of 17,500 lb (7,938 kg), it was designed to carry heavy loads: 17-pounder anti-armour gun and tractor; 25-pounder field gun and tractor; a light tank or two Bren carriers. With a crew of two, it was towed by either a Stirling or Halifax bomber and had a maximum towing speed of 150 mph (241 km/ph).

The first operational use of gliders by the British took place in November 1942 when 34 engineers from 1st Airborne Division were flown to Norway in two Horsas of the 1st Battalion The Glider Pilot Regiment, towed by Halifax tugs of 38 Wing RAF. Their mission was to attack the Norsk Hydro Plant at Vermork, in southern Norway, which produced heavy water for the Nazi atomic weapon development programme. Unfortunately, both gliders were forced to crash-land far from their objective and one tug crashed into mountains. Of the two parties of engineers, some were killed during the crash landings and the remainder executed by the Nazis.

The principal glider of US airborne forces was the Waco, known as the Hadrian when used by the British, which entered service in 1942. Constructed from tubular steel and wood with a fabric skin and wooden floor, it could carry fifteen fully equipped troops including the two crew. Normally towed by a C-47, it had a maximum towing speed of 125 mph (201 km/hr). The first major operational use of the Waco was in July 1943 during the invasion of *Sicily in which 1st Airborne Division took part. Eight Horsa gliders and 144 Wacos/Hadrians flew 1st Airlanding Brigade and gliderborne elements of the division's two parachute brigades to landing zones on the east coast of the island.

Unfortunately a combination of adverse weather, heavy anti-aircraft fire (some of it from Allied ships off the coast), and inexperienced tug pilots resulted in heavy losses within the division which nevertheless succeeded in taking its objectives.

The next major operation involving the use of gliders was the invasion of Normandy. On the night of 5/6 June a company group of 2nd Battalion Oxfordshire & Buckinghamshire Light Infantry, one of the battalions of 6th Airborne Division's 6th Airlanding Brigade, was landed in a successful *coup de main* operation on two bridges over the river Orne and Caen Canal. So accurate was the landing that the leading glider's nose was within feet of the location indicated to the pilot during the briefings. A further *coup de main* operation involving the use of gliders was carried out on the same night at Merville, on the Normandy coast, where a successful attack was carried out on an enemy gun battery.

Gliders featured largely in the main landings on 6 June of 6th Airborne Division and the 82nd and 101st US Airborne Divisions. Ninety-eight Horsas and Hamilcars brought in Headquarters 6th Airborne Division and support elements for 3rd and 5th Parachute Brigades, while a further 256 brought in 1st Airlanding Brigade and divisional troops in a subsequent lift. Meanwhile, 514 Wacos and Horsas were used to bring in the two glider infantry regiments and divisional troops of the two American divisions.

Two months later, gliders were used in BLUEBIRD and DOVE which formed part of DRAGOON, the landings in southern France in August 1944. Four hundred and three Wacos were used to transport airlanding elements of 1st Airborne Task Force. The landings were all successful, with 95 per cent of gliders reaching the landing zones successfully. Gliders were also employed extensively in MARKET GARDEN, the ill-fated *Arnhem operation in Holland in September 1944. A total of 1,295 were used to lift the airlanding and divisional troop elements of I Airborne Corps, comprising 1st Airborne Division and 82nd and 101st US Airborne Divisions. In March 1945 XVIII US Airborne Corps, comprising 6th Airborne Division and 17th US Airborne Division, led the assault during VARSITY, the crossing of the Rhine; 1,348 Horsas, Hamilcars, and Wacos took part but suffered very heavy casualties from enemy ground fire as they landed under fire on flat, grassy terrain in full view of the enemy. The operation was nevertheless successful and all objectives were taken by the end of the first day.

Japan produced a number of gliders but none saw operational service. The best was the Ku-7 which, with a maximum payload of 16,450 lb (7,461.7 kg), could carry a light tank or 32 fully equipped troops and was towed by either a Nakajima Ki-49 or Mitsubishi Ki-67.

The first Soviet glider was the Antonov A-7 which appeared in 1939. Carrying eight men or 1 ton of cargo, it was used to supply partisan units. After the war, Soviet development of gliders continued with the YAK-14 which had a maximum towing speed of 180 mph (290 km/ph), a pay-load of 7,700 lb (3,492.7 kg), and could carry 35 troops. Two other gliders, the TS-25 and IL-32, capable of carrying 25 and 35 troops respectively, were also produced.

Gliders played an important role in airborne warfare during WW II, transporting large numbers of troops, heavy weapons, and equipment. They also proved useful in *coup de main* operations, having the advantages of silence and the capability of landing within very short distances. However, they were vulnerable to attack from both the air and ground and, as landings were frequently under heavy fire, the costs in aircrew and aircraft were very high. During the post-war period, the role of the glider was gradually assumed by the helicopter which saw increasing operational use from the 1950s onwards.   HMPDH

Chatterton, Brig. George, *The Wings of Pegasus: The Story of The Glider Pilot Regiment* (London, 1962).

Harclerode, Peter, *Go to It! The History of The 6th Airborne Division* (London, 1990).

Otway, Lt Col T. B. H., *The Second World War 1939–1945: Army Airborne Forces* (London, 1990).

Wood, Alan, *History of The World's Glider Forces* (London, 1992).

Gneisenau, FM Graf August Wilhelm Neithardt von

(1760–1831). The son of a Saxon cavalry officer, Gneisenau served briefly in the Austrian cavalry before joining the Bayreuth-Anspach army, which sent him off to serve with the British in North America. He joined the Prussian army as a captain in 1786 and spent the next twenty years on garrison duty, rising no higher than major. Having fought at *Jena/Auerstadt, he distinguished himself in the siege of Kolberg in 1807, becoming a symbol of Prussian resistance to Napoleon. Taken up by *Scharnhorst, he was promoted major general and appointed to the Military Reorganization Commission. He worked tirelessly, in company with military reformers like Grolman and Boyen as well as civilian supporters like Stein and Konen. The officer corps was purged of the old and incompetent. Selection and promotion were opened up, although the fact that regiments continued to select their own officers partly nullified this measure. Service, either in the standing army or the Landwehr, was made compulsory, and when Napoleon restricted the size of the Prussian army the *Krümper* system was devised so that trained men could be sent on leave and their places filled by recruits.

Gneisenau became COS to *Blücher in 1813, and was ennobled after *Leipzig. After Prussian defeat at Ligny in 1815 he wanted to fall back on Liège, but Blücher arrived in the nick of time to order a concentration on Wellington's army, and the Prussian contribution to *Waterloo proved decisive. After the war his liberal views led him to resign when King Frederick William failed to implement a constitution. However, he returned to serve as governor of Berlin, was promoted field marshal in 1825, and in 1831 commanded the force sent to face the Polish insurgents. Like *Clausewitz,

his COS, he died of cholera in the epidemic sweeping Europe.

Gneisenau is one of the period's most attractive personalities. Brave, intelligent, and patriotic, he was a talented staff officer, whose style brilliantly complemented Blücher's own, as well as a skilled administrator. Ultimately the liberal wing he championed was to lose the military reform debate: the result was a Prussian army which combined a military effectiveness he would have admired with a social exclusiveness which he would not.   RH

Golan Heights, battles of

(1967, 1973). The high plateau of the Golan Heights stretches 45 miles (72 km) south from Mount Hermon, is up to 15 miles (24 km) wide, and dominates Israel's northern frontier with Lebanon, Syria, and Jordan, as well as the river Jordan—and therefore Israel's water supply. Because Syrian forces stationed on the rocky outcrops threatened the Galilee plain, which they had frequently shelled pre-war, the *IDF opened the Six Day War with a pre-emptive assault on the Heights on 9 June 1967. *Airborne forces delivered by helicopter subdued key Syrian garrisons, while armoured bulldozers preceded mechanized columns up steep mountain tracks. Attacking with seven brigades under Maj Gen David Elazar, within a day the IDF bundled the Soviet-trained Syrian forces off the Golan, inflicting losses of 7,500 killed and wounded with 100 tanks and 200 guns destroyed, for a loss of just over 400 Israeli soldiers.

In the October 1973 Yom Kippur (Day of Atonement) war, five Syrian divisions attempted to retrieve the Heights in an attack coinciding with an Egyptian strike in Sinai. The two armoured brigades of IDF defenders possessed only 180 Centurions and M-60s against the Syrian armoured forces' 1,300 tanks, including Soviet T-55s and T-62s, with *APCs in close support, while concentrations of SAMs kept the Israeli Air Force at bay. Achieving total surprise, Syrian tanks assaulted the Golan on 6 October but continuous fighting—which stretched the endurance of both sides' tank crews to the limit—resulted in an epic Israeli victory just four days later. The Israelis stood their ground, sustaining 90 per cent *casualties and the loss of all their armour, but 7th Armoured Brigade had destroyed over 500 Syrian vehicles in the northern sector ('the valley of tears') before its destruction and 188th inflicted similar damage in the south. Their sacrifices bought time for three reserve armoured formations to be mobilized and rushed to the area.

Forty-eight hours of solid fighting saw Syrian units across the Heights, at terrible cost, and approaching the Upper Jordan. There they were halted by the timely arrival of the IDF reserves, but further heavy fighting was required to stabilize the front. The reservists managed to surround and destroy massed Syrian armour in the Hushniya pocket, and on 10 October Israel went over to the offensive, pushing the demoralized Syrian forces back beyond their start line. Moroccan, Jordanian, and Iraqi forces tried in vain to stem the IDF counter-attack, and by the time of the UN-sponsored ceasefire (on 22 October) over 1,300 wrecked or abandoned Arab armoured vehicles choked the Golan Heights, while 10,000 of the attackers had been killed, wounded, or captured. The Israelis lost 250 tanks and 3,000 casualties, but the victory had been a very close-run affair. These battles affirmed the strategic importance of the Golan Heights, and the area now bristles with early warning *radar, IDF bases, and paramilitary Jewish settlements.

APC-A

Gonzaga, Marquis Francesco (1466–1519), high Renaissance prince of Mantua and *condottiere, outstandingly profligate and faithless even by highly competitive contemporary standards. His wife and match in every way was the notable art patron Isabella d'Este.

The French invasion of 1494 with a train of cannon that rendered old *fortifications obsolete created interesting times for all concerned. In addition to their own traditional internecine rivalries and those among the Holy Roman Empire, the Venetian republic, and the papacy, the northern Italian principalities now had to deal with France and Spain as well. Gonzaga was a master at obtaining stipends from them, usually to buy his neutrality. At various times he received payments from Venice, the papacy, France, Spain, and both the Holy Roman and Ottoman empires, which he spent on the principle that 'ostentation was power'. He raised his price by leading an army paid for by Venice to victory over the French at Fornovo in June 1495, but his inveterate scheming led to imprisonment by Venice in 1509. During his latter years syphilis eroded his mind and Mantuan affairs (*sic*) were handled by Isabella.   HEB

Simon, Kate, *A Renaissance Tapestry* (New York, 1988).

Gordon, Maj Gen Charles George 'Chinese' (1833–85). The fourth son of Lt Gen H. W. Gordon, he was educated at the Royal Military Academy, Woolwich. Commissioned in the Royal Engineers (1852), he served in the *Crimean war, participated in surveying the Russo-Turkish frontier, and served in the second *Opium war. He remained in China, reorganizing the 'Ever Victorious Army', and leading it to a series of brilliant victories over the *Taipings. He held several military commands, colonial postings and commissions thereafter, but served most notably as governor of Equatoria (1873–6) and governor-general of the Sudan (1877–9 and 1884–5), gaining acclaim for his efforts to suppress the slave trade. During the *Mahdist revolt he was sent to *Khartoum on 18 February 1884 with vague instructions from the Gladstone cabinet. Gordon evacuated some 2,600 civilians and soldiers before the city was blockaded in March. The *Gordon relief expedition failed to perform as named and he was killed on the steps of the governor's palace when the Mahdists stormed the place on 26 January 1885. The uproar in Britain nearly brought down the government and the *Egypt and Sudan campaigns were waged to avenge this prototypical Victorian Christian warrior-martyr. In his personal life he was very much more complex than the stereotype, but he was a shrewd tactician, a brave and energetic commander, and an indefatigable imperial administrator.   EMS

Trench, Charles Chevenix, *Charley Gordon* (London, 1978).

Gordon relief expedition (1884–5), under the command of *Wolseley, belatedly despatched (5 August 1884) to relieve *Gordon in *Khartoum. The commander's preferred route up the Nile had been contested in Whitehall and Egypt by advocates of the shorter Suakim–Berber route, but Berber fell to the *Mahdists, so the expedition proceeded by railway and steamer upriver. After the second cataract the 7,000 men and stores were conveyed by boats and camels to Korti, arriving in December and January. Wolseley split his force into river and desert columns, but, lacking sufficient camels, could only send the desert column (some 1,800 men) in a two-part movement across the Bayuda Desert to contact Gordon's steamers. The column fought two actions, Abu Klea (17 January 1885) and Abu Kru (19 January 1885), and lost its commander, Maj Gen Sir Herbert Stewart. Sir Charles Wilson assumed command and, on reaching the Nile, reconnoitred and overhauled the steamers before travelling upriver, arriving two days after the town had fallen. Although Wilson was made a scapegoat, the whole expedition lacked urgency and efficient staff work, discrediting both Gladstone and Wolseley.   EMS

Keown-Boyd, Henry, *A Good Dusting* (London, 1986).

Preston, Adrian (ed.), *In Relief of Gordon* (London, 1967).

Gort, FM John Standish Vereker, Viscount (1886–1946). John Vereker succeeded his father as 6th Viscount Gort in the Irish peerage while still at Harrow, entered the Grenadier Guards in 1905, and earned an outstanding reputation for bravery in WW I, winning the VC while in temporary command of 3rd Guards Brigade in 1918.

Thereafter, Gort rose steadily, as commandant of the Staff College, military secretary, and then CIGS in December 1937. Unsuited by temperament to military politics, Gort developed an intense dislike for the war minister, Leslie Hore-Belisha, despite the wide-ranging reforms the latter accomplished.

Consequently, on the outbreak of war in September 1939, Gort was delighted to escape to France as C-in-C of the Field Force. He fretted at military inactivity and friction with Allies during the 'Phoney war', and, when the war began in earnest on 10 May, promptly left his headquarters at Arras to command near the front. Gort quickly lost all confidence in his French and Belgian allies and, on 25 May, in defiance of his own government's orders, decided to withdraw to the Channel coast. This agonizing decision, correct from the British viewpoint but leaving the French to fight on alone, proved wise, for without it the evacuation from *Dunkirk would not have been possible, but he was never again to hold a field command. However, as governor of Malta (1942–4) he galvanized the defenders and made his greatest contribution to eventual victory. He was then appointed high commissioner in Palestine but was soon forced to return to London, terminally ill.

Gort's domestic life was unhappy, and rapid promotion above his ceiling brought nemesis in 1940, particularly because he had leapfrogged over *Alanbrooke and Dill who, between them, would control his career for the remainder of the war. Nevertheless Gort deserves to be remembered for the great moral courage he displayed in defying an out-of-touch government and making the 'miracle of Dunkirk' possible.   BJB

Goths A Germanic people whose origins lay along the lower Vistula (modern Poland), their southerly migration brought them into contact with the Roman empire in the 3rd century AD. In 238, Goths took Histria in the mouth of the Danube. From this base they launched naval raids on the Black Sea coast (255–7), penetrated the Aegean, even reaching Cyprus (268–9), and on land devastated northern Greece (270). Emperor Aurelian drove them out (271) but was forced to cede the trans-Danubian province of Dacia (modern Romania). This settlement lasted for a century, when pressure from the *Huns drove the Goths into the empire again, first as refugees and then as aggressors. At the battle of *Adrianople in 378 Gothic forces defeated the eastern Roman field army and killed Emperor Valens. Subsequently, like many other 'barbarian' groups, their leaders both served in imperial armies and raided Roman territory, depending upon political circumstance. In the 390s Alaric led his bands in attacks on Italy, followed in the crisis year of 405–6 by Radagaisus.

In the first two decades of the 5th century, the Huns arrived in central Europe and subjugated many Germanic peoples. When Attila was defeated in 453, by the Roman Aetius, Goths fought on both sides. The imperial regime collapsed in the 470s, enabling Euric to establish a western (Visigothic) kingdom in southern France and northern Spain, while Theoderic created the (eastern) Ostrogothic kingdom of Italy. Following defeat at Vouillé (near Poitiers) by Clovis's *Franks in 506, the Visigoths were pushed south of the Pyrenees. In the decade before his death in 526, Theoderic asserted in his rule in Spain, too. Goths in both kingdoms were considered heretics by their subject orthodox populations, which greatly outnumbered them, creating a strategic vulnerability in the face of invasion.

This came from Constantinople, where Emperor Justinian I (527–63) sought to recover imperial territories in the west. His general *Belisarius invaded Italy (536), seizing Naples and Rome, and beginning a twenty-year war. The Ostrogothic King Wittigis led several thousand men to besiege Rome (536–7). His troops consisted of armoured lancer cavalry supported by foot archers and spearmen. Although initially successful in battle, they were not equipped or trained for *siege warfare. In 538, another imperial general, the eunuch *Narses, arrived with reinforcements. Also, Burgundian troops, sent by the Frankish king, invaded northern Italy (539). Wittigis was unable to fight on two fronts and was surrounded and captured at Ravenna (540). Belisarius was then recalled to the eastern front against Persia, which enabled a Gothic revival under their new king, Totila. He defeated the Byzantines in a cavalry battle at Faventia and Mugello (542). In 545–6, Totila besieged and took Rome, despite Belisarius' return and attempted relief of the city (which changed hands twice again in 547 and 549). Totila's fleets then began an aggressive campaign attacking (and briefly occupying) Sicily and the Greek coast, although by 551 the Byzantines had gained the upper hand at sea. Also in 551, Narses reinvaded Italy, this time from the north, inflicting a decisive defeat upon the Goths in an epic encounter at Taginae, during which Totila was killed. The Byzantine forces included Lombards, Germanic cavalry recruited north of the Alps. It took until 555 for Narses to complete the conquest, and even then there were sporadic revolts. Italy was exhausted by war, and when in 568 the Lombards invaded under their King Alboin, resistance was short-lived.

In 552, Byzantine troops landed in Spain, seeking to exploit the possibilities of a royal succession dispute. They were initially successful and established an enclave which included the important city of Cordoba and the southern coast from Cadiz almost as far as Valencia. This was maintained for over seventy years, although Cordoba (577) was lost during the wars of King Leovigild (569–86). He effectively brought the whole of the Peninsula under his control by the end of his reign. In 589, the Visigoths converted to Catholicism and so strengthened their relationship with the subject population. Yet the kingdom fell swiftly following the Islamic invasion of a mixed Arab and Berber force in 711. Once again, the disputed succession of King Roderick (701) created political divisions and may have contributed to his crushing defeat and death near Medina Sidonia in July. Moving swiftly, the Muslim commander Tariq took the capital city, Toledo, unopposed. Within a few years the Visigothic nobility was either dead, dispersed, or assimilated and the Goths disappeared as a distinct people.

                                                                    MB

Boss, R., *Justinian's Wars* (Stockport, 1993).
Heather, P., *The Goths* (Cambridge, Mass., 1996).

Gough, Gen Sir Hubert de la Poer (1870–1963). Scion of an old military family, he was commissioned into the 16th Lancers in 1889. Gough earned a reputation for dash in the Second *Boer War and was appointed to command 3rd Cavalry Brigade at the *Curragh in 1911. In March 1914, fearing that troops would be used to coerce Ulster into a united Ireland, he determined to resign, as did most of his officers. Summoned to London, Gough remained obdurate until given a written declaration that opposition to Home Rule would not be crushed. The government repudiated part of this, and the Secretary of State for War, CIGS, and adjutant-general had to resign.

Despite this, Gough took his brigade to France in 1914 and was promoted to command 2nd Cavalry Division that autumn. A corps commander in mid-1915, he was given the Reserve (later fifth) Army in 1916. Initially designated to exploit the breakthrough achieved by Fourth Army, Gough soon found himself committed to the slogging match of the *Somme. In early 1917, as the youngest and most dashing of the army commanders, he was selected to command the offensive at the third battle of *Ypres. His slapdash staff work combined with dreadful terrain and unrealistic objectives to produce stalemate, and *Plumer, commanding Second Army, took over the major role.

In 1918 Fifth Army held the southern end of the British line. Gough pointed out that he was short of troops; that his positions, taken over from the French, were weak; and that his sector would be the focus of the imminent German offensive. On 21 March his army was pushed back with heavy loss, and he was replaced by Rawlinson on 27 March. In 1919 he briefly headed the Allied military mission to the Baltic and retired in 1922. Gough's arrogant manner and hot temper made enemies who were not sorry to see him fall. *Haig later admitted that a scapegoat was required in 1918, and 'the only possible ones were Hubert or me. I was conceited enough to think that the army could not spare me'. His brother John, a VC winner, served as Haig's COS and was killed in 1915.   RH

Goums originated in the 19th century as units of irregular troops (*goumiers*) recruited by the French in *Algeria for pacification campaigns. Later they were put on a more formal footing, and recruited from the hill villages of northern Morocco (see MOROCCO, FRENCH CONQUEST OF. A company-sized '*goum*' would be recruited from a village or group of villages—although losses might dilute the local emphasis—and three or four would form a battalion-sized *tabor* for larger-scale operations. Ideally led by specially selected Arabic-speaking French officers well versed in complex local customs and affiliations, and with a substantial complement of French *NCOs, the *goumier* excelled at patrolling, infiltration, and ambushes. He wore his own costume of undyed homespun woollen *djellaba* (a striped cloak), over trousers gaitered by woollen *tighiwines*, and even after the introduction of steel helmets often wore his *rezza* (small turban) in battle. He was generally given little

*drill or training, it being believed that *discipline might corrupt skills acquired in tribal feuding or even fighting the French. The result was that he could be as dangerous off the battlefield as on it, particularly towards women. Officially classified as auxiliaries, the *goumiers'* finest hour came when their skills were employed in large conventional formations in Italy in 1944. Specifically requested by French Expeditionary Force commander Alphonse *Juin, the 1st, 2nd, and 4th Groupement de Tabors Marocains, each made up of three *tabors*, their ponies and mule transport augmented with jeeps, radios, and heavy weapons, combined with a Moroccan infantry division to form the Corps de Montagne. During DIADEM in May 1944 this formation was instrumental in breaking the mountainous, apparently impassable centre of the Gustav and Hitler Lines and outflanking the defences around *Cassino.   DD

Graham, Dominick, and Bidwell, Shelford, *Tug of War* (London, 1986).

Porch, Douglas, *The Conquest of Morocco* (London, 1987).

Graeco-Persian wars (540s–330s BC). The Greeks first came into conflict with the Persians in Asia Minor, as a result of the conquest of Lydia by *Cyrus 'the Great', probably in 546 BC. Following an abortive Lydian revolt in which some of them participated, many of their towns were taken by assault, and the rest acquiesced in Persian rule.

In the early years of the 5th century BC there was a widespread rebellion from Byzantium to Caria, in which Cyprus, which had a substantial Greek population, joined. On the mainland of Asia Minor, with the advantage of 'interior lines' and superior numbers, the Persians were able to operate in more than one theatre at once, and to use the river valleys as a means of attack, whereas communications were more difficult for the Greeks. Five land battles are recorded, in four of which the Persians were victorious, but almost no details have survived, save that at Malene the Persian cavalry somehow played the decisive role; the one battle the Greeks managed to win was when they ambushed a Persian force at night. Meanwhile, despite a Greek victory at sea off the island, Cyprus was reconquered. The decisive Persian victory was also at sea, off Lade, which was followed by the capture of nearby Miletus, the heart of the revolt, probably in 494. Elsewhere resistance was crushed or petered out, and the Persians went on to conquer Thrace, including its Greek coastal cities, and now, if not before, to bring even Macedonia under their control.

Two mainland cities, Athens and Eretria, helped the Asiatic Greeks in the early stages of their rebellion, and this led, in 490, to the first Persian attack on Greece proper. A fleet of perhaps 600 ships, carrying possibly some 25,000 men, including cavalry, first subdued the Cyclades, then took Carystus and Eretria, in Euboea. But when it landed its troops at *Marathon, they were defeated by the Athenians with Plataean support.

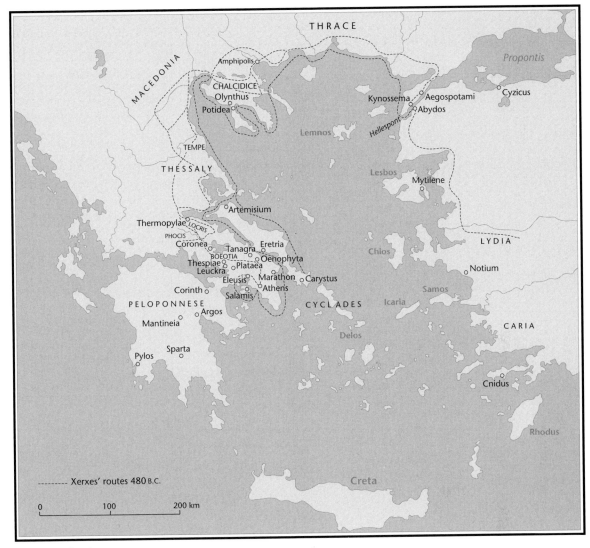

The **Graeco-Persian wars.**

Ten years later, in 480, the Persians were back, this time overland by way of Thrace and Macedonia, and led by King *Xerxes in person. The size of his forces is a notorious problem, but his army was perhaps something like 50,000–100,000 strong, and his navy perhaps contained over 1,000 warships. Resistance in Greece centred on *Sparta and her Peloponnesian allies, but Athens also joined the alliance, with a scattering of other states in central Greece and nearby islands, and at first other states as far north as Thessaly were willing to fight. Following an appeal from Thessaly, a force was sent to hold the pass of Tempe. But this withdrew after a warning of the size of Xerxes' forces, and realizing that Tempe could be turned. It was then decided to hold *Thermopylae, while stationing a fleet at Artemisium, some 40 miles (64 km) to the east, on the north coast of Euboea. Here for three days the Greeks more than held their own, although the losses they sustained and the fall of Thermopylae eventually compelled withdrawal.

Most of central Greece now more or less willingly went over to the enemy, but the people of Thespiae and Plataea in Boeotia took refuge in the Peloponnese, and now if not before, Attica, too, was evacuated. The Greek fleet took station at *Salamis, and it was here that the first decisive encounter of the war took place, when the Persian fleet ventured into the channel between the island and the mainland, perhaps as a result of a message from the Athenian commander, Themistocles, and was badly beaten. It still possibly had more ships than the Greeks, but its *morale had gone, and it now withdrew to Asia Minor, followed by Xerxes himself. Salamis certainly did not end the war, though in their euphoria the Greeks may have thought it did, making dedications for victory, and trying to decide who was to receive prizes for their part in it. But the Persian army still remained undefeated, and Xerxes probably left the bulk of his army behind, under his cousin, Mardonius.

Wintering in Thessaly, Mardonius tried by diplomatic means to woo Athens to his side, and when this failed, marched south again in late spring, compelling the re-evacuation of Attica. A second embassy, this time to Salamis, still failed to win the Athenians over, but Spartan procrastination almost succeeded where Persian diplomacy had failed, and at one point Athens actually threatened to make peace with the Persians. In the end the Spartans realized that their defences across the Isthmus would not save them if the Athenian navy passed under Persian control, and mobilized their army. Mardonius fell back to Boeotia, and it was here, just east of *Plataea, that the final encounter took place, probably in August, when the largest army of *hoplites ever assembled—eventually it totalled more than 38,000—under the Spartan regent Pausanias, annihilated most of Mardonius' Asiatic troops.

In the end, the Greeks won, not by brilliant strategy or tactics, or superior training and equipment, but because, in the two battles that mattered, the Persians allowed themselves to be drawn into a kind of fighting which did not suit them. At Salamis, their numerical superiority—if they still had it—and the speed and manoeuvrability of their ships were all nullified by the narrow waters in which the battle was fought. At Plataea, when he had the enemy on the run, Mardonius blundered into a close-quarter battle which suited hoplites far better than his own more mobile, missile-armed troops.

Supposedly on the same day as Plataea, a small Greek fleet destroyed Persian ships drawn ashore at Mycale in Asia Minor, and in the following years, now under Athenian leadership, the Greeks swept the Persians from the Aegean; possibly in 468, yet another victory was won at the Eurymedon. But attempts to liberate Cyprus and Egypt failed, and between 412 and 386 the Persians largely recovered control of western Asia Minor. It was left to *Alexander 'the Great' finally to bring the conflict to a close.   JFL

Burn, A. R., *Persia and the Greeks* (London, 1962).

Lazenby, J. F., *The Defence of Greece* (Warminster, 1993).

Graeco-Turkish wars (1897, 1921–2), two wars between the Greeks and the Ottoman *Turks, both of which resulted in Greek defeat. The first, also known as the Thirty Days War, was a result of a rebellion by local Greeks against Turkish rule in February 1896 on Crete. The Greeks sent arms and supplies to the insurgents. The Greek government then decided upon direct intervention and on 21 January 1897 mobilized the Greek fleet. The following month, Greek troops were landed on the island and a union with Greece proclaimed. However, the European great powers, fearing serious disturbances in the Balkans, blockaded the Greeks and prevented support being sent from the mainland. Thwarted by this, the Greeks sent an army led by Crown Prince Constantine against the Turks in Thessaly and Epirus. The Greek high command proved remarkably inept and were consistently beaten by the German-trained Turkish army. Yielding to international pressure, the Greeks withdrew from Crete and accepted an armistice on the mainland on 20 May 1897.

The second Graeco-Turkish war occurred in the aftermath of WW I. Under the Treaty of Sèvres of 1920, the Greeks had been assigned the right to administer Izmir. In the face of growing Turkish nationalism, the Greek government decided to send 100,000 troops into Anatolia ostensibly to protect the Greeks in the area in January 1921. The Turks under Kemal *Atatürk withdrew after some Greek successes. The Greeks, despite poor logistics, advanced on Ankara. They were checked by Atatürk at Sakkaria and fell back in the wake of a Turkish counter-offensive. Smyrna was captured by the Turks in November and the Greeks were finally driven out of Anatolia in the following year. Under the Treaty of Lausanne of 1923, the Greeks lost the major gains they had made after WW I and some 1.3 million Greeks were forced to leave Anatolia.   MCM

Granby, John Manners, Marquess of (1721–70). Eldest son of the Duke of Rutland, Granby was MP for Rutland when he joined the cavalry during the *Jacobite uprising of 1745. He served on the staff of the Duke of *Cumberland, being promoted major general in 1755. He was second-in-command of the Anglo-Brunswick cavalry at *Minden under Lord George *Sackville, when the latter notoriously refused to order his five regiments to charge the French. Replacing the *cashiered Sackville as lieutenant general, Granby commanded the British contingent at the battle of Warburg (1760). He lost his wig leading the decisive cavalry charge, giving rise to the expression 'going for it bald-headed'. He became a popular hero in Britain and his name still adorns a number of pubs. He was Master General of the Ordnance in 1763 and C-in-C from 1766 until his death.   APC-A

Grand Army of the Republic Generic term used to describe all Union land forces in the *American civil war. The Grand Army of the Republic encompassed all of the major ground forces on the Union side during the war, notably the Army of the Potomac in the east, and of the Cumberland and the Tennessee in the west. These forces were united only once in the entire course of their existence, on 23–4 May 1865, when they passed in review down Pennsylvania Avenue to celebrate their victory. There is some doubt over precisely how many men may have served in the Grand Army of the Republic. According to the Official

Records, enlistment in the various Federal armies totalled 2,672,341 men. However, there was a problem during the war with men enlisting more than once to obtain the generous bounties provided for volunteers, so these figures may be exaggerated. E. B. Long concludes that 'something over 2,000,000 would be as accurate a figure as possible'.

The Grand Army of the Republic was also a successful political lobbying organization for many years after the war, obtaining some benefits for *veterans as well as many for itself.   AH

Granicus, battle of the (334 BC). The first battle fought by *Alexander 'the Great' in his Persian campaign was fought in spring 334 BC at the Granicus river (modern Kocabas), shortly after Alexander crossed the Hellespont and marched east towards the provincial capital, Dascyleium. The Persian governors had assembled local Persian troops and a substantial contingent of Greek mercenaries. Although the mercenary Memnon of Rhodes recommended scorched-earth tactics until the Persians were better prepared, his strategy was dismissed as defeatist.

The Persians planned to hold the east bank of the Granicus; this is normally a small stream flowing in a broad bed between steep 6.5 foot (2 metre) banks, but was probably now in spate and so a more formidable obstacle. Alexander, arriving on the west bank in late afternoon, was urged by Parmenio to wait to find an alternative crossing. Most authorities agree that he rejected this and led his cavalry diagonally across the stream; he was nearly killed in a confused skirmish on the east bank as the Macedonians struggled out of the stream, but once the crossing point was secured the scratch Persian army crumbled. The Greek mercenaries were surrounded and either slaughtered or consigned to the Macedonian mines. Victory permitted Alexander to take over western Asia Minor.   LMW

Grant, Gen Ulysses S (1822–85), commander of Union armies at the end of the *American civil war and president 1869–77. Blessed with neither good political connections nor personal charisma, he is a classic example of a man redeemed from obscurity by the demands of an exceptional time.

He fought in most major engagements of the *Mexican war. Although awarded two brevet promotions for earlier performances, he was embittered not to receive a third for having smuggled a dismantled howitzer up a bell tower behind enemy defences in Mexico City. Post-war he was sent to inhospitable outposts on both coasts, where his 'binge' alcoholism first manifested itself. He resigned the day he received his regular captain's commission in order to make money, something he signally failed to do. At the outbreak of the civil war, refused a command by all normal channels, he only just managed to get on the escalator by election as

colonel of a troublesome Illinois militia regiment. Such was the need for senior officers in the rapidly expanding army that he was promoted to brigadier general a few months later.

His moment came when his superior *Halleck grudgingly ordered him to take half-finished Fort Henry on the Tennessee river. In what was to become a familiar theme, failure by subordinates to act with dispatch led to the escape of the garrison. Unaware that he was now outnumbered, Grant stretched his orders and pushed on to Fort Donelson, where Confederate commander Pillow virtually delivered the place to him by returning to the fort to collect equipment after having successfully breached the siege lines. He and his second in command then abandoned their army, leaving Grant's friend Buckner to surrender to him. After ten months of unbroken Union defeats, the fall of Fort Donelson was greeted with wild enthusiasm in Washington, and Grant was promoted to major general by a grateful *Lincoln. This did not improve relations with his mediocre theatre commander, who was determined to clip his wings.

After *Shiloh, Halleck made him his nominal second in command and excluded him from the chain of command. *Sherman won Grant's undying gratitude by persuading him not to resign and Lincoln resisted strong pressure to dismiss him, saying 'I can't spare this man, he fights.' When Halleck at last was called to Washington as general in chief, he broke up the western army rather than leave it in Grant's hands. The *Vicksburg campaign justified Lincoln's faith in him, and after he turned Union fortunes around even further at Chattanooga, Congress revived the rank of lieutenant general for him, previously held only by Washington.

When summoned to Washington to become overall commander, Grant did not remain in the capital but took to the field to seek a decision against *Lee. He did not take the opportunity to clean house, even retaining Halleck as his COS in Washington. This decision put Grant in limbo, neither directly commanding the Army of the Potomac, which continued under *Meade, nor properly placed to end the proliferation of independent commands under inept political generals like Sigel and Butler. A major criticism of Grant's generalship is that the suffering armies of the latter only achieved relief after further needless defeats. But he was the first of Lincoln's generals in chief to fully share his broad strategic vision that the North's human and industrial superiority would prevail if remorselessly applied, and who had the necessary ruthlessness to make it so.

By continuing to advance and to outflank him despite setbacks, Grant denied Lee any tactical freedom, but he committed serious errors nonetheless, in particular the bloodbath at Cold Harbor. The war might also have ended months earlier were it not for 'unconditional surrender', Lincoln's policy but Grant's phrase. Only by chance was he not in the box at Ford's Theatre when Booth came to assassinate them both. Post-war, his resentment at being used as a cat's-paw by President Johnson in his struggle with 'radical reconstructionists' led to his identification with the latter, and thus to selection as the successful Republican candidate in the presidential election of 1868.

Grant's tenure is indelibly stained by the financial scandals that wracked his second term and by the failure of belatedly humane policies towards the South and the Indians in the *Plains Indians wars. A poor judge of character, this weakness was compounded by his characteristic unwillingness to discard subordinates before they caused disaster. Overall, he was as unfortunate in his public life as he was in private affairs. Bankrupt and dying, he wrote among the best memoirs ever penned by a general, but his own bitter judgement was that he would not choose to live his life again. He is buried in an elaborate tomb in New York, a place he never liked. HEB

Perret, Geoffrey, *Ulysses S. Grant* (New York, 1997).

Great Northern war (1700–20). This was the second Northern war, engulfing the Baltic and much of eastern Europe, including parts of the Ottoman empire, which provided *Peter 'the Great' of Russia with his entrance to European power-politics and an opportunity to deploy his new, western-style army and navy. Begun as a reaction against earlier Swedish expansion and the arrogant and aggressive *Charles XII, the war was fought on an astonishingly wide stage, with Russian naval expeditions to Denmark, advances into what are now Poland and Ukraine, and against the *Turks as far south as Brailov on the Danube.

The Swedish involvement in the *Thirty Years War and the first Northern war of 1655–60 between Sweden and Poland had made the Baltic a 'Swedish lake' which antagonized neighbouring states and blocked Russia's access to the sea. In 1697 Charles XI died and was succeeded by his son Charles XII, aged 14. Perceiving weakness, the then united realm of Denmark-Norway initiated an anti-Swedish coalition with Poland-Saxony and Russia.

The war fell into four main periods. In the first (1700–6), Frederick IV of Denmark-Norway moved into Schleswig-Holstein in March 1700, after Augustus II 'the Strong', king of Poland and elector of Saxony, attacked Livonia. In October Peter 'the Great' laid siege to Narva. Charles XII, now approaching adulthood, attacked Denmark first, forcing Frederick to withdraw from the coalition in the Treaty of Trubenthal in August 1700. He then switched to attack the Russians besieging *Narva, and destroyed Peter's army on 30 November 1700. During the next six years he concentrated on knocking Poland-Saxony out of the war.

The second period began in 1707 when the Swedes renewed their attack on Russia, working their way south-east deep into what is now Ukraine. Severely depleted by a savage winter they were comprehensively defeated at *Poltava. Charles fled to the Turkish dominions, first to Ochakov on the Black Sea and then to Bendery on the Dniestr.

Thus the third period began in 1710. The Russians and their allies had seized Vyborg, Riga, Revel', and other Baltic strongholds and Charles persuaded the Turks that this was the time to declare war on Russia. The Russians launched the Pruth expedition in 1711, pushing south to Yassy and Brailov, on the Danube. The Mongols of the Crimean khanate, who were still independent, launched raids northwards as far as Kharkov and Belaya Tserkov, but the Russians managed to make peace at the price of ceding Azov to the Turks.

In 1713 Gen Menshikov took Stettin (Szczecin) and the Russians pushed far enough west to meet the Danes in Schleswig-Holstein. The Russians also defeated the Swedes in the naval battle at Hango (Gangut) in 1714, cutting them off from Finland, captured the Aland islands, and threatened Stockholm. At this point George I of Britain, who was also the elector of Hanover, and Frederick William I of Prussia joined the anti-Swedish coalition after the Swedes had rejected their promise of neutrality in exchange for territory.

In December 1715 Charles XII returned to Sweden and began negotiating for peace while surreptitiously expanding his armed forces. Russia, meanwhile, exploited its military success. Russian naval patrols reached Gotland in 1715 and Copenhagen and Stralsund in 1716, and ranged north to Stockholm and beyond from 1719–21. Russia also negotiated trade deals with the former Hanseatic cities of Hamburg, Lubeck, and Danzig (Gdansk) and concluded the Amsterdam agreement of 1717 with France and Prussia. Charles XII invaded south-east Norway in 1718 and was killed at the siege of Frederikshald in November 1718.

The final phase lasted from 1719–21. Russia and Sweden concluded peace at the Aland conference of 1718–19 but after Charles's sister Ulrika-Eleanora succeeded to the Swedish throne, hostilities were resumed. The British were on the verge of war with Russia, and sent a squadron into the Baltic under Adm Norris to destroy the Russian fleet, but Russian diplomacy headed off the conflict. The Russians again beat the Swedes in sea battles at Ezel' in 1719 and at Grengam, in the southern Aland islands, on 7 August 1720. The Russians were able to occupy the islands, securing St Petersburg against any further Swedish attacks. Sweden ceded Bremen to Hanover and Szczecin and part of Pomerania to Prussia. At the Treaty of Nystadt on 10 September 1721, Sweden ceded Estonia, Livonia, and a strip of Finnish Karelia to Russia, giving her the secure egress to the Baltic and the wider world she so coveted. As a result of the conflict, Sweden was destroyed as a major power and Russia emerged as a major player in European war and politics. CDB

Greek city-state wars (395–362 BC). Defeat of Athens in the *Peloponnesian wars ended the artificial order imposed on a normally fragmented Greece by the great alliances headed by Athens and *Sparta. What followed was a chaotic period in which Sparta, *Thebes, and a renascent

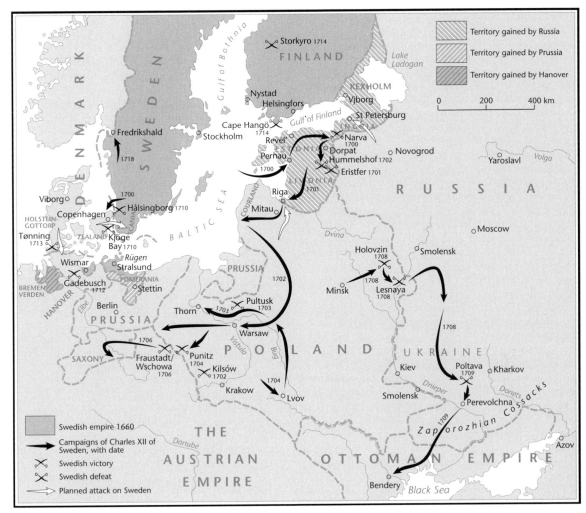

The **Great Northern war**, 1700–21.

Athens jostled for power, with Persia stirring the pot. Fear of any one state growing powerful enough to dominate the others is the key to understanding the shifting alliances.

Thus fear of Sparta was essentially the cause of the Corinthian war (395–386), in which her former allies, Thebes and Corinth, made common cause with Athens and Sparta's inveterate rival in the Peloponnese, Argos. In attempting to coerce Thebes before the rest joined in, Lysander was killed at Haliartus, in 395, but in 394 Sparta crushed coalition forces at the battle of *Nemea and King Agesilaus, returning from Asia Minor, thwarted an attempt to block his path at *Koroneia. Thereafter the war on land became increasingly desultory, fought largely in and around Corinthian territory—hence the name. One significant incident was the defeat, in 390, near Corinth, of a force of 600 Spartans by Athenian light troops under *Iphrikates.

In the end, the war was won and lost at sea. At first Persia, exasperated by Spartan interference in Asia Minor, culminating in Agesilaus' campaigns in 396–365, financed the building of a fleet. Under the command of the Athenian Conon, this defeated a Spartan fleet off Cnidus in 394, and rapidly removed all but a few vestiges of Spartan control in the Aegean. But the Persians, becoming alarmed at Conon's apparent revival of an Athenian empire, patched up relations with Sparta, and when a Spartan fleet, with Persian help, again cut Athens' supply line through the Hellespont, as Lysander had done in 405, the anti-Spartan coalition collapsed. The result was the notorious 'King's Peace', which, under cover of obliging all Greek states to respect each other's autonomy, in effect handed them over to the whims of a Persia-backed Sparta.

Sparta was now at the height of her power. Athens lost all her new-found empire, apart from some small islands;

Thebes had to submit to the break-up of the Boeotian League, and in 382 came under the control of a pro-Spartan government after her citadel, the Cadmea, had been captured in a surprise Spartan attack. Corinth was obliged to abandon her alliance with Argos, in which, interestingly, the citizens of each apparently had reciprocal rights when in the other, and elsewhere in the Peloponnese, Sparta disciplined recalcitrant allies such as Mantineia and Phlius. Finally, in the north, Olynthus was forced to accept the status of a subject ally.

But then all began to go wrong for Sparta. In the winter of 379/8 Thebes was liberated by patriotic exiles, and Athens, infuriated by an abortive Spartan attack on the Piraeus, invited the Aegean states to join her in a new confederacy, to which Thebes also adhered. Repeated Spartan invasions of Boeotia were ineffective, and with Athens increasingly dominant at sea, Spartan was increasingly hard put to hold her own. Although punctuated by a series of 'common peaces', the 370s were a decade of almost continuous warfare, culminating in the Theban defeat of the Spartans at *Leuctra, in 371.

The shattering of the myth of Spartan invincibility led to the break-up of the alliance through which she had dominated the Peloponnese for almost two centuries, and in 370 the Theban general, *Epaminondas, led an army into the Peloponnese, and on into the Spartan homeland. Although he avoided a direct attack on Sparta itself, he re-established the Spartan helots' long-suppressed state of Messenia, confining a consequently weakened Sparta into the south-east corner of the Peloponnese, cut off from allies still loyal to her such as Corinth and Phlius.

But Thebes overstretched herself in turn by seeking to dominate both Thessaly in the north and the Peloponnese in the south, and the removal of the fear of Sparta weakened the ties binding her allies to her—typical was Athens' cold response to the news of Leuctra. Eventually she found herself facing a coalition of Sparta and her erstwhile friends, including Athens, Corinth, and even some of the Arcadian states. At the second battle of *Mantineia, in 362, Epaminondas was killed in the moment of victory, and although Thebes remained the greatest military power in Greece for a number of years, her hegemony was effectively ended.

JFL

Buckler, John, *The Theban Hegemony 371–362 BC* (London, 1980).
Hamilton, Charles D., *Sparta's Bitter Victories* (London, 1979).

Greek civil war (1944–5 and 1946–9), a two-stage conflict in which Greek communists tried but failed to take over Greece. The German occupation of Greece during WW II had been resisted by two Greek *guerrilla forces, the communist EAM (Ethnikon Apeleftherotikon Metopon, 'National Liberation Front')—which had recruited, trained, and armed the ELAS (Ethnikos Laikos Apeleftherotikos Stratos, 'National Popular Liberation Army')—and the more moderate EDES (Ellinikos Dimokratikos Ethnikos Stratos, 'Greek Democratic National Army'). Upon the German withdrawal from Greece in October 1944, the British brought EDES and EAM/ELAS together in an uneasy coalition government. This quickly broke down and bitter fighting inspired by ELAS broke out in Athens on 3 December 1944 which the British forces managed to suppress. The communists accepted defeat at the *truce of Varkiza on 12 February 1945. However, they boycotted the election of the following March and a full-scale guerrilla war broke out again after a British-backed plebiscite voted in favour of re-establishing the monarchy.

The former ELAS commander Markos Vafiades created a 'democratic army of Greece in the North'. He received support from Tito's Yugoslavia, Albania, and Bulgaria. The commitment to defending Greece proved too much for the overstretched British who were forced to relinquish their Greek commitments. However, this burden was taken up by the US government when American Pres *Truman announced the Truman Doctrine on 12 March 1947. He made an open-ended commitment to protect friendly states against subversion, intimidation, and aggression and pledged $400 million to Greece and Turkey. This proved crucial: without US arms and advice, Greece might well have passed into communist control in the spring of 1947. The Democratic Army was eventually defeated in the field when the Greek Royalist Army under the command of Marshal Papagos trapped and destroyed the bulk of its forces on Mount Grammos, near the Albanian frontier on 30 August 1949. The communists announced the end of hostilities on 16 October 1949 and many of the remaining guerrillas fled across the mountains into Albania.

Quite apart from US military aid, the communists failed in the civil war because they did not succeed in gaining enough popular support to start a revolution successfully. This was largely due to Markos's methods of intimidation, which alienated the population and aroused popular hostility against the communists. The rupture between the Yugoslav leader *Tito and *Stalin further weakened the Greek rebels, because one of the results of the break was that Tito withdrew his support from Markos, who toed the Moscow line, in 1948. Finally, Markos's strategy was too ambitious. He attempted to seize and hold large towns as territorial centres for a provisional government. This exposed his forces to pitched battles with the regular national army, which was far better equipped for such conventional warfare. Estimates of the death toll of the Greek civil war range between 20,000 and 50,000, and possibly half a million Greeks were displaced by the fighting. This extremely bitter civil war left deep and long-lasting divisions in Greek society.

MCM

Greek historians Warfare was pandemic in the ancient world, and almost every ancient historian is a military historian. Among the Greeks whose works survive, Herodotus (*c*.484–424 BC) gives an account of the *Graeco-Persian wars including long digressions on peoples and places. His credibility has been questioned from his day to this, but what other evidence there is tends to bear him out, often in detail, and he shows much common sense in sifting evidence, giving different versions, and frequently confessing doubt. He has been particularly criticized for lack of military experience and naive views of warfare. But, although his accounts are dramatic and omit many things a modern historian may wish to know, it should never be forgotten that he stands at the very beginning of historical study, and had to depend almost entirely on oral evidence. His material may be presented in an unfamiliar way—strategy and tactics, for example, often discussed in speeches or conversations between protagonists—but enough is there, if we care to look, to enable us to understand what happened and why, at least in broad outline. As for his lack of military experience, that is true of most military historians, and his supposed naivety may accurately reflect the unsophisticated nature of the warfare of his time.

Thucydides (?460–*c*.390 BC) is very different, but he was contemporary with his main subject, the *Peloponnesian wars, and too much can be made of his military experience, which only certainly amounted to one campaign. Despite the existence of far more documentary evidence, most of the evidence he used was also oral, and we should not assume that he checked it more carefully than Herodotus just because he claims to have done so. Nevertheless, his accounts of military operations are more detailed and precise than Herodotus', and, although there are still many things we would like to know, one feels that one is dealing with something approaching proper military history, whereas reading Herodotus is like watching a good historical film. The danger is that Thucydides hardly ever gives alternative versions, and for better or worse we virtually have to accept his. His evident intelligence and precision are of some comfort, but he is clearly sometimes one-sided and tendentious. His style, too, is often tortuous and gnomic, and it can be almost impossible to see what he actually means, as the endless discussions of his analysis of the causes of the war show. Nobody could accuse Thucydides of being naive, but he was, perhaps, too intelligent for his own and our good.

Polybius (*c*.200–*c*.118 BC), like Thucydides, had some pretensions to military experience, serving as 'Hipparch' ('Vice-President') of the Achaean League in 170/169. But, although he wrote a lost work on tactics, he is not known to have taken part in any military operations, let alone exercised command. Through his friendship with *Scipio Aemilianus while in exile, he did witness the latter's operations at Carthage and Numantia, and he obviously liked to think of himself as a military man, sometimes, for example, using what look like technical terms. One can only be thankful that when so much of his work is lost, what survives includes so many important military events. He is not

as detailed and precise as Thucydides can be, but usually gives a clear, unpretentious, though somewhat pedestrian, picture of events.

Herodotus, Thucydides, and Polybius apart, one is left with a very mixed bag. The 'Library of History' of the Sicilian Diodoros, written between 56 and 30 BC, is the most extensive Greek historical work to have survived, even though we only have fifteen of its 40 books. Diodorus is the classic example of a historian who is only as good as his sources, his own contribution being perhaps only his moralistic and rhetorical tone. Thus he contributes little of value where we have Herodotus and Thucydides, but is sometimes a useful corrective to *Xenophon, for example, where he perhaps used the anonymous history of Greece known as the Hellenica Oxyrhynchia. He is invaluable where he preserves Hieronymus of Cardia on *Alexander's successors and, as one might expect, on the history of Sicily.

Plutarch (AD *c*.50–120) of Chaeronea is not really a historian at all, let alone a military historian, although his biographies of famous commanders inevitably contain much military material. Like Diodorus, he is full of moralizing and rhetoric, but he was a learned man who frequently refers to his sources, and occasionally he preserves interesting material.

Arrian (Lucius Flavius Arrianus, AD *c*.86–160), as governor of Cappadocia, would certainly have had military experience and works on tactics survive. But he is chiefly known for his account of Alexander the Great's campaigns, which, as its title *Anabasis* suggests, was modelled on Xenophon, but also harked back to Herodotus and Thucydides. Arrian's main sources were the contemporaries Ptolemy 1 and Aristobulus, but he also worked in later stories, and as a result, although detailed, his account is not wholly reliable.

Roughly contemporary with Arrian, Appian of Alexandria wrote a history of Rome mainly organized geographically. Of 24 books, only eleven survive complete, and it is clear that Appian not only reduced and reorganized his sources, but introduced rhetorical flourishes to suit his pro-Roman and monarchic views, He is chiefly valuable for his account of the *Roman civil wars, where he preserves material otherwise lost.

Polyaenus' collection of 'stratagems' was intended to assist Marcus Aurelius and Lucius Verus in the Parthian war of AD 162–6. Unfortunately, although the work preserves some valuable items, such as Philip's feint withdrawal at *Chaeronea, it contains obviously mythical and fictitious anecdotes as well as historical ones, and unless the source is clear, is of dubious reliability.

Finally, Cassius Dio (AD *c*.164–230) wrote a history of Rome from its origins to his own time, of which only the part covering the years 69 BC to AD 46 survives at all intact. He is particularly useful on the struggles for power, which destroyed the Roman republic and led to imperial rule, and can be perceptive, but devotes too much attention to the supernatural.   JFL

Hornblower, Simon, and Spawforth, Antony, *The Oxford Classical Dictionary* (3rd edn., Oxford, 1996).

Greek independence war (1821–32), rebellion of the Greeks against the *Turks which led to independence from the Ottoman empire and the establishment of the kingdom of Greece. Hellenism or a sense of Greek nationalism had long been fostered by the Greek Orthodox Church. This, coupled with a rediscovery of Greek culture, meant there was a common desire among Greeks of all classes for some form of independence. The Philiki Etaireia ('Friendly Brotherhood'), founded in Odessa in 1814, felt that the only way to achieve this was through violence. Therefore Alexandros Ypsilantis led a small force into Turkish Moldavia in March 1821. Although he was soon defeated, there were outbreaks of rebellion across the Peloponnese which seized a number of garrisons and key ports and the key fortress of Morea and also Athens. The Turks responded by putting down a Cretian rebellion and ravaging the whole island of Chios, massacring or enslaving the entire population, but they could not recapture Morea. The Greeks had further successes against the Turkish army which had invaded the peninsula north of the Gulf of Corinth. They were halted before the Greek fort at Missolonghi and forced to invest it. On 21 August 1822, 300 Greeks under Marco Bozzaris surprised Gen Mustai Pasha and routed 4,000 Turks at the battle of Karpenizi. In January 1823, the Turks lifted the siege of Missolonghi and withdrew. Instead of pressing their advantage, the Greeks eased their campaign against the weakened Turkish forces to set up a provisional government, but since this was fraught with difficulties a civil war erupted among the Greeks.

Taking full advantage of the respite this offered, the Turks made good use of the time to regroup. Sultan Mahmut II requested help from *Mohammed Ali, the pasha of Egypt. Mohammed sent his son Ibrahim with some 5,000 well-trained troops to the Morea against the much weakened Greeks. They soon captured the town and the peninsula. Meanwhile a new Turkish army under Reshid Pasha invaded from the north and took Missolonghi in 1826. The Turks moved on Athens and besieged the Acropolis the following year. The Greek cause had captured European interest. Lord Byron died at Missolonghi but his example was followed by a number of volunteer adventurers and idealists. Some of these men were experienced soldiers or sailors such as Adm Lord Cochrane and Gen Sir George Church who were placed in command of the Greek navy and army respectively. However, both were paralysed by Greek internecine intrigue. By June 1825, Reshid Pasha had captured the Acropolis and continental Greece was again under Turkish control.

Public opinion in Europe strongly supported the Greek struggle and the governments of Britain, France, and Russia signed a protocol agreeing to mediate between the Greeks and Turks. They also demanded that the Egyptians withdraw from Greece and the Turks sign an armistice; they both refused. A large Egyptian naval squadron landed reinforcements at Navarino on 8 September 1827, where a Turkish naval force also lay moored. The British, French, and Russians sent naval forces to help the Greeks and they arrived off the harbour of Navarino. On 20 October 1827, Adm Sir Edward Codrington, the senior allied commander, sailed the combined allied fleet into the harbour where the Egyptian-Turkish ships were at anchor and dropped anchor in the midst of the opposing fleet. When a Turkish ship fired on a British dispatch boat, Codrington ordered his ships to return fire and the French and Russians immediately joined in the battle. The Egyptian-Turkish fleet, which was heavily outgunned, was defeated, losing some three-quarters of its ships. Navarino essentially decided the fate of Greek independence. The Russians took advantage of Turkish difficulties and declared war on 26 April 1828, ostensibly in support of Greek independence, but mainly as an opportunity for further Russian expansion at the Ottoman empire's expense. The Russian offensives against the Turks in the Euphrates and in the Balkans further undermined Turkish power, and when a Russian army captured Adrianople and thus threatened Constantinople, the Turks sued for peace. The Treaty of Adrianople forced the Turks to give autonomy to Serbia, Wallachia, and Moldavia and resulted in considerable Russian territorial gains. Greece was also granted autonomy. The French landed an expeditionary force in Greece which supervised the evacuation of the Egyptians, which started on 9 August 1828. This was completed at the beginning of 1829 and essentially ended the war. Greece finally gained its independence from a reluctant Ottoman empire under the Treaty of London of 7 May 1832.   MCM

Greek tactical writers A designation applicable to various technical or theoretical writers on ancient Greek warfare and military procedures. Warfare itself is as inescapable in Greek literature—which for us begins with Homer's Iliad—as it was in Greek life, and *Greek historians of the 5th century BC such as Herodotus and Thucydides gave warfare a pride of place in mainstream historical writing that, as a legacy from Graeco-Roman historiography, defied challenge until almost the present day. Within this broad context more specialized genres emerged and flourished, between the 4th century BC and the 2nd AD (with later, Byzantine specimens to follow). Two main eras can be differentiated.

first, the 4th century BC itself saw the earliest handbooks on aspects of terrestrial military practice. (Sea power, oddly, seems to have generated nothing comparable.) Their authors, where known, are bringing their own personal experience to bear. Under this head belong two men in particular. One is the versatile Athenian *Xenophon, who besides stirring memoirs of his own campaigns penned a treatise on the duties of a cavalry commander. The other, and the more intriguing, is a certain Aineias—probably to be identified with a mid-4th-century Arcadian general of that name. Aineias' status as the first authentic *tacticus* resides in his authorship of an interconnected set of handbooks, perhaps half a dozen in all, on such topics as encampment and provisioning; but the only one extant is his *Siegecraft*. Although its (unofficial) subtitle, *How to Survive under Siege*, reflects the fact that its standpoint is for the most part not the besieger's but the besieged, it actually discusses most facets of campaigning which had as their objective *blockade rather than pitched battle. Modern readers find especial interest in Aineias' long chapter on the theory and practice of cryptography and for historians of the period his work as a whole offers unique insights into the stresses of life in small Greek towns vulnerable as much to internal treachery as external assault. At the time his advice (replete with concrete examples and object lessons) was intended mainly for those charged with the actual defence of such towns.

The second group of writers came later, from the 1st century BC onwards. Some of them would be classified, in ancient terms at least, as philosophers: Asclepiodotus (1st century BC), for example, whose treatise on battlefield dispositions reproduces the by-then conventional theoretical wisdom that a *phalanx of heavy infantry must contain, for arithmetical convenience, precisely 16,384 men. Onasander (1st century AD), known also as the author of a commentary on Plato's *Republic*, dedicated his *General's Manual* to Quintus Veranius, one of the earliest Roman governors of Britain, who may indeed have profited from its not uninsightful observations on the psychological as well as the military sagacity required in a commanding officer; Onasander himself expresses confidence that his work 'will be a training school for good generals and a delight to retired commanders'. Apollodorus of Damascus, a builder and architect in the service of Trajan and *Hadrian, wrote a *Siegecraft* from a more technological and logistical standpoint than Aineias'. (For this combination of interests compare the Roman Vitruvius, military engineer to Julius *Caesar as well as architectural treatise-writer.) The *Tactica* of Aelian (also 1st–2nd century AD) looks back, derivatively as well as anachronistically, to the infantry phalanx of the Hellenistic era. His contemporary Arrian (*c.*86–160) (see also GREEK HISTORIANS) is an altogether more important figure: a general and provincial governor in the eastern Roman empire and, as a writer, a conscious (and worthy) imitator of Xenophon. Arrian's *Tactica*, while similar in form to Aelian's, brought to bear contemporary field experience, especially in cavalry, and cited up-to-date illustrative material; and another short work, the *Order of Battle against the Alani*, recounted Gen Arrian's own tactics in repelling from his province a threatened invasion by those marauding nomads. The clientele for writing of this kind will also have enjoyed the stratagem genre, compilations of

strategic and tactical ploys culled from past and present. Two specimens survive: four volumes from the Roman Frontinus (1st century AD), better known for his invaluable study of the aqueducts of the city of Rome, and eight from the Macedonian Greek Polyaenus (2nd century AD). Polyaenus (see also GREEK HISTORIANS) cited almost every commander between the god Pan and the Emperor Augustus to prove the superior value of brains over brawn in overcoming an enemy.

The chronological gulf between Xenophon and Aineias in the 4th century BC and their late Hellenistic and Roman period successors is doubtless exaggerated by the accidents of loss and survival; a harder question is whether the works written were still intended and used as practical handbooks. Most of their authors, like Onasander (quoted above), claim that they were, so the difficulty for a modern age accustomed to other manifestations of didacticism becomes that of assessing the degree of truth behind the literary convention. When we ourselves read the likes of Asclepiodotus, Aelian, and in another vein Polyaenus, we seem to be in the world of the armchair general, his needs catered for by this plethora of military writings all more or less divorced from the inconveniences of warfare proper. The ancient world did not have our (by and large) clear-cut distinction between the military and the civilian, and seriously intended manuals of soldierly advice and accumulated wisdom would have circulated far beyond the ancient equivalents—had there been any—of Sandhurst and *West Point. Under the Roman empire if not before, 'Greek' military matters for some became part of an educational curriculum, for others a harmless exercise in private nostalgia; but if (in an age when slow technological change meant that the military theory and practice of times past was slow to lose its relevance) yet others wanted to prepare themselves for command by absorbing tactical expertise in written form, there was plenty of it to be had. DW

Aeneas, Tacticus, *Aineias the Tactician: How to Survive under Siege*, ed. and trans. David Whitehead (Oxford, 1990).

Campbell, Brian, 'Teach Yourself how to be a General', *Journal of Roman Studies*, 77 (1987).

Grenada, invasion of (1983). Following a bloody 19 October *coup d'état* against the repressive pro-Cuban government of Maurice Bishop by a harder line cabal, the Organization of Eastern Caribbean States requested US military intervention. URGENT FURY was launched on 25 October, using the pretext of rescuing American students. It has been alleged that the operation was mounted to distract popular attention from the contemporary destruction of the US Marine camp in Beirut by a suicide bomber, but in fact the invasion was ordered at least a week previously.

In the absence of good operational *intelligence, the decision to move fast in overwhelming force involved a high degree of improvisation, but when measured against the domestic and international problems inherent in a less precipitate approach, it was certainly correct. Strong resistance was expected from Cuban military advisers and construction workers, but in the event, given orders by *Castro to fight only if attacked, their performance was perfunctory. Nonetheless, they suffered 24 dead and 59 wounded, against about 50 dead and 150 wounded in the Grenadian army/ militia. Civilian casualties were at least as great. US casualties were 19 killed and 152 wounded.

Pres Reagan stated that URGENT FURY redeemed the military from post-*Vietnam demoralization, but the operation revealed continuing problems in the system. None escaped the attention of *Schwarzkopf, an acerbic observer, who was to be an unforgiving staff taskmaster during his conduct of DESERT STORM.   HEB

grenade (from Fr.: *grenade*, pomegranate). The earliest grenades appear to have been in use in China before AD 1000; their bodies were made of baked clay or tarred paper and so lacked a serious fragmentation effect. In the West, grenades in the form of hollow iron spheres, cast in two pieces and welded together, were in use in the medieval period during siege and *trench warfare. Containing *gunpowder and sealed with a waxed wooden plug, these early grenades were ignited with a lit fuse and hurled by specially trained assault troops who became *grenadiers; grenades' similarity in appearance to pomegranates gave rise to their name. By the late 17th century devices were being developed to fire grenades from the muzzles of *flintlock muskets. Grenades were not much used by the infantry after the early 18th century, being reserved for the engineers and artillery who were in charge of the science of siegecraft. The reintroduction of trench warfare after 1914 necessitated the reinvention of the grenade and brought about its widespread use. Many types of grenade were used and developed during WW I and the most effective were retained after 1918, such as the German 'stick-grenade' and the British Mills No. 36—both operated by time fuses. During WW II research was pursued into grenade effectiveness and role; grenades detonating on impact and specialist grenades, such as blast grenades, sticky grenades, and *anti-armour grenades all resulted. Rifle grenades were developed by all combatant nations and the modern infantryman is now equipped with personal weapons which can effectively fire a rifle grenade without prejudicing his primary role. Stun, *gas, and *smoke grenades—all developed during WW II—are now widely used in anti-terrorist operations and against rioters.   SCW

Courtney-Green, P. R., *Ammunition for the Land Battle* (London, 1991).

grenadiers were assault troops armed with *grenades. Soldiers trained to carry and throw them were equipped with a length of slow match with which to ignite their fuses. Since they were weapons of assault, those who were trained to throw them had to be highly motivated risk-takers; ideally, they were also large and agile, since length of arm and bodily strength contributed to the distance that the grenade could be thrown. These factors led to grenadiers becoming élite soldiers by the end of the 17th century and to their being dressed in ways reflective of this status.

Grenadiers first appeared in France: in 1667 four men per infantry company were trained as grenadiers and in 1671 one company per battalion was a grenadier company. Grenadier companies (see FLANK COMPANIES) were introduced in the British infantry in 1678 and in 1676 mounted grenadiers were created in Louis XV's household troops; in 1679 horse grenadiers were added to the British Household Cavalry and known as Horse Grenadier Guards. By the end of the 17th century each European nation had companies of foot or regiments of horse or foot armed and dressed as grenadiers. The grenadier company of a line infantry battalion was paraded on the right of the line, the place of *honour accorded to its status. In the 18th century, it became the practice, in time of war, for the grenadier companies to be grouped together to form battalions or larger formations: such units would be placed in the forefront of any assault. This practice continued in peacetime in some nations, France creating a regiment of grenadiers in 1748—Les Grenadiers de France—and Austria creating grenadier battalions in 1769. By this time though, the grenade itself had been largely dropped from the infantryman's armoury and grenadiers were simply soldiers selected for their appearance and height. These attributes were embellished, in the French army, by encouraging grenadiers to grow fierce moustaches; elsewhere, their height was exaggerated by 'mitre' or grenadier caps. These caps, close-fitting, tall, and pointed, developed from soft round hats which, for 17th-century grenadiers, replaced the broad-brimmed infantryman's hat. Such *headdress interfered less with their ability to sling their muskets and hurl their grenades overarm.

Grenadier companies were abolished in the British army in 1855 and in the French army in 1868, but the name lived on because the British 1st Foot Guards became the Grenadier Guards in 1815 in commemoration of their defeat of the Grenadiers of Napoleon's Imperial Guard at *Waterloo. The Grenadier Guards adopted the bearskin cap which, by 1815, marked grenadier companies out from battalion and light companies; subsequently the other regiments of British Foot Guards also adopted the bearskin cap. In WW II, regiments of *Panzergrenadieren* were attached to *Wehrmacht armoured divisions. These were assault-trained infantry; élite troops who accompanied tanks into battle as part of *blitzkrieg tactics and whose mobility was consequently enhanced. Although armed with grenades, like all German infantry, their name was a deliberate invocation of the original grenadiers' élite traditions.   SCW

Gribeauval, Jean-Baptiste Vaquette de (1715–89), French artillery general and gun designer. Gribeauval joined the French army in 1732 and was commissioned in 1735. During the *Seven Years War he was attached to the Austrian army. In 1765 he began reforming the French artillery after experience in the war. He achieved greater mobility by building lighter gun carriages, and having the guns and limbers drawn by paired horses rather than in tandem, as they had been before. The Gribeauval guns also had better ammunition, tangenet scales, and elevating screws, improving accuracy and rate of fire. He also standardized on 4-, 8- and 12-pounders. British iron-smelting processes, introduced to France in 1782, also improved the quality of barrels. Efficiency was also improved by having the field guns manned by soldiers—not hired civilians, as had been the case before. In 1776 he was made inspector of artillery, and was responsible for training artillery officers, including one *Napoleon Bonaparte. Gribeauval's technical improvements to artillery were the single most important change to weapon design in the 18th century (apart, perhaps, from the introduction of the socket *bayonet at the very beginning). Gribeauval's improvements to lethality and accuracy made artillery the biggest killer on the battlefield.   CDB

Grouchy, Marshal Emmanuel Marquis de (1766–1847). Most famous for his non-arrival on the fateful field of *Waterloo, Grouchy has been poorly served by posterity, which has largely ignored his previous career. A noble by birth, the young Grouchy was schooled in the pre-Revolution royalist cavalry, rising to a lieutenancy in the élite Compagnie Écossaise of the king's Garde du Corps. Disillusioned with the abuse of power and privilege, he became one of the many aristocrats who embraced the humanitarian ideals of the Revolution. He fought the royalist counter-revolution in the *Vendée and was embarked for the abortive invasion of Ireland in 1799.

He was wounded at Novi in 1799 while fighting the Russians in Italy, recovered, and went on to fight at Hohenlinden, Ulm, *Eylau, and Friedland. A brief sojourn in Spain was marked by his suppression, with *Murat, of the uprising in Madrid, the infamous Dos de Mayo of 1808. He discharged his duties as a cavalry commander with distinction in the 1809 Italian campaign under Prince Eugène de Beauharnais and performed useful service at the Piave and at Raab. Entering Austria with the Army of Italy, Grouchy was at *Wagram. His body and spirit seemingly broken by constant campaigning, he then went on extended leave until the Russian campaign of 1812, where he was in the thick of the action at *Borodino and commanded the Bataillon Sacré of officers that guarded Napoleon's person on the retreat. He spent 1813 recovering from the vicissitudes of Russia, but was recalled to lead the cavalry during the campaign of France in 1814, again showing his skill as a leader of cavalry, but was severely wounded at Craonne.

On Napoleon's return from Elba in 1815, Grouchy received his long-awaited marshal's baton and commanded the right wing of the army that was to pursue the Prussians after Ligny. He elected not to march to the sound of the guns, but caught the Prussian rearguard at Wavre, and was checked while Napoleon's agony was being played out some 10 miles (16 km) to the west at Waterloo. It is debatable whether his arrival would have reversed the result of the battle, but his force would certainly have provided a backstop, and minimized the scale of the disaster. It was an ignominious end to a distinguished career from which Grouchy's reputation never recovered.   TM

Guadalcanal, battle for (1942–3). A British possession since annexation in 1893, Guadalcanal is one of the largest of the southern group of Solomon Islands, and its occupation in early 1942 marks the limit of Japanese expansion in the south-west Pacific. The southern Solomons dominate New Guinea and in Japanese hands provided the springboard for an invasion of Australia; therefore their possession was vital for both sides. Just as the Japanese, with invasion plans in mind, started to move powerful forces into the area, a force of US Marines landed on Guadalcanal on 7 August 1942, seizing the adjacent harbour of Tulagi and the strategically valuable airfield the Japanese had constructed. In the fierce fighting that followed the Marines were introduced to the 'banzai' charge and to the fact that the Japanese were prepared to fight to the last man. The battle, which raged until February 1943, was decided by five sea battles fought in the vicinity, which began with US and Allied disasters, but ended with the Japanese loss of two battleships. The 'Tokyo Express' down 'The Slot', as the channel leading to Guadalcanal was called, came regularly by night (to negate US air superiority) to shell the airfield (Henderson field) and to land reinforcements. Defending the airfield perimeter, US Marines were locked in a bitter struggle with an enemy better trained and equipped to cope with the malaria-ridden jungle. Eventually US forces built up to an overwhelming 50,000 troops on the island, and the remaining Japanese were evacuated with one last run of the 'Tokyo Express'.   APC-A

Guam, battle for (1944). The largest, most populous, and southernmost of the Marianas island chain, with an excellent harbour and an important source of fresh water, Guam was demilitarized after the Washington Naval Limitation Treaty of 1922, and its defences were not restored in the 1930s, for fear of provoking Japan. It was occupied by Japanese forces immediately after *Pearl Harbor, which quickly overwhelmed the 500 defenders. When it came to be reinvaded by 55,000 Marines of III US Amphibious Corps on 20 July 1944, the Japanese defenders put up a stiff fight for three weeks, but over 10,000 (out of 19,000) were killed. The island is about 30 miles (48 km) long and 4–8 miles (6.4–12.9 km) wide, and covered with dense jungle, which made the going heavy, and gave the defenders an immense advantage. Maj Gen Geiger's solution was an extended naval and air bombardment which dislocated the defenders and bought time to clear away some of the beach obstacles. Once occupied, the island was then turned into a huge air and naval base, and squadrons of B-29 Superfortresses were stationed there to attack the Japanese mainland. Some defenders resisted for long afterwards, the last surrendering only in 1972.   APC-A

guards Forces raised to protect the monarch or head of state sometimes serving as shock troops in battle. Guards have played a political as well as a military role. After the accession of Augustus the Praetorian Guard, which had originated as a legion, remained in Rome, where it exercised remarkable political power, often acting as emperor-maker. The spectacle of guardsmen who rarely fought but used their monopoly of force in the capital to generate political clout has not been confined to Rome. In 1789 the defection to the insurgents of the Gardes Françaises was of profound significance. The Gardes Suisses, on the other hand, defended the Tuileries in 1792 with unavailing courage, underlining the point that the most effective guards have often been foreigners, less likely to become embroiled in domestic politics.

Guards often enjoyed a personal relationship with their monarch, constituting household troops in a literal sense. The *housecarls of Anglo-Saxon England were household warriors, maintained by their lord. Robert Abels has suggested that 'their obligation to fight did not arise from the cash nexus but from the bonds of lordship'. The Anglo-Saxon poem *The Battle of Maldon* makes much of the housecarl's duty not to leave the field if his lord had fallen:

> Steadfast warriors around Sturmere will have no cause
> to taunt me with words, now my beloved one is dead,
> that I travelled home lordless,
> turned away from the fight, but a weapon will take me . . .

King Harold's housecarls fought to the death about his body at *Hastings. 'They were few in number,' recorded the chronicler William of Malmesbury, 'but brave in the extreme.'

From the late 17th century guards in European armies assumed the form they were to retain, in most cases, until WW I. They grew to constitute at least several regiments apiece—in 1914 there were three full divisions of Russian foot guards, and even the much smaller British army fielded a Guards Division from 1915 and a Guards Armoured Division in WW II. They prized their links with the ruling dynasty. The two senior regiments of Russian footguards, the Preobrazhenskiy and Semenovskiy, originated in the boy-

hood friends *Peter 'the Great' had drilled, while *Napoleon, with an assortment of glittering *uniforms at his disposal, usually appeared dressed simply as a colonel of *chasseurs of his guard. Guards were exported to armies taught by European instructors: the Japanese Imperial Guard was modelled on the German.

In many armies the guard was socially exclusive, recruiting officers from the high nobility and sometimes enlisting private soldiers of gentle birth. When the Russian Chevalier Guard, the tsar's personal escort, was mauled at *Austerlitz, Napoleon remarked: 'Many fine ladies of St Petersburg will lament this day.' The memorial to the Queen Augusta Guards Regiment at Saint-Privat, where the Prussian Guard Corps lost heavily on 18 August 1870, includes two princes of Salm-Salm, and the panel commemorating the Grenadier Guards on the British Memorial to the Missing at Le Touret bears the names of four titled officers.

The standing of guards units was often reflected by allowing their members to hold higher *rank in the army than they did in their regiments. Until the mid-19th century British guards lieutenants ranked as majors in the line and captains as lieutenant colonels. Napoleon's guardsmen were paid as sergeants of the line, and so on up the hierarchy. Swedish household cavalrymen, known as *drabants*, ranked as captains in the line. British Household Cavalrymen are still addressed collectively as 'gentlemen', harking back to the 17th century when that is indeed what they would have been.

Alongside privileges in rank and pay went distinctive uniforms. Prussian guards uniforms featured the guards star and 'bear's-paw' lace. British footguards still wear a cap star, the stars on their officers' *badges of rank are of a different pattern to those in the line, and their uniform buttons are arranged so as to differentiate regiments. Although bearskin caps are not exclusive to guards regiments, they have often been favoured by guards, were worn by both the *grenadiers and chasseurs of Napoleon's Imperial Guard, and are retained by British and Danish footguards.

The social as well as the political standing of guards has made them suspect to some regimes. The USA has never had a guard proper (the extraordinarily smart 'Old Guard' is essentially a ceremonial unit) and republican France swiftly jettisoned the guard after the fall of the Second Empire, forming a smaller and less high-profile Republican Guard from the Garde de Paris, traditionally responsible for security in the capital.

Guards have served several purposes. The task of close protection often remained with a smaller, more ancient body like the Gentleman at Arms in England or the Royal Company of Archers in Scotland, or was entrusted to a specific group within the larger guard: monarchs of the *ancien régime* were protected by the Garde du corps (body guard) and *Napoleon III by the Cent-Gardes. Habsburg monarchs were defended by palace guard companies. There was no guard proper in the Austrian or later Austro-Hungarian armies: its nearest equivalent was the crack Hoch-und-Deutchmeister infantry regiment. Guards did duty at royal or presidential palaces, contributing to the dignity of state occasions, attracting tourists and contributing to the social (and sexual) life of the capital. They provided a source of emulation for the rest of the army. Napoleon's Imperial Guard grew steadily in size—it was a staggering 112,500 strong in 1814—partly in an effort to reward the pick of the conscripts of successive annual intakes and make conscription more tolerable. The Red Army dispensed with guards after the Revolution, but reinvented the title in 1941 as a means of rewarding units which performed well.

Guards have sometimes constituted a battlefield élite. Napoleon committed his guard as rarely as possible. Its splendid bearing in reserve wielded enormous psychological weight, and he was always conscious that such splendid soldiers could not be easily replaced. The Imperial Guard's repulse at *Waterloo was the battle's decisive moment: the spectacle of the guard retiring caused panic in the line regiments. Tension between guard and line is not uncommon. When the Scots Fusilier Guards fell back at the Alma in the *Crimean war, there were cries of 'Shame! Shame! What about the queen's favourites now?' Sir Colin *Campbell, commanding the Highland Brigade, made his own feelings characteristically clear: 'it were better that every man of Her Majesty's Guards should lie dead upon the field of battle than they should turn their backs upon the enemy'. Guards have been set high standards, and such is the store men set by reputation and *honour that they have often attained them. When *Tobruk was about to surrender to the Germans in 1942 the Coldstream Guards broke out: their commander argued that as a guards officer he had not been taught to surrender and did not propose to learn.

RH

Guderian, Col-Gen Heinz Wilhelm (1888–1954).

Guderian was born at Kulm in Prussia, son of an army officer. Although he was commissioned into the infantry in 1908, he took an early interest in the wireless, and in 1914 he went to war in France commanding the signals detachment of a cavalry division. An outburst of wrath (its astonished victim the divisional commander) saw him posted to HQ Fourth Army as assistant signals officer. He had begun a staff course before the war, and completed his studies during it, being posted to the *general staff in February 1918.

After the war, after serving as COS to the 'Iron Division' of the *Freikorps* in the Baltic states, he was tasked with investigating *mechanization to get around the Treaty of Versailles ban on tanks in the *Reichswehr. He read about British experiments in *armoured warfare, visited the USSR, and in 1929 experimented with mock-up vehicles, but even after *Hitler came to power he had to work hard to persuade the *Wehrmacht to see tanks as its 'principal weapon . . . supplied with fully motorised supporting arms

. . . permanently attached'. In 1935 he gained approval for the formation of the first three panzer divisions, and in 1937 he published *Achtung! Panzer!* which encapsulated his ideas on armoured warfare. These were neither wholly original nor part of a comprehensive official *doctrine, but they fitted in with the Nazis' fascination with the tough and the radical. Guderian's theories embodied some of the characteristics of the *manoeuvre warfare of a later generation. He argued that the panzer division should be used in 'short well timed operations launched by brief orders. The principle of surprise [is essential] in order to avoid or avert enemy defensive action.'

Guderian commanded one of the first panzer divisions, and in 1939 led a corps of one panzer and two motorized infantry divisions into Poland. His was a bravura performance: he led from the front, overcoming the doubts of his subordinates to earn the nickname 'Hurrying Heinz'. When Hitler, viewing the battlefield, asked whether the Luftwaffe had been responsible for some destroyed guns, Guderian replied: 'No! Our panzers.' In late 1939 he argued that the controversial *Manstein plan was indeed feasible, and in May 1940 his panzer corps struck the campaign's decisive blow, crossing the Meuse at Sedan. During the advance he led with characteristic verve and, no less characteristically, had a spectacular row with Kluge, his immediate superior. For the second phase of the campaign he commanded a two-corps *Panzergruppe* and was promoted colonel-general at its end.

When he heard of plans for the invasion of the USSR, Guderian sent his COS to protest. Guderian commanded a three-corps *Panzergruppe* during the invasion, but he forfeited the support of CGS Halder when he failed to press Hitler to make Moscow, rather than the Ukraine, the campaign's principal objective. His group was approaching Moscow when it was sharply counter-attacked. Guderian demanded freedom of action, again clashed with Kluge, and was dismissed on Christmas Day 1941.

Recalled to service as inspector general of armoured troops in February 1943, Guderian had the right of direct access to Hitler, and did his best to develop and train the panzer arm but he was unable to prevent serious mishandling of armoured forces. He declined to support the July 1944 bomb plot, arguing that his *honour as an officer forbade it. His honour did not prevent him issuing an order that all soldiers should regard themselves as Nazis when he was subsequently appointed CGS. No flunky, Guderian argued frequently with Hitler and in March 1945, after yet another quarrel, he was sent on leave, to surrender to the Americans on 10 May.

Guderian was not simply a notable theorist and organizer but a hard-driving armoured commander of rare talent: the Meuse crossing, a remarkable achievement, owed much to him. Yet he was headstrong and irascible, admired rather than liked, and, like so many German officers of the time, torn between the professional excitement of the wars

Hitler declared and the cost to his honour and his country of serving him.   RH

Guderian, Heinz, *Panzer Leader* (London, 1953).
Macksey, Kenneth, *Guderian: Panzer General* (London, 1975).

Guernica, bombing of (1937), infamous incident during the *Spanish civil war, the subject of a famous anti-war painting by Pablo Picasso. Twenty miles (32 km) from Bilbao, Guernica was regarded as the centre of Basque nationalism. At the time of the attack it was held by the Republicans and was an important communications centre, but it was also crammed with refugees and retreating Republican soldiers. The bombing was carried out by the Condor Legion of the German Air Command on 26 April. More than 1,000 people were reported killed, but modern research suggests only about 300 civilians died. The bombing shattered the defenders' will to resist and allowed the Nationalists to overrun it, facing little resistance and taking complete control by 29 April. Guernica was seen as an example of 'terror bombing' by western countries, and gave them the mistaken impression that the Luftwaffe was equipped and committed to such a policy. In fact Wolfram von Richthofen, the Condor Legion commander, had no idea of Guernica's political significance and saw it only as a military target.   AA2

Carr, Raymond, *The Spanish Tragedy* (London, 1993).
Corum, James, *The Luftwaffe: Creating the Operational Air War 1918–1940* (Lawrence, Kan., 1997).
Thomas, Hugh, *The Spanish Civil War* (London, 1988).

guerre revolutionnaire (Fr. revolutionary war). During the 1960s a group of French officers developed a comprehensive *doctrine for fighting insurgency, and employed it in the *Algerian independence war. It originated in French defeat in *Indochina, where many officers became convinced of the strength of a unified politico-military command and the vital importance of the civilian population. It was linked to a belief in a worldwide subversive threat, directed, not on an east–west axis, but, as Gen Allard put it, in 'a vast enveloping curve passing through China, the Far East, South-East Asia, the Middle East and North Africa in order to encircle Europe'. Supporters of the theory were nerved not merely by bitter experience of defeat, but also by disillusionment with the social and political realities of contemporary France.

Guerre revolutionnaire, as described by its theorists such as Charles Lacheroy and Roger Trinquier, embodied the destruction of armed opposition, the construction of an environment in which insurgents could not operate, and the use of *psychological warfare at all levels. The French sought to isolate nationalist *guerrillas in Algeria by sealing off the borders with Tunisia and Morocco, and providing a chequerboard of garrisons, backed up by a general reserve

to carry out anti-guerrilla sweeps. Tens of thousands of civilians were moved from vulnerable areas into villages that could be more easily defended: Special Administrative Sections (Sections Administratives Speciales, or SAS) of civil affairs officers, *NCOs, and civilians were responsible for their administration and political mobilization. A variety of local forces were recruited, some containing former insurgents. Both the military and civil affairs campaigns embodied psychological warfare, and psychological-warfare sections were made branches of the *general staff at regional and formation level in 1957.

Ultimately the doctrine proved a failure. Although the army effectively won the armed struggle, it was unable to convince the population of metropolitan France of the need for a continuing commitment to Algeria. There was tension between the activities of the SAS and those of fighting units, and some military successes were bought at too great a cost in relations with the population. The psychological warfare bureaux became involved in a variety of discreditable activities and were disbanded in 1960, while elements in the army became increasingly politicized and were moved, in 1958 and 1961, to take direct military action against the government.

Yet the theory had much merit. In common with successful *counter-insurgency doctrines it recognized both the centrality of the population and the need to fight a unified politico-military campaign. Officers attracted to it were often influenced by long-term currents in French military thought, such as the ideas put forward by *Lyautey on the social role of the officer. Their wholehearted, and often selfless, commitment to a lost cause, linked with profound regret at being forced to abandon their Algerian supporters, led many to imprisonment or exile: it was to take the French army years to recover.   RH

Paret, Peter, *French Revolutionary Warfare from Indochina to Algeria* (London, 1964).
Trinquier, Roger, *Modern Warfare: A French View of Counterinsurgency* (New York, 1964).

guerrilla warfare (*see opposite page*)

Guevara, Ernesto (1928–67), Argentine-born Cuban revolutionary and cultural ideal for a generation enamoured of style over substance, known as 'Ché' from a verbal mannerism distinctive of his native land. His contribution to military theory was the idea of a *guerrilla 'focus' to *create* revolutionary conditions by attracting the disaffected and provoking repression, a variant of the French Revolutionaries' *politique du pire* (the politics of painting things as black as possible), which overlooks the fact that ruthless repression usually succeeds.

Of Spanish-Irish descent, he grew up in a provincial bourgeois home. Although he suffered from asthma, he was

(*cont. on page 387*)

guerrilla warfare

GUERRILLA warfare is, at its simplest, a direct reversal of the logic of regular warfare. Where regular armies aim to concentrate force to achieve a decision with maximum speed, guerrilla forces disperse and conduct small-scale operations over an indefinite period of time. The strength of this form of warfare is its resilience; its weakness is the inability of small forces to confront regular armies directly. If a guerrilla strategy is to secure victory, this can only happen if it can debilitate the regular force, or if the guerrilla force can transform itself into a force capable of defeating the regular force in open battle. The former outcome is unlikely to occur in a physical sense. The arresting metaphor of fleas biting a dog to death (alluded to in the title of one of the most popular studies of guerrilla war, *The War of the Flea*) cannot be literally applied to human organizations like states and armies. But psychological debilitation is quite possible.

Guerrilla strategy and tactics are in one sense the most ancient form of warfare, but in the 20th century they have become one of the most sophisticated forms. Indeed for a whole generation in the third quarter of the century, there was a widespread assumption that they would neutralize all 'conventional' armies. The growth of this belief can be quite clearly traced. Even during the period of professional warfare, *skirmishers were maintained to conduct what was called 'la petite guerre' (the little war) on the flanks of the tightly controlled regular armies. But these forces were auxiliary and marginal. A big shift in perception came during the *Napoleonic wars, when irregular resistance both in Russia and in Spain played a substantial part in weakening the French invaders. It was the Spanish 'la guerra de guerrillas' (the war of little wars) as waged against the French in the *Peninsular war that gave the form its distinctive name and showed that it could work independently of regular war.

Observing the Napoleonic period, *Clausewitz perceived the significance of what he called 'arming the people' (*Volksbewaffnung*). Armed civilians, operating over an extended area and time, 'like a slow gradual fire', could 'destroy the bases of the enemy force'. Militarily, he saw such popular forces as still being auxiliary, but politically they were absolutely vital: they were the physical manifestation of the national spirit. Without patriotism, they would never take the huge risks involved. Clausewitz was profoundly aware of these risks: French reprisals against Spanish communities had been ferocious. But he suggested that careful selection of targets could nurture the spirit of resistance: occupying armies would have to detach small forces as guards and foragers, and as 'at some point the enemy is overpowered by sheer numbers, courage and enthusiasm grow'. This was the crucial dynamic for guerrilla warfare.

Ideology would prove to be the fuel for the eventual transformation of guerrilla warfare. After the fall of Napoleon there was to some extent a turning-away from the abyss of 'absolute war' that the French Revolution had opened up, but there were several indications that the return to 'limited war' was more apparent than real. The *American civil war generated less guerrilla activity than might perhaps have been expected, in the light of earlier American experience, and the leaders of both sides were as hostile to guerrilla war as most European regular soldiers. The reason for this hostility, and indeed fear, became clear in the *Franco-Prussian war, where an apparently decisive German victory in the first weeks of the war was followed by months of guerrilla resistance, known as the 'people's war'. This was a slight exaggeration of the level of popular involvement, but the struggle was hard enough to impress on the Prussian COS Helmuth von *Moltke 'the Elder' that the shape of future wars would change radically.

Guerrilla methods were of course ubiquitous in the imperial wars of the late 19th century, but they were seen as symptoms of inferiority, the only possible response of undeveloped societies to the overwhelming power of European armies, difficult and exhausting to deal with, but a nuisance rather than a real threat. Conventional wisdom took the same view of the more formidable guerrilla war waged by the Boers after the defeat of their main forces during the Second *Boer War, despite the respect accorded to some of the *commando leaders like de Wet and Smuts. The veld was hardly normal European territory; nor was the desert in which the *Arab revolt arose in 1916, but the latter produced something that no previous guerrilla war had: a charismatic theorist.

*Lawrence 'of Arabia' wrote a famous, highly coloured account of his role in the Arab revolt, as well as a compact and systematic analysis that set out what could be seen as a blueprint for national liberation movements everywhere (*The Evolution of a Revolt*, 1920). It held out the promise that imperial occupying powers were eminently defeatable; the apparent strength of their armies could be negated by careful use of guerrilla methods. His theory contained four key elements, which he called mobility, security, time, and *doctrine. A combination of their own mobility and the security provided by superior *intelligence information, an advantage which should naturally accrue from popular support, would render the guerrillas invulnerable. Time was on their side, so they could afford to limit their operations to those they were sure to succeed in. Success would bolster the popular support that doctrine, which for Lawrence was the cause of national liberation, ultimately guaranteed.

Although he recognized that irregular forces could not confront regulars in open battle, he argued that by harrassing, confusing, exhausting, demoralizing, and discrediting them, a guerrilla strategy could not only weaken or neutralize but actually overthrow a superior military power. This was a dramatic enlargement of earlier ideas. It was to some extent borne out by the success of the Irish patriots in the *Anglo-Irish war of 1919–21. They were numerically weak and chronically short of arms, but the use of guerrilla methods enabled them to paralyse key elements of the British administrative and legal system, and—crucially—to undermine the legitimacy of the state. By rendering local police posts untenable at an early stage of the fight, they effectively 'liberated' large areas of the country. The alternative government established by Sinn Fein after its election victory in 1918 achieved remarkable credibility. The use of modern publicity methods played an important part in maximizing the impact of small local operations, bearing out Lawrence's dictum that 'the printing press is the greatest weapon in the armoury of the modern commander'. Even in areas of heaviest British military presence like Dublin, the *IRA survived, thanks in part to the intelligence system built up by Michael *Collins. The British forces were never in any military sense defeated, but a substantial garrison (some 40,000 troops and 10,000 armed police) conspicuously failed to defeat the 3,000-odd active guerrilla fighters. The political damage caused by this failure was decisive. Though Britain conceded less than it appeared to, the impression that a major imperial power had lost a guerrilla war resonated throughout the world.

By the 1920s guerrilla warfare was poised to sweep into public and military consciousness. The final impulse was supplied by the revolutionary ideology that took power in Russia after 1917. For the next half-century socialism would combine with nationalism to generate a heady revolutionary cocktail. Though the Bolshevik leaders downplayed the significance of guerrilla action in winning the Russian civil war, the opposite was the case in China. After the failure of the communists to replicate a Russian-style urban insurrection in the late 1920s, they turned to the countryside. The Long March, which reduced the Red Army to barely a tenth of its orginal strength, also cemented the dominance of *Mao Tse-tung, who became the most influential of all guerrilla theorists. Mao had reservations about guerrilla action as such, with its potential for excessive decentralization or even anarchy, and preferred to speak of 'protracted war' to stress its essential logic. In protracted war the weaker side would adopt guerrilla tactics to harass and weaken the enemy, with the aim of building up forces that would eventually be capable of conventional fighting. Mao's famous triadic formula, with guerrilla operations during the phase of inferiority, mobile forces in the phase of contention during which the balance of strength would shift, preparing the way for a full-scale offensive, pointed up the difficulty of the central phase. The support of the people was vital. The revolutionaries needed to demonstrate not only that they could take on the enemy but that they could create a better social order—hence the stress that Mao, unusually among guerrilla theorists, laid on fixed base areas. Hence, too, his famous instructions governing the behaviour of the communist fighters, the 'Three Disciplinary Rules' and the 'Eight Points of Attention'. For Mao, party discipline was the only way of controlling a guerrilla campaign.

The eventual victory of the communists over the Chinese nationalist government in 1949 probably owed as much to the Japanese attack on China in 1937 as to Mao's theories. The effective and well-publicized resistance of the communist guerrillas damaged Japanese prestige and rallied patriotic support. The same patriotic credentials were a key asset for the Vietnamese communists who led the wave of post-war revolutionary movements inspired by the Chinese example. The guerrilla forces of the Vietminh led by Gen Vo Nguyen *Giap succeeded not only in fighting off a French effort to recover control of *Indochina between 1945 and 1953, but also a formidable US military intervention in support of the partitioned southern state in the 1960s. In the process they demonstrated that technological development favoured the guerrilla rather than the counter-insurgent forces. The whole tendency of modern weapons was to make firepower more portable. The *grenade launcher, for instance, transformed the striking power of small fighting groups; plastic explosives like Semtex were a similar boon. As against these, the stupendous increase in the destructiveness of *air power has been of limited utility in guerrilla war. The USA was able to inflict appalling collateral damage on *Vietnam, but not to inflict a decisive check on the Vietcong.

The post-war decade saw a dramatic burgeoning in guerrilla insurgency. Guerrilla successes seemed to outweigh failures like those of the MPLA (Malayan People's Liberation Army) in the *Malayan emergency, the Hukbalahap in the Philippines, or the *Mau Mau in Kenya. The campaign of the Zionist military groups against the British government in Palestine in the 1940s, and the miniature (at least by Chinese standards) EOKA (National Organization of Cypriot Fighters) campaign in *Cyprus in the 1950s demonstrated that declining imperial regimes could be persuaded to quit by relatively small threats. This was the bottom line in the extensive, vicious, and long-drawn-out *Algerian independence war that began in 1954. The military threat posed by the insurgent FLN (National Liberation Front) was gradually choked off by French *counter-insurgency measures (see GUERRE REVOLUTIONNAIRE); by 1961 the number of active guerrillas had been reduced from 40,000 in 1956 to around 5,000. But in the process French public opinion turned against the effort to keep the colony, despite the presence of a million French colons.

The most reverberant of all guerrilla triumphs came in 1959 in Cuba, when the government collapsed in face of a tiny insurgent force under *Castro. His apparently foolhardy invasion began in December 1956, and his original force of 80 was all but annihilated in its first battle. The survivors escaped to the southern mountains, the Sierra Maestra, and began a guerrilla campaign that survived the poorly organized efforts of the Cuban army to locate and destroy them. Until the very last phase of the war, rebel strength was no more than 300. The rapid collapse of the Batista regime astonished the world and seemed hard to explain. One explanation, not the most convincing but certainly the most romantic, was that offered by the revolutionaries themselves, and especially *Guevara, who argued that they had created a new paradigm for guerrilla strategy, a 'revolution in the revolution'. His international best-seller *Guerrilla Warfare* contained little that was new in military terms, but offered the prospect of success to small bands of dedicated revolutionaries. With the right moral qualities and physical toughness a dozen fighters could form a *foco insurreccional* whose actions would win public support. Unlike classical Marxists, who insisted that revolutions arose from objective circumstances, these soft Marxists said that revolutionary circumstances could be created by will.

The *foco* theory inspired a new wave of guerrilla insurgency in the 1960s, for example in Guatemala, Venezuela, Colombia, and Peru. None of these succeeded in generating the predicted mass support. The most striking failure was that of Guevara himself in Bolivia, hunted down and killed by US-trained Rangers in October 1967 amidst an indifferent peasant population. This was by no means the end of the line for guerrilla insurgency but by the early 1970s there was a noticeable shift towards what became known as 'urban guerrilla warfare', very different in its logic and method from the rural version. Pioneers of this new direction, like *Marighela in Brazil and the *Tupamaros in Uruguay, reversed the Guevarist geography and relied on *coups de théâtre* in major cities to convey their message. They operated in small anonymous groups, which could not grow and build up support in the way that earlier theories had required. The balance between military and propaganda elements in their campaigns was reversed; they became in effect terrorists.

The relationship between guerrilla warfare and terrorism was always complicated. Governments routinely branded all insurgents as terrorists, and most insurgents denied this label. In the abstract it is important to grasp the difference between the two, but in practice the dividing line can be blurred. All rebel organizations, like all states, use intimidation to maintain their security. They try to win public support but they also need to prevent public opposition. Their survival often depends on denying information to the state security forces. Terroristic violence was a salient part of most insurgencies—for instance the IRA in 1920–1 or the Vietminh in 1945–53—but guerrillas do not become terrorists unless they adopt an exclusively terrorist strategy. In some modern conflicts the balance has been very fine. Thus the *PLO, essentially a territorial nationalist guerrilla movement, turned to transnational terrorism in the 1970s to compensate for the loss of its territorial base. The reborn IRA in 1971 also had some territorial bases, but had no hope of conducting a classical guerrilla campaign, since the majority of the Northern Ireland population was deeply hostile to the nationalist programme.

Most of the 'urban guerrilla' movements which looked to be engulfing the world in the 1970s have subsequently died out. By the 1990s even long-lived groups, like the Shining Path in Peru and the Basque national liberation army ETA, seemed to be stalemated. But the strength of rural guerrilla warfare was again demonstrated in *Afghanistan, following the Soviet intervention in December 1979. By 1987 the Islamic forces opposing the communist government were in control of three-quarters of the country, and numbered some 100,000 guerrilla fighters. The inability of the USSR to contain or crush them was at first sight even more astonishing than the failure of the USA in Vietnam. It came to appear less remarkable in retrospect, as the political and economic weakness of the USSR—brought to a crisis by the Afghan campaign itself—became clear. Nonetheless, a global superpower with a shared land border and an undoubted strategic interest in supporting the People's Democratic Party of Afghanistan (PDPA), had failed. Defective counter-insurgency methods played a significant part in this, as did the weakness of the PDPA regime and the availability of foreign sanctuary and support for the rebels. But a key factor was the dedication of the insurgents, who saw themselves as mujahedin, holy warriors, going some way to bear out Lawrence's idealistic model.   CT

Fairbairn, Geoffrey, *Revolutionary Guerrilla Warfare: The Countryside Version* (Harmondsworth, 1974).

Laqueur, Walter, *Guerrilla: A Historical and Critical Study* (London, 1977).

Paret, Peter, and Shy, John W., *Guerrillas in the 1960s: A Background Study of Modern Guerrilla Tactics* (New York, 1962).

Taber, Robert, *The War of the Flea* (London, 1970).

Townshend, Charles, 'People's War', in Townshend (ed.), *The Oxford Illustrated History of Modern War* (Oxford, 1997).

a vigorous athlete as well as a scholar who travelled extensively in Latin America and was appalled by the poverty he observed. After completing his first medical degree he witnessed the 1954 *CIA-sponsored coup against the socialist Arbenz regime in Guatemala, which imbued him with an abiding hatred for the USA. Moving to Mexico, he met the *Castro brothers and joined their November 1956 expedition against Cuban dictator Batista in Cuba. Wounded in an ambush shortly after landing, he was one of the handful who made it to the Sierra Maestra mountains.

The only thing that can be said in defence of his inaccurate account of the *Cuban Revolution and the conclusions he drew from it is that he must have believed it, or else he would not have staked his life on repeating it elsewhere. It succeeded because revolutionaries in the cities absorbed Batista's attention, because his army was militarily useless, and because the USA cut off support. Once the dictator fled on 1 January 1959, the triumvirate of the Castro brothers and Guevara deliberately provoked the Americans to do their worst. When this proved to be the astoundingly inept Bay of Pigs invasion, the revolution was affirmed and Cuba's appeal both to the USSR as a beachhead in the western hemisphere and to wounded Latin American nationalism became irresistible.

Over the next years Guevara occupied key economic posts with an unbroken record of costly failure. Dogmatically committed to the idea that voluntarism could replace incentives, he preferred the glamour of propaganda and exhortation to the dreary work of trying to bring to completion the unrealistic projects he launched, and Cuba is still littered with rusting monuments to his crash industrialization programme. During his international forays he also trampled on Soviet sensibilities by questioning their world revolutionary leadership, but by 1964–5 Cuba was so deeply in debt to the USSR that its independence became tenuous and his own position untenable. Although his friendship with Fidel remained strong to the end, Cuba was also not big enough for two Messiahs.

In 1965 he resigned all offices and his citizenship in order to give Fidel a fig leaf of political deniability and went to Africa, where he led a Cuban contingent in the chaos of the ex-Belgian Congo, well after any possibility of making a difference had evaporated (see CONGO, UN OPERATIONS IN). Meanwhile Fidel had found himself obliged to make his renunciation letters public and Guevara found himself with nowhere to go. In the face of his desire to return to certain death in Argentina, Fidel persuaded him to lead an expedition to Bolivia as a means to that end, while convincing the Bolivian communists that the intention was to create a centrally located continental guerrilla training school.

Guevara made a bad start worse by his doctrinaire commitment to the 'focus' concept in the absence of any local preconditions, and by a desire to record every detail of what he believed was a fresh new chapter in the history of Latin America. Once its attention was drawn to his presence, the

Bolivian army had little difficulty in wiping out the 'focus' and capturing him. They shot him because he was less trouble to them dead than alive.

The dozens of idealistic Latin Americans who had already died seeking to emulate his example became thousands over the next decade. Internationally, he became the idol of the worldwide student revolts of 1968, for which his sexual promiscuity, undisciplined spontaneity, and massive ego made him an entirely appropriate icon.   HEB

Castañeda, Jorge, *Compañero* (New York, 1997).

Guibert, Jacques Antoine Hippolyte, Comte de

(1743–90). At the age of 13 the young Guibert followed in his father's footsteps and joined the French army, serving in the *Seven Years War. By 1788 he had risen to the rank of *maréchal de camp* (brigadier general) and sat on the Conseil de Guerre (War Council) of Louis XVI. He was both a philosopher and soldier—and in that he was typical of his generation—he had joined the Académie Française and published a few literary works. But it is his 1772 *Essai Générale de la Tactique* (General Essay on Tactics) with which we must concern ourselves here. With this work, and subsequently his later *Défense du Système de Guerre Moderne* (Defence of the System of Modern War) of 1779, he propounded some startling and original ideas. He claimed that the national character of the French soldier predisposed him to the attack rather than stoic resistance, and that the battle should be based on a mobile system that responded to the commander's appreciation of the enemy's likely course of action. The means by which this was to be achieved was the combination of troops into all arms divisions, which had been pioneeered by Broglie in the Seven Years War. These divisions could then rapidly deploy independently of each other to counter any given threat, without waiting for the whole army to catch up. As expressed, his system stressed speed and the abandonment of traditional defensive lines and fortifications, where the divisions of the army would transport everything they needed with them rather than relying on *magazines and extensive supply trains.

Once the troops were in a field action, de Guibert advocated the use of the line to deliver effective firepower, but recognized that *columns had their uses in the attack. His regulations of 1788 proposed an offensive based on massed skirmishers, and swift assaults in column. The French *règlement*, or *drill book, of 1791 incorporated many of these new ideas and de Guibert's influence on the armies of the *French Revolutionary and *Napoleonic wars was profound.   TM

Guiscard, Robert (also known as Roberto d'Altavilla) (c.1015–85), the son of a poor Norman knight who carved out what later became the kingdom of Sicily for himself by

force of arms. In *c*.1047 he followed his half-brothers to southern Italy, where they had already won Apulia for themselves from a decaying Byzantine empire. They sent him to do the same in Calabria, and by 1053 his band of Norman adventurers was strong enough to defeat a Byzantine/ papal army. His older siblings having died, he returned to seize Apulia from his nephews in 1057. In 1059, no longer a mere robber baron, he entered into a concordat with the pope to expel the Arabs from Sicily, a job he entrusted to another brother, Roger, while he consolidated his hold over most of southern Italy by defeating the Byzantines and first marrying into and then (1076) fiercely crushing a rival Lombard family. By 1083, after a bewildering series of political combinations, he had built a fleet and invaded Epirus, defeating a Byzantine/Venetian army, and intended to march to Constantinople and crown himself emperor. Recalled to rescue the pope from the Holy Roman Emperor Henry IV in 1084 and also to suppress rebellions in his own lands, he returned to his Adriatic campaign and died while besieging Cephalonia. See also BOHEMOND.   HEB

Pontieri, E., *Tra i Normanni nell'Italia meridionale* (Milan, 1964).

Gulf of Tonkin incident (1964). On 2 August 1964, the US navy destroyer USS *Maddox* was attacked in the Gulf of Tonkin by North Vietnamese torpedo boats while providing *radar cover for an amphibious raid into the North by the South Vietnamese. The attack was driven off by the *Maddox* and aircraft from the carrier USS *Ticonderoga*. Two days later, the *Maddox*'s jittery crew mistook radar returns from choppy seas for another attack and the Johnson administration responded by bombing a number of targets in North Vietnam and sending a resolution to Congress that was to become the basis for all future US involvement in the *Vietnam war.   DJJ/HEB

Gulf war (1990–1), a limited war in which a US-led coalition enjoying overwhelming technological superiority defeated the armed forces of Iraq in a six-week air campaign crowned with a 100-hour land campaign, with minimal coalition casualties. However, the coalition forces failed to destroy the Republican Guard, mainstay of the Iraqi dictator Saddam *Hussein, who remained a threat primarily because of his continued development of *nuclear and *chemical and biological weapons, leading to repeated aftershocks in the form of US and Allied air strikes throughout the 1990s.

The proximate cause was the Rumaila oilfield straddling the Iraq–Kuwait border. In mid-July 1990 Saddam claimed that Kuwait had stolen oil from this field by diagonal drilling and refused to pay back loans received from Kuwait to fund the recent *Iran–Iraq war, saying that he had been doing the Gulf monarchies' dirty work for them. Neither argument was completely without merit. He massed

armour on the frontier and after being told by the US ambassador that the USA did not wish to become involved in the dispute, at 01.00 local time on 2 August the Iraqi columns invaded.

Minds were concentrated and Pres Bush denounced the invasion, alarmed that the Iraqis would carry on into Saudi Arabia and thus control half the world's oil reserves. The *UN condemned the invasion in Resolution 660, demanding immediate and unconditional withdrawal and on 7 August the USA announced it was sending forces in a joint operation with Egypt and Saudi Arabia: DESERT SHIELD. The following day the UK announced it would send forces too, in GRANBY.

On 29 November 1990 the Security Council adopted Resolution 678, authorizing the USA-led coalition to use 'all necessary means' against Iraq to liberate Kuwait if it did not withdraw by 15 January 1991. Instead, the Iraqis reinforced their positions along the southern Kuwaiti border and by 8 January had an estimated 36 to 38 divisions, each nominally 15,000 strong but actually considerably less. The coalition eventually had about 700,000 troops in the theatre, with the main ground contributions coming from the USA and important contingents from the UK, France, Egypt, Syria, and Saudi Arabia, under the operational command of US Gen *Schwarzkopf. The maintenance of the coalition, in which Arab states were arrayed with infidels against another Arab state, was pivotal. It was therefore imperative to ensure that Israel—a target for Iraqi missile attacks— should stay out of the war. The Iraqis were known to have the means to deliver their chemical and biological weapons (CBW) with their al-Hussein missiles, which had a range of 373 miles (600 km), double that of the original Soviet *Scud missiles on which they were based.

At 02.38 local time on 17 January DESERT STORM began when US Apache *helicopters began attacking Iraqi air defence sites near the border to clear a corridor through which a massive air armada then passed, beginning a 43-day air campaign involving 100,000 sorties. The F-117A Stealth light bomber was very successful in striking key targets in heavily defended Baghdad, as were sea-launched cruise missiles. Early targets were the Iraqi air defences, electrical power, and command and control facilities, also suspected nuclear and chemical and biological warfare facilities. Although *precision-guided munitions got all the publicity thanks to the excellent TV pictures they sent back, the bulk of the ordnance delivered were conventional bombs. As the campaign continued, the Allies switched to Iraqi ground forces although the élite Republican Guard was less badly damaged than the poorer quality infantry in the forward positions. Schwarzkopf later explained that this was because of his strong concern to avoid his ground troops being held up and rained with CBW.

Early on 18 January Iraq responded to the air onslaught by attacking Israel, the coalition's most vulnerable point. A missile landed in Tel Aviv, initially reported to have a

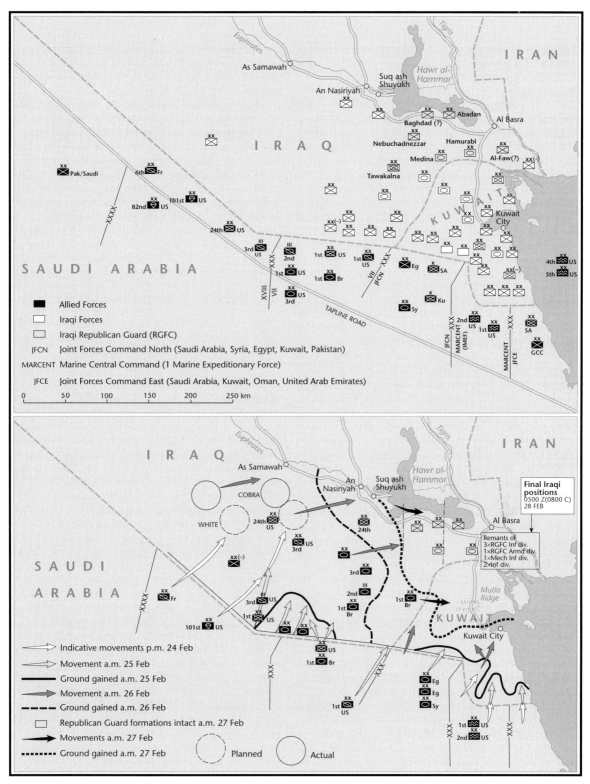

The **Gulf war,** 1991: the land campaign, 24–8 February. Top: positions of forces 24 February.
Bottom: Allied envelopment of Iraqi forces.

chemical warhead. The coalition later denied this but the relevant log, released after the war, recorded it carried cyclo-sarin, a particularly deadly nerve gas. Israel prepared to counter-attack, but was dissuaded when the USA promised to destroy the Scuds. As a result, a great deal of effort was diverted into the 'Scud hunt', although the mobile Iraqi missiles proved difficult to find. British and US *special forces were also sent in to find and destroy Scuds, with mixed results. The US also used the Patriot, originally an anti-aircraft system, to shoot down incoming missiles, the first time anti-missiles were used in the history of war. Very few incoming missiles were actually hit and those that were broke up, possibly doing even more damage than they would have otherwise. On 20 January, Iraq also began firing missiles at Riyadh, one of which hit a temporary US barracks and inflicted the worst Allied casualties of the war.

Schwarzkopf formulated a classic military plan of encirclement. While the Iraqis were to have their attention fixed to the south and on the coast by the US Marines, his main effort would be to the west of the main Iraqi forward defences, swinging round behind them and straight for the Republican Guard. The aim was 'to conduct a swift, continuous and violent air-land campaign to destroy the Republican Guard Force Corps while minimising friendly force casualties. Aim is to make Iraqi forces move so that they can be attacked throughout the depth of their formations'.

After several days of probing and artillery raids, the main ground attack began on 24 February with direct attacks into Kuwait from the south by the US Marines and two Saudi task forces. The next day, the outflanking forces swung into action, the main force being the US VII Corps including the 1st British Armoured Division, while the XVIII Airborne Corps including the French 6th Light 'Daguet' Division swung even wider to protect the left flank. The VII Corps hit its breach area with 60 batteries of artillery and Multiple Launch Rocket Systems, delivering more explosive power than the Hiroshima atomic bomb. Although Iraq was expected to use CBW, Saddam showed a little belated discretion and refrained, as there were a number of extremely unpleasant options the coalition held in reserve, including retaliation in kind or the destruction of Iraq's extremely vulnerable water-supply system. Late on 25 February he gave the order to withdraw from Kuwait, but the bulk of Iraqi armour was trapped between the Allies closing in from the south and west, and the Gulf and the Euphrates marshes to the east and north.

TV pictures of the comprehensively incinerated Iraqi column that had been attempting to flee Kuwait City raised fears of public revulsion and Pres Bush called a halt after only 100 hours of land campaign. There were also geopolitical considerations. Until the invasion, the West had been concerned to maintain a balance of power between Iraq and Iran in the region, and the Arab members of the coalition might have bolted if the land war had been extended into Iraqi territory. At 08.00 local time the guns fell silent, and Saddam was to be left with most of the Republican Guard and the freedom to use attack helicopters to crush the rebellions among the Sunni in the south and the Kurds in the north that the coalition had encouraged. Post-war, the extent and sophistication of his weapons development programmes came as a shock, and despite UN inspections and economic sanctions that affect mainly the civilian population, there is very little doubt that he has retained some CBW and possibly also some nuclear weapons. Nonetheless, Kuwait's territorial integrity was restored and most of Saddam's larger fangs were pulled. The war could only be considered unsuccessful if the hyperbole about human rights that accompanied it had ever been taken seriously by anyone involved. CDB

Bellamy, Christopher, *Expert Witness: A Defence Correspondent's Gulf War 1990–1991* (London, 1993).

Freedman, Lawrence, and Karsh, Efraim, *The Gulf Conflict, 1990–1991: Diplomacy and War in the New World Order* (London, 1993).

Gulf War Air Power Survey (2 vols., US Government Printing Office, Washington, 1993).

How the War was Won, Gen Schwarzkopf's final briefing on the conduct of the war, video (Castle, 1991).

gunpowder was the only *explosive until the mid-19th century and was used both as a propellant in firearms and as a bursting charge in *grenades and shells. The origins of gunpowder are unknown but evidence indicates that the Chinese first developed it, for pyrotechnic not propellant use, prior to AD 1000. Arabic sources suggest that it was in use in the Muslim world, for similar purposes, prior to its translation to the West in the 13th century. Both Roger Bacon (c.1214–92) and St Albertus Magnus (c.1200–80) are credited with recipes for gunpowder but these sources are compromised by doubts regarding their true authorship. However, the use of this explosive mixture of saltpetre, charcoal, and sulphur as a propellant for *bullets from firearms, and thus *gun*powder, is a western development and one which took place gradually from the 13th century. Early gunpowder was simply a powder and, because it burnt slowly, even in the confined space of a barrel's breech, early firearms were underpowered. By the end of the 15th century a process had been developed by which gunpowder was manufactured in grains of differing sizes; this powder was known as 'corned' gunpowder. It was more powerful than its predecessor powders since it ignited quicker thanks to air space between the grains and burnt quicker; it also produced less fouling for firearms barrels. Smaller-grained gunpowder, known as 'mealed' powder, was used in the priming pans of civilian sporting firearms, while larger grained powder was used in the main charge. Military muskets, being less refined and loaded from *cartridges containing only one type of powder, used the same 'corned' powder for both priming and charge but rifles, a more sophisticated weapon, maintained the difference. Recipes for gunpowder, relative to the proportions in the mixture of its three components, varied over the centuries of its use. Some nations, France for instance, varied the recipe dependent upon the type of firearm in which the powder was to be used. However, the proportion of saltpetre was consistently the highest of the three. British military gunpowder in the 18th century was 75 parts saltpetre to 10 parts sulphur to 15 parts charcoal. High quality, refined sulphur was preferred, as was charcoal made from willow or alder, although birch and beech were acceptable too. Gunpowder's chief limitations were its susceptibility to damp, which rendered it slow or impossible to ignite, and its volatility close to naked flame. On board ship the first problem tended to be countered by keeping powder in waxed canvas bags and often only mixing it immediately prior to use. The second problem was overcome by scrupulous care, in powder storehouses, over the use of candles and the wearing of clogs or felt slippers and, in the field, by the protection of the artillery train (in the 17th century when ordinary soldiers carried muskets fired by slow matches) by soldiers armed with *flintlock muskets. SCW

Partington, James R., *A History of Greek Fire and Gunpowder* (Cambridge, 1960).

Peterson, Harold L. (ed.), *Encyclopaedia of Firearms* (London, 1964).

Gurkhas A name derived from the village of Gurkha, originally settled by *Rajput immigrants from India, which is applied loosely to certain of the inhabitants of Nepal, including the Thakurs and Chettris, the Limbars and Rais of eastern Nepal, and in particular the Magar and Gurung tribes of western Nepal. In the course of the 18th century the Gurkhas took over the wealthy Katmandu valley and began a course of expansion which put them in control of all of Nepal by 1804. In 1814 they came into conflict with the English East India Company, were defeated, and surrendered some territory by the treaty of Segauli (March 1816). Three battalions of Gurkhas (the Malaun, Sirmoor, and Kumaon Rifles) had already been raised from prisoners of war by Lts Ross, Colquhoun, and Young, and by Maj Gen Sir David Ochterlony. Despite Nepal government discouragement until 1886, *recruitment was carried on via a recruiting station on the borders of Nepal at Gorakhpur.

Because of the rates of pay and other benefits, service was popular and Gurkha troops became a prominent element in the East India Company and, later, British Indian forces. They also served in the forces of the Lahore state and in Shah Shuja's Contingent in Afghanistan, where a battalion was destroyed at Charekar in 1841. Gurkhas were employed in the third *Maratha war, at the siege of Bharatpur in 1826, during the first *Sikh war, and during the *Indian Mutiny. During the latter, the 2nd (Sirmoor) Rifles (a unit mainly recruited in Garhwal) became famous for its successful defence of Hindu Rao's house at the siege of *Delhi, where the battalion lost 327 out of 490 men. Regular Gurkha forces from Nepal were also sent to suppress the mutiny. During the following years Gurkhas were extensively recruited and used, notably on the *North-West frontier but also in other areas.

By 1914 there were 26,000 Gurkha troops, mainly in the ten regular two-battalion *rifle regiments of the Gurkha Brigade (formed 1903). During the war 50,000 more men were recruited to the brigade and many more to other units; over 200,000 served between 1914 and 1918 in France, *Gallipoli, the Middle East, and in India. The Gurkhas made an even greater contribution during WW II when a total of 43 battalions were formed, winning nine VCs. The Gurkhas were riflemen and wore the characteristic green jackets with the Kilmarnock cap which was replaced for active service by the familiar slouch hat in 1901. Their best known arm was the long, curved-bladed *kukri*. They were commanded throughout the history of British India by British officers. In 1947 the Gurkha regiments were divided between India and Britain, six going to India and four to Britain. The British Gurkha regiments were rebased in Malaya, later in Hong Kong, and finally in Britain. They saw active service in the *Malayan emergency, the *Borneo campaign, and in the *Falklands. Superbly smart and with their own fine pipe band, they are a popular feature at *tattoos and on guard duty at Buckingham Palace, but the number of battalions was reduced from eight to two in 1995. MEY

Bolt, David, *Gurkhas* (London, 1967).

Farwell, Byron, *The Gurkhas* (London, 1984).

James, H. D., and Sheil-Small, D., *The Gurkhas* (London, 1965).

Gustavus Adolphus (correctly **Gustav Adolf**), **King of Sweden** (1594–1632). Gustavus Adolphus's death at the battle of *Lützen at the moment of victory was a fitting end for a man who devoted himself to war. As the ruler of a Protestant country he became involved in the *Thirty Years War in Germany, but he also fought against Denmark and Russia for control of the Baltic. He served his military apprenticeship in Poland, where he learnt valuable lessons about strategy and tactics, which he was later to employ in his German campaigns. Also, although not so often highlighted, as the ruler of a country with a seaborne tradition, Gustavus took a great interest in developing Sweden's navy to defend her shores and extend his authority over the Baltic Sea and its littoral.

Only 16 when he assumed the throne in 1611, Gustavus first had to defend his country against Danish invasion. He also became engaged in a war with Russia which lasted until 1617. In the 1620s he began a series of successful campaigns to win control of the southern Baltic shore. He captured Riga in 1621, after a siege of only eleven weeks. From 1626–9 he launched annual attacks upon Polish Prussia, winning his first victory in open field at Wallhof (1626). Despite a setback at Hammerstein the following year, when his German *mercenaries surrendered (18 May), Gustavus again defeated the Poles at Dirschau (8 August) although he was severely wounded in the neck. Helped by imperial Habsburg forces, the Poles were able to achieve a six-year *truce in 1629.

Gustavus learnt valuable lessons in his earlier wars which were to stand him in good stead for his invasion of Germany in 1630–2. First, he learnt not to rely entirely on mercenaries. Although the Swedish population was small, a system of conscription (*Utskrivning*), a tithe of the male population over 15 years old, organized by his chancellor, Oxenstierna (from 1617), yielded a field army theoretically up to 30,000 strong. In addition, mercenary troops largely recruited from Protestant Germans (but including a scattering of Scots and other exotic types) still played an important role, especially the 'Coloured Regiments' (Yellow, Blue, Red, and Green in order of seniority). The infantry were also reorganized tactically upon the model of *Maurice of Nassau. Company sizes were halved from 250 to about 140, with a 2 : 1 proportion of muskets to pikes (administratively eight companies to a regiment). In the field, they were deployed as small brigades of three or four squadrons (400–600 men) which anticipated later battalions. They were formed-up with one squadron thrown forward in a T-shape, which made the best use of their firepower, and allowed them to outmanoeuvre the larger *tercios of the Spanish manner still used by the Imperialists. Gustavus's experience against the Poles had taught him the value of a mobile cavalry at a time when *caracole tactics had reduced most western European horse to the role of mounted pistoleers. He taught them to charge with the sword, restoring their battlefield shock function. Finally, through the inspired developments of his master gunner *Tortensson, the artillery became lighter and more numerous. In addition, each regiment was given a pair of rapid-firing and mobile 4-pounders to boost its firepower.

In July 1630, Gustavus led only 13,000 men into Germany to rescue the Protestant cause, captured Stettin, and spent the rest of the year consolidating his position in Pomerania. The following spring, reinforced to 30,000 men, he swept south in a devastating campaign which included the destruction of enemy cavalry forces by night attack at Burgstall (27 July). In September he outmanoeuvred the imperial general *Tilly and forced a battle at *Breitenfeld. By now commanding over 40,000 men, including 10,000 Saxon allies, he matched Tilly's forces and outnumbered the enemy artillery by two to one (54 to 26 guns). Although the Saxons on the left wing were scattered by the charge of the imperial cavalry, the flexibility of the Swedish formations and their determination won the day. Galled by artillery fire, the imperial cavalry under *Pappenheim charged and was taken in the flank by Baner's quickly manoeuvred mixed squadrons of horse and *musketeers. Responding rapidly to the situation Gustavus advanced his foot and seized the enemy guns. When these were turned on the close-packed imperial foot, a massacre ensued. Tilly lost a third of his army. The following spring, after a brilliant and unexpected crossing of the river Lech, Gustavus defeated him again and Tilly was killed.

When Gustavus attempted to drive the imperial army, now commanded by the able *Wallenstein, from a fortified camp at Nuremberg, he suffered a bloody repulse (3 September). Wallenstein then outmanoeuvred the Swedes and forced Gustavus into a desperate encounter at Lützen (16 November), in which the Swedish king was killed leading a cavalry charge. Even without his leadership his army won another victory in 1633, but was defeated at Nordlingen (6 September 1634).

Gustavus's ambition and will to war had made Sweden, briefly, a major player on the European stage both on land and at sea, but at an unsustainable cost. The system of conscription, bringing over 10,000 men to the colours every year, saw numbers of men aged 15–60 fall by almost half in an already underpopulated nation. In a way the fate of his flagship the *Gustavus Vasa* symbolized the whole. Built by the top Dutch naval architect of the day, the ship sank on her maiden voyage in Stockholm harbour because her namesake had insisted on a weight of cannon that made her top-heavy.   MB

Brzezinski, Richard, *The Army of Gustavus Adolphus*, vol. i. *The Infantry*; vol. 2. *The Cavalry* (London, 1991).
Roberts, Michael, *The Military Revolution 1560–1660* (Belfast, 1956).

H

Hadrian's wall Running 80 Roman miles (73 modern miles, 118 km) across northern Britain from Solway Firth to the Tyne, Hadrian's wall is the most impressive defensive structure of an emperor who abandoned expansionism and aimed to consolidate the frontiers of the Roman empire. Hadrian(us) succeeded Trajan(us) as emperor in AD 117, having taken part in Trajan's conquests in the east, but immediately withdrew from the territories gained. He spent much of his reign travelling around the empire. After visiting Germany in 121 and erecting a timber palisade to mark the frontier line, he came to Britain in 122. There, he ordered the governor, Platorius Nepos, to construct the wall, partly in stone and partly in turf, just to the north of Trajan's frontier road. It was intended both as a defensive structure and to impress, but recent studies question its military effectiveness and suggest that its main function was to control trade and the movement of native populations. Soon after Hadrian's death in 138, the frontier was moved forward to the Antonine wall, running between the Clyde and the Firth of Forth. When this was abandoned about 155, Hadrian's wall was reoccupied together with outpost forts to the north and others in the Pennines to the south. After the campaigns of Septimius Severus in Scotland in the early 3rd century, the northern frontier remained quiet until the Pictish confederation increased pressure in the 4th century. The wall garrison was gradually weakened by withdrawals of troops to fight in Roman civil wars, but some military occupation continued into the early 5th century, when Britain ceased to be a Roman province. BR2

Birley, Anthony R., *Hadrian: The Restless Emperor* (London and New York, 1997).

Breeze, David J., and Dobson, Brian, *Hadrian's Wall* (London, 3rd edn., 1987).

Haig, FM Sir Douglas, 1st Earl Haig (1861–1928), British Field Marshal. Douglas Haig was C-in-C of the British Expeditionary Force on the western front from late 1915 until the end of WW I. He was the architect of the massive and costly offensives of the Somme (1916) and the third battle of Ypres (1917). Historians still argue whether he deserves censure for those offensives, or praise for the victory achieved in 1918.

Haig was born in Edinburgh on 19 June 1861, the son of John Haig, a Scotch whisky distiller from Fife. As a boy, he gave little indication of his eventual lofty achievements. It was at Sandhurst that he first revealed his considerable potential and fierce ambition. After leaving he joined the 7th (Queen's Own) Hussars. Stubbornly oblivious to the arm's impending obsolescence, he saw no other conceivable option than the cavalry.

Haig mirrored Victorian traditionalism: he was the product of an educational system that placed character before intellect and frowned upon science and technology. His faith in the cavalry meant that he viewed war according to immutable patterns of encounter, breakthrough, and charge. War was a moral contest in which superior character always prevailed. When he argued, rather controversially, that bullets would have little stopping power against a horse, he in fact meant that the superior moral force of the charging cavalryman would cause any foot soldier to lose his aim.

But Haig was also a progressive who shared the Edwardian obsession for efficiency. In Haig, the old and the new coexisted in weird harmony. Thus he assisted in the reform of the army from 1906–9, but blocked any change which might affect its elitist social structure or its traditional conception of war. The cavalry, thanks to his influence, enjoyed a nostalgic reintroduction of the lance, which had been scrapped in 1904. New weapons, be they machine guns or later tanks, were accepted enthusiastically by him, but forced into age-old tactical conceptions. In Haig's mind, form was always more important than content. If a battle did not succeed, its execution, not its objectives, were questioned.

Being of little imagination and even less flexibility, Haig could not have been expected to undergo a radical transformation during WW I, no matter how unique the challenges. He thought that the problems of the war seemed simple, it was merely a matter of applying 'old principles to present conditions'. When stalemate quickly ensued, he still sought a breakthrough so that the cavalry could be deployed.

When he was appointed C-in-C of the BEF in December 1915, he was certain of his worthiness for the assignment and confident that he alone knew the right way to victory. This self-assurance led to an extraordinary serenity, reinforced by his religious faith. 'I know quite well that I am being used as a tool in the hands of the Divine Power,' he wrote in 1916. 'So I am easy in my mind and ready to do my best whatever happens.' A man divinely directed did not seek the advice of mere mortals. Haig's subordinates were mostly sycophants carefully picked for their willingness to provide him reassurance and moral support. He kept close to his side a Church of Scotland padre, the Reverend George Duncan, who inadvertently reinforced his sense of divine inspiration. His intelligence officer, Brig Gen John Charteris, interpreted his function as being to gather data which would demonstrate that Haig's battles were a success. Haig consequently believed, from as early as the autumn of 1916, that the Germans were on the verge of collapse, and therefore susceptible to a knockout blow.

Haig has often been condemned for fighting a sterile war of attrition. His name will for ever be synonymous with the carnage and futility of the *Somme and third Ypres offensives. Yet he never accepted that this was a war of attrition. Nor should he be blamed for the fact that British soldiers spent four inconclusive years in the trenches of Flanders and northern France. Technology, not Haig, forced men into the trenches. His mistakes arose because he failed to realize that movement in this war was impossible. He tried to turn a siege contest into a mobile war.

Though he had very little effect upon the shape of the war, he nevertheless managed to impose his character upon it. The third Ypres offensive, in particular, was an expression of his personal ambitions: his wish to achieve a wholly British victory which he would not have to share with the despised French, his desire to embarrass PM David *Lloyd George who had earlier humiliated him, and his need to prove that the days of the cavalry had not passed. There is no doubt that men died needlessly because Haig pursued these ambitions. But this was not a war in which victory could ever have come cheaply.

Though Haig was the architect of victory, there were serious flaws in his design. He was undoubtedly the best commander available, but this reveals as much about the British army as it does about Haig. But issues of competence and culpability never bothered Haig. The serenity which he enjoyed on the western front was retained until his death in 1928. 'We lament too much over death,' he once wrote. 'We should regard it as a welcome change to another room.'

Haig answered his country's call and accomplished what he had been trained to do. In the Victorian age that would have made him a hero. But during his lifetime standards changed. When Britain became a people at war instead of simply an army at war, there was a corresponding shift in the definition of victory. It was no longer enough just to win. Costs and consequences became important. It was Haig's ironic fate that he was shaped by the ideals of one age and judged according to the very different standards of another.   GJDG

DeGroot, Gerard, *Douglas Haig, 1861–1928* (London, 1988).
Terraine, John, *Douglas Haig: Educated Soldier* (London, 1963).
Winter, Denis, *Haig's Command: A Reassessment* (London, 1991).

hair Mention of hair in its military context conjures up visions of the radical haircuts applied to generations of conscripts, to help treat head wounds, promote hygiene, aid identification of deserters, mark a man's transition from civilian to soldier, and underline the equality of recruits. 'I never saw so much hair in all my life,' wrote Vietnam veteran David Parks in *GI Diary*. 'It was all mixed up on the floor together, white hair, Spanish hair and soul hair, all going the same route.' The 1960s reaction against the short hair made common by WW II was in many ways a political as well as a counter-cultural phenomenon.

The military symbolism of hair is more complex. Usually, in common with uniform, it followed the dictates of fashion. Tenth-century warriors often wore their hair long in the Scandinavian style. The Normans shaved back and sides in a distinctive manner shown on the *Bayeux Tapestry*, but in the late 11th century longer hair, often worn with a beard, became fashionable once more. Knights going on a long campaign usually cut their hair short to help helmets fit snugly. A 'pudding-basin' cut, often seen on memorial brasses, shows hair thick but clear of the ears, probably to assist in cushioning the helmet.

The long but simply dressed hair of the early 17th century was succeeded by more elaborate fashions. Wigs, initially full-bottomed but neater as the 18th century wore on, were worn by officers, and soldiers had their hair pomaded, powdered, and drawn together at the back in a 'club' or queue. The queue generally disappeared in the early 19th century, though Napoleon's Old Guard retained it, a grenadier describing his 'six inch queue tied by a worsted ribbon with 2-inch ends and pinned with a silver *grenade'. It is commemorated in the British army by the Royal Welch (*sic*) Fusiliers, whose officers wear a ribbon on their collars to represent the ribbon binding the queue. As the queue declined, so side-whiskers (later called sideburns after the magnificent facial adornment of US Gen *Burnside) became popular. There were wide variations, from the braided lovelocks of French soldiers of the Revolutionary era to the bushy whiskers of Victorian officers.

Often, too, hair was part of an attempt to ape the successful or the warlike. Eighteenth- and early 19th-century *hussars tried to look like wild men from the great plain of Hungary, long plaits often weighted with pistol balls and long, waxed moustaches which were elaborately tied up at night. When young Marbot joined the French 1st Hussars in 1798 his mentor, Sgt Pertelay, had 'moustaches half a foot long waxed and turned up to his ears, on his temples two long locks of hair plaited, which came from under his shako and fell on his breast'. Marbot bought sham pigtails from the regimental barber, but as he was too young to grow a moustache, the helpful Pertelay used blacking to paint two huge hooks on his face.

The Turkish fashion of wearing a long tuft of hair atop an otherwise shaven head spread not only across many armies of the Muslim world, but also into Russian *Cossack irregular light cavalry. During the *Seven Years War they were sent to instil fear in the German population of East Prussia. 'They are an olive colour,' recorded an observer, 'and their faces full of wrinkles, with very little or no beard. They shave their heads, leaving only a tuft of hair on the crown.' The practice of wearing a scalp lock extended as far west as French hussars of the early 18th century.

*Grenadiers also cultivated facial hair. In Napoleon's Guard moustaches were a seasonal occurrence, shaved off on 1 December and not allowed back until 1 March: from 1806–7 they were worn all the time. Infantry units often included *pioneers (*sapeurs* in France) responsible for light construction or *demolition work, and they wore leather aprons (ostensibly to protect their *uniforms), carried axes, and often had full beards. Pioneer sergeants remain the only men in the British army normally allowed to sport beards. French *sapeurs* marched with the drummers as part of their regiment's *tête de colonne*, and very impressive they looked. A British soldier in the Peninsula wrote: 'Their hats, set round with feathers, their beards long and black, gave them a fierce look. Their stature was superior to ours: most of us were young. We looked like boys; they like savages.'

Although the moustache was not compulsory in the British army of the Edwardian era, shaving the upper lip was forbidden. An officer was successfully *court-martialled for shaving in 1916. When the sentence passed through the hands of Lt Gen Macready, adjutant-general of the British Expeditionary Force (BEF), on its way to the C-in-C for confirmation, Macready recognized the absurdity of the regulation and had it revoked. Facial hair retains symbolism even at the end of the 20th century: the gay community's affection for the moustache has dramatically reduced its popularity in the US army (see HOMOSEXUALITY AND THE ARMED FORCES). RH

halberds. See POLE ARMS/STAFF WEAPONS.

Haldane, Richard Burdon, Viscount of Cloan

(1856–1928), philosopher, lawyer, and army reformer who served as Secretary of State for War from 1905 to 1912. After the experience of the Second *Boer War, the British army required extensive reform but many of the measures introduced during or immediately after the war had proved costly, ineffective, incomplete, or politically contentious. Once in office, Haldane completed the institutionalization of a *general staff, appointed some key military advisers (Sir William Nicholson as CGS and *Haig as director of military training), and began his reforms.

He insisted that his advisers should formulate plans within the constraints of voluntary recruiting and a financial ceiling of £28 million, while sustaining the annual provision of drafts and reliefs for the overseas garrisons. He ensured thereby that the proposed creation of a British Expeditionary Force (BEF) of six large divisions and one cavalry division (160,000 men) would be accepted as a realistic and acceptable peacetime proposition. Using the requirements of a continental strategy (which were not made public), he organized the BEF into wartime formations, supported by drafts and ancillary services, and recognized that it would have to be ready for immediate despatch.

To provide the requisite support for the BEF, Haldane reorganized the auxiliary forces, the Militia and Volunteers, to form a second line (the special reserve), a broad base of expansion in the Territorial Force, and a potential supply of officers from school and university cadet corps, together forming the *reserve forces. Although he skilfully secured cabinet and parliamentary support for these measures, he found it more difficult to arouse popular enthusiasm for them. Despite immense recruiting efforts, propaganda campaigns, and speaking tours, the Territorials remained about a quarter short of their establishment (312,000 men), and, by September 1913, only 1,090 officers and 17,788 *NCOs and men had volunteered to serve abroad on mobilization. One outstanding exception was the *VAD, the first ever military organization for *women in peacetime, which built up a core of volunteers that handled a huge WW I expansion admirably.

Haldane became Lord Chancellor in 1912 and was optimistic that he had laid the foundations for mass mobilization. While he had concentrated on promoting the Territorial Force, he left his military advisers to reform matters of *doctrine and tactics, to oversee the training and regular manoeuvres of the home army, and, under Director of Military Operations Sir Henry *Wilson, to ensure that the BEF could mobilize quickly, cross the Channel, and deploy in northern France. When the BEF entered WW I in August 1914, it was widely regarded as the best-organized and trained expeditionary force to leave British shores. However, Lord *Kitchener, as the incoming Secretary of

State for War, preferred to raise his own army rather than rely on the Territorial Force. Haldane no longer had any influence over military matters: indeed, he would lose cabinet office in May 1915 because of allegedly pro-German sympathies. EMS

Beckett, Ian, and Gooch, John (eds.), *Politicians and Defence* (Manchester, 1981).

Spiers, Edward, *Haldane: An Army Reformer* (Edinburgh, 1980).

half pay It has never been easy for armed forces to cope with the conflicting demands of wartime expansion and peacetime shrinkage. Several 18th- and 19th-century armies and *navies placed unemployed officers on half pay (see also FENCIBLES) as a way of reducing the cost of the active establishment while retaining a nucleus of trained officers. The system played its part in the rise of standing armies, enabling a sense of careerism to develop as officers retained rank and status in peace as well as war.

Yet it had disadvantages. Penurious half-pay officers often became involved in discreditable activities, although few went as far as Lt J. Pieri RN who took to piracy and was hanged for it in 1817. In post-Waterloo France the 16,000 half-pay officers (*demi-soldes*) were a potential source of opposition to the new regime. They lived on meagre incomes, waiting for a recall that might never come, reminiscing vinously about the glories of the past, and helping pave the way for a Napoleonic revival.

Half pay almost disappeared as career structures and reserve systems developed in the late 19th century. It lives on in Britain, where field marshals, a disappearing breed, never formally retire. When they cease active service they are given what is in effect a pension, but is still known as half pay. RH

Halleck, Maj Gen Henry Wager (1815–72). Halleck, known with unconscious irony as 'Old Brains', was briefly commander of the Union armies during the *American civil war. He was educated at *West Point, where he excelled, graduating in 1839. He served as an ADC and engineer officer in California during the *Mexican war, but was better known at that time for his 1846 treatise *Elements of Military Art and Science* (see ART, THE MILITARY). When the civil war broke out Halleck was appointed a major general and given command of the Union forces in Missouri. Suspicious of *Grant, he tried to keep him from command and took over from him after *Shiloh, initiating a creeping advance against *Beauregard's army at Corinth, who could not stop him but had no difficulty in disengaging. In July 1862 Halleck was appointed general in chief of the US armies and chose to see it as a Washington desk job in which his organizational powers were effectively utilized. He was superseded by Grant in 1864, who took to the field and retained him as COS of the army, when in fact it was a division of the overall command functions into the spheres in which each was most comfortable. As the one entrusted with the often trickier political and logistical dimensions, Halleck deserves to be considered alongside Grant as the artisan of victory. AH

Hamilcar (*c.*270–228 BC). Known as Hamilcar Barca ('Lightning'), he commanded Carthaginian forces in Sicily during the first *Punic war. He was undefeated, though compelled to negotiate peace in 241 by the naval defeat off the *Aegates Islands. Returning to Africa, he crushed a *mutiny among the mercenaries and was then sent to Spain, where after conquering much of the south-east, he was drowned retreating from Helice in 229. He was succeeded in command of Carthaginian forces in Spain first by his son-in-law Hasdrubal and then, in 221, by his son *Hannibal.

His name was given to a WW II British *glider, appropriately first used during the invasion of *Sicily. JFL

Hamilton, Gen Sir Ian Standish Monteith (1853–1947). From a privileged military background, commissioned in 1872 and with experience of the Afghan, Egypt, *Burma, and Second *Boer wars, a COS to both *Roberts and *Kitchener, Hamilton was regarded by the Germans as the most experienced soldier in the world. Inspector general of Overseas Forces in 1910–14, he commanded the *Gallipoli operation indecisively until he was replaced in October 1915. Hamilton was an intellectual and a writer who, in old age, became something of an anti-war Liberal. He was the visionary force behind the creation of the British Legion (1921) and as a Germanophile advocated greater rapprochement with Germany, even in the Third Reich era, meeting *Hitler in 1938. *Liddell Hart believed that it was this Hamilton whom Rudolf Hess flew to see in 1941, and not the duke of the same name. (See also OPERATIONAL CONCEPTS and GENERAL STAFF). APC-A

Lee, John, *A Life of Ian Hamilton* (London, 1999).

Hamley, Gen Sir Edward Bruce (1824–93), soldier and scholar. Commissioned into the Royal Artillery in 1843, he saw action in the *Crimean war before becoming the first professor of military history at the British army Staff College, Camberley, 1859–65. The fruit of his six years lecturing there was *The Operations of War* (1866), which became a textbook in Britain and the USA. It was much influenced by *Jomini, with a tendency to be prescriptive rather than descriptive. However, at least one of its readers was saved from disaster by recalling a line from it. In 1914 FM *French was considering taking the British Expeditionary Force (BEF) to shelter under the guns of Maubeuge, and remembered being warned that a soldier who did such a thing was like a sailor who clutched hold of the anchor during a storm.

Hamley returned to Sandhurst as commandant, 1870–7, when he raised the profile of the college nationally, although he was very much a man of his times. It was said that he 'would as sooner find a student reading Jorrocks as *The Operations of War*, and would alter the programme of study to suit the convenience of those who would go a-hunting'. He held a field command in the *Egyptian campaign of 1882 when he was not generally deemed a success.   APC-A

Bond, Brian, *The Victorian Army and the Staff College, 1854-1914* (London, 1972).

Hankey, Maurice Pascal Alers, 1st Baron (1877–

1963), British civil servant. In 1908, while still an officer in the Royal Marines, Hankey was appointed assistant secretary to the *Committee of Imperial Defence (CID), a body established in 1902 to co-ordinate British strategy and defence planning. From this unpromising appointment he rose almost without let to a position of unparalleled influence in the inner councils of government. He was secretary to the CID, 1912–38; to the War Cabinet, 1916–19; and to the cabinet itself, 1919–38. Hankey had a genius for making himself indispensable. Successive political leaders came to appreciate his formidable memory and his discretion, but his influence was not only personal. He was also a man of systems and the architect of modern cabinet government, introducing agenda, proper record-keeping, and minutes. His views on defence matters were also often sought, less often acted upon, but always lucid, well informed, and sometimes far-sighted. During WW I, in particular, his co-ordinating role gave authority and substance to cabinet decisions. Without Hankey, declared Balfour, 'we should have lost the war'.   JMB

Roskill, Stephen W., *Hankey: Man of Secrets*, 2 vols. (London, 1970).

Hannibal (247–183/2 BC) was the son of *Hamilcar and

inherited command of Carthaginian forces in Spain. Whether or not he also inherited a vendetta with Rome is disputed, but certainly, when faced with an ultimatum not to attack Rome's ally Saguntum (Sagunto) at the end of 220, he did not hesitate, claiming that the Saguntans had been guilty of aggression against allies of Carthage. After taking the town in 219, he began to prepare for war with Rome. Probably in the late spring of 218 he marched an army from Spain to Italy, crossing the Alps to bypass Roman preparations, and went on to devastating victories at *Trebbia, *Lake Trasimene, and *Cannae.

After all three he released his non-Roman prisoners, proclaiming that he had not come to fight them, but Rome on their behalf. After Cannae, this propaganda began to bear fruit. Most of southern Italy came over to him, including Capua in 216 and Tarentum (Taranto) in 212. Meanwhile, in 215, he concluded an alliance with Philip V of Macedonia,

and in 214 Syracuse also joined him. But he could never break Rome's hold on the centre and north of the peninsula, and gradually her overwhelming manpower took effect. *Syracuse fell in 212 and Capua in 211, despite Hannibal's march on Rome itself to divert the besiegers. However, he remained supremely dangerous in the field, and attrition worked both ways. As late as 209, 12 of the 30 Latin colonies at the heart of Rome's alliance refused any longer to supply men for the *Roman army. The crisis came in 207 when his brother Hasdrubal reached Italy overland with a new army. But Hasdrubal was defeated and killed at the Metaurus before he could join Hannibal, and thereafter the latter was increasingly confined to the toe of Italy. In the end, when *Scipio 'Africanus' invaded Africa in 204 and defeated Carthage's principal ally Syphax in 203, Hannibal was recalled, and at *Zama not all his skill could save a now greatly inferior army from defeat.

It was now that he showed that he was not just a great soldier. Insisting that Carthage make peace, he busied himself with domestic affairs, and as chief magistrate for 196 was responsible for a number of reforms. But his enemies played upon Roman fears against him, and in 196 he fled to Antiochus III of Syria, whom he accompanied to Greece in 192 in the hope that he would give him an army to invade Italy. Instead he found himself commanding a fleet in his last battle and was defeated. Antiochus' peace with Rome forced him to flee again, this time to Bithynia, and it was there that he finally committed suicide, in 183 or 182, rather than be surrendered to Rome.

Hannibal was undoubtedly one of the world's greatest generals. He probably inherited from his father his professionalism and ability to keep superior forces at bay; possibly he also inherited the plan for attacking Italy, for his father had once raided Bruttium. His strategy has been criticized for failing to comprehend the nature of the Roman alliance and to ensure that adequate reinforcements came either by sea from Africa or by land from Spain. But Hannibal himself could not be everywhere, and there is no doubt that this was the only way that Carthage could ever have defeated Rome. The audacity of the march to Italy remains breathtaking, and one should not underestimate how near it came to success. At one point the three largest cities in Italy and Sicily, after Rome, were on Carthage's side, and possibly some 40 per cent of Rome's allies. His genius as a battlefield commander has seldom been questioned. It rested on a mixture of bluff and double bluff, and ability to use all types of troops to their best advantage. Cannae remains an ideal to which generations of subsequent generals have aspired.   JFL

Lazenby, J. F., *Hannibal's War* (Warminster, 1978).

Hašek, Jaroslav (1883–1923), Czechoslovak satirical

writer, author of *The Good Soldier Schweik* (*Dobrý voják Švejk*). Hašek started writing at 17, and the first Schweik story, based on a stoical but none-too-bright soldier in the Austro-Hungarian army, was published in 1912. Hašek was drafted into the army which he had satirized as a civilian, but was captured by the Russians. He joined the group of Czech prisoners which became the Czechoslovak Legion (see NORTH RUSSIA INTERVENTION FORCE), but later joined the Bolsheviks. He wrote four of six planned books for the Good Soldier Schweik series. Vladimir Voynovich, a Russian writer, later used the same situation comedy in his account of the exploits of Pte Ivan Chonkin—the Soviet Schweik.

CDB

Hašek, Jaroslav, *The Good Soldier Schweik* (London, 1930).

Hastings, battle of (1066). Fought on 14 October 1066, between the forces of *William 'the Conqueror', Duke of Normandy and King Harold (Godwinson) II of England, Hastings was one of the most decisive battles in the history of western Europe. William had a claim to the English throne and Harold expected him to invade, but William fortuitously landed on the Sussex coast when Harold was preoccupied with an invasion in the north. On hearing of William's arrival, Harold immediately began a forced march south from York, refusing to wait in London for re-inforcements, and arriving in the vicinity of Hastings on the night of 13 October. Less than three weeks earlier, at Stamford Bridge, he had defeated the army of Norwegian King Haraldr Harðráða, which he had caught completely by surprise. Now he hoped to repeat this successful strategy against William, but the latter was forewarned by his scouts and attacked Harold's force before a third of it was drawn up, forcing him into a strong but confined defensive position on Senlac ridge. Harold, moreover, had lost some of his best men in the earlier battles of Fulford Gate and Stamford Bridge on 20 and 25 September.

The Norman *archers, supported by heavy infantry, began the battle, but made little headway against the close infantry formations of the Anglo-Saxons, so densely arrayed, noted Duke William's biographer William of Poitiers, that the dead could not even fall. Assaults by the Norman cavalry initially fared little better, and the well-equipped *housecarls did terrible execution with their great two-handed axes. William's left, comprised of Bretons, broke in panic amidst rumours that the duke was slain, and William narrowly avoided catastrophe by rallying his fleeing men and removing his helmet to show he was still alive. Launching a counter-attack, the Normans cut down those Saxons who had broken ranks in pursuit, and, exploiting the efficacy of this manoeuvre, they executed several 'feigned flights' with considerable success. Renewed assaults by Norman archers and knights gradually thinned the remaining English formation, which lacked sufficient archers to neutralize the Norman missilemen. Harold's death effectively ended the battle; wounded first in the eye by an arrow, he was then cut down by Norman knights.

Hastings was by no means the inevitable triumph of *feudal heavy cavalry over 'outmoded' Germanic infantry; the battle raged from dawn to dusk, the Normans came close to complete disaster, and it was chance alone that Harold, not William, was slain. Contemporaries regarded the battle as so closely fought that only divine intervention could explain William's eventual victory. MJS

Bradbury, Jim, *The Battle of Hastings* (Stroud, 1997).
Brown, Reginald Allen, 'The Battle of Hastings', *Proceedings of the Battle Conference on Anglo-Norman Studies* 3, repr. in Matthew Strickland (ed.), *Anglo-Norman Warfare* (Woodbridge, 1992), and in Stephen Morillo, *The Battle of Hastings* (Woodbridge, 1995), a collection of articles on the battle.

Hattin, battle of (1187). On 2 July 1187 *Saladin attacked Tiberias with an army 30,000 strong including 12,000 cavalry. King Guy of Jerusalem gathered the entire army of the kingdom, 15,000–18,000 including 1,200 knights and many other cavalry, at Saffuriya. On 2 July the leaders, bitterly divided by personal and political feuds, debated whether to attack Saladin or to suffer the loss of Tiberias and wait for Saladin's army to fall apart. Guy decided to challenge Saladin, although his precise intentions are not known.

On 3 July the army marched east in three great divisions with the infantry protecting the cavalry for a fighting march. It was vital to reach water. All through 3 July Saladin harassed the crusaders, especially the rearguard under Balian of Ibelin. This forced the crusaders to camp with little water at Maskana. On 4 July the army deployed for battle close to the Horns of Hattin. Our sources are confused so it is impossible to reconstruct events but ultimately the demoralized infantry fled to the Horns of Hattin and the cavalry, despite valiant charges, simply could not break out of the trap in which they were held. The army of the kingdom was annihilated and King Guy captured, enabling Saladin to conquer the kingdom. JF2

Kedar, B. Z., 'The Battle of Hattin Revisited', in Kedar (ed.), in *The Horns of Hattin* (London, 1992).
Prawer, J., *Crusader Institutions* (Oxford, 1980).

Havelock, Maj Gen Sir Henry (1795–1857), British commander during the *Indian Mutiny. Havelock was considered to be the epitome of mid-Victorian 'muscular Christianity'. Just over 5 feet tall and white-haired, he appeared an avuncular figure but was aloof and arrogant. He was also able, ambitious, and brave, cutting his teeth in a series of Indian campaigns during which he had seven horses killed under him. He raised the siege of *Cawnpore early in July 1857, reaching Lucknow in late September. Here he was in turn besieged and, shortly after receiving news of his knighthood, died of dysentery. APC-A

Hibbert, Christopher, *The Great Mutiny* (London, 1978).

Hawkwood, Sir John (d. 1394), English soldier and proto-*condottiere. From 1359 Hawkwood led a *mercenary company in Europe, particularly Italy. He fought for a bewildering number of masters in the wars between Italy's city states, the papacy, and various foreign interlopers. In 1377 he entered the service of Florence and remained loyal until he retired, wealthy and admired, particularly for the neat way he sold out his own followers at the end. Before that he had paid them regularly and was therefore not troubled by the usual mutinies, earning a trust that enabled him to cash out at the opportune moment. A lost statue of him is the subject of a famous fresco by Paolo Uccello.

MCM

headdress, military The protection and embellishment of the warrior's head has preoccupied warriors themselves, as well as their armourers and hatters, since the earliest history of organized warfare. Since damage to the warrior's head incapacitated him far more quickly than did damage to any other part of his body, protection of that most vulnerable target loomed large as a priority in warrior societies. Once a level of practical protection was achieved, at least in terms of the available technology of the day, embellishment, in order to make the warrior look and feel larger, fiercer, and more intimidating to his opponent, followed quickly. Embellishment of certain types had a practical purpose too: in the heat, dust, and, eventually, *smoke of battle the ability to recognize leaders among one's friends or foes could be critical. All these factors, protection, decoration, and battlefield role, have guided the history of military headdress.

The earliest forms of military headdress date from pre-classical times and were caps or helmets of leather, stiffened cloth, and metal. From fragments surviving and from illustrations, often in the form of bas-relief sculpture, it is known that *Assyrian soldiers wore metal helmets and that those of ancient Egypt wore leather ones, stiffened with metal. Metal helmets were worn by *hoplites, the foot soldiers of ancient Greece, and elsewhere in eastern Mediterranean civilizations. In all forms of illustration, from bas-relief to classical statuary, the helmet symbolized the warrior and individuals wishing to be so remembered would deliberately be portrayed in helmets. The Roman soldier wore a variety of styles of helmet, styles dependent not only upon his battlefield role but also upon his place in the military hierarchy.

Roman helmets evolved into *Viking and Anglo-Saxon ones, which in turn became the conical types with nasal guards depicted on the heads of William's knights in the *Bayeux Tapestry* and, in the Middle Ages, the differing grades and types of western warrior were differentiated by their headdress: the knight with his all-enveloping great helm from the common foot soldier with his kettle-hat. The anonymity guaranteed by the helm, worn on the battlefield and for the *tournament, led to the adoption by knights of crests atop their helms—personal devices unique to them and one of the earliest of heraldic symbols. These led to the *badges and insignia on the headdress and hence to the modern cap badge.

Until the 17th century, the metal helmet—in its varying forms—was the principal headdress of the western warrior. In other cultures, particularly those innocent of metal or with less sophisticated means of dealing death, warriors' headdress remained less protective and more symbolic and this remained until the aborigines of the Americas, the Pacific, and the East made contact with the technology of the West from the 18th century.

In 17th-century Europe the increased power and effectiveness of the portable firearm began to make itself felt, with a concomitant gradual decline in the wearing of *armour. While helmets continued to be worn, particularly by those soldiers likely to feel the edge of a sword such as cavalrymen and *pikemen, the growing numbers of *musketeers eventually eschewed their Spanish-style morions and, by c.1630, were affecting broad-brimmed hats. These were often—in the case of officers or the more flamboyant among the German *landsknechts—adorned with flowing plumes. Some sagacious musketeers wore metal skullcaps, called 'secrets', beneath their hats. By the end of the 17th century the metal helmet had all but disappeared from the battlefield but, following the Classical tradition, soldiers wishing to be recognized as such would continue to have anachronistic close-helmets depicted by their sides in portraits. By 1700 the infantryman's headdress had become the wide-brimmed, low-crowned felt hat which, when 'cocked'—by having its brim caught up to its crown in three places—would become the tricorne cocked hat of the 18th-century foot soldier. Such hats lent themselves to the carrying of 'field signs': these were identifying symbols, often adopted close to the time of battle and often slips of coloured paper, or twigs, or feathers which enabled foe to be separated from friend and treated accordingly. Like heraldic crests, such field signs were the predecessors of cap badges and the formation signs of the 20th century.

As specialist troops emerged late in the 17th century—soldiers such as *grenadiers, *fusiliers, and *dragoons, all of whose battlefield roles required them to be able to sling their fusils or carbines over their heads—so headdress suited to their roles emerged, in the form of brimless caps. These, originally little more than low woollen, cloth, or leather caps, rapidly became taller and increasingly embellished as the 18th century advanced. Exotic forms of light cavalry were introduced into European armies in the 18th century too and these brought with them their native headdress, caps which would develop into the *hussar *mirliton* and then the fur cap—called a busby in Britain after its manufacturer—and the *lancer *czapska*. Britain had its own exotic natives too, Scots *Highlanders, who first appeared regimented in the British army in 1739 as the 43rd

Regiment, now famous as the Black Watch; these soldiers wore soft blue woollen bonnets which developed gradually into the tall feathered bonnets, with their diced woollen bands, now so inextricably associated with the Scots soldier.

By the second half of the 18th century a degree of uniformity of military headdress was visible in European armies. Cavalrymen generally wore tricorne hats, except for dragoons and light cavalry units which wore helmets or caps of native origin. In the infantry the tricorne was also generally worn except by grenadiers, who wore the tall 'mitre' cap; light infantry, who wore low leather peaked 'jockey' caps; and units such as Highlanders or *Jägers, who often wore a version of their native civilian headdress suited to their skirmishing role. On campaign, especially in the heat of India or the wilderness of North America, headdress and, indeed, uniform overall gave way to the exigencies of climate and the logistics of supply, and soldiers in practice wore whatever they could which would keep their heads protected. The 18th century saw a burgeoning of badges and insignia for headdress and the frontal plates or sections of the grenadiers, fusiliers, and light infantrymen's caps lent themselves favourably to the display of national, local, and personal heraldry and other significant symbols. Not until the old tricorne was replaced by the cavalryman's helmet and the foot soldier's shako late in the 18th century would badges be worn on their hats by the soldiers of the line.

Military headdress in the West in the 19th century was generally led by the examples of European nations. For much of the century the European and American line infantryman wore differing sizes, shapes, and designs of shako, or chaco, an originally peakless, cylindrical, felt hat introduced in Austria in 1769. Grenadiers and fusiliers continued, in general, to cling to their tall bearskin headdress and a variety of types of 'undress' cap was introduced for the soldier to wear when not in his full dress uniform. The infantrymen of some European nations wore helmets during the century but the helmet, especially in metal rather than in leather, remained principally the headdress of the cavalry. Bicorne hats, worn 'fore-and-aft' or across the head, continued throughout the century as the full dress headdress for some officers but, after c.1850, were principally worn by staff officers. Led by Prussia and Russia in the 1840s, styles of spiked leather helmets began to appear and gradually became popular further afield, even across the Atlantic. The British infantry adopted the spiked, cloth-covered cork helmet in 1878 and covered it in *khaki drill cloth for wear in hot climates—creating the first of the solar topis.

Undress caps became worn more and more frequently on active service. At first, they tended to be peakless soft round caps or folding blue bonnets, like the Scots glengarry, and by the end of the century most armies had softer and more comfortable caps to wear. These caps ultimately became the dress cap of the 20th century, once the realities of warfare

had reintroduced the steel helmet in 1915 and had disposed of the full dress headdress which had gradually developed during the previous three centuries. In the 1990s full headdress is still worn on appropriate occasions by units of the world's armies, principally by troops with a bodyguard role on state occasions, by musicians, and by the more tradition-conscious military *academies. The military headdress, when designed correctly in accordance with its inheritance, and when worn with a panache that would not disgrace a plumed landsknecht of the 16th century, still serves to set the serviceman aside from the more mundanely uniformed of his civilian or paramilitary colleagues—which is and was, after all, the original idea.   SCW

Edge, David, and Paddock, John M., *Arms and Armour of the Medieval Knight* (London, 1988).
Mollo, John, *Military Fashion* (London, 1972).

headquarters (HQ) The command element of any military unit or organization, originally named after the quarters which housed it. It has numerous functions, the most important the practical command of units and formations, a task facilitated by the rise of the *general staff from the 19th century, as part of a process in which headquarters, once consisting of the commander and a small number of aides and mounted messengers, became larger.

For much of history a headquarters was also a royal capital on the move, housing the monarch himself, often with a shoal of officials and flunkies to ensure his efficiency and comfort. The Prussian general staff was so finely honed by the time of the *Franco-Prussian war that its chief, *Moltke 'the Elder', was assisted by just three heads of sections, eleven officers, ten draughtsmen, seven clerks, and 57 other ranks. But this hard-working kernel was embedded in an unwieldy royal headquarters which included civil and military cabinets, *Bismarck himself, and foreign office officials together with the war minister and his own staff. And then came a crowd of foreign military observers and an assortment of princelings (*Schlachtenbummler*) who, as Michael *Howard puts it, 'in days when war was being turned into a science as dreary and exact as economics, still insisted on regarding a campaign as . . . a royal and seasonal sporting event'. Even when royal spectators had become a thing of the past, higher headquarters still attracted functionaries who often swamped the headquarters' war-fighting element. Although the WW II Supreme Headquarters Allied Expeditionary Force (SHAEF) had been conceived of as a small strategic headquarters which would make high-level decisions, it grew to such enormous proportions (including staff responsible, amongst other things, for the Allied military government of occupied territory) that it could not get a forward HQ to Normandy till August 1944, and even then it moved, inexplicably, to Granville on the western coast. It later moved into Versailles, where it took over the Trianon Palace Hotel and another 20,000 officers and men flooded into the town, leading disgruntled Frenchmen to call SHAEF the Société des Hôteliers Américains en France.

It is no easy task to preserve a balance between a head-quarters' war-fighting functions and the numerous administrative tasks which have fallen upon it in an age of mass armies and, most recently, coalition operations in the eye of the media. The Coalition command structure in the *Gulf war is a good example of the complexities of a modern headquarters. In 1983, the USA set up US Central Command (CENTCOM), a peacetime headquarters with responsibility for operations in the Persian Gulf area. When the crisis began in 1990, CENTCOM formed the headquarters for the Coalition forces. It had two chains of command, administrative and operational, both under the command of Gen Norman *Schwarzkopf, and had responsibility for all four US services as well as the forces contributed by seventeen other nations. This command of such a complex army required tremendous effort from the staff at CENTCOM. For instance, in order to co-ordinate the 1,820 combat aircraft from eleven different nations striking Iraqi targets, the air command component of CENTCOM issued an 'air-tasking order', which grew to 700 pages daily at the height of the bombing campaign.

Traditionally headquarters have often split into forward—or 'tactical'—and main. The reasons for this separation often concerned communications and reflected a commander's desire to command well forward where he could feel the pulse of operations. Some generals overdid this. In the *American civil war one always reported to *Lincoln 'from my headquarters in the saddle', leading the acerbic president to remark that he evidently had his headquarters where his hindquarters ought to be. In *North-West Europe in 1944–5 *Montgomery commanded from a tiny tactical HQ, supported by good communications and trusted young liaison officers (who acted as his 'directed telescopes' to report on what was really happening at the front), leaving his COS to run main headquarters. One of his staff rightly commented on 'the very real isolation from Main', and another observed that it was hard for his COS to keep in touch with 'what Master was thinking'. However, this sort of split will probably help the commanders of the future to retain their grip on the conduct of operations while retaining access to staff support for administrative, political, and media functions, all of which will form part of the legitimate concern of a modern HQ.   RTF/RH

Howard, Michael, *The Franco-Prussian War* (London, 1968).

Helder expedition (1799). This was the British army contribution to the Second Coalition in the *French Revolutionary wars. Plans for a decisive Austro-Russian campaign in Switzerland and Italy had been orchestrated by the British foreign secretary, Lord Grenville, who expected to overthrow the revolutionary government. He chose northern Holland as the British theatre for political reasons. Brit-ain had entered the war in 1793 to restore Dutch independence, but more immediately Grenville hoped that a British landing would encourage Prussia to join the coalition. Paradoxically however, the success of the British expedition depended on Prussian support, for the British army never operated effectively against France in western Europe except in direct conjunction with the army of a major continental power.

When Prussia drew back on the eve of the British landing, Grenville found a new political justification for proceeding. The Austrian army under Archduke *Charles withdrew from the decisive front in Switzerland and was moving northwards to retake Belgium, the former Austrian Netherlands. Grenville reasoned that a rapid British advance from Holland to occupy Belgium would lever the archduke back to the Swiss front.

The Helder expedition thus became a classic example of political desires prevailing over military advice. The military objections were strong. Apart from the inherent problems of a seaborne operation—the risks in an assault landing, the shipping restrictions on the size of the force as well as its horses and land transport, and the uncertainties of supply from the sea—the available force was of dubious quality, with many of the British regiments filled at the last moment with volunteers from the militia, and an unknown Russian contingent expected from the Baltic. But the warnings of the commander of the initial wave, Sir Ralph Abercromby, were brushed aside. Grenville asserted that the Franco-Dutch force was small and dissaffected, and would be swept aside by a Dutch insurrection: the British force could march unopposed through the country and occupy Belgium. PM William Pitt 'the Younger' boasted that all military difficulties were overruled.

Abercromby's landing on 27 August succeeded despite confused naval arrangements. The port of den Helder was captured, leading to the surrender of the Dutch fleet. On 10 September Abercromby repulsed a counterstroke by Gen Brune on the Zijpe dyke and with reinforcements raising the force to 34,000, the Duke of *York assumed command and took the offensive. Brune conducted a fighting withdrawal down the north Holland defile, with his reinforcements approaching. York fought three indecisive battles at Bergen (19 September), Egmond-an-Zee (2 October), and Castricum (6 October). The Russians' performance was disappointing; and after gaining 20 miles (32 km), autumn rain and storms at sea disrupted supplies. With winter approaching and sickness increasing, and with the Russian defeat in Switzerland releasing reinforcements for Brune, York withdrew to the Zipje position, where he signed the Convention of Alkmaar with Brune allowing him to re-embark.   PGM

Bunbury, Sir Henry, *The Great War with France* (1799–1810) (London, 1927).

Mackesy, Piers, *Statesmen at War: The Strategy of Overthrow, 1798-1799* (London, 1974).

helicopters The helicopter has emerged as an important addition to *air power and the conduct of military operations since the end of WW II, and has become crucial to modern-day armed forces. It offers tremendous flexibility and mobility to troops and has been particularly useful in *low-intensity operations and in providing support to units operating in dense terrain or terrain accessible only with great difficulty. The helicopter's ability to operate from hastily prepared clearings or in rugged country which would otherwise preclude the use of direct air support has been its greatest asset, although the helicopter has been deployed in a wide variety of roles for which its particular attributes make it well suited.

Although the helicopter has only come to prominence since the early 1950s, its gestation dates back to the time of the earliest fixed-wing powered flights. However, slow development has largely been due to the many and varied problems inherent in the helicopter's basic design. Compared to a fixed-wing aircraft, the helicopter is a much more complex piece of equipment in two basic ways. First, a sophisticated and precise transmission system is necessary, while secondly, the rotor blades have to be capable of operating effectively and safely over a wide range of speeds, as the central parts of the rotor move at relatively slow speeds while those nearer the tips move at near sonic speeds. Flawed rotor-blade design could result in aerodynamic vibrations as they travelled through the air, resulting in aerial buffeting, while an inadequate transmission would cause mechanical vibrations. These problems of design and engineering proved insurmountable for many decades, despite the fact that many of the mechanical hurdles were quickly identified.

Early efforts date back to the years leading up to WW I, but little lasting progress was made. Real breakthroughs came about in the inter-war era as a result of advances in mechanical engineering and aerodynamics, but the most basic problem confronting helicopter designers was the torque reaction. A single-powered rotor causes the body of the helicopter to turn in the opposite direction—this being the torque reaction. Much of the development between the wars was intended to solve this problem by having a second rotor which turned the opposite way, thus cancelling the torque effect. In France, Italy, and the USSR a number of multi-rotor helicopters were tested with limited and varying degrees of success. In France the control system developed by the Marquis de Pescara, an Argentine, proved highly successful and is now almost universally employed in modern helicopters. However, most designs still had two or more contra-rotating blades to solve the torque problem and this caused highly complex and unsound craft. There were also problems of engine-cooling and power-handling ratios.

More progress was made in the inter-war era in the development of the autogiro, which had an unpowered overhead rotor blade driven by the airflow from a conventional tractor propeller in the nose. Aside from an initial starting rotation the rotors were driven by the airflow only, and thus they autorotated. The main advantage of the autogiro was that it solved the torque reaction problem, but a failing was the need for a short take-off run—it could not lift off vertically, nor indeed hover effectively. Juan de la Cierva in particular pioneered the development of the autogiro, and much valuable information was gathered that was later fed into the design of the helicopter.

The first moderately successful helicopter design was the Breguet 314 of the mid-1930s, a model which incorporated a rotor-blade cyclic pitch system to tilt the rotor in flight, linked with collective pitch change for vertical control. This was followed by the Focke-Achgelis Fa61, still a contra-rotating design, but one which in 1938 was able to perform controlled hovering flight in the hands of a skilled pilot. During the war a tiny number of helicopters and autogiros were employed, sometimes actually seeing action, though success was sporadic at best.

However, the major breakthrough was spearheaded by Igor Sikorsky in the USA who was the first designer to conquer the torque problem. In 1940 his VS-300 design used a long tail boom with a small vertical rotor to counter the torque reaction. It was not a new idea but the system, now almost universally employed by helicopters, proved remarkably successful. Further development followed and by the closing stages of the war Sikorsky had orders from the US army and the Royal Navy. In the immediate post-war years the interest in the potential military and civil applications of helicopters caused a burgeoning of manufacture and design. By 1947 there were over 70 helicopter projects in the USA and companies such as Westland, Cierva, Saunders-Roe, Bristol, and Fairey in the UK all moved into the field. Similar interest was demonstrated in France, Italy, Germany, and the USSR.

During the mid-1950s a further major developmental step was taken when turboshaft engines began to be integrated into helicopter designs. Hitherto, helicopters had been powered by piston engines and this had brought many cooling problems. When turbo-engines became compact enough to be used in helicopters many benefits followed. Cooling problems were eased, more powerful engines could be used, and high power use, for hovering and lifting over long periods, was greatly facilitated.

The *Korean war also acted as a great boost to development. The war demonstrated the capability of the helicopter, first in operations to rescue and recover downed Allied aircrew, but additionally in the tactical movement of troops to enemy rear zones. With new and more powerful helicopters being designed and produced, the age of the helicopter was at hand. The *Vietnam war saw the helicopter truly come into its own, and it was deployed on a wide scale, undoubtedly the largest to date. Apart from US army formations, the USAF, the US Navy, and the US Marine Corps all employed helicopters in a variety of roles. In addition, the *CIA-sponsored Air America had its own helicopter fleet employed on extra-theatre operations in Cambodia and Laos, demonstrating the helicopter's value in covert operations.

The USSR also employed large numbers of helicopters in the *Afghanistan war to some effect. However, certain problems started to emerge. Helicopters were naturally vulnerable to fixed-wing enemy aircraft, and thus air supremacy or certainly air superiority was an essential prerequisite. However, little could be done about increasingly sophisticated ground-based anti-aircraft capability, notably surface-to-air missiles such as Stinger and Blowpipe. Helicopters employed defensive tactics such as NOE (nap of the earth) flying to minimize risk, but as with all types of battlefield air support, effectiveness decreases markedly in a hostile operating environment.

Nevertheless, the potential of the helicopter was clear and irrefutable. A whole host of helicopter designations and uses began to be formulated. For army support the helicopter is essentially now deployed in four basic roles. Observation helicopters (OH) are generally unarmed, small, fast, and manoeuvrable, and tasked with scouting and *reconnaissance duties. Versions have included the Coyote, Iowa, Sioux, Scout, and Gazelle. Attack helicopters (AH) are specifically designed for ground attack (see FIGHTER) and close *air support (CAS) operations. They are often armoured, present limited frontal profiles and silhouettes, and are armed with a variety of weapons such as cannon, rockets, machine guns, and technologically advanced missiles. Versions include the AH-1 Cobra, AH-64 Apache, and now the AH-64D Longbow Apache. The utility helicopter (UH) is the basic multi-purpose workhorse model, and is capable of carrying a squad or section of well-equipped troops or stores and supplies and if they are armed at all it is with door-guns. Versions include the Huey, Blackhawk, Lynx, and Puma. Cargo helicopters (CH) are heavier models capable of carrying 60 troops, lightly armoured vehicles, or underslung loads such as artillery and munitions. Types include the CH-46 Chinook and the CH-53.

Large-scale airmobile assaults can now employ all four types of helicopters, OHs to scout and reconnoitre ahead, gathering information and selecting targets for AHs. The AHs protect the main force from ground threat, prepare the landing zones, and provide close fire support for the landings themselves. UHs bring in the troops to secure the landing zones, take in cut-off forces for sweeps, prior to the main force being brought in by the CHs. This could include troops, artillery (or local fire support and air-defence), stores (offensive and defensive), and air-portable vehicles.

Most major world powers have formations based on the above aircraft, usually at brigade level. The US army pioneered the model with the 1st Air Cavalry in Vietnam, and then continued with the development of the 101st Airmobile Division and to a lesser degree the 82nd Airborne Division (also parachute-trained). What is clear is that helicopter-borne formations tend to be taking over from paratroop forces and *airborne or parachute units are training for the airmobile role.

Other powers have developed similar forces, though naturally on a more limited scale. The British have the 24th Airmobile Brigade with limited non-integral lift capability, the French the 4ème Division Aéromobile, and Germany the Luftlandebrigade with paratroops, airmobile infantry, and *anti-armour Fallschirmpanzerabwehr battalions.

In an offensive CAS role the helicopter certainly proved its worth in the *Gulf war, most famously with the AH-64A Apache attacks on the fleeing Iraqi troops on the Basra road. Again the caveat that air supremacy was assured throughout should be borne in mind when considering the true combat effectiveness of helicopters. In operations when air superiority might be contested or when ground-based AA fire could be sophisticated or intense, the helicopter would encounter serious tactical problems.

Nevertheless, the latest developments seem to be pushing the helicopter's CAS capability to new heights. The new AH-64D Longbow Apache is the latest leap forward, with claims being made that while a battalion of AH-64As could destroy an armoured regiment, a Longbow Apache (64D) battalion could wipe out a division. Stand-off capability where aircraft can loose off missiles from 2,187–3,281 yards (2,000–3,000 metres) from a target is nothing new and along with fire-and-forget ordnance have offered CAS huge advantages, but perhaps more importantly the Longbow is designed for 21st-century digital warfare. Longbows will be co-ordinated such that they will hunt over wide areas, three helicopters covering a 3.1 mile (5 km) front, for example. Any gathered information will be digitally disseminated to other Longbows which will then move into the most advantageous positions to prosecute the attack. The Longbow carries up to sixteen Hellfire anti-armour missiles which can independently seek out targets once located, along with 30 mm cannon and Hydra missiles. The US army has focused training in the 21st Cavalry Brigade to develop the sophisticated tactics and *operational concepts required to maximize the Longbow's potential.

Helicopters have also been enthusiastically adopted by world *navies. The helicopter provides an excellent platform for many maritime duties, especially anti-submarine operations. The helicopter can carry out the duties of a surface anti-submarine vessel by carrying underwater detection equipment and appropriate ordnance to deal with the threat once located. Helicopters can significantly extend the anti-submarine capability of a surface force at much smaller cost and risk than a surface vessel. They can also be used for ferrying personnel between ships or to shore and for air-sea rescue duties. The Sikorsky Sea King helicopter was specifically designed for anti-submarine operations and has become commonplace in the world's navies. It has been built under licence in Britain, Italy, and Japan, all by home-based firms and with minor modifications.

The impact of the helicopter on the conduct of military operations has been highly significant therefore, shaping capability in many ways from airlift, to ground support, to maritime duties. The inherent flexibility of the helicopter principle continues to play an important part in determining the nature of force structures in the future, and in the varied and complicated post-*Cold War environment the helicopter is an ideal tool. JDB

Fay, John, *The Helicopter* (London, 1987).
Mason, Tony, *Airpower: A Centennial Appraisal* (London, 1994).
Ripley, Tim, *Modern Military Helicopters* (London, 1998).

heliograph (from Gr: *hēlios*, sun, and *graphē*, writing). A heliograph was a *communications system consisting of two mirrors on a tripod used to flash signals with sunlight. The signals could be sent as messages or as Morse code using a combination of long and short flashes of light by opening and closing the shutter. Range was by line-of-sight and weather conditions affected heliograph operations.

The heliograph was invented by British scientist and engineer Sir Henry C. Mance, and the Mance heliograph was successfully tested in the second *Anglo-Afghan war of 1878–80. It was adopted by the British army and later widely used in India. An earlier version of the heliograph known as the heliotrope was used during the *American civil war. The heliograph was later used extensively by the US army in south-western USA during the *Plains Indians campaigns and also during the *Spanish-American war. The last significant use of the heliograph was during the Second *Boer War in South Africa, in which both sides used them. The US army kept some heliographs around until 1920. Some heliographs were kept at Corregidor in the Philippines as back-up communications in case of radio failure. Canada was the last major army to keep the heliograph as an issue item, retiring them in 1941.

The mujahedin *guerrillas in *Afghanistan were photographed using British pattern heliographs in their war with the Soviets. Given sunlight, it is an uncomplicated means of signalling, requiring no batteries or elaborate maintenance, and is not affected by electronic jamming. DMJ

Hemingway, Ernest (1899–1961), American big-game hunter, deep-sea fisherman, *war correspondent, and winner of the 1954 *Nobel Prize for Literature. Still a teenager, Hemingway volunteered for war work and was wounded on the *Italian front in 1918, the basis for his first major book *A Farewell to Arms* (1929). His fascination with 'grace under pressure' was explored in his treatise on bullfighting, *Death in the Afternoon* (1932), and he returned to Spain in 1937 to cover the *Spanish civil war, arriving in time for the end of the battle of Brihuega, part of the battle of Guadalajara, in which the Italians were stopped in a battle involving about 70 tanks. As war correspondents sometimes do, he overestimated its significance, reporting that 'Brihuega will take its place in military history with all the other decisive battles of the world'; but that was the way it was in Spain, sometimes, and he distilled the experience in his greatest novel *For Whom the Bell Tolls* (1940). In WW II he was a thrusting war correspondent with US forces in Europe. After the war he summarized his philosophy with marvellous economy in *The Old Man and the Sea* (1952). Repeated accidents and alcoholism sapped his vitality and he shot himself in 1961. CDB

Henri IV, King of Navarre and France (1553–1610). Henri IV was a direct descendant of the Capetian kings, married a Valois princess of the blood, and founded the Bourbon dynasty. He became king of Navarre upon the death of his mother in 1572 and of France in 1589 after his four Valois cousins/brothers-in-law, including Kings Charles IX and Henri III, had died without issue. Additionally he was raised a *Huguenot, converted to Catholicism to save his life in 1572, recanted and was excommunicated in 1576, converted again in 1593 to consolidate his claim to the throne, and brought 40 years of religious civil war to an end with the Edict of Nantes in 1598 (see FRENCH WARS OF RELIGION). Thus it borders on the churlish to point out that he was an indifferent military commander, and that when he said 'Paris vaut bien une messe' (Paris is well worth a Mass), the phrase was given added piquancy by the fact that he had signally failed to take the city by military means. The only time he came up against a really competent opponent (*Parma at Rouen in 1591–2) he was made to look like a dilettante, but since until the moment the Catholic fanatic François Ravaillac's stiletto ended his days he was a supremely lucky prince, his failings pale by comparison.

Henri inherited a bitterly divided nation, ravaged by international and civil war, beset on all sides by the mighty Habsburg empire, and bankrupt. He bequeathed to his son Louis XIII a unified nation, with a booming economy, and a burgeoning population, solid alliances, and able councillors. He paid off the national debt, encouraged the beginnings of the French empire in America, and built or completed some of the main architectural treasures of Paris. He sacked no towns, killed few men, conciliated formerly mortal enemies, and simply by stopping the self-destruction made France once again a power to be reckoned with in Europe and the world. HEB

Henry V, King of England (*c*.1386–1422) was a notable ruler and an outstanding soldier and commander. As a young man he gained wide experience helping to contain the revolt of *Glendower against the rule of his father, Henry IV. These campaigns taught him much about war against irregular forces, the importance of *siege warfare, and the necessity of maintaining supply routes by both land

and sea. Inheriting the throne in 1413, Henry decided to pursue English interests in France. In 1415 he invaded that country, besieged and captured Harfleur, and, on 25 October, went on to win a remarkable victory at *Agincourt. In 1417 he returned, his objective now being conquest. The ensuing campaign, which lasted over two years, was to reflect his understanding of the need to wage war in winter, and his determination to capture places which he besieged. His successes at Caen (1417), Rouen (1418–19), and Meaux (1421–2) are evidence of his mastery of the campaigns whose character he was dictating: Rouen was approached from the sea only after a long, circuitous movement by land had been completed, and a chain drawn across the river Seine above the city had effectively isolated it. Successful here, Henry advanced up the Seine valley, towards Paris. He would use the threat posed by his army, and the fear which it instilled in the population, to divide the enemy, divisions which were used to good effect to impose the terms of the Treaty of Troyes upon the French in 1420.

Henry showed many important military qualities. He appears to have been an exceptional, indeed charismatic leader, strict in disciplining his army, yet possessing a clear understanding, founded on experience, of what being a soldier involved; many of those whom he counted as his friends were themselves soldiers. He devoted much time and effort to detailed preparation for his campaigns. On his second expedition into France it is clear that he was exceptionally well prepared with cannon and other suitable weapons as only one who had learned from earlier experience could be. He was able to make the best of the rapidly evolving artillery of the time, a factor which contributed significantly to his successes in siege warfare. It is right to emphasize the flexibility of his approach to war which, as modern scholarship has stressed, included a fine appreciation of how his politico-military ambitions could be furthered by building ships, securing a measure of control at sea, and using rivers such as the Seine to bring men, provisions, and, in particular, heavy cannon to the very quayside of some of the cities (Caen and, in particular, Rouen) which he was besieging. CTA

Allmand, Christopher, *Henry V* (London, 1998).
—— 'Henry V the Soldier, and the War in France', in G. L. Harriss (ed.), *Henry V: The Practice of Kingship* (Stroud, 1993).

heraldry—hereditary shield emblems governed by rules of design and use—first appeared in western Europe in the second quarter of the 12th century. Its origins have been attributed to knights dressed in mail head coif and nasal helmet needing some form of identification.Recognition was perhaps the principal factor that produced this new phenomenon. Armorial bearings were to prove remarkably effective in distinguishing one knight from another, particularly in *tournaments where heralds, who announced the participants, quickly built up an expert knowledge of the subject. Later, after battles such as *Crécy in 1346, they identified the dead by their coats of arms. So successful was heraldry as a means of recognition that knights were able to enter tournaments and sometimes battles disguised in the arms of another person, or using bogus arms and therefore incognito. Ships, towns, and whole armies might fly or display false arms to deceive the enemy. Some leaders fought wearing the arms of others so they would not attract unwanted attention, or employed decoys bearing their own arms.

The fact that arms were initially very simple and easy to distinguish and were known as *connoissances* or *recognitiones* testifies to their role as emblems of recognition. In the mid-12th century the poet Wace wrote that at *Hastings the Normans 'had made cognizances so that one Norman would recognise another'. He was, in fact, describing the military practices of his own day. The Bayeux Tapestry contains no heraldry but does show that in 1066 knights wore much the same headgear—coif and nasal helm—as a century later and that recognition even then was a problem. In a famous scene *William 'the Conqueror' has to doff his helmet to prove who he is. Why then was there no heraldry by this date?

The answer lies in certain changes to the accoutrements and equipment of the knight in the century after Hastings, though these changes did *not* make them more difficult to recognize; helmets completely covering the face did not appear until the 1180s. The introduction of the pennon or 'gonfannon', the precursor of the heraldic banner, on the couched lance (no longer thrown as a javelin), the cloth surcoat, probably first used during the Crusades and to give its name to 'coats of arms' (and to some extent the equivalent horse caparison), and later the flat surface of the heater shaped shield, meant that for the first time knights could 'decorate' relatively large surface areas of their equipment with bold designs by which they could be easily identified. Even where not adopted for recognition such devices, if used consistently, quickly became associated with their owners thus helping identify them, and, in due course, their families and followers. Unlike rallying flags or war cries these distinguishing marks could be personal and not necessarily shared by whole armies or divisions. Hereditary shield devices had been born. AA1

Ailes, Adrian, 'The Knight, Heraldry and Armour: The Role of Recognition and the Origins of Heraldry', in C. Harper-Bill and R. Harvey (eds.), *Medieval Knighthood IV* (Woodbridge, 1992).
Barker, Juliet, *The Tournament in England, 1100–1400* (Woodbridge, 1986).

high explosive is a detonating explosive which can be subdivided into two groups: primary and secondary. Primary high explosive is detonated by impact, spark, or flame; secondary high explosive requires a separate detonator. Both types can be combined, and often are for military use.

Detonators are usually composed of primary high explosive combined with timing or percussion elements which ignite the primary explosive in order to detonate the main charge of secondary high explosive. Modern high explosives are developments of the last 150 years, which began with the discovery of nitroglycerine and the invention of nitrocellulose, or gun cotton, in the 1840s. Gun cotton became used as a shell-filler in the 1860s. Stabilized nitroglycerine was developed into dynamite by Alfred *Nobel, who combined this secondary high explosive with his detonator utilizing fulminate of mercury—the primary explosive—to produce a highly effective partnership. During the European arms race in the late 19th century, developments in high explosive produced the shell-filler picric acid—known in Britain as Lyddite—and trinitrotoluene or TNT, a shell-filler derived from nitroglycerine, in Germany. TNT filled German shells for much of WW I. In Britain, TNT was used initially but later replaced by Amatol, a compound of TNT and ammonium nitrate. Between the two world wars further developments in high explosive were pursued in Britain and Germany and, although both countries retained their preference for TNT and Amatol as shell- and bomb-fillers during WW II, other forms of high explosive were developed and used too. These were pentaerythritol or PETN, in Germany, and trimethylene trinitramine, or RDX, also known as Cyclonite, which was manufactured in Britain but had been invented in Germany. Tetramethylene tetranitramine, or HMX, also known as Octogen, was a British sophistication of Cyclonite and Torpex was a combination of TNT, RDX, and aluminium. Since WW II the majority of military high explosives have been combinations, in varying proportions, of PETN, TNT, RDX, and HMX, the proportions depending upon the envisaged role of the high explosive; naval mines, depth charges, and torpedoes, for example, use a combination of TNT, RDX, and aluminium to produce HBX—a compound which produces a blast suitable for shattering hard substances, such as armour plate.　　SCW

Bailey, A., and Murray, S. G., *Explosives, Propellants and Pyrotechnics* (London, 1989).

Cook, M. A., *The Science of High Explosives* (New York, 1966).

Highlanders Men from the Highlands of Scotland have been recruited into the armies of Europe since the Middle Ages. Men drawn from highland regions have proved to be hardy and intrepid. In this context, a historical survey of highlanders must include the *Gurkhas of Nepal and the *Pathans of the *North-West frontier, Italy's *Alpini, France's Chasseurs Alpins (see CHASSEURS), and the Tirolean *Jägers of Austria. But the Scots Highlander is probably the most recognizable of military icons.

The *clann* system of Highland Scotland prior to the mid-18th century required military service by able-bodied males. Although inter-clan warfare declined in the 16th century, the tradition remained, as did the raw material. Continental wars in the 17th century encouraged Scots, many of whom were Highlanders, to enlist in foreign armies, as their ancestors had done for over 400 years. Highlanders fought in the Scots armies during the *British civil wars of the mid-17th century and in the British army following its reconstruction in 1660 but in the latter force they were not distinguished by their native dress. The exile of their Catholic King *James VII (James II of England) in 1688 led to 60 years of *Jacobite-inspired disaffection in Britain, centred chiefly in Highland Scotland, and, in the early 18th century, independent companies of Highlanders were raised, dressed in the plaid and bonnet of their native areas, to police their neighbours. In 1739 these companies became the regiment now famous as the Black Watch, the first regiment of Highlanders in the British army. Other regiments of Highlanders came and went throughout the 18th century and the reputation of the Scots Highlander as a redoubtable soldier was made in India, in America, during the *Napoleonic wars, and ever after.

The British army continues to recruit Highland regiments, each with its traditions and *music, although these are increasingly drawn from the more populous urban areas of Scotland, rather than from the desolate and deserted mountains. Gurkhas and Scots Highlanders have always had a close mutual affinity and the Gurkha bagpipe and diced bonnet are directly drawn from those of their Highland comrades.　　SCW

Hill, Lt Gen Ambrose Powell (1825–65), Confederate general and corps commander in the Army of Northern Virginia. Hill was born in Virginia and educated at the US Military Academy at *West Point. He was commissioned into the US army just in time to see action in the final battles of the *Mexican war. When the *American civil war broke out Hill joined the Confederacy. Hill was an aggressive and sometimes impetuous commander, as epitomized by his performance as a brigade commander during the *Seven Days battles in 1862, and by the red hunting shirt he liked to wear in battle. Hill was promoted to command of a division in 1862, and his timely arrival after an epically fast march from Harper's Ferry saved *Lee at *Antietam. He was promoted lieutenant general in 1863 and rose from his sickbed to lead his corps at *Gettysburg. In the last two years of the war Hill was dogged by illness, but remained one of the most tenacious officers under Lee's command, fighting at the Wilderness, Spotsylvania, and Cold Harbor. He was killed on 2 April, while trying to rally his troops and stem the Federal breakthrough south of Petersburg. The Army of Northern Virginia surrendered one week later.　　AH

Hindenburg Line (1917–18), name given by the British to a defensive arc of fortifications along the line Lens–Noyon–Rheims, started by the Germans in winter 1916 and known to them as the Siegfried Line. Believing his army to have been 'exhausted' at *Verdun and the *Somme, *Ludendorff mounted ALBERICH, a strategic withdrawal from the 20 mile (32 km) bulge ('Ancre knee') of Army Group Crown Prince Rupprecht between Arras and Soissons. Troop withdrawals began on 15 March. The land left behind was stripped of all war material, tools, and food, wells were poisoned, streets mined, creeks dammed, railway sleepers ripped up, and all combustible material burned. The Allies, in Ludendorff's words, were 'to find a totally barren land, in which their manoeuvrability was to be critically impaired'.

ALBERICH was the war's greatest feat of engineering. More than half a million German workers and Russian POWs toiled for four months building the line; 1,250 trains hauled materials to construct the steel-reinforced concrete forts and blockhouses. The Hindenburg Line consisted of an elastic defence in-depth: an initial large antitank ditch yielded to a series of at least five barbed-wire barriers; next came a line of defence anchored by forts and blockhouses bristling with machine guns; and the final major barrier boasted an intricate system of zigzag trenches designed to prevent enfilading fire. Two lines of artillery were sited in the rear zone—on reverse slopes wherever possible, and later in trenches and tunnels. In time, the 300 mile (482 km) 'line' was extended to consist of five major defensive positions (Flanders, Wotan, Siegfried, Hunding, Kriemhild, and Michel Lines). Ludendorff judged that the Hindenburg Line freed up ten divisions as well as 50 batteries of heavy artillery, and shortened the front by nearly 30 miles (48 km). But it still required enormous manpower and in 1918, after his final offensives had used up his reserves, he saw his impregnable lines breached by the resurgent Allies.

HHH

Hindenburg, FM Paul von Beneckendorff und

(1847–1934). Hindenburg served during the wars of unification as a junior officer of the Prussian Guard and retired as a corps commander in 1911. Neither a scion of one of the great junker military families like the Kleists and the Bülows nor one of the 'new men' brought to power by the *general staff system and the industrial revolution, Hindenburg was widely respected for his integrity and force of character. Preferring service with troops to staff duty, he was nevertheless considered a possible candidate for both CGS and Prussian war minister. He was recalled to duty at the outbreak of WW I to command an Eighth Army falling back before an unexpectedly swift Russian onslaught into East Prussia, with *Ludendorff as his COS. The latter was sensitive, volatile, and arrogant, and someone calm was required to balance him; someone, moreover, who did not share Ludendorff's reputation of being too clever for everyone else's good. The solid Hindenburg was a logical choice.

The Hindenburg-Ludendorff team's success, first in de-

stroying one Russian army in the battle of *Tannenberg, then crippling another in the battle of the *Masurian Lakes, made Hindenburg a household word and a symbol of victory for a Germany facing a much longer, much harder war than had been expected. Hindenburg was more than a figurehead. Aware of his own limitations and his own qualities, he was able to provide, without resentment, a base and framework for Ludendorff's erratic brilliance while keeping his subordinate focused. As C-in-C of the *eastern front he received credit for a series of victories in 1915, most notably at Gorlice-Tarnow, whose operational virtuosity overshadowed their strategic sterility. As *Falkenhayn, Chancellor Bethmann-Hollweg, and not least Kaiser Wilhelm himself lost credibility in a stalemated war, Hindenburg's appointment as CGS in August 1916 surprised no one.

Even with Ludendorff as his deputy, Hindenburg was beyond his depth as de facto supreme commander of a state already in serious trouble. More committed to winning the war than to ruling Germany, he lent his prestige to a series of policies, including unrestricted submarine warfare, that overstrained Germany's resources and added the USA to an already long list of enemies. He participated in the intrigues that led to Bethmann's dismissal in July 1917 and kept his successors no more than figureheads. He accepted the increasingly unrealistic war aims of the German right and he allowed Ludendorff to squander what remained of the Reich's military resources in the futile offensives of March and April 1918. Only in October did the shrewd common sense that characterized his earlier career re-emerge. Instead of resigning with Ludendorff, he remained in office to lend his authority to the *Armistice his country now demanded.

He remained a national hero. Elected president of the Weimar Republic in 1925, he performed his new duties loyally and not ineffectively, albeit remaining a monarchist at heart. Advancing age limited his ability to cope with the Great Depression and the rise of National Socialism. Hindenburg's appointment of *Hitler as chancellor in January 1933 provided much-needed legitimacy for a man and a movement that eventually destroyed the Germany that Hindenburg served and tried to save. DES

Hiroshima and Nagasaki, bombings of (1945).

The atomic bombing of the Japanese cities of Hiroshima and Nagasaki in August 1945 represents arguably the most important and most sinister development in warfare in the 20th century. By the early 1940s scientists in Britain and the USA were rapidly developing the technology that would lead to an atomic weapon. It was research conducted under the deepest secrecy for fear that Nazi scientists would be able to obtain the necessary data to enable them to produce a weapon of their own. In mid-1942 a programme codenamed the *Manhattan Project was set up to develop a bomb. The scheme involved 100,000 persons and took three years to complete. On 16 July 1945 the first atomic bomb was tested at a site called Trinity in New Mexico. The blast that resulted was the release of energy equivalent to 20 kilotons of TNT. The steel tower on which the device was mounted completely vaporized, and the sand around melted to glass.

Hiroshima became the target of the first weapon at 08.15 on 6 August 1945. The all-clear had in fact sounded from an initial alert when the bomb was dropped. It was carried by a B-29 Superfortress called Enola Gay, and exploded about 602 yards (550 metres) over the city producing the equivalent of 15 kilotons of energy. Eyewitnesses reported seeing a parachute falling followed by a blast of intense heat. Between 130,000 and 200,000 people died, were injured, or disappeared. The Japanese government attempted to play down the impact and significance of this ominous development, which was followed a few days later by a second atomic bombing. This weapon had been destined for Kokura on the southern Japanese island of Kyushu, but cloud cover forced the crew to attack their secondary target of the shipyards of Nagasaki. The Nagasaki bomb was of about 20 kilotons but did less damage because of the local topography. It exploded above Urakami to the north of the port.

The injuries and destruction from the two bombs resulted from three factors: the intense blast, similar to that from conventional weapons but on a much larger scale; thermal radiation causing burns and producing fires; and nuclear radiation, which caused death and injury from damaged tissues. Each of the three effects was found on victims within 1 mile (1.6 km) from the epicentre, but the first two factors caused most deaths.

Even though more people died in the conventional bombing of Tokyo, the atomic bombings were significant because they caused death on a huge scale from one bomb dropped by one plane. Hiroshima and Nagasaki remain potent symbols and a sterile controversy over the use of the atomic weapons continues. In purely military terms the bombs proved decisive in persuading the Japanese government to think the unthinkable and accept defeat.

SRT/RH

Hitler, Chancellor Adolf

Hitler, Chancellor Adolf (1889–1945). Although *Stalin and *Mao-Tse-tung each killed more people, Hitler is in undisputed possession of the title of the most reviled man in a 20th century with more than its share of genocidal monsters. What heightens the appalled fascination is that he was in essence such an insignificant little man, driven by a need to compensate for his inadequacies. When the Soviets finally released the results of the autopsy performed on his half-incinerated corpse, it was revealed that the ribald words of the march 'Colonel Bogey' had been correct: he was monorchid. Additionally he had odd sexual quirks, had Oedipal feelings for his mother, and only felt comfortable showing love to animals and small children. His speech and writings are full of references to hygiene and cleansing with reference to the physical elimination (*sic*) of Jews and other 'subhumans'.

He was an outsider in every possible way. Not a German but an Austrian, he was born in Braunau, the son of a minor customs official with a much younger wife. A failure at school, his artistic aspirations were punctured when he was rejected by the Academy of Fine Arts in Vienna. There he imbibed the social Darwinism of the likes of Houston Stuart Chamberlain and the anti-Semitism of Karl Lürger, the dynamic mayor of the city. An aimless and friendless young man, embittered with his lot, a photograph exists of him amidst a joyful crowd in Munich welcoming the outbreak of war in 1914. He immediately volunteered, served as a battalion runner, was awarded both classes of the Iron Cross, for bravery (which he wore on his political *uniforms throughout the rest of his life), and was gassed in 1918.

Not only did his service at the front mark him, but it often gave him an edge over *general staff officers that he was never shy of exploiting. Significantly, it was in a Bavarian infantry unit of his beloved, adopted German army that he served, rather than in the Austro-Hungarian military. Perhaps the war gave him a sense of identity; it certainly provided him with a family and a hierarchy, which he admired until the end. Never promoted beyond corporal, he had no training for leadership or high command, but nevertheless, arguably, spent the rest of his days reliving the period of his life he found most fulfilling: making war.

Mein Kampf ('My Struggle'), a rambling outline of his inchoate political views, was written in gaol after his failed coup of 1923 and makes it clear that his war was a lifelong one, directed not just at external nations, but against the 'doubters' and 'outcasts' within Germany. The harsh terms of the Treaty of Versailles provided a general background of self-pitying resentment which he was able to exploit, and the feeling that Germany must somehow regain its lost preeminence was widespread. This partly accounts for his rise to power and the tacit support the *Reichswehr gave him. But he also, and this is very hard to explain but impossible to deny, had immense personal magnetism, which worked as effectively on individuals as it did on the large crowds he manipulated with carefully rehearsed gestures and choreographed responses from his strategically placed hard-core followers.

The Reichswehr still cultivated the attitudes of the old Prussian military, in which the importance of the oath of loyalty cannot be underestimated. Hitler knew this and used it, but even before he could do so, he bought the generals off with the prospects of rearmament and a chance to reverse the outcome of 1914–18. He also cold-bloodedly threw them the sop of the brown-shirted paramilitary Sturmabteilung (SA) that had won the streets from the communists and opened his way to power. In the 'Night of the Long Knives' (30 June 1934) he decapitated the SA using a new corps of bodyguards organized by the even more dysfunctional Heinrich Himmler, the black-clad *SS. On 2 August, following the death of *Hindenburg, the newly renamed *Wehrmacht swore an oath of loyalty, not to the state but to Hitler personally. Thereafter, in the perception of many including such stars as *Guderian, they were duty-bound to obey him.

The successful reoccupation of the Rhineland (1936), the Anschluss with Austria, and the annexation of the Czech Sudetenland (both 1938) were bluffs that could have been stopped by a moderate show of resolve by those affected. Much has been made of Chamberlain and Daladier selling out the Czechs at Munich, but the Czechs bore the main responsibility themselves. When Hitler visited the abandoned defences of the Sudetenland, his generals were appalled at their strength and told him they could not have taken them. 'It's not the guns but the men behind them', he replied, and this was the essence of his military leadership, very well expressed in the *blitzkrieg, which depended on sowing panic for success. It worked again against Poland in September 1939. For the campaign resulting in the fall of *France, Hitler took a more central role, backing a daring plan by *Manstein, in preference to more orthodox general staff proposals. The Wehrmacht's rapid and conclusive victory over the French convinced Hitler and not a few of his generals that he was a military genius. What he saw as the inevitable showdown between the Slav-Communists and the Aryan-Nazis was best not postponed. Stalin had disembowelled his officer corps and projections for Soviet rearmament showed a rapidly narrowing window of opportunity. He knew it to be a gamble, and it is significant that the 'final Solution', the systematic extermination of the *Untermenschen* (subhumans), was not implemented until he had made this highest-of-stakes throw of the dice. The opening weeks of *BARBAROSSA, perhaps fatally delayed by a sideshow in the Balkans, seemed to confirm the utter correctness of his instinct over the sober counsels of those few brave enough to urge caution upon him. Although it was the not-so-secret conceit of the German generals after WW II that left to their own devices they could have won the war, there were numerous occasions when Hitler's unschooled instinct was proved right and their less intuitive approach wrong. One such was the winter battle outside *Moscow in 1941 and *Kursk, spectacularly, another. Nor was his faith in fanaticism entirely misplaced: the Waffen *SS slowly grew to become a parallel army and often performed better than the Wehrmacht, especially in backs-to-the-wall situations like the second battle of *Kharkov.

In the absence of a quick victory, the latent power of the enemies he had challenged inexorably made itself felt and no amount of motivation or tactical brilliance could overcome the overwhelming *Materialschlacht* (battle of equipment) that crushed his armies on two fronts in 1944–5. Through it all and to the bitter end he continued to exert a strange fascination over his generals, as he did over the whole German people. It was not all mesmerism; his working methods were chaotic, keeping the officers of the Oberkommando der Wehrmacht (OKW) at his beck and call at all hours, and he frequently used his mastery of detail to make them feel uneasy about points which he had memorized but they had not. The failed attempt on his life by disaffected army officers on 20 July 1944 seems to have snapped whatever remaining links he had with reality and whatever restraints he still exercised over the sadism that drove him. Even if no other conflict in history deserves the title, the destruction of Hitler and his creed was surely a *just war. HEB

Rosenbaum, Ron, *Explaining Hitler* (London, 1999).

Stone, Norman, *Hitler* (London, 1991).

Weinberg, Gerhard L. *Germany, Hitler and World War Two* (Cambridge, 1996).

Welch, David, *Hitler* (London, 1998).

Zietelman, Rainer, *Hitler: The Policies of Seduction*, trans. Helmut Boger (London 1999).

Hittites The Hittites ruled in Anatolia from *c*.1600–1200 BC. Their capital was Hattushash (modern Bögazkoy) and their heartlands lay east of the river Marassantiya (classical Halys). In addition they dominated client states in Asia Minor: Kizzuwadna (Cilicia) and Tarhuntassa (Lycaonia), and also frontier zones, Gazga (north along the Black Sea coast) and Arzawa (later Ionia). At times they subdued Mesopotamia, and even pushed their rule into Syria and the Palestinian coast, bringing them into conflict with Egypt.

In *c*.1595 BC, Mursilis I destroyed the Babylonian empire of Hammurabi, but subsequently Hittite power waned in the face of the growth of Mitanni, and did not revive until the late 15th century BC under Tudhaliyas II (1430–1415 BC) and his son Arnuwandas I (1420–1400). They re-established Hittite rule by conquering the Cilician Plain in southern Asia Minor, and then subduing the Arzawa to the west. But the empire builder was Suppululiumas (1380–1340 BC), whose conquests are recorded by his son Mursilis II (1339–1306 BC) in histories entitled the 'Deeds' and 'Ten-year Annals'. Suppululiumas conquered Mitanni (based on the upper Euphrates and Tigris), and, using the Amorites as his spearhead, down these rivers and also west into Syria. As a result Muwatallis (1306–1282 BC) confronted Rameses II of Egypt at *Kadesh. In his account the pharaoh claims a decisive victory, although the battle was a Hittite ambush and probably ended in, at best, a draw for the Egyptians. Tudhaliyas IV (1250–1220 BC) campaigned in north-west Asia Minor, although this seems to have drained Hittite military resources, and the empire declined after 1200 BC. The war had also weakened the coalition in the region which included Troy, allowing successful Achaean expansion from across the Aegean under Agememnon.

Hittite military organization was based upon the military household of the sovereign, with a substantial royal guard. The Instructions for Military Governors survive (c.1440 BC) regarding the maintenance of military forces in the provinces, and demonstrate the risks of country life from enemy raiders such as the Gasgans. All fortifications were required to have a moat and be securely barred and bolted, with secure supplies of weapons, and food and protection for livestock. Garrison troops were not allowed to be away from their post for more than two days unless pursuing enemy raiders. Scouts were instructed to ensure that the roads and heights were free of enemy before the land-workers were allowed out into the fields. Because of the central role that religion played in Hittite war making, the governors were required to maintain the temples under their charge and also to ensure that the law was properly administered. They seem to have required a kind of *feudal military and labour service from the surrounding region. On campaign, the Great King was C-in-C, supported by his High Constable, the royal princes, and 'Lords of the Realm' as his generals. The army was raised from the provinces, client states, and allied countries of the Hittite empire; freemen serving oath-bound. The infantry were organized decimally in units of a thousand, with a company and section structure under designated officers.

Hittite strategy can be represented by Mursilis II's campaign against the Arzawa in western Asia Minor. For the first years of his reign he campaigned against the Gasgans to secure his northern border. Then he employed diplomacy to isolate the Arawan King Ukha-zitis from Achaean support. He then devastated Gasgan lands, drew them into battle, and defeated them. He was now free to move against Arzawa, with his ally the king of Kargamis. They defeated the Arzawans at Walma on the river Astarpa and pursued them to their capital Apasas (Ephesos). But Uhka-zitis had abandoned it and fled to the mountain fastness of Arrinanda. Mursilis invested the place in a winter siege and starved the defenders out. This campaign demonstrates the efficiency of the Hittite war machine and the degree of logistic support it must have enjoyed.

There are few illustrations of the Hittite warriors, but they seem to have worn a long wraparound 'Hurrian' robe (rather like a kaftan) and carried a spear and a waisted (violin-shaped) shield. The tall, pointed, and distinctively Hittite cap may have been reserved for officers and nobles, and although a helmet seems likely for the heavy infantry, contemporary Egyptian reliefs depict them as (conventionally) bareheaded. Side weapons included short sword, axe, and mace (possibly reserved for officers). The main strength of the army was in its *chariots, drawn by two horses, specially bred and carefully trained. A surviving document, known as Kikkulis' Horse Training Manual, details how this should be done. It describes how they should be fed, with a balance of grass and grain in carefully recorded quantities. There is also a training schedule. Part of this involves driving them over a distance of about 6.2 miles (10 km) (presumably as a kind of route march) to practise them for campaigning. But another section describes a

kind of interval training with bursts of galloping between longer, slower drives and rests. This can only have been preparation for battle manoeuvres, although no tactical details are given. Egyptian reliefs generally show Hittite chariots as heavier than their own, carrying a three-man crew. The charioteers, who bore the Hurrian title *mariyannu*, were an élite group given special privileges. The driver was protected by a shield-bearer; both were armoured in long scale tunics. The chariot also carried a spearman, who may have had the option to dismount in battle as a kind of 'chariot-runner'. Some lighter, two-man Hittite chariots are depicted, but whether these were adopted from the Egyptians or were of native Anatolian design is unclear. Numbers of Hittite armies are difficult to gauge, but Mursilis II claimed in his Annals to have captured 66,000 Arwazans in his two-year campaign against them (1332–1331 BC). (Egyptian) figures for the battle of Kadesh ascribe 3,500 chariots and 35,000 infantry to the Hittites opposing them, although these are probably exaggerated.   MB

Gurney, O. R., *The Hittites* (Harmondsworth, 1981).

Ho Chi Minh (1890–1969), leader of the Vietnamese communists and of the independence movement in that country in the decades following WW II. Ho was born Nguyen Tat Thanh in the Annam province, and was educated in Hué. In the 1920s and 1930s Ho operated in the murky underworld of the Vietnamese independence movement, and was a founding member of the Communist Party in Vietnam. During WW II, Ho and his communist group, which included the military leader Vo Nguyen *Giap, formed a base near the Chinese border and acted, with American support, against the Japanese occupation force. Ho also took the opportunity to solidify the position of the communists as the leaders and dominant force of the independence movement, which became widely known as the Vietminh.

The Vietminh was able to exploit the chaos which descended upon Vietnam at the end of WW II to seize power, and the Democratic Republic of Vietnam was proclaimed by Ho on 2 September 1945. However, the situation was far from stable. Kuomintang troops had flooded the city less than two weeks before, and the French government, recently restored to Paris, was already making plans to reassert control. The fragility of Vietminh control was quickly exposed in 1945–6, and Ho was forced to return to the communist stronghold near the Chinese border. The following eight years witnessed a monumental struggle on the part of the Vietnamese, to create an army and a logistical network capable of defeating the French, and to use that force effectively against the French forces in *Indochina. Giap's victory at *Dien Bien Phu in 1954 delivered such a victory, but Ho was disappointed by the peace conference which followed, and which granted the Vietminh control over only North Vietnam.

In spite of this setback, Ho was prepared to be patient. 'If we have the people,' Ho had once remarked, 'we will have everything.' In the years following Dien Bien Phu he set up a communist state apparatus in the north, and allowed communists in the south to agitate for reunification of the country. When war broke out again in the early 1960s Ho was already too ill to perform an active role, but remained an inspiration to those fighting the South Vietnamese and American forces. He died in Hanoi six years before the unification of Vietnam under the regime he had created.

AH

Fenn, Charles, *Ho Chi Minh: A Biographical Introduction* (New York, 1973).
Matthews, Lloyd J., and Brown, Dale E. (eds.), *Assessing the Vietnam War* (McLean, 1987).

Hoche, Gen Louis Lazare (1768–97). Son of a groom, Hoche was an assistant groom in the royal stables before joining the Gardes Françaises. A corporal in 1789, he rose rapidly in the *French Revolutionary wars: he was a captain by 1792 and a general of division within a year. As C-in-C of the Army of the Moselle he was beaten at Kaiserslauten on 28–30 November 1793 but defeated the Prussians at Froeschwiller and the Austrians at Geisberg in December, pushing the invaders back over the Rhine.

Imprisoned in 1794 as a result of intrigues by his rival Pichegru, he was released on the fall of Robespierre. Sent to repress the *Vendée rebellion which had spread to Brittany, he defeated the émigré force landed on the Quiberon promontory in June 1795, butchering royalists who could not be rescued by the British fleet. In December 1796 he commanded an expedition to Ireland, but his ship became separated from the others, waiting to land troops at Bantry Bay, and then the weather scattered the fleet. Hoche was commanding the Army of the Sambre et Meuse with distinction when he died of consumption at the age of 29. Quick-thinking, stern, and ruthless, he was a general of real talent, whose early death was a loss to France.   RH

Hofer, Andreas (1767–1810) a Tyrolean patriot who led an unsuccessful uprising against Bavarian control of the Tyrol in 1809, and was captured and executed. Austria, encouraged by Spanish success against Napoleon, began preparations to liberate Germany from France during January 1809. Archduke *Charles invaded Bavaria, then allied to France, on 9 April while Archduke John took an army of 50,000 men over the Julian Alps to invade Italy. The Austrians were attacked by Prince Eugène de Beauharnais, Napoleon's stepson, with 37,000 men at Sacile, east of the Tagliamento river but was repulsed 16 April. It was against this background that Hofer led a popular revolt against the Bavarian garrisons in the Tyrol. The rebels eventually succeeded in freeing most of the region with assistance from Archduke John. But after the Austrian defeat at *Wagram, the French under Eugène reconquered the region.   JR-W

Eyck, F. Gunther, *Loyal Rebels: Andreas Hofer and the Tyrolean Uprising of 1809* (Lanham, Md., 1986).

Hofkriegsrat The Vienna Court War Council. This came into being over the course of the 16th and 17th centuries as the directing body of the Habsburg standing army. A body of general officers and senior civil servants, the Hofkriegsrat controlled army appointments, *war finance, and deployment throughout Habsburg Europe. The Hofkriegsrat also provided both the civil and the military administration of the so-called 'military border' to Krajina in Croatia under terms approaching *martial law. While giving the appearance of the supreme Habsburg military body, the Hofkriegsrat never achieved a high level of either centralization or efficiency. It continually had to contend with rival agencies such as the Graz-based Hofkriegsrat, which largely directed Habsburg military policy in the south-eastern portion of the monarchy until the late 18th century. Also, the proprietary system of unit *recruitment limited the ability of the Hofkriegsrat to influence officer selection and professional development. Its unwieldy nature in directing the operational employment of the army in war led directly to the slow rise of a *general staff system in Austria. By 1848, viewed as hopelessly inefficient and bureaucratic, the Hofkriegsrat fell victim to the sweeping changes ushered in by the revolutions of that year and was abolished as an outworn symbol of royal power and modernized in the form of the constitutional Imperial/Royal Ministry of War.   SWL

Home Guard A civilian part-time armed force, first called Local Defence Volunteers, raised to help defend Britain from German invasion during WW II. The public response to the *War Office call for volunteers in the spring of 1940 vastly exceeded official expectations. By the end of the summer well over 1.5 million persons had come forward who were too young, old, or otherwise unable to serve in the regular forces.

Provided by the War Office with only armbands and a small number of surplus rifles imported from the USA in 1940, and given little or no guidance as to training or role, volunteers in the over-1,000 battalions that eventually formed equipped themselves with whatever private firearms and other weapons they could find and developed their own ideas concerning how best to meet the German parachute threat. The Home Guard was thus initially very much a populist affair. In 1941–2 military authority was gradually imposed on the force. Army-style ranks and organization were introduced, special sub-artillery and other weapons were provided, and training was set on a regular basis through the creation of official schools. Limited conscription was introduced in 1942, and in 1943 an official women's auxiliary was formed. The Home Guard was stood down late in 1944.

The effectiveness of the force in its anti-invasion role is questionable given its part-time nature and limited weaponry, especially in 1940–1 when the German threat was greatest, but there can be no doubt that the presence of Home Guards from 1942 onward on anti-aircraft sites helped free 100,000 regulars for other duties. The force as a whole was also an important means for the public to express its commitment to the war effort.   SPMack

MacKenzie, S. P., *The Home Guard: A Military and Political History* (Oxford, 1995).

homosexuality and the armed forces has not been an issue for much of history. It was tolerated and in the case of Ancient Greece actively encouraged, with the younger *hoplites at the back of the *phalanx and with the best opportunity to flee being held in place by the knowledge that their older lovers were in the front ranks. What men without women might get up to was certainly not regarded as the commander's business unless it gave rise to behaviour likely to undermine order, such as between officers and men. The idea that homosexuality is in some way related to *cowardice is a comparatively new one and has a great deal more to do with concepts of *gender than with pragmatic evidence. *Churchill once famously observed that the Royal Navy had three traditions, 'rum, sodomy and the lash', and one could go on indefinitely citing examples of notable warriors, *Alexander 'the Great' and *Richard 'the Lionheart' surely chief among them, who preferred male sexual partners.

What made it the issue that it is today was first the general tweeness about sex that gradually enveloped even previously uninhibited and bawdy societies such as the British during the 19th century, and more recently the drive by homosexual activists to win not simply tolerance but outright approval by political means. This involved trying to emulate the success of the women's movement in areas subject to government hiring and firing criteria. Hence, as with the issue of *women in the military, the armed forces have found themselves in the front line of a battle which is not really about them and their professional needs at all. But they should be used to that: they exist for a quintessentially political purpose and have always reflected the social prejudices of the regimes they serve.

In 1987, Sweden introduced legislation that prohibited discrimination in the military on the basis of sexual orientation. This was followed in 1992 by the courts in Canada ruling that the Armed Forces had to remove all restrictions based on sexual orientation, and in 1993 the *IDF implemented a far-reaching policy of non-discrimination, not only in *recruitment but assignments and promotion. Australia subsequently also introduced a similar policy. Initial evidence from these four nations does not substantiate claims that such action tends to undermine the cohesion, effectiveness, and *morale of military units.

The situation in the UK remained different until early 2000. Thereto homosexuals were barred from serving in the armed forces, and there was little support from within the forces to relax the ban. However, a pressure group called 'Rank Outsiders' was set up to help overturn this policy and helped a number of discharged homosexuals to present their case to the European Court of Human Rights. This ruled that the ban contravened European law; it was lifted in January 2000. A Code of Conduct, issued at the same time, wisely emphasized that sexual behaviour, rather than sexual orientation, was the real issue. One regular brigadier resigned over the issue, basing his action not on intolerance of homosexuality in itself, but on concern over the fact that an important national military matter had been decided by European legislation and reservations about the 'moral equivalence' between heterosexual and homosexual relationships that the change implied. Although his action was isolated, the new policy attracts suspicion from many servicemen who would have cheerfully accepted 'don't ask, don't tell'.

In the USA there has been a lot more noise. During the 1992 American presidential campaign, candidate Clinton pledged to lift the ban on homosexuals serving in the armed forces, but Pres Clinton has not delivered on the pledge. The compromise policy of 'don't ask, don't tell, don't pursue' has been denounced as hypocritical, but it does have some historical justification.   AA2/HEB/RH

Frost, Gerald (ed.), *Not Fit To fight* (London, 1998).
Kier, Elizabeth, 'Homosexuals in the US Military', *International Security*, 23 (1998).
Natzio, Georgina, 'Homosexuality: Can The Armed Services Survive It?', *RUSI Journal* (Dec. 1995).

Hong Kong, fall of (1941). In December 1941 the colony of Hong Kong island and its associated British-held territories were garrisoned by Maj Gen Maltby's six British-Indian and Canadian battalions and six companies of local volunteers, with six medium batteries and an assortment of *coast defence guns. He was supported by a tiny flotilla and five aircraft. It was recognized that sustained defence of Hong Kong was impossible, for half its water came from the mainland: Maltby was ordered to hold 'as long as possible'.

Maltby divided his force into the Mainland Brigade (Brig Wallis) and the Island Brigade (Brig Lawson) with three battalions apiece. With too few men to hold the Sham Chun river, the border with China, Wallis defended the Gindrinkers Line, running across the neck of the Kowloon peninsula. Although some defences had been constructed before 1938, and coast-defence guns on Stonecutters Island could provide supporting fire, the line was not ideal. There was a gap which obliged Wallis to commit his one reserve company, and it was so close to the sea that there was no room for another line behind.

Early on 8 December 1942 Japanese air attack destroyed all the British aircraft, and six battalions of the 38th Division began to cross the Sham Chun. A British covering force with light armour delayed them briefly, but they were up on the Gindrinkers Line late on 9 December. In the early hours of 10 December the commander of the Japanese 228th Regiment, acting without his divisional commander's approval, attacked and took the Shing Mun redoubt which dominated the ground in his sector. Wallis had no reserve available, and the local battalion commander was also unable to counter-attack. Wallis pulled back about 1 mile (1.6 km) on his left to compensate for loss of the redoubt, and was soon clear that the Japanese were so close to embarkation points that there was no alternative to evacuation, which was completed by early on 13 December.

Maltby reorganized his command into East Brigade (Wallis) and West Brigade (Lawson) with a two-battalion Fortress Reserve. An attempted crossing was repulsed on 15 December, but late on the 18th Japanese crossed Victoria Harbour and advanced inland. Lawson was killed defending the crucial Wong Nei Chong gap in the centre of the island, and there was some confusion as East Brigade withdrew prior to launching a counter-attack which was repulsed on the 20th. Despite some courageous local actions Maltby's position was impossible, and the governor, Sir Mark Young, authorized surrender which was completed on 26 December.   RH

---

honour or high respect, glory, credit and good name, and an adherence to what is right, has always been inextricably bound up in the conduct of warfare. To the medieval knight, his sense of honour was a controlling factor in battle which forbade flight before the enemy. The medieval ideal was personified in the *Song of Roland*. Roland accepted battle against overwhelming odds when he had the opportunity to flee. But being an honourable knight, he chose to fight, overcame his urge to escape, and died heroically. He gave his life for his cause and did nothing that would taint his honour. A knight's honour is a preoccupation of the *Song of Roland* because, to its writers, what a knight feared most was being denounced as a coward. However, practical experience and human nature showed that not everyone should allow themselves to die in battle once it became obvious the army was defeated. Lost battles do not necessarily mean lost wars, though this would be the case if the defeated side had allowed themselves to be killed on the battlefield. In such cases, honour had to be reconciled with the need to fight again and human safety and prudence.

In theory, knightly honour allowed only two alternatives, death or capture. During the Third *Crusade, the Master of the Templars refused to flee from battle when he still could,

and as a result was slain. He believed that had he fled it would have been a stain not only on his honour personally, but also on the honour of the entire order. However, distinction was made between an individual escaping during a battle while the outcome was still undecided and the retreat or collective flight of an army facing defeat. The Templars provided the generally accepted rule in such cases of defeat: once Christians were so near defeat that there were no banners left flying on the battlefield, the knight might escape to wherever he pleased.

By the early 19th century, the concept was not a great deal different. Certainly officers of Wellington's army did not look to sacrifice themselves needlessly. It was the way they faced death that most concerned them. It was an abstract idea, a matter of comportment, exposure to risk, acceptance of death if it should come, and of private satisfaction. Officers were most concerned about the figure they cut in their brother officers' eyes. This might be demonstrated by an officer's refusal to leave his post after receiving life-threatening wounds or the calm acceptance of an extremely hazardous order. For example, Major Howard of the 10th Hussars was ordered at the end of the battle of *Waterloo to charge a well-formed French square without infantry support. Howard's calmness in undertaking this order and his death at the edge of the French square seems to epitomize what honourable conduct was to British officers of the time. Officers demonstrated their fitness to hold *rank by their conduct in battle. They were very much individual gentlemen, their behaviour reflected on them, not necessarily that of their regiment. One hundred or so years later the officer's principal motivation and sense of honour was more likely to be defined in terms of 'duty to the regiment'.

Although *Frederick 'the Great' believed that only gentlemen should be officers because they alone were capable of being influenced by honour, it is clear that the definition of honour is rightly wider than this. The German army of the 19th and 20th centuries was able to foster a sense of soldierly honour which was not directly rank-related. Battlefield cohesion at the lowest level is promoted by men's desire to stick by their mates, and an abstract sense of honour is replaced by a very concrete desire not to let down those whose respect they value. A sense of honour binds men to military totems. The ex-soldier and radical politician William Cobbett observed that men would allow themselves to be 'sabred into crow's meat' in defence of a set of ragged *colours which, were they for sale in a market, would fetch only a few pence. A Russian officer at *Austerlitz urged his men not to leave their fine pieces to 'these enemies of Christ', and a British officer watched devoted Italian gunners hauling their elderly pieces over rough country after the defeat at *Caporetto, bound to them by a sense of honour which exceeded the weapons' real military value.

In WW II, Japanese soldiers had a very firmly rooted culture of honour to sustain them. For centuries, the *samurai warrior caste of Japan had emphasized the primary nature of honour and loyalty, and this code, called *bushido, 'the way of the warrior', had been kept alive by officers of the imperial Japanese army. Bushido was a concept of a heroic life that excluded frailty and was directed to perfect service and success. It produced a heroism that impressed those fighting them. Very few Allied units defended a position literally to the last man. But for the Japanese surrender, even in hopeless positions, was considered a disgrace. Therefore for the Japanese, fighting to the very end was routine and unwounded prisoners were a rarity. For example, only 216 of the 20,000-strong garrison of *Iwo Jima were taken prisoner. Conversely this produced the most revolting cruelty. Prisoners who by the harsh standards of bushido should never have been captured were routinely mistreated and civilian populations subjected to rape, massacre, and torture. Honour, which can produce the most noble behaviour on the battlefield and inspire acts of astounding courage, has also been guilty of provoking some of the worst atrocities committed by the military.   MCM

Keegan, John, *The Face of Battle* (London, 1976).

Pritchard, John, et al., *Total War*, vol. 2 (London, 1989).

honours of war The grant of the honours of war sometimes formed part of terms of *capitulation. Codified in the 17th century, they were intended to honour a surrendering garrison, which was permitted to march out of its battered stronghold with drums beating and *colours flying. *Musketeers were to have their matches lighted at both ends and to carry bullets in their mouths, showing that they were ready to fight. The terms might grant free passage to a specified friendly garrison, or they might confirm their surrender as *POWs.

Sometimes honours of war were used to induce a proud commander to capitulate rather than fight on to the last extremity, but they often showed genuine recognition of a gallant defence. Gen Joseph Barbanègre held Huningue until 27 August 1815—over a month after Napoleon's abdication—and his exhausted garrison marched out while the victorious Austrians presented arms. In 1870 *Bazaine was offered honours of war at Metz, but declined them, weakly claiming that his army was in too poor a state to parade with dignity. In June 1940 the Germans granted honours of war to the garrison of Lille, which paraded under arms with its own officers before entering captivity.   RH

Hood, Lt Gen John Bell (1831–79). Hood, a wealthy Kentuckian, graduated from *West Point in 1853 but resigned on the outbreak of war. A Confederate brigadier general within a year, he led the Texas Brigade at Gaines' Mill, second *Bull Run, and *Antietam. He lost an arm as divisional commander at *Gettysburg and a leg at Chickamauga. Promoted lieutenant general in February 1864, he

commanded a corps in the Army of Tennessee under *Johnston, from whom he took over. Promoted far above his ability, he failed to save Atlanta and then destroyed his army at Franklin and Nashville. A fellow officer compared him to Marshal *Ney, 'the bravest of the brave' but obdurately impetuous.   RH

Hooker, Maj Gen Joseph (1814–79). An aggressive corps commander in early battles of the *American civil war, Hooker restored *morale and cohesion in the Army of the Potomac following the disastrous tenure of *Burnside. He behaved atypically during the *Chancellorsville defeat, acknowledging that he 'just lost confidence in Joe Hooker', but withdrew in good order and shadowed the ensuing Confederate invasion. Although he resigned four days earlier, *Gettysburg was won by the army he shaped. Detached to assist Rosecrans, besieged at Chattanooga, under Grant's direction he seized Lookout Mountain on 24 November 1863 and along with *Sheridan took Missionary Ridge the next day. He was sidelined thereafter. His name is identified with the female *camp followers he favoured.   HEB

hoplites Greek heavy infantrymen during the period of the city state (c.700–300 BC) were known as hoplites, due to the cumbersome gear (*hopla*) that they wore into battle: corslet, greaves, and helmet; a double-grip, concave *shield with bronze veneer; a wooden spear 7 to 10 feet (2.1 to 3 metres) long, and a secondary short iron sword. The helmet, breastplate, and greaves were constructed entirely of bronze, reaching a thickness of about a half-inch (1.27 cm), which provided substantial protection from the entry of most swords, missiles, and spears.

The unusually large wooden shield of some 15–20 lb (6.8–9.1 kg) in weight, with a 3 foot (0.9 metre) diameter, covered half the warrior's body; its size and shape explain the nature of hoplite fighting itself. The infantryman depended on the man next to him to shield his own unprotected right side and to maintain the cohesion of the entire *phalanx, military service now reinforcing the egalitarian solidarity of the citizenry. Moreover, the shield's unique double grip allowed its oppressive weight to be held by the left arm alone, and its concave shape permitted the rear ranks to rest it on their shoulders as they pushed on ahead. Because of the natural tendency of each hoplite to seek protection for his unshielded right side in the shield of his companion on the right, the entire phalanx often drifted rightward in its approach.

The enormous weight of such an ensemble, ranging anywhere from 50 lb to 70 lb (22.7 to 31.7 kg), ensured that hoplite battle would be short and decisive, as infantrymen massed into the columns of the phalanx and charged each other head-on, soldiers seeking cover from the array of shields and victory through the sheer force generated by men pushing against the backs of those ahead. On flat ground and in dense formation, such heavily armed hoplites were invulnerable both to mounted assault and the harassment of lighter-armed skirmishers. By the 5th century BC they enjoyed a Mediterranean-wide reputation for infantry superiority. The battles of *Marathon and *Plataea are impressive testaments to hoplite dominance over an array of foreign infantry, while *Koroneia (394 BC) and *Leuctra demonstrate the sheer brutality of such engagements between similarly armed and equipped Greek hoplite armies.

The hoplite's presence on the battlefield was a reflection of his own free status in the polis community and thus reinforced his privileged position as a free yeoman farmer and voting citizen. Hoplite assemblies alone decided when and where to fight, and sought such engagements to protect their own land and families. Originally, hoplites, who provided their own weapons and *armour and met strict property qualifications regulating military service, comprised little more than half the adult population of their city states. Pitched and near *ritual infantry collisions during the day and in summer reflected their own parochial interests in keeping warfare amateurish, uncomplicated, and thus non-disruptive to the agrarian population at large.

However, after the *Graeco-Persian wars, with the rise of the maritime Athenian empire of the 5th century BC, the limitations of hoplite warfare in an increasingly Mediterranean-wide theatre of operations soon became apparent to the Greeks. Fighting on land and sea now required troops of all sorts, free and slave, citizen and foreigner, conscript and mercenary. The rise of taxation and the growing importance of capital, logistics, and *fortification and siegecraft spelled the end of the primacy of shock battles between farmers on inland plains. Gradually the hoplite lost his exclusivity as Greek warfare by the 4th century BC became a dynamic enterprise designed to storm cities, destroy communities, and acquire booty. Fighting became a science in its own right, now divorced from social concerns and ethical restraint. With the rise of Macedon, heavy pikes extended to nearly 18 feet (5.5 metres) and defensive armour diminished to ensure expendable mercenary troops greater mobility and offensive punch. Hoplites became merely one contingent of a complex fighting force of cavalry, light infantry, skirmishers, and missile troops. The ideal of hoplite warfare as an extension of civic agrarianism was lost, and with it the very autonomy of the Greeks and their old notion of the city state itself.   VDH

Hanson, V. D., *The Western Way of War* (New York, 1989).
—— (ed.), *Hoplites: The Ancient Greek Battle Experience* (London, 1991).

horse artillery was highly mobile, light artillery, used as a mobile reserve and to support cavalry. It differed from field artillery in that all its gunners were mounted. The concept was introduced by *Frederick 'the Great', who saw it as a mobile reserve to rapidly occupy those gun positions from which effective fire could be delivered. As virtually all fire was direct—that is, the guns had to see the target—it might be necessary to move artillery continuously to exploit opportunities to hit the enemy. The guns were usually 4- or 6-pounders. The support of cavalry started as a subsidiary role, because it was found that horse artillery had similar mobility and cross-country performance to cavalry. By the time of the *Napoleonic wars support of cavalry had become its principal role. At *Waterloo (18 June 1815), however, Sir Augustus Frazer, commanding the eight troops, each of six guns, of horse artillery used it far more intelligently. Two troops were detached to support the cavalry brigades, because they were some way away, leaving six, four of which had been up-gunned with 9-pounders and one, most unusually, with 5½ inch *howitzers. Lord Uxbridge, commanding the cavalry, agreed and 'offered him all the horse artillery to use as he wished'.

This unit, heavier than most horse artillery, was first of all moved to strengthen the centre of Wellington's position, which had been weakened out of concern for his right flank, at about 10.30. They were then moved to the right to strengthen that flank, at noon, then forward to help repel French cavalry charges at 15.30. Two troops 'advanced with an alacrity and rapidity most admirable'; Wellington exclaimed, 'that is how I like to see horse artillery move'. Finally, at 19.30, the troop on the left flank, which was unemployed, was moved into the centre to help retake La Haye Sainte as the victorious Allies counter-attacked.

Horse artillery played an important part in the fighting in India, but as ordnance generally became heavier its importance declined and the advent of *indirect fire removed one of the reasons for its existence: to get to places where it could see the enemy. Because of its fast movement and association with the cavalry, the 'horse artillery' acquired a certain social status and glamour. It had different, cavalry-style *uniforms and, in the Royal Artillery, 'ball buttons' as opposed to the common, flat kind. After its battlefield function had been subsumed by increasingly mobile field artillery, the title was retained for certain units within the Royal Artillery as a kind of élite. It was historically appropriate for *self-propelled (SP) guns, designed to keep up with and support armour, and in the 1970s 1st Regiment RHA (Royal Horse Artillery) operated SP guns while 3 RHA was given *anti-armour guided missiles. The 7 RHA was the parachute artillery regiment, which supported the *airborne brigade, armed with light pack howitzers, which could be dropped by parachute, along with the parachute-trained gunners. The Royal Artillery also maintained a mounted troop—the King's Troop—to gallop into position and fire ceremonial *salutes using immaculately maintained 13-pounders of WW I vintage. With its guns on parade the Royal Horse Artillery takes precedence over all other units in the British army, including the Household Cavalry.   CDB

horses were one of the earliest *animals to be domesticated, and their military use can be traced back to at least 1800 BC. The horses first used by man were altogether lighter than the ones known today: short in the leg and weak in the back, they were unsuitable for riding. They were limited in their usefulness as draught animals because of their weakness—the wild ass seemed a far better bet, and was used to drag a four-wheeled *chariot in about 2500 BC. At some time in the second millennium BC peoples in southern central Asia produced the two-horse chariot, and stallions no bigger than 14 hands were trained to pull it. Around 900 BC a bigger horse was bred, sturdy enough to be ridden astride by a man using weapons. The *Assyrians, who had been major chariot-users, initially used cavalrymen in pairs, one man using his *bow while the other controlled the horses. By the twilight years of their empire the Assyrians were using *cavalry proper, but their collapse was in part brought about by enemies who exploited the horse's potential more fully.

Nomads from the steppes of central Asia impacted on the civilized world under different names and guises for the next 2,000 years. The horse was not simply the key to their military capability, but central to their way of life. The steppe nomad spent his life in the saddle—it was said that the *Huns ate, drank, slept, gave judgement, and even defecated on horseback. Many of their horses were small—around 13 hands—but there is evidence, from grave burials, of 'powerful cantering animals' that were over 15 hands, and may have been the ancestors of the modern Akhal Teke horse. In modern tests Akhal Tekes covered 2,672 miles (4,299 km) in 84 days, 620 miles (998 km) of it through desert. The remarkable endurance of their steeds was at least one reason for the nomads' success. So too was their eagerness to augment and improve their own stock with captured horses. The Chinese had sent a costly expedition to Fereghana in 102 BC to obtain 'blood-sweating horses'—which seem to have been around 16 hands—and when the *Mongols took Peking in 1215 they captured most of the imperial herd, not simply depriving the Chinese of remounts but gaining the opportunity to improve their own stock. However, travellers noted that the Mongol pony was more robust than western horses: it could live out in all weathers, subsist solely by grazing, and dig for grass under the snow.

Such was the steppe horseman's mastery of his steed that the *stirrup meant far less to him than it did to the heavier, often armoured horsemen of the West. Yet the horse was as essential to occidental as to oriental society. In her ground-breaking work on the medieval warhorse, Ann Hyland notes the importance of 'destriers [warhorses], coursers, rounceys, palfrey and packhorses'. She has also demon-

strated that the *knight did not ride into battle on the ancestor of the modern heavy horse, but on something closer to the modern hunter: in experiments Norman horseshoes fitted an Arab of 15.1 hands, and the dimensions of horse transports used in the *Crusades suggest that 'early medieval destriers were of very moderate size'. Hyland estimates 'the build as stocky, and a height range between 15 and 15.2 hands'. Officers' chargers and the troop horses ridden by NCOs and men in succeeding centuries also tended to be small. The *dragoons of Napoleon's Imperial Guard averaged 15 hands, and Comanche, the charger of Capt Myles Keogh, which survived the fight on the *Little Bighorn (where his master fell), stands preserved at the University of Kansas and is 15.2 hands. *Frederick 'the Great' liked 'big, strong and handsome' horses, and his cuirassier mounts stood at least 16 hands tall. However, attempts to mount cavalry on big horses (as much for reasons of prestige as to give a weight advantage in the shock of the charge) both increased the logistic burden and risked expensive failure in inhospitable terrain. During the Second *Boer War the British army lost 326,000 horses, partly through poor horsemastership, but partly because many unsuitable horses were sent to that trying environment. By the end of the war local Basuto ponies were recognized as much more reliable than many imported horses which swiftly lost condition on the veld. Australian remounts from New South Wales—walers—had, however, a generally good reputation.

The armies of early modern Europe had an insatiable appetite for horses, and with the expansion of armies throughout the 18th century and into the 19th this hunger grew. Most continental states established state studs—that at Le Pin in Normandy, founded by Colbert in 1665, has magnificent buildings and is known as 'the horse's Versailles'—to improve the quality of breeding and to help meet military demands. However, during major wars demand usually exceeded supply, and *Napoleon rarely had enough horses to mount all his dragoons, some of whom were forced to revert to the infantry role in consequence. During the second half of the 19th century long-distance riding became popular amongst cavalry officers as a means of judging the best breed of horse for military use, and some astonishing results were achieved, usually by Arabs. Classical *equitation also had a military connection, with many of the actions of the *haute école* originating in training designed to teach horses to kick and bite opponents. Some needed no extra bidding. Baron de Marbot's vicious mare Lisette bit a Russian officer who grabbed her bridle at *Eylau. Marbot tells us that 'she seized him by his belly, and, carrying him off with ease, she bore him out of the crush to the foot of the hillock, where, having torn out his entrails and mashed his body under her feet, she left him dying in the snow'.

When war broke out in 1914 national preferences for horses varied. British line cavalry had horses 'of hunter stamp. Height 15.2 hands.' The Germans preferred solid Hanoverians and Trakheners, and one German officer commented on the 'cat-like Arab mounts' ridden by French *hussars. *Spahis rode tough little barb stallions, which they controlled with severe bits. Russian line cavalry rode mounts of the hunter stamp, but *Cossacks had tough little ponies that must have resembled the mounts of the steppe horsemen of old. However, all sorts of horses were rapidly pressed into service. Capt Walter Bloem, a German reservist, described them: 'Sturdy cart-horses, powerful runners, light hacks from gentlemen's stables, prancing thoroughbreds, steeple-chasers, blacks, browns, chestnuts, bays, all sorts and colours'. Traditionally regiments, or squadrons within them, tried to retain steeds of uniform colours, a practice remembered by the names of two British regiments, the Royal Scots Greys and the Queen's Bays. Just as trumpeters wore distinctive uniforms, so too they rode distinctive horses, usually greys, to aid recognition. The practice continued as late as 1914, through there were absurd attempts to dye greys with Condy's fluid or coffee to make them inconspicuous.

Once again supply could not keep pace with demand—in 1917 the British army had over a million animals, mainly horses and mules, on its strength—and good-quality horses became scarcer as the war went on. The terrible winter of 1917–18 killed many horses in their often-inadequate shelter on the western front. Losses amongst the big, steady Clydesdales that drew British heavy guns were especially serious. During the war the British army lost 484,000 horses, very roughly a horse for every two men.

The growing *mechanization of armies in the inter-war years reduced, but did not end, the military use of the horse. The Germans and Russians both maintained cavalry to the end of WW II, and horses were widely used for transport: in 1944 a German infantry division in *Normandy had some 5,000 on its strength. One abiding source of regret amongst many Allied close *air support strafing the *Falaise Gap was the plight of the horses in the retreating German columns. This reinforces a wider truth. The soldier's natural regard for what the French cavalry theorist F. de Brack called 'his legs, his safety, his honour, and his reward' has sharpened the pangs of war by putting another comrade at risk. Men who could cope with man's inhumanity to man often found man's inhumanity to animals too much to bear. One WW I British trooper called them 'Innocent victims of man-made madness. They broke your heart, especially when you passed the injured ones, left to die, in agony and screaming with pain and terror.' He lost his own horse at Néry on 1 September 1914, and his words underline a grief that wells up across the centuries. 'She was called Daisy. She was a lovely, docile, intelligent girl . . . I suppose she'd either been blown to bits or ended up as someone else's mount in another regiment.'

Some horses have left an enduring mark. Napoleon had a string of little Arabs, and his favourite, Marengo, was named after his 1800 victory. *Wellington had Copenhagen, captured from the Danes, who nearly brained his master with a well-aimed kick after a long and trying day at *Waterloo. *Lee on Traveller was a familiar sight to the Army of Northern Virginia. *Alexander 'the Great' loved his favourite charger Bucephalus such that after his death at the *Hydaspes, he was commemorated by the founding of the town of Bucephela (modern Jhelum in Pakistan).   JRHW/RH

Holmes, Richard, *Riding the Retreat* (London, 1995).

Hyland, Ann, *The Medieval Warhorse* (Stroud, 1996).

hospitals, military Military hospitals, like their civilian counterparts, are institutions comprising organized medical and nursing staff. They provide a range of services, now including surgery and intensive care. Many military hospitals are mobile (field hospitals) or semi-permanent (general hospitals), with an emphasis on the treatment of mass, critical casualties, and include the provision of *triage rather than an accident and emergency department. Often they exclude provision for maternity and childcare.

The origins of the modern hospital lie as far back as 400 BC when the temples of Greece were used as refuges for the ill, the injured, and the infirm. The *Roman army had hospitals in its frontier forts and along major routes. They were well designed, some with an airy entrance hall which served as a casualty clearing station, and wards consisting of small cubicles arranged off a central corridor. The *Byzantine army also had a sophisticated medical system, and even established hospitals for crippled soldiers or men with long-term medical conditions. In the West, monastic orders set up their own hospitals, hospices, and schools, and during the *Crusades the Knights Hospitallers—the Sovereign Military Order of the Hospital of St John of Jerusalem, of Rhodes, and of Malta—had brothers who fought as well as cured, and built castles and hospitals across Outremer.

The structure of military hospitals evolved into recognizable form in the 17th century. Renaissance armies had provided surgeons and assistants for units in the field, and treated the wounded in temporary field hospitals (the first tier) from which they were often simply discharged to the care of their friends and relatives. However, permanent military hospitals (the second tier) were gradually established across Europe: by 1674 France had them in Arras, Dunkirk, Calais, and Perpignan, and newly designed fortresses routinely included hospital space. However, poor standards of cleanliness, medical ignorance, and the slovenly habits of some staff combined to make hospitals dangerous places. Disease, for centuries a far greater *casualty-producer than steel or lead, swept through them. Even well-ordered medical arrangements, like those in the French army under Napoleon, collapsed under the sudden impact of major battle. At *Borodino in 1812 many of the wounded were packed into improvised hospitals, like that in the monastery at Kolotskoi, of which a commissariat official wrote: 'I had neither medical orderlies nor stretchers. Not only was the hospital full of corpses, but so were the streets and a number of the houses ... On my own I took away 128, which were serving as pillows to the sick and were several days old.' There was a growing recognition that hospitals were entitled to protection, and in 1747 *Frederick 'the Great' urged his generals to have 'a paternal care' for their own wounded, and 'do not be inhumane to those of the enemy'.

The third tier of hospitals—institutions concerned with the disabled and long-term sick—crystallized at much the same time. In 1603 the French introduced a system for the care of disabled soldiers, and this evolved, in 1676, into the Hotel des *Invalides in Paris, which could house up to 3,000 sick and disabled. Hospitals for disabled soldiers were built at Chelsea in England and Kilmainham in Ireland, with a hospital for sailors at Greenwich on the Thames.

The plight of British wounded in the hospital at Scutari during the *Crimean war, tellingly reported on by William Howard Russell, encouraged the government to send out Florence *Nightingale and her party of trained *nurses. She is often credited with pioneering military nursing, but in fact the Russians already had their own military nurses and, under their surgeon-general, Nikolai Ivanovich Pirogov, had established a chain of evacuation linking battlefield dressing stations with hospitals in safe areas. Initial battlefield treatment was confined to inspection, prioritizing according to the nature of the wound, and transferring the casualty to hospital. Pirogov's concept of prioritization and 'dispersion of casualties', or 'patch and dispatch', remains at the core of modern military medicine.

Nevertheless, the dreadful example of the Crimea was important. It generated reforms in Britain, where it led to the establishment of a corps of hospital orderlies. It also inspired the US Sanitary Commission, which inspected Union hospitals, lobbied for improvements and offered direct assistance to the wounded and their families during the *American civil war. The Commission's history concluded that 'a certain inflexible military routine' obstructed 'that zeal and enthusiasm for the welfare of the soldier' which characterized the people of a democratic state. The small size of the US regular army and its limited experience of large-scale operations meant that there were no general hospitals, and the largest post hospital, at Fort Leavenworth in Kansas, had only 41 beds. During the war, thanks largely to the efforts of Dr Jonathan Letterman, surgeon-general of the Army of the Potomac, front-line aid stations passed wounded back to mobile surgical field hospitals, whence they were evacuated by *ambulance, train, or hospital ship to general hospitals. There were 204 general hospitals in 1865, with a total capacity of 136,894 beds.

From the second half of the 19th century both hospital numbers and recovery rates rose. The introduction of anaesthetics and aseptic surgical practices helped increase survival, as did the development in 1890 of an anti-tetanus serum by a German medical officer, Emil von Behring. During the *Franco-Prussian war the Germans, whose lead over their opponents in medical matters matched their wider tactical and strategic superiority, placed particular emphasis on prompt life-saving treatment followed by eventual evacuation by railway to general hospitals in Germany. The British copied the system, using a system of field hospitals, 'stationary' hospitals, and general hospitals in the Second *Boer War. In WW I most combatants capitalized on the growing corpus of evidence to use an evacuation chain based—though national practices and terminology varied—on the regimental aid post, the advanced dressing station, the casualty clearing station (where surgery was routinely performed) to field hospital, and thence to the general hospital. The campaigns of WW II, sometimes fought at high tempo and in difficult terrain, encouraged the establishment of more easily transportable clearing stations, augmented by motorized surgical teams. Although the safety of hospitals was theoretically ensured by international agreement, they were bombed or shelled by accident from time to time and were occasionally subject to deliberate attack: there was a disgraceful example of this at Singapore in 1942 (see MALAYA AND SINGAPORE CAMPAIGNS).

Since 1945 the delay between the time of injury and the receipt of medical treatment has been reduced still further. *Air transport for wounded was routinely used by the end of WW II, and to an even greater extent in the *Korean war. The advent of the helicopter, with its ability to compress the chain of evacuation, helped get wounded in wars like *Vietnam and the *Falklands to a surgical facility more rapidly, often with the 'golden hour' after wounding. The improvements in military medicine from the mid-19th century were accompanied by the growth of uniformed, formally militarized medical and nursing corps and the building of military hospitals. This process may have begun to reverse. While there are now parts of the world in which military hospitals remain distinct from their civilian counterparts, and often enjoy better funding, there are signs that elsewhere the logic of air transport and rapid evacuation is encouraging governments to combine military and civilian general hospitals to reduce costs. Field hospitals will remain important, and increasing western concern for casualty limitation is likely to focus attention on their ability to receive wounded, often by helicopter, administer life-saving treatment, including surgery if required, and then stabilize the casualty for his journey, usually by air, to a general hospital at home. PMacD/RH

Hotchkiss *Machine gun with distinctive rigid strip ammunition feed invented by Benjamin Hotchkiss (1826–85) and used by the French, British, and US Armies during and after WW I.

housecarls (Old Norse: *húskarlar*). The Dane Knut Svensson ('King Canute') took the English throne in 1016 following the death of his rival Edmund 'Ironside', bringing in the élite of his own Viking troops for his personal protection and as a supplement to the English *fyrd. These warriors, known as 'housecarls', were heavy infantry armed in the Danish fashion with long, broad-bladed axes requiring the use of both hands to swing them effectively. Since this meant that they could not hold a shield, the housecarls were equipped with stout mail coats and helmets.

Romantic notions surrounded their closed warrior society in later tradition, although these are founded more in fantasy than fact. The housecarls were neither true *mercenaries nor *feudal vassals, but stipendiary troops fulfilling their military obligations in return for a fixed wage. Subsequent English kings found it useful to retain a similar body of men, and they are clearly depicted on the *Bayeux Tapestry*, illustrating the invasion of 1066, where they are shown in the English shield-wall in full mail *armour and with their *shields slung over their backs.   SJP

Abels, R, *Lordship and Military Obligation in Anglo-Saxon England* (London, 1988).

Howard, Sir Michael Eliot (b. 1922). Educated at Wellington and Oxford, Howard served in the Coldstream Guards in 1942–5, winning a MC in Italy. He held a series of appointments at King's College, London, and was Professor of War Studies 1963–8. He returned to Oxford, first as a fellow of All Souls, then Chichele Professor of the History of War, and finally Regius Professor of Modern History. In 1989–92 he held the chair of military and naval history at Yale.

His publications include *The Franco-Prussian War* (1961), *The Theory and Practice of War* (1965), *War in European History* (1976), *War and the Liberal Conscience* (1978), and he edited, with Peter Paret, the definitive translation of *On War* (1976) by *Clausewitz. Much of his time has been taken up with official history, including volumes on grand strategy and deception. Howard has done more than any other scholar of his generation to make military history and war studies respectable subjects for academic study in Britain, and he remains a highly regarded commentator on strategic issues.   RH

---

howitzer Developed as a cross between a mortar and a gun, the howitzer had qualities of both which fitted it for use during sieges and other work where the large calibre of the mortar and the manoeuvrability of the gun were needed. Howitzers probably originated in the *Hussite wars but were probably developed in Europe in the mid-17th century, the word entering English usage in 1695 from the Dutch *houwitser*, itself derived from the German *haubitze* meaning a catapult-like siege engine. *Marlborough is recorded as having howitzers among his artillery train in 1704, each needing eight horses to draw it, as compared to his 6-pounder guns, which required thirteen horses each; thus the British or Dutch howitzer of 1704 was smaller than the contemporary 6-pounder gun. It would have had a shorter barrel and a larger bore, probably of 8 or 10 inches (20.3 or 25.4 cm) diameter, and been used to lob explosive shells into besieged towns.

During the 18th century, the science of artillery developed rapidly, largely as a result of the reforms and innovations of the French general *Gribeauval, and howitzers were produced in a variety of calibres and in both brass and iron. Prussia adopted 10- and 18-pounder howitzers for its artillery in 1743 and 1744 and within two decades each Prussian infantry battalion had a 7-pounder howitzer attached to it. Such 'battalion guns' served as a versatile and quickly manoeuvrable means of laying down curtains of bursting shells either over relatively distant targets or beyond obstacles. In siege work, while standard heavy guns would pound holes in fortifications and static heavy *mortars lobbed exploding shells into the centre of towns or fortresses, the lighter and more versatile howitzers could be moved to engage likely targets as they presented themselves, such as groups of defenders attempting to repair masonry breaches. Howitzers were also used to provide covering fire during infantry assaults since they could be deployed rapidly, move up quickly behind the advancing assault troops, and fire safely and effectively over their heads. Light howitzers, around 5½ inches in calibre, were allocated as part of the *matériel* deployed by the units of *horse artillery which European nations established towards the end of the 18th century. This use magnified the manoeuvrability of the howitzer as a weapon against massed enemy formations and, until the advent of the machine gun, the light horse artillery howitzer, firing case, grapeshot, or bursting shells, could be deployed with much the same effect. At the second siege of Badajoz in Spain in 1812 three different sizes of howitzer were deployed: a 5.5 inch howitzer engaged a bastion with *ricochet fire, three 24-pounder howitzers bombarded the right face of the lunette, three more 24-pounder howitzers enfiladed the ditch in front of the principal breach in the wall and a battery of 12-pounder howitzers provided covering fire during the assault. Combinations of guns and howitzers continued to be used by the British artillery for siege work during the *Indian Mutiny. Howitzers in 12-pounder calibre, but weighing as little as 196 pounds, were issued to Indian mountain artillery units and transported, disassembled, by mule for use against entrenched tribesmen in the hills and mountains of India. The use of howitzers in the traditional way was continued by other European nations in the 19th century, by the French in their attack on *Antwerp in 1832 and by the Russians in their assault on Plevna in 1877. At Plevna the Russians' use of howitzers firing over the heads of their assault troops negated the *Turks superior infantry firepower—provided by

*Winchester rifles—by forcing the defenders to take cover against the bursting shells.

Howitzers of colossal size and range were used in WW I, Krupp's 'Big Bertha'—a mobile howitzer firing 17 inch (43.2 cm) calibre shells weighing almost a ton from a distance of 9 miles (14.5 km)—disposing very rapidly of the supposedly impregnable Belgian steel-clad forts defending *Liège. Britain relied largely on 12 inch howitzers, sometimes mounted on railways, as its principal heavy howitzer of the war but the 6 inch field howitzer was more versatile and widely used for pre-assault *barrages on the western front. Post–1918 howitzer development has taken the form of experiments with gun-howitzers, guns which fire large projectiles with high velocity and which can achieve a high parabolic trajectory; such weapons are now increasingly *self-propelled on tracked vehicles.   SCW

Hughes, Maj Gen Basil P., *British Smooth-Bore Artillery* (London, 1969).

Reid, William, *The Lore of Arms* (London, 1976).

Huguenots were French Protestants, the term possibly deriving from mispronunciation of the Swiss-German *Eidgenosse*, meaning sworn companion or confederate. They were at the centre of political and religious disputes in France in the 16th and 17th centuries. Under Henri II (1547–59) they formed a powerful group which included the king of Navarre and Gaspard de Coligny, Admiral of France, and was opposed by the Catholic party led by the Guise family. When Charles IX succeeded to the throne the Queen Mother Catherine de Medici first encouraged the Huguenots, to balance the power of the Guises. Then, fearing Coligny's influence on her son, she allied herself with the Guises and supported the Massacre of St Bartholomew (August 1572) in which thousands of Huguenots perished.

The massacre initiated the *French wars of religion, although the issues were more complex than a simple religious dispute. The weakening of royal authority after the death of Henri II; political, personal, and religious rivalry among a nobility anxious to profit from the crown's decline; and Spanish pressure on behalf of the Catholic party all helped prolong and intensify the dispute. After Huguenot victories at Arques (1589) and Ivry (1590) the Huguenot leader *Henri IV of Navarre became king of France in 1598. Although he converted to Catholicism, the religion of the majority of his subjects, he did not forget the Huguenots. In 1598 the Edict of Nantes granted them equality before the law and freedom of worship in specified strongholds, Protestant islands in a Catholic sea.

This independence was uncomfortable for a monarchy bent on increasing central control, but Louis XIII's chief minister Cardinal *Richelieu would probably have tolerated it had the Huguenots not forced the issue. In May 1625 the citizens of *La Rochelle rose in rebellion, hoping that Huguenots elsewhere would join them. The town was taken

in 1629 after a prolonged siege, and the Edict of Ales revoked the military clauses of the Edict of Nantes but confirmed its religious concessions.

*Louis XIV was less tolerant. Restrictions were imposed on their weddings and funerals, and Huguenots were bribed to convert to Catholicism. Marshal *Turenne, one of the most prominent, changed his faith in 1668. Pressure on the Huguenots mounted, and in 1685 Louis removed their religious liberties altogether by revoking the Edict of Nantes. The Duc de Saint-Simon in his Diaries declared that this, 'without the least pretext or any necessity, depopulated a quarter of the kingdom, ruined its commerce and weakened it in all parts'. Attempts at forcible conversion involved the quartering of troops—often *dragoons, hence *dragonnades*—on Huguenot households. Repression inspired revolts, like risings in the Cevennes in 1689 and 1692 and the Camisards war of 1702. Persecution included the execution of Huguenot ministers, the dispatch of laymen to the galleys, and the desecration of the dead. Huguenots were only granted freedom of worship in 1802.

The Revocation of the Edict of Nantes and the persecution which followed it encouraged perhaps 400,000 Huguenots to emigrate to Britain, Prussia, the Netherlands, and North America. They spanned the full spectrum of society, and they and their descendants made their mark on many professions: David Garrick the actor, the textile manufacture Samuel Courtauld, and the silversmith Paul de Lamerie were all of Huguenot descent.

They showed a particular aptitude for soldiering, and many of the 600 Huguenot officers who fled abroad resumed their old profession. The British army was full of Huguenots. The Duke of Schomberg, commander in Ireland for *William of Orange and killed on the *Boyne, had been a marshal of France. Other prominent Huguenots included Henri de Massue de Ruvigny, Earl of Galway, defeated commander at *Almanza; Louis Dejean, who commanded a regiment at *Culloden; and FM Jean Louis, Lord Ligonier, C-in-C of the army 1757–66. The martial tradition proved durable. Maj P. A. Charrier, commanding 2nd Royal Munster Fusiliers in August 1914, regarded the war as an excellent opportunity to get to grips with France's ancient foe, and was killed fighting a spirited rearguard action that month.

Huguenots were well represented in the Prussian army of *Frederick 'the Great'—they included the overbearing Gen de la Motte Fouqué as well as Lt Gens Hautcharmoy and Pennavaire—and their influence persisted. In 1870–1 Col von Verdy du Vernois was responsible for Moltke the Elder's *intelligence: a Frenchman described him as 'revenge for the *dragonnades*'. Huguenots appeared in several other European armies and in that of the USA. Their most recent distinguished representative was Gen Sir Peter de la Cour de la Billière, commander of British forces in the *Gulf.

                                                             RH

---

humour and the military Humour is used both within and about armed forces. Internal uses of humour range from the formal, like the revues and pantomimes staged behind the lines of the western front in WW I and the WW II 'concert parties' of servicemen with musical or thespian leanings depicted in the BBC television comedy series *It Ain't Half Hot Mum*, to the informal web of humour which permeates much of military life. Sometimes it lends spice to criticism. Many an officer cadet at Sandhurst has been told that he is 'as much use as an ashtray on a motorbike'. Sometimes it forms part of a language (see SLANG) designed to separate insiders from outsiders, in which aphorisms that were once (at least a little) humorous have simply become figures of speech. Thus: 'Jimmy had drunk so much that he was up and down like a whore's drawers all night', 'I've been out here since the Dead Sea first reported sick', or 'I've been flying since Pontius was a student pilot'. It sometimes goes much further, like the *brimades*, the coarse practical jokes used at the military *academy at Saint-Cyr: a favourite was drilling a hole in the victim's chamber pot. Such 'humour' has frequently been taken so far that its butts would identify it as nothing short of bullying. As an officer cadet, *Montgomery thought it amusing to set a fellow cadet on fire.

Dismissive humour is used to deal with unpopular groups, like the REMFs (Rear Echelon Mother Fuckers) in Vietnam, or individuals, like the testy WW I general *Allenby. He was nicknamed 'The Bull', and when he left his headquarters his helpful staff would signal in Morse code BBL, for 'Bloody Bull Loose' to warn units that might be visited. During the *Italian campaign of 1859 the French *intendant-général*, who seemed only able to supply ground maize to the troops, was christened duke of Polenta by the disgruntled soldiery as a play on *MacMahon's title duke of Magenta. The latter, not the brightest of officers, was himself known, in an untranslatable pun, as *mac-bête*. There are simple plays on words, as in 'duty burglar' for 'duty bugler', 'company ordures' for 'company orders', and 'camp comedian' for 'camp commandant'.

Humour often takes the form of avoidance joking, where combatants, faced with laughing or crying, try to laugh. The WW I *war correspondent Philip Gibbs thought that the more dreadful the situation, the more likely soldiers were to shout with laughter. 'The war-time soul', he wrote, 'roared with mirth at the sight of all that dignity and elegance despoiled.' One soldier complained that the severance of an arm protruding from the trench had left him nothing to hang his equipment on, and another observed that the accidental shelling of the regimental aid post during morning sick parade (killing the doctor and many of his patients) had done wonders for fitness as nobody subsequently reported sick. A WW II British soldier air-struck by friendly forces in Burma asked whether the Japanese had been lent the RAF 'to make it fairer?' An American soldier who had lost a foot in Vietnam quipped that he was actually a general, tasked with inspecting the hospital, who had blown his foot off as a convincing disguise.

This sort of humour rarely travelled. The WW I cartoonist Bruce Bairnsfather depicted his two characters, the gloomy and moustachioed Old Bill and the young and innocent Young Bill, contemplating a ragged hole in a ruined house. 'What made that 'ole?' asked the youngster nervously. 'Mice,' retorted Old Bill. When the cartoon was reproduced in a German military pamphlet which sought to explain British humour, its editor felt constrained to add: 'It was not mice. It was a shell.' In WW II the American cartoonist Bill Mauldin served as NCO in 45th Infantry Division. He described his two characters: 'Joe is in his early twenties and Willie in his early thirties—pretty average age for the infantry.' They point up many of the eternal truths of combat. An edgy Willie, unhappy (as soldiers often are) about facing air attack aboard ship, suggests to the crew: 'You guys oughta carry a little dirt to dig holes in.' The pair are in a trench in the rainy darkness, with Joe playing his harmonica. 'Th' krauts ain't following ya so good on "Lili Marlene" tonight, Joe,' says Willie. 'Ya think maybe something happened to their tenor?' Willie, bearded and filthy, confronts the company medic, who proffers him a medal. 'Just gimme a coupla aspirin,' he retorts. 'I already got a Purple Heart.'

The military's formalism and self-regard has often made it the butt of civilian humour. William Hogarth's *March to Finchley* shows the Guards marching out to confront the Jacobites in 1745, struggling with little success against the lure of women and drink, and Gillray and Rowlandson, painting a little later, focus on pompous militia officers, waistcoats and breeches bulging, leading ill-assorted yokels to the assault of the local dunghill. After the Allied occupation of Paris in 1815, French cartoonists lampooned the alleged indecency of Highland dress, showing French ladies swooning as kilted Scots stoop to ground their muskets. In Britain, once the French invasion scare of the 1860s had ceased to be a real concern, cartoonists had fiercely bewhiskered rifle volunteers pursued by urchins offering to 'Wipe the blood off your sword, general?' In 1865 *Fliegende Blatter* mocked military education. 'I want a globe,' demands a hussar officer. 'Terrestrial or celestial?' enquires the shopkeeper. 'Oh, no!' responds the officer. 'Don't you have any globes of Prussia?' A generation later, German cartoonists ridiculed the Reich's obsession with uniforms. In 1899 *Ulk* depicted an elderly gentleman in cape and wide-brimmed hat on a street where everyone—from schoolchildren to cab drivers and passers-by—is in uniform. 'A civilian! A civilian!' they cry.

Authors have trodden the same path. A Dorset *yeoman in Thomas Hardy's *The Trumpet Major* grows increasingly confused as he discusses whether he would use sword or pistol against an invading Frenchman. *Hašek's *Good Soldier Schweik* mercilessly satirized the Austro-Hungarian Army, and in Joseph Heller's *Catch 22* we have the drill-obsessed Lt Scheisskopf. Film and television has continued the process, from Phil Silvers's portrayal of the archetypal military fixer (few *QM stores are without one) in *Sergeant Bilko*, through the blimpish (a word itself deriving from David Low's cartoon character Col Blimp) Capt Mainwaring in *Dad's Army*, to Gen Melchett, Capt Blackadder, and Pte Baldrick in *Blackadder Goes Forth*. Clips from the latter are widely used to enliven lectures in the British army, and bases in the *Gulf were named after its characters. The use of humour to highlight political concerns found its clearest expression in the *film *M*A*S*H*. Made in 1969, its portrayal of the *Korean war was a thinly disguised reference to the contemporaneous conflict in *Vietnam.   JR-W/RH

Hundred Days, the (1815). Declared an outlaw by the Allies on his escape from Elba in March 1815 *Napoleon decided to take the offensive against the forces massing against him. The two nearest enemy forces were the Anglo-Dutch-German army under *Wellington and the Prussians under *Blücher, and he aimed to destroy them in detail before they could unite their forces.

Napoleon crossed the frontier into Belgium in the early hours of 15 June, surprising the Prussians and British, whose forces were still dispersed; an alarming gap threatened to open up between Wellington and Blücher. Napoleon divided his Army of the North in a right and a left wing under *Ney and *Grouchy, maintaining the reserve under his own command. After taking Charleroi, he sent Grouchy towards the Prussians at Fleurus, while Ney headed up the Brussels road.

On 16 June Napoleon joined Grouchy and attacked Blücher at Ligny. The Prussians fought stubbornly, but were defeated. But the battle was not a knockout blow and the *pursuit under the command of Grouchy was dilatory. They retreated to Wavre, from where on 18 June they were able to link up with Wellington at *Waterloo, despite Grouchy's efforts to interfere.

Ney's advance on 15 June was halted by a small force under the Prince of Orange at the key crossroads of Quatre Bras. Wellington rushed forces to the battlefield, and Ney's decision to delay attacking until the afternoon of 16 June bought the 'Iron Duke' more time. By the early evening Wellington had sufficient forces to drive back the French. Thanks to confused and incompetent command, D'Erlon's corps, which might have proved decisive at either Quatre Bras or Ligny, spent the day marching back and forth between the two battles without intervening in either. Wellington fell back on Waterloo, where on 18 June he met Napoleon in the climactic battle of the campaign.

Napoleon delegated command of his attack to Ney, and did not begin the battle until the ground had dried sufficiently to allow him to move his 12-pounders into a great battery facing Wellington's centre. He then allowed too many troops to get sucked into the fight for Hougoumont, on Wellington's centre right, and what could have been decisive attacks up the Brussels road were poorly co-ordinated. Grouchy was certainly not in his master's mind, and failed to prevent the Prussians from appearing in the afternoon. The battle was undeniably a close-run thing, but Wellington's well-judged defensive skill and the timely arrival of the Prussians proved too much for an emperor who was visibly past his best. After the Guard's last attack had failed the French army broke, and the Prussian cavalry was unleashed in pursuit. Napoleon's spell was broken, and he was again exiled, this time to St Helena.

Napoleon's strategy for the campaign was good in military terms (if poorly executed) but divorced from political reality; even victory at Waterloo would have probably only delayed his defeat at the hands of the Allies. Wellington was distinctly off-form at the beginning of the campaign. Recent suggestions by Peter Hofschroder that Wellington behaved in a devious way towards his allies notwithstanding, after a shaky start, the Anglo-Dutch and Prussian armies co-operated effectively to defeat the 'Corsican Ogre'.   GDS

Chandler, David, *The Campaigns of Napoleon* (London, 1966).
Hamilton-Williams, David, *Waterloo New Perspectives* (London, 1993).
Hofschroder, Peter, *1815 the Waterloo Campaign* (London, 1998).

Hundred Years War This is the term coined in France in the early 1860s to describe the wars between England and France from 1337 to 1453. In reality, there was not a constant state of warfare. Conflict was punctuated by several truces and by full peace between 1360 and 1369. Even in such periods there existed a type of 'cold war' between England and France, and their hostilities spilled over into conflicts waged within other lands, the best example, perhaps, being the civil war in Spain during the 1360-9 peace.

England and France had been at war on several occasions before 1337, most recently in 1294-7 and 1324-7, over the extent and conditions of tenure of the lands which the English kings held (or claimed) in France. By the early 13th century, Normandy, Maine, Anjou, and Poitou had been lost and only the duchy of Aquitaine remained in English control. The most important part of Aquitaine, especially because of the wine trade, was Gascony, whose capital was Bordeaux. At the Treaty of Paris in 1259 Henry III (1216-70) accepted that he held Aquitaine as a fief of the French crown and owed liege homage. This gave the French king the opportunity to intervene in the king/duke's lands, and the right to confiscate the duchy: this had led to the outbreak of war in 1294 and 1324.

Relations were already stormy, therefore, at the accession of *Edward III in 1327. In the very next year, Charles IV of France (1322-8) died without a direct male heir. The French crown passed to Philip VI (of Valois, 1328-50) as the nearest heir through the male line, but Edward also had a claim as

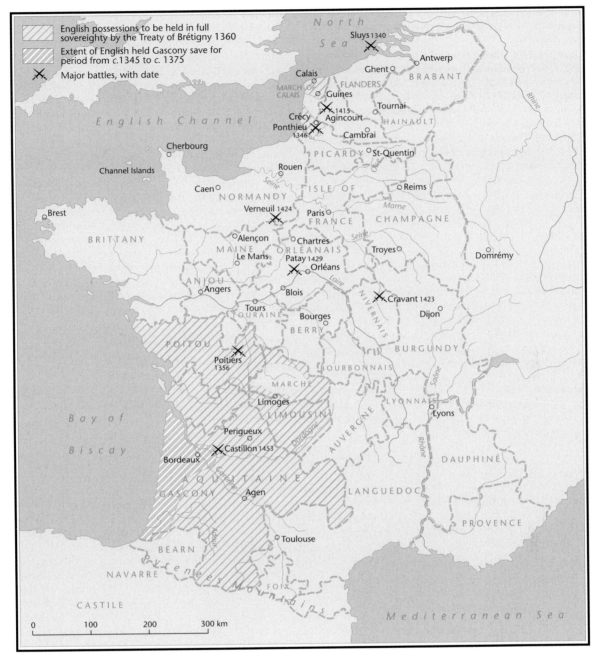

The legend reads:

- English possessions to be held in full sovereignty by the Treaty of Brétigny 1360
- Extent of English held Gascony save for period from c.1345 to c. 1375
- ✕ Major battles, with date

The **Hundred Years' War**.

the closest relative through the female line, being the son of Charles's sister, Isabella. Threats of the confiscation of his duchy of Aquitaine combined with a weak position at home forced Edward to pay homage to Philip in 1329, thereby effectively recognizing him as king of France. But the problems inherent in the tenure of part of France by the English king smouldered on, until Philip confiscated the duchy in 1337 and war began again. After some hesitation, Edward finally declared himself king of France in January 1340, and although he dropped the title between 1360 and 1369, as did *Henry V between 1420 and 1422, English kings otherwise all called themselves kings of France until 1801–2. Between

1337 and 1453 there were intensive periods of warfare over the claim to the French throne and over pre-existing territorial issues.

In the early stages of the Hundred Years War England and France largely fought each other by exploiting their alliances with other powers, alliances which they had built up during the 1330s as the likelihood of war mounted. The first campaign of Edward III is a good illustration of this. In 1338 he established a base at Antwerp, the capital of his ally the Duke of Brabant, and negotiated an alliance with the Holy Roman Emperor, Louis of Bavaria, which made him the imperial vicar general in Germany and France. The first attack on France, launched in September 1339, was thus in the Cambrésis, that part of France which lay within the boundary of the Holy Roman Empire. At Ghent in January 1340 Edward declared himself king of France in order to be able to exploit the military assistance of the Flemish townsmen who had rebelled against their pro-Valois count. The second campaign (July–September 1340) was thus against Tournai, a town in northern France which was claimed by the Flemish. For their part, the French conducted a series of raids on the south coast in 1338–9, but the threat to England and the Channel was reduced by the English naval victory at Sluys on 24 June 1340. The matter of Scotland also loomed large. English intervention there in the 1290s had prompted the Scots to ally with the French (see SCOTS WARS OF INDEPENDENCE). In the early 1330s Edward III had attempted to restore English royal authority through a puppet ruler. As a result, David II (Bruce) had fled to France in 1334, but was helped to return in 1341 so stirring up trouble for Edward on his northern frontier.

By the autumn of 1340 the wars had come to a stalemate and hence a temporary *truce: Edward was short of resources, and his allies were increasingly reluctant to assist. A new opportunity presented itself in 1341 with a succession dispute in Brittany. Edward offered military support to the de Montfort claimant, pouring in troops to the duchy and campaigning there in person in 1342. The English war effort became more adventurous in the mid-1340s. In 1345 the Duke of Lancaster expanded holdings in Aquitaine. In the following year Edward invaded Normandy, sacking Caen and marching inland almost as far as Paris. As he continued north he was intercepted by the French army at *Crécy (which lay within Ponthieu, a territory in English hands since 1279 through inheritance by Eleanor of Castile). His victory there on 26 August dealt a major blow to French *morale, as did the English victory over the Scots at Neville's Cross (17 October 1346), and the surrender of *Calais in the following year. Calais was subsequently developed as an English military and trading base, and was not retaken by the French until 1558.

The late 1340s saw a break in fighting due to the effects of the Black Death. Philip VI died in 1350 and his heir, John II (1350–64), afraid of an Anglo-Navarrese alliance and of further English successes, was more willing to negotiate than

his father had been. But papally sponsored negotiations at Guines in 1354 failed and the war began again in 1355. Edward, Prince of Wales (the *'Black Prince') carried out a raid across southern France from Bordeaux almost to the Mediterranean coast. In 1356 the Duke of Lancaster was active in Normandy and the Black Prince raided northwards. Forced to give battle at Poitiers, he won an emphatic victory, capturing John II. Edward launched what turned out to be his last major attack in 1359, probably hoping to take Rheims and to be crowned French king. But his plan failed and he agreed instead to a settlement (the Treaty of Brétigny, 8 May 1360). John was released in return for a *ransom of 3 million écus, Edward agreed to give up his claim to the French throne in return for an enlarged Aquitaine, Poitou, Ponthieu, and Calais, all to be held in full sovereignty, that is, without French overlordship or the need to pay homage. Although this settlement was confirmed by Edward and John at Calais on 24 October, the renunciation clauses (whereby Edward gave up his French title and the French surrendered sovereignty over his land acquisitions) were removed from the main treaty and were never effected: Edward was probably hoping to keep his options open.

This loophole in the treaty was exploited by Charles V in 1369, enabling him to confiscate Aquitaine and to send troops into Edward's lands. In revenge, Edward resumed his use of the title king of France. In the next period of conflict (1369–89) the English did badly, losing almost all of their recent gains. The French benefited considerably from an alliance with the Castilians which gave them supremacy at sea, enabling them to harass the English coasts. The English tried various forms of attack—raids through northern French territory, the attempted capture of bridgeheads on the French coast, alliances with the Flemish and the Duke of Brittany—but none met with marked success. The Papal Schism from 1378 to 1418 complicated the issue as the French and English supported opposing popes, and both kingdoms had minors as kings in the 1380s (Richard II, 1377–99, and Charles VI, 1380–1422).

The issues remained insoluble, and all that could be agreed in 1396 was a long truce (due to last to 1426), and the marriage of Richard II to Charles VI's daughter, Isabella. This situation was thrown into disarray by Charles's insanity which led to civil war in France between the Burgundian and Armagnac (or Orléanist factions), and by Richard II's deposition by his cousin, Henry Bolingbroke (Henry IV, 1399–1413). Although the long truce technically still applied, the French sent aid to Welsh rebels fighting against Henry, and attempted to take Calais and Gascony as well as to disrupt the Channel. By 1410, the French civil war had reached such a height that the two parties sought English assistance. This convinced the English that time was ripe for a new initiative in France. Thus in 1415 Henry V launched his first invasion which led to the capture of Harfleur and to victory at *Agincourt. Despite being severely outnumbered and weakened by an extended march, the English again defeated the French in emphatic fashion, taking Charles VI's nephew, Philip, Duke of Orléans, and many others prisoner.

Successes followed apace over the next few years not only due to the military genius of Henry V and his commanders but also due to divisions within France. Henry's second campaign, begun on 1 August 1417, was devoted to a systematic conquest of Normandy by means of sieges, the first time the English had tried this strategy on a major scale. Once Rouen fell in January 1419 after an eight-month siege, the duchy was effectively in Henry's hands and he began to march towards Paris. French attempts to unify came to an abrupt end when John, Duke of Burgundy, was murdered by the men of the Dauphin (who now headed the Armagnac group). This forced the Burgundians, who controlled the mad Charles VI, into alliance with Henry, who was now in a position to dictate terms. By the Treaty of Troyes (21 May 1420) he became heir to Charles VI (the Dauphin, later Charles VII, 1422–61, was disinherited) and Regent of France. As the treaty was not accepted outside the lands under English or Burgundian control, Henry and those acting on behalf of his son, Henry VI (1422–61, restored briefly 1470–1), who was only 9 months old at his father's death, had the difficult task of attempting to extend the area under their control. Victories in battle at Cravant (31 July 1423) and Verneuil (16 August 1424—a battle where the Dauphin's armies were boosted by Scots allies) assisted, and by 1428 the frontier had been pushed to the Loire. But the Dauphin's forces managed to raise the siege laid to Orléans, partly through the boost to morale given by *Joan of Arc. Charles's army went on to defeat the English at Patay (18 June 1429) and to recapture much of the land to the east of Paris, enabling the Dauphin to be crowned at Rheims a month later.

From then onwards the English were forced onto the defensive, even though Henry VI was crowned French king at Paris on 16 December 1431—the only king of England to realize the claim first put forward by his ancestor almost a century earlier. Their Burgundian ally defected in 1435 and in the following year Charles entered Paris. The English were left with Gascony, Calais, and Normandy, although control of upper Normandy was undermined by revolt in 1435–6 when even Harfleur was lost. Although it was subsequently recovered after a major siege (1440), Dieppe remained in French hands, causing the Channel and English coasts to be vulnerable once more. The English remained on the defensive into the 1440s, finding the war increasingly expensive to maintain. After the agreement of a truce in 1444 and the marriage of Henry VI to Margaret of Anjou, English defences in Normandy were scaled down, leaving them as easy pickings for Charles when he invaded the duchy with the assistance of the Duke of Brittany in 1449. What was left of English Normandy fell within a year, Gascony following suit in 1451. A rebellion against the French in Bordeaux in 1453 encouraged the English to send an army under the veteran Lord John Talbot, Earl of Shrewsbury, but both he and the English war effort met their death at the battle of *Castillon on 17 July.

War aims were certainly not consistent over the whole of the Hundred Years War: the claim to the throne was less significant after 1360 until it was given a new emphasis by the Treaty of Troyes. Strategy also varied. Generally speaking, the 14th century saw the dominance of the *chevauchée. This was a large-scale raid conducted into French territory, aimed at lowering morale, creating economic havoc, and collecting as much booty and prisoners as possible. This type of action was popular among English troops because of the rich pickings, and had a political significance in that it called into question the Valois's capacity to defend their lands and people. But it was of only temporary benefit to the English cause as a whole. Only by systematic conquest could the English translate their claims to territory, sovereignty, and the French crown into reality. Under Henry V and Henry VI, therefore, the predominant form of action was the siege. By this time too, of course, artillery was much more extensively used as both an offensive and defensive weapon in siege actions. But the 14th century did see sieges, the most obvious being that of *Calais, and there were chevauchée-style actions in the 15th century, such as that conducted by John, Earl of Somerset, into Brittany and Anjou in 1443. In both centuries there were many smaller skirmishes, raids and patrols, and the *fortification and garrisoning of strongholds were important for both sides. The French found it very difficult to penetrate far into English Gascony because its frontier was well protected by defensive structures. Because the English were waging a war overseas, naval activity was very significant, for the carrying of troops, for the patrolling of the Channel and trade routes to Gascony, and for actions at sea.

Both on land and sea full battles were few and far between, but the war will always be remembered for the three great English victories at Crécy, Poitiers, and Agincourt. All were fought in similar fashion, with the English dismounted and relying heavily on the withering effects of arrow fire to undermine the French charge. On all three occasions the English commander deployed his troops across a relatively narrow front. This created a funnel effect, limiting French freedom of action (all the more significant given that the French outnumbered the English threefold or more), making the arrow fire more telling in its impact, and leading to massive fatalities and captures on the French side. As the English had to send armies across the sea, they were inevitably small. Those of the 15th century, for instance, were rarely above 2,500 men (although troops were sent in almost every year from 1415 to 1450) and the chevauchées by the Black Prince of 1355 and 1356 were conducted with about the same number of English soldiers, although boosted by Gascons. Edward III probably had about 7,000 men at the battle of Crécy, and 10,000 on his 1359 campaign. While Henry V had also set off with 12,000 in 1415, sickness and the need to defend Harfleur had led to only about half the army being present at Agincourt. Although it is unlikely that Edward III did have an army as great as 32,000 for the siege of Calais that action probably did see the largest number of English troops.

Alliances remained important throughout the war—that of the French and Scots proving particularly enduring—and had a considerable military (and in the case of the Franco-Castilian link, naval) significance. Except for the first four years of the Hundred Years War the English relied mainly on troops from their own lands and not on foreign mercenaries. Most, and after 1369 all, troops used by the English were raised by the contract system whereby captains (including peers, knights, and esquires) indented to provide a certain number of men who received royal pay for the whole of their service. Many served only for short periods, six months or so, although the need for garrisons, most notably in 15th-century Normandy, did generate a form of standing army and extended lengths of military careers. In the 14th century the ratio of men-at-arms to archers was about one to one; from the Welsh wars of Henry IV, a ratio of one to three became common, recognition not only of the tactical value of archers but also of their relative cheapness and ease of recruitment. French armies were also based upon noble companies but there was a stronger element of feudal obligation and use of urban militias. Larger armies were thereby feasible, but lacked the degree of cohesion and professionalism found in English armies. The growing use of the longbow on the English side and of the crossbow on the French side, the development of the sword, and the trend towards dismounted actions led to the increasing predominance of full plate armour. Artillery was already beginning to make its mark in the second half of the 14th century and, by the end of the war, handguns and larger pieces were common on both sides: indeed the eventual French victory was much due to their increased use of artillery as well as to the reorganization and professionalization of the army which Charles VIII had ordered in the 1440s.   AC

Allmand, Christopher, *The Hundred Years War* (Cambridge, 1988).

Curry, Anne, *The Hundred Years War* (London, 1993).

—— and Hughes, Michael (eds.), *Arms, Armies and Fortifications in the Hundred Years War* (Woodbridge, 1994).

Sumption, Jonathan, *The Hundred Years War* (London, 1990).

Huns The reputation of the Huns as a warlike people is due to perceptions of their impact upon the late Roman empire. Under their greatest leader, Attila, they threatened to create an empire in 5th-century Europe. Contemporaries wrote of them with fear and loathing, characterizing their culture as primitive, and their behaviour as bestial. This image had a lasting impact on the Western imagination. Even in the 20th century the Germans of WW I were characterized as 'The Hun' for propaganda purposes. Yet surprisingly little is known for certain about a people whose natural habitat was the Asian steppe, impacting on China, India, and Persia, and whose supremacy in Europe lasted barely a century.

Steppe nomads had always been a threat to the settled agrarian societies. The Romans had been aware of the Huns at least as early as AD 200, when the geographer Pliny describes them; but it was not until the late 4th century that they had an impact on the empire. In the early 370s, Hunnic attacks on the previously all-conquering *Goths on the Eurasian steppe led to their king, Ermaneric, committing suicide in despair. The Goths then sought refuge over the Danube within the Roman empire, but were so badly treated that they rebelled and destroyed the army sent to pacify them at *Adrianople in 378. In the years that followed, Huns were found co-operating with other barbarian armies in looting an empire riven by civil war. They also served as mercenary troops for the Emperor Theodosius in 388, before ravaging the Balkans again in the 390s. As nomadic herdsmen, accompanied by their wives and families, they moved around continually seeking the best opportunities for grazing and plunder, but probably only numbered a few thousand. In 395, larger numbers of Huns attacked Persia, impelled by the loss of their herds through drought, and then drifted westward. By *c*.404, Hunnic leaders were negotiating with Emperor Honorius in Rome, and after 409 Huns served regularly in the *Roman army. They then disappear from history until 423 when Ruga is named as their king. He ruled for some ten to fifteen years and may have been ceded lands in Pannonia (modern Hungary) where the grasslands suited a nomadic lifestyle. It is only when Attila appears on the scene that the Huns seem to become a serious threat. In 441, the Huns broke into the western Balkan provinces and took Sirmium in 442. In 447, they devastated Thrace and threatened Constantinople. Outbreaks of plague were the only things to check their progress. Yet Attila was no world ruler along the lines of the later *Mongols, he ruled a defined territory from the mouth of the Danube west to Slovakia. In 451, the Huns crossed into Italy taking Aquileia, Milan, and Pavia, but were forced north of the Alps into Gaul by a combination of plague and Roman resistance led by the *magister militum* Aetius. He offered battle on the 'Catalaunian Fields' (*Châlons), both sides relying upon German support. Aetius drew up with his Visigothic allies on his right flank, who, despite the loss of their king, overran the Ostrogoths opposing them and gained control of a strategically placed hill. Meanwhile Aetius' Romans held off fierce Hunnic attacks on their own positions. Staring defeat in the face, Attila fell back into his camp, and allegedly prepared to die on a pyre of saddles, although his men's arrows kept the pursuing Romans at bay. Unable to sustain his strategic position, Attila withdrew to Pannonia and died in 435. No successor proved capable of creating such formidable force.

As warriors, the Huns were mounted archers, but this does not mean that they were necessarily dressed in skins or lightly equipped as is so often represented. Their equipment would have been much like other steppe-dwellers of whom evidence is available. Iron *Spangenhelm* (segmented) helmets, and lamellar (scale) *armour coats, reaching to waist or knee, with tall leather boots would be standard. The *bow was composite, made of wood, bone, and sinew (in a way that anticipated fibreglass), and very powerful, though probably most effective at relatively short ranges. They may have carried the long, two-handed lance also found on the steppe, but if not then their German subject warriors certainly did and acted in concert with the horse archers. The *Roman historian Ammianus Marcellinus describes their impact in 392: 'when provoked they fight singly, but they enter battle in ordered units ... they are lightly equipped for swift movements, ... they purposely divide suddenly into scattered bands and attack, rushing about in disorder here and there dealing terrific slaughter.' Clearly it was the rapidity and unpredictability of their manoeuvres which made the Huns so feared, combined with the showers of arrows with which they wound and kill. Ammianus also points out that they were not frightened of close combat though, fighting with swords 'regardless of their own lives' and also using lassos to entangle their enemies.

Whatever their individual fighting skills, from a military point of view, the Huns' lasting impact was the introduction of steppe fighting styles to the European theatre. The German tribes with which they first came into contact had already from another steppe culture, that of the Sarmatians, learnt to fight mounted in heavy armour, carrying a long lance (*kontos*). When used in conjunction with massed infantry this was a powerful formation (see also VANDALS). The Huns' contribution to the tactical mix was the well-armoured, mobile horse archer. The Romans had encountered heavily armoured, cataphract bowmen in the armies of Sassanid Persia from the 2nd century onwards; but these were generally deployed defensively. Contact with the Huns taught eastern Romans to develop a native cavalry which was both bow-and lance-armed, mobile and aggressively inclined. Such troops were the core of the armies sent out by Justinian I under his general *Belisarius to reconquer the western empire in the mid-6th century.   MB

Ferrill, A., *The Fall of the Roman Empire: The Military Explanation* (London, 1986).

Maenchen-Helfen, Otto J., *The World of the Huns* (Berkeley, 1973).

hussars Originally Hungarian *mercenary light cavalrymen of the late 15th century, recruited and paid when needed. Their ethnic roots were probably those of the *Mongols and their culture linked them to other central European light cavalry, such as the *Cossacks. During Hungary's wars for independence from Austria in the 17th century, standing regiments of these brave and hardy light cavalrymen were formed. But after the suppression of the movements for Hungarian independence, they became refugees and offered their services to a variety of other European nations in the late 17th century.

France made the first use of hussar regiments outside Hungary, recruiting a regiment of Hungarians and Germans in 1692, and the number of hussar regiments in the French army rose and fell for the next three centuries as the exigencies of war demanded. In 1789 there were six regiments, in 1793 twelve, in 1795 fourteen. All were dressed in the 'Hungarian' fashion, with tight-fitting braided or laced jackets, slung fur-lined jackets called pelisses, tight breeches, knee boots, sabretaches and—initially—a tall round brimless cap called a mirliton, soon replaced by the more familiar round fur cap, called a busby in English. This exotic appearance was reinforced by plaited hair at the temples and moustaches and by a devil-may-care attitude summed up by the saying 'a hussar not dead at 30 is a scoundrel'. By 1815 the number of French hussar regiments had shrunk to six and, although it rose to seventeen in 1915, it was back to four in the 1980s.

Prussia, Austria, and Russia also recruited hussar regiments in the first half of the 18th century and the British army encountered them during the War of the *Austrian Succession both abroad and at home; one of the *Jacobite regiments of the 1745 rebellion was called Bagot's Hussars. Britain began transforming certain of its own light dragoon regiments into hussars in 1807. Their role remained that of reconnoitring and hit-and-run skirmishing, and their *uniforms came to resemble those worn in continental European hussar regiments. 'Scimitar' swords were adopted by French officers in Egypt in 1800–1, an affectation copied by their British peers, who also followed their lead in elaborately decorative accoutrements and came to surpass them in extravagance. Hussars became the most expensively dressed of all British cavalry, reaching a peak of magnificence by the time of the *Crimean war of 1854–6, during which two British hussar regiments, the 8th and 11th, formed part of the doomed Light Brigade.

The 11th Hussars was one of the first British cavalry regiments to be mechanized, swapping its horses for *armoured cars in 1927, and by the 1990s British hussar regiments had dwindled through reductions and amalgamations from twelve to two. Hussar regiments now drive armoured vehicles and only vestiges of their former sartorial magnificence remain, leaving just the name to evoke the wild men of the eastern European plains who once made it famous.

SCW

Hussein, Saddam (1937–). Born on 28 April 1937 in Tikrit, after a career as an assassin and party enforcer, Hussein became the vice president of Iraq following the seizure of power by the Ba'th national-socialist party in a military coup in July 1968. Nine years later, in July 1979, he forced the resignation of his benefactor, Pres Ahmad Hasan al-Bakr, and took his place. With high revenues from oil pouring in, he embarked upon an ambitious and radical modernization of Iraq with preference shown to the military, which grew to be the largest in the Middle East.

In September 1980 he launched the *Iran–Iraq war with the double intention of crippling the militant Shi'a regime of Ayatollah Khomeini and asserting leadership over the Gulf Arab states. Eight years later he was only able to end the war by using *chemical weapons, having if anything strengthened the Iranian regime, paralysed his modernization programme, and become deeply indebted to the Gulf monarchies.

Saddam turned his sights to target Kuwait, his Gulf coast neighbour, and for a year waged an escalating diplomatic campaign with threats to force the Kuwaiti monarchy to bail him out of his financial predicament. When the latter refused, he invaded on 2 August 1990, and six days later annexed the emirate and began to dismantle its financial and economic assets and remove them to Iraq.

On 17 January 1991, after six months of futile attempts to bring about Iraq's peaceful withdrawal, a US-led international coalition waged the *Gulf war on Saddam and within six weeks inflicted a crushing defeat on his army and liberated Kuwait. Since the coalition did not attempt to topple him and even refrained from supporting Shi'a and Kurdish revolts against him, Saddam managed to survive. Although his ability to do harm was greatly reduced, well-founded suspicion that he retains not only chemical and biological but also *nuclear weapons programmes mean that economic sanctions remain in effect over eight years later.   EK/HEB

Hussite wars (1419–34). There were three elements in the 14th and early 15th centuries that signalled the decline of the armoured knight and the rise of infantry: *archers using the the longbow, the *Swiss pikemen, and the Hussite *wagenburg. While the first two are well known, at least in the West, the third remains somewhat obscure.

By means of truly revolutionary tactics the vastly superior forces of the Holy Roman Empire were beaten by a gang of uncouth peasants and freemen fighting for a cause they believed to be just. These victories can be ascribed to the one-eyed visionary Jan *Zizka. In an age not known for military innovation, he introduced *armoured warfare and massive firepower onto the battlefield by combining cavalry and infantry into a flexible formation impervious to the charge of armoured knights. All the more remarkable in that most of his followers were not military or noble at all, and were largely trained from scratch at Zizka's stronghold of Tabor in southern Bohemia. With a force of around 25,000 he was able to defeat forces two or even three times his own strength. Recognizing that the highly developed

and extensively used plate *armour of his enemies would defeat the crossbow, he trained a third of his men with handguns that could penetrate steel and cause a *morale effect out of all proportion to their numbers.

Moreover, the Hussites were highly motivated, even fanatical. Their strain of militant Christian fundamentalism, derived from the teachings of Jan Hus, gave them a firm conviction in the afterlife and an insouciance about leaving this one. With their strong attachment to their native Bohemia, and an iron *discipline born of faith and strict penalties for miscreants, the approach of the Hussite warhost, accompanied by echoing, dirge-like hymns, was enough to make even the bravest Catholic knight quake in his sabatons.

Although the idea of a defensive wagon laager was not new, its use as a mobile offensive weapon was. Furthermore these were no civilian ox-carts but stoutly built and fireproofed wheeled constructions, designed solely for war. They were iron reinforced, and liberally provided with loopholes from which the twenty or so crew could keep up an accurate and devastating fire, with the added luxury of having all their ammunition carried for them. In defence they could be chained one to another for added solidity. Other wheeled devices transported larger artillery pieces of varying calibres, two of which were Hussite inventions: the *tarasnice* and *houfnice*, translated in German as *Haufnitze* or *Haubitze*, from where we get the English *howitzer.

The whole body, wagons, guns, men, and horses, was trained to operate as a unit and could rapidly adopt any desired formation to meet an attack, or act as a pile driver forward into the enemy's ranks. There was also a mounted element of crossbowmen equally adept at *reconnaissance and pursuit. The only method to defeat the Hussites was to induce them to leave the safety of their vehicles where they were no match for the overwhelming numbers of the Catholic knights, who could reputedly muster over 100,000 men for a given engagement.

The Hussites were successful at Prague in 1419, where they repelled a frontal assault on a hill outside the city. The cleverly sited Hussite artillery caught their assailants in a withering crossfire. At Kuttenburg in 1422 the German knights were balked by the wagon forts, and a wild countercharge supported by the artillery firing for all they were worth utterly destroyed the enemy. After the death of Zizka, the Hussites were again victorious at Aussig in 1426 under *Procop 'the Bald', attacking with a combination of wagons and cavalry.

The Hussites had campaigned in Hungary, Silesia, Austria, Saxony, Bavaria, Thuringia, and Franconia, in a series of *spanile jizdy* (glorious rides). In 1431 Procop is supposed to have led 55,000 men accompanied by 3,000 wagons, although it must be noted that record-keeping was something of an inexact science at this time. Controversy over Polish-Lithuanian involvement and internal dissent split the movement into rival factions and it lost its single-mindedness of purpose that had brought it so many victories. Then when Zdnek of Sternberg led an anti-Hussite crusade from 1464 to 1471, many disreputable Bohemian *mercenaries were brought in to make up for a lack of numbers, and the true Hussite army was nothing but a glorious memory.

TM

Hydaspes, battle of the (326 BC). Alexander 'the Great' 's last major battle was fought in 326 BC by the river Hydaspes (modern Jhelum) as he advanced eastwards from Taxila to invade India. King Porus, ruler of the territory between the Jhelum and Chenab, deployed his army, which included numerous elephants, to thwart Alexander's crossing of the river, which was swollen by melting snows. For once Alexander was superior in numbers and, by splitting his army, feinting upstream and downstream, and exploiting the cover of various islands, he managed to transport part of his army across the river during a tempestuous night. Porus at once sent his son to confront him but the Indian cavalry and *chariots were brushed aside and Alexander marched downstream to meet the king. Porus relied on his elephants to disrupt the Macedonian cavalry and terrify the infantry, but Alexander already had experience of dealing with them and was able to force them back into the Indian ranks. Porus' army was encircled and massacred, although Alexander's historians preferred to depict a more epic encounter with Porus holding out bravely on the royal elephant. Alexander's beloved horse Bucephalus died of wounds after the battle.

LMW

Bosworth, A. B., *Alexander and the East* (Oxford, 1996).

identification of friend or foe. See IFF.

IDF (Israeli Defence Forces). The IDF is responsible for dealing with external and internal security threats to Israel and was established on 31 May 1948, two weeks after Israel's declaration of independence. In its early days the IDF was an amalgamation of former members of the British army's Jewish Brigade, pre-Independence Jewish security forces (Hagana and Palmach), and terrorist organizations (Irgun and Leshi). It has developed into one of the world's most effective military organizations, with army, navy, and air force closely integrated. During the past 50 years the IDF has fought six major *Arab–Israeli wars against neighbouring states: War of Independence (1948–9); Sinai War (1956); Six Day War (1967); War of Attrition (1967–70); Yom Kippur War (1973); and Peace for Galilee War (1982). In addition it has waged a prolonged *counter-insurgency campaign against the *PLO and, from 1987, an internal uprising (intifada) in the occupied West Bank and Gaza Strip. Although these demands have been muted since the 1991 peace settlement, the IDF continues to operate against other Islamic terrorist organizations within Israel and southern Lebanon. In the course of its brief history the IDF has achieved stunning military victories, such as in 1956 and 1967, but has also suffered occasional reverses, as in the opening days of the 1973 Yom Kippur war. Its approach to counter-insurgency has been heavy-handed and of dubious effectiveness, particularly in southern Lebanon since 1985. As guarantor of Israel's security the IDF's actions have quite often led to vociferous international criticism.

The organization and *doctrine of the IDF are the result of political, demographic, economic, and geographic circumstances. Historically, without military allies and surrounded by stronger and often hostile Arab states, Israel relies upon large military forces to guarantee her security. A small population and weak economy mean that IDF is organized as a militia rather than as a standing army. All able-bodied Jews and Druze over the age of 18 are required to do two–three years' military service followed by one month of annual reserve training until aged 42.

The IDF is divided into administrative and territorial commands which deal with all three services: army, air force, navy. The administrative commands are responsible for planning, manpower, and *intelligence. There are four territorial battle commands: Northern (Lebanon, Syria), Central (Jordan), Southern (Egypt), and Rear (created after the 1991 *Gulf war to protect civilian centres), each of whose commanders are responsible for the conduct of military operations. Administrative, territorial commands, and the three services come under the supervision of the COS (head of the IDF), who is appointed by the cabinet on the recommendation of the Minister of Defence.

The army is the largest of the three services and bears the brunt of action in general war. It is an all-arms formation designed to conduct high-tempo mobile operations. It is divided into sixteen corps/functional commands: armour, artillery, infantry, parachute, engineers, signals, ordnance, supply, general services, women's medical, military police, education, rabbinate, judge advocate, military intelligence, and Nahal (combining military and agricultural training to defend kibbutzim). The basic unit is the Brigade, grouped together on an ad hoc basis under a Divisional (Ugdah) headquarters according to the requirements of an operation. As a civilian army *discipline is more relaxed than in other armed forces, yet the paucity of *drill has not prevented it from becoming a highly trained and effective force.

The élite of the armed services is the Israeli Air Force (IAF), one of the best and most combat-experienced *air forces in the world. Its tasks are to defend civilian centres from air and missile attack, gain time for the mobilization of IDF reservists, neutralize enemy air defences, attain air superiority, and provide combat support to the other services; it is both the sword and shield of Israel. To carry out these tasks it is equipped with a large and varied inventory of the latest aircraft and aerial weapon systems and has a large attack and transport helicopter force for mobile operations. The IAF's crucial importance means it is maintained at maximum preparedness and has first priority in selecting IDF recruits.

The navy is the smallest service and until recently was largely neglected. It has concentrated upon acquiring small torpedo and missile attack boats, but has also acquired modest numbers of landing craft for *amphibious operations and a small submarine force. Its principal role remains coastal defence and raiding operations.

The size and proficiency of the IDF is above all one of *deterrence and in line with this policy it is known that Israel possesses *nuclear weapons, although it remains a 'nuclear opaque' state, never having declared them. In the event of war numerical and economic weakness combined with long indefensible frontiers and lack of territorial depth have made it unfeasible for the IDF to adopt a defensive posture in the face of Arab military threats. The result has been an emphasis upon pre-emptive attacks to seize the initiative, in order to carry the war onto enemy territory and swiftly overwhelm them. To achieve this the IDF is organized to carry out large-scale high-tempo armoured operations under the cover of a strong airforce. In the late 1960s an overemphasis upon the tank as the decisive arm of the ground forces led to the neglect of all-arms co-operation and consequently heavy losses in the 1973 war. The obsession with the offensive to the detriment of defensive techniques was also highlighted. Although steps were taken to remedy these force imbalances after the war the task of reorganization is not complete. In recent years civilian and some military commentators have argued that changes in the threats facing Israel mean that IDF doctrine is no longer appropriate. Some argue that long-range *precision-guided munitions and air mobility will allow the IDF to wage defensive operations. In response to this strong criticism in early 1999 COS Lt Gen Shaul Mofaz presented the first serious examination of IDF doctrine in 40 years. Fifty years after its creation the IDF is embroiled in a heated debate concerning the defence of Israel in the next century.

TJB

Hertzog, Chaim, *The Arab Israeli Wars* (London, 1982).
Hogg, Ian V., *The Israeli War Machine* (London, 1983).
Luttwak, E., and Horovitz, D., *The Israeli Army* (New York, 1975).
van Creveld, Martin, *The Sword and the Olive: A Critical History of the Israeli Defence Force* (London, 1998).

IFF (identification of friend or foe). The ability to discriminate between enemy forces and allies is of utmost importance to all members of all military units, be they sea, land, or *air forces. The need to avoid *friendly fire has driven development of advanced systems to attempt to overcome the difficulties. In modern warfare, the number of systems which make it possible to ascertain the presence of troops or machinery on the battlefield do not do anything to help lift the 'fog of war'; indeed, they may increase it. Targeting information provided by these systems makes it imperative that some form of accurately discerning friend and foe alike be in place. The task is enormously difficult, and even with advanced technology, the problem is not nullified and accidental engagement of friendly forces still occurs.

The earliest means of successful IFF was visual recognition, leading to banners and the gorgeous caparisons of medieval *heraldry. The visual aspect of identification remains important, but is most prone to error. The failure to recognize a piece of equipment or group of troops as being friendly occurs throughout history. Modern instances include the destruction of large numbers of Luftwaffe aircraft by German anti-aircraft guns during BODENPLATTE in 1945, the clash between British *special forces units in the *Falklands, and several incidents of fratricide during the *Gulf war, where some 20 per cent of US fatalities came from friendly fire. The culprit in almost all these cases was visual misidentification.

IFF is not a simple task. The confusion caused by combat can impinge upon the ability to discriminate between friend and foe. The conditions of the battlefield may degrade visibility, further complicating the issue. Finally, the range over which combat takes place has increased during the course of the 20th century, making visual identification problematic. The problem first became apparent to those responsible for air defence, since the development of *radar made it possible to detect aircraft at far beyond visual range. Detection is not the same as identification, and some means of ascertaining the identity of the detected aircraft was necessary. Furthermore, being able to determine whether an aircraft was hostile while at extreme visual range or beyond would give certain tactical advantages to the pilot able to make this distinction. This led to the introduction of the first IFF system, pioneered by the RAF from around 1939. An IFF system acts as a radio transmitter and receiver. It sends out continual radio signals made up of coded pulses. A friendly IFF system will recognize these codes when it receives them and will transmit further coded pulses which identify the aircraft to the interrogating IFF set. The system is still employed, albeit in a more advanced form, in all aircraft. While it is theoretically the perfect answer to the identification of friend or foe in the air, there are difficulties. If the IFF transponder is not functioning correctly, or if it has not been set to use updated codes, it will be registered as a hostile aircraft. With the development of radar-guided missiles which can be fired at beyond visual range, the malfunctioning of an IFF system can have serious consequences, even if such system failures have proved to be rare in practice.

IFF may reduce the risks in aerial combat, but pilots have still been subjected to attack by their own side, often from misdirected anti-aircraft fire on the ground. Numerous pilots ruefully complain that naval forces have a tendency to shoot first at approaching aircraft before trying (if at all) to establish identity. While this is a little unfair, there are sufficient instances of aircraft being engaged by their own naval units. During WW I, the Royal Flying Corps was often heard to complain that it was 'believed by none and fired on by all'. The root cause of this type of problem comes down to simple recognition. The failure to recognize friendly equipment is not the preserve of surface forces. Air forces have been known to engage their own side by mistake on countless occasions. Armoured vehicles can be terribly difficult to identify from the air, and this prompted them to be painted with recognition symbols. Although this was of assistance, it was more helpful to ground troops than to air forces. The increasing speed at which aircraft have been able to attack ground targets makes it essential that some form of highly visible recognition device is employed. These have included brightly coloured fabric panels attached to the tops of armoured vehicles, along with ever-larger painted symbols. They have not proved totally effective. The use of sensor systems and long-range engagements have increased the difficulties of positive identification. Thermal imaging sensors are particular sources of this difficulty, since they tend to give an image which lacks the definition to allow accurate identification; while it is clearly possible to identify a tank, identifying the type may be much more difficult, especially if the sensor's capabilities are degraded by battlefield conditions.

Solving the problem is far from simple. In the aftermath of the Gulf war, the USA took the decision to develop a digital battlefield recognition system. The long-term solution is felt to be to provide information-technology equipment which reduces confusion and provides users with real-time information. The acquisition of such systems is likely to be costly and fraught with short-term technical difficulties. The search for foolproof identification systems will take time to resolve, even with the most advanced technology. Eliminating fratricide through misidentification is unlikely to ever occur; the difficulties of identification are another of the unpleasant factors of war which have existed from the beginning and which will remain a constant difficulty. Recognition training and sophisticated equipment can reduce the problem immensely, but they can only do so much. **DJJ**

Cordesman, Anthony H., and Wagner, Abraham R., *The Lessons of Modern War*, vol. iv. *The Gulf War* (Boulder, Colo., 1996).

illuminants Warfare is not confined to daylight. Its prosecution at night is fraught with difficulties, most not-ably the inability of participants to see either their enemies or their colleagues. Prior to the invention of night vision devices operating in spectra beyond normal sight, simple illumination by artificial light had to be employed. This method still has value, since artificial light may be used to illuminate enemy aircraft, or to ensure that the approaches to defended areas are visible at night, preventing the stealthy approach of an enemy. Primitive illuminants, usually bundles of rags or wood soaked in an inflammable liquid, were used in ancient times. By the 17th century they were known as *carcases*, and were routinely employed in sieges. At Badajoz in 1812 the French used fireballs to illuminate the breaches, and one eyewitness described 'the wounded crawling past the fireballs, many of them scorched and perfectly black'.

The most common form of illuminant is the flare. The intense light provided by these devices enables vision, but only briefly. In land operations, the flare is often employed to illuminate attacking troops, to permit their engagement by all those without night vision equipment. Prior to such devices being created, the flare, often attached to a small parachute to slow its descent, and the artillery-fired star-shell provided the only means of rapidly illuminating a wide area. Night photography by aircraft relied upon powerful flares to light the area of interest, but since the light also illuminated the aircraft to the enemy, this practice was abandoned when *infra-red devices became widely available. Trip flares, attached to low pickets, can be placed around a position or in an ambush site, and may either be fired when an enemy touches a tripwire or initiated by the defender or ambusher.

The searchlight has great utility for target illumination. This applies especially to air defence, where powerful searchlights make it possible for attacking aircraft to be illuminated for engagement by optically aimed anti-aircraft artillery. Searchlights have uses in maritime operations, particularly the detection of surfaced submarines. This technique was of great value in WW II, with devices such as the Leigh Light proving their worth on many occasions. Maritime patrol aircraft such as the British Aerospace Nimrod and Dassault Atlantique continue to employ powerful airborne searchlights for anti-submarine operations. It is also not uncommon for *helicopters used in internal security operations to be fitted with searchlights for the illumination of the ground or of individuals when operations are in progress. Such devices include the aptly named Nitesun, which can be attached to most military helicopters with little modification to the airframe.

The use of illuminants in land warfare has not been without its difficulties. Their use can provide the enemy with a suitable target to aim at, and destroys surprise. Using searchlights has proved dangerous in land operations, since although they can dazzle the enemy, they provide a perilously illuminated backdrop to the attacking troops. Searchlights have been mounted on armoured vehicles, particularly main battle tanks, but the use of such lights invites retaliation. While in defensive situations illuminants can be most valuable, in offensive situations, their use for *surveillance and target acquisition can be counterproductive. Only in maritime operations has their offensive use been truly successful, and even here this has been slightly qualified by the inescapable problem that the source of illumination becomes as visible as the target itself once it has revealed itself through the use of an illuminating device.   DJJ

---

imperial policing is a term coined in the 1930s and reflects the change from traditional methods of control for conquered lands and peoples to cheaper policies following WW I, particularly by the UK. While on the ground it included patrolling by *armoured cars, the principal innovation was the use of *air power to manage and overawe areas of the globe which had hitherto required garrisons. Imperial policing was also an important factor in the survival and development of the independent RAF, since it was used by *Trenchard as a method of demonstrating the cost-effectiveness of the air force to British imperial policy in the financially stringent inter-war years.

Air power proved to be an effective arm in imperial operations in the post-1918 era, initially because local populations had little defence against it. The British in particular were faced with a series of imperial problems and the first campaign where aircraft proved their worth was the third *Anglo-Afghan war in 1919. Aircraft bombed Kabul, Jalalabad, and Dakka and dropped leaflets designed to undermine *morale. In 1920 a rising in Somaliland led by Muhammad bin Abdulla Hassan also saw the RAF being deployed effectively. However, the most famous example of aerial imperial policing came in the ex-Ottoman empire between 1922 and 1925. A rebellion had broken out in newly formed Iraq in 1920 and the British, as the occupying power, were forced to deploy ever-increasing numbers of troops to deal with the problem. Aware of the escalating costs Chief of the Air Staff Trenchard and *Churchill (then the minister responsible) proposed a policy of 'substitution', in effect, deploying the RAF to police these troublesome regions at much lower cost than the army. The impact was considerable and costs were cut from £22.36 m in 1921–2 to £7.81 m in 1922–3. By 1927 the figure for policing the region had been cut to just £3.9 m. The RAF was also used in Transjordan (now Jordan), Aden, Palestine, and in ex-German East Africa. In areas of open country air power proved highly effective, but in urban centres it was less so for obvious reasons.

The imperial policing role was critical to the survival of the RAF in the early-to-mid-1920s as both the RN and the army were at the time advocating the reabsorption of the RAF into ground and maritime support air arms. Trenchard argued that the theory of strategic bombing and the policy of imperial policing were too important for the RAF to be dissected. To the British government of the 1920s, driven by the desire to cut costs and balance the books, the saving provided by the RAF's imperial policing rather than theories of air superiority was the critical factor in ensuring the RAF's survival as an independent arm.

Other powers also deployed air forces in imperial policing roles during this period. The French and Spanish were involved in long and drawn-out operations against Abd-el-Krim in Morocco in the Rif war (1921–6). The Spanish initially used aircraft sporadically, but when a systematic policy of bombing crops, villages, and livestock was introduced, along with the use of poison *gas, success increased dramatically. The French used aircraft more effectively when Abd al-Krim moved from Spanish to French Morocco in 1925, deploying them in concert with small mobile ground units. The USA also used air power in imperial operations between 1927 and 1933 when US troops were deployed in support of the puppet *Nicaragua government. US Marine Corps aircraft were employed in a variety of duties against the Sandinista rebels, most notably in the battle of Ocotal where dive-bombing was first used.

Although not technically imperial policing, the most extreme example of aerial activity against a non-western power came in the Italian–Abyssinian war of 1935–6. Almost 900 bombing operations were undertaken by the Regia Aeronautica, many infamously dropping poison gas bombs. Air power was as important an aid to the Italians in conquering their new empire as it was to others in maintaining theirs. It proved itself a highly effective weapon against local populations unused to aircraft, the psychological impact invariably outweighing the physical. Such operations had little impact on the metropolitan air forces, although it might be argued that the development by the British of long-range aircraft and the failure of the Germans to do so reflected the different imperatives prevailing in the two nations between the wars. It might also be argued that the USAAF's B-2 stealth bomber with a worldwide range and a technology that puts it beyond the reach of 'lesser breeds outside the law' represents the final expression of the concept of imperial policing.

Although imperial policing occupies an important position in the development of air power, as a concept it had far wider implications. In 1934 Maj Gen Sir Charles Gwynn published *Imperial Policing*, which considered the army's doctrine when it found itself 'the chief agent for maintaining law and order and for the restoration of the authority of the civil power'. He established the important principle of 'minimum force', arguing that 'the hostile forces are fellow citizens of the Empire, and that the military object is to re-establish the control of the civil power and secure its acceptance without an aftermath of bitterness'. He also argued in favour of civil supremacy and the need for civil–military co-operation, and emphasized the importance of timely action. While his principles have lasting importance, in other respects Gwynn was a creature of his times, arguing that 'machine guns can be usefully employed without any suspicion of ruthlessness'. The large paramilitary police forces raised by colonial powers not only made their own contribution to imperial policing, but, as in the case of the Indian police, extended a tradition of *gendarmerie-style policing beyond Independence.   JDB/RH

Gwynn, C. W., *Imperial Policing* (London, 1934).
Hallion, R., *Strike from the Sky* (Washington, 1989).
Omissi, D., *Air Power and Colonial Control: The RAF 1919-1939* (Manchester, 1990).

Imphal, battle of (1945). In 1944 Imphal was the capital of Manipur state, India's eastern province. A scattering of villages rather than a real town, it lies in a plain 20 miles (32 km) long by 20 broad, with hills all around. It formed the main British base in the area, held by IV Corps of Gen Slim's Fourteenth Army. The corps commander, Lt Gen Scoones, expected to be attacked, and planned to draw in his outlying troops and supply a defensive box around Imphal by air. However, the difficult country and poor communications made his task difficult. Lt Gen Mutaguchi's Japanese Fourteenth Army attacked in March 1944, sending a division against Imphal from the south while two others hooked around to cut Scoones's communications with his railhead at Dimapur. One took most of the little hill station of *Kohima, which became the scene of some of the war's fiercest fighting.

The British held Imphal, greatly assisted by command of the air and artillery superiority. Mutaguchi's logistic plan relied on captured British supplies, and when these were not forthcoming his men starved. The offensive was called off by Lt Gen Kawabe of Burma Area Army in July. The Japanese suffered 55,000 casualties at Imphal, the British 12,500. Louis Allen described the battle as 'the biggest defeat the Japanese army has sustained in its whole history', and it paved the way for Slim's successful *Mandalay/Meiktila offensive.   RH

Allen, Louis, *Burma: The Longest War 1941–1945* (London, 1984).
Evans Lt Gen Sir Geoffrey, and Brett-James, Antony, *Imphal: A Flower on Lofty Heights* (London, 1954).

INA. See INDIAN NATIONAL ARMY.

Inchon, landing at (correctly Inch'on) (1950), battle of the *Korean war. In August 1950 the North Korean People's Army (NKPA) had pushed South Korean and UN forces into a defensive perimeter around *Pusan in the south-east corner of the peninsula. *MacArthur, the C-in-C, was short of troops but possessed air and sea supremacy. While first reinforcing Pusan, he kept back the 1st US Marine and 7th Infantry Divisions (X Corps) to cut NKPA communica-

tions with an *amphibious landing 200 miles (322 km) behind the battle zone at the port of Inchon.

This offered surprise, on which he relied, while the national capital Seoul lay nearby on the main road and railway routes. But access to the port basin lay through channels where the tide fell 32 feet (9.75 metres) twice daily. This factor and the distance from the Japanese bases prompted the US chiefs of staff to advise a less ambitious plan, but MacArthur insisted on his audacious one. The fleet carrying X Corps under Lt Gen Edward Almond sailed early in September, despite delays imposed by successive typhoons. Meanwhile, the USAF continued to attack the NKPA around Pusan.

During preparations, the US navy had surveyed the Inchon approaches by night, and had posted a small observation team to watch the port area from an offshore islet. At high risk, the team leader ignited the seaward light there on 14 September. US naval and Marine Corps aircraft supported the landings in complement to American and British *naval gunfire. Inchon exuded smoke as the assault began at 06.15 on 15 September. The marines' assault echelon had three hours to offload before tidefall threatened to beach their ships.

Absolute surprise was achieved and the landing forces secured the harbour defences and a third of the town by midnight. A relieved MacArthur, who had suffered an hour of doubt following an early misreport of failure, informed Washington that 'the whole operation is proceeding on schedule'. By 20 September, 50,000 troops were ashore fighting for Seoul and meanwhile, preceded by an intense air and land bombardment, the UN and South Korean forces at Pusan shattered the NKPA and began to drive northwards. On 26 September, a divisional column joined elements of X Corps close to Seoul. By then, NKPA remnants were joining *guerrilla bands in the south or filtering northwards across the 38th Parallel, incapable of forming a comprehensive line at any point. MacArthur was at the peak of his reputation but the complete success of the operation fed his hubris and led to the adoption of an overambitious strategy which carried him into a defeat.   AF-H

Heinl, Robert Debs, *Victory at High Tide* (New York, 1968).
Manchester, William, *American Caesar* (New York, 1978).
Rees, David, *Korea: The Limited War* (London, 1964).
Schnabel, James F., *US Army in the Korean War, Policy and Direction: The First Year* (Washington, 1972).

Indian army In 1600 Elizabeth I granted a charter to 'The Company of Merchants of London trading into the East Indies', the origin of what was to become the Honourable East India Company (EIC) and enjoy a monopoly of British trade with the area between the Cape of Good Hope and Cape Horn. This arrangement meant that the government could profit from mercantile activities while maintaining a useful distance from its merchant adventurers.

The Portuguese and the Dutch were already established but it was the French, also aggressive interlopers in an area which till then had a low level of European penetration, that most seriously challenged the EIC. Beginning with the achievements of *Clive, a policy of divide and rule accompanied by military action that was sharp in both senses of the word gradually won territorial dominance in the pursuit of trade. Much policy did indeed find itself in orbit between Mars and Mammon, as Douglas Peers's account of army and the state in India 1819–35 suggests. The separation of company and government was more apparent than real throughout this period, but if the empire was not won in a fit of absence of mind, it certainly did not grow according to any grand design. Like the later French experience in *Algeria, or the conquests of *Caesar in Gaul, it was the work of adventurers at the periphery who tended to present the metropolitan capital with faits accomplis.

The EIC consolidated its position until, by Victoria's coronation in 1837, it ruled directly, or through alliances with local potentates, an area of 1.6 million square miles (4.1 million sq km), which stretched from the Indus in the west to Burma in the east. It encompassed high mountain ranges, sweltering lowland plains, and humid jungles and a population of some 400 million people as diverse as the geography. As the EIC's writ spread across the subcontinent, it gradually became more akin to an agent of imperial rule than a commercial enterprise. Nonetheless, its military requirements plus its desire for independence from political oversight meant that it had to recruit, train, and equip its own armed forces, and in the process the Indian army was born, eventually to outnumber its British equivalent two to one.

As V. G. Kiernan has observed, 'on the whole the slowly evolved European military pattern proved strikingly adaptable' to India, and what emerged was a cultural composite. On the one hand it embodied traditions that pre-dated British arrival (most notably that of *mercenary service), and sanctified practices that the occupier had little real chance of changing. These were most obvious in matters like uniform and rank titles, but went deeper. Regimental durbars, semi-formal councils, enabled men to air complaints outside the usual hierarchy, and in WW I Indian soldiers on the western front were issued with the narcotic hemp they were accustomed to chew. The mercenary tradition meant that discussions over pay and allowances sometimes induced what the British might ill-advisedly regard as *mutinies, but were often closer to labour disputes. On the other it showed how 'Entry into a powerful army, or respected regiment, even in the service of foreigners, could satisfy a craving, by conferring a share in a common purpose and spirit, heightened by martial music, banners, uniforms.' Generations of British officers were transformed by their own experience of the Indian army, and the relationship between officers and men, when it worked well, as it so often did, embodied close familial links. When *Roberts

was C-in-C he retired to his quarters after an inspection, only to be waited on by senior Indian officers, who wished 'as private persons to have a confab with the War Lord'. Told that this was impossible, they replied: 'But we know him privately. Know him well and he knows us; even our families he knows.' They felt that he was their *bhaiband*, their brother in arms. The system had its darker side, and George Orwell, serving in the Burma police, complained that he was 'a creature of the despotism, a pukka sahib, tied tighter than a monk or a savage by an unbreakable system of tabus'.

EIC authority was indirectly subject to the British government and it ruled India through the three presidencies of Bombay, Madras, and Bengal, each of which maintained forces for internal and external defence. The backbone of the EIC military system was the Indian regular soldier or sepoy (from the Persian *sipahi*), serving under mainly British officers and mainly Indian NCOs. British officers, trained at the EIC's 'military seminary' at Addiscombe, held their *commissions from the EIC's court of directors and enjoyed the right of command over British troops, though only as long as they were east of Suez. Indian officers were commissioned from the ranks, and the most senior Indian officer ranked below the most junior British. The symbiosis of British and EIC government was illustrated by the fact that regular British army units were required to serve in India, at the EIC's expense, and were distinguished from EIC troops by being known as king's or queen's regiments. This system meant that greater numbers of regular units could be employed than London was prepared to pay for, and in time Indian army troops became the backbone of Britain's imperial military and sustained the empire, serving throughout the globe, though their use against enemies of European stock was often contentious. It was the issue of overseas service that contributed to the pivotal challenge faced by the British in India.

The proximate cause of the *Indian Mutiny was a *cartridge used in the Enfield rifle supposedly coated in pig and cow grease, offensive to both Muslims and Hindus. In fact the celebrated cartridge was just the tip of the iceberg as far as discontent was concerned. The matter of caste-threatening service overseas was also important, exacerbated by the religious proselytism that accompanied a new generation of self-conscious imperialists, combined with concerns over service conditions, growing racism among whites, and fury among local princes at their loss of power to the EIC. The mutiny was confined to the Bengal army and was largely suppressed by units from the others, particularly from the quite recently conquered 'martial races' like the Sikhs (see SIKH WARS).

After the mutiny Britain assumed direct rule over the subcontinent through a governor-general, often (though without constitutional foundation) termed the viceroy. EIC native regiments transferred their allegiance to the crown, the EIC's European troops were re-formed as British regiments, and the regular army was posted to India with greater frequency to diminish over-reliance on native troops. This resulted in many British soldiers serving a proportion of their enlistment in India even with the introduction of the short-service system in 1870: service in India was to leave an enduring mark on the British army's *slang. The Indian regiments were also reorganized, and the number of men under arms reduced. The old Bengali army in particular saw attempts to mix different castes together in regiments in order to prevent high-caste men from a particular locality dominating units. Company artillery was quietly subsumed by the Royal Artillery, most Indian army artillery units were disbanded, and for the remainder of the 19th century the infantry was generally equipped with a firearm only after the British army had discarded it for an improved weapon. The separate presidency armies were combined in 1895, and regiments were renumbered to produce a unified list.

By this time recruitment had been modified to conform with the 'martial races' theory, popular with Roberts, which suggested that men from central, northern, and western India were by nature liable to make the best soldiers. There was abundant evidence to the contrary. One experienced officer protested: 'I cannot admit for one moment that anything has occurred to disclose the fact that the Madras sepoy is inferior as a fighting man. The facts of history warrant us in assuming the contrary.' Gradually regiments and companies recruited from classes which Roberts did not approve of were replaced by those he did, and men like Pathans, Sikhs, Jats, Dogras, and Rajputs filled the army's ranks. Even if the theory which underpinned the recruitment of 'martial races' was false, there is abundant evidence, even in letters written by Indian soldiers serving in the unfamiliar misery of the western front in WW I, of the importance of class or family military traditions in promoting cohesion.

The Indian army was regularly engaged in combat and was a source of operational feedback to the less tested British, for example in the introduction of *khaki uniforms. It was routinely preoccupied with the suspected Russian threat to India, long a defining feature of sometimes disastrous policy towards *Afghanistan and the *North-West frontier. The Indian army formed the bulk of Britain's imperial troops and fought in Egypt (see EGYPTIAN AND SUDANESE CAMPAIGNS), and in the *Burma and *Opium wars. However, despite reforms introduced by *Kitchener in the early 20th century the Indian army was not well suited for use in major war. During WW I an Indian corps served in France in 1914–15 and a cavalry corps remained there throughout the war. The campaign in *Mesopotamia involved a majority of Indian troops, and in all nearly 1 million Indians served outside their own country. Their performance was patchy, often first-rate, but sometimes less so, partly because of the unfamiliar terrain and climate in France and the problem of producing sufficient officer re-

inforcements who could speak the language of their men. Discipline sometimes wavered, most seriously when a battalion mutinied at Singapore in February 1915: 47 of its members were shot.

Following the end of WW I the Indian army returned to peacetime garrison duties and intermittent fighting on the frontier, and began to show some of the strains resulting from the Congress Party's demands for Indian independence. Ironically the *Amritsar massacre was largely carried out by Indian troops. The years 1923–32 witnessed a spate of political assassinations and terrorist activity, while Gandhi began his second campaign of civil disobedience, all of which put pressure upon an army often called upon to assist the *civil power. The slow process of 'Indianizing' the officer corps had already begun when, in 1917, ten places at the Royal Military College Sandhurst were set aside for Indian cadets. In 1923 it was decided to concentrate Indian officers into eight units, a policy which was eventually abandoned in favour of granting Indians commissions more widely.

The outbreak of WW II saw the army again called on to deploy outside India. Indian divisions were committed to Eritrea against the Italian army in the East African campaign, and served as part of the Eighth Army in the *Western Desert and later in the *Italian campaign, where they played a gallant part in the bitter fighting at *Cassino. With the Japanese entry into the war in December 1941 the land defence of the subcontinent became the priority, and there was an early setback in Malaya with the surrender of Singapore (see MALAYA AND SINGAPORE CAMPAIGN) and capture of many Indian troops, most of them from units whose quality reflected the demands which had already been placed on the Indian army.

On the grounds that my enemy's enemy is my friend, the Bengali politician Subhas Chandra Bose recruited the *Indian National Army (INA) from Indian army POWs in Japanese hands, having first helped form the Indian legion for the Germans in Europe from those captured in North Africa. During the war, a famine with one of the largest death tolls in history was permitted to devastate Bengal, an event that is seldom given the attention it deserves by British historians. If the aim was to ensure that the civilian population would not have the energy to rebel, it certainly succeeded, although there is little evidence that Bose's appeals reached a mass audience. It also greatly complicated morale and logistical problems for the Indian army on the eastern frontier, since food convoys had to be escorted through the afflicted area. Yet the defection of some Indian soldiers to the INA was only part of the story. The captured 3rd Cavalry held together in captivity largely because of the influence of two of its Indian officers. Capt Hari Badwhar was confined in an iron cage in which he could neither stand up nor stretch out. Captive Gurkhas were so impressed that they asked that he should be made an honorary officer in their regiment.

The *Burma campaign was fought under the most difficult of environmental conditions, and the Indian army played a major part in it. Despite considerable early difficulties the Indian army rose to the occasion, and by 1944–5 its fighting achievements were consistently impressive. Indeed, many saw the *Mandalay/Meiktila attack as its apotheosis, and John Masters, regular officer turned accomplished novelist, who movingly described this collection of races and religions going down to the assault through the choking dust, paid tribute to 'the largest volunteer army the world had ever known'.

After the Japanese *capitulation in September 1945 there was no real hope of returning to business as before in India. The dramatic events of the preceding six years and the blow that these had inflicted on British prestige, coupled with the near-bankruptcy of the metropolitan power, meant that the best that could be achieved was graceful withdrawal, a difficult task performed controversially under *Mountbatten. With independence on 14 August 1947 the Indian army ceased to be an adjunct to the British empire and provided large, experienced, and well-equipped forces for both India and Pakistan. However, the process of partition was agonizing, not least for British officers witnessing the division of the force they had spent their careers in, and which often represented a long tradition of family service. Perhaps a million and a half lives were lost, and the scars inflicted on the subcontinent by partition and subsequent armed clashes have yet to heal.

As India moved out of Britain's orbit in the following decades her army began to form a separate identity and structure, particularly in the formation of paramilitary and heavily armed police units for internal security purposes. Increasing use was made of Soviet weaponry such as T-55 and T-72 tanks and BMPs and BRDMs (*APCs) although western European weaponry in the form of Carl Gustav and Abbot *self-propelled (SP) artillery was also deployed. The army's use of equipment from both blocs during the *Cold War reflected India's position as a leader of the non-aligned nations.

Conflict with Pakistan and China has been a long running feature of Indian politics since independence and has occasionally spilled over into armed confrontation in the *Sino-Indian and *India-Pakistan wars. The invasion of East Pakistan to set up the independent client state of Bangladesh in 1971 was even in its own way imperialist. Continuous low- to medium-level conflict in Kashmir has meant that the independent Indian army has been involved in fighting for much of its lifetime and has developed awesome expertise in *arctic and mountain warfare. India is also one of the few admitted nuclear powers, with short- and medium-range missiles. Pakistan has developed a similar capability and as of writing if the world is ever to see the use of tactical nuclear weapons in war, it is most likely to occur in the subcontinent. With the sharp shrinkage of the Russian army, the all-volunteer Indian army, at 980,000

strong, is now the world's second largest, after China, with five regional commands, four field armies, and eleven corps and a martial tradition equalled by few.   JR-W/RH

Heathcote, T. A., *The Indian Army* (Newton Abbot, 1974).
Kiernan, V. G., *Colonial Empires and Armies 1815–1960* (London, 1982).
Mason, Philip, *A Matter of Honour* (London, 1974).
Omissi, David, *The Sepoy and the Raj* (London, 1995).
Peers, Douglas M., *Between Mars and Mammon* (London, 1995).
Yapp, M. E., *Strategies of British India* (Oxford, 1980).

Indian Mutiny (1857–8). This was a climactic point in British imperial history, encapsulating the best and the worst of the Victorian era. By the time of Queen Victoria's coronation (1837) the East India Company (EIC) had effectively become an agent of the British government and ruled India through three self-contained presidencies, Bombay, Madras, and Bengal, with the last Mughal emperor, Bahadur Shah II, a company puppet in his powerless court at Delhi.

The mutiny was confined to units of the the Bengal army stationed along the Ganges river valley and near the Grand Trunk Road that ran from Calcutta to Delhi. This consisted of 10 regular and 18 irregular regiments of cavalry, 74 regiments of infantry, and 22 artillery batteries. The Bengal army was the backbone of the *Indian army and although not all regiments mutinied, had there been unity of purpose and command the British could scarcely have withstood it. It was above all a traditionalist revolt against a wave of administrative, technological, and social reforms and became focused on the perceived British attack on the Hindu caste system, distilled by the fact that the Bengal army sepoys were largely high-caste Brahmins. Contemporary accounts also stress that the quality of people sent out from Britain had declined, with a greater incidence of racism and contempt for local customs. The chairman of the EIC himself declared that 'Providence has entrusted the empire of Hindustan to England in order that the banner of Christ should wave from one end of India to the other.' Past and present governor generals Ellenborough and Canning both warned of the mortal danger to British rule posed by proselytizing officers, but they were not heeded.

The proximate cause was the General Service Enlistment Act of 1856 which required troops to serve overseas, itself a threat to caste, as well as involving voyages by sea where the risk of contamination in confined quarters from those of lower caste by shared messing and sanitary facilities was ever present. The famous greased (in fact waxed) *cartridge introduced the same year proved to be the last straw. It was rumoured that they were lubricated with grease from cattle (holy to Hindus) or pigs (unclean to Muslims). On 29 March sepoy Mangal Pandy of the 34th Native Infantry ran amok on the parade ground at Barrackpore and not only he but also a native officer who had failed to stop him were hanged. Thereafter the mutineers were known to the British troops as 'pandies'.

On Sunday 9 May 1857, after some troopers had previously refused the new load and been *drummed out, the 3rd Light Cavalry and 11th and 20th Native Infantry at Meerut (Mirath), near Delhi, opened fire on their officers at church parade. In the absence of prompt action by the local British commander, they massacred British families and then marched on Delhi, where the garrison also mutinied and massacred the Europeans. They proclaimed the bemused and aged Bahadur Shah restored to power, and under pressure from his sons he agreed to serve as their nominal leader. A similar sequence followed at Agra and at Jhansi, where on 8 June 66 British men, women, and children who had held out for five days were butchered after surrender. It was at this time that Nana Sahib, adopted son of the deposed Maratha Peshwa, and Lakshmibai the maharanee of recently annexed Jhansi, came forward to provide some direction to what was otherwise a spontaneous and leaderless explosion of resentment.

Both at the time and since the earlier massacres were overshadowed by what followed at *Cawnpore, where Gen Wheeler commanded a small force of soldiers with around 330 women and children in a hastily constructed defensive position outside the city. Having negotiated safe passage with Nana Sahib, Wheeler led his force and dependants down to the river Ganges and into waiting boats. Whether the attack was ordered or the result of the tension of the moment has never been established, but the embarkation was brought under heavy fire. One boat managed to escape but Wheeler and most of the soldiers were killed, leaving only some 200 women and children to be taken prisoner. When news reached the rebels of an approaching relief force under *Havelock and Brig James Neill, itself committing systematic atrocities, they massacred the prisoners and threw their dismembered bodies into a well, which became and remains the cause célèbre of the mutiny.

Even before this, the reaction of the badly frightened British had been sanguinary and included a revival of the old Mughal punishment of tying captured mutineers over the mouths of cannon and blowing them apart. After it, something akin to bloodlust became commonplace, especially among irregular units such as Hodson's Horse. September saw the British retake *Delhi after an extremely fierce fight in the city streets where no distinction was made between non-combatants and mutineers. Bahadur Shah and his sons were captured, the latter being murdered by the infamous Hodson despite or perhaps because of the payment of a large *ransom. Fighting continued throughout the following year with the British and loyal Indian forces under two able commanders, the methodical Sir Colin *Campbell and the less well-known but perhaps more brilliant Sir Hugh Rose. The former entered the Victorian pantheon by his relief of Lucknow, where an earlier relief column under Havelock was besieged, overcoming odds of ten to one, while Rose overcame the same numerical disadvantage to defeat the rebels' last important field

army under Tantia Tope, their only general of merit, at Betwa on 1 April 1858. Lakshmibai was killed while leading cavalry in June, and Nana Sahib mysteriously disappeared, allegedly to Russia whose agents also played a part in the mutiny.

Lord Canning declared the mutiny officially over on 8 July 1859, but before that the long reign of the EIC was over. The company was dissolved and the British government took over direct administration of India, which was ruled until 1949 by a viceroy. The Indian Mutiny was one of those conflicts, like the *American civil war, where so many of the vital threads of history came together and in which so many remarkable people took part that it repays study without offering any prospect of a definitive answer to all the questions it raises. The experience of India was formative not only for the British army but for British society as a whole. It was in many ways far more significant than the legacy of empire in the subcontinent itself where, as the mutiny revealed, deep-seated cultural forces retained an authority that was never more than subdued by the latest in a long series of conquerors. HEB

Hibbert, C., *The Great Mutiny: India 1857* (London, 1978).

Indian National Army (INA) A force recruited by Indian nationalists from Indian *POWs, principally from the 55,000–60,000 captured by the Japanese in Malaya (see MALAYA AND SINGAPORE CAMPAIGN). About 25,000 volunteered for the INA, some from ideological conviction, some from a feeling that British rule in Asia was doomed, but most probably from a justified fear of exposure to much worse conditions in Japanese labour camps (of the 40,000 Indian POWs who did not join the INA 11,000 died). The original force was formed by Capt Mohan Singh, a Sikh (see SIKH WARS), but he soon became disillusioned by the Japanese attitude towards the INA and on 21 December 1942 ordered its dissolution. Singh was imprisoned and his place taken by a prominent Bengali nationalist politican, Subhas Chandra Bose, who had previously helped to raise an Indian force in Germany from Indian POWs taken in *North Africa and known as the Indian Legion (eventually employed on occupation duties in south-west France where it disintegrated). Bose revived the INA whose numbers had sunk to about 8,000 in early 1943, recruiting more POWs and many Indian civilians, and eventually two weak divisions were sent to Burma (see BURMA CAMPAIGN) to be employed chiefly on line of comunications duties, although the first INA division took part in the battle of *Imphal, suffering heavy casualties especially from disease and starvation and from *desertion. In 1945 INA *morale collapsed: of 15,500 INA troops in Burma 7,000 were captured and 5,000 surrendered or deserted. The military significance of the INA, which was intended to be a revolutionary force, was very small but its political significance was great. During the war the British authorities had endeavoured to cloak the circumstance that a number of Indian troops had gone over to the enemy but at the end of the war it was decided that the most serious offenders must be tried. Nationalist politicians hailed them as national heroes and the sentences were suspended and the trials abandoned. Today INA *veterans are more honoured in the subcontinent than those who fought for the British during WW II.

Ghosh, K. K., *The Indian National Army* (Meerut, 1969).
Gordon, Leonard, *Brothers against the Raj* (New York, 1990).
Hauner, Milan, *India in Axis Strategy* (Stuttgart, 1981).
Toye, Hugh, *The Springing Tiger* (London, 1959).

India–Pakistan wars Relations between the states of India and Pakistan have been blighted since the two states gained their independence in 1947. The Hindu states of British India formed the new country of India, while those states with a Muslim majority became part of Pakistan. The geographic-religious breakdown of the population meant that Pakistan was divided by India into West and East Pakistan. Those states ruled by local princes were permitted to join either India or Pakistan. The whole process led to a legacy of ill feeling between the two countries, and this was exacerbated by the situation in Kashmir. The Hindu ruler decided that his religiously divided state should join India, in spite of the large Muslim population of the area. Indian and Pakistani troops immediately confronted one another across Kashmir's borders, a situation which continues to this day.

In 1962, a brief border war between China and India resulted in India's defeat, encouraging Pakistan's government to believe that they might be able to win a conflict between the two countries, in spite of the numerical advantage enjoyed by India. In January 1965, a border dispute over the poorly marked frontier of the Rann of Kutch escalated into conflict, although this was ended by agreement in June. In August, tension over Kashmir rose, culminating in further border clashes and claims by each side that the other had violated its territory. An advance by Indian troops was countered by a Pakistani advance, and a full-scale war ensued. By 23 September 1965, both sides were running low on ammunition after a *UN embargo had been imposed, and a ceasefire was agreed. In January 1966, both sides agreed to return to the positions they had occupied before the war broke out.

Tension between the two countries remained, and again developed into war in 1971. The Bengali population of East Pakistan had become increasingly disillusioned with rule from West Pakistan, and in elections on 7 December 1970, the Awami League, which demanded Bengali autonomy, won 160 of the 162 seats allocated for the East in the Pakistani National Assembly. This provoked the president of Pakistan into postponing the meeting of the National Assembly. The Bengali leader, Mujibur Rahman, called on the Eastern Pakistanis to go on strike. In response, a curfew was imposed. Negotiations broke down, and some 60,000 Pakistani troops commanded by Gen Tikka Khan were left to suppress the East, which proclaimed itself to be the independent state of Bangladesh. Pakistani troops embarked upon a wave of repression, which led to an enormous refugee crisis. The number of refugees increased daily, until it was estimated that between nine and fifteen million, or one in five of the Bangladeshi population, had fled to India. By September 1971, it was calculated that the monthly cost of feeding the refugees stood at $200 million. This placed a financial burden upon India which it could not hope to sustain; consequently, it was in India's interest for the crisis to be resolved. Protests to the UN regarding the atrocities being committed by Pakistani forces in Bangladesh did not lead to a satisfactory outcome, and geopolitical considerations meant that it was most unlikely that India could stand aside to allow Pakistan to reassert its authority over the new state.

The conclusion of the monsoon season allowed Bangladesh to be infiltrated by some 30,000 Bangladeshis of the Mukti Bahini (Liberation Forces), trained by the Indian army. The Mukti Bahini undertook *guerrilla activity, concentrated along the frontier with India. Awareness in Pakistan of the co-operative attitude of the Indians toward the Mukti Bahini had serious repercussions. Tension greatly increased, and in November, the governments of both states announced that their forces were to be permitted to cross their frontiers if necessary. This made war an increasing possibility. It came on 3 December, when Pakistan launched air strikes against twelve Indian airfields. India struck back the following day, attacking both towards Bangladesh and Pakistan itself. The advance went well for India, which was able to recognize the new state of Bangladesh on 6 December. Three days later, Jessore was liberated, and six days later, Pakistani forces in Bangladesh surrendered.

Although this marked the last serious fighting between the two, small-scale fighting continues at high altitude in the Himalayas. These ongoing clashes over Kashmir, which greatly increased tension in 1999, coupled with the fact that both sides have developed and tested *nuclear weapons, mean that India and Pakistan remain embroiled in their own local semi-cold war, with no conclusion in sight.

DJJ

indirect fire is usually carried out by artillery, *mortars, rockets, and missiles but also by tanks and machine guns, at targets which cannot be seen directly from their own position. The fire, which may come from any number of weapons, can be controlled if necessary by one observer who can see the target and whose instructions may be passed back to the firing systems by flags, *telephone, *radio, or datalink, or may be entirely 'predicted', using the co-ordinates of the weapons and the target and meteorological information alone. Indirect fire was the most important aspect of the *military revolution that shaped WW I, but its impact has been poorly grasped by historians.

For centuries, field artillery could not hit what it could not see. Primitive systems of indirect fire had been in use by siege and fortress artillery for hundreds of years, but they depended on a line of stakes or other markers between the gun and a point from which the target could be seen. In the siege of *Sevastopol in the *Crimean war the Russians used some very good system of signalling to enable the fortress artillery to hit British forces in dead ground. Nevertheless, it was not until the *Franco-Prussian war of 1870–1 that the need for guns to be concealed became pressing. The problem became more acute with the advent of *smokeless powder—modern, cordite-like propellants—in the 1880s. The *smoke which had helped conceal the guns disappeared, leaving them in full view of enemy riflemen and machine guns. The range of guns was increasing, too, but could not be used to the full because of the limitations of human eyesight and the folds of terrain.

Systems of markers worked in siege warfare, but were quite unsuitable for use in field combat requiring rapid lateral shifts of fire. What was needed was a way of swinging the guns in any direction to fire at map co-ordinates or in response to orders from a 'spotter' or 'forward observation officer' with the forward troops. The answer was remarkably simple. In the 1890s European artillery arms began using primitive 'dial sights', initially part of a circle, then a full circle, in combination with an aiming point visible from the gun position. These were called *Richtfläche* (German), *goniometer* (French, British), and *uglomer* (Russian). The pointer on the plate was moved through the desired angle (in the opposite direction), and then brought back onto the aiming point by moving the gun. The range could be set from tables using the elevation of the barrel and charge. All that was then needed were fine corrections passed from the observer, at first by flags but by the time of the *Russo-Japanese war by telephone. From then on, artillery could hit any target within range, a profound change in the use of artillery catalysed by a simple device.   CDB

Bellamy, Christopher, *Red God of War* (London, 1986).

Indochina, French campaign in (1946–54). In the
immediate aftermath of WW II, France faced the challenge of recovering her colonial possessions not only from the hands of former enemies, but also from indigenous *resistance movements that had grown up in 1941–5. In French Indochina, guerrilla resistance to the Japanese by the Vietminh had become organized and united under the leadership of *Ho Chi Minh, and perforce had to be defeated if French authority was to be restored.

At this time more than 80 per cent of Indochina was classified as forested, much of it dense and humid jungle. The problems for any force attempting to carry on a campaign in such terrain are obvious, and in the case of Vietnam these difficulties were exacerbated by the peculiar weather patterns which prevail in the region. The southwest monsoon, for example, limited the campaigning season to what the Vietnamese described as winter–spring, stretching roughly from October to mid-May. During the remainder of the year it was almost impossible, and certainly imprudent, to move troops because the smallest logistical problems would be magnified many times over by the torrential and destructive rains which swept across the country. The political context of the war is also crucial to an overall understanding of its shape and outcome. The Vietminh under the operational direction of *Giap began with significantly inferior resources, but after 1949 were able to draw wholehearted support from newly communist China. The defeat of the Kuomintang by *Mao Tse-tung was crucial to the Vietnamese insurgents' success in the years that followed. By contrast the French government received only some support from the USA, torn between its traditional anti-colonialism and a more recent appreciation of the communist threat, and was also indecisive, bureaucratic, and largely half-hearted about the campaign in Indochina. Various military commanders were sent to the troubled colony, but they were given limited resources and scant encouragement from home.

The French campaign in Indochina began with a few skirmishes with the Vietminh, and some controversy as to who actually fired the first shot. The French were intent upon undoing the fragile hold the Vietnamese had taken on the apparatus of state after the capitulation of Japan, and they rapidly asserted control in the major cities. The Vietminh had great sympathy among the population, but little strength in 1946, and were soon pushed back into their stronghold, the Vietbac, which is an almost impenetrable region of steep valleys and caves near the Chinese border. In 1947 Gen Jean Valluy, the French commander, having taken time to marshal his resources, attacked this area. Operation LEA, as it was known, met with initial success, but the plan—drawn straight from the European theatre of WW II—became bogged down in the difficult terrain. French units were isolated, and the Vietminh leadership was able to adapt to circumstances much more rapidly than the French. In the end the French managed to extricate themselves from an increasingly dangerous situation, while the Vietminh remained intact and with soaring *morale.

The next two years of the French campaign were marked by small battles and French indecision. Valluy was replaced by Gen Roger C. Blaizot in 1948, and Blaizot was, in turn, replaced by Gen Marcel Charpentier a year later. Charpentier took over just before Giap's first major offensive in 1950 and was outgeneralled. After some vicious fighting shortly before the monsoon, the resumption of campaigning in the early winter months saw the Vietminh capture the key supply base at Dong Khe. Charpentier counter-attacked by sending two columns, which were ambushed and defeated

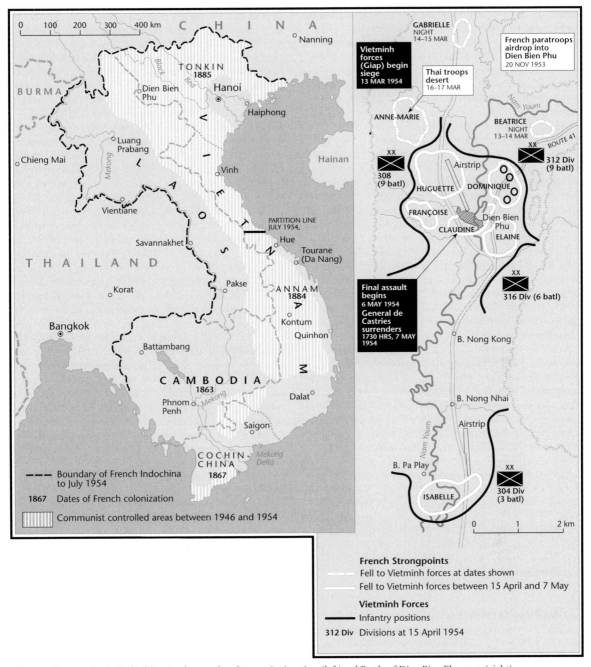

The French campaign in **Indochina**. Background and strategic situation (left)and Battle of Dien Bien Phu, 1954 (right).

in detail by an enemy with intimate knowledge of the terrain.

Gen Jean de Lattre de Tassigny, Charpentier's successor, enjoyed rather more success against Giap's second offensive in 1951. French forces repulsed the Vietminh at Vinh Yen, Mao Khe, and during the Day River battles. De Lattre built up the Vietnamese National Army to provide support for the French, and used these troops to man the de Lattre Line, a series of forts and bases. This freed French troops for an offensive at Hoa Binh in November 1951, but Vietminh counter-attacks forced a withdrawal from that position three months later. Illness forced de Lattre to return to

441

France in late 1951 and his replacement Gen Raoul Salan carried on the pattern of limited offensives and counter-offensives, winning a victory at a pitched battle at Na San in November 1952. Giap enjoyed some degree of success in the Black River campaign of 1952, and his Laotian campaign a year later was thwarted only because his troops advanced so far so quickly that they outran the limited Vietminh logistical capacities.

The success of the Laotian campaign opened the way for a final Vietnamese victory. Gen Henri Navarre became the latest French commander, and began to plan a major battle to give the French a strong bargaining chip in ongoing peace negotiations. When this set-piece battle began, however, it was on Giap's terms. Navarre had believed he could maintain an 'airhead' at Dien Bien Phu, near the Laotian border, but when serious fighting broke out around the position on 12 March 1954, the French were outgunned, outnumbered, and fatally placed in a valley with Vietminh artillery all around them. The garrison held out for two months, but the outcome was a foregone conclusion once Vietminh guns had smothered the French artillery and closed the airfields. On 7 May the last defenders surrendered and the French delegation at the peace conference in Geneva was compelled to capitulate.

Most of the fighting had been in the North and, prompted by the USA, a separate, non-communist state of South Vietnam came into being. Ho Chi Minh and Giap were not to be denied and although it took them a further twenty years, they eventually consolidated their hold on territory they had already won once from the Japanese and again from the French—an epic of tenacity, courage, and endurance that will live for as long as warfare is studied.

AH

Currey, Cecil B., *Victory at any Cost: The Genius of Vietnam's Gen. Vo Nguyen Giap* (London, 1997).
Davidson, Philip B., *Vietnam at War: The History, 1946–1975* (London, 1988).
Kelly, George A., *Lost Soldiers: The French Army and the Empire in Crisis, 1947–1962* (Boston, 1965).

infantry (*see opposite page*)

information warfare (IW). There have been many attempts to define IW, but at the time of writing authorities disagree on the boundaries of the term. All war, as *Sun-tzu said, is based on deception—a form of IW—and has been since the dawn of history. In the military context IW embraces and overlaps with 'command and control warfare' at the *tactical, *operational, and *strategic levels. However, the term is also used to refer to grand-strategic attack on, and defence of, the information infrastructure of a modern state, including stock markets, banking, telecommunications, air traffic control, and electric power. Modern states, increasingly dependent on computers, are ever more vul-nerable to such attacks, and an IW attack could have the same paralysing effect as a nuclear strike. Furthermore, it may be very difficult to find out who launched it. IW might be waged by a nation state, a faction within a state, a terrorist or criminal group. Its unique nature is illustrated by the fact that in the UK defence against IW is now the responsibility of the Cabinet Office, not the Ministry of Defence.

Nowadays the term IW is often used to refer to 'cyberwar', from the Greek for a governor or controller. A neat definition, though probably too simple, is that IW is war in a new element, cyberspace, in which electronic messages and 'viruses' are introduced into the enemy's computers, either to disable them or to plant false information, either through existing communication lines or, in future, by lasers or other electromagnetic transmissions. 'Trojan horses' may be introduced which nestle undetected in an enemy computer system until activated by the user. 'Logic bombs' may sabotage the software. Thus IW may take three forms: physical attack such as bombing against an information system; a computer-based attack on a physical objective, for example, disabling an aircraft's controls; or an information attack from one information system against another—proper cyberwar.

Some authorities consider the term to have a wider application and to refer to any form of attack on the commander's mind and *morale, including *psychological warfare, electronic warfare, ruses, and deception. Others consider this to be 'indirect' IW, as it depends on commanders' perceptions, whereas direct IW involves attack and defence of the information systems on which commanders and military forces increasingly depend. The appearance of information systems as a new level between the commander's mind and physical combat provides a neat parallel with the appearance of the operational level of war between strategy and tactics.

IW has become a fashionable subject in the US military, which aims to achieve 'information dominance' in any future conflict. However, the adversary may be far less dependent on information than US forces or their western allies. In the future, as Ferdinand Otto Miksche suggested when writing about atomic war, the advantage may lie with the side which keeps its communications and equipment robustly simple, and eschews dependence on complex information systems.

CDB

Adams, James, *The Next World War* (London, 1998).
Freedman, Lawrence, *The Revolution in Strategic Affairs* (Adelphi Paper, 318; Oxford, 1998).
Libicki, Martin, *What is Information Warfare?* (Washington, 1995).
Miksche, F. O., *The Failure of Atomic Strategy* (New York, 1958).

infra-red devices employ the wavelength just beyond the red end of the spectrum, and provide their users with the ability to acquire targets in darkness or low-light conditions.

(*cont. on page 446*)

infantry

THE foot soldier is as old as man, whose ability to make weapons compensated for lack of lethal teeth and claws: these weapons formed two categories which still define the infantryman today. Projectile weapons, initially the stick, stone, arrow, or throwing spear, enabled him to strike at a distance, while he fought hand-to-hand with shock weapons, like the club, stabbing spear, and sword. The fragility of his body, so evident in infantry combat, encouraged him to protect himself with shield, helmet, and body *armour. The relationship between the weight of weapons and equipment, and the mobility generated by human muscles has been his lasting preoccupation. Initially his tactics were an extension of the hunt: he ambushed, raided, and swept enemies against a human cordon or natural barrier. He was essentially a warrior, whose skills were individual, and not yet a soldier with collective skills.

From about 2500 BC the infantry of Mesopotamian city states made this crucial transition. They were armed alike, with shield and spear, and went into battle in massed *phalanxes which required simple drills. Although the infantryman's status might be eclipsed by that of charioteers or horsemen, he played a key role in many of the great armies of the ancient world. The cities of classical Greece produced the *hoplite, so called from the *hoplon*, the bronze shield he carried. Hoplite armies met in battles whose duration was limited by the physical difficulty of plying spear and shield for very long. Though they usually had little to fear from cavalry, they were vulnerable to *light troops who might hover outside their reach, and it was often clear that assertive democracy did not make for military effectiveness. Nevertheless, the Spartans, the most martial of the Greeks, displayed a high level of organization: Plutarch (see GREEK HISTORIANS) describes them advancing 'in step to the pipe, leaving no gap in their line of battle and no confusion in their hearts'. The infantrymen who formed the core of the *Macedonian army under *Alexander 'the Great' were more lightly equipped than hoplites, and carried the *sarissa*, a 15-foot (4.5-metre) pike. Their basic unit, the *syntagma*, consisted of 256 men formed 16 deep, and was combined with others into the phalanx, flexible enough to open up to allow Persian *chariots or Indian war-elephants to pass harmlessly through.

The Roman legion, developed during two major wars against Carthage in the 3rd century BC, possessed even greater flexibility. Its organization, with the 8-man *conturbernium*, the 80-strong century, the 6-century cohort, and the 10-cohort legion, reflected ageless truths about the bonding process and the span of command. The legionary carried a throwing-spear, the *pilum*, which he used to disorganize the enemy's ranks before he charged with sword and shield. Rigid *discipline, hard training, and standard operating procedures accounted for much of the legion's success. The Romans, recognizing that no army could live by heavy infantry alone, recruited cavalry and missile-armed troops from their allies. There were always dangerous foes even for the legion, and the combination of overconfidence and unsuitable terrain could prove fatal. In 53 BC Parthian mounted *archers defeated Crassus at *Carrhae, and in AD 9 a Roman army was wiped out in the trackless *Teutoburger Wald.

The decay of the legion's recruiting base, as much as tactical obsolescence, caused its decline. The Emperor Valens was defeated at *Adrianople by Gothic cavalry which caught his infantry tired and straggling, and pressed in to throw spears from close quarters. For the next thousand years the cavalryman was to predominate. From the East came swarms of steppe horsemen, while in the West the armoured knight emerged as the dominant military instrument. The link between social status and military effectiveness, which had told in favour of the foot soldier in the era of hoplite and legionary, now told against him. Not only were infantrymen despised by mounted warriors, but any increase in their effectiveness was a threat to the knight's status. Armies of the Middle Ages were often little more than a rabble of mounted gentility, with their foot soldiers as low in military value as social status.

One major threat to the knight came from the *Swiss, some of whose sturdy and egalitarian soldiers plied the 18-foot (5.4 metre) pike at shoulder level, while others, posted behind the hedge of pikes, rushed out to swing axes, two-handed swords, or clubs. The Swiss usually gave battle on ground that did not favour cavalry, and in the 14th and 15th centuries won a series of victories over *feudal opponents. They were eventually eclipsed by the development of pike-armed *landsknechts in Germany and the improvement of cannon in the 16th century.

If the pike was a classic shock weapon, the second major threat to the knight was just the opposite. In the 13th century the longbow had become the characteristic weapon of English infantry, although much 'English' infantry was in fact Welsh. English archers fought with knights and spearmen as part of a combined-arms force, and their effect upon armoured cavalry or unsupported infantry could be devastating. At *Falkirk in 1298 they riddled *schiltroms of Scots spearmen with their arrows. At *Crécy in 1346 they demolished a French army which attacked mounted. The French deduced that they had failed because chargers had been maddened by arrows, but when they attacked dismounted at *Agincourt in 1415 the result was no less calamitous.

Social as well as military pressures played their part in the decline of the longbow. It was not until the 1800s that firearms could match it in range, accuracy, or rate of fire. But the archer was the product of years of training, and the bowyers and fletchers who supported him were craftsmen whose skills could not easily be duplicated. The monarchs of the 15th and 16th centuries set great store by modernity, and noisy, up-to-date *gunpowder weapons emphasized their status.

The 16th and 17th centuries drew together the threads represented by the Swiss on the one hand and the English on the other. The infantry of early modern Europe combined the fire of gunpowder weapons—first the arquebus and then the *matchlock musket—and the shock of cold steel. At first it was the Spanish *tercio, literally a third of an army, that ruled the roost. It drew up in deep formations with pikemen in the centre and 'sleeves' of *musketeers at the corners. Both *Maurice of Nassau and *Gustavus Adolphus improved the effectiveness of infantry by making units smaller and thus more flexible, and by increasing the proportion of musketeers to pikemen. The process accelerated in the *Thirty Years War and the *British civil wars. By 1691 pikemen formed less than a quarter of the strength of the English regiments which left for Flanders.

Towards the end of the 17th century the matchlock was superseded by the *flintlock, more convenient to use but more expensive to manufacture. The invention of the *bayonet sounded the death knell of the pike, although for many years infantry officers and sergeants carried staff weapons as a symbol of authority. The first bayonets plugged into the musket's muzzle, and the weapon could not be fired with the bayonet fixed. This, as British government troops discovered when charged by the Scots at *Killiecrankie, was no small inconvenience. In the early 18th century the socket bayonet, which fitted round the musket's muzzle, came into general use.

Infantry of the line now formed the bulk of armies, and decided most battles by the regularity of their fire and the cohesion of their ranks. The musket was inaccurate: in the late 18th century a Prussian battalion, engaging a target 6 feet (1.8 metres) high and 100 feet (30.5 metres) long, scored 25 per cent of hits at 225 yards (206 metres), 40 per cent hits at 150 yards (137 metres), and 60 per cent hits at 75 yards (69 metres). Under the stress of battle the proportion of hits fell dramatically. Many of the most successful commanders of the age, like Frederick and Wellington, were men who trained their infantry carefully and used them well. There were lengthy debates about the efficacy of *column and line, the former best suited for movement and shock and the latter for fire. Although there were national preferences—*French Revolutionary armies often used columns, with *tirailleurs skirmishing ahead—mixed order, with deployed battalions firing and others, in column, ready to reinforce them or to charge with the bayonet, usually brought best results.

Bayonet fights were relatively rare, usually because one side fled before contact, and determination to close with the enemy—the product of discipline, patriotic fervour, or soldierly emulation—was a battle-winning quality. Cohesive infantry could usually see off cavalry, but a skilful commander could unhinge an opponent by threatening him with cavalry, thus forcing his infantry to form square, engaging the squares with artillery, and bringing on the cavalry again if the infantry tried to open out to offer a less attractive target.

These tactics had limitations. Rifle-armed opponents could cause heavy casualties even if resolute infantry pushed on through their fire: the British lost 1,150 men, nearly half the infantry engaged, at Bunker Hill in 1775. The threat of light troops encouraged the formation of light companies, each usually paired with a grenadier company, whose soldiers originally carried hand *grenades, to form a battalion's *flank companies. Specialist light or rifle battalions were raised, sometimes by the *recruitment of woodsmen or gamekeepers.

In the 19th century technological change accelerated. The simple and reliable *percussion lock replaced the flintlock from the 1830s; rifles became standard in the 1850s; and the *Franco-Prussian war was the first in which the infantry on both sides carried breech-loaders. Heavy infantry casualties of the period owed much to the fact that these new weapons were used in old-fashioned massed tactics: the Prussian Guard lost over 8,000 men at Saint-Privat (see REZONVILLE/GRAVELOTTE, BATTLES OF). The machine gun also appeared, and within a generation this 'concentrated essence of infantry' would make the battlefield even more lethal.

By 1871 there were clear signs that infantry could achieve best results by fire and manoeuvre, one company providing fire to cover the movement of another, and that artillery could do much to shake the cohesion of infantry, whether attacking or defending. These lessons were underlined in the Second *Boer War, where British infantry lost heavily making frontal assaults on positions held by riflemen whose weapons now used *smokeless powder. In the years before 1914 there was renewed emphasis on close-order offensive tactics, because of fears that the conscript infantry composing European armies would lose cohesion if allowed to spread out on the 'empty battlefield' dominated by the rifle.

WW I brought suffering and transformation to the infantryman. The most numerous of the war's soldiers, he was its beast of burden, trudging along laden with rifle and pack, suffering the privation, tedium, and danger of *trench warfare, and enduring the enemy's artillery. In the process he received old and new weapons and equipment. Hand grenades, *mortars, and helmets were rediscovered, light machine guns were new. Although the battlefield was dominated by artillery, the infantryman found his rightful place upon it, in looser formations than ever before, his movement linked to the fire of artillery and mortars. German storm troops, used to such effect in 1918, underscored his transformation.

It was a transformation which was only partial, and infantry in WW II retained elements of the ancient set alongside the modern. *Mechanization, begun in the inter-war years, saw some infantry carried in *APCs and integrated, like German panzer grenadiers or Soviet motor riflemen, into the mobile all-arms battle. The proliferation of weapons continued, with *anti-armour weapons like Panzerfaust or bazooka entering the inventory and automatic weapons becoming ever more numerous. The spread of radio sets made tactical separation easier and improved the control of artillery and mortar fire. But infantrymen still marched long distances, and the impact of terrain and climate, from the jungles of *Burma to the mountains of Italy and the steppes of Russia, was ever-present. Sometimes this terrain was man-made, and the fighting at *Stalingrad in 1942–3 was but one example of the value of infantry in the urban environment.

These tensions have persisted since 1945. The introduction of infantry fighting vehicles, like the US *Bradley* or British *Warrior*, continues to stitch infantry into the combined-arms battle, at the risk, as Gudmundsson and English observe, of 'converting them to something other than infantry'. In the casualty-conscious 1990s, when the dismounted infantryman, even with helmet and body armour, seems dangerously vulnerable, such vehicles have proved useful in peace support operations, as well as, of course, relieving the foot soldier of at least part of his traditionally crushing burden of *equipment. Alongside this runs a demand for light infantry, quickly deployable, usable on terrain which restricts the deployment of armour, in circumstances where heavy weapons may be politically unusable. As western nations ponder the risks of asymmetrical war against an enemy who chooses not to offer targets for their technology, they may conclude that the requirement for first-class infantry will increase—perhaps at a time when their societies find it harder to produce those tough and resourceful foot soldiers who have for so long provided the backbone of their armies.   RH

English, John A., and Gudmundsson, Bruce I., *On Infantry* (rev. edn., Westport, Conn., 1994).

Infra-red is used for a variety of military purposes, particularly for sighting systems and *reconnaissance purposes. The first infra-red sights employed active detector systems, emitting beams invisible to the human eye which bathed the target in infra-red light. Reflections from the target were focused on a converter unit containing a photocathode, which provided the viewer with a reconstructed image. The first infra-red sights were bulky, and image quality was lacking. Nonetheless, such sights provided advantages to the user, in that whereas the enemy had been cloaked by poor light or darkness, he was now visible, even if not with the utmost clarity. Technological advance enabled the size of such sights to be reduced, although it did not overcome the fundamental difficulty that infra-red sights of this nature are emitters, and can thus be detected by an enemy with suitable equipment.

This drawback gave rise to passive systems, which have evolved into the thermal imager. As the name suggests, the thermal imager creates images based on heat (the most common infra-red source on the battlefield), enabling clear definition of objects against the cooler background. Infra-red photography and imaging systems, used both in aircraft and by ground systems, enable the provision of 'round-the-clock' reconnaissance information, while modern targeting systems, such as the British Thermal Observation and Gunnery System (TOGS) for tanks and the Thermal Imaging and Laser Designation (TIALD) pod for aircraft, employ similar technology for finding targets in poor light conditions or darkness. In the latter case, the combination of a laser designator and thermal imager allows the aircrew to acquire their target in low-light conditions, and to then designate it for attack by laser-guided bombs.

Further employment of the infra-red spectrum may be found in aerial combat with the infra-red homing missile. These missiles, such as the AIM-9 Sidewinder, use a seeker to detect heat from enemy aircraft. The first such missiles had to be fired from the rear at the enemy aircraft's engine, but refinements have increased the sensitivity of the seeker, to permit all-aspect engagement even of the friction over a wing. Although technological advances have increased the capabilities of sighting systems, air-to-air missiles, and reconnaissance capabilities immensely, the fundamental technology remains the same as it was in the 1940s when infra-red first became a military tool.   DJJ

intelligence, military (*see opposite page*)

interdiction is a general term for isolating a part of the battlefield or theatre of war to prevent the enemy reinforcing his troops there. It is also used more specifically of artillery fire with this aim, which may take place along the sides of a planned operation or deep behind the enemy, and may use *smoke, *chemical weapons, or remotely delivered mines as well as high explosive to achieve the effect.

The classic example was the Allied air attacks on the French rail network in 1944 to interdict German troop movements that might interfere with the *Normandy landings. Another was given by Gen Colin *Powell, summarizing the strategy to be employed against the Iraqi army in the *Gulf war: 'We're going to cut it off, then we're going to kill it.' Interdiction was accomplished by air attack on routes

(*cont. on page 449*)

intelligence, military

AMONG the hoariest military jokes is that these two words are a contradiction in terms. Military intelligence means information, usually but not exclusively about the enemy, and without both information and the cerebral intelligence to make proper use of it, any commander is halfway to defeat. Among the obstacles that good intelligence must overcome in order to be applied are prejudice, as in US Secretary of State Stimson's statement that 'gentlemen do not read each other's mail', preconceptions in the commander's mind that will shut it out, as with *Montgomery when planning *Arnhem, and a sycophantic desire to reinforce those preconceptions and/or not to be the bearer of bad news, as with *Haig's intelligence officer Charteris. But the most common problem is information overload, when so much undifferentiated intelligence pours into the decision-makers that they are unable to discern what it means. This may be deliberately exacerbated by the enemy through *information warfare.

The main input categories are by direct observation, easily the oldest and most trusted, by the collation of a number of indications none of which by itself offers a true picture, by inference from past behaviour or known constraints upon the enemy's freedom of action, and by actually knowing what the enemy is going to do by intercepting oral or written communications or by having an agent placed in his headquarters. Apart from direct observation by the commander himself, certainly the mainstay of all generals until well into the 19th century, all the others require specialist staff to collect, corroborate, evaluate, and sythesize information before presenting it to the commander.

Throughout most of history generals themselves usually organized the collection of their own information, working through ad hoc means and a few trusted aides—European armies of the 18th and 19th centuries frequently assigned this task to their *QMG. States sometimes created ad hoc bureaux to handle secret intelligence tasks for a decade or two, as the Admiralty did during the *Napoleonic wars, but these vanished when the crisis passed. To a large extent, the essence of strategy and tactics has always been to force the enemy to react to your own initiatives, putting the onus of intelligence gathering and evaluation on him and thereby slowing his reaction time. Surprise in war is achieved by doing the unexpected and the avoidance of unpleasant surprises is what military intelligence is all about. *Wellington put it exactly: 'All the business of war, and indeed all the business of life, is to endeavour to find out what you don't know by what you do; that is what I called guessing what was at the other side of the hill.'

The key word here is 'guess', something that less gifted or intuitive commanders hate with uniform passion. This fear of the unknown can produce paralysis, as in the case of *McClellan during the *American civil war, whose natural caution was fed by exaggerated enemy troop strength estimates from Pinkerton until at last, even when Lee's written plans and troop dispositions were found wrapped around some cigars in a field, and even when he had him backed up against the Potomac river, and even though he outnumbered him two to one, he was unable to deliver the *coup de grâce*. In war there can be too much intelligence of the cerebral as well as the informational kind, indeed *Clausewitz argued that on the battlefield 'most intelligence is false', more likely to weaken a commander's will than to guide his actions.

Actually seeing what is on the other side of the hill was not something commanders could hope to do before the advent of aerial *reconnaissance, from which have followed satellite surveillance and battlefield drones sending back pictures in real time. Before that, it was the province of the light cavalry both to report on enemy movements and to 'screen' the activities of their own army. *Frederick 'the Great' complained that the Austrian cavalry covered his 'army like a cloud and let nobody pass', a service that the French light cavalry performed brilliantly for *Napoleon in his campaigns. He could more easily replace the men he lost in Russia in 1812 than the horses, and part of his declining performance as a general thereafter can be attributed to loss of the light-cavalry dominance he had enjoyed previously.

Really accurate, detailed *maps were rare until quite recently, but when available they provided an inestimable advantage to whatever side possessed them. Napoleon was always poring over large-scale plans with *Berthier and the brilliant campaign waged by *Jackson in the *Shenandoah Valley was built upon the work of a local cartographer who enabled him literally to run rings around the larger armies sent to crush him. Again, the intelligence alone without a commander with the confidence and the will to use it would have been sterile. An eye for terrain has been the signature of great commanders from *Alexander 'the Great' to Chief Gall of the victorious Sioux at *Little Bighorn, and neither of them had maps.

The modern age of intelligence began in 1914. Aerial imagery and radio interception, joined to greatly improved *communications and the *general staff system, produced more powerful means to collect, assess, and use intelligence. During August–October 1914, radio interception enabled the Germans to shatter the Russians at *Tannenburg and the *Masurian Lakes, but aerial reconnaissance revealing an open flank lay behind their defeat on the *Marne. *SIGINT twice gave the Royal Navy the opportunity to trap the German High Seas fleet, but on both occasions the execution by Adms Beatty (Dogger Bank) and Jellicoe (see JUTLAND) let them get away. At an even higher level, the British interception and decipherment of the 'Zimmerman telegram' in which Germany offered Mexico an offensive alliance against the USA may have helped to bring the Americans into the war, even if doubt as to its authenticity may make it a better illustration of information warfare.

British intelligence successes during WW II including *ULTRA and FORTITUDE, the highly elaborate deception plan that preceded the invasion of Normandy, are now well known, as is the cryptographic intelligence that enabled *Nimitz to deploy his remaining assets to such telling effect at *Midway. But here again one may seriously doubt that a lesser admiral would have dared to risk everything on one throw of the dice in this manner. It gave him a chance to take the great *Yamamoto by surprise, but his confidence in his own judgement and in the US navy's men, equipment, and *doctrine did the rest.

In the final analysis, the one place not even the most modern and sophisticated intelligence systems can penetrate is the human mind. Sometimes, as in the case of the *Falklands, so many better options are available to an opponent (blockade, hit and run, etc.) that when he does the only thing that delivers him into your hands, there is a perceptible pause while incredulity wrestles with the facts. Battalions of intelligence experts predicted that Saddam *Hussein would not be so rash as to invade Kuwait when he could achieve his political and financial objectives by sabre-rattling, and they went on to predict that he would not be so stupid as to sit still while the Allied *Gulf sledgehammer was built up. But he did both. The old saying 'bullshit baffles brains' might be modified to read 'the human mind is unfathomable and for as long as it directs human affairs, there is no knowing exactly what is happening on the other side of the hill'.

HEB

into the theatre, particularly the destruction of bridges over the Euphrates. The air attacks on the former *Yugoslavia in 1999 were similarly an interdiction operation, designed to cut off federal Yugoslav forces in Kosovo from resupply and make their political leadership decide to cut its losses and withdraw them.   CDB

Invalides, Hôtel des By an ordinance of 26 February 1670, *Louis XIV founded the Hôtel Royal des Invalides, an ambitious scheme to house poor crippled *veterans. Those admitted to the Hôtel were aged, wounded, or infirm veterans, of at least twenty years' service. The best architects and craftsmen working on the royal palace at Versailles were employed to complete the enormous range of buildings. This led directly to Charles II creating the *Royal Hospital at Chelsea in 1682, and similar establishments in Dublin, Vienna, and Prague. With the evolution of France's mass conscript army, the relevance of supporting a few cherished veterans declined, as a national military welfare scheme was developed. Les Invalides became the home of the French Artillery Museum in 1871, but returned briefly to housing casualties during WW I before becoming the French National Army Museum in 1945. It still remains the headquarters of the French national veterans association, and houses a few disabled pensioners. Les Invalides is most well known today as the spiritual home of the French army, with permanent and temporary exhibitions of *uniforms, paintings, and cannon, and a fine collection of regimental *colours. A specially constructed rotunda holds the remains of *Napoleon, *Foch, and *Turenne, among other national heroes.   APC-A

Iphrikates (b. c.413 BC), Athenian general who first won distinction by boarding an enemy ship during the engagement off Knidos (394 BC). Commanding mercenary *peltasts, it was his destruction of a Spartan *mora* (brigade) outside Corinth that earned him everlasting fame (390 BC). Redeployed, with his command, to the Hellespont by the Athenian authorities, he eliminated Anaxibios of Sparta (388 BC). Following the King's Peace (387 BC) he married the sister of the Thracian chieftain Kotys, spending the next decade in Thrace before joining an unsuccessful Persian invasion of Egypt (374 BC).

Having quarrelled with Pharnabazos, he returned to Athens. Awarded a generalship he sailed to check Spartan interference on Corcyra, which prompted *Sparta to negotiate for peace (371 BC). Again named general, he aided Sparta against *Epaminondas of Thebes (369 BC). Next, in the north, he secured the Macedonian throne for his adoptive brothers—including Philip II—but failed to recapture Amphipolis (368 BC). Recalled home in disgrace, he sided with Athens' enemies and thus aided Kotys (365 BC). Although pardoned, it was to be several years before he reap-

peared in Athenian service. The Embata debacle (356 BC) ruined his career, although a robust defence secured his acquittal. In serving Athens or a foreign power, this self-made cobbler's son invariably provided for his own interests. Nevertheless, he was a commander who achieved victory and did so by using his brains: his ingenuity was the subject of many later anecdotes.   NF

Best, J. G. P., *Thracian Peltasts* (Gröningen, 1969).
Pritchett, W. K., *The Greek State at War*, pt. 2 (Berkeley, 1974).

Ipsos, battle of (301 BC). This was the largest of *Alexander's successors' wars. On one side Antigonus 'the One-Eyed' and his son Demetrius deployed 70,000 infantry, 10,000 horse, and 75 elephants; on the other Ptolemy and Seleucus had 64,000 infantry, 10,500 horse, between 400 and 480 elephants, and 120 *chariots. The armies deployed conventionally, in the centre a *phalanx of pike-armed heavy infantry flanked on both sides by cavalry. Demetrius opened the battle with a furious cavalry attack on the Antigonid right which swept away the opposing enemy horse; unfortunately he lost control of his men who rode off in pursuit. Seleucus in the meantime deployed a chain of elephants, which may have been held in reserve for such a contingency, between the exposed left flank of the allied phalanx and Demetrius' victorious cavalry. Horses were notoriously frightened of elephants and, after rallying, Demetrius' command was unable to approach the centre of the battlefield and influence events there. Seleucus harassed the Antigonid phalanx, possibly with horse archers, and in time large numbers defected to the allies. Finally, Antigonus was killed by a javelin and his army collapsed. The battle's outcome was decisive, Seleucus becoming leader of Syria and Mesopotamia, Ptolemy king of Egypt.   SWN

Diodorus, 20. 113–21. 2.
Plutarch, *Life of Demetrius*, 28–9.

IRA (Irish Republican Army). The IRA emerged out of the Irish Volunteer organization established in 1913 to exert pressure on the British government to grant Home Rule for Ireland. After 1914 it was taken over by an older revolutionary nationalist organization, the Irish Republican Brotherhood (IRB), dedicated to the establishment of a unitary Irish republic by force of arms. In the 1916 *Easter Rising the rebel forces were declared to be the Army of the Irish Republic, but the term IRA did not come into use until after the Declaration of Independence in 1919. Officially the organization remained Ogláich na hÉireann (Irish Volunteers). Under the leadership of Michael Collins, Richard Mulcahy, and Harry Boland, the traditional IRB policy of insurrection was replaced by a guerrilla strategy. The keystone of the organization was the local company or battalion; brigades (one to three per county) were shadowier formations, and the divisions introduced in 1921 existed mainly on paper. Local energy in pursuit of weapons, skill in the use of explosives, and determination to engage the British police and military forces, were indispensable. Despite chivvying from Headquarters in Dublin, many if not most areas of Ireland remained quiescent—usually pleading shortage of arms and ammunition—throughout the fighting that lasted from the ambush at Soloheadbeg in January 1919 to the Truce in July 1921. The most aggressive units were in the south-west (Cork, Kerry, Tipperary, Limerick, Clare) and in Dublin itself.

The IRA campaign impelled the government to negotiate but could not compel it to concede Irish independence. When the Anglo-Irish Treaty was signed, accepting partition and non-republican status for the Irish Free State, a number of local IRA commanders believed that they could still fight on to achieve a unitary republic. The IRA split over the issue, and civil war followed. The IRA Council emerged as the ultimate republican authority.

Defeat in the civil war reduced the IRA to sporadic attempts to restart its campaign in the 1930s and 1950s. The eruption of the conflict in Northern Ireland in 1969 caught it unprepared, and in 1971 a breakaway group—the Provisional IRA (PIRA)—returned to the traditional policy of force. In Belfast and Derry, rural-style guerrilla operations were difficult and the PIRA devoted much of its energy to urban bombing. Its old territorial organization was partly replaced with a cellular structure. After a campaign lasting over 25 years, it reversed its longstanding repudiation of politics, declaring a 'cessation of operations' to allow its political wing Sinn Fein, under the leadership of Martin McGuinness and Gerry Adams, to participate in constitutional negotiations. At the time of writing the future of the peace process seems uncertain, with the issue of the 'decommissioning' of IRA weapons and explosives a stumbling block in negotiations. The process has emphasized the IRA's insistence that it is indeed an army whose campaign has been legitimate, and whose premature relinquishing of weapons would smack of surrender.

CT/RH

Iran-Contra affair (1985–92), a rare non-venal political scandal in which high officials of the Reagan administration were discovered to have used funds raised by covert arms sales through Israel to Iran in order to finance the activities of the 'Contra' revolutionaries against the Sandinista regime in Nicaragua, every step of which violated declared government policy, domestic law, or international law—or all three. Ramifications included fund-raising from friendly Arab states and the employment of British *mercenaries for *commando raids.

Before 'mission creep' asserted itself, it was a modest operation conducted by Reagan's National Security Adviser McFarlane, assisted by Casey, the director of the hamstrung *CIA, to prolong the war between Iran and Iraq in order to

exhaust both, with the (unfulfilled) hope of obtaining the release of hostages held by pro-Iranian terrorists in Lebanon. But the large amounts of untraceable money this left in Swiss bank accounts proved too tempting to an administration wedded to realpolitik and frustrated by a hostile and highly partisan Congress. The key actors and/or scapegoats were Lt Col North and McFarlane's successor Poindexter. A special investigator obtained convictions against them and six other top officials, all either overturned on appeal or pardoned by Pres Bush.

HEB

Iran–Iraq war On 22 September 1980, Iraqi forces crossed the Iranian border in strength, igniting what was to become one of the longest, bloodiest, and most costly armed conflicts in the post-WW II era. By the time fighting ended on 18 August 1988, there would be no victor or vanquished: only a million war casualties, untold economic dislocation, and widespread destruction on both sides.

It has become a commonplace to view the invasion as a natural offspring of the aggressive personality of the Iraqi president, Saddam *Hussein, and his unbridled regional ambitions. These ranged from the occupation of Iranian territories (the Shatt al-Arab waterway and the oil-rich province of Khuzestan) to the desire to assert Iraq as the pre-eminent Arab and Gulf state. Conversely, the invasion has been explained as an excessive reaction by Saddam to the lethal threat posed to his personal rule by the revolutionary Shi'a regime in Tehran, headed by the militant Ayatollah Ruhollah Khomeini, which sought to substitute its own version of an Islamic order for the existing status quo in the Persian Gulf.

Be that as it may, the Iraqi war strategy was fundamentally flawed. Instead of dealing a mortal blow at the Iranian armed forces, Saddam limited the war operations to the Shatt al-Arab and a small part of Khuzestan, in southern Iran, committing less than half of the Iraqi army: five of twelve divisions. Far worse, rather than allow his forces to advance to a natural stopping point, Saddam voluntarily halted their advance within a week of the onset of hostilities and announced his willingness to negotiate a settlement. This decision proved catastrophic, saving the Iranian army from a crushing defeat and giving Tehran a vital respite to seize the initiative and move onto the offensive.

In January 1981 Iran carried out its first major counter-offensive since the beginning of the war, and by the end of the year Iraq had been dislodged from most of its strongholds in Khuzestan. In one of his wisest strategic moves during the war, Saddam decided to withdraw from Iranian territory still under Iraqi control and to redeploy for a static defence along the international border. This move failed to appease the clerics in Tehran and on 13 July 1982, following a bitter debate within the Iranian leadership, a large-scale offensive was launched in the direction of Basra, the second-most important city in Iraq.

From now on the war would become a prolonged exercise in futility, reminiscent of the *trench warfare of WW I, in which successive Iranian human-wave attacks would be launched against the formidable Iraqi lines of defence, only to be repulsed at a horrendous human cost. It would be only in February 1986, after nearly four years of costly attacks, that Iran would gain its first significant foothold on Iraqi territory by occupying the Fao peninsula in the southern tip of Iraq and retaining it despite ferocious Iraqi counter-attacks.

By this time, the spectre of an Iranian victory had brought a group of the most unlikely bedfellows to do their utmost to ensure that Iraq did not lose the war. The USSR and France armed Iraq to its teeth, while the USA provided vital *intelligence support and economic aid; numerous European companies were building Iraq's arsenal of non-conventional weapons, the Arab Gulf monarchies were financing the Iraqi war effort, and a million Egyptian workers were servicing the overextended Iraqi economy.

Meanwhile Iran, starved of major weapons systems and subjected to a punishing economic *blockade, was showing growing signs of war-weariness. Intensifying discontent among the poor who constituted the mainstay of the regime's support was particularly disconcerting for the clerics, as was the sharp drop in the number of war volunteers. Seeing the light at the end of the tunnel for the first time since the early months of the war, in April 1988 Saddam ordered his troops onto the strategic offensive, after nearly six years on the defensive. Within 48 hours of fierce fighting the Iraqis recaptured the Fao peninsula from the demoralized and ill-equipped Iranian troops, thus signalling the final reversal in the fortunes of the war.

This was soon followed by a string of military successes. In May Iraq drove the Iranians out of their positions east of Basra, and a month later dislodged them from the Majnoon islands, held by Iran since 1985. In early July Iraq drove the remaining Iranian forces out of Kurdistan and later that month gained a small strip of Iranian territory in the central front. Confronted with these setbacks, the mullahs in Tehran were desperately urging Ayatollah Khomeini to drink the 'poisoned chalice' and order the cessation of hostilities. After a year of evasion and hesitation, Iran accepted UN Security Council Resolution 598 for a ceasefire and a month later the guns along the common border fell silent.

EK

Irish campaign of William of Orange This, the British phase of the *League of Augsburg war, was a result of an attempt by *James II to regain his kingdom, *William of Orange's to prevent him, and the desire of *Louis XIV to expand the war into the British Isles. James landed with a small force in March 1689 and most of the country rapidly fell to him. William landed at Carrickfergus in June 1690 with a large army composed of seasoned Dutch, Danish,

French Huguenot, and English troops. They joined forces with William's existing troops in Ireland under the command of the Duke of Schomberg, bringing the total of troops under his command to 40,000. James's army, encamped near the Boyne river, was further reinforced by additional French contingents under the command of the Duc de Lauzun, raising his army to 21,000 by March 1690. James, refusing the advice of his senior staff to withdraw to the Shannon, offered William battle. In the ensuing battle of the *Boyne, James weakened his centre to meet a flank attack and duly lost the battle against William's main force. The Jacobites defended themselves creditably, despite heavy losses, and staved off total disaster, withdrawing in reasonable order. James's resolve did not survive, and he fled to France, never to return.

In 1691 William appointed Godert de Ginkel as his field commander and Ireland now fell to his advancing army, driving remaining resistance to the west and south-west of the country. Ginkel now advanced to besiege Athlone, which fell on 10 July. St Ruth had been appointed to command the Jacobite forces in Ireland in James's absence, and he decided to meet Ginkel at Aughrim on 12 July. In the ensuing very hard-fought battle, St Ruth was killed and the French-Irish army collapsed, and along with it James's war effort in Ireland. Nevertheless, it was not until 3 October 1692 that Limerick, the final centre of resistance, fell. Subsequent negotiations resulted in the Articles of Limerick which provided for the freedom of religious belief in Ireland, the voluntary transporting of Irish troops to France, and a general amnesty. The treaty, although recognized by the English Parliament, was rejected by the mainly Protestant Irish Assembly who introduced harsher anti-Catholic penal laws.

JDB

Irish rebellions There have been many. The Anglo-Norman intervention into Irish dynastic politics and the subsequent increased English military presence in Ireland led to large areas of Ireland falling to the hands of the English barons. In 1171 King Henry II successfully asserted his lordship over his subjects who had gone to Ireland and also many of the Irish kings, thus adding Ireland to the lands of the English king. According to historian Robert Kee, eight centuries of conflict were to flow from the Anglo-Norman Invasion of 1169–73. Although subsequent expansion was achieved largely through economic colonization rather than military conquest, there was sporadic resistance from the Irish kings: Brian O'Neil was proclaimed king of Ireland in direct challenge to the colonists, but he was defeated at the battle of Down in 1260.

English power was far from uniform across Ireland and many of the Irish dynasties survived. By the end of the 15th century English lordship extended over the eastern 'Pale' around Dublin, east Munster, and some scattered enclaves in the north. The new English Tudor dynasty was determined to end this state of affairs and impose modern centralized government across Ireland. However the Earls of Kildare had been the cornerstone of English rule, and Henry VIII's fitful policy of reform was met by considerable indifference by Gerald, the 9th Earl. His imprisonment in 1534 provoked a rebellion led by his son Lord Offaly, 'Silken Thomas'. Thomas besieged Dublin castle and proclaimed a Catholic crusade in an effort to exploit the resentment felt at Henry's expropriation of the Church. The revolt was put down by an English army the following year and Henry introduced direct rule through an English governor and garrison.

Although the Tudor governors tried to persuade the local lords of the advantages of administrative reform, common law, and land tenure, the standing army under their control meant they often used the military option to coerce the population. A whole series of rebellions followed. The Geraldine League demanded a restoration of the house of Kildare and rejected Henry's ecclesiastical supremacy. It was decisively beaten at Bellahoe in 1539. The Fitzgerald earldom of Desmond revolted against the Tudor demands for centralization twice from 1569–73 and 1579–83. The latter rebellion, proclaimed as a holy war, was supported by a papal invasion force and suppressed all the more brutally because of this. The Baltiglass rebellion of 1580–1 in the Pale was also aggressively crushed.

Hugh O'Neil, Earl of Tyrone, although initially loyal to the crown, realized that the spread of English administration into his lands in Ulster represented a challenge to his position. He, therefore, chose to head a confederacy of Ulster chieftains against the English. O'Neil's army was well trained and equipped and therefore inflicted a number of defeats on the English forces which were surprised at the discipline of the Irish troops. O'Neil's Rising, also known as the Nine Years War, was largely defensive and the Earl of Essex's forays against him were largely ineffectual, although Lord Mountjoy brought renewed efficiency to the English campaign. When a Spanish expedition landed at Kinsale in 1601, O'Neil risked all by marching to their aid and was comprehensively defeated in open battle. O'Neil signed a generous peace treaty in 1603 but he fled Ireland four years later. The war was as costly as any of Elizabeth's continental wars but it gave England complete control of Ireland for the first time since the Anglo-Norman invasion.

As constitutional and economic crises racked Charles I's government, on the evening of 22 October 1641 a group of Ulstermen under the leadership of Sir Phelim O'Neil seized Charlemont castle. The conspirators were demanding improvements in property rights and they were probably fearful of the virulently anti-Catholic English parliament. They pushed southwards and a series of sectarian massacres followed. That these were brutal there is no doubt, but stories about them lost nothing in the telling back in horrified England, where they did much to heighten war mood. The Old English Catholic gentry sided with the rebels as the in-surrection spread across Ireland. The issue was further confused by the outbreak of the English civil war (see BRITISH CIVIL WARS). The Irish insurgents took advantage of the weakened royalist position in Ireland to establish a Catholic confederacy around Kilkenny. The war rumbled on through ceasefire, truce, and sporadic outbreaks of fighting until the execution of Charles I in 1649 united the confederates and the royalist Dublin government against parliament. This provoked a parliamentary invasion and an efficient if brutal campaign by *Cromwell to bring Ireland under parliament's control.

The *Irish campaign in 1689–91 between the supporters of Catholic *James II and *William of Orange cannot really be classified as a rebellion. James fled from England to France in 1688. He landed in Ireland backed by considerable French support the following year and began a campaign against Protestant enclaves loyal to William. William was unwilling to intervene in Ireland but the presence of James and particularly French troops forced his hand and he landed in Ireland with an army. He defeated James's forces over the following year.

Although the following century appeared largely peaceful, the widespread nature of the 1798 rebellion indicated that elements of the population were highly politicized and sectarian divisions still ran deep. The United Irishmen initially campaigned for reform of the representative system but from 1795 they became increasingly revolutionary. Nationalist Wolfe Tone made considerable efforts to gain French support but their attempt to land support was disrupted by bad weather. The authorities took the opportunity to launch an aggressive campaign of disarmament, thus when the rebellion eventually broke out in 1798 they were able to suppress it with relative ease.

By the later part of the century Irish nationalism was a powerful political force, as demonstrated by the popularity of Charles Parnell's Home Rule Party. Its revolutionary strand in the shape of the Young Ireland movement attempted a half-hearted rebellion in 1848. However, the Fenian movement (see FENIAN RAIDS INTO CANADA) and particularly their successors the Irish Republican Brothers (IRB) were of more consequence. The IRB leadership saw their opportunity for action in 1916 and launched the unsuccessful *Easter Rising. The clumsy government reaction to the Rising gave momentum to the Irish Volunteers, increasingly known as the *IRA, and their 1919 *guerrilla campaign against British rule resulted in the *Anglo-Irish war and Irish independence.   MCM

Connolly, S. J. (ed.), *The Oxford Companion to Irish History* (Oxford, 1998).

Duffy, Sean (ed.), *Atlas of Irish History* (Dublin, 1997).

Guy, John, *Tudor England* (Oxford, 1988).

Kee, Robert, *Ireland: A History* (London, 1991).

Irish Republican Army. See IRA.

Ironside, FM Edmund, 1st Baron Ironside of Archangel (1880–1959). Ironside provided John Buchan with a model for his character Richard Hannay, hero of *The Thirty-Nine Steps* and other novels. Broad as well as tall, 'Tiny' Ironside was a good all-rounder sportsman, fluent in seven languages, and he made rapid progress in the army from humble beginnings. Commissioned into the Royal Artillery in 1889, he did well in the Second *Boer War and Staff College in 1913–14 positioned him for high office during WW I. In 1918–19 he commanded the Allied *North Russia intervention, and was later commandant of Staff College. His career stagnated during the inter-war years and he expected to retire as governor of Gibraltar. Surprised when the war minister Hore-Belisha appointed him as inspector general of Overseas Forces in early 1939, he was stung when *Gort, his junior, was made C-in-C of the British Expeditionary Force (BEF) at the outbreak of WW II. Ironside instead became CIGS, but was unsuited to the role and completely at odds with his minister. He found *Churchill's continual interference in military affairs exasperating and was relieved to be replaced by Dill, becoming C-in-C Homes Forces instead, in May 1940. He retired shortly afterwards. APC-A

Bond, Brian (chapter), in Keegan (ed.), *Churchill's Generals* (London, 1991).

Ismail I (also spelt Esmail), **Shah of Iran** (1487–1524). Founder of the Safavid dynasty, Ismail converted Iran from Sunni to the Shi'a sect of Islam. At the age of 14, Ismail took over as head of the Kizilbash (Red Heads) and soon established himself in north-western Iran. In 1501, he captured Tabriz in Azerbaijan which he made his capital and from there he proclaimed himself shah of Iran. Ismail spent the first twelve years of his reign expanding his territory. In 1508 he captured Baghdad and in 1510 overwhelmed the Sunni Uzbeks at a battle near Marv. He brought all of the geographical area of modern Iran and some of Iraq under his control.

Ismail made Shi'a the state religion. This provoked the Sunni Ottoman *Turks and Sultan *Selim I sent Ismail a series of belligerent and provocative letters. Ismail however, had no desire for war with his powerful neighbour. Nonetheless, the Ottomans invaded north-west Iran in 1514. Ismail was defeated outside Tabriz and Selim captured the capital, but was forced to withdraw by a *mutiny in his army. Ismail managed to recover his strength and although there were numerous border skirmishes, the Ottomans were unable to repeat their earlier successes. MCM

Israeli Defence Forces. See IDF.

Issus, battle of (November 333 BC), the second major battle of the Persian campaign of *Alexander 'the Great' and his first encounter with Persian King Darius, fought on the narrow coastal plain between the Mediterranean and Amanus mountains, just north of modern Iskenderum (south-east Turkey), named after him. Darius had mobilized a large army and advanced to Damascus, where he was reinforced by Greek mercenaries previously attached to his navy. He then moved north-west through the Amanus Gates (Bahçe Pass) into Cilicia. Simultaneously, Alexander marched south-east across the Syrian Gates (Belen Pass) and only at the summit of the pass did he discover that the Persians were now behind him. He at once turned back and hurried to confront Darius, who deployed his forces defensively on the north bank of the small Pinarus stream (probably the modern Payas). Alexander strengthened his left wing on the Mediterranean shore, where Parmenio confronted the bulk of the Persian cavalry, while he occupied the right with his Companion Cavalry. While his outnumbered *phalanx struggled in the centre, Alexander drove in around the main battle and forced Darius to flight, whereupon his army disintegrated, leaving only the Greek mercenaries to die fighting. LMW

Bosworth, A. B., *Conquest and Empire* (Cambridge, 1988).

Italian campaign (1859). *Napoleon III had long been anxious to foster Italian unification, and in 1858 he met Cavour, PM of Piedmont, to agree how best to expel the Austrians from northern Italy. In mid-April 1859 he felt obliged to accept a British suggestion of a congress to discuss the Italian question, but Austria presented an ill-judged ultimatum to Piedmont, and Cavour and Napoleon III had their war.

Although Napoleon had anticipated war his army was ill-prepared and the formation of four corps in addition to the Imperial Guard produced chaos. Two corps were to go by land and the Guard and two others by sea, but they were not concentrated until early May. A swift Austrian offensive might have crushed the Piedmontese, but Gyulai, the Austrian commander, moved too slowly. Napoleon was in personal command, with the 70-year-old Marshal Vaillant as his COS. He disembarked at Genoa on 12 May and, despite repeated assertions that the army was not ready to move, decreed that the campaign would start at once.

The French set off for Piacenza, but on 19 May Napoleon was persuaded that he had insufficient *pontoons to cross the Po, and decided to march on Vercelli by way of Casale. On the following day an Austrian *reconnaissance in force was repulsed by Forey's division at Montebello in an action which set the tone for the campaign: French infantry pushed on with such vigour that the fire of Austrian rifles could not stop them. The clash at Montebello persuaded Gyulai that the French were still heading for Piacenza, and he strengthened his left flank at exactly the moment that the Allies marched laboriously across his front to fall on his right flank. On 3 May the Piedmontese took Palestro and

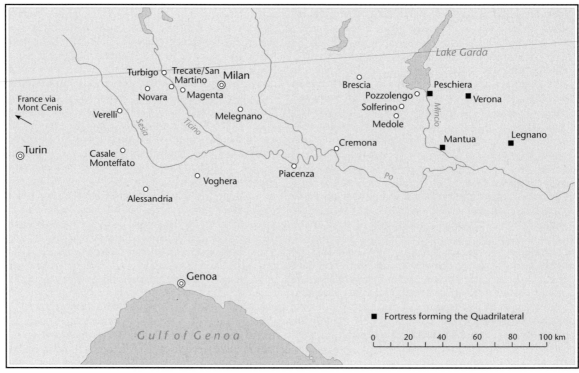

Area of the **Italian campaign**, 1859.

the crossings of the river Sesia around Vercelli, and when the Austrians counter-attacked the next day they ran into Canrobert's corps and were soundly beaten.

Napoleon reached Novara on 2 June and issued orders for the crossing of the Ticino. One crossing was secured at Turbigo and another at San Martino, despite some inept staff work and the proximity of the Austrians. On the 4th the French, advancing in two large columns, stumbled on the Austrians near Magenta: both sides had about 50,000 men. The southern column was in difficulties when the northern column, headed by MacMahon's corps, swung in on the Austrian flank. Magenta was cleared house by house, with a French divisional commander killed in the mêlée, but by nightfall the Austrians were in full retreat.

Gyulai gave up Milan and fell back eastwards, breaking contact as he did so. On 8 June a three-corps attack on Melegnano misfired when Baraguey d'Hilliers attacked prematurely with his own corps. The battle persuaded the Austrians to continue retreating, and all units south of the Po were ordered to cross the river and head for the *Quadrilateral, the fortresses of Verona, Mantua, Legnano, and Peschiera, gateway to Venetia. The Emperor Franz Josef I arrived to take personal command, and fell back across the Mincio on 20 June. But on the 23rd, believing that the Allies were so widely dispersed as to be vulnerable, Franz Josef pushed forward to a line from Pozzolengo through Solferino to Medole.

After taking Milan the Allies had two possible lines of advance, a southerly route along the Po and a northern road through Brescia. They chose the latter, entering Brescia on 16 June and then moving south-east, convinced that the Austrians were on the far side of the Mincio. Both armies issued orders for a routine advance on the 24th, and collided in the hills around Solferino. The village itself was the epicentre of the battle: six French attacks on the cemetery were repulsed until artillery was brought up to breach the walls and a *Zouave regiment went roaring through. Although his flanks still held, Franz Josef realized that his position was untenable; a sudden rainstorm enabled him to recross the Mincio. He had lost more than 13,000 men to about 10,000 French and 5,000 Piedmontese, and the scene around Solferino shocked many who saw it, particularly Napoleon and a young Swiss, Henri *Dunant, who was to found the *Red Cross.

The Austrians fell back within the Quadrilateral and the Allies were preparing for siege operations when Napoleon concluded an armistice. Prussia had mobilized, and he told Cavour: 'With our present military organization, it is impossible for us to wage a war on two fronts'. The campaign had shown that the French army was ill-suited for war against a first-rate adversary, despite Napoleon's efforts to reform it. Not for nothing did Count Hübner call the war 'The first step on the road to *Sedan.'   RH

Italian front (WW I) If it were not for Hemingway's novel *A Farewell to Arms*, few English-speakers would know, or care very much, about the Italian contribution to WW I. This is unfortunate, because the war fought on the north-east frontier against the Austro-Hungarians, reinforced on occasion by the Germans, was one of the nastiest in a very nasty war and witnessed the use of deliberately provoked avalanches to kill thousands of Italian troops, a 'natural disaster weapon' unique in the history of warfare. It was also the reason why Austria-Hungary did not drop out of the war over a year before the end, and created the medium that spawned fascism. It killed 600,000 Italians, who emerged from the war with an undeserved but lingering reputation for cowardice, about as many Austro-Hungarians, and was the only front on which Allied troops set foot on the territory of the Central Powers before the *Armistice. Not bad for a backwater.

The diplomatic background was suitably Byzantine. Italy had belonged to the Triple Alliance since 1882, which committed her and Germany to aid each other militarily if either were attacked by France, and promised neutrality if Austria-Hungary went to war with Russia, freeing the latter from the prospect of a war on two fronts or, since she chose to attack Serbia, three. When WW I broke out none of the conditions of the treaty compelled Italy to act, so she negotiated with both sides to see the best deal she could get, dubbed 'sacro egoismo' by foreign minister Sonnino. The Central Powers grudgingly offered the Trentino, but the Entente, in the secret Treaty of London in April 1915, promised South Tyrol, Trieste, Gorizia, Istria, and northern Dalmatia as well, to be carved out of the Austro-Hungarian empire after the war was won. There was also, certainly, a powerful current of opinion in Italy that a major war would bring the disparate elements of the new Italian nation together and forge a new and improved identity. It was while the ministers who had negotiated the London treaty were trying to sell the war (without mentioning the treaty) to a chamber of deputies largely opposed to it, that Entente funds were secretly passed to Benito *Mussolini, expelled from his post as editor of the Socialist Party's newspaper because of his pro-war views, to found the rabble-rousing *Il popolo d'Italia* which was to be his sounding board for the ideas that later became fascism, and provided him with his post-war power base.

In late May 1915, the war party had its way and a desperately ill-equipped, untrained, and badly led Italian army set out to attack up some of the steepest mountains in Europe, where artillery spotters could bring down accurate indirect fire on them (and, in winter, on the snow and ice slopes above them) in perfect comfort and safety. The C-in-C Cadorna was an unimaginative pounder, but he could see that to attack along the narrow coastal strip towards Trieste was an invitation to cut him off that even the Austro-Hungarians could not resist. Accordingly, he launched ten consecutive uphill offensives on the Izonso front, exhaust-

ing the morale of troops who mostly did not understand what they were fighting for and compounding his brutal ineptitude by never getting his logistics properly balanced, so that the men were also ill-clothed and ill-fed.

Nor was Austro-Hungarian policy much better. Austria's long-term relationship with Italy—part of which had been under Austrian rule for much of the 19th century—meant that, as Gordon Brook-Shepherd points out, 'The Italian front . . . became the only really "popular" one.' The CGS, *Conrad von Hotzendorf, had argued in favour of a preventive war against Italy or Serbia before 1914. When Italy entered the war his focus on the Balkans and the Adriatic made it impossible for the Germans to achieve a consistent strategic approach in which the eastern front was properly of far greater significance than Italy.

As the third miserable winter of the war grew closer, a combined Austro-German counter-offensive fell upon the Italians at *Caporetto and they broke, surrendering by the thousand or fleeing to the Piave river where some semblance of a line was restored with a stiffening of eleven Anglo-French divisions rushed from the western front. But before this, in one of history's greater might-have-beens, peace feelers from the new Austro-Hungarian Emperor Charles through Prince Sixtus of Bourbon-Parma and the Swiss had been rejected by the Entente because of the terms of the Treaty of London, which of course could only be imposed on a totally defeated Austria. The treaty was also to cause problems with US Pres Woodrow Wilson who was shocked to discover the grubby material reasons for which his new allies were fighting. He was, nonetheless, to consent to the handing over of half a million German-speakers to Italy after the war.

At the battle of the Piave in June 1918, the reinforced Italians under their new C-in-C Armando Díaz defeated a renewed offensive, and in October they returned the favour for Caporetto by shattering the Austro-Hungarians in the battle of *Vittorio Veneto, after which they surged back to the pre-war frontier and in the last days before the Armistice finally entered enemy territory. At the Treaty of Saint-Germain in 1919, the Italians received South Tyrol (Alto Adige), the Trentino, Trieste, and Istria, but not north Dalmatia or the largely Italian-speaking city of Fiume in Croatia. The result was that Italy, along with Japan, was both on the winning side and felt she had been stabbed in the back, laying the foundation for the WW II Axis.　　HEB/RH

Brook-Shepherd, Gordon, *The Last Habsburg* (New York, 1968).

Italian independence wars (1821–70), also known as il Risorgimento (It., resurgence). Following a period of semi-independence from the Habsburgs, the Bourbons, and the pope at the point of French bayonets, in 1815 the Italian peninsula reverted to the pre-war tripartite division with the newly revitalized Austrian empire holding Venetia and Lombardy in the north, the backward Papal States in the middle, and the retrograde kingdom of the Two Sicilies in the south, with assorted semi-autonomous principalities scattered around. Additionally there was the north-western kingdom of Sardinia, or Savoy, or Piedmont (we will use the last designation), which was possessed of the sense of nationalism that was the great legacy of the *French Revolutionary wars.

Among the riots and revolutions that convulsed the continent in 1848 were two quite serious popular uprisings in Lombardy and Venetia. King Carlo Alberto of Piedmont believed that Austria would be too distracted to oppose him and invaded in support of those he declared were fellow Italians. He was decisively defeated at the first battle of *Custoza by a numerically inferior Austrian force under *Radetzky, fell back to his own lands, and was to be forced to abdicate in favour of his son, who became 'il re galantuomo' Vittorio Emanuele II. The noisy patriot Giuseppe Mazzini and the less noisy but equally patriotic soldier of fortune *Garibaldi seized Rome in February 1849 and announced the formation of the Roman republic, which was promptly suppressed by troops from France, Austria, and Naples.

In 1858, Count Camillo Cavour, the Piedmontese foreign minister, negotiated a treaty with *Napoleon III which promised French assistance in freeing northern Italy from Austrian rule, and the following year he encouraged revolts in Venetia and Lombardy to precipitate a war with Austria. At the battle of Solferino (24 June 1859), a combined Franco-Piedmontese force defeated the Austrians and in the peace that followed, Austria was forced to cede most of Lombardy (except for the important fortresses of Peschiera and Mantua) to Piedmont. In addition the duchies of Parma, Tuscany, Modena, and Romagna, anxious not to be part of a confederation under papal rule as desired by the French, agreed to union with Piedmont. As agreed, in return for her assistance France annexed Nice and Savoy.

In April 1860, King Francis II of the Two Sicilies bloodily suppressed revolts in Naples and Sicily and in response Garibaldi led his 'Thousand Redshirts' (with the covert support of Piedmont) in an invasion of Sicily in May 1860. Gathering supporters as he went, he chivvied the Neapolitan army out of Sicily and crossed the Straits of Messina on 22 August with the help of the Royal Navy. Naples fell on 7 September and Garibaldi marched north, defeating the last Neapolitan army at the battle of Volturno (26 October). It was perfectly clear that he intended to march on Rome, and it was equally clear that if he did Napoleon III, self-appointed guardian of the papacy, would intervene. So the Piedmontese army marched south, defeating a papal army at Castelfidardo on 18 September but carefully skirting Rome, and interposed itself between Garibaldi and his objective. On 17 March 1861 a united Kingdom of Italy was proclaimed, its capital in Florence and Vittorio Emanuele its first constitutional monarch.

Garibaldi was unreconcilable and in August 1862 gathered another army of patriots and marched on Rome. The same reasons that led him to the Volturno in 1860 caused Vittorio Emanuele to block him, and this time there was a battle at Aspromonte where the great patriot was wounded and after which he had to flee the country. He tried again in 1867 and was again defeated, this time by the French.

In April 1866, Italy signed a treaty with Bismarck's Prussia against Austria and attacked across Lombardy towards Venetia at the outbreak of the *Austro-Prussian war. Things did not go well. The Italian army was defeated at the second battle of *Custoza and its technically superior navy was trounced at Lissa. Nonetheless, the Prussian victory at *Königgrätz was sufficiently overwhelming to dictate terms that included giving Venetia and the Lombard fortresses to Italy.

There remained the matter of the vestigial Papal State around Rome, guarded by Napoleon III with a devotion worthy of a better cause. The *Franco-Prussian war caused France to withdraw her garrison and Italian troops entered the city on 20 September 1870. It was not to be until the Lateran Treaty of 1929 signed by Mussolini that matters of territoriality and compensation were finally to be agreed between the papacy and the first united Italy since the time of the Roman empire. RTF/HEB

Italian wars, French (1494–1559). The invasion of Italy in 1494 by King Charles VIII of France (1483–98) sparked a series of wars that sporadically involved all of western Europe. Charles claimed the kingdom of Naples and hoped to seize it by force of arms, and at first his advance swept all aside. In the process he offended the Holy Roman Emperor, the pope, and most dangerously Ferdinand, monarch not only of Sicily but now joint monarch of a newly unified Spain that was about to send out its surplus warrior population to conquer the empire. It was an army of these hardened soldiers commanded by Ferdinand's 'Gran Capitán' Gonzalo de *Córdoba that threw the French out of Naples and rescued Pope Alexander VI, winning Ferdinand and Isabella the title of 'Most Catholic'.

Charles's successor Louis XII (1498–1515) invaded Naples again in 1500 having taken the precaution of hiring the *Swiss (see also MERCENARIES) and once again ran into the Spanish under Córdoba, who handed them resounding defeats at *Cerignola and at Garigliano in 1503. The French did not return to Italy in force again until Gaston de *Foix, whose father had been killed at Cerignola, himself died defeating imperial and papal forces at Ravenna on 11 April 1512. The last assignment of Ferdinand's 'Gran Capitán' was to restore the allied situation.

Under *François I (1515–47), the conflict broadened. He had the misfortune to ascend to the French throne one year before the Habsburg *Charles V became king of Spain and eventually also Holy Roman Emperor. Henry VIII of England also fought against François, who began well when his artillery smashed the Swiss, now hired to fight against him, at the battle of Marignano on 13–14 September 1515. But that proved to be the high point for French arms and over the next 30 years France found herself as often as not defending her own frontiers, at one point in 1544 having to fight the Spanish in Italy, an invasion by an imperial army across the Rhine, and losing Boulogne to the English.

During the last phase of a struggle whose main theatre was no longer Italy, Henri II (1547–59) devoted his entire reign to war. Earlier he seemed to be reversing the tide and even took Calais, England's last continental possession. But a series of Habsburg successes, culminating at the battle of Gravelines on 13 July 1558, finally led him to conclude the Peace of Câteau-Cambrésis with Philip II of Spain in 1559, ending the wars.

This interminable conflict drained France, established the pre-eminence of Spain in Europe, and brought a marked change in warfare. Artillery had transformed *siege warfare and an entirely new style of *fortification, the bastioned artillery fortress, came into being. Field artillery had also come of age. The Spanish solved the problem of mating individual firearms with pikes and artillery in the *tercio, which ruled the battlefield for a further century.   JAL

Oman, Charles, *The Art of War in the 16th Century* (London, 1937).

Parker, Geoffrey, *The Military Revolution: Military Innovation and the Rise of the West, 1500–1800* (Cambridge, 1988).

Italo-Turkish war (1911–12), one of the several small wars sparked by the crumbling of the Ottoman empire that immediately preceded WW I. Italy coveted the Turkish possessions of Cyrenaica and Tripolitania (modern Libya), and issued an ultimatum on 28 September 1911. She occupied the coastal districts expecting support from the local *Senussi, but encountered resistance instead. Italian forces occupied Derna and Benghazi and used aeroplanes to bomb the Turks, a historical first just pre-empting the Bulgarians, who also bombed the Turks from the air. More concerned with the *Balkan wars, Turkey sought peace and the Treaty of Lausanne on 18 October 1912 ended the war. The Senussi continued fighting into the 1930s, but this partial success gave Italy the base from which to launch the invasion of *Abyssinia in the 1930s and exposed her to humiliating defeats there and in the Western Desert when she entered WW II in 1941.   CDB

Italy, campaign in (WW II) This was the result of the US acceptance of a British strategy in 1942. The British favoured an 'indirect approach', fighting in the Mediterranean theatre. By contrast, the Americans preferred to build up their forces in England and attack the Germans by the shortest route, a cross-Channel assault on occupied France. They invaded French North Africa in November 1942 and with the collapse of Axis resistance in Tunisia the following

May, Anglo-American forces were no longer in contact with the enemy. Logistic realities meant that it was not possible to return these troops to England and launch an invasion of France in 1943 and the only alternative was to attack Italy.

On 10 July 1943, Fifteenth Army Group under *Alexander, consisting of the US Seventh Army under *Patton and Montgomery's British Eighth Army, landed in *Sicily. The Sicilian campaign showed the Allies in a bad light. Poor combat performance and lack of co-ordination permitted the evacuation of over 100,000 Axis troops, 40,000 of whom were Germans, with much of their equipment. Bitter inter-Allied and inter-service rivalries, failures to make best use of *ULTRA, the painfully slow advances of Eighth Army, and the skill and tenacity of the German defenders all contributed to the disappointing result of the campaign.

*Mussolini was deposed in July 1943 and the new Italian government opened negotiations to surrender, keen for the Allies to occupy as much of their country as possible to forestall German moves. But while the Anglo-Americans hesitated the Germans did not, rushing troops into Italy and ensuring that the Allies would have to fight every step of the way. Eighth Army landed unopposed at Reggio di Calabria on 3 September, and Clark's US Fifth Army (which included British troops) landed at *Salerno on 9 September. The strategy of Kesselring, the German commander in Italy, was to conduct a forward defence, forcing the Allies to fight every step of the way. He held a series of strong defensive lines and turned the campaign into a grim war of *attrition. SHINGLE, the Allied attempt at *Anzio in January 1944 to use sea power to outflank his Gustav Line before the landing craft were withdrawn for the *Normandy invasion, was a miserable failure that never broke out until the main force advanced from the south.

Between 12 January and 18 May 1944 the Allies launched the four battles of *Cassino, akin to a *Passchendaele fought up a steep mountain. Before the second offensive the battlefield-dominating 6th-century Benedictine monastery, previously used by the Germans only for artillery-spotting, was bombed to rubble, which made it an even better defensive position than when it was intact. The fourth battle (DIADEM) was rather better planned and executed than previous efforts and the forces of two of the smaller Allied powers played a starring role. Anders's II Polish Corps captured the ruins of the monastery and Juin's French Expeditionary Corps breached the outlying Hitler Line. On 25 May the Anzio force, which had been penned into the beachhead since January, finally linked up with the advancing Fifth Army. There was a fleeting chance that the retreating Germans might be surrounded, but a combination of Alexander's weak leadership and Clark's egocentric determination to take Rome before the Normandy landings denied him the prospect of headlines let the last chance for a decisive victory slip away. Instead the Germans fell back to the

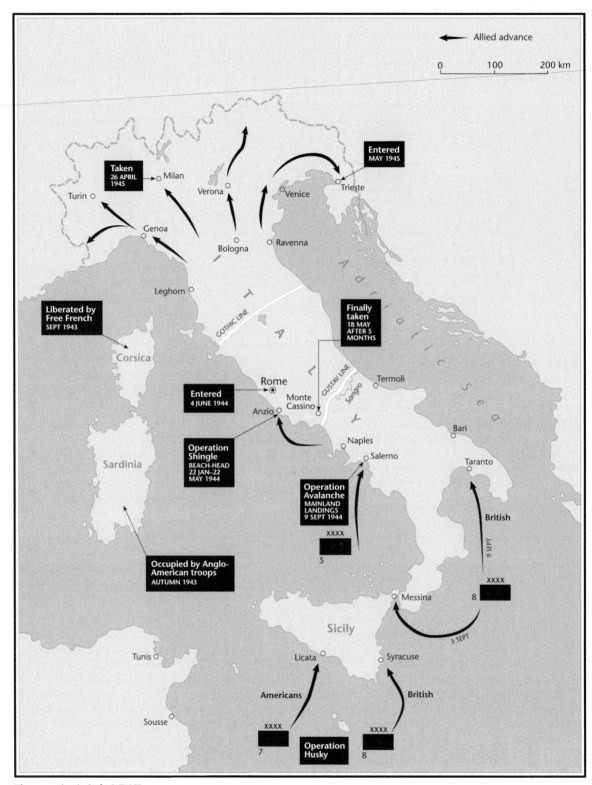

The campaign in **Italy, WW II**.

Gothic Line, which wound from Ancona to south of Bologna via Pisa and Florence.

After D-Day in Normandy, Italy became very much a secondary front, with six divisions taken away to take part in the largely ceremonial landings in the south of France. In September 1944 the Eighth Army under Gen Leese launched OLIVE, an offensive on the Adriatic coast which turned into the now usual attrition. The Eighth (now under McCreery) and the US Fifth Army (now under Truscott) had to contend with a second bitter winter facing a still formidable enemy in well-chosen and ever-hardening positions.

In March 1945, with the Third Reich collapsing, Gen von Vietinghoff assumed command of German forces in Italy. This coincided with the preparations for GRAPESHOT, the final Allied push. On 9 April McCreery began Eighth Army's final offensive, and on 14 April the US Fifth Army joined in. Von Vietinghoff's forces began to crumble, and on 25 April Eighth and Fifth Armies linked up at finale in Emilia. On 2 May 1945, the German forces in Italy surrendered after twenty months of resistance.

Opinions differ on the usefulness of the Italian campaign to the Allied cause. Its defenders argue that it tied down German forces and resources that could have been deployed in more decisive theatres, and as a battle of attrition it was fairly cost-effective, inflicting 434,000 casualties in exchange for 312,000. By contrast the US official history fairly questions who was tying down whom. The performance of Allied forces in Sicily was fairly dismal even under the command of the 'A' team of Montgomery and Patton. Under less prominent commanders it did no worse against much tougher defences and with greatly reduced resources.

While a campaign in the Mediterranean was all that was available in 1942–3 and may have been of crucial importance in working out the modalities of inter-Allied co-operation and *doctrine for the later Normandy campaign, it is probable that after the failure at Anzio a more limited campaign might have been just as successful in tying down German forces. Although the troops under *Slim in the *Burma campaign called themselves the 'forgotten army', it was a description that could be claimed with equal justification by the men who fought their way up Italy against geography and one of Nazi Germany's best field commanders.   GDS

Graham, D., and Bidwell, S., *Tug of War: The Battle for Italy, 1943–1945* (London, 1986).

Ivan IV 'the Terrible', Tsar of Russia (1530–84). Ivan 'Grozny' was the first Russian ruler to take the title tsar (from Caesar). *Grozny* means 'terrible' or 'awesome' and he deserved that title more. He became prince of Muscovy at the age of 3 on the death of his father and grew up under the guardianship of the boyars (nobles) who were not anxious to have a strong ruler. It was a time of intrigue and constant

danger which moulded his ruthless and suspicious nature. It took him 30 years, but by a process first of tactical alliances and then by physical elimination he gradually won absolute personal power, cemented with the creation of the black-clad Oprichnina, a private army or secret police force whose members owed everything to Ivan and could be relied on to conduct a reign of terror against the boyars.

Ivan's military and foreign policy had two main goals: continuation of the struggle against the *Mongol Golden Horde, whose yoke Russia had shaken off in 1480, but who remained a threat, and access to the Baltic Sea. In 1552 he captured the Tartar city of Kazan and in 1556 Astrakhan. The Crimean Tartars repaid the favour by burning Moscow in 1571. His campaigns in the west during the Livonian war (1558–83) were less successful and ended in defeat and renewed isolation from the West.

Ivan's armies were split into five corps, or *polk* ('regiments'): the main body (*bol'shoy*), left and right flanking (*levy* and *pravy*), the advance guard (*peredovoi*), which also provided scouts and forces for *pursuit, and the rearguard (*zasadny*), each commanded by a high-ranking boyar who had an Ivan loyalist and more professional lieutenant general to advise him. For fighting on the steppe, the Russians devised the *gulai-gorod* or 'running castle'—a wagon fort akin to the one made famous by the *Hussites.

Ivan was particularly interested in artillery, possibly because it was the only system that outranged the powerful Tartar composite bows, and enjoyed watching firepower demonstrations in which earth bunkers were flattened to see what his gunners could do. Foreign observers were greatly impressed with Ivan's firepower. During his reign the body of the *strelsty or musketeers was created and the artillery chancellery was extant by 1581.   CDB

Berry, Lloyd, and Crummey, Robert, *Rude and Barbarous Kingdom: Russia in the Accounts of 16th Century English Voyagers* (Madison, Wisc. 1968).
Yanov, Alexander, *The Origins of Autocracy: Ivan the Terrible in Russian History* (Berkeley, 1981).

IW. See INFORMATION WARFARE.

Iwo Jima, battle of (1945), penultimate island invasion of the *Pacific campaign and possibly the most intense battle of WW II, where *Nimitz said that 'uncommon valor was a common virtue'. A quarter of all the Congressional Medals of Honor awarded during WW II were won there. Japanese commander Kuribayashi negated US firepower by sheltering his 22,000 men in 1,500 bunkers linked by 16 miles (26 km) of tunnels, enabling them to strike in areas believed to be secure. He turned the whole 8 square mile (21 sq km) island, not merely the infamous hill given the name, into a meat grinder. USMC casualties between 19 February and 25 March were 26,000. The defenders swore there would be 'no Japanese survivors' and 99 per cent of them kept their word. Aerial kamikaze attacks also sank an escort carrier and damaged several other ships.

The emblematic event of the battle was the raising of the US flag atop extinct volcano Mount Suribachi on 23 February, the subject of the most famous battle photograph of all time by Associated Press photographer Rosenthal and the model for the US Marine Corps memorial at Arlington National *Cemetery. Secretary of the Navy Forrestal commented that the flag-raising guaranteed an independent Marine Corps for 100 years.   HEB

Jackson, Gen Thomas J. 'Stonewall' (1824–63), hard-driving, Cromwell-like Confederate general, and sole undisputed military genius of the *American civil war. Convinced that God intended him for some great purpose, he became a terror to the Union and an inspiration to the Confederacy by his implementation of the axiom 'move swiftly, strike vigorously and secure *all* the fruits of victory'. He graduated from *West Point in 1846, but left the army to teach at the Virginia Military Institute in 1851. Appointed a Confederate brigadier general in 1861, he earned his nickname at first *Bull Run where his brigade was described as standing like a stone wall. After the 1862 *Shenandoah Valley campaign he was marked for greatness and became *Lee's principal lieutenant.

As *Fuller put it, he 'possessed the brutality essential in war'. More even than *Sherman, he did not wish merely to defeat but to *punish* the enemy. There was none of Lee's courtliness in his make-up, and his own men were either useful to his purposes or not worthy of consideration. He was impatient with weariness or even illness, harshly unforgiving of *desertion, and inclined to attribute any battlefield failure to *cowardice. On several occasions he gave battle with subordinate commanders awaiting *court martial. Apart from a weakness for fresh fruit, his only passion was to fulfil the predestination of his implacable God.

During the Shenandoah campaign he refined an ability to 'mystify, mislead and surprise' not only the enemy but his own officers and men. Aware of his inability to convince others of the rightness of his ideas, he used ambassadors to advocate his strategic concepts with his superiors, without success. His most persuasive argument was the fait accompli, notably at *Chancellorsville where he improved on Lee's bold concept of a flank march by announcing that he would take two-thirds of the army from his momentarily nonplussed commander. Many judged that he took insane

risks, but more than any other Confederate commander he was acutely aware that these were necessary to overcome the imbalance of forces.

Although without peer in the conception of battle, he was not a tactical innovator. At first and second Bull Run he made use of the reverse slope to protect his badly outnumbered men, but on other occasions he exposed them to needless casualties, and he was slow to learn that the increased range of rifle fire made the forward deployment of artillery suicidal. Like other Confederate commanders, he paid little attention to training or to assembling the staff that he needed more than most to bring about the co-ordination and ruthless execution that so often escaped him. He believed that natural selection—or as in his own case, divine dispensation—would provide, and it seldom did.

His greatest success also encompassed the most glaring failure of his secretive style of generalship, when at Chancellorsville his mortal wounding aborted his plan to cut off the Union retreat. It is doubtful that it would have produced the annihilation he intended, but he appears to have been alone in appreciating that only thus could the war be won. Lee's last message to him said that for the good of the country he would have chosen to be struck down in his stead. His own last words resonate poignantly over the years: 'Let us cross over the river and rest under the shade of the trees.'   HEB

Robertson, James, *Stonewall Jackson* (New York, 1997).

....

Jacobite risings is a term generally applied to the rebellions in 1715 and 1745–6 ('the Fifteen' and 'the Forty-Five') against the Hanoverians by mainly Scots supporters of the exiled Stuart 'Old Pretender' (James Edward, son of *James VII and II) and his son the 'Young Pretender'

(Bonny Prince Charlie). They were claimants to the throne of what became from 1707 Great Britain, although *William of Orange also had to defeat a Jacobite force in his *Irish campaign.

Of the two, the second was more spectacular, but the first presented a more serious threat. George I, the first of the house of Hanover to rule Great Britain, had only been in England a year when 'the Fifteen' began. There was much discontent with the new regime, particularly from Scots who resented the Treaty of Union. The Stuart standard was raised north of the border by the Earl of Mar and he rallied substantial support, some eighteen lords bringing with them 5,000 men. Since government troops in Scotland scarcely numbered 1,500 at the start of the uprising, a determined move by Mar at this stage could have been decisive. Instead he delayed, waiting for reinforcements, and the government was able to concentrate its efforts on drawing the teeth of Jacobitism in England. An Act was passed empowering the king to imprison any person suspected of conspiring against him. The first arrest was made in September when an officer in the Guards was arrested for enlisting men for the Pretender. Six MPs were also rounded up, including Sir William Wyndham who was suspected of plotting a rising in the west of England. Another MP, Thomas Forster, did lead a rising in the north with the Earl of Derwentwater, and together they marched about 2,000 men south to Preston, where they were intercepted by Gens Carpenter and Wills and surrendered on 14 November. The day before that, Mar with 10,000 troops had engaged 3,500 government forces under the Duke of Argyll at the battle of Sheriffmuir. The outcome was indecisive, but it was enough to herald the defeat of the Jacobites. By the time James himself arrived in Scotland in December, Mar's forces were depleted while Argyll's had been strengthened with troops which included a Dutch contingent. James, realizing that the cause was lost, left Scotland taking the Earl of Mar back to France with him.

James Edward never returned, but his younger son Charles Edward landed in Scotland in July 1745 to raise his standard again. Although initially he only had seven supporters, within weeks the last feudal host to be raised in Europe had answered the call of its clan chieftains and he had an army of 1,500 men to confront Hanoverian troops under Sir John Cope numbering about 4,000. Cope marched north from Stirling to intercept the Jacobite forces but found them entrenched on the Corrieyairack pass in an impregnable position and diverted instead to Inverness. This allowed Charles to proceed to Edinburgh where he took the town but not the castle. Cope, meanwhile, sailed his forces from Inverness to the Firth of Forth and engaged the Jacobite army at Prestonpans on 21 September, where he was routed. On 3 November Charles led his troops, now some 5,500 strong and including elements of Scots and Irish regiments in French service, south to Carlisle, thus avoiding Gen Wade who was stationed at Newcastle with superior

forces including 6,000 Dutch soldiers. Wade tried to intercept the Jacobites but got no further than Hexham, his route being blocked by snow. The Jacobite army proceeded south, reaching Derby by 4 December. There was then no army between them and London, *Cumberland being at Lichfield, having been tricked by the prince's Lt Gen Lord George Murray into believing that the Jacobites were heading for Wales.

Four thousand regulars who were in the capital were mobilized to protect the northern approach to the city at Finchley, but perhaps fortunately for them on 6 December the prince and his advisers decided to retreat to Scotland. Some at the time and since have maintained that if they had advanced they could have taken London. Others claim it was a sound decision, since few recruits had joined them in their march through England—they left more men to garrison Carlisle than they had been able to recruit subsequently. Also Cumberland was no more than a day's march away, while Wade was at Wetherby, threatening their retreat north. Whatever the second-guessing, it was the high water mark of the rebellion and the Jacobites were hotly chased by Cumberland, his advance guard encountering their rearguard in a skirmish at Penrith, the last battle to be fought on English soil. The bulk of the Jacobite army reached Scotland and even defeated Hanoverian troops at *Falkirk in January, only to be decisively beaten at *Culloden in April 1746.

Despite persistent attempts to portray the risings as Scots versus English, the truth is more complex. There were many Scots in Cumberland's army, and some of the worst excesses in the suppression of 'the Forty-Five' were perpetrated by Lowland Scots officers. There were some flickerings of Jacobitism in the Highlands after 1746, despite the government's ruthless repression, which included the deportation of thousands to the West Indies, from whence few returned, and the banning of traditional Highland dress and tartan. London also abolished the hereditary, essentially feudal jurisdictions which had helped create the army that perished at Culloden, but it was the Highland chieftains themselves who completed the process by dispossessing their tenants, driving yet more thousands to emigrate to Ireland and to America.   WS

Black, Jeremy, *Culloden and the '45* (Gloucester, 1990).
Lenman, Bruce, *The Jacobite Risings in Britain 1689–1746* (London, 1980).

Jägers German *light troops, whose name—like *chasseurs in French—means huntsmen. They began in the 18th century as quite literally that. When *Frederick 'the Great' raised his Feldjäger-Corps zu Fuss in 1744 he recruited it from foresters and gamekeepers, as did many of his fellow-sovereigns. Prussian Jägers, in common with those of other German states, carried heavy hunting rifles which made them very effective skirmishers, although the facts that they were not fitted with *bayonets and took longer to load than muskets made them vulnerable to cavalry. Jägers were among the German troops used by the British during the *American independence war, and influenced the British army's approach to *rifle regiments. The Honourable Artillery Company (perversely not a company at all, but a regiment) was amongst the units to call its light company the Jäger (sometimes anglicized as Yager) company.

An assortment of Jäger units fought in the *Napoleonic wars. In 1914 the imperial German army had eighteen Jäger battalions, doubled with reserve units on mobilization, which, in a reflection of their light traditions, were expected to operate with the cavalry. As the German army developed storm-troop tactics during WW I, Jäger battalions which, like similar light troops elsewhere, had long emphasized toughness and self-reliance, were converted into assault battalions. Jägers wore grey-green rather than field-grey uniforms, and a flat-topped shako rather than a spiked helmet. Their *waffenfarbe* (arm of service colour), used as piping round epaulettes, was light green.

There were also Jäger ski-battalions, known as *gebirgsjäger*, which wore a distinctive Edelweiss badge. The Wurttemberg Jäger battalion, in which Rommel served, enjoyed a particularly high reputation in WW I. German *mountain troops performed some spectacular feats in WW II, among them the capture and defence of Narvik by Gen Dietl's division in 1940 and the ascent of Mount Elbrus, highest peak in the Caucasus in 1942.

The Germans had no real equivalent to French *chasseurs à cheval*, but the Prussian army did raise *Jäger zu pferd* (horse Jäger) squadrons in 1897, based on *Meldreiter* (dispatch rider) detachments which had been formed in 1895. The squadrons became three regiments in 1905, and more were raised to make a total of thirteen by 1914. They did not survive WW I. RH

James, King, VII of Scotland and II of England

(1633–1701). Second son of Charles I, James Duke of York was exiled after the *British civil wars. He served in the French army under *Turenne, who thought highly of him, changed sides when his brother concluded an alliance with Spain in 1656, and commanded part of the Spanish army at the battle of the Dunes in 1658.

On Charles II's restoration in 1660 he became Lord High Admiral, and did much to improve the navy's efficiency. He was far less successful as a commander, failing to pursue the Dutch fleet after the battle of Lowestoft, and being beaten by de Reuter at Sole Bay. James became a Catholic in 1669, was forced to retire as Lord High Admiral in 1672, and there were moves to exclude him from the throne. When he became king in 1685 he set about remodelling the army to improve its efficiency and pack it with supporters. It fought well for him at *Sedgemoor in 1685, but when *William of Orange landed at Torbay in 1688 James displayed an indeci-

sion which encouraged many officers to desert him. At the crucial moment he fled, only to be captured and allowed to escape to France.

Ireland remained largely in the hands of his Lord Deputy, Tyrconnell, and in 1689 James landed there. When William arrived in Ireland in June 1690 James met him on the *Boyne and took up a good position, but weakened his centre to meet a threat to his left flank and was soundly beaten. He soon left the country, reviled as 'Seamus an Chaca', James 'the Shithead', while his supporters fought on with bravery worthy of a better cause. James died in exile at St Germain, leaving his son James Edward ('the Old Pretender') as the *Jacobite hope. Tactless and obdurate, James was capable of great personal courage but lacked the poise and self-discipline needed for high command. RH

janissaries (Turkish: *yeniçeri*, new troops), the name given to the formidable soldiers of the infantry created by the Ottomans as early as the 14th century, who remained the terror of Europe until the mid-17th century. The janissaries were drawn from *devşirme* (collection or round-up) of Christian boys of conquered territories of the Balkans. Generally between the ages of 12 and 18, these boys were unmarried, converted to Islam, slaves of the sultan, and educated in special schools which graduated both the disciplined, fighting force and many of the high officials, including the grand vizier, of the early empire. Five to ten per cent served in the palace; the rest of the recruits were attached to the *acemioğlan* (cadet) corps. The janissaries were created to counterbalance the cavalry, fief-based troops (*sipahi*, hence the English 'sepoys', or *timariots*) of the Turkish aristocracy, acting as the private standing army of the sultan. The effective fighting force under *Suleiman 'the Magnificent' (1494–1566), was 20,000; that figure rose to as high as 80,000 by the end of the 17th century.

The janissary corps was called the *ocak* (hearth), and divided into 196 distinct regiments (*orta*), varying in size from 100 to 1,000 depending on the period, and lodged in barracks (*oda*) in Istanbul. Their skill in the use of firearms, unique uniforms, and extensive privileges distinguished the corps from all other Ottoman troops. The chief officer was the *ağa*, appointed by the sultan. *Discipline remained the prerogative of the corps itself, one of the persistent problems of the later empire. Janissaries of the 16th century were described as the most disciplined, ascetic, and fierce infantry troops Europe had ever encountered. By the mid-16th century, janissaries served throughout the empire, manning fortresses and battlefronts, guarding cities, and quelling internal violence. At sustained sieges they were unparalleled, as in 1683, when they literally came within inches of breaking through the walls of *Vienna. Their importance to the spread of Ottoman power cannot be exaggerated.

By the beginning of the 17th century, janissary recruits came from the Muslim population, even from sons of the janissaries themselves. *Devshirme* style recruitment lapsed after the 1660s. By 1800, everybody was a janissary, as the corps was swollen to as many as 400,000 names, based on corrupt and marketable muster rolls, which supported a process of gentrification of the janissary families. Probably 10 per cent of that number could be counted upon to defend the empire. The Ottomans evolved different means of recruitment through state-funded militias, both cavalry and infantry, to defend the Danubian fortress system, and other battlefronts. They replaced the timariots, whose presence on Ottoman campaigns was insignificant after 1700, and were the antecedents to the new style regiments (*nizam-i cedid*) of Selim III (1761–1808). The militias were organized side by side with the janissaries, a corps which represented both the chief obstacle (and source of profit) to reforming sultans and bureaucrats, now challenged by the successful western military system.

Mahmut II (1785–1839) put an end to the corps in 1826, when loyal artillery troops surrounded the barracks, and shot down those remaining janissaries who had rebelled against his creation of the new trained and disciplined *eşkinci* corps. Thereafter, the Ottomans created an army more closely aligned to western models. VHA

Goodwin, Godfrey, *The Janissaries* (London, 1997).

Huart, C. 'Janissaries', *Encyclopedia of Islam* 2nd edn. (Leiden, 1987).

Stiles, Andrina, *The Ottoman Empire, 1450–1700* (London, 1989).

javelins. See POLE ARMS/STAFF WEAPONS.

Jena/Auerstadt, battles of (1806).

In August 1806 the Prussian government, humiliated by Napoleon's actions since his victory over Austria and Russia at *Austerlitz the previous year, decided to declare war on France. The French army had at least 160,000 men quartered in southern Germany, and although the Prussians and their Saxon allies could produce rather more, the Prussian army was 'a walking museum piece' which had changed little since the days of *Frederick 'the Great'. In September the Prussians began a hesitant advance, initially confident that Napoleon would stand on the defensive. They were beset by divided counsels, with both Prince Hohenlohe and the Duke of Brunswick favouring different plans which an irresolute King Frederick William III did his best to balance.

*Napoleon decided to concentrate on his extreme right and push swiftly through the difficult Thuringerwald into the area between Dresden and Leipzig. If the Prussians advanced he would outflank them, and if they fell back he hoped to catch them at a disadvantage on one of a number of river lines. He crossed the Saxon frontier on 8 October behind a cavalry screen with the Guard and six corps, a *bataillon carré* (lit., square battalion) of 180,000 men moving in lateral columns close enough to offer mutual support. Prince Louis of Prussia, commanding a division

watching the south-west approaches to the Prussian concentration area, was caught and killed at Saalfeld. On the 13th Napoleon reached Jena, where reports from *Lannes, commanding his leading corps, suggested that the whole Prussian army lay on the lofty Landgrafenberg feature in front of him, though thick fog prevented accurate *reconnaissance. He was confident that he would be able to move his corps up to concentrate in overwhelming strength over the next 24 hours, and decided to attack. That night he set about securing the Windknollen feature, highest point of the Landgrafenberg.

On the morning of the 14th Napoleon duly attacked, and a combination of French élan and Prussian command errors soon gave him enough room to deploy his troops as they came up. By late morning Hohenlohe realized that he was dealing with the main French army and did his best to concentrate to meet it. The turning point of the battle came when 20,000 Prussian infantry drew up outside the village of Vierzenheiligen, under merciless fire from French in the village, until, as Maj Gen Maude says: 'In places the fronts of companies were marked only by individual files still loading and firing, while all their comrades lay dead and dying around them.' A general advance, begun at about midday, pushed the Prussians from the field.

Unbeknown to Napoleon, he was in fact only facing part of the Prussian army: Brunswick's 60,000 men were at Auerstadt, 12 miles (19 km) to the north. Two French corps under *Davout and *Bernadotte had hooked to the east of Jena, making for Hohenlohe's rear, and collided with Brunswick early on the 14th. Davout fought a masterly battle against the odds, unsupported by Bernadotte who turned a deaf ear to his appeals for help and was lucky to escape *court martial for it. The Prussians were routed and Brunswick himself was killed. Auerstadt was a prodigious achievement, a tribute to the 'Iron Marshal' and his troops.

The double battle of Jena/Auerstadt cost the Prussians 25,000 prisoners and 200 guns. The towering reputation of the Prussian army was demolished, and French defeat at *Rossbach avenged: Napoleon entered Berlin on 26 October. The Prussians had been hamstrung by disunited command, fatal for an army which worked by order, not by reflex. Although Napoleon's advance had been skilful, he had made a significant error of judgement on the night of the 13th and was saved from its consequences by Prussian hesitation, by Davout's talent, and by the superb fighting qualities of a French army at the very peak of its form. RH

Chandler, David G., *Jena 1806* (London, 1993).

Maude, Maj Gen., *The Jena Campaign* (London, 1906).

jerrycan (or jerrican), robust metal or, later, plastic container with rounded corners for carrying fuel, oil, or water. A German design—hence its name—it was copied by British and US forces in WW II. CDB

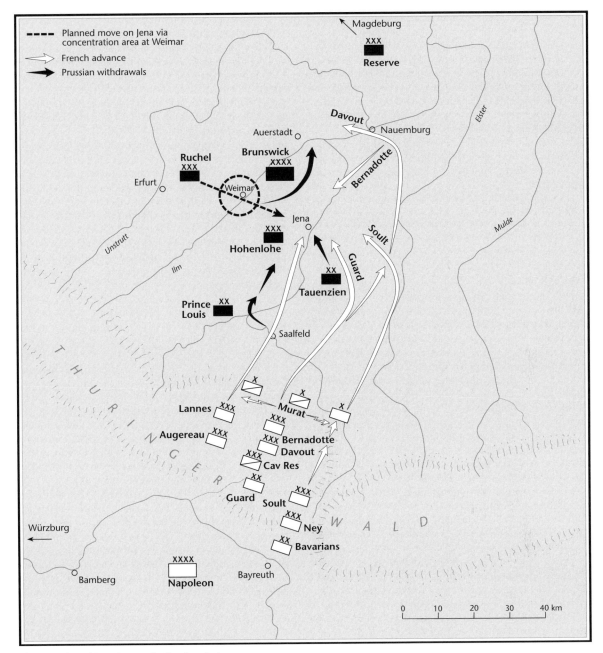

The campaign of **Jena-Auerstadt,** October 1806.

Jerusalem, siege of (1099). The First *Crusade had been inspired by the idea of delivering the Holy Sepulchre from the infidel so when the crusaders besieged Jerusalem on 7 June it was not a military objective but the emotional mainspring of the whole undertaking. The 0.62 mile (1 km) long north wall, unlike the east and west walls which crowned steep slopes, lacked natural defences but was pro-tected by an outer wall and ditch. Level land outside made Zion Gate, which was shielded only by a ditch, vulnerable. Religious exaltation and fear of a relief force impelled the crusaders, with no siege equipment, to a doomed attack on 13 June.

When a crusader fleet landed supplies at Jaffa on 17 June the army began to erect two siege towers. The northern

465

French built one, with a ram to breach the outer wall, at the north-west corner of the city, while the Provençals constructed theirs outside Zion Gate. On the night of 9/10 July the northern tower and ram were moved from the west to the east end of the north wall, surprising the defenders. A two-pronged attack was launched on 13 July. On 15 July after very fierce fighting the northern French broke into the city causing the garrison to surrender to the Provençals in the south in order to avoid massacre. The inhabitants were less fortunate, and almost all were butchered, an act which was to erect a lasting barrier to good relations between Christian and Muslim. Not for the last time, one fanaticism awoke another.
JF2

France, J., *Victory in the East: A Military History of the First Crusade* (Cambridge, 1994).

Prawer, J., 'The Jerusalem the Crusaders Captured: A Contribution to the Military Topography of the City', in *Crusade and Settlement in the Latin East* (Cardiff, 1985).

Jewish revolts (66–73 and 132–5). The first and second Jewish revolts were responses to Roman control of Judaea and Samaria, and both revolts can be compared to modern *guerrilla insurgencies. The Roman general *Pompey conquered the Jewish homeland of Judaea and Saman'a in 63 BC and these lands became a Roman protectorate. In AD 44, the region was placed under the direct rule of Roman procurators. Roman rule resulted in religious and political tensions, and a rise in nationalistic feeling among the Jews.

In AD 66, sporadic Jewish discontent culminated in a revolt by Jewish extremists against Roman rule. These extremists, or 'zealots', seized the city of Jerusalem and drove out the Roman garrison. A Roman relief force headed by the imperial legate of Syria, Gallus, was overwhelmed by the Jews in the pass of Beth-Horon, leaving the Jews free to establish a revolutionary government. In response, Emperor Nero despatched a force headed by Vespasian and accompanied by Titus, Vespasian's son. Vespasian had proved himself as a first-class general and administrator in Germany, Britain, and Africa, and under his command the Romans set about suppressing the Jewish revolt. To this end, Vespasian deployed four legions, 25,000 auxiliaries, and a siege-train of 340 catapults. In a three-year campaign, Josephus, a historian, led the desperate Jewish resistance to Vespasian's counter-insurgency campaign. When Vespasian became emperor in AD 69, Titus took charge of the final phases of the suppression of the revolt. In the end, the might of the Roman legions proved too much and in AD 70 Jerusalem was recaptured. The Romans then burnt the Jewish temple and the nascent Jewish state collapsed.

The first revolt was remarkable for the continued resistance of the Jewish mountain-top stronghold of *Masada by the Dead Sea. Between AD 72 and AD 73, the Romans laid siege to this last symbol of Jewish resistance. Rather than surrender to the Romans, the 900-strong Jewish garrison, headed by Eleazar ben Yair, committed collective suicide.

When the Romans finally entered the fortress they found only seven survivors: two women and five children.

Following the suppression of the first revolt, intermittent clashes continued across the Roman province of Palestine. Misrule by Tinnius Rufus, the Roman governor of Judaea, exacerbated matters and Roman-Jewish tension grew. Emperor *Hadrian then attempted to romanize Jerusalem by restricting Jewish religious observance and establishing a Roman settlement in the city. This led to a renewed Jewish revolt in AD 132, this time led by Bar Kochba. As in the first revolt, the Jews were initially successful but Jewish rebels were no match for Roman strength and firepower. Hadrian personally commanded Roman operations during the second revolt and methodically and ruthlessly set about reducing Jewish resistance. Roman legions finally suppressed the revolt in AD 135 and ended any hopes that the Jews had of restoring their temple in Jerusalem. Following the second revolt, Jews were forbidden to enter Jerusalem and many Jews were dispersed (the 'diaspora') to other parts of the Roman empire.
MH

---

jihad (Arabic: *jihād*, 'striving, exerting oneself'). Some classical Islamic writers distinguished between 'the greater jihad', a spiritual struggle against the evil within oneself, and a 'lesser jihad', physical effort in the cause of Islam, but it is the latter which is our concern here. It has meant in practice military action for either the spreading of Islam or its defence, following on from the idea of the universality of Islam and the consequent necessity of strenuous and continuous action for the furtherance of the faith. The basis of the doctrine is found in the Koran, and in strict Islamic law jihad is a duty on all adult free male believers until Islam has attained universal domination; hence there can be no permanent peace with unbelievers but only limited truces.

In medieval times, feelings of jihad lay behind fighting for the defence of Islam in the Mediterranean basin, such as during the *Crusades in the Levant and during the Christian *Reconquista of the Iberian peninsula. It was also used for the spreading of Islam outside the heartlands, e.g. into sub-Saharan Africa, in the Indian subcontinent, and in Indonesia. Typical manifestations of this last in West Africa were the Fulani Jihad led by Usumanu dan Fodio (d. 1817) in Hausaland and jihads by Umar al-Futi and Samori Ture in other parts of black West Africa in the 19th century, aimed primarily at spreading the faith among local animists. In Muslim India, notable was the movement of the mujahedin or 'fighters for the faith' of Sayyid Ahmad Brelwi (killed 1831), primarily against the *Sikhs in the Punjab, and other similar movements against the British which continued throughout the century and into the present one, especially along the *North-West frontier. In pre-modern times jihad was not invariably directed against the outside, non-Islamic world; at various times, the slogans of jihad were employed in campaigns against heterodox or dissident

Muslims, such as the Ismailis, during the Mongol period and just afterwards.

In the 20th century, the term jihad has increasingly become part of the political vocabulary of certain Muslim elements in the Middle East, sometimes as a justification for warfare in fact based on essentially secular and nationalistic considerations, such as during the Iraq–Iran war of 1980–8, sometimes for warfare based at least in part on religious considerations, such as the periodic *Arab–Israeli wars. Fundamentalist and Islamist groups have a fondness for styling their movements jihads and their members mujahedin, often with the implication that the object of their jihad is secularized Muslims who are lax in the observance of religious law, to be regarded as not true believers. This is noticeable at the present time in countries like Egypt and Algeria, where such a jihad has assumed a violent form; it was a member of the 'Islamic Jihad' movement who in 1981 murdered Pres Sadat.   CEB

Esposito, John L. (ed.), *The Oxford Encyclopedia of the Modern Islamic World* (Oxford, 1995), art. 'Jihad'.

Khadduri, Majid, *War and Peace in the Law of Islam* (Baltimore, 1955).

Peters, Rudolph, *Islam and Colonialism: The Doctrine of Jihad in Modern History* (The Hague, 1979).

Joan of Arc (*c*.1412–31) remains an enigmatic figure in the context of the *Hundred Years War and of warrior women (see GENDER). The daughter of a prosperous tenant farmer of Domrémy in eastern France, she was fiercely patriotic. Inspired by voices she journeyed to Chinon where she persuaded Charles VII to let her accompany his army to raise the siege of Orléans. French success here and at the battle of Patay on 18 June 1429 led to Charles's coronation at Rheims on 17 July, serious blows to English power in France. Although mounted and armed it is unlikely that she was much involved in fighting, but was rather a source of religious inspiration as the bearer of the banner of Christ and the Virgin. Once crowned Charles soon distanced himself from her, afraid of the charge that he had gained his throne by diabolical means. She overreached herself in a failed attack on Paris and was subsequently captured by the Burgundians who sold her to the English. She was tried for heresy, admitted her fault, but then relapsed, being burned at Rouen on 31 May 1431. It was at the French-sponsored Process of Rehabilitation of 1456 that stories of her military prowess began to be advanced. Over succeeding centuries she became an icon for French national identity and was canonized in 1920 by a pope anxious to encourage the revival of Catholicism in France.   AC

Warner, Marina, *Joan of Arc: The Image of Female Heroism* (London, 1981).

Joffre, Marshal Joseph Jacques Césaire (1852–1931), C-in-C of the French armies, 1914–16, the eldest of eleven children of a provincial cooper. He made his way on merit in a technical branch of the army, the engineers, forging a modest pre-war reputation as an efficient officer largely in colonial campaigns. It was his lack of objectionable political or religious affiliations, however, which secured him promotion to CGS in 1911. In this capacity he was responsible for the near-disastrous Plan XVII, the all-out assault on Germany through Alsace-Lorraine, with which France began WW I. Joffre's claim to greatness as a commander lies principally in his ability to recognize the plan's catastrophic failure, to redeploy his armies, and to counterattack the German right wing. The battle of the *Marne was as much a triumph of character as intellect. Joffre's strength was his ability to remain calm in a crisis and to retain the power of decision. In 1915, displaying the iron resolution he demanded of his troops, he launched massive attacks against the German defences in the Champagne and Artois with severe losses for paltry reward. The German offensive at *Verdun in February 1916 caught him by surprise and found the historic defences denuded of guns on his orders.

Joffre's autocratic character became more pronounced as the war developed; in the generously defined 'Zone of the Armies' he exercised almost dictatorial powers. But colossal French losses at Verdun, the failure of the Anglo-French attack on the *Somme to achieve decisive results, and the fall of Bucharest to the Germans on 6 December emboldened France's civilian leaders and he was relieved of command on 13 December. He spent the rest of the war in ceremonial appointments consoled by his promotion to marshal of France.   JMB

John III (Jan Sobieski), **King of Poland** (b. 1629, ruled 1674–96). In 1668 Jan Sobieski became Hetman of the Poles (see also COSSACKS). He defeated the *Turks in the Turco-Polish war of 1672–6. In 1672 he led a thrust towards Istanbul which penetrated 280 miles (450 km), and he also won at Khotin in 1673 and Lwów in 1675. In 1683 the Turks launched their last great offensive against the West, almost reaching *Vienna. Sobieski's heavily armoured Polish cavalry arrived in the nick of time and played a major part in the battle, but so did firepower from mounted carabiniers using the *caracole. In 1683 he concluded the 'Eternal Peace' with Russia, which later history proved was anything but.   CDB

Johnston, Gen Joseph Eggleston (1807–91). A Virginian, Johnston graduated from *West Point and served in the artillery for eight years before resigning to become a civil engineer. He returned to the army as a topographical engineer a year later, and was promoted brevet colonel during the *Mexican war. *QMG of the army with the rank of brigadier general in 1860, he resigned on the outbreak of the *American civil war. Regaining his rank in the

Confederate Army, he was the senior officer at first *Bull Run, where he yielded command to *Beauregard, and was then promoted full general to command the Army of Northern Virginia. Badly wounded at Fair Oaks in May 1861, he took over the Department of the West in November 1862. Jefferson *Davis countermanded his order for the evacuation of *Vicksburg, and, as he had feared, he proved unable to relieve the city. He took over the Army of Tennessee from *Bragg, falling back before Sherman's advance on Atlanta and winning a battle at Kennesaw Mountain. Davis, tired of constant retreat, replaced him by *Hood, who was duly beaten. In February 1865 he was restored to command of the scattered Army of Tennessee, and manoeuvred with skill before being forced to surrender to *Sherman in April. He went into business after the war and served a term in Congress. Johnston was a pessimist and a difficult subordinate, but showed real talent in holding outnumbered armies together in retreat.   RH

Jomini, Baron Antoine-Henri de (1779–1869), Swiss-born French and Russian soldier and strategic theorist. Jomini was the most influential of many 19th-century military writers who believed they had found, in the campaigns of *Napoleon, a basis for establishing the conduct of war on a scientific footing.

In the course of his long life, Jomini produced dozens of volumes on the history and theory of war, of which the best remembered is his *Summary of the Art of War* (1837–8). Everything he wrote was oriented toward a common theme: that the conduct of war was governed by a small number of fixed principles and that among these the most important were first, that one should seek a line of operations capable of threatening the communications of the enemy while protecting one's own; and second, that the key to victory lay in massing one's forces at what he famously called 'the decisive point'.

Jomini's confidence that warfare answered to its own inherent logic did not save him from inconsistencies. He believed that Napoleon had demonstrated the superiority of the offensive, and the necessity of seizing the initiative and dominating the enemy. Yet Jomini's emphasis upon concentrated forces and secure communications also made him a proponent of fighting on 'interior lines', a relatively cautious approach by which one sought to place one's united forces between divided opponents, in order to defeat each in detail, almost as though *Frederick 'the Great' had been his model. Although Napoleon might as easily have exemplified the advantages of an enveloping attack on 'exterior' lines, Jomini thought the dangers implicit in such methods could rarely be justified. He stressed the value of surprise, but also the importance of planning and methodical deployment. He regarded the destruction of the enemy army as the natural objective of a military campaign, yet he usually portrayed the results of victory in terms of expanded territorial control. Strategy, he said, was the art of making war upon a map. It was often the lay of the land or the distribution of rivers and roads, rather than the actions of the enemy, that determined for him where the 'decisive point' should be.

Jomini never grasped the spirit of fierce improvisation that animated Napoleon's most characteristic campaigns. As a theorist, he owed a great deal to pre-Revolutionary writers, especially the Englishman Henry Lloyd, whose history of the campaigns of Frederick 'the Great' Jomini admired as a young man. Like Lloyd, Jomini was disposed to conceive of warfare in terms of abstract spatial relationships, and to identify strategic excellence with carefully deliberated manoeuvre and the avoidance of defeat. Indeed, much of Jomini's appeal lay not in his having plumbed Napoleon's genius, but on the contrary in his assimilation of the Napoleonic experience to the conservative, risk-averse strategic traditions of the *ancien régime*.

The Europe in which Jomini came to be regarded as an authority was dominated by small, regular armies, tailored to the conduct of wars whose scale and violence were limited by the great powers' shared commitment to a stable international order. He was even more influential in the USA, where his teachings were at the core of the *West Point syllabus. But when his ideas were put into practice in the *American civil war, where mass armies of citizen soldiers grappled for the highest stakes, they had less reassuring implications: not swift decision on scientific principles, but grinding *attrition. His views were further discredited by the *Austro-Prussian and *Franco-Prussian wars, in which victory had gone to the side that forsook the advantages of mass, security, and interior lines, in favour of energetic, independent manoeuvre by multiple detached forces.

Jomini's reputation would eventually be eclipsed by that of his contemporary *Clausewitz. For Clausewitz war was not a scientific enterprise, but a violent clash of wills, driven by deep springs of political and social energy, in which the play of friction, chance, and genius must inevitably exceed the bounds of prescriptive theory. His was, without question, the more encompassing and intellectually demanding vision—though his interpretations of specific historical episodes were often closer to Jomini's than he was inclined to admit. It would be wrong, in any case, to imagine that Jomini's influence ceased to count once his personal fame began to fade. On the contrary, Jomini's faith that the chaos of war must somehow be subsumed by a few principled guides to action has been shared by generations of soldiers. All modern armies accept that there are *principles of war, upon which they continue to base their most essential training and *doctrine. If Jomini is no longer a name to conjure with among students and practitioners of war, it is in part because his point of view has been so widely adopted, even by those unaware of his work.   DM

Howard, Michael, 'Jomini and the Classical Tradition', in *The Theory and Practice of War* (London, 1965).

Shy, John, 'Jomini', in Peter Paret (ed.), *Makers of Modern Strategy* (Princeton, 1986).

Juárez, Benito (1806–72), Mexican president and resistance leader. Despite prejudice against him as a full-blooded Indian, he was appointed justice minister after the Liberal revolution of 1856 and abolished clerical and military legal privileges (*fueros*). He became substitute president and led Liberal resistance after the 1858 Conservative counter-revolution. Confirmed in office on return to Mexico City in 1861, his suspension of payment on foreign debt led to the French *Mexican expedition. Juarista forces eventually retook the country and he was re-elected in 1867. He had himself declared re-elected in 1871 and died as he lived, embroiled in civil strife. HEB

Juin, Marshal Alphonse Pierre (1888–1967). Son of a *gendarme, Juin was born at Bône in Algeria and commissioned from Saint-Cyr, where he was a classmate of *de Gaulle. He fought as an infantry officer in Morocco in WW I, and was captured commanding a division in 1940. Released in 1941, he became military governor of Morocco under Vichy but went over to the Allies in 1942. He commanded the first-rate French Expeditionary Corps in the campaign in *Italy, and was COS of the National Defence Committee in 1944–7. Resident-general of Morocco in 1947–51, he was appointed marshal in 1952, the last to be granted the honour while still living, but broke with de Gaulle over his policy during the *Algerian independence war and retired in 1960. RH

Junger, Ernst (1895–1998), German soldier, writer, and scientist. Junger was considered a true Renaissance man in his lifetime. His literary output—over 60 books—covered a wide range of topics, from science to philosophy, politics, and fiction, but he first achieved fame as a WW I storm trooper. Enlisting in 1914, he served four years at the front: at *Ypres, on the *Somme, and in the March 1918 offensive. Wounded fourteen times, he was awarded the highest imperial *decorations. In 1920 he published *The Storm of Steel*—an account of his war. In it, he glorified in the severity of battle, the comradeship of soldiering, and saw war as the true test of man, while describing combat scenes with an accurate, icy detachment. It is considered the most arresting personal account by anyone of WW I trench fighting, and a complete antithesis to the *pacifism of Remarque's *All Quiet on the Western Front* (1929). Later, similar works included *The Battle as Inner Experience* (1922), *Fire and Blood* (1925), and *Copse 125* (1930). A German patriot, his positive attitude to WW I appealed to *Hitler, who greatly admired his work. Although he avoided close contact with the Nazis, he served in the *Wehrmacht in France, 1940–4.

Close to the Stauffenberg conspirators, he was dismissed from the army in 1944 following the abortive July bomb plot. Under the Nazis, he developed an abhorrence of totalitarianism and in later years became a convinced European and was courted by Chancellor Kohl of Germany and President Mitterrand of France. Until his recent death at the age of 102, he was the last surviving holder of the imperial German Pour le Mérite. APC-A

Nevin, Thomas, *Ernst Junger and Germany: Into the Abyss 1914–1945* (London, 1997).

Junot, Gen Andoche, Duc d'Abrantes (1771–1813). Junot enlisted into a volunteer battalion in 1791 and, as a sergeant, was Bonaparte's secretary at the siege of Toulon in 1793. His star rose with *Napoleon: he was a major on his staff at the start of the 1796 Italian campaign, a colonel at its finish, and a general two years later. He was disappointed not to be appointed marshal in 1804, but was sent on an independent mission to Portugal in 1807 and took Lisbon, covering the last 300 miles (483 km) in fourteen days and only narrowly missing capturing the Portuguese royal court. This achievement brought him his dukedom, but he was soon beaten by *Wellington at Vimiero, captured, and repatriated. A corps commander in 1812, he was censured by Napoleon for letting the Russians escape from Smolensk in August. His baton lost for ever, he became deeply depressed and committed suicide by jumping from a window. RH

just war is a concept closely associated with Christian thinking regarding the resort to and conduct of war, but all the world's major *religions have addressed the issues associated with warfare and have contributed to the development of notions of restraint and discrimination. The modern concept of just war draws not only upon these religious traditions, but also upon more recent approaches to the question of the *laws of war. In the 19th and 20th centuries, thinking about the morality of war became as much a problem for secular ethicists, international lawyers, and advocates of universal human rights as for religious thinkers.

Early Christians were fundamentally pacifist. Accepting no distinction between murder and killing in war, they were convinced that any killing—even in self-defence in war—was wrong. A fundamental shift began when *Constantine converted to Christianity and then, in 313, made the Roman a Christian empire in the Edict of Milan. As the 'official' religion of a martial empire, Christianity began to move away from the seeming unworldliness of absolute *pacifism and began to wrestle with the possibility that war might, in certain circumstances, be both politically necessary and morally justifiable. The idea of fighting a 'Christian war' took several centuries to develop, and it was not until the end of the Dark Ages that the first indications of just-war thinking began to emerge. Relatively quickly thereafter, the two strands of just-war thinking began to emerge: *jus ad bellum*, concerning the resort to war, and *jus in bello*, concerning conduct in war.

Drawing upon the work of St Augustine and particularly St Thomas Aquinas in the 13th century, the concept of *jus ad bellum* has been elaborated over the centuries and requires that several conditions be met before resorting to war. First, there must be a just cause or right intention. That is, the purpose of the war must be to right a wrong which has been committed (self-defence against unlawful aggression would be considered just), and the ultimate objective must be peace. Second, the use of armed force must always be considered a last resort. Third, the resort to war is the preserve of legitimate authority; an arbitrary act of an individual cannot be considered just. Fourth, there must be good prospects; no matter what the grievance, if war is likely to be a wasted effort, it should not be undertaken. And finally, there should always be a sense of proportion between means and ends, in that the good to be achieved through war must outweigh the damage and harm to be endured.

Jus in bello thinking concentrates primarily on the effect of the conflict and is expressed in two different approaches to the regulation of armed conflict (see GENEVA AND HAGUE CONVENTIONS). The Hague approach concerns hostilities in general, the conduct of combat, and the concepts of occupation and neutrality while the Geneva approach addresses the protection and humane treatment of *POWs, those made hors de combat through wounding or otherwise, and the status of non-combatant civilians and medical personnel. *Jus in bello* in its evolved form thus presents two key principles. First, conduct should be proportionate and belligerents cannot assume unlimited rights to injure an opponent. Second, there must be discrimination between combatants and others.

In early 1999 NATO's bombardment of Serbia on behalf of Kosovar Albanians was frequently debated in just-war terms. As so often in the past the concept was not able to produce an unequivocal and universally agreed judgement on NATO's action. There are indeed many criticisms to be made of the just war, on moral, legal, and political grounds. But perhaps the most eloquent critique was that offered by the British historian A. J. P. Taylor: 'Bismarck fought "necessary" wars and killed thousands, the idealists of the 20th century fight "just" wars and kill millions.'   PC

---

justice, military All military forces require a code of laws and regulations for the maintenance of *discipline and good order. This may be considered military law which should not be confused with the term *martial law. Military law has now come to be the special body of rules applicable to the armed forces of a state governing the terms of service, discipline, and military *punishment of specific service offences which are often not considered criminal by the ordinary law of the land.

In Rome, military law derived from the imperium of magistrates in their capacity as commanders of the Roman military forces. It was initially somewhat arbitrary and harsh depending very much on the individual commander. However, Roman military law became much more formalized under the digest and codex of the Emperor Justinian. In the Middle Ages in England, the maintenance of discipline was administered by the court of the *constable and the *marshal who applied the ordinances and articles of war as issued by the sovereign or the commander appointed by the king. The earliest examples of these are the charter drawn up in 1189 by *Richard 'the Lionheart' for the regulation of his forces going on the Third Crusade.

The European armies of the 16th and the 17th centuries tended to be a multinational mixture of *mercenaries, thus each contingent usually applied the rules of the army's supreme commander according to their own procedures. The articles of war of *Maurice of Nassau and *Gustavus Adolphus, served as the basis of most forms of military justice until the 19th century. Their ideas were spread by the many men whom they commanded. During the *British civil wars, the ordinances of the royalist and parliamentary commanders were both based on these continental ideas and therefore almost exactly the same. The impressive discipline of the *New Model Army was not due to an improved code of military justice but due to the fact the articles were so rigorously enforced.

In England, as mentioned above, military justice originated in the courts of the constable and marshal, but the government began to take over the drawing up of codes of rules of the military from 1642 onwards. In 1689, the jurisdiction of the constable and marshal courts was declared obsolete and military law was legalized by the introduction of the Mutiny Act, normally passed annually, to which the prerogative articles were subordinate. In 1777, the power to make articles of war was embodied in the Act. In the British army, the articles of war were replaced in 1881 by the Army Act. The Army Act is an Act of Parliament dealing with the discipline, *court martial, and enlistment of the army and has in itself no permanent operation. It is annually brought into operation by the Army Act (which was reformed in 1955 to become the Army and Air Force Act). By this system of annual acts, parliament retains control of the land forces of the Crown. The Army and Air Force Act is part of the statute law of England and is construed in the same manner and carried out under the same conditions as the ordinary criminal law of the country, although discipline is administered by courts martial, not the civil courts. The articles of war continued to be in use by the Royal Navy until 1957.

The first Congress of the USA established courts martial to enforce the discipline of the army and navy. In 1775 and in 1806, articles of war were adopted modelled on the British Mutiny Act and articles in force at the time. Military law is now administered in the USA under the Uniform Code of Military Justice adopted in 1951.

The jurisdiction of military law is not necessarily confined to the discipline of members of the armed forces. It extends in varying degrees under different countries' systems to all offences committed by members of the military and offences that damage discipline committed by civilians. In countries which operate a system of conscription, soldiers who fail to answer their initial call-up are liable to military jurisdiction. Civilians become subject to military justice in a number of ways. In Italy and Turkey, treason and rebellion can be dealt with under the military code. In Norway, breaches of the *Geneva Conventions are dealt with under military law. In a number of countries, civilians in a war zone or theatre of active operations can come under military jurisdiction. In other countries, only civilians associated or working with the armed forces come under Service Law. Under British military law, civilians accompanying armed forces stationed in a foreign country, including civil servants and war correspondents, can be tried for offences against the military community. In some countries, such as France, Germany, and Austria, civil courts deal with all crimes, military or civil, during peacetime.

The logic and practice of military justice have come under increasing attack. There have been assertions that both summary military justice, meted out by commanding officers, and courts martial themselves are inherently prejudiced against the defendant. Most western armed forces have liberalized their systems of military justice in recent years by such measures as reducing the scope of summary jurisdiction and improving the quality of defendants' representation at courts martial.   MCM/RH

Jutland, battle of (31 May 1916). Fought between the British and German fleets in the North Sea about 75 miles (121 km) from the Danish coast, Jutland was the biggest naval battle of WW I, and in terms of the forces engaged, close to being the largest naval battle ever fought. Vice Adm Reinhard Scheer, the German High Sea Fleet Commander, aimed to reduce the overall quantitative superiority of the Royal Navy by ambushing part of the Grand Fleet, perhaps Vice Adm Sir David Beatty's battlecruiser force. For his part, Adm Sir John Jellicoe hoped to bring the whole of his Grand Fleet to bear and to destroy the German fleet, once and for all. Jellicoe needed to be cautious, however, for, as *Churchill said, only he 'could lose the war in an afternoon'. The German battlecruiser force under Rear Adm Hipper engaged Beatty at 15.48 and was joined 55 minutes later by the rest of Scheer's fleet. Beatty's losses were unsurprisingly heavy but he drew the whole German Fleet behind him as he fought his way towards the British Grand Fleet speeding south towards the battle. When Scheer realized he had now encountered the whole of the British fleet, he sought to extricate himself from this perilous situation and eventually, aided by a combination of British signalling blunders, cautious tactics, and luck managed to escape under cover of darkness. Inadequate shells, design faults in the British battlecruisers, and their lack of effective damage control, made for a disappointing result for the British, who lost 3 capital ships (all battlecruisers), 3 cruisers, and 8 destroyers, and 5,069 dead. The Germans lost 2 capital ships (1 battleship and 1 battlecruiser), 3 cruisers, 5 destroyers, and 2,115 dead. But the losses were proportionate to those engaged, and the force ratio for the Germans the day after the battle was worse than it had been before. The strategic situation in the North Sea, which made a German defeat eventually inevitable, was confirmed. Nonetheless the British, expecting another *Trafalgar, were grievously disappointed at the battle's outcome.   GT

Kabul to Kandahar march Between 9 and 31 August 1880 Lt Gen Sir Frederick *Roberts marched a distance of 300 miles (483 km) with 10,000 men, 7,800 *camp followers, and 18 guns from Kabul to the relief of the British garrison at Kandahar which was besieged by a claimant to the Afghan throne, Ayub Khan, the governor of Herat. Ayub raised the siege before Roberts's arrival and retired with 5,000 troops, 8,000 irregulars, and 32 guns a short distance west of the city near the Arghandab river where Roberts, his artillery reinforced from Kandahar, attacked and defeated him on 1 September. Although it was not a more remarkable feat of arms than Roberts's own advance to Kabul in 1879 or the march of Sir Donald Stewart from Kandahar to Kabul in the spring of 1880, this campaign in particular captured the imagination of the British public and made him the national hero of the second *Anglo-Afghan war.   MEY

Kadesh, battle of (1300 BC). Ramesses II, Pharaoh of Egypt (1304–1237 BC) defeated the *Hittites of King Muwattallish (1315–1296) outside the strategically important city of Kadesh on the river Orontes, in northern Syria. The conquest of the state of Mitanni in the late 14th century by the Hittites had created a crucial border zone between their empire and the Egyptians. Ramesses led four divisions north, each of 500 *chariots and 5,000 men, against 15,000 Hittites. His vanguard division, 'Amun', was already encamped against Kadesh when the pharaoh arrived. The Hittites had planned an ambush which caught their enemy by surprise. From their camp on the far side of the Orontes river, and using a wood as cover, the Hittite chariot force, recorded as 2,500 strong, swung south and behind the advancing Egyptians. Fording the river, still undetected, they fell upon the Egyptian rearguard division and destroyed it. Ramesses then counter-attacked and drove them off.

Neither side's infantry took part, perhaps because they could not get across the river. Ramesses claimed the victory from this drawn fight, celebrated in monumental funerary temple reliefs still visible at Thebes on the Nile.   MB

Healy, M., *Qadesh 1300 BC* (London, 1993).

Kaffir wars Nine conflicts in South Africa arising from the tension between Boer/British expansion and the tribes of the powerful pastoral Xhosa nation, characterized by slow British adaptation to *guerrilla warfare in dense subtropical bush. The first two (1780–1 and 1793) were fitful operations against the Xhosas by the ailing Dutch East India Company, as was the third (1799) (in which the Khoikhoi (Hottentots) also fought), the first by the British. The fourth (1811–12) saw the Xhosa driven across the Fish river, and the fifth (1818–19) the defeat of the united tribes at Grahamstown, with perhaps 1,000 killed for a British loss of only 3. A failed Xhosa invasion reduced the sixth (1834–5) to a war of *attrition, while the seventh (1846–7) saw Chief Sandile refuse to give battle to British columns marching fruitlessly through his Amadola mountains stronghold. The eighth (1850–3), though the longest and costliest (16,000 Xhosa and 1,400 British/colonial dead), was decided at the outset by the Xhosa's failure to overrun weak Amadola outposts and prolonged by British incompetence. The ninth (1877–8) saw the Gcaleka and Ngqika, shattered by the auto-genocide of the 1850s cattle-killing, lose 3,680 killed against 193 British in a last act of defiance.   DD

Mostert, Noel, *Frontiers* (London, 1992).

Kalashnikov, Mikhail Timofeyevich (b. 1919), Soviet weapons designer, creator of the most widely manufactured series of *small arms in history, used by at least 55

nations and by *guerrilla forces across the world. Born at Alma-Ata (now Almaty) in Kazakhstan, Kalashnikov joined the Red Army in 1938. He got on his company commander's nerves by asking constant questions about military equipment, and was promptly put on an armourers' course. He then trained as a tank driver, and invented a device for measuring fuel consumption. Recalled in 1941, he was badly wounded in the battle of *Vyazma-Bryansk and spent six months recovering, during which he started designing weapons. In 1942 he was part of a team, along with the well-known designers Georgiy Shpagin and Georgiy Degtyarev, working on a new *sub-machine gun. His energy and originality attracted attention and in 1949 the Soviet army adopted his Avtomat Kalashnikova (Kalashnikov automatic rifle) AK-47 as standard. Firing a 7.62 mm × 39 mm rimless *cartridge from 30-round magazines, it was cheap to manufacture, using sheet metal rather than castings for the receiver, and formidably rugged. It became the best-known automatic or 'assault rifle' in the world. In 1959 a modified version, the AKM, was introduced. Many of the same parts went into the 1961 RPK section (squad) machine gun, and the Dragunov sniper rifle. AK-47s and AKMs were also copied or produced under licence in China, from the mid-1950s, in most east European states, and in Egypt, Israel, and Finland. In the early 1970s the basic design was given a new lease of life with the AK-74 firing a 5.45 mm round. Even smaller than the 5.56 mm standard NATO round, it is probably as lethal because it is designed to tumble when it hits flesh. About 50 million Kalashnikovs or derivatives have been manufactured since the appearance of the AK-47.

CDB

Ezell, Edward C., *The AK-47 Story: Evolution of the Kalashnikov Weapons* (Harrisburg, Pa., 1986).

Karadjordje (born Djordje Petrovich, also known as Karageorge, George Petrovich) (1762–1817). Soldier and leader of the Serbian people in their struggle for independence from the *Turks, his nickname comes from Kara (black) and Djordje (George).

Born in Serbia, Karadjordje emigrated to Austria where he joined the army and served with distinction against the Turks. In 1804, with Karadjordje at their head the Serbs rose against *janissaries of the Turkish army who occupied Serbia. They were quickly victorious and demanded autonomy from the Turkish sultan, Selim III. When it was refused Karadjordje launched a war of independence. He managed to seize Belgrade in 1806 and established practical Serbian independence. The first Serbian constitution appointed Karadjordje supreme and hereditary ruler.

The Serbs joined the Russians in war against Turkey in 1809 and a combined Serbian-Russian army defeated the Turks at Varvarin in 1810. However, Napoleon's invasion led the Russians to make peace with the Turks. The sultan, with all his forces freed for action, launched a massive invasion

of Serbia in 1812–13, crushing all opposition and forcing Karadjordje to flee. He returned to Serbia two years after the successful 1815 revolt but was murdered on the orders of the leader of the rebellion, Milos Obrenovich, who feared him as rival.

MCM

Karbala', battle of (680). Karbala' lies to the south of modern Baghdad in Iraq, and was the site of an engagement between the forces of the Umayyad Arab Caliph Yazid I and Husayn, son of the former Caliph 'Ali and grandson of the Prophet Muhammad. The Umayyads had come to power on 'Ali's assassination and the abdication of his elder son Hasan (661), but Husayn seems to have felt that he had a right to the throne through hereditary succession and, as his later partisans, the Shi'a, were to maintain, through divine designation. Husayn refused allegiance to Yazid in 680 and raised a revolt with some 50 supporters. The actual battle, on 10 October, seems to have been merely a series of skirmishes, but Husayn was killed. The event had a disproportionate significance, since Husayn's fate aroused widespread sympathy among many Muslims. He was subsequently made into a martyr by the Shi'a, to be mourned as the central, suffering figure in the *ta'ziyas* or Shi'ite 'Passion Plays' of recent times, with his richly endowed tomb at Karbala' becoming the major pilgrimage goal for Shi'ites. CEB

Halm, Heinz, *Shiism* (Edinburgh, 1991).
Momen, Moojan, *An Introduction to Shi'i Islam: The History and Doctrine of Twelver Shi'ism* (Oxford, 1981).

Kasserine Pass, battle of (1943). The TORCH landings in *North Africa in 1942 meant that Axis forces there were squeezed between Eighth Army under *Montgomery in the east and the US forces under *Eisenhower in the west. In February 1941, *Rommel, who was facing Montgomery, decided to launch a pre-emptive attack against an Allied threat to his communications with von Arnim, further north.

He sent one column through Sidi bou Zid to the Kasserine Pass and another further south. The Germans attacked in the best *blitzkrieg style, armour supported by aircraft. The US 1st Armoured Division was caught flat-footed, its piecemeal counter-attacks roughly handled. On 18 February Rommel broke through the Kasserine Pass and pressed northwards to the Western Dorsal Range, threatening the supply base at Tebessa. Eisenhower rushed reinforcements into the sector, Allied units steadied to their task, a thrust by von Arnim failed to materialize, and the attackers ran out of steam. Rommel then swung back to meet Montgomery, but received a bloody nose at Medinine.

The Allied reverse was in part a consequence of inexperience: the British, in a parody of a best-selling book, quipped, 'How Green was our Ally'. More culpably, it was the result of overextension and poor co-ordination. It

473

produced a command shake-up, with *Patton taking over the US II Corps from Fredendall, and *Alexander assuming command of Eighteenth Army Group.   RH

Kautilya (also known as Kautalya, Canakya, Chanakya, or Visnugupta) (active *c.*300 BC). Hindu statesman, philosopher, and writer of the *Arthasastra*, the classic ancient Hindu political text. Kautilya was the PM and chief political adviser to Chandragupta, ruler of the Magadha empire from 320 BC to *c.*297 BC. Under Kautilya's guidance, Chandragupta consolidated his dynasty, defeated Seleucos Nicator's attempt to claim the heritage of *Alexander 'the Great' in India, and expanded his empire. However, Kautilya is more important for the political theories expounded in the *Arthasastra*.

The central idea of Kautilya's doctrine was the prosperity of king and country and the king's struggle for victory against his rival neighbouring states. The king had to try to defeat one after another of his enemies. Kautilya identified seven factors of power, which affected his ability to do so. These factors were first, the qualities of the king, then of his ministers, his provinces, his city, his treasure, his army, and his allies. The aim of the *Arthasastra* was to instruct the king on how to improve the qualities of these factors and undermine those of his enemies. He provided detailed instruction for spies and agents and showed great understanding of the weakness of human nature, earning himself comparison with *Machiavelli.   MCM

Kulke, Hermann, and Rothermund, Dietmar, *A History of India* (London, 1986).

khaki is an Anglicized transliteration of a Hindi adjective meaning 'dusty' or 'dust-coloured'; it derives from the Persian noun transliterated as *khāk*, meaning 'earth' or 'dust'. It entered English in 1857 as a descriptive word for the light drab or brown *uniforms which appeared in elements of the British *Indian army in the first half of the 19th century. Debate has ensued on the earliest date when khaki uniforms were worn (it was probably in the late 1840s), but they were certainly in common use during the *Indian Mutiny. The recipe for the colour has also been a matter for debate and little consistency of shade seems to have been achieved much before the 1880s, by which time its use was established for British troops overseas. In 1902 a khaki service dress uniform for British troops in Europe was authorized and it had ousted scarlet full dress for other ranks, except musicians and the Household Brigade, by WW I. Although originally British, khaki uniforms were gradually adopted by most nations, initially for combat use and then for general use, but some countries, Germany—for instance—with its *feldgrau*, adopted other shades of drab cloth. In the British army, khaki uniforms exist in a variety of shades and cloth, pale khaki drill for wear in hot climates and dark khaki barathea for the service dress of Guards officers being two examples. As *camouflage or disruptive pattern materials became usual for combat wear, so khaki—in many armies—has become the standard secondary dress worn on semi-formal occasions when smartness is required. Thus, from being one of the first camouflage shades to be worn in the field, khaki has become an acceptable dress for soldiers on non-combat duties at home.   SCW

Mollo, John, *Military Fashion* (London, 1972).

Khalkin-Gol, battle of (1939). Also known as the battle of Nomonhan, this was an exemplary encirclement by Soviet forces of Japanese troops within a defined and disputed area, leading to a decisive Soviet victory which protected the USSR from a two-front war after the German invasion in 1941. It was also a formative experience for *Zhukov, later the pre-eminent Soviet commander in WW II.

The boundary dispute over Khalkin Gol (Halha river) was 200 years old. The Japanese claimed the river Khalkin Gol itself as the border: the Soviets and their Mongolian allies claimed it lay 15.5 miles (25 km) to the east, passing through Nomonhan. On 28 May 1939 a Japanese force tried to encircle a Soviet-Mongolian force in the disputed area. The Japanese then pushed forward not only to the river, which they claimed as the border, but beyond it. On 2 June Zhukov was summoned to see *Voroshilov and ordered to Mongolia. Zhukov decided to launch an attack with LVII Special Corps, later renamed First Army Group, to destroy Japanese forces in the disputed area. It had to be decisive, even spectacular, in order to work and neutralize the Japanese as a threat in the region. *Stalin approved the plan, and Zhukov reported directly to him.

The area was 404 miles (650 km) from the nearest railhead. A conveyor belt of trucks brought supplies forward, including materials to build defences. This was an important part of Zhukov's deception, to convince the Japanese that the Soviets had no intention of attacking. Zhukov built up a force of 65,000 Soviet and Mongolian troops against 28,000 Japanese and Manchukuoan (from the puppet state the Japanese had created in Manchukuo). Soviet troops began pressing forward on both flanks on 19 August. The battle followed what would become a classic pattern of Soviet encirclement: establishing an outer front of mobile forces (tank and mechanized brigades) while an inner front, largely infantry, worked to destroy the trapped enemy. The Japanese divisional commander and 400 survivors just managed to escape. On 3 September the Japanese emperor, aware of the crisis in Europe as WW II began, ordered the incident to be resolved. The USSR admitted 18,500 casualties in the battle, and claimed to have inflicted 61,000; the Japanese admitted 18,000. As Shtern, the Far East Army commander who worked with Zhukov, was quick to recognize, 'I think it will become the second perfect battle of encirclement (after *Cannae) in all history.'   CDB

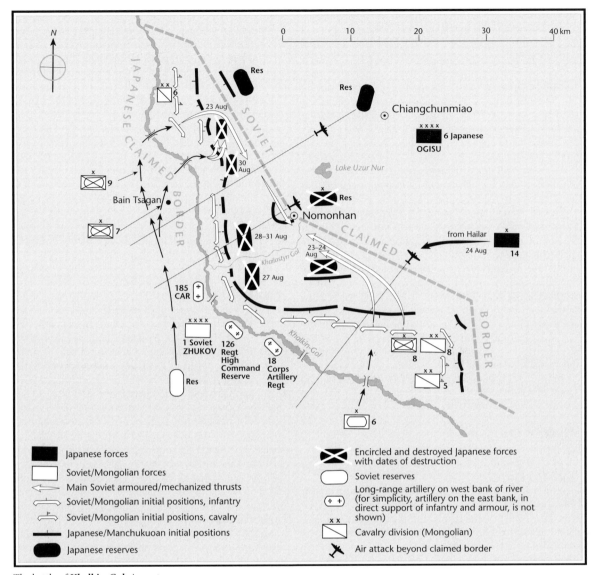

N

0   10   20   30   40 km

Res

Res

Chiangchunmiao

xxxx
6 Japanese

OGISU

23 Aug

XX
6

30 Aug

x
9

Bain Tsagan

x
7

Lake Uzur Nur

x
Res

Nomonhan

CLAIMED

from Hailar

24 Aug

x
14

28–31 Aug

Khailastyn Gol

23–24
Aug

27 Aug

185
CAR

xxxx
1 Soviet
ZHUKOV

126
Regt
High
Command
Reserve

18
Corps
Artillery
Regt

Khalkin-Gol

x

xx
8

8

xx

5

Res

x
6

BORDER

JAPANESE CLAIMED BORDER

SOVIET

Japanese forces

Soviet/Mongolian forces

Main Soviet armoured/mechanized thrusts

Soviet/Mongolian initial positions, infantry

Soviet/Mongolian initial positions, cavalry

Japanese/Manchukuoan initial positions

Japanese reserves

Encircled and destroyed Japanese forces
with dates of destruction

Soviet reserves

Long-range artillery on west bank of river
(for simplicity, artillery on the east bank, in
direct support of infantry and armour, is not
shown)

Cavalry division (Mongolian)

Air attack beyond claimed border

The battle of **Khalkin-Gol,** August 1939.

Coox, Alvin, *Nomonhan: Japan against Russia 1939* (Stanford, Calif., 1985).

Zhukov, Georgiy, *Reminiscences and Reflections* (Moscow, 1985).

Kharkov, battles of (1942–3). Kharkov, in the Ukraine, had fallen to the Germans relatively easily at the end of 1941, and became one of the 'hedgehogs' in which the Germans held fast during the winter. In May 1942 Soviet forces in the Izyum salient to the south-east and Volchansk to the east launched a concentric attack to recapture the city, but Gehlen, the new chief of Fremde Heere Ost, the German *intelligence organization, predicted it, and it was defeated.

In February 1943, after the battle of *Stalingrad, the Red Army's Voronezh and South-West Fronts (army groups) launched an offensive to destroy the main forces of the German Army Group B, and recaptured Kharkov as a bonus on 16 February. *Manstein, commanding the German Army Group South, immediately launched a counter-offensive. On 7 March Fourth Panzer Army attacked north-east towards Kharkov, aiming, once again, not so much to capture the city as to destroy the Soviet forces there. Golikov's Voronezh Front and Vatutin's South-West fought the 'Kharkov defensive operation', but lost the city on 14 March and were pushed back 93 miles (150 km). Manstein's attack is a classical example of a defender counter-attacking 'on the backhand', first letting his enemy's attack swing past him to its culminating point, and then striking back.

CDB

Khartoum, siege of (1884–5). This took place during the *Mahdist uprising. *Gordon, despatched by the Gladstone cabinet and serving as governor-general of the Sudan, arrived in Khartoum on 18 February 1884. Having evacuated some 2,600 civilians and soldiers, he found the city blockaded by 12 March. He strengthened the landward defences of his triangular perimeter, bounded on two sides by the White and Blue Niles, and employed ten steamers and some barges to carry communications, make foraging raids, and attack enemy positions. Until September the Mahdists did not invest the city closely, but they tightened the siege thereafter, defeating Muhammad Ali, one of Gordon's best generals, killing 1,000 men (5 September), and murdering Lt Col J. D. H. Stewart and the British and French consuls, who had been sent downriver. On 5 January, they seized Fort Omdurman. After the *Gordon relief column failed to appear, and the receding Nile waters weakened Khartoum's defences, as confirmed by a deserter, the city was successfully stormed on 26 January and Gordon was killed.

EMS

Holt, P. M., *The Mahdist State in the Sudan* (Oxford, 1958).
Marlow, John, *Mission to Khartum: The Apotheosis of General Gordon* (London, 1969).

Khitans (Qidans in Pinyin romanization), a little-studied people of Mongolia who founded the Liao dynasty, rulers of eastern Mongolia, Manchuria, and parts of north China, c.916–1125. They appear, to judge from what is understood of their language, to have been related to the *Mongols who achieved world prominence in the 13th century. They were a semi-nomadic, tribally organized confederation led by an imperial clan, the Yeh-lü. Like many successful conquest dynasties in China, they straddled the steppe and the sown, combining the military effectiveness of an army of nomad mounted *archers with a willingness to rule their Chinese sedentary territories so as to maximize the productiveness of the agricultural sector. They had five capitals: supreme (in Mongolia), central, western, eastern, and southern (near the site of modern Beijing). They occupied only a small part of China proper, which was governed according to the traditional ways of the Chinese bureaucracy. The much larger nomadic and semi-nomadic lands to the north were ruled in the equally traditional tribal fashion. Their army of nomad cavalry was organized on a decimal basis, as was common in Asian steppe polities and as the Mongols after them were also to do.

By 1125 they had been displaced by their former vassals, the Jurchen of Manchuria (ancestors of the Ch'ing, the last Chinese dynasty), who founded the Chin dynasty, which many Khitan notables were prepared to serve faithfully. One group of Khitans, headed by a member of the imperial family, Yeh-lü Ta-shih, declined to submit and headed west, to found a new empire, Qara-Khitai (Western Liao in official Chinese usage). This survived until its conquest by the Mongols in 1218. In 1141 Yeh-lü Ta-shih defeated the Seljuk *Turk Sultan Sanjar in battle near Samarqand, a battle which seems to have helped give rise to the enduring European legend of Prester John, the Christian king of the East who was coming to the aid of Christendom against the Muslims (Yeh-lü Ta-shih was in fact a Buddhist). Khitans who entered Mongol service in the early 13th century were influential in helping to set up the institutional basis of the Mongol empire. The word Cathay (for China) in English and other European languages, is derived from the Khitans' realm, Khitai.

DOM

Wittfogel, K. A., and Fûng, C. S., *History of Chinese Society: Liao 907–1125* (Philadelphia, 1949).

Khubilai Khan (sometimes spelt Kublai or Qubilai) (1215–94) was the *Mongol Great Khan (1260–94) and Emperor of China; founder of the Yüan dynasty. He was a grandson of *Genghis (Chinggis) Khan, and one of four sons of Tolui, the youngest of Chinggis's four principal sons. Until his thirties he was one Mongol prince among many; but in 1251 his elder brother Möngke seized the imperial throne from an elder branch of the Chinggisid family. After Möngke's death in 1259, the throne was contested between Khubilai and his brother Ariq-Böke: Khubilai emerged victorious by 1264. The legitimacy of his rule was contested in central Asia throughout the reign by Qaidu, a member of the branch of the royal house ousted by Möngke. After 1264 Khubilai devoted himself to completing the conquest of the Sung empire of south China which Möngke had begun. Hang-chou, the Sung capital, fell in 1276 and resistance ceased in 1279.

Khubilai's reputation as a ruler is a high one. He did not devastate south China, and he worked hard to secure acceptance by his Chinese subjects as a legitimate emperor. In 1272 he founded a new imperial capital (on the site of modern Beijing), constructed on traditional Chinese lines, and adopted a Chinese dynastic title, Yüan, 'the origin'. His reputation as a military leader is, by Mongol standards, less illustrious, although his successful conquest of China tends to be underrated. This was the more remarkable in that south China could not be conquered by the customary Mongol approach to warfare, that of the cavalry archer. The extensive waterways, rice paddy fields, and vast walled cities of the Sung empire could not be taken by cavalry. Khubilai proved adaptable in employing infantry (by 1279 most of the so-called Mongol armies in China were probably mainly composed of Chinese soldiers fighting in their traditional way), and in using warships on the great rivers and along the Chinese coast.

His military adventures outside China were much less successful. He made little progress in the Indochinese peninsula or in mounting an expedition to Java. But his greatest failure was in his two amphibious assaults on Japan. Khubilai no doubt shared the customary Mongol view that the world and the Mongol empire were conterminous; so an attempt to incorporate Japan into the empire was probably inevitable. The first expedition, in 1274, can perhaps be regarded as a large-scale *reconnaissance; but the expedition of 1281 was a disaster on the grand scale. The Japanese, no doubt warned of the need for adequate preparation by the 1274 invasion, mounted an effective defence which was conclusively assisted by a typhoon, the 'kamikaze' or divine wind. Few Mongol soldiers were able to struggle back to China. Khubilai, member of an imperial family unaccustomed to military defeat, took this to heart. Nevertheless his long reign provided a newly, and permanently, united China with a welcome period of stability and reasonably benevolent rule.   DOM

Morgan, David, *The Mongols* (Oxford, 1986).
Rossabi, Morris, *Khubilai Khan* (Berkeley, 1988).

Khyber Pass One of the principal *North-West frontier passes connecting Pakistan with Afghanistan, the Khyber Pass was notable throughout history as a road for trade, communications, and conquest as well as for the fighting abilities of the Afridi tribes who are its principal inhabitants. From Jamrud in the east to Torkham on the Afghan frontier in the west the Khyber Pass is about 45 miles (72 km) long. The pass lies along stream beds and in places is very narrow and the hills almost vertical, notably at the midway point of Ali Masjid, the site of a 19th-century fort. Subsequently forts were built at Shagai and at the highest point of the pass at Landi Kotal 3,500 feet (1,067 metres). All rulers of northern India experienced difficulties in the Khyber Pass although we know little of its history until the time of the Mughals. Among conquerors it was probably not used by *Alexander 'the Great' but probably was exploited by the Ghaznevids. The Mughals, who also ruled in Kabul, needed the pass and under *Akbar 'the Great' a road was built. Sometimes the Mughals fought in the pass (and were heavily defeated in 1672) but mainly they paid for transit.

The capture of the pass by *Nadir Shah on his way into India in 1738 was exemplary, and Russian military analysts later studied it as part of their own plans for the invasion of India. He sent engineer detachments to improve the approaches to it and give the impression he planned a frontal attack, but by night he sent his cavalry through narrow gorges to the south. They covered 50 miles (80 km) in eighteen hours and appeared behind the Mughal army, cutting it off from its base at Peshawar.

It was the *Anglo-Afghan wars that gave the pass its special celebrity. During the first, the British forced the pass in 1839 and again, under Gen Pollock, in 1842. In 1878 the refusal of passage to Gen Chamberlain precipitated the second, which led to the eventual incorporation of the pass into British India. Following the third war in 1919 a railway (opened in 1925) was constructed through the pass.   MEY

Killiecrankie, battle of (1689), *Jacobite victory over a government army of about 4,000 men under Gen Hugh Mackay. This was marching from Perth to occupy Blair Castle when it was ambushed by a smaller force of *Highlanders led by John Graham of Claverhouse, 1st Viscount Dundee. Four miles (6.4 km) south of Blair, by the deep gorge of Killiecrankie, they charged downhill at the English, whose plug *bayonets stuffed into the muzzles of their muskets prevented effective volleys. The Highlanders pushed the English back into the gorge, killing half their number. Mackay retreated to Stirling to regroup, but the irreplaceable 'Bonnie' Dundee had been killed.   APC-A

King's shilling The shilling—for many years a soldier's daily pay, before stoppages—was given to recruits in the British army of the 18th and 19th centuries. By 'taking the shilling' a man agreed to serve as a soldier, and all sorts of tricks, most involving strong drink, were used by recruiters to press the shilling on unsuspecting victims. The man did not formally become a soldier until attested before a Justice of the Peace, and could still escape his fate by paying his recruiter 'smart money' before attestation. In the 1840s this amounted to £1, a sum most recruits were unlikely to have to hand.   RH

Kissinger, Henry (b. 1923), American rags-to-riches paradigm and statesman who between 1969 and 1977 articulated US foreign policy in terms of clearly defined national interests instead of nebulous and non-binding idealism. Born Heinz Kissinger to a German-Jewish family that fled to the USA in 1938, he served in the army in WW II and during the occupation of Germany. As a specialist in defence matters at Harvard University he became a consultant to government agencies and in 1960 warned of a spurious 'missile gap', a significant factor in the election of Kennedy. Freely on offer in the political bazaar, his views on realpolitik found resonance with Nixon, who appointed him assistant for national security affairs in 1968, head of the National Security Council in 1969, and Secretary of State in 1973. He survived the disgrace of his patron with enhanced authority and served to the end of Ford's term. After the moralizing and ineffectual Carter interlude, he hoped for a return to power under Reagan, but the latter declined to employ a potentially over-mighty servant.

Kissinger's achievements during his years of power included negotiating a face-saving formula for extracting US forces from *Vietnam, 'shuttle' diplomacy to bring about a territorial settlement between Egypt and Israel following the 1973 *Arab–Israeli war, and the *Strategic Arms Limitation Talks of 1972. The insurmountable problem his policies encountered was the American item of faith that the USA is great because she is good. Kissinger's view, shared by most foreign observers, is that she is immensely powerful and has abused that power a great deal less than she could have, which is about as 'good' as you can get in international relations. Under his direction, the axis of US foreign policy moved away from irksome and highly selective preachiness and legalism for the first time since the presidency of Theodore *Roosevelt. It was his misfortune to be associated with one of the most personally unappealing and finally discredited presidents in US history, and to have charge of clearing up the social and political mess created by his Messianic predecessors' pursuit of unlimited objectives with limited means.

In his negotiations with the implacable North Vietnamese, for which he unwisely accepted a joint *Nobel Peace Prize sensibly declined by his Vietnamese counterpart, Kissinger laboured under the constraints imposed by an impatient public and a shamelessly pandering Congress. He and Nixon were compelled to devise the 'mad dog' tactic of portraying him as all that stood between an unpredictable president and the total destruction of North Vietnam, which involved 'escalating' the war by striking at previously off-limits Hanoi and mining Haiphong harbour. As in *Korea, only the credible threat of fully unleashing US military power brought an end to a stalemate that served enemy interests.

As a caste traitor in the eyes of envious 'liberal' intellectuals, he has been assailed in print for many years. This has greatly enhanced his millionaire income as a consultant on the inner workings of the US government. HEB

Kissinger, Henry, *Diplomacy* (New York, 1994).

26,000 British, Egyptian, and Sudanese troops, made steady progress down the river Nile and on 2 September 1898 the Mahdist forces were overwhelmed at the battle of *Omdurman.

The victory established Kitchener's reputation as the empire's greatest soldier and paved the way for further honours. During the Second *Boer War he was COS to *Roberts and then C-in-C, but it was to be his last command in the field. Between 1902 and 1909 he commanded the army in India and in 1911, by then a field marshal, he returned to Egypt as British Agent.

With retirement beckoning he was unexpectedly made Secretary of State for War in August 1914. Although PM Herbert Asquith admitted that appointing a soldier to the cabinet was a dangerous experiment, Kitchener's prestige inspired the nation's confidence and he impressed his colleagues with his prediction that the war would last three years and would require a million volunteers. Under Kitchener's guidance a huge recruiting drive (in which Kitchener's portrait on the recruiting poster, proclaiming 'Your country needs you', remains an enduring image) achieved that figure by the end of the year. However, like most of his contemporaries Kitchener failed to understand the realities of modern industrialized warfare and in 1915 he was made a scapegoat for the shortage of artillery shells during the spring offensives on the western front. Later that year he also had to take some responsibility for the failure of the *Gallipoli campaign.

With the cabinet eager to be rid of him, yet anxious to retain his great name, Kitchener was despatched to Russia on an ill-fated fact-finding mission: the cruiser taking him to Archangel struck a mine off Orkney on 5 June 1916, drowning him and most of the crew. TR

Magnus, Philip, *Kitchener: Portrait of an Imperialist* (London, 1958).

Royle, Trevor, *The Kitchener Enigma* (London, 1985).

Kitchener, FM Horatio Herbert, Earl Kitchener of Khartoum and of Broome (1850–1916). With his luxuriant moustache and commanding presence Kitchener was an indefatigable organizer who understood the absolute necessity of consolidating resources before striking a decisive blow.

Born in Ireland, he was commissioned into the Royal Engineers and saw service in Palestine and Cyprus. However, he was destined to make his name in the Sudan where fundamentalist Islamic forces, known as *Mahdists, had taken control of the country. Having been seconded to the Egyptian army in 1883 Kitchener's name became linked inextricably with the *Egyptian and Sudanese campaign. In 1892 he was appointed sirdar (C-in-C) of the Egyptian army and developed a painstaking invasion plan which included the construction of a railway to ensure logistical support. Escorted by armed river steamers his army, consisting of

knighthood and chivalry began its rise to social and military prominence in the 10th century when, with the decline of Frankish royal power and the political fragmentation of society, local castellans gathered around them groups of heavily armed horsemen to enforce their newly appropriated rights of lordship, law-making, and taxation. These knights (known in Latin sources as *milites*), gradually rose in status from being lowly, even in some cases unfree, warrior servants of the nobility, to a lesser aristocracy in their own right. At the same time, the nobility, who had always been a martial élite, assumed the title of knight, depicted themselves on their seals as heavily armed warriors, and gloried in common membership of the *militia* or knighthood. By the 12th century not all knights were great men, but all great men were knights. Hence Henry 'The Young King' (d. 1183), eldest son of Henry II Plantagenet, could be praised by the troubadour Bertran de Born not so much for his royalty, but because he was 'the best knight there was of any nation'.

What bound great lord and lesser knight together was their costly equipment and method of fighting, with the great social gulf being between cavalry and infantry. Higher status was conferred by possession of lance, sword, shield, helmet, and above all, a mail shirt or hauberk, the essential piece of defensive *armour and the legal prerequisite of holding a fief. The knight's warhorse or destrier was far more valuable than other horses; it was not the great, lumbering beast of common misconception, but more akin to a cob or hunter, highly trained and ridden only in battle itself, being led at other times by a squire. With the development of plate armour from the later 13th century, a knight's equipment became still more expensive, and this, combined with burdensome administrative duties imposed by the crown, led to a sharp decline in the number of men willing to accept the title of knight. As knighthood became more exclusive, the title of squire (*armiger*) which had formerly denoted a trainee knight in a lord's service, was adopted as a rank in itself by the lesser gentry, and contemporaries now spoke of lords, knights, and squires simply as men-at-arms (*homines ad arma*), distinguished by armour and *heraldry.

Rigorous training from boyhood was required to master the skills of cavalry combat, and hunting as well as the mock combat of the *tournament, which emerged in the later years of the 11th century, played a crucial role in developing both horsemanship and bonds between members of a lord's household. Against a mounted opponent, the knight's chief form of attack was with the couched lance, whereby the lance was tucked under the right arm and, with the rider secured by a high-backed saddle and long *stirrups, the blow was delivered with the full impetus of charging horse and rider. The resulting impact was capable of penetrating mail and running an opponent through.

Yet although knighthood was intimately connected with horsemanship (the word chivalry derives from the French *chevalier*, a horseman), the knight throughout the Middle Ages was a flexible professional warrior, just as capable of fighting effectively on foot whether in siege or open battle. Several engagements of the Anglo-Norman period such as Tinchebrai (1106), Brémule (1119), and the Standard (1138) reveal dismounted knights, supported by cavalry and sometimes by archers, as highly effective, particularly in defensive formations. The same adaptability can be seen in crusading warfare, while the battle-winning tactics deployed by the English during the *Hundred Years War depended on the archers having the protection of a solid core of dismounted knights, who often bore the brunt of the hand-to-hand fighting. As a result of the massed deployment of archers, the French dismounted a greater part of their knights at battles such as Poitiers and *Agincourt, although they were always at a disadvantage when taking the offensive because of the weight of their armour. Cavalry

warfare itself enjoyed a renaissance in the later 15th century, as witnessed by the campaigns of Charles 'the Bold', Duke of Burgundy, and the *Italian wars of the French King Charles VIII.

Chivalry, the knighthood's corporate value system, had at its core the timeless values of almost all warrior élites; courage in combat, loyalty to one's lord and brothers in arms, and largesse in the distribution of arms, booty, and other fruits of victory. Whereas in Anglo-Saxon and Viking warfare noble opponents might be killed precisely because of their rank and martial function, the Normans and French did not sell *POWs into slavery, and in many (though not all) cases, aimed to spare knightly enemies. Such clemency reflected the religious and cultural homogeneity of French aristocratic society, ties of kindred and marriage, and respect for fellow knights, not to mention a desire for rich *ransom. The same potent mixture of pragmatism and a shared profession of arms led to the development of *laws of war governing payment of ransom, the profits of war, and behaviour in a siege. Garrisons, for example, might frequently negotiate terms whereby if they were not relieved by their lord within a specified number of days, they could *capitulate without incurring disgrace or dishonour, and be allowed to go free by the besieger with their horses and arms.

Other distinctive features of European chivalry included a Christian dimension and, from the 12th century, the role of romance and courtly love. After the success of the first *Crusade, churchmen taught that to achieve salvation knights no longer had to abandon their arms and assume the monastic habit, but could gain spiritual merit by fighting in clerically sanctioned wars against the infidel or heretic, provided they fought for justice not booty. Crusading struck a powerful chord with many of the knighthood of western Europe, and some even devoted themselves to *military monastic orders like the Templars and Hospitallers, which combined a quasi-monastic rule with military action against the Muslims in the Holy Land. As warriors had done from the earliest days of the conversion of the Germanic peoples to Christianity, and indeed long before, knights continued to invoke the protection of the deity in war, inscribed weapons with religious talismans, took mass and made confession before battle, carried relics and holy banners (see COLOURS, BANNERS, AND STANDARDS) into combat, and made votive offerings after victory.

The growth of Arthurian romance in the 12th century, fostered by writers such as Chrétien de Troyes, had an equally profound influence on chivalry. Knights now had to be more than just brave warriors, but also polished courtly gentlemen, able to converse with and entertain ladies. Increasingly lavish tournaments re-enacted Arthurian tales, while kings such as Edward I and *Edward III skilfully manipulated the imperial symbolism of Arthur for their own political aims. Monarchs sought to create close bonds with their nobles by establishing *orders of chivalry such as the

English Order of the Garter, or the Burgundian Order of the Golden Fleece, modelled on Arthur's brotherhood of the Round Table, while other 'votal' orders dedicated themselves to the service of ladies. Later medieval chivalry has been criticized for being decadent and other-worldly, yet it never lost touch with the changing military dimensions of war nor was blind to its bloody realities. A complex and often paradoxical set of values, chivalry at its best sought to ameliorate the brutality of war. It remained nevertheless very much an arrangement among aristocrats and knightly consideration was seldom extended to the common soldier.

The western ideal of chivalrous behaviour in warriors, now extensive to all soldiers, continues to be honoured centuries after the disappearance of the armoured knight. Admiration for the fighting quality of the *enemy, clemency and moderation in victory, and the hope of decent treatment in defeat descend in large part directly from medieval chivalry and are quite often absent in non-western warrior cultures.   MJS

Barbour, Richard, *The Knight and Chivalry* (Woodbridge, 1996).

Coss, Peter, *The Knight in Medieval England, 1100–1400* (Stroud, 1993).

Flori, Jean, *L'Essor de la chevalerie, xie–xiie siècles* (Geneva, 1986).

Keen, Maurice, *Chivalry* (Yale, 1984).

Strickland, Matthew, *War and Chivalry: The Conduct and Perception of War in England and Normandy, 1066–1217* (Cambridge, 1996).

Kohima, battle of (1944). Kohima was linked to the larger action at *Imphal, a defensive battle fought by the British against the major Japanese offensive launched in early 1944. The hill station of Kohima stood on the road connecting the main British forward base of Imphal with the railhead at Dimapur, 46 miles (74 km) to the north. Its garrison, commanded by Col Richards, consisted of 2,500 men, about 1,000 of them non-combatants, with Lt Col Laverty's 4th Royal West Kents as its most effective unit. The British were expecting Imphal, 80 miles (129 km) to the south, to be attacked, and although they thought that the Japanese would hook northwards to cut the road at Kohima they judged that only a regiment would be given the task. Lt Gen Sato's 31st Division, after a difficult march across country, attacked it on 3 April, greatly outnumbering the defenders.

For the next fortnight the Japanese mounted attacks on the string of defended localities running along the road. They took GPT (General Purpose Transport) Ridge early on, gaining control of the water supply, and pushed the garrison back into a small area around the district commissioner's bungalow and the FSD (Field Supply Depot) area to its south. The fighting was some of the worst in the war, with wounded being hit again as they lay on stretchers, and the smell of unburied bodies polluting the position. LCpl

Martin Coles Harman of the Royal West Kents was awarded a posthumous VC for repeated valour.

Kohima was relieved on 20 April, but fighting went on in the area for another two months. Overall casualties there amounted to 4,000 British and almost 6,000 Japanese. The British memorial at Kohima bears the poignant words:

> When you go home
> Tell them of us, and say:
> For your tomorrow,
> We gave our today.   RH

Campbell, Arthur, *The Siege: A Story from Kohima* (London, 1956).

Swinson, Arthur, *Kohima* (London, 1966).

Kolchak, Adm Alexander Vasilevich (1874–1920), with Lt Gen Anton *Denikin and Lt Gen Peter Wrangel', one of the principal leaders of the 'White' counter-revolutionary movement against the 'Reds' in Russia during the 1917–20 Russian civil war. The aquiline-featured Kolchak commanded a destroyer and then a shore battery in the *Russo-Japanese war, then served on the newly established naval *general staff. In WW I he served with the Baltic Fleet and, from 1916, commanded the Black Sea Fleet. After the March Revolution he escaped to Britain and the USA and was brought back to Russia in October 1918, when he was appointed defence minister in the so-called 'Siberian Government'. His name is synonymous with the cruelty of the White regime, although the Reds were little, if at all, better. During 1919 the Red Army pushed Kolchak's forces eastward, back to Omsk and Irkutsk, and on 27 December he was taken prisoner by the Czech Legion and handed over to the Bolsheviks, who shot him on 7 February 1920. CDB

Koniev, Marshal Ivan Stepanovich (1897–1973). Colleague and sometimes rival of Georgiy *Zhukov, Koniev was the victor in the final battle of the European war and, from 1955 to 1960, first commander of the military forces of the *Warsaw Pact alliance. Conscripted into the imperial army in 1916, Koniev served as an NCO and after the November 1917 *Russian Revolution became a political commissar. He just escaped Stalin's purges of the 1930s, like Zhukov, because he was in the Far East. He commanded the Steppe Front (the reserve army group) at *Kursk in July 1943 and won renown for his reconquest of the Ukraine and southern Poland in 1944–5, commanding First Ukrainian Front. In April 1945, *Stalin pitted Koniev's Front against Zhukov's in the race for Berlin. Although Koniev did better, swinging up from the south after Zhukov's frontal attack stalled, Stalin let Zhukov capture the Reichstag. Koniev then seized Prague in the last battle of the European war. He was governor of the Soviet occupation zone in Austria (1945–6). Although he played second fiddle to Zhukov (but only just) during the war, after it he commanded the Warsaw Pact forces from 1955 to 1960 and served as inspector general of the Soviet Ministry of Defence until his death.   CDB

Königgrätz (Sadowa), **battle of** (1866), the decisive clash of the *Austro-Prussian war. On 3 July 1866, Austria's North Army of 240,000 men under *Benedek stood on rising ground between the village of Sadowa and the fortress of Königgrätz. They awaited the approach of 245,000 Prussian troops grouped in three armies under the nominal orders of Prussia's King Wilhelm I and the operational command of *Moltke 'the Elder'.

Whereas the Austrians arrived at Königgrätz by chance, the Prussians had planned to fight there. In June, Moltke had deployed Prussia's three armies on a 310 mile (500 km) arc from Halle in the west to Breslau in the east precisely so that he could rapidly invade Bohemia and sweep Benedek's densely concentrated, slow-moving North Army into a 'pocket' (*Kessel*) on the Elbe. The plan succeeded admirably. Descending from the north-east, Moltke's Second Army inflicted a sequence of bloody defeats on the Austrians in the last week of June and herded Benedek's increasingly ragged army westward into the grasp of Moltke's first and Elbe Armies, descending from the north-west. Trapped, Benedek decided to fight a defensive battle at Königgrätz.

Moltke intended Königgrätz to be a classic 'pocket battle' (*Kesselschlacht*). Heavy rain on 3 July nearly ruined his plans. His First and Elbe Armies arrived before Sadowa wet and exhausted. Second Army did not reach the field until late afternoon. Benedek therefore enjoyed a considerable advantage for most of the battle. He had 240,000 men against just 135,000 Prussians. Yet Benedek did nothing with this advantage, and stopped an attempt by a subordinate (Gen Anton von Mollinary) to swing North Army's right wing forward to encircle the two Prussian armies at Sadowa before the arrival of the third. This Austrian flanking attack, pushed forward by Mollinary and pulled back by Benedek, foundered in Swib Forest, where small parties of Prussian riflemen lacerated the confused columns of Austrian infantry filing in and out of the wood.

Saved by Benedek's inaction, Moltke had time to await the arrival of the Prussian Second Army, which struck Benedek's weakly guarded right flank at dusk. Hit from all sides, North Army dissolved in a defeat which the gallantry of its cavalry and artillery rearguards mitigated but could not avert. Königgrätz ought indeed to have been the classic pocket battle, a 'second *Cannae'. With the Elbe at his back, Benedek had no line of retreat. Yet Moltke's *pursuit was too slow. Prussian reserves of infantry and cavalry were stuck in a muddy knot of wagons behind the lines, and did not come up in time to seal shut the pocket at Königgrätz. Most of Benedek's army escaped across the Elbe in the night. However, the Austrians lost 44,000 men in the course of the day, compared with Prussian losses of just 9,000. North Army retreated to Vienna in such a weakened,

demoralized state that the Austrian emperor had no option but to agree to an armistice on 22 July 1866.   GDWW

Craig, Gordon A., *The Battle of Königgrätz* (London, 1964).
Wawro, Geoffrey, *The Austro-Prussian War* (Cambridge, 1996).

Korea, Japanese invasions of (1592, 1597). The first Japanese invasion of Korea in 1592 was ordered by *Toyotomi Hideyoshi as the first stage of a plan to conquer China. The Japanese troops landed at Pusan, and three armies proceeded northwards, taking Seoul with ease. The Japanese use of the arquebus was a considerable element in their success. P'yŏngyang fell within weeks, but several factors then came into play which halted the Japanese progress. The first was a vigorous Korean resistance movement whose irregular troops conducted a *guerrilla war. The second was the Korean navy under the leadership of Adm Yi Sun shin, whose 'turtle boats', manoeuvrable oared vessels protected by iron spikes, played havoc with the Japanese lines of communication. The third factor was the intervention of Chinese troops. One Japanese division crossed briefly into Manchuria, but were driven back by the winter and lack of rear support. Another division were defeated at Haengju, and forced to evacuate Seoul in spite of a victory at Pyŏkje, a bloody pitched battle at which the superior Japanese swords came into their own. The progress of the Chinese forced the Japanese from the north of Korea into a series of fortified camps in the south where they remained for the winter and evacuated the peninsula in 1593. The second invasion followed in 1597. Adm Yi had been replaced and the Japanese troops landed unopposed. They first took Namwŏn, but their progress was restricted again by the Chinese and the Korean guerrillas. Once Yi was reinstated as Korean admiral the Japanese armies became progressively isolated. A major pitched battle was fought at Sa'chŏn, but by now Hideyoshi was dead, and the Japanese armies were withdrawn. The departing transports were intercepted by Adm Yi, who was shot and killed as the invaders escaped.   SRT

Korean war (1950–3). In 1945, the Japanese colony of Korea was divided 'temporarily' between the USSR and the USA along the line of the 38th Parallel of latitude. Some five years later the division persisted, despite repeated efforts at reunification by the UN. *Stalin established a satellite state under Kim Il-sung in North Korea, while in the south the Republic of Korea (ROK) was formed under an autocratic right-wing coalition, elected under UN supervision. Its president was Syngman Rhee, a fiery old patriot. The leaders of both North and South Korea wished to unite the country by force of arms. Neither the Americans nor Stalin were minded to supply the means to do so. Chafing, each side skirmished indeterminately along the 38th Parallel.

On 9 February 1950, perceiving that US support for the ROK was declining, Stalin at last assented to an invasion of the south and the new ruler of China *Mao Tse-tung concurred. War stocks including tanks, artillery, and aircraft were delivered from Siberia to the North Korean People's Army (NKPA). Mao returned a host of seasoned Korean soldiers serving among his armies to their homeland. Soviet staff officers in Kim's headquarters completed a plan of operations.

With complete surprise, the offensive was opened in summer showers on 25 June 1950. It was a Sunday; many of those in the southern defence lines were away on weekend leave and the ROK army took US forces with them in headlong retreat. Although the attack was immediately condemned by the USA, Britain, Australia, Canada, New Zealand, and South Africa, followed by a majority of UN members, it was only the fact that the USSR was boycotting the Security Council that permitted the passage of a UN resolution not merely condemning it, but authorizing the formation of a multinational force to combat the aggression. Gen Douglas *MacArthur, the US *shogun in Japan following WW II, was appointed C-in-C. Two US divisions were rushed to Korea from Japan under strong air and sea cover, but these were unfit, untrained occupation troops who were roughly handled by the hardy and well-drilled NKPA. Eventually five divisions were fed into the peninsula as they arrived, mostly US but including a British-led Commonwealth brigade. Formed as the Eighth Army under the US Lt Gen Walton H. Walker, these troops along with the ROK army remnants held a perimeter around *Pusan, the principal southern port.

Meanwhile MacArthur was building up a reserve corps in Japan consisting of the 1st Marine and 7th Infantry Divisions and launched them in an *amphibious landing at the port of *Inchon on the west coast of the peninsula, 200 miles (322 km) behind the battle front. It was a hazardous venture, but successful. In mid-September, the marines captured the port and were joined ashore by the 7th Division to liberate Seoul, the national capital of Korea. Apprehensive of such a landing, Mao had earlier reinforced the Fourth Field Army (in fact an army group) in north-east China with two divisions. Now anticipating the destruction of the NKPA, he discussed countermeasures with Stalin.

From 22 September 1950, Walker's Eighth Army and the resuscitated elements of the ROK army began to break out of the Pusan perimeter. Shattered by intensive air as well as ground action, the NKPA filtered away through the central mountain chain. On the 27th, the American I Corps linked up with 7th Infantry Division near Seoul. MacArthur asked Washington for instructions: was he to stand on the 38th Parallel or cross it in *pursuit?

While *Truman considered this, Chinese PM Chou Enlai gave warning through Indian diplomatic channels that 'if the American authorities decided to cross . . . China will be forced to act accordingly'. The British chiefs of staff took this to mean Chinese military intervention, a response to be avoided at all costs while Stalin threatened in Europe. The

US and British governments, in close consultation, disagreed; likewise a majority in the UN. China might be bluffing and to hold back would surely offer Kim an opportunity to raise new forces and strike again. Against the protests of the communist bloc in the UN, where the USSR had resumed its place, the decision was taken to occupy North Korea as a preliminary to uniting North and South following democratic elections.

China was not bluffing. As the UN and ROK armies advanced, Gen P'eng Te-huai marched 130,000 soldiers of the Fourth Field Army into Korea, a host represented as 'volunteers' to establish the pretence that China remained aloof from the struggle. Stalin had promised them air cover, but withheld it as the march began, believing that Soviet fighters could not operate under a similar pretext—a Soviet pilot shot down and captured would discredit claims to neutrality. Mao collapsed temporarily with a nervous breakdown. P'eng responded more positively by restricting all movement to the winter nights. This simple stratagem paid a high dividend.

Crossing the Yalu river into north-west Korea, his veterans emerged from the darkness on 26 October, unexpected because undetected by the UN air force, to encircle and penetrate the UN and ROK formations approaching them. Usually fighting at night, sometimes in snowstorms, P'eng's light infantry bore in, shifting their axes of attack frequently, until on 6 November, they had swept so far afield that it became essential to draw them back, laden with plunder from the retreating UN forces, to regroup.

The governments of the UN alliance were stunned by this setback so soon after the defeat of the NKPA. Seeking at least to stabilize the battlefield, a *truce was suggested as a preliminary to reaching an accommodation with their foes. The creation of a buffer zone was contemplated. All this was 'wind past the ear' to the Chinese. When, at MacArthur's insistence, his troops, rebalanced and reinforced, advanced again on 24 November, Walker deployed eight UN and four ROK divisions. They were assailed almost at once by 30 of the Chinese. Despite considerable supporting firepower, the Eighth and ROK armies were still unable to withstand the close actions forced upon them selectively by P'eng's forces across the front from coast to coast. Gen Walker decided to break contact while he maintained some measure of control. He withdrew his line 150 miles (241 km) south below the Han, abandoning Seoul. Almond's X Corps in the north-east began a closely contested withdrawal to the coast. Many in the UN Command believed that they would be driven out of Korea altogether.

The UN forces moved in trucks. The Chinese marched. When the latter again closed on the UN and ROK positions in January 1951, they were suffering from exposure in temperatures often below 20 °C at night, lacking proper clothing and supplies. P'eng asked for a pause but Mao urged him on. Lt Gen Matthew *Ridgway, replacing Walker who had been killed in an accident, brought his subordinate

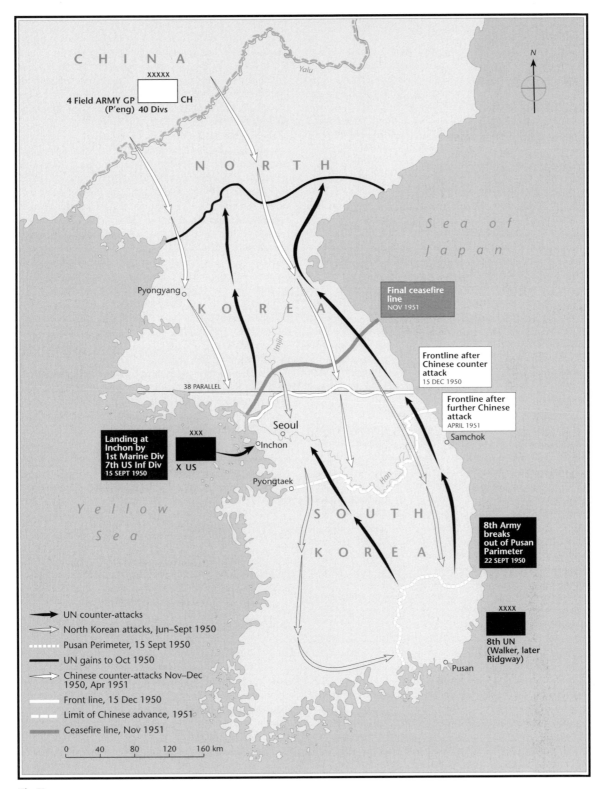

CHINA

XXXXX
4 Field ARMY GP
(P'eng) 40 Divs
CH

Yalu

N O R T H

Sea of Japan

K O R E A

Pyongyang

Final ceasefire line
NOV 1951

Imjin

Frontline after Chinese counter attack
15 DEC 1950

Frontline after further Chinese attack
APRIL 1951

38 PARALLEL

Seoul

Samchok

Landing at Inchon by 1st Marine Div 7th US Inf Div
15 SEPT 1950

XXX

X US

Inchon

Pyongtaek

Hon

Yellow Sea

S O U T H

K O R E A

8th Army breaks out of Pusan Parimeter
22 SEPT 1950

XXXX

8th UN (Walker, later Ridgway)

Pusan

UN counter-attacks
North Korean attacks, Jun–Sept 1950
Pusan Perimeter, 15 Sept 1950
UN gains to Oct 1950
Chinese counter-attacks Nov–Dec 1950, Apr 1951
Front line, 15 Dec 1950
Limit of Chinese advance, 1951
Ceasefire line, Nov 1951

0   40   80   120   160 km

The **Korean war,** 1950–1.

483

commanders to order. The Eighth Army was to stand and fight. As the Chinese ardour waned, the spirits of the Eighth Army waxed. They held the line and, encouraged, counter-attacked. Now P'eng was forced to withdraw. By mid-April 1951, Ridgway's line commanded the 38th Parallel. Its numbers had risen: battalions and brigades from eleven nations had joined the Eighth Army and even the ROK army was maturing. A new strategy had been implemented whereby they would roll with the punches in the event of a new Chinese offensive.

As the winter ended, P'eng was indeed preparing to strike again. Forty assault divisions were available to him. The march to contact began on 21 April, directing principal thrusts across the Imjin and Kap'yong rivers, areas held by chance by the 29th British and 27th Commonwealth brigades. Both held firm while the UN line 'rolled' back unbroken, drawing out the enemy. Sustaining high casualties, running short of supplies due to widespread air attack, P'eng's 40 assault divisions were unable to maintain their momentum. They drew off never to engage in a strategic offensive again. Manoeuvre was succeeded by costly but localized *trench warfare, using the tactics of WW I, employing the weapons of WW II. Seven American, one British Commonwealth, and eleven ROK Divisions held the line, together with battalions and a brigade from fourteen other nations. It scarcely moved for the remaining two years of the war.

This change was occasioned by the opening of armistice talks, nominally between the opposing commanders-in-chief. Stalin was content to play a waiting game. Mao was more or less persuaded that Korea offered no further triumphs for him. The American public was unwilling to back uncertain prospects of victory when peace was an option. A ceasefire might have been agreed in 1951 but for American and British Commonwealth insistence that no *POW would be returned against his will, a condition that affected only the Chinese and North Koreans. The UN prisoners and ROK prisoners had been treated so shamefully by their communist captors that all but a handful opted for repatriation.

In the POW camps in the South, Chinese who nursed preferences for Nationalist China on Taiwan, or NKPA members disenchanted with Kim Il-sung's regime, demonstrated their preferences vehemently. Communist zealots rioted in opposition. The American camp authorities lost control of the compounds periodically. Essentially, the Beijing regime could not accept any admission that there could be Chinese who preferred the Nationalist camp. Armistice prospects declined.

American air commanders sought during the stalemate to win the war by bombing the enemy into submission, attacking troops, industries, and communications repeatedly. Inevitably, many civilians were among the casualties. The full effect of their offensive was limited by UN rules forbidding attacks on targets in China or any use of atomic weapons—for good reasons; it would have been counter-productive politically and ineffective militarily. But in North Korea the capacity to survive exceeded the bombers' capability for destruction. UN naval forces maintained their domination of the sea flanks in all seasons but lacked the means to break the massed ranks of the Chinese and NKPA remnant.

Fortunately a common factor militated for peace: the costs of war. By the time Stalin died in March 1953, these were becoming intolerable to the Chinese. *Eisenhower, succeeding to office in 1953, was also anxious to end the expense of a protracted holding action. He declared that he would resume active operations in Korea if the armistice negotiations remained unproductive and hints emerged from Washington that atomic weapons might be used. In this climate, negotiations came to life; sick and wounded prisoners were exchanged. Thereafter, with the adoption of a screening system for prisoners, contrived to save Chinese sensitivities, the basic obstacle to an armistice was overcome. Despite the arbitrary release of many NKPA prisoners by Syngman Rhee and late operations by the communist forces to secure ground of tactical advantage, an agreement was completed. Hostilities ceased on 27 July 1953, some three years after they began.

This first military operation by UN forces failed to reunite the Korean nation but saved those in South Korea from the tyrannical and incompetent government of Kim Il-sung. It exposed to members of the Chinese People's Liberation Army flaws in Mao's military leadership which had far-reaching consequences. No less, the victory won in Korea, albeit qualified, encouraged a powerful section of American opinion to believe that the USA could win any war of its choice in Asia. The *Vietnam war lay ahead.

AF-H

Fehrenbach, T. R., *This Kind of War* (New York, 1963).
Hastings, Max, *The Korean War* (London, 1987).
O'Neill, Robert, *Australia in the Korean War*, 2 vols. (Canberra, 1981 and 1985).
Pannikar, K. M., *In Two Chinas* (London, 1955).
Tu P'ing (also Du Ping), *In the headquarters of the CPV* (Beijing, 1989).

Koroneia (Coronea), battles of (447 and 394 BC). Commanding the narrow neck between the foothills of Helicon and Lake Copais, Koroneia was the scene of important battles during the *Peloponnesian and *Greek city-state wars. In the first an Athenian army on its way back from recovering Chaeronea from Boeotian rebels, was defeated by an army of Boeotians, Locrians, and Euboeans, and in order to recover the prisoners, Athens was forced to withdraw from central Greece.

In the second, King Agesilaos of *Sparta, returning from Asia Minor to face a growing crisis in Greece, found his way barred by a combined army of Boeotians and their allies. As so often happened in *hoplite battles, both sides won on their right, but when Agesilaos was informed that the Thebans who had formed the enemy right were now in his rear, he countermarched his *phalanx, and met them head-on as they tried to rejoin their defeated allies on the slopes of Helicon. Eventually the Thebans broke through, albeit with considerable losses. Strategically the battle represented a victory for Sparta, but the breaking of a Spartan phalanx by Thebans in close order was ominous for the future.   JFL

Lazenby, J. F. *The Spartan Army* (Warminster, 1985).
Xenophon, *Hellenika*, 4. 3. 15–20.

Kosovo (1389, 1999). The most important battle in Serbian history took place at Kosovo Polje (Kosovo field) on St Vitus day, 28 June 1389 (or 15 June according to the old Orthodox calendar) between armies led by the Serbian Prince Lazar and the Ottoman *Turk Sultan Murad. The result, though inconclusive, has been celebrated since in Serbian epic *poetry as a defeat of great mystical significance, ushering in the end of Serbia's independence and the start of four centuries of Ottoman, Muslim domination. No accounts by participants in the battle survive, though it is accepted that both Murad and Lazar were killed. Recent historians put the strength of the armies at about 30,000 on the Ottoman side and 15,000–20,000 on the Serb side. Serb oral legend has it that Lazar chose defeat, after being offered a choice between a heavenly and an earthly kingdom on the eve of the battle. In terms of strategy Kosovo field was probably less important than an earlier Christian battle with the Turks on the Marica river in Bulgaria in 1370, which enabled the Ottomans to break through into the centre of the Balkans.

The 600th anniversary of the battle was celebrated with great pomp by the Serbian strong man Slobodan Milosevic (see YUGOSLAVIA, OPERATIONS IN FORMER) and was one of the main reasons given for Serb intransigence in 1999 when required by *NATO to pull their forces out of the province of Kosovo. An air campaign against a variety of targets in the province and in Serbia itself, carried out against a backcloth of press and public controversy outside Kosovo and 'ethnic cleansing' within it, was followed by a Serb withdrawal and, on 13 June, occupation by NATO ground forces. Some commentators have suggested that the campaign represents the first ever triumph of unsupported *air power. However, it is likely that the air campaign, linked with diplomatic pressure (not least by Russia) and the growing likelihood of a land attack all combined to encourage Milosevic to back down.   MGT/RH

Ksatriya (Sanskrit) (also known as Kshatriya), the second highest of the four varnas, or social classes, of Hindu India. The Ksatriya has traditionally been the military or ruling class. Early Vedic texts make a distinction between the ordinary members of the Aryan tribe that had sub-jugated much of northern India and the warrior nobility referred to as the Ksatriya. Initially they came first in the developing varna or caste system that the Aryans used to classify their society between priests, warriors, and free peasants or traders. A hymn of the Rig-Veda contains first evidence of this new system. It concerns the *sacrifice of Purusha and the creation of the universe and four varnas:

When they divided Purusha how many portions did they make?
What do they call his mouth, his arms? What do they call his thighs and feet?
The Brahman was his mouth, of both arms was the Rajanya [Ksatriya] made
His thighs became the Vaishya, from his feet the Shudra was produced.

At the top of this hierarchy were the first two estates or castes: the Brahmin priests and, as so clearly described by the Rig-Veda as the arms of society, the Ksatriya or warrior nobility. The second level was the Vaishya, the free Aryan peasants and traders, and the third level was the Shudra, the labourers, slaves, and artisans from the indigenous people.

The Ksatriya formed a ruling class which was often resented and led to social conflict. For example, a contemporary text states, 'Whenever the Ksatriya feels like it he says, "Vaishya bring me what you have hidden from me." He pillages and plunders. He does what he wants.' There was also considerable conflict between the Ksatriya and the Brahmins as they vied for superiority. According to legend, the Ksatriya were destroyed for their tyrannous behaviour by the Parasurama, the sixth reincarnation of Vishnu. Some scholars believe this reflects the long struggle between the priests and the warrior caste which ended in victory for the Brahmins. By the end of the Vedic era they were supreme and the Ksatriya held merely second place. In modern times, the Ksatriya varna contains a broad swathe of caste groups of differing status headed by the aristocratic *Rajputs.   MCM

Kursk, battle of (1943), the greatest tank battle in history, but also an important air battle, which took place on the *eastern front in WW II between 5 and 23 July 1943. Soviet successes in early 1943 and German counter-attacks had left a huge bulge or salient sticking out into German-held territory round Kursk in Ukraine. *Hitler had once postponed ZITADELLE, the plan to cut out the salient, but on 18 June 1943 decided to go ahead in order to achieve a crushing victory over the Red Army which had so humiliated the *Wehrmacht at *Stalingrad. The Germans concentrated 70 per cent of their tanks and 65 per cent of their aircraft from the entire eastern front. The German forces totalled 900,000 men, 2,700 tanks and *assault guns, and 1,800 aircraft. The battle would demonstrate the differing qualities of German and Soviet technology. The Germans had been seeking an answer to the successful Soviet T-34, and produced the Panther, which first appeared in May

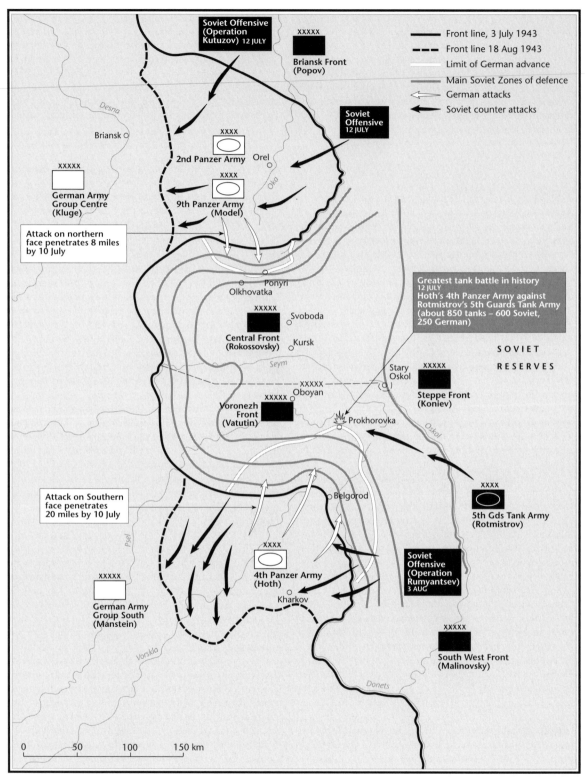

The battle of **Kursk,** July 1943.

1943. It had a 75 mm gun and thick frontal armour, but was unreliable. The Soviets, meanwhile, had begun up-gunning the T-34 from 76 mm to 85 mm. The Germans also had the massive Tiger tank with an 88 mm gun and 100 mm of armour and the Ferdinand assault gun on a Tiger chassis. It was in some ways to be a ritualistic contest, between heavy, armoured German knights and fast-moving Soviets. But more important, the Soviets knew the Germans were coming and built a huge defensive network 150–200 miles (241–321 km) deep. There were five to six defensive 'belts,' each 2–3 miles (3.2–4.8 km) deep. Most of the engineering effort went into the first 20 miles (32 km)—the 'tactical zone', with field defences, mines, and anti-tank guns.

The German plan envisaged the Ninth Army under *Model with five corps attacking the salient from the north, southwards from Orel, and Hoth's Fourth Panzer Army, also with five corps, from the south, around Belgorod. The Soviet *Lucy* spy ring discovered the rough timing of the attack: 3 to 6 July. Battlefield *intelligence refined this to 02.00 on 5 July. The Soviet artillery therefore fired the biggest artillery 'counter-preparation'—smashing up enemy forces as they are concentrating for the attack—in the history of war.

At 05.00 Hoth's panzers, already shaken, pressed forward in wedge formations into a waiting arc of fire. Many of the Panthers broke down. The heavy Ferdinands and Tigers pressed on, to be met by *Pakfronts*, whole batteries of anti-tank guns which would blast a single tank, then move to the next. By 10 July the southern pincer had stalled, not having penetrated the 20 mile (32 km) tactical zone. The same happened in the north, where the Germans only penetrated 8 miles (12.9 km). Now the Germans had stalled, the Soviet tank armies were committed. Hoth's Fourth Panzer tried to penetrate the Soviet defences near the village of Prokhorovka. They collided with Pavel Rotmistrov's Fifth Guards Tank Army. In the general area there were 1,200–1,400 tanks, but only 850 (600 Soviet and 250 German) actually clashed on the Prokhorovka field. Among them the Germans had 100 Tigers. On 12 July, under a sky full of thunderclouds, the titans clashed, the Soviets under orders to close with the Tigers to negate the latter's advantage in range. The outcome was a stand-off, although *Guderian recalled he had 'never received such an overwhelming impression of Soviet strength and numbers as on that day'. Soon, T-34s were streaming 'like rats over the battlefield'.

The Germans lost 400 tanks and 10,000 men. The Soviets lost more, but they could afford them more. In the entire battle, which equated to the armoured actions on both Israeli fronts in the 1973 *Arab–Israeli war, the Red Army claimed to have killed or captured 500,000 Germans and destroyed 1,500 tanks. The Germans claimed to have destroyed 1,800 tanks on the south face alone. Through an inferno of blazing armoured vehicles and scorched and shattered bodies surrounded by shell-cases and stale bread, the Soviet counter-attack—the BELGOROD-KHARKOV

operation—began. In the air, and on the ground, the fundamental balance of forces had shifted in favour of the USSR. It had been Germany's last chance to win the war.

CDB

Erickson, John, *The Road to Berlin* (London, 1982).
Manstein, Erich von, *Lost Victories* (London, 1958).
Glantz, David, and Orenstein, Harold (eds.), *The Battle for Kursk 1943: The Soviet General Staff Study* (London, 1999).

Kusunoki Masashige is revered as the epitome of *samurai loyalty to the emperor. He was the follower of Emperor Go-Daigo, who attempted to overthrow the government of the *shogun in 1333. Masashige maintained the imperial cause from the fortress of Akasaka, in the wooded mountains of the Kii peninsula, and resisted several attempts to dislodge him. When Akasaka finally fell Masashige retreated to the more remote and formidable Chihaya, where he withstood a long siege. During the fighting both sides used several ingenious stratagems, such as movable bridges to cross ravines and dummy troops to fool the attackers. While Masashige held the shogunate forces at bay other allies destroyed their base at Kamakura, but instead of leading to the intended imperial restoration, another dynasty of shogun, the Ashikaga, was established, and moved against Masashige. When their armies threatened Masashige advised withdrawing once again to Chihaya, but the emperor was determined to fight a pitched battle. Masashige knew that their cause was hopeless, but met the Ashikaga forces at Minatogawa in 1336. Defeated on the battlefield, he committed suicide. At the time of the Meiji Restoration in the 19th century Masashige was held up as an example of imperial devotion.

SRT

Kut Al Amara, siege of (1916). In May 1915 Gen Sir John Nixon, GOC the Mesopotamian Expeditionary Force, sent Maj Gen Charles Townshend up the Tigris with a divisional-sized force. Townshend took Kut in late September, but his communications were fragile. Under political pressure to take Baghdad, Nixon ordered Townshend forward: checked at Ctesiphon, he fell back on Kut. In 1895 Townshend had successfully defended the outpost of Chitral on the *North-West frontier, and hoped to repeat the achievement.

Townshend was encircled on 7 December. Relief attempts failed in January and March 1916, and, his supplies exhausted, Townshend surrendered with 10,000 men in late April. His defeat dealt a serious blow to British prestige. Many of Townshend's soldiers perished in their harsh captivity. He himself lived in comfortable confinement in a Black Sea resort, and received a knighthood during his captivity. Although he was well received in 1918, he was rightly given no further military employment.

RH

Kutuzov, Marshal Mikhail Illarionovich (1745–1813), Russian military commander and diplomat, the wily old general of *War and Peace*. Kutuzov served his military apprenticeship under the great FM Pyotr Rumyantsev, in the Russo-Turkish war of 1768–74, and FM Aleksandr *Suvorov, in the Crimea and at the capture of Izmail in 1790, where Kutuzov commanded one of the assaulting *columns. He was a tactical innovator and discarded line formations in favour of the columns introduced during the *French Revolutionary wars. He retired in 1802 but was recalled in 1805 to command one of the two Russian armies sent into Austria. Unable to effect a junction with the Russians, the Austrians were defeated at Ulm. Kutuzov managed to extract his forces but, against his judgement, was ordered to make an attack which resulted in Napoleon's great victory at *Austerlitz.

When Napoleon invaded, Kutuzov was made C-in-C of the Russian armies on 20 August 1812. He adopted a 'scorched earth' policy to exhaust the invaders' logistics during the long retreat into Russia, and gave battle only at the gates of Moscow. On 7 September the armies met at *Borodino, the bloody battle that destroyed the myth of Napoleonic invincibility. Kutuzov was also behind the decision to burn Moscow, to mobilize extensive support from partisan units, and to harry Napoleon's army on its icy long retreat, 'war to the knife'. Kutuzov's approach to war went beyond the strategy of single, decisive battles between regular armies. He sought total annihilation of the enemy, employing every resource at his disposal. As such, he might be considered the grandfather of *total war.

CDB

La Rochelle, siege of (September 1627–October 1628). In one of the most famous sieges of French history, an army led by Louis XIII and his first minister, Cardinal *Richelieu, took the Protestant seaport of La Rochelle during the last of the *French wars of religion. In order to deny La Rochelle supplies or relief by the English fleet, royal forces constructed a barrier across the narrow bay on which La Rochelle was situated. After its surrender and royal victory in the war, Louis XIII allowed the *Huguenots to practise their faith, but stripped them of their fortresses and ability to make war. JAL

Lafayette, Marie-Joseph du Motier, Marquis de (1757–1834), key figure in both the *American independence war and the *French Revolutionary wars. He travelled to America in 1777 and joined the staff of *Washington, with whom he developed a father–son relationship. In 1779 he returned to Paris in representation of the hard-pressed rebels and was instrumental in obtaining French land and naval support, which won the culminating battle at *Yorktown in 1780.

In the pre-revolutionary 1789 French Estates General he led the liberal aristocrats and advocates of constitutional monarchy. As commander of the National Guard he saved Louis XVI from the mob at Versailles, but was compelled to resign in July 1791 after firing on a crowd calling for abdication. Ambivalently in command at Metz when France went to war with Austria in 1792, he defected when the French monarchy was overthrown and to escape trial for treason. The Austrians nonetheless imprisoned him for five years.

He kept a low profile during the Empire and as a deputy under Louis XVIII, but his return to the USA in 1824–5 was a revitalizing apotheosis. Again commanding the National Guard, in 1830 he helped to overthrow Charles X and replace him with the constitutional monarch Louis-Philippe. HEB

Lake Trasimene, battle of (217 BC). The battle, fought on 21 June 217 BC, was an ambush on a huge scale. *Hannibal, with probably about 60,000 men, trailed his coat before the Consul Flaminius, at Cortona, before disappearing into the narrow passage north of the lake. Flaminius, probably with about 25,000 men, followed and was caught between the hills and the lake, either between Pieve Confini and Passignano or between the latter and Magione. Some 6,000 Romans in the van managed to escape, only to be rounded up later, but the rest, including Flaminius, were annihilated. JFL

Lazenby, J. F., *Hannibal's War* (Warminster, 1978).
Livy, 22. 4–7.
Polybius, 3. 81–4.

lancers were light cavalrymen armed with and trained in the use of a lance. In the medieval period, the term 'lance' was also used to describe a knight plus a small band of retainers. Lancers first appeared in Europe as organized light cavalry in the early 18th century and were Poles in the Army of Saxony, but before that the lance was widely used in the Middle East from the earliest days of Islam. These Polish troops, called *Uhlans*, also served in the French army as part of a contingent of Saxon volunteers during the War of the *Austrian Succession, 1742–8, and were armed with pennon-tipped lances. In the French service they wore helmets with horsehair crests but in Saxony they wore the square-topped national cap of Poland called a *czapska*. Both *uhlan* and *czapska* derive from Turkish and clearly associate the Polish lancers with origins in Turkey. Austria first used lancers in 1781 and formed a regiment in 1791, Russian utilized lancers from the 1770s, and in 1797 lancers joined the French army of Italy, under the Polish Gen Dombrowski. Lancers became a part of the French imperial army, with the title Chevaux-légers-polonnais, in 1807 and the Lancers of the Imperial Guard were formed in 1810.

By 1810, most of the combatant European powers' armies included regiments of lancers, the troopers of which, in addition to their swords, *pistols, and carbines, all carried similar lances with ash shafts varying in length from 7 to 10 feet (2.1 to 3 metres), tipped with a steel point and often having a metal shoe at the butt-end. Britain introduced lancers into its light cavalry in 1816 and by the end of the 19th century had six such regiments armed with lances 9 feet (2.7 metres) long and, after c.1868, of bamboo rather than ash. In British India, *Maratha fighting traditions led gradually to the introduction of the lance and, by 1918, there were sixteen lancer regiments in the Indian army. In America, the lance had long been the hunting and war weapon of the Plains Indian but, in the early years of the *American civil war, 1861–5, at least one regiment of Federal Cavalry, the 6th Pennsylvania (Rush's Lancers), were equipped with 10 foot (3.04 metre) fir lances.

The long-range *breech-loading rifle contributed strongly to the obsolescence of the lancer by the late 19th century and the advent of the machine gun finished the process. Lancers continued to be retained, and armed with lances, in some European armies, notably the British, French, and German, throughout WW I and several cavalry actions were fought with lances in its opening months. The figure of the lancer, particularly the German *Uhlan*, was in the forefront of British propaganda during WW I, British lancers being commonly depicted as the last embodiment of *knighthood in action and their German counterparts as baby-killers. After 1918, lances have been retained for ceremonial purposes and have appeared in *tattoos and military *tournaments carried by cavalry regiments of varying designations, not always lancers, in 'musical rides'. The bodyguards of the presidents of India and Pakistan are still armed with them for ceremonial purposes, tracing this practice to the romantic figure of the 19th-century Bengal lancer.   SCW

landsknecht The very epitome of the 16th-century military freebooter and vagabond, the landsknecht was rightly feared wherever he went. Their garish, ripped, and rakishly padded costume, and improbably large weaponry, meant that the landsknechts presented an awe-inspiring sight to friend and foe alike. An unwholesome appetite for plunder and strong drink, and blood-curdling cries of 'Hut dich Bauer, ich komm', made them feared by the civilian population in the regions where they campaigned. And indeed they fought in almost every campaign in every region of Europe from 1486 to their decline at the end of the 16th century.

Originally, they had been raised by the Emperor Maximilian, who had no army of his own, as a cheap and efficient way of raising troops by contract with individual *mercenary captains. However, having taken up a career of military entrepreneurship, the captains of the landsknecht bands found that the emperor's wages were insufficient and infrequent, and rapidly cast about for the opportunity to serve elsewhere. They were not short of attractive offers, and despite the fact that they were prohibited from fighting against the emperor, many did. The French hired the infamous landsknecht Black Band for service at Pavia in 1525, where it was cut down to a man.

The landsknechts were at times truculent and untrustworthy employees, they were prone to strike for higher pay at the most inopportune moments, and often embarked on escapades of private enterprise like the sack of Rome in 1526. But if well provisioned with gold, food, and drink, they could perform useful service, and in the 1550s a good half of the French infantry was landsknecht in origin. The landsknecht Capt Empser had already shown his loyalty to a foreign flag under *Foix at Ravenna in 1512, where he ignored a letter from the emperor recalling him and his company from French service and went to glory and a better life hereafter for his employer.

The captains of the landsknecht bands would recruit in northern Germany and the Low Countries, offering promises of gold and plunder to prospective recruits. Each candidate was expected to provide his own weapons and armour and to prove his fitness by jumping a stand of three pikes or halberds before his name was entered in the roll. The landsknecht companies were mainly pike-armed and supposed to be about 400 strong, including about 100 *Doppelsöldener* (double pay men) who were daredevils armed with close combat weapons such as 6 foot (1.82 metre) two-handed swords, and who would rush into the attack ahead of the main body in order to break up the enemy formation. Between 25 and 50 of the company would be *Schützen* armed with crossbow or arquebus who skirmished ahead of the pikes. Between ten and eighteen companies made a regiment, which would combine with three other regiments to form a massive phalanx, fronted by the men with the best armour. There was also a *Blutfahnen* (Blood flag) of suicide troops that could sally out of the block to take a strong enemy position, or disrupt a particularly stubborn enemy formation.

The landsknechts' deadly enemies were the *Swiss, and when German fought Swiss no quarter was given or expected—the 'Bad war'. Most contemporaries rated the landsknechts as inferior to the Swiss, but considered them the equal of the Spanish foot, and definitely superior to any other infantry in Europe.   TM

Lannes, Marshal J., Duc de Montebello (1769–1809). Jean Lannes, born to a farming family in the Gers in 1769, was elected second lieutenant in a volunteer battalion in 1792, learnt his trade fighting the Spaniards, and was a colonel in 1794. In Italy in 1796 his outstanding dash brought him to Bonaparte's (see NAPOLEON) attention and earned him promotion to general. He served with Bonaparte in Egypt (see EGYPTIAN EXPEDITION, FRENCH), becoming commander of the Consular Guard after the Brumaire coup.

Lannes led the advance guard into Italy in 1800 and distinguished himself in the campaign. A loan from *Augereau saved him from punishment for unauthorized expenditure on the Guard, but he had to relinquish command. He represented France in Portugal in 1801–4, and was appointed marshal in 1804. Lannes shone as a corps commander in the *Austerlitz campaign, and in 1806 routed Prince Louis of Prussia at Saalfeld, going on to triumph at *Jena/Auerstadt and Friedland.

Sent to Spain in 1808, Lannes reduced Saragossa after a terrible siege. He then commanded a corps of the Army of Germany, leading the assault on Ratisbon with the words: 'before I was a marshal I was a grenadier, and I am one still.' Mortally wounded at Essling in May 1809, he was the first marshal to fall. Despite disagreements, usually over money, Lannes was devoted to Napoleon, who called him 'the most distinguished general in my army, and a companion in arms for sixteen years who I considered my best friend'.   RH

Larrey, Baron Dominique Jean (1766–1842). Larrey began his career as a naval surgeon and joined the French army in 1793, rising to become Napoleon's chief surgeon. In a career which spanned 60 battles and saw him wounded three times, Larrey was enormously influential both as a surgeon and a medical administrator. He advocated primary amputation, and practised the debridement of necrotic tissue, subsequently leaving the wound open, a policy revived with success during the *Falklands campaign of 1982. Unusually for his age, he insisted on hygiene, ordering his subordinates to change their clothing frequently and wash with vinegar water. He developed a mobile ambulance corps, using specially designed light *ambulances manned by properly trained personnel, and allocated medical detachments, with ambulance units bringing wounded to advanced dressing stations, to each of the army's field divisions. Larrey was supremely practical: on one occasion he used the breastplates discarded by unhorsed *cuirassiers to boil the flesh of their mounts and feed the wounded. At *Eylau he operated for 24 hours in weather so cold that his assistants could not hold the instruments, and at *Borodino he carried out 200 amputations on the day of battle alone. He was also a prolific author of memoirs and medical works.   RH

last post From the 17th century drums and trumpets sounded *tattoo, originally an instruction to turn off the taps of beer or wine-barrels, to call men back to quarters at the end of the day. Musicians marched from post to post as they played, and ended at the last post. The 1915 edition of *Trumpet and Bugle Sounds for the [British] Army* lists both 'Tattoo: first Post' and 'Tattoo: Last Post'.

In the US army the last post is known as 'taps', and owes much to Union general Dan Butterfield, who was dissatisfied with the army's bugle-call for lights out, and composed something which, he felt, symbolized a darkening camping ground with men settling down to a peaceful night's sleep. The British version is similar, and both are played at military funerals. On Remembrance Day the last post is followed by a period of silence, and then by the *reveille—the day's first bugle-call—to symbolize death and resurrection.   RH

Lawrence ('of Arabia'), Thomas Edward (1888–1935), widely known, not least because of the writings of the American journalist Lowell Thomas, and Peter O'Toole's 1962 film portrayal, as simply Lawrence of Arabia. The illegitimate son of an Anglo-Irish baronet who had eloped with the family governess, Lawrence was educated at Oxford where he took a first in history, thanks in part to a distinguished thesis on crusader castles. He had already visited the Middle East, and after graduation worked on the excavation of the Hittite city of Carchamish, learning useful lessons in how to motivate Arab villagers without formal authority.

Commissioned in 1914, he worked in the geographical section of the *general staff in London before being posted to the *intelligence branch in Cairo, where his responsibilities included collating information on Arab nationalist movements in areas under Turkish rule. He was sent on a fact-finding mission to the Hedjaz in October 1916, meeting Sherif Hussein of Mecca, who had rebelled against the Turks, and establishing a close rapport with his son Emir Feisal. Appointed liaison officer to the Arabs, he helped arrange support which enabled Feisal to advance up the Red Sea coast to Wej, where he threatened Turkish communications. He then developed a strategy for attacking the Hedjaz railway, the Turkish supply line. In mid-1917 he helped develop a plan for the capture of Akaba, thus enabling the Arabs to be supplied for operations striking up into Syria. He played an important role in 1918, operating against the Turkish rear while *Allenby attacked northwards after his victory at *Beersheba, and entered Damascus in October.

Lawrence served in the British delegation at the Paris peace conference, working hard to promote Arab unity and independence. By now a colonel, with a CB and DSO he never formally accepted, he was swept to fame by Lowell Thomas's 'travelogue', unusually courting the publicity in order to promote the Arab cause. However, he was embittered by the allocation of Syria, Palestine, and Mesopotamia to Britain and France as mandated territories, and retired to Oxford where he worked on *The Seven Pillars of Wisdom*, the most important of his books. Briefly recalled to government service, he helped establish the kingdoms of Iraq and Trans-Jordan (later Jordan). However, under severe mental pressure he sought obscurity by joining the ranks of the RAF under the assumed name of Ross. Discovered by the press, he speedily re-enlisted, this time as Pte Shaw of the Tank Corps. He managed to return to the RAF, and ended his service helping with the development of air-sea rescue launches. In May 1935 he was fatally injured in a motorcycle accident near his home, Clouds Hill, near Bovingdon in Dorset.

Lawrence's reputation has ebbed and flowed. Not all his writings are wholly accurate, and his enigmatic personal behaviour and ambivalence about publicity has led some of his many biographers to accuse him of charlatanism. The verdict now seems more benevolent. While he was never the leader of the Arab revolt (a position he never claimed), he did much to ensure its victory over the Turks, and made an influential contribution to planning for attacks on the Hedjaz railway, the capture of Akaba, and operations against Turkish communications in Syria. *The Seven Pillars of Wisdom* is not merely an important literary work in its own right, but embodies profound thoughts on the nature of *guerrilla warfare, not least the importance of casualty-avoidance in a society where deaths sent 'rings of sorrow' through the community.   RH

Wilson, Jeremy, *Lawrence of Arabia* (London, 1992).

laws of war (*see opposite page*)

Le Cateau, battle of (1914). On 23 August the British Expeditionary Force (BEF) under FM Sir John *French fought the battle of *Mons. Although it succeeded in holding a frontal attack by the German First Army, by midnight it was clear that it would have to retreat. On 25 August the BEF was divided by the Forest of Mormal, with Smith-Dorrien's II Corps passing to its west and *Haig's I Corps to its east. Smith-Dorrien had been told that the retreat was to continue, and at 22.15 he issued orders for a retirement the following morning. At about midnight he heard that the Cavalry Division had pulled back off the long ridge to his north: unless he was away by first light the Germans would be upon him. Smith-Dorrien concluded that if he tried to withdraw as planned he would be caught in the open by superior forces. He decided to stand and administer 'a stopping blow' and then to continue the retreat.

This was a courageous decision, for Smith-Dorrien got on badly with the C-in-C. French's COS had collapsed from overwork that night, and French himself was preoccupied with the threat to I Corps at Landrecies rather than II Corps at Le Cateau. Smith-Dorrien spoke to GHQ on the phone and was given grudging permission to stand. *Allenby of the Cavalry Division, not formally under Smith-Dorrien's command, agreed to fight under his orders, as did Maj Gen Snow, whose newly arrived 4th Division had come up on his left. The British were fortunate in that a French cavalry corps appeared on the left flank, where its 75 mm field guns made a useful contribution to the battle.

There was no time to lay out a defensive position. Most of Smith-Dorrien's men fought close to where they had spent the night, and were in action soon after dawn. The Germans, with no clear idea of British positions, launched repeated assaults. For many of the British the battle resembled Mons: determined infantry assaults prepared by heavy shellfire, met with accurate rifle fire. Smith-Dorrien's artillery commanders had decided that the infantry might not stand without intimate gunner support, and many batteries fought close to the front line.

The most vulnerable point in Smith-Dorrien's position was the knoll on his right above Le Cateau, and in the early afternoon Smith-Dorrien ordered a withdrawal, beginning with the hard-pressed right. It was difficult to get the guns out: three VCs were won in the process. The battle cost the British 7,812 men killed, wounded, and captured, as well as 38 guns, most of them from 5th Division, on the right. German losses were around 5,000. Smith-Dorrien's decision to stand and fight had paid off: the German *pursuit was not quite so pressing again.   RH

Le Marchant, Maj Gen John Gaspard (1766–1812). Although he never held high command, Le Marchant had a lasting influence on the British army. A Channel Islander, he was commissioned into the cavalry and took serious interest in tactics, arguing that charges succeeded because of physical impulsion, not because of damage done by swords. He argued that cavalry swords should be designed for slashing, and the heavily curved 1796 pattern Light Cavalry sword owed much to him. He also became convinced that the *education and training of officers should be taken more seriously, and was the founding father of the Royal Military College Sandhurst. He was lieutenant-governor of the college in 1801–12 before going to Spain, where he was killed leading the decisive charge at *Salamanca.   RH

League of Augsburg war (1688–97), also known as the Nine Years War or the War of the Grand Alliance. After having the first eighteen years of his 72-year reign dominated by his political mentor Cardinal Mazarin and by his struggles with the nobles of France, *Louis XIV decided to take the reins of state into his own hands when Mazarin died in 1661. His subsequent desires for a powerful France

(*cont. on page 496*)

laws of war

T HE laws of war are rules governing the conduct of armed conflict and the protection of victims of war. They have also sometimes been called in the post-1945 period 'international law of armed conflict' or 'international humanitarian law'. The classical name of the laws of war, often still used today, is *jus in bello*. This body of law is distinct from the rules governing the resort to armed conflict (*jus ad bellum*). The laws of war have for centuries encompassed a wide range of matters, including rights and duties of neutrals, treatment of *POWs and of those wounded in battle, administration of occupied territories, negotiation and implementation of truces, limitations on means and methods of warfare, and *war crimes.

The idea that the conduct of armed hostilities is governed by rules can be found in almost all societies. The Greeks and Romans customarily observed certain humanitarian principles. The Christian tradition placed emphasis on restraints on the conduct of war within the context of *just-war theology in the works of such writers as St Augustine of Hippo (354–430) and St Thomas Aquinas (1226–74). In the Middle Ages, a law of arms was developed in Europe to govern *discipline within armies as well as to regulate the conduct of hostilities. From the 15th century onwards, early European writers on international law such as Legnano, Victoria, Gentili, and Grotius wrote extensively on the laws of war. Ideas of restraint in the use of force also had a place in *poetry and drama.

For centuries, the customary rules regarding the conduct of armed hostilities have been enunciated not only in the writings of individuals, but also in official statements of various kinds, including in military codes. From at least the early 17th century neutrality in war, especially at sea, was frequently addressed in bilateral treaties. The paradox that one of the first areas of international law to be developed was that which concerned war is partly explained by the fact that peaceful relations can often be regulated on an *ad hoc* basis, whereas wars repeatedly pose questions of a general character which cannot be settled at the time by agreement between adversaries, and therefore need to be addressed earlier.

In the second half of the 19th century the idea of the multilateral treaty, open to any state to accept, became the main focus of international law-making. The laws of war had a pioneering part in this process. The 1856 Paris Declaration on Maritime Law, which (at the conclusion of the *Crimean war) laid down general rules on relations between belligerent and neutral shipping in wartime, has a strong claim to be regarded as the first modern multilateral treaty. In 1864 the first of what was to be a long stream of *Geneva Conventions was concluded, for the 'Amelioration of the Condition of the Wounded in Armies in the Field'. This spelt out the principle that those helping the wounded, on or off the battlefield, were to be recognized as neutral and to be protected from attack. The *Red Cross was to be used as a symbol of humanitarian work and a guarantee of immunity.

A classic statement of the purposes of the laws of war as seen at this time was in the 1868 St Petersburg Declaration prohibiting explosive *bullets. This said that 'the only legitimate object which States should endeavour to accomplish during war is to weaken the military forces of the enemy'. This statement conveys a vision of war as a struggle between the uniformed armies of states, rather than between governments or peoples.

The laws of war were further developed at international conferences at The Hague in 1899 and 1907, particularly in the 1907 Hague Convention IV 'Respecting the Laws and Customs of War on Land' and annexed regulations, covering such matters as treatment of POWs, protection of *hospitals, *truce negotiations, and the conduct of armies in occupied territories. These rules, based on a justified fear that the 20th century would be one of *total war, remain formally in force a century after they were drawn up.

WW I cast a shadow over this process of law-making. The many violations of the law had exposed its fragility, and the propaganda war about atrocities had shown how law could exacerbate mutual hostility. More fundamentally, much of the slaughter in *trench warfare had been technically in accord with the Hague Regulations, exposing law as an inadequate means of limiting war. At the end of the war, governments were not much interested in further refining the *jus in bello*, but sought rather to prevent war altogether.

In the inter-war years, there was some further codification of the international law of armed conflict. Apart from agreements on the treatment of prisoners and of those wounded in war, the most important development was the 1925 Geneva Protocol prohibiting the use of *chemical and biological weapons. This treaty, a rare example of a reasonably successful prohibition of use of a particular class of weapon, played some part in limiting the resort to these weapons in major international conflicts, including WW II. Its effectiveness is partly due to threats of retaliation in kind: many states, on becoming parties to the Protocol, declared that it would cease to be binding in relation to any enemy state which failed to respect it.

In WW II, many of the principles of the laws of war were violated, especially by the bombing of cities, the ruthless treatment of many POWs, and the massacres of Jews, gypsies, and others in Axis-occupied territories. The International Military Tribunals at Nuremberg and Tokyo immediately after the war, and many other courts as well, sought to punish leading Axis figures involved. Allied war practices went largely unexamined. This contrast fuelled the argument that the war crimes trials delivered 'victor's justice'.

In the immediate aftermath of WW II there were hopes that, since the resort to force was severely restricted under the UN Charter, there would be no need for substantial further development of the *jus in bello*. However, a succession of wars in subsequent decades impressed on governments the need to update the law. At least twelve major treaties on the laws of war have been concluded since 1945. (Numbers of states parties as at 12 August 1999 are indicated in brackets):

- 1948   UN *Genocide Convention (129).
- 1949   The four 1949 Geneva Conventions (188). These seek to protect four categories of victims under the power of the enemy: wounded and sick on land; wounded, sick, and ship-wrecked at sea; POWs; and civilians.
- 1954   Hague Cultural Property Convention (95). Two protocols, concluded in 1954 and 1999, address the export of cultural property from occupied territory, and measures to improve implementation of the convention's provisions in civil as well as international wars.
- 1976   UN Convention on the Prohibition of Military Use of Environmental Modification Techniques (65).
- 1977   Protocol I Additional to the 1949 Conventions, and Relating to the Protection of Victims of International Armed Conflicts (155).
- 1977   Protocol II Additional to the 1949 Conventions, and Relating to the Protection of Victims of Non-international Armed Conflicts (148).
- 1980   UN Convention on Prohibitions or Restrictions of the Use of Certain Conventional Weapons (73). The Protocols annexed to the Convention (including two adopted in 1995 and 1996) address non-detectable fragments, landmines, incendiary weapons, and blinding laser weapons.
- 1997   Ottawa Convention Prohibiting the Use, Stockpiling, Production, and Transfer of Anti-Personnel Mines (84).

- 1998   Rome Statute of the International Criminal Court (4). Articles 5 to 8 contain an important summary of the crimes of genocide, crimes against humanity, and war crimes.

None of these agreements mentions the term *nuclear weapons. The question of whether the threat and use of these could ever be compatible with the laws of war was addressed directly in an Advisory Opinion of the International Court of Justice on 8 July 1996. All fourteen judges agreed that the laws of war were applicable to nuclear as well as to other weapons, but not on the consequences that flowed from that proposition. All fourteen wrote separate statements, illustrating the difficulty of reaching a consensus view on this question.

So far as actual wars are concerned, the application of the laws of war does not depend upon the recognition of the existence of a formal state of 'war'. Many treaties concluded since WW II refer to 'armed conflict' rather than 'war'. The laws of war are applicable to all international wars, but there has been a problem regarding civil wars.

The extent to which the laws of war apply to civil wars has long been a matter of varied opinion and practice. Historically, governments have often been reluctant to treat rebels as legitimate belligerents entitled, for example, to POW status; and treaties on the laws of war have generally specified that they apply to international wars, without mentioning civil wars. However, certain rules are applicable in civil wars, including the prohibition on genocide; Article 3 in each of the four 1949 Geneva Conventions, which specifies some minimal rules to be applied in civil wars; and the 1977 Geneva Protocol II. In the 1990s, in response to the carnage of civil wars, there was further pressure to place legal limits on the actions of belligerents in civil wars. Both the 1997 Ottawa convention on landmines and the 1998 Rome Statute of the International Criminal Court, contain extensive provisions applicable in civil wars.

The case for applying the laws of war to internal armed conflicts has been strengthened by the fact that a high proportion of the wars of the 20th century, and especially of the post-1945 period, were internationalized civil wars, in which local belligerents gained the support of outside powers. In such cases, the simultaneous application of two sets of rules, for civil and international wars, poses problems. Some armed forces as a matter of policy train their troops to follow the rules for international armed conflict in all circumstances.

In general, the rules appear to work best when there is some degree of understanding and respect between belligerents. The rules regarding treatment of prisoners and others in the hands of the adversary have sometimes operated more effectively than the rules relating to the conduct of hostilities. In the conflicts of the post-1945 era implementation has been uneven. Often one side was unwilling to admit the legitimacy of the adversary's existence or status as a belligerent. Especially in civil wars, the distinction between the soldier and the civilian, basic to the modern laws of war, was not nearly as clear in practice as in theory. Extreme nationalism and ideological zeal militated against observing rules of moderation. Some violations of basic rules went unpunished.

Yet many limits were observed. In most wars, military prisoners received reasonable treatment. In the 1982 *Falklands war, and the 1991 *Gulf war, there was much (though not complete) observance of the rules. Such observance did not hamper, and may have positively assisted, the efficient professional conduct of operations.

In the 1990s, in the face of repeated and major violations of the laws of war, attempts were made to improve implementation. The UN Security Council's decision to establish the International Criminal Tribunal for the former *Yugoslavia in 1993, and that for Rwanda in 1994, illustrated the trend, but the experience of the two tribunals also exposed some of the difficulties of trying to apply the law supranationally. In particular, the number of cases they dealt with in the first five years of their existence was very small when compared with the scope of the problems addressed. In 1998, a UN-convened conference in Rome adopted a treaty for the establishment of an International Criminal Court: 60 states must become parties before it enters into force. While international implementation is beginning, states and armed forces, with all their virtues and defects in this regard, remain the main mechanism for implementation and enforcement of the laws of war. AR

Best, Geoffrey, *Humanity in Warfare: The Modern History of the International Law of Armed Conflicts* (London, 1980).
—— *War and Law since 1945* (Oxford, 1994).
Howard, Michael, Andreopoulos, George J., and Shulman, Mark R. (eds.), *The Laws of War: Constraints on Warfare in the Western World* (New Haven, 1994).
Keen, Maurice, *The Laws of War in the Late Middle Ages* (London, 1965).
Roberts, Adam, and Guelff, Richard (eds.), *Documents on the Laws of War* (3rd edn., Oxford, 2000).

governed by a strong central government under the direction of a monarch who ruled by divine right led him to undertake a series of wars aimed at garnering glory and at expanding the borders of his realm.

The decay of the Spanish monarchy in the late 17th century resulted in squabbles over the various Spanish possessions and influence in Europe and provided Louis with opportunities to reach his goals. As the son-in-law of Philip IV of Spain and king of one of the most powerful nations in Europe, Louis waged a number of wars between 1665 and 1714 to press his claims to a number of territories. The first of these conflicts began in 1667, two years after the death of Philip IV, when Louis claimed the entirety of the Spanish Netherlands as part of his inheritance. This 'War of Devolution' lasted until 1668 and resulted in France gaining a number of fortresses in Flanders, but not the Netherlands. Four years later, Louis again took up arms to win the Netherlands. The resulting Dutch war lasted until 1678 and drew in Brandenburg and the Holy Roman Empire allied with Spain against France. A series of treaties between August 1678 and June 1679 ended the conflict and gained France border fortresses and minor territories, but again Louis did not obtain the Netherlands. Over the next few years, Louis continued to expand his realm by unilaterally annexing some western border areas from the Netherlands and from the Holy Roman Empire.

By the mid-1680s, the other powers of Europe feared Louis was attempting to secure French hegemony over the continent and indeed France was in a good position to do this. By 1680, France had a population of 19 million, three times that of Spain or England. As such a large nation, the French economy was largely independent of foreign trade. Further, under the direction of two capable ministers, the Marquis de *Louvois and Jean Baptiste Colbert, the French army and navy had become the largest and best organized

in Europe and Louis had proved more than willing to use these instruments in pursuit of his goals.

Spurred on by fear of Louis's expansionism, the Holy Roman Emperor, the electors of Bavaria, Palatinate, and Saxony, and the kings of Sweden and Spain created the League of Augsburg in 1686 to resist Louis's policies. Louis met this coalition, soon reinforced by Savoy, Brandenburg, Hanover, and the Netherlands and England united under *William of Orange, when he laid claim to the Palatinate and invaded Germany in September 1688. The League of Augsburg war had begun. Given this Grand Alliance arrayed against him, Louis's France was surrounded by enemies and was forced to fight on several fronts, including Spain in the south, Italy in the south-east, Germany in the east, and Flanders in the north-east. Additionally, the war was carried on in the European colonies in the New World.

Although the war was fought primarily on land, *naval power played a role. Louis determined to support an Irish rebellion seeking to reinstall the deposed Catholic *James II to the English throne. But after his first attempt to reinforce the Irish was halted by the drawn naval battle of Bantry Bay on 1 May 1689, he did not follow through. The French gained temporary command of the seas after their victory at the battle of Beachy Head in July 1690, in which a French fleet of 78 ships under the command of Adm de Tourville decisively defeated a combined Anglo-Dutch force of 56. But by that time James had been defeated at the *Boyne, so it availed Louis little. By 1692, the Anglo-Dutch had regained control of the seas and the French were limited to privateering, Jean Bart in particular inflicting such damage on Anglo-Dutch shipping as to provoke the introduction of *convoys.

Like the war at sea, the war in the New World colonies was merely a sideshow to the main conflict on the continent of Europe. In North America, where the war was known as

'King William's war', French and British forces, each reinforced by Native American allies, raided each other's settlements, but with no decisive results. Additionally French and Spanish forces raided each other's settlements in the Caribbean.

The land war in Europe was marked by a similar indecisiveness. Only a few major battles took place, with the French more often than not emerging victorious, but without achieving a crushing enough victory to be able to dictate peace terms. In many ways, it was a war of logistics, starting with Louis's decision to ravage the Palatinate to deny it as a source of supply to his enemies without having to expose his forces to the cost of retaining it. The armies of this period expanded considerably in size, with Louis being able to keep 440,000 men under arms in 1693. Field armies of 100,000 men were not uncommon. These large armies demanded great amounts of supply. For instance, an army of 60,000 required an average of 198,414 lb (90,000 kg) of bread per day, or 94,806,400 lb (43,000,000 kg) over a six-month period. As there were few areas of Europe sufficiently developed to supply such an army locally, an intricate supply network had to be established. In preparation for a campaign, food and munitions would need to be stocked and concentrated in *magazines near the theatre of war. Armies would draw upon these for their logistical needs rather than stripping the area in an effort to live off the land. This dependence upon a fixed logistical structure limited, of course, the strategic mobility of armies. No army dared to advance more than a week's march from its supply magazines for fear of starvation.

This logistical structure had a major impact on strategy. Tied as it was to its magazines, an army was extremely vulnerable to having its lines of communication cut. Thus, a commander did all he could to protect his supply lines and to cut the lines of his enemy. This situation resulted in a characteristic manoeuvring of armies for position, forcing an enemy army to withdraw rather than seeking a decision of the battlefield. The war of logistics also resulted in the large number of siege operations. In addition to being sited to protect borders, fortress towns tended to be situated on key road or river junctions and their possession was often vital to the smooth supply of an army. Following the teachings of *Vauban, *siege warfare during this period both expanded greatly and became more formalized. Fortresses were redesigned to take advantage of the defensive potential of modern firearms and techniques for besieging and reducing fortresses were refined. As they played such an important role, the capture of a particularly important fortress might decide an entire campaign.

Nonetheless, battles were fought. The land war opened with a minor Alliance victory at Walcourt (25 August 1689) in Flanders. An Alliance army of 35,000, including 8,000 English troops under John Churchill, then Earl of *Marlborough, inflicted 2,000 casualties on the French army under d'Humières while only suffering 300 themselves. The defeat resulted in d'Humières being replaced by Luxembourg, who would emerge as one of the most successful commanders of the war.

The next major engagement took place in July 1690, when Luxembourg's 45,000 troops defeated Waldeck's Alliance army of 37,000 at the battle of *Fleurus in the Low Countries. The French force suffered 2,500 casualties to the Alliance's 6,000 dead and 8,000 prisoners, but Luxembourg was unable to exploit his victory by driving into the Netherlands, as Louis ordered him to co-ordinate his army with other forces manoeuvring against Alliance armies on the Meuse and Moselle rivers.

The French continued their winning streak the next year, emerging victorious on all fronts. Despite Louis's constraints, Luxembourg managed to win another series of engagements in the Low Countries. On 8 April 1691, he took the fortress of Mons and followed this up by seizing Halle in June. Perhaps his greatest success was the routing of Waldeck's army in September. Through the use of a bold night march, Luxembourg was able to catch Waldeck's army unprepared at Leuze as it retired for winter quarters and inflict heavy casualties. At the battle of Staffarda on 18 August, a French force commanded by Catinat defeated the army of Victor Amadeus II of Savoy, allowing the French forces to capture most of Savoy. In September, French armies under Duc Anne-Jules de *Noailles seized Riploi and Urgel on the Spanish front.

The French were again largely victorious in 1692. The campaign season opened with the capture of the fortress of *Namur in June, an operation supervised by Vauban but under Louis's direct command. Luxembourg was also successful against the Alliance army, now commanded by William of Orange. At daybreak on 3 August, William's 63,000 men attacked Luxembourg's fortified camp at Steenkerke. After initial successes, the French, numbering around 57,000, were able to drive off the Allies in a savage close-quarter battle. William ordered the British Guards to cover the withdrawal of his army, and in the rearguard action, they lost Gens Mackay and Lanier. The Alliance lost 8,000 and the French 6,800.

The year 1693 saw the last large-scale battles of the war. The war's biggest battle occurred on 29 July 1693 at Neerwinden. There, Luxembourg attacked William's entrenched army of 50,000 with a force numbering 80,000. After eight hours of hard fighting and three assaults, the French were able to drive the Alliance troops from the field. The French suffered 9,000 casualties, while the Alliance lost 19,000 killed or wounded. Given the damage suffered by his own army, Luxembourg was unable to exploit this victory.

While the French had a number of minor successes in Italy and Spain later in the year, Neerwinden convinced Louis, who was already sceptical about the merits of large-scale battles, to avoid great engagements in the future. After Neerwinden, the war became almost totally one of manoeuvre and siege, with neither side willing to risk high losses in battle. It became a war of relatively minor *attrition, with each side hoping the other's will and financial ability to resist would give out first.

Despite some success in 1695, it was the Alliance that first began to crack. Savoy was the first to drop out of the war. In June 1696, the Duke of Savoy signed the Treaty of Turin with Louis. The French returned all their Italian conquests and transported their 30,000-man Italian army to the Low Countries to face William. Bottled up in the Netherlands, he too decided to seek peace in early 1697. William was joined in the summer by the Holy Roman Emperor and between 20 September and 30 October the powers negotiated a peace settlement. The Treaty of Ryswick ended this indecisive conflict by restoring the captured territories, including colonies, to their original owners. While the Alliance had not defeated Louis, it had stopped him from achieving his expansionist objectives. The peace was merely a prelude in which both sides gathered strength for renewed conflict in the War of the *Spanish Succession. RTF

Black, Jeremy, *European Warfare, 1660-1815* (London, 1994).

Delbrück, Hans, *The History of the Art of War*, vol. iv. *The Dawn of Modern Warfare* (London, 1985), trans. from German orig. (1920).

Parker, Geoffrey, *The Military Revolution: Military Innovation and the Rise of the West, 1500-1600* (Cambridge, 1988).

Lebanon (1958, 1975–90). Lebanon was created in the post-WW I peace settlements. In 1920, France received the League of Nations Mandates for Syria and Lebanon; she then redrew the boundaries of Lebanon to create an artificial, 'greater' Lebanon. This Lebanon was formed at the expense of Syria, and included within its borders a multiplicity of religious communities: Christians, Muslims, and Druzes. France relied heavily on the Christian Maronite community, the largest single religious group, to run the country. In 1943, three years prior to France's departure from Lebanon, a 'National Pact' confessional system of politics attempted to share out power in the Lebanon between the different communities on the basis of a census taken in 1932.

As long as Lebanon was untouched by internal or external forces, this system was viable. However, once the system was put under pressure it was liable to collapse. Four factors, two internal, two external, threatened Lebanon after WW II and led to civil war in 1958 and from 1975 to 1990. First, demographic change eroded the Maronites' dominance as they had a lower birth rate and higher emigration rate. Secondly, economic change favoured certain groups, particularly the Christians, at the expense of groups such as the Shi'ite Muslims who became second-class citizens. Thirdly, the rise of pan-Arabism in the form of 'Nasserism' spread to Lebanon. Fourthly, the *Arab–Israeli wars spilled over into Lebanon as Palestinian *guerrillas and Israeli and Syrian troops fought out a series of small wars in Lebanon.

In 1958, the uneasy peace was shattered when Lebanon erupted into civil war following the call of Egypt's president, Gamal abd al *Nasser, for revolutionary Arab unity. Camille Chamoun, the Christian president of Lebanon, fearing a Nasserite takeover, appealed for help. In response, in July 1958, the Americans sent in 14,300 troops to defend Chamoun's pro-Western administration.

The Americans left in October 1958 but Lebanon's basic problems remained unresolved. Intermittent clashes continued through the 1960s and early 1970s as Palestinian fighters from the *PLO arrived in Lebanon to continue their war against Israel. As Palestinians launched raids across Israel's northern border, Israel launched retaliatory strikes into Lebanon. Both Israel and Syria were dragged into supporting different sides in Lebanon: Israel backed the Maronite Phalanges militia, while Syria supported different Muslim militias and, on occasion, the Palestinians. In April 1975, a trivial incident was the excuse for a full-scale civil war between Christian, Palestinian, and Muslim militias that was only brought to a temporary end in 1976 by the intervention of the Syrian army. In 1978, Israel attacked as far as the Litani river in a raid to push the Palestinians away from its border.

Like the Syrians, once involved in Lebanon, the Israelis found it difficult to extricate themselves. On 6 June 1982, following the wounding of an Israeli diplomat in London the Israelis launched an all-out invasion of Lebanon with three division-sized formations (PEACE FOR GALILEE) with the objective of driving the Palestinian fighters from Lebanon. This invasion took the Israelis up to the Lebanese capital, Beirut, and brought the Israelis face-to-face with Syrian forces in the Bekaa valley. Following a prolonged bombardment of the city by Israeli artillery, the PLO fighters left Beirut in August–September 1982 under the supervision of a multinational peacekeeping force of 1,200 troops apiece from America, France, and Italy. However, from 16–18 September, as the last PLO fighters were departing, Christian Phalangist militia under the supervision of Israeli forces massacred some 400 Palestinian civilians at the Beirut refugee camps of Sabra and Shatilla (some estimates put the number killed at 1,000). This action forced Israel to reconsider its role in Lebanon and by 1985 it had withdrawn its forces to a security zone in southern Lebanon. The international peacekeeping force in Beirut then became a target in the civil war, and in October 1983 suicide car bombers killed 241 US marines and 56 French paratroopers. Meanwhile, in Lebanon, the civil war continued as Islamic fundamentalist groups such as Hezbollah ('Party of God'), which rejected the disadvantaged position of groups such as the Shi'ites, took up the struggle. Lebanon fragmented further as rival factions turned on one another. Finally, exhaustion after fifteen years of civil war allowed the Syrians to move into the vacuum and restore a semblance of peace in 1989–90 following accords signed by the different Lebanese factions at meetings held in Taif in Saudi Arabia. MH

Cobban, Helena, *The Making of Modern Lebanon* (London, 1985).

Deeb, Marius, *The Lebanese Civil War* (New York, 1980).

Fisk, Robert, *Pity the Nation: Lebanon at War* (London, 1990).

Leclerc, Marshal Philippe François Marie, Vicomte de Hauteclocque

(1902–47). Fighting as Capt de Hauteclocque, Leclerc was wounded in the fall of *France and escaped via Spain in July 1940 to continue the fight against Germany under *de Gaulle. Having left his wife and six children behind in France, he adopted the pseudonym of Leclerc to protect them against reprisals. Dispatched initially to rally Free French support in Cameroon and Gabon, he found fame for a number of morale-boosting military exploits in North Africa. His troops captured Koufra Oasis, supporting the advance by *Wavell into Libya in March 1941, whereupon de Gaulle appointed him commander of French troops in Equatorial Africa, based in Chad. He led a column north to link up with Montgomery's Eighth Army in January 1943, and commanded a formation (Force 'L', later 2nd French Armoured Division) in the Tunisian campaign.

After training in England, Leclerc's division landed in Normandy in August 1944 as part of Patton's Third US Army, and entered the annals of French history as the liberators of Paris during 23–5 August. Dubbed 'the jerk Leclerc' by *Hemingway, he was in fact a great deal less arrogant than his master. Leclerc led his division through tough fighting in Lorraine and the Vosges, liberating Strasbourg in November, and arrived, eventually, at Berchtesgaden in May 1945. He was sent to *Indochina as C-in-C French Forces Far East, but recalled in 1946 to be inspector general of French Forces in North Africa. His death in an air crash in 1947, aged 45, robbed the French army of a steady hand when it needed it badly. APC-A

Lee, Gen Robert E.

(1807–70), aristocratic Confederate commander in the eastern theatre of the *American civil war and 'Lost Cause' icon. He was at heart a Unionist who, despite owning slaves, believed the practice was a moral and political evil. But he despised northern demagoguery and declined an offer to command all Union forces in 1861 in order to 'go with his people'.

The fecklessness of his father, independence hero 'Light Horse Harry', ensured an early life of genteel poverty. Himself a conscientious and detail-oriented officer, he seemed to value these qualities less than blood and breeding in others, a weakness compounded by his refusal to replace underperforming subordinates. This caused major battlefield errors, becoming more serious as the war progressed. His background similarly coloured his strategic vision, limiting it to events immediately affecting his beloved Virginia. Both before and especially after the war, his repu-

tation was due above all to being the epitome of an officer and a gentleman, and the emblematic image of the civil war was Brady's photograph of him in impeccable uniform, surrendering to the mud-spattered *Grant at Appomattox.

On the staff of *Scott, he performed *reconnaissance and co-ordination duties with distinction during the *Mexican war but was only a cavalry colonel when Scott called him to Washington and offered him overall field command in the midst of the secession crisis. For the Confederacy he first commanded in north-west Virginia and in South Carolina, emerging with the not entirely unmerited nickname of 'Granny Lee'. Subsequently appointed Davis's military adviser, he deserves some credit for the *Shenandoah campaign, during which he negotiated considerable freedom of action for *Jackson, no easy task. After *Johnston was wounded at Seven Pines and his second in command collapsed, Lee assumed command when the threat of fighting on two fronts was relieved by the retreat of McDowell, leaving him free to browbeat *McClellan in the *Seven Days battles.

Comparison with Jackson is inevitable and casts Lee in a less favourable light. At second *Bull Run and at *Antietam, *Fredericksburg, and *Chancellorsville, he should have learned that his own and his outnumbered army's strength lay in counterpunching, and when circumstances forced him onto the defensive he was indomitable. But his Mexican experience convinced him that offensive tactics could best compensate for inferior numbers, and *Longstreet was to comment on a characteristic 'subdued excitement, which occasionally took possession of him when the hunt was up, and threatened his superb equipoise'. To put this in context, 'subdued excitement' in Lee was the equivalent of killing rage in a less tightly controlled man, the only logical explanation for costly frontal assaults at Malvern Hill and elsewhere, and for his fatal insistence on launching Pickett's unsupported charge at *Gettysburg.

Lee was fortunate that McClellan, Pope, *Burnside, and *Hooker were generals seemingly designed by nature to make him look good, and that he possessed in the *Confederate States Army a remarkable instrument for war. His ability also shines by comparison with the performance of the other Confederate full generals and their C-in-C Davis, but he shared with them a deep conservatism in all things. Because they believed in a natural human hierarchy, they failed to develop professional staffs to mobilize Confederate resources systematically, or to match the pragmatic command experimentation that transformed the Union war effort.

In his crowning moment at Chancellorsville Lee suffered the first major symptoms of the congestive heart condition that eventually killed him. He knew it had diminished him, but although he asked to be relieved after Gettysburg he did not recommend a successor, a judgement both on the sincerity of his modesty and on his ability to nurture talent among his subordinates. Nonetheless, among civil war generals exercising independent command, only Jackson and *Sheridan ever elicited comparable devotion from their troops. Grant, who was not given to making excuses for his own shortcomings, judged that knowledge of Lee's arrival at Petersburg alone halted a near-certain 1864 break-through.

Revisionism can identify his many errors, but it cannot explain away his charisma. Even those who hated him have contributed to his legacy: the historic estate he acquired by marriage at Arlington was vengefully turned into a burial ground for Union dead, but became the national shrine to American valour. He leads Jackson and Davis in the huge bas-relief equestrian sculpture carved into Stone Mountain, Georgia, his gaze averted from the vulgar commercialism all around.　　　　　　　　　　　　　　HEB

McKenzie, John, *Uncertain Glory* (New York, 1997).

Thomas, Emory, *Robert E. Lee* (New York, 1995).

Leipzig, battle of (1813). After a series of defeats suffered by his marshals, and the defection of the Saxons and Bavarians, *Napoleon concentrated his forces around Leipzig. Three Allied armies, some 300,000 strong, converged on this point under Schwarzenberg, *Blücher, and *Bernadotte. The resulting clash, fought over three days (16–19 October), became known as the battle of the nations, as there were Germans, French, Poles, Russians, Swedes, and even a few British troops involved. Napoleon initially attacked Schwarzenberg to the south of the city, but was forced to concentrate in and around Leipzig, and eventually to withdraw across the river Elster to his rear. French losses would have been fewer had the Lindenau bridge not been blown prematurely: 20,000 men were cut off in the city.

This was the decisive battle of the *Napoleonic wars. The French had lost around 60,000 bringing total losses in the 1813 campaign to around 500,000. These men could not be replaced and Napoleon was forced to abandon Germany entirely, and prepare for a last-ditch defence of France the following year. Leipzig was the largest European battle until 1914 and represented the limit of what could be achieved by armies commanded by messages sent by courier and lacking *mechanization.　　　　　　　　　　　　　　TM

---

lend-lease Following the fall of *France, *Churchill bombarded his friend and contemporary Franklin D. *Roosevelt with increasingly desperate requests for help. Though sympathetic, with an election looming the latter knew that his critics would excoriate any action that might lead to US involvement in another European war. The fear of the British fleet falling into German hands galvanized him into more concrete measures to support Britain. In July 1940, arguing that it was in the national interest, he agreed to swap 50 obsolete destroyers for 99-year leases on a number of British bases in the western Atlantic. Although in retrospect this was indeed the thin end of the wedge his opponents denounced, he argued that it enhanced US national security, and that supporting Britain would help keep America *out* of the war. After winning the November 1940 election, and after consultations with Churchill by his personal envoy, Harry L. Hopkins, he introduced a 'Lend-lease' Bill into Congress in January 1941 empowering him to sell, transfer, exchange, lease, or lend war supplies to any nation whose defence was deemed vital to US security. Though bitterly contested by isolationists, the bill became law in March 1941, and ten US Coastguard cutters were transferred to the Royal Navy. In July, when American troops relieved the British garrison in Iceland, US destroyers and aircraft began to escort *convoys to and from the island, and by September the US Navy was escorting convoys in the western Atlantic, leading to hoped-for clashes with U-boats. After the launching of operation *BARBAROSSA, he extended material aid to the USSR as well, after which opposition from the US left was muted. The Lend-Lease Act must be seen in the context of Roosevelt's very delicate balancing act to reverse hostile US public opinion and bring it around to active support for Britain, a process that was far from complete when *Pearl Harbor and Hitler's declaration of war obviated the need for further subtlety.　APC-A

Edmonds, Robin, *The Big Three* (London, 1991).

Lash, Joseph P., *Roosevelt and Churchill 1939-1941* (London, 1977).

Lenin (né Ulyanov), Vladimir Ilych (1870–1924), Russian socialist and architect of November 1917 *Russian Revolution. His destiny may have been carved in stone in 1887 when his elder brother Alexander was executed for complicity in a plot against the life of Tsar Alexander III. When Vladimir enrolled in the Legal Faculty of Kazan University the same year he was promptly arrested for taking part in student revolutionary activity and expelled. He moved to St Petersburg in 1893 but two years later he was arrested again and sent to Siberia where he produced some 30 polemical works including *Tasks of Russian Social-Democrats* and *The Development of Capitalism in Russia*.

In July 1900 he went into exile and founded the Marxist newspaper *Iskra* (Spark), in which in December 1901 he published his first article under the pseudonym by which he would be known to history. In 1903, the Second Congress of the Russian Social Democratic Workers' Party (RSDWP) resolved that it would become a Marxist revolutionary party. From the beginning, Lenin's views were sharply at variance with the orthodox Marxists, who foresaw a need to ally with bourgeois parties to bring about a democratic revolution, which would then be followed in due course by a proletarian socialist revolution. Lenin was adamant that the proletariat had no allies except the peasantry, and that the RSDWP must play a leading role in both revolutions, exacerbating contradictions during the first and leading the second. After the revolutionary events of 1905, he went further and argued that if the western European industrial proletariat, which he saw as far more ripe for revolution, should proceed to the second stage, then Russia could omit the bourgeois democratic stage altogether and proceed directly to the dictatorship of the proletariat and peasantry. It was a vision from which he would not waver, and it is important to remember that he maintained his views over a prolonged period when the rest of European socialism departed from its commitment to social revolution. WW I revealed this clearly, as the socialist parties in general expressed nationalist solidarity with the governments leading Europe into what, pre-war, they had agreed was an imperialist conflict to be opposed and exploited to bring about the revolution.

Not Lenin. Even before the war he had split the RSDWP irrevocably by his doctrinal rigidity. The factions, which became in effect rival parties each with their own organizations, were the Mensheviks (which means the minority, which they were at the 1912 Prague conference where the split occurred, but not in the membership) and the Bolsheviks (the majority). The latter founded the newspaper *Pravda* (Truth), with Lenin as editor, and the one consistent feature of the publication over the next 80 years was that it rarely published a truthful word. However, it did provide a platform for Lenin, and although his intensity emanates from his writings, even in translation, it cannot convey the personal authority that accrued to him as almost the only man in Europe who lived the revolution 24 hours a day. He had a mesmeric effect on people: some would go away convinced, others repelled, none indifferent.

WW I not only split European socialism into majority pro- and minority anti-war factions, it divided the latter into the merely pacifist and a tiny minority within a minority, which included Liebnecht, Luxemburg, Lenin, and a few others, that advocated transforming the imperialist war into civil war. His views were set out in his (later) most influential work, *Imperialism, the Highest Stage of Capitalism* (1917). That it might have been convincing at the time is understandable, but to this day there are still those who believe that it represents an accurate analysis and illustrates Lenin's gift for tapping into the human need for simple, Manichaean explanations for complex realities. The war, he wrote, was a product of the expansionist nature of imperialism, the final stage of monopoly capitalism. Thus he held that colonialism, in fact an economically insignificant by-product of world dominance by the industrially developed West, was essential for the survival of capitalism. He completely missed the significance of the cosy cartels into which the world's largest industrial and financial institutions had settled and, more damningly, failed to see that even though presided over by kings and emperors, WW I owed both its ferocity and duration to the fact that it was a bourgeois war par excellence. The majority socialists were not, as he de-

clared, a 'labour aristocracy' bribed by the imperialists to betray the proletariat at home and the even more exploited sub-proletariat abroad, but true representatives of their own super-patriotic lower middle class. *Mussolini, another prominent socialist editor, perceived this far more accurately and rode the bandwagon to power and eventual infamy. Lenin required the prior services of the imperial German army, not only to put him in Petrograd (formerly and now St. Petersburg) at the opportune moment in the famous 'sealed train', but also to atomize Russian society to such an extent that his tiny faction was able to seize power in the *coup d'état* of 7–8 November 1917.

Thereafter there is no denying that his ruthless clarity of purpose affirmed the *Russian Revolution. Others might say the words 'peace at any price' but he saw the absolute objective need for it, threatening to resign unless the Bolsheviks accepted the Treaty of Brest-Litovsk, surrendering 60 per cent of European Russia and one third of the pre-war population. His realpolitik certainly saved the Bolsheviks from going the way of the tsar and the bourgeois Kerensky government, which had persisted in the war beyond all reason. Thereafter his enemies did as much to consolidate his dictatorship, the 'White' Russians seeking to impose traditional landownership on a peasantry that would otherwise have turned against the harsh impositions of the Bolsheviks, and foreign invasions reawakening the great power of Russian patriotism. Operationally, *Trotsky was both the architect of the *coup d'état* and of victory in the civil war that followed, as well as being the father of what became the Red Army; but strategically, both in the mobilization of at times barely enough resources to survive and later in launching a disastrous offensive into Poland, Lenin's will was paramount.

Like any successful revolutionary, Lenin was an opportunist. Circumstances, unimaginable at the time he formulated his political philosophy, made it possible for him to preside over a sequence of events that permit one, in retrospect, to perceive a guiding principle. There was none except survival. However influential his views were to become, especially among the colonized peoples of the world, they were tactical in nature and related to seizing power. What he did with it embodied the worst of the Russian political tradition, with appalling consequences not only for Russia but also for the second Russian empire won in blood and maintained in cruelty and savage repression by his successor.   HEB

Szamuely, Tibor, *The Russian Tradition* (London, 1974).

Leningrad, siege of (1941–3). Russia's stunningly beautiful second city, formerly and now St Petersburg, but known as Leningrad 1924–91, has had a unique character since *Peter 'the Great' built it as his window on the west at the start of the 18th century. As Petrograd (1914–24) it witnessed the *Russian Revolutions of 1917, but the '900 days' of the siege of Leningrad were one of the most moving, stirring, and horrific tales of human ingenuity and endurance in military history.

When the Germans invaded the USSR in *BARBAROSSA, Army Group North had Leningrad as its objective. From the west, the Finns also closed in to recover Karelia, lost to the Soviets pre-war, but they did not push any further, to the disgust of the Germans and the probable salvation of the city. In mid-July the Germans were within 60 miles (97 km) and they virtually encircled it by 15 September. The first long-range artillery shell had fallen on 1 September. At this time there were 2.6 million people in the city—100,000 of them refugees—and there was only enough food for one to two months. Any meat went to fighting troops, and the Leningrad Scientific Institute discovered a way of making flour from shell-packing and the paste from stripped wallpaper. With all these measures and the consumption of horses, dogs, cats, and rats, each working man got about a tenth of the normal calorific intake. Yet in spite of this, Leningrad's many arms factories and scientific research institutes kept working.

A small amount of food was brought across Lake Ladoga, but on 9 November the Germans captured Tikhvin, cutting the route to the lake and establishing an effective *blockade. The Soviets started building a lifeline road further north, through the forest, and at the end of November the lake froze, permitting the first relief *convoy to reach the city on 26 November over the ice with 33 tons of food—one-third of the daily requirement. The forest road was eventually finished on 6 December, but three days later the Soviets recaptured Tikhvin, reopening the shorter route. On 25 December the bread ration was raised slightly but 3,700 people died on that day alone.

Attempts to relieve the siege continued from January to April 1942, but without success. The Baltic fleet played an important part in the city's defence with aircraft, coastal artillery, and warships. During the siege the Germans fired 150,000 shells at the city and dropped more than 4,600 bombs. The sewage system broke down under the bombing and shelling, but in the northern winter the excrement froze, reducing the risk of infection. On 12 January 1943, Soviet formations from inside the city (Sixty-Seventh Army) and outside (Second Shock army) began ISKRA (SPARK) to break the siege. On 18 January 1943 forward units met at one of the housing estates outside the city. They forced a corridor 5–7 miles (8–11.3 km) wide, through which they built a railway and a road in seventeen days. The blockade was broken in one place but the Germans were still close. The 900 days ended in February 1944, when the Red Army dislodged Army Group North. The official Russian death toll in the siege was 632,000, mostly civilians, although the real number was probably nearer a million.   CDB

Salisbury, Harrison E., *The 900 Days: The Siege of Leningrad* (New York, 1985).

Leo VI, 'the Wise', Byzantine Emperor (866–912). It is ironic that Leo VI has a place in military history. He was an emperor who rarely ventured beyond Constantinople and who never campaigned in his life, despite the intense military problems that marked his reign. This witnessed an aggressive Bulgarian kingdom as well as significant Arab naval success, of which Thessalonica was a casualty in 904. Leo's contribution lies in the theoretical sphere. In his youth he produced the *Problemata*, a text composed of extracts from the 6th-century *Strategikon* of Maurice, which Leo quotes in answer to questions he has posed. He also compiled a book of extracts on warfare, and commissioned a work on imperial military expeditions. However it is Leo's *Taktika* which has earned him his fame in the sphere of military history. It was intended as a manual of advice for the generals (*strategoi*) of the empire, is couched in legal language, and consists of an introduction, twenty 'constitutions', and an epilogue. Subjects addressed include the character of the general, the division of the army, weapons and *armour, marching, encampments, the stages of battle, *siege warfare, and foreign nations. Much of the *Taktika* is based on earlier works, especially the *Strategikon* of Maurice, and this has bearing on its value for understanding the *Byzantine army in the 9th century. However, contemporary concerns are reflected in the *Taktika*. The topic of the Arab threat is addressed for the first time in the genre, and Leo states that he wrote his work because of this very problem. Indeed it has been argued that the *Taktika* demonstrates that the emperor was keen for the Byzantine army to copy traits of the successful Arab military system. Leo also tackles the topic of naval warfare, the constitution of which he composed from information supplied by his naval officers. Leo's work led to a significant revival in the genre of the military manual, reflected by a host of 10th-century successors. Most notable of these are those associated with the soldier-emperor Nikephoros II Phokas (963–9), whose grandfather, fittingly enough, had served Leo VI as a commander.   ST

Karlin-Hayter, P., ' "When Military Affairs were in Leo's Hands": A Note on Byzantine Foreign Policy (886–912)', *Traditio*, 23 (1967).
Tougher, S., *The Reign of Leo VI (886–912)* (Leiden, 1997).

Leonardo da Vinci (1452–1519), Florentine Renaissance man, genius, artist in all media, architect, military engineer. Possibly the most brilliantly creative man in European history, he advertised himself, first of all, as a military engineer. In a famous letter dated about 1481 to Ludovico Sforza, of which a copy survives in the Codice Atlantico in Milan, Leonardo asks for employment in that capacity. He had plans 'for bridges, very light and strong', and 'plans for destroying those of the enemy'. He knew how to cut off water to besieged fortifications, and how to construct bridges, mantlets, scaling ladders, and other instruments. He designed cannon, 'very convenient and easy of transport', designed to fire 'small stones, almost in the manner of hail'—grape- or case-shot (see AMMUNITION, ARTILLERY). He offered cannon 'of very beautiful and useful shapes, quite different from those in common use' and, 'where it is not possible to employ cannon . . . catapults, mangonels and *trabocchi* [trebuchets—see SIEGE ENGINES] and other engines of wonderful efficacy not in general use'. And he said he made 'armoured cars, safe and unassailable, which will enter the serried ranks of the enemy with their artillery . . . and behind them the infantry will be able to follow quite unharmed, and without any opposition'. He also offered to design 'ships which can resist the fire of all the heaviest cannon, and powder and smoke'.

The large number of surviving drawings and notes on military *art show that Leonardo's claims were not without foundation, although most date from after the Sforza letter. Most of the drawings, including giant crossbows (see BOWS), appear to be improvements on existing machines rather than new inventions. One exception is the drawing of a tank dating from 1485–8 now in the British Museum— a flattened cone, propelled from inside by crankshafts, firing guns. Another design in the British Museum, for a machine with scythes revolving in the horizontal plane, dis-membering bodies as it goes, is gruesomely fanciful.

Most of the other drawings are in the Codice Atlantico in Milan but some are in the Royal Libraries at Windsor and Turin, in Venice, or the Louvre and the École des Beaux Arts in Paris. Two ingenious machines for continuously firing arrows, machine-gun style, powered by a treadmill are shown in the Codice Atlantico. A number of other sketches of bridges, water pumps, and canals could be for military or civil purposes: 'dual use technology'.

Leonardo lived at a time when the first artillery fortifica-tions were appearing and the Codice Atlantico contains sketches of ingenious fortifications combining bastions, round towers, and truncated cones. Models constructed from the drawings and photographed in Calvi's works re-veal forts which would have looked strikingly modern in the 19th century, and might even feature in science fiction films today. On 18 August 1502 Cesare Borgia appointed Leonardo as his 'Military Engineer General', although no known building by Leonardo exists.

Leonardo was also fascinated by flight. Thirteen pages with drawings for man-powered aeroplanes survive and there is one design for a helicoidal helicopter. Leonardo later realized the inadequacy of the power a man could gen-erate and turned his attention to aerofoils. Had his enor-mous abilities been concentrated on one thing, he might have invented the modern glider. CDB

Calvi, Ignazio, *L'architettura militare de Leonardo da Vinci* (Milan, 1943).

—— *L'ingegneria militare di Leonardo da Vinci* (Milan, 1958).

Popham, A. E., *The Drawings of Leonardo da Vinci* (London, 1973).

Lepanto, battle of (1571). This was the largest ever sea battle in the Mediterranean, fought between the Ottoman *Turks with about 275 ships and the Holy League of Venice, the Habsburg dominions, Malta, Genoa, and other Italian states led by the papacy, with about 210. Sultan Selim 'the Sot' had a passion for Cyprus wine, and in 1570 the Turks captured the island. The west's reaction was unprecedented. A massive and well-appointed fleet was formed under the command of Don Juan of Austria, a bastard son of *Charles V. He sighted the Ottoman fleet off Lepanto (Navpaktos) on the Gulf of Patras, in western Greece. Almost all the ships were galleys but the League also had six galleasses, big hybrid ships between a galley and a galleon, with oars and guns along the broadside. The Turkish galleys were rowed by slaves: some of the Christian ships were rowed by volun-teers. Whereas the Turks still favoured ramming, the Chris-tian galleys had large guns pointing forward above the ram, and were well protected against the Turkish arrows. In the ensuing carnage, up to 200 of the Turkish ships were sunk or captured, as against just 15 of the League's galleys, the Turks' first major defeat in two centuries and the largest number of sinkings in any sea battle. The near-complete destruction of the Ottoman fleet resounded round Europe. Miguel de Cervantes, author of *Don Quixote*, was there and said it was the end of the myth of Turkish invincibility. But the western states reckoned without the efficiency of Ottoman admin-istration. The Turks cut down a forest and rebuilt their fleet within a year, and held on to Cyprus when the war ended in 1573. Lepanto was also an evolutionary dead end for naval warfare. The Turks had been slow to move with the naval innovations introduced by Atlantic states, the massive and heavily gunned Spanish, English, and Dutch sailing ships designed to ride the Spanish Main. The naval museum in Madrid has a splendid gallery devoted to the victory of Lep-anto. There is only a small display devoted to the 'unsuc-cessful expedition against England' in 1588. CDB

Lettow-Vorbeck, Gen Paul Emil von (1870–1964), commander of German military forces in the campaign in *German East Africa during WW I. Although he never had more than 3,000 German and 11,000 African troops (Aska-ris) under his command, he tied down Allied armies almost ten times as large through aggressive hit-and-run tactics, proving himself a master at motivating his motley army and of improvising to compensate for his material inferior-ity. He remained undefeated at the time of the *Armistice and surrendered on 25 November 1918 only when news of this reached him. JMB

Hoyt, Edwin P., *Guerrilla: Colonel von Lettow-Vorbeck and Ger-many's East African Empire* (New York, 1981).

Leuctra, battle of (371 BC), fought during the *Greek city-state wars. Near a small hamlet in central Greece in 371

BC the Theban general *Epaminondas and his Boeotian confederates crushed the Spartan army. The battle marked a dramatic end to three centuries of Spartan infantry superiority and prompted four subsequent Theban invasions of the Peloponnese itself. Ancient sources disagree over what led to this astounding victory, but modern students emphasize Epaminondas' mass column of 50 shields deep on the Theban left wing that ploughed through the Spartan élite right, killed their king, and left nearly a thousand Lacedaemonians dead on the battlefield.   VDH

Anderson, J. K., *Military Theory and Practice in the Age of Xenophon* (Berkeley, 1970).

Lazenby, J. F., *The Spartan Army* (Warminster, 1985).

Leuthen, battle of (1757). After *Rossbach, *Frederick 'the Great' of Prussia, with a force of 36,000, encountered the 80,000 strong Austrian army under Daun at Leuthen in the snows of 5 December 1757. The Austrians were formed up in a strong position 4 miles (6.4 km) wide, in an area of rolling country, with the village of Leuthen at their centre, and their flanks protected by marshy ground. Frederick feinted toward the enemy right, driving in their piquets and effectively blinding them, and then marched right around the enemy's left flank, protected from view by a range of low hills. He then proceeded to form his army at right angles to the Austrian line. The Austrians could only watch amazed at this rapid redeployment, and mocked it by calling it the 'Potsdamer Wachtparade'—the changing of the guard at Potsdam. They were in for a rude awakening.

Daun could not react swiftly enough and despite a determined cavalry counter-attack, his army was torn apart by Frederick's 'walking batteries' of well-drilled infantry, losing 7,000 casualties and 20,000 prisoners. This was Frederick's finest hour. Napoleon called it a 'masterpiece of movement, manoeuvre and resolve' and said that this victory alone placed Frederick in the ranks of the greatest generals of all time.   TM

levée en masse (Fr., mass levy) (23 August 1793). Responding to continued military crisis during the *French Revolutionary wars, the National Convention sought to call up more troops to defend the new republic. Appeals for volunteers had gone out in 1791 and 1792, and limited conscription had been applied since then, but more recruits were needed again by the summer of 1793. After debate, the Representatives in the Convention declared a *levée en masse* in the following terms: 'Young men will go to battle; married men will forge arms and transport supplies; women will make tents, uniforms, and serve in the hospitals; children will pick rags; old men will have themselves carried to public squares, to inspire the courage of the warriors, and to preach the hatred of kings and the unity of the Republic.'

This was more than conscription; it mobilized an entire nation. The practical effect was to send all able-bodied unmarried men aged 18 to 25 to the front, an infusion of some 300,000 new recruits who raised the official strength of the army to 1,000,000 men. However, the impact of the *levée en masse* went beyond this, for it announced a new era of warfare in which peoples, not simply rulers, fought.   JAL

Bertaud, Jean-Paul, *The Army of the French Revolution*, trans. R. R. Palmer (Princeton, 1988).

Lynn, John A., *The Bayonets of the Republic: Motivation and Tactics in the Army of Revolutionary France, 1791–1794* (Boulder, Colo., 1996).

Lewis gun Invented by the American Col Isaac Lewis (1858–1931) in 1911, the Lewis light machine gun was the first to be fired from an aeroplane and was used in both aerial and ground roles in .303 calibre by Britain during WW I. With its 47-round drum magazine, it was issued four to a battalion in the British army in 1915. A 97-round magazine increased its firepower and it was widely used by a variety of countries.   SCW

Thompson, James, *Machine Guns: A Pictorial, Tactical and Practical History* (London, 1990).

Truby, J. David, *A Pictorial History of the Lewis Gun* (Boulder, Colo., 1976).

Lexington and Concord, battles of (1775), first battle of the *American independence war. On receipt of peremptory orders from London on 19 April the military governor of Massachusetts Gen Gage reluctantly sent a force of 700 soldiers from Charlestown to seize militia stores in Concord, followed by a support column out of Boston. An earlier expedition to Salem had retreated in the face of threatening Minutemen (militia who undertook to be ready 'at a minute's warning') and Gage knew that his orders made a showdown inevitable.

Signal lamps and mounted couriers, including the now-legendary night ride of Paul Revere, gave warning. Minutemen made a demonstration on Lexington Green, but they were dispersed with a loss of eight killed and ten wounded. By the time the main column arrived at Concord, the stores had been removed or destroyed, and at the North Bridge Minutemen fired the 'shot heard around the world', the first time any British soldiers were killed. In imminent danger of being cut off, the column retreated under heavy sniping. Order broke down in the face of guerrilla tactics for which the troops were unprepared and the rout continued until they came under the guns of the support brigade at Lexington. For the remainder of the retreat the redcoats gave as good as they got, but lost 273 men in exchange for no more than 95 rebel casualties.

Never was it more true that the first clash in a war tends to set the tone. Lexington and Concord emboldened the rebels to besiege Boston/Charlestown and to stand at the battle of Bunker Hill in June, after which *Washington took over as commander of what was now the Continental Army. Gage's successor Howe evacuated the isolated garrison to attack New York the following year.   HEB

Liddell Hart, Capt Sir Basil Henry (1895–1970). Liddell Hart, British military historian, critic, journalist, propagandist, controversialist, archivist, adviser, exemplar, and thrower of stones, was not the *Clausewitz of the 20th century, as he and others were wont to claim; but he was, perhaps, the next best thing. A war poet in prose—his interwar writing carried a comparable charge—he wrote no great book, no timeless synthesis, finished or unfinished. *Thoughts on War* (1944) is the skeleton of such a work, *The Revolution in Warfare* (1946) the sketch, *Strategy: The Indirect Approach* (4th revised and enlarged edn., 1967) the simulacrum. His output is staggering—dozens of books, hundreds of articles, thousands of letters—but his output is not so much an oeuvre as an aggregation, and very often (too often) a repetition. Yet his influence was and is enormous. There is hardly a military writer of repute in the western world who was not touched in some way by this prodigal, indomitable lighthouse of a man. He survives, still, as a climate of ideas. Liddell Hart is the Bertrand Russell of his field: he is all-pervasive.

He described himself as 'border', meaning something more than geography, and always felt a certain distance from the social and intellectual heartland of England, a distance he worked uncommonly hard to close. He was born in Paris, where his father was minister of the Methodist church. He had a conventional upbringing, peripatetic on the Methodist circuit. A series of prep schools led eventually to St Paul's in London in the wake of a rather backward boy by the name of *Montgomery. His school career was undistinguished; he rose laboriously through the Pauline ranks more by the passage of time in each form than by any sign of intellectual distinction. In 1913, after some frantic cramming, he went up to Corpus Christi College, Cambridge, to read for the History tripos. His university career was, if anything, even more undistinguished; many years later, when asked to contribute to a survey on 'What I Owe to Cambridge,' he put first a taste in food and wine. In the examinations at the end of his first year he recorded a dismal third.

On the outbreak of war Liddell Hart was one of the many young men unconscionably eager for action. On a temporary commission in the King's Own Yorkshire Light Infantry, he went to this war three times, a persistence of which he was achingly aware. These were short stints, abruptly curtailed by injury; in each case a certain ambiguity surrounds the curtailment. The first was for about three weeks, in September–October 1915, in a quiet sector near Albert. The second was for a few beleaguered days in November 1915, very much in the thick of things, in the water-logged lines of the *Ypres salient. The third was again for about three weeks, in June–July 1916, for the Big Push on the Somme, in the Fricourt sector, where he was traumatized in Mametz Wood. That was enough, but that was all. In spite of himself, Liddell Hart was never a true *grognard*.

Officially 50 per cent disabled from *gas poisoning, and prey to 'soldier's heart', he was relegated to the half-pay list in 1924. He left the army, sorrowfully, three years later, bearing his famous, galling, eternal rank. With the passage of time that lowly station became a kind of inverted status symbol, epitomized in Yigal Allon's graceful compliment to 'The Captain Who Teaches Generals'. Henceforth, he lived by his pen and he lived well. He was first a sports correspondent, producing in short order four different accounts of the same match for four different outlets, and an early *succès d'estime*, *Lawn Tennis Masters Unveiled* (1926), an intriguing anticipation of *Great Captains Unveiled* (1927). He was also a leading authority on fashion—women's fashion, in particular tight-lacing. Liddell Hart had a sophisticated appreciation of *l'artillerie de nuit*. He was adept at literary cross-dressing. He wrote strategic accounts of lawn tennis, fashion-conscious accounts of strategy, and games-playing accounts of war. Like all great artists, his best ideas were other people's, made matchlessly his own. He had a gift for the expressive phrase—he called them parables—'the man in the dark' theory of war (1920), his early metaphor of personal combat; 'the expanding torrent' system of attack (1921), derived Newton-and-apple-like from nature, and later adapted to the *blitzkrieg. His biggest idea, 'the indirect approach', was announced in 1927, first developed in book form in 1929, supplemented by a compendium flagging 'the British way in warfare' (a parallel gestation) in 1932, and four times further elaborated by its restless author, in 1941, 1946, 1954, and 1967. As a strategy, the indirect approach is both devious and vaporous. Normally, it is an eccentric manoeuvre, literally and figuratively, directed at the enemy's rear. Robert Graves, a close friend, suggested 'The Art of Out-flanking' as a catchpenny title. But the indirect approach is more an attitude of mind than an arrow on the map. The essence of the idea 'is not so much to seek battle as to seek a strategic situation so advantageous that if it does not of itself produce the decision, its continuation by a battle is sure to achieve this'. For Liddell Hart, *contra* Clausewitz, 'strategy has for its purpose the reduction of fighting to the slenderest possible proportions. . . . The perfection of strategy would be, therefore, to produce a decision without any serious fighting.' Of what use is decisive victory in battle, he asked, if we bleed to death as a result? A secure peace is better than a pyramid of skulls.

Liddell Hart's theses seem to live, stubbornly, no matter how many times their tails are salted. The salting itself has immensely enriched military discourse. Used as a vademecum by various statespersons, numberless strategists, and the militarily curious of many lands—a Chinese edition of the book came out in 1994—the indirect approach continues to live an active and inspirational life to this day, not least in 'the manoeuvrist approach' of official British defence *doctrine. Indeed, the dissection and exhibition of Liddell Hart's work is now almost epidemic. A negative wave of exegesis is followed by a positive one. This is entirely in keeping. As the Germans (keen students) noted in 1936, 'like Zeus's sun light and rain he bestows . . . praise and blame on the leaders of the armoured formations'. That was his currency. Praise and blame: great captains and over-promoted ones.

He was inordinately fond of lists. Among his last, a Christmas challenge, was the seven people in history he would like to assemble for a dinner party: Socrates, Confucius, Galileo, Bacon (or Shakespeare), Montaigne, Voltaire, and Zola. He could not resist adding to the general list a professional one: *Sun-tzu, *Xenophon, *Scipio 'Africans', *Belisarius, *Saxe, *Napoleon, and, perhaps in reconciliation, Clausewitz. If 'who is the greatest' is the question of the child stretching out its hand for the moon, as his prophetic friend and rival *Fuller said, Liddell Hart aged remarkably little. He lived to be 74, but he was forever 14. Throughout his life he was always stretching out his hand for the moon.

There was a strong journalistic streak in him. Between 1924 and 1939 he was defence correspondent to, successively, the *Morning Post*, the *Daily Telegraph*, and *The Times*, and at least part of the repetition in his works was caused by an understandable desire to recycle for profit. Many of his ideas were repolished notions from the past, set out attractively for an audience attracted as much by their glitter as their substance. The indirect approach owed much to Sun-tzu, and the British way in warfare, far more apparent in the writings of Liddell Hart than in a broader reading of history, struck a powerful chord with a readership anxious to believe that a strategy of limited liability was indeed possible. His ideas were certainly tank-using—in 1925 he wrote that tanks should be 'concentrated and used in as large masses as possible'—but popular imagination continues to accord him a greater role in their paternity than modern studies of armoured warfare justify.

He was acutely conscious of his own place in history; his relationship with Fuller reflected this. The two enjoyed an effective partnership from the mid-1920s, but while Liddell Hart acknowledged Fuller's intellect as 'the profoundest that has been applied to military thought this century', the occasional tussle between them reflected basic differences of ideology and outlook (Liddell Hart was a liberal and Fuller a fascist) as much as specific disagreements over the relative importance of tanks and infantry in the broadly similar tactics they both advocated: Fuller was sceptical of the oversimplifications he believed to be inherent in the indirect approach. On the eve of WW II Liddell Hart served as adviser to the reforming war minister, Leslie Hore-Belisha, and helped the army shed some 'over-aged and under-talented' generals. However, his opposition to a con-

tinental commitment for the army helped undermine the logic underpinning the very armoured forces he advocated. In later life he suggested that the use of *nuclear weapons crossed a threshold into purposeless war, littered with its own pyramids of skulls.   AD/RH

Bond, Brian, *Liddell Hart: A Study of his Military Thought* (London, 1977).

Danchev, Alex, *Alchemist of War: The Life of Basil Liddell Hart* (London, 1998).

Gat, Azar, *Fascist and Liberal Visions of War* (Oxford, 1998).

Mearsheimer, John J., *Liddell Hart and the Weight of History* (London, 1988).

Liège, sieges of The Belgian city of Liège has figured prominently and frequently in wars from the Middle Ages to the 20th century. In a border location and an important manufacturing centre with, at least during the Middle Ages, a very independent citizenry, the town of Liège has often found itself under attack. In 1345, the Liégeois rebelled against their ruler, Prince-Bishop Engelbert de la Marck, who advanced on the town and was met by the rebels at Vottem, a suburb of Liège, where they conclusively beat him.

At the end of the *Hundred Years War, the French King Louis XI was forced into a reluctant alliance with Charles 'the Bold', Duke of Burgundy. Together, they attacked Liège. Operations were undertaken during the winter and deep mud around the gates hampered the attackers. The Liégeois made unexpected sorties and nearly captured the king and duke. The city was finally stormed by surprise attack on a Sunday, in defiance of the belief that the sabbath should be treated as a *truce day.

The fortifications of Liège were remodelled by *Brialmont in the 1880s, and outlying forts were added to keep an attacker at arm's length from the city. In 1914, the *Schlieffen plan meant that the Germans needed to capture the twelve forts around Liège so that their armies could pass between the 'Maastricht appendix' of Dutch territory and the Ardennes on their wide encircling march into France. The attack began on 5 August and the forts were battered into submission by massive siege guns, the last falling on 16 August. Any delay was harmful to the success of the plan, and although the forts were expected to hold out much longer, their defence added sand to the German machine and contributed to its eventual failure. They were able to contribute far less during WW II. At the outset of the battle leading to the fall of *France in 1941, the Germans occupied Liège within three days of their invasion of Belgium and the forts either surrendered or fell easily to specialist assault units.   MCM

Bradbury, Jim, *The Medieval Siege* (Woodbridge, 1992).

light troops is a phrase used throughout military history to distinguish unencumbered, agile soldiers by contrast with the 'heavy' or line infantry and cavalry. Modern usage first rose to real prominence during the great conflicts of the 18th century, notably the War of the *Austrian Succession, the *Seven Years War, the *American independence war, and the *French Revolutionary wars. The backbone of western armies during this period comprised heavy infantry who were trained to fight in close-order linear formations, normally three ranks deep. Musketry was delivered in salvoes, with more emphasis being placed on the rate of fire than on its accuracy, if only because smoothbore flintlocks were rather imprecise weapons with a maximum range of around 109 yards (100 metres). Orchestrating volleys and manoeuvring such ponderous, unwieldy formations called for a rigid system of command and control. Initiative on the part of individual soldiers was suppressed in favour of unquestioning compliance with instructions. Elaborate, ritualistic manual *drills were devised, with, for instance, the loading and firing of a musket requiring as many as 30 distinct moves, each regulated by the beat of a drum. This training was underpinned by punitive disciplinary codes; troops were drilled, flogged, and caned into being more afraid of their officers than they were of the enemy. Indeed, *Frederick 'the Great', who was to carry linear tactics to perfection, once summarized his notion of the ideal infantry regiment as a 'moving battery'.

When troops of this kind were pitted against opponents who fought in accordance with the same Frederician principles, the system worked well enough. However, in the War of the Austrian Succession, the Habsburg empire mobilized large numbers of auxiliaries, both horse and foot, from Hungary, Croatia, and Romania who were normally utilized for border and local defence missions. These irregulars were unsuited to, and largely incapable of, fighting in the disciplined, geometric formations employed by regiments of the line. Nevertheless, they were regarded as having a valuable contribution to make to the so-called *petite guerre* (little war)—the mercurial conflict waged on the fringes of armies and which consisted of outpost and *reconnaissance duties, ambushes, raids, and skirmishes.

This concept attracted ever more attention from military theorists as the century progressed. Experience in colonial conflicts, notably in America, where regular European soldiers found themselves fighting in enclosed, wooded, or mountainous terrain alongside auxiliary units often recruited from among trappers, hunters, and Native indian tribes, underscored the growing need for van, flank, and rearguards. In Europe, too, agricultural reforms and increasing prosperity gradually led to a topographical transformation which had major implications for battlefield tactics. The growth in urbanization, afforestation, and enclosure broke up the terrain, making much of it less than ideal for traditional close-order, linear formations. As a result, skirmishers acquired a role on the battlefield proper as well as in the peripheral *guerre des postes* (war of outposts).

With their gaudy attire, hefty packs, bulky weaponry and staid, inflexible tactics, soldiers of the line were ill-suited to the *petite guerre*. Light troops—the term denoting their tactical function still more than the mass of their equipment—who exploited cover and *camouflage and combined the characteristics of the scout with those of the marksman, were what was called for. Indeed, the procedures and trappings of the hunt were adapted for military purposes. Dubbed 'rangers', *chasseurs, or *Jägers, odd companies and battalions of riflemen and other *sharpshooters were raised. Deployed in open order, often across broken terrain and beyond the immediate supervision of their commanders, the manoeuvres of these soldiers were controlled by signals relayed by bugles and horns. Dressed in brown or dark green *uniforms designed with ease of movement and other practical considerations in mind, they were primarily intended to act as free-moving, free-firing skirmishers, but the best were also capable of acting in rudimentary shoulder-to-shoulder formations when circumstances demanded. These versatile, all-purpose infantry were often combined into 'legions' in which they would serve alongside a few squadrons of light cavalry, usually *dragoons who could fight on foot or horseback, and a handful of small, highly mobile artillery pieces.

In many senses, these units were the precursors to the combined-arms brigades and divisions into which *Napoleon was to divide the entire French army in 1800 and from which modern armies continue to be structured. However, armed forces reflect the societies which spawn them and, in the 18th century, there was considerable resistance to the widespread introduction of light troops and many of the innovations associated with them. Within Europe's socially stratified armies, where officers were appointed more often than not on the basis of their social standing as aristocrats or affluent gentlemen, and where the rank and file were often recruited from the very dregs of society, common soldiers were often dismissed as mindless ruffians at the best of times. The disdain with which light troops were regarded was frequently still more intense. One Line officer serving in the American independence war dismissed them as 'for the most part young and insolent puppies, whose worthlessness was apparently their recommendation to a service which placed them . . . in danger, and in the way of becoming food for powder, their most appropriate destination next to that of the gallows'. Their unglamorous, some would say scruffy, attire and unorthodox tactics inevitably encouraged the view among the British redcoats and their counterparts that light troops were a rabble who, lacking *discipline and *honour, were not to be compared to proper soldiers who, deployed in serried ranks, braved the enemy's fire like real men instead of shooting from under cover and running around 'like lamp lighters'. Respectable society could only agree. But this sort of prejudice was not based merely on the opinion that the tactics of light troops were those of the coward. In a military system where unthinking obedience to one's betters formed the very basis of order, the ethos of the skirmisher with its emphasis on initiative and free movement seemed like dangerous heresy, one that could not only undermine the tactical efficacy of the armed forces but also have unsettling political ramifications for society as a whole.

The *levée en masse* of the French Revolutionary wars seemed to underscore this very point. The thousands of conscripts who were drafted into the French army lacked the training and discipline necessary to perform intricate, close-order manoeuvres with any finesse. However, as the embodiment of Rousseau's concept of free, natural men they had the appropriate psychological outlook to make marvellous skirmishers; all they required was some basic military instruction. So it was that, alongside the highly professional units of chasseurs that the French army had been developing for some time, there appeared a great mass of *tirailleurs and *voltigeurs who played an important part in the victories of the Republic over the armies of the *ancien régime*.

France's enemies gradually concluded that the only way to counter these soldiers was by developing more light forces of their own. Reformists such as the Duke of *York and Lt Gen Sir John *Moore in Britain, the Archduke *Charles in Austria, and Gerhard von *Scharnhorst and Karl von Tiedemann in Prussia all urged their respective countries to raise more light troops and train them accordingly. Instructing them revolved as much around psychological preparation as it did around tactical training. Since men from feudalistic societies tended to be unaccustomed to using their own initiative and there were political objections to giving them too much liberty, the success of these experiments varied considerably. Nevertheless, substantial numbers of light troops were incorporated into the armies of all the major powers in the course of the *Napoleonic wars, many units, such as the British 95th Rifle Regiment, acquiring formidable reputations.

Light forces continued to have considerable utility for the rest of the 19th century and beyond. However, as the face of war changed under the impact of new technology, many of the old distinctions between heavy and light forces began to disappear. Infantry became versatile, general purpose troops and, once mechanized *armoured warfare established itself as the most intense form of land combat, the terms 'light' and 'heavy' came to refer more to the mass of equipment employed by a given unit and less to its tactical function. While today the British army, for instance, still has several battalions which have the words 'light infantry' in their titles, they are essentially indistinguishable from other mechanized and armoured infantry units. Traces of the modus operandi of the light infantry of old still live on amidst *special forces such as the *SAS.   DG

Gates, D., *The British Light Infantry Arm* (London, 1987).

Paret, P., *Yorck and the Era of Prussian Reform* (Princeton, 1966).

Lille, siege of (1708). This 120-day siege was a costly success for *Marlborough. Following his victory at Oudenarde in July 1708, he and Prince *Eugène of Savoy moved south to besiege the French stronghold of Lille, reckoned one of Vauban's finest fortress towns, ringing the city with trenches containing 100,000 men. The siege opened on 12 August, and despite two French attempts to sever the besiegers' line of supply to Ostend, and some costly assaults, the outer lines gradually succumbed, whereupon the defenders withdrew into the citadel, requiring a second siege. Marshal Boufflers eventually surrendered his 16,000 garrison on 10 December.   APC-A

Liman von Sanders, Gen Otto (1855–1929), German general and Turkish field-marshal. The Germans had reorganized the Ottoman army in 1883–95, a process in which Colmar von der Goltz played a leading part. However, their poor showing in the first *Balkan war of 1912 encouraged the Turks to request further assistance. Liman von Sanders, a cavalry officer with an apparently poor future (*Seeckt thought him unfit to command German troops) and a recently acquired title (his new name was the result of adding the Scottish name of his late wife to his own), was sent out in December 1913. Initially appointed inspector-general of the army, friction with *Enver Pasha, added to French and Russian protests (for although pro-German, Turkey was still neutral), saw him packed off to command the Turkish First Army in August 1914. In 1915 he commanded the Fifth Army on *Gallipoli, and although he misjudged the initial Allied landings, his dogged determination, which contrasted with *Hamilton's lack of grip, inspired the defence. In February 1917 he was given the impossible task of defending Palestine, with inadequate resources, against a British attack which became irresistible once *Allenby arrived. He emerged from the war with a far better reputation than most German generals whose pre-war promise had earned them appointments on the western front.   RH

Lin Piao, FM (correctly Lin Biao) (*c*.1907–71), Chinese minister of defence, 1959–71. He was born in Hupeh (correctly Hubei) province to a local factory owner and entered the Whampoa military *academy. A member of the Socialist Youth League at school, in 1927 he deserted the Kuomintang army and joined the communists. A protégé of *Chu Teh, he commanded the First Army Corps during the Long March of 1935–6 before heading the Red Army Academy. He fought during the Sino-Japanese war (1937–45) and the Chinese civil war (1945–9). In 1955, he was made a marshal and his loyal support of *Mao Tse-tung continued in the late 1960s when, as minister of defence, he initially supported Mao during the Cultural Revolution. However, he also used the upheavals across China to advance his power base and this brought him into conflict with Mao. He is said to have plotted against Mao with a view to seizing power in a military coup ('Project 571'). The plot was uncovered and in September 1971 he died, purportedly in an aeroplane crash while attempting to escape to the USSR.   MH

Lincoln, Abraham (1809–65), US President and *American civil war leader. His election was the proximate cause of the conflict and his political views shaped it. He was adamant that slavery was not the issue, but rather whether his vision of a unified continental empire would prevail over his opponents' traditional belief in a free association of sovereign states. Fort Sumter controlled the port of Charleston and symbolized his commitment to tariffs and economic autarky, bitterly opposed by the free-trading South. By deliberately provoking hostilities there, he accepted that most of the 'upper eight' slave states would secede or, like Kentucky, Missouri, and Maryland, adopt a hostile neutrality because of his policy.

The length, cost, and ferocity of the war can also be attributed largely to him. He defined the conflict as between the USA and traitorous individuals in which the states had no standing, because to do otherwise would admit that the Union was not perpetual and that secession was constitutional. There could be no peace negotiations, no compromise, only unconditional surrender to a lawful police action. Lincoln's position predicated the grinding, exhausting struggle it was to become and from the outset, even when most believed in a prompt outcome, he implemented the 'Anaconda Plan' devised by army commander *Scott for the slow suffocation of secession by sea and river.

He was an 'accidental' president, virtually unknown nationally before 1860 and elected with only 40 per cent of the popular vote because the Democrat Party split. Far from being the unquestioned leader of his own party, he was a compromise candidate, expected to be dominated by powerful cabinet members and congressional leaders. His lack of a personal political base forced many undesirable compromises on him, perhaps the most damaging being the appointment of the corrupt Cameron, owed a favour from the Republican Convention, as his first war secretary. But within a year he had replaced him with the fanatically honest Stanton and by various means he gradually brought the rest to heel.

Lincoln's subsequent achievement must be measured from the baseline that he began his presidency with scant experience of even local government. He lacked personal standing and was contemptuously dubbed 'the baboon' by Washington society. Not least, his erratic wife only with charity may be called a liability. He assumed power without even the physical means to enforce his authority, the first troops summoned to garrison the capital being compelled to bypass hostile Maryland. His military experience was confined to a short non-combatant stint with the militia during the Black Hawk war of 1832, and he inherited a tiny

pre-war regular army, scattered along the frontier. In addition the senior officers were mainly southern, including *Lee who declined an offer to command Union forces and went with Virginia.

His performance as C-in-C was far from perfect, but he handled mobilization much more skilfully than his opposite number Davis. Both sides had their share of political officers, but Lincoln was cursed not only with politically irresistible demands by local politicians to be given command over 'their' militias, but also by generals who were convinced they could replace him to advantage. Among the former was Sickles of *Gettysburg infamy, probably the only general in history to be appointed *after* he was found legally insane. Among the latter was *McClellan, the officer he appointed to succeed Scott and who later stood against him in the 1864 presidential elections.

This does not acquit him of overestimating his own competence as strategist in early 1862, when he dispersed forces and permitted his armies to be defeated in detail. In mitigation, he was ill-served by field commanders who either lacked the killer instinct or made grandiose plans that unwisely assumed the enemy would do what was expected of them. After he learned his own limitations, much of what his generals regarded as 'meddling' was his insistence that they close with the enemy to make the Union's great numerical and industrial superiority felt. Once he found in *Grant and *Sherman a pair of bulldogs who ignored setbacks and would not let go, his 'meddling' diminished.

Overall, it is difficult to fault his performance. After early 'learning' errors he made the best of whatever human material was to hand and backed winners wherever he could find them. Above all, he rallied an uncertain Union and made full use of its preponderant financial and industrial resources to settle fundamental issues left unresolved since the birth of the republic. In the process, he created a new nation.   HEB

Donald, David, *Lincoln* (London, 1995).

linstock Mentioned in Act III of *Henry V*—'the nimble gunner with linstock now the devilish cannon touches'—the linstock was a pole of varying length mounting a clamp on one end which held the slow match or hot wire used by the gunner to ignite the primary charge in the touch-hole of a muzzle-loading cannon. Ignition caused a back-blast up the touch-hole so distance from it was advisable and this the linstock provided. Flintlock firing devices began to supplant the linstock in the late 18th century.   SCW

Blair, Claude (ed.), *Pollard's History of Firearms* (London, 1983).

literature and drama, the military in Given the dramatic nature of warfare and the inherent tragedy within it, it is not surprising that the military has been the subject, direct or indirect, of a vast amount of literature whose sheer size and scope means that only a cursory survey, concentrating on the western literary tradition, is possible here. Although ancient Greece is often considered the cradle of western civilization, the *Greek city states were constantly at war with each other or outside powers, and their literature is full of violence and tragedy. Indeed the two most famous pieces of classical Greek *poetry, Homer's two epics *The Iliad* and *The Odyssey* (probably mid-8th century BC), both concern the Greek military élite. The *Iliad* tells the story of the Trojan wars and addresses the important themes thrown up by warfare: life and death, victory and defeat; the nature of heroism and *honour. To quote *The Oxford History of the Classical World*, 'The *Iliad* is not so much concerned with what people do, as with the way they do it, above all the way they face suffering and death.' As Hector says before his death in combat with Achilles: 'Let me at least not die without a struggle, inglorious, but do some big thing first, that men to come shall know of it.' As an antidote to this, Aristophanes' (c.445–385 BC) play *Lysistrata* shows the warring Greeks as buffoons finally brought to their senses by a sex strike by the Athenian *women.

The *Greek historians also created the western tradition of history writing. Herodotus of Halicarnassus (c.484–424), 'the father of history', produced the earliest Greek book in prose on the wars between the Greeks and Persians. His work was a memorial to that generation of Greek warriors, 'so that the achievements of men should not be obliterated by time'. The Romans' major contribution to literature concerning the military was also in the field of history rather than fiction. Historians of Rome such as Polybius, Julius *Caesar, Livy, and Tacitus paint a full picture of what Tacitus felt ought to be the subject matter of historians: 'vast wars, the sack of cities, the defeat and capture of kings, or in domestic history conflicts between consuls and tribunes . . . the struggles of the aristocracy and plebs.' Virgil was an epic poet in the Homeric tradition, with his *Aeneid* telling the story of a survivor from Troy. Horace, who had himself fought at *Philippi and had seen death on the battlefield, nevertheless coined what the WW I poet Wilfred Owen called 'the old lie': 'Dulce et decorum est pro patria mori' (It is a sweet and seemly thing to die for one's country).

In the Dark Ages, the northern European élite remained a warrior caste. Therefore much of the little literature that emerged was tailored to their beliefs and ideals. The most important old English poem, *Beowulf*, completed in the 8th century AD, is a monument to a great and perfect warrior hero. The warriors in the poem are either feasting or fighting and the epic heroism of Beowulf in his glorious life and tragic death provided an example of the perfect fighting king. This type of behaviour is mirrored in the Viking sagas, which are of a similar age although written down much later. The men depicted in the *Egil's Saga*, written in 1230, probably by Snorri Sturluson (1179–1241), are also happiest when fighting, usually showing considerable non-

chalance when meeting their violent ends. As Christianity established itself in Europe, the main protagonists remained heroic idealized warriors, but they had a new and worthwhile cause. This is probably best illustrated by the 12th-century French *Song of Roland*, where Roland is the last to fall fighting hordes of savage infidel Saracens (even though Roland had in reality died fighting the Basques at *Ronceval).

The idealized view of the soldier survives into the 14th century with Geoffrey Chaucer's (c.1340–1400) depiction of the Knight 'as a verray, parfit gentil knight' in the Prologue of the *Canterbury Tales* and into the 16th century with Torquato Tasso's *Gerusalemme Liberata* (Jerusalem Liberated, 1581) which deals with the Crusades. The knight has been traditionally viewed as the perfect Christian soldier who had 'fougten for oure feith' in the *Crusades. About two hundred years later a far more complex and rounded picture of the military appears in the work of William Shakespeare (1564–1616). Probably his best-known play with an explicitly martial theme is *Henry V* (1598). Quite apart from some of its stirring speeches, the play provides some of the most convincing scenes of the eve of battle capturing the tension and fears of both the common soldiery and highest generals before *Agincourt. While King Henry remains a largely heroic character (scarcely surprising given the play's nature as propagandist history), not all Shakespeare's military characters are quite so admirable. Indeed, the contrast between public rank and private flaws makes them apt subjects for tragedy. In *Othello* (1604), an excellent and intelligent soldier is brought down by jealousy of his wife and in *Coriolanus* (1609), the eponymous hero, quite possibly Shakespeare's most formidable military figure, brings destruction on himself and the Romans through his intolerant pride. Shakespeare's military observations are so acute that one commentator suggested that he had been a soldier—'Sergeant Shakespeare'—and A. D. Harvey's penetrating survey of the literature and art of war took, from *Henry V*, the fitting title *A Muse of Fire*.

If the *British civil wars generated little in the way of literature (though, in the shape of Richard Lovelace, at least one swashbuckling poet) the nearly contemporary *Thirty Years War inspired Grimmelshausen's *Simplicissimus*, a largely autobiographical account of the horrors of campaigning. Lawrence Sterne's *The Life and Opinions of Tristram Shandy* (1760) waxed eloquent on the difficulties of the hero's Uncle Toby in recalling the details of his experiences at the siege of *Namur. Sterne elaborated on 'the almost insurmountable difficulties he found in telling his story intelligibly, and giving such clear ideas of the differences and distinctions between the scarp and counterscarp—the glacis and the covered-way—the half-moon and ravelin—as to make his company fully comprehend where and what he was about.'

In the early years of the 19th century while Europe was in the throes of the *Napoleonic wars, Romantic authors such as Sir Walter Scott (1771–1832) craved the apparently more honourable and chivalrous days of warfare in the past. Scott, arguably the creator of the historical novel, produced books such as *Rob Roy* (1818) and *Ivanhoe* (1820) whose characters were impossibly heroic. Dumas père was another important exponent of the historical novel with works such as *The Three Musketeers*, and *La Reine Margot* includes a graphic description of the Massacre of St Bartholomew (see FRENCH WARS OF RELIGION). The Napoleonic wars were the subject of what is regarded by some critics as the best novel ever written. *Tolstoy served as an officer with the Russian army during the *Crimean war which provided him with the experience which so informs the extraordinary battle scenes of the Napoleonic campaigns against Russia in *War and Peace* (1864). Henri Beyle, writing as Stendhal, had served in the French commissariat in the Napoleonic wars, and balanced military (scarlet) against clerical (black) life in *Scarlet and Black* (1831). That direct military experience is no hindrance to writing well about the experience of warfare is illustrated by Stephen *Crane's seminal novel of the *American civil war *The Red Badge of Courage*. Émile Zola (1840–1902) set new standards for research on weapons, tactics, and the experience of the French soldier in the only strictly historical novel of his Rougon-Macquart series, *La Débâcle* (*The Downfall*, 1892), set during the *Franco-Prussian war of 1870 which includes a vivid description of the battle of *Sedan. The *Dreyfus affair was transformed into fiction in Zola's *Vérité*.

The best chronicler of the British army in India in the later part of the 19th century was Rudyard Kipling (1865–1936) who knew it as a journalist who was prepared to listen to soldiers. His collections of short stories *Plain Tales from the Hills* and *Soldiers Three* sometimes catch the very essence of military life, with its snoring barrack rooms and scorching parade grounds. His feel for the ground is deft: 'the turn of the pass [see KHYBER PASS] fornist Jumrood and the nine-mile [14.4 km] road on the flat to Peshawar.' He captured the experience of marching (in the Second *Boer War) remarkably well in his poem 'Boots'. George MacDonald Fraser credits Kipling with producing the 'best comment on infantry war, the best philosophy and above all the best advice' in four lines:

> When first under fire and you're wishful to duck,
> Don't look nor take heed at the man that is struck,
> Be thankful you're living, and trust to your luck,
> And march to front like a soldier.

MacDonald Fraser's own *Flashman* series of novels, based on the supposedly discovered papers of Harry Flashman, a notorious bully in *Tom Brown's Schooldays*, provides an entertaining and informative account of most of Britain's Victorian wars and numerous other conflicts.

WW I put an end to any notions of the honour and glory of war. The experience of the western front produced perhaps the best wartime literature of the English language. Although the poetry of Rupert Brooke and Julian Grenfell saw war in rather conventional heroic terms, the most famous wartime British poets such as Siegfried Sassoon, Edmund Blunden, Robert Graves, and Wilfred Owen produced images of such horror and disgust at the waste of war that they have become embedded in the British consciousness. Graves and Sassoon also wrote two of the definitive prose accounts—both at least part-fictionalized—of the experiences of WW I in *Goodbye to All That* and *Memoirs of Infantry Officer* respectively. The German experience of the western front inspired both Remarque's profoundly anti-war *All Quiet on the Western Front* and the 'patriotic realist' works of Ernst *Junger. Henri Barbusse's *Under Fire* and Frederic Manning's *Her Privates We* both, in common with so many books inspired by the war, concentrated on the experience of the group—not a group, like Kipling's three heroes, of professional soldiers, but of ordinary men projected into an extraordinary situation.

WW II did not produce the same flowering of British literature as WW I, probably because it did not prove quite such a traumatic experience for the British people. Perhaps the best novels to come out of the British war were Evelyn Waugh's *Officers and Gentlemen* series (1952–61). Yet somehow the experiences of the trilogy's hero, a 35-year-old member of the Catholic aristocracy, did not really speak for a generation in the way WW I authors had. In fact the best English-language literature of WW II came out of the American experience, notable American war novels being Norman Mailer's *The Naked and the Dead* (1952), Joseph Heller's *Catch 22* (1955) which captured the insanity of war and gave a new phrase to the English language, and Kurt Vonnegut's *Slaughterhouse 5* (1969). The infinitely more bitter German experience was reflected in characters like Hans Helmut Kirst's cynical Gunner Asch, and the experience of the war helped Alexander Solzhenitsyn address an earlier conflict in *August 1914*.

The wars of the 20th century have provided a fruitful source for contemporary authors. The *Vietnam war provided writers—commentators as well as veterans—with a rich seam to mine, and at least two books about it, Philip Caputo's *A Rumor of War* (1977) and Michael Herr's *Dispatches* (1978), are of lasting importance. As the century neared its close, however, several authors looked back to what seemed its defining conflict. Pat Barker's prize-winning *Regeneration* (1991–5) used fictional and real protagonists such as Siegfried Sassoon and Wilfred Owen; Sebastian Faulk's *Birdsong* (1994) produced a harrowing portrayal of life in the trenches and was especially evocative of the subterranean war of mine and counter-mine. On a somehow more cheerful note, despite the grimness of so much of its subject matter, an Axis-occupied Greek island in WW II was the setting of Louis De Bernières's *Captain Corelli's Mandolin* (1994), which became obligatory British holiday reading.   MCM/RH

Boardman, John, Griffin, Jasper, and Murray, Oswyn, *The Oxford History of the Classical World* (Oxford, 1986).

Harvey, A. D., *A Muse of Fire* (London, 1998).
MacDonald Fraser, George, *Quartered Safe Out Here* (London, 1993).

Little Bighorn, battle of (1876), second defeat (the first was of Crook's column at the Rosebud on 17 June) of an attempt by the US army to trap rebellious Lakota and Arapaho/Cheyenne on their Montana hunting grounds. On 25 June *Custer sent part of his 7th Cavalry under Reno to 'beat' the hostiles out of their encampment, while led by Crow scouts he hooked around to drive off their pony herd and envelop them, a standard Indian-fighting tactic. On 25 June he was outmanoeuvred and his detachment of 215 men was annihilated between an anvil led by the Hunkpapa Gall that cut off his retreat and a head-on mounted hammer led by the Oglala *Crazy Horse. The rest of the regiment lost a further 100 men when Reno was forced back upon the reserve elements under Benteen in the hills along Custer's line of advance, where they were besieged for 36 hours. Coming nine days before the centenary of the USA, the battle immediately assumed mythic status and it is probably the most written-about skirmish in military history. The lonely battlefield, with poignant white markers showing where Custer's men fell, is among the most visited US National Parks.   HEB

Lloyd George, David (1863–1945), British PM, 1916–22. A remarkably energetic and dynamic politician, Lloyd George (like his close colleague *Churchill) was a political maverick. A Liberal MP from humble origins, the eloquent 'Welsh Wizard' first made his name as a solicitor before entering parliament in 1890, retaining his seat until 1945. He served as President of the Board of Trade (1905–8), Chancellor of the Exchequer (1908–15), Minister of Munitions (1915–16), and was thereafter Secretary of State for War and PM.

Lloyd George, the radical social reformer who introduced the 'People's Budget' of 1909 which provided funds for social services, was once at loggerheads with the very notion of war. He had opposed the Second *Boer War, and was likewise initially hostile to the concept in August 1914. Yet within days he embraced the fact of war, and was circulating memos on strategy before the year's end. In December 1916, he was able to overthrow the less single-minded Asquith and become PM with Conservative support, due to his promise of 'a more vigorous prosecution of the war'.

He was a habitual and not particularly constructive schemer. His relations with senior British commanders, notably *Haig and *Robertson, were poor, the more so after his surprise subordination of Haig to Nivelle in February 1917. The six volumes of his *War Memoirs* (1933–6) were a shameless exercise in self-justification, where blame for the controversial aspects of WW I was shifted onto the shoulders of his generals. In them (the popular edition was a best-seller), Lloyd George rewrote history, exaggerating casualty figures and bitterly criticizing Haig, who had conveniently died in 1928.

There were times when Lloyd George's stubbornness bore fruit, when, for example, he forced a reluctant Admiralty into adopting the *convoy system for merchant shipping in May 1917 and losses to U-boats dropped overnight. It was once believed that his organizational skills shone when as munitions minister he perceived the requirements of a war economy, copied American manufacturing methods, built National Munitions factories, and recruited female labour to work in them, but most historians now agree that his impact even in this sphere was not as great as he claimed. He put enormous energy into satisfying his equally large ego, advocating the creation of a Welsh army corps and being instrumental in the formation of a Welsh division for the *Somme, with his son ADC to its GOC.

Lloyd George flirted with both 'eastern' and 'western' strategies. He supported some 'sideshows' as a way of breaking the deadlock on the western front, believing that to knock away the 'props' of Germany's allies by successful campaigns away from France would put Germany out of the war. His strategies for such operations varied enormously, from an Allied thrust up the Danube in 1914 to joint offensive in Italy in early 1917 or attacks in Macedonia (1917) and Palestine (1918). However, in the autumn of 1916 he demanded a 'knockout blow' on the western front and he backed the desperate *Nivelle offensive of 1917. He was unable to push through a coherent strategy later that year: although he feared that Haig's Flanders offensive would not achieve the desired result, he could neither find a replacement for Haig (though he tried) nor compel Haig to abandon Flanders in favour of Italy. He supported the creation of the Allied *Supreme War Council, partly as a means of controlling Haig, and although he eventually disposed of Robertson, it was at the cost of replacing him with the scarcely less difficult *Wilson.

In the post-war general election he publicly pursued a vindictive anti-German policy, but in private his natural Liberal sentiments once more rose to the fore, and he warned against too harsh terms against the Germans at Versailles. The treaty was not as vindictive as France would have liked, nor as moderate as Lloyd George wished, but Lloyd George was handicapped by his own election pledges and speeches, and his conciliatory tone at Versailles shocked the British electorate, who thereafter mistrusted him. Resigning as premier in 1922 he led his dwindling party from 1926 to 1931, and was created Earl Lloyd George months before his death in 1945.   APC-A/RH

logistics (*see opposite page*)

logistics

LOGISTICS is a relatively new word used to describe a very old practice: the supply, movement, and maintenance of an armed force both in peacetime and under operational conditions. Most soldiers have an appreciation of the impact logistics can have on operational readiness. Logistic considerations are generally built in to battle plans at an early stage for without them the tanks, APCs, artillery pieces, helicopters, and other aircraft are just numbers on a table of organization and equipment. Unfortunately, it often seems that high-profile weapon systems have had greater priority in resources than the means to support them in the field, be it ammunition, fuel, or spares. For it is logistics that will determine the forces that can be delivered to the theatre of operations, what forces can be supported once there, and what will then be the tempo of operations.

Logistics concerns not only the supply of *matériel* to an army in times of war, but also the ability of the national infrastructure and manufacturing base to equip, support, and supply the armed forces—the national transportation system to move forces—and its ability to resupply those forces once deployed. Thus it has been said that 'logisticians are a sad race of men, very much in demand in war, who sink back into obscurity in peace. They deal only with facts but must work for men who merchant in theories. They emerge during war because war is very much fact. They disappear in peace, because in peace, war is mostly theory.'

The practice of logistics, as understood in its modern form, has been around for as long as there have been organized armed forces with which nations have tried to exert pressure on their neighbours. The earliest known standing army was that of the *Assyrians at around 700 BC. They had iron weapons, *armour, and *chariots, were well organized, and could fight over different types of terrain and engage in siege operations. The need to feed and equip a substantial force of that time, along with the means of transportation (i.e. horses, camels, mules, and oxen), would mean that it could not linger in one place for too long. Considerable numbers of followers carrying the *matériel* necessary to provide sustenance and maintenance to the fighting force would provide essential logistic support.

Both *Philip of Macedon and *Alexander 'the Great' improved upon the art of logistics in their time. Philip realized that the vast *baggage train that traditionally followed an army restricted the mobility of his forces, so he did away with much of it and made the soldiers carry much of their equipment and supplies. He also banned dependants. As a result the logistics requirements of his army fell substantially, as the smaller numbers of animals required less fodder, and a smaller number of wagons meant less maintenance and a reduced need for wood to effect repairs. Added to that, the smaller number of cart drivers and lack of dependants meant less food needed to be taken with them, hence fewer carts and animals and a reduced need to forage. Alexander was slightly more lenient than his father as regards women and allowed his men to take their women with them. This was important, given the time they spent away on campaign and also reduced disciplinary problems. He also made extensive use of shipping, with a reasonable sized merchant ship able to carry around 400 tons (406 tonnes), while a horse could carry 200 lb (91 kg) (but needed to eat 20 lb (9.1 kg) of fodder a day, thus consuming its own load every ten days). He never spent a winter, or more than a few weeks on campaign, away from a sea port or navigable river. He even used his enemy's logistics weaknesses against them, as many ships were mainly configured for fighting but not for endurance, so Alexander would blockade the ports and rivers the Persian ships would use for supplies, thus forcing them back to base. He planned to use his merchant fleet to support his campaign in India, with the fleet keeping pace with the army, while the army would provide the fleet with fresh water. However, the monsoons were heavier than usual, and prevented the fleet from sailing. Alexander lost two-thirds of his force, but managed to get to Gwadar where he reprovisioned. The importance of logistics was central to Alexander 'the Great''s plans, indeed his mastery of it allowed him to conduct the longest military campaign in history. At the furthest point reached by his army, the river Beas in India, his soldiers had marched 11,250 miles (18,101 km) in eight years. Their success depended on his army's ability to move fast by depending on comparatively few animals, by using the sea wherever possible, and on good logistic intelligence.

The Romans made few genuine innovations in logistics, but they profited from applying their characteristic organization to logistic policy and from keeping an army's non-combatant element to a minimum. Their logistics were helped, of course, by the superb infrastructure, including the roads they built as they expanded their empire. However, with the decline in the western Roman empire in the 5th century AD, the art of warfare degenerated, and with it, logistics was reduced to the level of pillage and plunder. It was not until the coming of *Charlemagne, and his use of large supply trains and fortified supply posts called 'burgs', that logistics was again taken seriously in the West.

The Byzantine empire did not suffer from the same decay as its western counterpart. It adopted a defensive strategy, recognizing that expansion of territory is costly in men and material. Thus their logistics problems were simplified—they had interior lines of communication, and could shift base far more easily in response to an attack than if they were in conquered territory. They used shipping and considered it vital to keep control of the Dardanelles, Bosporus, and Sea of Marmara. On campaign they made extensive use of permanent warehouses or *magazines, to supply troops.

In the West, feudalism was a means to provide for the logistic support of the armoured horseman in peacetime. However, when medieval armies took the field their logistic provision was usually scanty. During the *Crécy campaign of 1346 an English knight wrote: 'we have lived off the countryside with great difficulty and much harm to our men.' The *chevauchée was a tactic which enabled a force to sustain itself by moving through enemy territory, thereby solving its own logistic problems and stripping its opponent of resources. Sieges posed particular problems. While the besieged would generally have a stock of provisions, the besieger would usually eat up his rations quickly, and then have to send foraging parties ever wider to find more.

Medieval armies were generally small: the English force beaten at *Bannockburn was, at 20,000, unusually large. Armies this size could generally cope by a judicious mixture of living off the land and carrying some of their provisions with them. But as armies grew bigger in the 17th century so their problems multiplied. Primitive logistics turned the armies of the *Thirty Years War into huge destructive maggots that gnawed their way across the countryside, biting ever deeper if others had passed that way before. Well might Cardinal Richelieu write that 'History knows more armies ruined by want and disorder than by the efforts of their enemies.'

By 1700 an army of 60,000 men needed 45 tons (45.7 tonnes) of bread a day, the product of 60 portable bread-ovens and 200 wagonloads of fuel. Its 40,000 horses ate 500 tons (508 tonnes) of fodder a day in the campaigning season, falling to 250 tons (254 tonnes) in winter quarters. The French war administrator Michel le Tellier took the lead in calculating the ration requirements of an army, arranging for civilian contractors to supply food, and setting up a wagon train with provision reserves. His son *Louvois developed the magazine system, already used since classical times, to ensure that frontier fortresses were well stocked with supplies which could be moved out to the armies by wagon or barge. Yet although the French established a corps of intendants to supervise supply and expenditure, the system still depended on contractors who required payment, and upon civilian drivers who were not proof against war's alarms. Moreover, the need to feed horses made war a largely seasonal affair: not for nothing did Mars, the Roman god of war, give his name to the month when campaigning could traditionally start.

*Napoleon was able to take advantage of the better road system of the early 19th century and the increasing population density, but ultimately still relied upon a combination of magazines and foraging. While many Napoleonic armies abandoned tents to increase speed and lighten the logistic load, the numbers of cavalry and artillery pieces (pulled by horses) grew as well, thus defeating the object. The lack of tents actually increased the instance of illness and disease, putting greater pressure on the medical system. Despite careful preparation, Napoleon failed the logistics test when he crossed the Nieman in 1812 to start his Russian campaign. He started with around 450,000 men and reached Moscow with just over 100,000 excluding stragglers. The battle of *Borodino only partly explains the shortfall. He had known the logistics system would not sustain his army on the road to Moscow and keep it there. He gambled that he could force the Russians to the negotiating table and dictate terms. He failed, and so had to retreat, a venture which logistic breakdown (as much as the weather or Russian pursuit) turned into a rout. The pursuing Russian army did little better, starting at Kaluga with 120,000 men and finally reaching Vilna with 30,000.

The *American civil war foreshadowed future warfare, particularly as regards logistics. Both sides were determined, with large populations to draw recruits from, and (more notably in the case of the North) the means to equip them. This laid the foundations for a long war, one which would not be determined by one or two battles but by several campaigns, and which would hinge upon the will to sustain the war-fighting capability (material and *morale). This meant that a logistics infrastructure would have to be set up to cater for the movement of large armies, as well as the supply of food, ammunition, equipment, spare parts, fresh horses and their fodder, and the evacuation of casualties (of which there would be greater numbers than ever).

Strategy took into consideration not only the combatants' own logistic requirements, but those of the enemy as well. That principle meant that *Grant was able to fix *Lee in Virginia and enabled *Sherman to march to Atlanta to destroy the Confederates' major communications and supply centre, and hence on to Savannah. Lastly, it was the first major war in which *railways played an important part, speeding up the movement of troops and supplies. But it also warned of the consequences of having a large army tied to the railway system for the majority of its supplies, as *McClellan found out in both the Richmond peninsular campaign and after the battle of *Antietam. Most European observers had lost interest in the war early on, but a few were impressed with the support given by the Union navy to the Union army in tactical and logistic terms, and the use of railway repair battalions to keep the rail systems functioning. The two lessons they missed or forgot were the growing importance of *field fortifications and the increasing rate of ammunition expenditure.

During the second half of the 19th century, partly in response to failures like those in the *Crimean war, the logistic services of armies became increasingly militarized, staffed by officers and men accountable to the chain of command. It was evident that maintaining a nucleus of transport officers to manage hastily drafted peasant carters would not meet the demands of modern war. Service corps troops drove and maintained wagons, specialist railway troops were responsible for the maintenance and repair of the permanent way, and as the internal combustion engine made its presence felt in the early 20th century so service corps troops took that in their stride.

The age-old disdain of combat troops for those who supplied them was reflected in the nicknames service troops received (see SLANG). In Britain the Army Service Corps was known, after a popular music hall character, as Ally Sloper's Cavalry, and the initials of the Royal Indian Army Service Corps were alleged to stand for Really I am So Common. The German army of WW I coined the unkind expression *Ettappenschweine* (lines of communication pigs), and the French army of the 19th century had a long and acrimonious dispute over whether officials of its *Intendance* (military commissariat) might be regarded as 'proper' officers.

WW I was unlike anything that had gone before it. Not only did the armies, particularly the Germans in 1914, outstrip their logistic systems with the amount of men, equipment, and horses moving at a fast pace, but they totally underestimated the ammunition requirements (particularly for artillery). Once the war became trench-bound, supplies were needed to build fortifications that stretched across the whole of the western front. Added to that were the scale of the casualties involved, the difficulty in building up for an attack (husbanding supplies), and then sustaining the attack once it had gone in (if any progress was made, supplies had to be carried over the morass of no man's land). It was no wonder that the war in the west was conducted at a snail's pace, given the logistic problems. It was not until 1918 that the British, learning the lessons of the last four years, finally showed how an offensive should be carried out, with supply tanks and motorized gun sledges helping to maintain the pace of the advance, and to maintain supply well away from the railheads and ports. It was no longer true to say that supply was easier when armies kept on the move. From 1914, the reverse applied, because of the huge expenditure of ammunition, and the consequent expansion of transport to lift it forward to the consumers.

This of course, was a foretaste of WW II. The conflict was global in size and scale. Not only did combatants have to supply forces at ever-greater distances from the home base, but these forces were fast moving, and voracious in their consumption of fuel, food, water, and ammunition. Railways again proved indispensable, but sealift and airlift made ever greater contributions as the war dragged on (especially with the use of *amphibious and *airborne forces, as well as underway replenishment for naval task forces). The large-scale use of motorized transport for tactical resupply helped maintain the momentum of offensive operations, and most armies became more motorized as the war progressed. The Germans, although moving to greater use of motorized transport, still relied on horse transport to a large extent—a fact worth noting in the failure of *BARBAROSSA. After the fighting had ceased, the operations staffs could relax somewhat, whereas the logisticians had not only to supply the occupation forces, but also relocate those forces that were *demobilizing, repatriate *POWs, and feed civil populations. The principal logistic legacy of WW II was the expertise in supplying far-off operations.

With the end of WW II, the tensions that had been held in check by the common goal to defeat fascism finally came to the fore. The *Cold War started in around 1948 and was given impetus by the Berlin *blockade, the formation of NATO, and the *Korean war. The period was characterized by the change in the global order from one dominated by empires to a roughly bipolar world, split between the superpowers and their alliance blocs. The deadlock between *NATO and the *Warsaw Pact in Europe made battlefield logistics relatively simple. The principal logistic requirement would be to keep open the transatlantic sea lines of communication. However, the continued activity by both blocs in the Third World meant that both sides continued to draw on the experience of power projection from the war. East and West continued to have to prepare for both limited conflicts in the Third World, which would vary between *low-intensity operations (*Aden, Central America, *Malaya, *Mau Mau, and *Afghanistan) and 'medium-intensity' conventional operations (Korea, the *Falklands) often conducted well away from the home base, and an all-out confrontation involving high-intensity conventional and/or nuclear conflict. Both sides had to deal with the spiralling rate of defence inflation, while weapon systems increased in both cost and complexity, having implications for the procurement process, as defence budgets could not increase at the same rate.

The ending of the Cold War has had profound effects upon the philosophy of, and approach to, military logistics. The long-held approach of stockpiling of weapons, ammunition, and vehicles at various strategic sites around the expected theatre of operations and in close proximity to the lines of communications which was possible when the threat and its axes of attack were known, is no longer the optimum method in the new era of force projection and *manoeuvre warfare. 'High tech' weapons are also difficult to replace. Even the USAF started to run short of smart munitions during the 1999 attacks on the former *Yugoslavia.

With pressure on defence budgets and the need to be able to undertake a (possibly larger) number of (smaller) operational tasks than had previously been considered there has been a closer examination of the approach of commercial organizations to logistics. The total-process view of the supply chain necessary to support commercial business is now being adopted by, and adapted within, the military environment. Hence initiatives such as 'Lean Logistics' and 'Focussed Logistics' as developed in the US Department of Defense and acknowledged by the UK Ministry of Defence in the so-called 'Smart Procurement', recognize the importance of logistics within a 'cradle to grave' perspective. This means relying less on the total integral stockholding and transportation systems, and increasing the extent to which contractorization logistic support to military operations is farmed out to civilian contractors—as it was in the 18th century. Force projection and manoeuvre warfare blur the distinction between the long-held first-, second-, and third-line support concept of the static Cold War philosophy and link the logistics' supply chain more closely with the home base than ever before.

One of the reasons for the defeat of the British in North America in 1776 was the length of time involved in replenishing the forces from a home base some 3,000 miles (4,827 km) away. The same was true of Russia's defeat in the *Russo-Japanese war, with a 4,000 mile (6,436 km) supply line along a single track railway. While the distances involved may still be great in today's operational environment, logistic philosophies and systems are being geared to be more responsive in a way that could not have been previously envisaged.

The five principles of logistics accepted by NATO are foresight, economy, flexibility, simplicity, and co-operation. They are just as true today as they were in the times of the Assyrians and Romans. The military environment in which they can be applied is considerably different, and, as can be seen in the Balkans in the late 20th century, adopting and adapting military logistics to the operational scenario is an essential feature for success. As FM *Wavell said in 1946: 'A real knowledge of supply and movement factors must be the basis of every leader's plan; only then can he know how and when to take risks with these factors, and battles and wars are won by taking risks.'   DMM

Christopher, M., *Logistics and Supply Chain Management* (London, 1992).

Foxton, P. D., *Powering War: Modern Land Force Logistics* (London, 1994).

Lynn, John A., *Feeding Mars: Logistics in Western Warfare from the Middle Ages to the Present* (Oxford, 1993).

Sinclair, Joseph, *Arteries of War: A History of Military Transportation* (Shrewsbury, 1992).

Thompson, Julian, *Lifeblood of War: Logistics in Armed Conflict* (London, 1998).

Van Creveld, Martin, *Supplying War: Logistics from Wallenstein to Patton* (Cambridge, 1995).

Longstreet, Lt Gen James (1821–1904), Confederate corps commander whom *Lee called his 'old war-horse'. He was commissioned from *West Point in 1842 into the infantry, and was badly wounded in the *Mexican war. He resigned from the US army to become a Confederate brigadier general in 1861, rising rapidly through division and corps command to emerge, after the death of *Jackson, as Lee's principal lieutenant. He is the preferred scapegoat of 'lost cause' romanticists because he was a reluctant secessionist, because he delayed Pickett's Charge at *Gettysburg, because he was a friend of *Grant and joined the Republican party after the war, and because he criticized Lee in his memoirs.

By contrast with Jackson, he showed little ability in independent command, but he fully shared Stonewall's belief that assaults were only justified when manoeuvres had put the Union army at a disadvantage. Just such opportunities were achieved at second *Bull Run and at Chickamauga, and on both occasions Longstreet's corps delivered the decisive attacks. He was no less effective on the defensive, and at *Fredericksburg his corps inflicted appalling casualties on Union frontal assaults. Proof that he had not lost Lee's confidence after Gettysburg was shown when he recalled him to duty in 1864 before he had recovered from his severe wounding at the Wilderness. Those who judge that as a South Carolinian he was out of place in an army dominated by Virginians ignore the opinion of Lee and of his own troops, who trusted him implicitly to the end.　　HEB

Loos, battle of (1915). In the summer of 1915 the French C-in-C *Joffre planned a repetition of the strategy used that spring, an assault on each flank of the great German salient in the centre of the western front. His Tenth Army was to attack in the Vimy sector, and he pressed Sir John *French, C-in-C of the British Expeditionary Force (BEF), to support this by attacking around Loos, to the immediate north. French looked at the ground in July and was not impressed by the numerous mines and miners' cottages, which he believed to be well suited to defence. However, Lord *Kitchener, Secretary of State for War, made it clear that the French were to be supported even if the British suffered 'very heavy casualties' by doing so.

French then seemed to warm to the scheme, in part because he hoped that the use of chlorine *gas on a large scale would paralyse the German defence. The attack was entrusted to the First Army under *Haig, which was to attack with two corps, each of three divisions, side by side on a front running from Loos to La Bassée. French decided to keep the general reserve, two of whose divisions were inexperienced 'New Army' formations, at his own disposal rather than to entrust it to Haig, probably because he feared that it might be committed prematurely.

The battle began early on 25 September, and although the gas was not as successful as had been hoped the attack went well in the south and Loos was taken. However, the reserves were too far back to reinforce success, and the German second position—constructed following the experience of receiving British offensives at Neuve Chapelle and Aubers Ridge that spring—remained untouched. When the reserves appeared on the 26th, after a difficult approach march, they could make no impression on it and lost heavily. Although the battle did not end until 4 November, there was no real prospect of success after its first day. The British lost over 60,000 casualties to about 20,000 German. Three British major generals were among the killed, as was the only son of the poet Rudyard Kipling. The failure inspired serious disappointment in Britain, and the issue of the reserves became a cause célèbre. Haig used official papers, some of them shown to the king, to demonstrate French's unfitness for high command, and succeeded as C-in-C in December.　　RH

Louis XIV, King of France (1638–1715). Louis, the greatest king of France's *grand siècle*, was only a small boy when he succeeded his father in 1643. Because of his youth, real power passed to his mother Anne of Austria as regent and to the Italian-born first minister, Cardinal Mazarin. When Mazarin died in 1661, Louis refused to appoint another first minister and instead grasped the reins of government himself, never to relinquish them so long as he lived. During this 'personal reign', France exercised pre-eminent power on the continent of Europe.

Louis, who adopted the sun as his symbol to become the 'Sun King', displayed the splendour of his reign by constructing his opulent and vast palace at Versailles. There his dazzling court strutted and bickered, while Louis reserved real authority for himself. Louis is reputed to have claimed 'I am the state', and although this statement may be apocryphal, his will was, indeed, the will of the state in matters of military matters and foreign policy.

During the second half of the 17th century, French troops proved themselves virtually invincible on the battlefield. Phenomenal growth of his army multiplied its effect. French forces during the *League of Augsburg war climbed above 400,000 men on paper, and may have attained 340,000 in reality. Administrative reforms carried out by war ministers Michel Le Tellier and his son, the Marquis de *Louvois, provided a more regular provision of food, equipment, and pay, making such large forces possible.

Louis regarded being a soldier as an essential attribute of kingship, and he devoted himself very much to military affairs. During wartime, he regularly went to the field until the infirmities of age kept him from doing so, yet he never commanded in battle. He had a penchant for sieges and attended over twenty of them. In contrast to his identification with the army, Louis never harboured equal concern for his navy. Although it expanded mightily by 1690, he later allowed it to decline in order to concentrate resources on land.

As befitted the tone of the age, Louis cared much for his *gloire*, best translated as fame or reputation, but that does not mean that his foreign policy was vainglorious. Historians have often argued that the wars he fought during his personal reign, like those of Napoleon a century later, resulted from a desire to annex much of the continent. Yet Louis's goals were more modest and reasonable.

Early in his personal reign, the young king lusted to establish his reputation as a warrior-king by conquest. His Spanish wife had renounced her claims to the domains of her father, Philip IV, contingent upon delivery of a huge dowry which was never paid. Therefore, when Philip died in 1665, Louis insisted that parts of the Spanish Netherlands should go to, or 'devolve' upon, his wife, setting off the War of Devolution (1667–8). An alliance led by the Dutch imposed an end to this brief struggle, and although Louis received twelve important fortress towns, he believed himself cheated. In the Dutch war (1672–8), Louis intended to punish the Dutch and gain a free hand in the Spanish Netherlands. French armies invaded the Dutch Netherlands, but failed to impose their terms. As the alliance against Louis grew, he had to withdraw south in 1674.

At mid-course during the Dutch war, Louis gave up his dream of adding the Spanish Netherlands to his kingdom and, instead, came to associate his *gloire* less with conquering more territory than with protecting what he already held. *Vauban, Louis's great military engineer, urged Louis to create a double line of fortresses, known as the *pré carré*, to seal off his northern border. But he also advocated creating a more defensible frontier to the east by seizing additional strong points. After the close of the Dutch war, which netted him more fortresses in the Netherlands plus the entire province of Franche-Comté, Louis resolved to take still other key towns, particularly Strasbourg and Luxembourg, in a series of land grabs known as the 'Reunions'. The climax of this process was the brief and profitable war of that name (1683–4).

When Louis demanded European recognition of all his territorial gains—and did so by invading German lands to compel such recognition—he precipitated the League of Augsburg war in which he faced the 'Grand Alliance' of the English, Dutch, Spanish, and Austria, along with several lesser German states and Savoy. During this war Louis's army won all its major battles and enjoyed the upper hand in *siege warfare, but the struggle so exhausted France that Louis sacrificed some of his earlier acquisitions to secure a peace settlement.

Louis's last great war came with the inevitability of sunset, when Charles II, the childless king of Spain, died in 1700. Before Charles's death, Louis tried to hammer out an agreement with other rulers to avoid a major war by dividing the Spanish inheritance. However, all prior arrangements dissolved when Charles stipulated on his deathbed that everything should go to Louis's grandson, Philip of Anjou. Louis really had little choice but to accept the dying declaration, but he should have avoided the series of ill-considered acts that alarmed his foes, who once again formed a Grand Alliance to oppose him in a final cataclysm, the War of the *Spanish Succession. Two brilliant allied commanders, *Marlborough and Prince *Eugène of Savoy, won a series of battles and sieges that nearly exhausted Louis's strength. But he refused to capitulate and eventually outlasted his enemies. When Queen Anne removed Marlborough from command and British forces from the war, Louis's armies reasserted French power, defeated Eugène, and established a settlement that did not require Louis to sacrifice territory and that also left his grandson Philip on the Spanish throne. JAL

Lossky, Andrew, *Louis XIV and the French Monarchy* (New Brunswick, NJ, 1994).
Lynn, John A., *The Wars of Louis XIV* (London, 1999).
Wolf, John B., *Louis XIV* (New York, 1968).

Louisbourg, siege of (1758). Situated on Cape Breton Island, the fortress of Louisbourg protected access to French Canada, via the great waterway of the St Lawrence river. It was the most formidable *fortification in North America, but it had fallen once before, in 1745, to a combined British operation. In July of 1758, a British force of 11,600 under Amherst was able to capture it again after a sustained land and naval bombardment weakened the defences. The French garrison surrendered and 5,600 prisoners and 239 guns were taken. Cutting off communications between France and the still very active and hitherto successful French forces in the interior, it was a turning point in the *French and Indian war. TM

Louvois, François-Michel Le Tellier, Marquis de (1639–91). As the highly effective, though heavy-handed, war minister of *Louis XIV, Louvois provided the invaluable administrative support that made possible Louis's large armies and impressive victories. Louvois was preceded in office by his father, Michel Le Tellier, who at first shared responsibility with his son and then passed the burden entirely to him in the 1670s. Le Tellier designed many of the reforms later carried out by Louvois; the father played the role of architect and the son of builder in erecting the edifice of French military administration. Among his other accomplishments, Louvois organized a more regular and permanent system of *magazines to supply armies in the field. By gathering and storing foodstuffs and, particularly, fodder, Louvois made it possible for French armies to begin campaigning in the spring before their enemies could take the field. But this was simply one of his many administrative accomplishments. For all his ability and power, Louvois was never accepted as the social equal of the commanders who carried out his orders. The great *Turenne dismissed Louvois as little better than a valet or clerk. But Louvois was by nature thick-skinned and bull-headed, characteristics he needed to make himself obeyed, although they hardly endeared him to the court. While Louvois's influence on military administration was highly beneficial, his influence on state policy was far less so. He encouraged Louis's brutal conduct during the 1680s. Louvois advocated the seizure of frontier fortresses, aided in the persecution of Protestants, and argued for the use of bombardment as a political tool. Finally he facilitated reprisals during the War of the Reunions and the devastation of the Palatinate that began the *League of Augsburg war. Still, it can be argued that the military machine never ran as smoothly after his death. JAL

Lynn, John A., *Giant of the Grand Siècle: The French Army, 1610–1715* (Cambridge, 1997).

low-intensity operations A formula made famous by Col (later Gen Sir) Frank Kitson in his book of 1971. It deals with the diffuse and ill-defined forms of conflict—his sub-title instanced 'subversion, insurgency and peacekeeping'—that may be said to lie somewhere between peace and war. By the 1970s these kinds of unconventional operations had become the most common military business for the British army and many others, but doctrinally they remained in a kind of limbo. The difficulty of reaching a clear military analysis lay in the highly political nature of the issue; the early stages of insurgency could not be dealt with by straightforward military methods. Unless *martial law was declared, military action in aid of the *civil power had to follow the old common-law rule that the force applied must never exceed what is reasonably necessary, and had to take place within the civil administrative and judicial frame-work. In Kitson's experience (which included the *Malayan emergency and *Mau Mau uprising), the civil authorities invariably underestimated the threat posed by subversive movements. Military aid was always hampered by depend-ence on police forces that had by definition already failed (otherwise the army would not have been required) but which would have to be reconstructed if a stable pacifica-tion was to be achieved. The crucial problem that Kitson dealt with was how to involve the army more closely with-out pushing the conflict over the brink into outright war. The answer lay in systematic civil-military co-operation at all administrative levels (historically, difficult to achieve) and the development of more effective *counter-insurgency techniques by the army. In particular the army would have to throw itself wholeheartedly into the burdensome task of *intelligence-gathering, which offered the only prospect of linking 'background' with 'contact' information to make engagement with the insurgent forces possible. The point of the concept 'low intensity' was that such operations would depend on the energy and initiative of small units, and indeed every individual soldier, in a way that regular operations did not. Whether the phrase 'low intensity' pre-cisely expressed Kitson's complex and sophisticated model may perhaps be doubted. When the term eventually crossed the Atlantic it was in the significantly different phrase 'low-intensity conflict', with the implication that it was defined in terms of the weight of weaponry employed (on a spec-trum ranging through 'medium' to 'high' intensity, the lat-ter being nuclear war) rather than what may be called the politicized use of violence   CT

Corr, Edwin G., and Sloan, Stephen, *Low-Intensity Conflict: Old Threats in a New World* (Boulder, Colo., 1992).

Kitson, Frank, *Low Intensity Operations: Subversion, Insurgency and Peacekeeping* (London, 1971).

Ludendorff, Gen Erich von (1865–1937), a personally violent and abrasive officer whose bulldozer skill in mili-tary operations and organization paved the way, at horrific cost, for the realization of his strategic ideal of *total war and militarized, mass politics in the industrial age. Born of bourgeois background and commissioned into the infantry, Ludendorff soon made his reputation in the Prussian *gen-eral staff. From 1904 until 1913, he served in the mobiliza-tion and operations department, the section which he headed from 1908 until 1913. He participated in *Moltke 'the Younger''s modifications to the *Schlieffen plan, as well as helping to draft the laws and operational procedures re-quired to increase the size of the army in the years prior to war. He soon saw such plans become a reality. As DCOS of the Second Army in the German operation against Belgium he assumed a field command in the siege of *Liège, after which Moltke shifted him to the *eastern front to become COS of the Eighth Army under *Hindenburg. Together they turned back the Russian armies invading East Prussia at *Tannenberg and the *Masurian Lakes.

His strategic and operational successes in the east led him into conflict with the Army COS *Falkenhayn over the centre of gravity of German strategy. Once the latter was broken by failure at *Verdun, Hindenburg and Ludendorff were appointed to assume supreme command of the army in August 1916. Ludendorff emerged as a national figure with an unprecedented impact on the face of war and the character of German society until 1918 and beyond. His re-vamping of tactics, operations, and *doctrine adjusted battlefield practice to the realities of *trench warfare with modern weapons. Simultaneously, his reforms of the home front vastly increased supplies of munitions and *matériel*, and he put in hand such measures as the 'Hindenburg Pro-gramme' of munitions, an economic super-agency for the mobilization of all sectors of society for war work. The Russian collapse, starting in 1917 and helped along by his dispatch of *Lenin to Petrograd (formerly and now St Petersburg), seemed to reward his efforts. However, an-other aspect of total war, unrestricted submarine warfare, caused the USA to enter the war and to a degree negate suc-cess in the east.

The reorganized German war machine was hurled west in the *Ludendorff offensive of 1918, which achieved great tactical success but not the necessary breakthrough. He suffered a loss of nerve amounting to a nervous breakdown and left the stage already blaming the politicians for his fail-ures. Emerging from the chaos of defeat and Swedish exile, Ludendorff became a prolific author of apologia for the way he had waged war, while wallowing in the maelstrom of *völkisch*, militarist Bavarian politics. His brief, violent alli-ance with *Hitler and the National Socialists ended blood-ily in the Munich putsch in November 1923, where he appears to have been the only one not to take cover. There-after he withdrew from active political life to devote himself to verbose political, strategic, and cosmological writings until his death in 1937.   DA

Ludendorff offensive (1918), Germany's final bid for victory on the western front between 21 March and 15 July;

officially code-named MICHAEL. In fact, the offensive was divided into a series of smaller operations: Army Group Crown Prince Rupprecht opened the campaign with an advance on both sides of the Scarpe river (MARS); Gen Otto von Below's Seventeenth Army pushed toward Bapaume (MICHAEL I); Gen Georg von der Marwitz's Second Army advanced south-west from Cambrai (MICHAEL II); and Gen Oskar von Hutier's Eighteenth Army drove forward on both sides of St Quentin (MICHAEL III). Gen Hans von Boehn's Seventh Army was held in reserve south of the Oise river. It was primarily an infantry operation as the Germans were outnumbered in aircraft (4,500 to 3,670), guns (18,500 to 14,000), trucks (100,000 to 23,000), and especially tanks (800 to 10).

*Ludendorff, holding the post of 1st QMG and effectively in charge of the whole German war effort, was convinced that unrestricted submarine warfare had failed to defeat Great Britain and that Germany had used up its last manpower reserves. On 11 November 1917 he decided to play his 'last card', that is, 'to deliver an annihilating blow to the British before American aid can become effective'. He selected 44 full-strength 'mobile' divisions for MICHAEL, and equipped them with the best available machine guns, trench *mortars, and *flame-throwers; he also shifted more than 40 largely reserve divisions from Russia to France. The assault forces were trained in infiltration tactics according to Capt Hermann Geyer's manual, *The Attack in Position Warfare*, and patterned on Capt Willy Rohr's *storm troops. No deep strategic/operational design lay behind MICHAEL. Instead, Ludendorff opted simply to 'punch a hole' into the Allied line. 'For the rest, we shall see.'

The western front erupted in a hurricane of thunder and fire at 04.00 on 21 March as 6,608 guns and 3,534 trench mortars announced the opening of MICHAEL. Five hours later, 76 German divisions assaulted the Allied lines between Arras and La Fère. By the third day, they had opened a 50 mile (80 km) gap in the Allied lines and were heading into open fields. In the process they sent *Gough's Fifth Army reeling and drove the British 40 miles (64 km) behind the Somme. During the next three days, the Germans advanced another 20 miles (32 km). *Haig's armies were pushed back behind the Somme battlefield of 1916 and special 'Paris guns' with a range of 75 miles (121 km) shelled the French capital. But Ludendorff failed to sever the British from the French and on 28 March Gen John J. *Pershing reluctantly agreed to release American formations to plug the holes in the Allied lines.

Ludendorff had asked too much of his troops and MICHAEL degenerated into position warfare north of the Somme. Starving German troops all too often had stopped the advance to raid rich Allied supply depots. They became demoralized as victory receded from view. Nonetheless, Ludendorff mounted five more assaults: against Arras (29 March), the Lys river (9 April), the Chemin des Dames (27 May), the Oise river (9 June), and Rheims (15 July). In the

meantime, the Allies had appointed *Foch C-in-C of the Allied armies in France. On 18 July Foch launched a counter-attack near Villers-Cotterêts that caught the Germans unprepared. Allied forces quickly ruptured the German front and penetrated deep behind the lines, while Allied aircraft mercilessly strafed the retreating Germans.

This second battle of the *Marne formally ended the German advance in France. Step by step, they fell back upon the *Hindenburg Line. Cases of *desertion skyrocketed. Some soldiers openly refused to obey orders; entire units lost any sense of discipline; others wildly fired their weapons out of moving trains; countless thousands simply surrendered to the Allies. The German army had given its all for MICHAEL. Skeletal divisions manned by badly clothed and undernourished soldiers and powered by emaciated horses had driven the best-equipped and best-fed armies of Britain and the empire, France, and the USA back to the very gates of Paris. Yet all they had achieved, in the words of the German official history of the war, were 'ordinary victories'. Nowhere had they possessed sufficient manpower to turn it into the extraordinary breakthrough that Germany required.   HHH

Herwig, Holger H., *The First World War: Germany and Austria-Hungary 1914–1918* (London, 1997).

Luger (Pistole 08). This automatic pistol was known to its users as the P 08 or, from the name of its *cartridge, the Parabellum: the term Luger is Anglo-American. Designed by George Luger in 7.62 mm calibre in 1899, it was adopted by the Germans in 9 mm in 1908. It was produced in many versions, including a long-barrelled artillery model which took a detachable shoulder stock and a 32-round drum magazine, but the most usual had an 8-round magazine and a 102 mm barrel.

The Luger had several defects. Its working parts, pulled back by a toggle mechanism on top of the action, allowed dirt and moisture to enter; its trigger-pull was irredeemably rough; and it was not well suited to mass manufacture. It was phased out in 1943, but lives on, especially on the screen, as the quintessential German pistol of the two world wars.   RH

Walter, John, *The Luger Story: The Standard History of the World's Most Famous Handgun* (London, 1965).

Lusitania, sinking of the (1915) At 32,000 tons, the RMS *Lusitania* was the flagship passenger liner of the Cunard Line. A floating luxury hotel, she was the fastest and largest liner on the transatlantic run. While crossing from New York to Southampton on 7 May 1915, she was hit off the southern coast of Ireland by a lone torpedo fired without warning, and sank within twenty minutes. She took with her 1,192 passengers and crew, including 128 then-neutral Americans. Both Germany and Great Britain exploited the event for their own ends, for at stake was US intervention in WW I. Germany emphasized that newspaper advertisements in the USA had warned passengers of the perils of sailing in wartime, but more importantly that *Lusitania* had virtually exploded on being hit, as though she was carrying ammunition. Great Britain highlighted the fact that U-20 had fired without warning and that nearly 2,000 civilians had died, especially neutral citizens. *Lusitania* was in fact carrying a small quantity of ammunition, which in theory made her a legitimate naval target, but recent marine archaeology suggests that it was coal dust in her near-empty bunkers, triggered by the torpedo, that blew a cavernous hole in her side.   APC-A

Lützen, battle of (1632). *Gustavus Adolphus caught up with the imperial army under *Wallenstein entrenched at Lützen on 16 November. The latter had split his force, sending the best of his cavalry under *Pappenheim to Halle, and Gustavus seized the opportunity. The ground around Lützen was flat on either side of a road running east to west, with a ditch on the northern side, and further north there were three large windmills. Wallenstein had drawn up his forces, some 12,000–15,000 strong, between the road and the windmills, with a large body of *camp followers in the rear to give the impression of greater numbers. Gustavus came up to the south of the road. Both armies faced each other from 08.00 until about 10.00, while the artillery kept up a harassing fire. Gustavus opened the proceedings leading an attack with his right-wing cavalry, breaking the imperial horse, driving them through their own guns, and panicking the camp followers in the rear. On the opposite flank the imperial *Croatian cavalry, covered by *smoke from the burning village of Lützen, conducted a spirited attack against *Bernhard of Saxe-Weimar's men.

Sometime after midday, and accounts disagree as to the exact time, Pappenheim rejoined the army, summoned by an urgent despatch from the beleaguered Wallenstein. His *cuirassiers plunged into the thick of the fray at once, driving the Swedes pell-mell back across the ditch and road. Pappenheim was shot and killed and Gustavus's horse was seen careering about the field riderless. When the Swedes learned that their king was down, they boiled forward in an unstoppable attack. After dark, Gustavus was found dead from a number of wounds, which made it an excessively expensive victory.   TM

Lyautey, Marshal Louis Hubert Gonsalve (1854–1934). Lyautey was born to well-to-do parents in Nancy, and traced his roots to the Norman nobility. Commissioned into the cavalry, he led a conventional career of regimental and staff appointments, enlivened by fashionable social and political contacts. Ambitious but disappointed in an army which seemed to be moving too slowly, in 1891 he published an article on the social role of the officer in the influential *Revue des deux mondes*. He complained of an officer corps which had not adapted to universal military service and whose members knew their horses better than their men. Lyautey saw the army as the one genuinely national institution that could unite all Frenchmen.

In 1894 he was posted to Indochina and came under the spell of *Gallieni, working to elevate his plan for military pacification into a broader scheme which would reconcile narrow colonialism with his own idealism and patriotism. In an article published in 1900 he described the colonial role of the officer as more than purely military: he was administrator, farmer, and engineer. Colonialism, he argued, led to progress, and it was best achieved through collaboration with indigenous élites to establish a gentle but civilizing protectorate. He saw the colonial army as much more than simply a French army in the colonies: it needed to be free of metropolitan bureaucracy to get on with its own essential tasks.

In 1903 Lyautey was appointed to command a military district on Algeria's border with *Morocco, where he attempted 'economic penetration' by setting up posts which were designed to become local trading centres. However, the experiment was not wholly successful. His irregular *Goums had mixed results in the struggle against dissidents, and he was driven to use reprisal raids, the *razzias* that had traditionally formed part of warfare in North Africa. When France decided to annex Morocco he was appointed her resident-general there, and continued his attempt to achieve 'a fraternal union between two peoples to vanquish sterility and misery'. Such was his charm, diplomacy, and essential humanity—with a good leavening of solid military skill—that he brought stability to Morocco. However, the results of French annexation were mixed, and if local leaders profited from it not all citizens did: even Lyautey could not prevent Abd el Krim's very damaging Rif rebellion in 1925. Appointed marshal in 1921, Lyautey is rightly regarded as the most distinguished of France's colonial soldiers.   RH

M is the model designation (followed by the date) of weapons originally employed by the US armed forces, and the practice continues in the German and other armies today.

The US government created national armouries at Springfield and Harpers Ferry in 1794. In 1795 Springfield began production of the Model 1795 musket. This was the first standard government issue firearm and the beginning of the long tradition of US military *small arms manufacture. US military weapons were usually referred to according to the year they entered service, such as the Model 1842 musket for example. However, this method of classification was not absolutely uniform, as weapons were also named by their calibre and place of manufacture, such as the .58 calibre Springfield rifle musket, the standard weapon of the Union army of the *American civil war.

The practice became more uniform by the 20th century. So when the US army was re-equipped with a new Springfield rifle in 1903 it was officially known as the Magazine Rifle Caliber .30 Model of 1903, but this was usually abbreviated to Model 1903 or simply M-1903. The famous .45 Colt Automatic Pistol of 1911 was technically known as the Pistol Automatic Caliber .45, M-1911. The custom of identifying a model of weapon by the year it entered service persisted until a new generation of weapons introduced from about 1930 were classified even more simply. The first self-loading rifle ever to be accepted for military service was an extraordinarily successful design called the Rifle Caliber .30, M-1. The Garand, as it was almost universally known after its designer, gave excellent service from 1932 until 1957 when it was replaced by the M-14, which was little more than a M-1 Garand updated to take a new 20-round box magazine and a selective fire mechanism.

The M-14, although popular with the troops, was a heavy, bulky weapon firing a large 7.62 mm *cartridge. As the US army found itself embroiled in jungle warfare, it became obvious that a lighter rifle was needed. They turned to a commercial design, the Armalite AR-15 which introduced the 5.56 mm cartridge and which, under the designation M-16, entered service in 1961. The weapon had performed well in tests and troops were told when issued with the M-16 that it was so efficient it did not require cleaning. But the propellant in the early 5.56 mm ammunition left a sticky residue that when cooled became solid and jammed the mechanism, especially the bolt head. Under normal circumstances this fouling would have been serious enough, but with the lack of cleaning it was a disaster. As a result of complaints during the early years of the *Vietnam war and after a congressional investigation, a rigorous cleaning regime was introduced and a manual bolt closure device was added to the rifle in 1966. These problems overcome, the M-16 became an excellent service rifle, light, easy to handle, and capable of producing high volumes of fire. It has been the standard US assault rifle for over thirty years, has sold widely, and is particularly popular with *special forces worldwide. The M-16A2 has recently entered service with a heavier barrel to take the NATO 5.56 mm SS109 cartridge.

The M designation in the USA also lost all connection with date or calibre for other weapons: the M-1A1 is a main battle tank, while the M-109 and M-110 are 155 mm and 203 mm *howitzers respectively.   MCM

MacArthur, Gen Douglas (1880–1964). MacArthur began his career in the US army with an enviable military pedigree. His father retired as the army's senior general and had won a Congressional Medal of Honor during the *American civil war. Commissioned from *West Point as top of his year (1903) into the prestigious Engineers, he served on the staff in the Philippines, where his father had been civil and military C-in-C during the *Philippines insurrection, and was later appointed ADC to Pres Theodore Roosevelt. He came to prominence as the commander of the 42nd (National Guard) Division during the closing months of WW I, having also served as the Rainbow Division's COS and a brigade commander. A brigadier general in 1918, he was an extremely influential commandant of West Point in the 1920s and by 1930 he was a full general and US army COS. That he was an extremely bright and zealous officer there is no doubt, but the key to his accelerated promotion in the inter-war years was his supreme self-confidence, spilling over into arrogance. He collected around him bright young staff officers (including *Eisenhower), and courted media attention. In 1935 he returned to the Philippines and notionally retired from the US army in order to accept the post of field marshal and director of national defence in the newly created commonwealth.

With war threatening, MacArthur formally returned to US service in July 1941, but like everyone else he was caught by surprise by Pearl Harbor and simultaneous, crippling air attacks in the Philippines. In the Japanese invasion that followed, he was hampered by the inadequate spending of the 1930s on the local defence force, and the best he could manage was a delaying action while withdrawing to the Bataan peninsula. On being appointed Supreme Allied Commander South-West Pacific in February 1942, MacArthur was ordered to escape to Australia by Franklin Roosevelt and made his famous 'I shall return' pledge. He felt sidelined by the 'Germany first' priority in WW II, but employed his distinct blend of charm, flamboyance, insubordination, and contemptuous manipulation on politicians, the media, and superior officers to get his way.

It must be borne in mind that during the *Pacific campaign he was not only competing for resources with the European theatre, but also with the US navy's drive across the central Pacific. From his HQ in Brisbane, MacArthur first launched a counter-offensive in New Guinea, and then embarked on an economical 'island-hopping' advance that bypassed areas of strong Japanese concentration such as Rabaul, leaving them to wither on the vine. In this he made good use of *intelligence deriving from the blind faith of the Japanese in their *Enigma machine enciphering systems. It may at first have been dictated by a shortage of troops and amphibious craft, but it was a bold strategy that paid off handsomely not only in terms of objectives achieved with minimal casualties, but also in making sure his theatre and the army in the Pacific did not become relegated to backwater consideration.

Both *Nimitz and the Joint Chiefs of Staff argued, correctly, that the Philippine island chain had no strategic value and should be bypassed. But MacArthur had a promise to redeem, a humiliation to avenge, and a paternal legacy to live up to, and his essentially political arguments trumped the military concentration of forces argument.

Preceded by a swarm of *photographers, he waded ashore at Leyte in October 1944 and scored a great publicity and morale victory in the USA, while the US navy was less photogenically pounding the Japanese fleet into scrap when it tried to ambush the landing. Roosevelt, who never liked him, nonetheless went with the flow and made him a five-star general of the army along with Eisenhower two months later.

Nominated Supreme Commander Allied Powers for the invasion of Japan, revenge was sweet on 2 September 1945, when he received the Japanese *capitulation on board the USS *Missouri* in Tokyo Bay. But there was nothing petty or vindictive about his role in the resettlement and reconstruction of Japan as Allied commander of the occupation during 1945–51, when he became *shogun in all but name, a role to which his autocratic nature and imperial bearing were particularly well suited.

The last, unexpected chapter in his military career came with the *Korean war when, long past retirement age, he was called upon to take command of UN forces to repel the invasion of the South by the Russian and Chinese-backed North Koreans. He fought a holding action while building up forces around *Pusan, then struck at the overextended North Korean lines of communication with the daring landing at *Inchon. The North Korean army dissolved and he drove north, under orders to create the conditions for a unified Korea after democratic elections. He was not alone in discounting Chinese warnings, but bears the main responsibility for the fact that they managed to insert a very large army between the two prongs of his advance and send them both reeling. This time his cavalier attitude towards the concentration of forces had been severely punished, and although the troops under his command rallied to hold South Korea, he did not take it well.

He also overplayed his hand with his C-in-C, Pres *Truman, thinking that he could obey the orders that suited him and, as always, use the media to get the ones he disliked changed. Among the latter was a prohibition on the public discussion of extending the war to China and the mention of *nuclear weapons, both of which MacArthur broached in a press conference not long after returning from meeting the president in Guam, where he patronized him abominably. Truman had no doubts about his authority and summarily sacked him. His last public act was a shamelessly tear-jerking speech at a joint session of Congress where he promised to 'fade away'. This he did, mainly because his political ambitions found no resonance in the Republican party, which had the far more popularly appealing Eisenhower in its sights.

MacArthur was a towering figure in the US army, in the Pacific theatre of WW II, in post-war Japan, and in the Korean war. That the manner in which he departed public life was somewhat undignified does not diminish his stature nor detract from his many achievements.

APC-A/HEB

James, Clayton, *The Years of MacArthur*, 3 vols. (New York, 1970–85).

Hastings, Max, *The Korean War* (London, 1987).

Manchester, William, *American Caesar* (New York, 1978).

McClellan, Maj Gen George Brinton (1826–85), Union commander in the *American civil war. McClellan graduated second in his class from *West Point and served as an engineer, winning two brevets in the *Mexican war, before transferring to the cavalry. An observer in the *Crimean war, he designed a new cavalry saddle on his return. He resigned in 1857 to become a railway engineer, and was president of the Ohio and Mississippi Railroad when war broke out. Appointed a volunteer brigadier general in April 1861 and a regular major general a month later, he assumed command of the Department of the Ohio and quickly secured west Virginia. Posted to what was to become the Army of the Potomac, demoralized by defeat at first *Bull Run, he reorganized it and restored its confidence.

McClellan succeeded *Scott as general-in-chief in November, but proved reluctant to attack until pressed by *Lincoln. His *amphibious Jamestown peninsular campaign, brilliant in conception and potentially war-ending both in terms of the numbers under his command and their location so close to the Confederate capital, was undone by a caution bordering on paralysis. Extending a flank to reach out to a secondary Union advance from the north under McDowell, he was checked at Seven Pines, sat still for three weeks, and was then driven back to the water's edge by *Lee during the *Seven Days battles, showing a skill in retreat conspicuously absent from his hesitant advance to contact. His failure left Union hopes riding on the sagging shoulders of Pope, whose advance from the north was resoundingly repelled at second *Bull Run. When Lee followed this by invading Maryland, a copy of his campaign plan fell into the hands of McClellan, now back from the peninsula with much of his army. Such was the Confederate commander's contempt for him that he offered battle at *Antietam, outnumbered nearly two to one and with his back to the Potomac river. Once again McClellan let a golden opportunity slip through his fingers and an exasperated president replaced him with the even less competent *Burnside.

He ran against Lincoln in the 1864 presidential election and was roundly defeated. Handsome and popular, McClellan was extremely self-regarding and was prematurely nicknamed 'Young Napoleon' by an enthusiastic press. In truth he was an excellent organizer and motivator of men; unfortunately for the Union, he seemed to believe that he could win the war mainly by manoeuvre and totally lacked the killer instinct. RH

Macedonian army Until the accession of *Philip II of Macedon in 359 BC, powerful neighbours and internal conflicts had kept Macedonia from achieving its full military potential. During his first five years Philip suppressed the latter and developed the most effective fighting force in the Greek world to coerce the former. Innovation, training, and first-class leadership were the key.

Philip created a solid infantry core for his army in the *phalanx: men with relatively light body *armour wielded a long pike (*sarissa*) and so constituted a mobile hedgehog. The relative cheapness of the equipment meant that large numbers could be recruited, probably on a local basis into regional brigades, while intensive training ensured that the resulting formation was moderately mobile. The royal bodyguard formed the élite infantry element, the Hypaspists; equipped with large shield and spear, like conventional *hoplites, they could protect the flanks of the phalanx in battle and undertake demanding special missions. The army's striking force was provided by the Companion Cavalry, who wielded spears of tough cornel wood.

Their numbers were greatly expanded as Philip acquired good land from the coastal Greek cities to allocate to his followers; units appear to have been recruited locally, with squadrons (*ilai*) attested from Amphipolis, Apollonia, Anthemus, and Bottiaea. Ample money from Thracian mines allowed mercenaries and experts such as siege engineers to be employed as needed. What struck outsiders, like the Athenian Demosthenes, was the rapidity of Philip's actions and his ability to sustain year-round campaigning, quite unlike the Greek cities. The troops were trained to carry the bulk of their own equipment, but not unnecessarily: Philip once commented that he pitched camp to suit the needs of his baggage animals. The mercenaries were kept under tight control (a Tarentine commander was dismissed for taking a warm bath) and *morale was high, since the king set an example in battle and bravery was rewarded.

*Alexander 'the Great' inherited a formidable fighting machine, ready for the conquest of Persia. The perfection of the troops' training was revealed when a display of parade-ground *drill helped to extricate the army from a trap in the Balkan mountains. They were trained to cope with the unusual, whether heavy wagons rolling downhill in Thrace, scythe-chariots at *Arbela, or elephants at the *Hydaspes. Different units were superbly co-ordinated, so that Alexander could withdraw his army under pressure across a river in Illyria by deploying catapults and missile-throwers to cover the retreat of the infantry and cavalry.

The Macedonian army formed the core of his expedition against Persia in 334. He had about 15,000 Macedonian infantry, 3 brigades of Hypaspists, of which one was the formal bodyguard (*agema*), each about 1,000 strong. The main phalanx was organized into 6 brigades, 1,500–2,000 strong; within the brigade the key small-scale unit was the file, sixteen strong (though known as a *decad*), of which the file leader, second- and third-rankers, and rear marker had enhanced status and pay; *decads* were grouped into *lochoi*. The Companion Cavalry was organized into eight squadrons, each of 225–50 men, while there were a further four squadrons of scouts armed with a *sarissa*. Allied troops and mercenaries provided a number of important specialist skills. Among units repeatedly detailed for hard tasks, in company with the Macedonian Hypaspists, were the Agrianian javelin men and Cretan *archers; the contingent of Thessalian cavalry, 1,800 strong in 334, was also of top quality and was awarded the prize for valour at *Issus.

Alexander regularly received reinforcements, collected and dispatched by Antipater in Macedon, but numbers are not fully recorded in the sources (just as there are no figures for losses from sickness or incapacitation through wounds). However, numbers increased to a peak at Arbela with the new recruits being incorporated into existing units. In 331 the cavalry squadrons were subdivided into two units (*lochoi*), perhaps in response to their increasing size but perhaps too with the political motive of undermining the links between regional commanders and local units. In 330 political factors caused further changes in the cavalry command structure: after the elimination of Philotas, who had led the cavalry since 334, command was divided between two Hipparchs, Hephaestion and Clitus; by 326 and the invasion of India the Hipparchs had increased to eight.

The most significant development under Alexander was the progressive incorporation of oriental troops, initially in separate national units, especially cavalry units from Bactria and Sogdiana. He began to introduce orientals into mixed cavalry units, and accorded them the coveted title of Companion. With regard to infantry, Alexander commissioned the recruitment and training in Macedonian ways of 30,000 oriental youths, who arrived at court in 324 to form a new phalanx. At the same time, the Macedonian phalanx was reshaped to incorporate oriental recruits in the inner ranks of each file: the resulting units would have had three *sarissa*-wielding Macedonians at the front and one in the rear, with the central ranks composed of missile-firing easterners. There is no evidence whether this hybrid formation was ever put to the test.

Under *Alexander's successors the Macedonian army lost some of its flexibility. Recruitment caused problems and both Ptolemies and Seleucids had to draft in native troops; these might be extremely competent, but they changed the nature of the army as an élite institution. Reliance was placed on elephants, which Alexander had found easy to counter. The cavalry lost its effectiveness as a strike force, so that the phalanx, whose *sarissas* now reached 18 feet (5.5 metres) in length, became the main aggressive arm: in encounters with Roman armies it remained a formidable sight, but its inflexibility and problems in coping with rough terrain rendered it vulnerable.   LMW

Bosworth, A. B., *Conquest and Empire* (Cambridge, 1988).
Hammond, N. G. L., *The Macedonian State* (Oxford, 1989).

maces. See PERCUSSION WEAPONS.

Machiavelli, Niccolò (1469–1527). Florentine political thinker, writer, and historian, and also military thinker. Although he is popularly known as a scheming political spin doctor of satanic cynicism and subtlety, an examination of Machiavelli's work in the context of the brutal politics of the Italian city states and emerging nation states of the time suggests he was merely an accomplished practitioner and advocate of realpolitik. His best-known works are *The Prince* (1513–16), and *The Discourses* (1513–19). His *Art of War* (1519–20) seems to have arisen from the *Discourses*, and from 1520 Machiavelli became preoccupied with the *Florentine History*. *The Prince*, by far the most famous, was written to gain the attention of the Medici, rulers of Florence, after Machiavelli had been dismissed from the civil service jobs—one of them that of secretary to the committee responsible for military and diplomatic affairs—he held from 1498 to 1512. It includes three short sections on military organization, dismissing *mercenaries and composite armies as 'useless' and advocating a citizens' militia. 'The first way to lose your state', he tells the Prince, 'is to neglect the art of war; the first way to win a state is to be skilled in the art of war.'

His *Discourses* on Livy (see ROMAN MILITARY HISTORIANS), which inevitably included Roman military organization, led to the *Art of War*. A great admirer of the Romans, Machiavelli asked what had changed since Roman times which might make their exemplary military organization obsolete. There was only one real candidate: *gunpowder, and the most charitable view of Machiavelli's *Art of War* is that it was the first-ever attempt to wrestle with the results of a technological *military revolution. The book takes the form of a civilized dialogue between a group of prosperous citizens and a renowned professional soldier, Fabrizio Colonna, in the garden of Cosimo Rucellai. The superiority of citizen armies over mercenaries is asserted, and Machiavelli dismisses artillery on the battlefield as an ineffectual nuisance, which can only fire one salvo, usually inaccurately, before it is overwhelmed. Therefore, Machiavelli concludes, artillery does not prevent modern armies following the well-tried methods and close formations of ancient times. He favours swordsmen, who move nimbly among *pikemen and cut them to pieces. In all this, history proved him wrong. The French had won Marignano in 1515 with firearms, and the Spanish had developed the *tercio, with pikes and firearms only. None of Machiavelli's recommendations bore any relation to the subsequent evolution of weapons and tactics. He deserves recognition, however, for defining the concept of *virtù*, a kind of active citizenship which embodied the willingness to subordinate personal safety and interest to the good of the state. *Engels thought Machiavelli was the 'first military writer of the new epoch'. He was partly right, for if Machiavelli's regard for classical antiquity made him backward-looking, his notion of *virtù* has formed an important component of morale to the present day.   CDB

Machiavelli, Niccolò, *The Chief Works and Others*, trans A. Gilbert (Duke, NC, 1965).

Anglo, Sidney, *Machiavelli* (London, 1969).

Oman, Sir Charles, *The Art of War in the 16th Century* (London, 1937).

machine guns The concept of a gun able to fire multiple shots rapidly and without constant reloading is as old as the history of firearms in warfare and was experimented with throughout firearms' early history. Volley guns, with multiple barrels arranged in parallel, in a fan shape, or in a tubular cluster were the best that the *flintlock and muzzle-loading age could produce, and it rapidly became clear that the best multiple-shot gun would have to be a form of breech-loader. As with the history of *breech-loading weapons, the invention of the self-contained *cartridge proved to be a conclusive milestone in the development of machine guns since, while the percussion system lent itself better than did the flintlock system to multiple shots, it was still severely limited.

A combination of the percussion cap and self-contained cartridge was utilized in a variety of American-designed hand-cranked early machine guns invented in the 1850s and 1860s, perhaps the most successful being Wilson Agar's 'coffee-mill', 50 of which were bought and used by the Union army during the *American civil war for the defence of Washington; its nickname was derived from the hopper atop the weapon from which were fed steel tubes filled with powder and ball and primed with percussion caps—essentially reloadable cartridges. Agar's 'coffee-mill' gun was superseded by the far more effective *Gatling gun, invented in 1861 and used in limited quantities, and in defensive positions during the war. Like the Agar gun, and like all machine guns for the next 30 years, the Gatling was operated by a hand-crank. Unlike the single-barrelled Agar, the Gatling had six barrels arranged around a central core; these revolved as the crank was operated and cartridges were chambered, fired, and extracted one barrel at a time.

Prior to the invention of the automatic firing machine gun by *Maxim in the 1890s, most inventors experimented with multi-barrelled hand-cranked weapons. Aside from the well-known Gatling, other hand-cranked machine guns included the Gardner gun, invented by William Gardner of Toledo, Ohio; the Lowell gun, invented by De Witt Farrington of Lowell, Massachusetts; and the Nordenfelt gun, invented by a Swedish engineer, Heldge Palmcranz, but financed by a Swedish banker, Thorsten Nordenfelt. The Gardner gun initially featured two side-by-side barrels contained in a tube and was fed vertically from a tall clip atop the chamber, the rounds being inserted, fired, and extracted by a hand-turned crankshaft; it was adopted with some success by the Royal Navy in the 1880s. The Lowell gun was four-barrelled with a feed similar to that of the Gardner but, despite small sales to Russia and the US navy, was never

successful. The Nordenfelt generally featured ten side-by-side barrels, although combinations of two to twelve barrels existed too; it was gravity-fed from a hopper, operated by a crank and lever, and capable of firing 100 rounds per minute per barrel—1,000 rounds per minute from the ten-barrelled version. The Nordenfelt was manufactured in a large variety of calibres and adopted by the Royal Navy in two versions: five-barrelled .45 inch for anti-personnel use and four-barrelled 1 inch calibre for defence against torpedo boats. Britain's Royal Navy thus made use of three types of hand-cranked machine gun in the 1870–90 period: the Gatling, the Gardner, and the Nordenfelt. Significantly, they were used aggressively and defensively.

Across the English Channel, similar developments in multi-barrelled weapons in Belgium and France resulted in the invention of the *mitrailleuse, perfected by the Belgian Joseph Montigny and sold to the French government. Originally a 37-barrelled weapon, it was later refined to 25 barrels and was capable either of firing all its barrels almost simultaneously or firing them slowly: it all depended upon the speed at which its crank was operated. But it was sited and used as field *artillery during the *Franco-Prussian war and was not a success in this role, many being destroyed by German counter-battery fire. But when a single mitrailleuse was used as an infantry support weapon at the battle of *Rezonville/Gravelotte, it caused over 2,600 Prussian casualties, or more than 50 per cent of the troops opposing it: the Prussians may have learned more lessons than the French from this experience. France also adopted the *Hotchkiss 37 mm revolving cannon in the 1880s, as did the navies of Denmark, Germany, Greece, the Netherlands, and Russia. This weapon operated similarly to the Gatling and had also been an American invention successful in the European arms race of the late 19th century.

The 1880s were the decade of transformation for the machine gun and, as with the Gatling and—to a lesser extent—the Hotchkiss, it was a transformation wrought by an American but adopted successfully in Europe. Hiram *Maxim (1840–1915) was born in Maine of Huguenot stock and was a successful and versatile inventor in the USA before settling in England in the early 1880s. The machine gun which came to bear his name was developed by him between 1883 and 1885 and demonstrated by him, using the .45 inch drawn brass *Martini-Henry rifle cartridge, to British staff officers in 1885. His machine gun was fully automatic in that it utilized the recoil power of the barrel and its attached sliding breech-block, generated by the blast from the fired cartridge, to eject the empty cartridge case, chamber a new cartridge, and cock and fire the weapon. Once initially cocked and fired, the gun would then continue to fire, except when interrupted by the very rare jam, until the gunner's finger was released from the trigger. Capable of firing 600 rounds per minute, the Maxim's single barrel was encased in an oil-filled cooling jacket and the rate of fire harnessed to the rate of oil flow so that the barrel could not overheat and distort. Chambered for the .303 rifle cartridge, Maxim's machine guns were adopted by the British in 1889 and first issued to infantry battalions in 1891. By 1899 Germany had adopted them, as had Russia: both nations manufactured them under licence and Russia first employed its Maxims with devastating effect in the *Russo-Japanese war. Britain's combat use of the Maxim was necessarily confined to colonial wars against less well-equipped opponents and accounts of the slaughter they inflicted exist from the Gambian campaign of 1887, through the Matabele war of 1893–4, to the Chitral campaign on the *North-West frontier in 1895 and at *Omdurman. Both the British and their enemies used Maxims in the Second *Boer War of 1899–1902, a conflict less easily won by the British.

Maxim's machine guns did not suffer from lack of competition. Other automatic systems were developed almost contemporaneously, notably by John Moses Browning (1855–1926), whose gas-operated machine gun—which used barrel combustion gases to effect what in the case of the Maxim was effected by recoil—was perfected by Colt in 1895. In the same year Hotchkiss developed a gas-operated machine gun invented by an Austrian; it was adopted by the French army in 1897. In Austria Skoda developed a machine gun in 1888 on the 'blowback' principle; its breech was blown back by propellent gases, ejected the spent cartridge, and rammed a fresh one into the breech. By the end of the 19th century, therefore, the three principal automatic firing systems had been developed into operating machine guns available to or adopted by those nations who would be the main combatants fourteen years later during WW I: recoil, gas-operated, and blowback.

Problems which remained with machine guns were centred upon weight and thus manoeuvrability, versatility, and battlefield role. In 1914 both Britain and Germany went to war with versions of the Maxim: the British *Vickers Mk.I and the German MaschineGewehr (MG) Modell 1908. The Vickers weighed 34 lb (15.4 kg) and the MG 08 44 lb (19.9 kg), without their tripod mountings and other equipment, including such essential features as the ammunition belts. While both guns proved devastatingly effective, and the British learned several hard lessons in the role of machine guns in the relatively static warfare of the trenches, both were limited in their tactical value by their weight and, to an extent, by their need to be operated by a team. Light machine guns were quickly developed, the British adopting the Lewis and the Germans modifying the MG 08 in 1915 by fitting a shoulder stock and bipod and redesignating it the MG 08/15. Both weapons, although lighter than the Vickers or MG 08, were still heavy and both were operated more effectively if the gunner was accompanied by a loader.

The French army adopted both the Chauchat and the Hotchkiss and both, particularly the former, were issued to the US army in Europe after 1917. In the USA Browning continued the development of machine guns, eventually producing the Model 1917 water-cooled heavy machine gun

which came into land service in France in 1918; it was derived from a gas-operated machine gun developed for aircraft use. Aircraft during WW I generally mounted lightened and air-cooled versions of machine guns developed for land use, with—as appropriate—their cyclic rate modified to be interrupted in order for them to be fired through the arc of the propeller. The lightened Lewis machine gun was particularly popular as an observer's weapon, fitted on co-axial mounts, in the rudimentary turrets of light and heavy RAF bombers.

Lessons learnt by the Prussian army in its war with France 1870–1 underlie the debate which occupied European military thought in the 1880–1918 period over the tactical use of the machine gun. It was clearly ineffective when used as artillery, and only the German army of 1914 seems to have understood the enormous defensive capabilities of the machine gun when used to provide cones of intersecting fire which were all but impassable by advancing troops. As the supreme defensive weapon, the machine gun effectively created the stalemate of *trench warfare, before being itself countered by the tank.

Developments in machine guns since 1918 have focused upon questions of weight and power. Both became increasingly relevant as wars of swift movement involving ground–air co-operation replaced the brief experience of relatively static conflict of 1914–18. High-powered machine guns were developed for aircraft use, most importantly the American .50 inch Browning—which was used in fighters' wings, in the turrets and fuselages of bombers, and mounted on the turrets of tanks. Armour-piercing ammunition was also introduced for machine guns. Germany led the way with the development of both light and *sub-machine guns, adopting the MaschineGewehr 1934 (MG 34) a year after Hitler's assumption of power. The arms race of the late 1930s produced that great friend of the British soldier, the Bren gun: a light machine gun developed from a Czech design, chambered for the .303 British rifle cartridge and weighing only 22 lb (9.9 kg). The German MG 34 was replaced after 1942 by Mauser's MG 42, a gas piston-operated light machine gun firing 1,200 rounds per minute and notable for both its cheapness—being manufactured from mass-produced pressed steel components—and its adaptability. A paratroop version was designated the FallschirmGewehr, or FG, 42 and the MG 42's descendants are still in use worldwide. Most nations now have a version of light machine guns developed during the 1940s and differences between them are small and matters of detail. There remains a role for the heavy machine gun, often the tried and tested .50 inch Browning and its derivatives. The general purpose machine gun, or GPMG (of which the German MG 34 was the first), has been increasingly developed to bridge the gap between the heavy and light machine gun. Modern tendencies have leant towards light machine guns which are nearer to bipod-mounted assault rifles or personal weapons than machine guns in the traditional sense.

Aside from the infantryman's use of machine guns, automatic weapons have been developed in the past 40 years for tank and helicopter use. Derivations of the multi-barrelled Gatling principle became the American GE Minigun. 'Chain guns' have been experimented with in both tanks and *helicopters, utilizing electrically driven roller chains to drive the weapons' bolts and achieving high rates of fire.   SCW

Blair, Claude (ed.), *Pollard's History of Firearms* (London, 1983).

Hobart, F. W. A., *Pictorial History of the Machine Gun* (London, 1971).

Hogg, Ian V., *The Complete Machine Gun* (London, 1979).

—— and Weeks, John, *Military Small Arms of the 20th Century* (London, 1985).

Mackensen, FM August von (1849–1945). Mackensen served as a volunteer in the *Franco-Prussian war and was subsequently commissioned into the 1st Hussars. He became its regimental colonel, and even as a general often wore its uniform, with its death's-head badge on the busby. He served on the *eastern front throughout WW I, first as an army, and then as an army group, commander. Ably assisted by Hans von *Seeckt, his COS, he achieved the great breakthrough at Gorlice-Tarnow in May 1915, defeated Serbia, and was overall commander for the defeat and occupation of Romania in 1916.

Promoted field-marshal during the war, after it Mackensen, by then an old man, was paraded by *Hitler in an effort to legitimize National Socialism. He had allegedly boasted of his Scots ancestry before WW I, but after 1939 it was suggested that his name derived from a German village called Mackenhausen. It has been suggested, without any real foundation, that he was actually Maj Gen Hector Macdonald—'Fighting Mac'—a British hero who killed himself in 1903 rather than face *court martial.   RH

Mackinder, Sir Halford (1861–1947), British political geographer, exponent of geopolitics. Mackinder was reader in geography at Oxford, director of the London School of Economics, and a key figure in the creation of the federal University of London. In 1904 he outlined his idea of the 'heartland' in a paper to the Royal Geographical Society. He argued that the greater mobility made possible by *railways had made Asia and eastern Europe (the heartland) the strategic centre of the world island. The heartland stood in opposition to the maritime or oceanic lands, and would triumph. 'Those who control eastern Europe dominate the Heartland: those who rule the Heartland dominate the World Island (that is, Eurasia): those who rule the World Island dominate the world.' Mackinder's views clashed with the US strategist Alfred Thayer Mahan, whose views on the importance of sea power supported the idea that the oceanic powers would win any conflict. WW I tended to support Mahan, and Mackinder shifted his views. In 1924 he first mooted the idea of the Atlantic community, one of a number of 'regional organizations' of minor powers. Two years after his death, the idea came into reality, with NATO. His work, of course, is of great interest to the Russians.
CDB

MacMahon, Marshal M. E. P. M., Duc de Magenta (1808–93). Like so many other distinguished French soldiers, MacMahon was of Irish ancestry. Commissioned into the infantry from the academy at Saint-Cyr, he rose to fame in *Algeria and commanded a division in the *Crimea. In 1855 he stormed the Malakoff, one of the strongest parts of the defences of Sevastopol, laconically proclaiming 'j'y suis, j'y reste' (here I am, here I stay). In the *Italian campaign of 1859 his corps took the village of Magenta (hence his ducal title) and fought hard at Solferino.

Governor-general of Algeria when the *Franco-Prussian war broke out in 1870, he commanded the superb I Corps, composed of North African troops. Beaten at *Wörth on 6 August he fell back on Châlons with the defeated right wing, reorganizing it, with reinforcements, as the Army of Châlons. Ordered eastwards to relieve *Bazaine at Metz, he was trapped at *Sedan, where his army was destroyed: he was wounded and captured.

In 1871 he organized the Versailles army which recaptured Paris from the *Commune, though he was not responsible for its excesses. He replaced Thiers as president in 1873, largely because monarchists in the National Assembly thought him favourable to their cause. But a pretender visited him in 1874 and was deeply disappointed: he had hoped to find a *constable of France, he remarked, but found only a village policeman. In difficulties with the radical left, he resigned after the republicans won the 1877 elections.

Like many of his comrades in arms MacMahon was formidably brave but had no grasp of the higher art of war. He was famously thick-headed, with the untranslatable punning nickname 'Mac-bête'. The right word often eluded him: when visiting a flooded area he could think of nothing better to say than 'que d'eau' (what a lot of water).   RH

McNamara, Robert Strange (b. 1916), US Secretary of Defense during the war in *Vietnam. Born in San Francisco and educated at Berkeley, McNamara studied and then taught at Harvard University in the early 1940s. After a stint in the US Army Air Corps during WW II, he achieved technocratic fame for his incorporation of systems analysis into management at the Ford Motor Company, where he became president in 1960.

McNamara was appointed Secretary of Defense by John F. Kennedy in 1961 and was closely associated with the think-tank theology that produced MAD (mutually assured destruction) and other attempts to make sense of the *nuclear weapons dilemma (see WOHLSTETTER). But his principal claim to infamy rests on the arrogance of his and other members of the 'best and the brightest' who so totally mismanaged US involvement in South-East Asia. Misled by optimistic military and *intelligence assessments, he initially believed that US participation could be limited to support for the South Vietnamese forces. He soon found himself supervising the deployment of ever-larger US resources, which he and his team of systems analysts attempted to direct from Washington, down to the choice of targets and the bomb loads for individual air strikes. By October 1966 he had reached the blindingly obvious conclusion that the North Vietnamese had adopted 'a strategy of keeping us busy and waiting us out (a strategy of attriting our national will)'. Having no answers to people, his own as well as the Vietnamese, who did not respond according to his mathematical computations, by 1967 he had soured on the war to the point of calling for an immediate bombing halt and a stand-down in ground operations. But by that time he had committed the USA too deeply and wars, unlike investments, cannot simply be walked away from. His resignation made little impact and he went on to further demonstrate his lack of sympathy or understanding for human nature at the World Bank. Recently he has produced his long-awaited *mea culpa* for Vietnam, which unsurprisingly concentrates on the stategic errors for which he was only partially responsible while skating over the ineffable hubris of his attempt to micro-manage the war tactically.

AH/HEB

McNamara, Robert S., with VanDeMark, Brian, *In Retrospect: The Tragedy and Lessons of Vietnam* (New York, 1995).

....

Mafeking, siege of (1899–1900), one of three major sieges that began the Second *Boer War. A British force of about 1,200 (mainly irregulars) under Col *Baden-Powell was besieged at Mafeking, just inside the border of Bechuanaland, by a Boer force of about 7,000 at first. The siege was loosely maintained for 217 days, from 13 October 1899 until relief on 16 May 1900 by a British column under Col B. T. Mahon. Uproarious popular rejoicing in Britain on 'Mafeking Night' accompanied the news and the verb 'to maffik' briefly entered the language. SDB

Pakenham, Thomas, *The Boer War* (London, 1979).

....

magazines (from Fr.: *magasins*) are stores for equipment, provisions, arms, and ammunition. By extention the word also came to mean the usually detachable containers for *cartridges in rapid fire weapons. Although the concentration of provisions for an army in a few places was not new, it came to dominate warfare in Europe following the *Thirty Years War, during which one of the more telling of the innovations introduced by *Gustavus Adolphus had been an integrated logistics system combining pre-stocked warehouses and compact supply trains with orderly requisitioning.

However, his armies had been relatively small. During the 1640s and 1650s the French administrator Michel Le Tellier established the beginnings of a system on a much larger scale, using civilian contractors both to provide supplies to *magasins* and to transport them between stores or in the traditional baggage train with the army. His son the Marquis de *Louvois established larger *magasins généraux* to meet the needs of Louis XIV's huge field armies, and also ensured that the network of frontier fortresses had sufficient supplies to resist a siege for at least six months. Within France this was designed to relieve the local population of the impositions of a large army, while outside her borders the theatres of operations might already be picked clean. The ravaging of the Palatinate at the start of the *League of Augsburg war was intended to deny the area to enemy armies, limiting the number of fronts Louis's armies had to cover.

The degree to which armies were ever completely weaned from foraging can be overstated, not least because of cash limitations in symbiosis with the near-crippling corruption that came to characterize the state's relationship with civilian contractors. But in the absence of a parallel revolution in transport, what the magazine system certainly did was to impose severe strategic limitations. During the League of Augsburg war and for the following century armies rarely ventured more than a week's march from their nearest magazine, and manoeuvres to get across the lines of supply of armies in the field came to be far more common than battles. Accompanying this was the evolution of *siege warfare to capture the impressive fortifications surrounding the larger *magasins généraux*, the loss of which could deny an army the possibility of operating in a given area.

Although more given than many contemporary commanders to the battlefield decision, *Frederick 'the Great' would bring this about by getting across his enemies' lines of supply and once remarked that 'the masterpiece of a successful general is to starve the enemy'. With all their limitations, for as long as fear of *desertion and a totally centralized system of rigid command and control dictated that armies march as one huge unit, magazines were indispensable. It was the advent of the highly motivated *French Revolutionary armies, which could be trusted to disperse for foraging on the march and concentrate for battle, that exposed the strategic and tactical poverty of the older style armies and restored mobility to European warfare. Magazines remained of great importance, but their absolute centrality to the conduct of wars declined. JR-W/HEB

....

Magdeburg, sack of (1631), a widely publicized 'atrocity' during the *Thirty Years War. The imperial Catholic general *Tilly placed the town of Magdeburg, a centre of Lutheranism, under close siege in March 1631, reinforcing *Pappenheim who had been there since the previous November. The imperial force of about 22,000 was resisted by a small force of Swedes commanded by von Falkenburg. The approach of a relief army under *Gustavus Adolphus precipitated the all-out assault of 20 May. After fierce resistance lasting two hours during which von Falkenburg was killed, the town was taken. *Croatian and other *mercenaries serving the emperor ran riot, venting their anger and frustration at the privations they had suffered during the siege and killing thousands. Although this was the custom of the time when a fortress declined to *capitulate, the unusual scale of the slaughter gave rise to the term 'Magdeburg quarter' for merciless killing. In fact, many more inhabitants died in the resulting fire, such that of a population of 30,000 only about 5,000 survived.

Broadsheets describing the horror of Magdeburg were distributed in the capitals of Europe and throughout Germany, to show how the emperor treated his recalcitrant Protestant subjects. This led to widespread revulsion and contributed to the United Provinces and Saxony entering the Thirty Years War.   TM

Maginot Line This much-maligned defensive work was arguably misnamed. André Louis René Maginot (1877–1932) was the most visible, but not the most influential, advocate of static French frontier defences. Wounded at Verdun in 1914, he was unrelentingly hostile to Germany. He opposed the Versailles and Locarno Treaties and voted to send French troops into the Ruhr in 1922. But once Germany began to recover her former strength, as war minister from November 1929 to January 1932 he secured the funding for the frontier defences built between 1930–5 that would bear his name. More credit should have gone to his predecessor Paul Painlevé, who guided the crucial negotiations between the government and a highly sceptical Superior War Council.

Few artefacts of military history have been as misunderstood. Rather than an expression of tactical defensive-mindedness, they were a reflection of military, political, diplomatic, and financial circumstances. France was weaker than Germany and needed to be able to concentrate her armies. True defensive-mindedness would have extended the line along the Belgian frontier to the coast. The overriding aim was to channel rather than stop a German advance, while providing proof that France did not herself intend a war of aggression. Construction also protected while stimulating the economy of Lorraine and Alsace, only recovered from Germany in 1919. Finally, it was the only major military expenditure acceptable to French voters.

When first proposed by Painlevé, most French generals preferred fortified sectors designed to support offensive as well as defensive operations, but there was no political support for turning eastern France into a prepared battlefield. The line would also be cheaper and held out the promise of rendering French soil inviolable. It was not really a line at all, but a state-of-the-art use of military *engineering to prevent any broad invasion, backed up by mobile forces. Extending from Luxembourg to the Swiss border, it was a string of concrete forts spaced at roughly 3 mile (5 km) intervals and separated by smaller casemates. Both types were deeply buried, with only observation domes and gun turrets visible. At least in theory, the forts were screened by advanced warning posts, *anti-armour obstacles, barbed wire, and mines. Their garrisons ranged in size from 12 to 30 men in the casemates and from 200 to 1,200 men in the forts. The latter were virtual subterranean towns equipped with *barracks, kitchens, power plants, *magazines, and even electric railways to transport men and ammunition.

The line was relatively under-gunned. Interval casemates contained only machine guns and a single 47 mm anti-armour gun, the heavy artillery being concentrated in the larger forts. Because they could not be subterranean, there were no anti-aircraft batteries. Notwithstanding its weaknesses, the Maginot Line did indeed deter a direct German attack. When ordered to cease resistance on 25 June 1940, only the small fort at La Ferté, its crew asphyxiated after a ventilation failure, had fallen to enemy action. The other garrisons refused to depart until granted the traditional *honours of war.   ECK

Hughes, Judith M, *To The Maginot Line* (Cambridge, Mass., 1971).
Kemp, Tony, *The Maginot Line* (London, 1981).

Magnesia, battle of (189 BC), Roman victory that ended the Syrian war with the Seleucid King Antiochus III. Antiochus' expedition to Greece had been defeated at Thermopylae in 191. In 190 a Roman army of c.30,000 men under Lucius Cornelius Scipio, accompanied by his brother, *Scipio 'Africanus', crossed the Dardanelles and invaded Asia. They advanced to meet Antiochus' army of 60,000 infantry, 12,000 cavalry, with a force of scythed *chariots and 54 elephants near Magnesia. After eleven days of skirmishing and manoeuvre, in which the Romans gradually moved closer to the Seleucid camp, Antiochus was forced to fight. He stationed his *phalanx in the centre with elephants in the gaps between its units. After the battle had opened with an ineffective charge by the scythed chariots, the main lines clashed. Antiochus, leading his cavalry on the right, achieved a breakthrough, but was driven back by the Roman troops left to guard their camp, supported by a tactical reserve. Elsewhere the Romans had pushed back the Seleucids and soon the entire army was in flight. The Romans claimed to have killed 53,000 of the enemy, and captured 1,400 with 15 elephants, while losing only about 350 themselves.   AKG

Mahdi the honorific (Expected Guide) was Muhammad Ahmad (1844–85), a carpenter and boat-builder by training, which enabled him to travel widely, making contacts and

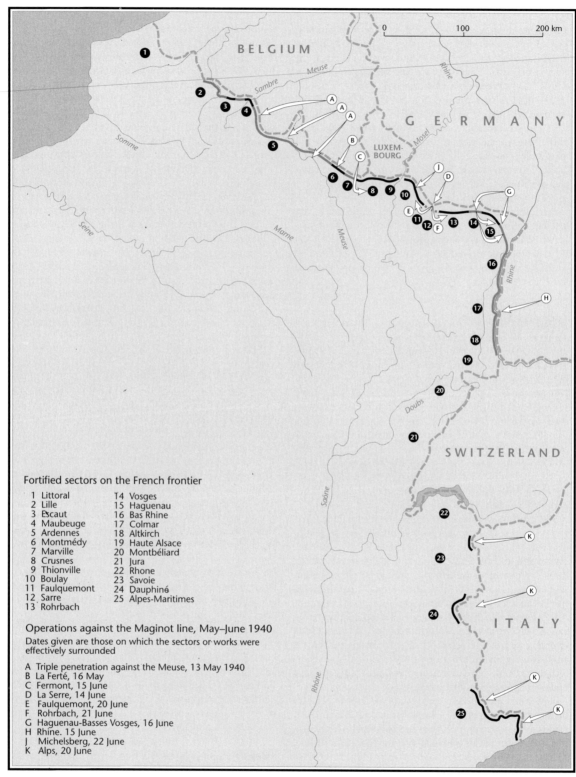

Fortified sectors on the French frontier

1	Littoral	14	Vosges
2	Lille	15	Haguenau
3	Escaut	16	Bas Rhine
4	Maubeuge	17	Colmar
5	Ardennes	18	Altkirch
6	Montmédy	19	Haute Alsace
7	Marville	20	Montbéliard
8	Crusnes	21	Jura
9	Thionville	22	Rhone
10	Boulay	23	Savoie
11	Faulquemont	24	Dauphiné
12	Sarre	25	Alpes-Maritimes
13	Rohrbach		

Operations against the Maginot line, May–June 1940

Dates given are those on which the sectors or works were effectively surrounded

A Triple penetration against the Meuse, 13 May 1940
B La Ferté, 16 May
C Fermont, 15 June
D La Serre, 14 June
E Faulquemont, 20 June
F Rohrbach, 21 June
G Haguenau-Basses Vosges, 16 June
H Rhine. 15 June
J Michelsberg, 22 June
K Alps, 20 June

The **Maginot Line** and operations against it in 1940.

gathering *intelligence. On 29 June 1881 he proclaimed himself 'the Mahdi' and exhorted his followers to wage a *jihad and overthrow the Egyptian authorities. Despite lacking any formal military training, he led his army of devoted followers to a succession of victories in battles and sieges. Although lacking modern weapons or foreign allies, they defeated or killed some 40,000 Egyptian troops, including an expeditionary army of over 10,000 soldiers and camp followers under English Col William Hicks near El Obeid (5 November 1883). The Mahdists also engaged British forces in northern and eastern Sudan, killing Maj Gen *Gordon in the storming of *Khartoum, and gained control over some 1 million square miles (2,590,000 sq km). The Mahdi died on 22 June 1885 before British retaliation made itself felt, but he had laid the foundations of a new state, uniting his people and reforming their religion.   EMS

Holt, P. M., *The Mahdist State in the Sudan 1881–1898* (Oxford, 1958).

Theobald, A. B., *The Mahdiya* (London, 1951).

Maiwand, battle of

Maiwand, battle of (1880). In June 1880, the governor of Herat, Ayub Khan, left Herat with a small army, intent on seizing the throne of Kabul left vacant by the British deposition of his elder brother, Yakub Khan. A British brigade was despatched from Kandahar to intercept him and the two forces met on 27 July 1880, near the village of Maiwand some 45 miles (72 km) west of Kandahar. The British force under Brig Gen Burrows was outnumbered but trusted to the firepower of the *Martini-Henry rifle. But it was also ineptly handled and overwhelmed, suffering casualties of nearly 1,000 killed. The survivors, amounting to some 1,500, retreated in confusion to Kandahar and with the rest of the garrison were besieged there by Ayub Khan until relieved by *Roberts in his famous *Kabul to Kandahar march of August 1880.   BR1

Malakand Field Force

Malakand Field Force The Malakand Pass on the *North-West frontier connects Peshawar with the Swat valley, and was the scene of several revolts in the turbulent history of this rocky frontier area between British India (now Pakistan) and Afghanistan. In 1895, a small force of native troops at Chitral was besieged by a force of Pathan tribesmen caused by the traditional Indian problem of a disputed ruling succession. A British expeditionary force under Gen Sir Robert Low mounted a relief operation, relieving another besieged garrison at Malakand on the way, killing about 500 rebels, and routing the rest. Subsequently a fort was established at Malakand to guard the Chitral road and monitor local rebels, which, along with the *Khyber Pass, became one of the targets of the risings of 1897–8, which occurred all along the North-West frontier.

This time an estimated 12,000 Swati-Pathan tribesmen surrounded Malakand, and the neighbouring fort of Chakdara. The garrisons—native troops commanded by British officers—held out and were relieved after a week of day and night assaults. A relief force of three brigades was formed under Gen Sir Bindon Blood to mount punitive expeditions against the local tribesmen, in which the 22-year-old Lt *Churchill served. Shamelessly seeking glory, he accompanied the force as war correspondent for the *Daily Telegraph*, as there was no room on Blood's staff, and his own regiment, the 4th Hussars, was not involved. The expedition was over within weeks, but Churchill collated his accounts into *The Story of the Malakand Field Force* (1898). This was his first published work and a considerable success, establishing his reputation as a writer. In view of his subsequent fame, the book, with its vivid descriptive style, has ensured that this otherwise minor colonial campaign has risen above the mists of obscurity.   APC-A

Malaya and Singapore campaign

Malaya and Singapore campaign (1941–2). The British acquired trading settlements on the Malay peninsula in the 18th century, and early in the 19th colonized Singapore island at its southern tip. Singapore became an important trading centre, and Malaya exported rubber and tin. After much debate the British decided to build a naval base at Singapore to counter the threat of Japanese expansionism. Heavy guns were put into position on Singapore island to defend it against attack from the sea. In the 1930s there was recognition that Singapore and Malaya could best be defended from the air, and new airfields were built. By 1938 it was accepted that the defence of Singapore must involve that of Malaya and its airfields, but with the outbreak of war in Europe, aircraft and warships which might have been sent to the Far East were more urgently needed elsewhere. The threat posed by the Japanese, who saw the capture of Singapore as part of seizure of the 'Greater South Asia Co-Prosperity Sphere', was not fully grasped. There was a general failure to recognize the fighting quality of Japanese troops and the excellence of some Japanese equipment like the Zero fighter.

In October 1940 ACM Sir Robert Brooke-Popham was recalled from retirement to become C-in-C Far East: he was 62 and lacked recent operational experience and knowledge of the area. Sir Shenton Thomas was governor of Singapore and the Straits Settlement on the mainland, and each service had its own commander: Lt Gen Arthur Percival arrived as GOC Malaya in May 1941. Brooke-Popham had demanded more resources, but was told by *Churchill in January 1941 that 'The political situation in the Far East does not seem to require, and the strength of our air force by no means permits, the maintenance of such large forces in the Far East at this time.'

When Japan entered the war in December 1941 Malaya was defended by the two understrength divisions, 9th and 11th, of Lt Gen Heath's III Indian Corps. Maj Gen Simmons, GOC Singapore Fortress, was responsible for the defence of

Singapore and the southern tip of Johore, and his force included the leading brigade of the 8th Australian Division under *Bennett. The RAF had only 158 first-line aircraft, mostly old and vulnerable. The Japanese invasion was well prepared, with landings at Singora and Patani in Thailand and Khota Bharu in Malaya. The British considered mounting MATADOR, a pre-emptive move into Thailand to hold the peninsula at its narrowest point, and although this was cancelled there was an ill-starred attempt to send a column into Thailand to seize an important defile.

The pattern of the campaign emerged quickly. The Japanese soon gained air superiority, and three divisions under Lt Gen *Yamashita moved rapidly southwards, attacking along the axis of main roads but hooking into the jungle to outflank the defenders and establish road blocks behind them. The British lost successive battles at Jitra (11 December), Gurun (15 December), Kampar (2 January 1942), and Slim River (7 January). Kuala Lumpur fell on 11 January.

In October 1941 the British decided that the brand-new battleship *Prince of Wales* and the equally new aircraft-carrier *Indomitable* would join the old battlecruiser *Repulse* in the Indian Ocean. The carrier was damaged during working-up trials, but the other vessels, known as Force Z, under the command of Adm Sir Tom Phillips, reached Singapore. On the evening of 8 December Phillips put to sea in an effort to engage the Japanese landings, and on the 10th was attacked by aircraft based in Indochina: both his capital ships were sunk by torpedo-bombers, and he was among over 800 men lost.

Disasters on land and sea encouraged the Allies to establish a unified American-British-Dutch-Australian (ABDA) Command, with the British Gen *Wavell at its head. Wavell visited Malaya, revised Percival's plans, and warned him to prepare defences in case he had to withdraw to Singapore. The commitment of the Australian division could not prevent the fall of Johore, and on 31 January the causeway linking Singapore to the mainland was blown.

Percival was ordered by Churchill not to contemplate giving up until 'after protracted fighting among the ruins of Singapore city', but his position was already difficult. Singapore's population was swollen by refugees, and two-fifths of the city's water had come in pipes from the mainland. Early on 9 February the Japanese landed on the north-west shore, and made good progress, rapidly reaching the reservoirs in the island's centre. The newly arrived 18th Division, committed to battle without preparation, could do little to stem the flow, and after consulting his senior commanders Percival surrendered on 15 February. Yamashita was desperately short of ammunition, and in no position to fight a protracted battle.

Churchill was right to call it 'the worst disaster and largest capitulation in British military history'. Of the 140,000 British and Commonwealth engaged, some 9,000 were killed and about 130,000 captured. The Japanese committed 55,000 men and lost 3,500 killed. The defeat struck an irreversible blow to European prestige in the Far East. Although British performance was generally lacklustre, the real origins of the catastrophe lay in a pre-war defence policy which failed to balance commitments with resources.

RH

Allen, Louis, *Singapore 1941–1942* (London, 1977).
Kirby, Maj Gen S. Woodburn, *Singapore: The Chain of Disaster* (London, 1971).

Malayan emergency Also known as the communist insurrection in Malaya. For the Malayan Communist Party (MCP) it was the start of the armed struggle to overthrow colonial rule, while for the government it was a state of emergency in which the army was acting in support of the *civil power. When it began in 1948 three British infantry battalions and an artillery regiment, six understrength battalions of *Gurkha Rifles, and two battalions of the Malay Regiment were reinforced from Hong Kong and with a Guards Brigade from the UK. In the meantime, 9,000 police and a hastily raised force of 20,000 special constables were the first line of defence for the country's rubber estates and tin mines.

Insufficient in number and largely unprepared for *counter-insurgency, the army was nevertheless able to prevent the *guerrilla forces of the MCP from disrupting the country's economy, overrunning small towns, or establishing significant 'liberated areas'. Formed, with British support, as the Malayan People's Anti-Japanese Army after the fall of Singapore in 1942, it was formally demobilized in 1945 and renamed the Malayan Races Liberation Army (later Malayan People's Liberation Army). The armed guerrillas would eventually reach a strength of some seven or eight thousand, 90 per cent ethnic Chinese. Their advantage lay in their close connection with the rural Chinese communities in Malaya, at least half a million of whom lived without or beyond government control on the jungle fringes. Their weakness lay in the limited appeal of communism for the two-and-a-half million Malays and the threat they posed to Malay political supremacy.

In the long run, accommodation between Malays and Chinese was the political problem to be solved in the process of decolonization. In the short run, the strategic problem was how to withstand a renewed and reinvigorated guerrilla assault in 1950 and 1951, and at the same time deprive guerrillas of the indispensable support of perhaps 100,000 Malayan Chinese. Opinions differed on the actual target: the guerrillas themselves or their supporters in the Min Yuen, the Masses Organization. In any case, FM Slim observed that the bandits were simply being chased round and round, without any substantial reduction in numbers. In Singapore, Gen Harding commented on the enormous amount of military effort that was absorbed in will-o'-the-wisp patrolling, jungle-bashing, and air bombardments. None of which, said Harding, made much difference in the absence of *intelligence for which the Services had to depend almost entirely on the police. The police, in turn, depended on the confidence of the people—especially the Chinese—the civil administration generally and its power to protect them, and also on a thoroughly efficient Special Branch organization.

Having identified the problem, the solution lay with two soldiers, both of whom, paradoxically, were to act in an essentially civilian role. The first, retired Lt Gen Sir Harold Briggs, was appointed in April 1950 as director of operations: in effect as co-ordinator rather than commander. A system of state and district war executive committees was to focus and integrate the emergency effort throughout the country. A framework of troops and police was to cover all populated areas. On this framework the army was to superimpose striking forces in each state which would dominate the jungle up to five hours' journey from likely guerrilla supply areas. Briggs's emphasis was on civil administration, including police, on the breeding grounds, as he put it, rather than on the mosquitoes themselves, but his plan to clear Malaya from south to north unfortunately began in the state of Johore, a guerrilla stronghold, and soon ran into difficulties.

The major problem was still intelligence, something that was unlikely to be generated by a largely Malay police force which, in any event, was heavily involved in the fighting, deploying some 500 paramilitary Jungle squads. Army patrolling sometimes generated its own intelligence. Eight-or ten-man ambushes, where successful, quite often led to the recovery of useful documents, but at the end of 1951 the cabinet in London was told that 'the communist hold on Malaya is as strong, if not stronger today than it has ever been'. The Labour government in London seemed to have run out of ideas.

The high commissioner in Malaya, Sir Henry Gurney, had probably done the same when, in October 1951, he was ambushed and killed in a spectacular but fortuitous guerrilla success. At this point, however, again fortuitously, everything began to change. The MCP decided to change course and, while continuing military operations, placed more emphasis on political activity. In London the new Conservative government put Malaya at the top of its overseas agenda. Of the old team Gurney was dead, Briggs had retired, the director of intelligence had resigned, and the surviving commissioner of police was removed.

The way was now open for the appointment of Lt Gen Sir Gerald *Templer as high commissioner and also as director of operations. Concentration of power in Templer, total integration of civil and military functions, and dynamic co-ordination of policy allowed security forces to function at maximum efficiency. And yet, as Templer said, 'the shooting side of the business is only 25 per cent of the trouble'. Templer's achievements were as much civil as military, but as soon as the effective Special Branch began producing operational intelligence, the key to military success lay in

food-denial operations. By now, half a million 'squatters'—Chinese peasant farmers—had been resettled into 500 'new villages' and the guerrillas, often on the point of starvation, were forced to approach them through areas saturated by soldiers and police. Many surrendered; large numbers starved; even more were killed. Special operations involving *SAS and armed aborigine scouts pursued dwindling numbers of insurgents into the deep jungle but it was not until the MCP's political organization, the District Committee in particular, was penetrated and destroyed that the insurgency as a whole became vulnerable. In 1955 the MCP tried to negotiate a settlement with Malayan political leaders on the brink of independence. Their failure was followed by Malayan independence in 1957 and in 1960 the emergency was declared to be at an end.

Casualty figures reveal the nature of the conflict. Regular police and the army each lost just over 500 men; but over 800 special constables and auxiliary police were killed. Over 3,000 civilians, mainly Chinese, were dead or missing. Almost 7,000 guerrillas were killed, 1,300 captured, and 2,700 surrendered—500 in 1958, many of them financially induced. Approximately 500 British and Commonwealth soldiers, including Gurkhas, were killed, as were about 100 British civilians, most of them planters. Essentially it was a small-unit war in which patrols of under a dozen men, a high proportion of them national servicemen, spent up to a thousand hours in the jungle before a contact was made. *Air support for the greater part of the emergency, was given over to supply drops, occasional bombing, casualty evacuation, and troop movement when *helicopters became available. Offensive helicopter operations were unknown and lack of targets usually limited air attack of any kind. The guerrillas themselves, although perhaps on the point of attaining critical mass at the end of 1951, were never quite strong enough on their own to challenge the government in the populated areas. In notable contrast to *Vietnam, they were never supplied with men or significant numbers of weapons from outside Malaya. Having to depend on their own resources, in particular weapons which they had to capture, they were unable to maintain a military effort long enough to drain the combined resources of increasingly effective civil-military government.   AS

Coates, John, *Suppressing Insurgency* (Boulder, Colo., 1992).

Mackay, E. D. R., *The Malayan Emergency 1948–1960: The Domino that Stood* (London, 1997).

Short, Anthony, *The Communist Insurrection in Malaya* (London, 1975).

Thompson, Robert, *Defeating Communist Insurgency* (London, 1966).

Maldon, battle of (991). One of the most serious encounters between *Vikings and Englishmen during the late 10th-century wave of Viking attacks took place on the banks of the Blackwater river near Maldon, Essex. A Viking force had first sacked Ipswich before being confronted on 10 or 11

August 991 by the levies of Essex under their ealdorman Byrhtnoth. Details of the ensuing battle are provided by the Old English poem generally entitled *The Battle of Maldon*, which survives substantially only in an 18th-century transcript. There is no agreement as to the historicity of its account, but it is clear that the English were defeated and Byrhtnoth slain. Shortly afterwards, the English made their first payment of Danegeld (£10,000) to the Vikings in an attempt to buy them off. MC

Cooper, J. (ed.), *The Battle of Maldon: Fiction and Fact* (London, 1993).

Scragg, D. G. (ed.), *The Battle of Maldon* (Manchester, 1981) [poem].

—— (ed.), *The Battle of Maldon AD 991* (Oxford, 1991) [articles].

Malplaquet, battle of (1709). Malplaquet was the most costly and least useful of *Marlborough's four great victories. In August 1709 he and Prince *Eugène de Savoy took Tournai and moved on to besiege Mons. Villars, ordered to raise the siege, approached from the south-west with 80,000 men. He took up a strong position north of Malplaquet, where a main road to Mons passed between thick woods, and Marlborough advanced against him with 110,000 Allied troops. He hoped to repeat his favourite ploy of attacking his enemy's flanks to persuade him to weaken his centre. However, the late arrival of a force from Tournai meant that he could not make his left as strong as intended.

He attacked on 11 September and made slow progress on his right, while on his left the Prince of Orange launched two costly attacks to little effect. Villars eventually thinned his centre to support his left, and was wounded shortly afterwards. Orkney's infantry then advanced through the French redoubts in the centre, and the Allied horse moved up into a bitterly contested cavalry battle. Boufflers, who had succeeded to command, eventually fell back, in good order, on Le Quesnoy, having lost 17,000 men to the Allies' 25,000. Mons surrendered in October, but it was a prize too dearly bought. RH

Malta, Great Siege of (1565). In 1564 *Suleiman 'the Magnificent' ordered his general Mustafa Pasha to seize Malta, which dominated the narrows between Sicily and Africa. La Sangle, who was Grand Master of the Knights of Malta (see MILITARY MONASTIC ORDERS) from 1553–7, and Jean de la Valette who succeeded him and who gave his name to the harbour he defended in 1565 were great builders. They had strengthened the harbours and surrounding heights according to the most modern principles of artillery fortification. These included the fort of St Elmo between the two main harbours, and St Michael and St Angelo south-east of the Great Harbour, on either side of the galley harbour. The Turks were helped by the pasha of Algiers, whose Barbary pirates would benefit from the elimination of the Maltese base.

On 18 May 1565 130 galleys and 50 transports carrying 30,000 troops hove in sight of what is now Valetta. They landed some distance away, ignored the town where most of the civilian population fled for shelter, and moved straight for the naval base. Valette had 500 Knights of Malta, 1,300 *mercenaries, 1,000 marines normally employed on war galleys, and 4,000 local Maltese levies. The Turks bombarded St Elmo for a month, and after it fell on 24 June the defenders' bodies were floated in the harbour, bloody crosses scored on their chests. But the capture of St Elmo had cost 8,000 Turkish troops to 130 Knights and 1,200 rank-and-file defenders. 'If the child has cost me so many casualties,' mused Mustafa on losing nearly a third of his force, 'how many will remain when we have done with the parent?' However, the Turks were then able to put guns directly opposite St Angelo, firing across the Grand Harbour. The viceroy of Sicily was assembling a relief force, but moved slowly. Hassan, Pasha of Algiers, arrived in early July to reinforce the Turks but on 6 September a Spanish-Sicilian fleet arrived from Toledo with 10,000 Spanish infantry. By this time the Turks had lost half their strength and abandoned the siege. Their total losses are reported as 24,000, against 240 Knights of Malta and 5,000 rank and file. With the defeat at *Lepanto six years later, the Turks were no longer a threat to the western Mediterranean, and Malta became the centre for operations against the Barbary pirates. CDB

Oman, Sir Charles, *A History of the Art of War in the 16th Century* (London, 1937).

Mamelukes (Arabic: *mamluk*, slave). From the 9th century onwards, Muslim rulers increasingly used slaves, mostly of Turkish origin, as the backbone of their military forces. Also known as *ghulams* or pages, these *slave soldiers were purchased young and brought up in the households of their masters. Many became skilled professionals and were highly valued for their military prowess and their loyalty to their masters since they had no local or family ties. Some also became extremely powerful and in 1260 the Mameluke Baybars seized the throne of Egypt, beginning a pattern of rule by monarchs of slave soldier origin which continued until the Ottoman conquest of 1517. Initially the Mamelukes were mostly Qipchaq Turks from the steppe lands north of the Black Sea but from 1382 onwards the rulers were mostly Circassians from the Caucasus. Though Mameluke politics were marked by intrigue and violence, the regime was very successful. Militarily they were the only power able to defeat the *Mongols, at the battle of Ain Jalut in 1260, and they put an end to the crusader occupation of the Holy Land with the conquest of Acre in 1291. Both economically and culturally, Mameluke rule was the most successful period in the history of medieval Egypt.

The Mamelukes remained a force to be reckoned with until their defeat by *Napoleon at the battle of the Pyramids in 1798. Some French and British officers who had served in

Egypt took to wearing captured Mameluke swords, whose design still influences the dress swords carried by British generals—and by US Marine Corps officers, although in their case Tripoli, not Egypt, was the source of inspiration.

HK/RH

Manchurian campaign (1904–5). See RUSSO-JAPANESE WAR.

Manchurian campaign (1945), final campaign of WW II, in which the Soviet Far Eastern Command destroyed the million-strong Japanese 'Kwantung Army' in the Japanese

puppet state of Manchukuo between 9 August and 2 September. The campaign began the night before the dropping of the second atomic bomb on Japan on 9 August, which has led some historians to question its importance. However, on 9 August a Japanese theatre command with 3 army groups ('area armies'), 1 million men, 5,000 guns, 1,100 tanks, and 1,800 aircraft was still intact, and it fought on until the end of the month. Although many of the troops were trainees and included non-Japanese units, they fought fanatically. Furthermore, the Soviet operation was considered by *Cold War military analysts to be the prototype for a future Soviet theatre strategic operation in, for example, western Europe. The theatre was the size of Europe and the terrain very varied, including the Gobi desert, the

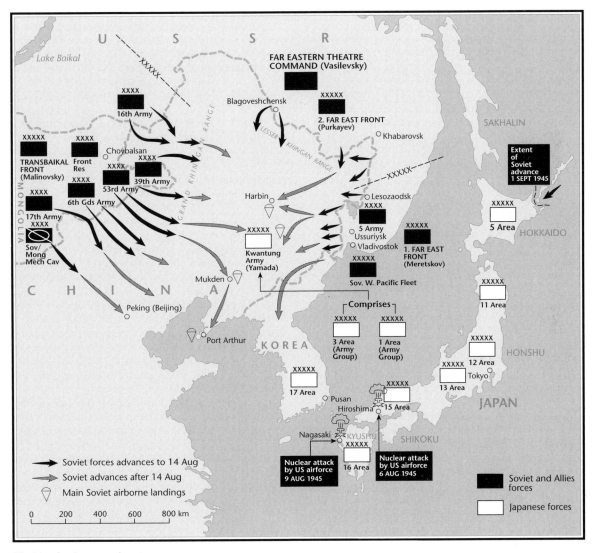

The **Manchurian campaign**, August 1945.

Greater and Lesser Khingan mountain ranges, melted permafrost, and swamp.

In April 1945 the USSR indicated it would not renew the non-aggression treaty signed with Japan in April 1941 when it expired in April 1946. The Japanese concluded, correctly, that the USSR would attack as soon as it had finished with Germany. At Yalta, *Stalin promised he would attack three months after victory in Europe. That came for the USSR on 9 May 1945 and Stalin was true to his word.

Three months after defeating the Germans in Europe, the Red Army was at its most powerful. In firepower, mobility, communications, support, and even battle experience (their veteran troops mostly having died in the *Pacific campaign) the Japanese were no match for the three Soviet Fronts (army groups) gathered round Manchuria: First and Second Far Eastern on the Pacific and the Transbaikal Front in Mongolia. Units which had experience against German defences in East Prussia were drafted in to deal with similar defences near Vladivostok. The Second Far Eastern Front, with most of the lower quality formations, stood mainly on the defensive north of the Amur river. An independent force, equating to an army, in the Gobi Desert was Issa Pliev's Soviet-Mongolian cavalry mechanized group. This secured the right (south-western) flank and moved to threaten Peking (Beijing).

The Japanese had seriously misjudged how far the Soviet army had come in conducting 'deep operations' (see OPERATIONAL CONCEPTS). They believed any Soviet offensive would have to halt for resupply after 250 miles (402 km) and planned to use this breathing space to marshal their forces for a defensive battle on the central Manchurian plain. In fact, the Soviets and Mongolians penetrated much deeper without halting. They made extensive use of *airborne forces to seize airfields and communications centres ahead of the main advancing columns. They also captured the puppet emperor of Manchukuo—the last emperor of China.

The Transbaikal Front advanced through the mountains to the central plain covering an astonishing 560 miles (901 km) in eleven days—virtually unopposed because the Japanese had not thought the Soviet-Mongolian forces would be able to advance through the mountains because of resupply problems. As the Soviet columns bit deeply into Manchuria the Kwantung army, following an order from Tokyo, surrendered at Khabarovsk. Soviet forces also advanced south from Kamchatka and northern Sakhalin to occcupy southern Sakhalin and the Kurile islands. Soviet and Japanese troops continued to fight until the day before Japan's formal capitulation on 2 September.   CDB

Glantz, David, *August Storm: The Soviet 1945 Strategic Offensive in Manchuria* (Fort Leavenworth, 1983).

Manchus (also called Ching or Quing). The Manchus conquered China and established an imperial dynasty which ruled between 1644 and 1911. At first an energetic and powerful ruling dynasty, the Manchus trebled the size of the Chinese empire.

The Manchu dynasty was first established in 1636 in Manchuria. They were not powerful enough to conquer China alone, but took advantage of the opportunities of the civil war that racked the last years of the Ming dynasty. When rebel leader Li Zicheng (1605–45) captured Peking (correctly Beijing), Ming Gen Wu Sangui enlisted the help of the Manchus and together they defeated Li Zicheng. The Manchus took advantage of the power vacuum in Beijing to seize the city and install the first Manchu emperor in 1644.

The first thirty years of Manchu rule were restricted to northern China; the south remained in the hands of Wu Sangui and others who supported a variety of Ming pretenders. Had the Chinese quickly united under Wu Sangui they might well have succeeded in dislodging the rather tenuous Manchu hold on power. However, by the time Wu Sangui raised his banner against the new dynasty, the new and energetic Emperor Kangxi (1662–1722) was on the throne. He crushed Wu Sangui and extended Manchu control over southern China, the last Ming bastion falling in 1683.

The acquisition of China and its vast resources allowed the Manchus considerable scope for expansion. Kangxi met and countered Russian penetration along the Manchurian border and forced the Russian stronghold at Albazin to surrender. Under the Treaty of Nerchinsk of 1689 the Russians withdrew from Albazin and the area north of the Amur river. The Manchus conquered Outer Mongolia in 1697 and to the west their armies took Turkestan before 1700, Tibet in 1720, and Zungharia in 1757. Their expansion into the steppe was of lasting strategic benefit to China because it finally ended the ancient menace of nomad raiders. To the south the Manchus re-established suzerainty over Burma and Vietnam.

The Manchus, a minority within the 250 million Chinese population, ensured control over the administration by reserving half of all civil service posts for themselves. This led to a considerable degree of complacency among the Manchus who needed no exceptional talents to gain office while able Chinese candidates, particularly in the south, were continuously frustrated. This frustration could lead to open revolt—indeed the most serious, the *Taiping rebellion, was started by a failed civil service candidate. However, the growing crisis within China was largely economic. The population of China had grown dramatically yet food production and industry had not kept pace. Popular unrest followed, further exacerbated by famine. Rebellion after rebellion had to be put down and the embattled dynasty was forced to rely increasingly on Chinese militia as the standard of the purely Manchu units had declined dramatically.

The Taiping rebellion was by far the most serious of these. In terms of human life, it is the costliest civil war in history and second bloodiest war of any kind, being only exceeded in casualties by WW II. Between 20 and 30 million people died during its fourteen-year course from 1850 to 1864. Inspired by Hung Hsiu-chuan and drawing on his own personal interpretation of Christianity, the rebels sought to sweep away the Manchus. They captured Nanking, which was established as the revolutionary capital. In 1860 a revitalized government aided by the 'Ever Victorious Army' under *Gordon began to regain the territory lost to the rebels and Nanking was retaken in 1864.

The British involvement in the rebellion was indicative of the other problem facing the corrupt and inward-looking Manchus. The clash between the dynasty and British traders led to Chinese defeat in the *Opium war. The shock of capitulation to such a small British force was considerable and demonstrated the fragility of the Manchu empire to the world. Further conflict followed over the opium trade between 1856 and 1858 culminating in a surprisingly good Chinese showing at the Taku forts. However, hostilities were renewed resulting in a decisive Anglo-French victory in 1860. Taking advantage of Manchu difficulties the Russians seized the vast territories along the Amur river. In 1885 Britain took over *Burma and France Vietnam. The Japanese invaded *Korea in 1895. The repeated defeats and humiliating concessions granted to foreign powers coupled with a failure effectively to reform or modernize underscored the bankruptcy of the Manchus which was only underlined by the hopeless failure of the *Boxer rebellion of 1900. The dynasty was finally swept away by a republican revolution in 1911. The last emperor became a WW II Japanese puppet in Manchukuo (Manchuria), where it all started.   MCM

Cotterell, Arthur, *China: A History* (London, 1988).

Mandalay/Meiktila, battles of

(1944). In mid-1944, after the failed Japanese attack on *Imphal, *Mountbatten, C-in-C of South-East Asia Command, issued orders for CAPITAL, an offensive into Burma by Slim's Fourteenth Army, with thrusts by the Chinese on its left and into the Arakan on its right. Rangoon was to be taken by an amphibious landing, DRACULA. The linked battles of Mandalay and Meiktila were part of Fourteenth Army's offensive.

Slim had two corps available for his attack, Messervy's IV and Stopford's XXXIII. Divisions were shifted between them as the battle developed, but each usually comprised at least two infantry divisions and a tank brigade. Slim's opponent, Lt Gen Kimura of the Burma Area Army, had been ordered to hold southern Burma, and to interfere as much as he could with Allied links with China. His three armies were understrength, and he was badly outclassed in the air. He hoped to hold a line from Lashio to Mandalay and on down the Irrawaddy south of Mandalay.

Slim sought to defeat the Japanese, not merely to capture ground, and sent XXXIII Corps against Mandalay while IV headed south and then swung eastwards to Meiktila. The Japanese 15th Division had been ordered to hold Mandalay

to the last man, and both Fort Dufferin and Mandalay Hill, to its north, were splendid defensive positions. But 19th Indian Division, well handled by Maj Gen Rees, duly crossed the Irrawaddy and took the town in early March 1945 while Stopford's other divisions encircled the city. The IV Corps, meanwhile, crossed the Irrawaddy opposite Meiktila, and pushed its armour out of a bridgehead seized on 17 February. Meiktila was first invested, and then assaulted, by Maj Gen Cowan's 17th Indian Division. Fierce fighting followed, and when the Japanese fell back at the end of March they were intercepted by 20th Indian Division and suffered heavily.

Slim failed to encircle the bulk of Japanese forces holding Mandalay and Meiktila, and the balance of casualties did not seem to tell heavily in his favour. However, only 2,600 of his 18,000 casualties were killed, while the Japanese lost 6,500 dead from total casualties of 13,000. They also lost most of their tanks and guns, and were in no position to resist Slim's subsequent breakout towards Rangoon.   RH

Manhattan Project

Code name for the Anglo-American project to develop the atomic bomb. In June 1943 *Churchill and Franklin D. *Roosevelt agreed that development should be based at the top-secret research establishment of Los Alamos in New Mexico. Brig Gen Groves was appointed to oversee the project, but the scientific director was Robert Oppenheimer and there were other Soviet intelligence assets involved, so the details were well known to *Stalin from the beginning. The first live test of an atomic bomb was on 16 July 1945.   JR-W

Mannerheim, Marshal Karl Gustav Emil

(1867–1951). Finnish military and national leader, responsible for the formidable belt of fortifications named after him built across the Karelian isthmus 20 miles (32 km) from Leningrad. From 1889 to 1917 he served in the Russian army, as Finland was then a grand duchy within the Russian empire. In 1918 he commanded the White Finnish army, allied with the Germans. Made a field marshal in 1938, he commanded the Finnish armed forces in the Russo-Finnish war and in the so-called 'continuation war', when Finland allied with the Germans to recover Karelia, but did not press the siege of *Leningrad. Made president in 1944, he prudently withdrew from the war before the Soviets could return the favour and had to give up Karelia again.

The 'Mannerheim Line' was built from 1927 to 1939 with advice from British, French, German, and Belgian experts. It was 84 miles (135 km) long and 56 miles (90 km) deep, and comprised about 2,000 installations, some of earth and wood, some of concrete. The Soviets literally had to tear it out of the ground with overwhelming artillery firepower to break through.   CDB

manoeuvre warfare (*see opposite page*)

Manstein, FM Erich von (1887–1973). Manstein was

commissioned into 3rd Foot Guards, *Hindenburg's old regiment, in 1906, and during WW1 he fought at *Verdun and the *Somme. In 1937 he became DCGS, but was sent off to command a division after the replacement of Fritsch as C-in-C. He served as COS of *Rundstedt's army group during the *Polish campaign, and went on to be COS of Army Group A in the West. He objected to the unimaginative plan for the invasion of France and the Low Countries, and drew up a more ambitious version, designed, as he put it, to force 'a decisive issue by land', which threw the weight of the attack through the Ardennes. Although he was posted to command a corps in the east—his reward for being 'an importunate nuisance'—he met Hitler and helped persuade him to adopt the plan (see FRANCE, FALL OF).

He was an outstanding success on the *eastern front, commanding Eleventh Army which captured the Crimea, and was promoted field-marshal in 1942. In November he was sent to command Army Group Don (later South) to the west and south of *Stalingrad, where the German Sixth Army had just been encircled by the Russians. Arguing that Sixth Army should break out of the Soviet encirclement as soon as possible, he feared that the moment had already passed, and emphasized that it could only hope to hold out if guaranteed adequate air supply. He mounted Operation WINTER STORM in an effort to reach the Stalingrad pocket, and might have succeeded had *Paulus been allowed to break out to meet him.

After the fall of Stalingrad he carried out a brilliant counter-attack at Kharkov in February–March 1943, carried out 'on the backhand' against an attacker who had swept beyond his northern flank, and briefly regained the initiative. It was lost for ever at *Kursk, in an attack he initially supported, but believed had been delayed too long by Hitler. 'The whole idea', he wrote, 'had been to attack before the enemy had replenished his forces and got over the reverses of winter.' He was relieved of command in March 1944 because his concept of fluid defence offended Hitler.

In 1950 he was sentenced to eighteen years' imprisonment for *war crimes, but served only three. The title of his dignified book *Lost Victories* (dedicated to his son and all who, like him, had died for Germany) sums up the frustration of so many Germans in fighting so well but yet being beaten. He is widely regarded as one of the ablest practitioners of *armoured warfare, and *Liddell Hart, in his foreword to Manstein's book, declared that 'he had a superb sense of operational possibilities and an equal mastery in the conduct of operations . . . In sum, he had military genius.' RH

Manstein, Erich von, *Lost Victories* (London, 1958).

Mantineia, battles of (418, 362, and 207 BC). These

three battles spanned the whole development of Greek warfare from a typical *hoplite battle to the appearance of catapults. The first was during the *Peloponnesian wars and was fought between a largely Spartan and Tegeate army, and a combined army consisting largely of Mantineians, Argives, and Athenians. Having the larger army, the Spartan King Agis II attempted to cover the enemy overlap on his left by shifting his left wing outwards and plugging the gap with units from the right. But his orders were disobeyed and the enemy right exploited the gap to defeat his left. On the centre and right, however, the Spartans carried the day, and wheeled left past the retreating Athenians and the gap left by the flight of most of the Argives, to take the enemy right in its shieldless flank as it streamed back across the battlefield. The victory restored Spartan *morale and reinforced her control in the Peloponnese.

The second battle came at the end of the *Greek city-state wars and was brought about by the collapse of the *Thebes-inspired anti-Spartan coalition in the Peloponnese. It was fought between a Boeotian, Euboean, Thessalian, and Arcadian army, commanded by *Epaminondas, against a combination of Mantineians, Spartans, Eleans, and Athenians. Epaminondas massed his left as he had done at *Leuctra, but it was a charge by cavalry mixed with light infantry, trained to run into battle with cavalry, that broke the enemy right. A decisive victory was prevented by the death of the great Epaminondas himself.

The third battle, finally, saw the Spartan 'tyrant' Machanidas defeated and killed by Achaean League troops led by Philopoemen, in a typical Hellenistic engagement, in which all types of troops, and catapults, were used. JFL

Buckler, J., *The Theban Hegemony, 371–362 BC* (London, 1980).
Lazenby, J. F., *The Spartan Army* (Warminster, 1985).
Walbank, F. W., *Historical Commentary on Polybius 2* (Oxford, 1967).

Manzikert, battle of (1071), a hinge event in Middle

Eastern history. It took place near Manzikert (Malazgird) some 25 miles (40 km) north of Lake Van in what is now eastern Turkey. The most valuable account of the battle is that of the Byzantine historian Attaliates who was an eyewitness. The battle is also mentioned in Armenian, Syriac, Islamic, and western European sources. In the battle the Byzantine Emperor Romanus IV Diogenes, campaigning on his eastern borders to counter the Seljuk *Turk threat, met a depleted army under Sultan Alp Arslan. Few details of the actual battle are known. The Byzantine rearguard left the battlefield at nightfall and the Seljuk army was able to lure them into ambushes. The terrain favoured the Seljuk mounted *archers and the *Byzantine army was wracked with internal dissension. Although Romanus's army was superior in numbers, its composition was heterogeneous,

(*cont. on page 545*)

manoeuvre warfare

THE term 'manoeuvre warfare' has become a mantra. Its original meaning is the movement of forces on the ground into advantageous positions which facilitate the destruction of the enemy or may of themselves induce the enemy to surrender. In recent years this has been extended to include surprise, deception, and being able to act faster than the enemy can respond, to the point where it has embraced the 'indirect approach'. At the start of the 21st century the US and British armies are committed to 'the manoeuvrist approach', which appears to mean all things good, as opposed to *attrition, which means all things bad. However, a serious study of military history reveals that, like attack and defence, manoeuvre and attrition are always interlocked in a form of creative tension rather than the absolute polarity sometimes identified. Manoeuvre is of value—maybe decisive value—because it increases the ability, actual or potential, to inflict attrition. Conversely, attrition may be necessary to restore manoeuvre. Manoeuvre warfare derives essentially from the practice of land operations. At sea and, above all, in the air, the manoeuvre–attrition polarity is more apparent.

*Sun-tzu wrote that the acme of skill in war was to subdue the enemy without fighting. That is the manoeuvrist approach in its purest form: it may be likened to checkmating an opponent's king in chess. Some have gone so far as to assert that there are two opposed and mutually exclusive schools of thought: 'manoeuvre theory' and 'attrition theory'. That is wrong. War is an act of force, ultimately manifested in the ability to destroy or immobilize the enemy's forces and render them incapable of effective resistance. That is attrition. Manoeuvre means moving one's forces in such a way as to multiply their effectiveness and ability to inflict attrition. Mobility is the ability of a force to move, not only in terms of whether it is on feet, hooves, wheels, tracks, wings, or rotors, but in terms of how much fuel it has, the condition of the roads, soil, and so on. Manoeuvre is moving so as to gain an advantage over the enemy, whether getting into a better firing position, or getting astride his communications, perhaps forcing him to attack in unfavourable circumstances. But manoeuvre without the ability to strike is an illusion. As Alfred Thayer Mahan (1840–1914), the greatest US strategist, said in his *Lessons of the War with Spain*, 'force does not exist for mobility but mobility for force. It is of no use to get there first unless, when the enemy arrives, you have the most men—the greater force'.

Sun-tzu encapsulated the idea of manoeuvre as being similar to water: avoiding heights and hastening to the lowlands. That is what a manoeuvrist commander does, avoiding strength and striking weakness, but the power of water is nonetheless overwhelming. The *Mongols may have imbibed ideas about manoeuvre warfare from captive Chinese, but it is more likely they did it by instinct. Mongol armies were not only highly mobile, they also manoeuvred, avoiding cities, leaving them like so many uncracked nuts to be returned to later. They also moved so fast that their victims vastly overrated their numbers, leading to tales of vast Mongol 'hordes'. In fact, they were usually numerically inferior to their opponents.

The relation between manoeuvre and attrition mirrors that between the notions of attack and defence. As *Clausewitz pointed out, the latter notions are unstable states: the defender is actually well placed to surprise the attacker by counter-attacks.

Throughout military history, the most favoured manoeuvre has been envelopment. A force deployed to fight in one direction is always more vulnerable when attacked from the side. The overlapping or outflanking movement can be taken further, to reach the enemy rear. It is then called an envelopment. A variant of the envelopment was perfected by *Frederick 'the Great', the so-called 'oblique attack'. Frederick's superbly drilled army was able to execute such a movement faster than his opponents could respond.

Envelopment has four cardinal advantages. First, there is the surprise factor of appearing behind the enemy: this is both psychological and practical, in that he will have to redeploy to deal with the new threat. Second, his reinforcements and supplies are cut off. Third, his retreat is cut off and, fourth, one's own movement in the desired direction is accomplished more economically because one has gone round the enemy rather than had to fight through him.

If the enemy is enveloped from both sides, it is called a 'double envelopment' or, more popularly, a 'pincer movement', for obvious reasons. The archetype of this movement is Hannibal's victory at *Cannae in 216 BC. The great warrior nation of the Zulus turned double envelopment into a drill (see ZULU WAR). Their formation was based on the fighting bull buffalo, with horns, head, and loins. The enemy was drawn in to meet the head, which then dispersed to form the horns. The enemy continued towards the loins, but was encircled by the horns, and destroyed. This is what happened to 1,500 British and native troops at Isandhlwana on 22 January 1879. It can be achieved either by having the wings remain static while the centre falls back (Cannae) or by having the centre stand firm but advancing the wings (Isandhlwana).

If the enemy is completely prevented from withdrawing, he is said to be encircled. This does not necessarily mean completely surrounded: it is merely necessary to cut all practicable routes for retreat and supply. However, when there are other groups of enemy forces around this is not enough, for they may attack and try to break the encirclement. Therefore when executing encirclements an inner front, facing the encircled enemy, and an outer front, to prevent other forces reaching him, need to be established.

The two faces of any encirclement must not be confused with the term double encirclement, which is when one encirclement is followed by or conducted within a wider and deeper one. The classic example here is the battle of *Stalingrad, with Operations URANUS, the smaller encirclement, and then LITTLE SATURN, the larger. In this case the encircling forces have not two but four faces: the inner and outer fronts of the inner encirclement, and the inner and outer fronts of the outer one.

An encircled enemy may fight bitterly, and it may be better to encourage him to withdraw. In this case he can be left an escape route, known as a 'golden bridge'. He may be easier to cut down and destroy as he is withdrawing, than when concentrated in an encircled position.

In the 20th century the term vertical envelopment has come into use, where the enveloping force (or part of it) is delivered by parachute, *glider, transport aircraft, or helicopter. The archetypes of this three-dimensional manoeuvre warfare are the German assault on Fort Eben Emael in 1940; the later, albeit sometimes unsuccessful *airborne operations of WW II; the Israeli raid on Entebbe in 1976; and the Soviet seizure of Kabul in 1979. Envelopment can also take place by sea, notably MacArthur's landing at *Inchon in 1950.

As armies became bigger and the ranges of weapons extended, it was not always possible to envelop the enemy. In WW I, which began with a huge, attempted envelopment—the *Schlieffen plan—the armies spread to form a continuous line from the Alps to the sea, partly as a result of their attempts to envelop each other. No WW I general adopted an attrition strategy from choice. Attrition was necessary to restore manoeuvre. Instead of enveloping the enemy, they would have to blast a hole through the continuous line, splitting it in two (the much sought-after breakthrough) and then envelop—outwards. This can be described as an 'envelopment from within' or an 'eccentric movement'. This is the principal form of large-scale modern operations, perfected by the Red Army in WW II and executed successfully as part of the campaign in the *Gulf war.

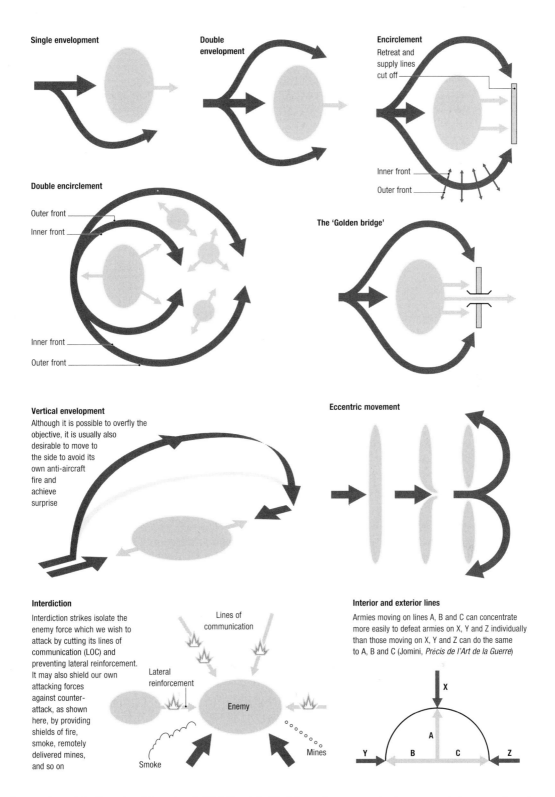

Single envelopment

Double envelopment

Encirclement
Retreat and supply lines cut off

Inner front

Outer front

Double encirclement

Outer front

Inner front

Inner front

Outer front

The 'Golden bridge'

Vertical envelopment
Although it is possible to overfly the objective, it is usually also desirable to move to the side to avoid its own anti-aircraft fire and achieve surprise

Eccentric movement

Interdiction

Interdiction strikes isolate the enemy force which we wish to attack by cutting its lines of communication (LOC) and preventing lateral reinforcement. It may also shield our own attacking forces against counter-attack, as shown here, by providing shields of fire, smoke, remotely delivered mines, and so on

Lines of communication

Lateral reinforcement

Enemy

Smoke

Mines

Interior and exterior lines

Armies moving on lines A, B and C can concentrate more easily to defeat armies on X, Y and Z individually than those moving on X, Y and Z can do the same to A, B and C (Jomini, *Précis de l'Art de la Guerre*)

X

A

Y   B   C   Z

From Cannae, through Stalingrad to Schwarzkopf's 'Hail Mary', the ideal form of manoeuvre has been to attack the enemy from the side or rear, where he is more vulnerable, and to cut him off from supply, reinforcement—and hope. But where conditions do not permit envelopment, attrition has to be used to blast a gap before manoeuvre can be reintroduced. Interior lines can confer advantages, but at some point those advantages may give way to the great disadvantage of being encircled.

The Gulf campaign illustrates the interaction and mutual dependence of manoeuvre and attrition. The air campaign was pure attrition, to the point where Iraqi ground forces were cut to about half their original strength, in terms of numbers of tanks and artillery. The ground campaign embodied all the classic elements of manoeuvre war. The Allies swung west of the main Iraqi forces, some heading for the Republican Guard far behind the front line, others—the British 1st Armoured Division—in a tighter envelopment behind the Iraqi front line. The Allied forces blasted a hole in the Iraqi front line (attrition) through which the 1st Armoured Division was inserted (manoeuvre). Artillery fire and air attack also rained down on the Iraqi forward troops, to prevent them stopping the Allied attack on the wire—attrition to permit manoeuvre. *Schwarzkopf summed it up at his final briefing on 27 February 1991: 'Once we got through this and we're moving, then it's a different war. Then we're fighting our kind of war. Before we get through that, we're fighting their kind of war, and that's what we didn't want to have to do.' That is what manoeuvre war is all about.

Current US and British military *doctrine stresses the 'manoeuvrist approach'. *British Defence Doctrine*, published in 1996, defines the manoeuvrist approach to war as 'one in which shattering the enemy's overall cohesion and will to fight, rather than his *matériel*, is paramount'. Manoeuvre warfare is invariably joint; it aims to apply strength against identifiable weakness; significant features are momentum and tempo which in combination lead to shock action and surprise. Emphasis is on the defeat and disruption of the enemy—by taking the initiative and applying constant and unacceptable pressure at the times and places the enemy least expects—rather than attempting to seize and hold ground for its own sake. It calls for an attitude of mind in which doing the unexpected and seeking originality is combined with a ruthless determination to succeed. The manoeuvrist approach is equally applicable to all types of military operations. Such an approach offers the prospect of rapid results or of results disproportionately greater than the resources applied. Hence it is attractive to a numerically inferior side, or to a stronger side which wishes to minimize the resources committed. A key characteristic of the manoeuvrist approach is to attack the enemy commander's decision-making process by attempting to get inside his decision-making cycle. This involves presenting him with the need to make decisions at a faster rate than he can cope with, thereby paralysing his capability to react.

Whatever the lip-service paid to the manoeuvrist approach, it is not always practicable to employ it. Measured against the above criteria, the NATO attack on the former *Yugoslavia in March–June 1999 appears strongly attritional. The methodical dismantling of the Yugoslav military and to some extent civil infrastructure was pure attrition and did little to achieve the stated aim of protecting Kosovar Albanian refugees. Pres Milosevic of Yugoslavia, on the other hand, proved highly manoeuvrist. Unable to respond effectively to NATO *air power, he nevertheless made great capital out of a downed US F-117 Stealth fighter-bomber, aiming for a weak spot—NATO's confidence in its technological superiority. And the moment the bombing started, his troops intensified their attacks on the Kosovar Albanian population—NATO's weakest point. He got inside his enemy's 'decision-making cycle' because he could expel refugees faster than NATO could degrade his military forces. NATO troops were not initially committed to a ground offensive, and so Milosevic could not easily attack another vulnerable point—their concern about casualties. However, he managed to capture three US servicemen in Macedonia, striking at 'the times and places the enemy least expects'.

Manoeuvre warfare is therefore potentially a means of achieving decisive results with minimal casualties. But it is not the exclusive preserve of those who advocate it. And sometimes, as on the western front in WW I or in modern operations, constrained by political and media pressure, there may be no 'room for manoeuvre'. When that happens, attrition comes into its own.   CDB

Bellamy, Christopher, *The Evolution of Modern Land Warfare: Theory and Practice* (London, 1990).
British Defence Doctrine (HMSO, London, 1996).

containing many foreign *mercenary contingents. The ultimate humiliation was the capture of Romanus himself. The sources agree that he was honourably treated by Alp Arslan and released after a few days. Byzantine prestige was seriously damaged by this defeat. The disaster at Manzikert has been seen as a convenient point from which to date the decline of the eastern Byzantine empire and eventually the Turkification of Anatolia. The battle has also been viewed as one of the mainsprings of European involvement in the Levant in the *Crusades.   CH

Mao Tse-tung (correctly Mao Zedong) (1893–1976), Chinese revolutionary leader and theorist of people's war, was born in Shaosan, Hunan province, in central China, the son of relatively affluent peasants. As a student in Changsha, he became involved in radical politics. In 1921, Mao became one of the founders of the Chinese Communist Party (CCP), and rapidly became one of the leaders of the movement. The alliance between the CCP and the ruling Kuomintang (KMT) broke down in 1927. In that year the KMT leader, *Chiang Kai-Shek, bloodily purged the communists and the CCP carried out a series of abortive uprisings. The Chinese civil war had begun.

By 1931 the CCP established fifteen base areas in the countryside; the Kiangsi soviet was established in November. Mao was at this stage only one among a number of CCP leaders, engaged in a battle for power with rivals, but his success in building up CCP administrations in the base areas brought him to prominence. Mao was a dedicated revolutionary who suffered personally as a result of his commitment.

It was the Long March which established Mao as the leader of the CCP. The fifth KMT offensive threatened to extinguish the CCP, so the communists marched some 6,000 miles (9,654 km) to Yenan from October 1934 to the summer of 1935. Even then, had it not been for Japanese invasion of China in 1937, the KMT forces might have defeated Mao. Instead, an uneasy alliance was patched up between the rivals allowing all Chinese to concentrate on the common enemy.

Mao was a theorist as well as a practitioner of revolutionary war, writing *On Protracted War* in 1938. His experiences in the 1920s convinced him that the Russian model of revolution was inappropriate for China; given the overwhelmingly agricultural nature of Chinese society, the revolution had to be based on the peasant, not the industrial worker. Mao realized that the solution had to be in part military, as 'power grows from the barrel of a gun'. The problem Mao faced was how to defeat the conventional KMT forces with a *guerrilla army. His solution was to look to the intangible (as opposed to material) factors of time, space, and will. The communists would trade space for time (as in the Long March) and use the time bought to create political will, to indoctrinate and mobilize the people. In a famous analogy, Mao saw the guerrillas as fish swimming in the sea of the peasantry. The peasants sustained them, just as the sea sustained the fish. Thus it was essential for the Red Army to behave correctly in its relations with the peasantry, which came as a pleasant surprise to peasants used to the behaviour of other armies.

In addition to its military role the Chinese Red Army was a political instrument of revolution. The establishment of base areas allowed the CCP to set up as an alternative government and begin to win over the peasants by a mixture of judicious reforms (concerning landholding, rents, and the like) and education. With the 'sea' of peasants mobilized, Mao believed, the enemy would be swept away in the resulting human tidal wave.

Mao's achievement was to take the elements of irregular warfare that would have been familiar to the Spanish guerrillas of 1808 to 1814 and link them to a specifically revolutionary political aim. He identified three phases of war. In the first, the guerrillas were on the strategic defensive, seeking to disperse their forces to avoid presenting a target to the enemy. The aim was to begin to mobilize the population. Mao's tactics were influenced by *Sun-tzu. In 1930, Mao summarized his tactics as 'Divide our forces to arouse the masses, concentrate our forces to deal with the enemy. The enemy advances, we retreat; the enemy camps, we harass; the enemy tires, we attack; the enemy retreats, we pursue.' Mao's approach has been described as the 'war of the flea'. The analogy is with a large, shaggy dog, which, bitten by the nimble pest, puts up his hind leg to scratch the flea bite, only for the flea to jump away and bite the dog somewhere else. The dog, like the conventional army, is always reacting to actions initiated by the flea/guerrilla. Conversely, a major feature of many successful *counter-insurgency campaigns has been the building up of an effective *intelligence system to allow government forces to seize the initiative.

Mao's second phase was when a stalemate was reached: the guerrillas were not yet strong enough to win the insurgency but were too strong to be destroyed by the opposition forces. In the final stage, they turned themselves into a conventional army and defeated the enemy forces, at least in part, in open battle.

The *truce with the KMT broke down in the summer of 1946. The CCP had made good use of the previous nine years: by this time it claimed to have a 900,000-strong army, backed by a militia of over 2,000,000, drawn from a communist-controlled population of 90,000,000. The communists equipped themselves with Japanese arms, captured by Soviet forces in the brief Soviet campaign in Manchuria in August 1945. Mao's forces then employed a mixture of guerrilla and conventional warfare against the KMT forces, which numbered about 3 million. The communists won a major campaign in Manchuria in October 1948, followed by the Hsuschow campaign in north China (November–December 1948). Mao entered the capital, Beijing, on 21

January 1949 and founded the People's Republic of China (PRC) in October of that year.

Mao's leadership of the PRC falls outside the scope of this article, although it should be noted that if it were not for *Stalin he would be the greatest mass-murderer in history. He represents one more swing of the millennial Chinese pendulum between ferocious centralization and anarchy, although his Cultural Revolution of the 1960s, echoing the *Taiping rebellion of a century earlier, was a bizarre effort to combine both. As a military leader, Mao was one of the greatest theorists and practitioners of revolutionary guerrilla war in history—if not the greatest. His style of insurgency, while not infallible, has proved to be eminently exportable and capable of being adapted to non-Chinese circumstances.   GDS

Mao Tse-tung, *Selected Readings from the Works of Mao Tse-tung* (Beijing, 1971).

Ellis, John, *A Short History of Guerrilla Warfare* (London, 1975).

Maori wars (1845–72) (also known as New Zealand wars; the 1860–72 period is also known as *te riri pakeha*, white man's anger). These were conflicts between Maori tribes of the North Island and the British authorities, imperial and colonial. The cause was the usual tension between land-hungry settlers and the natives, compounded by the British assumption that they had acquired full sovereignty over the Maori by the Treaty of Waitingi in 1840, and the Maori conviction that their autonomy persisted. The first major clash was the Northern war (1845–6), also known as Heke's war (after Maori leader Hone Heke) or the Flagstaff war, fought in and around the Bay of Islands. The result was inconclusive, despite the eventual deployment of 1,300 British troops. Clashes between the British and elements of the Ngati Toa alliance followed at Wellington, in 1846, and Wanganui, in 1847. The net effect of the wars of the 1840s, which were localized and small in scale, was to confirm that Maori autonomy persisted in most areas. Maori disadvantages in numbers and resources were balanced by the transformation of their traditional fortified villages (*pas*) into trench-and-bunker earthworks capable of withstanding artillery bombardment and requiring besiegers to take them by *sapping.

Conflict again broke out in Taranaki in 1860–1, with British forces totalling 3,500 opposing local tribes supported by warriors from the Maori King Movement, established to consolidate resistance in 1858. The first Taranaki war too was drawn, with each side winning a couple of battles. Maori autonomy remained intact, but faced a full-scale onslaught in 1863 when the British launched a well-prepared invasion of the Waikato, the core territory of the King Movement. The invasion was masterminded by Gov Sir George Grey and the able Scots Gen Duncan Cameron. The British mobilization, including colonial units and allied Maori, amounted to about 20,000 troops. Despite unprece-

dented intertribal co-operation, the resisting Maori could muster no more than 5,000. The Maori were able to delay, but not halt, a continuous British push south from Auckland into the central Waikato. Some 230 Maori did inflict a shock defeat on 1,700 British troops at the battle of Gate Pa, near Tauranga, on 29 April 1864. By late 1864, it was clear that the British had won the second Taranaki war on points, but they had been unable to destroy the King Movement, or Maori independence beyond the frontier. Imperial troops conducted two further campaigns in the Wanganui-South Taranaki area in 1865–6, then left the remaining fighting to colonial troops and their Maori allies, known as *kupapa*.

From April 1864 a new conflict erupted, involving followers of a series of Maori prophetic leaders, beginning with Te Ua Haumene, who fought a *guerrilla war. Internecine conflict between and within tribes increased, as did the killing of non-combatants by both sides. Fighting died down in 1867, then rekindled in 1868 with the remarkable resistance efforts of two Maori prophet-generals, Titokowaru and Te Kooti. Their victories almost brought the colonial government to its knees by the end of the year, but it was saved early in 1869 by a victory over Te Kooti at Ngatapa and by the collapse of Titokowaru's forces due to an internal dispute. Government forces were unable to capture either leader, but kept trying until 1872.

The wars shattered traditional Maori society, but left a legacy of treaties that their descendants have used in recent years to claim back large parts of North Island. Their formidable *pas* and their military skill made the Maoris a rare example of an indigenous people very nearly holding the imperial tide at bay.   JB

------

maps For much of history commanders were impeded by lack of topographical information. 'Bela IV of Hungary and Ottokar II of Bohemia were in arms in 1260,' wrote Sir Charles *Oman, 'and both were equally bent on fighting, but when they sighted each other it was only to find that the River March was between them.' Before the battle of Kolin in 1757 *Frederick 'the Great' told his generals: 'Gentlemen, many of you must still remember this neighbourhood from the time we stood here in 1742. I am certain I have the plan somewhere, but Major von Griese cannot find it.'

Early maps were drawn on stone, wood-bark, and hide, and an example from about 500 BC, impressed on a clay tablet, shows the world with Babylon in its centre. Both Romans and Greeks saw the world as a flat disc with the Aegean in its centre and the east uppermost, surrounded by sea. The Romans had trained geometers (*agrimensores*) and surveyed their roads, many of which led to distant garrisons. Few maps of the period have survived, but among them is a Roman shield bearing a map of part of the Black Sea coast.

The maps of medieval Europe, influenced by the Church's view of a flat earth, reflected first Roman and

Greek, and then Islamic and Byzantine cartography, including Ptolemy's *Geographia*. World maps remained inaccurate, but detailed work, based on observation and survey, was surprisingly good: by the 15th century coastal and harbour charts were available. The first printed maps were produced then, and the great discoveries of the next century improved the quality of world maps, with globes appearing in the 16th century and consideration being given to ways in which the detail of a round earth could be projected onto a flat map.

By the 17th century most governments regarded mapping as an essential component of the modern state. In 1683 England's Chief Engineer was expected 'to be well-skilled in all the parts of the Mathematicks, more particularly in Stereometry, Altemetry, and Geodoesia. To take distances, Heights, Depths, Surveys of Land . . . to draw and design the situation of any place'. In Britain surveying was in the hands of the Board of *Ordnance, which also controlled the artillery and the engineers: maps are still produced by the Ordnance Survey. The French *ingénieurs-géographes*, absorbed into the engineers proper in 1831, were responsible for mapping, and their products were housed in the Dépôt de la Guerre, which combined the functions of an *intelligence bureau with those of a map and statistical service. The USA had its Topographical Engineers, and its General Survey Act of 1824 further blurred the distinction between military and civilian engineering by encouraging the use of military engineers on a variety of projects, including the exploration and mapping of the West.

It was not until the mid-19th century that maps were available to armies in useful quantities. During the *Napoleonic wars commanders procured maps from a variety of sources, and in the *Hundred Days one British general used a historical map, stuck to linen to give it durability. Strategic blunders were reflected in map issue. In 1870 the French army had a sketch map of 'routes leading to the Rhine' but few maps of eastern France in which it actually fought.

The whole of Europe was accurately mapped by the end of the 19th century, and colonial powers had turned their attention to Africa, Asia, and India. In 1881 the British *War Office began numbering its maps in sequence, and in 1909 nomenclature changed to include the annotation Geographical Section, General Staff, which survives as the abbreviation GSGS on modern British service maps. Standardization appeared only gradually. For example, British cartographers favoured showing height by means of contour lines while the French preferred hachures. Scales varied, and while maps like the 1 : 250,000 series of South Africa were valuable for planning, they were less useful for navigation. When operations during WW I became static, maps reflected this by becoming more detailed. The British army took 1 : 80,000 maps to France with it, but was soon using trench maps with a scale of 1 : 10,000.

During WW I armies improved cartographic techniques, using air photographs to supplement survey. They also became adept at producing maps for issue right down the chain of command: when the Canadian Corps (see CANADIAN EXPEDITIONARY FORCES) took *Arras/Vimy Ridge in 1917 it had on average one map for each of its soldiers. Britain alone issued about 34 million maps for use on the western front. Maps enabled artillery to produce accurate *indirect fire, and the techniques developed by the then Brig Gen Tudor in 1917, which involved the accurate survey of the gun position, reduced the need for preliminary 'registration' of targets. Maps had long been gridded with lines of latitude and longitude, and the practice of gridding them in accordance with their scale and numbering these lines (northings and eastings) enabled users to give references to indicate locations on the map.

Subsequent developments have both increased the accuracy of maps and enabled armies to produce them more rapidly. Not least among the achievements of *Patton's army, which swung north to counter-attack during the battle of the *Bulge in 1944, was the manufacture and issue of thousands of maps of the new sector. Even at the end of the 20th century, when Global Positioning Systems make accurate navigation far easier than ever before and the partial automation of indirect fire has reduced dependence on maps, they still play a fundamental role in military affairs.

RH

Oman, C. W. C., *The Art of War in the Middle Ages* (Ithaca, NY, 1953).

Maratha (Mahratta) **wars** Name given to three wars fought between 1775 and 1818 involving the English East India Company (EIC) and the confederacy of Maratha chiefs in western and northern India. Maratha power had begun as a Hindu challenge to Mughal domination of India during the 17th century and by the latter part of the 18th century had become the dominant force in northern and western India and the principal rival of the EIC. The Maratha confederacy consisted of the fiefs of many semi-independent chiefs, of whom the most prominent were Holkar, Sindhia, the Bhonsla of Berar (Nagpur), and the Gaekwar of Baroda, grouped under the leadership of the Peshwa in Poona (Pune).

The first Anglo-Maratha war arose out of the interference of the EIC's Bombay government in Maratha affairs in the hope of obtaining some territorial advantage following *Panipat. Bombay supported Raghunath Rao, a contender for power in Poona, and in 1778 Gov Gen Warren Hastings despatched a force from Bengal under Col Leslie, who was succeeded by Col Goddard. Before Goddard's arrival, an EIC force from Bombay force had attempted to penetrate to Poona, failed, and had been obliged to sign a convention abandoning all territorial gains (1779). Hastings, who had hoped to gain control over the Maratha confederacy, now found himself at war with the whole of it and with the states of Mysore and Hyderabad as well. After two years of desultory campaigning in which Goddard obtained some victories, peace was made at Salbai (May 1782) in which the EIC relinquished all gains since 1776.

The Treaty of Salbai was followed by twenty years of peace between the Marathas and the EIC during which time Sindhia rose to pre-eminence by virtue of his extensive conquests in northern India and his disciplined infantry and artillery trained by a French adventurer, Benoit de Boigne. (The traditional Maratha military system had been based on light cavalry, raids, and attacks on enemy communications.) The second Anglo-Maratha war began when the governor general, then Lord *Wellesley, saw an opportunity to establish British control over the confederacy by a treaty with the Peshwa (Bassein 1802). The Bassein arrangement was resented by the other Maratha chiefs and Wellesley became involved in a war which took the form of extensive connected operations throughout India. There were four theatres of operations. In Orissa operations against the Bhonsla gave Britain territory which enabled the Bombay and Madras presidencies to link up. In Gujerat Broach was seized from Sindhia. But the main operations were in central India where the governor general's brother Arthur (later *Wellington) defeated the forces of Sindhia and the Bhonsla (battles of *Assaye and Argaum) and in northern India where the C-in-C, Lord Lake, attacked the French-trained forces of Sindhia in the Ganges-Jumna Doab and was victorious at Delhi and Laswari.

By the end of 1803 these victories and conquests were consolidated in peace treaties with Sindhia and the Bhonsla. Holkar was not included and in 1804 war commenced against his forces in Hindustan and the Deccan. The EIC forces suffered two heavy reverses, first when, after an imprudent advance, Col Monson retreated precipitately and lost his guns and many men, and, second, in January and February 1805 when Lake failed to take Bharatpur by assault and suffered considerable losses. Although it seemed probable that Holkar would eventually be defeated, London had had enough of war. Lord Wellesley resigned and was replaced by Lord Cornwallis with instructions to make peace and abandon the attempt to extend British power beyond the river Jumna and to control the Marathas.

In the following years the Maratha territories increasingly became a refuge for plundering bands of irregular cavalry known as *Pathans and Pindaris. British indignation at the activities of the bands eventually boiled over and in 1816 Gov Gen Lord Hastings set in motion an extensive plan to bring them under control. This plan involved allying with some of the Marathas and the *Rajput states beyond the Jamna and launching military operations against the Pathans and Pindaris from the north and the south. Inevitably the war spread and the main Maratha chiefs were drawn in and duly defeated: the Peshwa at Kirkee (6 November 1817), the Bhonsla at Sitabaldi (27 November 1817), and Holkar at Mahidpur (21 December 1817); the first were two brilliant defensive actions and the last an

expensive charge straight at the enemy guns. The danger from the Pathans and Pindaris was eliminated by a mixture of military action and conciliation. By the conclusion of hostilities in 1818 Britain was paramount throughout India as far as the borders of the Punjab and Sind.   MEY

Bhattacharyya, Sukumar, *The Rajput States and the East India Company* (London, 1972).
Roberts, P. E., *India under Wellesley* (London, 1929).
Roy, M. P., *The Origin, Growth and Suppression of the Pindaris* (London, 1973).
Sen, S. N, *The Military System of the Marathas* (London, 1928).
—— *Anglo-Maratha Relations* (London, 1961).

Marathon, battle of (490 BC). Fought during the *Graeco-Persian wars, Marathon was the first encounter between Persian and Greek troops on the mainland of Greece, and an earnest of things to come. The Persians, led by Datis and Artaphernes, had perhaps some 25,000 troops, including cavalry, the Athenians with their Plataean allies, perhaps 10,000. Though one of the ten Athenian generals, Miltiades, was later given much of the credit, the titular Greek commander was Callimachus, the polemarch (warleader). After some delay, the Persians possibly began to move on Athens, and the Greeks who had probably been waiting for the Spartans, encamped near the southern exit from the plain, were forced to fight. Thinning their centre to cover the longer Persian line, but leaving their wings strong, the Greeks advanced, probably breaking into a jog-trot when they came within bowshot. On each wing, the Persians were routed, and probably their flight carried away their cavalry, which apparently played no part in the struggle. In the centre, the Persians forced the Greeks back, but were then probably taken in both flanks when the victorious Greek wings wheeled inwards. Allegedly, 6,400 Persians were killed for only 192 Athenians.   JFL

Lazenby, J. F., *The Defence of Greece, 490–479 BC* (Warminster, 1993).

March to the Sea (Sherman's) Punitive 1864 'scorched earth' campaign through the south-east towards the end of the *American civil war. There are still places in the South where to whistle 'Marching through Georgia' is an invitation to violence. After the drawn-out Atlanta campaign of May–September, *Sherman was delayed a further two months by *Hood's attacks on his supply lines, but did not yield to the temptation of pursuing him into Tennessee, leaving his subordinate Thomas to destroy him. Sherman divided 62,000 men between the Armies of Georgia under Slocum and of Tennessee under Howard. Ordering Atlanta to be levelled after his departure, on 7 November Sherman advanced with his four corps in parallel across a 50 mile (80 km) front, destroying railways and living off the land with a vengeance. There was little fighting involved in a forthright war on the civilian population, during which Union soldiers were encouraged to burn what they did not pillage. The rape of white women was discouraged, a restraint not extended to the liberators' treatment of blacks.

The only serious resistance was posed by Hardee with 10,000 men behind fortifications defending the long-blockaded port of Savannah. It was well within Sherman's capability to cut him off, but he left him with an escape route across the river. This Hardee took on 21 December, permitting the Unionists to occupy the city unopposed. In a Christmas Eve message Sherman 'presented' it to *Lincoln along with 150 heavy guns and 250,000 bales of cotton. Technically this was the end of the March to the Sea, but the same approach was adopted in the subsequent campaign through South Carolina, hated as the cradle of secession, which included the sack of Columbia. The campaign was the logical outcome of Lincoln's definition of secession as a criminal act by individuals, not states.   HEB

Marighela, Carlos (1911–69), Brazilian communist who came to the theory and practice of urban *guerrilla warfare comparatively late in a life devoted to clandestine activity. A mulatto, he joined the Brazilian Communist party (PCB) in 1929 and was imprisoned in 1932 and 1939–45, eventually becoming a member of the executive committee. He was radicalized by the *Cuban Revolution and moved away from PCB orthodoxy, the final break coming in 1967 when he accepted an invitation the party had refused to the Latin American Solidarity conference in Havana and broadcast a call for armed struggle.

He formed the Açao Libertadora Nacional (National Liberating Action) and preached an urban variant of the *Guevarist concept of an armed nucleus providing a 'focus' for social discontents, enshrined in his rudimentary *Mini-Manual of the Urban Guerrilla*, which became required reading at the US *counter-insurgency School of the Americas. Its shortcomings as *doctrine and his own as a practitioner were underlined when the repression provoked by his robberies and kidnappings proved to be ruthlessly effective, in particular the conversion to political purposes of the police vigilante 'Death Squad'. Marighela himself was an early victim, betrayed and killed from ambush in São Paulo on 4 November 1969.   HEB

Marines are naval infantry trained and organized to carry out *amphibious operations and to fight from ships. A widely used definition in the USA is 'My Ass Rides In Naval Equipment' and the British equivalent is 'Muscles Are Required: Intelligence Not Essential'. In fact, Marines stress not only fitness but cunning in the conduct of operations and are the most naturally joint of the services, conducting the most complex land, sea, and air operations.

Throughout the history of naval warfare soldiers have fought on board warships, but in the 17th century many *navies formed their own infantry units to carry out two roles: fighting on board ship and amphibious operations. Arguably the former was the more important role and it has only been during the 20th century that their organization as an élite spearhead for conducting landing operations has become their principal role.

It is possible to accurately identify soldiers fighting aboard warships and conducting amphibious operations in the wars fought between the Greeks and the Persians over 2,500 years ago. In 480 BC the Athenian Themistocles ordered the formation of heavily armed sea soldiers to fight aboard his ships against the Persian invasion, while the Roman republican navy possessed its own naval infantry. In general, Marines were simply regular army troops serving aboard warships during wartime who returned to their parent service when no longer required. Their function has been significantly influenced by the technology and tactics of naval warfare at particular periods in history. Before the availability of artillery the emphasis upon close-quarter battle in naval warfare meant that seaborne soldiers were used to board, and repel, boarders. They remained important in galley warfare in the Mediterranean.

The organization and role of Marines underwent major changes in the 17th century. The Royal Marines, established by King Charles II on 28 October 1664, were the first modern regular corps of naval infantry. They were separate from the army, being administered by the Royal Navy exclusively for use with its warships. The majority of Marine regiments were still disbanded in peacetime and it was not until 1755 that a large permanent standing corps of Royal Marines was established. Other nations quickly imitated the British: the Dutch created a marine regiment in 1665; the Russians in 1705; the US Marine Corps (USMC) in 1775. In general most navies have established Marine forces.

The role of Marines in the mid-17th century changed dramatically when developments in naval gunnery meant that fleets now fought in line of battle (each ship astern of the one in front) in order to defeat the enemy with firepower. With diminished call for boarding attacks, Marines were now also employed as *sharpshooters against the exposed top decks of enemy vessels or to assist in firing the ships' guns (the Royal Marine artillery was established in 1804). They also carried out a provost role to maintain order and quell *mutiny on board ships.

The relationship between changes in naval warfare and the role of Marines continued in the 19th century. Marines were involved in a variety of tasks such as suppressing slavery and piracy and expeditionary operations, often in support of the main army. In the latter half of the century the development of armoured warships with crews under cover below deck removed the need for sharpshooters, so Marines now concentrated upon manning a number of specific gun turrets (always the smartest) and acting as landing parties.

In the 20th century Marines have regularly been used as élite infantry and gunners in major land campaigns. The Royal and US Marines fought on the western front in WW I, and the USMC repeated this role in the *Korean, *Vietnam, and *Gulf wars. The employment of Marines in this fashion is seen by themselves, and many other commentators, as a misuse of their specialist amphibous capabilities. Complaints during the Second *Boer War of the frittering away of Royal Marines in land actions led to them being returned to shipboard duties. While Marines still retain a provost role on board ship, and many of the tasks they undertake are no different from the army (quelling civil disorder, disaster relief, *peacekeeping) their main purpose has come to be the conduct of amphibious operations.

Historically this has always been their niche, but arguably it was only in the mid-20th century, with the dominance of the assault landing (one made against defended positions), that it evolved as their primary specialist role. In previous centuries the small size of armies in relation to long coastlines meant that forces could usually land unopposed. This did not exclude the need to develop methods for conducting operations in an organized and cohesive manner (the British developed a system in the 1740s), but it did not require an organization specifically trained to carry out amphibious operations. Instead Marines were assigned to individual warships from which they could be grouped to take part in landings, but they were rarely employed as a large spearhead force.

The vast size of armies in the 20th century meant that unopposed landings were rare, and the more dangerous and risky assault landing became the dominant form of attack. The high casualties and limited success of these operations in WW I (*Gallipoli and the Zeebrugge raid of 1918) discredited amphibious operations, with Marines being restricted to on-board ship duties and small landings. Only the Japanese and the USMC, looking out on an ocean of strategic islands, kept faith with the concept. While the Japanese developed a method for conducting largely unopposed night landings, the USMC developed a *Tentative Landing Operations Manual*, which solved the problems of the assault landings by exploiting new technology and innovative techniques, and served as the basis for all their future island assaults.

The complexity of these operations demanded a force trained and organized to carry it out with specialist equipment. This has meant that while Marines have continued to carry out many traditional duties, they have been formed into self-contained all-arms formations dedicated to amphibious operations. In the case of the USMC, it possesses more personnel (171,300 in 1999), aircraft, and ships than many nations' entire armed forces. In the 1990s, the USMC was made the 'lead service' for the development of so-called 'non-lethal' weapons, a somewhat incongruous role, given its history. The requirement for specialist amphibious troops and the ability of seaborne troops to deploy in strength rapidly to crisis points around much of the globe means that Marines continue to play an important part in present military operations, and will probably do so for the foreseeable future. As Adm David D. Porter commented, 'A ship without Marines is like a garment without buttons.'

TJB

Bartlett, M. L., *Assault from the Sea* (London, 1983).
Millett, Allan R., *Semper Fidelis* (New York, 1980).

Marius, Gaius (*c*.157–87 BC). Of undistinguished family, Marius came to the attention of *Scipio Aemilianus through his conspicuous service at Numantia. He went to Numidia in 109 as the senior subordinate of Metellus Pius in the war against Jugurtha. In 107 he was elected consul and succeeded Metellus in his command. He began attacking Numidian cities and successfully provoked Jugurtha into battle at Cirta, defeating him. However, the war was only concluded when the Romans subverted Jugurtha's ally, Bocchus of Mauretania, into betraying him in 105. Returning to Rome, Marius was elected consul for five years consecutively and given command against the migrating Cimbri and Teutones, who had inflicted a series of defeats on the Romans and were threatening Italy. After several years spent training and disciplining his army, he defeated the Germans at Aquae Sextiae (102) and Vercellae (101). He commanded armies in the *Social War, and in 88 provoked the ensuing Civil War by trying to take command of the war against Mithridates from *Sulla. He died in 87 soon after capturing Rome.

Many reforms of the *Roman army have been associated with Marius, but the justification for this is keenly disputed. He may simply have improved the efficiency and *morale of the army without changing its structure. AKG

Marlborough, John Churchill, Duke of (1650–1722). The son of Winston Churchill, a West Country gentleman impoverished after supporting Charles I, Marlborough was brought up in modest circumstances. With the Restoration, Marlborough's father was knighted and given a post at court. However, he died a debtor, and the experience of poverty marked Marlborough. In 1665 his sister Arabella was appointed maid of honour to the Duchess of York, eventually becoming mistress to James Duke of York (later *James II). Marlborough became a page to the duke shortly afterwards.

In 1667 Marlborough was commissioned as an ensign in the guards. He served in the garrison of Tangiers and with a naval expedition before returning to court, when he had an affair with Lady Castlemaine, the king's mistress, once escaping through a window when the king appeared. Charles forgave him, saying: 'You do it to get your bread.' He served with the fleet during the third Dutch war and in 1673 transferred to the Duke of Monmouth's Regiment in French service, and fought under *Turenne. In 1678 he was appointed a colonel in the British army, being expanded for what seemed an imminent war against France. Marlborough was sent on a diplomatic mission to *William of Orange, but war did not materialize, and he found himself in Europe accompanying the Duke of York, unpopular in England because of anti-Catholic hysteria and in danger of being excluded from the succession.

Marlborough prospered after Charles's victory over the Exclusionists in 1681, becoming a baron in the Scots peerage and colonel of the Royal Dragoons. When James came to the throne in 1685 he was given an English peerage, and later that year played a leading part in the *Sedgemoor campaign, although most of the credit went to the indecisive C-in-C, the Earl of Feversham. When William landed at Torbay in 1688 Marlborough was Feversham's lieutenant general, and at a crucial *council of war advised James to advance to attack the invaders. Feversham recommended a retreat, and when James decided to fall back Marlborough deserted to William. He was motivated by self-interest mingled with realism. Although he owed everything to James, his early life had shown him the risk of being on the losing side, and James's conduct did not inspire confidence.

Marlborough was confirmed as lieutenant general, elevated to earl of Marlborough in 1689, and tasked with reconstructing the army. He was then sent to Flanders with 8,000 men for the Prince of Waldeck's allied army. He led the decisive counter-attack at Walcourt, inducing Waldeck to tell William that 'Marlborough in spite of his youth has displayed in this one battle greater military capacity than do most generals after a long series of wars.' In 1690 he was granted independent command, and led an expedition which took Cork and Kinsale from the *Jacobites, prompting William to declare that 'No officer living who has seen so little service as my Lord Marlborough is so fit for great commands.'

In 1692 Marlborough was dismissed from all his posts and imprisoned in the Tower. He had remained in contact with James II, leading William, who had harboured doubts about his reliability after his conduct in 1688, to suspect him of treachery. Marlborough was soon released, but his rehabilitation was gradual. In 1695 the death of Queen Mary, an implacable enemy, allowed him to return to court, and he was reconciled with William by 1698. But he missed the *League of Augsburg war, including the battles of Steenkirk and Neerwinden and William's triumphant siege of *Namur.

William died in 1702, and Marlborough stood high in the favour of his successor Anne, the staunchly Protestant daughter of James II. Marlborough's wife Sarah had been in James's service when he was duke of York, and had become Anne's close friend. In their private correspondence Anne was 'Mrs Morley' and Sarah 'Mrs Freeman'. Sarah dominated the royal household, and was to play an important part in maintaining the power of Marlborough's Whig political

associates. Even if William had survived there was little doubt that Marlborough would play a leading role in the War of the *Spanish Succession, and Anne's succession left him in a position of unrivalled power, with the office of captain general.

Marlborough's long absence from the military stage did not encourage Dutch confidence. In 1702 he chafed at Dutch slowness in prosecuting the siege of Venlo and was unable to persuade the Dutch to attack the French, briefly at a disadvantage, but by the end of the campaigning season he had captured several important fortresses, including Liège. His successes had to be set against Allied failures in southern Germany and Spain, but they ensured him promotion to a dukedom. The queen had granted him £5,000 a year from Post Office revenues and although an attempt to persuade parliament to settle the sum on him and his successors failed, the marriages of their daughters helped knit the Marlboroughs into the Whig aristocracy. They lost their only son Jack to smallpox in early 1703, and Marlborough set off for the new campaigning season with a heavy heart.

The campaign went badly. Marlborough had conceived a 'Grand Design' of manoeuvring Villars out of the Lines of Brabant, fortifications running from the Meuse to Antwerp, but its inherent fragility combined with awkward Dutch generals to produce stalemate. That summer he considered a more ambitious project for the following season, marching to the Moselle to put pressure on Franco-Bavarian troops who had beaten imperial forces and were threatening Vienna. His political allies were under pressure from Tories who argued that resources should be concentrated on Spain and the fleet, and it took all his skill to persuade the government, the queen, and the Dutch of the need to support the empire. By the spring of 1704 it was clear that the Moselle would not do: he would have to march to the Danube.

The conduct of the *Blenheim campaign, when Marlborough had to move an Allied army of over 40,000 men, rising to about 60,000 as other contingents joined, for more than 250 miles (402 km), reveals his mastery of organization. Capt Robert Parker opined: 'Surely never was such a march carried on with more order and regularity, and with less fatigue to both man and horse.' He set off from Bedburg, near Cologne, on 20 May, and on 10 June met the imperialist commander Prince *Eugène of Savoy at Mundelsheim, south-east of Stuttgart. On 2 July he stormed the Schellenberg, key to Donauworth, which left Bavaria open before him. He spent the next weeks uncharacteristically laying waste the country rather than seeking a battle, but on Eugène's urgent summons he marched to join him near Blenheim where, on 13 August, he beat Tallard in the campaign's conclusive battle. It was typical of him to tell his wife the good news first: 'I have not time to say more but beg you will give my duty to the Queen, and let her know Her army has had a Glorious Victory, Monsieur Tallard and two other Generals are in my coach and I am following the rest'.

Blenheim saved the empire, destroyed the myth of French invincibility, and, as the Duc de Saint-Simon declared in his Diaries, left *Louis XIV 'with this ignominy and loss . . . reduced to defending his own lands'. The following year, campaigning on familiar territory, Marlborough pierced the Lines of Brabant near Tirlemont and pushed on to confront Villeroi near what later became the battlefield of Waterloo, but Dutch hesitation deprived him of a battle. In 1706 he moved through the destroyed section of the Lines to meet Villeroi at *Ramillies, where he won another major victory. As usual he did not spare himself. His horse threw him in a cavalry mêlée, and an equerry who helped him remount was decapitated by a cannon ball as he did so. He went on to overrun the Spanish Netherlands, but the success did not bring a prompt end to the war, for although Louis offered peace on terms that the Dutch might have accepted, the English would not.

The allied cause did not prosper in 1707: in Spain, the allies were beaten by Marlborough's nephew Berwick at *Almanza, and Eugène's attack on Toulon failed. At home Marlborough's grip on favour slackened as Abigail Hill began to supplant Sarah in the queen's affections, and Godolphin, his closest political ally, barely retained power. In 1708 Marlborough beat *Vendôme and Burgundy at Oudenarde, and went on to take *Lille after a long siege. There was no peace and Marlborough, anxious for an end to the war, found himself increasingly out of sympathy with his Whig supporters. He defeated Villars at *Malplaquet in 1709 in what he described to Godolphin as 'a very murdering battle'. Yet he had lost none of his old skill, for in 1710 he manoeuvred Villars out of the Lines of Ne Plus Ultra and took Bouchain. It was his last victory. Sarah had been dismissed, Godolphin had fallen, and Marlborough was dismissed from the post of captain general.

In 1713 the Treaty of Utrecht ended the war in Allied favour, although better terms might have been obtained in 1709. Parliament voted that some of the payments made by Marlborough had been illegal, but he was not impeached. On the accession of George I in 1714 he was restored to the post of captain general, but he was crippled by a stroke in 1716 and died after another in 1722.

Marlborough has good claim to being Britain's greatest soldier. As a tactician he was keen-eyed and quick-thinking, with a knack for putting an opponent off balance, and it was this, rather than real innovation, that brought him success on the battlefield. His personal courage was a beacon to others. Not only were his campaign plans brilliantly conceived, but they demonstrated a mastery of logistics that helped endear him to soldiers who felt he had their interests at heart. They nicknamed him 'Corporal John', and responded when they knew he needed all their efforts and heard that 'My Lord Duke desires that the foot should step out.' As an alliance manager and generalissimo he was un-

rivalled, always able to flatter with the impression of sincerity. He bore a political and military burden shouldered by few of his countrymen before or since.

Marlborough was notoriously tight-fisted, regretting an annuity made to a clerk who had saved him from capture. He hoped to receive a sweetener of 2 million livres from Louis for promoting peace, and happily made money from most of his offices. Yet his perseverance shines out across the centuries. A victim of severe (probably stress-related) headaches, after Ramillies he pursued the French long into the night with a splitting head, and when he lay down to rest on his cloak he offered half of it to a Dutch representative. RH

Barnett, Correlli, *Marlborough* (London, 1974).
Chandler, David, *Marlborough as a Military Commander* (London, 1973).

Marmont, Marshal Auguste Fredéric Louis Viesse de, Duc de Ragusa

(1774–1852). An artillery officer in the old royal army, Marmont saw service with Bonaparte at Toulon in 1793, and joined the Army of Italy as a brigade commander for the 1796 campaign. Although he had assisted Bonaparte during the coup of Brumaire, he was not included in the first batch of Napoleonic marshals in 1804, a slight for which he never forgave the emperor. He was a corps commander in the *Austerlitz campaign and went to govern Dalmatia for France from 1806–8. He played a significant role in the 1809 Danube campaign, and was present at *Wagram where his contribution finally earned him his marshal's baton.

He was then posted to the graveyard of French commanders, the Iberian theatre, and was defeated and severely wounded during his defeat by *Wellington at *Salamanca. He went on to command VI Corps in the 1813 and 1814 campaign but surrendered his corps to the Allies on 5 April, helping to bring about Napoleon's abdication. His title, duke of Ragusa, thus passed into the French language as *raguser*, to double-cross someone, a somewhat ignominious legacy. TM

Marne, battles of the

(1914, 1918). The stately Marne, which joins the Seine on the edge of Paris, offers a barrier to invaders entering France from the north: it saw fighting in the *Champagne campaign of 1814. In 1914 the German invasion plan initially went well, but by the beginning of September was in difficulties, partly because of the weakness of *Moltke 'the Younger', the German commander, and partly because of the effects of a long advance upon his troops. The Germans had planned to send their westernmost army (Kluck's First) west of Paris, but a counter-attack by the French Fifth Army at Guise on 29 August persuaded Moltke to edge it eastwards to support Bülow's Second Army, and subsequently to order it to follow in echelon behind Second Army—east of Paris.

*Joffre realized that the main threat was to his left, around the Marne, and drew troops from his right to form two new armies, Manoury's Sixth and Foch's Ninth. An aviator from the Paris garrison brought news of Kluck's wheel in front of Paris, and Joffre planned a counterstroke, with Sixth Army attacking the German flank north-east of Paris, the armies in the curve of the salient standing firm, and in the east Third Army jabbing in across Champagne.

The battle did not go as planned. *Gallieni, governor of Paris, sent troops to join Sixth Army in taxicabs, but Kluck, fighting with remarkable skill, swung round to check the attack. In the east the attack failed to materialize, and in the centre, in the stifling valley of the Marne, the fighting was fierce but inconclusive. Joffre was not helped by the fact that the British Expeditionary Force (BEF), sandwiched between Fifth and Sixth Armies, was not under his command, and Sir John *French, bruised by previous French failures, required a direct order from his government to remain in the line.

The battle hung in the balance when Moltke sent a trusted staff officer, Lt Col Hentsch, to the front with 'full powers to act on my own initiative'. Persuaded, by pessimism at Second Army and the chaotic state of the rear areas, that a retreat was essential, Hentsch ordered First Army to fall back to conform with Second. Most historians agree that the battle could have gone either way, and that it was a failure of nerve in the German high command that lost it. The Germans withdrew from the Marne and made a stand on the Aisne: they were to remain there for four years.

The second battle of the Marne was the result of operations BLÜCHER and YORCK, components of the *Ludendorff offensive which began on 21 March 1918. The Germans had made tactical gains but no strategic success, and on 27 May they attacked the French Sixth Army on the Chemin des Dames, above the Aisne, driving it back to the Marne. Although *Pershing had decreed that his American Expeditionary Force would only fight united, he was prepared to commit formations piecemeal to meet the Allied crisis. The first Americans were committed at Cantigny on 28 May, and, more significantly, at *Château-Thierry/Belleau Wood on the Marne and to its north in May and June. Just as the Marne had proved the high water mark of German success in 1914, so it did in 1918. RH

marshal/field marshal is the highest *rank in most armed forces, the equivalent in the USA and armies that follow its lead of a five-star general of the army. It began humbly, from the Frankish-Latin *mariscalcus* and from the Old High German *marahscalh* meaning 'horse-servant', the title of the man who tended and shoed the horses. This became, first of all, the title of a holder of high office in the royal household and, in time, of high military rank, much like the parallel title of *constable. By the mid-13th century in England and the 14th century in Scotland the *marescal* or *mareschal* in England was a high officer of state, a title bestowed on an earl or a duke. The title was first used as a military rank in 1300. It later referred to a C-in-C, perhaps through the parallel evolution of the verb to marshal—to set or arrange, and thus to gather forces together. By 1450 the king of Hungary was referred to as the 'marshal of Christendom against the heathen', and by 1560 the office of marshal of France, technically a dignity of state rather than a military rank, had been established.

In the 17th century the office of marshal or field marshal came to surpass that of general, although through a somewhat haphazard process, with wide national differences in policy and terminology. In Germany the rank, used until the end of WW II, was termed *Generalfeldmarschall*. It was always felt that it should reward success on the battlefield, and *Ludendorff, in old age, declined the honour, saying: 'An officer is promoted field-marshal on the battlefield, not at a tea-party in time of peace.' The Austrian army used the same rank, but also had the oddity *Feldmarschall-leutnant*, equating to major general. In 1736, the Duke of Argyll and the Earl of Orkney were appointed the first field marshals of Great Britain. The rank of marshal had been used under the *ancien régime* and was revived by *Napoleon who often gave his marshals independent authority to command armies of their own as well as major components of the Grande Armée when assembled. It disappeared after the Second Empire, but was revived again for *Joffre to sweeten his dismissal in the winter of 1916–17, and has been granted sparingly (and sometimes posthumously) since.

When the RAF was founded as an independent service in 1918 it needed distinctive ranks comparable with the various grades of admiral or general. The ranks of air vice-marshal (rear admiral or major general), air marshal (vice admiral or lieutenant general), and air chief marshal (admiral or general) were introduced. Marshal of the RAF equated to field marshal. The US army never espoused the term. Until after the *American civil war it did not promote much above major general. *Grant was eventually appointed general of the army, a rank later held by *MacArthur and Eisenhower, among a few others.

The Russian tsarist army had field marshals including *Suvorov, but the rank, like all the old military ranks, was abolished in 1917. In 1935 the rank of marshal of the USSR was introduced for five officers, including *Tukhachevskiy, recalling Napoleonic precedent. During the 1941–5 Great Patriotic War, marshals commanded Fronts (army groups) and acted as representatives of Stavka—the supreme command group. Marshals of arms—of aviation, artillery, or armour, for example—equated with army (full) generals, and chief marshals of arm to marshals of the USSR. The rank was later abolished but in 1997 Pres Boris Yeltsin reintroduced the rank of marshal (of Russia) for his defence minister.

In most contemporary armies, including the British, the rank is in abeyance, although it may be revived in wartime.

Throughout military history it has been the ultimate military distinction and it is ironic that its etymology has nothing to do with 'martial', a word that sounds the same and derives from Mars, the Roman god of war.   CDB

Marshall, Gen George (1880–1959), US army COS during WW II, appointed general of the army in 1944, Secretary of State in 1947–9, and Secretary of Defense in 1950–1. Author of the Marshall Plan for European recovery in 1947 and *Nobel Peace Prize laureate in 1953, he was the most prominent member of a generation of austere and selfless public servants who shaped American policies at the time of her greatest relative world power.

From an old Virginia family, he entered the army via the Virginia Military Institute rather than *West Point. His first service was during the *Philippines insurrection in 1902–3. He was operations chief of the 1st US Division in France in 1917 and of the First Army during the 1918 *Meuse-Argonne offensive. He was one of the 'inner circle' around *Pershing and served as his ADC 1919–24. From 1927 to 1933 he was in charge of the infantry school at Fort Benning and became COS on the day Nazi Germany invaded Poland to begin WW II.

Like Franklin D. Roosevelt, his efforts at first were devoted to preventing further weakening of an army that many, *Hitler among them, regarded as irrelevant. Starting from a baseline of less than 200,000, by mid-1941 Marshall was able to organize war games with twice that number, during which *Eisenhower, whom he was to promote over the heads of 366 senior officers to command US forces in Europe, first caught his eye. He also recalled his far-better-known predecessor *MacArthur to active service in the Philippines and was to show great forbearance in handling him and other prima donnas like *Patton and *Clark during the course of the war.

After *Pearl Harbor he directed the largest military build-up in history, training and equipping a citizen army that eventually numbered nearly 8.5 million men and women. In the face of an achievement on such a scale there is a tendency to overlook serious deficiencies in both the training and equipment with which the American host was sent to war. The selection and training of infantry officers was particularly poor, an odd lapse considering Marshall's background, while the massive commitment to the under-gunned, under-armoured *Sherman tank, known to the Germans as 'the Ronson', was a choice of quantity over quality with a horrible human cost.

He shared a common US suspicion of British motives in seeking to postpone the cross-Channel invasion, and seriously underestimated the fighting power of the *Wehrmacht. Had the invasion been launched in 1943 as he wished, it would almost certainly have been defeated with untold consequences for the shape of post-war Europe. As it was, a doctrinaire hostility towards geopolitical considerations, allied to the knowledge that whoever got there first was going to pay a high price, led him to divert the main American drive away from Berlin towards a chimerical 'southern redoubt'. The consequences of this decision during the *Cold War were to be painful, but it faithfully reflected the views of Roosevelt and cannot be attributed solely to Marshall.

He played a central role in the policy of containment developed when he was Secretary of State under Roosevelt's successor *Truman. The *Berlin airlift; the European Recovery Programme; military assistance to Greece, Turkey, and Israel; and the preliminary discussions that eventually led to the formation of NATO all took place during his watch. Until Britain confessed to bankruptcy in early 1947, American policy assumed that London must take care of security concerns in Europe. The 'Truman Doctrine' was not merely an awakening to geopolitical realities; it was a philosophical revolution involving a commitment to 'overseas entanglements', the avoidance of which had hitherto dominated US diplomacy.

He resigned because of ill health in 1949, to be appointed Secretary of Defense a year later to provide political cover for Truman after the outbreak of the *Korean war revealed deplorable military unpreparedness. It is difficult to imagine that Truman would have been unmoved by a protest against the manner in which the army was run down from a man he respected to the point of awe but that, to Marshall, was not his province. Nor did he feel it necessary to defend himself when Sen McCarthy accused him of being the mastermind of a communist conspiracy, although he did resign a few months later. The unkindest cut of all was when, in a shameful ethical lapse, the Republican presidential candidate and his protégé Eisenhower was prevailed upon not to defend him from McCarthy's odious slander.

HEB

Marshall, Brig Gen Samuel L. A. (1900–77), military theorist best known for the 'Ratio of Fire' theory from his fourth book, *Men against Fire* (1947). Marshall claimed that only 25 per cent of US infantrymen fired their weapons in combat and argued that the key to making the fighting soldier more effective was to concentrate on improving this 'Ratio of Fire'. His conclusions were apparently based on his thousands of post-combat interviews of infantry companies in the Pacific and European theatres in WW II. His combination of scientific method, confident proselytization, and field experience—as a soldier in both world wars and a journalist in Latin American brush fire wars—was convincing, and his idea gained extraordinary currency. But companions present at those interviews could not recall the subjects ever being asked if they had fired their weapons, while his notebooks showed no sign of the statistical computations needed to build his theory. Nevertheless, his 30 books are a swift economical read and were instrumental in restoring the ordinary soldier as the focus of the study of war. Many veterans of infantry combat agree that even if Marshall's methodology is flawed, his conclusions are—very broadly—correct.   DD

Marshall, S. L. A., *Men against Fire: The Problem of Battle Command in Future War* (Washington, 1947).

Spiller, Roger J., 'S.L.A. Marshall and the Ratio of Fire', *RUSI Journal* (Winter, 1988).

Marston Moor, battle of (1644). Marston Moor was the largest and most important battle of the *British civil wars, although its results were not immediately decisive. A strong Scots army, commanded by the Earl of Leven, crossed the Tweed in January 1644 and advanced southwards, first meeting parliamentarian forces under Lord Fairfax and his son Sir Thomas *Fairfax, and then being joined by the Earl of Manchester's forces from East Anglia. The Marquess of Newcastle, royalist commander in the north, fell back into York. Charles I regarded the city as crucial to his cause, and told his nephew Prince *Rupert of the Rhine to relieve it at all costs. Rupert duly crossed the Pennines and outmanoeuvred the allies to join Newcastle.

The allies decided to block Rupert's route south, and on 2 July their rearguard was on Marston Moor, south-west of York, when it became clear that the royalists had marched out of the city to offer battle. Not all royalist commanders shared Rupert's wish to fight. Newcastle's infantry was slow in arriving, and this prevented Rupert from attacking the allies while they were strung out on the line of march. Both armies were drawn up by late afternoon, their foot in the centre and their cavalry on the flanks, with the Long Marston–Tockwith road between them and a ditch and some cultivated ground just in front of the royalists. The allies, with around 27,000 men, outnumbered the royalists, with perhaps 17,000.

A desultory cannonade began at about 14.00, and as it seemed likely that there would be no battle that day Newcastle retired to his coach. But at about 19.00 the allies advanced, their attack providentially screened by a shower which impeded the royalist *musketeers in the ditch. On the allied left *Cromwell's cavalry beat their opponents after 'a hard pull of it'. On the allied right, however, most of Fairfax's horse were beaten by Goring, and their defeat dragged some of the infantry back too. The royalist infantry had rather the better of the fighting in the centre (and but for the dogged action of two Scots regiments might have won altogether), persuading several allied generals, and not a few of their men, to leave the field hurriedly.

Cromwell still had his victorious cavalry in hand. Fairfax, already wounded, had made his way behind the royalists to join him, and they now came in against the royalists from the rear. One of Newcastle's regiments fought to the end in the Hatterwith enclosures, on the north-east edge of the battlefield. A parliamentarian captain admitted that 'he

never in all the fights he was in, met with such resolute brave fellows'. Some isolated parties of royalist horse stayed in the field until midnight, but the battle was clearly lost. Rupert had allegedly been forced to take refuge in a bean field as Cromwell's men swept past, and his dog Boy was among the killed. The royalists lost at least 4,000 killed and 1,500 captured, the allies perhaps 2,000 killed. Newcastle 'would not endure the laughter of the court' and went into exile. Rupert got away with perhaps 6,000 men, and York surrendered on terms on 16 July.   RH

Newman, Peter, *Marston Moor 1644* (London, 1981).

Martel, Charles (*d.* 741), mayor of the palace of the Merovingian Frankish kings, son of the mayor Pippin II and his second wife or concubine Alpaida. After Pippin's death in 714, Charles wrested control of his father's inheritance from Pippin's first wife Plectrude. He defeated an opposing aristocratic faction led by King Chilperic II and his mayor Ragamfred at the battles of Amblève (716) and Vinchy (717), and again in 719 when they had allied with Eudo, Duke of Aquitaine. These successes did not win for him the overwhelming power in the Frankish kingdoms implied by the Carolingian sources, but did allow him to begin judiciously to engineer a redistribution of power among his supporters, sometimes at the expense of the Church. Thus secure in the Frankish heartland, Charles could turn his attention to peoples traditionally subordinate to the *Franks. He campaigned against the Saxons in 724 and again in 738, when he made them tributary, and against the Frisians in 734. In 725 he invaded Alemannia and Bavaria, capturing and marrying, as his second wife, a member of the Bavarian ruling house. Charles faced his greatest threat in 733 or 734 when the ruler of Arab Spain, Abd ar-Rahman, crossed the Pyrenees and defeated Duke Eudo of Aquitaine. Responding to Eudo's plea for help, Charles defeated the Arab army at or near *Tours. This victory allowed Charles to intervene south of the Loire, establishing his supporters in Burgundy and Provence, where he put down a revolt in 737 and 738. Charles's failure to install a replacement for the Merovingian King Theuderic IV (721–37) indicates the extent of his power by this time. Though he was not, as has been claimed, the architect of a new type of mounted cavalry, he was a uniquely successful general who laid the foundations for the Carolingian empire built by his son Pippin III and grandson *Charlemagne. The byname Martel ('Hammer') is attested from the 9th century.   MC

Jarnut, J., Nonn, U., and Richter, M. (eds.), *Karl Martell in seiner Zeit* (Beihefte der Francia, 37; Sigmaringen, 1994).

Wood, I. N., *The Merovingian Kingdoms, 450–751* (London, 1994).

martial law is government by military authorities when the normal machinery of civilian administration has broken down as a result of disaster, invasion, civil war, or large-scale insurrection. It is not to be confused with military law. Any trial of civilians held by military authorities under martial law would not enjoy the status of a *court martial.

In the Middle Ages, martial law meant law administered by the court of the *constable and marshal and from that court originated both the martial and military law of today. In Britain, it now means the law applicable by virtue of the royal prerogative to foreign territory occupied for the time being by the armed forces of the British Crown. Except insofar as the ordinary courts of the occupied territory are permitted to continue to exist and administer, justice is administered by military tribunals according to rules established by the military authorities of the occupying forces.

Martial law may also be established within a state itself in substitution for the ordinary government and legal system during serious disturbances. Again, in this event, justice is administered by military tribunals. Usually while the military authorities are restoring order, their conduct cannot be called into question by the ordinary courts of law. After the restoration of order, the legality of the military's actions might well be theoretically capable of examination. In Britain, this has not occurred since the 17th century. It cannot be declared in time of peace and it is uncertain whether martial law may be declared in emergency by act of royal prerogative or whether it always requires the approval of parliament. In either case, as mentioned above, the civil courts cannot interfere with the acts of the military in pursuance of their powers.

In other countries, a state of war has not necessarily been a prerequisite to a declaration of martial law or, more commonly, a 'state of siege'. In April 1989, students, teachers, and human rights activists began demonstrating in Tiananmen Square in Beijing. The demonstrations took place against the communist regime in China, against a backdrop of reform in other communist countries. Over the following months the number of demonstrators swelled to over one million people. Deng Xiao Ping evidently believed that this constituted a serious threat to his government and declared martial law on 20 May 1989; 300,000 troops, largely from rural areas in China, were sent to Beijing. The People's Liberation Army put an end to the occupation on 3–4 June: up to 3,000 people lost their lives, as many as 10,000 were wounded, and there were countless arrests. This brutal use of martial law incensed world opinion but firmly re-established the hard-line Chinese regime.

Another example of a communist regime that used the tool of martial law to suppress internal dissent was Gen Wojciech Jaruzelski's Polish government in 1981. Although he used considerable force to crush the Solidarnosc (Solidarity) Trade Union, the morality of this imposition of martial law is less clear cut. The Solidarity movement was the most serious challenge to the Soviet system since the Prague Spring (in 1968). The Soviet government was worried by the Polish Communist Party's apparent willingness

to compromise with the dissident movement and even though Stanisaw Kania, head of the Polish party, assured Moscow control could be maintained, the KGB believed otherwise. Thus, the Soviet army held some very threatening manoeuvres on the Polish border. Kania and Jaruzelski, who had become PM, visited Moscow and were told 'the socialist community is indivisible and its defence is the concern of not just each individual state, but the socialist coalition as a whole'. This was a very explicit warning. Jaruzelski declared martial law in December 1981 and used the army and police apparatus to quash, albeit temporarily, the Solidarity movement. He also arrested many of its leaders. It is not clear whether he imposed martial law out of a genuine desire to suppress Solidarity or to forestall an imminent invasion by the Soviet army, thus avoiding both turning Poland into a battleground like Hungary in 1956 and having a Soviet-imposed regime whose repression would have been much worse. If the latter is the case, this is an example of using martial law for a political end vital to the continued independence of the country. In February 1996 a parliamentary committee leaned to the latter interpretation, recommending that Jaruzelski should not face prosecution for declaring martial law in 1981.   MCM

Martini-Henry rifle The British army's first *breech-loading rifle was the *Snider, chosen because its action could be fitted to muzzle-loading Enfield rifles. It was only a temporary expedient, and in 1867 a committee studied purpose-built breech-loaders, selecting a weapon combining a breech designed by Frederick von Martini and a barrel designed by Alexander Henry.

Adopted in 1871, it was a single-shot weapon, with an under-lever falling-block action and a calibre of .45 inch. The *cartridge was first made of rolled sheet brass, but this often caused difficult extraction and a drawn brass case replaced it. The rifle was later made for the .303 round used in the Lee-Metford, the army's first magazine rifle. The .303 Martini-Henry was used by the *Home Guard in WW II, and the .22 version was a popular target rifle. The Martini action was used in the Peabody-Martini rifle which, in Turkish hands, caused most of the 37,000 Russian casualties incurred in the assault on Plevna in 1877.

The Martini-Henry bore the brunt of Victorian imperial campaigns. Its heavy bullet could stop determined warriors in their tracks, though faulty deployment prevented the 24th Regiment from taking full advantage of it at Isandhlwana in 1879, and over-reliance on its firepower encouraged the British to take on a powerful Afghan army and thus contributed to the disaster of *Maiwand in 1880.   RH

Masada, siege of (AD 73), one of the final acts of the *Jewish revolt against Rome which began in AD 66. Masada, a high outcrop of rock by the Dead Sea, had been fortified in the mid-2nd century BC and again by Herod the Great in the 30s BC. It was seized early in the revolt by the Sicarii sect of alleged assassins led by Eleazar ben Yair. In AD 73, with Jerusalem captured and the rest of the province subdued, the Roman governor, Flavius Silva, laid siege with Legion X Fretensis. The account by the turncoat Jewish leader and historian Josephus claims to have been derived from the two women survivors, but is regarded as heavily embroidered (though confirmed in outline by archaeological excavation in the 1950s and 1960s). Over several months Silva constructed a siege wall, with towers and eight camps, right round the plateau, and then an assault ramp up which he rolled a massive siege tower equipped with a battering ram and artillery. The final assault, on the day after the defences had been breached and fired, revealed that the 960 defenders had taken their own lives. BR2

Josephus, *The Jewish War*, 7. 275–406.
Yadin, Yigael, *Masada* (London, 1966).

Masséna, Marshal André, Duc de Rivoli, Prince d'Essling (1758–1817). Born at Nice in 1758, Masséna served fourteen years in the ranks of the infantry, leaving in 1789 to join a volunteer battalion which elected him its commander in 1792. A general in 1793, he trounced the Austrians at Rivoli in January 1797 and went on to defeat the Russians at Zurich. Given command of the battered Army of Italy, he held Genoa for two months, surrendering on terms. His stout defence distracted the Austrians, helping Bonaparte (see NAPOLEON) to invade northern Italy and beat them at Marengo.

Genoa broke Masséna's health, but he was made marshal in 1804 and commanded a corps in Poland in 1807. Napoleon peppered him at a shooting party in 1808, costing him an eye. Masséna did well in the war against Austria in 1809, and was sent to command the Army of Portugal in 1810. He was accompanied by a lady, unconvincingly disguised as a dragoon officer, which led to unpleasantness amongst his corps commanders. Following *Wellington into Portugal, he found only scorched earth in front of the Lines of *Torres Vedras. Wellington beat him at Busaco in September and Fuentes de Oñoro in May 1811. Masséna was replaced shortly afterwards: he had told Napoleon that he was past his best, and was undoubtedly right. RH

Masurian Lakes, battle of (1914). The destruction of the Russian Second Army at *Tannenberg left another Russian army deep in East Prussia, with the Germans badly out of position to deal with it. Even before the last Russian prisoners were counted in the south, *Ludendorff, *Hindenburg, and their brilliant operations officer Max Hoffmann began co-ordinating redeployment. Eighth Army, reinforced by two corps drawn from the western front during the Tannenberg crisis, now consisted of thirteen divisions, two cavalry divisions, and about five more divisions' worth of fortress and garrison troops. The Russian First Army, under Gen Pavel Rennenkampf, had fourteen divisions, a rifle brigade, and five cavalry divisions. Supporting it on the left, moving into the hole created by Second Army's defeat, was a new Tenth Army with the equivalent of a half-dozen first-line divisions—and more en route.

Eighth Army's command team saw their best chance as concentrating against First Army's left wing, in the air since Tannenberg. The German *operational concept was based on a right hook through the Masurian Lakes, driving northeast against the Russian lines of communication while the rest of the army fixed the Russians in place by a frontal attack. Rennenkampf had held his ground partly because he did not believe the Germans could redeploy as quickly as they did. Instead, replicating their earlier performances, the Eighth Army staff and the railways within a week mustered eight divisions on First Army's front and five more, with two cavalry divisions, for the flank attack.

This relatively even division of forces suggests willingness to accept Russian retreat, as opposed to thinking in terms of a *Cannae or a *Chancellorsville. On 7 September, three divisions drove in the Russian left against scattered opposition, but the cavalry, blocked by the leading units' supply trains, could not get forward. The XVII Corps, expected to support the initial advance, was stopped by determined Russian resistance, as were the four corps that went against the First Army's front. The flank attack's commander responded on his own initiative by swinging two of his divisions hard left, routing the Russians in front of XVII Corps. The way to First Army's rear seemed open, but Rennenkampf reacted with an energy and decision in sharp contrast to his earlier lethargic behaviour. On 10 September he committed two divisions to a counter-attack that bought the rest of his army time to disengage.

Marching over 20 miles (32 km) a day in brutally hot weather on roads blocked by their own transport, the Russians managed to run faster than the Germans could chase them. Ludendorff, expecting a general battle, kept his flanking force close to the main army on the 10th. Given more latitude on the 11th, they were too tired and too disorganized to do more than push the Russians across the frontier in the face of determined rearguards. The Russian Tenth Army made no significant effort to intervene. By 14 September, the battle of the Masurian Lakes was over. The Russians had lost over 125,000 men and around 200 difficult-to-replace guns. They had not lost the war. Having defeated two armies in a month, the Germans would find they had not yet begun to fight in a theatre that, from first to last, gave nothing back. DES

Matabele Warlike people in southern Africa, suppressed during the colonization of Rhodesia in the 1890s.

matchlock was the earliest mechanical means of firing a firearm and seems to date from the early 15th century. In the matchlock system, a length of smouldering slow match, instead of being held in the hand, was held in the jaws of a swivelling double-curved bar called a serpentine and brought to the touch-hole by operating a trigger. Further sophistications of the basic system involved introducing a sear-spring either to hold the match in the pan (itself a development of the touch-hole inspired by the invention of the matchlock) when the trigger was pulled, or to hold it out of it; thus the trigger could be used either positively or negatively. In the West matchlock muskets were superseded for military use by flintlocks by the end of the 17th century but they remained popular in the Orient, particularly in Japan, and in northern India until the 19th century. Matchlock muskets tended to be heavy and, in the case of 16th- and 17th-century arquebuses, needed to be placed on a forked musket rest to be fired. SCW

Blair, Claude (gen. ed.), *Pollard's History of Firearms* (London, 1983).

Peterson, Harold L. (ed), *Encyclopaedia of Firearms* (London, 1964).

Mau Mau uprising (1952–6). This uprising in Kenya was defeated by tactics learned in *counter-insurgency campaigns elsewhere during the retreat from empire. The regrettable truth of the matter is that the violence that spotted this process was not anti-colonialist per se, although presented as such, but rather a competition among local factions for who was going to rule once the British pulled out. Kenya was a prime example. After 1945 the most probable decolonization scenario would have left the white-settler minority as the main beneficiaries of imperial devolution. This prospect met with rebellion among the Kikuyu, one-fifth of the population. As the largest source of labour for the white farmers, they were the most displaced by post-war mechanization and suffered the worst urban poverty. Conversely, they enjoyed the best education and grew much of the urban food supply. Of all ethnic groups, therefore, the Kikuyu were most deeply divided between the constitutional politics of hope and the militancy of despair. This intimacy of disagreement obliged Kikuyu militants—the so-called 'Mau Mau'—to coerce kinsmen into keeping secret their plans to drive white settlers from their lands. Conflict within the insurgents ensured Mau Mau's defeat as much as British counter-insurgency.

Defeating the Mau Mau took four years, a long time considering the inequality of the fighting forces. The British fielded three brigades at the height of the campaign, in 1954–5, in which British infantry balanced the white-officered King's African Rifles. The loyalist Kikuyu Guard was much larger but was dispersed and immobile in its village keeps. The police also expanded. Mau Mau *guerrillas may have numbered up to 15,000 in late 1953 and 25,000 in all

over the four years. Less than one in five of them carried precision firearms however, and their casualties were heavy; over 10,000 died. Of the security forces, 164 died: 100 of these were African, largely Kikuyu auxiliaries.

Nonetheless the campaign started disastrously. After a few shocking atrocities during attacks on isolated white households, racial panic and poor *intelligence fostered a blind brutality that terrorized many Kikuyu into the arms of the Mau Mau. Forgetting the lesson of the utility of minimum force taught by the *Anglo-Irish conflict, the authorities were also slow to accept the example of the *Malayan emergency on joint military and civil command, convinced that the Mau Mau would soon give in. When in mid-1953 Gen Erskine arrived with such powers, his troops were at first wasted in penny-packet farm guards and large but ineffective sweeps. The answer lay in combining the urban techniques used in Palestine and the rural civil action employed in Malaya. The early 1954 ANVIL cleared suspect Kikuyu out of Nairobi in emulation of AGATHA eight years earlier in Tel Aviv. Meanwhile the concentration of the rural population in defended villages at last followed the Malayan example and forced the Mau Mau out of concealment to obtain supplies. This was accompanied by small-unit penetration of Mau Mau mountain-forest strongholds.

In time, almost all the forest-fighting patrols were made up of 'pseudos', that is captured or surrendered Mau Mau 'turned' by very much more decent treatment than they had been receiving from their own leaders, among them Dedan Kimathi who was captured and hanged. The precise role of post-independence leader Jomo Kenyatta in the rebellion was never satisfactorily established, but the Mau Mau certainly served to make him look like a moderate and to become the main beneficiary of independence. JL

Maurice of Nassau, Prince of Orange (1567–1625), succeeded his assassinated father *William 'the Silent' in the midst of the protracted and deadly *Netherlands revolt against the Habsburg empire. A military thinker and innovator of the first order, it was his fate to be matched against first *Parma and later *Spinola, the two most talented generals of the period, a misfortune somewhat balanced by the fact that the Spanish court emasculated both by denying them the funds to finish him off. Even amid the hammer blows of defeat, he found time to 'professionalize' his forces. He created a system of proper military training for officers, particularly in the technical branches of engineering and gunnery, and began to move away from the dense column of the omnipotent Spanish *tercio towards a more extended and manoeuvrable formation. He equipped his cavalry with *pistols, abandoning the obsolete lance, and began to concentrate standardized artillery pieces in batteries. Perhaps most significantly, he put supply, training, and pay on a regular footing.

The doom of the tercio, finally confirmed at *Rocroi, was presaged at Nieuport in 1600 where in an even contest Maurice's all-arms formation prevailed. The advent of Spinola reversed the trend for a while, but the Twelve Years Truce of 1609–21 was in part a tacit admission of greatly improved Dutch performance on the battlefield. It did not save Maurice when war resumed in 1621 and he died trapped in Breda. Maurice's legacy was a Dutch army he had transformed into the modern fighting force that enabled his brother Frederick Henry to secure eventual independence from Spain. So important were these reforms that they were adopted by most European armies, most notably that of *Gustavus Adolphus, who further refined and improved Maurice's tactical system.   RH

Maxim, Sir Hiram Stevens

(1840–1916), inventor of the world's most successful *machine gun. Born in the USA of *Huguenot stock, Maxim was self-educated and had already invented a mousetrap and the world's first automatic fire-sprinkler when, on a business trip to Europe, he was advised by a fellow-countryman: 'If you really want to make a pile of money, invent something that will enable these Europeans to cut each other's throats with greater facility.' A sore shoulder after firing a rifle suggested to him that recoil could be put to profitable use, and in 1883–4 he developed a rifle which used the recoil to eject the spent round and chamber a new one. A recoil-operated, belt-fed machine gun with a rate of fire of 600–700 rounds per minute soon followed, and Maxim dealt with the problem of the barrel overheating during sustained firing by surrounding it with a water-filled jacket. The Maxim's reliability and durability commended it to a score of armies. First used, by the British, in the *Matabele war of 1893, it was adopted by every major power around the turn of the century. There were national variations, such as the British *Vickers-Maxim and the Russian sledge-Maxim, so-called from its sledge-like mounting. Although most of his weapons took rifle-calibre ammunition, a 37 mm version fired shells whose distinctive explosions earned it the name 'pom-pom'. Maxim died, loaded with cash and honours, as his inventions cut a swathe through European manhood.
                RH

Meade, Maj Gen George Gordon

(1815–72). Born in Spain of American parents, Meade was commissioned into the artillery from *West Point but left the army in 1836 and spent six years as a civil engineer before rejoining, this time as a topographical engineer. He served with distinction in the *Mexican war and was promoted captain in 1856. Appointed brigadier general of volunteers in August 1861 he was wounded during the *Seven Days battles but recovered to fight at second *Bull Run and *Antietam, where he took over Hooker's corps when its commander was wounded.

Promoted major general of volunteers in November he was given command of V Corps in December and led it at *Chancellorsville in May 1863. Unusually among senior Union officers he had no driving ambition and, no less important, was no political threat to *Lincoln, who nominated him to succeed *Hooker in command of the Army of the Potomac. He accepted reluctantly, and only days later was engaged in a difficult defensive battle at *Gettysburg, from which he emerged victorious. Although he failed to press Lee's retreat, Meade was appointed brigadier general in the regular army and voted the thanks of Congress.

Meade headed the Army of the Potomac throughout the war, although when *Grant was appointed commander of all Union forces in March 1864 he stationed himself at Meade's headquarters, greatly reducing his independence. Yet the arrangement worked well: Meade proved a skilful collaborator through the grinding campaigns of 1864–5 and was promoted major general in the regular army in August 1864. He stayed on in the army after the war. Meade was not a brilliant general, and his filthy temper made him a difficult man to serve. However, his dogged determination and high principles gave him a strength which served the Union well.   RH

mechanization

was the next logical step in the substitution of chemical for muscle power once small and light enough power sources became available. Although men had dreamt of creating armoured fighting vehicles since at least the days of *Leonardo da Vinci, the impact of steam power was largely limited to *logistics and the naval environment, where power to weight and space considerations were not so crucial. Only the advent of the internal combustion engine allowed the dream to become reality on land and in the air, with its full expression in *armoured warfare.

The first area of warfare utterly transformed by mechanization was at sea, where the pace of technological advance greatly outstripped *doctrine and even the understanding of a visionary like *Fisher, who thought he had to sacrifice armour to combine speed and hitting power, when within a very few years all three were successfully combined in the *Warspite* class of fast battleships. Mechanization opened up the third dimension in warfare by permitting the development of purposeful *air power, which was well advanced before the first mechanically unreliable *tanks rolled into battle on the *Somme in 1916.

Between the wars mechanization stood at the forefront of the military debate. The apostles of armoured warfare, *Fuller and *Liddell Hart, pressed for mechanization, although they disagreed over the speed at and process by which it might be accomplished, as well as over the function of infantry in the mechanized force. Liddell Hart recognized the need for them, and sketched out the armoured infantry of the future in what he termed 'tank marines', while Fuller (although himself an infantryman) relegated them to duties like guarding bases or lines of communication. J. P. Harris has suggested that the British army's real problem was organizational and tactical: 'getting the right balance between units of different arms … and getting them to work together in the right way'.

The process was complicated, in Britain, France, and the USA, by financial stringency, industrial constraints, and lack of a clear strategic question to which mechanized forces were the answer, as well as the resistance (neither surprising nor ignoble) of military culture to the most profound change since the introduction of firearms. In Britain the emphasis on *imperial policing scarcely encouraged mechanization, while in France preoccupation with positional defence and the dominance of fire had a similar effect. The debate was rarely as clear-cut a collision between boneheaded conservatives and incisive radicals as is sometimes portrayed. Even in Germany, where *Guderian borrowed heavily from British and French theory and practice, there was widespread recognition that emphasis on *blitzkrieg would be likely to result in partial mechanization, with a two-tier army, part old and part new: this is precisely what happened. The British army that fought in *France in 1940 was fully motorized—though not mechanized in the sense described by Fuller and Liddell Hart—something the German army never achieved during the entire war.

Mechanization has unquestionably had profound effects. It has largely removed the pack and draught *animal from armies, and has greatly reduced the daily grind for the average infantryman. During the 20th century he has evolved from a warrior defined by the most basic means of propulsion, to (under most but by no means all tactical circumstances) a passenger in a vehicle who disembarks to fight and, in the case of armoured infantry in *MICVs, may even fight mounted. That it seems to have introduced no fundamental change in the military *art is suggested by the fact that the inspiration for US AirLand battle doctrine came from the *Howard-Paret translation of *Clausewitz, and the fact that the largely mechanized armies at the end of WW II still moved more slowly than the *Mongols. But that it has changed the face of war in less than a century is beyond question.   RH

Harris, J. P., and Toase, F. N. (eds.), *Armoured Warfare* (London, 1990).

mechanized infantry combat vehicles. See MICVs.

media and war (see also WAR CORRESPONDENTS). In 1995 the former BBC journalist Martin Bell, a distinguished inhabitant of the media–war interface, stated that 'the media and the military are partners in the same enterprise'. This might at first glance be interpreted as meaning that both deal with the cutting edge of policy decisions, but it really points to the unsettling truth that for cultures enjoying the full impact of the digital revolution, war has become just another aspect of show business. Just how true this is became apparent during the *Gulf war, when millions safely at home thrilled to images from cameras in laser designating aircraft showing the tiny minority of bombs that were both 'smart' and accurate destroying bridges, buildings, and vehicles—or more exciting yet, the pictures transmitted by TV cameras in the noses of the bombs or missiles themselves. The latter were particularly open to comparison with video games, in that the consequences of their impact were not, of course, even vicariously experienced. When the real business end of war was broadcast towards the end of the war with footage of the charred wreckage and *casualties along the Mutla ridge, north of Kuwait City, it persuaded Pres Bush and his advisers that the public might be revolted if they continued to 'pour it on' and was one of the reasons given for bringing combat operations to an early halt. But there is no evidence that the viewing public shared this jejeune equation of war with a sporting event, or that people in general are more upset by real gore and destruction on screen than by the fictionalized version, and this consideration may not be so influential in future.

Indeed one of the problems the media have with covering war is that reality cannot compete with the 'ultra-realism' of films like *Saving Private Ryan*. To capture the same thing in action would require large numbers of suicidal TV crews and even then could not deliver the choreographed impact of the same event when staged, where the consequences of getting a scene wrong may be expensive but are not fatal. Although moving pictures were produced as early as the Second *Boer War and in WW I, they were often posed after the event and were not shown to the public until much later. The British film of the battle of the *Somme was, unusually, shown when that operation was at its height. Even action footage, although it awoke the public to some dim idea of what hell the soldiers were going through on the western front, showed men just falling down untidily when hit and could not begin to convey the intimate agony involved. Technological advance made it possible for movie crews to be very much nearer the action during WW II, but even the extremely dedicated German cameramen, at a very high cost to themselves, were seldom in the right place at the right time. Still *photographers actually produced the more telling images of the physically and psychologically wounded (the now-clichéd 'thousand yard stare'), as well as moments of high drama if not of high danger like the raising of the stars and stripes at *Iwo Jima. One notable exception was the film coverage of the liberated Nazi *concentration camps, which captured a reality far beyond the ability of normal people to imagine and hardened public attitudes towards the perpetrators—not enough, perhaps, but more than words could have achieved.

It is conceivable that at some not-too-distant time, 'virtual reality' may tap into the brain itself and only then will non-participants be able to experience the full overwhelming impact of the sights, sounds, smells, and above all the bowel-loosening terror of war. Until that time media coverage of combat will remain essentially voyeuristic, titillating rather than satisfying, and will be handled as such by those conducting military operations. The influence of the international news media on governments' willingness or otherwise to initiate military operations and on their conduct has become a detailed and significant part of any western military planning. The RAF's *Air Power Doctrine* of 1991 states that 'the conduct of war is affected by group passions, cohesion and determination. A significant war effort cannot be sustained by a democratic state in the face of public hostility or indifference.' US *field manual FM 100–5 (*Operations*) similarly recognizes that the importance of understanding the impact of raw television coverage is 'not so that commanders can control it, but so they can anticipate adjustments to their operations and plans'. These are poignant words.

The nadir of media coverage of 'bang-bang' may well have been plumbed during coverage of the civil wars in Central America during the 1980s, where the rights or wrongs of the conflicts were decided in the bars of comfortable hotels in the capital cities and hinged entirely on which side made it easiest for the TV crews and journalists to get their required combat footage in time for the evening news programmes. Media management tended to be better managed by the insurgents and there is always the unspoken consideration, very noticeable over the last 25 years in the coverage given to the motives of men of blood such as the *IRA, that reporters who do not toe the *terrorists' line may not merely lose access to the 'decision makers' but also their lives. This consideration is not, of course, absent from the calculations of politicians. By assassinating *Mountbatten and Airey Neave, and by nearly blowing up PM Thatcher and her cabinet at Brighton, a definable predisposition to see their point of view was achieved.

Even with micro-miniaturized cameras transmitting events via satellite in real time to faraway studios, the impact of media coverage grows up the chain of command. It is never going to influence the handling of a particular situation by a given platoon, but it may cause colonels, generals, and even presidents or prime ministers to give orders that will affect how another platoon in a similar situation will react. In 1993 former British Foreign Secretary Douglas Hurd said that 'the public debate is run not by events, but by the coverage of events', but most in the business are wary of politicians seeking to share their responsibility with the media. A government with a clear policy in which it has confidence is not swayed by media coverage and indeed makes sure that its own case is properly presented. What the media can unmask mercilessly is a politician or a military spokesman fudging the issues, as it did most tellingly in *Vietnam, showing that if indeed there was 'a light at the end of the tunnel' it was a very dim one, and the tunnel

extremely hazardous. Far more often there is an unhealthy symbiosis between governments and those who wish to preserve access to decision-makers for cheap, easy, and mutually beneficial interviews where the hard questions are not asked and the absence of answers is not revealed.

The impact of television was increased by the appearance in the 1980s of 24-hour news channels, broadcasting constantly. The 'CNN factor', named after the Cable News Network based in Atlanta, Georgia, was recognized by military leaders and politicians alike, and by the mid-1990s commentators joked that CNN occupied the sixth permanent seat on the UN Security Council. Other satellite channels with a global audience were British Sky Broadcasting and BBC World Television. Large media organizations can have news teams deployed on both sides of a conflict, with analysts in the newsroom back home to interpret and comment on events, fundamentally altering the position occupied by the media in earlier generations, when reporters were the hostages of one side or the other.

But the media are not monolithic, and neither is their target audience. Print and broadcasting, broadsheet and tabloid newspapers, photojournalism, TV, and radio are all different. So are reportages that give individual correspondents' views at a particular place and time, general news reporting, features, and expert analysis. Military operations and *exercises are good for television, but require vivid pictures to earn a place in a news programme, whereas descriptions of the evolution of military *doctrine, tactics, or strategy may be limited to specialist magazines or, with luck, find a place in broadsheet newspapers. The media target audience and that for 'media operations' also varies. There are four main categories: the reporter's own country; an international audience; the 'host nation'; and the 'enemy'. A military force has to do more than keep the public at home informed. A higher priority in media operations, especially in a *peacekeeping situation, is to influence the local media in the area where it is operating. In this case, media operations become intertwined with *psychological warfare.

The choices made by media organizations are often extremely arbitrary, affected by the personal interests of correspondents and editors, by the natural life of a story; boredom soon sets in and there is competition from other stories. Media organizations also have to make hard choices based on what they can afford. The principal reason why the flight of Kurdish refugees in northern Iraq in April 1991 received much media coverage, which probably influenced western states into trying to help them, was that equipment and personnel were still in the area from the *Gulf war. Bosnia received wide coverage because it was relatively easy to get to: contemporary conflicts in Africa, Afghanistan, Chechnya, and elsewhere in the former USSR were much more difficult and expensive to cover, and received less attention.

Most unusually for a major war, there was a strong group of western correspondents in Baghdad at the outset of the

Gulf war, who provided film of the first Allied air strikes simultaneously with the announcement that hostilities had begun. The Iraqis decided it was in their interest to allow an international media presence, not least because the basement of their hotel provided one of the few command and control centres not likely to feature in the nose camera of a bomb. They also manipulated the media presence, for example with the alleged bombing of a 'baby milk factory', complete with a sign in English proclaiming it as such. But conversely the broadcasts from Baghdad provided the Allied command with useful additional *intelligence throughout the war. Media coverage of the more apparent-than-real success of Patriot anti-missile missiles in Israel and Saudi Arabia was also militarily significant. The presence of more than 2,000 media persons in Saudi Arabia could have betrayed the coalition plan for the envelopment of the Iraqi forces from the west, but the nature and scale of the movement was carefully disguised as a training exercise. Meanwhile Gen Schwarzkopf's headquarters staff were assiduously briefing the media on *amphibious operations, helping to keep Iraqi attention on the US Marines offshore rather than the opposite direction.

The use of the media to influence one's own side is as old as communications. Julius *Caesars's accounts of the *Gallic wars were manifest propaganda, and Douglas *MacArthur notoriously used the press to influence decision-makers during WW II, although it went less well with him when he tried the same technique on *Truman during the *Korean war. There was much sniggering when the US Marines stormed ashore into the teeth of whirring cameras and clicking shutters in *Somalia in 1992, but no one was laughing when MacArthur waded ashore at Leyte in 1944. This was partly because the latter was a legitimately dramatic moment, but the two incidents do illustrate the high and the low side of using the media to draw attention to oneself. There can be no argument but that subsequent media coverage of dead US Rangers being dragged through the streets of Mogadishu after a failed raid was the clearest expression of the role of the fourth estate in war, correctly posing the question of whether US national interests were sufficiently involved to be worth the cost.

Coverage of fighting in the Balkans represented the state of the art both in terms of the technology involved and the commitment of resources. Unusually, it also aroused passions usually kept under professional wraps. It may yet come to be seen as a defining event for many young intellectuals who were there, much like the *Spanish civil war nearly 60 years earlier. The terrain in the war zone was rugged, the climate treacherous, and the divisions between the warring sides unclear. In the first year, reporters suffered heavy casualties, mainly among locally recruited television camera operators who had to get close to the action to obtain pictures. They learned rapidly, acquiring body armour, cross-country and armoured vehicles, satellite communications (the terrestrial *telephone network had been disrupted), and expert local guides, known in the trade as 'fixers'. They worked closely with the UN forces, particularly the British, who realized the media were essential to maintain public interest and support at home, and could also affect their mission. One British commander admitted that when negotiating with local factions, a television crew was a valuable adjunct, as the factions would know their conduct would be reported, worldwide. The media was sometimes the only means of recording agreements, and agreements made on camera are less easy to repudiate.

Media coverage of war is, if ever the cliché were justified, a two-edged sword. It may be useful to a commander in obtaining intelligence, in influencing public and political opinion, or in misleading the enemy. Or it may betray his plans and otherwise highlight his lack of the qualities necessary for command. Generalship has always demanded competence in a very broad range of activities from its practitioners; handling the media sensibly and positively is merely one of them, and by no means the most demanding.

CDB/HEB

Bell, Martin, *In Harm's Way* (London, 1996).

Bellamy, Christopher, *Expert Witness: A Defence Correspondent's Gulf War* (London, 1993).

Knightley, Phillip, *The First Casualty: The War Correspondent as Hero, Propagandist and Mythmaker* (London, 1978).

medicine, military (*See opposite page*)

Megiddo, battles of (*c.*1468 BC, 609 BC, and AD 1918) (see also ARMAGEDDON). Tel Megiddo, in the fertile coastal strip of Palestine, now Israel, was the site of the first battle of which we have record of battle tactics, of another of which we know little except that the Israelites did poorly, and of the culminating battle of the Palestine campaign in 1918. It stands at a vital crossroads from Egypt into Mesopotamia and from the coastal plain into Galilee. The earliest settlement was built in the early 4th millennium BC and was occupied until *c.*450 BC.

In around 1476 BC Egyptian Pharaoh Thotmes (Thutmosis) III led perhaps 10,000 men in a rapid march against rebel Palestinian chieftains. They had sent outposts to hold the Megiddo pass, a covering force which was easily scattered leaving the king of Kadesh to face the pharaoh on the Megiddo plain. Thotmes' army advanced in a concave formation, its southern wing enveloping the rebels while the northern wing was driven between them and the town of Megiddo itself. They used surprise, shock action (*chariots) and firepower (archers), cut communications, and enveloped the enemy.

Solomon built a fort on the site and in 609 BC King Josiah of Judah was killed there when opposing the march of the Egyptian King Necho II towards Assyria.

(*cont. on page 567*)

medicine, military

WARFARE and disease have always gone hand in hand. Disease affects armies, and armies spread disease. It seems probable that the first surgeons were military, treating the results of single combat or of tribal raids. The *Roman army was the first for which there is much written and archaeological evidence of organized medical services. It was as much exposed to disease as any other, but because the troops were better fed and had better organized sanitary arrangements, strictly enforced, they suffered less than their opponents. Despite this, barely half the enlisted legionaries lived to complete their eighteen-year service. Rather fewer auxiliaries survived, but this was still a higher proportion than that for civilians.

The Romans felt that medical practice was suitable only for Greeks and slaves, so most, if not all, army doctors were Greek. Such tombstones, or altars, that have survived are of Greeks. In the legion, the doctor (*medici*) had under him orderlies (*medici ordinarii*) and dressers (*capsarii*) who seem to have been the equivalent of stretcher-bearers. They treated wounded in the battle lines, and evacuated them to safer areas. There is a scene on Trajan's column where an auxiliary is having his wounded thigh dressed.

Legionary fortresses were provided with a large hospital, containing many rooms, arranged round a courtyard and verandah. The larger auxiliary forts were also provided with smaller *hospitals, of which several in Great Britain have been excavated. The best known of these is at Housesteads, on *Hadrian's wall. Each hospital had a large room, occupying the full width of one end of the building, which seems to have been an operating theatre. The equipment of military surgeons has been found, and there are descriptions of the treatment of particular kinds of wounds. Split reeds were used to extract arrowheads, and a metal blade-like instrument was used for extracting larger missiles. Celsus (25 BC–AD 50), in *De Re Medicina*, describes a number of such operations, including limb amputations, carried out, of course, without anaesthesia. Herbal remedies were known and rather coarse antiseptics, such as pitch and turpentine, often accompanied by religious incantations, were widely used.

The first great figure of military surgery of whom much is known was Ambroise *Paré, the greatest surgeon of the Renaissance. He served for almost 30 years in the armies of the French kings, with practice in Paris in the peaceful intervals. He left graphic descriptions of a vast array of wounds, with advice as to their treatment and the instruments to be used. Thomas Gale, a contemporary, published a treatise of gunshot wounds and their treatment in 1563, and William Clowes, who served in the Elizabethan navy, wrote on burns caused by *gunpowder in 1591.

In the British army, organized military medicine began with the raising of a standing army in the 1660s. The army was organized on a regimental basis, and permanent commissions were given to regimental surgeons. They were not highly regarded, and career advancement for medical men was very uncertain. A surgeon and assistant surgeon formed part of each regiment, to run a small hospital and treat the sick. A few non-regimental doctors served on the administrative staff for general and field hospitals. Some distinguished medical men served in the forces. John Hunter (1728–93), the father of modern scientific surgery, served in both the army and the navy, and in 1790 was appointed surgeon general to the land forces, and inspector general of hospitals.

The *Napoleonic wars produced many great medical figures. James Guthrie (1785–1856) joined the army at the age of 13, and became a Fellow of the Royal College of Surgeons at 16. He was bitterly opposed to the routine amputation of damaged limbs, and realized the necessity of rapid casualty evacuation. His textbook *Commentaries on the Surgery of War 1808–1815* was a standard work for decades. Sir James McGrigor (1771–1858) was director general of the Army Medical Department from 1815 to 1851. He was a fine administrator, and quite early appreciated the dangers of cross-infection between wounds and infective fevers. He was even able to disagree with the Duke of *Wellington and survive.

A worthy successor to the work of Ambroise Paré was Dominique Jean *Larrey, who served in the French navy, the Republican army, and the Napoleonic army. He introduced *ambulances volantes*, light, two-wheeled, sprung vehicles, drawn by two horses, for the rapid evacuation of the wounded. He was a meticulous surgeon, who served in Egypt, Russia, Germany, and at *Waterloo.

During the *Crimean war, the appalling conditions of the sick and wounded caused a public outcry. In that war 1,761 British soldiers died of wounds and 16,497 died of disease—almost ten times as many. The main causes of death were cholera, typhoid, and typhus, due principally to a total neglect of hygiene. Chaos reigned in the main hospital at Scutari, an old Turkish *barracks, where, in the space of eight weeks, over 2,000 men died of infections acquired in hospital. That remarkable woman Florence *Nightingale took charge, and produced dramatic changes. She was autocratic and strong-willed, and needed to be, given the incompetence and obstruction of the medical and administrative staff. Surgery during the campaign remained fairly primitive, with wholesale limb amputations and a high rate of post-operative infections.

The *American civil war took place on a vaster scale than the Crimean war, but the problems were much the same, although they were more efficiently tackled. Once again, disease was the major killer of soldiers. Of the approximate total of 618,000 deaths on both sides, about 414,000 were from disease and non-battle injuries, and 204,000 from wounds. Although anaesthesia in the form of ether and chloroform was available for operations, because of the vast numbers of casualties, supplies sometimes ran out before all the wounded were treated. The Confederate forces were even worse off in this respect because their supply system was worse. Infectious diseases, by crippling armies, delayed some campaigns, and prevented others starting at all. The main killers were cholera, typhoid, dysentery, malaria, and tuberculosis, but there were also serious outbreaks of smallpox and measles, against which many troops had no immunity. In early battles, many wounded might lie out for two to three days, but by *Gettysburg, at the end of each day the casualties had been cleared. Nearly all wounds became infected, the infection often being transmitted by the surgeons' unwashed hands and instruments. In the Union army, mortality from chest wounds was 62 per cent, and from abdominal wounds 87 per cent. An Ambulance Corps, to speed casualty evacuation, was formed in the Union army in 1862. As the war progressed, hospital arrangements became better, with many around Washington, and scattered throughout the Union states. Emulating Florence Nightingale, many women worked in hospitals, caring for the sick and wounded, and improving their lot considerably. Of the large number of *POWs who died in camps, the vast majority died of dysenteric diseases, due to grossly deficient hygiene.

Following the Crimean war, an Army Hospital Corps was formed in the British army, but general medical care remained in the hands of regimental surgeons. The Army Nursing Service was formed in 1881, and the Royal Army Medical Corps (RAMC) was formed as a separate entity in 1898, in time for the medical chaos of South Africa. The Second *Boer War once again proved the overwhelming importance of hygiene and sanitation in armies. In the British and empire forces there were 26,750 battle casualties with 7,994 deaths (29.8 per cent mortality) and 404,126 non-battle casualties with 14,448 deaths (3.5 per cent mortality). The much lower death rates showed the significant advances in medicine, but the spread of disease was largely preventable. Once again, the sickness and deaths were due to cholera, typhoid, and dysentery, as many Boer war memorials will testify. The British army was said to be fully prepared to fight the Crimean war again in 1899, but the medical services were even worse, being understaffed, inadequate, and unprepared. Large numbers of very well-paid civilian specialists had to be employed to treat the sick and wounded. At one stage, the sickness was 958 per 1,000 troops. In the so-called *concentration camps, organized by *Kitchener, to hold Boer women and children, things were even worse. There were 20,000 deaths among 117,000 inmates, partly due to inefficiency, unpreparedness, and lack of supplies, and partly due to the Boers being un-used to living in close communities.

WW I was expected by most combatant nations to be over in a few months. Few people had planned for the enormous number of men, or the enormous number of casualties, that would be in-volved. This applied particularly to the medical services, who were at first overwhelmed by the sheer number of battle casualties confronting them, and later, by the even larger number of sick soldiers. In all the worldwide theatres of war, disease admissions to hospital reached staggering proportions, considerably outnumbering wounds. During the *German East Africa campaign for example, ad-missions to hospital reached 240 per cent of troops in the theatre, mainly from malaria and dysen-teric illnesses, with wounds accounting for only 3 per cent of admissions. Areas like Macedonia and *Mesopotamia were almost as bad. Even on the western front, among British and Dominion troops, battle casualties were only 39.5 per cent of admissions. Mortality rates fell to less than 1 per cent for disease, and less than 8 per cent for wounds, a great improvement on previous wars.

Improvements in the treatment of wounds and disease were astonishing for the time, under the pressure of warfare, with the prospects for a sick or wounded soldier improving steadily throughout the war. The hard-won experience of WW I surgeons and physicians proved a very sound basis for the continuing improvements which occurred in later wars. The medical advances made in this war were the greatest in any conflict, and vastly improved not only military but also civilian practice. The type of wound and the bodily area of wounding changed from previous conflicts. It was very much an artillery war and in the British army shells, *mortars, and *grenades accounted for 61 per cent of all wounds, with *bayonet wounds accounting for only 0.3 per cent. Wounds of the limbs made up the greater part of the treated casualties, revealing the poor survival of chest and abdominal wounds. Patients with wounds to the head and neck survived better than had been expected, due to improved surgery, with an astonishing 82 per cent being subsequently fit for some form of duty.

A considerable amount of research, often under front-line conditions, went on into the problems of shock, fluid replacement, blood loss, and wound infections. There was close co-operation between the British, Dominion, French, and later American medical services on all these topics, and on others of common interests as well. Blood transfusion, which was rarely used pre-war, became routine later in the war. At first, blood had to be fresh, with direct transfusion from man to man, but by 1916–17 blood could be stored for several days, and stocks could be moved where needed. Blood groups were unknown, but a simple agglutination test was performed to check that blood was suitable for the re-cipient. Early in the war, blood transfusion could only be given in base hospitals, but by early 1918, a blood transfusion service existed, so that blood could be provided as far forward as the Advanced Dressing Station. Fluid replacement proved invaluable in the treatment of dehydration, due to cholera and dysenteric diseases, but intravenous fluid had to be made up fresh, and all equipment had to be boiled at every use. The problems of wound infections were attacked with great vigour and much bacteriological research was undertaken. By opening wounds, cleaning out and removing dead and damaged tissue, infection was controlled to some extent, but healing was delayed. A large, open wound could be observed and dressed more readily. The twin terrors of tetanus and gas gangrene, due to fighting over heavily manured ground, were diminished compared with many previous conflicts, and were rare away from the western front. Both of these diseases thrived in deep wounds, in the absence of oxygen. In the British army, and probably in all forces, infections from gas gangrene occurred in 10 per cent of all wounds in 1914–15, but had fallen to 1 per cent by 1918. Mortality was 22 per cent in 1918, the same figure as in British forces in North-West Europe in 1944–5, despite the use of antibiotics in the latter campaign.

One problem, which all forces had, was the comparatively primitive state of anaesthesia. Although dramatic changes had taken place in surgery in the previous 40–50 years, anaesthesia had not kept pace. General anaesthesia, using the agents then available, was hazardous for shocked casualties, so that more and more local anaesthesia, mainly Novocaine, was used in British units, even for chest and brain surgery. Other armies had different views, the Americans, for example, swearing by inhaled nitrous oxide. Most branches of surgery received tremendous impetus from the Great War, particularly surgery of the chest, brain, and plastic and reconstructive surgery. Dentists had first been attached to medical units, to treat jaw injuries, during the Second Boer War, and co-operation between dentists and plastic surgeons during WW I laid the groundwork for modern plastic surgery. The surgery of limb wounds made dramatic strides, with the amputation rate for upper and lower limbs falling to 3 per cent, which would have astonished Crimean or American civil war surgeons.

Casualty evacuation, which had been such a problem at the third battle of *Ypres and the *Nivelle offensive in 1917, had been improved by 1918, with a corresponding improvement in survival rates. The problem of psychiatric *casualties, victims of what is now called combat stress, was gradually tackled on a systematic basis, so that by 1917–18 a well-developed hospital procedure was in place. Treatment and convalescent regimes meant that the vast majority of cases could be returned to duty, but not all to front-line service. Recurrence rates in some groups remained high. Of the 341,025 soldiers discharged unfit from the British army by April 1918, only 6 per cent were for war neurosis, a lower figure than popularly supposed. After the war, large numbers of pensioners, no longer fit for service or full-time work, had to be provided for. The fact that disease was still more important than wounds was shown by the Ministry of Pension's figures for 1919–20, when pensions for disease were 63 per cent, wounds 35 per cent, and *gas poisoning 2 per cent.

WW II showed further reductions in sickness rates and in mortality from wounds. There were several reasons for this. The availability and storage of blood was further improved, and ready sterilized and packaged intravenous fluids were supplied. There were, in addition, further improvements in casualty evacuation and a great improvement in anaesthesia. Advances in the diagnosis, prevention, and treatment of disease, particularly tropical disease, made a great difference. Antibiotics were available and their importance was very great, but this can be overemphasized except in the treatment of *venereal diseases where it was outstandingly effective. Large numbers of men died, or were invalided, during WW I because of chest infections, particularly forms of pneumonia. Penicillin made a great difference to these in WW II. The results of treatment of abdominal wounds, which had been disappointing during WW I, improved, partly due to improved surgery and anaesthesia, but largely due to the control of infection. One problem which occurred after surgery, particularly of the upper abdomen, was the development of pneumonia due to breathing being restricted. The same thing had happened with chest wounds, not only in the affected lung, but also in the opposite one. Antibiotics made a great difference to this complication, with improvement in survival. Although the infection rate with tropical disease was bad, particularly malaria, for example during the *Burma campaign, it was never quite the problem it had been in the German East Africa campaign in 1914–18. Casualty evacuation in Burma, New Guinea, and some of the Pacific Islands was as great a problem as it had been in Flanders, until air evacuation became a practical possibility.

One attempt to provide surgery as close to the action as possible was the Forward Surgical Unit (FSU), developed in Libya in 1941. A later development at the FSU was the provision of post-operative beds for supervision in the dangerous time after surgery. The developed FSU became standard practice later in the war, in all theatres. During the *Normandy campaign the problem arose of how to evacuate wounded before there was sufficient room to set up hospitals ashore. This was solved temporarily by converting some LSTs (Landing Ship, Tank) to take about 300 patients. They proved adequate in calm weather, but rolled appallingly in rough seas. The problem was solved permanently when airstrips became available for air ambulance evacuation. Psychiatric casualties were expected in WW II, and during the campaign in Europe over 13,000 cases were seen in the British forces, but adequate provision had been made beforehand.

The *Korean war, and later wars, continued the progress made before. The widespread use of *helicopters for rapid evacuation of casualties to specialized surgical units, revolutionized the outlook for the wounded. The first recorded helicopter casualty evacuation was in Burma in 1945, but the increasing availability of numbers of helicopters made them, by far, the best form of evacuation. Further improvements in anaesthesia and antibiotics also helped. The outlook for a casualty was much improved compared with 35 years earlier. Disease was not absent from Korea, as shown by American casualty statistics. They suffered in 1950–3 33,629 killed or dead from wounds and 20,617 non-battle deaths. There were also 10,218 listed as missing or prisoners.

The *Vietnam war confirmed the importance of air evacuation: 372,947 Americans and Allied troops were carried to hospital by helicopter in 1965–9. The USAF evacuated, to facilities in South-East Asia or the USA, 406,022 patients, including 168,872 battle casualties in 1965–73. The type and causation of wounds suffered by US personnel differed somewhat from previous conflicts, with 16 per cent of wounds and 51 per cent of deaths caused by *small arms, there being much less artillery used by their opponents. Seventeen per cent of wounds and 11 per cent of deaths were caused by various forms of booby trap, which came as a very unpleasant surprise. The lightweight, high-velocity, small-arm rounds caused significant entrance and even larger exit wounding, with massive tissue damage. On another front, penicillin-resistant venereal diseases announced the return of an old enemy.

The *Falklands war and the *Gulf war were largely continuations of previous wars, from the medical standpoint. The Gulf war was somewhat different, in that fear of Iraqi *chemical and biological weapons caused many thousands of troops to be immunized, and given antidotes against every eventuality. This caused significant medical problems later.   FGAN

Grant, Michael, *The Army of the Caesars* (London, 1974).
Guthrie, Douglas, *A History of Medicine* (London, 1945).
McLaughlin, Redmond, *The Royal Army Medical Corps* (London, 1973).

Here also, between 19 and 21 September 1918, British and Commonwealth forces under *Allenby defeated Turkish forces under *Liman von Sanders. Following the loss of Jerusalem in December 1917 the Turkish Seventh and Eighth Armies had regrouped on a well-fortified line from Jaffa to the Jordan. Allenby deceived Liman into believing that the attack would fall inland, whereas he attacked on the left, on the coastal plain. An intense artillery bombardment opened a breach for the British XXI Corps, through which Allenby then pushed his cavalry, the Desert Mounted Corps. Local Jewish settlers helped by showing them the way through the marshes, enabling them to penetrate the Turkish positions and then exploit the breakthrough using cavalry, *armoured cars, and aircraft. The RAF attacked the retreating Turkish columns, and helped force the Turks back to the Jordan. In just under a month the British and Commonwealth forces destroyed three Turkish Armies (Seventh, Eighth, and Fourth, to the east), advanced

350 miles, and took 36,000 prisoners at a cost of only 853 dead. CDB

Wavell, Col Archibald, *The Palestine Campaigns* (London, 1928).

memoirs An account of historical events as viewed by a participant or contemporary. These take various forms, depending upon the events being described, the rank and perspective of the writer, and the motives for the production of such an account. Military memoirs may be divided, broadly, into two categories: those produced by politicians and generals, offering an insight into key decisions and a top-down view of events; and those of the officers and men who witnessed front-line action, or of ordinary people who were in some way affected by war.

Since the late 19th century it has become common for the politicians and generals involved in a major conflict to publish personal account of the campaigns or decisions in which they were involved. It is often the case that such works emerge from the desire of the author to justify his part in the conflict, or to explain why particular decisions were taken. The memoirs of *Lloyd George, for example, presented a very distinct picture of the British high command in WW I. Lloyd George was highly critical of *Haig and many others. There was, of course, more than an element of truth in such criticism, but Lloyd George was also keen to portray his own efforts in the most favourable light. Thus his memoirs, while providing useful information on the British high command and his role within that command, must be viewed through the lens of the author's manifest self-interest.

The wish to justify one's action after the event appears in a number of modern memoirs. Indeed, it is not unknown for quarrels begun during a war to be carried on in print long after the final shot has been fired. Generals *Johnston and *Hood, for example, continued their vitriolic debate concerning the final year of the *American civil war for fifteen years after the Confederate surrender. The debate was cut short only by Hood's death in 1879. Memoirs tainted by such vendettas inevitably lose some of their value, as it becomes clear that only one side of a story is being presented. Even so, such works provide invaluable insight into the mind of the author, and can help a reader to understand the problems and contradictions that so quickly appear when the 'fog of war' descends.

Many memoirs begin with less polemical objectives. Some politicians or generals wish to leave a didactic account of the events through which they passed with the aim of helping others to learn from their experiences. Others simply wish to provide an account of their battles and trials in order to preserve the memory of those events, and the people involved, for future generations. Often an author may combine these elements, such as in the case of *Panzer Leader* by *Guderian, published shortly after WW II. Guderian hoped not only to restore his faltering financial position in the immediate aftermath of the war, but also to examine the development of the tank and its part in the conflict. *Sherman began his memoirs with a note to his 'comrades in arms', in which he expressed the hope that his reminiscences might be of use to future historians, and to future Americans, who 'may learn that a country and government such as ours are worth fighting for, and dying for'. The USSR produced a remarkable collection of more than 130 war memoirs by senior officers. Many were heavily edited and some were written with the aim of heading off criticism, but they present a remarkable combination of personal reminiscence and analysis of military planning and operations. The memoirs of major historical figures can, therefore, provide valuable information for a wide audience, but must always be read within the context of the time at which they were writing, and the motives which prompted the author to take up his pen. Increasingly these reflect self-justification: few Napoleonic generals wrote memoirs; by WW II most did.

This is, to a slightly lesser extent, also the case with the reminiscences of ordinary men and women who, having passed through the ordeal of war, chose to recount their own thoughts and deeds on the events in which they participated or which they witnessed. Such accounts fill an important position in the source material available to any student of warfare. As the historian Correlli Barnett has noted, neither official documents nor the memoirs of politicians and generals tell us what it was like to live and fight in the front lines. The memoirs of common soldiers can help scholars to understand not only how troops reacted to combat, but also how they lived on a day-to-day basis, how they reacted to great events, and how they perceived their leaders, their enemies, and their objectives.

The memoirs of private soldiers, NCOs, and junior officers became increasingly common during and after the *Napoleonic wars. The British army of the *Peninsular war is seen clearly through the writings of Rifleman Harris and Lt Kincaid, while Napoleon's 1812 campaign is illuminated by the likes of Capt Coignet, Sgt Bourgogne, and even 'Cornet Aleksandrov'—the Russian 'cavalry maiden' Nadezdha Durova. Subsequent conflicts like the American civil war and the *Franco-Prussian war swept thousands of educated men into the ranks, and this flowering of memoirs was eclipsed only by the outpouring from the two world wars. The complexities of the *Vietnam war were reflected in accounts like Philip Caputo's *A Rumor of War* and David Mason's *Chickenhawk*, while Bob Stewart's *Broken Lives* is a telling account of the anguish of the former Yugoslavia—and the book's author.

An increased regard for family history at the close of the 20th century has helped ensure that many works which were never designed as formal memoirs, but were written to enable a veteran to put his own service into perspective or leave an account for his relatives, have been rescued from obscurity. Personal accounts like this, published or not, constitute a vein of source material which no military historian can afford to ignore. Sometimes they shake received wisdom. 'The Somme raised the morale of the British army,' wrote Capt Charles Carrington. 'We were quite sure we had got the Germans beat: next spring we would deliver the knock-out blow.' And often they remind us that battle is but one element of a life in which more mundane factors predominate. CSM Ernest Shephard reminds us that whatever else may have happened on the first day of the Somme, it was 'A lovely day, intensely hot.' AH/RH

Fussell, Paul, *The Great War and Modern Memory* (London, 1975).

Zhukov, Marshal Georgii, *Reminiscences and Reflections* (Moscow, 1985), trans. Vic Schneierson from Russian orig. (1974).

Guderian, Heinz, *Panzer Leader* (London, 1952).

Sherman, William T., *Memoirs of Gen William T. Sherman* (New York, 1984).

memorials (*see page 570*)

mercenaries, medieval It would be wrong to categorize all paid troops as mercenaries in the medieval period. Pay was widely used, and many who served under some form of obligation were paid to fight. There were also true mercenaries, professional soldiers, who were prepared to serve under any master. Their reliability was sometimes suspect but their skill was rarely in doubt. They were the product of periods of endemic warfare.

In the 11th and 12th centuries the Low Countries were a prime recruiting ground for mercenary troops, or *routiers*. *William 'the Conqueror' hired large numbers when invasion was threatened from Scandinavia in 1085. Robert de Bellême used mercenaries when he rebelled at the start of Henry I's reign. The civil war in Stephen's reign in England provided employment for many such men, 'utterly steeped in craft and treachery', who used castles as bases from which to terrorize the countryside. William of Ypres, illegitimate son of the Count of Flanders, brought many with him when he fought for Stephen. Many of the evils of the Anarchy were blamed on the activities of mercenaries. Their expulsion from England was an important element in the restoration of order under Henry II. 'They seemed to disappear in a moment, like phantoms.'

Mercenaries from the Low Countries found employment easy to obtain in the second half of the 12th century. The German Emperor Frederick *'Barbarossa' hired many in 1166 for his invasion of Italy. Flemings and Brabançons were employed by Henry II of England during the rebellion of 1172–3, and were hired again by Barbarossa in 1176. Southern France and Spain were also significant recruiting grounds. *Richard 'the Lionheart', John of England, and Philip II of France all took on mercenaries, under such leaders as the Provençals Mercadier and Lupescar. King John in particular relied extensively on mercenary troops.

In 1210 he had at least 65 knights from the Low Countries with him on his Irish campaign, while a muster list from 1215 names 375 foreign knights in the king's service. John had substantial financial resources and was prepared to offer significant rewards. The Spaniard Martin Algais, for example, prospered from service in John's cause. His booty was protected, his merchants excused payment of customs, and he became seneschal of Gascony and Périgord.

Mercenary troops depended on their reputation as well as their skill for their livelihood. At Robert de Bellême's castle at Bridgnorth in 1102, his mercenaries objected strongly to a *capitulation accepted by the local men; rather than punish them for their refusal to make terms, Henry I acknowledged that they had acted properly and allowed them to depart with their horses and arms. If they were not paid, however, mercenaries could prove disobliging, as the future Henry II discovered on his first expedition to England in 1147, when the troops he took with him failed him and fled.

The mercenaries comprised soldiers of very different types. Some were knights, but the majority were foot soldiers. The weapon that made them especially feared was the crossbow. The *routiers* were hated not simply because of their skill in war, but also for their cruelty and lack of respect for many of the conventions of a Christian society. They were 'shamelessly guilty of murder and pillage and various abominations'. Many of them were younger sons, some illegitimate, impoverished figures on the fringes of society. They were condemned in the Third Lateran Council of 1179, but did not in the end pose the threat to the fabric of society that many considered them to be. Nevertheless, in 1215 Magna Carta demanded the expulsion of the mercenaries from England, and after the end of the civil war in 1217 few remained in the land.

Mercenaries continued to find employment in the 13th century, but not on the scale of the previous century. In Italy the wealthier cities began to stiffen their militia forces with hired professional soldiers. In 1277 Florence was even employing a hundred English troops. German mercenaries were brought south through the presence of the German Hohenstaufen dynasty in southern Italy and Sicily. It was not until the 14th century that the great mercenary companies emerged, dominating warfare above all in Italy and the Levant.

The first, and in some ways the most remarkable, of these companies was the Catalan Grand Company, formed by veterans of the wars of the *Sicilian vespers, and led by Roger of Flor. It was hired by the Byzantine Emperor Andronicus II in 1302, and operated in Greece where it achieved major successes. The Company remained together after Roger's murder in 1305. It had formal statutes, and possessed its own seal. Its success was assured after it defeated the Duke of Athens at the battle of Kephissos in 1311, and the Catalans remained dominant in Greece until the 1380s.

(*cont. on page 575*)

MEMORIALS have been a feature of the commemoration of war since early recorded history. They were once largely triumphalist. The pharaoh Tuthmosis III (1479–1425 BC) erected two obelisks to proclaim his victory over his enemies in Asia, and the Roman Emperor Trajan had his victories depicted on the column which bears his name. By the 19th century memorials also celebrated the idea of nationhood: the Arc de Triomphe in Paris celebrates Napoleon's victories, and the Victory Column in Berlin commemorates the defeats of Denmark, Austria, and France in 1864–71 which were fundamental in bringing about German unity. Sometimes these memorials were retrospective: Germany commemorated *Leipzig a century after the battle, and France erected a memorial at *Malplaquet two centuries after the battle was fought, gently obscuring the fact that it was a French defeat, although a hard-fought one.

Memorials often recognized sacrifice as well as proclaimed victory. On *Frederick 'the Great' 's battlefield of Kolin (1757) stands a distinguished eagle-topped pillar which remembers the Walloon dragoons, the Austrian regiment whose charge decided the battle. Individual noblemen or senior officers might receive individual commemoration: the blind king of Bohemia is remembered by a cross on the field of *Crécy (1346). The walls of English cathedrals glisten with marble plaques commemorating the paragons of a hundred campaigns: at Canterbury ensigns Tritton and Jones of the 31st Regiment are remembered on a memorial beneath the *colours they died carrying against the *Sikhs at Sobraon in 1845.

The involvement of growing numbers of ordinary folk in the wars of the 19th century saw the proliferation of memorials, and the battlefields of the *American civil and *Franco-Prussian wars are strewn with them. Generally they commemorate individual regiments, and typically list a regiment's dead on the ground where they fell. Thus a row of memorials to the Guard Corps and the individual regiments of the Prussian Guard tops the ridge at Saint-Privat (see REZONVILLE/GRAVELOTTE), acknowledging the appalling loss inflicted by the breech-loading rifles of the French defenders on an ill-advised frontal assault.

The memorials of WW I, however, are altogether more numerous, and still dot the landscapes of the combatant nations. They were built in three waves: during the war, in the first five years after the *Armistice, and in the period from 1928 to 1932, when a more universal meaning was sought for the terrible loss of life in the 1914–18 war. After August 1914, commemoration was an act of citizenship. To remember was to affirm community, to assert its moral character, and exclude from it those values, groups, or individuals that placed it under threat. This form of collective affirmation in wartime identified individuals and their families with the community at large, understood both in terms of a very localized landscape and a much broader and more vaguely defined national entity under siege or threat. The first event commemorated was the call to arms. The fact that mass armies were mobilized in all combatant nations without any significant opposition or obstruction was remarkable enough. Monuments were built early in the war to celebrate this unprecedented response. Where the prompting of notables stopped and popular initiatives began is very difficult to determine. Proud citizens of a working-class district in East London marked the voluntary enlistment of 65 men in a street of 40 houses in one cul de sac by setting up what they called a 'street shrine'. The religious echo was one they chose, possibly reflecting the strength of Irish Catholicism in the area, but also blending in well with general views of the war as a conflict of the sons of light against the sons of darkness. According to the bishop of London the Anglican rector of South Hackney helped create the shrines, which were visited by the queen in 1917. In Australia and New Zealand, celebrating the act of volunteering was also central to commemoration. The lists engraved in stone during the war of those who had joined up helped encourage further enlistment; later lists formed a permanent and immediate chastisement of those who chose not to go.

As soon became apparent, the war the men of 1914 engaged to fight was nothing like the war that developed after the battle of the *Marne. Henceforth, the focus of commemoration shifted away from the moment of mobilization to the stupendous character of the world conflict itself. One form of such commemoration was the collection and preservation for posterity of the ephemera of war. This was by and large a civilian operation, although many soldiers were collectors as well. It was also a patriotic act, and led (unintentionally at times) to the creation of what remain to this day the most important public repositories of artefacts and documents about the war. In Britain, an officially sponsored Imperial War Museum was formed in 1917, ironically enough on the grounds of the former 'Bedlam' lunatic asylum. It houses many military objects and records, as well as an invaluable collection of photographs, manuscripts, books, and works of art. In France, the initiative was private. What is now known as the Bibliothèque de Documentation Internationale Contemporaine started its life as the repository of wartime records, collected by the Leblanc family in their apartment in avenue de Malakoff, but intended from the start as a state museum. In the trench journal *Taca Tac Teuf Teuf*, soldiers on leave were encouraged to visit the collection, which ultimately was indeed passed on to the City of Paris, and then the University of Paris, in one of the outlying campuses of which it remains to this day. The Australians established a 'War Museum' (not the Australian War Memorial) in October 1917 and soldiers were invited to submit objects for display.

A more austere parallel is the private initiative of a German industrialist, Richard Franck, which led to the creation of the Kriegsbibliothek (now the Bibliothek für Zeitgeschichte) in Stuttgart. The director of the Historical Museum in Frankfurt was responsible for yet another German collection of documentation and ephemera related to the Great War. On a smaller scale, the Cambridge University Library, spurred on by the University librarian, gathered together a war collection of printed books and other documents. Similar efforts produced war collections in the New York Public Library. Most of these acts of preservation were intrinsically valuable. They were the work of civilians, many too old to fight, or with sons in uniform, and determined to preserve the dignity and honour of their country's war effort. By their very nature, they both glorified the war effort and contained, at least initially, little about the appalling character and costs of trench warfare. This was in part a function of *censorship, but it also reflected some features of the mystification of warfare, especially in the press, whose 'eyewash' struck many soldiers as absurd or dangerous. Commemorating the war in this ill-informed and blatantly non-combatant manner took on the air of propaganda, as indeed some intended it to do. And like most propaganda, it did not dwell on the sadder facets of the war: the maimed, the deformed, the dead, the widows, the orphans, and the bereaved.

After the war, the character of such collections was mocked by the pacifist activist Ernst Friedrich, who set up an Anti-War Museum in Berlin in 1924. Its collection of documents and gruesome photographs showed everything the patriotic collections omitted. By displays of savage images of the mayhem caused by war, Friedrich pointed out graphically the dangerous selectivity of the patriotic collectors of wartime memorabilia, documents, and books. It is important to note that even though Friedrich's monument to the victims of war was more unsparing and (in a sense) more truthful than the pro-war collections, both arose out of prior political commitments. Commemoration was a political act; it could not be neutral, and war memorials carried political messages from the earliest days of the war.

The mobilization of popular culture on behalf of the nation's war effort occurred in all combatant countries, and was bound to mark commemorative forms. Each nation developed its own language of commemoration, but some features were universal. One was the tendency to locate the men of 1914–18 in the long history of martial virtue. There is hardly any difference between the treatment of *Marlborough in Blenheim palace, *Nelson in Trafalgar Square, and, a century later, Hindenburg in Berlin, except that Hindenburg was immortalized in gigantic form while the war was still going on. The victor of Tannenberg became a towering figure, whose lofty achievements were symbolized by a three-storey model placed prominently in the Tiergarten in the heart of Berlin.

The celebration of military or naval commanders was one way in which to glorify national military traditions. In some countries a more egalitarian language was used to proclaim the virtues of the martial spirit. In Australia and New Zealand, generals and admirals did not bear this symbolic weight; the common soldier or sailor was the link with the past. In France, both elevated and obscure soldiers celebrated the Gallic military tradition. What cities did on a grand scale, individual households could replicate in a more domestic manner, thanks to the emergence of the thriving industry of wartime kitsch. Commemorative images were marketed on the mass scale in WW I. Iron Hindenburgs were available in many materials and sizes.

Whether on the level of national celebration or domestic ornamentation, each nation adopted its own distinctive commemorative forms. One excellent example is the German phenomenon of 'iron nail memorials'. These objects decorated sculptures, plaques, and domestic items like tables, and have (as far as we know) no equivalent in France or Britain. We can learn much about them from an instruction book prepared by two public-spirited Germans early in the war. They were made of 'Ready for use materials' and were ideal 'for patriotic undertakings and ceremonies in schools, youth groups and associations'. These objects were described both as 'war landmarks' and as war memorials, but the distinction between the two was rarely clear. In each case, the figure or image to be celebrated or sanctified was outlined or described by a series of nails. The iron cross was the most popular choice for such objects, requiring according to the handbook between 160 and 200 nails per cross. Among the images they displayed were iron crosses embellished by the imperial initial or the date, but other nail memorials picture the turret or outline of a U-boat, Teutonic floral designs, swords, and mosaic designs for table tops.

Austrian examples of this form of patriotic art may also be found, but it would be a mistake to assume a common Catholic origin for it. Indeed, Crucifixion images and motifs were probably more prevalent in Protestant than in Catholic art, especially in Germany, where Marian and other saintly iconography proliferated. Furthermore, the culture of popular nationalism in imperial Germany was essentially Protestant. *Sedan day was to a degree an anti-Catholic festival, and the ambiguous place of Catholics within the state was never resolved before 1914. Iron-cross nail memorials fit in much more closely with Protestant celebrations of the Prussian military genius and the grandeur of the Kaiserreich.

Ceremonies at which these iron nail memorials were created or displayed enabled patriots of whatever faith to show their commitment to the cause. Some paid for the privilege of nailing by contributing to a war charity or benevolent organization. Others introduced schoolchildren to the nobility of sacrifice in war by the declamation of lofty poetry. We can get some idea of the deliberate medievalism of this practice by citing but one of these poems:

> From whistle of lead, the bloody wound
> A warrior falling
> A red cross on the white ground
> A trusted arm;

> Leaning and leading in the heat of battle
> A red cross arm
> A good bed is made
> Warm and comfortable . . .

And so on into a misty, medieval past remote from the ugliness of industrialized war.

A 24-part ceremony surrounding such poetic affirmations was outlined for school or other civic use. It was replete with the choreography of uplifting allegorical Teutonic plays, songs, and noble poetry. Items 22–4 were the following: 'Deutschland über alles', a 'Pledge of Truth and Faith in Victory', and a round of 'A mighty fortress is our God', Luther's hymn. The imagery of cleansing through the shedding of blood is repeatedly invoked, further suggesting the militarized Christianity of the memorial itself. It is not at all surprising that such objects, and the ceremonies surrounding them, soon framed lists of the fallen.

This is indeed the commemorative art of *Tannenberg, not *Verdun, and we can almost see the idealized form of *Hindenburg, presiding in spirit over these ceremonies, just as he had done after his famous victory. Here is his own version of it, written just after the war:

In our new Headquarters at Allenstein I entered the church, close by the old castle of the Teutonic Knights, while divine services were being held. As the clergyman uttered his closing words all those present, young soldiers as well as elderly 'Landsturm', sank to their knees under the overwhelming impression of their experiences. It was a worthy curtain to their heroic achievement.

Some of the central themes of commemoration are visible in these early wartime rituals and the legends surrounding them. The need to reaffirm the nobility of the warrior by an appeal to 'ancient' tradition, the tendency to highlight soldiers' sacrifice and civilian debt, and the consequent unending duty of dedication to some noble communal task: all are expressed here in a romanticized form which described a war which changed rapidly after August 1914—so rapidly indeed that these rituals and the verse they inspired were bound, as Siegfried Sassoon put it, 'to mock the riddled corpses' of whatever nationality 'round Bapaume'.

The phenomenon of 'nail memorials' is but one example of the initial phase of commemorative art, in which the glorification of sacrifice was expressed in a deliberately archaic language, the cadences of knights and valour, of quests and spiritualized combat. The problem with this language was that it was too unreal, too uplifting, too patriotic, and insufficiently sensitive to the desolation of loss. For this reason, other forms of commemorative art emerged, both during and after the war. These objects and rituals expressed sadness more than exhilaration, and addressed directly the experience of bereavement. These two motifs—war as both noble and uplifting, and tragic and unendurably sad—are present in most post-war memorials; they differ in the balance struck between them. That balance was never fixed; no enduring formula emerged to express it, though traditional religious images were used repeatedly to do so.

Both religious and lay communities devoted themselves to the task of commemoration after 1918. The resulting monumental art provided a focus for ceremonies of public mourning beginning in the decade following the Armistice, and continuing to this day. The languages, imagery, and icons adopted varied considerably according to artistic convention, religious practice, and political conviction. They also reflected more mundane considerations, such as the ability of the community to pay for monuments. Consequently, some plans were scrapped and others had to be scaled down or redesigned to suit the means of the donors. Despite powerful currents of feeling about the need to express the indebtedness of the living to the fallen and the near universality of loss in many parts of Europe, commemoration was and remained a business, in which sculptors, artists, bureaucrats, churchmen, and ordinary people had to strike an agreement and carry it out. Certain general lines of iconography may be identified. These objects were by and large non-triumphalist. They were ambivalent about the war; it would have been jarring to remember only the heroism and not the horror. And too many of the lame, the crippled, and the blind were there, on the street corners, in the railway stations, in the nursing homes and hospitals, reminding any who sought an easy grammar of imagining the human price of 'glory'.

War memorials were indeed reaffirmations of the symbols of decency, comradeship, and sacrifice expressed by millions of soldiers during the war. This attempt to reconfigure the symbols of brotherhood is part of the history of commemorative forms. It is not possible in a brief essay to do justice to this many-faceted exercise in symbolic resurrection, the fruits of which are part of the landscape of contemporary Europe. But perhaps one or two salient points about commemoration, more than 80 years after 1918, may be pertinent.

Within that history of healing and grief, these sites of memory rest on a discourse which was profoundly traditional. These statues, paintings, poems, plaques, buildings, and other commemorative forms reflect the backward gaze of so many writers, artists, politicians, soldiers, and everyday families in this period. They inhabited a world in which bereavement was virtually universal. Everyone had lost someone; many had lost everyone. No one can understand the heavy gloom of the end of 1918 without recognizing this simple and tragic reality.

In this atmosphere, and throughout the inter-war years, there flourished a complex traditional vocabulary of mourning, derived from classical, romantic, or religious forms. These gestures and modes of expressions were the language in which ordinary people mediated bereavement. The power of this cultural configuration has been ignored in much writing on the cultural history of the Great War. Some hold that 'modernism', a portmanteau for languages of irony, abstraction, and experimentation, was the language best configured to express the chaos and horror of the war. Through the validation provided by soldiers' memoirs, the argument goes, some modernist modes of writing and visualizing the war were granted a kind of post-war authenticity, the imprint of the direct experience of the men in the trenches. Thus the first industrialized war provided a new way of looking at the world, an ironic vision suited to the even larger catastrophe to come. And that war was seen through the lenses fashioned twenty years earlier at Verdun, the Somme, and Passchendaele.

There is much of value in this position, but it leaves out as much as it explains. Above all it omits the cultural significance of commemoration and the traditional languages in which it was expressed. Modernist modes of expression, while profound and exciting in many ways, could stir, disturb, inspire, but they could not heal. Like a giant star flaring up just before it disappears, this grammar of compassion inspired the commemorative movement during and after the war. It captured the final phase of a culture of consolation, a culture through which meaning could be ascribed even to an event as terrifying as the war of 1914–18. That culture was soon to be engulfed by an even more terrible war. And after that disaster, there was no going back. After Auschwitz and *Hiroshima, there could be no full return to the commemorative forms, so redolent and so moving, which still reach out to us now, more than 80 years after the end of the catastrophe we call the Great War.

WW II memorials made some attempts to strike old chords. The Royal Air Force Memorial at Runnymede resembles the cloister-style memorials used to commemorate the missing on WW1 battlefields, and the marine corps memorial of the raising of the US flag on Iwo Jima catches the heroic determination of an earlier age. Amongst attempts to use the war's ruins as memorials were the incorporation of the ruins of Coventry cathedral as a narthex to the new one, and the preservation of the truncated spire of the Kaiser Wilhelm Memorial Church in Berlin. Russian war memorials were often on a gigantic scale, like the huge Soviet soldier in Berlin's Treptow park, and the battlefield of

*Kursk houses a panorama, a popular 19th-century form of battle commemoration. Alan Borg is generally right, however, to suggest that WW2 memorials 'are seldom executed by artists of the first rank'.

There are memorials to many post-1945 conflicts, amongst them the gigantic Martyrs Memorial in Baghdad and the Martyrs Fountain (with its blood-red water) in Tehran. The Vietnam wall in Washington DC, which bears the names of the dead incised in black marble, is more modest, but permits comrades or relatives to trace the names with their fingers and reflects the viewer's image. Its construction embodies part of America's coming to terms with the experience of *Vietnam, and it remains a place of pilgrimage. As the 20th century ends there is no sign that humanity's desire to commemorate war has lessened. War memorials are still being built on the western front. In recent years the Accrington Pals have been commemorated by an enigmatic brick memorial near Serre on the Somme, and a few miles away a dragon embodying 38th Welsh Division glares out towards Mametz Wood. From the nationalist triumphalism of Bagdhad to quieter commemoration on the Somme, the traditional functions of war memorials remain.   JW/RH

Borg, Alan, *War Memorials* (London, 1991).

In Italy in 1339 the Company of St George, formed of Swiss, Germans, and Italians, came close to defeating Milan. The Great Company, founded in 1349 by Werner of Urslingen, had a continued existence under several leaders until 1363. Large profits were made from booty and *ransom, and by exacting protection money from the cities. Even defeat at the hands of Florence did not destroy a formidable force. The Anglo-French conflict of the *Hundred Years War, which opened in 1337, offered some good opportunities for mercenaries further north. The Hainaulter Walter Mauny did well serving *Edward III, as did others from the Low Countries such as Eustace d'Aubrichecourt. The peace between England and France made at Brétigny in 1360 released many experienced soldiers onto the mercenary market. D'Aubrichecourt chose to enter the service of the king of Navarre, and continued to fight in France. He was accused by his former master Edward III of 'seizing, robbing and ransoming the people, burning and destroying buildings, violating and ravishing widows, virgins and other women'.

Italy, not France, was the prime haunt of those who sold their military services in the 14th century. The celebrated White Company, largely formed of veterans of Anglo-French warfare, began its operations in Italy in 1361, and defeated the Great Company two years later. The company took its name from the 'white', or polished metal, *armour its members wore, and its striking successes were in part due to use of the tactics developed by the English in France under Edward III. Dismounted men-at-arms fought with *archers equipped with longbows in support. The first leader of the White Company was a German, Albert Sterz,

but its most notable commander was the English knight, Sir John *Hawkwood, one of the most notable of the foreign mercenaries operating in Italy. A highly professional and formidable soldier, he built up a great reputation, largely in Florentine service. The companies were international in composition, but by the late 14th century Italians were increasingly coming to the fore.

Alberigo de Barbiano who established a new Company of St George in the late 1370s is often taken as the first of the Italian *condottieri. This term derived from the contracts, or *condotte*, which the companies made with the Italian cities. These set out the number of troops to be provided for a given period, and the payment due. Increasingly, the individual condottiere came to dominate Italian warfare, rather than the corporate great companies. Some were great men. Bartolomeo Colleoni, who commanded the Venetian armies from 1455 to 1475, was not only a formidable soldier, but also a man of culture, an important patron of art and sculpture. There was an obvious relationship between the employment of mercenaries and the power of states to raise money. It was in cash that mercenaries wished to be paid, and it was no coincidence that new forms of taxation were introduced in England in the late 12th and early 13th centuries at a time when mercenaries were extensively used. The widespread use of mercenaries in later medieval Italy was made possible by the commercial wealth of the cities.

Mercenaries thrived in periods of endemic warfare and in regions where political authority was relatively dispersed. They played a very significant role in medieval warfare. The employment of such men, tough and reliable (as long as they were paid), usually conferred a distinct advantage in war on a ruler or a city, which outweighed the unpopularity that resulted from the way in which they might disregard some of the conventions of war. They were international, and helped to spread advances and changes in military technique from region to region, most notably by introducing the methods used by the English in the Hundred Years War into Italy. Above all, the medieval mercenaries made war a profession. MCP

Contamine, P., *War in the Middle Ages* (Oxford, 1984).

Mallett, M., *Mercenaries and their Masters: Warfare in Renaissance Italy* (London, 1974).

Prestwich, M. C., *Armies and Warfare in the Middle Ages: The English Experience* (London, 1996).

mercenaries, modern Modern mercenaries shun easy definition. Simply describing them as hired soldiers misses the point, for there is an important mercenary streak in most national armies, whose members might resent being termed mercenaries but are motivated, at least in part, by the *pay that they receive. The profit motive played a notable part in the English armies of the *Hundred Years War, and prize money materially assisted motivation in the Royal Navy during the Napoleonic period. Narrowing the definition to include only soldiers who serve a foreign power for pay will not do, for while it might accurately describe, say, the *Swiss and German regiments (and the later *French Foreign Legion), which played such a distinguished part in the French army, it would be inadequate for the voluntarily exiled Catholics who fought in France's Irish Brigade and little less than insulting to the thousands of volunteers who served in the International Brigades during the *Spanish civil war. Moreover, until relatively recently the very notions of 'national' and 'foreign' were at best ill-defined. The tendency to revile mercenaries as 'the dogs of war' is an ancient one. Sir Walter Ralegh wrote 400 years ago that they were 'Seditious unfaithful disobedient destroyers of all places and countries whither they are drawn as being held by no other bond than their own commodity'. But this, similarly, is an oversimplification, for mercenaries have often shown high standards of discipline and behaved better to prisoners and civilians than other members of the armies of which they formed part.

Anthony Mockler's definition of a mercenary is a useful start: 'a soldier who fights with money as his main objective', thus defining him by motive rather than status. The *condottieri might seem a clear-cut case, yet some became not only successful rulers but notable patrons of the arts. Mockler goes on to add, 'the real mark of the mercenary— devotion to war for its own sake'. Given that some mercenaries, like those so reviled by *Machiavelli, knew enough about battle to avoid it if at all possible, even this addition still falls short. It is wisest to recognize that while pay lies at the centre of a mercenary's relationship with his employer, other identifying characteristics are also important, though not all may be present in each case. Mercenaries generally serve foreign powers and, in recent years, 'non-state actors' like insurgent groups or even commercial companies: the African activities of Sandline International attracted much press comment in the 1990s. In many cases this service may also reflect (as it does with the British army's *Gurkhas) long-term bonds of loyalty. Although some mercenaries have shown a disturbing interest in violence for its own sake, others have not and have often been more devoted to the discipline and order of military life than to war itself.

Modern mercenaries often prefer the term 'soldiers of fortune', and that is indeed a fair description of many of history's mercenaries: men who embarked upon a military career because there was no realistic alternative. Areas where families were large, the soil poor, and notions of personal honour powerful were fertile nurseries of mercenaries. Wales, with its tough and proud minor gentry, made a substantial contribution to English armies of the Hundred Years War. Scotsmen and Irishmen served in dozens of foreign armies, and their names still stand out in army lists: Gordon and Keith in Russia, and Lacy, O'Donnell, and O'Reilly in Austria. At least two French marshals had Irish backgrounds, Macdonald under the First Empire and *MacMahon under the Second. Surnames sometimes weathered with the passing generations to produce strange combinations, like Campbell von Craigmillie in the Prussian service and Lally-Tollendal (a corruption of O'Mally of Tollymally) in the French. Travelling warriors often inflated their status as they went—the Austrian military was especially uncritical in its acceptance of applicants' self-certified genealogy. Even *Frederick 'the Great', so insistent on noble status as a prerequisite for commissioned rank, employed a Turkish adventurer rejoicing in the name of Major Ludwig von Steinmann, while his Gen Rupert Scipio von Lentulus, who actually came from Switzerland by way of Austria, claimed Roman ancestry.

The export of European military techniques provided literally golden opportunities for soldiers of fortune. The Sikhs, for instance, owed their formidable artillery and well-drilled infantry to foreign experts (see SIKH WARS). Some of these men had careers for which chequered is too gentle a term. Alexander Gardner was born in North America, and may have served in the British army before becoming a brigand in central Asia and, at least by his own account, serving the ruler of Afghanistan. He helped train the Sikhs in gunnery and was photographed for his (probably unreliable) memoirs wearing a costume, including a plumed turban, made from Scots tartan.

Many soldiers of fortune were political or religious exiles. The Revocation of the Edict of Nantes forced *Huguenots to leave France in their thousands, and many of them took service in the armies of the states they fled to. The defeat of the *Jacobite cause in the British Isles instituted the same process in reverse, causing the 'Wild Geese' to take flight. The Treaty of Limerick, which in 1691 ended the

Williamite war in Ireland, allowed safe conduct to Jacobites who wished to serve abroad. The triumph of the Protestant cause deprived Catholics of an important source of gentlemanly employment: unable to serve in the British army, they served with distinction in others. A brigade of Irish exiles thereafter formed a valuable part of the French army. At *Fontenoy in 1745 the six Irish regiments—Clare, Dillon, Bulkeley, Roth, Berwick, and Lally—were commanded by Charles O'Brien, Earl of Thomond, Viscount Clare and lieutenant general in the French service, and their counterattack played an important part in checking the advance of the British infantry.

Soldiers of fortune served in 17th- and 18th-century armies on a comparatively large scale, either as individuals or in foreign-raised units. The latter enabled a cautious monarch to limit the impact of war on his own subjects. Sometimes one state might contract to provide soldiers for another: the British obtained German troops for service in the *American independence war by commercial agreements with German princes like the Duke of Brunswick and the Margrave of Hesse-Cassel: in all some 30,000 were to serve in North America. These processes meant armies which were national in name might be substantially foreign in terms of recruitment. One-sixth of Prussian generals were foreign in the period 1740–63, and during Frederick 'the Great''s reign outsiders consistently outnumbered native-born Prussians in his army. Families were sometimes split: at Kolin in 1757 the Prussian Lt Col von Gemmingen found himself fighting his father, an Austrian lieutenant general. However, there was increasing unease about the use of foreigners in national armies, especially when—like the Germans in North America—their services were procured for hard cash.

States also became increasingly reluctant to accept that men born within their borders could legitimately serve in the ranks of hostile armies. As we have seen, in 1691 the British government allowed Jacobite Irishmen free passage to France to serve in a hostile army, and in 1746 it regarded officers and men of the Irish Pickets (detachments from regiments in the Irish Brigade) and the Royal-Ecossais Regiment serving with the Jacobite army as legitimate combatants, treated as POWs rather than criminals when captured. But by the end of the century attitudes had hardened. In the Irish rebellion of 1798 Irish-born officers in the French service were treated as traitors when captured. The Irish leader Wolfe Tone claimed that it was 'an indignity' against 'the honour of the French army' to put him in chains, and was tried wearing a French colonel's uniform. Recognizing the inevitability of a death sentence, he demanded to be shot like a soldier not hanged as a criminal, and committed suicide after this appeal was denied.

Sometimes mercenaries gained value and reputation from mastery of particular weapons or tactics. In the ancient world, the Persians employed Greek *hoplite infantry, and *Xenophon's account of the march of the 10,000 is a classic description of the ebb and flow of mercenary fortunes. The Romans used *archers from Crete, *slingers from Rhodes, and a variety of auxiliary cavalrymen, to supplement their own heavy infantry. In the Middle Ages mercenaries (see MERCENARIES, MEDIEVAL) were widely used: both Genoese crossbowmen and German handgunners were highly regarded. The Swiss became almost 'a nation of mercenaries' gaining their reputation through their formidable *pikemen who neither gave nor expected quarter. They were so widely used that the phrase 'point d'argent, point des Suisses' (no money, no Swiss) remains in the French language. Mercenaries were widely used as guards (French monarchs once had, and the pope retains, a Swiss Guard) because of their lack of involvement in domestic politics and loyalty to their employer. In the second half of the 20th century mercenaries have been employed, notably in Africa, because their training, discipline, and cohesion often gave them the edge over indigenous forces.

Fighting in Africa brought mercenaries to the world's attention. The mercenary leaders Mike Hoare, Jean 'Black Jack' Schramme, and Bob Denard all fought in the *Congo in the 1960s, and the Irish-born Hoare's Five Commando gained a formidable reputation. Mercenaries were employed in the civil war in *Angola. An ex-British soldier, Costas Georgiou (alias Callan) led a mercenary force against the Movimento Popular de Libertação de Angola and its Cuban allies, showing a vicious flair for the fighting. Already widely reviled for having ordered the execution of some of his own men, he was captured by government forces. At his trial he took responsibility for the deeds of his men, refused to answer any questions, and faced the firing squad bravely. The Diplock commission, set up to review mercenary enlistment in Britain in the wake of these events, suggested in 1976 that 'A spirit of adventure, an ex-soldier's difficulty in adjusting to civilian life, unemployment, domestic troubles, ideals, fanaticism, greed—all these may play some part in the individual's motivation.' This is not a bad definition of the spectrum of mercenary motivation across history—and seems likely to remain so in the future.

RH

Mockler, Anthony, *Mercenaries* (London, 1969).
Tickler, Peter, *The Modern Mercenary* (London, 1987).

Mesopotamian campaign (WW I). On 6 November 1914, a force of Indian and British infantry landed at the head of the Persian Gulf ostensibly to protect imperial oil interests, now threatened by Turkey, who had joined the Central Powers on 28 October. Oil had been discovered in the area just prior to 1914, and the sandy wastes swiftly assumed strategic importance as the Anglo-Persian Oil Company began to develop the first oilfields. Moreover, as Briton Cooper Busch has shown, Britain was anxious to preserve her established position in the Gulf, to prevent Turkish agents from stirring up trouble amongst

Mesopotamian campaign

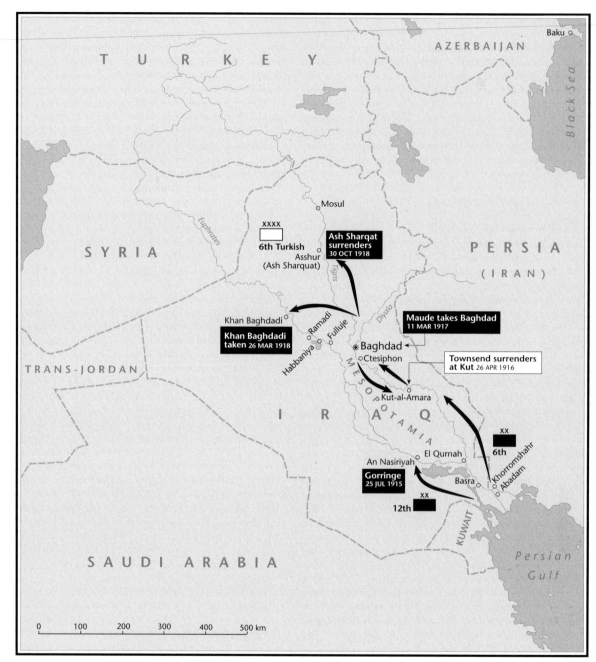

The **Mesopotamian campaign** in WW I.

India's Muslims, and to encourage Arab resistance to Turkish rule.

Until early 1916 the campaign was directed by the government of India, which left much of the decision-making to its own military authorities and to the C-in-C, Gen Sir John Nixon, who took over in March 1915. Both recognized that as long as they retained only a toehold in Mesopotamia the Turks were at liberty to move down the Tigris and Euphrates against them, and early successes encouraged them to believe that an advance inland would be easy. Political motives remained blurred. An inter-departmental committee in London produced a list of desiderata which included the development of 'a possible field for Indian colonisation', and some officials argued in favour of wide territorial annexation.

Despite the campaign's lack of clear strategic focus, its early signs were promising. Basra (which the Turks had already evacuated) was taken on 22 November, and El Qurnah, at the junction of the Tigris and Euphrates, fell on 9 December. Nixon was told to 'retain complete control of the lower portion of Mesopotamia'—defined as the province of Basra, which he had not fully secured—and to submit plans for an advance on Baghdad. In May 1915 two British columns moved off, one following each river upstream. The 6th Indian Division under Maj Gen Charles Townshend moved up the Tigris towards Baghdad, while Maj Gen Gorringe took his 12th Indian Division to An Nasiriyah on the Euphrates, which fell on 25 July.

These easy successes encouraged Nixon to aim for Baghdad. His *logistics were never robust, and it became increasingly difficult to supply the advancing troops: as his supply line grew longer, that of the Turks grew shorter. Nixon was convinced that he could take Baghdad, though Townshend disagreed. The latter's men were unused to the local climate and had begun to tire after the long advance. Despite pleas for reinforcement, 6th Division was ordered to continue along the Tigris, and took a series of river towns before reaching *Kut Al Amara. The Turks evacuated their 10,000-strong garrison, and Townshend occupied Kut, just 120 miles (193 km) from Baghdad, on 28 September 1915.

Opinion on the wisdom of an advance on Baghdad remained divided. Although in October 1915 a joint War Office–Admiralty memorandum warned against the diversion of troops to a campaign 'which cannot appreciably influence the decision as between the armies of the Allies and those of the Central Powers', the same month the cabinet concluded that success in Mesopotamia would offset failure in *Gallipoli. 'We are therefore in need of a striking success in the east,' it announced. 'Unless you consider that the possibility of eventual withdrawal is against the advance . . . we are prepared to order it.' Although Nixon knew that the Turks had been reinforced, he told Townshend to press on.

Townshend resumed his advance, and though he had to wait six weeks to resupply, by 22 November he was 24 miles (39 km) from Baghdad, where he attacked a strong Turkish defensive line at Ctesiphon, losing over 4,000 men, one-third of his force. Townshend had pushed his luck too far. He was without reserves, and, faced with the arrival of fresh Turkish troops, was obliged to fall back on Kut Al Amara, where he was besieged. Meanwhile, Nixon had remained 300 miles (482 km) distant in Basra, and was unable to appreciate the gravity of the situation, while the Allied evacuation from Gallipoli allowed the Turks to further reinforce their forces in Mesopotamia. Three attempts at relief failed and on 26 April 1916, his force starving and riddled with disease, Townshend surrendered 2,000 British and 6,000 Indian soldiers. The failure of the relief attempts, which had cost a further 21,000 casualties, allied to the surrender at Kut caused a storm of indignation in England.

In August 1916 Gen Sir Stanley Maude took over as C-in-C and resumed the offensive up the Tigris in December with two corps, an impressive force of 166,000. By 25 February, he had retaken Kut, and pressed on to the prize, Baghdad, which his main force entered on 11 March 1917. Now Turkish forces began to be stretched in turn, as the British successes at *Gaza made demanding calls on their manpower. To secure Baghdad, Maude formed three columns, and sent them further up the Tigris, Euphrates, and Diyala rivers, with the aim of destroying the Turkish field army. Each column won a series of engagements, but Maude died of cholera on 18 November and was succeeded by Lt Gen Sir William Marshall. In January 1918, a small British force under Maj Gen Dunsterville (Dunsterforce) moved north from Baghdad in a race with the Turks to seize the Russian oilfields at Baku, some 500 miles (805 km) distant, which had been vulnerable since Russia's withdrawal from the war, following the November *Russian Revolution. Dunsterforce arrived only in August, and had to withdraw the following month after Turkish attacks.

Back in Mesopotamia, the river advances continued throughout 1918, but some of the British force was withdrawn to Palestine to replace troops sent to France to repel the *Ludendorff offensive. Five thousand Turkish prisoners were taken in an engagement on the Euphrates at Khan Baghdad on 26 March, and Turkish troops gradually lost their enthusiasm for fighting. In late October 1918, faced with an impending Turkish armistice, a British force under Cobbe pushed up the Tigris to seize the oilfields at Mosul, fighting their last battle with the Turks near the ruins of the ancient Assyrian city of Asshur. The armistice with Turkey of 30 October brought about the surrender of Asshur (Ash Sharqat), but Cobbe moved on to occupy Mosul in early November. In 1918 Mesopotamia assumed its modern name of Iraq, under a British mandate, and imperial forces remained garrisoned there to subdue dissident tribesmen. The campaign, which had begun and ended with the seizure of oilfields, cost the British army 27,000 men, 13,000 of whom died of disease. It was indeed a sideshow, conducted without proper strategic control: the courage of the troops engaged, who fought in what were often appalling conditions, merited deeper thought on the part of their leaders.   APC-A/RH

Barker, A.J., *The Neglected War: Mesopotamia 1914–1918* (London 1967)

Busch, Briton Cooper, *Britain, India and the Arabs 1914–1921* (London 1971).

Messines, battle of (1917), the preliminary battle of the third *Ypres campaign. Meticulously planned by *Plumer, whose Second Army had held this sector for two years, its aim was the removal of the Germans from the Wytschaete-Messines ridge, which ran due south from Ypres for 5 miles (8 km) and overlooked Ypres sector. Plumer was noted for his caution in planning attacks and his concern to minimize casualties. From early 1916, 22 tunnels were dug under German positions on the ridge by Royal Engineer tunnelling companies and 470 tons of explosives laid in them. One mine was discovered by the Germans and blocked, but at 03.10 on 7 June 1917, the rest were fired. Nineteen actually exploded on time, causing a shock wave felt in London. The twentieth was accidentally triggered by a bolt of lightning 38 years later in 1955, while the twenty-first remains unaccounted for. The mines had been preceded by a seventeen-day *bombardment of unprecedented ferocity, and as the earth was still falling, the IX, X, and II *Anzac Corps of Plumer's Second Army attacked, supported by *gas and tanks. The ridge itself was seized straight away: the town of Wytschaete fell to the combined efforts of 16th (Irish) and 36th (Ulster) Divisions, and in 1998 a *memorial commemorating this symbolic joint effort was unveiled. The New Zealand Division took Messines, and by mid-afternoon, the reserve divisions and tanks had leapfrogged through to ward off counter-attacks. Some 7,000 prisoners were taken, but fewer guns than had been expected, largely because the plan was not amenable to easy variation. This was Plumer's finest hour, and he took the title 'Plumer of Messines' when elevated to the peerage in 1929. Tragically, the British were slow in following up this impressive victory. The third battle of Ypres did not begin until 31 July and by then the Germans were ready for it.

APC-A

Passingham, Ian, *Pillars of Fire* (London, 1990).

Meuse-Argonne offensive (1918), part of the overall Allied offensive of late 1918 to defeat the German army before the onset of winter. It was fought by the US First Army under *Pershing, under overall co-ordination of *Foch. Its aim was to break through the *Hindenburg Line in the 35 mile (56 km) sector of hills and forest west of Verdun, and extending northwards from the Argonne forest to Sedan. The major component of the attacking force was 22 US infantry divisions, only 3 of whom had previously seen

action, and 6 French divisions (totalling 500,000 men), plus tank support.

The offensive came hard on the heels of the *Saint-Mihiel battle, and American units fighting in the former, through slick staff work, were speedily redeployed in night moves to the Meuse-Argonne front, some 65 miles (105 km) away. In the planning phase, to maintain secrecy US officers wore French uniforms when visiting the front. During their four years of occupation, the Germans had created four successive, mutually supporting defensive lines, linked by trenches and interlocking arcs of fire.

Preceded by a three-hour bombardment, US troops attacked at 05.30 on 26 September in thick fog but made little headway in the centre. However, the flanks broke through, and Lt Col *Patton, commanding nearly 200 little Renault FT tanks, steamed ahead of the infantry he was supposed to be supporting. The German first lines were overrun, but between 27 and 30 September Gen *Ludendorff reinforced the sector with over twenty divisions, supported by excellent artillery, his last reserves, who mounted a vigorous series of counter-attacks.

Due to inexperience, American transport and communications broke down initially, with the result that some scattered US units received no food or ammunition for four days. The weather was unfriendly, reinforcements scarce, and thus the momentum slowed. Pershing resumed the advance on 4 October, keen to demonstrate the power of his army, and hard fighting continued until 29 October, when the Germans finally fell back to the west bank of the Meuse. The attack was renewed on 1 November and by 6 November Sedan had been taken. A further advance began but was halted by the *Armistice. Of the 115,000 US casualties, an unusually low 15,000 were killed.   APC-A

Mexican expedition, French (1861–7), an attempt to counter Protestant Anglo-Saxon influence in the Americas that gave birth to the term 'Latin America', and which included the battles of Puebla and *Camerone, anniversaries still celebrated by Mexico and the *French Foreign Legion.

Wracked by civil wars, Mexico suspended payment on its international loans in 1861 and in retaliation a joint Anglo-Spanish-French force seized Vera Cruz. The others withdrew when they realized that *Napoleon III had wider plans involving his dream of a 'Latin League', encouraged by his Spanish wife, by exiled Mexican conservatives, and by US preoccupation with its own civil war. Although much of *Juárez's army was tied up by conservative forces elsewhere, the first French advance towards Mexico City was stopped at the Puebla pass on 5 May 1862, where about 5,000 men commanded by Zaragoza repelled a rash attack by an élite force of 6,500. This was the first Mexican victory over a foreign enemy since independence, and stands as the moment when a truly national identity first began to take form.

Napoleon III dispatched 30,000 reinforcements under Forey, who besieged a Mexican army of 20,000–25,000 men at Puebla. After it capitulated on 17 May, large-unit resistance ended and Forey marched into the capital on 10 June. He directed an assembly of conservative and clerical 'Notables' to issue an invitation to the Habsburg Archduke Maximilian, Napoleon III's handpicked candidate, to become emperor of Mexico. He then returned to France, leaving *Bazaine with the thankless task of pacifying a people with a long tradition of *guerrilla warfare. Maximilian was duly installed in mid-1865 while Bazaine's troops chased Juárez in the north and Porfirio Díaz in the south. The French controlled the cities, but in the countryside their authority was limited to where they stood. In anticipation of this, from 1863 they countenanced the operations of a ruthless irregular force of *mercenaries under Dupin and attempted to recruit bandit gangs. These added little to military effectiveness and greatly to the suffering of the Mexican people.

The original pact between Napoleon III and Maximilian specified a force of 10,000 European troops to remain as the nucleus of a new Mexican army, and consideration was given to transferring the Foreign Legion. But the occupation proved costly and with the end of the *American civil war it became a serious liability, underlined when Juárez took refuge against the border beneath the protection of an 'army of observation' under the aggressive *Sheridan. In February 1866 Napoleon III agreed to withdraw his troops by November 1867, but the growing threat from Prussia in Europe advanced the date and in March 1867 an embittered Bazaine embarked his 29,000 men for return to France, destroying supplies to deny them to Maximilian. The hapless Habsburg felt honour-bound to make a last stand at Querétaro with a small Austrian contingent and an unreliable Mexican conscript army. Betrayed, he and his two remaining Mexican generals were shot on 14 June 1867.   HEB

Garfias, Gen Luis, *La intervención francesa en México* (México, 1988).

Mexican war (1846–8), the first successful international war of USA 'manifest destiny' imperialism, in which Pres Polk provoked a border dispute in order to seize the New Mexico territory (all of today's south-western states) and California. Mexico had not accepted the independence of Texas, still less its claim to the strip between the Nueces river and the Rio Grande. Following American annexation of Texas in early 1845, a US army of 'observation' under *Taylor moved from Louisiana to the Nueces strip. In May 1846, 3,700 Mexicans attacked Taylor's 2,300. Repulsed at Palo Alto and defeated at Resaca de la Palma, they fell back behind the Rio Grande. The USA declared war on the 13th.

In a murky episode which could well have defined the course of the war, Polk's agents encouraged the return to Mexico of exiled dictator Santa Anna in August 1846. He agreed to a face-saving formula whereby the USA would occupy Saltillo, Tampico, and Vera Cruz, after which he would sell the territories Polk wanted for the $30 million earlier refused by the Mexican government. Once back in power he demonstrated his unique ability to finance and raise armies, but to the end of his life he hoped for a payment of $3 million, fuelling suspicion that his military operations were designed to enforce the agreement. If so, his need to act the role of national saviour believably was discounted or misinterpreted, an expensive error. The USA was to pay or forgive over $20 million in 1848 and a further $10 million in 1854, plus the $70 million direct costs of the war itself.

The New Mexico and California territories fell early to a small expedition under Kearny. To his rear a revolt of Pueblo Indians and unreconciled Mexicans was crushed by Price in January 1847, while Doniphan with 600–700 Missouri volunteers overawed the powerful Navajo. The latter then rode into Mexico over appalling terrain, defeating a more numerous and entrenched enemy outside Chihuahua, after which he rode east to join the main army with captured guns in tow.

On the Rio Grande front, the Mexican commander ignored Santa Anna's order to fall back on Saltillo and fortified Monterrey. Taylor successfully assaulted the town in September, but permitted the defenders to retreat on terms including an undertaking that US forces would not advance for eight weeks. Taylor was convinced that an invasion from the north to Mexico City was not viable and underlined his conviction by delay. His army suffered most of the 9,000 *desertions during the war and lost at least as many more who refused re-enlistment or were sent home because of indiscipline.

Probably aware of this and informed that part of Taylor's army was being withdrawn for a seaborne expedition to Vera Cruz, Santa Anna attacked in February 1847 with 15,000 men. At Buena Vista, south of Saltillo, he drove back Taylor's 5,000 by sheer weight of numbers and would certainly have prevailed the next day. Instead he chose to retreat. Thereafter the theatre subsided into guerrilla warfare.

The navy duly captured Tampico and army commander *Scott led the expedition to Vera Cruz, landing where Santa Anna had recommended in March 1847. The port fell to bombardment twenty days later. At Cerro Gordo in mid-April, a strong position designed by Santa Anna to keep the Americans in the lowland yellow-fever belt was outflanked with minimal casualties. No further organized resistance was encountered until the Americans approached Mexico City, where on 20 August Santa Anna's forces were defeated at the battles of Contreras and Churubusco, the latter featuring fanatical resistance by Irish deserters and volunteers organized in the San Patricio regiment. Last-ditch resistance was overcome at Molino del Rey on 8 September and at the fort of Chapultepec five days later, whose defenders

Mexican war

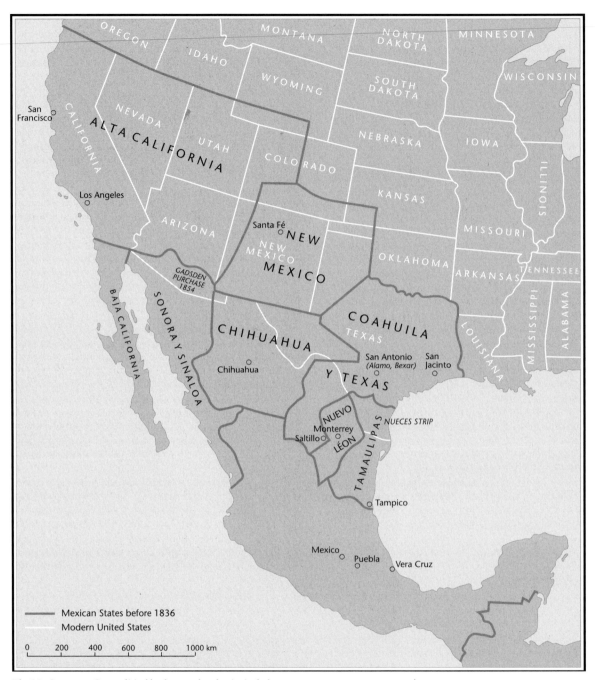

The **Mexican war:** Geo-political background and principal places.

included a group of boy military cadets, the *niños heróicos* of Mexican folklore.

In these later battles fewer than 11,000 Americans overcame 30,000 defenders, inflicting 7,000 casualties and capturing a further 3,000, for a loss of only 3,100 killed, wounded and missing. Overall, US forces suffered 5,800 battle casualties and 11,500 deaths by disease, 22 per cent of all involved. The Duke of *Wellington, no less, said the Vera Cruz campaign showed Scott to be the greatest soldier living. Polk thought otherwise and denigrated his achievement, keeping him in Mexico while Taylor rode the victory bandwagon to the presidency, an objective that was to elude his superior in every respect four years later.   HEB

Bauer, K. Jack, *The Mexican War 1846–1848* (New York, 1974).

Mexico, conquest of (1518–21). See CORTÉS, HERNÁN and CONQUISTADORES.

MIA (missing in action). While *casualties are normally thought of as either dead or wounded, a third category exists, the MIA. A soldier is so listed if he cannot be located after combat. This could be the result of temporary separation from his unit, of *desertion, or, as was often the case for those shot down over enemy territory, of the period of limbo before advice was received of the death or capture of the missing airman. The increased power of weapons in the 20th century added another gruesome category to this list. During WW I, it was found that soldiers could be completely destroyed or buried by artillery fire, leaving no remains behind for identification. The names of 54,000 such British soldiers are inscribed on the Menin Gate *memorial in Ypres. Most countries buried a symbolic *Unknown Soldier in a place of maximum honour. In Britain the Unknown Soldier is buried at the centre of the nave of Westminster Abbey, the resting place of monarchs.

Countless men have died while recovering the bodies of fallen comrades and proper accounting for human remains is an extremely emotive issue. The issue of MIAs in *Vietnam continued to bedevil efforts to normalize diplomatic relations 25 years after the last US soldier was evacuated.

RTF

MICVs (mechanized infantry combat vehicles) are armoured, usually tracked, vehicles designed to transport infantry soldiers, either to deploy on the battlefield or to provide a protected environment from which to fight. There are those who regard them as a monstrous hybrid, akin to Fisher's battlecruisers, with the difference that they do not even have a heavy punch to compensate for their extreme vulnerability to *anti-armour weapons. The scandal surrounding over-elaboration and cost inflation for the Bradley MICV in the USA may have been merely one of many examples of western arms procurement 'gold-plating', but it also reflected a shift in *doctrine while it was being developed.

During WW II, particularly on the *eastern front, the Germans possessed motorized infantry that was able to advance with the fast tank forces, but for most of the war the Soviets did not. They found that tanks were vulnerable whenever they outstripped their infantry and developed the *APC to enable them to keep up. When they went a step further and created armoured vehicles from which the infantry could fight without having to dismount and expose themselves to enemy fire, the MICV was born.

In the years after WW II, nations increasingly mechanized their armed forces, with the USSR taking the lead. Unlike the WW II armoured formations, these new units had tanks, APCs, and *self-propelled (SP) artillery. At their heart, these formations had the concept of close infantry support for tanks, and by the 1970s these vehicles were deployed in large numbers. But there remained the drawback that under many tactical circumstances, APCs would be likely to disgorge their infantry straight into enemy fire. Returning to the WW II Soviet experiment, MICVs were introduced in the 1980s to enable the infantry to fire from within the vehicle, which acquired many of the characteristics of a light tank. An example is the British Warrior, a tracked vehicle armed with a 30 mm cannon and a 7.62 mm machine gun. It carries a section of eight soldiers and has a maximum road speed of 47 mph (75 km/h).

MICVs have not been universally well received by soldiers on the grounds that they are neither fish nor fowl, too lightly armed and armoured to be deployed alongside tanks, yet carrying too few infantry for an individual vehicle to make a sufficient impact on its own. Traditionalists argue that the use of MICVs diminishes the combat effectiveness of the troops thus deployed. But they are much lighter than main battle tanks, hence easier to airlift and deployable in areas where tanks may be too heavy: a Warrior weighs 54,022 lb (24,500 kg) loaded compared to 13,781 lb (62,500 kg) for a Challenger tank. This means MICVs have been used extensively in *peacekeeping operations against comparatively lightly armed opposition, limiting the possibility of attrition by the traditional tactics of irregular forces.

RTF

Midway, battle of (3–7 June 1942), turning point of the *Pacific campaign. On 2 June 1942 the Japanese combined fleet under the direction of *Yamamoto on the superbattleship *Yamato* was committed to an elaborate ocean-wide operation with three objectives. The first was to seize an outer perimeter including the undefended Aleutian islands in the north and the well-garrisoned atoll of Midway, with its important airbase, in order to prevent a repetition of the raid on Tokyo by a flight of B-25 bombers led by Gen Rickenbacker, launched from the aircraft carrier *Hornet* a few months earlier. The second was thereby to disperse what was left of the US Pacific fleet after *Pearl Harbor and the battle of the Coral Sea. The third was to draw the remaining US carriers towards Midway to counter the attack by four large carriers under Vice Adm Nagumo, while the main battle fleet sailed to the north to cut them off.

US naval intelligence was achieving considerable success against the Japanese naval code then in use and *Nimitz was well informed of his opponent's intentions, but not of the full danger he faced. Of his four fleet carriers, *Hornet* and *Enterprise* were intact, but the *Yorktown* had been severely damaged in the Coral Sea, where he had lost the *Lexington*. The damaged carrier was made battleworthy in 48 hours and sailed to form the heart of one battle group under R Adm Fletcher, while *Hornet* and *Enterprise* under R Adm Spruance formed the other.

The invasion force making for Midway was ineffectually attacked on 3 June, and Midway was heavily bombed on the following day. Nagumo was preparing for a second attack on Midway when the Americans found him. Their torpedo bombers were massacred and scored no hits, but the result was to pull down the Japanese carriers' fighter cover, and the US dive-bombers had the further good fortune to catch the carriers with their decks loaded with fully armed and fuelled bombers awaiting launch against the US carriers. *Akagi*, *Kaga*, and *Soryu* were set on fire from stem to stern within minutes at around 10.30, all to be sunk later by their escorts. *Hiryu*, the sole survivor, got off a strike that found and damaged the *Yorktown* (later to be finished off by her escorts after a Japanese submarine also hit her) but she was herself found and set ablaze at 17.00. The US navy lost 150 aircraft and 300 men. The Japanese lost their entire front line of naval aviators, 250 aircraft, and their crews, as well as the carriers that had been running wild in the south Pacific for six months. Yamamoto ordered a withdrawal and the combined fleet never regained the strategic initiative.

HEB

militarism is defined as the prevalence of military sentiments among a people, or the tendency to regard military efficiency as the paramount interest of the state. Defined in this way, it is a not-very-useful term that covers most societies in history until the present day. The need to defend oneself is a prerequisite for any stable society, and for most of history a degree of militarism was a necessity, not a choice. It is notable that the tradition of non-militarism among the English-speaking peoples emerged in countries where the danger of invasion was limited or non-existent over nearly a millennium.

As a more refined term of political analysis, the term has been traced back to the memoirs of Madame de Chastenay, who used it with reference to Napoleon's glorification of war and the trappings thereof. After that the word fell into disuse until the 1860s when Proudhon revived it to attack the authoritarian mentality that viewed war as means of mobilizing man's best energies. The concept gained wide acceptance and appeared as a neologism in contemporary European encyclopaedias and journals. Over the next decades the term took on two meanings. On the one hand, it was used, in a narrow sense, to describe the intrusion of military considerations into the process of political and diplomatic decision-making. Thus a particular country's (foreign) policy was deemed 'militaristic' if policy-formulation had become dominated by the military. On the other hand, there emerged a broader notion of 'social militarism' which was seen to exist in countries in which military values and mentalities had percolated into civilian society and had permeated the political culture. It was with these two meanings that scholars subsequently employed the concept for analysing certain types of political systems and societies.

The notion of a dichotomy dividing two different types of socio-political systems and indeed entire societies not only informed all scholarly discussion of 'militarism' throughout this century, but also was probably implied from the very beginning. Still, it assumed sharper conceptual contours only at the end of the 19th century, when sociologists and political economists joined the debate. One of the earliest systematizers was Herbert Spencer. In his *Principles of Sociology* he identified a 'militant type of society' which he defined as one in which 'all men fit for fighting act in concert against other societies'. Insofar as those 'other societies' were not themselves of the 'militant type', Spencer sharply contrasted them as 'industrial' societies in which the defence of man's 'individuality becomes the society's essential duty'. In the latter, 'life, liberty and property are secure and all interests justly regarded'. For the same reason they did not require 'a despotic controlling agency'. Spencer appreciated that the lines between these two types of society were occasionally blurred and that 'militant' societies could be engaged in industrial production. But his point was that they were merely 'industrially occupied, not industrially organised'. Ultimately Spencer advanced his taxonomy both to buttress a liberal-evolutionary view of human history and to demonstrate that the industrial states would inevitably replace the more backward 'militant' systems. To him, industrialism was of course synonymous with modern capitalism.

Other scholars subsequently tried to refine Spencer's scheme. One who was directly inspired by him was the influential German constitutional historian Hintze, who introduced an epochal and geographic differentiation. His work on militarism is furthermore significant because he designed his arguments explicitly to rebut the Marxist line on the subject. If militarism for Spencer and Hintze was a manifestation of pre-industrial and pre-capitalist societies, for Marxists all pre-socialist systems were basically militaristic. In other words, while they, too, developed a grand scheme of societal change over time, contrary to the liberals they believed that capitalist-industrial societies were just as prone to produce militarism as pre-industrial and pre-capitalist ones.

The Marxist argument took two forms. Some, like Hilferding and *Lenin, integrated the concept into their theory of capitalist imperialism and viewed it as part of Europe's violent expansion abroad. Others, like Rosa Luxemburg, focused on the domestic angle of arms manufacturers and the arms races they sponsored, postulating that militarism represented the means of economic exploitation and political repression of the proletariat. Armaments, Luxembourg believed, secured the domestic status quo against workers' protests and demands for fundamental change. And they kept the population in a state of tension, excitement, and fear about an impending foreign war in which working-class men would be the cannon fodder.

Theory and practice being inseparable in Marxism, the insights gained into the workings of capitalism were to be used in the struggle to overthrow it. The working-class movements of Europe were not only to fight for a transformation, by revolution or by radical reform, of the existing socio-economic order, they were also to fight against 'militarism', which they saw as a basic evil in capitalist-industrial societies. In Germany, which had the largest and best organized working-class movement in Europe, agitation was stepped up not only against the brutal treatment of recruits and the militarization of politics, but also against the arms race and the kaiser's adventurist foreign policy. Karl Liebknecht was one of the most impassioned anti-militarist speakers at Social Democratic rallies. All of this vanished like mist before a strong wind when war broke out and all thoughts of international proletarian solidarity went out of the window. The socialist international never recovered.

The debate about militarism revived with the emergence of fascism and Nazism and it was not about whether or not they were militaristic. Of course they were, proudly and openly. Marxists were concerned to link the phenomenon to bourgeois capitalism and to what they thought to be its worsening crisis after WW I. Some, it is true, saw fascism as an outgrowth of a backward capitalism typical of post-WW I Italy, but *Hitler looked to many Marxists more like a henchman of an advanced capitalist system. A similar difference of opinion emerged with regard to Japan and its militarism in the 1930s and early 1940s. The crucial point is that whatever internal variations there may have been, for Marxists militarism became even more directly associated with capitalism than it had been before 1914.

The problem was that both fascism and Nazism presented themselves as a 'third way', not merely anti-communist but also anti-capitalist and anti-liberal. It was because of this self-representation and of the repressive policies that stemmed from it that liberals, pursuing Spencer and Hintze's arguments, argued in an evolutionary-developmental vein that militarism could occur only in societies that had not fully industrialized and did not have a parliamentary-representative political system and civic culture. The association of militarism with relative backwardness was further refined following 1945, when it merged with modernization theory, particularly as elaborated by American social scientists.

If there is one generalization to be made about the use of the concept of militarism in public and scholarly debate during the 20th century, it is that the two schools of thought continued to argue their respective cases across the ideological fence that separated them on every issue. After 1917 the liberals also began to raise the question of a Bolshevik or 'red' militarism and linked the concept to an expanded notion of backwardness which included not merely pre-capitalist, pre-industrial, or industrializing societies, but also socialist ones. This assumption gained its greatest popularity during the *Cold War and became not merely an explicit propaganda weapon but also a means of understanding the power structures of the Soviet system. In connection with the western debate on the emergence of an American Military-Industrial Complex (see EISENHOWER) in the 1960s and 1970s, Vernon Aspaturian tried to identify a similar phenomenon in communist societies and discerned 'a polarisation of men and institutions into a security-producer-ideological grouping and a consumer-agricultural-public services grouping'.

After the collapse of the USSR the question of a 'red militarism' lost its significance as an ideological weapon and is now being treated as a purely historical phenomenon, as scholars delve into the Soviet archives in their attempt to reconstruct what made the Soviet system tick. The questions to be answered are whether the Soviet marshals ever occupied a position powerful enough to challenge the primacy of the Soviet Communist Party and the Kremlin leadership ('political militarism'), and whether the militarization of Soviet society in WW II and during the Cold War amounted to 'social militarism'?

Owing to this approach there is one final twist to the non-Marxist discussion of militarism. It arose with regard to countries of the Third World. Since quite a few of them were run by military regimes, in the 1950s and 1960s social scientists began to debate how far the professional officers, having seized power in these countries and particularly in Latin America, in fact acted as modernizers. It was also central to the argument that contrasted temporary, superficial 'authoritarian' regimes with deep-rooted 'totalitarian' regimes which aimed at permanently altering a society and perpetuating themselves. The notion that the military could act as stewards was never widely accepted and is now seldom heard.

With the end of the Cold War, the concept of militarism has lost most of the ideological steam that seemed to make it worth discussing. It is rarely used to describe present-day systems and policies but instead is seen as a phenomenon of the past to be examined with the tools of the historian. What may have been lost thereby is the study of militarism as merely one aspect of the whole 'ask not what your country can do for you but what you can do for your country' philosophy to which many subscribe who would be appalled to be described as militarists.   VRB/HEB

Aspaturian, Vernon, on the Soviet Military-Industrial Complex, *Journal of International Affairs*, 26 (1972).

Berghahn, Volker R., *Militarism: The History of an International Debate, 1861–1979* (New York, 1981).

Gillis, John R. (ed.), *The Militarization of the Western World* (New Brunswick, NJ, 1989).

Stargardt, Nicholas, *The German Idea of Militarism: Radical and Socialist Critics, 1866–1914* (Cambridge, 1994).

Vagts, Alfred, *A History of Militarism* (London, 1938).

military monastic orders came into being after the First *Crusade. Hugh de Payns and a small group of knights elected themselves the guards of pilgrims visiting Jerusalem and the River Jordan *c.*1119 and were given quarters in the al-Aqsa mosque or temple of Solomon, from which they drew the name Knights of the Temple or Templars. In 1129 at the Council of Troyes they were recognized by the papacy and given a Rule partly written by the greatest crusader preacher of the day, St Bernard of Clairvaux. His Latin version taught them how to live as monks in poverty, chastity, and obedience, while French additions dealt with military organization and tactics. The Templars quickly became an invaluable part of crusading armies. Their Master saved the French Second Crusaders from destruction in Anatolia in 1147 by instructing them in how to conduct a fighting march. The order also became rapidly enormously wealthy by virtue of pious donations. Alfonso I, king of Aragon, even tried to will it a third of his kingdom.

The Templars were probably intended to complement the Order of St John of the Hospital or Hospitallers who, since the 1080s, had been part of the monastery of Santa Maria Latina, where they ran a hospital dedicated to St John the Baptist. The Hospitallers were accepted as an independent order *c.*1113, although not militarized until later, probably in the 1130s. Both orders created a network of western commanderies, which sustained their military and charitable activities in the Latin East. In 1193, following the Third Crusade, German knights made up the Teutonic Order. The Teutonic Knights were formed around a hospital at Acre, but in 1198 they adopted military functions modelled on the Templars. Two smaller orders followed similar paths: St Lazarus, a hospitaller order caring for lepers since the 1130s, and St Thomas of Acre, a house of regular canons founded *c.*1190, both became militarized in the 1220s. The international financial base of the orders enabled them to construct and maintain expensive *castles beyond the means of secular lords. Krak des Chevaliers (Hospitaller), Atlit (Templar), and Montfort or Starkenberg (Teutonic) are just three of the grandest in the Holy Land.

New monastic orders were created in other crusading zones. In Iberia there were the orders of Calatrava (1158) and Santa María de España in Castile (1270s); Santiago (1170) and Alcántara (*c.*1176) in León; Mountjoy (*c.*1173), Alcalá (1174), and San Jorge de Alfama (*c.*1200) in Aragon; and Avis (*c.*1176) in Portugal. In eastern Europe the orders of the Swordbrethren (1202) and of Dobrin (*c.*1228) were absorbed by the Teutonic Knights in the 1230s. Finally there were short-lived anti-heretical orders such as the Militia of the Faith of Jesus Christ and the Order of the Faith and Peace in Languedoc from the 1220s, and the Order of the Blessed Virgin Mary in Bologna and Florence from 1261.

When driven from the mainland in 1291, the Teutonic Knights established a sovereign state in Prussia, from which they orchestrated crusades against Lithuania. Their domination of the region was ended by their defeat at *Tannenberg in 1410. The Templars, who had become successful bankers, were destroyed by the greed of the French King Philip IV who arrested them in 1307 and charged them with heresy, obscenity, and satanism. Pope Clement V was sceptical but nevertheless ordered their arrest elsewhere. He finally decided that they were too defamed to continue and at the Council of Vienne in 1312 he suppressed the order and transferred its possessions to the Hospitallers. The latter retired to Cyprus and then *Rhodes, where they constructed a sophisticated fortress and conducted fierce attacks upon the Ottoman *Turks. Expelled by *Suleiman 'the Magnificent' in 1523, they withdrew to *Malta, which they famously defended in 1565. They held the island until 1798, but were no longer of military significance by the time *Napoleon expelled them while on his *Egyptian expedition. They retain a headquarters in Rome, the view through the keyhole on the main gate which frames St Peter's being a well-known tourist attraction.   MCB/HEB

Barber, Malcolm, *The New Knighthood* (Cambridge, 1994).

Christiansen, Eric, *The Northern Crusades: The Baltic and the Catholic Frontier 1100–1525* (London, 1980).

Forey, Alan, *The Military Orders: From the Twelfth to the Early Fourteenth Centuries* (Basingstoke, 1992).

Riley-Smith, Jonathan, *Atlas of the Crusades* (London, 1991).

military police are soldiers detailed for duties concerned with the maintenance of *discipline and upholding the *laws of war. In WW II the British military policeman's slogan was 'guide the responsible, check the irresponsible and incarcerate the incorrigible'. Military police is a wide term, which can refer to troops belonging to dedicated units or to soldiers temporarily carrying out policing duties, for instance at unit level or in garrisons. Troops have carried out such duties in many armies in history. It has been claimed that the household sergeants-at-arms of *Richard 'the Lionheart' were the first English military police, and the English army of the 16th century had a few 'tipstaves' who exercised limited powers. From the creation of modern standing armies in the 17th century onwards, most armies had small numbers of troops who performed policing duties, assisting the *provost marshal or his equivalent.

A principal role of military police has been to apprehend deserters and to prevent soldiers straggling or running from the battlefield; troops deployed in the latter role are often termed 'battle police'. Twentieth-century mechanized armies demand sophisticated traffic control, which has become an important role for many military policemen. In addition, on occasions regular troops have performed policing duties in support of the *civil power, especially in the era before the establishment of standing police forces, and various paramilitary bodies, especially during the British Raj, were given the somewhat misleading title of 'military police'. Military police also have an important role in processing and guarding *POWs. Many military police forces have adopted distinctive items of dress: the German gorget (hence the nickname 'chained dogs'), the American white helmet (Snowdrops), the British red cap.   GDS

Sheffield, G. D., *The Redcaps* (London, 1994).

military revolution Military revolutions have taken place throughout history, and one of the greatest may be underway now. They involve major changes in the conduct of war and in military organization and administration, both reflecting and further influencing wider technological, political, administrative, and social change. For historians of the early modern period in Europe and its colonies, the 'military revolution' means the creation of recognizably modern armies and navies in the period 1500 to 1800, and centres on a debate initiated by the historian Michael Roberts in his article on 'The Military Revolution 1560–1660', first published in 1956. More widely, 'military revolution' embraces earlier and subsequent changes pivoting on fundamental shifts in technology and social organization and attitudes. These other 'military revolutions' include the advent of potential nuclear missile war in the mid-20th century and the 'revolution in military affairs' involving *precision-guided munitions, and changes in views of national sovereignty and *information warfare which some believe to be underway—or getting underway—now.

In his article, revised in 1967, Roberts was the first to admit that other military revolutions were 'turning points in the history of mankind' and that the century and geographical area on which he focused might seem of 'inferior importance'. The other revolutions he listed were the advent of the sword and mounted warrior in the middle of the second millennium BC (see CHARIOT and CAVALRY), the triumph of the heavy cavalryman resting on the *stirrup in the 6th century AD, and what he called 'the scientific revolution in warfare' (see NUCLEAR WEAPONS) of his own day. Nevertheless, Roberts contended, the revolution which he associated with *Gustavus Adolphus of Sweden stood 'like a great divide separating medieval society from the modern world', and had a wider influence on European society at large.

His period certainly saw a military-technical revolution which might, in current parlance, be termed a revolution in military affairs. The huge Spanish *tercios, 3,000 strong, and massive square formations gave way to line formations designed to maximize the effect of small-arms fire—although the advent of the *bayonet, which made the pike obsolete, came after Roberts's chosen time frame, as did the perfection of mobile artillery. More importantly, however, Roberts noted a move towards greater initiative and flexibility on the battlefield, necessitating a vast increase in the number of *officers and *NCOs. It is true that there was a general increase in the number of these people and the grades into which they were divided (see RANK), although this had begun earlier and continued later. Roberts's comments did not always endear him to military historians. Drill, reflecting a more absolute subordination of the soldier to his superior, implied that 'it might not be the soldier's business to think, but he would at least be expected to possess a certain minimal capacity for thinking'. Armies, he continued, were no longer 'a brute mass in the *Swiss style, nor a collection of bellicose individuals in the feudal style'. An army was to be 'an articulated organism' of which each part responded to impulses from above. This military-technical revolution led to—or perhaps coincided with—a dramatic increase in the size of armed forces. Whereas Philip II of Spain had dominated Europe with a professional army of perhaps 40,000, *Louis XIV needed ten times the number a century later.

Roberts made the interesting observation that the great military revolutions throughout history generally coincided with the predominance of mercenaries. They possessed the necessary discipline and professional skill to create a revolution, but had to be promptly stepped on. The military revolution was also characterized by a sharp tightening of civilian control over the military—exemplified by *Peter 'the Great''s destruction of the *streltsy. Secretaries of state for war and war offices—recognizably modern defence administration—proliferated. And out of the horror of the *Thirty Years War, and in recognition of the need to keep the increasingly potent military instrument within legal and ethical bounds, came the first works on the laws of war. Roberts concluded that in this period 'the conjoint ascendancy of financial power and applied science was already established in all its malignity . . . The road lay open, broad and straight, to the abyss of the twentieth century'.

But others thought the revolution went wider. Geoffrey Parker, historian and geographer, in his Lees-Knowles lectures at Cambridge in 1984 argued that the military revolution had been bigger, and had been the key to the West's success in creating the first truly global empires between 1500 and 1800. This argument, resting on the development of navigation, big ships, sails, and guns, had also been made earlier by Carlo M. Cipolla. Parker had begun by challenging Roberts in his Cambridge Ph.D. The tactical developments described by Roberts could not alone have been the cause of the gargantuan armies which came to stalk Europe. Parker was then alarmed to find that, with typical academic sadism, Cambridge had appointed Roberts to be his external examiner. No matter: Roberts conceded that Parker had made a valid criticism. Parker argued that the revolution had its roots as far back as 1430, began in 1530, and extended forward to 1730.

Others added a third element: the development of the *trace italienne*—of artillery *fortifications and siegecraft. While medieval *castles had been defended by tiny garrisons, the capacious new fortresses also forced an increase in the size of armies and treasuries.

The historians' debate on the early modern military revolution coincided with another one, the first to be labelled a 'Revolution in Military Affairs', by the Soviet Union. By 1960 it was clear that the advent of nuclear weapons, in particular thermonuclear weapons, and ballistic missiles to deliver them, created the potential for a completely new kind of warfare: push-button, nuclear-missile war. A study, *Problems of the Revolution in Military Affairs*, was set in type while Khrushchev was still in power and published, with all references to him removed, in 1965. Like the Roberts revolution, this one went much further than weapons technology. A whole new branch of the armed forces, the Strategic Missile Forces, was set up in 1959, sweeping to pre-eminence over the army, navy, and air forces, and the whole country was fortified to withstand a nuclear rocket war which threatened instantaneous destruction. The term features prominently in the third edition of Marshal Vasiliy Sokolovsky's *Military Strategy*, published in 1968.

But are military revolutions really revolutions? The great military historian Cyril Falls warned that observers constantly define the warfare of their own age as marking a revolutionary breach in the normal progress of methods of warfare. But, he said, it is a fallacy, due to ignorance of the technical and tactical military history, to suppose that methods of warfare have not made continuous and, on the whole, fairly even progress. But if the methods of warfare change by evolution rather than by revolution, social organization and attitudes may still progress jerkily to catch up. A period of evolution in military technology may cause a head of water to build up which will then create a more sudden change in organization and attitudes—the realization that major war is unwinnable, for example.

This view concurs with that of the futurists Alvin and Heidi Toffler, who, in their book *The Third Wave*, concluded that there had only been two full-scale military revolutions—the agricultural, at the dawn of organized warfare, and the industrial—and that we are now entering the third great military revolution—the informational.

The argument that so-called military revolutions are, in fact, evolution applies with particular force to the revolution in military affairs (RMA) widely believed to be underway now. After the 1991 *Gulf war, the technological advances and associated tactical, operational, and strategic opportunities were labelled a 'military technical revolution' (MTR) in the USA. By the mid-1990s, however, the pre-

ferred term was RMA, reflecting the belief that technology should not be overemphasized. Most of the technologies associated with this so-called RMA went back a long way. The first precision-guided munitions were used in 1972. Satellites were used for *reconnaissance in 1961 and for *communications in *Vietnam in 1965. Information warfare has been around as long as warfare itself, and the widespread employment of information systems may not be so revolutionary. The 1991 Gulf War, rather than being the epitome of a military revolution, as many believe it is, may actually have been the last, consummately perfect manifestation of a style of warfare towards which planners strove in WW I and WW II.

In addition to the technological components which are commonly thought to make up the present RMA—precision-guided weapons, information systems, instant communications, faultless navigation, and 'transparency of the battlespace' through all-seeing reconnaissance—there are wider factors. The emergence of non-state actors, greater willingness by governments and the international community to intervene in other people's wars but far less willingness by developed states to accept casualties, and yawning differences in technological capacity to wage war will lead the disadvantaged to turn to asymmetric solutions. These wider factors create a bigger shift—wider than a MTR, wider than a RMA, which Lawrence Freedman called the 'revolution in strategic affairs'. But is a new term needed? Or is this greater shift, in fact, a true military revolution? CDB

Black, Jeremy, *A Military Revolution? Military Change and European Society 1550–1800* (London, 1991).

Cipolla, Carlo M., *Guns, Sails and Empires: Technological Innovation and the Early Phases of European Expansion* (New York, 1965).

Falls, Cyril, *A Hundred Years of War, 1850–1950* (London, 1953).

Freedman, Lawrence, *The Revolution in Strategic Affairs* (IISS/Oxford, 1998).

Parker, Geoffrey, *The Military Revolution: Military Innovation and the Rise of the West, 1500–1800* (Cambridge, 1989).

Roberts, Michael, 'The Military Revolution 1560–1660' (1956), repr. in *Essays in Swedish History* (London, 1967), 195–225.

Rogers, Clifford L., *The Military Revolution Debate: Readings in the Military Transformation of Early Modern Europe* (Westview, 1995).

Toffler, Alvin and Heidi, *The Third Wave* (New York, 1980).

—— *War and Anti-War* (Boston, 1993).

militia is a term which has varied meanings. It has been commonly used to characterize a military force recruited directly from civilians who would not otherwise be liable to serve in a state's regular armed forces, and upon whom a military obligation is imposed by the state in certain circumstances. Usually this obligation is imposed for the purposes of local or home defence although, on occasions, such militias have been employed abroad. In the past, both Britain and the USA had citizen militias of this kind, that in

Britain existing on an organized basis from 1558 until 1908. A second use of the term is to describe any unorganized military force drawn from within a civilian population and which has taken up arms. Thus, in modern *Somalia the armed followers of different warlords have been characterized as militias.

Military obligations were imposed on free men in both Carolingian Europe and Anglo-Saxon England and, throughout the medieval period, communal defence was widely regarded in Europe as a civic virtue. However, as modern state systems began to emerge by the 16th century, permanent professional standing regular armies were increasingly preferred by rulers as a more reliable means of making war. Citizen militias were often regarded at this stage as a possible constitutional safeguard against absolutism by representing an alternative to the trained military manpower available to the state. In England, for example, a dispute between crown and parliament over the control of the militia was the actual catalyst for the outbreak of the English civil war in 1642 (see BRITISH CIVIL WARS). As the constitutional significance of the militias disappeared, they became utilized mainly as a manpower supplement to the national army in the event of war. In many cases, as in Sweden in 1682 and Prussia in 1733, the obligation to the citizen militia was actually replaced by conscription for the national army. Moreover, as conscription was increasingly extended throughout Europe, new kinds of *reserve forces were substituted for militias such as the Landwehr in Prussia and the National Guard in the USA. By contrast, Britain maintained a system of voluntary enlistment for its regular army until 1916 but, paradoxically, its militia was raised by compulsory ballot from 1757 until 1831. Uniquely, in the case of Switzerland, the militia obligation has remained the basis of military organization for all its armed forces.

The militia obligation itself usually required a commitment to undertake a certain period of annual training in peacetime with a more permanent embodiment in the event of war. In the case of England, only a portion of the militia was customarily called out for such training between 1573 and 1663, hence the use of the term 'trained bands'. In colonial North America, the supposed instant readiness of the militia to take up arms was reflected in the currency of the term 'Minutemen', and it was these who distinguished themselves at *Lexington and Concord. The second amendment to the US Constitution reads: 'A well regulated Militia, being necessary to the security of a free State, the right of the people to keep and bear Arms, shall not be infringed.' Significantly, various contemporary groups of armed citizens in the USA, united only in their belief that the state has become despotic, all designate themselves 'militias'.   IB

Beckett, Ian, *The Amateur Military Tradition, 1558–1945* (Manchester, 1991).
Mahon, J. K., *The History of the Militia and National Guard* (New York, 1983).

Minamoto Yoshitsune (1159–89) is one of the most celebrated names in *samurai history. As a child, following the defeat of his family in the Heiji Rebellion, he was placed under the guardianship of the Kurama temple, but instead of adopting the life of a monk he studied martial arts, and left the temple for northern Japan, where he sought the protection of a Minamoto sympathizer called Fujiwara Hidehira. He joined his brother Yoritomo in his rebellion against the Taira (see GEMPEI WARS), although their first actions were fought against their cousin Yoshinaka, whom they defeated in 1184. Yoshitsune entered Kyoto, and attacked the Taira at Ichi no tani. When they escaped to the sea Yoshitsune pursued them to Yashima, and then to Dan no Ura, where he inflicted a third major defeat upon them. The victory over the Taira secured the post of *shogun for his brother Yoritomo, but Yoritomo turned against him and tried to have him killed. Yoshitsune escaped but was pursued by Yoritomo's armies until he was defeated and committed suicide at Koromogawa along with his celebrated companion the monk Benkei. Legend has it that he did not die but escaped to Mongolia where he became *Genghis Khan.   SRT

Minden, battle of (1759), fought during the *Seven Years War in Westphalia. A 37,000-strong Anglo-Hanoverian force under Prince Ferdinand of Brunswick met a French army of 44,000 commanded by the Marshal de Contades and skirmishing and artillery exchanges began at about 05.00. The French front was eventually pierced by a remarkable attack (launched as the result of a linguistic misunderstanding) by a brigade of British infantry, which shrugged off cavalry attacks and artillery fire, but suffered one-third casualties. But when the Allied cavalry of five regiments was called to charge in support, Lord George *Sackville thrice refused to give the order to advance, and thus lost an opportunity to influence the battle. Sackville's conduct has never been satisfactorily explained. At a crucial moment, the Anglo-Hanoverian heavy artillery (30 guns) was moved to the left flank by a concealed route, and quickly repulsed an attack from that quarter, exploiting their mobility to the full. The same guns were then pushed forward, accompanying the final Allied attack that decided the battle. The battle lasted for about five hours during the early morning, and was over by about 10.00. The French suffered a resounding defeat, losing between 7,000–10,000 men, while the Allied casualties were fewer than 3,000.

APC-A

Cole, Howard, *Minden* (London, 1972).

mines were just that, originally, and a common feature of *fortification and siegecraft. *Oman described the process as follows: 'The besieger removed as much earth as he could carry away from beneath some exposed corner of the fortifications, and shored up the hole with beams. He then filled the space between the beams with straw and brushwood, and set fire to it. When the supports were consumed, the wall crumbled downwards into the hole, and a breach was produced.' Over time *explosives added to the effects of this technique and mining of the traditional sort continued into WW I. Mining was particularly important in the *Messines ridge attack of 1917. Because of the similar purpose, any submarine or subterranean explosive device came to be known as a 'mine'. At sea they became extremely effective means of denying a passage to the enemy, sinking several warships at *Gallipoli, or, as used in the *Russo-Japanese war, to channel an attacker into machine guns' lines of fire. The indiscriminate use of naval mining at *Port Arthur during this war caused damage to neutral shipping and resulted in the 1907 Hague Convention (see GENEVA AND HAGUE CONVENTIONS) 'Relative to the Laying of Automatic Submarine Contact Mines'. It was to be several decades before another type of mine was to figure so prominently in debate about the conduct of warfare.

With the advent of 'land ships' (*tanks) to land warfare, the use of mines to disable them was a logical extension of their naval role. By the middle of WW II, the use of mines had become a central feature of land warfare and continued to figure prominently in the operational *doctrine of armies through much of the 20th century. Mines, be they *anti-armour, anti-vehicle, or anti-personnel, could have a variety of uses. They might be laid on a key area or feature, such as a hill or a road, in order to deny any operational advantage to the enemy or to delay movement. They might also be laid sporadically in order to harass enemy vehicles and troops and, once again, to slow down movement. But the prime use of mines would be to provide 'protective' or 'tactical' minefields. A protective minefield is one which would be laid in front of a key defended position and form part of the overall defensive plan. A tactical minefield is one which would block an enemy's advance and canalize his movement towards a 'killing area' observed by the defending force. In mine warfare, it is considered essential for both protective and tactical minefields to be covered by the direct and *indirect fire weapons of the defending force in order to preserve the integrity of the feature. During the *Cold War, the deployment of nuclear *demolition mines was designed to block or otherwise eliminate possible enemy lines of advance entirely.

Anti-personnel mines (APM) originated as anti-handling devices attached to larger anti-armour or anti-vehicle mines. With only a little further effort, the anti-handling device became a weapon in its own right. If covered by fire, APMs could help to prevent or delay enemy breaching. They could also immobilize the crews and occupants of tanks and infantry fighting vehicles crippled in the minefield. Depending on the type of APM, the target might be an individual enemy soldier or a small group. In a macabre way, the effect of APMs could be maximized when the resulting *casualties were wounded rather than killed: a soldier with his foot blown off is just as ineffective as a dead one, but his injury and distress might also have a psychological effect on his comrades. Furthermore, some of the victim's comrades would have to leave the battlefield in order to evacuate the casualty, who then became another burden on the enemy's medical and logistic services. While commanding the Eighth Army in *North Africa in 1943, *Montgomery accepted anti-armour mines as inevitable but saw that the APMs would require a 'very robust mentality' on the part of vulnerable infantry. APMs are hated by foot soldiers, and attrition by Vietcong mines set the stage for the atrocity at *My Lai.

Easy to manufacture and deploy in huge numbers, but extremely difficult to map and recover, the APM presented a major challenge to international humanitarian law of armed conflict and the principles of discrimination and non-combatant immunity. The first attempt to regulate the use of APMs, the 1980 UN Convention on 'Prohibitions or Restrictions on the Use of Certain Conventional Weapons Which May Be Deemed to Be Excessively Injurious or to Have Indiscriminate Effects', failed to solve the problem. During the 1990s, a popular international campaign to ban the production and use of APMs resulted in the December 1997 Ottawa Convention on the 'Prohibition of the Use, Stockpiling, Production and Transfer of Anti-Personnel Mines and on their Destruction'.   PC

Oman, C. W. C., *The Art of War in the Middle Ages* (Oxford, 1885).

Minié rifle   Popularized as 'Minnie rifle', this was the term adopted in the English-speaking world to describe a muzzle-loading percussion rifle firing a cylindro-conoidal *bullet with a concave base containing a cup. This type of bullet was patented by Capt Claud-Etienne Minié of the French army in 1849 from an idea by his fellow countryman, Gustave Delvigne. The bullet had greased grooves running horizontally around its base, which facilitated its loading into a rifled barrel. When fired, the skirts of the bullet expanded to fit the rifling, resulting in improved accuracy and range. Adopted in Britain as the Pattern 1851 Rifle-Musket, the British Minié rifle had a 39 inch barrel of .702 inch calibre and fired a 680 grain Minié bullet; fitted with its triangular-section socket *bayonet, it weighed 11 lb (5 kg) and stood 6 feet (1.82 metres) from butt-plate to bayonet-tip; it was superseded in 1853 by the Pattern 1853 Rifle-Musket. The Minié bullet was adopted by many nations in their earliest forms of muzzle-loading service rifle and it accounted for a large proportion of the casualties during the *American civil war of 1861–5.   SCW

Peterson, Harold L. (ed.), *Encyclopaedia of Firearms* (London, 1964).

Roads, Dr Christopher H., *The British Soldier's Firearm 1850–1864* (London, 1964).

miquelet is a Catalan word, sometimes spelt *miguelet*, indicating irregular *mountain troops armed with local styles of *snaphaunce muskets; it came to be applied to the locks of the muskets themselves in the late 19th century. Miquelet lock muskets, popular in Spain, Italy, and other areas of the Mediterranean rim from the 15th to 19th centuries, had forms of snaphaunce lock typical in their external mainspring, combined pancover and steel, and with dual sear springs allowing both full- and half-cock positions; local variations followed either Italian or Spanish styles.   SCW

Blair, Claude (gen. ed.), *Pollard's History of Firearms* (London, 1983).

missiles have been around since the first thrown stone, but today the word is reserved for rocket-powered guided weapons systems. These have had a revolutionary effect on almost every area of military activity, changing the nature of aerial and maritime combat, close *air support (CAS), and strategic air war. *Nuclear weapons provided the method of mass destruction on a wholly new scale, but missiles, in the shape of land-based intercontinental ballistic designs and similar submarine launched models, presented the means of delivery. By the 1960s concepts of mutually assured destruction (MAD), four-minute warnings, and nuclear *Armageddon had pervaded strategic thinking, all brought about by the vast destructive potential of missiles combined with nuclear warheads.

The development of modern missiles dates back to before WW II, but it was with the German V-1 cruise missile and the V-2 ballistic rocket that the missile age truly began. The weapons had limited success but the long-term potential was irrefutable. There were even plans for an intercontinental German missile to strike New York in 1946. Today there are a wide range of strategic level weapons from intercontinental ballistic missiles (ICBM) to contour-hugging Tomahawk cruise missiles. Apart from such large-scale weapons, missiles have also been developed to act in the tactical role, from early bazooka-type *anti-armour weapons to modern-day air-to-air Sidewinder and Phoenix missiles.

The most infamous form of missile is the ICBM, equipped with a nuclear warhead. A ballistic missile is accelerated by rocket propulsion and guided by internal controls, though once its fuel is spent it then coasts to its target. The curved or ballistic trajectory takes the missile to the outer reaches of the earth's atmosphere or even beyond it in the case of intercontinental types. Ballistic missiles may be launched from hardened silos, submarines, or mobile land platforms. They can be either single or multi-staged. Single-stage types include the German V-2 and Soviet Scuds, while multi-stage missiles have two or three sections and when the fuel from a given stage is spent, it is discarded. Missiles with ranges of less than 932 miles (1,500 km) tend to be single-stage devices, those with ranges up to 3,418

miles (5,500 km) double-stage, while intercontinental types have three stages. The velocity imparted by ballistic missiles is much greater than that attained by aircraft or cruise missiles and thus decreases markedly the ability to track and destroy them. Modern guidance systems are very precise, but in earlier models the use of nuclear warheads was held to lessen the requirement for accuracy. Missile accuracy was usually phrased in terms of Circular Area Probability (CEP), defined as the 50 per cent or greater likelihood of a missile falling within a given distance of the aiming point, a fairly loose indication of capability.

The first ICBMs were tested by the USA in 1958 and they rapidly replaced the manned strategic bomber during the 1960s. Such was the potential destructive force of nuclear missiles that no defence was considered truly viable and even anti-ballistic missiles (ABMs) could only provide the survivability of counterstrike missiles, thus negating the possibility of surprise first-strike attacks. Since the 1970s many ICBMs have been equipped with multiple independently targeted re-entry vehicles (MIRVs), which allow a number of nuclear warheads to be delivered at a variety of targets from a single missile, thus greatly escalating the potential for nuclear holocaust and undermining still further spurious notions of survivability. In reality, superpower nuclear missiles effectively stalemated each other in the *Cold War and their influence on the confrontation was actually quite limited.

Tactical missiles with conventional warheads have in fact had a much greater influence on the conduct of warfare in the latter stages of the 20th century. Air war has been shaped markedly by the widespread introduction of missiles. The US Sidewinder, a supersonic guided missile, was the first air-to-air design to bring down an enemy aircraft. The US Navy's Phoenix air-to-air missile has a range of some 100 miles (161 km). Modern aircraft are fitted with a variety of weapons, but missiles predominate to such an extent that developments in vectored thrusting and manoeuvrability to enhance dogfight capability have been questioned, as they are unable to defeat enemy missiles, the principal method of engagement. The surface-to-air missile (SAM) has also greatly affected *air power. Cheap but potent SAMs, such as the Stinger, have dramatically decreased the battlefield survivability of CAS aircraft and *helicopters, Afghanistan being a case in point. Stealth technology is one countermeasure but is extremely expensive.

Naval warfare has also been altered by missile technology, and surface-to-surface missiles, such as the Harpoon, as well as air-launched varieties have effectively replaced surface gunnery as the method of naval engagement. Missiles, even equipped with nuclear warheads, offer large carrier battlegroups considerable military capability, but large surface vessels also offer tempting targets to enemy nuclear missiles. During the Cold War, the survivability of carrier task forces was extremely dubious.

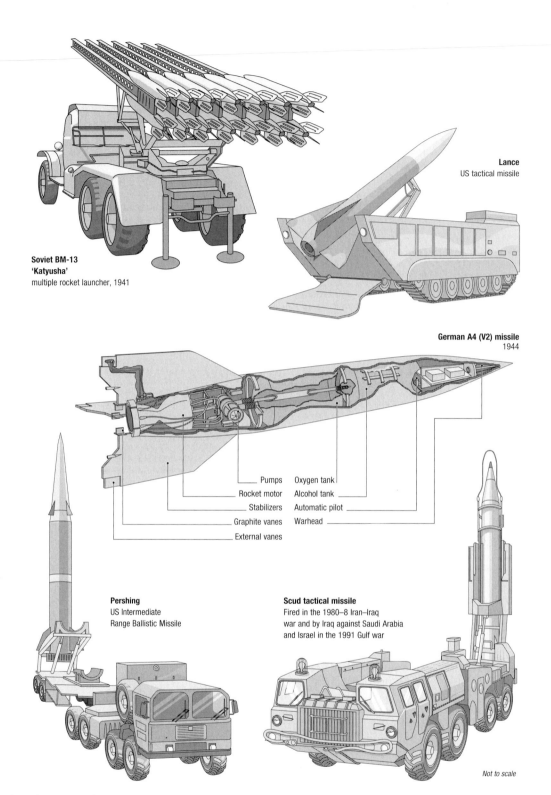

Soviet BM-13 'Katyusha'
multiple rocket launcher, 1941

Lance
US tactical missile

German A4 (V2) missile
1944

Pumps
Rocket motor
Stabilizers
Graphite vanes
External vanes

Oxygen tank
Alcohol tank
Automatic pilot
Warhead

Pershing
US Intermediate
Range Ballistic Missile

Scud tactical missile
Fired in the 1980–8 Iran–Iraq
war and by Iraq against Saudi Arabia
and Israel in the 1991 Gulf war

Not to scale

In the 20th century rocket systems were widely used in war – and in deterring it. In modern parlance, a 'rocket' is unguided once it leaves its launcher: a 'missile' is guided. The Soviet BM-13 'Katyusha' ('Little Kate'), which first saw service in 1941, and its German counterpart, the *Nebelwerfer*, were a prominent feature of the artillery war on the eastern front. The A4 or V2 (*Verwältungswaffe* – 're-venge weapon') liquid-fuelled ballistic missile was used against southern England in 1944. Captured V2s were fundamental to the post-war missile programmes of both the US and the Soviet Union, leading to missiles like the Pershing and Scud.

Missiles may also doom the main battle *tank (MBT), for so long the king of the battlefield. When one infantryman with reasonably steady hands can destroy a million-dollar MBT, not to mention the expensively trained crew, with a missile costing a few thousand, the cost–benefit arguments are extremely convincing. The US Hellfire missile mounted on helicopters was particularly effective during the *Gulf war.

The Tomahawk cruise missile has provided a new dimension to military capability, solving many operational issues and those of particular pertinence in the post-Cold War environment. The Tomahawk is an all-weather submarine/surface-launched anti-ship or land-attack cruise missile. The land-attack version of the Tomahawk has an inertial and terrain contour matching (TERCOM) guidance system which uses a stored map reference to compare with the actual terrain, and if required, a course correction can be made to place the missile on course to the target. In the climate where western forces are likely to be called upon to carry out precise air strikes, with emphasis being placed both on avoiding own losses and on very limited 'collateral damage'. the Tomahawk is an ideal delivery system.　JDB

Brodie, Bernard, *Strategy in the Missile Age* (Princeton, 1959).

Lee, R. G., *Guided Weapons* (London, 1988).

Carus, W. Seth, *Ballistic Missiles in Modern Conflict* (London, 1991).

missing in action. See MIA.

mission command. See DIRECTIVE CONTROL.

Mitchell, Gen William (1879–1936). Billy Mitchell is widely regarded as one of the great visionaries of *air power, and a prime mover in establishing the aeroplane at the forefront of American military thinking. In many ways his importance is overstated, especially in the field of theory, and his place in the development of an independent *air force is best viewed as a prophet or advocate rather than as a system builder.

Mitchell, already commissioned in the army, quickly recognized the potential of the aerial dimension in the years leading up to WW I, and became involved in the development of US aircraft, writing a number of articles on the subject. Indeed, in 1912 after being appointed to the army *general staff in Washington he wrote a report on the need for an army air arm. Following the entry of the USA into the war in 1917, he was despatched to Europe where he was undoubtedly influenced by MRAF Hugh *Trenchard, the founding father of the RAF. Mitchell began an abrasive and uncompromising campaign in favour of a similar US service, which earned him resentment and hostility from fellow officers who did not share his vision. After the

*Armistice he expressed disappointment that the war had ended before air power could prove its true worth.

In the post-war period Mitchell was appointed assistant chief of the US Army Air Service and did nothing to endear himself even among those who shared his enthusiasm. In 1921 he was allowed to bomb US navy surplus or captured German warships and proved conclusively that even a near miss could sink them. It did not move the navy brass, who held that a ship underway and properly handled would be an impossible target. Mitchell's superiors attempted to keep him out of trouble, to no avail. In 1925 he released a scathing report on the state of US preparation for aerial warfare that employed phrases such as 'criminal and treasonable negligence', and was promptly *court-martialled. He resigned from the army in 1926 but continued his crusade until his death.　JDB

Hurley, Alfred, *Billy Mitchell: Crusader for Air Power* (Bloomington, Ind., 1975).

MacIsaac, David, 'Voices from the Central Blue', in Peter Paret (ed.), *Makers of Modern Strategy* (Oxford, 1986).

mitrailleuse is a French word translating as 'grapeshooter' and still used in France to mean 'machine gun'. The original mitrailleuse was developed by a Belgian, Joseph Montigny, into a 37-barrelled mechanical machine gun and it was adopted by the French army in the late 1860s. Loaded with separate iron breech-plates containing thirty-seven 11 mm *cartridges, it was fired by turning a crank with a rate of fire of 444 rounds per minute. Used as though it were an artillery piece during the *Franco-Prussian war of 1870–1, it was a success only when occasionally used in the close support role. The French were not impressed, but the Germans were.　SCW

Hobart, F. W. A., *Pictorial History of the Machine Gun* (London, 1971).

Miyamoto Musashi. See MUSASHI MIYAMOTO.

mobilization traditionally consists of the measures taken to bring the armed forces of a nation to war footing, and includes the calling up of reserves and organizing the supplies and equipment necessary for active operations. In recent years, this process has also included taking the necessary steps to prepare a nation's economy and population for war.

The modern concept of mobilization dates from the rise of mass armies and the professionalization of the military which took place in the late 19th century. In the *Franco-Prussian war, the Prussian-led German Confederation was able to expand its peacetime army of around 300,000 to over 1 million men and deploy this force within three weeks. This accomplishment was due to the combination of detailed planning undertaken during peacetime by the Prussian *general staff, under the direction of *Moltke 'the Elder', and the introduction of permanent corps-level commands that served as assembly points for recalled reservists.

The speed with which it had been able to assemble and deploy such a conscript army conferred upon the German Confederation an advantage over the French, who struggled to get a smaller army into the field over a longer period of time. The Germans, who possessed the initiative, were able to invade France and fight on their own terms. After the French defeat, the major powers of Europe (with the notable exception of Great Britain) introduced conscription and general staff systems based on the Prussian model. With all the nations of continental Europe employing conscript armies, speed and efficiency of mobilization became of paramount importance. In the years before WW I, each nation developed more sophisticated mobilization and deployment plans and utilized a greater percentage of its population in an attempt to outdo the others.

A significant, perhaps indeed the most significant, factor in the Gadarene rush to war in 1914 was the rigidity that these mobilization imperatives introduced into both diplomatic and military calculations. When Russia mobilized against Austria-Hungary in defence of Serbia, she perforce mobilized against Germany as well. Germany was committed to a mobilization that concentrated forces first against France and to a plan that involved the violation of Belgian neutrality, thus giving the British government a *casus belli* to honour pre-war commitments to the French. No country wanted to be 'out-mobilized' by another, and so by August around 4 million Frenchmen, 4 million Germans, 3 million Austro-Hungarians, and 6 million Russians were committed to war.

The duration and demands of WW I caused the government of each belligerent to mobilize not just the military strength of the nation but also the industrial potential. Initially, personnel from industries that contributed to the war effort were exempt from military service. As the war continued and the demand upon industry increased, some nations conscripted personnel into the workforce. All governments found it necessary to manage the economic resources of their nation in some way. WW I convinced most nations that mobilization for a future major war would need to include industry as well as the military. This belief was reinforced by WW II, which required an even greater exploitation of the manpower and economic strength of the belligerents. To this day, although the threat of large-scale war has receded, most nations maintain comprehensive mobilization plans.   RTF

Feldman, Gerald F., *Army, Industry, and Labor in Germany, 1914–1918* (Princeton, 1966).
Kennedy, Paul (ed.), *War Plans of the Great Powers* (London, 1979).

Model, FM Walther (1891–1945). Model was born near Magdeburg, son of a music teacher. Commissioned into the infantry in 1910, he won the Iron Cross in 1915 and served on the *general staff towards the end of WW I. One of the 4,000 officers selected for the *Reichswehr, he became a technical expert and visited the USSR to discuss rearmament. A convinced Nazi, he was promoted major general in 1938 and was a corps COS in Poland in 1939 and an army COS in France in 1940. Promoted lieutenant general, he commanded a panzer division in the invasion of the USSR, doing so well that he was given command of XLI Panzer Corps that October in the rank of *General der Panzertruppen*. In January 1942 he took over the threatened Ninth Army at Rzhev, where he won a desperate battle and was promoted colonel-general.

Model voiced misgivings about ZITADELLE, the *Kursk offensive, in which his army suffered heavy losses. He took over Army Group North in January 1944, becoming the army's youngest field marshal shortly afterwards, and going on to head Army Group North Ukraine in the chaotic summer of 1944. Transferred to the western front as C-in-C in August, he reverted to command of Army Group B, helping crush the landing at *Arnhem and exercising overall command of the *Bulge offensive in December. He committed suicide in the Ruhr pocket in April 1945.

Nicknamed 'the Führer's fireman', Model was aggressive and energetic, with real flair for command in the armoured battle. Famously blunt, he was one of the few generals who stood up to *Hitler.   RH

Mohacs, battle of (1526), decisive defeat of Hungarian forces by the Ottoman *Turks, effectively destroying the Hungarian monarchy. *Suleiman 'the Magnificent' demanded tribute from a failing Hungarian state. When it refused to pay, he advanced, capturing Sabac and Belgrade (then lying within the Hungarian dominions). The Hungarian King Louis II assembled a puny army of 20,000 and advanced from Buda (one of the twin cities which became Budapest). On 29 August 1526 he stupidly attacked 100,000 well-armed, -trained, -paid, and -motivated Ottoman Turks. He was killed and his army annihilated. Suleiman took Buda but then withdrew, taking 100,000 prisoners as slaves. Hungary was no threat to him now, and he left it alone. Transylvania and eastern Hungary became autonomous provinces of the Ottoman empire. Hungary herself collapsed into civil war from 1526 to 1538.   CDB

Moltke, FM Graf Helmuth Karl Bernhard von, 'the Elder' (1800–91), the pre-eminent military figure in European history since *Napoleon. He created the *general staff that became the basis for Germany's formidable modern armies, and the model for similar organizations throughout Europe. He also guided the armed forces of

Prussia and Germany to victories over Denmark, Austria, and France, making possible *Bismarck's creation of a unified German state.

Moltke was born in Mecklenburg in 1800. His family, of ancient nobility but modest means, settled in Denmark a few years later, where it was further impoverished when its property was plundered by the French. Moltke entered the Danish cadet corps at the age of 11. He transferred to Prussian service in 1822, and was admitted shortly thereafter to the Allgemeine Kriegsakademie in Berlin. Following graduation he devoted himself to the characteristic tasks of staff officers in that era—surveying and mapmaking—at which he became proficient: one of Moltke's maps is still included in the German Ordnance Survey for Gross Zöllnitz. He also found time to exercise his gifts as a man of letters, publishing minor works of fiction under a pseudonym, and contracting, in 1832, to translate Gibbon's *Decline and Fall of the Roman Empire* in order to be able to buy a horse. In 1835 he was seconded to Turkish service, and directed the Turkish artillery at the battle of Nezib (1839), a losing encounter with the forces of *Mohammad Ali that proved to be Moltke's only battlefield command.

Thereafter Moltke's career evolved into a series of increasingly senior staff appointments, which afforded a comprehensive view of a military environment on the verge of far-reaching technological change. He was among the first European soldiers to take an interest in railways—he became a director of the Hamburg–Berlin Line in 1841—and also among the first to recognize that rifled infantry weapons (introduced in the Prussian army that same year) would place an increasing premium on enveloping forms of attack. He also acquired an appreciation of Prussia's military deficiencies. Alone among the great powers, Prussia fought no military campaigns in the 1840s or 1850s. It did mobilize repeatedly in response to political crises always with lamentable results. By the time Moltke became COS in 1857, there was reason to doubt whether the Prussian army could support an independent foreign policy worthy of a major state.

Part of the solution—increasing the number of men under arms—would be the work of Moltke's colleague, the Prussian war minister, Albrecht von *Roon. Moltke, for his part, recognized that a larger army would mean nothing if men and equipment could not be brought onto the field smoothly. He also saw that armies of a size made possible by modern conscription—and necessary by the lethality of modern weapons—could not be moved or sustained logistically except as detached corps. He developed an exacting system of rail-based mobilization and communications, whose continuous refinement and rapid implementation became essential staff functions.

He also transformed the staff itself. When Moltke took over as chief, the general staff possessed little prestige, and stood outside the wartime chain of command. Under his leadership, it became the brain and nervous system of the army: at once a centralized planning agency, and a decentralized command and control system. The latter was the more daring conception. No plan, as Moltke once observed, could survive contact with the enemy for long. It was at that moment that an incisive, far-seeing intelligence was necessary, and that was what Moltke's staff officers were intended to provide. Moltke selected and trained his men in his own image, emphasizing breadth of learning and mental agility, and instilling a shared instinct for mutual support in battle that stood in marked contrast to the cautious, rule-bound orthodoxy of the day.

It took time for Moltke's influence to be felt. During the war with Denmark in 1864 he remained in Berlin, and went forward only after his plan to cut the Danes off from their coastal islands had miscarried for lack of execution. His arrival transformed the situation, which he resolved by organizing an amphibious assault on Alsen, after which the Danes sued for peace. This confirmed Moltke's standing in the eyes of the king. Within the army he remained relatively unknown. When, in anticipation of war with Austria in 1866, he was given the right (for the first time) to issue operational orders, mild confusion ensued: one division commander remarked that the instructions he had received 'were entirely in order, but who is Gen von Moltke?' Four weeks later, three Prussian armies operating under Moltke's direction converged to crush the Austrians at *Königgrätz, as bold and decisive an operation of war as Europe had seen in half a century. The question would not be asked again.

It is a tribute to Moltke's self-discipline that, confronted with the challenge of war with France a few years later, he resisted the temptation to relive his earlier triumph. Strategy, he once said, was a system of expedients, to be developed in light of changing circumstances. Against France, a stronger and more dangerous opponent than Austria, Moltke adopted a more compact scheme of manoeuvre, in which his armies sought contact with the enemy while remaining within supporting distance of each other, only then turning against the adversary's flanks and rear. Such tactical responsiveness was made possible by the staff structure Moltke had put in place over the previous decade. In 1870, every Prussian commander had at his shoulder an officer trained by Moltke, who knew enough of his chief's intentions to act effectively on the basis of general instructions. No comparable means of harmonizing the actions of dispersed forces existed on the French side, and the result was a swift Prussian victory, against an opponent that had been regarded as the most militarily gifted in Europe.

Moltke remained COS until 1887. Personally taciturn, he was said to have been 'silent in seven languages'. No such reticence afflicted him as a writer, however: his collected works run to 24 volumes, all of which testify to the profound realism that was his outstanding characteristic.   DM

Craig, Gordon, *The Battle of Königgrätz* (London, 1965).
Holborn, Hajo, 'The Prusso-German School: Moltke and the Rise of the General Staff', in Peter Paret (ed.), *Makers of Modern Strategy* (Princeton, 1986).

Howard, Michael, *The Franco-Prussian War* (London, 1961).

Rothenberg, Gunther E., 'Moltke, Schlieffen, and the Doctrine of Strategic Envelopment', in Paret (ed.), *Makers of Modern Strategy.*

Moltke, Gen Helmuth von, 'the Younger' (1848–1916).

Moltke 'the Younger' grew up and lived his life in the shadow of his famous uncle, known as 'the Elder'. Decorated for combat in the *Franco-Prussian war, afterwards he became the military comrade and drinking companion of Crown Prince Wilhelm. From 1882 to 1891 he was part of his uncle's official entourage. When the latter died and Prince Wilhelm became German kaiser, Moltke was appointed to high military posts which kept him in Berlin and close by: he was one of the kaiser's best friends. In 1906, upon the retirement of *Schlieffen, Moltke was appointed CGS. Although he worked at it, he was unsuited to fill his predecessors' boots, as he himself admitted. Lethargic and lacking self-confidence, he was a quiet dreamer, with interests in theology, art history, and oriental religions. He maintained an atelier where he painted and practised the cello. Although he did pay careful attention to the logistic aspects of the Schlieffen plan, in August 1914 he failed to respect Schlieffen's basic principle to 'only make the right wing strong'. More culpably (for the plan's feasibility remains a matter of controversy) he failed to give firm and consistent direction to his army commanders. He suffered a nervous breakdown, resigned in September 1914 (though he had to remain at HQ for a while to preserve the fiction that all was well), and died two years later.   AB3

Bucholz, Arden, *Moltke, Schlieffen and Prussian War Planning* (Oxford, 1993).

'Moltke, Helmuth von (The Younger)', in Dieter K. Buse and Juergen C. Doerr (eds.), *Modern Germany: An Encyclopedia of History, People and Culture, 1871–1990* (New York, 1998).

Hull, Isabel, *The Entourage of Kaiser Wilhelm II* (New York, 1982).

Monash, Gen Sir John (1865–1931),

an Australian of German-Jewish parentage, an active and proficient citizen-soldier before 1914, and a highly successful engineer in civil life. He commanded the 4th Brigade at *Gallipoli and was promoted to major general in June 1916 and given command of the 3rd Division, then forming and training in England. As a result he missed the *Somme offensive and he and his formation were able to digest the lessons of that year's fighting before going into the line in November.

Monash commanded at *Messines where he impressed *Haig and others with his thoroughness and preparations. He repeated this performance at Broodseinde in October. *Birdwood recommended that Monash succeed him in command of the Australian Corps in May 1918, and he led the Australians through their most successful phase of the war until the *Australian Imperial Force was withdrawn for rest in October 1918. The assault at Le Hamel in July was a model of its kind and was completed in 93 minutes, and Monash drove the Australians forward after the victory at *Amiens in August, certain that the Germans were losing even defensive capabilities. After the *Armistice he supervised the efficient repatriation of his countrymen.   JG1

Mongols

or Moghuls were one of the Turkic tribes which inhabited the vast steppe lands of central Asia, north of the Gobi desert and the Great Wall of China and south of the Siberian forests. It was a hard land for humans but perfectly suited to the raising of the tough and hardy horses, which provided the livelihood of its peoples. It was said that Mongol children learned to ride before they could walk and their preferred weapon was the short but powerful composite *bow, fired from horseback. Tribal rivalries meant that every male Mongol was brought up to be able to fight and hunting expeditions formed the ideal training ground. Traditionally, these steppe lands had no cities, permanent houses, or fixed frontiers. There was no established religion: most of the people adhered to a sort of Shamanism, although Nestorian Christian, Muslim, and Buddhist missionaries were active. Kinship and personal relations remained much more important than religious affiliation,

In the second half of the 12th century, the Mongols were simply one of a number of nomad tribes, the Tatars, Kereits, and Naimans being others, who inhabited this area. Temujin or Temuchin, later known as *Genghis Khan, was born *c.*1162 in a family which had enjoyed a high status among the Mongols but which had fallen on hard times after the death of his father. By a mixture of brute force and clever alliances, the young Temuchin secured the leadership of the Mongols and then went on to lead his followers to victory over the neighbouring tribes, including the Tatars. Ironically the Mongols were often known by this, the name of a people they had defeated.

In 1206 Genghis Khan was acknowledged as the leader of all the central Asian Turkic peoples at a great Kuriltay (meeting) on the Onon river. According to the Mongol accounts, it was at this assembly that Genghis promulgated the great Yasa or Mongol law code and established the Yam or postal service, which was to connect his far-flung domains. However, his new empire was inherently unstable, it had either to expand or break apart, as so many steppe powers had done before. Genghis directed his first attacks against China, an alien culture and both the traditional enemy and cultural model of the steppe peoples. Between 1211 and 1215 he succeeded in reducing most of northern China, though the Sung dynasty remained in control of the south where the canals and irrigation canals made movement for the Mongol horsemen very difficult.

Mongol attacks on the lands to the west only began after 1218 when agents of the Khwarazmshah (Khorezonian Shah), an eastern Iranian ruler, killed merchants trading under the protection of Genghis Khan. In the years that followed, the Mongols systematically destroyed the flourishing cities of north-east Iran: both contemporary observers and the archaeological evidence, confirm the picture of widespread slaughter and the destruction of urban life and cities like Merv, Nishapur, and Balkh never recovered their former prosperity. Terror was used as a weapon and civilian as well as military populations were massacred. The death of Genghis in 1227 hardly interrupted their progress. In 1240 they launched a devastating attack on southern Russia which destroyed the ancient city of Kiev and the neighbouring lands, indirectly opening the way for the expansion of Muscovy. The next year they attacked Germany and defeated Henry of Silesia at the battle of Liegnitz before the army heard of the death of the Great Khan Ugeday in distant Mongolia and broke off the offensive. Western Europe was spared any further attacks and, indeed, popes and crusading monarchs like St Louis of France tried to make alliances with the pagan Mongols against their common Muslim enemies in the Middle East.

The expansion of the empire continued in the next generation. In the east, *Khubilai, who was generally accepted as Great Khan, completed the conquest of China but at the same time assimilated traditional Chinese culture and founded the Yuan dynasty, moving his capital from Karakorum on the steppes of Mongolia to Beijing. In the west, his brother Hulegu led another expedition into the Middle East which culminated in 1258 in the capture of Baghdad and the destruction of the Abbasid caliphate, which had provided leaders of Sunni Islam since 750. In the second half of the 13th century the Mongols' domains drifted apart and four main khanates emerged: China, the Chaghatay in central Asia, the Il-Khanate in Iran and Iraq, and the khanate of the Golden Horde in Russia. Until around 1300 there was still a sense of unity and a Pax Mongolica which allowed trading expeditions across its whole extent from Europe to China, as Marco Polo found, but the days of military expansion and conquest were over.

The reasons for the military success of the Mongols have been much debated. Both contemporaries and later historians have noted their hardiness and the extraordinary mobility which Mongol armies enjoyed. Soldiers were trained in vast hunting expeditions where co-ordination and teamwork were developed. Mongol soldiers needed no supply trains or *camp followers since they lived off and with their horses. After 1206, the Mongols and the other Turkic tribes functioned as a nation in arms. Among their enemies, like the Chinese and the Iranians, the military were a specialist group, highly trained and well equipped, but fairly small in number. Furthermore, Mongol armies tended to grow in numbers as they spread out and many Turkish peoples in eastern Iran and southern Russia joined them. The Mongols were especially concerned to recruit siege engineers in both China and Iran so that the fortifications, which had resisted many attackers, were taken. A combination of their military skills as mounted *archers, their rigorous *discipline and toughness meant that the Mongols rapidly created one of the most continuous and extensive empires the world has ever seen.
                                                                    HK

Monongahela River, battle of (1755). This was an incident in the *French and Indian war where some 224 French troops accompanied by approximately 600 Indian warriors enveloped the front of a British column of 1,400 regulars and 700 colonials, commanded by Maj Gen Edward Braddock with *Washington as his ADC. The British were marching on Fort Duquesne in western Pennsylvania when ambushed. It is taken as a classic example of the unwisdom of employing European tactics in the forests of North America, but it was really a failure of scouting and *intelligence, in both senses of the word, for Braddocks's firepower might have proved decisive if sensibly deployed. In the crossfire over 400 men, including Braddock, were killed and a similar number wounded. Washington rallied the survivors and, although still outnumbering the French, the demoralized survivors retreated to Fort Cumberland in Maryland.
                                                                    MCW

Mons, battle of (1914). In late August 1914 FM Sir John French's force of a cavalry division and two corps advanced into Belgium on the left of the French Fifth Army. Sir John was unaware that the French offensive was in difficulties, and that German armies were moving through Belgium in strength. On the evening of 22 August his westernmost II Corps, under Gen Smith-Dorrien, arrived on the Mons-Condé canal east and north of Mons, with Lt Gen Haig's I Corps echeloned back on its right. Gen von Kluck's First Army, in superior strength, was approaching the canal from the north, but neither side had much knowledge of the other's dispositions.

Early on 23 August the Germans mounted courageous but disconnected attacks: most foundered in the face of fierce rifle fire. Smith-Dorrien recognized that the troops on his right, where the line bulged out north of Mons, risked being cut off, and in the afternoon pulled back south of Mons. On the following day the British Expeditionary Force (BEF) began its long retreat to the *Marne. The battle cost the BEF 1,642 casualties, and the Germans up to 10,000. It gave early proof both of the quality of the BEF's soldiers and the shaky state of its staff work. The British army's first two VCs of the war were won by Lt Dease and Pte Godley on the Nimy railway bridge north of Mons.
                                                                    RH

Montecuccoli, Raimondo (1609–80), imperial officer and distinguished military theorist. Born in northern Italy, Montecuccoli entered the imperial army and became a successful cavalry leader in the *Thirty Years War, defeated the Ottoman *Turks in the battle of St Gotthard (1664), and successfully manoeuvred against *Turenne in the Rhine campaigns of 1673 and 1675. As president of the *Hofkriegsrat, he led the creation of a professional standing army. He also performed diplomatic missions and was heavily involved in power struggles both in court and within the army. Montecuccoli was regarded in the 18th century much as *Clausewitz has been in the 19th and 20th, as the most distinguished modern military theorist. A true military intellectual, he gave expression to the ideas of the late humanists and was an enthusiastic student of the occult, alchemy, and natural magic. These were central to the evolving scientific enterprise of the 16th and 17th centuries and were widespread among the Habsburg empire's élite. Montecuccoli's intellectual world informed his quest to formulate a general theory of war. This produced three major and largely parallel studies: *Treatise on War* (*Trattato della guerra*), *On the Art of War* (*Del arte militare*), and the celebrated *On the War against the Turks in Hungary* (*Della guerra col Turco in Ungheria*) or *Aphorisms*. Only the last two works were published, posthumously, at the beginning of the 18th century, and were widely translated and reprinted. AG1

Montecuccoli, Raimondo, *Ausgewälte Schriften des Raimun Fursten Montecuccoli*, ed. A. Veltze, 4 vols (Vienna and Leipzig, 1899–1900).

Barker, Thomas, *The Military Intellectual and Battle: Montecuccoli and the Thirty Years War* (New York, 1975).

Gat, Azar, *The Origins of Military Thought from the Enlightenment to Clausewitz* (Oxford, 1989).

Rothenburg, Gunther, 'The 17th century', in Peter Paret (ed.), *Makers of Modern Strategy from Machiavelli to the Nuclear Age* (Princeton, 1986).

Montfort, Simon (IV) de, Lord of Montfort

(*c*.1160–1218), scion of a large martial family originating in Montfort l'Aumary on the eastern borders of Normandy. He played a leading part in the Fourth *Crusade (1202–4), and also participated in the *Albigensian Crusade, commanding the force which remained when the larger crusading army split up after its victories in 1209. He defeated and killed Peter II, King of Aragon, at Muret in 1213, but was himself killed besieging Toulouse five years later. His younger son, also called Simon de *Montfort, rose to even greater prominence. His brother Guy sired Philip de Montfort, Lord of Toron and Tyre, a major figure in 13th-century Outremer and an early victim of an *Assassin. RH

Montfort, Simon de, Earl of Leicester (*c*.1208–65),

Henry III's most redoubtable opponent in the *Barons' wars. Born in Montfort, he was well received by Henry when he arrived in England in 1230, allowed to claim the earldom of Leicester, and married the king's youngest sister Eleanor. He went on crusade in 1240–1, and in 1248 was appointed the king's deputy in Gascony, where he put down a

revolt with severity. After his return to England in 1253 he became a central figure in the baronial opposition, helping impose the Provisions of Oxford which greatly reduced royal authority. He emerged as sole leader of the opposition in 1263, but his position had weakened, for many magnates suspected him of having designs on the throne. The Provisions of Oxford were referred to Louis IX of France for arbitration, and when, in 1264, Louis declared in favour of Henry, war broke out.

Although the campaign began badly for Montfort, he transformed it by besieging Rochester to draw the king south, and united his own divided forces to beat the king at Lewes. Henry and his son Edward surrendered by an agreement which reimposed the Provisions of Oxford but allowed some of Montfort's most committed opponents to escape. Virtually ruler of England, Montfort provoked dissatisfaction amongst some of his most notable supporters: Edward escaped and war broke out again. Edward surprised one of Montfort's armies, under his son Simon, outside the Montfort stronghold of Kenilworth. Montfort himself was caught, outnumbered, at Evesham. As he watched his foes converge, he is reported to have said: 'may God have mercy on our souls, for our bodies are theirs', but he and his men 'proceeded courageously to meet the multitude of their enemies'. Montfort fought valiantly, hoping that his son would arrive in time. He was killed and mutilated, but such was his reputation—he had a flair for attracting popular support, especially in London—that miracles were soon associated with his tomb in Evesham abbey.

Montfort was a skilled commander, and deserves admiration for overcoming the strategic disadvantage of divided forces at the start of the first Barons' war. At Lewes he showed a sharp eye for the ground, and got his army onto the downs above the town by night, no easy feat. He had a good grasp of fortification and siegecraft: the improvements he had made to Kenilworth castle enabled it to undergo a long siege after his death. RH

Montgomery, FM Sir Bernard Law, 1st Viscount

(1887–1976). A bishop's son, Montgomery was educated at St Paul's School and Sandhurst, where he was demoted for setting a fellow cadet on fire, burning him badly. Commissioned into the Royal Warwicks, for he had not passed out high enough to join the cheaper Indian army, Montgomery was wounded in 1914. He finished WW I a lieutenant colonel, having spent some instructive time on the staff of one of *Plumer's corps.

His wife's early death impelled him more deeply into his profession, and in the fall of *France in 1940 his 3rd Division was the model of well-trained competence. A corps commander in England after *Dunkirk, he was given command of Eighth Army in the Western Desert when Gott, who was to have succeeded *Auchinleck, died in an accident. He arrived in August 1942 to find an army which remained unhappy, though its position had been stabilized by his predecessor. Aided by reinforcements and his own flair for publicity, he bolstered its confidence, and thwarted *Rommel's attack at Alam Halfa. He beat the Germans and Italians in a methodical battle at *Alamein, though cautious *pursuit drew some criticism. After the Axis surrender in *North Africa he led Eighth Army into the *Italian campaign before being appointed land commander for the invasion of Normandy.

Montgomery immediately realized that the planned attack was too weak, and the success of D-Day owes much to him. His role in the subsequent fighting was controversial, in part because of his insistence that Allied success was preplanned, whereas it contained genuine opportunism. His personal style was often abrasive, and he came close to being sacked by *Eisenhower. He was right to argue that an advance to the Ruhr on a narrow front was the best policy (though difficult to achieve within the alliance), but his badly planned and executed *Arnhem operation (so uncharacteristic as to suggest a temporary mental aberration), which might have made it possible, was a disaster. After the war he served as both CIGS and Deputy Supreme Allied Commander Europe.

Montgomery's self-confidence, showmanship, and practical efficiency made him popular with his troops, but did not always endear him to allies, whose point of view he rarely grasped. He was at his best as an army commander, and his lack of political finesse handicapped him at higher levels.   RH

Montrose, James Graham, Marquess of (1612–50). Montrose was educated at St Andrew's and travelled in Europe. He helped draw up the National Covenant in support of Presbyterianism, and fought in both Bishops' wars against Charles I. Briefly imprisoned at the behest of the Marquess of Argyll, who mistrusted his moderate views, he went to England, but Charles I did not turn to him until the Scots had thrown in their lot with parliament. In early 1644 he was created captain general (C-in-C) in Scotland but given only a handful of men. He raised more troops and began a dazzling campaign against more numerous enemies, beating Elcho at Tippermuir and going on to rout the Campbells at Inverlochy in February 1645. In rapid succession he won Auldearn, Alford, and Kilsyth, and occupied Edinburgh. On his way south he was beaten by David Leslie at Philiphaugh: his men were butchered then or executed later.

Montrose escaped but, repudiated by Charles in return for Scots support, had to flee abroad. He returned when he heard of Charles's execution, but was beaten at Carbisdale and betrayed to his enemies. Already stripped of his title and proclaimed traitor, he was hanged from a 30 foot gallows in Edinburgh. Montrose was charming and gallant, a superb natural soldier with a rare ability to get the best out of his tiny army of ill-equipped *Highlanders.   RH

Moore, Lt Gen Sir John (1761–1809). Born into a prominent Glaswegian family, after spending much of his childhood at school in Geneva and in touring Germany, France, and Italy, in 1776 Moore obtained an ensigncy in the 51st Foot, serving with it in Minorca. Appointed lieutenant in the 82nd, he then saw action in the *American independence war. Thereafter Moore, a Pittite, was returned as MP for the Peebles group of boroughs, a position he retained until 1790.

In the interim, his military career developed apace. He became lieutenant colonel of the 51st, with which he subsequently saw extensive service in the Mediterranean. Thereafter, he commanded brigades in the West Indies and in Ireland before participating in the *Helder and French *Egyptian expeditions.

In 1803, he took command of a brigade based at Shorncliffe, the linchpin of south-east England's defences, where he and like-minded officers notably Col (later Lt Gen Sir) Kenneth Mackenzie trained Britain's first permanent light infantry regiments (see LIGHT TROOPS). Knighted and made lieutenant general, Moore was then posted to Sicily before leading an abortive expedition to Sweden. Thereafter he was sent to Spain and made a bold thrust into the heart of the peninsula in support of local resistance. Confronted by Napoleon in person he retreated to *Corunna, where he was mortally wounded covering the evacuation.

DG

---

morale is an imprecise term. It is related to the moral qualities of the individual (indeed, in earlier times it was often spelt 'moral') and may be defined, in the words of Irvin L. Child, as 'pertain[ing] to [the individuals'] efforts to enhance the effectiveness of the group in accomplishing the task in hand'. This definition links the morale of the individual with that of the larger organization. The relationship between the two can be described as follows: unless the individual is reasonably content he will not willingly contribute to the unit. He might *mutiny or desert, but is more likely simply to fail to work wholeheartedly towards the goals of the group. High group morale, or cohesion, is the product in large part of good morale experienced by members of that unit. The state of morale of a larger formation such as an army is the product of the cohesion of its constituent units. The possession by an individual of morale sufficiently high that a soldier is willing to engage in combat might be described as 'fighting spirit'.

In his book *On War*, the 19th-century Prussian soldier and military philosopher *Clausewitz differentiated between professional armies which possess such attributes as *discipline, experience, and skill, and non-professional armies which have 'bravery, adaptability, stamina and en-thusiasm'. He divided what we might call morale into two components, 'mood' and 'spirit', and warned that the two should never be confused. An army's mood is a transient thing, which can change day by day or even minute by minute depending on whether troops are hungry or well fed, warm or cold, and the like. An army with 'true military spirit' keeps 'its cohesion under the most murderous fire' and in defeat resists fears, both real and imaginary. Clause-witz argued that military spirit is created in two ways, by the waging of victorious wars and the testing of an army to the very limits of its strength: 'the seed will grow only in the soil of constant activity and exertion, warmed by the sun of victory'. Thus in 1861 a Union army of inexperienced vol-unteers marched out to the first battle of the *American civil war at *Bull Run with superficially high morale, only later to flee from the field, defeated and its morale shat-tered. Four years later, the fatalistic veterans of the Union Army of the Potomac wrote their names and addresses on slips of paper which they pinned to their uniforms, so that if they were killed in the coming battle their families might learn of their fate. Their mood might have seemed to indi-cate low morale: but as their dogged fighting during the battles of *attrition in 1864 demonstrated, these veterans, some of whom might have fought at Bull Run, had true military spirit. Similarly, Napoleon's nickname for the in-fantryman of his élite Imperial Guard was *grognard* ('grum-bler').

During WW I, the unending nature of the fighting took a heavy toll on military morale. A decline in French morale resulted in widespread mutinies in 1917, although it re-covered somewhat during 1918. German military morale underwent a partial collapse in the autumn of 1918, while the British army's morale remained remarkably high; these two factors help to explain why the war should have ended in November. Generally speaking, a swift and decisive vic-tory can only be achieved if one adversary is greatly inferior to its opponent in terms of 'fighting power', a term that en-compasses such factors as training, tactics, weapons, and morale (see OPERATIONAL CONCEPTS). French civilian and military morale was noticeably poor in 1940, as were other aspects of its army's fighting power. During the *Vietnam war, effective American tactics, logistics, and the like were undermined by a collapse of morale among its troops, which was in turn related to the decline of support for the war on the US home front.

In the era of *total war civilian morale became as important as military morale. Basing their views on the ex-perience of German bombing of British cities during WW I, *air-power theorists and governments alike during the inter-war period believed that civilian morale was likely to crumble under sustained air attack. In fact, as the experi-ence of Britain in 1940–1 and 1944 and Germany in 1942–5 demonstrated, civilian morale proved to be remarkably re-silient under aerial bombardment.

Research into what makes western armies 'tick' suggests that high military morale depends on a number of factors. These include: belief in a cause; good training; trust in lead-ers; *honour; good logistics, which ranges from everything from hot baths and dinners to an efficient postal service; pride in the unit; and a sense of being treated fairly. The 'primary' or 'buddy' group, the small clique of friends who provide a substitute family for the soldier, is widely per-ceived as being of vital importance, for soldiers do not usu-ally fight for queen, cause, or country, but rather so as not to let down their mates. However, it would be unwise to as-sume that the same factors also apply to the morale of sol-diers drawn from very different cultures, such as the communist North Vietnamese Army or the Islamic Iranian Pasdaran.

Being attentive to the morale of the troops does not automatically make one a successful commander. *McClel-lan was renowned for his care for his men but scarcely rates as a great general. However, the achievements of *Slim and *Montgomery in rebuilding the morale of the British Four-teenth and Eighth Armies respectively during WW II rate among their finest achievements. The military leader at all levels has a vital role in ensuring that the aims of the group—which might be simply survival—are congruent with those of the army. Research also suggests that high personal and group morale can retard, although not pre-vent, the onset of psychiatric *casualties.   GDS

Clausewitz, C. von, *On War*, ed. and trans. M. Howard and P. Paret (Princeton, 1976).

Holmes, Richard, *Firing Line* (London, 1985).

Morocco, French conquest of (1907–34). By 1900 France regarded expansion into Morocco as the logical conclusion of her policy in North Africa. Diplomacy helped ensure the acquiescence of other great powers, and the for-eign ministry emphasized that Moroccan interests would be safeguarded. The country was sunk in debt and anarchy, with the weak Sultan Moulay Abd el Aziz challenged by rivals: some Moroccans supported foreign intervention.

Murders in Casablanca in 1907 encouraged *Lyautey, commanding the neighbouring Oran military district, to cross the border, and by mid-1908 the area had been secured. The sultan was deposed by his brother Moulay Hafid: in return for French recognition he ordered the ces-sation of resistance. France's grip grew stronger. The Span-ish increased their efforts to pacify northern Morocco, and a new road between Fez and Rabat aided French penetra-tion. In 1911 the French intervened to protect Moulay Hafid from a rising, and the following year the sultan, again hard-pressed, accepted a French protectorate. Germany, which had sent a gunboat to Agadir, had been bought off by the grant of land in French Equatorial Africa.

Lyautey arrived as resident-general and suppressed the rebellion. He persuaded Moulay Hafid to abdicate in favour of another brother, Moulay Yussuf, and methodically extended French control. Where possible he favoured 'peaceful pacification', using 'oil stain' tactics in which pacified areas spread outwards. Converging columns moved against hostile groups to emphasize the futility of resistance. Sometimes military subjugation was severe, and not all French-backed local leaders proved worthy of their trust. However, French rule generally brought with it peace and cohesion.

Despite the respect in which Lyautey was held, in 1925 Abd-el-Krim, whose power base in the Rif straddled French and Spanish Morocco, invaded. It required both Spanish co-operation and the commitment of six divisions before he was subdued. Fighting went on elsewhere until 1934.

RH

Porch, Douglas, *The Conquest of Morocco* (New York, 1984).

mortars are weapons typically designed to fire in the high trajectory (over 45 degrees) and have generally been smooth-bore and muzzle-loaded systems with short, light tubes, relatively low muzzle-velocities, and a high rate of fire. They lack recoil systems, transferring the force of the recoil into the ground. Although the US Department of Defence defines a mortar as being muzzle-loading, automatic breech-loaded mortars appeared 40 years ago in fortresses, and in the 1980s the USSR produced a breech-loaded mortar to fire in both the low and high angle.

Mortar bombs have a lower velocity than artillery shells and are subject to lesser forces on firing. They can therefore contain a higher proportion of explosive, but being of low velocity and not directly aimed at a target, mortar bombs are least effective against armour, and most potent against soft area targets. They are also effective against targets such as entrenchments. The time of flight of a bomb is longer than that of a shell and mortar fire is therefore subject to greater meteorological variation, making it less accurate than shelling by guns or *howitzers and less likely to hit a moving target. Emerging technology is now redressing some of the mortar's disadvantages. Mortars have tended to be cheap and simple but mortar bombs can now be given rocket assistance, increasing their range without requiring significantly greater weight or expense in the mortar itself. Mortars have been most easily located by *radar calculating the point of origin of the bomb by comparing two points on its trajectory, but bombs which have a trajectory distorted by rocket assistance should be harder to detect. Mortar bombs with terminally guided 'smart' fuses can now hit armoured vehicles with precision from above, a hard-target kill capability to rival more expensive and sophisticated weapon platforms.

Mortars were originally developed for *siege warfare to lob munitions over walls and other fortifications. They were first used by the *Turks at the siege of *Constantinople in 1451 to attack the enemy fleet. They tended to be heavy and immobile, but in the *American civil war were transported for the first time on railway mounts. Mortars were used in coastal defence to attack armoured battleships from above and were also mounted in ships to attack shore fortifications, for example the bombardment by the Royal Navy of the Russian fort of Sweaborg in August 1855 and the attacks on Russian river forts by the British and French in October 1855. By the beginning of the 20th century, the siege mortar had been transformed into a short-barrelled, breech-loaded howitzer. Giant mortars/howitzers, usually mounted on railways, were used by the Germans to reduce the fortress of *Liège in 1914 and in the siege of *Sevastopol in 1941–2. By the mid-1980s the USSR had deployed *self-propelled (SP) mortars of up to 240 mm designed to demolish NATO strong points.

In WW I, armies developed lighter infantry mortars for use in the trenches, based on the British 3 inch Stokes mortar of 1915. These became standard issue in most armies and thereafter a distinction was made between artillery mortars and infantry mortars. High explosive shells were largely ineffective in cutting wire in WW I and in the British army this became the major task for mortars from the battle of *Arras/Vimy Ridge, April 1917, onwards. Between the world wars, the infantry of most nations sought to introduce their own *anti-armour guns and mortars to provide what *Wavell called 'self support, not close support'. The British army was so impressed by the German use of mortars in France in 1940 that it trebled the number in its own battalions. By 1944, Allied artillery had largely mastered German artillery and the mortar, which was more mobile and harder to detect, became the greatest threat to Allied infantry in Normandy, accounting for an estimated 70 per cent of British casualties. The Germans usually placed their 81 mm mortars 547–875 yards (500–800 metres) short of their opponents' positions, making it hard for the Allies to return fire with artillery or mortars without endangering their own men. A sophisticated counter-mortar organization was developed and for VERITABLE, the battle for the Reichswald in February 1945, this linked observers, detecting radar and counter-fire units. The Soviets made great use of mortars in WW II, the Germans having nothing to match their 160 mm piece. When attacked by it for the first time, they believed that they were under air attack. Mortars were so useful in the *Burma campaign that, after April 1945, many anti-tank units of the British army were converted to 3 inch and 7.2 inch mortars. US Under Secretary of State for the Army E. D. Johnson claimed that mortars caused most of the casualties in the *Korean war.

Where artillery support cannot be guaranteed, mortars have come to be regarded as the infantry's organic source of fire, particularly for parachutists, *mountain troops, and irregulars who lack heavy equipment. Where the infantry has been mechanized, so mortars have been mounted in armoured vehicles or towed by trucks to accompany them. The ranges of these heavier mortar systems now rival light artillery, reaching over 10 miles (16 km). The tactical mobility, range, and lethality of mortars have made them ideal weapons for *guerrilla warfare in numerous African conflicts, during the *Vietnam war, in *Afghanistan in the 1980s, and by all sides in the Bosnian conflict of the early 1990s. Home-made mortars have also been the most effective weapon employed by the *IRA against British security installations in Northern Ireland since the 1970s and, on one occasion, against the British PM's house in Downing Street. JBAB

Bailey, J. B. A., *Field Artillery and Firepower* (Oxford, 1989).
Bellamy, C., *Red God of War, Soviet Artillery and Rocket Forces* (London, 1986).
Fowler, W., 'Mortars—The Infantryman's Artillery', *Defence*, 17/8 (Aug. 1986).
Kershaw, A., *Weapons and War Machines* (London, 1976).

Moscow, battle of (1941), the first defeat inflicted on the *Wehrmacht in WW II. In spite of the spectacular success of the German armies after invading the USSR on 22 July 1941, by October they were falling behind schedule and victim to the muddy autumn Russian roads. TAIFUN, the attack on Moscow, involved two converging attacks, beginning on 30 September, that turned into the encirclement battle of *Vyazma-Bryansk. By mid-October Soviet government ministries began preparing to leave Moscow, now under increasingly heavy German air attack. But at the beginning of November the German high command admitted they would not be beating the USSR in 1941—meaning they were committed to a war in the Russian winter they were ill-equipped to fight.

The defence of Moscow was entrusted to the Western Front (army group), under *Koniev until 10 October when he was replaced by *Zhukov. In mid-November the Germans were 40 miles (64 km) from Moscow, but Soviet resistance was ferocious and the Germans encountered a new weapon, the remarkable Soviet T-34 tank. On 15 November they attempted to encircle the city from Tula in the south and Kalinin in the north, but made slow progress. The onset of a severe winter froze the mud but German equipment was not designed to cope with minus 30°C.

*Stalin's counterstroke was made possible by *intelligence from the Sorge ring in Tokyo that the Japanese, sobered by their punishment at *Khalkin-Gol, had no intention of attacking in Manchuria. He was therefore able to move armoured divisions west into European Russia and had the patience to wait until they were fully assembled and the freeze came. On 30 November the Soviets had fallen back to their final defence line at kilometre 22—near Moscow's international Sheremetevo airport, the point now marked by a monument in the shape of a giant *anti-armour obstacle. There were two Soviet counter-attacks on 4 December and then on 6 December the main counter-attack began with First Shock Army and Twentieth Army attacking north of Moscow, and Tenth Army attacking from the south, past Tula. The Soviet reserves, well equipped

against the winter cold, struck German forces that were exhausted, paralysed by the bitter cold, and at the limit of their lines of supply. Large areas were still held by *partizans behind the German lines, and the Soviet forces tried to link up with them using *airborne forces. The Red Army recaptured thousands of villages—crucial shelter in the cold—and the German salients north and south of the city were driven back. Airborne and cavalry corps penetrated the German rear areas, notably IV Airborne Corps on 20 January, near Vyazma. The Red Army pushed the German lines back 93–248 miles (150–400 km). In total, the Germans lost 500,000 men, 1,500 tanks, 2,500 guns, and 15,000 trucks—many of them immobilized by the cold.

Compared with anything the Germans had experienced before, the scale of their losses and the scope of the Soviet counter-offensive were staggering. The Red Army launched the overambitious second phase of its winter campaign in mid-January, attempting to encircle Army Group Centre. The concept was excellent but the Russians lacked the resources to maintain the offensive deep into the German-held areas, under heavy attrition from *Hitler's 'stand and fight' order, given in defiance of his generals' advice, but which proved to be the salvation of the Wehrmacht, leaving it poised to resume offensive operations in the spring.

CDB

mountain troops (see also ARCTIC AND MOUNTAIN WARFARE). These are specialists trained and equipped to operate in mountainous environments. Western Europe has a number of locally raised units, traditionally linked with the mountains. Germany's Gebirgsjäger, Italy's Alpini, and France's Chasseurs Alpins all tend to be highly distinctive and individual in nature. The armies of Austria, Switzerland, the former Yugoslavia, and Greece also have a tradition of mountain-trained formations. Dedicated mountain troops are a relatively new phenomenon. Prior to the last century the high alpine areas of central western Europe, for instance, were considered protection enough from invading neighbours. However, Italy began forming specialist mountain companies in 1872 and by 1882 had raised six Alpini regiments plus specialized mountain artillery, prompting France to create twelve similar regiments, initially termed Chasseurs-Alpins, in response.

The bitter experience of fighting French mountain troops in the Vosges mountains (1914) led to Germany creating the 1st Bavarian Ski Battalion to operate in that area. This soon expanded to a corps-size formation, the Alpenkorps (1915), which immediately began operations on the *Italian front in the Dolomites. By early 1916 all countries bordering on the Alps realized that dedicated mountain and winter warfare troops were essential.

Between the two world wars, mountain warfare units continued to expand in number. By 1938 the *Wehrmacht had three mountain divisions. The Gebirgsjäger saw action

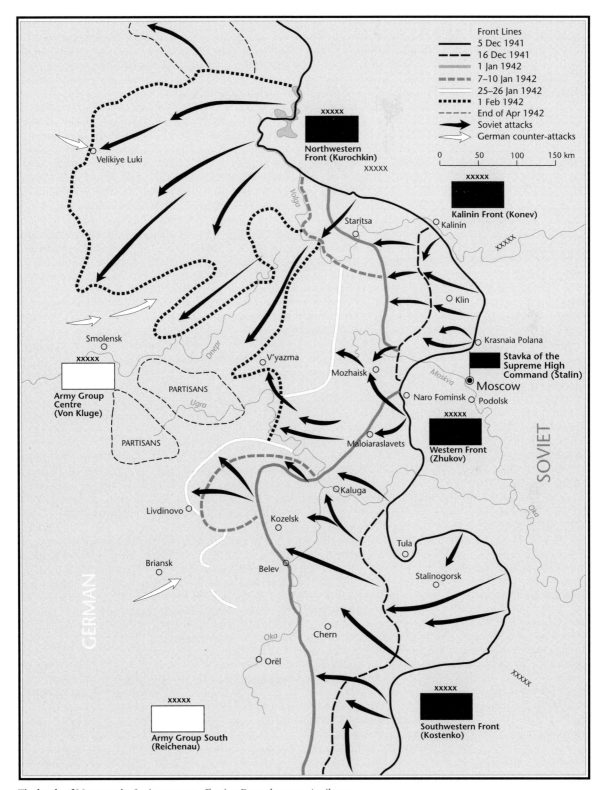

Front Lines

——	5 Dec 1941
– – –	16 Dec 1941
——	1 Jan 1942
– – –	7–10 Jan 1942
——	25–26 Jan 1942
····	1 Feb 1942
- - -	End of Apr 1942
➤	Soviet attacks
➪	German counter-attacks

0   50   100   150 km

Northwestern Front (Kurochkin)

Kalinin Front (Konev)

Velikiye Luki

Staritsa

Kalinin

Volga

Klin

Krasnaia Polana

Smolensk

Dnepr

V'yazma

Mozhaisk

Moskva

Stavka of the Supreme High Command (Stalin)

Moscow

PARTISANS

Ugra

Naro Fominsk

Podolsk

Army Group Centre (Von Kluge)

PARTISANS

Maloiaraslavets

Western Front (Zhukov)

Kaluga

SOVIET

Livdinovo

Kozelsk

Oka

Briansk

Belev

Tula

GERMAN

Stalinogorsk

Oka

Chern

Orël

Army Group South (Reichenau)

Southwestern Front (Kostenko)

The **battle of Moscow:** the Soviet counter-offensive, December 1941–April 1942.

during the conquest of Poland (1 September–5 October 1939) and during the fall of *France. During the latter operation, they distinguished themselves at the Maas, Aisne, and Loire river crossings before being withdrawn to prepare for the planned but subsequently aborted invasions of Great Britain and later Gibraltar. The latter would have required six mountain divisions.

The advantages of specialist training and equipment were dramatically revealed during the Russo-Finnish war of 1939–40, where well-trained and equipped Finnish ski troops initially trounced a Soviet force which outnumbered them five to one. German successes during the *Norwegian campaign prompted British interest in mountain warfare training and led to the creation of the Mountain and Snow Training Camp first in Scotland, later in north Wales, which was primarily designed to promote similar specialist skills, especially within the newly formed British *commandos. The defeat of British and empire forces in Greece and *Crete owed as much to the fighting ability of the Gebirgs-jäger as it did to their airborne (Fallschirmjäger) counterparts. It is interesting to note that after this operation the concept of massed airborne assaults was shelved—the casualties were considered too high—while the success of the Gebirgsjäger in this and their earlier campaigns led to the creation of additional Wehrmacht mountain divisions, a total of eleven by 1945.

Their successes further served to reinforce the need for troops experienced in mountain warfare techniques. The US army reacted with the creation of the highly specialized joint US–Canadian Special Service Force (SSF) (1942) which underwent its initial training in the mountainous terrain around Helena, Montana. This unique unit, comprising both American and Canadian servicemen, went on to distinguish itself in the assaults of Monte La Difesa and Monte La Remetanea in Italy (1943) before being the first Allied formation to enter the city of Rome. Now known as the 'Devil's Brigade', the SSF advanced as far as the river Tiber before being selected to spearhead the Allied landings in southern France, in ANVIL-DRAGOON in August 1944.

While the SSF was effectively an airborne commando unit with a mountain warfare capability, the US army also set about creating a specialist mountain formation: the 87th Mountain Infantry Battalion—at Fort Lewis, Washington. Training began on 16 December 1941 around Mount Rainier and continued until September 1942. After conducting a series of trials, the US army established a Mountain Warfare Center (MWC) during the winter of 1942/3 at Camp Carlson in Colorado. The MWC then moved to Camp Hale, also in Colorado and suitably located at an altitude of over 9,000 feet (2,743 metres). By July 1943 the US army activated the 10th Light Division (Alpine) at Camp Hale. It was manned by carefully selected soldiers, most with previous mountain and/or skiing experience. A significant proportion of the volunteers came from the National Ski Patrol

System, which was a non-military organization. This new division's mission was to train to attain ultimate combat efficiency in high mountain warfare; to operate in mountains and primitive terrain where road networks were poor or non-existent, and under adverse and extreme weather conditions.

Since the end of WW II, those countries with mountain troops and those with a likelihood of having to deploy soldiers into areas dominated by mountainous terrain have retained or established units capable of operating at high altitude. Additionally the special forces' units of most of the world's major military powers have a mountain warfare capability. Mountainous terrain favours the use of small, lightly equipped, independent manoeuvre groups. The nature of the terrain will normally afford these elements good cover and concealment against air attack, supplemented with shoulder-launched SAM missiles such as the 'Stinger', used to such good effect by the mujahedin in *Afghanistan.

A number of conflicts post-1945 have required such specialist skills. These include *counter-insurgency operations by the French in Morocco (1953–5) and during the *Algeria independence war; by the British in Yemen and the Radfan (1963–7) and *Oman; and by the Soviets in Afghanistan. Often, conventional mountain-trained troops found themselves facing irregular *guerrilla forces with generations of experience in mountain warfare, albeit often tribal in nature. Mountain fighters, be they Dhofari Jebalis, Afghan Gilzais, Scots *Highlanders, or Nepalese *Gurkhas, tend to be fierce and the wars they wage are often as brutal as the environments in which they fight.

The most competent major power in high altitude warfare in the modern era is India, which has no fewer than nine mountain divisions and has engaged in protracted conflict with Pakistan in the Himalayas, extending as far up as the Siachen glacier. Mountain troops, like their counterparts in airborne and commando forces, have tended to adopt distinctive headgear. The Edelweiss and long-peaked Feldmütze or forage cap was adopted by the Gebirgsjäger, and the Chasseurs Alpins continue to wear their traditional large berets or tartes. The development of specialist winter-warfare clothing during 1939–45 has benefited subsequent generations of soldiers, and special weaponry was devised, particularly mountain artillery, capable of being dismantled into small, portable loads.   PMacD

Mountbatten of Burma, Adm Louis, Earl (1900–79), related by blood to the British royal family and the son of a First Sea Lord, then Battenberg, who had been hounded out of office in WW I by public hostility towards those of German descent, something that caused the royal family to change its name from Saxe-Coburg to Windsor. Mountbatten followed in his father's footsteps and chose to make the navy his career. He was a glamorous officer with the Mediterranean fleet, first specializing in signals and then commanding a succession of destroyers before becoming ADC to Edward VIII and George VI before WW II.

While it is possible that his royal connections and the wealth he enjoyed through marriage were not instrumental in advancing his career, this was not the opinion of his superiors, who resented him. Doubts about his competence were fairly raised when the destroyer HMS *Kelly* under his command was, most unusually for the type, sunk by dive-bombers off *Crete in May 1941. But he showed great courage during the episode, which inspired Noel Coward's 1942 film *In Which We Serve*. Thereafter he was appointed to command Combined Operations in October 1941, over the heads of many. The appointment was largely socio-political, although *Churchill may also have been influenced by the common touch Mountbatten had revealed during a propaganda visit to the USA in mid-1941. Combined Operations also needed a 'fixer' who could steer between inter-service rivalries, and Mountbatten's independent status fitted the role well.

He bears heavy responsibility for the fiasco of the August 1942 *Dieppe raid, but arguably something similar along the north French coast would have to have taken place in 1942 in order to learn lessons for the seaborne invasions that, starting with TORCH that November, culminated in OVERLORD. His tenure was considered a success and he was appointed Supreme Commander South-East Asia. A similar style was needed there, that of a behind-the-scenes diplomat rather than a field commander. He and *Slim complemented each other perfectly, and his semi-royal status was an advantage in India. He eased relations with the Americans, although 'Vinegar Joe' *Stilwell was no more impressed by Mountbatten than he was by anyone else ever put in authority over him.

His tour at SEAC (South-East Asia Command) highlighted his love of luxury and ostentation, in sharp contrast to the bare-bones functionality of local military commands. But the post was really a political one, and extended into post-war decolonization, including his appointment as India's last viceroy. His love of pomp and elaborate uniforms and the liaisons formed by his active wife were appropriate to the place and time and helped smooth an extremely edgy transition, although not to prevent the violent partition of the subcontinent at independence.

He was a catalyst in the romance between his relative Philip and the later Queen Elizabeth II, was appointed First Sea Lord in 1956–8 and finally Chief of the Defence Staff in 1959–65, when he played a key role in the creation of an integrated Ministry of Defence. He was killed together with two young boys by an *IRA booby trap on the pleasure craft he maintained in Ireland. India and Pakistan expressed the most forceful regrets and both their own and many other heads of state joined the entire royal family at his state funeral.   APC-A

mounted infantry The practice of putting infantry on horses to increase their mobility is an ancient one. Medieval English *archers were sometimes mounted to enable them to keep pace with men-at-arms, and *dragoons, who eventually became cavalry proper, were initially foot soldiers mounted on cheap nags.

During the 19th century the improvement of firearms led to demands that mounted infantry (or mounted rifles, as they were sometimes called) should replace conventional cavalry in whole or in part. The case for mounted infantry was strong in armies engaged in colonial campaigning where horses were an aid to mobility off the battlefield, but when accurate shooting on it was more valuable than the charge. French and British infantry were often mounted, usually in units formed for particular campaigns, though *compagnies montées* were regular features of French North Africa. During the British occupation of *Burma in the 1880s, for example, a mounted infantry corps was formed from men mounted on local ponies. On the *Gordon relief expedition of 1884–5 some British infantry were mounted on camels. In 1888 mounted infantry training schools were set up at Aldershot and the Curragh, creating a nucleus of trained personnel who returned to their battalions able to serve on horseback.

The terrain of South Africa encouraged growing demands for mounted infantry. The 91st Regiment had a mounted company at the Cape in 1796–1802, and in 1875 the 24th Regiment created one. The British made extensive use of mounted infantry during the Second *Boer War, with some units drawn from regular infantry. A company of mounted infantry was formed from each battalion and combined with companies from other battalions in the brigade to form a mounted infantry battalion. They were known as MI in contemporary slang and in Rudyard Kipling's poem of the same name:

I wish my mother could see me now, with a fence-post under my
    arm,
And a knife and spoon in my putties that I found on a Boer farm,
Atop of a sore-backed Argentine, with a thirst that you couldn't
    buy.
I used to be in the Yorkshires once
(Sussex, Lincolns and Rifles once)
Hampshires, Glosters and Scottish once!
But now I am MI.

Other units were formed for the war as mounted infantry. Thorneycroft's MI was raised from local volunteers, while Canadian and Australian units, often composed of men who could already ride and shoot, had come much further. Erskine Childers, who served with a British volunteer unit, thought that mounted riflemen from the colonies had unique frontier qualities: they 'seemed by intuition to grasp the possibilities of a union of the rifle with the horse'. Some saw the war as proof, as FM *Roberts put it, 'that all attacks can be carried out far more effectually with the rifle than the sword'. Others, like Gen *French, argued that 'it is only by the employment of "shock tactics" and the superior morale of the highly trained horseman wielding sword and lance, that decisive success can be achieved'. The cavalry lobby eventually triumphed, but there was compromise in the process, and in 1914 British cavalry was far more proficient in dismounted action than its allies or opponents.

The logic of mounted infantry has not disappeared. Even in the second half of the 20th-century infantry have used horses in exceptional circumstances. More commonly, lorries, half-tracks, and *APCs have carried the infantryman onto the battlefield, and the *MICV can now carry him across it. RH

Anglesey, Marquess of, *A History of the British Cavalry 1816–1919*, vol. 4 (London, 1986).

Childers, Erskine, *War and the Arme Blanche* (London, 1910).

Mozambique By 1508 Portugal had brought the area of south-eastern Africa now known as Mozambique under its influence but it was only in the late 19th century during the 'scramble for Africa' that the interior was occupied against fierce resistance. Portuguese colonial control was only fully established in Mozambique between 1913 and 1915. It was *Lettow-Vorbeck's lifeline and part of his area of operations during the *German East Africa campaign, also the site of a particularly brutal 'pacification' campaign in 1918. The Portuguese colonial regime was one of the harshest on the continent. Mozambique's resources were ruthlessly exploited and the use of forced labour was only abandoned in 1961. The Portuguese authorities made little effort to produce an indigenous élite and illiteracy stood at 91 per cent in 1961.

The success of decolonization movements in the British and French African colonies coupled with the exploitative nature of the Portuguese colonial regime provided fertile grounds for rebellion in Mozambique. Certainly the refusal of the Portuguese dictator Antonio Salazar even to consider any negotiations regarding a peaceful transition towards self-determination made any peaceful solution unlikely. In 1962 a number of exiled nationalist organizations combined to form FRELIMO (Frente de Libertação de Moçambique, Mozambique Liberation Front) to oppose Portuguese rule by violent means. Under the leadership of Eduardo Chivambo Mondlane, FRELIMO opened its *guerrilla campaign in Mozambique on 25 September 1964. Already facing rebellions in *Angola from 1961 and Guinea from 1963, yet fearing another serious loss of face following the invasion of Goa by India in 1961, the Portuguese reinforced their 20,000-strong garrison in Mozambique and began what Gen Spinola called a total colonial war.

The war remained at a low intensity and at comparatively low cost in contrast to the conflicts in *Indochina and *Algeria, but even so Portugal's colonial wars imposed severe strains on its weak economy. Meanwhile, increasingly well armed by the USSR, China, and other eastern bloc countries and with its experience in *guerrilla warfare growing, FRELIMO was becoming an ever more effective force. Soon it began to inflict heavy losses on the overstretched and demoralized Portuguese army. As the army became more desperate, so did the brutality of the conflict. The massacre perpetrated by Portuguese troops at Wiriyamu on 16 December 1972 received widespread press coverage and did much to further turn world opinion against the Portuguese. These tactics could not halt the successes of FRELIMO and by 1974 it controlled over a fifth of Mozambique and the Portuguese were facing the possibility of defeat in the north of the country.

Nonetheless FRELIMO was not prepared for the speed of the collapse of the colonial position in Mozambique following the successful military coup in Portugal on 25 April 1974. The new Portuguese regime pushed through a rapid decolonization programme and Mozambique became independent on 25 June 1975. FRELIMO immediately formed the new government with Samora Machel, FRELIMO's leader since 1968, as its first president. He proclaimed the country a communist People's Republic. Given the ravages of ten years of guerrilla war, Mozambique needed some years of peace to recover. It did not get it.

The white-ruled state of Rhodesia (now Zimbabwe) had provided the Portuguese with much military support during the war of decolonization and following the Portuguese collapse in Mozambique, the Rhodesians attempted to destabilize their now hostile neighbour. They set up RENAMO (Resistancia Nacional Moçambicana, Mozambique National Resistance), as an armed opposition to the FRELIMO government. With the end of white rule in Rhodesia, support for RENAMO fell to South Africa. It was essentially a negative force, existing solely to attack the infrastructure of Mozambique and to terrorize the population. It was never a viable political alternative to the FRELIMO government. By 1989 it had destroyed threequarters of the country's education system and numerous hospitals. Between 1975 and 1989 perhaps 50 per cent of Mozambique's children died directly and indirectly as a result of the civil war and RENAMO is estimated to have killed over one million civilians. This campaign, coupled with occasional direct South African military intervention, led Machel to seek an accommodation with the South Africans. Under the Ntomati Accord of 1984, he ceased supporting liberation movements in South Africa and removed ANC (African National Congress) bases from Mozambique, although South Africa continued to supply RENAMO. However, by the mid-1980s the international community was increasingly supportive of the Mozambique government. The British armed FRELIMO's forces, the USA provided financial aid, and Mozambique's neighbour Zimbabwe contributed direct military support. Following Machel's death, the new president Joaquim Chissano sought compromise with the RENAMO rebels, a process much facilitated by the end of the apartheid regime in

South Africa. RENAMO, after accepting the decommissioning of 90 per cent of its troops in a gesture mirrored by FRELIMO, took part in the democratic elections of 1994 and peacefully accepted second place.   MCM

Birmingham, David, *A Concise History of Portugal* (Cambridge, 1993).

Cann, John P., *Counterinsurgency in Africa: The Portuguese Way of War, 1961–1974* (London, 1997).

Muhammad Ali, Pasha (*c*.1769–1849), ruler in Egypt 1805–48. Originally from Macedonia, he became nominally governor of Egypt for the Ottoman sultans in Istanbul but in practice an autonomous ruler, styling himself khedive, and founded a hereditary line which was to endure until 1952. He embarked on an independent, expansionist policy, humbling the Wahhabis of Arabia, aiding the sultan against the Greek rebels, occupying Syria and the Levant for ten years, and moving southwards into the Sudan. Such ambitions required a modern army. He first formed an army of Sudanese *slave soldiers and then one of conscripted Egyptian peasants trained by Col Sèves, an ex-Napoleonic army officer, and training schools for the navy and the army, plus their technical arms, were established on European lines. Agricultural reforms, heavier taxation, and pioneer industrial enterprises, including munitions factories, supplied the material backing. Student missions were sent to western Europe. Not all his enterprises endured, but Muhammad Ali ranks as a pioneer westernizer and centralizer in the Near East and his policies brought Egypt into the spheres of international diplomacy and markets.   CEB

Dodwell, Henry, *The Founder of Modern Egypt: A Study of Muhammad Ali* (Cambridge, 1931).

al-Sayyid Marsot, Affaf Lutfi, *Egypt in the Reign of Muhammad Ali* (Cambridge, 1984).

Mukden (also called Shen-yan), battle of (1905), final and biggest land battle of the 1904–5 *Russo-Japanese war and harbinger of WW I. The Russian Manchurian Army under Kuropatkin had been withdrawing northwards up the railway toward Harbin. The fall of *Port Arthur in January enabled the Japanese commander, Marshal Oyama, to redeploy Gen Nogi's besieging Third Army and with the creation of a new Fifth Army under Gen Kamura, the Japanese concentrated five to attack Kuropatkin's three. The Russian forces totalled 293,000 men with 1,494 guns, and 56 machine guns: the Japanese had 270,000 men, 1,062 guns, and 200 machine guns. The Japanese attacked on 19 February attempting to envelop and destroy the Russian force, but failed in the face of artillery, machine guns, and barbed wire. The Russians lost 89,000 men and the Japanese 71,000 on a continuous front 96 miles (155 km) wide with fighting to a depth of 50 miles (80 km), in a battle lasting nineteen days until 10 March. The Russians then withdrew to prepared positions at Sypingai 109 miles (175 km) to the north. It was the shape of wars to come.   CDB

Murat, Marshal Prince Joachim, King of Naples (1767–1815). Son of a village postmaster, Murat was educated in a seminary. He joined the cavalry in 1787 and speedily won promotion to sergeant major. After ups and downs in 1790–2 he was commissioned, and, having enabled *Napoleon to seize the cannon with which he administered a 'whiff of grapeshot' to Paris in 1795, was promoted colonel. He served under Napoleon in Italy and accompanied him on the French *Egyptian expedition, leading the decisive cavalry charge at Aboukir on 25 July 1799.

Confirmed as general of division on his return to France, Murat commanded the *grenadiers who saved the day when Napoleon's 18th Brumaire coup faltered. He married Napoleon's pretty and intelligent sister Caroline in 1800, and was appointed marshal in the first creation of 1804. His cavalry performed well in the campaign and battle of *Austerlitz. Murat's *pursuit reaped the reward of *Jena/Auerstadt in 1806, and the massed cavalry charge he led, dressed in a *uniform consisting mostly of gold braid, saved the day at *Eylau in 1807. He was created grand duke of Cleves and Berg in 1806 and showered with foreign orders in 1807.

Sent to Spain in 1808, he brutally put down the Dos de Mayo rising. Recalled when Joseph Bonaparte was appointed king of Spain, he was installed on Joseph's throne of Naples. Soon at odds with Napoleon, he joined the Grande Armée for the Russian campaign, commanding it when Napoleon left. He returned to his kingdom as soon as he could, resisted Allied attempts to win him over, and rejoined Napoleon in 1813. After *Leipzig he went back to Italy and struggled hard to retain his throne. Hearing that Napoleon had escaped from Elba he went to join him, but was denied even an audience. He returned to Naples, now in Bourbon hands, and was shot by firing squad. Murat characteristically declined a blindfold and gave the order to fire.

Murat was handsome, burly, and a devoted (if noisily irascible) husband and father. An archetypal cavalryman, with a taste for extravagant self-designed uniforms, he had enormous courage and a penetrating tactical eye, but no strategic or common sense at all.   RH

Murphy, Lt Audie (1924–71), US hero and film star. A poor country boy from Texas, he enlisted as a private in 1942 and served in 1943–5 with the 3rd US Infantry Division, ending the war as the most decorated soldier in the US army. He saw almost continuous action in *Sicily, at *Anzio where he was commissioned, and in France, where he earned the Congressional Medal of Honor for bravery at Holtzwihr in January 1945. Murphy epitomized the American ideal and by 1948 had made the transition to

Hollywood actor. His autobiography of the war *To Hell and Back* appeared in 1950 and was made into a melodramatic *film starring him in 1958. He made 40 other films, mostly Westerns, and died in a plane crash.   APC-A

Musashi Miyamoto (full name Shinmen Musashi no Kama, Fujiwara no Genshin) (1584–1645) was a famous Japanese *samurai and artist of the early Tokugawa period. A masterless *ronin, he made his reputation in over sixty duels between the age of 13 and 29, and thereafter made a living teaching swordsmanship. He is credited with inventing the *nitoryu* technique of fighting with two swords. Nerveless and with the reflexes of a scorpion, he ceased using swords towards the end of his duelling career and still killed his opponents with whatever came to hand. It is said that he never combed his hair, never took a bath, and, unsurprisingly, never married. His monochrome paintings of birds are national treasures and his *The Book of Five Rings*, written in 1643, contains the distillation of his combat experience. A recurrent phrase is: 'this should be given careful and thorough consideration.' Indeed.

Musashi was the name given to one of Japan's three super-battleships laid down before WW II (the others were the *Yamato* and the *Shinano*, the latter completed as an aircraft carrier and sunk by the USS *Archerfish* on her maiden voyage). Built to be superior to any US battleship (because of the size limitations imposed by the Panama Canal), she never got the chance to prove it, being sunk by swarming torpedo and dive-bombers in 1944.   HEB

Musashi Miyamoto, *The Book of Five Rings*, trans. T. Cleary (Boston, 1994).

---

museums, military Military museums began in Europe and it is on that continent that the greatest strides in their development have been made. Outside Europe, military museums have been established in many countries, notable ones being found in Australia, New Zealand, Canada, and South Africa, but in the USA, despite a multiplicity of regimental corps and academy museums, there is as yet no national museum to enshrine that nation's long military tradition.

Military museums fall into two principal categories, with a third category whose status is ill-defined. The two principal types are national military museums and regimental, or site-specific, museums of a non-national nature, such as those at the Royal Military Academy Sandhurst, and at the US Military Academy *West Point. The third category contains military collections which are themselves a significant part of larger collections, often with a site-specific or parochial focus, such as military items in stately homes or in municipal museums.

The earliest military museums were *arsenals, but since many of these have since become famous military museums it is expedient to regard them as the forerunners of the genre. Visitors are believed to have been first admitted to the White Tower of the Tower of London in 1489 in order to see the arms and *armour displayed there, but an alternative view puts the date of such admissions as two centuries later, in the 1680s, by which time, certainly, museums which would be recognizable as such today had begun to be established as part of 17th-century antiquarianism. Similar armouries to that at the Tower of London appear to have admitted visitors during the 17th century, notable ones being those in Stockholm and Madrid, and the museums now descended from these royal armouries can claim not only to being among the oldest museums in the world but also, perhaps a little less convincingly, to being the world's first military museums.

Museums of artillery appear to have led the way in the history of the military museum per se, although, of course, many of the royal armouries contained artillery too. In France, a museum of artillery was established in 1684; it was one of the foundations of the Musée de l'Armée when that institution (now fittingly and magnificently housed in the Hôtel des *Invalides) was created in 1905. In Britain, a museum of artillery was founded in 1778 at Woolwich, southeast of London, which still exists today. Like the West Point museum, founded in 1854, such early museums had, as part of their brief, a training role for contemporary servicemen. This role continues to be played, not only by regimental museums but also by national museums which are funded by Departments of Defence.

In the 19th century, museums in general multiplied and military museums were a part of the process. In Britain, a Naval and Military Library and Museum was founded in London in 1831. This became the Museum of the Royal United Services Institution (RUSI) in 1860 and its collections were all there was in Britain to reflect British military history in a national context prior to 1914. Regimental and local military museums grew up in Britain and elsewhere in the same century, that of the Royal Engineers, again with an important training role, dating from 1875 and that of the imperial Tirolean Jäger Regiment being founded in Austria earlier in the century. Small military museums were established, too, in garrisons such as Aldershot, as part of the British army's drive to educate its soldiers away from their traditional pastimes of drink and fornication. In the Germanic world by 1914 museums with varying pretensions to being military existed; some, like the Zeughaus in Graz, resembled the armouries that their titles suggested, some, like the Zeughaus in Berlin, were closer in content and interpretation to the RUSI Museum in London; others were museums reflecting the military history of individual states within the German empire. All national European military museums had one common factor: their establishment reflected a perceived need to rescue and interpret the material evidence of past glories for the edification of their visitors.

To an extent, this common factor still remained after 1918 but an additional important ingredient was added: that of commemorating *sacrifice (see also MEMORIALS). This was particularly so in Britain and in its imperial outposts and the need to commemorate the recently dead manifested itself in the post-war period with the foundation of the Imperial War Museum in England, the Scottish United Services Museum in Scotland (now the National War Museum of Scotland), and with museums in Australia and Canada which significantly included the word 'war' in their titles: each museum was a memorial first and a museum second. Regimental museums also burgeoned in the inter-war period, often being centred on the regimental headquarters where the regimental family lares et penates could be seen by the cultural and, often, familial descendants of those who had donated them. Municipal museums raked in WW I souvenirs, their custodians sympathetic guardians of objects which their curatorial descendants in the 1960s would seek to throw out. After 1945 the trend continued in Britain, but in a more socially aware sense in the national context, with the foundation of the National Army Museum in 1960 and of the RAF Museum in 1963; four museums for the Royal Navy date from the same epoch. Small military museums have multiplied in the West since 1945 and the national ones in Germany have rejoined each other following reunification. As museums, national heritage sites, and 'heritage centres' vie with each other in the 1990s for a steadily increasing audience, the role of the military museum has been to interpret its collection in ways more intelligible to the general visitor with little or no knowledge and no longer to cater only to the specialist and the well-informed enthusiast.   SCW

Thwaites, Dr Peter, *Presenting Arms: Museum Interpretation of British Military History* (London and New York, 1996).

....

music, military The role of music as a mood-changer or mood-enhancer is appreciated in all human activities. In a military context, music can serve to create and maintain a warlike spirit, act as a means of *communication, assist movement, and enhance *morale. Music produced by the human voice has been used for such purposes by fighting men of many different countries, times, and cultures. In the armies of classical Greece, the paean or war-chant was the standard opening to set-piece battles. The *Roman military historian Tacitus recorded that the Germanic war-bands of his day, after assembling in response to horn-blasts, moved to the accompaniment of their own voices. During the religious wars in the Germany of the 17th century, Protestant armies sang hymns to raise their spirits as they went into battle, as did the parliamentarians in the *British civil wars of the 1640s. On one occasion, psalms bellowed by the advancing *Hussites alone caused an imperial army to flee.

Singing on the line of march was encouraged in European and American armies of the 19th and early 20th cen-turies, but faded out when the advent of *mechanization meant that infantrymen moved on their feet only in operational conditions. The lyrics of such marching songs tended to enhance group cohesion by appealing to the local, national, or ideological sentiments of the singers, reminding them of the heroic achievements of their predecessors, or emphasizing the justice of their cause. Examples of all these may be found in songs such as 'The British Grenadiers' (UK), 'Dixie' and 'The Battle Hymn of the Republic' (USA), 'The Watch on the Rhine' (Germany), 'Sambre et Meuse' (France), or 'Peasants and Workers are One' (People's Republic of China). Songs by minstrels, bards, or other popular entertainers have at all periods raised the morale of their audiences and inspired appropriate martial sentiments. Such performers frequently join armies in the field or even go into battle with them. One well-known instance is that of the Norman *jongleur* Tallifer who sang what was probably an early version of the *Chanson de Roland* (Song of Roland) as he rode to his death among the English axes at the battle of *Hastings.

The drum, the simplest of musical instruments, was still in use for various military purposes by tribal warriors in Africa, Asia, and North America at the close of the 19th century. Its earliest use by the troops of civilized states appears in wall-friezes depicting the armies of Ancient *Egypt, who may have adopted the drum from their campaigns in the Sudan or Ethiopia. Drums were not used by the *Roman Army but European soldiers were reintroduced to them in the *Crusades, when the presence of kettledrums and other percussion instruments was noted in the Saracen battle line. Such instruments were a feature of the Ottoman *Turk armies and were taken up by western armies from the 16th century onwards as 'Turkish music'. With the regimentation of battle tactics and the increasing importance of the need to keep step, drummers became an essential part of European armies. They not only beat time but also used recognizable rhythms to signal orders such as the alarm, the charge, retreat, parley, etc. Increasing sophistication of construction allowed the development of complicated drum tunes, played in combination with tonal instruments such as fifes or bagpipes. Among cavalry units, kettledrums provided the percussion, followed by mounted trumpeters, horn-blowers, and other wind instrumentalists.

Trumpets of various types were used in organized armies from Ancient Egypt onwards, to give signals in camp or battle and to sound fanfares on ceremonial occasions. The bugle, a smaller and less shrill instrument, emerged in the mid-18th century as the trumpet of light infantry, who found that the infantryman's drum was not suited to a body of rapidly moving skirmishers. Their origins lay among the huntsmen and foresters who had for long used horns, either animal or metal, as a way of communicating in wooded areas. Such instruments, especially when grouped together and supported by percussion, could play simple tunes on the march, but it was not until the full development of valves and keys in the early 19th century that brass instruments realized their full musical potential.

Woodwind instruments were more melodious and mostly capable of a fuller scale of notes. In battle, the armies of classical Greece moved to the sound of the flute. In Saracenic armies, bands composed of reeds and pipes of various sorts played during combat to encourage their own troops and to show that the line remained unbroken. The first military band in the modern sense, made up of uniformed musicians forming part of a regimental establishment, was that of the *janissaries, the élite regular troops of the Ottoman empire, first raised in 1326. Such bands were formed in all western armies in the course of the 18th century to provide music not only for marching but also for general entertainment and social occasions. During the 19th century, the emergence of new instruments such as the saxophone (invented in 1845) gave military bands the potential to become, in effect, walking orchestras. They then had the full diatonic scale of conventional western music, rather than the simpler pentatonic scale of folk instruments such as bagpipes.

Careful scoring allowed bands to play all kinds of music. Military bandmasters were able to arrange pieces to suit their players and instruments, and many became composers themselves. Among the most famous was John Philip Sousa, 'the March King' and conductor of the US Marines Band between 1880 and 1892, who wrote over a hundred military marches together with other works. Evocative tunes from earlier periods, such as 'The girl I left behind me' and 'Garryowen', and their equivalents in other countries, remained popular. By the late 19th century, military bands had disappeared from the battlefield, but, a century later, technical advances in sound recording, broadcasting, and reproduction systems meant that martial music could once again accompany the soldier in combat as in ceremonial parades. The worldwide commercial success of the pipe and brass rendition of 'Amazing Grace' in 1971 gave testimony to its continued ability to move and inspire. Strauss 'the Elder''s *Radetzky march, the piece of music most identified with the old imperial Austrian army, is played each year as the finale to the Vienna Philharmonic's New Year's Concert.   TAH

Arnold, Denis, *The New Oxford Companion to Music* (Oxford, 1983).

Farmer, Henry George, *Military Music* (London, 1950).

....

musket (from Fr.: *mousquet*). The term seems first to have become current in the mid-16th century as indicating a heavy firearm fired from the shoulder and, at that time, with its barrel supported by a forked rest planted in the ground by the musketeer. Such weapons were used in wars in Italy and in the Netherlands in the mid-1500s and, by the end of the 16th century the musket was in wide use with European armies and used in the Americas by both colon-

ists and *conquistadores. When used at sea in the 1590s, muskets are thought to have fired incendiary arrows.

The dimensions of military muskets varied very little between the 1580s and 1630s, most being about 62 inches (157.5 cm) long, with 48 inch barrels of 12 bore. As the 17th century progressed, muskets became lighter, the forked musket rest was jettisoned, and manoeuvrability improved. By the end of the 17th century, most European military musket barrels were about 46 inches (116.8 cm) long, with calibres of .75 inch. The use of the term persisted well into the 19th century and only became redundant when *breech-loading rifles superseded muzzle-loading smooth-bored or rifled muskets in the 1860s. In the 18th century British army such weapons, the *flintlock land pattern muskets, were often called 'firelocks'; by the end of that century, the affectionate term *'Brown Bess' was in common usage. Muskets spanned the transition from *matchlock, through *wheel lock and flintlock, to percussion. In 18th-century France the flintlock came to be called a *fusil*, *mousquet* being reserved for the matchlock.

Tactical use of the musket in war was significantly affected by the military reforms of *Gustavus Adolphus of Sweden during the *Thirty Years War. Building on a system of battlefield deployment of infantry developed by *Maurice of Nassau during the Dutch wars against Spain in the final decade of the 16th century, Gustavus Adolphus substituted the musket for the arquebus and reduced the number of ranks of his *pikemen and *musketeers, thus widening the front of a deployed regiment and increasing its rate of fire. Volley firing remained the principal battlefield use of the musket until its supersession in the 19th century, since its relative inaccuracy combined with its simplicity meant that sustained rolling volleys of musketry, fired largely unaimed but with automaton-like regularity by well-trained and steady troops, could put an unending hail of lead into the general area of the opposing ranks of an enemy. In the 17th century, the musketeer and his relatively sophisticated weapon was protected from being ridden down by cavalry by protective screens of pikemen. The invention of the socket *bayonet and the development of volley firing made steady formations of musket-equipped infantry, notably in the British square, invulnerable to cavalry and susceptible only to long-range artillery and to *snipers or *skirmishers equipped with the more accurate rifle.   SCW

Blackmore, Howard L., *British Military Firearms 1650–1850* (London, 1961).

Blair, Claude (gen. ed.), *Pollard's History of Firearms* (London, 1983).

....

musketeers were soldiers distinguished by being equipped with the *matchlock. For the use of musketeers in battle, see MAURICE OF NASSAU and GUSTAVUS ADOLPHUS. Although the weapon appears first to have been used militarily by the Spanish in the *Netherlands revolt in 1567, its name seems only to have entered English usage in 1587, its use being common from 1590. Both were drawn from the French *mousquet*, thus *mousquetaire*. Early musketeers, of the late 16th and early 17th century, were noted not only for the flamboyance of their dress but also as élite foot soldiers, armed with the latest in death-dealing technology, the matchlock. Wearing little in the way of body *armour, the *mousquetaire* was characterized in the 17th century by a broad-brimmed hat adorned with feather plumes. He also carried a sword and wore a cross-belt, from which hung short wooden cylinders—usually twelve in number—each containing an individual powder charge; the musket balls were carried separately in a belt pouch before the days of made-up *cartridges which carried both powder and ball.

While the musketeer's uniform of broad-rimmed hat and long coat developed into the European infantryman's uniform of the 18th century, the musketeers became *fusiliers as the *flintlock *fusil* replaced the cumbersome and less reliable matchlock *mousquet*, both confusingly known in English as 'muskets'.

The musketeers romantically portrayed by Alexandre Dumas in the 19th century reflected the flamboyance and panache expected of them and their kind. Mounted musketeers existed in two regiments in the French Maison du Roi: the Mousquetaires Gris, raised in 1622, and the Mousquetaires Noirs, raised in 1667; both regiments comprised one squadron. The former regiment wore a grey sleeveless surcoat and the latter regiment a black one. Neither regiment lasted until the Revolution of 1789 but both were revived after the Bourbon Restoration in 1815. Mounted musketeers, whose firearm would have been a carbine or *musketoon, were experimented with in other European armies but the equipping of cavalry with flintlock firearms by the second half of the 17th century rendered the term obsolete except in the very tradition-conscious army of *ancien régime* France. In the 20th century the only musketeers to have survived are those of re-enactment groups and in the Honourable Artillery Company of London whose pikemen and musketeers, dressed in their 17th-century uniforms, provide the bodyguard to the Lord Mayor of London on state occasions.   SCW

musketoon (from Fr.: *mousqueton*). The term was first recorded in English in 1627 in Sir Thomas Kellie's *Pallas Armata*. The term's meaning became modified during the two centuries or so that it was in use. In the 17th century it seems to have been synonymous with the term 'dragon' as indicating a short musket of full musket bore, not of reduced bore like a 'carbine'. However, in English usage and by the early 18th century it had come to refer to types of blunderbuss of the type issued in quantity to the Royal Navy for use on board ship and in dockyards. The flaring mouths of these weapons were not, as is commonly supposed, to achieve a scattering effect, but to assist in loading loose

shot. Burgoyne's 23rd Light Dragoons, raised in 1781, armed its flankers with small, short blunderbusses with elliptical muzzles referred to as musketoons. Probably the last European military use of the term was with the Modèle 1874 Gras musketoon issued to French artillery and engineers; it was a bolt action, *breech-loading, single-shot short version of the Gras rifle of 1874–86. In the USA, the 1842 Massachusetts Light Dragoon Musketoon was probably the last American military *flintlock.   SCW

Blackmore, Howard L., *British Military Firearms 1650–1850* (London, 1961).

Blair, Claude (ed.), *Pollard's History of Firearms* (London, 1983).

Mussolini, Benito Amilcare Andrea (1883–1945), also known as 'Il Duce' (the Leader) and founder of fascism who as PM (1922–43) created the modern Italian state. A thug from childhood, he was also a brilliant organizer and a spellbinding orator who came late to the idea of creating the sense of nationhood not achieved by the *Italian independence wars. Before the outbreak of WW I he was the violently anti-war and anti-nationalist editor of the main newspaper of the Socialist Party, but soon became the foremost advocate of Italian participation as a unifying struggle. Expelled from the party, he was set up with his own newspaper, *Il popolo d'Italia*, by pro-war interests. After being wounded on active service with the élite Bersaglieri on the *Italian front, he returned home to promote the theme that Italian soldiers had been stabbed in the back by his erstwhile comrades, and to advocate the need for a dictator to clean up Italian politics.

With financial backing from employers weary of being squeezed by violent trade unions and rapacious politicians, he developed a strong following among disenchanted leftists and, especially, *veterans of the war whom he organized into a black-shirted militia called the Fasci di Combattimento after the symbols of office (fasces) of the Roman lictors. In the summer of 1922 the communists and socialists called for a general strike and in an elaborate political bluff he threatened a converging march on Rome by his followers unless the king summoned him to form a plenipotentiary government. In the face of mass popular revulsion against rampant political disorder, incompetence, and corruption, the traditional political parties caved in.

Until he invaded *Abyssinia in 1935, he enjoyed almost unqualified approval at home and abroad as 'the man who made the trains run on time'. Among his admirers was *Hitler, who introduced the 'Roman Salute' among his own followers and dressed his bodyguard in black shirts. Nazi Germany alone supported Italy when the League of Nations imposed irritating but not disabling economic sanctions, and from this emerged the double entendre Pact of Steel (Italy lacked the raw materials and the infrastructure to sustain a modern war). Half in thrall to and half in rivalry with his German counterpart, Mussolini dragged his unenthusiastic country into WW II by declaring war on France after she was defeated, which led to military humiliation at the hands of Commonwealth forces during the campaigns in *Abyssinia and the *Western Desert. Both in North Africa and after he invaded Albania and Greece in 1941 without consulting Hitler, his hapless armed forces had to be rescued by the Germans, and he became an ever more junior partner in the Axis.

When the Allies invaded *Sicily his own fascist grand council declared him deposed and thus precipitated a German counter-invasion and the long-drawn-out and deeply destructive *Italy campaign. Rescued from imprisonment by German *special forces he was the head of a puppet government in northern Italy until captured by communist *partisans while trying to escape to Germany, shot, and hung by his ankles in a public square in Milan.   HEB

---

mutinies (*see opposite page*)

My Lai, massacre of (1968), a military atrocity carried out in *Vietnam. On 16 March 1968, 'C' Company of the 20th US Infantry Brigade was ordered to attack a Vietcong battalion in the village of My Lai. The American unit had been mauled over the previous weeks by booby traps, *snipers, and *mines, and the company commander told his men they were about to 'get even' with the enemy. Although there was no opposing fire, the infantrymen advanced into the village shooting everyone they saw. Despite the fact that no Vietcong were found, the villagers—male, female, of all ages—were shot, bayoneted, or beaten to death. Some women were raped and later a platoon commander, Lt Calley, ordered 150 civilians to be herded into a drainage ditch, where they were killed by automatic fire. Accompanying news *photographers recorded the grisly events, which resulted in perhaps 400 civilian deaths. The *Tet offensive intervened, but afterwards photographs of the massacre were eventually published and led to a public outcry. Several senior officers were reprimanded and Calley sentenced to life imprisonment, although he was soon quietly released when a remarkably unanimous public opinion judged him a scapegoat for the merely reprimanded senior officers and for the US army in general. This war crime was symbolic of several others known to have been committed, for which perpetrators were never brought to justice, and of the poor quality of low-level leadership that the theatre commander *Westmoreland himself admitted was prevalent by this time.   APC-A

---

mutinies

'**A**NY army', wrote Richard Watt, 'is but a flicker away from becoming an armed gang. The only thing that prevents this is military discipline, which is actually an incredibly flimsy institution, if its subjects but knew it.' Mutinies happen when discontented soldiers collectively challenge *discipline, usually with considerable awareness of its flimsiness. Just how and why mutinies occur has been subject to considerable change over time. But at the heart of any mutiny is the relationship between the acts of collective disobedience and the military and political authority structures around it. The demands of mutineers have often been quite specific and more practical than explicitly ideological—complaints over food, *pay, leaves, officers, disputes over regulations of various sorts. But any mutiny by definition involves a challenge to one of the most fundamental institutions of state, the army. No mutiny, therefore, is completely 'non-political', in that no army can ignore the fact that it is simply an instrument of political power. Mutinies could and regularly did disrupt the functions of state policy when the armies were small, but once mass conscript armies of citizen-soldiers replaced armies of *mercenaries and long-term volunteers drawn from society's outcasts, mutinies became more 'political' still.

Under the old regime, Watt's adage was an open secret and soldiers for hire were notoriously unreliable. By definition, they served who paid them. Their officers might endeavour to put down mutinies or might help lead them, depending on how they perceived their own interests. The practice of provisioning and housing soldiers 'off the land' led to a brutal approach to campaigning that once unleashed was not easily controlled. Unstable armies made for unstable policy. Mutinies among the Spanish forces during the *Netherlands revolt from 1573 to 1576 exposed the weakness of the Spanish state and of the Spanish imperial enterprise itself. Mercenaries employed by Spain had one eminently practical demand, and their mutinies could be considered a particularly violent form of strike because Spanish units were often two to three years behind in pay, with some light cavalry units claiming as many as six years' arrears. The estimated cost of maintaining the campaign in the Netherlands was 1.2 million florins/month, yet the military treasury received only one-quarter that amount from Spain. The deficit, it was presumed, would be covered by collections from the local populace in the form of taxes, loans (forced or otherwise), and simple plunder. On top of this, administrative incoherence and systemic corruption made it impossible to determine precisely what was spent where. A 1574 mutiny in Antwerp was settled along lines recognizable to labour negotiators in modern times, by splitting the difference. The crown agreed to pay half of the mutineers' demands, in exchange for an admission on the part of the soldiers that they had already extracted the other half one way or another from the countryside. Yet this sort of resolution helped give the Spanish the worst of all worlds: an empty treasury, a sullen and rapacious army, and an enraged populace in the Netherlands.

The ever-present potential for mutiny on the part of mercenary armies led European powers to develop professional armies staffed by long-term volunteers. While this made some forms of mutiny much more manageable, it also created the sort of remote and professionalized military society that *Clausewitz warned about after the *French Revolutionary wars. Although it emerged from the East India company's military subculture, the *Indian Mutiny could not possibly be construed as simply a strike. The rebellious sepoys directly challenged imperial rule based on the deepest beliefs of local peoples and many believe that the war it sparked marks the first emergence of a sense of Indian nationalism that transcended local identities. The imposition of direct rule from London certainly marks the beginning of an *Indian army as opposed to the various company divisions under which it was previously organized, and this has remained a unifying institution in a fragmented and vastly diverse land.

In the 20th century, mutiny had its most profound political impact during WW I. Between 1914 and 1918, the theoretically irresistible force of military discipline ran up against the immovable object of the stalemated war of the trenches. All of the major European protagonists suffered some form of major military crisis attributable at least in part to temporary or permanent collapses of *morale. Military collapse as a form of 'hidden mutiny' occurred in the Italian army at *Caporetto in November 1917, the British army in March 1918, and in the German and Habsburg armies in the autumn of 1918. Open mutiny occurred in the imperial Russian army in February 1917, the French army in May and June 1917, and in the German navy in the autumn of 1918. Mutiny, in short, helped shape the outcome of the war.

In May and June 1917, in the wake of the failed *Nivelle offensive along the Chemin des Dames, constituent units of about half of the divisions in the French army refused at one point or another to take up positions in the front lines. Guy Pedroncini provided the classic 'military' explanation of the mutinies, and placed Gen Philippe *Pétain at the centre of resolving them. Pétain, according to Pedroncini, repaired the French military effort through particular reforms in leave and food policy and, most importantly, through tacitly agreeing not to initiate any more general offensives until tanks and American reinforcements gave France an unquestionable military superiority. The soldiers, according to Pedroncini, had wanted nothing more all along. Some historians have identified this mutiny as a form of strike, a matter of soldiers temporarily downing tools for less horrible working conditions. Soldiers, according to this point of view, brought with them to the front practices of protests learned from the civilian workplace. Other historians dispute this, on the principles that soldiers are not workers and that war is not production, quite the reverse. Most strikes have established scripts and all of the protagonists know that the strikers will return to work eventually. This, indeed, was the underlying assumption even of the mutineers of Antwerp in 1574. But, some historians argue, such an assumption cannot be made when citizen-soldiers, whose personal morale and commitment to the struggle is essential to the waging of modern *total war, challenge such a fundamental institution of state so directly.

An alternative explanation focuses on the particular dynamic of the mutinies and on the political identity of French soldiers as framed by the Third Republic. Pétain, and the senior command in general, are seen more as responding to a political situation fundamentally determined from below. The moment of explicit defiance of command authority came most often at railway depots or other embarkation points. Groups of soldiers would refuse point-blank to advance into the front lines, and would hold anti-war demonstrations instead. Initially, and from Pétain down, the French high command chose not to confront the demonstrators directly. At no point did the command structure have enough reliable troops to hand to repress the mutinies by force, even if it had chosen to. In the absence of external coercion, only internal suasion kept the mutinies from going further than they did.

According to this point of view, the French army mutinies are best understood in the context of soldiers working out two paradoxical components of their identity as citizen-soldiers: direct democracy and representative government. Direct democracy authorized resistance and wide-ranging political expression, as it had in the many French revolutions since 1789. Relatively mundane demands for better food and a more fair leave policy existed alongside demands for an immediate peace and for 'liberty'. Soldiers' demands were riddled with curious inconsistencies, such as the fact that immediate peace would have made a more fair leave policy irrelevant. Yet the demands of the soldiers also showed the importance to them of representative government. Soldiers demanded that their commanders tell their representatives in the Chambers of Deputies of their plight. The significance of soldiers asserting their identities as citizens can scarcely be exaggerated. In doing so, they affirmed the basic legitimacy of republican institutions, and of the deputies representing them. The Third Republic as a representative democracy existed in each of them, and informed their very conception of what power and politics were all about. The Third Republic demarcated the boundaries of the mutineers' political imagination. Republican identity carried within it the means of its own internal coercion. It authorized obedience as well as mutiny.

In its outcome, the contrast with the mutinies of 1917 in the imperial Russian army could not be more stark. The tsar's soldiers of August 1914 brought with them two ancient and often conflicting images of authority. Soldiers came overwhelmingly from the countryside, where they grew up in the confined power relationship between peasant and landlord. Obedience in the tsar's army was a replication of this relationship, with the officer replacing the landowner. The officer's authority was as irresistible as it was capricious; the soldier could only submit and hope for better, most probably in the next world. Against this image of authority lay that of the tsar, the very good but very mysterious 'little father' of his peoples, who had his will constantly thwarted by the likes of landlords and officers, those who exercised immediate authority. Little change occurred through reformist efforts over the course of the 19th century to motivate soldiers along 'modern' lines by giving them some sort of otherwise unobtainable civil status. In the revolution of 1905–6, soldiers had mutinied one day and repressed workers' strikes the next, depending on which ancient image of authority they thought the stronger. Imperial Russian soldiers entered the war fundamentally unincorporated into any national community as westerners understood it.

In Russia, the old-regime conception of political identity proved ill-suited to a protracted and total war of nation states. Tsar Nicholas II made a bad situation worse in 1915, when he assumed personal command of his armies. In so doing, he nailed the flag of his autocracy to the tottering mast of Russian military performance. The 'little father' became very real and very fallible, as Nicholas undercut the mystical distance so important to his own legitimacy. The result was a mutiny that invoked the demise of the monarchy. External coercion ceased to exist as the Tsar's regime collapsed. The issue became putting into place the means of internal suasion.

Despite a generally deteriorating military situation, mutiny in the Russian army had no connection to any particular calamity on the battlefield. Rather, it was provoked by a subsistence crisis in the large cities of the interior. Nicholas precipitated the disintegration of his own authority at the end of February 1917, when he ordered garrison units to fire on the civilian population to end the foot riots. He could scarcely have chosen a more volatile situation or a less reliable instrument. Urban garrisons comprised two varieties of soldiers: recuperating wounded veterans and semi-trained recruits. Both could be counted on to have more immediate links to the suffering people in the interior than to those ordering them to shoot. The garrisons refused wholesale to fire on the crowds, provoking a crisis that in a matter of days led to the tsar's abdication.

With the collapse of the regime and the systemic question of authority within the army that followed, soldiers ceased to have any clear notion of what or to whom they were loyal. Whoever could remobilize soldiers' military and civilian identities would stand a good chance of gaining power in Russia. Alexander Kerensky, the leader of the provisional government, was a superbly educated 'European' Russian. As such, he had in mind the image of the French armies of the Year II of the French Revolution. In 1793–4, the Revolution had called into being the most impressive military machine the world had ever seen. Kerensky tried to make history repeat itself by transforming the tsarist soldier into the citizen-soldier of an emerging Russian republic in a matter of months. His effort collapsed in part because an alternative source of authority emerged within the army more or less simultaneously to that of the provisional government—the soldiers' councils, more commonly known as soviets. The soviets dealt with matters as diverse as food distribution, military *justice, and whether and how to take up positions in the front lines. In this sense, the soviets constituted something of an institutionalized mutiny. Kerensky also overplayed a weak hand by ordering, incredibly, another offensive in June 1917, just as the French army mutinies were calming down. In the summer of 1917, Kerensky placed far greater demands on his newborn citizen-soldiers than the French on theirs, on a far more uncertain basis. By the autumn, the Provisional Republic had gone the way of the tsar.

Only the Bolsheviks, led by *Lenin, another superbly educated European Russian, understood the delicate interplay between the microdramas of military authority and the macrodramas of keeping and holding state power. To the majority of Russian soldiers in 1917, loyalty meant mostly loyalty to home and village. Land and peace meant more to them than whether 'Russia' lost the war. Indeed, by the summer of 1917, 'Russia' ceased to have much coherence at all. The Russia of the tsar had been swept away, and no new Russia existed yet, at least not one responsive to their profoundly local concerns. The Bolsheviks understood that by delivering land and peace immediately, they could consolidate their hold on state power and could mobilize soldiers to resist a return of the old regime, as in fact happened during the civil war. Later, the Bolsheviks could proceed to the construction of the new citizen and the new citizen-soldier, of their own design. As the USSR took shape, soldiers as much as workers became the vanguard of the proletarian dictatorship.

Large-scale and overt mutinies have not occurred in western armies since WW I. The second world conflict never produced the combination of ideological ambiguity and military stalemate that proved so volatile in the first. The so-called Salerno mutiny, Britain's only troop rebellion during 1939–45, was caused by the inept management of convalescing soldiers who should have been sent home, but were diverted to strange units instead (see SALERNO LANDING). It is intriguing to contemplate what might have happened in the second half of 1945 had large numbers of Allied troops been transferred from Europe to fight a protracted ground war in China or Japan. Soldiers have certainly resisted authority since 1945, often on overtly political grounds. French officers in *Algeria plotted against the civilian authorities in 1958 and 1961, and indeed helped provoke the transition from the Fourth to the Fifth Republic. It is now widely recognized that the most violent form of protest on the part of American troops fighting in *Vietnam involved *fragging, in which an overly zealous officer or NCO would be 'taken out' of an equation of discontent. But in general war in the 20th century has become more intensive in terms of capital and less intensive in terms of personnel. High technology has meant increased professionalization, and perhaps the creation of the Clausewitzian ideal soldier. Mutiny in its historically recognizable forms, either as strikes or as preludes to revolution, seems to have declined accordingly. LS

Hibbert, Christopher, *The Great Mutiny: India 1857* (Harmondsworth, 1978).

Parker, Geoffrey, *The Dutch Revolt* (London, 1985).

Pedroncini, Guy, *Les Mutineries de 1917* (Paris, 1967).

Smith, Leonard V., *Between Mutiny and Obedience: The Case of the French Fifth Infantry Division during World War I* (Princeton, 1994).

Watt, Richard, *Dare Call it Treason* (London, 1964).

Wildman, Allan K., *The End of the Russian Imperial Army* vol. 1. *The Old Army and the Soldiers' Revolt (March–April 1917)* (Princeton, 1980); vol. 2. *The Road to Soviet Power and Peace* (Princeton, 1987).

NAAFI Britain's Navy, Army and Air Force Institutes, founded in 1921 to formalize the variety of facilities like canteens and leave centres run for servicemen during WW I. The NAAFI on most military bases was essentially a junior ranks *canteen, although facilities gradually improved. For many years the official trading organization of the armed forces in peace and war, the NAAFI lost its contract to provide food in 1997. NAAFI still offers retail and leisure facilities to the armed forces at home, in permanent bases abroad, and on deployment throughout the world, with operations that include fast food outlets, amusement arcades, and community pubs. In operational theatres its personnel are transformed into uniformed members of the Expeditionary Forces Institute (EFI). The butt of much (often unfair) humour, NAAFI was alleged to stand for 'No Ambition And Fuck-all Interest'. The British 1939–45 service star was sometimes called the 'NAAFI gong'. RH

Nadir Shah (c.1688–1747), King of Persia, was probably the last great Asiatic conqueror in the tradition of *Genghis Khan and *Timur, and consciously imitated the latter. He started life as a shepherd boy, rising through domestic service to high household office and then state leadership, though like Genghis, and unlike Timur, he remained illiterate. He has also been compared with his near-contemporary *Frederick 'the Great' as the master strategist of his state, for his extensive recruiting beyond the frontiers of his country, the careful training of his men, and all-pervading belief in the importance of mobility. Like other great captains of Asia, his forces covered great distances with 'supernatural speed', and excelled at the swift cavalry attack from an unexpected quarter. His heavy artillery was weak but his light artillery was the best in Asia, although this owed much to French and Russian experts whom he employed.

Nadir was sometimes impetuous. On 19 July 1733 he attacked a Turkish position on the Tigris, losing 30,000 dead and all his artillery and baggage. He proved himself a great leader, rebuilding his army from nothing in two months. From 1736–8 he reconquered Kandahar, from 1738–40 conducted his Indian campaign, reaching Delhi, and from 1740–1 invaded Turkestan, reaching Khiva. His capture of the *Khyber Pass on the way to India in 1738 was masterful, and Russian military analysts later studied it as part of their own plans for the invasion of India. On 17 November Nadir sent engineer detachments to improve the approaches to it and give the impression he planned a frontal attack. But on the night of the 18th a force of cavalry set out through narrow gorges to the south of the pass. They covered 50 miles (80 km) in eighteen hours, probably without *maps and, being mid-November in the Himalayas, in bitter cold. The next day his cavalry appeared behind the opposing army, cutting them off from their base at Peshawar.

Nadir Shah also appreciated the value of infantry and the precise application of firepower. He had a corps of specially trained marksmen called *jazayirchis*. Like all great commanders he was renowned for his ability to size up a situation quickly. He also restored the *morale that the Persians had lost under a series of incompetent commanders. Under Nadir, the Persians were able to fight and beat ferocious and martial races like the Afghans and Turks. Like Frederick, Nadir brought many foreigners into the army's ranks, notably Afghans and Uzbeks. By rigid *discipline and *drill, like Frederick again, he turned the Persian army into a formidable fighting machine. His charisma as a leader was enhanced by his ability to recall all the principal officers in his numerous army by their names.

Although brought up far from the sea, Nadir also had an instinctive understanding of the value of *naval power. With help from European advisers, he built up a navy in the

Gulf and a small fleet in the Caspian Sea. His army then crossed the Gulf and campaigned in Oman. However, his dependence on western gunners and sailors was an indication of how Europe was now pulling ahead in the sphere of military technology. CDB

Bellamy, Christopher, 'Land War in Asia', in *The Evolution of Modern Land Warfare: Theory and Practice* (London, 1990).
Lockhart, Laurence, *Nadir Shah: A Critical Study* (London, 1938).

Nagashino, battle of (1575). The celebrated battle of Nagashino was fought between the army of *Oda Nobunaga, who came to raise the siege of Nagashino castle, and the army of Takeda Katsuyori, son of the late Shingen, who was attacking it. The Takeda army that laid siege to Nagashino castle consisted of 15,000 men, of whom 12,000 took part in the subsequent battle. They were therefore well outnumbered by the Oda and *Tokugawa Ieyasu force of 38,000 which advanced to meet them, whose positions looked across the plain of Shidarahara towards the castle. About 328 feet (100 metres) in front flowed the little Rengogawa, which acted as a forward defence for the positions Oda Nobunaga had chosen.

Oda Nobunaga also had the advantage of a unit of 3,000 *matchlock men, but realized that they would need some form of physical protection, so his army built a palisade halfway between the forested edge of the hills and the river. It was a loose fence of stakes, staggered over three alternate layers, and with many gaps to allow a counter-attack. Nobunaga's plan was for the matchlock men to fire rolling volleys as the Takeda cavalry approached. For the majority of the Takeda troops, their first sight of the enemy came when they moved out of the woods to the east of Shidarahara. From this point it was 656 feet (200 metres) at its narrowest to the Oda/Tokugawa line, and at its broadest only 1,312 feet (400 metres). There were three matchlock men in the Oda lines for every four Takeda mounted *samurai charging at them, but Takeda Katsuyori hoped that his horsemen would be upon the *ashigaru* as they tried to reload, to be followed within seconds by the Takeda foot soldiers.

At 06.00 on 28 June 1575, Takeda Katsuyori ordered the advance. The three vanguards of the Takeda cavalry under Yamagata, Nait, and Baba swept down from the hills on to the narrow fields. Horses and men carefully negotiated the shallow riverbed, to pick up speed again as they mounted the far bank. At this point, with the horsemen within 164 feet (50 metres) of the fence, the volley firing began. All along the line his horsemen in the vanguards, and the attendant foot soldiers who had advanced with them, were falling in heaps. The samurai, with their shorter spears, took the fight to the Takeda in small group actions. The battle lasted until mid-afternoon, when the Takeda began to retreat, and were pursued. Takeda Katsuyori left behind

him on the battlefield 10,000 dead, a casualty rate of 67 per cent. Out of 97 named samurai leaders of the Takeda at Nagashino, 54 were killed and two badly wounded. Eight of the veteran 'Twenty-Four Generals' of the Takeda were killed. SRT

Najera (Navarette), battle of (1367). When the Treaty of Brétigny (1360) halted fighting between England and France, their rivalry continued in other theatres. Both sides intervened in the war between King Peter the Cruel of Castile and his illegitimate brother, Henry of Trastamara, who in 1365 gained the support of *mercenaries led by Bertrand *Du Guesclin. Peter riposted by allying with Edward the *'Black Prince', who in early 1367 led a battle-hardened force from Guyenne to Peter's aid and defeated Henry and his allies at Najera on 3 April. Using the classic English tactic of dismounted men-at-arms and *archers, they won the day but their bloody success was reversed two years later when Henry murdered Peter and seized the Castilian crown. MJ

Russell, P. E., *English Intervention in Spain and Portugal in the Reigns of Edward III and Richard II* (Oxford, 1955).

Namur, sieges of (1692, 1695). The two sieges of Namur during the *League of Augsburg war illustrate very well the clash between the *fortification and siegecraft of the two great contemporaries *Vauban and *Coehoorn. The importance of Namur lay in the fact that it straddled the great waterways of the Sambre and the Meuse, thus controlling riverine access to the south and east of the Spanish Netherlands.

Namur was an immensely strong fortress overlooked by an extensive citadel that incorporated the natural waterways to complex man-made defences and obstacles. Outside the main defences lay large outworks such as the Terra Nova and Fort William. In 1692 some of the defences were under construction when the French army and siege train arrived on 25 May. Besiegers numbering 120,000 led by *Louis XIV and the Duke of Luxembourg confronted a mixed garrison of some 6,000 Dutch, Spanish, German, and English troops. Coehoorn himself defended his own handiwork, Fort William.

Vauban constructed massive batteries and, under the watchful eye of the king, quickly established a lodgement on the enceinte around the town, which surrendered on 5 June. The remains of the garrison retreated to the citadel, while the French stormed the redoubt of La Cachotte that lay several hundred yards outside the main position. Then Vauban sapped forward toward Fort William in atrocious muddy conditions, and when the parallels were close enough to launch a storming, Coehoorn dug his own grave to show that he meant to fight and die there. An exploding bomb rendered him hors de combat and, deprived of their do or die commander, the garrison surrendered on 23 June.

The two great engineers exchanged a few sharp words when Coehoorn was ushered into Vauban's presence. The remainder of the defenders in Terra Nova retreated to the old medieval castle, and were granted the *honours of war on 30 June. Vauban had captured Namur with very light casualties by a patient, painstaking approach and liberal use of the shovel.

In 1695 the Allies attempted to retake Namur, which had been strengthened and improved, and was held by 13,000 men commanded by the veteran Marshal Boufflers. On 2 July the Allied commander Athlone invested the town and by the 18th the lunettes protecting the south-eastern side had been stormed and taken. On 27 July English and Dutch *grenadiers under the leadership of *William of Orange himself gained a foothold on the defences proper, and by 2 August the French were induced to abandon the town and head for the Citadel which came under intense fire directed by Coehoorn from the town itself at the weakest part of the defence. However, things were progressing too slowly, and on 30 August English grenadiers and *fusiliers launched a costly assault which barely managed to hang on to the outer edge of the Citadel by its fingernails. This act of derring-do persuaded Boufflers to *capitulate rather than undergo another storming. Coehoorn had used the different strengths of the Allied army to their best advantage, undermined the defenders' *morale with a fierce bombardment and a savage storm, and had taken the fortress faster than Vauban had confidently predicted. The latter was heard to sniff that the assault had been unnecessarily bloody. The siege formed the basis of Uncle Toby's rambling recollections in Lawrence Sterne's *Tristram Shandy* (see LITERATURE AND DRAMA, THE MILITARY IN). TM

Nanking, rape of (correctly Nanjing) (1937). Japanese troops captured Nanking in December 1937 after *Chiang Kai-Shek was forced to abandon it. The city became the scene of the worst atrocities of the war as Japanese soldiers were left free to murder, rape, burn, and loot at will. Several hundred thousand civilians were killed and brutalized. The officers responsible were hanged after 1945, but the Japanese government only very recently permitted mention of it in school textbooks and, elliptically, apologized for it. It did not even succeed in its intention of encouraging other Chinese cities to capitulate, but rather hardened resistance. SRT

napalm An incendiary compound, developed because WW I experience showed that petrol often burned too quickly, when used in *flame-throwers, to ignite enemy equipment. In 1942 US scientists mixed napthaline and palmitate (hence napalm) with petrol to produce a brownish sticky syrup. This was mixed in various proportions to produce fuel for American and British flame-throwers and

to fill some incendiary bombs. A later version, napalm-B, used 46 parts of polystyrene and 21 parts of benzene to 33 of petrol, producing a more stable mixture which burns at 1,000°C rather than the 675°C of petrol.

Napalm's employment in the *Vietnam war attracted particular obloquy. It was delivered by aircraft, often in the BLU-32 500 lb bomb, and its horrifying effects on Vietnamese villages and civilians were widely reported. A character in the *film *Apocalypse Now* memorably philosophized: 'I love the smell of napalm in the morning—it smells of . . . victory.' RH

Napier, Gen Sir Charles James (1782–1853), forceful and eccentric personality and brother of the historian William. Charles was with Sir John *Moore at Shorncliffe and at *Corunna, and served with the Light Brigade in the *Peninsular war. He combined political radicalism with benevolent despotism as Resident in Cephalonia (1822–30), and in the northern district when confronting Chartism (1839–41). Arriving in India in 1842, he crushed the emirs of Sind at Miani (1843). Although Sind's annexation aroused considerable controversy, Napier was appointed C-in-C in India in 1849. He disputed his powers with the governor-general and resigned. *Punch* attributed to him (wrongly) the shortest (and wittiest) battle report ever telegraphed, the one word *peccavi*—'I have Sin[ne]d'. HFAS

Napier, W. F. P., *The Life and Opinions of Sir Charles James Napier G.C.B.* (4 vols., London, 1857).

Napier, FM Robert Cornelis, 1st Baron Napier of Magdala (1810–90). A veteran of much mid-19th-century campaigning in India, Napier was the son of an artillery major and sailed, aged 18, to join the Bengal Engineers. He was a competent military commander as well as a good sapper and at Ferozeshah (1845) had a horse shot from under him and was wounded in the infantry charge. He was present at Gujerat (1849), and was military secretary to Sir James Outram's force for the relief of Lucknow in the *Indian Mutiny, which earned him the rank of brigadier general and a KCB. In 1860 he led 2nd Division to conquer Peking, and subsequently mounted the brilliantly successful expedition to *Abyssinia in 1867–8 to release hostages taken by King Tewodrus (Theodore) II. He was rewarded with a peerage, named after Tewodrus's stronghold.

APC-A

Smith, Peter C., *Victoria's Victories* (London, 1987).

Napier, Sir William Francis Patrick (1785–1860), British soldier and military historian. Napier, a Dubliner by birth, arrived in the military as an ensign aged 15. He served in the Light Brigade (43rd, 52nd, and 95th Light Infantry) under *Moore and was present at most of the principal battles of the *Peninsular campaign as a regimental officer in the 52nd. He was thrice wounded and eventually retired in 1819, but took to writing to supplement his pension. His major legacy is the six-volume *War in the Peninsula and the South of France 1807–1814*, which appeared between 1834–40. In it, he admires Napoleon, 'the greatest man of whom history makes mention', and is scathing in his criticism of British officers and politicians. His comments caused much discussion, ensuring wide circulation and commercial success. APC-A

Napoleon I (Napoleon Bonaparte), **Emperor of France** (1769–1821) (see also NAPOLEONIC WARS). Born Napoleone Buonaparte in Ajaccio, Corsica, the second son of an impecunious lawyer, Napoleon lost his father when he was only 15 and quickly assumed much of the burden of supporting his mother and numerous siblings. Educated at Autun and Brienne, he distinguished himself in mathematics and science in particular. Having entered the École Militaire in 1784 he was, a year later, commissioned into the artillery. In between discharging his professional duties and visiting his impoverished family in Corsica, he undertook an intensive study of military history and theory. Indeed, on moving to Auxonne, France's premier artillery school at the time, Bonaparte became acquainted with, among other military thinkers, the commandant, Baron du Teil, a celebrated gunner who, recognizing his potential, took a keen, paternal interest in his training.

Although once an ardent Corsican nationalist, Bonaparte was gradually alienated by separatist sentiments and eventually moved his family to France. In the interim, he witnessed the fall of the Bourbons in 1792, developing an ever deeper loathing for the disorder that followed the storming of the Tuileries. On the other hand, the *French Revolutionary wars provided Capt Bonaparte with the perfect opportunity to make a name for himself. His skilful handling of the artillery at the siege of Toulon in 1793 compelled the British invaders to relinquish their conquest, and he was duly rewarded with promotion to brigadier general. He quickly fell from favour, however. A friend of Robespierre's brother, he was arrested following the *coup d'état* of 9 Thermidor and imprisoned for a time. Thereafter, he found himself unemployed and was considering emigrating when the political pendulum swung in his favour. A Directory member, Paul Barras, ordered Bonaparte to defend the Convention from a hostile crowd. This he did with a show of force, dispersing the mob with a 'whiff of grapeshot'.

Initially, a grateful Directory rewarded the young general with the command of the Army of the Interior. Early in 1798 he was appointed to lead the Army of Italy, which he did with conspicuous success. His victories induced the Austrians to conclude the Peace of Campo Formio (1797), and Paris turned its attention to Britain. Having judged the Royal Navy's mastery of the Channel to be incontestable, an invasion was deemed impracticable, but a blow against British trading interests through an *Egyptian expedition seemed to have much to recommend it. Accordingly, in 1798, forces under Bonaparte sailed from Toulon, captured Malta, and landed in Egypt. Defeating the *Mamelukes at the battle of the Pyramids, Bonaparte took Cairo only to have his maritime communications severed by Nelson's destruction of the French flotilla at Aboukir Bay. Invading Syria in 1799, he endeavoured to capture Acre before turning back into Egypt, where, at Aboukir, he routed a Turkish army which had recently arrived from Rhodes.

This strengthened the French grip on Egypt. However, Bonaparte had concluded that there were bigger fish to fry and, leaving his army, secretly returned to France, which was being menaced by the forces of the Second Coalition. Publication of the news of his recent triumph at Aboukir raised his standing with the public still further—so much so that, on his return, the Directory, corrupt and discredited, felt threatened by him. Their fears were not to prove groundless: in the *coup d'état* of Brumaire 1799 they were overthrown and Bonaparte became one of three consuls. He wasted no time in establishing himself as first Consul and persuading the other two to withdraw into private life, leaving him as France's de facto ruler.

Realizing that if he were to consolidate his own position and reinvigorate his war-weary country he would have to secure her a period of peace, in 1800 Napoleon set out in search of a decisive confrontation with France's principal opponent, Austria, and embarked on a second Italian campaign. It was a mercurial, brilliant affair which culminated in his victory at Marengo. Defeated in Germany, too, the Austrians ratified the Treaty of Lunéville, dismembering the Second Coalition. Britain's PM, William Pitt 'the younger', resigned and his successor, the recapture of Egypt notwithstanding, quickly sought an agreement with France.

With the signing of the Peace of Amiens, ten years of incessant conflict came to an end and Napoleon's popularity reached new heights. Freed from the distractions of war, he was now able to embark on a series of important domestic reforms: the state bureaucracy was overhauled, improving the efficiency of the administration in general and the government's ability to exploit the country's manpower and other resources in particular; a Concordat with the Pope was reached, restoring some legitimacy and tranquillity to France's relations with Rome and, by extension, to those between Napoleon's Catholic subjects and his regime; a scientifically uniform and versatile set of weights and measures was created; the Bank of France was established to support business and regulate the state's finances; a metal-based currency, with the franc's value fixed at 5 grains of silver, replaced the Revolutionary *assignats*; French law in its entirety was codified; international industrial exhibitions were staged and economic development encouraged; and the control of education was centralized, with emphasis being placed on the creation of élitist secondary schools—the *lycées*—which drew their pupils primarily from middle-class families and prepared them for a life of public service as doctors, functionaries, and officers.

All of this helped strengthen Napoleon's own position. A pragmatic rationalist, a child of the Enlightenment who subordinated rights to efficiency where necessary, he successfully replaced the chaos of the Revolution with order and, for a time at least, with peace. *Le peuple* proved suitably thankful. A plebiscite made him consul for life, while several royalist-inspired assassination attempts only helped reinforce popular support for a hereditary succession. Believing that the Bourbons had debased the title of king, and anxious to avoid any association with the *ancien régime*, Napoleon, who in any case saw himself as the successor of *Charlemagne, now proposed the establishment of the French empire. The necessary legislation was passed by the enfeebled Tribunate and, given popular endorsement through a plebiscite, Napoleon was proclaimed emperor, his coronation taking place in December 1804. In 1805, he was to be proclaimed king of Italy, too, while his siblings and marshals were likewise to be granted titles and lands as part of his policy of creating a new, imperial aristocracy. The dynasty was further underpinned by the institution of a system of civil and military awards, notably the Légion d'Honneur.

Amiens yielded but a brief, peaceful interlude in the continuing rivalry between Europe's great powers. Britain resumed hostilities against France in 1803 and, over the next ten years, orchestrated the formation of a further four coalitions against her. The first three of these were shattered by Napoleon in a series of dazzling campaigns which firmly established him as the pre-eminent commander of his age and as one of the greatest military leaders in history. So spectacular was his success that by the beginning of 1810, he found himself presiding over the largest empire Europe had seen since Roman times.

Domestic reforms followed in the wake of his conquering armies. Although its application was inevitably uneven, the Code Napoléon was intended to serve as a universal set of principles founded on reason. Extended to an ever-greater area of Europe, its impact lingers in many regions to this day. In parallel to this, Napoleon's unprecedented style of waging war compelled his enemies to adapt and modernize not only their armed forces but also every other organ of state power. Even semi-feudalistic Russia and the multinational Austrian empire were obliged to try to arouse and exploit rather dangerous concepts like nationalism and patriotism in a bid to counter the passions unleashed by the French Revolution and harnessed by Napoleon.

Napoleon thus posed a threat to the whole European order. His opponents, particularly Britain, were unwilling to grant him a lengthy period of peace in which to consolidate his gains and France found herself in an *attritional struggle which proved unsustainable. The 'Spanish Ulcer' of 1807–14 (see PENINSULAR WAR) was already bleeding France white when the Russian debacle of 1812 jeopardized the whole of Napoleon's gains in central Europe. Victorious at *Leipzig, the Sixth Coalition's armies invaded France in 1814, securing Napoleon's abdication and restoring the Bourbons.

Exiled to Elba, Napoleon staked all on one last desperate gamble. Landing in France in March 1815, he deposed the Bourbons in a bloodless revolution. A renewal of the war was unavoidable, and the Allies promptly formed the Seventh Coalition. Although the campaign of the *Hundred Days began well, Napoleon was defeated at *Waterloo, abdicated a second time, and was confined on St Helena where he remained until his death. Victorious in nearly all of the 50 battles he fought in his career, for contemporary soldier-theorists, notably *Clausewitz and *Jomini, Napoleon was the very 'God of War', an operational commander of the premier rank.

His personality, like his achievements, both dazzles and repels. A fearless and charismatic leader, he had the knack of inspiring an extraordinary degree of devotion. His nickname, 'the little corporal', reflected not merely an easy informality but the use of strong language that real corporals sometimes found surprising. Yet when he chose to be formal he was utterly chilling: in 1810 he stood for fifteen minutes, wordlessly staring at the floor, with a cloud of assembled dignitaries, French and foreign, frozen into immobility around him. His personal tastes were simple: he liked potatoes fried with onions, and was partial to *poulet à la provençale*, washed down with a little Gevrey Chambertin. When not on campaign, he fluctuated between frenzied activity and languid repose. He enjoyed long, early-morning baths; cheated shamelessly at cards; whittled chair-arms with a penknife, and was a notable opera buff—but sang badly. He drove his staff as hard as he did himself, and would often dictate several letters to his secretaries simultaneously.

His affairs (often managed, in a very businesslike way, by Christophe Duroc, Grand Marshal of the Palace) were legion. During the Egyptian campaign he took a young officer's wife as his mistress, he had a brief affair with his brother Joseph's future sister-in-law, and a longer one with the Polish countess Marie Walewska. In 1796 he married Joséphine de Beauharnais, widow of a general guillotined during the Terror. The marriage was childless and, despite very real affection, he divorced her to marry the Austrian princess Marie-Louise, whose hand was part of the 1809 peace settlement, telling Josephine bluntly: 'I need a womb.' Establishing a dynasty mattered enormously to him, and when his son was born he announced: 'He has my chest, my mouth and my eyes. I trust that he will fulfil his destiny.'

DG/RH

Collins, I., *Napoleon: First Consul and Emperor of the French* (London, 1986).

Geyl, P., *Napoleon: For and Against* (London, 1964).

Markham, F., *Napoleon* (New York, 1963).

Napoleon III, Emperor of the French

Napoleon III (Louis Napoleon Bonaparte), Emperor of the French (1808–73). Napoleon III was born Charles Louis Napoleon Bonaparte, son of the great Napoleon's brother Louis, King of Holland, and Josephine's daughter, Hortense Beauharnais. He served in the Swiss artillery, reaching the rank of captain and publishing a textbook on artillery. The deaths of his brother and Napoleon's son left him Bonapartist pretender to the French throne. He tried to subvert the garrisons of Strasbourg in 1836 and Boulogne in 1840. Imprisoned after the latter venture, he escaped in 1846 and returned to France after the 1848 Revolution, being first elected to the Assembly and then, in December, becoming president of the Second Republic.

By cultivating the support of leading officers, whose careers were to profit from the venture, he staged a coup in December 1851. One plebiscite supported increased presidential powers, and another approved the conversion of Second Republic into Second Empire in December 1852. He immediately formed an Imperial Guard and restored the eagle to *uniforms. Conviction that he understood military matters was aligned to a dynastic need to show martial prowess, but his attempts to do so by telegraphing instructions to his army in the *Crimea were unhelpful.

He married the devoutly Catholic Eugénie de Montijo in 1853, but was to have numerous mistresses. In 1858 he met Cavour, the Piedmontese premier, and agreed to support Piedmont against Austria in the cause of Italian independence (see ITALIAN INDEPENDENCE WARS). He commanded the army which fought the *Italian campaign the following year and won the scrambling victories of Magenta and Solferino. The experience shocked him, and he made peace at Villafranca sooner than the Italians wished, obtaining Nice and Savoy for France.

For the next decade he juggled the conflicting demands of extending liberalism at home with maintaining an ultra-Catholic and forward foreign policy. His *Mexican expedition was part of a grand plan to counter 'Anglo-Saxon' dominance in the Americas and indeed his concept of a 'Latin League' lives on only in the (English) term 'Latin America'. He was successful in placing his candidate on the throne, less so in pacifying the country, and Union success in the *American civil war and the crystallization of the Prussian threat, starkly demonstrated in the *Austro-Prussian war, caused him to abandon the enterprise. He supported the introduction of the *chassepot breech-loader and used his own money to help develop the *mitrailleuse machine gun, but his attempts to reform the French army failed.

On the outbreak of war in 1870 he tinkered with the mobilization plan in order to have a single army to command, for as a Bonaparte he could do little else. However, the war's first battles speedily proved what he already guessed: he was not up to the task, and agonizing kidney stones made clear thought almost impossible. The Bonapartist tradition meant that he had groomed no military successor. Having handed over the Army of the Rhine to *Bazaine, he accompanied the Army of Châlons on its journey to *Sedan, spent the day courting death, and surrendered, with antique courtesy, to the king of Prussia. His regime collapsed immediately and he died in exile in England. His only son, the plucky Prince Imperial, accompanied British forces to the *Zulu war of 1879 and was killed in action.

Napoleon III's reign embodied more good intentions than settled policy, more misjudgement than malice. Yet it was not without considerable economic progress, notably in the 1860s, and saw Paris remodelled to the plans of Baron Haussmann. Part of his tragedy was that he came to believe his own propaganda, and was ensnared by a military tradition he never fully understood.   RH

Napoleonic wars (1803–15). The Napoleonic wars were a series of conflicts, all involving France, that dominated European history at the start of the 19th century, and cast a long shadow over most of its remainder. The Treaty of Lunéville and the Peace of Amiens sought to conserve the balance of power which had emerged in Europe in the course of the *French Revolutionary wars. While not entirely satisfactory for all concerned, it was not unbearable either: Britain was war-weary and evincing signs of a willingness to barter with France; Austria, though keen to reassert herself in Italy and Germany, was also exhausted and prepared to compromise in return for peace with security; Russia, with an invulnerable sphere of influence in eastern Europe, was also a guarantor of the Lunéville settlement and thus enjoyed a prominent role in the West; while France, enlarged and reinvigorated, had regained her former standing.

It is possible then that these treaties might have formed the basis of a more durable peace, had the powers been willing to honour them in both spirit and letter. However, tension between, initially, Russia and Britain had ineluctable ramifications for other international relationships. Soon, France and Britain were again at loggerheads, culminating in the latter declaring war in May 1803.

As France's first Consul, Napoleon had made the most of the respite granted by the short-lived Peace of Amiens. In order to revitalize his country and consolidate his own position, he had begun implementing a range of economic, administrative, and military reforms. Besides increasing France's overall robustness and prosperity, these were intended to permit the state to mobilize its resources with unprecedented efficiency. Military strength, for instance, was largely dependent upon the availability of manpower and money, which in turn called for efficacious conscription and taxation systems, all of which had to be administered by a suitably competent bureaucracy. This called for talent to be blended with vocational and professional training. Accordingly, Napoleon's meritocracy channelled the gifted and diligent into an educational system which was geared to serving the needs of the regime. Though never completely eradicated, the nepotism and reliance on cronies which was a feature of so many European courts, armies, and governmental machines during this period came to be recognized as a potentially fatal flaw.

Indeed, in waging war against Napoleon, his opponents learned the hard way that they too would have to imitate at least some of his methods if they were to have any hope of success. This suggested the need for reforms which went beyond modifications to their armed forces; change in the latter would necessitate the transformation of the very societies they were seeking to shield from the dangerous ideas unleashed by the French Revolution. This was an alarming paradox for some of France's adversaries. Nevertheless, they were compelled to adopt Napoleon's methods to some degree or face annihilation.

Some of the most striking changes occurred in the size and organization of armies. Whereas at the start of the Napoleonic wars European armies were unitary forces which were assembled on an ad hoc basis using infantry battalions, cannon, and cavalry squadrons as basic building blocks, as early as 1800 Napoleon had devised a permanent structure for the French army consisting of *corps d'armée* which subdivided into divisions and brigades. Divisions were self-contained, comprising a mixture of artillery, infantry, cavalry, engineers, and logistic troops. The notion of semi-autonomous combined-arms units was not new, but Napoleon, refining the theories of others in the light of his own practical experience, developed the concept to an unprecedented degree. Skilfully co-ordinating skirmishers, heavy infantry, cavalry, and guns—the latter two in particular being employed en masse in an unprecedented fashion—he derived the maximum synergy from these complementary arms. The enhanced flexibility of his forces at the tactical level also yielded benefits on the strategic plane. Each of his corps formed a small army in its own right. Capable of independent manoeuvre along several axes, and expected to live off the land, Napoleon's forces shook off the constraints of 18th-century warfare, with its emphasis on positions, magazines, and protracted campaigns. Ever larger, yet endowed with an unprecedented capacity for strategic mobility, they manoeuvred rapidly over what were often vast tracts of Europe, cornering their opponents and compelling them to fight or surrender. Indeed, in contrast to almost all 18th-century commanders, for Napoleon the goal of strategy was to destroy the enemy's means to resist through battle, not *attrition.

Napoleon exploited this early form of *blitzkrieg as far as his immense skill and the technology of his time would permit. However, with the range of the largest field gun being no more than 1,094 yards (1,000 metres), armies had to be brought into close contact with one another for an engagement to occur. Napoleon was an unsurpassed exponent of manoeuvre warfare. Nevertheless, fought over relatively vast theatres and comprising forced marches

punctuated only by pitched battles, his campaigns called for the mobilization of armies of unheard-of dimensions. For every casualty on the battlefield, several soldiers were killed or invalided by disease, exhaustion, or malnutrition. Likewise, thousands of horses perished in the course of the various campaigns. Indeed, as Napoleon's adversaries mobilized more and more of their own resources in order to confront him on more equal terms, the war was to take on an increasingly total nature.

To begin with, the geostrategic situation imposed considerable limits on the scope and complexion of the conflict. Having declared war on France, Britain was quite unable to deal her a decisive blow. While, as an island, Britain was difficult to invade, it was equally hard for her forces to influence affairs on the continent. Although the Royal Navy quickly bottled the French fleet up in its ports and harried the enemy's merchantmen, there was a persistent fear that a hostile armada might jeopardize the British Isles or key trade outlets. The blockade was strategically indispensable, but it stretched naval resources to the limit.

Britain's army was committed to defending the motherland, colonial possessions, and pivotal bases, notably in the Mediterranean, leaving comparatively few soldiers for expeditions on the European mainland. Moreover, in order to move troops overseas, Britain needed ships. Entrusted with the defence of the home waters and the foreign trade on which Britain's prosperity and, ultimately, her ability to pay for the war depended, the Royal Navy already faced too many demands on its resources and tonnage was in short supply. Even the triumph of *Trafalgar in 1805 was to fail to dispel Britain's basic strategic problems; her naval supremacy was a necessary condition for France's defeat, but it was not a sufficient one. Indeed, although Britain, relying on the flexibility of *naval power, was to execute a number of raids on the littoral of the European continent during the course of the struggle with Napoleon and was even to sustain a sizeable army on the Iberian peninsula after 1807, it was evident that she herself could never muster sufficient military might on land to counter France. Only the great powers of central and eastern Europe might do that.

They, on the other hand, lacked the wherewithal to do this, at least initially. They were still as interested in competing with one another as they were in containing French power, and they lacked both the money and the incentive to commit themselves to another war. By the end of 1804 Russia and Austria had been sufficiently alienated by French actions in Germany and Italy to enter into a coalition with Britain. She, as the world's only industrialized country and most prosperous power, was far better placed to provide her partners with specie and equipment, which she did on a lavish scale, than with troops, but she did undertake to commit most of her army to expeditions against Hanover and Naples.

So it was that the Third Coalition was born. Napoleon, who had been proclaimed emperor in December 1804,

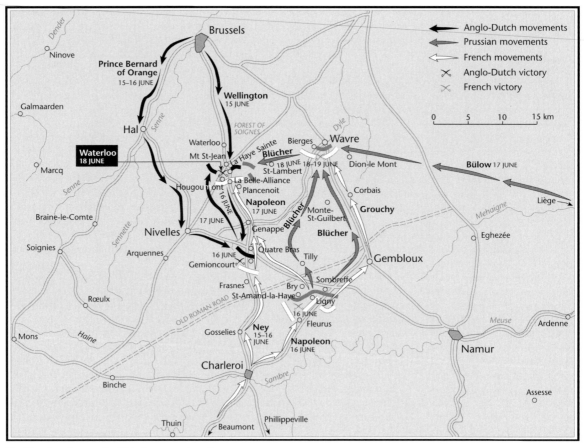

The **Napoleonic wars**: the Waterloo campaign, 1815.

assembled an army along the Channel coast in preparation for an invasion of England. He hoped to gain at least local naval supremacy for the duration of the crossing, but it soon became clear that the Royal Navy would continue to bar his flotilla's path. Aware of the preparations that Austria and Russia were making for war, he resolved to strike at them and, thus, indirectly at Britain; he too realized that, without continental allies, 'Perfidious Albion' would be almost impotent.

Accordingly, amidst conditions of great secrecy, he wheeled his forces, now dubbed the Grande Armée, towards the Rhine. Advancing at tremendous speed, they pounced before the Russians could reach the theatre. Encircling an unsuspecting Austrian army at Ulm, they compelled it to surrender before marching on Vienna. The Russian vanguards recoiled before them. Retiring to *Austerlitz, they were joined by reinforcements from Russia and a contingent of Austrians, bringing their strength up to some 89,000 men. After eight weeks of ceaseless operations which had taken them nearly 621 miles (1,000 km) from their homeland, the French, badly outnumbered, tired, and

apparently dispirited, seemed at the end of their tether. However, when the Allies fell on them on 2 December 1805, Napoleon launched a brilliant riposte which swept his adversaries from the field with crippling losses.

Although Nelson's victory at Trafalgar in October had ended any French maritime threat to Britain for the time being, Austerlitz gutted the Third Coalition and the Austrians sued for peace. Napoleon proceeded to redraw the map of Germany. Rewarding various princes who had supported him against Austria with titles and land, he abolished the ancient Reich and replaced it with the Rheinbund. This was to vary in size over the coming years as new territories were assimilated and others were transferred between polities, but, in substituting around 30 sizeable states for the hundreds of entities which had constituted the Reich, it transformed the geopolitics of the region, laying the foundations of modern Germany.

This alarmed and offended Prussia, Austria's traditional rival in the region. Uncertain how to react in the face of developments, Prussia had remained neutral during the war of the Third Coalition. She had been on the verge of giving

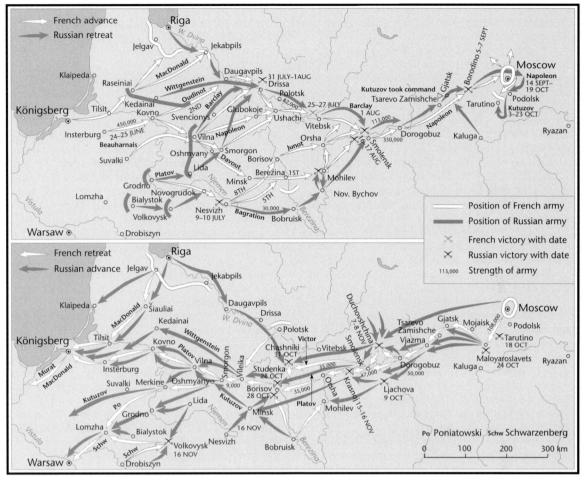

The **Napoleonic wars**: Napoleon's disastrous 1812 campaign against Russia and the retreat from Moscow (bottom).

Napoleon an ultimatum when, quite unexpectedly, he had triumphed at Austerlitz. At this, the Prussian emissary had sought to change horses in midstream, but he failed to impress the emperor who was well aware of Berlin's machinations in recent months. Napoleon demanded that Prussia join him in an exclusive pact against Britain and surrender many of her possessions in southern and western Germany to France or her ally, Bavaria. In return, Prussia would receive Hanover.

With Austria defeated, Russia's armies withdrawing eastwards, and Britain increasingly suspicious, Prussia now found herself isolated and exposed to the full might of the French empire. After a bout of dubious diplomacy, which was largely an attempt to buy time in which to mobilize their forces, the Prussians issued Napoleon with an ultimatum in October 1806. He had been hoping that war might be avoided: a Russian envoy had accepted a draft peace treaty, Britain had appeared a little more conciliatory

of late, and he doubted that Prussia would be so rash as to challenge France alone. Provoked by Berlin's demands he again unleashed the Grande Armée.

The ensuing campaign was a catastrophe for Prussia. Her army, thought to be the finest in Europe, was antiquated and proved no match for the French forces on the battlefield. Strategically, too, Napoleon dazzled and overwhelmed his opponents with a series of brisk, bold manoeuvres. Outmarched, the Prussians were also outfought in battles which occurred simultaneously at *Jena and Auerstadt on 14 October. Thereafter, Napoleon's troops commenced what was to become one of the most thorough and rapid *pursuits in military annals. Engulfed by the French tide as it surged towards Berlin, the remnants of the dejected Prussian forces surrendered en masse. So great was the demoralization that formidable fortresses capitulated to mere cavalry units. Whereas the supposedly rickety Habsburg empire had managed to survive years of war and defeat at

France's hands, within four weeks of the start of Napoleon's campaign against her, Prussia had experienced almost total military and political collapse.

As King Frederick William III took refuge in Königsberg, the few remaining units of his army linked up with the Russians in Poland and launched a counter-offensive. On 8 February 1807, Napoleon brought them to battle at *Eylau, but was held off in a gory confrontation that took place in atrocious weather. Licking his wounds, he reduced Danzig while awaiting the enemy's next move. In early June, the Allies again took the offensive, only to be repelled by Napoleon's counterstroke which culminated in the battle of Friedland. Roughly half of the Russian army was killed or wounded as Napoleon swept it into the river Alle.

This catastrophe prompted Tsar Alexander I to make peace, regardless of the consequences for his Prussian ally. Indeed, contemptuously excluded from the proceedings, Frederick William could only look on as his realm was dismembered by Napoleon and his erstwhile partner. The Treaty of Tilsit altered the map of Europe dramatically. Burdened with reparations and occupied, Prussia ceased to be a great power; her Polish provinces became Napoleon's grand duchy of Warsaw and all of her lands west of the Elbe were transferred to the new kingdom of Westphalia. The demise of the Fourth Coalition climaxed with Russia becoming France's ally, joining both Napoleon's anti-British maritime league and his Continental System.

Unable to bring his military power to bear against her, Napoleon had resolved to subdue his most implacable opponent, Britain, through economic strangulation. Late in 1806, he issued the Berlin Decrees, closing all European ports and coastlines under French control to British trade. Further decrees refined the Continental System as it was known and, over the next few years, it was extended to an ever larger area of Europe through alliance or conquest. However, it was apparent that such a *blockade could only have much prospect of success if it, first, genuinely involved all the continent and, second, was applied long and consistently enough. Moreover, the British retaliated with orders-in-council which regulated neutral trade with the French empire and its vassal states. This placed the USA and the unaligned countries of Europe in an invidious position. They were effectively compelled to choose between being either the enemies or the allies of France or Britain; neutrality became meaningless. So it was that in 1807, as the British attacked Denmark, destroying her fleet and bombarding *Copenhagen, Napoleon turned his attention to Lisbon.

Bent on compelling Portugal to join the Continental System, Napoleon concluded the secret Treaty of Fontainbleau with Spain. This envisaged the partition of Portugal. However, within months of their troops occupying the kingdom, the Allied powers turned on one another. Seriously misjudging the popular mood in Spain, Napoleon, with a mixture of intrigue and brute force, sought to remove the Bourbons and replace them with one of his brothers. An insurrection flared up, which, supported by Spanish, Portuguese, and British regular troops, turned into a war that raged across Iberia until the French were finally driven out in late 1813.

The 'Spanish Ulcer', as Napoleon dubbed the *Peninsular war, was to cost him dear, not least in terms of its wider ramifications. Believing him to be preoccupied by events in the peninsula, Austria joined a new coalition, the fifth, and suddenly launched an offensive into southern Germany in April 1809. Having learnt from her earlier defeats and having reformed her armed forces accordingly, she proved a more formidable opponent than in past conflicts. Napoleon saved the situation with his customary skill and resourcefulness, but he suffered his first serious repulse at *Aspern-Essling and, although ultimately victorious at *Wagram, the largest battle yet seen in the gunpowder age, he could not drub Austria into submission until as late as mid-October. In the interim, an abortive British landing at *Walcheren highlighted both the vulnerability of his empire's littoral to amphibious attack and the limitations of Britain's military capabilities.

By 1812, her endeavours to control neutral trade with France had embroiled Britain in a distracting war with the USA. However, Russia and France also found themselves on a collision course over the Continental System and other divisive issues. Invading Russia at the head of a colossal army, Napoleon sought to encircle and annihilate the Russian forces within three weeks. But his quarry eluded him. Obliged to venture ever further east over scorched earth, he failed to clinch a decisive victory at *Borodino and, after having captured Moscow, had it burned around his ears. The retreat that followed was a holocaust.

With the Grande Armée all but obliterated in Russia, first Prussia and then Austria turned on Napoleon, who, drawing on France's last reserves of manpower and other resources, clung to Germany throughout 1813, securing several major if indecisive victories at the head of his improvised and outnumbered army. Finally cornered and defeated at *Leipzig, his remaining allies began abandoning him as the triumphant forces of the Sixth Coalition converged on France. For all his talents, he could not keep such overwhelming numbers at bay for long. Paris fell, his marshals virtually mutinied, and he abdicated in favour of his infant son on 6 April 1814. The child had no chance.

France had been at war almost incessantly for over twenty years. She had lost millions of men and her colonies, her overseas trade was strangled, and she was virtually bankrupt. Although she was treated far more leniently by the Allies than she had much right to expect, the restored Bourbons could scarcely cope with the problems they inherited. Popular disenchantment soon set in. Napoleon, seizing his chance, escaped from exile and overthrew the monarchy. His reckless gamble lasted but a *Hundred Days, culminating in *Waterloo and his second abdication. The

French, their country defeated and occupied, also lost any hope of national reconciliation.

The Napoleonic wars were over, but their ramifications were to continue. In fact, having engulfed most of Europe, claiming millions of lives and touching yet more, having necessitated the mobilization of so much of the states' manpower and other resources, and having included the largest battles yet seen, the conflict was, until supplanted by that of 1914–18, widely known as the 'Great War'. Many of its socio-economic, artistic, political, and diplomatic repercussions continued to be felt for decades, as did its influence on military thought and *doctrine, while, to this day, armed forces retain the pyramid architecture that was first adopted during this harbinger of 'total' war. **DG**

Chandler, D., *The Campaigns of Napoleon* (London, 1966).
Esdaile, C., *The Wars of Napoleon* (London, 1995).
Gates, D., *The Napoleonic Wars, 1803–1815* (London, 1997).

Narses (*c.*480–*c.*574), a Persarmenian eunuch at Justinian's court in Constantinople, gained his first military experience during internal unrest. After the regime-threatening Nika riots of 532 (an early example of sports hooliganism, in which the Blue and Green chariot-racing factions ran amok), he led a unit which assaulted the fans falsely gathered for a race in the Hippodrome, a massacre in which forces loyal to Justinian led by *Belisarius, allegedly killed 10,000. In 535 Narses was sent to Alexandria to impose a heretical bishop on the city, which led to virtual civil war for sixteen months. Finally, in 538, he received a foreign command when he was sent to Italy against the *Goths. Narses brought 5,000 men to Belisarius and together they raised the siege of Arminium (Rimini). But he soon disputed his commanders' authority because of disagreements on strategy and caused a split in the army. Mediolanum (Milan) fell as a direct result and Narses was recalled to Constantinople in 539. Six years later, while on a mission to encourage the Heruli to rejoin the war in Italy, he led these federates in a victory over a large barbarian raiding party in Thrace.

Narses returned to Constantinople until 551 when he returned to Italy as supreme commander. At last the Byzantines had sufficient men and money to resolve the deadlock and Narses defeated Totila's forces at Busta Gallorum in June 552, their king dying in battle. He took Rome in July and inflicted another defeat on the new ruler, Teia, at Mons Lactarius in October. Nevertheless many cities and forts still held out and he was forced to besiege several including Lucca, Cumae, and Campsa (Conza). Moreover, while he was entangled with the Goths, the *Franks and Alamanni invaded northern Italy. Although he beat them convincingly in spring 554, the Franks continued to menace the north and sometimes co-operated with the Goths. Not until 562 did he finally take Brixia (Brescia) and Verona from the Goths and inflict a crushing defeat on the combined Frankish and Gothic armies.

In 566 the Heruli, a contingent of Narses' army, rebelled but he swiftly crushed them and in 568 the new emperor, Justin II, recalled him to Constantinople. Before he could return, the Lombards invaded Italy and he hastened to Rome at the request of the Pope. However, he never actually marched against the Lombards and is believed to have died in 574 in Rome. **SMcC**

Fauber, L. H., *Narses Hammer of the Goths* (New York, 1990).

Naseby, battle of (1645). This was the occasion in the *British civil wars when the *New Model Army under the command of *Fairfax was blooded, when *Cromwell's 'Ironsides' confirmed that parliamentarian cavalry could now meet and defeat royalist horse, and when the weaknesses and rivalries that had bedevilled Charles I's cause finally doomed him. The royalists, under the command of Prince *Rupert of the Rhine, were significantly outnumbered (approximately 10,000 to about 16,000) although enjoying near-parity in cavalry. Not waiting for a detached force under Goring or the bulk of their artillery to join them, they offered battle with much of their cavalry under Rupert himself on their right, while Langdale's troopers covered the left on terrain that restricted the enemy advance.

Rupert did not give time for the parliamentarian artillery to be a factor and despite being outnumbered by Ireton's cavalry and taken in the flank by *dragoons posted by Cromwell behind a hedge along their line of advance, his troopers broke through and, had he been able to rally them, could have decided the battle by falling on the rear of the parliamentarian foot, hard pressed by the determined attack of the outnumbered royalist infantry. He could not, however, and the impetus of the charge led instead to the enemy baggage train and a fatally wasted two hours.

Meanwhile on the right, Cromwell kept his men well in hand, overthrew Langdale, and turned to take the royalist infantry in the rear. The king wished to lead his reserves forward, but courtiers pulled him away and they were never committed. Thereafter the parliamentarians' greater numbers and steadiness remorselessly prevailed. Recent research, based on the discovery of musket balls on the battlefield, proves that the infantry battle covered a wider area than was previously believed, suggesting that the royalist foot fought on long after the day was lost. The wonder is not that the royalists were defeated, but that they came so near to snatching victory from a situation they should have avoided. After Naseby, the king's cause was doomed. **RH**

Foard, Glenn, *Naseby: The Decisive Campaign* (Whitstable, 1995).

Nasser (correctly Nasir), Gamal Abd al (1918–70), president of Egypt 1954–70. Nasser led the first radical revolution in the Arabic-speaking world that, in 1952, toppled King Farouk of Egypt and established an administration of military officers from the Free Officers' Society. In 1954, Nasser formally assumed power as president.

He was born the son of a postal clerk. He had an unsettled childhood and, like many ambitious Egyptians of limited means, in 1937 he chose a career in the army. He subsequently fought in the *Arab–Israeli war of 1948–9, where he served with distinction and was wounded. In 1949, Nasser was a founding member of the Free Officers' movement. The average age of the Free Officers was 33, all held the rank of major or lieutenant colonel, and all were the sons of small landowners or minor government officials. The Egyptian revolution of 1952 brought to power a new social class, swept away the established system of rule by notables, and marked the beginning of the end of the old political order across the Middle East.

While Nasser was determined and bold, he was too junior an officer to lead the revolution. Therefore a figurehead, Gen Muhammad Neguib, took charge following the coup of July 1952. In November 1954, Nasser seized control from Neguib and was proclaimed president. Internally, Nasser's period in office had two main features: first there was the replacement of the old landed notable order with a new class of military officers; secondly, there was a major shift of political, economic, and social control to the state. Externally, Nasser pursued a radical foreign policy that brought him into conflict with the West, Israel, and the conservative Arab world. Nasser's clash with the West began when, in July 1956, he nationalized the Anglo-French-controlled Suez Canal Company.

In response, in November 1956 an Anglo-French force invaded Egypt in the *Suez campaign, in conjunction with an Israeli invasion of the Sinai peninsula. Defeated militarily, Nasser survived the invasion politically enhanced and emerged as the Arab leader who had resisted the West. Nasser's reputation in the Arab world soared and soon Nasserite revolutionary movements for Arab unity spread across the Middle East. In 1958, this revolutionary wave threatened to overturn the conservative Arab regimes of the region, and America and Britain sent troops to *Lebanon and Jordan to prevent Nasserite takeovers. In 1958 Egypt joined with Syria in the United Arab Republic, a symbol of pan-Arabism (the union only lasted until 1961). In 1956 and 1967 Nasser fought, and lost, two more Arab–Israeli wars, although his control over Egypt was such that they did him little political damage.

His legacy was one of awakening and then wasting Arab nationalism on an unwinnable war, and an alliance with the USSR that brought little material gain for Egypt. Nasser's schemes for Arab unity all foundered and it was his successor, Anwar al-Sadat, who made peace with Israel, recovered the Sinai, and established handsomely subsidized closer ties with the USA. For which, in due course, he was assassinated.   MH

Woodward, Peter, *Nasser* (London, 1992).

Nasution, Gen Abdul Haris (b.1918). Nasution was pivotal in the foundation, development, and political activities of the Indonesian Armed Forces. A Muslim Batak from north Sumatra, his Bandung Military Academy education and Dutch colonial army service made him one of the few professionally trained officers in the nascent Indonesian military. He was a hero of the independence struggle and conceived and planned the overall strategy of the successful 1948–9 *guerrilla war directed by *Sudirman, which drove the Dutch to a negotiated handover.

Made army COS in 1950, he was forced out in 1952 when he requested new elections to overcome civilian opposition to an essential but unpopular military rationalization plan. His reappointment in 1955 and the implementation of his reforms provoked rebellions in Sumatra and Sulawesi, an abortive coup, and *martial law. The latter saw the army assume key administrative, business, and political tasks in tune with Sudirman's 'Middle Way' idea of a 'dual function' (political and military) army, central to but not dominating the state. But the army's increasing political power under 'Guided Democracy' meant Pres Sukarno increasingly turned to the Communist Party (PKI) as a counterweight, setting him on a collision course with the anti-communist military. Somewhat marginalized after losing operational control of the army in 1962, Nasution escaped assassination in the abortive coup of 1 October 1965, but Sukarno dismissed him as minister of defence in 1966, thereby indirectly leading to his own removal. From 1966 to 1971 Nasution held the prestigious but powerless post of chairman of the Provisional People's Consultative Assembly. Widely respected (as well as distrusted) for his personal incorruptibility, he saw the army as an arbiter, but this led to outright military dominance of the state.   DD

Crouch, Harold, *The Army and Politics in Indonesia* (Ithaca, NY, 1988).

Kahin, Audrey and George, *Subversion as Foreign Policy* (New York, 1995).

Sundhaussen, Ulf, *The Road to Power* (Oxford, 1982).

NATO (North Atlantic Treaty Organization). This alliance of sixteen sovereign Euro-Atlantic countries is dedicated to the proposition of maintaining democratic freedom by means of collective defence. The Atlantic Alliance, as it is also known, has been the dominant feature of European security and defence for half a century and remains at bottom a device designed to guarantee continuing US military commitment to western European defence. Latterly it has begun to find a new role in *peacekeeping. Like the UN, it has been an expression of a US foreign policy based on ideals believed to be intrinsically favourable to US interests and will continue to exist as long as it serves that purpose.

NATO began with the Washington Treaty of 4 April 1949, drafted upon the basis of the Brussels Pact of March 1948 (UK, France, Belgium, Netherlands, and Luxembourg), and is a landmark of the start of the *Cold War. Primarily intended to deter Soviet expansionism, it was also a response to the questions of collective security that did not find satisfactory answers in 1919–39 and rested upon Article 51 of the UN Charter, which gives UN members the right to individual and collective self-defence. It had three fundamental objectives: to reduce the possibility that Soviet military threats would reduce western Europe to client status, to counter US isolationism, and to co-ordinate the armed forces of western powers occupying Germany. Later it was to provide a safe framework within which Germany herself might rearm.

Consisting of a preamble and fourteen clauses, the Washington Treaty embodied the will of the signatories to further democratic values and to reduce economic conflict (Article II); to share the burdens of defence individually and collectively (Article III); to consult together in the face of threats (Article IV); to regard an attack upon one member as an attack upon all, and, in concert with one another and as individuals, to assist the victims of attack (Article V). The Washington Treaty delineates the geographical boundaries of the alliance (Article VI); creates the North Atlantic Council to implement the treaty (Article IX); provides for the accession of new members (Article X); governs ratification according to constitutional processes (Article XI); makes provisions for review of the treaty (Article XII). With the signing of the treaty, a new struggle began in the 1950s to put teeth into these clauses through effective organization.

From the outset, the composition of alliance membership and the geographical limits of the treaty area have caused controversy among NATO members. The twelve signatories of April 1949 (UK, France, the BENELUX countries, Norway, Denmark, Iceland, Portugal, Italy, USA, and Canada) were joined by Greece and Turkey in 1952 to secure the Mediterranean and Near Eastern flanks; years of diplomatic haggling between the USA, UK, and France preceded the accession of the Federal Republic of Germany in 1955, while the accession of Spain in 1982 had to follow the restoration of democracy after the 40-year hiatus under *Franco. Despite the objections of the Russian Federation and the doubts of some foreign-policy experts in the west, in July 1997 the sixteen NATO members invited Poland, the Czech Republic, and Hungary to join the alliance by the spring of 1999.

The civil and military organizations of the North Atlantic Treaty emerged during 1949–54 and the basic arrangement has remained in place since then. The civilian headquarters for the North Atlantic Council (NAC) originated in 1950 on a small basis in London; a larger headquarters opened in Paris in 1952, which later moved to Brussels-Evere in 1967 after France withdrew from the integrated military structure. The NAC stands at the pinnacle of the NATO civil entity as the highest decision-making body of the alliance. The NAC's overall tasks are delineated in the Washington Treaty itself. The Secretary-General chairs the council, as

well as oversees the work of the International Staff (IS). The various nations dispatch Permanent Representatives (Ambassadors) to the council, who are supported by their own civil and military staffs. The council offers the forum for diplomatic consultation and the co-ordination of strategy and policy. All member countries have the right to express their views around the council table. The allies take decisions based upon the collective will of the member governments determined by common consent. The NAC meets at the ministerial level twice a year, while summit meetings attended by heads of state occur as circumstances of grand strategy require.

The Secretary-General also chairs the Defence Planning Committee (DPC) which deals with aspects of collective defence planning. The DPC normally consists of the Permanent Representatives, but also meets at the Defence Ministerial level twice a year. The DPC provides guidance to NATO's Military Authorities to perfect common measures of collective defence and military integration. From the mid-1960s until the end of the Cold War, the Nuclear Planning Group (NPG) assumed prominence as a subsidiary body that formulated alliance nuclear policy and strategy for the NAC. Since 1991, the North Atlantic Co-Operation Council (NACC), supplanted in 1997 by the Euro-Atlantic Partnership Council (EAPC) within the 'Partnership for Peace' (1994), as well as the NATO–Russia Permanent Joint Council, came into existence as adjuncts of the NAC. These new bodies around the NAC symbolized how NATO embraced its former opponents and sought a modus vivendi with the Russian Federation and successor states of the defunct USSR.

The pivotal importance of the civilian organization notwithstanding, soldiers and weapons arrayed under NATO's compass banner bulk largest in the public image of the alliance. The Military Committee stands at the top of NATO's military pillar. The Military Committee originally met in Washington, only to move to Brussels in 1967. It is subordinate to the NAC and consists of the chiefs of staff of the member nations, who advise the NAC on all military matters and who oversee the measures necessary for the common defence of the North Atlantic area. The Chairman of the Military Committee is a four-star (lieutenant) general chosen by the member nations. The International Military Staff (IMS) supports the work of the Military Committee which meets twice a year at chiefs of staff level, and at other times at the so-called National Military Representatives level designated by the general staffs of the members' armed forces.

The perfection of common military structures, forces, and mutual efforts within the integrated military structure has stood at the centre of NATO's military organization since 1949–50. The annual review of military policy and force structure (Defence Planning Questionnaire) forms a major aspect of this effort, as does the system of international, integrated commands. From its creation in 1950–1, this system exists in peacetime to provide the strategic and *operational framework for the defence of the treaty territory via a network of major and subordinate military commands. Best known of these major NATO Commands is Allied Command Europe with its Headquarters Allied Powers, Europe (SHAPE) created in 1951 near Paris by Gen *Eisenhower and moved to Casteau, Belgium, in 1967. Such other commands included Allied Command Atlantic (Headquarters, Supreme Headquarters, Allied Command Atlantic, Norfolk, VA) and Allied Command, Channel, (dissolved 1994/5). Integration has meant in practice improvements in the quality of collective command and control, the speeding-up of reaction times, the equitable sharing of the alliance defence burden, and increases in alliance combat power. During the Cold War, the alliance differentiated the mass of forces assigned to NATO as (1) remaining under national command in peacetime, while (2) in crisis and war, coming under direct command of SHAPE's Supreme Allied Commander, Europe (SACEUR), a US four-star general officer.

Since its inception in 1949, the alliance has faced repeated trials and turmoil arising from the course of the Cold War; the imperative to adapt collective defence to allied, democratic statecraft; and the need to master the challenges of technology and defence. The making of NATO strategy among the sixteen democracies has never been especially easy, but this undertaking has proceeded better than the dark expectations of NATO's critics would have suggested. From the outset of the alliance, NATO members had to address the perceived imbalance of forces, in which the Atlantic countries could muster but 14 active divisions against 175 Soviet divisions. This circumstance grew all the more troublesome with the outbreak of the *Korean war in June 1950, which worsened fears that war could spread to Europe.

The NAC meeting at Lisbon of February 1952 saw the alliance agree to a conventional build-up of some 50 divisions and 4,000 aircraft by the year's close and 96 divisions by 1955. At the end of 1952, NATO put forward a new strategic concept, the so-called MC 14/1. This *doctrine of massive conventional defence as well as long-range nuclear strikes against the USSR underlay the planned 96-division force. Such strategy required the armament of the Federal Republic of Germany, but the cost and practicality of MC 14/1 doomed it almost from the start. Following a British lead, in 1953–4 the administration of Pres Eisenhower drastically cut the conventional forces and opted for nuclear deterrence. The USA preferred to rely on light atomic projectiles as well as the new hydrogen bombs within the strategy of 'massive retaliation'. The nuclearization of NATO followed during the latter half of the 1950s with the strategy of sword (nuclear air and missile power, MC 70) and shield (conventional ground forces, MC 14/2). The need to reinforce NATO's nuclear strength became especially intense after the Anglo-French-Israeli combined operation of 1956

against the Egyptian takeover of the *Suez Canal led to Soviet nuclear threats against France and the UK.

Nuclear crises of 1958–62 over Berlin and Soviet nuclear forces on Cuba pointed to the need for a more graduated strategy than that of all-out nuclear war. The administration of Pres John Kennedy embraced a strategy of 'flexible response' in 1961–3, which led to a conventional build-up in Europe and US demands for the NATO allies to follow suit. This development combined with Franco-American disagreements over the manner of alliance governance since the late 1950s caused French Pres *de Gaulle to withdraw French forces from the integrated military structure in 1967. In December 1967, NATO adopted MC 14/3, a doctrine of a flexible conventional and nuclear response in the face of Soviet escalation. The NAC also embraced a grand strategy that sought a 'stable relationship' with the *Warsaw Pact and the resolution of the underlying causes of tension on the basis of 'adequate military' strength, a policy that came to be known as 'Harmel' doctrine.

The final challenge to NATO from the USSR-led Warsaw Pact came in the mid-to-late 1970s when the Soviets deployed large numbers of intermediate range missiles in the theatre. Amid the orchestrated clamour of *peace movements, NATO members found the resolve to permit the stationing of Pershing II and Ground-Launched Cruise Missiles in West Germany, the UK, the BENELUX, and Italy. The emergence of less confrontational leadership in the USSR amid signs of national exhaustion led the Warsaw Pact and NATO to scrap these missiles at the end of the 1980s.

The 'underlying causes' of political tension in Europe seemed to evaporate with the collapse of communist regimes in central and eastern Europe and the disappearance of the Warsaw Treaty Organization in 1990–1. Despite the abrupt disappearance of the monolithic Soviet bloc threat, NATO continued to exist because of the perceived need to retain a US presence in Europe and to preclude the renationalization of security and defence policies in Europe. In mid-1990 the alliance announced its willingness to embark on a policy of co-operation (London Declaration) with former opponents, followed in turn by the creation of the North Atlantic Co-Operation Council in late 1991 and the promulgation of a new strategic concept that foresaw a NATO collective security role in crisis management and rapid reaction expeditionary forces.

The new doctrine was developed and tested in the new countries of former *Yugoslavia during the 1990s, in the face of armed attempts to retain hegemony by Serbia, employing tactics with a sinister echo of Nazism. Despite bombast about how Europe alone would deal with the problem from such influential personages as the prime minister of Luxembourg, the Serbs continued to test the resolve of the alliance and find it wanting until in 1995 a tacitly NATO approved counter-attack by Croatia and a short but intense display of US *air power under the NATO umbrella raised the price to the Serbs sufficient to make them accept a ceasefire and a partition of Bosnia that has proved surprisingly stable.

A further crisis in *Kosovo was again characterized by brinkmanship until mainly US bombers were set loose to attack Serb troops occupying the territory and to destroy infrastructure within Serbia. The Serbs unexpectedly held out for six weeks while collateral damage mounted, and the broken terrain and uncertain weather rendered airstrikes surprisingly ineffective even against armoured units. UK, US, German, and French ground forces subsequently moved in unopposed in a peacekeeping role, with a Russian airborne contingent rolling in at the last minute to secure the airport at Pristina, the capital of the province. Details have emerged of a serious dispute between SACEUR and the British ground force commander over whether or not to confront the Russian force, while revenge killings by ethnic Albanians against ethnic Serbian Kosovars continue to complicate the situation.

Two seeds for future trouble in the alliance were sowed: the first was that it reminded Russia forcefully that NATO remains an organization antagonistic to her traditional interests (the defence of Serbia was, after all, the reason for her entry into WW I); the second was that certain European leaders irritated an important segment of US public opinion by presuming too much, seeking to define NATO policy as though it did not remain primarily an expression of US military power. The degree to which European leaders may be able to use that strength in the furtherance of newly expanded definitions of continental collective security interests will be the main problem facing NATO into the 21st century.   DA/HEB

---

naval gunfire support (NGS) is the provision of heavy seaborne artillery in support of land operations. The emphasis here is on 'heavy', in that warships have always been able to move massive concentrations of guns more easily than land forces, particularly where roads are poor or non-existent. An early example of NGS occurred during the battle of Pinkie on 10 September 1547 when English warships in the Firth of Forth fired on Scots troops manoeuvring near the coast. The latest in a long tradition was the use of the 16 inch guns of the WW II vintage *New Jersey* class of battleships during the *Gulf war.

The limitations have always been range, something now overcome by the deployment of cruise missiles on warships, such that the big guns of the *New Jersey* class have been retired, probably for the last time. But in the era of wooden ships, shore batteries could employ ship-killing heated shot, and the advent of the submarine *mine was equally deterrent to the use of ironclad capital ships close inshore, as illustrated particularly at *Gallipoli. But NGS remains a core element in *amphibious and other maritime operations in the projection of *naval power. It has long been a feature of British and US military theory, and indeed a classic illustration of the importance of NGS was when the temporary loss of control of the surrounding Chesapeake Bay led to the capitulation of the British army at *Yorktown in October 1781. The threat of NG alone was used to overawe coastal states during the 19th century and NGS gave the Union a considerable unilateral advantage during the *American civil war, for example in support of Federal landings on Hilton Head Island on 7 November 1861, at the siege of *Vicksburg in 1862, and in operations off Charleston and in Mobile Bay in August 1864.

The same advantage was enjoyed by the western Allies during WW II. It was crucial during the *Normandy campaign where German troops dreaded NGS above all other forms of *bombardment. It played a vital role in US amphibious operations against Japanese-held islands such as Tarawa, Saipan, and *Iwo Jima, which were in effect *siege warfare with NGS providing the battering train. *Artillery fire control techniques rapidly improved as front-line naval units were deployed to direct supporting fire. Targeting was refined by aerial photography, and accuracy improved to the point where fire could be brought down within yards of friendly troop positions. Offshore gunfire was complemented by close support by rocket-firing landing craft. In the case of the British, combined operations bombardment units were established in April 1941, while American forces in Europe established naval shore fire control parties.

NGS proved moderately effective in *Vietnam and the Israelis used NGS in 1982 to support their advance on Sidon. The British used NGS extensively during the *Falklands war, counter-attacking ahead of the ground forces and taking a psychological toll of Argentine troops out of proportion to the number of rounds fired. In September 1983 the US navy bombarded the Shouf Mountains in the *Lebanon and NGS supported the invasion of *Grenada a month later.

NGS retains the advantage of strategic and tactical mobility in coastal theatres of operations. The limitations remain vulnerability to air attack and fire from the shore, now extended by *missiles such as Exocet and Harpoon. Submarine-launched cruise missiles provide an answer, but these weapons systems are not navy-specific.   JBAB

Bailey, J. B. A., *Field Artillery and Firepower* (Oxford, 1989).

Heinl, R. D., 'Naval Gunfire Support in the Pacific', *Field Artillery Journal* (Oct. 1945).

Kline, J., 'Firepower from the Sea', *Field Artillery Journal* (Mar. 1985).

Morgan, M. J., 'Naval Gunfire Support for Operation Corporate, 1982 *Journal of the Royal Artillery* (Sep. 1983).

Pocock, T., *Battle for Empire* (London, 1998).

---

naval power (*see page* 632)

---

naval power

NAVAL power is the projection of force by *navies. Although it has been a feature of warfare since the earliest days, the difference it makes to the waging of wars and to the rise and fall of nations has only been seriously addressed over the past century or so. The US Adm Alfred Thayer Mahan was one of the first in the field really to analyse the nature, extent, and requirements of naval power in a variety of books that became very popular and influential at the turn of the century.

He believed that strong navies conferred power in a form that had many advantages over land power. It was fast-moving, flexible, and cost-effective. In peacetime, strong navies could provide the conditions for the merchant marine to carry on the levels of international trade upon which national prosperity and security depended. Naval power afforded the means of acquiring foreign markets, supplies, and colonies. In wartime naval power conferred the ability to protect your trade against the attacks of your adversary and to attack his. It meant that expeditions against the most vulnerable parts of the enemy's land mass could be mounted in the form of *amphibious operations. He concluded: 'Control of the sea by maritime commerce and naval supremacy means predominant influence in the world . . . [and] is the chief among the merely material elements in the power and prosperity of nations.'

Mahan's views on the nature and the prospects of naval power were somewhat moderated by the other main naval theorist of the time, Sir Julian Corbett. A lawyer by training, Corbett was a prominent thinker on the nature of naval power in Britain before WW I. He had a much more judicious sense of the limitations of naval power than Mahan, so much so in fact that he tended to avoid the word. Instead he talked about 'maritime power', a phrase he adopted in order to give some emphasis to the need for navies to work with armies. Corbett was the author of *Some Principles of Maritime Strategy* and a friend of the main naval decision-makers of the time, especially *Fisher.

Corbett's conclusions about naval, or maritime, power were twofold. First, he believed that a maritime policy in which Britain's sea concerns were given some prominence would suit the country's interests and national policy best. Naval power was not an end in itself, but more a means to a political end. The type of strategy chosen by the navy should reflect the national objectives for which the war was fought. He explored the idea of limited maritime wars (for narrowly defined economic or geographic objectives) where the investment costs were few, the price paid small, but the gains disproportionately large. With this approach, military power could be made particularly cost-effective. Britain's historic success was founded on such principles. It was Britain's naval power and the consequent ability to command the sea that explained how it was that a small country with a weak army should have been able to defeat Napoleon and gather to herself the most desirable regions of the earth as overseas possessions.

Secondly he believed that Britain needed a balanced, amphibious type of strategy, with the kind of army and enfolding military doctrine that could exploit the strategic opportunities yielded by naval supremacy. Corbett was deeply sceptical of the growing tendency of his time to develop an army whose structure and habits of thought were becoming increasingly optimized for large-scale war on the continent of Europe. Britain should, on the contrary, leave that to its allies who did not, in most cases, have Britain's luxury of choice. In this he echoed the views of Thomas More Molyneux who wrote as long ago as 1759 that 'The Fleet and army, acting in conjunction seem to be the natural bulwark of this kingdom.'

On the basis of his study of the success of the British in the 18th century, Corbett concluded that naval power offered the prospect of avoiding the huge drains of resources associated with large-scale continental campaigns. Where necessary, these costs would be met by Britain's allies whose geographic circumstances would deprive them of maritime alternative. The British had contented themselves with limited engagements on the continent of Europe and had shown themselves able to use the flexibility and mobility afforded by their naval supremacy to launch spoiling attacks on the weakest points of the enemy's land mass. The enemy had been exhausted by virtue of the fact that he could not know where such an attack was coming and had therefore to guard the whole of a coastline rendered potentially vulnerable everywhere by the strength of Britain's navy. Britain's naval power had also enabled British maritime trade to proceed unhindered, while the enemy's was strangled; it allowed the British to seize their enemies' colonies and bases, devastating their war economies while protecting their own. All this seemed to show quite conclusively that naval supremacy, properly exploited, was the means to economic prosperity, possessions, and influence around the world and the ability to manage the international balance of power.

After WW I, Corbett's views were developed by *Liddell Hart into a philosophy of war that came to be known as 'The British Way in Warfare'. In this, both built on earlier ideas espoused by another military dissident Charles *Callwell. For all of them, naval power was the basis for a distinctively cost-effective and inherently limited approach to the business of war.

Mahan and Corbett were both clear about how nations should aim to increase their relative naval power. Obviously, it would be easier for nations that had the requisite characteristics to become naval powers. These characteristics included a national geography that provided access to the sea, sufficient ports, and a lively sense of the importance of the sea to their prosperity and their security amongst the ordinary population. Governments with the good sense, the administrative competence, and the financial and industrial resources to translate all this into an effective maritime policy, with strong and appropriately designed navies, stood the best chance of developing significant naval power. In the light of the technological challenges articulated by the likes of Halford *Mackinder, Corbett, in particular, was well aware of the fact that sea dependence could be at least as much a source of weakness and vulnerability as of strength if the country in question did not recognize this fact and act accordingly.

With a strong navy, a term which navalists understood to encompass ships (with all their weapons), trained personnel, sufficient bases, and the harbour and industrial facilities to support them, the nation could then seek to increase its power at sea. The physical destruction of the adversary's fleet in some grand-fleet encounter (such as *Jutland) was the quickest and most convenient way of achieving this happy result. More normally naval supremacy was achieved through the effect of a number of less than totally decisive battles added together over a period of time (such as the battle of the *Atlantic). In their era this was largely a matter of heavy-gun warships battling each other on the open ocean. Later mines, submarines, aircraft and aircraft carriers, and small torpedo boats came in to complicate the calculations of admirals.

But, for the weaker side, it would be foolish to agree to a battle on such terms, and the vastness of the oceans made it possible for the second-best fleet (measured in terms either of size or quality or maybe both) to indulge in a naval defensive, usually called a fleet-in-being strategy. This was designed to extract as much strategic benefit from the circumstances as possible by keeping the fleet safe from major encounters with a stronger adversary but nonetheless able to challenge the adversary's capacity to use the sea as he might wish. In WW I, the German High Sea Fleet sought to avoid full-scale battle with the Grand Fleet but to attack Britain's weaker points. Thus the British were forced to keep their fleet on constant alert should the Germans sally forth, isolated squadrons were constantly menaced, the exposed coastline constantly threatened, and individual warships and merchantmen sailing about the sea always liable to unpredictable destruction.

Confronted by a weaker adversary resorting to such an operational philosophy, the stronger party would need to fall back on the strategy of *blockade. Naval forces would seek effectively to seal the adversary's main naval forces from the sea by deploying forces off his harbour entrances or positioning them in his region in such a way as to maximize the chances of an unwanted and deadly encounter should he seek to reach the open ocean. This strategy could be implemented in two ways, close and distant, which differed only in the amount of sea room they allowed the weaker side. Although it could be a way of seeking to force a battle on a reluctant adversary, blockade was more normally the best way of neutralizing an enemy fleet by sealing it off from the open ocean.

All three approaches (the pursuit of decisive battle, the fleet-in-being strategy, and blockade) could be the means by which adversaries sought to control or command the sea. A fleet which had command of the sea could exploit it as a source of transportation of both warlike and economic goods, and at the same time deny the adversary equivalent possibilities. The more command of the sea was enjoyed, the more able would its possessor be to mount or defeat amphibious operations, to send economic and war supplies and military personnel across the oceans while preventing the adversary from doing likewise, and to be able to use the sea for general strategic purposes.

For a naval power, command of the sea was in other words a means to an end, but as far as navalists like Mahan and Corbett were concerned, these ends were strategically crucial to the outcome of wars and to world power. By following these suggestions nations could build up their naval power and become able to enjoy a level of prosperity and strategic influence, possibly quite disproportionate to their own, home-grown resources. Although both Mahan and Corbett wrote with their own nations, the USA and Britain, very much in mind, they were in fact universalists too. Although they both took Britain's maritime experience as the material from which their theories were developed, they both believed that what they had to say was relevant to other countries in other times as well. Other countries would need to adapt and amend according to their circumstances, but most of them would be able, at least to some degree, to take advantage of navalist ideas—provided they had the sense to see the advantages of doing so.

But, of course, naval power faced its challenges and its sceptics too. One of the most celebrated of these was Halford Mackinder. His view on naval power was quite clear. The Columbian age, in which for the past several hundred years European naval powers had been able to dominate the world's affairs, was over. Now better able, with the help of modern technology in the form of *railways and so on, to exploit their huge latent economic resources, land powers like Germany and Russia were apparently becoming steadily less susceptible to maritime pressure in the shape of economic blockade. Increasingly they would be able to find ways of getting round it.

Much the same applied to the threats of amphibious assault and coastal bombardment. Even Charles Callwell was concerned that technology in the shape of railways and the internal combustion engine would increase the land defender's capacity to move around behind threatened coastlines and to bring powerful defences (increased by the advent of long-range artillery, machine guns, and so on) against threats from the sea wherever they eventually materialized. Thus Corbett's stress on amphibious assaults around the edge of the adversary's land mass seemed likely to lead to costly disasters with little real impact on the war's outcome, such as Gallipoli in WW I and the *Norwegian campaign in WW II.

Worse still, for their part, the naval powers seemed to be increasingly vulnerable to the hostile attention of continental powers, especially when the latter chose to put to sea with navies that were essentially in the negative business of sea denial. Being maritime could in fact be a source of dangerous vulnerability. Britain's PM Ramsay MacDonald put it like this in 1929: 'In our case, our navy is the very life of the nation. We are a small island. For good or for ill, the lines of empire have been thrown all over the face of the earth. We have to import our food. A month's blockade, effectively carried out, would starve us all in the event of any conflict. Britain's navy is Britain itself and the sea is our security and our safety.'

New technology in the shape of the modern submarine able to mount savage assaults on merchant-shipping at sea, and long-range air power capable of devastating ports and harbours, hugely increased the threats that continental land powers could mount against the naval powers. Many naval powers were vulnerable to overland attack. Soviet naval power was, for example, quite undermined by the eastward advance of the *Wehrmacht in 1941. And even the island kingdoms of Britain and Japan were open to aerial attack.

Despite all this, the experience of the 20th century shows that naval power continues to be effective as a means of increasing the security and prosperity of the nations that possess it. The degree of its effectiveness of course depended on circumstances. In both world wars against continental Germany, the naval power of Britain had an enabling function. It ensured that Britain was not defeated and it provided the conditions in which the other services, and the other services of other countries, could win the war. This meant that Britain and its allies won the battle to keep the shipping going that was necessary both for immediate survival and for eventual counter-attack. During WW I, the British naval blockade was sufficiently effective to create serious food shortages in the Central Powers, an important and some would say the decisive factor in their collapse in 1918.

In WW II, the battle of *Britain was fought so that German *air power could counter British naval power, a precondition for a cross-Channel invasion. When this could not be achieved, naval power preserved the integrity of the UK as the base from which Allied *air forces and invading armies could project military power against the German-held continent. In the war against Japanese expansionism, while land campaigns in China, *Burma, and latterly in *Manchuria were significant, it was US maritime operations in the *Pacific campaign that put the dagger to the heart of the island empire, sinking its entire merchant fleet and enabling the *coup de grâce* to be delivered at *Hiroshima and Nagasaki

In the same way, the battle for sea transportation was both offensive and defensive. Sea dependence brings its own vulnerabilities, especially when it is exploited by a technologically advanced and resourceful adversary. In both world wars the naval power of Britain faced one of its greatest challenges when seeking to counter the savage attacks of the German U-boats. In both cases, this defensive campaign was won but it took huge resources to do so. This defensive victory, however, conferred enormous offensive possibilities. Indeed it could almost be regarded as a war-winning campaign in its own right. At the grand strategic level the Axis powers totalled only some 193 million people and 17 per cent of the world's manufacturing capacity. The Allies on the other hand amassed 359 million people and some 60 per cent of the world's manufacturing capacity. Other things being equal, by ensuring that a vast international coalition could act as such and eventually bring the whole of its potential to bear against a weaker adversary, naval power could be said to have had a war-winning function at the level of grand strategy.

The same could, in some theatres, be said at the *operational level too. In the Mediterranean campaign, for example, control of the central sea area between Italy and the North African coastline helped determine the outcome of the North African campaign, since the armies in contention there depended in large measure on the supplies brought by sea. Here the effects were clear and followed events at sea directly. But the effect of the battles for the Arctic *convoys was much more hard to trace for the outcome of the Nazi–Soviet struggle on the *eastern front, where so many other factors had a bearing too. Operations against the shore were both defensive and offensive too. Against a maritime power like Japan, amphibious operations were clearly decisive in that they were the means by which superior land, sea, and air power could be projected eventually against the Japanese homeland itself. The issue in regard to continental powers like Germany was less simple. On D-Day there were 154 divisions on the eastern front, the quintessential continental campaign, but 128 elsewhere defending Germany from attack from the sea, or engaged in theatres such as *Italy which were supported from the sea. When it came, *Normandy changed the course of the war and hastened its end considerably, but clearly naval power had made a major contribution towards that end.

By 1945, then, the strategic effectiveness of naval power had been subjected to a number of conceptual, theoretical, and technological challenges. The geographic context and the leading characteristics of the main adversary meant that naval power was probably more strategically decisive in its own right in the Pacific war, but even in the European war, the expectations of orthodox navalists such as Mahan and Corbett were largely confirmed. Nonetheless, by the end of WW II new challenges to traditional concepts of naval power were already making themselves manifest. Particularly in the Pacific war the aircraft carrier had replaced the battleship as the navy's 'capital ship' and had thereby drawn a line under the experience of several centuries in which the long-range gun had dominated naval warfare. Submarines, in the shape of the U-boat arm of the German navy, had shown they could inflict severe damage on the strongest naval power by avoiding battle altogether and attacking commerce directly.

Perhaps the gravest challenge of all was the advent of *nuclear weapons. Strategists around the world concluded that major wars in the nuclear age would be short either because such weapons were used or because of the fear that they would be used unless military operations were ended quickly. Either way, it was far from clear what the function of naval power would then be, since it was by tradition slow-acting. What, for example, was the point of preparing for a major onslaught on the adversary's sea lines of communications, or to defend them against such an assault, if the war was only likely to last a few days? Adm Gorshkov, of whom more later, called this the 'atomic shock' and realized, as did many other professional sailors, that the whole function and value of naval power was now in question.

Allied to this was a recurrence of a view that had first appeared between the two world wars in the shape of the 'bomb v. the battleship' debate. At that time the RAF believed itself to be at the cutting edge of new technology and able to offer cheaper and more effective ways of performing such strategic functions as the defence of territory against invasions, the defence or attack of coastwise convoys, and so on. Surface warships appeared to be much more vulnerable to attack than they were before the advent of aircraft, and the vital functions they performed seemed also threatened. These views reappeared strongly in the late 1940s in the form of a ferocious conflict between the US navy and air force over the former's proposed carrier construction programme, but found echoes in many other countries as well. In brief, some advocates of air power claimed that aircraft could perform the tasks of naval power much more easily and cheaply.

There were other technological puzzles and concerns as well. For example, over the years, harsh experience had shown that the traditional convoy strategy was the best way of defending shipping. But in the post-war era there were many naval professionals who seriously doubted whether that was still true, given the advent of nuclear-powered submarines guided by surveillance satellites and potentially armed with area attack weapons. Perhaps the experience of naval power in the past was irrelevant, even misleading?

To this set of technological challenges were soon added others of a political and legal nature. One of the hallmarks of traditional naval power was its political utility in peacetime. As *Nelson once

remarked, 'a fleet of British ships of war are the best negotiators in Europe'. But the increased political sensitivities of the international community in the nuclear age seemed to make gunboat diplomacy quite unacceptable. By the traditional standards of naval power, for example, Britain should
have won the Icelandic Cod 'wars' (1958, 1972, 1975) since her naval forces far outweighed the Icelandic
opposition. But she did not.

Moreover, the leading characteristics of naval power which had made them so useful in war, peace,
and the twilight situations between the two included their controllability, mobility, flexibility, and
relative invulnerability, given the size and opacity of the oceans. Now there were many who concluded that new developments in the law of the sea could seriously threaten these attributes. For example, the extension of the territorial sea from 3 to 12 miles (4.8 to 19.3 km) and the prospect of
jurisdiction gradually being extended over the 200 mile (322 km) Exclusive Economic Zone could
make it much more difficult for navies to move about as freely as they used to, and so could reduce
the value of naval power.

To this varied set of challenges, there was a multitude of responses, most particularly from strategic thinkers associated with the Soviet and US navies. Despite the somewhat spotted history of the
Russian/Soviet navy, perhaps the most thoroughgoing response came from Adm Sergei Gorshkov
who was C-in-C of the Soviet navy from 1956 to 1985. In 1979 his *The Sea Power of the State* first appeared in the West. In this weighty (if difficult) volume, Gorshkov argued two key points. First, he
believed that many of the traditional functions of naval power were still valid, even though the advent of new technology meant they might be performed in different ways. For example, he believed
that there had been a shift in naval firepower away from surface ships and towards submarines and
aircraft, although this did not stop him building notably effective ships such as the *Sovremenny* class
destroyers or the *Kirov* class nuclear battlecruisers. 'Operations against the Shore' could still be conducted in a nuclear environment; indeed, since the threat of nuclear weapons could be said to force
the dispersion of defending forces, they might actually make the conduct of landing operations
easier.

Secondly, Gorshkov argued that naval power had become more influential in that some of its older
functions were now relatively much more important and that, on top of this, naval power could perform new and vital functions too. Gorshkov, and his American equivalents, put much more stress on
the peacetime functions of naval power in winning friends and influencing people around the world.
Navies had reach, mobility, and flexibility and could go to places that their sister services could not.
In the sensitive *Cold War era, peacetime naval diplomacy had a special value. Whereas in the past
this had been regarded as something of a bonus, something to do with navies when there were no
wars for them to fight, it was now a core function that justified their existence and helped determine
their design and composition.

More dramatically, and as had been realized by the British and US navies before the end of WW
II, the advent of *missiles and nuclear weapons provided them with a strategic nuclear function that
made them more important than ever they had been before. Strategic nuclear weapons could be deployed at sea in missile-firing submarines which would need to be protected by open fleet and hunted
by another. With such weapons, navies could deter or determine the outcome of wars much more immediately than ever.

Similar views were espoused in the US navy by a variety of strategic thinkers which included Adms
Elmo Zuwalt and Stansfield Turner and the largely anonymous authors of the US navy's *The Maritime Strategy* of 1986. They vigorously argued that naval power was at least as effective strategically
as it had always been, and that during the Cold War, it provided the 'forces of choice' for many peacetime situations of threat in the Third World. Moreover, navies had adapted to the new technological

circumstances sufficiently to be able to make their particular strategic contribution to the outcome of wars.

Such claims can be investigated by considering the three types of conflict in which naval forces have been involved since 1945. The first was the potential full-scale world war between *NATO and the *Warsaw Pact. This would have been a war encompassing the whole world, but its naval aspects are best understood by looking at its application to the waters surrounding north-west Europe. Naval power in the shape of NATO's Strike Fleet had first of all a key role in dissuading the USSR from regarding the Norwegian Sea as a Soviet lake in which it could do what it liked and of persuading allies in advanced positions (most obviously Norway) that significant help would be available were the Soviets not to be deterred.

In the event of a conflict in that area, NATO's Strike Fleet and the supporting naval forces of north-west Europe would have mounted a determined sea-control campaign featuring the local inshore defence of Norway's fiords and the Baltic approaches, the imposition of a modern blockade in the shape of so-called 'barrier operations' across the Greenland–Iceland–UK (or GIUK) gap, and offensive operations by carrier and submarine forces looping around the top of Norway to attack the Soviet navy in its own waters, and its infrastructure ashore. Securing sea control by this means would have greatly facilitated the extension of naval support (including landing operations and the provision of close *air support ashore) to the conduct of the land campaign in Scandinavia and northern Germany. At the same time, NATO's nuclear posture (whether to use or merely to threaten the use of such weapons) would have been sustained by offensive and defensive strategic nuclear operations at sea. Finally, the land and air campaigns in the NATO area as a whole would have been sustained by another battle of the Atlantic in which war supplies and reinforcements would have been fought across the Atlantic against Soviet submarine and air attack. The outcome of such a Homeric contest is, of course, pure speculation, but its putative importance was demonstrated by the huge efforts that both sides devoted to their naval power during the Cold War era.

There is much more certainty about the contribution made by naval power to the conduct of the second more common because more limited type of conflict that has unfortunately characterized the last 50 years. The *Falklands war of 1982 was a very maritime war in the sense that the objective and the main theatre was maritime. Accordingly, it would not have surprised the likes of Corbett that the key contest was for the capacity to control the seas around the disputed islands. Sea control was assured for the Royal Navy by its demonstrated capacity to use its submarines and its aircraft against the Argentine fleet and by its capacity to reduce the Argentine submarine and air threat, if not completely, then at least to manageable proportions. The consequent degree of sea control meant that Argentine forces on the islands were largely cut off from all but inadequate air supply and that the British could accumulate, land, and support the land and air forces that eventually retook the islands.

In some ways, the *Gulf war of 1990–1 was more significant in that this was clearly not a maritime theatre. The main disputants (and their allies) were territorial neighbours. The maritime area of operations was not the open ocean so familiar to the likes of Mahan and Corbett but a narrow and constrained sea area almost entirely surrounded by land and air bases. Nonetheless, the contribution made by naval power was unique and indispensable. First and foremost, the war could only be conducted once international and domestic opinion had been reconciled to its necessity. Even though it failed to persuade Iraq to leave Kuwait, the extensive sea-based UN sanctions campaign had a vital function in rallying world opinion and in constructing the international coalition that would eventually go on to conduct the war. Equally essential, huge military supplies and forces needed to be transported into the area. This depended on the Coalition's being able to locate the necessary ships. Many observers have since commented on the impact that the declining fortunes of the West's merchant-shipping fleets might have on the capacity to conduct such a vast operation in the future. Less obviously, success depended absolutely on the degree of sea control exerted by the Coalition. As it turned out, there was no significant challenge to this outside the Gulf (although even a minor threat might have made a tremendous difference) and the potential danger posed by Iraq's missile armed fast-attack craft inside it was quickly disposed of by American and British *helicopters and warships.

Once sea control was assured and the forces assembled, military operations could be mounted. As it turned out, amphibious operations were not found to be necessary although the Coalition's very obvious preparations for them undoubtedly persuaded the Iraqis to devote significant forces to the defence of the Kuwait coastline, well away from the main axis of the Allied advance. Naval power was projected ashore in the form of cruise missile and aircraft attack, supplementing the more extensive efforts made by Coalition air forces operating from shore bases. And once the conflict was over, naval forces were needed to take many of the forces home, to clean the detritus of war from the sea and the beaches, to engage in an extensive mine-clearance operation, and of course to maintain sufficient forces in the area to guard against further aggression.

Finally, throughout the Cold War era and increasingly since then, naval power has been deployed in support of humanitarian and peace-support operations that range from hurricane relief in the West Indies to the support of peace-support operations in Bosnia. It would appear from this review that one of the most notable characteristics of naval power is its capacity over the years to adapt to changing circumstances.   GT

Corbett, Julian S., *Some Principles of Maritime Strategy* (London, 1911).
Friedman, Norman, *The US Maritime Strategy* (London, 1988).
Gray, Colin, *The Leverage of Sea Power* (London, 1992).
Grove, Eric, *The Future of Sea Power* (London, 1990).
Mahan, Alfred Thayer, *The Influence of Sea Power upon History, 1660–1783* (Boston, 1890).
Till, Geoffrey, *Maritime Strategy and the Nuclear Age* (London, 1984).

navies are the means whereby *naval power may be exerted. A handful of ancient and medieval powers (notably Athens and Venice) were able to maintain something like a national navy for long periods, while others assembled squadrons of warships, often privately owned, for particular campaigns, or improvised fleets out of merchant ships carrying soldiers. The only true warships were galleys, fitted with rams in classical times, but in the Middle Ages essentially fast troop-carriers were mainly used for short-range *amphibious operations. In northern waters a similar style of warfare was conducted by the *Vikings over much longer ranges, using ships owned by individuals or localities but sometimes assembled in national fleets. Outdated in Scandinavia by the 14th century, such 'Viking' ships were still active in the Hebrides in the 17th century. Elsewhere on the Atlantic coasts of Europe, France, Castile, and Portugal at various periods in the 13th and 14th centuries maintained galley squadrons, but the 'navies' of most countries were improvised from armed merchantmen.

With the adoption of heavy guns, first in galleys in the late 15th century, and later in sailing ships, the cost of navies rose markedly. The possession of modern warships was a primary mark of power and status in Renaissance Europe, but even the richest princes struggled to organize and finance a permanent fleet, which presented challenges financial, technical, and managerial which strained the resources of the early-modern state to the limits. At the end of the 16th century only Venice, Denmark, England, and (on a small scale) the papacy possessed permanent state navies with effective infrastructure. Spain, the superpower of the age, had several regional squadrons, but did not succeed in establishing a permanent national fleet until the 18th century. The Dutch became the leading naval power of the 17th century by assembling provincial, local, and private fleets into a national navy. In England the financial and political strains of sustaining a navy contributed to the fall of the Stuarts, and it was the fleet built by the military regime of the 1650s which gave England the status of a great power.

Soon afterwards *Louis XIV of France began the construction of a navy more or less from nothing, which by the 1690s was briefly the most powerful in the world. The strain of war revealed that this imposing force lacked the necessary financial, political, and industrial foundations, and by the Peace of Utrecht it was in rapid decline.

By then it was clear that the possession of a modern navy was essential to participation in the rich oceanic trade which was transforming the advanced economies of Europe. For Britain, alone among European states, the navy was also a guarantor of national integrity. Politically unstable, with an apparently weak government and an undoubtedly weak army, Britain had no real defence apart from her navy. For this reason all parties united in supporting it, and the British navy enjoyed a solid, long-term political commitment unequalled in any other country. To sustain an effective fleet required heavy investment in dockyards, stores, and industrial plants spread over many years; it called for a ceaseless effort of shipbuilding to match the continual decay of wooden ships; and all this would be useless without a large seafaring population to provide skilled crews for the ships. With the largest merchant fleet and the most resilient system of public credit in Europe and above all with the political will to sustain a powerful navy, Britain was able to win a decisive victory in the naval arms race of the late 18th century. Having beaten off a dangerous challenge from the united fleets of France and Spain during the *American independence war, the Royal Navy enabled Britain not only to survive but to prosper while every other European state was more or less devastated during the *French Revolutionary and *Napoleonic wars.

The other major 18th-century navies all suffered from a lack of one or more of the basic components of naval power. The Dutch fleet, still in the first rank in 1688, declined rapidly after 1715 for want of adequate funds. The French navy, painfully rebuilt in the 1770s and 1780s, suffered badly from the effects of the French Revolution. At its best it was always beset by industrial and financial weakness, inconsistent state policy, and inadequate skilled manpower. The Spanish navy grew to be in many respects a formidable force by the 1780s, but was always crippled by shortage of seamen. Other 18th-century navies, notably those of Russia, Sweden, Denmark, Turkey, Algiers, and the Two Sicilies, belonged to the second rank, exercising an important influence only in particular areas and periods.

The basic unit of sea power was the ship of the line or battleship, mounting a minimum of 40 or 50 guns (in 1688), and 100 or more (by 1815), capable of taking its place in the line of battle. Because warships mounted almost all their guns on the broadside, and were vulnerable to fire from ahead or astern, actions were usually fought in line ahead. This was a strong defensive formation, especially as ships' means of propulsion (masts and sails) were much more exposed than their hulls, and they were often stopped or disabled before they could come to close quarters. The meeting of two competent fleets in roughly equal numbers usually resulted in an inconclusive action. Ultimate victory tended to go to the navy which could mobilize and deploy overwhelming numbers fastest, which placed a premium not only on numbers of ships, but on logistical and technical resources, on reserves of skilled manpower and the means to draw on them, and on the political will to begin the very lengthy mobilization process in good time. Only during the Napoleonic wars did new tactical methods allow equal or even inferior fleets to win overwhelming victories, and these were developed by the Royal Navy, drawing on a strength of seamanship and *morale conferred by overall strategic naval dominance.

Fleets and squadrons were employed to escort *convoys of merchant ships; to cover raiding, expeditionary, and invasion forces; and in the case of Britain in particular, to defend the country against threats of invasion. Where the only main roads ran along the coast (notably in the western Mediterranean), naval gunfire might hinder or even block the movements of armies ashore. Lesser squadrons and individual ships fulfilled some of the same functions, besides cruising for the defence and attack of trade, and assuring supplies to any place accessible by sea. Smaller warships such as frigates and sloops were employed as cruisers, escorts, and scouts for the battle squadrons; bomb vessels deployed heavy *mortars for shore bombardment; schooners and cutters maintained communications; gunboats of various types operated inshore; and a huge fleet of storeships, transports, hospital ships and other auxiliaries supplied and sustained the fleets.

In all its aspects naval warfare was above all the warfare of technology and capital, and its characteristic form was *attrition. Decisive battles were difficult to achieve, and did not confer control of the sea in the way a victory on land might gain territory, but when ships were more often captured than destroyed, a victory might sharply alter the balance of forces, and enormously speed the process. The costs of maintaining even a small fleet greatly exceeded those of a large army ashore, they had to be borne over a much longer period to achieve useful results, and they called for the resources of an advanced economy. The number of men in a fleet, though not negligible (a fleet of 30 sail in the 1780s called for about 25,000), was small by comparison with armies, but a large proportion of them were highly skilled and scarce. The firepower of a single battleship exceeded that of all the artillery of a large army, and on the occasion when *naval gunfire support could be given to land operations, the results were usually decisive. The flexibility and power of navies, capable of being deployed over huge distances, presented problems of strategy, command, and communications many of which the 18th century never completely solved.

For states with the capacity to develop effective naval power, a navy offered opportunities as a diplomatic instrument in peacetime, as well as a means of waging war, which even the largest army could not equal. Limited or altogether useless against landlocked powers, navies could be used effectively and sometimes decisively against any state with a coast, and especially any which depended to any extent on foreign trade or colonies. As the world economy grew more connected and sophisticated during the 18th century it depended increasingly on seaborne trade as an engine of prosperity in general, and a generator of liquid investment capital in particular. Naval power enabled states to gain access to this means of economic growth, and eventually enabled Britain to dominate the world economy in the 19th century. The Royal Navy for most of this century maintained only small seagoing forces (except briefly during the *Crimean war), backed with large reserves and sustained expenditure on infrastructure, research, and development. During the 1840s and 1850s the British fleet was entirely reconstructed, all classes being fitted with auxiliary screw *steam propulsion. At the same time large 'steam factories' were added to the major dockyards. Starting in 1860, Britain and France began to build armoured battleships, *breech-loading guns firing explosive shell were introduced about the same time, and over the next 30 years warship design evolved very rapidly. The introduction of compound engines in the 1870s made it possible for seagoing warships to dispense with masts and sails. At the same period the early Whitehead torpedoes offered the possibility of striking armoured warships at their most vulnerable point—below the waterline; new types of small warship and new tactical methods were developed to exploit it. In the 20th century the submarine was to prove the most effective of them all.

Until about 1890 British technical superiority was never effectively challenged, and British private shipyards built a high proportion of the world's warships. At that time an unprecedented peacetime naval arms race hugely increased the size of the Royal Navy, which remained more than equal to its two nearest rivals (France and Russia) combined. In the long term Britain's strategic situation was fatally undermined by the rise of major naval powers outside Europe. This meant that for the first time in 300 years, the fleet maintained in home waters for home defence could not at the same time ensure superiority worldwide. In the short term an alliance with Japan and friendship with the USA sufficed to maintain Britain's position and allow a concentration against Germany. After WW I Britain was forced to choose between the USA and Japan, opening the possibility of having to fight a war in Europe and the Far East simultaneously. That threat became a reality in 1941.

By 1945 the USA represented nearly half the productive economy of the world, and the US navy was clearly the major world fleet, as it has remained. It has not been able to assume the position formerly held by the Royal Navy, since with significant naval powers in every part of the world, global superiority can only be maintained by a global system of alliances. In other respects the fundamentals of naval power remain in the late 20th century much as they always

have been. Aircraft and missiles enable land forces to project power seaward and warships to strike further inland than before. The economic importance of seaborne commerce and the economic dominance of coastal over inland regions has greatly increased as the bulk of the world's population comes to work in trade and industry rather than on the land. Modern warships are widely available even to relatively minor powers, as they were even in the 18th century, but effective navies, whether on a large or small scale, still require years of sustained investment in training and infrastructure. The expense and difficulty of maintaining an effective navy remain as great as they have ever been, but the rewards in terms of direct control of the world's trade, and indirect power over a large proportion of its population and economic resources, continue to justify the effort.

NAMR

Navy, Army and Air Force Institutes. See NAAFI.

Nazi auxiliary units (WW II) There was no overall policy for the formation of auxiliary units. Most were formed after the invasion of the USSR on 22 June 1941 because of manpower shortages in the *Wehrmacht and, later, Waffen *SS but rapidly acquired political significance. The origins of Hitler's policy towards the USSR and occupied territories (Ostpolitik) could be found in *Mein Kampf* and rested on the assumption that Slavs were *Untermenschen* (subhumans). The length of the campaign and the population's response to Nazi policies forced the military to argue for changes.

Between June and November 1941, the Germans took 3,800,000 POWs and some of these began to be used in auxiliary capacities. These Hilfswillige (Hiwis) worked at first in non-combatant positions—drivers, ammunition carriers, etc.—and gradually in military capacities as local militia, in partisan combat, and as regular units with German officers. Statistics were inaccurate and designed to mislead the authorities as to the extent of non-Aryans in the armed forces. On 15 December 1942 Gen Heinz Hellmich was appointed *General der Osttruppen* and in 1943, Gen Ernst Köstring replaced him. On 1 January 1944 the position was renamed *General der Freiwilligeverbände* (volunteer units). It is estimated that by the end of the war there were more than 800,000 Soviet nationals in the Wehrmacht.

Many auxiliaries considered themselves members of the Russkaya Osvoboditel′naya Armiya (Russian Liberation Army) under the command of captured Red Army Lt Gen Andrey Andreyevich *Vlasov and sewed badges on their uniforms to indicate their allegiance. This army never existed although it was mentioned in propaganda, beginning with the Smolensk Manifesto of December 1942. In June 1943, at the Berghof conference, *Hitler forbade further attempts to form a Russian army and Vlasov was kept under virtual house arrest until the summer of 1944 when after further discussions the Komitet Osvobozhdeniya Narodov Rossii (the Committee for the Liberation of the Peoples of Russia, KONR) was formed. The publication of the Prague Manifesto in November 1944 signalled the creation of two divisions numbering initially about 10,000 men recruited from POW camps and not the Wehrmacht. The 1st Division fought with the Czech nationalists against SS troops and the Wehrmacht in Prague in May 1945. The 2nd KONR Division never saw active service. When it became clear that the Americans were not going to enter Prague, the division tried to enter the American zone. Refused permission to do so, the army disbanded and many were captured by the Red Army.

In contrast to the controversy surrounding the creation of a Russian army, the formation of the *Ostlegionen* was sanctioned in 1941 and was fostered by Rosenberg in the Ostministerium. The Armenian, Azerbaijani, Georgian, North Caucasian, Turkestan, and Volga Tartar legions were formed. There was a cavalry corps of Kalmyks and a Volga Tartar formation. Sizes of formations varied and most were stationed on the *eastern front. *Cossacks were allowed to have their own military formations because some of their émigré leaders had supported Hitler in the 1920s for his anti-Bolshevism. Consequently they were considered to be 'Goths' and not *Untermenschen* Slavs. However, numbers are unclear as the terms 'Cossack' and 'Ukrainian' were widely used to describe Soviet citizens. Nazi policy was inconsistent and attempts to create self-governing Cossack areas never came to fruition. On 15 April 1942, a Cossack division under the command of Lt Gen Helmuth von Pannwitz was formed with regiments from the Don, Kuban, Terek, and Siberia. The émigré Gen P. N. Krasnov headed a directorate of Cossack forces created in March 1944 and refused to join Vlasov; his men moved south and surrendered to the British in Italy.

The other significant auxiliary formation was the Spanish Blue Division. Ostensibly despatched to the Soviet front in gratitude for help during the *Spanish civil war, and as part of Franco's campaign against communism, the division was perhaps part of the price *Franco felt he had to pay to deny Hitler the right to roll through Spain to take Gibraltar or in some other way commit him irrevocably to the war on the Axis side. Formed in 1941, commanded by Maj Gen Augustín Muñoz Grandes and from December 1942 by Maj Gen Esteban Infantes, it originally numbered 17,692 men. It became the German 250th Infantry Division with 262nd, 263rd, and 269th Regiments and 250th Artillery Regiment. It saw action in the USSR in October 1941 on the Volkhov, and later was involved, ironically, in surrounding Vlasov's Second Shock Army. Part of the *Leningrad front, it was recalled in late 1943 with the smaller Spanish Legion remaining until spring 1944. Approximately 47,000 served with the division: 22,000 were casualties and 4,500 were killed or died.   CA

Andreyev, C., *Vlasov and the Russian Liberation Movement* (Cambridge, 1987).

Dallin, A., *German Rule in Russia* (2nd edn., London, 1981).

Hoffmann, J., *Die Ostlegionen* (Freiburg, 1976).

Kleinfeld, G., and Tambs, L., *Hitler's Spanish Legion: The Blue Division in Russia* (Carbondale, Ill., 1979).

Longworth, P., *The Cossacks* (London, 1969).

NCO (non commissioned officer). In 1642 Sgt Nehemiah Wharton referred to his regiment's *officers and sergeants collectively as 'we officers'. However, as military ranks formalized in the 17th century a clear distinction developed between 'commission-officers' who held a *commission, increasingly granted by the monarch, and NCOs, who did not. Despite historical evolution, and differences between and within armies, the distinction survives to this day. Petty officers in *navies have many of the characteristics of NCOs.

For much of history NCO rank stemmed from a lesser authority than that of commissioned officers: NCOs were appointed and promoted by their colonel. Their rank was more fragile than that of commissioned officers, and they might lose it with fewer legal niceties. NCOs were promoted from the ranks and worked their way steadily upwards. All too often a barrier separated them from commissioned rank, and the ambitious NCO has proved a source of political as well as military tension, most notably in the French army.

NCOs received better pay and allowances than private soldiers. Though national customs varied, sergeants messed separately from the men—and corporals often had a special 'bunk' with more privacy than the barrack-room—enhancing their status. In many armies the distinction between officers and NCOs was social as well as functional. NCOs were responsible for minor administration, *drill, and *discipline, and were not expected to exercise command on anything but a small scale. Though 'gentleman rankers' were never uncommon—François de Chevert in the French army, *Robertson in the British, and Courtney Hodges in the American all began as privates—NCOs in general were not reckoned gentlemen. The fortune of war often demolished such distinctions, and NCOs not infrequently took command when all their officers had fallen.

The British army, and many others influenced by it, begins its NCOs with lance-corporal and corporal. The term corporal probably derives from the Latin *corpus*, for body (of troops): in 1598 the corporal was described as 'a degree in dignitie above the private soldier'. The expression lance-corporal—originally *lancia spezzada*, broken lance, in Italian, leading to the obsolete *lancepesad*, dates from the late Middle Ages, when a cavalryman who had lost his horse and served on foot would retain higher status than infantry privates. Equivalent ranks in the Royal Artillery are lance-bombardier and bombardier, harking back to the ancient rank of bombardier, a species of trained artilleryman. They are junior NCOs, distinct from senior NCOs, sergeants, and above. The *caporal* in the French army and the *gefreiter* in the German were not regarded as NCOs proper but as senior soldiers.

The term sergeant derives from the Latin *serviens* (servant) and in the Middle Ages described a heavy horseman below knightly status. In 1813 the British army introduced the rank of colour sergeant to reward sergeants of good standing, and for the next century the colour sergeant was the senior non-commissioned member of a British infantry company, equivalent to the US army's first sergeant. Sergeants on the staff of a battalion were termed staff sergeants, and *QM sergeants (both company and regimental) were responsible for stores and equipment. The British Household Cavalry does not use the rank of sergeant, but substitutes the ancient term Corporal of Horse.

The senior non-commissioned member of a British unit is its regimental sergeant major (RSM). This began as an NCO rank, but attained *warrant officer status in the 19th century. When British infantry battalions were restructured from eight companies to four in 1913 the rank of company sergeant major (CSM) was created. The colour sergeant then became the second senior member of his company, carrying out the role of company QM sergeant (CQMS). With the creation of the rank of CSM, RSMs became Warrant Officers Class 1 and CSMs Warrant Officers Class 2.

The German army traditionally distinguished between *Unteroffiziere ohne Portepee* (NCOs without a sword knot) and *Unteroffiziere mit Portepee* (NCOs with a sword knot). The former, corporals and sergeants, roughly equated to British NCOs, whereas the latter, who, in both world wars, might command platoons or their equivalents, were closer to British warrant officers.

The effectiveness of many great armies of history has depended heavily upon their NCOs, who drilled and trained the men and steadied their ranks on the day of battle. They were not always popular: an 18th-century Prussian soldier compared his NCOs to oriental eunuchs, polite to their superiors but taking out their frustrations on their subordinates. Yet Kipling was not far wrong when he wrote: 'The backbone of the army is the Non-Commissioned man.'

RH

needle gun A rifle which was fired by driving a long needle-like firing pin through a paper *cartridge to strike the detonator, placed in the middle of the propellent charge to ensure even combustion. Early needle guns were muzzle-loading but the most well known was the *breech-loading Dreyse *Zündnadelgewehr*, adopted by the Prussian army in 1841. As propellent quality improved, the detonator was moved to the base of the charge and the needle system was replaced by a spring-loaded short firing pin within the bolt head.

SCW

Peterson, Harold L. (ed.), *Encyclopaedia of Firearms* (London, 1974).

Nelson, Vice Adm Horatio, Viscount Nelson (1758–1805). Nelson first distinguished himself at the battle of St Vincent in 1797, turning out of line without orders, and leading the boarding parties which took two Spanish ships. Next year he pursued Napoleon's expedition to *Egypt, found the French fleet at anchor in Aboukir Bay at the mouth of the Nile, and sank or captured all but two of the enemy battleships. He now based his squadron at Naples, and when the French overran the city in December he evacuated the royal family to Palermo. He remained at Palermo for much of the next twelve months, ignoring direct orders to rejoin the main fleet. His liaison with Lady Hamilton was by now notorious, and damaged his reputation. Returning to England, he sailed in February 1801 as second-in-command of a squadron intended to break up the 'Armed Neutrality' of Baltic powers. Nelson led the smaller ships of the squadron to attack the Danish fleet before *Copenhagen. The battle was desperate, but at the critical moment Nelson deliberately ignored a signal to withdraw, and was rewarded with a costly victory. On the return of war in May 1803 he took command of the Mediterranean squadron blockading Toulon. When Villeneuve's squadron escaped in March 1805 Nelson followed him across the Atlantic and back. On 21 October Nelson finally caught the Franco-Spanish fleet off Cape *Trafalgar, where he was killed in the moment of a crushing victory.

Nelson's vanity and scandalous private life disgusted many who did not know him, but in the navy he was adored, and the success of his eclectic tactics owed much to delegation to trusted subordinates, inspired by the example of an admiral who always led from the front. His death in the hour of victory left a heroic memory which time has not dimmed.

NAMR

Nemea, battle of (394 BC), fought during the *Greek city-state wars. Though called after the river Nemea, the battle was probably actually fought near Rachiani (Longopotamos) to the east. Here, perhaps some 24,000 Boeotians, Corinthians, Argives, Euboeans, and Athenians faced between 18,000 and 19,000 Spartans and their allies, in possibly the greatest *hoplite battle ever fought. In the advance, both sides edged to the right, as had occurred at *Mantineia in 418. Perhaps on this occasion it was not just because, as Thucydides (see GREEK HISTORIANS) says, hoplites tended to seek the protection of their right-hand neighbour's shield, but in a deliberate attempt to outflank the enemy left. As a result, both armies were defeated on the left, but whereas the Boeotians and their allies streamed off in disorderly *pursuit, the Spartans, as usual under perfect control, fell upon the shieldless side of the enemy right as it tried to retreat. According to *Xenophon only eight Spartans fell, but this may have just been the full citizens of *Sparta itself. Diodorus (see GREEK HISTORIANS), however, gives the losses among the Spartans and their allies as 1,100, for 2,800 on the other side.   JFL

Diodorus, 14. 83. 1–2.
Lazenby, J. F., *The Spartan Army* (Warminster, 1985).
Xenophon, *Hellenika*, 4. 2. 15–23.

Netherlands revolt (1567–1648), or Eighty Years War. The long struggle that eventually gave birth to the nationality called 'Dutch' in English is complicated by the fact that

the identity itself did not exist before the war. The seventeen provinces of the Netherlands were first united under Philip of Burgundy in the 15th century and inherited by the Habsburg Emperor *Charles V, but each province and even each of the great merchant cities had different political and religious customs, and jealously treasured their individual prerogatives. For as long as imperial authority was exercised lightly, the only desire they had in common was to trade and enjoy steadily increasing prosperity.

Under Philip II, self-appointed leader of the Counter-Reformation, the delicate balance of tacit religious toleration was disturbed, a process exacerbated by an outbreak of Calvinist iconoclasm in 1566. The main figures in the early

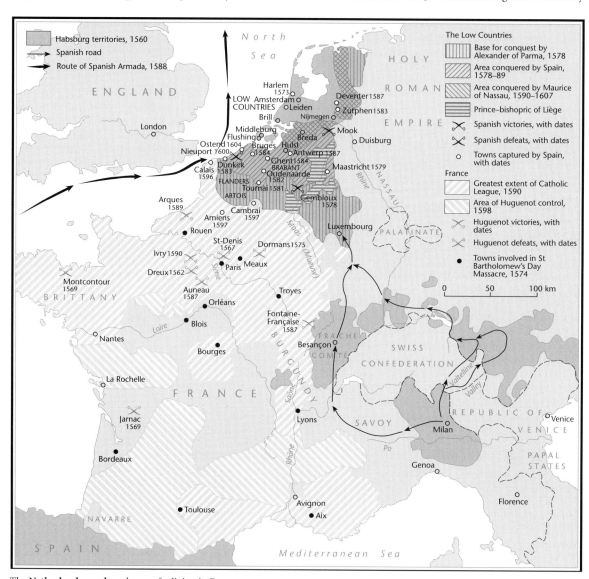

The **Netherlands revolt** and wars of religion in France.

part of the revolt were the enigmatic *William 'the Silent', whose diplomatic skill and tenacity more than compensated for his many military failures, and Philip's captain general the Duke of *Alba, whose competent generalship was accompanied by a brutal oppression that gave the provinces a common cause against Habsburg rule. By the dispossessions of the infamous Council of Blood (1567–74), Alba made an enemy of the previously temporizing William and created a class of embittered lesser nobility and fanatical Calvinists who became the 'Geuzen' ((Sea) Beggars), privateers operating from England into the maritime provinces of Zeeland and Holland. By simultaneously imposing a 10 per cent sales tax, he also united Catholic and Protestant merchant magnates. Finally, by the judicial murders of counts Egmond and Hoorne he removed William's principal rivals for leadership of all Netherlands factions.

The first phase of the revolt witnessed military failures by William and his brothers, and growing success in the *guerrilla campaign waged by the Sea Beggars from bases in England. Evicted from these in 1572, they seized Brielle and the maritime provinces rose in spontaneous revolt, inviting William to lead them, which he did to a string of almost unbroken defeats on land. At sea it remained another matter, and one of the features of the campaign was the manner in which the rebels could flood terrain to halt the advance of Spanish armies. It was a grinding war of sieges, among the more notable being the heroic resistance of Leyden for eleven months in 1573–4, but imperial brutality such as the 'Spanish Fury' in Antwerp, where 7,000 inhabitants were killed, preserved rebel unity.

The second phase began when disorder among the Spanish emboldened all the provinces to proclaim William their stadtholder, neatly reaffirming his imperial title while underlining their relative independence. This unity did not survive the appointment as imperial captains general of the two ablest generals of the period, Don Juan of Austria and his diplomatically as well as militarily gifted successor Parma. It was the great misfortune of *Maurice of Nassau that the latter was his opponent when he succeeded his assassinated father, and by 1579 the provinces were divided into the Protestant (Dutch-speaking) northern provinces allied by the Union of Utrecht and the Catholic (French-speaking) south that acquiesced to continued imperial rule by the Union of Arras.

Once again only topography and the unlimited scope of Habsburg ambition saved the now United Provinces. England, uneasy about helping a rival in maritime trade, was an undependable ally even after the *Spanish Armada fiasco of 1588, although this had the beneficial effect of demoralizing the Spanish and removing the deadly Parma from the scene. Maurice enjoyed a period of military success until his bad luck resumed with the appearance of the brilliant Genoese soldier of fortune *Spinola to breathe new life into the imperial cause. Happily for the Dutch, the Spanish court distrusted him and despite an unbroken string of victories he was obliged by lack of funds to agree to the Twelve Years Truce in 1609, which de facto recognized the independence of the United Provinces.

The third phase formed part of the greater *Thirty Years War. Maurice died while besieged by Spinola at Breda in 1625, the fall of which was immortalized by Velázquez and reckoned to be among the most remarkable military achievements of the period. Once again the Spanish court sabotaged its brilliant field commander and let the United Provinces off the hook. The tide finally turned when the Dutch won a crushing victory against the Spanish fleet at the battle of the Downs in 1639, while French intervention ensured that they made no headway on land. In 1648, as a part of the Treaty of Westphalia, the exhausted Habsburgs wrote off 80 years of ruinous expense and persistent strategic vulnerability, and at last gave *de jure* recognition to the fact of Dutch independence.   RH

New Model Army The Long Parliament created the New Model Army in early 1645 as a response to the nearly disastrous loss of momentum in the English civil war with the king (see BRITISH CIVIL WARS). The previous December the Commons had adopted a Self-Denying Resolution aimed at removing Members of both Houses from all offices, military or civil, for the duration of the war. Blocked by the Lords, it was not passed as an ordinance for another four months. In the meantime the Commons outflanked the Lords' opposition by creating a new army as if the Self-Denying Ordinance were already law. An amalgamation of the three existing armies of Essex, Manchester, and Waller, the New Model was composed two-thirds of infantry—most of whom were conscripts—and one-third of cavalry—all of whom were volunteers. It numbered 22,000 men, in addition to 2,300 officers. Its creation marked a victory for the war party over the peace party led by the Earl of Essex.

*Fairfax was named captain general (C-in-C), apparently because of his excellent military record in the north, and his lack of involvement in the political infighting that had plagued the southern armies. The peace party tried unsuccessfully to alter his officer list, but they did not forget their resentment against *Cromwell. When the Commons majority tried to override the Self-Denying Ordinance by naming him lieutenant general (second in command) of the cavalry, the peace party peers balked. Only the New Model's stunning victory at *Naseby obliged them retroactively to approve Cromwell's appointment.

The triumph at Naseby owed not a little to the king's great blunder in attacking a force nearly twice as large as his own. Even then the battle was a close thing. But the rest of the first civil war was essentially a mopping-up operation. By June 1646 the king had surrendered. In the previous fifteen months the New Model had not lost so much as a skirmish; indeed, it would lose no important engagement throughout the second civil war (1648) and the invasions of Ireland (1649–52) and Scotland (1650–1).

How are we to explain this formidable battlefield record? A major factor was the New Model's generous financing through the monthly assessment. Secondly, it had access to a great economic powerhouse—London. Vast quantities of clothing, gunpowder, pikes, halberds, swords, and muskets poured out of the workshops of the metropolis. *Religion was another factor in the army's success. It galvanized men to risk their lives in battle, and furnished them with the confidence that they would win. A high proportion of the officers were devout Puritans who stamped the army with their own conviction that they were fighting the warfare of heaven. The practical result was to breed in the soldiers the courage to perform many acts of daring and improvisation.

In the spring of 1647, to defend themselves from disbandment or exile to Ireland, the rank and file revolted by seizing the king, calling for a rendezvous of the army, and securing the creation of a General Council of the Army to oversee political affairs. The council comprised the higher officers, and representatives or 'agitators' elected by each troop or company. It was this body that debated the Leveller Agreement of the People at Putney in the autumn of 1647.

The royalist, Scots-supported uprisings of 1648 were easily snuffed out by the New Model's battle-seasoned veterans. The key encounter occurred at Preston when Cromwell outmanoeuvred and shattered a joint force of English and Scots royalists. Angered at parliament's continued negotiations with the king, the army now began denouncing him as 'that man of blood', and demanding that he be brought to justice for his crimes against the people. The army then purged parliament of moderate MPs and oversaw the trial and execution of the king. Once the republic had been proclaimed the officers set about to organize the invasion of Ireland in the summer of 1649. To the accompaniment of massacres at Drogheda and Wexford, the Catholic Irish were beaten into submission, though their formal surrender required another three years of intense warfare and a continually increasing commitment of troops from England. Cromwell had to leave Ireland in May 1650 to deal with a resurgent royalist threat from Scotland.

Under his leadership at Dunbar (1650) and Worcester (1651) Charles II was driven out and the New Model clinched its mastery of the three kingdoms. From that point it fought no more battles on British soil. Its political interventions—expelling the Rump, engineering the dissolution of Barebone's Parliament (both in 1653), and vetoing Cromwell's acceptance of the crown (1657)—testified to its power, if not to its political imagination. Ironically, the army which had forced the execution of one king in 1649, was instrumental, thanks to Gen George Monck, in restoring that king's son in 1660. By inviting Charles II back the army had brought the revolution full circle.　　　IG

Firth, Charles H., *Cromwell's Army* (4th edn., London, 1962).

Gentles, Ian, *The New Model Army in England, Ireland and Scotland, 1645–1653* (Oxford, 1992).

Kishlansky, Mark A., *The Rise of the New Model Army* (New York and Cambridge, 1979).

Ney, Marshal Michel, Duc d'Elchingen, Prince de la Moskowa (1769–1815). A red-headed cooper's son from Saarlouis, Ney enlisted in the hussars in 1787, became regimental serjeant major in April 1792, and was commissioned that autumn. He made his reputation commanding cavalry in the Army of the Sambre et Meuse, and confirmed it by marrying a protégée of the future Empress Josephine. Appointed marshal in 1804, he commanded IV Corps with distinction in 1805–7, and was created Duc d'Elchingen in 1808. Sent to Spain in 1810, he fell out with *Masséna, who sent him home in disgrace. Speedily re-employed, he led III Corps with distinction in 1812, and his conduct during the retreat earned widespread admiration. He was amongst the last out of Russia, on foot, musket in hand: *Napoleon called him 'the bravest of the brave'.

The experience helped unbalance Ney, who grew increasingly jealous of other marshals. Though his courage never faltered, his judgement was poor, and at Bautzen he misunderstood Napoleon's intentions and botched his plan. Although he fought gallantly in 1814, when he saw the cause was hopeless he demanded Napoleon's abdication on behalf of the other marshals. Given immediate employment by the Bourbons, he was sent to arrest Napoleon at the start of the *Hundred Days, but went over to him. Belatedly given command of the left wing for the *Waterloo campaign, he failed to clinch victory at Quatre Bras. Entrusted with the main attack at Waterloo, Ney proved typically gallant but headstrong, and had four horses shot under him. Even when the day was lost he sought to rally men with the cry: 'Come, and see how a Marshal of France can die!' Arrested by the Bourbons, he was shot by firing squad at the Luxembourg Gardens. Like his comrade *Murat, he himself gave the order to fire.　　　RH

NGS. See NAVAL GUNFIRE SUPPORT.

Nicaragua, US military intervention in (1926–33) (see also IRAN-CONTRA AFFAIR). American military involvement in Nicaragua dates back to a civil war in 1910–12, when 2,300 US sailors and Marines were landed to protect American lives and property, and to decide the outcome against the revolutionaries. A 100-man Marine 'embassy guard' remained in Managua until 1925.

In 1926 another revolution provoked American fears of communist influence. By accepting the unpopular government's invitation to intervene on its behalf, they made themselves the target of a patriotic reaction led by Sandino, one of the rebel officers. In July 1927 he directed an assault on a US Marine and Nicaraguan guard post at Ocotal, which was only defeated by the first dive-bombing attack in aviation history. A peak of 5,000 US sailors and Marines were involved in the ensuing *guerrilla war, the last being withdrawn in 1933.

They left behind a well-equipped National Guard under 'Tacho' Somoza, a loathsome man of no military ability who used his good command of English to curry favour with American officers and diplomats. It was of him that Franklin *Roosevelt commented, 'he may be an SOB, but he's *our* SOB'. In 1934 Somoza assassinated Sandino after tricking him to come to Managua for peace talks, and from 1936 he and his sons ruled, brutally and venally, until 'Tachito' was overthrown by latter-day Sandinistas in 1979, to be assassinated in Paraguay the following year.

During the campaign, famed US Marine 'Chesty' Puller won two Navy Crosses when commanding a company of the National Guard. Unlike the rest of the Guard and the occupying forces, which were committed to garrison duties, Puller patrolled guerrilla territory aggressively, earning the nickname 'El Tigre' (The Tiger) and a price reluctantly put on his head by Sandino, who admired him as a fellow warrior.   HEB

Nigerian civil war (1967–70). This was an attempt at secession by the Ibo-dominated Eastern Region of Nigeria suppressed by the federal Nigerian authorities in a bitter three-year civil war. Nigeria achieved independence from Britain as a federal state in 1960. Her 430 different ethnic groups were dominated by three peoples: the Islamic Hausa-Fulbe in the north, the Yoruba, and the Christian Ibo (Igbo) in the south-eastern part of Nigeria. Under British colonial rule, the Ibos had become an educated élite and after independence there was much resentment of them. In 1966 thousands of Ibos living in the north were killed in ethnic rioting, and as a result many Ibos fled their homes and moved to traditional Ibo territory in the south-east of Nigeria.

In 1966, after two successive military governments, power passed to Lt Col (later Gen) Yakuba Gowon, who was immediately faced with a move by the Ibo-dominated Eastern Region to break away. In May 1967, the military governor of the Eastern Region, Lt Col Odumegwu Ojukwa, declared an independent state of 'Biafra'. The Biafran army then went on the offensive in a push towards Lagos. Gowon's federal troops stemmed this advance and counter-attacked. In the ensuing civil war, Gowon had the advantage of international recognition and continued to receive regular supplies of arms from abroad. He was determined to bring the oil-rich region back into Nigeria and his troops began a systematic reduction of Biafra. Without Biafra's oil, the financial viability of Nigeria seemed in doubt. The Biafrans, while garnering much international sympathy, received little official recognition for their nascent state. While Biafra was determined to resist federal rule, without international recognition it was at a serious disadvantage. European *mercenaries, international aid agencies, and a trickle of supplies on flights from friendly neighbouring states helped keep Biafra in the war, but by 1968 the rebels were landlocked, having lost their coastline and Port Harcourt to federal troops. The cost of the war was immense: the federal *blockade and the dislocation of the war led to widespread famine that killed some one million Ibos. Biafran resistance finally collapsed following a series of engagements in late 1969 and early 1970. Ojukwa fled to Ivory Coast and in January 1970 Gowon's 'police action' ended.   MH

Jorre, John De St, *The Nigerian Civil War* (London, 1972).

Nightingale, Florence (1820–1910), army nursing and hygiene reformer. She began her association with British military health during the *Crimean war in October 1854 when she led female *nurses to the *hospitals at Scutari (Shkodër). She improved cleanliness, organization, and cooking. The male orderlies who did the bulk of the actual nursing were smartened up, while Nightingale's private stores of clothing, bedding, and food enabled her to disregard army parsimony. For her, hospital management was simply good housekeeping. She answered enquiries from kin and wrote condolences to families of common soldiers. Roving journalists and her family publicized her labours. 'The Lady with the Lamp' symbolized compassionate duty and efficiency amidst a bungled war.

Her experiences at Scutari convinced her that the impediment to maximal military capability was illness. This waste was remediable through common-sense reforms. These included army provisioning rather than dependence on local suppliers; *commissariats freed from red tape; land transport under clear military control; sanitary officers to advise on encampments; hospital management clarified and strengthened; an army medical school; comprehensive rules for victualling, canteens, washing, soldiers' wives, nurses, wage stoppages; fuller sickness statistics and their use towards improvement. She was not the only begetter of this programme, but she dramatized its urgency.

Nightingale, an irregular by disposition and circumstance, conspired with reformers in the army, parliament, bureaucracy, and court to fight the diehard Horse Guards and stingy ministers. Privately, she manipulated the memberships, evidence, and reports of royal commissions into the sanitary condition of the army (1858) and the army in India (1863). Publicly she reinforced these investigations with critical surveys of army mortality (1858), army sanitary administration (1862), and sanitation in India (1863, 1864). She held a miasmatic explanation of disease and urged fresh air and cleanliness. Her interest had turned to the subcontinent after the *Indian Mutiny. She perceived that the new white, costly army required to hold the dominion could be maintained only by sanitary reform. As at home, she drove up Indian public spending in good causes.

Nightingale's huge cosmopolitan correspondence with eminent persons established female nursing and sanitary works as goals for nations. The International *Red Cross appropriated her in the 1860s, despite her distrust of international conventions and supranational relief services. The world heroine had rendered her causes morally imperative and essential to national military power.   FBS

Nimitz, Adm Chester

Nimitz, Adm Chester (1885–1966), commander of US forces in the *Pacific campaign during WW II. In terms of the resources under his operational command and the strategic vision required of him, he was arguably the greatest admiral in history.

Appointed following the attack on *Pearl Harbor, he made daring use of his aircraft carriers to halt further Japanese advances at *Midway, while unleashing a campaign of unrestricted submarine warfare that eventually sank more warship tonnage than all other arms combined. Despite the intense partisanship of King, his own C-in-C, and of his imperious subordinate *MacArthur, he kept inter-service rivalry under control during the many combined operations that followed. A key factor was the lack of personal vanity he showed in letting MacArthur take the lead during the Japanese capitulation aboard the USS *Missouri*, confident that the battleship herself made a sufficiently clear statement about the navy's preponderant role in the victory.

Although honoured by his own countrymen, the Japanese respect him as a *samurai on a par with their own great Adm Togo, whom he greatly admired. Behind his Texas birthplace there is a replica of the latter's garden, donated in gratitude for Nimitz's leading role in the restoration of Togo's flagship *Mikasa*.   HEB

ninja

ninja (otherwise *shinobi no mono*, men of secrecy) were the assassins, spies, and secret agents of Japan at the time of the *samurai. Legend has greatly embellished accounts of their activities, which, together with popular movies and comic books, has created a myth of the ninja as an invincible and deadly secret warrior. Pictorial representations of them, which date from the early 19th century, have reinforced a visual image of them as superior warriors who dressed from head to foot in black, although this is likely to be no more than an artistic convention as there are no contemporary references to such costumes, and accounts of surprise attacks often mention the assailants dressing in such a way as to blend in with their victims. Nonetheless, reports of assassinations carried out by men who climbed into castles or fortified camps reinforce the authenticity of the profession, even if the 'superman' image may be readily

discarded. The chronicle of the Hōjō family also makes reference to such men being used to cause confusion in an enemy camp before an attack, and spies were certainly used during the siege of Hara castle in 1638.   SRT

Nivelle offensive

Nivelle offensive (1917), named after its architect, the charismatic French Gen Robert Nivelle, who succeeded *Joffre as C-in-C of the French army in December 1916. Nivelle sang a siren song to both the British premier *Lloyd George and French politicians, disillusioned with static war and heavy casualties. His fluent English (learnt from his English mother) helped him persuade Lloyd George to put *Haig under his command for the duration of the battle, in order to mount a diversionary attack at *Arras/Vimy Ridge.

Nivelle's plan was based on tactics he had used on a much smaller scale at *Verdun. It involved mass infantry attacks on a broad front, supported for the first time by tanks, and preceded by a swift, rolling artillery *barrage, unlike previous assaults which had been heralded by long *bombardments. He had been a good army commander and his plan might have had some chance of success—though not on the enormous scale he hoped for—had not the Germans withdrawn suddenly in the spring of 1917 to the *Hindenburg Line. This move, relinquishing territory but taking up a much shorter and cunningly sited defensive line, left Nivelle's plans dangerously up in the air, but he did not change them. His tactics had been much discussed within France, and Nivelle, swept along by the tide of his own rhetoric, had championed them more vigorously than the evidence warranted. News of the threat reached the Germans, who fortuitously captured a copy of the plan. They widened their trenches in the crucial Aisne sector to confound the French tanks, built extra concealed machine-gun bunkers, posted additional artillery nearby, and circulated information which would enable them to shell French trenches at their most crowded.

The 'lightning' bombardment fell on a 25 mile (40 km) stretch of front between Rheims and Soissons on 5 April 1917, but the infantry attack was postponed several times due to the weather. French troops eventually slithered out of their trenches in appalling conditions on 16 April, by which time the Germans were fully alerted. The French tanks were halted and destroyed by artillery fire and the 'creeping' barrage moved forwards too fast for the accompanying infantry. German machine guns and artillery exploited the window of opportunity after the hurricane of shells had passed, and caused 134,000 French casualties between 16 and 29 April, 80 per cent during the first day's fighting. Penetrations were made in some places and 11,000 prisoners taken, but the 48 hour victory was undeliverable.

Nivelle's failure caused troops in 68 of France's 112 scattered infantry divisions to *mutiny, first expressed in a refusal to return to the front by troops rotating from rear areas. Nivelle's failure was the latest in a string of costly defeats, the last straw for the war-weary *poilu*. The government, alarmed by the scale and consistency of the mutineers' grievances, summoned *Pétain, the hero of Verdun, to take command of the army. Nivelle, sacked on 15 May, was packed off to command French forces in North Africa. Although Haig was not aware of its scale, the French breakdown reaffirmed the need for the British to take the initiative, and this played a part—though it remains impossible to be sure how much of a part—in persuading him to fight the third battle of *Ypres three months later.   APC-A

Noailles family Titled French family with a long and distinguished military, clerical, and scientific tradition. The Noailles can be traced back to the 13th century. Anne (d. 1678), grandson of the first count, Antoine de Noailles, was created first duc de Noailles and a peer of France in 1663. A successful soldier, he became premier captain of Louis XIV's bodyguard in 1648 and was made captain general (governor) of the newly captured province of Roussillon. The head of the house was usually appointed to this title thereafter.

Anne's son, the second duke, Anne-Jules (1650–1708), fought with distinction in the War of the *Spanish Succession, and was made a marshal of France in 1693. The third duke, Adrien Maurice (1678–1766), also served *Louis XIV during the War of the Spanish Succession and was made a marshal of France, as such commanding French forces with considerable skill in the War of the Polish Succession (1733–8). However, he was less successful in the War of the *Austrian Succession and was defeated by the Hanoverians and British at *Dettingen. He was succeeded in 1766 by his son the fourth duke, Louis (1713–93), who served in most of the wars of the 18th century with no particular distinction but was still made a marshal of France.

Louis Marie, Vicomte de Noailles (1756–1804), was one of the most distinguished military members of the family. He served with great élan under *Lafayette during the *American independence war and was the officer who negotiated the capitulation of *Yorktown. He emigrated to the USA during the French Revolution and accepted a command against the English in San Domingo. It did not prosper and he was forced to escape with his men to Cuba, but their ship was attacked by an English frigate and he was killed.
MCM

Nobel, Alfred Bernhard (1833–96), Swedish chemist who amassed one of the largest fortunes of his day as the inventor of dynamite. Uncertain of a career, the young Nobel discovered an aptitude for chemistry and engineering. A year spent travelling around Europe, the USA, and Russia also gave him a commercial perspective, and he settled down on his return to study explosives. Concentrating his attention on nitroglycerine, he developed it into a safer version for handling, which he patented as dynamite in 1862. He later combined nitroglycerine with gun cotton to create a clear jelly, patented in 1867 as Blasting Gelatin. He also invented a *smokeless powder called ballistite. On the arrival of the similar cordite in 1889, he unsuccessfully sued the British government for infringement of one of his 355 patents. By then he had also devised detonators incorporating fulminate of mercury, which allowed his other explosives to be set off at will. The military applications of his inventions were significant, for they coincided with the move from muzzle-loaders to *breech-loading weapons, which required ammunition with more powerful explosive in a self-contained capsule. His blasting powders and fuses were also instrumental in the revival of the hand *grenade shortly after his death. He died disillusioned with his inventions, and, having no family, left his fortune in trust for the establishment of five prizes—today's Nobel Prizes for Physics, Chemistry, Physiology or Medicine, Literature, and, always controversially, Peace.   APC-A

Nogi, Gen Marusuke (1849–1912). Nogi was declared a 'war god' after the *Russo-Japanese war. Following a landing in Korea the Japanese under Nogi took *Port Arthur in June 1904 after a vicious siege with the loss of 100,000 Japanese troops. The victory released Nogi's forces for an advance on *Mukden, which was taken following a fierce frontal assault. Despite the accolade given to him, Nogi was ashamed of his performance and wanted to commit suicide. The Meiji emperor denied him permission, so Nogi had to wait until the death of his sovereign before expiating his guilt.   SRT

non-commissioned officer. See NCO.

Normandy campaign (1944). The western Allies had long agreed that continental Europe should be invaded as soon as practicable, and the Soviets vigorously demanded a second front to reduce German pressure in the east. However, the British, with imperial commitments and the painful legacy of WW I, were more cautious than their allies. In August 1942 a raid on *Dieppe by a Canadian division failed with heavy casualties, but by illustrating the problems of cross-Channel assault it gave planners an early indication that specialized armoured vehicles and landing craft would be required for a subsequent attack. At the Casablanca conference in January 1943 *Churchill and Franklin D. Roosevelt agreed that the Allies would develop operations in the Mediterranean and continue with the bombing of Germany. Although there was as yet no supreme commander for the operation, the British Lt Gen Morgan, COS Supreme Allied Commander (Designate) (COSSAC), began

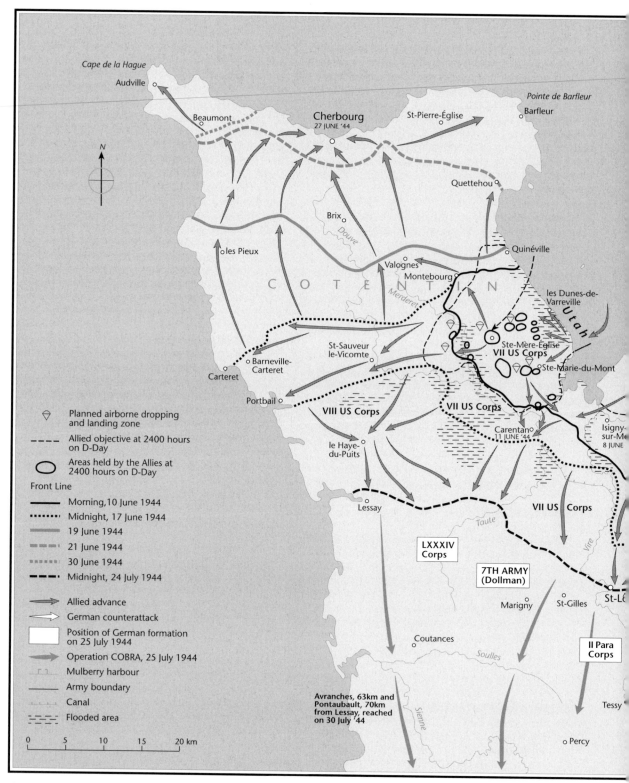

Cape de la Hague

Audville

Beaumont

Cherbourg
27 JUNE '44

St-Pierre-Église

Pointe de Barfleur

Barfleur

N

Quettehou

Brix

Douve

les Pieux

Valognes

Montebourg

Quinéville

C O T E N T I N

les Dunes-de-
Varreville

Merderet

Utah

St-Sauveur
le-Vicomte

Ste-Mère-Église

VII US Corps

Barneville-
Carteret

Ste-Marie-du-Mont

Carteret

Portbail

VIII US Corps

VII US Corps

Isigny-
sur-M

le Haye-
du-Puits

Carentan
11 JUNE '44

8 JUNE

Lessay

VII US   Corps

Taute

Vire

LXXXIV
Corps

7TH ARMY
(Dollman)

St-Lô

Marigny

St-Gilles

Planned airborne dropping
and landing zone

Allied objective at 2400 hours
on D-Day

Areas held by the Allies at
2400 hours on D-Day

Front Line

Morning, 10 June 1944

Midnight, 17 June 1944

19 June 1944

21 June 1944

30 June 1944

Midnight, 24 July 1944

Allied advance

German counterattack

Position of German formation
on 25 July 1944

Operation COBRA, 25 July 1944

Mulberry harbour

Army boundary

Canal

Flooded area

Coutances

Soulles

II Para
Corps

Tessy

Avranches, 63km and
Pontaubault, 70km
from Lessay, reached
on 30 July '44

Sienne

Percy

0   5   10   15   20 km

The **Normandy campaign,** June 1944: the Normandy landings, Operation OVERLORD.

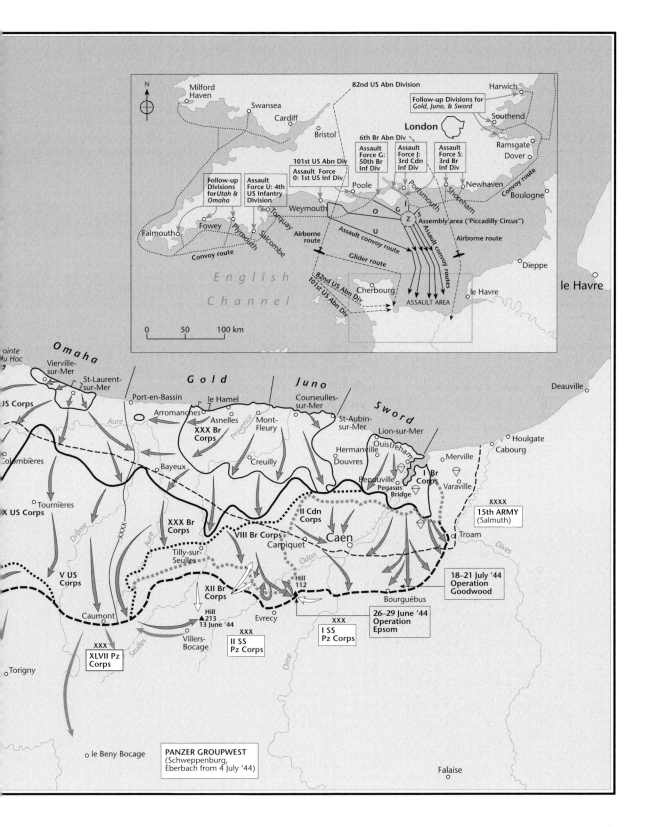

N

Milford
Haven
Swansea
Cardiff
Bristol

82nd US Abn Division

Harwich

Follow-up Divisions for
Gold, Juno, & Sword

London

Southend

Ramsgate
Dover

6th Br Abn Div

101st US Abn Div

**Assault Force
G:
50th Br
Inf Div**

**Assault
Force J:
3rd Cdn
Inf Div**

**Assault
Force
S:
3rd Br
Inf Div**

Poole

Portsmouth
Shoreham

Newhaven

Boulogne

**Follow-up
Divisions
for** *Utah &
Omaha*

**Assault
Force U: 4th
US Infantry
Division**

**Assault Force
O: 1st US Inf Div**

Weymouth

Torquay

O

G
J
S

Z

Assembly area ('Piccadilly Circus')

Convoy route

Falmouth
Fowey
Plymouth
Salcombe

**Airborne
route**

Assault convoy route

U

Assault convoy routes

Airborne route

Dieppe

*English
Channel*

Glider route

82nd US Abn Div

101st US Abn Div

Cherbourg

ASSAULT AREA

le Havre

le Havre

0   50   100 km

Omaha
Pointe
du Hoc
Vierville-
sur-Mer
St-Laurent-
sur-Mer

Gold

Port-en-Bassin

le Hamel

Juno

Courseulles-
sur-Mer

Sword

Deauville

US Corps

Arromanches
Asnelles
Mont-
Fleury

St-Aubin-
sur-Mer

Houlgate
Cabourg

Colombières

Bayeux

**XXX Br
Corps**

Creuilly

Lion-sur-Mer

Hermanville
Douvres

Merville

Ouistreham

**I Br
Corps**

Varaville

X US Corps

Tournières

XXXX

Aure
Drôme
Aure
Provence

**XXX Br
Corps**

Tilly-sur-
Seulles

VIII Br Corps

Carpiquet

**II Cdn
Corps**

Caen

Bénouville
Pegasus
Bridge

Troam

Dives

**XXXX
15th ARMY
(Salmuth)**

V US
Corps

Caumont

**XII Br
Corps**

Odon

Hill
112

Evrecy

Hill
▲213
13 June '44

**XXX
II SS
Pz Corps**

**XXX
I SS
Pz Corps**

Bourguébus

**18–21 July '44
Operation
Goodwood**

**26–29 June '44
Operation
Epsom**

Torigny

**XXX
XLVII Pz
Corps**

Seulles

Villers-
Bocage

Orne

le Beny Bocage

PANZER GROUPWEST
(Schweppenburg,
Eberbach from 4 July '44)

Falaise

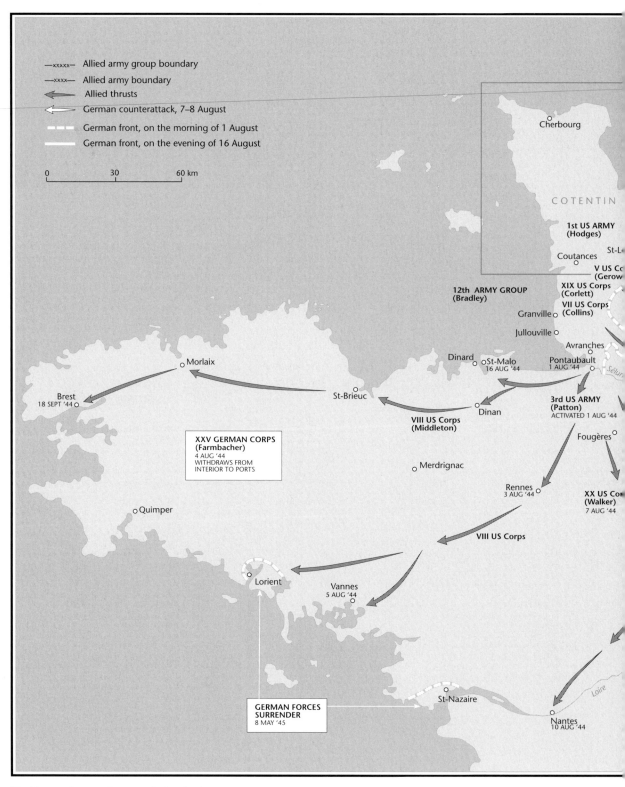

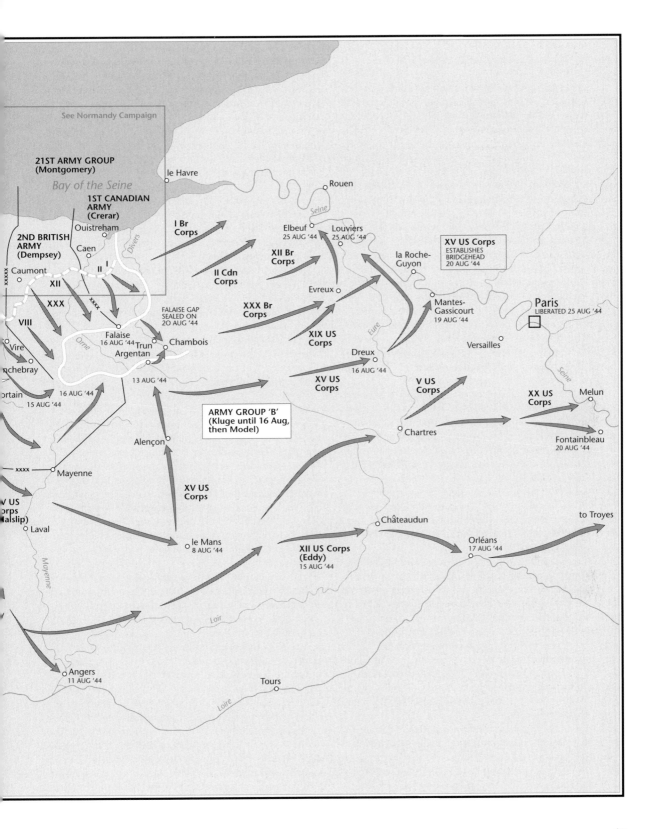

See Normandy Campaign

21ST ARMY GROUP
(Montgomery)

Bay of the Seine

1ST CANADIAN
ARMY
(Crerar)

Ouistreham

2ND BRITISH
ARMY
(Dempsey)

Caen

Caumont

XXXX

XII

XXX

VIII

Vire

nchebray

ortain

15 AUG '44

16 AUG '44

Orne

Falaise
16 AUG '44

Trun

Argentan

Chambois

13 AUG '44

le Havre

Rouen

Seine

Elbeuf
25 AUG '44

Louviers
25 AUG '44

la Roche-
Guyon

I Br
Corps

XII Br
Corps

II Cdn
Corps

Evreux

XXX Br
Corps

XIX US
Corps

Dreux
16 AUG '44

XV US Corps
ESTABLISHES
BRIDGEHEAD
20 AUG '44

Mantes-
Gassicourt
19 AUG '44

Eure

Versailles

Paris
LIBERATED 25 AUG '44

FALAISE GAP
SEALED ON
20 AUG '44

XV US
Corps

V US
Corps

XX US
Corps

Melun

Seine

ARMY GROUP 'B'
(Kluge until 16 Aug,
then Model)

Chartres

Fontainbleau
20 AUG '44

Alençon

XXXX

Mayenne

XV US
Corps

to Troyes

Châteaudun

Orléans
17 AUG '44

V US
orps
alslip)

Laval

Mayenne

le Mans
8 AUG '44

XII US Corps
(Eddy)
15 AUG '44

Loir

Angers
11 AUG '44

Tours

Loire

653

planning an invasion, and a target date of 1 May 1944 was set.

COSSAC staff considered two main invasion sites: the Pas de Calais, across the Channel at its narrowest point, and Normandy. They decided on the latter. It was less obvious and less heavily defended; the port of Cherbourg might be captured early on; and, although Normandy was further away than the Pas de Calais, it was well within range of fighters based in Britain and conveniently placed for the many ports and anchorages on the south coast. Morgan believed that it would take two weeks to capture Cherbourg, and in the meantime the Channel weather might make it difficult to land supplies: work was begun on two huge floating sectional harbours (Mulberries) which would be towed to France. Maj Gen Hobart, a pioneer of *armoured warfare, had been brought back from retirement to command an armoured division composed of 'funnies', specialist vehicles which would help the attackers get ashore and fight their way through the beach defences. In addition to the naval plan for the invasion (NEPTUNE) and the invasion itself (OVERLORD), a comprehensive deception plan (FORTITUDE) would seek to persuade the Germans first that the Pas de Calais would be attacked and second that the invasion of Normandy was simply a diversion.

In December 1943 *Eisenhower was appointed Supreme Allied Commander, with a British deputy, ACM Tedder. The component commanders were all British. Naval forces would be commanded by Adm Ramsay, ground forces (Twenty-First Army Group) by *Montgomery, and *air forces by ACM Leigh-Mallory. Montgomery decided that the COSSAC team had allocated too few troops to the initial attack, and directed that five divisions—from east to west British, Canadian, British, and two American—would form the first wave, their flanks protected by three *airborne divisions, the British 6th to the east and the US 82nd and 101st to the west.

Concurrent activity proceeded on a massive scale. Intelligence on the invasion area was gleaned from the French Resistance, air *reconnaissance, and even holiday postcards requested by the BBC. Air attacks wreaked havoc on German road and rail communications, though in such a way that the invasion sector was not especially favoured. The Mulberries and landing craft were built, and as Montgomery's plan demanded more of the latter the invasion date slipped to 5 June. FORTITUDE gained momentum, persuading the Germans that an American army group under *Patton was in south-east England, ready for a descent on the Pas de Calais.

The Germans knew that invasion was likely. Their forces in France and the Low Countries, under C-in-C West *Rundstedt, comprised Army Group G, in southern France, and *Rommel's Army Group B. The latter's Seventh Army held Normandy, with the Fifteenth responsible for the Pas de Calais, Belgium, and the Netherlands. The Germans had been at work on the defences of the Atlantic wall since 1942,

and Rommel pushed the work ahead as quickly as he could. His own experience in *North Africa persuaded him that the textbook solution for dealing with amphibious invasion—identifying its main thrust, and then concentrating reserves to meet it—would not work in Normandy because of Allied air power. He was convinced that the invasion would have to be stopped on the beaches, and that, for Allies and Germans alike, the first day would be the longest. Both Rundstedt and the commander of *Panzergruppe* West, Gen Geyr von Schweppenburg, disagreed. The argument was made more complex by the fact that most German armoured divisions in Normandy could not be moved without Hitler's personal authority. When the invasion came Rommel had only one usable armoured division, 21st Panzer, in the immediate area.

The west played second fiddle to the *eastern front, and the bulk of German combat-ready divisions were there. Many divisions in the west were understrength and still relied on horse-drawn transport. There were many foreign troops, most of them former Soviet *POWs who spoke little German. Allied bombing wore down the German arms industry, forced the diversion of manpower and material to the air defence of the Reich, and had already done serious damage to the Luftwaffe.

Bad weather compelled Eisenhower to postpone the invasion for 24 hours, and even on 5 June the forecast was uncertain. Early that morning Eisenhower, in his headquarters at Southwick House near Portsmouth, took the brave decision to go ahead on the 6th, which was to become D-Day. Almost 5,000 ships set out, and parachutists and *glider troops prepared to board their aircraft. The first blow fell just after midnight on the 6th when a company of 2nd Oxfordshire and Buckinghamshire Light Infantry secured the bridges over the Caen canal and the river Orne just north of Caen. Shortly afterwards the airborne divisions began to arrive, and although they were widely spread, with some men lost in the sea or flooded rivers, their arrival helped confuse German commanders. German response was not helped by the fact that Rommel was on leave in Germany and many senior officers were on their way to a war game at Rennes.

The British and Canadian landings on GOLD, JUNO, and SWORD beaches went much as planned, although exploitation inland was somewhat disappointing, and the British 3rd Division, in the east, failed to capture Caen. Although the American landing on UTAH beach went well, at OMAHA beach the Americans ran into a strong defence and, with most of their amphibious tanks swamped offshore and lacking the specialist armour used in the British sector, they suffered heavily before wresting a toehold. The results of D-Day were impressive enough. Over 150,000 Allied soldiers were ashore, and the expected German counter-attack had failed to materialize: even 21st Panzer Division, dangerously close to SWORD beach and the British airborne landings, had not been committed until it was too late.

Over the days that followed, the Allies linked up their beachheads and, while the Americans swung up the Cotentin peninsula towards Cherbourg, Montgomery made the first of several attempts to take Caen. The 7th Armoured Division, with desert experience but uneasy in the very different terrain of Normandy, was checked at Villers-Bocage on 12–14 June. Cherbourg fell at the end of June, but the harbour was so thoroughly damaged that it took months to repair. On 24–30 June the British launched EPSOM, another attempt to outflank Caen from the west, and made slow progress in very heavy fighting.

The characteristics of the battle for Normandy, where the intensity of the fighting at times resembled that on the western front in WW I, were already clear. The Allies enjoyed superior resources, and sustained themselves despite a storm which destroyed the American Mulberry and damaged the British. Their air power played havoc with German units on their way to the front and made movement in the battle area risky. But they lacked relevant experience, and sometimes their morale wavered. The *bocage* terrain of western Normandy favoured the resolute defender, and there was growing concern at an invasion which seemed to have stuck fast. Yet German commanders were no more sanguine. Hitler replaced the gloomy Rundstedt with FM von Kluge, who arrived filled with a confidence which soon evaporated. Rommel was wounded in an air attack on 17 July, and three days later the bomb plot increased the tensions between Hitler and his senior commanders.

Montgomery's role remains controversial. He was to maintain that his master plan involved fixing German armour in the east to allow the Americans to break out in the west, while his critics have suggested that he was in fact more opportunistic. He was under pressure to take decisive action when, on 18 July, he launched three armoured divisions east of Caen in GOODWOOD. The attack was preceded by a strike by Allied heavy bombers, and it may be that the need to secure the support of the strategic bombing force induced Montgomery to oversell the operation to Eisenhower. It cost almost 6,000 casualties and 400 tanks, and produced no breakout. Montgomery argued that this did not matter, for he had attracted German reserves, giving *Bradley, in command of the US First Army, the chance to break out.

On 25 July Bradley mounted COBRA, west of Saint-Lô. Its initial aims were modest, but Lt Gen Collins, commanding the assaulting corps, realized that he had achieved a breakthrough and hustled on towards Avranches. It had been planned that when the Americans had sufficient forces in theatre they would activate the US Third Army under *Patton, with Lt Gen Hodges taking over First Army while Bradley became commander of Twelfth Army Group. Patton, ideally suited to fighting a mobile battle, sent some of his troops to Brittany but swung others eastwards. The British and Canadians continued the long slog around Caen, the former taking Mont Pincon and the latter mounting two methodical attacks, operations TOTALISE and TRACTABLE, down the Caen–Falaise road. Hitler insisted on a counter-attack at Mortain with the intention of cutting off Patton, but despite initial progress on 7 August it foundered in the face of Allied air attacks.

German forces in Normandy were squeezed into a pocket around *Falaise, with the Americans curling round from the south while the British, Canadians, and a Polish armoured division, thrust down from the north. Although the Allies were slow to seal off the pocket, enabling many determined Germans to escape, it was the climax of the campaign. The Germans lost most of their guns and vehicles, mainly to Allied air attack. Paris was liberated on 25 August, and the tide of war rolled away. German defeat in Normandy was serious in itself, and on the eastern front operation *BAGRATION destroyed Army Group Centre: Germany's strategic position, parlous three months before, was now impossible.   RH

d'Este, Carlo, *Decision in Normandy* (London, 1983).

Hastings, Max, *Overlord: D Day and the B battle for Normandy* (London, 1984).

Keegan, John, *Six Armies in Normandy* (London, 1982).

Normandy, English loss of (1204). King John's loss of Normandy was probably inevitable in view of the scale of the resources that King Philip II of France could put into its capture. John lacked the calibre of his brother *Richard 'the Lionheart', although he had an early success in 1202 when he relieved Mirebeau and resoundingly defeated his enemies. Rumours that he had his nephew Arthur of Brittany murdered did nothing for his popularity. In the following year his supporters began to desert him. A bold attempt to send supplies to Château Gaillard failed, and John's sack of Dol in Brittany was his only achievement. His reliance on *mercenary troops added to his unpopularity. In March 1204 the storming of Château Gaillard by the French, when John was in England, spelled the beginning of the end. On 24 June Rouen surrendered, and English rule of Normandy came to an end. John's failure to hold the duchy was at least as much political as military, but the lack of clear strategy and effective leadership did nothing to aid the English cause. The Normans had no enthusiasm to fight for a ruler whose efforts to defend the duchy appeared so half-hearted.
                                                                    MCP

Powicke, F. M., *The Loss of Normandy* (Manchester, 1913).

North Africa campaign (1940–3). During WW II there was fighting along much of the North Africa littoral. It was in essence a single theatre of war with two linked campaigns: a British campaign in the *Western Desert, and an Anglo-American campaign, beginning with the TORCH landings in French North Africa in November 1942, and going on to link up with the British advance and eventually

The **North Africa campaign,** WW II: theatre of operations.

overwhelm Axis forces in Tunisia. The see-saw campaign in the Western Desert eventually brought German-Italian forces under *Rommel within striking distance of Alexandria facing a British Eighth Army depressed by defeat. At *Alamein the new British army commander *Montgomery methodically applied superior force and then followed Rommel back across Cyrenaica towards Tunisia, taking Tripoli on 23 January 1943.

A few days after Alamein an Allied invasion force under *Eisenhower landed in French North Africa. There was some fighting with the French before Darlan, a senior minister in *Pétain's Vichy government, who happened to be in Algiers, ordered a ceasefire. Having secured Oran, Algiers, and Casablanca, the Allied First Army advanced eastwards, taking Bone on 12 November before being stopped at Mejez el Bab, just 30 miles (48 km) south-west of Tunis. *Hitler had reacted swiftly to the invasion, sending his troops into the Unoccupied Zone of France and reinforcing his troops in North Africa with what was to become Arnim's Fifth Panzer Army.

Arnim, anxious to prevent the Allies from cutting him off from Rommel, who was withdrawing before Montgomery, stopped First Army in hard-fought battles at Tebourba and Longstop Hill, and then counter-attacked in January 1943, knocking it off balance. When Rommel, who had now fallen back into southern Tunisia, joined in the following month and attacked into the *Kasserine Pass the Allies were even more badly rattled. Eisenhower was preoccupied by political concerns and lacked relevant experience, and many of his troops and their commanders were green. *Alexander was appointed to command an army group

consisting of First and Eighth Armies in order to improve co-ordination.

It was fortunate for the Allies that the Axis forces had problems of their own. Rommel was unhappily under the authority of the Italian *commando supremo* (CGS of the Armed Forces), while Arnim was directed by Kesselring, the German C-in-C South-West. On 23 February Rommel was given command of Army Group Africa: his old German-Italian Panzer Army was retitled First Italian Army under Messe. Rommel was still very dangerous, and planned to use all three of his armoured divisions against Montgomery, who was now approaching the Mareth Line, a pre-war French defensive system, which had been designed to prevent the Italians moving from Libya into south-eastern Tunisia. On 6 March Rommel made an unsuccessful jab at Medenine, just east of the line, and was flown home, a sick man, three days later. Although Montgomery's frontal attack on the Mareth Line failed, he outflanked it from the south, and Messe fell back on Wadi Akarit.

By now Arnim's position was worsening daily as the Allied sea and air blockade throttled him. While Eighth Army took Wadi Akarit and advanced northwards to Sousse and Enfidaville, First Army fought its way towards Bizerta and Tunis. Arnim's men fought hard to the end, but Bizerta and Tunis were both captured on 7 May and the last Axis troops surrendered on 13 May. The Allies took 238,000 prisoners, and had at last won the campaign in North Africa.

Some historians have seen the campaign as a strategic irrelevance for both sides. However, such was the importance of Egypt and the Suez Canal to Britain that it is hard to see how the war in the Western Desert could have been averted.

If the TORCH landings and the advance into Tunisia did not contribute directly to the Allies' main strategic goal, the invasion of *North-West Europe, they certainly provided the Allies with invaluable experience. Given their showing in some battles in the winter of 1942–3 it is difficult to resist the conclusion that the Allies were not ready for a cross-Channel invasion then. However, the theatre was a low strategic priority for both sides. The British would have fared better had they not diverted troops to Greece and the Far East, while far more Germans surrendered in Tunisia than Rommel ever commanded in the Western Desert.

RH

Carver, Michael, *Dilemmas of the Desert War* (London, 1986).
Jackson, William, *The Battle for North Africa* (London, 1975).

North Atlantic Treaty Organization. See NATO.

North Russia intervention force (1918–19), international US, British, French, and Canadian force of all three services inserted into north Russia through Archangel and Murmansk as part of the muddled and unsuccessful intervention in the 1917–20 Russian civil war by the WW I Allies. The *Russian Revolution of November 1917 and the Peace of Brest-Litovsk on 3 March 1918 removed Russia from the war against Germany and Austria-Hungary. The Russian army's contribution to the Allied war effort against the Central Powers had been immense, holding down, even at the end, 160 German and Austro-Hungarian divisions. Now there was nothing to prevent the Germans flinging them against the western front. Nor was there much to keep Germany out of Russia with its vast resources of wheat, oil, coal, and iron. The enormity of Russia's 'defection' from the war helps explain the Allied reaction. On 23 December the British and French agreed to divide south Russia into 'spheres of influence' for activity against Germany. At the same time, the first flames of civil war flared at Rostov on the Don, in December, with action by the Volunteer Army, the 'Whites', or counter-revolutionaries, against the 'Red' forces of the Bolshevik government.

The Allies' first concern was a huge dump of 600,000 tons of war supplies which had been poured into Vladivostok in the Far East as aid, mainly American, to the imperial Russian army, including vast quantities of ammunition and 1,000 motor vehicles. The thought of this falling into the hands of German and Austro-Hungarian prisoners wandering around chaotic Russia and being passed to Germany focused Allied attention on Vladivostok, leading to the landing of US and Japanese troops in Siberia, where 70,000 Japanese and 9,000 US troops were ultimately deployed.

The port of Murmansk had been created in 1915 to bring Allied aid to Russia. Murmansk and Archangel had been the only European Russian ports open to the Allies and here, too, there were thousands of tons of war supplies. By February 1918 the Bolsheviks had taken control of Archangel and were removing them. The British sent a force under Adm Kemp, since Russia was not yet at peace with Germany. On 28 February *Trotsky, believing the peace negotiations had failed, ordered the Murmansk Soviet to do everything to protect the Murmansk railway against the Germans. They did, and on 6 March 130 Royal Marines landed at Murmansk, the first of the North Russian intervention force, at the invitation of Trotsky, a charge *Stalin later held against him.

The importance of the north Russian ports was increased by the presence, somewhere in Russia, of the so-called Czechoslovak Legion. This was 70,000 Czechs and Slovaks, originally Austro-Hungarian *POWs taken by the Russians, who had then been organized, using Allied money, into a force to fight against the Central Powers in order to obtain national independence. The plan was to extract the force, well armed, along the trans-Siberian railway to Vladivostok and then ship it to the western front. In March the French asked their representative at Murmansk if the Czechs and Slovaks could be extracted via that northern port, instead of making the long trek to Vladivostok with the risk that on the way the Bolsheviks would dissuade them from fighting for the Allies. Then, as the force trickled east, the British thought of splitting it. Those already east of the Urals would carry on to Vladivostok; those west of them would travel north. When the Czechs and Slovaks received the order, they thought they were being split to weaken them and, on 14 May, they rebelled and took over Chelyabinsk. Trotsky ordered 'every armed Czech' to be shot, and on 26 May clashes between Czechs and local Bolsheviks broke out all along 3,000 miles (4,827 km) of the trans-Siberian railway. These competent soldiers found themselves the foci of numerous anti-Bolshevik risings, and were the catalyst that really set off the Russian civil war. The Bolsheviks believed they had been paid by the Allies to start the insurrection: in fact, it was just an accident.

The Allies hoped the Czechs were making their way north, and may not have realized they were busily fighting the Bolsheviks. In May Maj Gen F. Poole arrived in Murmansk as 'British Military representative in Russia'. A month later Maj Gen Maynard arrived with 600 men, and completed securing Murmansk. Then they turned to the other port, Archangel.

Here, on 2 August Poole landed a force of 1,500 men in one of the most complex operations in military history. The main elements were a British battalion, a French colonial battalion, some Royal Marines, and 50 US sailors. The British battalion consisted entirely of men unfit for service in France. The three services, including the new RAF, were involved. The British sent seaplanes, which had belonged to the Royal Naval Air Service but now belonged to the RAF, and the seaplane tender *Nairana*. Because Poole's force was not strong enough to take the town by storm, an anti-Bolshevik rising had to be organized in the town and co-ordinated with the landing. In spite of all the complexities, which make it a remarkable early example of a 'combined joint task force' intervening in the chaos of a collapsed state, it worked. But Poole now had 1,500 men to defend an area six times the size of England.

News of the landing reached Moscow on 4 August. No one had any idea how big it was and some estimates put it at 100,000. Like later interventions, the landing provoked increased repression and terror by the Bolsheviks. Foreigners, including diplomats, were arrested, and the landing achieved precisely what it was designed to prevent: an alliance between the Germans and the Bolsheviks.

Murmansk and Archangel remained separate commands, as the Allied strength was built up to 30,000 US, British, French, Canadians, Italians, Russians, Finns, Poles, and Serbs. Half of these (4,000 US, 6,000 British, 2,000 French, and 3,000 Russians) were at Archangel, the rest at Murmansk under Maynard. At Archangel, the seat of the White regime in north Russia, a new commander was appointed, *Ironside, who was also COS to Poole. He arrived on 1 October, in time for the terrible winter campaign of 1918/19. In the summer, the weather was hot; in winter the temperature dropped to −30 °C or −40 °C. The few locals effectively hibernated for the winter; the soldiers had to fight. An American officer, John Cudahy, wrote of the 'vast stretches of cheerless snow reaching far across the river to the murky, brooding skies and the encompassing sheeted forests, so ghostly and so still, where death prowled in the shadows . . . strong men were made cowards by the cumulative depression of the unbroken night'. The troops were often of poor quality and with large supplies of whisky, sold on to the Russians at exorbitant prices, drunkenness was a problem. Ironside confirmed several death sentences.

The irony was that the 11 November *Armistice should have made this intervention, designed to guard against Germany, unnecessary. But it was only after it that intervention in Russia seriously got underway. The main focus for Allied intervention was in south Russia. In Transcaucasia and on the Caspian Sea the British, with their interests in the Middle East and India, and with an eye on the Baku oilfields, intervened. The French intervened in the Ukraine, and were trapped in Odessa by the Bolsheviks. Meanwhile, the north Russian force fought off Bolshevik attacks and sent patrols down the railways and rivers into the endless forests, some of which did not return.

*Churchill was acutely aware of the vulnerability of the force. The US resolved to pull its troops out in February, although because of the ice this would not be possible until June. On 4 March 1919 the British cabinet also resolved to withdraw their forces in June, but to keep them properly reinforced and supplied in the meantime. The main effort of the intervention would be shifted to support *Kolchak and later *Denikin.

The force's departure was delayed. In June, Ironside was ordered to march south from Archangel to link up with one

of Kolchak's armies advancing from the east. Ironside launched a number of successful operations, the last on 10 August, but British politicians were increasingly concerned about casualties in a war which seemed to have no coherent aim. As one Labour MP said, echoing *Bismarck on the subject of the Balkans, 'there is nothing in the political and . . . economic condition of Russia that justifies the sacrifice of another British soldier'.

On 1 September 1919 the evacuation began. The troops were withdrawn in a leapfrogging operation, which ended on 27 September, leaving the head of the Archangel government, a White Russian general called Miller, to his fate. They offered to take Russian refugees, but only 6,000 wanted to go. They also destroyed all the military supplies, in case they fell into Bolshevik hands, to the White Russians' dismay. On 12 October the last transport left Murmansk. British casualties in the campaign were 327 killed and 615 wounded, to no purpose. CDB

Ironside, FM Lord, *Archangel 1918–1919* (London, 1953).
Silverlight, John, *The Victors' Dilemma* (London, 1970).

North-West Europe campaign (1944–5). This was fought across France, the Low Countries, and Germany, beginning with the invasion of *Normandy on 6 June 1944 and ending with the unconditional surrender of Germany on 7 May 1945. The Allied commanders were grimly aware that the *Wehrmacht was a mighty engine of war, even at this late stage and after the appalling *attrition of the *eastern front, and the sum of their generalship was to so arrange matters that their immense material advantage (the German generals called it *Materielschlacht*) could be brought to bear, sparing themselves the human losses that would otherwise be the inescapable price of victory. Much criticism of the conduct of the campaign fails to bear in mind that the British were war-weary and at their manpower limit very soon after the breakout from Normandy, that the Americans were institutionally very weak at the junior infantry officer level, but above all that man-for-man and tank-for-tank, even reserve German units heavily diluted with non-Germans often beat the best the Allies had to throw at them. They were often better equipped and usually better trained, and they were directed by an officer corps that worshipped the military *art and grimly obeyed to the bitter end the orders of a man many of them despised, simply because they had sworn an oath of loyalty to him.

Neither at the time, nor even in their memoirs did *Eisenhower, *Bradley, or *Montgomery dwell upon this embarrassing fact, but it was certainly never far from the front of their minds throughout the campaign. There is no cheap way of defeating a courageous, skilled, and determined enemy, but insofar as it could be done, they did it. However, whenever they permitted themselves to believe that they had the enemy on the run, he turned and savaged them, on the defensive at *Arnhem and, to the stupefaction of a supreme command enjoying not only total air superiority but also the advantage of what was by this time a steady stream of *ULTRA decryption, on the offensive at the *Bulge. It was akin to beating a venomous snake with a large stick, working up from the tail. At any time it might whip round and strike and the danger was not over until the head was finally immobilized and cut off.

There were also political and geopolitical constraints on the Allied commanders' freedom of operation. The French had to be treated with respect (no easy task in view of previous difficulties with *de Gaulle) because, whatever their weakness at the moment, a strong and friendly France was the key to US and British hopes for a stable post-war Europe. Thus a largely symbolic diversion of resources to liberate the south of France (DRAGOON) had to be mounted, at the expense of the *Italian campaign. And after the Forces Français de l'Intérieur had launched an assault on the remaining German occupiers in Paris, the 2nd (French) Armoured Division under *Leclerc had to be diverted to make an emotive entry into their capital and prepare the way for de Gaulle to walk down the Champs-Elysées amid popular ecstasy.

The operational problems facing Eisenhower were seriously complicated by the fact that Montgomery and *Patton were both forceful characters who hated each other, and that the former made no secret in public or in private of his belief that he should be the supreme commander. As late as the Bulge, he threw away the goodwill he had generated by promptly and efficiently coming to the assistance of Bradley with a bombastic claim to have directed the whole counter-attack and to make one more demand for overall command. Despite the tensions it would have caused within the alliance, there were times when he was close to dismissal. Patton, who already had been sacked once, at least restrained his public utterances. It is important to bear in mind that the indulgence shown to the French was also extended, for many good military as well as political reasons, to the British who by the end of the campaign were very much the junior partners.

In Eisenhower's favour was the fact that Hitler was by this time a physical ruin, poisoning himself with quack medicines, and that after the 20 July bomb plot his tenuous hold on reality slipped still further. Much is made of Hitler giving orders for the movement of non-existent units in 1945, but it should be borne in mind that at no time did he waver from his ferocious commitment to the war to the death with the Slavs on the eastern front. It is easy to deride his 'no retreat' policy in Normandy in the months after D-Day, and to observe that by the time the *Falaise gap was closed the Germans had lost 1,500 tanks, 3,500 guns, 20,000 vehicles, and nearly 500,000 men and with it all hope of stopping the Allies before the Rhine. But this is to overlook the fact that, like *Rommel, he knew very well that the Allied advance had to be stopped at the water's edge. His only hope of personal salvation lay in buying a year while the Al-

lies regrouped back in Britain, in order to turn his full attention back to the war that really mattered to him. He was right; even as the Allies' OVERLORD struggled, the Soviets' *BAGRATION was tearing the heart out of the Wehrmacht.

Another point is that every day the likes of Rommel, *Model, and Kesselring bought for their diseased overlord saw his other great obsession nearer to completion. The extermination camps were operating at full capacity during 1944–5 and for Hitler, this remained an important objective. However, the roots of continued German resistance were far more deep-seated and reflected, *inter alia*, a strong martial tradition, robust tactical leadership, training which (at least until mid-1944) was better than that of the Allies, and the recognition that if France was lost the next battle would be fought in Germany. Some of the blame must lie with the Allies' formula of unconditional surrender. The Germans, Nazis or not, knew very well what unconditional surrender to them had meant for other peoples, and could only assume the worst. US Treasury Secretary Morgenthau seriously proposed reducing Germany to a purely agrarian economy post-war, while the Soviets did, of course, do precisely that to the area they occupied. Cornered rats fight viciously.

This, then, was what Eisenhower and his subordinates had to deal with. The element of good luck came from the fact that like many gamblers, Hitler believed in doubling his bets. Thus in Normandy he sacrificed all hope of waging a fighting retreat across northern France, and at the Bulge he squandered the mobile reserves that might have made the taking of the Siegfried or the Rhine Lines very much more costly. This was seen very clearly at Arnhem, a mere 30 days after Falaise, where the grossly outnumbered Luftwaffe managed to regain a degree of temporary air parity; but it was even more tellingly shown in the miserable experience of the US First and Ninth armies in the Hürtgen Forest before the Ardennes offensive. WACHT AM RHEIN was a doomed enterprise even before the weather cleared and the ground-attack fighters came out in force. Although the Allies were surprised in the battle of the *Bulge, in the end the attack told greatly to German disadvantage.

Early 1945 saw the battle for the *Rhineland conclude with another stroke of good fortune when the 9th Armoured Division of the US First Army captured the almost intact Ludendorff railway bridge over the Rhine at Remagen. Before it fell to water and air attacks ten days later, several First Army divisions had made it across. The capture of the bridge resulted in the dismissal of *Rundstedt as C-in-C West and his replacement with Kesselring, but this was just shuffling deckchairs on the *Titanic*. Between 22 and 26 March, all the Allied armies crossed the Rhine, involving the British, who had to cross in the north where it was a greater obstacle, in a set-piece assault combining large-scale amphibious and airborne operations.

Eisenhower was concerned that the Germans planned an Alpine redoubt, and accordingly directed the US armies to

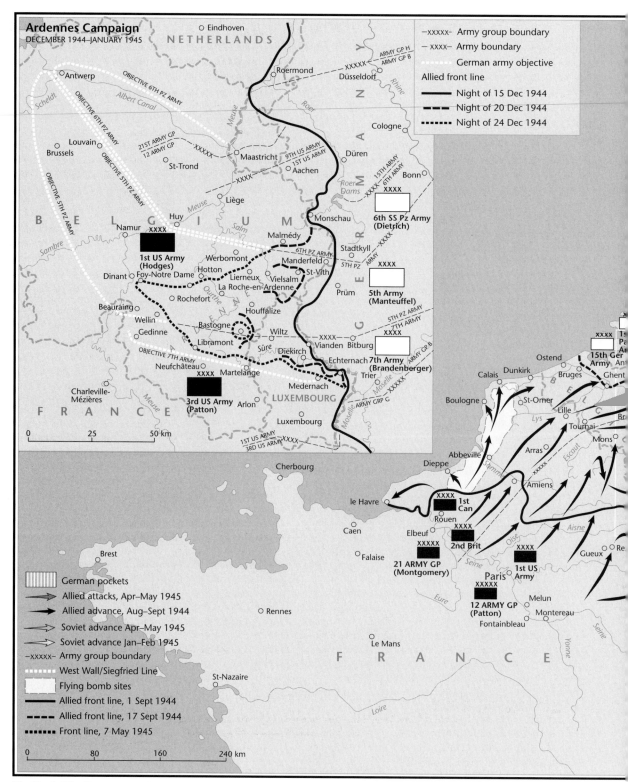

Ardennes Campaign
DECEMBER 1944–JANUARY 1945

Legend:
- –xxxxx– Army group boundary
- – xxxx – Army boundary
- German army objective
- Allied front line
  - Night of 15 Dec 1944
  - Night of 20 Dec 1944
  - Night of 24 Dec 1944

Inset map labels:
NETHERLANDS
Eindhoven
Roermond
Düsseldorf
ARMY GP H / ARMY GP B
Antwerp
Rhine
OBJECTIVE 6TH PZ ARMY
Albert Canal
Scheldt
Roer
Cologne
Louvain
Brussels
21ST ARMY GP
12 ARMY GP
St-Trond
Maastricht
9TH US ARMY
1ST US ARMY
Aachen
Düren
Roer Dams
15TH ARMY
6TH ARMY
Bonn
OBJECTIVE 6TH PZ ARMY
OBJECTIVE 5TH PZ ARMY
Liège
Meuse
6th SS Pz Army (Dietrich)
Huy
Monschau
OBJECTIVE 5TH PZ ARMY
Namur
1st US Army (Hodges)
Malmédy
Salm
Stadtkyll
5th Army (Manteuffel)
Werbomont
Manderfeld
6TH PZ ARMY
5TH PZ
Dinant
Hotton
Foy-Notre Dame
Lierneux
Vielsalm
St-Vith
La Roche-en-Ardenne
Prüm
Rochefort
Ourthe
Houffalize
Beauraing
Wellin
Bastogne
Wiltz
Gedinne
Libramont
Sûre
Diekirch
Vianden
Bitburg
5TH PZ ARMY
7TH ARMY
OBJECTIVE 7TH ARMY
Neufchâteau
Martelange
Echternach
7th Army (Brandenberger)
ARMY GP B
Trier
Charleville-Mézières
Meuse
3rd US Army (Patton)
Arlon
Medernach
Moselle
ARMY GRP G
FRANCE
LUXEMBOURG
Luxembourg
1ST US ARMY
3RD US ARMY
0   25   50 km
B E L G I U M
G E R M A N Y
A R D E N N E S

Main map labels:
Cherbourg
Calais
Dunkirk
Ostend
Bruges
Ghent
15th Ger Army
1st Par Army
Boulogne
St-Omer
Lille
Tournai
Mons
le Havre
Dieppe
Abbeville
Somme
Arras
Amiens
1st Can
Rouen
Elbeuf
Aisne
Caen
Falaise
21 ARMY GP (Montgomery)
2nd Brit
1st US Army
Oise
Gueux
Re
Seine
Paris
12 ARMY GP (Patton)
Melun
Montereau
Fontainebleau
Eure
Brest
St-Nazaire
Rennes
Le Mans
F R A N C E
Loire
Yonne
Lys
Escaut

Main legend:
- German pockets
- Allied attacks, Apr–May 1945
- Allied advance, Aug–Sept 1944
- Soviet advance Apr–May 1945
- Soviet advance Jan–Feb 1945
- –xxxxx– Army group boundary
- West Wall/Siegfried Line
- Flying bomb sites
- Allied front line, 1 Sept 1944
- Allied front line, 17 Sept 1944
- Front line, 7 May 1945

0   80   160   240 km

The **North-West Europe campaign,** 1944–5 and (inset) the Ardennes campaign of December 1944 ('Battle of the Bulge').
For preceding and concurrent events see also NORMANDY CAMPAIGN and EASTERN FRONT.

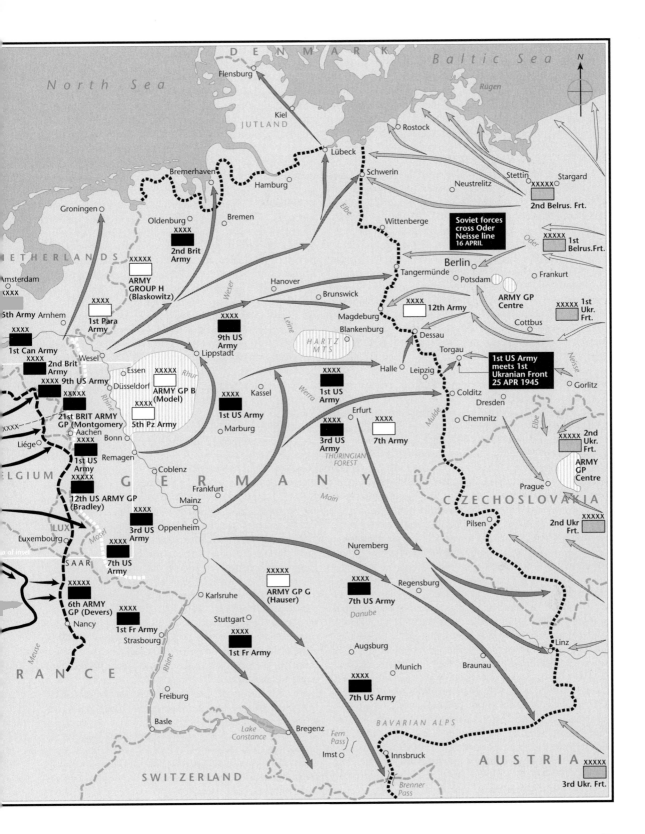

DENMARK

Baltic Sea

North Sea

Flensburg

Kiel
JUTLAND

Rügen

Rostock

Lübeck

Schwerin

Stettin   Stargard

Bremerhaven

Hamburg

Neustrelitz

2nd Belrus. Frt.

Groningen

Oldenburg

Bremen

Wittenberge

Soviet forces cross Oder Neisse line 16 APRIL

Oder

1st Belrus.Frt.

NETHERLANDS

XXXXX

2nd Brit Army

Tangermünde

Berlin

Potsdam

Frankurt

XXXX

XXXXX

ARMY GROUP H (Blaskowitz)

Weser

Hanover

ARMY GP Centre

1st Ukr. Frt.

Amsterdam

XXXX

5th Army Arnhem

XXXX

1st Para Army

Brunswick

Magdeburg

XXXX 12th Army

Cottbus

XXXXX

XXXX

9th US Army

Leine

Blankenburg

Dessau

HARTZ MTS

Torgau

1st US Army meets 1st Ukranian Front 25 APR 1945

Neisse

1st Can Army

XXXX

Lippstadt

Halle   Leipzig

Wesel

XXXXX

Essen

Rhur

Werra

Colditz

2nd Ukr. Frt.

2nd Brit Army

Düsseldorf

ARMY GP B (Model)

Kassel

Dresden

Elbe

9th US Army

Rhine

5th Pz Army

1st US Army

Chemnitz

ARMY GP Centre

21st BRIT ARMY GP (Montgomery)

Bonn

Marburg

XXXX

1st US Army

Erfurt

XXXX

7th Army

Prague

Aachen

XXXX

Liége

1st US Army

Remagen

XXXX

3rd US Army

THURINGIAN FOREST

CZECHOSLOVAKIA

Pilsen

2nd Ukr. Frt.

BELGIUM

GERMANY

Coblenz

Frankfurt

Main

12th US ARMY GP (Bradley)

Mainz

LUX

Luxembourg

XXXX

3rd US Army

Oppenheim

ARMY GP G (Hauser)

Nuremberg

7th US Army

Regensburg

Mosel

SAAR

XXXX

7th US Army

Karlsruhe

Danube

Linz

XXXXX

6th ARMY GP (Devers)

Nancy

XXXX

1st Fr Army

Stuttgart

Augsburg

Munich

Braunau

Strasbourg

XXXX

1st Fr Army

XXXX

7th US Army

Meuse

Freiburg

Rhine

FRANCE

Basle

Lake Constance

Bregenz   Fern Pass

BAVARIAN ALPS

Imst

Innsbruck

AUSTRIA

XXXXX

3rd Ukr. Frt.

SWITZERLAND

Brenner Pass

strike deep into the mountains of southern Germany and Austria, which they did with comparative ease. The redoubt turned out to be a chimera, but at this stage he was rightly concerned that the meeting with the Red Army should be as carefully orchestrated as possible. His political masters had already defined zones of occupation and he knew that such glory as could be had in taking *Berlin was going to be very dearly bought. And it was, by the Soviets.

By 1 April, Model's Army Group B had been surrounded when the pincers of the US Ninth and First Armies closed at Lippstadt. Three hundred thousand men surrendered and their commander shot himself. Hitler also shot himself as the Soviets fought their way into Berlin, a process completed by 2 May. Montgomery's Army Group reached Hamburg on the following day and between 4 and 5 May the surrender of German formations in the west was negotiated, Montgomery taking that of units in north-west Germany, Denmark, and Holland, while *Dönitz surrendered what was left of German forces to Eisenhower at his HQ in Rheims on 7 May. The campaign and the European war officially ended at midnight on 8 May 1945.   APC-A/RH

North-West frontier Designation applied to the frontier of British India, as established in 1849, bordering the chain of mountains separating the provinces of Punjab and Sind from Afghanistan. Until 1901 the northern part of the region came under the authority of the Punjab government and was divided into four trans-Indus districts (Peshawar, Kohat, Bannu, and Dera Ismail Khan) and one district (Hazara) on the east of the Indus and into five tribal agencies (Malakand, Khyber, Kurram, and north and south Waziristan). In 1901 the whole was formed into a new province, the North-West Frontier Province under a chief commissioner. The logic behind the scheme was to introduce a dedicated regime to accommodate the mainly Pathan population of the frontier, to deal with the special problems caused by the activities of the independent tribes of the mountains, and to allow the supreme government in Delhi direct control over the frontier region with its international problems.

The historical problem of the North-West frontier incorporated two elements: the first the question of stopping or at least controlling tribal raiding from the mountains into the more peaceful settled lowland districts; and the second the question of strategy, namely how to prevent an overland invasion of India from the north-west and how to insulate British India from disturbances originating in regions beyond the frontier. There was a close connection between the frontier and the maintenance of British power in India, a link summed up in the word 'prestige'. It was thought that Britain could not afford to be flouted by frontier tribes; British prestige must be vindicated, the power of British arms demonstrated. Therefore costly expeditions must be sent out, even when it was believed that little or no

direct purpose would be served, in order that the people of India in general should continue to believe in the overwhelming power and will of the British Raj.

At different times the border or strategic elements predominated: broadly speaking from 1849 to 1876 the border element was to the fore but from 1876 to 1919 the strategic question was often uppermost in the minds of policy makers. In the first period it was thought most convenient to have as little to do with the tribal regions as possible, to manage the tribes, and to punish them by expeditions when they offended. This system, favoured by the Punjab government, was usually designated the Close Border system or, by its critics, the 'Butcher and Bolt' policy. It was contrasted with a policy developed on the Upper Sind frontier which involved more active intervention in tribal affairs and which led into what was called the Forward policy and eventually, under the direction of Sir Robert Sandeman, contributed to the advance to Quetta and the assumption of control over Baluchistan. During the 1890s a systematic attempt with very mixed results was made under Richard Bruce to introduce the same policy on the Punjab frontier in Waziristan. This new Forward policy was justified both in relation to border policy as giving greater control over the tribes and in relation to the strategic question as giving Britain control over the heads of the passes leading to British India and enabling the British forces the better to anticipate any hostile movement against British India. In this strategic view the advance was connected with the *doctrine of the scientific frontier, a term much vaguer than it sounds but which was usually used to denote the Kabul–Ghazni–Kandahar line towards which it was thought British forces should move in the event of an attack on British India. The opponents of the Forward school argued that such a move would mean that British forces would have to rely on vulnerable lines of communication through the Suleiman mountains and that it was far better to wait on the line of the Indus and allow the enemy to struggle with the problem of passing through the mountains with their wild inhabitants. And they believed that tribal management could be more cheaply accomplished by reliance on the old Close Border policy and by distant friendship with Afghanistan. The ultimate solution of the strategic problem, they argued, lay with the government in London: either to fight Russia elsewhere or to make an agreement with Russia as was indeed done in 1907, partly because of the escalating costs of the Forward policy. Russia was always the chief enemy to be feared: only briefly in the two world wars were Ottoman and German activities the cause of frontier concern.

So much for broader questions; to most readers the phrase 'North-West frontier' stands for all the romance and adventure of frontier fighting as celebrated in many novels, short stories, and poems as well as in numerous memoirs and regimental histories. Before considering some of the principal expeditions, it should be noted that military expeditions were regarded as a last resort only to be employed when other methods failed. These other methods included the use of constabulary forces and militias such as the Tochi Scouts and the Khyber Rifles, blockades and reverse blockades, fines, seizures of goods, and suspensions of allowances paid allegedly to guard passes. Nearly all these methods were employed during the first disastrous British involvement in the *Khyber Pass during the first *Anglo-Afghan war in 1839–42, but they were greatly refined in later years and did, apparently, reduce the perceived necessity for expeditions.

During the first ten years after 1849 there were seventeen larger military operations but only five or six a decade during the following three decades (leaving aside the special operations linked to the second Afghan war in 1878–80. The typical expedition during these years consisted of 2,000–5,000 men mainly drawn from the Punjab Frontier Force and local levies supplemented as thought necessary by British troops and *Gurkhas. The forces were predominantly infantry with some cavalry, mountain guns, and light field artillery. Their objectives were usually the destruction of crops, forts, and villages so as to compel the tribe concerned to surrender criminals or make redress for crimes. The adoption of the Forward policy led to an escalation of violence during the 1890s culminating in the great frontier uprising of 1897 when almost all tribes rose and there were major military expeditions in Waziristan, the Swat valley, against the Mohmands, and especially against the Afridis in their stronghold of Tirah, an expedition which involved 34,500 troops.

The character of frontier warfare underwent a change in the 1890s. Hitherto the tribesmen had been armed with *matchlocks, daggers, and swords and had relied especially on the sudden charge from ambush and on cold steel. From about 1890 they acquired modern rifles and modified their tactics to include long-range sniping which caused British forces to alter their own system of fighting. In the years which followed, technical innovation also improved the British capability with the increased use of machine guns (Maxim and, later, *Lewis guns), improved mountain guns and *smokeless powder, better signals, and eventually *air power, first used in 1917 in support of land operations but from 1925 employed on its own to bomb villages and destroy crops. Some flexibility was lost with the decision to amalgamate the Punjab Frontier Force with the regular Indian army under the *Kitchener reorganization of the early 1900s, a scheme which gave priority to defence against invasion rather than control of the frontier.

WW I led to increased violence on the frontier, partly as a result of German and Turkish propaganda and partly because of the withdrawal of British forces. In 1919 the third Afghan war led to a general outbreak on the frontier, the evacuation of posts, the collapse of some of the frontier militia forces—notably the Khyber Rifles which was disbanded—and to several expeditions. The largest problems were concentrated in Waziristan which from 1914 onwards became the major frontier problem. Apart from the Afridi expedition of 1930–1 and the Mohmand expedition of 1935 all the major expeditions were sent against the Wazirs and especially the Mahsuds of south Waziristan.

The situation in Waziristan was the result of several factors including the Forward policy of the 1890s and the influence of two remarkable religious leaders, the Mulla Powindah (d. 1913) and the Fakir of Ipi (d. 1960) who contrived to organize opposition to British authority on a much larger scale. During the 1920s it was determined to try to assert close control over Waziristan and in particular, after the extensive campaigns of 1921–2, to establish a permanent regular army base at Razmak from which to dominate the country. The long lines of communication through difficult country became a target for tribal attacks and there were more or less continuous kidnappings, murders, and fighting, punctuated by major expeditions such as that of 1936–7. The number of troops involved constituted a very serious drain on resources. To maintain the Razmak position and other garrisons required on average twelve battalions in Waziristan and four extra infantry brigades were introduced in 1936–7. In September 1947 the new Pakistan government resolved on a complete change of policy and evacuated all regular army units from Waziristan.

MEY

Caroe, Olaf, The Pathans (London, 1958).
Davies, C. Collin, The Problem of the North-West Frontier (Cambridge, 1932).
Elliott, Maj Gen J. G., The Frontier, 1839–1947 (London, 1968).

Norwegian campaign (1940). Norway and Sweden, having opted to remain neutral in 1939, found themselves key suppliers of iron ore and other metals, vital for the Axis war machine. Difficulties arose when the ore was transported through Norwegian territorial waters (chiefly the port of Narvik) using German shipping, which went against the prevailing conventions of war. Britain and France resolved in early 1940 to mine Norwegian inshore waters and land troops at Narvik and other ports to strangle this flow of raw materials. Suspicions were afoot that Germany was in any case planning to occupy Norway, to protect her economic interests.

The mining went ahead directly, but before Allied troops could be landed, the Germans invaded Denmark on 8 April and Norway on the 9th, but were surprised to encounter opposition since the collaborator Vidkun Quisling had suggested that Norway might fall without a fight. The cruiser *Blücher* covering an amphibious landing force was sunk off Oslo, but Norway's capital fell to the first ever combat use of *airborne forces, which captured the airport and then the city. Other airborne troops seized Stavanger, while Bergen (though with the loss of the cruiser *Königsberg*), Kristiansand (with the loss of the *Karlsrühe*), and Trondheim were also captured. Narvik, where ten German destroyers quickly landed 2,000 *mountain troops under Lt Gen Eduard Dietl' fell almost without a struggle.

Before the German warships could leave, a Royal Naval destroyer force attacked them, sinking two and damaging five. Three days later another flotilla, led by the battleship *Warspite*, sank the remaining vessels, crippling the tiny Kriegsmarine (which had possessed only 22 destroyers) and stranding Dietl. Although the powerful Royal Navy deployed several vessels off the Norwegian coast to support the mining, German *air power proved decisive: the first occasion in which air power cancelled out *naval power. In mid-April, in poorly planned operations, Anglo-French forces landed 12,000 men at Namos and Andalsnes, north and south of Trondheim respectively, but were unable to be resupplied due to the attentions of the Luftwaffe, and were driven back by German ground troops. Both were evacuated by 2 May. Another overwhelming Allied force landed to retake Narvik on 13 May but was more frustrated by disagreements between army and navy commanders than by any opposition from Dietl's mountain troops. Although the port was captured a fortnight later, Dietl had been supplied by air (Norway was the first campaign where aerial supply was an influential factor) and managed to tie down a large Allied-Norwegian force. Under constant Luftwaffe bombardment and unable to sustain the Narvik force due to the invasion of France, all Allied troops were evacuated from Narvik on 8 June, but much valuable equipment and stores had to be left behind.

The Norway campaign was the first genuinely tri-service campaign to be fought by either side, and the Wehrmacht high command (OKW), really for the only time in the war, provided an effective tri-service command and planning organization. By contrast, Anglo-French command and control in Norway was disastrous, with little tri-service co-operation. But the German surface fleet suffered such crippling losses as to virtually remove it from consideration during the planning of SEALION, the 'river crossing' for which the aerial battle of *Britain was a necessary preamble. The next German tri-service operation, in *Crete, was to lead to yet more shocking losses despite once again enjoying aerial superiority, and they abandoned the form of warfare in which they were the pioneers and which had shown such promise. The British learned the lessons and returned the favour in *North-West Europe. The Norwegian campaign redounded little to the credit of the Allies. It was, however, to their advantage that it provoked the replacement of PM Chamberlain by *Churchill, and that it left the Germans with a northern flank which swallowed up a large garrison for the whole war.   APC-A

nuclear weapons derive their explosive power from the fission (splitting) and fusion (combining) of atoms. Fusion devices need to be combined with a nuclear fission weapon to generate the intense heat necessary to begin the still more powerful process of fusion. Fusion weapons—the 'H' (hydrogen) bomb—can be a thousand times more powerful than fission weapons and these opened the horrific possibility of global destruction through nuclear missile war. Many early 'fusion' weapons were in fact 'boosted fission devices', gaining most of their power from the fission explosion with a fusion component to enhance its efficiency. Military requirements have also led to enhanced radiation/reduced blast weapons, the so-called 'neutron bomb', in which the immediate radiation is multiplied in order to kill troops rather than destroy installations.

The idea of a source of enormous energy for motive power or weapons featured in the work of 19th-century science-fiction writers including Jules Verne, George Earle Bulwer-Lytton, and H. G. Wells who talks of atomic bombs in *The World Set Free*. By 1914 the Newtonian view that the universe consisted of lumps of indestructible matter had given way to the realization that matter could be transformed into energy. It was not until the eve of WW II that the practical possibility of a nuclear weapon was understood. On 2 August 1939, Albert Einstein signed a letter to Pres Franklin D. *Roosevelt, saying that recent work in France and the USA had indicated the possibility of setting up a nuclear chain reaction in a large mass of uranium. This new phenomenon could 'also lead to the construction of bombs and it is conceivable—though much less certain—that extremely powerful bombs of a new type may thus be constructed. A single bomb of this type, carried by boat and exploded in a port, might very well destroy the whole port, together with some of the surrounding territory. However, such bombs might very well prove too heavy for transportation by air.' He was wrong on the last point, and six years and four days later the US dropped the first atomic bomb over *Hiroshima, the result of the *Manhattan Project.

The first test bomb ever to be exploded, at Alamogordo in the New Mexico desert on 16 July 1945, 'the Gadget', was an 'implosion' device, with a hollow plutonium core weighing about 8.3 lb (6.1 kg), compressed to critical density by about 4,866 lb (2,270 kg) of high explosive. The 'yield'—the size of the explosion—was 22 kilotons. Nuclear weapon yields are measured as kilotons (each 1,000 tons of TNT) or megatons (one million tons of TNT).

The first bomb to be dropped on Japan on 6 August was of a different type—a 'gun-assembly' device called 'Little Boy'. It was cruder than the Gadget—132.3 lb (60 kg) of highly enriched uranium in two pieces, one of which was fired at the other down a gun-type barrel, producing a far less efficient yield of 12 to 15 kilotons. The US B-29 bomber *Enola Gay*, named after the pilot's mother, carried the bomb to Hiroshima from its base at Guam, escorted by two other planes carrying observers and instruments. The bomb had been brought from the USA by the cruiser *Indianapolis*, which was to be sunk by a Japanese submarine on its return trip. The city was obliterated.

Atomic or fission bomb

Nuclear fission occurs when a uranium or plutonium nucleus is struck by a single neutron. It releases energy, more neutrons and two lighter nuclei.

The released neutrons bombard more nuclei, in turn producing more neutrons and so on. If enough material is present (a super-critical mass), a nuclear explosion occurs.

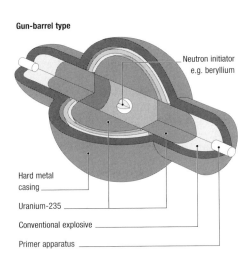

Neutron

Uranium-235 or plutonium-239

Neutrons

Fragments of nuclei

Hydrogen or fusion bomb

Nuclear fusion occurs when deuterium and tritium (two gases) are exposed to a temperature of 10^7 °C. The two nuclei fuse together, forming an unstable isotope of helium and at the same time releasing a single neutron and a huge amount of energy. Although no gamma radiation is produced, the fast moving electrons are harmful.

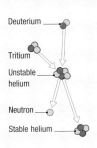

Deuterium

Tritium

Unstable helium

Neutron

Stable helium

Gun-barrel type

Neutron initiator e.g. beryllium

Hard metal casing

Uranium-235

Conventional explosive

Primer apparatus

Implosion type

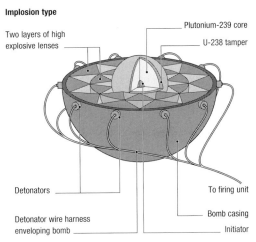

Two layers of high explosive lenses

Plutonium-239 core

U-238 tamper

Detonators

Detonator wire harness enveloping bomb

To firing unit

Bomb casing

Initiator

Thermal and blast effects of a nuclear explosion

The diagram below shows likely effects resulting from the explosion of a 20 KT (kiloton) bomb. A 1 KT bomb has the explosive power of 1,000 tons of TNT and a 1MT (megaton) bomb is equivalent to 1 million tons of TNT

Diagrammatic representation of a fusion weapon

High explosive lens

Tamper U-238

Fusion material

Fission trigger

Detonators

To electric exploder

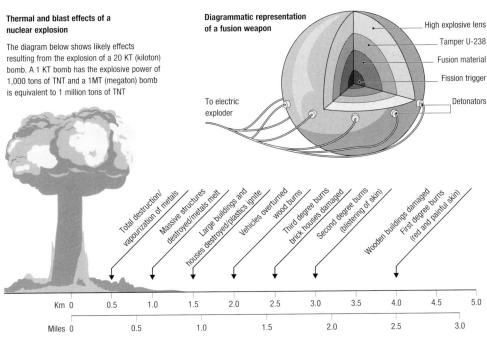

Total destruction/vapourization of metals

Massive structures destroyed/metals melt

Large buildings and houses destroyed/plastics ignite

Vehicles overturned wood burns

Third degree burns brick houses damaged

Second degree burns (blistering of skin)

Wooden buildings damaged First degree burns (red and painful skin)

Km 0 0.5 1.0 1.5 2.0 2.5 3.0 3.5 4.0 4.5 5.0

Miles 0 0.5 1.0 1.5 2.0 2.5 3.0

Although simple in principle, nuclear weapons are difficult to engineer in practice. The 'gun assembly' type is less efficient but more robust and favoured for artillery shells. The implosion type is more difficult to build and more fragile, but is more efficient and is essential to exploit the advantages of fusion.

The second operational bomb, 'Fat Man', dropped on Nagasaki on 9 August, was of the same type as the Gadget. Implosion devices are more efficient than the gun type and do not require high-grade uranium, but they are more complex in their design and more delicate, requiring precise co-ordination of the timing for the detonation of the surrounding explosive charges, and are unsuitable to withstand the stress of being launched from a gun. For this reason, gun-assembly devices retain their importance as nuclear artillery shells, while implosion devices tend to be carried on rockets.

The detonation of a nuclear weapon produces an incandescent 'fireball' in which everything is vaporized. Being hot, the fireball climbs upwards, generating the characteristic 'mushroom cloud' as it pulls debris from the ground up with it. Nuclear weapons have five main effects. The first is heat, or 'flash', causing burns and eye damage far from the immediate source of the explosion. The second is blast, caused by a shock wave moving outwards from the fireball at about the speed of sound. Third is immediate radiation travelling at the speed of light-neutron radiation at shorter distances, and gamma radiation further out. Most of the latter is generated after the explosion, so a dive for cover may still be worth while. Fourth is residual radiation: the neutrons from the explosion make other material radioactive, which falls back to earth as fallout. Fifth is electromagnetic pulse (EMP), which burns out electronic apparatus. A multi-megaton weapon burst high above the earth, outside the atmosphere, would not have perceptible flash-and-blast effects but could knock out power grids and electrical equipment over a wide area.

After the explosion of the bombs over Japan, some thought the nuclear weapon would render traditional forms of war obsolete. Others were sceptical about the bomb's power, although some used this to try to discourage its development. As early as October 1945, Sir George Thompson, participating in the revision of the British Tizard report on future warfare, foresaw that the bomb's very potency might preclude its use. Whereas the tendency had been to wage war more and more unrestrictedly, it was possible that the nuclear weapon might reverse this trend. Therefore Britain should keep 'pre-atomic defence forces'. The first atomic bombs were very large, could only be delivered by large aircraft, and were also very rare. Therefore, like other new weapons in military-technical revolutions, they were only suitable for use against strategic targets. Tizard's revised report noted 'the bombing of towns and industry now give a far greater return for war effort expended and may therefore become the most profitable type of war'.

By contrast, the effect of a Hiroshima- or Nagasaki-type bomb on military targets appeared to offer little return on investment. In 1946 Tizard estimated that when detonated at 300 feet (91 metres) above the ground such a bomb would disable tanks and guns out to 400 yards (366 metres) and soft-skinned vehicles out to 800 yards (732 metres), while in battlefield conditions it would disable troops in the open out to 1,200 yards (1,097 metres) immediately and 1,800 yards (1,646 metres) with delayed action. A 1953 assessment drew similar conclusions. All that was likely to be accomplished was the destruction of 120 to 140 vehicles over a length of 4 miles (6.4 km) or so. Atomic weapons would tend to create obstacles in front of advancing columns, rather than destroy them. Whereas fighting troops, dug in, were very robust in the face of nuclear weapons, large staging areas and ports were vulnerable. *Amphibious operations like D-Day, would clearly be a lucrative target for nuclear strikes.

As nuclear weapons became more plentiful, the possibility of using them on the battlefield grew, and by 1955 both the USSR and NATO, now arrayed against each other in Europe, were contemplating their use in this way. In 1954 the Soviet army conducted winter manoeuvres in the Carpathians, in which an 'attacker' succeeded in penetrating the high mountain passes near Czernowitz. Both sides were assumed to be using nuclear weapons and to be about equal in strength. Each side concentrated its strikes on the opponent's lines of communication and supply centres. The umpires declared that, because of this, operations had ground to a standstill.

The talented military thinker Ferdinand Miksche, a Czech émigré, believed that nuclear weapons would, like other increases in firepower, lead to a 'bogging down of the fighting'. He was also aware of the effect of electromagnetic pulse. If all high-frequency apparatus within 4 miles of a nuclear blast burned out, he reasoned, what were the implications for land forces? Nuclear weapons might give rise to a development 'entirely different from the one foreseen by armies at present'. Simpler weapons and equipment would be more dependable than complex systems, which would be powerless without the extensive, rear services. It might be that in nuclear warfare 'only material and tactical methods of the simplest kind will retain their value'.

Nonetheless, the opposing blocs had to reckon with nuclear weapons on the battlefield as well as strategically. In 1953 the USSR and the USA exploded the first fusion bombs, which, combined with the development of ballistic missiles, appeared to shift the emphasis away from armies towards a new form of war. During the late 1950s the USSR concluded that a 'revolution in military affairs' had taken place, expressed in Sokolovskiy's *Strategy*. By 1970, when Sidorenko's *The Offensive* was published, the vision of the future battlefield was truly apocalyptic. 'A new characteristic of the offensive in nuclear war', he wrote, 'is the conduct of combat actions under conditions of the presence of vast zones of contamination, destruction, fires and floods.'

This vision led western powers, whose territory was likely to be the scene for such vast zones of destruction, to try to refine the effects of nuclear weapons. In an enhanced radiation/reduced blast weapon, such as the US W-79 8 inch artillery round, the burst of prompt nuclear radiation (neutrons and gamma rays) is enhanced by minimizing the fission yield relative to the fusion yield. Small enhanced radiation weapons can kill by radiation well outside the range of the blast: with ordinary nuclear weapons, the blast and heat usually kill first. Because there is little residual radiation, friendly troops could then operate in the area very soon afterwards.

The Soviet emphasis on *armoured warfare may have owed as much to the characteristics of nuclear weapons as to the lessons of the *eastern front in WW II. Tanks and armoured fighting vehicles were heavy and low and did not blow away easily in a nuclear storm, they could be hermetically sealed against fallout, and their armour was good protection against immediate radiation.

Similar considerations influenced Israel, India, and Pakistan. Israel probably had nuclear weapons by the time of the 1973 *Arab–Israeli war, and might have used them if overrun, but has never admitted it publicly. India and Pakistan were the foremost 'threshold' nuclear powers until 1998, when each conducted multiple nuclear tests, although India had set off a 'peaceful' nuclear explosion back in 1974. The Indian and Pakistani armies both placed great emphasis on armour as the arm of choice on a nuclear battlefield, and discussed nuclear warfare extensively. The use of nuclear weapons exploded below ground as *demolition charges in the Himalayas has also been discussed.

The development of *precision-guided munitions and improved conventional area munitions has, arguably, made battlefield nuclear weapons obsolete. The first are conventional bombs able to strike their targets so accurately they could perform the same military tasks as nuclear weapons. The second distribute mines or a fuel-air explosive cloud over an area similar to that seared by a nuclear device, but far more efficiently. Nuclear weapons are wasteful, and it is almost impossible to imagine any circumstances in which their use could possibly be justified. But to some Third World dictators, the bomb is still the ultimate status symbol.

A number of 'third-generation nuclear weapons' are under development in the USA and Russia, however. These include diverting the rays from a nuclear explosion and pumping it out in a beam, or very low-yield nuclear weapons to destroy missiles or electronics with radiation alone. Over the past half-century, nuclear weapons have had enormous influence on the design of conventional military forces. But, apart from the two bombs on Japan which ended WW II, they were seen as too terrible to use. *Clausewitz said that war 'tended to the extreme', but that there were always limitations in practice. With nuclear weapons, it seems the limitations became overriding; let us hope that they remain so.   CDB

Cochran, Thomas, Arkin, William, and Hoenig, William, *Nuclear Weapons Databook* (5 vols., Cambridge, Mass, 1984).
Glasstone, S., and Dolan, P. J., *The Effects of Nuclear Weapons* (Washington, 1977).
Grace, Charles, *Nuclear Weapons: Principles, Effects and Survivability* (London, 1994).
McNaught, L. W., *Nuclear Weapons and their Effects* (London, 1984).
Miksche, Ferdinand Otto, *Atomic Weapons and Armies* (London, 1955).
Sidorenko, Col A. A., *The Offensive* (Moscow, 1970); trans. and ed. USAF (Washington, 1976).
Sokolovsky, Vasily, *Soviet Military Strategy*, ed. Harriet Fast Scott (3rd edn., London, 1975).
Tizard, Sir Henry, *Examination of the Possible Development of Weapons and Methods of War*, PRO Defe II TWC 1252 (46)3(Revise), 30 January 1946.

nurses, military (see also MEDICINE, MILITARY). The connection between nursing and the military is a long-established one. In earlier centuries, extra-familial nursing provision was most commonly provided by volunteers with little or no training, usually by men and women belonging to monastic orders, or by laypersons associated with them. However, during the *Crusades certain *military monastic orders were established which also provided nursing care. Most notable among these orders were the Knights Hospitallers, who were also known as the Knights of St John of Jerusalem. Members of the *sangha* sect, a Buddhist religious order, have likewise traditionally adopted the responsibility for the care of the sick and injured in Buddhist countries. However, in post-Reformation Europe the role of nurse, with its close association with the dead and the dying, was generally regarded as a low-status occupation.

Modern nursing practice began in the mid-19th century. The German pastor Theodor Fliedner began one of the first formal training programmes for nurses in 1836, at Kaiserswerth, for the Order of Protestant Deaconesses. While other religious orders provided formalized nurse training in 19th-century Europe, Fliedner's school remains notable for having trained Florence *Nightingale, Britain's most noteworthy nursing reformer. Kaiserswerth provided her with the impetus to organize proper nursing care during the *Crimean war and to later establish a nurse training programme at London's St Thomas's Hospital. The Nightingale Training Schools for nurses and their founder's reputation, based on the battlefields of the Crimea, transformed the nurse's status and provided the foundation upon which the modern profession has been built.

Nurse education and training is traditionally based in *hospitals, although in Britain and the USA there is now an increased emphasis on external college-based training. Typically nurse training prior to qualification lasts around three years, involving general training in medicine in addition to practical experience on wards, caring for patients under supervision. The standard of medical education for nurses in North America and western Europe is now high, while Britain in particular is noted for the high medical content of its courses. Many nursing duties are technical in nature. They range from implementation of complex treatment regimes to operating life-support systems in intensive care units. Some duties are dependent, under the direction of a qualified doctor or dentist, but there are many independent functions which nurses perform based on their own professional judgement. It can be argued that military nurses, like their doctor colleagues, tend to have greater licence than their civilian counterparts, especially during wartime. Since WW II there have been significant advances in medical practice and health care. The post-war explosion of technical knowledge in the field of health care has led to increased nurse specialization. Such areas include surgery, dentistry, and psychiatry.

Military and civilian nursing, like many other aspects of health care, are both complementary and interlinked. The American model, in particular, provides a good illustration of nursing development within the military sphere. The establishment of the Continental Army (later the US army) on 14 June 1775 saw the seeds sown for what became the US Army Nursing Corps. Shortly after, Maj Gen Horatio Gates reported to his C-in-C *Washington that within his force 'the sick suffered for Want of good female nurses'. Washington appealed to Congress to authorize a matron to supervise nurses to attend the sick and injured. On 27 July 1775 the scheme was approved and led to the creation of a hospital (medical department) providing one nurse for every sick or injured soldier, with a matron for every hundred patients. These women tending sick and wounded during the *American independence war were not professional nurses in the modern sense, but they helped establish the path for recognized schools of nursing which began with the creation of civilian hospitals in America.

Following the war the size of the military establishment was greatly reduced with limited provision at regimental/garrison level, while patient care was handled by soldiers drawn from companies. There was little by way of a formal medical department until the *War of 1812. In 1818 a Surgeon General, Dr Joseph Lovell, was appointed. By the start of the *American civil war in 1861 a modern military Medical Department was well established, with patient care provided by stewards who equated to *NCOs. It was not until the appointment of Dorothea Lynde Dix on 10 June 1861 as Superintendent of Women Nurses for the Union army, that female nurses re-entered the frame. Miss Dix was aided in her endeavours by Dr Elizabeth Blackwell, the first woman to receive a medical degree in the USA, who trained a number of women nurses prior to their engagement with the army. Throughout the American civil war, many women served as nurses in both Union and Confederate hospitals, including a large number of Catholic sisters.

After the war, soldiers continued to perform patient care duties and nursing functions in military hospitals as enlisted hospital stewards and privates in a part of the Army Medical Department. In 1891 formal instruction was introduced for members of the Hospital Corps at Fort Riley,

Kansas, and with the onset of the *Spanish-American war, congressional authority was again given to appoint contract women nurses. Military nursing had been almost dormant since the civil war. Many nurses were still members of religious orders.

In the years when the US military was not involved in conflict, nursing numbers were drastically reduced. However, a proper structure for military nursing was established. In August 1898 a Nurse Corps Division had been established and this was formalized by Congress in February 1901, when the Nurse Corps (female) became a permanent corps of the Medical Department, with an authorized strength fixed at a mere 100 nurses. This remained unchanged for ten years after which it increased to 125 (1912) and to 150 (1914). Rules, regulations, conditions of service, salaries, uniforms, and training had all been introduced by April 1917, when the USA entered WW I. At this time there were 403 nurses on active duty. In comparison, by 30 June 1917 there were 1,176 nurses on duty and one year later, 12,186 nurses (2,000 regular army and 10,186 reserve) were on active service at 198 stations around the world.

When, on 8 September 1939, a state of Limited Emergency was declared because of the war in Europe, there were just 625 regular army nurses on active duty. In response the authorized Army Nurse Corps (Regular) establishment was raised to 949 while a further 15,770 nurses, enrolled with the first Reserve of the American Red Cross Nursing Service, were, it was hoped, available for service if required. In May 1941, the increased threat of a global conflict led to the declaration of a state of National Emergency and once more it became necessary to activate reserve nurses.

On entering WW II, the US faced a critical shortage of registered nurses. It was deemed more expedient and more economical to bolster those instructors and facilities of existing civilian nursing schools rather than to reconstitute the Army School of Nursing or raise from scratch similar military hospital-based schools. In addition the Cadet Nurse Corps was established. It comprised student trainees, who were neither a part of the armed forces nor the civil government. Nor did their training and effort constitute federal service, and thereby qualify them for future benefit. The Corps' pledge 'to be available for military or other Federal, governmental, or essential civilian services for the duration of the present war' was not legally binding but rather a statement of intent. A total of 169,443 joined the Cadet Nurse Corps of which 124,065 graduated in this remarkable scheme involving 1,125 of America's 1,300 nursing schools. It was only by adopting such measures that the US army was able to field the huge number of nurses that it did.

Developments in Britain were similar. In 1860 Florence Nightingale established a training school for military nurses at the Royal Victoria Hospital, Netley. The Army Nursing Service was founded in 1881 and Princess Christian's Army Nursing Reserve in 1897. During the Second *Boer War 1,400 nurses, most of them reservists, served in 22 general hospitals. Post-war reforms saw the formation, in 1902, of Queen Alexandra's Imperial Nursing Service. Its members, reinforced with reservists and volunteers—like the unqualified nursing assistants of the WW I Voluntary Aid Detachments—served with much distinction, and at no little risk, in two world wars. The service was reorganized to form Queen Alexandra's Royal Army Nursing Service ('QAs' for short) in 1949, and its members gained formal military rank—rather than simply 'equivalent status'—the following year. Non-commissioned members were recruited in 1950, and in 1992 male nurses—previously part of the Royal Army Medical Corps—were transferred to the corps.

Military nurses, their corps formalized in a similar manner to that which characterized the nursing services in the British and United States armies, served widely in both world wars and in the hundreds of conflicts which have marked the world since 1945. On the one hand they play an essential part in the provision of effective medical care which, in itself, gives a powerful boost to *morale. But on the other their contribution is more primal. They have provided charm and romantic attachment in areas where both are conspicuously lacking: as US sailors in the musical *South Pacific* sing, 'There is nothing like a dame.' FM *Montgomery was not alone in maintaining that the presence of female nurses had a palpable effect on morale: no male, he argued, could nurse quite like a woman. Geneviève de Galard-Terraube, a French Air Force nurse, was marooned at *Dien Bien Phu after her plane was destroyed. She worked tirelessly in the underground hospital, changing filthy dressings, cleaning maggots from wounds, and soothing the dying. Maj Paul Grauwin, the senior medical officer, was sure that men remembered their self-respect and bore their pain more stoically when she was present. WW I nurses were affectionately nicknamed 'The Roses of No Man's Land', and in just the same way Galard-Terraube earned her own place in the affection of survivors.

PMacD/RH

Conde, Marlette, *The Lamp and the Caduceus* (Washington, 1975).

Flikke, Col Julia O., *Nurses in Action* (Philadelphia, 1943).

Grauwin, Paul, *Doctor at Dien Bien Phu* (London, 1955).

O'Connor, Gen Sir Richard Nugent (1889–1981). Son of an army officer, O'Connor was commissioned into the Cameronians (Scottish Rifles) in 1909, fought in WW I, and was a temporary lieutenant colonel at its end. In 1940 he commanded 7th Armoured Division in Egypt, and at Wavell's behest was given command of the Western Desert Force. In December 1940 he launched COMPASS, rolling the Italians back across the *Western Desert and taking 130,000 prisoners. While on *reconnaissance he was captured by the Germans and imprisoned in Italy. Escaping when Italy concluded an armistice, he commanded VIII Corps in Europe in 1944–5. Adjutant-general of the army after the war, he resigned on a point of principle in 1947. Famously tiny and tough, O'Connor was nevertheless past his best in Normandy, and Maj Gen 'Pip' Roberts, the youngest of his divisional commanders, regretted that he 'did not understand the proper handling of armour on a European battlefield'.   RH

Oda Nobunaga (1534–82) is one of the pivotal figures in Japanese history. He was only 15 when his father died, and rose to national prominence with his stunning victory of Okehazama in 1560, when he defeated the powerful army of Imagawa Yoshimoto. In 1564 he defeated the Saitō family and made his capital at Gifu. Campaigns against the Asai and Asakura followed, including the battle of Anegawa in 1570. In 1571 he destroyed the temples of Mount Hiei, ending for ever the influence of the *sōhei (warrior monks). Other religious rivals caused him more problems. His campaign against the Ikkō-ikki at Nagashima and Ishiyama Honganji lasted a decade. In 1575 he fought the decisive battle of *Nagashino, famous for the large-scale and controlled use of firearms, but it took a further seven years for him to destroy the Takeda family. In 1576 he built Azuchi castle, and towards the end of his career conducted successful campaigns in Ise and Iga provinces. As a ruler he was tolerant towards the spread of Christianity in Japan and encouraged foreign trade. In 1582 he was murdered in a surprise night attack on the Honnōji temple in Kyoto by his general Akechi Mitsuhide.   SRT

Office of Strategic Services. See OSS.

officer A person holding authority in the armed forces. Although the term subsumes commissioned officers, *warrant officers, and *NCOs, it is only specifically applied to those holding *commissions. The military hierarchy and its ranks became established with the advent of modern armies around the 17th century. In land forces there were three levels of officer rank: company officers (*officiers subalternes*) including ensign (cornet in the cavalry), second lieutenant, lieutenant, and captain; field officers (*officiers supérieurs*), majors, lieutenant colonels, and colonels; and general officers, brigadier general, major general, lieutenant general, and general. The rank of field marshal (or *marshal) is the most senior, and in France was regarded as a dignity of state rather than a specifically military rank.

There were inevitably differences, which can only be touched on here (see RANK). The Austrian army called the rank of general *feldzugmeister* and lieutenant general *feldmarschall leutnant*. In the French army of the old regime there were two grades of general officer, *maréchal de camp* (equivalent to brigadier general) and *lieutenant général*, roughly and confusingly equivalent to major general. After the Revolution these were replaced by *général de brigade* and *général de division*, with the full range of general officer ranks, including *général de corps d'armée* and *général d'armée* coming only after WW I. In many armies a brigade might be commanded by the senior colonel of the regiments comprising it or, as was often the case in the German army, by a major general. The British army abolished the rank of brigadier general after WW I, replacing it briefly with the hybrid colonel-commandant and then with brigadier without the 'general'. There is now a greater degree of standardization across most armed forces, with the term 'one star' describing brigadiers, brigadier generals, commodores, and so on; to 'four star' for full generals and their equivalent; and 'five star' for those forces which still retain field marshals or their equivalents.

In most 18th- and 19th-century armies there was a close association between social class and commissioned rank. This was rarely simple or straightforward, as most armies commissioned men who had little real claim to gentle birth. This increased in wartime when the demand for officers was greater. *Frederick 'the Great' disliked bourgeois officers, but was prepared to tolerate them, especially in units at the lower end of the social scale. Even he could be persuaded that a man's conduct was so markedly honourable as to justify elevation to the nobility. David Krauel, a 50-year-old private soldier who was first to storm into the Zizkaberg at Prague in 1744, was ennobled as Krauel von Zizkaberg. However, in the Prussian army of 1786 there were only some 700 bourgeois in an officer corps of 7,000, and all but 22 of them were company officers.

The Austrian army was more liberal, and was easily impressed by some odd pedigrees advanced by younger sons from Scots and Irish families. The French army, relatively liberal at the beginning of the 18th century grew less so as it wore on. The Ségur edict of 1781 required candidates for commissioning to produce evidence of four degrees of nobility, and the strengthening of the aristocracy's grip on officer rank helped alienate ambitious NCOs on the eve of the Revolution.

If gentle birth helped gain commissioned rank the reverse could also be true. In 1757 Maria Theresa decreed that all commoner officers with 30 years' meritorious service should be raised to the hereditary nobility. In the British army, the fact that John Elley's father was an eating-house keeper did not prevent Elley from commanding the Royal Horse Guards, being knighted, and establishing his descendants as gentlemen. The route to commissioned rank and, through it, to gentle status was made easier in the British army, which permitted the purchase of commissions: many a family put new money into a commission, as Thackeray's odious Mr Osborne demonstrates.

This association between officer rank and social status continued until well into the 20th century. In the German army of WW I social strictures on officer-recruiting remained rigid: although the number of reserve officers increased eightfold, the number of regular officers only doubled although three-quarters of the total became casualties. The British army commissioned 500 NCOs and warrant officers in the first month of the war, but relatively few of the survivors retained regular commissions after the war. And while it was easy for boys who had been to public (that is, in Britain, fee-paying) schools to gain direct commissions, especially at the start of the war, as the author R. C. Sherriff discovered, the path was far steeper if one's school did not feature on the approved list. The US army has good reason to be regarded as a meritocracy and places at *West Point were traditionally in the gift of elected representatives, but its officers become gentlemen by Act of Congress.

Alongside the liberalization of social requirements for commissioning went the professionalization of officer corps, with academic and professional entry standards and specified rules for promotion. The process was subject to considerable variation, for while Austrian officers were expected, from the 1750s, to attend military *academies like the Theresianische Militarakademie in Wiener-Neustadt or the Ingenieursakademie in Vienna, the purchase of commissions in the British army was not abolished until 1871. At much the same time the profession broadened its base, as medical officers and *commissariat officials in most armies were admitted to commissioned status.

Although most armed forces would argue that they offer careers open to men (and, increasingly, *women) of talent regardless of social background, there is widespread belief that commissioned rank demands personal qualities as well as military skills. Its holders must retain standards of behaviour, on and off duty, which do not compromise the trust vested in them or the status they hold. Some military sociologists have emphasized the 'narrowing skill differential' between officers, especially those in supporting services, and civilian managers, and suggested that societal pressures, and in particular the shift from institution to occupation, will inevitably chance the nature of officership. Others have identified the characteristics of corporateness, expertise, and responsibility as fundamental to any genuine profession, and have argued that these have specific and lasting relevance to the military officer.   RH

Huntington, Samuel P., *The Soldier and the State: The Theory and Practice of Civil-Military Relations* (Cambridge, Mass., 1957).
Moskos, Charles C., and Wood, Frank R., *The Military: More than Just a Job?* (London, 1988).

Oman campaign (1962–75). The British withdrawal from *Aden in November 1967 and the creation of the People's Democratic Republic of Yemen led to a marked increase in irregular warfare in neighbouring Dhofar. Dhofar, the southernmost province of the sultanate of Oman (formerly Muscat and Oman), was a breeding ground for nationalist activity. Poor and oppressed, distanced culturally and geographically from Oman proper (some 621 miles (1,000 km) to the north) the mountain-dwelling Jebalis were natural *guerrilla fighters. The Dhofar Liberation Front (DLF) began a *low-intensity conflict in 1962, and between then and 1967 had carried out a series of small-scale attacks against the main track leading from Salalah to Thumrait.

Ineffective action by the ill-equipped Sultan's Armed Forces (SAF) allowed hostile numbers to increase to some 6,000 before the old sultan was replaced by his son in July 1970. Qaboos bin Said, a Sandhurst-trained progressive and exquisite, set about a programme of welfare reforms, aided and abetted by British Army Training Teams (BATTs), supplied by 22nd SAS Regiment. With the help of *SAS organized *firqat* (local *counter-insurgency forces), seconded British officers, and Iranian and Jordanian troops, the SAF finally ousted the insurgents from Dhofar. While the insurgency was declared over and official British involvement ceased in December 1975, incursions by Dhofari rebels based in Yemen continued until 1983.   PMacD

Oman, Sir Charles William Chadwick (1860–1946), British historian. Born in colonial India, Oman was sent to England to be educated. He developed a wide range of interests, extending from the ancient world through medievalism to Welsh castles, coins, and 19th-century historical topics. Elected to a fellowship at All Souls College, Oxford, in 1883, he was to publish several diverse books, among them *The Art of War in the Middle Ages* and *The Art of War in the 16th century*. He is principally remembered for his vast and authoritative *A History of the Peninsular War* (7 vols., Oxford 1902–30), with which military history in the form of pure campaign narrative reached its apogee.   DG

Omdurman, battle of (2 September 1898), the decisive battle in the reconquest of the *Sudan by *Kitchener. His Anglo-Egyptian army (some 26,000 men) defeated a *Mahdist army almost twice its size in a morning, suffering only 48 fatalities and 382 wounded while killing 11,000 Mahdists and wounding an estimated 16,000. The battle inspired Hilaire Belloc to write:

> Whatever happens we have got
> The Maxim gun and they have not

Anglo-Egyptian firepower annihilated massed frontal charges, and hand-to-hand fighting occurred only when the 21st Lancers (including *Churchill), having failed to reconnoitre, charged into a substantial force of enraged Mahdists concealed in a wadi and were roughly handled.
                                                            EMS

Spiers, Edward M. (ed.), *Sudan: The Reconquest Reappraised* (London, 1998).
Zulfo, 'Ismat Hasan, *Karari* (London, 1980).

---

omens are related to divination, foretelling, premonitions, apparitions, and prophecies and are no strangers to ancient and modern battlefields. The uncertainty of war makes military enterprises especially open to the interpretation of omens and divination, and soldiers remain the most superstitious of men. Omens are passive phenomena requiring interpretation whereas divination is ritual practice designed to interrogate fate and is first recorded in Ancient Mesopotamia. The Greeks and Romans used divination to determine the outcome of war (see RITUAL WARFARE), particularly through oracular utterance and by *augury* (observing, among other phenomena, the flight or behaviour of birds) or *haruspices* (studying the entrails of animal *sacrifices).

Theodosius I outlawed divination in AD 391, the practice having survived in the nominally Christian army. Omens remained potent and Constantine's victory at the Milvian Bridge in AD 312 was famously preceded by the appearance of Christ's cross and the words 'In hoc signo vinces'. In 1066, despite being in possession of papal authority to suppress heresy in England, *William 'the Conqueror' drew on an older tradition by pointing to the appearance of Halley's comet as an augury of divine blessing on his enterprise. He also turned to advantage his legendary stumble on the beach at Pevensey, telling his followers that by this act he took possession of his rightful kingdom. Medieval chroniclers recorded omens at all great events; for example, *Froissart noted a heavy thunderstorm, an eclipse of the sun, and a hovering circle of crows before the battle of *Crécy in 1346.

The Angel of Mons and the Golden Virgin of Albert provided sustaining inspiration to the Allies in WW I. The legend that the war would end badly if the latter fell off the basilica tower was taken so seriously that French military engineers quietly secured her in place, until the whole tower came down in 1918. During WW II, lucky rabbit's feet and other good luck charms were endemic among aircrew, the loss of which often led to fatalistic acceptance that the next flight would be their last.   BB

Bushaway, Bob, 'Name upon Name: The Great War and Remembrance', in Roy Porter (ed.), *Myths of the English* (London, 1992).

---

operational concepts (*see opposite page*)

---

operational level of war A metaphoric realm of military action lying between strategy and tactics. The latter are ancient concepts, referring on the one hand to the highest forms of military command (Gr.: *strategos*, the [art or office of] general-in-chief), and on the other to the methods and means of combat (Gr.: *taktika*, matters pertaining to arrangements). The 'operational' level of war, in contrast, is a reflection, at the level of theory, of the decentralized command structures made necessary by the expansion of
(*cont. on page 676*)

operational concepts

THERE are three components of military power: the moral, which motivates soldiers and makes them fight; the physical, the way they are armed and supplied; and the conceptual. The conceptual component of military power is the cheapest, in terms of financial investment, but acts as a powerful 'force multiplier' to the other two.

During the 20th century a number of broad operational concepts have shaped the way armed forces are designed for battle and the way campaigns have been conducted. They relate to both the *strategic purpose they strive to achieve and the *tactics that make them up. Some of the first ideas which could be described as 'operational concepts' were part of naval strategy, 'open' and 'close' *blockade, for example, and even such abstract concepts as 'the fleet in being' or 'command of the sea', although in modern terms these were strategic rather than operational. *Air power has also come up with operational concepts, for example the 'big wing' advocated by AM Leigh-Mallory during the battle of *Britain.

If there was an 'operational concept' at work in armies at the outbreak of WW I, it was the *doctrine of the offensive. The paralysing effect of modern artillery, rifle, and machine-gun fire, recognized in the Second *Boer War and *Russo-Japanese war, and the 'softness' of modern youth, which was not expected to bear privations as stoically and self-sacrificingly as its forefathers, led to a reaction. The French school was led by Col Louis de Grandmaison (1861–1915), the Director of Operations, who put forward his views in two lectures in 1911. 'It is more important', he said, 'to develop a conquering state of mind than to cavil about tactics.' Two years later he drew up the *Regulations for the Conduct of Major Formations* of October 1913, which declared 'the French army, returning to its traditions, recognizes no law save that of the offensive'.

In Germany there was a similar reaction against cautious tactics and by 1903 regulations emphasized the offensive. The *Schlieffen plan gave operational/strategic form to these tactics, although it was assailed by Gen Friedrich von Bernhardi, who preferred breakthrough to envelopment as an operational concept. In Britain Gen Sir Ian *Hamilton, a highly sensitive and intelligent man, also dismissed the belief expounded by Jan Bloch in his book *Future War*, that armies would be paralysed by fire. 'The best defence to a country', wrote Hamilton, 'is an army formed, trained, inspired by the idea of attack.'

The primacy of the offensive had universal appeal, whether to professional soldiers, who believed it to be the preserve of dedicated professional armies, or the radical left, who saw it as a product of popular will. It also fitted nicely with the views of Henri Bergson, the French philosopher, and those of Nietzsche and even of Darwin. In terms of the three components of military power, it represented a massive reliance on the moral, with far less emphasis on the necessary physical and very little on the conceptual.

In 1914 all the armies went on the offensive. However, it would be a mistake to link the terrible casualties of WW I too closely with the doctrine of the offensive. Given the mismatch between firepower and the means of mobility, huge casualties were inevitable. After the initial casualties British, French, and Germans all worked hard to minimize their own casualties by meticulous preparation and the use of new technology.

As the WW I armies chewed away at each other, unable to encircle one another in a single bite, images of eating or nibbling became popular. The emergence of the *operational level of war, under circumstances where a single battle could not be decisive but formed a stepping stone to a greater end, provided the ground in which modern operational concepts began to emerge.

The first concept that springs to mind—*blitzkrieg—was never formulated as an operational concept. It was not even a German military term but appears to have been invented by a US journalist after the 1939 *Polish campaign. One school of thought sees the initial German successes in 1939–41 as the result of a coherent blitzkrieg strategy or operational concept. The theory goes that in order to maintain consumer production at a high level *Hitler planned a series of short, mobile campaigns by tanks and aircraft (themselves to a large extent spin-offs from the civilian tractor and aircraft industries), with pauses between to replenish stockpiles. But, as Williamson Murray has argued, 'a closer examination of the evidence . . . points to an uncertain and unclear grand strategy in which the Germans put the military pieces together at the last moment, with serious doubts and in considerable haste'.

The first panzer division was improvised in the summer of 1935. The Germans' striking success at the start of WW II was therefore probably the product of a very transitory set of advantages. They had produced suitable equipment in the mid–1930s so it was well tried and tested and the troops well trained when war came; they had a primitive but effective system of close *air support, tested in the *Spanish civil war, and a command and control network which was tailored to coping with more rapid manoeuvre than any opponent could reasonably expect to achieve (see also MANOEUVRE WARFARE).

Whereas the German approach was therefore ad hoc, the Soviet approach was highly conceptual. Following on from work on 'deep battle', in the late 1920s, designed to break through the tactical crust of a WW I-style army, the Soviets began to develop the idea of the deep operation in the 1930s, probably the first true 'operational concept' and the origin of others since. It was the brainchild of *Triandafillov, *Tukhachevskiy, and Marshal Aleksandr Yegorov (1883–1939). The deep operation aimed to accomplish 'simultaneous destruction of the enemy through the entire depth of his deployment', by smashing through the tactical zone (12 miles (20 km) deep) and then introducing a 'breakthrough development echelon' comprising army and front mobile groups and *airborne forces. In the mid–1930s a deep operation was envisaged as that of a shock army or Front (army group). There would be an attack echelon (EA), a breakthrough exploitation echelon (ERP), reserves, air forces, and paratroops. The attack echelon comprised rifle corps with tanks and artillery, in order to break through the tactical zone. The exploitation echelon, comprising mobile groups formed from mechanized or cavalry corps, would then break out and convert tactical success into operational. A shock army would attack on a 31–50 mile (50–80 km) wide front, and penetrate to a depth of 43–62 miles (70–100 km).

The Red Army's *Field Service Regulations for 1936* (PU-36) only include provisions for deep battle but by the early 1940s Soviet military theorists had concluded that the larger deep operation might be conducted, not by one Front, but by several, and bring in naval forces. Such an operation might reach to a depth of 124 or 186 miles (200 or 300 km). These ideas were modelled on paper and by *exercises in the Kiev (1935), Moscow, Belorussian, and Odessa (1936) military districts, and also practised, on a smaller scale in the operations at Lake Khasan (1938) and *Khalkhin-Gol.

By the end of WW II a Front deep operation could involve a 373 mile (600 km) advance in twelve days, a six-day pause, and then another 600 km in twelve days, which remained the Soviet pattern of operation for the *Cold War. By the 1980s Soviet planners were envisaging a single, 22-day Theatre Strategic Operation (TSO) to cover 746 miles (1,200 km).

The prospect of a massive Soviet invasion, probably trying to avoid the use of *nuclear weapons and to overrun *NATO before it could take the political decision to use its own, led to a resurgence of conventional operational concepts in the 1970s. It is still unclear which came first: the renewed Soviet emphasis on so-called Operational Manoeuvre Groups (OMGs) or NATO's concept of

Follow-On Forces' Attack (FOFA). In order to stop a massive *Warsaw Pact offensive, it was necessary to tear away at forces far behind the forward troops, slowing and thinning them to the point where NATO's front line could engage them successfully. The OMG was a variant of the WW II forward detachment and mobile group, and comprised a resilient, fast-moving formation which would be inserted into a gap in the NATO deployment and run amok deep behind NATO forward positions. Its missions might be to destroy, disrupt, or capture nuclear weapons, airfields, command, control and communications, logistic support, and the lateral communications needed to move NATO troops to counter a Warsaw Pact breakthrough. It might also prevent NATO withdrawal and seize or isolate key political or economic objectives. Because OMGs and NATO forces would be mixed up, this might also discourage NATO from using nuclear weapons. When the OMG was first publicized in an open western journal in October 1982, the Soviets linked it with remarks the previous week by Gen Bernard Rogers, NATO's Supreme Allied Commander Europe, about FOFA. This interacted profoundly with the OMG concept since the OMG might actually remove the follow-on forces that FOFA hoped to attack.

Another concept, which evolved in response to the Warsaw Pact threat, was the US doctrine known by the fused syllables of 'AirLand battle'. The 1976 edition of the US FM 100–5 *field manual *Operations* had taken to heart the lessons of the 1973 *Arab–Israeli war and stressed the increased tempo of the modern battlefield. In 1977 Gen Donn A. Starry took over command of the US Army Training and Doctrine Command (TRADOC) at Fort Monroe, Virginia, and began a series of initiatives which led to the evolution of AirLand battle. A study called *Division 86* (later *Army 86*) began to explore the idea of a deeper battlefield or, from 1980, 'extended battlefield'. This involved the use of air power and *helicopters. It was summarized in the phrase 'AirLand battle', formally announced in 1981 and embodied in the September 1981 draft of the new FM 100–5 field manual published in 1982. FM 100–5 provided for three types of battle: the deep battle (against enemy follow-on forces), the close-in battle, and the battle in one's own rear area against *special forces (Spetsnaz).

FM 100–5 enunciated US army AirLand battle doctrine. It should not be confused with the futuristic study *Air Land Battle 2000*, a quite different document, although it often was. Whereas FM 100–5 field manual dealt with contemporary conditions, *Air Land Battle 2000* endeavoured to look 20 years ahead. A subsequent study called *Focus-21* developed the air-land battle theme further and was then combined with *Air Land Battle 2000* to produce a new concept of future operations called Army-21.

AirLand battle took a 'nonlinear view of battle'. It enlarged the battlefield area, stressing unified ground and air operations throughout the theatre. The war the USA and its Allies fought in the *Gulf in 1991 was AirLand battle, in particular the use of XVIII Airborne Corps with its assault by 300 attack helicopters of the US 101st Airborne Division. It is debatable whether AirLand battle would have worked in the crowded, wooded counterpane of Europe, for which it was originally intended. It did succeed in the broad vastness of the desert, which provided ideal conditions. FM 100–5 did include a substantial section on desert operations, but AirLand battle and the equipment designed to fit in with this concept—Abrams tanks, Bradley *MICVs and Apache helicopters—had originally been designed to fight the USSR, not Iraq, although the latter opponent obligingly used Soviet equipment and some Soviet tactics.

Since the Gulf war, information technology has multiplied and the latest US operational concept, Army After Next (AAN), looking to 2020, envisages a war in which the US enjoys total vision of the 'battlespace'. The armoured divisions of the Gulf war contained about 100,000 tons of equipment each and needed another 100,000 to keep them supplied. The average speed was little faster than that in WW II—20 mph (32 km/ph). AAN aims to cut the weight of a division to a quarter of this, which its authors believe is possible because total information dominance will permit precise strikes on enemy targets. Vehicles could also be less heavily armoured as they should be able to avoid hostile forces. AAN also aims to increase a new-style division's speed tenfold to 200 mph (322 kmph)—a true AirLand force. But this will be enormously expensive and the USA may only be able to afford one division of this type. Furthermore, who will be the USA's allies? It is unlikely that any other country will be able to field a similar force. The wars of the 21st century are likely to be asymmetric and dirty, with a lot of old-fashioned equipment and belligerents who may not be impressed by information dominance and are adept at operating without it. Operational concepts may be a valuable force multiplier, but there has to be force—physical and moral—to multiply.   CDB

Bellamy, Christopher, *The Evolution of Modern Land Warfare* (London, 1990).
—— *Expert Witness* (London, 1993).
Howard, Michael, 'The Doctrine of the Offensive', in *Makers of Modern Strategy* (Oxford, 1990).
Murray, Williamson, 'Forces Strategy, Blitzkrieg Strategy and the Economic Difficulties', *RUSI* (Mar. 1983).
Simpkin, Richard, *Race to the Swift* (London, 1985).
—— *Deep Battle* (London, 1987).

military institutions in the industrial era. In the middle decades of the 19th century, military writers began to refer to complex military tasks as 'operations', a term that initially did little more than capture the technocratic spirit of the age. In time the word became associated with the actions of large but subordinate military commands. In the 1920s Soviet theorists, influenced by German precedents, coined the expression 'operational art' to refer to the handling of formations above a division, and to the conduct of campaigns as distinct from battles. In 1939 the US army appended the term 'Operations' to the title of its capstone publication, the FM 100–5 *field manual—though it was only in 1982 that it officially accepted the 'operational level of war' as coequal to strategy and tactics.

The rising significance accorded the operational level of war reflects the degree to which military success has become associated with the co-ordinated action of independent, mobile forces; with the use by senior commanders of aircraft and other deep-strike weapons to avert tactical stalemate; and with *logistics, *intelligence, planning, and staff work as core military functions. Tasks like these resist the kind of prescriptive solutions that are normally applied to tactical problems. Yet they are distinctly military in character, and exist at some perceptible remove from the exigencies of policy and strategy, both of which, in the modern era, have been dominated by civilians. It is thus at the operational level of war that military officers have increasingly sought their professional identity. It is, proverbially, the level where generals fight.

This is less true of admirals or air marshals. *Navies and *air forces have paid far less attention to the operational level of war than armies have, in part because they have envisioned themselves exerting direct strategic influence of a kind that is supposed to make the application of operational art unnecessary. Much of the current interest in 'joint' operations, in which land, sea, and air forces act in close co-operation with each other, has been stimulated by the apparent vanity of such hopes, and by the realization that operational effectiveness on land requires mastery of all the media in which combat can occur. In the final analysis it is hard to say whether the idea of an operational level of war represents a permanent improvement in our understanding of war, or a response to transient conditions. The massive military organizations created by the industrial revolution and the advent of the mass mobilization, which called the operational level of war into existence, may themselves be supplanted by other military forms, employing such fine-grained communications technologies, or such precise and devastating means of attack, that abstract distinctions between strategy, operations, and tactics will lose their saliency.   DM

Opium war (1840–2), Anglo-Chinese conflict which ushered in a century of enforced exploitation of China, and a still-emotive symbol for Chinese resentment of the West. Four decades of mutual misunderstanding and disrespect meant that reciprocal humiliations in 1839–40 related to the illegal opium trade (the confiscation of Britons' property, their enforced expulsion from Macao, and outsiders' refusal to pay even lip-service to Chinese edicts) provided a tinderbox. This was lit on 4 September 1840 when Chinese attempts to stop supplies reaching a refugee flotilla off Hong Kong ended with the sinking of four war junks by the Royal

Navy. A letter of protest was sent to Peking, underlined by the *blockade of Canton and the occupation of Chusan. The emperor repudiated the subsequent Convention of Chuenpi, signed by his representatives on 20 January 1841, for giving away too much, and prepared for war. The British—commanded surprisingly effectively by a naval/military/civil committee—struck pre-emptively, eventually occupying the heights commandinge Canton, from which they withdrew on payment of $6 million. The British attacked Amoy in August and went into winter quarters at Ningpo and Chinhai, where they easily repelled attacks in the spring. Counter-attacking, they seized the forts guarding Hangchow, occupied Shanghai in June, and marched to the gates of Nanking. British demands were now more intransigent and imperial commissioners could only obtain terms far more severe than those of the 1841 Convention. The Treaty of Nanking gave Britain $21 million, the right to trade in five ports (opium was not mentioned), legal jurisdiction over her own nationals, and the island of Hong Kong. Humiliatingly one-sided, the war provided a little-heeded wake-up call to the complacent imperial *Manchu court.   DD

Fairbank, John King, *The Great Chinese Revolution* (London, 1987).

Farwell, Byron, *Queen Victoria's Little Wars* (London, 1973).

order, tactical Tactical order is how troops deploy for combat and can be divided into two categories: close and open order. While close order has today been relegated to the parade square, it was the predominant battlefield formation through most of history. Close order, where soldiers fought shoulder to shoulder in set tactical bodies (usually battalions), provided the mass needed for shock tactics and the concentration needed to employ inaccurate firearms. Further, it gave the commander the ability to control his soldiers on the battlefield. By the beginning of the 19th century, there were four basic close-order formations: the column, the line (see COLUMN AND LINE), the *ordre mixte*, and the square, each of which had its specific tactical uses.

Until the mid-19th century the main infantry weapon was the musket, normally only effective to 55 yards (50 metres). Given this, infantry had to concentrate on the battlefield in order to accumulate the volume of fire necessary to do damage to their opponent. This concentration was accomplished by deploying the infantrymen in ranks, either two or three deep; a formation called the 'line'. On a battlefield, the two combatants would face each other in parallel lines and fire away. Once their commander believed the other side was ready to break, he would order a charge to complete the process. Very seldom did it ever come to close-quarter *bayonet fighting, as one side or the other preferred to recall an appointment elsewhere.

As a unit attacking in line was highly vulnerable to cavalry attack and difficult to move across country, a 'column'

would be used to cover intermediate ground. The column consisted of a unit deployed in deep lines perpendicular rather than parallel to the enemy's front. This way, a battalion of 700 men would face the enemy with a front of only about 27 yards (25 metres), but would have a depth of about 164 yards (150 metres). This formation was, however, more vulnerable to artillery and unless deployed opportunely could be brought to a halt by fire from a steady line (for the moral impact of the column was considerable), bringing hundreds of muskets to bear on the column front. When *Wellington deployed his men on the reverse slope to protect them from artillery, he also achieved tactical surprise over French columns, which would often crest the slope still in columns and have to deploy into line under concentrated fire.

A combination of the line and column, called the *orde mixte*, was developed in the French army and was favoured by *Napoleon: two battalions in column formation flanked a battalion deployed in line in the centre. The *orde mixte* proved to be extremely flexible on the battlefield, as it combined the advantages of both formations: concentration of fire and shock.

The 'square' consisted of an infantry battalion (although large units could form the square as well) formed into a square (or sometimes diamond-shaped) formation with several rows of soldiers on each side. Squares could be formed so that the fire from each face would rake the flank of any attack upon a neighbouring square. These formations provided excellent protection from enemy cavalry, as the glittering lines of bayonets were an obstacle into which horses could rarely be made to charge. But squares were extremely vulnerable to field artillery and the textbook means of dealing with them was to use the threat of cavalry to force infantry to move from line into square, then shatter them with artillery, and then charge home.

Oblique order, more accurately termed oblique attack, was a ploy which enabled a commander to bring overwhelming superiority to bear on one wing of an enemy army. Used to great effect by the Theban general *Epaminondas, it was much discussed in early modern Europe and brought to perfection by *Frederick 'the Great'. While his advance guard headed for the chosen end of the enemy line, the remainder of his army followed with successive regiments 'refused', with each marching just behind, and slightly to the flank of, that in front. The enemy, confronted by an apparently solid Prussian line, found it hard to see exactly what Frederick was up to, but once the attack was under way the refused regiments marched slant-wise to concentrate on the chosen sector. It did not always work as planned. At Kolin (1757) the refused wing made an unsuccessful attack of its own, but at Zorndorf (1758) this wing (its commander anxious not to repeat the mistakes of Kolin) resolutely declined to engage. However, at *Leuthen (1757) the oblique attack went like clockwork, with successive Prussian units moving like automatons first to destroy the Austrian left wing and then to roll up the Austrian army from the flank.

As accurate long-range firearms came into general use in the late 19th century, close-order formations began to disappear from the battlefield. The great volume of accurate fire that could be generated by the individual infantryman meant that what had once been the preserve of élite troops, open order, now became standard. Instead of advancing in tight ranks, units now spread out in an effort to avoid enemy fire. Building on the tactics of skirmishers, open-order tactics possessed only loose tactical formations. The battalion ceased to be the prime tactical unit, as companies and sometimes platoons were dispersed across the battlefield, relying on the firepower of the individual rifleman, rather than on concentration or mass.

The transition to open-order tactics was not smooth. Despite the indisputable evidence of the deadly volume of fire of modern weapons offered by the wars of the second half of the 19th century, many officers (see FOCH) still clung to the belief that close-order tactics were necessary both for control and also for their moral effect. A very high level of motivation in the infantryman was required for open-order tactics to prevail in attack, and the apparently pig-headed survival of faith in semi-close-order formations not only illustrated a lack of confidence in their men by the officers in question but also reflected the well-known tendency of troops to bunch together under fire, something that still requires in-depth training to overcome. *Machine guns eventually won the argument.   RTF/RH

Boguslawski, Albrecht von, *Tactical Deductions from the War of 1870–1871* (Minneapolis, 1996), trans. from German orig. (1872).
Griffith, Paddy, *Forward into Battle* (Novato, Calif., 1990).
Gudmundsson, Bruce, *Stormtroop Tactics* (New York, 1989).
Lynn, John, *The Bayonets of the Republic* (Chicago, 1984).
Showalter, Dennis, *The Wars of Frederick the Great* (Harlow, 1996).

orders of chivalry first appeared in the 14th century as secular orders of *knighthood which were clearly distinguished from the earlier *military monastic orders. They were associations of knights identified by the wearing of a particular device or badge, bound together by solemn vows of loyalty to their sovereign or master (usually the founder of the order and his heirs after him) and of companionship toward one another. Admission was nominally elective, but usually followed the sovereign's preferred choice: elevated birth and proven military achievement were the crucial qualifications. Besides the great princely orders, the late Middle Ages witnessed the foundation of many lesser knightly orders or confraternities with their own regulations and special devices. We hear also from this time of a number of 'votal' orders, temporary associations whose statutes and emblems committed their companions to achieving certain stipulated deeds of arms, usually in the tourneying lists and in honour of ladies.

The most famous and long lived of the princely orders were the Garter, founded by *Edward III of England, probably in 1348, and the Golden Fleece, founded by Philip 'the Good', Duke of Burgundy, in 1430. Numerous other foundations of the 14th and 15th centuries included the Order of the Band and of Castile (1330), of the Star in France (1351), of the Knot of Naples (1352), of the Ermine of Brittany (1381); the Orders of the Dragon of Hungary (1408) and of the Swan of Brandenburg (1444); René of Anjou's Order of the Crescent (1448); and King Louis XI of France's Order of St Michael (1469).

The Burgundian writer Olivier de la Marche (1426–1502) lays down as a principle that for an association of knights with an identifying device to be properly called an order, its statutes must provide for regular chapter meetings, and for a limit on the number of companions admissible. An association of knights which had a badge or emblem but lacked one or both of these requirements he classified as a confraternity or a devise, and as of lesser status. The Garter and the Golden Fleece typified for him orders proper, their statutes providing for regular chapter meetings and limiting the number of companions, to 26 (including the sovereign) in the Garter's case, and originally to 25 in that of the Golden Fleece (raised to 31, including the sovereign, in 1433). Some other orders had a substantially larger companionship; papal letters concerning the foundation of the French Order of the Star speak for instance of 'a congregation of 200 knights'.

The communal and ceremonious activities of the orders naturally loom large in their statutes, which commonly included sumptuary regulations (the robes, mantles, and *badges and insignia of the order): directions for chapter meetings (usually at the feast of the order's patron saint, for example St George for the Garter) and for the liturgical offices and the banquet accompanying these meetings; regulations for providing masses for recently departed companions; procedures for election to vacancies and rules about qualifications for candidature. Other matters recurrently regulated by the statutes of orders have a sharper military and political tone. Loyal service, and in particular armed service, to the sovereign was expected of every companion. If for honourable reason he was unable to discharge it, he would be expected to resign the order and return its badges and insignia, as the French Knight Enguerrand de Coucy returned his Garter in 1377 because of his overriding obligation to King Richard II's enemy, the king of France. At chapter meetings the conduct in the field of individual companions was closely scrutinized; thus in 1433, for instance, the chapter of the Golden Fleece ruled that Jean de Montaigu must resign the order in consequence of his flight from the battle of Anthon. Conversely, several orders, including the Star, the Knot, and the Crescent, maintained a 'book of adventures' recording acts of special prowess of individual companions (none have survived).

The mottoes, badges, and insignia of princely orders illuminate the military and political purposes of their founders. Thus the Garter motto, 'honi soit qui mal y pense', asserted the justice of Edward III's cause in his war with France, 'retorting shame and defiance upon him that should dare to think ill of so just an enterprise' (the story of the king at a ball picking up the fallen garter of the Countess of Salisbury is late and apocryphal). The sash of Alfonso XI's Order of the Band was given to knights 'who had done some good deed of arms against the enemies of the King . . . in such a way that each one of the others wanted to do well in chivalry to gain that honour and the King's good will'. Thus the purpose behind the foundation of the great chivalric orders was the desire of princes, through these honorific companionships, to bind to their service and policies individual members of the aristocracy, and so enhance their own dignity and repute in the eyes of their mightier subjects and of the chivalrous world at large. Membership of their orders was not restricted to their subjects and vassals, and the election of 'stranger knights' could be significant, diplomatically as well as chivalrously. The admission of a fellow sovereign to a princely order was an important symbol of commitment to alliance. Under Edward IV no fewer than eight foreign sovereigns came in this way to be admitted to the Garter, including Charles 'the Bold' of Burgundy and Ferdinand of Spain. A number of the greater princely orders long survived the Middle Ages, but most lost in time their knightly military significance.

MK

Boulton, D'Arcy Jonathan Dacre, *The Knights of the Crown* (Woodbridge, 1987).

Keen, M., *Chivalry* (New Haven, 1984).

Kruse, H., Paravicini, W., and Ranft, A., *Ritterorden und Adelsgesellschaften im spätmittelalterliche Deutschland* (Frankfurt, 1991).

Vale, J., *Edward III and Chivalry* (Woodbridge, 1982).

Vale, M., *War and Chivalry* (London, 1981).

Ordnance, Board and Master-General of

The Board of Ordnance was responsible for the British army's train of artillery, comprising guns and engineer services, and came under the control of the Master-General of the Ordnance. This post dates back to the 15th century and was originally entitled Master of the Ordnance from 1414 to 1597 when the title Great Master of the Ordnance came into use. The present title of Master-General of the Ordnance dates from 1603.

Until the early 1700s, there existed a considerable anomaly in the organization of the British army. While the cavalry and infantry came directly under the commanding general in the field, the artillery and engineers remained the responsibility of the Master-General, who was tasked with the supply of all guns, even to the Royal Navy. Although a serving officer, his was very much a political appointment. This had serious implications for the army's operational efficiency. It was fortunate that the captain general commanding British and allied forces during the War of the *Spanish Succession, the Duke of *Marlborough, combined both the positions of commander of the army and Master-General of the Ordnance. In 1716 he requested that the immediate predecessor of the Royal Regiment of Artillery be created and bring the guns into the main army organization. This was one of Marlborough's last and most important services to the army.

The responsibilities of the Board grew to include the upkeep of military buildings although it was notoriously sluggish in this role. Its abolition was proposed before the *Crimean war, and it was eventually wound up in 1854-5 and its duties taken over by the newly established Secretary of War and the C-in-C.

In the modern British army, the Master-General is the fourth military member of the Army Board. He is responsible for the identification of future weapon systems needed by the army and the actions taken to meet those needs.

MCM/RH

organization, military (*see page* 680)

Osaka castle, sieges of

(1614-15). Following the establishment of the Tokugawa shogunate in 1603 the opposition to *Tokugawa Ieyasu centred around Toyotomi Hideyori, the son of the late *Toyotomi Hideyoshi. In 1614 Hideyori fortified himself inside Osaka castle with over 100,000 troops, many of whom were *ronin, dispossessed *samurai whose masters had perished in battle. The Tokugawa army began a long siege during the winter of 1614-15, but the castle, under the inspiration of Sanada Yukimura, resisted successfully. The Tokugawa tried negotiation, backing up their demands with a fierce artillery bombardment. The conclusion was a spurious peace, and the Tokugawa began to demolish the walls and fill in the moat. Alarmed by these developments Hideyori again increased his garrison, and the summer campaign of Osaka began. At first the Osaka troops tried to defeat the individual Tokugawa units before they had the chance to regroup outside the weakened walls, but defeats at Domyoji and Wakae made them seek safety within the castle walls. In June 1615 the Osaka garrison marched out for a pitched battle at Tennoji. Driven back by the Tokugawa the defenders tried to hold the castle, but the keep was bombarded and burned as Hideyori committed suicide.

SRT

OSS

(Office of Strategic Services), an *intelligence organization set up in the USA in late 1941 along similar lines to Britain's *SOE. Based on existing US government departments and initially titled the office of Co-Ordinator of

(*cont. on page* 682)

MOST modern military forces tend to have organizational and structural similarities, reflecting not only common origins but also the practical span of command and the nature of the bonding process. There is usually a difference between the organization and strength of an army in peace (peace footing or peace establishment) and in war (war footing or war establishment), and history suggests that armies which adapt most successfully to the demands of war are those in which the war establishment is a logical reflection of the peacetime structure. Individual regiments are generally known as units, and the larger structures into which they are combined as formations: the basic component of a regiment, the company or its equivalent, is styled a subunit. That said, terminology varies between nations and between arms of the service. The infantry subunit is a company composed of platoons, while in the cavalry it is usually a *squadron composed of troops, and in the artillery a battery composed of sections or troops.

Modern armies can trace their origins back to the mercenary bands of the 15th century. The basic unit of the period was the company—where *mercenaries were concerned, as much a commercial enterprise as a military force—command by a captain, whose principal officer, the lieutenant (Fr.: *lieutenant*, taking the place), was so called because he could take the captain's place when required to do so. A junior officer carried the company's ensign, and his *rank bore its title. Companies were combined under the rule, or regiment, of a colonel, and during the 16th and 17th centuries the state strengthened its control over colonels, with their *commissions increasingly being signed by the monarch. Uniforms and regimental *colours initially embodied the colonel's armorial bearings and livery, but soon took on the state's symbols. The link is exemplified in the British army, whose infantry regiments still carry a regimental colour and a queen's colour.

The fact that the infantry company, for much of history around 80 men, was a similar size to the Roman *centurium* is no accident, nor was the fact that the eight-man Prussian messing group, the *Kameradschaft*, looked much like the Legion's ten-man *conturbernium*. Such groups gained their cohesion from the routine of daily life, and were easily commanded by one man, although it was not until the 19th century that they began to gain a tactical significance which matched their administrative and psychological importance. They are the ancestors of the modern rifle section or squad.

By the 17th century regiments were brigaded, usually under the colonel who was 'eldest', that is senior by his date of commission. Just as a regiment was roughly similar to a Roman cohort, so the brigade had something in common with the legion. Experience demonstrated that commanders could deal most effectively with three or four senior subordinates, and there was a tendency to reduce the span of command within the regiment, either by subdividing regiments into battalions or by reducing the number of companies per battalion. Not least among the military skills of *Gustavus Adolphus was his recognition of the realistic span of command: he organized Swedish infantry into 150-man companies, with four companies to a battalion and three battalions to a brigade.

Regiments could be titled in a number of ways. Initially they took the name of their proprietary colonel, often a senior officer who 'owned' the regiment (and might indeed make a profit from it) but would be unlikely to command it in battle. Thus Howard's, Barrell's, and Munro's were among the government regiments at *Culloden in 1746, while 18th-century Prussian regiments included those of Markgraf Heinrich, Graf von Anhalt, and Prinz von Preussen. Regional titles were also common: the Régiment de Picardie was the oldest regiment of French infantry, and the Régiment d'Auvergne proudly described itself as 'stainless Auvergne' ('Auvergne sans tache').

The country regiment emerged as a fundamental element of organization in the British army after the *Cardwell reforms, and by WW I a unit like the Hampshire Regiment would have two regular battalions, usually with one at the depot and one abroad, a Special Reserve battalion to supply drafts to the regular battalions, and two or more Territorial battalions. Giving battalions such weight within the regiment was idiosyncratically British, for in most armies they had no distinct identity and were rarely separated from their parent regiment. Finally, regiments were often numbered, sometimes with 'of the Line' added to their number to distinguish them from light or *rifle regiments.

In the 17th and 18th centuries there was no permanent tactical organization in the infantry below company level. The term platoon referred either to groups of 'commanded' *musketeers interwoven, sometimes rather hazardously, into the ranks of the cavalry to provide it with fire, or to ad hoc designations of small groups within the regiment or battalion—like 'platoons of the first firing'—to establish a pattern of rolling volley fire. As linear tactics broke down platoons gained permanent identity and tactical function, and in many armies they became the lowest level at which an officer—lieutenant or second lieutenant—routinely commanded. By WW I platoons were established in most major armies, and one of the British army's most successful trainers and tactical innovators, Lt Gen Sir Ivor Maxse, emphasized that platoon training was the key to success.

Organization above brigade level took great leaps forward in the 18th and early 19th centuries. Subdividing armies into divisions comprising several brigades made them easier to move, as they could use different routes, their baggage trains would be less encumbering and it would be easier to requisition food and fodder. Divisions were used in the 18th century, but they were either ad hoc or administrative, although the work of *Guibert, Bourcet, and Broglie pointed the way ahead. All-arms divisions, typically consisting of twelve battalions of infantry, a regiment of cavalry, and 32 guns, were used in the armies of revolutionary France, and the example was widely copied.

The French army also led the way in grouping divisions into the *corps d'armée*, variously translated as corps or army corps. Each corps consisted of two to four infantry divisions, a brigade or division of light cavalry, together with artillery, engineers, and transport. *Napoleon placed the corps at the very heart of his system, as he wrote in 1809: 'Here is the general principle of war—a corps of 25,000–30,000 men can be left on its own. Well handled, it can fight or alternatively avoid action, and manoeuvre according to circumstances without any harm coming to it, because an opponent cannot force it to accept an engagement but if it chooses to do so it can fight alone for a long time.' The *Jena/Auerstadt campaign of 1806 shows the corps system working at its best, with individual corps moving in what Napoleon called his 'square battalion' (*bataillon carré*) through the Thuringerwald to fall on the Prussians.

The next major innovations did not appear for another century. The mass armies swept into being by conscription might comprise a number of field armies—like the German First, Second, and Third in 1870. The experience of 1914 showed that it was difficult for a C-in-C to deal effectively with the headquarters of several armies, and on both the western and *eastern front armies were combined into army groups, which were usually given a geographical or functional title, like Army Group Centre or Reserve Army Group, or named after their commander, like Army Group Crown Prince. In Russia the term Front—as in Steppe Front, first used during WW I—had the same meaning as army group.

During the later 20th century military organization continued to evolve. Divisional structures became more varied, and armoured, motorized, and mechanized infantry, parachute, mountain, and marine divisions appeared. During the *Cold War both *NATO and the *Warsaw Pact had permanent military structures in the central region of Europe, and generations of NATO soldiers exercised within the 'layer cake' structure of national corps within multinational army groups. As part of the quest for a European defence identity after the Cold War a Franco/German/Spanish Eurocorps was created, while the corps-sized Allied Rapid Reaction Corps combines forces from most NATO nations around a British framework. At the turn of the millennium the lack of clearly defined threats but the multiplicity of risks encourages defence planners to think increasingly in terms of modular force structures which can be assembled to fit particular tasks. This may result in the eclipse of some of the larger structures of yesteryear, but it will be surprising if the familiar building blocks of companies, batteries, and squadrons do not retain their traditional importance, for they say as much about human nature as about armed forces.

RH

Information (COI), the OSS was formally activated in June 1942 under the leadership of Maj Gen William 'Wild Bill' Donovan, a Franklin D. *Roosevelt confidant from his clandestine relationship with *Churchill during the 1930s.

Like the SOE, the OSS was tasked with undertaking unconventional warfare (UW) as well as intelligence gathering and evaluation, which included psychological operations, sabotage, *guerrilla warfare, and the co-ordination of resistance activity behind enemy lines.

Divided into three operational branches: Intelligence, Special Operations, and Operational Groups, the OSS remained a cellular organization, with individual groups knowing little of the others. The operational groups (OGs) each consisted of 30 enlisted men and three officers, divided into two 15-man sections, and tasked with a particular region or country. Because of the need for linguists, volunteers were recruited from a wide range of backgrounds, many without any previous military connections.

Training was similar to that carried out by the *commandos, with emphasis placed on raiding, *sentry elimination, ambushing, cross-country night navigation exercises, and target attacks. With the exception of *demolitions training, there was little in the way of literature to aid either the students or their instructors, and in the early days the OSS lacked the experienced directing staff that later operations would provide.

Further training for OSS operators destined for western Europe was provided in conjunction with already-established SOE units in Scotland and the Midlands. Special units known as 'Jedburgh' teams were raised, as part of a tripartite effort by the SOE, OSS, and the French Bureau Central de Renseignements et Action (BCRA). Consisting of an officer from either the OSS or the SOE, plus a French officer and a radio operator, the four-man Jedburgh teams were parachuted into occupied countries in advance of conventional forces. The first Jedburgh force numbered some 350 of all ranks and nationalities, and more were to follow.

From 1941 until the Allied invasion of Normandy in 1944 the Jedburghs operated in occupied Europe in ever-increasing numbers, providing Supreme Headquarters Allied Expeditionary Force (SHAEF) with strategic information for the preparation of the *Normandy landings. They conducted both passive and active sabotage campaigns against transport targets and, on receipt of the invasion signal, maximized their activities to delay Axis reinforcements reaching Normandy. The crack *SS *Das Reich* armoured unit, for example, had to travel from southern France by road because of the disruption of the railway system, committing atrocities as it went, in response to harassment from the emboldened French Resistance.

While a significant proportion of the French population were sympathetic to the Allied cause, only an estimated 2 per cent were actively involved in resistance. Some 10,000 French civilians were killed, either as a direct result of resistance activity or by German reprisals. Insignificant in the overall holocaust of WW II, these losses must also be measured against the gains in terms of enemy soldiers committed to garrison and guard duties throughout the occupied territory, and in material damage. Aerial bombing was still very clumsy and the Jedburghs were a very cost-effective means of 'throwing sand in the works' by destroying railway tracks and, particularly, switching points.

Both the SOE and OSS sent thousands of agents into occupied western Europe, Italy, and the Balkans. However, the two organizations did not always agree on policy, as their differing attitudes towards the Vichy authorities in French North Africa testifies. The Balkans too proved to be a sensitive area, with two distinct resistance groups being supported initially, before the royalists were dropped in favour of *Tito's communist Partisans. Tito was successful in creating diversionary actions responsible for tying-up over two Axis divisions, denying their deployment elsewhere, and preventing Germany achieving full control of *Yugoslavia.

The area of OSS operations was extensive, and extended across the world, with two main exceptions: Central and South America, which was covered by the Federal Bureau of Investigation (FBI); and the Pacific area, where Gen Douglas MacArthur's own organization conducted OSS-type operations. OSS Detachment 101, which operated behind Japanese lines in the *Burma campaign, is accredited with over 5,500 enemy killed and a further 10,000 wounded, at a cost of only 15 OSS operators lost. This detachment was also responsible for the repatriation of 215 downed Allied aircrew. While rescuing shot-down pilots represented a small area of OSS operations, it provided a morale booster to the men of Allied air forces. Of those airmen brought down over occupied Europe, over 5,000 were brought out by the OSS, in itself a significant achievement that contributed much to the Allied war effort.

Post-war the OSS was disbanded, only to be reborn three years later as the *CIA. One enormously ironic legacy was the help and equipment it provided for resistance to the Japanese in Vietnam, one of the reasons that *Giap was able to field 5,000 Vietminh regulars in August 1945 and go on to defeat the French during the *Indochina war and, later, the USA herself.   PMacD

Oudinot, Marshal Nicolas Charles, Duc de Reggio (1767–1847). Oudinot was introduced to Tsar Alexander by Napoleon as the Bayard of his army, a fitting description of an officer wounded in action 22 times. A brewer's son from Bar-le-Duc, he served in the ranks of the old army and was commissioned after the Revolution, rising rapidly to command a brigade in 1794. He earned real distinction commanding a force of picked *grenadiers who rushed the key Danube bridge at Vienna on 12 November 1805, and fought with distinction at *Austerlitz and Friedland. Appointed marshal and duke in 1809, he was charged with the occupation of Holland in 1810. Entrusted with the smallest of the Grande Armée's corps in the Russian campaign of 1812, he was wounded and came close to capture on the retreat, but organized fifteen companions and drove off his opponents. He was not a success in command of a large and widespread force in Germany in 1814, but fought hard at *Leipzig, characteristically swimming the Elster at the battle's conclusion, a feat which cost his comrade *Poniatowski his life. In 1814 he fought a rearguard action of typical determination after Arcis-sur-Aube. Showered with honours after the Second Restoration, he commanded the Spanish expedition of 1823.   RH

Pacific campaign (1941–5). The roots of the Pacific conflict lay in the Japanese unwillingness to accept a status quo dictated by the USA and Britain. Following what most thought was a crushing victory in the *Russo-Japanese war, Japan felt cheated by the ensuing peace brokered by Theodore *Roosevelt. Nor was she happy at her share of the German Far Eastern possessions following WW I, when she was the least remembered of the Allies. The Washington Conference (1921–2) limitation on naval armaments, which purported to lock Japan into naval inferiority vis-à-vis the USA, was perceived as a further insult. The collapse of the world economy in 1929 played into the hands of extreme chauvinists, some civilian but primarily within the army, who were hostile to the West and anxious to build up an autarchic economic empire, and Japanese policy became overtly aggressive and expansionist. In time this led to an alliance with Nazi Germany and fascist Italy (the Axis), two other regimes dissatisfied with the 'new world order' following 1914–18 and determined to change it in their favour.

In 1931 the Japanese army in Manchuria seized the whole province. Border incidents with China were provoked until in 1937 full-scale war broke out, which led to the Japanese conquest of much of northern China by 1941. French defeat in Europe in 1940 permitted the Japanese to move into Indochina without firing a shot. Although she had a long-declared interest in China, a strangely proprietory attitude born of a century-old missionary commitment, the USA was slow to react to Japanese expansion, while the European colonial powers did almost nothing to obstruct it from fear of provoking a Pacific war they could not afford. But by 1940 Franklin D. *Roosevelt felt strong enough to do more than merely provide economic and semi-official military aid to China, and began a more forceful economic campaign against Japan. In July oil and scrap-metal exports

were restricted and, following Japan's occupation of Indochina, a tighter oil embargo was imposed.

The oil factor prompted Japanese military leaders to plan a 'southward advance' to seize the oil and other resources of the Dutch Indies and British Malaya. They believed that war with the USA was inevitable, but calculated that seizing oil supplies would allow the Japanese navy to hold a 'southern perimeter' in the Pacific around their new empire which Americans would lack the will or ability to penetrate. After the failure of diplomatic negotiations with the USA in the autumn of 1941, the emperor finally approved the plan to seize the southern area on 1 December 1941. *Yamamoto, C-in-C of the Combined Fleet, knew the economic power of the USA and was not sanguine about the army-driven policy, but devised a plan whereby naval aircraft flown from a powerful group of aircraft carriers would neutralize the American Pacific Fleet while the southward advance was completed.

As Yamamoto had predicted, the Japanese ran wild for the first six months. Quite by chance, the US aircraft carriers did not share the fate of the battleships at *Pearl Harbor, but the southward advance proved unstoppable against weak or poorly prepared defences. *Hong Kong fell on 25 December and the conquest of Malaya was complete with the fall of Singapore on 15 February 1942 (see MALAYA AND SINGAPORE CAMPAIGN). US forces in the Philippines were quickly cornered and finally surrendered on 6 May, while the Dutch East Indies, the Solomon Islands, and most of New Guinea were in Japanese hands by March. British, Dutch, and US naval and air forces in the theatre had been destroyed, but a US carrier force inflicted the first check on Japanese expansion at the battle of the Coral Sea (5–7 May 1942). After a raid on Tokyo by American carrier-launched medium bombers, Yamamoto was ordered to secure the ocean perimeter, an operation he combined with a plan to lure what was left of the American Pacific Fleet into a battle of annihilation.

The Pacific theatre became a chiefly American responsibility, as British Commonwealth forces struggled to contain Japanese pressure through Burma towards India. Though Roosevelt favoured priority for the European theatre following German declaration of war on 11 December 1941, the Anglophobe US navy chief Adm King (and much of American opinion) favoured emphasis on the Pacific. Forces were rushed to the southern Pacific to hold the remaining islands and to protect Australia, but the quantity of material and trained men available left a thin shield until American rearmament reached higher levels in 1943.

The turning point was the failure of the Japanese grand naval plan to achieve strategic dominance of the mid-Pacific at *Midway between 4 and 6 June, where a US carrier force under Adm Spruance sank four Japanese carriers and destroyed the cream of Japan's naval aviators. Exhibiting none of the kamikaze spirit that was to characterize Japanese resistance later, when it made no difference to the final outcome, Yamamoto turned his huge battle fleet around and went home. Even given that his opponent *Nimitz was intercepting his signals, something that was to lead to Yamamoto's aerial assassination a year later, his decision to withdraw was illogical. He knew that he was coming to the end of the window of opportunity before US industrial power inexorably began to crush Japan, yet he did not play his battleship trump card when it might still have been decisive.

While the USA devoted the bulk of its army to the war in Europe, the Pacific was by far the main theatre for the navy and US Marines, while *MacArthur was successful in his public and private lobbying to ensure that the army also got enough resources to compete. The strategy was to assault (or bypass) key island strongholds while unrestricted submarine warfare gnawed away at Japanese trade and military supply lines. The Japanese were reduced to holding on to what had been seized and trying to conserve sufficient naval and air reserves to counter the American advance. The material contest was a very uneven one. In 1943–4 Japan launched 7 aircraft carriers, the USA 90. Japanese naval aircraft were soon technically inferior to their US counterparts, while by January 1944 they had only 4,050 aircraft with which to oppose 11,442. But even more significant was their loss of trained pilots, with 50 per cent of sorties not returning to base in 1944. Meanwhile US submarines reduced the Japanese merchant fleet from over 5 million tons in 1942 to a mere 670,000 in 1945, and sank a warship tonnage of over 2 million.

During 1944 the US advance northwards from New Guinea and the Solomon Islands and westwards across the Pacific from the Marshall and Gilbert and Ellice Islands was speeded up in order to secure bases from which American long-range bombers, and in particular the new B-29 'Superfortress', could attack the Japanese home islands. In June 1944 the US navy was in a position to attack and seize the Mariana Islands, including Saipan, from which sustained air attack could be conducted. Japanese leaders were determined to hold on to what they saw as the critical area of the Pacific theatre. Adm Ozawa gathered a force of 9 aircraft carriers and 450 aircraft, but was greatly outnumbered by the 15 carriers and 902 aircraft available to the US task force. In what became known as the 'Great Marianas Turkey Shoot' US aircraft destroyed the Japanese carrier force and all but 35 Japanese aircraft. The battle of the Philippines Sea was an overwhelming US victory and paved the way for the successful occupation of Saipan by 10 July and Guam by 8 August. On every island Japanese soldiers refused to surrender, which made conquest a longer and more costly process than the balance of material forces suggested. In savage fighting almost all the 27,000 Japanese troops on Saipan were killed.

Not to be outdone, MacArthur was making a virtue of necessity by 'island-hopping' around areas of Japanese strength, and used political and sentimental arguments to insist on the strategically irrelevant invasion of the Philippines. In October the largest task force of the Pacific war sailed for the island of Leyte to begin the reconquest of the archipelago. The Japanese navy calculated that a triple-pronged counter-attack making use of the channels between the islands and the remains of their land-based air power might offer a last chance of success, but they simply lacked the strength to make their brilliant conception work. The battle of Leyte Gulf was the largest naval engagement in history and despite luring away Adm Halsey's main battle fleet, there were enough ships left to withstand the Japanese attack and US submarine and air dominance was decisive. The Japanese lost 28 warships to 6 and were finished.

Conquest of the Mariana Islands allowed US bombers to be deployed for a concerted attack on the Japanese war economy. The Twenty-First Bomber Group, which had been prepared for operations from mainland China, was transferred to Saipan from where operations were launched from November 1944. The Japanese war economy was already crippled by lack of raw materials because of the submarine campaign, but the American Joint Chiefs ordered the air force to attack Japanese aircraft and shipping industries, and to undertake urban area bombing as in Europe. From March 1945 Gen Le May undertook the firebombing of vulnerable Japanese cities as gloatingly predicted by *Mitchell, and between May and August a schedule of 58 cities was drawn up for destruction from the air. As has since become their habit, American air leaders argued that bombing alone would decide the issue, blithely ignoring the fact that without the US navy they would not even have got within range.

Nonetheless preparations began for a massive amphibious assault on Japan, code-named OLYMPIC, for which the US navy allocated 90 aircraft carriers and 14,000 combat

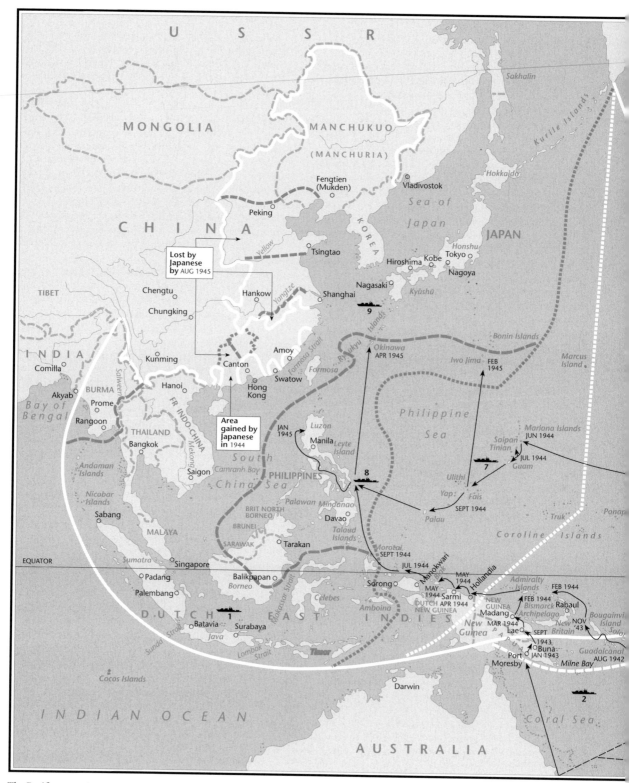

The **Pacific** campaign, 1941–5.

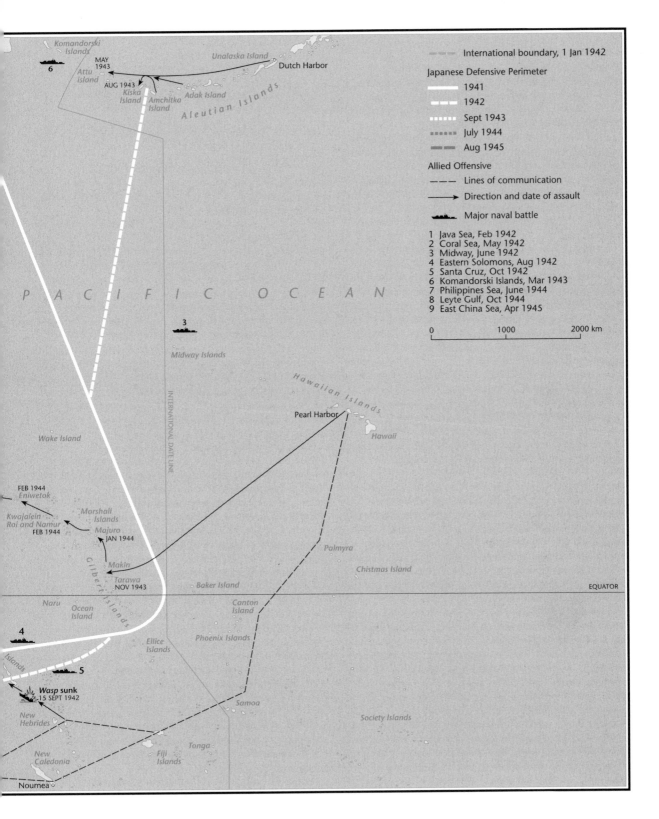

International boundary, 1 Jan 1942

Japanese Defensive Perimeter
- 1941
- 1942
- Sept 1943
- July 1944
- Aug 1945

Allied Offensive
- Lines of communication
- Direction and date of assault
- Major naval battle

1 Java Sea, Feb 1942
2 Coral Sea, May 1942
3 Midway, June 1942
4 Eastern Solomons, Aug 1942
5 Santa Cruz, Oct 1942
6 Komandorski Islands, Mar 1943
7 Philippines Sea, June 1944
8 Leyte Gulf, Oct 1944
9 East China Sea, Apr 1945

0   1000   2000 km

PACIFIC OCEAN

Komandorski Islands
MAY 1943
Attu Island
AUG 1943
Kiska Island
Amchitka Island
Adak Island
Unalaska Island
Dutch Harbor
Aleutian Islands

6

3
Midway Islands

Hawaiian Islands

Pearl Harbor
Hawaii

Wake Island

INTERNATIONAL DATE LINE

FEB 1944
Eniwetok
Kwajalein
Roi and Namur
FEB 1944
Marshall Islands
Majuro
JAN 1944
Makin
Tarawa
NOV 1943
Gilbert Islands
Baker Island
Palmyra
Chistmas Island

EQUATOR

Naru
Ocean Island
Canton Island
Phoenix Islands

4

5
Ellice Islands

Islands

Wasp sunk
15 SEPT 1942
New Hebrides
Samoa
Society Islands

New Caledonia
Fiji Islands
Tonga

Noumea

aircraft, larger than the force deployed for the *Normandy campaign. The Japanese military prepared for a last-ditch defence of the motherland, building thousands of primitive miniature submarines for suicide missions, and converting their remaining aircraft into one-way flying bombs for kamikaze attacks. It was the fear of massive casualties from the conquest of the home islands that encouraged the American government to launch attacks with two atomic bombs developed by the summer of 1945. Horrific though they were, the casualties inflicted by the atomic attacks on *Hiroshima and Nagasaki were no greater than those killed by Le May's firestorms. Japan might have capitulated earlier, but US insistence on unconditional surrender prolonged the war.

By August 1945 Japan was in ruins, and the political conflict between hard-line militarists and civilian capitulationists was resolved by the emperor, who made his first-ever broadcast to his people on 15 August, announcing in one of history's greater understatements that the war had 'not necessarily developed in a manner favourable to Japan'. By this time the last major Japanese armies had been effectively destroyed in the *Burma campaign and by the Soviet-Mongolian *Manchurian campaign. Even before this, the Japanese would probably have capitulated if they had been assured that they could keep their emperor, which in the end they did.

The Pacific war was fought with a ferocity and barbarism matched only on the *eastern front. It was a clash of cultures alien to one another in which profligate displays of extraordinary courage were commonplace on both sides. The single most disturbing thing for the Allies was that the Japanese code forbade surrender, meaning that even hopelessly surrounded and outnumbered garrisons fought to the death, and that Allied *POWs were barbarously treated. Even after the end of the war, Allied aircraft had to drop leaflets on the remaining pockets of resistance scattered throughout Japan's short-lived island empire, explaining what surrender meant in the western context. Unconvinced, the last Japanese soldier did not give himself up for a further quarter-century.

Although the outcome was US Pacific hegemony, the war also destroyed the moral underpinnings of European empires in the region, from which Holland, France, and Britain extricated themselves with varying degrees of skill. This ranged from the outright disastrous French attempt to reverse the tide in *Indochina, to the more measured departure of the British having defeated insurgency in the Malayan and Indonesian campaigns. Perhaps more significantly, the Russians were now a major presence in the Far East after a 40-year hiatus, and the Japanese had so weakened the Kuomintang regime of *Chiang Kai-Shek that *Mao Tse-tung and the communists were able to take over a third of the world's population in 1949. These changes led to the *Korean war, and ultimately the *Vietnam war, of which it might be said that it, too, did not necessarily

develop in a manner favourable to the main apparent victor in the Pacific campaign.   RO/HEB

Dower, J., War without Mercy: Race and Power in the Pacific War (New York, 1986).

Iriye, A., The Origins of the Second World War in the Pacific (London, 1987).

Rhodes, R., The Making of the Atomic Bomb (London, 1986).

Thorne, C., The Far Eastern War: States and Societies, 1941–1945 (London, 1986).

Vat, D. van der, The Pacific Campaign: The US–Japanese Naval War, 1941–1945 (London, 1992).

Werrell, K. E., Blankets of Fire: US Bombers over Japan during WW II (Washington, 1996).

pacifism covers a broad range of ideas and practices, but the common denominator is opposition to force and *militarism at the individual, societal, and international levels. In its purest form this opposition is absolute, unequivocal, and unconditional, and no resort to any violence whatsoever is condoned, for any reason. Absolute pacifists would reject *just-war theology, arguing that there are no circumstances in which war can be morally acceptable. The Lord Buddha so argued, and his followers have proved remarkably resilient in the face of invasion and oppression. The satyagraha protests organized by Gandhi against British rule in India, and King's civil rights protests in the USA in the 1960s, illustrate the use and efficacy of non-violent protest.

Approaching this but not rejecting violence in self-defence is the anarchist tradition that rejects the initiation of violence and thus most forms of government, based as they are on force or the threat of same. Because anarchism became associated with bomb-throwers in the late 19th century, and with some of the wilder elements on the Republican side during the *Spanish civil war, this tradition continues under the name of libertarianism and has developed a corpus of *political economy theory which states that the ultimate reason governments engage in war is to extend their ability to coerce their own peoples.

When pacifist movements are more conditional than that, it is difficult to see how they can still claim the title, but they do. The slogan 'the war to end all wars', belatedly thought up to justify the carnage of WW I, springs to mind; also the use of the euphemism 'pacification' to describe laying waste a territory in order to force the inhabitants to give up whatever struggle they are engaged in. In principle, means and not ends define pacifism, and this precludes the use of violence or coercion even in the enforcement of domestic law. Thus properly pacifist convictions are a matter of strictly private moral preference rather than a question of public policy, since the latter ultimately depends on coercion.

*Conscientious objection based on unconditional pacifist convictions has tended to be respected even during the total wars of the 20th century, but not when it is more selective. The *peace and anti-war movements that object-ively served the cause of the USSR during the *Cold War and earlier are a case in point. While attracting many genu-ine pacifists, their purpose (often invisible to the rank and file) was to increase the relative international power of one of the most coercive regimes the world has ever seen, thus they were at the core intellectually negligible and morally bankrupt.

Early Christian pacifism came from a clear reading of the Scriptures: 'Thou shalt not kill'; 'love thy neighbour as thy-self'; 'blessed are the peacemakers'; 'love thine enemies'; summed up in the so-called Golden Rule: 'Therefore all things whatsoever ye would that men should do to you, do ye even so to them'. Early Christians were therefore con-vinced that any killing was murder, even in self-defence, and died in large numbers to prove the sincerity of their convictions. But the absolute pacifism and conscientious objection of early Christianity foundered when *Constan-tine converted to Christianity. Now the official religion of a vast and powerful empire, the essentially subversive quality of Christian pacifism became an embarrassment. From St Augustine of Hippo to the present, Christian thinkers have sought a way to balance the dictates of their faith with the realities of a coercive and violent world, distilled surpris-ingly early in just-war theology.

The way forward came from the belief that, as well as rev-elation, human reason could also provide the parameters for moral conduct. War and violence per se could be seen to be wasteful, unproductive, intemperate, irrational, and therefore immoral. The Stoics, from whom a good deal of Christian theology was borrowed, argued that the capacity for reason made all human beings equal; a brotherhood of man resting upon a universal moral law against which war was a gross infringement. The natural law thinking of the medieval Scholastics sought to blend ancient philoso-phy and rationalism with Christian theology, and to show that human reason need not be the antithesis to revealed religion, but could be a means by which to perceive and understand more closely the nature and purpose of divin-ity. While St Thomas Aquinas, the greatest of the Scholastic philosopher-theologians, could not be described an absol-ute pacifist, his writing (particularly on just war) did estab-lish firmly the principles of moderation and proportionality in warfare and self-defence, and in that sense contributed to the development of conditional pacifism.

During the Renaissance, humanist philosophers and the-ologians such as Erasmus took a more absolutist line, re-jecting the justification of war devised by Aquinas and arguing that it was repugnant, degrading and contrary to human nature, and that it both should and could be pre-vented. The 17th-century humanist Grotius, the founder of modern international law, saw war as a violation of univer-sal, natural law and a denial of the natural human desire to associate peacefully with others. If war was to be under-taken, it could only be as a last resort and should be mod-erated on humanitarian grounds. The notion of war as an impediment to man's achievement of his full potential was taken up by Enlightenment philosophers such as Rousseau, who saw human nature as inherently good and war as a perversion, and by Kant for whom war could be prevented by the spread of democracy.

In the eighteenth and nineteenth centuries a more prag-matic approach to the philosophical discussion of war and peace came to the fore, with renewed emphasis on its con-sequences and costs (direct and opportunity) as a means by which to judge the morality of conflict and organized viol-ence. Utilitarian philosophers such as Bentham and Mill (*père*) argued that their goal of reformed, civilized societies would result in a world in which war and conflict would be unnecessary and at worst an infrequent occurrence. This argument was amplified by the free-trade movement of the mid-19th century and J. S. Mill's argument that 'commerce . . . is rapidly rendering war obsolete'. Cobden took the argument further by insisting that peace should be the pur-pose, rather than a mere attribute, of free trade. All of these arguments have proved durable and are occasionally repro-duced with a flourish by contemporary thinkers, presented as though they had some new insight to offer.

Pacifism encompasses so broad a range of often contra-dictory views that it cannot be considered a discrete and coherent school of thought. The absolute rejection of coer-cion remains deeply subversive of all governments and by definition cannot express itself in terms of public policy. Conditional pacifism does not have to be hypocritical, and acts as the principal moral moderator where the use of military force is concerned. It challenges old and new as-sumptions which inform debate and policy in such areas as nuclear deterrence, the concept of 'surgical' air attacks, and all the other ways in which violence is camouflaged with neutral words or even positive jargon. Whether absolute or conditional, pacifism provides an essential moral reference point and a counterweight to militarism and the glorifi-cation of war and violence.   PC/HEB

Palestine Liberation Organization. See PLO.

Panipat, battles of (1399, 1526, 1556, 1761). Panipat is now a town, still with a fort and a wall with fifteen gates, in the Haryana province of northern India, in the Ganges-Jumna basin to the north of Delhi. It lies in a corridor, be-tween the southern foothills of the Himalayas and deserts of Rajasthan, through which the Ganges and Jumna flow, one much used by invaders from Afghanistan and hence of strategic significance. It was the site of four battles, all deci-sive for the fate of Muslim India.

The first came in 1399, when *Timur defeated the sultan of Delhi with great slaughter, and sacked the city. The sec-ond was in 1526 when the Turco-Mongol adventurer *Babur was invited into Hindustan from Kandahar by dissident members of the Delhi Sultan Ibrahim Lodi's family. In a battle on 20 April, Babur's troops were heavily outnumbered, but he managed to gain a decisive victory, end the 75 years' rule of the Lodi dynasty, and lay the initial foundations for Mughal rule, although this was only consolidated a generation later by his grandson *Akbar 'the Great'. The victory has been attributed to Babur's use of some primitive cannon, lashed together with bull's hide and placed at intervals along a wagon line, and he also had *musketeers using *matchlocks.

The third battle was on 5 November 1556, when Bayram Khan, on behalf of the newly acceded Akbar, defeated the usurping Hindu minister Hemu, who had assumed the regal title of Raja Vikramaditya. He was then able finally to vanquish the last ruler of the preceding line of Suri sultans and consolidate Mughal power in India.

The fourth battle was fought on 14 January 1761 when the Afghan ruler of Kabul, Ahmad Shah Durrani, entered northern India for the fourth time in an attempt to oust the Hindu, fiercely anti-Muslim *Marathas from the Punjab and north-western India, and thereby to preserve the shrinking authority of the Mughal emperors, now essentially reduced to the area round Delhi (which the Marathas had in fact recently occupied). The Afghans crushed Sardashiv Rao, uncle of the Peshwa of the Marathas, inflicting great losses. Although Ahmad Shah returned to Afghanistan and Maratha power revived, being only reduced by the East India Company in the early 19th century, the battle had important and lasting consequences in the rise of a Muslim state in Mysore under Haydar Ali, while the British in Bengal were granted a respite to consolidate their power *pour mieux sauter*.   CEB

Gupta, Hari Ram, *The Marathas and Panipat* (Delhi, 1961).
Irvine, William, *The Army of the Indian Moguls* (London, 1901).
Pasokar, R. D., *Babur: A Study in Generalship* (Poona, 1971).
Spear, Sir Percival, *The Oxford History of Modern India 1740–1947* (Oxford, 1965).

Pappenheim, Graf Gottfried Heinrich von (1594–1632).

A Catholic convert, Pappenheim was perhaps the most famous *mercenary cavalry leader of the *Thirty Years War. He had learnt his trade with the Poles, and from them he borrowed their favoured tactic of the charge with cold steel as opposed to the convoluted cavalry *caracole tactics then in favour in western Europe.

Pappenheim was a truculent subordinate whose appetite for plunder made him difficult to control. However, in 1623 he gained his own *cuirassier regiment, whose black *armour and dashing commander soon gained them a fearsome reputation. He went on to play a leading part in the sack of *Magdeburg.

At *Breitenfeld, Pappenheim came up against the Swedish horse for the first time and found them tough and disciplined opponents, while skirmishing infantry deployed in support of the cavalry shot his troopers out of the saddle. He covered the retreat with skill and in 1632 he became an imperial general under *Wallenstein.

At *Lützen, Pappenheim found himself detached from the main army, and urgently summoned to Wallenstein's assistance. Riding pell-mell into the thick of the action, his men began to force the Swedes back, but Pappenheim was hit by a cannon ball at the height of the fighting and carried off to the rear. His cuirassiers retired, much dispirited by his death, and consoled only by the fact that *Gustavus Adolphus had also been killed at virtually the same moment.
                                                                TM

paratroops, generic term for *airborne forces.

Paré, Ambroise (*c.*1510–90). 'The father of modern surgery' and of military *medicine, Paré was born of humble parents at Bourg Hersent in France, studied as a barber-surgeon, and joined the army in 1537. Although he became surgeon to four French kings, Henri II, François II, Charles IX, and Henri III, Paré is best known for developing techniques for improving the battlefield amputation of limbs, increasingly necessary as gunshot wounds became more frequent. It was believed that such wounds were poisonous, and that the stumps of amputated limbs should be cauterized with a hot iron or boiling oil. Paré noticed that many of the patients thus treated died of shock and revived the ancient practice of tying off veins and arteries rather than cauterizing them. He treated the limb with a mixture of egg yolk, oil of roses, and turpentine, and also applied similar poultices to gunshot wounds. Paré concluded that these were not inherently poisonous, but that infection was carried into them from the outside. He recommended *débridement* (opening and cleaning of the wound) to assist the process of healing, a technique revived with spectacular success during the *Falklands war of 1982.

In several other respects Paré was ahead of his time. He suspected that flies carried disease, experimented with artificial limbs and eyes, and used astringent red wine as an antiseptic. His *Method of Treating Gunshot Wounds* (1545) became an important textbook.   RH

Paris, siege of (1870–1). This took place during the *Franco-Prussian war. Following its victory at *Sedan the Prussian army reached and besieged Paris from 19 September 1870. The city was ringed by a well-built bastioned enceinte and ditch with several self-contained forts. It contained a large garrison of regular troops, National Guard, and the hastily recruited Garde Nationale Mobile. The governor, Gen Trochu, made three unsuccessful attempts to break the siege in November, December, and January.

Eventually, the only way in or out was by *balloon, and in an early instance of *psychological warfare, leaflets were dropped by French balloonists over German lines, in an attempt to persuade the Germans to desert. German efforts were boosted when the defenders of Metz surrendered in October 1870, releasing more troops for siege duty around Paris. An artillery bombardment which began on 5 January 1871 failed to break civilian morale. Starvation, and the failure of the Armies of National Defence in the provinces, led to an armistice on 28 January 1871. The peace terms allowed the Germans a triumphal march through the city. The rigours of the siege were soon followed by the *Commune uprising, harshly repressed by the French regular army under *MacMahon. Siege and Commune between them left an enduring mark on this 'modern Babylon', pointing the way to some of the worst features of 20th-century warfare. APC-A/RH

Parma, Alessandro Farnese, Duke of (1545–92).

The Farnese were prominent *condottieri and Pope Paul III created the duchy for his illegitimate son, Alessandro's grandfather, in 1534. Alessandro was the survivor of twins born to the union of the second duke and the illegitimate daughter of *Charles V.

As a child he was sent to the court of his half-brother Philip II in Brussels and later Madrid, and was married to the Portuguese Infanta María in 1565. He preferred campaigning to her company and to Parma, not even returning to rule after the death of his father in 1586. He learned soldiering under Don Juan of Austria, fighting under his command at *Lepanto in 1571, and again when he became governor-general of the Netherlands. He distinguished himself in the rout of Dutch rebels at Gembloux in 1578 (see NETHERLANDS REVOLT) and succeeded to overall military command when Don Juan died later that year. Not without problems of precedence with his mother, previously regent of the Netherlands, he initiated a policy of reconciliation with the southern Catholic provinces culminating in the Treaty of Arras, while delivering a heavy blow to *William 'the Silent' and his Union of Utrecht by taking Maastricht in 1579.

The terms concluded at Arras included the withdrawal of Spanish troops and of Parma himself, but he contrived to remain at the head of fewer than 15,000 locally raised forces and to inflict further defeats on William. He established his capital at Tournai in 1581 and in 1582 he persuaded Philip II and the southern provinces to consent to the return of substantial Spanish and Italian forces. At the head of a seasoned army four times the size of his previous force, he embarked upon a campaign of reconquest in the north.

Having consolidated the line between the Catholic south and the rebellious north, he set about quartering the United Provinces by capturing strategic towns in a long succession of sieges. Finally he moved to cut off Antwerp from the sea by gaining control of the Scheldt river, also capturing Bruges and Ypres to complete the encirclement. With Dutch resistance temporarily in disarray following the assassination of William in mid-1584, the final and justly celebrated siege of *Antwerp lasted for thirteen months, culminating in its capitulation in August 1585.

The land campaign was now put on hold while Spain prepared what it hoped would be the knockout blow against the Dutch and their English allies. Their warships were known to be greatly superior to the galleases and galleons of Spain, but after long delays in 1588 the *Spanish Armada carrying 16,000 troops successfully sailed up the English Channel, intending to cover a crossing from Flanders by Parma at the head of a further 30,000. He began embarkation as soon as he learned that it had arrived, but the Armada was attacked and dispersed almost immediately. He was among those blamed for the defeat by the courtiers responsible, but died before they could achieve his recall.

HEB

parole (Fr.: *parole*, word) has two meanings in its military context. As word of *honour it had wide application until the end of the 19th century. The assumption was that officers were gentlemen and thus men of their word. When captured, they might be released on parole, allowed to return home on undertaking not to bear arms against their captor or his allies during current hostilities. Other arrangements could be practised, such as retaining officers as *POWs but allowing them to live privately, provided that they undertook not to escape. Officers might be paroled on capture and allowed to make their own way to a specified location.

An officer who breached parole to escape could expect strict imprisonment if recaptured, and even if successful might discover that brother officers looked askance at his 'ungentlemanly' conduct. Should he breach parole conditions through no fault of his own—for instance, by being liberated by his own side while proceeding to an enemy garrison to which he had undertaken to report—he might insist on fulfilling parole conditions. His superiors, recognizing a matter of personal honour, would be unlikely to interfere.

Parole became inappropriate as wars reflected powerful national emotions. The terms surrendering the French army at *Sedan in 1870 allowed liberty to officers promising 'not to take up arms against Germany nor to act in any way prejudicial to her interests until the close of the present war'. Five hundred and fifty officers took advantage, only to discover that their countrymen regarded them, not as chivalrous gentlemen, but as privileged deserters.

Parole also described the password given out daily to assist sentries in challenging those approaching them. Practice for issuing and using the parole varied over time and between armies: often it was paired with a countersign, uttered in response. In the Prussian army of *Frederick 'the Great', for instance, the parole was issued by the king when briefing the major generals of the day. It was passed down the chain of command, together with other orders, and at the end of the process the senior royal aide-de-camp repeated the parole to the king as proof that the army's commanders had indeed been properly briefed.   RH

partisans/partizans In English, originally the name of a medieval *pole arm, similar to a bill, designed to pull knights from their horses, but more well known as a *guerrilla fighter behind enemy lines in eastern Europe, rendered in Russian in its latter form, with a 'z' (from Fr.: *partisan*, one taking sides). Partisan formations existed in Ukraine during the German occupation in 1918 but the term came into widespread use during WW II. One of the downsides of the Germans' rapid invasion of the USSR in *BARBAROSSA was that huge military formations and civilian populations were encircled but not destroyed. Partisan districts were set up at the end of 1941 and by April 1942 there were eleven. In 1943–4 the number expanded to twenty. The government in Moscow worked to maintain liaison with the units through air resupply, whether by landing aircraft, which was possible, given the vastness of the terrain, or by parachute. There were partisan detachments of 20 to 200 fighters, regiments, brigades comprising hundreds and thousands of fighters, and partisan formations, comprising ten or more brigades, numbering 5,000 to 19,000 fighting men and women. After the war, *Stalin sent most of them to the gulags, presumably because they had developed abilities that might threaten his despotism. This was a correct appreciation, as illustrated in Yugoslavia, where *Tito's Partisans, having defeated the Germans and the *Chetniks, were strong enough to secure their country from Soviet imperialism.   CDB

Passchendaele Village north-east of Ypres, whose name officially describes one component action of the third battle of *Ypres (1917) but is often used to describe the whole dreadful battle.

Pathans is a name given to speakers of Pashtu (Pakhtu) living in Afghanistan and more particularly on the *North-West frontier of British India and to their descendants living in India, notably in Rohilkhand. They played an important part in the history of India supplying three dynasties which ruled in Delhi and mercenary soldiers in many areas, as well as forming a large part of invading forces. During the British period the name was especially applied to the warlike and independent tribes of the frontier, among the most important of which were the Yusufzays of Swat, the Mohmands of the Kabul river, the Afridis of the

Khyber, the Waziris of north Waziristan, and the Mahsuds of south Waziristan. The original weapons of the Pathans were the composite *bow and long dagger; later they acquired *matchlocks and at the end of the 19th century modern rifles with which they became even more formidable adversaries both to each other and to any who sought to penetrate their country. Divided as they were into tribes, septs, and clans and penetrated by family feuds they had little central organization but in times of crisis rallied under a war leader, often a religious figure such as the Waziri Faqir of Ipi. They observed a social code known as Pashtunwali. Their economy was based upon animal herding supplemented by trading, raiding, blackmail levied on caravans, and allowances paid by governments to keep them quiet. Some settled inside the British administrative frontier and took up agriculture. Pathans were recruited into sepoy regiments from an early period but more generally into regular and irregular units from the time of the first British occupation of the Punjab in 1846. In the last years of British rule some Pathans were given King's Commissions. After 1947 they formed (after the Punjabi Muslims) the second largest group in the Pakistan army and supplied three of the first four C-in-Cs. Many Pathans migrated to the larger cities of Pakistan, especially Karachi, and became involved in business ventures, notably transport, and, not infrequently, in violent crime.   MEY

Ahmad, Akbar S., *Pukhtun Economy and Society* (London, 1980). Caroe, Sir Olaf, *The Pathans* (London, 1958).

patronage is an element of civilian and military *politics. Since the world descended into the age of ideologies it has been less easy to discern, but a key task of government remains the ability to reward supporters, preferably at the expense of opponents, but at all times to increase the number of persons beholden to it. This is patronage, and it does not matter whether the source of legitimacy is God, birth, limited franchise, or universal right democratic elections; any government that fails to nurture its power base will not last. Lest the first be considered a blasphemous flippancy, for much of world history *sacrifices to placate the gods and the interpretation of divine will through *omens accompanied all important human undertakings, and for most of that time there were few activities as important as war.

Thus from earliest times, patronage in the broadest sense of the powerful seeking to bind to them other sources of power has lubricated the interface between governments and armed forces. Until quite recently, there was no dichotomy and rulers naturally led their armies and rose or fell in accordance with their performance. A dynasty might be founded by a great warrior, but the reason why the hereditary principle was adopted by most cultures was to avoid the costs and disruptions of battles over the succession. *Alexander's successors' wars are an example of the generally dire alternative. Athenian democracy and Roman republicanism only provided an alternative for small, homogenous polities, and neither survived for long once their boundaries spread. It was precisely because the hereditary principle required the tacit suspension of individual ambition by other powerful individuals that patronage became so important. A hereditary ruler who failed to honour and reward this forbearance would soon find this early form of social compact crumbling and civil war would ensue. Feudalism evolved to make clear the rules of the game, and it was immensely powerful, best illustrated in the West when the Emperor Henry IV was obliged to do homage to Pope Innocent III at Canossa because his authority came from a greater lord than Henry. Thus *feudal service was a very elaborate but fundamentally pragmatic system of patronage.

'Lop-sided friendship', which is how patronage is more narrowly defined, dominated the period from the mid-17th to the mid-19th centuries, when the feudal system no longer conveyed legitimacy and before contract became formalized as the basis for service and reward. Social advancement as a result of preferment by the powerful represents the transitional stage between the two, lacking the spiritual as well as temporal power of the former, but retaining the element of an intimate interpersonal bond that imposed obligations on both parties. Limited governments disposed of limited patronage, but it was most clearly shown in the armed forces which were, after all, practically the only area where government spending was both recognized as necessary and of paramount importance to those involved and to the social and economic systems they defended. (For a discussion of the theory that war has been the key means whereby government writ and exactions have steadily extended see POLITICAL ECONOMY.)

It was as good a system as any other for the simple reason that it was not in the interest of a patron to waste his authority on advancing the career of an incompetent. The hereditary nobility still enjoyed what we now call the 'inside track', but if they were wise they delegated operational matters to others. One reason why the hereditary principle survived as long as it did was that the aristocracy by blood constantly co-opted able commoners like *Marlborough to strengthen its ranks. That people are still made peers or awarded membership of *orders of chivalry, and are often very anxious to be so distinguished, is a reminder of how strong that supposedly pre-modern system of patronage remains. The reason for this is that it worked so well. The Royal Navy that enabled a small island off the north-west coast of Europe to dominate half the world was built on patronage, with the elements and the enemy quickly weeding out the unsuitable.

It should not be supposed that patronage was antidemocratic; on the contrary, so-called Jacksonian democracy in the USA was in fact a vast system of patronage, the saying 'to the victor the spoils' in fact being coined in 1860 to describe Pres Andrew Jackson's insistence that every public office should be filled by either a supporter or someone for whom a supporter wanted to do a favour. Admission to *West Point was by patronage, and without patronage *Sherman would have lived in obscurity. For that matter, it was the deadlock between far more powerful members of his own party that permitted the almost unknown *Lincoln to be elected, and his conduct of the war effort was seriously compromised by the need to find places in his cabinet for his patrons.

If patronage has been a means of linking military to political leaders, it has also played its part within armies, although the term is often assigned an opprobrium that it does not always deserve. Many of the personal bonds linking officers reflect a common experience in services or individual units, military academies, staff colleges, or on specific operations. These are often crucial in determining appointments and promotions, and most armies have contained interest groups like the Bonapartist generals who dominated the early years of the *French army of the Second Empire, the *Wolseley ring which proved so influential in the late Victorian army, or the 'Ginger group' which focused on the reforming FM Sir Nigel Bagnall in the 1980s and gained its punning title from his red hair. Patrons do not usually support the advancement of incompetent clients, although close personal regard may blur the clarity of their vision. *Haig retained his intelligence officer, Brig Gen John Charteris (who had served with him since he was a captain) longer than was wise. Haig himself had enjoyed the patronage of *French, on whose staff he had served, which made the break between them in December 1915 all the more painful. As armies strive to be more transparently meritocratic, so they will continued to refine reporting systems designed to eliminate patronage. But the fact remains that when a difficult military job has to be done, both politicians and senior officers will tend to favour the man they know above one they don't.   RH

Patton, Gen George Smith (1885–1945). 'Larger than life' is a sobriquet applied to several military figures, but in this case the title is just. Few generals in history have been the subject of a flattering *film, but the hagiographic *Patton* (1970) revived interest in this charismatic officer 25 years after he died. Inevitably it dwelled on his flamboyance—the polished riding boots, whip, and pearl-handled revolvers—at the expense of the expertise and flair he brought to *armoured warfare.

He was in many ways a throwback, a man from a landed, wealthy family who adored military history and embodied the southern/cavalier military tradition at a time when others of his class no longer chose to serve in the armed forces. He attended the Virginia Military Institute, built around the cult of its old artillery instructor Stonewall *Jackson, and then went to *West Point where, like *Grant, he was top of his class in *equitation. He represented his country at the 1912 Olympics and served in the last campaign of the old boots-and-saddles US Cavalry in northern Mexico. He impressed *Pershing, who took him on his staff to Europe in 1917. Patton embraced the *tank without the reservations that might have been expected of such a tradition-minded officer, and saw action in Renault FTs at *Saint-Mihiel and *Meuse-Argonne.

Between the wars he was a tactful and effective advocate of armoured warfare and by 1940 had more experience in the field than any other officer, being given command of the new 2nd Armoured Division in 1940. As the senior US armoured commander in North Africa after the TORCH landings, he was appointed to replace Fredenall in command of II Corps after the debacle at the *Kasserine Pass in March 1943. In a whirlwind of inspections and meetings with individual units, he restored morale and combat efficiency before handing over to *Bradley to prepare for the invasion of *Sicily. Promoted lieutenant general and given command of Seventh Army, he drove it to Palermo and then to Messina at a speed that surprised his own people as well as the Germans. The run to Messina was a piece of one-upmanship at the expense of *Montgomery and laid the basis for a poisonous rivalry.

At a stop at a field hospital, he slapped the face of a *shell-shocked soldier and accused him of *cowardice. When word leaked out, the US press excoriated him and *Eisenhower relieved him of command. The German high command simply did not believe that the finest field commander the US possessed could be disgraced over such a trivial matter, which added greatly to the credibility of his next assignment. This was commanding an entirely notional army group in south-east England as part of FORTITUDE, the deception operation that kept German units awaiting an invasion at the Pas de Calais even after the *Normandy landings, where *Bradley commanded the First US Army that would have been Patton's were it not for the slapping incident.

Highly political though he was, Eisenhower knew there was only one man to command the Third US Army in the breakout from Normandy, and Patton did not disappoint him. He charged across France, his flanks wide open, grabbing supplies destined for other formations, and even so his advanced units sometimes ran out of petrol. It made him the only exponent of *blitzkrieg the western Allies produced during WW II and to the quibble that he encountered no organized resistance he would have replied, rightly, that this was a consequence of the speed of his advance. Doubts about his competence in positional warfare emerged before Metz in October–December 1944, but he turned his army through 90 degrees to counter-attack during the battle of the *Bulge in inimitable style.

By this time the press had nicknamed him 'Old Blood and Guts', prompting his soldiers to comment 'Yeah, our blood and his guts'. But they were intensely proud to serve

under him and he proved able to get performances that few other US commanders could approach. He continued to drive them mercilessly until the end of the war, reaching Czechoslovakia in early May, having received his fourth star a month earlier. He was disgusted to be ordered to withdraw and let the Soviets take possession of land he felt he had won, and was not assuaged by his appointment as military governor in Bavaria. The press eventually provoked him into criticizing US policy with regard to de-Nazification and relations with the Soviets. Dismissed for the last time in October 1945, while still in Germany he died in a car accident in December.

He had said that a warrior should die from the last bullet in the last battle of the war, and he came close to fulfilling that ideal. His style of heroic leadership was already giving way to the managerial approach while he lived, and he would have been disgusted at what happened to his beloved army after the war. He was not a man of the people and did not pretend to be, which makes his achievement all the more remarkable. He took a citizen army from a not very martial culture and brought it to share his warrior spirit, with the help of profane pep talks.   APC-A

Irving, David, *The War between the Generals* (London, 1981).
Patton, George S., *War as I Knew It* (Boston, 1947).

Paulus, FM Friedrich (1890–1957). Born to a lower middle-class family in Hesse, Paulus failed to gain admission to the navy and was commissioned into the infantry. For part of WW I he served with the élite Alpenkorps. He stayed on in the *Reichswehr, commanding a motorized battalion in 1934 and being promoted major general in 1939. An army COS in Poland in 1939, he was posted to the German army high command (OKH) as chief of the operations section in 1940, and played a leading role in planning *BARBAROSSA. In January 1942 he was given command of Sixth Army in south Russia, a surprising choice in view of his lack of command experience. He came close to capturing *Stalingrad, but was encircled by the Soviet counterstroke and surrendered in January 1943. *Hitler had promoted him to field marshal shortly before, in the expectation that he would commit suicide.

Paulus broadcast support for the German Resistance after the bomb plot of 20 July 1944, but he was not released until 1953. He was a talented staff officer but an uninspiring commander: a morally braver man would have pressed harder to be allowed to withdraw from Stalingrad before the pincers closed, saving part of his army.   RH

pay, military The very word 'soldier' means 'paid', from the Latin solidus, originally a gold coin worth 25 denarii (pence), and the Old French *soulde*. Although pay has therefore been at the centre of the military ethos since Roman times, soldiers were frequently disappointed. They went unpaid for months, sometimes years, and their *discipline and effectiveness suffered proportionately. The armies of the Ottoman *Turks were so effective, in part, because they were paid regularly and their *morale and discipline were maintained accordingly, in contrast to the levies of western powers. If soldiers were unpaid, they were even more likely to go off in search of plunder. 'Constant pay' was a frequent demand of soldiers, on both sides, during the *British civil wars.

The introduction of standing armies at the end of the 17th century brought little improvement. An 18th-century British soldier was paid sixpence a day but there were deductions for food, clothing, and in some armies soldiers had to buy their own lead to make *bullets. Pay increased exponentially with *rank: the commander of a 16th-century Spanish *tercio received 40 escudos a day, his major 20, a captain commanding a company 15, a staff captain 12, and a lieutenant 6. Officers also received far greater shares of prize money, and this was particularly attractive to naval officers, who could reap substantial rewards from capturing ships. However, most of the time the higher pay did not compensate for the greater costs of an officer's existence which arose and in many armies a private income was essential. A year's pay for an 18th-century private soldier would hardly pay for the wig worn by his officer. When *Churchill became a second lieutenant in the British cavalry in 1895 his pay was £120 a year but a private income of at least double that was necessary to maintain horses and equipment.

As the 18th century wore on armies tended to be more regularly, though generally badly, paid, and to fill their ranks with men who were subject to what a 20th-century British commentator was to call 'the compulsion of destitution'. As long as there was an adequate supply of the unemployed, the disadvantaged, or the adventurous, pay did not need to be substantial to act as an inducement. And when conscription became the norm in most European states in the 19th century there was no need for such inducement. Many conscript armies maintained two pay scales, one for conscripts and a better one for those who signed on as regulars, and many a conscript retained an abiding memory of his service being marked by shortage of money. 'My saddest memory of the war', wrote George Coppard of WW II, 'is my continual state of poverty.' Although the immediate cause of the French army's mutiny in 1917 was the failure of the *Nivelle offensive, low pay (especially when compared with the wages paid munitions workers) was a constant irritant. In 1917 a correspondent to a trench newspaper asked its readers: 'Do you know how much I got paid for my first two months at war? 0.25 francs. That's it, five sous ... and here is the pay-slip. Battle of Charleroi: 0.05 francs. Battle of Guise: 0.05 francs. The retreat: 0.05 francs. The Marne: 0.10 francs. Total: 0.25 francs.'

Officers who were expected to survive on their pay—as was the case in the French and Prussian armies—often lived out an existence of genteel poverty. Many observers noted that this system worked only as long as the officer enjoyed high social status. *Ardant du Picq complained of the French army of the 1860s that 'today none turn to the army, because it is poorly paid'. In contrast, *de Gaulle wrote of the officer during the army's 'golden age' after the *Franco-Prussian war that 'though his pay is meagre, everyone treats him with respect'. As the status of the army dropped in the years after the *Dreyfus affair, so officer recruitment fell and resignations increased.

The British army, in contrast, has only recognized relatively recently that officers should be able to live on their pay. A 1903 committee pointed out that it was folly to expect to find young men who had both education and private means. It suggested that a line infantry officer needed £160 per annum to supplement his pay, while a Guards officer needed at the very least £400. A cavalry officer needed £600–700, eight times a second lieutenant's annual salary and twice a lieutenant colonel's. On the eve of WW I it was just possible for a British officer, in the right regiment, to live on his pay. It was, however, to take at least another generation for this to become the norm.

Post-1945 the armies of developed states have increasingly found themselves competing in a market place where military status confers dwindling benefits and pay looms increasingly large. As their appetite for the technologically aware and computer-literate grows, so pay and allowances gain in importance. The maintenance of pay-scales which enable them to compete with civilian jobs which, in the nature of things, may impose less serious demands in terms of physical fitness, personal risk, or the disruption to family life become increasingly important. The Russian army finds itself in the worst of all worlds. It has lost the status that it once enjoyed, and finds the cost of maintaining adequate pay-scales prohibitive. The historical precedents, for its own cohesion and its political involvement, are not encouraging.   AA2/RH

peace and anti-war movements For the purposes of this entry, these are not a manifestation of the *pacifist and *conscientious objection traditions, but were those movements in western Europe that campaigned for unilateral disarmament between the world wars and during the *Cold War. They could be sponsored openly by the local communist parties, or as 'front' organizations set up by the Soviet state security apparatus (NKVD Narodny Kommissariat Vnutrennykh Del, the People's Commissariat for Internal Affairs, MGB (Ministerstvo Gosudarstvennoy Bezopasnosti, Ministry of State Security), KGB), or could simply be semi-spontaneous organizations of what the Soviets called 'useful fools'. The most successful was the anti-Fascist Popular Front stategy pursued by the Comintern in the 1930s, which elected centre-left governments in Spain, France, and elsewhere until *Stalin reversed course in 1938, executed the Comintern organizers, and directed a rapprochement with Nazi Germany culminating in the Molotov-Ribbentrop Pact in 1939. The least, although still impressive in their demonstration of the KGB's ability to turn the useful fools on and off like a light switch, were the widespread protests against the deployment of US *Pershing and cruise missiles in Europe in the 1980s, which fizzled out as soon as Moscow changed diplomatic tack, a last reminder of the realpolitik that lay behind the 'great betrayal' of 1938.

Although after WW II the standing joke was that the Communist Party of the USA would collapse if all the deep-cover FBI agents resigned their memberships, before the war Soviet/Comintern influence was not only well placed in Roosevelt's inner circle, but also betrayed itself in the 'light switch' response of prominent isolationist organizations and media, which changed their tune without preamble the day that *Hitler invaded the USSR. However, the Soviets could take no credit for either initiating or maintaining the 'Peace Movement' in the USA in the late 1960s and early 1970s, which was largely a misnomer for a protest against the possibility of being sent to fight in the *Vietnam war and deflated as soon as that possibility faded, although the war continued.

Ambrose Bierce's definition that to do a favour is to make an enemy comes to mind when considering the subculture of anti-Americanism that the Soviets were able to tap into among western European leftish intellectuals. Perhaps as a manifestation of wounded pride that their continent had so comprehensively sabotaged itself between 1914 and 1945, they demonstrated a knee-jerk willingness to side against the USA in any international conflict. This was not only in and of itself immensely helpful to the USSR, it also led the *CIA to mount its own covert efforts to influence public opinion which, being discovered, were grist to the moral equivalence mill. Thanks very largely to the Vietnam war, it was the USA that was denounced as being a *militarist regime and a unilateral threat to world peace, while the peaceful Soviets crushed Czechoslovakian freedom, forced the Poles to crush their own, and finally were imprudent enough to invade *Afghanistan. While all this was going on, an organization known as Physicians for Social Responsibility continued to campaign against the build-up of *nuclear weapons, for which somehow the USA alone was responsible, which culminated in their being awarded the *Nobel Peace Prize, courtesy of Soviet lobbying. And nobody laughed.

Perhaps the clearest illustration of this bias, whether a manifestation of subconscious resentment or the product of manipulation by the very clever men and women of the V Directorate of the KGB, or a bit of both, was the hysterical reaction to Pres Reagan's so-called 'Star Wars' initiative, on the face of it a defensive system that a pacifist might approve of. Suddenly remarkably uniform articles about the essentially aggressive nature of the initiative surfaced in newspapers and magazines all over the world. Not that the

argument lacked merit, merely that the same reasoning was never applied to the Soviets' own development of an ABM (Anti Ballistic Missile) capability, or to their deployment of intermediate range nuclear missiles in the European theatre, and so on and on. Four legs good, two legs bad.

HEB

peacekeeping (*see opposite page*)

Pearl Harbor (1941). The attack on Pearl Harbor of 7 December 1941 was at one level simply a repeat of the Sunday surprise attack with which the Japanese navy opened the *Russo-Japanese war. It was intended to cripple the US Pacific Fleet at its base in Oahu, Hawaiian islands, and thus give Japan an early advantage in the *Pacific campaign of WW II. The attack was ordered by *Tojo and planned by *Yamamoto when it became evident that negotiations between Japan and the USA, focusing on Japan's activities in China, were proving fruitless.

A task force under V Adm Nagumo, which included six aircraft carriers and two battleships, sailed from Japan on 26 November and from 250 miles (400 km) north of the island launched some 350 aircraft before dawn. Surprise was complete, 8 battleships and assorted other warships were sunk or disabled, and 186 aircraft were destroyed, mostly on the ground. The Japanese lost 29 aircraft and 6 submarines, 5 of them ineffectual midgets. However, the attack did not find the US fleet carriers in port and Nagumo showed the fear of land-based aircraft that was to be fatal at *Midway seven months later, and withdrew without sending in a third strike to destroy crucial oil storage facilities.

The episode remains deeply controversial. Although V Adm Kimmel and Lt Gen King, the senior US naval and military commanders in Hawaii, were unwise in allowing normal peacetime routine to prevail at a time of tension (and both had to resign in consequence), they were not provided with intelligence deriving from intercepted radio messages (see SIGINT), which would have altered their view of the risk. Some have accused Franklin D. *Roosevelt of deliberately permitting the attack to take his forces by surprise so as to bring the United States into the war. He cannot be convicted on the surviving evidence, though puzzling inconsistencies remain.

The disaster provoked an outburst of anti-Japanese hysteria in the United States, and welded the nation together in its determination to obtain revenge. It is ironic that Yamamoto recognized the long-term economic supremacy of the United States, and feared that a pre-emptive strike, however successful, would only buy time for Japan. Nagumo thought that all he had done was 'to waken a sleeping giant, and to fill her with a terrible resolve'. His point was well made: except for the battleships *Arizona* and *Oklahoma* all

(*cont. on page 699*)

peacekeeping

PEACEKEEPING is a term mainly used to describe actions sponsored by the *UN. Peacekeeping operations are authorized by the Security Council, endowed by the UN Charter with primary responsibility for maintaining international peace and security. The *Congo intervention was the only occasion where the UN tried to act as an independent power in its own right.

A traditional peacekeeping operation is established when parties to a conflict, typically two states, agree to the interposition of UN troops to uphold a ceasefire. Limited numbers of lightly armed troops are introduced and situated between the combatants, and they provide a symbolic guarantor of the peace. The Security Council maintains authority over the operation, expressed through the Secretary-General of the UN and the military commander, authorized under Chapter 6 of the Charter, although the term 'peacekeeping' is conspicuous by its absence. UN troops, voluntarily provided by member states, can use force in self-defence or in defence of their mandate. They are to be impartial throughout the operation and derive their legitimacy from representing the international community as a whole.

Examples of traditional peacekeeping operations include the operations in Cyprus, which have separated the Greek and Turkish communities (UNFICYP, established in 1964); in the state of Jammu and Kashmir, disputed by India and Pakistan (UNMOGIP, 1949); and in the *Golan Heights, between Israel and Syria (UN Disengagement Observer Force, 1974). Often referred to as 'Blue Berets' or 'Blue Helmets', the military units in peacekeeping operations remain members of their own national armies with their own command and control, but serve under a UN-appointed local commander. For a peacekeeping operation to succeed, it needs to secure not only the co-operation of the conflicting parties, but also of the international community, including regional and non-governmental organizations, donors, and member states.

Since 1948 there have been 49 UN peacekeeping operations, the majority since 1988. Over 750,000 military personnel and thousands of civilians have served in peacekeeping operations, while approximately 1,500 peacekeepers have lost their lives while serving in missions. The funding for peacekeeping operations is handled separately from the overall UN budget. The 1997–8 peacekeeping budget was approximately US $1.3 billion, which was a significant reduction from the previous few years.

Since the end of the Cold War, superpower constraints no longer hinder effective execution of policy at the UN and international intervention now encompasses the issues of common concern and collective security as originally intended in the UN Charter. Concurrently there has been a drastic increase in civil conflicts, with 90 per cent of deaths being civilian. This increase in civil conflicts has prompted member states to request involvement in a range of disputes that would have been considered distinctly domestic during the Cold War, although not in all of them for financial and political reasons. Correspondingly, the number of Security Council resolutions on peacekeeping around the world has also increased significantly. In the 41 years between 1947 and 1988 there were a total of 348 resolutions on peacekeeping, an average of 8.5 per year, while in the short six-year time span covering 1989 to 1994, there were 296 resolutions, or 49 per year.

Peacekeeping today therefore comprises a wider range of activities, which has prompted the introduction of new terms in military, political, and academic circles. The evolution began with the Namibian operation (the UN Transition Assistance Group, 1989), which was mandated with more authority than previous missions. UNTAG monitored the withdrawal of South African troops, registered voters, and managed the 1989 elections, which led to Namibia's independence.

Subsequent operations have used even more robust *rules of engagement, often in situations where there is no ceasefire nor a peace to keep. Here, the term 'peace enforcement' has been used to describe these operations, complying with the notion of 'collective security', as described in Chapter 7, Article 42, of the UN Charter: 'the Security Council . . . may take such action by air, sea, or land forces as may be necessary to maintain or restore international peace and security. Such action may include demonstrations, *blockade, and other operations by air, sea, or land forces of members of the United Nations'. Peace enforcement thus takes place when the Security Council authorizes member states to use 'all necessary means' to prohibit or check acts of aggression, and deal with armed conflict or threats to peace, and not always with the consent of the parties on the ground. Examples include one Cold War exception, Korea (1950), and more recently in Kuwait (1991), at the Iraq–Kuwait border (UNIKOM, 1991), Western Sahara (MINURSO, 1991), Bosnia and Herzegovina (UNPROFOR, 1992), Somalia (UNITAF, 1992; UNOSOM II, 1993), Georgia (UNOMIG, 1993), Haiti (UNMIH, 1993), Liberia (UNOMIL, 1993), Rwanda (UNAMIR, 1993), and Tadjikistan (UNMOT, 1994).

Some peace-enforcement missions have been controlled by leading states, as the USA initially did in Haiti and *Somalia, or France in Rwanda. Peace enforcement operations are authorized by the Security Council only as a last resort, when all other peaceful means have been exhausted. Command and control issues become more critical, as does co-ordination with a wide array of actors, and can account for success or failure of a mission, as was learned in Somalia during UNOSOM II.

Today's complex missions incorporate political, military, and humanitarian activities—depending on the needs and mandate of the operation—which have built upon traditional UN peacekeeping. UN troops now have increased responsibility to undertake tasks as diverse as preventing the outbreak of hostilities, as in Macedonia (UNPREDEP 1995); disarming, demobilizing, and reintegrating troops to secure the conflict area, creating buffer zones, and monitoring troop withdrawals as in Somalia, Mozambique (ONUMOZ 1992), and Cambodia (UNTAC 1992); providing security for repatriation of refugees and for elections, and helping to rebuild infrastructure as in Cambodia, El Salvador (ONUSAL 1991), Haiti, Mozambique, and Namibia; protecting and delivering humanitarian relief as in Bosnia, Rwanda, and Somalia; guaranteeing free access or denying such access to belligerents, as in Somalia and Bosnia; and clearing landmines as in Cambodia, Mozambique, and Somalia. Civilian police trainers, electoral observers, human-rights monitors, and others have also joined military UN peacekeepers in some operations, and they too participate in peace-building and peacemaking activities.

In 1996, the UN Transitional Authority in Eastern Slavonia, Baranja, and Western Sirmium (UN-TAES), was mandated to reintegrate 'the territory and people of Eastern Slavonia into the sovereign institutions of Croatia'. UNTAES successfully accomplished its mandate before shutting down in January 1998. In some respects, UNTAES resembled the Trusteeship period when the UN administered colonies during the transition to independence. Since the end of the Cold War the UN has been reluctant to assume such responsibility. Responsibilities like UNTAES are rarely part of UN peace-enforcement operations and are accepted only in exceptional circumstances.

Another term that is used to describe the current array of military options in complex political environments that require several simultaneous responses, is 'peace-support operation'. This term subsumes traditional Chapter 6 peacekeeping operations and Chapter 7 peace-enforcement operations, since many missions now incorporate both. A final term utilized to describe operations that are situated between defensive peacekeeping and intensive peace enforcement is 'peace maintenance'. This term incorporates political negotiations, humanitarian assistance, the use of force, and the rebuilding of civil society.   KVonH

Bellamy, Christopher, *Knights in White Armour: The New Art of War and Peace* (London, 1997).
Chopra, Jarat (ed.), *The Politics of Peace-Maintenance* (New York, 1998).

Mackinlay, John (ed.), *A Guide to Peace Support Operations*, Thomas J. Watson, Jr. (Institute for International Studies, London, 1996).

UN, *Blue Helmets: A Review of United Nations Peacekeeping* (3rd edn., New York, 1996).

the US vessels were returned to service, while of the Japanese only the destroyer *Ushio* survived the war.   RH

Peking, siege of (correctly Beijing) (1900). This was part of the *Boxer rebellion.

Peloponnesian wars (*c.*460–446, 431–404 BC). The first of these periods of warfare, sometimes called the first Peloponnesian war, although the second is never so designated, was sparked by Athenian aggression in the Argolid and the Saronic Gulf. It was complicated by Athens' continuing involvement in anti-Persian operations down to 450, and by Sparta's inability to strike overland at Attica due to the defection of Megara.

Athens began well, winning two sea battles off Aegina, before laying siege to the island's chief town, and twice defeating the Corinthians in the Megarid. Even when, in 457, a Spartan army crossed the Corinthian Gulf and defeated her at Tanagra, Athens' response, after the Peloponnesians had gone home, was to invade Boeotia, defeat the Boeotians at Oenophyta, and bring all Boeotia, Phocis, and Locris under her control. Shortly afterwards, Aegina surrendered, and perhaps in the summer of 456, an Athenian fleet sailed triumphantly round the Peloponnese, raiding as it went.

In 454 Athens' success was cut short by defeat in Egypt and growing unrest among her Aegean allies, and probably in 451–450 a five-year *truce was negotiated with *Sparta. Then, in 447, there was a revolt in central Greece, and after defeat at *Koroneia, Athens abandoned Boeotia, Phocis, and Locris. Worse still, in the early summer of 446, Euboea revolted, and later that summer, after Megara had rejoined the Spartan alliance, a Peloponnesian army invaded Attica. Although it withdrew after ravaging the plain of Eleusis, Athens had had enough and a thirty-year peace was concluded.

In the spring of 431, this peace was broken by a Theban attack on Athens' ally, Plataea, and 80 days later by a Peloponnesian invasion of Attica. The causes of the war are controversial, but there is no good reason to doubt Thucydides' view (see GREEK HISTORIANS) that the fundamental cause was Sparta's fear of Athens. Twice before the war of 460–446 she had tried to do something about it, and although the events of 447–446 had seriously weakened Athens, there were signs that she had by no means learned her lesson. In 440–439, for example, she had crushed Samos, and Sparta would evidently have gone to war then but for the opposition of Corinth. In the 430s Corinth fell out with Athens over Kerkyra (Corcyra) (now Corfu) and Potidea, and another important ally, Megara, added her voice to the clamour for war.

Now able to invade Attica through the Megarid, Sparta did so five times down to 425, only desisting when Athens captured a number of her citizen *hoplites on Sphakteria and threatened to kill them. At first, on Pericles' advice, the Athenians took refuge inside the walls surrounding the city and the Peiraeus, and responded to the Spartan ravaging merely by minor cavalry operations, raids on the Peloponnese, and biennial invasions of the Megarid. But after Pericles' death in 429 and the crushing of the Mytilenean revolt in 427, Athens adopted a more daring strategy, establishing bases on the Peloponnesian coast, notably at *Pylos in Messenia. She also countered Peloponnesian operations in Acarnania, and twice attempted to knock Boeotia out of the war by over-elaborate, two-pronged invasions, the second of which ended in defeat at *Delium, in 424.

In the same year, the Spartan *Brasidas marched overland to Chalcidice and by a mixture of persuasion and threats succeeded in winning over a number of Athens' allies, including Amphipolis. His own death in battle outside the city, in 422, and that of the Athenian demagogue Cleon, led to the conclusion of peace.

The peace was unsatisfactory to many of Sparta's allies, and this and the ending of a peace between Sparta and Argos was exploited by the Athenian Alcibiades to create an anti-Spartan coalition in the Peloponnese. At the battle of *Mantineia in 418, as Thucydides says Alcibiades claimed, the Spartans were forced to fight for their all on a single day. Although they were victorious, one has only to remember what happened after *Leuctra to realize that this was the only way that Athens could ever have defeated Sparta, as opposed to merely 'winning through', the result Pericles had promised his strategy would achieve.

With Sparta's position in the Peloponnese once more secure, Alcibiades turned elsewhere for a field in which to exercise his talents, and, principally at his urging, in 415 Athens sent an expedition to Sicily, with himself as one of

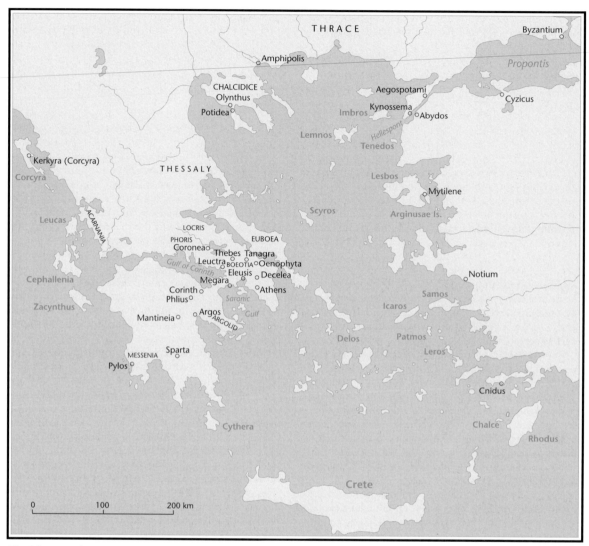

The **Peloponnesian war**, 431–404 BC.

three commanders. The object is unclear, but it was either a pre-emptive strike to prevent Syracuse taking control of the island and then throwing her weight behind the Peloponnesians, or an extension of a long-held Athenian interest in the island which had already led to naval forces being sent there in 427–424, or a combination of the two. But the expedition became bogged down in a siege of *Syracuse and ended in total disaster in 413. Whether it would have succeeded if Alcibiades had remained in command is doubtful, but in any case he was recalled early to answer charges of sacrilege, and rather than risk condemnation fled to Sparta.

Meanwhile mainland Greece had once more slipped into war, with the Athenians raiding the Peloponnese and the Spartans not only invading Attica in 413, but, on Alcibiades' advice, seizing a permanent base at Decelea in the foothills

north of Athens. But the loss of so many ships and trained crews in Sicily changed the nature of the war. The Spartans were encouraged to try to match Athens at sea, while Athens' allies in the Aegean were in revolt and the king of Persia, infuriated by Athenian support for a rebel satrap, supported Sparta in the hope that his reward would be the Greek cities in Asia Minor which Athens had 'liberated' after 479.

The Spartans appreciated that the way to defeat Athens by sea was to win control of the Hellespont (Dardanelles) and Propontis (Sea of Marmara), through which essential supplies came to the now even more beleaguered city, and by 411 the conflict became increasingly focused in that area. Athens made a remarkable recovery but was at first hampered by internal problems, culminating in the overthrow of the democracy in June 411. However, the oligarchs who seized power were never able to reconcile the fleet at Samos to their rule, and in September they in turn were overthrown. At first only a limited form of democracy was restored, full rights being confined to the hoplite class, but the victory near Cyzicus, in 410, led to the restoration of the old system.

One paradoxical result of all this was the return of Alcibiades. After making Sparta too hot to hold him, he had fled to the Persians and started the train of events by suggesting that he might be able to win the Persians round if the democracy was replaced by a more congenial regime. Although the oligarchs soon dropped him, the fleet, at loggerheads with the new regime and all the more anxious to win Persian support, recalled him to Damos and elected him one of its commanders, despite his failure to deliver the promised Persian support. He played no part in the Athenian victory off Kynossema in the Hellespont in 411, but arrived in time to take part in the subsequent victory off Abydos, and another near Cyzicus in the following year. After further success in the north, including the recovery of Byzantium in 408, he returned triumphantly to Athens in 407, and was soon given supreme command of the Athenian navy on the west coast of Asia Minor.

But the new Spartan commander in the area, Lysander, was not to be lured into premature battle, and while Alcibiades was absent, his lieutenant was drawn into a scrambling fight off Notium, in which he lost his life and a number of ships. Furious, the Athenians sacked Alcibiades, who fled to Thrace. When Lysander in turn was superseded, the new Spartan commander, having succeeded in bottling up the Athenian fleet in the harbour of Mytilene, was then himself defeated off the *Arginusae in 406. The Persians and Sparta's allies in western Asia Minor then demanded Lysander's reinstatement, and it was he who won the decisive battle at *Aegospotami in 405. Athens held out to the spring of 404, but, now blockaded by both land and sea, was eventually compelled to surrender.

In the end the Spartans won primarily because Persian gold enabled them to build more ships when battles were lost, and to outbid Athens for mercenaries. But Sparta also recognized from the first that Athens would have to be beaten by sea, because she depended on seaborne supplies, whereas, apart from Alcibiades perhaps, the Athenians do not appear to have realized that Sparta could only be beaten by land. It took the Theban *Epaminondas to show the way by his victory at Leuctra and subsequent invasion of the Spartan homeland. JFL

Kagan, Donald, *The Outbreak of the Peloponnesian War* (Ithaca, NY, 1969).
—— *The Archidamian War* (Ithaca, NY, 1974).
—— *The Peace of Nicias and the Sicilian Expedition* (Ithaca, NY, 1981).
—— *The Fall of the Athenian Empire* (Ithaca, NY, 1987).

peltasts were javelin-equipped soldiers who derived their name from their shield, the *pelte*. Peltast was a term originally used for Thracians. The *pelte* was smaller and lighter than that used by a *hoplite, lacking a rim or any kind of bronze facing. Either of simple wickerwork or of wood and covered with the skin of a sheep or goat, it was of crescent shape, a segment being cut out of the top edge to allow the peltast unobstructed vision while casting his javelin. Often the front of the *pelte* would be painted with some kind of good luck symbol, the most popular being a stylized face. Although contemporary vase paintings suggest that Pesistratos employed them (*c.*540 BC) it is Thucydides (see GREEK HISTORIANS) who first remarks on the presence of peltasts, and he does so in connection with the *Peloponnesian war (431–404 BC). More effective as skirmish troops than the standard Greek javelin man, who lacked a shield, they could wear a *phalanx down by missile fire if they kept their distance, as at Amphipolis. Their greatest exploit was under the command of *Iphrikates when they annihilated a *mora* (brigade) of Spartan hoplites outside Corinth (390 BC). He had taken care to combine a high level of individual training and *discipline—vital ingredients if skirmishers are to be of use on the battlefield—with a strong *esprit de corps*. NF

Best, J. G. P., *Thracian Peltasts* (Groningen, 1969).
Snodgrass, A. M., *Arms and Armour of the Greeks* (Edinburgh, 1967).

Peninsular war (1808–14). The Iberian Peninsular war, known in Spain as the Guerra de la Independencia, formed a part of the *Napoleonic wars. By late 1806, Napoleon's establishment of the Rheinbund and his defeat of Prussia had opened up new possibilities in his continuing struggle with Britain, the paymaster of his continental adversaries. Unable to overcome the Royal Navy's domination of the Channel and thus bring his military strength to bear directly against London, he was obliged to resort to other instruments of policy. Hoping to 'conquer the sea by the power of the land', he resolved to bring 'Perfidious Albion' to her knees through economic strangulation. Britain's war effort was ultimately founded on her prosperity, which, in turn, depended upon her overseas trade. Consistent with prevailing physiocratic and mercantilist thinking, Napoleon believed that the European mainland, although predominantly still at the proto-industrialization level of development and massively dependent upon agriculture, would, because of its superior resources and population, prevail in any economic competition with a comparatively tiny state which relied upon its commercial and maritime strengths. By endeavouring not so much to end as to control Britain's trade with the European continent, he hoped to induce her capitulation; without a favourable trading environment, 'the nation of shopkeepers' would fall victim to bankruptcy, mass unemployment, and possibly even revolution.

However, any embargo on British merchandise would, Napoleon realized, have to be applied in a sufficiently uniform and enduring fashion: the entire coastline of Europe would have to be sealed off.

The Berlin Decrees of 1806 were the first in a series of sanctions against Britain's trade known collectively as the Continental System. She responded by enacting orders-in-council aimed at controlling neutral trade with the burgeoning French empire. These competing measures placed the USA, a neutral country with a substantial and lucrative export and carriage trade, and hitherto unaligned European states in an invidious position; they had to take sides in the contest between their more powerful neighbours. Thus, while Britain squabbled with the USA and attacked Denmark in 1807, the French turned their attention to Portugal, which was an important entrepôt.

Tempted by the prospect of territorial gains, Spain joined with France in occupying the almost defenceless kingdom. The Portuguese royal family and fleet, escorted by British warships, were evacuated to Brazil, but Napoleon was now able to incorporate the entire Iberian peninsula into the Continental System.

His relationship with Spain soon took a disastrous turn for the worse. He had been meddling in the political intrigues at the Bourbon court for some time, and had been gradually persuaded that the Spaniards would not object to the removal of their feeble, corrupt, and divided ruling house. On the pretext of supporting the operations in Portugal, he steadily increased his forces in Spain. In February 1808, these soldiers, with a mixture of trickery and force, wrested several key fortresses and towns from their astonished Spanish 'allies'. Thousands more French troops then swept over the Pyrenees with impunity.

In the political turbulence that ensued, the Bourbons endeavoured to leave for the Americas, but were stopped by a riotous crowd of citizens and soldiers. An unholy alliance between a mob and disaffected aristocrats toppled the old order; the PM was deposed and King Charles IV abdicated in favour of his son, Ferdinand.

This revolution alarmed Napoleon. He was hoping to transform Spain into a modern state which would be both politically and socially compatible with France and her other vassals. Determined to oust the Bourbons altogether, he lured the quarrelsome family to Bayonne to resolve the matter. Charles, insisting that his abdication had been obtained under duress by a treacherous son, repudiated it. Ferdinand was compelled to return the crown to his father, who then quite happily surrendered it to Napoleon. The emperor, in turn, proclaimed his brother Joseph the new king of Spain.

By 6 May, the formalities for this transfer of power had been completed. However, while Napoleon could place his brother on the throne, he could not give him popular support. Tension had already been rising across Spain for some time when, on 2 May, the population of Madrid turned on the French garrison. Though suppressed as rapidly as it was savagely, this rising sparked off a general insurrection which quickly engulfed the entire country. Although its revolutionary nature horrified many civil functionaries and military commanders, and most of the ruling élite questioned the wisdom of challenging France's military might, urged on by extemporized provincial juntas, thousands of ordinary Spaniards took up arms on behalf of the captive Ferdinand, 'El Deseado', their fatherland, and their Catholic faith.

As the uprising spilled into neighbouring Portugal, the British glimpsed an opportunity to establish a toehold on the European continent. An expedition was duly despatched to Portugal and, on 21 August, it inflicted a sharp defeat on the occupying French forces at Vimiero. Judging the situation to be hopeless, the French commander *Junot concluded the Cintra Convention with his British counterpart. In accordance with this, and the sensitivities of the Portuguese and Spaniards notwithstanding, Junot, his troops, and all their equipment (and booty) were repatriated, leaving the British in undisputed control of Portugal. Meanwhile, the French armies in Spain had sustained a still more shocking setback. Encircled at *Bailén by Spanish regulars, a corps of some 20,000 men had been compelled to surrender. This was the first defeat and capture of a French army in the field since the beginning of the Revolutionary wars. It did immense damage to the reputation for invincibility that Napoleon's legions had acquired and so panicked King Joseph that he ordered a general withdrawal to the Ebro, thus compounding the impression of a French debacle.

Infuriated, Napoleon now withdrew fresh troops from Germany and hurried across the Pyrenees to redeem the situation. Arriving in early November, he unleashed a devastating counterstroke against the astonished Spanish armies, scattering them to the winds. Madrid fell and, by mid-December, the French had reoccupied the heart of the peninsula and were preparing to march on Lisbon.

The reconquest of Portugal was prevented essentially by a timely foray mounted by a British column under Sir John *Moore. Their forces' earlier successes had aroused great hopes within the British cabinet; Spain, it was believed, might follow Portugal in being completely cleared of the enemy. However, like their Spanish allies, they had not reckoned with Napoleon's reaction to developments. Moore, unaware of the strength of the hostile forces confronting him, was preparing to fall on a seemingly isolated corps around Burgos when he was alerted to the approach of Napoleon himself. Diverting his army from its march on Portugal, the emperor was seeking to get behind the redcoats, sever them from the coast, and annihilate them. He all but succeeded. Slipping away, Moore went into precipitate retreat for *Corunna. Napoleon, alarmed by Austria's preparations for a renewal of the war, turned the *pursuit over to Marshal *Soult and hurried back to Germany. Repulsed at Corunna on 16 January 1809, Soult failed to

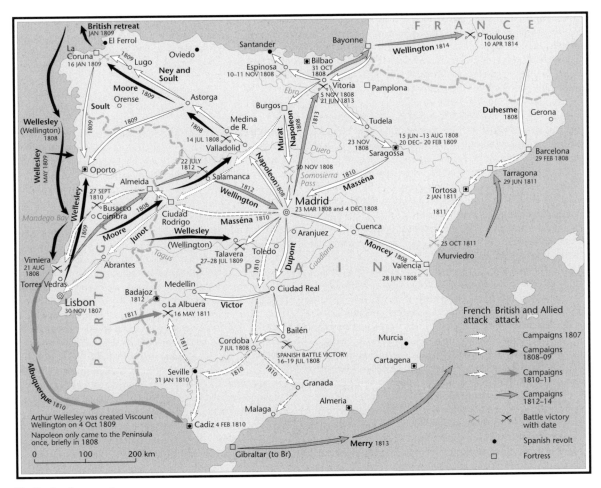

The **Peninsular war**, 1807–14.

prevent the British evacuation, but Moore was killed and his force, which comprised much of Britain's available army, had been badly mauled.

Nevertheless, Portugal had been saved from immediate reoccupation, giving the British and the Portuguese, who completely subordinated themselves to their powerful allies throughout the war, time to prepare their defences. Soult slowly moved south, taking Oporto, while his colleague, Marshal Victor, having destroyed a Spanish army at Medellin on 28 March 1809, ventured down the Guadiana. The new British commander, Arthur Wellesley (see WELLINGTON, DUKE OF), had some 23,000 redcoats at his disposal and was having some 70,000 Portuguese regulars and militia trained by British officers under *Beresford. Despite Moore's predictions, he was confident that he could cling to Portugal; with a new war looming in Germany, Napoleon would simply not be able to spare sufficient men for a successful invasion of the kingdom.

This surmise was to prove correct. Having attacked Soult at Oporto and driven him northwards, Wellesley was free to join with the Spanish in a concentric advance on Madrid. After holding off a counterstroke by Victor at Talavera in July 1809, the British were compelled to retreat back into Portugal once Soult threatened their rear, while the Spanish armies, their efforts poorly co-ordinated, were subsequently defeated. Moreover, the Talavera campaign highlighted the importance of adequate logistical support in the barren peninsula; Wellesley's troops suffered badly because of shortcomings in this regard. As the French had already discovered to their cost, living off the land in such an inhospitable environment was rarely feasible, making their own mercurial style of warfare impracticable; once concentrated for action, large forces starved whereas small ones risked defeat. Indeed, the Peninsular conflict was to take on many of the traits of 18th-century warfare, which accentuated secure communications, adequate depots, and strong positions, notably fortresses. In fact, during the Napoleonic wars as a whole, sieges were almost unheard of outside the peninsula.

By the time that Napoleon had defeated Austria and another French invasion of Portugal seemed practicable, Wellesley, now Wellington, had prepared a series of concentric defences, the Lines of *Torres Vedras, to protect Lisbon. He also had an army which was equal if not greater in size to that available to his opponent, Marshal *Masséna. King Joseph had committed many of the 300,000 troops at his disposal to seizing Andalusia rather than to the all-important mission of ejecting the British interlopers. Masséna, after reducing the fortresses of Ciudad Rodrigo and Almeida, advanced into Portugal to find that Wellington had scorched the countryside. Checked at Bussaco on 27 September 1810, he circumvented the Allies' position and resumed his advance on Lisbon only to find his path barred by the impregnable Lines.

With his men and horses dying from starvation, Masséna lingered before Lisbon from October until March, hoping to entice Wellington into attacking him. When he did not, the marshal retired on Almeida, gingerly followed by his adversary. A series of clashes along the Portuguese-Spanish frontier ensued as Masséna, and his successor Soult, together with Marshal *Marmont, sought to prevent the Allies seizing the fortresses commanding Spain's northern and southern gateways, Ciudad Rodrigo and Badajoz respectively. However, early in 1812, Wellington succeeded in storming both of these before the French field armies could concentrate and come to their relief. Should an opportunity present itself, he was now poised to advance into the peninsula's very heart.

Just as Napoleon's attention and resources were turning to the invasion of Russia, the French position in Spain was becoming dire. True, considerable progress had been made against the insurrectionists, but, aided and encouraged by the British especially, they showed no sign of abandoning the struggle. After destroying the Tagus bridge at Almaraz so as to cut the communications between Soult's army in Andalusia and Marmont's in Leon, Wellington fell on the latter, scattering it at *Salamanca. He then thrust deep into the interior, capturing Madrid and besieging Burgos. Only the arrival of Soult retrieved the situation. Burgos was relieved and, by mid-November, Wellington had retreated beyond the Huebra. However, the following May, his forces returned in overwhelming strength, took Burgos, and, on 21 June, heavily defeated Joseph at Vitoria.

Their forces in northern Spain having been pushed back to the Bidassoa, the French were also obliged to evacuate Valencia and Aragon. With Wellington investing San Sebastian and Pamplona, Soult led an ultimately futile counter-offensive to try to save the fortresses. Subsequently levered out of defensive positions on the Bidassoa, Nivelle, and Nive, his battered army was worsted again at Orthez in February 1814, and driven from Toulouse on 11 April. The tid-

ings of Napoleon's abdication arrived hours later, bringing the campaign to its end.   DG

Lovett, G., *Napoleon and the Birth of Modern Spain*, 2 vols. (New York, 1965).

Oman, C. W. C., *History of the Peninsular War*, 7 vols. (Oxford, 1902–30).

percussion lock   This system of firearms ignition replaced the *flintlock in the early 19th century. One of the limitations of the flintlock was the delay between the flash of the priming powder in the pan and the explosion of the main charge in the barrel; this caused frustration for sportsmen whose targets, alerted by the flash, had moved by the time of the discharge. The explosive properties of chemical fulminates had been identified in the 17th century but were not harnessed until the Revd Alexander Forsyth (1768–1843) combined mercury fulminate and potassium chlorate to form a priming charge capable of igniting the main charge so quickly as to make the two explosions virtually simultaneous. Forsyth developed his new primer for dispensing from a series of styles of magazine which replaced the flintlock's steel and pan; since his primer was exploded by being struck, a hammer replaced the flintlock's cock. His percussion system was patented in 1807 and is most associated with his 'scent-bottle' magazine which housed about 40 primings, each of which was dispensed by simply inverting the magazine. The separate percussion cap, in which the priming was contained in the crown of a copper cap shaped like a hat, was invented c.1814 and other percussion systems, like pill, pellet, and tape primers, were developed over the following 40 years. Initially avidly accepted by sportsmen and civilians, the percussion system only ousted the flintlock for military use in the 1830s, two decades after it had been invented. Britain, France, Sweden, and the USA were the first to adopt the percussion system militarily. Percussion firearms dominated the military world from their eventual adoption until their replacement by breech-loaders in the late 1860s.   SCW

Blair, Claude (gen. ed.), *Pollard's History of Firearms* (London, 1983).

Peterson, Harold L. (ed.), *Encyclopaedia of Firearms* (London, 1964).

percussion weapons   These weapons, such as clubs, maces, axes, and hammers, are as old as warfare and are certainly the oldest form of weapon wielded by man and his ancestors. Such weapons have appeared on the battlefield in both functional and symbolic forms since the earliest times and still exist in the significantly different styles of baton carried by field marshals and by riot policemen.

The club, equally well adapted from a tree branch or a redundant human femur, must have been the first weapon. From it, all forms of percussion weapon have sprung, the mace, the axe, and the war hammer being the three principal types, each offering a differing kind of damage to the recipient of their blows. The club itself is more than merely an instrument of destruction. Like the other percussion weapons types, it has a symbolic role too, perhaps the earliest example being that of the club carried by Hercules and so indicative, by its size, of his strength and virility. A wooden club with wicked metal spikes known with grim humour as the Godentag (good morning) was still in use among Dutch levies painted by Breughel.

The mace is most obviously derived from the club and, while clubs are known in all cultures, the mace, as it developed in the knightly culture of the West, differs from the club in that it is principally of metal, originally iron. Maces were known in the Arab world too, as well as in the China of *Genghis Khan but, apparently, were not used in Rome or on the Celtic fringe. Against a foe clad solely in mail a club could be disabling without damaging the mail as it broke bones or stove in skulls by sheer percussive effect: plate *armour changed this and so maces were developed with heads which were capable of piercing or splitting thin plate or damaging armour at its joints.

Maces of the late 15th and 16th century often had multi-flanged heads shaped in the Gothic style. Maces with spiked heads, either fixed or pendant from a chain and known as Morgenstern or morning star types, were less used in the West than is popularly believed but remained in use in Persia and India until the 19th century. Maces with flanged but rounded—sometimes onion-shaped—heads were popular in eastern Europe, especially in Poland, and in other areas affected by Turkish influence. The end of armour spelt the end of the mace as a fighting weapon (except in the trench warfare of WW I) and the beginning of its symbolic life as an indicator of its owner's rank or status. From the 16th century onwards, maces have come to symbolize authority, either as batons of command or as civic maces—used in boroughs, cities, universities, and parliaments.

The war axe is obviously derived from the earliest unhafted hand axes but, once hafted, the axe became as effective a weapon of war as it had been a domestic tool. Like the mace, it was depicted in use in Ancient Egypt and was also used in Mycenae and Crete; it was, similarly, not used in Rome but widely used by Rome's enemies, especially those from northern and eastern Europe. Axes were wielded by both infantry and cavalry and, in cultures such as the *Viking and Anglo-Saxon which developed the design of the fighting axe considerably, were often thrown efficiently too. Small axes were carried by English *archers during the *Hundred Years War, as much for fashioning their protective wall of sharp stakes as for finishing off armoured knights felled by their arrows. At the other end of the scale, axes were used as knightly weapons, notably by Robert *Bruce of Scotland, who slew the English Henry de Bohun at *Bannockburn in 1314 with his battleaxe. Axes have retained their functional role into modern times as the tool of

the pioneer and are carried symbolically by these troops on ceremonial occasions.

The war hammer was just that: a large, long-hafted hammer with a spiked top and rear and a blunt head. Principally carried by armoured knights, like the mace, the war hammer was used from the 14th century, against mail, to the end of full plate armour and was an effective weapon in stunning and disabling an opponent. Often highly decorated as well as brutally functional, war hammers retained a symbolic role towards the end of their life on the battlefield, but not to the extent of the mace or the axe.   SCW

Edge, David, and Paddock, John M., *Arms and Armour of the Medieval Knight* (London, 1988).

Oakeshott, Ewart, *European Weapons and Armour* (London, 1980).

Pershing, Gen John Joseph 'Black Jack'

Pershing, Gen John Joseph 'Black Jack' (1860–1948). One of the very few US five-star generals of the army, Pershing's life spanned the *American civil war to WW II and he served in most of the US wars in between. In 1886 he graduated from *West Point, where he later returned as an instructor, and served in the *Plains Indians and *Spanish-American wars. He was military attaché in Japan and an observer of the *Russo-Japanese war, and later served with such distinction at the end of the *Philippines insurrection that Pres Theodore *Roosevelt promoted him from captain to brigadier general, bypassing 862 other candidates. He was the commander of the last expedition by the traditional US Cavalry against Pancho Villa in northern Mexico in 1916–17 and after the US declaration of war on the Central Powers in April 1917, Pres Wilson appointed him to command the American Expeditionary Force, initially to be based on the National Guard structure. In June he shook the political establishment with a report requiring an army of one million men by 1918 and three million by the following year which was, nonetheless, accepted.

The next two years were a test of his drive and tenacity, for he was initially pressured to feed American divisions as they arrived into the existing western front command structure, to which his government would have acquiesced and which would have enabled them to gain combat training and experience from veterans. Although dependent on the French for much of his equipment, Pershing was determined that the (white) US army should only take the field unified under his command, while releasing *African-American troops who performed with distinction under French tutelage. He did release white troops to help the French stem the German MICHAEL offensive of March–April 1918, and it was not until 12 September 1918 that he was able to direct 500,000 men of the First US Army in the battles of *Saint-Mihiel and *Meuse-Argonne. He, his staff, his unit commanders, and his men all learned the hard way the lessons that the battered British and French might have taught them at very much lesser cost. The domestic impact of these casualties was magnified by the fact that National Guard units were recruited from individually limited geographical areas, thus certain communities suffered disproportionately. The influx of fresh and ignorantly enthusiastic troops was nonetheless felt on both sides of the front, and contributed significantly to the Germans' reluctant acceptance of the need to seek terms.

It is not easy to acquit Pershing of putting his pride and desire for glory above the lives of his men, and the beautiful *cemeteries on the Meuse-Argonne would have been smaller if he had behaved differently. It was a rare lapse in the US tradition of civilian control that permitted him to define US military policy. MICHAEL was launched nearly a year after the US entry into the war and was postulated on getting in a killer blow before the US presence could make itself felt, eloquent comment on the effects of Pershing's policy. He was nonetheless fêted on his return home in September 1919, awarded five-star rank and served as COS between 1921–4 before retirement.   APC-A/HEB

Pershing missile Family of intermediate-range US nuclear *weapons, first deployed to West Germany in 1964 and upgraded from 1983 onwards amid the clamour of a carefully orchestrated *peace and anti-war campaign.

Persia, German activity in (WW I). The Central Powers and their Turkish allies, the latter of whose territories in Mesopotamia (what is now Iraq) marched with Persia, hoped to take advantage of anti-British and anti-Russian feeling in Persia. They were able to achieve little militarily against the Russians in their northern Persian sphere of influence: a pre-emptive strike against the Russian troops at Tabriz in January 1915 did not prevent the latter from massing in Transcaucasia, advancing as far as Erzerum (February 1916), and hurling back a Turkish invasion of western Persia (spring 1917).

The Germans were more successful in southern Persia, the British sphere of influence. They hoped, first, to extend Turco-German arms towards the Gulf, threatening communications with India and endangering British oil interests in south-western Persia (the Anglo-Persian Oil Company had a contract to supply the Royal Navy); and second, to bring Persia into the war or, at least, to compel its ruler, Ahmad Shah Qajar, to allow passage of German and Turkish troops across Persia towards Afghanistan. This last was then to be the launching-pad for an invasion of India, in conjunction with a rising within the subcontinent of nationalist elements which would sweep British rule into the sea.

The network of German consuls (who also functioned as *intelligence gatherers) expanded in southern Persia and the Gulf region in the years before the war. Local anti-court Persian elements and German agents, with the tacit support of the pro-German Swedish officers of the Persian *gendarmerie, captured and looted several of the British consulates and telegraph stations by the end of 1915, and numbers of armed Germans and Austrians were infiltrating from Turkish Iraq. The man who was to prove the sharpest thorn in the British side in 1915 and early 1916 was Wilhelm Wassmuss, 'the German Lawrence', who raised the Qashqai and other tribesmen of southern Persia, always hostile to central government control, and held out there, completely cut off from contact with Germany and moneyless, until the end of the war.

Wassmuss's mission was originally part of a grand design to induce Afghanistan to attack India by sending a joint German-Turkish mission across Persia to Kabul. In the event, the mission was a purely German-Austrian one, with a Bavarian soldier, Oskar Niedermayer, in charge of getting the party to Kabul, and a diplomat, Werner Otto von Hentig, to be in charge of the negotiations on arrival there. A smaller German military group left for Kirman in southeastern Persia. The main group reached Kabul in September 1915 after an epic journey in summer heat across the central Persian deserts, slipping through the Russo-British cordon sanitaire in eastern Persia, but found the Emir Habibullah could not be dislodged from his treaty and financial connections with British India. By spring 1916, the Germans recognized that their mission was hopeless, and made their ways circuitously homewards. German efforts in south-east Persia also collapsed, the south of the country now being secured by the newly formed South Persia Rifles and a military expedition from Baluchistan into the Sarhadd region under Brig Gen Dyer of later *Amritsar notoriety.   CEB

Hopkirk, Peter, *On Secret Service East of Constantinople* (London, 1994).

Sykes, Christopher, *Wassmuss: The German Lawrence* (London, 1936).

Vogel, Renate, *Die Persien und Afghanexpedition Oskar Ritter von Niedermayers 1915–1916* (Osnabrück, 1976).

Persian expedition (1856), an expedition sent to the Persian Gulf as the sole military operation of the 1856 Anglo-Persian war. Contrary to previous pledges Persia attacked Herat in Afghanistan and captured the city on 25 October 1856. Persia might have been persuaded to withdraw by diplomatic means but at the time British diplomatic relations with Persia were severed due to Persian accusations of misconduct made against the British minister in Tehran. The British government in London ordered a reluctant East India Company (EIC) administration in India to send an expedition to the Gulf rather than attempt the risky enterprise of acting directly at Herat, although the EIC did take the occasion to conclude an agreement with the ruler of Kabul.

The expedition initially was directed against the Persian town of Bushir and consisted of 5,670 troops of which 2,270 were European under the command of Maj Gen Foster Stalker. War was declared on 1 November and after very little resistance the troops captured Bushir on 10 December. It was then decided to adopt the capture of the Persian port of Muhammerah (modern Khurramshahr) as a second objective, for which reinforcements (three infantry battalions, including one European, together with cavalry and artillery) were required and the enlarged expedition was put under the command of Sir James Outram. The reinforcements arrived at Bushir in January 1857 and Outram elected to attack the Persian forces north of the town. It was a confused engagement: Outram, having failed to bring the Persians to battle, was retiring on Bushir when the Persians launched a night attack on his rearguard; the battle of Khoosh-ab (8 Feb 1857) was fought the following day and was won by the action of the 3rd Bombay Light Cavalry, which rode down a Persian infantry square. The Persians broke and fled suffering heavy losses in the rout. On 26 March Outram attacked Muhammerah: a naval bombardment silenced the Persian guns and facilitated an unopposed landing, and this forced a Persian retreat.

On 4 April news was received that peace had already been signed at Paris on 4 March, before Outram had even moved his force to Muhammerah. Under the terms of peace the shah apologized to the British minister and recognized the independence of Herat, the same terms in fact which had been agreed before hostilities commenced. A curious feature of the expedition was that both Stalker and the naval commander shot themselves. The most interesting aspect of the expedition was that it provided a test of a long-held strategic theory, namely that Persia could be controlled by operations from the Persian Gulf where Britain had naval mastery. The results of the test were inconclusive but the expedition demonstrated the difficulties of bringing Persian forces to a decisive engagement on the coast and the perils of operations conducted inland at some distance inland. MEY

English, Barbara, *John Company's Last War* (London, 1971).

Outram, Sir James, *Lt. General Sir James Outram's Persian Campaign in 1857* (London, 1860).

Peru, Spanish conquest of. See PIZARRO, FRANCISCO and CONQUISTADORES.

Pétain, Marshal Henri-Philippe Omer (1856–1951). Born to a prosperous peasant family in the Pas de Calais, Pétain was commissioned into the infantry from Saint-Cyr. After attending the École Supérieure de Guerre he served on the staff of the military governor of Paris during the *Dreyfus affair, but slow promotion endemic in the army of the Third Republic saw him a major only in 1900. He was an instructor at the École de Guerre where, in contradiction to official *doctrine, which emphasized the superiority of moral qualities over firepower, he taught that fire killed. Promoted to command the 33rd of the Line (a young *de Gaulle was one of his officers), in 1914, still a colonel, he commanded a brigade at Saint-Omer.

Pétain was saved by the war. His brigade was in Lanrezac's Fifth Army, and some of Pétain's mistrust of the British may have been learnt from him. On 31 August he was promoted *général de brigade* and given a division: his general's stars were taken from an old tunic found in a house on the line of march. He was given another step in October, becoming *général de division* and taking command of a corps. His deft handling of his corps, which advanced 2 miles (3.2 km) and captured 3,000 prisoners at Souchez in May 1915, brought him command of Second Army in Champagne. When the Germans attacked *Verdun in February 1916 *Joffre sent for him.

Pétain was unmarried, but an aide ran him to earth on the night of 24–5 February in the Hôtel Terminus at the Gare du Nord. Outside the bedroom door stood his boots and a pair of lady's shoes. Pétain announced that he would report in the morning: meanwhile the night imposed its own duties. Briefed by Joffre, he set off for Verdun, a slow journey in filthy weather. He reached the local commander's headquarters at Dugny, where he heard that Fort Douaumont had fallen, and then returned to Souilly, on the little road from Bar-le-Duc which constituted Verdun's only link with the outside world, and set up his headquarters in the Mairie. Joffre's deputy *Castelnau met him there, and gave him a written order to hold both banks of the Meuse and take over at midnight.

Pétain telephoned senior officers to tell them that he was in command, but he awoke on the 26th with pneumonia. Using trusted staff officers as emissaries, he gathered the reins of battle into his hands. He was to tell a visitor that 'artillery now conquers a position and infantry occupies it', and made it clear that this was a gunner's war. He began telephone conversations by asking: 'What have your batteries been doing?' The Germans felt the effect of his policy as French guns, tucked in behind the ridges on the left bank of the Meuse, raked slopes opposite with their fire. He recognized that the defence hinged on a single fragile line of supply along the road still known as La Voie Sacrée (the Sacred Way). Never a man for bombast, he caught the mood of the moment in an order of the day which proclaimed: 'Courage: on les aura!' ('Courage—we'll get 'em').

The crisis past, Pétain's refusal to take the offensive persuaded Joffre to move him upwards to command Army Group Centre. Nivelle took over at Verdun, where his success brought him appointment as C-in-C of the French army. With the failure of the *Nivelle offensive and subsequent mutinies in the spring of 1917 Pétain took over as C-in-C and restored morale by a judicious mixture of stick and carrot, putting down indiscipline but improving leave conditions, food, accommodation, and the distribution of decorations. When attacks were resumed they were characteristically methodical: Fort Malmaison was slickly recovered in October.

By now his caution was overriding, and he was convinced that the Allies should wait for the Americans before taking the offensive. When the Germans attacked in March 1918 he muttered that they would defeat the British in open field and then go on to beat the French. Subordinated to *Foch, the newly appointed Allied C-in-C, Pétain commanded the French army for the remainder of the war and was appointed marshal at its end. A doctor found him unbelievably fit, and he married in 1920.

Between the wars Pétain held a series of major appointments. He took charge of the operation which crushed Abd-el-Krim's revolt against the French conquest of *Morocco, watched over the planning of the *Maginot Line, served as minister of war, and in 1939 went to Madrid as ambassador. Recalled when the Germans attacked in 1940, he became deputy PM, and then, as premier, negotiated the armistice.

He went on to replace the Third Republic by the État Français based at Vichy, presenting French officers, not least his old subordinate de Gaulle, with a painful crisis of conscience. His regime did reflect a feeling amongst the upper bourgeoisie and high officials that defeat was the penalty for political as well as military failure and, in his dour and impassive person, Pétain somehow seemed a credible head of state. Yet his political grasp was never firm, and the problems facing him were enormous. By the time the Germans responded to Allied landings in *North Africa by moving into the Unoccupied Zone, Vichy was 'little more than an agency for the German exploitation of France'. The acts of some of Pétain's subordinates, notably Laval, brought lasting discredit on his regime. In 1944 it moved to *Belfort and eventually to Germany, and a dazed Pétain gave himself up to stand trial. He was sentenced to death, and then reprieved, to die in prison on the Île d'Yeu, where he was buried.

Pétain lacked the resilience and inspiration to be a great general, but his grasp of war in 1914–18 and his understanding of the common soldier mark him out as a good one. The last decade of his life was unrelieved tragedy: some of his countrymen now argue that time should expunge this last failure, permitting Pétain to lie where he wished, among his soldiers at Verdun.   RH

Griffiths, Richard, *Pétain* (London, 1994).

petard (from Fr.: *pétard* and It.: *petardo*). The term first appeared in the late 16th century as signifying a small mine placed against a door in order to destroy it and permit entry by besiegers. Such mines were, apparently, originally encased in metal and bell-shaped. Their fuses may have had a reputation for unreliability since, in 1604, Shakespeare was able to comment, in *Hamlet*, Act III: 'for 'tis the Sport to have the engineer | Hoist with his own Petard.' The term

was also used as a verb and, in the days of its currency, a petardier was the individual charged with the explosion of the petard. Clearly linked in its etymology with the French verb *péter* (to fart), the term may be an indication of the robust *humour associated with soldiers and their trade.

Petards were an important part of early *siege warfare since, as walls became stronger in order to resist the increasing power of artillery, so only the doors or gates of a fortress—themselves very heavily defended—remained as the most vulnerable points on its perimeter. Mining, sapping, and efficient *mortars eventually rendered petards obsolete by the 18th century.   SCW

Peter 'the Great' (1672–1725), **Tsar** (1682) **and Emperor** (1721) **of Russia** Statesman, military leader, and diplomat, founder of Russian power and influence in Europe, of the regular Russian army and fleet, and of a national arms industry. Born Peter Alekseyevich Romanov, the son of Tsar Aleksey Mikhaylovich by his second wife, Peter was in constant danger from his half-sister Sofia and in 1682 he and his mother retreated to the village of Preobrazhenskoy near Moscow. Young Peter was fascinated by militaria and was soon drilling his own *poteshnye*—'play soldiers'—recruited from his friends and experimenting with an old sailing boat, the origin of the Russian navy. In 1687 the *poteshnye* were reinforced by drafting men from the old *streltsy regiments of Moscow and formed into two new, western-style regiments of the Imperial Guard, the Preobrazhenskiy and Semenovskiy.

In 1695 and 1696 Peter and his evolving army made two expeditions to the Turkish-held stronghold of Azov, in the south, the second of which was successful, establishing Russian power on the Sea of Azov. From March 1697 to July 1698 Peter made his famous incognito trip to the west, visiting Sweden, Prussia, Holland, and England and building up a vast store of naval, military, and scientific knowledge for his later reforms. His trip was curtailed by news of the final streltsy revolt. Peter then completed the transformation to a modern regular army on the western model, which had begun under his father, Tsar Aleksey. His strategic focus also shifted west, towards Europe and access to it via the Baltic, with the *Great Northern war. Peter's new army saw its first action against the Swedes at Narva in 1700, but clearly had much to learn. They surrounded the Swedish fortress with about 34,000 troops but the Swedish relief force, emerging from the woods, only 11,000 strong, tore into them, killing up to 8,000 and capturing all their artillery. Although Narva was a disaster, Peter continued his strategy of dominating the Gulf of Finland and securing access to the sea. By 1703 the Russians had the eastern end of the Gulf, and on 16 May the foundation stone of the Petropavlovsk—Peter and Paul—fortress was laid on the estuary of the river Neva. The growing settlement around was called Sankt Peter Burk, in Dutch: St Petersburg.

At *Poltava on 27 June 1709, the first battle where Peter took personal command, the new Russian army scored its first victory over a western army, and one of Russia's greatest military triumphs. The Swedes, led by *Charles XII, by now outnumbered nearly two to one and short of ammunition, nevertheless attacked a strongly defended Russian camp, and lost about half their strength killed and wounded. Historically, the Russians had been considered cowardly, lazy, and better at *siege warfare than in the open field. This battle announced a new style.

In the ensuing years, Russia grew stronger, and foreign observers, including the Hanoverians and the English, newly joined, expressed anxiety about the growth of Russian power. Towards the end of his reign, Peter again turned south, seizing Derbent in 1722 and Baku and Reshut in 1723, gains recognized by the Persians and the *Turks. The creation of three new fleets reflected the strategic direction of Peter's campaigns: the Baltic, the Azov, and the Caspian. The Baltic was the biggest and, by the end of the Great Northern war, had 124 Russian-built craft and 55 taken from the Swedes, including twenty sail of the line. Because the waters of the Baltic and the Sea of Azov were often shallow, galleys proved especially useful and Peter had 416 by the end of the Northern war. Although Peter drew much from foreign advisers, especially Scotsmen like Patrick Gordon, James Bruce, and G. B. Ogilvy, and the Swiss Franz Lefort, he also thought profoundly and wrote at length about the art of war. The *Code of 1716* and *Rules of Combat* (1708) were his own work and drew heavily on his own experience. By the end of his reign Russia, according to a French diplomat writing to *Louis XIV in 1723, 'whose very name was scarcely known, has now become the object of attention of the greater powers of Europe, who solicit its friendship'. CDB

Duffy, Christopher, *Russia's Military Way to the West* (London, 1981).

Peterloo massacre (1819). An unhappy example of military aid to the *civil power, the Peterloo massacre was so called in ironic reference to Waterloo. On 16 August 1819 a large crowd gathered at St Peter's Fields, Manchester, to listen to an address by Henry 'Orator' Hunt, the radical agitator. The local magistrates had decided to arrest Hunt and other leaders, who were prepared to be detained peaceably.

Col Guy L'Estrange commanded a force of some infantry, two guns, six troops of the 15th Hussars, and six of Cheshire *Yeomanry. The magistrates retained a troop of Manchester and Salford Yeomanry, and while L'Estrange deployed his own troops with discretion, the yeomanry, their horses not used to working together, pushed on towards the speakers' platform. Cheers and jeers frightened horses and excited men, and after the arrests were made there was a shout of 'Have at the flags' which encouraged some yeomen to slash at the crowd while trying to ride down its banners.

The magistrates ordered L'Estrange to disperse the meeting and rescue the yeomanry, and the 15th Hussars charged. Although troopers tried to use the flat of their swords, there were inevitably casualties as horses crashed into the crowd. There were widely conflicting versions of events, whose enduring significance still divides historians. Perhaps a dozen people were killed, and many more injured. The poor training of the yeomen and horses was partly responsible for the affair, and the fact that many of the yeomen were well-to-do tradesmen with an animus against the reformers did not help. RH

Read, Donald, *Peterloo: The 'Massacre' and its Background* (London, 1958).

Walmsley, Robert, *Peterloo: The Case Reopened* (London, 1969).

PGMs. See PRECISION GUIDED MUNITIONS.

phalanx Classical Greek infantry customarily fought in *columns for shock encounters, head-on against a similarly arrayed enemy. Such mass fighting was not original, Mycenean and Near Eastern armies had done it for centuries. But the Greeks of the early *polis* (700–500 BC) refined the earlier loosely organized mob into neat lines and files (the original meaning of phalanx may have been 'log' and then 'row' or 'rank'), each propertied citizen now claiming an equal place in the phalanx, a voice in the assembly, and a plot in the countryside.

Outside *Sparta, the general, an amateur and elective public official, usually led his troops on that wing to spearhead the attack; in defeat he normally perished among his men. Because of the limited tactical options open to a phalanx once battle commenced, complex manoeuvre and tactics were problematic and rarely attempted. Often a phalanx simply tried to win the battle outright on the stronger right side before its own inferior left wing collapsed and eroded the cohesion of the entire army.

The phalanx usually stacked eight men deep; only the spears of the first three rows could extend to the enemy, the rear five lines pushed on the men in front. If they kept their nerve and formation, the armour and the length of their spears made the *hoplite fighters of the phalanx *on level ground* invulnerable to cavalry charges and skirmishers alike. On rare occasions, the phalanx could be defeated by mixed contingents, but almost always this was accomplished through manipulation of terrain, or ambush and encirclement, not decisive engagement or shock tactics.

The contrived and ritualized nature of classical phalanx battle should not suggest an absence of mayhem and savagery. The initial collision was horrific, as each side stumbled blindly ahead into the enemy mass, attempting to create some momentum, through stabbing, pushing, clawing, or kicking, that might fragment the opposing formation.

This traditional practice of phalanx battle persisted well into the 5th and 4th centuries BC until the Greek states routinely embraced skirmishes, sea battles, and sieges where military dynamism not ethical protocol determined the time and space of fighting. By Macedonian times, the phalanx simply denoted a body of densely arrayed spearmen, enhanced by cavalry, light-armed soldiers, and missile troops, a column no longer reflective of the unique cultural and political matrix of the *polis*.   VDH

Adcock, F. E., *The Greek and Macedonian Art of War* (Berkeley, 1957).

Anderson, J. K., *Military Theory and Practice in the Age of Xenophon* (Berkeley, 1970).

Hanson, V. D., *The Western Way of War* (New York, 1989).

Pharsalus, battle of (48 BC). This was the great victory of Julius *Caesar over his rival *Pompey. Pompey fielded 45,000 infantry and 7,000 cavalry against Julius' 22,000 and 1,000, and massed his horse on the left, intending to sweep around the enemy flank. Julius stripped one cohort from the third line of each of his legions and concealed them behind his right flank as a fourth line. Pompey's cavalry crashed through Julius' outnumbered horse, but was then surprised and stopped in its tracks by this reserve force. In the centre Julius' veteran infantry prevailed and killed thousands for the loss of only 230 of their own.   AKG

Philip II of Macedon (382–336 BC) ruled Macedon from 359 and transformed it from a backward region on the northern periphery of Greece into the director of Greek affairs. Philip began as regent for his nephew Amyntas, but military crisis, with Illyrian tribesmen dominating the western marches, Greek cities controlling the coastal lands, and royal rivals supported by Athens and others, required decisive leadership. While reforming the *Macedonian army, Philip secured his northern and western frontiers through a mixture of diplomacy and force, and obtained recognition from the Athenians in return for supporting their claims to Amphipolis, a city on Macedon's eastern border and key to the Thracian gold and silver mines. Having secured his throne, Philip snatched Amphipolis and left the Athenians without reward. Control of this region provided him with funds to hire mercenaries, engage in effective diplomacy, and pursue territorial ambitions.

Marriage to Olympias of Epirus consolidated his western borders and a son, the future *Alexander 'the Great', was born in 356. Philip now set about reducing the Greek cities along the Macedonian coast (including Methone, where he lost his right eye), which provided good lands to allocate to supporters. This reinforced his control of Macedon, since the nobility of border cantons were firmly attached to the royal court at Pella by prospects of rich patronage, while the women might enter the royal harem and their sons be educated in Macedonian ways as royal pages, thus providing hostages for current good behaviour and well-inclined leaders of the next generation.

Lack of strong leadership in Thessaly and the protracted Third Sacred War against the Phocians permitted Philip to move south; he had himself elected leader of the Thessalians, and so gained command of their powerful cavalry. Philip now suffered his only military defeat, when the Phocian Onomarchus lured him into range of an artillery trap, but Philip was victorious in 352. The Athenians were becoming increasingly wary of the rise of Macedon, and, urged on by the orator Demosthenes, unsuccessfully attempted in 348–347 to thwart Philip's designs on Olynthus, the last Greek outpost in the north.

In 346 the Peace of Philocrates briefly ended hostilities, but the constant growth in Macedonian power and Philip's interests in eastern Thrace, which he needed to control as a preliminary to the Persian expedition that now loomed larger in his plans, raised Athenian concerns about their grain supply through the Bosporus and Dardanelles. In 340 Philip detained the Athenian grain fleet during abortive sieges of Byzantium and nearby Perinthus; conflict with Athens resumed, to be ended at *Chaeronea in 338. In 337 Philip established the League of Corinth which embedded Macedonian hegemony over Greece and provided a vehicle to attack Persia in revenge for the invasion by *Xerxes in 480. An advance guard landed in Asia in 337, but Philip was murdered at Aegae while finalizing arrangements for the campaign, which Alexander inherited. Philip's rich tomb and cremated remains were recently discovered at Vergina; they are now displayed in the Archaeological Museum at Thessaloniki.   LMW

Cawkwell, George, *Philip of Macedon* (London, 1978).

Hammond, Nicholas, *Philip of Macedon* (London, 1994).

Philippi, battles of (42 BC). These ended the unsuccessful struggle to save republican government at Rome. After the assassination of Julius *Caesar and seizure of power by the Second Triumvirate, Brutus and Cassius were left commanding republican forces in the east. In 42 BC, they crossed to northern Greece to confront Mark *Antony and Octavian. The armies met east of Philippi and the first battle took place in early October. Brutus on the republican right defeated Octavian and captured his camp. Octavian himself was ill and escaped by hiding in nearby marshland. On the republican left Antony personally took the camp of Cassius who, unaware of Brutus' victory, fell on his sword. After three weeks of inactivity, with both sides suffering supply problems, Brutus decided to fight again on 23 October. This time he was routed with heavy losses. He and other republican leaders committed suicide, though some surrendered or escaped, and their army went over to the triumvirs. Antony emerged triumphant and the dominant partner of the triumvirate, while Octavian's seeming cowardice caused a severe if temporary setback to his ambitions. BR2

Syme, Ronald, *The Roman Revolution* (Oxford, 1939).

Philippines insurrection (1899–1902), continuation of the Filipino creole struggle for independence (1896–8) after America assumed sovereignty following the *Spanish-American war. Not to be confused with the centuries-old resistance of the Muslim *Moros* (Sp, Moors), which continues to this day.

Aguinaldo became leader of the resistance by his treacherous execution of the more popular Bonifacio in 1897. Outraged at being excluded from Manila after the Spanish capitulation, he organized his followers into a semi-regular army of approximately 80,000, half of it around the capital. Despite orders to the contrary, American commander Otis provoked hostilities in February 1899 and routed the Filipinos during a first period of conventional warfare. By November, they had reverted to guerrilla warfare under local leaders. His authority destroyed by his murder of charismatic general Luna, Aguinaldo retreated to a mountain hideout.

Otis was psychologically unsuited to irregular warfare and widely despised. Having deprived himself of any justification for keeping it by premature declarations of victory, the volunteer half of his army of 30,000 went home in mid-1899, to fill newspaper columns with atrocity stories and denunciations of his ineptitude, while the War Department sent replacements over his objections. He was recalled (at his own request and to a hero's welcome) in May 1900.

Arthur (father of Douglas *MacArthur), the new military governor, increased the occupation force to a peak of 70,000. He was also to reap the benefits of a traditional colonial policy of divide and rule begun by Lawton, a general much publicized for gung-ho exploits inappropriate to his rank. After seeking approval directly from the War Department, he began recruitment of Filipino scouts among the Macabebe, bitter rivals of the rebellious Tagalog, in mid-1899. With well-orchestrated press support, Lawton would probably have replaced Otis if he had not been killed in December leading a scouting patrol.

MacArthur implemented a policy based on the carrot of amnesty for surrendered guerrillas and civic action in pacified areas, and when this did not prosper he followed with the stick of *concentration camps, confiscation of property, and ruthless retaliation in areas where resistance persisted. Aguinaldo was captured in a daring March 1901 raid led by Funston, another publicity-hungry general, and was clever enough to negotiate a pension for himself in exchange for swearing fealty to the USA and appealing to the guerrillas to follow his lead, something they had not done since 1899.

Once again the war was pronounced won and after an uneasy power-sharing interim, in July 1901 MacArthur handed over civilian authority to Taft, who revived the carrot, and military command to Chafee. The latter applied the stick so vigorously that it led to a congressional investigation and the court martial of one of his brigade commanders, who had boasted of the prisoners he had shot. So had Funston, but he was saved by a cover-up directed by Pres Theodore *Roosevelt himself.

The figures speak for themselves: 4,234 US troops were killed and 2,818 wounded, against an estimated 20,000 Filipino deaths in 'combat' and perhaps 200,000 civilians, mostly from disease and privation. HEB

photographers The modern image of war begins with war photography. The first known photograph had been taken in 1826 but it was thirteen years before Louis Daguerre began commercial photography in his Paris studio. The odd blurred photograph survives from the *Mexican war of 1846, but the first war to be recorded on camera was the *Crimean. The first cameras could record static objects and people posing, but no movement, and were extremely bulky, thus the first war photographs were either of camp life or of the dreadful legacy of battle—the spent cannon balls in the 'Valley of Death' after the Charge of the Light Brigade. Even so, these photographs illustrate the power of the photograph. The camera records more than the human eye and brain, which filter out what they do not want to see.

After *war correspondent William Russell's reports of the conduct of the war began appearing in *The Times*, the British government sent Roger Fenton to make a more favourable photographic record. The camp scenes, with bearded soldiers, some wives, and *cantinières*, or the many-masted ships riding at anchor in the harbour at Balaclava, instantly transport us to the scene in a way that no painting ever can. The battle scenes had to be staged, however. The *Indian Mutiny produced similar group pictures and recorded the aftermath of hard fighting.

By April 1861, when the *American civil war began, photography had advanced with the introduction of glass plate negatives. Mathew Brady, a successful celebrity photographer, packed a mobile darkroom in a horse-drawn wagon and headed for the first battle of *Bull Run. He compiled *Incidents of War*, a photographic history of the conflict. The results were dramatic. Brady's photographs of the devastation after the battle of *Antietam did much to temper war fever. His shots of Confederate dead, their bodies swollen, their trouser buttons undone as the wounded had fumbled to see if they had received wounds to the gut, told of the disgusting reality of conflict. As the *New York Times* reported, 'Brady has done something to bring home to us the terrible reality and earnestness of war.' This was the beginning of photo-journalism. Brady's work was, and is, recognized not only as a superb historical record, but as a form of art. He was the civil-war combat photographer par excellence, but he was not alone. His assistant Alexander Gardner's *Photographic Sketchbook of the War* includes the deeply moving photograph 'Home of a rebel sharpshooter', a young Confederate sniper lying dead between the rocks in July 1863, the shining barrel of his well-maintained rifle so real you can almost touch it.

In the 1870s technicians produced a dry plate with silver salts in a gelatine base which did not need to be sensitized in liquid but was ready to use and could be developed long afterwards. The new developments ensured even better coverage of the Second *Boer War and the *Russo-Japanese war. The British dead packed in their trenches on Spion Kop mirror the dead in Brady's photographs, but now that such photographs were easier to take, a reluctance to show them began to emerge. By the time of WW I box cameras were within the reach of every soldier. Paradoxically, because reporting and photography were so tightly controlled, and because photography—including air photography—was now part of *intelligence gathering and *surveillance and target acquisition, WW I did not give rise to any first-rate human-interest war photographers. Photographs of dead and mutilated soldiers were suppressed. But there were millions of photographs.

The *Spanish civil war ushered in a new era in which the civilian population was enmeshed in the conflict. Robert Capa, born André Friedmann in Budapest, understood and recorded this change. After working in Berlin he moved to Paris in 1933 where he met Henri Cartier-Bresson, the artist, photographer, and film producer. In 1935 he adopted his famous name and began collaborating with Gerda Taro, who was killed in Spain in 1937. Capa's coverage of Spain appeared regularly in *Vu, Regards, Ce Soir, Weekly Illustrated, Picture Post*, and *Life*. His 'Death of a Loyalist soldier', taken in 1937, first appeared in *Vu* and was then picked up by the US *Life* and the UK *Picture Post*. Capa's photographs were the subject of hyperbole: *Picture Post* billed a set of photographs titled 'This is war!' as 'the finest picture of front line action ever taken', by 'the greatest war photographer in the world'. Although the pictures might seem tame to a generation accustomed to horrific pictures of conflict, they did have a great impact at the time. *Picture Post* felt it necessary to point out the photographs were not propaganda but, in accordance with the new philosophy of war correspondents of the time, 'simply a record of modern war from the inside'. The photographers also showed that the battlefield was now everywhere: Capa's picture of a mother and child watching as bombers circled overhead, or those of Barcelona being bombed taken by Chim/Szymin (David Seymour).

It was clearly impossible to impose WW I-style restrictions on photographers of this standard. Instead, Allied governments needed their support. After the fall of *France in 1940 all pretence at objectivity was abandoned. Capa and his British colleague George Rodger became part of the Allied war effort, as did fine British photographers who joined the Army Film and Photographic Unit. WW II generals were aware of the power of photography and often dressed for the part, notably *Clark, *Montgomery, *Patton, and above all *MacArthur. Capa and several other top US photographers joined Clark's forces in Italy, and Capa went ashore with the Americans in Normandy, moving with them in their advance through Europe. The Red Army also had excellent photographers, notably Yevgeniy Khaldei, who took the famous re-enactment of raising the Red Flag over the Reichstag in the battle of *Berlin. One of the Russian sergeants was wearing two looted watches on each wrist, which the censors duly painted out.

The end of WW II did not make the world a safer place—not for war photographers, at any rate. Capa was killed on 25 May 1954 in Thai Binh, *Indochina, after stepping on a landmine. His colleague Chim was killed on 10 November 1956 by Egyptian machine-gun fire near the Suez Canal. Both had been founder members of the Magnum photographic agency. The Overseas Press Club's annual Robert Capa Award is given for 'superlative photography requiring exceptional courage and enterprise abroad'.

The greatest photographer of the post-war period is probably Don McCullin, who worked for *The Sunday Times* and for Magnum. McCullin photographed in *Vietnam—notably the 1968 *Tet offensive—Northern Ireland, and Cyprus. Larry Burrows also took outstanding photographs for *Life* including the emblematic Vietnam shots of a weeping US helicopter gunner and of a white soldier coming to the aid of a wounded black comrade. Gilles Peress photographed Bosnia, Northern Ireland, and Rwanda. James Nachtwey photographed Northern Ireland, Nicaragua, El Salvador, Lebanon, Afghanistan, Bosnia, Sudan, and Rwanda and has gained many awards including the Robert Capa Gold medal in 1983, 1984, 1986, and 1994. Luc Delahaye photographed Bosnia, Rwanda, Chechnya, and Haiti for Magnum and won the Capa award in 1993. Corinne Dufka photographed Nicaragua, Bosnia, and post-modern chaos in many countries in Africa for Reuters. By the nature of their work, war photographers are exposed to danger. Due to restrictions on what can be shown on television, and the nature of the medium, still photographers remain able to capture the most graphic images of the horrors of combat, conflict, and its consequences, and continue to record the most vivid and concise images of war.   CDB

Manchester, William, *In Our Time: The World as seen by Magnum Photographers* (New York, 1989).

Piccolomini, Prince Ottavio (1599–1656). Although an Italian aristocrat by birth, Piccolomini served the imperial cause faithfully throughout his military career. He fought against the renegade Hungarian Protestant Bethlen Gabor at the siege of *Vienna in 1619, and in 1627 after a brief spell in his homeland, he joined *Wallenstein to command his lifeguard, having earned a reputation as a dashing cavalier of some audacity and courage. He used his influence at the court in Vienna to support Wallenstein's rehabilitation in 1631, after the Swedish invasion. At *Lützen he charged a total of seven times with his *cuirassiers, losing five horses and stopping six musket balls, but fought on and eventually rolled the stubborn Swedes back.

For reasons that no doubt seemed compelling, Piccolomini was involved in the conspiracy to murder Wallenstein in 1634 and was disappointed when he did not receive an army command. After a period of inactivity he entered Spanish service, beating the French at Thionville in 1639. Philip IV of Spain heaped honours on him and he was induced to return to imperial service, commanding the army defeated by *Tortensson at *Breitenfeld, after which he again went into semi-retirement in disgrace. He was recalled in 1648 to face the French advance into the Habsburg heartlands and skilfully negotiated himself out of a precarious situation and brought about a peace. Made a prince of the Holy Roman Empire in 1650, he retired to live out his life in Vienna.   TM

Picton, Lt Gen Sir Thomas (1758–1815), a Welshman who spent almost his entire life soldiering, being gazetted ensign in the 12th Foot at 13 years of age. He served in the West Indies, where he acquired a reputation as a brutal disciplinarian, and in 1810 he was posted to Iberia to command the 3rd Division under Wellington. He developed a uniquely eccentric style of leading his men from the front amid a cloud of profanity, dressed in black civilian coat and top hat. His division acquitted itself magnificently in many of the major battles of the *Peninsular war and Wellington came to depend on him to handle demanding assignments. Rather pathetically, he begged to be excused service during the *Hundred Days, writing that he was no longer sure he could control his nerves, but the duke would not be denied and gave him command of the 5th Division. He displayed all his old fire and determination at Quatre Bras, where he was wounded. Keeping his injury a secret, he was leading his division to crush D'Erlon's attack on the Allied centre at *Waterloo when shot through the head. His last words were said to have been, 'Come on you rogues, you rascals.' It is unlikely that any of his men loved him, but they respected him and Wellington valued him above all his other divisional commanders.   APC-A

pikemen Seventeenth-century infantry consisted largely of pikemen and *musketeers. By the 1640s the pikemen's main weapon was 18 feet (5.48 metres) long in theory, but often shorter in practice, for soldiers sometimes cut off a foot or two to make it more manageable. They also carried a sword, though this was generally of poor quality. At the beginning of the century pikemen wore a rimmed helmet

('pikeman's pot'), breast- and back-plate, and articulated tassets covering the thighs, but *armour was discarded as the century went on. The pikemen of the *New Model Army seem not to have worn body armour, and Sir James Turner reported that in 1671 pikemen were 'naked'—that is, unarmoured—everywhere save in the Netherlands.

The pike was at first regarded as a more honourable weapon than the *musket. Shakespeare's character Pistol asks the disguised *Henry V who he is. 'I am a gentleman of a company,' replies the king. 'Trailst thou the puissant pike?' asks Pistol. 'Even so', is the reply. It required greater physical strength than the musket, so the sturdiest soldiers became pikemen. An index of the determination of infantry was their preparedness to come 'to push of pike'. *Cromwell wrote that at Worcester (1651) 'the dispute was very long, and very near at hand, and often at push of pike'.

The proportion of pikemen to musketeers shrank steadily. Early in the century there were perhaps two pikemen to one musketeer. This ratio was reversed by the time the English civil wars broke out in 1642 (see BRITISH CIVIL WARS), and by 1691 English regiments that left Ireland for Flanders had only fourteen pikemen per company, less than a quarter of their strength. The 17th-century soldier Sir James Turner had already complained that there was 'an universal contempt for the pike'. Although the pike was effectively rendered redundant by the invention of the *bayonet which, in effect, made every musketeer his own pikeman, it lingered on well into the 18th century, and *Saxe retained a lasting affection for it.

Pikemen made an occasional reappearance in armies denied more potent weaponry. A participant in the *Irish rebellion of 1798 recorded that 'Every man had a fire-arm of some sort, or a pike. The latter weapon was easily had at the time, as almost every blacksmith was a United Irishman.' In 1940 many members of the British *Home Guard carried pikes, often made from bayonets attached to poles.   RH

pillbox Term for a cylindrical *fortification, first used in the Second *Boer War, when many British blockhouses were circular. It gained wide currency in WW I, and was applied to concrete bunkers built by Allies and Germans alike, though most were rectangular and so ceased to resemble the traditional round chemist's box. They played an important part in the German defensive system, providing shelter for machine-gunners and artillery observers. Most could resist hits by field artillery, and were often captured by assault, with attackers posting *grenades through firing slits to kill or demoralize their garrisons. They remain durable features of the French and Belgian landscape, and are often used as animal shelters or tool sheds. Pillboxes were widely constructed in Britain in WW II, and many, with their polygonal outlines, again resembled the box for which they were named.   RH

Pilsudski, Marshal Jozef (1867–1935), Polish general and politician, leader of the first independent Poland for 123 years after WW I. Pilsudski was one of the founders of the nationalist faction of the Polish Socialist Party in 1906. At that time Poland was part of the Russian empire, but Polish nationalists sided with Russia's adversaries, such that Pilsudski commanded the Polish legion which fought with the Austro-Hungarian army during WW I. Despite backing the losing side, Pres Wilson's insistence on self-determination as a principle of the Treaty of Versailles and Allied hostility to the Bolsheviks in Russia enabled Pilsudski to be proclaimed head of state of the newly independent Poland, with dictatorial powers. In 1920 he launched the *Russo-Polish war and captured Kiev on 7 May. When the Soviet First Cavalry Army struck behind him, he was initially dismissive of a manoeuvre he described as 'almost in the manner of nomadic peoples', but soon found it necessary to fall back on Warsaw, where he rallied his forces and defeated *Tukhachevskiy.

A militarist and an anti-Semitic extreme Catholic nationalist, he was again dictator in 1926–8 and from 1930 until his death. Although it was all too obvious what a resurgent Nazi Germany and Soviet Union meant for Poland, instead of seeking an alliance with similarly threatened Czechoslovakia, his foreign minister and eventual successor Józef Beck pursued irredentist claims.　　CDB/HEB

pioneer is a word with a complex military etymology. It has the same Latin root as *peon*, meaning a humble labourer and also pawn with its implication of expendability, but by the 17th century the full word meant one who goes ahead and prepares the way for others, not necessarily in the military context, and who is worthy of honour. Very broadly speaking, in most armies the low-status pioneers, sometimes not even regarded as soldiers, did the work and the *engineers got the credit. To confuse things further, there is the intermediate category of *sappers to be considered. Although the separately named functions only came much later, there is a hint of things to come in the *Roman army, where all legionnaires dug, ditched, built roads, ramps, and ramparts, directed on occasion by *mensores* (surveyors) and even *artifices qui fossam faciunt* (ditch-digging specialists).

In the British army a Royal Pioneer Corps was raised in 1762 but disbanded the following year. By contrast the Corps of Royal Engineers was founded in 1787 and has existed ever since. The WW I non-combatant Labour Corps for *conscientious objectors and others not judged fit to be killed in the front lines was also known as the pioneers and was disbanded in 1919. In 1939 a similar Auxiliary Military Pioneer Corps was formed, like its predecessor explicitly to free soldiers for front-line duties. Simply the Pioneer Corps by 1940, it finally regained the 'Royal' prefix in 1946 and four years later ceased to be classified as an auxiliary force and became part of the regular establishment. In 1993 it was amalgamated with the Royal Corps of Transport, the Royal Army Ordnance Corps, and the Army Catering Corps to form the Royal Logistics Corps. The Royal Pioneer Corps' motto was 'Labor Omnia Vincit' meaning 'work conquers all'—except, that is, the professional snobbery of the engineers. This distinction was even more pronounced in the land of the free, where engineers traditionally were the crème de la crème of the US army. The Navy Construction Battalions (Seabees), on the other hand, were combat pioneers in the highest and most honourable sense of the word.

The German army was somewhat less troubled by these social nuances, and pioneers had an active combat role. In the USSR, the Young Pioneers were the shock troops of the Komsomol, the party youth organization, devoted to spying on their family, friends, and neighbours. An ambivalent word, best left alone.　　MCM/HEB

pistols and revolvers Scholars have yet to decide upon the etymology of 'pistol', but it first appeared in the 1540s in its French version *pistolet*, said to be derived from the Italian *pistolese* and referring to arms produced in Pistoia. An alternative derivation ascribes it to the Bohemian word *pistala*, meaning a pipe or whistle and apparently used to describe a light cannon. The pistol is a development in the history of firearms which only became feasible during the era of the *wheel lock, since the term denotes a small firearm capable of being held and fired with one hand. There are very early exceptions, one of which is a unique 16th-century *matchlock revolving pistol in the Palazzo Ducale in Venice. One-handed matchlock pistols were made in Japan and the gun-shields made for Henry VIII in the mid-1540s incorporated *breech-loading matchlock pistols, but the development of the true pistol began in the early 16th century and utilized the wheel lock system.

German gunmakers dominated the development of the pistol in the 16th century, the earliest of which date from the 1530s. These wheel lock pistols were often shaped like muskets in miniature but the pistol-butt developed during the second half of the century in two forms: one resembling a fishtail and almost in line with the barrel; the other ending in a ball and at a sharp angle. The carrying of pistols by soldiers (French heavy cavalrymen carrying a pair in saddle-holsters) has been dated to 1549 and the pistol rapidly became a popular firearm for European cavalrymen. Belt pistols, equipped with a long flat hook, became popular at the same time and, by c.1600 the pistol, increasingly sophisticated, decorated, and therefore expensive, had become linked with the cavalry and the commander: it was a military firearm of high status. By c.1600 too, the original short, fat pistols of large bore were beginning to be replaced by longer, more elegant designs, probably of French origin, with smaller bores and oval, or lemon-shaped pommels. The pistol continued its élitist position on the battlefield throughout the 17th and 18th centuries, generally carried in pairs in holsters forward of the saddle.

*Snaphaunce and *flintlock pistols joined wheel locks by c.1600 and the European wars of the 1630s and 1640s resulted in munition-quality flintlock pistols for use by cavalry troopers. Both the wheel lock and flintlock systems lent themselves to experiments with revolving pistols, the earliest known flintlock revolving pistol surviving in the Kremlin Armoury in Moscow from 1616 to 1625. By 1700 the European cavalryman's flintlock pistol was likely to have a barrel of about 14–16 inches (35.5–40.6 cm) long, with a calibre of about .24 inch to .30 inch, but these statistics varied from nation to nation. The martial pistol became gradually standardized during the 18th century, its pattern changes paralleling those of military muskets. Naval pistols generally featured belt-hooks and some nations investigated separate shoulder stocks for their cavalry and artillery pistols. In mid-century, *Highlanders of the British army carried metal belt pistols of distinctively Scots design, but often made in England. Officers carried personal pistols little different, except—traditionally—in their subdued decoration, from those bought for self-defence by civilians. By 1800, the European military flintlock pistol had a barrel of 8–10 inches (20.3–25.4 cm) and a calibre of about .50 inch; again, details varied between nations. The introduction of the *percussion lock in the early 19th century did little for the design of the military pistol and it was being replaced by the carbine by mid-century, pistols being reserved solely for issue to senior *NCOs. Such pistols as were issued were increasingly likely to be rifled.

The revolver had little military use prior to the mid-19th century and revolving pistols tended to be carried by officers. Most would have had clusters of revolving barrels rather than a single barrel and a revolving chamber, although such weapons date from the 17th century. It is now generally accepted that Samuel Colt (1814–62) perfected the first practical and efficient military revolver. Colt's earliest revolvers—rifles and pistols—were used in limited numbers by the US army during the Seminole war of 1838 and the *Mexican war of 1846–7. These early revolvers were loaded with powder and ball into the cylinder from the front and fired with percussion caps. The majority of mid-19th century revolvers were variations upon this theme but Colt was the first to have his revolvers made on a factory basis, using machine tools and employing interchangeable parts: this was a vital development in the mass production of weapons. Colt's revolvers were very popular with officers, as were those of his American and British rivals—such as Remington and Starr in the USA and Tranter and Webley in Britain. Revolvers firing pin-fire *cartridges were developed in the 1840s and 1850s by Lefaucheux, père et fils, in France and adopted by the French navy in 1858. Revolvers firing first rim-fire and then centre-fire cartridges dominated the last forty years of the 19th century and many dozens of makers produced models, first in single-action

and then double-action, which were bought by military and naval officers. Despite the advent of the self-loading, or 'automatic', pistol in the last decade of the century, the revolver remained the officer's accepted sidearm in many countries until the mid-20th century.

The self-loading pistol was principally developed in the 1890s and utilized a recoil system to eject the fired cartridge and chamber a fresh one. Although there were experiments in gas-operated self-loading pistols, most—in the last century—have used variations on the recoil system and individual designs by household names such as Mauser, Browning, Mannlicher, Luger, Savage, and Beretta are modifications on this essential theme, utilizing different locking and loading systems. Self-loading pistols have had widespread military and paramilitary use for the past century, often being carried as an additional side arm by both officers and soldiers.

The pistol's tactical use has always been limited by its comparatively short range and, although of value in an assault role, its principal military employment has been as a defensive weapon. Its small size has made it attractive to 20th-century *partisans and terrorists for assassination and a pistol remains an essential part of an airman's survival kit.

SCW

Blair, Claude (gen. ed.), *Pollard's History of Firearms* (London, 1983).

Chickman, Col A., *United States Martial Pistols and Revolvers* (Buffalo, NY, 1944).

Taylerson, A. W. F., Andrews, R. A. N., and Frith, J., *The Revolver 1818–1865* (London, 1968).

——— *The Revolver 1865–1888* (London, 1966).

——— *The Revolver 1889–1914* (London, 1970).

Pizarro, Francisco (c.1475–1541), *conquistador of Peru. Already an old man by contemporary standards, during a 1526–8 expedition down the Pacific coast with Almagro, he learned of the Inca empire. Staying behind while his partner sailed back for supplies and reinforcements, he drew a line in the sand with his sword in front of his dispirited men and asked those desirous of wealth and glory to cross it. With only thirteen followers he continued south, collecting evidence of abundant treasure. Sent back to Spain to legitimize the partners' position, he obtained a marquisate and viceroyship over the still to be won province, relegating Almagro to a subordinate position. In 1531, accompanied by four half-brothers and later joined by Soto, he returned to Peru.

The Inca empire was newly wracked by a civil war in which Atahualpa defeated his half-brother Huascar, but Pizarro made none of the local alliances that elsewhere proved so useful and advanced into the Peruvian highlands with 60 cavalry and 100 infantry, equipped with twenty crossbows and a few firearms. Losing many horses on the way, he passed through several narrow defiles where he could easily have been stopped to arrive in November 1532 at Cajamarca, where Atahualpa with an army of some 30,000 awaited his homage. The Inca accepted an invitation to dine and entered Cajamarca with a retinue of about 5,000, only to be captured in an ambush in which half his escort was killed.

Pizarro's only thought was to extort a *ransom of priceless artefacts, melted down to about 6 tons of gold and 12 of silver. Still with only a few hundred men under his command, he chose to murder the source of his authority in August 1533. He ignored the symbolic importance of the Inca capital at Cuzco and founded Lima in one of the worst locations ever chosen for a capital city. In his absence, the puppet Inca Manca Capac escaped to rally his people, reducing Spanish authority to Lima and Cuzco, the latter besieged from February to August 1536.

No sooner had the Incas dispersed to plant for the coming year than a wrathful Almagro returned from a horrendous exploration of northern Argentina and Chile and seized Cuzco, imprisoning Gonzalo and Hernando Pizarro. He defeated one army sent by Pizarro and another under Manca Capac before marching on Lima. Once there, he naïvely accepted an undertaking by Francisco to recognize his claim to Cuzco and released Hernando, until then a hostage. The latter returned with an army to defeat and execute him in April 1538.

Francisco spent two years in Cuzco trying to subdue the Manca Capac rebellion before returning to Lima. The chaos in Peru was so notorious that the Crown sent out a commissioner to restore order, but before he arrived Pizarro had been assassinated by Almagro loyalists, whom he had gratuitously insulted. A mummified body falsely believed to be his was on display in Lima cathedral for centuries.

HEB

Plains Indians wars (1860s–80s) (see also AMERICAN INDIAN WARS). These were uprisings by the 'hostile' tribes of the Great Plains horse and buffalo cultural area, excluding the Apache of the south-west and the Utes and others of far west and mountain zones. They were subdued by a strategy of exterminating the buffalo and winter campaigning devised by *Sherman. The main hostiles with their approximate ranges stated in terms of modern US states were

- *Northern Cheyenne/Arapaho*: Algonquian-speaking tribes in Wyoming and Montana
- *Southern Cheyenne/Arapaho*: in Colorado, Kansas, Oklahoma, and Texas
- *Comanche*: Uto-Aztecan speaking people, from Kansas to Mexico inclusive
- *Kiowa*: Kiowa-Tanoan speakers in Kansas, Oklahoma, and Texas
- *Kiowa-Apache*: Athapascan speakers in Texas and New Mexico

- *Santee Sioux* (Mdewkanton, Sisseton, et al.): Siouan speakers in Minnesota and Wisconsin
- *Teton Sioux* (Brulé, Hunkpapa, Mineconjou, Oglala, Sans Arc): spread over the Dakotas, Wyoming, and Montana

The Canada border-area hostile Algonquian-speaking Blackfoot tribe is included among the Teton Sioux. Because of tribal enmity or prudent calculation, many of the Caddoan Arikara and Pawnee, the Siouan Crow and Osage, and the Uto-Aztecan Shoshoni allied with the whites against the hostiles—when, that is, they were not raiding on their own account amid the swirling confusion of a frontier war where the autumn hostiles could be the winter reservation Indians and back out on the warpath in the spring.

Like the Yankton/Yanktonai Sioux, the Santee grudgingly accepted 'concentration' in 1858. In August 1862, a corrupt Indian agent of the government denied them treaty supplies and one of his soon-to-die confederates suggested they eat grass. Led by the previously accommodationist Mdewkanton Little Crow, the Santee went on an orgy of raiding that spread into Wisconsin until defeated at Wood Lake on 23 September. Two thousand surrendered and 303 were condemned to death by courts martial, but *Lincoln personally reviewed the sentences and reduced the number to 38. The Sisseton and some Teton Sioux were chased into Dakota, where the last battle took place at Killdeer Mountain in July 1863.

For the southern hostiles, the moment when resisting the whites finally took absolute precedence over fighting each other came with the massacre of Black Kettle's trusting Cheyenne at *Sand Creek. The 'Cheyenne-Arapaho war' of 1864–5, 'Hancock's Campaign' of 1867, and 'Sheridan's Campaign' of 1868–9 were basically one long spasm of related uprisings. In the first, raids by the Cheyenne and Arapaho joined by some Teton Sioux ravaged Colorado until battles at the North Platte and Powder rivers in late 1865 bought a year's relative tranquillity. When raiding revived in 1867, Hancock drove them out of Colorado, to spread terror through western Kansas.

Although he signed the Treaty of Medicine Lodge in 1867 and withdrew to a reservation in Indian Territory (now Oklahoma), the hapless Black Kettle could not control the élite Dog Soldiers of his own tribe, who joined a Kiowa and Comanche uprising the next year, once again provoked by withheld supplies. In September, 50 troopers held off 600 Oglala and Dog Soldiers at Beecher's Island in Kansas, killing their leader Roman Nose. On 27 November, Black Kettle and 102 others, mostly old men, women, and children, were killed in Sheridan's Campaign when *Custer attacked their camp at Washita River. On Christmas Day, Dog Soldiers and Kiowa were defeated at nearby Soldier Spring. After a further defeat in July 1869 when fighting alongside the Northern Cheyenne at Summit Springs in north-east Colorado, surviving Dog Soldiers surrendered.

The Kiowa rebelled again in May 1871. Satanta and other leaders were captured and condemned to death, but their sentences were commuted—unwisely, because they led the Kiowa war faction to join the Comanche again in the 'Red River war' of 1874, which tore up the Texas panhandle. After defeats at Adobe Walls and Palo Duro Canyon, Satanta surrendered to Miles in October. Sporadic raiding continued, but the southern Plains Indians wars are considered to have ended when the feared half-breed Comanche Quanah Parker surrendered in June 1875.

Their northern brethren, particularly the Teton Sioux, gave the overstretched US army even more trouble. Always ready to join the uprisings of others to the east and to the south, under remarkable leaders such as Spotted Tail of the Brulé, his nephew *Crazy Horse and Red Cloud of the Oglala, and Sitting Bull of the Hunkpapa, the defeats they inflicted on the regular army were unique in the Plains wars saga. In 1854 after the Brulé wiped out a 30-man punitive column under Grattan near Fort Laramie, the ensuing punishment persuaded Spotted Tail to become an advocate of negotiation. The same pattern of winning prestige in battle first and then accepting the inevitable was followed by Red Cloud after his successful 1866–8 war against the Bozeman Trail in Wyoming. Sent to build three forts through the heart of the Teton's range in 1866, the army encountered fierce resistance. On 21 December a party of Oglala led by Crazy Horse lured to destruction an 80-man column out of Fort Kearny under Fetterman, who had boasted he could ride through the whole Sioux nation with precisely that number. In the face of constant harassment, the Trail was abandoned by the Fort Laramie Treaty of April 1867.

The northern Plains Indians' last stand was provoked by a treaty-violating ultimatum to surrender their sacred Black Hills (*Paha Sapa*), where an expedition under Custer discovered gold in 1874. In June 1876, driven by converging army columns, a unique concentration of Sioux and Cheyenne/Arapaho in southern Montana first repulsed a 1,000-man column under Crook at the Rosebud and then destroyed Custer's command at *Little Bighorn. The concentration dispersed and the ensuing winter campaign broke the back of the resistance, with battles at Slim Buttes and Wolf Mountain. One by one the war bands surrendered or followed Sitting Bull to refuge in Canada. The last battle was Miles's destruction of the Mineconjou at Muddy Creek in May 1877 after their chief Lame Deer had died trying to kill him in a personal gunfight.

The Plains Indians wars effectively ended within a year of the Indians' greatest victory at Little Bighorn, which finally goaded Washington into providing the resources necessary to crush them. There were two subsequent clashes. In 1878 the Northern Cheyenne, desperate to return, were almost exterminated, an act which aroused pity and an unusual concession to their wishes. The pathetic Ghost Dance revival was drowned in blood at Wounded Knee in December 1890. HEB

Utley, Robert, *The Indian Frontier of the American West* (Albuquerque, N. Mex., 1984).
Waldman, Carl, *Atlas of the North American Indian* (New York, 1985).

Plassey, battle of (1757). The victory at Plassey gave the East India Company control of Bengal. Following the attack by the independent Mughal nawab (governor) of Bengal, Siraj al-Dawla, on the British settlements in Bengal in the summer of 1856, a force commanded by Col Robert Clive was sent from Madras. In March 1757 Clive forced the submission of the French settlement at Chandernagore and then marched against Siraj al-Dawla's forces, having first suborned his principal commanders who remained inactive during the battle which took place on 23 June 1757 on the banks of the Bhagirathi river. Clive was very heavily outnumbered and outgunned, but the battle resolved itself into an artillery duel which the nawab lost when his powder was soaked by rain. Clive's total casualties numbered only 63. MEY

Plataea (Plataia), battle of (479 BC). The battle which marked the defeat of *Xerxes' invasion of Greece, Plataea was fought about 5 miles (8 km) east of the ancient town, near the modern Erythrai. After defeating the Persian cavalry at the foot of Cithaeron, the Greeks under the Spartan regent Pausanias, and eventually over 38,000 *hoplites strong, moved down to a position along the Asopos. Here, however, they were increasingly harassed by Persian mounted archers, and eventually attempted to withdraw at night. But this led to the army dividing, the centre back near Plataea, the Spartans on the right, the Athenians on the left. The Persian commander, Mardonius, perhaps as he had intended, had got the enemy on the run, and should have been content with a moral victory which might have brought about the disintegration of the fragile Greek alliance. But whether because he lost control of overenthusiastic men or because he thought he saw a chance to annihilate the Spartans, who, being on higher ground, were all the enemy in view, he made the mistake of engaging them in hand-to-hand battle and was routed. Meanwhile, the Athenians managed to successfully fight off the Boeotians on the Persian side. JFL

Herodotus, 9. 19–70.
Lazenby, J. F., *The Defence of Greece* (Warminster, 1993).

PLO (Palestinian Liberation Organization). The PLO was founded in 1964, as an umbrella organization for groups dedicated to the foundation of an independent Palestine. It is organized into three main bodies: the eighteen-strong Executive Committee serves as the decision-making body of the PLO and includes members from the major fedayeen, or *commando, forces; the Central Committee, which advises the Executive Committee and is made up of 60 members; and the Palestinian National Council (PNC) which is the legislative body of the PLO and elects the Central Committee. The 483 delegates of the PNC are elected or appointed, depending upon the condition under which the members' constituents live. Its functions are assumed by the Central Committee when the PNC is not in session.

In the aftermath of the 1967 *Arab–Israeli war, when the Gaza Strip, the West Bank, and the *Golan Heights were occupied by Israel, the PLO assumed the role of a Palestinian 'government in exile'. In 1968, Yasser *Arafat was elected to the chairmanship of the Executive Committee. He proceeded to centralize power and become the undisputed leader of the Palestinian diaspora. Under his direction, the fedayeen organizations under PLO control launched bloody terrorist attacks in Israel and on Israeli interests abroad from their bases in Jordan.

International reprisals forced Jordan to outlaw the PLO and forcibly eject the organization from Jordanian territory in 1970. Most of the PLO fled from Jordan to Lebanon, from where they continued their raids on Israel for the next twelve years. By the mid-1970s international pressure had forced the PLO to limit most of its terrorist activity to Israel and the Occupied Territories. The PLO raids from Lebanese territory provided Israel with a good excuse to invade *Lebanon in 1982. This invasion weakened the PLO greatly. Splits within the organization were intensified as its members were forced into exile in several Arab countries. The Central Committee relocated to Tunisia.

Perhaps the most successful action taken under PLO leadership was the intifada, or uprising, unleashed in the Gaza Strip in 1987. This war of *attrition contributed to the political agreements in the early 1990s, which granted the Occupied Territories self-rule.

Although it was condemned as a *terrorist organization, the PLO was also recognized as the political organization representing Palestinian interests. In October 1974, it was formally recognized by the UN General Assembly as the representative of the Palestinian people and was granted UN observer status. In 1988, Arafat publicly announced that the PLO renounced terrorism and recognized the right of Israel to exist, and the PLO was diplomatically recognized by the USA.

Intensive negotiations resulted in the signing of the Oslo Accords in 1993. This agreement paved the way for self-rule in the West Bank and the Gaza Strip. In January 1996, the Palestinians conducted their first democratic election to choose representatives for the Palestinian Authority (PA), which comprises an 88-member council and a president. Yasser Arafat was elected first president of the PA with 83 per cent of the vote. The PA is staffed largely with PLO members and members of the former fedayeen make up the PA's security forces.   RTF

Cobban, Helena, *The Palestinian Liberation Organisation: People, Power and Politics* (Cambridge, 1984).

Livingstone, Neil C., and Halevet, David, *Inside the PLO* (New York, 1990).

Plumer, FM Herbert Charles Onslow, 1st Viscount

(1857–1922). With his red face and white walrus moustache, Plumer might have been the inspiration for the cartoonist Low's Colonel Blimp. Appearances were deceptive, for Plumer was an extraordinarily successful army commander. Educated at Eton, he was commissioned into the infantry in 1876 and went to Staff College in 1885. He proved an enterprising commander of irregular horse in Rhodesia in 1896, and went on to lead his Rhodesians in the Second *Boer War. Promoted major general in 1902, he was successively *QMG, a divisional commander, and GOC Northern Command before going to France to head V Corps.

He took over Second Army in the spring of 1915. In June 1917 he captured *Messines ridge in a meticulously planned attack, and, given responsibility for the *Passchendaele battle in the wake of Gough's failure, produced some solid gains in appalling circumstances. Sent to Italy that winter after the disaster at *Caporetto, he helped stabilize the situation and returned to the western front just in time to face part of the *Ludendorff offensive, which he did with his customary deftness.

Part of Plumer's achievement rested on close co-operation with his very capable COS Sir Charles 'Tim' Harington. But he was always his own man, and was less inclined to be bullied by Haig than other army commanders. He understood, as *Montgomery did in WW II, that a largely civilian army required methodical handling. Irreverent young officers called him 'Drip' because of his perpetual sinus problems, but his soldiers called him 'Daddy', an index of their regard for him.   RH

poetry of war

(see also LITERATURE AND DRAMA, THE MILITARY IN). Poetry of war is of two kinds: poetry written about war by poets who may or may not have direct experience of it and poetry written by soldier-poets. The latter are very much a 20th-century phenomenon as whole societies were mobilized for *total war. But poems about war are as old as poetry itself, beginning with the greatest poem in European culture, Homer's *Iliad* composed in the 8th century BC telling the legendary tales of *Troy and war between Greek and Trojan. The poem is clearly based on much older oral forms. Virgil's *Aeneid*, written in the 1st century BC, tells the story of the Trojan Prince Aeneas and his adventures after the fall of Troy. Other civilizations also recorded war in poetic form from the earliest times.

The great Indian epic the *Mahabharata* tells of the futility of war between kin groups feuding over power and wealth. Among the earliest Hebrew poetry are poems on the wars of the Israelites. Early Celtic poems, although dating from the 6th century AD, refer to much older oral forms concerning their legendary wars in the heroic age. Poems such as the Welsh *Gododdin* testify to the celebration of the warrior ideal and its powerful attraction for poets.

Chinese civilization provides the earliest evidence of a continuous poetic tradition and from the 4th century BC poems about war are to be found. From ancient times, poets were fully aware of both the glories of heroic military action and its consequences in grief and destruction. Epic poems lauded both the warrior's courage and noble ideals as well as deploring the horror of war and its wastefulness. War poems were both reminders of past glories and awful warnings for the future.

The designs on the shield of Achilles, in Book XVIII of the *Iliad*, contrast scenes of peace and harmonious governance, harvest and the vintage with scenes of war and battle. The Roman poet Horace might, when prompted by his patron Caesar Augustus, construct odes to celebrate the ideal that to die for one's country is a 'sweet and noble thing' ('dulce et decorum est pro patia mori') but Roman poetry leaves us in no doubt that Cicero's peaceful good life is to be preferred.

Poetry in the heroic age established the ideal of the noble warrior. *Beowulf*, written in the 8th century AD, celebrated the achievements of a Scandinavian hero and his eventual death in combat with a dragon. The Anglo-Saxon fragment *The Battle of Maldon*, concerning a minor skirmish with the Vikings fought in AD 991 on the coast of Essex, makes personal loyalty the key quality of the warrior élite even in hopeless circumstances.

The full flowering of the ideals of *knighthood and chivalry is found in poetry in the high Middle Ages. Chaucer's Knight in the *Canterbury Tales* embodies both martial valour and humility: 'He loved chivalrye, Trouthe and honour, freedom and curteisye'. The revival and elaboration of Arthur's Camelot reach their most complete evocation in Sir Thomas Malory's great cycle *Morte D'Arthur*, first published by Caxton in 1485. How far chivalry can be interpreted as providing rules for war during European conflicts such as the *Hundred Years War or in the many *Crusades from the 11th century onwards is a matter of dispute among military historians, but among western poets the chivalric ideal was the main poetic convention during the Middle Ages. War poetry arose in similar *feudal societies in the East such as Japan where the *samurai code was also the subject for poets. Like their European counterparts samurai themselves were expected to be practised in the fine arts including poetry, composing five-line verses known as tanka when not actually fighting.

It might be suggested that the coming of *gunpowder curtailed chivalric war poetry as the experience of the *Thirty Years War and other conflicts in the 17th century provided evidence enough of the fearsome impact of firepower as an addition to war's grim reality. However, there is an exception: Tasso's *Gerusalemme Liberata* (Jerusalem Liberated), one of the most important works of Italian literature, deals with the Crusades and was written in 1581. Shakespeare's dissolute Falstaff condemned honour in war as merely a 'word' in *King Henry IV, Part I*, but the protagonist embodied it. The sentiments lingered in the verses of the cavalier poets in Britain and only fizzled out at the beginning of the 18th century, save in the descriptions of the Royal Navy's sea fights where the ideal of the noble warrior continued to be embodied in the deeds of Britain's sea captains. Professional soldiers of this age did not appear to have time for verse.

Poets in the age of Romanticism revived the ideal of the noble warrior especially when inspired by the defence of liberty or new nationalist or revolutionary fervour, although Wordsworth's 'Happy Warrior' is offset by Coleridge's reminder in 'Fears in Solitude', written in 1798, that no soldier who fell in battle 'passed off to Heaven, translated and not killed'. To him war remained a horrific business and should make us tremble even if it is necessary for our self-defence.

As the features of modern 'industrial' war became discernible in the 19th century, so contemporary poets tried to clothe them in classical respectability. Tennyson's 'six hundred' were a modern-day equivalent to the Spartans at *Thermopylae save that 'someone had blundered' and their *sacrifice was unintentional. The fratricidal bloodshed of the *American civil war was mourned by James Lowell and Walt Whitman. Time brought reconciliation and death united enemies, but as Julia Howe put it in *The Battle Hymn of the Republic*, God's purpose remained 'to make men free' after Christ's example.

Poets began to accept that war might be worth it when the cause was justified, which explains why the outbreak of war in 1914 was greeted with such apparent enthusiasm in verse. Rupert *Brooke was not alone in seeing war as a consummation and it misrepresents his individual and often ironic poetry to view it as the result of naïve and youthful innocence. What is more, his generation, throughout Europe, had been prepared beforehand to describe their sentiments in poetic form. Catherine Reilly has identified details of 2,225 published poets in English during this period. This can be matched by enormous poetic output across Europe. The nature of modern conscripted mass armies which faced each other provided the reason why it is WW I which sees the specific coining of the phrases 'war poet' and 'war poetry', as Robert Graves points out, himself one of the foremost 'poets in arms'. On all sides soldier-poets could be found; men and women in the ranks (including army, navy, air, and support services) who were themselves poets or who used poetry as a medium for expression, as distinct from civilians who only wrote poetry *about* the war. The most famous and moving of the latter was W. B. Yeats.

A familiar list of British poets was given critical acclaim, mostly after the war, in the framework of a developing critique which saw a transition from youthful innocence in 1914 to knowing and outright condemnation in 1918. Beginning with Brooke, the roll passes through Robert Graves, Edmund Blunden, and Siegfried Sassoon, and ends with Isaac Rosenberg and Wilfred Owen. Of these, only the middle three lived to tell the tale and could only escape from their post-war reputations in various forms of self-imposed exile. The public taste for 'war poets' was insatiable, especially for published collections of poets who had fallen in the war.

Their work had an oracular or prophetic immediacy for a civilian population generally starved of real news about the war. More recently, other poets have been 'discovered' and admitted to the roll, such as Edward Thomas and Ivor Gurney. Other European powers also produced war poets in their own right who became involved in the war. These included George Trakl and Yuan Goll writing in Germany, Guillaume Apollinaire in French, and Giuseppe Ungaretti and Gabiele d'Annunzio in Italian. It is possibly the nature of the war on the western front which produced such a volume of war poetry. The *eastern front produced far less although the Russian poet Valery Brysov, working as a *war correspondent, wrote a good deal. Other Russian war poets were Nikolai Gumilev and Velemir Khlebnikov. Russian poetry tended to the apocalyptic and visionary rather than preoccupation with the blood and ruin of the real war.

So strong was the desire for the insights of the soldier-poet that it inspired new outpourings in the 1930s during the *Spanish civil war and, at the beginning of WW II, the question 'where are the war poets?' was answered in work of at least as high a standard as that of Owen and Sassoon, including the poetry of Keith Douglas, Alun Lewis, Frank Thompson, John Pudney, Henry Reed, and Alan Ross, to select only a small number. WW II produced little poetry of suffering in the West perhaps because of its nature, perhaps because it was seen as a 'good war'. The greatest volume of poetry in this war came from the country which suffered most: Russia, notably the poetry of Anna Akhmatova and Aleksey Tvardovsky.

The lasting achievement of the 'war poets' in the 20th century is that they demonstrated that poetry should not follow blindly the political causes of the moment, should not serve the state or provide the new rallying cries, but should remain critical. Poetry about war since 1945 has embraced this rich and diverse legacy. From the therapeutic and popular poetry of *Vietnam veterans, to be found in profusion on the internet, to the mannered criticisms of the *Cold War and beyond in the work of the Liverpool Poets and Bob Dylan, or to the lyricism of Seamus Heaney's *Requiem for the Croppies*, the democratization of war poetry is sadly a reflection of the scale, frequency, and universality of the experience of war in our time.   BB

Bowra, Sir Maurice, *Poetry and the First World War: The Taylorian Lecture 1961* (Oxford, 1961).

Cross, Tim, *The Lost Voices of World War 1* (London, 1988).

Featherstone, Simon, *War Poetry: An Introductory Reader* (London, 1995).

Harrison, Michael, and Stuart-Clark, Christopher (eds.), *Peace and War: A Collection of Poems* (Oxford, 1989).

Reilly, Catherine W. *English Poetry of the First World War: A Bibliography* (George, 1978).

Stallworthy, John (ed.), *The Oxford Book of War Poetry* (Oxford, 1984).

pole arms/staff weapons As spears, these were used by man's earliest ancestors in their hunting. As warfare developed, so the spear and its varying derivatives developed too, usually as the weapon of the common soldier on horse or foot. Like other weapons which have their roots at the beginning of man's story, pole arms are still with us, principally in a symbolic or ceremonial role, but, only 60 years ago in a time of national emergency, Britain's Local Defence Volunteers were hurriedly armed, as had been their predecessors of the 1790s, with crudely fashioned pikes. It is probable that the little morale-building effect that the pikes had in 1940 would, itself, be recognizable as an emotion to the medieval peasant *pikemen, similarly armed and confronted with apparently superior technology. Most pole arms were derived either from the basic spear or from implements, such as the scythe or bill-hook, in common use for agricultural purposes; many types of pole arm have differing names to describe the same weapon.

Few ancient civilizations eschewed the spear in their armies and, both short and long, it is known to have been used in Egypt and by the Persians, Greeks, and Romans. While the Macedonian *phalanx was noted for its effective use of the thrusting spear, in the 3rd century BC, the *pilum*, or throwing spear, of Rome was equally effective. Tactically, the Macedonians' use of the pike, both as a weapon for the charge and for the defensive 'hedgehog', was little different from its use by the Swiss in the 16th century or by the Scots *schiltroms in their war of independence of the late 13th and early 14th centuries. Javelins, or throwing spears, are as old as pikes and were used by both the Greek and Macedonian armies but the Roman *pilum* appeared in the 3rd century BC and was perfected over the following century to become a 7 foot (2.1 metre) light javelin, half wooden shaft and half iron rod. Its design was such that, thrown from a distance of about 60 feet (18.3 metres), usually in volleys, it would snap or bend on impact and render its targets, transfixed body or penetrated wooden shield, either incapacitated or unwieldy. The *pilum* served equally efficiently as a short thrusting pike and could have its accuracy enhanced by being thrown using a wound cord which imparted a spin; if the angle of impact was greater than 45 degrees it was capable of penetrating contemporary *armour.

The thrown spear did not survive competition with the longbow, crossbow, and firearm in the West but it continued in cultures innocent of *gunpowder. In the hands of the infantry, the long spear became the pike and survived until the musket and socket *bayonet combination rendered it obsolete, apart from brief anachronistic appearances in 1793 and 1940. Towards the end of its active life, by the early 17th century, the pike, generally shortened to 12 feet (3.65 metres) from its earlier length of 18 feet (5.5 metres), was widely regarded, perhaps inevitably, as a more gentlemanly weapon than the noisy, dirty, rather technical interloper of the musket. With this attitude in mind, it is easy to comprehend how the half-pike of 8 or 9 feet (2.4 or 2.7 metres), called an *esponton* or spontoon from the mid-17th century, could remain the weapon of junior infantry officers into the late 18th century; in the British army it survived as a subaltern's weapon until 1786 and was then carried by sergeants—to replace their traditional halberd—from 1792 to 1830. Half-pikes remained as anti-boarder weapons in most *navies until the mid-19th century.

The halberds of European infantry sergeants, carried as a symbol of their authority and used not only to dress the ranks but also as the components of a flogging triangle, were derived from a weapon called, in Swiss-German, a *hallembart* and known to have existed in the 13th century; it may have derived from *Frankish and *Viking war axes. In its most developed form, the halberd was a long-shafted axe with a broad head, sharp rear pick, and long spike continuing the line of the shaft. During its ancestry it spawned many derivatives, such as the poll axe, the long-shafted war hammer, the bill, the glaive, the Jedburgh staff, and the Lochaber axe: all were, essentially, long-shafted axes with a rear pick or hook ideal for unseating horsemen and all represented fearsome weapons in the hands of muscular infantry.

Offshoots from the development of the half-pike and the halberd in the medieval period were the long-shafted, broad-bladed thrusting weapons of which the partisan is the most well known. Remaining today as the ceremonial weapon of the Vatican's Swiss Guard and the British monarch's Yeomen of the Guard, the partisan resembles a winged, broad-bladed spear. Variations on this theme were weapons such as the rawcon, the langdebeve (or *langue du bœuf*), the fork, the *chauve-souris*, and the *couseque*: the vulnerable parts of an armoured knight or man-at-arms were favoured targets for their searching, incapacitating thrusts.

For mounted troops the long spear evolved into the lance. Only in central Europe did lances survive the end of armour but they were reintroduced into European warfare by Polish *lancers in the early 18th century and widely employed after *c.*1780, being used in cavalry charges, often against far superior technology, into the 20th century. Outside Europe, the lance remained an important weapon for the American Plains Indians and in both the Middle East and India. Its role as a significant weapon in the medieval *tournament is continued today, symbolically, by 'musical ride' teams in military tournaments and *tattoos, especially those influenced by the British army. The mounted bodyguard of the president of India still carry lances on state occasions, echoing their history and that of the Bengal Lancers.   SCW

Blair, Claude, *European and American Arms* (London, 1962).

Edge, David, and Paddock, John M., *Arms and Armour of the Medieval Knight* (London, 1988).

Oakeshott, Ewart, *European Weapons and Armour* (London, 1980).

Polish campaign (1939). The invasion of Poland in 1939 may have been very likely, sandwiched as she was between Germany and Russia when both were under the absolute dominion of the most ruthless rulers in their histories; but it was not inevitable. The iconic view is that Nazis, in pursuit of *Lebensraum* in the east, were certain to roll over Poland once 'the West' in the form of British PM Chamberlain and French PM Daladier had 'sold out' Czechoslovakia at Munich in 1938. But this is to acquit the rulers of both Czechoslovakia and Poland, whose job it was to preserve their nations' integrity. The Czechs were militarily prepared, and the elaborate defences they surrendered in the Sudeten could well have inflicted a reverse on the Germans, had Hitler's bluff been called. The Poles were not even militarily prepared and what we may only with charity call their diplomacy between the world wars meant that they were without useful allies when their turn came. Specifically, under *Pilsudski and his foreign minister and eventual successor Col Józef Beck, the Poles not only pursued a dispute with Czechoslovakia over Cieszyn, but also took advantage of its dismemberment to seize the disputed territory. Non-aggression pacts with the Soviets in 1932 and the Nazis in 1934 were pieces of paper, and the Poles knew it. The Polish regime was if anything even more anti-Soviet than the Nazis, but lacked the wit to see that by 1939 neutrality between her two neighbours was not an option. Without a Soviet alliance, Beck was not in a position realistically to deny the Nazi demand for a solution to the absurdity created by the Treaty of Versailles that put Poland in the way of the territorial unification of East Prussia with the rest of Germany. He settled for a vapid alliance with Britain on top of the known-to-be-useless alliance with France instead.

The failure of Beck to accept the need to buy off one of his over-mighty neighbours by accepting one set of territorial concessions created the circumstances for them to pursue the realpolitik he refused to accept. *Stalin and *Hitler concluded the Molotov-Ribbentrop pact, a non-aggression pact whose secret clauses dealt with the dismemberment of Poland, and a week later after a fabricated border clash involving concentration-camp inmates dressed in Polish uniforms, the Germans introduced Poland and the world to *blitzkrieg. WEISS involved Army Groups North, with 15 divisions in East Prussia and Pomerania under Gen Fedor von Bock, and the main Army Group South with 26 divisions in Silesia under *Rundstedt. Between 1 and 6 September the Luftwaffe destroyed the Polish air force (a remnant fled to Romania) and thereafter Stuka dive-bombers flew

Polish campaign

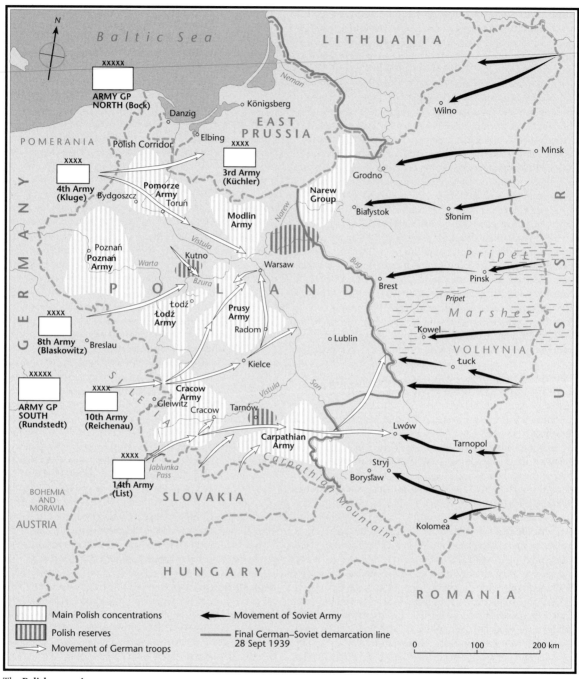

The **Polish campaign**, 1939.

freely over Polish territory, hammering communications neural points and any sign of organized resistance ahead of the two panzer-led pincers that encircled and destroyed the Polish army.

Correctly calculating that the *Maginot Line and the mentality that produced it precluded a direct advance by France into Germany, and that Belgian neutrality would inhibit any other incursion, Hitler denuded his western frontiers and committed his military forces to a campaign designed to achieve swift results. Britain's ultimatum and declaration of war on 3 September was discounted in advance and on 17 September another reason for swiftness was revealed when the Soviets attacked Poland on the Belorussian and Ukrainian fronts. The partition of Poland had been agreed in the Molotov–Ribbentrop Pact, but each party judged it prudent to occupy its allotted territories before the other could get there.

Things did not all go the Germans' way. The fast-moving mechanized columns proved vulnerable to flank attacks, and the Poles managed one such on 9–12 September at Kutno, mauling a division from Blaskowitz's Eighth Army before themselves being defeated. By contrast, the Red Army encountered little opposition, having waited until the Poles were committed (and defeated) before rolling in to pick up the spoils. Warsaw held out until 27 September and technically the campaign continued until 5 October, but it was really all over by mid-September. A nation of 35 million people under authoritarian and even militaristic leadership had succumbed in two weeks. There are no accurate estimates of Polish losses, but the Germans had only 8,000 dead among their 50,000 casualties. The Polish campaign confirmed Hitler's instinctive preference for swift, daring military action over the necessary mobilization of Germany for the protracted war to which he eventually committed her. It also laid bare the chasm between the stated objectives of France and Britain and their ability to enforce them. The poor quality of Soviet soldiers occupying eastern Poland was also noted, so that after another lightning success against France in 1940, he doubled his bet once too often and launched *BARBAROSSA.

Many of the Polish officers who fell into the hands of the Soviets were herded together and murdered by Stalin's NKVD (People's Commissariat for Internal Affairs) in the Katyn forest. Tens of thousands of Polish patriots fled to Britain by various routes and provided among the highest motivated units in the battle of *Britain and later in the campaigns in *Italy and *North-West Europe, with Monte Cassino, *Falaise Gap, and *Arnhem among their many battle honours. This was to no avail, for in 1945 their nation was occupied once more by the Soviets for a further 35 years. Once again, 'guarantees' from the West proved tissue-thin in the face of the geopolitical realities within which this unfortunate nation has been enclosed since the emergence of Russia and Prussia as imperial powers.　　HEB

political economy and war (see page 724)

politics, the military in When *Clausewitz suggested that war was a political instrument, he was addressing the theory of strategy, not the practice of civil–military relations. And yet his dictum's resonance has been particularly powerful in late 20th-century liberal democracies, in part at least because for them it reflects norms of government in peace as well as in war. Serving soldiers should not be involved in active party politics, and armed forces should be subordinated to civil control.

The theoretical underpinnings of these assumptions were established in the 1960s, and were a product of two phenomena. First, the institutionalization of the *Cold War required the world's premier liberal democracy, the United States, to sustain a large army in peacetime. Concerns that its existence could unbalance the workings of the constitution were reinforced by the second consideration, the frequency of military coups, especially in Latin America and Africa. Explanations that rested on the comparative political and economic immaturity of some of the affected states were not sufficiently reassuring. The army was frequently the best organized, the best educated, and technologically the most sophisticated component of a newly independent African state. It therefore had a greater capability for intervention than did an army in a European state, where other government agencies probably had the edge in every respect save that of the monopoly of arms. But means had proved to be only one element in determining an army's behaviour; intention and opportunity proved as important. In the 1960s the recent histories of many developed countries suggested that military intervention in politics was not the prerogative of the Third World.

At the beginning of the decade, French generals plotted an anti-Gaullist coup. France's history gave the republic good grounds for fear. A general, Napoleon Bonaparte, had used the army to subvert the French Revolution and seize power in 1799; the army had supported revolution in 1830 and suppressed it in 1848; and its equivocation towards the Third Republic, whether motivated (as it claimed) by legitimate professional concerns or inspired by clericalism and royalism (as the left asserted), culminated in the Dreyfus affair. *Dreyfus, a Jewish captain, was wrongly convicted of treason in 1894. The army's reluctance to revisit the verdict rested in part on anti-Semitism and in part on its determination to sustain its inner unity against the fissiparous tendencies of individualism. Professionalism had rendered it a state within a state.

Continuities, however, were less important in determining the French army's politics in the early 1960s than the withdrawal from *Indochina and then Algeria (see ALGERIAN INDEPENDENCE WAR). The relevance of this for the theorists was twofold. First, other armies were similarly being
(cont. on page 728)

political economy and war

INSOFAR as any of the social sciences deserves to be considered on a par with the natural sciences, economics comes the closest to being a discrete discipline in which hypotheses may be formulated and tested ('falsified') in the quest for general applications, significantly known as 'laws'. But whereas the laws of natural science are universal, those of social science are man-made, and there's the rub. The Moses of modern economics was Adam Smith, whose *Inquiry into the Nature and Causes of the Wealth of Nations* (1776) aimed to set out 'the general principles of law and government' and was a work in which economics, as narrowly defined today, merged seamlessly with history, philosophy, and legal theory. In the same year, Jefferson managed to substitute the concept of 'happiness' for what everyone else thought was the more self-evidently natural pursuit of property in the US Declaration of Independence, a sentiment echoed in Jeremy Bentham's *Defence of Usury* (1787). Because of its undeservedly lasting influence, Thomas Malthus's crude *Essay on the Principle of Population as it Affects the Future Improvement of Mankind* (1798) must be mentioned, while the similarly bleak-minded David Ricardo put a name on the emerging philosophy in *Principles of Political Economy and Taxation* (1817). Karl Marx and Friedrich *Engels considered themselves to be political economists, their philosophy consisting of an (unattributed) marriage of Malthus's theory of population with Smith's concept of surplus value. Their contemporary John Stuart Mill set out what events have proved to be the more valid historical interpretation in *Principles of Political Economy* (1848).

All of the above studied history in a diagnostic, not prescriptive, mode. Thus although they were not averse to hurrying the process along, Marx and Engels saw the triumph of socialism as evolutionary and inevitable, while redefining the Smith tradition of laissez-faire economics as 'capitalism'. Somewhere in between developed the now-discredited theories compiled in *The General Theory of Employment, Interest and Money* (1936), written by John Maynard Keynes, who never claimed to be an economist, but which gained an enormous following among those anxious to preserve and extend the role of government after WW II. It has not been difficult for rulers to choose between a doctrine that concentrates ever-greater power in their hands and another that regards government as at best a light-handed arbiter in the interplay of natural forces. If one considers this to have been the central dynamic of modern history, then the importance of war becomes apparent.

It is a big 'if', but as a form of philosophical enquiry it provides an interpretative tool that permits a review of the actions of rulers through the ages from a new perspective. It also helps to explain the apparent contradiction of popularly based regimes being some of the most bellicose, because it simply is not true that democracy and war are antithetical, as many fondly believe. From *Genghis Khan and earlier to some of our contemporary statesmen, hugely popular leaders have tended to be Messianic and to find the role of war leader both personally irresistible and politically rewarding.

Thus far the *mise en scène*, and a bridge to Clausewitz's generally misquoted dictum that 'war is nothing but the continuation of politics with the admixture of other means'. It is indeed, and nothing shows it more clearly than the manner in which war has been persistently used to expand the share of the economy that governments control and reapportion, to the point that today a number of thinkers who might once have been considered of the 'left' and of the 'right' have come to agree that this was the real purpose of, for example, the *Cold War. From *Megiddo in 1485 BC to *Kosovo in AD 1999, this argument runs, the only thing all wars have had in common has been to increase governments' powers of convocation and coercion. There is obvious merit in this point of view: as we have seen most dramatically in the last 60 years, war both centralizes power and facilitates the process whereby those exercising power can conflate their personal and sectional advantage with the 'national interest', be it in terms of economic advancement or the no less significant but murkier area of social and psychological compensation.

To deal summarily with the last item first, it is the only link that may be made between, for example, *Hitler and *Churchill, the former compensating for his humble origins and personal inadequacies, the latter reclaiming a leading role for his marginalized class and for himself as the direct descendant of *Marlborough, arguably England's greatest general. Without war, neither would have been much more than a footnote in history, and both of them knew it. The degree to which that subconsciously made them relish war can be debated, but that they did is unarguable. Flawed personalities (in general, *cherchez la mère*) seek to impose their will on others to deaden the psychological 'noise' that envelops them, and the sycophants that power attracts like flies serve to massage their vulnerable egos. In his *Psychology of Military Incompetence*, Dixon has pointed out that the armed forces, on the face of it an arena that should be repulsive to individuals with a deep-seated fear of failure, can be perversely attractive to precisely such people for many reasons that actively militate against military effectiveness.

To make the leap from individuals to whole classes or sections is a bold one, but let us make it and see where it takes us. The bridge, quite possibly too far, is the pursuit of power as an act of social and psychological compensation, as opposed to being a natural extension of the restless expression of a winning attitude that drove mothers' favourites and (highly) sexually functional individuals like *Alexander 'the Great', *Napoleon, and *Wellington. The approach to the bridge is built on the likes of the chauvinist schoolteacher in Remarque's *All Quiet on the Western Front*, but the main span emerges from the apparent contradiction between the spread of mass democracy and the growth of government power. Tocqueville feared that freedom could not survive once the majority discovered it could vote itself money from the public purse; but even he did not foresee the manner by which the process could be extended almost indefinitely. Milton Friedman's analogy is taking a cent from each of a hundred people, giving a dollar to one, and repeating the process as many times as necessary. The loss of each cent is barely felt, the 'gift' of a dollar much appreciated. Even if none of the money were kept, to increase the amount collected is to increase the transactional power of the collector/distributor, hence it is to be assumed that rulers and the bureaucrats who serve them, regardless of ideology, will strive constantly to do precisely that. And so they have, particularly during wars.

Until comparatively recently, expenditure on what we now prefer to call 'defence' was virtually the sole justification for taxation, wonderfully illustrated by the French aristocracy's self-exemption from taxation on the grounds that they paid an *impôt de sang* in war, a delicate consideration not extended to the politically powerless peasantry, obliged to pay by far the greater part of both forms of tax. A study of *war finance shows that once the cost of war exceeded any likely financial gain from conquest, proto-Keynesian considerations about the stimulus that war gave to a nation's economy began to emerge, along with a bureaucracy dedicated to harvesting some (at times most) of the surplus thus generated for 'affairs of state'. But the slow emergence of what we now call liberal democracy was based on a very early illustration of the principle that it is more difficult to turn power into money than vice versa. The introduction of *scutage in place of *feudal service amounted to a tax, one furthermore that King John, following the profligate *Richard 'the Lionheart' who had sold the royal patrimony at a discount, could use to hire *mercenaries and thus recover some of the power lost to the nobles—hence the Magna Charta, the foundation stone of a parliamentary tradition that would have appalled all at Runnymede had they foreseen where it would lead.

The process is symbiotic; while it is easy to see that a civil war is about who rules, it is perhaps less easy to perceive that when *Caesar and *Pompey created the Roman empire, their primary intention was to increase their own power. The Roman republic recognized and institutionalized the process in the office of *dictator and Caesar was, in fact, the last person to be so designated. His successors had no need of it because between an army that was no longer an expression of citizenship and the vastly increased power of *patronage they controlled, it was relatively easy to brush aside the corrupt remnants of republicanism and rule as emperors.

Although Freud persuasively argued that Akhenaton and his priest Moses were the first to perceive the political advantage of monotheism, ideology might be said to have become a permanent part of the equation with the conversion of *Constantine to Christianity. Constantine's genius lay in seeing that a single *religion with a single god could be a powerful unifying factor in an empire of disparate cultures, and in realizing that he could co-opt what was until then a *pacifist and subversive doctrine into an instrument of state power. The prophet Muhammad had the same clarity of vision 300 years later, with explosive consequences among what had been until then a disunited and fractious people. The frontier between these two Messianic creeds became for hundreds of years the preferred arena for rulers on both sides to increase their power through *crusade and *jihad. From the popes who convoked Christendom to retake the Holy Land as part of their temporal struggle with the Holy Roman Empire, through Charles V who used the Ottoman threat to consolidate the Habsburg empire, to Imam Khomeini calling for a jihad to reunite the Muslim world under his Shi'a leadership, monotheism and war have gone hand in hand to extend and to sanctify the centralization of power. Charles I's 'divine right of kings' was a late and rather silly confusion of cause and effect, promptly corrected by the realpolitik of such as *Cromwell.

When Philip IV of France expropriated the *military monastic order of the Templars in 1307, it was as much to eliminate an alternative source of power as to lay hands on the Order's wealth. This was seen even more clearly when Henry VIII, a great centralizer, dissolved the monasteries in what has been called the 'Tudor revolution in government'. The appearance of 'pure' mercenaries as major actors in warfare coincides precisely with the emergence of the Italian city states, able to generate great wealth without the agricultural lands and populations that previously defined military and hence political power. It has been argued that the main reason for the decline of the Habsburg empire was that the silver pouring in from the Americas was the equivalent of a modern state printing unlimited amounts of currency, in that it unleashed an inflation that destroyed commerce and strangled manufacturing, above all in Spain. Certainly, nobody doubts that by persecuting the Moorish and Jewish *conversos* who constituted their commercial and financial class, the Habsburgs attacked their own ability to finance their wars. Conversely, in the *Netherlands revolt, the House of Orange was discovering the power of protracted war to assemble a new kingdom from the dozens of disparate sources of economic power represented by the great trading cities of the region. The successive immigrations of groups persecuted for their religion as a means of expropriating their wealth in the Netherlands and Spain, as well as the French *Huguenots, laid the foundation for the astounding commercial success of England, then Britain, and finally the USA.

The USA provides one of the clearest illustrations of the tight link between war and statism. The four great centralizers in her history were Abraham *Lincoln, Woodrow Wilson, Franklin D. *Roosevelt, and Lyndon Johnson, not coincidentally associated with the four greatest wars the nation has fought. Theodore *Roosevelt was of a similar persuasion, but all he could manage was the imperial adventure in the Philippines (see PHILIPPINES INSURRECTION), so we cannot know what he might have done given the chance. There is no chance here of confusing cause and effect—all were firmly committed to the growth of federal government control over the economy *before* getting involved in war. More controversially, all can also be said to have conspired to bring war about as a means of achieving their objective. To this day, among those who admire their legacy, there remains a marked tendency to declare unwinnable 'wars', such as those on poverty and narcotics, to justify previously unthinkable intrusions into the pockets and the private lives of citizens.

To the idea that socialism is intrinsically pacifist, one has only to examine the intellectual trajectory of the French socialist Jean Jaurès, whose examinations of the *French Revolutionary and *Franco-Prussian wars led him to develop the appalling doctrine of 'the nation in arms'. The idea that the individual is enhanced rather than diminished by marching in step with millions of others is the common thread linking socialism with *militarism. It is worth remembering that *Bismarck, to many the epitome of 'blood and iron', was also the architect of the beginnings of a welfare state far more comprehensive than anything France or Britain had in 1914. Extending government favour to the industrial working class, like his short, sharp limited wars, was a means to an end, namely the unification of Germany under a strong central government. *Moltke 'the Elder', a far less radical individual, towards the end of his life came to deplore the social and political consequences of the mass mobilizations that had put such effective weapons in his hands. Juárez and many other socialists before and since have welcomed it for precisely that reason.

The politicization of private life, foretold by Orwell in *1984* and Vonnegut in the prophetic stories of *Welcome to the Monkey House*, is not the least of the entirely intentional results of rallying peoples to great national causes. For as long as people continue to rejoice in the dollar they receive from on high and do not appreciate that it is simply their own money, recycled, then as Sowell gloomily observes there is no logical stopping point on the road to consensual tyranny, what he calls 'totalitarianism from within'.

If by 'totalitarian' we understand a philosophy that claims to have the answers to all the questions of existence and which will seek to impose that philosophy through indoctrination and coercion, the three great totalitarian systems of our time have been Soviet Marxism-Leninism, German-Italian National Socialism-Fascism, and Anglo-American Progressivism. Of these the last and least overtly offensive has proved the most durable. All three have depended on not so much a class as a type of person for whom a world without clear direction from above is unendurable. All three have fought to the death among themselves, but have been united in their hostility towards traditional economic liberalism. This is not surprising, for laissez-faire means leaving people alone, and if you do that they may not think and act in the approved manner. The power of Messianic creeds lies not in their lip-service to a better afterlife, but in their promise to improve things in the here and now, and Adam Smith's 'invisible hand' of the market not only works too slowly, but also gives more importance to those who produce wealth than to those who merely collect, spend, and distribute it. Seen in that light, war is the antithesis of progress not just because it destroys and kills, but because whatever the high-flown reasons given for fighting ('a world fit for democracy' springs to mind), its political legacy is oppression. HEB

Dixon, Norman, *On the Psychology of Military Incompetence* (London, 1976).

Friedman, Milton, *Capitalism and Freedom* (Chicago, 1962).

Hayek, Friedrich, *The Road to Serfdom* (London, 1944).

Higgs, Robert, *Crisis and Leviathan: Critical Episodes in the Growth of American Government* (New York, 1987).

Jones, E. L., *The European Miracle* (Cambridge, 1981).

Porter, Bruce, *War and the Rise of the State* (New York, 1994).

Sampson, Geoffrey, *An End to Allegiance* (London, 1984).

Sowell, Thomas, *The Vision of the Anointed* (New York, 1995).

asked to hold colonies and then give them up. Secondly, in countering insurgencies, armies were meeting ideas with ideas. By engaging in 'hearts and minds' campaigns, they were using weapons that were more political than military, and they were developing techniques applicable at home as well as abroad. By 1968 the temptation to intervene seemed almost overwhelming. The student demonstrations in Paris and Berlin, the anti-Vietnam protests in the USA, and the civil rights movement in Northern Ireland all challenged the established domestic order. The very threats which the armies of the West had confronted in the colonies seemed to be re-emerging in their parent states.

The fears were exaggerated. The army seized power in Greece in 1967, and in Portugal in 1974. Both interventions were comparatively short-lived; and Britain escaped entirely. By 1990 the end of the Cold War confirmed liberalism's security. Nonetheless the subsequent restructuring of armed forces was debated in terms which often owed more to the issues of political subordination than military effectiveness. Conscription might be the legacy of the mass army designed for major European war but it ensured that the army reflected the society from which it was drawn, and so guaranteed its political compliance. The professional army was in danger of separating itself from society, of developing its own mores and thus its own politics.

This was not how Samuel P. Huntington had seen professionalism in his primer on civil–military relations, *The Soldier and the State*, published in 1957. A true professional would accept it as his duty to obey orders despite the fact that they were politically uncongenial. If an order was illegal, the soldier should have recourse to the judiciary, and if it was militarily unwise the fault was the politician's. What Huntington's argument failed to take on board, as Morris Janowitz recognized in *The Professional Soldier* (1960), was the careerism which professionalism generated. Long-service regulars were committed to the prestige and promotion of their own calling, and this could involve lobbying for a larger defence budget or for a new equipment programme.

Both Huntington and Janowitz looked at armies in intrinsic terms; it was a British scholar, S. E. Finer, who looked at them from the outside in, and did so in terms which were less concerned with the American experience and more driven by establishing a theory of universal application. As a result, *The Man on Horseback: The Role of the Military in Politics* (1962) achieved a level of abstraction sufficient to ensure it a continuing validity. Finer described four ascending levels of intervention: influence, blackmail, displacement, and supplantment. He thus accepted Janowitz's argument that professionalism can promote politicization: all armies, at the very least, seek to influence their governments, and on occasion blackmail them too. Whether they remove them in favour of another government depends less on their own political inclinations than on the legitimacy of the existing government and its constitution. A coup, or

supplantment, is thus only the most extreme in a range of options. Amos Perlmutter's *The Military and Politics in Modern Times* (1977) rests on Finer's emphasis on the primacy of the political order, since Perlmutter explicitly states that 'the military cannot take a neutral political stance'.

This body of thought is Anglo-American, the fruit of liberal democracies on the one hand and of the modern nation state on the other. It therefore presupposes that the need to reflect on and manage civil–military relations is a consequence of functional specialization, the product of standing armies and the democratization of politics. There could be no institutionalized tension between the military and the political for *Frederick 'the Great' or *Napoleon as they embodied supreme control in both. But such an interpretation merely serves to highlight the limitations of political science for the historian. Both Frederick 'the Great' and Napoleon enjoyed more absolute powers than their predecessors. In the seventeenth century, and before, power resided in the military, but the state did not have the monopoly of armed force. The crown relied on the nobility to bring men. If the monarch endeavoured to raise taxes in order to ensure his independent ability to raise forces, as Charles I did in Britain, then he ran the risk of clashing with the nobility and gentry. Not only in the subsequent *British civil wars but also in the Fronde in France, the crown's struggle to centralize administration and to assert its authority over the entrenched local powers of the aristocracy pivoted on the control of armed force. So fragmented were the components of the Holy Roman Empire during the *Thirty Years War that power resided with the commander of the troops rather than with imperial authority. *Wallenstein raised his own taxes, conducted his own diplomacy, and even extracted an oath of personal loyalty from his officers.

The depredations inflicted on society by uncontrolled armies in the seventeenth century, and the alternative, the authoritarianism of military government (England, for example, was administered at the local level by major-generals in 1655), were not unfamiliar to the scholars of the Enlightenment. They knew that the ability of the generals to subvert their governments by dint of their conquests and their control of armies had wracked the Roman republic with civil war and culminated in the triumph of Julius *Caesar. Caesar's imperial successors had, however, not escaped the same vulnerabilities. Their answer, the creation of the Praetorian Guard as a form of protection against an internal coup, rendered them in turn dependent on the guard's loyalty. Both 'Caesarism' and 'praetorianism', like 'Bonapartism', have entered the vocabulary of civil–military relations.

The combination of civil war in the first half of the 17th century and of humanist scholarship in the second made the control and use of armed force a pressing problem for political thought. In 1688 *James II was ousted from the British throne in favour of *William III, not least because a large element in the army, led by John Churchill (see MARL-BOROUGH), changed sides. The subsequent settlement met the soldiers' needs insofar as it authorized the existence of a standing army, but it did so on the sufferance of parliament. The effect was to divide the control of the army between two authorities, the crown and parliament. Effectively, the ability of any component in this triumvirate to operate independently was thwarted. Although the so-called 'Glorious Revolution' of 1689 became the building block for subsequent liberal thinking on the army's constitutional status, in reality the patterns of control were slow to emerge. Throughout the 18th century, and indeed well into the twentieth, there was no bar on serving officers sitting in the House of Commons, and many did so. Moreover, the civilianization of the ministerial control of the army in Britain did not become a fixed principle until after the Napoleonic wars. However, by the 19th century it had become an axiom of British government that the army was kept in its proper place by the division of military from civilian authority: the former was pre-eminent on the battlefield, the latter in the debating chamber. Crucially, however, the Secretary of State for War was simultaneously a civilian, a Member of Parliament, and a minister of the crown.

Although this solution satisfied the constitutionalists, it made less strategic sense in the volatile areas of the empire or in time of war. Then command needed to be united, not divided. Moreover, the defence of late Victorian Britain was not restricted to the War Office and the Admiralty, but was also within the remit of the foreign office, the India office, the colonial office, and the home office. In 1904 Britain created the Committee of Imperial Defence. A subcommittee of the cabinet, it lacked executive powers, but it brought into one forum all those ministers concerned with defence, and included soldiers and sailors. Effectively, it recognized both the truth of Clausewitz's dictum and its limitations. War did indeed have to be set in a political context, but the formulation of strategy was not a purely political activity: it had to be grounded in military reality. Thus the British model developed in the 20th century on two lines. First, the principle of civilian supremacy was rarely challenged, the most significant exception being the so-called *Curragh 'mutiny' of March 1914. Secondly, the business of defence embraced the integration of professional and civilian. On the outbreak of WW I the Committee of Imperial Defence went into abeyance, and the formulation of strategy became a matter for the cabinet as a whole. But by 1916 the War Cabinet, a small group of ministers supplemented by professional advisers, became the engine of strategy, and a model for subsequent thought.

The casualty of this form of civilianization was democracy. Wide-ranging debates on the army, which had characterized not only the 19th-century House of Commons but also the French National Assembly, became subsumed by internal discussion in ministry councils. Generals who spoke out publicly were seen to be motivated by 'Caesarism'

or 'praetorianism' rather than by the needs of national security. When the British director of military operations, Frederick Maurice, wrote to the press in 1918 to complain about Lloyd George's presentation of the army's manpower position and its effect on the western front, he had no option but to resign. Charles *de Gaulle, in advocating tanks and professionalism rather than conscription in the 1930s, became a demon of the left not a potential saviour of France. The danger that confronted liberalism was that the scope for public and parliamentary debate was limited by ignorance, and that forceful professional critics became typecast as political mavericks.

Britain and the United States were able to embrace liberalism because of their geographical advantages. In neither case was the army central to national survival, and in both cases it found employment on the periphery (in the case of the American West) or overseas. The liberal model of civil–military relations, however, could not take root so easily when the army played a central role not only in the formation of the nation state but also in its defence against predatory neighbours.

In the eighteenth century the Prussian state was, in many respects, embodied in the army. Moreover, in 1864–71, the army was the instrument of German unification, and by 1914 the army was the nation's principal bulwark against France to the west and Russia to the east. Military values permeated society, but their political implications were held in check by the authority of the monarch. The army's dilemmas arose when the monarch was weak. Its reaction to the crown's subservience to the French after *Jena and to its surrender to the Berlin revolutionaries in 1848 was to distinguish between the monarchy as an institution, to which its loyalty was unconditional, and its loyalty to the king as an individual, which was not. In 1870–1, when *Moltke 'the Elder' as chief of the general staff clashed with Bismarck over the conduct of the war with France, he was kept in check by Wilhelm I. But in 1914–18, his grandson, Wilhelm II, lacked the authority or the stamina to coordinate civil and military in this way. Until 1916 *Falkenhayn remained CGS against the wishes of the chancellor, Bethmann Hollweg, because he continued to enjoy the support of the kaiser, but when he lost that support he was replaced by *Hindenburg. With a succession of weak chancellors, the German high command extended its authority into the war aims, economics, politics, and labour relations of Germany. Its authority rested on a form of populism that subverted not only the civilian government but also the kaiser himself. Wilhelm II abdicated in November 1918 not because of the revolution but because the army told him to do so.

Hans von *Seeckt, the army's professional head between 1920 and 1927, stressed that its loyalty was to the state and not to any political party. But such a doctrine, although outwardly conforming to Huntington's model, contained a double danger in the circumstances of Weimar Germany. First of all, it left the definition of the state to the army itself—to the point where indeed it could become the embodiment of the state. Secondly, democratic party politics required the army to give its loyalty to the elected government of the day, regardless of its policies. At best Seeckt rendered the army politically naïve. At worst, it was bound to be attracted by a government that promised to revoke the humiliation of the Versailles Treaty and to undertake Germany's rearmament. In WW II the *Wehrmacht became the willing executor of Hitler's strategy. In careerist terms, the war gave the army's generals the victories that had eluded their predecessors 30 years previously. More significantly, in ideological terms, the army identified wholeheartedly with the war against Bolshevism on the eastern front, and was deeply implicated in the atrocities to which the front's barbarization gave rise. The German army of 1871 to 1945 enjoyed a reputation for professional excellence in the operational and tactical sense. But the political context into which this was set was paradoxical. In terms of global strategy, Germany proved unable to relate war to politics, to set objectives consonant with its means. And in terms of Huntington's definition of professionalism, it proved sadly deficient. Its high command became the tool of Nazism; it did not even have the excuse of a Seecktian detachment.

What the Wehrmacht shows is that totalitarian regimes have devised methods of subordinating their armies that are every bit as effective as those of liberal governments, and that their claims to represent strong government and to ready the nation for war can facilitate the process. The French armies of the 1790s became the tools of the revolution at both top and bottom. *Commissaires aux armées* accompanied generals into the field and removed those whose policies were suspect: 67 were executed in 1794 alone. In the ranks, songs, pamphlets, and public addresses became the vehicles of ideology. Broadly speaking the Soviet Union did the same. In time of war the political imperatives of the commissar might become subordinated to the professional needs of the field commander, but the concession was only temporary. Stalin's sensitivity to the power of the army was amply manifested in his purge of the officer corps in 1937–8, and even his most successful field commanders, such as Zhukov, were regularly put in their place rather than given the opportunity to convert military triumph into political authority. When the Cold War ended, the defence ministers of the former Warsaw Pact countries were staffed by soldiers rather than civilians, but this implied subordination not independence: the vast majority of officers were party members. In their subsequent efforts to liberalize and democratize their civil–military relations, the states of eastern central Europe looked to the West German idea of *innere Führung*, which attempted to counter the legacy of its own army's past by stressing the individual rights of soldiers and the civic education of the armed forces.

One component in ensuring the army's compliance and subordination has been its need for prestige. Every British

campaign of colonial withdrawal ended in political defeat, in that Britain acknowledged the colony's right to independence, but nominal victory. Neither the American army in *Vietnam nor the Soviet army in *Afghanistan had the same good fortune. The effects on the civil–military relations of both countries were deleterious. In the United States, the army used the memory of Vietnam to drive up its demand for resources, and to undermine the wishes of its political masters and so dictate the manner of its own employment. In Russia, the army remained loyal to the government throughout the 1990s, but it became alienated from its parent society despite—or even because of—conscription. Defeat in Chechnya and moral defeat in the Cold War robbed it of the status it enjoyed under communism. For the other armies of NATO and the UN Security Council, the peacekeeping and peace-enforcement missions which dominated their operational activities in the 1990s honed political skills to the detriment of military. Moreover they have done so outside the aegis of national structures. At one level the end of the Cold War marked the triumph of a liberal consensus, but at another it imposed fresh strains on the civil–military aspects of that inheritance. HFAS

Poltava, battle of (1709), at which *Peter 'the Great' of Russia defeated *Charles XII of Sweden during the *Great Northern war. After an appalling Russian winter the Swedes, whose military reputation was high and their self-esteem more so, marched south-east into Ukraine with about 22,000 men and 32 guns and besieged Poltava, a supply depot with a 6,700 strong garrison. Peter, at the head of a relief force of 42,000 men and 72 guns, approached and built fortifications behind the besiegers. Charles being sidelined by an infected wound received earlier while scouting, the Swedes launched a pre-dawn attack in four columns directed by Rehnskjold, a veteran commander but one neither as inspiring nor as obeyed as the king would have been. The attack on the Russian fortifications succeeded after fierce fighting, but the Swedes then had to advance 656 yards (600 metres) under withering artillery fire before closing with the Russian infantry, which outnumbered them two to one. Seven thousand died in the battle and 2,500 were captured, to be joined by the 10,000 who retreated in good order but were cornered a few days later against the Dniestr river. Charles was carried off in a stretcher towards Turkey. By destroying the previously almost invincible Swedish army and separating Charles from his kingdom, Peter won the war and signalled the arrival of Russia as a military power in Europe. TM

Pompey 'the Great' (correctly Gnaeus Pompeius Magnus) (106–48 BC) may have owed his honorific to an act of malicious irony by *Sulla following easy success in a campaign in Sicily and Africa. Nonetheless, he was very good at organizing large armies and along with *Caesar laid the foundations of the Roman empire. An aristocrat, he served in the *Social war under his father Pompeius Strabo, and supported Sulla in the ensuing Civil War, raising three legions from Strabo's veterans and clients (83). After the victory in Italy, Sulla sent him to clear Sicily and Africa of opposition, and dubbed him 'Magnus' after he returned, perhaps unduly pleased with himself. In 77 he played a major role in suppressing the revolution led by Lepidus, after which he was sent against *Sertorius in Spain. Pompey suffered several reverses and felt that he was not receiving sufficient replacements and logistical support from the Senate, but when his rival was assassinated he quickly defeated his less able successor. By 71 it was all over and Pompey returned to Italy, where he took most of the credit for bringing to an end the *Gladiators' war, largely won by Crassus. The two of them were elected consuls in the year 70 and Pompey was awarded a triumph for his Spanish conquests.

In 67 Pompey was given an extraordinary command to combat the problem of endemic piracy in the Mediterranean. His authority extended not just on the sea, but 50 miles (80 km) inland. Dividing the command into thirteen regions, Pompey mounted an aggressive campaign against the pirate strongholds. Pirates who surrendered were treated leniently and resettled in peaceful communities. The whole operation was a triumph of organization, completed in less than three months. In 66 Pompey went to complete the third Mithridatic war, already substantially won by Lucullus, whom he replaced. Defeating Mithridates, he campaigned extensively throughout the east, intervening in a Judaean civil war and capturing Jerusalem after a three-month siege (63).

Pompey did not take the field again until the *Roman civil war against Caesar. Ironically, given his earlier career, he allied with the traditionalist republicans in the Senate. Many notable senators went to his camp, and their presence and interference may explain his somewhat lacklustre performance. He did show his accustomed organizational ability by his rapid creation of a large army, but although he won at Dyrrachium, he was utterly defeated at *Pharsalus. Fleeing to Egypt, he was assassinated by erstwhile supporters who hoped thereby, in vain, to gain credit with the approaching Caesar, who had them put to death. AKG

Poniatowski, Marshal Prince Josef Anton (1763–1813).

Born in Vienna to a noble family—his uncle was elected king of Poland in 1764—Poniatowski was commissioned into the Austrian cavalry in 1780. Wounded fighting the *Turks in 1788, he was summoned by his uncle in 1789 and appointed major general in the expanding Polish army. He commanded in the Ukraine during the Russian invasion of 1791, fighting bravely but without success. When his uncle agreed to place the kingdom under Russian protection Poniatowski resigned. He was exiled shortly afterwards, only to return to fight for Kosciuszko's patriots.

Exiled after the collapse of the revolt, in 1807 Poniatowski accepted Napoleon's offer of command of the Polish army, and fought a skilful campaign against the Russians in 1809. In 1812 his army formed V Corps of the Grande Armée and fought at Smolensk and *Borodino. After the retreat from Moscow the corps was reduced to 3,500 men, and Poniatowski seriously considered suicide. He commanded VIII Corps in the 1813 campaign, and was awarded his marshal's baton on 15 October. On the 18th, as Napoleon's army retreated from *Leipzig, he perished trying to swim his horse across the Elster. Poniatowski was a brave and honourable soldier, and a patriot who strove to preserve an independent Poland in impossible circumstances. RH

Pontiac's rebellion (1763–6),

misnomer for an uprising by American Indian tribes of the eastern Great Lakes region. Pontiac was an Ottawa chief, but the Delaware, Shawnee, and Seneca were more significant. During the *French and Indian war they wrung land recessions from the English in treaties which neither side intended to respect, underlined when Amherst discontinued buying peace with gifts in 1760.

The rebellion was also inspired by the revivalist preaching of a Delaware prophet and started with a botched attack on Fort Detroit by Pontiac in May 1763. A number of small forts in today's New York, Pennsylvania, and Michigan fell soon afterwards and some 2,000 settlers were killed. Apart from the innovative device of giving the besiegers of Fort Pitt smallpox-infected blankets, Amherst had no answers and he was replaced by Gage in November.

In December, Scotch-Irish settlers in Pennsylvania murdered Christianized Conestoga and Delaware Indians in the Paxton Riots, but the uprising had petered out by then. Pontiac tried to spread rebellion to Illinois and Ohio, but tribes fell away steadily, the last surrendering in July 1764 in Ohio. Pontiac himself signed a peace treaty at Oswego in July 1766. He was murdered three years later. HEB

pontoon bridge

This is one of a number of obstacle-crossing devices employed by military *engineering. Probably the largest military pontoon bridge ever constructed was used by *Xerxes to cross the Hellespont in 480 BC on the way to his ill-fated invasion of Greece. The *Greek historian Herodotus decribed 676 ships anchored and moored together in parallel lines, with a wooden roadway laid over them. *Alexander 'the Great' is said to have crossed the Oxus on a bridge laid over floats, but his usual technique was to use rafts. The Romans were great bridge builders and twice used the technique to cross the Rhine. In more modern times, Gonzálo Fernández de *Córdoba used pontoons to outflank the French on the Garigliano river in 1503, and the fact that it was his skill in installing them quickly and secretly that was commented upon suggests that the technique itself was well known.

The first use of what we now call a pontoon bridge, namely the assembly of prefabricated parts specifically accompanying the army for the purpose, was by *Gustavus Adolphus in 1632 when he had a 109 yard (100 metre) bridge constructed across a river near the village of Rain in Bavaria, allowing his army to cross supported by artillery fire and a screen of *smoke. The technique was widely copied and the French gave it its name c.1676. It consisted of stretching a cable across the obstacle and attaching flat bottomed boat-like pontoons to it one after another and poling them across, then laying a roadway across them with timber beams. Military engineers would choose the site, but specialists known in the British army as 'tin boatmen' because of the metal sheathing of the pontoons would construct it. The floats themselves accompanied the army on a train of wagons and were 17–20 feet (5.2–6.1 metres) long.

At the end of Napoleon's disastrous Russian campaign of 1812, a careless order resulted in the destruction of the retreating army's pontoons, requiring his engineers to build bridges across the Berezina from demolished houses. It required a prodigious display of courage and skill, plus more good luck than anyone had a right to pray for, to save the remains of the Grand Armée from annihilation. Fifty years later a failure to measure the channels they would have to float down resulted in a three-week delay in the arrival of pontoons for Burnside's plan for a surprise crossing of the Rappahannock; he went ahead anyway and his engineers somehow bridged the river in the face of a well-prepared defence. It would have been better for the Union army if they had failed, as the ensuing battle of *Fredericksburg was their most lop-sided defeat of the war.

One of the most successful versions of the pontoon bridge was the 'Birago' bridge (1841), named after its inventor. It consisted of two pontoons that could be carried on trucks with all other equipment necessary for its construction. It was introduced into all German-speaking armies, and was the basic design for all subsequent military bridging until WW II. Although WW II saw the introduction of the Bailey bridge and mechanized bridgelayers for shorter spans, an invading army once more crossed the Rhine on pontoon bridges in 1945. Like all good designs, it is simple and flexible and refuses to grow old.   JR-W/HEB

Port Arthur, siege of (1904–5). Port Arthur was the focus of the *Russo-Japanese war. It was a warm water naval base snatched by the Russians from under the nose of the Japanese after the latter's successful war against China in 1894–5. It was therefore fitting that Port Arthur should have been the place where the war started during the night of 8–9 February, with a night attack by torpedo boats on the

Russian fleet moored in the harbour, prior to a formal declaration of war.

Having ensured the safe passage of the Japanese armies, Adm Togo continued offshore, fighting several battles against Russian sorties and trying without success to sink block ships in the harbour mouth. On 5 May the Japanese Second Army landed north of Port Arthur, cutting it off from the Russian Manchurian Army, followed by Third Army under *Nogi which invested the place on 26 June. For six months there was a dress rehearsal for WW I, with trenches, *dugouts, sometimes electrified barbed wire, *machine guns, both the old and the new types of *mines, trench *mortars, and *indirect fire by heavy artillery, the largest on the Japanese side being secretly acquired Krupp 11 inch siege howitzers. It was also a bloodbath, with the Japanese suffering 14,000 casualties in their repeated frontal assaults (there being no alternative) on the dominant feature known as Hill 203.

The Russian command was divided between Stoessel, the despised governor, and Smirnov, the generally respected military commander. After one of the Japanese 'portmanteau' shells killed Gen Kondratenko, the heart and soul of the defence, Stoessel prematurely surrendered 22,500 soldiers and sailors with a further 15,000 sick and wounded out of an original garrison of 50,500. He thereby freed Togo and Nogi to attend to other Russian army and naval units and was to be sentenced to death by court martial for so doing. The sentence was not carried out, but he spent many years in prison.

The Japanese had suffered nearly 58,000 killed and wounded, while disease raised the total to 91,500. Nogi, his two sons killed under his command, sadly wrote:

> His Majesty's millions conquer the strong foe
> Field battles and siege result in mountains of corpses.
> How can I, in shame, face their fathers?
> Songs of triumph today, but how many have returned?

CDB/HEB
Warner, Denis and Peggy, *The Tide at Sunrise* (London, 1974).

---

post exchange. See PX.

Potemkin, Prince Grigoriy Aleksandrovich (1739–91), Russian diplomat and military reformer. Potemkin was born in Yassy (now in Romania). He enlisted as a trooper in the Horse Guards where he had a chance meeting with Empress Catherine II who was impressed by his energy, passion, and colossal height, and was appointed an officer in her personal bodyguard. He remained a favourite and personal adviser throughout her reign, 'the only man that the Empress stands in awe of', according to one contemporary.

He served in the 1768–74 Russo-Turkish war, rising rapidly to the rank of general. He was ennobled in 1774 and put in charge of irregular forces. He proved a talented if unorthodox administrator and commander and suppressed the *Pugachev revolt the following year. In 1776 he was made governor of Novorossiysk, Azov, and Astrakhan and in 1783 realized his aim of incorporating the Crimea into Russia, for which he was made 'Tauride (*Tavricheskiy*) Prince', after the ancient Greek name for the tribes of the region. He presided over the development of the area including the great naval base of Sevastopol and the development of the Russian naval and merchant fleets on the Black Sea, for which historians have dubbed him 'the Russian Nelson'.

The apocryphal tale of his erecting false house fronts to deceive Catherine about the success of his colonization efforts in the Ukraine (hence 'Potemkin villages') contains a grain of truth, in that his plan was too grandiose and poorly executed. However, he did radically reform the appearance and comfort of the Russian army, doing away with the pigtails and powder and maintaining that uniforms were for 'dressing a soldier and not for loading him with a burden'. The workmanlike uniform, with a short dark green tunic and round black leather cap, was much admired by foreign observers.   CDB

POW (prisoners of war) are combatants captured by the opposing side and confined until freed at the end of hostilities or some other disposition is made of them. The latter has included slaughter, exchange, *ransom, *recruitment into the enemy's armed forces, or simply being abandoned to look after themselves. The first hurdle, of course, has always been to have a surrender accepted in the heat of battle. Thereafter treatment of POWs has varied from appalling degradation to reasonably humane treatment. It has often hinged on the circumstances of their capture and the resources available to their captors.

For much of history, POWs were slaughtered for the same reason towns were sacked and burned—*pour encourager les autres*—and this continued to be one of the rules of war for many centuries: submission might save your life, unsuccessful resistance meant death. It is not always appreciated that the sack of towns after the garrisons obliged the besiegers to take them by storm was an accepted rule of war, as was the taking of hostages and their execution in reprisal for the acts of irregular forces up to and including WW II. Even so, there was a recognized if ill-defined line between what the out-of-control soldiers of a *forlorn hope might do after storming a breach (their officers could very well be killed themselves if they tried to stop them), and the systematic rapes of *Magdeburg and *Nanking, centuries apart in time but alike in cold-blooded beastliness.

The traditional alternative was enslavement, much practised by the Romans, sometimes after marching their POWs through the streets of Rome along with other booty, and thus clearly giving them some value as property if not as human beings. Many cultures also sacrificed captives to their gods, but only the Aztecs of Mexico fought wars specifically to capture large numbers for *sacrifice, their weapons being crafted not to kill but to disable. The horse peoples, of course, could not allow prisoners to slow them down, and this has remained a characteristic of the cavalry; *tanks find it hard to take prisoners, too.

The cash value of a POW was appreciated under the *feudal system, and a *knight might expect his surrender to be respected by an opponent of his class who also knew that his family or kinsmen would pay a suitable *ransom. It took the Scots twenty years to raise the required ransom for King David II after his capture in the battle of Neville's Cross in 1336, but one suspects that they were not trying very hard. The common soldier, being of no monetary value, could expect no such consideration. The *Swiss, when fighting for themselves, and the *Hussites very particularly reversed the formula and killed any enemy knights they captured. The slaughter of the flower of French chivalry captured at *Agincourt may have been a tactical necessity, their numbers being too great to control, but it represented a great financial loss to the English soldiers which *Henry V promised to compensate.

Following the excesses of the *Thirty Years War, more humane treatment of POWs began to be a feature of European warfare during the rest of the 17th and into the 18th centuries. Captured officers, who were still usually of 'gentle' birth, would be offered the chance to give their *parole. An officer on parole was often treated more like a guest than a prisoner and could look forward to being exchanged for a prisoner of like rank taken by his own army. We see here the beginnings of a new, pragmatic reason for more humane behaviour, in that even common soldiers were spared. Admittedly they could expect to be confined in cramped, insanitary conditions such as prison hulks moored in estuaries, but the glimmer of the idea that it made military sense to encourage surrender was beginning to illuminate the minds of commanders. This could certainly be taken too far: under the 1808 Convention of Cintra, Junot's defeated French army in Portugal, all 26,000 of them complete with arms, equipment, and loot, were shipped home on British ships, on parole that they would not fight in Portugal again.

The problem illustrated by the poor deal struck at Cintra was that a large number of prisoners could become an insufferable burden to their captors, who could themselves be suffering from serious shortages. The only Confederate soldier hanged for *war crimes after the *American civil war was the commandant of the POW camp at Andersonville, Georgia, and he was very much a victim of circumstances beyond his control. The stockade was designed to hold 10,000 prisoners and the first Union soldiers to arrive were housed and fed decently. But by August 1864, after the prisoner exchange system broke down because of the South's refusal to treat *African-American soldiers as such, the camp's population had swelled to over 32,000. Overcrowding quickly led to a terrible deterioration in conditions and the hard-pressed Confederate commissariat simply did not provide the necessary *rations. Twelve thousand, nine hundred and twelve men died during Andersonville's fourteen-month period of operation and the spectacle that greeted the Union soldiers who liberated the camp was truly appalling. Be it said that the Union, with an abundant commissariat, ran its own death camp at Elmina in New York state, known as the 'Andersonville of the North', which was designed to hold 5,000 prisoners but at one point contained 9,400. Some 3,000 Confederate POWs died there.

Irregular warfare created the worst problems. The Spanish in Cuba, the British in the Second *Boer War, and the US in the *Philippines insurrection all employed concentration camps to mop up the 'crowd cover' used by the guerrillas. Overcrowding and disease killed hundreds of thousands, although it should be noted that the situation on the veld was so appalling that some Boers actually sent their families to the British for internment. Prior to the fortified-villages strategy in the post-WW II *Malayan emergency and *Mau Mau uprising, no nation developed an answer to this problem that was both humane and militarily effective, and whether the fate of non-combatants in these situations is blamed on the irregulars who use them as cover or on the regulars who must perforce remove that cover to get at them depends entirely on one's point of view.

The proper treatment of POWs was not formally addressed until the *Geneva and Hague Conference and Conventions of 1864, 1899, and 1907, which declared that soldiers who lay down their arms were to be decently treated. WW I was thus the first major war to be regulated by some form of international agreement for the treatment of prisoners and this, along with the activities of the International *Red Cross, ensured that treatment of POWs was generally humane. One notable exception was the treatment received by British and Indian prisoners at the hands of the Turks after the siege of *Kut Al Amara in 1916. Many of these POWs died on the long marches they were forced to make on their way to inadequate prison camps, but their treatment was not much worse than that received by the average Turkish soldier, and this illustrated a further problem.

The Geneva Convention of 1929 stated that prisoners of war were to be housed and fed no worse than garrison troops of the capturing power. Although the Japanese general responsible was later hanged for it, the unfortunates on the infamous 'Death March' of surrendered US and Filipino soldiers from Bataan to their POW camp were, in fact, fed standard Japanese army rations. In a sense their fate was that of the garrisons who held out for too long in earlier sieges, only now they were so weak and exhausted after their long and hopeless resistance that they lacked the strength to endure an ordeal they would have survived had their commanders surrendered opportunely.

This is not to acquit the Japanese of bestial behaviour. They believed that surrender was a disgrace and therefore treated the Allied soldiers they captured with utter contempt. No attempt was made to house and feed them adequately, medical attention was non-existent, and many died in the appalling conditions of the prison established in the Changi barracks in Singapore. Many more died while working on the Burma–Thailand railway, although it should be noted that the use of POWs for manual labour was specifically permitted under the Geneva Convention. Starving them, beating them, and using them for sword practice was not.

On the *eastern front both sides treated POWs abominably. Of the 5.7 million Red Army soldiers taken prisoner, over 3 million died from disease, starvation, and ill-treatment. Captured Germans (in a war in which neither side was much given to taking prisoners) fared little better, 45 per cent of them dying in captivity. Both sides put their POWs to hard labour, and the same grim statistic about survival being intimately linked with how fit they were when captured applied: of the 100,000 men taken captive after the prolonged and bitter battle of *Stalingrad, only 5,000 ever returned to Germany.

The right to escape and not be punished unduly (30 days' solitary confinement) was enshrined in the Geneva Convention. For most POWs escape has been impossible but for Allied prisoners in German camps during WW II, an escape attempt gave at least some relief to the boredom of prison life. The most famous attempt was the 'Great Escape' which involved a multinational team of 600 POWs at Stalag Luft 3 in Germany. Three very long tunnels were dug during 1943–4 and on 24 March 1944, 76 prisoners managed to escape from the camp. This mass escape infuriated *Hitler who ordered an estimated 5 million German police, soldiers, and Hitler Youth to recapture the prisoners. Only three men made it back to Britain and the rest were all recaptured within two weeks. Tragically, 50 of them were then murdered by the Gestapo on Hitler's express orders.

POWs have continued to experience mixed treatment at the hands of their captors, notwithstanding a new Geneva Convention, signed in 1949. Allied prisoners held by the Chinese during the *Korean war were kept in very poor conditions and subjected to 'brainwashing' in order to convince them of the communist cause and turn them into vehicles for Chinese propaganda during the war. Similar methods were used against the 651 American prisoners captured by the North Vietnamese during the *Vietnam war. The harsh conditions suffered by these prisoners led to the return and even rescue of American POWs becoming a major political issue in the USA during the peace negotiations of 1972–3. The manner in which US Pres Jimmy Carter permitted himself to become obsessed with hostages held in Tehran towards the end of his presidency gave terrorist groups and regimes leverage to use against the USA. It is to be noted that when they tried the same on the Soviets, selective lethal retaliation or the very credible threat of massive reprisals caused their citizens to be released promptly. During the *Gulf war the Iraqis used coalition prisoners and civilian internees as human shields to protect important targets from air attack, and similarly in 1994 UN troops were captured by Serb forces and used as human shields during the Bosnian conflict. Just as in the past, humane treatment of POWs remains dependent on the circumstances, the resources, and the disposition of their captors.   NB/MCM

Barker, A. J., *Prisoners of War* (New York, 1975).
Garrett, Richard, *POW: The Uncivil Face of War* (London, 1981).
Marvel, William, *Andersonville: The Last Depot* (Chapel Hill, NC, 1994).

Powell, Gen Colin (b. 1937), *African-American chairman of the Joint Chiefs of Staff during the *Gulf crisis and war. His family was from Jamaica but moved to the USA when he was a child. By his own admission he was the beneficiary of 'affirmative action' (positive discrimination) and rose to the highest command without any combat experience. A born diplomat, he held the line between his irascible theatre commander *Schwarzkopf and the other politicians outside and in the armed forces. His economically expressed war strategy was to 'cut off and kill' the Iraqi forces in the Kuwait theatre of operations and to reduce their overall strength so that they were no longer a threat to the region.   CDB

precision-guided munitions The development of precision-guided munitions (PGMs) is perhaps the most significant factor in air warfare since aircraft first began to carry bombs. While bombing has proved of considerable military value, it has always been gravely hampered by one key factor, namely a lack of accuracy. Precision-guided weapons, while not providing the 'one target, one bomb' equation supposed by popular opinion, greatly enhance the tactical effectiveness of attack aircraft, and have become particularly important in modern warfare with the increased concern over the avoidance of civilian casualties. With the increase in the number of weapons with guidance systems, it is important to define what PGMs are. They may be regarded as weapons which are air launched and guided to their target through the use of laser, electro-optical sensors, global positioning systems, or inertial navigation systems. Some *anti-armour missiles, such as the American TOW system, are highly accurate and guided, but they do not quite fall into the category of PGMs. The term does not normally encompass weapons which are fired from the ground or sea, and generally, but not exclusively, applies to unpowered bombs with guidance systems attached.

The first precision weapons were employed in WW II. Most of the development occurred in Germany and the USA. The two key German weapon types were the Ruhrstahl/Kramer X1, or Fritz X, and the Henschel Hs 293,

both used for anti-shipping purposes. The Fritz X was a guided glide bomb, while the Hs 293 was powered by a small rocket motor for the initial stage of its journey, gliding the rest of the way. Both were guided to their targets by *radio signals. The Hs 293 was the first into action, sinking the sloop HMS *Egret* on 27 August 1943. The Fritz X was first employed the following month. Both systems had the disadvantage that the launch aircraft were required to fly at slow speed, loitering in the target area, which made them vulnerable to attack by enemy fighters or anti-aircraft fire.

The development of guided weapons on the Allied side has been curiously ignored by historians. The first guided bomb, the GB-1, was perversely not guided, simply being a bomb with wings to enable it to glide to the target. The GB-series of bombs were little used, but began the principle of precision guidance being made available to aircrews. The GB-4 was guided through the use of a television camera system; GB-6A possessed an *infra-red seeker; GB-8 was a visual-controlled glide bomb and GB-12 was an over-water light-contrast weapon. Derivations of these methods of control are to be found in modern PGMs. As well as the winged GB-series, the US employed the VB (Vertical Bomb) system, which did not possess flying surfaces, only tail assemblies with guidance systems to adjust the tail fins. The only one to be used in WW II was the VB-1, also known as the Azon, a contraction of Azimuth Only. This meant that while the bomb aimer had control of the bomb through wireless, he could not adjust its trajectory to prevent the bomb from falling short of the target or overshooting it; he could only control its horizontal position over the target. Although trials demonstrated that the Azon was 29 times more accurate than unguided ordnance, under combat conditions, results were patchy. A development of Azon, the enormous 12,000 lb (5,443 kg) Tarzon, proved equally disappointing in Korea, even though it did destroy a number of bridges. Precision-guided weapons were not to be seen in large numbers until the *Vietnam war.

The first types of PGM employed in Vietnam were the laser-guided Paveway system and the electro-optically guided bomb. These types have been greatly refined, and the laser-guided bomb is the most well-known and currently the most important type. The Paveway system, on which all western laser-guided bombs are based, was a simple kit to be fitted to ordinary bombs. The kit involved a guidance system to be mounted on the nose of the bomb, and control surfaces. A target is designated by laser, either from a ground observer or from a podded laser system carried by the aircraft or a companion ('buddy lasing' in the latter instance). The laser-guided bomb is then tossed or dropped into the inverted cone of laser light reflected from the target. The seeker system detects the laser light and its guidance computer corrects the angle of the control surfaces to ensure that the bomb arrives on or near to the point of the cone of laser radiation. The system has been highly effective, and has been used to equip several thousand bombs weighing between 500 lb and 2,000 lb (between 226.8 and 907 kg) in weight. Although much more accurate than unguided weapons, the laser-guided bomb does not guarantee complete accuracy. The figures are greatly disputed, particularly since the qualifications for accuracy change from assessment to assessment, but it is estimated that a laser-guided system, if used under adequate conditions, can achieve in the region of 80 per cent of bombs dropped hitting within 10 to 30 feet (3 to 9 metres) of the designated spot.

The electro-optically guided bomb has been less successful. The first to see widespread use were the US navy's Walleye and the USAF's GBU-8 HOBOS in Vietnam, followed into US service by the GBU-15 glide bomb and the AGM-130 rocket-assisted weapon. Soviet forces employed a number of similar weapons, and development of the type continues in Russia. The principle behind such weapons is simple: the pilot or weapons system operator acquires the target through the weapon's electro-optical seeker, locks the seeker onto the target, and then launches the weapon. The newer weapons can have corrections sent to them through a data-link pod to ensure accuracy, but many of the older types broke lock through the failure of the seeker to maintain the contrast between the target and the background. This has led to the use of imaging infra-red seekers as alternatives to the optical systems on the GBU-15 and the AGM-130. The major difficulty with acquiring electro-optical PGMs is their cost; the sophisticated seeker equipment is considerably more expensive than laser-guided types.

Laser-guided and electro-optical weapons have a major obstacle to their effective utilization, and this is the weather. Both rely upon visual acquisition of the target so that it can be designated. Increasingly sophisticated designation pods such as the British TIALD are not proof against this problem, and when conditions of visibility are poor, it is not unknown for missions to be aborted. This leaves dependency upon intertially guided systems which are highly expensive, and are to be found only in cruise missiles. These did not originate as conventional weapons, but were designed to deliver nuclear warheads to a target over long ranges. The two key types in use are the American Tomahawk Land Attack Missile and Conventional Air Launched Cruise Missile. Both rely upon terrain profile matching, so that they navigate by matching the contours of the ground beneath the missile with pre-installed navigational instructions. This gives the weapons their famed ability to turn at key road junctions as if navigating along the highway beneath; they do not rely upon the presence of the road, but on the contours along which it runs. The addition of Global Positioning System (GPS) equipment makes the weapons even more accurate. Essentially, GPS enables the missile to communicate with satellites so that it can work out exactly where over the earth's surface it is. When the satellite systems tell the weapon that it is approaching or over the tar-

get's co-ordinates, the weapon adjusts its control surfaces so that the PGM hits the target. The order of accuracy may be measured in a few feet.

The use of GPS would appear to be the way forward for PGMs. It means that they can be employed in any weather, and conventional bombs can be modified relatively inexpensively with the fitting of a fixed aerodynamic jacket around the bomb body to keep it falling at a constant angle, and a tail unit with GPS equipment and movable fins. The GPS-guided munitions currently in service are the USA's GAM-84 and GAM-113, deployed on the B-2 bomber.

PGMs are essential tools for modern war. The political implications which now attach to civilian casualties mean that their use will increase. The search for the PGM which hits its target every time will be eternal; however, the purpose of the PGM is not to ensure 100 per cent accuracy, but to ensure that targets are much more likely to be destroyed or damaged, increasing the effectiveness of the aircraft employing them and reducing the risk of civilian casualties on the ground. In spite of their expense when compared to unguided weapons, they are a worthwhile investment, and desirable acquisitions for all military services. They will not replace unguided ordnance entirely, but PGMs will be the air weapon of choice in the future.   DJJ

Cordesman, Anthony H., and Wagner, Abraham R., *The Lessons of Modern War*, vol. iv. *The Gulf War* (Boulder, Colo., 1996).
Gunston, Bill, *The Illustrated Encyclopedia of Aircraft Armament* (Salamander, 1987).

present arms is the act of presenting or aiming a weapon or firearm, and also the position of the weapon when so presented. The act of presenting arms is a central part of *drill, that is the series of prescribed and formalized movements that are used to prepare soldiers for battle. Although classical armies were often extremely well drilled, *Gustavus Adolphus reintroduced drill to European warfare to make more effective use of improved weapons and he was copied throughout Europe. To make the most effective use of muskets, volley fire had to be concentrated, requiring rigidly maintaining battle lines under fire and simultaneous fire on command. Thus all musket-armed infantrymen went through a series of movements taking them through loading to being ready to fire. 'Present' was the penultimate command at which the soldier took aim prior to the order to fire.

As the range, accuracy, and rate of fire improved, parade ground drill manoeuvres disappeared from the battlefield, as soldiers were trained to spread out and use cover. Parade-ground drill, or close-order drill as it is known, remained, quite apart from its ceremonial use, because it develops a sense of *discipline. Present arms now means to hold a rifle vertically in front of the body as a *salute. In many armies the positioning of the soldier's hands and feet at the 'present' shows that the modern version of this drill movement is very closely derived from the old act of aiming the weapon: the soldier simply needs to throw forward his left arm and left foot to bring his weapon to the 'aim'.

MCM/RH

***

Primo de Rivera y Orbaneja, Gen Miguel, Marqués de Estella (1870–1930), Spanish general and effective dictator of Spain from 1923 to 1929. Although his authoritarian regime was overthrown, it formed the basis for the subsequent revolution by *Franco which led to the *Spanish civil war. Primo de Rivera graduated from the military *academy at Toledo in 1888 and served in Morocco, Cuba, and the Philippines. In 1915 he became military governor of Cadiz, and moved on to Valencia and then Barcelona. In 1923 he staged a *coup d'état and dissolved parliament. He ended the Moroccan war against the Rifs in 1927, which was popular, but was forced to resign after the army refused to support him. He is buried in the great vault of the imposing if tastefully dubious monument to the Spanish civil war in the Valle de los Caídos (Valley of the Fallen), north of Madrid, along with his son, José Antonio, the founder of the Spanish fascist Falange, who was assassinated at the outbreak of war in 1936. CDB

***

principles of war The American acronym KISS (keep it simple, stupid) is of military origin. The advantages of KISS in the stress, uncertainty, and exhaustion of battle are obvious, but if taken above a certain level, the final S may become lapidary. *Frederick 'the Great' warned that one should not follow rules 'as a blind man follows a wall', and like all successful military commanders he ignored the accepted principles of war when instinct and experience spoke otherwise. We do tend to read more about those who break the rules and succeed, because those who break them and fail tend to have very brief careers.

The first 'principles of war' were probably enunciated by *Sun-tzu, in the 4th century BC. He listed five 'factors': moral influence, weather, terrain, command, and *doctrine. Other principles which emerge from reading his *Art of War* are deception, speed, know your enemy, and that to win without fighting is the acme of skill.

*Clausewitz was acutely aware of the dangers of imposing rules. The genius, he wrote, rises above all rules and laughs at them. But military history has produced no more geniuses than any other sphere of human activity and for the rest he enunciated four principles: employ all available forces with the utmost energy; concentrate where the decisive blow is to be struck; lose no time and surprise the enemy; follow up success with the utmost energy. He also enunciated three general principles for defence, fourteen for offence, eight for troops, and seventeen for use in terrain. Today he is revered, but for much of the 19th century his rival *Jomini, a far more superficial and emotional

writer, was very much more influential: the triumph of style over substance.

WW I produced a demand for principles which could help prevent a repetition of the disastrous waste of life and resources in that conflict. *Beaufre suggested that the one principle of war, based on the writings of *Foch, was to reach the decisive point thanks to freedom of action gained by sound economy of force, warning against an overcommitment to one course of action until the decisive moment arrives. *Fuller wrote of three groups of principles: mental principles—direction, concentration, and distribution; moral principles—determination, surprise, and endurance; and physical principles—mobility, offensive action, and security. These prefigure the modern British army 'components of fighting power'—conceptual, moral, and physical (see OPERATIONAL CONCEPTS and MANOEUVRE WARFARE).

The US and British forces have similar principles of war, though expressed slightly differently. What the USA succinctly calls the 'objective', the British call 'selection and maintenance of the aim'; these are followed by maintenance of *morale, offensive action, surprise, security, concentration of force, economy of effort, flexibility, co-operation, and administration. The equivalent Soviet principles in the *Cold War period were mobility and high tempos of combat operations; concentration of main efforts and creation of the necessary superiority at the decisive place and time (mass, concentration); surprise, combat aggressiveness, and energy (offensive action); preservation of the effectiveness of one's own troops (security); adjust the end to the means (economy of force); and co-operation (unity of command). It will be noted that the Soviet principles are not only nearer to the KISS ideal, but also more Clausewitzian in nature.

The primary 'objective' in the *Gulf war was the expulsion of Iraqi forces from Kuwait; the second was to degrade Iraq's ability to conduct future regional offensive action. A third, unwritten for political reasons and thus unfulfilled, was to destroy the Republican Guard and deprive Saddam *Hussein of the foundations of his repressive regime. Other than that, operations proceeded according to both sets of principles listed above, against an enemy who had ignored most if not all of them.

In the 1990s greater emphasis on *peacekeeping and peace enforcement ('operations other than war') begged the question as to whether these operations required different principles. Still, it seemed self-evident that the first principle, 'objective', remained paramount. Thus the NATO attack on the former *Yugoslavia in March 1999 fell at the first fence. The stated objective was to protect the Kosovar Albanians, but the operation resulted in an intensification of Yugoslav action against them which, in spite of the promises made by the advocates of *air power, NATO proved powerless to stop and for which it had made no provision. Attacks on Yugoslavia's infrastructure were so dramatically counter-productive as regards the stated objective that they gave rise to intense speculation as to what the 'real' objective might be. It should not need saying that the principles of war must be respected by the politicians who start wars as well as by the soldiers who fight them.   CDB

Alger, John, *The Quest for Victory: The History of the Principles of War* (New York, 1982).

Beaufre, Andre, *Introduction to Strategy* (London, 1965).

Clausewitz, Carl von, *On War* (1831), ed. and trans. M. Howard and P. Paret (Princeton, 1976).

Fuller, John F. C., *Foundations of the Science of War* (London, 1925).

Lider, Julian, *Military Theory: Concept, Structure, Problems* (Swedish Studies in International Relations, Aldershot, 1983).

Savkin, V. Y., *Basic Principles of Operational Art and Tactics* (Moscow, 1972), trans. USAF (Washington, 1982).

Sun-tzu, *The Art of War*, trans. Samuel B. Griffith (Oxford, 1963).

prisoners of war. See POWS.

Procop, Andrew (*c*.1380–1434), also known as Prokop the Bald or Procopius the Great, Bohemian warrior priest and military leader of the Hussites, a heretical religious movement from 1424. Pope Martin V declared a general crusade against Hussites in 1419 and there followed a bitter series of wars in which the Taborite Hussites proved remarkably successful under the leadership of *Zizka (see HUSSITE WARS). Their military achievements continued under Procop. He repulsed a whole series of German invasions between 1426–31 and also led repeated expeditions into Hungary and Germany. Procop was killed at the battle of Lipany, after which an accommodation was reached with the pope.   MCM

Procopius (Prokopios) **of Caesarea** (?500–?562) wrote several histories in the reign of the Byzantine Emperor Justinian I. His major work is the *Wars* (in eight volumes) which describes the campaigns of Justinian's attempt to reconquer the lands of the defunct western empire. One of Justinian's greatest generals in this effort was *Belisarius, whom Procopius served as secretary and legal adviser from 527. He is an invaluable eyewitness since he accompanied his master on campaign until 540, and remained an informed observer afterwards, writing his histories in the 550s. Belisarius scored some brilliant successes in Africa, against the *Vandals (533) and initially against the Ostrogoths in Italy (535–40). But during his second Italian campaign (544–50) Justinian grew impatient with his general and replaced him. Although he is inclined to stereotype the 'barbarian' adversaries that the Byzantines faced, Procopius has a good eye for detail. He provides some clear descriptions of battles, sieges, tactics, weapons, and equipment as well as an essential narrative chronology. His translated works are still in print in Loeb translations and provide profound insights into the warfare of his age.   MB

Cameron, Avril, *Procopius and the 6th Century* (Berkeley, 1985).

Procopius of Caesarea, *History of the Wars*, trans. H. B. Dewing (Cambridge, Mass., 1935–40).

propaganda (*see opposite page*)

provost marshal an officer of *military police. The word provost probably comes from the Latin *praeponere* (placed before, to superintend) via the Old English word Prafost; or alternatively, from *proepositus* (a chief or governor). The first recorded provost marshal in English history was Henry Guylford (*fl.* 1511) although it is possible that such an office had existed much earlier. Certainly, the duties of the provost marshal—maintaining military *discipline, punishing offenders, policing armies—had previously been carried out by the two principal law officers of the army, the marshal and *constable, in medieval times. It has been conjectured that at the beginning of the 16th century the provost marshal came into being, taking on some of the duties associated with a deputy of the earl marshal.

Over the next two centuries the provost marshals proliferated and lost a good deal of their military prestige. From the mid-16th century, 'civil' provost marshals were used to carry out a policing role within England; such men had authority over civilians as well as soldiers. The standing army created in 1660 initially had provost marshals at regimental level, this post often being combined with that of the *QM. During the 18th century this position was to vanish. Marlborough's army had a senior officer who acted as provost marshal general; his responsibilities including controlling foraging parties. During the 18th century, once again, the rank and prestige of the provost marshal declined, with *NCOs often being appointed on an ad hoc basis. *Wellington on arrival in Portugal in 1809 appointed NCOs as assistant provost marshals to support the provost marshal as part of a general tightening up of discipline.

Provost marshals appear to have had the right to carry out summary military *punishments, including executions, if the offender was caught red-handed (as in the case of the aftermath of the sack of Badjoz in 1812). This power was taken away by the Army Act of 1879. Provost marshals are recorded as carrying out summary floggings as late as 1854, during the *Crimean war.

Most armies acquired provost marshals, or as in the case of the 18th-century Austrian *General-Gewaltiger* an official with a different title performing duties that in Britain or the USA would be given to the provost marshals. Armies that sprang from the British tradition tended to use the title of provost marshal, such as both the Union army in the *American civil war (which appointed a provost marshal

(*cont. on page 741*)

propaganda

PROPAGANDA is a word derived from the Vatican's establishment of the *Sacre Congregatio de Propaganda Fide* in 1622. It is a process of persuasion designed to induce ideas, opinions, or actions beneficial to the source. As a process, it is value-neutral although the word has acquired pejorative meaning. Analysis of propaganda would more profitably benefit by examination of intentions. In, for example, the case of combat propaganda, more usually termed *psychological warfare, the intention is to persuade enemy soldiers to defect, desert, surrender, or otherwise influence their behaviour on the battlefield with a view to defeating them. As such, these 'munitions of the mind' have become increasingly more sophisticated with advances in psychology and communications, especially during the course of the 20th century.

Before 1914, propaganda was usually associated with *religion and the implanting of ideas to be cultivated in support of existing beliefs and 'faith'. Its wartime applications, in the *Napoleonic or the *American independence wars, were confined largely to calls to arms, lampooning the enemy, glorifying victory, and sustaining *morale. The intention by the few to impress the many can be traced back to the ancient world in art, architecture, and symbolism. The advent of printing in the 14th century shifted the emphasis from script to print. In wars of religion, propaganda from the pulpit remained a potent method of swaying emotions, hence the Vatican's *Sacre Congregatio*. Massive advances in communications technologies in the 19th century, the development of a global cable network, and the arrival of the mass media by the end of the century extended propaganda to a global audience.

The Great War of 1914–18, a *total war which industrialized warfare and made the home front as important as the fighting front, altered the nature of popular involvement and introduced domestic morale as a military asset. It also discredited the word 'propaganda' which henceforth came to be associated with the manipulation of opinion, by foul means rather than fair, with lies or half-truths, and with deceit. In particular, the popularization of atrocity propaganda through the relatively new mass-circulation press and the increasingly popular silent cinema discredited the relationship between propaganda and 'truth'. It was this manipulative power over human emotions which *Hitler identified as being a weapon that could be of enormous value for his purposes.

In the new USSR also, propaganda was seized upon as a device that could serve the state, by extending revolutionary ideas to the illiterate masses and, more innovatively, into the international class struggle. With the advent of radio broadcasting in the 1920s, the ability to transmit propaganda across frontiers and appeal directly to foreign audiences undermined traditional notions about non-interference in the internal affairs of other countries. A series of radio 'wars' prompted the League of Nations in 1936 to pass a convention attempting to outlaw the use of broadcasting for these purposes. More honoured in the breach as the Nazi and Fascist regimes positioned propaganda as a central feature of their domestic and foreign policies, the BBC ideal that 'Nation Shall Speak Peace Unto Nation' fell victim to the ideological conflict that was to produce both WW II and the subsequent *Cold War.

By the outbreak of WW II, the sound cinema had also become an important medium for disseminating propaganda. The British Ministry of Information (the choice of words reflecting the nervousness of democratic countries in eschewing propaganda) recognized that 'for the film to be good propaganda it must also be good entertainment'. Once the USA entered the war, the formidable American motion-picture industry ('Hollywood') was mobilized in support of wartime propaganda themes: 'why we fight', 'know your enemy', 'unity is strength', and so on. The wartime democratic alliance evolved a 'Strategy of Truth' towards their propaganda, which did not mean that the whole truth was told. But the reputation for credibility which organizations like the BBC were able to develop in their broadcasts to Nazi-occupied Europe was a serious corrective to the propaganda output of Josef Goebbels' Ministry of Propaganda and Public Enlightenment encapsulated by the phrase the 'Big Lie'.

While propaganda by press, poster, radio, and *film was used extensively on the domestic fronts to sustain popular morale through the harsh realities of war, bombing, rationing, victories, and defeats, on the fighting fronts it was used as an adjunct to military tactics. Millions of leaflets were dropped over enemy lines, mobile loudspeaker teams shouted out messages, and radio transmissions attempted to sow seeds of confusion, doubt, and defeatism. It is axiomatic that successful propaganda must go hand in hand with policy. The Allies in this respect shot themselves in the foot with the insistence on unconditional surrender following the Casablanca Conference of 1942. By announcing that all Germans in defeat would be treated in exactly the same way, this policy fused the fate of the German people with that of the Nazi Party in a way undreamed of by a grateful Goebbels. It enabled him to launch his own drive for total war, it pre-empted the Allied use of such inducements as 'surrender or die' since any German soldier would be treated as a war criminal, and it partly helps to explain why the German people kept fighting to the bitter end.

Words by themselves did not win the war. But in the ideological confrontation between the USSR and the USA in the years that followed, they were to become significant weapons in the Cold War. Overt propaganda by the US Information Agency or by Radio Moscow was supplemented by covert activity and disinformation by the *CIA and KGB. Propaganda continued to be employed in the low-intensity conflicts of Korea or in the 'hearts and minds' campaign in the *Malayan emergency, but it was its escalation into a strategic weapon in the global battle for allegiances in disputes over *nuclear weapons, the *space race, even medical advances or the Olympic Games, which made it an all-pervasive feature of the Cold War.

With the advent of television in the 1950s and 1960s, a new medium of enormous propaganda potential was quickly recognized. The *Vietnam war was fought out nightly in the living rooms of middle America and, as the 'first television war', raised the spectre of whether democracies would be able to sustain popular support in wartime under its prying lens. A myth emerged that the US military lost the Vietnam war not due to military incompetence but because it had been stabbed in the back by a hostile media on the home front. It is important to remember that Vietnam was the most uncensored war of recent military history and, in light of the lack of restrictions imposed on journalists, the tendency was to shoot the messenger for the bad news it carried.

Nonetheless, the belief that the media could become (to use Churchill's phrase about the BBC) an 'enemy within the gates' for democracies, which would always therefore be at a disadvantage in conflicts against authoritarian regimes, gave rise to the belief that restrictions on reporting were essential in wartime. In the 1980s, as the system of media 'pools' was being developed, the British showed the way during the *Falklands war. Only 30 journalists (all British) were allowed to accompany the Task Force and they were dependent on the military not only for transportation to the combat theatre but also for communications from it. Indeed, it took longer for one Independent Television News despatch to reach London than it had taken one of William Howard Russell's despatches for *The Times* 150 years earlier during the Crimean war.

Developments in new communications technologies during the 1980s, such as the portable satellite phone, the laptop computer, and digital data transmission meant that such military control of the information environment would never be possible again. However, as the *Gulf war of 1991 indicated, propaganda had not been confined to the dustbin of history. An increasingly sophisticated US military information policy was able to secure a desired view of warfare through the release of video-tapes showing missiles hitting (not missing) their targets with unprecedented accuracy, and through live television press conferences which bypassed the traditional role of the media as mediator. Despite the unprecedented effort by the Iraqis to counter this propaganda of a 'clean' and 'smart' high-tech war by permitting correspondents from Coalition countries to stay behind in the enemy capital under fire, the military information agenda succeeded in dominating the media coverage. Democracies had indeed demonstrated that they could wage war in the presence of more than 1,500 journalists, and thereby sustain public support in the process.

The Gulf war has been described as the first 'information war'. Indeed, the emphasis in contemporary military thinking on 'Command and Control Warfare' places great emphasis on *information warfare or 'information operations'. As such, propaganda is redefined as a non-lethal weapon, a combat force multiplier which saves lives and empowers the individual to make decisions he/she might not otherwise have done—all to the benefit of the source.   PMT

Ellul, J., *Propaganda: The Formation of Men's Attitudes* (New York, 1965).

Pratkanis, A., and Aronson, E., *Age of Propaganda* (New York, 1991).

Taylor, Philip M., *Munitions of the Mind: A History of Propaganda from the Ancient World to the Present Era* (Manchester, 1995).

general in 1862) and the contemporary US and Australian armies. Other services, such as the US navy and the RAF, also use the title of provost marshal, although in some cases this title carries a meaning rather different from that of the army.

With the establishment of permanent bodies of military police—in Britain, this dates from 1855—provost marshals began to assume their modern form, as officers commanding such troops. In the British army, the provost marshal (army) carries the rank of brigadier. The Military Provost Staff Corps runs the military prisons.   GDS

Sheffield, G. D., *The Redcaps* (London, 1994).

---

psychological warfare Largely because of political sensitivities, psychological warfare has had several names during the 20th century, including propaganda, political warfare, and psychological operations (psyops). It encompasses activities to weaken the enemy's will, reinforce loyalty, and gain the military or moral support of the uncommitted, usually through the control and management of news and information. Its rise in importance is directly related to the development of print and other media, particularly in the last 100 years. Put simply, it is perception management. The aggressive needs of psychological warfare in a world war have since given way to the different aims of psychological operations in times of peace. Although the distinction between it and propaganda is often indistinct, the former is based on presenting a version of the truth (or perceived truth) to an enemy, whilst propaganda has come to mean peddling a lie, often to one's own side.

Although handbills appeared in the *American independence war and were dropped by balloon on Prussians besieging *Paris in 1870–1, modern psyops can be traced back to the Second *Boer War. Following widespread criticism in the world's media of British conduct of the war, which had resulted in the deaths of some 20,000 Boer civilians, many nations came to support their own war effort in WW I with psyops activity. This included recruitment posters, and—with government encouragement—newspapers interwove truth and fiction in a deliberate effort to focus national hate against a common enemy. Incidents like the German execution of British nurse Edith Cavell and the sinking by a U-boat of the liner *Lusitania in 1915, together with atrocities committed against the civilian population of Belgium, were inflated in an effort to manipulate public opinion.

*Balloons and aircraft dropped newspapers to civilians living behind enemy lines containing summaries of news otherwise censored. Strategic themes in leaflets dropped over enemy trenches included despair—supporting the idea that a defeat was inevitable—and hope—inviting the soldier to surrender and thereby save his life. Other literature suggested that those at home were living in luxury, despite poor rations at the front. Deserters were also used to persuade their comrades at the front to surrender. By 1918, deserters, supported by aerial leaflets, were used by most armies with varying degrees of success. After the war, senior commanders, including *Ludendorff, acknowledged that the British leaflet campaign of 1918 was very effective in sapping their soldiers' will to fight.

The growth of adult literacy and expansion of radio broadcasting during the 1930s altered significantly the importance of psyops during WW II. All BBC broadcasts to occupied Europe commenced with 'V' (for Victory) in Morse, and the letter was chalked on walls all over occupied Europe. Stations broadcast daily to all European occupied countries, using native speakers who had escaped the invasion of their homelands. Broadcasts contained a mixture of news and current affairs as well as coded messages to resistance movements. All sides in the European and Pacific campaigns sponsored stations that broadcast a mixture of news (a blend of truth and falsehood) and popular music. True news stories were usually items that could be checked independently by the listener, thus giving the lie credence also. Such broadcasting encompasses three categories: white (the origin is known), grey (the origin is unknown or concealed), and black (where the origin is faked). All combatant nations placed heavy emphasis on recruitment posters and the security of information, and in Britain the 'Careless Talk Costs Lives' theme was promoted throughout the war. Using images of Adolf Hitler, the Germans demonstrated the effectiveness of the personality cult via poster campaigns as a unifying weapon.

Vehicle-mounted and manpack amplifiers were deployed in many theatres by front-line troops. The Germans and Russians used propaganda companies with combat troops, and loudspeakers were also used in the Pacific. These broadcast pre-recorded and live messages relating to the local tactical situation. They could also be used as a force multiplier, broadcasting sounds of troops or armour. All sides dropped leaflets encouraging soldiers to surrender during 1939–45. These took the form of a safe conduct pass signed by a senior commander. In total, the Allies dropped over 1.5 billion leaflets, emphasizing the importance attached to psyops during WW II.

Psyop techniques have been used in every war and emergency since 1945. They have been particularly successful in the 'bush fire wars' of the 1950s and 1960s, when broadcasting and distributing leaflets by air to rebel tribesmen, guerrillas, and terrorists was the most effective means of communication or persuasion. The success of these techniques in the *Malaya emergency and the 1952 *Mau Mau uprising convinced field commanders that psyops were an essential component of modern low-intensity Operations, particularly if fully integrated into the activities of government. In *Vietnam, over 10 billion leaflets were airdropped or distributed by hand throughout the war.

In response to Iraq's invasion of Kuwait in August 1990, both sides instigated a psyops campaign, Iraqi radio stations trying to divide the Arab coalition forces in Saudi Arabia. The Coalition eventually dropped 29 million leaf-

lets by air, whilst psyops troops operating on the battlefield induced surrender or withdrawal. However, the term is becoming politically unacceptable, so much so that in Bosnia, psyops were known by the euphemism 'information operations'. Undoubtedly, the use of psyops against an enemy offers an alternative, or essential precursor, to combat and casualties, while its application to allies or domestic populations will strive to reinforce public support. It will grow in importance, and the omnipresence of the media gives enormous scope for its use.   APC-A

....

Pugachev, Emelian Ivanovich (*c.*1742–75), leader of the most dangerous peasant revolt in Russian history. A Don *Cossack with charismatic gifts, Pugachev served in the *Seven Years War and against the Turks. He deserted in 1771 and began wandering through southern Russia and the Urals. He was arrested in 1772 and 1773 but escaped both times. He then claimed to be the dead Tsar Peter III, who had freed the nobles from their state service obligations and, so his supporters assumed, would do the same for the peasantry. He attracted a following of peasants, Old Believers, Ural mineworkers, and non-Russians such as Bashkirs and Kalmyks. In August 1773 Pugachev formed a detachment of 300 cossacks from Yaitsk (later Ural'sk), which rapidly expanded to about 25,000. Because the main Russian forces were fighting the Turks, Pugachev's insurgents were able to seize Kazan, Penza, and Saratov and besiege other towns. But he was defeated by *Potemkin near Kazan in the summer of 1774 and fled to the Urals. His supporters then handed him over to the Russians, and he was executed in Moscow on 10 January 1775. The Pugachev rebellion was the setting for Pushkin's novel *The Captain's Daughter.*   CDB

....

Punic wars (264–241, 218–201, 149–146 BC), three wars between Rome and Carthage, so-called from the Latin for Carthaginian, which effectively decided the struggle for mastery of the Mediterranean world. Before the first war, Rome was still a purely Italian power, not even in control of northern Italy; after the last, her writ effectively ran from the Levant to Spain and from the Alps to Tunisia.

The first war was sparked by an incident involving Messina in Sicily, then held by Campanian mercenaries, calling themselves the 'Mamertini' or 'Men of Mamers', their equivalent of Mars. Threatened by King Hiero of Syracuse these first asked Carthage for help, but then turned to Rome. After some hesitation, the Romans accepted their appeal, and when the Carthaginians and Hiero joined forces to attack them, the Roman Consul Appius Claudius Caudex first issued an ultimatum and, when this was rejected, daringly crossed the straits and lifted the siege.

Behind this action probably lay Roman fears, however exaggerated, of a Carthaginian presence in eastern Sicily,

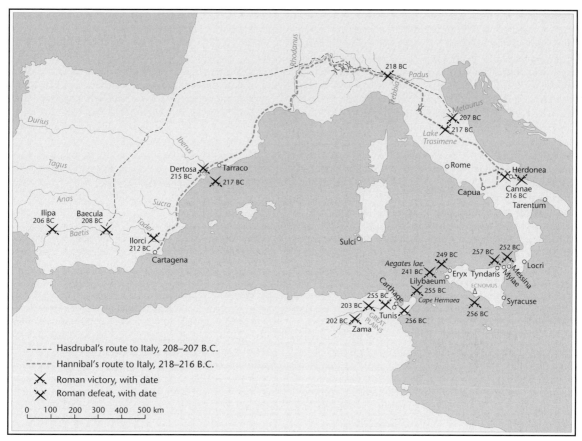

The **Punic wars**, including Hannibal's campaigns.

particularly so soon after their conquest of southern Italy, while neither Carthage nor Hiero were prepared to allow Roman interference in Sicily. The situation was complicated by the fact that Rome and Carthage had hitherto been on friendly terms, whereas Syracuse and Carthage had been enemies for centuries. But there is no reason to doubt that Rome saw Carthage as the principal danger from the first, and neither Hiero nor Carthage can be entirely absolved of blame for what happened.

Rome first concentrated mainly on Syracuse, but once Hiero had made his peace in 263, the war became essentially a conflict between Rome and Carthage for control of the rest of Sicily. Mostly fought out in and around the island, apart from a brief Roman foray to Africa, it was the greatest naval war in ancient history, and at least in numbers of men and ships one of the greatest ever fought. Indeed, it was chiefly remarkable for the way in which Rome, which began the war with virtually no navy, consistently outbuilt and outfought what was then the most powerful naval state in the Mediterranean. Beginning with Mylae (Milazzo) in 260, which saw the first use of the *corvus*, Rome not only won a series of victories—Sulci (258), Tyndaris (257),

*Ecnomus, and Cape Hermaia (255)—but used her new-found sea power to strike at the enemy homeland in 256/5.

After defeat in Africa, overconfidence and lack of experience led to disasters through bad weather in 255, 253, and 249, and in the last year Carthage won her sole naval victory at *Drepana. But by that time Carthaginian forces had been confined to the west of Sicily, where only Eryx (Monte San Giuliano), Drepana (Trapani), and Lilybaeum (Marsala), the last two under siege, remained in their hands. Thereafter there was stalemate in Sicily, where *Hamilcar commanded Carthaginian forces in the north-west, until a Carthaginian fleet bringing reinforcements and supplies was heavily defeated off the *Aegates Islands in 241, and Carthage made peace. She had lost the war because she lacked the resources, particularly in manpower, to outslog Rome, and had failed even to use her sea power to prevent the Romans landing in Sicily and Africa, let alone to carry the war to Italy.

The second war may have been deliberately engineered by Hamilcar and his son as a war of revenge, and clearly owed much to the legacy of bitterness left by the first, particularly Carthaginian anger at the way Rome seized

743

Sardinia when Carthage, weakened by war with her mutinous mercenaries, was in no position to intervene. *Hannibal, who had succeeded to his father's command in Spain eight years after the latter's death, may also have inherited his father's belief that Rome could only be defeated in Italy. At all events, when warned by Rome not to attack Saguntum in the autumn of 220, Hannibal, who claimed that the town had been guilty of aggression against Carthage's allies in the area, showed no hesitation. He took it in 219, and then seized the initiative by his audacious march to Italy, and the devastating victories at the *Trebbia, *Lake Trasimene, and *Cannae. Thereafter much of southern Italy, including the two largest cities after Rome—Capua and Tarentum—came over to him, and Syracuse and Macedonia also joined what appeared to be the winning side.

But after Cannae, Rome returned to the strategy, first introduced by *Fabius Maximus, of refusing to fight Hannibal in the field while aggressively defending strategic bases such as Nola and Beneventum, denying him a seaport in Campania, and retaking places when he was elsewhere. The turning point came in 212–211 when first *Syracuse and then Capua fell. Hannibal was still dangerous in the field, as he demonstrated in the two battles of Herdonea (if there were two) in 212 and 210, and the strain on the loyalty of Rome's allies was amply demonstrated by the refusal of twelve of the 30 Latin colonies to supply their quotas of men in 209. But Hannibal only once received any reinforcements by sea, in 215, and when his brother, Hasdrubal, arrived in northern Italy overland in 207, he was defeated and killed at the Metaurus. Thereafter, the Carthaginians were increasingly confined to the toe of Italy, until Hannibal was recalled to Africa in the winter of 203/2.

Meanwhile in Spain, following the death of his father and uncle who had commanded there since 218, the young Publius Cornelius *Scipio ('Africanus') had carried all before him. Landing in 210 at Tarraco (Tarragona), he first put his army through rigorous training and then in 209 made a lightning strike at Cartagena, the capital of Carthaginian Spain. This was followed by a victory at Baecula (Baylén) over Hasdrubal, which led the latter to depart for Italy, and a final victory over the new Carthaginian commander, Hasdrubal Gisgo, at Ilipa near Seville in 206. After dealing with a mutiny and mopping up Celtiberian resistance in the Ebro valley, Scipio returned to Italy and triumphant election as consul in 205.

He seems to have been determined from the first to carry the war to Africa, and after some opposition from senators led by Fabius, he was duly assigned to Sicily, with the option of using the island as a springboard for the invasion of Tunisia. Because of renewed opposition sparked by an ugly incident involving one of his lieutenants at Locri, and also because he needed to train his men, he did not actually proceed to the invasion of Africa until the summer of 204, and even then it was a year before he broke out of his beachhead to win the battle of the Great Plains, and to bring direct pressure on Carthage by occupying Tunis, while his lieutenants overran Numidia (Algeria).

Carthage now sued for peace, and negotiations had probably reached a fairly advanced stage when an attack on Roman supply ships, carried to the vicinity of the city by bad weather, precipitated a renewal of the conflict. Carthaginian attitudes may also have hardened as a result of the return of Hannibal with some of his veteran troops during the negotiations. At all events, military operations were resumed by Scipio with great vigour, and eventually Hannibal was compelled by the clamours of his fellow countrymen to confront his rival inadequately prepared. The decisive encounter, known as the battle of *Zama, took place in October 202 and resulted in a complete victory for Rome, following which Hannibal insisted that peace be made.

The peace stripped Carthage of her navy and of Spain, but left intact her main strength, which had always been commerce. This attracted the fearful envy of such as Marcus Cato, who returned from an embassy *c.*153 convinced that 'delenda est Cathago' (Carthage must be destroyed), which he declaimed regularly thereafter in the Senate. Rome had created a rival to Carthage in the Numidian King Massinissa and he encroached on Carthaginian territory, knowing that Roman envoys sent to arbitrate would be prejudiced in his favour. Finally, in 150, Carthage's patience snapped and Rome was presented with an excuse to declare war when a Carthaginian army invaded Numidia in defiance of the treaty with Rome. Realizing that they stood no chance, the Carthaginians formally surrendered, but when ordered to move their city at least 10 miles (16 km) from the sea, determined to fight after all. After a series of incompetent generals had failed to take the city, command was finally given to *Scipio Aemilianus, grandson of the consul killed at Cannae and adoptive grandson of Scipio 'Africanus'. It was he who finally took the city in 146, razed it to the ground, sowed salt in the ruins, and sold the inhabitants into slavery. JFL

Caven, Brian, *The Punic Wars* (London, 1980).

Lazenby, J. F., *The First Punic War* (London, 1996).

—— *Hannibal's War* (Warminster, 1978).

punishments, military These have in general been distinguished from their civilian equivalent by the fact that they are very task-specific. In the *Roman army, the first military organization which we know to have had a formal code of *discipline, if a *sentry was found guilty of being asleep on duty or absent without cause he was sentenced to the *fustuarium*. The sentenced man was then set upon by soldiers of his own unit with cudgels and stones and usually killed. The severity of this punishment had a certain military logic to it because a sentry who sleeps endangers the lives of all his comrades. The same punishment was also imposed for theft in the camp, giving false testimony, and on any soldier found guilty of the same minor offence four times. If a unit was found guilty of *cowardice, the men were paraded in front of the legion and every tenth man subjected to the *fustuarium*, a process known as decimation (the origin of this much-misused word in English).

The *fustuarium* illustrates a basic function of military punishment. It has to serve as retribution for an offence, as a deterrent to the offender and his fellows, and it must serve to reinforce unit cohesion. It is also part of a necessary process of brutalization, so that soldiers will not if possible even feel the second part of the fight or flight instinct in the presence of the enemy. *Frederick 'the Great' declared that 'the common soldier must fear his officer more than the enemy', and his army inflicted a wide range of savage punishments to errant soldiers. These included 'riding the wooden horse' in which the offender sat astride a sharp-backed wooden horse with weights attached to his feet. Recalling the *fustuarium* was 'running the gauntlet' where the prisoner had to walk between two ranks of soldiers who lashed him as he passed. A Prussian general noted that those sentenced to 36 runs usually died, and a 'flogging around the fleet' in the Royal Navy was equally fatal, with the macabre added touch that the corpse would continue to be flogged beside every ship until all had witnessed the butchery. The Piedmontese military code, the basis for Italian army discipline until WW II, included the provision that cowards would be shot in the back, yet another example of the harsh logic of military punishment.

For two thousand years or more, armies and navies relied heavily on corporal punishment, ranging from 'starting' with a cane for minor errors in drill or deportment, to spreadeagling and exposure to the mockery of one's fellows, to whipping for more important offences. Serious offences against military discipline, especially in the face of the enemy, carried the *death penalty. All of these punishments were performed in the presence of the offenders' military unit and were seen simply in terms of minatory retribution and deterrence. But military justice was also personal and often tempered by the fact that the more persistent offenders, especially in matters of *alcohol, were often known to be excellent combat soldiers.

Prisons of any kind are a relatively recent phenomenon, military prisons reflecting (and usually lagging behind) changes in perceptions of appropriate punishments for crimes in the broader society. With the advent of penology, the concept of incapacitation, which in earlier times had meant mutilation (amputation or branding) was extended to incarceration and by the 1840s prisons were being built in much of Europe and the USA. Previously, as in the notorious prison hulks rotting in the estuaries of England, people were incarcerated only because their sentence of deportation was never carried out and in the rare event that they survived, they would be released at the end of the term imposed. Prisons were seen as a humane alternative and eventually the reforming tide swept over the military.

With penology and prisons came the idea of rehabilitation, again somewhat inappropriate given the difference in civilian and military perceptions of undesirable character traits. Thus military prisons, universally known as 'glasshouses' from about the turn of the century, stuck to retribution and deterrence. They were physically harsh, but did not indulge in the subtler tortures that characterized civilian prisons run by enlightened reformers. The basic urge of the military is to rid its ranks of undesirables and today serious offenders are sent to civil institutions, while the *provost staff corps runs the military prisons. Famous military prisons include the one outside Alexandria in WW II on which the film *The Hill* was based, while the US Marines featured in *The Brig*. The most famous US military prison is in Fort Leavenworth, Kansas, not far from the US army General Staff College, a source of much ironic commentary over the years.   MCM/RH

Punjab is the English rendition of Panjab, the source of some of the finest soldiers in the *Indian army as well as the most tenacious resistance to British rule. See NORTH-WEST FRONTIER, SIKH WARS, and PATHANS.

pursuit is the most demanding—and often most neglected—phase of war. Most casualties occur not in the initial clash of arms but when one side breaks and runs. However, once the initial fury of the assault is spent, the incentive to expend more effort pursuing a fleeing enemy rapidly evaporates. Pursuit is going that extra mile—or hundreds of miles—to ensure the enemy is either trapped or utterly destroyed and cannot reassemble to be a threat again.

The *Mongols were probably the greatest exponents of pursuit, not stopping until the enemy was hunted down and annihilated. After their first encounter with the Russians, at the river Khalka in 1223, they pursued the Russian survivors ruthlessly. After the defeat of the *Mamelukes at the battle of Salamiyet, pursuing Mongol troops were seen as far south as Gaza, some 311 miles (500 km) from the battle. This may have been because, to the Mongols, land was not important. It was just an element across which one moved, like the sea. As in naval warfare, therefore, it was not enough just to drive the enemy from the field, or into port. He had to be pursued, fixed, held in place, and eliminated. This may be one reason for the tremendous emphasis on pursuit in the Asiatic and, by connection, Russian and Soviet style of war. *Timur, like his distant forebear *Genghis Khan, also understood the importance of pursuit. He personally pursued Sultan Ahmed into Baghdad, and then out of the kingdom. Pursuit seems embedded in the Russian and Soviet style of war. *Trotsky, even when exiled, was still hunted down and killed in 1940.

Cavalry was the arm best able to conduct pursuit, the harrying of the Prussian army after *Jena/Auerstadt being a classic modern example. But it often failed to perform this function. The *American civil war Confederate cavalry commander *Stuart, for example, was criticized for never conducting 'a pursuing raid after a victorious battle', in other words letting the enemy off the hook. By contrast his colleague *Jackson fought to the principle 'move swiftly, strike vigorously and secure *all* the fruits of victory'. Students of *armoured warfare will recognize that the latter and not the former understood the crucial interaction of breakthrough, exploitation, and pursuit.

At the end of the 19th century, partly as a result of the lessons of the American civil war, special attention was paid to 'strategic raids' by cavalry and its role in pursuit. Because pursuit on the battlefield, now disrupted by trenches and accurate rifle fire, was expected to be very difficult (which proved totally correct), strategic pursuit by cavalry was of greater importance than ever. Furthermore, pursuit would ideally be conducted in parallel with the retreating enemy on one or, ideally, both flanks, so as to continually threaten to envelop him and thus prevent him establishing new lines of defence. To pursue—and draw parallel with—a retreating enemy, and threaten envelopment required speed, above all, and the ability to cover great distances. See MANOEUVRE WARFARE.

During WW I, pursuit became as difficult as the pre-war military writers had all predicted. Armies dependent on *railways could hardly move across the tactical zone beyond the railheads, never mind into territory vacated by an enemy who had thoughtfully destroyed every vestige of the transport infrastructure. This was the fundamental problem which affected the Allied forces in WW I. Having turned the ground into a quagmire with artillery fire and either bombed the railways and roads behind to oblivion or invited the withdrawing enemy to do so, it was hard enough to advance, never mind pursue. In the Middle East, it remained possible, and Allenby's offensive at *Megiddo in September 1918 was a rare example of breakthrough, exploitation, and pursuit, the latter accomplished, in part, by the RAF which savaged retreating Turkish columns. At *Amiens, in August 1918, the British and Commonwealth forces had also managed to pursue to some extent. The Australians caught a German corps headquarters withdrawing and the corps commander made his escape just in time. The Australian battalion commander noted: 'our men killed the lot (using 3,000 rounds) and left them there; four staff officers on horseback shot also.'

The lingering idea that gentlemanliness has a place in war can be seen in the 1991 *Gulf war. The Iraqis who had raped Kuwait were retreating with some hostages and much booty, and the Allied air forces caught them on the Mutla ridge. The expected effect of the images of the massacre on public opinion was such that one of the muted objectives of the war—the destruction of the Iraqi Republican Guard—was abandoned. It was considered (possibly wrongly) that 'public opinion' would not tolerate the con-

tinued destruction of defeated troops clearly on the run. Thus prompt media coverage and political squeamishness meant that pursuit, without ceasing to be the only way to secure *all* the fruits of victory, was curtailed.   CDB

Pusan perimeter (1950). The outbreak of the *Korean war saw the North Korean army drive the US and South Korean armies to the south-eastern corner of the peninsula. Hard fighting, chiefly by American troops under Lt Gen Walton H. 'Bulldog' Walker, supported by absolute US air superiority, held a perimeter around the port of Pusan while reinforcements were rushed to the theatre. The build-up proceeded until US forces were able to mount a devastating counter-attack against the overextended North Koreans to coincide with the *amphibious landing at *Inchon that severed their supply lines. Caught between the two pincers, they dissolved.   SDB

Halliday, John, and Cumings, Bruce, *Korea: The Unknown War* (New York, 1988).

PX (post exchange). The current system in the USA dates back to July 1895 when the war department issued General Order 46 directing army post commanders to establish an exchange at every post where possible. This general order set the standard for the concept and mission of today's exchange service.

The term PX was first used in 1919. In January 1942, the first supply ships arrived in Northern Ireland and the Army Exchange Service supported troops in all war theatres. In July 1948, the Army Exchange Service was redesignated as the Army and Air Force Exchange Service (AAFES) and it has supported US forces on a wide variety of deployments from *Korea to the former *Yugoslavia. The Air Force refers to its exchange stores as the Base Exchange (BX).

AAFES is a non-appropriated fund activity (NAF) of the Department of Defense, which funds 98 per cent of its operating budget (civilian employee salaries, inventory investments, utilities, and capital investments for equipment, vehicles, and facilities) from the sale of merchandise, food, and services to customers. The only US congressionally appropriated money spent in AAFES comes in the form of utilities and transportation of merchandise to overseas and for military salaries. AAFES has its headquarters in Dallas, Texas. The AAFES system operates 10,878 facilities worldwide, in 25 countries and overseas areas, and in every state of the union. These include 1,423 retail facilities and 218 military clothing stores on army and air force installations around the world. AAFES also employs some 54,000 personnel.

The Navy Exchange System, or NEXCOM, was officially established in April 1946. NEXCOM's roots can be traced back to the merchant 'bumboats' of the 1800s. At that time, sailors relied on bumboats for their daily needs.

Independent stores cropped up aboard ships and ashore with no standard of conduct until finally in 1946 the system was legitimized. NEXCOM supports and manages four programmes: Navy Exchanges, Navy Lodges, Navy Uniforms, and Ships Stores. With the exception of the Ship Stores programme, activities of NEXCOM operate as non-appropriated fund activities. They are self-supporting and all dividends are reinvested to support morale and welfare programmes and reinvestment in Navy Exchange buildings and equipment. NEXCOM headquarters is located in Virginia Beach, Virginia. NEXCOM employs some 18,000 personnel who work at one of the 114 Navy Exchanges including 123 navy uniform stores. The US Marine Corps has its own exchange system known as the Marine Corps Exchange. For the British equivalent see NAAFI.   DMJ

Pydna, battle of (168 BC), the decisive battle of the third Macedonian war (171–168 BC) in which the Romans led by L. Aemilius Paulus inflicted a crushing defeat on the Macedonians of King Perseus. Neither side had planned to fight on that day, but a bickering between their outposts escalated as more and more supports were committed, until both armies were drawn in. After a series of running fights between detachments, each side managed to form a battle line. The Macedonian pike *phalanx had, as a result of its hasty advance, fallen into disorder, breaking up into its constituent units. The Roman legions encouraged far greater initiative in its junior officers, the centurions in charge of each maniple. The centurions began to infiltrate the Macedonian phalanx with small groups of men, isolating sections of it and attacking the pikemen in the flank. The Macedonians were encumbered by their long pikes, and had no reserves to confront these breakthroughs. In only an hour the phalanx collapsed and was cut to pieces. The Romans claimed that they killed 20,000 Macedonians and captured 11,000, for the loss of only 100 dead and a greater number of wounded.   AKG

Pylos, battle of (425 BC) fought during the *Peloponnesian war. Pylos was the headland at the north-west corner of Navarino Bay seized by the Athenian Demosthenes in 425. *Sparta recalled its army from Attica, but failed to take the position by a land and sea assault. Worse still, 420 *hoplites placed on Sphacteria, the island south of Pylos, in order to deny it to the enemy, were trapped when Athenian ships arrived in force and defeated the Spartan fleet in the bay. When negotiations failed, the Spartans kept them supplied by boat and swimmer, until Demosthenes was joined by specialized light troops brought by Cleon. Demosthenes then landed on the island in overwhelming strength, with 800 hoplites and the rest divided into easily controllable groups of about 200. The guards at the southern tip of the island were taken by surprise and annihilated, and when the main body of Spartans tried to close on the Athenian hoplites, they were deluged with missiles by the light troops to flank and rear. Eventually they retired to the north end of the island, but were compelled to surrender when an enterprising Messenian climbed the supposedly inaccessible cliffs behind them.   JFL

Kagan, Donald, *The Archidamian War* (Ithaca, NY and London, 1974).

Thucydides, 4. 2–6, 8–23, 26–41.

Pyrrhus of Epiros (319–272 BC). Pyrrhus was king of Epiros in northern Greece and a soldier of fortune of the early Hellenistic period. He was rated as the foremost general in history by no less an authority than *Hannibal and is known to have written a treatise on warfare, now lost. His extensive military career started in *Alexander's successors' wars, but he is most famous for his costly Italian victories over the Romans at Heraclea (280), Asculum (279), and Beneventum (275) from which we derive the term Pyrrhic victory. He was killed in street fighting in Argos in 272 BC.   SWN

Plutarch, *Life of Pyrrhus.*

Quadrilateral was the name given to the three fortified cities of Mantua, Peschiera, and Legnago and an entrenched camp at Verona, in the province of Venetia in north-eastern Italy, which were the dominant strategic feature in the *Italian independence wars. While essentially defensive in nature, the works at Mantua and Legnago also provided protected bridgeheads across the Po river, enabling swift attacks to be launched.

Built at great expense between 1833 and 1849, the Quadrilateral was based on the ideas of Archduke *Charles concerning key geographical locations, and represented the Austrian empire's rejection of Napoleonic offensive strategy. Instead, the Austrians opted for a strategy which aimed at barring key invasion routes around the empire. While other states, particularly Prussia, were embracing strategic speed and flexibility in the form of railways, the Habsburg empire went in the other direction.

In the 1859 *Italian campaign the invading French decided that discretion was the better part and did not attack the Quadrilateral, in a war that left the feature at the frontier of the reduced Austrian holdings in Italy. During the *Austro-Prussian war, the Piedmontese were roundly repulsed by the army of Archduke Albrecht operating from the fortress system. It had proved its worth, but defeat by Prussia forced Austria to surrender the Quadrilateral and the rest of Venetia.   RTF

quartermaster/quartermaster general. See QM/ QMG.

Quebec, battle of (1759). The capture of Quebec was the culmination of the British campaign in Canada during the *French and Indian war. In June 1759 a *convoy of ships carrying 8,500 British troops headed down the St Lawrence and set up a base of operations on the Île d'Orléans, opposite Quebec. To the east the banks of the river were heavily defended against a landing, but scouting revealed a cove on the banks of the St Lawrence west of the city, below the dominant Plains of Abraham, that could be used for an amphibious assault. On 13 September, the British commander *Wolfe led a force of 1,700 to seize this vital point and scramble up the cliffs. Once on the high ground above the city the British mustered 5,000 men and the French, preceded by swarms of Indian and French-Canadian *sharpshooters, deployed to meet them. A brisk firefight ensued, in which both Wolfe and the French commander Montcalm were mortally wounded. Wolfe expired knowing that victory was in his grasp: the city surrendered on 17 September 1759, the beginning of a run of victories that temporarily secured North America for the British crown.   TM

QM/QMG (quartermaster/quartermaster general) was the title originally given to the officer entrusted with providing armies with accommodation (quarters) as well as food and equipment. It became a prefix to some NCO ranks (thus company QM sergeant, etc.) to denote their particular responsibility with regard to supply.

In most countries, particularly in Prussia and Austria, the entire concept of a *general staff grew up around the office of the QMG, in recognition of the fact that warfare is, above all, a matter of *logistics. At an early stage, again in most armies, other specialist functions such as *engineering and *intelligence tended to gravitate to the department. The pressure of campaigning meant that, for example, the *Indian army QMG was well ahead of its English equivalent in performing the tasks of a general staff. During WW I *Ludendorff took the title '1st QMG', a fitting title for a post which gave him extraordinary political as well as military power, although *Hindenburg, as CGS, was senior.

At the regimental level the role of QM (S4 in the US system) is invested with a great deal of responsibility, and is usually given to an officer with a proven record of reliability and strong organizational skills. Traditionally the British army gives the post of regimental QM to an officer commissioned from the ranks. The QMG remains among the top ranks of most armies. AH/RH

radar has had a considerable impact on warfare since its development in the 1930s, most significantly in aerial and maritime operations. Radar (radio direction and ranging) functions by reflecting ultra-high frequency *radio waves off objects back to a detecting source, thereby ascertaining the target's range, direction, and altitude. Although by the late 1930s the Germans were more technically advanced, it was the British under the aegis of Robert Watson Watt who first put radar, or RDF ('radio direction finding' as it was initially known in Britain), to practical operational use as part of a package of measures to provide early warning and interception capability for the RAF against the Luftwaffe prior to WW II. As Britain prepared for war a series of radar stations was set up across southern England, and radar was an important factor in the winning of the battle of *Britain in 1940. Other powers were also developing radar and a critical scientific war began as each side attempted to produce new innovations that might gain a short-term advantage.

In order to avoid enemy fighters zeroed in by ground radar, bombers began using the cover of night to avoid detection, but this had been anticipated and defenders began fitting smaller short-range radar sets into two-seater night fighters. The Germans adapted a whole range of aircraft to meet the challenge of the RAF's night-time bombing offensive of 1941–5. RAF Bomber Command also developed radar equipment to aid bombing and measures to confuse German defences, the most notable example being the dropping of 'window', aluminium strips (an early form of 'chaff') designed to blind German radar. The Allies took a lead in the radar war with the development of centimetric radar which greatly increased efficiency and capability. In the final year of the war the RAF's radar-assisted bombing often proved to be more accurate than the USAAF's precision air raids using visual methods.

Radar was also used in the maritime war to hunt German U-boats both from the air and from the surface, and, moreover, proved to be an essential tool for surface fleets as early warning against air attacks. Advanced radar technology conveyed considerable advantage to US forces fighting the Japanese whose radar capability was much less developed.

Radar development post-war has enhanced navigation, bombing accuracy, and co-ordination capabilities in attack (AWACS (Airborne Warning and Command System) for example). Radar has also been an important factor in modern tactical engagement techniques with great reliance being placed on guided missiles and methods to defeat them, both passive and active. Nevertheless, radar appeared to have negated the element of surprise in conventional air attacks and much effort has been invested in defeating radar detection, the most famous and expensive example being the Lockheed F-117. Such stealth technology projects as this, the Northrop B-2, the Joint Strike fighter, and the new F-22 undermine radar by using radio-absorbent materials and low-reflective silhouettes.   JDB

Bowen, E. G., *Radar Days* (Bristol, 1987).
Murray, Williamson, and Millett, Allan R., *Military Innovation in the Interwar Period* (Cambridge, 1996).

Radetzky von Radetz, FM Count Josef (1766–1858), perhaps the greatest soldier ever produced by Austria. He came to prominence in the Habsburg army during the *French Revolutionary and *Napoleonic wars and in the aftermath of the failed *Wagram campaign of 1809, he became COS to Count Karl Schwarzenberg when he replaced Archduke *Charles as head of the army. In this capacity Radetzky directed the operations of the Austrian army at the battle of *Leipzig in 1813 and throughout the subsequent campaign in Germany and western France the following year. Entrusted with the command of the Habsburg Italian army, he suppressed nationalist revolts on several occasions through the 1820s and 1830s. Made a field marshal in 1836, he maintained his army in the highest state of readiness, and conducted the first large-scale peacetime manoeuvres in the the history of the Habsburg army to keep the skills of officers and men honed. This preparation bore fruit during the uprisings of 1848, when empire-wide insurrection threatened to topple the dynasty. Radetzky not only put down the Italian insurrection quickly, he also twice defeated the army of Sardinia-Piedmont, which had invaded Habsburg territory in the hope of unifying Italy under its banner. Radetzky retired from active duty in 1857 at the age of 91, forced out by imperial favourite Count Karl von Grünne, who replaced Radetzky with the much less capable Count Franz von Gyulai, loser of the *Italian campaign of 1859. Commemorating his great victories in 1848–9, Austrian composer Johann Strauss 'the Elder' wrote the 'Radetzky March', probably the single piece of *music most identified with old, imperial Austria and its army, and which is played each year as the finale to the Vienna Philharmonic's New Year's Concert.   SWL

radio is the basis of the 20th-century *communications revolution. It first became a possibility when the English physicist Michael Faraday demonstrated in 1831 that an electrical current could produce a magnetic field. In 1864, James C. Maxwell, a professor of experimental physics at Cambridge, proved mathematically that electrical disturbances could be detected at considerable distances. In 1888, a German, Heinrich Hertz, demonstrated that Maxwell's prediction was true for transmissions over short distances. The Italian physicist Guglielmo Marconi then perfected a radio system that in 1901 transmitted Morse code over the Atlantic Ocean from England to Newfoundland. The Royal Navy was an enthusiastic customer of the company Marconi formed to develop radio communications. Similarly, the German armed forces were among the first buyers of AEG and Siemens radio equipment. This new type of technology was well known but still cumbersome at the beginning of WW I.

The western front became a trench war, fought at close range, which made visual signalling perilous. Although field wireless sets were available in small numbers, they were heavy and imperfect. The open spark gap radio and the crystal receiver could not be fine-tuned in the transmission-glutted combat zone. *Telephone and *telegraph were used as the backbone communications systems, and *trench warfare exacted a heavy toll on signal personnel who installed and repaired the lines. As radio was developed, the ability of the enemy to eavesdrop on radio messages (such as before *Tannenberg in 1914) brought about the development of codes and ciphers. Efforts were also made to use

radiotelegraph and radiotelephone between aircraft and ground headquarters. The closing stages of the war saw many planes equipped with voice radio, which proved of particular value for the control of artillery fire, but it was never wholly satisfactory or reliable.

Two inventions in the 1920s transformed not only military communications but also strategy and tactics. The first was the short-wave transmitter, which could be used to communicate at great distances but was small enough to fit into an aircraft or tank. The second was the cipher machine, beginning with the German *Enigma and later with the American SIGABA, and the British TYPEX, which could be operated by minimally trained personnel, yet were (falsely) considered invulnerable to eavesdropping. During the inter-war period, smaller, more robust radio sets, some with crystal tuning, were developed. This meant that vehicles and aircraft could be equipped with radios, giving both the army and air force true mobile radio communications. It was quickly appreciated that voice radio was the only realistic way to control large numbers of personnel and vehicles. Higher frequencies were developed which improved reception. The *armoured warfare of WW II would have been impossible without the installation of lightweight and reliable radios in the majority of fighting vehicles.

Military communications in WW II benefited from pre-war integration of civil communications systems. Radio relay, developed out of a requirement for mobility, became one of the outstanding developments of WW II. It was first used by the Germans and later used by the British at their headquarters in Normandy and London. Radio relay, telephone, and teletypewriter circuits spanned the English Channel for the Normandy invasion and later furnished important communications after the Allied breakout from the beachhead. Short-wave radio allowed tactics such as submarine wolf packs, massive bombing raids, and co-ordinated *blitzkrieg attacks. Frequency-Modulated (FM) radio was used for local communication, such as between ships in *convoy. The need for command control took priority over the risk of interception. Push-button crystal-controlled FM radios provided relatively static and interference-free communications for combat units at the tactical level.

Electronic communications proliferated in the late 20th century. After WW II, innovations such as replacing tubes with transistors and wires by printed circuits, drastically reduced the amount of power the receiver needed to operate and allowed for components to be miniaturized. Two-way mobile radio communications on a large scale revolutionized warfare, allowing for mobile operations co-ordinated over large areas. Technology today has revolutionized the means in which military units communicate with each other. Many of today's combat net radios have been enhanced to carry data in addition to voice. Military trunk systems today are the equivalent to a telephone network that can be moved around the battlefield, providing voice, fax, or data/email links.

Increases in the mobility of armies on land, at sea, or in the air as well as growing demands, as far as the quantity and quality of information transfers are concerned, forced the introduction of automated equipment for the conveyance of messages. Satellites have contributed to the development of sophisticated signal systems. Information technology is advancing at a breakneck pace in a worldwide market place, driven not by military requirements but by the industrial and consumer sectors.   DMJ

Raglan, FM FitzRoy James Henry Somerset, 1st Baron (1788–1855). Younger son of the Duke of Beaufort, FitzRoy Somerset served on *Wellington's staff in the *Peninsular war and lost an arm at *Waterloo. Appointed secretary to Wellington as Master-General of the *Ordnance in 1819, he found that Wellington's many responsibilities meant that he did much of the work. He was promoted major general in 1825. In 1827 Wellington became C-in-C, and Somerset his military secretary. Wellington grew increasingly infirm, and again much of the work was done by Somerset. He came close to succeeding Wellington as C-in-C in 1852, but was appointed Master-General of the Ordnance instead, and was ennobled.

Given command of the British force sent to the *Crimea in 1854, Raglan won the battles of the Alma and Inkerman, but was heavily criticized for the administrative failings of his army as it wintered before *Sevastopol. He died in June 1855, allegedly of cholera, though recent evidence points to the impact of severe strain. Raglan was more the victim of a long peace and financial retrenchment than guilty of incompetence. Unfailingly courteous, even in adversity, he keenly felt the misfortunes of his men.   RH

railways The prospect of land forces being transported further, faster, and more efficiently than on foot or on horseback pre-dated the appearance of working *steam railways. The precursors of the railways, the canals, had already shown what might be possible. In December 1806, British troops bound for Dublin were taken from London to Liverpool by barge which took only seven days, rather than the fourteen they would have taken to march, and with 'comparatively little fatigue'. Steam locomotives became a practical proposition when George Stephenson's *Rocket* won the prize at the Rainhill locomotive trials in 1829. The following year the London and Manchester railway carried a regiment of soldiers 34 miles (55 km) in two hours. Under contemporary planning assumptions it would have taken a military unit two days to march that distance. In 1832 Gen Lamarque told the French Chamber of Deputies that the strategic use of railways would lead to 'a revolution in military science as great as that which had

been brought about by the invention of gunpowder'. By an extraordinary coincidence with profound repercussions for the conduct of war, the electric *telegraph appeared the same year (see also COMMUNICATIONS). The following year a Westphalian, Frederick Wilhelm Harkort, made the first serious proposal for the strategic use of railways, a railway from Weder to Lippe and one on the right bank of the Rhine from Mainz to Wesel, running alongside a telegraph line. This would permit rapid concentration of forces, making a Rhine crossing by the French impossible. The Germans, who lacked the advantages enjoyed by powers with sea lines of communication, were first to grasp the railway's strategic potential.

However, it was another generation before that potential was fulfilled. In 1846 the Prussian VI Army Corps of 12,000 men was moved by rail to Cracow and in 1849 a Russian corps of 30,000 was moved from Poland to G'oding in Moravia where it effected a junction with the Austrian army to help suppress one of the revolutions which had convulsed the continent the year before. But it was not until the French *Italian campaign of 1859 that railways were used to transport thousands of men directly to the battlefield. Writing in 1861, a British officer described how the visitor to *Magenta, scene of one of the terrible battles of the war, would see, close to the railway platform, rough mounds and black crosses marking the graves of hundreds of men. 'This first employment of railways in close connexion with vast military operations', he wrote, 'would alone be enough to give a distinction to this campaign in military history.' In 86 days between 19 April and 15 July the French moved 604,000 men and 129,000 horses by rail, peaking at 8,421 men and 512 horses a day at the end of April. Furthermore, the troops were going straight to the front. As *The Times* reported from Pavia, 'from the heights of Montebello the Austrians beheld a novelty in the art of war. Train after train arrived by railway from Voghera, each train disgorging its hundreds of armed men and immediately hastening back for more.' Railways were now clearly part of the war and both sides attacked track, bridges, and tunnels to deny them to the enemy.

The use of public railways to deploy troops required special measures to run them and a special organization to deal with damage to track and rolling stock by the enemy and to inflict such damage upon them. The *American civil war, fought over an area the size of Europe, could hardly have been fought at all without railways. Much of the land was not well-enough cultivated to enable armies to live off it and it was only by rail that the new vast armies could be supplied.

An experienced railway man, Daniel Craig McCallum, a Scot, was immediately appointed Military Director and Superintendent of Railroads in the USA by order of Pres *Lincoln, with the honorary rank of colonel (later brigadier general). In 1861 the USA enjoyed no fewer than six railway gauges: 6 feet (183 cm), 5 feet 6 inches (167 cm), 5 feet (152 cm), 4 feet 10 inches (147 cm), 4 feet 9 inches (144 cm), and 4 feet 8½ inches (143 cm) (the standard British gauge, later adopted as uniform). In spite of the problems, the combatants adapted and exploited railways to an astonishing degree. In September 1863 the Union wanted to send reinforcements from the Army of the Potomac to eastern Tennessee. McCallum calculated that he could move 23,000 men with guns and ammunition 1,200 miles (1,931 km) in seven days, a distance it would have taken them three months to march. In December 1864 Gen Schofield's corps of 15,000 men was moved the other way, from Tennessee to the Potomac by river and rail, a distance of 1,400 miles (2,253 km) in eleven days.

For all its strategic significance, the 'iron road' was terribly vulnerable, and its rails were made of precious steel that was also needed for ordnance and ammunition. The first destruction of a railway line for military purposes had been by the Venetians, during their insurrection against the Austrians in 1848. In April 1862 the USA formed a rail construction corps under Herman Haupt to make good damage done to the Richmond–Washington railway by the Confederates. The USA became brilliant at replacing destroyed bridges, spanning huge gaps with raw timber, like the Potomac Creek bridge which was 414 feet (126.2 metres) long and 82 feet (25 metres) high. They also developed prefabricated bridges with 60 foot (18.3 metre) spans. During his *March to the Sea, *Sherman destroyed hundreds of miles of railway track, while at the same time US construction troops reopened 300 miles (483 km) of railway in North Carolina ready to receive and supply the Union force.

In the 1870–1 *Franco-Prussian war both sides deployed by rail (the Germans with infinitely greater efficiency), but a new threat which had been oddly rare in the American civil war emerged—sabotage by civilian resistance fighters. From the start, European armies came down very heavily on anyone trying to sabotage their rail communications. In 1866 the Prussians advertised 'the terror of reprisals'. In France, where after the defeat of the field armies war became more diffuse, the Germans deployed 100,000 troops to protect 2,000 miles (3,218 km) of French railway line with detachments at each station and signal box.

The Russians, observing all this, hit upon an admirable defensive ploy. They made their rail gauge 5 feet, as opposed to the usual 4 feet 8½ inches used by Germany. This meant that if Germany invaded Russian territory (which then included Poland) they would either have to build their own railways or build special rolling stock able to run on Russian lines which would still mean having to trans-ship supplies from one train to another at the border. However, in 1877–8, when the Russians were largely on the offensive against Turkey, they suffered a disadvantage, as they had to trans-ship their supplies on the Romanian–Turkish border.

As German strategic railways expanded towards the Russian frontier before 1914, the German ability to deploy beyond the border became problematic. Observers noted that the main lines approached the border, and that there were then numerous branches, which stopped on the frontier itself. The only explanation was that these were jumping-off points for military light railways, which the Germans would then construct across conquered territory. Observers just before the war reported 'diminutive little engines and rails in sections so that they could be bolted together and even bridges that could be put across ravines in a twinkling'—and were promptly invited to leave the country.

In addition to using the civil main lines, railways were constructed for purely military purposes, with no commercial value. The first was one of the earliest used in war, the 7 mile (11 km) line from the port of Balaclava to the Allied camp at Sevastopol. The most striking example was probably the line constructed during the British expedition to *Abyssinia in 1867–8 on the orders of Sir Robert *Napier. Intent on rescuing British prisoners held by Emperor Theodore at Magdala, the British planned to build a railway to cover part of the 63 mile (101.4 km) journey. In October 1867 the advanced brigade arrived at the start point, but work did not begin until January 1868. The line, built by Indian labourers, was of the 5 foot 6 inch Indian gauge. It clung to a hillside in country which was largely timberless and waterless. Six locomotives were imported from Bombay. For four months they laboured on 11 miles (18 km) of railway (12 miles (19 km) if sidings are included). At the end of April they decided not to complete it as Magdala had by then fallen. Instead, they strengthened it to carry the troops coming back.

Trains were also developed as weapons of war themselves. During the 1859 invasion scare in Britain, there were plans to build a circular track at a 15 mile (24 km) radius from the centre of London and mobile artillery mounted on trains was an attractive option for *coast defence. The problem was how to get a big gun to fire at right angles to the direction of travel without tipping the train off the track. In the American civil war it did not take long for a proposal to reach Herman Haupt for 'an armor-clad car, bullet proof and mounting a cannon'—the origin of the armoured train which proved a prominent instrument of war in numerous subsequent conflicts including the Second *Boer War and the Russian civil war. Trains, protected by railway sleepers and metal plates, were used—also in the Franco-Prussian war when four were fitted out to defend Paris during the siege. During the Second Boer War the British brought control of the railways to a fine art, and also used armoured trains which, as *Churchill observed from bitter personal experience, while formidable, could be brought to the fighting efficiency of a beached whale if derailed.

The railway—or lack of it—was not only the cause of Russia's failure to achieve a decisive land victory in the *Russo-Japanese war. It was also the cause of the war. Parsimony about building a line round the north of the Amur river bend led to a decision to put a railway across a more direct route, which precipitated hostilities. The Russian achievements in keeping their one single-track trans-Siberian line open were remarkable, but ultimately inadequate.

By the end of the 19th century bringing 'million-strong' armies to battle along railway lines had become the apotheosis of war planning. As A. J. P. Taylor observed, the war came about, in part, because the railway timetables decreed it. The problems of different gauges encountered in the east may have confounded German plans for victory over Russia, while in the west, ironically, the rail timetables mandated an ultimately fatal clash with Britain, as well as France (in their quest for rapid victory, the Germans violated Belgian neutrality, thus bringing Britain into the war).

The appearance of the automobile, tank, and truck revolutionized war at the tactical and *operational levels, but strategic mobility on land continued to be by rail. In WW II major operational movements were conducted by rail, especially on the *eastern front. German reinforcement to attack the *Normandy landings would come, overwhelmingly, by rail, and before D-Day the British and Americans diverted their strategic bombers to attack the French rail network to *interdict the invasion area. And even in the *Cold War, rail gauges—and rail tunnels—remained the ultimate determinant of strategic mobility. The dimensions of the main battle tank were ultimately limited by their ability, mounted on rail flats, to pass through European rail tunnels. When Russia started removing its forces from eastern Germany at the end of the Cold War, they went by rail. And when Britain wanted to send Challenger tanks to Bosnia to enforce the 1995 Dayton agreement, complete with their additional armour packages to further overawe the Bosnian Serbs, they were—unlike the basic tanks—too big to go through the tunnels from Germany through Hungary to Bosnia. So they had to be taken by sea. Right up to the end of the Cold War, and beyond, when tactical and operational mobility belonged to the petrol engine, the jet engine, the helicopter, the track, and the road wheel, strategic mobility on land was still dependent on the railway.

CDB

Pratt, Edwin A., *The Rise of Rail Power in War and Conquest* (London, 1915).

Taylor, A. J. P., *War by Timetable* (London, 1969).

Terraine, John, *White Heat* (London, 1983).

Rajput is a name employed in three ways: to indicate members of the *Ksatriya (warrior) Hindu caste; to denote in a loose racial sense much of the population of northern India, part of which was converted to Islam or to Sikhism (see SIKH WARS); to denote particularly inhabitants of Rajputana (roughly corresponding to the Indian province of Rajasthan). From the 7th to the 12th centuries Rajput chiefs ruled much of northern and western India until they were subdued by Muslim invaders *c.* AD 1200. Under the Mughals a modus vivendi was struck and many Hindu Rajputs served in the Mughal army. Rajputs were recruited to the East India Company's sepoy forces as infantry and cavalry from an early period and Rajputs (and Brahmins) from Bihar and Oudh, because of their fine physique, became the principal recruits sought by the Bengal army prior to the *Indian Mutiny of 1857. Many were also recruited by the Bombay army. After the mutiny the emphasis shifted away from these traditional sources of recruits towards the Punjab but Rajputs were still recruited, especially those from the Himalayan region, notably the Garhwal, Kumaon, and Dogra hills. The hillmen usually found their way into the 17th Dogra Regiment, the 18th Royal Garhwal Rifles, the 19th Hyderabad (Kumaon) Regiment, and into Dogra companies in Punjabi regiments. Rajputs from Rajasthan usually entered the 6th Rajputana Regiment (which included battalions from the old Bombay army) and the 7th Rajput Regiment (which also recruited in the traditional areas of Bihar and Oudh and which embraced the debris of many of the regiments of the old Bengal army). Recruitment was conducted with great care: the Dogra recruitment handbook lists 420 subdivisions of Rajputs suitable for recruitment ranked in four grades. Many Rajputs also served in the armies of princely states; cavalrymen from these forces served with the British and Indian army forces in many campaigns, especially during the two world wars.

MEY

Mason, Philip, *A Matter of Honour* (London, 1974).

Tod, James, *Annals and Antiquities of Rajasthan*, 2 vols. (1829; repr. Calcutta, 1972).

Ramesses II (1304–1237 BC), Pharaoh of Egypt who defeated the *Hittites at the battle of *Kadesh in *c.*1300 BC.

Ramillies, battle of (1706). In 1705 *Marlborough's Allied army—largely British, Dutch, and Danish—penetrated the Lines of Brabant, *field fortifications intended by the French to defend the frontier of the Spanish Netherlands, and destroyed a section between Zoutleew and Merdorp. The following spring, anxious to bring Villeroi to battle before he was reinforced, Marlborough advanced through the damaged section. Villeroi at once raised the siege of Zoutleew and marched to meet him. Early on Whit Sunday, 23 May, Marlborough's scouts found the French in a good position on open countryside behind the marshes of the Little Geet with their right on the river Mehaigne and the village of Ramilles in their centre. Both armies were equal, at around 50,000 men apiece, and the French, *uniforms pristine in start-of-campaign whiteness, were unusually confident.

Marlborough's guns opened on the French centre at about 13.00 and he struck at both flanks shortly afterwards.

He pushed back the French right, and though he made poorer progress against the French left, Villeroi reinforced it with troops from his centre. Nevertheless, the centre remained very strong, and Marlborough could make little impression on it. In mid-afternoon he withdrew troops from his right, using a re-entrant to enable them to move unseen, and their unexpected arrival gave him the decisive advantage. The French right was pushed back, and by 18.00, although Villeroi still had troops facing a non-existent threat to his left, he had none spare to reinforce Ramillies, which was taken after heavy fighting. He tried to form a second line but Allied cavalry swept him away: by dawn on the 24th only about half his army was intact. Marlborough had lost just 4,000 men, and exploited success by taking Louvain, Brussels, and Antwerp and shepherding the French field army back to the Flanders frontier.   RH

rank All military forces depend for their operation on a strict, unambiguous organizational hierarchy which has usually been reflected in distinctive *uniforms, *badges, and insignia. Attempts to create 'classless' armed forces without visible rank distinctions have been short-lived. Even the People's Liberation Army (PLA) of Red China had two pockets for junior ranks and four pockets for officers, and finer rank distinctions could also be deduced from the quality and cut of the uniform. Recently, the PLA has reintroduced a conventional rank system recognizable anywhere. After 5,000 years of evolution, the rank structures of armies, *navies, and *air forces around the world are extraordinarily consistent. The universality of the system is striking, particularly with regard to general officer grades. In addition to the shoulder badges and insignia shown, generals around the world usually wear oak leaves in some form on their collar patches.

Recent attempts to 'flatten' the hierarchy in western armies in accordance with current management practice, reducing the number of layers, have failed, for example, the Bett Report in the UK in the 1990s. As those consulted explained, in the confusion of battle there is not time to work out who is the most senior of the five soldiers or officers crouched in a foxhole. A full range of ranks is needed. Military ranks evolved in relation to the command of specific organizations. The smallest, equating to the British section or the US squad, consists of eight to ten soldiers. The commander may be a corporal or (in the USA) sergeant, and he needs a clearly identifiable deputy—a lance-corporal or corporal. The smallest entity commanded by a commissioned officer is usually a platoon of about 30 men although the German army has a tradition of using senior *NCOs as platoon commanders. In modern armies companies of 100 men or so are usually commanded by captains or majors, although the Romans used centurions—who were promoted from the ranks—to command centuries.

Although ranks owe their origins to the command of certain sizes of unit, they are also borne by staff officers who are not commanding troops directly, but need to interrelate to field commanders at an appropriate level and to be recognized as senior planners. Thus, a division may be commanded by a major general; his deputy and chief-of-staff may be brigadiers or colonels, as will his brigade commanders. There has also been a noticeable 'inflation' in the ranks required to do jobs throughout history. British majors now command companies or their equivalents, while the RAF rank of squadron leader no longer defines the officer who commands a squadron, for that task is now entrusted to a wing commander.

One of the most important distinctions is the difference between commissioned and non-commissioned officers. Commissioned officers receive their appointment from the head of state, traditionally in a *commisson once signed in person. NCOs are appointed, in turn, by those officers, and can therefore be promoted or demoted much more quickly and easily. In Frederick 'the Great' 's Prussian army, every officer, from the highest general to the lowest ensign, wore the 'king's coat', promoting cohesion and mutual loyalty. In modern armed forces there are also *warrant officers (WOs), who come between NCOs and officers and form part of the permanent, professional hierarchy.

The relationship between NCOs and officers reflects not only different responsibilities, but also career structures. Some military ranks are clearly 'training grades'. The lowest officer rank, second lieutenant or ensign, is one: officers once began their careers by carrying the ensign, or colour. Senior NCOs and WOs who are awarded commissions often skip the most junior officer grades.

In the regular British and US armies there are parallel hierarchies. Although a second lieutenant—the lowest form of officer life—is technically senior to a sergeant or even a CSM or RSM (in Britain, WO Class II or Class I, respectively) he or she would usually be ill-advised not to heed their advice. In conscript armies the relationship has been rather different. Officers and senior NCOs are the career professionals; junior NCOs are selected from among the conscripts. As many of these armies try to become all-professional, the relationship will have to change.

In the *Roman army the distinction between NCOs and officers was clear and the rank structure highly developed. The first promotion, to *immunis*, brought exemption from fatigues. Centurions—commanding 'centuries' (in fact, companies of 80 men)—were usually senior NCOs, although they were sometimes commissioned directly. In Caesar's time they seem to have been distinguished by armoured greaves protecting the shins and a deep plated belt. Above the centurions within each legion there were then five junior tribunes (*tribuni augusticlavii*) and one senior tribune (*tribunus laticlavius*). These were staff officers who were members of the Roman aristocracy and recognizable by muscled *armour and purple stripes on their garments.

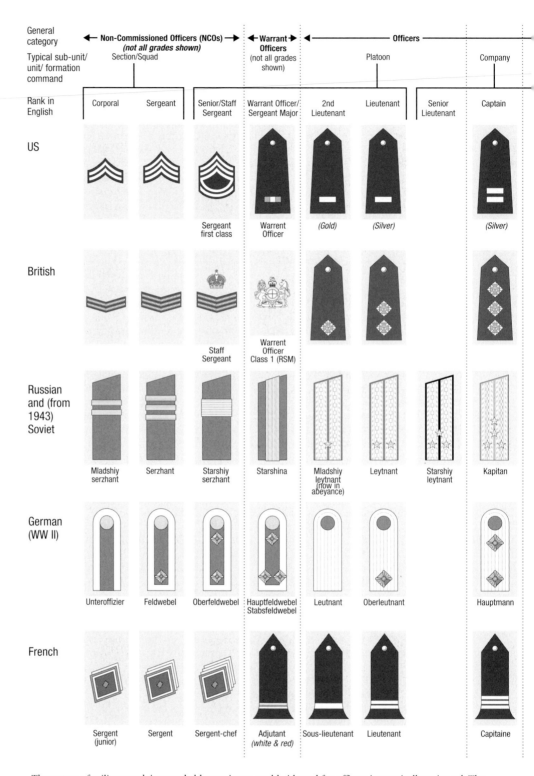

General category	Non-Commissioned Officers (NCOs) *(not all grades shown)*			Warrant Officers (not all grades shown)	Officers			
Typical sub-unit/ unit/ formation command	Section/Squad				Platoon			Company
Rank in English	Corporal	Sergeant	Senior/Staff Sergeant	Warrant Officer/ Sergeant Major	2nd Lieutenant	Lieutenant	Senior Lieutenant	Captain
US			Sergeant first class	Warrent Officer	*(Gold)*	*(Silver)*		*(Silver)*
British			Staff Sergeant	Warrent Officer Class 1 (RSM)				
Russian and (from 1943) Soviet	Mladshiy serzhant	Serzhant	Starshiy serzhant	Starshina	Mladshiy leytnant (now in abeyance)	Leytnant	Starshiy leytnant	Kapitan
German (WW II)	Unteroffizier	Feldwebel	Oberfeldwebel	Hauptfeldwebel Stabsfeldwebel	Leutnant	Oberleutnant		Hauptmann
French	Sergent (junior)	Sergent	Sergent-chef	Adjutant *(white & red)*	Sous-lieutenant	Lieutenant		Capitaine

The system of military rank is remarkably consistent worldwide and for officers is practically universal. The five major systems of insignia illustrated here provide a rough guide to those in use in most of the world's armed forces in the 20th and 21st centuries. The British system has been widely adopted, with some modifications, in the Middle East, Africa, and south Asia. The Russian, with its origins in the Tsarist army and navy and re-adopted by the Soviet Union in 1943, is widely used with small modifications in eastern

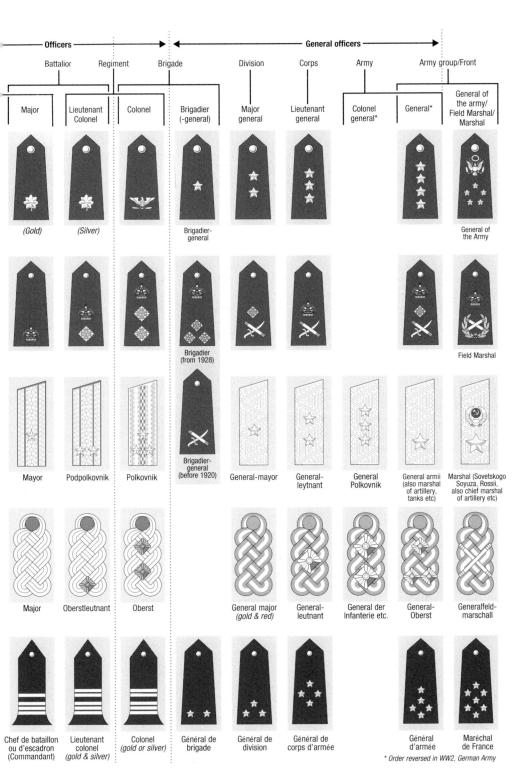

	Officers				General officers				
	Battalion	Regiment	Brigade		Division	Corps	Army		Army group/Front
	Major	Lieutenant Colonel	Colonel	Brigadier (-general)	Major general	Lieutenant general	Colonel general*	General*	General of the army/ Field Marshal/ Marshal

(Gold) | (Silver) | | Brigadier-general | | | | | General of the Army

Brigadier (from 1928) | | | | | | | | Field Marshal

Mayor | Podpolkovnik | Polkovnik | Brigadier-general (before 1920) | General-mayor | General-leytnant | General Polkovnik | General armii (also marshal of artillery, tanks etc) | Marshal (Sovetskogo Soyuza, Rossii, also chief marshal of artillery etc)

Major | Oberstleutnant | Oberst | General major (gold & red) | General-leutnant | General der Infanterie etc. | General-Oberst | Generalfeld-marschall

Chef de bataillon ou d'escadron (Commandant) | Lieutenant colonel (gold & silver) | Colonel (gold or silver) | Général de brigade | Général de division | Général de corps d'armée | Général d'armée | Maréchal de France

Order reversed in WW2, German Army

Europe and east Asia, including China, Korea, and Vietnam. The German system shown is from WW II: that used in WW I was similar, and these insignia continued in use with the East German armed forces (NVA) until 1990. The British, US, and French armies have a number of senior NCO and warrant officer ranks: for simplicity, only one example is shown here.

Above the senior tribune was the *legatus legionis*, a senior officer and aristocrat, commanding a legion of more than 5,000 men. The tribunes therefore roughly equated to a modern brigade staff.

Modern rank titles originated in the Middle Ages. One of the most ancient, 'admiral', comes from Arabic and entered western languages during the Mediterranean clashes between Christendom and Islam. An *amir*, or *emir*, was a commander, and *al-* is the definite article, leading to titles such as *amir-al-bah*, commander of the sea. The ranks of *constable and *marshal both began as humble titles for the head groom, in charge of the horses, but enjoyed a parallel rise to become the titles of the principal officer of the royal household or C-in-C of the army. The rank of sergeant (or serjeant) originated as an attendant, or servant, but by the 14th century was used for a soldier below the rank of knight and roughly equal to an esquire—an apprentice knight. By the 16th century the rank of sergeant-major had appeared, more senior than now, usually an officer ranking above captains and below the lieutenant colonel—a modern major. Many modern ranks are based on Italian, Spanish, or French words of this period. A colonel commanded a small column, *colonello* in Italian.

Originally, the word 'general' was an adjective applied to high-ranking officers holding other titles, thus 'captain-general'. In time, 'general' became the noun. The word lieutenant means, simply, 'taking the place of' or 'deputy': the lieutenant was the deputy to the captain, the lieutenant-colonel to the colonel. Cromwell's army gave rise to one of the more confusing idiosyncrasies of modern military rank. Although a major is senior to a lieutenant, a lieutenant general is senior to a major general. This is because the latter is an abbreviation for *sergeant*-major general, whereas a lieutenant general is, simply, a 'deputy general'.

The US system of rank badges and insignia, introduced in the early 19th century, is highly distinctive, and instructive. Junior officers, who are 'cogs in the machine', wear geometrical shapes—bars. Field officers—majors and lieutenant colonels—wear an oak leaf, perhaps an expression of their position at the core of a living human organization. Colonels, overseeing this organic structure, wear an eagle. Generals, part of the higher direction of war, are distinguished by stars.

After 1917, and the foundation of the Red Army in 1918, Soviet Russia attempted to introduce a utilitarian rank system eschewing traditional titles, badges, and insignia. Officers were called simply 'platoon commander', 'company commander', and so on, and from 16 January 1919 were distinguished by geometrical shapes: triangles for NCOs, squares for junior and field officers, and rhomboids (diamonds) for general officer equivalents, starting with one for a brigade commander (*kombrig*). The system became progressively more elaborate and in 1935 the USSR introduced the rank of marshal, complete with big gold stars on red collar patches and a gold star and chevrons on the sleeve. On 13 July 1940 they reintroduced the term 'general', with a system of stars similar to the USA. In 1943, after the victory at *Stalingrad, they reintroduced the gold shoulder-boards worn by the tsarist army, slightly modifying the tsarist system. This included the rank of colonel-general (*general-polkovnik*), unknown in the tsarist army. In the German army, a colonel-general (*Generaloberst*) was above a general; in the Red Army, the positions were reversed.

Until 1920, the British army, like most others, had brigadier generals to command brigades. After the Great War, there was concern that the *demobilization of the mass army was going too slowly, and that there were 'too many generals'. The answer was simple: the rank of brigadier general was replaced by 'colonel-commandant' wearing a colonel's insignia with an extra 'pip'. In 1928 'brigadier' was reintroduced, but *tout court*—minus the 'general', and retaining the cumbersome three 'pips' and a crown of the short-lived colonel-commandant. The insignia of major generals, the crossed sword and baton and a star, remained unchanged. The old British brigadier general insignia survives in the Israeli army, in the form of a sword crossed with an olive branch—the latter a symbol of peace.

In order to stress the independence of the new RAF, the British invented a new set of ranks although the officer ranks, badges, and insignia, were modelled on the naval system. One interesting anomaly arose. The chief of the air staff was only a 'three-star' officer, whereas those of the army and navy were one grade higher. However, in order to disguise this distinction he was made an air marshal, to sit beside a full admiral and full general. As the air force grew in size and importance, it became necessary to introduce the rank of air chief marshal, equating to a general or admiral. Most air forces, including the US, kept army ranks, badges, and insignia.

General officers in armies and most air forces, 'flag officers' in navies, and 'air officers' in those air forces which have adopted the British system are normally known according to a system of 'stars', derived from the American. Brigadiers (-general) are 'one star', major generals two, lieutenant generals three, and full generals four. The 'five star' ranks of general of the army (US) or field marshal, or equivalent, have been generally abolished except in time of full-scale war. The system used by Russia and her former allies is very similar, although many of these armies do not have the rank of brigadier (-general). A major general therefore wears one star, although he may still be doing a job appropriate to a NATO major general (two-star). However, these armies often have the rank of 'colonel-general', wearing three stars, between lieutenant general and full general, so the mismatch is ironed out. Furthermore, many communist and former communist countries, such as Vietnam and China, have the rank of 'senior colonel', which effectively equates to brigadier (-general).

Many countries in the Middle East, including for example Saudi Arabia and Iraq, follow the British system, although they may substitute an eagle for the crown. There are some curious hybrids. Israel's system of badges and insignia follows the US pattern up to captain, multiplies the major's single leaf to produce two leaves for lieutenant colonel and three for colonel, and then follows the British system from brigadier general upwards. CDB

ransom (from Old Fr.: *ransoun*) is the practice of releasing prisoners taken in battle in exchange for money. During pre-history and ancient times when conflict was conducted between individuals or relatively small groups, the taking of prisoners was rare. As conflict grew and developed into warfare, victory in a battle usually resulted in the slaughter of opponents. By the time that the Greeks and Romans achieved military ascendancy in the Mediterranean, battlefield captives were usually enslaved, although massacres still occurred. Although during the period of internecine Greek wars the ransoming of prisoners was not uncommon, it was during the Middle Ages that this practice became significant.

The age of *knighthood and the importance of key family members to a noble dynasty provided the circumstances for the re-establishment of ransoming as a feature of European warfare. This process was applied only to knights; the ordinary foot soldier, archer, or pikeman could still expect death or slavery following capture. The ransom itself was demanded, owed, and collected by individuals involved in the defeat and capture of an enemy and bypassed the state entirely. This said, in 1194 England, in the shape of Prince John, paid 100,000 marks for the release of *Richard 'the Lionheart'. Richard had been returning from the *Crusades in the Holy Land when he was captured by the Duke of Austria and handed to the Emperor Henry VI. He was held in Germany between December 1192 and February 1194, and John levied taxes on revenue at a staggering 25 per cent. The sum paid, however, was only one-third of the king's ransom demanded. At a lower level, ransom was part of the profit motive interwoven into medieval war. Successful warriors like the Hainault knight Sir Walter Manny could make fortunes.

The practice of *parole became another feature of ransom during this period. An individual would be released after giving his word that he would not take up arms again until after the ransom had been paid in full. This again was an option available only to the nobility whose oath could be trusted.

By the close of the *Thirty Years War in 1648 prisoners had become custody of the state rather than their individual captors. Concurrent with this development was the custom of exchanging *POWs once hostilities had ceased. Prisoners could also be exchanged during the war. This was carried out on a man-for-man basis between combatants of equivalent rank or on a scale where a lieutenant would be worth four privates for example. The last occasion that this was carried out was probably during the *American civil war. JR-W

Raphia, battle of (217 BC). At Raphia a Seleucid army, led by Antiochus III 'the Great', of 62,000 infantry, 6,000 cavalry, and 102 Indian elephants was defeated by a Ptolemaic force, led by Ptolemy IV, of 70,000 infantry, 5,000 cavalry, and 73 African forest elephants. Both armies deployed in typical fashion with pike-armed infantry in the centre and cavalry, screened by elephants, on the flanks. The Seleucids echeloned their right cavalry wing forward to gain tactical advantage. The battle opened with a fight between the two elephant corps, the Seleucids coming off the better due to the greater size and ferocity of their Indian beasts. This was swiftly followed by cavalry actions on both wings, each army's right being victorious and pursuing the enemy from the field. The decisive clash came with the push of pike in the centre. The Ptolemaic army was victorious due to the personal leadership of Ptolemy IV and the greater size of their *phalanx which had been bolstered by raising native Egyptians to supplement the Macedonian settlers who traditionally wielded the pike, or sarissa, in Hellenistic battles. Antiochus, who had ridden from the field with his victorious cavalry, returned just in time to see his infantry collapse. SWN

rations A daily allowance of food and drink provided for military personnel. The provision of food is essential for any military campaign, the more so as military activity is physically strenuous and takes place in the cold and open air. Without sufficient rations the performance and *morale of any military unit will be adversely affected—soldiers will have less energy to march and fight, and more reason to become depressed and querulous. This much is obvious. The points at issue, throughout history, have been what should rations consist of, and how should they be delivered to the troops for whom they have been collected.

Rations have been a part of military existence for as long as records have been kept. Even when an army has travelled through a fertile region and elected to 'live off the land', this has been viewed as a temporary state. When Sherman's army cut its supply lines and embarked upon the *March to the Sea in 1864, living off the land, it was on the understanding that ships laden with rations would be awaiting them at Savannah. Moreover, for an army to make such a march exceptional circumstances must first be in place. Not only must the region being traversed be fertile, it must be relatively unguarded by any sizeable enemy force. Foraging for food requires manpower, and entails dissipating the mass of the armed force—a dangerous act should an enemy army be in the vicinity.

The composition of rations alters from country to country according to the benefits to the consumer, availability, durability, and the ease with which the foodstuffs may be carried and moved. Food that can be moved over significant distances, or carried in a knapsack for several days, may not always taste as good as fresh fruit or vegetables, but sustenance and nutrition invariably take precedence over taste when an army is on campaign. Nevertheless, a soldier must eat a reasonably balanced diet in order to avoid fatigue, and the diseases which can run rampant through the camps of undernourished troops.

Rations have always been dependent upon the ability of the authorities to supply them. Extensive rail networks, and then airdrops, have made the supply of food more rapid in the past century, but for thousands of years before these developments troops were dependent upon what could be dragged behind the army in wagons, supplemented by what the troops could forage from the regions they were passing through. The armies of ancient Greece serve as a good example in this regard. Lazenby has suggested that, 'depending on circumstances Greek troops would evidently eat almost anything'. Various meats and bread baked from wheat or barley seems to have formed the basis of their diet, to which would be added any fruit or vegetables the foragers could acquire. Such foods were sometimes bought directly from merchants as the troops passed through town, on other occasions they might be simply picked from the trees or pulled from the ground. Fish and dairy products appear to have filled a comparatively small part of the diet for the ancient Greek armies. The former could, of course, only be eaten when caught, and to catch enough fish to supply the army through regular channels simply could not work. Fish would, therefore, only be eaten when the men could find the time to catch and cook them. Cheese and dairy products tend to receive little mention, and were simply unknown or unpopular. In addition, both fish and dairy products have a comparatively short 'shelf life', and would spoil very quickly in warm climates.

The limited availability and durability of certain products have determined that they would be seldom used by military organizations particularly when a force is required to move over any significant distance. Thus, while the arrival of rail networks sped the movement of supplies from bases to the front in the 19th century, dietary staples remained similar to those consumed by the ancient Greeks: the *American civil war was the first war in which food supply was significantly aided by rail network, yet the food delivered to the Federal troops who fought far to the south of their home states was not markedly different from that eaten by the Greeks. Throughout most of war the federal soldier could expect to receive a daily ration of 12 oz (340 g) of pork or bacon, or 1 lb 4 oz (567 g) of beef. Bread was also a constant in his diet. During the winter months troops could expect soft bread (usually 1 lb 6 oz (624 g)) from ovens set up near camp; while on campaign hard bread, a biscuit-like substance which soldiers had to soak in coffee to make edible, was more common. 'Hardtack', as the sol-

diers called this, represented the zenith of comestible durability and the nadir of taste. But it is clear that bread and meat continued to be the basic staples in the late 19th century as much as they had done hitherto. For men undertaking arduous physical work, carbohydrates—bread, potatoes, and biscuits—are crucial. Fats keep out the cold, but protein, though desirable, can wait.

In the 20th century the advent of *air transport and greater nutritional information have brought still greater speed to the delivery of food to the troops, and highlighted the importance of a balanced diet for military personnel. The variety of food has consequently increased. Food packaging has also improved. Meat was preserved in tins in the Napoleonic period and known as *bœuf bouilli*, the origin of the English description of corned beef as 'bully beef'. By the end of the 19th century tinned and desiccated rations were widely available, and durability remains a key factor in determining the composition of rations. Rather than any fundamental change in the components involved, the most important development in recent times has been the incorporation of vitamins and drugs into daily consumption. Vitamins can provide an important and portable supplement for troops on a rapid march or when detached from their logistical support. The potential for the use of drugs in warfare—for example, in sleep management—has also come to the fore in recent years, and may soon make up a key component of any basic ration.

Rations have always been crucial to the performance of military personnel, and the search for the ideal combination of durability, portability, and nutritional value will continue. AH

Lazenby, J. F., 'Logistics in Classical Greek Warfare', *War In History*, 1/1 (Mar. 1994).

Offer, Avner, *The First World War: An Agrarian Interpretation* (Oxford, 1989).

Wiley, Bell I., *The Life of Billy Yank: The Common Soldier of the Union* (Baton Rouge, La., 1986).

reconnaissance/reconnoitre (from Old Fr.: *reconnoître*, to recognize). The art of reconnaissance may be said to pre-date all military combat. It is hard to imagine that the first two combatants in war, whoever they might have been, embarked upon conflict without attempting to gain some knowledge of the capabilities of their enemy. The Chinese military philosopher *Sun-tzu noted as much in *c*.500 BC, claiming that 'what enables a good general to strike and conquer . . . is foreknowledge'. This fundamental point is ignored by a senior officer at his peril. The method of obtaining information through reconnaissance has changed over time thanks to technological advances, but the underlying principles remain the same.

The collection of *intelligence can be performed by the oldest form of military technology, the human eyeball, or the most advanced, including satellite systems. It is carried out in all theatres of war, on land, at sea, and in the air. It may be conducted within a short distance of the enemy or with the opposing sides many miles apart. Reconnaissance may not lead to combat, since it may simply keep commanders appraised of enemy capabilities; it may be the precursor to attack; or it may follow an attack to assess the effectiveness of operations.

Obtaining reconnaissance information is obviously of the highest importance. As a result, it is desirable that the units employed to collect information return to convey what has been learned, and it is unusual for reconnaissance units to seek contact with the enemy. Reconnaissance is normally conducted by small groups, individual aircraft, or naval vessels detached from their main force. Trying to define a specific paradigm for reconnaissance is impossible, since the gathering of information of all types is useful. A section of infantry, operating within a short distance of their lines, may be used to carefully advance to seek out but not to engage the enemy. Cavalry, by virtue of its mobility, proved to be a valuable source of information, a principle continued by this arm today, albeit in light armoured vehicles. Again, it would be unusual for cavalry on reconnaissance to seek to engage the enemy, since the value of reconnaissance units lies not in the damage they can inflict upon the enemy, but the provision of information which permits commanders to plan how to damage the opposition to best effect. However, there are times when information must be fought for, and sometimes an enemy's strength may be tested by reconnaissance by battle.

As technology developed and the range over which battles were fought increased, it became increasingly difficult to obtain the necessary intelligence. This was particularly true during WW I. Static warfare prevented observation of anything beyond the front line by ground forces, which could not hope to outflank the enemy to observe unseen. As a result of this, reconnaissance had to be provided by the nascent technology of the aircraft. Although initially compelled to rely upon the human eye, the development of suitable photographic equipment enabled air services, particularly those of Britain, France, and Germany, to obtain information at a great distance behind the enemy lines. The importance of aerial reconnaissance was enhanced as longer-ranged aircraft were developed, allowing flights over enemy territory. This remained the case throughout WW II, in spite of increased opposition from anti-aircraft artillery. The fundamental problem faced by reconnaissance aircraft in the modern era has been the increasing sophistication of air defences, which has led to the refinement of equipment to allow the aircraft to acquire imagery from long range at oblique angles. In addition, reconnaissance has moved into the non-visual spectrum, with electronic reconnaissance. The monitoring of enemy signals traffic and *radar networks by specialized aircraft has increased. The development of the satellite has moved photographic and electronic reconnaissance into a new sphere. Satellites can provide images or information at regular intervals thanks

to their orbit, or can remain fixed above a certain target to monitor developments. Their invulnerability to interception makes them a worthwhile addition to the reconnaissance armoury of any nation which can afford them.

Although of considerable use, aerial and satellite reconnaissance cannot provide all necessary information. The gathering of information on the ground is still essential: technology has not made redundant the more traditional forms of acquiring intelligence. Simply knowing an enemy's deployment or technical capability may not be enough: human intelligence (HUMINT) helps provide a judgement of his morale and fighting efficiency. Intelligence gleaned from monitoring enemy communications—*SIGINT—also has a valuable part to play. A commander may be able to fight successfully even when lacking in certain areas such as numbers or equipment, but a commander deficient in information is heading for disaster. This is as true now as it ever was.
DJJ

Reconquista (Sp.: *reconquista*, reconquest) is the name given to the long process in which the Christians drove the Muslims out of the Iberian peninsula. The Muslim conquest of what is now Spain and Portugal was extremely swift. After the first invasion of 711, the Muslim forces, mostly made up of Berbers from North Africa but largely led by Arabs, swept through the country. By 716 they had achieved some sort of control over the entire peninsula, with the exception of the mountainous areas of the Asturias and the southern valleys of the Pyrenees. Until 732 they also raided deep into France.

It was only slowly that the poor and isolated Christian enclaves to the north could do more than survive. Progress was fastest in the west. Here Muslim settlement never extended further north than the Guadarrama mountains and central Portugal. By 900 the Christians of the Asturias and Galicia had been able to occupy and fortify the almost deserted lands of the Duero valley and the plains to the north, establishing a new capital at Leon. Further east, in the Ebro valley, Muslim settlement reached the foothills of the Pyrenees while in Catalonia the Christians were unable to advance much south of Barcelona.

The strategic position changed dramatically with the collapse of the caliphate of Cordoba in the years after 1010 and the fragmentation of Muslim Spain into small Taifa kingdoms. The Christians, with their heavily armoured cavalry, were able to take immediate advantage. In 1085 Toledo fell to Alfonso VI of Castile, in 1118 Saragossa was taken by Alfonso I ('the Battler') of Aragon while in 1147 Lisbon fell to Alfonso I of Portugal, supported by *crusaders from Britain and the Low Countries.

After the fall of Toledo and the Christian occupation of the Tagus valley, Muslim Spain was not viable on its own. Its survival was due to the intervention of North African Muslim powers, the Almoravids (1086–1145) and the Almohads

(1145–*c*.1230). The Muslims paid the price of subjection to berber rulers whose main interests lay not in al-Andalus, but in their North African territories. From their capital of Marrakesh, both Almoravid and Almohad rulers were able to launch major campaigns against the Christians. They were much less able to defend the lands they did possess or to reconquer lands they had lost. The Christian military effort was led by the kings of the various states but greatly aided by the *military monastic orders and town militias. The latter, raised by the *concejos* or town councils, were especially important in the 12th century and the armies of cities like Avila played a major part in resisting both Almoravids and Almohads. The Spanish military orders, notably the Knights of Calatrava and Santiago, held the castles of the plains of New Castile against the Almohads in the crucial period between 1195 and 1212.

The climax of the Reconquista came at the end of the 12th century. In 1195 the Almohads decisively defeated the army of Alfonso VIII of Castile at Alarcos but they were unable to take advantage of the victory to retake Toledo or any of the cities which had been lost in the previous century. The Almohad caliph retired to North Africa and it was not until 1211 that another major campaign was launched. This new Almohad invasion united the fractious Christian powers, whose quarrels with each other had frequently occupied more of their energies than the struggle against the Muslims. With the support of the pope, a combined Christian army led by Alfonso VIII inflicted a major defeat on the Almohad army at Las Navas de Tolosa in 1212.

Despite the overwhelming victory, the Christians did not immediately advance into Andalusia but the death of the Almohad Caliph al-Nasir in 1213 and the subsequent succession disputes meant that the Muslims were unable to use the respite to repair their defences. When Ferdinand III, now king of reunited Castile and Léon, resumed the Christian advance, neither the local Muslims of Andalusia nor the various pretenders to the Almohad throne could mount a serious resistance. Cordoba fell in 1236 and Seville in 1248. In the east, Jaume I of Aragon-Catalonia took Majorca in 1230 and Valencia in 1236. In the west, the Portuguese had taken control of the Algarve by 1250.

Muslim Spain was now confined to the kingdom of Granada, based on the southern mountains from Algeciras to Almería. The sharply defined border with the Christian sector was known as *la frontera* and many Spanish towns, including Jerez, the home of sherry, bear that postscript. Despite its small size, the kingdom was able to survive for another two and a half centuries until 1492. This was partly due to the mountainous terrain which favoured the defenders and the fact that the kingdom was densely populated, partly with refugees from areas to the north. Until their defeat at the battle of the Rio Salado in 1340, the Muslims of Granada also enjoyed the support of the Merinid dynasty, the new rulers of Morocco. The kings of Castile, now the only Christian state with a common frontier with Granada,

were content to accept the tribute the Nasrid kings paid rather than trying to launch costly invasions. The frontier lands became an area where chivalrous knights could show their prowess and their achievements be recorded in ballads.

This position changed with the accession of Queen Isabella of Castile in 1474 and her marriage to Ferdinand of Aragon. The new monarchs were determined to use the holy war to confirm their position and justify the unification of their kingdoms. Faced with determined Castilian pressure, and lacking any support from fellow Muslims, the Granadans inexorably lost ground until on 1 January 1492 Granada itself was finally taken and the Iberian Reconquista was over. The same year, however, a Spanish-funded expedition landed in the West Indies. The militant ethos of the Reconquista continued in the overseas Spanish and Portuguese empires. HK

---

recruitment (from Old Fr.: *recrute*) originally meant reinforcement, but came to mean any enlistment of personnel for military purposes. This is one of the few immutable factors in warfare. To initiate any type of large-scale conflict, be it on the basis of ideology, *religion, nationality, or even financial gain, a leader must first muster a force sufficient to execute his plans. When an armed force is divided according to how its personnel was recruited, we may expect to find career soldiers, volunteers, and conscripts, while the proportions of each may be expected to vary greatly depending upon the purposes, nature, and scale of a war.

The success of any campaign to induce volunteers or force conscripts into an army will be decided, to a large extent, by circumstances. The recruitment of professional soldiers is less variable. The factors involved have changed very little since the medieval *mercenaries, and centre on *pay. Yet this alone has rarely been enough, other than to attract those seeking to escape destitution. Beyond this, the recruit may hope to develop a career within the armed forces, or he may expect to enjoy the lifestyle provided. It is not uncommon to read of young men joining the army or navy in the hope of seeing the world. The case for those receiving a *commission has generally been a little different. Career development is a common goal for professional officers, and this has often been closely linked to social standing. The practice of purchasing commissions, which was widespread in the 18th and early 19th centuries, was very much a reflection of this link.

The distinction between career soldiers and volunteers is not always clear. After all, most professionals choose their career; they act under their own volition. Moreover, in some cases, soldiers have volunteered on the understanding that they will share in whatever spoils are won before returning to civilian life. The *Vikings are perhaps the best example of this volunteer mercenary. More recently volunteers have joined the colours for more altruistic reasons than plunder and booty, although 'proffing' remains an attraction. This kind of recruitment is often at its height in the first months of a war, particularly if men feel their nation, ideology, or community is threatened. Such motivations are, nevertheless, further exploited in most cases. Before more technologically oriented media became available, those attempting to recruit soldiers might make inspiring, patriotic speeches in a town square. In the medieval period the church was sometimes used as a means both to transmit information on political developments and to direct the response of the population to those developments. The *Crusades are the most obvious example of this, but the link between Church and State was often sufficiently close that the Church became involved in national wars.

As technology has become more advanced, more avenues of recruitment have opened up. In the 20th century newspapers, radio, television, and posters have all served to aid recruitment. Perhaps the most famous single image in this regard is the poster featuring the face and pointing finger of *Kitchener, which invited British civilians to enlist in 1915–16, with the words 'Your country needs you.' News coverage supplemented such propaganda with details of alleged atrocities and aggression. Posters and newspapers have effectively advertised modern wars in the opening months of a conflict, and induced thousands to enlist. Such recruitment plays upon existing motivations in the minds of recruits, primarily, nationalism, patriotism, and certain ideologies. During the *Cold War these factors blended together in support of recruitment to the armed forces of both sides.

Whatever the motivation that brings a volunteer into the ranks, the military authorities must be prepared to deal with the practicalities of recruitment. The authorities are expected not only to accept those who have agreed to fight, but also to provide uniforms, equipment, and training facilities. Since these cannot be created immediately, the actual recruitment process commonly stretches over several weeks, the volunteer being ordered to report at a certain place and time when facilities will be available to begin the process of training him as a soldier. From the point of view of the authorities, *mobilization involves very much more than simply inviting men to join up, but even the recruitment side of it involves a great deal of logistical work to provide the volunteers with uniforms and equipment, to feed them, and to move them to training camps.

In prolonged wars, such as the world wars or *Vietnam, the early willingness to volunteer eventually dries up or, a particular problem during the US wars of the 19th century, they fulfil their term of enlistment and wish to return home. This leaves any armed force with a major shortage in personnel, particularly if the war expands. It is at this point that even those governments who have shunned it in peacetime resort to the third method of recruitment, conscription.

Conscription, defined as the forced recruitment of men into the military, has long been established as a means of supplying troops. The *Roman army included large numbers of *auxiliares*, men drawn from conquered territories. In order to promote loyalty among such troops, the promise of promotion and possibly even Roman citizenship was provided as an incentive, thus blurring the distinction between conscription and professional soldiering. Such blurring may be found in other periods in history. For example, *feudal recruitment depended upon the relationship between suzerain and vassal. Thus a monarch might ask his leading nobles, who held land from the Crown in return for providing military service, to furnish him with troops; these noblemen would then require knights, who held land from them, to provide military service, usually for a specified period. At the local level landowners might effectively coerce their tenants to join them in arms. The element of outright coercion was often intermingled with ties of loyalty and obligation and, increasingly, reinforced by the prospect of pay and plunder. Even in 17th-century England these old bonds still proved enormously strong. In 1642 the Royalist Sir Bevil Grenvile raised a fine regiment of foot (whose men wore the Grenvile blue and silver and fought beneath colours emblazoned with the family's griffin badge) from his hardy Cornish tenantry. He made it clear, however, that any tenant who chose not to follow the griffin would have no roof over his head.

Conscription became more formalized in modern armies. *Frederick 'the Great' conscripted a proportion of the Prussian male population (and made wide use of mercenaries) in order to offset the numerical advantages held by his enemies and diminish the demographic cost of the war. The *French Revolutionary government, and later *Napoleon, conscripted vast numbers of unwilling troops when volunteers became scarce. Indeed, the *levée en masse* introduced by the French Revolutionary government in August 1793 established the practice of large-scale conscription which set the stage for the large scale of warfare in the 19th and 20th centuries.

Conscription appeared again during the *American civil war. Both sides conscripted a significant proportion of their armies despite the antipathy for conscription among both soldiers and civilians. In the South, where manpower problems were acute, the government was forced to conscript men to war-related industries as well as to the army, and by the latter stages of the conflict the Confederacy was moving towards some form of national mobilization. Conscripts were often reluctant soldiers, of course, and *desertion rates climbed following the introduction of conscription in both North and South, just as it had done in France. The North was able to introduce conscription while exempting those involved in vital economic activities (or with the money to hire a substitute), but for the South, even with slaves to perform much of the agricultural work, there was a trade-off involved that was never satisfactorily resolved. The highly divisive issue of exempt status in wars involving conscription continues to dog the heels of today's US politicians, many of whom found some way of not being sent to Vietnam.

In the generation before 1914 large, conscript armies had replaced smaller, professional forces in most of Europe. Since 1870 France, Russia, Germany, Austria-Hungary, and Italy had collectively doubled the strength of their forces through short-term, mandatory military service for adult males. We can see the emergence of a symbiosis between war planning and mass conscription in the development of the *Schlieffen plan, both made conceivable by greater numbers and at the same time demanding more. Schlieffen's fulcrum was that the German armies 'would have to secure a quick victory and would therefore have to attack. Otherwise the absence of so many able-bodied men from productive occupation . . . would cause economic collapse'. Events proved him wrong, but by then the damage arising from this false postulate was done.

Of the major European powers, only Britain did not maintain a large conscript army in the years leading up to WW I—primarily because the British did not expect to become involved in a continental war and were prepared for colonial conflicts instead. Yet the expansion of the war in its first two years, and the horrific casualties taken by both the British Expeditionary Force and the French army in 1914–15, prompted Britain to introduce conscription in 1916. The last two years of the war then saw manpower being stretched between domestic and military demands in all of the major European nations. The difficulty of balancing manpower resources gave a tremendous fillip to those who believed in central planning, which indeed proved necessary for full mobilization during the world wars. Men were subtracted or added to industry, agriculture, or the armed forces on the basis of skills and experience. Oddly, even at the very end it cannot be said that Nazi Germany was fully mobilized: for example, the Nazis failed to mobilize women to anything like the extent that the Allies did, and in terms of quality control or outright sabotage their use of slave labour may well have substantially diminished overall productivity.

What is likely to remain as the clearest example of how mass recruitment—for all purposes—can enable a smaller nation to defeat one that, on paper, should crush it flat, was the Vietnam war. The North Vietnamese, having already defeated the French, developed into a true nation in arms, in which there was no line between volunteer and conscript because even small children had war work to do. By contrast the US 'draft', riddled with classist and political exemptions, divided the nation, while by refusing to declare, still less mobilize, for war, Pres Johnson unleashed major inflation. The contrast between the morale of the even more corruptly conscripted South Vietnamese army and the all-volunteer Vietcong guerrillas was stark enough, but when the former came up against the North Vietnamese army without overwhelming US *air support, the results were predictably humiliating. That the dedicated and ruth-

less Marxists who won the war subsequently proved unable to deliver prosperity to their long-suffering people by using the same methods is another matter. For the singular purpose of waging *total war, their doctrine was the stronger.

AH/HEB

Milward, Alan, *The German Economy at War* (Cambridge, 1965).
Strachan, Hew, *European Armies and the Conduct of War* (London, 1993).

Red Cross/Crescent/Star of David Revulsion at the conduct of war had long encouraged attempts to establish rules which would make it less terrible. The medieval Church had sought to protect churchmen, peasants, and the helpless, and to prohibit wars during planting and harvest, with its Peace of God (998) and Truce of God (1095) as milestones. During the French *Italian campaign of 1859 Jean-Henri *Dunant was shocked by the suffering of the wounded. He wrote *Un souvenir de Solférino*, demanding the formation of voluntary relief societies in all countries. In 1863 a committee of five for 'succouring the wounded' was established in Geneva. Several national societies were formed soon afterwards. The first *Geneva Convention of 1864 dealt chiefly with the care of the wounded, and subsequent conventions widened the scope.

The Geneva-based International Committee of the Red Cross (ICRC), the founding body, is an impartial, neutral, and independent body of 25 Swiss citizens which strives to protect the lives and dignity of victims of war and violence. It is linked with the International Federation of Red Cross and Red Crescent Societies and with the national societies themselves, but the latter are independent, and the ICRC has no formal authority over them.

The Red Cross is not simply concerned with the protection of wounded, though the fact that military *ambulances, hospital, personnel, and hospital ships bear prominent red symbols is one of its the most obvious manifestations. The red cross itself is the Swiss flag reversed, and although it is emphasized that the sign has no religious significance, in Islamic countries it is represented by a red crescent and in Israel by a red Star of David. The Red Cross organizes visits to *POWs, provides them with relief supplies, arranges exchanges of sick and wounded and captured medical personnel, and helps ensure the passage of mail and information. It is now also concerned with the relief of natural disasters.

The Red Cross has helped mitigate some of war's worst effects. Even during WW II, when it had no powers of compulsion with countries that had not signed the 1929 Geneva Convention, it was often able to use considerable moral leverage.

RH

Reichswehr (1919–35), the armed forces of the first German republic (Weimar Republic) later expanded by the

Nazis into the *Wehrmacht. Despite burdens of defeat in 1918 and the restrictions of the peace in 1919, the Reichswehr revived German military professionalism, assumed a pivotal role in the state, and laid the basis for rearmament and for a renewed push for German power in Europe. At the same time, the army played an at times loyal, at times baleful role in foreign and domestic politics, while its senior leadership contributed to the collapse of German democracy from 1930 to 1933. The November 1918 alliance between COS Wilhelm Groener and the socialist chancellor (later president), Friedrich Ebert, assured that the German professional soldier would endure in the first German republic and doomed to failure attempts to establish a new force on a liberal or revolutionary basis.

The preliminary Reichswehr (1919–21) comprised a transitional force manned by demobilized *veterans returned to service amid civil disorder and along the contested eastern borders of the Reich. The *arms control clauses of the Versailles peace settlement limited the Reichswehr to 100,000 troops, abolished the *general staff, and denied it such weapons as armour, heavy artillery, aircraft, and modern heavy battleships.

Once the first defence minister, the socialist Gustav Noske, and COS Gen Walter Reinhardt had used the provisional Reichswehr to quell the domestic communist threat in 1919, the reconstruction of the army began under the liberal defence minister Otto Gessler and COS Hans von *Seeckt as a large army in miniature. This process combined the ethos of the Prussian general staff (reconstituted and hidden in various locations and led once more by officers from the nobility and educated middle class) with innovative operational ideals of air–land battle. Seeckt's cadre force would form the basis for wartime expansion by relying upon various paramilitary organizations.

The Reichswehr ministry consolidated the functions of strategic planning and management within its walls, with covert sections of the general staff located in other ministries such as transport. The army had two corps headquarters and seven divisions of infantry and cavalry, once again, all established upon an expansible basis. The officer and NCO corps embraced high intellectual and physical standards as well as sharpened training, tactics, and operations in order to master technological developments. Strategic and operational thinking foresaw France and Poland as Germany's opponents in the next war. The navy relied upon units left over from 1918; the need to update the pre-*Dreadnought* battleships with a type of pocket-battleship (Armoured Cruiser 'A') provoked parliamentary controversy in 1929.

The relationship between the army and the republic never fully escaped the impact of defeat and counter-revolution (1919), the Kapp putsch (1920), the French occupation of the Ruhr, and the Bavarian uprising (1923). Seeckt sought to banish partisan politics from the ranks, while, devoid of a democratic ethos, the army served first the state and secondly the republic. Parliamentary forces of the 1920s failed to integrate the Reichswehr fully into the executive branch of the Weimar Republic, despite the pro-military sympathies of the right-of-centre parties.

The Reichswehr broke the Versailles Treaty with clandestine military-to-military contacts that culminated in secret air and armour training in Soviet Russia, disguised design and arms manufacture and production in the Netherlands and Spain, and the so-called 'Black Reichswehr' of paramilitary auxiliaries. The latter units stood along the Polish border as a reserve for the overstretched regulars. This semi-independent military policy aroused the concern of the left-of-centre parties, and, combined with Seeckt's cult of monarchist martial tradition and his own political ambitions in the era 1923–6, drove him from office. His successor, Gen Wilhelm Heye (1926–30), and defence minister Wilhelm Groener brought the Reichswehr closer to the republic, which soon fell into a profound crisis of state, society, and economy. These events drew the Reichswehr once more into domestic politics, where Groener and COS Kurt von Hammerstein-Equord tried vainly to protect aspects of democratic statecraft, only to be undone, in part, by the sleight of hand of Gen Kurt von Schleicher, whose failed policies of 1932–3 did much to facilitate Hitler's chancellorship on 30 January 1933. As one observer said, 'soldiers presided over the birth of the republic and had a hand in its burial'.

DA

reiter (Ger., horseman, though the word was conscripted straight into English and converted into the French *reître*). The reiter was an armoured cavalryman of the 16th and 17th centuries, German in origin though imitated elsewhere. He carried a sword and a pair of long *wheel-lock pistols, and often used the *caracole, a manoeuvre which enabled formations of reiters to maintain a steady volume of pistol fire. Reiters played an important part in the *French wars of religion, when John Casimir, son of the Elector Palatine, brought many to support the *Huguenots. Improvements in infantry firepower sounded (all too literally) the reiter's death knell.

RH

reivers A term from the same Old English root as 'ruffian'. Reivers were disparate groups and families of outlaws in the Anglo-Scots borders between the 13th and 17th centuries. They lived in the overpopulated buffer zone between two hostile neighbours, Scotland and England, where employment and farmland were limited. Organizing themselves into highly efficient bands of light horsemen they took advantage of the remoteness of national law, order, and justice. Indeed, in many cases, neither country acknowledged responsibility for the 'debatable land' between them. Attempts to govern the border regions and introduce law and order were made. In 1249 the governments of Scotland and England came to an agreement, known as the Laws of the Marches (the word 'Marches' also referred to the Anglo-Welsh borders). Both sides were divided into three zones—west, east, and middle Marches. These were each to be administered by a March warden, who was responsible for all judicial and martial matters. The wardens were to liaise with their opposite numbers on the other side on a monthly basis, on 'truce days', in order to solve the problems arising from the implementation of the border laws and to dispense justice where needed.

Although the reivers acted in their own interests, they could respond to the call to arms of their respective countries. Recruited as 'staves', their role was the same as their everyday activities, with the addition of scouting, ambushes, and patrolling. They saved the English left wing at *Flodden in 1513 and gained a victory against a vastly superior Scots army at Solway Moss in 1542.

By the end of the reign of Elizabeth I of England, the reivers' reign of terror had reached new heights. This was their undoing. The new king, James VI of Scotland and I of England, ruled both countries and was striving for a united kingdom and a pacified border region. Both were a high priority. The border Marches were renamed the Middle Shires and the border laws replaced with 'Jeddart Justice', where summary executions were common. Many old reiver families, such as the Elliots and Armstrongs, were now forced into military service in either Ireland or the Low Countries. The ownership of quality horses and carrying weapons was made illegal, and reiver numbers began to dwindle dramatically. Despite a brief revival during the *British civil wars, the reivers had disappeared by the end of the 17th century. They are partially and appropriately remembered in the word 'bereaved'.   JDB

---

religion and war (*see opposite page*)

---

reserve forces Armed forces need to be larger in war than peace and use reserves to help achieve the transition. As modern armies evolved and *feudal duties weakened, the obligation to serve in a part-time *militia usually survived. These were used to support professional forces, either serving alongside them or furnishing them with recruits. Although militias had limitations, such as regionalism, the reluctance of men to serve, and inferior training and equipment, they had some advantages: they were cheaper than professionals and often more reliable than *mercenaries. Sometimes they retained real value, military or political. The Grenzers, free peasants settled along the Habsburg frontier, could be called out to produce a force of tough irregulars. In Britain the militia, the 'constitutional force', provided a counterbalance to the regular army and ensured that defence was not simply left to the professionals. In Post-Revolutionary France it was believed that the generally middle-class National Guard was likely to defend property against insurgents with a zeal sharpened by self-interest.

From the 19th century reserve forces followed two distinct paths. Most European nations introduced conscription, and after German victory in the *Franco-Prussian war it was clear that only conscription followed by reserve service could generate mass armies. National policies varied, but the Prussian system of 1895 provides a good example. Between the ages of 17 and 20 young men were liable for service in the Landsturm (home guard). At 20 they spent two years in the regular army and five in the reserve—three and four years respectively in cavalry and horse artillery. At the age of 27 the reservist joined the first class of the Landwehr, transferring to its second class at 32 and going back to the Landsturm between the ages of 39 and 45. Because there were more young men than the regular army needed, many did not serve full-time but went on to the Ersatz Reserve, carrying out part-time training and going to the Landsturm after twelve years. The system was made attractive to the middle classes by allowing well-educated young men to serve for only a year with the colours, usually passing on to the reserve as officers.

The French system was broadly similar—the French equivalent of the Landwehr was called the Armée Territoriale—but reserve training obligations were enforced far less rigidly than in Germany. The 'Common Army' of Austria-Hungary was supported by two national armies, one Austrian and one Hungarian, and while the Austrians used the German term Landwehr for part of its reserve, the Hungarians termed theirs the Honved.

Nations like Britain and the USA, which had no conscription, followed another path. They found part of their reserve by ensuring that ex-regulars retained a reserve liability: in pre-1914 Britain, generally seven years with the colours and five with the reserve, with variations for Guards, cavalry, and artillery. In Britain the militia, its rank and file recruited by ballot, survived throughout the 19th century, and was often used as a back door to a regular commission. Alongside the militia stood the Volunteers, raised to meet the threat of French invasion in the 1790s and revived since, notably with the invasion scare of the 1860s. The militia composition was similar to that of the regular army, with gentry as officers and men who were too poor to pay for a substitute, while the Volunteers were altogether more middle class. Mounted troops of *yeomanry had been raised during the *Napoleonic wars. Originally intended for home defence, they were increasingly used for internal security.

As part of the *Haldane reforms of the British army after the Second *Boer War the reserve forces were restructured, the Volunteers and Yeomanry into a Territorial Force (TF) intended primarily for home defence and the militia into a Special Reserve to provide drafts for the regular army.

(*cont. on page 770*)

religion and war

N its frequency, its conduct, and its consequences, warfare has always been a matter of great significance to the world's major religions, and the study of warfare in human history has often led to the conclusion that religious differences lie at the heart of many or most conflicts. There has been nothing approaching a consensus either among the faith traditions collectively, or within each one individually, as to how war should be viewed from a religious perspective. Many religions have a strong strand of *pacifism and at times have rejected and condemned war as spiritually misguided and morally wrong, but just as often have acknowledged that since war nevertheless takes place, the mere act of condemnation may be redundant, could open the faith tradition to the criticism that it prohibits the defence against evil and aggression, and may risk excluding moral and spiritual considerations from subsequent debate on war and its effects. This realization has drawn the various faith traditions into the more instrumental discussion of the rights and wrongs of the resort to war and its conduct. The development of Christian thinking on *just war offers a useful illustration.

War has not always been considered a problem, however. On many occasions war has been seen as an opportunity and has been actively promoted by religious and spiritual leaders. For example, in the 1970s Imam Khomeini of Iran looked forward to the success of the Islamic revolution in Iran as the first step in a holy 'war of conquest whose final goal is to make Koranic law supreme from one end of the earth to the other'. It was rhetoric of this nature, with its similarities to the medieval Christian *Crusades, which led to the growing fear in the West of aggressive 'Islamic fundamentalism'. And there have also been occasions when military commanders have found a space for religion in their armoury, either on spiritual grounds or for more pragmatic reasons. Philip II of Spain (1556–98) and leader of the Roman Catholic Counter-Reformation was convinced, throughout his campaigning life, that he was doing God's work and saw no distinction between religious and strategic goals. Ultimately, his religious zeal caused a loss of strategic judgement when he attempted to crush English Protestantism, and failed. Cromwell, parliamentarian general in the *English civil wars and then Lord Protector of the Commonwealth, was a devout Calvinist who believed profoundly in the involvement of divine providence in all that he did both as a soldier and as a politician.

The search for a single, synoptic view of the relationship between religion and war must be fruitless. What the world's major faith traditions do have in common is a profound debate on this subject, with conclusions and teachings which prove to be ambivalent to varying degrees. In Hinduism, the moral repudiation of actions which deliberately injure other living beings, is set alongside a socio-religious structure in which the warrior occupied a recognized class or estate, and had certain obligations to fulfil. The tension between non-violence on one hand and the warrior's duty to fight on the other is explored in the *Bhagavadgita*, Hinduism's most important sacred text. Here, the Lord Krishna teaches the warrior Arjuna that a devout man is one who is 'without hatred for any creature, friendly and compassionate', and who 'does not afflict the world'. But in the same text, Krishna advises Arjuna to fight because it is his inherent duty to fight, and that in so doing he will be acting as God's instrument: 'Recognising your inherent duty, you must not shrink from it. For there is nothing better for a warrior than a duty-bound war'. Other Hindu texts and codes contain writings which approximate closely to what was to become the *jus in bello* strand of Christian just-war thinking. Thus, the *Mahabharata* requires both proportion, in that it prohibits excessive injury to an enemy, and discrimination, in that it condemns the killing of the disabled, women, boys, and old men. The choice of weaponry was also a matter of concern: battles should not be fought with concealed weapons, or with weapons which are barbed or tipped with poison.

With its mendicant and ascetic traditions, Buddhism has always been associated with non-violence, non-confrontation, and the inner or spiritual life. However, Buddhism has also always engaged with the real world, and has placed clear emphasis on hierarchy and the political and moral ordering of society, and has always been conscious of the tendency to violence in international and national life. It would be wrong to describe Buddhism as a martial religion, nevertheless it is significant that one of the most ardent champions of Buddhism was the Indian Emperor Ashoka in the 3rd century BC, famed for his conquest of much of the Indian subcontinent. In the 20th century, Buddhism became closely and often militarily involved in resistance to colonial domination and imperialism in such countries as Sri Lanka, Burma (Myanmar), and Vietnam. Zen Buddhism, the variant of Buddhism introduced into Japan in the 7th century, saw its role, in part, to help defend the state and teach the martial arts. *Bushido, the code of conduct of the *samurai warrior class, reflected most closely the relationship between Zen spirituality and the Japanese martial spirit.

In the Judaic tradition, the martial connection is especially strong. Yahveh, the God of the Israelites who revealed his name to Moses, was Yahveh Sabaoth, the God of armies. The God of Moses was both martial and partial, siding with his chosen people in their great conflicts. The Old Testament offers plenty of apocalyptic and warlike visions, and called for crusades against the heathen. It is hardly surprising, therefore, that *milmahah* (Hebrew, war) occurs more than 300 times in the Old Testament account of God's involvement with his chosen people the Jews. Yet, awesome and magnificent though he was, Yahveh was also the God of all creation who demanded restraint even in crusades against the heathen. In Deuteronomy, Israelite soldiers are instructed that while they may eat fruit from captured Canaanite orchards, they should not destroy the orchards, while in the Second Book of Kings, the Israelites are urged to care for their prisoners rather than slaughter them.

Beginning in northern India in the late 15th century, *Sikhism combined a tendency towards pacifism, mysticism, and asceticism as found in the teachings of the first guru, Nanak, with a more worldly and martial approach. In the early 17th century, the sixth guru, Hargobind, threatened by Moghul authorities, sought refuge in the mountains where he learned the skills of hunting and warfare, and thereafter became both a spiritual and a military leader. The synthesis of spiritual and military leadership was perfected by the tenth and final guru, Gobind Singh, who is known to Sikhs as the 'soldier-saint'.

Having begun as an absolutely pacifist religion, early in the 4th century Christianity began to take on a more militant and activist character. Christianity's contribution to thinking about warfare was twofold and in certain respects self-contradictory: on the one hand the early and medieval Christian Church developed doctrines of restraint and discrimination, while on the other hand the brutal and bloody crusade became the preferred means by which to spread the faith and punish non-believers. Some historians have also argued that the Christian Crusades were little more than early demonstrations of the European tendency to hegemony and imperialism. But for their part, the crusaders seem to have been convinced that they had God on their side. The First Crusade, proclaimed by Pope Urban II in 1095, had as its holy objective the liberation of *Jerusalem and was at one point directly assisted in battle by a divine cavalry force.

The Crusades brought Christianity into a direct conflict with Islam, though not for the first time. The prophet Muhammad was a successful military commander and Islam had been spread by the sword, including the conquest of Spain at the beginning of the 8th century. A religious war by Muslims against unbelievers is called a *jihad. Those who died in the service of the one God would go straight to paradise. It was a simple doctrine, and similar to the Christian view. Whereas restraints then applied in war between Christians, or between Muslims, there was less in war between Christian and Muslim. Yet in spite of the fanatical beliefs of both sides, there were examples of restraint and even of chivalry in the Crusades. This must be put down to the natural respect which soldiers have for brave and competent opponents, which may override uncompromising religious attitudes. The Crusades also provided many examples of Christian fighting against Christian. The schism between eastern and western Christendom was often replicated in friction between crusaders and the Byzantine authorities, and on their way to the Middle East the crusaders sacked Constantinople. Crusades were also mounted against east European peoples, some of whom were still pagan, but some of whom, including the Russians, were Christian orthodox. The Teutonic Knights—a medieval *military monastic order—went from the Holy Land to a mission of pacification and conversion in the region. The split between Shi'a and Sunni Muslim, leading to the establishment of Shi'ism as state religion in Persia in 1512, provided a similar division within Islam. The hatred of Shi'a for Sunni found its most violent expression in the wars between Persia and its neighbours, and especially in the 1980–8 *Iran–Iraq war.

However, in Europe and the Middle East religion, as a motive for war, was also inextricably entwined with politics and national self-interest. When combatants were of exactly the same faith, as in the 14th- and 15th-century wars between England and France, they could be conducted according to Christian rules. The *Hussites, on the other hand, who broke away from the Holy Roman Empire in both political and religious senses, were heretics. After Martin Luther nailed his theses to a church door in 1520, beginning the Reformation, the scene was set for new levels of barbarism. The Counter-Reformation—the Catholic reaction—got going in the 1560s, giving rise to orders like those to the Duke of *Alba to kill every Protestant in the Netherlands and to the Massacre of St Bartholomew in France (see FRENCH WARS OF RELIGION).

The struggle between Reformation and Counter-Reformation was compounded by the strengthening of the nation state, and it is impossible to separate the two in the wars of 16th- and 17th-century Europe. This explosive combination climaxed in the *Thirty Years War which was both a religious war and a war between ambitious nation states. The Peace of Westphalia which ended it tried to prevent wars being waged for religious purposes only on the principle of 'cuius regio, eius religio' (their religion is that of their ruler). This principle, which underlines the reluctance, until recently, to interfere in the internal affairs of nation states, was never fully respected. Furthermore, it did nothing to prevent religion being a cause of civil wars.

Nevertheless, religion largely ceased to be a cause of interstate conflict in western Europe in the 18th century. In the 20th century the rise of communism and its establishment in Russia, then China and Vietnam, had similar effects to that of a new, militant religion, although in theory communist states rejected the idea of exporting communism by force of arms. The establishment of the state of Israel—a Jewish state in the middle of Muslim states—also led to a series of wars which, while primarily secular in their motivation—the Israelis were seen as occupying land which belonged to Arabs—inevitably had a religious element. Religion also played its part in the long-running conflict in Ireland (see IRISH REBELLIONS), although, not surprisingly, it became woven into a deeper social and political dispute in which Catholicism or Protestantism seemed little more than a tribal marking.

The end of the *Cold War in 1989 brought about a resurgence in religious conflicts, though again, primarily internal. The so-called 'ethnic' conflicts in the Balkans (see YUGOSLAVIA, OPERATIONS IN FORMER) are not really ethnic, since most of those involved are Slavs, but religious. The Bosnian Muslims, who originally converted to Islam to work with their Turkish overlords, are distinguished from the Catholic Croats and the Orthodox Serbs by religion more than blood. Muslims from more militantly Islamic countries such as Afghanistan came to help, in small numbers. But in the case of the expulsion of Kosovar Albanians (Muslims), from the former Yugoslavia in 1999, Muslim countries such as Turkey and Saudi Arabia expressed little interest or concern and it was left to the infidels to come to their rescue. As usual, religious considerations could not be separated from political and strategic interests.

PC/HEB

Despite familiar complaints that part-timers could not master relevant skills—and familiar problems in doing so—the TF, although understrength and part-trained, put the first of its units into the field in October 1914 and by the end of the year the British Expeditionary Force's (BEF) C-in-C was to admit: 'We could not have held the line without them.' The TF was revived as the Territorial Army (TA) after the war, merged with the regular army during WW II, re-established its identity afterwards, and remains a valuable part of the defence establishment.

In the USA the National Guard sprang from the militia, whose ethos took some time to recover after the *American civil war, and in 1877 the Guard was ill-prepared to confront the nationwide strike. A period of revival followed: state militia codes were revised between 1881 and 1892 and the National Guard Association was formed to lobby Congress in 1879. By the early 1890s the Guard was over 100,000 strong, and was widely used during industrial disputes. When America entered WW I she introduced conscription, but already had 185,000 National Guardsmen available to reinforce her 133,000 Regulars. Since then the Guard, under state control until federalized, has retained a concern with internal security and disaster relief, but has also produced units which played a distinguished part in WW II and the *Gulf war.

Nations with conscription use ex-conscripts to provide their reserve, and in a state like Israel, where the necessity for military service is widely understood, the system has generally worked well. Those without it find some reservists from their ex-regulars, but also maintain a volunteer reserve. The latter is subject to national idiosyncrasy: the USA, for instance, has a National Guard and a US Army Reserve, the latter distinct from the reserve obligation of ex-regulars. There are, in addition, reserves, regular and volunteer, for the other services. Many of the old tensions remain. Volunteer reserves often enjoy powerful political support, springing from their strong community links, which themselves help bind armed forces to the society they protect. They may find their skills and motivation assailed by regulars on the one hand and humorists on the other. However, non-conscript armies cannot fight major wars without them, and forget this at their peril.

RH

Reserve Officers Training Corps (ROTC) is a programme that provides college-trained officers for active duty branches of the US military services and for the reserve components. It offers military science courses at American private and state colleges and universities.

ROTC is more than a college programme. It is a tradition dating back over 175 years. The first civilian institution of higher learning in the USA to actually incorporate military *education into its curriculum was the American Literary, Scientific, and Military Academy—now Norwich University in Vermont. Capt Alden Partridge, former superintendent of the US Military Academy at *West Point, founded the school in 1819 at Norwich. Modern ROTC traces its heritage back to this institution, which became the prototype for all ROTC training. ROTC was formally established by the US National Defense Act of 1916.

ROTC programmes exist to commission college-educated officers into the army, air force, navy, and Marine Corps in sufficient numbers to meet the requirements of these services. In fact, it is the single largest source of officers for the US Armed Forces today. ROTC's objectives are to provide an understanding of the principles of military, aerospace, and naval science; to develop comprehension of associated professional knowledge; to build attitudes of integrity, honour, and individual responsibility; and to encourage appreciation of national security. College students earn college credit for ROTC courses. ROTC is an elective course of study, taken in conjunction with any academic major that, upon graduation, leads to a reserve commission as a second lieutenant in the army, air force, or Marine Corps or an ensign in the navy.

The ROTC programme consists of two parts: the Basic Course and Advanced Course. The Basic Course is usually taken in the first two years of college and requires no military obligation by the student unless the military has provided the student a scholarship. Scholarship students receive tuition fees, books, uniforms, and a stipend. The Advanced Course is designed for leadership development, organization and management, tactics, ethics, and professionalism. There is a requirement for a summer camp of six weeks between the junior and senior year of college conducted at a military post, camp, or station. Those enrolled in the Advanced Course receive $150 per month for subsistence, and their uniforms and military textbooks are also furnished. Once the Advanced Course is completed and a college degree obtained, the student is commissioned as an officer and required to serve a period on active duty or in one of the reserve components.

The army and air force also offer a Junior ROTC-level programme, which teaches self-reliance, self-discipline, and citizenship training in US high schools.   DMJ

Crocker, Lawrence P., *Army Officer's Guide* (47th edn., Harrisburg, Pa., 1996).

---

resistance movements (WW II) Resistance activities encompass a wide range of activities against an occupying army, from the traditional *guerrilla tactics of harassment, sabotage, and ambushes, to the writing, printing, and distribution of underground *propaganda and the passive resistance of factory go-slows and non co-operation. Such opposition can also take the form of moral and intellectual resistance, not just against an occupying power, but against one's own government, as in the case of citizens in Nazi Germany. Although the term is associated commonly with the activities of WW II groups, acts of resistance have been recorded through history. The Jews resisted Roman rule in the first and second centuries AD, while *Jacobites in Britain and various groups in Revolutionary France practised active and passive resistance. Spaniard resistance to Napoleonic rule in the Peninsula campaign gave birth to the word *guerrilla* itself, and similar movements sprang up among militant Zionists in pre- and post-WW II Palestine, while activities against the communist regimes of *Cold War eastern Europe also fall into this category.

With this long-established pedigree, it was not surprising that the Nazi regime found itself at the receiving end of resistance activities in mainland Europe. Eastern and western European resistance movements differed in character and, until the invasion of the USSR in June 1941, communist resistants outside the USSR were torn between loyalty to the Moscow line (there was a Nazi-Soviet non-aggression pact (the Molotov-Ribbentrop pact) in force until broken by *BARBAROSSA) and patriotism to their own invaded homelands. This helps explain, for example, the early lack of co-operation between different groups in France, and the lingering suspicion between them throughout and after the war. Eastern European movements tended to reflect the Soviet creed of the mass-mobilization of the people, and were violent in character from the start. Large *partisan bands operated behind German lines, the term spreading to

*Tito's men in Yugoslavia, who became known as Partisans. German reprisals against them were particularly vicious, and were often implemented by locally recruited units, with their own ethnic and other private scores to settle. Polish resistance culminated in the heroic but doomed *Warsaw uprising of August 1944.

In western Europe, much initially spontaneous resistance activity came to be co-ordinated through Britain and the *SOE and the later the American *OSS, who supplied arms, equipment, and radio operators. The SOE was conceived by *Churchill as a means of hitting back at the Germans, and resistance movements established invaluable escape-chains enabling shot-down Allied airmen to evade capture and return to the United Kingdom and resume their war. In southern France organized groups were known as the Maquis, originally composed mainly of young men avoiding compulsory labour service in Germany. Two major resistance activities were incorporated into the planning for the invasion of *Normandy in June 1944. The first was the provision of intelligence about German defences (and later about V-weapon sites), the second was the disabling of communications, sabotaging railways, and generally delaying the movement of reinforcements and supplies to the Normandy region. These activities certainly saved the lives of many civilians who would otherwise have been injured in bombing raids, but cost the lives of others shot in reprisal or deported to Germany (some 90,000 French men and women died in this way). The French Resistance army (FFI) also liberated their capital, Paris, before the arrival of regular (French) troops, and the Belgian underground similarly managed to take over Antwerp and prevent the destruction of its port—a valuable strategic resource—in early September 1944, as Canadian troops drew near. Belgium and Denmark also established popular underground newspapers, while Danish groups were particularly successful at aiding their own Jewish community to escape.

The terrain and dense settlement in Holland prevented the operation of a Maquis, as in France, but an underground newspaper (*Je Maintiendrai*) was especially successful, and the Protestant and Catholic Churches sponsored much passive resistance in the form of general strikes. Some workers and ex-servicemen simply went into a perpetual underground existence for the duration (known as 'submarines'), but the Dutch resistance was infiltrated by the *Abwehr and thus hampered until late 1943. Dutch and Norwegian resistance was focused by loyalty to their monarchs, who actively encouraged revolt. In Norway there was widespread passive non-co-operation particularly against Quisling's collaborators, and active SOE-sponsored sabotage. The Norwegian group which sabotaged the hydroelectric plant at Rjukan and then sank a ferry carrying heavy water (essential for Germany's atomic weapons programme) may possibly have saved London from joining *Hiroshima and Nagasaki on the short list of cities destroyed by an atomic bomb.

In Greece as in Yugoslavia, a small communist underground had operated prior to WW II, in opposition to the monarchy, so it was already organized (if not well equipped) when the Germans invaded in 1941. The monarchist, republican (EDES), and communist (ELAS) resistance movements rarely co-operated, though when they did, such as in the SOE-co-ordinated destruction of a viaduct carrying the Salonika–Athens railway (November 1942), the results were spectacular. However, by the war's end a bitter civil war had broken out between the two. The German occupation of Greece and northern Italy (after the September 1943 armistice) was characterized by some vicious anti-partisan reprisals by regular German formations, including the army, and assorted Kriegsmarine and Luftwaffe ground troops, giving the lie to the belief that such acts were perpetrated exclusively by the Field Police, *SS, SD (Sicherheitsdienst), or Gestapo. Aided by geography, the Balkan resistance movements in Italy, Greece, and Yugoslavia were some of the strongest in Europe, though all were reliant on the SOE for arms and, to a degree, co-ordination. In each of these three countries, local communist groups saw military resistance as a route to peacetime power, with resultant troubles in 1945. In Yugoslavia over one million died, underlining the bitter fratricidal strife between different resistance, collaborationist, and ethnic movements, while 40,000 Italians died as a result of resistance activities or in reprisals.

Many communists readily formed resistance movements in 1940–1, some already living off the land, leading the life of outlaws. In the USSR, such partisan bands (perhaps numbering as many as 250,000 to 500,000) were treated cautiously by *Stalin, who perceived them (probably correctly) as a political threat, and quickly placed them under NKVD (People's Commissariat for Internal Affairs) control, attaching political commissars to each formation. They aided the regular forces in the collection of intelligence, but were not necessarily supplied by the native population who, for example in the Ukraine, welcomed German liberation from Soviet oppression. Germany's failure to capitalize on this must be accounted a major strategic error.

There was much intellectual resistance to Nazism within Germany (the Widerstand), but the movements were scattered, uncoordinated, and received no aid from Britain. A 'White Rose' student movement suffered the execution of its leaders, while groups within the Protestant clergy under Dietrich Bönhoffer, the Abwehr under *Canaris and Hans Oster, the Foreign Office with Ülrich von Hassell, and civilian politicians such as Karl Gördler, a former mayor of Leipzig, all maintained anti-Nazi sympathies. Their only major activity was the bomb plot of 20 July 1944, led by Count Claus von Stauffenberg, Ludwig Beck, and other senior officers of the Reserve Army, which failed because a table-leg fortuitously deflected the blast from Stauffenberg's bomb away from *Hitler. The Gestapo then used this as an excuse to eliminate all known opponents to the regime

(and some of their families), whether implicated in the July plot or not. Perhaps 5,000 perished in this way, among them men and women who once believed that Hitler might lead Germany to greatness rather than squalor and defeat. As Jürgen Förster has written: 'The men, women, and adolescents of the resistance saved the honour of the German people, but their courage should no longer be used as an alibi for the compliant attitude of the great majority.'

APC-A

Förster, Jürgen, et al., 'Germany', in *The Oxford Companion to the Second World War* (Oxford, 1995).

reveille (from Fr.: *reveillez*, wake up, you). Generations of soldiers have been roused reluctantly from the mists of sleep by reveille, the signal by drum, bugle, or human voice to troops that it is time to rise. First recorded in English usage in 1644, it was particularly relevant in *bivouacs. It has now become a generic term in English-speaking armies for 'get your . . . out of bed'.

APC-A

Rezonville/Gravelotte, battles of (1870), the decisive engagements of the *Franco-Prussian war. They arose as Marshal *Bazaine's Army of the Rhine, over 160,000 strong, retreated through Metz and across the Moselle towards Châlons, where the defeated French right wing was being reconstituted. Two German armies were involved, Steinmetz's First, advancing on Metz, and Prince Frederick Charles's Second, moving to its south.

On 16 August most of Bazaine's force was ready to move off for Verdun. Forton's cavalry division was at Mars la Tour and Vionville, with Frossard's II and *Canrobert's VI Corps around Rezonville. Le Boeuf's III Corps was at Verneville and the Guard at Gravelotte, while Ladmirault's IV Corps marched up from Metz. Bazaine's sloth confused *Moltke 'the Elder', the German COS. The right wing of Second Army—Rheinbaben's cavalry at Puxieux, Voigts-Rhetz's X Corps at Thiaucourt, and Alvensleben's III Corps, marching up from Gorze—had no idea that it faced the main French force. Rheinbaben shelled Forton out of Mars la Tour at about 09.00, but when Alvensleben arrived he realized what he was dealing with. Recognizing that only determined action would deter an attack, he engaged II Corps, taking Flavigny and Vionville, but was soon fought to a standstill.

Early in the afternoon Alvensleben sent Bredow's cavalry brigade charging north of the Verdun road. It overran VI Corps' gun-line, and helped assert moral superiority over Bazaine. Yet French infantry made good progress towards Verdun, and it was more Bazaine's failure to inspire his corps commanders than German resistance that stopped them. A cavalry mêlée north of Mars la Tour ended the day. The Germans lost almost 16,000 men to almost 14,000 French, but cut the Verdun road. Bazaine, worried about ammunition shortages, ordered his exasperated men to fall back to restock.

The French adopted a strong position above Gravelotte, with II and III Corps to the south, IV in the centre, VI in the north at Saint-Privat, and the Guard in reserve. On the 18th Moltke sent Second Army to the north while First Army pushed in from Gravelotte. Steinmetz's assault was a bloody failure, and further north the Prussian Guard, attacking VI Corps, lost over 8,000 men in an early demonstration of the effectiveness of the *breech-loading rifle in defence. Bazaine neither counter-attacked the shaken First Army, nor committed the Guard in time to reinforce Canrobert, eventually outflanked by the Saxon Corps. When Canrobert's men broke they took the Guard with them, and Bazaine had to retire on Metz. The Germans lost over 20,000 and the French at least 12,000 men, but the battle sealed Bazaine's fate: he capitulated in October.   RH

Rhineland, battle of

Rhineland, battle of (1945), the name given to a series of battles fought by the Allied armies to capture terrain up to the west bank of the Rhine river, from 8 February until the crossings of mid-March 1945. In the northern sector, also known as the Reichswald battle, *Montgomery planned to seize the land ahead by a pincer movement, advancing from the line of the Roer river westwards towards the Rhine. VERITABLE began on 8 February with the most concentrated British-Canadian artillery barrage of the war: 6,000 tons of shells were fired in the first 24 hours to support the advance of II Canadian Corps moving south-east, while XVI US Corps of Simpson's Ninth Army moved north-east to meet it. Horrocks's British XXX Corps held the front between the two, but the Germans breached local dykes to create large flooded areas, and with foul weather, notoriously difficult terrain, and the stiffening resistance of the German First Parachute Army of Army Group B, the Allied advance was stalled.

To the south, fierce German resistance at Düren and Jülich on the Roer, and the use of floodwater from the Schwammenauel dam delayed the progress of Simpson's Ninth and Hodges's First US Armies. By 23 February the water levels had subsided sufficiently for the Americans to resume, and the Canadian-American pincers in the north closed at Geldern on 3 March. By 7 March all troops had come up to the west bank of the Rhine, and were preparing to cross. Elements of the eight German divisions under *Model in Army Group B fought in the Rhineland battle, which was characterized by its unfriendly weather and hard terrain, and suffered about 45,000 killed, wounded, or captured, while Allied losses were 15,000.   APC-A

Rhodes, sieges of

Rhodes, sieges of (1480–1 and 1522). The largest of the Dodecanese islands in the eastern Aegean Sea, Rhodes was one of the central strategic points during the long series of

wars between the Ottoman *Turk empire and other Mediterranean powers.

The first siege of Rhodes (1480–1) followed the revival of the Ottoman empire under the reign of Muhammad II (1451–81, 'the Conqueror'). The capture of *Constantinople in 1453 saw the end of the Byzantine empire and the ascendancy of the Turkish galley fleet over the Venetian and Genoese in the Aegean. This superiority allowed the Ottomans to seize islands and other coastal colonies one by one and helped ensure their control over areas of southern Europe and the Levant. The nature of galley warfare in the Mediterranean at this time put a premium on key strategic bases, one of which was Rhodes. Rhodes had been a bulwark for Christendom against the Turks since its capture by the *military monastic order of the Knights of St John (Hospitallers) in 1310. Muhammad II began the siege of Rhodes in 1480. The Hospitallers held out until the following year when the Ottomans were ultimately driven off with heavy loss of life. Muhammad's death was followed by the reign of Bayazid II (1481–1512). Bayazid's reign began with a civil war against his younger brother, Djem, who took refuge on Rhodes, and ended with him being forced to abdicate by his son Selim who had just won another civil war over his two brothers. Selim was possibly the greatest military practitioner of the Ottoman sultans and although he died preparing for another expedition against Rhodes, he concentrated his campaigns in the east.

Selim's son and heir, *Suleiman 'the Magnificent', continued his father's plans and laid siege to Rhodes in 1522. By this date the island's defences were probably unmatched anywhere in the world. The port was guarded by strong tower forts at the entrance to the harbour. Entry by sea was further complicated by huge bronze chains. The city itself was defended by a new type of bastion fortress, with a broad ditch and a glacis; in some places there were two interior walls. The Grand Master Phillip Villiers de L'Isle Adam commanded some 700 Knights, well-placed artillery which was to prove devastating, and some 6,000 auxiliary cavalry, *pikemen, arquebusiers, and marines.

Suleiman landed at the end of June with an army of 100,000 and a month later the siege opened with an artillery duel under which were conducted extremely hazardous mining operations. The Knights had the advantage of pre-ranged targets but the engineers managed to breach the wall in several places. During September and November the Ottomans repeatedly attacked the breaches but were repulsed with terrible losses. The defenders were losing irreplaceable men and were running short of powder. Suleiman offered honourable terms of *capitulation but was rebuffed and by the middle of December the Turks had penetrated the fortress. Negotiations resumed on 20 December and honourable terms of evacuation were agreed. Only 180 Christian knights and 1,500 other troops were left, while Suleiman had lost as much as half his army.   JR-W

Rhodesia war (1965–79). Ian Smith, Rhodesia's PM, announced his country's Unilateral Declaration of Independence (UDI) from Great Britain on 11 November 1965. The former British colony of Southern Rhodesia rejected British moves towards majority rule, citing its existing semi-autonomy dating back to the country's foundation by the explorer and entrepreneur after which it was named, Cecil Rhodes.

With a total area of 150,873 square miles (390,746 km) Rhodesia (now Zimbabwe) is a landlocked country in southern Africa, sharing its borders with Zambia (north-west), Mozambique (north-east and east), Botswana (west and south-west), and South Africa (south). The most prominent geophysical feature is the Highveld, the great plateau of southern Africa running north-east to south-west with an average elevation of 5,000 feet (1,524 metres). Following the UDI the country's white minority (270,000) withheld political power from the black majority (5,400,000) despite economic sanctions imposed by Britain, the USA, and most African nations. On 9 May 1968 the UN Security Council ordered a trade embargo on Rhodesia, and on 2 March 1970 Rhodesia declared itself a republic, thus precipitating a war with black nationalist groups seeking independence under majority rule. Rhodesia remained a republic until the multi-party elections of April 1980 when Rhodesia formally became the independent Republic of Zimbabwe.

A rich country in terms of mineral deposits, which elicited clandestine multi-national corporate support especially during the early years, Rhodesia's main problem centred on providing manpower to police rural and border areas from *guerrilla incursion. Pressured by Britain, Smith's government released nationalist leaders, most notably Robert Mugabe and Joshua Nkomo who had been interned within Rhodesia for ten years. Mugabe and Nkomo led the Zimbabwe African National Union (ZANU) and the Zimbabwe African People's Union (ZAPU) respectively. Together these political parties combined to form the Patriotic Front (PF) in exile in Zambia, where they established guerrilla training camps from which they mounted operations into Rhodesia.

As guerrilla activity increased inside its borders, Smith's Rhodesian Front (RF) security forces conducted a *counter-insurgency campaign, initially with great success. The first proper ZANU incursion was mounted from Zambia with just fourteen guerrillas in April 1965. In August 1966 a combined force of 90 ZAPU and ANC (African National Congress) insurgents deployed to Rhodesia, followed by a further two groups (of 123 and 91) over the next year. None of these groups met with anything more than limited success and by the end of 1968 had lost 160 killed against 12 from the security forces.

However, Rhodesia's manpower resources were limited. In 1969 the army's strength stood at 4,600 regular troops, of which over 1,000 were black, mostly belonging to the Rhodesian African Rifles (RAR). These forces were backed up by 6,400 police regulars, both black and white, known somewhat confusingly as the British South Africa Police (BSAP). Over the next ten years these figures increased but not commensurate with the rise in guerrilla numbers. Despite national service and the annual call-up of reservists (both involving whites only) the Rhodesian government remained short of men for the remainder of the war.

In the face of increased external pressure and the lessening of support from South Africa, Smith attempted a coalition government with the black moderate Bishop Muzorewa. When this failed to attract popular support the only viable option was a British-brokered agreement with the PF, effected in London and signed on 21 December 1979. Britain resumed temporary control, overseeing open elections and *demobilization, resulting in a ZANU political victory in February and independence for Zimbabwe on 17 April 1980.

PMacD

Richard I 'the Lionheart', King of England (1157–99), whose equestrian statue stands outside the Houses of Parliament of a country he cared little about, is one of the more remarkable examples of the triumph of *propaganda over reality. He was a virtual parricide, a profligate monarch, a faithless vassal, a rancorous ally, and a devoted homosexual, yet the balladeers made him into the *beau ideal* of *knighthood, complete with all the trappings of courtly love and nobility of spirit. He doomed the Angevin empire in France by performing *feudal homage for all the Angevin holdings in France, including Normandy, to Philip II (Augustus) in 1188 to enlist his support in his civil war against his father, Henry II. Upon assuming the throne of England a year later, he sold off his considerable patrimony at discount prices (including the sale of the shrievalty of Nottingham that the Robin Hood myth blames on his brother John) in order to finance his participation in the Third *Crusade. Pausing only to mortally offend the Holy Roman Emperor Henry VI by recognizing a rival claimant to the throne of Sicily, he conquered Cyprus to establish a logistics base and then took Acre (1191) along with Leopold V of Austria and Philip Augustus, both of whom he insulted and threatened. The latter went home to set in motion the campaign that ended in the Angevin loss of *Normandy, while the former was to seize him on his way back from the Crusade in late 1192 and hand him over to Henry VI, who held him for a swingeing ransom (and compelled him to do feudal homage even for England) until early 1194.

During 1191–2 he appears to have done most things right militarily, in particular by restraining the knights of his heterogenous army and so inflicting a rare defeat in a marching engagement on the great *Saladin at *Arsuf. Without first bothering to conquer the city, the cream of European knighthood fell to murderous dispute among themselves as to who should be the king of Jerusalem, and although it seems he did not order the murder of Conrad of Montferrat in order to make way for his own candidate, the German contingent thought he had. It was therefore a rare act of prudence on his part to conclude an armistice with Saladin and set out on the return journey rendered perilous by his blood-feuds with all whose lands he might have to cross. We can only be sure that he was in England for two months as an adult, on the occasions of his first and second coronations, the second being necessary to reaffirm the rights voided by his homage to Henry VI. After five years fighting his (now) liege lord Philip Augustus, he was killed by an archer while besieging the castle of Châlus in order to obtain a hoard of gold reputed to have been dug up by a local peasant.   HEB

Richelieu, Armand Jean du Plessis, Cardinal-Duc de (1585–1643), the greatest of a series of clerical first ministers who organized the *war finances of the French kings. He dominated French foreign and military policy under Louis XIII from 1624 until his death, but his preference lay in diplomacy and intrigue rather than war. In his *Political Testament* he advocated negotiations 'everywhere without cease, openly and secretly'. In 1624 he arranged the Treaty of Compiègne with the Dutch, and in 1625 he arranged the marriage of Charles I of England to the French Princess Henrietta Maria, who is said to have been influential in the king's alleged secret conversion to Roman Catholicism and much of his subsequent folly.

In Germany Richelieu fomented rivalry between the German princes and the emperor at the Diet of Ratisbon in 1630, and persuaded *Gustavus Adolphus of Sweden to intervene militarily after 1631 with a large subsidy. He also seriously undermined the position and credibility of *Wallenstein and possibly helped arrange for his assassination. In the continuing saga of Franco-Habsburg rivalry it seemed that he had discovered the secret of success by using surrogates to fight the wars, while French military forces concentrated on internal security and were only committed abroad in peripheral theatres such as the Valtelline in northern Italy.

From 1635 events compelled him to get more directly involved in the *Thirty Years War before adequate preparation had been made, following the defeat of the Swedes at Nördlingen the year before and the Peace of Prague between Saxony and the empire. France suffered some serious reverses when the Spanish invaded in 1636, but Richelieu put in hand the organization that eventually bore fruit in one of the turning points in military history, the victory of *Rocroi which he did not live to see.   TM

---

ricochet Although the etymology of this French word is unknown, the concept is familiar to all who have seen any film involving firearms. In such films, the rebounding of a projectile from any suitable surface, such as a wall, water, or armour plating, leads to the round missing its intended target and noisily departing the scene. In the reality of combat, the situation differs. The ricochet's result is indiscriminate and unpredictable, placing all in close proximity in danger. For those involved in internal security operations, a ricochet striking an innocent bystander can have major political consequences. This has led to the development of special rounds which are designed to break up on contact with an unyielding surface.

In spite of its hazards, ricochet is not without value. It was used in both field and siege operations to bounce cannon balls through an enemy's tightly packed ranks or along a defended rampart, enhancing their effect. The latter technique seems first to have been employed by Vauban in 1688. The practice of low-level skip bombing, particularly employed in attacks on shipping during WW II, relied upon ricochet for its effect. The bomb would be dropped ahead of the target and then ricochet from the surface into it. The technique simplified bomb aiming, and allowed alternative attack profiles to be flown by aircrew. Then again, the bomb might detonate under the aircraft and destroy it. In general ricochet is an element of combat which all participants would be safer without.   DJJ

Ridgway, Gen Matthew Bunker (1895–1993), US airborne forces leader and UN commander in Korea. *West Point-educated Ridgway missed service in WW I and held a series of high profile staff jobs during the inter-war years under *George Marshall. His opportunity came in 1943, when he was appointed to plan the US airborne assault on *Sicily in July that year, which sustained high losses, but valuable lessons were learned for the *Normandy campaign. Succeeding *Bradley as commander of the 82nd Airborne Division, Ridgway jumped with his division on the eve of 6 June 1944 over Normandy, and under him the 82nd came to regard itself as a hard-fighting élite. He later commanded US XVIII Airborne Corps in the *Arnhem operation and in the battle of the *Bulge. Stagnating in Washington, in December 1950 he found himself overnight in command of all UN ground troops in *Korea after his predecessor, Walker, was killed in a traffic accident. He rallied the UN forces whose morale was at a low ebb following a bitter winter and heavy casualties, and four months later, was selected to replace MacArthur as Supreme Commander Far East, after the latter had been sacked by *Truman for his public statements in favour of attacking the Chinese mainland. Ridgway saw this episode as 'a clash of wills bordering on insubordination' and did his job without presuming to influence policy. In 1952 he succeeded *Eisenhower as SACEUR (Supreme Allied Commander Europe), and then served as US army COS 1953–5. He found himself continually at odds with Pres Eisenhower over military cuts and was happy to retire. A soldier's soldier, he liked to be photographed in a combat jacket festooned with *grenades and found his four-star commands frustrating.   APC-A

Riel's rebellions (1870, 1885), uprisings by the Métis against the encroachment of English-speaking settlers on their lands. Their leader was Louis Riel (1844–85), a Méti from Manitoba. During the 19th century the Métis, of mixed French and Canadian Indian descent, had developed a vigorous national identity and distinctive culture. They particularly resented the expansionist aspirations of the Canadian government. In 1870 Riel led the Métis in a rebellion against the incorporation of Manitoba into Canada. It was quickly suppressed and Riel was forced to flee to the USA.

Riel remained politically active and upon his return home even managed to be elected to the Canadian House of Commons. He continued to campaign for the rights of the Métis. Frustrated by the Federal government's lack of interest, the increasingly unstable and religiously fanatic Riel decided to rebel again. On 19 March 1885 at Saint-Laurent he formed a provisional government, although Riel himself was not a member, as this would have been inappropriate to his role as prophet by divine sanction. The charismatic Riel, however, was the undisputed leader of the rebellion.

The first serious clash occurred when 300 Métis under Riel's military leader, Gabriel Dumont, encountered 100 men of the North-West Mounted Police. Their commander, Superintendent Leif Crozier, impetuously attacked the Métis who held the higher ground and were well protected by natural cover. He lost twelve men killed and eleven wounded and would have probably been annihilated had Riel not ordered his men to stop fighting.

Where the rebellion failed was in Riel's inability to recruit support from various Native American groups. Although some Native Americans such as those led by Wandering Spirit undertook occasional acts of violence, such as his attack on the town of Frog Lake on 2 April, the chronic factionalism among them and lack of co-ordination meant they made little contribution to Riel's cause. The attack on Frog Lake provoked the Canadian government into action. Maj Gen Frederick Middleton marched with 800 men on Riel's capital at Batoche. While Dumont wanted to conduct a guerrilla campaign, Riel refused, deciding to stand and fight with the 175–200 men available to him. Middleton won a convincing victory on 9 May and Riel surrendered six days later. He was tried in Regina in front of a hostile jury and despite his evident mental illness, he was found guilty of treason, sentenced to death, and hanged on 16 November.   MCM

---

rifle Makers of arrows and throwers of spears had early identified the stability which spin imparts to a fired or hurled projectile. Arrow fletchers fixed their split goose feathers at a slight angle to the arrow shaft and Roman *pilum* throwers discovered that if they wound a cord around the shaft and threw the *pilum* with a flick of the cord at the moment it left the hand, it flew truer. Early firearms fired darts which were little more than short arrows and which probably spun as they flew and so, from the earliest days of firearms, constant experiments were made in how to impart spin to the *bullet in order to make it fly true. Spiral grooving from breech to muzzle was developed as the solution in the Germanic world at the end of the 15th century but opinions remain divided as to whether it was invented in Vienna, in Nuremberg, or in Leipzig; it became called 'rifling' from the Low German word *riffel*, meaning a groove, and its English pronunciation derives from the Flemish *riffel*, with the same meaning. Rifles, generally using the *wheel-lock system, were developed in Germany, Austria, Scandinavia, and Switzerland during the 16th century for sporting purposes, those areas being rich in the types of large game hunted at comparatively long distance.

Military use of rifles was attempted and experimented with during the 17th century but not on any large scale. Corps and bodies of riflemen appeared in Denmark in 1611, in some German states by mid-century, and in France under both Louis XIII and *Louis XIV. The results were not so remarkable that rifles were adopted by any state's army and there were sound and explicable reasons for this. Rifles were slower to load than muskets; their delicate and important rifling fouled more quickly than did the muskets' smooth bores, and thus not only rendered them little different from muskets after six or seven shots but also necessitated their detailed cleaning and resultant removal from action. They were expensive, compared to muskets, and they were less soldier-proof and thus more liable to damage in the hands of any but well-trained riflemen. Such arguments, essentially negative, conservative, and thus immediately attractive to many military minds, militated against the widespread military use of rifles until significantly into the 19th century.

The hunting use of rifles, especially in Germanic countries, continued and increased, as did the rifles' technology, throughout the 17th century and by 1700 such rifles had become known by contemporaries by the German word *Jäger*, meaning hunter. Significantly for the military history of the rifle, such weapons were exported to the American colonies, either alone or when their German or Swiss owners emigrated there, in the early 18th century. They developed, with inevitable local variations, into the American long rifles, of which the Pennsylvania school, centre of early German settlement in North America, was one of the best known. The typical European Jäger rifle was a short weapon with a large bore. It had an octagonal barrel of about 30 inches long with a calibre averaging .60 inch, deep multiple rifling, basic sights, a heavy—often intricately carved—wooden stock, and was usually fitted with a sling for carrying over the shoulder; it was accurate up to about

200 yards (183 metres) and its large ball had considerable stopping power against large game. Such weapons were arming corps of riflemen in most German states by the mid-18th century and in use in Scandinavia similarly. Rifles were experimented with in the British army during the *Seven Years War of 1756–63. It has been suggested that the earliest British units to use the Jäger rifle were drawn from Scots *Highlanders whose hunting traditions were not dissimilar to those in the mountains of Switzerland.

The *American independence war was the first in which rifles were used to any significant effect and, although both sides possessed rifles, the combination of the American long rifles and their users' sniping tactics had repeated and devastating effects on the battlefield. Although the lessons learned in America were quickly forgotten by the British, they were rapidly relearned during the twenty years of wars with France between 1793 and 1815 and all combatant states in those wars utilized rifles and skirmishing tactics. During the battle of New Orleans in 1814 the British suffered again at the hands of accurate American sharpshooters with whom their skirmishers, armed with equally good rifles, could not cope. The USA had adopted a military rifle in 1803, a few years after the *Baker rifle had been adopted for the use of the newly raised British Corps of Riflemen, and both the British and US armies retained rifles from this point, with other nations gradually following suit. All the early military rifles fired spherical lead bullets, often of smaller size than the musket ball, and no significant improvement in accuracy appeared until the development of the cylindro-conoidal expanding bullet in the 1840s. This, the *Minié, transformed the rifle from a specialist firearm into one generally used by all troops and from the late 1840s nations began to equip their armies with rifled weapons in all arms of their services.

From the development of the Minié ball, it was but a short step to the *breech-loading rifle firing a self-contained *cartridge and from that to the repeating rifle, the semi-automatic rifle, and the assault rifle and machine gun. From the mid-19th century all military weapons had rifled barrels and the term rifle was restricted to the long-barrelled weapon of the infantryman. With recent developments in personal weapon technology, the military use of the rifle tends now to be confined to the sniper, as the ordinary infantryman has reverted to being less of a marksman and more of a highly mobile sub-machine gun carrier.

SCW

Blackmore, Howard L., *British Military Firearms 1650–1850* (London, 1961).

Blair, Claude (gen. ed.), *Pollard's History of Firearms* (London, 1983).

Peterson, Harold L. (ed.), *Encyclopaedia of Firearms* (London, 1964).

Roads, Christopher H., *The British Soldier's Firearm 1850–1864* (London, 1964).

rifle regiments first appeared in quantity in the armies of European nations in the first half of the 18th century. At first, riflemen—known as *Jägers from the German word for hunters—were recruited and employed in small units within the armies of Hesse and Bavaria in the 1630s and 1640s and proved to be effective skirmishers. Although rifles and their trained marksmen were considered of value, their role was also considered peripheral to the principal use of the infantry arm in Europe, which involved large-scale use of rolling volleys of smooth-bored musketry in which rapidity of fire was of greater importance than long-range accuracy. Opinions began to alter during the wars of the mid-18th century and military riflemen appeared in most combatant nations' armies, albeit in small numbers. The first corps of riflemen in the French army was Grassin's Régiment des Arquebusiers, raised in 1744, to be followed by *chasseurs in due course. During the *Seven Years War in Europe, 1756–63, Austrian Tirolean Jägers fought Prussian troops to such effect that a battalion of Prussian Jägers was formed: this remained the sole Prussian rifle regiment until the 1790s. In 1788, the last year of *ancien régime* France, the six battalions of *chasseurs à pied* were doubled in number to twelve and so, with the notable exception of Britain, most European nations had at least one regiment of riflemen by the outbreak of war in Europe in 1792.

The US army had included companies of riflemen ever since Congress had raised ten companies from the states of Pennsylvania, Maryland, and Virgina in 1775; these companies had been the first outside New England to join the new Continental Army and they represented a recognition of the well-known skills of the American frontiersman and his long rifle. In that war, Britain had made use of riflemen too: German *mercenaries armed with Jäger rifles, Highland skirmishers armed with short rifles, and *Ferguson's corps of riflemen armed with his *breech-loading rifle. Ferguson's men were all picked for their skill and marksmanship and so were those recruited by Col Coote Manningham for the Corps of Riflemen he was authorized to raise in 1800. This corps copied its continental counterparts in its chasseur dress of green and rifle regiments throughout the 19th century retained this earliest form of *camouflage, together with other traditions of their role on the battlefield such as a rapid marching pace, the use of bugles and whistles for the giving of commands, and the lack of regimental *colours: all these differentiated them from line infantry and helped give them élite status.

By the end of the 19th century, the breech-loading rifle had made all infantrymen riflemen and only the rifle regiments' historic traditions and *uniforms differentiated them from the infantry of the line. The British found that the *Gurkha regiments of the *Indian army were particularly suited to the role of riflemen in the mid-19th century and so trained and dressed them as such, thus exporting the ethos of the rifle regiment outside European culture. SCW

ritualized warfare All warfare is ritualized to a degree. Even the late 19th-century *Geneva Convention, which is intended to impose some restraints upon modern conflicts, is a form of ritualization. In laying down, for example, that in order to be recognized as proper soldiers and receive the prescribed treatment as *POWs, combatants should wear a recognized uniform, the Convention imposes a dress code upon participants. Of course, when thinking of ritualized warfare, most commentators cite examples from intertribal conflicts in cultures such as Papua New Guinea. Here, even in the 20th century, it has been possible to observe the kind of battles depicted in Neolithic cave paintings. Groups of warriors, all decked out in paint and feathers, perform the kind of manoeuvres not far removed from a dance. True, some may be killed by spears or arrows, but the main intention is to impress the opposition and then come to an agreement as to which side should pay the other a tribute in pigs. Such battles are crucial for the transition from boys to men which warrior societies demand.

To a modern audience this may seem very distant from 'civilized' behaviour, but even in ancient Greece, seen as the ancestor culture for the western world, city-state warfare had ritualized aspects. In the campaigning season the citizen *hoplite armies of spearmen would parade between the two cities involved, burning crops and carrying off cattle as a demonstration of force. Sometimes, but not always, there would be a confrontation in the open field, in which the two *phalanxes strove to overcome one another in a shoving match. Upon the outcome of this endeavour depended the resulting treaty between the two parties. In common with practice throughout the ancient world, *auguries* (see OMENS) were taken before battle. After the engagement a trophy was erected from a hoplite panoply (see ARMOUR, BODY) on a wooden frame set to decay in time—a symbolic statement about the temporary nature of human endeavour in the military sphere.

Throughout all warfare the importance of a parade through enemy territory has been recognized. This might be in the form of a cattle raid found in all cultures and celebrated in *poetry. The 'Cattle Raid of Cooley' is one of the Irish language's most famous pieces. The warring kingdoms of Ireland used these raids as a way of establishing status; the most successful ruler became High King in a constantly fluctuating polity. In the medieval period the *chevauchée, literally a ride through enemy territory during which damage was inflicted upon the territories in the form of ravaging, also had a symbolic aspect. The disgrace suffered by the lord whose subjects had to endure such treatment unprotected could result in him losing influence over lands and their population.

In battle itself, there has been a great deal of ritualized behaviour. A notable example from 19th-century America was the clash of culture between Europeans and the aboriginal population. It was customary for the Plains Indians, lightly equipped horsemen, in their skirmishes associated with raiding, to carry a long stick with which they could 'count coup', which is to say to tap an opponent without injury (see PLAINS INDIANS WARS). This was seen as a grave loss of face for the recipient. Needless to say, European soldiers simply shot the deliverer of the blow, to the dismay of the Indians. In medieval Europe a defeated nobleman could expect more mercy, however. If in fear of his life, he could, by handing over his glove as surety, surrender and be held for *ransom. Often this lasted for years, the prisoner giving his *parole that he would not try to escape. Thus, the whole risk of warfare was ritualized for a privileged élite. In medieval Europe and other cultures it was also possible to make a challenge to personal combat or to send out a champion, with the decision of the battle between two armies (theoretically at least) resting on the result of the individual duel. The contest between Robert *Bruce and Bohun before *Bannockburn was one such. Had Bohun succeeded, the Scots might have lost heart.

In Meso-American cultures the reason for engaging in battle was not necessarily for territorial aggrandizement or the tribute, but specifically for the taking of prisoners. In Aztec culture these were known as 'flower wars'. The captives were then used as sacrificial victims to the gods of the victor; one ritual feeding another. More usually in warfare designed to capture the opposition, the defeated side became the slaves of the victors, as in Classical Greece and Rome.   MB

Divale, W., *War in Primitive Societies: A Bibliography* (Santa Barbara, Calif., 1973).

Roberts, FM Frederick Sleigh, 1st Earl, of Kandahar, Pretoria, and Waterford (1832–1914). Perhaps the ablest British field commander since Wellington, Roberts was born at Kanpur, the son of an East India Company officer, Abraham Roberts, who rose to be a full general. Frederick Roberts joined the Bengal artillery in 1851. On the outbreak of the *Indian Mutiny he was posted as a staff officer to the Punjab Movable Column and took part in the siege and capture of *Delhi, subsequently winning the VC. He served in the Indian army's QMG department from 1859 until 1878, seeing service in the Ambeyla expedition (1863), the *Abyssinian expedition (1867–8), and the Lushai expedition (1871). On the outbreak of the second *Anglo-Afghan war in 1878, he commanded the Kurram Column; when that war reignited in 1879, following the murder of Cavagnari, he was appointed to command the force which occupied Kabul in October 1879, remaining in command there until succeeded by Sir Donald Stewart in May 1880. Roberts then commanded the force which marched from *Kabul to Kandahar in August 1880 to relieve the garrison at the latter, where he defeated the Afghan besiegers under Ayub Khan.

He was C-in-C Madras (1881–5) and C-in-C India for the unprecedented period of eight years, from 1885 to 1893. He then became C-in-C Ireland from whence he superseded *Buller in command of the Second *Boer War in 1899. Before he arrived, his only son Freddie was killed trying to save the guns at Colenso, an action for which he received a posthumous VC. Although Roberts's logistical arrangements have been criticized by some modern historians, he succeeded in a few months in reversing the situation and occupying both Boer capitals. When he returned to England in 1901, the issue of the war was no longer in doubt, even if the *guerrilla tactics of the Boers succeeded in prolonging it for another eighteen months. He was C-in-C of the British army from 1900 until 1904, when the post was abolished.

In retirement, Roberts became a leading exponent of National Service and supporter of Ulster rights. He died in France in 1914 from pneumonia contracted when visiting the Indian troops there. He is buried in St Paul's Cathedral near the Duke of *Wellington.   BR1

Robertson, FM Sir William Robert, Baronet

(1860–1933). 'Wully' Robertson's career was a classic rags-to-riches story. He enlisted as a private in the 16th Lancers in 1877, gained a commission, and was the first ranker to pass through Staff College, of which he later became commandant (1910–13). A rival and contemporary of Wilson (whom he followed as commandant at Camberley), he was a hard-working professional officer, when such types were rare. COS to the British Expeditionary Force in 1915, he later became CIGS, until succeeded by Wilson in 1918. Robertson was made a baronet in 1919 and commanded the British occupation of the Rhineland 1919–20, afterwards being promoted field marshal.   APC-A

Robertson, W. R. *From Private to Field Marshal* (London, 1921).

---

rocket

A form of *missile first used in ancient China strictly for pyrotechnical display. Its first military application was in the early 19th century when the erratic Congreve rocket was deployed in the British army and struck terror into the heart of friend and foe alike. It was this that provided the 'rockets' red glare' of the US national anthem when failing to make any impression on Fort McHenry during the attack on *Baltimore. It has become considerably more reliable since then.   HEB

---

rocket-propelled grenade. See RPG.

Rocroi, battle of

(19 May 1643). During the *Thirty Years War, the 22-year-old Duc d'Enghien (see CONDÉ, LOUIS II DE BOURBON) with 23,000 French troops defeated a Spanish army numbering 25,000 under Francisco de Melo at Rocroi. Melo had advanced from the Spanish Netherlands to besiege Rocroi, where Enghien decided to attack the Spanish quickly before they could receive reinforcements. Enghien took considerable risk in approaching through narrow forest defiles, but was in position in the open country before Rocroi by the evening of 18 May. Enghien initiated the battle the next morning by personally leading a charge by the cavalry of his right wing against the squadrons of the enemy's left. There Enghien's troopers succeeded, but on the other flank, French cavalry also attacked in contravention of orders and was repulsed. Learning that a crisis loomed on his left, Enghien marshalled his victorious horsemen and rode through the rear of the Spanish army to collide with the Spanish right-wing cavalry and drive it from the field. This success isolated the infantry of Melo's centre. At first, the Spanish infantry, which enjoyed a reputation as invincible, defied the French. However, facing the full fury of French artillery, the Spanish foot finally requested to surrender late in the day, but when someone mistakenly fired on Enghien, his infuriated troops attacked the Spanish, charged into their midst, and cut down most of them before taking the rest prisoner. More than any other single battle, Rocroi stripped the Spanish *tercio of its aura of invincibility and presaged the military pre-eminence of France. The young Enghien would soon succeed his father as the prince of Condé, and be known as 'the Great Condé' because of his victories.   JAL

Godley, Eveline, *The Great Condé: A Life of Louis II de Bourbon, Prince of Condé* (London, 1915).

Rogers, Robert

(1731–95), soldier and explorer in pre-independence America who raised and led a crack force known as Rogers' Rangers in the *French and Indian war and *Pontiac's rebellion. His services rejected by *Washington during the *American independence war, he formed and led the Queen's Rangers for the Loyalists and later formed the King's Rangers, commanded by his brother. In financial difficulties for much of his life, Rogers died in poverty in London.

His common-sense 'Standing Orders' include the following immortal precepts:

don't forget nothing; see the enemy first; don't never lie to a Ranger or officer; don't never take a chance you don't have to; march single file, far enough apart so one shot can't go through two men; on soft ground spread out abreast; keep moving till dark; don't sit down to eat without posting sentries; half the party stays awake while the other half sleeps; don't sleep beyond dawn; keep prisoners separate till we have time to examine them; take a different route home; don't cross a river by a regular ford; keep a scout 20 yards [18 metres] ahead, on each flank, and in the rear so the main body can't be surprised; in action take cover, wait till the enemy's almost close enough to touch, then let him have it.   HEB

Roman army

One of the most successful and long-lived armies of antiquity, it developed standards of *discipline,

779

organization, and efficiency that would not be seen again in western Europe until the late 17th century. It began as the small warbands of aristocratic war leaders, but by the end of the 6th century BC it had developed into a *phalanx of heavily armoured *hoplites fighting in dense array and carrying round *shields. The core of the army was composed of all citizens with the property to pay for a panoply. Poorer citizens served as light infantry or servants. As in Greece, the army was designed for short campaigns in the less busy periods of the agricultural year.

By the late 4th and early 3rd centuries BC, the army began to assume the familiar form of the manipular legion. This was described in its classic form by the *Greek historian Polybius, writing in the 2nd century. Each legion consisted normally of 4,200 infantry and 300 cavalry, but in times of emergency this could be increased to 5,000 infantry. Its main strength was the heavy infantry, divided into three lines (the *triplex acies*) each of ten maniples. The first and second lines, the *hastati* and *principes* respectively, each consisted of 1,200 men armed with two heavy javelins, or *pila*, while the third line, the *triarii*, mustered 600 spearmen. Recruitment to the heavy infantry was based on property qualification and membership of each line on age and experience, the *triarii* consisting of veterans. All heavy infantrymen wore body *armour, ranging from a mail corselet to a simple disc-shaped chest protector, carried the oval, semi-cylindrical body shield (*scutum*), and used the short thrusting sword (*gladius*). In support were 1,200 light infantry or *velites*, armed with a bundle of light throwing spears and a round shield. Maniples were commanded by centurions and deployed in a chequerboard formation (*quincunx*) so that the maniples in the second line covered the intervals between those in the first, while the third line covered the gaps in the second. The legion was commanded by six tribunes. Each of the two consuls, the annually elected senior magistrates of the Roman republic, were normally given command of two legions and a similar number of allied troops, divided into two wings (*alae*) with 4,000–5,000 infantry and 900 cavalry. The pick of allied troops, about one third of their overall number, were formed into the cohorts of *extraordinarii*, kept at the immediate disposal of the consul.

Consular armies of two legions plus allies fought most of the wars in the 3rd and 2nd centuries BC, finally beating *Hannibal and crushing the armies of the Hellenistic kingdoms. Sometimes the armies of both consuls were concentrated, in which case the consuls commanded on alternate days. The manipular legion proved very effective in fighting pitched battles. Armies moved rapidly into contact, but then spent days or weeks close to the enemy, jockeying for a favourable position. Another characteristic was the great care taken to build a highly ordered camp every night, giving it a secure base for this manoeuvring. In battle the manipular formation proved far more flexible than the rigid phalanx still employed by Hellenistic pikemen.

Prolonged campaigning against Spanish and *Gallic tribal armies probably provided the impetus for the next major reform of the Roman army. Traditionally associated with *Marius, the changes are now thought to have been more gradual, reaching fruition near the end of the 2nd century BC. A citizen militia was unsuitable for long service as garrisons in the provinces, so increasingly the army came to consist of professional soldiers, men drawn from the classes lacking the minimum property qualification formerly required for service. Dependent on their commanders during their service and upon retirement, this broke the allegiance of the army to the Roman state that had previously been such a source of political stability.

After the *Social and Civil Wars and the extension of Roman citizenship to most of Italy the allied *alae* vanished and all Italians were henceforth recruited into identically armed and organized legions. When the property qualification was abandoned, so were the distinctions of equipment within the legion. The *velites* disappeared and all legionaries were now heavy infantrymen, armed with the *pilum*. The basic subunit of the legion became its ten cohorts of 480 men each, composed of one maniple from each of the three lines, each divided into two centuries of 80 men commanded by a centurion.

The legion of ten cohorts was more flexible than the manipular legion. As adept at fighting pitched battles, its structure allowed it to operate effectively in the smaller scale fighting common against the politically disunited tribes of the western empire. The growth of professionalism and permanence of units improved the army's overall quality and in particular its abilities in specialist tasks such as engineering and siegecraft. These were the armies with which *Caesar and *Pompey added vast territories to the empire. They were also the armies which they and other commanders turned against each other in the civil wars which destroyed the republic and led to the establishment of a principate under Caesar's adopted son, Augustus.

The army of the principate was shaped in the period from Augustus to Claudius, building on the developments of the last centuries. Legions became permanent units with their own numbers and names and many were to remain in existence for centuries. Each consisted of ten cohorts of 480 men in six centuries of 80, each commanded by a centurion, and a small cavalry force of 120 riders. At some periods, some legions had a larger first cohort of 800 men in five centuries. Legions included large numbers of specialist personnel, ranging from armourers to administrators, catapult crewmen to engineers. Soldiers were Roman citizens who served for 25 years, the last five with the veterans who were exempt from most duties. Each legion was commanded by a legate supported by a senior tribune, Roman aristocrats whose career included a range of both civilian and military tasks and who served with a legion for a few years. Greater continuity and professionalism was provided by the corps of centurions, some of whom were promoted from the ranks. Supporting the legions were the non-citizen troops of the *auxilia*. The infantry were organized into cohorts of 480 or 800 men, the cavalry in *alae* of 512 or 768. There were also units (*corhortes equitatae*) composed of a mixture of infantry and cavalry. The *auxilia* included units of archers and light troops, but most seem to have been equipped with mail armour, helmet, and shield and armed with a sword and various types of spear/javelin. At the end of their 25 years' service these auxiliaries were granted citizenship.

The army's strategy and tactics were highly aggressive, attempting to seize and maintain the initiative in any conflict. It was also flexible enough to adapt to the local situation. This, combined with the usually high quality of its units and sound logistical support, gave the army an advantage over all its opponents. The army of the principate remained in essentially this form until the 3rd century AD. Many of the details of the organization of the later Roman army are now obscure. More units were created, but the units themselves seem to have been much smaller, legions perhaps being reduced to as little as 1,000 men. There was also a move away from deploying almost all of the army in the frontier provinces as had been the practice throughout the principate. This culminated in the division between the troops deployed on the frontiers (*limitanei*), and the units of the field armies (*comitatenses*). The *comitatenses* were not involved in local policing and administration and so were not tied to one region. They formed central reserves against both external threats and political rivals from within the empire.

The units of the later Roman army were potentially as efficient as they had ever been, but political weakness often made it harder to muster and supply a large army in the field. The army still won most of the battles it fought, but its doctrine had become less confident, less aggressive, and increasingly reluctant to risk open battle. Considerable use was made of foreign troops fighting under their own leaders, and traditionally it has been assumed that the barbarization of the army led to decline in quality, but this is now fiercely debated. Even so, the Roman army in the west disappeared in the 5th century when the political and economic infrastructure to support it collapsed, not as a result of military defeat.   AKG

Elton, Hugh, *Warfare in Roman Europe AD 350–425* (Oxford, 1996).

Goldsworthy, Adrian, *The Roman Army at War 100 BC–AD 200* (Oxford, 1996).

Keppie, Lawrence, *The Making of the Roman Army* (London, 1984).

Webster, Graham, *The Roman Imperial Army* (London, 1985).

Roman civil war (49–30 BC). The final bout of the civil wars of the 1st century BC began as a conflict between *Caesar and *Pompey, previously allies, and between those who clung to the ideal of collective senatorial rule and others who liked the smack of firm government in the form of a *dictator. It ended with a duel between Caesar's surviving political heirs, Octavian and Mark *Antony, to decide who should be emperor. These aristocratic struggles were possible because, for many thousands of Italians, service in the army of one or other of the military dynasts was very greatly more profitable than agrarian pursuits. Ominously, in the *Roman army there was now more to be gained through loyalty to individual generals than to the state.

The foundation for civil war was laid with the formation of the unofficial first Triumvirate in 60 BC, in which Caesar, Pompey, and Crassus agreed to pool their wealth and influence to dominate Roman politics for their own ends. Julius extended the provinces of Gaul to include all of modern France and Belgium, and built up a superbly efficient army entirely responsive to his will. Meanwhile, Pompey and Crassus controlled domestic politics in Rome, and had their own armies in Spain and Syria respectively. But while Pompey remained just outside Rome and governed his province through deputies, Crassus went east, invaded the Parthian empire, and met with defeat and death in 53 BC at *Carrhae.

With Crassus gone, Pompey made a tactical alliance with diehard republicans and they instituted a series of manoeuvres to weaken Julius politically. Facing the threat of prosecution as soon as he lay down his command, Caesar crossed the river Rubicon (in northern Italy, precise location unknown) in January 49, and marched on Rome at the head of a single legion. Pompey was forced out of Italy and fled to Greece, but Caesar first dealt with his rival's military power base in Spain. Only after defeating Pompey's forces there did he cross to Greece in January 48. After an unsuccessful siege of Dyrrhachium (now Durrës, Albania), he was able to rout Pompey, reinforced by the army of Syria, at *Pharsalus in northern Greece on 9 August. Pompey fled to Egypt, where he was murdered on 28 September by the followers of the boy-king Ptolemy XIII. Caesar advanced through Asia Minor to Alexandria, where he dallied with Ptolemy's sister Cleopatra while affirming his control over Egypt.

He now faced a dual threat, from the republicans, regrouped in Africa under Metellus Scipio and Cato, and from Pharnaces, ruler of the Crimea, in Asia Minor. He defeated Pharnaces at Zela in August 47 (the occasion of his famous despatch to the senate: 'I came, I saw, I conquered') before marching through Greece and Italy to invade Africa in October. Cato was besieged at Utica and Metellus Scipio defeated at Thapsus on 6 April 46. Both committed suicide, and the remnants of the republican army withdrew to Spain under Pompey's sons, Cnaeus and Sextus Pompeius. Caesar followed them there and on 17 March 45 won a final victory at Munda. Cnaeus was executed but Sextus escaped.

Caesar returned to Rome, but his assumption of the dictatorship for life and rumours that he was aiming at kingship led to his assassination on the Ides (15th) of March 44. While the assassins and their republican supporters tried to re-establish control, Caesar's lieutenants Mark Antony and Lepidus gathered their own forces. His 18-year-old nephew, Octavian, adopted as his son in Caesar's will, now entered the fray. Having collected a small army of his political father's veterans, he was attached to the republican army sent to northern Italy to deal with Antony. But when both consuls were killed defeating Antony near Mutina (now Modena), Octavian took command, marched on Rome, and demanded the consulship for himself. He then changed sides and formed the legally ratified Second Triumvirate with Antony and Lepidus, effectively a triple dictatorship.

While Lepidus held Rome, Antony and Octavian invaded northern Greece to confront the republican forces of Brutus and Cassius in two battles at *Philippi in October/November 42, after which both republican leaders took their own lives. Antony took control of the east, with its opportunities for amassing wealth and military glory fighting the Parthians, while Octavian received the west, with the difficult task of settling tens of thousands of veterans on confiscated land in Italy and dealing with Sextus Pompeius, who had seized Sicily and Sardinia and was raiding the Italian coast. Lepidus, always the junior partner, was confined to Africa. Octavian then survived an armed uprising against him in Italy, misguidedly led by Antony's wife and brother, in part because of the reluctance of Caesar's veterans to fight each other. He emerged from the peace agreement at Brundisium (now Brindisi) in 40 a much more equal partner with Antony.

Octavian then turned his attention to Sextus Pompeius and, with the aid of his lieutenant Marcus Agrippa, defeated him at sea after many setbacks and captured Sicily in 36. Lepidus' vain attempt to take over Sextus' forces only led to his removal from power. Meanwhile, Antony had only limited success against the Parthians, losing 32,000 men to the Armenian winter in 37/6, and alienated popular support in Italy when he distributed Roman possessions to his mistress Cleopatra and their children in 34. After an intensive propaganda war, Octavian declared war on Cleopatra in 31, and on 23 September, his fleet, under Agrippa, defeated Antony and Cleopatra off *Actium in western Greece. The lovers were pursued to Egypt and committed suicide the next year. Having settled the veterans of both sides, Octavian became Augustus in 27, basing his lasting power on the standing, professional Roman army that his adoptive father had brought to a peak of efficiency. BR2

Brunt, Peter A., *The Fall of the Roman Republic and Related Essays* (Oxford, 1988).
Cambridge Ancient History, vols. 9 and 10 (Cambridge, 1994 and 1996).
Gruen, Erich S., *The Last Generation of the Roman Republic* (Berkeley, 1974).
Syme, Ronald, *The Roman Revolution* (Oxford, 1939).

Roman military historians The Romans were at least as warlike as the Greeks, and their historians and biog-

raphers also, sooner or later, found themselves writing military history. Here only the more important will be discussed. The earliest surviving works with a military content are the lives of various generals, including, for example, Miltiades and Hamilcar, by Cornelius Nepos (c.110–24 BC). But these are slight and eulogistic and show little insight. More important is Sallust (Gaius Sallustius Crispus, 85–36 BC), one of whose surviving works is a monograph on the Jugurthine war. But Sallust was mainly interested in the impact the war allegedly had on the contemporary political scene and the moral decline of Rome's ruling class, and the military narrative is secondary.

Unfortunately Sallust's moralizing and rhetorical attitude set the tone for his successors, and one looks in vain in Roman writers for the precision and perception of a Thucydides or a Polybius (see GREEK HISTORIANS). The most important for the republican period is Livy (Titus Livius, probably 59 BC to AD 17), who wrote a history of Rome from its foundation to 9 BC, of which 35 out of an original 142 books survive, with summaries of the rest. Apart from his unhistorical approach, Livy has also been attacked for failing to be critical of his sources, particularly Roman annalists. But although his stories of Rome's early wars are obviously partly legendary, there was probably little hard evidence, and his accounts of later wars, if one discounts the rhetoric, do not suffer too badly from comparison with Polybius. If we only had Livy's account of *Cannae, for example, we would still know what happened. Livy also has the merit of preserving details of the political background and of Roman dispositions, and where Polybius' narrative is lost, he is invaluable.

Born in 20 or 19 BC, Velleius Paterculus summarized the history of his world from Greek mythology to AD 29. As a soldier himself, he sometimes provides invaluable evidence, for example on Tiberius' campaigns in the Balkans, but the narrative is so compressed that his quality as a military historian can hardly be assessed.

Quintus Curtius Rufus, possibly the suffect-consul of AD 43, wrote a history of *Alexander 'the Great' in ten books, of which much is missing. He is valuable on Macedonian customs and in preserving parts of the lost work of Clitarchus which was probably based on first-hand accounts and the source of the so-called 'vulgate' tradition also lying behind Diodorus (see GREEK HISTORIANS). But Curtius also used other material and tended to hop from source to source in the interests of his own rhetorical approach to history, with disastrous results.

Sextus Iulius Frontinus, three times consul between AD 73 and 100, wrote a lost book on military science of which he was inordinately proud, and a collection of military anecdotes under the title *Stratagems* which he hoped would be of practical use to soldiers. Whether they would have been is dubious, but they contain a fund of historical information, some of which is interesting. A younger contemporary of Frontinus was Cornelius Tacitus (AD c.56–c.120), of whose five surviving works, three deal in part with military events. Thus the life of his father-in-law, Agricola, contains an account of the latter's campaigns as governor of Britain from AD 77 to 84. Since this is biography, indeed eulogy, we should not expect too much, but even so it is disappointing, lacking any real precision or awareness of the military problems.

Better are Tacitus' two historical works, the *Annals* and the *Histories*. The former originally contained an account of the period from Tiberius to Nero, but substantial sections are missing, and Tacitus was more interested in events in Rome than on the frontiers. When he does include military events, he tends to use them to point a contrast with the often lurid goings-on at the centre, and he makes little or no attempt to explain overall imperial strategy. Nevertheless, within limits, the narrative is reasonably detailed and comprehensible, though some of the descriptions of battles seem to be modelled on earlier writers.

The *Histories*, written before the *Annals*, were originally an account of the period from AD 68 to 96, but only the beginning, covering the civil wars of AD 69—the 'Year of the Four Emperors'—and the following year, survives. This, too, has been severely criticized for lack of both chronological and topographical precision. But enough is there to enable us to follow the campaigns without too much difficulty, and modern research has confirmed the essential accuracy. In any case, such is the pace and brilliance of the narrative that one feels that one can forgive the author almost anything.

Suetonius (Gaius Suetonius Tranquillus, AD *c*.70–*c*.130) deserves a mention because of the evidence he provides for 1st-century imperial campaigns, though he is a biographer first and foremost. But it was left to Rome's twilight to produce perhaps her best military historian, Ammianus Marcellinus (AD *c*.330–95). He saw service all over the empire from Gaul and Germany to Mesopotamia, and also travelled widely before finishing his history in Rome in the 380s. This originally covered the period from AD 96 to his own time, but the first thirteen books, taking the narrative to 353, are lost. The surviving books deal with the period 353 to 378, culminating in the disastrous battle of *Adrianople. Much of the military narrative is still marred by imaginative rhetoric, but where Ammianus uses eyewitnesses, and particularly where he was present himself, it is detailed and analytical.

Finally, contemporary with Ammianus, was Eutropius who wrote a summary of the history of Rome to AD 364 in ten books, using Livy for the republic, a lost work on imperial history which also lies behind some of Ammianus, for example, for the empire, and his own experience for later events. Despite its brevity, Eutropius' work is generally sensible, and is particularly useful where Livy is lost.   JFL

Hornblower, Simon, and Spawforth, Antony, *The Oxford Classical Dictionary* (3rd edn., Oxford, 1996).

Rommel, FM Erwin (1891–1944). Known to the British as the 'Desert Fox', Rommel received the following encomium from *Churchill: 'We have a very daring and skilful opponent against us, and, may I say across the havoc of war, a great general.' Of middle-class stock and no military background, he was decorated for his leadership in a string of combat actions during WW I, culminating in a Pour le Mérite won on the *Italian front (originally awarded to another, he had to lobby to receive the honour himself). During the inter-war years, he was an instructor and wrote a memoir-textbook, *Infantry Attacks*, in 1937.

The book came to Hitler's notice and Rommel was promoted to command his bodyguard in 1939–40. He took over 7th Panzer Division in February 1940, and with no previous experience of armour, he led it to war in France on 10 May. With an instinctive feel for handling a mobile formation, he outperformed his contemporaries in boldness and speed. In a six-week campaign 7th Panzer was credited with taking 100,000 Allied prisoners and over 450 tanks. He may have lacked the operational flair of *Manstein, but he was a superb practitioner of *blitzkrieg.

In January 1941 he received a new command and promotion, landing in Tripoli with the advance elements of two divisions: the *Afrika Korps. He had an independent command, far away from feuding contemporaries, and led literally from the front, as he had done in France. His arrival was Hitler's token effort to save his Axis partner *Mussolini from defeat at the hands of an inferior British force in Libya. Without waiting to consolidate and against Wehrmacht high command (OKW) orders, he struck and caught the British off balance in March, retaking all of Cyrenaica, except *Tobruk. Promoted general that summer, commanding Panzer Group Africa—a mixture of eight German and Italian divisions—he held out against British counterattacks, before being forced to withdraw in November. Luftwaffe dominance of the Mediterranean allowed reinforcements and supplies to arrive, and in a series of offensives culminating in the *Gazala battles he regained all the lost ground and captured Tobruk. A grateful Führer rewarded him with a field marshal's baton on 22 June. Lured into the conquest of Egypt, he was halted by *Auchinleck at the first battle of *Alamein in July, checked again by *Montgomery at Alam Halfa in September, and decisively beaten at Alamein again in October. His army was suffering from extreme fuel shortages and he himself had flown back to Germany for treatment of a mixture of ailments. Rommel returned and masterminded an orderly withdrawal—against Hitler's orders—but the TORCH landings forced him into a campaign on two fronts.

Rivalries between Rommel and Arnim, both commanding sizeable Axis armies in Tunisia, prevented strategic success there, despite the tactical victory at *Kasserine Pass in February 1943 against inexperienced US troops. Too late, Rommel was promoted to command Army Group Africa, over Arnim, but unable to defeat Montgomery at

Medenine in March, he flew to Germany on extended sick leave.

With the Allies triumphant in Tunisia, he was recalled as C-in-C Army Group B in August 1943, to plan for operations in northern Italy. After the invasion of *Sicily and the *Salerno landing, Kesselring withdrew slowly to enable Rommel to secure his rear. But they disagreed on how best to defend the peninsula, the former winning with proposals for forward defence and being made C-in-C Italy. On Hitler's orders, Rommel took his Army Group B headquarters to France in November 1943 to direct the defence of the west against invasion. He strengthened the Atlantic wall, inventing beach obstacles ('Rommel's asparagus'), but clashed with *Rundstedt, his superior in France, who demanded that a strategic armoured reserve should be held back, while Rommel wanted his panzers close enough to the coast to immediately destroy any lodgment. Both tried to stem the Allied advance following the Normandy landings and in vain sought more operational flexibility than Hitler would allow them. On 17 July an RAF fighter strafed Rommel's staff car and he was severely wounded. This was three days before the assassination attempt on Hitler. The July plotters had long maintained informal contact with Rommel, whose public and military reputation might have helped secure an early end to the war, and he was offered the choice of poison or a show trial. Unsurprisingly, he took the former course on 14 October 1944.   APC-A/RH

Fraser, David, *Knight's Cross* (London, 1993).
Irving, David, *The Trail of the Fox* (London, 1977).

Ronceval (Roncesvalles) is a high Pyrenees pass and the site of a defeat suffered by *Charlemagne on 15 August 778. Among the *Franks who died was Roland, a high-ranking aristocrat, who was later immortalized as the subject of a superb Old French poem, *The Song of Roland*, the surviving manuscript of which dates from *c*.1100. The *Song* tells an epic tale of *honour, loyalty, and betrayal against the backdrop of Christian–Muslim conflict. Its value lies in the vivid insights it allows into the aristocratic mentality of the age in which it was composed; it can add nothing to our knowledge of the historical Roland.

The campaign of 778 was a response to an embassy received by Charlemagne from the Muslim ruler of Barcelona in 777. A large army which was assembled from across Charlemagne's empire at Easter 778 crossed the Pyrenees by two separate routes, before reassembling outside Saragossa, where there were protracted negotiations with the Muslims. In early August Charlemagne suddenly decided to withdraw: Frankish claims of substantial successes in the Ebro valley must be taken with a pinch of salt. The problems of conducting a campaign in a hostile and strange countryside distant from the Frankish heartland are well illustrated by the disaster of 15 August. As the Frankish army reached the heights of the Pyrenees, they were ambushed by Basque forces seeking plunder (all contemporary accounts agree that the Franks' opponents were the Basques, not the Muslims of *The Song of Roland*). With the Frankish formation drawn out by the pass, the Basques cut off and then butchered the Frankish rearguard and baggage-train, before melting into the hills. These tactics put the Franks, heavily armed and used to pitched battle not skirmishing, at a disadvantage.

Beyond this outline information is scarce, largely because of the embarrassment of Frankish authors; the death of trusted aristocratic commanders, including Charlemagne's chamberlain, made this a serious defeat.   MI

rōnin (Jap.: *rōnin*, wave man) was a masterless *samurai, an unemployed warrior. A favourite subject of literature and folklore, at one extreme he appears as a knight errant, driven on by a desire for *honour and sense of adventure, while at the other he is a bully and a braggart. The subjects of Akira Kurosawa's film *Seven Samurai* are in fact rōnin, and the western gunfighters in its derivative, *The Magnificent Seven*, strike the right comparative chord. There were always rōnin in old Japan, and many thronged the country in the 17th century, after the confiscation of so many fiefs following the victory of *Tokugawa Ieyasu at *Sekigahara in 1600. The garrison of *Osaka castle, which defied Ieyasu in two separate sieges in 1614–15, was composed largely of rōnin, thousands of whom perished.

The popular *Tale of the Forty-Seven Rōnin*, describing events of 1701–2, tells us much about the values of samurai society. The Lord Asano, *daimyo* of a fief at Ako in the province of Harima, was provoked into attacking an official, Lord Kira, within the precincts of the shogun's palace and in consequence ordered to commit seppuku. With his death his retainers became rōnin, and 46 of them, led by Kuranosuke Oishi, agreed to secure Lord Kira's death. They adopted a louche lifestyle to put Kira off guard, and on one occasion a Satsuma samurai, finding Oishi lying drunk in the street, spat on him. Eventually they stormed Kira's house and, when he declined to kill himself, stabbed him to death. They delivered his head at the temple where Asano was buried and then surrendered to the authorities. After a long debate—for their deed was recognized as one akin to filial piety—they were ordered to commit suicide, and buried with their lord in the Sengaku-ji temple. The samurai who had spat on Oishi apologized before his tomb, committed seppuku, and was buried beside the others.

RH

Roon, FM Graf Albrecht Theodor Emil von (1803–79). Born near Kolberg in Prussia, son of an officer, Roon was commissioned in 1821 and attended the Kriegsakademie in Berlin in 1824–7. He was military tutor to Prince Frederick Charles, and served with Prince William of

Prussia, who became regent in 1858. That year Roon submitted a memorandum warning that the standing army was too small, while the Landwehr, the citizen militia which provided the reserve, was both 'politically false' because it no longer impressed potential adversaries and 'militarily false' because it was poorly trained and lacked discipline. William appointed Roon chairman of a military commission, which was to draft a reform bill. Bonin, the war minister, opposed many key demands and, when William supported Roon, he resigned.

Roon became war minister and developed a bill which doubled the standing army, reduced the Landwehr, and brought it firmly under regular control. A political crisis followed, with conflict between crown and chamber leading some observers to fear revolution: it was resolved only after Bismarck became minister-president in 1862. Roon got the army he wanted: a conscript was liable for seven years' service, three with the colours and four with the reserve, and he remained in the Landwehr, a second-line reserve to the regular army, for another five years. Roon created the instrument which won the *Austro-Prussian and the *Franco-Prussian wars, and is not least among the architects of imperial Germany.

Roon was large and brusque, with a *Gardeleutnantsmanier* (Guard lieutenant's manner) that routinely affronted members of parliament. He was supported by a determined monarch, by the talented CGS *Moltke 'the Elder', and by Bismarck, the towering political figure of his age. Made a count after the Franco-Prussian war, he was promoted field marshal in January 1873 and retired later that year.   RH

Roosevelt, Franklin Delano (1882–1945), US president 1933–45 during the Great Depression and WW II. He served four and a half years longer than any other, and if the monumental busts of the four greatest presidents were to be sculpted on Mount Rushmore today, his would join those of *Washington, Jefferson, and *Lincoln by acclamation, replacing his distant cousin and youthful inspiration Theodore, whose niece Eleanor he married in 1905. She was to prove a formidable political asset throughout his career; less welcome was her self-appointed role as his social conscience.

Nothing FDR did as president is quite as remarkable as the fact that he won the office at all, despite being an aristocrat and wheelchair-bound after an attack of polio in 1921. Like Theodore before him, early in his career he sparred with his own New York party's corrupt urban 'machine', but unlike him he won two terms as governor (1928 and 1930) against a country-wide Republican tide, during which time he matured and learned the virtue of accommodation. The platform that bore him to the presidency in 1932 in the midst of the Great Depression was for further deflation and austerity, but once in power he implemented the 'New Deal', a greatly expanded version of the programme advocated by his opponent Hoover, doomed by incumbency when industrial production fell by 40 per cent and there were 13 million unemployed.

Although it was WW II that brought the economic depression to an end, the New Deal and FDR's reassuring radio broadcasts were effective in countering the no less significant psychological depression gripping the country. He was never a Keynesian and the money his numerous new 'Alphabet Agencies' (FERA, CCC, RFC, AAA, NIRA, WPA, etc.) poured into the economy was incidental to his main aim of restoring hope and confidence. The most abidingly popular of his measures was the provision of a state pension scheme with the Social Security Act of 1935, but his main ambition was crowned by winning various test cases before a generally hostile Supreme Court, which affirmed almost unlimited federal power to regulate the economy.

With characteristic insouciance, he campaigned for his unprecedented second re-election in 1940 with the promise to keep America out of the wars engulfing the rest of the world, while conducting what can only be called a conspiracy with *Churchill to do the opposite in Europe, and pursuing a policy actively hostile to Japanese expansionism in the Far East. Once re-elected, he subverted his own Neutrality Acts and aligned the USA firmly on the side of Britain against Germany with the *Lend-Lease Act and by taking over *convoy escort duties in the eastern Atlantic. He anticipated a Japanese attack in south-east Asia and the Philippines but was outraged when they also struck at *Pearl Harbor, after which Germany and Italy did Britain and the USSR the enormous favour of declaring war on the USA in solidarity with their Axis ally.

FDR had, barely, managed to keep conscription ('the draft') in being and had quietly organized agencies to direct a war economy, such that overwhelming American industrial and manpower resources were promptly mobilized and rapidly deployed under the brilliant direction of *Nimitz in the Pacific and *Marshall in Europe. Being better served by his military commanders, FDR was not tempted to exercise operational control, unlike Churchill or his own great predecessor Lincoln. He did adopt the latter's formula of 'unconditional surrender' with greater justification, given the very real criminality of Nazi Germany and imperial Japan and the need to maintain unity among allies who might otherwise have been tempted to make deals at each other's expense.

His vision for the post-war world was based on the 'five policemen' concept in which the USA, Britain, France, China, and the USSR would work together to preserve peace through the UN. Reluctant to admit that he indulged in appeasement, apologists argue that ill health undermined his faculties and permitted *Stalin to 'bamboozle' him at Yalta in February 1945. This is to deny ample evidence that he regarded Churchill as the greater obstacle to his vision of a post-war world advancing to harmony through the pursuit of the 'self-evident' principles of the US Declaration of Independence. It remains a quintessentially American mystery how such a shrewd politician could have believed with such heartbreaking sincerity that events in China would develop favourably to his vision, or that bankrupt Britain could long sustain an independent worldwide role, or that the Soviet dictator would sincerely espouse principles that self-evidently undermined his own power.

HEB

Roosevelt, Theodore (1858–1919), soldier, explorer, prolific author, and USA president 1901–9. Known as 'Teddy', from whence, after an apocryphal incident in which he spared a cub, comes the term 'teddy bear'. Despite asthma and extremely poor eyesight, he was a serious naturalist and outdoorsman who founded the National Parks system, and in general brought 'vigah' to bear on everything he did. Although a Republican with an aristocratic background, his presidency was populist and he used the office as a 'bully pulpit' to reach out to the people over the head of an outraged political and economic establishment.

He was also an egomaniac who split his own party and let in only the second Democrat president since the *American civil war, and a flagrant racist who was forced to retract lies about the performance of *African-American troops at the battle of San Juan Hill, who as president dealt viciously with them after a disturbance in Brownsville, Texas, and who preached the crudest social Darwinism from that bully pulpit. He was high-handed with 'lesser breeds' abroad as well, waging an atrocity-ridden campaign against the *Philippines insurrection and instituting temporary colonial rule over the Dominican Republic in 1905 and Cuba in 1906, as well as organizing the 1903 secession of Panama from Colombia in order to obtain the Panama Canal Zone cheaply.

There was a 'Boys' Own' quality to his many adventures, in particular his participation in the *Spanish-American war, for which he raised and led the 'Rough Riders' regiment of western irregulars. During the assault on Kettle Hill, he led from the front and on a horse until he encountered wire. In sum, he was a protean high Victorian figure with all the vices and virtues of the type, and does not fit into any of today's political or social pigeon-holes.

Because of his war hero status, the powerful New York Republican machine anointed him for the governorship of New York in 1899, with a private understanding that he would refrain from attacking corruption. Once elected, his personal popularity enabled him to renege on this agreement and to make a start on cleaning the Augean stables of New York politics. His choice as the vice-presidential candidate for the party in 1900 came about because by then the machine wanted him out of the governor's mansion at any price. It was not a good day for politics as usual when Pres McKinley fell to an assassin's bullet in September 1901 and

Roosevelt became the youngest president. Of his successors, only John Kennedy in 1961 was younger.

For those who rate presidents according to the degree they have extended the power of the office, Theodore stands shoulder to shoulder with his distant cousin Franklin and with *Lincoln, without their advantage of a tangible national crisis to strengthen his hand. He did this by auditing and breaking up large corporate combinations, exploiting the interstate commerce clause of the constitution, and using the powers granted to the federal government by the 1890 Sherman Anti-Trust Act, previously applied only to trade-union activity. What is so remarkable about his performance is that the Republicans were unequivocally the party of big business and his 'trust-busting' of 44 major corporations over the next seven years bypassed a conservative Republican congress disinclined to give him the inch it knew he would turn into a mile.

During Roosevelt's presidency the USA, already possessed of the most powerful economy, began to play a commensurate political role in world affairs, as symbolized by his own role in mediating the end of the 1904–5 *Russo-Japanese war, for which he won the 1906 *Nobel Peace Prize. The Japanese correctly perceived his prejudice against them, strengthened when he restricted 'oriental' immigration in 1907. The festering resentment caused by these, along with his acquisition of a hostage to fortune in the Philippines, can be seen to lead directly to the death struggle of 1941–5. That war was to be won by the mighty blue-water navy that Roosevelt was also instrumental in creating.

After leaving the White House in 1909, he toured Africa and Europe and returned to the USA over a year later to play a deeply divisive role in the politics of the Republican party, including the formation of a Progressive party as a vehicle for his own presidential aspirations, the final outcome of which was the election in 1912 of the sanctimonious Democrat Wilson, who was personally everything Roosevelt despised.

HEB

Roses, Wars of the Once applied to the whole of the 15th century, the name is now given to the sequence of plots, rebellions, and battles that took place between 1455 and 1487. They are so called because of the notion that, being fought between the dynasties of Lancaster and York, Lancaster was represented by a red rose, York by a white. The identification of the roses with the rival dynasties first became prominent in the reign of Henry VII. He adopted the red rose as one of his *badges; his wife Elizabeth of York the white. The idea of the warring roses, brought to an end by the marriage of the two, was developed by Henry VII for propaganda purposes after he had seized the throne in 1485. He claimed that the union of the two houses brought peace, order, and prosperity after the civil war, anarchy, and ruin of the preceding decades. The idea of the warring roses thus quickly entered historical tradition, although the modern phrase 'the Wars of the Roses' did not appear until the early 19th century.

There were three distinct phases: between 1455 and 1464, between 1469 and 1471, and between 1483 and 1487. The first began as a conflict between rival factions for control of the kingdom under the weak and vacillating Lancastrian King Henry VI, but became a war for possession of the crown in 1460, settled for a brief period in favour of Edward IV of the house of York. The second was similar in pattern to the first, in which factional conflict led eventually to renewed dynastic war between Edward IV and supporters of Henry VI (briefly restored). The third was entirely dynastic and led to the accession of Henry VII.

The wars can be said to have begun when Richard, Duke of York, supported by the Neville Earls of Salisbury and Warwick, defeated the Duke of Somerset at the first battle of St Albans on 22 May 1455. York secured control of the king and the government for a short while. He rose once more in rebellion in 1459. Although he was outmanoeuvred at the rout of Ludlow in September 1459, his son, Edward, and Warwick 'the Kingmaker' recovered power at the battle of Northampton on 10 July 1460. Thereafter York was declared heir to the throne by the victorious faction. But York was himself defeated and killed at the battle of *Wakefield on 30 December and Warwick defeated at the second battle of St Albans on 12 February. The Yorkist cause was saved by Edward of York, who, only 18, having first defeated a Lancastrian army at Mortimer's Cross in the Welsh Marches, seized London, made himself king, and finally defeated the main Lancastrian army at *Towton on 29 March. Sporadic war continued in the far north until 1464 and Harlech remained in Lancastrian hands until 1468.

By 1468 Edward IV had fallen out with Warwick, his principal supporter. In 1469 Warwick took to arms and destroyed his enemies at the battle of Edgecote on 26 July. He proved no more successful in ruling by force than the Duke of York ten years earlier. A second rebellion failed in the spring of 1470 and he fled to France. There he made his peace with the remaining Lancastrians led by Henry VI's queen, Margaret of Anjou. With French support Warwick landed in the autumn in the name of Henry VI. Deserted by his troops Edward IV fled to the shelter of his brother-in-law the Duke of Burgundy. Henry VI, who had been a prisoner in the Tower, was restored to the throne. But Edward IV returned in the spring of 1471, and, in a brilliant campaign defeated his divided enemies, first Warwick at Barnet on 14 April and then Margaret of Anjou at Tewkesbury on 4 May. At Tewkesbury the heir to Lancaster was killed. His death sealed the fate of Henry VI.

The wars would have come to an end in 1471 had not Edward IV's youngest brother, Richard, Duke of Gloucester assumed the throne in June 1483 because the legitimacy of Edward IV's sons was denied by canon law as being the product of a bigamous marriage. It was at this point that Henry Tudor, Earl of Richmond, who had a remote claim to the throne, emerged as the candidate of those opposed to Richard III, both displaced Yorkists and diehard Lancastrians. He defeated and killed Richard at *Bosworth and survived a challenge at Stoke-by-Newark in 1487. Although he faced further threats co-ordinated from abroad, he successfully held his throne.

Most battles were short and sharp, often no more than skirmishes. Armies were formed largely by raising levies who would only serve for short periods; trained soldiers and indentured retainers provided only the nucleus of any force. They were usually small, being no more than 5,000 strong and often less. Only at Towton were significant numbers engaged. These were not wars of conquest. For this reason there were few sieges. The intention of rival commanders was to get at their enemies as quickly as possible and kill them, either during or after battle. Both Northampton and Bosworth ended abruptly once this had happened. After Edgecote and Towton, the fleeing commanders were hunted down and killed. Strategy and tactics were uncomplicated. The normal pattern was for armies to march straight towards each other, seeking on contact to secure the more favourable ground. It was usual for armies to be drawn up in three divisions, known as 'battles', facing each other and for one to launch a frontal attack. Battles were fought on foot, armoured horsemen dismounting. Horses were usually deployed for flight or *pursuit. Warwick 'the Kingmaker' was caught and killed according to one account as he was trying to mount his horse; Richard III did *not* call for a horse, as Shakespeare would have us believe, but rather died fighting in the thick of it. Artillery was used, but mainly as an alternative to archery to disrupt the enemy formation before engaging hand-to-hand. Often the lie of the land or the unexpected led to a confused mêlée in which the outcome was determined as much by luck as judgement. Barnet was fought in thick fog and the lines became so confused that Lancastrians found themselves fighting each other.

The level of casualties and the extent of disorder caused by these wars was much exaggerated by Tudor writers and later historians. At Northampton the order was issued by the Yorkist commanders to spare the commons. But the death rate among the gentry and aristocracy participating could be high; this was especially so at Towton. On the other hand many of the knightly class avoided entanglement if they possibly could. The wars as a whole, with the exception of 1460–1, did not embroil the entire political nation. The most intense period of warfare occurred between July 1460 and March 1461, but in total there were barely more than two years' military activity throughout the 32-year period. Civilian casualties and physical damage were light. The greatest amount of destruction was caused by the army from the north with which Margaret of Anjou campaigned in January–March 1461, but the havoc caused may have been exaggerated by excitable chroniclers and Yorkist propaganda. Even at the height of fighting it was possible for most people to go about their normal business. Direct disruption of the economy was therefore slight; indirectly, by taking men away from work and dislocating overseas trade, the wars and the attendant political crises did have a greater effect. But for ordinary men and women the second half of the century witnessed a period of growing prosperity and rising standards of living upon which the wars barely impinged.

The general direction of 20th-century scholarship has been to play down the military significance and character of the wars. They are seen primarily in political terms as a late medieval crisis. Thus the origins and causes have been much discussed. Some, arguing that in 15th-century politics everything rested on the fitness of the king to rule, have laid the blame on the feebleness of Henry VI. Others have seen additional deeper causes in the social, economic, and political trends of the era, which suggest that any monarch in the mid-15th century would have faced severe problems. Nevertheless the recovery from the wars was rapid and no profound social or political changes are immediately discernible; the *feudal aristocracy did not destroy itself and no middle class emerged to take its place. Apart from the emergence of the house of Tudor as the ruling dynasty, the most lasting impact of the wars has been on the historical imagination. They have come to symbolize an anarchy which the English have congratulated themselves on subsequently avoiding.   AJP

Goodman, Anthony, *The Wars of the Roses* (London, 1981).
Pollard, A. J., *The Wars of the Roses* (London, 1988).
Ross, Charles, *The Wars of the Roses* (London, 1976).

Rossbach, battle of (1757). Following the defeats of Kolin on 18 June 1757 and Gross-Jägersdorf on 30 July during the *Seven Years War, Prussia was invaded by Austrian, French, Russian, and Swedish armies heading for Berlin. *Frederick 'the Great' decided to deal first with the Franco-imperial army, commanded by *Soubise, and met them near Leipzig in Saxony. On 5 November, the Franco-imperial army attempted to envelop Frederick's left flank by marching around it in five giant *columns totalling 40,000 troops. Frederick observed their approach, and, concealed by the dominating position of the Janus hill, turned his entire army to face them and simultaneously launched a massive cavalry counter-thrust led by the redoubtable Seydlitz, that brushed aside the Allied horse and went on to scythe into the unprepared Franco-imperial infantry. This was followed by an echeloned attack by the Prussian foot. In one and a half hours the Allies lost 8,000 to Frederick's few hundred.

French military prestige was shattered, and the scale of the defeat prompted a rethinking of French military doctrine which ultimately led to the work of *Guibert. The victory enabled Frederick to turn about and deal with the fresh threat posed by the Austrians in Silesia, where he defeated them at *Leuthen.   TM

ROTC. See RESERVE OFFICERS TRAINING CORPS.

Royal Hospital Chelsea Established by King Charles II for the care of veteran soldiers. The original idea was suggested by the King's Paymaster General, Sir Stephen Fox, in 1681 and was probably inspired by the Hôtel des *Invalides in Paris and a similar institution for the Irish army. Christopher Wren, designer of St Paul's Cathedral, was appointed architect for the project. The site itself had been an unsuccessful theological college in the early years of the century after which the government used the buildings to house Dutch and Scots *POWs. The king laid the foundation stone in 1682 and 476 pensioners were admitted in 1689. The building work itself was completed three years later and, save for minor alterations made by Robert Adam in 1765–82 and Sir John Soane in 1814, remains more or less unchanged to this day.

Gen Whitelock was *cashiered at the hospital in 1807 after his *court martial for surrendering the fortress of Montevideo. The Duke of *Wellington lay in state here between 10 and 17 November 1852. The crowds that gathered to file past his coffin and pay their respects were so numerous that two of them were killed in the crush.

The in-pensioners, usually about 420 in number, are organized into six companies. Men over 65 (55 if unable to earn a living) are housed, fed, clothed, cared for when ill, and receive a small weekly allowance. The pensioners wear a distinctive three-quarter length uniform coat, navy blue in winter and scarlet in the summer, which dates from the 18th century. A three-cornered hat is also worn on special occasions and ceremonies. Oak Day (29 May) is held in the central quadrangle and marks their royal founder's birthday. Foliage is draped on the statue of Charles II and the pensioners carry sprigs. A harvest festival also takes place in the autumn.   JR-W

RPG (rocket-propelled grenade). The WW II US bazooka and the German Panzerfaust were the first RPGs, used to give infantrymen the firepower to damage tanks, although only at extremely close range and usually from the back or side. Designing them is difficult. The launcher needs to be a reasonable length to allow the rocket to gain speed, but all the fuel must be spent before it emerges, otherwise it will burn the firer's face. This means their launch speed and hence range is limited—to about 219 yards (200 metres). The Soviet RPG-7, used around the world including the Middle East, *Afghanistan, Chechnya, and the former *Yugoslavia is a most ingenious design. It has a small charge to throw the *grenade well clear of the firer and only then does the rocket motor ignite and drive it to its target. This design permits a relatively large warhead and a light, thin launcher, but at some cost to accuracy. The US LAWS (light anti-tank weapons system) was a single-shot cardboard tube with a smaller warhead. As their value against armour declined (Australian Centurion tanks in *Vietnam survived a hail of RPG-7 hits), RPGs retained their usefulness against bunkers. In principle *anti-armour guided weapons such as those used to crack Argentine positions in the *Falklands war are in the RPG family, but the term is now reserved for lighter weapons.   CDB

---

rules of engagement The conduct of war is governed by laws and conventions. Among these are rules laid down by governments and command authorities governing the circumstances in which their armed services may use force, and to what degree. Rules of engagement are designed to prevent the inadvertent escalation of a situation, and strive to follow general precepts of law. These presuppose that aggressive action will not be instigated against the forces of another state, or against armed groups within a state, without careful observance of guidelines laid down by governments. The inherent difficulties of rules of engagement lie within the conflict which often arises between political and military necessity. This can lead to vital targets being declared off limits to attack, ensure that friendly forces are placed at a disadvantage or in grave danger, and create confusion owing to ambiguities.

The difficulties pertaining to rules of engagement vary according to situation. In an internal security situation, it is desirable that a government provides clear rules of engagement to the military personnel deployed. Although they are not fail-safe, these rules ensure that military force is only employed as a last resort, and within the confines of national law. The most obvious examples of such rules of engagement can be found in the British army's presence in Northern Ireland since 1969. The rules of engagement, laid out in the so-called 'yellow card', make explicitly clear when a soldier may employ lethal force. The rules are not so rigid as to be utterly proscriptive, since soldiers are required to utilize their initiative, with the rules of engagement providing them with suitable guidelines. A further consideration is that the rules of engagement in a civilian arena are governed by national law; thus, in Northern Ireland, the principle that only the minimum force necessary may be used is enshrined in the regulations. Where it is deemed that this principle has been breached, prosecutions under civil law have taken place.

In situations where military forces confront one another, rules of engagement are laid down to prevent escalation of hostilities or their premature commencement, but they must not be so prescriptive as to impinge upon necessary action. America's prosecution of the *Vietnam war was at times hindered by the rules of engagement, which, for example, negated the technological sophistication of its equipment, thus placing the advantage in the hands of its enemies. Since rules of engagement are essentially the responsibility of national governments, it is no easy task to harmonize them in the context of alliance or coalition operations, a point that has caused increasing concern in an era of multinational *peacekeeping and peace-enforcement operations.

Rules of engagement must be varied to take account of changing situations. While they are vitally important to ensure that military force is not employed too early or to extremes, they must be flexible enough to allow some freedom of action. Command and control systems must be flexible enough to permit swift passage of orders regarding changes in rules of engagement. While it is correctly perceived that democratic, civil control over armed forces is desirable, governments have a responsibility to ensure that they do not prescribe rules which place their forces at a disadvantage.   DJJ

Rundstedt, FM Gerd von (1875–1953), perhaps the leading soldier of the Third Reich, and the last Prussian officer of the Second. Gerd von Rundstedt, C-in-C West at several times during WW II, epitomized the old Prussian military élite, and struggled to rationalize its code of conduct with that of *Hitler. He had been always destined for the military, entering the army at 16, was a graduate of the Berlin Kriegsakademie, and saw service during WW I on the *general staff in France, Poland, and Russia. Serving in the inter-war *Reichswehr, he maintained strict neutrality towards politics, unlike several colleagues, and was thus seen as a safe pair of hands, perpetuating the old values. By 1933, he was a full general, C-in-C of the First Army Group (the senior command), but privately (though never publicly) reviled the Nazis. At Nuremberg, Rundstedt interpreted his military role as being to execute orders to the best of his ability, but never to moralize to his superior. This personal inability—or reluctance—to distinguish between right and wrong prevented the military from putting an effective brake on Hitler's military ambitions.

Rundstedt was happy to retire after the Sudetenland occupation of 1938, but was recalled to plan and execute the invasion of Poland, as C-in-C Army Group South. He took over Army Group A which led the invasion of France through the Ardennes, to a plan formulated by his COS *Manstein. The Fall of *France gained Rundstedt his promotion to field marshal, although he was a conservative and reluctant convert to *Guderian's use of armour. He was C-in-C of Army Group South for *BARBAROSSA in June 1941, and remains culpable for transmitting the 'Commissar Order' (which authorized the immediate killing of captured commissars) down to his subordinate commands. Hitler dismissed Rundstedt on 1 December for withdrawing from Rostov against orders, but it is significant that he later apologized for doing so—at the behest of *SS Gen Sepp Dietrich.

Replaced by the brilliant von Reichenau, who died of a stroke shortly afterwards, Rundstedt was recalled as C-in-C West in March 1942, and was joined by *Rommel in a subordinate command in November 1943. The two differed over the strategy of how to defeat an Allied invasion, and in practice Rundstedt had little effective control. In the strategic disaster that developed after the *Normandy landings, Rundstedt was again sacked on 2 July—a fortuitous time at which to bow out—but was recalled to preside over the odious courts of 'honour' in the aftermath of the July plot, and eventually again as C-in-C West on 4 September. He oversaw the Ardennes offensive, by then a 69-year-old figurehead. He was 'retired' for the fourth time on 11 March 1945 after the capture of the Remagen bridge over the Rhine, replaced by Kesselring, and captured in May. That he retired or was sacked four times, but always returned to serve Hitler, is evidence of the moral blind spot the old Prussian military had about serving their country, right or wrong. Never a sycophant—as Keitel and Jodl were—to Hitler's military pretensions, he was detained until 1949 and died four years later.   APC-A

Blumentritt, Gunther, *Von Rundstedt: The Soldier & the Man* (London, 1952).

Ziemke, Earl F. (chapter), in Correlli Barnett (ed.), *Hitler's Generals* (London, 1990).

Rupert of the Rhine, Prince

Rupert of the Rhine, Prince (1619–82). Rupert was born in Prague, son of the 'Winter King' Frederick V and Elizabeth, Charles I's sister. He developed his martial skills as an imperial cavalry commander in the *Thirty Years War, before coming to England to fight for Charles I and the royalist cause during the *British civil wars. The popular perception of Rupert's military career is one of impetuosity, rashness, and wanton glory-seeking. The reality was somewhat different. He was a popular commander and military organizer with a real flair for cavalry tactics and, moreover, was an intelligent linguist and artist. Nevertheless, his popularity resulted in resentment at court and despite many successes such as Charlgrove Field (1645) and Newark (1644) he was increasingly to become a scapegoat for the decline of royalist fortunes, particularly after *Marston Moor and *Naseby. Charles eventually relieved Rupert of all responsibilities and ordered him into exile. Although they were later reconciled, Rupert did not regain a field command.

During the interregnum he served as a royalist admiral, and after the restoration he played a leading part in naval reform, commanding the fleet against the Dutch in 1673 before retiring to spend his time in scientific research. He never married, but fathered a daughter with the engaging if giveaway name Ruperta. Dogs were his lifelong passion and his beloved 'Boy' was one of the casualties of Marston

Moor. The *London Gazette* of the 1660s has frequent advertisements for the return of lost dogs 'belonging to H. H. Pr. Ru.'.   JDB/RH

Russian army

Russian army The land forces of imperial Russia before 1917 and of the new state of Russia after 1992 were known as the Russian army; from 1918 to 1946 the land forces of Soviet Russia and (from January 1924) the USSR were officially the 'Workers' and Peasants' Red Army' (RKKA), usually abbreviated to the 'Red Army', and from 1946 until the dissolution of the Union in December 1991, the 'Soviet army'. Because of the strong element of continuity throughout the period, this entry covers them all. Although always variable in quality and at times cursed by poor leadership, rigid tactics, lack of initiative, and occasionally indiscipline which led to atrocities, the Russian and Soviet armies often surprised their critics, and those who underestimated them—including *Napoleon and *Hitler—paid a terrible price. They have also made remarkable contributions to the development or adaptation of military technology, of *tactics, *operational concepts, and the military *art throughout the last three centuries. As the German general and military theorist Hugo von Freytag-Loringhoven said of the imperial army on its exit from WW I, it remained, 'to the end a redoubtable adversary'. Winston *Churchill, no Russophile, paid his great ally the highest compliment: 'The guts of the German army', he said in 1944, 'have been largely torn out by Russian valour and generalship'.

The Russian army was born under the 'Tartar yoke', the two-and-a-half centuries of Mongol suzerainty in Russia from 1240 to 1480. Under the command of Genghis Khan's grandson, Batu, with Subedei as COS, the *Mongols seized the heart of what is now European Russia in two swift campaigns (1237–8 and 1240), deliberately choosing to attack in winter because the rivers and ground would be frozen. The Mongols exercised power through Russian princes, who were responsible for raising troops. Russian princes were therefore part of the Mongol military system and could hardly fail to be impressed by it. In 1380 Prince Dmitry of the Don defeated the Tartar Khan Mamay at Kulikovo field, with an army raised on the Mongol conscription system and using Mongol tactics. In 1382 the Mongols retaliated, capturing and burning Moscow which was defended, for the first time in Russia, by artillery. The Mongol influence persisted after the end of the Tartar yoke. Giles Fletcher, Elizabeth I's ambassador to Russia in 1588–9, wrote that the Russians were at war with 'the Tartars' nearly every year and that they were the neighbours 'with whom they have greatest dealings and intercourse, both in peace and war'. The Mongol legacy can be traced to this century, for example, in the *lava*—a Cossack formation, an open-order cavalry attack. *Lava* is from the Mongol word *lau*, which expresses the idea of convergence. It was employed against the French in 1812 and in 1912 was adopted as the standard formation for Russian cavalry, and was widely used in the Russian civil war. So a Mongol formation with a Mongol name survived for 700 years, right into the Soviet period.

The Russians' great emphasis on artillery, in which the Russian army has always had a tradition of excellence, may also date back to fighting the Mongols. Russian writers commented that artillery was the one thing that really frightened the Mongols, and it was the only weapons system that gave the Russians the crucial advantage of range over their powerful composite bows.

The Asiatic component of the Russian army and its experience of campaigns in the Caucasus and central Asia, combined with its schizophrenic position on the edge of Europe, sometimes playing a European role, sometimes not, gave it many characteristics which it shares with the British army.

Under *Ivan 'the Terrible' professional units of gunners (*pushkary*) and musketeers (*streltsy) were formed, although the Russian army remained a predominantly cavalry force on the oriental model until the 17th century. Then Russia began to look to the west, a process which began in earnest under Tsar Aleksey Mikhailovich in 1645–76. After the *Thirty Years War and the *British civil wars there were plenty of *mercenaries for whom Russia offered both safety from reprisals and opportunity, including Scotsmen like Gen Patrick Gordon, who entered Russian service in 1661.

Russia exerted a fascination on western intellectuals which has continued to this day. John Milton and Daniel Defoe both wrote about it. Milton noted that the Russians fought 'without order, nor willingly give battail but by stealth or ambush; of cold and hard Diet marvellously patient', an assessment with which the *Wehrmacht in 1941–5 would probably have agreed. An early 18th-century assessment of the Russian fleet similarly stressed Russian cunning and their expertise at 'a handsome defence, ever a Russian's masterpiece'.

The process of westernization accelerated under *Peter 'the Great', who created a regular army on the western model, based on a system of conscription. The Russians learned by their mistakes, losing to the Swedes at Narva in 1700 but winning at *Poltava in 1709. The army regulations (*Ustav voinskiy*) of 1716 established a regular army of 112,000 men, comprising 70,000 infantry, 38,000 cavalry, and 4,000 artillerymen.

By the mid-18th century the Russian army had expanded to 331,000, ready for Russia's appearance as a major player in European politics in the *Seven Years War. At the battle of Kunersdorf on 12 August 1759 a Russian-Austrian army under Russian Gen Saltykov defeated *Frederick 'the Great', and the following year a Russian cavalry raid reached Berlin. The Russians introduced excellent new artillery including the 'unicorn' *howitzer and at the battle of Paltsig (modern Pałcł in Poland) used a form of *indirect fire. Russia was now a great European power, and would remain so. In 1763 the Russian *general staff was formed. During this

period the main European powers had moved towards characteristic uniform *colours, though with many exceptions, and the Russians adopted a very practical dark green.

Russia's double-headed eagle continued to face east—or south—as well as west, however. There were a total of nine Russo-Turkish wars (1676–81, 1686–1700, 1710–13, 1735–9, 1768–74, 1787–91, 1806–12, 1828–9, and 1877–8), not counting the *Crimean war and WW I, the first of which began against Turkey and the second of which included large-scale action against Turkey on the Caucasus front. The fifth and sixth Russo-Turkish wars provided a hard school for many 18th- and early 19th-century Russian commanders, including Rumyantsev, *Suvorov, and *Kutuzov.

A key figure in the development of the Russian army was *Potemkin, who established a Russian trend for practical, comfortable, but stylish uniforms. Potemkin's easygoing uniforms were discarded under mad Tsar Paul, who ruled 1796–1801 and ordered a return to Prussian-style *drill and uniforms and pigtails. The Russian army which goose-stepped into battle at *Austerlitz in 1805 was still run on the lines laid down by Paul. After the defeat at Austerlitz the Russians discarded the Prussian system and began training their troops to conduct aimed fire and make use of natural cover. In 1809 a new 0.7 inch musket was introduced. The war ministry had also been founded in 1802 (from 1802–12 it was called the 'Ministry of Land Forces') and officers began undertaking field training and staff rides. As a result, the Russian army was much better schooled and equipped to take the field against Napoleon in 1812.

During the 'long peace' which followed the *Napoleonic wars the European Russian army ossified, reflecting the backward state of the economy. However, in the Caucasus the Russians were fighting a vicious war against local tribes (1817–64) including the great *guerrilla leader *Shamyl, an experience similar to that of the British in India or the US army in the west at the same time. Furthermore the 1848 revolutions gave the Russian army an opportunity to deploy the first force ever sent on operations (as opposed to on *exercises) by *railway. The 'Eastern war', as the Crimean war was known in Russia, showed the backwardness of the Russian army, still equipped with smooth-bore muskets, compared with the French and British who had the new *Minié rifle. Their inferiority was even more apparent at sea, where the Russian wooden fleet declined to give battle to the iron-framed, steam-powered vessels of Britain and France. However, for the Russians the Crimean peninsula (where Turks and Piedmontese were also employed) was a minor theatre: the main potential theatre was in central Europe and they also fought a war with the Turks in the Caucasus with Shamyl at their back.

It was obvious that what would later be called a 'revolution in military affairs' was taking place, and the Russians determined to do something about it. The liberal war minister Gen Dmitry Milyutin set in train a series of military reforms between 1860 and 1870. Most remarkable was the invention of the system of Military Districts (MDs), from 1863, which survived into the Soviet period. Russia was so vast—it stretched from Poland more than halfway round the world to Alaska, which was not sold to the USA until 1867—that the only way to defend it was to make each MD able to fight a war on its own. This happened twice in the Soviet period, though in both cases a single MD was not quite up to it. The Leningrad MD fought the war with Finland in 1939–40 and the Turkestan MD was responsible for the invasion of *Afghanistan in 1979. Milyutin's reforms included examination of the movement of troops by rail and water (1864) and of Russia's strategic railways (1866). Both were chaired by Gen Mikhail Ivanin, a veteran of the central Asian expedition to Khiva in 1839–40 and an expert on the Mongols. In 1874 Russia also introduced a modern system of universal short service conscription, to replace the older system where certain peasants had been called up for long periods of service.

In 1877 Russia was drawn into war with Turkey in support of her Orthodox and Slavic kinsmen in Serbia and Bulgaria. Volunteers had been going to the Balkans for some years before. The Russian army, reformed by Milyutin, performed brilliantly. In the battle of Avliyar-Aladja, they used the *telegraph to co-ordinate an attack on a wide front, and pushed Lt Gen Yuri Gurko's forward detachment through the little-used Khainkoi Pass through the Balkans to take the main Shipka Pass in the rear, and then to cut Turkish communications. It was the prototype of the Great Patriotic war 'forward detachment' and 'mobile group', and of the 'operational manoeuvre group' which caused NATO analysts such alarm in the 1980s. The Russian army stopped, in part to avoid clashing with the British who did not want them to seize Istanbul.

It was also in the 1870s that the Russian army began its extraordinarily rigorous and academic exploration of the likely character of future war. More than the other great European powers, they took the lessons of the *American civil war seriously, particularly with regard to cavalry 'raids', known as *Americanskiy reyd*.

The Russian army which went to war in the *Russo-Japanese war of 1904–5 was, in spite of the common impression, a good one. The Russians were well equipped, especially with artillery, and fought well. There were two problems: Gen Kuropatkin, the former war minister, tried to bring about a single decisive battle, in an era when battlefronts had extended to make this impossible, and the Russian army had to be supplied along an incomplete single-track railway over about 4,000 miles (6,436 km). In spite of that, Kuropatkin was optimistic that the Russians could win, until the 1905 revolution in European Russia forced the government to end the war.

The Russians were similarly unlucky in 1914. Between 1908 and 1915 the Russian army was reorganized under the CGS, then war minister, Vladimir Sukhomlinov. He responded correctly to the lessons of the Russo-Japanese war, but his reforms were not complete when war started. During this period a group of bright young officers, who would later join the Red Army, including Aleksandr Neznamov, began working on a unified military *doctrine. The Russians mobilized faster than the Germans expected, and won their first battle, at Gumbinen. They had prepared for a short, sharp, mobile war—the wrong war. As in the west, they rapidly experienced a shell shortage. A number of western journalists were with the Russian army and their reports indicate they were generally impressed. Despite defeat at *Tannenberg and the *Masurian Lakes, the Russians held the Germans and regularly bested the Austrians. The *Brusilov offensive in June 1916, timed to coincide with the British *Somme offensive, was brilliantly planned and came close to achieving a breakthrough. The Russians attempted a final great offensive, the 'Kerensky offensive' of summer 1917, but it failed. Contrary to *Lenin's statement that the Russian army 'voted for peace with its feet', the evidence indicates that many Russian units stood their ground until the November revolution (see RUSSIAN REVOLUTIONS). Freytag-Loringhoven was right. The imperial Russian army remained, to the end, a redoubtable adversary.

Some officers, including the brilliant Gen Mikhail Alekseyev, joined the 'White' forces, opposed to the revolution, in the Russian civil war that followed. But some 50,000 imperial officers—often those from Moscow or Petrograd—joined the new Red Army, founded by a decree of 28 January 1918 since it became obvious that the revolution would have to defend itself. By the end of April 1918 the Red Army was 196,000 strong. By autumn 1920, at the end of the main phase of the civil war, it was 5.5 million. Although led at the highest level by *Trotsky, the mechanics of fighting were left to ex-imperial Russian army officers under political supervision—the origin of the commissar system—while imperial army *NCOs formed the next generation of senior officers. Very senior officers like Brusilov, the CGS during WW I, Nikolay Mikhnevich, and Maj Gen Aleksandr Svechin moved into teaching positions; more junior officers like *Tukhachevskiy and Boris Shaposhnikov rapidly assumed senior command and staff positions. It was the latter officers who were mainly killed in the great purge of 1937, allowing the tsarist NCOs like *Zhukov and Konstantin Rokossovskiy to take command and become marshals during the 'Great Patriotic War' of 1941–5. Shaposhnikov, a tsarist cavalry officer who had completed the General Staff Academy in 1910, survived, uniquely, to be CGS at the beginning of the 1941–5 war and a Deputy People's Commissar of Defence. *Stalin said it was because Shaposhnikov did everything he was told.

The continuity between the imperial army and the Red Army was underplayed, though acknowledged, in the Soviet period. Neznamov, who had worked on military doctrine before WW I, now began publishing and during the 1920s the Red Army developed its understanding of the *operational level of war. An enormous effort went into military *education, to provide new working-class commanders with the knowledge and education needed to handle large military formations, and to enlist them into the communist party.

During 1924–5 the *Frunze military reforms took place, leading to the creation of a 'mixed' system with a small professional army at the core of a territorial militia which could be called up in war. During the late 1920s and early 1930s, the Red Army was responsible for some of the most original and far-reaching developments in military theory on the conduct of *total war and the development of deep battle, especially the work of Aleksandr Svechin, *Triandafillov, and Tukhachevskiy. By 1935 it was clear that technological advances made it essential to have a 'high quality mass army'—an ambition the USSR struggled to achieve, probably bankrupting itself in the process.

In 1937 the Soviet armed forces, including the army, were devastated by Stalin's great purge. The army lost 3 out of 5 marshals, 3 out of 5 'army commanders first class' (generals), all ten second class, 50 out of 57 corps commanders, 154 out of 186 divisional commanders, and 401 out of 456 colonels. Although these figures were not published until 1987, foreign observers at the time knew enough of what had happened to believe the Red Army had been decapitated and would prove easy meat in a future war. The way the Red Army looked in the invasions of eastern Poland in 1939, the Baltic States in 1940, and its performance in the 1939–40 Russo-Finnish war suggested they might be right. By this time the Red Army was receiving some remarkable new equipment but appeared unable to use it.

*BARBAROSSA, the invasion of the USSR on 22 June 1941 that began the war on the *eastern front, was the most devastating attack in the entire history of war. The Red Army, supported and sometimes disciplined by the troops of the People's Commissariat for Internal Affairs (NKVD), fought stubbornly, and inflicted the first great defeats on the German armies at *Moscow and *Stalingrad. The conceptual studies of the inter-war years bore fruit in vast operations of staggering scale and scope. The old tsarist *badges and insignia were reintroduced, and victory over Nazi Germany and imperial Japan brought glory to Russian arms. Although it was very variable in quality, sometimes guilty of atrocities, and maintained in battle by a combination of patriotism, courage, and coercion, the Red Army's reputation soared. In 1946 it was renamed the Soviet Army.

The 'revolution in military affairs' brought about by the nuclear weapon and the ballistic missile to carry it led to the creation of a new armed service in 1959—the Strategic Missile Forces (RVSN), avoiding the awkward problem which faced western governments in deciding whether to give the new weapons to the army, navy, air force, or all three. A strategic air defence force (PVO) had been created in 1941, operating both aircraft and anti-aircraft guns and missiles, creating a structure with five armed services rather than the traditional three. The army was last in the queue for recruits—the best went to the high-tech services. We will never know how it would have performed against NATO but it would have been formidable. The Soviets made mistakes in Afghanistan in 1979–89, but learned from experience. The lack of a tradition of doctrine for operations short of major war—it had focused totally on large-scale armoured and nuclear warfare—proved a major disadvantage.

On 8 December 1991 the USSR broke up and shortly afterwards the new Russian army was formed. Its uniforms, badges, and insignia were little changed apart from the reintroduction of the double-headed eagle, facing east and west. The financial crisis of the 1990s meant that soldiers and officers went unpaid, and it was difficult to attract recruits. In 1996 President Yeltsin announced to intention to end conscription by 2000—this was hastily pushed back to 2005 and then 2015. At the time of publication, Russia cannot afford professional armed forces, though it would like them. The army's performance in Chechnya was variable, but it was ultimately successful. Its most professional troops—the *airborne forces—have performed very creditably in Bosnia. The Russian army will no doubt rise from its present crisis as it has before. It will always be a 'redoubtable adversary'. Or, preferably, as it was to America and Britain in much of two world wars, a mighty ally and friend.

CDB

Bellamy, Christopher, 'Seventy Years On: Similarities between the Modern Soviet Army and its Tsarist Predecessor', *RUSI Journal* (Sept. 1979).

—— 'Heirs of Genghis Khan', *RUSI* (Mar. 1983).

—— 'Antecedents of the Modern Soviet Operational Manoeuvre Group', *RUSI* (Sept. 1984).

Duffy, Christopher, *Russia's Military Way to the West* (London, 1981).

Erickson, John, *The Soviet High Command, 1917–1941* (London, 1967).

—— *The Road to Stalingrad* (London, 1975).

—— *The Road to Berlin* (London, 1982).

Milton, John, *A Brief History of Moscovia and other Countries Lying Eastward of Russia as far as Cathay* (1682; repub. London, 1929).

Sovetskaya voyennaya entsiklopediya (Soviet Military Encyclopedia), vol. 7 (Moscow, 1979).

Russian Revolutions (March and November 1917). The two revolutions of 1917 took Russia out of WW I. They led to the creation of the world's first communist state and, in December 1922, to the formation of the USSR, which lasted until December 1991. Historically, the revolutions were called 'February' and 'October', because until February 1918 the Russians still used the old Julian calendar, which, by the 20th century, was thirteen days behind the modern calendar. Thus, the main events of the first revolution took place from 23 to 27 February, Old Style, or 8 to 11 March. The armed insurrection in Petrograd (formerly St Petersburg), the beginning of the 'Great October Socialist

Revolution', began on 24 October, Old Style, or 6 November.

Both revolutions were metropolitan, carried out with little reference either to the armies at the front or to the countryside. The first revolution brought about a brief period of parliamentary democracy under the provisional government led by lawyer Alexander Kerensky, which remained committed to the war effort. But that led quickly to a second—a well-organized coup by a disciplined minority, the Bolsheviks, led by *Lenin whom the Germans helped return to Russia in April 1917, in a successful bid to knock Russia out of the war.

In November 1916 military chiefs of the Entente—France, Britain, Russia, and Italy—met at Chantilly and in the third week of January 1917, Entente politicians met in Petrograd. Both meetings declared that 1917 would be the year of victory over the Central Powers. The Entente now enjoyed a 60 per cent superiority over the Central Powers on all fronts—including the Russian front. But by the beginning of 1917, most of the imperial Russian army, which was still holding down half the Central Powers' forces, showed little interest in fighting, although reports of its disintegration were premature. The initial cause of the Revolution was the collapse of the Russian monarchy, weakened by the influence of Rasputin. On 8 March Petrograd workers demonstrated against the tsarist regime, the war, and food shortages. Fights with the police and army followed but many soldiers sided with the revolutionaries who took control of the capital. On 12 March the 'Soviet' (council) of Soldiers and Workers' Deputies created during the 1905 revolution was re-established and on the 15th the tsar abdicated. A provisional government was set up in the Tauride palace, which it shared with what was effectively a rival government, the Petrograd Soviet. The reaction of Russian troops at the front varied: some wept openly, others demanded the imperial monogram be removed from their colours before they would take an oath to the new government. They all expected the war to continue and fighting continued on the Caucasian front where the Russians had been performing well against the Turks. By mistake, an order from the Petrograd Soviet establishing its authority over the Petrograd garrison was sent to the whole army, with the result that officers had to consult local soldiers' soviets before giving orders. The Duma (parliament) and the Soviet also sent 'commissars' to the front to explain what was going on, but they were often Bolsheviks who took the opportunity to undermine military authority and criticize the provisional government. Liberal measures, including abolition of the death penalty, intended to calm the situation, had the opposite effect.

Had the Germans attacked at this time, the Russians would probably have fought back. Instead, the Germans realized they might be able to bring about the collapse of the Russian army more cheaply. Russian attempts to make contact with the Germans to spread revolutionary propaganda

to their fellow workers provided a conduit for German government propaganda to get back to the Russian soldiers. The Germans also allowed Lenin to return from exile in Switzerland in April in the famous 'sealed train'.

Much of the workforce was now on strike, which hampered resupply of the armies at the front. In April, 130 factories were closed in the capital. Britain stopped supplying war materials until the situation was resolved. In May Alexander Guchkov, the war minister, resigned and was replaced by Kerensky. Notwithstanding the turmoil, the government remained committed to continuing the war, and so did many Bolsheviks, including, at this stage, *Stalin. But the provisional government felt increasing resentment at pressure from the western Allies to mount an offensive. On 21 March the Russian C-in-C, Gen Mikhail Alekseyev, received a telegram from Nivelle, his French opposite number, asking him to launch an offensive 'around the beginning or middle of April', which, under the circumstances, provoked astonishment (see NIVELLE OFFENSIVE). Alekseyev said he could not, and the Allies, attacking on the western front and encountering fierce opposition, started to threaten sanctions, which Russia could not afford. Kerensky, the new war minister, made a speech-making tour of the front, to whip up new enthusiasm. But the number of *desertions was rising: between March and May it was 34,000 a month, five times the average during the war before that. The Russians began preparations for a new offensive, launched on 30 June. The observation posts were crammed with journalists, political commissars, and soldiers' delegates as the Kerensky offensive—the old Russian army's last—began. The Germans were using new tactics of defence in depth developed in the west, and the Russian offensive ground to a halt with appalling casualties.

On 13 July *Brusilov, who had replaced Alekseyev, was in turn replaced as C-in-C by Lavr Kornilov. After failing to restore discipline, Kornilov turned his forces round to try to overthrow the provisional government from 7 to 13 September. In late August reports of a Bolshevik coup against the provisional government gave Kornilov an excuse to march on Petrograd. Sympathetic officers were spread out along the front and the route back, and Kerensky soon heard of Kornilov's planned coup. Kerensky, who was now PM, denounced him as a counter-revolutionary, dismissed him, and took the post himself—thus becoming a virtual dictator.

But the provisional government was now in crisis. Some Bolsheviks had made an abortive attempt at revolt in July. Now Lenin, who had then fled for his life, was determined that a well-organized coup would bring him to power. On 23 October a secret meeting of the Bolshevik Central Committee adopted a resolution calling for an armed revolt, and on 25th a Revolutionary staff was set up. Trotsky did most of the detailed planning; Lenin did not return to Petrograd from Finland until 29th. In Petrograd, the Bolsheviks could count on 20,000 'Red Guards' (*krasnogvardeytsy*)—

card-carrying, armed members, up to 150,000 soldiers, and 80,000 sailors of the Baltic fleet.

At 21.40 on 7 November a blank shot fired from the Baltic Fleet cruiser *Aurora* signalled the start of the assault on the Winter Palace, the seat of the provisional government. At 02.10 on 8 November the Bolsheviks seized control. The provisional government was arrested. The next night the gathered representatives of the soviets passed decrees on peace and land, and set up the Soviet of People's Commissars, headed by Lenin. On 15 November the new Soviet government moved to the old Russian capital, Moscow. On 21 November, a radio message ordered all Russian army units to begin armistice negotiations with the Germans and Austrians. The Revolution had taken Russia out of the Great War, but three years of foreign intervention and civil war had already begun.   CDB

Russo-Japanese war (1904–5), major but ultimately indecisive war, noted for its political consequences—the first (1905) Russian revolution—but most important militarily as a full dress rehearsal for WW I. It was a war of extended fronts and protracted battles, leading to the emergence of the *operational level of war, *trench warfare, the use of *machine guns, *mortars, *grenades, land and sea *mines, submarines, barbed wire (sometimes electrified) and *indirect fire, *radio transmission and even electronic warfare (jamming). Foreign observers from the USA, UK, France, and Germany were present on both sides and their detailed and perceptive reports help make it the best-documented war up to that time.

In 1898 Russia leased the Kwantung peninsula from Japan and set up its naval base at *Port Arthur. In autumn 1900 it occupied Manchuria. In 1902 the Japanese concluded an agreement with Britain and began preparing for war. Russia's ability to influence events in the region was dependent on the trans-Siberian *railway, first discussed in 1860, studied in 1875, and begun in 1891. By 1896 the western section, through Irkutsk to Lake Baikal and from its eastern shore to Sretensk near the Amur river, was built. However, the Russians then decided not to follow the great bend of the Amur round to the north but to cut straight across Manchuria from Chita, 300 miles (483 km) east of Baikal, via Harbin to Vladivostok—the Chinese Eastern railway. The occupation of Manchuria upset the Japanese even more, so the line by which the Russian troops would have to be supplied was itself a cause of the war, and it was single track, with lightweight rails and badly laid.

At the outbreak of war Russia had the world's largest standing army—1,350,000 men—but most of it was in Europe. In the Far East Russia had two corps totalling 98,000 men, plus 24,000 local troops and 198 guns, scattered across Manchuria, the Pacific coast, and the trans-Baikal region. The Russian Far Eastern Fleet comprised 63 warships including seven battleships and 11 cruisers, mostly obsolete.

Japan, much nearer to the theatre of war, had an army of 375,000 on mobilization, with 1,140 guns and 147 machine guns, and 80 warships including six battleships and 20 cruisers. The Russian army in the west—5,000 miles (8,045 km) away—was re-equipped with the 76 mm M-1900 and M-1902 field guns, described by foreign observers as 'really excellent' and 'the most powerful field gun in the world' respectively. However, most of the fortress artillery in Port Arthur was antiquated. Russia was not ready for war with Japan in the Far East, and the Japanese knew it. The Russian plan, sensibly enough, was to delay the Japanese while they built up their own strength in the Liao-Yang area, bringing forces south from the Chinese Eastern railway at the top of the 'T' at Harbin.

Neither were the Russian command arrangements ideal. The commander of the Manchurian Army, Gen Aleksey Kuropatkin, a highly academic general and former war minister, was appointed in February 1904, but as such he was junior to the C-in-C Far East, Adm Yevgeniy Alekseyev, which led to friction. Kuropatkin was made C-in-C in October 1904, but after the battles of Liao-Yang and *Mukden he was demoted to command First Army.

On 6 February 1904 Japan cut off diplomatic relations with Russia and two days later launched a surprise attack before declaring war—a technique repeated in 1941. On the night of 8/9 February Japanese torpedo boats attacked the Russian squadron in Port Arthur and the following day sank two Russian warships at Inchon, Korea. In spite of heavy losses, the Port Arthur squadron remained a threat and was blockaded, permitting the Japanese to transport its armies to the peninsula. These deployed for a land offensive under Marshal Oyama and at the end of April Gen Kuroki's 45,000–strong Japanese First Army, which had advanced north through Korea, met the Russians at the river Ya-lu. The Russians withdrew, the first of many withdrawals under Kuropatkin's probably overcautious command. On 5 May Gen Oku's Second Army, with 35,000 men, landed on the Liao-dun peninsula, cutting Port Arthur off from the Russian Manchurian Army. After an unsuccessful attempt by the Russian I Siberian Corps to re-establish communications at the battle of Wafangkou (Telissu) on 14–15 June, the Japanese laid siege to the fortress, shipping in the new Third Army under *Nogi with 60,000 men and 400 guns. Second Army meanwhile tried to push the Russians north up the railway line, in the battle of Tashichao (23–4 July). The Russians fought the Japanese off but Gen Kuropatkin nevertheless ordered a withdrawal north. Here, from 24 August to 3 September the great battle of Liao-Yang took place. Once again the Russians, dug in on a wide front, and exploiting the emerging supremacy of the defensive, held the Japanese but again Kuropatkin ordered withdrawal. On 6 September the Russians pulled back to the Shah-ho, where Kuropatkin intended to build up his strength further and then counter-attack. By this time the Manchurian Army was 214,000 strong with 758 guns against total Japanese

Russo-Japanese war

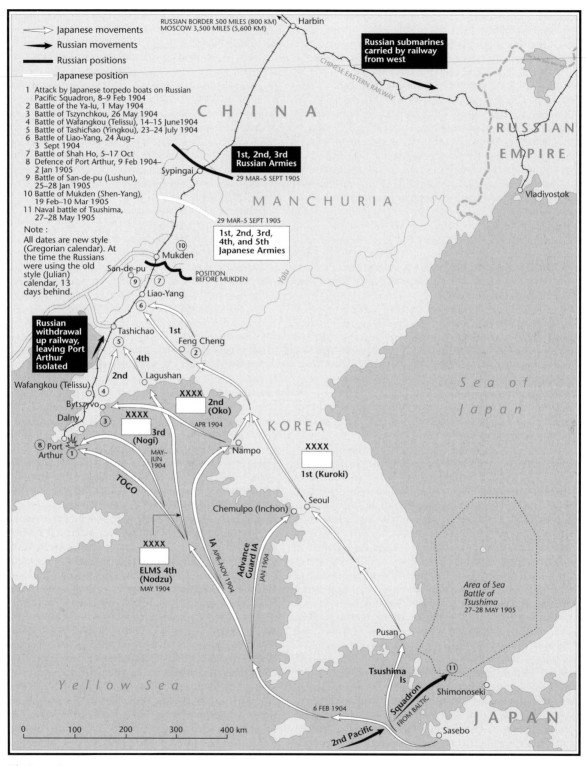

Japanese movements
Russian movements
Russian positions
Japanese position

1 Attack by Japanese torpedo boats on Russian Pacific Squadron, 8–9 Feb 1904
2 Battle of the Ya-lu, 1 May 1904
3 Battle of Tszynchkou, 26 May 1904
4 Battle of Wafangkou (Telissu), 14–15 June 1904
5 Battle of Tashichao (Yingkou), 23–24 July 1904
6 Battle of Liao-Yang, 24 Aug–3 Sept 1904
7 Battle of Shah Ho, 5–17 Oct
8 Defence of Port Arthur, 9 Feb 1904–2 Jan 1905
9 Battle of San-de-pu (Lushun), 25–28 Jan 1905
10 Battle of Mukden (Shen-Yang), 19 Feb–10 Mar 1905
11 Naval battle of Tsushima, 27–28 May 1905

Note :
All dates are new style (Gregorian calendar). At the time the Russians were using the old style (Julian) calendar, 13 days behind.

RUSSIAN BORDER 500 MILES (800 KM)
MOSCOW 3,500 MILES (5,600 KM)
Harbin

Russian submarines carried by railway from west

CHINESE EASTERN RAILWAY

C H I N A

RUSSIAN EMPIRE

1st, 2nd, 3rd Russian Armies
29 MAR–5 SEPT 1905
Sypingai

M A N C H U R I A

Vladivostok

29 MAR–5 SEPT 1905
1st, 2nd, 3rd, 4th, and 5th Japanese Armies

Mukden (10)
San-de-pu
(9) (7)
POSITION BEFORE MUKDEN

Yalu

Liao-Yang
(6)
1st
Feng Cheng
(2)

Russian withdrawal up railway, leaving Port Arthur isolated

Tashichao (5)
4th
2nd
Lagushan

Wafangkou (Telissu)
Bytszyvo (4)
Dalny (3)
(8) Port Arthur (1)

XXXX
2nd (Oko)
APR 1904

XXXX
3rd (Nogi)
MAY–JUN 1904

Nampo

K O R E A

XXXX
1st (Kuroki)

Sea of Japan

TOGO

XXXX
ELMS 4th (Nodzu)
MAY 1904

IA APR–NOV 1904

Advance Guard IA JAN 1904

Chemulpo (Inchon)

Seoul

Area of Sea Battle of Tsushima 27–28 MAY 1905

Pusan

Tsushima Is

(11)
Shimonoseki

J A P A N

Yellow Sea

6 FEB 1904

Squadron FROM BALTIC

2nd Pacific

Sasebo

0   100   200   300   400 km

The **Russo-Japanese war** 1904–5.

forces of 170,000 with 648 guns. Kuropatkin, who still believed in the possibility of a decisive battle, decided the time was now right to go over to the offensive. However, the encounter engagement on the Shah-ho proved indecisive and a continuous front 37 miles (60 km) wide developed, just as it would in WW I, giving rise to a positional battle from 5 to 17 October.

After the Shah-ho battle there was a lull in the fighting. In January 1905 the Russians launched Mishchenko's raid, round the left (western) flank of the Japanese to cut the railway supplying their troops in the front line north of Liao-Yang. The raid by a force of 7,500 *Cossacks cut the line in several places—a classic 'strategic' cavalry raid and prototype of the Soviet manoeuvre group (see OPERATIONAL CONCEPTS).

Realizing that the Russians were gaining strength, Oyama decided to reduce Port Arthur, which had been blockaded since February and under land attack since May, in the shortest possible time and switched his main effort to achieving this, increasing the besieging force from 70,000 to 100,000. Two attempts by Russian squadrons to break in from the sea, on 23 June and 10 August, failed. The 50,000 Russians, well dug-in, repelled numerous land assaults, using, among other things, trench mortars and hand grenades, but on 2 January 1905 the commander, Gen Anatoliy Stoessel, surrendered the fortress. The Russians claim to have inflicted 60,000 casualties on the Japanese in its defence. The siege of Port Arthur was certainly not taken to suggest that fortresses were obsolete but, on the contrary, that they could hold up huge armies for periods of time unacceptable to the enemy.

Following a Russian attempt to outflank the Japanese at San-de-pu from 25 to 28 January 1905, the final land battle at Mukden lasted nineteen days and nights from 19 February to 10 March 1905. This was the shape of future war. Both commanders tried, in Napoleonic fashion, to destroy the other army. Both failed. From the middle of March active military operations ceased on land.

The main Russian forces, meanwhile, had been supplied and reinforced along the trans-Siberian and Chinese Eastern railways—a distance of 4,000 miles (6,436 km) from European Russia and 5,400 miles (8,689 km) from their main bases, most of it single track. The section around Lake Baikal, the largest freshwater lake in the world, had not been built. The ingenuity and effort shown by the Russians in overcoming these problems attracted the admiration of foreign observers. Lake Baikal froze over at the end of January 1904, just in time for the war. When the ice reached a metre and a half in thickness, a 25 mile (40 km) railway was laid over it, and the supplies were carried across. Meanwhile, the Russians pushed ahead with the circum-Baikal section at a cost equivalent to £52,000 per mile (1.6 km)—£20,000 a mile more expensive than usual in Russia. It was completed at the end of September 1904. Down this single line the Russians carried vast quantities of munitions, barbed wire, and

all the requisites for a fully modern war. They even brought submarines, built in St Petersburg, by rail, to Vladivostok, where they launched them into the Pacific.

Kuropatkin maintained that even after the bloody but indecisive battle of Mukden he was still gathering strength. By the end of the war he had a million men, two-thirds of whom had not yet seen action, and new machine guns, artillery including howitzers, with growing numbers of shells and even wireless supplies.

Meanwhile, there had been a revolution in European Russia, starting with the massacre of peaceful protesters in St Petersburg on 22 January 1905. Protest, which began with industrial workers, spread rapidly to the army and fleet. Kuropatkin, understandably perhaps, blamed the 1905 revolution for his failure:

What single authority would have admitted a few years ago the possibility of concentrating an army of a million men 5,400 miles [8,689 km] away from its base of supply and equipment by means of a poorly constructed single-line railway? Wonders were effected but it was too late. Affairs in the interior of Russia for which the War Department could not be held responsible were the cause of the war being brought to an end at a time when decisive military operations should have only just been beginning.

Japanese control of the sea was a major problem for the Russians and in October 1904 and February 1905 Russian squadrons were sent from the Baltic fleet round Europe, Africa, and Asia to the Far East to form the Second Pacific Squadron. Shortly after leaving the Baltic, the Russians were panicked by some British North Sea trawlers, which they thought might be Japanese torpedo boats, and opened fire, causing outrage. On 27 May 1905, after half circumnavigating the world, the Russian fleet was surprised by the Japanese in the Straits of Tsushima between Korea and Japan. Vice Adm Zinoviy Rozhdestvenskiy commanded the Russian force. His eight battleships, nine cruisers (only one of them armoured), three coast defence monitors, and an assortment of other ships ran into Adm Togo's four battleships and 24 cruisers, eight of them armoured. The Russians had 228 guns to the Japanese 910 but their strength in big guns—8 to 12 inch—was almost equal, with 54 Russian to 60 Japanese. At 07.00 on 27 May the Russians spotted a Japanese cruiser. At 13.15 the Russians encountered the main Japanese fleet trying to cross their bows, and at 13.49 they opened fire at a range of 38 cables (more than 7,000 yards (6401 metres)). In the battle that followed the Russians lost all eight battleships and their armoured cruiser, and one of the monitors, plus a number of other ships. The cruiser *Aurora*, which later signalled the storming of the Winter Palace in the *Russian Revolution of November 1917, made it to Manila, but only one cruiser and two torpedo boats reached Vladivostok. The Russian fleet had been utterly destroyed.

The destruction of the Russian fleet was one setback too many. As the 1905 protests at home gathered strength, the Russians sued for peace. At Portsmouth (USA) on 5

September the Russians recognized Korea as lying within the Japanese sphere of influence and gave up southern Sakhalin island and the lease of the Liao-dun peninsula, Port Arthur, and Dalny. Both sides withdrew their forces from Manchuria. After the 1917 revolution the Soviet government agreed to honour the peace terms, but after the occupation of Manchuria by Japan in 1931, which violated it, the peace treaty became irrelevant.

The Russo-Japanese war is sometimes cited as an example of the backwardness of the Russian armed forces, and this is true of the navy, but the foreign observers who were there with the Russian army were impressed by its performance and equipment, and particularly its artillery and the way it utilized indirect fire—the first time these techniques were generally used in war. 'The army as a whole', one wrote, 'is distinctly a good one, and presents many points worthy of imitation.' It could have won, had the home front not collapsed behind it.   CDB

Kuropatkin, Gen A. N., *The Russian Army and the Japanese War*, trans. Capt A. B. Lindsay, ed. Maj E. D. Swinton, 2 vols. (London, 1909).

Reports of British Observers attached to the Russian and Japanese Armies in the Field (General Staff, London, 1907).

US Official Reports on the Russo-Japanese War (War Department, Washington, 1906).

Russo-Polish war (1920), short but violent war in which two outstanding military commanders, Polish Marshal *Pilsudski and Russian General, later Marshal, *Tukhachevskiy, clashed before Warsaw. The Poles' victory at Warsaw was seen at the time as the salvation of European democracy in the face of communism. Soviet historiography regarded the war as part of the final phase of the 'civil war and military intervention in Russia', which ended in November with the defeat of Wrangel in the Crimea. Poland had been part of the Russian empire during the 19th century but the 1919 Treaty of Versailles established an independent state with new borders, led by Pilsudski who had commanded the Polish Legion on the Austro-Hungarian side in the Great War. In January 1920 the Russian government began negotiations with the Poles on the new frontier. Conscious of their military weakness, the Russians were prepared to cede territory east of the Curzon Line, the frontier established by Versailles in December, but the Poles wanted all the territory which had belonged to Poland before 1772, and withdrew from the talks on 7 April.

On 25 April they attacked with five armies, organized and supplied with the help of the Great War Entente, which had unsuccessfully intervened in Russia itself. These armies were grouped in two fronts on a frontage of 311 miles (500 km): the north-east (First and Fourth) aimed at Belorussia and the south-east (Third, Second, and Sixth) at Ukraine, where the main attack was directed. The Poles planned to destroy the forces of the Soviet South-West Front (army group) first, capturing 'right bank Ukraine' (as seen from the north-west of the river Dnieper), and then turn north to take Belorussia. The Poles would be helped by forces loyal to the anti-Soviet Ukrainian leader Simon Petlyura, and their attack coincided with renewed activity by Wrangel's White Russian forces in the Crimea.

The Poles quickly pushed 124 miles (200 km) into Ukraine and took Kiev on 7 May. In June, Wrangel broke out of the Crimea, and the Soviet Republic mobilized 1.5 million men and concentrated forces in right-bank Ukraine including the First Cavalry Army. On 12 June they recaptured Kiev and pressed forward to take Novograd-Volynsk on 27 June. The successful counter-attack in Ukraine then allowed the Soviet Western Front to go on the offensive in Belorussia and on 11 July the Soviets recaptured Minsk.

The Soviet Western Front commanded by the 27-year-old Tukhachevskiy, then drove on to Warsaw, reaching Grodno on the 23rd, the beginning of the 'Warsaw operation'. The Soviet C-in-C, Sergey Kamenev, a former tsarist colonel, ordered Tukhachevskiy to pursue the Poles without pause, and he reached the gates of Warsaw on 13 August. It was a daring bid to seize the Polish capital, and almost succeeded, but was frustrated in what the British military theorist *Fuller later recognized as one of the decisive battles of the western world. As Tukhachevskiy reached the end of his stretched communications, without supplies or reserves, the Soviet South-West Front was suffering heavily in the battle for Lvov, to the south. The Poles, helped by the French, managed to regroup and exploited the lack of co-operation between the western and south-west fronts. They managed to get between them and hit the Soviet Western Front forces, whom they outnumbered two to one, in the southern flank between 16 and 25 August. By now, the Soviet forces were exhausted and were forced to fall back to a line running roughly south of Grodno by 25 August and roughly level with Minsk by 12 October, when an armistice was signed at Riga. This enabled the Soviet government to switch their effort to the Crimea, which *Frunze invaded after his breakthrough at the Perekop isthmus on 7 November and defeating Wrangel's forces in the peninsula itself during the following week.

A Polish-Soviet peace treaty was signed at Riga on 18 March 1921, establishing the frontier some 155 miles (250 km) east of the Curzon Line (the line which the Soviet Republic had been prepared to accept before the war). The armistice gave the Soviet Republic a breathing space to complete the destruction of 'White' forces deep in its own territory. Poland held western Ukraine and Belorussia for just eighteen years. In September 1939 the USSR invaded again.   CDB

Fuller, John F. C., *The Decisive Battles of the Western World*, vol. 3 (London, 1956).

Pilsudski, Marshal Jozef, *Year 1920 and its Climax, Battle of Warsaw during the Polish-Soviet War 1920, with the addition of M Tukhachevskiy's March beyond the Vistula* (London, 1972).

Sackville/Germain, Lord George, Viscount Sackville

Sackville/Germain, Lord George, Viscount Sackville (1716–85), British general and statesman. Known as Lord George Sackville until 1770, he was *court-martialled for equivocal conduct at the battle of *Minden and branded as unfit to serve in any military capacity. As Secretary of State for the American colonies 1775–82 and director of the war in the western Atlantic, he was blamed for the loss of America. In reality, he displayed energy, resolution, and a degree of strategic originality, for which he received a viscountcy in 1782. **PGM**

Mackesy, Piers, *The Coward of Minden* (London, 1979).
—— *The War for America, 1775–1783* (London, 1964).

sacrifice Propitiation of the gods before battle by means of sacrifice was common throughout the ancient world. Animal sacrifice was a central part of early religious practice, having several stages: dedication of the sacrifice, confession of sins, slaughter of the sacrifice, spilling of blood upon the altar, consumption of the sacrifice by fire or by those offering the sacrifice. In the case of the augurs or haruspices of Rome, the animal was sacrificed to permit contemplation of the entrails for prophetic purposes.

Evidence of human sacrifice in the ancient world is not plentiful. Rome abhorred the practice and rooted it out when encountered among others, although when writing of the druidic rituals of the Celts and the taking of heads for trophies they probably exaggerated for propaganda purposes. Across the Atlantic, wholesale Aztec human sacrifice is well documented and additionally their 'flower wars' were fought specifically to gather captives for evisceration on the temples of the Sun. In many Amerindian cultures cannibalism, with or without sacrifice, seems to have been a spiritual rather than a dietary custom.

At an early stage, warrior societies recognized the importance of self-sacrifice battle. In a funeral oration for Athenian war dead in 431 BC, Pericles established the link between religious sacrifice and death in war, while Horace wrote 'dulce et decorum est pro patria mori', a useful precept for politicians and generals ever since. Examples of heroic self-sacrifice are enshrined in the annals of humankind, from Leonidas' Spartans at *Thermopylae, to Byrhtnoth and his retinue at *Maldon, Roland at Roncevaux, and the Light Brigade at Balaclava. The military outcome is not relevant. We do indeed 'remember the *Alamo'. Sacrifice can take the form of conscious martyrdom as with the defenders of *Masada or Gordon at *Khartoum. Military ends are transcended by a higher purpose or, at least, an act of desperation can be given moral meaning as with the self-immolating kamikaze in the final phase of the *Pacific war against Japan.

Although Christian Communion symbolically embodies sacrifice, much theological ink has been spilled to get around 'thou shalt not kill'. At the time of the Protestant schism, the link between *religion and state power was made explicit in the saying 'cuius regio, eius religio'. Perhaps its saddest manifestation was the holocausts of the 20th century. Perhaps the most pathetic manifestation was the cult of remembrance which arose during WW I, especially in Britain, when the experience of battle was directly equated to the sufferings of Christ and soldiers were said to have died in a state of grace. This heresy, known as patripassionism, was quietly denounced after the war, but 'greater love hath no man than this' was carved not only on war memorials but also into the hearts of their grieving families. **BB**

Bushaway, Bob, 'Name upon Name: The Great War and Remembrance', in Roy Porter (ed.), *Myths of the English* (London, 1992).

St Barbara Patron saint of armourers, fortifications, and artillery. In Spanish the word *santabárbara* means an explosives depository. St Barbara is invoked against thunder, lightning, and all accidents involving *gunpowder. She is the armed Pallas or Bellona of mythology reproduced in the form of a Christian martyr. There is no mention of her in early Christian references and veneration of her was not common before the 7th century.

Tradition has it that she lived in Heliopolis, the daughter of Dioscorus who was rabidly hostile to Christianity and kept her locked in a tower to preserve her virtue. Contemplation caused her to reject pagan gods and she managed to communicate with the Christian teacher Origen. She refused to renounce her faith and in AD 303 was martyred when her father beheaded her for her conversion. He was consumed by fire for his actions.

Alternatively, she was the daughter of Alypius who had learned the secrets of naphtha and saltpetre from a fakir while on military service in the east. He devoted his life to study and with the help of Barbara invented an explosive mixture. Barbara rejected many suitors and entered the convent of St Perpetua in Hippo. In AD 430, the *Vandals besieged Hippo. Barbara helped Alypius to position jars of their mixture in defence of the city, but he was killed and it fell to Barbara to direct the pyrotechnic defence of the city. Her mixture burned the pestilential corpses that threatened the defenders and her illuminations at night thwarted Vandal attacks. She also manufactured incandescent globes which were hurled from catapults. The city eventually fell, and as the attackers tried to capture her, she set off a subterranean explosion in which she and her foes perished.

It was said that those devoted to her might die safely without receiving holy sacraments and she is often depicted carrying a sacramental cup. Early gunners were at high risk from the sudden explosion of bursting gun barrels and she became their patron saint. The cannoneers of Lille recognized her as their saint in 1417, describing themselves as the 'Confrères de Sainte Barbe'. In 1448 Henry Kock was nearly burned to death, but it was believed that her intervention kept him alive long enough to receive the last sacrament. This story did much to popularize her. The powder room of a French warship has traditionally been called 'Sainte Barbe'.

The most famous painting of St Barbara is by Palma Vecchio over the altar of St Barbara in the church of Santa Maria Formosa in Venice. The feast of St Barbara is celebrated by the Greek and Roman calendars on 4 December; the 9th-century martyrologies cite 16 December which is the traditional English date for the festival. In May 1969 she was deleted from the liturgical calendar by Pope Paul VI. It was once suggested by a Major Hanson that the grounds for St Barbara being the patron saint of artillery are rather insubstantial and that St Joan, who used artillery very effectively in sieges of English fortresses, should replace her. The US artillery has an order of St Barbara, awarded to those who have performed conspicuous service as artillerymen. It is traditional among gunners of most western armies to celebrate St Barbara's Day with a dinner.   JBAB

Anon., 'St Barbara', *Field Artillery Journal*, 10/6 (Nov.–Dec. 1920).
Anon., 'Some Legends of St Barbara', *Field Artillery Journal*, 35 (Dec. 1945).
Fort Sill Home Page: usaa@sirinet.net
Hanson, J. M., 'A Candidate for the Position of Patron Saint of Artillery', *Field Artillery Journal*, 11 (Jan. 1921).

Saint-Cyr, Marshal Laurent Gouvion, Marquis de (1764–1830). Saint-Cyr, an artist by trade and inclination, joined the army in 1792 and subsequently rose very rapidly to become a divisional commander. He saw service at the siege of Mainz, and with the Army of the Rhine and Moselle. Saint-Cyr received his marshal's baton from Napoleon after his sterling performance in taking over from the wounded *Oudinot at the battle of Polotsk on 18 August 1812, but he was generally a slow and cautious commander. He saw service in the Spanish theatre in 1808 and 1809 (see PENINSULAR WAR), fighting at Rosas, Barcelona, Molinos del Rey, and at the siege of Gerona, but left his post there without orders and was recalled in disgrace. His health prevented him from participating in the early stages of the 1813 campaign, but he commanded XIV Corps at *Dresden, holding the city until 11 November.

Saint-Cyr swore loyalty to the Bourbon Restoration and led a force that unsuccessfully tried to stop Napoleon's return from Elba. At Bourges on 24 March 1815 his troops deserted but, unlike *Ney, he did not and wisely played no part in the *Hundred Days. He became minister of war under Louis XVIII, and was made a marquis, retiring to devote himself to painting and music in 1819.

The town of Saint-Cyr was where the École Spéciale Militaire (very roughly the French Sandhurst or *West Point) was established in 1802, and where it stayed until after WW II when it moved to Coëtquidan in Brittany.   TM

Saint-Étienne is a city in central France located in a small basin at the foot of the Massif du Pilat. The river Furan runs through it, and this provided energy for the area's industrial activities. The mills powered by the Furan provided the basis for the growth of metallurgy and arms smithery. Arms smithery turned to gun smithery as early as the 16th century, and arms manufacture was central to its economic success.

Saint-Étienne's expansion in the 19th century was based on coal mining. This industrial boom led the further development of the city's arms industry. The Manufacture d'Armes et de Cycles (Gun and Bicycle Manufacture), nicknamed 'la Manu' by its workers, was founded by Étienne Mimard in 1885. In partnership with another arms manufacturer Pierre Blachon, la Manu became one of the largest arms concerns in France. During WW I the arms industry expanded rapidly and Saint-Étienne became the *arsenal of France, earning the nickname 'Armsville'. Because of the rapid collapse of France in 1940, the town's contribution was less important although the Germans attempted to maintain production. This persuaded the USAAF to bomb Saint-Étienne on 26 May 1944, killing almost 1,000 people. Post-war la Manu went into decline, closing in 1973.

MCM

St George, James of (c.1250–1308). In 1278 Edward I recruited a Savoyard master mason, James of St George, into his service. James is known to have worked at Yverdon and elsewhere for the Count of Savoy, and Edward probably first encountered him as he returned from *crusade in 1273. Edward gave James general responsibility for the *castle-building programme during the conquest of *Wales; accounts show that he was directly responsible for the design and construction of Flint, Rhuddlan, Conwy, Harlech, and Beaumaris. Such details as the use of spiral scaffolding and the design of latrine chutes, demonstrate the strong Savoyard influence on these castles. Beaumaris, concentric in plan and symmetrical in design, is the finest example of his art. James's service was recognized by his appointment as constable of Harlech, a post he held from 1290 to 1293. He served Edward in Scotland in the final years of the reign; a contract survives for the works he undertook at Linlithgow. Financial stringency meant that he was unable to build in Scotland on a similar scale to his great works in Wales, which stand as perhaps the finest surviving example of medieval military architecture.

MCP

Taylor, A. J., *Studies in Castles and Castle-Building* (London, 1985).

Saint-Mihiel, battle of (1918), the first major offensive by the US army in WW I. *Pershing had consistently resisted Allied attempts to feed his divisions into the front piecemeal, under foreign command, although he was prepared to commit them to meet genuine emergencies, like that on the *Marne. The US First Army, with five French and fifteen US divisions, was activated on 10 August 1918. South of Verdun the German-held Saint-Mihiel salient followed the eastern bank of the Meuse, and in their four years of occupation the Germans had tunnelled extensively into the hilly and wooded terrain, creating a defensive system which, at the end of the 20th century, remains one of the best preserved on the western front. Pershing hoped to pinch out the salient and then, if German resistance faltered, to push on against the defences around Metz. *Foch, the Allied C-in-C, persuaded him to adjust his aim, mounting the Saint-Mihiel offensive as a discrete operation before moving north to attack into the Argonne.

Pershing planned to use the US I and IV Corps to drive northwards from the southern flank of the salient while V Corps attacked its western flank. Two divisions of the French II Colonial Corps would advance across the nose of the salient to take Saint-Mihiel itself. The Americans were inexperienced and required considerable French tank and air support, but the determination of their assault would not be denied, and they secured all their objectives, taking 16,000 prisoners and 443 guns for the loss of 7,500 men. Pershing thought they could have gone on, though his staff doubted it.

RH

Saladin (correctly Salah al-Din ben Ayyub) (1138–93) was a Kurd and the nephew of Shirkuh, who had conquered Egypt for Nur ad-Din in 1169. Saladin secured Egypt on the death of his uncle, fought off crusader attacks and in 1171 ended the Fatimid caliphate and founded the Ayyubid. Saladin quarrelled with Nur ad-Din whose death in 1174 enabled him to seize Damascus; henceforth he portrayed himself as the champion of Islam against the Christians, though he always faced Muslim enemies, notably the Zengids whom he fought many times before finally gaining Aleppo in 1183.

In 1177 he invaded Jerusalem from Egypt but was surprised and defeated by Baldwin IV at Mons Gisardi. In June 1179 he returned the favour at Marj Uyun and in September destroyed the new strategic castle at Jacob's Ford. After fighting in Mesopotamia he mounted a major attack on Jerusalem in 1183 which failed because the Christians refused battle and two attacks upon Kerakin in 1184 also miscarried. After a final war with the Zengids in 1187 Saladin invaded Jerusalem, attacked Tiberias with a huge army, and lured King Guy of Jerusalem into battle at *Hattin where on 4 July the European knights were annihilated. Saladin seized Jerusalem, Acre, and most of the kingdom, offering clemency to all who surrendered. But at Tyre Conrad of Montferrat rallied resistance and Saladin did not press the siege. He took inland strongholds and in 1188 moved against Tripoli and Antioch, though without challenging their chief cities. Perhaps he hoped, by picking off weak places, to encourage the strong to *capitulate, but new crusaders were arriving from the West. King Guy was released by Saladin, perhaps to divide the Christians, and after a quarrel with Conrad he led the arriving crusaders to besiege Acre in August 1189. Saladin's inaction in these months was partly a result of declining health and partly because of discontent within his army, although the two were related.

The arrival of the Third Crusade at Acre in 1191 provided a trial of Saladin's skill, but despite his efforts the city surrendered in July. Under *Richard 'the Lionheart' the crusaders marched south to establish Jaffa as a base from which to capture Jerusalem. Saladin attacked the march, but cautiously because he recognized that Richard was seeking to trap him into a battle; after a final spasm at *Arsuf on 7 September his army retreated intact and was able to deter Richard from attacking Jerusalem. In the fighting during

1191–2 Richard won most of the prestige, notably in battle at Jaffa and in a daring attack on a Muslim caravan, but Saladin preserved his forces and in 1192 the Third Crusade ended having restored only a rump of the old kingdom of Jerusalem on the coast of Palestine.

Saladin has been criticized because his indecision immediately after Hattin robbed him of the fruits of his victory, but it should be noted that his style was to provoke his enemies until they did something that delivered them into his hands. This was how he won at Hattin and this was why even a battlefield defeat like Arsuf left his army intact and able to limit the territorial gains of the Third Crusade.   JF2

Lyons, M. C., and Jackson, D. E. P., *Saladin: The Politics of Holy War* (Cambridge, 1982).

Salamanca, battle of (1812).

This was an encounter battle in the *Peninsular war which has been hailed as 'Wellington's Masterpiece' and ended a brief period of shadow-boxing between *Wellington and *Marmont, each with about 50,000 men. On 22 July the rival armies were marching westwards, parallel with one another south of Salamanca, across flat ground dominated by two hills, the Greater and Lesser Arapile. Marmont occupied the Greater, hoping to pin Wellington's army to its position while he hooked around its western flank, cutting Wellington's communications with Portugal. In the process his divisions, marching across Wellington's front, became too extended to provide mutual support.

Wellington, watching from the Lesser Arapile, seized his opportunity, and ordered his leading division, under his brother-in-law Edward Pakenham, to attack the French advance guard. He then fell on Marmont's divisions in succession, and a cavalry charge by *Le Marchant, who was killed in the moment of victory, helped clinch the French defeat. Marmont was wounded by a shell, and although Foy's division preserved his army from rout it was very roughly handled, losing about 14,000 men to Wellington's 5,000. The battle led King Joseph to abandon Madrid, but Wellington was threatened by superior forces under *Soult and compelled to make a difficult retreat towards Portugal. Nonetheless the battle showed that he was more than just a good defensive general and struck a lasting blow at French morale and prestige.   RH

Salamis, battle of (480 BC).

This was the decisive naval encounter of the *Graeco-Persian wars. Following three days of indeterminate skirmishing off Artemisium, the Greek fleet fell back to the island of Salamis, and it was here, in the channel between the modern Ambelákia on Salamis and Pérama on the coast of Africa, that the reckoning with Xerxes' navy took place. It is possible that the Persian fleet was induced to move into the channel, at night, by a mes-

sage from Themistocles, but the Greeks were informed by a deserter and were ready at dawn. It is unclear exactly what happened, and even numbers are uncertain, though the Greeks appear to have had 300–400 ships and the Persians rather more. Persian morale may have been low both after a night at the oar and because they had thought the Greeks would not fight. It seems probable that the Greeks initially outnumbered the leading or right-wing Persian squadrons, and were able to cut them off and drive them ashore before turning on the left wing and driving it out to sea. All that we know for sure is that the Persian fleet was defeated and the survivors withdrew to Asia Minor.   JFL

Herodotus, 8. 40–94.
Lazenby, J. F., *The Defence of Greece* (Warminster, 1993).

Salerno landing (1943).

On 9 September 1943, after the invasion of *Sicily, the downfall of *Mussolini on 24 July, and the subsequent Armistice with Italy, the Allies launched a two-pronged invasion of southern Italy at Taranto and Salerno. AVALANCHE involved landing one US and two British divisions of Clark's US Fifth Army along a 26 mile (42 km) stretch of coast in the Gulf of Salerno, 40 miles (64 km) south-east of Naples. The aim was threefold: to cut off German forces in the south, capture the port of Naples, and reach the Volturno river.

Kesselring, the German commander in Italy, had disarmed Italian troops in the area and manned coastal defences just prior to the invasion and counter-attacked with elements of six divisions, supported by artillery in the surrounding hills. *Naval gunfire and reinforcements from the sea alone could not stem the German attack, which was halted with the deployment of US paratroopers and massive *air support. By 16 September the British and US forces had linked up and the crisis had passed, with Naples falling on 2 October. On 20 September, 300 British troops had refused orders to move inland. The Salerno *mutiny, Britain's only troop rebellion during 1939–45, was defused, but had been caused by the inept management of convalescing soldiers who should have been sent home, but were diverted to strange units at Salerno instead.   APC-A

Salonika campaign (1915–18).

A Balkan campaign was seriously discussed in both Britain and France at the beginning of 1915 as part of the reassessment of military strategy which followed the onset of deadlock on the western front. Many saw it as the best way to persuade the various states in the area to throw in their lot with the Allies. When a campaign based on the Greek port of Salonika finally got underway in October of that year, it did so as a last-minute expedient, ostensibly designed to bring aid to the hard-pressed Serbian army, but in large part the result of the determination of the French government and high command to find gainful employment for the politically troublesome Gen Maurice Sarrail, who had recently been relieved of his command on the western front.

The Anglo-French army arrived too late to assist the Serbs, whose forces escaped to Corfu, and throughout its duration the campaign was opposed by the British military hierarchy, who believed that it was doing nothing to win the war against Germany. Most leading British politicians were also sceptical, though *Lloyd George was a notable exception in his enthusiasm for a Balkan strategy. In the last resort the British government was always prepared to accept the argument that the continuation of the campaign was essential to the stability of the French government and that its ending might lead to a grave crisis in Anglo-French relations. It was certainly true that the Salonika expedition was enmeshed in political intrigue, revealing in particular continuing divisions in French political life, notwithstanding the declaration of a Union Sacrée at the outbreak of hostilities. Sarrail enjoyed significant backing in left-wing circles in Paris. At a time when the majority of the army hierarchy was suspected of right-wing, clerical, and even royalist sympathies, Sarrail stood out as a general whose commitment to the republican ideal could not be questioned. In addition, and much to the irritation of British observers, Sarrail became deeply involved in Greek politics and was widely seen as the leading agent of a French drive to establish a post-war sphere of influence in the eastern Mediterranean.

As the months passed the Allied commitment to the Salonika campaign steadily increased with the addition of the reconstituted Serbian army as well as Italian, Romanian, and, after the Allies had deposed King Constantine in June 1917, Greek forces. At its peak the Allied army numbered some 600,000 men. By contrast, the Germans progressively withdrew from the campaign. In March 1916 *Falkenhayn abandoned plans for a large-scale offensive in the Balkans in order to concentrate on the attack at *Verdun. The practical effect was to leave a largely Bulgarian force of about 450,000 men to make use of the difficulties of the terrain to hold down the numerically stronger Allies. The grateful Germans thus came to look upon Salonika as the largest internment camp of the war. The campaign was largely irrelevant to the outcome of the war, at least until the last few weeks of fighting. Then, in mid-September 1918, an advance under the new Allied commander, Franchet d'Espérey, produced a rapid disintegration in the Bulgarian forces, which the German commander *Ludendorff concluded had been a decisive factor in his country's defeat. But the campaign is probably more important in the diplomatic sphere, revealing enormous tensions in the Anglo-French alliance and highlighting the problems of fighting a war as a coalition, particularly in the absence of an inter-allied decision-making machinery. DJD

Dutton, David, *The Politics of Diplomacy: Britain and France in the Balkans in the First World War* (London, 1998).

Palmer, Alan, *The Gardeners of Salonika: The Macedonian Campaign 1915–1918* (London, 1965).
Tanenbaum, Jan Karl, *General Maurice Sarrail 1856–1929: The French Army and Left-Wing Politics* (Chapel Hill, NC, 1974).

SALT/START. See STRATEGIC ARMS LIMITATION/REDUCTION TALKS.

salute The formal military gesture of greeting. In military and nautical terms, it is a prescribed or specified movement of the hand or of weapons or of flags of recognition. In its simplest form, it is merely a simple greeting between soldiers, usually in modern armies by raising the right hand to the forehead. This probably originated with medieval knights who raised visors so they could be recognized, also showing that the hand in question did not contain a weapon. At its most formal and elaborate, a salute can be accompanied by appropriate military *music and can include the discharge of a prescribed number of guns as a formal or ceremonial sign of respect.

Salutes have been common in armies since at least Roman times. The most common Roman salute was to strike their chests with their forearms, indicating that their hearts were true. Another was an outstretched right arm, which was to be copied by Mussolini's fascists and Hitler's Nazis. In neither of these countries did it replace the conventional military salute. The Nazi salute was a particularly potent symbol. When the English football team played against Germany in Berlin in 1938—in keeping with British policy at the time it was advised by the British Embassy to give the Nazi salute during the German national anthem. Although the team was unhappy about it, its members did as they were asked, producing one of the most shameful images of English football. They did, however, beat the Germans 6 : 3. MCM

samurai were the members of the military class of old Japan. The word is first used from about the 8th century AD, and is derived from the verb *sabarau*, which means 'to serve'. The original service rendered was as guards to the imperial palace or on police duties in the provinces. Many samurai families originated from imperial princes settled in lands far from the capital. They grew in local influence, and learned considerable military skills through fighting the *emishi*, the aboriginal Japanese, or from conducting campaigns against rivals or rebels. In the latter case commissions were awarded to samurai by the central government, who rewarded them well. The hallmark of these early samurai was the possession of a horse and skills at handling *bow and arrow. By the 12th century the samurai clans became powerful enough to challenge the imperial authority themselves, which culminated in the *Gempei wars. The shogunate established by Minamoto Yoritomo was a government of the samurai class. From this time on the rank of samurai became more closely defined as an élite group supported by lowly foot soldiers. By the 13th century the samurai sword achieved prominence over the bow, and by the beginning of the Sengoku-jidai ('The Age of the Country at War') the period of civil wars that lasted from 1467 to 1615, bows had been completely abandoned for *edged weapons. Samurai now fought in large armies, either on horseback or on foot, commanding well-drilled troops of *ashigaru* (foot soldiers) who were armed with arquebuses, spears, or bows. With the establishment of peace under *Tokugawa Ieyasu the status of samurai was firmly defined and included the foot soldiers who became its lowest ranks. No other social classes were allowed to wear the characteristic two swords which the samurai wore through his belt. Many samurai, *Musashi Miyamoto being the prime example, became master swordsmen and travelled the country as teachers of swordsmanship, a tradition from which much of samurai legend is derived. They also developed the *bushido code, the 'way of the warrior'. The samurai class was formally abolished in 1876 with the establishment of Japan's national conscript army. Sword-bearing was restricted to the army, and the characteristic topknot hairstyle forbidden. The Satsuma clan, who had rebelled furiously against this, turned around to become the dominant force within the armed forces (see SATSUMA REVOLT). The ethos lived on.

SRT

Sand Creek massacre (1864), among the most egregious atrocities committed by Anglo-Americans against the Indians and one of the darkest episodes of the *Plains Indians Wars. The Colorado territory governor, rebuffed when he tried to buy Cheyenne/Arapaho hunting grounds, ordered militia commander Chivington, an ex-preacher who had performed creditably against the Confederates in New Mexico, to provoke incidents to justify their forcible removal. To combat the crisis thus created, the governor and Chivington raised the 3rd Colorado Cavalry among mining camp scum. As winter approached and the term of enlistment for this unit was near to expiry, Cheyenne Chief Black Kettle requested a meeting and was told to surrender his arms at a military outpost, and to camp nearby. Obediently, he camped at Sand Creek some 30 miles (48 km) from Fort Lyon with 600 followers. On 29 November Chivington and his rabble surrounded it, opened fire with *howitzers and then charged. One to two hundred mainly old men, women, and children were killed and many were scalped and sexually mutilated. The heroes were cheered when they displayed these souvenirs at the Denver opera house. Even in the midst of the *American civil war, this incident and the Plains-wide war it provoked were too much for Washington legislators to stomach. Chivington (but not the governor) was denounced during a congressional investigation

and forced to resign. Black Kettle died during an attack by *Custer on his Washita river camp in 1868.   HEB

San Martín, Gen José de (1778–1850), equal of *Bolívar among the liberators of South America from Spanish rule. Born in what was later Argentina, he returned to Spain at the age of 6 and eventually became an officer. He joined the patriotic uprising against Napoleon and fought at *Bailén and Albuera in the *Peninsular war. In 1812 he joined revolutionaries in Buenos Aires, winning a skirmish at San Lorenzo in February 1813. Convinced that final victory required the defeat of royalist forces in Peru, he formed an expeditionary force to link up with patriots under O'Higgins in Chile. Although the royalists retook Chile, he marched his army over the Andes, through passes up to 12,000 feet (3,658 metres) high, between 18 January and 8 February 1817, and defeated them at Chacabuco four days later. The liberation of Chile was confirmed at Maipú in April 1819, after which with Cochrane he organized sea transport to Peru. When the royalists abandoned Lima, he entered and was proclaimed protector in July 1821. Disowned by Buenos Aires and uncertain of Peruvian support, a year later he met Bolívar in Guayaquil. Precisely what transpired is unknown, but he resigned all offices and spent the rest of his life in Europe, dying in Boulogne.

HEB

sapper The term sap originated in the Middle Ages, and first defined a trench dug to undermine a castle wall. By the 17th century it referred to the zigzag trenches driven forward from the parallel trenches dug by the besiegers of a fortress (see FORTIFICATION AND SIEGECRAFT). Sappers had the dangerous job of digging these zigzag trenches. Their work made them the targets of concentrated hostile fire, and they often wore heavy helmets and *armour to afford them some protection. In the British army a Royal Corps of Sappers and Miners was formed in 1772, and later absorbed within the Royal Engineers. The British-Indian army preserved the term sappers and miners, with a corps for each of the presidencies of Bombay, Bengal, and Madras, to the end of its existence.

In Britain private soldiers in the Royal Engineers are styled sappers, and the term is applied generally to any military engineer—what would in America be termed a combat engineer. It makes the useful point that much military engineering is inherently dangerous. When the British stormed Delhi in 1857 the Kashmir gate was blown in by engineers (fittingly two officers, four sergeants, and seven sappers of the Bengal Sappers and Miners, most of whom were killed by heavy close-range fire), and the successful German airborne attack on Fort Eben Emael in 1940 was the work of assault engineers. It is small wonder that Royal Engineers pride themselves on the aphorism: 'Follow the sapper.'

The French army's *sapeurs* were similar to (and often as famously bearded as) regimental pioneers in the British army, while the expression *sapeur du génie* defines a private soldier in the engineers. And one who both digs and pumps is a *sapeur-pompier*—a fireman.   RTF/RH

Saratoga, battle of (1777), the key engagement of the *American independence war. It consisted of two engagements: a British attack on American positions on 19 September, and an assault on Bemis Heights on 7 October. Lt Gen 'Gentleman Johnny' Burgoyne was marching down the trackless wastes of the Hudson valley from Canada in an abortive attempt to link up with Sir Henry Clinton's forces marching north from New York. This strategy was an attempt to split the economic base of New England from the seat of the rebel Congress in Philadelphia, along the axis of the Hudson. It was a bold and ambitious plan that took no account of the terrain or local conditions.

Burgoyne found his way barred by American forces at Bemis Heights, and the British came under a harassing attack at Freeman's Farm on 19 September. They withdrew in some disorder to construct a fortified camp and await developments. When the prospects of relief by Clinton faded, Burgoyne ordered a major assault on the American position on the heights on 7 October, but this attack was repulsed. On the 17th, surrounded and outnumbered, he capitulated. The defeat handed the strategic initiative to the Americans in the region and strengthened the embassy of *Lafayette, which helped to bring about the entry of France into the war, which in turn sealed the fate of the British effort in North America.   TM

SAS (Special Air Service) is the principal *special forces formation of the British army. Formed by Lt (later Lt Col) David Stirling of the Scots Guards in July 1941 at Kabrit, initially as L Detachment SAS Brigade but subsequently redesignated 1st SAS Regiment (1 SAS), it carried out raiding operations behind enemy lines in the *North Africa campaign. In April 1943, A Squadron was redesignated the Special Raiding Squadron (SRS) and subsequently redeployed to Sicily, while B Squadron became the Special Boat Squadron (SBS) and departed for the Aegean under the command of Maj The Lord Jellicoe.

April 1943 also saw the formation at Philippeville in Algeria of 2nd SAS Regiment (2 SAS), under Lt Col Bill Stirling, which subsequently took part in operations in North Africa, Sicily, and Italy. In early 1944 it returned to Britain to join 1 SAS, reconstituted from the SRS and under command of Lt Col 'Paddy' Mayne, with which it formed the SAS Brigade, commanded successively by Brigs Roderick McLeod and Mike Calvert, together with the 3rd and 4th French Parachute Battalions, the Belgian Independent Parachute Company, and F Squadron Phantom. In June 1944 all units were deployed on operations in France, subsequently seeing service in the Low Countries, Germany, and Scandinavia before disbandment in 1945.

In 1946 the SAS was re-formed as a Territorial Army unit: 21st SAS (Artists') Regiment (21 SAS). In 1952 a regular army regiment was raised in Malaya as 22 SAS, being formed from a squadron of volunteers from 21 SAS and the Malayan Scouts, the latter comprising volunteers from British army units on operations in the country at the time.

In 1959 a second Territorial Army regiment, 23 SAS (TA), was formed from the Reserve Reconnaissance Unit. During the early 1960s, Headquarters SAS Group was established and all three regiments, together with two SAS signals squadrons, thereafter came under its direction. More recently, it has been redesignated Headquarters Special Forces with all British special forces, including those of the Royal Marines, placed under it.

C (Rhodesian) Squadron 22 SAS and the New Zealand SAS Squadron were formed in 1951 and 1955 respectively, serving with 22 SAS in the *Malayan emergency. After return to Rhodesia and disbandment, C Squadron was later re-formed and subsequently expanded to become the Rhodesian 1st SAS Regiment, ultimately being disbanded in 1980. In 1957 the 1st SAS Company (Royal Australian Infantry) was formed, subsequently being expanded and redesignated the Australian SAS Regiment (SASR) in 1964. Together with the New Zealand SAS, it subsequently served in the *Borneo campaign and *Vietnam. More recently, the SASR has been deployed in the Middle East and Bosnia alongside 22 SAS.

The 22 SAS, based in Hereford, has had worldwide influence through its intensive and highly practical training system, based on secondment to the regiment itself. These included the founders of the US Special Forces Green Berets, among them the legendary Dick Meadows who married the regimental sergeant major's daughter. It has also seen active service in almost every campaign in which the British army has taken part, prominently in the *Falklands and the *Gulf wars. In addition it fought a war on its own during the 1970s in *Oman against *guerrillas in the Dhofar. The regiment has also carried out a number of other roles, including the provision of a counter-terrorist team and the training of similar teams for other armed forces overseas.

In 1980 it performed a copybook assault on the Iranian embassy in London, held hostage by terrorists, which fortuitously appeared on live TV. The commander of the regiment in that operation, previously highly effective against the *IRA until the British government lost its nerve, and later in the Falklands, became Gen Sir Michael Rose, UN commander in Bosnia. It is a peculiarity of the regiment that the permanent establishment is NCOs and troops only, the officers. being seconded from their parent regiments and returning to them. The result is that special forces' abilities and to a certain extent mentality are more diffused through the British army than any other. Rose, for example, became commandant of the staff college, while the *Huguenot descendant Gen Sir Peter de la Cour de la Billière, GOC British forces in the Gulf, always proudly wore his beige SAS beret.   HMPDH

Baker, W. D., *Dare To Win: The Story of The New Zealand Special Air Service* (Melbourne, 1987).

Cole, Barbara, *The Élite: The Story of The Rhodesian Special Air Service* (Transkei, 1984).

Geraghty, Tony, *Who Dares Wins: The Special Air Service 1950 to the Gulf War* (London, 1992).

Horner, D. M., *SAS: Phantoms of The Jungle. A History of The Australian SAS Regiment* (Sydney, 1989).

Kemp, Anthony, *The SAS at War 1941–1945* (London, 1991).

Satsuma revolt (1877), an incident peculiarly illustrative of the conflict between the old and the new after the Meiji restoration in Japan. Takamori Saigō, a hero of the Restoration wars, had argued that unemployed *samurai should be used to invade Korea, and when this was rejected he retired to Satsuma, heartland of his clan of that name on Kyushu island. From there he viewed with rising fury the introduction of conscription and the abolition of the samurai monopoly of bearing arms. The revolt he led became something of a clan civil war, with his followers defeated by the new conscript army led by his cousin Oyama Iwao. In February Saigō captured Kagoshima, the provincial capital, then laid siege to the city of Kumamoto. Oyama relieved the siege and drove his old chieftain back on Kagoshima, where he made his last stand on Castle Hill. Blasted out by artillery, on 24 September Saigō was wounded in a last sortie and committed seppuku assisted by a faithful follower, who then killed himself. Oyama went on to become war minister and along with other Satsuma raised the money to put up bronze statues to Saigō in Tokyo and Kagoshima. After the *Russo-Japanese war of 1904–5 he, Adm Togo, Gen Kuroki, and other Satsuma went to report their victory to the latter. The revolt marks the end of the clan-based samurai tradition and the transfer of its ethos to a national rather than a sectional force.   HEB

Saumur A pleasant wine-producing town on the Loire, Saumur is the spiritual home of the French cavalry. In 1764 Choiseul established five military equitation schools, but that at Saumur was the only one to survive the budgetary reductions of 1771. Between 1767 and 1770 the architect Jean de Voglie designed elegant *barracks for the school and the resident regiment, the Carabiniers. The school's title changed from time to time, but for many years it was the École d'Application de la Cavalerie. Cavalry officers were sent there for their special-to-arm training after commissioning, and there were also courses for *NCOs. With the French military revival after the *Franco-Prussian war a school was established at Saumur to train cavalry NCOs

destined for commissions. Saumur took on tank as well as cavalry training between the world wars, and on 18–20 June 1940 its officers and cadets gallantly held the crossings of the Loire against superior German forces.

The school moved to Tarbes under Vichy, but returned to Saumur after the war. The École Nationale d'Equitation was established at Saumur in 1972 to train civilian riding instructors, and is distinct from the cavalry and armour school. In 1984 the instructors from the cavalry school moved there, retaining the name, deriving from their dark uniforms, of Cadre Noir. The town has a museum of the horse, a tank museum, and a cavalry museum.   RH

Saxe, Marshal Maurice de (1696–1750), also known as Moritz of Saxony, French military commander and thinker, the greatest European general and military intellectual between the times of *Marlborough and *Eugène of Savoy at the start of the 18th century and *Frederick 'the Great' in its second half. Hermann Maurice/Moritz was born in Goslar in Germany, the illegitimate son of King Frederick Augustus I of Saxony and later Augustus II of Poland (see GREAT NORTHERN WAR). He began his military career as a boy serving under Eugène in 1709–10. His father made him count of Saxony, or, in its French form Saxe, in 1711.

Although Saxe could equally have fought against the French, he joined their service in 1719 and attracted attention through his unusually comprehensive training methods. In 1726 he was elected duke of Courland and would have married the future Empress Anna Ivanovna of Russia had it not been for Russian and Polish opposition. During the War of the Polish succession (1733–5), Saxe fought for France against Saxony, plus Russia and Austria, an indication of the slight national ties which bound members of the European aristocracy of that time. France came off worst, but Saxe was made a lieutenant general. He returned to France where he wrote his famous *Mes rêveries*, published in English as *Reveries upon the Art of War* in 1757. The work is not just one of military theory, but also a treatise on military life, which he lived to the full.

During the War of the *Austrian Succession, Saxe captured Prague in 1741 in a surprise night attack. In 1744 he was made marshal of France. On 11 May 1745 he led 40,000 French troops into action at *Fontenoy, now in Belgium, against an Austrian–Dutch-Hanoverian force of 50,000 under *Cumberland. The French occupied Fontenoy and fortified it. They beat off the Allied attack, inflicting 14,000 casualties while sustaining about 6,000 of their own. Cumberland, hitherto hailed as the greatest British general since Marlborough, hastened back to take on less well-led opposition at *Culloden.

Fontenoy gained control of the Austrian Netherlands for France. Saxe won victories at Raucoux (Rocour) in 1746 and Maastricht in 1748. Made marshal-general of France by Louis XV, he retired to the royal chateau of Chambord, where he died. He had many mistresses, and through one of hem was an ancestor of the French writer George Sand.

His *Reveries upon the Art of War* drew heavily on Machiavelli. Although a talented commander in the field, Saxe's view of warfare was highly formalistic, and he believed (probably rightly, in the context of his time) that an army of 46,000 troops was about the limit that one commander could control. Like Frederick, he combined massive practical experience with limited dabbling in military theory. Over the next hundred years, the theoretical component of military power and military thought would gain weight. His work was still highly regarded a hundred years later.

CDB

Paret, Peter (ed.), *Makers of Modern Strategy* (Oxford, 1986).

Saxe-Weimar. See BERNHARD, DUKE OF SAXE-WEIMAR.

Scharnhorst, Gen Graf Gerhardt Johann David von

(1755–1813). Commissioned into the Hanoverian artillery in 1788, Scharnhorst fought with distinction under the Duke of *York in Flanders in 1793–4. However, his middle-class background seemed a bar to promotion, and he transferred to the Prussian service in search of better prospects. Promoted Lt Col and ennobled, he taught at the Kriegsakademie in Berlin, where *Clausewitz was one of his students, before serving as COS to the Duke of Brunswick for the *Jena/Auerstadt campaign. Wounded at Auerstadt, he was subsequently captured but exchanged, and served with the Prussian contingent at *Eylau. Promoted major general in July 1807, he was appointed minister of war and chief of the *general staff, set up the Military Reorganization Commission, and, with *Gneisenau, Grolman, Boyen, Stein, and Hardenberg, worked to rebuild the Prussian army. A French decree banning foreigners from serving in the Prussian army obliged him to leave it in 1810, but he was recalled in 1812 to act as COS to *Blücher. He was wounded at *Lützen in 1813 and, sent to Prague to negotiate Austria's entry into the war, died from blood poisoning caused by the wound.

Scharnhorst was an accomplished staff officer and administrator, whose notion of universal military service was to have lasting importance. His untimely death was a cruel blow to the cause of liberal military reform in Prussia. RH

Scheldt, battle of the

(1944). The history of the campaign to clear the Scheldt estuary is the tale of lost opportunities. On 4 September 1944, to both the Germans' and Allies' surprise, the port of Antwerp was taken by the local *resistance, preventing the German garrison from destroying the harbour facilities. The Allies badly needed a large working port by late 1944, their logistic tail still stretching back to the artificial port at Arromanches (none of the well-demolished French ports were functioning yet). *Montgomery might have concentrated on clearing the Scheldt estuary from Antwerp to the sea, but instead he launched MARKET GARDEN, in the hope of taking a short cut into Germany. The defeat at *Arnhem removed any hopes of gaining Rotterdam or Amsterdam as alternative ports and belatedly he ordered Simonds's First Canadian Army to clear the Scheldt. The estuary mouth was dominated to the north by the garrisoned island of *Walcheren, and to the south by a defensive perimeter around Breskens. Second Canadian Division attacked along the north bank from 2 October, and eventually overran the Beveland peninsula, with the help of 52nd (Scottish) Division, allowing an *amphibious assault to be made against Walcheren in early November. On the southern bank, 3rd Canadian Division attacked towards the coast, taking Breskens on 21 October, and reaching Zeebrugge by 3 November. The reduction of Walcheren by 8 November allowed the Scheldt to be swept of mines and obstacles and by the end of the month the first Allied ships arrived in Antwerp. APC-A

schiltrom (shield ring). The dependence of the Scots army on its infantry, or rather its lack of cavalry, ensured that developments in military strategy revolved round the foot soldier. The spear has, of course, an ancient place in military tactics, as well as a long history in Scotland. However, the schiltrom is associated predominantly with the wars with England. At the battle of *Falkirk in July 1298, the Scots guardian Sir William *Wallace arranged his men in four or five semicircular groups of around 1,000 spearmen each, hemmed in with ropes; each man held his iron-tipped spear outwards across his chest. A small force of Scots *archers were interspersed in between, with the cavalry at the back. This intrinsically defensive formation succeeded in repulsing the initial English cavalry charge, but was then destroyed by the archers. King Robert *Bruce adapted this technique by training his men to move offensively in schiltrom formation; at *Bannockburn this prevented an English cavalry unit reaching Stirling and played an active role in the battle itself. The schiltrom disappeared from Scots battle tactics with the arrival of the long pike. FW

Barrow, Geoffrey W. S., *Robert Bruce and the Community of the Realm of Scotland* (Edinburgh, 1992).

Nicolle, David, *Medieval Warfare Source Book*, vol. 1, *Warfare in Western Christendom* (London, 1995).

Schlieffen, FM Graf Alfred von

(1833–1913). The son of an army officer, Schlieffen was destined for the law but enlisted as a one-year volunteer in 1853 and was commissioned in 1854. He attended the Kriegsakademie in 1858–61 and joined the *general staff, serving on it in the *Austro-Prussian and *Franco-Prussian wars. Commanding 1st

Guard Uhlans in 1876–84, thereafter he served on the staff, being promoted major general in 1866 and lieutenant general in 1868. He succeeded Waldersee as CGS in 1891 and held the post until retirement in 1906.

Schlieffen was the epitome of the single-minded staff officer, and his wife's early death left him even more chilly, with no outlet but work. He spent much of his time concocting a solution for the strategic problem facing Germany: a war on two fronts against France and Russia. Recognizing that he could win only 'ordinary victories' against the Russians, who would withdraw into their vast empire, he decided to leave a holding force in the east and to throw most of his army against France. The French had fortified their border, and a frontal attack was not to Schlieffen's taste. He decided instead to send the right wing through Belgium, violating Belgian neutrality, to swing behind the French armies and fight a decisive battle in Champagne.

'The Schlieffen plan' was a series of yearly memoranda, whose changes reflected staff rides and war games as well as recent military events. With retirement looming, he drafted 'War against France', a detailed guide for his successor, which emphasized the need for a decisive offensive war. Much influenced by the battle of *Cannae, he dwelt on the need for the left wing to fall back before the French, drawing them deeper into the trap. Having won a decisive victory in the west, Germany could then use interior lines to shift armies to the east to beat the Russians, who would then sue for peace.

Schlieffen's desire to control in detail rather than to give broader direction to his armies was a break with *Moltke 'the Elder''s precepts, although, in fairness, any advance on the scale he planned would demand a greater degree of centralized control. He endeavoured to use planning to mitigate the effects of what *Clausewitz called friction, suggesting that 'a modern Alexander' could make full use of the *telegraph, *telephone, and wireless to achieve a greater degree of control than ever before. Schlieffen recognized that the right wing faced a difficult task, and was concerned about the need to mask Paris. He was over-optimistic about capturing railways intact, underestimated logistic requirements, and ignored the long-term effects of British entry into the war.

Schlieffen's scheme was not feasible in the terms its author proposed, but brought Germany close to victory in 1914. His successor, *Moltke 'the Younger', should not be blamed for tinkering with it but for failing to win when victory was attainable. Ultimately Schlieffen did his country little service in bequeathing it a plan he recognized as risky but whose existence was to distort political decision-making on the eve of war.   RH

Rothenberg, Gunther E., 'Moltke, Schlieffen and the Doctrine of Strategic Envelopment', in Peter Paret (ed.), *Makers of Modern Strategy* (Oxford, 1986).

Schmeisser One of military history's many misnomers, the term Schmeisser is often applied to the German MP 38 *sub-machine gun and its similar derivative the MP 40. These simple but effective 9 mm weapons were designed by Erma-Werke of Erfurt, made of steel and plastic, and took a 32-round magazine. Over a million MP 40s were produced.

Schmeisser was the designer of the MP 18, the Bergmann, with its characteristic 'snail' or drum magazine and wooden stock, which was produced in time to see service in 1918. It is a mystery how his name remains attached to the MP 38 and MP 40.   RH

Schwarzkopf, Gen Norman H. (b. 1934), commander of US Central Command and hence of all the Allied forces in Saudi Arabia, Iraq, and Kuwait in the 1990–1 *Gulf crisis and war. Born in Iran, son of the police officer who produced the evidence that condemned Hauptmann in the Lindbergh kidnapping case, he was a battalion commander in *Vietnam and this experience made him determined that future wars would be fought hardest on the officers. Known as 'Stormin' Norman' or 'the bear', with a build to match, he was a formidably impressive four-star general and 'ate major generals for breakfast'. His handling of the Iraqi *capitulation at Safwan on 3 March 1991 was chivalrous. His masterly management of the Allied sea–air–land campaign and handling of the *media showed that in high-tech war charismatic leadership had not only not lost its importance, but was probably more significant than ever.

                                        CDB

science and technology in war (*see opposite page*)

Scipio Aemilianus (*c*.185–129 BC), in full Publius Cornelius Scipio Africanus Minor. He was the adoptive grandson of *Scipio 'Africanus' and served with distinction under his father, Aemilius Paulus, at *Pydna, and later in 151 in Spain. The only Roman commander to emerge with credit from the disasters at the start of the third *Punic war, he was elected consul by popular demand, despite being below the legal age, and sent to take command against the Carthaginians. Through caution and careful preparation he concluded the siege of Carthage, razing it to the ground in 146. After a series of Roman humiliations he was sent to Spain in 134 where he starved the stronghold of Numantia into submission.   AKG

Scipio 'Africanus' (236–183 BC), in full Publius Cornelius Scipio Africanus Maior, Roman general, consul 205/4 BC and 194/3 BC. Having fought at the Ticinus—where he
(*cont. on page 813*)

science and technology in war

E VER since Archimedes devised defensive engines and 'burning glasses' for the defence of *Syracuse against Roman attack in 212 BC, scientists and engineers have been closely involved in the conduct of war, but their involvement really took off during the Renaissance. It is to be emphasized that both *Leonardo da Vinci and Michelangelo regarded themselves as primarily military engineers. From the early 16th century onwards, and most spectacularly during the last 150 years, scientific advances have accelerated progress in military technologies. This phenomenon has not been confined to firepower and weapons development. Machine power, manifested in *steam, internal combustion, and jet engines, provides strategic and tactical mobility and logistic lift to armed forces. Industrial power and *mass-production techniques have shovelled copious offerings into the mouth of war since the mid-19th century. Over the last 100 years *communications and information technology has transformed the command and control of armed forces.

While the *American civil war is seen by some as the first industrial war, the first true demonstration of what modern war would entail was given during the *Russo-Japanese war. As *Fuller observed in *The Conduct of War*, the outstanding tactical lessons of that war included 'the failure of frontal attacks . . .; the enormous defensive power of field entrenchments and wire entanglements; the increasing deadliness of the machine gun; and most marked of all, the power of quick-firing artillery'.

Many understood that the greater lethality and range of modern weaponry had tipped the scales heavily in favour of the defence, but a Warsaw banker called I. S. Bloch put this into a socio-economic context in his *The War of the Future in its Technical, Economic and Political Relations*, the sixth and concluding volume being published in English in 1899 under the title *Is War Impossible?* Bloch thought that the burden of *war finance would bring militarily stalemated wars to an end, but he overlooked the *political economy considerations that made it advantageous for rulers to persist beyond apparent reason.

Science and technology came of age fully during WW I, when nations threw all their intellectual and productive energy at each other. In just one military generation, dramatic advances in the firepower, mobility, and protection of armed forces on land, air, and sea were achieved, at a staggering human and economic cost. WW II moved the military world further along the road with *armoured warfare, *air power, and a cascade of electronic innovations adding new dimensions on land and sea. As a result of the multibillion dollar scientific *Manhattan Project, came the development in just under three years of *nuclear weapons that directly threatened the lives of ruling élites, on the basis of which a latter-day Bloch might well conclude that at last wars among technologically advanced nations have become, to put it conservatively, unlikely.

While scientists involved in Nazi *genocide plumbed the depths of inhumanity, military *medicine was transforming the incidence of disease and the treatment of *casualties. Affecting the cutting edge perhaps more fundamentally, scientific 'operations' analysis and research was applied to the assisted planning and conduct of war. Since the war, the pace of technological development fed by both pure and applied science has become exponential. But all this needs to put into historical perspective: some of the military technology we recognize today can be traced back to the 16th century, when we can see that the process became irreversible after the long hiatus of the Middle Ages.

What happened in the Renaissance was the beginning of synergy, where breakthroughs in one field would feed into another with the birth of what we now call 'lateral thinking'. Advances in chemistry produced more reliable *gunpowder and metallurgy, which produced effective *cannon, which in turn rendered the old high-walled *castle built in a prominent location obsolete. Thus military *engineering grew to require sophisticated mathematics and geometry to design the new lower and less vulnerable polygonal defensive works. In turn, the attacker needed heavier guns and new techniques such as *ricochet fire, as well as tried and tested *mines and the carefully calculated trenches that advanced inexorably upon a work, such that by the 17th century *Vauban was to set a prescribed number of days after which a given fortification was certain to fall, permitting *capitulation with an *honour now based on scientific calculation rather than heroism.

While on land the engineers and generals needed reliable topographical surveys and maps to conduct campaigns, at sea the advent of a reliable chronometer ushered in one of the most profound technology-driven revolutions of all time by permitting sailors to calculate longitude. The Royal Navy, with a worldwide remit, set out to chart the oceans and many of the soundings made then are still in use today. By contrast the emancipation from wind, current, and tide represented by steam power pales into near insignificance. It is of vital importance to understand that delivery is the key to military effectiveness, something perceived by Mahan over a century ago. This was illustrated when a British nuclear submarine sank the cruiser *Belgrano* with a WW II vintage torpedo during the *Falklands war, but even more strikingly by the nuclear devastation of *Hiroshima and Nagasaki, rightly described as a blow delivered by the US navy, which had brought the B-29s into range.

More mundanely, by reducing the weight, recoil, and the upper-body strength required to use infantry weapons effectively, technology has made it possible for *women to participate in combat on an equal footing with men. The remaining problems are sociological, and that illustrates another of the crucial factors in the impact of science on warfare: since the Renaissance, it has been the ability of the human mind to adjust to the possibilities and not the technology itself that has dictated the rate of innovation. The weapons employed on land and sea during the *Napoleonic wars were largely the same as those used 100 years earlier. What changed war beyond recognition was their application in mass formations moving faster and further than ever before, and this in turn powered the escalation of ever-increasing numbers moving more and more rapidly over ever-greater distances equipped with ever-improving weapons produced by arms manufacturers whose profits were swollen by the regular obsolescence of entire categories of weapons, a process that may be said to have reached a natural limit during WW II, the only truly *total war involving the major world powers. While one of the *principles of war is the economical application of force, one of the fundamentals of war is the application of economy in its broadest sense. Until the 20th century, it simply did not occur to rulers that they could second every aspect of national life to the pursuit of their policies of which, as *Clausewitz epigrammatically observed, war is merely a continuation. Once they realized it, there was no stopping them.

In what he called the constant tactical factor, once again it was Fuller who identified the inescapable leapfrogging effect of technology in the eternal see-saw between offence and defence in *The Dragon's Teeth* (1932):

Every improvement in weapon-power (unconsciously though it may be) has aimed at lessening terror and danger on one side by increasing them on the other; consequently every improvement in weapons has eventually been met by a counter-improvement which has rendered the improvement obsolete; the evolutionary pendulum of weapon-power, slowly or rapidly, swinging from the offensive to the protective and back again in harmony with the speed of civil progress; each swing in a measurable degree eliminating danger.

Thus the battles between surface ship and submarine, *tank and *anti-armour weapons, aircraft and anti-aircraft gun, *radar and electronic countermeasure. But he also indicated a more general trend in method of distancing the weapon-firer from the place of impact of his projectile, presaging the advent of modern 'fire and forget' missiles. Yet the constant tactical factor applies not only to weapon-power and protection. The mobility of an armoured vehicle is directly related to its all-up weight, itself a function of armament, ammunition, engine, and fuel, and the degree of protection provided. Thus there is a triangular relationship between firepower, mobility, and protection that has been the subject of considerable scientific and engineering research. Further, the heavier the vehicle, the greater the load on bridging, which in turn leads to greater engineer personnel and *matériel* resources being required.

Mathematical research supporting tank design also indicated that overall success in tank engagements depended on a number of linked probabilities. As Ogorkiewicz has demonstrated, the first is that the tank must arrive in time within striking distance of the target; the second is to survive engaging the target; the third is to inflict lethal damage on the target. In turn, 'kill probability' is a function of hitting the target; perforating the target's armour given a hit; providing lethal damage given a perforation; and the probability of the weapon system functioning correctly. Yet success also depends on the tactical skill of the tank commander in the way he exploits ground and his tank's mobility to best advantage. Although 'get there firstest with the mostest' is falsely attributed to *Nathan Bedford Forrest, who was not that unlettered, it sums up a principle as old as war itself, and technological sophistication of and by itself is no substitute for being at the right place, at the right time, and in sufficient strength to make it count.

The same basic problem of balancing speed, range, weapon load, survivability, and reliability applies equally to sea and air-based platforms. Further, adding effective protection in terms of earth, steel, and concrete to improve the survivability of land forces, fortifications, or other military or civil installations against attack from sea, land, or air-based weapon systems requires huge investment. Providing active defences against aircraft and missiles is also very costly, and such resources that are available may have to be spread thinly. Therefore considerable scientific research has been undertaken to improve the quality of passive defences that range from dispersion, *camouflage, and deception to elaborate physical and electronic decoys such as radar reflectors. But some of the simplest of techniques remain effective. In the 1991 *Gulf war the Iraqis fooled Allied air forces into attacking pick-up trucks armed with telegraph poles that looked like artillery pieces.

In general the greater the degree of technological sophistication of weapons and their platforms, the greater the amount of logistic, electrical, and mechanical repair effort required to support them. By D-Day, it was estimated that for each British fighting division ashore in *Normandy (averaging 16,000 men), approximately 25,000 men in corps, army, GHQ, and line of communication troops would be required. Thus the 'gross division' or 'divisional slice' represented 41,000 men. Every additional non-fighting unit places its own logistic demands, is vulnerable and needs protection, and compounds the problems of mobility. When one adds that each division was accompanied by 4,000 RAF personnel, the overall logistic demands in fuel, food, and ammunition increased further. During the US involvement in *Vietnam it was (very) conservatively estimated that for every soldier, sailor, or airman committed to combat, there were ten in support. Are we to suppose that the one man on the cutting edge was eleven times more effective as a result of all this 'support', or was it not rather the peripheral detracting from the central purpose?

Providing sufficient trained manpower to fight has always been a problem and one that has affected all armed forces in both world wars. Thus scientific research in order to improve efficiency in terms of improving the output, expressed as fighting power for the same (or preferably, less) personnel input, has been at a premium. For example, Soviet tank design following WW II was based on the use of automatic loaders to save one crew member. Western armies remained wedded to heavier four-man tanks with a higher silhouette. Progress at reducing manpower through labour-saving technology has been more marked in the air and at sea. For instance, the work of the Lancaster bomber with its seven-man crew is now done by a Tornado fighter-bomber with only a pilot and a navigator which can carry the same bomb-load but deliver it far more accurately. Such aircraft and all complex weapons systems today rely on electronic support for communications, position-finding, and targeting. Thus the financial and technological investment required is measured as much in software as in any hardware terms. However, the job of training the operators and developing their tactics and mission support systems remains, as does the maintenance of the weapons systems themselves, and these continue to be manpower-intensive activities. Thus 'high-tech' warfare works from another direction to decrease the number of 'teeth' while reducing neither the cost nor the manpower.

Even a cursory study of the development of science and technology in war reveals that new advances have tended to cancel each other out. This is the way of many so-called military *revolutions, they simply raise the ante for all participants so that warfare continues at a higher intensity and cost, without either side gaining any permanent advantage. The same is not true, of course, of human talent, courage, and commitment, without which a technological advantage may be very much more apparent than real, nor of *doctrine that may not be adequate to employ it properly or on the receiving end may be adapted in order to neutralize it. *Guerrilla tactics are a case in point. There is also the matter of the political will to make a military advantage felt. At the higher end, the ability to fight war at all can depend on both sides refraining from employing a given technology. A classic contemporary illustration of this was the 'willing suspension of disbelief' that permitted navies to act out nuclear warfare exercises when everybody knew that underwater nuclear explosions would crush every submarine and rip the bottom off every surface ship over a considerably greater range (thanks to the incompressibility of water) than the effective blast from similar detonations on land.

One cannot avoid the impression that the tactical or operational impact of technical revolutions is more often overestimated in retrospect than underestimated at the time of their first fielding. The German combination of forward commanders with abundant individual drive and initiative, supported by reliable *radio communications and directing armoured formations, radically increased the tempo of land operations at the beginning of WW II. But the panzer forces themselves could neither be sustained at the appropriate strength nor their tactical advantage maintained for the rest of the war. New tactics and heavier land- and air-based weapons were developed to counter them. Faced with the immense resources and strategic depth of the USSR, the *blitzkrieg, so successful in the short campaigns in *Poland and *France, met its due nemesis. So in considering conflicts of any duration, the quest to obtain a decisive technological superiority or information dominance would appear to have been illusory. As Martin van Creveld has argued persuasively:

Using technology to acquire greater range, greater firepower, greater mobility, greater protection, greater whatever, is very important and may be crucial. Ultimately it is less critical and less important than achieving a close 'fit' between one's own technology and that which is fielded by the enemy. The best tactics, . . . are based on bypassing the enemy's strengths while exploiting the weaknesses in between. Similarly, the best military technology is not that which is 'superior' in some absolute sense. Rather it is that which 'masks' or neutralizes the other side's strengths, even as it exploits his weakness.

Thus overwhelming strategic and industrial resources coupled with immense tactical firepower provide no guarantees of success in war, as the American experience in Vietnam showed. The technologically advanced *Gulf war indicated to many observers a revolution in military affairs with media-friendly *precision-guided munitions, but as Keaney and Cohen have observed: 'air power is an unusually seductive form of military strength because, like modern courtship, it appears to offer the pleasures of gratification without the burdens of commitment.' Therefore we should be careful about drawing simplistic lessons for other conflicts with quite different strategic conditions and terrain, as operations both in Bosnia and Kosovo have indicated. Thus while science and technology will continue to play a very important part in the planning, preparation, and conduct of war, other factors will determine its origins and outcome.

The frills and furbelows of technical innovation should never be permitted to obscure first principles. The long *Cold War represented a brute application of economic power, of which technology was simply one aspect, until the weaker side gave way. Had we a time machine with which to bring *Epaminondas to the present, he might observe that it differed only in scale from the battle of *Leuctra.   RAMSM/HEB

Bidwell, Shelford, and Graham, Dominick, *Fire-Power* (London, 1982).
Creveld, Martin van, *Technology and War* (London, 1991).
Dupuy, T. N., *The Evolution of Weapons and Warfare* (Fairfax, Va., 1984).
Fuller, J. F. C., *The Conduct of War 1789–1961* (London, 1961).
Guerlac, Henry, 'Vauban: The Impact of Science in War', in Peter Paret (ed.), *Makers of Modern Strategy* (Oxford, 1986).
Keaney, Thomas A., and Cohen, Eliot A., *Revolution in Warfare? Air Power in the Persian Gulf* (Annapolis, Md., 1995).
Macksey, Kenneth, *Technology in War* (London, 1986).
Ogorkiewicz, R. M., *Design and Development of Fighting Vehicles* (London, 1968).

supposedly saved the life of his father, the consul—and at *Cannae, Scipio leapt to prominence in 210 when he was appointed to command in Spain after the deaths of his father and uncle the previous year, although he had never held any of the higher offices. In four short years he conquered Carthaginian Spain, capturing its capital (now Cartagena) in 209, and winning decisive victories at Baecula (Bailén) in 208, and Ilipa, north of Seville, in 206.

Returning to Rome, he was elected consul and after some opposition was assigned to Sicily from where, in 204, he launched the invasion of the Carthaginian homeland (now, roughly, Tunisia), landing on Cap Farina (Rass Sidi Ali el Mekki). After wintering on the site now occupied by Kalaat el Andelous, he surprised and burned the camps of the Carthaginian forces gathered to oppose him, and then broke out of his beachhead to win a decisive victory at 'Campi Magni' ('Great Plains', possibly Souk el Kremis, near Bou Salem). Leaving part of his forces to overrun the kingdom of Carthage's principal ally, Syphax of Numidia (in modern Algeria), he himself took up a position at Tunis. Carthage now sued for peace, and although the peace process collapsed, possibly because of Carthaginian treachery, one result was the recall of *Hannibal from Italy. In October 202 Scipio won the decisive encounter, usually known as *Zama, and peace was made.

Although Scipio's prestige after Zama was enormous, and he became successively censor in 199/8, *princeps senatus*, and consul for the second time in 194, the rest of his life was an anticlimax. He and his brother came increasingly under attack from their enemies in the 180s, and eventually, in order to avoid trial, he retired into voluntary exile in Campania, where he died.

As a general Scipio combined charisma with careful planning based on good use of *intelligence and attention to training, and was not afraid to use innovatory tactics, often based on the element of surprise. His strategy of striking at Carthaginian forces in Spain, and letting the conquest of ground take care of itself, was brilliant, and was a complete contrast to that of his predecessors. But although he has been extravagantly praised for his strategy in invading Africa, this had been the Roman plan since 218, and appears pedestrian in comparison with Hannibal's daring invasion of Italy and rapid succession of victories. Both men were fine tacticians but Ilipa, Scipio's most tactically sophisticated battle, appears ponderous when compared with Cannae. Hannibal himself is supposed to have said that, if he had won Zama, he would have rated himself even better than *Alexander 'the Great'. That is debatable, but few would agree with *Suvorov that Scipio was the better general, even though he won it.   JFL

Lazenby, J. F., *Hannibal's War* (Warminster, 1978).
Scullard, H. H., *Scipio Africanus: Soldier and Politician* (London, 1970).

Scots wars of independence

Scots wars of independence (1296–c.1357). Despite previous close relations between Scotland and England, the dynastic crisis following the death of Alexander III of Scotland in 1286 allowed Edward I to push strongly defined claims of English overlordship on the new King John Balliol. In 1295, the Scots negotiated a mutually defensive treaty with Edward's enemy, King Philip of France, as a prelude to regaining independence by force.

The first engagements were profoundly traditional, resulting in a Scots *capitulation following their defeat at Dunbar in April 1296. However, fear of English 'big government' soon provoked spontaneous revolts throughout Scotland. Co-ordination was subsequently provided by Andrew Murray and William *Wallace, who led a Scots infantry army to victory against an overconfident English force at Stirling in September 1297, exposing shortcomings in the English cavalry.

The Scots then employed *guerrilla tactics to drive out English garrisons and provoke terror across the border until Wallace was defeated by Edward himself at *Falkirk in July 1298. The deadly effect of longbowmen warned the Scots off traditional set-piece battles. Falkirk was no Dunbar and the war became one of attrition: the English campaigned to capture castles and extend their effective control beyond south-eastern Scotland; the Scots harassed English armies and garrisons. The Scots wearied first, submitting in 1304, although England was also exhausted. However, two years later Robert *Bruce, Earl of Carrick, seized the throne and reopened hostilities.

Initially, the Bruce failed against the combined might of England and Scots outrage at his violent usurpation of kingship. A pleasing legend describes him sheltered in a cave, while he watched a spider triumph over repeated failure to climb to the roof: the indomitable spider was his inspiration and he kept his cause alive until the death of Edward I provided political relief. English political divisions in the early years of Edward II's reign allowed the Bruce to deal with his enemies in Scotland by all possible means, including the 'fiery cross'.

The following years were spent reducing enemy castles by employing all kinds of trickery, often involving local communities in a piecemeal, though co-ordinated, popular form of warfare. Most of the forts were then razed. *Bannockburn crowned this success but did not win the war. Attempts to force Edward II to accept Scots sovereignty subsequently centred on the systematic raiding of the north of England and the opening of a second front in Ireland. Neither strategy worked directly, but may have contributed to the circumstances leading to Edward's deposition and murder in 1326.

The ensuing political turmoil brought a peace treaty from the regency government, but a few years after the Bruce's death in 1329 the claims of those who had lost out relaunched the war, ostensibly under the leadership of Edward Balliol, son of the King John ousted by the Bruce. *Edward III gave covert, and then overt, support to the so-called 'disinherited' but ultimately the *Hundred Years War drew his attention away from Scotland. The wars left an enduring legacy of enmity between the two kingdoms; they also proved that guerrilla tactics, good leadership, and luck could combine successfully against even the English war machine, which also learned sufficient from its Scots experience to cut a swathe through the *knighthood of France.   FW

Barrow, Geoffrey W. S., *Robert Bruce and the Community of the Realm of Scotland* (Edinburgh, 1992).
Prestwich, Michael C., *The Three Edwards: War and State in England 1272–1377* (London, 1990).

Scott, Gen Winfield (1786–1866), American general in three wars, commander of the army 1841–61, and unsuccessful presidential candidate in 1852. During the *War of 1812 he was captured, exchanged, and later won fame at Lundy's Lane in July 1814. He supervised the near-genocidal removal of the Cherokee from their ancestral homeland to Oklahoma in 1838. During the *Mexican war, he led a seaborne expedition to Vera Cruz and directed it to an unbroken series of victories, culminating in the capture of Mexico City. *Wellington judged the campaign to be 'unsurpassed in military annals'. Many of the general officers on both sides during the *American civil war won their spurs under his command. He lost the 1852 election to a Democrat nonentity chiefly because of the division over slavery that in the end extinguished his Whig party. A serious student of warfare, at the start of the American civil war his 'Anaconda Plan' for the suppression of Southern secession was perceptively predicated on the control of the coasts and inland waterways to fragment and suffocate the Confederacy. Accepted by *Lincoln but derided by everyone else, the failure of Unionist field armies to deliver a decision soon proved its wisdom.   HEB

Scud NATO name for Soviet short-range nuclear capable *missile. Widely distributed to the USSR's clients and used by Egypt in the 1973 *Arab–Israeli war and Iraq in the *Gulf war, when its destabilizing ability to reach Israel led to energetic but rarely successful 'Scud-hunting' by Coalition special forces and aircraft.   CDB

scutage It was normally possible to make a payment, known as scutage or shield money, in place of performing *feudal military service. The practice is best documented in England. The earliest reference to scutage dates from 1100.

A normal rate in the reign of Henry I was 30 shillings for each knight's fee, but this could be varied, and did not necessarily directly reflect the cost to the crown of hiring paid soldiers in place of service. In John's reign scutage became a major political issue. No fewer than eleven scutages were collected in his reign, effectively becoming taxes rather than an alternative to service. As new, radically reduced, quotas of service were developed, fines were demanded from those who chose not to serve, but scutage calculated on the traditional assessment of knights' fees continued to be paid as long as feudal summonses were issued. By Edward I's reign there was much argument, as tenants-in-chief resented being asked to pay scutage on the old assessment of knights' fees, when they had in fact provided service based on the new reduced quotas. At the same time, tenants-in-chief benefited from scutage themselves, for they could, and did, collect it from their own tenants. See POLITICAL ECONOMY AND WAR. MCP

Holt, J. C., *Magna Carta* (2nd edn., Cambridge, 1992).

Scythians A people who lived in the Pontic region (north-east of the Black Sea) from the 7th to 3rd century BC, the Scythians have left little in written record but a rich archaeological heritage displays their military tradition. Grave finds of horse and rider, with a full complement of harness, weapons, and *armour, enable historians to make detailed reconstructions of their equipment. They fought in the steppe nomad tradition as mounted *archers, yet they were not lightly armed. Their armour, including Greek helmets and greaves, Persian-style scale corslets had a great deal of gold decoration demonstrating their wealth.

The Scythians are first recorded in the early 7th century. They attacked Assyria in the 670s BC, only being bought off by the marriage of their king, Partatua, to an Assyrian princess. A generation later, King Madyes led an expedition as far as the borders of Egypt, seemingly being able to ride unopposed through the empires of the Near East. Pharaoh Psammetichus I (663–609 BC) paid a heavy tribute to prevent invasion. In the second half of the 7th century BC, the Scythians played a senior role in partnership with the Medes, and together they overthrew the Assyrian empire with the destruction of Nineveh (612 BC). They were then driven back north of the Caucasus by their erstwhile allies. The *Greek historian Herodotus, the only (and not too reliable) source for the period, blames Median treachery at a feast, but it may be that Scythian social organization was too loose to enable them to engage in empire building.

Certainly, when the Persian successors to the Medes sought to counter Scythian raids in the late 6th century BC, their military capacity had not declined. In a campaign *c.*514–512 BC, *Darius, the most powerful of the Persian kings, led an army north of the Danube (into modern Ukraine). The Scythian nomads outshot even the Persian bowmen, and avoided a pitched battle. Suffering heavy casualties, Darius abandoned his baggage and wounded to escape back across the river, totally humiliated. Subsequently the Scythians attacked Thrace and as both allies and individual warriors became involved in the Greek wars of the 5th and 4th centuries BC. From *c.*350 BC, as they became a more sedentary people, they came under pressure from the Sarmatians, another group of nomads living on the east bank of the Don. In 339 BC, their king, Atheas, was killed in battle against *Philip of Macedon (in modern Romania), although in 330 BC they routed *Alexander 'the Great''s general Zopyrion near Olbia. Squeezed from both east and west, the Scythians retreated into the Crimea. Here they were defeated (*c.*110–106 BC) by Mithradates Eupator, King of Pontus, and absorbed into his large, if short-lived, Black Sea empire.

The glories of Scythian military culture have been uncovered by the work of Russian archaeologists in the 19th and 20th centuries. Many warrior graves have been excavated. The horse was vital to Scythian war-making and many skeletons survive. They are sturdy animals of around 14 hands, shown as stallions by surviving artistic representations. In addition harness, lavishly decorated with gold, and horse armour for head and chest (of scale on leather) have been found. The warrior's equipment was first his *bow, of composite construction and only 31½ inches (80 cm) long, but enormously powerful and capable of being shot rapidly. It was carried in a combined bow and quiver known as a gorytus. In addition, a fully equipped warrior carried a lance, with side arms of a long, straight sword, and axe or mace (which indicated status). He also wore a helmet, which might be of the traditional pointed, 'Scythian cap' shape, in leather, covered in scales. There are also many examples of Greek helmets, some cut down to give better vision, or with added scale neck-guards. The torso was covered with scale armour, extending down to the thighs, and full suits survive which include scale-armoured chaps. The lower legs were usually protected by greaves, often of Greek manufacture, and also modified for use on horseback by having the knee-piece removed or articulated. Exquisite works of Greek manufacture, like the Sokhala comb, show exactly how the equipment was worn. Although there were many lighter-armed mounted archers in a Scythian force, this all goes to show that they possessed a significant heavy cavalry for close-order charging. Scythian nobles were equipped to the standard described in the ancient world as cataphracts, and the number and quality of their hand weapons show that they were more than capable of close fighting. MB

Cernenko, E. V., *The Scythians* (London, 1983).

SDI (Strategic Defense Initiative) was launched in 1983 by US Pres Ronald Reagan to explore the possibility of protecting the USA against incoming ballistic missiles using layered ground-, sea-, air-, and *space-based defences. Until then, it had been assumed, rather as it had been about bombers in the 1930s, that *missiles would 'always get through' and anti-missile defences—to shoot incoming missiles down—had been banned under the Anti-Ballistic Missile (ABM) Treaty (see ARMS CONTROL). They were viewed as destabilizing in the context of the nuclear balance of terror. Strategic thought favoured *deterrence, not defence. However, by the early 1980s, new technologies appeared which might make it possible to develop effective countermeasures. These included lasers, charged particle beam weapons, which are effectively a stream of tiny bullets—atoms or subatomic particles—and electromagnetic guns, which fire projectiles faster than is possible with chemical propellants. These systems would be mounted in ships, aircraft, orbiting space platforms, and on the ground. The best time and place to knock out missiles is in the boost phase soon after launch, when the engine is still burning, but it was theoretically possible to intercept them in space or on the way down.

The initiative was announced in 1983 and was immediately dubbed 'Star Wars', after the science fiction film. Preliminary feasibility studies indicated the system would be impossibly expensive and the expense would arguably be wasted if even a few nuclear missiles got through. The USSR reacted angrily—understandably, as it committed them to a new arms race which they could not afford. Amid national and international obloquy and mockery, progress could only be made very discreetly.

The end of the *Cold War gave SDI a new lease of life. While it would probably have been impossible to build a shield against a determined nuclear strike by either superpower, the prospect of a rogue Russian general or a Middle Eastern potentate with a limited number of *nuclear weapons launching one 'out of the blue' appeared real. The 1991 *Gulf war showed that incoming ballistic missiles could be intercepted (though not as reliably as people were told at the time). *Scud missiles fired at Israel and Saudi Arabia were engaged by Patriot missiles. It might be more feasible to provide 'Global Protection Against Limited Strikes' (GPALS) or 'Theatre High Altitude Air Defence (THAAD), to protect an armed force deployed in a distant theatre against short-range attack by Scud-type missiles. The USA has successfully tested lasers mounted in Boeing aircraft designed to intercept missiles in flight. The UK launched a £5 million study into ballistic missile defence before the 1997 general election, and it was supposedly examined in the 1998 Strategic Defence Review, but the cost appears to have frightened the government. For the near future, deterrence will remain the preferred option, although the USA revived the idea, now called National Missile Defense (NMD) in 2000.   CDB

Sedan, battle of (1870). During the *Franco-Prussian war, the 120,000-strong French Army of Châlons under *MacMahon and accompanied by *Napoleon III retreated to the vicinity of Sedan, on the Meuse near the Franco-Belgian border, after an initial attempt to support the breakout of the main field army under *Bazaine, which was bottled up in Metz. They were driven there by the Prussian Third Army under Crown Prince Friedrich Wilhelm and the Army of the Meuse commanded by the Crown Prince of Saxony, totalling 250,000 men and 500 modern, rifled, *breech-loading guns. The Germans (for such they would soon declare themselves to be) attacked Sedan at first light on 1 September. Overlooked and under accurate fire from artillery on the surrounding heights which outranged their own, the French were soon in difficulties, though the gallant defence of the outlying village of Bazeilles by their *Marines showed that this was still a force to be reckoned with.

MacMahon was wounded by shellfire early on and named Gen Ducrot, the senior commander, as his successor. Ducrot ordered a withdrawal, but Gen de Wimpffen, who had been appointed to take MacMahon's place by the war minister, arrived and countermanded this. The Germans, meanwhile, completed the encirclement of Sedan by midday. After final, desperate cavalry charges seeking to break out to the west in which the Chasseurs d'Afrique distinguished themselves, by 18.30, with 41,000 French killed or captured, a *truce was arranged to negotiate capitulation.

The Prussian King Wilhelm I, his military commander *Moltke 'the Elder', *Bismarck, their staff, and foreign observers, including Russell of *The Times*, had watched the battle from a clearing above Frenois. Wimpffen surrendered at the Château de Bellevue the following morning, and the remaining 83,000 French, including Napoleon III, became prisoners. The Prussians lost just 9,000, despite the superiority of the French *chassepot rifle over their Dreyse *needle gun.

After just two months of campaigning, the victory at Sedan and Napoleon's capture precipitated the fall of the Second Empire and the proclamation of the Third Republic. The area was overrun by another generation of Germans in WW I and in 1940 Guderian's XIX Panzer Corps breached French defences here and crossed the Meuse by the Bellevue Château in its drive to the coast. The town was the boyhood home of the great *Turenne, but of late it has not been a happy name in French history.   APC-A

Howard, Michael, *The Franco-Prussian War* (London, 1961).

Sedgemoor, battle of (1685). When the Catholic *James II succeeded to the throne in February 1685, his half-brother the Duke of Monmouth was pressed to lead a rising which would be synchronized with a rebellion by the Earl of Argyll in Scotland. Monmouth landed at Lyme Regis on 11 June and was proclaimed king in Taunton. Local men—but few notables—flocked to join him, and he had the best of a clash with the Earl of Feversham's royal army on the 27th. He then heard that Argyll had been executed, and fell back to Bridgwater. Feversham followed, establishing himself at Westonzoyland. He had about 2,700 regulars (including the future Duke of *Marlborough) to Monmouth's 3,500 largely untrained men.

Monmouth decided on a night attack, but his men were detected by a cavalry vedette and discovered that a wide drainage ditch, the Bussex Rhine, lay between them and Feversham. Although they fought with courage they were no match for the firepower of the royal infantry, and as they broke Feversham's horse cut many of them down. The rebellion was suppressed with a savagery still remembered in the West Country. Monmouth himself was captured, and executed by a headsman who botched his job.   RH

Seeckt, Gen Hans von (1866–1936), second COS of the *Reichswehr, 1920–6, organizer of the inter-war German military, whose ideal of the apolitical soldier in the state and whose institutional/operational reforms reshaped German military professionalism. After company-level service in the crack Kaiser Alexander Guard Grenadiers, Seeckt entered the Prussian *general staff in 1897, where, as COS at the corps and army group level (1914–18), he achieved successes on the eastern and Balkan fronts.

Once the upheaval of defeat in 1919–20 swept away Defence Minister Gustav Noske and his COS Walter Reinhardt, Seeckt, as new COS, built the 100,000 strong Reichswehr into an effective cadre force, despite limitations of size, composition, and armament. His act of military reconstruction, through rigorous standards of personnel, comprehensive training, and the depoliticization of the ranks subordinated the new army to the republic, whose partisan politics he nonetheless disdained. He concentrated command, control, and administration within his branch (*Heeresleitung*) of the defence ministry amid ongoing external threats and civil disturbances. In 1923 these perils reached a climax with Franco-Belgian occupation of the Rhineland and extremist uprisings, whereupon Pres Friedrich Ebert assigned emergency powers to Seeckt and his commanders. Seeckt toyed with the idea of taking a yet more prominent role in the government, but handed back the reigns of power to Ebert in 1924.

Fearful that the intellectual horizon of the Reichswehr officer would atrophy within the confines of the lightly armed 100,000-man army, Seeckt brought education, training, and manoeuvres to a high degree of perfection. This ideal was codified in his field service regulations of 1921, *Command of Combined Arms Combat*, a classic of modern military *doctrine, and the intellectual basis for German operational and tactical success in 1939–41.

Once *Hindenburg became president in 1925, Seeckt's power weakened considerably as political normalcy took hold in national life. In the autumn of 1926, Defence Minister Gessler removed Seeckt from office for allowing a member of the Hohenzollern dynasty to visit a regimental

manoeuvre, which critics regarded as an affront to the republic. In retirement, Seeckt briefly belonged to parliament as a member of the Deutsche Volkspartei, wrote his memoirs as well as several political volumes, allowed himself to be courted by the Nazis, and became briefly a military adviser to *Chiang Kai-Shek.   DA

Sekigahara, battle of (1600). This was fought between *Tokugawa Ieyasu (the 'Eastern Army') and Ishida Mitsunari (the 'Western Army'), and was one of the most decisive battles in Japanese history. Ishida had carried out a night march to Sekigahara. His plans were that the main body would hold the Tokugawa in the centre while others would attack them in the rear. Early in the morning of 21 October the Western Army was fully in position. In the centre were the divisions under Ukita Hideie and Konishi Yukinaga. To the left of them was Ishida Mitsunari himself. On the right wing, straddling the Nakasendō road, were various contingents including Kobayakawa Hideaki.

By daybreak the Eastern Army had advanced along the Nakasendō to meet them on as wide a front as the narrow valley would allow. There was a thick fog which persisted until about 08.00, when the fighting started. The central divisions were the first to engage, the first shots of the battle probably being fired by Ukita's troops at those of Ii Naomasa of the Eastern Army. Ukita was successful in driving the Easterners back, but they rallied and the fight swayed one way and then the other. All the main divisions were now engaged, and Ishida thought the moment opportune to light the signal fire that would bring Kobayakawa down from Matsuoyama. But Kobayakawa turned traitor and assaulted the flank of Ōtani. Ieyasu then ordered a general attack along the line, and further contingents of the Western Army changed sides.

In the meantime Kobayakawa's men swept through the defeated Ōtani troops, round the rear of Ukita, and attacked Konishi from behind. The Western Army began to break up. Only the army of the Shimazu clan were left intact. Putting himself at the head of 80 survivors Shimazu Yoshihiro succeeded in cutting his way through the Eastern Army. Unfortunately this route took them south-west of Mount Nangu where Ishida's reserve troops were stationed. Some had already decided to join Ieyasu, others were wavering, unsure what to make of the noise they could hear and the garbled reports they were receiving. The battle was already lost, so the very contingents who might have been able to reverse Ishida's defeat turned and marched away from Sekigahara. Ieyasu's victory enabled him to become *shogun, establishing the Tokugawa dynasty which lasted until 1868.   SRT

self-propelled (SP) gun *Horse artillery might be said to be the first SP equipment, given that its purpose was to provide highly mobile artillery support in forward areas using a dedicated power source. More usually, an SP gun is taken to be one mounted on its own automotive system, rather than one designed to be towed. These may be soft-skinned or more usually armoured. The need for such pieces became evident during WW I and early tanks were, in essence, merely SP, direct firing *assault guns. It was also clear that *indirect fire field artillery also needed an SP capability to keep up and exploit success in a breakthrough battle across shattered terrain.

The first British SP equipment was the experimental gun-carrying tank of January 1917, a tank chassis with a 6 inch gun. The French produced 220 mm pieces mounted on the Renault FT light tank chassis. Recommendations flowing from battlefield experience did not survive long in peacetime. The French inspector general of artillery had suggested that all medium and heavy artillery should be SP, but majority opinion was against him and all development was stopped. The US army developed SP artillery based on the Christie chassis but work on this was halted in 1922. The British army persisted for a time and produced the 18-pounder Birch Gun which was tested on exercise in 1925 with the Experimental Mechanized Force, but most influential opinion was against the SP and there were no further trials after 1930. The essential problem was seen to be one of logistics—how could the weight of ammunition which artillery required be supplied in a fast-moving tank battle? It was also argued that as tank armament became more powerful, tanks did not need artillery support. The British army, like most others, entered WW II with no SP guns of any type. The experience of war rapidly changed perceptions. The French appreciated the value of SP artillery and in 1936 decided to introduce five SP battalions, but when war broke out they had only some experimental equipment.

SP equipment was fielded rapidly once the need became clear. They included families of assault guns, *anti-armour guns, field guns, *howitzers, and anti-aircraft guns. The British mounted a 25-pounder on a Valentine tank and adopted the Canadian Sexton, based on a medium tank. In 1940, US Gen McNair devised a controversial anti-armour *doctrine which was to guide US tank development throughout WW II, but which was eventually found to be flawed. He envisaged the SP tank-destroyer, rather than the tank, as the primary anti-armour system and the most common of these US tank-destroyers was the M10. The Germans' first Panzerjäger was a 47 mm gun on a Mk I tank chassis, but this was followed by the heavier 88 mm Ferdinand Elefant of 1943 and the Hetzer of 1944–5. German SP field artillery included the 105 mm Wespe and the 150 mm Hummel howitzer. The Soviets developed SP artillery as an integral part of their design for offensive armoured operations and placed them under command of the tank forces rather than the artillery. The most notable Soviet systems were the SU-85 and SU-100 dual-purpose tank-hunters which only left Soviet service in 1957. An amphibious SP gun, originally called the Amtank, was developed by the USA, primarily for use in the *Pacific campaign. It would open fire from its landing craft at about 4,374 yards (4,000 metres) and continue firing while swimming ashore. It would then revert to its indirect fire role with the divisional artillery.

By the 1960s, the tank-hunting role in most armies had been taken over by the tank itself, but SP equipment remained popular in the field artillery where its protection and cross-country performance were well suited to modern *armoured warfare. The Soviets introduced a comprehensive family of SP field artillery in the 1970s, including the 122 mm 2S1 and the 152 mm 2S5. For 30 years from the mid-1960s, the US 155 mm M109 was the mainstay of *NATO field artillery. Currently this is being replaced by a number of national ventures offering autonomous navigation, automatic loading, burst fire capability, and increased protection.   JBAB

Bellamy, C., *Red God of War* (London, 1986).

Gabel, C. R., *Seek, Strike and Destroy: US Army Tank Destroyer Doctrine in WW II* (Fort Leavenworth, 1985).

Kurowski, F., and Tornau, G., *Sturmartillerie 1939–1945* (Stuttgart, 1978).

Perrett, B., *Allied Tank Destroyers* (London, 1979).

Zaloga, S. J., *US Tank Destroyers of the Second World War* (London, 1985).

Selim I, Ottoman Sultan of Turkey

Selim I, Ottoman Sultan of Turkey (*c*.1470–1520), nicknamed *Yavuz*, meaning 'the Grim'. One of the most able military leaders of all the Ottoman sultans, in his brief reign Selim hugely expanded the borders of the Ottoman empire. The son of Bayazid II, Selim soon rebelled against his father. Although Selim was defeated and forced to flee, his father soon abdicated in favour of his more martial son. One of Selim's first acts as Sultan was to invade Persia with 60,000 men, both to deal with the biggest threat to the Ottoman empire and to stamp out the 'heresy' of the Shi'ite Persians. In the summer of 1515, he defeated a 50,000 strong Persian army at the battle of Chaldrian and was able to seize the capital of Shah *Ismail at Tabriz in September. He could not hold it however, as his *janissaries mutinied and he was forced to withdraw. However, he had gained useful footholds on both the upper and middle Euphrates.

The following year, while preparing to attack Persia once again, Selim learnt of the threat of an imminent attack by the *Mameluke Sultan Kansu al-Gauri, so he invaded Syria instead. Making a forced march around the Taurus mountains, he surprised the Mamelukes at the Merj-Dabik in August 1516. He decisively defeated them and followed up his victory by beating the army of the new Mameluke sultan, Touman Bey, at Yaunis Khan near Gaza. His forces then crossed the Gaza desert and advanced on Cairo. The first major clash inside Egypt took place at Ridanieh on 22 January 1517. Touman Bey was once again defeated and Selim occupied Cairo, but Touman Bey launched a desperate attempt to recapture his capital, resulting in several days of bloody street fighting. It was to no avail and Selim subsequently proclaimed himself sultan and caliph. He then launched a campaign to occupy Mecca and the western Arabian coast, leaving a Turkish governor general behind in Cairo.

In his last years, Selim crushed minor religious risings in Anatolia and Syria. In 1519, Selim accepted the homage of Khair ed-Din, bey of Algiers, in return for Selim's support against Spain. Khair ed-Din provided a fleet in return. Therefore, by the time of his death near Corlu on 22 September 1520 while preparing an expedition against *Rhodes, Selim had not only doubled the size of the Ottoman empire, but also had provided with it a fleet which would dominate much of the Mediterranean.   MCM

Sellasia, battle of (222 BC). At Sellasia a Macedonian-led coalition army under Antigonus Doson defeated a Spartan army under their king, Cleomenes III. The battlefield was dominated by two hills, separated by the Oenus stream, which were occupied by 20,000 Spartan infantry, predominantly pike- or *sarissa*-armed. Cleomenes strengthened his position further by erecting a palisade in front of his right. Antigonus, with 28,000 infantry—of which approximately 13,000 were *sarissa*-armed *hoplites—and 1,200 cavalry, launched an assault on his right with a combined force of missile-armed light troops and Illyrians supported by heavy infantry. They shot into the Spartan left and forced it to advance downhill. A flanking attack on Antigonus' troops from Spartan light infantry stationed in the Oenus valley was thwarted by an aggressive cavalry attack led by the Achaean general Philopoemen. As the Spartan left advanced it became disorganized by the rough terrain and was defeated. Watching these events unfold Cleomenes decided that he had to abandon his defensive position on the right and attack if he were to save the day. His troops were defeated after becoming disordered by their advance down the steep and broken hillside into an especially deep Macedonian *sarissa* *phalanx.   SWN

Polybius, 2. 65–9.

---

semaphore The semaphore is a visual *communications system, which usually uses flags or lights to spell out letters. In 1792, Claude Chappe, a French engineer, devised an optical semaphore system that could carry a message 143 miles (230 km) from Lille to Paris in two minutes. It was designed with a set of arms that pivoted on a post. The positions of the arms determined the meaning of the message. The arms were attached to towers that were spaced 5–10 miles (8–16 km) apart. Messages were read by a *telescope at each tower. Other nations adopted Chappe's invention which was not superseded by the electric *telegraph until about 1850.

Hutton Gregory, a telegraph engineer on the British railways, developed a modified version of Chappe's semaphore for railroads in the early 1840s. His system employed moving metal arms or rows of lights, mounted on towers to signal trains. This system is still in effect today.

Semaphore also remains in use for maritime communications. The flags are usually square, red and yellow, divided diagonally with the red portion in the upper hoist. The flags are held, arms extended, in various positions representing each of the letters of the alphabet or numbers. The arms are kept straight when changing from one position to another. This system is used for short distance signalling. Use of semaphore flags was limited to within range of telescopes in earlier days and binoculars today. The colours were chosen for long-distance visibility. Ships also use flashing lights between vessels—the Aldis lamp—as another means of semaphore signalling.   DMJ

---

sentry A soldier responsible for guarding a military building, camp, or deployed unit. The duties of a sentry are crucial to security, and once the penalty for sleeping on sentry duty was death. In *barracks sentries are usually furnished by the unit's guard, a detachment of soldiers on duty for a 24-hour period, who live in the guardroom or guardhouse. They are often provided with sentry boxes to protect them against inclement weather, and the posting and relief of sentries is often the subject (particularly in the case of public buildings in national capitals) of elaborate ritual. The sentry will challenge individuals who approach, sometimes using a prescribed form of words—traditionally (but no longer) 'Halt: Who goes there?' in the British army—and perhaps inviting the challenged person or party to reply with a password. Depending on his *rules of engagement, he may detain, or even fire upon, intruders.

In the field sentries were traditionally visited by the orderly officer—'rounds'—or by the field officer of the day—'grand rounds'—to ensure that they were awake. French sentries repeated the cry 'sentinelle, garde à vous!' for the same reason. British soldiers, besieging the French-held fortress of Badajoz in Spain in 1812, mistakenly believed that they were shouting: 'All's well in Badahoo!' For many of the campaigns of history sentries, or larger security parties constituting infantry pickets or cavalry vedettes, did not habitually fire on one another. To do so was regarded as wasteful cruelty, since it could not affect the fortunes of the campaign. Prior to a formal attack sentries might be brushed aside, in a process called 'driving in the pickets' and remembered in the doggerel:

> They're at it already! I hear by the din
> Boot and saddle, the pickets are in.

Attacks on sentries were regarded as legitimate if a covert assault was intended. At Prague in 1741 Col François de

Senussi

Chevert briefed the grenadier chosen to lead his storming party:

Do you see that sentry over there?
Yes, colonel.
He will shout out 'Who goes there?' You will say nothing in reply, but just keep going.
Yes, colonel.
He will fire at you and he will miss.
Yes, colonel.
You will then cut his throat. I shall be there to back you up.

In the very recent past technological developments have introduced some changes to the manner and means by which sentry duties are carried out. First, a sentry need no longer be a soldier standing at the entrance to a camp with a pike, or a rifle. In modern warfare a small tank unit may be positioned to protect and stand post for other tank units while the crews sleep or prepare for renewed fighting. Secondly, the sentry is no longer wholly reliant upon what he or she can see in the immediate vicinity. Technological supports, such as *infra-red equipment, can enable the sentry to be informed as to the approach of vehicles or troops at greater distances. Finally, in the near future, sentries may commonly be monitored for alertness via sleep/activity equipment linked to a local command and control centre. These developments may further ensure that the highly important duties carried out by sentries are executed with maximum alertness and efficiency. Yet there was something attractive in 'sentinelle, garde à vous!'   AH/RH

Senussi (also Sennusiya) were a mystic Muslim Sufi brotherhood established in 1837 by Said Muhammad ibn 'Ali al-Senussi. One of the Senussi leaders, Said Muhammad Idris al-Senussi, became the king of Libya (King Idris I) in 1951. The Senussi were a missionary order that aimed to return to the simple faith and life of early Islam. By the turn of the 20th century, many Bedouins and oasis dwellers in the desert Sahara regions of Egypt and Libya were converted to the Senussi faith. The order was strongest in the Cyrenaica province of Libya where it integrated its religious lodges with the existing tribal system to the extent that it was able to marshal its members as a religious fighting order. When the Italians conquered coastal Libya during the *Italo-Turkish war, they were faced with Senussi resistance as they attempted to push inland. During WW I, the Senussi uprising spread over the border to British-controlled Egypt. While the British suppressed the Senussi revolt in the deserts of Egypt, the Italians were unable to extend their authority into Senussi-controlled areas and so by the peace of Arcoma in 1917, the Senussi leader Idris secured a ceasefire and confirmation of his position. A further agreement in 1919 established a Cyrenaican parliament and an Italian financial grant to Idris. However, he was unable to disarm his militant Senussi followers and in 1922 an Ital-

ian invasion forced him to flee to Egypt. The Italian pacification campaign against the Senussi in the 1920s was brutal, involving the widespread use of detention and *concentration camps. Idris re-emerged in 1942 when he returned to Libya with the British forces driving the Italians from the country. Idris was made king of Libya in 1951 but was forced to stand down when a military coup in 1969 brought Muammar al-Gaddafi to power, with a philosophy that recalled the old Sufi mysticism.   MH

Seringapatam (Srirangapatan), **siege of** (1799), last episode of the four wars fought between the British East India Company (EIC) and the Muslim adventurer Hyder Ali who (c.1761) had made himself ruler of the Hindu state of Mysore (modern Karnatka), and his son Tippu Sultan. In 1766 the EIC Madras presidency joined the Nizam of Hyderabad in a war with Hyder Ali. The Nizam dropped out and the EIC was happy to escape without penalty. In about 1780 Hyder Ali joined the Marathas (whom he had previously combated) (see MARATHA WARS) and troops had to be sent from the Calcutta presidency. French help arrived but Hyder Ali died and Tippu made peace in 1782 in return for recognition as sultan. In 1789 Tippu started the war but by 1792 he had been driven back on Seringapatam and made peace at the expense of half his kingdom. His further dalliance with the French decided the governor general (later Marquess *Wellesley) to finish him and in 1799 he sent 21,000 British and EIC troops under Maj Gen Harris from Madras while a further 16,000 strong Hyderabadi contingent advanced under the direction of his brother Arthur (later *Wellington). After artillery had opened a practicable breach, Tippu refused to surrender and was killed fighting the storming party.

Sertorius, Quintus (c.126–73 BC), one of the most able Roman generals, who displayed a particular genius for leading armies of irregulars. In 105 he was wounded at the Roman disaster at Arausio. He served under *Marius against the Cimbri, disguising himself as a barbarian to spy on the enemy. He also fought in Spain and in the *Social War, during which he was wounded and lost an eye. Siding with *Marius during the ensuing Civil War, he continued the struggle against *Sulla longer than any other leader, first in Spain, and then in Mauretania, before returning to Spain. There he assembled a highly disciplined force raised from Italian settlers and Lusitanian tribesmen. He displayed a mastery of *guerrilla tactics, harassing the far larger armies sent against him, but avoiding combat altogether when unsure of victory. From 80–73 he inflicted reverses and serious defeats on commander after commander sent against him. He came to dominate much of the Spanish Peninsula and allied himself with Mithridates of Pontus and the Cilician pirates, posing a major threat to the powers at Rome.

Metellus Pius and *Pompey slowly wore down his strength, but Sertorius eventually fell to treachery, murdered by his subordinate, Perpenna, who was then brought to battle and defeated by Pompey.   AKG

Servile Wars. See GLADIATORS WAR.

Sevastopol, sieges of (1854–55, 1941–2). Sevastopol in the Crimea (formerly in Russia and now in the Ukraine) is a perfect natural harbour, and was selected by *Suvorov as an ideal base for the Russian fleet. In the *Crimean war, the Russian fleet, which was wooden and sail-powered, dared not venture out to fight the steam-powered iron ships of France and Britain, and sheltered under the guns of the naval base. The capture of Sevastopol and neutralization of the Black Sea fleet was therefore the objective of the Crimean war expedition. The fortress was prepared to defend against a seaborne attack, but not against one from the land. On 25 September 1854, 67,000 British, French, Turkish, and Sardinian troops began besieging the garrison of 7,000, rising to 43,000 during the course of the siege. The Russians constructed elaborate defences and the siege lasted so long that the British public became impatient and there was a proposal to put the siege out to contract. On 8 September 1855, after the fall of the Malakoff redoubt, Sevastopol surrendered (see TOLSTOY).

By 16 November 1941 the Germans had captured all the Crimea apart from Sevastopol. Eleventh Army and elements of Third Romanian Army ringed the fortress. Sevastopol was surrounded by forts with armoured emplacements buried deep in concrete and rock. With troops who had escaped the Germans and had fallen back on Sevastopol, the garrison numbered 106,000. The Germans began to bombard the fortress on 17 December. They brought up the fearsome 31½ inch Gustav Gerät, known as 'Big Dora', the largest calibre gun ever built until Saddam *Hussein's 1 metre supergun in 1990, to help flatten it. The Red Army and navy attempted to relieve the city with a huge amphibious assault, the Kerch-Feodosiya operation, on 25 December. They captured Feodosiya but were then dislodged.

The assault went in on 7 June and the Soviets fought on for 27 days. The Germans used toxic *smoke to kill them in their underground installations, one of the few times in WW II when *chemical weapons were used. At the very end, some top Soviet officers and officials were taken out by submarine. Sevastopol fell, after 250 days, on 4 July. The Soviets recaptured it on 9 May 1944, after a campaign to recapture the whole of the Crimea lasting a month.   CDB

Seven Days battles (1862), series of battles in which 60,000 Confederates newly under *Lee chivvied 100,000 Unionists under *McClellan away from a position of

imminent threat to Richmond and back against the James river, from where they were eventually evacuated. Convinced he was outnumbered, McClellan had crawled up the Jamestown peninsula, hoping to combine with an advance by McDowell from the North. After repulsing a Confederate attack at Seven Pines (31 May–1 June), he did little while Lee replaced the incapacitated Joseph *Johnston and recalled Jackson's army from the *Shenandoah. A dangerous Union probe at Oak Grove (25 June) nearly disrupted Lee's plans, and his first attack at Mechanicsville (26 June) was a draw, but McClellan began to retreat, hurried on his way at Gaines' Mill (27 June). The Union army again held its own at Savage's Station (29 June) and White Oak/Glendale (30 June), and severely mauled Lee's final frontal assault at Malvern Hill (1 July). Including Seven Pines, McClellan had inflicted nearly 27,000 casualties in exchange for less than 21,000 of his own more numerous and better equipped army. But he was mastered by his fears and Lee's relentless aggressiveness, and his promising campaign came to nothing.   HEB

Seven Years War (1756–63). This was in reality two separate conflicts, the first fought in Germany and central Europe between Prussia and a coalition headed by Austria, France, and Russia, and the second overseas between Britain and France, latterly assisted by Spain. The two struggles were linked principally by France's involvement in both, though as the war continued this link became increasingly fragile. Both conflicts were to prove decisive, albeit in different ways: that in Europe established Prussia and Russia as great powers, while in the maritime and colonial sphere Britain overwhelmingly defeated the two leading Bourbon monarchies and secured a dominant position by 1763. The principal loser in both struggles was France, whose standing as the leading continental power was destroyed for a generation and would only be restored by the armies of the French Revolution during the 1790s.

The European conflict had a clear-cut beginning which the colonial war lacked. On 29 August 1756 *Frederick 'the Great' led his troops across the border into neighbouring Saxony. He was convinced that he would be attacked in the following spring by a coalition assembled by the Austrian Chancellor Wenzel Anton von Kaunitz, which aimed to recover the former Habsburg province of Silesia, seized by Prussia during the War of the *Austrian Succession. This powerful alliance now contained not only Austria but France and Russia, and would subsequently be extended to include the declining second-rank state of Sweden and contingents of soldiers provided by the Holy Roman Empire. In the period before the Seven Years War Frederick's foreign policy was pacific; he believed that any further conflict could only imperil his possession of the rich and well-populated territory of Silesia. But he recognized the military threat posed by Saxony, which could serve as a

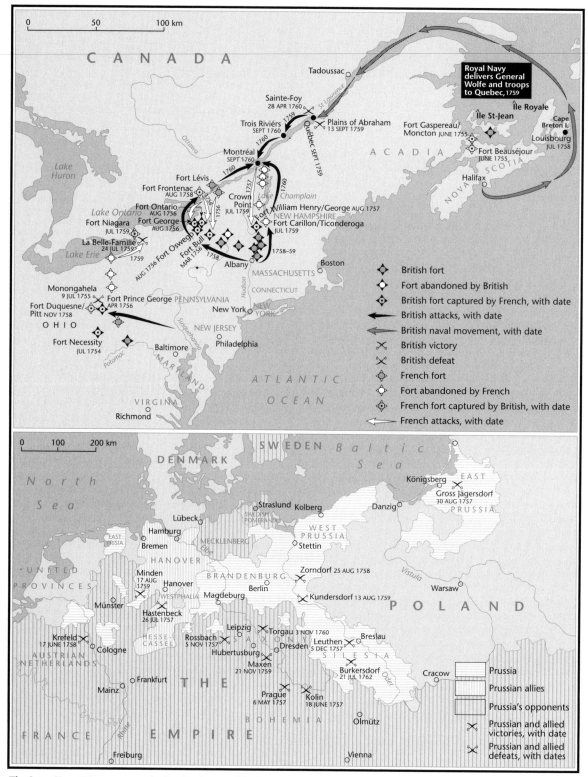

The **Seven Years War**, 1756–63, and related actions worldwide. This 'world war' overlapped with continuing British–French colonial conflicts in America (top) and India (right), but at its centre was the Prussia of Frederick the Great and its fight for survival (bottom).

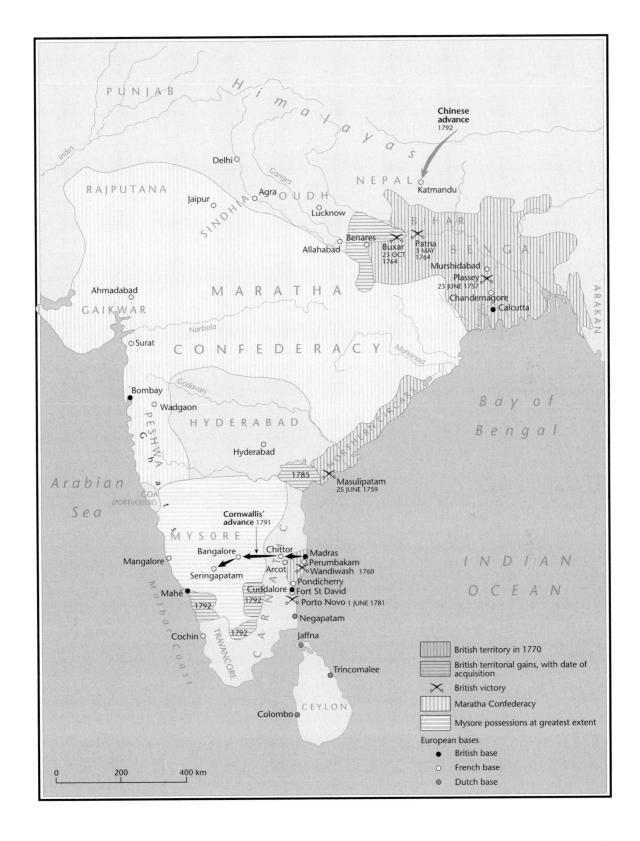

PUNJAB

Himalayas

Indus

RAJPUTANA

Delhi ○

Jaipur ○

Ganges

Agra ○
SINDHIA

OUDH

Lucknow ○

NEPAL

Katmandu ○

**Chinese
advance**
1792

Benares ○

Allahabad ○

Buxar
23 OCT
1764

Patna
3 MAY
1764

BIHAR

BENGAL

Murshidabad ○

Plassey
23 JUNE 1757

Chandernagore ○

● Calcutta

ARAKAN

Ahmadabad ○

GAIKWAR

MARATHA

Narbala

Surat ○

CONFEDERACY

Mahanad

Godavari

Bombay ●

Wadgaon ○

PESHWA

HYDERABAD

Hyderabad ○

NORTHERN CIRCARS

*Bay of
Bengal*

*Arabian
Sea*

GOA
(PORTUGUESE)

1785

Masulipatam
25 JUNE 1759

ghats

**Cornwallis'
advance** 1791

MYSORE

Mangalore ○

Bangalore ○

Chittor ○

Madras ●

Seringapatam ○

Arcot ○

Perumbakam
Wandiwash 1760

Pondicherry ○

*INDIAN

OCEAN*

Mahé ●

1792

CARNATIC

Cuddalore ○
Fort St David ●

1792

Porto Novo 1 JUNE 1781

Malbar Coast

Negapatam ○

Cochin ○

TRAVANCORE

1792

Jaffna ○

Trincomalee ○

CEYLON

Colombo ○

	British territory in 1770
	British territorial gains, with date of acquisition
✕	British victory
	Maratha Confederacy
	Mysore possessions at greatest extent

European bases
● British base
○ French base
○ Dutch base

0   200   400 km

bridgehead for an invasion of Brandenburg, the core of the Hohenzollern monarchy. The river Elbe bisected both territories and would be used to move supplies, while his capital Berlin was only some 50 miles (80 km) from the exposed frontier with the Saxon electorate. Though ostensibly neutral, the electorate was firmly in the political orbit of Austria and France and a Saxon princess was married to the heir to the French throne. Believing he would inevitably be attacked by Austria and Russia in the spring of 1757, Frederick took the initiative and invaded Saxony at the very end of August 1756.

His action was, at first sight, successful. The Saxon army was speedily surrounded and disarmed. Its officers were permitted to go into exile with the ruler and his court, which moved to Warsaw (the Elector Augustus was also king of Poland), and the rank and file was incorporated into Prussian regiments, though most of these unwilling recruits subsequently deserted. An attempted Habsburg counter-attack was repulsed, confirming Frederick in his disdainful view of Austrian military power. The political repercussions of his invasion were more serious. It ensured that France would fight actively to defeat Prussia, and enabled Kaunitz to transform his defensive alliance into an offensive coalition, which confronted Frederick in the campaign of 1757.

Encouraged by his early success and anxious for a short war (because of Prussia's very limited resources, particularly when measured against the overwhelming advantage which his enemies seemed to enjoy), Frederick went on the offensive in this first campaign. He invaded Bohemia, winning a hard-fought victory at Prague (6 May) but suffering a severe reverse at Kolin (18 June), in a battle which forced him to acknowledge the progress which the Austrian army had made since the defeats of the 1730s and 1740s. Simultaneously the Russians advanced upon isolated East Prussia, the source of the Hohenzollern royal title but cut off from the dynasty's heartlands by several hundred miles of Polish territory. Two months after the reverse at Kolin, Russia's troops inflicted a serious defeat on the Prussians at Gross Jägersdorf (30 August). Prussia's first crisis of the Seven Years War in autumn 1757 was overcome by Frederick's comprehensive victory at *Rossbach over a Franco-imperial force twice his own strength and, a month later, by an even more impressive success over the Austrians at *Leuthen.

Rossbach was the war's most decisive battle, because of its enormous repercussions within France. Louis XV's monarchy was Europe's leading military power and had not expected such a shattering reverse, particularly at the hands of an upstart such as Prussia. It was also involved in a worldwide struggle with the rising British empire, its colonial and commercial competitor throughout the 18th century. The outbreak of the colonial war was far less clear-cut than the European. Britain and France were neighbours as well as rivals in North America, and the peace settlement which had ended the previous conflict, that over the Austrian succes-

sion, at Aix-la-Chapelle (1748), had been only a *truce. The two colonial powers competed for territory and influence, especially in the Ohio river valley, and the *French and Indian war had been underway throughout the 1750s. Britain's actions in sending a force under Gen Braddock in December 1754 to punish the French for an earlier attack and her seizure of French ships on the high seas in 1755, signalled a sharp deterioration in relations, though these initiatives were viewed in London as responses to earlier provocations. After the French destroyed Braddock on the *Monongahela the two states were openly at war, even if it was not formally declared until May 1756.

The Anglo-French war in Europe began with important French victories, especially the capture of Britain's Mediterranean base of Minorca in June 1756, her defeat in Germany at Hastenbeck (26 July 1757), and the capitulation by *Cumberland at Klosterseven (10 September). This proved a false dawn for France. The rout at Rossbach in November destroyed French military power for a generation and undermined the confidence of her generals and statesmen. Throughout the 18th century France's strategic Achilles' heel had been that even the great resources available to her were insufficient to support two simultaneous wars: that with the Habsburgs on the continent and with Britain overseas. The rivalry with Austria had apparently been ended by the first Treaty of Versailles signed in May 1756, one purpose of which had been to enable French resources to be concentrated on the overseas struggle, now widely seen in France as the greater priority. Frederick's invasion of Saxony had frustrated this intention, and Rossbach demonstrated the disastrous consequences of attempting to fight two wars. Thereafter France's commitment to the continental struggle was scaled down, being formally reduced by the third Treaty of Versailles (March 1759), after which French troops fought only in Westphalia, where they engaged in indecisive operations against the so-called Army of Observation. This treaty was concluded by the Duc de Choiseul, who had become foreign minister in December 1758 and who was determined to concentrate available resources on the colonial struggle with Britain.

France's changed priorities proved decisive in the continental war. Prussia's desperate struggle was reduced in scale, becoming primarily a war against Austria and, increasingly, Russia. Sweden, though a member of the anti-Prussian coalition, contributed little to the struggle and her military effort was viewed disdainfully by Frederick. Meanwhile Britain, where William Pitt 'the Elder' had secured real authority in 1757 after the early defeats, moved to support Prussia effectively. From 1758–61 London provided an annual subsidy of £670,000, which contributed almost one-fifth of the total costs of Prussia's war effort, and more practical help in the shape of the so-called 'Army of Observation' which protected Prussia's vulnerable western flank for the remainder of the war and which was financed and in part manned by Britain. The stalemate on the Westphalian front, together with the ineffective Swedish military effort, significantly reduced the threat of encirclement which Frederick had faced in 1756–8.

The war now became a less unequal struggle than it had been initially. Frederick's exposed geographical position did not become a strategic liability. The provinces of the Hohenzollern monarchy sprawled across northern Europe, from the Rhineland in the west to the Niemen far to the east. Territorial dispersal had long been a problem facing rulers in Berlin. During the Seven Years War the king abandoned the outlying possessions: those in Westphalia were under French occupation from the first campaign of the struggle, while East Prussia was occupied by the Russians from January 1758 onwards. Instead he concentrated upon his compact central position, adopting a strategy of interior lines and fighting the war in Brandenburg, Saxony, Silesia, and Bohemia. The Prussian offensive in 1757 had, for a time, seemed likely to end in disaster. Thereafter Frederick adopted a strategy of *attrition, striking first against one opponent and then against another, with the aim of preventing his enemies, with their massively superior resources, from uniting and delivering the decisive blow which he feared. This was successful, though along the way he lost as many battles as he won: his towering military reputation after the war reflected more his survival, in the face of overwhelming odds, than his battlefield successes.

This survival owed much to non-military factors. The Prussian home front proved stronger than that of its enemies. Despite its officials being unpaid for extended periods during the war, Prussia's famed administration was able to scrape together the men, money, and *matériel* needed to sustain the struggle. Though the quality of recruits declined during the second half of the war, the *canton system of territorial *recruitment proved more able to provide soldiers than its Austrian counterpart. The brutal and haphazard conscription of the Russian empire provided more soldiers than were available to Frederick, and the continental war became a life-and-death struggle between Prussia and her powerful rival in north-eastern Europe.

In its middle years no clear decision was evident in the war for Silesia. Despite a series of reverses, particularly at the hands of the Russians—a bloody tactical draw at Zorndorf on 25 August 1758, serious defeats at Kay (Paltzig) on 23 July 1759 and especially at Kundersdorf on 12 August of that year—Frederick retained the ability to win sufficient victories to keep the struggle going. Though he had lost Hochkirch to the Austrians (14 October 1758), decisive victories at Liegnitz (15 August 1760) and Torgau (3 November) broke Habsburg will to sustain the conflict. In 1761 Austria was forced to reduce the size of her army, though the fighting continued, and embark upon the further administrative changes which were essential. Vienna had contributed to its own failure. Though Austrian troops had fought bravely, earning Frederick's respect, Habsburg generalship was at best mediocre and frequently did not rise to that level. The French alliance had not produced the expected contribution, in men and money, to the war effort, while Russia was too much of a political rival in eastern Europe ever to be a comfortable partner: the military co-operation of the two powers, upon which so much rested particularly during the second half of the war, was beset by mutual suspicion and distrust.

The indecisive, though bloody, struggle in central Europe was in sharp contrast to the clear-cut outcome overseas. France's concentration on the war against Britain from 1759 onwards did not bring success: on the contrary defeats soon began to mount up in this theatre as the British war effort, now directed by William Pitt, gained purpose and momentum. Britain was far superior at sea, and this was underlined by decisive victories in European waters during 1759 at Lagos (July) and in Quiberon Bay (November). Maritime supremacy was the basis of a series of British successes which destroyed 18th-century French imperial power for ever. The losses in the French and Indian war were particularly striking. There Britain's objective in 1758–60 was the conquest of the French colony of Canada, and this was achieved in stages. The vital base of *Louisbourg on Cape Breton island in the Gulf of St Lawrence was captured in July 1758, and Fort Duquesne (renamed Fort Pitt, now Pittsburgh) in December. In the following year *Quebec was taken, after the dramatic scaling of the Heights of Abraham by *Wolfe. The British conquest of Canada was completed by the seizure of Montreal in September 1760. In the Indian subcontinent France's position was undermined by a series of British successes. Victory by *Clive in the small-scale but decisive battle of *Plassey gave Britain, or rather her East India Company, control of Bengal, while subsequent successes at Wandiwash (January 1760) and Pondicherry (January 1761) weakened the French position on the Carnatic coast in the south-east. Other colonial trophies were seized from the near-prostrate French monarchy, above all the West Indian Islands of Guadeloupe (May 1759) and Martinique (February 1762).

As Britain's gains mounted up in the *annus mirabilis* of 1759, Horace Walpole famously remarked that so numerous were the successes the church bells were worn out ringing for victories. Whether these gains were the result of a clear-cut strategy, so much as superior *naval power and *war finance, better generals and admirals, and experience of previous successful struggles with France, must be doubted. Pitt was an energetic and, more important, a lucky war leader, rather than a strategist of genius. His reputation, at the time and since, owes much to the skilful way he was careful to exploit the successes and ring the bells of victory: his greatness rested on his undoubted abilities as a propagandist.

By 1760 Britain had comprehensively won the Anglo-French Seven Years War. The scale of that victory was reduced by a series of events during the next two years.

George III's accession in October 1760, and the coming to power of his minister-favourite, the Earl of Bute, in the following year seriously reduced British willingness to pay for a 'German war' which appeared to be deadlocked and, more important, did not appear to be contributing to Britain's struggle with France. Anglo-French peace negotiations in 1761 failed to produce a settlement. Choiseul, from that year Louis XV's leading minister, now broadened the war by signing the so-called Bourbon Family Compact with Spain. During the reign of Ferdinand VI (1746–59) Madrid had remained neutral, but the accession of the anti-British Charles III (1759–88) opened the way for a Franco-Spanish alliance, concluded in August 1761. Pitt favoured an immediate attack upon Spain and its vulnerable empire and, when his cabinet colleagues refused support, resigned (October 1761). Spain entered the Anglo-French war in January 1762, but this only enabled the victorious British forces to win a further series of victories, especially the capture of Havana and of Manila later in that year.

The continental war was effectively decided by the death of Frederick's implacable foe, the Russian Empress Elizabeth, in January 1762. Her successor was the pro-Prussian Peter III, who immediately concluded first an armistice and then a peace treaty with his Prussian hero. Austria continued to fight for one further campaign, in the course of which Frederick won a final tactical victory at Burkersdorf (July 1762). Though preparations for the next campaign went ahead, neither state had either the will or the human and material resources to continue fighting. Peace negotiations between Austria and Prussia began on 30 December 1762, and were quickly concluded. By the peace of Hubertusburg (15 February 1763), signed at the Saxon elector's hunting lodge, the continental war was ended on the basis of the territorial status quo. Seven years of intensive and at times desperate fighting had produced a settlement which merely restored the position which had prevailed before the war began. Frederick famously compared his own predicament during the conflict to that of a trapeze artist who was always one step from disaster. By 1763 he had safely reached the end of the high wire, an outcome which had been in doubt for much of the struggle.

The Anglo-Bourbon peace settlement took far longer to conclude, though it was signed in the same month. During complex and prolonged negotiations in 1762–3 Choiseul's skilful diplomacy, together with Britain's war-weariness, limited Bourbon losses: the final settlement was more generous to France and Spain than the prevailing military situation might have required. Yet the terms of the Peace of Paris (10 February 1763) were still a serious defeat for the Bourbon allies. France was excluded from the North American mainland, retaining only a precarious foothold in the Newfoundland fisheries through the possession of the islands of St Pierre and Miquelon, while her position in the Indian subcontinent was effectively destroyed. Her ally Spain handed over Florida to Britain, subsequently receiving Louisiana from France in compensation. The Seven Years War had thus established Britain's maritime and colonial dominance over her Bourbon rivals, and after 1763 she was clearly Europe's leading commercial and imperial power. Within Europe, by contrast, no such clear-cut result was apparent. Yet the political consequences of the continental fighting were in some ways even more momentous. The survival of Prussia and the military victories won by Russia established these two states as continental great powers. France by contrast had been defeated in both struggles, while the war's enormous cost was a major source of the massive financial problems of the Bourbon monarchy during the next generation which made a major contribution to the outbreak of the French Revolution of 1789.   HS

Dorn, W. L., *Competition for Empire, 1740–1763* (New York, 1940).

Duffy, Christopher, *Frederick the Great: A Military Life* (London, 1985).

Middleton, Richard, *The Bells of Victory: The Pitt-Newcastle Ministry and the Conduct of the Seven Years' War, 1757–1762* (Cambridge, 1985).

Peters, Marie, *The Elder Pitt* (London, 1998).

Showalter, Dennis E., *The Wars of Frederick the Great* (London, 1996).

Seversky, Alexander Prokofiev de (1894–1974), Russian born, US naturalized aviation designer and *airpower theorist. In a career presenting remarkable parallels with that of Igor Sikorsky, the Russian designer of the Ilya Muromets heavy bomber who came to the USA after WW I and designed *helicopters, Seversky began as a pilot in the Russian Naval Air Service. He worked as a test pilot and founded the Seversky Air Corporation in 1922, and later headed several aeronautical firms including the Seversky Aircraft Corporation from 1931 to 1939. He invented an automatic bombsight patented by the USA and in 1936 designed an all-metal trainer and high-speed fighter. In 1938 he designed a fighter around the Rolls-Royce Merlin engine which became the P-47 Mustang, the key to air superiority over Germany in WW II. In 1942 he published *Victory through Air Power*, an influential book on the subject.

CDB

Shaka, Chief (1787–1828). The result of a liaison between the Zulu chief Senzangakhona and a woman from another tribe, Shaka's name was a contemptuous reference to an intestinal beetle. First a protégé of Dingiswayo, leader of the Mthethwa confederation, Shaka's astonishing rise was based on the radical changes he made to Zulu military techniques. Zulu society was already disciplined, with age groups organized on military lines. Shaka's 'Regiments' had no fixed establishments but were drawn from these age groups, reducing the risk of clan-inspired rivalry. Shaka hardened his soldiers by long, barefoot marches, and inflicted the death penalty for the least failure. He believed that battles were won by pressing to close quarters and replaced the throwing spear, traditionally the principal weapon, by the broad-bladed stabbing spear and the light shield with a larger, heavier one designed to hook away the opponent's and expose him to the killing stroke. Shaka developed, though he did not invent, the crescent-shaped deployment, which he likened to the buffalo: the horns enveloped the enemy and the chest 'ate him up'. A reserve, the loins, could be committed as required.

Shaka first served Dingiswayo, who gave him the resources to establish himself as leader of the Zulus. Over the ten years following Dingiswayo's assassination in 1816 he expanded a small state into a vast empire. The process was called *mfecane* (crushing), and perhaps 2 million people may have died during it. Shaka's ruthlessness, at first calculated, grew increasingly uncontrolled. On his mother's death in 1827 he killed thousands for failing to show proper grief, and even banned the planting of crops. He had embarked on a campaign against the European settlers of the Cape when his increasingly vulnerable half-brothers, led by Dingane, murdered him. Shaka's army was a remarkable creation: in the *Zulu war of 1879 it became one of the few indigenous forces to inflict a defeat on a well-armed European opponent in the open field.   RH

Shamyl (1796–1871), the leader of Islamic resistance to Russian penetration of Dagestan in the eastern Caucasus in the mid-19th century. Of Avar tribal origin, his traditional Islamic education and military talents fitted him to become the leader of a *jihad against the relentlessly advancing Russians, and in 1834 he was recognized as imam or religio-politico-military leader. He soon came to control the mountain areas of Dagestan, and established within them an Islamic polity. With his *murids* or dedicated warriors, he achieved several striking successes against the Russian troops, fighting as they were in an alien environment, at times compelling them to sue for peace, and he extended eastwards into Kabardia or Circassia. However, the end of the *Crimean war in 1856 enabled the tsar to concentrate efforts against Dagestan. Chechnya, to its north, was pacified and Shamyl gradually encircled, so that he was compelled to surrender in 1859. He was treated leniently and honourably, dying in 1871; one of his sons became a general in the imperial Russian army.   CEB

Baddeley, John F., *The Russian Conquest of the Caucasus* (London, 1908).

Gammer, M., *Muslim Resistance to the Tsar: Shamil and the Conquest of Chechnia and Daghestan* (London, 1994).

sharpshooters are skilled marksmen, also known as *Jägers and *tirailleurs. The term is often synonymous with *sniper, but in the *American civil war referred specifically to sharpshooter regiments raised by both sides. In 1861 Col

Hiram Berdan raised the 1st US Sharpshooters, and a second regiment followed shortly afterwards. Originally issued with the unreliable Colt revolving rifle, the sharpshooters soon received the deadly Sharps *breech-loaders. They often reported direct to a division, tended to fight as skirmishers, not in the line of battle, and wore the regulation infantry uniform, but in dark green cloth. The regiments withered in 1864 as enlistment terms expired, and eventually disappeared in February 1865. The Confederacy also raised sharpshooters, but simply as state regiments which generally took their place in the line with others, and were not used to full advantage.

In England the 3rd County of London Yeomanry (Sharpshooters) was originally raised from volunteers in 1899 to fight in South Africa. The regiment's title is preserved within a squadron of the Royal Yeomanry, part of the Territorial Army.   AH/RH

shell-shock WW I soldiers who became psychiatric *casualties were generally diagnosed as suffering from shell-shock in the belief that their brains had been concussed by the explosion of a nearby shell. A 1922 *War Office committee recognized that breakdown was far more complex than this: although there were some cases caused by concussion, battle exhaustion and other war neuroses were far more frequent.   RH

Shenandoah Valley campaign (1862), mobile campaign waged by the heavily outnumbered 'Stonewall' *Jackson to protect the 'breadbasket' of Virginia, which also fatally disrupted Union strategy in the east. The valley lies between the Blue Ridge and Allegheny mountains and is formed by the north and south forks of the Shenandoah river, which flow north-east on either side of the Massanutten mountain, until they join near Front Royal and run into the Potomac river through a deep ravine at Harpers Ferry, an important Union railway junction and *arsenal. For the strategic implications see CONFEDERATE STATES ARMY.

During the winter Jackson, displaying his trademark fanaticism, marched a corps west of the Alleghenies through pro-Union west Virginia. Soldiers deserted in droves and many senior officers became convinced he was insane. Of a paper strength of 13,750 only 5,400 were present in early March, but Jackson had found in Ashby a charismatic local irregular cavalry commander and along with local militia drafts he acquired a brilliant cartographer who knew the valley intimately.

The situation facing the Confederacy was ominous. The Union *blockade had begun to bite and coastal areas were being lost, the army in the west was in retreat and had lost Nashville, but above all Jackson's *West Point classmate *McClellan had assembled and polished an army of 150,000 around Washington to strike at Richmond. In a situation analogous to that of *Grant at Fort Donelson, Jackson was to deliver good news to a leadership badly in need of it.

He began by assaulting Shields, who was holding Winchester while the rest of Banks's army of the northern Shenandoah redeployed east of the Blue Ridge. Although repulsed at Kernstown on 23 March, the attack deepened the concerns *Lincoln entertained that McClellan's plan to take Richmond by a seaborne invasion up the Jamestown peninsula would leave Washington exposed. This had resulted in the detachment of troops to armies under McDowell (covering Washington), Banks (in the valley), and Frémont (west of the Alleghenies). Jackson did not cause this dilution of Union strength, but his campaign was to keep these armies from operating in concert, while depriving the peninsular campaign of the overwhelming numerical superiority McClellan felt he required.

He did this by marching his troops so rapidly over such long distances that they called themselves his 'foot cavalry', while by achieving local numerical superiority he multiplied his troops in the minds of the bemused Union commanders. When McClellan disengaged after Kernstown, Washington believed he was abandoning the valley and detached Shields to join McDowell for an advance on Richmond from the north. Jackson redeployed to the southwest, defeating Frémont's advance guard at McDowell on 8 May, and then marched back up the northern Shenandoah turnpike towards Banks, well entrenched at Strasburg.

On receipt of urgent if initially contradictory orders from *Lee and *Johnston, resolved by an insubordinate appeal to the former over the head of the latter, his priority became to prevent further reinforcement of McDowell by Banks, and to draw troops away from the two-front advance on Richmond. To achieve this he cut across the Massanutten and the southern Shenandoah in mid-valley to join Ewell's Corps. The combined force of perhaps 17,500 drove between the two Union armies, taking the vital river crossings at Front Royal on 23 May and manoeuvring Banks out of Strasburg. They fell on the Union rearguard and defeated Banks at Winchester on 25 May, drove him north across the Potomac, and then seized Harpers Ferry, sending shock waves to Washington.

By now, without changing his austere and secretive leadership style, Jackson's apotheosis was at hand. After he arrested the commander of his old brigade for disobedience at Kernstown, his officers learned not to second-guess his orders. Ewell wryly commented: 'I never saw one of Jackson's couriers approach without expecting an order to assault the North Pole.' But he would have done so, and his men would have believed it possible if they knew 'Old Jack' thought it was. The alchemy of command turned a ragged rabble of ill-equipped, often unshod, and always hungry and tired individualists into a proud army which delivered performances that in their wildest dreams few generals in history have asked, still less expected, of their men.

Lincoln, at the time acting as commander of the armies, reversed McDowell's advance on Richmond and detached Shields's 20,000 to return to the valley in an attempt to trap Jackson's army in the north by a mid-valley pincer movement in combination with Frémont from the west. The results of this were uniformly disastrous for the Union in Virginia. Instead of facing armies converging on two fronts, Johnston was left to deal only with McClellan, who had furthermore rendered his right wing vulnerable by overextending it to link up with McDowell. On 31 May–1 June the Confederates attacked and halted McClellan's advance at Seven Pines, a setback made all the more significant when Johnston was severely wounded and replaced by the far more aggressive Lee.

Back in the Shenandoah, Jackson had to scramble to extract his army from Union encirclement, prevented by his earlier precaution of fortifying the Allegheny passes, which forced Frémont to march well to the north before entering the valley, where Ewell hit him at Strasburg, buying further time. But at the end of the first week of June Jackson turned to face Frémont's and Shield's armies, which together greatly outnumbered him, advancing on either side of the south fork of the Shenandoah at the southern end of the valley, with a reinforced Banks advancing in support. A Union breakthrough would have put them behind the already outnumbered Lee.

At the battles of Cross Keys and Port Republic on 8–9 June, the Union armies were defeated in detail by Ewell and Jackson and retreated up the valley. Freed to join Lee, the Army of the Shenandoah and its exhausted leaders performed poorly during the *Seven Days battles, but it was largely thanks to their efforts that by then a near-certain Confederate defeat had been averted.   HEB

Tanner, Robert, *Stonewall in the Valley* (Mechanicsburg, Pa, 1996).

Sheridan, Gen Philip H. (1831–88), along with *Sherman, the officer most associated with mercilessness against the South in the *American civil war and the Plains Indians thereafter (see PLAINS INDIANS WARS). Of poor Irish immigrant stock, he won a place at *West Point by chance and was still a lieutenant at the outbreak of war. He earned promotion from colonel to brigadier general with a victory against odds at Booneville, followed by promotion to major general of volunteers for steadiness at Perryville in October and for holding the Union centre in the face of repeated attacks at Stones River over New Year 1863. Outside Chattanooga, he shared fully in the near rout at Chickamauga in September, but redeemed himself under *Grant by directing an unexpected break-through at Missionary Ridge in November.

When Grant was called east to assume overall command he appointed Sheridan to head the cavalry of the Army of the Potomac. After the battle of the Wilderness, in May 1864 he overcame the opposition of his immediate superior *Meade to massed cavalry tactics and defeated the South's legendary cavalry general *Stuart, killed at Yellow Tavern. In August, following Early's advance up the Shenandoah to the outskirts of Washington, Grant gave him an independent command, with instructions to clear the valley and to destroy its capacity to support any future Confederate offensive.

Union generals were regularly humiliated in this theatre, which was further complicated by savagely effective mounted *guerrilla warfare. His predecessor Hunter burned the Virginia Military Institute in retaliation, but Sheridan also burned the unharvested crops. At the hard-fought third battle of Winchester in September his plans to trap the outnumbered Early went badly awry, but he retrieved a victory with great battlefield leadership. At Cedar Creek in October he was surprised away from his army when a newly reinforced Early attacked. The situation was potentially disastrous until he returned, his appearance cheered as he galloped, blaspheming memorably, in front of the whole line. No other Union commander ever received such a tribute from his men in battle.

With the thanks of Congress and his rank made regular, Sheridan led 10,000 cavalry and artillery through Virginia to join Grant at Petersburg. He directed the war's final chapter, cutting off *Lee at Five Forks and bringing him to bay at Appomattox. Immediately afterwards, Grant appointed him military governor of Louisiana and Texas, with the double objective of pacification and to demonstrate against the French *Mexican expedition. In 1867, what President Johnson regarded as his high-handed implementation of what came to be known as 'radical reconstruction' led to reassignment to the department of the Missouri, exchanging places with Hancock and inheriting the southern Plains Indians uprising.

Sheridan's aphorism that the only good Indians he ever saw were dead has clung to his memory, with some justification, although the directing intelligence was Sherman's, whom he succeeded as army commander in 1884. After a series of heart attacks, Congress hastily voted him his fourth star, the rank of general, shortly before his death.

HEB

Morris, Roy Jr., *Sheridan* (New York, 1992).

Sherman, Gen William T.

Sherman, Gen William T. (1820–91), second among *American civil war Union generals and architect of the post-war pacification of the western frontier. Undistinguished in battle, Sherman owed his advancement to powerful family political connections and to his close friendship with *Grant. He is remembered for the aphorism 'war is all hell' and for his adamant refusal to run for president, unusual among successful US generals.

Named Tecumseh after the Shawnee leader, he was rechristened William in a Catholic ceremony at age 9, after he was informally adopted by a prominent Ohio politician when his father died. His surrogate father later became secretary of the interior, and Sherman was to marry his daughter. A graduate of *West Point, he served in the Seminole wars and in California, resigning to pursue a disastrous career in finance. On the eve of the civil war he was superintendent of a Louisiana military academy.

He obtained a colonelcy through the influence of his Senator brother, but fared so badly at first *Bull Run that on promotion to brigadier general he asked *Lincoln to keep him 'in a subordinate capacity', an early indicator of a lifelong propensity to depression. Posted as second in command in Kentucky, he took over when his superior resigned because of the 'mental torture of his command' in October 1862. A month later Sherman asked to be relieved for the same reason.

For any less well connected officer this would have spelled the end, but he was given a second chance as one of Grant's divisional commanders in Tennessee. At *Shiloh, the mood pendulum swung the other way and he ignored repeated and specific warnings of an impending attack. Once it struck, he behaved with great coolness in salvaging the situation and although principally responsible for the near defeat, he was promoted to major general. When Grant was blamed by northern newspapers and sidelined, Sherman's solidarity and his influence with his patron *Halleck persuaded Grant not to resign and defined the rest of both their military careers.

During the mid-1863 *Vicksburg campaign, at Chickasaw Bluffs he failed to get his subordinates to act in concert and suffered an expensive defeat. He had no confidence in Grant's manoeuvre to the south of the city, but played his assigned part well, showing considerable talent in the battle for Jackson. Moving with Grant to Chattanooga, he directed an unsuccessful attack by the Union left on Tunnel Hill and the battle was won by Thomas and *Sheridan in the centre and *Hooker on the right. Despite this, Sherman's political connections ensured a congressional vote of thanks for him. After his December relief of Knoxville, he responded to a rebuke about the behaviour of his men in words that defined his emerging military philosophy: 'War is cruelty. There is no use trying to reform it; the crueller it is, the sooner it will be over.'

Left in command of the western theatre when Grant went to Washington, he advanced slowly towards Atlanta with three armies totalling 98,000. Sherman repeatedly manoeuvred 60,000 Confederates under *Johnston out of defensive positions until he risked an all-out assault at Kennesaw Mountain in June, suffering a bloody repulse. When *Hood replaced Johnston and took the offensive, Sherman's armies dealt him a series of defeats, finally capturing Atlanta in early September, a ray of light for the otherwise stalemated and war-weary Union which helped to make Lincoln's re-election resounding. Sherman coolly let Thomas handle Hood's desperate invasion of Tennessee and embarked upon the *March to the Sea, as cruel a campaign as any during the war.

When Grant became a full general in 1866, Sherman was promoted to lieutenant general, rising to command of the armies when his friend became president in 1869 and holding the office until 1884. Although Sherman's cavalier treatment of blacks and his later policy of 'vindictive earnestness' against the Plains Indians have earned him a modern reputation as a racist, he was not unusually prejudiced by contemporary standards. What he foresaw was that both groups would be exploited by government agents for their own power and enrichment. Writing to Halleck early in 1865 he presciently commented: 'Poor Negro—Lo, the poor Indian!' HEB

Hirshson, Stanley, *The White Tecumseh* (New York, 1997).

Sherman tank The M4 US Medium Tank, the Sherman, was the workhorse of Allied armoured divisions during WW II and afterwards worldwide. Nearly 50,000 Shermans were built, production beginning in July 1942. It was first bloodied at *Alamein when some 270 Shermans arrived in time to assist the British Eighth Army in October 1942. Considered highly manoeuvrable, it weighed 30 tons and was powered by a nine-cylinder 400 hp radial engine, giving a speed of 25 mph (40 km/ph), and a range of 85 miles (137 km). At the time of introduction, the Sherman was a big improvement on British models, but that was not saying much. Its dual-purpose 75 mm gun, which could fire both armour-piercing (AP) and high-explosive (HE) ammunition, started to challenge equivalent German tank guns in range and muzzle velocity. But its lightly armoured petrol tanks meant that Shermans often caught fire when hit, and were not unsurprisingly dubbed 'Ronsons' (after the cigarette lighter) by crews and German anti-tank gunners alike. In the Western Desert, the *Afrika Korps called them 'Tommy cookers'. For the invasion of Normandy, the British modified one Sherman in four into a 'Firefly' packing a powerful 17-pounder gun. This made it superior to the Mark IV Panzer, the most numerous German tank of the period, but it remained appallingly inferior to both the 'Tiger' and 'Panther'. Shermans were also used as the basis for some ingenious specialist armour, of which the 'DD' (Duplex Drive) swimming tank, the 'Crab' minefield flail, and the M10 'Wolverine' Tank Destroyer were prime examples. By 1945, an improved model (M4A3E8) had entered service with the US army, with a power-traverse turret mounting a 76 mm gun, improved suspension and a wider body, but weighing 35 tons. This version saw service in Korea, before replacement in 1955. Prior substantial modification including up-gunning and the replacement of the lethal petrol with diesel engines. The last major conflicts in which the type was involved were the *Arab–Israeli wars.

APC-A

shields The most common and simple defensive armament carried by soldiers from prehistory to the end of the Middle Ages was the shield. Prehistoric cave paintings portray wooden shields carried in the hands of hunters as a means to ward off attacks. Bronze Age shields were stronger and larger. The Greek *hoplite was named after his shield, the *hoplon*. The *hoplon* was wooden, rounded, and concave, although its size could vary depending on the length and strength of the bearer's arm, and by the 5th century BC a solid, thin bronze sheet covered it. The Greek shield had a special grip, which distributed the weight along the entire left arm. The large Roman shield (*scutum*) was constructed from three layers of glued plywood, each made of strips, with the outer pieces laid horizontally and the inner piece laid vertically, and covered in canvas and calf hide. A long wooden boss ran the entire length of the shield.

This shield changed in shape and construction, although not in size, during the 2nd and 3rd centuries; it became much more rectangular in shape and curved to fit the body. It also was rimmed by metal and covered in leather, on which were fastened bronze decorations and a metallic boss. The most common early medieval shield was convex, round, or elliptical and was made from strips of wood covered by leather. It also contained a large and heavy metal boss, and some were decorated with symbolic figures and ornaments. The main defensive armament of the Carolingian army remained the shield; it was also the least expensive armour, and all soldiers were required to carry it. Carolingian shields were round, concave, and made of wood, and some were covered by leather. They were rimmed with metal, and metal strips were sometimes added for extra strength. A dome-shaped metal boss was set in the middle of each shield with a grip running across the underside and attached both to the boss and to the wood. These shields were also much larger than earlier medieval shields.

For the next three centuries, shields followed the Carolingian standard in shape, size, and construction. This began to change in the 11th century, when almost all shields became long, narrow, and kite-shaped with rounded tops and pointed bottoms. Kite-shaped shields were constructed of wood and covered by leather with a metal boss and a metal rim. These shields were gripped by a series of leather straps which were riveted onto their insides. The size, shape, and material of the shield remained unchanged until the 13th century, when it became lighter, shorter, and more triangular. After the turn of the 15th century, the triangular cavalry shield was supplanted by a variety of shapes and sizes. The most common of these was oblong, either rounded or pointed on the lower edge, and often bent forward at the top and bottom. All cavalry shields of any shape were usually made of metal.

However, by the mid-15th century, shields began to fall into disfavour among the cavalry, already well protected by body armour. This trend continued until *c*.1450, when the shield continued to be used only in jousts. Three styles of late medieval infantry shields developed: the target or targe, which was large, flat, and equipped with a number of leather straps for gripping by the forearm and hand; the buckler which was small with a hollow metal boss and gripped by a crossbar across the inside; and the pavise which was a large oblong shield generally propped up by a wooden brace to provide protection to *archers and crossbowmen. Most infantry shields continued to be made of leather-covered wood, and all styles were used well into the 16th century. The last serious military force to use shields were the *Zulus who used them as offensive as well as defensive weapons.   KDeV

Oakeshott, R. Ewart, *The Archaeology of Weapons: Arms and Armor from Prehistory to the Age of Chivalry* (New York, 1960).

Shiloh, battle of (1862), first battle of the *American civil war involving casualties that were to become commonplace. Following the loss of the Tennessee–Kentucky line, Confederate commander Albert Sidney Johnston concentrated 45,000 men at the Mississippi–Tennessee border. *Grant advanced by river with 48,000 while Buell with 18,000 marched from Nashville to join him. On 6 April Johnston surprised *Sherman and drove his corps and the rest of the Union army back on Pittsburg Landing. Next day, with his own divisions concentrated and reinforced by Buell, Grant broke an attack under the fallen Johnston's successor *Beauregard and reclaimed the field. There were 13,050 Union casualties to the Confederates' 10,700.

No general emerged with credit. Grant and Sherman were caught unprepared, while Johnston was persuaded by Beauregard and *Bragg to weaken his envelopment of the Union right and to pound it up the middle. Thereafter he exercised little control and died leading a regiment. Bragg wasted momentum with frontal assaults on the Union rearguard, until others took the initiative and deployed massed artillery. Beauregard failed to regroup for either attack or defence the following day. The battle surrendered the vital Tennessee river and prefigured the poor leadership of the western *Confederate States Armies throughout the war.
                                                HEB

Daniel, Larry, *Shiloh* (New York, 1997).

---

shogun Title of the military rulers of Japan from 1192 to 1868. Following a succession of civil wars between various clans vying for power and influence Minamoto Yoritomo (1147–99) became virtual dictator of Japan in 1185. Although ruling in the name of the emperor, the reality was that the shogunate was government of the samurai by the samurai for the samurai. Yoritomo took the title of shogun (barbarian-subduing C-in-C), which had been a temporary commission from the emperor, and made it a permanent hereditary office. It was only handed back on 4 January 1868.

The Minamoto clan held the office from 1192 until 1333, a period known as the Kamakura shogunate. During this period Mongol invasions from Korea were repulsed. In 1274 and 1281 separate invasions were defeated in part through the Mongol fleet being damaged by the kamikaze, the divine wind sent by the gods to protect Japan.

For the next three centuries Japan was riven by factions and civil wars. The Ashikaga clan held the shogunate from 1336 to 1573 but it was under the influence of three great rulers that order was restored during the period 1570–1615: *Oda Nobunaga, *Toyotomi Hideyoshi, and *Tokugawa Ieyasu.

Ieyasu defeated his rivals at the battle of *Sekigahara in 1600. His army of 74,000 troops decisively defeated a coalition of 82,000 that was riven by internal disputes. Three years later Ieyasu established the Tokugawa shogunate at Edo that would last until the re-establishment of imperial rule in 1868.

Contact between Japan and Europe had been established in 1542 when Portuguese traders arrived but during the 17th century Japan expelled all foreigners allowing only the Dutch to trade. During the 1850s the USA insisted on opening trade relations. It was this issue which led to the abdication of the last shogun and the installation of a nationalist, modernizing regime in the Meiji restoration.   JR-W

Shutzstaffeln. See ss.

Sicilian vespers (1282), an uprising of native Sicilians against the French and Provençals who had occupied the island of Sicily on behalf of Charles of Anjou, king of Sicily since 1266. It began outside the church of Santo Spirito in Palermo on Easter Monday, 30 March, when an enraged husband stabbed to death a French soldier who had made advances to his wife. As the bells of Santo Spirito and other churches began the call to vespers, the incident quickly escalated into a slaughter of all the French throughout the city. Anti-French feeling was sufficiently deep-seated for other towns to follow, including Corleone, Trapani, and Caltanissetta, and, after some hesitation, Messina, the administrative centre of Angevin rule. The major towns established themselves as communes and placed themselves under papal protection.

Charles at once set about crushing the revolt, backed by Pope Martin IV, who had no sympathy with the Sicilian appeals. Then, on 30 August, Peter III, king of Aragon, who had been stationed at Collo in North Africa with a large fleet, ostensibly for a crusade against Tunisia, landed at Trapani. He had come in response to a request from the Sicilians, but he had always intended to invade once an opportunity arose, as his wife, Constance, was the daughter of Manfred, the Staufen ruler of the kingdom whom Charles had defeated and killed in 1266. Peter's intervention changed the whole perspective from a localized revolt to a war which had repercussions throughout the entire Mediterranean, for Charles had been the champion chosen to rid Italy of the Staufen dynasty with which the papacy had been in intermittent conflict since the 1150s. Moreover, when the vespers occurred Charles, together with his Venetian ally, had been about to launch an attack against the schismatic Greeks. In the face of this Angevin threat, the Byzantine Emperor Michael VIII Palaeologus had allied himself to the Aragonese.

Although the rising itself was probably spontaneous, both these powers had been trying to destabilize Angevin rule on the island since at least the late 1270s. The military and political implications were far-reaching, for the war with Aragon destroyed Charles's imperial pretensions, saved Constantinople from a new Latin attack, divided the island of Sicily from the mainland, and preoccupied the papacy to the detriment of its other priorities, most notably the crusade to the Middle East.   MCB

Dunbadin, Jean, *Charles I of Anjou: Power, Kingship and State Making in Thirteenth-Century Europe* (London, 1998).
Runciman, Steven, *The Sicilian Vespers* (Cambridge, 1958).

Sicily, invasion of (1943). HUSKY had been on the agenda ever since the Casablanca Conference of January 1943. The success of the TORCH landings in French *North Africa the previous November had encouraged Franklin D. *Roosevelt and *Churchill to plan for a seaborne assault as soon as the Axis had been defeated in Tunisia. Although TORCH had been virtually unopposed, Sicily was reckoned to be a tougher nut to crack, with the Italians fighting on their home ground, stiffened by good German troops. But the mood was optimistic. A blend of the battle-hardened men of Eighth Army under *Montgomery, the profusion of US war *matériel*, and American troops of the Seventh Army under *Patton were considered enough to overwhelm the island garrison and bring the war to mainland Italy.

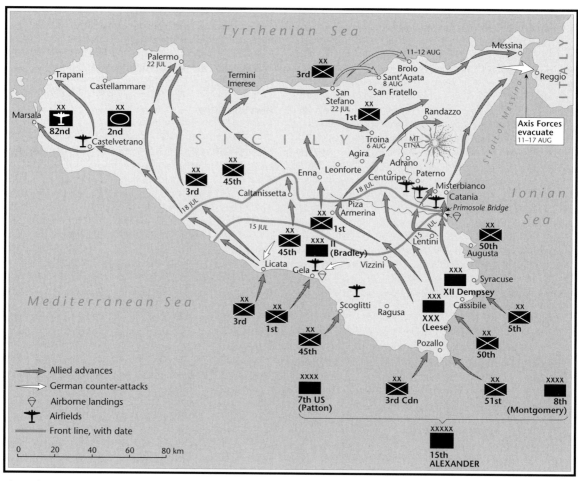

The **Sicily invasion,** 1943.

*Amphibious ships and landing craft were the resource that defined Allied military strategy in 1943–4, and it took six months to assemble enough for the main component of HUSKY, an operation involving 150,000 men and 3,000 ships.

The two Allied armies were to attack on 10 July, landing on two separate 40 mile (64 km) strips of beach, in a mutually supporting operation. *Eisenhower was the theatre commander and *Alexander at the head of Fifteenth Army Group was the operational commander. The British Eighth Army of one airborne and six infantry divisions, plus one infantry and two armoured brigades, and three Royal Marine Commandos, was to land in the south-east. Their objective was to clear the eastern half of Sicily, including Syracuse and Messina. The US Seventh Army of one armoured, one airborne, four infantry divisions, and one commando was to assault in the south and take the western part of the island, including Palermo. Nearly 4,000 Allied aircraft ensured local air supremacy, although there were 1,500 German and Italian aircraft in the theatre. In refusing to evacuate North Africa, *Hitler had lost many first-rate troops in Tunisia, and the Axis could muster only ten Italian divisions of dubious quality and two dependable German formations with which to counter any landings. Furthermore, a deception plan had encouraged the Germans to expect an attack on Sardinia. In one of the murkier episodes of WW II, the gangster 'Lucky' Luciano had been released from prison in New York and was shipped back to Sicily to use his influence among the local mafiosi in support of the Allies, although there is no evidence that he did.

Driving winds and poor weather disrupted the first-ever large-scale deployment of Allied *airborne forces by parachute and *glider. The worst affected were the 144 gliders carrying the British 1st Airborne Brigade: only 54 landed in Sicily and the majority ditched in the Mediterranean, drowning their occupants. The gale also played havoc with the invasion fleet, but the rough seas caused the defenders to relax their watch. They were woken up by *naval gunfire support from a bombardment fleet including six battleships, while the few airborne units scattered behind the coastal defences distracted attention and hampered the arrival of reinforcements. The Seventh Army had a rougher reception than the Eighth, but by the end of the first day the Americans held nearly 40 miles (64 km) of beach between Scoglitti and Licata, while the British held a coastal strip from Pozallo to Syracuse, having captured the latter port intact.

Recovering quickly from the initial shock, German forces counter-attacked at Gela and Licata and were repulsed only within sight of the coast, while heavier opposition halted Montgomery around Catania. After much hard fighting, Canadian units reached Enna in the centre of the island on 20 July, and two days later Patton's troops had taken Palermo after a lightning strike across the island. Seventh Army then turned eastwards, Patton having decided to cap-

ture Messina ahead of the slower Montgomery. Italian resistance collapsed rapidly and the locals were friendly once the danger of turning their villages into battlefields was past. Nonetheless, the broken landscape favoured the Germans, commanded by the energetic Gen Hube, who defended a series of stop lines, counter-attacking with armour when the terrain suited. But once his main position at Adrano had been captured, Montgomery advanced towards Messina on either side of Mount Etna. Kesselring, the German C-in-C in Italy, was determined not to see another army thrown away and prepared to evacuate his best forces from the island in defiance of Hitler. He concentrated them in the north-east corner and lined both shores of the narrow Straits of Messina with anti-aircraft artillery.

By the time Patton occupied Messina a few hours ahead of the indignant Montgomery, Kesselring had evacuated 40,000 German and 60,000 Italian troops to the mainland, along with much valuable armour, from under their noses. The success of this German Dunkirk was to have serious repercussions for the Allies in Italy later on, and represents a glaring failure to apply near-total air and sea superiority. Patton's advance into Messina was politically questionable, but a lot of Americans were tired of being patronized by more experienced British officers, and Patton was also keen to complete the rehabilitation of the fighting spirit of his troops after the defeat at *Kasserine Pass in February. On 17 August, after 38 days' fighting, the whole of Sicily was in Allied hands. The Eighth Army had suffered 9,000 casualties and the Seventh 7,000. The Axis losses were 160,000, including 30,000 Germans. The invasion of Sicily prompted King Vittorio Emanuele III to order the arrest of *Mussolini, while Marshal Badoglio negotiated an armistice with the Allies.   APC-A

side arms are weapons that may be hung from the waist such as *pistols or a variety of *edged weapons.

siege engines were devices designed to reduce the time taken to capture a besieged *castle or other *fortification. There were a number of different types, the most prominent and certainly the simplest to construct being the battering ram. In its primitive form this was little more than a large beam or tree trunk that could be propelled continually against a wall or gate until a breach was made. It was frequently capped with metal (sometimes a symbolic ram's head) to strengthen the striking surface, and the survival of those operating it was greatly enhanced when it was covered by an armoured roof structure, from which it could also be suspended to improve impact frequency and accuracy. The digging machine was developed to aid *sappers to undermine walls and usually consisted of a rotating beam equipped with an iron head which could drill through earth, stone, and mortar, again under an armoured roof.

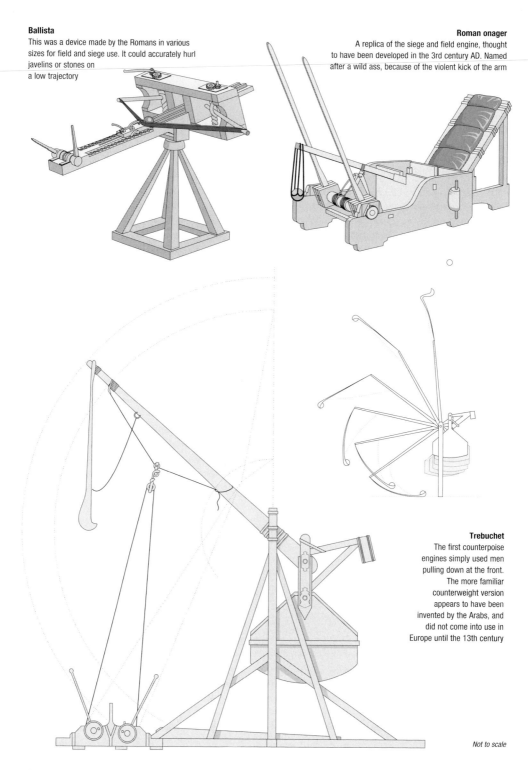

Ballista

This was a device made by the Romans in various sizes for field and siege use. It could accurately hurl javelins or stones on a low trajectory

Roman onager

A replica of the siege and field engine, thought to have been developed in the 3rd century AD. Named after a wild ass, because of the violent kick of the arm

Trebuchet

The first counterpoise engines simply used men pulling down at the front. The more familiar counterweight version appears to have been invented by the Arabs, and did not come into use in Europe until the 13th century

Not to scale

Torsion and counterpoise engines of war were widely used by the Greeks and Romans and throughout the Middle Ages by Europeans, Chinese, and Arabs and, following their example, the Mongols. Although smaller engines like the ballista were sometimes used in the field their principal function was to attack fortifications. Trebuchets could throw the biggest projectiles, although the most powerful catapults achieved greater range, velocity, and accuracy.

The latter developed into a siege engine in its own right, with wheels or rollers and with sloping sides covered with leather or metal.

But the most technologically complicated siege engine was the siege tower or *beffroy*, built to be taller than the walls of the work under attack and consisting of an elevated platform from which *archers could bring the ramparts under fire and ramps lowered to permit an assault. The bigger siege towers contained internal stairs so that once in place they could pour a continual flow of assaulting soldiers onto the ramparts, obviating the need for a breach. These too would be made of wood and covered with leather, water-soaked skins, or wicker to protect them against projectiles and fire, and were advanced on rollers or their own wheels.

Before the advent of *gunpowder, siege artillery went by the generic name of catapults and worked on torsion, traction, or counterweight. The earliest were torsion catapults, derived in the 4th century BC Syracusan *gastraphetes* or 'belly-bow'. The *gastraphetes* was a large, powerful, and flexible crossbow mounted on a heavy stock. Although it could propel a projectile further than the composite *bow, it was still too weak to breach walls or gates. To gain this needed power, ancient engineers constructed torsion springs made of tightly twisted sinew to which they anchored two rigid bow arms. Mounted onto a stock with the addition of a winch, ratchet apparatus, and trigger mechanism, much further distances and much greater ballistic forces were achieved. *Philip II of Macedon and *Alexander 'the Great' used them to capture many towns in Greece and the Middle East. The Romans and Carthaginians continued to use torsion artillery, making some improvements in the housing of the springs and in the stock. The Romans also made them smaller and portable. Using the same torsion technology, they also created the *onager*, the familiar single-spring, one-armed catapult used to launch larger projectiles.

Torsion catapults continued to be built into the time of the barbarian invasions when they were superseded by a traction artillery piece, the trebuchet. Diffused westward from China, where they were invented some time during the 5th to 3rd centuries BC, trebuchets were designed with a rotating beam placed unevenly on a fulcrum which was supported by a wooden tower and base. On the longest side of the rotating beam was hung a sling in which projectiles would be placed; on the opposite side were hung between 40 and 125 ropes which, when pulled in unison, would propel a projectile with great ballistic force. These were used from the early to the high Middle Ages. It was also the principal siege weapon used by both Christians and Muslims during the *Crusades. Toward the end of this period, in the mid-12th century, the trebuchet also underwent a significant change by the substitution of the pulling ropes with a fixed counterweight. This counterweight, which was little more than a box filled with stones, sand, or other heavy material, provided the power to discharge any large missile. By the mid-13th century all trebuchets had counterweights.

In the early 14th century, gunpowder artillery developed in Europe and Asia and by the end of that century they were in use in *siege warfare. Initially, these were very large weapons made of iron bars held together by iron rings. They were immensely heavy, difficult to operate, and slow to fire, and their size diminished as greater muzzle velocity permitted smaller projectiles to produce the same effect. By the 17th century all such weapons were made in cast iron or bronze. Gunpowder was also employed in sieges in the form of *petards placed against a gate or other obstacle. The last use of siege engines in a major engagement was in April 1945 when US forces used a siege tower on a specially adapted landing craft to assault Fort Drum, the 'concrete battleship' in Manila harbour. They disabled the gun cupolas with satchel charges (the descendants of the petard), poured 10,000 gallons of gasoline into the ventilation shafts, lit fuses, and hastily retired to a safe distance. It burned for a week, amid secondary explosions that completely wrecked it.
KDeV

Bradbury, Jim, *The Medieval Siege* (Woodbridge, 1992).
De Vries, Kelly, *Medieval Military Technology* (Peterborough, 1992).
Hogg, Ian, *Fortress* (London, 1975).
Landels, J. G., *Engineering in the Ancient World* (Berkeley, 1978).

siege warfare *(see page 836)*

SIGINT (signals intelligence) is the monitoring, collection, and analysis of *communications intelligence and covers the monitoring of *radio and *telephone message traffic and the decryption and analysis of coded messages. The related but separate activity known as electronic intelligence (ELINT) mainly covers the detection and analysis of *radar, telemetry, and other non-communication signals to discover performance parameters and develop countermeasures.

During WW I, listening to and jamming enemy signals became routine. SIGINT enabled the German army to crush the Russians at *Tannenberg and the *Masurian Lakes, and also enabled the British Admiralty to intercept the German High Seas fleet at the Dogger Bank and *Jutland. The opposing armies were so close to each other on the western front that with primitive crystal-set receivers they could pick up the traffic passing over telegraph and telephone wires through electrical induction. Personnel on both sides were responsible for locating enemy transmitters, monitoring transmissions, and intercepting and deciphering enemy traffic.

During WW II, *ULTRA gave the Allies an inestimable advantage over the Axis, although the *Abwehr also broke the Royal Navy codes. The US Army Signal Corps developed

(cont. on page 838)

siege warfare

THROUGHOUT history, the desire to capture a fortified position in order to acquire territory has generally taken precedence over battles, raids, and other military adventures, especially in ancient, medieval, and early modern times. Because of this, specific tactics and technology were continually being devised and refined in order to diminish the time it took to wage a successful siege. The attack and defence of fortresses did not simply demand the techniques of *fortification and siegecraft, but shaped a form of warfare in which the siege played a central role.

Before *gunpowder weaponry altered the time required to conduct a siege, there were four means of successfully capturing a fortified site. The first, and least violent, was the negotiated *capitulation, to take place should a relief army not appear by a certain date. Negotiation occurred when the besieger either did not necessarily wish to capture the besieged site, but wished instead to use the siege as leverage to force a battle against the army of the site's owner, or when the besieger knew that no relief army would be able to come to the aid of the besiegers and wished to lessen his own losses and minimize damage to the fortress. An example of the former occurred in 1314 when Robert *Bruce used the siege of Stirling castle to provoke the battle of *Bannockburn against Edward II; examples of the latter were seen in the sieges of numerous Norman castles by *Henry V in 1417–20, most of which submitted to him when no French relief army appeared before the day negotiated for their capitulation.

A second means of forcing the surrender of a fortification was through starvation by *blockade. Eventually, should those delivering supplies not be able to evade the blockade, hunger would force those besieged to surrender. While the most frequent means of capturing a fortification, starvation often required a lengthy siege, sometimes lasting longer than a year, such as at *Calais in 1346–7. The process could easily misfire, for the besieged might well have stocks of provisions which the besiegers lacked: sometimes it was the latter who starved. A military commander (the governor) might expel 'useless mouths' from his fortress in order to conserve supplies, but a harsh besieger might refuse to let them depart.

A third means of capturing a fortification was the *bribery* of one of the besieged to open a gate or otherwise to assist the entry into the fortification by the besiegers. This generally became an option only when the inhabitants had some reason for accepting the bribe, a relationship with the besiegers, or when suffering from starvation, they became desperate to end a siege. Bribery is credited with the surrender of Rome in 410, *Antioch in 1098, and Château Gaillard in 1204.

The most costly, in terms of casualties among the besiegers, but perhaps the most quick means of capturing a besieged site, was the *assault*. Should a besieger not wish to spend the time required to force submission by starvation, to find an opportunity for bribery, or to negotiate a capitulation, an option was to attempt to take the besieged place by force. This could be achieved by going under, through, or over the walls or gates of a fortress. Going under required *mines. A tunnel, supported by wood, would be dug beneath the walls, and then the wooden supports would be burnt, causing the wall above to collapse. Successfully countering this generally required a counter-mine. Mining is generally credited with the fall of Jericho to the Israelites in *c.*1350 BC. Going through the walls or gates of a fortified site generally required a means of breaching those fortifications (see SIEGE ENGINES) to create a breach in a wall or gate through which attacking besiegers might gain access to the fortified site. To prevent such an assault, defenders were forced to attack the siege engines or their operators to prevent a breach in their fortifications. *Constantinople was captured in 1453 after Ottoman *Turks breached that city's strong walls.

Finally, going over the walls of a besieged fortress generally required scaling ladders or a siege tower. By using these devices, besiegers would climb over the walls and gain access to the site and its inhabitants. This was a particularly risky means of concluding a siege as the attackers using ladders would be continually assailed from above on their climb up the walls. A covered siege tower did provide some protection for the attackers, but even with this protection did not often prevent the first attackers from meeting stiff opposition to their assault. Still, going over the walls by means of siege towers is credited with causing the fall of *Jerusalem in 1099.

The advent of gunpowder weapons signalled great changes. By the end of the 14th century, cannon were able to demolish the high walls which had previously resisted attack. In an effort to counter the new weapons, gunports and artillery towers were added to old fortifications, while new ones were built in the lower, more angular style of the *trace italienne*. With the advent of artillery fortification, sieges once again became long-drawn-out affairs, although the development of associated techniques of siegecraft meant that an attacker who knew his business and was not dislodged by a relieving army, would generally be able to proceed methodically towards the reduction of a fortress.

The advent of artillery fortification, with the bastion as its defining feature, saw the development of techniques which saw the besieger establish himself outside the fortress and then proceed methodically, through systems of parallel trenches linked by zigzag saps, to breach the ramparts by mining or the fire of heavy guns and either deliver an assault or accept capitulation. The siege was a major feature of campaigns in 18th-century Europe, and many of the battles of the era were focused on the desire of the adversaries to maintain or raise a siege. Thus in 1709 *Marlborough was besieging Mons when a French army threatened him from the south: he went out and beat it, though at terrible cost, at *Malplaquet. In 1745 *Saxe was battering Tournai when *Cumberland marched to its relief, only to be beaten at *Fontenoy.

As artillery fortification spread, unsurprisingly, to the overseas possessions of European powers, so too did siege warfare. For example, in 1761 Eyre Coote took Pondicherry, noting that the defences were in no fit state to stand a formal siege, while the Spanish fortress of Havana on the island of Cuba was taken by the British in the following year after a sharply contested siege which ended with capitulation and the *honours of war. In North America, Montcalm took Fort Oswego by siege in 1756 (the unlucky governor was decapitated by a roundshot), and proved, as Christopher Duffy has written, that 'meticulously-planned advances and formal siege attacks were as effective in backwoods warfare as in the plains of Flanders'.

By the time of the *French Revolutionary wars, sieges had ceased to be the central business of warfare and the style of warfare which featured them had begun to change. Duffy suggests that it was not simply the improved power of attack that was responsible, but that the bigger armies of the late 18th century, subject to increasingly effective central authority, made it easier for an invader to flow between fortresses, masking them if he chose to, to push his attack deep into the heart of the enemy's country. Nevertheless, if sieges had lost much of their former importance, and no longer shaped the wars of the 19th century as they had those of previous centuries, they remained a part of warfare. During the *Peninsular war Wellington besieged and stormed Badajoz and Ciudad Rodrigo, and Spanish defence of Saragossa in 1808–9 was a mark of popular resistance to the French; Paris, surrounded by a bastioned wall built in the 1840s, was besieged during the *Franco-Prussian war; the siege of *Port Arthur played a central part in the *Russo-Japanese war; *Leningrad was besieged, at extraordinary cost, in WW II, and from 1992 to 1995 Sarajevo was besieged. Sieges have often demanded as much from the beleaguered population as from their defenders, and in recent sieges popular determination, rather than the siting of breaching batteries or the defence of bastions, has been the deciding factor.   KDeV/RH

Aeneas Tacticus, *How to Survive under Siege*, ed. and trans. David Whitehead (Oxford, 1990).

Bradbury, Jim, *The Medieval Siege* (Woodbridge, 1992).

Duffy, Christopher, *Siege Warfare: The Fortress in the Early Modern World, 1494–1660* (London, 1979).

—— *The Fortress in the Age of Vauban and Frederick the Great* (London, 1985).

Kern, Paul Bentley, *Ancient Siege Warfare* (Bloomington, Ind., 1999).

an automatic machine for enciphering and deciphering Morse messages called SIGABA which, unlike *Enigma and the Japanese system, was never broken. Another US development was the radio telephone system called SIGSALY. A third security system developed during the war was the SIGTOT and the British TYPEX which permitted two-way teletype conferences—both were reserved for senior commanders.

The Achilles' heel of SIGINT arises both from the perishability of the product and the fact that if it is acted upon too openly, the source will likely dry up as the enemy finds less vulnerable means of communication. This was a major difficulty in the use of the information provided by ULTRA (see CRETE, BATTLE OF).

During the latter part of the *Cold War, thanks to the treachery of the Walker family and friends, the Soviets could read all US navy traffic, which might have been an advantage akin to ULTRA if it had ever become hot. All other nations must work on the assumption that major SIGINT and ELINT establishments such as those maintained by the USA, Russia, and the UK can read all their communications if they wish to. In general any machine encipherment system can be broken if sufficient computer time is devoted to it, hence modern military communications are protected only for the notional length of time (against computer attack) necessary to preserve operational secrecy. This can be quite brief.   DMJ/HEB

Bauer, F. L., *Decrypted Secrets: Methods and Maxims of Cryptology* (New York, 1997).

Kahn, David, *The Codebreakers: The Story of Secret Writing* (rev. edn., New York, 1996).

signals intelligence. See SIGINT.

Sikh wars (1845–6 and 1848–9), in which the British East India Company (EIC) destroyed the independent Sikh state of Lahore and annexed the Punjab (Panjab) to British India. The Sikhs were by origin (*c.* AD 1500) a puritanical Hindu sect which flourished among the Jat population in northern India and developed distinctive attributes. Members of the Sikh community, known as the Khalsa, were recognized by the five Ks: uncut hair (*kes*), a comb (*kangha*),

knee length breeches (*kach*), a steel bracelet (*kara*), and a sabre (*kirpan*) (see also RELIGION AND WAR). Under Ranjit Singh (1780–1839) several of the various Sikh communities were united and formed the basis of the Lahore state which also embraced Hindus and Muslims. The expansion of the state towards British India was checked in 1809 on the river Sutlej but the state was extended to include Kashmir (1819) and Peshawar (1834). Britain was content to leave the Lahore state as a valuable buffer on her *North-West frontier, insulating British India from the Muslim peoples of central Asia, but the Punjab fell into increasing disorder after the death of Ranjit Singh and there was evidence of mutinous conduct in the Sikh regiments which were run by their own councils (*panchayats*). Fears became reality in December 1845 when Sikh forces crossed the Sutlej and invaded EIC-protected territory.

The Sikh army was the most formidable military opponent Britain encountered in India. Trained by French and other European *mercenaries, it included *c.*50,000 disciplined infantry, 10,000 disciplined artillerymen, and 6,000 regular cavalry as well as irregular formations. Because of previous fears of provoking just such an attack, EIC forces were comparatively unprepared, but Sir Hugh Gough marched rapidly to the relief of the garrisons on the Sutlej and encountered an advanced Sikh force at Mudki on 18 December, where he fought a bloody, confused, and indecisive battle. The advanced party retired on Firuzshah where they joined the main Sikh force. There a second battle took place on 21 December. As at Mudki, Gough attacked when there was insufficient daylight and when fighting was broken off he feared defeat on the morrow, when Sikh reinforcements were expected. Instead the Sikh army abandoned the field and the reinforcements did likewise when they learned of this. Gough was left in possession of the field and 73 captured guns. His casualties were severe—2,415 out of 16,000 engaged—and were especially heavy among his British regiments, which had borne the brunt of the superior Sikh artillery. Consequently he elected to wait for reinforcements, especially of heavy guns. In the meantime Sir Harry Smith carried out a series of skilful manoeuvres to protect British garrisons along the Sutlej, collect scattered forces, and defeat the Sikhs at Aliwal (28 Jan 1846). On 10 February Gough attacked the Sikhs in their last remaining position east of the Sutlej at *Sobraon where in another hard battle he gained a complete victory taking 67 guns and inflicting c.10,000 casualties while suffering 2,300 casualties among his own forces. The Sikhs then sued for peace. Gov-Gen Hardinge decided not to annex the Punjab but stripped it of some territories, disbanded part of the army, and set up an EIC-controlled regency in Lahore.

The settlement was inherently unstable and in 1848 friction culminated in an uprising at Multan in August 1848. At first the EIC was inclined to regard the uprising as a matter for the Punjab government but it was drawn into operations against Multan and into a formal siege which lasted from October into January 1849. The Army of the Punjab was formed under Gough who crossed the Sutlej on 9 November but proceeded cautiously, waiting for reinforcements. There followed a period of manoeuvre, punctuated by an indecisive cavalry engagement at Ramnuggur, before Gough encountered the main Sikh force at Chillianwala (13 Jan 1849). The Sikhs had some 30,000 men and 62 guns against the 12,000 Gough managed to put into the field. A struggle in jungly terrain ensued in which Gough suffered 2,331 casualties and once more the excellent Sikh artillery pounded the British infantry. Both sides pulled back and when battle was rejoined at Gujerat near the river Chenab, Gough's newly arrived artillery silenced the Sikh guns and a complete victory was obtained. The Sikhs surrendered at Rawalpindi on 14 March and the Punjab was formally annexed.

Although the Sikh forces during the second war were much weaker than during the first, they had fought with their customary tenacity and the British victory was not cheaply obtained. Sikhs subsequently became and remain important elements in the *Indian army. Recruiting had begun in 1846 and after 1849 Sikh regiments were raised for the Punjab Irregular Force (later the Punjab Frontier Force) and the numbers were considerably increased during and after the *Indian Mutiny. Sikhs were particularly targeted for recruitment during WW I, their numbers rising from 35,000 at the beginning of 1915 to over 100,000 by the end of the war, amounting to about a fifth of the army. This made it all the more poignant that the post-war *Amritsar massacre was perpetrated against an unarmed Sikh demonstration.

In 1947 partition divided their homeland and those finding themselves in Pakistan suffered terrible losses making their way to India. Subsequently they became among the most prosperous of independent India's populations and are still disproportionately represented in the military: although only 2 per cent of the population they provide 10 per cent of the soldiers and many senior officers. But there remained a strong sentiment among the more traditional (and economically backward) Sikhs for an independent state (Khalistan—'Land of the Pure') and from the early 1980s a typical ultra-nationalist movement emerged and began to employ terrorist tactics against the Hindu popula-

tion. PM Indira Gandhi did her best to temporize and even nominated a Sikh to be president, but armed insurgents seized the Golden Temple in 1984 and defied her authority. She sent in the army and the temple was stormed with heavy loss. In October Indira was assassinated in her garden by two of her Sikh bodyguards and Hindu mobs, incited by leading members of her party, massacred Sikhs in Delhi in the worst religious riots since partition.

Cook, Hugh, *The Sikh Wars* (London, 1975).

Featherstone, Donald, *At Them with the Bayonet* (London, 1968).

Singh, Kushwant, *A History of the Sikhs*, 2 vols. (Princeton, 1963–6).

Yapp M. E., *Strategies of British India* (Oxford, 1980).

Simpkin, Brig Richard (1921–86), British army officer and military thinker, author of several influential works of military history and theory which are similar in theme and bear comparison with the works of *Fuller. Commissioned into the Royal Tank Regiment, he served in the Middle East in WW II, was awarded the MC, and taken prisoner. A student and instructor at both the army staff college and the Royal Military College of Science, he headed the equipment branch in the Ministry of Defence responsible for the development of the Chieftain main battle *tank and the Scorpion and Scimitar family of light tanks. He commanded 1st Royal Tank Regiment from 1963 and took early retirement in 1971 to set up a language consultancy. Fluent in Russian and German, he translated Gerd Niepold's *Battle for White Russia: the Destruction of Army Group Centre June 1944* and was keenly interested in the Soviet military system and *manoeuvre warfare. *Race to the Swift* is a profound, though sometimes demanding, evaluation of the nature of combat and of cycles in the development of armies. His last work was a study of *Tukhachevskiy entitled *Deep Battle*, and was completed during his last illness.   CDB

Simpkin, Richard, *Race to the Swift: Thoughts on Twenty-First Century Warfare* (London, 1985).

Singapore, fall of (1942). See MALAYA AND SINGAPORE CAMPAIGN.

Sino-Indian war (1962). On 20 October 1962, China invaded India in a short, sharp border war that lasted a month before Chinese troops unilaterally withdrew to prehostility positions on 21 November 1962. The war was fought along the Sino-Indian border in the heights of the Himalayan mountains in Ladakh and Aksai Chin (in northern Jammu and Kashmir province) in the west, and in the North-East Frontier Agency (NEFA) (now Arunachal Pradesh province) in the east. The Himalayan frontier zone had always been an area of great geopolitical importance. The strategic significance of the Tibetan plateau to Indian security had long been recognized by the British, who spent much time and effort preventing Russian incursions into the region. In 1904 Britain invaded *Tibet to ensure a friendly regime in the capital, Lhasa, and in 1907, Britain and Russia established a neutral belt from Persia (now Iran) across to Tibet to separate the two empires. When the British left south Asia in 1947, these strategic priorities remained to trouble the newly independent Indian government. To compound matters, long stretches of the Sino-Indian border had never been agreed. In particular, the Chinese rejected the 'McMahon line' along the NEFA border.

As long as China was weak and distracted by internal and external pressures, the question of the border was unimportant. However, once the communists unified China in 1949, the authorities in Beijing wanted Tibet restored to central control. In 1950–1, People's Liberation Army (PLA) forces moved into Tibet and occupied Lhasa. This move by the Chinese brought PLA forces up against Indian army posts along the poorly demarcated common frontier. Against the advice of his military advisers, the Indian leader, Jawaharlal Nehru, adopted a forward policy designed to establish Indian control over the disputed border areas in Ladakh and the NEFA. Nehru, like the British before him, did not want a powerful country like China to control Tibet, but unlike the British, Nehru did not have the military force to control Tibet. In 1956–7, Chinese engineers constructed a road across the disputed Aksai Chin. This highway connected recently conquered Tibet to Sinkiang in western China. The road was a vital part of Chinese strategy to link Tibet to China and provided for military access to Tibet and the sensitive border region. The remoteness of the area was shown by the fact that the Indians were unaware of the road until the Chinese announced its completion in September 1957. In 1958–9, a Tibetan revolt against Chinese rule led to the flight of the Tibetan leader, the Dalai Lama, to India. The suppression of the Tibet revolt by the PLA polarized attitudes in Delhi and Beijing, and reduced chances of a peaceful solution to the border dispute. From the summer of 1959, armed clashes between Indian and PLA units escalated. In late 1959, Chou En-lai, China's premier, suggested a mutual withdrawal in the NEFA to 12.4 miles (20 km) behind the McMahon line. Meanwhile, forces would remain *in situ* in Ladakh/Aksai Chin in the west. The proposal proved China's priorities: it was willing to concede the McMahon line in the east if India conceded Aksai Chin (and China's strategic highway) in the west.

Unfortunately, Nehru pursued an increasingly intransigent line and rejected the Chinese offer. India then looked to the USSR for military aid and an alarmed China launched a full-scale invasion in Ladakh/Aksai Chin and the NEFA on 20 October 1962. In the NEFA, 20,000 PLA troops poured across the border and advanced towards the plains of India. The Indian troops in the Himalayas were hopelessly outmatched. Nehru had ignored the military realities of fighting at high altitude, and poor lines of communications left Indian posts without supplies and isolated. On 21 October, the Chinese launched a third front by attacking down the Lohit valley near the Burmese border in eastern NEFA. All along the frontier, Indian units fell back under the pressure of the PLA assault. On 29 October, a beleaguered Nehru asked for American aid but before this was needed the PLA unilaterally fell back to the old border on 21 November.

As in the *Korean war, the Red Chinese displayed a disconcerting lack of nuance (to diplomats of the wordy western school), putting their military money exactly where their mouth was. The war secured Aksai Chin in exchange for recognizing the McMahon line and the NEFA as Indian, but this could have been agreed without bloodshed. Chinese casualties for the war are unknown, but Indian casualties (including POWs) exceeded 7,000.   MH

Maxwell, Neville, *India's China War* (London, 1970).

Sino-Japanese war (1894–5), known in Japanese as the Nisshin Sensō. At the root of the conflict was what both countries saw as their competing rights in Korea, particularly with regard to the market for cotton, which from about 1892 had begun to favour China. Anti-government uprisings in Korea provided the pretext for a Japanese invasion, and troops landed in 1894, where they soon met a Chinese army in a series of battles favourable to Japan. In September P'yŏngyang was captured, followed shortly by a naval victory in the Yellow Sea. The Japanese took *Port Arthur in November, and Weihaiwei fell in February 1895. The Chinese fleet surrendered to the Japanese later the same month and an armistice in March led to the signing of the Treaty of Shimonoseki. As a result China recognized Korea's independence and ceded the Liaotung peninsula and Formosa (Taiwan) to Japan. International diplomatic intervention forced Japan to relinquish her claim to the Liaotung peninsula, and Russia obtained it, creating such resentment that it made the *Russo-Japanese war a certainty unless the Russians chose to behave with less arrogance, which they did not.   SRT

---

skirmishers is the generic term used to distinguish agile troops who either because of their natural inclination, or through training, enjoyed greater freedom to observe and harass an enemy army in advance of their own main force, whose movements they masked. Ancient skirmishers could be *slingers, *archers, or just allied tribes whose method of warfare did not coincide with, say, the Greek or Roman preference for massed battlefield shock. Outside Europe the distinction was never so pronounced.

In Europe during the 18th century, armed with *rifles and expected to use their own initiative (which the line infantry emphatically was not), most armies developed specialist *sharpshooters, *Jägers, and *light troops, and the French (who made the most systematic use of them) had their *chasseurs à pied* (see CHASSEURS), *tirailleurs, and *voltigeurs.

With the widespread introduction of accurate, rapid-fire infantry weapons during the 19th century, the distinction between line infantry and skirmisher disappeared as the old close-order formations (see ORDER, TACTICAL) that had dominated the battlefield for so long became suicidal.

HEB

Skobelev, Gen Mikhail (1843–82), flamboyant Russian commander in Russia's colonial wars in central Asia and the Russo-Turkish war. Skobelev completed the *general staff academy in 1868 and took part in the Khiva expedition in 1873. From 1876 he was governor-general and commander of the Fergan district. In the 1877–8 Russo-Turkish war he commanded a *Cossack brigade and distinguished himself at the battles of Plevna and Shipka-Sheynovo. Skobelev always wore a white uniform, which made him a prominent target, but like some participants in recent wars he believed it was lucky, and bullets missed him. His presence was therefore an inspiration to his soldiers, and with his role in the liberation of Bulgaria from the Turks, he achieved great popularity both there and in Russia. A fervent believer in Russia's Asiatic roots, expansion, and destiny, in 1878 he authored a plan for the invasion of India. Among other things, he planned to organize 'hordes of Asiatic horsemen, who, to a cry of blood and plunder, might be launched against India as the vanguard, thus reviving the days of *Timur'. Such plans filled the British Indian *intelligence staff with dread. In 1880, Skobelev commanded Russian forces in the Akhal Tekke campaign against Turcoman tribes.

CDB

slang, military Military slang reflects views on *rank, arm of service, race, gender, and hostility, and, through the use of acronyms and catchwords, marks soldiers from civilians and helps distinguish insiders from outsiders. Reviewing his own experience in WW I, Henri Barbusse wrote of how language 'made up of a mixture of workshop and barrack slang, and patois, seasoned with a few newly-coined words, binds us, like a sauce, to the compact mass of men who, for several seasons, have emptied France to concentrate in the north-east'. More recently, in *Dress Gray* Lucian Truscott described a military language: 'fuelled by cigar smoke and mess hall coffee, greasy fatigues and scuffed boots, afternoons spent ghosting at the motor pool . . . full of aphorisms and clichés discarded by others, which [take] on new life and meaning in the coarse texture of a sergeant's timing and delivery'.

Soldiers favour a collective nickname, sometimes descriptive like the Roman *mulus marianus* (Marius' mule),

the French *poilu* (hairy, meaning virile as well as unkempt), the WW I American 'dough foot' (from his muddy feet) and 'doughboy', or the more recent 'grunt' (from the sounds emitted while marching heavily laden). The German soldier, across several generations, was a *landser*, and his British opponent a Tommy (see ATKINS, TOMMY), more recently a 'Tom', or the slightly deprecating 'squaddie' or 'swabbie', like the French *bidasse*. To their officers soldiers were often their 'boys' or 'children'. Old FM von Schwerin was killed at Prague in 1757 rallying his regiment with a shout of 'Heran mein Kinder!', while at *Rezonville/Gravelotte in 1870 *Bazaine trotted his horse ahead of a shaky battalion, saying: 'Allons, mes enfants, suivez votre maréchal.'

Civilians are at best dismissed as 'civvies' or *pékins*. At worst they are slackers and profiteers, like the *embusqués* pilloried by French trench newspapers, or the mythical American character Jody who avoided conscription and got the draftee's job, car, and girl. US army cadence calls, used on the march, are known as 'Jody calls', and often explore Jody's fate when the draftee returns. The front-line soldier resents others who do not share his danger. He may call them *Ettappenschweine* (lines of communication pigs), 'remfs' (rear echelon mother-fuckers), or 'ponti' (people of no tactical importance). A German soldier assigned to administrative duties was a *Schreibstubenhengst* (office stallion), and his French counterpart a *buveur d'encre* (ink drinker). American rear echelon personnel were also the rhyming (in American) 'clerks and jerks' or 'chairborne rangers'. Members of the French *train des equipages* were *hussards à quatre roues* (four-wheeled hussars), and British infantrymen unkindly maintained that the initials of the Royal Army Service Corps really stood for 'run away someone's coming'.

The graduation of nicknames within armies is a subculture in itself. French recruits were *Marie-Louises* (after Napoleon's empress), the surprisingly durable *bleus* (from National Guard blue as opposed to old army white), or, especially if ungainly, *jeanjeans*. Old soldiers were *briscards* because they wore *brisques*, long-service stripes. Infantrymen in general were *fantassins* or *biffins*, line infantry were *lignards* or, from their red trousers, *culs rouges* (red arses), while their *chasseur comrades were *chasse pattes*. Cuirassiers were variously *coquillards*, *gros frères* or (more cautiously) *gros lolos*; the Chasseurs d'Afrique were *chass d'aff*; spahis, from their red uniforms, were *cavaliers rouges*; marine infantry and gunners respectively *marsouins* and *bigorres*. The disciplinary battalions of *infanterie legère d'Afrique* were *joyeux*, *zephyrs*, or *zefs*, while Zouaves were *zouzous*.

A gunner has been a 'cannon cocker' or 'redleg' to the Americans, somewhat bitterly a 'dropshort' or 'long-range sniper' to the British, and *bumskopf* (bang head) to the Germans. Non-airborne personnel are 'straight-legs' or simply 'legs' to US paratroopers, 'crap-hats' to the British, and *culs de plomb* (lead arses) or *poireaux* (leeks) to the French.

Weapons were often given affectionate nicknames, like 'Katyusha' (little Katie) for the Soviet multi-barrelled rocket launcher), 'Puff the Magic Dragon' for the Vulcan revolving cannon (thus 'Dragon's Lair' for the AC-47 gunship), and Rosalie for the French Lebel bayonet. Rosalies also had the descriptive nicknames *vide-boche* and *tue-boche*, though a *coup de baionnette* (bayonet thrust) had marital as well as martial implications. Avoidance joking encouraged WW I British infantrymen to call a heavy shell, which burst in thick black smoke, a 'coal box' or (from the black boxer) 'Jack Johnson'; to a German it was a *Schwarze Maria*; and to a Frenchman a *gros noir*.

Until recently a British soldier might call his rifle a *bundook*, reflecting the widespread raiding of Indian terminology which included *jildi* (hurry, quickly), *charpoy* (bed), *bint* (female), and *char* (tea.) Adding *wallah* defined a trade, as in *char-wallah* for teaboy or *dhobi-wallah* for launderer. A special affinity with India could be implied by using *log* as in *badmash-log* (bad people) or *gora-log* (working-class whites) as opposed to *sahib-log*. The French borrowed from their own colonial experience to nickname the commanding officer *caïd* or *kebir*.

The commander might be the *chef* to a German and 'the old man' to a British or American soldier, regardless of age. The regimental sergeant major was the *spiess* to a German, and a warrant officer *le juteaux* to a Frenchman. A company sergeant major or first sergeant was the *chien de compagnie* in France and 'top kick' or 'first shirt' to an American. The canine analogy produced *chien du régiment* for regimental adjutant and 'orderly dog' for orderly officer, as well as *officier chien* for martinet. Slang for rank might reflect the nature of its badge, as in 'butterbar' for a US second lieutenant or 'bird-colonel' for a full colonel.

A British conscript might keep a 'chuff chart' to mark the gradual expiry of his service. His French counterpart, looking forward to *la quille* (*demobilization), might enquire 'combien tu pête?' (how many farts left in you?) to receive the response, from a man with ten days left to serve, 'je pête dix!' A newly arrived conscript in *Vietnam was a 'cherry' (virgin) or FNG (fucking new guy). A British Territorial would once (though rarely now) have rejoiced in the nickname 'terrier' but been less pleased with 'weekend warrior'. To regular soldiers' assertions that he was a 'stab' (stupid TA bastard) he might retort that they were simply 'arabs' (arrogant regular army bastards). Other acronyms are official, like 'Awol' (absent without leave), Flak (Fleiger Abwehr Kanone), Pak (Panzer Abwehr Kanone), 'fiscal' (fire support co-ordination line), and 'feba' (forward edge of battle area), and unofficial, like 'fubar' (fouled up beyond redemption/recognition), snafu (situation normal, all fouled up), and 'buff' (big ugly fat fucker) for the B-52 bomber.

Food and drink feature prominently in slang. A German mobile field cooker was *Gulaschkanone* (goulash cannon). To the French, *bidoche* (meat) easily became *barbaque* (bad meat) or even tinned meat, called *singe* (monkey) from its supposed origin. To the British soldier corned beef is 'corned dog' and the infamous 'cheese, processed' is 'cheese, possessed' (just as 'drawers, cellular' are inevitably 'drawers, Dracula'). The allegedly alcoholic propensities of German junior NCOs produce *Schnapser* for gefrieter and *Oberschnapser* for obergefrieter.

Nicknames for an enemy often reflect a sneaking regard. If the German were *boches* to the French, they were 'Fritz' or 'the Hun' to the British. The Vietcong soldier was 'Victor Charlie', simply 'Charlie', and sometimes 'Sir Charlie'. Even the racist 'gook' had a warm derivative: a notorious and much-shelled sniper at Khe Sanh was called 'Luke the Gook'. The British soldier's propensity for mispronunciation led to enemy commanders receiving unlikely names: Sang-ko-lin-sin, whose troops defended the Taku Forts in 1860, was popularly believed to be an Irishman called Sam Collinson.

Swear words are interwoven throughout military slang, doing duty for most parts of speech. Glenn Gray suggested that 'The most common word in the mouths of American soldiers had been a vulgar expression for sexual intercourse.' A WW II British driver announced as follows that his truck would run no more: 'the fucking fucker's fucked.' A German linked briefly overstaying his leave for carnal pleasure with receipt of *dicken* (confinement in the guardroom), writing on its wall: 'Halb stunde ficken-drei tage dicken.' This sort of thing was all too much for a Belgian priest, who wrote: 'I have looked it up phonetically in my little English dictionary (fah-ke) and find, to my surprise, that the word "fake" means "false, unreal or not true to life." Why the soldiers should refer to us in this way is difficult to understand, and yet everywhere one hears them talk of "fake Belgium" and "fake Belgians" . . .'.   RH

slave soldiers The inherent power of a military man might seem to contrast paradoxically with the unfree legal status of a slave. Yet there have been frequent examples of the employment of military slaves throughout history, from ancient times up to the *American civil war. Usually, this was a response to crisis and only a temporary measure. In the post-Roman west until the 12th century a class of military serfs did exist and in Islamic societies slave soldiers became a social and military institution at the heart of government which endured for a millennium (8th–19th centuries).

In ancient Greece and Rome, societies which depended upon the economic productivity of slaves, they were generally excluded from military activity. Indeed the Corinthian Pact of 338 BC specifically stated that no signatories were allowed to offer freedom (manumission) in return for military service. Slaves performed as body servants and did menial jobs around the camp. This role was common in all slave-owning societies up to the abolition of slavery in the 18th and 19th centuries. Roman penal legions during the

*Punic wars were not recruited from those born slaves and were a quickly abandoned crisis measure. The name 'servile' was given to the *Gladiators wars of Spartacus because it involved the arming of slaves, something so threatening to the established social fabric that those involved were crucified rather than returned to their previous owners, a substantial capital loss.

In the Roman successor states of western Europe, the *feudal system contained a hint of servility in the act of homage that liege lords found it unwise to presume upon. The evidence is confused, but the military caste known as the *ministeriales* in the 10th-century Ottonian German empire may have been more like bondsmen, while in Muscovy the retainers of the boyars were even more so. Military manpower crises led to the liberation of serfs in Russia and slaves in Brazil, while the American civil war had much the same effect. Thus the entire history of the West, pre- and post-Christian, was marked by a presumption that only free men, however relative their freedom was, should bear arms.

By contrast slave soldiers were a characteristic of Middle Eastern dynasties. Their first large-scale use was under the Abbasid Caliph al-Mutasim of Baghdad in 838, when 4,000 *Turks served on an Egyptian campaign. Such troops were known as *ghulams*, or later as *Mamelukes, and there were several institutional features which differentiated them from other societies. First, they were deliberately recruited from what were considered warrior populations of the Islamic world. In the Near East, Turks were popular, as were Kurds and Circassians, and also Christian populations, such as Armenians. In the west, Berbers also fulfilled this role. Secondly, they were trained to a very high standard of fighting ability, as mounted *archers. Often they were recruited as young boys, and given a sternly Muslim spiritual and military *education. Under the Ottoman empire this system was called *devshirme* and was bitterly resented by Christian populations, although the individual benefited enormously from the social promotion. This was because, thirdly, the role of slaves in Islamic governments enabled them to hold the highest positions of state, including military command. In Egypt, the Mamelukes of the Ayyubid dynasty (founded by *Saladin) actually seized power. As a result of the crisis caused by St Louis's *Crusade in 1250, the sultan was assassinated and replaced by the Mameluke Qutuz. Under his successor Baibars the Holy Land was recovered from the Christians (by 1291). The Mameluke dynasty continued in Egypt until the Ottoman conquest of 1512, and the military caste lasted until it lost credibility at the hands of Napoleon in 1798. *Abbas of Persia also employed *ghulams*.

The Ottoman Turks employed perhaps the most famous slave soldiers, the *janissaries, formed in the late 14th century to provide a body of good quality infantry to supplement the numerous, but often lightly equipped Ottoman cavalry. The janissaries stormed *Constantinople and destroyed the Hungarians at *Mohacs. Initially armed with the *bow, they later became efficient *musketeers. As the Ottoman tide ebbed they took on a Praetorian role, making and deposing sultans, but they were not disbanded until 1826.   MB

Pipes, D., *Slave Soldiers and Islam* (New Haven, 1981).

Slim, FM William (Joseph), 1st Viscount of Yarralumla and Bishopston (1891–1970). Slim and *Montgomery, both commissioned into the Royal Warwickshire Regiment, are two of Britain's outstanding commanders of WW II, and could not be more different. Slim had none of the flair or PR skills of Monty, and initially, little of the self-confidence that might have been bestowed by a more comfortable background, like that of *Alexander. His core skill—which took him to the top—was his ability to manage men. Slim, of a lower middle-class urban parentage, was a product of the University Officer Training Corps (OTC) system, which taught basic military skills to the better-educated with a view to a Territorial commission. Commissioned in August 1914, Slim was wounded at *Gallipoli and in *Mesopotamia, where he gained an MC. He was rescued from his fear of returning to an uninspiring office life in Birmingham by transfer to the Indian army, where he gained a permanent commission and could live on his pay. His inter-war career was slow (as it was for all between 1919 and 1939), but he attended staff college and commanded a Gurkha battalion.

As commander of 10th Indian Infantry Brigade, Slim took part in the conquest of *Abyssinia in 1940. The campaign did not go well for him, either as a commander, or physically—he was wounded again in January 1941. Later that year, as its COS, he accompanied an Expeditionary Force to attack Vichy French units and native pro-Nazi forces in Iraq. Within days, the GOC of 10th Indian Division had fallen ill, and Slim replaced him. He was a success at this level of command, and in March 1942 was promoted to command the Burma Corps, who had been chased out of Rangoon by the Japanese (see BURMA CAMPAIGN). Here, he was able to employ his best talents—that of talking to soldiers and restoring their morale. Ever since Gallipoli, Slim had possessed the 'common touch' of being able to level with his men, and get them to do his bidding.

Although he still had to conduct a 900 mile (1,448 km) retreat to India, Slim turned it from a disorderly panic into a controlled military withdrawal. By May his force had reached India, but he suffered from a difference of style to his superior, the patrician Alexander. This disagreement and the fact that the reconquest of Burma was a low priority for *Churchill meant that it was not until April 1943 that Slim's next command, XV Corps, saw action in the Arakan. Despite the setback there, he was promoted in October 1943 to command of the Eastern Army (later renamed Fourteenth Army), as a result of the arrival of *Mountbatten as Supreme Commander South-East Asia. The new supremo recognized in Slim a tenacity and aggressiveness lacking in his contemporaries. Both as XV Corps and Fourteenth Army commander, Slim emphasized jungle warfare training for all his men—even the HQ staff; early Burma garrisons had been little more than a colonial gendarmerie. This provided his soldiers with a new-found confidence, while his pep talks (his only common ground with Monty) added the motivation. Here his service in Gurkha battalions paid off, for his ranks contained many with whom he conversed in their own language. Slim later reckoned that as a senior commander, one-third of all his time was spent talking to his men.

He undertook a partially successful attack into the Arakan region (February 1944) on the Burma–India frontier, and then, in the battles of *Imphal and *Kohima, he repelled a major Japanese drive to invade north-east India. He devised new tactics adapted to cope with a style of war that had no fixed front lines, and used aerial resupply for formations that were surrounded, or advancing through difficult terrain. Rangoon fell on 3 May 1945, but days later, he was effectively sacked by Leese, who offered him a lesser command. Slim held his ground and requested retirement while his Fourteenth Army rumbled dangerously. Eventually *Alanbrooke intervened, and it was Leese who was sacked, Slim taking his place as C-in-C Allied Land Forces, South-East Asia Command.

After the war he served as CIGS and was promoted field marshal in 1949. Between 1953 and 1960 he was governor-general of Australia. His memoirs, *Defeat into Victory*, which appeared in 1956, were a best-seller, and in their humility and lack of pomposity are as unlike Montgomery's as they could be. Slim is a good example of how in both world wars, a class-ridden British army was blessed with an egalitarian streak, enabling its less privileged, but equally able commanders to rise to the top.   APC-A

Anderson, Duncan (chapter) in John Keegan (ed.), *Churchill's Generals* (London, 1991).

Lewin, Ronald, *Slim the Standard Bearer* (London, 1976).

slingers were ancient *skirmishers who employed a simple but, as the biblical Goliath discovered at the hands of David, effective weapon. The sling is simply a piece of material held as a loop in the hand. The missile sits in the centre of the loop, which may be wider or strengthened to hold it better. Energy is imparted to the missile by the slinger swinging the sling around his head, releasing one end at the crucial moment so that the missile flies out with optimum velocity and direction. Assyrian bas-reliefs of *c*.700 BC show armoured slingers at a siege, though generally slingers depended on their agility to stay out of trouble. In 5th-century Greece the Rhodians were most renowned, outranging bows by reputedly shooting up to 383 yards (350 metres). Other famous slingers came from the western Mediterranean Balearic Islands, fighting for Carthage from

the 5th to the 2nd century BC, and later for Rome. They carried three slings of different sizes and different missiles for use depending upon the range. They were a composite of rushes, animal hair, and sinew bound together. When not in use the sling was wound around the forehead as a headband. The missiles could be stones, but were frequently ceramic or lead. Lead slingstones have been found with simple messages cast into them like 'Take That!' Slingstones were acknowledged to inflict fearful wounds, penetrating the flesh, which closed around them. Every Roman legionary was supposed to carry the weapon, and in the late empire, a staff-sling (on a pole) was developed which threw even heavier shot, developing in due course into a *siege engine. As such, slings continued in use throughout the Middle Ages until replaced by cannon. In the New World, the *Conquistadores found them the most dangerous weapons they faced and as late as 1987 a party of Peruvian journalists left photographic evidence that their collective demise was occasioned by highland Indian slingers.   MB

Connolly, Peter, *Greece and Rome at War* (new edn., London, 1998).

small arms is a term first recorded in use in English in the early 18th century and used to define firearms capable of being carried in the hand. The exact etymological position of heavy and medium *machine guns in this context is unclear, but they are now generally included within the term, to the exclusion of ordnance and machine guns and cannon mounted on aircraft and ships, but including *anti-armour weapons and light, portable *mortars. Essentially a military term, the development of small arms has generally been stimulated by warfare, driven by technological advances, and has accompanied significant changes in battlefield tactics.

Notwithstanding the first use of the term *c*.1718, a chronological survey of the history and development of small arms must begin 400 years before that, with the earliest known use of *gunpowder as a propellant in a military portable firearm. *Cannon are first referred to and illustrated respectively in a Florentine decree and an English illuminated treatise of the late 1320s, and from the 1340s European manuscript references to guns, cannon, firearms, and other descriptive terms multiply, many references containing the implication that firearms had been around for some time previously. By the mid-14th century, the references include mention of implicitly small cannon—later called handguns—with rudimentary stocks or tillers; this was in the year 1346, in which the English victory over the French at *Crécy occurred, although it was rendered decisive by the English longbow rather than the English handgun. Before the end of the century, references exist to handguns having separate chambers, an indication of the earliest experiments with types of breech-loader. The term 'handgun' itself, now so inevitably associated with the

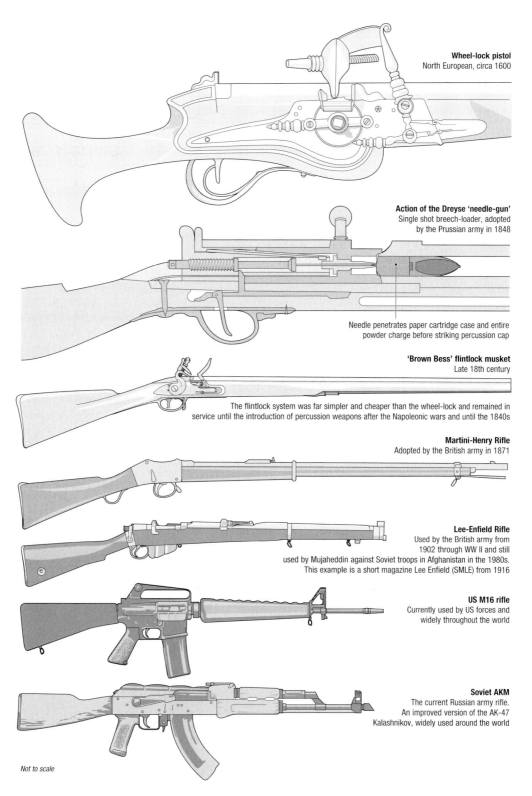

Wheel-lock pistol
North European, circa 1600

Action of the Dreyse 'needle-gun'
Single shot breech-loader, adopted
by the Prussian army in 1848

Needle penetrates paper cartridge case and entire
powder charge before striking percussion cap

'Brown Bess' flintlock musket
Late 18th century

The flintlock system was far simpler and cheaper than the wheel-lock and remained in
service until the introduction of percussion weapons after the Napoleonic wars and until the 1840s

Martini-Henry Rifle
Adopted by the British army in 1871

Lee-Enfield Rifle
Used by the British army from
1902 through WW II and still
used by Mujaheddin against Soviet troops in Afghanistan in the 1980s.
This example is a short magazine Lee Enfield (SMLE) from 1916

US M16 rifle
Currently used by US forces and
widely throughout the world

Soviet AKM
The current Russian army rifle.
An improved version of the AK-47
Kalashnikov, widely used around the world

Not to scale

Hand-held firearms – 'small arms' – have retained the same basic shape for half a millennium. Even if the use of chemical energy to propel a heavy metal projectile is superseded by directed energy, the shape of the human body and the relationship of arm, eye, and shoulder are likely to ensure that future weapons would remain recognizable to anyone from 1500 or 2000.

popular press and thus shunned by the scholar, appeared first in 1388.

The earliest surviving such gun, less than 12 inches (30.5 cm) long, bottle-shaped, and with a calibre of 1.4 inches, dates from the 1300–50 period and is now in the National Historical Museum in Stockholm; it may, originally, have been intended to be set into a heavy wooden tiller-shaped stock but this has not survived its interment and subsequent excavation. From this rudimentary form developed handguns with truer cylindrical barrels, similarly stocked and often with hooks below their barrels which, when the barrel was rested on a parapet, reduced the inevitable and uncomfortable recoil; such hooked guns became known in German as *Hakenbüchsen*, or hook-guns. Ignition of these guns would have been achieved by the application of a lighted match or heated wire to their touchholes—inevitably a hit-and-miss process not guaranteed to ensure the relaxation of the gunner. Early in the 15th century rudimentary *matchlock systems appeared, in which the match was held in the screwed jaws of a hinging S-shaped lever, now called a serpentine, and brought to the touch-hole by hinging the serpentine downwards. By 1500 triggers had been developed, which remotely operated the serpentine and thus removed the gunner's hand from the area of the touch-hole. By 1500 too, shoulder-held long guns had reached a stage of appearance and development that they were to retain, in essentials, for the next 350 years: muzzle-loaded with powder and *bullet, fired from the shoulder—usually the right shoulder, the concept of a left-handed soldier being a relatively modern concept—by pulling a trigger which ignited a primary charge to fire the main charge in the chamber of the barrel. *Breech-loading systems had been experimented with and rifling, although probably not for soldiers' weapons, was in its infancy. The 16th century saw the refinement of the military long arm into types: the arquebus or heavy carbine; the somewhat heavier caliver; the currier, a long caliver; the petronel, another heavy carbine; and the carbine proper. All took up their places in the military armoury beside the *musket, the largest and heaviest of all of them.

During the course of the 16th century the invention of the *wheel-lock system of ignition greatly facilitated the development of the *pistol. It also, for the first time, widened the use of the firearm from being merely the tool of the ordinary foot soldier to becoming not only a weapon suitable for use by mounted officers but also one desired by sportsmen. During the 16th century the gunmaker became a craftsman, designer, innovator, and artist, spurred on by an increased interest in small arms by the rich and powerful. Although such developments as occurred took time to trickle down to the military level, their encouragement by those in power, who often held military office, inevitably resulted in the soldier eventually obtaining increasingly sophisticated firearms. Few common soldiers were allowed close to the delicate and complicated mechanism of the wheel-lock, however, and its military use tended to be restricted to pistols carried by officers or horsemen who, for the first time, were provided with a firearm usable from the saddle. Aside from the necessity of training horses to bear the noise of firearms fired close to their ears, the availability of the pistol to the cavalry not only gave them a back-up weapon to their sword and lance but also changed their tactical role as—very gradually, since it was so well entrenched—the headlong charge gave way to the more circumspect *caracole, in which ranks of horsemen would advance, fire their pistols, and then wheel to the rear to reload. By 1700 the caracole, initially so fashionable, was obsolete and the cavalryman's pistol—by that time a *snaphaunce or *flintlock—was reserved for the mêlée or as just another item in the horse soldier's armoury.

The development of the snaphaunce and then the flintlock systems in the late 16th and 17th centuries brought up-to-date, and soldier-proof, technology to the armies of the West and the flintlock system dominated warfare in Europe, and wherever else Europeans fought, throughout the 18th century. Military small arms multiplied in type in a century of wide-ranging, large-scale, and almost constant wars or rumours of wars in Europe and across the increasingly discovered globe. The musket remained the standard arm of the infantry soldier, although he might occasionally be equipped with a metal socketed cup for its muzzle, from which to launch *grenades. The carbine, a shortened musket of smaller bore, was a popular cavalry weapon and one much modified, reinvented, and improved upon as the cavalry's use of firearms continued to attract the scrutiny of governments, the interference of cavalry regiments' colonels, and the innovations of gunmakers. Cavalry pistols were improved upon and sometimes fitted with removable shoulder-stocks, in the hope of their replacing the carbine and thus simplifying the trooper's weaponry. For seamen, special patterns of musket were introduced and the *musketoon, or blunderbuss, became a shipboard weapon useful for discouraging both boarders and putative mutineers. *Rifles began to appear in military units from the Urals to the Appalachians and, by the end of the century, had achieved—largely through their much-publicized success in the hands of the rebellious American colonists—the kind of notoriety, as sniper's weapons, that crossbows and their operators had enjoyed on medieval battlefields. Wall guns (debatably not small arms per se) and swivel guns, which were really no more than huge versions of the military musket and musketoons, became used in fortifications and on board ship; volley guns, multiple-barrelled weapons, joined them as part of the arms chests of a number of navies. Rocket-firing muskets were experimented with towards the close of the *Napoleonic wars but not pursued.

During the 19th century, no less than in the previous hundred years, warfare stimulated military and sporting small-arms development and, in the case of the percussion system and many other firearms developments, the requirements of the sportsman led to the equipment of the soldier. The effects of the industrial revolution, a burgeoning of scientific experimentation and development either side of the Atlantic, and a constantly bubbling cauldron of national aggressions in Europe took small arms from the musket to the machine gun in well under a century. The US army adopted the rifle in 1803. The Prussian army adopted the Dreyse *needle-gun bolt-action breech-loading rifle in 1841, at a date when every other European infantry soldier loaded his smooth-bored musket with powder and ball from the muzzle, as his predecessors had been doing for three centuries. American soldiers used Colt's revolving-chamber pistols and rifles against the Seminoles in 1838 and the Mexicans in 1847. British officers took Colt's 1851 pattern Navy revolver, and its British competitors, to the Crimea in quantity in 1854; of the soldiers they led, many were still using smooth-bored muzzle-loading muskets, although some had rifles firing *Minié bullets. While the *American civil war produced the Gatling machine gun, most of its soldiers fought with muzzle-loading rifles; in 1870, on the Franco-German border, the soldiers of France, Prussia, and Bavaria used breech-loading rifles firing self-contained *cartridges and France had its own version of the Gatling, the Montigny *mitrailleuse.

In the final quarter of the 19th century most of the technical developments familiar in modern small arms were experimented with and essentially perfected. Rifles became breech-loaders, then repeaters, then with reduced bore and increased velocity, then with *smokeless powder; semi-automatic or self-loading rifles became a not-too-distant possibility. Pistols, initially large-bore revolvers, became smaller bore, higher velocity, and self-loading, or 'automatic'. Machine guns developed from being hand-cranked and firing big, fat, black powder cartridges to being fully automatic, liquid-cooled and capable of firing 600 rounds a minute. All these developments had a profound effect upon battlefield tactics but these, for the most part, had to be learned the hard way in the early years of WW I. Every infantry soldier was encouraged to become a marksman, now that he had the technology to be one; every cavalry soldier had to relearn his role and fight as an infantryman (but, with the tank, his time would come again). The operation of machine guns became a study in the mastery of the battlefield and, as they became lighter, more portable, and more personal, so the *sub-machine gun—introduced too late for widespread use in WW I—became the ancestor of the modern soldier's personal weapon. Grenade launchers reappeared, their projectiles ideally suited for *trench warfare, and the appearance of the tank on the battlefield in 1917 inevitably produced the first of a family of portable anti-armour weapons: just as predictably, it was a scaled-up infantryman's rifle, the 13 mm calibre version of the Mauser Gewehr 1898. Trench mortars were developed and became the ancestors of the modern light and portable infantry weapons.

Small-arms developments since 1918 have focused upon lightness and versatility, factors in which Germany led the way, closely followed by the USA, prior to and during WW II. The mass-produced German assault rifle, or Sturm-Gewehr, adopted in 1944, is the ancestor of modern such weapons, notably the Avtomat *Kalashnikov, or AK, models of 1947 and 1974. The light, air-cooled, and very fast-firing machine gun was born with the MaschineGewehr 1934 and 1942; later versions of the MG 42 are still in use worldwide. The self-loading rifle became familiar with the American M1 Garand and the personal sub-machine gun with the Maschine Pistole 1938 and 1940 and the American M-3 or 'greasegun'. Developments since 1945 have concentrated upon calibre-reduction and, recently, on caseless ammunition and weapons employing plastic components: all these contribute to reducing the carrying load of the soldier who, however small his arms become, still has to carry them and their ammunition. SCW

Blackmore, Howard L., *British Military Firearms* (London, 1961).
Blair, Claude (gen. ed.), *Pollard's History of Firearms* (London, 1983).
Cormack, Alexander J. R., *Small Arms: A Concise History of their Development* (Windsor, 1982).
Reid, William, *The Lore of Arms* (London, 1975).
Roads, Christopher H., *The British Soldier's Firearm, 1850–1864* (London, 1964).

smoke Between the introduction of firearms on a large scale in the 16th century and the invention of smokeless powder at the end of the 19th, battlefields were often smoky places. A royalist officer, Capt Richard Atkyns, wrote of Lansdown (1643) that 'the air was so darkened by the smoke of the powder, that for a quarter of an hour . . . there was no light seen but what the fire of the volleys of shot gave'. Col Lyman, a Union officer, described the field of *Chancellorsville as 'smoke and bushes'. So great was the smoke produced by cannon and muskets that wind direction conferred tactical advantage: troops with the wind to their backs would have the smoke of their discharges blown into the enemy's faces, while they themselves could aim and fire unimpeded. At sea aggressive captains would often lay their vessels alongside an opponent, fire a last broadside, and then board him in its smoke.

Smoke could also be created deliberately. Crops or buildings were often fired so that the smoke blew back to inconvenience an enemy, or screened the movement of friendly troops. In WW I smoke was delivered in shells fired by artillery, or laid by hand-held smoke candles. It was widely used, usually by an attacker who sought to deny his opponent the advantage of the observed fire of artillery and machine guns. In WW II smoke delivery improved. 'Base-ejection' artillery and mortar rounds emitted smoke gradually, while white phosphorous rounds burst to produce an instant smokescreen—and to cause terrible injuries to troops or civilians splashed by the phosphorus. Smoke *grenades followed the same lines, with some emitting smoke and others bursting to disgorge phosphorus. Smoke generators, burning fuel oil to create a dense and evil-smelling cloud, were able to screen targets from air or ground attack for extended periods. When the Americans crossed the Moselle at Arnaville, near Metz, in the autumn of 1944 a smoke generator company kept the crossing-site screened for several weeks. Coloured smoke was used to identify friendly units or mark targets. Some tanks could emit smoke, while warships often deliberately made smoke to conceal or confuse.

Smoke remains useful for concealing movement on the battlefield, and can still defeat the light-intensifier sights beloved of *snipers, although providing no protection from *infra-red or ground radar detection.   RH

---

smokeless powder From the first appearance of firearms on the battlefield until the late 19th century their presence was marked by clouds of acrid white smoke: the more firearms and the more fire, the more smoke. On a windy day it cleared rapidly but in calm conditions the smoke from cannon and muskets would produce enveloping and swirling clouds that quickly obscured details of the action from its participants, its directors, and its recorders. Tell-tale puffs of white smoke also revealed the position of *snipers.

Smokeless powder was the first firearm propellant to replace gunpowder and was perfected by *Nobel in the late 1880s on a base of nitrocellulose, which had been discovered in 1846. Smokeless *explosives such as cordite, first produced in England in 1889, used gelatinized nitrocellulose, or gun cotton, mixed with minerals and nitroglycerine; stabilizers were later added. Quickly adopted by the world's armies in the 1890s, the new type of powder removed much of the obscuring smoke from the battlefield and, combined with high-velocity ammunition and increasingly accurate rifles, made the long-range sniper all but invisible.   SCW

Bailey, A., and Murray, S. G., *Explosives, Propellants and Pyrotechnics* (London, 1989).

---

snaphaunce The snaphaunce lock appeared in Europe in the mid-16th century and was the earliest form of *flintlock firearms ignition system. It was later differentiated from the 'true' flintlock by firearms scholars for whom the 'true' and original snaphaunce lock had a steel separate from the pan cover and a cock incapable of the half-cock safety position. The pan cover either slid open automatically upon the trigger being pulled or had to be slid open manually first. Snaphaunce locks seem to have been invented by the Dutch, who gave them the name *snaphaan*, meaning 'snapping hen'. They likened the flint-bearing hammer to a cock bird (*Hahn* in German, *Haan* in Dutch) and *Haan*, when translated into English as 'cock', came to

mean the hammer, which struck the steel with its flint to ignite the primary charge. Differing styles of snaphaunce developed in the Low Countries, in Britain, Spain, Italy, and North Africa. As a system it remained popular in Spain, the Balkans, and North Africa into the 19th century, where it was the ignition system principally found on *miquelet muskets.   SCW

Blair, Claude (gen. ed.), *Pollard's History of Firearms* (London, 1983).

Snider rifle Named after the American inventor of its breech-block, Dr Jacob Snider, the Snider was the British army's first *breech-loading firearm and was produced, after 1865, as a rifle and a carbine. A modified Pattern 1853 rifle-musket, the Snider featured a solid breech-block incorporating an integral rod. This block, hinged on its left, swung open to reveal the chamber. Closing the block sealed the chamber. When the hammer fell on the exposed end of the rod, the enclosed end struck the detonator.   SCW

Blair, Claude (gen. ed.), *Pollard's History of Firearms* (London, 1983).
Roads, Dr Christopher H., *The British Soldier's Firearm 1850–1864* (London, 1964).

---

snipers are picked marksmen who shoot, usually from a concealed position, with the aim of killing key enemy personnel. The concept is probably as old as missile weapons themselves: during the *Hundred Years War selected *archers were used to engage difficult targets. Snipers in the modern sense appeared after the development of firearms. In the *British civil wars Lord Brooke, a parliamentarian commander, was picked off by a crack shot while observing the siege of Lichfield Close.

Initially there was no clear distinction between snipers and rifle-armed *light troops whose fire was effective at greater range than that of their musket-armed comrades. A British veteran of the *American independence war observed that 'provided an American rifleman were to get a perfect aim at 300 yards [274 metres] at me, standing still, he most undoubtedly would hit me unless it was a very windy day'. During the *Peninsular war Tom Plunkett of the 95th Rifles sniped a French general, and in the siege of Sevastopol marksmen in 'rifle pits' ahead of the siege lines sniped Russian soldiers who exposed themselves and fired into the embrasures of guns. Both sides in the *American civil war raised regiments of *sharpshooters; Union recruits had to place ten shots in a 10 inch (254 mm) circle at 200 yards (183 metres) to be accepted, but they tended to be used as skirmishers, not snipers. Sniping was usually carried out by experienced marksmen found in both armies: during the siege of Port Hudson, Louisiana, there is an early example of a sniper taking on a target identified by a spotter with a *telescope.

Sniping assumed great importance during WW I, especially where *trench warfare was prevalent. The distinction between the trained sniper and the ordinary rifleman became clear. Snipers had telescopic sights and were sent on courses which emphasized both marksmanship and fieldcraft. They often worked in two-man teams, one man spotting with telescope or binoculars. Sniping demanded not merely skill and patience, but willingness to kill an enemy who might pose no threat. It helped inject hostility into quiet sectors, and snipers often found themselves mistrusted by their own side. Billy Sing of 5th Australian Light Horse, who sniped more than 150 Turks at *Gallipoli, was nicknamed 'the Murderer' by his comrades.

Similar principles prevailed during and after WW II. Sgt Harry Furness, an experienced sniper in Normandy, said, 'All snipers (on both sides) if captured were shot on the spot without ceremony as snipers were hated by all fighting troops; they could accept the machine gun fire, mortar and shell splinters flying around them . . . but they hated the thought of a sniper taking deliberate aim to kill by singling them out.' Snipers not only killed large numbers of the enemy—Ludmilla Pavlichenko, a female history student turned sniper, was credited with 309 kills—but, by picking off commanders and radio operators, degraded fighting effectiveness.

Some snipers rationalized their action by concentrating on enemy leaders. A US Marine remarked: 'you don't like to hit ordinary troops, because they're usually scared draftees or worse . . . The guys to shoot are big brass.' Sometimes snipers brought a personal edge to their craft. Sgt Brennan was chief cook of 7th Australian Light Horse, also at Gallipoli, but went sniping in his spare time: if he killed a Turk he was 'as happy as Larry all day'. Snipers were prominent in the fighting that followed the break-up of the former *Yugoslavia. During the siege of Sarajevo Serb snipers, on the high ground around the city, targeted civilians in the streets below.

Sniping is undoubtedly effective: in the first six months of 1969 US snipers in *Vietnam achieved 1,245 confirmed kills at an average of 1.39 bullets per kill. It helps demoralize potential targets, and significantly reduces combat efficiency. During the *Gulf war the .5 inch Barrett sniper rifle deployed by the US Marines even knocked out light armoured vehicles at ranges of around 2,187 yards (2,000 metres). Most armies pay insufficient attention to snipers in peacetime. Peter Staff argued that this was partly because of revulsion at their task: after every war 'the US Military rushes to distance itself from its snipers. The same men called upon to perform impossible missions during combat quickly find themselves to be peacetime pariahs.'

RH

Sobieski, Jan. See JOHN III, KING OF POLAND.

Sobraon, battle of (1846), the final and decisive battle of the first *Sikh war, fought on 10 February between British and Sikh forces on the eastern bank of the river Sutlej in north-west India. The Sikhs were in entrenched positions with their backs to the river. After a heavy exchange of artillery fire, the British infantry breached the Sikh left. The bridge of boats securing the Sikh retreat collapsed, turning defeat into rout. Losses on both sides were severe, the Sikhs suffering between 8,000 and 10,000 dead. As a result of the defeat the threat from the Sikhs was contained, but not yet eliminated.

JMB

Social and Civil Wars (91–82 BC). The Social War was the last occasion in which a substantial number of Italian peoples fought against Rome. It led directly to a civil war at Rome, in which *Sulla was eventually to emerge triumphant. The Social War was caused by dissatisfaction among Rome's allies who had shared much of the burden of conquering the empire, but gained few of the benefits, in particular being denied citizenship. Discontent came to a head when a Roman politician who pledged to extend the franchise to the Italians was assassinated. The massacre of a Roman magistrate and his staff at Asculum signalled open warfare.

Only some of the Italians joined the open rebellion, but they swiftly mobilized 100,000 men, the largest contingents being supplied by the Marsi under Poppaedius Silo, and the Samnites under Papius Mutilius. The Allies set up a rival state with a capital at Corfinium, renamed Italia. Virtually all of Rome's Latin allies, who enjoyed greater privileges than the Italians, stayed loyal, while other groups, such as the Etruscans, were mollified by the swift grant of citizenship. Each side fielded armies that were very similar in tactics, organization, and equipment, and both used African and Gallic auxiliary troops. The normal directness of Roman warfare made many of the battles very costly affairs.

The war divided broadly into two theatres. In the north, in Picenum along the Adriatic coast, the fighting focused in particular on the siege of Asculum, and in the south the Samnites made large-scale raids into neighbouring Campania, Apulia, and Lucania. Much of the early fighting was on a relatively small scale, as each side attempted to organize its armies, but the campaigns swiftly escalated. In this early fighting the Romans suffered a number of serious reverses, both consuls for the year 90 being defeated. At one stage the Senate was forced to conscript slaves to provide an immediate source of manpower. On another occasion, disturbed by the extravagant public displays of mourning which greeted the arrival of the bodies of a consul and most of his staff, it decreed that senior offices should be buried where they fell.

Rome may have come very close to defeat, but the presence with her armies of several experienced and able commanders did much to stabilize the situation. *Marius and Cnaeus Pompeius Strabo, father of *Pompey, did much to restore the situation in the north during 90. Strabo returned there as consul in 89, continuing the siege of Asculum and inflicting a massive defeat on an army of 60,000 sent to its relief. Once Asculum surrendered the rising in the north was effectively over. In the southern campaigns Sulla embarked on a major offensive in 89, capturing enemy strongholds and defeating any armies sent to confront him. The Samnites maintained a determined resistance, but the result of the war was no longer in doubt and the last strongholds were gradually mopped up. The cost of the war had been massive in terms of human losses and damage to the agrarian prosperity of much of Italy.

Sulla gained considerable prestige through his campaigns against the Italians and easily secured the consulship for 88, and command in the war against Mithridates of Pontus. A keen rivalry then developed between Sulla and Marius, the latter supporting a radical tribune, Sulpicius, in an effort to gain the eastern command for himself. After rioting during which he was forced to take refuge in Marius' house, Sulla fled the city, and a law was passed giving his command to Marius. Although this action was scarcely legal, Sulla's was even less so: he joined his army and led it against Rome. None of the senior senators on his staff went with him. Rome had no garrison and Marius no time to raise an army to oppose him. He was chased out of the country, and Sulpicius was executed. Sulla declared his legislation invalid, carried out a few reforms, and then left to fight an eastern war.

Lucius Cornelius Cinna, elected consul for 87, mustered an army after Sulla left and joined with Marius. Cnaeus Octavius, the other consul, and Strabo attempted to defend Rome, but were defeated. Octavius was executed and Strabo died of disease soon afterwards. Marius and Cinna declared themselves consuls for 86 and freely massacred suspected opponents, but Marius too died of natural causes early in the year. There was a lull in the fighting in Italy while Sulla prosecuted the war against Mithridates. One of Cinna's associates was sent east with an army, ostensibly to co-operate in operations against Pontus, but failed to achieve much and was murdered by one of his subordinates (86). By 85 Sulla was close to victory and Cinna prepared to lead an army into Macedonia to confront him, but was killed when his own soldiers mutinied.

Cinna's consular colleague Cnaeus Carbo was in overall command of the forces arrayed against Sulla when he landed at Brundisium in 83. Men who had suffered because of Marius and Carbo, notably Pompey who proceeded to raise troops from his father's veterans, rallied to Sulla and augmented his forces. He defeated the First army sent against him, and then persuaded the soldiers of another, led by Lucius Scipio, to desert to his cause. Winter ended the active campaigning and both sides spent the next few months preparing their armies. Carbo enlisted the assist-

ance of Marius' nephew in an attempt to use his uncle's reputation to inspire their supporters. In 82 a series of battles were fought, almost all significant victories for Sulla. He showed a particular vindictiveness against the Samnite troops which his enemies had raised in large numbers, evoking an echo of the Social War. Sulla took Rome and then faced the last major Marian army in the field. On 1 November 82, he defeated this 70,000-strong army at a battle fought outside the Colline gate. The war was over in Italy, but fighting continued in Africa, Sicily, and Spain before all resistance was defeated. Sulla was elected *dictator, executed his opponents and reformed the state, before resigning to return to private life in 80.   AKG

SOE (Special Operations Executive) was formed at the personal insistence of *Churchill in July 1940 as the only immediate means other than *air power of hitting back at the Germans after *Dunkirk. Its activities encompassed *intelligence, subversion, sabotage, and the creation of armed *resistance movements in all countries occupied by the Germans and later the Japanese. The catalyst for SOE's creation was originally the impression that the 1940 German victories in the west had been made possible by significant SOE-type infiltration by the Axis prior to invasion, but there is little evidence that this was so. Under the political direction of the Minister of Economic Warfare, initially Hugh Dalton until early 1942, thereafter Lord Selbourne, SOE unsurprisingly found itself in competition with the British security (MI5) and secret intelligence (MI6) services, with whose functions it overlapped, and later with the American *OSS, formed in emulation of SOE.

The lack of clear distinction between these agencies and also the Political Warfare Executive arguably restricted the potential of SOE, but it is also the case that Churchill preferred to bypass the regular ministries whenever he could do so. Although it was slow to produce results, it survived due to his enthusiasm for intrigue and irregular warfare. By 1944, it had evolved into a heterogenous force of over 10,000 personnel, including many *women. Starting from an 'old-boy' network of supposedly trustworthy officers, it recruited actively among linguists and foreign nationals, establishing separate cells for each occupied country, though France merited several such branches. SOE trained radio operators and specialist saboteurs to work with resistance units and despite RAF reluctance, several squadrons were engaged in ferrying agents and equipment to and from the occupied countries, and dropping weapons. SOE-trained resistance groups in France made a valuable contribution to the *Normandy landings, both in pre-invasion intelligence-gathering of troop dispositions and mapping the Atlantic Wall, and in post-invasion sabotage of the rail network. By contrast in Holland *Abwehr infiltration completely negated all SOE efforts and cost the lives of many agents and sympathizers because the controllers in London chose to ignore the agreed duress signals sent by captured radio operators.

The SOE was important in Europe not only for training and equipping resistance groups, but in terms of morale, as a demonstration of British support, and also as an outside agency capable of unifying resistance groups with different political leanings. In Greece, Italy, *Yugoslavia, and France, for example, communist-led groups frequently refused to work with those of the political right, to the detriment of the war against the Germans. SOE sponsored links to Norway by trawler (the 'Shetland bus'), where the German production of heavy water, vital for an atomic weapon, was severely disrupted and Czechoslovakia, where the Sicherheitsdienst (SD) chief Heydrich was assassinated, and co-operated with the production in London of aerial leaflets, part of the Allied contribution to *psychological war.

The contribution made by SOE to the war effort is hotly debated. While some historians contend that the resources, personnel, and finances it tied up could have been better used by conventional forces, and that its influence on the course of the war was negligible, there is a strong argument that SOE activities also tied down vast numbers of German resources and troops, guarding installations and searching for spies. Certainly there was a German perception of agents behind every bush, fostered by SOE activities, and Gestapo reprisals were brutal. In the *Burma campaign, SOE encouraged the revolt of the Karen tribe against Japanese rule and then trained them as a *guerrilla army. The arming of nationalist movements by SOE was to have post-war repercussions in Indochina, the *Greek civil war, the *Malayan emergency, and elsewhere, but in Yugoslavia it cemented good post-war relations with the former Partisan commander, *Tito, until the latter's death in 1980.

SOE was a typical 'talented amateur' organization and recruited some notable eccentrics and a large number of past and future writers, such that although it was disbanded in 1946 amid glad cries from all the regular services, it has lived on in the world of fiction and in the fantasy lives of millions. On balance it did more good than harm, and throughout its brief life it bore the imprint of the energetic, talented, but undisciplined spirit of the man who called it into being.   APC-A

sōhei (literally, 'priest soldiers'; often translated as 'warrior monk') refers particularly to the fighting men associated with the ancient Buddhist foundations of Enryakuji on Mount Hiei near Kyoto and its daughter temple Onjōji (Miidera) near Otsu, or the temples of Nara to the south: Kōfukuji and Tōdaiji. There are references to Buddhist temples arming themselves as early as the 10th century, and for the next 200 years armies of sōhei were to be used, either in disputes between temples, in disagreements between them and the imperial court, or in alliance with a particular *samurai family or faction.

Contemporary illustrations tend to portray the sōhei as rough characters, implying that many were not ordained priests but warriors recruited by the temples. Their traditional weapon was the naginata, a form of glaive, but they were also proficient in archery and swordsmanship. When in arms against the imperial court the sōhei would reinforce their presence by carrying into Kyoto the sacred omikoshi (portable shrine) in which the kami (spirit) of the temple was believed to dwell.

The first major conflict involving sōhei and samurai took place at the first battle of Uji in 1180. During the action two sōhei from Miidera fought celebrated single combats on the broken bridge across the river. Following the defeat of the Minamoto the Taira attacked Nara and caused great destruction. This effectively ended the Nara sōhei involvement in the war, although sōhei from Mount Hiei assisted in defending Kyoto against Minamoto Yoshinaka. We may also note the presence of a religious contingent from Kumano, a Shinto shrine, at the battle of Dan no Ura in 1185.

Sōhei from Mount Hiei were involved in the fighting of the Shōkyū war in 1221, and provided military help during the attempt at imperial restoration by Emperor Go-Daigo in 1333. For the following two centuries the sōhei were to be sporadically involved in war, culminating in support for the Asai and Asakura families in 1570 against *Oda Nobunaga. Nobunaga's reaction to sōhei intervention was a massive raid on Mount Hiei during which the entire temple complex was set ablaze and possibly 20,000 people killed.

                                                                    SRT

Sokolovsky, Marshal Vassiliy (1897–1968), Soviet wartime commander and military thinker, who gave his name to the definitive work *Strategy* in the 1960s which announced the 'revolution in military affairs' brought about by the ballistic missile and *nuclear weapons.

Sokolovsky joined the Red Army in 1918 and in 1921 became one of its first 'red commanders' (see TROTSKY). From February 1941 he was DCGS, he commanded the Western Front (army group) in 1943–4, and was COS and deputy commander of the first Ukrainian and first Belorussian Fronts. After the war, from 1946, he commanded the Group of Soviet Forces, Germany; from 1949 he was first deputy minister of defence; and CGS from 1952 to 1960. It was in this period that his thoughts on the revolution in military affairs germinated, assisted, no doubt, by many subordinates. *Strategy*, the first work to bear the name since Svechin's book of the same name in 1926, was first published in 1962 and republished in 1963 and 1968. For many years it was the 'bible' on the Soviet approach to war, but was superseded in the 1980s as the Soviet *general staff began to look away from all-out nuclear-rocket war.   CDB

Sokolovsky, Vasily, *Soviet Military Strategy*, trans. and ed. Harriet Fast Scott (3rd edn., London, 1975).

Somalia, operations in (1992–5). In the late 1980s, a full-scale civil war erupted in Somalia, which led to the end of Muhammad Siad Barre's dictatorship and the collapse of the Somali state. The war was responsible for a man-made famine, and caused hundreds of thousands of refugees, internally displaced persons, and civilian deaths from hunger. Because of this large-scale humanitarian tragedy, the USA, together with the UN, intervened militarily to protect the delivery of food supplies and thereby stop the famine. The intervention also necessarily entailed plans to rebuild the state in order to prevent the situation on the ground from reverting to that which caused the conflict in the first place.

The famine was successfully relieved, yet the international community did not rebuild the Somali state during the three Somali operations: the UN operation in Somalia (UNOSOM I); the US-led, UN-sanctioned RESTORE HOPE (also known as Unified Task Force, or UNITAF); and UNOSOM II, the last two of which ran from April 1992 until March 1995. UNOSOM I was a small *peacekeeping operation that could not provide adequate security for food delivery, which is why the US government in December 1992 sent 37,000 of its troops on a peace-enforcement mission to assist in the task. UNITAF in turn handed-off to a multinational, peace-enforcement operation, UNOSOM II, in May 1993 (the USA withdrew in March 1994). Difficulties were encountered throughout, partly because this was the first post-*Cold War peace-support operation in a collapsed state and proper procedures for co-ordinating such a massive operation had not been standardized.

The abiding image of these interventions remains the pictures of the bodies of US Rangers being dragged through the streets after a failed raid seeking to capture a prominent warlord. Somalia will be remembered for its complexity, for the influence of the media on the operation, for the loss of lives of 156 peacekeepers and many more Somalis, and for tasking the UN with more than its resources could realistically accomplish.   KvonH

Clarke, Walter, and Herbst, Jeffrey (eds.), *Learning from Somalia* (Oxford, 1997).

UN Development Programme, *Somalia Human Development Report, 1998* (New York, 1998).

Somme, battle of the (1916), WW I campaign in northern France. Battalions from every infantry regiment in the British army at some stage were stationed here, thus the Somme has a unique place in British social and military history. Although *Haig would have preferred to attack in the north, he was persuaded to mount a major attack with the French on the Somme, where the Allied armies joined. However, the Germans attacked *Verdun on 21 February, forcing France into an *attritional, defensive battle. The Somme battle was therefore launched early, to draw German pressure off Verdun, and never involved as many French troops as had been intended. Bisected by the Al-

bert–Bapaume road, the battleground was a series of gentle chalk ridges, into which the Germans had dug extensive fortifications. Haig's plan was for Rawlinson's Fourth Army to break through in the centre, capturing the Pozières ridge-line, while Gough's Reserve Army (later renamed the Fifth Army), including cavalry, exploited this gap and rolled up the German defences and took Bapaume. Allenby's Third Army was to mount a diversionary attack on Gommecourt, to the north.

Massive preparatory bombardment to destroy the German defences started at 06.00 on 24 June: 1.7 million shells were fired, while tunnelling companies hollowed out chambers under the key German strong points and filled them with explosives. Perhaps 30 per cent of the shells did not explode, while others failed to destroy the barbed wire or *dugouts. The shelling started on 'U' Day, continued throughout the subsequent days, and the assault should have gone in on 'Z' Day, 29 June. Heavy rainstorms, which made the approach roads, trenches, and crater-ridden no man's land too wet and muddy to keep up with the strict timetable of advance, meant that 'Z' Day was postponed until 1 July.

As the attack went in, seventeen large mines were exploded under German strong points, and the guns lifted and fired further forward. Behind the creeping *barrage infantry followed. Although there were local gains—36th Ulster Division was briefly successful near Thiepval, and on the southern end of the line Montauban was taken—the picture was bleak by the day's end. The British had lost 57,470 officers and men—19,240 of them killed, 2,152 missing, the rest wounded. This casualty rate was an unprecedented experience for the British army. Martin Middlebrook has identified 32 battalions that lost over 500 men on 1 July. Twenty of these were New Army battalions of 'Pals' or 'Chums' units—groups of friends who enlisted together. Seven New Army divisions attacked, alongside three Territorial and four Regular ones, making 1 July a fairly even-handed affair. The French attack on the British right, although smaller in scale than initially planned, went relatively well, and the preponderance of heavy guns in the French sector proved a real help to adjacent British formations.

The images of 1 July tend to cloud the overall Somme campaign. The British army's casualties of that day need to be seen against its overall losses for the 142 days—some 415,000 men. The perception is of disproportionate British casualties; in fact, the Germans are calculated to have suffered much more—possibly 650,000. Spread over the 142 days, therefore, the average British casualty rate was under 3,000 per day. John Terraine argues persuasively that 1 July should be seen as a freak day of battle, an unrepresentative snapshot of 1916, and certainly not a typical day of war.

There were twelve separate battles that together constitute the 1916 Somme campaign, which ended on 18 November 1916, when the 51st Highland Division took Beaumont

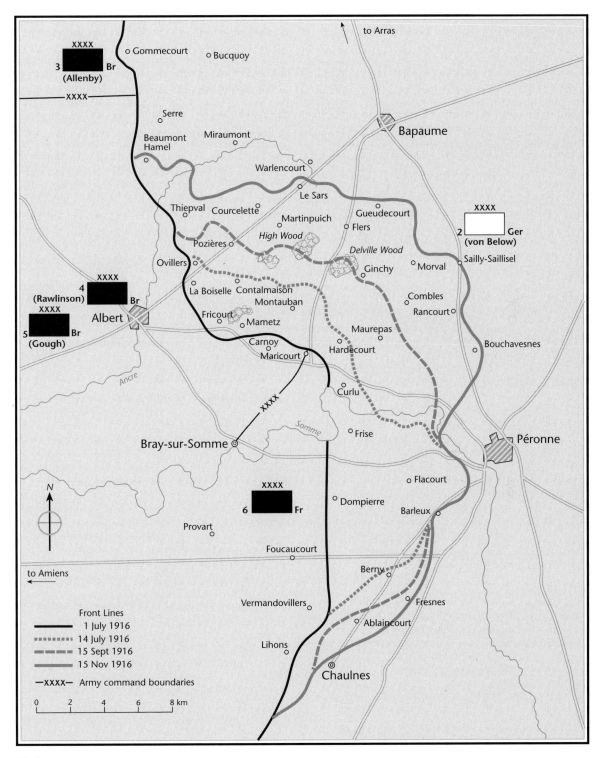

The **Somme**, 1916.

Hamel (which had been a Day One objective). After the initial setback, *Gough's Fifth Army took over attacking Pozières in the north, while Rawlinson's Fourth concentrated on securing a series of ridgelines in the Mametz-Montauban area, to the south. The 38th (Welsh) Division suffered particularly taking Mametz Wood, and fighting up to 13 July cost the Fourth Army 25,000 more men. Longueval and Bazentin fell to a well-conducted night attack on the 14th, opening a hole in the German second line, but Delville Wood took longer to subdue, the South African Brigade suffering heavily. However, German reserves arrived in time to hold a line between High Wood and Delville Wood, on the crest of Longueval Ridge, and remained there for the rest of the summer. On 15 September, *tanks made their first-ever appearance in war, supporting the attack on Flers-Courcelette. This led to the capture of High Wood, and the break-in to the German third line. While 1 July did not bring the breakthrough expected by Haig, by November he could claim a victory, though only in attritional terms. Territory had been taken, and the Germans pushed back and badly mauled: one officer called the Somme 'the muddy grave of the German field army'. That eleven French divisions also fought on the Somme between July and November is often overlooked, along with the 200,000 casualties they sustained.

The battle remains deeply controversial. Paddy Griffith emphasizes that the British army that emerged from it was a better-trained instrument of war than that which entered it, and John Terraine points out that the 'true texture of the Somme' included failed German counter-attacks as much as failed British attacks. However, it is impossible to exonerate Haig and Rawlinson from having fundamentally different conceptions of the battle: the latter had initially advocated modest 'bite and hold' tactics, and had little real confidence in the breakthrough he was bidden to achieve. There was also a distressing lack of grip by Fourth Army for much of the battle, when the same objectives were repeatedly attacked, with too little originality, behind too light a barrage. In principle Haig had no alternative but to fight on the Somme; but in practice it was not a well-handled battle.

APC-A/RH

Brown, Malcolm, *The Imperial War Museum Book of the Somme* (London, 1996).

Griffith, Paddy, *Battle Tactics of the Western Front: The British Army's Art of Attack 1916–1918* (London, 1994).

Middlebrook, Martin, *The First Day on the Somme* (London, 1971).

Prior, Robin, and Wilson, Trevor, *Command on the Western Front* (Oxford, 1992).

Terraine, John, *The Smoke and the Fire* (London, 1980).

Soubise, Marshal C. de Rohan, Prince de (1715–87).

The unfortunate Soubise was more of a courtier than a general, and his talents lay in the salon rather than on the field of battle. A protégé of Louis XV's favourite, Madame de Pompadour, he was appointed to command an army—part of the Franco-imperial Reichsarmee with D'Estrées in the spring of 1757. D'Estrées had no time for the prince and refused to discuss military affairs with him. Ignored by the war ministry, despite repeated requests for troops and supplies, Soubise's army was in pitiful shape by the time it encountered the Prussian soldier automatons at *Rossbach. The numerically superior Franco-imperial army was utterly routed, and scurrilous ditties did the rounds at the court of Versailles:

I've lost my army—wherever can it be—oh thank goodness!
I see it coming towards me—horrors! It's the enemy!

The courtiers also joked that Soubise had let his home while he attended military school as a cadet, and that he would build a new house from the stones thrown at him by the Paris mob. To be fair, Soubise had shown personal bravery during the battle and could not really be held to blame for the misfortunes of his shambling army, its soldiers memorably summarized by Christopher Duffy as 'decent, sleepy, and peaceable'. His reputation was protected by La Pompadour, who engineered his rehabilitation at court. Soubise went on to win two victories in Germany, with the very competent Chevert, at Sandershausen and Lutzelberg in 1758.

TM/RH

Soult, Marshal Nicholas Jean de Dieu (1769–1851).

Soult was born into a merchant family in the south of France and grew up a stocky and hardy young man, enlisting in the army in 1785 to help the family out of poverty after the death of his father. He left the army during the Revolution and attempted to start a bakery, but the hard work did not agree with him, and he returned to his regiment in 1791 as a corporal. He then rose swiftly through the ranks establishing his reputation as a first-class battalion officer with the Army of the Moselle in 1793 and 1794, transferring to the experienced Army of the Sambre et Meuse, where he served until 1799. Soult by now had gained exceptional combat experience with France's crack formations and commanders, notably André *Masséna, under whom he served in the Zurich campaign of 1799.

A wound received during the subsequent Italian campaign prevented him from being present at Marengo, and left him with a permanent limp. Promoted marshal in 1804, he commanded IV Corps for the *Austerlitz campaign, where he took the commanding Pratzen heights, securing victory for Napoleon. He was present at *Eylau in 1807, but his command was too shattered to take part at Friedland. His exploits earned him the title of duke of Dalmatia (to be corrupted to 'Damnation' by British troops) and great personal wealth was bestowed on him by the emperor.

In 1808 he was posted to Spain, and drove *Moore's army to *Corunna in January 1809. However, it escaped by sea, having buried its beloved commander on the ramparts of the town. In March of the same year he led the invasion of Portugal and captured Oporto, but proved unable to go on and take Lisbon. Soult then went on to set up a French protectorate in northern Portugal and was suspected of setting up a private kingdom, a charge that was also levelled against him during his governorship of Andalusia from 1810–12.

Recalled by Napoleon for the 1813 campaign, he fought with valour and distinction at Lützen and Bautzen, but was urgently sent to Spain to pick up the pieces after Joseph's defeat at Vitoria. He fought a masterful defensive action in the Pyrenees, but it was only delaying the inevitable. Napoleon persuaded Soult to join him as COS for the *Hundred Days campaign of 1815, but he was no *Berthier. He warned Napoleon that Wellington was a dangerous opponent, but the emperor pooh-poohed him, and despite the defeat of the French army Soult stayed loyal until the final moments. He lived in exile in the Rhineland after Waterloo, and was rehabilitated in 1830, becoming minister of war in 1832 and the author of the major military service law, the Loi Soult, which influenced the *French army, for the next 40 years. He was appointed marshal-general in 1847, a title only awarded thrice before—and never again.   TM/RH

SP gun. See SELF-PROPELLED GUN.

space, military implications of Throughout history, one of the most important terrain types to occupy in battle was high ground of some sort, be it a hill or a ridge line. In the 20th century, the new 'high ground' is space, and since the end of WW II, the race has been on to exploit this new medium for military advantage.

On 3 October 1942 Nazi scientists launched an A-4 rocket that travelled a distance of 118 miles (190 km) and reached an altitude of 50 miles (80 km). But it was not until the 1950s that the true potential of space began to dawn on both the politicians and the military. On 4 October 1957 the West was stunned to learn that the USSR had placed an artificial satellite (Sputnik-1) in orbit around the Earth, and that the object weighed 183 pounds (83 kg), dwarfing the 20 pound (9 kg) package that the US navy was planning to send up on its Vanguard rocket. A double blow ensued with the launch of Sputnik-2, which carried into orbit a dog called Laika, on 3 November 1957 and weighed 1,120 pounds (508 kg).

The American space race started with the launch of the small 10½ pound (4.8 kg) Explorer-1, on a Jupiter rocket on 30 January 1958, discovering the Van Allen radiation belts. This was followed up by the launch of SCORE (Signal Communication by Orbiting Relay Equipment) on an Atlas rocket on 18 December 1958 (it carried a taped Christmas greeting from Pres *Eisenhower) and Discoverer-1 on 28 February 1959, not from Cape Canaveral, but from Vandenberg Air Force Base.

The 1960s saw an intensification of the space race, as both sides by now realized its potential. While the USA had some notable achievements such as having the first *reconnaissance, meteorological, communications, and navigation satellites, the Soviets had even greater successes with the first manned space capsule in orbit (Yuri Gagarin in Vostok-1 on 12 April 1961), as well as the first space walk by Alexei Leonov, from Voskhod-1, in March 1965. The fact that the Soviets seemed to be ahead dented American pride, and was also a cause for concern since it also implied a lead in heavy missile capability as many rockets were modified ICBMs and could therefore be used to strike targets anywhere on the globe. John F. Kennedy stated in October 1960 while running for the presidency: 'Control of space will be decided in the next decade. If the Soviets control space they can control Earth, as in the past centuries the nations that controlled the seas dominated the continents.' As its Gemini and then Apollo programmes progressed, the USA began to rehearse the techniques and test the equipment with which it would send a manned vehicle to the moon. Finally, on 21 July 1969, Neil Armstrong became the first man to set foot on the moon.

During the 1960s and 1970s the number of launches per year by both sides increased to a peak of 55 for the USA and 66 for the USSR, and then gradually tailed off, as satellites became more reliable and had longer endurance. Both countries continued sending probes out to the far reaches of the solar system; both started to develop a manned space station programme (Skylab and Salyut) and look at the possibility of a lifter that could be reused time and time again. This culminated in the launch of the US Space Shuttle on 12 April 1981. The space shuttle rode into orbit on booster rockets and then re-entered the Earth's atmosphere to land like a conventional aircraft.

The main military use of space has been to field increasingly sophisticated satellite systems to support operations on Earth. In many ways, satellite-based systems have superseded their ground-based counterparts, causing these other systems to atrophy. This is because space-based systems can accomplish the mission in a superior manner and are more economical. Indeed, the *Gulf war, which could be seen as the first 'space war', confirmed that space-based technology gave the western powers a substantial force multiplier. Military activity is now almost unthinkable without the exploitation of space-based systems for surveillance, navigation, and targeting.

Orbital dynamics depends upon gravity, and so Newton's Law of Universal Gravitation comes into play. In simple terms, the force of gravity affecting an object is proportional to how far away it is. To stay in a circular orbit, the speed a satellite needs to reach depends upon its distance from the Earth. The lowest orbits require a velocity of 5 miles/sec (8 km/sec) while that of 60 Earth radii (the distance of the moon) would only require a velocity of 0.6 miles/sec (1 km/sec). Alternatively, the satellite could be launched into an elliptical orbit, with the closest point to the Earth known as the perigee, and the furthest, the apogee. Both types of orbits have to operate under Kepler's laws of orbital motion. The first law states that the orbit of a satellite is an ellipse, and that one of the foci of the ellipse must be located at the centre of the Earth. The second of Kepler's laws states that a satellite in orbit will have an imaginary line joining it to the centre of the Earth that sweeps equal areas in equal time. The satellite will thus be altering its speed at different times in its orbit and will have a maximum speed at perigee and minimum at apogee. Of course, all would be fine if the Earth was a perfect sphere, but it is in fact a slightly flattened sphere. This introduces complications in determining the best orbit for a satellite.

Space-based assets are not available to all countries, and are not evenly spread among those who have them. Space technologies are complex and well beyond the budget of most countries, in that developing a reasonable military communications satellite system could cost in the region of £1 billion. In the era of shrinking budgets, space systems have to compete with front-line equipment, research and development, and personnel costs. The two superpowers are the only two that acquired the full range of space capabilities (and Russia still matches the USA for this). There are a number of distinct uses that satellites can be put to. Communication satellites provide tactical and strategic real-time communications with forces around the world, and as sensors and weapon-system ranges increase so this importance will continue to grow. In fact, over 70 per cent of America's overseas military communications is relayed by satellite. The main systems in this area are the USA's Defense Satellite Communications System; US air force and navy's AFSATCOM and FLTSATCOM and the Satellite Data System; the Soviet Molniya ('Lightning'), and Volna ('Wave') systems; and Britain's Skynet (Skynet 1, being the first geostationary military communications satellite, launched in November 1969). Most communications satellites use 'geostationary' orbits which entail a highly elliptical orbit, and involve an apogee of 22,370 miles (36,000 km) which is approximately six Earth radii. At this distance, the satellite appears to stay in the same position when viewed from Earth. These systems use a variety of frequency bands, UHF (300 MHz–3 GHz), SHF (3–30 GHz), and EHF (30–300 GHz), each of which has certain advantages and disadvantages. Reconnaissance satellites cover the areas of photo-reconnaissance, ocean reconnaissance, and *SIGINT. Photo-reconnaissance satellites cover much of the electromagnetic spectrum (*infra-red, ultra-violet, *radio, *radar, and visible light) and the resolution that these satellites are capable of is the most important feature, and one that has been improving constantly. SIGINT satellites are known as 'ferrets' and try to locate radio transmitters, eavesdrop on radio communications, and monitor telemetry from missile tests. The best-known systems are the USA's Keyhole and 'Bigbird' satellites and the Soviet Kosmos system.

Weather satellites carry a battery of sensors to record atmospheric conditions, including a line-scanning radiometer (which records visual and infra-red imagery), infra-red temperature-moisture and microwave sounders (to measure precipitation), a precipitating electron spectrometer (for forecasting the location and intensity of the aurora borealis), and an ionosphere sounder (to measure the electron distribution in the upper atmosphere). Early warning satellites include those designed for the early detection of ballistic missile launches and those that detect nuclear explosions. They tend to have focal-plane array telescopes with infra-red sensors to detect the heat exhaust of a missile, or atmospheric burst sensors which detect the visible light, x-ray, and electromagnetic pulse emissions of a nuclear explosion. The USA operates these systems on the DSP (Defense Support Program) satellites in geosynchronous orbit and the new Navstar navigation satellites, while the Russians have a constellation of nine satellites in a highly elliptical orbit inclined 63 degrees to the equator. Finally, navigation satellites have been in use since the early 1960s, initially for warships and submarines (the American systems known as Transit and Nova, while the Soviets used Navsat). The early satellite systems have been superseded, however, by a new generation (Navstar GPS and Glonass) which travel in circular semi-synchronous orbit, in six groups of four, each in a different plane with an inclination of 55 degrees. The Global Positioning System (GPS) made possible the large-scale desert movements of the Gulf war; in an earlier era, they would just have got lost. GPS has also made possible GPS-guided bombs, which navigate themselves to the desired point in three dimensions without the need for an external guidance source such as a laser, and are thus effective in all weathers.

As satellites have proved to be indispensable for the military in operations on Earth, it is very probable that these very satellites may start to be targeted by adversaries who wish to degrade the 'force multiplier' available to those forces that have them. This can be done by what is known as 'cyber warfare'; that is, attacking the software in the computer systems that control the satellite itself, or those on the ground that rely on them, or by a physical assault on the satellites themselves, by ASAT (anti-satellite) weapons. Although ASAT weapons were first researched in the late 1950s and 1960s, neither side has been keen to really fund an extensive ASAT programme, probably as a result of budgetary pressures and the fear of opening up another strand in the arms race. As such, these weapons could be projectile or kinetic-kill weapons (such as an electromagnetic rail gun), lasers (such as the chemical, excimer, free electron, or x-ray types), particle beam weapons, or conventional missiles. They could either be based on Earth or launched into orbit, but some weapon types are more suitable to Earth- or orbit-based deployment than others. Alternatively, such weapons could be used for other purposes, such as a ballistic missile defence, as was the hope of Ronald Reagan's *SDI or 'Star wars'. Finally, although satellites can be thought of as relatively vulnerable (being fragile and packed with sensitive electronics), they are small, at great distances from the Earth, and travelling at high speed, and there are a great number of them to keep a track of. PDA

Dutton, Lyn, et al., *Military Space* (London, 1990).

Hayward, Keith, *British Military Space Programmes* (London, 1996).

Hobbs, David, *An Illustrated Guide to Space Warfare* (London, 1987).

Kirby, Stephen, and Robson, Gordon, *The Militarisation of Space* (Brighton, 1987).

Peebles, Curtis, *Battle for Space* (Poole, 1983).

Stares, Paul B., *Space and National Security* (Washington, 1987).

spahis were native cavalry raised by the French in North Africa. The term derives from the Turkish *sipahi* (soldier), also the root of sepoy, the word used by Europeans for native Indian soldiers. Spahis were raised in *Algeria during the French conquest, and were subsequently recruited in *Tunisia and *Morocco as well. Officers and NCOs were both French and North African, and troopers largely native. The spahis tended to attract Arabs of good family, and French ability to offer commissions to the sons of local magnates played a useful part in the pacification of Algeria. Their counterparts were the Chasseurs d'Afrique, raised from the white settler population.

Although the spahis did not fight in the *Franco-Prussian war, a provisional regiment of Algerian light cavalry, which was sent to France, included many spahis. The spahis had a distinguished record in both world wars, first as cavalry and latterly as armour. A spahi mounted brigade's defence of the village of La Horgne against German tanks in May 1940 was a remarkable, though unavailing, feat of arms.

The spahis were perhaps the most colourful of France's North African units, wearing a red and white burnous and riding little barb stallions with traditional North African horse furniture. The name and traditions of the spahis have been preserved in a French armoured regiment. RH

Spanish-American war (1898), imperialist conflict in which the USA extended its formal authority over the Caribbean and across the Pacific, achieved on the back of long-standing insurgencies in Cuba and the Philippines, which traduced America's self-image and created many future complications. The American establishment wanted to establish American hegemony and to acquire naval bases in both places, but President McKinley shrank from embarking upon the necessary war. It was forced upon him by popular clamour whipped up by the yellow press and by Spanish intransigence.

American public opinion strongly sympathized with the nationalist *guerrillas in Cuba, particularly after the Span-

ish military governor introduced a system of *concentration camps (the origin of the term) in which as many as 100,000 died. The flashpoint was the publication on 9 February 1898 of a dispatch by the Spanish ambassador in Washington, purloined by a Cuban revolutionary sympathizer, which spoke contemptuously of McKinley, followed six days later by the sinking of the battleship *Maine* in Havana harbour. Post-war investigation showed that it sank from an internal explosion, but at the time an American court of enquiry blamed it on a mine. Popular agitation led to a US ultimatum and Spain declared war on 23 April.

Already possessed of a two-to-one advantage in warship tonnage, the US navy spent over $30 million acquiring 131 new vessels and doubling its manpower between March and August. By contrast, the Spanish possessed neither the means to add significantly to their fleet, nor the diplomatic clout to obtain coal in foreign ports for the ships they had. Their armoured cruisers were designed as ocean-going raiders and certainly not to engage their heavier armoured and gunned American counterparts, built for coastal defence. They were to be sacrificed by the Madrid government, which incorrectly calculated that it could survive a heroic defeat.

In a classic demonstration of 'mission creep', Commodore Dewey of the Pacific squadron based in Hong Kong set out to neutralize the obsolete Spanish naval presence in Manila and ended by adding the Philippines to the US empire. In a one-way battle during the morning of 1 May, he sank or disabled the outgunned enemy squadron at Cavite. The Spanish admiral could have run to maintain some kind of 'fleet in being', or he could have anchored under the heavy guns of nearby Manila. He chose instead to bring about 'heroic defeat' sooner rather than later.

There were about 26,000 Spanish regulars and 15,000 local militia facing about 30,000 insurgents throughout the archipelago. With the exception of the 12,000 Manila garrison, the rest soon fell to the insurgents. That this was due mainly to Spanish defeatism is illustrated by the tiny outpost at Baler, which held out beyond the end of the war to June 1899. Once 11,000 American ground forces had landed, Manila surrendered on 13 August after symbolic resistance. By conspiring with the Spanish governor to bring this about while excluding the rebels, who had done most of the fighting, the American military commanders set in motion the second *Philippines insurrection.

There were 70,000 Spanish 'effectives' in Cuba (27,000 more were in hospital) with perhaps 30,000 local militia. These were also scattered around the island and, as in the Philippines, pressure from the insurgents made concentration of forces impossible. Havana was strongly held, but the poorly provisioned garrison at Santiago numbered less than 12,000. What made it the prize of the campaign was the arrival there on 19 May of the Spanish Atlantic squadron under Cervera, who believed he had nowhere else to go. This was fortunate, because it took the blockading fleet under Sampson ten days to locate him. An unsuccessful attempt was made to sink a blockship in the narrow mouth of the harbour on 3 June, and US Marines seized Guantánamo Bay to provide a sheltered anchorage in mid-month, but a decision awaited the arrival of the expeditionary force under Shafter.

After a rushed and chaotic embarkation at Tampa, followed by landings on open beaches at Daiquirí and Siboney, where it proved impossible to bring heavy equipment ashore, some 17,000 US troops were available for the battles around Santiago. Much of the fighting was done by a spearhead formed by highly motivated dragoon units, including the *African-American troops of the 9th and 10th regiments and the 'Rough Riders', the 1st USA Volunteer Cavalry, at Las Guásimas on 24 June and at El Caney, Kettle Hill, and neighbouring San Juan Hill on 1 July. Shafter failed to follow up, but the positions won were sufficiently menacing to force Cervera to steam out of Santiago harbour to annihilation on 3 July.

Pausing to satisfy 'honour' and to obtain repatriation at American expense, the Spanish commander surrendered the whole province and 23,000 men on 17 July at a ceremony from which the leader of the Cuban insurgents, hitherto working in close concert with the Americans, was excluded. Further operations in Cuba and those of army commander Miles in Puerto Rico ended with the suspension of hostilities on 12 August. By the Treaty of Paris, the USA annexed Puerto Rico, Guam, and the Philippines, paying $20 million compensation for the latter, and Cuba exchanged Spanish rule for an independence subject to US intervention.

In a war that ended in bitter mutual recrimination among American commanders ashore and afloat, the popular hero was the Rough Riders' dynamic Theodore *Roosevelt, who had already played a significant role in the mobilization as assistant secretary of the navy. He led on horseback up much of Kettle Hill and culminated a day of outstanding temerity by charging from there to take San Juan Hill.

It was to be called 'a splendid little war', and while the first adjective is debatable, there can be no argument about the second. US combat casualties were 385 dead (2,061 more by disease) and 1,662 wounded. While the financial cost was considerably higher than the *Mexican war 50 years earlier, it was greatly inflated by the crash naval expansion and the enrolment of 308,000 men, most of whom never left training camp.   HEB

Trask, David, *The War with Spain in 1898* (New York, 1981).

Spanish Armada The voyage of the *Gran Armada* in the summer of 1588 is the subject of controversy on both the strategic and tactical levels. The Spanish plan, devised largely by Philip II himself between 1586 and 1588, involved an *amphibious operation in which a fleet from Spain commanded by Medina Sidonia would occupy the anchorage in the Downs off the Kentish coast and protect a landing by an expeditionary force from the army of Flanders under *Parma. The English, faced with a number of potential invasion sites, adopted a counter-strategy of intercepting the Armada in Iberian waters, but several attempts to do so between May and July 1588 were driven back by storms. Later in July the Armada (122 ships) sailed past the English fleet (66 ships) replenishing in Plymouth harbour. The running battle up the Channel was inconclusive (two Spanish ships lost through accident) and only the English fireship attack on the Armada's anchorage off Calais broke the stalemate. The Armada lost four important warships at this point, but the rest had to cut their cables and the prevailing wind drove them into the North Sea. They were then obliged to sail around the British Isles to return home, at the cost of 35 of the weaker ships.

The 1588 campaign was a major English propaganda victory, but in strategic terms it was essentially indecisive.
SA

Martin, Colin, and Parker, Geoffrey, *The Spanish Armada* (London, 1988).
Rodger, N. A. M., *The Safeguard of the Sea: A Naval History of Britain*, vol. 1, *660–1649* (London, 1997).
Rodríguez-Salgado, M. J., and Adams, Simon (eds.), *England, Spain and the Gran Armada 1585–1604* (Edinburgh, 1991).

Spanish civil war (1936–9), conflict precipitated by a failed military *coup d'état* in July 1936, itself provoked by violent social and anticlerical disorders following the election of a Popular Front government. It became a protracted struggle between two uneasy alliances of traditionalist and fascist 'Nationalists' and the socialists, communists, Trotskyites, anarchists, and separatists known as 'Republicans'.

The Nationalists were assisted by some 60,000 Italian, 20,000 Portuguese, and 15,000 German 'volunteers' sent by their governments, plus about 2,000 French monarchists and Irish Catholics. They were further aided by an effectively one-sided Anglo-French-American policy of non-intervention. The Republican cause attracted 40,000 international volunteers in all: 15,000 French, 5,000 German, 4,000 Italian, 3,000 US, 2,000 British, and 1,000 each from Canada, Yugoslavia, Hungary, and Scandinavia. The Soviets, who acquired disproportionate political influence as well as Spain's gold reserves, were seldom more than 500 at any time. Although they provided many senior officers and much of the Republic's air, armour, and artillery, their contribution was curtailed in 1937 when *Stalin recalled all his Comintern agents and most of his army officers and executed them as part of the great purge.

Although long portrayed as a dress rehearsal for WW II, it is best understood as a uniquely Spanish phenomenon, fought mainly by Spaniards in their own archaic military tradition and for very idiosyncratic reasons. With the exception of some experiments by the German Condor

Legion in close support of infantry operations by fighter aircraft, the conflict cannot be seen as a proving ground for WW II tactics. The Republican cause attracted intellectuals from all over the world, whose idealized view of the conflict did not survive exposure to its realities. Like other 'lost causes,' an oversimplified myth has tended to obscure the less black-and-white history.

The rebels included virtually the whole regular army officer corps and the long-service Army of Africa, plus the bulk of the rural paramilitary Guardias Civil. These were soon joined by the well-trained Navarrese *Carlists and a larger number of fascist Falangist (political movement) volunteers. The Republic retained the support of most of the urban paramilitary Guardias Asalto and of variously armed and organized trades unions and revolutionary groups. It was the latter, in the face of the government's timid refusal to summon a *levée en masse* or to release arms to the spontaneous popular uprising against the coup, which provided the necessary leadership to thwart barracks revolts in Barcelona, Valencia, and Madrid, while closely besieging Nationalist garrisons in Oviedo and the *alcazar of Toledo.

Once the coup failed, political leadership became decisive. The early deaths of possible rivals, including the Falange's charismatic founder José Antonio *Primo de Rivera, left *Franco unchallenged and he maintained unity of purpose on his side, including the Italians and Germans despite their impatience at his deliberate generalship. By contrast, Republican leadership was divided and rancorous, unable to command respect at home or abroad. The Basque provinces and Catalonia had their own separatist agendas while the rival leftist parties fought ferocious internal civil wars.

The Nationalists quickly gained control of a northern swathe encompassing all of Galicia and Navarre, most of León and Old Castile and half of Aragon and Extremadura. They established their capital at Burgos and their first attempt to advance on that front towards Madrid was halted in the first major battle of the war in the Guadarrama mountains. In the south, Seville, Cordoba, and Granada were seized and soon consolidated by the vanguard of the Army of Africa, airlifted by German transports. While half remained to garrison Morocco, the rest followed by ship under Italian fighter cover. After an early Republican counter-attack towards Cordoba was defeated and a coastal strip around Malaga was eliminated by Italian armoured troops in January 1937, the southern front became a backwater for the duration.

In the centre, the *Spanish Foreign Legion spearheaded a Nationalist advance from Seville into Extremadura marked by characteristic atrocities. It then relieved the alcazar of Toledo and pushed on towards the capital, being stopped inside the city limits by militia and a small Soviet armoured unit. Although the defence of Madrid captured the imagination of sympathizers all over the world, the Republican government set a lamentable example by fleeing to Valencia. During the 1936/7 winter a Nationalist attempt to sever Madrid's communications with the Guadarramas failed and in February the newly formed International Brigades checked the Army of Africa in the Jarama mountains. In March an Italian armoured division, rendered overconfident by success against light opposition and on more suitable terrain around Malaga the year before, was humiliatingly repulsed near Guadalajara. In July the Republicans launched a bloodily unsuccessful counter-offensive at Brunete, but thereafter a vicious stalemate prevailed around Madrid.

In the north, the Nationalists under Mola advanced from Navarre to close the Basque provinces' French border in August–September 1936. Oviedo was relieved in October, many of the dynamite-throwing Asturian miners having gone to defend Madrid. Starting in late March 1937, Mola again attacked the Basque provinces from the east and Bilbao fell to his ponderous advance in mid-June. Santander fell in August and the conquest of Asturias was completed in October.

In the east, the revolutionary armies of Barcelona twice launched broad offensives in Aragon, but the Nationalists held the major towns, including a vulnerable salient at Teruél where savage fighting took place during the winter of 1937/8. Starting in March the Nationalists counterattacked with heavy artillery preparation followed by short infantry advances across northern Valencia, severing the land-link with Catalonia in mid-July. Republican strength was shattered in a desperate battle on the Ebro in July–October and Catalonia collapsed early the following year. The Republican rump, torn by another internal civil war, fell to Nationalist advances from all sides in March.

The Nationalists had about 600,000 under arms to the Republicans' 450,000. They lost 110,000 and 175,000 respectively in battle, but 80,000 Nationalist sympathizers were caught on the wrong side of the lines and executed, while 40,000 Republicans were also executed during and after the war.   HEB

Spanish Foreign Legion (Sp.: Tercios de extranjeros). Despite the name, a primarily Spanish unit founded in 1920 for service in Morocco by Lt Col Millán Astray, after an attachment to the *French Foreign Legion. His greeting to the first *bandera* (regiment) was ominous: 'There is nothing finer than to die with honour for the glory of Spain, as you will soon learn.' The Legion's signature war cries became: '¡Abajo la inteligencia!' (Down with intelligence!) and '¡Viva la muerte!' (Long live death!).

Maj *Franco was put in charge of the new depot at Dar Riffien outside Ceuta, soon known as the best in the army. The Rif war exploded when Abd el-Krim directed the 1921 massacre of thousands of Spanish soldiers retreating from Anual, reducing Spanish control in eastern Morocco to a small garrison at Melilla. Rushed there, the Legion mounted

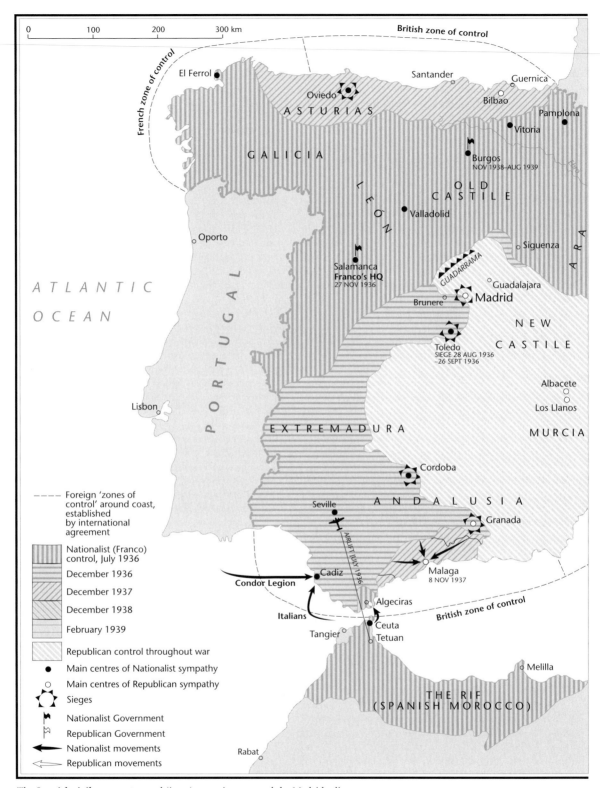

The **Spanish civil war**, 1936–9, and (inset) operations around the Madrid salient.

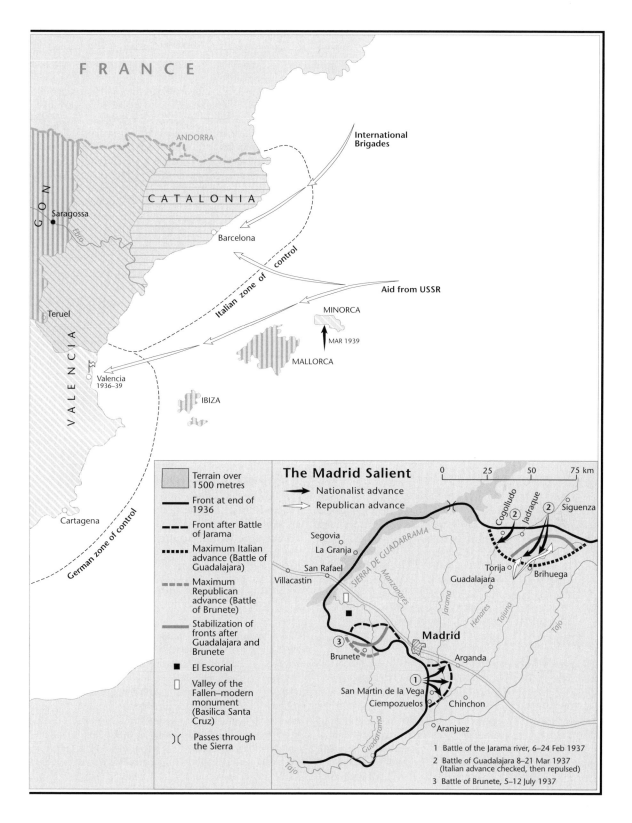

FRANCE

ANDORRA

CATALONIA

Saragossa

GON

Ebro

Barcelona

International
Brigades

Italian zone of control

Aid from USSR

Teruel

MINORCA

MAR 1939

VALENCIA

MALLORCA

Valencia
1936–39

IBIZA

Cartagena

German zone of control

Terrain over
1500 metres

Front at end of
1936

Front after Battle
of Jarama

Maximum Italian
advance (Battle
of Guadalajara)

Maximum
Republican
advance (Battle
of Brunete)

Stabilization of
fronts after
Guadalajara and
Brunete

El Escorial

Valley of the
Fallen–modern
monument
(Basilica Santa
Cruz)

)(Passes through
the Sierra

The Madrid Salient

➤ Nationalist advance

⇨ Republican advance

0   25   50   75 km

Segovia

La Granja

San Rafael

Villacastin

SIERRA DE GUADARRAMA

Manzanares

Cogolludo

Jadraque

②

②

Siguenza

Torija

Guadalajara

Brihuega

Madrid

Jarama

Henares

Tajuna

Tajo

③

Brunete

Arganda

①

San Martin de la Vega

Ciempozuelos

Chinchon

Aranjuez

Guadarrama

Tajo

1 Battle of the Jarama river, 6–24 Feb 1937

2 Battle of Guadalajara 8–21 Mar 1937
(Italian advance checked, then repulsed)

3 Battle of Brunete, 5–12 July 1937

the first of many punitive forays. During the 1924 retreat from Chaouen to Tétouan in west Morocco, a disaster even greater than Anual, it fought a month-long rearguard action under Franco.

In a combined operation with a French offensive from the south, Spanish and Moroccan troops led by Franco and the Legion landed at Alhucemas in September 1925 and fought their way to the rebel capital of Axdir, which they destroyed. Abd el-Krim surrendered to the French in 1926, Franco was made brigadier general, and the much-wounded and now one-armed Col Millán Astray resumed command, only to be shot through the face with the loss of an eye in March. The following year he was promoted away from the Legion (although remaining honorary colonel for life), having led it in 62 of 845 engagements in which it suffered over 2,000 dead, 6,100 wounded, and only 285 missing. By contrast, desertion to the enemy from its French equivalent was notorious.

The Legion and the Moroccans, collectively the Army of Africa, added to their fearsome reputation by the ruthless suppression of the Asturian miners' revolt in 1934, again under the direction of Franco. At the start of the *Spanish civil war they were the only combat-tested regulars in a short-service conscript army. Under Yagüe, the Legion secured Morocco before flying to the mainland in the first airlift in history. Less publicized than the Republic's International Brigades, a significant number of foreign volunteers were incorporated into the Legion. Most were Italian Black Shirts under their own officers, but French monarchist volunteers formed their own Joan of Arc *bandera*. Used as shock troops throughout, the Legion suffered over 37,000 casualties.

After the war, it returned to Spanish Morocco, its last major battle honour being won at Ifni against the Sahara Liberation Army after Moroccan independence in 1956. Post-Franco and after Spanish Sahara was relinquished in 1976, it survived calls for disbandment and its three *tercios evoked Spanish imperial grandeur at her vestigial overseas outposts, 'Gran Capitán' (*Córdoba) at Melilla, 'Duque de *Alba' at Ceuta, and the rapid reaction 'Don Juan de Austria' at Fuerteventura in the Canary Islands.   HEB

Scurr, John, *The Spanish Foreign Legion* (London, 1985).

Spanish Succession, War of the (1701–14). While the Treaty of Ryswick may have ended the *League of Augsburg war in 1697, it did nothing to alter the underlying tensions within the European balance of power. The war had demonstrated that France under *Louis XIV could only be contained by the strenuous efforts of the remaining European powers. Thus anything that could extend the strength of France even further was resisted by the other powers of Europe, especially Louis's great rivals, *William of Orange and the Habsburg Holy Roman Emperor Leopold I. Thus, when Louis claimed the crown of Spain in the name of his grandson, Philip, Duke of Anjou, France was met by a revived Grand Alliance of powers who objected to a Bourbon reigning in Madrid.

Louis's moves to create a Bourbon Spain had begun as far back as 1659, when he agreed to marry King Philip IV of Spain's eldest daughter, Maria Teresa. By the terms of the marriage contract, both Louis and Maria Teresa renounced any claims upon the Spanish crown in return for a considerable dowry. However, Louis used the fact that the Spanish never paid the promised dowry in full as a pretext to declare the agreement void. When Charles II acceded to the throne of Spain, Louis had to put off his goal of unifying the two crowns temporarily. Louis kept up his diplomatic pressure and by 1700 had convinced the Spanish that a French candidate should follow Charles upon his death. Accordingly, when Charles died on 1 November 1700, Louis's grandson, Philip IV's great-grandson, was proclaimed Philip V, King of Spain.

On 7 September 1701, another Grand Alliance against Louis was formally brought into being, consisting of the Habsburg Empire, England, the Netherlands, Brandenburg-Prussia, and most of the other German states. Louis could count on the support of Savoy, Mantua, Cologne, and Bavaria, in addition, of course, to Spain.

Upon the crowning of Philip, Louis marched his troops into the Spanish Netherlands, the prize for which he had fought so long, and provoked the Habsburg empire to declare war. The first moves of what would again be a multi-front war were taken in Italy, as Louis sent an army under the command of Catinat to occupy Rivoli. The French intention was to prevent the Austrian army of Prince *Eugène of Savoy from entering Italy. However, the extremely capable Eugène was able to outmanoeuvre Catinat, in part by violating Venetian neutrality, and his arrival in Vicenza on 28 May 1701 forced the French to withdraw westwards. Through the spring and summer, Eugène, although outnumbered, continued to outmanoeuvre Catinat in Lombardy, forcing the French to withdraw to the Oglio and abandon a third of their territory in Italy. Louis replaced Catinat with Villeroi, who in turn was captured by an Austrian raid at Cremona on 1 February 1702 and replaced by *Vendôme.

The remainder of the campaign in Italy is an excellent example of the manoeuvring that dominated much of early 18th-century warfare. Tied to lines of supply and unwilling to risk their expensive armies in combat, both Vendôme and Eugène went to great lengths to avoid battle. Instead, the war in Italy consisted mainly of attempts to cut the enemy off from his supplies and to occupy and exploit as much of the enemy's territory as possible. Operations there, however, had an impact on the war as a whole. The Habsburg successes caused the Duke of Savoy to abandon his alliance with France and join the Grand Alliance in 1703. Further, the campaigns in Italy tied down French troops that were needed elsewhere.

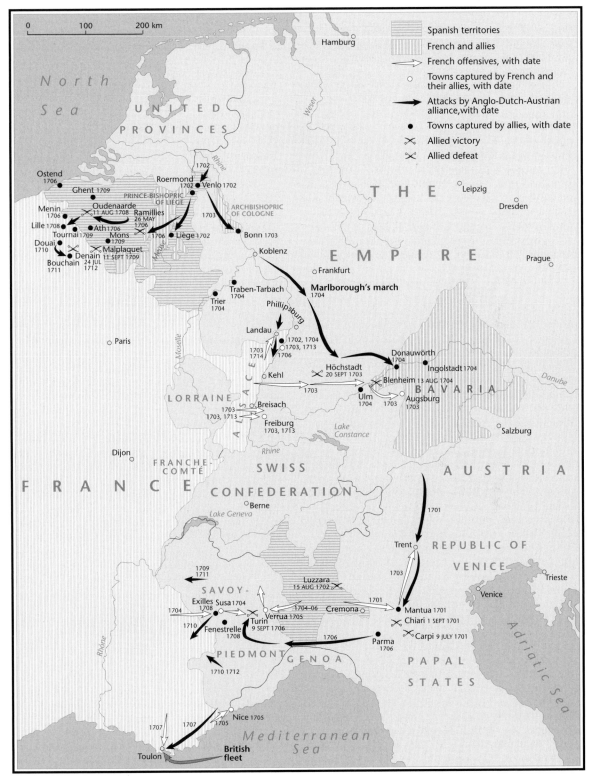

North
Sea

UNITED

PROVINCES

Hamburg

Leipzig

Dresden

THE

Spanish territories

French and allies

French offensives, with date

Towns captured by French and
their allies, with date

Attacks by Anglo-Dutch-Austrian
alliance, with date

Towns captured by allies, with date

Allied victory

Allied defeat

Ostend
1706

Ghent 1709

PRINCE-BISHOPRIC
OF LIEGE

Menin
1706

Oudenaarde
11 AUG 1708

Ramillies
26 MAY
1706

Lille 1708

Ath 1706

Tournai 1709

Mons
1709

1706 ● Liège 1702

Bonn 1703

ARCHBISHOPRIC
OF COLOGNE

Roermond
1702 ● Venlo 1702

1702

Rhine

Weser

Douai
1710

Malplaquet
11 SEPT 1709

Denain
24 JUL
1712

Bouchain
1711

Koblenz

EMPIRE

Prague

Frankfurt

Traben-Tarbach
1704

Trier
1704

Phillipsburg

Marlborough's march
1704

Paris

Landau

1702, 1704

1703, 1713
1706

1703
1714

Donauwörth
1704

Ingolstadt 1704

Höchstadt
20 SEPT 1703

Blenheim 13 AUG 1704

Danube

Kehl

1703

BAVARIA

LORRAINE

Breisach

1703
1703, 1713

Freiburg
1703, 1713

Ulm
1704

Augsburg
1703

1703

Salzburg

Lake
Constance

Rhine

Dijon

FRANCHE-
COMTÉ

SWISS

CONFEDERATION

Berne

Lake Geneva

AUSTRIA

1701

Trent

REPUBLIC OF

VENICE

Trieste

1703

Venice

1709
1711

SAVOY-

Luzzara
15 AUG 1702

Exilles
1708

Susa 1704

1704

Verrua 1705

1704-06 Cremona

1701

Mantua 1701

Chiari 1 SEPT 1701

Adriatic
Sea

1710

Turin
9 SEPT 1706

Fenestrelle
1708

1706

Parma
1706

Carpi 9 JULY 1701

PIEDMONT GENOA

PAPAL

Rhone

1710 1712

STATES

1707

1707

1705

Nice 1705

Toulon

British
fleet

Mediterranean
Sea

0   100   200 km

The war of the **Spanish Succession,** 1701–14.

The main theatres during the long war consisted of the Low Countries and Germany. In contrast to the war in Italy and the previous League of Augsburg war, the conflict in these theatres saw the armies increasingly being employed aggressively, resulting in a greater number of large-scale battles. However, the armies of this war were still constrained by the same limitations that had plagued those of the previous war, the most important of which was the continued dependence on *magazines. Consequently, these large-scale battles generally had only local, temporary results.

The Alliance began the war aggressively in 1702. In July, the Austrians invaded Alsace with an army under the direction of Prince Louis, Margrave of Baden. While this army threatened Alsace, an Anglo-Dutch force under the command of John Churchill, then only the Earl of *Marlborough, captured the French fortresses along the Meuse river between 15 September and 15 October (for which he was created a duke).

However, French diplomacy scored a notable success which helped negate the Alliance successes. In September, Louis concluded an alliance with Bavaria, who declared war on the Habsburg empire. Bavarian troops quickly seized Ulm and forced Louis of Baden to withdraw from Alsace to protect his territory. Baden was pursued by a French army under Villars, and defeated at the battle of Friedlingen on 14 October 1702. These events allowed Louis the possibility of threatening the Habsburg empire directly. In the spring of 1703, Villars advanced through the Black Forest to meet Maximilian of Bavaria at Ulm with the intention of driving on Vienna. Villars desired to advance on Vienna immediately, but the Bavarian elector decided that it would be better first to seize the Tyrol and link up with Vendôme's Italian army. The resulting expedition was a disaster for the Bavarians. Although they were able to occupy the Tyrol, by August the Austrians were able to throw them out with the help of the local population. Vendôme's army was also held back, preventing any linking of the two forces.

While Maximilian was engaged in his abortive invasion of the Tyrol, Villars had remained in the Danube valley to hold off the Alliance armies of Louis of Baden and Styrum. Villars manoeuvred successfully to keep the two armies from unifying and defeated each in detail at the battles of Munderkingen on 31 July and Hochstadt on 20 September. Villars once again urged Maximilian to join with his army in a drive on Vienna, but Maximilian demurred and operations came to a halt for the year. The clash of opinions between the two commanders resulted in Villars being replaced by Marsin.

By the beginning of 1704, the Franco-Bavarian forces were well positioned to invade Austria and take Vienna. Maximilian and Marsin had collected around 55,000 men at Ulm and this force was to be reinforced by Tallard's army of 30,000 for the invasion. Thus, the main task of the Alliance was to prevent this from happening and to drive the French from Germany. To accomplish this, they determined on several diversionary operations designed to draw off French forces from the main theatre and to unite their armies in Germany to overpower the Franco-Bavarian forces there. The first of these resulted in the British capture of Gibraltar in August. The second step resulted in one of the largest battles of the war.

In May, Marlborough advanced with an army of 35,000 down the Rhine valley to meet the army of Louis of Baden (30,000 men) and the army of Eugène (10,000 men) at Mondelsheim. The three commanders agreed that Louis of Baden and Marlborough would advance down the Danube valley to deal with the armies of Maximilian and Marsin, while Eugène prevented French reinforcements from reaching the Franco-Bavarian force.

By August, a French army under Tallard had worked its way around Eugène's observation force and had united with the Franco-Bavarian force at Ulm, which had successfully avoided Marlborough's attempts to bring it to battle. With a force of about 60,000 men, the French and Bavarians now decided to force the Alliance armies away from their lines of communication. Marlborough and Eugène decided to unite their armies to meet this threat. The two armies met at *Blenheim in what was the most crushing defeat suffered by France during the war. The French and Bavarians lost 38,600 men, including 6,000 dead and 14,000 prisoners and Tallard himself was taken prisoner. The Alliance armies suffered 4,500 dead and 7,500 wounded.

With this battle, the safety of Vienna was assured and the French armies were driven from Germany. Maximilian was forced into exile and his state was annexed by the Austrian empire. Exhausted by the campaigns of 1704, both sides were incapable of great effort in 1705. By 1706 the Alliance was again attacking the French forcefully. Marlborough with 62,000 met a French army of 60,000 at *Ramillies in the Low Countries. He attacked Villeroi's fortified camp on 23 May, drove the French from the field, and undertook a vigorous pursuit. The French suffered 8,000 casualties and 7,000 prisoners, while the Alliance lost 4,500 dead and wounded. This victory enabled Marlborough to occupy the entire Spanish Netherlands over the course of the next few months.

The French faced a similar defeat in Savoy, where Eugène was able to outmanoeuvre and outfight Vendôme and drive his army from Italy. The French war effort never recovered from the defeats of 1705 and 1706. French attempts to retake the Spanish Netherlands in 1708 resulted in another severe defeat for the French at the battle of Oudenarde (11 July 1708), after which Louis sued for peace. However, the negotiations broke down over Louis's refusal to join the Alliance against his grandson, Philip of Spain, and in 1709 he made a final effort to regain the Netherlands. Again he was defeated in the war's bloodiest battle, in which the French army of 90,000 men faced an Alliance army again under Marlborough and Eugène at *Malplaquet. Despite losing 12,500 casualties to the Alliance's 20,000, the French were driven from the field and Louis was forced to give up his attempt to reconquer his lost territory.

After several more years of indecisive manoeuvring, the principals again entered into peace negotiations. The death of the Emperor Joseph I in 1711 had brought Charles VI to the Austrian throne. As Charles was also the Habsburg claimant to the Spanish crown, Britain (which England and Scotland became in 1709) feared an Alliance victory would substitute potential Habsburg for French hegemony. Consequently Marlborough was withdrawn from the continent at the end of 1711 and the remainder of the British contingent was withdrawn in May 1712.

In the meantime, the agents of the powers had been negotiating for a general solution to the war and on 11 April 1713 the Treaty of Utrecht was signed between all the participants, save the Habsburg empire. Under its terms, Philip V was recognized as king of Spain, but France had to agree that the crowns of Spain and France would never be joined. France also recognized the Protestant succession in Britain and gave her parts of French colonial possessions in North America. Additionally Britain retained Gibraltar and Minorca. The duchy of Savoy received Sicily and a number of other minor territories and Prussia was recognized as a kingdom. The Spanish Netherlands and the Spanish territories in Italy were also to be ceded to the Habsburg empire. After resisting the terms of the treaty for a time, the Habsburgs were finally forced to submit by the Treaties of Baden and Rastatt signed in March and September 1714.

The War of the Spanish Succession had finally settled the balance-of-power tensions which had divided Europe for several decades. French power was contained and even reduced. Although Louis had gained the crown of Spain for the house of Bourbon, he had been forced to cede the territories he so desired: the Spanish Netherlands. Further, the decline of Spain as a major power on the continent was completed. The crown was forced to surrender its remaining territories in the Netherlands and in Italy. Perhaps the ultimate victor of the wars was Britain, with the Protestant succession seemingly guaranteed (but see JACOBITES) and important overseas possessions gained. Further, the rise of British *naval power and the continuing eclipse of the Dutch navy during the war meant that Britain was confirmed as a major trading nation and one of the strongest economies of Europe.   RTF

Chandler, David, *The Art of Warfare in the Age of Marlborough* (New York, 1976).

Delbrück, Hans, *The History of the Art of War*, vol. 4. *The Dawn of Modern Warfare* (London, 1985), trans. from German orig. (1920).

Kamen, Henry, *The War of Succession in Spain, 1700–1715* (London, 1969).

Sparta Lying some 30 miles (48.3 km) from the sea, in the lovely valley of the Eurotas, Sparta was a state unique in the ancient world. For a start it had two kings, drawn from separate royal families, one of whom, in normal circumstances, commanded the army. But it also had some quasi-democratic institutions: an assembly which all citizens were entitled to attend, and an elected council and officials. The most important of the latter, the five annually elected *ephors*, had exceptionally wide and apparently unchallengeable powers during their year of office, though they could only hold the office once. However, the full rights of citizenship were confined to an increasingly narrow group of landowners, who had to pay dues in kind to their military mess, relying on helots to do the work.

But it was the state-run system of training boys and the semi-professional army which attracted most attention. The training was clearly designed to produce tough and disciplined soldiers, though details are mostly lacking, the sources mainly emphasizing such things as that the boys were expected to wear the same clothes, summer and winter, go barefoot, and steal to supplement their meagre *rations, being flogged if caught, not for stealing, but for being caught. At the age of 20, they were elected to a mess, and were then expected to dine there, except when on campaign, every night, and to sleep there until they were 30, visiting their wives only by stealth.

This system will have produced a magnificent *esprit de corps*, and the army was also evidently unique in being articulated down to units of only 40 men, giving a Spartan *phalanx more flexibility than usual and a proper chain of command. Thus the Spartans were able to carry out manoeuvres thought too difficult for other armies, and tended to remain under command, when others became an ill-disciplined rabble.

Spartan devotion to duty 'unto death' is, perhaps, best expressed by the epitaph of those who fell at *Thermopylae: 'Friend, go tell the Spartans that here we lie obeying their commands.' But Spartans were neither automata nor berserkers. Though clearly highly disciplined, they regarded themselves as 'equals' (*homoioi*), and stories suggest they had a real, if grim, sense of humour, and a cheerful irreverence for those in authority. They were perhaps closer to Royal Marine Commandos or paratroopers than 18th-century Prussian guardsmen.   JFL

Cartledge, P. A., *Sparta and Lakonia* (London, 1979).

Lazenby, J. F., *The Spartan Army* (Warminster, 1985).

Special Air Service. See SAS.

special forces exist to conduct special operations, irregular and *guerrilla warfare, *counter-insurgency, and counter-terrorist operations. They were first conceived in the modern context just prior to WW II by the Germans who had studied the Allied use of irregular forces during WW I. In October 1939 a unit was formed by the *Wehrmacht at the city of Brandenburg under the aegis of the *Abwehr. Initially given the cover name of 800th Special

Purpose Construction Training Company, it soon became better known as the 'Brandenburgers'. Expanded to battalion strength and redesignated the 800th Special Purpose Training Battalion Brandenburg, it eventually became a regiment and ultimately a division.

The Brandenburger concept, of highly trained men capable of carrying out long-range deep-penetration missions, can be considered the blueprint for today's special forces. Training, conducted at two training schools at Brandenburg and Düren, included fieldcraft, tactics, combat survival, training on German and foreign weapons, marksmanship, silent killing, close-quarter combat, small-boat handling, *demolition and sabotage, *radio communications, *intelligence gathering, foreign languages, and the study of foreign armed forces, their equipment, and orders of battle. Parachute training was carried out at the Luftwaffe parachute school at Spandau. Brandenburger units saw action in *Poland, *France, *Norway, Denmark, *Italy, *Yugoslavia, *North Africa, Persia, the Aegean, and on the *eastern front.

In April 1943, the Waffen-*SS formed its own special forces unit. Located just north of Berlin at Friedenthal, it was designated the Friedenthal Special Duties Battalion (later the 502nd SS Special Service Battalion) and was commanded by *Obersturmbannführer* Otto Skorzeny. At first volunteers were recruited only from the Waffen-SS but subsequently it included Brandenburgers, the 500th SS Parachute Rifle Battalion, and other specialist units. Training was similar to that of the Brandenburgers and elements of the battalion also qualified as combat swimmers. Air support came from Kampfgeschwader 200, the Luftwaffe special operations squadron.

In September 1943 502nd SS Special Service Battalion, reinforced by Luftwaffe paratroopers, carried out its first mission successfully, rescuing the deposed Italian dictator Benito Mussolini from imprisonment on the Gran Sasso in Italy's Abruzzi mountain range. Subsequently expanded to a training centre and four battalions, the SS special forces saw service in many places, most notably behind US lines in the battle of the *Bulge.

At the end of 1943, the German navy also formed its own special forces in the form of the Klein Kampf Verbände, better known as 'K' units. This formation comprised a headquarters, three naval assault detachments, and a training school. Each detachment consisted of one officer and 22 other ranks, all highly trained combat swimmers expert in the use of small craft, explosive motor boats, midget submarines, human torpedoes, explosives, and mines against naval targets. In addition, each man underwent intensive military training similar to that of the Brandenburgers and 502nd SS Special Service Battalion as well as instruction in naval engineering, seamanship, navigation, and foreign languages. 'K' units first saw action in July 1944 on the coast of Normandy and thereafter in southern France, Italy, Holland, Denmark, Norway, and northern Germany.

The Italian navy pioneered underwater special warfare with its Decima Flottiglia Mas (10th Light Flotilla), a combat-swimmer unit specializing in the use of explosive motor boats, human torpedoes, and limpet mines. This unit carried out a number of successful attacks against Allied naval vessels in the harbours of Gibraltar, Algeciras, Algiers, and Alexandria, severely damaging two battleships in the latter operation and, had they known it, giving the Italian navy local superiority. But the warships sank on an even keel, and aerial photography did not detect that they were disabled.

The British entry into the world of special warfare commenced in 1940 with the formation of the *SOE which was tasked with organizing and supporting resistance in enemy-occupied countries. Special Training Schools (STS) were established throughout Britain, each specializing in instruction in the different skills in which SOE agents were trained. Similar establishments were also set up overseas, some as far afield as India, Ceylon (now Sri Lanka), Australia, and Singapore. SOE operated in different countries under various cover names such as Force 133, Force 136, and the Inter Services Research Department. One of its offshoots was the Small Scale Raiding Force which devoted itself to raiding operations along the French coast and on the Channel Islands.

In June 1940 the Long Range Desert Group was formed with the role of carrying out deep-penetration reconnaissance operations in the *Western Desert, and July 1941 saw the formation of the *SAS. Other wartime British special forces included the Special Boat Sections who pioneered the use of canoes and other small craft for special operations; the Royal Marines Boom Patrol Detachment whose swimmer/canoeists carried out the successful 'Cockleshell Heroes' raid against German shipping in Bordeaux harbour in December 1942; the Special Boat Squadron which carried out raiding operations in the Aegean and the Adriatic; Popski's Private Army whose jeep-mounted patrols raided enemy lines of communication in North Africa and Italy; and the Combined Operations Pilotage Parties which conducted clandestine reconnaissances of enemy-held coastlines.

The principal American wartime special forces organization was the *OSS, which performed a similar role and was initially trained by the SOE. The Special Operations division deployed missions and detachments in Europe, the Middle East, North Africa, *Burma, Siam (now Thailand), and China. OSS personnel also provided the American element in Jedburgh groups: Allied three-man teams, comprising two officers and a radio operator, which were dropped into German-occupied territories prior to D-Day in *Normandy.

In the *Pacific, Australian coast watcher teams monitored the movement of Japanese shipping and troops while Australian independent companies and the British/Australian 'Z' Special Unit carried out guerrilla operations in Borneo, Balikpapan, New Guinea, the Celebes, Portuguese Timor, and Indonesia. Meanwhile SOE's Far Eastern arm, Force 136, dropped agents into Burma, Malaya, Sumatra, Siam, and French Indochina to organize resistance and conduct guerrilla warfare. Other units which operated in Burma included 'V' Force, formed for the conduct of fighting patrols and collection of intelligence behind enemy lines, and the Sea Reconnaissance Unit which carried out coastal and riverine intelligence tasks prior to landings by the British Fourteenth Army.

The period immediately after the war saw reductions and disbandments of special forces but post-war conflicts soon saw their return and since then they have been retained in the orders of battle of most armed forces. Britain's 22nd SAS Regiment (22 SAS) and Royal Marines Special Boat Service (SBS) have seen action in almost all of the post-war conflicts in which the country has been involved. During the last twenty years, considerable expertise has been developed by British special forces in the areas of counter-terrorist operations and covert surveillance with one unit, 14 Intelligence Company, being formed for the latter role.

During the *Vietnam war special forces played an important role. Among their number were the US army's 5th Special Forces Group, Long Range Reconnaissance Patrol (LRRP) units, the Military Assistance Command—Vietnam—Studies & Observation Group (MAC-V-SOG), US navy Sea Air Land (SEAL) teams, US Marine Force Reconnaissance units and USAF Air Commandos, special operations squadrons, and combat control teams of forward air controllers. Elements of the Australian SAS Regiment and New Zealand SAS Squadron also saw service in South Vietnam, along with special forces units of the Republic of Korea.

The 1980s saw a major expansion of American special forces and the formation in 1987 of the US Special Operations Command which incorporates the US army Special Forces, Rangers, civil affairs and psychological operations units, US navy SEALs and support elements, the 160th Special Operations Aviation Regiment, and USAF special operations units. Within that formation exists the Joint Special Operations Command which incorporates the US army's DELTA Force, the navy's SEAL Team 6, a specialist Ranger unit, an intelligence unit, and a helicopter force. The years 1983 and 1989 saw US special forces deployed in action in *Grenada and Panama respectively and in Iraq during the *Gulf war of 1991, along with British and French units. Two years later they saw action again in *Somalia.

The USSR placed great emphasis in the use of special forces and, with other members of the *Warsaw Pact, created a large number of Spetsnaz formations which would have spearheaded any assault on the West. Many have since disappeared since the collapse of the eastern bloc but Russia's Spetsnaz forces still comprise eight brigades, each specializing in operations in specific areas of the world.

Other countries which maintain sizeable special forces include France with its 13ème Régiment de Dragons Parachutiste, 1er Régiment de Parachutistes d'Infanterie de Marine, and the Commando Hubert naval combat swimmer unit. In the Middle East, Israel has its Sayeret Matkal General Staff Reconnaissance Unit, Sayeret Shaldag LRRP unit, Sayeret Hadruzim Druze Muslim reconnaissance unit, and Flotilla 13 naval special operations unit. In South-East Asia, Thailand maintains a special forces division comprising four regiments, a psychological operations battalion, long-range reconnaissance company, and special warfare training centre, while the Republic of Korea maintains seven complete special forces brigades.   HMPDH

Beaumont, Roger, *Special Operations & Élite Units 1939–1988: A Research Guide* (Westport, Conn., 1988).
Foot, Michael, *SOE: The Special Operations Executive 1940–1946* (London, 1984).
Moon, Tom, *This Grim and Savage Game: OSS & the Beginning of US Covert Operations in WW II* (Los Angeles, 1991).
Seymour, William, *British Special Forces* (London, 1985).
Skorzeny, Otto, *My Commando Operations* (Atglen, Pa., 1995).
Waller, Douglas C., *Commandos: The Inside Story of America's Secret Soldiers* (New York, 1994).

Special Operations Executive. See SOE.

Spinola, Ambrogio, Marqués de Balbases (1569–1630), outstanding general and master of *siege warfare in the service of Spain during the latter half of her 150-year military ascendancy in Europe. Born into a wealthy Genoese family, in 1602 he raised and led an army under contract to the Netherlands, where he repeatedly defeated *Maurice of Nassau. Kept deliberately short of funds by courtiers who doubted his loyalty, in 1606 he sought to confirm his good faith by pledging his entire fortune to bankers to obtain a loan for Philip III to continue the war. It was spent elsewhere and the following year he had to negotiate the Twelve Years Truce with Maurice. Two years into the *Thirty Years War he seized the Palatinate, a Protestant barrier along his Rhine supply route, and renewed the war in the Netherlands. His most famous victory was the capture of the Dutch fortress of Breda in 1625, immortalized by Velázquez. Faced with an abler opponent in Frederick Henry and undermined by Olivares, regent for the boy-king Philip IV, he returned to Spain in 1628 and was given a meaningless marquisate. Ruined, he accepted a commission in Italy where he died at the siege of Casale.   HEB

spit and polish Many armies have pursued a smartness which goes well beyond the need to keep clothing, weapons, and equipment in clean and serviceable condition. Sometimes this reflected wider fashion: Napoleonic officers cursed with spindly legs might wear false calves to improve appearances, and art often aided nature in the matter of moustaches. Sometimes it embodied narrower military dandyism, as men sported rolled silk handkerchiefs instead of sword knots, slashed the seams housing the peaks of their caps to make them lie flatter, or shrank berets to eliminate floppiness. One of Kipling's old sweats tells us how:

> I carried my slops to the tailor; I sez to 'im 'None of your lip!
> You tight 'em over the shoulder, and loose 'em over the 'ip,
> For the set of the tunic's 'orrid.

For most soldiers the required standard of smartness was the product of drudgery. Blemishes in leather were massaged away with a hot spoon, a process easily overdone. The leather was then treated with saliva and boot polish (water, placed in the lid of the polish tin, took over when spit ran out) applied in tiny circles until the shine was deep enough to reflect colour—but ruined by an ill-placed heel. Brasswork was once polished with moistened whiting, and later with a variety of patent preparations. Until the early 19th century the barrels and locks of muskets (with much other metalwork) were polished with dampened brick-dust, resulting in complaints that arms were made unsafe by excessive scouring.

The buff leather of cross-belts and accoutrements was daubed with dampened pipeclay, thus the 14th Light Dragoons in the *Peninsular war lampooned:

> Bad luck to this marching, pipe-claying and starching
> How neat one must be to be killed by the French

When webbing took over early in the 20th century it was anointed with blanco in half a dozen shades. Neither pipeclay nor blanco reacted well to rain, and many men who fought at *Waterloo, where it rained heavily the night before the battle, had uniforms streaked with pipeclay. The British Household Cavalry, smart to the last, sent grubby fellows to the rear.

Harness was treated with saddle-soap and polish in a daily routine brought to naught by steaming horses. The British army's stable belt, now itself the bright source of dandyism, originated in an attempt to keep more vulnerable belts away from the horse, its by-products and the ingredients needed to keep the beast and its tack in good order.

It was only after WW II, when chromium plate or anodized aluminium did away with the need to polish metal daily, and the conditions of conscription progressively ameliorated, that the lives of men in barracks were not shrouded in a fog of polishing and pressing. The psychologist Norman Dixon suggests that what the British army calls bull—routine tasks or discipline—is a substitute for thought. Spit and polish did more than produce a smart appearance: it helped inculcate a corporate spirit. Many of those toiling to achieve glossy leather or shiny brass saw their task as repetitive, only to be surprised, against their

better judgement, by the almost tribal sense of unity the whole otherwise pointless process fostered.   RH

squadron Originating in 16th-century Italy as *squadrone*, a group of soldiers drawn up in square formation, the term squadron has application to war on the land, at sea, and in the air. It describes a subdivision of a naval fleet deployed for a particular purpose—'the China Squadron'—or a grouping of similar vessels—'the Battlecruiser Squadron'. It is the basic administrative and tactical grouping of *air forces.

In land warfare it defined a cavalry subunit composed of two or more troops. From the 16th century the troop, a captain's command, was the basic subunit in the cavalry. Troops could be combined, initially on an ad hoc basis, under the command of one of the regiment's field officers or a senior captain, to create a more substantial grouping, the squadron. During the 19th century squadron organization became permanent in most armies. In the process troops lost their former importance, generally becoming subalterns' commands. The British army is among those which have retained the term squadron to describe subunits of armoured regiments. In the US army an Armoured Cavalry Squadron is an altogether larger and more powerful unit within the brigade-sized Armoured Cavalry Regiment.   RH

SS (Shutzstaffeln) (Ger., protection squads), the name reflecting its origin as a protection force for *Hitler. The SS was commanded from April 1929 by Heinrich Himmler who had served towards the end of WW I, qualified as an agricultural chemist in 1922, and taken part in the Munich putsch. He was convinced by theories of ethnic superiority advocated by Rosenberg and Darré, and had an obsessive interest in heredity. Although his receding chin, poor eyesight, and pear-shaped body made him an unlikely champion of Nordic manhood, Himmler sought to make the SS racially exclusive, and during its expansion from 400 to 50,000 between 1931 and 1933 rejected candidates if they had one filled tooth.

In 1933 Himmler was appointed police president in Munich, and extended power by gaining control of police forces in other states. He set up a concentration camp at Dachau, and staffed it by Totenkopf (death's head) guards. He had already set up an armed Stab Wache (Staff Guard), under the command of Sepp Dietrich, an ex-NCO and early Nazi, and it soon became Hitler's black-clad guard with the title Liebstandarte Adolf Hitler.

The status of the *Reichswehr was threatened by Hitler's early paramilitary Sturmabteilungen (SA) which embodied the old *Freikorps* traditions and had incorporated thousands of ex-servicemen. In the 'night of the long knives' in 1934 he used the SS, with army logistical support, to eliminate the SA leadership. On the death of Hindenburg, Hitler fused the offices of president and chancellor, and required servicemen to swear an oath to him. The army, already compromised by its support for the purge, was now bound by *honour to obey, while the SS was granted the status of 'an independent organization within the National Socialist Workers' Party'.

In 1935 Himmler raised the Verfügungstruppe (Reserve Force), ancestor of the Waffen-SS (Armed SS). The SS now looked increasingly like an alternative army, with its own officer cadet school at Bad Tolz and a programme based on rigorous military training, physical fitness, and political indoctrination. In early 1938 the Waffen-SS received formal approval for 'special internal political tasks or for use with the wartime army'. Although they were to come under army command when deployed, Himmler, as *Reichsführer SS*, was responsible for recruitment, administration, and peacetime control. The SS developed its version of the army's field-grey combat uniform, with its own distinctive badges of rank on the collar, retaining black for full dress.

SS units served in Poland in 1939, and in the 1940 campaign regiments (*Standarten*) fought under army command. Their performance gave an indication of what was to come. Standarte Deutschland carried out a courageous assault crossing of the river Lys, but SS men massacred British *POWs at Le Paradis and Wormhoudt. By early 1941 the Waffen-SS had four divisions, one of which, Wiking, was raised from volunteers (*freiwilligen*) from Norway, Denmark, and the Low Countries, and two brigades. Expansion continued throughout the war, and no fewer than 38 divisions had been raised by 1945. Many never attained full strength, and some were composed of foreign volunteers whose enlistment made a mockery of notions of racial purity.

Courage on the battlefield was matched by severity off it. Three SS panzer divisions, Leibstandarte, Totenkopf, and Das Reich, participated in Manstein's counterstroke at *Kharkov, suffering 12,000 casualties in the process and taking few prisoners. In Normandy Das Reich and Hitler Jugend (65 per cent of the latter were 18 years old) formed Dietrich's I SS Panzer Corps. The Corps' historian tells how 'The combined effects of brave officers and senior NCOs and brave, dedicated soldiers made for an extremely formidable military machine. Wounds were to be borne with pride and never used as a reason to leave the field of battle; mercy was seen as a sign of weakness and normally neither offered nor expected.' Battlefield performance was impressive but atrocities were commonplace: on the way to Normandy one of Das Reich's regiments murdered 642 civilians at Oradour-sur-Glane.

After the war the SS was declared a criminal organization, and many of its members were prosecuted for *war crimes. On the one hand its best divisions were superb, though they often had better equipment than army counterparts, and, like other élites, frequently lost more men than was necessary. On the other its reputation is poisoned by its racist murderousness. Although research has shown that the *Wehrmacht was also involved in murder, the record of the SS was especially shocking. Apologists suggest that units like the Dirlewanger and Kaminski brigades, rather than the Waffen-SS proper, carried out the worst atrocities like the reduction of Warsaw in 1944. There has even been a suggestion that the *concentration camp personnel were somehow distinct from the Waffen-SS, a patently false distinction. As Bernd Wegner observes: 'the Waffen-SS cannot be considered in isolation from the history of the SS as a whole, which in turn is inseparable from the story of national socialism.'   RH

Reynolds, Michael, *Steel Inferno: 1st SS Panzer Corps in Normandy* (Staplehurst, 1997).

Sydnor, Charles, *Soldiers of Destruction* (Princeton, 1977).

Wegner, Berndt, *The Waffen SS* (Oxford, 1990).

Stalingrad, battle of (1942–3). This entered the realm of legend almost as soon as the guns fell silent in the vast industrial city on the river Volga on 2 February 1943. As the closest and bloodiest battle on the *eastern front, it was a German disaster and a Soviet triumph.

The principal German objective for the 1942 summer campaign had been the Caucasus oilfields. Only later did the city acquire an equally important operational status for the Caucasus region and a symbolic value for both dictators. *Stalin decided to hold parts of Stalingrad regardless of the cost and *Hitler openly assured Germans that the city would be taken. As late as 17 November 1942, his Sixth Army under *Paulus tried to reach that objective, while aware of the weakness of its flanks mainly defended by Allied troops. Chuikov's Sixty-Second Army was successful in holding four shallow bridgeheads on the left bank of the River Volga. Mobile operations had long been replaced by urban fighting in which both sides bled heavily for a few dozen ruined city blocks while Stalin and Red Army commanders planned to counter-attack.

Both the high command and Sixth Army had anticipated a Soviet attack against its vulnerable flanks but underestimated an encircling offensive on the massive scale prepared by the Red Army. German generals were soon to learn the bitter lesson that their counterparts had become as proficient in the art of mobile armoured warfare as their former tutors. On 19 November, the South-western Front (army group) under Lt Gen Vatutin began its long-prepared counter-offensive (URANUS), attacking the Third Romanian Army north of Stalingrad. One day later, the Stalingrad Front, under Col-Gen Eremenko, joined in against Fourth Romanian and Fourth Panzer Army south of Stalingrad. Soviet superiority was absolute in the main penetration sectors. After the spearheads had linked up at Sovetsky south-east of Kalach on 23 November, Soviet forces established an inner encirclement around Sixth Army, one corps

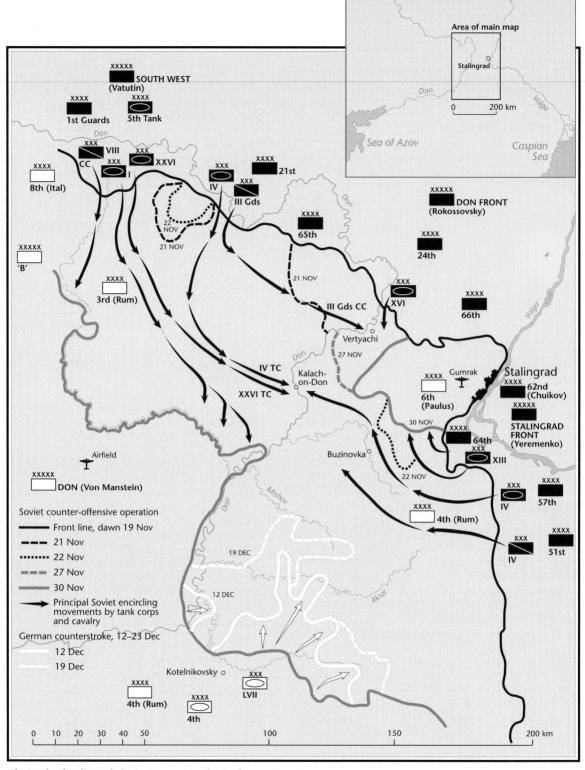

The **Battle of Stalingrad**: the Soviet counter-offensive from 19 November 1942.

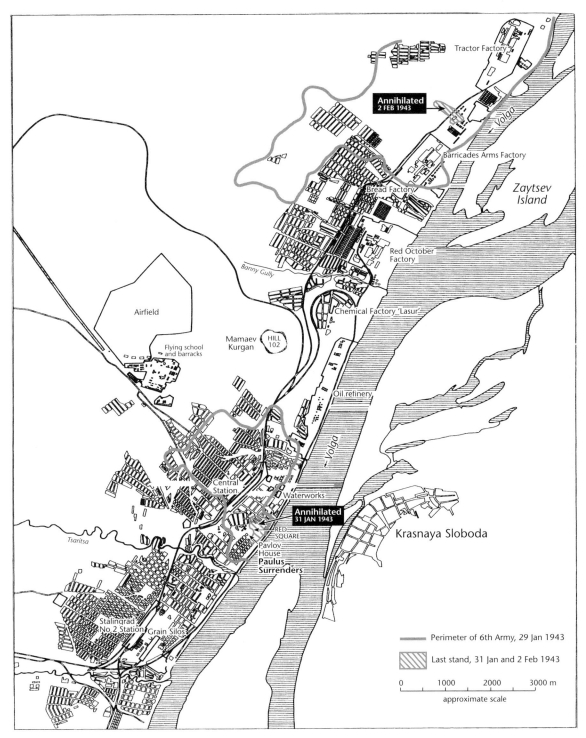

Stalingrad: the city, held by Chuikov's Sixty-Second Soviet Army, and the end of the trapped German Sixth Army, January–February, 1943.

of Fourth Panzer Army, and Romanian remnants totalling 250,000 men, including 195,000 Germans (among them one Croatian infantry regiment), 50,000 Soviet auxiliaries, and 5,000 Romanians.

While Hitler refused to contemplate withdrawing from Stalingrad, Paulus did not possess the logistical strength to break out unassisted. His regrouped Sixth Army lacked fuel, ammunition, and transportation. While the Sixth Army was (inadequately) supplied by the Luftwaffe a relief force was assembled. Although all available transport was concentrated, the airlift hardly ever met the army's needs. In addition, its troops had been exhausted and undernourished before the siege.

Alongside the outer encirclement, the Red Army did everything to disrupt envisaged German relief operations. It succeeded in allowing only one thrust from Kotel'nikovskij (100 km/62 miles). It began on 12 December (WINTERGEWITTER). While the LVII Panzer Corps struggled forward to link up with Sixth Army, the South-western Front continued its Winter Campaign (LITTLE SATURN) and penetrated deep into the rear of Army Group Don. When LVII Panzer Corps had given its best, Paulus was too short of motor fuel, ammunition, and rations to implement the breakout (DONNERSCHLAG). The Sixth Army's leaders knew by the end of December that it was doomed. While self-sacrifice and fatalism were growing at the top, the troops were ordered to hold out against all odds.

The end began when the Don Front under Lt Gen Rokossovsky executed RING on 10 January, after Paulus, after consultation with his senior generals, had rejected an offer to *capitulate. Seven days later, the Stalingrad pocket was reduced to half its size and Sixth Army had lost its last major airfield. On 22 January, Paulus asked Hitler in vain for permission to cease fire. By 26 January, the Sixth Army was confined to two small pockets in Stalingrad. Paulus was unwilling to put a formal end to the fighting although the remnants of 297th Infantry Division had already surrendered. On 31 January he surrendered himself, despite his last-minute promotion to field marshal, but refused to order the northern pocket to do the same. It fought until 2 February. According to recent estimates 60,000 Germans died in Stalingrad and 110,000 went into Soviet captivity, of whom only 5,000 returned home, including the dishonoured Paulus.   JF1

Beevor, Antony, *Stalingrad* (London, 1998).

Förster, Jürgen (ed.), *Stalingrad: Ereignis, Wirkung, Symbol* (Munich, 1992).

Glantz, David M., and House, Jonathan, *When Titans Clashed: How the Red Army stopped Hitler* (Lawrence, Kan., 1995).

Stalin, Josef Vissarionovich (né Djugashvili) (1879–1953). Along with *Hitler and *Mao Tse-tung, Stalin was one of the three *genocidal monsters of the 20th century. Soviet dictator and war leader, supreme commander in the

1941–5 'Great Patriotic War' and one of the 'big three' with Franklin D. *Roosevelt and *Churchill. In 1945 he appointed himself *generalissimus* (general of generals), a title only previously awarded to the great *Suvorov.

Born in Georgia and the son of a shoemaker, Josef started training as an Orthodox priest, which undoubtedly influenced his public style. In 1899 he became a revolutionary and was expelled from the seminary in Tbilisi (once Tiflis). He adopted the name Stalin (man of steel) and in 1902 was arrested for conspiracy for the first time. He was arrested many more times, but managed to extricate himself by betraying his comrades. He took part in the 1905 Russian revolution in the Transcaucasia region. In 1912 he moved to St Petersburg (1914–24 Petrograd, 1924–91 Leningrad) and became one of the first editors of the Bolshevik newspaper inaccurately named *Pravda* (the truth). He was sent to Siberia for life in 1913 but allowed to return in the amnesty after the March 1917 Revolution. After the November Revolution (see RUSSIAN REVOLUTIONS) he was made People's Commissar for Nationalities. During the civil war he helped organize the defence of Tsaritsyn (1926–61 *Stalingrad, now Volgograd), with *Voroshilov and Aleksandr Yegorov, which fused a powerful clique.

Despite a belated attempt by *Lenin to prevent it, he turned the originally administrative post of general secretary of the communist party into a monolithic power base, consolidated after Lenin died by a ruthless purge of *Trotsky and his supporters from all offices, a process that continued to the point of editing him out of all photographs of the revolution. The process of eliminating all other sources of power continued within the party through a series of purges that continued until he died, by the forced collectivization of agriculture and the extermination of the merely productive peasant kulaks, by the use of political slave labour to implement his wasteful industrialization five-year plans, and by the 1937 decapitation of the Red Army by the purge of *Tukhachevskiy and any other senior officer who showed signs of thinking for himself.

Internationally, Stalin pulled the strings of the Popular Front and other anti-fascist *peace movements through the Comintern and provided some support for the Republicans in the *Spanish civil war (taking Spain's gold reserves in return) until he realized that the western powers were seeking to channel Hitler's malign energies towards him. Prior to the recall and execution of the Comintern agents of his previous policy, he engineered the diplomatic revolution of the August 1939 Molotov-Ribbentrop Pact, under the terms of which his armies rolled into eastern Poland and the Baltic States.

He rejected *intelligence warnings of *BARBAROSSA, believing them to be a western deception operation, and after the blow landed he physically hid for a week, exhibiting surprising moral cowardice in such a hard man, emerging only to try to take credit for the fact that the Red Army, in spite of being left exposed and unprepared entirely because of his attempts at appeasement, resisted with obstinate courage. Even before he formally turned his back on internationalism, Stalin had been experimenting with appeals to traditional Russian patriotism, and now he went all the way, reviving old ranks and symbols and even slackening his persecution of the Jews and the Church. He made himself president of the State Committee of Defence (GKO) on 30 June 1941, People's Commissar for Defence on 19 July, supreme C-in-C of the armed forces on 8 August and, from 10 July 1941, president of the Stavka of the Supreme Command (from 8 August of the Supreme High Command). The Stavka (an old Russian word for a warrior chief's *council of war) was the tightly knit body that ran the war at the front line. The State Committee of Defence coordinated all aspects of the *total war, including industry.

There are many parallels between Hitler and Stalin, not the least of them being their conviction that they were great generals, their utter indifference to human suffering, and their wastefulness of lives. By far the greatest contribution Stalin made to Soviet victory was made pre-war, when he moved much heavy industry out of European Russia and thus out of the reach of BARBAROSSA. The next biggest contribution was made by Hitler, who failed to recognize the importance of the fact that his armies were initially greeted as liberators in Belorussia and the Ukraine. By implementing a brutal policy of racialist repression, he rallied the peoples of the Soviet empire around the leadership of Stalin *faue de mieux* and even so hundreds of thousands of Russians and subject peoples served in the German armies. After the German advance chewed up dullards like Stalin's favourite Buddeny, a new generation of senior officers rose to the challenge, men like *Zhukov, *Koniev, and Rokossovsky, the last plucked from a punishment camp. There was nothing new or attributable to the leadership of Stalin in Russian determination to defend the homeland, or in their stoicism and vengeful determination. He said, 'it takes a brave man to be a coward in the Red Army', but this had always been the case.

On the diplomatic front, Roosevelt played right into his hands at the Allied conferences in Tehran in 1943 and Yalta in 1945, where he was greatly assisted by the fact that Soviet intelligence agents were well placed in both the British and US governments. One cannot escape the suspicion that his constant pressure for a 'second front' was more than just a plea to relieve the pressure on the eastern front, but also embodied the hope that the invasion of Europe would be launched prematurely and fail. As it was, the Red Army rolled well beyond the old imperial borders and there is little reason to doubt the insight *Patton had: it only stopped because the western Allies were strong enough to dissuade it from continuing. By the time he died, Stalin's Soviet empire extended further and with greater effective control than the tsars had ever dreamed of.

Of the many evil creatures who sprang to do Stalin's bidding, the great survivor (for his predecessors were all executed after show trials) was his last secret police chief and fellow Georgian, Lavrentiy Beria. Because the nuclear programme was based on the Soviet intelligence services' comprehensive penetration of the *Manhattan Project, Beria directed the development of *nuclear weapons, which rapidly caught up with the USA. He also directed intensified internal repression, including a vicious campaign against the leaders of the heroic city of *Leningrad and the purge of all those who had been involved in *partisan activity.

When Stalin died, incredible though it may seem after the horrors he had perpetrated, he was mourned by scores of millions of Soviet people, for whom he had been a 'little father' like the tsars of old. They wept in the streets, unable to imagine a future without him. His successors could. They quickly put Beria out of their misery, and only three years after his death, Stalin's crimes were denounced in a not-so-secret party plenum by Khrushchev, beginning the period known as the 'thaw' during which his monstrous 'archipelago' of punishment camps was gradually dismantled. Demographic evidence shows very clearly that many times more people died at his hands before BARBAROSSA than subsequently at the hands of Hitler's minions. It is a shattering judgement on his successors, and a powerful reflection on the loss of international status he did so much to establish, that his despotism is looked back to as the 'good old days' by millions of ordinary Russians at the turn of the century he polluted.   CDB/HEB

Bullock, Alan, *Hitler and Stalin: Parallel Lives* (London, 1998).

Erickson, John, *The Road to Stalingrad: Stalin's War with Germany* (London, 1975).

—— *The Road to Berlin* (London, 1982).

stealth technology has as its fundamental principle the prevention of detection by the enemy, and applies not only to aircraft as is commonly assumed, but also increasingly to naval vessels and to armoured vehicles, although in the latter cases, it is nascent technology upon which comment must be reserved. Stealth technology, therefore, does not simply mean the evasion by aircraft of *radar through the reduction of radar signature. It also encompasses the reduction of an aircraft's visibility in other spectra, most notably acoustic, visual, and *infra-red. Consequently the popular term 'stealth technology' would perhaps be better referred to as 'low-observable technology'.

The only known operational equipment relying upon low observable technology is found in the inventory of the USAF. The Lockheed F-117 Nighthawk and the Northrop B-2 Spirit are both designed to penetrate sophisticated air-defence systems to attack key targets with *precision-guided or *nuclear weapons. Their utterly contrasting designs demonstrate that the principles of low observability may be obtained in a number of ways. The fundamental goal of stealth technology is to reduce the radar cross-section of an aircraft to an absolute minimum, so that it does not stand out on a radar screen. The term 'radar cross-section' refers to the amount of radar energy reflected from a body. The most obvious reflector on an aircraft is the flat plate surface, and the design of the F-117, so-called 'faceting', reduces such reflectors to an absolute minimum. The elimination of vertical control surfaces in the B-2 'flying wing' design is not new; a flying wing was built by Northrop immediately after WW II. The novelty lies in the advance of computer technology which enabled far superior wing and fuselage algorithms to be developed than was possible when the F-117 was created, while both make extensive use of radar-absorbent materials.

Stealth technology provides its users with a number of tactical advantages. As well as allowing the penetration of heavily defended airspace, it enables single aircraft to carry out attacks in a manner impossible for conventional aircraft, which require a large number of support aircraft to conduct similar missions, including escort, defence suppression, and electronic warfare types. A conventional aircraft 'package' may employ up to 40 aircraft, while a stealth aircraft can conduct the mission by itself. This naturally requires the use of precision-guided weapons to ensure that the single aircraft has a high probability of success.

Stealth is not without its drawbacks. The cost of the technology is enormous, and it is hard to envisage that its eventual employment in maritime and land operations will ever be obtained at a price comparable to conventional technology. Nonetheless, precisely because of its elevated cost it does emphasize the economic power of the USA as well as its immense advantage in *science and technology over the rest of the world.   DJJ

---

steam power propelled first Britain and then the world into the industrial revolution and into the increasing *mechanization of all aspects of human endeavour, warfare of course included. Steam affected warfare in three respects. Two were in the field of motive power both on land with the *railways and also at sea where it replaced sail. In addition to this it revolutionized industry and made possible the growth in arms manufacture necessary for the equipping of modern mass armies.

The adaptation of railways to military use dramatically increased the strategic mobility of armies. Before railways the strategic tempo of operations was limited by the speed at which armies could march; utilization of railways extended the range and sustainability of armies in the field. Prince Wilhelm of Prussia (later King and Emperor Wilhelm I) issued a memorandum in July 1851 establishing a 'train cadre' for each of the nine corps of the Royal Prussian army. When mobilization came each cadre would provide five provisions columns, field bakeries, a horse depot, and field hospitals. By 1860 the railway provided rapid and inexpensive communication between all the major cities in western Europe and became the heart of all *mobilization plans.

At sea the introduction of steam gave a freedom of manoeuvre to *navies that they had not enjoyed since the days of galley warfare. Independence from the prevailing winds dramatically changed naval warfare. Although tactical movement was enhanced, at the strategic level the requirement to coal limited ships endurance and tied them to key bases. The Royal Navy was able to exploit its possession of global bases as coaling stations. In contrast when the tsar sent a fleet from the Baltic to the Pacific during the *Russo-Japanese war, denied coaling facilities by Britain it had to overburden itself with coal wherever it could find it, reducing its already inferior sailing and battleworthiness.

The first steam-powered warship was developed by the Americans in response to their worsening situation in the *War of 1812. The *Demologos* was an unseaworthy twin-hulled floating battery with her paddle wheels carried internally, designed to protect New York harbour. The much-touted duel between the steam-powered USS *Monitor* and the CSS *Virginia* (ex Merrimac) during the *American civil war was between ironclads of similarly limited use. A few years before the French had launched *La Gloire*, an iron-sheathed wooden, steam-driven warship. They intended the fourth of her class to be entirely iron but were beaten to the punch by the British. In 1860 the Royal Navy launched HMS *Warrior*, a steam-powered, shell-firing, all-iron warship. Masts and yards continued to be installed for decades, becoming increasingly vestigial, but the die was cast.

The main drawback of steam power was its poor power to weight ratio, which limited its applications. Landships and aircraft had to await the arrival of the internal combustion engine, and although there were some interesting hybrids that used steam on the surface and electrical power underwater, it was not until the diesel-electric combination power source was developed that the submarine began its progress to becoming the new capital ship of the seas. Railways and ships were still mainly steam powered into the 1950s, but the era of 'steam warfare' was over by then.

JR-W

Sten gun A British WW II *sub-machine gun, its name derived from the names of its inventors Shepherd and Turpin and the *small arms factory at Enfield Lock. It was a very cheap, mass-produced weapon, its action worked by the recoil of its 9 mm round. The Mk I, issued in 1941, cost about £2.50 to produce. It had a metal skeleton butt, a tubular action housing the bolt and return spring, and a barrel surrounded by a perforated jacket tipped with a compensator intended to limit the weapon's tendency to climb when firing bursts. A single-column magazine, entering on the action's left, was prone to cause stoppages, especially if the firer gripped it with his left hand. The Mk 2, workhorse of the Stens, was smaller and simpler.

The weapon's shoddiness, tendency to jam, and habit of firing accidentally if struck sharply or dropped made it less than universally popular. The Mk 5 was better looking, with a wooden butt and pistol-grip. The Mk 6, issued in small numbers, had a silencer. By 1945 nearly 4 million Stens had been produced, and many were distributed to *resistance groups, who had no choice but to use them.   RH

Stilwell, Gen Joseph Warren (1883–1946). With thirteen years in various postings in China during the inter-war years, Stilwell was considered the US army's senior Chinese expert. As such, he was posted as COS to *Chiang Kai-Shek, when China became an ally after *Pearl Harbor, and immediately he took control (if not command) of the Chinese forces fighting a rearguard action during the *Burma campaign. Effective command eluded him, not least because he found the Chinese inefficient and riddled with corruption and intrigue at every level; while he forged them eventually into a fighting force, he never managed to address the culture of corruption. Also acting as a conduit for US military aid to China, his responsibilities multiplied, and from 1943, he was additionally Deputy Supreme Commander South-East Asia, under *Mountbatten. He took personal command of the battle for northern Burma in 1943–4, controlling three Chinese divisions, 'Merrill's Marauders', and the *Chindits. The latter two formations greatly detested his command style, not helped by his brusque, no-nonsense manner and Anglophobia, which earned him the nickname 'Vinegar Joe'. He was recalled to the USA at Chiang's request, following a dispute over control of operations against the Japanese in October 1944.   APC-A

Romanus, Charles F., and Sunderland, Riley, *Stilwell's Command Problems* (Washington, 1985).

---

stirrups probably originated as the addition of a wood, rope, or metal tread or toehold at the end of a strap descending from a saddle. But its impact on *cavalry warfare far exceeds its simple technology. Before the stirrup's introduction, the cavalry soldier was forced to stay on his horse by pressing his knees into its sides and could at best be a mounted *archer or fight dismounted. The stirrup meant that the horseman could thrust a lance or swing a sword with more power and direction, and after the development of the high cantel (rear) and pommel (front) saddle, he was able to couch the lance and use it to transmit the power of his horse to the enemy.

The earliest stirrup appeared in southern Siberia during the 1st century AD. It was found in China by the 5th century AD and in Korea and Japan a century later. About the same time the stirrup was used by the *Huns and Avars. It is perhaps from these peoples that European horsemen adopted

the stirrup. Alternative theories suggest that the stirrup was introduced to Europe by Middle Eastern or Iberian soldiers during the 7th or 8th centuries AD. European cavalry began using the stirrup in mounted shock combat in the 11th century, from whence emerged the concepts of *cheval*-ry and *knighthood that persist long after the horse has been retired from warfare.   KDeV

DeVries, Kelly, *Medieval Military Technology* (Peterborough, 1992).

Littauer, Mary Aitken, 'Early Stirrups', *Antiquity*, 55 (1981).

---

storm troopers were originally special assault troops developed most notably in the German army during WW I. The concept was in fact more widespread, and the French Capt André Laffargue wrote of it in 1915, but it is now clear that German preparations were well in hand by this time. On New Year's Eve 1914 the Prussian Guard Rifle Battalion had pioneered fluid attack techniques to retake a lost trench, and in March 1915 the first half-battalion sized assault unit was created, soon coming under the command of Capt Willy Rohr of the Guard Rifles. He developed tactics based on section/squad-sized 'storm troops' supported by mortars, machine guns, and flame-throwers, trained to force a gap in enemy trench lines and then roll up defences by flank attack, making wide use of grenades. The experience of *Verdun, where Crown Prince Wilhelm became an admirer of storm troops, persuaded the Germans to increase these detachments into storm battalions, with a mix of infantry, machine-gun, flame-thrower, and artillery companies, and to create more of them, often by the wholesale conversion of *Jäger units whose traditions already favoured dash and initiative. There were also smaller storm-troop detachments in conventional regiments. These units contained the 'princes of the trenches', the brightest and best that the German infantry could produce.

Storm troops were used to attack behind a short and ferocious artillery barrage at Riga on the eastern front in 1917, and later the same year they were used with notable success in the German counter-attack at *Cambrai. They pushed deep into weak spots in the defence, with 'infantry accompanying batteries' following them and 'assault blocks'—battalion-sized teams of infantry, mortars, and machine guns—hard on their heels to exploit success. *Ludendorff was convinced that this was the way ahead, and storm-troop tactics were at the heart of his plans for 1918. During the *Ludendorff offensive they did very serious damage to the British army, but were ultimately unable to convert tactical success into a strategic victory. As has so often been the case with élite troops, the enormous losses they suffered weakened the rest of the army materially and morally.

The concept of the storm trooper rapidly had ideological overtones. The soldier-poet Franz Schauwecker wrote of 'a new kind of man, a man in the highest exaltation of all manly qualities and so harmonised and from a single caste that one sees a man in the word "fighter" '. In the inter-war years the notion was exploited for political reasons: the Nazi Brownshirts were styled *Sturmabteilungen* (storm detachments), and some ranks of the *SS often included a reference to the storm detachment that their holders notionally led, as in *Hauptsturmführer* for captain.   RH

Gudmundsson, Bruce I., *Stormtroop Tactics: Innovation in the German Army 1914–1918* (Westport, Conn., 1995).

Strategic Arms Limitation/Strategic Arms Reduction Talks (SALT/START) are the negotiations between the USA and the USSR (latterly Russia) to limit and reduce their arsenals of strategic (that is, intercontinental) offensive nuclear weapons. The first attempts to limit nuclear weapons in the context of the wider *UN Disarmament Commission, created in 1952, demonstrated that bilateral negotiations between the superpowers were essential to limit their growing stocks of *nuclear weapons.

The first signal to the West that the USSR might not be able to sustain development of its nuclear arsenal came in a speech by PM Georgi Malenkov in March 1954. Khrushchev, First Secretary of the Communist Party, denounced him, but adopted his policy line. By 1955 both superpowers had successfully detonated sophisticated thermonuclear (hydrogen) bombs with the explosive power of millions of tons of TNT. The USA had the B-47 intercontinental bomber and the B-52 was due in service the following year. In 1957 the USSR countered by launching the first artificial satellite, Sputnik, creating a panic in the USA over the 'missile gap'. It was in both sides' interest to avoid a cripplingly expensive and potentially cataclysmic arms race, and in 1958 both governments took the first steps in the direction of negotiated arms control. Prior to this there had been ritualistic—and totally unrealistic—calls for 'general and complete disarmament' but now the pattern was broken. A 'conference of experts'—US, Soviet, and British—conferred on monitoring nuclear weapons tests, a little-appreciated turning point in post-war diplomacy. A ban on testing in the atmosphere, under the ocean, and in space was signed in Moscow in August 1963. It remains in force today.

During the period 1957–62 the Kremlin appeared to move towards détente with the West and to try to gain a position from which to dictate to them. Both were probably true. Meanwhile Pres John F. Kennedy had taken office in January 1961. The strategy of mutually assured destruction (MAD) associated with his Secretary of Defense, Robert *McNamara, implied that above a certain threshold—reached in 1964–5—additional nuclear weapons were of marginal utility. The *Cuban missile crisis of October 1962 warned of the dangers of nuclear confrontation but its resolution ended two and a half years of US–Soviet tension and reinforced the view that a nuclear exchange could not

be won. Both superpowers now sought a limited détente in the form of the limited test ban and the establishment of the hotline, designed to prevent accidental nuclear war.

In the wake of these tentative attempts to make the world a safer place, in January 1964 the USA suggested a bilateral verifiable freeze on the number and characteristics of both nations' strategic nuclear offensive and defensive vehicles. Meanwhile other developments threatened to upset the fragile strategic nuclear balance. Other nations had fielded nuclear weapons: the UK in 1952, France in 1960, China in 1964. In 1966 the USSR introduced Anti-Ballistic Missile (ABM) defence, followed by the USA in 1967, but discussion between the two superpowers continued. In June 1967 Pres Lyndon B. Johnson met Soviet Premier Aleksey Kosygin in New Jersey for discussions on ABM systems. Johnson and McNamara warned that the USA might be forced to respond in kind to Soviet efforts, setting off a new round in the arms race that would leave both sides worse off than before. On 1 July 1968, at the signing of the Non-Proliferation Treaty, Pres Johnson announced that the USA and the Soviet Union had agreed to negotiate limiting and reducing strategic nuclear weapons and ABM defences.

Delayed by the Soviet invasion of Czechoslovakia, the first series of Strategic Arms Limitation talks (SALT I) finally began in Helsinki in November 1969. Such was the emphasis placed on strategic stability—reflecting US and, to a lesser extent, Soviet doctrine—that the first product of the two different strands of negotiation was a Treaty on the Limitation of Anti-Ballistic Missile (ABM) Systems, in May 1972, and an Interim Agreement on limiting strategic offensive arms, freezing the number of intercontinental missiles for five years while negotiations continued: SALT II. The thinking was that anti-ballistic missile systems, possibly able to shoot down incoming missiles, were 'destabilizing': they upset the delicate balance of terror. This thinking has pervaded opposition to other initiatives such as the *SDI of 1983 and the subsequent less ambitious anti-missile programmes which may now have become feasible. SALT I was possible because of increased political confidence between Moscow and Washington. SALT I undoubtedly symbolized détente, but other problems in the shadow of potential global nuclear war—such as Soviet and US ventures in the Middle East—provoked dissent in the USA.

The SALT II negotiations resulted in the Treaty on the Limitation of Strategic Offensive Weapons, signed in June 1979. The Treaty included reductions in nuclear arms and restraints on the development of new weapons, but it was not ratified by the US Senate, and the arms race continued. However, in December 1987 US President Ronald Reagan and Secretary of the Soviet Communist Party Mikhail Gorbachev signed the Intermediate-range Nuclear Forces (INF) Treaty, calling for the elimination, rather than just the limitation, of an entire class of nuclear weapons delivery systems. The Treaty was ratified by both countries in 1988.

Meanwhile, Strategic Arms Reduction Talks (START) on long-range arsenals began in 1982, and a treaty (START I) was finally signed in July 1989. After the disintegration of the Soviet Union, START I was ratified by all the new (successor) states with offensive strategic nuclear forces: Russia, Belarus, Kazakhstan, and Ukraine. The last three nations are committed fully to eliminating their nuclear stockpiles, but Russia has retained most of the USSR's strategic nuclear forces, though with greatly reduced resources to maintain them. Two years after the ratification of START I, the USA and Russia signed a second agreement, START II, further reducing each country's arsenal of long-range nuclear weapons to one-third of their 1990 levels. The US Congress ratified START II in 1996, but the Russian Duma (parliament) has, at the time of going to press, yet to agree to do so, for political rather than financial or military reasons. Russia's existing strategic nuclear force is becoming obsolete, and Russia cannot afford to retain the parity with the USA agreed under START I. Indeed, Russia would have much difficulty maintaining parity with the USA at the lower levels of START II, which limits arsenals to single warhead missiles only. Russia would actually have to increase its holdings to achieve the permitted START II levels of 3,000 to 3,500 warheads. This lay behind the March 1997 Presidential Summit Declaration committing both sides to negotiate further reductions to between 2,000 and 2,500 warheads apiece (START III), once START II has been ratified. With START II thus stalled, US–Russian relations are proceeding under START I.

Other strategic nuclear arms reductions are proceeding outside START, notably those in US tactical nuclear weapons. However, the wider international situation is increasingly complex. The UK and France have maintained their arsenals at a 'minimum' nuclear deterrent level. But Israel, too, has nuclear weapons, India and Pakistan both tested multiple, sophisticated nuclear devices in May 1998. and China has said it will only join the strategic nuclear disarmament process 'at the appropriate time', related, among other criteria, to when the US States and Russian stockpiles each fall to below 1,000, implying, perhaps, a future, trilateral START.

The future is further complicated by other, so-called 'rogue' nuclear states, by the possibility of non-state nuclear terrorism, and by the spread of other (chemical and biological) weapons of mass destruction. The SALT/START process has proved effective in an essentially bilateral, bipolar context during and after the Cold War. It remains to be seen if mechanisms can evolve to deal with the new challenges of a multipolar, disordered, nuclear, biological, chemical, and information-armed world.   SJLR

Blacker, Coit D., *Reluctant Warriors: The US, the Soviet Union and Arms Control* (New York, 1987).
Bloomfield, Lincoln P., et al., *Khrushchev and the Arms Race: Soviet Interests in Arms Control and Disarmament 1954–1964* (Cambridge, Mass., 1966).
Freedman, Lawrence, *The Evolution of Nuclear Strategy* (New York, 1989, 1996).
Gray, Colin, *The Soviet-American Arms Race* (Lexington, Ky., 1976).

Strategic Defense Initiative. See SDI.

strategic hamlets In 1961, PM Ngo Dinh Diem of South Vietnam initiated the strategic hamlet programme to construct fortified villages to isolate the rural population from the Vietcong *guerrillas. Based loosely on the recommendations of British *counter-insurgency expert Sir Robert Thompson from his experience in the *Malayan emergency and headed by Diem's brother Ngo Dinh Nhu, the programme resembled Diem's earlier effort to increase his regime's presence in the countryside (the *agroville*). The strategic hamlet programme barely inconvenienced the Vietcong, but it did underline the corruption, political weaknesses, and increasing military ineffectiveness of the Diem regime, developments that fuelled growing US participation in the effort to suppress communist insurgents in South Vietnam.

The hamlets were supposed to deter Vietcong attacks and activity by facilitating local self-defence. Forming a defensive network, the fortified villages would be reinforced in case of concerted attack. Like *agrovilles*, strategic hamlets were intended to bolster South Vietnamese nationalism by allowing villagers to help defend their own homes. By providing educational and medical services, the programme also was intended demonstrate the Diem regime's commitment to the countryside.

A variety of problems prevented the realization of these goals. In practice, the programme was used by Saigon to exert physical control over its rural population and to leverage resources from its US patron. Village life was greatly disrupted by the effort to construct and settle strategic hamlets. At least 750,000 peasants were moved during the four years of the programme. Instead of building support for the Saigon regime, forced peasant labour and agricultural dislocation created resentment against the Ngos. Once relocated, peasants were often left without military equipment or training. For the average villager, the strategic hamlet represented another nuisance imposed by distant government officials.

The Diem regime, seeking grandiose claims of success, designated thousands of villages as strategic hamlets, a number that vastly exceeded available resources. Often based on quantitative measures of material expended, claimed achievements bore little resemblance to actual improvements in village security. The appearance of progress in Saigon was more important than the construction of a small yet realistic programme in the countryside.

US officials offered mixed evaluations of the programme. Some argued that strategic hamlets reflected a demoralizing defensiveness, while others saw them as a logical first step in reversing the Vietcong's gains in the countryside. The Vietcong seemed to ignore the programme, rarely expending resources to attack the hamlets in frontal assaults. Instead, Vietcong cadre infiltrated strategic hamlets, using persuasion and coercion to gain effective political control of the local population.   JJW

---

strategy (*see opposite page*)

---

strategy, medieval Many elements are involved in military strategy. Essential elements include the co-ordination and direction of armies and allies on a large scale, the planning of appropriate logistical arrangements and of supply routes, and the matching of fighting methods to the overall objectives of war. It is a common view that none of this was possible in the Middle Ages, that tactics and personal prowess were all that mattered in war, and that armies could not be effectively controlled by commanders who did not even possess *maps. In fact, there was much thought given to strategy. A theoretical basis was provided by the late classical work of *Vegetius, *De Re Militari*, which was widely read throughout the Middle Ages and commanders put its broad concepts into practice.

There is much evidence that campaigns were planned in quite a modern sense. The *Crusades saw consideration of such eminently strategic matters as whether or not to move against Damascus or against Egypt, and whether an alliance could be made with the *Mongols to co-ordinate military efforts. Richard 'the Lionheart''s participation in the Third Crusade shows a strategic mind at work, with much care taken to maintain supply routes, and a refusal to be diverted by the romantic goal of Jerusalem. In Britain, the 12th-century writings of Gerald of Wales also display strategic thinking. He advocated the imposition of an economic *blockade on Wales by the English, advised that internal divisions among the Welsh should be fostered and that lightly armed troops would be more effective than heavy cavalry. A century later Edward I's conquest of *Wales saw a clear strategy along these lines put into striking effect. The Anglo-French wars, above all the *Hundred Years War, saw both sides adopt grand strategies. Each constructed complex international alliances, though it has to be admitted that these were often hard to bring into action. Memoranda reveal the careful way in which the supply of arms, equipment, and foodstuffs was planned by *Edward III and his councillors.

Fighting methods were matched to overall objectives. The widespread destruction of territory was not aimless violence; medieval commanders deliberately used fire and sword as a highly effective way of compelling opponents to negotiate and come to terms. The *chevauchée was a powerful weapon. Advice set out by Sir John Fastolf in 1435

on how to conduct war in France stressed the advisability of avoiding sieges, the need to burn and destroy the land, and the necessity of maintaining control of the sea. It was to be the French and not the English who were to demonstrate their command of strategy, when Normandy was captured by three well-co-ordinated armies in just over a year.

MCP

Contamine, P., *War in the Middle Ages* (Oxford, 1984).
Prestwich, M. C., *Armies and Warfare in the Middle Ages: The English Experience* (New Haven, 1996).

Straussenburg, Baron Arthur Arz von (1857–1935), Austro-Hungarian general. Having joined the army in 1878, he began WW I as a divisional commander, but by 1916 was commanding an army. He was chosen by the new Habsburg emperor to replace *Conrad von Hötzendorf as the Austro-Hungarian CGS on 1 March 1917. Straussenburg was not chosen because of his military brilliance, rather Emperor Karl wanted a man who would not overshadow him in his efforts to direct the empire's war on his own. He served loyally in this capacity until the monarchy was dissolved at the end of the war.   RTF

---

streltsy (Russ., 'musketeers'), the first permanent and professional military force in Russia, created by *Ivan 'the Terrible' but disbanded after a series of unsuccessful revolts against *Peter 'the Great', the last in 1698.

Ivan established the first permanent detachment of 3,000 streltsy in 1550. Most were infantry, armed with *matchlock muskets and halberds, although there was also a small force of cavalry. By 1681 there were 55,000, half of them in Moscow serving as police and palace guards as well as soldiers. With the introduction of western-style regiments and the influx of foreign 'advisers' the streltsy began to feel resentful and threatened and in the 1680s some streltsy units were remodelled on western lines.

In 1682 the streltsy broke into the Kremlin, terrifying the 10-year-old Peter 'the Great', the first of a number of such revolts. In 1698, four streltsy regiments, about 4,000 men, who had been left in Azov after the campaign of 1695–6, were ordered to proceed to Velikye Luki instead of returning home to Moscow. Some deserted and made contact with Peter's rivals—his half-sister Sofia Andreevna and Prince Golitsyn—at the Novodevichy Monastery, near Moscow. Peter sent his newly formed Preobrazhenskiy and Semenov Guards regiments, which engaged and defeated the streltsy at the New Jerusalem (Voskrasensky) Monastery 34 miles (55 km) west of Moscow on 18 June. The streltsy revolt was crushed: 57 were hanged, some also drawn and quartered, the rest exiled. Peter, just returned from abroad, took no chances and purged the remaining regiments, executing 1,182 and exiling 600. Some were suspended outside the

(*cont. on page 883*)

strategy

S TRATEGY is an ancient concept that has eluded precise definition. The word derives from the Greek *strategos*, a civil-military official elected by the citizens of Athens to assume leadership in time of war. Most attempts at definition have turned upon a contrast with 'tactics' (*taktika*), the art of making arrangements, or of putting things in position. There is a superficial practicality in the idea, put forward by one 18th-century observer, Heinrich von Bülow, that strategy should refer to any military measures taken beyond the range of the enemy's weapons, while tactics referred to those taken within that range. Yet the original etymology is a useful corrective to the tendency to assume that strategy refers simply to the conduct of military operations on a large scale. Its most essential meaning points to the intellectual and practical reconciliation of military means and political ends. For *Clausewitz, strategy was 'the use of combats for the purposes of the war'. *Liddell Hart, similarly, said it was 'the art of distributing and applying military means to fulfill the ends of policy'.

In recent times, as the ends of policy have become more complex and diverse, it has become common for strategy to encompass non-military means as well; though one might argue that for great polities like the Roman empire or the Ming dynasty it has always done so. Expressions like 'national strategy' and 'grand strategy' typically refer to the full range of methods by which states act internationally, including non-coercive diplomacy, trade, peacetime alliances, humanitarianism, and so on, as well as the actual use or threat of force—the concern of military strategy strictly understood. The adoption of the word 'strategy' by private organizations to refer to any deliberate, long-term plan, has further blurred its conceptual distinctiveness.

At a minimum, it seems fair to insist that, as applied to the conduct of states, a strategy is a course of action in which the use of force is not excluded as a matter of principle. Strategic action can be readily distinguished, for instance, from actions governed by market relationships, which are essentially rule-bound and, as a consequence, susceptible to a kind of abstract analysis that has eluded theorists of war. For all its competitive pressures, the market place is a far less confounding environment than the battlefield. The latter, as Hobbes said, is the domain of 'force and fraud', which admit no limits in principle, nor any sort of mutually transparent rationality to help ensure that the conduct of one antagonist is understandable to the other.

If strategy is made necessary by the inherent chaos of the international system, it is made possible by the human capacity to anticipate and organize against adversity; to detect—in the conclusion of a pact of friendship between formerly rival cities, or the arranged marriage of an obscure princess to a neighbouring prince, or the discovery of new and fertile lands overseas, or a thousand other contingent events—some remote or proximate threat, to which a forceful response may someday be required. Such responses may be simple or elaborate, cunning or bold, bellicose or pacific; but all will be shaped by deeply rooted geographic, social, economic, and cultural facts, as well as by whatever immediate interests are thought to be at stake. If strategy is, proverbially, a realm of uncertainty, it is because it must account for fundamentally unpredictable behaviour, shaped by assumptions that are rarely fully understood even by those most directly concerned. *Moltke 'the Elder', one of modern war's greatest practitioners, doubted that strategy could ever be more than a 'system of expedients'.

All the expedients of strategy nevertheless share a common purpose: to reach military results that alter the political calculations of the belligerents. If there is a central idea around which serious strategic analysis must revolve, it is decisiveness. One might well say, more simply, victory; but the latter is a less useful idea, because it is too prone to be interpreted in purely military terms, and to attribute exaggerated importance to dramatic episodes on the battlefield. The capture of a town, the successful defence of a hill, the destruction of the enemy army in front of you—these are all undeniably victories, to be admired as such. Yet nothing is more common in war than strategically barren victory—meaning military achievements that, however impressive in their own terms, nevertheless fail to alter the political context in which they occur. Such disconnection can be demoralizing to those who fight, and is a common source of civil-military discord, if not, indeed, of defeat. More than a few of history's most skilful soldiers—*Charles XII, *Napoleon, *Lee, the German High Command of both world wars—have single-mindedly pursued tactical success all the way to strategic ruin; while others less gifted by prevailing military standards—*Washington, *Blücher, *Haig, *Giap—have achieved strategic decisions favourable to their causes despite tactical results conventionally deemed mediocre, or worse. Among the virtues that strategy can lend to tactics, persistence and the long view are among the most underrated.

Strategic possibilities are always influenced by the means employed to raise the armed forces intended to achieve them. The ancient *phalanx and the medieval host were brought to the battlefield by a complex web of social relationships that were only partly military in character. Such armies might be capable of tremendous violence when brought into contact with each other—a formidable task in itself—but they were also temporary structures, called into existence by immediate threats or opportunities, or in response to some cultural imperative (personal honour, civil obligation, etc.). Such forces had exceedingly limited capabilities, and could engage in sustained combat for only a few hours at a time before losing cohesion. The strategic *pursuit or 'exploitation' necessary to capitalize upon tactical success did not exist, and wars were accordingly decided, as often as not, by simple exhaustion, or impatience with futility. The standing armies of early modern territorial states possessed greater military efficiency—they could train more regularly, and their officers, although still drawn from a vestigial *feudal élite, were more professional in outlook—but their strategic significance lay chiefly in the fact that they existed all year round, and were more firmly at the disposal of the crown. Although it would be wrong to imagine that anything like 'strategic planning' existed before the 19th century, standing armies allowed governments to estimate their own strength, and that of potential allies and opponents, more consistently, and so (in theory at least) to integrate military means and political ends more effectively than in the past.

Nevertheless, the tactical limitations of even the best pre-industrial armies were sufficient to restrict feasible strategic objectives to the seizure of a province, the ravaging of a border district, and so on. If such actions might occasionally have far-reaching results, it was a reflection of the fragility of the political base upon which armies, and the governments that employed them, rested. For most governments at most times, the perils of defeat have been more vivid than the promise of victory. Until relatively recently, this asymmetry found expression in the systematic *fortification of cities and towns, a genuinely strategic practice demanding much foresight, expense, and protracted effort. From the Bronze Age to the industrial revolution, the 'typical' military engagement has in fact been a siege—*Marlborough conducted 60, in addition to the four pitched battles that made him famous—and much of what passed for strategy, on land at least, consisted in bringing them about on favourable terms, by fortifying every vital place.

Somewhat different considerations arise for traditional societies that rely on *navies to advance their interests. If the goal of strategy is to influence political decisions by force of arms, it is obviously a matter of some importance that political decisions are made on land. Navies have usually achieved their strategic effects less directly than armies, by attacking an adversary's seaborne trade or overseas possessions, or by supporting harassing operations against his coast—for either of which purpose it might, of course, be necessary to suppress (or, for the weaker side, to elude) the enemy navy first. It is historically rare for such measures to achieve decisive results by themselves. When combined with major operations on land the effects of maritime power on an opponent could be profound. Few countries have ever possessed the need, or the means, simultaneously to maintain armies and navies of the first rank. For continental states, immediate threats across land frontiers necessarily predominate, while geographically isolated or island nations like Great Britain and the USA have tended to find large standing armies an unnecessary and politically dangerous burden. The simultaneous application of land and sea power has thus been accomplished for the most part by strategic alliances; and it is perhaps not by chance that maritime powers have often found themselves with exaggerated reputations for artful, if not duplicitous, diplomacy.

These basic strategic patterns were significantly altered, though not, indeed, abolished, by the industrial and democratic revolutions of the late 18th and 19th centuries, which created new means of organizing society for war, and of adapting new scientific and managerial methods to warfare. The strategic possibilities of the modern era have been largely defined by the interactions between mass social mobilization and technological change. Neither was viewed with anything like equanimity by those who first confronted them. The advent of the *levée en masse, which made Napoleon's career possible, struck his opponents and successors as a profoundly dangerous development, in which seeds of atavistic escalation and incipient social revolution were clearly visible. Better to rely upon small armies of tactically proficient, politically reliable professionals. Only they, it was thought, could deliver an effective attack; and it was only by well-modulated offensive operations that strategic decisions could be reached at an acceptable social cost.

This prudent consensus was eroded by the increasing lethality of modern weapons. By the middle decades of the 19th century, it was clear that the modern battlefield could only be mastered by mass armies far larger than any country could afford to maintain in peacetime. Regular armies became training organizations for vast streams of conscripts, whose rapid mobilization and dispersed deployment became central to the military *art. Such forces were regarded as wasting assets. Although railways and the *telegraph made their mobilization possible—which in turn made intensive, continuous military planning necessary—their staying power under fire was open to question; and once concentrated for battle, the difficulties of moving, supplying, and manoeuvring armies numbering in the hundreds of thousands quickly become intractable.

It was, moreover, reasonable to assume that wars to which a large proportion of society's able-bodied men were committed could not go on for long before being brought to a halt by economic failure or social unrest at home. To be politically useful, strategic decisions had to be obtained quickly. For this purpose, two prospects stood out: pre-emptive attack, in which the enemy's forces might be engaged and destroyed before their mobilization or deployment was complete; and strategic envelopment, which sought to mitigate the effects of modern firepower by directing large forces against the flanks and rear of the enemy, far more rapidly and deeply than small, slow-moving armies of even a generation before could have contemplated. These methods, continuously modified by technological advance, dominate the conduct of land operations in the era of the world wars, and in most other major conflicts to this day. Yet the modern strategist's governing ideal of swift, decisive results, achieved by rapidly evolving, intensely violent, well-controlled manoeuvre, has remained elusive, largely because it rests upon a foundation of what has proven to be an unjustified social pessimism. Advanced societies at war are not fragile machines, prone to economic breakdown and revolutionary decay. Once aroused, their military energies have proven extraordinarily resistant to strategic manipulation, or to defeat by other than *attritional means—a strategy in itself, to be sure, but one with scant appeal to professional soldiers.

The impact of industrialization on naval warfare has been equally complex. The emergence of an integrated global economy rapidly increased the value of water-borne trade, and hence of those things that navies were best suited to attack. Few advanced societies at the turn of the 20th century were producing all the necessities of life within their own borders, and their resulting dependence on unfettered access to the oceans appeared to present a profound strategic opportunity, which even traditional continental powers sought, for a while, to seize. At the same time new technologies conspired to produce warships of enormous tactical power, but limited strategic range and endurance. The great steam-and-steel fleets of the day were poorly suited to the classic missions of *blockade and *guerre de course*, and were shockingly vulnerable to underwater weapons when brought close to shore. The proliferation of railways and paved highways also reduced the relative advantage of mobility that seaborne forces had enjoyed in the past. The maturation of submarines and naval aviation, both deeply suspect at first appearance, have combined to assure that naval forces remain an essential source of modern military strength, most decidedly so when a state's strategic interests span the globe. Yet the promise that *naval power might somehow suffice to dominate events on land, or render the grinding clash of armies unnecessary, has gone unfulfilled.

Navies were the first military institutions to confront the dilemmas of technological change on a scale capable of altering strategic calculations. As late as the 1840s, the working life of a first-class warship could reasonably be expected to exceed that of the men who sailed her. Thirty years later, such comforting assumptions had been displaced by the realization that some new method of laying guns, or designing engines, or compounding armour plate, could require a generation's military investment to be discounted at sickening rates. It is the fear, as much as the fact, of technological obsolescence that matters. Precisely because significant technologies almost always arise first in civil society, it is rare for any state to remain at a technological disadvantage to its competitors for long. Military advantages based upon technical means are notable mainly for their evanescence—which only heightens the need to keep up. The fortress-builders of the pre-industrial world did not fear that some device might arise to render their life's work irrelevant. Such anxieties, while easily exaggerated, are no longer completely absurd. They have made the 'arms race', a metaphor first employed in connection with naval building programmes, a distinctive feature of the modern strategic landscape.

No new technology has had more far-reaching strategic consequences than the aeroplane, and the ballistic missiles that have followed in its wake. Those who embraced what immediately became known (in imitation of the navalists) as *air power, did so for two competing reasons. To some, air power offered the last increment of technological proficiency necessary to preserve industrialized war as a plausible instrument of policy. Aeroplanes could see what could not otherwise be seen, strike what could not otherwise be struck, and so break the bloody stalemate that always threatened to emerge whenever modern armies came within weapons' range of each other. Aeroplanes, in these terms, were simply the most recent in a series of technological advances that would finally make modern warfare swift and efficient. Others doubted that the leavening effects of 'tactical' air power could be that great. As an independent, strategic weapon, however, the aeroplane's possibilities seemed unlimited. By providing a means of striking directly at the social and political fabric of the adversary, strategic air power captured the quintessence of what 'strategy' was always supposed to mean—the maximally effective application of military force for political ends. By dissolving all meaningful distinction between armed forces and the civil societies they protected, war in the air would make war as conventionally understood a thing of the past. Above the enemy's cities, strategy and tactics would become one.

It would be vain, in the shadow of *nuclear weapons, to declare the apocalyptic pretensions of strategic air power disproved; though it is fair to say that the expectations of those who conceived of *air forces as components of modern combined arms operations have been more fully vindicated by events. Nevertheless, the unique possibilities afforded by war in the air continue to exert enormous sway. At the end of the 20th century, strategic air power—meaning the independent use (or threat) of air strikes to achieve direct political effects—dominates both ends of the conflict spectrum. Nuclear *deterrence remains the ultimate guarantee of security for most of the large countries in the world, who either possess such weapons themselves or have allies that do. At the same time, *precision guided munitions and *stealth technology have made air weapons the preferred instruments for the conduct of low-intensity conflict and coercive diplomacy by advanced societies.

Whether this last, superficially surprising adaptation of air power will justify the hope that has been placed in it by its political masters remains to be seen. The history of strategy in the industrial era has been dominated, to a degree that is perhaps not easily appreciated, by the need to control the escalatory pressures that arise in societies at war, for the most part by technical and managerial means that are supposed to make war less destructive (if only by ending it quickly), more efficient, and more predictable in its political effects. The record, to say the least, is mixed. The quest for decisiveness that is at the heart of strategic decision-making has always concealed elements of desperation, not to say despair. In this sense, all strategic choices are bad choices. Yet the consequences of dispensing with them entirely remain unfathomable.   DM

Bond, Brian, *The Pursuit of Victory* (Oxford, 1996).
Murray, Williamson, Knox, MacGregor, and Bernstein, Alvin (eds.), *The Making of Strategy* (Cambridge, 1994).
Paret, Peter (ed.), *Makers of Modern Strategy* (Princeton, 1986).
Strachan, Hew, *European Armies and the Conduct of War* (London, 1983).

window of the room where his half-sister was to spend the rest of her life.   CDB

Stuart, Maj Gen James Ewell Brown ('Jeb') (1833–64).

An inspirational Virginian cavalry leader and *beau sabreur* of the *American civil war, Stuart served in the pre-war US cavalry and, like his mentor *Lee, resigned to join the *Confederate States Army when Virginia seceded. He distinguished himself at first *Bull Run and was promoted brigadier general, emerging as a cavalry general of real ability. In June 1862 he rode around the Union army during the Jamestown peninsular campaign and was promoted major general to command all Army of Northern Virginia cavalry by Lee, who called him the 'eyes of the army'. Those eyes found the open Union right flank at *Chancellorsville, enabling *Jackson to launch his crushing attack. In June 1863 he was surprised by a Union cavalry attack at Brandy Station and fought one of the war's few wholly cavalry battles to a finely balanced draw. Immediately afterwards, sent to raid around the Union army, he failed to maintain contact with Lee in the days before *Gettysburg, depriving him of vital *intelligence. In May 1864 he was mortally wounded at Yellow Tavern when blocking a move by *Sheridan towards Richmond. Famously flamboyant in dress (nicknamed 'Beauty' by old friends and 'Jeb' by his men), his late arrival at Gettysburg must be balanced against the fact that it was largely thanks to him that the Union cavalry took so long to make its numbers felt.   RH

Student, Gen Kurt (1890–1978),

modest creator and commander of German WW II *airborne forces. The young Student had commanded a fighter squadron in WW I and served in the (disguised) *general staff in the early inter-war years. Director of Luftwaffe technical training from 1933, and inspector of airborne forces in 1938, a small force of his *glider troops knocked out the Belgian Eben Emael fortress in a spectacular *coup de main* in May 1940. He himself commanded two divisions in Holland in May 1940, where he was severely wounded by a sniper. A year later, his XI Fliegerkorps took *Crete, though with heavy losses. Thereafter, *Hitler lost interest in airborne assaults, and Student's carefully trained élite were misused as ground troops, though with a fearsome reputation. *Churchill ordered the formation of British airborne forces in emulation.

                                                                APC-A

Hackett, Sir John (chapter), in Correlli Barnett (ed.), *Hitler's Generals* (London, 1990).

sub-machine gun is a hand-held, fully automatic weapon firing pistol ammunition and designed to be used for close-quarter action. Developed during WW I, it was a fully automatic refinement of the self-loading pistol fitted with a shoulder stock and a large capacity magazine. There are claims that the original sub-machine gun was designed by an Italian, B. A. Revelli, and manufactured by the Villar Perosa company as their Model 1915, but this twin-barrelled automatic weapon was really a light machine gun. The ancestor of all sub-machine guns was the German MaschinePistole 1918, or MP 18, developed by the inventor *Schmeisser for Bergmann. It had a short, air-cooled barrel, a wooden stock, and a 'snail-drum' magazine containing 9 mm pistol ammunition. It was issued in limited numbers to assault troops in the closing months of WW I.

In the period 1919–28, the sub-machine gun was synonymous with the name Thompson, whose design, manufactured by the Auto-Ordnance Corporation in .45 inch calibre and fitted with drum magazines of 50- or 100-round capacity, was purchased worldwide by those interested in crime and its deterrence; the Thompson's only military use, and even there the term is debatable, was with the *IRA. In the late 1920s Germany and the USSR were surreptitiously co-operating on weapons development, the former in order to evade the terms of the Versailles Treaty of 1919, the latter to take advantage of Germany's technological development. Sub-machine gun development was included and, by the late 1930s, both the German and Soviet armies were equipped with the results: the German MP 38 and the Soviet Degtyarev PPD. German use of the sub-machine gun was a major contributory factor to the effects of *blitzkrieg and its army's successes in 1940–1. After 1940 the cheaper MP 40 replaced the MP 38.

The impact of the MP 38 and MP 40 caused Germany's enemy, Britain, to take two steps in remedying the situation: large quantities of the expensive Thompson were bought from the USA and development immediately began on a British sub-machine gun. The result of the latter step was the *Sten, in every way different from the Thompson: it cost one-twentieth as much and was lighter, less complicated, and much more quickly and easily made. Although profoundly limited in many aspects, the Sten was widely used by Britain and its allies in WW II and for many years afterwards. Its American equivalent was the M-3, or 'grease-gun'; cheaply made in .45 inch calibre, it could quickly be converted for the 9 mm ammunition widely available in the European theatre. In the USSR, the PPsh 41 and PPS 42/43 7.62 mm drum-magazined sub-machine guns equated to the Sten and M-3 as being cheap, mass-produced, and effective. In Australia, the Owen and Austen sub-machine guns represented an independent alternative, the latter weapon combining the best elements of the MP 40 and the Sten.

Effective though the cheap and mass-produced sub-machine gun was, it tended to be underpowered for long-distance use and its ammunition was heavy, limiting the quantities that the soldier could easily carry. German experimentation provided the answer in the form of the SturmGewehr 1944, SG 44, or assault rifle. This fired the smaller 7.92 mm shortened rifle cartridge, with higher velocity and lower mass than the 9 mm pistol. It was a powerful, long-range sub-machine gun capable of firing single shots or fully automatically and it was the ancestor of most modern assault rifles, notably the Avtomat *Kalashnikova, AK-47, and its descendants.

Developments in sub-machine guns since 1945 have concentrated on bringing them closer to assault rifles and shrinking them in size. The advantages of the former have been in the standardization of ammunition, an important factor in military terms; those of the latter have greater appeal for the use of the sub-machine gun by paramilitary units, specialist military forces, and by criminals and terrorists. The distinction between the assault rifle and the sub-machine gun has become blurred by these developments and the sub-machine gun of the 1990s tends to be, like the Uzi or the Ingram, little more than a large pistol capable of fully automatic fire and fitted with a large capacity magazine. SCW

Blair, Claude (ed.), *Pollard's History of Firearms* (London, 1983).
Cormack, Alexander J. R., *Small Arms: A Concise History of their Development* (Windsor, 1982).
Hogg, Ian V., and Weeks, John, *Military Small Arms of the 20th Century* (London, 1985).

Sudirman, Gen (1912–50), Indonesian general known as *bapak tentara* (Father of the Army), and first commander of the independent Indonesian army. A former teacher and devout Muslim, he was elected commander in November 1945 largely by fellow Javanese officers impressed with his traditional values, his lack of Dutch links, and his use of his Japanese-trained militia battalion against his former patrons and the British alike. He saw the army as an embodiment of a state, not a political ideology, and tried to keep it above the partisan strife of the revolution. A unifying commander of the armed forces from June 1946, his near-legendary status principally rests on his last year. In December 1948 a Dutch offensive took the capital of Jogjakarta and while his government chose surrender, Sudirman, stricken with tuberculosis, left his sickbed to retreat to the hills and direct the skilful *guerrilla campaign that drove the Dutch to the negotiating table. Although opposed to the August 1949 ceasefire, he preserved unity by leading his forces back to barracks. He died in January 1950, a month after the transfer of sovereignty, but his legacy lived on in *Nasution. DD

Crouch, Harold, *The Army and Politics in Indonesia* (Ithaca, NY, 1988).
Sundhaussen, Ulf, *The Road to Power* (Oxford, 1982).

Suez campaign (1956). Anglo-French interests in Egypt dated back beyond their financial support and construction of the Suez Canal, completed in 1869. After the death of *Muhammad Ali in 1848, European control over Egypt increased and following the country's bankruptcy in 1876 an Anglo-French commission took over Egypt's finances. Then in 1882, following a failed attempt by the Egyptian army to end foreign interference, British troops occupied the country.

Egypt remained under British control, as the Suez Canal became an integral part of Britain's strategic policy in the Mediterranean and the Middle East, providing as it did a short route to India. Britain, with French connivance, remained in illegal occupation until *Nasser took control of the country in 1956. He had been involved in the abolition of the monarchy and in the negotiated withdrawal of British troops, but his dream was to build the high Aswan Dam, and he wanted the revenues from the canal to pay for it. In pursuing a policy of nationalization and negotiations with the USSR, he gave the British government what it thought was an opportunity to recover lost ground. Attempts to prevent him nationalizing the canal failed and Britain conspired with both France and Israel to repossess it. On 29 October 1956 Israeli forces under the command of *Dayan, citing the need to destroy *guerrilla camps in the Sinai desert, crossed the frontier and drove back four Egyptian divisions before them.

The invasion of Egyptian territory permitted London and Paris to issue a twelve-hour ultimatum, calling for the cessation of hostilities. While Israel agreed, the Egyptian refusal to compromise provided the excuse for Anglo-French action. This came in the form of air attacks from 31 October, which effectively destroyed the Egyptian air force on the ground.

There followed a delay of four days, resulting from poor planning, allowing for a consolidation of world (and domestic) opinion against the Anglo-French response, with the USSR and the USA leading the protests. Unwisely ignoring these, the British and French governments launched an invasion, mounted from Cyprus. The airborne operation, code-named MUSKETEER, began on 5 November and was conducted in conjunction with an amphibious assault by Royal Marine Commandos, under cover of a naval bombardment.

The 3rd Battalion The Parachute Regiment, carried out an operational parachute descent onto El Gamil airfield. The Egyptian defenders, although supported by light armour, assault guns, machine guns, and mortars, were unable to prevent the lightly equipped paratroop battalion from reaching all its objectives within hours of landing. By 6 November both Port Said and the airfield were under Anglo-French control, but amid the rattling of the nuclear sabre by the USSR and economic threats from the USA, on 7 November they acceded to UN demands for a cease-fire.

Suez is an episode the British would rather forget. It effectively ended Anthony Eden's tenure as PM, causing such controversy that he resigned the following January. Egypt had lost some 3,000 troops killed and a further 7,000 were taken prisoner, compared to Anglo-French losses of 33 dead and 129 wounded, with the Israelis losing only some 180 killed in an advance to within 30 miles (48 km) of the canal. Nasser had sunk blockships in the canal and it did not reopen until March 1957, under UN control.

PMacD

Suleiman I, 'the Magnificent' (1494–1566), Ottoman *Turk sultan who ruled from 1520, when Ottoman power was at its zenith. Lord of 'the realms of the Romans, the Persians and the Arabs', his empire stretched from Algiers to Azerbaijan and from Moldova to Yemen. One Venetian ambassador reported fancifully, if not inaccurately, that his empire bordered those of Spain, Persia, and, of Prester John (the fabled emperor of Abyssinia).

Suleiman succeeded his father, Selim 'the Grim', on 1 October 1520. At first, the Christian West welcomed the accession of a man renowned as a scholar. But never would the Ottoman empire be as admired or feared as under Suleiman. He inherited a superb military machine which worked because, unlike western European armies of the time, the forces were promptly paid and supported by a superb administration. He could put an army of 100,000 into the field centred on the professional corps of *janissaries, Christian-born men from the Balkans, carefully selected and superbly trained, particularly in military—and therefore general—engineering. He was also helped by the schism in the Christian Church which coincided with his accession. The same year, Luther set the Reformation in train. Unlike Selim, who had directed Ottoman expansion east and south, Suleiman sensed it was time to move west. In 1521 he took Belgrade and moved against *Rhodes, which had been an unwelcome Christian strong point in the eastern Mediterranean for 200 years. The knights withdrew to Malta on New Year's Day, 1523. In a characteristic aside, Suleiman said he was sad to make the Grand Master, an old man, leave his home and his belongings. In 1526 he defeated a foolhardy attack by the Hungarian army at *Mohacs, and captured Buda, but delayed the formal annexation of Hungary for twenty years, allowing the Hungarians to squabble among themselves. In 1532 he perhaps met his match in the Holy Roman Emperor and King of Spain, *Charles V. The Ottoman army was held up unexpectedly by the stubborn resistance at Guns, 70 miles (113 km) south-east of Vienna, and Charles did not make the mistake of moving out to meet the Ottomans, as the Hungarians had.

The Ottoman army possessed some of world's most powerful artillery, but still preferred the powerful composite *bow to the muskets now becoming dominant in western European armies. Suleiman's last campaign in 1566 was

885

another incursion into Habsburg territory, with the largest army he had ever assembled. On 7 September he died in his tent, among his troops, in the siege of Szigeth. His grand vizier kept his death secret, embalmed the body, and carried it home as if it were alive. He was succeeded by his bibulous son Selim II, 'the Sot'. CDB

Goodwin, Jason, *Lords of the Horizons* (London, 1998).

Sulla, Publius Cornelius (*c*.138–78 BC). Of an old, but recently undistinguished, family, Sulla entered politics relatively late and saw his first military service in 107 BC as *Marius' *quaestor* in North Africa, where he made a reputation for himself by arranging the capture of Jugurtha through treachery. He then served in the defeat of the migrating Cimbri and Teutones. Having fought with distinction and increasingly high responsibility in the *Social and Civil Wars, he was elected consul in 88 and given command in the war against Mithridates VI of Pontus, who had overrun Rome's eastern provinces. When his rival Marius attempted to take over this command himself, Sulla used his legions against his political opponents. This was the first time that a Roman army had marched on the city of Rome. Leaving for the east, Sulla stormed Athens and defeated the large, but poor quality Pontic army at the battles of *Chaeronea and Orchomenus in 86. Having made peace with Mithridates in 85, he invaded Italy in 83 and fought a series of successful battles against his opponents, culminating in a battle fought outside the Colline Gate of Rome. The victorious Sulla was made *dictator and exercised his power by massacring his opponents, but retired to private life in 80. AKG

Sumerian warfare Mesopotamia produced one of the earliest civilizations, based on competing city states, which sometimes became united into kingdoms. Before 2500 BC, these states were capable of far-reaching campaigns employing *phalanxes of drilled spearmen, ass-drawn battlewagons, and fortified garrison posts. A carved stone known as the Vulture Stela from the city state of Lagash shows the infantry in close order behind large *shields led by their king in his battlewagon. A beautifully decorated lyre from Ur depicts similar figures in lapis lazuli and shell. The soldiers wear studded leather cloaks for protection and metal helmets. Weaponry consisted of battleaxes, thrusting spears and daggers for the infantry, while the leaders in their battlewagons carry sheaves of javelins. Battle tactics between two similarly armed armies probably consisted of the ass-drawn wagons skirmishing with each other and the opposing phalanx, seeking to create gaps which could be exploited by the heavy infantry.

The technology of warfare was already quite well developed. The battlewagons were drawn by four asses and were constructed of wicker and leather, mounting a driver and

warrior. They are shown with four solid wheels, which suggests that they could not have been a particularly rapid form of transport. They must have been clumsy and difficult to manoeuvre as well. Models of lighter, two-wheeled *chariots from grave finds suggest that there were alternative modes of transport, but these may not have been used in war. Perhaps surprisingly, there is little evidence of the employment of missile weapons in the depictions of battle. *Slings are occasionally shown, but there is only one surviving depiction of a *bow. This is a composite bow on a victory stela of King Naram-Sin (*c*.2254–2218 BC). Archaeology has revealed the existence of great stone curtain walls, which seem designed for defence by archery. Strangely, there are no depictions of *siege warfare, although this would seem likely to have taken place between city states. It is possible that the technology to construct *siege engines was not available to the Sumerians. Although Sumerian states did keep documentary records, in which war featured strongly, there is nothing to compare with the kind of information, both visual and the written record, which survives for the later Mesopotamian empires such as the *Assyrians. MB

Hackett, Gen Sir John, (ed.), *Warfare in the Ancient World* (London, 1989).

Yadin, Yigael, *The Art of Warfare in Biblical Lands* (London, 1963).

Sun-tzu (Sun-pin or Sun-wu) (pronounced 'Soon-dzer') (active 400–320 BC), Chinese general, military theorist, and philosopher. Author of the world's first and potentially most long-lived work of military theory, *The Art of War*, also known as *The Thirteen Chapters*. Although it is quite possible that 'Sun-tzu' might be a combination of different writers, the author of the pre-eminent translation of the ancient texts into English, the scholarly US Marine Col Samuel B. Griffith, was convinced the structure of the work indicates it was written by 'a singularly imaginative individual who had considerable practical experience in war'. In the 1980s *The Art of War* was adopted by Tokyo, Wall Street, and the City of London as a text for students of business strategy, and became fashionable dinner-party conversation for the so-called 'yuppies' of the time.

Sun-tzu probably wrote in the period of the *Warring States in the 4th century BC. It has been suggested that the work might be by Sun Wu and date from the late 6th century BC, but there are repeated references to crossbows, invented in China in around 400 BC. Furthermore, there is no mention of cavalry, which appeared around 320 BC, only of *chariots. We can therefore be tolerably sure this first and most universal work on the art of war dates from 400–320 BC.

Like many great works of military thought, *The Art of War* is a mixture of profound philosophy and detailed and dated tactical prescriptions. The opening sentence of *The*

Thirteen Chapters is clear enough: 'war is a matter of vital importance to the state; the province of life and death; the road to survival or ruin. It is mandatory that it be thoroughly studied.' Probably its most lasting observation is to do with *information warfare. 'All war is based on deception. Therefore, when capable, feign incapacity; when active, inactivity. When near, make it appear that you are far away; when far away, that you are near.' Sun-tzu was the first to enunciate the 'indirect approach' in war; indeed, he coined the phrase. He who was master of both the direct and the indirect approach would be victorious, a reflection of the interaction of regular and partisan forces which was a characteristic of war in Sun-tzu's age. Mao and the Vietnamese followed this tradition. Sun-tzu likened an army to water, 'for just as flowing water avoids the heights and hastens to the lowlands, so an army avoids strength and strikes weakness'.

Sun-tzu was the first to set out what we would now recognize as *principles of war: moral influence, weather, terrain, command, and *doctrine. The first meant the trust of people in their leaders. By 'command', he meant the qualities and ability of the general and by 'doctrine' he meant organization, command and control, and logistics.

The first translation of Sun-tzu into a western language was by Father Amiot, a French Jesuit missionary, published in Paris in 1772, but Sun-tzu attracted little attention in France. Had the French studied it, they might have done better in *Indochina. Sun-tzu was immensely influential on *Mao Tse-tung and on the Soviet military system. Mao's writings evince a clear debt to Sun-tzu. His 'four slogans' coined at Ching Kang Shan bear a remarkable resemblance to several of Sun-tzu's verses. Sun-tzu was translated into Russian in 1860, and several times thereafter, and retranslated into German for the East German Ministry of Defence. Although Sun-tzu was introduced to Japan in the 8th century AD, and extensively studied thereafter, the Japanese understanding of it appears to have been superficial. At Pearl Harbor and in their initial campaign in *Malaya the Japanese followed Sun-tzu's precepts, knowingly or unknowingly. But later they showed themselves to be obstinate fighters who were unable to cope with unorthodox methods applied by the Allies, including the Chinese.

The biography of Sun-tzu in the official Chinese records (*Shih-Ch'I*) relates the story of Sun-tzu commanding a parade of the concubines of the king of Wu, in an experiment to test the general's ability to command. In spite of repeated clear instructions, the girls responded to the orders by giggling. Eventually, Sun-tzu had the two girls who had been appointed as commanders beheaded, much to the king's dismay. Many commentators have dismissed the episode as unlikely, but it raises another intriguing possibility. There were women generals in ancient China. Could it be that Sun-tzu was a woman?   CDB

Sun-tzu, *The Art of War*, trans. Samuel B. Griffith (Oxford, 1963).

supply. See LOGISTICS.

Supreme War Council (SWC), the co-ordinating body created by the western Allies towards the end of WW I. For much of the war there was no formal machinery for co-ordinating the strategy and actions of the French and British armies. Strategy was settled by conferences between British and French commanders and politicians, a slow and cumbersome process.

The idea was first proposed by *Lloyd George, acting on the advice of Wilson, at the Rapallo conference of 7 November 1917. Both men wanted to curb the power of the British C-in-C *Haig and the timing was propitious, as the Italians had just suffered a heavy defeat at *Caporetto and there was a patent need for the British, French, Italians, and Americans to co-ordinate the response. The other national representatives agreed and the SWC was established at Versailles.

It faced a number of problems. Its deliberations slowed down the decision-making process even further by providing for a military talking shop, and not an Allied C-in-C, which Haig would not accept, while the British CIGS *Robertson also resented the fact that his role as chief military adviser to the government was under threat. *Clemenceau, the French PM, regarded the SWC as an unsatisfactory halfway house on the way to unity of command. An Executive War Board, chaired by *Foch, was supposed to control an Allied reserve, but Haig and *Pétain would not release troops to him and *Pershing, probably correctly, saw it as an attempt to use his troops piecemeal, which he opposed utterly. The *Ludendorff offensive of 21 March 1918 made everybody sober up, and suddenly both Haig's objections to unity of command and Pershing's reservations vanished. Foch's appointment as Allied generalissimo rendered the SWC irrelevant.   GDS

Philpott, William James, *Anglo-French Relations and Strategy on the Western Front, 1914–18* (London, 1996).

surrender (from Fr.: *se rendre*, to give oneself up). Compare with *capitulate.

surveillance and target acquisition is, loosely, another variable in the all-encompassing term *reconnaissance, but it is a specific function. Surveillance will take place at a distance away from the front line or the battle area, and is particularly relevant to air warfare and to the use of artillery to enable the accurate acquisition of targets.

The decision by the Japanese during the *Russo-Japanese war to deploy their artillery on reverse slopes at the battle of Sha-ho on 1 September 1904 marked a significant development in warfare. Out of sight of the enemy, the guns required assistance from forward observers, who conducted surveillance of the target and corrected the fire of the artillery. This *indirect fire became key to the battles of WW I, but could not be conducted without accurate surveillance of targets which were out of sight of the guns which were to engage them.

The advent of aircraft enabled spotting to take a giant leap forward and artillery observation flights became part of the daily work of the early *air forces, both to identify targets and to observe the fall of shot. But weather could ground the aircraft or obscure a target area, while enemy fighter action and *camouflage made this less than a panacea, so other means of surveillance and target acquisition evolved, namely flash-spotting and sound-ranging. In the first, forward observers would take a bearing on the flash of an enemy gun and report it to a central control. The intersection of several bearings would establish the location of the gun for counter-battery fire to be ordered. Sound-ranging took time to develop as an effective system, since the noise of the battlefield and weather conditions could make it difficult to differentiate among sounds, but technological innovations enabled the system to develop by using microphones to detect the sound of an enemy gun firing and extrapolating the range and bearing from the sound intensity.

These technologies remain in use, although flash-spotting has declined. A more significant development has been that of *radar systems to locate the source of enemy fire. Soviet artillery, before the demise of the USSR, employed highly effective target acquisition systems combining inertial navigation systems and laser rangefinding and direction-finding equipment. It was advancing towards what was termed a 'reconnaissance-destruction complex', a system whereby the automated surveillance and acquisition of targets followed by their immediate engagement would be possible. It is hard to exactly assess how the collapse of the USSR has hindered this development, but there can be little doubt that the system is less formidable now than it might have been. A similar automated system, the Stand-Off Target Acquisition System (SOTAS), is employed by the US army.

The sophistication of radar means that it is now possible to acquire the positions of enemy *mortars through the use of systems such as the British Cymbeline, while the introduction of Uninhabited Air Vehicles (UAVs)—formerly Remotely Piloted Vehicles (RPVs)—exemplified by the Israeli Pioneer, enables artillery units to acquire targets for engagement with near real-time transmission of information. Similar technology is employed by naval units. In the *Gulf war of 1991, 57 per cent of targets engaged by the US battleships *Missouri* and *Wisconsin* were located from the air by UAVs.

Surveillance of the aerial environment has become of ever-increasing importance. Radar early warning enables enemy aircraft to be located and with adequate communications, friendly fighters can be despatched to engage them. This technology began to be seen in the later 1940s, particu-

larly in carrier air wings, but it was not until the late 1960s that the system became truly effective. The development of the Boeing E-3 Sentry Airborne Warning and Control System (AWACS) started a new trend, with highly capable radar systems coupled with advanced communication facilities being employed to provide management of air battles. The information provided by AWACS aircraft allows fighter aircrews to plan in advance what tactics they will employ. It also makes the setting of traps using decoy aircraft impossible, since the AWACS sees the big picture and there is nowhere to hide.

As well as providing an aerial battle management facility, radar has led to the development of airborne systems to survey the progress of the land battle. The systems extant for this purpose can be found in the E-8 JSTARS (Joint Surveillance Target Attack Radar System). This enables ground commanders to be furnished with a 'God's-Eye' view of the disposition of their own and enemy forces, an exponential improvement over all previous systems that will make JSTARS and AWACS the priority target for any commander who can find some means of attacking them.   DJJ

Bellamy, Chris, *The Red God of War* (London, 1986).
Bidwell, Shelford, and Graham, Dominick, *Fire-Power: British Army Weapons and Theories of War 1904–1945* (London, 1982).

sutler (from early modern Dutch: *zoeteler* (now *zoetelaar*), a small vendor, petty tradesman victualler, soldier's servant). The word has fairly negative connotations as the Low German *suttler* or *sudeler* from the verb *suetelen* means to befoul or perform low duties, especially with regard to the army. Essentially a sutler was a *camp follower who sold provisions to the soldiers, part of early *logistics.

The French had the *cantinier* or the preferred female *cantinière*, derived from the Italian word *cantina* meaning wine cellar. A *cantinier* would provide liquor for the troops. Although usually a civilian, a *cantinier* might well be a moonlighting soldier or the *cantinière* his wife, seeking to supplement his meagre income. Given that drinking has always been one of a soldier's most popular forms of recreation, the *cantinier* was an important institution though thoroughly frowned upon by many military reformers. Apart from selling the troops provision, they would also undertake domestic tasks such as washing and repairing clothes. Many soldiers' wives supplemented their income in this role. Even on campaign sutlers made up a large proportion of the great train that trailed behind the armies of the 17th to 19th centuries. The demise of the sutler came with the militarization of supply and transport services in the 19th century. However, the variety of 'soldier's homes' and station canteens that sprang up during WW I were a more orderly reflection of an old practice, providing extra comforts to men for whom issue rations were unavailable, inadequate, or simply unappetizing.   MCM

Suvorov, Generalissimus Aleksandr Vasil'evich

(1730–1800), the greatest Russian military commander in history. Never defeated, Suvorov was tiny, wiry and eccentric, but, as with *Wolfe or *Wingate, this signalled physical toughness and determination. He was loved by his men, whom he called 'brother' and with whom he shared every hardship. His reputation survived all subsequent rewriting of history under the USSR. He remains the idol of the Russian armed forces today, and his portrait presides over most commanders' offices. 'Presidents come and go,' one airborne brigade commander said recently, 'but Suvorov—he is always there.'

Suvorov was the son of a general who compiled the first Russian military dictionary. In common with practice of the time, he joined the ranks aged 12, enabling him to reach officer rank by 24. His military career began in earnest in the *Seven Years War, when he served in the battles of Kunersdorf and in the capture of Berlin in 1760. From 1776–9 he commanded in the Crimea. He instantly spotted the potential of the great natural harbour at Sevastopol, and began its development, a manifestation of the quality of *glazomer*, the 'ability to judge by eye', which he said was essential in a commander.

In 1791 Suvorov commanded the Russian assault on the Turkish fortress of Izmail. He combined land artillery with warships to concentrate a hurricane of fire. When the Russians entered the city, they massacred virtually all the 40,000 inhabitants in house-to-house fighting. Suvorov reported his victory to Empress Catherine 'the Great' in doggerel verse, but later confided that afterwards he wept.

A collection of Suvorov's aphorisms was later published, called *Nauka pobezhdat* (the Science of Victory), probably compiled in 1795–6. It includes his famous saying 'the bullet is a fool—the bayonet is a good chap'. He never really believed that, but maintained a bluff façade, presenting the results of detailed and careful planning as 'inspiration'. In 1799 he led a joint Russian-Austrian army in the extraordinary north Italian and Swiss campaign, in which steppe Russians ended up fighting, and winning, a high-altitude battle in the St Gotthard Pass.

Asked the names of the greatest commanders of history, Suvorov named *Alexander 'the Great', *Scipio 'Africanus', and—he smiled—a young and then little-known French general, Napoleon Bonaparte (see NAPOLEON). Suvorov and Napoleon never met in battle and it is one of the fascinating though unprofitable 'ifs' of history to speculate who would have won if they had. It was left to his pupil *Kutuzov to tear the guts out of Napoleon's army. Stories about Suvorov abound. He hated it when soldiers said 'I don't know', and this soon got around the army. On one occasion, he was inspecting troops, and asked a sergeant 'how far is it to the moon?' The sergeant had not a clue, but answered smartly, 'For Suvorov, two campaigns.'   CDB

Duffy, Christopher, *Russia's Military Way to the West* (London, 1981).

Longworth, Philip, *The Art of Victory: The Life and Achievements of Generalissimo Suvorov, 1792–1800* (London, 1965).

Swiss attract the attention of military historians most for their role in what are called the French *Italian wars of the 16th century—despite the fact that these were also fought on the Rhine, the Pyrenees, and the English Channel—from which derived their fame as *mercenaries. Their martial skills were forged in an epic struggle for their own independence against the Habsburgs that began with the mutual assistance pact agreed by three Alpine peasant communities in 1291 and did not formally end until the 1648 Peace of Westphalia closed the *Thirty Years War. Of the three, the Schwyz won undying repute and their name came to be given to the whole confederation because in 1315, at the ambush battle of Morgarten, their humble spearmen killed several thousand knights, characteristically taking no prisoners. Thus 31 years before *Crécy, the knell of military and social supremacy based on *knighthood sounded. From the start their preferred weapons were *pole arms and their preferred tactic was to advance at the trot in compact columns. We have no way of ascertaining how these became so firmly established. All we can say for sure is that they did not remain on the defensive, and that population pressure and a sort of aggressive collective consciousness (for they were fiercely egalitarian and had no 'leaders' as the term is generally understood) produced a highly expansionist policy until the first half of the 16th century, at which point they began to cultivate the (heavily armed) neutrality that remains the signature of Switzerland to this day.

Swiss aggression was felt by neighbours at all points of the compass, and their merciless rivalry with the German *landsknechts is notorious. The threat from the Habsburgs was mainly latent, and the Swiss confirmed their reputation as a savage hedgehog best left alone at Morat in 1476, where they checked the pretensions of Charles 'the Bold' to revive the Burgundian kingdom, and by killing Charles himself and many of his knights at Nancy the following year. History does not record another occasion in which a small polity overthrew one much larger so completely that it never recovered. The decline of the Swiss as the rulers of the battlefield tends to be ascribed to field artillery and musketry, as though they were too stupid to adapt. They were not invincible even before French guns blasted bloody furrows in their ranks at Marignano in 1515—the Spanish *gran capitán* *Córdoba defeated them at Cerignola in 1503. But what happened after 1515 was that *François I had the wit to behave generously towards them, granting them free trading privileges that were to be the foundation of Swiss prosperity. It also bound them to the French interest, such that they shared in the defeats at Bicocca (1522) and Pavia (1525), and red-coated Swiss regiments served the French monarchy faithfully until 1791.

They never evolved cavalry, and their expertise with the crossbow (hence the myth of William Tell) made them slow to adopt firearms, but it was not the Swiss as fighting men who were eclipsed at Bicocca and Ravenna. Rather it was the closure of the brief period when the dynastic rivalries of Europe permitted the Swiss as a nation to play a significant role in the affairs of the continent. As to the careless use of the term 'mercenary' as an epithet, to deny a soldier his pay is to refuse the *honour due to him and implicit in the contract under which he takes service. The Swiss did not believe in promises and if pay day came around and it was not duly counted out, they would simply leave, no matter what the situation their patron might find himself in. Thus to this day the phrase *point d'argent, point des Suisses* (no money, no Swiss) persists in French usage. The pope still retains a Swiss Guard.

HEB

Syracuse, sieges of (416–413 and 213–210 BC). Syracuse was the principal city of the rich grain-producing area of Sicily, but it appears that it was an unhealthy spot, for both of these sieges were all but decided by the outbreak of epidemics. During the 431–404 BC *Peloponnesian war against *Sparta, Athens launched an expedition to seize Syracuse under Nicias, whom the Athenian historian Thucydides (see GREEK HISTORIANS) represents as both unwilling and incompetent. He also records that Nicias' force was '100 triremes and 5,000 hoplites', with archers and Cretan *slingers in proportion. The Athenians cut off Syracuse with two forts, and began a twin circumvallation, but left their northern walls incomplete, which was to prove disastrous. After two attempts to build counter-walls were defeated, the Syracusans appealed for Spartan help, which was refused. But Gylippus, a Spartan general, managed to raise 3,000 men for an independent relief effort and he landed and captured the unfinished northern fortifications, and built a wall from there to the city. Nicias changed the axis of his attack to the south and built three more forts, but an outbreak of disease forced him to give up the struggle. Since Gylippus had blockaded the harbour where the Athenian fleet lay, the Athenians attempted to escape overland, but were run down by Syracusan light troops and forced to surrender. This was Athens' greatest reverse and a turning point in the war.

During the second *Punic war between Rome and Carthage, Syracuse was held by the mercenary Hippocrates for the Carthaginians. In 213 Marcellus, a renowned soldier but with only three legions at his disposal, began a siege. He directed his main attack on the Northern 'Little Harbour', deploying 60 quinqueremes for a naval assault. Pairs of galleys were lashed together to carry a sliding assault ladder called a *sambuca* (harp) invented by Heracleides of Taras. But the city was defended by Archimedes, a greater inventor, whose 'burning glasses' and other counter-engines destroyed the attackers' *siege engines. Hearing the news of a Carthaginian relief force under Himilco, Hippocrates slipped out of the city to join him, but he was surprised by Marcellus and his forces dispersed. The following year Marcellus exploited the fact that the defenders were drunkenly celebrating the feast of Artemis to seize a gate and the dominant Epipolae plateau. A Carthaginian relief force was defeated in two assaults and then fell victim to disease, and Syracuse surrendered.

MB

Caven, B., *The Punic Wars* (London, 1980).
Thucydides, *The Peloponnesian War*.

Syria campaign (1941). Following the fall of *France, the British attempted to neutralize the powerful French Mediterranean fleet by bombardment at Oran and Mersel-Kebir. At the other end of the Mediterranean the situation became even more fraught after defeats in Greece, *Crete, and *North Africa in March–May 1941. At the post WW I division of the Ottoman empire, the French had obtained the mandate for Syria and Lebanon, while the British got Palestine, Transjordan (now Jordan), and Iraq. From the last, Britain obtained much of her oil, while ever since *Megiddo Palestine has been the military crossroads between Egypt and Mesopotamia. Thus when Vichy granted the Germans facilities in Syria, this was seen as a fang poised over the British jugular.

In addition, German and Italian agents had been very active in the area, and while Prince Abdallah of Iraq was pro-British, his PM Rashid Ali was pro-Nazi and brought tensions to a head in early May 1941 by attacking British garrisons at Basra and Habbaniya and inviting the Germans to establish an airbase in the oil town of Mosul, on the Tigris. This was dealt with briskly, but the situation in Syria was much more serious. Pan-Arabist and anti-British sentiment was being stoked by Shukri-al-Kuwatli, while the 35,000–strong Vichy forces stationed there threatened to tilt the balance of power in the Mediterranean in Germany's direction. There was a real danger that if the Germans were given time, they would be able to develop a twin-pronged threat to Iraq and to the forces defending Egypt against *Rommel.

*Wavell could not accept the risk and ordered a four-pronged pre-emptive invasion of Syria from Palestine and Iraq by 20,000 men under the command of Gen Sir Henry (Jumbo) Wilson, begun on 8 June 1941. These were the British 1st Cavalry Division (some of whom were still on horses), an Australian infantry division, an Indian motorized infantry brigade, and some Free French units, as well as volunteers from the Jewish settlements in Palestine including *Dayan, who was to lose his eye in this campaign. The main objectives were to seize Damascus, Beirut, and Palmyra, and it was hoped that the Vichy forces, including elements of the *French Foreign Legion, would not resist.

They did, ferociously, in great measure to show that despite the humiliation of 1940, French soldiers could still fight. Little opposition was encountered at first, but resistance stiffened along the Litani river and Vichy troops counter-attacked at Merjayun and Kuneitra. Gradually they gave way, but the Indian brigade was so severely mauled attacking Damascus that it was out of action for six months afterwards. Damascus was taken in a second attack on 21 June by Free French forces under Gen Georges Catroux, a civil war with friends and family members fighting each other. Battles continued for five weeks until Beirut fell on 11 July and the Vichy commander Gen Henri Dentz surrendered. Honour satisfied, a minority of Dentz's troops subsequently transferred to Free French command under Catroux and saw action in the North Africa, *Italy, and *North-West Europe campaigns.   APC-A

tactics (*see opposite page*)

Taiping rebellion (1851–64). This rebellion in China was the bloodiest civil war and, until WW II, the bloodiest war of any kind in history. An estimated 11 million, mostly non-combatants, were direct victims of the conflict and including the victims of famine the total exceeded 30 million. What makes it all the more staggering is that it was a mainly *small arms war and, while not challenging *Cannae for the one-day total, the 100,000-plus killed in the three-day battle of Nanking in 1864 will probably never be exceeded.

It was a spasm of rejection of the *Manchu dynasty sparked by the unlikely figure of Hung Hsiu-chuan who, if he was not insane at the start, very rapidly became hopelessly so as the war progressed. After failing the civil service exam in *c*.1844, he had a vision in which he spoke with God and the 'elder brother' Jesus Christ, who appear to have told him to throw the Manchus and their idols out of China and establish Taiping Tienkwo (the Heavenly Dynasty of Perfect Peace). He attracted four able generals known as *Wangs* (kings) who were either killed in action, murdered each other, or were executed for so doing by 1856. By that time they had seized Nanking and controlled a quarter of Chinese territory and perhaps half the population.

They never seized a port and seem to have expected the Christian West to favour them without their making any diplomatic overtures. Nor did they develop any kind of civil administration, and the depradations of their well-drilled and disciplined armies achieved the wildly improbable result of making most Chinese and all foreign powers regard the Manchu as the better of two evils. This did not stop the British and the French from mounting what one might call an armed diplomatic expedition against Peking in 1860 to obtain extortionate treaty rights, burning the huge imperial Summer Palace complex in retaliation for the torture and murder of several of their number.

The Taipings preached but did not practise sexual and social equality. What they did enforce, massively, was the death penalty for any infringement of a strict disciplinary code forbidding fornication, wine, gambling, and, above all, 'indulgence in the fumes of opium'. Their forces were organized into armies of 13,000, but their real strength always fell far short of that and this may account for the unbelievable numbers of troops reported. They had four auxiliary armies: 'earth battalions', very important in the numerous sieges; 'water battalions', very important in the numerous riverine operations; the 'Young Boys' Army'; and the 'Women's Army', the last reportedly 100,000 strong.

After the fall of Nanking the talented imperial general Tseng Kuo-fan, known as 'Tseng the head-chopper', began to restore some order. In 1860 a Taiping expedition under Li-Hsiu-ch'eng (Loyal Prince Lee) threatened the great foreign emporium at Shanghai. With money from Chinese merchants, the US adventurer Frederick Ward recruited a small army of mercenaries which became the 'Ever Victorious Army', taken over by *Gordon after Ward was killed in 1862, and which crushed the rebellion in co-operation with Tseng. Nanking eventually fell on 19 July 1864 and the rebel leaders either took poison or were executed, although the fighting continued well into 1866. The rebellion had a profound influence on Sun Yat-sen, who once described himself as 'the new Hung Hsiu-chuan'. But it took *Mao Tse-tung to exceed the slaughter in his extermination of the independent peasant class, and there was much about his Cultural Revolution in the 1960s that eerily echoed the madness of the Taiping experience.   CDB

tactics

Tactics is a term used to describe the art of fighting on or near the battlefield. Ever since man began to organize armed groups for the purpose of combat, the way in which warriors have been organized and employed—as much as their personal bravery and the arms and armour they carry—has to a large extent defined their effectiveness in war. In ancient times an increasing diversity and sophistication of weaponry led to differing structures to optimize the efficiency of each arm. Associated tactics arranged, disposed, and integrated these arms in contact with the enemy. In this way the actions of variously equipped *infantry could be combined with each other and with those of assorted *cavalry on the battlefield, and these joined by *artillery, broadly defined. Until the 20th century added the aerial dimension (with a mention for earlier *naval gunfire), these were the core tactical factors.

Over the ages the tactical military *art has been concerned with four closely related battlefield functions: hitting (or firepower), mobility, protection (or security), and shock action. Command (involving leadership, decision-making, and control—including information gathering and *communications) is a separate function in combat. The standing requirement for timely and accurate *intelligence drives the need for *reconnaissance. In battle, troops fight by a combination of firepower and manoeuvre; tactics regulate the sequence and balance. Manoeuvre is defined in NATO as 'the employment of forces on the battlefield through movement in combination with fire, or fire potential, to achieve a position of advantage in respect to the enemy in order to accomplish the mission'. Forms of manoeuvre can be grouped into the broad categories discussed under *manoeuvre warfare. The co-ordination of forces in time and space is known as synchronization, which is one of the essential requirements of successful tactics. 'Grand tactics'—a term largely gone out of use—refers to the planning and conduct of large formations in or between battles, in the pursuit of campaign objectives. Nowadays this level of conflict is subsumed by the *operational level of war.

Supporting military activities such as supply, transport, and the provision of medical care that provide the means to fight and to sustain forces in battle are covered under the general rubric of *logistics. In contrast to the more glamorous combat arms, the vitally necessary logistic organizations are known as supporting services. But if insufficient account is taken of them in the planning or conduct of a campaign, no tactical, operational, or strategic scheme of manoeuvre is likely to succeed. Both Napoleon's and Hitler's disastrous forays into Russia demonstrate this point, illustrating the *Clausewitz concept of 'culmination', whereby an attacking force is no longer able to sustain its offensive and the pendulum of advantage swings to the defender.

Military *engineering, a combat support arm, straddles both arm and service functions in providing armies with the ability to live, move, and fight on the battlefield. The enduring roles of the military engineer to overcome natural and artificial obstacles in the offensive and to create them in delaying and defensive operations have remained an important adjunct to tactics for thousands of years. Indeed, one of the most complex military operations on land, and that at which engineers are always at a premium, is the breaching or crossing of an opposed obstacle. Special equipment, tactics, techniques, and procedures involving 'all arms' need to be developed, as demonstrated repeatedly during the 1944–5 Allied campaign in *North-West Europe.

The development of tactics has reflected a shifting balance between the complementary functions of hitting power, mobility, protection, and shock action; between 'dominant arms' represented on the battlefield and, perhaps more fundamentally, between firepower and manoeuvre. Various models have been proposed to illustrate the connections between these factors. In *The Dragon's Teeth*, *Fuller maintained that in each of the classical and Christian epochs there were three great tactical cycles. For the Christian period he argued that a 'shock' cycle took place *c*.650–1450, a 'shock and projectile' cycle *c*.1450–1850, and a 'projectile' cycle from *c*.1850 onwards. In 1943, Tom Wintringham proposed six chronological periods linking the development of armour, mobility, and protection. This methodology can be developed to indicate the dominance of particular arms and to highlight associated tactical trends.

Period	Dominant arm	Tactical trends
First unarmoured period, to *Plataea (479 BC)	*None*, both infantry and cavalry are relatively lightly armed, chariots provide a measure of shock	Egyptian, Persian, and Greek armies become better organized and equipped
First armoured period, to *Adrianople (AD 378)	*Infantry*, *phalanx, and Roman Legion. Use of elephants for shock not a success	Armies and casualties increase significantly, introduction of siege and field artillery by Romans
Second unarmoured period, to Charlemagne's victory at Pavia (774)	*Light cavalry*, horse *archers, and shock action defeat infantry	Mobility rules until checked by armoured cavalry
Second armoured period, to Morgarten (1315) and *Crécy (1346)	*Heavy cavalry*, the effect of the *stirrup and armour	Expense limits numbers of armoured cavalry, Swiss infantry and English longbow redress the balance
Third unarmoured period, to *Cambrai (1917)	*Infantry*, through steadily increasing firepower	Combined arms, with artillery becoming increasingly dominant
Third armoured period, to the present	*Armoured forces* restore mobility	Armoured combined arms countered by air power and infantry anti-armour weapons

Close-range striking or longer-range missile or projectile weapons provide tactical hitting or firepower. With advances in technology, the emphasis has shifted from the former to the latter with steady increases in the range of missile and projectile weapons. However, it would be a mistake to overrate the contribution of missile or of infantry-delivered firepower in battle until the mid-19th century. Despite the introduction of more flexible tactical formations such as the French column, the limited range, poor accuracy, and low rate of fire of muskets in the early 19th century precluded decisive engagements by fire alone. The shock effect of well-controlled volley fire on a formed body of troops, coupled with the often far more devastating impact of artillery, more often than not swung the battle. In *Forward into Battle*, Paddy Griffith concluded of the *Peninsular and *Hundred Days campaigns:

The real secret of the British volley was not that it was delivered particularly well or accurately, but rather that it could be delivered at all at such close range; almost at bayonet range, in fact. Waiting without firing until the enemy came close enough to charge must have been a nerve-racking business which tested the coolness and discipline of the troops to the limit. Having delivered the volley, it took yet more steadiness not to reload, but to launch immediately into the assault.

The proportion of troops armed with more accurate, but slower firing, rifles remained low. *Light troops such as the French *tirailleurs or British *rifle regiments, useful enough in finding, fixing, and disrupting the enemy, could not bring down a sufficient weight of fire to strike him hard.

The employment of the mass-produced rifled musket in the *Crimean and *American civil wars and the rifled *breech-loader in the *Austro-Prussian and *Franco-Prussian wars enabled fire that could inflict significant casualties at longer ranges. Both Pickett's charge at *Gettysburg in 1863 and the Prussian Guard's attack at Saint-Privat in 1870 were broken up by defending fire. With greater weapon ranges and therefore flatter trajectories and improving accuracy, the 'beaten zone' that an attacking force has to cross widened from less than 109 yards (100 metres) to 656 yards (600 metres) and further. Not surprisingly, casualties increased commensurately. Thus attacks without covering artillery fire (and later machine-gun fire) to suppress the defence became increasingly difficult. Various methods have been employed to assist the infantryman in reaching and fighting through his objective. WW I saw the introduction of the creeping *barrage, infiltration, or *storm-trooper tactics, often termed Hutier tactics after the German general who first used them at Riga in 1917, and 'intimate' *tank support. During WW II the first generation of armoured infantry fighting vehicles appeared. Adequate fire must be employed to fix and blind a defending enemy while an attacking force can move into contact and strike him decisively. No doubt with fresh memories of WW I in mind, *Liddell Hart stressed the importance of 'fixing' in *Infantry Tactics Simplified*: 'The act of fixing can only be neglected if the enemy commits some mistake of supineness or the neglect of his own security by which he fixes himself without our intervention and so exposes himself to an immediate knock-out blow.' Unfortunately this enduring tactical lesson, which applies equally well to the conduct of attacks by armoured forces, was often forgotten by Allied forces during WW II.

Mobility determines the rate at which an army and its constituent parts can move to, across, and from the battlefield. From the days of *Alexander 'the Great', mobility was strictly regulated by the marching pace of the foot soldier, together with his supporting trains of pack mule, horse, and bullock. Rarely could an army better an average of 20 miles (32 km) in a day. Only small bodies of specially trained 'light' troops and cavalry could exceed this norm. While the advent of the *steam engine and the development of a *railway network in the 19th century revolutionized strategic mobility in Europe and America, tactical mobility at the outbreak of WW I remained that of *Caesar's legions. Only the introduction of armoured tracked vehicles powered by reliable internal combustion engines improved tactical mobility sufficiently to offer the prospect of decisive manoeuvre in 1917–18. Despite the limited successes of the tank in WW I, the full promise of tactical and operational mobility was not achieved until WW II. Even then, such is the enduring myth of *blitzkrieg that it is often forgotten that during the fall of *France in May–June 1940, the seventeen German panzer and motorized divisions constituted less than a fifth of the total order of battle. This very sharp pointed lance had a long and brittle shaft, vulnerable to counter-attack.

Since the classical period, personal *armour has provided a measure—but no guarantee—of individual protection, which may also be extended to a soldier's mount (whether horse or vehicle). The tactical effectiveness of armour through the ages has been limited by its weight and correspondingly deleterious effect on mobility and human endurance. And if a heavily armoured medieval knight could protect himself against the majority of striking and missile weapons, he and his horse remained relatively vulnerable to longbowmen, and later to crude firearms. Largely discarded in the 18th and 19th centuries, personal armour made a limited comeback in WW I with the introduction of steel helmets and, on a much smaller scale, body armour. After WW II 'flak jackets' became commonplace, particularly in western armies. Fortifications, either 'fixed' or 'field', not only provide collective protection but also enhance the power of the defence by the formation of obstacles. 'Field defences' and barriers may also bring tactical advantage by compensating, for example, for a defender's shortages of manpower, providing that obstacles are adequately covered by fire, a tactical lesson often relearned the hard way.

Shock action aims as much at psychological impact as physical damage. In battle, shock effect has been provided 'at the charge' not only by well-trained groups of assaulting foot soldiers (whether Roman legionaries or German storm troopers) but also by heavier and speedier means. Chariots, elephants (the tanks of the ancient battlefield), cavalry, and armoured vehicles provide momentum to the assault. Shock action can also be applied by skilled forces in defence. The drenching arrow fire of longbowmen at the battle of *Agincourt in 1415 caused horses to panic and contributed to French knights turning and running down their own infantry. As we have seen, the tactical *column and line issue of the *Napoleonic wars involved a tactical effect greater than that produced by weight of fire alone. In WW II, German machine-gun and tank-gun fire, coupled with well-observed indirect mortar and artillery fire, often broke up Soviet, British, or American attacks on the 'forming up place' or 'start line' before they got moving, or caused them to break down once started through casualties inflicted on key subunit leaders. In both cases, the cumulative 'shock' effect on the units concerned, particularly if this course of events were to be repeated a number of times, was often greater than might be expected from the physical casualty list alone, adding a new dimension to the term 'battle shock' in the form of psychiatric *casualties.

The art of orchestrating various arms to work together (including ground-attack *fighters) towards a common tactical or operational objective, is known as combined arms tactics. Thus a broad measure of tactical effectiveness is the extent to which arms, including *air forces, integrate their actions on the battlefield as combined arms teams. Historically, this aim has proved easier to theorize about than to realize in practice, and the formation of effective combined arms organizations typically has had a history of costly and painful development. The contrasting experience of the German and British armies in WW II is instructive. The key organizational principle recognized by the Germans—and belatedly by the British—is that all components of combined arms teams need identical mobility and sufficient protection and firepower if their total tactical potential is to be realized. But, above all, all arms on the battlefield must train together in order to fight successfully.

In the 20th century, *air power has brought a fundamental change to tactics, the seeds of which were sown in the closing stages of WW I. By WW II, close *air support had matured and complemented greatly the striking power and shock action of ground manoeuvre. In addition to providing information through tactical air reconnaissance, indirect air support provides protection to troops by defeating hostile air forces (offensive and defensive counter-air action) and by the *interdiction of opposing land forces. Air power also brings considerable benefits in terms of troop and supply lift, enhancing the tactical, operational, and strategic range, mobility, and sustainability of land forces. The benefits and inherent risks of air supply were demonstrated in various battles in WW II. The German failure to resupply *Stalingrad in the winter of 1942–3 contrasts vividly with Allied success at *Kohima and *Imphal. Since WW II, rotary-winged aviation has become an arm in its own right in most armies. Support *helicopters provide integral tactical lift and attack helicopters offer great striking power, increasing the tactical flexibility of land forces and the tempo of operations. However, all types of aircraft, and particularly those flying at low to medium altitudes, remain to some extent vulnerable to ground-based air defences. In hostile environments, attacking aircraft must face a combined challenge from air defence artillery equipped with guns and missiles and from air defence aircraft. The vulnerability of ground-attack aircraft to air defence systems was illustrated by the crippling losses of 60 per cent endured by the RAF in attacking the Meuse bridges at Sedan in May 1940, while the Israeli Air Force suffered similarly during the opening days of the October 1973 Yom Kippur war.

Much tactical and operational flexibility is promised by vertical envelopment or 'air assault' operations by parachute, *glider, or helicopter-borne troops. Such operations remain at high risk in view of the inherent dangers of insertion on to the battlefield. Once landed, a lack of mobility, protection, and heavy armament may limit critically the fighting power of the troops involved, as demonstrated at the battle of *Arnhem in September 1944. In *Vietnam, the helicopter gave US forces enormous reach, firepower, and a sure means of evacuating casualties. However, 'air cavalry' tactics often proved costly as the North Vietnamese lured the Americans into deeper and more protected parts of the jungle, and ambushed remote landing zones.

*Science and technology has made its most vital contribution to tactical communications, but the impact of the more photogenic *precision-guided munitions is in practice more limited. In particular the difficulties encountered in finding suitable strategies and tactics to employ against *guerrilla forces on their own, often close, terrain have haunted regular armies. *Callwell concluded in his famous work *Small Wars*: 'Since tactics favour the regular troops while strategy favours the enemy, the object to be sought for clearly is to fight, not to manoeuvre, to meet the hostile forces in open battle, not to compel them to give way by having recourse to strategy.'

Yet it has been the standing aim of irregular forces to avoid that 'open battle' and to harry regular forces and civilians at their points of vulnerability—initially targeting isolated rural outposts and lines of communication and, with growing success, bringing the war into urban centres of population: asymmetric conflict. The British and French retreats from empire after WW II show that fighting *counter-insurgency wars is a long and painful process. Tactics based on firepower alone cannot win. First the enemy has to be found, by no means an easy task; then he has to be fixed (if he does not melt away after first contact) before he can be struck. But the enemy will return to fight the long fight. As *Ho Chi Minh said to the French in *Indochina, 'You can kill ten of my men for every one that I kill of yours. But even at those odds, you will lose and I will win.' In this sort of small war, small-unit leaders often bear a disproportionate weight of combat. Eventual success depends on low-level tactical skills, a long-term campaign plan sustained by sufficient resources, and an overarching strategy that addresses the roots of the conflict.

In conclusion, it is a prime function of a nation's military theorists and practitioners to promote and develop superior tactics to those of its prospective opponents. Less well understood is the requirement to maintain organizational coherence between arms and services in order to provide the right balance of material and personnel resources on the battlefield and to support its activities. As weaponry, tactics, and operational methods evolve, that balance may need to shift. A failure by a party to an armed conflict to recognize that such a shift is required may herald military setback at best, or failure at worst. The experience of Polish, French, and British forces in 1939–40 in response to blitzkrieg surely demonstrates this. But while superior tactics are usually important in determining the shifting scales of engagement or battle, they are not necessarily sufficient for success in a campaign or war. A tactically or technically advantaged force may be beaten by a tactically inferior but numerically superior enemy. The tactical advantage on either side might be quite transitory, as shown by the contrasting British failure and success against the *Zulus at Isandhlwana and at Rorke's Drift on 22–3 January 1879. Disappointingly, the hard-won tactical lessons of actions in small- or medium-scale wars do not necessarily reap due rewards in larger conflicts. The professional volunteer British army emerged from the Second *Boer War and subsequent *Haldane reforms well organized for a limited war. Its infantry tactics, musketry, and organization (including cavalry and horse artillery) were second to none in 1914, but the British Expeditionary Force (BEF) was nonetheless outclassed by a conscript German army. Quantitatively superior in numbers of troops and heavy guns, and also qualitatively in terms of grand tactics and the work of its *general staff above divisional level, the Germans had the operational advantage.

Above the tactical and operational levels, national strategy, intelligence capability, industrial resources, and not least the supply of trained manpower may contribute as much to the final outcome of any lengthy armed conflict. Thus the Allied victory over Germany and Japan in WW II was based largely on marked strategic advantages as opposed to any decisive tactical superiority at land, air, or sea. The one exception is perhaps the application of Allied air power which achieved air superiority in most theatres by 1943–4. Also, armed forces with supposedly 'superior' battlefield or combined arms tactics may not necessarily win in the long run, even if they achieve an initial operational advantage and win the opening campaign. 'Easy' tactical gains, while offering the alluring prospects of victory, may not translate into strategic success. When *Manstein rued *Lost Victories*, he was concentrating on the tactical level and underplaying strategic failure. If a conflict is of sufficient scale and duration, lessons can be learned during the war and tactics can be modified accordingly, but the next conflict may be totally unexpected with little time to learn the hard way. Therefore new tactics must be anticipated, developed, and rehearsed during peacetime. The huge investment in combined arms tactics training facilities, backed up by realistic combat simulation, paid off handsomely for US, British, and French forces in the *Gulf war. Saddam *Hussein's strategic calculation that the alliance would not hold together if confronted with high casualties was not misplaced, but his forces were not sufficiently well equipped or trained at the tactical level to inflict them. This merely illustrates how tactics and strategy are inseparably interwoven. As one component of the art of war, tactics are but part of the whole; the complex, costly, and messy business of war must be seen in the round.

RAMSM

Bellamy, Christopher, *The Evolution of Modern Land Warfare* (London, 1990).
Callwell, Charles E., *Small Wars: Their Principles and Practice* (London, 1906).
Fuller, J. F. C., *The Foundations of the Science of War* (London, 1925).
—— *The Dragon's Teeth* (London, 1932).
Griffith, Paddy, *Forward into Battle* (Swindon, 1990).
Liddell Hart, B. H., *A Science of Infantry Tactics Simplified* (London, 1923).
Strachan, Hew, *European Armies and the Conduct of War* (London, 1983).
Weller, Jac, *Weapons and Tactics* (London, 1966).
Wintringham, Tom, and Blashford-Snell, J. N., *Weapons and Tactics* (London, 1973) (incorporating Wintringham, *Weapons and Tactics*, (London, 1943)).

Tamerlane. See TIMUR.

tanks A term coined in 1915 in a coy attempt to conceal the true purpose of early 'landships', which has stuck. The concept dates back at least as far as *Leonardo da Vinci, but in the modern era it was the Austrian Gunther Burstyn and the Australian Lancelot de Mole, in 1911 and 1912 respectively, who produced designs that were tanks in all but name, only to be ignored. British interest in landships was fostered by the Admiralty at the insistence of *Churchill, then First Lord of the Admiralty. Most of the early designs were for vehicles that would transport infantry across no man's land although to begin with designers could not decide whether tracks or huge wheels represented the best means of propulsion. The adoption of the design as we know it was due largely to the engineers Walter Wilson and William Tritton, but nothing would have been achieved without the driving force of Albert Stern, secretary to the Landships Committee.

The earliest British tanks were little more than mechanical battering rams, designed to cross a few hundred yards of rough ground, crush wire, and suppress opposition, enabling the infantry to gain their objective. Slow speed and poor manoeuvrability rendered them unsuitable for more subtle tactics or wide-ranging operations, while their firepower was restricted by their side-mounted gun sponsons. Male tanks carried a pair of 57 mm guns, females only machine guns. There was parallel development in France, largely due to the efforts of Col Estienne of the artillery, but their early designs were more like *self-propelled (SP) guns, with poor cross-country capability. Nonetheless the first tank worthy of the name, in the modern sense, was probably the two-man Renault FT-17. It was the first tank to see active service that carried a fully rotating turret and the first to feature the combination of rear mounted engine and final drive which is now almost universal. It was, of course, intended for a more mobile form of warfare, beyond the trenches, and designed to be used in quantity, in theory compensating for lack of protection by overwhelming the defence.

Tanks developed dramatically over the two years from their creation. By the end of WW I Great Britain had produced a dozen different models including SP artillery, an *APC, and engineer tanks adaptable to clear mines, place *demolition charges, or lay bridges under fire. The British answer to the Renault was the Medium A, or Whippet, which had a separate engine and gearbox for each track, making it notoriously difficult to drive. The Germans, by contrast, were slow to start tank development and the results were not impressive. Their A7V model, of which just twenty examples were built, had a poor cross-country performance and demanded a crew of eighteen. As the war ended they were constructing a monstrous machine, which would have weighed 148 tons had it been completed, a mistake they were to repeat.

The end of the war found Great Britain developing the Medium D, a high speed, amphibious tank of impossible complexity, intended to match the tactical theories of *Fuller, while the French, now saddled with hundreds of the little Renaults, were building a 70 ton giant with turrets at each end. Italy, Japan, the USSR, and the USA, meanwhile, developed the Renault with minor variations. Britain took the lead again in 1923 with the so-called Vickers Medium, a turreted tank designed specifically to fight other tanks while on the move, in accordance with Royal Tank Corps *doctrine. This was followed by a veritable land battleship with five turrets, known as the Independent, which never got beyond the prototype stage. However, it did create an international fashion for multi-turreted tanks which lasted far too long. The Experimental Armoured Force of 1927/8 placed Britain in the forefront of tactical thinking. It was the first step in the creation of the armoured division but it aroused considerable opposition among the traditional arms, which provided the British government with an excuse to scrap it. Economy also gave rise to tiny tracked vehicles such as the Carden-Loyd Carrier which was influential worldwide, despite being almost useless. The Carden-Loyd also spawned a vast range of two- and three-man light tanks of little practical value which, nevertheless, formed the basis of Vickers-Armstrong's success as a manufacturer and exporter of armoured fighting vehicles.

In the USA J. Walter Christie produced a range of high-speed tanks based on the revolutionary suspension system that bears his name. His work had considerable influence in Russia and Britain, but his abrasive personality caused rejection in his own country, and America developed more pedestrian types that reflected French thinking to some extent. They were mechanically well designed, but were overly wedded to the machine gun. France was producing a range of tanks for infantry and cavalry support which all suffered from a preoccupation with small, one-man turrets that rendered them almost unfightable. Even so the French made considerable strides in the development of cast armour and produced some interesting transmission systems. The Italians also favoured light tanks, which were mechanically sound but crudely constructed to save cost.

In the years leading up to WW II, Britain lost its lead. A new doctrine classified tanks by role: light tanks, little better than tracked *armoured cars for *reconnaissance; slow, heavily armoured tanks for direct infantry support; and thinly armoured 'cruiser' tanks for wide-ranging operations. With another European war in view the British army concentrated on the problems of *trench warfare and gave priority to the production of infantry tanks. Along with the Americans, they continued to produce riveted tanks while the Germans and the Soviets were welding theirs, and in addition there was a fundamental difference of approach between the Americans, who made extensive use of machine tools and mass-production techniques, and the British, who tended to rely upon their traditional arms-manufacturing system.

German advocates of *armoured warfare were obliged to develop their ideas in secret—during the 1920s in co-operation with their future adversaries, the Red Army. Yet their early work laid the foundations of an impressive striking force that combined tanks with SP artillery and APCs. Likewise in secret the Soviets created a massive tank force which relied extensively on American and British technology but promoted firepower and the employment of armour en masse.

The various national choices of tank technology and doctrine were put to the test in 1940–1, with disastrous early results for both the French and the British at the hands of the Germans, who had found an ideal combination of speed, protection, and hitting power in the Pkw III and IV, fundamentally good designs that proved capable of accepting additional armour and larger guns without suffering any great loss of performance. By contrast the British 'cruisers' were neither strong enough to carry additional armour nor designed with enough latitude to accept larger guns, even when these became available. German doctrine also stressed firing when stationary, giving them greater accuracy than the British, trained to fire on the move. In North Africa, *Rommel was to demonstrate that, properly handled, even Italian armoured units (the bulk of his force) could be winners, while the absolute superiority of the Afrika Korps tanks became embarrassingly apparent. British tanks were deployed in larger numbers, but they were unreliable and unimaginatively handled, their difficulties compounded by the practice of stowing ammunition in unprotected racks.

A stopgap solution was provided by the American M3 Medium (its different versions known as Grant and Lee to the British), which combined a heavy, hull-mounted gun with a lighter one in a turret, at last giving the long-suffering British tank crews the ability to fire armour-piercing or

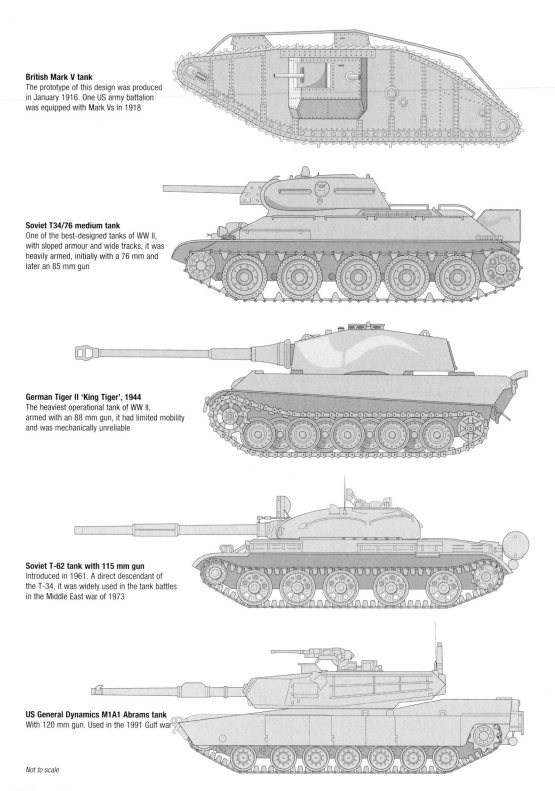

British Mark V tank
The prototype of this design was produced in January 1916. One US army battalion was equipped with Mark Vs in 1918

Soviet T34/76 medium tank
One of the best-designed tanks of WW II, with sloped armour and wide tracks, it was heavily armed, initially with a 76 mm and later an 85 mm gun

German Tiger II 'King Tiger', 1944
The heaviest operational tank of WW II, armed with an 88 mm gun, it had limited mobility and was mechanically unreliable

Soviet T-62 tank with 115 mm gun
Introduced in 1961. A direct descendant of the T-34, it was widely used in the tank battles in the Middle East war of 1973

US General Dynamics M1A1 Abrams tank
With 120 mm gun. Used in the 1991 Gulf war

Not to scale

Initially designed as an armoured bulldozer to overcome barbed wire and trenches, the tank quickly evolved into a system designed not only for breakthrough but also for exploitation and pursuit. Some variants, like the Soviet T-34, were simple, rugged and built in vast numbers: others, like the German Tiger, were highly engineered but produced in small numbers. Although the tank is often seen as the epitome of land warfare in the late 20th century, tanks have only ever been effective as part of combined-arms teams.

high-explosive shells from the same gun. The silhouette was too high and the hull mounting was cumbersome, but at last they could confront German tanks from a sensible range, although no answers were found then or later to Rommel's most potent weapon, the dreaded 88 mm anti-tank gun.

Arriving in Tunisia in 1942 the US army brought with it a doctrine which, in theory, allocated tanks to infantry support while enemy armour was dealt with by dedicated anti-armour vehicles, called tank destroyers. In practice it proved impossible to arrange matters in such a tidy way: tanks fought tanks while tank destroyers proved vulnerable on account of their thinner armour and open tops. The Tunisian campaign also saw the last of British tanks for a while. When the Allies invaded *Sicily and in the subsequent *Italian campaign, British and Commonwealth forces were equipped with the American *Sherman tank and not before 1944 did the British Churchill appear, still inadequate but less inclined to burn than the Sherman.

In the summer of 1942 Germany introduced the 57 ton Tiger armed with the 88 mm anti-armour gun, and later the superb Panther, which outclassed every other tank on the battlefield. The Allies overwhelmed them with numbers, production of the Sherman coming close to 50,000 against less than 9,000 of all the heavier German machines. But the best all-round design both in terms of battlefield performance and ease of manufacture was unquestionably the Soviet T-34, produced in greater numbers even than the Sherman, backed up by heavier machines designed to counter the Tiger. The Soviets in WW II pioneered the commonality of parts among combat vehicles which has characterized their approach to armoured warfare to this day, while the West has moved towards the smaller numbers of unique and technologically 'gold-plated' designs after the frightful experiences of the hapless Sherman tank crews at the hands of the Germans. Britain developed a number of specialist armour applications based on the ponderous but dependable Churchill, but it was on the immensity of the *eastern front that the Germans and Soviets pioneered the use of early APCs and even *MICVs.

By 1945 the Soviet T-34 was carrying a larger gun (85 mm) and it was backed up by the sleek, futuristic, and well-armed Stalin. The USA was building larger machines with a respectable 90 mm gun and Britain was on the point of producing the excellent Centurion. In Germany tank production was crushed under the weight of Allied *air power and pursued peculiar lines such as the 140 ton Maus. In a sense this increase in size and firepower appeared to vindicate pre-war British theories. Tank guns were, once again, dedicated anti-armour weapons while the adoption of weapon system stabilizers permitted an effective return to the practice of firing on the move.

Post-war, new projectiles such as discarding sabot (APDS) and high explosive anti-tank (HEAT) improved armour penetration and introduced new ways of destroy-ing tanks, but it would be some time before these developments could be matched by improved means of *surveillance and target acquisition. Yet the lessons of WW II did not result in immediate consensus. The Americans were developing larger tanks, with cast-armour hulls and turrets, better guns, and air-cooled diesel engines. In Britain policy centred upon a multi-purpose tank in the form of Centurion while the Soviets stuck to their wartime preference for mass production and simplicity in the shape of their T-54/55 and T-62 models. Since the USSR also continued to develop heavier tanks, Britain and America countered with the massive Conqueror and M103. Yet when West Germany revived its tank-building industry the emphasis was on mobility. France tended to follow German thinking and its AMX-30 was even lighter. Britain was now almost alone in staying with petrol engines and not employing torsion bar suspension but the Centurion was so well designed that it was twice up-gunned while in British service and became a major export success.

Other countries were expanding tank production to ensure survival in an ideologically divided world rendered more dangerous by the advent of *nuclear weapons. Switzerland produced its own tanks and in Sweden the highly original S-Tank appeared—an almost flat turretless tank destroyer which elevated and depressed its gun by adjusting its suspension. Japan, which only built tanks for home defence, tended to follow American practice while the Chinese simply copied the Soviets. Post-war light tanks ranged from the innovative, air-portable French AMX-13, one of the first tanks to feature an automatic loader, to the technically advanced American M551 Sheridan which, like the simpler Soviet PT-76, was capable of amphibious operation. Britain preferred to rely on armoured cars at this stage but it did continue to develop its experience of specialized armour to a far greater extent than any other nation. APCs were now almost universal, among which the American M113 must be singled out as the most widely deployed.

The appearance of the British Chieftain in the sixties marks a key stage in the development of the tank. In many respects, in terms of multi-fuel power unit, weapon mountings, and reclining driver's position it was highly innovative and may be regarded as the first of the true main battle tanks. At the same time it was the last of a generation of tanks that relied on conventional armour to resist the effect of kinetic energy projectiles. It was the development of new projectiles, notably anti-armour guided missiles, that led to the invention of so-called Chobham armour in Britain and the adoption of reactive armour panels elsewhere. But such developments were not entirely passive. Solid state technology enhanced the effectiveness of surveillance and target acquisition and tanks were now designed to survive on a nuclear battlefield.

Another development of the sixties was the family of armoured fighting vehicles with commonality of parts. An excellent example is the British FV100 series, typified by

Scorpion and Scimitar—in effect light tanks—which includes ambulance, recovery, personnel carrying, and anti-armour guided weapon vehicles. In theory the anti-armour guided missile sounded the death knell of the tank. Highly destructive, readily transported, and accurate, they were supposed to be the ultimate ground-based antidote to the tank. In fact the majority of these weapons demand certain conditions to be ideal before they can be used to full effect and have not yet supplanted the high-velocity tank gun.

If trends can be identified in post-war developments then it may be said that Britain and the USA favoured the big gun and thick armour which, in German hands, had caused such carnage during the war. The Germans, on the other hand, now promoted mobility to the point that Leopard 2 is probably the fastest main battle tank in the world while the Soviets simply confirmed their belief that quantity mattered a good deal more than quality. The results of the *Arab–Israeli and *Gulf wars seem to call this into question, but it seems undeniably right in principle.

Current trends, in addition to a wider adoption of Chobham-type armour, include the use of a gas turbine engine in the US M1A1 Abrams. It delivers 1,500 hp (against 1,200 hp for the Perkins diesel in Challenger) but consumes fuel in prodigious quantities and produces a considerable heat signature. Germany pioneered the use of a smooth-bore 120 mm gun in their Leopard 2, which fires fin-stabilized projectiles to compensate for the lack of rifling. Various nations have adopted automatic loading systems for their guns but the Russians have created a system that works in a conventional, rotating turret. The human loader is a tank designer's nightmare. Effectively he can only work standing up which inevitably affects the overall height of the tank. Thus the Russian T-72 has the lowest profile of all modern main battle tanks, but the loading equipment is temperamental at best and, like British tanks in WW II, the ammunition in the crew compartment increases its vulnerability to fire.

British engineers developed a hydro-pneumatic suspension system for Challenger, which works in conjunction with an automatically adjustable idler that maintains correct track tension without the normal hard labour associated with this task. But if one seeks a design worked out in the hard grind of bitterly won battlefield experience, the highly innovative Israeli Merkava takes the prize: it is the only main battle tank in the world with its engine ahead of the fighting compartment, a feature which not only enhances crew protection but enables them to escape through a back door in an emergency rather than clambering out the top, in full view of the enemy.

There remains the possibility that wheels could supersede tracks. The South African defence industry has produced an eight-wheeled vehicle known as the Rooikat which is virtually a wheeled tank. Progress in tyre technology, in conjunction with suspension developments, could soon produce a wheeled vehicle that would rival the versatility of tracks without the complications of transmission and power waste. Any vehicle that could equal the performance of a tank across country, yet travel rapidly by road without the need for a transporter, would have both tactical and strategic implications along with considerable economic advantage. Finally, when considering the future, one can only point to the rapid rise of the MICV, which combines firepower with the ability to transport its own infantry. If one can visualize a situation where major wars are a thing of the past, then existing tanks, suitably modernized, should be sufficient for battlefield superiority, while MICVs should prove more than adequate for international security duties.   DF

Macksey, Kenneth, *Tank versus Tank* (London, 1991).
Ogorliewicz, Richard M., *Technology of Tanks* (1991).
Simkin, Richard, *Tank Warfare* (London, 1979).
Stern, Sir Albert, *Tanks 1914–1918: The Logbook of a Pioneer* (London, 1919).

Tannenberg, battle of (1410), also known as the battle of Grünwald, the decisive engagement of the 'Great War' of 1409–11, in which Polish-Lithuanian-Russian forces defeated the *military monastic order of the Teutonic Knights, who ruled the region from their vast, forbidding castle-monastery at Marienburg (Malbork). The Polish King Wladislaw II Jagello led a multinational force of about 30,000 Poles, Lithuanians, Russians, Czechs, and even *Mongols towards Marienburg. On 14 July, moving northwest, they encountered the Grand Master of the Teutonic Order, Ulrich von Jungingen, commanding a slightly smaller force between Grünwald and Tannenberg (Stembark). His knights, with some Swiss and English *mercenaries, took up position on a crest. The battle began with a salvo from the Teutonic Order's bombards but, like most artillery of the time, that had little effect in the open field. The Tartar cavalry then attacked the order's right flank, but was driven off. The Lithuanian Prince Vitovt attacked but was repelled and the knights began to pursue. The Russians held the centre, however, and the Poles then attacked, again from the right, this time breaking the knights' formation. All the order's senior officers, including the Grand Master, were killed in a crushing defeat that halted the order's eastward advance permanently. The decisive defeat of the Teutonic Knights also gave encouragement to the *Hussites in their struggle against the Holy Roman Empire.   CDB

Tannenberg, battle of (1914). The first major encounter between the German and the Russian empires in WW I ended in a major tactical victory for the Germans whose mythic significance (revenge for the destruction of the Teutonic Knights in 1410) was arguably greater than its military importance. The *Schlieffen Plan allowed only token forces to be left for the defence of East Prussia against a Russian army whose significant improvement since the

*Russo-Japanese war encouraged the belief that it could defeat Germany and Austria-Hungary simultaneously instead of concentrating against one at a time. On the outbreak of war the Russian First Army advanced west from the Nieman river; the Second moved north-west from the Narew. Co-ordination between them was poor, due to inadequate communications, bad staff work, and the geographic barrier of the Masurian Lakes. Nevertheless the Russian plan of using their significantly superior numbers to encircle the German Eighth Army had good prospects of success, especially when German commanders panicked after being defeated by the First Army at Gumbinnen on 20 August. The First Army, however, failed to follow up its victory while poor logistics and worse *intelligence handicapped the Second's advance. As a result the Eighth Army's new command team of *Hindenburg and *Ludendorff was able to implement plans, already outlined by the Eighth Army's staff officers, to concentrate their entire force against the Russians coming from the south.

The German railway network merits the credit it received for its rapid movement of men and supplies between the theatre's two sectors. A bit of insubordination was involved as well. The commander of the German I Corps refused to attack until his artillery arrived, a delay that gave the Russians two more days to push forward into a tightening German noose. On 27 August I Corps crushed the Second Army's left wing. Two more corps, who had reached their position by hard marches in the August heat, drove in the Russian right. The Second Army's commander saw neither of these local defeats as decisive and sought to master the situation by driving forward with the five divisions of his centre. The Russians came closer to success than is generally realized, but proved unable to break through their opponents. By the evening of 28 August, German forces advancing on the flanks had closed a circle around Second Army. The final balance sheet showed 50,000 Russians dead or wounded and another 90,000 POWs.

The adversaries in the Tannenberg campaign were reasonably well matched. The Russian failure was less a consequence of general institutional incompetence than of an attempt to employ a concept of manoeuvre warfare their field forces could not execute. While Russian losses in men, material, and morale were severe, the battle had negative consequences for the Germans as well. It established a model of decisive victory that discouraged realistic assessment of what could be achieved by military means under the conditions of 1914–18.　　　　　DES

Tarain, battles of (1191–2), also known as the battles of Taraori, a series of engagements, the last of which resulted in a decisive Muslim victory which opened all of northern India to Muslim conquest. Sent forth by his elder brother Ghiyas al-Din to extend their Ghur territories, Muizz al-Din Muhammad was soon drawn to the vast wealth of India. He proclaimed a *jihad against the infidel Hindus and his initial campaigns met with considerable success, capturing Sind in 1182 and Lahore and the Punjab in 1186.

He was checked for the first time on the plain of Tarain, about 62 miles (100 km) north of Delhi, in 1191. The Hindu *Rajputs seeing the common threat Muhammad posed, for once managed to unite and put a vastly superior force into the field. Led by Prithviraja, king of Delhi, and supported by Jai Chand of Kanoaj, the Rajput coalition soundly defeated Muhammad who was to fortunate to escape the battlefield with his life.

Muhammad returned to the plains of Tarain with a new army the following year. Once again he was heavily outnumbered, his 12,000 men facing an alleged 100,000 Hindus. Muhammad conducted a masterly mobile battle against the largely static defenders. Employing Turkish tactics to which the Hindus had no adequate response, his cavalry harried the Rajput flanks and showered their ranks with arrows while eschewing the hand-to-hand combat at which the Rajputs excelled. The Hindus were unable to chase the elusive cavalry without dangerously exposing themselves and thus were forced to endure the attrition of the Muslim arrows. When Muhammad finally judged his enemy sufficiently worn down, he charged their centre and routed them. Prithviraja died in the mêlée. The battle proved decisive and Delhi was captured in 1192–3. The whole of northern India fell to the Muslims within twenty years.　　MCM

Tartars/Tatars. See MONGOLS.

tattoo The term tattoo now refers to a military pageant, often held at night. It originated in the 17th century, when drums or trumpets sounded to call troops back to quarters in the evening. It derived from the Dutch *doe ten tap toe*, an instruction to innkeepers and *sutlers to turn off the tap of the wine- or beer-barrel.

Tattooing the skin by pricking and staining with dye reflects the use of woad by Celtic warriors, warpaint by North American Indians, and tattooing by Maoris. In the age of black powder soldiers and sailors tattooed one another using needles and *gunpowder. Tattooing was particularly associated with colonial service, and lavish oriental designs were popular. Dragons and geishas vied with the names of sweethearts, regimental insignia, and the flags of Allied nations. One future admiral, in a moment of youthful unwisdom, had a fox-hunt tattooed down his back, with the fox disappearing into its earth.　　　　RH

Taylor, Gen Zachary (1784–1850), commander of US forces during the first phase of the *Mexican war and later president. He commanded troops in the *War of 1812 and the Black Hawk war (1832), and won promotion to brigadier general at Lake Okeechobee (1837) during the Seminole wars.

In command of an army provocatively sent by Pres Polk into the disputed Nueces Strip, he twice defeated a larger Mexican force in May 1846. An easygoing officer, he was bedevilled by non re-enlistment and desertion, while the savage behaviour of the hard-bitten Texas contingent was a constant concern. Despite this, he took Monterrey in September in brilliant style, but the generous truce he granted the surrendered garrison snapped Polk's patience. With his best troops withdrawn to join *Scott at Vera Cruz, he beat off a half-hearted February 1849 attack at Buena Vista by four times his number of Mexicans under the ambivalent Santa Anna.

He returned home a hero and became the winning Whig candidate in the 1848 presidential elections. He died after sixteen miserable months of rancorous disputes over the admission of new states carved out of the conquered territories, and humiliated by revelations of flagrant corruption in his cabinet. HEB

telegraph (from Gr.: *tēle*, far, and *graphē*, writing). In 1832, Baron Schilling, a Russian diplomat, linked the Summer Palace of the tsar in St Petersburg to the Winter Palace using a telegraph with rotating magnetized needles. In 1833, Germans Karl F. Gauss and Wilhelm Weber made significant experiments with an electric telegraph. Englishmen William F. Cooke and Charles Wheatstone patented the five-needle telegraph in 1837 with a panel imprinted with letters and numerals to which the five needles pointed singly or in pairs. The Wheatstone telegraph linked Liverpool with Manchester, England, in 1839.

The development of the electromagnet about 1837 provided the American Samuel F. B. Morse with a way to transmit and receive electric signals. Together with Alfred Vail, Morse developed the simple operator key and refined their signal code, which became Morse code. Morse inaugurated a telegraph link between Baltimore, Maryland, and Washington, DC in May 1844. Probably the best-known group of codes was 'SOS', the international distress code—Save Our Souls. Vice Adm Philip Colomb's flash signalling adopted by the Royal Navy in 1867 was an adaptation of the Morse code to lights. The British in the *Crimean war made the first application of the telegraph *communications in war in 1854. In the *Indian Mutiny the newly established telegraph, which was controlled by the British, was an important factor in the outcome of the conflict.

In the *American civil war, wide use was made of the electric telegraph by both sides. The North equipped special telegraph wagon trains with insulated cable and poles that linked those lines with permanent civilian telegraph systems where messages could be transmitted. During the Austro-Prussian and *Franco-Prussian wars, the field telegraph enabled *Moltke 'the Elder', the Prussian COS, to exercise command over his distant armies. The British would, soon after, organize their first field telegraph trains in the Royal Engineers.

With growing telegraph traffic, improvements were required. The duplex circuit, developed in Germany, made it possible for messages to travel simultaneously in opposite directions on the same line. Thomas Edison devised a quadruplex in 1874 that permitted four messages to travel at once, two going in either direction.

The telegraph was more suited to long-distance fixed communications than for relay of messages and orders over short distances or on the battlefield. Telegraph lines were vulnerable to being cut and could not be erected at the speed of marching and manoeuvring armies. By the end of the 19th century, the world was criss-crossed by telegraph lines, including numerous cables beneath the Atlantic Ocean. The invention of the teletypewriter and its development of the teleprinter, linked to the telegraph system, added a further dimension to communications. Teleprinter circuits would later be used extensively during WW II. The telegraph was the first instrument to transform information into electrical form and transmit it reliably over long distances. With the advent of electronic mail and faxes, the telegraph has all but been replaced in today's world of electronics. DMJ

telephone (from Gr.: *tele*, far, and *phone*, sound). In 1861, a German scientist, Philip Reis, achieved renown for very nearly inventing the simple telephone. He used an animal ear membrane to receive signals from an oscillating galvanic inductor. The apparatus could only send sounds of constant pitch such as those produced by a single musical note. Reis could not arrange for any financial support nor could he get a patent for his efforts.

The American Alexander Graham Bell achieved a functional telephone system while seeking a way to make sound waves visible to deaf people. His telephone consisted of a microphone and a speaker and he patented it on 14 February 1876, two hours before Elisha Gray of Chicago filed a similar patent. After a long legal battle, the US Supreme Court upheld Bell's patent. Almon Strowger, an undertaker, invented the first automated telephone exchange in 1892 in Kansas City, and his switches were used until the 1970s.

It was some years before the telephone became dependable and portable enough to be adopted by the military, but it was used by the US army in the *Spanish-American war, by the British in the *Second Boer War, and by the Japanese in the *Russo-Japanese war. During WW I field telephones and switchboards were developed. Both sides laid telephone lines involving thousands of miles of wire. The static conditions of *trench warfare allowed for extensive telephone use. The chief problem lay in the maintenance of the miles of cable, always disrupted by shellfire and the threat of security from the enemy tapping into the lines and listening to conversations. The telephone had a significant impact on warfare. Larger forces could be controlled from the rear and massed artillery fire could be controlled directly by a forward observer in the trenches.

The weakness of the telephone emerged once mobile warfare became more general in WW II. Troops in the south Pacific had telephone troubles right through 1943. There was a shortage of switchboards, field wire, open wire, insulators, construction troops, and teletype machines. US army field telephones were superior and lighter than German units, but German field switchboards were superior to those of other countries. Great Britain maintained excellent telephone communications from the start of the war. The major German improvements to the telephone in WW II included technical improvements to equipment. Multi-conductor cables were provided for wire communications. They could be reeled out rapidly and as many as four conversations could take place on them at one time. The Germans were the first to use this type of military long-range cable, and they were followed by both British and US forces.

Telephone instruments became more robust and the use of multi-core cable and more sophisticated portable telephone exchanges meant that telephone communication could be relied upon under even the most adverse conditions. Major telephone switchboards of much greater capacity were needed. They were developed, manufactured, and issued for use at all tactical headquarters to satisfy the need for the greatly increased number of telephone channels required to co-ordinate the movements of field units whose mobility had been expanded many times.

The problem of wire maintenance and the possibility of tapping remained, as illustrated by the Anglo-US operation in Berlin in the 1950s, when the main Soviet telegraph and telephone cables were tapped by means of a clandestinely excavated tunnel. On the other hand, landlines were more generally secure than *radio, as the success of *ULTRA testified. It is a trade-off that continues into the era of digital cellular telephones.   DMJ

telescopes and binoculars The telescope increases the apparent size of distant objects, so making them to appear nearer. A crude form was in use before 1570. In 1608, two Dutch spectacle makers, Jansen and Lippershey, designed and built three instruments 'for seeing at a distance'. Galileo improved on these by using double concave eyepieces. He built his first optical instrument, to which he gave the name 'telescope', in 1609. Galileo immediately turned his telescope on the heavens, but the military applications for something that provides a magnified view of things far off were obvious.

Sailors seized on the telescope's possibilities almost at once. However, the term 'telescope' was not in naval use until 1744 when Murdoch Mackenzie referred to the instrument in his treatise on surveying. The telescope, usually re-

ferred to in the navy as a glass, extended the effective range of vision of the lookouts who were so vital to naval warfare since spotting the enemy in the midst of a vast ocean was a necessary prelude to avoiding or bringing the enemy to battle. It made the observation of the signals, the principal method of ship-to-ship communication, more effective—or not, in the case of Adm Horatio *Nelson. During the battle of *Copenhagen of 1801, Nelson's superior Sir Hyde Parker signalled the recall imperilling the success of the British fleet. Nelson put his telescope to his blind eye and murmured: 'I really do not see the signal!' and ignored it, turning possible disaster into triumph. Telescopes were also widely used in land warfare.

The principle of the telescope has also been adapted to other military uses. A terrestrial telescope with sharply defined markings placed in one of its image planes can be fitted to a weapon to offer magnification of the target and enhance accuracy. Such 'telescopic sights' are a feature of sniper rifles.

A refinement of telescope is the binocular telescope or binoculars as they are more common called. The binocular consists of two similar telescopes provided with two prisms, one for each mounted on a single frame. A single thumb-screw may control the focus of both telescopes simultaneously and provision may be made for focusing each separately to allow for varying characteristics in the two eyes. Compact, handy, and allowing better stereoscopic effect, that is depth perception to greater distances than the telescope, the binoculars have become an absolutely standard piece of military equipment, commonly carried by officers and vehicle commanders.   MCM

Templer, FM Sir Gerald Walter Robert (1898–1979). Commissioned into the infantry, Templer served in WW I, and was awarded the DSO as a company commander in Palestine in 1916. A staff officer with the ill-fated British Expeditionary Force (BEF) in 1940, he commanded a division at *Anzio. He is, however, best known for his service as high commissioner and C-in-C in 1952–4 during the height of the *Malayan emergency. He took major political initiatives and vigorously pursued *counter-insurgency warfare by pulling the administration, police, and army firmly together. As CIGS (1955–8), he proved anachronistic in opposing the reduction of the army's size, the increasing integration of the three services, and the consolidation of the Minister of Defence's role and powers. He supported intervention in *Suez, but resented the politicization of the operation. He objected to an over-reliance on nuclear strategy and pressed unsuccessfully for retaining a capacity to wage conventional war outside the NATO area. His Malayan techniques were later perverted by the South Vietnamese in their *strategic hamlets programme.   BC

Cloake, John, *Templer: Tiger of Malaya* (London, 1985).

tercio (Sp.: *tercio*, a third) was a fighting formation developed by González de *Córdoba to exploit firearms protected by *pikemen, although only given the name in 1534, perhaps to contrast with the similar 'legions' of *François I. It became a byword for Spanish military power. Unlike earlier formations, the tercio only comprised pikemen and arquebusiers, with none of the 'sword and buckler men' whom *Machiavelli had so admired. A development of the medieval division of an army into three parts—the van, the main battle, and the rear—the new 'third' was a regiment or brigade equivalent, 3,096 strong on paper and commanded by a *maestre de campo*—a colonel—part of a staff of nineteen officers controlling twelve companies. At the time it represented a step forward in battlefield flexibility, but it was gradually overtaken by the tactical innovations introduced by *Maurice of Nassau and others who followed his example. Its demise as a formation is generally considered to have come with the destruction of the Spanish army at *Rocroi in 1643 by a combined arms assault.　　CDB

terrorism is the deliberate creation and exploitation of fear through violence or its threat. Although ancient, it has become a common feature of the late 20th century, when it has raised a host of complex moral and practical issues. Terror, inflicted by the wholesale slaughter of populations who resisted, was used by *Assyrians and *Mongols alike to achieve the rapid collapse of enemy resolve, and was embodied in the practice (defended by *Wellington even after the Napoleonic wars) of butchering the garrisons of fortresses which held out to the last extremity. Although terrorism is generally seen in the context of being employed against a government or its agencies, its use is not necessarily anti-governmental. The French Revolutionary 'Reign of Terror' was exactly that, and many subsequent regimes—like those of *Stalin in Russia, *Hitler in Germany, and Pol Pot's Cambodia—have used terror against their own citizens. The use of coercive power by governments—'state terrorism'—has itself been used by terrorists to justify their own activities, even when the level of repression used by the government in question might appear to fall well short of terrorism. Albert Camus's 1949 play *Les Justes*, set in late 19th-century Russia—whose regime was indeed repressive—turns on the relationship between the damage terrorists necessarily inflict on the innocent and the greater political goal that they pursue. It underlines the point that the whole issue is extraordinarily subjective: one man's bomber-pilot is another's terror-flier, one man's freedom fighter another's terrorist.

One of the first recorded doctrinaire terrorists was Carlo Pisacane, Duke of San Giovanni, who renounced his aristocratic birthright to further the cause of Italian nationalism. Employing the revolutionary language of a century later, he argued that 'ideas result from deeds, not the latter from the former and the people will not be free when they are educated but educated when they are free'. Pisacane was killed in 1857, but his ideas were taken up in Russia twenty years later by the revolutionary organization Narodnaya Volya (The People's Will), a group dedicated to achieving political change by the assassination of high-profile individuals associated with the state. Their adherence to the principle of committing acts of violence only against specific individuals contrasts with the relatively random acts of violence perpetrated by many modern terrorist groups, for whom society itself has become the target.

That terrorist groups began to emerge in late 19th-century Europe was no accident. The era was characterized by the growing pains of a new and often disadvantaged urban class, and by new weaponry such as breech-loading pistols and rifles, and the invention of dynamite by *Nobel in 1862. This malleable form of high explosive was relatively safe to carry and plant, while the contemporary invention of mercury detonators enabled a charge to be set off at will. Similar social change, in this case the shift of populations from the countryside to the towns, and the ready availability of plastic explosive, had similar effects in South America a century later.

The relationship between the terrorist and the *guerrilla is complex. Not all guerrillas are terrorists: many have striven to represent themselves as irregular forces fighting a regular war, while their opponents have consistently sought to portray them as terrorists in order to deprive them of legitimacy. Yet the guerrilla's military weakness and his dependence on popular support both tend to drive him towards terrorism. The former encourages him to get the maximum publicity—especially in and beyond the media-rich 1960s—from the meagre means at his disposal, and the latter drives him to use both stick and carrot in his dealings with the population. The communists in China and the Vietcong in *Vietnam both dealt harshly with civilian supporters of the hostile regime. Vietcong attacks on the civil service and local administration during the *Tet offensive, often exemplified by the brutal murder of whole family groups, did much to destabilize South Vietnam. Independence campaigns against colonial rulers, like those in *Cyprus and *Algeria, usually embodied elements of terrorism. It is profoundly ironic, in view of Israel's subsequent experience of terrorism, that some of the groups who pursued Israeli independence used some of the very methods their successors now condemn.

Urban guerrillas, like the Brazilian Carlos *Marighela, argued that gangster actions like bank raids and kidnappings would provoke the government into action which would turn the population against the government, rather than against the perpetrators of the original violence, but the process rarely worked that way. In Uruguay the *Tupamaros—as judicious and responsible in their actions as any urban guerrillas can hope to be—simply polarized opinion against them and were duly crushed.

Although there had been connections between national anarchist groups in the 19th century, the internationalization of terrorism really occurred after 1945, as the Soviet bloc and its clients actively supported terrorist groups with training, equipment, and safe havens; the role of Libya has been particularly suspect. International terrorism took a new turn in 1968. The *PLO had been founded in 1964 from Palestinian pressure groups who wished to recover their homeland. Israeli victory in the Six Day War of June 1967 resulted in the Jordanians losing Jerusalem and the West Bank of the Jordan, swelling the number of Arab refugees. The more radical elements of the PLO reacted violently, beginning in July 1968 with the hijacking of an El Al airliner. The Israelis released sixteen Arab prisoners, but this only encouraged more hijacks, and the PLO (and its splinter groups) mounted ever more daring and bloody attacks. These culminated with the kidnapping of Israeli athletes at the 1972 Munich Olympics, where all eleven hostages and five terrorists were killed. It is arguable whether the latter act caused an invitation to be issued to Yasser *Arafat to address the UN General Assembly, but within eighteen months Arafat had spoken to the UN, and his PLO had been awarded 'Special Observer Status'. Despite the success of the Israeli *commando raid at Entebbe in 1976, which released over 100 hostages held by German and Palestinian hijackers, it is hard to resist the conclusion that it was the use of terrorism that brought the PLO to its prominent position on the world's stage.

The spread and sophistication of modern communications has ensured that modern terrorists have an effect out of all proportion to their numbers, a factor which has been crucial to late 20th-century terrorists for whom publicity is indeed oxygen. In Europe, the *IRA in the UK and the Basque separatists ETA in Spain both generated publicity out of all proportion to the number of activists engaged. The nationalist splinter group that detonated the bomb at Omagh in Northern Ireland in 1998 probably killed more people than it had activists. Similarly, although the terrorist groups of the 1970s, like the Baader-Meinhof gang in West Germany, the Italian Red Brigades, and the Japanese Red Army Faction, consisted of very few individuals with little popular support, their activities were nothing if not headline-grabbing. They saw themselves as 'class warriors', directing their venom at international businessmen, national government, or representatives of the US military. In a similar nihilistic vein are the Japanese religious cult behind the Sarin *gas attack in Tokyo (March 1995) and the perpetrators of the Oklahoma City federal office block attack of just one month later, which resulted in 168 deaths.

Other extremist groups, such as animal rights campaigners, anti-abortionists, and some extreme ecologists, have also used terrorism, justifying it with the familiar 'state terrorism' arguments already described. Though there is little evidence that 1990s terrorist groups are as interlinked as those of the 1970s and 1980s, their rise may be due in part to widely published studies of the techniques of terrorism and its effectiveness. Modern crime gangs and drug barons—'non-state actors'—have also acquired the resources to wage terrorist-type campaigns. Though the methods may be identical, the motivation is financial, not political—in this sense they are merely imitators, 'quasi-terrorists'. The fall of the Iron Curtain in 1989 and the resultant numbers of automatic weapons and explosives in circulation are partly responsible for this development. The portrayal of destruction and terror by the media underlines the core function of terrorism, which continues to be achieved by a tiny minority of zealots. Some commentators have now identified 'cyber terrorism', where no physical violence is threatened (or implied) to humans, but rather information systems themselves are the target. A computer virus circulated via the Internet is, in its way, as newsworthy as a traditional terrorist bomb.

Terrorism has caused many nations to develop specialist anti-terrorist units in the military or police, though the distinctions between the traditional functions of each sometimes became blurred in the process. In the British model, troops were used in support of the civil power, well demonstrated in 1980 with the storming by the *SAS of the terrorist-held Iranian Embassy in London. The internationalization of terrorism generated an international response, particularly in terms of the pooling of police intelligence, although the old question of value judgements continues to enable one state's terrorists to emerge as another's political refugees. Most visibly, terrorism has resulted in the tightening-up of security at ports, airports, and public buildings, with concomitant delays and frustrations. In this respect its consequences may prove more enduring than those of many aspects of conventional warfare, for they will remain with us. APC-A/RH

Tet offensive (1968). Because it turned out that way, some have suggested that this was a politico-military operation designed to undermine US domestic support for the war in *Vietnam and at the same time bring the southern Vietcong cadres out in the open where US firepower could destroy them. The evidence is that, both in this and at the ongoing siege of Khe Sanh, *Giap had not fully understood that US *air power was an order of magnitude greater than anything he had encountered before. The offensive was intended to spark an insurrection among South Vietnamese civilians and military forces, destroying the US-backed regime in Saigon and isolating the US main military presence concentrated to the north, thus forcing the Johnson administration to seek a negotiated end to the war. The US area commander *Westmoreland was not the only one who let memories of *Dien Bien Phu cloud his judgement.

Early on 31 January 1968, North Vietnamese and Vietcong forces attacked 27 of South Vietnam's 44 provincial capitals and scores of villages. Timed to take advantage of a *truce declared for the annual lunar New Year celebrations, it utterly failed to prompt an uprising, although government supporters were methodically massacred in a telling use of *terrorism. With the exception of the battles of Saigon and Hué, US and South Vietnamese forces quickly defeated the attacks and Vietcong units indigenous to South Vietnam were indeed decimated. But the Tet offensive was a brilliant political success for Hanoi. Believing that progress was being made in the war, members of the Johnson administration and the American public were shocked by the scope and intensity of the offensive. On 31 March, a haggard Lyndon Johnson announced that he would not seek re-election and the long process of disengagement began.

JJW

Teutoburger Wald, battle of (AD 9). Rome's first emperor, Augustus, feared that the rich province of Gaul was too vulnerable to German attack from across the Rhine and determined upon the Elbe and Danube as the empire's northern boundaries. He sent his able son Tiberius to campaign in the region in AD 4–5, which he achieved through an effective combined operation with a fleet on the northern coast of Germany. In AD 6 Tiberius was recalled to deal with a revolt in Pannonia and the responsibility for consolidating his work fell to the legate P. Quinctilius Varus, commanding five legions and German auxiliary forces. Prominent among his auxiliary commanders was Arminius, a chief of the Cherusci tribe. In AD 9 Varus was conducting operations with three legions in central Germany, east of the Weser near modern Minden. Arminius had planned a rebellion, and, although warned of this, Varus still trusted him. Setting out to return to winter quarters, the Romans, 12,000–15,000 strong, with many dependants, had to march through the mountainous and heavily wooded Teutoburger Wald. Near modern Detmold, Arminius and his following deserted, and the Romans became subject to *guerrilla attacks. Varus continued the march despite the problems his unwieldy column was experiencing in the terrain. The attacks grew more severe, and, although we cannot be certain of the details, the soldiers and all their families were massacred and Varus committed suicide. Tiberius stabilized the military situation and in AD 13 his younger brother Germanicus led an expedition to the Elbe again. In AD 16, he finally defeated Arminius (who was assassinated by rivals in AD 21) and recovered the legions' lost eagles (see COLOURS); but Augustus, who had been shocked by the defeat, decreed that there should in future be no effort made to extend Roman authority beyond the Rhine.

MB

Keppie, L., *The Making of the Roman Army* (London, 1984).

Thebes The prominence of Thebes in early Greek myth reflects the Boeotian city's Mycenean status as one of the great citadels of the late Bronze Age. In Classical times, the city was notorious for joining the Persians against the Greeks during the *Xerxes invasion of 480–479 BC, and igniting the later internecine *Peloponnesian war by a night attack on the nearby neutral town of Plataea. Its rich agriculture, Boeotian allies, and federated political organization gave the Thebans natural military advantages, and it was eagerly courted for much of its history by both Athens and *Sparta to tip the fragile balance of power among the Greek states. By the 4th century under *Epaminondas and Pelopidas, Thebes and its Boeotian confederacy achieved a brief but unquestioned pre-eminence among the city states after the battle of *Leuctra (371) after which a further campaign freed the Spartan helots and ensured autonomy from Spartan hegemony for most of the cities of the Peloponnese.

Leuctra was won by stacking *hoplites in an unprecedentedly deep *phalanx on the left wing of the battle line, where it smashed the élite enemy right. After the death of Epaminondas at the battle of *Mantineia (362), Thebes' hegemony was short. In a futile effort to stop Macedonian aggrandizement, it anchored the Greek right wing at the battle of *Chaeronea (338), where the Sacred Band, an élite corps of 300 Theban fighters, was slaughtered to the man. On the death of *Philip II of Macedon, Thebes revolted against the Macedonian yoke, only to fall to *Alexander 'the Great', who destroyed the city and sold the inhabitants into slavery, an act of terror that shocked Greece and ended centuries of uninterrupted political and military eminence.

VDH

Buckler, J., *The Theban Hegemony 371–362 BC* (Cambridge, Mass., 1980).
Demand, N., *Thebes in the 5th Century* (London, 1982).

Thermopylae, battle of (480 BC). In antiquity the pass of Thermopylae ran between Mount Kallidromon and the sea, which has now receded. Here a force of perhaps some 6,000 Greeks, under Leonidas, one of the kings of *Sparta, held off the army of *Xerxes for three days, until a local offered to guide the Persians to their rear by a mountain track. Informed of this by deserters and scouts the Greeks divided, probably under orders, some withdrawing and the surviving Spartans, Thespians, and Thebans remaining to act as a rearguard. The Thebans possibly surrendered at the last, but the rest were annihilated. JFL

Lazenby, J. F., *The Defence of Greece* (Warminster, 1993).

Thin Red Line Often used as a classic description of British infantry, the phrase 'thin red line' is in fact a misquotation. On 25 October 1854 the British base at Balaclava in the *Crimea, defended by the 93rd Highlanders, was threatened by Russian cavalry. *The Times* correspondent W. H. Russell wrote: 'gathering speed at every stride, they flew towards that thin red streak tipped with steel.' The *Highlanders fired and the cavalry fell back, though the 93rd's surgeon put Russian dead at 'no more than twelve'. 'Streak' soon became 'line', Robert Gibb's painting showed horsemen only feet from Highlanders, and the episode had been duly overdramatized.   RH

Thirty Years War (1618–48). The Thirty Years War had its roots in the dynastic and imperial ambitions of the house of Habsburg and its leadership in the Counter-Reformation. For the rest, the religious aspects should not be overstated because princes would readily trade religious conviction for political advantage; Catholic France in particular was eager to support Protestant states against the Habsburgs.

By the beginning of the 17th century there was parity between the faiths among the small principalities that made up Germany. Of the larger states, three of the electors of the Holy Roman Emperor were Protestant, another three Catholic, and the seventh and final one was the emperor himself, in his capacity as king of Bohemia. This apparently stable majority for Habsburg ambition was undermined by the fact that the majority of Bohemians were Protestant, and therein lay the spark of the Thirty Years War.

This came in 1617 when the Emperor Mathias placed his heir apparent Ferdinand on the throne of Bohemia to ensure his succession to the imperial title. Ferdinand was a known Catholic zealot and his subject nobles urged him to exercise restraint in the proclamation of religious edicts. When Ferdinand ignored their entreaties, a group of Protestant nobles burst into the royal palace in Prague in May 1618, and threw his advisers out of a window into the moat/midden. The 'Defenestration of Prague' was the signal for a Protestant uprising in Hungary, Transylvania, and Bohemia, which was a direct threat to the continued prosecution of war against the Dutch, who would doubtless find new allies among the truculent Protestant population of central Europe in their struggle against the Spanish Habsburgs. Yet no single prince was willing to set himself up as a rival king of Bohemia in opposition to the legitimately constituted sovereign.

In 1619 Ferdinand succeeded to the imperial throne on Mathias's death, and Frederick of the Palatinate rashly agreed to stand as a rival king of Bohemia. The Palatinate bordered on the Spanish Netherlands and Catholic Bavaria, providing two further flashpoints in addition to Bohemia itself, and Spanish troops soon occupied the Lower Palatinate while the Bavarians occupied the north. The Dutch and English, both supposed champions of the Protestant cause, were reluctant to become involved, sensing a lost cause in the making. German Lutherans stayed neutral for the time being, leaving their rivals, the Calvinists, to their fate. Hence Frederick's army was crushed at the battle of the *White Mountain outside Prague in 1620. Rebellious Bohemia was thoroughly ravaged by the imperial mercenary army, and forcibly restored to the Catholic faith.

The Habsburgs seemed to have settled matters in their favour, therefore the Protestant princes belatedly began to cast around for allies. A grand Protestant league was formed consisting of some German states, England, and Holland, secretly supported by France, and led by the imprudent Christian IV of Denmark, who began the attack in 1626. The Danes were run ragged for three years by the more numerous imperial and Bavarian armies, led by the Bohemian mercenary *Wallenstein, and by 1629 they had had enough of fighting without effective support from their allies, and sued for peace. The alliance collapsed, and it seemed that Protestant hopes were lost, particularly when Ferdinand attempted to return to the state of affairs that had existed at the time of the Peace of Augsburg in 1555, demanding the return to Catholicism of lands that had subsequently converted to the Protestant faith by issuing the Edict of Restitution. For once Calvinists and Lutherans were united in their opposition to this draconian policy.

But by seeking to exploit their victory over the Danes to obtain an outlet to the Baltic, from which to strike at Dutch maritime commerce, the Habsburgs provoked their nemesis. *Gustavus Adolphus of Sweden, offended by Habsburg behaviour and rescued from an inconclusive war against the Poles by French mediation, declared war in 1630. By this time the cost of the war had exhausted the imperial treasury, and Ferdinand's policies had weakened his alliances within the empire, so the Swedish invasion came at the moment when the empire was least prepared to repel it. The Swedish army was tough and battle-hardened and won two stunning victories at *Breitenfeld in 1631 and *Lützen in 1632, although Gustavus was killed during the latter. But so too was the imperial cavalry leader *Pappenheim while Wallenstein, who had made himself prince of Mecklenburg, was assassinated in 1634. It is not clear whether this was because he no longer seemed able to win, because Ferdinand was afraid of him, because *Richelieu paid his lieutenants to do it, or a combination of all three.

Constant campaigning and *attrition had deprived the Swedes of their best native troops, who had been replaced by inferior local freebooters, and this contributed to their defeat at Nördlingen in August 1634, where the Swedish Gen Horn and the new champion of Protestantism, *Bernhard of Saxe-Weimar, were roundly defeated by the veteran Spanish-imperial army with the loss of 14,000 men, and all their artillery. The last hope for the Protestant German princes was that Catholic France, fearing Habsburg hegemony, would come to the rescue. Thus the ascendancy gained by the Habsburgs after Nördlingen was destined to be short-lived.

Meanwhile, the Dutch were able to roll back the Spanish, who were crippled by an economic collapse and revolt at home. The Spanish Atlantic fleet was destroyed by the Dutch Adm Tromp at the battle of the Downs in 1639, and

Portugal declared herself independent in 1640. The Spanish tried to renew the offensive, but were decisively defeated by the French at *Rocroi. War exhaustion now led to a desire for peace, but there was no consensus on how this was to be achieved, and the fighting dragged on. The breakthrough came in 1648, when Spain and Holland concluded their 80-year war, which had become enmeshed in the wider conflict of the Thirty Years War, and the other combatants followed suit and settled their differences one after another.

These agreements were rolled up into the Treaty of Westphalia, which was to condition the political map of Europe for over a century. Sweden gained a foothold on the southern shores of the Baltic, France had secured her borders, and the Dutch had achieved nationhood. Overall the Protestants had secured their position in Germany, and Bavaria and Brandenburg (Prussia) were to emerge as significant independent states. The Holy Roman Emperors were left with little influence or control over German affairs, as the principle of the Peace of Augsburg, 'cuius regio, eius religio', was restored: each state would follow the faith of its ruler.

The Thirty Years War had a lasting impact. One of its most obvious effects was the loss of life. Perhaps 8,000 of the imperialist troops at Breitenfeld were killed, while almost half the Swedish force of 25,000 was killed at Nördlingen. Civilians also suffered appallingly: some parts of Germany were laid waste, and the population may have fallen from around 20 million to around 16–17 million. However, depredations tended to be concentrated around the areas of greatest fighting—the cities of the north-west actually prospered—and disruption has lent itself to exaggeration by partisan commentators. Thousands were displaced rather than killed, and often the peasantry was permanently weakened, usually to the advantage of the landed nobility. Yet there is no absolute consistency, for the war enabled some humble men to rise. The peasant Peter Melander commanded an army and became a count; his daughter married a reigning prince. During the war, Grotius had published *De jure belli ac pacis* arguing that individuals deserved protection against the ravages of war, and one of the war's legacies was a desire by rulers, as well as their subjects, to make war less destructive.

Although the *military revolution thesis is now widely questioned, war did change during this period—though arguably even more significantly after it. If the relationship between evolving armies and evolving states was less direct than the thesis suggests, it was nonetheless important. Armies grew bigger—Wallenstein may have commanded as many as 150,000 men and Gustavus perhaps 120,000—and were often better organized, with a premium attached to the marshalling of infantry firepower and the improvement of artillery. They became notably more costly: the French army cost about 16 million *livres tournois* in the 1620s and over 38 million after 1640. Many senior commanders were commercial entrepreneurs, with their subordinates subcontractors in a commercial venture: it is unsurprising that

the infantry subunit was called a company. Disgust at some of the more extreme effects of this encouraged hesitant steps towards the professionalization of officer corps, more marked at sea than on land, and increasing government control over armies. Although *uniforms would have seemed multiform to the drillmasters of a later age, they were beginning to establish themselves, and regimental *colours and standards increasingly bore unmistakable national symbols.   TM/RH

Parker, Geoffrey, *The Thirty Years War* (London, 1984).
Steinberg, S. H., *The 'Thirty Years War' and the Conflict for European Hegemony 1600–1660* (London, 1966).
Wedgwood, V., *The Thirty Years War* (London, 1938).

Tibet, British expedition to (1904). Suspecting that Russia proposed to establish an agent at Lhasa, capital of Tibet, then loosely under Chinese control, in 1903 the Indian government sent Col Younghusband to negotiate with the Tibetans. Denied access, he was given an escort of some 2,000 troops with four light guns. The force set about crossing some of the most difficult country in the world in poor weather, and Brig Gen Macdonald, the escort commander, clashed with Younghusband, maintaining that it was unwise to continue. On 31 March 1904 a deadlock with Tibetan troops at Guru turned into a battle which left over 600 Tibetans dead and half a dozen British and Indians wounded.

Younghusband reached Gyantse, his authorized destination, and was besieged in nearby Chang Lo, indulging in squabbles by messenger and *telegraph with his political masters and Macdonald. On 6 July the escort stormed Gyantse fort, and on the 14th the force set out for Lhasa, arriving there in early August. A treaty dealt with frontier issues and declared that Tibet was to have no dealings with foreign powers without Britain's consent. Younghusband was later censured for exceeding his authority, although both he and Macdonald were knighted.   RH

Fleming, Peter, *Bayonets to Lhasa* (London, 1961).

Tilly, Graf Johann Tserclaes von (1559–1632). A Fleming schooled in the wars of the Low Countries, Tilly was a thoroughgoing professional who did much to preserve and advance the Catholic cause during the *Thirty Years War. Serving under *Spinola, Tilly was present at the capture of *Antwerp in 1585, and learned much from his commander about the need for meticulous preparation and the importance of a rock-solid infantry in military operations.

When the Army of Flanders began to suffer serious reverses at the hands of Maurice of Nassau, Tilly sought his fortune in imperial service, fighting the Turks at Kerestes in 1596. In 1610 he transferred his allegiance to Maximilian of Bavaria and joined the army of the Catholic League, which he did much to reform. At the head of the army, Tilly faced the Bohemian rebels under Frederick, the Elector Palatine at the battle of the *White Mountain in 1620. Tilly was victorious and began the subjugation of Germany. He was checked by Mansfeld at Mingolsheim in 1622, but crushed the Protestants at Wimpfen and Höechst that same year. At Stadtlohn the next year he utterly destroyed Christian of Brunswick's army, the last threat to imperial power in Germany.

Then in 1626 Tilly co-operated with *Wallenstein, and routed the Danes at Lutter. When Sweden entered the war, Tilly found a far more formidable opponent in *Gustavus Adolphus and desperation at his approach may have been a factor in the brutal sack of *Magdeburg. A year later his army was broken by the Swedes' new tactics at *Breitenfeld, a defeat from which his troops did not recover. He retired to Bavaria to defend the river Lech for the Catholic League. He was mortally wounded defending the river line against Gustavus and died on 20 April 1632. The 74-year-old 'warrior monk' had outlived the style of war he knew so well.

TM

Timoshenko, Marshal Semyon (1895–1970), Soviet military commander and state official. A tsarist NCO, he joined the Red Army in 1918 and the Communist Party the following year, and commanded a cavalry regiment in the civil war. In the late 1930s he commanded the North Caucasus, Kharkov, and Kiev Special Military Districts. He directed the final offensives in the 1939–40 Russo-Finnish war and was made a marshal in 1940. He was in command for the critical battle of *Moscow. As vice-commissar for defence under *Stalin he was a member of Stavka (the Supreme High Command HQ) and he also commanded the Western, South-Western, Stalingrad, and North-Western Fronts (army groups). He was a somewhat unimaginative pounder, but he survived many abler men. He impressed Sidney Keyes, the British poet, who wrote a poem about him. Like many generals in this book, 'in a rage of love, and grief, and pity, he made the pencilled map alive with war'.

CDB

Timur (1336–1405), also Timur Lenk, hence Tamerlane, was a Turco-Mongol conqueror who created in Samarkand a city which even in ruins reveals a love of delicate beauty that is difficult to reconcile with the known nature of its creator. Claiming to be a distant relative of *Genghis Khan through the female line, Timur was not a *Mongol himself, but from the Turkic Barlas tribe in Transoxania, now Uzbekistan. His name means 'iron' in Turkish—like Genghis's original name, Temujin. The pejorative suffix 'Lenk' means 'the lame' in Persian—which he was as the result of an arrow wound—but Asian historians call him Amur Timur Gurigan—Lord Timur the Splendid.

Timur's trajectory began with a three-year struggle to achieve dominance in Transoxania at the end of which in

1370 he proclaimed himself not merely emir of Samarkand but khan of the Chagatai and inheritor of Genghis's Mongol empire. For the next decade he made this grandiose claim a reality, alternately defeating rival khanates or assisting them against outsiders, notably the Russians and the Lithuanians who had rebelled against the Golden Horde. Between 1383 and 1399 he conquered the Caucasus, Persia, and Iraq, having to turn back twice to deal with the khan of the Golden Horde who invaded first the Caucasus and then Transoxania. While he was thus engaged, the Persians rose in revolt and it was during his repression of this starting in about 1396 that he levelled towns, destroyed irrigation systems, and built his trademark pyramids of skulls. For an encore he invaded India in 1398 on the pretext that the Muslim sultan of Delhi was being too tolerant of his Hindu subjects. Burning and massacring as he went, he defeated the sultan at *Panipat and then sacked Delhi so comprehensively that it took a century to recover.

Between 1399 and 1403 he laid waste Azerbaijan (a sequel to the Golden Horde invasion) then rode west to defeat the *Mamelukes and sack Aleppo, Damascus, and Baghdad, shipping their artisans to Samarkand and killing everyone else. He then turned his baleful attention on the Ottoman *Turks, destroying their army near Ankara in 1402 and in passing taking Smyrna from the Knights of Rhodes. The sultan of Egypt and the Byzantine emperor made submission and he received ambassadors from as far away as England. Timur returned to Samarkand in 1403 and immediately set about preparing an invasion of China, on which he had embarked when he fell ill and died. His body was embalmed and such was the awe surrounding his name that it lay unmolested in his beautiful mausoleum in Samarkand until Soviet archaeologists opened it in 1941, shortly before the Germans invaded Russia.

The differences between Timur's style and Genghis's are instructive. Genghis trusted his generals to execute the plans he had sketched on the broadest of canvases, communicating with his widely dispersed armies using his system of 'arrow' messengers. Timur exercised much more rigid control, concentrating his armies and leading them in person. This may simply have been a difference in style, or it may have been that Genghis had better lieutenants such as Subedei and Jebe, or both. None of Timur's generals were first-rate commanders in their own right. He was even more meticulous in planning and preparation than Genghis, personally drawing up the requirements for equipment for each soldier and writing detailed regulations for setting up camps. But once a campaign had started he could be impetuous; in 1388 he rode into Baghdad with a small band of followers and personally pursued the sultan out of the kingdom. In 1400 Timur met the great Arab historian Ibn Khaldun outside Damascus in one of the most fascinating encounters in military history. Timur asked him to write a detailed description of Egypt and territories to the west 'in such a manner that when the conqueror read it, it would be as if he were seeing the region'. The historian prudently completed the assignment in a few days, but North Africa was to be spared a visit by a man who would very likely have made the ecological damage done by drought and goat pale by comparison.

Additional to his attention to *logistics and *intelligence requirements, Timur was also a master of the oriental philosophy of war that emphasizes treachery and sowing dissension among your adversaries. If he made an alliance, it was to make the ally drop his guard, and if he sent an emissary to an enemy camp it was to distribute money and promises (seldom kept) so that the enemy general would be betrayed by his own lieutenants. He was the complete master of every aspect of war in the Mongol style and led from the front in countless battles. A single exquisite city is not much to put in the balance against the fact that he crushed the fragile edifice of civilization everywhere else.

CDB/HEB

Bellamy, Christopher, 'Swift Flight of the Parthian: Great Captains of Asia', *Military Review* (July 1987).

Gale, Gen Sir Richard, *Kings at Arms: The Use and Abuse of Power in the Great Kingdoms of the East* (London, 1971).

Lamb, Harold, *Tamerlane the Earth Shaker* (London, 1929).

tirailleur (translatable as skirmisher, *sharpshooter, or rifleman) has had a variety of meanings in the French army. It applied to specific units, particularly to those raised in the colonies, such as *tirailleurs algériens* (popularly known as *Turcos), *annamites* and *tonkinois* (from what is now Vietnam), and *senégalais*.

In a wider context tirailleurs were infantry skirmishers. They played an important part in the 'tactics of common sense' advocated by many French officers who were dissatisfied with the formalism of the 1791 drillbook, and which reflected suggestions made by *Guibert as early as 1772. Poor training and difficult terrain between them limited the battlefield effectiveness of *drill, and there was often a wide gulf between drillbook theory and tactical reality. We must not make too much of assertions that the British always fought in line and the French in column. A column, screened by a swarm of tirailleurs, was a handy way of moving troops, and often these *columns found themselves too close to the enemy to deploy and so attacked as they were. By preference the French often employed *l'ordre mixte*, with one of a regiment's battalions deployed in line to generate fire, and the other two battalions in column. One company from each battalion—usually its light or *voltigeur company—would skirmish ahead of the line. An enemy line would find itself galled by the fire of tirailleurs long before it faced the French main body.

Many authorities, after the *Napoleonic wars as well as during them, argued that there was something particularly French about tirailleurs. Skirmishers filled with patriotic ardour and individual resolve, keen shots who made good

use of the ground, could pave the way for the decisive attack. As late as 1854, in instructions issued for the *Crimea, Marshal St Arnaud wrote: 'The action of tirailleurs must always precede that of masses.' And in response to a German suggestion that French infantry attacks would be broken by the fire of breech-loaders, in 1866 a Frenchman responded that 'For all Frenchman, battle is above all an individual action, the presence of dash, agility and the offensive spirit'.

RH

Tito, Marshal Josip Broz (1892–1980), leader of the Yugoslav *Partisans and subsequently president; a revolutionary activist inspired, trained, and funded during the inter-war period by Moscow. According to Fitzroy Maclean, head of Britain's military mission to the Partisans during 1943–5, Broz was known from his early revolutionary days as a dominant leader, always ordering his subordinates to 'do this', or 'do that', which translates as *tito*. Always on the move, and taking several pseudonyms or nicknames, 'Tito' eventually stuck and was adopted as his permanent name.

Having already served the cause of communism in the *Spanish civil war, Tito was fully committed to clandestine life even before the German invasion of April 1941 (see YUGOSLAVIA IN WW II), but he refrained from overt resistance activity while the Nazi-Soviet non-aggression pact was in force. Nonetheless he anticipated the German invasion of the USSR and had already taken to the hills with a small band of followers to combat Mihailović's *Chetniks as well as the Germans and their allies the *Ustashe.

Tito collected disaffected Catholic Croats, Muslim Bosnians, and Orthodox Serbs into his force, and created a broader base of support than Mihailović, though the latter was in receipt of British arms, and was recognized by the Yugoslav government-in-exile. Tito also sought to indoctrinate his Partisans (a title, not a description) with communism, which (to a degree) successfully overcame the ethnic and religious divisions that had traditionally dogged Yugoslav politics and would do so again after his death.

The Partisans survived several campaigns against them by the German-Ustashe forces in 1942–3, keeping on the move and losing a quarter of their troops and half their equipment. By this time Tito was portraying himself as general of a national liberation army, rather than leader of a communist resistance group, and had initiated a Pan-Yugoslav Council of Unity in Bihac (November 1942) as a means of appealing for more support. The decision in 1943 to divert all support to Tito, at the behest of Fitzroy Maclean, and confirmed by the 'Big Three' at Tehran, enhanced his status considerably. A second Council of Unity at Jajce in central Bosnia gave him the rank of marshal and it was also agreed that the post-war future lay not with a monarchy, but with communism, which was very much what *Stalin wanted to hear. But the war was a long way from over, a fact underlined in May 1944 by the German *special forces assault on Tito's new HQ in Drvar. Though many of his staff perished, he escaped and was brought by the British to Vis, one of the western chain of islands off the Croatian coast in their possession. Thereafter he commanded from Vis, aided considerably by the RAF in the form of the Balkan Air Force, which engaged in a systematic campaign of aerial *interdiction against German ground and sea forces, as well as the supply of the Partisan columns. Tito also paid a secret visit to Moscow to arrange for Soviet military assistance and to co-ordinate his plan to take over the country with the arrival of the Red Army on Yugoslavia's eastern frontier.

Thanks to these arrangements Belgrade fell to Tito on 20 October 1944, and thereafter he consolidated his control over the country he had won, the only *resistance leader to liberate his own country without the significant intervention of foreign troops. In some ways what he did thereafter was even more remarkable. He defied Stalin in June 1948, and then became a leader of the non-aligned nations. One may speculate whether he might have used his benign dictatorship to achieve greater integration among the heterogenous and mutually antagonistic peoples of Yugoslavia, but the fact remains that while he lived there was inter-communal peace and relative prosperity. The wheel turns, and in 1999 as in 1914 the Russians recovered their traditional role as the protectors of the Serbs amid the ruins of Tito's federation.   APC-A

Tobruk As a deep-water port on the North African coast in Cyrenaica, sheltered on the landward side by high ground, Tobruk was of immense significance in the battle for *North Africa. Its 27,000-strong Italian garrison first surrendered to Australian troops on 22 January 1941 during the *Wavell offensive into Libya. *Rommel disembarked at Tripoli a month later and launched a ground offensive that regained most of the ground lost the previous year. He failed to capture Tobruk, and for over a year the isolated garrison held out against all attempts to take it. For both sides it assumed a propaganda role that outweighed even its great strategic value: Goebbels referred to its defenders as the 'rats', which in characteristic British fashion the whole army proudly adopted as their title, thus *Desert Rats, and the port became a symbol of resistance when the war was going badly for Britain. When it fell and 25,000 men surrendered to an armoured assault on 21 June 1942, *Churchill said it was 'one of the heaviest blows I can recall during the war'. *Hitler promoted Rommel to field marshal, but the triumph was short lived and during the retreat after *Alamein he abandoned the port without a fight, British troops marching into Tobruk for the last time on 21 November 1942.   APC-A

Heckstall-Smith, Anthony, *Tobruk* (London, 1959).

Tojo, Gen Hideki (1885–1948). Tojo was the son of a general in the Japanese army, and was called Eiku Tojo until becoming premier in 1941. He graduated from the Japanese military academy in 1905 and in 1915 completed his studies at the war college. Greatly influenced by the lessons of WW I he espoused the theories of *total war, and appreciated the need for Japanese military strength to be based on a sound and strong economy. During the 1930s he argued for the reorganization of the Japanese army and the economic integration of the resources provided by Manchuria. He served as chief of police affairs for the Japanese army in China and became its COS in 1937. In May 1938 he became vice minister of war, then minister of war in July 1940. It was in this capacity that he drafted a mobilization strategy that put Japan on course for war with the USA. In October 1941 he became premier, effectively a military dictator, and ordered the attack on *Pearl Harbor. He was forced to resign when the USA recaptured Saipan on 9 July 1944. When Japan surrendered he attempted suicide and was despised by his later co-defendants for failing to achieve what he had ordered millions of others to do. Nursed back to health, he was condemned to death by the International Military Tribunal sitting in Tokyo and hanged.   SRT

Tokugawa Ieyasu (1542–1616) had an unpromising childhood as hostage of the Imagawa, for whom he fought as a young man against *Oda Nobunaga. His first experience of battle was at the siege of Terabe. When Imagawa Yoshimoto invaded Nobunaga's territories Ieyasu played a distinguished role in the capture of the fortress of Marune, where he made use of concentrated arquebus fire. Following the death of Imagawa Yoshimoto at the battle of Okehazama in 1560 Ieyasu allied himself to Oda Nobunaga and fought loyally at Azukizaka (1564) against the Ikkō-ikki sectarians. Ieyasu took part in the battle of the Anegawa (1570), when his army took much of the brunt of the fighting. He was defeated by Takeda Shingen at Mikata ga hara (1572), but avoided the loss of Hamamatsu castle by a tactical withdrawal and a night attack. He also accompanied Nobunaga in the relief of Nagashino castle in 1575, which led to the famous battle of Nagashino. The death of Nobunaga placed Ieyasu against *Toyotomi Hideyoshi, but through adroit political skills Ieyasu avoided the fate of other rivals, and their major conflict at Nagakute (1584) ended in stalemate.

Following the defeat of the Hōjō in 1590, Ieyasu received their territories and transferred his capital to Edo (Tokyo). As his army had avoided service in Korea he was in a strong position when Hideyoshi died, and challenged the Toyotomi family for the succession against a powerful alliance under Ishida Mitsunari, whom he defeated at the epic *battle of Sekigahara. Tokugawa Ieyasu became *shogun in 1603, and finally vanquished the Toyotomi heir, Hideyori, with the long and bitter siege of *Osaka castle in 1614–15. He died peacefully in bed, having established a dynasty that would last for two and a half centuries. Tokugawa Ieyasu is remembered as a skilled general and statesman, who laid the foundations for the long rule of his family.   SRT

Tolstoy, Count Leo (1828–1910), Russian soldier, later pacifist, environmentalist, writer, *war correspondent, and author of *War and Peace*, regarded by some as the world's greatest novel and also a work of great historical, political, and military insight.

Born on the family estate at Yasnaya Polyana, 100 miles (161 km) south of Moscow, Tolstoy dropped out of Kazan University, aged 19. As a young man he possessed enormous physical strength and agility, with a limitless appetite for vodka and women, and he could not be bothered with studies. In 1851 he joined his soldier brother Nikolay in the Caucasus where the Russians were engaged in a protracted war with the great guerrilla commander *Shamyl and his Chechen and Dagestan supporters. He enrolled as a volunteer in an artillery unit and, after taking part in a raid, later described in *The Raid*, was invited to join the regiment as a potential officer. *The Cossacks* was also a tale based on the Caucasus experience and in early 1852 he narrowly escaped being captured which laid the foundations for his story *The Prisoner of the Caucasus*. The Chechen *guerrillas used to hide in the forests in the flat country round Grozny, so the imperial Russian army methodically cut it down, and his story *The Wood Clearing* describes such an expedition.

He was commissioned early in 1854 and in April 1855 was sent to Sevastopol during the *Crimean war as an artillery officer—the élite of the Russian army. He had already decided a professional military career was not for him, but nevertheless resolved to see his service through. He was nominated for the Cross of St George twice, but on one occasion he was absent from the parade where the medals were presented, and on the other he gave it up in favour of an old soldier for whom the medal would mean a higher pension. Both events were fully in character.

At *Sevastopol, the horror of war really hit him. While young Russian ladies still strolled in the besieged city, Tolstoy, on the ramparts above, trod on pale, rotting, liquefying bodies, which he described in his *Sevastopol Stories* 1855–1856. He also witnessed the French attack on the Malakoff redoubt. His experience at Sevastopol, and especially of fighting the French, in conditions not far different from *Napoleonic warfare, gave him the insight to write *War and Peace*, published in six volumes in Moscow in 1868. The novel is an epic description of the campaign of 1812 with real characters such as Napoleon, *Bagration, and *Kutuzov as well as fictional ones. Most would argue that *Anna Karenina*, published in 1878, is a better novel, but for a military historian there is no contest.

After *Anna Karenina* he went through a period of despair and emerged from it a fundamentalist Christian who rejected all churches and all authority. Had he not been a national icon and a count, he would no doubt have been imprisoned as an anarchist. This was combined with a belief in the mystical bond between the Russian soil and people that was indistinguishable from the views of the *narodniki* who also populated the tsar's prisons. His extreme *pacifism was to reach out to a most unlikely convert in Gandhi, who also shared his views on abstinence. Tolstoy spent his last years as a recluse, writing religious tracts and railing against the *Russo-Japanese war.   CDB

Tolstoy, Leo, *War and Peace*, trans. Rosemary Edmonds (London, 1957).

—— *The Cossacks*, trans. Rosemary Edmonds (London, 1960).

Doroshenko, S. S., *Lev Tolstoy, voin i patriot* (Leo Tolstoy, Soldier and Patriot) (Moscow, 1966).

Torres Vedras, Lines of A stratagem adopted by *Wellington at the crucial early stage of his *Peninsular campaign. In autumn 1809 he reconnoitred the area between Lisbon, Torres Vedras, the Atlantic coast, and the river Tagus accompanied by Col Richard Fletcher, his chief engineer. He had been forced out of Spain, and wished to site *field fortifications to help him to hold Lisbon if the French followed up. The positions were constructed over the next year. Forts and batteries on hills commanded all likely approaches, with lengths of rampart between them to impede enemy advance. *Semaphore towers enabled the defenders to communicate. There were three lines: the first, running for 29 miles (47 km) through Torres Vedras itself, between the Tagus at Alhandra and the coast south of the Ziandre estuary; the second, rather stronger line some 6 miles (9.7 km) to the south; the third, centred on Fort St Julian on the Tagus estuary, secured an embarkation beach in case all else failed. The first line proved to be sufficient.

Wellington withdrew into the Lines in October 1810. The French commander *Masséna had no knowledge of them, and could neither attack them nor supply his army if it remained before them. He soon fell back about 30 miles (48 km), but his men grew increasingly hungry, and terrorized the inhabitants in their quest for food. In March 1811 Masséna retreated at last, and Wellington pursued. The character of the war had changed. With Portugal secure, Wellington was now free to attack 'the keys of Spain', the fortresses of Badajoz and Ciudad Rodrigo.   RH

Tortensson, Lennart (1603–51). Tortensson, the father of modern artillery, was given command of the reformed Swedish artillery, the most modern in Europe, at the age of 27. He had served under *Maurice of Nassau and had a clear understanding of the need for the standardization of calibres for ease of resupply and the requirements for battlefield mobility, in order that firepower might be applied at the point of decision.

At *Breitenfeld his guns decisively outperformed the imperialists' and were able to keep up with the infantry in the final assault. As a result of this service he was made a general and played an important role at the Lech and Alte Veste in 1632, but was captured and held prisoner for a year, missing the battle of Lützen.

From 1635 to 1641 he campaigned with Baner in eastern Germany, taking over command reluctantly upon the latter's death. The ranks of the Swedish army by now contained many adventurers and dubious *mercenaries, and it was a shadow of its former self. He set about restoring discipline and was victorious at Leipzig in 1642. Even by the standards of the time, his campaign against the imperialists in Bohemia during 1644 was considered notably ruthless. He met a Bavarian-imperialist army at Jankow in 1645, and blew it apart with his mobile guns that moved to different firing positions several times during the battle. But by now his health was broken by years of constant campaigning and he retired the following year.   TM

---

total war is one in which the whole population and all the resources of the combatants are committed to complete victory and thus become legitimate military targets. With few, mostly 20th-century, exceptions, all the other wars in history have been limited, in that they have engaged less than the entire energy of the societies involved and have stopped short of unconditional surrender by one side. Total war can be unilateral, bilateral, or multilateral and is characterized by an absence of rules or restraint in the conception and execution of military action in pursuit of unlimited political objectives. It precludes *capitulation, so there is no incentive to cease fighting even when defeat is objectively inevitable. Practically by definition, total war is or becomes ideological in nature at an early stage, not least because the ruled need to be reassured that the sacrifices they are called upon to make are for a worthwhile cause and not, as is invariably the case, to increase the power of the rulers.

It is thus a term to be used sparingly. The annihilation of Carthage at the end of the *Punic wars was total in its effect, but the proportion of the overall resources of the Carthaginian empire committed to prevent this outcome was minor. The principle of total war was contained in the proclamation of the *levée en masse on the eve of the *French Revolutionary wars, but the wars were still waged with very much less than the full resources of the state. The term 'unconditional surrender' was coined by *Grant, and *Lincoln made it his policy but, once again, only a limited proportion of the entire resources, even of the Confederacy, were mobilized during the *American civil war. A notable theorist of the 'nation in arms'—a theory which envisaged wholesale male mobilization—was the French socialist Jean Jaurès. This has encouraged some theorists to draw a distinction between the nation in arms and total war, but the differences are semantic only as to theoretical ends; in practice the means inexorably predominate.

*Clausewitz lived only at the beginning of an age which saw the power of the state increase immeasurably through war. He died in 1831, before *railways made mass mobilization practicable and before even the advent of *breech-loading artillery and rifles. It is unhistorical, therefore, to cull *On War* for phrases that prefigure total war, since the philosophical parameters were those of a general European society that was still primarily pre-industrial both in fact (France only became more than 50 per cent urban in 1948) and, even more to the point, in ethos. He wrote about *absolute* war, by which he meant not much more than that moderation in the prosecution of war was folly. What he predicated was the use of means unconstrained by rules to achieve defined and achievable political ends. Implicit in his philosophy was that there were natural, not man-made limits on those means, and he explicitly declared that war was the servant and not the dictator of policy. The war he wrote about represents the mid-point between the peasant who, when warned that the battle of *Marston Moor was about to be fought over his plot was surprised to learn that king and parliament had fallen out, and the peasant in Flanders after WW I, who could not even find the landmarks that would enable him to establish where his plot had been.

Thus the wars of *Bismarck and *Moltke 'the Elder' were indeed Clausewitzian. Modern game theory, with its penchant for reinventing the wheel, would term them 'mini-max', in that the party enjoying the maximum advantage after the trial of arms was satisfied with gains much less than could have been imposed on the loser. The annexation of Alsace and Lorraine after the *Franco-Prussian war was a breach of the mini-max principle and was opposed by Bismarck until the continued futile resistance directed by the demagogue Gambetta made his objections untenable. This was indeed a breach of the German chancellor's fabled realpolitik and created the festering sore of French *revanchisme* that certainly contributed to further wars. The malignant genie of nationalism let out of the bottle by the *Napoleonic wars rendered such transfers of territory anachronistic and Bismarck probably knew that a less browbeating settlement would have better served the long-term interest of his newly recreated German Reich.

By contrast the 20th-century world war, its two greatest outbursts divided by a twenty-year armistice, has been likened to a man whose tie gets caught in a mangle, from the imperatives of the rigid mobilization schedules that dictated events in August 1914 to the firestorms that consumed whole cities in 1944–5, of which the atom bombs dropped on *Hiroshima and Nagasaki were merely a more efficient means to the same end. In between the two acts of this fatal drama, none other than *Ludendorff coined the phrase 'total war' in his 1935 book *Der totale Krieg*, drawing on his experience as the virtual dictator of the German war effort in 1917–18. By comparison with the harm he had already done by lending his prestige to the upstart *Hitler, the book is little more than a curiosity and there is no evidence that it had any influence. It is far more interesting for the glimpse it gives us into the technocratic German officer mentality in which the military means were fatally detached from the political ends they served, without which the evil that Hitler stood for might never have extended beyond the truncated borders of Germany. Ludendorff's book was an elaborate *apologia per vita sua* and perforce specifically rejected Clausewitz. He was entirely correct in pointing out that Germany was never mobilized internally on a scale commensurate with her geopolitical ambitions, but it does not seem to have crossed his mind that the fault lay in the latter.

Although the concept of total war is indissolubly associated with German *militarism, the most ringing declarations were made by *Clemenceau in 1917 and Churchill in 1940. The statement of war aims made by the latter after the fall of *France was unequivocal: 'Victory at all costs, victory in spite of all terror, victory however long and hard the road may be; for without victory there is no survival.' Wonderful rallying cry though it was, it was also patently based on a false postulate. Britain could have withdrawn from the war at that point relatively painlessly; Hitler was counting on it and insofar as he thought anything through, he wanted Britain to sustain her empire to counterbalance the USA. But just as Ludendorff had been unable to comprehend that Clemenceau would not negotiate while an inch of French territory was occupied by Germany, so Hitler failed to understand that Churchill would not compromise with the evil he represented. The result was that France in WW I and Britain in WW II mobilized far more completely than Germany.

Darwin might not have proposed a theory *On the Origin of Species* in 1859 had he known that less thoughtful men would apply his themes of the struggle for existence to whole societies. Social Darwinism allied to nationalism has been the true ideology of total war, and although it is most clearly identified with the Axis in WW II, its influence was very strong in the USA. Theodore *Roosevelt and Woodrow Wilson were strident social Darwinists, with all the racism and cultural imperialism it implied. Seeking moral equivalence is a slippery and usually pointless exercise, but it is relevant to mention that the forcible sterilization of the mentally incompetent for which Nazi judges were condemned at Nuremberg was practised in the USA in the 1920s and 1930s, with the blessing of the Supreme Court. Practically the only good thing that can be said about the horrors perpetrated by Hitler is that they discredited, one hopes for all time, the idea that there is some genetically 'natural' ruling élite.

Nuclear war introduced an element of caution as the rulers of the major powers grappled with the sobering thought that they would very likely be early casualties in an all-out war. An early and contemptible response was to dig themselves elaborate secret shelters where they might sur-

vive while the common herd got irradiated, the existence of which has still to be fully revealed. Suffice to say that more by good luck than judgement all the theories of limited nuclear war were never put to the test. But even all-out nuclear war would not have meant the end of the world, or even of humanity, any more than the various other doomsday scenarios of anthropogenic *Armageddon with which the political élites seek to justify the immense powers that total war permitted them to accumulate. What it did do was threaten them directly and reduce their options. Rulers were never happy with the iron logic of *deterrence based on mutually assured destruction (MAD) and in some ways the much ballyhooed *Strategic Arms Limitation/Reduction Talks can be seen as a way to make limited war between the powers possible again.

At the more practical level, assymetrical total war in *Vietnam and a number of other post-imperial conflicts revealed a *principle as old as time, namely that military might alone cannot substitute for an absence of *doctrine and of properly thought-out policy. If the total wars of the 20th century taught nothing else, they underlined the wisdom of Clausewitz in pointing out that once war is embarked upon, the urge to win means there is no natural resting point in what we now call 'escalation'. It therefore behoves those who might start them to consider, very carefully, whether the ends are sufficiently important to justify flirting with means that may consume them.   HEB

tournaments The mock battles of *knighthood, nicely defined by the chronicler Roger of Howden as 'military exercises carried out not in the spirit of hostility but solely for practice and the display of prowess'. An uncertain tradition ascribes their origin to a knight of Anjou, Geoffrey de Preuilly, who was killed in 1066: their later description by English writers as *conflictus gallicus* seems to confirm their French origin. In the course of the 12th century they became extremely popular all over western Europe. The mêlée tournaments of this period were extremely rough affairs. Those taking part were usually divided into two teams, often on the basis of *feudal allegiance (such as French v. Angevins): the site of the tournament would cover a wide area, permitting the mock fighting to range over the countryside. The principal weapons were lance and sword; prisoners were taken and expected to pay a *ransom as forfeit. Fatal casualties were common. These, together with the damage and expenditure involved, were no doubt the grounds of the Church's hostility to tournaments, which were condemned by the Second Council of Clermont in 1130; but this did not much dent their popularity with the martial class.

From the 13th century onward, tournaments became progressively less dangerous and more ceremonious. 'Rebated' (blunted) weapons came into more frequent use; a coronal, a crown-shaped piece, replaced the sharp point of a tourneying lance. Jousting, when two opponents charged one another from opposite ends of the lists, grew in popularity and made for better spectator sport. So did the growing taste for the introduction of an element of theatre; at the tournament at Hem in 1279, for instance, the participants took on the parts of knights of Arthur's Round Table. Tourneying meetings became occasions of much festivity, and often formed part of the celebrations accompanying royal marriages, the knighting of a prince's heir, or returns from victorious campaigns. The famous Burgundian *pas d'armes* of the 15th century (as those of the Tree of Charlemagne, 1443; or the Golden Apple, 1468) were lavish jousting festivals with a courtly theme, often an amorous one (from the early 13th century it had become fashionable for jousting combatants to pose as champions of their chosen ladies, and to bear their tokens).

Late in the Middle Ages, the invention of the tilt, a barrier running the length of the lists on either side of which jousters charged one another, further reduced the hazards of the sport, as did the development of special tourneying *armour, heavier and more expensive than war armour. The requirements for admission to tourney, in terms of noble birth, also became more demanding: the rules of the 15th-century German tourneying societies were especially exacting in this respect. By the beginning of the 16th century tourneying had thus become an aristocratic art with little relation to true martial skill, and soon after its popularity began to wane. By the close of the century, the tournament's day was past.   MK

Barber, R., and Barker, J., *Tournaments, Jousts, Chivalry and Pageants in the Middle Ages* (Woodbridge, 1989).
Barker, J., *The Tournament in England 1100–1400* (Woodbridge, 1986).
Cripps-Day, F. H., *The History of the Tournament in England and France* (London, 1918).
Fleckenstein, J. (ed.), *Das ritterliche Turnier im Mittelalter*, 2 vols. (Göttingen, 1985).

Tours, battle of (733 or 734). Charles *Martel, the mayor of the palace of the Frankish kings, stemmed the advance into northern Europe of Arab forces under Abd ar-Rahman at or near Tours in 733 or 734. The traditional location and date of this battle—at Poitiers in 732—are due to misinterpretations of the near-contemporary Frankish continuation of the Chronicle of Fredegar. That source states that, having burnt Poitiers, the Arab army was advancing towards Tours when it was met by Martel's force. It also implies that the battle took place in the year before the death of Eudo, Duke of Aquitaine, commonly accepted as 735. On both points this account is supported by the Mozarabic Chronicle of 754, which, however, disagrees with the continuator of Fredegar in its account of the aftermath: far from 'scattering them like stubble before the fury of his onslaught', it alleges that Martel allowed the Arabs to slip away by night.   MC

Staudte-Lauber, A., '*Carlus princeps regionem Burgundie sagaciter penetravit*: Zur Schlacht von Tours und Poitiers und dem Eingreifen Karl Martells in Burgund', in J. Jarnut, U. Nonn, and M. Richter (eds.), *Karl Martell in seiner Zeit* (Beihefte der Francia, 37; Sigmaringen, 1994), 79–100.
Wallace-Hadrill, J. M. (ed. and trans.), *The Fourth Book of the Chronicle of Fredegar and its Continuations* (Oxford, 1960).
Wood, I. N., *The Merovingian Kingdoms, 450–751* (London, 1994).

Towton, battle of (1461). This battle confirmed Edward IV on the throne of England. Fought over two days, 28–9 March, it involved the largest numbers and was the bloodiest engagement of the Wars of the *Roses. Fighting began when Lord Fauconberg, a veteran from the wars in France, forced the passage of the Aire at Ferrybridge. Edward IV followed up the following day, his initial success assisted by flurries of snow driving into the enemy. The battle was long and hard, decided late in the day when the Duke of Norfolk came up with fresh troops on the Yorkist side. Many died in flight trying to cross the beck behind the Lancastrian lines. There were many notable casualties, both killed on the field and massacred afterwards, but contemporary estimates of 28,000 killed are probably too high.

AJP

Toyotomi Hideyoshi (1536–98) was born in humble origins at Nakamura near Nagoya, but rose to be the first of the *daimyō* (warlords) to rule the whole of Japan, and is often referred to as 'the Napoleon of Japan'. He first served *Oda Nobunaga, joining his army originally as a foot soldier and fighting beside his master at all of Nobunaga's battles. He distinguished himself at *Nagashino and at the taking of Gifu (1564). The opportunity for Hideyoshi came with Nobunaga's death. At the time he was conducting the siege of Takamatsu castle when the news of Nobunaga's murder was brought to him. He avenged the assassination by marching rapidly to Kyoto and defeating the army of Akechi Mitsuhide at the decisive battle of Yamazaki (1582). Taking control, he proclaimed Nobunaga's infant son as heir, which brought him into conflict with the old Oda supporters, whom he defeated one by one, culminating in the battle of Shizugatake in 1583. Only *Tokugawa Ieyasu now opposed him in central Japan. A battle between the two, at Nagakute (1584), was indecisive, and a *truce was called. Toyotomi Hideyoshi then proceeded to make himself master of Japan. He pacified Shikoku island in 1585, and Kyushu island in 1587, where he defeated the Shimazu family. Hideyoshi was a consummate general with superb strategic and tactical skills, and was particularly successful in siegework. He won the castles of Takamatsu (1582) and Ota (1585) by flooding them through ingenious dyke systems which diverted rivers. Other fortresses were overcome by mining (Kameyama 1582) or starvation (Tottori 1581). In

1590 a long siege brought about the surrender of the Hōjō's Odawara castle, and the remainder of the northern *daimyō* soon submitted to him. Hideyoshi overreached himself only with the invasions of Korea which ended in failure.

SRT

Trafalgar, battle of (1805). This, along with the defeat of the *Spanish Armada and the battle of *Britain, rightly occupies the first place in Britain's historical consciousness, because all three decisively ended a threat of invasion. On all three occasions unbeatable armies were camped across the Channel requiring only a brief period of localized maritime supremacy. With Napoleon's Grande Armée at Boulogne, the threat in 1805 was probably the most serious of the three. Although Adm Lord Jervis had drily said, 'I do not say they cannot come, I only say they cannot come by sea', the 'Corsican Ogre' revealed a good grasp of naval strategy on this, the only time he turned his attention to it. He ordered his new Adm Villeneuve to lure the British fleet to the West Indies and then head straight back across the Atlantic to combine with the Brest fleet and escort his invasion barges across the Channel. Villeneuve completed the first part and *Nelson duly chased across the Atlantic after him, but on his return the French admiral was unnerved by a skirmish with Adm Calder off Cape Finisterre in July and he sailed not east to Brest but south to Vigo, and thence to join the Spanish fleet in Cadiz. Meanwhile Britain's other weapon of *war finance was at work and Napoleon decamped to chastise the Austro-Russian armies in the *Austerlitz campaign.

The combined Franco-Spanish fleet included several of the most powerful warships afloat, but enforced inactivity under British *blockade had eroded the skills and the morale of officers and sailors alike. Petulantly, Napoleon ordered Villeneuve to seek battle even though the strategic justification was gone, and he duly sailed on 20 October with 33 ships of the line. He anticipated Nelson's tactics and had made provision by putting his faster ships under Dumanoir in the rear, to sail up and close the gaps when the British ships broke his line. But when he reversed direction the next day before the engagement, he threw his line into confusion and put Dumanoir in the van, from whence he played a culpably limited role in the battle. It is doubtful whether it would have made any difference in the face of greatly superior British ship handling and gunnery. The British lost 449 killed and 1,214 wounded out of 18,000 engaged on 29 ships, but the price of epaulettes was high: Nelson was killed and 22 per cent of the captains and 19 per cent of the lieutenants fell. The carnage on the other side was indescribable: Villeneuve's flagship alone suffered 546 casualties and 18 ships surrendered, many to sink in the storm that followed, while one blew up.

Jervis was right: they could not come by sea. Nelson's inspiration and tactical boldness may be said to have been the crowning touch, but it was the long years of blockade that built the edifice, with a little assistance from an exasperated Napoleon, who threw away an arm whose value he never fully appreciated.

HEB

Keegan, John, *The Price of Admiralty* (London, 1988).

transport. See LOGISTICS.

Trebbia, battle of (218 BC). This was the first great Italian victory of *Hannibal during the *Punic wars. By sending his Numidian cavalry to harass the Roman camp on the right bank of the river Trebbia, he provoked the Roman commander Sempronius Longus into crossing to his side. The Romans had some 36,000 foot in the usual triple line, skirmishers in front, and 4,000 cavalry on the wings. Hannibal had 20,000 African, Spanish, and Celtic infantry in a single line behind a screen of 8,000 skirmishers, with elephants in front of the wings, Celts in the centre, and his 10,000 horsemen equally divided on either flank. His cavalry easily routed their Roman counterparts and then fell on the flanks of the Roman infantry in co-operation with the skirmishers, who had fallen back through the main infantry line. Assailed in front and flank, the Roman infantry wings began to crumble and fled when Hannibal's brother Mago and 2,000 men who had been placed in ambush to one side of their line of advance, fell on their rear. But in the centre, 10,000 Roman infantry managed to break through Hannibal's Celts and eventually made their way to safety at Placentia (Modern Piacenza).

JFL

Lazenby, J. F., *Hannibal's War* (Warminster, 1978).
Livy, 21. 54–6.
Polybius, 3. 70–4.

Trenchard, Marshal of the RAF Sir Hugh (1873–1956), a crucial figure in the early development of British *air power, though mainly as a shrewd political fighter rather than as a theorist. He achieved his wings shortly before his 40th birthday and was one of twenty pilots included in the Royal Flying Corps in 1912. By 1918 Trenchard had become chief of the air staff of the newly created RAF and was reappointed to the position in 1919 to guide the RAF through the retrenchment of the 1920s. Trenchard believed that strategic bombing was the future of warfare, but recognized that in fiscally stringent times such thinking was not popular. Instead he developed the policy of cost-effective aerial *imperial policing to stave off efforts from the army and the navy to second the RAF to their purposes. When Trenchard retired in 1929 the independence of the RAF was secure, but so was the fatally grandiose *doctrine that strategic bombing could win a war unaided. He was the first officer to hold the five-star rank of marshal of the RAF. His nickname 'Boom' referred to his loud voice, not to the products of his bombers.

JDB

Ferris, John, *The Evolution of British Strategic Policy, 1919–1926* (London, 1989).

Gooch, John, *Airpower: Theory and Practice* (London, 1995).

trench foot was caused by having wet feet for a long period, common in WW I trenches. One immersion, followed by 24 hours during which boots were not removed, could be enough to cause it. Symptoms resembled those of frostbite, and there was risk of gangrene: toes or a whole foot might have to be amputated. It caused almost 75,000 hospital admissions, including 41 deaths, among British forces on the western front.

It could be averted by ensuring that soldiers dried their feet as often as possible, had dry socks to change into, and rubbed a suitable preparation—whale oil was used in the British army—into their feet. Its avoidance required constant vigilance by regimental officers, and its incidence was often regarded as indicative of a unit's morale.   RH

trench warfare Although regarded as a defining characteristic of the western front in WW I, trench warfare was far older. It formed part of *siege warfare, when attackers dug trenches to protect themselves from the fire of the besieged. Both the terminology and techniques of trench warfare have roots in the 17th century. Trenches advancing towards the enemy were known as saps—and the men who dug them as sappers. Trenches parallel to the defence works were traced by engineers, and usually dug at night by infantry under engineer supervision, with other infantrymen providing covering parties to protect them. In the *American civil war the sieges of *Vicksburg and Petersburg saw trench warfare on a localized scale, and the same was true of the siege of *Port Arthur in the *Russo-Japanese war. Armies might also dig defences to strengthen positions in open field, and by the mid-19th century both 'rifle pits' and longer trenches were used.

What was genuinely new about WW I was the scale and duration of trench warfare. This was a consequence of the manpower available to the combatants, the proliferation of firepower which made open warfare costly, and, especially in areas like the western front and *Gallipoli, the ability of armies to fill the entire combat frontage with troops so as to leave no assailable flank. Trench warfare began on the *Aisne in September 1914, and after the 'Race to the Sea', with both armies extending their flanks northwards, spread from the Swiss border to the North Sea.

Variations of terrain and tactical circumstance meant that there was little consistency across the front. If trenches were hard to dig, either because the ground was boggy or rocky, then defences might be built up rather than dug down. Countryside which offered long field of fire, might mean that opposing trenches were far apart and the no man's land between them was wide. In close country trenches could be so close together that sentries had to speak in whispers so as not be overheard. The trench line slashed capriciously across the landscape, running through the mines and mining suburbs west of Lille (the battlefield of *Loos), over the chalk and limestone of Artois, Picardy, and Champagne, through the Argonne forest and the Meuse uplands, to the hills of Alsace. Farms, factories, villages, and estates might be divided, with buildings forming strong points: part of the strength of the German first line on the *Somme stemmed from the fact that it linked villages like Serre and Thiepval, their solidly built houses provided with deep cellars. At Mametz, on the Somme, a German machine gun was dug in below the crucifix of the village cemetery, its robust plinth providing the gunners with overhead cover.

Trenches were initially simple. They were sometimes short, disconnected trenches designed to shelter a few men or, especially if civilian labour had been conscripted for the work, longer lines of straight trench. To start with, neither side favoured much sophistication, the Allies because they believed that trench warfare was simply a prelude to a war-winning offensive, and the Germans because tactical *doctrine emphasized only a single defensive line. However, as a result of Allied offensives in early 1915 (the British attack at Neuve Chapelle was especially significant) the Germans extended their front trench system to form three or more trench lines with communication trenches linking them. Further back, ideally behind an intervening ridge, a similar second position was dug, and it was this that enabled the Germans to repulse the British at Loos in September 1915 after the front system had been penetrated. By mid-1916 the Germans had two positions dug on the Somme and a third in active preparation, and by 1917 their defences were even more sophisticated.

The fact that many German defences were prepared behind the front line and thus in relative security—this was especially true of the *Hindenburg Line, to which the Germans withdrew in the spring of 1917—enabled them to excavate deep *dugouts, often using 'cut and cover' techniques to replace earth on top of a thick concrete roof, and to construct concrete *pillboxes whose fire dominated the area. These defences were difficult to destroy: some deep dugouts were effectively impervious to artillery, and pillboxes could shrug off hits by field guns. German trenches tended to be more comfortable to live in than those used by the Allies. Some on the Somme were supplied with piped water, and dugouts were often panelled with wood taken from French villages.

By 1915 both sides dug fighting trenches that followed a Grecian key pattern, to minimize the damage done by a shell bursting in the trench and to make it easier for the defenders to seal off penetrations. Some shelters and dugouts opened off front-line trenches, and communication trenches led back to a second trench, perhaps 44 yards (40 metres) behind the first, that contained more. Third or subsequent trenches were further behind, and in the German case there were communication trenches leading back to the second position. Saps were driven forward from front-line trenches. They might house listening posts, artillery observers, *snipers, or trench *mortars. The latter were unpopular with the infantry, for having taken on a target they often decamped to safety, leaving the infantry to bear the brunt of retaliation. Flooding was often a problem. A sump was dug in the bottom of each trench to accommodate water, and duckboards covered the sump. Sometimes pumps were installed in an effort to make trenches more habitable, but all too often they were wet and muddy.

A soldier walking along the duckboards would be safe from hostile view. To look out across no man's land he would climb up onto the fire-step, a raised step running along the enemy side of the trench, and peer cautiously (a variety of periscopes made this safer) across a stout earth berm known as the parapet. Behind him on the other side of the trench, was a similar berm called the parados. A captured trench had to be 'reversed', with a new fire-step dug, before it could be used effectively by its captors.

Each side strung barbed wire in front of trenches. This needed to be deep enough to prevent attackers from getting within grenade-throwing range, but was often much deeper: belts of wire 33–44 yards (30–40 metres) deep were not unusual. The area between Allied and German wire was known as no man's land, and varied in depth from a few metres to several hundred metres. Patrols and raiding parties crossed it at night, sometimes in an effort to capture prisoners so that *intelligence staffs could ascertain enemy units and gauge morale, sometimes to provide covering parties while new trenches were dug or damaged wire was repaired, or simply at the behest of staffs who feared (often not without reason) that the sector had become quiet and sought to stimulate fighting spirit.

The procedure for holding trenches varied. By and large both sides kept only a proportion of their men in front-line trenches, and rotated units so that periods of front-line duty were interspersed with time spent in reserve or at rest. Battalions would move up by night to carry out 'relief in the line', met, on their way forward, by guides from the unit being relieved. Commanders would establish contact with their opposite numbers, trench stores would be handed over, and the departing unit would then slip away, hoping that the process had not attracted the attention of enemy gunners. Before first light men would stand to their arms, manning their allocated sectors. This was standard procedure for beating off attacks that were often delivered around dawn or dusk, and also helped commanders at all levels ensure that their men were in hand for the next phase of work.

Unless there was a battle afoot, most soldiers spent the day on *sentry duty, or resting in dugouts or simpler shelters where they tried to keep boredom at bay by playing cards, carving brass shell-cases to produce trinkets now termed 'trench art', writing letters, or simply dozing. At night sentries were doubled, and most men found themselves on carrying parties, going back along communication trenches to bring up barbed wire, sandbags, ammunition, or trench-mortar bombs. Hot food, usually an all-in stew or what the French army called *soupe*, might be brought up in insulated 'hay boxes' after dark, and both sides often enjoyed cooked breakfast, frying tinned bacon or sausages in front-line trenches.

Trench warfare was uncomfortable, boring, and often frightening. It imposed what staffs called 'trench wastage', but for the average battalion this might amount to relatively few officers and men killed or wounded on a tour in the trenches. When men left their trenches, going 'over the top', they were far more vulnerable. There were instances of trench warfare during WW II and subsequently in the *Korean and *Iran–Iraq wars, but never anything on the scale of the western front.   RH

Ashworth, Tony, *Trench Warfare 1914–1918: The Live and Let Live System* (London, 1980).

Brown, Malcolm, *The Imperial War Museum Book of the Western Front* (London, 1993).

Ellis, John, *Eye-Deep in Hell* (London, 1976).

triage is a system employed in military *medicine for the evaluation and classification of *casualties. Its primary purpose is to categorize the wounded for treatment and further evacuation where necessary. In effect, triage consists of two main elements. First, the immediate sorting of casualties according to the nature and seriousness of their wounds and the likelihood of their ability to survive them, with or without intervention and with consideration of the available resources. Second, the establishment of priorities for treatment and subsequent evacuation, in order that medical care is provided for the greatest benefit of the largest number of casualties.

Accurate assessment is a vital component of triage. In battle, both confusion and large number of casualties means that speed is of the essence, so assessment systems have been adopted to simplify the task. Using the procedure adopted by most NATO armies, the wounded are generally divided into four groups by casualty type. The highest priority, P1, are those whose breathing has stopped; P2, casualties with severe bleeding; P3, casualties with broken bones; and P4, casualties with burns. These priorities are of course adjustable, dependent on the severity of the injury. While breathing and heartbeat are vital, and therefore casualties suffering from cessation of either require immediate attention, the categories P2–P4 are more flexible. A soldier may present extensive burns, possibly more serious than the loss of one to two litres of blood from a moderate wound. Such a soldier might require P2 treatment rather than P4.

Current civilian assessment practice now centres on the ABCD method (Airway, Breathing, Circulation, and Disability) to categorize injuries by the level of severity and this may be used in conjunction with, or instead of, the first model. However, the importance of experienced and knowledgeable personnel manning triage, be they medical assistants, technicians, corpsmen, *nurses, paramedics, doctors, or surgeons, cannot be overstated. They will assess the wound, prioritize the patient for treatment, stabilize, transfer, or evacuate.

The term triage may be applied to such actions being performed at various levels. Subunit medics or corpsmen, at platoon or possibly section/squad levels, will probably be the first troops to assess the nature and severity of a colleague's wounds. There are a number of simple, basic rules that may be applied in, for example, the assessment of blood loss or the degree of burns. Essentially triage is what surgery is not, its aim being to stabilize rather than repair.

PMacD

Triandafillov, Lt Gen Vladimir (1894–1931), Russian and Soviet officer and military theorist, responsible for the development of the concepts of 'deep battle' and 'deep operations'. Born in Kars district, now in Turkey, Triandafillov joined the Russian army as an ensign in 1915, rising to command a battalion as a staff-captain. He joined the Red Army in 1918 and during the civil war rose to command a brigade, fighting on the eastern, southern, and south-western fronts. From 1923 until 1931 he was head of the operations directorate of the Red Army *general staff, commander and commissar of a rifle corps, and, finally, deputy chief of Red Army Staff with the *rank of *komkor* (lieutenant general). Triandafillov's study of WW I led him to develop the idea of a simultaneous attack on the entire depth of the enemy's deployment, using long-range artillery, armour, and air. His work closely paralleled that of *Fuller in Britain, particularly *Plan 1919*. Like Fuller's, his early work focused on the penetration of the tactical zone—up to the zone of the enemy's guns—some 6.2–7.5 miles (10–12 km) deep, using three different types of tanks for close support of infantry (NPP), for destroying machine guns (DPP), and for destroying artillery (DD). In *The Scale of Operations of Modern Armies* (1926) and *The Character of the Operations of Modern Armies*, first published in 1929, Triandafillov had begun to explore the possibility of deeper and more expansive penetration-deep operations, although this was not fully developed until after his death, in the temporary Field Service Regulations for 1936 (PU-36).

His work on the scale of operations of modern armies and the *operational level of war drew on that of earlier writers, especially Aleksandr Neznamov (1872–1928). Triandafillov, like most Soviet military theorists, focused on the next big future war (*budushchaya voyna*), against a great capitalist coalition. He therefore concurred with Svechin that the USSR needed armed forces 'of high quality and in sufficient numbers'—the 'high quality mass army' which was probably unattainable.

On 12 July 1931, Triandafillov was due to fly to Kiev to read a paper on 'new forms of deep battle' to a command conference of the Kiev Special Military District—used as a laboratory for studying new forms of warfare. The plane crashed on or shortly after take-off. Foul play is not suspected. His ideas were vindicated during WW II, and his remains are now fittingly interred in the Kremlin wall.   CDB

trooping the colour is a British military ceremony which dates back in its present form to 1755 but has older origins. It derives its name from the musical troop, or tune, that was played whenever the *colours were lodged in safe custody. Originally each infantry company possessed its own colour, but now British infantry battalions possess two, the Queen's (or King's) Colour, and the Regimental Colour. They are flags, one of which is a Union Flag, while the other bears the royal crown, regimental badge, motto, and *battle honours. During the ceremony, the colours are paraded in slow time along the lines of troops. This originated with the requirement to show the men their colours, that they might recognize them in battle as a rallying point. The term is often applied to the annual Queen's Birthday Parade.   APC-A

Gordon, Lawrence, *Military Origins* (London, 1971).

troopship There has long been a need to transport fighting troops over the sea. The regular exchange of British units in India and other possessions was a feature of military life in the 19th and early 20th centuries. The process accelerated in wartime, when the demands—and resources—of the empire saw troopships moving to and from the Antipodes, the Far East, the Middle East, South Africa, and North America. Sea transport was usually undertaken in whatever was at hand and seaworthy, and the use of old fighting vessels or the hiring of civilian ships has long been a feature of British practice. The number of floating hulks laid up after the *Napoleonic wars provided the basis of the shipping used to transfer British soldiers to the *Crimea following the outbreak of war with Russia.

Long journeys by troopship were as inevitable as they were unpleasant. Soldiers (and often families too) were packed aboard; accommodation was uncomfortable; food was monotonous; shipwreck was a constant danger, especially before the opening of the Suez Canal, when the route to India was by way of the Cape of Good Hope. The loss of the troopship *Birkenhead* on a reef off the coast of South Africa in February 1852 had a particular poignancy: the troops formed up on the deck, in a remarkable example of steadiness in the face of adversity, to allow women and children to fill the lifeboats first. All too often there was more boredom than danger, with added irritations stemming from the rigid discipline often imposed on board, and a marked inequality of accommodation which might have officers and their ladies living in relative comfort and soldiers and their wives in cramped squalor.

In contrast the USS *Henderson* was designed to meet the expanding needs of the US Marine Corps prior to America's entry to WW I. She had room for 1,500 men and 24 mules, was capable of 14 knots, and was armed with eight 5-inch guns, two 3-inch guns, and two 1-pounders for self defence. Within a month of her commissioning she made her first voyage to France in June 1917 and by the end of hostilities had made nine such trips. After the *Armistice she brought more than 10,000 troops back from Europe. *Henderson* saw service in the Pacific in WW II and eventually became a hospital ship.

During WW II six ocean liners in the Atlantic transported some 200,000 troops from the USA to Britain in only six months, on occasion a division at a time. Among their number were the two largest ships in the world: the *Queen Elizabeth* (84,000 tons) and *Queen Mary* (81,000 tons). These monster liners could attain 30 knots and were well able to outpace any submarine, and therefore sailed without escort. Lesser ships were not so fortunate. On the night of 12 September 1942 the liner *Laconia* was some 500 miles (805 km) north of Ascension Island in the South Atlantic. She was a former Armed Merchant Cruiser turned troopship of 19,700 tons. *Laconia* had around 2,600 men on board, including 1,800 Italian POWs on their way to internment in America from Libya via the Cape of Good Hope. She was fatally damaged by a torpedo from *U156*; 1,350 Italians died as a result despite the attempts by *U156* and two further submarines *U506* and *U507* to effect a rescue operation. In addition the Allies lost the liners *Oronsay*, *Orcades*, and *Duchess of Atholl*, each of over 20,000 tons, within quick succession. The worst attack on a 'troopship' (also carrying refugees) from East Prussia occurred in the Baltic in 1945 when a Soviet submarine sank the German liner *Wilhelm Gustloff* with the loss of perhaps 7,000 lives—the worst ever sea disaster.

Ships Taken Up From Trade (STUFT) again provided the British with the wherewithal to move troops during the *Falklands war of 1982. The passenger liners *Canberra* and *Queen Elizabeth II* were both pressed into service along with other merchant Roll-on/Roll-off ferries. JR-W/RH

Trotsky (or Trotskiy), **Leon** (real name Lev Bronstein), (1879–1940), Jewish Russian agitator, journalist, revolutionary, and Soviet People's Commissar for War, founder of the Red Army and architect of its military victory in the 1917–20 Russian civil war, which he had helped start. He then fell out with *Stalin, was exiled, erased from Soviet accounts of the civil war and the formation of the Red Army, and even from photographs, and ultimately murdered by a Soviet agent in Mexico City in 1940. Years of Soviet propaganda never managed completely to obscure his key role in creating the Soviet armed forces.

Born near Elizavetgrad, Trotsky began his military career as a *war correspondent in the 1913 *Balkan war. He avoided service in the Russian army in WW I but returned to Russia in May 1917. He joined *Lenin and the Bolsheviks and was active in organizing the November 1917 *Russian Revolution. Arrogant and inclined to overdramatization, he was nevertheless an outstanding orator. Because of his long experience abroad he was first made People's Commissar for Foreign Affairs but in March 1918 swapped this post for Commissar for War. He created the basic outline of the Red Army and its early command structure. In April and May 1918 he issued a number of decrees creating the machinery to transform the nascent Red Army into a regular military force. Trotsky then started the Russian civil war, probably accidentally, by ordering the Czechoslovak Legion to be disarmed (see NORTH RUSSIA INTERVENTION FORCE). He realized that professional military men were needed to help run the Red Army and recruited 55,000 *voyenspets* (military specialists), 50,000 of them former tsarist officers, and, to the Red Army's longer term benefit, 214,700 tsarist *NCOs. He also began training 'red commanders'—former NCOs and civilians who could read and write—who filled some of the officer vacancies. Trotsky also took a direct part in restoring the situation on the *eastern front in autumn 1918.

The *voyenspets* policy was violently opposed by the Stalin-Voroshilov group which successfully defended Tsaritsyn (1926–61 *Stalingrad, now Volgograd) against the Whites, but Trotsky successfully defended it as a matter of pragmatic necessity at the Eighth Party Congress in 1919. Star among the *voyenspets* was the young *Tukhachevskiy, whom Trotsky personally picked out from his post training troops in the Moscow district to command First Red Army in June 1918. His critics were not slow to note the appointment of a Russian aristocrat to such a responsible post, and the association with Trotsky was to have fatal consequences for Tukhachevskiy nineteen years later.

Trotsky was a pragmatist and dismissed the thought that there was a distinct 'proletarian style' in war, or that this led to the 'manoeuvrist strategy' of the civil war. The best invention the proletarians had come up with was the *tachanka*, a light horse-drawn wheeled carriage with a machine gun on it, to accompany cavalry. Any further military-technological advances, he sneered, would need bourgeois military science to help achieve it. There was lengthy debate over Red Army organization and doctrine after the civil war, and Trotsky came into conflict with *Frunze and *Voroshilov and some of the new 'red commanders' over Red Army organization and the balance between a militia and a regular army. The first Cavalry army clique, led by Budenny, eventually succeeded in ousting him. His tenure at the War Commissariat was first undermined by interference with his staff, then he was replaced by Frunze in 1925.

Frunze was killed soon afterwards. Trotsky later said he believed this may have been because he tried to protect the army against the overzealous security services. He launched a bitter attack on the handling of defence and military affairs by Voroshilov and Stalin in 1927. Trotsky still believed in international revolution, led by Russia, but also that Russia's best chances lay in conducting coalition warfare, while Stalin had fixed on the development of 'socialism in one country'. In January 1928 Trotsky was exiled to Alma-Ata and then banished from the USSR in 1929.

He founded the fourth International to compete with Lenin's Comintern, now become a tool of Stalin, but his influence was limited. Nonetheless it suited Stalin to exaggerate the threat he posed and membership of the international Trotskyist conspiracy was a convenient catch-all accusation for those purged during the 1930s, including Tukhachevskiy and the leadership of the Red Army in 1937. On 20 August 1940 the NKVD (People's Commissariat for Internal Affairs) secret agent Mercader infiltrated Trotsky's entourage in Mexico and murdered him with an ice-axe.

CDB

Trotsky, Leon, *My Life* (London, 1930).
—— *The Revolution Betrayed* (London, 1930).
Erickson, John, *The Soviet High Command: A Military-Political History 1918–1941* (London, 1962).

Troy, siege of (mythical?). According to legend, Paris, prince of Troy—or Ilium (Ilion) as it was also called—carried off Helen, wife of Menelaus of *Sparta, whereupon a confederation led by Menelaus' brother, Agamemnon, king of Mycenae, was formed to recover her, and over a thousand ships assembled to carry the heroes to Troy. But the siege dragged on for nine years, and in the tenth, after quarrelling with Agamemnon, Achilles, the greatest Greek hero, withdrew from the fight. In his absence, the Trojans, led by Paris' brother, Hector, carried all before them, at one point even threatening to burn the Greek ships. But Achilles returned to the fray when Hector killed his friend Patroclus, and took his revenge. Achilles himself was later killed by Paris, but Troy was eventually taken by a trick. The Greeks pretended to abandon the siege, but left behind a wooden horse containing a force of men who emerged at night to open the gates, after the Trojans had dragged the horse into the city as a trophy.

The Greeks accepted this as history, and from at latest about 700 BC located Troy/Ilium at a hill now called Hisarlik, in north-west Anatolia. Excavation of the site has revealed a series of settlements dating from the early Bronze Age to Roman times, including an extensive lower town. Troy VI, destroyed in *c.*1270, is the favoured candidate for the 'Homeric' Troy. Archaeology has revealed that it was in contact with Greece, where a flourishing and warlike civilization existed, centred on Mycenae, and including most of the places from which the heroes supposedly came. Hittite records also possibly suggest an involvement of these people in western Anatolia at about the right time.

But although epic tales tend to have a kernel of historical truth, they also distort and exaggerate historical events beyond recognition—compare, for example, the *Chanson de Roland* and the battle of *Ronceval. In the case of the Trojan war, it is a far cry from the archaeological evidence to believing in a ten-year war, involving over 100,000 Bronze Age Greeks led by men called Agamemnon and Achilles, and the Trojan war should not be regarded as on a par with, for example, the Graeco-Persian wars, even if Troy VI really was destroyed by contemporary Greeks. JFL

Hope Simpson, R., and Lazenby, J. F., *The Catalogue of the Ships in Homer's Iliad* (Oxford, 1970).
Wood, Michael, *In Search of the Trojan War* (rev. edn., London, 1996).

truce is the cessation of hostilities on a temporary basis. A state of truce is created by an agreement between two antagonists to cease operations against one another. It is normally brought about through communication between senior officers on each side. This is termed an official truce. When the troops themselves arrange a truce it is described as an unofficial truce. Such arrangements are commonly denounced by commanders as fraternization, and are discouraged.

In most cases a truce is agreed for a set period of time determined by the commanders involved. This may be to permit negotiations for peace to be carried out, as was the case in 1918 when the *Armistice brought operations in WW I to an end. However, if negotiations prove unsuccessful fighting is expected to resume. Sometimes a truce may be called for simple expediency rather than for peace negotiations, and in these cases the period set for the truce is comparatively brief. For example, evacuation of women, children, or wounded from a besieged position is widely regarded as an act of humanity, and such evacuations may be facilitated by a short truce. In at least one instance, during the *American civil war, such a truce was held to forcibly evacuate civilians from Atlanta following the capture of that city by *Sherman. Hostilities may also be halted for a short period after a battle to allow medical staff to reach the wounded, or remove the dead. More fleeting still are truces called to allow communications between adversaries. These are often indicated simply by the bearer lofting a white flag, and proceeding towards enemy lines. This type of truce is localized to the area in which the bearer may be readily seen, and, unless an alternative arrangement is made, ends upon his return to his own lines.

It is, of course, an act of trust and bravery to proceed toward enemy lines relying upon the honour of an opponent not to fire on men bearing a flag of truce. The Para officer killed at Goose Green on such a mission during the *Falklands war was hit by a machine gun crew unaware that the rest of its unit had ceased firing. This illustrates the problems involved in arranging an unofficial truce. A truce is a tenuous arrangement in mutable circumstances even when created through official channels. When the truce is unofficial, when it amounts merely to an undertaking among soldiers themselves, the opportunity for deceit or misunderstanding is obvious, and although the latter is the more likely reason for an unofficial truce to be breached, broken truces inevitably escalate hostility.

The best-known example of an unofficial truce occurred during WW I when troops from both sides emerged from their trenches to celebrate Christmas in 1914. Official disapproval of this fraternization, and the increasingly brutal nature of the war, meant that the event was not repeated in the following years. The Christmas truce was sufficiently widespread to attract attention, but in most cases an unofficial truce tends to be small and localized, and may be disguised by desultory firing. Where troops faced extended periods in contact with the enemy, a 'live-and-let-live' agreement was sometimes an acceptable substitute to a truce for troops on both sides.   AH

Truman, Harry S. (1884–1972), US president 1945–53. No other US president is so easy for his countrymen to identify with while remaining so enigmatic to foreigners. The product of probably the most corrupt of all the many urban Democratic party 'machines', surrounded by crooks and fixers throughout all his public life, he was personally honest. A failure at every business he tried to start, he provided the seed money for the whole western European economy after WW II and was prepared to do the same for the USSR, even though he knew from personal acquaintance that *Stalin was the enemy of everything he held dear. Chosen as the vice presidential candidate for the certain third re-election of Franklin D. *Roosevelt, he met the great man twice, briefly, before he died and left him with the world to run, not even knowing about the *Manhattan Project or any other of the high secrets of state. The list continues, but the longer it gets, the greater the wonder that a man who had shown no signs of aspiring even to mediocrity for 61 years, stepped into the giant shoes of his predecessor on 12 April 1945 and calmly, competently, and humanely directed the affairs of the world's most powerful state during the eight years of her greatest strength relative to the rest of the world. Furthermore he did this without indulging in any of the imperial trappings that have unbalanced so many of his successors, and at the end he went home by train with the wife to whom he had been faithful for 33 years, with the tickets paid from his own pocket, and was surprised and moved to find a large crowd waiting to say goodbye. The new America needed such a man, but only the old America could have produced him.

While he had more experience of Washington upon becoming president than *Lincoln (so, for that matter, has every other president), he was held in similarly low esteem, particularly by the courtiers of his predecessor. In quick

succession he had to launch the *UN, deal with the surrender of Nazi Germany, meet Stalin and Attlee at Potsdam, and then order the bombing of *Hiroshima and Nagasaki to end the war in the *Pacific. He then submitted a programme to Congress designed to ward off the possibility of a depression consequent on the *demobilization of millions of servicemen and -women and the inflationary pressures of war spending, only to see it ripped to shreds and the Republicans take control of Congress in 1946. He fared better in foreign policy, in 1947 announcing the 'Truman Doctrine' with reference to the *Greek civil war, and reversing an earlier decision to scrap the US *intelligence services by authorizing the creation of the *CIA. In 1948 he signed the *Marshall Plan of financial aid for European economic recovery and called Stalin's bluff with the *Berlin airlift. But he was such an underdog going into the 1948 elections that the day after polling day several newspapers incorrectly headlined that his opponent had won.

In 1949 he set up *NATO, and instituted a programme of aid to underdeveloped countries, while his opponents yapped that he had 'lost' China to *Mao Tse-tung and bayed for the blood of the crypto-communists in his administration who they said were responsible. They were right about the Soviet agents of influence, but blinded by partisanship attacked men like Acheson and Marshall, two stalwart anti-communists and probably the finest public servants the USA was ever blessed with. Finally, when the North Koreans with Soviet encouragement launched the *Korean war, he did not flinch from fighting for a land he personally viewed as of no importance to the USA, and when the mighty *MacArthur attempted to use the same techniques to dictate policy that had worked with Roosevelt, sacked him and weathered yet another storm of vituperation, holding the USA to a deeply unpopular war as part of a worldwide policy of containment that prevented any further Soviet adventurism on a similar scale—a very real possibility during his terms of office.

To understand Truman, one must understand that upright and unassuming though he was in private, he was a ferocious and ruthless competitor in all aspects of public life. Thus he cheerfully permitted his supporters to blacken his political opponents' reputations with false accusations and innuendo, but refused to use information about their private lives that would have destroyed them. Hence his ambivalence about the CIA. As the sign on his desk said: 'The Buck Stops Here.' From whatever wells of strength a Midwestern everyman draws upon, he had an instinctive feeling for what was right and what was merely expedient.
                                        HEB

Tukhachevskiy, Marshal Mikhail Nikolayevich (1893–1937), Russian and Soviet commander and military thinker. Born into down-at-heel Russian aristocracy, he graduated with the highest marks ever awarded from the

Aleksandrovsk officer training school in 1914. A second lieutenant with the Semyonov Guards regiment, he was captured by the Germans in 1915 and spent two years as a prisoner. He escaped, returning just in time for the November 1917 *Russian Revolution. He was not the only aristocrat ever to find revolution to his taste or advantage, probably realizing that the new Bolshevik government was then Russia's best hope, domestically and on the world stage.

In 1918 he joined the Communist party and was one of the *voyenspets* (military specialists) recruited into the Red Army. *Trotsky personally picked him out from his post training troops in the Moscow district to command First Red Army in June 1918, and he led it in fighting in the Volga region, then in the Caucasus during the civil war from January to April 1920, and then in the *Russo-Polish war from April to August 1920. His plan to take the Polish capital was a daring one, but the Red Army outpaced its logistics, suffering defeat at the hands of *Pilsudski before Warsaw. The 27-year-old Tukhachevskiy then put down the Kronstadt *mutiny outside Petrograd (now St Petersburg) and returned to the Tambov region to finish off the 'White' counter-revolutionaries there. His views on dealing with 'bandits' were uncompromising: *chemical weapons were recommended.

After the civil war he headed the Red Army Military 'Academy' (Staff or War College) and played an active part in the 1924–5 *Frunze reforms. From 1925 to 1928 he was Red Army COS, beginning a period of far-reaching creative work on the character of future war and its impact on the armed forces' organization and technology. In the late 1920s Tukhachevskiy produced his massive study *Future War*, in 1931–2 *New Questions of War*, which was not published until 1962; and also, in 1931, the introduction to the Russian translation of J. F. C. Fuller's *The Reformation of War* (1923). In 1931 he became People's Commissar for Armaments, a post in which he was able to indulge his own inventiveness and passion for gadgets. His concept of 'deep battle' led him to sponsor the first large-scale experiments with paratroops, film of which made a big impact in the West in 1935 and 1936, and extraordinary 'flying tanks'. He was fascinated by *air power, particularly the long-range bombers being developed in the USA. Tukhachevskiy appears to have stolen many of his best ideas from Maj Gen Aleksandr Svechin (1878–1938), and then put him in prison. Tukhachevskiy, meanwhile, was made one of the first five marshals of the USSR in 1935, aged 42.

Tukhachevskiy appears schizophrenic. In 1928, German Gen Werner von Blomberg, who visited the Red Army as part of its co-operation with the *Reichswehr, described him as 'cultured, likeable, a person to note'. In 1936 the Soviet ambassador to London noted his diplomatic ability. A year later, the British secret service reported he was 'noted for his taciturnity with foreigners . . . believed to be a cocaine addict'. He was artistic, made violins as a hobby, and, like *Fuller, had an interest in the occult.

He represented the USSR at King George V's funeral in January 1936, and met senior British officers who were impressed by their first encounter with a Red marshal. But in May 1937 he was demoted and on 10 June arrested along with several others, accused of 'anti-state connections with the leading military circles of a foreign power'—presumably Germany. On 12 June, after a brief trial, it was announced he had been shot, the start of Stalin's great purge of the Soviet army. After the advent of glasnost in the mid-1980s reports surfaced that he had secretly been kept alive until 1941, entirely possible given Soviet treatment of others accused of treason and espionage.　　　　CDB

Bellamy, Christopher, 'Red Star in the West', *RUSI Journal* (Dec. 1987).

Erickson, John, *The Soviet High Command 1918–1941* (London, 1968).

Tunisia, French conquest of (1881–1911). French motives for entry into Tunisia were much the same as for her annexation of *Morocco: Tunisia was bankrupt and anarchic, and there was always the risk that if France did not act another colonial power might. In March 1881 anti-French agitation produced a border incident, and the French responded by sending Gen Forgemol de Bostquenard into north-west Tunisia with 30,000 men while Gen Breart landed at Bizerta with 8,000. The bey of Tunis agreed to accept a French protectorate, but some of his subjects proclaimed a holy war and continued a fierce resistance. The bey then called for French support, and three French columns, totalling some 35,000 men, were deployed. The French neglected the wise precepts, developed in *Algeria by Bugeaud, of using light 'flying columns', and although battlefield losses were light almost 2,500 men died of disease. A military administration, established after occupation, attracted controversy and was replaced, except in border areas, by civilian officials. French did not occupy some border areas, especially those south of Bir Djeneien, until after the Convention of Tripoli with Italy.

After occupation the French raised troops in Tunisia, among them *tirailleurs and *spahis tunisiens*. Tunisian units formed part of the French Expeditionary Corps in Italy in 1943–5, and earned particular renown on the Colle Belvedere north of *Cassino.　　　　RH

Tupamaros A Uruguayan urban *guerrilla group of the 1960s and 1970s. Tupamaros is the abbreviated form of Movimiento de Liberación Nacional Tupac Amaru (National Liberation Movement) named after the leader of an 18th-century Inca revolt against Spanish rule. It was formed in 1963 by Raúl Sendic, a law school drop-out, Socialist party activist, and labour agitator, inspired to armed action by the *Cuban Revolution.

Uruguay was an early welfare state, with a bloated public sector and broad social services financed by the profitable beef trade with Europe. The result was a static society offering declining prospects for a burgeoning population. After a boom during WW II, Europe's agricultural protectionism eroded the economic underpinnings of 'the Switzerland of Latin America', a changed reality that the corrupt, power-alternating Blancos and Colorados parties were unwilling to address.

For five years the Tupamaros devoted themselves to stealing from the rich and distributing to the poor. Starting in 1967–8, as part of a continent-wide escalation orchestrated by Havana whose centrepiece was the doomed *Guevara expedition to Bolivia, they shed their Robin Hood image and embarked on a campaign of assaults on police and government officials, kidnappings, and other forms of extortion. They achieved international notoriety with the kidnapping of British ambassador Jackson in 1969 and the 1970 kidnap-murder of Dan Mitrione, a US police adviser believed to be an expert in interrogation techniques. The latter episode was fictionalized in the 1972 movie *State of Siege* and led to a US government decision to end all overseas police advisory missions.

In 1971 Sendic and more than 100 others escaped by tunnelling out of Punta Carretas prison. In the face of growing military participation in police activities, the Tupamaros made the fateful decision to attack military installations and 'expropriate' arms, something they had previously been careful to avoid. Exasperated by the lack of civilian political will and facing revolt from below, the generals increased pressure on the president until in 1973 he dismissed Congress to rule as a military puppet.

Uruguay pioneered the successful and much-emulated 'dirty war' *counter-insurgency techniques of 'disappearing' suspects, ruthless interrogation (they broke the recaptured Sendic by threatening to execute his mother), and a purge of leftists from the university system. In 1985, as a condition for restoring civilian government, the military obtained a general amnesty for all political crimes. In consequence Sendic and other Tupamaros survivors were released and formed a legal political party, which did not prosper.   HEB

Turcos France made widespread use of colonial troops. Native infantry were usually termed *tirailleurs and were raised in *Tunisia, *Morocco, Senegal, Annam, and *Algeria, but it was the *tirailleurs algériens*, known as Turcos, who somehow epitomized them. Raised in 1841, partly from members of a *bataillon turc* in French service, there was a battalion each for the provinces of Algiers, Oran, and Constantine. Officers and NCOs were French and native, rank and file wholly Algerian. They served in the *Crimean war and, as a three-battalion regiment, in the *Italian campaign of 1859.

In the *Franco-Prussian war there were three regiments, which fought fiercely at Wissembourg and *Wörth, in their distinctive short light-blue tunics. A French doctor saw their dead lying so thickly that 'a little hill was blue with turcos . . . From the distance it looked like a field of flax.'

During WW I Turcos fought in France, the Dardanelles, Salonica, and the Levant. In WW II they took part in the 1940 campaign, and later formed part of the French Expeditionary Corps in Italy, whose performance at *Cassino earned them widespread admiration. North Africans who fought so nobly for France did not feel that their sacrifices were properly recognized, and many became involved in the *Algerian independence war. Ahmed ben Bella, first PM of an independent Algeria, had been a warrant officer in the Turcos. The Turcos were disbanded when France relinquished Algeria in 1962.   RH

Turenne, Vicomte Henri de La Tour d'Auvergne

(1611–75). Turenne was born to a Protestant family in 1611, the nephew of *Maurice of Nassau. His military training therefore combined the best of the French and Dutch traditions. In 1630 he took command of the recently revived family regiment of infantry and served in Piedmont and Lorraine. He distinguished himself at the storming of La Mothe and was promoted to the rank of *maréchal de bataille*.

After the Swedish defeat of Nördlingen in 1634, France entered the *Thirty Years War to combat Habsburg hegemony, and Turenne was sent to Heidelberg to spy out the land for *Richelieu. In the spring of 1635 he met *Bernhard of Saxe-Weimar and the two formed a friendship from which urenne was to learn much. Bernhard's army was now to fight under French sponsorship and Turenne covered himself with glory at the storming of Saverne, before being despatched to the northern frontier, from where he returned to lead his Weimarians across the Rhine in 1638. The rigours of campaigning laid him low in 1639 and he returned to Paris.

In 1642 he was wounded at Turin and was made marshal of France by Cardinal Mazarin. An emergency in 1644 meant Turenne's recall to the Rhine front where he was to soldier with *Condé, the victor of *Rocroi. The two went on to fight at Freiburg on 3 August against Mercy's Bavarian army. Turenne favoured the indirect approach to the strong enemy position, but Condé was for the all-out attack. Condé's plan faltered, and on 5 August Turenne's flanking attack succeeded and the French grip on Lorraine was tightened.

In 1645 Turenne crossed the Rhine with a refitted army in an attempt to link up with *Tortensson, only to have to face Mercy at Mergentheim, where his army was caught unprepared and he was forced to flee. This was the first serious defeat of his career and he never forgot its harsh lessons. Joined by reinforcements, Turenne again faced Mercy at Nördlingen where an impetuous attack by Condé nearly lost the day for the French, but the imperialists were driven from their defences and Mercy was killed.

In 1646 Turenne managed to effect a junction with Wrangel's Swedes and carried fire and the sword into Bavaria, frustrating the imperialists with the now famous strategy of *le style indirect*. Maximilian was confounded and abandoned the imperial alliance, but Turenne was ordered to return to France when the Dutch made peace in 1647, to guard against a threatened Spanish incursion. However, Maximilian thus freed from the Protestant threat had taken up arms once more and Turenne and Wrangel again marched on the Danube. They caught the imperialists at Zusmarhausen, defeated them, and headed into Bavaria forcing an end to hostilities in October 1648.

In 1658 Turenne met his erstwhile colleague Condé, now a rebel and leading a Spanish army, at the battle of the Dunes and beat him convincingly. In 1672 he commanded the French armies in Germany, but was killed at Sasbach.

TM

Turks, Seljuk and Ottoman The Turks stemmed originally from what is now Mongolia. They migrated into Transoxania (the region of the former Soviet Central Asia) and what became the Chinese province of Sinkiang or eastern Turkestan from the 8th century onwards, in the former region coming within the borders of the Islamic world. Large numbers of originally pagan Turks were brought there as slaves and employed as servile soldiers in the armies of the Abbasid caliphs in Baghdad and the provincial dynasties which succeeded them in Persia and Afghanistan and in the lands of the Fertile Crescent. From their origins as typical steppe warriors, these Turks were mounted *archers using the composite *bow as their main weapon and also the lance, and they speedily achieved a reputation in the Islamic world as the martial race par excellence, hardy, brave, and loyal to their new masters.

In the early 11th century, a family of chiefs from the Oghuz or Ghuzz tribe of Turks, the Seljuks, by now Muslim, appear as auxiliaries of the local Muslim powers of Transoxania and north-eastern Persia. Under a dynamic leader, Toghril Beg, they took over power for themselves, eventually overrunning the whole of Persia and Iraq and raiding into Syria and Anatolia. Assuming the title of sultan, Toghril inaugurated the Great Seljuk Sultanate (1040–1194), relegating the caliphs essentially to a role as moral and religious heads. Other members of the family set up branches in south-eastern Persia, Syria, and central Anatolia, these after the *Byzantines had been defeated at the battle of *Manzikert and pushed westwards. This Seljuk sultanate of Rum, based on Konya, was to endure for two centuries until the time of the *Mongol invasions, with its rulers, like the Syrian Seljuks, frequently clashing with the Frankish *Crusades.

The Seljuk sultans depended both on their tribal contingents, lightly armed mounted archers and, increasingly, on a multi-ethnic standing army, many of these troops being *slave soldiers, comprising Arabs, Kurds, Armenians, Georgians, etc.; these professionals comprised heavily armed and armoured cavalrymen and infantrymen with swords and spears. For them a system of land grants grew up, on whose revenues the warrors, their mounts and weapons could be supported. The spread of this system through much of the northern tier of the Middle East had significant effects on land tenure and utilization, and there was probably a trend towards the pastoralization of areas of northern Persia and eastern Anatolia favourable to horse and sheep grazing—a trend which was to be accelerated by the subsequent invasions of a further wave of nomads from Inner Asia, the Mongols.

Amongst the Oghuz nomads entering Anatolia in the wake of the Seljuks of Rum was apparently the family of Othman, though the origins of the dynasty are shrouded in legend. The Ottomans or Osmanlis established themselves in north-western Anatolia, expanding at the expense of Byzantium and the Italian trading colonies of the Aegean shores. They then overran much of the Balkans, extinguishing ancient monarchies there, and forming these lands into the province of Rumelia, European Turkey. Their advance was delayed for a generation by an incursion by *Timur, but in 1453 Mehmet II 'the Conqueror' captured *Constantinople. The extinction of the Byzantine empire alarmed Christian Europe, but disunity amongst the powers and the onset of the Reformation and its attendant wars prevented any concerted effort to stem the momentum of Ottoman conquest.

The sultans of the 16th century went on to conquer further territory, and seemed unstoppable to contemporary Christians. *Selim I marched into the Arab lands of Syria and Egypt (1516–17), and *Suleiman 'the Magnificent' annexed much of Hungary and went on to besiege *Vienna in 1529, with his cavalry raiding into Bohemia and Bavaria. Suleiman's reign marks a peak of Ottoman culture and power, although in the next century the Ottomans recovered Iraq from the Persians and were still able to capture Crete from the Venetians; and they only just failed at Vienna again in 1683. It was in the 18th century that there began a slow decline for the empire, and the Christian belief in Ottoman invincibility began to wane. The Habsburgs and Russia now exerted a relentless pressure on the Turks in south-eastern Europe. Greece and almost all the Balkans were lost by 1913, and Turkey's ill-judged entry into WW I on the side of the Central Powers sealed the empire's fate. The Arab lands were lost by the Treaty of Sèvres (1920) and the integrity of what is modern Turkey was only secured by the military genius and political leadership of Mustafa Kemal, the later *Atatürk, who finally abolished the Ottoman sultanate and caliphate in 1922 and 1924 respectively.

The early Ottomans were a minority, a military ruling class, in the extensive lands which they had acquired. Their fellow tribesmen had to be supplemented by more professional and reliable troops. Land grants were made to Turks in Anatolia and the Balkans and also to members of the Slav and Bulgarian landed classes of the conquered lands, with the obligation to provide troops and horses when called upon to campaign; these were the *sipahi* or *feudal cavalrymen. The Christian manpower of the Balkans was tapped by the institution of the *devshirme* or periodic 'collection' of Christian boys who were taken to Istanbul for training in the palace school, inevitably becoming Muslims if only for advancement purposes, and who then followed careers either in the palace service and civilian bureaucracy or as soldiers. Hence many Ottoman viziers were of non-Turkish ethnic origin, including Greeks, Albanians, and even Italians. The soldiers formed the celebrated corps of the *janissaries (Turkish *Yeni cheri*, 'new troops'). These infantrymen took to the use of handguns in the form of arquebuses and, later, the more manageable early forms of musket. By their *discipline and *esprit de corps* in battle they terrified their Christian opponents during their heyday of the 15th and 16th centuries. The Ottomans also adopted the use of static cannon, at first cast on the spot for sieges but later mounted on mobile gun carriages, probably as early as the first quarter of the 15th century, although it was only later that technical advances made an effective Ottoman field artillery possible. In this development of artillery and other weapons like *mortars, bombs, and *grenades, the Ottomans relied heavily on Christian experts, at first from occupied provinces like Serbia and Bosnia but later from further afield such as Hungary, Germany, and Italy; reliance on outsiders in the technical arms was to remain a permanent feature of Ottoman military practice.

But the Ottomans eventually failed to keep pace with the development in military techniques and weaponry which occurred in Europe, and suffered from incompetent high command, ineffective artillery, and ignorance of modern formations and tactics; valour and enthusiasm were no longer enough. The janissaries declined into an indisciplined and reactionary element in the capital, reluctant to go out on campaigns, and hostile to any new ideas. Attempts at military reform, mainly short-lived, were made in the 18th century, again with the help of foreign specialists. Thus the corps of bombardiers was trained on European lines by a renegade French officer, the Comte de Bonneval. In 1793 Sultan Selim II created his *nizam-i jedid*, 'new order' of trained troops with modern weapons parallel to the older, forces and with foreign advisers who also supervised *arsenals, dockyards, and fortifications, only for it to be swept away in a traditionalist reaction of 1807 which also led to the sultan's overthrow and death. It was not until 1826 that Mahmut II felt strong enough bloodily to suppress the janissaries, and from 1839 onwards the empire entered on the *Tanzimat* ('new organizations') reform era in the spheres of administrative and legal structures, in considerable part a response to pressure from powers like Britain and France who hoped to revitalize what had become the 'Sick Man of Europe' against Russian ambitions. These reforms had a mixed success, but there was real progress in the military sphere. In the 1830s the sultan turned to Prussia and Austria for help in training a new army which would have western-type discipline, *drill, and *uniforms together with a corps of competent officers; the youthful Helmuth von *Moltke 'the Elder' was one of these advisers, and the Turkish army henceforth acquired a long-lasting strong Germanic tradition. The Ottoman army acquitted itself creditably in the wars in the Balkans, Crimea, etc. of the later 19th century. But no amount of increased efficiency could save an empire which was multi-ethnic and multi-religious but yet still dominated by Muslims who felt a supreme contempt for all non-Muslims, and which had become an anachronism in an age of newly discovered nationalisms.   CEB

Bosworth, C. E., in *Cambridge History of Iran*, vol. 5. *The Saljuq and Mongol Periods* (ed. J. A. Boyle) (Cambridge, 1968).

Cahen, C., *Pre-Ottoman Turkey* (London, 1968).

Cook, M. A. (ed.), *A History of the Ottoman Empire to 1730* (Cambridge, 1976).

Lewis, Bernard, *The Emergence of Modern Turkey* (London, 1961).

Shaw, S. J., and Kural, Ezel, *History of the Ottoman Empire and Modern Turkey*, 2 vols. (Cambridge, 1976–7).

U-2 incident (1960). The U-2 spy-planes, flying at over 70,000 feet (21,336 metres), were a marvel of 1950s aeronautical achievement. The USA used them to conduct surveillance of the USSR during the *Cold War and was still using them in the 1991 *Gulf war. On 1 May 1960 Soviet air defence forces shot one down, reportedly with the last of seventeen specially enhanced SA-2 missiles fired at it, one of which downed a MiG fighter pursuing it. The US representative at the UN denied responsibility for the flight and so the humiliation was complete when on 7 May Premier Khrushchev announced that the pilot, Gary Powers, had parachuted out and been captured. The USA then said the plane had been used to survey weather conditions, but Powers told his interrogators he had taken off from Peshawar in Pakistan with orders to photograph military installations in Sverdlovsk, Kirov, and Archangel. The Soviets sentenced him to ten years but he was exchanged for the Soviet master spy Rudolf Abel on 10 February 1962.   CDB

ULTRA (in full 'TOP SECRET ULTRA'), British code name for the most secret *SIGINT gained in the first place by the attack on the *Enigma machine encipherment system widely used by the Axis. The product of the Allied attack on the different Japanese systems was code-named MAGIC in the US. Other code names used in this context included the cover name of BONIFACE for a fictional *intelligence agent supposedly supplying much of the material, and LUCY on which more below. For the most part it was gained by decryption of radio signals and thus could be negated by a radio blackout, as occurred before the battle of the *Bulge.

Growing success against Enigma began with the Luftwaffe, most of whose instructions were sent by radio. ULTRA provided critical intelligence during the battle of *Britain and in the sinkings of Italian supply ships in the Mediterranean, contributing heavily to the defeat of *Rommel. ULTRA permitted the location and sinking of U-boat tankers and wolf packs, and was instrumental in winning the battle of the *Atlantic. In order to conceal the source, ULTRA was fed to the Soviets through the LUCY spy ring based in Switzerland, but, despite the fact that he had well-placed agents in the British diplomatic, intelligence, and SIGINT services, *Stalin often refused to believe it, most disastrously with reference to warnings about *BARBAROSSA.

The decryption of the Japanese diplomatic cypher throughout the war was enormously helpful. For example Ambassador Oshima reported from Berlin in detail on the defences of the Western Wall in 1943–4, and the Japanese military attaché to Vichy reported on the defences of the south of France. Bletchley Park also intercepted messages from the Japanese military attaché in Berlin concerning the shipping of uranium oxide from Germany to Japan as early as 1943. The Allied leaders, with the *Manhattan Project underway, could evaluate that with great precision and attacks on the German nuclear weapons development programme followed although in fact the Germans abandoned the programme in 1943.

In 1941 the Germans introduced the Lorenz double encipherment machine which was used to send messages from the German high command (OKW) to generals in the field. This complex device was decrypted by the development (1943–4) of the Colossus computers, the world's first large electronic logic machines, which had all the features of a modern computer save an internal memory. The last of these seems to have been working as late as 1960.

The main problem, which the ULTRA distribution system was designed to answer, was that carelessness or worse in the field would betray this priceless resource. In Italy,

*Clark was so contemptuous and careless in his handling of ULTRA that he was nearly dropped from the distribution list. On the other hand Freyburg in *Crete may have been so concerned with preserving the secrecy of ULTRA that he failed to make dispositions to counter known German intentions.

It is a miracle that the secret was kept from the Axis leadership during the war. That secrecy continued for decades thereafter simply enabled some individuals to claim more credit than they deserved; the Soviets knew all about it, so the only people kept in the dark were the citizens of the West. Perhaps the reason was expressed by one veteran of the *Western Desert when the story was first published: 'Since we knew so much about their plans, so early on, how on earth did we do so badly for so long?'　　PJ/HEB

----

uniforms (*see opposite page*)

UN (United Nations) (see also PEACEKEEPING). The UN was established by charter in San Francisco on 26 June 1945, as a voluntary association of sovereign countries, and came into existence on 24 October 1945, 'United Nations Day'. According to the preamble of its charter, the UN's principal objective is 'to save succeeding generations from the scourge of war'.

Under Chapter 7, Article 51 of its charter, the UN accepts that countries have a right of individual and collective self-defence if attacked. Chapter 8 of the charter also recognizes the legitimacy of regional security organizations (such as NATO). Otherwise, the UN regards all forms of war as illegal, and asserts its own right to intervene to preserve peace. In this, the UN has a mixed record since 1945. Most countries have wanted the UN to be effective, but not so as to threaten their own interests. One view of the UN, strongly held by many members, is that it is nothing more than the sum of its member countries; another is that it has developed, and will develop, into something more with genuine international authority. But it was neither structured nor intended as a world government.

The term 'United Nations' was first used in WW II, in the 'Declaration by the United Nations' on 1 January 1942 when 26 countries pledged to oppose the Axis. It was the hope particularly of Franklin D. *Roosevelt that the major Allied powers—the USA, USSR, Great Britain, France, and Nationalist China—would continue as the 'five policemen' of the world to maintain peace after WW II. To this end the UN (unlike its failed predecessor the League of Nations) was structured to recognize political realities as well as international law.

The UN headquarters in New York has three main components: the Security Council, the General Assembly, and the Secretariat. The Security Council consisted originally of the 'five policemen' as permanent members, plus a further six members (increased to ten in 1965) drawn from the General Assembly for two-year terms. A Security Council resolution requires a simple majority of votes to pass, with each of the five permanent members having a power of veto. Nationalist China (Taiwan) kept the Chinese permanent seat on the Security Council until 1972, when the USA recognized communist China. In 1991 Russia succeeded to the defunct USSR's permanent seat. The political effectiveness of the Security Council was greatly restricted by superpower rivalry in the *Cold War, and it failed to act over some wars involving the superpowers either directly or indirectly, including the *Vietnam war and the *Iran–Iraq war.

The General Assembly consists of all sovereign member countries of the UN, each with one vote. The original membership of 51 increased to 185 by 1999. Membership is by election and countries can be expelled or resign, but the UN charter regards its authority as binding even on non-members. For a resolution to pass the General Assembly requires a simple majority in most cases, but a two-thirds majority in important cases. The role of the General Assembly in diplomacy, providing a point of contact for many countries, was very important in the decolonization era.

The UN Secretariat is headed by the Secretary-General, a five-year renewable appointment by the General Assembly on the recommendation of the Security Council. The role of the Secretary-General and Secretariat has expanded chiefly because of the Cold War paralysis of the Security Council. As with the UN itself, some Secretary-Generals have been more proactive and ambitious than others, and controversy has resulted when they have pursued UN policies at variance to those of the major powers.

Other than self-defence under Article 51, the UN charter covers two broad areas related to peace and military force. Chapter 6 deals with the peaceful settlement of disputes, in which all sides seek a solution. Chapter 7 deals with 'Action in respect of threats to the peace, breaches of the peace, and acts of aggression'. Under Article 39 of this chapter, the Security Council may determine that a threat to international peace and security exists, and under Article 42 it 'may take such action by air, sea, or land forces as may be necessary to maintain or restore international peace and security'. No enforcement operation would be possible against a major power without a major war, and the UN would have failed in its purpose should this happen. But other than this, the Security Council may authorize a very wide range of actions, from unarmed policing to a regional war. This has also helped prevent direct superpower military confrontation, particularly over conflicts in the Middle East.

It was intended under Chapter 7 that the UN would have its own armed forces supplied by member countries, to be agreed by a Military Staff Committee. Cold War rivalry, and the reluctance of countries to place their forces under direct UN control, meant that this never happened. Instead,

(*cont. on page 935*)

uniforms

THE weapons and dress of the serviceman are what distinguishes him from civilians; differences in those weapons and dress, often only discernible to the initiated, are what distinguishes friend from foe. While uniform, in the sense of a national military costume principally fashioned from cloth and codified according to regulations, is a comparatively modern concept, warriors have, since the earliest beginnings of warfare, worn costumes which identified them as warriors and differentiated them, as a group, from their enemies: since such aims were uniform so, to an extent, might their dress be described.

Although it is important to make the distinction between the uniform costume and body *armour, there are areas where the two concepts meet. Although most elements of armour were common throughout its development from the medieval period in western Europe, this very commonality necessitated national and local distinctions being made, in order to avoid fatal mistakes. Few items of early armour rendered the wearer quite so anonymous as being dressed from head to foot in mail, especially if a cylindrical helm completely covered his head. The earliest form of national uniform developed from this anonymity in western Europe in the late 12th century, as a result of the multinational *Crusades and the need to differentiate between the warriors of the different nations. Long flowing overgarments, called surcoats, had begun to be worn by mail-clad knights in the mid-12th century. While these probably served to protect the knight a little from both sunshine and damp, they also had an important additional function: they could be decorated with symbols identifying the man beneath. Just before the Third Crusade, in 1188, the rulers of England, France, and Flanders met at Gisors in north-eastern France and decided how their knights should be identified, nation by nation: the English were to wear white crosses—presumably on a darker ground—the French red crosses, and the Flemings green ones. It is assumed that these crosses would have been worn, in front and behind, on their surcoats by the knights and presumed that the knights' retainers and men-at-arms contrived some similar means of proclaiming their national identities and allegiances. It is probable that such nationally distinctive colours were only worn on appropriate occasions, such as on foreign service.

The development in the 13th century of the art of *heraldry in Europe led to surcoats, and their shorter, sleeved successors—called cyclasses and jupons—being used as vehicles for the portrayal of the wearer's armorial bearings. As heraldry expanded from its initial simplicity, so personal *badges and charges on an individual's shield of arms became granted: these could be worn in replica by a knight's retainers, who might also wear his livery colours (the principal colours of his coat of arms) and from these heraldic beginnings the concept of regimental uniform grew.

These two systems of quasi-national and personal livery uniform existed side by side until the 17th century and the growth of national permanent or 'standing' armies. Not that there was no standardization of military uniform before that; there was just no national standardization, except when the troops of one nation were fighting in the territory of another. The combination of the *feudal system—which lasted in attitudes long after it had ceased to function economically—and the growth of heraldry, together with the generally shaky nature of internal national politics in Europe and in multinational allegiances until the 16th century, meant that the period from 1200 to c.1580 was marked all over the continent by conflicts undertaken by armies made up of small groups of differently dressed soldiers, each group having a different parochial allegiance, led by powerful and influential individuals whose allegiances were, generally, intensely personal and selfish. The small groups making up these armies would, as we have seen, wear their lord's livery and sometimes a personal badge too; if part of a larger formation or alliance they might assume a badge symbolic of that alliance, such as the red rose of the house of Lancaster or the white rose of that of York during the English 15th-century Wars of the *Roses. Increasingly powerful monarchs sought, with varying degrees of success, to end such a chaotic system of parochial military units with short-lived allegiances and, at the same time, instituted corps of personal bodyguards—wearing the royal livery—to protect themselves. Such bodyguards were, necessarily, uniformly dressed, their liveries reflecting the royal heraldic colours and, often, these royal livery colours became the basis for part, or all, of the eventual national military uniforms which would spread across Europe in the 17th century.

For the first half of the 17th century, there was little difference between the dress of soldiers and that of civilians in Europe, except for the obvious one of the protective clothing worn and weapons carried by soldiers. If there was an exception to this rule it would be in the case of the *landsknechts, German mercenary *pikemen and *musketeers renowned for their swagger, menace, and exaggeratedly flamboyant dress. As professional (and thus full-time) soldiers, European *mercenaries of the late 16th and early 17th centuries were unlike most soldiers, except royal bodyguards, who were recruited when needed and disbanded as soon as possible thereafter. Mercenaries had a greater financial stake in their appearance and their trade than did part-time soldiers and thus their clothing, within a considerable range of styles and clothing, became almost a form of uniform.

During the *Thirty Years War, 1618–48, and the *British civil wars, 1638–52, regiments were formed in Europe which often adopted colours as part of their titles; these referred to the colours of their regimental flags and often to the colours of their cloth coats too. While uniformity of clothing was known within regiments—usually among the infantry and then only for the musketeers, who wore no armour—national military uniforms did not develop until the end of the 17th century. At *Edgehill in 1642 it is recorded that regiments on both sides were dressed in a variety of colours and it was at this period that coloured sashes began to appear for officers—the colours often denoting allegiances. During the Thirty Years War, for example, Swedish officers wore blue sashes, the Dutch orange, the French white, Habsburg troops wore red sashes, and those of Saxony green ones. In Britain, royalist officers wore red sashes and parliamentarian ones wore tawny—although no assumption should be made that this practice remained consistent for the whole of the British civil wars. Such regimental uniforms as existed, those—for example—which had been established in France in the 15th century for the *compagnies d'ordonnance*, were really only continuations of the medieval practice of wearing livery, although the growing fashion for wearing coloured sashes and that of assembling large formations and dressing them in similar colours presaged national uniforms—which was the next logical step in both the history of military uniforms and that of armies.

From c.1660 for the next century or so, the dress of the European gentleman closely paralleled that of the European soldier, and particularly the foot soldier. Each influenced the other as civilian fashions changed or as military advances inspired alterations in uniform. The long coat, called the *justaucorps* in France, appeared in Europe as a civilian garment, copied from the oriental kaftan, after c.1660; it had voluminous skirts, full sleeves, deep cuffs, and no collar and it was rapidly adopted by the armies of Europe which were, inexorably, becoming 'standing' or full-time, national forces. From this change in status developed the concept of national uniforms, a concept actively pursued in the armies of France and Britain. France's army, directed by the reforming war minister *Louvois, was assiduously reformed and a national uniform emerged, its principal colour for the infantry's coats being white—the ground of the French royal arms. White, or greyish-white, cloth was the cheapest and most common type, being almost the natural colour of undyed wool, so the colour had an economic base too. French regiments were allowed regimental distinctions denoted by their coats' linings and these, when eventually turned back on the skirts, cuffs, and lapels, would form the basis for the 'facing' colours still so important to defenders of regimental traditions. In Britain the French styles and reforms were noted and developed simultaneously, Charles II having been influenced during his exile by the growing power, style, and ambition of *Louis XIV. Red had long been a colour favoured for military coats, scarves, and other apparel in Britain and regiments on both sides in the British civil wars had worn it before it was standardized for the *New Model Army of the late 1640s; indeed, the monarch's personal bodyguard—the Yeomen of the Guard—had worn red coats laced with gold (the royal livery colours) since its foundation in 1485. The red coat of the British infantry soldier was not unique in Europe's rainbow of full dress military uniforms either: it was worn by the Swiss and Irish regiments in France and ultimately by Denmark, Hanover, and Saxony (until 1734). Like the French infantry, British regiments of foot signified their regimental distinctions through their facing colours and through the increased wearing of regimental badges on their grenadier caps, drums, and accoutrements. Regiments designated as 'Royal' adopted blue facings, blue being another principal colour of British royal heraldry and of the national flag.

By the end of the 17th century, most nations had adopted the national uniform colours that would remain constant until either the end of full dress uniforms or a significant change of regime. Apart from France's white and Britain's red, Prussia wore dark blue and Austria pearl-grey. In the cavalry regiments, less national uniformity was observed and what there was largely dissolved in the 18th century as the cavalry fragmented into heavy and light: *dragoons, *chasseurs-à-chevaux*, hussars, *lancers, horse grenadiers, and mounted musketeers. No sooner had national uniforms evolved than the old regimental and arm-of-service rivalries resurfaced to shatter the uniformity and create the military kaleidoscope of dress that burgeoned, despite occasional pruning, until 1914.

For much of the century between 1689 and 1789 most conflicts in Europe were caused by real or perceived shifts in the balance of power on that continent as alliances formed, broke, and re-formed and, although it is too simplistic to identify the principal power blocs as Protestant and Catholic ones, it seems apparent that the armies of Protestant nations wore dark-coloured uniforms while those of Catholic ones wore pale uniforms. Countries following the lead of France or Austria generally wore white; those occasionally allied to Prussia favoured either dark blue or another dark colour. The Russian army, for no apparent reason, but uniquely, wore green—except for its scarlet-coated artillery. As the 18th century progressed, so the cut of the original long, full-skirted coat gradually reduced. Its length was shortened, then its skirts were fastened back, then it became cutaway at the front; it grew a collar and sprouted epaulettes. On campaign, especially in hot or wooded countries, the skirts would be cut off and the coat converted into a jacket or short-tailed coatee. Exotic eastern European uniform appeared, like the clothing of the hussar—elements of which were copied in non-hussar units, like *rifle regiments. The Celtic fringe became represented by the appearance of the British army's Scots *Highlanders who, originally derided as outlandishly costumed savages, rapidly became patriotic and noble ones as their native plaids and flat blue woollen bonnets gradually developed into the kilt and feather bonnet now so well known. Troops trained in skirmishing, sniping, and other agile manoeuvres requiring great mobility or concealment were allowed uniforms which promoted both and the dark green jacket of the *Jägers and *chasseurs à pied* accompanied the short coat and helmet of the *chevaux-légers* and the light dragoons by the 1760s. In the newly formed USA, the Continental Army's most favoured colours of blue with buff facings—affected for civilian coats and waistcoats by some British supporters of the USA too—were accompanied by a variety of other colours as the *American independence war developed. Although dark blue remained the principal full dress colour of the US army, it was by no means uniform—any more than was any other 'national colour'.

Coats, jackets, and other garments became increasingly embellished during the 18th century as epaulettes, loops, lace, and aiguillettes all appeared. Epaulettes and aiguillettes were created by the plaiting together of the old 'arming laces' on the shoulders of padded garments worn beneath the cuirass and used to secure the armour; such laces also appeared on the shoulders of the 17th-century buff leather coats and were quickly plaited in a decorative manner. Breeches and waistcoats became more important in their uniformity as more of them was revealed by the turning back of coat skirts, and long gaiters began to be worn, only to be shortened by the 1770s. Buttons ceased to be purely decorative and began to feature regimental designs. Belts were standardized, the cross belts of the infantry—supporting *bayonet and cartridge pouch—characterizing the last half of the 18th century and lasting until well into the next, the brass plate securing the bayonet belt being used to carry increasingly complex regimental badges. Magnificence symbolized the officer, just as assiduous use of pipeclay, blacking, hair-grease, and brick-dust were the daily round of the ordinary soldier as his uniform, ever more complicated, tightly fitting, and—apparently—suitable only for the parade ground, advanced uncomfortably into the 19th century. Trousers increasingly replaced breeches and gaiters towards the end of the century and a variety of footwear emerged at the same time, including boots of differing styles dependent upon battlefield role. The calf-length boot, worn under trousers strapped beneath the instep and called 'overalls' eventually became called the *Wellington boot, after its most famous adherent.

Practicality, comfort, and efficiency remained matters for overseas campaigns in countries with extremes of climate as far as military uniform was concerned, especially for the European armies, until the late 19th century—although great and sensible strides were made in these three directions by the East India Company's Indian armies after the 1840s. Indian experience produced *khaki uniforms, a shade and style invented by the British and widely copied by other nations. By mid-century, the old coatee, not worn by civilians except on formal court occasions, was being replaced by the tunic and frock coat—waisted, skirted, and regarded as more practical, even if they were equally as constrictive as the coatee.

Along with khaki, experiments were made with other drab colours, especially by corps of volunteer riflemen in Britain, but the European wars of mid-century, from the *Crimean to the *Franco-Prussian, were still fought in full dress uniforms. In the USA, comfort and practicality vied with splendour for acceptance and—contrary to popular belief—dark 'Federal' blue and butternut 'Confederate' grey were worn by both sides during the civil war.

Insignia of *rank appeared and regimental badges mushroomed. The *breech-loading long-range rifle (especially in the hands of the trained *sniper) and machine gun, capable of dealing in death at long distance, led inexorably to the decline of full dress, although it was a closely fought rearguard action and one that only succumbed to the brutal reality of the casualty lists of 1914–15. Military uniform died in magnificence in the mud and dust of WW I, the French scarlet-trousered *poilu* being one of its first casualties, and the mud necessitating the invention of the trenchcoat and the rubber 'gumboot'. Khaki became opposed by *feldgrau* and allied to *bleu d'horizon* as the combatants exchanged brightness for drab. Despite efforts to revive it in the inter-war years, especially in nations still nursing or newly pursuing imperial ambitions, full dress was a hopeless anachronism—much mourned—by 1918. The fighting clothing of WW II completed the process, with battledress and *camouflage smocks forcing service dress into the position of becoming the principal smart uniform, rather than the combat dress it had been designed as originally.

Functionality and frugality have ruled military uniform since 1918. In an area in which tradition is most sensitively felt, and vigorously defended—especially in the military sphere—changes have been hard fought and more honoured in the breach than in the observance. *Navies and *air forces have, equally traditionally, taken a more practical view of what they—objectively—regard as working attire than have armies, many navies actually having no uniform as such until the 19th century and most air forces embracing with considerable circumspection the admittedly anachronistic concept of a dress uniform for such a highly technological service. Uniforms adopted a century or more ago for working dress (like mess dress and service dress) are now worn on formal occasions and soldiers go to their duties in comfortable, functional clothing suited to their roles. Significantly, perhaps, and certainly timelessly, it continues to be the case that personnel often find privately purchased kit—like the all-important footwear—superior to anything provided free by their masters. Uniform and uniformity has always been a touchy subject in a society as guided by pride, tradition, hierarchy, and competition as the military world and this shows little sign of abating. In most of the more successful of the world's armed forces, one of the few things which has been, and still is, uniform is lack of uniformity in dress: such is the value of morale-breeding individuality and such has it always been. The pride in the uniform, rather than the uniform itself, is what has made the serviceman.   SCW

Carman, William Y., *British Military Uniforms from Contemporary Pictures* (London, 1957).

Knötel, Richard, Knötel, Herbert, and Sieg, Herbert, *Uniforms of the World* (London, 1980).

Lawson, Cecil C. P., *A History of the Uniforms of the British Army*, 5 vols. (London, 1940–67).

Mollo, John, *Military Fashion* (London, 1972).

member countries are invited to contribute forces to UN operations. This has also enhanced the role of the Secretary-General, who is responsible for the administration, organization, and daily operation of such forces. However, member countries have sometimes failed to contribute the forces necessary for UN success.

The first case of the Security Council determining a threat to international peace under Article 39 came in 1947 over the boundaries of the new state of Israel. The result was the deployment in 1948, under the authority of Chapter 6, of a UN monitoring contingent, the UN Truce Supervision Organisation (UNTSO), which lasted until 1987, and set a precedent for many such contingents. For many years the only UN Chapter 7 operation was the Korean war. In July 1950 the Security Council passed resolutions condemning the North Korean invasion of South Korea and establishing a UN command, so that the war was fought under UN badges and insignia. The USSR, which had temporarily boycotted the Security Council, regarded these resolutions as unconstitutional, and blocked further Security Council action. In response, in November 1950 the General Assembly passed its historic and controversial 'Uniting for Peace' resolution, which declared that if the Security Council failed to carry out its function then the General Assembly could act instead. A Cold War criticism of the Security Council was that its resolutions simply legitimized the interests of the USA. Gen *MacArthur, the commander in Korea 1950–1, later described his UN command as 'entirely notional'.

The next major UN development came in October 1956, at the end of the *Suez campaign. When Britain and France vetoed resolutions in the Security Council, the 'Uniting for Peace' mechanism was invoked to transfer the issue to the General Assembly. This accepted a Canadian proposal for a multinational UN Emergency Force (UNEF I) to deploy with mutual consent on the border between Egypt and Israel, and in the Canal Zone. This enabled the British and French to withdraw, and avoided superpower involvement. UNEF I became the prototype for Chapter 6 peacekeeping forces established by the Security Council.

Between 1948 and 1998 there were 49 UN peacekeeping operations including observer missions, 36 of them created in the last decade. The terms of peacekeeping operations are defined by Security Council resolutions, and UN command of troops is negotiated with their country of origin. Most troops wear their national uniforms with UN badges and insignia, most particularly the distinctive UN light blue headgear, and vehicles are painted white. UN peacekeeping forces are lightly armed, and depend on consent for their presence. Since 1948, altogether 118 countries have contributed more than 500,000 troops to peacekeeping operations, and some countries such as Canada and Fiji have taken part in almost every one. Until 1991 it was almost unknown for the permanent five members of the Security Council to contribute troops to a peacekeeping operation (the exception being British participation in UNFICYP on Cyprus since 1964). Being drawn from many countries, peacekeeping forces are not structured or equipped to cope with major military operations or high levels of fighting. The UN priority is peace rather than a settlement acceptable to all sides, and many peacekeeping deployments have lasted for decades. The UN pays countries $1,000 per soldier per month, plus equipment charges, for peacekeeping forces, and is reimbursed by member countries. Costs of peacekeeping peaked in 1993 at almost $4 billion, while member countries owe the UN $1.75 billion in unpaid peacekeeping dues. In 1988 the UN peacekeeping forces were collectively awarded the *Nobel Peace Prize.

Under Dag Hammarskjold, Secretary-General 1953–61, the UN Secretariat argued for a notional 'Chapter 6½' of the charter: military action that was more than peace but less than a war. The closest to this was ONUC (1960–4), the UN involvement in the civil war in the newly independent *Congo, which saw in June 1960 the first use of Article 99 of the charter (allowing the Secretary-General to warn the Security Council of a threat to peace), and a further use of the 'Uniting for Peace' mechanism in September. From this experience Hammarskjold (who was killed in an air crash in the Congo in September 1961, being posthumously awarded the Nobel Peace Prize) developed principles for UN peacekeeping that are still in existence. The view emerged that the UN could mount peacekeeping, but that 'peace enforcement' should be left to national forces with UN authorization.

Chapter 1 Article 2(7) of the charter forbids the UN to intervene in matters 'within the domestic jurisdiction' of any country. However, UN internationalism, peacekeeping, and the problem of civil wars have increasingly reduced the definition of 'domestic jurisdiction', together with the argument that some countries' behaviour is so outrageous as to constitute a threat to international peace. This was invoked for the first time in 1966 by the British over the unilateral declaration of independence by Rhodesia (now Zimbabwe) the previous year (see RHODESIA WAR), leading to the first case of the Security Council imposing mandatory trade sanctions.

A major change in the effectiveness of the UN came with the end of the Cold War. In November 1990 the Security Council authorized, for the first time since Korea, a full-scale Chapter 7 operation, which became the 1991 *Gulf war against Iraq. This time there was no overall UN command structure, and contingents fought on a national basis. With the Security Council no longer deadlocked, Chapter 7 resolutions have been passed since 1991 in support of several smaller operations, such as the American use of force to restore the government of Haiti in 1995.

Following the Gulf war, in 1991 the Security Council passed a historic series of resolutions stipulating Iraqi conduct, rejecting the argument that these fell within Iraqi domestic jurisdiction. In 1992 Secretary-General Boutros Boutros-Ghalli (1992–7) argued that a new era of 'collective sovereignty' was emerging, giving the UN a new mandate. A UN *doctrine of international legal authority—or even

obligation—for intervention in countries in crisis or civil war rapidly emerged. This was followed by a number of controversial UN operations that—as with ONUC in the Congo—exposed the problems of 'Chapter 6½' and the gap between UN ambition and political reality, These included UN involvement in the disintegrating former *Yugoslavia, in Rwanda (1994), and in *Somalia. The civil war in Yugoslavia also saw increasing co-operation between the UN and NATO, in a new role as a force for regional peacekeeping. This led in 1995 to a NATO peace enforcement contingent replacing the UN peacekeeping force in Bosnia.   SDB

Bellamy, Christopher, *Knights in White Armour* (London, 1996).
Hillen, John, *Blue Helmets* (Washington, 1998).
Parsons, Anthony, *From Cold War to Hot Peace* (London, 1995).
The Yearbook of the United Nations (New York, 1947–   ).

United Nations. See UN.

United States army In the closing year of the *American independence war, *Washington wrote his views of a proper military (land forces) policy for the new United States of America. Washington's 'Sentiments on a Peace Establishment', completed in May 1783, not only reflected the experiences of the colonial period and the war for independence, but also identified the enduring factors that would shape American armies well into the 20th century. From his experience in two North American wars, Washington did not believe that Americans would ever tolerate the cost or political threat of a large regular army raised and commanded by a strong central government. 'Altho' a *large standing Army in time of Peace hath ever been considered dangerous to the liberties of the Country, yet a few Troops, under certain circumstances, are not only safe, but indispensably necessary. Fortunately for us our relative situation requires but few.' Washington knew that the state governors and assemblies jealously guarded their control of the *militia, the citizen-armies of white male homeowners-voters-taxpayers that had defended their villages and farms since the early 17th century. He also knew that the state forces and his own Continental Army had great difficulty using any sort of conscription system. Such drafts usually meant opening service to 'the lower sort' and offering them rewards of land, money, and political rights.

Washington also recognized that militia-based land forces had one military function: the defence of localities and states from direct attack, whether from the sea by Europeans or from Native American warriors, often abetted by Europeans. With a vast new nation to defend, thinly populated away from the Atlantic seaboard, no conceivable national army could protect the western settlers by itself. Even if Congress provided some sort of army to police and protect the national domain, most conspicuously the Northwest Territory beyond the Appalachians and north of the Ohio river, this army would be too small to replace the militia. The difficulty with any militia force was that it included the males who formed the backbone of America's agricultural population, the largest and most important part of its free labour force. Thus, state authorities—let alone a national officer—were unlikely to call out the militia for greater than a 30–60-day period of compulsory service; expeditions that left a state and/or remained in the field for a longer time would have to be raised as volunteers under either national or state authority. These volunteers would insist, like the militia, in selecting their officers (meaning gubernatorial appointment) and establishing their own regulations. They also presented the same problems as the militia in terms of discipline and effectiveness.

Like Washington, the other military experts and political leaders of the post-independence period agreed in principle that (1) the USA still faced threats of internal unrest and foreign invasion and (2) the nation's economic health and political liberties demanded a mixed force of long-service volunteer 'regulars' called the US army and state-controlled militia organized for emergency 'calling forth' by national and state authorities. Like many other aspects of the American federal system, embodied in the Constitution and the Bill of Rights (Amendments 1–10), the power over the use of military force and the creation of military institutions rested in the hands of many levels of political sovereignty and (in one interpretation of the Second Amendment) in the hands of citizens themselves, who retained the 'right to bear arms'. This 'right' in Great Britain had rapidly disappeared in the face of laws designed to disarm Celtic rebels and disgruntled rural mobs. While the national government had the power to form armies (granted to the Congress in Article 1, Section 8 of the Constitution) and command these armies through the President as C-in-C (Article 2, Section 2), the states bore the principal responsibility for maintaining their own defence forces as they saw fit.

As the land forces developed in the Federalist and Jeffersonian periods (1789–1816), the US army and the militia forces of the states and federal territories exhibited the very strengths and weaknesses that Washington and other nationalists predicted in the 1780s. The US army performed four major functions: expanded the western frontier; manned coastal fortifications with heavy artillery around major harbours or estuaries; developed and produced military ordnance like cannon and muskets; and provided officer-experts in exploration, cartography, and civil engineering, all essential to westward settlement. The territorial and state militias had the duty of mounting an immediate response to invasion, whether by a British army or a Shawnee war party, and of suppressing rebellion, whether it came from slaves, a new immigrant urban working class, or unhappy farmers. Any major conflict, dignified by Congress as a 'war', would probably force an expansion of the US army, the formation of volunteer units under national and state authority, and the compulsory call-up of the militia for federal (limited to 90 days a year) or state service. The Militia Act of 1792 expressed this concept, amplified by further legislation in 1808 that promised that the states could share an annual appropriation of $200,000 for the purchase of muskets if the states could prove they had an organized militia.

The *War of 1812 demonstrated the best and worst of the characteristics of America's armies. The regular US army was too small and too dispersed to deter Great Britain; it was too ill-equipped and poorly commanded to either wage offensive operations or even hold its own posts along the Canadian border in 1812. It could, however, expand from 6,000 to 33,000 by 1815, and it performed on a few occasions up to European standards against British regulars along the Canadian frontier in 1813 and 1814. Yet the regular army alone could not meet all the military challenges. State governments, usually those most directly threatened, could and did form volunteer units to take the field. Some of these units of infantry, cavalry, mounted infantry, and artillery reached 'professional' standards, but they seldom served for longer than six to twelve months. Their effectiveness almost always depended on the charismatic leadership of a local warrior-hero like Andrew Jackson of Tennessee, Richard H. Johnson of Kentucky, or Samuel Smith of Maryland. At one time or another almost 500,000 citizen-soldiers served in the 1812–15 war, and they contributed to some notable successes like the Creek campaign of 1813 and the defences of Plattsburg, *Baltimore, and New Orleans in 1814–15. They also suffered their share of defeats, the sack of Washington (1814) being the most dramatic.

For the rest of the 19th century, American land-force policy endured despite fundamental changes in the conduct of war like the development of *breech-loading ordnance and steam-powered transportation as well as the institutional growth in Europe of professionalized officer corps and *general staffs. The regular army and the state forces continued to perform their traditional missions with relative effectiveness; their only major failure in maintaining the authority of the national government occurred in 1860–1, and became the *American civil war.

The *Mexican war had shown how flexible the system might be, especially adaptive to the political realities of a war that divided citizens on party and regional lines. The regiments and batteries of the US army increased in strength through bounty-driven volunteering from 7,400 to 42,400; this wartime expansion included the formation of ten brand-new regiments, rich in officer commissions. Nineteen out of 29 state governments provided 61,000 men in 27 volunteer regiments, enlisted for one year's service or more. The War Department later concluded that 12,600 militia had also served under involuntary call-up, but these Texas and Louisiana units were probably volunteers in state service and served for very short periods. Some entered federal service to cross state or national boundaries as the Texas Rangers did under *Taylor in the army in northern Mexico or the Mormon battalion and New Mexico militia who participated in Gen Alexander W. Doniphan's expedition into north-central Mexico. In retrospect, the regular regiments fought and won the war's major battles, three in Texas and northern Mexico under Taylor in 1846 and six under *Scott in the campaign that eventually captured Mexico City. In only one battle (Buena Vista, February 1847) did state volunteers bear the brunt of battle. The regular army also endured the preponderance of combat casualties, 1,100 of 1,700 dead and 2,745 of 4,102 wounded in action. The war demonstrated—as the War of 1812 had not—that the USA could bring most of its wartime army to bear upon the enemy, even in an overseas expedition.

In terms of land-force policy, the civil war proved little except that mass American armies could kill and maim each other by the hundreds of thousands over a four-year period. Despite some creative myth-making during and after the war about the superior generalship of regular officers (*West Point graduates like *Lee, *Grant, and *Sherman) and the staunch service of small contingents of US army 'regulars'—really wartime enlistees—the war from start to finish was a bloodletting inflicted by citizen-armies upon each other. Of the four million officers and men who served in either the Union or Confederate armies, fewer than 100,000 had seen service in the regular US army, fought in the war with Mexico as volunteers, or participated in pre-1860 military training as volunteer militia, a category of citizen-soldier that had grown after the 1812–15 war. These units protected or attacked urban ethnic groups, provided ceremonial units in state capitols, satisfied the martial urges of upper middle-class gentlemen, and trained expatriate revolutionaries who wanted to free Ireland, Hungary, and various states in Germany. If one counts every man who had a uniform and took part in military training on a regular basis in 1860 (the US army and the volunteer militia), the total land forces of the USA on the eve of its bloodiest war (both in absolute and population-proportional terms) might have been 56,000.

A handful of Union army officers, incorporated back into the post-war US army, saw two major lessons in the American civil war: (1) the wartime army like the peacetime army must be run by professional officers, embodied into a general staff and devoted to wartime contingency planning; (2) efficient and timely wartime mobilization required a federal reserve force untainted by state politics that would enlarge the regular US army quickly and provide new units if necessary. After 1871 the German model attracted great interest, but the Swiss system of universal military training also had its attractions. In the meantime, the post-war army went back to its coast defence and frontier forts, numbering only 37,200 by 1870 and 27,300 in 1890.

After a decade of war-weariness and sectional strife, the states rebuilt their volunteer state militias (although compulsory service remained a legal option) in the 1870s, in part as a response to racial and labour unrest. In 1890 the

volunteer militia, which had largely adopted the title National Guard, may have numbered 100,000 in units that drilled once a week for a few hours and sometimes went to the field for a week in the summer, both training periods without pay. (States paid Guardsmen only when called to state duty, usually for riot control and disaster relief.) The national government did little to support the Guard other than transfer and sell arms and military equipment under existing federal law.

Some army and Guard officers thought that greater federal subsidies would improve the Guard as a first-line reserve for wartime mobilization, and some states successfully lobbied to have regular officers assigned as Guard advisers and to get federal funds to build armouries. More wartime soldiers, particularly junior officers, might come from the 'Land Grant' universities and colleges, established by the Morrill Act of 1862, which required that any state receiving Morrill Act land sales profits had to offer military training for student-volunteers at its new Land Grant university. By the 1890s the students who had received such training might have numbered as many as 100,000.

Before various military reforms could be established, the USA fought the *Spanish-American war, which led to the *Philippines insurrection. Waged well beyond the continental USA, the two wars revealed the limitations of the mixed land-force system. Although the War Department wanted to fight Spain with a 64,000-man all-regular army, supplemented if necessary with federal volunteers, Congress responded to National Guard champions and dictated that state volunteers (under their own officers) be allowed to enter federal service first. The only exceptions were three federal volunteer cavalry regiments, an engineer brigade, some specialist troops, and ten regiments of white and black troops that were supposed to be proof against yellow fever and malaria ('the Immunes'). The 130 state volunteer regiments (200,000 officers and men) usually included no more than one-quarter of its soldiers with any sort of prior service, but it was the state governors who commissioned the officers, about 40 for every 1,000-man regiment. Fewer than half of the state volunteers deployed to the Caribbean or the Philippines; their disease deaths in poorly organized camps in the USA (around 4,000, compared with fewer than 300 combat deaths) dramatized the fact that the war department had not prepared its support departments and services for wartime expansion.

In the less than twenty years before the USA entered WW I, the military policy of the nation underwent dramatic, but unfinished reform. One factor was the growing appreciation of the impact of new military technology on warfare; in this short period the US army and the National Guard converted to modern magazine rifles, experimented with machine guns, began to use automobiles and trucks, formed aviation units, modernized their artillery, adopted field telephones and primitive radios, and developed motor-powered field engineering. Another development was the awareness that the management of a modern army required extensive pre-war planning and officer education; by 1917 the US army had an officer education system in place to provide European-style commanders and staff officers for large field forces. The greatest challenge was to create a politically legitimate system for raising a wartime army. Just defending the new overseas possessions (Puerto Rico, the Panama Canal Zone, Hawaii, and the Philippines) required far larger regular forces, and the active army reached a peacetime strength of over 100,000 by 1905, supplemented by Filipino regulars (the Philippine Scouts) and National Guard units in Puerto Rico and Hawaii. To back up this force the War Department and Congress again turned to the National Guard.

In collaboration with the War Department, Congress attempted to reform the National Guard with two major laws, the Militia Acts of 1903 and 1908, and began the 'nationalization' of the National Guard as an unlimited federal reserve force, completed by the end of the century. The lever of reform would be federal appropriations for armouries, weapons and equipment, advisers, access to special *education and training courses for officers and men, and pay for annual summer field training. The only omitted subsidy was drill pay, and this became a federal responsibility in 1916. The difficulty was some legal uncertainty over whether the federal government could call the National Guard to compulsory service for expeditions abroad for unlimited ('duration of the emergency') periods of service. When the War Department examined the issue in 1912, it received an advisory opinion from the US Attorney-General that the federalized National Guard could not be sent abroad unless its members volunteered for such service as individuals. This problem forced the War Department to examine again the feasibility of establishing a federal reserve force, and in 1912 Congress approved a provision that regular enlisted men might volunteer for a reserve corps. The number of soldiers who chose this option would not have formed a company in 1916.

Concerned about the possibility of a war with Mexico after the outbreak of revolution in 1910 and anxious about its security in a world now disordered by WW I, Congress in 1916 passed a National Defence Act. This legislation reflected conflicting sentiments: a generalized interest in 'preparedness', the Wilsonian pledge to maintain neutrality yet pressure the Allies and the Central Powers into a compromise peace, and a fear that the USA would soon intervene in the European war. The National Defence Act represented the first peacetime effort to deal with organizing wartime armies and to link those forces to the management of military procurement through a Council of National Defence or 'war cabinet' whose authority might extend to economic regulation. The legislation recognized the importance of a ready US army, expanding it to 175,000 in 111 regiments of infantry, cavalry, and artillery. The National Guard (planned at 400,000) would become the first

source of trained reserve manpower in tactical units, unleashed from potential legal problems by the requirement that any Guardsman receiving federal money would have to take a federal oath that obligated him to overseas service for such a period as the Congress might determine. The mobilization of the Guard for service on the Mexican border proved that Guardsmen would accept this obligation.

Although the Guard lobby and Congress could block any move to create a federal reserve force of units, they conceded that a wartime army would be likely to require the formation of other citizen-soldiers (volunteers and conscripts) into wartime divisions (roughly calculated at around 20,000 officers and men) and much-enlarged army service and support units. The National Defence Act of 1916 focused on identifying and training officers in peacetime for wartime service either as combat leaders or staff specialists; the legislation created an Officer Reserve Corps (subdivided by combat arms and staff departments) that would come from graduates of university-based university cadet programmes, the summer training camps organized and run by the army since 1912, and from already-licensed professionals like doctors, lawyers, dentists, and engineers. Another unstated assumption was that the War Department would for the first time create officer-training courses in wartime that would supply combat arms leaders to the expanded army. This concept, which assumed the possibility of forming an army of two million, did not reflect any plan to intervene in the European war, but the possibility of a later war with Japan or some future European enemy.

American entry in WW I in April 1917 tested every aspect of the nation's land-forces policy and found it barely satisfactory. Upon entry into the war, the Wilson administration and Congress accepted with great reluctance the reality that the war would be won or lost on the western front. To influence that outcome the USA would have to form a massive American Expeditionary Force (AEF), which eventually numbered over two million. The only way to conserve on shipping and speed up the American reinforcement was to arm the AEF with French and British weapons and equipment. Such adjustments cut almost a year (from both German and American estimates) from the time required to form an American army in France. In the crisis the US government turned to wartime conscription and Congress passed a 'Selective Service' Act in May 1918. This law first stirred volunteering for the regular US army and federalized National Guard in 1917 and later in the same year provided a foundation for the creation of a 'National Army' of draftees. The legitimacy of the system rested in the decentralization and civilization of the induction process; the locus of deciding who served and who received exemptions and deferments rested in 4,648 local boards staffed by civilians, not the despised military officers used by the Union and Confederacy in the civil war. Voluntary enrolment for the draft produced more than 24 million names and fewer than 1 million avoiders. By war's end two-thirds of

America's soldiers (2.8 million) had entered the army through the draft.

The performance of the AEF left a set of ambiguous lessons for the post-war review of land-force policy. The AEF had found plenty of brave junior officers and enlisted men in its ranks; both regulars and temporary officers (Guardsmen, reserves, and graduates of the officer-candidate schools) had performed with unexpected expertise, a credit to their own intelligence and the AEF school system. Most of the AEF's problems on the battlefield stemmed from poor staff work, primitive transportation logistics, and the inadequate use of supporting arms. No doubt some of these problems might have been eased had the AEF not existed but had been treated like British Commonwealth and French colonial divisions; that is, amalgamated into a larger national army. Such a solution was not congruent with Wilson's diplomacy nor *Pershing's national and institutional pride. The AEF, which suffered most of its 55,000 dead in a span of only fifteen weeks in 1918, had struggled until the war's last week. If less traumatized than their civil-war forebears, army officers returned from France full of ideas on how to modernize and organize American land forces.

Land-force policy and army politics felt the impact of new forms of warfare: the employment of military aircraft of various types for a wide range of missions. The Air Service AEF, an organizational stepchild of the Signal Corps, performed almost every modern airwar mission except strategic bombardment. Army aviators, flying French and British aircraft, protected their own forces, raided German airbases and installations, bombed transportation systems, took photographs, spotted artillery targets, carried messages, and strafed and bombed front-line positions. At the war's end the Air Service numbered 200,000 officers and men, one-quarter of them in Europe. One group of army aviators, rallying around the charismatic AEF air combat leader *Mitchell, argued that the army's aviation force should be an independent service with strategic bombing its primary mission; other air and ground officers believed that army aviation should be integrated with the ground forces in order to insure rapid, decisive battlefield victory. Although they did not use the term 'air-land battle', that is exactly what these moderate reformers envisioned. After 1918 any attempt at military reform invariably had to cope with the contentious issue of the future of army aviation.

Reflecting its understanding of the lessons of WW I, Congress passed the National Defence Act of 1920 on the assumption that the mixed armies it created in 1916 and 1917 needed little change. The regular army and National Guard still would provide infantry-artillery divisions (each about 25,000 soldiers in 1920) while the Officers Reserve Corps would train peacetime officers for an expanded wartime army. One new concept in the 1920 Act was the creation of army Reserve divisions manned in only cadre status (1,000 or fewer officers and NCOs); these federal reservists would prepare for their wartime role of training divisions of draftees for combat. The continental USA was divided into nine corps areas whose commanding generals would train one US army division, two National Guard Divisions, and three army Reserve cadre divisions. All of the divisions would be organized and equipped the same (at least on paper), which allowed National Guard divisions to form tank companies and aviation squadrons, the latter units eventually becoming the Air National Guard in 1947. The Congress intended that the regular army and the National Guard would number about 715,000 officers and men in peacetime while all elements of the new 'Army of the United States' would be used as the foundation for a wartime army of 5–7 million. Congressional economizing, deepened by the economic depression of the 1930s, reduced the actual strength of both armies by 1939 to only 380,000.

The failure to man and train the Army of the United States (AUS) in the 1930s reflected two major problems. The first was the lack of equipment modernization, which the war department and combat arms commanders recognized; equipment shortages (and the growing obsolescence of the WW I weapons) meant that much of the army could not be combat-ready for at least two years. One option was to limit investment in new weapons like tanks; another was to develop prototypes of new weapons (like the 105 mm howitzer and the M-1 semi-automatic rifle) but not field them. The army pursued better mobility, especially for its service and supply units, through comprehensive motorization, but the willy-nilly purchase of trucks and cars made automotive maintenance difficult and costly, which made Congress unhappy.

The other problem was the new popularity of the Army Air Corps, established as an equal arm in 1920 and then as a super-arm with special allowances to develop aircraft, train pilots, build airbases, and manage its own affairs, all assured in the Air Corps Act of 1926. The Air Corps may have dominated one-quarter of all army spending in the 1930s, and it enjoyed close and co-operative relations with American commercial aviation. In 1931 the army and navy agreed that the Air Corps had an important role in coast defence, which justified the highest priority development of the XB-17, a long-range bomber. In 1935 the emerging bomber force had its squadrons unified under the commanding general, GHQ Air Force. This change meant that much of the Air Corps no longer supported the ground army (the armies and corps), but prepared to wage war by strategic bombardment, smashing the will and industrial might of any future enemy by direct attack on his cities and economic assets.

Concerned with the lack of readiness of all elements of the AUS, Gen Malin Craig, the COS, decided to focus his scarce resources on portions of the US army and the National Guard; after 1935 the army would train and equip a 400,000–man field army named the Initial Protective Force. Equipment shortages restricted the training of this grouping of 'minuteman' divisions; Craig estimated that he needed an additional $4 billion to arm and equip the force. This sum was eight times the army's entire budget in 1935.

The Japanese invasion of China in 1937 and the Nazi–Soviet conquest of Poland in 1939 did not change the army except to accelerate some procurement and modernization plans. When the War Department tried to put its plan for more urgent procurement into effect, the Industrial Mobilisation Plan, the Congress rejected the plea for army modernization. The fall of *France in 1940 created a new sense of crisis, and the Congress approved the federalization of the National Guard and the enactment of a new Selective Service Act to draft men for peacetime military training. The fundamental concern was to deter Japan from using German successes to seize the European colonial empires in South-east Asia and the Philippines.

The War Department general staff drafted the 'Victory Program' of 1941, a blueprint for the creation of a wartime army of 8.8 million officers and men, a force (as planned) that would produce a ground force of 213 divisions, about half of them mechanized or motorized, and an air force of 195 groups, half of them bombers. In the same summer the Air Corps became the Army Air Forces (USAAF), whose operational forces would be assigned to a theatre commander, not a ground forces general. The Commanding General, USAAF, would be the DCOS of the army, answerable only to the COS, US army. Two years later the army's authoritative doctrinal manual on the conduct of operations stated that army aviation had a co-equal role with the ground forces in winning wars. The USAAF planners in 1941 also drafted their version of an air campaign against Germany; this war of strategic bombardment would ensure air superiority and crush the industry that supplied the Axis ground forces. None of these hopes would materialize completely or in quite the way the planners imagined, but the plans represented a dramatic shift away from massing resources in a large ground army to focusing on an élite, technologically advanced, and capital-intensive air force in order to spare lives in conventional ground battles.

The AUS met its greatest test in the two-front struggle with the Axis in WW II. The AUS split into three functional groupings: Army Ground Forces, Army Air Forces (USAAF), and Army Service Forces (ASF). In terms of numbers and training quality of personnel, the Army Ground Forces took second place to the USAAF Air Forces and ASF; of the 11 million soldiers who served in WW II, only one-third served in the ground forces, principally the 89 divisions formed and deployed abroad. The USAAF absorbed 2.5 million army airmen, and the ASF, faced with global transportation and base-building challenges, grew to three million officers and men. Early in the war army COS George *Marshall pledged that the army would produce the best soldiers, armed with the best weapons, in the world. This goal proved to be beyond the army's means. The massive investment of money and quality manpower in the USAAF remains controversial, but it is hard to imagine the army fighting the *Wehrmacht in Europe without the benefits of its strategic bombing campaign and the direct support of tactical aviation. In quantitative terms the army directed two-thirds of its combat power against Germany and Italy and one-third against Japan.

The *demobilization after WW II and the subsequent development of *Cold War military challenges posed by the USSR in central Europe brought more changes to the army. First, it lost almost all its pilots and aircraft (and the guarantee of close *air support) to the US Air Force (USAF) in the National Security Act of 1947. By 1949 its principal civilian official, the Secretary of War, had become the Secretary of the Army, subordinated to the Secretary of Defence and stripped of cabinet membership. The army COS became a member of the Joint Chiefs of Staff, eventually (1986) subordinated to a powerful Chairman invested with special access to the Secretary of Defence and the President. Fundamentally organized and equipped for a mechanized war with the USSR as part of the *NATO collective defence alliance, the army, nevertheless, fought two extended ground wars in Asia, neither of which brought it much public acclaim. Instead the wars in *Korea and *Vietnam used up lives, morale, money for continued modernization, and a good deal of the public sympathy given the army in WW II. The most positive benefit of the two wars was the re-emergence of army aviation as a helicopter force for airmobile warfare.

The Cold War army retained much of its WW II organizational character with an active force that varied between 500,000 and 1.6 million officers and men formed into between ten and twenty divisions, reinforced with corps troops and separate brigades. The army Reserve and the army National Guard shared the role of providing deployable units with the Reserve stressing service and support units and the Guard combat units, most of which shrank from divisions to brigades by the 1990s. Both reserve components provided units and individuals for the expanded wartime armies of the Korean and Vietnam eras, although the compulsory mobilization of the Vietnam war did not occur until 1968, too late to influence the course of the war. The Korean war mobilization, on the other hand, rebuilt a strategic reserve in the USA, provided veterans for combat service in Korea, in Germany in 1951–2, and allowed the creation of the Seventh Army. The *Gulf war also required the army to mobilize Reserves and Guardsmen to strengthen the US Third Army, principally with artillery and support units. Of the 381,000 soldiers who fought Iraq, 134,300 male and female soldiers came to the war from federalized reserve units. The subsequent reduction of the active army in the 1990s had one happy benefit, the release of experienced soldiers to reserve units and the equipping of these units with first-line weapons and equipment.

The army also grappled with several manning changes that changed its character. None of the changes came without organizational stress. One fact of life was that the Cold

War ground forces could not be manned in sufficient strength without peacetime conscription, enacted in 1948 and continued until 1973. This army of true volunteers, coerced volunteers, and conscripts meant a high turnover, heavy training load, and an irreducible minority of 'summer soldiers'. The army also tried to balance its emphasis on ready forces, especially in Germany and Korea, with the maintenance of a vast training establishment designed for wartime expansion. By its own admission it retained too many bases, stored too much equipment, supported officer commissioning programmes that could not be justified on cost grounds, and created an active duty officer corps that lacked cohesion and common values. Many army 'warriors' sought refuge in élite units: rangers, special forces, attack helicopter squadrons, parts of the armoured forces, and technically advanced artillery and air defence units. The creation of an all-volunteer force in the 1980s and 1990s helped build 'one army' in the functional sense, but other factors brought stress from other directions.

One way the army had always justified its existence was to argue that it served as an employer of the American underclass and an agency of assimilation for immigrants, dispossessed farmers, and unemployed, unskilled workers. After WW II this social function, which was real if difficult, received a stern test. First, conscription and (later) the high wages of the volunteer army brought young men into the army with few skills, unfinished education, and no taste for authority and discipline. The drug use of the 1960s and 1970s (pandemic in the army) reflected a rootless youth culture that made training difficult.

This problem was further exacerbated by a presidential decision (long overdue) in 1948 to give African-American soldiers wider opportunities as officers and senior enlisted men, including the command of whites, and to provide meaningful training to black enlistees to the best of their abilities, not just assign them to segregated units with minimal combat and logistical missions. This policy paid real dividends until the 1970s when unemployed black youths flooded the army and went into direct battle with their officers and NCOs and their white comrades. Only by reducing the army and applying higher enlistment standards to all recruits could racial violence be reduced, essential in an army that is now one-third black. Just as this problem subsided, the army found itself accepting the fact that almost 12 per cent of its force would be female, a trend started in 1948. It accelerated in the 1970s when male recruits came in short supply and the Congress accepted the argument that 'equal opportunity' had gender as well as racial meaning. The American army of men, women, soldiers of many races and ethnic origins, and even soldiers with unconventional sexual tastes, is a wonder of the world at the end of the 20th century. Optimists believe it will eventually produce the élite androgynous 'starship troopers' of the future, adept with wizard weapons and full of traditional warrior virtues detached from old notions of masculinity. Pessim-

ists believe that the army will mirror the experience of the Roman legions, weakened by too-long service abroad, divided by nationalities and deviant subcultures, and devoted to its own comfort and perpetuation, not defence. The past of the American army suggests that it will endure, but that the process will be difficult and test the devotion of those men and women who will try to sustain its honour.

AM

Hagan, Kenneth J., and Roberts, William R., *Against All Enemies: Interpretations of American Military History from Colonial Times to the Present* (New York, 1986).

Mahon, John K., *History of the Militia and the National Guard* (New York, 1983).

Millett, Allan R., and Maslowski, Peter, *For the Common Defense: A Military History of the United States of America* (rev. edn., New York, 1994).

Washington, George, 'Sentiments on a Peace Establishment', May 1783, repr. in Walter Millis (ed.), *American Military Thought* (Indianapolis, 1966).

Weigley, Russell F., *History of the United States Army* (New York, 1967).

unknown soldiers Most of the men who have died in battle have been buried anonymously, if at all. The deliberate burial of an unknown soldier could not arise until the idea that common soldiers ought to have individual graves had arisen. The linkage of military service and citizenship during the 19th century created the military *cemetery which in turn gave rise to tombs of unknown soldiers.

The earliest example is in Arlington cemetery in Virginia (1866), which contains the remains of unidentified Union soldiers killed during the *American civil war. What marks this ossuary out from the traditional mass grave is that the bodies were placed there *because* they could not be identified. During this war for the first time, it was generally assumed that the families of dead soldiers had the right to expect that the bodies would be buried individually. When the state took on the power to conscript from the general population, it was inevitable that the public would demand that the state would provide soldiers a decent burial.

Modern weapons mutilate horribly, and battlefields are confused and extensive. At the time that the demand for individual burial arose, the problem of identifying the dead was starting to become more difficult. As the expectation that soldiers would be buried in marked graves spread across the USA to Europe, the realization arose that for a substantial minority of soldiers this would prove impossible. In the aftermath of the *Franco-Prussian war, there were calls in France that the unknown soldier, *representative* of those with no marked graves, should be buried with state honours. The proposal was not implemented, but the idea persisted. During WW I, at least one-third of the war dead were unidentifiable. The British army *chaplain, David Railton, is often credited with the idea of the Tomb of the Unknown Warrior, after burying Londoners killed on the *Somme. In reality, the idea probably had a French source. In 1920, both Britain and France decided to bury a representative unidentified corpse with full honours. Both nations staged elaborate ceremonials choosing the body to guarantee anonymity. In the French case, an infantry soldier chose one coffin from six. In the British case the choice was from four bodies from the 1914 battlefields of *Ypres, *Mons, the *Marne, and the *Aisne. On 11 November, the second anniversary of the *Armistice, a British soldier was interred in Westminster Abbey and a French soldier beneath the Arc de Triomphe. The British use of the word 'warrior' rather than soldier was supposed to indicate symbolic inclusiveness for all armed forces and for the empire.

The USA followed suit the next year. In Italy, the soldier buried in 1921 became a focus for emerging fascism. Germany, politically divided by the war, took much longer to adopt the idea, burying an unknown soldier only in 1930. By this time, the idea had taken on new force as a symbol of nationhood. Poland buried an unknown soldier of the Russo-Polish war. The link between Unknown Soldiers and nationhood is inescapable: the decision to bury an unknown Australian soldier of WW I in 1994, at the Australian War Memorial in Canberra, was an implicit statement that the body in Westminster Abbey could no longer represent Australia.

The advent of DNA testing now makes it at least theoretically possible for a remains to be identified, as was the case in 1998 when an unknown soldier from *Vietnam was identified as a USAF lieutenant. But there remained the problem of the *MIAs.   AG2

Inglis, K., 'Entombing Unknown Soldiers', *History and Memory*, 5 (1993).

Lloyd, D., 'Tourism, Pilgrimage and the Commemoration of the Great War in Britain, Australia and Canada', unpublished PhD (Cambridge, 1995).

Mosse, G., *Fallen Soldiers* (Oxford, 1990).

Ustashe The Ustashe movement, or Ustashe Croatian Revolutionary Movement, was an ultra-nationalist organization founded in January 1929 in the Croatian capital Zagreb by Ante Pavelic. The Ustashe (from *ustanak*, an uprising) were a direct response to the establishment of a royal dictatorship by King Alexandar. Rejecting the moderate tactics of the Croatian Peasants Party, they demanded the destruction of the Yugoslav state and a greater Croatia that included all of Bosnia. Forced into exile, Pavelic's Ustashe forged closer ties with anti-Serbian Macedonian émigrés and in 1934 the two groups organized the assassination of King Alexandar in Marseilles.

The Ustashe opposed the *Sporazum* (agreement) of 1939 between the Yugoslav government and the Croat moderates, which granted Croatia autonomy. Their moment arrived on 6 April 1941, when Germany invaded Yugoslavia (see YUGOSLAVIA IN WW II). The Ustashe seized power in Croatia with *Mussolini's support and proclaimed the Independent State of Croatia (Nezavisna Drzava Hrvatska, or NDH) with Pavelic as *Poglavnik* (dictator).

The Ustashe state was a dependency of the Axis powers. It introduced Nazi-style racial laws against Jews, gypsies, and Serbs, along with *concentration camps, most infamously at Jasenovac. It exterminated most of the NDH's urban Jews and gypsies, but pogroms against Serbs, who made up 30 per cent of the NDH population, only fuelled a rural rebellion. From mid-1941 it confronted the pro-communist *Partisans led by *Tito. The Partisans won support among many Croats after Pavelic conceded parts of Dalmatia to Italy in May 1941. After Tito entered Belgrade in November 1944 the NDH began to crumble and on 8 May 1945 Pavelic fled to Austria, eventually reaching Argentina.

After Croatia declared its independence from Yugoslavia in 1991, the Serb-led army justified its war against Croat independence as a struggle against a revived Ustashe, a claim the Croats naturally rebutted (see YUGOSLAVIA (FORMER), OPERATIONS IN).   MGT

VAD (Voluntary Aid Detachment), a voluntary nursing organization established in 1909 as part of the British Territorial Force (TF), the product of the *Haldane reforms. The VAD was a remarkable innovation, being the first time that *women were given military organization and training in peacetime. The TF (renamed Territorial Army in 1921) amalgamated the existing volunteer units into a coherent reserve force for the British army. The VAD was designed to supplement the TF's medical services in time of war and was likewise organized on the county system. It was realized that if the TF needed to be expanded in time of war, there would be the necessity for greatly increased military *medicine personnel, and the VAD scheme was designed to fill this gap. Before joining, volunteers had first to obtain a medical certificate, typically from the St John's medical service. In war, the VADs would release trained *nurses from the more routine medical tasks.

During WW I, the VADs, men and women serving in separate units, proved their worth as the strains of war demanded a massive increase in medical provision. They staffed field and clearing *hospitals, and ambulance trains close to the front, as well as hospitals back in Britain. From 1914 to 1918, VADs set up in every country involved supplied the British and empire forces with 23,000 nurses and 15,000 orderlies. The British *Red Cross Society, founded in 1905, also registered their detachments as VAD units. Work was tedious, hours were long, and pay was poor. Night shifts of twelve hours ran uninterrupted for stretches of two months, and remuneration was only £20 per year plus a small clothing allowance. Although the majority of female nurses came from middle- or upper-class homes, their parents frequently opposed their joining and refused to help support them.

Their work in the VAD was a unique experience of independent living. Vera Brittain, feminist and author of *Testa-ment of Youth* (1933), spoke for many when she wrote that service as a VAD nurse was a release from a previously cloistered existence. While most VADs returned to a more traditional lifestyle after the war, some VADs found it difficult to return to the pre-war social order and ex-VAD nurses were involved in the women's movement of the 1920s. For them as for many other *veterans, there could be no return to the *status quo ante bellum.* MH

Brittain, Vera, *Testament of Youth* (London, 1933).
Summers, Anne, *Angels and Citizens: British Women as Military Nurses, 1854–1914* (London, 1988).

Valmy, battle of (1792). At Valmy on 20 September, French troops repelled a Prussian/Austrian invasion that threatened to extinguish the French Revolution in the late summer of 1792 (see FRENCH REVOLUTIONARY WARS). When war broke out the previous April, French recruits had performed poorly, often breaking in panic. The Duke of Brunswick, who commanded the Allied invasion, incorrectly expected his opponents to run again, but this was not to be. With elements of the Army of the North, Charles-François Dumouriez marched against Brunswick, skilfully manoeuvred, and held up the enemy advance at the Argonne forest. This bought time for François-Christophe Kellermann to bring his Army of the Centre to Valmy. Brunswick, after finally penetrating the Argonne, wheeled south with 30,000–34,000 Prussians to confront Kellermann's 36,000 republican troops.

*Cannon decided the battle. The day began with an intense artillery duel, during which the French guns demonstrated their superiority. Although the Prussian infantry advanced a few times, it turned back rather than be decimated. After seeing how steady the French remained, Brunswick calculated that he could ill afford the casualties

of a frontal assault and called off his attack. After a week-long face-off, Brunswick began a disastrous retreat to the Rhine.   JAL

Bertaud, Jean-Paul, *The Army of the French Revolution*, trans. R. R. Palmer (Princeton, 1988).

Vandals were a Germanic people who came into contact with the Roman empire during Emperor Marcus Aurelius' Marcomannic wars (166–80). By the 3rd century, in common with many German tribes, they had adopted the military instrument of the western steppe peoples, lance-armed cavalry. Divided into two groups, the Asdings and Silings, they were usually mentioned together with the Alans. In the 290s, they were living on the Hungarian Plain and in alliance with the Gepids against the Gothic Tervingi. Like the *Goths, whom they seem to have resembled, they were driven westward by the Hunnic attacks of the 370s, and played a role both as enemies and soldiers of the empire. Stilicho, the Roman *magister militum* (C-in-C) in the 390s, was half-Vandal. He was the most successful opponent of the Gothic attacks on Italy, neutralizing Alaric and defeating and killing Radagaisus (406). The western Emperor Honorius feared his ambition and had him captured and executed (408).

At the end of 406, the Vandals and Alans, in conjunction with the confederated Suevi, crossed the river Rhine at Mainz, and swarmed into a Gaul largely abandoned by the imperial government. They devastated the country for three years before crossing into Spain. Here they settled, mostly in the south and west, for a generation. The Siling group was dispersed by Visigoths in alliance with the Romans c.416–18, and this may have persuaded the Asdings to transfer to Africa in 429. Their king, Gaiseric, proved himself an able conqueror and great strategist. He soon seized Mauretania and Numidia (by 435), capturing Carthage in 439. He took full advantage of the city's position and resources. First, he put pressure on the Roman government to recognize his title in return for assuring the North African grain supply upon which the Italian cities depended. Secondly, he constructed fleets which enabled him to carve out a sphere of influence in the western Mediterranean. The Balearic Islands, Sicily, Corsica, and Sardinia fell under Vandal control. Extensive naval raiding against imperial territories included a sack of Rome (455). Byzantine attempts to reconquer Africa in the 460s were beaten off, and in 474, a treaty with the eastern Emperor Zeno reaffirmed Vandal legitimacy. Gaiseric established a dynasty which lasted as long as their rule in Africa.

Although a very mixed group ethnically, being composed of the Asdings and remaining Silings, Alans, Goths, Suevi, and some Hispano-Romans, the Vandals formed a narrow social élite. They were divided from the local population by their adherence to the Arian form of Christianity, and by their military status. Gaiseric provided public lands, known as the *sortes Vandalorum* to support the warrior caste. They could fight in alliance with the local Mauri tribes, who provided light cavalry and infantry, but these had drifted out of allegiance by the early 5th century because of Vandal military decline. Reliance upon a small group of lance-armed cavalry, however socially élite and well equipped, was to prove inadequate in the face of more flexible forces. In 533, as the first stage of Justinian's plan to reconquer the western empire, the Byzantine general *Belisarius invaded Africa with an expeditionary force. A fleet of 92 swift two-decker craft kept the Vandal fleet at bay. He had just 10,000 infantry and 5,000 cavalry (although these included his 1,000-strong bodyguard troops and Hunnic mounted archers. Against them the Vandal King Gelimer could probably only muster comparable numbers, all cavalry. Belisarius landed five days' ride from Carthage and advanced upon the city. He did not expect Gelimer's rapid response and was surprised in line of march at Ad Decimum (the tenth milestone from Carthage). Initial Vandal success was halted by the death of the king's brother Ammatas, and resulted in them being driven off. Gelimer then withdrew, allowing the Romans to occupy Carthage, which he blockaded. The decisive encounter took place when Belisarius emerged from the city, leading only his cavalry to attack the Vandal camp at Tricamerum, 18 miles (29 km) away. Gelimer instructed his men to charge, sword in hand for close combat, but their attack was impeded by a stream. The trained Byzantine troops responded better to the situation, fought back skilfully, and once again killed the Vandal general, Tzanon. Procopius, the Byzantine historian, records the losses as 50 for his own side and 800 of the enemy. This was the end for the Vandal army in Africa. They were organized into five regiments, the Vandali Justiniani, each 400 strong, and shipped off to fight on the Persian frontier. MB

Boss, R., *Justinian's Wars* (Stockport, 1993).

Vauban, Marshal Sebastien le Prestre de (1633–1707). Vauban was the leading military engineer of his own age and arguably the best known of any, whose impact on *fortification and siegecraft was enormous. Indeed, although there were many other successful engineers in the era of artillery fortification, somehow the star-shaped bastioned trace tends to take his name. His military career began inauspiciously. Born to a poor family of Burgundian gentry, he served as a cadet under *Condé during the Fronde and was promptly captured. His captor, who had noted his promise, induced him to join the royal army and gave him a commission in his own regiment. He was appointed a 'king's ordinary engineer' in 1655, and fought under *Turenne in the Low Countries: he directed the siege of Gravelines, which brought him a captaincy in the senior line regiment, Picardy. During the War of Devolution (1667–8) he helped take Douai, Tournai, and Lille, and at its conclusion assisted *Louvois in his reform of the army.

Vauban was assisted by the fact that *Louis XIV took engineering very seriously. He was to be present at nineteen of the sieges directed by Vauban, partly because, as Christopher Duffy observes, a grand siege was his favourite operation of war, 'a magnificent spectacle in the baroque style, at once vigorous and theatrical'. With royal support Vauban sketched out his plan for the famous *pré carré*, a defensible frontier zone based on two lines of fortresses running across France's northern border. The outer line was eventually to run from Dunkirk on the coast through Ypres, Lille, Tournai, and Valenciennes to Dinant on the Meuse, while the inner belt stretched from Gravelines through Arras and Cambrai to Charleville. His fortresses would contain *magazines for French armies on campaign, and would present enemies with obstacles which could only be reduced by costly and time-consuming formal sieges. The building of 33 new fortresses and the remodelling of hundreds of others was to consume much of his time. In addition, he built fortified naval bases at Dunkirk, Brest, Le Havre, Rochefort, and Toulon to support Colbert's plans for the creation of a powerful navy.

Vauban wrote extensively about his craft, with his *Treatise on Sieges and the Attack of Fortresses* (1704) discussing attack and *Treaty on the Defence of Fortresses* (1706) defence. His correspondence with Louis and Louvois testified both to the minutely detailed quality of his unrelenting work and flashes of genuine humanity. In 1699, for instance, he asked Louvois to compensate a poor man with eight children whose land had been eaten up by the citadel of Pinerolo.

The details of his techniques evolved from his 'first system', essentially the bastioned trace inherited from Pagan, which he used in normal circumstances throughout his life; through bastion towers which lay at the heart of his 'second system'; to the addition of casemated shoulders or flanks to these towers, his 'third system'. The last combined the familiar advantages of the bastioned trace with formidably strong internal works intended to seriously disrupt the latter stages of the attack.

Vauban miraculously contrived never to find himself besieged—which in some respects is a pity, for he maintained that he had discovered an infallible method of defending a fortress, but never disclosed what it was. As a besieger, however, he had few equals, and at Maastricht in 1673 he developed what became the standard method of attack in the age of artillery fortification, moving forward by successive parallels connected by zigzag saps until the rampart could be breached at close range and an assault delivered—or, more commonly, capitulation agreed. Vauban never spared himself during the process, and was always on hand, muttering away in a Burgundian dialect littered with forceful neologisms. When the breach was reported practicable, he would always try to check it himself, scrambling back to report, 'that's ripe!' or 'that's not ripe!'

When not designing fortresses, a process which consumed the winter months in Paris, Vauban was on the road,

surveying, inspecting, and checking. He also found time to pioneer the use of the socket *bayonet, and to develop the use of *ricochet fire.

Appointed *commissaire générale des fortifications* in 1678, Vauban became a lieutenant general (then the highest rank of general officer in the French army) in 1688 and marshal of France in 1703. He died in 1707, having sustained eight wounds and directed 48 sieges. Evidence of his handiwork still litters France, and the town of Maubeuge, its northern side still snug behind rampart and ravelin, boasts a block of flats, a stationery shop, and, most importantly, a bar named after the old gentleman.   RH

Duffy, Christopher, *The Fortress in the Age of Vauban and Frederick the Great* (London, 1985).

Vegetius (correctly Flavius Vegetius Renatus) (active *c*.390), Roman military writer. The author of the only Roman military manual to survive complete was not a soldier, but a senior civilian administrator who advocated a return to the discipline of the 'old legion'. Vegetius reconstructs its recruitment and organization, field strategy and tactics, siege and naval warfare, by using many sources of different dates, an antiquarian approach which makes his *De Re Militari* a difficult text for modern students. It largely ignores the 4th-century army, and did not influence imperial policy, but it gained a wide readership in the Middle Ages and Renaissance. His influence extended into the 18th century, linking with the Enlightenment and its 'scientific' approach to military thought.   RSOT

Vegetius, Renatus Flavius, *Vegetius: Epitome of Military Science*, trans. and ed. N. P. Milner (Liverpool, 1993).

Vendée revolt (1793–4). Once the French Revolution degenerated into a bloody tyranny as the heads of monarchists and republicans alike rolled, any opposition to what was going on in Paris and the larger urban centres, where resistance was suicidal, perforce had to be armed. Thus it was that the Revolution was threatened not only by foreign armies on its borders, but by armed revolt inside France as well. As in the later Russian Revolution, the white armies seemed at one point in a position to strangle the revolutionary regime, but failed for lack of unity.

The main foci of revolt were in south-eastern France—Lyons and Toulon—but above all the Vendée in the west. Regional uprisings or *chouanneries* were a feature of the period from 1791 to 1815, but the revolts in the Vendée were easily the most important. The announcement of the *levée en masse* in 1793 provoked a wave of riots the like of which had never been seen, and the revolutionary regime sent in troops. In the west resistance to conscription was identified with powerful religious sentiment, and soon large areas of Brittany and the Loire were in open revolt. Republican government collapsed in the Vendée and by the end of March

1793 all the towns in four *départements* were in rebel hands amid large-scale executions of revolutionary sympathizers. In early April the Royal and Catholic Army was formed and emissaries were despatched to seek British help.

There was a bitter campaign of skirmishes, sieges, and field actions ultimately leading to the defeat of the Royal and Catholic Army under d'Elbée at Cholet in October 1793, and the Virée de Galerne where the Vendéens crossed the Loire into Brittany and Normandy. British help was not forthcoming and the Vendéens struck north to seize the port of Granville in the hope of linking up with the British fleet. The failed siege of 14 November disheartened the Royal Army and the republicans harried them ceaselessly toward the south and into the interior. The inspiring Comte de Rochejacquelein, who had succeeded the executed d'Elbée, was killed in the process. Finally the Vendéens were routed at Savenay on 23 December. There followed summary trials and executions of suspected and actual royalists, in the wake of Gen Turreau's infamous *colonnes infernales*, where up to 2,000 people were shot at a time, and there were mass *noyades* or drownings of Vendéen prisoners in the Loire in response to the threat of a British landing.

The Vendéens rebelled again in 1795. However, this time, abandoned by the émigrés and feebly supported by the English fleet, they were crushed at Quiberon in July. This still required an enormous effort by *Hoche, one of the best Revolutionary generals, and even then insurrection continued in the *bocage* of Brittany and Normandy until 1804. There was another revolt during the *Hundred Days of 1815, led by Louis de Rochejacquelein, whose brother had fallen in 1794. The revolts in the Vendée failed, but the divisions in French society that they so powerfully underlined persisted, some believe to this day.   TM

Vendôme, Marshal Louis Joseph, Duc de (1654–1712). Vendôme, great-grandson of *Henri IV of France, served in the early wars of *Louis XIV, performing well under Luxembourg at Steenkirk in 1695 before going on to command in Catalonia, where he captured Barcelona in 1697. In the War of the *Spanish Succession he replaced Villeroi on the Italian front, where he held *Eugène of Savoy to a draw at Luzzara in 1702, took Vercelli two years later and blocked Eugène again at Cassano in 1705. He was then sent to the northern front, arriving in the wake of *Marlborough's victory at *Ramillies. In July 1708 he was beaten at Oudenarde after a hard-fought battle made more difficult by clashes with his joint commander the Duke of Burgundy. Failure to relieve *Lille, taken by Marlborough after a costly siege, led to his temporary disgrace.

Re-employed in 1710, he was sent to Spain, where he demolished his allied opponents in detail, first beating Stanhope at Brihuega and the following day defeating Starhemburg at Villaviciosa. Repeated over-indulgence, for which he was notorious, sapped his strength, and he died a month later, leaving his successor Berwick to complete his work. Vendôme was brave, brusque, scruffy, and probably the ablest general of the latter part of Louis's reign.   RH

---

venereal diseases (VD) is the common term for infections spread by sexual contact, and the politically correct term (avoiding the sexist reference to Venus) is Sexually Transmitted Diseases (STDs). Several of these are epidemic, including genital herpes virus, genital warts (*condyloma acuminata*), scabies (mites), and the big two: syphilis and gonorrhoea (non-gonococcal urethritis or, if it's an officer, non-*specific* urethritis). Their impact on armed forces was considerable. In WW I just over one-quarter of the diseases for which British soldiers were hospitalized were venereal.

A soldier's terms and conditions of service, unless he were a devout member of a *military monastic order, have rarely demanded of him a life of abstinence and celibacy. Some believe that soldiers noted for their strong religious beliefs had a lower incidence of STDs, but until fairly recent times all armies were fertile cultures for infections and contagions of all types. The concentration of so many men and *camp followers promoted the outbreaks of cholera, diphtheria, dysentery, typhoid fever, typhus, bubonic plague—and venereal diseases.

Because the first outbreaks coincided with it, most medical authorities believe that syphilis was introduced to Europe upon the return of Columbus's first expedition to America where they had left smallpox in exchange. However, it may have existed in a less virulent form for centuries and been confused with leprosy At a time when many did not even understand the relationship between sexual intercourse and procreation, it can be of no surprise that the link between the sexual act and diseases transmitted through it was not fully realized. This lack of understanding allowed such diseases to flourish unchecked and, in certain cases, reach endemic proportions.

The first recorded outbreak was in Naples in 1495, whence it spread rapidly across Europe. The virulence of this outbreak argues strongly that, was a new disease attacking a population lacking antibodies. The new 'malady' infected the invading army of France's Charles VIII and was just one of the significant consequences of the French *Italian wars. The French called it the Neapolitan disease while the latter referred to it as the French disease. What the *Swiss and the Spanish, not to mention the papal, forces called it is unknown but probably unprintable. The tendency to attribute unsafe or at least unsavoury sexual practices to one's opponents in war is universal. So is the fact that the prospect of or relief from mortal danger alike increase the desire to fornicate.

Despite the appalling and sometimes decisive *casualties that disease could inflict on armies, until the 19th century there was not much military *medicine could do to treat them. Prevention was the only option available and the more enlightened military commanders enforced essential hygiene procedures. The better organized and disciplined armies invariably suffered the least. Measures such as collective field cooking and proper sanitary arrangements remain little changed to date, and much of what is now taken for granted, with regard to the principles of hygiene, was pioneered by the military.

The special problem posed by STDs was not so much that they were a source of ribald mockery from one's fellows, but that such treatments as were available included putting a red-hot needle up the urethra. Consequently there was a very low probability of an infected individual reporting it to higher authority. Although Casanova is reputed to have used a condom made of sheep's gut and tied with a ribbon, the general application of that approach to prevention had to await technological advances in the field of elastic materials. Until then, prophylaxis could only be practised by militarizing prostitution. Thus the French and Italians created military brothels under medical supervision (French field brothels endured the siege of *Dien Bien Phu), as did the German army with red lights for other ranks' and blue lights for officers' brothels. In WW I the British army experimented with brothels staffed with medically inspected prostitutes: one at Rouen accommodated 171,000 men in the first year, with only 248 reported cases of VD. In WW II, the British and Americans were more strait-laced, compounding their folly by placing civilian brothels out of bounds, making the contraction of STDs a chargeable offence, or worse still threatening to treat it as a self-inflicted wound. The result was that their soldiers often refused to report infection even after effective treatment became available and their armed forces suffered a higher number of venereal casualties than their continental equivalents. *Montgomery was once reprimanded for recommending the application of common sense, and no US general dared to do so.

Only relatively recent advances in medical science, especially with regard to chemical therapies, coupled with wider health awareness and improved personal hygiene, have done much to improve the lot of both soldier and civilian alike. The spirochaete responsible for syphilis was only isolated in 1905 by the German zoologist Fritz Schaudinn. In 1906 the German bacteriologist August von Wassermann developed the first blood reaction diagnostic test and in 1909 the German bacteriologist Paul Ehrlich discovered the first effective treatment: the arsenic-containing compound Salvarsan. It was only in 1943 that the antibiotic penicillin was shown to be highly effective and it is still the preferred treatment in the battle against both syphilis and gonorrhoea.

However, in *Vietnam penicillin-resistant strains emerged and today STDs that do not respond to antibiotics (including AIDS) are among the most dangerous health problems facing soldiers of all nations. Pre-service and in-theatre screening, counselling from army *chaplains and medical officers, and the free issue of condoms, disinfectants, and antiseptics are all measures which appear to have only limited effectiveness. The main problem remains human nature. In Joseph Heller's novel *Catch-22*, Capt Yossarian USAAF, the central character, is hospitalized after being brought down by 'a burst of clap while on a low-level mission over a WAC' (member of the Women's Army Corps). The pun is improved if one understands that the title refers to the fact that anyone who does not wish to fly missions and risk death or injury by flak is clearly sane, hence compelled to continue flying, while anyone who likes to fly such missions is clearly insane, therefore likely to be grounded. A 'love wound' incurred in a low-threat encounter leading to hospitalization in relatively comfortable surroundings and away from immediate danger is not unattractive to a reluctant serviceman.   PMacD

Vercingetorix (d. 46 BC), the chieftain who interrupted *Caesar's conquest of Gaul by uniting his tribe, the Arverni, with other *Gallic tribes in revolt in 52 BC. Taking advantage of the tribesmen's superior knowledge of their home terrain, he was able to wage an effective *guerrilla war against the Romans. For reasons unknown he decided to concentrate his forces at *Alesia (now Alise-Sainte-Reine), permitting Julius to crush the uprising in an epic siege. He surrendered and after being exhibited in chains during Caesar's triumph (46 BC) in Rome he was strangled.   RTF

Verdun, battle of (1916). In terms of casualties and the sheer suffering of combatants, Verdun has good claim to being one of the most terrible battles of history. The little town of Verdun lies in a circle of hills where the main road to Paris crosses the river Meuse. The Germans took it after a long siege in 1870, and in the 1880s it became a keystone of the new Franco-German frontier. Its forts were modernized before 1914, but the destruction of the *Liège forts encouraged the French to remove most of their guns. By 1915 Verdun formed a quiet salient jutting into German lines.

Late in 1915 the German CGS *Falkenhayn decided to attack Verdun. He later claimed that he selected a spot of such importance that the French would have to 'throw in every man they have. If they do so the forces of France will bleed to death'. However, no original copy of this memorandum survives. It is possible that he sought to justify a lost battle, and that he either meant to take Verdun or hoped that by attacking there, where it would be easiest to supply his gunners with shells, he would unbalance the Allied armies and open the way for an offensive elsewhere.

The state of Verdun's defences alarmed not only Gen Herr, its governor, but also Lt Col *Driant, a parliamentarian commanding two *chasseur battalions in the Bois des Caures on the right bank of the Meuse. A commission was

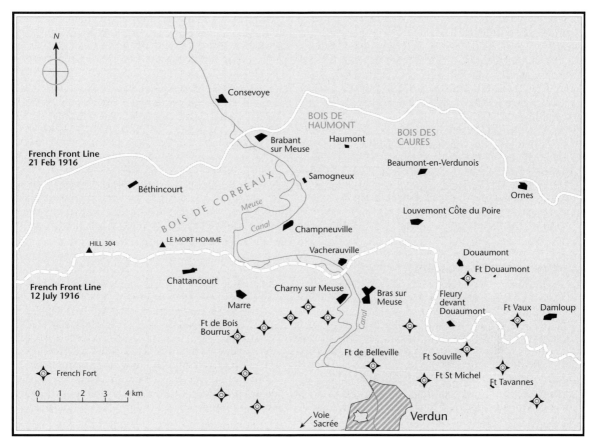

Verdun, 1916.

sent to Verdun as a result of Driant's protests, but *Joffre, the French C-in-C, angrily dismissed its findings.

Bad weather forced the German Fifth Army under Crown Prince Wilhelm of Prussia to delay its attack until 21 February. It began with a carefully orchestrated bombardment in which some guns reached out to destroy distant targets while others knocked out batteries and smashed infantry positions. When the infantry went forward of the right bank that afternoon they made good progress everywhere save in the Bois des Caures. Driant was killed when it fell the next day, and soon the German tide was lapping against the ridge crowned by Douaumont, strongest of Verdun's forts. It fell to a small detachment of Brandenburg *grenadiers on the 25th, its caretaker garrison unreinforced after a crucial order went astray.

Joffre decided that Second Army would be sent to hold Verdun, and his deputy, *Castelnau, went to see things for himself. Gen Philippe *Pétain a big, wintry infantryman, close to retirement when the war broke out, was given command. Castelnau suggested that he should be ordered to hold both banks of the Meuse—a withdrawal from the right had been considered—and Pétain set up his head-

quarters at Souilly on the Bar-le-Duc road late on the 25th. Next morning he awoke with pneumonia, but had put in train the techniques which saved Verdun: no more costly counter-attacks, and the use of artillery to take the strain. The Bar-le-Duc road became an artery pumping lifeblood into Verdun. In the week beginning 28 February 190,000 men and 25,000 tons of supplies passed along it, and troops worked almost shoulder-to-shoulder to keep it open. It richly deserved its title 'la Voie Sacrée' (the Sacred Way).

Checked on the right bank, in March the Germans attacked on the left. In April they assaulted both banks at the same time, and though they took the heights of the Mort Homme and Hill 304 on the left, there was no breakthrough. The importance of artillery observation gave new emphasis to the war in the air, and above the battlefield fighters struggled for a superiority eventually won by the French.

Losses were now so serious that the crown prince would have discontinued the attack had he not been pressed to continue. There were also divisions in the French leadership, and in April Pétain was promoted away and replaced by Gen Robert Nivelle. The Germans launched more attacks. On 7 June they took little Fort Vaux after a heroic defence, and in July a final burst took them momentarily to the top of Fort Souville, within sight of Verdun. But they could not continue: on 1 July the Allies attacked on the Somme, and on 23 August Falkenhayn was dismissed. That autumn the French retook the lost ground, and Nivelle's recapture of Douaumont on 24 October marked him as the army's rising star.

We cannot be sure of casualties, but each side lost more than 300,000, the French rather more than the Germans. Verdun epitomized the dogged defence of French soil against the invader: Pétain's slogan 'Ils ne passeront pas' (They shall not pass) enjoyed wide and lasting currency.
RH

Denizot, Alain, *Verdun 1914–1918* (Paris, 1996).
Horne, Alistair, *The Price of Glory: Verdun 1916* (London, 1962).

vertical take-off and landing (VTOL). One of the most significant failings of the *helicopter is the high power level required to sustain lift, which in consequence limits that available for forward thrust. In view of this a number of initiatives were undertaken to develop a so-called 'convertiplane' which would be able to convert its available power to horizontal thrust once airborne. Such a weapon would offer the tactical and operational flexibility of the helicopter alongside the high performance of the fixed-wing aircraft. A distinction should be made between VTOL and its cousin STOL (short take-off and landing). The latter was intended as an independent development in aircraft design that would maximize wing lift to enhance short take-off capability. WW II *reconnaissance and artillery-spotting STOL aircraft, such as the Fieseler Storch and the Piper Grasshopper, were able to operate close to the front line and were little hindered by operating conditions that would have flummoxed conventional aircraft. Modern STOL aircraft such as the De Havilland Canada DHC series offer much-enhanced capability.

However, VTOL, which by way of a by-product also provides STOL capability, has proved a more significant *air power development. Early VTOL designs during WW II were based on the 'tail sitter' concept. These aircraft were pulled into the air nose first by a large propeller and when airborne would level out into horizontal flight, thus using all power for upwards and then forward movement. However, these designs were hindered by the inadequate propeller thrust for vertical lift, especially when landing. The major breakthrough came with the advent of the turbojet, which provided sufficient thrust to push much heavier loads into the air.

The first jet lift aircraft was the famous 'flying Bedstead' of 1953, a curious experimental piece which used two horizontally facing turbojets to provide lift by deflecting the force downwards by special plates. Movement was controlled by downward-pointing nozzles which could be dir-

ected by the pilot. By 1957 Shorts had produced the SC.1 which was powered by five specially designed turbojets, four for vertical thrust and one for horizontal flight. The SC.1, however, had to shut down most of its power (the four downward-facing jets) when switching to forward flight, and it was not until the development of the vectored thrust system that true high-performance VTOL aircraft emerged. This innovation allowed the downward-thrusting jets to be turned to face the rear thus providing high-performance forward thrust.

The development programme which was to culminate in the famous Hawker Siddeley Harrier dated back to the 1950s, but its forerunner, the P.1127, first flew in 1960 and this was superseded by the Kestrel. The Harrier's ability to operate away from vulnerable airfields was a major factor in initially eliciting military support, though by the time the first Harriers went into service in 1969 this had become less of an issue and the aircraft was developed as a close support and reconnaissance aircraft to which its attributes were naturally well suited. The USA ordered the aircraft for the Marine Corps and McDonnell Douglas later acquired the production rights and went on to sell the type to Spain. In the late 1970s the inherent flexibility of the Harrier resulted in it being adopted by naval forces. The Royal Navy adopted the Harrier in the FRS1 version and both this and the RAF ground-attack version proved their worth in the *Falklands war. The Harrier allowed effective jet combat aircraft to be operated from much smaller aircraft carriers than hitherto, adding still further to the reputation of the aircraft's military flexibility. The Soviet navy noted the advantages of V/STOL naval aircraft and developed the Yak-36 Forager, a very similar aircraft to the Harrier.

There have been many other VTOL designs, but none has thus far been developed to the same degree as the Harrier. The French Dassault company attempted to develop a VTOL version of the Mirage which would have been capable of Mach 2 speeds, but this was abandoned. The German Dornier company attempted to develop a large military VTOL transport aircraft, the Do 31, in the late 1960s but this again failed. However, Boeing and Lockheed Martin are currently developing designs for the British and American Joint Strike Fighter (JSF) which will be equipped with vectored thrusting jets and may well mirror the Harrier's capabilities. In financial terms the fighter programme is already the largest in history at over $100 billion.   JDB

Davies, Peter, and Thornborough, Anthony, *The Harrier Story* (London, 1996).

veterans is a term more used in the USA than in Britain to describe people who have served in the armed forces. The USA celebrates 11 November (*Armistice Day in Britain and the Commonwealth) as Veterans' Day to honour all men and women who have served in the US armed forces, without implying that they have seen active service.

Those who have are to be found in the organizations called VFW (veterans of foreign wars). In Britain, the term 'ex-service' is used to denote a person who has served in the armed forces and 'veterans' refers only to those who have been involved in campaigns. In battles through the ages, the numbers and deployment of veterans—that is, soldiers with previous combat experience—has very often been the deciding factor, but the focus of this entry is on what happened to them afterwards.

In the ancient world, a veteran did not necessarily have a special status within society. Military service in ancient Greece was seen as a mark of manhood as all free men were required to serve their city state. Thus veterans were neither unusual nor considered different to other citizens. Roman noblemen considered successful service with the army as an important route for a political career and imperial Rome, with its standing army of Legions, did accord veterans a special status after serving their statutory 30 years. Completion of service in the army could confer the rights of citizenship on the veterans and such old soldiers were often settled on farms in border regions where they were expected to provide stability to the area.

Throughout the Dark and Middle Ages, veterans did not expect or receive special treatment, but ex-soldiers with military experience could have an influence upon their societies. In the 1450s and 1460s, the large numbers of veterans of the *Hundred Years War who returned to England had a destabilizing effect on the country and provided a ready supply of fighting men during the Wars of the *Roses.

The same destabilizing effect was felt in Europe during the *French wars of religion and the *Thirty Years War in the 17th century. However, the English parliament's treatment of the *New Model Army after the *British civil wars provides the clearest example of the problems for veterans in peacetime. With the war over, parliament had no need for the army and no longer wished to pay the large sums necessary to keep the army together. This caused enormous resentment among the soldiers who demanded better treatment from the government and was instrumental in provoking the army's intervention in politics. Governments have invariably been suspicious of veterans as men trained for war who seem to have no place in a more settled society once the firing stops. As Kipling wrote later in *Tommy* (see ATKINS, TOMMY):

'It's Tommy this, an' Tommy that, an' "Chuck him out, the brute!"
But it's "Saviour of 'is country" when the guns begin to shoot.'

The development of proper standing armies in the latter part of the 17th century brought about a minor change in the status of veterans. Most European monarchs set up military *hospitals to care for veterans of exceptional service and loyalty. *Louis XIV of France established the Hôtel des *Invalides while Charles II established the *Royal Hospital Chelsea for old soldiers and the Greenwich Hospital for old sailors in Britain.

However, the fate of most veterans during the 18th and 19th centuries was to be returned to an unsympathetic civilian society with no assistance from the government. After the *Napoleonic wars, the large numbers of men discharged from the services caused the British government much alarm in a period of radical discontent, while the clamour of veterans of his Grande Armée was a major factor in Napoleon's decision to attempt to regain his throne in 1815 during the *Hundred Days.

The aftermath of the *American civil war saw the development of some of the first powerful veterans' organizations. The *Grand Army of the Republic, established in 1866, became a strident voice within the Republican Party until the turn of the century. By 'waving the bloody shirt' the Grand Army of the Republic demanded generous pensions for war veterans and often swung the outcome of elections in the northern states. Although not limited to Confederate veterans, the Ku Klux Klan also picked at the scabs of the civil war, much to the detriment of the social and political development of the South.

However, it was WW I, involving as it did millions of men who fought for their nations and wider ideals, which really altered the status of veterans within societies across the world. The veterans' organizations established after 1918 derived great strength from the huge numbers of veterans demobilized, and the great sacrifices made by each nation's manhood made it difficult for governments to ignore the many grievances of veterans on their return to a bleak post-war world.

Thus, the inter-war period saw the first mass organizations of veterans. In the USA the American Legion, formed in 1919 by veterans who had fought in France, became a powerful political voice for the fair treatment of returned soldiers. The same was true in France of a number of competing organizations, all of which demanded better treatment for French veterans. The British Legion was founded in 1921 out of a number of rival organizations and, although it never became as powerful politically as its sister organizations in Canada, Australia, or New Zealand, it nevertheless became a major social movement which worked for the unemployed and disabled veterans, widows, and orphans left as a result of the war. The British Legion enshrined, as did all veterans' organizations worldwide, the comradeship which soldiers had felt during their service and worked to increase the meagre pensions allotted to veterans after the war.

The British Legion adopted the Flanders poppy as the symbol for its main fund-raising event, thus the anniversary of the Armistice became Poppy Day, and this meant that the organization became intimately connected with the rituals of remembrance, the powerful emotional response of remembering the sacrifice and loss of WW I. Many pilgrimages to the battlefield *memorials and *cemeteries of the war were organized by veterans' groups as one way to come to terms with the grief caused by war. In

Australia and New Zealand, veterans' organizations play a crucial role in *Anzac Day, which remembers the contribution of their countries' troops in the two world wars.

However, it was German and Italian veterans' movements after WW I which had the greatest influence on world events. Italian fascism began among dissatisfied Italian veterans, and Benito *Mussolini used their support for his dramatic 'March on Rome' in 1922 when he seized power. In Weimar Germany, veterans' groups assumed considerable political importance, with the right-wing Stalhelm and republican Reichsbanner both contributing to the increasing political violence within the country. *Hitler derived a great deal of strength from disaffected WW I veterans and the Nazis used the idea of the *Frontkampfer* (a veteran who has been at the front) as a powerful political rallying cry.

One of the most idealistic elements of veterans' organizations after WW I was their belief in the idea of the 'Brotherhood of the Trenches'. Many veterans believed that all soldiers who had fought in the war—even on opposing sides—shared a special bond and could work together for peace to ensure that such a terrible war never happened again. While the many meetings between veteran movements in the 1930s did not secure world peace, the idea of a special bond between fighting men is still a powerful concept even today.

After WW II, the importance of the special needs of veterans was recognized in proper planning for the reintegration of fighting men back into society. The *GI Bill in the USA was the most famous of such programmes which offered veterans job training, education, grants for businesses, and other help in establishing a stable civilian life. Similar measures enacted in Britain and elsewhere proved that veterans had become an important factor in government planning. Unfortunately the Veterans' Administration in the USA became a byword for corruption and inhumanity only rivalled by the bureau set up to deal with the Native Americans, which had a head start of nearly a century.

The treatment of *Vietnam veterans demonstrated that the traditional suspicion of returned soldiers could still assert itself. Soldiers from this war were neither deployed nor returned home en masse, as their fathers and grandfathers had been, thus deliberately reducing the possibility of politically embarrassing action. This worked even better than planned, as the returning veterans absorbed much of the indiscriminate hostility from a civilian population disaffected by the war. The ostracism of the Vietnam veterans by government and people alike remains among the most unsavoury episodes in US history.

Many veterans of the *Gulf war have had to fight to gain recognition of the serious medical problems they have suffered as a result of 'Gulf War Syndrome' which covers a wide range of symptoms and has yet to be properly explained but may well be a result of prophylactic injections given in preparation for *chemical and biological warfare.

Veterans today can still find reintegration into civilian society a long and hard process but the organizations established after WW I are still very active and can offer much-needed support to returning soldiers.　　　　NB

Dearing, Mary, *Veterans in Politics: The Story of the G.A.R.* (Baton Rouge, La., 1952).

Diehl, James, *Paramilitary Politics in Weimar Germany* (London, 1977).

Wootton, Graham, *The Official History of the British Legion* (London, 1956).

Vickers machine gun This .303 inch calibre machine gun was used by Britain from 1912 until the 1960s. Water-cooled and mounted for land use on a tripod, it was based on an original design by Hiram *Maxim. A heavy, slow-firing weapon (450 rounds per minute) it was used (lightened and air-cooled) on aircraft during WW I, and more widely on ships, in tanks or trains, and in an anti-aircraft role. It was manufactured by Vickers' Sons and Maxim (later Vickers-Armstrong Ltd) and in Royal Ordnance factories.　　　　SCW

Hogg, Ian V., and Weeks, John, *Military Small Arms of the 20th Century* (London, 1985).

Vicksburg campaign (1863). Vicksburg was the last major Confederate stronghold on the Mississippi whose capture on 4 July, Independence Day and the day after *Gettysburg, marked the turning point of the *American civil war. The terrain along the 120 mile (193 km) stretch between 'the Gibraltar of the West' and Port Hudson to the south made it an appallingly difficult gap to close. Against competent defence, it might have been impossible.

Although Confederate forces in the theatre were numerically superior, they were widely scattered and their leadership was Byzantine. *Johnston was the nominal theatre C-in-C, but lacked the confidence of Pres Jefferson *Davis and did nothing to deserve it, refusing to exercise coordinating authority even when pressed to do so. By contrast, Davis had a blind spot for the many failings of Pemberton at Vicksburg and *Bragg in Tennessee, who were disesteemed by nearly everyone else.

This does not detract from the pragmatic genius of *Grant. During winter manoeuvres he learned from cavalry raids around his rear that he could survive without lines of supply. This was a key calculation in his 1863 offensive, immediately preceded by a massively disruptive cavalry raid through Mississippi. With forces out of Baton Rouge threatening Port Hudson and *Sherman making a demonstration from the north, Grant crossed to the western bank with 40,000 men and marched 30 miles (48 km) south of Vicksburg. There a flotilla that had run the gauntlet of Vicksburg's guns transported him back over the mile-wide (1.6 km) river. Once Sherman rejoined him, Confederate forces were defeated in detail, preventing Pemberton's

32,000 from linking up with Johnston's 7,000, driving the latter out of Jackson and the former into Vicksburg. Early assaults failed, but after 48 days the garrison *capitulated on *parole, to spread word of the defeat, followed five days later by Port Huron. A delighted *Lincoln commented: 'The Father of Waters again goes unvexed to the sea.' HEB

Victor, Marshal Claude Victor, Duc de Bellune

(1766–1841). Born Claude Victor Perrin, son of a bailiff, Victor served in the ranks of the royal army, earning the nickname 'Le Beau Soleil' (Handsome Sun) before leaving in 1791 to become a grocer. Re-enlisting almost at once, he distinguished himself at the siege of Toulon, where he attracted the notice of *Napoleon, and was a brigadier general within three years. Although Victor fought well at Marengo, he languished in unimportant appointments until 1807, when his performance as a corps commander at Friedland earned him his baton. He spent the next three years in Spain, and was not amused when Napoleon made him duc de Bellune (Handsome Moon) in punning reference to his nickname. He covered Napoleon's withdrawal across the Berezina in 1812. Dismissed but then recalled to command the Guard, Victor was wounded at Craonne in 1814. He did not join Napoleon for the *Hundred Days, but served the Bourbons until 1830. RH

Vienna, sieges of (1529, 1683).

The Ottoman sultan *Suleiman 'the Magnificent' defeated and killed Louis II of Hungary at *Mohacs in August 1526, and again invaded Hungary in 1528–9, adding the greater part of that realm to the Ottoman empire. He then went on to besiege the Habsburg capital Vienna and ravaged its suburbs (27 September–15 October 1529), but the early onset of winter plus lack of supplies and armaments compelled him to lift the siege and return to Istanbul.

Vienna was not threatened again until 1683, when Sultan Mehmet IV's Grand Vizier Kara Mustafa Pasha besieged it (14 July–12 September), but a staunch defence plus the timely arrival of Jan Sobieski (later *John III of Poland) with a relieving force compelled the Turks to retire, and the vizier paid for his failure with his life. This second and last siege marks the apogee of Ottoman success in central Europe, and Turkish power now began slowly to recede in the Balkans. CEB

Barker, Thomas M., *Double Eagle and Crescent: Vienna's Second Turkish Siege and its Historical Setting* (Albany, NY, 1967).
Coles, Paul H., *The Ottoman Impact on Europe* (London, 1968).
Stoye, John, *The Siege of Vienna* (London, 1964).

Vietnam war

refers to the US political and military continuation of the French Campaign in *Indochina that followed the signing of the 1954 Geneva agreements, which divided Vietnam along the 17th Parallel, and which ended when the People's Army of Vietnam (PAVN) occupied Saigon on 30 April 1975. A continuation of the Vietminh's effort to free Vietnam from foreign domination, this isolated conflict was slowly transformed into the bloodiest battleground of the *Cold War.

Following the Geneva accords, relative calm descended on Vietnam. In Hanoi, the Vietminh, who had come under the control of the Vietnamese Lao Dong (Communist) Party by the time of the French defeat, consolidated their power under the leadership of *Ho Chi Minh, collectivized agriculture in the north (which sparked a bloodily suppressed peasant uprising in 1956), and debated how to gain control of South Vietnam. In Saigon Bao Dai, the French-backed emperor, was deposed in a referendum by the US-supported Ngo Dinh Diem in late 1955. Diem, a Catholic in a predominantly Buddhist country, was a committed anti-communist. Bolstered by increasing economic and covert aid from the USA, Diem launched an anti-communist sweep of South Vietnam. By the late 1950s, the hard-pressed Vietminh cadres who had remained in the South, derisively dubbed Vietcong by Diem, appealed to Hanoi for reinforcement and greater support.

Although Hanoi had ordered the formation of Vietcong military units in the Mekong Delta as early as 1957, North Vietnamese leaders debated if the time was ripe to intervene more directly in the South. At a May 1959 meeting of the Lao Dong Party, they decided to support 'armed revolution' against Saigon: 4,500 'regroupees' (a southern communist cadre who had come to North Vietnam following the Geneva accords) began to stream down the 'Ho Chi Minh Trail' between North and South Vietnam to help form Vietcong units. In December 1960, Hanoi announced the creation of the National Liberation Front (NLF), a collection of southern groups opposing the Diem regime, to bolster the North Vietnamese contention that the revolt against Saigon was an indigenous movement.

This reversed the military situation and by the early 1960s Saigon was under enormous pressure. Diem's campaign against the communists increasingly was directed against all political dissent, bringing local and US calls for him to reform his government. In November 1960, Diem narrowly avoided being overthrown in a military coup. Vietcong terrorist incidents against the regime surged. In 1959 the Vietcong killed about 1,200 government representatives, in 1961 this had risen to 4,000. Vietcong units also began inflicting a string of defeats on the Army, Republic of Vietnam (ARVN). Diem, who generally turned to family members for their political reliability, now relied increasingly on his brother Ngo Dinh Nhu to eliminate political opposition.

The Ngos overstepped the bounds of US patience in 1963 when they forcefully suppressed a series of Buddhist protests against their regime. Madame Ngo Dinh Nhu's characterization of a Buddhist monk's self-immolation as a 'barbecue show' only increased the Kennedy administration's disenchantment with Diem. The Ngos had undertaken a delicate balancing act between receiving enormous quantities of US economic and military aid to the *civil power (15,000 US military advisers were in South Vietnam at the end of 1963) while resisting what they perceived as US meddling in South Vietnamese affairs. By 1963 many officials in the Kennedy administration had come to perceive Diem and his brother Nhu as obstructionists. The US diplomatic mission in Saigon gave tacit approval to, if it did not actually orchestrate, a November 1963 *coup d'état* that resulted in the assassination of Ngo Dinh Diem and Ngo Dinh Nhu.

The coup caught Hanoi by surprise, but the removal of Diem, recognized as a nationalist throughout Vietnam, invited further North Vietnamese intervention. After his murder, Saigon was rocked by a series of military coups, which produced political instability and battlefield lethargy. Hanoi quickly capitalized on this opportunity: by the end of 1964, Vietcong units had been organized into division-size formations and entire PAVN regiments had infiltrated into South Vietnam. As Vietcong/PAVN activity spread, more US personnel became casualties in the conflict. On 3 February 1964, the Vietcong attacked the US advisers' compound in Kontum City. On 7 February, a bomb blew up in a Saigon theatre, killing three Americans. In May, the USS *Card* was sunk by Vietcong *commandos in a Saigon harbour. In November, the Vietcong attacked the US airbase at Bien Hoa and on 24 December they claimed credit for a bombing at the Brinks Hotel in Saigon where US officers were billeted.

A controversial incident in the *Gulf of Tonkin would have a profound impact on the war. Early in the morning of 2 August 1964, the US destroyer *Maddox*, while patrolling along North Vietnamese territorial waters, was attacked by three North Vietnamese torpedo boats. The *Maddox* returned fire and was quickly supported by aircraft from the USS *Ticonderoga*. During the night of 4 August, the *Maddox*, now joined by the destroyer *C. Turner Joy*, initially reported a renewed attack, although officers at the scene quickly determined that the North Vietnamese vessels were nowhere to be found and that inexperienced crewmen had simply responded to sonar and *radar anomalies. The Johnson administration, uninterested in validating initial reports and indifferent to the probability that Hanoi might have been responding to South Vietnamese amphibious attacks (30–1 July OPLAN 34A raids) against the North Vietnamese coast, ordered retaliatory air strikes against the torpedo-boat base at Vinh. The Johnson administration also gained congressional approval for increased US military action in South-East Asia. Although critics have long believed that the Johnson administration manipulated public and congressional sentiment by not divulging complete details of the incident, the Gulf of Tonkin Resolution provided the administration with carte blanche to take military action to defend US personnel and interests in South-East Asia.

By 1965, the nature of the war was changing. No longer just a Vietcong effort to overthrow the Saigon regime through a 'People's war', the conflict became a deadlock between the USA and North Vietnam, which was backed by its Soviet and Chinese allies. Hanoi hoped that the USA would not resist a PAVN invasion of South Vietnam; while Washington hoped that Ho Chi Minh and his followers would be deterred by a demonstration of US military might. The 7 February 1965 Vietcong attack on the US airbase at Pleiku prompted US retaliatory air raids against North Vietnam (FLAMING DART); on 13 February Pres Johnson ordered a 'program of measured and limited air action', against North Vietnam, which came to be known as ROLLING THUNDER.

To protect the US airbase at Da Nang from Vietcong retaliation for US air strikes against North Vietnam, the Johnson administration dispatched two battalions of US Marines to guard the base. More US troops soon followed, initially to protect other US installations, but US military commanders viewed this initial 'enclave' strategy as ineffective. On 27 June 1965, Gen *Westmoreland, Commander of the US Military Assistance Command, Vietnam (MACV), ordered the first US offensive ground operation of the war. The 'Big-Unit war' had begun.

As US troops streamed into the country, Westmoreland faced his first major challenge: preventing the collapse of South Vietnam and a successful PAVN occupation of the northern sections of the country. In November 1965, the battle was joined in the Ia Drang valley in the Western Highlands, a hard-won victory for the US 1st Cavalry Division. As US troop strength grew, Westmoreland went on the offensive. Launching a series of large-scale 'Search and Destroy' operations, US and Allied forces targeted Vietcong operating bases. Vietcong and PAVN units often managed to evade Allied forces by fading into Cambodian and Laotian sanctuaries, but continuous attacks took their toll, especially on Vietcong forward-supply bases.

By mid-1967, the war had reached a turning point and officers at MACV began to proclaim 'light at the end of the tunnel'. US *attrition objectives were being achieved: Vietcong and PAVN units were apparently losing more forces in South Vietnam than could be replaced through *recruitment or infiltration. Policy-makers in Hanoi also came to the conclusion that the war was stalemated and that battlefield trends were not in their favour. In response, they called for a 'Tong Cong Kich, Tong Khai Nghia' (General Offensive, General Uprising). Known in the USA as the *Tet offensive, because it occurred during the celebration of the Chinese lunar New Year, the countrywide attacks were intended to spark an insurrection among South Vietnamese civilians and military forces, destroying the Saigon regime. The North Vietnamese hoped to leave US forces isolated along the South Vietnamese border, forcing the Johnson administration to negotiate an end to the war. Hanoi even planned to re-enact the siege of *Dien Bien Phu; by January

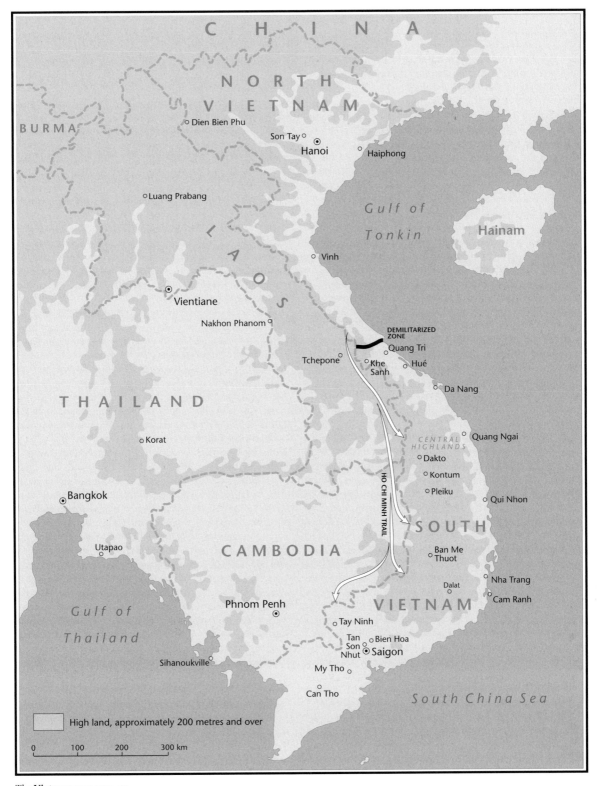

The **Vietnam war**, 1959–75.

1968, 40,000 PAVN soldiers were laying siege to the firebase at Khe Sanh and its garrison of 7,000 US Marines.

The Tet attacks failed to prompt a southern uprising and military mutiny. With the exception of the battles of Saigon and Hué, Allied forces quickly repelled attacking Vietcong units. At Khe Sanh, the US Marines, supported by thousands of air sorties, stood firm and inflicted enormous casualties on PAVN. But the Tet offensive was a brilliant political success for Hanoi. Believing that progress was being made in the war, the Johnson administration and the US public were shocked by the scope and intensity of the offensive. On 31 March 1968, Lyndon Johnson announced that he would not seek re-election as his administration reassessed its policies toward South-East Asia.

Following Tet, US policy-makers became increasingly determined to devise an exit strategy that would not simply abandon South Vietnam to PAVN. In terms of diplomacy, US and North Vietnamese negotiators began meeting in Paris in May 1968, but their talks made little progress. On the battlefield, the Nixon administration implemented a policy, called 'Vietnamization', to bolster ARVN. The USA began turning the war over to ARVN while gradually withdrawing US combat troops from South Vietnam.

Vietnamization came none too soon. Domestic opposition to the war mounted in the aftermath of the Tet offensive, reaching a peak in May 1970 following a US-ARVN raid into Cambodia. Launched to buy time for Vietnamization by destroying PAVN base areas, the Cambodian raid sparked nationwide student protests and tragedy at Kent State University when four students were shot and killed by the Ohio National Guard. In South Vietnam, morale among US troops plummeted as soldiers became preoccupied by the prospect of becoming the last casualty in a war that was winding down. By 1971, over 7,000 troops in Vietnam faced charges related to heroin (out of a force that numbered about 225,000), insubordination, and *fragging incidents (attacks against officers and NCOs), and *courts martial soared. Vietnamization continued, but ARVN remained incapable of holding its own against PAVN: in spring 1971, ARVN launched Lam Son 719, a raid into Laos to destroy PAVN base areas, but was saved from disaster only by the massive use of US *air power. In the spring of 1972, during the so-called 'Easter-Offensive', Saigon was again saved from disaster by a massive US air effort. Although PAVN, which by now resembled a conventional military force complete with armoured vehicles and ample large-calibre artillery, suffered devastating casualties, it succeeded in bringing western portions of South Vietnam under complete communist control.

By late 1972, Hanoi and Washington, moved along by secret negotiations conducted by Henry *Kissinger and Le Duc Tho, were near agreement on a negotiated end to the fighting in South Vietnam. When South Vietnamese Pres Nguyen Van Thieu objected to several portions of the proposed agreement, particularly that North Vietnamese troops would be allowed to stay in South Vietnam, Hanoi began back-pedalling on previously settled issues. The Nixon administration, seeking to break this diplomatic impasse, informed the Thieu regime that the USA would sign the agreement; the only hope of continued US military support to Saigon was in response to Hanoi's violation of the peace accord. To persuade Hanoi, Nixon initiated LINEBACKER II, also known as the 'Christmas Bombing'. Although aircraft loses were significant, the USA dropped over 20,000 tons of bombs on the North between 18 and 29 December 1972, causing enormous damage and completely exhausting North Vietnam's air defences. This surge in military-diplomatic pressure finally produced agreement: ceasefire accords were formally signed in Paris on 27 January 1973. The Paris agreement turned out to be a short-lived *truce. Saigon forces collapsed in the face of an eight-week offensive launched by PAVN in March 1975. Americans, who had mostly come to the conclusion that US involvement in the war had been a mistake, were in no mood to intervene to prevent Hanoi's victory.

Military victory against the *total war waged by North Vietnam was only attainable with US economic and military *mobilization, but the decision was taken instead to sell the war in small increments. To minimize the political fallout, the National Guard was not engaged (except to put down domestic disorders) and the children of the influential were exempted from conscription. Secretary of Defense *McNamara devised a process of feeding troops in and rotating them out again as individuals, directly attacking unit cohesion and *esprit de corps*, while the military high command devalued the *honour of combat medals by awarding them to non-combatants, and put careerism ahead of combat effectiveness by allowing senior officers to 'ticket punch', that is to rotate in and out of combat commands too quickly to bond with their men or to lead them effectively. The impact of the *media was twofold, at once feeding domestic outrage at what was being done and demoralizing the troops in Vietnam by showing them the contempt with which *veterans were being treated back in 'the world'. In particular, the effect of live TV coverage of the race riots in the late 1960s on *African-American troops was devastating. And, as always, the promises of the air power enthusiasts proved over-optimistic. Bombing the jungle is possibly the least cost-effective form of warfare ever devised by man.

Twenty-five years after the fall of Saigon, much has changed in the world. Relations between reunited Vietnam and the USA are slowly improving, complicated by the issue of *MIAs but helped along by tension with China that briefly erupted into a shooting war in 1978. The USSR got into its own Vietnam in *Afghanistan and finally could no longer sustain the costs of the Cold War. In South-East Asia the dominos did not fall, although it was only the armed intervention of PAVN that put an end to the genocide of Pol Pot in Cambodia after it was hopelessly destabilized by the neighbouring war. There are 58,000 names inscribed on the immensely moving war *memorial in Washington, while over 2 million dead Vietnamese are largely forgotten. The US military has not yet come to terms with the loss of the war, preferring to nurture a 'stab in the back' explanation, but in due course it undertook a reformation of organization and *doctrine that was stunningly effective in the *Gulf war. Just as the full social and political significance of the *American civil war took nearly a century to be appreciated, it may well be that by the middle of the 21st century the Vietnam war will be seen to have been just as important a turning point in the development of the USA.   JJW

Herr, Michael, *Dispatches* (New York, 1991).

Herring, George, *America's Longest War* (New York, 1996).

Lewy, Gunter, *America in Vietnam* (Oxford, 1978).

Lind, Michael, *Vietnam: The Necessary War* (New York, 1999).

MacLean, Michael, *The Ten Thousand Day War* (New York, 1981).

Palmer, Dave R., *The Summons of the Trumpet* (Novato, Calif., 1978).

Vikings In 793, a group of Scandinavian warriors sacked the monastery at Lindisfarne, off the north-east coast of England, unleashing two and a half centuries of turmoil on western Europe. Scandinavia already had close ties with its North Sea neighbours: trade links were strong between Swedish, Danish, Frisian, and English merchants, and East Anglia may have had kings of Swedish origin. The wealth of western Europe eventually tempted some to take what they could not barter for.

The causes of the 'Viking Age' (in England, *c*.793–1066) are disputed but include such factors as a worsening climate in Scandinavia making agriculture more difficult; poor prospects at home for younger sons who stood to inherit little; a religion (see below) promoting aggressive self-reliance; political consolidation in Denmark and, later, Norway which uprooted many earls and their followers, whose only skills were in warfare. The technological breakthrough which made Viking raids possible was in shipbuilding; the typical Viking craft was a low, sleek, clinker-built vessel, designed with a prow at either end for rapid relaunching and fitted with a sail, but capable of being rowed (or even carried short distances overland) by its crew of between 40 and 60 men. In small groups they were fast enough to evade detection, to make a sudden raid from a beach landing and put out to sea again before land forces could be mustered against them. The decisive Viking advantage was the ability to make a sea-crossing without hugging the coasts, so maximizing the element of surprise.

The early raids were mostly hit-and-run attacks, but in 864–5 a Danish force (known as *se micla here*, 'the Great Army') decided to winter over in England. From this point on, the character of Viking activity changed: a more mature leadership saw the benefits of a settled life in the west over the perils of transporting plunder back to Denmark or Norway. The Vikings moved into the north-east of England,

Ireland, the Hebrides, and Orkneys as settlers, changing the political geography of these regions. At about this time, Norwegian adventurers discovered Iceland and within a few decades permanent settlements had been established. They also, of course, 'discovered' America 500 years before Columbus.

If fast-moving raiders were hard to deal with, warlords determined to overthrow the existing hierarchy and install themselves as leaders were even harder. The coasts of northern Europe were defended by a variety of measures. In France, bridges over navigable rivers were strengthened with towers at either end, and town defences were refurbished. Viking attacks destroyed one English kingdom after another until only Wessex survived in the south-west of the country. There, King Alfred (849–99) devised a system of *burh* strongholds which provided static points of defence for the countryside. He also reformed the pattern of military service to make better use of his resources and designed ships which could match those of his foes. After years of struggle, a treaty of 886–90 between King Alfred and the Danish leader Guðrum (d. 890) ceded the north and east of England to Danish control, an area known as the 'Danelaw'. It fell to Alfred's son, Edward (*c*.872–924), and grandson, Æðelstan (*c*.894–939), to recapture this territory also.

Viking control continued in Dublin and there was even a short-lived Scandinavian 'Kingdom of York' under the exiled Norwegian King Eirikr Blóðox ('Eric Bloodaxe') who was killed at Stainmoor, Yorkshire, in 954. In 911 Norsemen were granted territory on the coast of northern France where they set up a buffer state; this province of Normandy eventually proved a troublesome neighbour and, of course, the source of the last successful invasion of England 155 years later.

Viking interest was not confined to western Europe, and Swedes navigated the rivers draining into the eastern Baltic in search of trading opportunities and sources of silver, the principal medium of exchange. Viking kingdoms based on Novgorod and Kiev were established in the 10th century through trading contacts with the Slavs, although within a century the Swedish rulers had forsaken their separate identity and adopted Slavonic names and customs. The Slavs called these Scandinavians 'Rus', which may be the origin of the name 'Russia'. They also traded along the great rivers down to the Black Sea, and some enlisted as *mercenaries with the Byzantine emperor, providing him with the élite Varangian Guard. Others sailed through either around Spain or along the rivers of France to raid in the Mediterranean, forming a permanent settlement in Sicily. The archaelogical indicators that Vikings once cruised offshore are the watchtowers built along the coasts of Spain, France, and Italy by people anxiously looking out for their signature longships.

From the late 980s a fresh wave of raiding from Scandinavia hit western Europe; these were larger forces led by determined men such as Olaf Tryggvason (968–1000), later king of Norway. The English King Æðelred II Unræd (*c.*966–1016) (Ethelred 'the Unready') saw one of his best generals slain at *Maldon, Essex, in 991 and on the advice of his churchmen decided to buy the Vikings off. Taxes were raised to pay this 'Danegeld', but the payments only encouraged raiding by other groups. Thus began an ignominious period in English history during which the nation paid taxes to raise armies against itself. Æðelred went into exile in Normandy in 1013–14 with his Norman wife, Emma, leaving the country to the Danish leader, King Sven 'Forkbeard'. Æðelred's third son, Edmund Ironside, led a bold, determined, but ultimately unsuccessful resistance to Sven's son, Knut ('King Canute'), whose reign proved a period of reconstruction and consolidation.

The last great Viking leader must be Haraldr Harðráða (1016–66), sometime king of Norway and leader of the Byzantine emperor's Varangian Guard, whose invasion of the north of England was crushed by Harold (Godwinson) II's Saxons at Stamford Bridge, a battle that may have weakened them sufficiently to make the difference at *Hastings 21 days later against the Normans, themselves of Viking stock.

The size of Viking armies is difficult to assess; English sources refer for example to '250 ships', but there is no agreement as to what this means in terms of battlefield army size. A surviving Viking warship from Gokstad had provision for 32 oarsmen, but it is not clear whether this was the entire ship's company and, furthermore, what proportion of the crew would be non-combatants or watchmen to guard the craft. Were all the 250 vessels warships, or were some cargo vessels with a large hold and correspondingly less room for warriors? It seems safe to conclude that armies (better, ad hoc groupings) numbering some thousands could be assembled by charismatic leaders.

Viking techniques of warfare were in the mainstream Germanic tradition of mobile infantry engagements. Generally, Viking armies, whose main advantages were speed and surprise, avoided open battle, preferring the swift raid against a wealthy, unsuspecting target followed by orderly withdrawal. When reluctantly brought to battle, leaders used standard 'shieldwall' formations of front-rank men standing shoulder to shoulder with their *shields before them, wielding long (6–8 foot (1.8–2.4 metre)) thrusting spears to break up enemy formations as they advanced to within striking distance. Hostilities began with an exchange of missiles (arrows and throwing spears) followed by one side charging the other's line; if the defenders' shieldwall held, the attackers were beaten back onto their own second rank, while if the attackers broke through, the shieldwall fragmented into a series of isolated battle groups. A general mêlée followed, where confidence and determination must have been as important as skill at arms.

Body *armour and weapons were very personal items, and the wealthy chose them as much for display value as for technical effectiveness. Characteristic Viking hand weapons included swords, the slashing blades often of Rhenish workmanship, tapered and up to 3 feet (0.9 metre) in length; narrow, single-edged, sharply pointed knives; long-shafted, broad-bladed axes, and shorter, single-handed forms such as the 'bearded axe' (Norse *skeggox*). Shields were usually circular (occasionally kite-shaped), up to 3 feet (0.9 metre) in diameter, with a conical, central iron boss covering the hand. Viking warriors commonly used bows and arrows, as well as other missile weapons such as throwing-spears and axes. Armour consisted of a knee-length mailshirt, a helmet with faceplate, and iron-banded protection for forearms and lower legs (although these latter are only attested from the earlier Vendel period). Leather, hide, and fur garments formed a cheaper and warmer alternative—an important factor when crossing many miles of open sea.

An aspect of Norse society which contributed to the success of its warriors was its religious background. Much is made of the cult of Óðinn (Odin), the one-eyed master of death and magic whose handmaidens, the Valkyrjar (Valkyries), welcomed fallen warriors into his hall, Valhöll (Valhalla); worshippers of this god actively sought battle death, regarding anything less as unmanly. Devotees of Óðinn included the notorious *berserkir* and *ulfheðnir*, who fought unprotected except by bear- or wolf-skin respectively, without regard for personal safety. Impressive though these specialists were, the majority of Vikings were worshippers of Þórr (Thor) whose cult centred round the weather and the agrarian cycle. The irascible, red-bearded giant-killer protected men and their livelihoods against the savage elements of the northern winter; his hammer, Mjolnir, was a popular amulet and continued even into the period of contact with Christian belief. In time, Vikings gained knowledge of Christianity during their activities in the west and many accepted the 'White Christ' into their pantheon, but without abandoning their older gods.

For all the immense distances they covered and their qualities as warriors, the Vikings made no lasting cultural impact on western Europe and were ultimately absorbed into the host populations wherever they settled.   SJP

Foote, P., and Wilson, D. M., *The Viking Achievement* (London, 1970).

Vittorio Veneto, battle of (1918). Masterminded by Gen Alberto Díaz, this was the last offensive on the WW I *Italian front, mounted to assault the Austrian forces sitting astride the Piave river in north-east Italy. During the night of 26–7 October the Twelfth (Franco-Italian), Tenth (Anglo-Italian), and Eighth (Italian) Armies, totalling 41 divisions (22 forward, 19 in reserve), began to throw bridges across the Piave at eleven places. Engineers had earlier occupied a midstream island, but a heavy rise in the river had delayed the assault by 24 hours. The 33 Austrian divisions (23 in line with another 10 in reserve), formed into two armies and fought well in some places, though Tenth Army (two British and two Italian divisions) under the Earl of Cavan had advanced 2 miles (3.2 km) on a 4 mile (6.4 km) front by the 28th. This was the greatest success, as floodwater destroyed the bridges of Eighth and Twelfth Armies. Eventually the Eighth Army commander detached a corps to cross by the British bridges in the early hours of the 28th and manoeuvred around to clear the Eighth Army's front. By the close of 29 October the bridgehead for the three Allied armies measured 10 miles (16 km) wide and 4 miles (6.4 km) deep, a wedge had been driven between the Fifth and Sixth Austrian Armies, and 33,000 prisoners were taken. Now the attack began to yield results, as an Italian column took the town of Vittorio Veneto that evening. The Austrian withdrawal became a rout on 30 October, and senior Austrian commanders began requesting an armistice, which was eventually signed on 3 November, coming into force at 15.00 on the following day. Allied casualties amounted to over 35,000, but the final Austrian prisoner count alone was over half a million, full revenge for *Caporetto.   APC-A

Vlasov, Lt Gen Andrey Andreyevich (1900–46), Red Army officer with an exemplary pre-war career. He was one of the key defenders of *Moscow, before being made commander of the Second Shock Army on the Volkhov front and captured during the Volkhov encirclement. Enraged by what he saw as a betrayal, he lent his name to the formation of an anti-Stalinist Russian Liberation Movement recruited among fellow *POWs. This existed mainly for propaganda purposes and by the end of the war Vlasov was fighting against the Germans once more. He and his men tried to surrender to the Allies but were handed over to the Soviets. He was tried and hanged on 1 August 1946, but no such formality accompanied the executions of the men who had followed his lead.   CA/HEB

Andreyev, C., *Vlasov and the Russian Liberation Movement* (Cambridge, 1987).

voltigeurs (Fr.: *voltigeurs*, vaulters) were a type of French light infantry soldier. In the second half of the 18th century there had been various experiments with light infantry, and during the *French Revolutionary wars the French made good use of swarms of light infantry *tirailleurs moving ahead of heavy *columns. Like most European infantry, French line infantry battalions had two élite *flank companies, one each of *grenadiers and voltigeurs as well as a number of centre companies. Light infantry also had flank companies, though their grenadiers were known as carabiniers. There were full regiments of voltigeurs in Napoleon's Young Guard, their soldiers hoping for promotion into the *chasseurs of the Middle or Old Guard.

Commanding officers tried to select lithe, nimble men as voltigeurs, and might use them to screen the unit's front as it advanced or to skirmish in front of its line. They wore yellow embellishments, and both they and the grenadiers had fringes to their epaulettes. The French army retained voltigeurs until the abolition of flank companies in 1868, though by then the distinction between them and the centre companies was honorific rather than tactical.   RH

Voluntary Aid Detachment. See VAD.

Voroshilov, Marshal Kliment (1881–1969), senior Soviet state and party official. He joined the Communist Party in 1903 making him, along with *Stalin, one of the senior communist officials. He helped form Red Guard units before the November 1917 *Russian Revolution and commanded an army in the Russian civil war. In 1921–4 he commanded forces in the north Caucasus, rooting out *guerrilla opposition to the Soviet regime.

He was one of the first five *marshals of the USSR created in 1935 and one of only two (with Budenny) to survive into WW II, on the basis of dog-like devotion to Stalin. On the outbreak of war he was a member of the State Defence Committee (GKO) and was given the north-west 'strategic direction' in 1941, controlling multiple Fronts (army groups). As a former revolutionary, he found a more natural place as adviser to the *partizan movement and briefed *special forces commanders personally before their insertion behind enemy lines. He took part in the Tehran Conference (1943) and after the war was president of the Soviet control commission in Hungary. He became president of the USSR on Stalin's death, but Khrushchev forced him into retirement in 1960.   CDB

VTOL. See VERTICAL TAKE-OFF AND LANDING AIRCRAFT.

Vyazma-Bryansk, battle of (1941), vast battle of encirclement immediately preceding (October 1941) the great battle of *Moscow. The Soviet Western Front (army group) under Col-Gen Ivan *Koniev and the Reserve Front under Marshal Semyon Budenny attempted to prevent the German Army Group Centre breaking through towards Moscow and buy time for the build-up and concentration of reserves. The German attack began on 2 October, forcing back elements of Nineteenth, Twentieth, Twenty-fourth, and Thirty-second Soviet Armies and encircling them with elements of two other armies west of Vyazma. Third and Fourth Panzer Armies linked up on 7 October to form the Vyazma pocket. This great battle of encirclement continued until 23 October, with several attempts by the Soviets to break out. In three weeks the Germans netted 700,000 prisoners. However, the onset of the autumn rains and the need to clear the pockets, which kept fighting, slowed the German advance. Meanwhile, Guderian's Second Panzer Army, swinging up from the south, captured Orel on 3 October and Bryansk on 6 October. The resistance of the main Soviet forces on the Tula, Kalinin, and Mozhaisk defensive lines was equally stubborn, further slowing the German advance. Moscow was put under a 'state of siege' on 19 October and the remnants of the Western and Reserve Fronts were combined in one Front under *Zhukov.　　CDB

wagenburg A mobile fort assembled by drawing wagons into a defensive circle, like the Wild West wagon circle or the *Boer laager. The first references are from the time of Julius *Caesar, when the Helvetii and the German tribes are reported to have used them, the latter in 55 BC. Byzantine armies frequently used such a formation, and the Russians developed it to provide a defensible locality in the middle of the flat and featureless steppe, which they called the *gulai-gorod* ('running castle'). The Teutonic Knights also retreated into a wagenburg after their defeat at *Tannenberg in 1410. When *Zizka developed the technique for the *Hussites, it was not, therefore, a new idea, but in the period 1419 to 1435, when they held off three imperial Crusades against them, they improved it with specially built wagons which could be chained together. Sometimes used in combination with earthworks, the wagenburg proved highly effective against armoured cavalry. However, when different Hussite factions fought each other—the Utraquist Hussites allied with the Roman Catholics against the extreme Hussite Taborites—they both used the wagenburg, and the result was a very immobile battle. The wagenburg proved an excellent way of exploiting crossbows and handguns, but would not have lasted long in the face of the field artillery which appeared later. The technique was rediscovered by the white settlers in South Africa, where the Boers made laagers against the indigenous inhabitants, and in the American West. But once again, neither the *Zulus nor the *Plains Indians had artillery.   CDB

....

Wagram campaign (1809). By early 1808 the Austrians were anxious to reopen hostilities against France (see NAPOLEONIC WARS), though some leading figures like Archduke *Charles, effectively C-in-C, urged caution to give the army time to prepare. Although Napoleon was not surprised, he had troops tied down in Spain, and the Austrians moved faster than expected, invading Bavaria on 9 April. Napoleon reached Donauworth on the 17th to find his army widely spread. He planned to concentrate and then move against Charles's left flank and rear, but misjudged both Austrian strength and his corps commanders' ability to move quickly enough. On 20–2 April *Davout and Lefêbvre had the better of difficult fighting at Abensburg and Eckmühl, and Charles fell back through Ratisbon towards Bohemia. *Lannes took Ratisbon by storm, and Napoleon advanced on Vienna, which fell without a fight.

He now found himself facing Charles's army across the Danube east of Vienna, and knew that Austrian reinforcements were on their way. He determined to cross the river to deal with Charles, and took Lobau island to secure Aspern and Essling on the far bank. On 21 May Charles counter-attacked and after two days of bitter fighting the French fell back onto the island. Each side had lost more than 20,000 men: Lannes was among the dead.

Napoleon was badly shaken by *Aspern-Essling, but two months later renewed his attack, this time crossing the Danube from the eastern edge of Lobau island. Early on 5 July the French crossed and secured a bridgehead, and on the 6th fought the campaign's deciding battle around the village of Deutsch-Wagram. Napoleon rose brilliantly to the numerous crises of the day. Davout took the village of Markgrafneusiedl, key to the Austrian left, but when Macdonald attempted to roll up the Austrian right with a huge column his men were slaughtered. The French were too exhausted to pursue Charles when he fell back. The French lost at least 30,000 men and the Austrians rather more. An armistice was agreed on the 12th, and the peace treaty, signed on 14 October, was much to Austria's disadvantage.

RH

Epstein, Robert M., *Napoleon's Last Victory and the Emergence of Modern War* (Lawrence, Kan. 1994).

Wakefield, battle of (1460), an early battle of the Wars of the *Roses. Based at Pontefract, the Lancastrian army under command of Henry Beaufort, Duke of Somerset, and Henry Percy, Earl of Northumberland, were half-heartedly besieging the Yorkists, under Henry VI's son Richard Plantagenet, Duke of York, and grandson Edmund, who were bottled up in Sandal castle. Richard and Edmund were enticed into an ambush on 10 December, possibly by Lancastrians masquerading as Yorkist troops, and both were killed in the battle and subsequent pursuit. Edmund's brother Edward (killed at Tewkesbury in 1471) succeeded as duke of York to lead the Yorkist cause.   APC-A

Walcheren campaigns (1809, 1944). This diamond-shaped island about 9 miles (14.5 km) in each direction lies on the northern edge of the Scheldt estuary, jutting out into the North Sea, and dominates all shipping moving in and out of the port of Antwerp. Much of Walcheren is below sea level, and a protective rim of sea walls, sand dunes, and dykes surrounds the whole. The British expedition to this reclaimed marsh in 1809 is remembered mainly because it lost over 23,000 men to disease while suffering only a little over 200 *casualties from combat, one of the worst disasters ever to overtake a British army.

In 1944, with his supply lines stretching back to *Normandy, *Montgomery was presented with the windfall that Antwerp had been seized by the local *resistance before the Germans could sabotage the port as they had every other along the Channel and North Sea coast. After *Arnhem he turned to clearing the *Scheldt in order for his Twenty-first Army Group to be able to use the port for its forthcoming advance into the *Rhineland.

The Germans defended the island in strength, with 10,000 men and eighteen major batteries in concrete bunkers, extensive minefields, and beach obstacles. The RAF was entrusted with the preliminary *bombardment during October and breached the sea walls to flood some of the German defences. Few of these were below sea level, unlike the Dutch civilian population that had not acted upon warning leaflets with sufficient alacrity.

In the meantime nearly 200 landing and support craft had been assembled for amphibious assaults on Westkapelle and Vlissingen (Flushing). Supported by battleships, INFATUATE was launched in the early hours of 1 November in poor weather. The shore batteries took a heavy toll of the landing craft, particularly at Westkapelle, and supporting armour bogged down in the soft clay. The planned close *air support was initially impossible due to the weather. Elements of 4 Commando Brigade stormed Westkapelle, suffering heavy losses, while infantry battalions from 52nd Division and 41 Commando assaulted Vlissingen. By 8 November, they had taken the island and linked up with 2nd Canadian Division, advancing along the South Beveland peninsula. Minesweeping operations began immediately to clear the river, and the first convoy entered Antwerp on 27 November.   APC-A

Denis, W., and Whitaker, Shelagh, *The Battle of the Scheldt* (London, 1985).

Wales, conquest of (1277–95). Norman penetration of Wales began in the 11th century, but true conquest was not achieved until the reign of Edward I. Southern Wales came under the sway of the Anglo-Norman marcher lords, but the north was a different matter. Despite the scale of the resources he could muster, Henry II was largely unsuccessful in his campaigns in north Wales, while in the early 13th century Llywelyn the Great took full advantage of the political difficulties faced by King John. Although it was said that Henry III aimed at conquest in 1225, a series of campaigns in his reign yielded no more than a formal agreement with the rulers of Gwynedd in 1245. The events of the *Barons' war in England provided Llywelyn ap Gruffudd with a fresh opportunity to assert the power of Gwynnedd.

Edward I's initial campaign in 1277 was intended to curb Llywelyn's power, and to make it clear that the Welsh prince owed homage to the English king. These aims were easily achieved. The king advanced from Chester to Flint, and eventually to Rhuddlan and Deganwy. A force was sent by sea to take Anglesey. Edward imposed a humiliating treaty on Llywelyn. The English king's reluctance to reward those Welshmen who had supported him in 1277, notably Llywelyn's brother Dafydd, combined with disputes over the use of English or Welsh law, led to rebellion in 1282. Dafydd was joined by Llywelyn in this rising; English-held castles in north Wales fell to surprise attacks. A massive campaign was organized and Edward again advanced from Chester to Flint and then on to Rhuddlan, while marcher lords operated in mid- and south Wales. A bridge of boats was constructed, linking Anglesey to the mainland, to provide another attack route. An English force was defeated in November as it attempted to return to Anglesey across the bridge, but a month later, on 11 December, Llywelyn was killed at the battle of Irfon Bridge when he made a move into mid-Wales. Dafydd's forces held out until the following year, but the conquest was complete.

There was a small-scale rebellion in the south in 1287 and a far more serious uprising in 1294, which required another major royal campaign. Once again the royal army advanced from Chester, and wintered at Conwy. Other forces mustered at Montgomery and Carmarthen. The Welsh leader Madog was captured at the battle of Maes Moydog by the Montgomery army under the Earl of Warwick in March 1295, and the rebellion collapsed.

The conquest was not achieved by imaginative generalship. Edward's strategy of advancing along or near the coast varied little. The Welsh were reluctant to fight major battles and those that did take place were little more than skirmishes between relatively small forces. It was the sheer weight of resources that the English were able to deploy that was crucial in the conquest; in 1294–5 Edward was able to send some 30,000 men to Wales and each phase of the conquest was followed by fortification on an impressive scale. New *castles such as Flint, Harlech, Conwy, and Caernarfon were sited so that supply by sea would be easy, while they were built on a massive scale so that they could provide bases from which substantial forces could operate. It was also important that Wales was not a united country. In 1277 Edward was able to capitalize on divisions within the ruling house of Gwynedd, and he was always able to recruit extensively in south Wales for his campaigns in the north.

Edward's campaigns, and the political settlement that followed them, transformed Wales. The old ruling families were destroyed, and a new administrative structure introduced. This was a true conquest, and the English achievement was not undone by rebellions such as those of Llywelyn Bren in 1316, or Owain Glyndwr (*Glendower) in the early 15th century.   MCP

Davies, R. R., *Conquest, Coexistence and Change: Wales 1063–1415* (Oxford, 1987).

Morris, J. E., *The Welsh Wars of Edward I* (Oxford, 1901).

Prestwich, M. C., *Edward I* (London, 1988).

Wallace, Sir William (*c*.1270–1305), younger son of a very junior branch of the Wallace family. He led a revolt against Edward I's government in south-western Scotland in 1297, contributing to a countrywide, spontaneous attempt to restore *Scots independence using less orthodox tactics than those which had failed at the battle of Dunbar in 1296. As revolt spread, Wallace joined up with Andrew Murray from the north-east and defeated an overconfident English army at Stirling Bridge, attacking before the English were in proper battle formation. Most English garrisons were then expelled and the north of England was raided.

Edward I led the army himself in 1298, prompting the Scots to burn south-eastern Scotland. Wallace, now guardian of Scotland, engaged the starving English at *Falkirk. Occupying a defensive position on a hill, the Scots *schiltroms rebuffed an ill-disciplined English cavalry charge but were subsequently decimated by *archers. The defeat ended Wallace's political career, though he rejoined the noble-led Scots army in 1303. When English rule was accepted in 1304, Wallace soldiered on but was captured and executed barbarously for treason in 1305. Hailed subsequently as a great patriot and *guerrilla fighter, Wallace remains a powerful enigma, whose military qualities, while undoubtedly in-

cluding charismatic leadership, cannot be construed as particularly innovative.   FW

Barrow, Geoffrey W. S., *Robert Bruce and the Community of the Realm of Scotland* (Edinburgh, 1992).

Fisher, Andrew, *William Wallace* (Edinburgh, 1986).

Wallenstein, Albrecht E. W. von, Duke of Friedland and Mecklenburg (1583–1634). A typical military entrepreneur of the 17th century, the Bohemian apostate Protestant Wallenstein is a complex and somewhat mysterious figure. He acquired some considerable wealth and estates in Moravia by an advantageous marriage to a wealthy widow. When his wife died in 1614, he raised a cavalry regiment for imperial service in the war against Venice, and after the Protestant defeat at the *White Mountain in 1620 he bought up the lands of the vanquished rebels at nominal cost, eventually ruling vast tracts of land in the north-east of Bohemia which he ran as a semi-independent fiefdom.

In 1625 he rose to the command of the new imperial army funded by the Holy Roman Emperor Ferdinand II for service in the *Thirty Years War against the Protestant princes of Germany. Wallenstein was victorious against Mansfeld at Dessau in 1626, and went on to defeat the Hungarians and Danes on behalf of the emperor. For these services he demanded and obtained the duchy of Mecklenburg. Thereafter he began to pursue his own designs, unilaterally laying siege to Stralsund in 1628. His ruthless exaction of tribute from the areas where his army operated led to his dismissal at the demand of the German electors in 1630. Shortly thereafter the new model Swedish army invaded the empire commanded by the talented *Gustavus Adolphus.

After *Tilly was defeated at *Breitenfeld and later killed, the emperor recalled Wallenstein, who fared no better at *Lützen although Gustavus was killed. During the following lull, Wallenstein dealt himself an independent hand in the politics of Germany (see POLITICS, THE MILITARY IN), entering into a complicated intrigue with Saxony, Sweden, Brandenburg, and France. He became too powerful and too clever for his own good, because while it is not easy to establish whether the emperor, *Richelieu, or the Protestant electors paid for it to be done, he was assassinated by his own men.   TM

war and economic growth (*see page 964*)

war art is that which has been developed and executed (1) by *artists officially commissioned either to spend varying periods of wartime under fire or to be present at nearly every kind of military activity, in order to record them; or (2) by servicemen-artists responding to powerful inner (*cont. on page 969*)

war and economic growth

MILITARY historians usually ignore detailed investigations into the economic consequences of wars, concentrating upon investigations into the origins, political effects of wars, or the process involved in waging war. Generalizations about the economic impact of war seem difficult to validate with reference to empirical evidence which might represent a measurable difference that active involvement in armed conflict with rival powers made to the long-term progress of a nation's economy.

Counterfactuals are clearly implicit in the enquiry. What might have occurred without participation in war is a question that arises for every sector of any national economy we begin to consider. War may delay, accelerate, arrest, or totally transform economic development. Occasionally (and this may be the case for 'smaller' wars) its influence will turn out to be neither here nor there.

Counterfactual modes of reasoning emerge explicitly in the economists' methods of dealing with connections between war and economic progress. Impatient with history, they cut through detailed investigation by positing the continuation of pre-war trends in rates of growth for national income, industrial production, and consumption per head. They then assert that (1) in the absence of war these trends would have persisted; (2) deviations from trends are imputable to the malign effects of war; (3) observed differences between postulated trends and actual values represent the costs of war; and (4) that the influence of war ceases once national economies are back on their pre-war trends. These methods are used to support the assertion of Arthur Lewis that the world 'lost' four and a half years' industrial output and five years' agricultural output from WW I; they led Claudia Goldin and Frank Lewis to suggest that as late as 1913 per capita consumption in the South remained seriously depressed by the effects of the *American civil war. Such procedures enabled Simon Kuznets to separate countries that did well out of WW II from those that fared badly.

Historians are unlikely to be convinced that trends in production or consumption can be defined in any 'scientific way' or extrapolated forward on the basis of accessible information for runs of so-called 'typical' pre-war years. They will not be inclined to accept assumptions that the influence of war 'ceases' when an economy is back on some kind of normal growth path. They will insist upon investigating the enduring economic impact of war step by step, sector by sector, institution by institution. Nevertheless macro-statistical exercises performed by economists draw attention to the fact that war usually reduces a country's capacity for steady growth; that deprivation (measured in terms of private consumption foregone) rises to a maximum in wartime but then steadily diminishes as recovery carries economies forward again; and that wars are accompanied by shifts in the relative positions of national economies within the global economy at large. Furthermore choices of time periods for the analysis also predetermine the assessment of historical outcomes. Some attempt at a clear separation should be made between short and enduring effects of war. During and immediately after hostilities, war clearly disrupts 'normal' economic activity. By no means everything that occurs during 'years of conflict and transition' (peace to war and back to normal again) has significant long-run economic effects upon the growth of national economies; this entry is concerned exclusively with trends and proposes to bypass the ups and downs of economies in wartime.

For the analysis of trends and structural change cost-benefit analysis (as developed by modern economics) provides us with an illuminating taxonomy and vocabulary: what were the 'costs' of war, how are they best defined and added up, what were the economic benefits, and how can they be quantified are the most relevant questions to pursue. Most literature on the impact of wars is concerned with their costs. Economic benefits are generally ignored because liberal scholars are reluctant to admit that engagement in war can actually pay. In the mercantilist era positive connections between the successful prosecution of war, political stability, state building, and commercial success were well understood by European statesmen and intellectuals. Latterly, the only material gain that has sustained historical interest is the link between war and technological breakthroughs. Yet not much of that discussion is or could be definitively settled. Spin-offs from military to civilian technology appear to be limited in scope. When set against the redeployment of limited supplies of scientists and engineers and the huge sums of public money allocated to military research and development, it is difficult to make a positive technological case for war without invoking an implausible counterfactual, namely that civilian demand would always be too weak or too diffuse to have imparted a comparable stimulus to technological progress.

Estimates of total costs of war can be found in many books dealing with the question. They operate with commonsensical definitions and offer straightforward balance sheets. Obviously the costs are imputed to those who actually paid the bills; for example, the costs to Italians from their government's decision to participate in WW I. The sums spent by governments on their armed forces are published in their budget accounts and can be refined, moreover, to include only incremental expenditures from engagement in war. Here the easiest assumption to work with is to subtract pre-war expenditures (growing at a certain rate) from actual war and immediate post-war expenditures. The net figures can then be deflated to produce estimates in constant prices for a group of years before a war or discounted from an investor's perspective to produce totals expressed in terms of present or pre-war values. Totals of budgetary expenditures can then be converted to a common currency (dollars or ducats) in order to render total outlays on war comparable across countries.

Two other direct costs are often included in publications dealing with the total costs of war: human casualties and the value of productive assets destroyed and damaged by enemy action. Neither seem easy to define, let alone measure. For example, the published figures on army, navy, air force, and civilian casualties occasioned by war need to be refined in several ways. First, civilian deaths (which turned out to be huge during and immediately after both global wars of the 20th century) must be scaled down to take account of epidemics, famines, and normal death rates among national populations. Furthermore, and since the deaths and wounding of large numbers of soldiers, sailors, and airmen also occurred at some remove from actual combat, figures of dead and wounded personnel as recorded by the armed forces also need to be adjusted for 'normal' death and accident rates among the relevant age groups. Finally the gross totals need to take account of 'birth deficits' flowing from diminished conception rates, contingent upon the mobilization of young males (and females) into the armed forces. Birth deficits are clearly complex to estimate and if family size was restored (as it was by the baby boom in several belligerent countries immediately after WW II) the allowance for this factor could turn out to be small.

Research and careful calculations might produce rough national totals of the dead and wounded and also of unborn men and women imputable to war. There certainly is considerable interest in comparing these estimates across countries and through time war by war. Just how 'bloody' was WW I? Is it true that on a per capita basis more British personnel died in order to contain *Napoleon than to defeat *Hitler? What was the economic value of all those dead, wounded, and unborn people? The answers rest upon rather simplistic calculations. For example, the arithmetic of such exercises involves (1) converting wounded into dead people by counting two wounded as equal to one dead soldier; (2) estimating the average years of working life potentially available at the time of death, thus a young man killed in the Somme at age 20 hypothetically lost 45 years of employment—assuming full employment for the years after 1918; (3) assessing the value of the skills lost in wartime;

(4) multiplying human casualties by appropriate sets of national wage rates, which implies that in 1918 a dead American could be calculated as four to five times the sum imputable to a dead Serb. If these calculations ever became feasible, historians would then be in a position to offer considered estimates of the economic values of 'lost generations'.

Alas, to estimate how a nation's productive assets (machinery, social overhead capita, housing, transport, equipment, etc.) might have been affected by war seems equally complex. Leaving aside the possibly insurmountable problem of finding usable statistical information, conceptually historians are required to draw up balance sheets of how wars operated to decrease or to increase the pre-war value of capital stocks owned by different societies. On the minus side would be listed the values of destroyed, damaged, and enforced transfers of property to the enemy; reduced rates of repair and maintenance; losses related to lower rates of civilian capital formation in wartime—and that can only be calculated with reference to a posited trend rate of capital formation for the pre-war period. On the positive side the balance sheet should include gains from reparations, from the capture of enemy territory and other assets, from the demise of competition and the enhanced security of capital flowing from victories over enemy powers. For example, success in the battle of *Britain, 1940–1, made the world safer for British capital and that should in theory have been reflected in the values of Britain's capital stock from 1942 onwards.

Clearly it looks almost impossible to draw up comprehensive balance sheets of gains and losses on the nation's 'capital account'. What precisely was the value of Malta acquired by Britain at the Treaty of Vienna in 1815? By how much was the value of the productive wealth of the USA appreciated by the demise of Japanese and German competition in 1945? How far were the transaction costs of protecting commerce and capital reduced from 1815 to 1914 by the British naval supremacy following from Nelson's victory at *Trafalgar in 1805? What we can construct (with the aid of data included in reports from reparations commissions and other official sources) are estimates for the costs of damage and destruction to property—particularly to houses, transport equipment, and livestock. Historians appreciate from studies of reconstruction (now available for some modern wars) that stocks of capital could be restored to pre-war levels fairly rapidly after the cessation of hostilities. They are, however, some way from measuring national capital gains and losses imputable to war.

The rough and ready and incomplete 'guesstimates' now in print for the total costs of wars (which include estimates for governmental expenditures on war together with some best 'guesses' of the net values of human and physical capital destroyed by military conflict) still remain difficult to interpret. For example, there are numbers which suggest that total global costs of WW I came to somewhere between $300 and $400 billion, that Britain spent £600–700 million to defeat Napoleon, and that the American civil war cost something like $10 billion. War might be compared with war, by expressing total costs as multipliers of pre-war national incomes. For example, the American civil war cost 1.2 times the American gross national product for 1861; to defeat France, Britain spent 4 to 5 times its national income for 1801; and WW I used up 5 times Europe's national output for 1913. Historians have not yet calculated the costs of global warfare from 1939–45 but that war was almost certainly 'more expensive' than its predecessors. Such costs could be expressed in dollars per head of population country by country. The figures could then be compared with average incomes at the time and reviewed across countries to ascertain, for example, if the British or the French made 'greater sacrifices' to defeat the Germans and juxtaposed to see whether Hitler was a more expensive menace to restrain than Napoleon.

Interesting exercises, but for purposes of connecting the outcomes of wars to the long-term economic progress of participating nations, the figures remain conceptually flawed, and underspecified. They do not, for example, include the 'opportunity costs' (or output forgone or gained) from the manpower and investible funds used to wage war. Manpower in the form of statistics for the numbers of civilian workers recruited into the army and navy can be considered. Such numbers (less *mercenaries and foreigners) are normally expressed as proportions of a national workforce. For example, by 1810–11 the British government had mobilized some 4 to 6 per cent of its male workforce. In 1917 that proportion was much larger—30 per cent at least. Such ratios are revealing but what historians wish to establish as another cost of war is the net loss of output that flows from the reallocation of civilians into the armed services. That depended upon how easily normal peacetime output was made up: by *recruitment from the ranks of the unemployed and from among those normally classified as outside the labour force (particularly women), by lengthening the work year, by skill dilution, and by increased mobility of labour. Substitutions for men at the front tended to occur only in circumstances of war but they compensated for potential bottlenecks in production. National economies rarely entered wars in states of full employment. War not only operated to take up 'the slack', it increased participation rates particularly among women and inculcated skills and attitudes which in several ways enhanced the long-term efficiencies of the post-war workforces. Such conjectures will be difficult to quantify but it is not clear that recruitment into the services during wars fought from 1793 to 1945 seriously depleted the supplies of productive labour available to national economies. For countries the effect of war on labour as a factor of production could have been positive for long-term growth.

Turning to capital, the relevant question is what were the effects of war on the rate at which societies accumulate stocks of assets for long-term civilian production? The effects of damage, destruction, enforced transfers, and changes in the security of property (both malign and benign) still seem unmeasurable. It is also clear that urgent military demands stimulated the formation of productive capacity, some of which is useful only for the specific purposes of combat and becomes surplus, with limited scrap value after the ending of hostilities. Historians do not know how much capital (created for the armed services) was reallocated into civil production at the end of wars, or continued to be used by the forces for the protection of a nation's security and its wealth. Expenditure on war cannot be simply represented as 'unproductive' for long-run growth.

Thus assessments of connections between investment and warfare turn largely on the contested issue of what happened to net civilian capital formation during and after major wars. How far was private investment depressed by the demands of states for the funds required for enlarged military expenditures? In some theoretical models of the wartime fiscal process, borrowing by governments crowds out capital formation for the civilian economy. States bid away available supplies of investible funds and private capital formation slumps. By the end of hostilities the economy is left with a depleted stock of capital compared to the level it would (counterfactually) have attained in the absence of government borrowing undertaken to engage in warfare.

Damaging qualifications can be made to the crowding-out hypothesis in its more extreme forms because net capital formation clearly continued in several but not all sectors of wartime economies. Rates of private savings which flowed as loans to the state or continued to support gross domestic investment expenditures tended to rise in wartime and private investment has no clear inverse relationship to government borrowing over the short run. Economists have protected their models with counterfactuals which postulate that (in the absence of war) the share of gross investment to gross national income could have risen but this defence seems difficult to substantiate and the rise in national savings ratios seems too large to be explained away by some latent investment potential creamed off to *war finance. Furthermore, after wars mini-booms and the rather rapid recovery of production do not suggest that stocks of productive capital had been 'severely' depleted by the reallocation of investible funds into expenditures on the armed forces.

Instead of crowding out there may be a paradox to explain: how did it come about that flows of savings for state and private investment could be maintained at surprisingly high rates both in wartime and over the immediate post-war years? Historians now expect to find elements of an explanation in two general observations. First, public expenditure on rearmament and war carried several economies to full employment. In some industries wartime demand led to more intensive and efficient use of resources and to the more rapid diffusion (not, however, to discovery) of advanced technology in order to cope with pressures on existing capacity. Thus, to some extent funds borrowed for the armed forces came from the extra output that had emerged as a response to intensified military demands. In this Keynesian perspective, war pays for itself and potentially adverse effects of crowding out are mitigated. Secondly, savings rates appear to have been unusually responsive to rather modest upswings in interest rates; although prospects for longer term capital gains also helped—provided governments could maintain confidence in victory or a satisfactory peace treaty. Patriotism (or, as the economists might prefer, the heightened need for the protection of private wealth) operated to increase savings by the rich. Wartime taxes on luxuries and shortages of imports and other goods, normally consumed by the affluent classes, also reinforced propensities to save.

Furthermore, and here the argument ventures into the realms of *political economy, wartime taxation is regressive in its social incidence. Thus any accumulation of public debt redistributed income from social groups with lower to those with higher propensities to save and invest. While wartime inflations (which result from failures by states to raise anything but a small proportion of the money required to pay for wars by taxation) tended to be marked by the lag of wages behind prices which again exercised regressive effects on income distribution and positive influences upon investment. Finally financial intermediation often improved in wartime. Banks and other institutions operating within a framework of an unconstrained expansion in the money supplies attracted and channelled savings more efficiently into the coffers of governments without rationing credit to businessmen. Institutional innovation managed to tap latent potential for savings.

To sum up: in time of war a state's overall economic strategy seems simple to represent. Governments endeavour to maximize the growth of national income and to acquire the largest possible share. Consistent with that objective statesmen and their advisers implement war finance policies designed to squeeze consumption and to maintain investment upon which future loans and tax revenues depend. Expressed as a share of gross national expenditure private consumption is normally severely depressed and remains so for several years after the war while governments endeavour to reconstruct economies and clean up the mess left by wartime inflations and the accumulation of national debts. Investment is usually less constrained than consumption, continuing the socially regressive trend.

Economic outcomes flowing over time from participation in wars between states cannot be meaningfully analysed just in terms of the impact on labour, capital formation, and technological progress within particular belligerent countries. Between 1688 and 1939 national economies were no longer autonomous entities. Increasingly they operated within an international economy and became steadily more integrated through flows of trade, capital, labour, and technology across frontiers. The relative significance of these interconnections for particular countries can be estimated in the form of ratios of foreign trade to total outputs.

Wars dislocated international commerce in familiar ways by blockading, attacking, and effectively constraining foreign trade. Armed conflict promoted autarky and the substitution of domestic production for imports. Except on a limited scale and largely for military purposes, flows of capital and labour across frontiers dried up in wartime. Finally the fiscal and financial processes deployed by governments to fund their engagements in armed conflict damaged the international monetary system upon which global commerce depended. After every international war, in circumstances of recrimination, heightened tendencies towards autarky, and radical changes in the structure of trade (often precipitated by conflict), an international economic order needed to be restored. For long-term development the reconstruction of that order can be represented as more urgent in 1945 than it was in 1648 and it was probably of the greatest historical importance in 1918.

To conclude: wars and particularly major wars from 1630 to 1939 represent major discontinuities in history that have exercised profound influences on the political, social, and economic development of nations. The origins and causes of these great power conflicts seem less difficult to analyse than their effects. Their longer term economic outcomes for national economies and the world economy as a whole seem problematical both to conceptualize and to measure. Classical political economy is marked by a laudable bias against armed conflict but liberal economists are prone to exaggerate the malign effects of war on manpower and capital formation. War also clearly disrupted and dislocated international economic relations and pushed national economies away from specialization. Since none of the macro-elements of the connections between wars and long-term economic growth have been or could be properly measured, historians may be inclined to speculate that losses from unrealized but potential gains from trade may have been the most extreme economic outcome of global wars in the 20th century. That same effect could also have been the most malign consequence of the *French Revolutionary and *Napoleonic wars.   PO'B

Goldin, Claudia, and Lewis, Frank, 'The Economic Cost of the American Civil War', *Journal of Economic History*, 35 (1975).

Kuznets, Simon, *Postwar Economic Growth* (New Haven, 1954).

Lewis, Arthur, *Economic Survey, 1919–1939* (London, 1953).

O'Brien, Patrick K., 'The Impact of the Revolutionary and Napoleonic Wars, 1793–1815, on the Long Run Growth of the British Economy', *Review*, 12 (1989).

Silberner, Edward, *The Problem of War in 19th Century Economic Thought* (Princeton, 1946).

urges to depict direct war experience; or (3) by sensitive onlookers; or (4) by a combination of all of these. The purest, most profound war art is not always the oil, fresh from the studio, but the preliminary drawing, in pencil, charcoal, chalk, or a combination of each; or the painting in water-based media (watercolour or gouache), made near the action. It happens that these are the defining (but not exclusive) features of much 20th-century war art, for no earlier epoch can boast so many artistic witnesses to so much violence.

This cannot be said of battle painting, a branch of art which began during the High Renaissance, featured regularly in the European academies from *c.*1770–1880, and has waned since. Here an overlap with the earlier entry military *artists must be tolerated, since great artists have also been commissioned to paint war art. Battle painting mirrors the fluctuations of imperialism, and, together or apart, its major constituents—nationalism, heroic (often sentimental) narrative, and commemoration—are easily visible in the best examples. Among its most important generic

benchmarks are *The Battle of San Romano* (1454–7) by Paolo Uccello (1397–1475), three famous, colourful decorations for the Medici now in the Uffizi, in Florence, National Gallery in London, and the Louvre in Paris, and *The Surrender of Breda* (1634–5) painted by Diego Velazquez (1599–1660), now in the Prado in Madrid. All were painted retrospectively, but it is fair to say that without these images, military painting would not have progressed, and war art would have atrophied. Uccello's imaginative scenes developed technical and compositional devices, including scientific perspective, while *The Surrender of Breda* remains unsurpassed in its representation of courtly sentiment and chivalry.

Its component figures inspired many battle painters, among them 18th- and 19th-century luminaries like the Americans Benjamin West (1728–1820) and John Singleton Copley (1738–1815), the Frenchmen Antoine, Baron Gros (1771–1835) and J. L. E. Meissonier (1815–91), and the very British Lady Elizabeth Butler (1846–1933). Irrespective of their virtues, their pictures remain academic re-enactments rather than representations resulting from direct experience: images for the Officers' Mess. Often painted years after the events they portray, they can and often do lack the vitality of immediacy, a feature transmitted to a healthy school of imitators. The same symptoms also afflicted most of the excellent, but idealized, magazine illustrations that typify mid-19th- and early 20th-century pictorial journalism in the USA and in every European country. There are very few exceptions, but one of the earliest, most memorable, and arguably the most unusual was the artist Francisco de Goya y Lucientes (1746–1828).

Goya was no journalist, but was remarkable for the way in which—unlike other Romantic painters—he straddled the categories of war art and battle painting. In the former category are his famous *Disasters of War*, an acerbic series of etchings developed during 1810–13 (but only fully published in 1863), and, in the latter, the oil paintings *2 May 1808* and *3 May 1808* (c.1814; in the Prado, Madrid). Goya's overall theme was the wanton destruction and brutality wrought by both sides in the wake of the Napoleonic invasion of Spain. Each etching is a giant blow, a testimony to the absence of Victory, graphic in every sense, none much larger than 6 × 8 inches (15 × 20 cm), with at least one claimed by Goya to have been directly observed. However, in *2 May* and *3 May* Goya redefines battle painting. These two oils, from which chivalry and honour are entirely absent, and within which barbarism is unrestrained, were executed after the expulsion of the French, under whose regime Goya was a passive collaborator. They show the Spanish revolt in Madrid and the French reprisals on consecutive days. Together, the etchings and paintings summarize Goya's contribution to war art per se. No mention of Goya should pass without citing Otto Dix (1891–1961). Without Goya's example, Dix's great WW I etched saga *Der Krieg* (The War, 1924) would probably not exist, and its didactic truths would be denied to war art as a whole.

Did the fundamentally graphic nature of war art owe its origin to Goya? Either way, that it fell to Great Britain to become the seat of commissioned war art was as much due to accident as to design. In 1916, the British government's Department of Propaganda (in 1917 MoI, Ministry of Information) established an Official War Artist Scheme following criticism that its propaganda photography seemed too posed. Just why officialdom rejected an established scientific technique in favour of a variant of the graphic reportage rendered uncertain by the Defence of the Realm Act (1914) remains unclear, but the inherent (and anarchic) violence of Italian futurism proved exciting and persuasive to some in authority. As a system of patronage the Scheme's philosophy was flawed, but its purpose was clearly and officially defined: to provide images 'for the purposes of propaganda at the present time, and for historical record in the future'. The first Official Artist arrived fortuitously. Muirhead Bone (1876–1953) was an internationally respected Scots draughtsman who, at 41 years, was eligible for call-up

under the 1916 Conscription Act. Wanting to do his patriotic duty, but being rightly fearful of becoming cannon fodder (his own phrase), he sought sanctuary through an influential contact. By September 1916 Bone was an honorary second lieutenant, drawing the *Somme battles, and within months his direct drawings of the main British battle areas graced *The Western Front*, an official propaganda publication, as intended. Bone became indispensable, and would eventually execute over 500 drawings of army, Royal Navy, and munitions subjects for the MoI, before overwork triggered a nervous breakdown and curtailed his output. He was followed to France and Flanders by British artistic talent old and young. Many artists were ex-servicemen, and two by two, in accord with the demands of GHQ, they made maximum use of their restrictive six-week official commissions. Most were consummate draughtsmen in khaki. Professor Henry Tonks (1862–1937) would head a list of Slade School alumni, among them William Orpen (1878–1931), Stanley Spencer (1891–1959), and, representing the Slade's avant garde, Percy Wyndham Lewis (1884–1956), William Roberts (1895–1980), Paul Nash (1889–1946), and C. R. W. Nevinson (1889–1946). Eric Kennington (1888–1960) and James McBey (1883–1959) typified young independent artists whose war drawing and etching gained them deserved reputations.

By the Armistice the Imperial War Museum existed (in name at least) to house the 3,000 works (plus the trophies) accumulated for the nation by some 300 artists, nearly every one a person with a valid statement to make. Although some nations within the British empire established fine collections of war and battle art as war *memorials (notably Canada and Australia), war art in the other combatant nations tended to remain a matter of personal response, and therefore outside official control.

Among the better-known figures in France were Fernand Léger (1881–1955), Marcel Gromaire (1892–1971), and Félix Valotton (1865–1925), and in Italy Gino Severini (1883–1966) and Giacomo Balla (1871–1958), who all managed to survive cubism, futurism, and the war. In Germany, with or without official sanction, Ernst Ludwig Kirchner (1880–1938) and Kathe Kollwitz (1867–1945) responded harshly to the business of life and death. The biting, satirical paintings and prints by Georg Grosz (1893–1959) and Otto Dix ridiculed the descent of Europe. Whatever their artistic affiliations before 1914, and however abstract their styles, by November 1918 most young European artists were either under arms or dead. The survivors eschewed extreme avant-garde tendencies and reverted to figurative images to render their experiences and relate them.

In some ways the *Spanish civil war heralded WW II, and so it was with war art also. One of the most memorable war paintings of all time, *Guernica* by Pablo Picasso (1881–1973), records his outraged, emotional response to the bombing by the Condor Legion of an undefended Spanish town. *Guernica* (1937, now in the Prado, Madrid) is painted in the visual language of cubism, and its scale—at least equal to the biggest battle painting—belies its speedy execution. It is a cornerstone of 20th-century war art, and a monument to the development of the art of that period in general.

In artistic terms WW II prompted myriad graphic images from every embattled country. Art had caught up with society. Only in Britain were there traces of surrealism—such a feature of the 1930s—in works by Paul Nash, Henry Moore (1898–1986), and Graham Sutherland (1903–80), and in Britain also the War Artists Advisory Committee ensured that every facet of the war would be recorded, on terms much the same as those of 1914–18. Once more, artists were commissioned to work in areas where they had expertise. A few, like Bone, were great war artists; most were not. Anthony Gross (1905–84) made hundreds of superb drawings, etchings, and paintings of the British forces around the world, while Leslie Cole (1910–77) and Edward Bawden (1903–89) drew and painted ennui, fear, and the aftermath of war, in Malta, the Middle East, and at the liberation of *concentration camps. They had their counterparts throughout the British empire and in the USA. By 1945 some British war artists had died on active service, notably Eric Ravilious (1903–42) and Albert Richards (1919–45), the one flying off Iceland and the other in action with the Airborne Division on the Rhine. In this war also, women artists fought official prejudice to have their images accepted. In Britain the excellent drawings of Laura Knight (1877–1970) go unremarked, and she is best known for her prosaic oils. Her contemporaries Doris Zinkeisen (1898–1991) and Ethel Gabain (1882–1950) were at least her equals. In Russia, the Party machine commanded the services of many excellent and versatile artists, who created an extraordinarily credible balance between record and propaganda. Their imagery moved freely between socialist realism and emotional, figurative expression, and, perhaps surprisingly—despite a cultural gulf—similar works were executed in Australia and Canada also. For the opposition, German artists supplemented Nazi propaganda photography with sound, factual drawings, especially on the *eastern front, providing posterity with an interesting contrast to the rhetoric and heroics of Nazi neoclassicism.

War art did not cease on VJ day 1945. In the USA, pop art collided with the *Vietnam war, and many civilian artists such as Edward Kienholz (1927–94), Claes Oldenburg (b. 1929), George Segal (b. 1927), James Rosenquist (b. 1933), and Martha Rosler dealt with it sparingly. More important, many *veterans still use art as therapy to defuse their worst experiences of that conflict. In Britain war art is still commissioned by the Imperial War Museum, whose Artistic Records Committee sent Linda Kitson (b. 1945), John Keane (b. 1954), and Peter Howson (b. 1958) to record British service participation, or presence, in wars in the *Falklands, the *Gulf, and in Bosnia. The validity of these images, and of every image executed as a direct result of experience of

warfare, must go unquestioned, however partial and subjective they may be. They remain records, and their marks, on paper or canvas, are as vital for future generations as any words.   JDF

Cork, Richard, *A Bitter Truth: Avant Garde Art and The First World War* (Yale, 1994).
Harries, Susan and Meirion, *The War Artists* (London, 1982).
Lippard, Lucy, *A Different War* (Seattle, 1990).
McCormick, K., and Perry, H. Darby (eds.), *Images of War: The Artist's Vision of WW II* (New York, 1990).
Ross, Alan, *Colours of War* (London, 1983).

war correspondents William Howard Russell, the first war correspondent, described himself as 'the miserable parent of a luckless tribe'. Not so luckless: among his offspring have been *Churchill, H. H. Munro (Saki), Rudyard Kipling, Edgar Wallace, Ernest *Hemingway, and Evelyn Waugh, who all honed their imaginations, literary ability, and knowledge of human nature, as well as their reputations, as war correspondents.

Russell (*c*.1820–1907) reported on the *Crimean war for *The Times* and went on to report on the *Indian Mutiny, the *American civil war, the Paris *Commune, and the *Zulu war. His career coincided with the beginning of the golden age of the war correspondent. This was a result of the near-simultaneous appearance of the *railway and the *telegraph, combined with a massive expansion of the popular press which benefited from the technological advances because it could get reporters where they were needed, get their copy back quickly, and therefore sell more newspapers.

Before the Crimea, newspapers tended to print the generals' or admirals' official despatches: both *Trafalgar and *Waterloo were reported in this way. In the middle of the century, newspaper editors experimented with luring junior officers serving with a military force to file copy between their other duties, but this was unsatisfactory. It clearly conflicted with military regulations and the military ethos, and the officers did not know how newspapers worked or what made a good story. *The Times* tried Lt Charles Nasmyth first and then, in February 1854, sent staff reporter Russell out with the Guards.

Russell found the British army in an appalling state and almost immediately asked his editor, John Delane, 'am I to tell these things or hold my tongue?' War correspondents have wrestled with the same question ever since. The solution arrived at was for Russell to file everything and those despatches which Delane judged unsuitable for printing were circulated to the cabinet. In spite of Delane's tact and circumspection, *Raglan accused Russell of breaches of security. On 23 October 1854, for example, he recorded the number of guns, ammunition requirements, and a shortage of round shot, a report which the Russian embassy undoubtedly telegraphed from London to St Petersburg the day it appeared.

Russell is often credited with alerting Britain to the appalling conditions of the wounded at Scutari, leading to the intervention of Florence *Nightingale, but in fact this honour goes to Thomas Chenery, *The Times*'s constitutional correspondent. Crimea was the first campaign in which the British army had been subject to independent scrutiny, and they did not like it. In an attempt to counter the perceived 'negative' coverage, the government sent the war photographer Roger Fenton, who produced comforting images.

The Crimea was thus the birth of modern war reporting and official responses to it. Raglan's successor issued the first military *censorship order on 25 February 1856, forbidding publication of details of value to the enemy and authorizing the ejection from the theatre of war of correspondents who transgressed. By the time his order reached Britain hostilities had ceased, so it did not become an issue.

The American civil war, only five years later, showed how the idea of 'independent' coverage had taken hold. There were 500 correspondents on the Union side, fewer on the Confederate, but this was still an enormous expansion in such a short time. There were now 50,000 miles (80,450 km) of telegraph wire in the theatre of war, making coverage more extensive and immediate. But few of the correspondents distinguished themselves, neither those from the Union or Confederate states—who were biased in the extreme—nor the foreign reporters, including Russell and *Clemenceau of *Le Temps*, although Russell was alone in reporting the first battle of *Bull Run as a Union defeat, for which the Union promptly turned against *The Times*. None of the reporters melded coverage of day-to-day detail with an awareness of the gigantic political, economic, and historic forces at work around them, ultimately the test of a great war correspondent.

The following years, until WW I, probably marked the zenith of the war correspondent. Between 1880 and 1900 the number of newspapers in Britain doubled, and the continued improvement of communications, combined with the slow introduction of organized censorship, helped. So did the fact that the wars did not directly affect or threaten Britain or the USA, and often took place in wild and exotic places—a situation repeated a hundred years later. War correspondents themselves took risks and paid with their lives. Mark Kellogg, of the American agency Associated Press, died at *Little Bighorn and Frank Le Poer of *The Times* died with *Gordon.

The *Franco-Prussian war witnessed the beginning of 'pool' arrangements, where journalists agreed to cover for each other. Archibald Forbes of the *London Daily News* and George Smalley of the *New York Tribune* made such an arrangement. By this time, newspapers were prepared to pay a fortune to get a story. Smalley telegraphed his account of the battle of *Rezonville/Gravelotte and then sent the works of Shakespeare in order to deny the sole telegraph office to his competitors, a telegram which cost $5,000.

The tragic events in the Balkans in the late 1870s provided opportunities for disturbing talents, much as they did more than a century later. H. H. Munro (Saki), the epitome of conciseness, reported from the Balkans for the *Westminster Gazette*. Forbes reported the atrocities that led to outrage over the Bulgarian massacres, and gained a 'scoop' when he was the first reporter to send news of the Russian victory at the battle of the Shipka Pass in 1878. He rode for three days and three nights to reach the telegraph office at Bucharest. He could hardly stay awake, but claimed that he ordered a bottle of champagne and, suitably refreshed, telegraphed four columns which appeared the next day. Soon afterwards, he was back in action, dodging the enraged Zulu survivors as he rode through them to the telegraph office to report the battle of Ulundi.

Churchill, who both fought and reported from the Sudan (see EGYPTIAN AND SUDANESE CAMPAIGNS) and the Second *Boer War, trod a dangerous path by mixing being a serving officer with being a war correspondent. When he was hired by the *Morning Post* to report on the latter, he was paid £250 a month, believed to be the highest sum ever paid until then for a journalistic assignment. In November he went on his fateful ride on an armoured train into Boer territory and when it was ambushed he played an active role in its defence. After the Boers captured the train, he was lucky not to be shot as a civilian taking an active military role, but this did not stop him asking the long-suffering Boers to release him because he was a journalist and not a soldier, and soon he escaped, making news and reporting it at the same time. On 26 December *Buller wrote to Lady Londonderry that Churchill had turned up again, revealing a common military attitude to war correspondents: 'I wish he was leading irregular troops instead of writing for a rotten paper. We are very short of good men, as he appears to be, out here'. Churchill then became a lieutenant in the South African Light Horse, but Buller allowed him to remain a correspondent. Not only did he fight in the battles of 1900, he also continued to report on them for the *Morning Post*.

An outstanding war correspondent of this period was the Italian Luigi Barzini, who reported the *Boxer rebellion and the *Russo-Japanese war. Barzini's reporting did not focus on heroics or adventure, but only on slaughter. He took 700 pages of notes on the latter conflict, which he correctly appraised as being of immense significance for the development of warfare with its extended and static fronts, battles continuing for many days, the vast numbers of troops involved, and the increasing dominance of technology.

When Russell died in 1907, he believed that increasing military censorship had already killed the profession he had helped to found. The Defence of the Realm Act of 1914 introduced a system of severe censorship whose legacy lingers to the present. Newspaper proprietors accepted the new controls on the altar of *total war and co-operated in disseminating government *propaganda. *The Times*, for example, accepted that its role was to increase the flow of recruits and was not receptive to reports giving unpleasant accounts of what happened to recruits after they become soldiers. At first, there were no official war correspondents but in June 1915 five official war correspondents, wearing officers' uniforms without badges and insignia but with green armbands and the nominal rank of captains, arrived in France. They wrote stoically about life in the trenches, but kept quiet about the slaughter.

On the *eastern front, Valeny Bryusov, the Russian symbolist poet, followed the Russian forces into Germany in 1914 as special correspondent for the newspaper *Russkiye vedomosti*. Based mainly in Warsaw, he reported Russian successes and how the ebb and flow of the armies reflected the continuous or cyclical nature of European history. It was on this front that the best British war correspondent from this period emerged, Morgan Philips Price of the *Manchester Guardian*, who did not suffer from the same constraints as his colleagues on the western front. He filed reports of some of the first large-scale Russian *desertions, in August 1917, and sent the first account of the Bolshevik seizure of power in November. He stayed on, in spite of the difficulty the *Guardian* had supporting him because the Bolsheviks closed all the banks. He said he decided he was in the middle of 'perhaps the biggest thing that had happened to the world', and that it was worth risking his life to stay on.

Even when reporters managed to get a 'scoop', newspaper editors were reluctant to publish. Immediately after the *Armistice five American reporters succeeded in getting into Germany and arranging an interview with FM *Hindenburg. They were met by his COS, who said he had 'just lost a world war' and had a headache. By the time the story was sent, it was considered 'stale' and was never printed.

Other people's wars were easier to report objectively. The Italian invasion of *Abyssinia was covered by Evelyn Waugh, and the *Spanish civil war by Drew Middleton and Herbert Matthews of the *New York Times* and by Hemingway, who pioneered a new style of reporting, still trying to be objective, but siding openly with one side. This style of reporting, in which the public is told about every facet of the war and especially its effects on the individual, is essentially that used by the media today. The war also saw the first and so far the greatest woman war correspondent, Martha Gellhorn, unfairly overshadowed by her brief marriage to Hemingway.

During WW II correspondents were more tightly controlled than ever, although there was some splendid reporting, especially from Edgar Snow and Alexander Werth of *The Sunday Times* and Curzio Malaparte of *Corriere della sera*, reporting from the USSR. Well-known war correspondents like Hemingway and Gellhorn were courted by the US generals, most of whom realized they had to play to a domestic audience. *Patton nearly saw his career truncated by war correspondents who blew up the incident where he

cuffed a shell-shocked soldier out of all proportion, while *Clark was amazingly indiscreet in his efforts to get his photograph into the newspapers. *MacArthur systematically used war correspondents to influence policy, a technique that boomeranged on him later in the *Korean war, and so did *Montgomery, to the fury of his C-in-C *Eisenhower.

The individual war correspondent's freedom to report and his or her ability to encompass the events of a war were both under threat from greater military and state control and the scale of operations. Furthermore, other *media, more immediate and more graphic, had now entered the fray. During WW II radio reporters played an important part in conveying the immediacy of events to listeners at home. CBS reporter Ed Murrow did much for the British cause in the USA by conveying sympathetic understanding of Britain's plight under air attack, and BBC correspondents like Richard Dimbleby—who flew more than twenty combat missions and was the first reporter into Belsen—brought the war home in the most vivid way. Even in the *Falklands war of 1982, by which time TV had already established itself, it was Brian Hanrahan's radio account of an air attack flown from a British carrier—'I counted them all out, and I counted them all back'—that caught the mood of the moment.

Although *Vietnam produced some first-rate print journalism (Michael Herr's book *Dispatches* has proved remarkably durable) it was, in the main, a television war. The future Gen Colin *Powell recalled the impact of watching, as a staff college student in the USA, the fighting in Saigon during the *Tet offensive, and one of the war's most painful images was that of a tearful Vietnamese girl running, naked, with napalm burns. More recent conflicts have been flashed to peaceful living rooms with remarkable speed and impact. On the one hand TV pictures of famine in *Somalia helped persuade the USA to intervene there, while on the other harrowing shots of a dead American being dragged through the streets of Mogadishu brought pressure for withdrawal. During the *Gulf war Baghdad-based TV reporters broadcast with cruise missiles streaking past and anti-aircraft fire illuminating the sky behind them, while the BBC's Kate Adie, with her trademark pearl earrings, reported from amongst troops waiting in the desert. After WW II, with the increased number of small wars reported by war correspondents from nations not directly involved or whose interests were not directly threatened, the war correspondent, whether print, photojournalist, or TV, once again had more freedom. However, the spread of TV coverage, with large, well-organized, and well-resourced teams and TV crews, had an ironic spin-off. The writing correspondent, alone and armed only with a notebook, became more vulnerable to charges of spying than the large and very obvious TV crews. The introduction of satellite telephones in the 1990s made his or her job easier, however, and writing correspondents can get to places and report faster than TV which also needs time to edit broadcasts and facilities to transmit. Correspondents like the *Independent's* Robert Fisk still provide lone, courageous, and sometimes politically unwelcome reporting, in the best war correspondent tradition.   CDB/RH

Gellhorn, Martha, *The Face of War* (London, 1993).

Knightley, Phillip, *The First Casualty: The War Correspondent as Hero, Propagandist and Myth-Maker* (London, 1978).

Royle, Trevor, *War Report: The War Correspondent's View of Battle from the Crimea to the Falklands* (London, 1987).

war crimes (*see opposite page*)

war finance (*see page 978*)

War of 1812 Known at the time as 'Madison's war' after the US president who prosecuted it so badly. This war was a failed attempt by the young USA to seize Canada while Britain was engaged fighting Napoleon in Europe. It might better have been called 'the Republicans' war', for it was this party, and in particular the 'war hawks' who dominated the House of Representatives thanks to the leadership of Henry Clay of Kentucky, that most wanted it. It was remarkable in that the alleged reason for the war, the British Orders in Council designed to counter Napoleon's Continental System, had been repealed before the USA declared war, and the principal victory won by American arms, by Andrew Jackson at New Orleans in January 1815, was won after peace terms had been agreed. Many attribute this to slow communications, but what the episodes underline is that the US government was determined on war in 1812 and desperate for peace in 1815. It is, finally, a classic illustration of the principle of *political economy that wars are fought to increase the domestic power of those who wage it, because the Republicans, while achieving none of their stated war objectives, decisively won the political battle with their opponents the Federalists.

The flashpoint was the stopping of US shipping by the Royal Navy, allegedly to recover *deserters but actually impressment by captains desperate for seamen, as they always were—there were five sailors admitted to be American on board HMS *Victory* at *Trafalgar, as there were French, Spanish, Dutch, Danish, and Italian, and we may be sure that few of them were there voluntarily. Thus it was fitting that the war was decided at sea by an imperfect *blockade that nonetheless strangled US commerce, bankrupting among others ex-president Thomas Jefferson, who was in many ways the grandfather of the war. He it was who reversed the prudent policy of accommodation with the ocean-dominating British that permitted US exports to treble 1794–1801, who rejected a British offer of what would now be called 'most favoured nation' status in 1806 and imposed his own 'continental system' that had no significant impact on Britain but reduced US exports from $108 million in 1807 to $22 million in 1808.

On paper it was no contest. The USA had a population of about 7.5 million and a regular army of 12,000 against 500,000 and less than 7,000 in Canada. Her navy, now with seven 'super frigates' that outgunned their British equivalents, had acquitted itself well in an undeclared naval war with the French in 1794–1801, the national debt was minuscule thanks to the Federalists, and her flanks were covered. Indeed the one territorial gain to come from the war was West Florida, acquired by sending in agents to proclaim independence from Spain and then request US protection, a technique that also nearly worked in Texas in 1813. This was part of Secretary of State Monroe's forward policy in the matter of western expansion, later to be called 'manifest destiny'. The USA had ample supplies of powder and two efficient *arsenals at Harpers Ferry and Springfield. What it did not have was functional systems of *recruitment or supply, the former based on short-term volunteers because of the collapse of the *militia and the latter based on notably corrupt contracts with *sutlers who added insult to injury by providing short-weight and condemned food to troops already restive because their inadequate *pay was invariably months in arrears. Additionally, since 1808 they had been fighting a *guerrilla war with Indian tribes loosely confederated by the great Shawnee chief Tecumseh. Although the westerners blamed them for this uprising, in fact one of the greatest lost opportunities of the war was that the British once again failed to exploit the usefulness of Indian allies as systematically as they easily could have.

This does not mean that the role of the Indians was minor; to the contrary, both in the battles along the Canadian border and in tying down US troops all along the western frontier their contribution ensured that the land war started very badly for the USA. A three-pronged invasion of Canada ended with the surrender of armies at Detroit, Frenchtown, and Queenston, while the capitulation of Fort Dearborn was followed by a massacre of the defenders by the Potawatomi, who had some scores to settle. By contrast, the war at sea went spectacularly well, with USS *Constitution* sinking HMS *Guerrière* and HMS *Java*, and the USS *United States* capturing HMS *Macedonian*. The US navy also took 50 merchant ships, while privateers took a further 450. As both Theodore *Roosevelt and Mahan were later to point out in their outstanding studies of the war, the python-like effect of British sea power was slow to make itself felt, but even so 150 of the fast commerce raiders were taken, writing on the wall for those who could read it.

The year 1813 saw a more sober US strategy of winning control of the Great Lakes, the key to their defeats of the previous year. A US force took York (modern Toronto) and Newark, looted them, and burned the government buildings, something they were to regret. In September under Cdre Perry they won by far the most significant naval

(*cont. on page 982*)

war crimes

ALTHOUGH an exact definition of this much-used expression is not possible, largely because the term refers to a variety of different transgressions, war crimes could be said to be the violation of national and international laws and customs regarding the resort to war and the conduct of war, and other activities associated with war. Since the Nuremberg and Tokyo trials of 1945–8, it has been accepted in international law that war crimes include at least three types of activity: crimes against peace; crimes against the laws and customs of war (see LAWS OF WAR); and crimes against humanity.

At the end of WW I there was some talk about putting the German war leaders on trial, particularly the hated kaiser, but a tacit recognition prevailed that it might not be such a good idea to delve too deep into who did what to whom and when. Having whipped up popular sentiment with *propaganda about German baby-killers and the like this was awkward, but embarrassment is never a sentiment of much weight in *information warfare and anyway the general populace was mentally exhausted. However, failure to follow through was to have serious repercussions for the British trying to engage popular sympathy in the USA prior to *Pearl Harbor, where the not entirely unfounded suspicion remained ingrained that the USA had been tricked into WW I by British disinformation.

During WW II, the Allied powers had on several occasions made clear their intention to pursue and punish alleged war criminals. The war had seen appalling murders, persecution, and other outrages carried out against combatants and civilian populations alike, the most notorious being the systematic murder of several million people (mainly Jews) in Nazi Germany's death camps, and Japanese mistreatment and murder of *POWs and civilians. There was general determination that those responsible should be brought to justice and that any future atrocities should also be punished.

In due course, the great majority of war criminals were tried under a national jurisdiction. In a small number of cases a different process was required, either because of the excessive nature of the crimes, or because the crimes took place outside any one geographical area and could therefore not readily be tried under a national jurisdiction. On 8 August 1945, three months after the surrender of Germany, the USA, Britain, France, and the USSR signed the London Agreement for the 'Prosecution and Punishment of the Major War Criminals of the European Axis' and nineteen other states later subscribed. The London Agreement provided for an International Military Tribunal, which would sit in Nuremberg in Germany. The trials began in November 1945 and concluded in October 1946. There were 24 original defendants, one of whom committed suicide, one was declared unfit for trial, three were acquitted, four sentenced to lengthy prison terms, three sentenced to life imprisonment, and twelve sentenced to death by hanging. A similar process was held in Tokyo. The International Military Tribunal for the Far East sat from May 1946 to November 1948. Two of the 25 Tokyo defendants received prison sentences, sixteen were sentenced to life imprisonment, and seven were sentenced to death by hanging.

Article 6 of the August 1945 Charter for the Nuremberg Tribunal defined the three categories of crime. Crimes against peace related to violations under *jus ad bellum* (laws governing the legitimacy of war) and were defined as 'planning, preparation, initiation, or waging of a war of aggression, or a war in violation of international treaties, agreements, or assurances, or participation in a common plan or conspiracy for the accomplishment of any of the foregoing'. Crimes against peace were difficult to prove, and the attempt to do so was thought by some to be an example of retroactive legislation. Nevertheless, with the Kellogg-Briand Pact of 1928 and other treaties and resolutions, there were sufficient grounds to try acts of aggression as infringements of international law.

Jus in bello (laws governing the conduct of war) thinking, on the other hand, drove the prosecution of crimes against the laws of war, which were defined in the Nuremberg Tribunal Charter as 'murder, ill-treatment, or deportation to slave labour or for any other purpose of civilian population of or in occupied territory, murder of ill-treatment of prisoners of war or persons on the seas, killing of hostages, plunder of public or private property, wanton destruction of cities, towns, or villages, or devastation not justified by military necessity'. In addition, it was accepted that violations of the laws of war could include other acts, such as the use of banned weapons or the misuse of the flag of surrender, which were not explicitly mentioned in the Charter but were covered elsewhere. Indeed, given that there already existed a sizeable body of international law, particularly the *Geneva and Hague Conventions, against which the conduct of combatants could be tested, the prosecution of violations of the law of war were in many respects the least contentious aspects of the war crimes trials.

The Nuremberg Tribunal Charter defined crimes against humanity as 'murder, extermination, enslavement, deportation and other inhumane acts committed against any civilian population before or during the war, or persecutions on political, racial or religious grounds'. As such, crimes against humanity were, like crimes against the laws of war, derived more from the *jus in bello* tradition. The war crimes tribunals were at their most adventurous where the prosecution of crimes against humanity were concerned. Since crimes against humanity could be committed 'before or during the war', and since 'any civilian population' (including, therefore, that of the offending state) was henceforth to be protected against such crimes, the Nuremberg and Tokyo tribunals tried a new and very broad category of offences. In this respect, the tribunals represented a serious challenge to the traditions of state sovereignty and non-interference; previously, a state had been more or less entitled to treat its citizens as it wished. There was also the defence of *ex post facto* legislation to contend with; those on trial for crimes against humanity argued that these new developments in international law could not logically or fairly be applied to actions and events which had already taken place.

The international military tribunals established a number of principles, central to the development of international law in the 20th century. One of the most significant of the 'Nuremberg Principles' was that war crimes, as defined in the Charter of the Tribunal, were an offence against customary international law and as such were subject to universal jurisdiction. In other words, when a state found that it could not exercise domestic jurisdiction over the national of another country who chose not to present himself for trial, it was entitled to bring a prosecution under international law. What was lacking, of course, was an appropriate method by which the alleged criminal could be brought to trial, a deficiency which did not begin to be addressed until the 1990s. Another principle was that private individuals (and not, therefore, just governments of states) could be tried under international law, and as criminals. This was a revolutionary development, the implications of which were still being realized as the 20th century came to a close. In the words of the Nuremberg Tribunal, 'Crimes against international law are committed by men, not by abstract entities, and only by punishing individuals who commit such crimes can the provisions of international law be enforced.' Furthermore, it was not acceptable for an individual accused of committing war crimes to claim in his defence either that he had acted under superior orders (and perhaps, therefore, under duress or even fear for his own life) or that he had acted out of military necessity (being required to act in certain ways in order to carry out an otherwise just and legal military mission). War crimes, in these respects, were absolute and there could be no plea in mitigation.

Whatever the lawyers said, and it is to be understood that all professions seek at all times to generate complexity so that they may be seen as indispensable, the populations of the defeated nations and not a few among the victors knew that there was nothing new in all of this. *Vae victis* (woe to the vanquished) is a very old principle indeed, and many of the crimes for which the defendants at Nuremberg and Tokyo were condemned had been committed by the victorious Allies. That a Soviet judge handpicked by *Stalin should be involved in condemning anyone for genocide was particularly poignant, and US Adm *Nimitz gave testimony in defence of Adm *Dönitz on the subject of unrestricted submarine warfare, to no avail. But when the US representative, later Supreme Court Justice, Telford Taylor pointed out that the 'poisoned chalice' being fashioned for the defendants was being also held to the lips of their judges, he knew of what he spoke.

The Nuremberg and Tokyo processes both invigorated the post-war development of international criminal and humanitarian law, and prompted wider efforts to bring about the prosecution of acts of inhumanity. In December 1946 the General Assembly of the UN unanimously adopted the Nuremberg Principles. In the 1950s the UN's International Law Commission also adopted the Nuremberg Principles and began its long-running attempt to establish a 'Code of Offences Against the Peace and Security of Mankind'. In 1968 the UN attempted to remove the statute of limitations from war crimes. In addition, the corpus of international war crimes law was steadily augmented, with the *Genocide Convention of 1948, the four Geneva Conventions of 1949, the two Additional Protocols of 1977, and the 1981 UN Weaponry Convention being of particular note.

Individual governments also acted to reinforce or extend the precedents set at Nuremberg and Tokyo. In 1960 Adolf Eichmann, a leading participant in the Nazi 'final solution', was tracked down in Argentina by Israeli agents and secretly abducted to Israel. Eichmann was tried in Jerusalem in 1961 for his crimes against the European Jews, found guilty, and sentenced to death by hanging. In 1971 in the USA a young army officer, William Calley, was tried as a war criminal for ordering the *My Lai massacre in Vietnam. In 1986, also in the USA, Ivan Demjanjuk, a Ukrainian accused of war crimes committed on behalf of the Nazis, was extradited to Israel, where he was sentenced to death in 1988, although doubts about his identity led to a later reversal. In 1987 a French court tried Klaus Barbie, a leading Nazi figure in the German occupation of France, for crimes against humanity, and sentenced him to life imprisonment. And in April 1999 in Britain, Anthony Sawoniuk was found guilty of murdering Jews in Nazi-occupied Belorussia in 1941. Sawoniuk received two life sentences for his crimes against the laws of war, becoming the first person to be convicted of war crimes in a British court. Taken together, these cases contributed to the development of international war crimes law by showing that individual crimes against international law could be tried nationally, by allowing in certain cases for the exercise of extraterritorial jurisdiction, and by making it impossible for an alleged war criminal to find refuge behind a statute of limitations.

The 1990s saw progress made in arguably the most important and most contentious aspect of war crimes law and practice: the international prosecution of individual breaches of international law. In May 1993 the UN Security Council established an International Criminal Tribunal for the former *Yugoslavia. The tribunal, based in The Hague, began to prepare indictments for war crimes committed by the various sides in the Yugoslav conflict, and in April 1995 an alleged Bosnia Serb war criminal—Dusko Tadic—became the first occupant of a new UN detention centre while awaiting trial for outrages committed in the Omarska prison camp. Tadic was later sentenced to 20 years' imprisonment for crimes against humanity. Radovan Karadjic, the Bosnian Serb leader, together with other Serbs, Croatians, and Bosnian Muslims, were also later indicted. Following the recrudescence of genocide and 'ethnic cleansing' in Kosovo in early 1999, the Hague tribunal began preparing evidence for another round of indictments.

A second UN International Criminal Tribunal was established in Arusha, Tanzania, to hear cases arising from the atrocities carried out in Rwanda in 1994. The Rwandan president, Juvenal

Habyarimana, was killed when his aircraft was shot down over Kigali in April 1994. In the months of violence which followed, over one million Tutsi and Hutu people were massacred, mainly by extremist Hutu *interahamwe* militia groups. In September 1998, one of the accused, Jean-Paul Akayesu, the Hutu mayor of Taba in central Rwanda, was convicted on nine counts of genocide, torture, rape, murder, crimes against humanity, and breaches of the 1949 Geneva Conventions. Sentenced to life imprisonment, Akayesu became the first person ever to be convicted of genocide by an international court. The judgement also established that rape and sexual violence could be considered genocidal (see GENDER AND WAR).

The Yugoslav and Rwandan tribunals, although far-reaching, are nevertheless ad hoc tribunals in the model of Nuremberg and Tokyo, dealing with crimes committed in specific conflicts by specific (and weak) regimes or individuals. Since the end of WW II there have been calls for the investigation and prosecution of war crimes to be managed in a genuinely international and more systematic manner. That goal came close to being realized in July 1998 in Rome, when the statute for the establishment of the International Criminal Court was opened for signature. When the preparatory work and negotiations have been completed, the Rome statute will see the creation of a permanent, free-standing court, able generally to hear cases of war crimes wherever and whenever they may have been committed. The International Criminal Court will also have its own, independent prosecutor. But one may entertain a modest doubt that the poisoned chalice will ever be held to the lips of those upon whose funding it will depend.   PC

war finance

As Marshal Trivulzio wrote to Louis XII of France in 1499, 'To carry out war three things are necessary: money, money and yet more money.' Regrettably we do not know what his majesty replied, but we may safely assume that it was terse. A year earlier he had inherited the throne from Charles VIII but he also took over the French *Italian wars, whose financing gave birth to the beginnings of today's omnipresent French bureaucracy. Hoping to avoid the cost of a standing army, he hired the *Swiss, only to see them defeated at *Cerignola. He had the misfortune to be a contemporary of Ferdinand and Isabella of Spain and Pope Julius II and at one point faced military threats from Spain in Italy and southern France, the Holy Roman Empire in Italy and across the Rhine, and England across the Channel. His need for 'money, money and yet more money' made Cardinal George d'Amboise the first of the great French finance ministers who made the French wars of the next three centuries possible.

The cost of the artillery train and professional soldiery was such that even if Louis had been a more skilled diplomat his conquests would not have paid for themselves. He was also up against the Sforzas and the Borgias, people who understood money in a way that he did not, and who to his fury used it to thwart his ambitions. Once war became an enterprise without even the prospect of being self-financing, it became even more of a two-edged sword; a ruler might find his power diminished not only by defeat but even by a successful campaign, in that it increased the degree to which he was beholden to others (see POLITICAL ECONOMY AND WAR). In the case of France, thanks to the skill of successive finance ministers, the day of reckoning was postponed for nearly three centuries. In England, where the monarchy enjoyed a much smaller personal income thanks to the completeness of *feudal delegation following the Norman Conquest, a degree of accountability appeared early, in the Magna Charta of 1215. While compacts without the sword are but words, the exception that proves the rule is the compact governing the sword, and after the hiatus that minister Thomas Cromwell won for Henry VIII with the expropriation of the monasteries, parliament enforced the compact against the hapless Charles I in the *British civil wars.

The matter was not fully resolved until the 1689 Act of Settlement which enshrined power-sharing in the form of an annual vote by the legislature on the financing requested by the executive. Since the former could be expanded reasonably painlessly to incorporate new sources of power and revenue, the British monarchy sailed through the storms of the following centuries that saw all the more apparently powerful monarchies shipwrecked. The *American independence war was less of an exception than the slogan 'no taxation without representation' would make it seem. The colonies were being required to pay the cost of their own defence, but with the *French and Indian threat contained, the once clamoured-for British troops were perceived as an occupying army—which, since many were German *mercenaries, is precisely what they were. This would not have been tolerated anywhere in the British Isles and it was the failure of London to respect the colonists' rights as Britons, along with the desire of Yankee merchants to make money wherever they saw fit and keep it, that caused the English-speaking peoples to part ways.

Although the financial power of Britain had already made itself felt over the wars of the preceding century, it was to be during the *French Revolutionary and *Napoleonic wars that France was to be reminded of the lesson imperfectly taught to Louis XII by the Sforzas and Borgias: money could be turned into power more easily than power could be monetized. Pitt 'the Younger' was able to appropriate a part of the war-fuelled economic and industrial revolution in Britain through the novel income tax, but the real strength of Britain lay in the sale of long-dated government bonds (consuls), which had a threefold benefit. First, by affirming the Hanoverian dynasty against the *Jacobites, they tied together the interests of the regime and the financially powerful; second, they created a broad national commitment to prosecuting the wars to a conclusion; third, inflation could be used to reduce the debt (until, that is, people woke up and started demanding compound instead of simple interest, too late for all the patriotic purchasers of war bonds during the two world wars). A century later George Bernard Shaw observed that the taxpayer had 'to be half cheated, half coerced into paying [taxes]', and this was Pitt's great legacy, compared to the art of plucking a live goose: the trick was to obtain the maximum of feathers with the minimum of hissing.

Napoleon, in so many other ways a fountain of innovation, did not understand the power of money to the same degree, with the result that the despised nation of shopkeepers gave financial weight to the coalitions that defeated him and went on to a century of prosperity, while France was left cracking the gnawed bones of *gloire* to retrieve the marrow of psychological compensation for what was a comprehensive defeat. The flexibility of the Pitt-inspired method of financing war meant that principal could be sought from foreign investors and even governments. Thus *Lincoln was not only able to use the *American civil war to introduce easily devalued paper money, he was also able to counter 'King Cotton', the weapon the Confederate States believed would compel foreign diplomatic recognition, by tying European financial interests to the Union. The reverse was to happen during WW I when Woodrow Wilson, previously 'too proud to fight', went to war to protect massive US investment on the Allied side. He was also able to institutionalize the income tax that Lincoln had only been able to impose for the duration of his war.

What can be seen as the completion of the 1688 English revolution came after the scandals of the *Crimean war and the *Indian Mutiny with the 1866 Exchequer and Audit Act, designed to prevent the *War Office and the Admiralty from circumventing annuality by selling assets without reference to parliament. The Act established that all income should be paid directly to the Treasury and not accumulated in discrete accounts under departmental control, and that at the end of any year all outstanding cash balances in departmental accounts should revert automatically to the Treasury. That this was a matter of political economy rather than housekeeping will be evident to anyone who has observed departments frantically trying to spend all the money allocated to them before the end of the financial year.

It is important to appreciate that not merely war financing but government revenue raising in general is considered criminal activity if practised by private individuals, resting as it does on the two sturdy legs of extortion and fraud. But like any protection racket, it is vulnerable to external threats to the stability promised in return for regular levies, thus the need to protect what criminal gangs would call their 'turf'. The canard that the arms manufacturers precipitated WW I is based on a total misunderstanding; the war in fact shattered the extremely profitable cartel they had established and thereafter government became an active partner. When *Eisenhower belatedly warned about a 'military-industrial complex' in 1961, he knew, but his listeners failed to appreciate, that what he was talking about was the appearance, thanks to the *Cold War, of a phenomenon previously observed only during major shooting wars. Because it is not subject to commercial accountability, government procurement has historically been characterized by staggering corruption, and periodic scandals about bribery and overcharging simply serve to remind the semi-plucked geese of this eternal verity.

In modern societies financial support for war, actual or potential, comes from the output of the rest of society. As war moves closer an increasing proportion of productive capacity is devoted to financing it. Eventually this means real resources, men and material, have to be deliberately shifted into the war effort. This decreases the tax base at a time when the state needs more revenue. This problem is compounded by the events that occur before war even begins. The international community relies on trade and this depends on confidence that bills will be settled and the passage of goods unimpeded, both of which are threatened by major wars. The mere prospect of such wars destroys confidence first in the reliability of the combatants as prospective payers, second in their capacity to physically deliver on uncompleted contracts, and finally on the future accessibility of any funds deposited in their financial systems. The threat of war thus disrupts financial markets and non-belligerents will try to move resources away, as will the belligerents' own nationals if they can. Thus governments in anticipation of a war will impose exchange controls and other actions preventing the free movements of both physical and financial assets. Once war is declared they will seize any assets or financial instruments deposited in their country by enemy nationals, while neutral countries may freeze the assets of belligerents. This confirms the worst fears of those involved in trade and commerce and further undermines trust in the continuing integrity of the system.

Since the British were the pioneers and most sophisticated practitioners of modern war financing, it is instructive to examine how the City handled the financial crunch of 1914, when the sterling commercial bills from which most international trade was financed had either fallen due or were being been discounted back into the London market, creating a worldwide liquidity problem. The solution was to issue an increasing number of 90-day Treasury Bills at whatever rate the market would bear. In 1914 the British government and its citizens had destrainable assets outside the immediate area of conflict worth some £4,000 million. In addition they had a strong reputation for reliability and financial integrity so even in the circumstances of war these bills could be sold. They quickly replaced the liquidity lost as a result of the disappearance of sterling commercial bills. Thus was created a system of UK government financial management that continues to this day: the London Discount Market based on Treasury Bills with the Bank of England as lender of last resort.

None of the wars of national unification fought in Europe in the century after Waterloo could compare either in length, ferocity, or financial demands with the twenty years that preceded it. Likewise the minor 19th-century wars of repressive imperial pacification could be financed out of current revenues or ordinary borrowing. The *Russo-Japanese war was a harbinger, stretching both combatants' ability to raise finance at home and abroad to the limit, the only area where the Russians were able to make their greater latent strength felt. But the two world wars represented an order of magnitude change in war financing. WW I bankrupted Russia and the Allies' post-war military interventions had much to do with the Bolsheviks' repudiation of overseas debt. Eighty years later, the issue is still alive: you may expropriate and cheat your own citizens to your heart's content, but woe betide you if you fail at least to genuflect at the altar of sovereign debt. Britain went from being the world's creditor to being one of its larger debtors with £2,000 million in liabilities. Germany could have renegotiated the demands for financial reparations but chose instead to inflate her way out of her obligations, while the apparent winners in the conflict in financial terms narrowed down to one. The USA had neither the institutions nor the wisdom to handle the responsibilities of her own equally abrupt change from being the world's greatest debtor to greatest creditor, and thanks to her reversion to crude mercantilism what might have been merely a severe recession following the great boom after WW I degenerated into the Great Depression, the culture in which virulent *militarism prospered, most notably in Italy, Japan, and Germany, who all felt cheated by the post-war settlement.

After WW II, by then a greater economic power and creditor than the rest of the world combined, the USA had a shrewder appreciation of its interest and the *Marshall Plan was in stark contrast to the village banker's mentality of Calvin ('they hired the money, didn't they?') Coolidge as the world teetered on the edge of financial collapse in the 1920s. While the French and the British continued to strangle their own economies by retaining wartime economic and financial controls into the 1960s, if indeed they can be said to have relinquished them even then, the Germans and the Japanese turned their backs on autarchy and the primitive imperial mercantilism that had led them to defeat, and prospered. A state at war imposes trade restrictions, exchange controls, and high import duties in order to direct resources to the state by stifling domestic private demand. Meanwhile by injecting cash back into the economy in order to pay for the materials of war, incomes will rise and the inevitable consequence is inflation. For this reason governments are doubly interested in financing the war by borrowing, to soak up excess demand. John Maynard Keynes in a sequence of papers and exchanges with other economists and bankers in 1939 and 1940 even proposed that this reality should be fully recognized and savings made compulsory. The attractiveness of this to governments without the constraints that the Constitution and an independent judiciary imposed on the USA meant that coercive financial devices only previously conceivable in times of dire national emergency continue in force half a century after WW II. Oddly enough, even the natural efforts of the populace to evade these impositions works to increase the power of government. An inevitable consequence of income and price controls is a black market, for the suppression of which governments can vote themselves ever-greater police powers.

BH/HEB

engagement of the war against a British flotilla of equal strength on Lake Erie, enabling them to reverse the land results of the previous year. Two British invasions of Ohio failed and at the battle of the Thames east of Detroit, the Americans caught up with the retreating Anglo-Indian army and trounced it, killing (and skinning) Tecumseh, who had earlier suggested that the British commander should wear petticoats. Elsewhere skirmishing characterized by incompetence when not treasonable corruption left the British controlling much of the frontier.

In the south, with little assistance from the British save for the use of Pensacola as a base of operations for escaped slaves and Indians, later to be called Seminoles, some of the Creek people fought their own war 1813–14 until Andrew Jackson instilled some order in the militia rabble under his command by executing one of them, and destroyed the Creeks at Horseshoe Bend in March 1814. Among those under his command were *Crockett and Sam Houston, later heroes of Texas independence.

But 1813 had witnessed the turning point at sea, with the British sailing in *convoys and sending several new squadrons, one of which ravaged the Chesapeake Bay area. The blockade began to bite and unleashed violent inflation in the USA, while the commander of the USS *Chesapeake* chose to accept a challenge to single combat by HMS *Shannon*, which unknown to him had been up-gunned, and was defeated and killed in a 15-minute engagement. The USS *Essex* was also tracked down and captured in the Pacifics after a very successful year of commerce-raiding, but it was the privateers who kept the stars and stripes on the high seas, boldly sailing around the British Isles and capturing merchant ships by the hundred and even defeating the occasional small warship.

With the abdication of Napoleon in April 1814, the British were able to release more ships and regular troops for the war in America, their numbers rising to about 40,000. But the US army was able to match these numbers and, under the pressure of war, had shed incompetent commanders and promoted able ones such as Winfield *Scott who, although he was nearly killed at Lundy's Lane in July, had drilled his men so well that they fought the British regulars to a standstill. Things went less well elsewhere, with a punitive *amphibious operation in the Chesapeake returning the favour for Newark and York by burning Washington and then bombarding *Baltimore. More significant was the capture of eastern Maine and the unilateral surrender of a number of New England islands and ports, which were delighted to be able to resume trade in exchange for swearing an oath of allegiance to the crown or otherwise betraying their country. US public finance had collapsed and the Royal Navy, paying in cash, was better able to supply itself from American farmers and merchants than were the US forces offering promissory notes.

The peace negotiations at Ghent that ran from August until Christmas Eve 1814 were a game of bluff and counter-bluff. *Wellington, asked to command the forces in America, put his finger on the loss of control of the Great Lakes as the Achilles' heel of the British position, so naturally the British mounted their last big offensive in the south under the command of his brother-in-law Pakenham, who launched a frontal attack across a river and into *field fortifications manned by men who could shoot, and was killed along with 1,500 of his men (a further 500 surrendered) at the battle of New Orleans on 8 January 1815. On 21 February the last men to die in the war were the ringleaders of a *mutiny by Tennessee militia in September the previous year, shot by the implacable Jackson, although by that time Congress had hastily ratified the Treaty of Ghent, which restored the *status quo ante bellum*. HEB

Hickey, Donald R., *The War of 1812: A Short History* (Urbana, Ill., 1995).

War Office The principal administrative agency for the British army from 1683 until 1964, although it was not until 1855 that all administrative functions were centralized within it. After having several London homes, the War Office was located at the Horse Guards building in Whitehall from 1722 until 1858. It then moved to Pall Mall but it was only in 1906 that the office was moved to purpose-built accommodation in Whitehall. The War Office originated with the appointment of William Blathwayt as Secretary at War in 1683. Two predecessors had acted as clerks to the army's C-in-C but Blathwayt greatly extended his functions to include most of the routine day-to-day administration. However, the Secretary at War remained a minor official within government and, in war, strategic policy was directed by the principal secretaries of state presiding over the northern and southern departments. In 1782 the former became the Foreign Office and the latter the Home Office while, in 1801, overall responsibility for military and colonial affairs was vested in a new Secretary of State for War and Colonies. Responsibility for war and colonies was separated in 1854 and the new Secretary of State for War then absorbed the office of the Secretary at War in 1855.

Under the new arrangements, there was a duality of power between the Secretary of State for War and the army C-in-C but, as part of the *Cardwell reforms, the latter was made subordinate to the Secretary for War and in 1871 the office of the C-in-C was symbolically moved from the Horse Guards to Pall Mall. In practice, the C-in-C retained considerable influence through the sheer permanence of the Duke of Cambridge, who held the office from 1855 until 1895, while war ministers were subject to the vagaries of the electoral system. A War Office Council was established in 1890 to widen the range of professional advice reaching the Secretary of State but the continuing defects in War Office organization apparent during the Second *Boer War led to the recommendations by the Esher Committee in 1904 to abolish the C-in-C and appoint a chief of the *general staff.

A *Committee of Imperial Defence (CID) had also emerged in 1902 as a forum for the discussion of wider defence issues. The advantages of the establishment of a general staff were lost during WW I when *Kitchener, the only soldier ever to become Secretary of State, virtually dismantled it. After 1918 the CID became increasingly important and the appointment of a Minister for Co-ordination of Defence in 1936 and Churchill's decision to assume the post of Minister of Defence as well as that of PM in 1940 were indicative of the declining significance of the War Office. A single Ministry of Defence absorbing the War Office, Admiralty, and Air Ministry was then created in 1964.   IB

warrant officers are a grade of officer, generally found in all three services, whose authority stems from a warrant, usually signed by a government minister or representative of a service board. As such they rank below commissioned *officers but above *NCOs or petty officers. Warrant officers originated in the 17th century, as 'standing officers' on warships—like the sailing master, carpenter, and gunner—appointed because of specific technical skills and holding Navy Board warrants.

Their use extended into armies in two ways. First, as in the naval context, to emphasize particular skills, especially in logistic and administrative areas: for many years the British army's senior warrant rank was that of Conductor in the Army Ordnance Corps (later Royal Army Ordnance Corps). Secondly, to grant added status to individuals whose functions were clearly more important than those of NCOs but could not be granted commissioned rank. The rank of *adjutant* (not to be confused with the post of adjutant, held by a commissioned officer in the British army) was introduced into the French army in the 18th century, and in the 19th the British Regimental Sergeant Major (RSM), initially simply the most senior NCO, became a warrant officer.

The British army created the warrant rank of Company Sergeant Major (CSM) in 1913: CSMs ranked as Warrant Officers Class 2 and RSMs as Warrant Officers Class 1. The rank of Warrant Officer Class 3, Platoon Sergeant Major, was introduced just before WW II to produce warrant officer platoon commanders, but was not a success and was allowed to lapse. Here the British were influenced by the success of German *Unteroffiziere mit Portepee* ('NCOs with (an officer's) sword knot') in WW I, but the notion did not transplant into the British army where distinctions between commissioned and non-commissioned rank were often as much social as military.

The use of warrant officers by the US army reflects the older use of the rank as a means of giving pay and status to an individual whose technical skill may not be mirrored by a need to exercise wide command responsibility. Warrant officers were recruited in large numbers during the *Vietnam war to fly *helicopters.

The status of warrant officers is reflected by their uniforms and *badges of *rank which are often more like those of officers than those of NCOs and men: in the British army the break point comes between WO1 and WO2. In some forces they mess with the officers and, like them, are saluted.
                                                          RH

Warring States period (453–221 BC), chaotic and violent period in China contemporary with Classical Greece, *Alexander 'the Great', the *Peloponnesian wars, and the early *Punic wars in southern Europe. In this period Chinese armies were first commanded by professional generals including the first military theorist, *Sun-tzu, iron weapons were first introduced on a large scale, and the first version of the Great Wall of China was built at the beginning of the 3rd century BC.

Confucius, the Chinese philosopher, died in 479 BC. A quarter of a century later the leaders of the Wei, Han, and Chao clans attacked the ruler of Chin and defeated him at Chin Yang (modern Taiyuan, in Shanxi Province) in 453 BC, dividing his realms among themselves. He was beheaded and his skull used, as was the custom, as a drinking cup. At this time there were eight large states in China, but Yen in the north and Yüeh in the east played no decisive part in the wars which raged for the next two and a quarter centuries. The states involved were therefore Ch'I, Ch'u, Ch'in, and and the three Chin states—Wei, Han, and Chao. A dozen smaller principalities were rapidly absorbed into the 'big six'.

It was one of the most chaotic periods in China's long history. The still extensive forests, swamps, and reed-edged lakes provided cover for gangs of bandits, robbers, and deserters. Yet in spite of this, the cities were prosperous. Lin Tzu, the capital of Ch'I, had 70,000 households—likely to have represented more than half a million people. Society was controlled by a draconian legal code, with five grades of punishment ranging from tattooing or branding the face, through cutting off the nose, amputating the feet, castration or (for women) claustration, to death. Sun means 'the footless', suggesting that Sun-tzu may have suffered the third grade of punishment.

Iron was known in China before 500 BC but it was very rare and valuable. By about 400 BC a form of mass production had been introduced and individual ironmasters were employing hundreds of workers. Soon after, Ch'u low-steel lance points were said to be 'sharp as a bee's sting'. As with the introduction of cannon in the late Middle Ages in Europe, the large foundries were the property of state rulers, increasing their power relative to their unruly vassals. This centralization of weapons manufacture was paralleled by administrative centralization.

Before the Warring States period warfare was conducted on a *feudal and somewhat ritualistic basis. By the middle of the 5th century BC large armies were embarking on distant campaigns which required state direction. The temporary levies of the earlier period were replaced by standing armies, officered by professionals, comprising élite or shock troops plus conscripted peasants. The former, known as *guards, wore *armour and carried crossbows, introduced about 400 BC.

Samuel B. Griffith, the translator of Sun-tzu, believed that the Chinese of this period would have been able to cause Alexander 'the Great' 'a great deal more trouble than did the Greeks, the Persians or the Indians'. When not campaigning, the army laboured on public works projects, including, probably, the Great Wall—as it does in modern China. It was into this environment, as war became more violent and began to be directed by professional generals, that Sun-tzu was born. CDB

Sun-tzu, *The Art of War*, trans. and ed. Samuel B. Griffith (Oxford, 1963).

Warsaw Pact (or Warsaw Treaty Organization)

(1955–91), military alliance comprising eight states—Albania, Bulgaria, Czechoslovakia, East Germany, Hungary, Poland, Romania, and the USSR—led by the USSR and throughout its 35-year history the principal opponent of and military threat to *NATO.

Following the occupation of central Europe at the end of WW II, the USSR set up tame national armed forces in the countries it had occupied. Those of Poland were commanded, initially, by Marshal Konstantin Rokossovsky, a Soviet marshal of Polish stock. Although some national characteristics were retained—and later became more pronounced—the armed forces of the states in Soviet-occupied zones were equipped and organized entirely on Soviet lines, were under Soviet command, and had Soviet occupation troops alongside them. In western Europe, the countries liberated at the end of the war retained their own armed forces, but these joined together voluntarily in 1949 as the NATO Alliance. At the Paris Conference in 1954, the Western European Union (WEU) was formed as a European pillar of NATO, and West Germany was invited to join, which it did the following year.

Partly in response to German accession to NATO, eight of the east European socialist countries met in Warsaw on 11 May. Yugoslavia did not attend and never joined. The Pact was signed on 14 May and came into effect on 5 June. Although nominally an alliance between sovereign states, the Warsaw Pact was quite different from NATO. The latter was, and remains, a voluntary alliance which requires consensus to act, although the USA is unquestionably the dominant power. The Warsaw Pact was run by the USSR and used as a cordon sanitaire. Its working language was Russian and the first C-in-C of Warsaw Pact armed forces, appointed in 1956, was the Soviet *Koniev.

The Warsaw Treaty stressed the maintenance of international peace and security (Article 1). It proposed effective *arms control measures (Article 2), and obliged member states to consult each other on all aspects of international relations (Article 3). Other alliances prejudicial to the interests of the Warsaw Pact were banned (Article 7). In the event of attack on any Warsaw Pact states they would have the right to individual or collective defence under Article 51 of the UN Charter (Article 4). This clause was cited to justify the invasion of Hungary in 1957 and of Czechoslovakia in 1968. In effect, this was the same as NATO's 'an attack on one is an attack on all'. Like NATO, the Warsaw Pact was declaredly a defensive alliance. NATO never believed this, but it was NATO which expanded after the Pact dissolved, and which first attacked a sovereign state outside its own borders in 1999.

The Pact's military organization comprised the committee of defence ministers (KMO), the combined armed forces (OVS) and the combined command (OK). In addition to the combined command, there was a military committee of the combined armed forces, a combined armed forces headquarters—in Moscow—and a technical committee (TK). Commonality of equipment—all Soviet-designed, although some was later adapted and improved by the 'Non-Soviet Warsaw Pact' (NSWP) states—and of training and organization would probably have given the Warsaw Pact the advantage on the battlefield. By the 1980s the NSWP states were increasingly acquiring their own style and equipment. The Poles played a leading role in developing the idea of the *operational manoeuvre group, while the Czechoslovaks built their own multiple rocket launchers and *self-propelled (SP) guns. Following the collapse of the Berlin wall in 1989 and the unification of Germany, the Warsaw Pact was defunct—East Germany had been a member. In 1990 it was announced that it would be dissolved and the USSR ratified the decision at the end of 1991. CDB

Warsaw uprising

(1944), tragic attempt by the Polish 'Home Army' (Armija Krajowa) to overthrow the German occupation as the Red Army closed on Warsaw. By 28 July 1944 citizens of Warsaw could hear the sounds of the battle between the *Wehrmacht and the Red Army. The Soviets were concerned about a German counter-attack and ordered their troops onto the defensive on 1 August.

The Home Army was sponsored by the British and the Polish government in exile in London, but the British turned down requests for active assistance from RAF aircraft and the Polish Parachute Brigade because Warsaw was beyond normal aircraft range and lay within the Soviet sphere. The USSR had its own plans and government-in-waiting, Rada Narodowa, and sponsored a different Polish army, the Armija Ludowa, which was unified with the Polish army that had been formed in the USSR. Nonetheless, the charge that the Soviets sat back and waited for the Germans to crush the uprising is baseless; there were four German armoured divisions between them and the city and Marshal Rokossovsky, commanding the Soviet First

Belorussian Front (army group), needed to regroup before continuing the offensive. The lamentable fact is that the uprising was intended to present the advancing Soviets with a fait accompli and was launched without prior consultation with either London or Moscow. It should also be noted that the Home Army did little to support the equally heroic and doomed uprising of the Jews in the Warsaw Ghetto in April 1943.

On 1 August Home Army underground units opened fire inside Warsaw, beginning two months of bitter fighting. The lull in Soviet operations permitted the Germans to send in overwhelming force, backed up by *Einsatzgruppen* extermination squads, and even if the Soviets had cooperated with earlier British efforts to airdrop supplies, it would not have made much difference. The Soviets themselves dropped supplies in the second half of September, but much of it fell into German hands. By 24 September the Germans had forced the isolated Polish units into small pockets and escape through the sewers was the only option. Fifteen thousand fighters of the 30,000–40,000-strong Home Army were dead, and 120,000–200,000 civilians were killed. On 2 October the fighting stopped, the remaining Poles were rounded up for slavery or extermination, and the Germans began razing Warsaw to the ground.   CDB

Washington, Gen George (1732–99), first president (1789–97) and the founding father of the USA. He stands as one of the three men—the others being *Lincoln and Franklin *Roosevelt—who came to power at the most critical moments in US history, and perforce shaped the nation in his image.

Washington's military career dated back to the *French and Indian war, which gave him ample opportunity to assess the strengths and weaknesses of the British army. Twenty years later this background, plus New England's desire to make common cause with his home state Virginia, made him the unanimous choice to command the newly formed Continental Army, besieging Boston. Eventually he bluffed Howe into evacuating the city with some heavy artillery brought from Fort Ticonderoga, and a large number of dummy cannon. Moving to New York, he suffered a series of defeats that would have broken the spirit of a lesser commander. Half his army was routed at Brooklyn Heights with a loss of 5,000 men, and the other half simply ran away at Kip's Bay. After further setbacks he was compelled to retreat into New Jersey, with *desertion reducing his forces to no more than 6,000 men. He was not well served by his subordinates, and at Christmas 1776 he himself led a successful attack on Trenton with only 2,500 men, capturing 1,000 prisoners. When this drew Cornwallis at the head of 8,000 men, Washington performed a flank march by night to win another stinging victory at Princeton.

During 1777, while Gates was defeating Burgoyne's invasion from Canada at *Saratoga, Washington confronted a larger British force at Brandywine Creek on 11 September, trying to prevent the capture of Philadelphia. Pinned by Howe's main force, he was outflanked by Cornwallis and nearly surrounded. That he salvaged the bulk of his army was probably his finest military achievement, but the congressmen forced to flee Philadelphia at short notice were not inclined to appreciate this. Washington survived the following winter at Valley Forge, without the means to pay or even clothe his men and undermined by a cabal of opportunists seeking to replace him with Gates. He did this mainly by force of personality, but he also built a 40 foot (12 metre) gallows to emphasize that there was force as well as personality involved.

In June 1778, after his protégé *Lafayette helped to bring about a French alliance to balance the strategic equation, Washington's plan to cut off British forces under their new commander Clinton, retreating from Philadelphia to New York, failed because of behaviour akin to treachery by Charles Lee at Monmouth Courthouse. This was one of the very few occasions where Washington was seen to lose his legendary self-control, and Lee came close to being suspended not only from command, but from the neck as well.

With Clinton bottled up in New York it was patience that brought the war to a successful conclusion: patience with dilatory French assistance; patience with an army that mutinied twice; patience with a Congress that demanded but did not provide; patience while Greene lost the battles but won the war in the south; patience that was at last rewarded when the French navy briefly won control of the sea around *Yorktown, enabling Washington to deliver the *coup de grâce*.

There being little dispute that his austerity and personal modesty put an abiding stamp on the quasi-monarchical office of president, created with him very much in mind, criticism of him tends to focus on his military leadership. All that needs to be said in rebuttal is that he won, and it is unlikely that anyone else could have maintained unity of purpose among the secessionists, during a very protracted struggle. One has only to compare his performance to that of the similarly situated *Davis in 1861–5 to see how easily sectional interests could have prevailed, and doomed the rebellion.

By refusing to serve more than two terms, he set an example followed by all his successors save Franklin Roosevelt, and since 1951 enshrined in the 22nd amendment to the Constitution. George III observed that his retirement and his resignation as army C-in-C fourteen years earlier 'placed him in a light the most distinguished character of the age'. Upon his death, Congress unanimously voted his memory the eloquent encomium proposed by 'Light Horse Harry' Lee (father of Robert E. *Lee and not to be confused with Charles of that ilk): 'first in war, first in peace and first in the hearts of his countrymen'.   HEB

Brookhiser, Richard, *Founding Father* (New York, 1996).

Waterloo, battle of (1815), last battle of the *Napoleonic wars, fought on 18 June, towards the end of the *Hundred Days. After defeating *Blücher at Ligny while *Ney tangled indecisively with a late-arriving *Wellington at Quatre Bras on the 16th, *Napoleon fielded 72,000 men and 346 guns to attack an Anglo-Dutch-Belgian army of 68,000 men and 156 guns under Wellington, drawn up along the Mont St Jean ridge and blocking the road to Brussels.

The numbers are deceptive: although smaller than many armies he had commanded in the recent past, Napoleon's force included a high proportion of *veterans and morale was high. By contrast the Allied force was heterogeneous, with a mixture of British, German, and Dutch–Belgian units and part of it deserted in the course of the battle. However, Napoleon was not well served by his subordinates: *Grouchy failed to keep Blücher away, *Soult was no *Berthier, and Ney was well past his best. But Wellington had to cope with the loss of much of his cavalry and with the feckless Prince of Orange, who nearly threw the battle away. The crucial difference was certainly that Napoleon's generalship had been declining for years and on this day he was also suffering from cystitis and prolapsed haemorrhoids, whereas Wellington—who had been caught flat-footed at the campaign's opening—was now at the peak of his form and spent fourteen hours in the saddle, riding to every crucial point to direct the battle personally.

Drenching overnight rain dictated a delay for the ground to dry out for his cavalry and in particular his artillery to be able to manoeuvre, so Napoleon spent the time deploying his army for maximum visual effect, which did indeed dishearten some of the troops facing him across a long shallow valley. It was late morning before his younger brother Jérôme advanced to attack the fortified farmhouse complex of Hougoumont anchoring Wellington's right flank. His purpose was to draw in Allied reserves from the centre, where the main assault was to go in, but he failed to achieve this and by attacking unsuccessfully seven times between 11.30 and 19.30 he reversed the equation and drew in French troops neeeded elsewhere.

At 13.00 Napoleon's grand battery of 84 guns opened fire on the Allied centre, but as usual Wellington had deployed most of his men on the reverse slope and it had little effect. D'Erlon's Corps then attacked to the right of the Brussels–Charleroi road, with his two centre divisions in a formation he believed solved the *column and line problem, two giant columns 150 men wide and 25 deep. As they passed La Haie Sainte farm, their left came under fire from the 95th Rifles and the King's German Legion (KGL), but their right managed to take Papelotte at the left end of the Allied position. The attack in the centre came close to succeeding because of its sheer weight, but was eventually halted by concentrated point-blank volleys. *Picton was killed at the head of his division and then, at the crucial moment, the British cavalry brigades under Ponsonby and Somerset drove the French back, breaking both of D'Erlon's centre divisions.

But the horsemen got carried away and charged across the valley to attack the grand battery unsupported. After French *cuirassiers and *lancers had counter-attacked, Ponsonby was dead and a sad remnant on blown horses limped back to be of no further use to an exasperated Wellington. Meanwhile La Haie Sainte was besieged and the defenders were running out of ammunition when the Prince of Orange sent part of the KGL forward in line, to be ridden down by French cavalry that everybody except he had realized was lurking in the *smoke. The farm complex eventually fell and Wellington's centre was desperately vulnerable, but Napoleon let the opportunity slip away.

This was because, from mid-afternoon, Ney was deceived, when he saw stragglers and ammunition wagons moving back, into believing that Wellington was close to breaking. He led massed cavalry advances against the left of centre, thinking to precipitate a rout. Disabused by steady fire from unbroken British squares, he nonetheless persisted in cavalry-only attacks. Had be brought up horse artillery or even ordered his troopers to spike the touchholes or to break the wheels of the British artillery, which the gunners had to abandon to shelter in the squares every time the cavalry rode up, it would have made sense. But he did not and appears to have succumbed to something close to the berserk rage that his nickname 'Ginger' suggested. When La Haye Sainte fell and he asked for infantry to advance and attack the weakened centre, an understandably sceptical Napoleon refused.

Napoleon had other worries beside the successive failures of his brother, D'Erlon, and Ney. On his right, Grouchy had not appeared but the Prussians had. He dispatched Lobau and the Young Guard to clear them out of the village of Plancenoit and secure his right flank, which they did with commendable efficiency, preventing the union of the Allied armies until the end. This came at 19.30, when Napoleon himself led out (to be hastily led back by his staff) the Old and Middle Guard to attack up the slope littered with the bodies of Ney's troopers. The attack evolved into an assault by several distinct columns, one of which collided with Maitland's Guard Brigade, with Wellington himself to hand. He ordered 'Up Guards! Make ready! Fire!', directing what were perhaps the day's decisive volleys.

The sight of the Guard falling back stunned the French, and Wellington waved his hat and what was left of his army surged forward. The mainspring of Napoleon's army snapped at last, and it was *sauve qui peut*. Wellington's army was exhausted, but Blücher's cavalry had scores to settle and a *pursuit as vigorous as they had endured after *Jena/Auerstadt prevented all hope of an organized fighting retreat. Protected by the remnants of his Guard, Napoleon left the battlefield and at 21.30 Wellington and Blücher were embracing in the courtyard of the farmhouse that had been Napoleon's HQ, La Belle Alliance. It would have made a far more appropriate name than Waterloo, which was miles away, but the duke decided otherwise, as was certainly his right after winning 'the nearest run thing you ever saw in your life'.

Napoleon could certainly have won the battle had he been at the peak of his form. It is, however, pointless to cavil that Wellington was somehow saved by the Prussians: he had given battle on Blücher's promise of Prussian support, a promise he kept despite *Gneisenau's reservations and Grouchy's ill-directed efforts to stop him. Peter Hofschröer's recent work is right to emphasize the scale of the German contribution to the victory, though his suggestions that Wellington behaved duplicitously to his allies have generated as much heat as light. More work must be done on the Dutch–Belgian contribution, by no means as poor as some historians suggest. HEB

Uffindell, A., and Corum, M., *On the Fields of Glory: The Battle-fields of the 1815 Campaign* (London, 1996).

Haythornthwaite, Philip J., et al., *Napoleon: The Final Verdict* (London, 1996).

Hofschröer, Peter, *1815: The Waterloo Campaign: The German Victory* (London, 1999).

Wavell, FM Archibald Percival, 1st Earl (1883–1950). Wavell was educated at Winchester, commissioned into the Black Watch, and served in South Africa and India. In 1917 he was sent to represent the CIGS on *Allenby's staff in Egypt and became an admirer, later writing his biography. In 1939 he was appointed C-in-C Middle East, and it was under his command that *O'Connor routed the Italian army, driving it from Egypt and across Libya. He could have concluded the campaign in *North Africa had *Churchill not ordered him to send troops to Greece. Having done so he then had to cope with the arrival of German forces under *Rommel. Sent to the Far East in July 1941 he discovered a lack of trained men and modern aircraft, and when the Japanese attacked in December found himself presiding over a disaster. He remained C-in-C until June 1943, when he was appointed viceroy of India, retaining the appointment for the remainder of the war.

Famously taciturn, which induced Churchill to suspect his powers of decision, Wavell was in fact intelligent and sensitive. An outburst of ill temper on hearing of British collapse in the *Burma campaign was entirely uncharacteristic. He wrote numerous books, and compiled a *poetry anthology called *Other Men's Flowers*. When lecturing on generalship at Cambridge in 1939 he began with a definition from Socrates, and regarded *Belisarius and *Marlborough as prime examples of successful generals. He wrote that 'the best soldier has in him . . . a seasoning of devilry'. Yet his historical grasp was not matched by real enthusiasm for making war, and he lacked that very seasoning of devilry which might have made him a great general. RH

Wayne, John (1907–79), screen persona created by and for the actor Marion Morrison that embodied American idealization of a heroic past. That his portrayals were neither historically accurate nor reflected his own private behaviour is beside the point, because Morrison became Wayne, and Wayne became a symbol of vanishing manliness at a time of uncertain national identity.

He achieved star status in director John Ford's *Stagecoach* (1939) and played the lead in many of his other films, notably *Fort Apache* (1948), *Rio Grande* (1950), and the very much darker *The Searchers* (1956) and *The Man Who Shot Liberty Valance* (1962). Another long collaboration with director Howard Hawks produced such classics as *Red River* (1948), *Rio Bravo* (1959), and *El Dorado* (1967).

Wayne suffered a severe personal setback when he directed a treasured project about the siege of the *Alamo and ran it over time and budget. Hostile reviews and disappointing attendance figures revealed that the popular mood was turning against his brand of unquestioning patriotism. This was unkindly underlined when in an attempt to replicate his rousing *Sands of Iwo Jima* (1949) he made *The Green Berets*, released to near-universal scorn during the *Vietnam war. Unrepentant, he continued to advocate an America strong abroad but lightly governed at home, beliefs he was convinced were shared by the Republican Party. He campaigned vigorously for his similarly motivated friend Ronald Reagan, but did not live to see him win the presidency.

Towards the end of his career, he broke with the stereotype and played a fat, drunken, one-eyed marshal in *True Grit* (1969) which won him a long-sought Oscar, and memorably opposite Katharine Hepburn in *Rooster Cogburn and the Lady* (1975). Echoing his own long struggle with lung cancer, his last role was as a dying gunman in *The Shootist* (1976). HEB

Wehrmacht (Ger.: *Wehrmacht*, defence power) refers to the German armed forces of WW II. In 1935 *Hitler announced the existence of the air force and the reintroduction of conscription, both prohibited by the Treaty of Versailles. The Wehrmacht thereafter comprised the army (Heer), the navy (Kriegsmarine), and the air force (Luftwaffe). Each had its own headquarters, OKH (Oberkommando des Heeres) for the army, OKM (Oberkommando der Marine) for the navy, and OKL (Oberkommando der Luftwaffe) for the air force.

On Hitler's birthday, 22 April 1936, the army C-in-C Col Gen Werner von Blomberg was promoted field marshal and appointed war minister and head of the Wehrmacht. He proposed the creation of an Armed Forces General Staff, based on the nucleus of the existing Wehrmachtsamt (Armed Forces Office), but ran into opposition from single services who feared loss of authority, and was forced to resign in January 1938 after contracting an unsuitable marriage.

Something of his scheme bore fruit. In February the war ministry was abolished and the Wehrmacht high command,

OKW (Oberkommando der Wehrmacht), was established. Hitler became C-in-C, and Gen Wilhelm Keitel, who had headed the Wehrmachtsamt, became its chief, a post he was to hold throughout the war. Keitel was promoted field marshal in July 1940 after victory over France, something to his embarrassment. He proved a tireless executor of Hitler's wishes, although personal notes confess to much inner tribulation. Never fully trusted by Hitler, he was known as 'Lakeitel' (from *lakei*, lackey) by many brother officers. The OKW operations staff was headed by another gunner, Alfred Jodl, an energetic staff officer who gave substance to many of Hitler's schemes. The main body of OKW was based at Zossen, on the outskirts of Berlin, though it provided staff for Hitler's headquarters, Wolfschanze, (wolf's lair) in East Prussia, and Werwolf in the western Ukraine. Jodl described life there as a mixture of cloisters and concentration camp: smoking and drinking were taboo, and women out of the question.

OKW was never really a proper joint planning headquarters. It only functioned as such once, for Operation Weserubung, the invasion of Denmark and Norway in 1940. After the invasion of Russia Hitler took personal command of the army, and distributed responsibilities so that OKH was responsible for the eastern front while OKW dealt with all other matters. Single-service commanders were amongst those who had right of personal access to Hitler, and generally championed the vested interests of their own services. Göring, Reich aviation minister as well as head of the Luftwaffe, enjoyed a wide measure of independence. It was in Hitler's nature to divide and rule, in defence as in much else, and he never allowed OKW to co-ordinate or evaluate the views of individual services. As the war went on Hitler became increasingly involved in the day-to-day conduct of military operations, using OKW as his mouthpiece. His conviction that he understood war better than his generals (reinforced by successes achieved in the face of military advice in 1939–41), together with the progressive effects of strain and ill health, made him increasingly disinclined to take advice, and his conferences often became little more than ranting monologues.

Not only was the Wehrmacht's command structure fatally flawed, but its expansion, from the 100,000 men allowed by the Treaty of Versailles to the 4.5 million men under arms in 1939, imposed an enormous strain on trained manpower. The procurement system could never keep pace, and exhibited the same lack of strategic consistency which characterized the command structure itself, with fashionable projects consuming resources better diverted elsewhere. It was not until 1942 that Speer was given control over the war economy, and only in 1944 that Germany was fully mobilized for total war. Thus although Germany led the way with development of armoured warfare (see BLITZKRIEG), she retained a two-tier army, with panzer divisions fighting alongside infantry who retained horse-drawn transport until the war's end.

Given these disadvantages the Wehrmacht's achievements are all the more astonishing. The army generated a combat performance which was consistently 20–30 per cent better than that of British and American units facing it. Martin van Creveld called it 'a superb fighting organisation . . . [which] probably had no equal among twentieth-century armies'. Because of Hitler's strategic errors, from 1942 Germany fought an increasingly attritional struggle against powerful opponents, but even after the tide of war had turned against them German armed forces continued to astonish their opponents by dogged defence sprinkled with rapid counter-attacks. In April 1945 a single German tank destroyed fourteen Russian tanks in a day while covering the evacuation of the Vienna bridgehead, and the most surprising thing about the battle of the *Bulge, the Ardennes offensive of December 1944, is not that it failed, but that it did such damage in its first dew days.

Cultural factors like national character and the status enjoyed by the armed forces within society played their part in promoting a performance which, in victory and defeat, remains remarkable. There were also a number of specifically military factors. Until the training and replacement system broke down under the impact of defeats in east and west in mid-1944 German soldiers were not simply better trained than their opponents, but were delivered from the Replacement Army to the front line by way of 'marching battalions' which gave regiments a strong incentive to polish the training of their own replacements, who were often trained by the officers and NCOs who would lead them in battle. Officer and NCO training was well ahead of that in Allied armies: in *Normandy it is no exaggeration to say that the average German senior NCO was better trained than the average Allied junior officer, while German officer training routinely incorporated periods of front-line service.

Military organization was designed to maximize combat power at the expense of logistic support. In a given theatre, combat troops represented 84.5 per cent of the total in the German army but only around 50 per cent in the US army. Troop indoctrination played its part in maintaining morale, especially on the eastern front, where, as Omer Bartov has shown, there is good reason for doubting the primacy of the standard view of the primary group as the foundation of combat morale. There the impact of casualties was such that these groups were constantly disrupted, and indoctrination helped meet the perceived need for the war to have some purpose. Both stick and carrot—the efficient distribution of awards and (see below) draconian punishment for failure all helped. And even though the Wehrmacht eventually incorporated a wide variety of non-German auxiliaries, as well as, latterly, the very old and the very young, at its core lay a notion of soldierly honour which helped sustain it to the very end of what was evidently an unwinnable war. It was as well for the Allies that this formidable machine was not directed by a better co-ordinated command structure or a wholly rational brain.

There was unquestionably a darker side to all this, sometimes neglected by those historians dazzled by the glitter of the Wehrmacht's performance on the battlefield. The Reichswehr had slipped easily from showing 'benevolent neutrality' to anti-communist Nazi brutality into overt support for Nazism. In July 1933 Blomberg declared that it was the army's task 'to serve the national movement with the utmost dedication', and national socialist symbols were speedily incorporated into military insignia. Greater compliance soon followed. Hitler saw the struggle against Russia as a carefully planned war of extermination, and demanded that the armed forces share his world-view encompassing race, autarky, and living space. In December 1938 the army's C-in-C, Col Gen von Brauchitsch, had demanded an officer corps which would be unsurpassed 'in the purity and genuineness of its National Socialist Weltanschauung'. In 1941 Halder, the army's CGS—who himself harboured significant doubts about its relationship with Hitler—wrote that 'Bolshevism equals antisocial crime . . . We must get away from the standpoint of soldierly comradeship . . . It is a war of extermination.' Jürgen Förster concludes that 'the armed forces did not confine themselves to 'normal' warfare . . . Total exoneration of the army is no more of an aid towards the understanding of this chapter in German history than is total condemnation.'

The armed forces involved in this process were not only politicized but rigorously invigilated. As Manfred Messerschmidt has observed, 'military justice became a strong link between the National Socialist system and its armed forces'. During WW I 150 German soldiers were sentenced to death by military courts, and only 48 were actually executed. Messerschmidt suggests that in WW II at least 17,000 were executed, and to these must be added the thousands sent to penal battalions, which suffered very heavy casualties. The Wehrmacht's motivation was in part traditional, and its members fought for victory, survival, comrades, and families: but they also fought for Nazism and all it meant. 'The transformation of Germany's workers into Hitler's soldiers,' writes Bartov, 'was a measure of the regime's success in mobilising the whole nation to fight its war of conquest and destruction.'   RH

Bartov, Omer, *Hitler's Army* (Oxford, 1991).
Diest, Wilhelm (ed.), *The German Military in the Age of Total War* (Leamington Spa, 1985).
Kitchen, Martin, *A Military History of Germany* (London, 1975).
van Creveld, Martin, *Fighting Power: German and US Army Performance 1933–1945* (London, 1982).

Wellesley, Richard Colley, Marquess of (1760–1842), the East India Company's (EIC) governor general of India, 1797–1805. Although overshadowed by the achievements of his younger brother Arthur, the Duke of *Wellington, Wellesley was an important figure in his own right, especially in expanding British imperial power. During his

governor generalship he redrew the map of India through a combination of diplomacy and military annexation, a process to which his brother's military victories made a formidable contribution. Mysore, Hyderabad, Tanjore, Surat, the Carnatic, and Oudh were either partially annexed or subordinated to EIC rule. French power in India suffered a major blow and Wellesley refused British government orders to restore French territory under the provisions of the Treaty of Amiens (1802), an act of insubordination which was soon justified by events. Wellesley's ambition, his expansionist policy, and the huge cost of his military arrangements alarmed the directors of the EIC in London. He was recalled in 1805 and threatened with impeachment, but survived. He remained politically important, serving as ambassador to Spain in 1808 and as foreign secretary, 1809–12. His later years were soured by jealousy of his younger brother's increasing fame.   JMB

Butler, Iris, *The Eldest Brother: The Marquess Wellesley 1760–1842* (London, 1973).

Wellington, Arthur Wellesley, Duke of (1769–1851). Born Arthur Wesley (the family later changed the spelling), second son of the Earl of Mornington, Wellington was commissioned at the age of 17. Influence gained him appointment as ADC to the viceroy of Ireland, and he was promoted lieutenant in 1787. He was elected to the family seat of Trim in 1790, and promoted captain the following year. Loans from his elder brother, now Lord Mornington (later Marquess *Wellesley), purchased a majority and lieutenant colonelcy in the 33rd Regiment in 1793. He resigned his seat and took the 33rd to Flanders in 1794. He complained that 'no one knew anything of the management of an army' and admitted that the episode taught him much. 'The real reason why I succeeded in my campaigns', he wrote, 'is because I was always on the spot—I saw everything; and did everything for myself.'

He regained his seat on his return, tried to obtain a government post, and, now a colonel, sailed for India. His brother was governor general, and he was given command in Mysore and promoted major general on the India list. In 1803 he beat the *Marathas at *Assaye. Years later, when asked what was 'the best thing' he did in the way of fighting he unhesitatingly replied 'Assaye'. He lost 1,500 of his 7,000 men, one of his horses was shot and its replacement piked. He went on to win another battle at Argaum and take the fortress of Gawlighur (Gwalior).

He returned home in 1805, was knighted, took a brigade on a brief expedition to the Elbe, and then married Kitty Pakenham, who had rejected him over ten years before. On their wedding day he muttered, 'She has grown ugly, by Jove', privately admitted that it was a mistake, and was to have a series of characteristically discreet affairs. He sat unhappily on the backbenches until appointed Chief Secretary for Ireland in April 1807. Shortly afterwards he commanded a brigade in an expedition to Denmark, returning to Dublin after the capture of *Copenhagen.

In the spring of 1808 he was promoted lieutenant general and sent to Portugal with a small force. On arrival he heard that the French were stronger than expected and the force would be increased: he would be superseded by Sir Hew Dalrymple, with Sir Harry Burrard as his second-in-command. In the meantime he faced *Junot at Vimeiro. He checked the attack with skirmishers at the foot of a ridge and kept the bulk of his force concealed behind it to take on French *columns at close range. The French had begun to break when Burrard arrived, but Wellington could not persuade him to pursue. Dalrymple and Burrard agreed the Convention of Cintra, which allowed the French passage home in British ships. A court of enquiry whitewashed all three generals, but neither Dalrymple nor Burrard held active command again.

Without military employment during the *Corunna campaign, he returned to Portugal in 1809. He quickly secured Oporto, and within a month Portugal was cleared of French. He complained that 'The army behave terribly ill. They are a rabble who cannot bear success any more than Sir John Moore's army could bear failure. I am endeavouring to tame them'. In uneasy collaboration with the Spanish, he pursued the French into Spain, only to have them turn on him at Talavera. On 28 July the French launched attacks on his line and came close to breaking it, but in the nick of time he plugged what he called an 'ugly hole'. He lost a quarter of his force and was in no state to pursue. Talavera brought him a peerage, and he chose the title Viscount Wellington of Talavera and (for the family originated in the West Country) Wellington.

Hearing that Austria had made peace, Wellington knew that the French would be free to deal with him, and fell back into Portugal while French reinforcements flooded in, taking Ciudad Rodrigo and Almeida. On 27 September 1810 *Masséna lost heavily attacking him on the long ridge at Busaco, but Wellington, outnumbered, retreated to the Lines of *Torres Vedras, impervious to French attack. After a cold and hungry winter Masséna withdrew from Portugal in March 1811.

Wellington hoped to take Badajoz and Almeida, and left *Beresford besieging Badajoz while he moved on Almeida, defeating Masséna at Fuentes de Oñoro in May, though the escape of the Almeida garrison took the gilt from the victory. Beresford, meanwhile, beat a relieving force under *Soult in a bloody action at Albuera, and Wellington abandoned the siege of Badajoz shortly afterwards.

In January 1812 Wellington took Ciudad Rodrigo by storm, which brought him an earldom, and went on to assault Badajoz in April. The attempt nearly failed, and when the attackers at last fought their way in, discipline collapsed completely. Wellington lost 5,000 men, and wrote to London: 'The capture of Badajoz affords as strong an instance of the gallantry of our troops as has ever been displayed.

But I greatly hope that I shall never again be the instrument of putting them to such a test'. In July he beat Masséna's successor *Marmont at *Salamanca, in a brilliantly timed attack, rightly regarded as his masterpiece. He followed up the victory by entering Madrid, rising another notch in the peerage by doing so, but failed to take Burgos. Slipping back into Portugal with Soult close behind him, he congratulated himself on getting out of 'the worst scrape I was ever in', but launched a merciless attack on indiscipline, gripping his army with what he called 'A HAND OF IRON'.

In May 1813 he again advanced into Spain, meeting Napoleon's brother Joseph, its puppet king, at Vitoria in June. With almost 80,000 men Wellington outnumbered the French, and tried to pin Joseph to his position by a frontal attack while turning his flank. Although the attack did not go according to plan Joseph narrowly escaped capture and all his baggage and 151 guns were taken. Victory brought Wellington a field marshal's baton, sensitively designed by the Prince Regent himself. Wellington stormed San Sebastian and crossed the Bidossa into France in October. He beat the French at Orthez, but a subordinate's error marred the *pursuit. Wellington reprimanded the officer so stiffly that he rode into a skirmish and was shot. Some thought that Wellington blamed himself, but as Sir William Napier said, 'He has always kept to that system of never acknowledging he was wrong'. The war's last battle, at Toulouse on 10 April 1814, was what Wellington called 'a very severe affair'. Although he drove Soult from the town, he lost more men than the French, and both sides claimed victory. Wellington was dressing for dinner in Toulouse when he heard that Napoleon had abdicated.

Created a duke, Wellington visited Paris before returning home to a tumultuous welcome, not much to his taste. Dispatched to Paris as ambassador, he was then sent to be senior British representative at the Congress of Vienna. On 7 March 1815 he heard that Napoleon had escaped from Elba, and a fortnight later he was appointed C-in-C of British and Dutch-Belgian forces in the Low Countries. He arrived in Brussels on 1 April to undertake the sternest test of his career, the campaign of the *Hundred Days.

Wellington recognized that this was not the old Peninsular army, but 'an infamous army, very weak and ill equipped'. He knew that the campaign would hinge on collaboration with his Prussian allies, assuring the diarist Creevy that 'Blücher and myself can do the thing'. On 15 June he heard that Napoleon had crossed the frontier, but did not identify his main thrust correctly. He was at the Duchess of Richmond's ball in Brussels—giving the impression of normality, but with his senior officers to hand—when he heard that Napoleon was moving up from Charleroi. Admitting that 'Napoleon has humbugged me' he decided to concentrate at Quatre Bras, but planned to fight further back, on the ridge at Mont St Jean.

He reached Quatre Bras on the morning of 16 June, thought that the young Prince of Orange had things in hand, and then rode eastwards to confer with *Blücher near Ligny. He confirmed that he would join Blücher, 'provided I am not attacked myself', and rode back to Quatre Bras. Although Wellington checked *Ney at Quatre Bras, Blücher was beaten at Ligny by Napoleon, and Allied fortunes hinged on the old Prussian's gallant decision to march north-westwards to join Wellington rather than fall back, as *Gneisenau suggested, on his lines of communication.

Wellington laid out his position near *Waterloo on 17 June, making the most of slopes which allowed him to conceal much of his infantry. When Napoleon attacked on the 18th the duke was everywhere, plainly dressed in blue coat and white breeches, slipping on a blue cape with each of the many showers. He sent precise orders to the garrison of Hougoumont, congratulated Capt Mercer on the handling of his troop of artillery, and, when the Imperial Guard came up the trampled slope, was on hand to give Maitland's Guards Brigade the order to fire. It was a long and dreadful day, and at 18.30 he muttered: 'Night or the Prussians must come.' He had repulsed Napoleon's last attack when he saw that Blücher's men had bitten deep into the French right flank, and waved his hat to signal a general advance. That night he gave his bed to a mortally wounded staff officer, and tears furrowed his cheeks when he heard of the losses. 'Well, thank God,' he said, 'I do not know what it is to lose a battle, but certainly nothing can be more painful than to win one with the loss of so many of one's friends.'

Wellington commanded the Allied armies of occupation, and returned home in 1818 to become Master General of the *Ordnance with a seat in Lord Liverpool's cabinet. Appointed C-in-C in 1827, he resigned when Canning became PM, but was persuaded to become PM himself in 1828. He spent two unhappy years in office, bravely introducing Catholic Emancipation but losing ground over parliamentary reform, to which he was steadfastly opposed. He was reappointed C-in-C in 1842, casting a long conservative shadow over the army for the last decade of his life.

Wellington was a brilliant defensive tactician, with a sharp eye for ground and clear understanding of the men who held it. His campaigning in India and Spain shows him as a skilled manager of armies, with a flair for manoeuvre in attack, prepared to risk but never to gamble. He was no manoeuvrist in the modern sense. Orders were orders, and officers deviated from them at their peril. He was personally rather chilly, and many felt him stingy with praise, but his quiet 'gentleman-like' demeanour inspired regard often denied the more flamboyant. 'We would rather see his long nose in a fight than a reinforcement of ten thousand men any day', wrote an officer, while a private of the 7th Fusiliers asked, in Tyneside vernacular, 'Whore's ar Arthur? Aw wish he wor here.' RH

Longford, Elizabeth, *Wellington*, vol. 1. *The Years of the Sword* (London, 1969); vol. 2. *Pillar of the State* (London, 1972).

West Point US Military Academy. Built on a beautiful escarpment overlooking the Hudson river, the academy was founded in 1802 by Jefferson partly to fill a void in technical education, but also with the idea that a standing army would be more acceptable if military engineers could perform public works. This put a unique stamp on the US army. Despite its apartness from a society that regards its concepts of *honour and service as, at best, quaint, it never developed a praetorian mentality and has produced a number of successful politicians. This may be partly because political *patronage long governed admission to West Point, but it is also because Congressmen have traditionally valued the army for 'pork barrel' projects in their districts, giving officers a sound grounding in the essence of democracy.

The character of the academy was set in stone by Superintendent Thayer between 1817 and 1833, modelled on the French *École Polytechnique. He introduced a curriculum in which each student was assessed every day by his instructors, and a system of cumulative 'demerits' to enforce strict standards of deportment. French was the only foreign language taught, and there was a taste for formalism, for the Napoleon described by *Jomini rather than by *Clausewitz. This was reinforced but modified in unique ways by Mahan, professor of engineering 1832–71, and much *American civil war generalship reveals his influence, from the odd emphasis on holding key points rather than seeking to destroy the enemy army, to posing for photographs with one hand tucked into the tunic. Two hundred and ninety-one Union and 151 Confederate generals were West Point graduates, but Mahan's favourites were *Halleck and *McClellan, who appeared to believe that the war could be won by manoeuvre alone.

Once West Pointers achieved sufficient seniority, they commanded in all of America's wars save one. Miles, a hero of the American civil and *Plains Indian wars, was army commander during the *Spanish-American war and like many another outsider, he believed that military *academies produce self-serving cliques. While certainly correct, his appreciation missed the deeper significance of the self-selection that draws a certain personality to a military career, one which is deeply unsuited to the unorthodox warfare at which he excelled. Engineering remained West Point's forte and its supreme expression was the on-time, under-budget construction of the Panama Canal by Goethals. Despite Superintendent MacArthur's 1919 effort to inject more life into the curriculum, leadership per se was not a specific subject before *Eisenhower requested it in 1946, which suggests he may have noted a deficiency in this area.

Along with the military in general, West Point fell into popular disrepute during the *Vietnam war, which had its Mahanite moments and also heavily underlined Miles's long-forgotten strictures. Along with a declining emphasis on abusive male bonding rituals, inevitable after the admission of *women in 1976, West Point has shared in the general rediscovery of *doctrine by the US army since Vietnam, and it is pleasing to fancy that Clausewitz, at long last, has been allowed to elbow aside the ghosts of Jomini, Thayer, and Mahan.   HEB

Western Desert campaigns WW II It is arguable that the North African theatre, in its constant changes of fortune, was unlike any other during WW II. Both sides prolonged their campaigns there unintentionally, due to the demands of other theatres which were considered more important by their political masters—thus the British diverted forces to the Far East and Greece at crucial moments, as did the Germans to Russia. For both sides also, the campaign stressed the tensions of coalition warfare. The British effort from the start involved her whole empire, with South Africans, Indians, New Zealanders, and Australians fighting under British command, later joined by Free French and, after Operation TORCH in November 1942, Americans. The Germans had to contend with the wildly variable Italian army, and a highly political command structure based in Italy. As the Allied and Axis forces in North Africa relied on air cover to protect their Mediterranean shipping convoys and ground troops in the desert, at a strategic level joint co-operation was vital. The Allies eventually mastered this, but the Axis failed to effectively integrate an air campaign to support movement on the ground or across the Mediterranean.

With the Italian invasion from Libya eastwards into British-protected Egypt on 13 September 1940, the desert war began. The Italians halted at Sidi Barani after three days, establishing a series of colonial-type fortified camps which were too far apart to provide mutual assistance. *Wavell's tiny Western Desert force of two divisions from Mersa Matruh counter-attacked on 9 December, and within two months—greatly to his surprise—pushed the Italians out of Egypt, and across Cyrenaica destroying 10 Italian divisions and taking 130,000 prisoners, for a British loss of 2,000 killed and wounded. *Mussolini appealed to *Hitler for help and a relatively unknown lieutenant general was despatched with two divisions to North Africa. *Rommel's arrival in Tripoli on 12 February 1941 altered the course of the desert war. Without waiting to build up his forces, he attacked on 24 March, and over the next 30 days drove the British from El Agheila right back across Cyrenaica and into Egypt at the Halfaya Pass. The port of Benghazi fell on 4 April, but Rommel was unable to take *Tobruk, which remained isolated 100 miles (161 km) behind the front, and whose continued resistance assumed a symbolic significance for the British when the war elsewhere was going appallingly. Rommel had actually been forced to pause before Tobruk due to petrol and other logistical shortages: such problems dogged the rest of his war in North Africa, and dominated the whole campaign over the waterless desert wastes for both sides. Wavell launched the unsuccessful Operation BATTLEAXE to relieve Tobruk in June, but by the time the British launched their next offensive, their commanders had changed. *O'Connor, commanding the Western Desert Force, had been captured in April and was replaced by Cunningham (whose admiral brother commanded the RN Mediterranean fleet), whilst an impatient Churchill sacked the unfortunate Middle East commander, Wavell (who had also to contend with the abortive operations in Greece and *Crete), replacing him with *Auchinleck. With both sides reinforced, Cunningham's renamed Eighth Army struck back at Rommel's Afrika Korps on 18 November 1941 in Operation CRUSADER. The British outnumbered Rommel in CRUSADER, but individual German units within the Italo-German army were better led, and possessed much greater initiative and resourcefulness, with the result that the campaign subsided into a series of inconclusive battles between the Egyptian frontier and Tobruk. Whilst Rommel withdrew west all the way back to El Agheila, Cunningham was replaced by Ritchie.

With the arrival of fresh forces in Tripoli, Rommel immediately counter-attacked on 21 January 1942, retook Benghazi on the 29th, and in three weeks had rolled Ritchie's Eighth Army back east to *Gazala, close to Tobruk. The British southern flank at Bir Hacheim was held by a Free French brigade under Koenig, which had fought its way up from Chad, and provided the first evidence that *de Gaulle's Free French units could play a role in the war. Rommel again attacked at Gazala on 28 May, and with good Italian support eventually broke through after vicious fighting. Ritchie ordered a withdrawal into Egypt on 13 June, and on the 21st Tobruk fell, seeming to underline the British failure in North Africa. Churchill took the blow badly, whilst Rommel was rewarded with a field marshal's baton.

By this stage, Eighth Army morale was suspect, especially as regards the relationship between infantry and tank units, whilst reinforcements were being diverted to the Far East, and the logistical tail through the Mediterranean was under severe German and Italian air and U-boat attack. But Rommel, too, had outrun his lines of supply, and was surviving only on what had been captured in Benghazi and Tobruk. Auchinleck took the opportunity to remove Ritchie and assume command of the Eighth Army himself. However, he was still forced to retreat before Rommel, first at Mersa Matruh on 28 June, and thence on 7 July to a fortified line on the Alam Halfa ridge, between the railway station at *Alamein and the Qattara depression 30 miles (48 km) to the south. The series of minor battles between the armies' arrival at Alam Halfa and 22 July, collectively known as first battle of Alamein, proved the exhaustion of both forces and Rommel's inability to advance further without substantial reinforcement. Consequently both sides paused, but now the British were able reinforce quicker, whilst Auchinleck was replaced by *Alexander, and Gott was nominated to take over Eighth Army. The latter's death in a plane crash resulted in *Montgomery assuming command of Eighth

Army on 13 August. Rommel attacked the Alam Halfa ridge on 31 August, but was blocked from breaking through by 7th Armoured Division and, under aerial attack and short of fuel, withdrew. Rommel then departed for Germany with a catalogue of medical ailments, the result of exhaustion, whilst throughout September and October Montgomery built up an overwhelming force of tanks, artillery, and men. Second *Alamein proved Montgomery's ability as a field commander, justified his elaborate and time-consuming logistic and deception plans, and was an important psychological blow both to Rommel (who quickly resumed command on 25 October), and to Berlin. As Alexandria lay only 60 miles (97 km) east of Alamein, Egypt and the Suez Canal had been in grave danger, but Montgomery's victory lifted this threat for good, and restored Eighth Army morale just when needed.

Although the British lost almost as many tanks as Panzer Army Africa, Rommel could not replace the losses he sustained at Alamein, and the TORCH landings at Casablanca, Oran, and Algiers in French North Africa to his rear (which followed Montgomery's victory by a mere four days) altered completely the nature of the campaign (see NORTH AFRICA CAMPAIGN). By November 1942 Hitler was preoccupied exclusively with the struggle for *Stalingrad which was nearing a climax, and the 'stand-and-fight' order issued to Rommel immediately after Alamein demonstrated Berlin's complete lack of understanding of the situation, or the nature of desert war. Rommel began his retreat on 4 November 1942 anyway. Thereafter his withdrawal westwards was swift, and Montgomery was slow to exploit the pursuit. Nevertheless by 17 December the Eighth Army had reached El Agheila, from whence Rommel had set out 21 months previously, in March 1941. The Axis supply base of Tripoli fell on 23 January 1943, and, although the port was partially wrecked, it started taking shipping within a week. Montgomery's logistics remained a nightmare, though, all the way into Tunisia, which he entered on 4 February, two days after Stalingrad fell.

In strategic terms the Western Desert campaigns were never going to affect the course of the war for either side. Both Hitler and Churchill realized this: the war would be decided by land battle in Europe and Russia. However, for the British the Western Desert battles initially provided cheap victories, when the news from elsewhere was grim, and were proof that Britain could hit back against the Axis. During 1941–2 when the commitment was greater, armed with ULTRA intercepts which indicated just how precarious Rommel's grip in the theatre was, the prospect of beating a high-profile German general provided the incentive to commit greater resources, which resulted in success at Alamein. As with many campaigns it was a combination of good intelligence work and the work of Bletchley Park that told against the Afrika Korps. For the Germans, North Africa was only ever a sideshow. Rommel never received the backing from Berlin in terms of resources that he really needed, and suffered from the continued interception of his supply convoys, courtesy of ULTRA. The defeat of Malta might well have altered this imbalance in his favour. Eventually, the eastern front absorbed German attention and resources and Rommel was effectively marginalized, leading to his inevitable defeat. APC-A

Westmoreland, Gen William (b. 1914), commander of US forces in *Vietnam during the build-up of 1964–8. Echoing Secretary of Defense McNamara's policy of treating soldiers like inputs of industrial production, he measured success in tons of ordnance delivered and 'body counts'. He was blamed for the institutional failure of an army characterized by 'ticket-punching', in which combat command was regarded as one of several necessary credits for promotion, not as the military *raison d'être*.

During WW II he commanded a battalion of artillery in *North Africa and *Sicily and was a divisional staff officer in *North-West Europe. He commanded an *airborne brigade in the *Korean war, and subsequently an airborne division and corps. In 1957 he became the youngest major general in the army and in 1961 he was appointed superintendent of *West Point, where he had been captain of cadets.

In Indochina he judged that the South Vietnamese army was too rotten to redeem and recommended 'Americanizing' the war. Like the rest of the military hierarchy, he was convinced that technology and firepower rendered the old rules for irregular warfare obsolete. Within a framework of battalion-sized 'search and destroy' sweeps, he pioneered the development of helicopter-borne forces and of airlifting artillery to detached fire bases, beyond the range of which only the *special forces were permitted to patrol. In combination with a historic US tendency to regard infantry as the bottom of the barrel, these tactics led to the demoralization of the bulk of the forces under his command.

The bankruptcy of this approach was revealed when he permitted a false analogy between the siege of the Marine fire base at Khe Sanh and the French defeat at *Dien Bien Phu to dominate his thoughts before, during, and after the country-wide *Tet offensive. His successor *Abrams belatedly encouraged company-sized patrols while concentrating on orthodox population control and implemented 'Vietnamization', a face-saving attempt to revitalize the South Vietnamese army, by now worse than ever and hopelessly dependent on departing US firepower.

Westmoreland retired in 1972 as army COS. In 1984 he sued for libel after CBS News accused him of lying about enemy troop strength in 1967. Faced with the network's superior firepower he withdrew the suit, not before reviving debate about whether the USA lost the war politically or militarily. That he still believed the two could be considered separately does much to explain the failure of overall US policy in Vietnam. HEB

Weygand, Gen Maxime (1867–1965). Weygand twice featured at the centre stage of history. Commissioned into the cavalry in 1885, he served from the outset of WW I as aide to *Foch. When the latter became Supreme Allied Commander in 1918, he made Weygand his COS. He deputized for Foch on the *Supreme War Council and took part in the *Armistice negotiations, reading out the principal clauses to the German delegates, and oversaw the signing on 11 November. In 1920–1, while serving under *Pilsudski, he displayed his ability to handle formations on his own account, directing the defence of Warsaw against *Tukhachevskiy. He retired after a tour as inspector general of the French army in 1931–5. In 1939 he was recalled to command French forces in Syria and Lebanon and, aged 73, he succeeded Gamelin as C-in-C in France on 20 May 1940 (the same day that *Pétain joined the government). There is evidence that Weygand had started to restore French military morale, but in the face of continued German victories PM Reynaud considered replacing him with Huntziger. After governmental discussions on 11–12 June, despite Churchill's pleas to the contrary, Reynaud opted for an armistice, signed (by Huntziger) in the very railway carriage where Weygand had stood so sternly in 1918. After Pétain took over on 16 June, Weygand served under him as defence minister, and later in North Africa. The unlucky Weygand was never a collaborator and was later imprisoned by the Germans. Nonetheless after the war his fellow-countrymen charged him with treason, of which he was rightly acquitted.   APC-A

wheel lock was an expensive and sensitive firearms mechanism with limited military use, principally in cavalry *pistols of the late 16th and early 17th centuries. The system worked by a wheel, with a serrated rim, within the lock being wound up against a spring with a key. The cock, holding a piece of iron pyrites, was brought down to make the pyrites touch the wheel rim. When the trigger was pressed the wheel was released, it revolved and struck sparks from the pyrites into the pan of priming powder which ignited the main charge.   SCW

Blair, Claude (gen. ed.), *Pollard's History of Firearms* (London, 1983).

White Mountain, battle of (1620), fought at Bila Hora, west of Prague. On 8 November during the *Thirty Years War a 48,000-strong Bavarian-imperial army of the Catholic League defeated a 33,000-strong Protestant force. The latter mostly comprised foreigners who had no particular interest in defending the Czech people. As a result of the defeat what is now the Czech Republic came under the rule of the Habsburg empire for 300 years.   CDB

Wilhelm II (1859–1941), Kaiser of Germany, Wilhelm helped lay the foundations for WW I, and in consequence gambled away his throne, bringing to an end the German empire—the Second Reich—established by his grandfather and namesake in 1871. His father, Frederick, had married Queen Victoria's namesake daughter, which was probably the origin of his love–hate relationship with Britain (and his uncle Edward VII and cousin George V). Plagued with insecurities and physically fragile (he had a withered arm), he perceived his father's liberalism as a weakness and resolved to rule with a firm hand. Had Frederick not died of throat cancer just months into his reign, he and Victoria might well have established a constitutional monarchy, which Wilhem would have found difficult to undermine.

Within two years of ascending the throne Wilhelm had forced the departure from office of *Bismarck, his grandfather's long-serving chancellor, adviser, and architect of the Second Reich. Bismarck, as Europe's senior statesman and diplomat, had engineered the security of Germany through a complicated series of alliances. Wilhelm's dismissal of him began to remove the props of peace, while his provocative naval rearmament strengthened the diplomatic and military ties between Britain and France. He was no judge of character and selected the nervous, sensitive *Moltke 'the Younger' as CGS in 1906, in the hope that he could outperform the achievements of his uncle in a future war. He was not really military-minded at all, but rather a superficial *militarist, obsessed with trappings and ceremonies. Additionally his temperament alternated between patronizing arrogance (which won him the detestation of Tsar Nicholas II of Russia) and debilitating self-doubt.

Two scandals in 1908 did significant (and arguably deep-seated) damage to his authority. He was certainly not in command of the events of July–August 1914, and as the war went on his real power declined still further. In early November 1918 he talked of leading his army personally to crush the reported outbreaks of Bolshevik mutiny, yet by 9 November he had abdicated without a whimper and fled the country with his family. He spent the rest of his life in retirement on his estate at Doorn in Holland, and maintained a mutual antipathy with the Third Reich, whose armies swept past his estate in 1940 without a sidelong glance.

Wilhelm was certainly not the first leader to be seduced by the siren calls of nationalism and militarism, or to discover that leading a cavalry charge on manoeuvres (an annual ritual in his case) is not the same thing as presiding over a beleaguered state engaged in *total war. However, he lacked the strength of character and consistency of purpose which his role demanded, and if he cannot be blamed for leading Germany into war, he may be more justly censured for what one historian has called 'a childlike flight from reality' in the crisis of July 1914.   APC-A

William of Orange (1650–1702). Prince William Henry of Orange and King William III of England (1688–1702) was the hereditary stadtholder of the United Provinces of the Netherlands, grandson of King Charles I of England and, despite being deformed, beloved husband of Mary, the daughter of *James II. But above all he was a robust champion of Protestantism at a time when his father-in-law compounded the Stuart family propensity for religious folly by his overt Catholicism. Thus in 1688 he and Mary were invited to become joint rulers of England while James II fled to the court of his patron *Louis XIV, and three centuries of involvement in the wars of continental Europe began.

It was also thanks to Louis XIV that William was able to exercise authority over the Netherlands. The latter had decided that no future ruler should be both the political (stadtholder) and military (captain general) leader, but when in 1672 Louis and Charles II of England declared war and the French overran three provinces, minds were concentrated. William at first could only defend, but after he rebuilt the Netherlands army and allied with the Holy Roman Emperor and the elector of Brandenburg, the provinces were recovered. The invitation to co-rule in England came at the end of the only prolonged lull the aggressive Louis granted him, and he never regarded England as much more than an added resource in his lifelong struggle against the Sun King. During the *League of Augsburg war there was a brief moment when, if Louis had considered it worthwhile, England could have been invaded, but instead James II was sent to put himself at the head of an *Irish and *Jacobite rebellion in 1790 and to be defeated by William's *Irish campaign culminating at the *Boyne. William's generalship was dogged, not inspired. In 1792 he not only failed to save *Namur from Louis and *Vauban, but was also trounced at the battle of Steenkirk. Mary died in 1694 without issue, so England was even less of a priority for the remainder of William's life. He recaptured Namur in 1695 and the League he did so much to keep together managed to contain Louis; but five years later it was business as usual with the outbreak of the War of the *Spanish Succession, and a year later William died. In his absence party politics evolved in England, which has kept the oligarchy entertained ever since.   HEB

William 'the Conqueror' (1028–87), also known as William 'the Bastard', Duke of Normandy and King William I of England. As the only (if illegitimate) son, he succeeded Duke Robert at the age of 7 in 1035. During his minority Normandy fell into bloody anarchy during which three of his guardians were killed and his kinsmen murdered his personal tutor, which is perhaps why William remained illiterate. He began to assert his authority from about 1045, calling upon his *feudal lord King Henri I of France to assist him in subduing rebellious barons, finally defeating their assembled forces near Caen in 1047. He is described as of average but robust build, tending to corpulence as he grew older, and of the savage and despotic disposition necessary to impose his will on a duchy in which, perhaps because of *Viking blood, there was a high state of latent or actual violence.

He also had a peasant's Christian faith and founded several monasteries, although his use of prelates as his representatives was politically shrewd. In 1049 the pope, at the behest of the western emperor, declared his marriage to the daughter of Baldwin of Flanders incestuous and among other penances he undertook was to go on a crusade. So it was that his invasion of England, where the church was schismatic, was officially a crusade and a papal banner flew over the Norman knights at *Hastings. The dynastic background to the invasion was complex and its prelude was the subject of propaganda of which the *Bayeux Tapestry* forms an enduring part. William had been promised the throne by the childless Edward 'the Confessor' (1042–66), who may have subsequently changed his mind: it was said that on his deathbed he supported the succession of Harold Godwinson, Earl of Wessex. Harold himself, however, was alleged to have sworn an oath on holy relics to support William's claim. This made his assumption of the throne on Edward's death, in the eyes of William and his supporters, an act of blasphemous usurpation which earned papal blessing for the invasion of England.

The invasion served three purposes: it united his fractious nobles in a cause dear to their warlike hearts, it bought a blessing from the pope on his marriage and legitimacy for his children, and—one should not underestimate the contemporary power of this—it enforced the homage done to him by the usurper Harold. It certainly would appear that his venture had divine blessing, for he failed in his first attempt to cross and thus landed a week after Harold had defeated Haraldr Harðráða, the last of the great Viking invaders, and his own brother Tostig, at Stamford Bridge. Thus it was a tired and depleted Saxon army that William only just defeated. Had he landed first, he would probably have fared as ill as Harðráða. The subjugation of England went on for the rest of his reign, punctuated by rebellions and intrigue among his own relatives and nobles on both sides of the Channel. In 1072 he invaded Scotland and in 1081 Wales, and he had the brilliant idea of settling his more turbulent vassals in the northern and western 'marches', where they could indulge their combativeness while protecting the rest of the kingdom.

By eliminating the native aristocracy, the Normans achieved something akin to *Sparta in subjugating Messenia: they created a huge helot class that left them free to hone their martial skills. The Channel, and the fact that William owed no man homage for his new kingdom, meant that the social structure thus created proved very durable. He was owed homage for every inch of his new kingdom, and the famous Domesday Book was an inventory of his new property. But he did not value it particularly highly—he spent the bulk of the rest of his life fighting in France and left England to his second son, while the eldest got Normandy and Maine. HEB/RH

William 'the Silent' (correctly 'the Prudent') (1533–84), the figure around whom the *Netherlands revolt coalesced. Ruler of the county of Nassau-Dillenburg in Germany and of the principality of Orange in Provence, also the largest landholder in Brabant, he was brought up under the tutelage of the Emperor *Charles V. His son Philip II made William a councillor of state in 1555, governor (stadtholder) in Holland, Zeeland, and Utrecht in 1559, and in Franche-Comté (where he also had extensive lands) in 1561. With so much to lose he was indeed careful, but events forced him into a role for which he was unprepared by training or temperament. A Lutheran, he suppressed Calvinist disorders in Antwerp in 1566 and strove to maintain peace between Catholics and Protestants, but he was pushed into rebellion by the Duke of *Alba's infamous Council of Blood, which declared his lands forfeit and seized his son. In 1568 Alba crushed one mercenary army under William's brother Louis and evaded battle with the second, led by William himself. As always out of money, he withdrew to France, where he made peace with the local Calvinists (*Huguenots) before returning to his lands in Germany.

William prepared a co-ordinated attack for 1572, but the St Bartholomew's Day massacre in France dashed his hopes of support from that quarter. Generalized revolt was in fact sparked by the capture of Brielle by the 'Sea Beggars' as a result of being driven out of their havens in England. Most of Holland and Zeeland declared for William, later joined by Gelderland and Friesland. For the next four years he led the maritime provinces' resistance to the Spanish, his brothers Louis and Henry falling at Nijmegen in 1574, the same year he gave up trying to tame Calvinist fanaticism and joined the Reformed Church.

In 1576, taking advantage of disorder among the Spanish, he achieved the Pacification of Ghent in which the Habsburgs' own states general, exceeding their authority, restored his lands and confirmed his status as stadtholder. This arrangement did not survive the arrival of the new captain general, Don Juan of Austria, and the lid was nailed down by Don Juan's successor *Parma, who drove a permanent wedge between the Catholic south and the Protestant north. William's last efforts were to bring in the French to counterbalance the Spanish, on his terms, but he was assassinated before the plan bore fruit. RH

Wilson, FM Sir Henry Hughes (1864–1922), British WW I general and inveterate intriguer who was involved behind the scenes in the *Curragh mutiny, in the removal

of *French in 1915, and the appointment of his pre-war friend *Foch over the head of *Haig as Allied C-in-C in 1918. A garrulous and ambitious Irishman, he entered the Rifle Brigade via Marlborough and was later an influential Staff College commandant (1906–10). Perceptive enough to anticipate war and as an ardent Francophile anxious to support the French, as director of military operations (1910–14) he formulated plans that ensured an efficient deployment to France of the British Expeditionary Force (BEF) in August 1914. He accompanied the BEF as its vice-COS, and was notably influential in 1914 before being sent to the French HQ as a liaison officer. Wilson succeeded *Robertson as CIGS in early 1918 and was remarkably duplicitous in betraying the things said to him in confidence by Haig to *Lloyd George, whom he despised, and vice versa. He gained his field marshal's baton and a baronetcy in the 1919 Peace Honours and remained CIGS until 1922, throughout the *Anglo-Irish war. Immediately after he retired he entered parliament to speak out on the Irish question and was assassinated on his doorstep, in the full-dress uniform he had worn to an official function. It is said that he went for his sword, which would have been entirely characteristic. APC-A

Callwell, C. E. (ed.), *Life and Letters of Sir Henry Wilson* (2 vols., London, 1927).

Winchester rifle The Winchester Repeating Arms Company was established in New Haven, Connecticut, and in 1866 began producing the repeating rifle that made it famous, based very closely on the Henry rifle of 1860. A rugged .44 calibre lever-action rifle with a tubular magazine beneath the barrel, the 1873 model was bought by Turkey and used very effectively in the Russo-Turkish war of 1877–8. It was also one of many types employed by the Cheyenne and Sioux at *Little Bighorn. Winchester rifles were bought in limited quantities for the US army and navy, and the Royal Navy used them for a period in the 1890s. SCW

Blair, Claude (gen. ed.), *Pollard's History of Firearms* (London, 1983).

Wingate, Maj Gen Orde (1903–44). Wingate was born in India on 26 February 1903 and educated at Charterhouse school and the Royal Military *Academy at Woolwich, where he was picked upon by his peers but ultimately respected for his physical and mental toughness. He served in the Sudan from 1928 to 1933 and was sent as special adviser to the Jewish settlements police in Palestine. He helped train the 'special night squads', later the *Palmach*, and became such a devoted Zionist that he was recalled. In 1940 he was sent to advise the Ethiopian patriots to form what he called the 'Gideon force' in *Abyssinia and became the trusted adviser to the Emperor Haile Selassie. Once again he was judged to have 'gone native' and not only recalled but demoted. He seems to have been a manic depressive, and this along with malaria and exhaustion led him to attempt suicide in June 1941 while in Egypt. While he was recovering in Britain, his old commander *Wavell requested that he join him in his new command in the *Burma campaign and eventually promoted him major general. Wingate is best remembered for the pioneering concept of creating strongholds behind enemy lines to create disruption, and the *Chindits were the outcome. He was killed in an air crash during their second deployment. Neither *Slim nor *Stilwell shared Wavell's high opinion of him, though *Churchill did, and most Anglo-Saxons distrusted an enthusiasm bordering on religious fanaticism.   CDB

Royle, Trevor, *Orde Wingate: Irregular Soldier* (London, 1995).

Sykes, Christopher, *Orde Wingate* (London, 1959).

Wittstock, battle of (1636). This was fought around a little village on the Dosse river some 58 miles (93 km) north-west of Berlin on 4 October by the Swedish army under Johan Baner to keep open its communications with the Baltic. Baner enticed an imperial, Saxon, and Bavarian army of 20,000 under John George of Saxony out of its entrenchments, while Scots *mercenaries in Swedish service conducted a wide encircling movement, hitting the imperialists in the flank and rear and routing them, inflicting 5,000 casualties and capturing all their artillery. The Swedes lost about 3,000 of 15,000 engaged.   TM

Wohlstetter, Albert (1913–97), brilliant pioneer thinker in the field of 'thinking the unthinkable' with reference to *nuclear weapons. He joined the Rand Corporation in 1951 where he worked as a senior policy analyst and carried out a research project about the selection and use of Strategic Air Command's (SAC) bases, revealing the vulnerabilities of the SAC to surprise attack. This resulted in a change of SAC's basing policy so that its aircraft were located further from the USSR and better protected. Wohlstetter's paper also influenced Secretary of Defense *McNamara to develop the US nuclear deterrent around the concept of first-strike survivability based on Wohlstetter's dictum, 'a force cannot deter an attack which it cannot survive'.

Wohlstetter became central to US diplomatic and military strategy from about the Johnson presidency (1963–9) onwards. His career as a strategic analyst was guided by a number of principles, including his belief that the USA should control its military forces in such a way as to permit flexibility in the American response to foreign aggression according to the specific circumstances. The goal of this was to ensure that the USA was not forced to mount a first-strike nuclear attack on the USSR but have a variety of options instead, very much a move away from the strategy of massive retaliation.

He is credited with the thinking behind Pres Reagan's 'end game' with the USSR during the *Cold War, including the 'Star Wars' initiative. He was generally less interested in the diplomatic and economic side of geopolitical thinking.   MCM

Wolfe, Maj Gen James (1727–59). Son of a general, Wolfe joined his father's regiment in 1741 and was its adjutant at Dettingen (1743). A brevet major at *Culloden, he declined an order from Lt Gen Hawley, on whose staff he was serving, to pistol a wounded *Jacobite officer. A colonel by 1750, Wolfe turned his regiment into one of the best-trained in the army. 'I have a very mean opinion of the infantry in general,' he told his father. 'I know their discipline to be bad, & their valour precarious. They are easily put into disorder & hard to recover out of it; they frequently kill their Officers thro' fear, and murder one another in their confusion.' His regimental orders warned: 'A soldier who quits his rank, or offers to flag, is instantly to be put to death by the officer who commands that platoon'.

In 1757 Wolfe took part in the abortive expedition to Rochefort, but performed so well that he was sent, as a brigadier, on the *Louisbourg expedition to North America. Here he covered himself with glory, and was promoted. Given command of the attack on *Quebec, Wolfe made slow progress, and fell seriously ill. Recovering, he asked his brigadiers for advice. They recommended a landing upstream of the city, and he duly slipped a force onto the Heights of Abraham. His adversary, Montcalm, came out to meet him, and both were mortally wounded in a firefight won by superior British musketry.

Wolfe was a strange mixture. His romantic streak led him to declare that he would rather have written Gray's *Elegy* than take Quebec, but there was nothing romantic in his views on *discipline. His fierce energy blazed from a weedy frame, with weak chin and pointed nose. Had he escaped French musketry he would have died of the galloping consumption that was already eating him away.   RH

Wolseley, FM Garnet Joseph, Viscount Wolseley
(1833–1913), the inspiration for the 'very model of a modern major general' in Gilbert and Sullivan's operetta *The Pirates of Penzance*, Wolseley was popularly described by the Victorians as 'Our Only General'. Lacking means to purchase his commissions, Wolseley sought to advance in the army through gallantry. In less than eight years he rose to brevet lieutenant colonel but at the cost of a severe leg wound in *Burma and the loss of his left eye in the *Crimea. His wider military reputation was established by publishing a practical guide to soldiering, *The Soldier's Pocket Book*, in 1869 and leading an expedition against a rebellion on Canada's Red River in 1870. He then commanded another expedition to punish the *Ashanti in West Africa, his

capture of their capital at Kumasi in February 1873 being rewarded with his major generalcy. He was British high commissioner in both Natal in 1875 and on Cyprus in 1879 before returning to South Africa to conclude the *Zulu war in 1879. He became *QMG of the army in 1880 and adjutant-general in 1882. His great military achievement was the occupation of Egypt in the latter year, culminating in the battle of Tel-el-Kebir. Wolseley was promoted general and elevated to the peerage as a result but, three years later, his relief expedition failed to reach *Khartoum in time to rescue Charles *Gordon from the *dervishes. Advancement to a viscountcy was small consolation for failing to save his friend. He was promoted field marshal in 1894. Though a political conservative, Wolseley was regarded as dangerously radical in terms of his advocacy of military reform and his advancement was strongly opposed by the army's C-in-C, the Duke of Cambridge and his cousin, Queen Victoria. Wolseley's reliance on a small group of handpicked subordinates in his campaigns—the so-called Ashanti Ring—also bred resentment within the army among those excluded. Nevertheless, Wolseley became C-in-C in 1895 but ill health impaired his performance and he was blamed for the early failures of his protégés in the Second *Boer War. He retired in 1900 and his influence contributed to the professionalization of the army that he had been too old to achieve.   IB

Lehmann, Joseph, *All Sir Garnet* (London, 1964).

----

women in the military *(see opposite page)*

World War I (1914–18). Now usually abbreviated 'WW I', to the British it was until recently always 'the Great War'. It was the first major conflict between European coalitions since 1815. Individual powers were not defeated in seemingly decisive battles because each had allies to take up the fight. Ranged against the Central Powers (Austria-Hungary and Germany, joined in November 1914 by Turkey and in September 1915 by Bulgaria) were those of the Entente. Originally consisting of Russia, France, and Britain, they were reinforced by Japan in August 1914, Italy in May 1915, Portugal in March 1916, Romania in August 1916, and Greece in June 1917. When the USA entered the war in April 1917, the nations of South America followed suit, as did China. Much of the rest of the world were colonies of the belligerents, thus it was indeed a global war.

Austria-Hungary declared war on Serbia on 28 July 1914 in a bid to reassert its authority as a Balkan power. Its determination was buoyed by the knowledge that it enjoyed the backing of its ally, Germany. But Serbia was supported by Russia, and Germany therefore confronted the danger of a war on two fronts, as Russia was allied to France. Determined to deal with France first, Germany needed Austria to engage Russia in Galicia. The result was that Austria-Hungary divided its forces, and suffered defeat on both fronts. The situation was partially redeemed by the Germans' defeat of two Russian armies in East Prussia. The Germans then shifted their efforts to the south, so as to give direct aid to the Austrians, and the two allies advanced into Poland in October. The offensive miscarried, partly owing to lack of co-ordination, but principally because the Russians crossed the Vistula westwards with comparable designs.

In the west the main German advance, swinging through Belgium in order to envelop the French, began on 18 August. The French, redeploying round Paris, together with the British, checked the now extended German armies on the *Marne. Thereafter each side sought to get round the other's flank to the north. By October they had filled the space to the coast and heavy fighting around *Ypres between then and mid-November failed to result in breakthrough.

The principal priorities of the British and French outside Europe were to contain the war by destroying the Germans' network of wireless stations and cruiser bases. Conversely, by extending the war to the Islamic peoples of central Asia and North Africa, Germany could threaten the colonies of their enemies. Her ally Turkey declared a *jihad on 14 November 1914, while Britain had already landed an expeditionary force in *Mesopotamia, and in March and April 1915 British sea and land forces attacked the Dardanelles. The Turks countered both threats, causing the British to evacuate the *Gallipoli peninsula at the end of 1915, and forcing the advanced elements of the Mesopotamian force to surrender at *Kut Al Amara on 29 April 1916.

In Germany, Falkenhayn's first instinct was to renew the offensive in the west in 1915, but the need to support Austria-Hungary, the greater fluidity of the eastern front, and the pressure of Hindenburg and his supporters resulted in a concentration in the east. A joint Austro-German offensive at Gorlice-Tarnow (2 May 1915) unlocked Russian Poland and the tsar's shattered armies fell back to the Pripyat marshes. Falkenhayn hoped that the Russians would accept a separate peace so that the Germans could concentrate on the west. But alliance loyalty held. Moreover, the entry of Italy on the Entente side in May prompted the Austrians to divert their already inadequate forces to a third front on the river Isonzo. By September the German advance into Russia had exhausted itself, and Falkenhayn switched his attention to the Balkans. With Bulgaria as an ally, the Central Powers outflanked and overran Serbia. Britain and France finally sent troops to *Salonika in October, too late to influence Bulgaria and too distant to give aid to Serbia.

Although the Germans had not won on the eastern front, they had gained sufficient breathing space to allow them to turn their attention back to the west. On 21 February 1916 they attacked the *Verdun salient. Their initial target was

(cont. on page 1002)

women in the military

O F the many reasons the military developed as a male preserve, the first was human sexual dimorphism and the greater upper-body strength required to wield clubs and swords, to shoot an arrow with killing velocity, and to bear the weight of body *armour. This is a sine qua non for relatively few tasks in the modern military. The second, emergent from this, was that women were prey, not predators, thus in time to be seen as part of the property men fought to preserve or to seize from the enemy. The modern cliché that rape is not a violent expression of sexuality but a sexual expression of violence is apposite. The third reason was the belief that women were naturally softer and gentler by nature, in fact a culturally defined assumption by no means common to all human societies over time. Western chivalry combined these factors, the putting of (upper-class) women on a pedestal going hand in hand with denying them freedom and the rights enjoyed by men. The fact that until very recently there could be no way of knowing who the biological father of a child might be has undoubtedly contributed to this.

This remained little changed until the 20th century, and especially its last three decades, during which time women's role in armed forces has become transformed. In many countries, from playing key roles in the non-combatant support arms and services (for example, during WW II), women now serve in an increasingly wide range of mainstream military jobs. These include combat roles in some *air forces and *navies, as illustrated by the employment of women combat pilots in the RAF and the USAF, and in the Royal Navy (which does not in any case distinguish combat from non-combat ships). However, there is still a powerful norm that women are excluded from the combat arms of armies; that is, the infantry, armour, and artillery (except in administrative supporting roles). Even in the USSR, where during WW II women played active roles as combat pilots, tank crew, and even in the highly specialized killing role of *snipers, once the emergency was over the military reverted to using women primarily in supporting arms, as in the West.

This last example suggests that the driving force for women's full integration into the armed forces has been manpower shortage. This was an imperative for the USSR facing the German onslaught (although the Germans themselves were culturally inhibited from tapping into womanpower resources even at the bitter end), and remains a relative consideration for modern volunteer armies trying to recruit from a population that no longer greatly respects martial values. According to this argument, the reduction of standards of physical strength and endurance now required, for example, in the US armed forces, is not so much a function of ideologically suspect legislation as of a pragmatic need to find the numbers necessary to maintain institutions that have become just one bureaucracy among many. Despite the film *GI Jane*, not only are the units most likely to get involved in serious hand-to-hand fighting resistant to the admission of women, women themselves seem to find little attraction in military specializations that combine extremes of hardship in training with a higher probability of getting killed in war.

There remains a great variation among nations, even among the nations of NATO, in the extent to which women serve in the armed forces. In some countries women are excluded, or have limited involvement, as in Germany and Spain. In others all or almost all military positions (including, in some cases, those with direct combat functions) are open to them, as in Canada, the Netherlands, Norway, and, more recently, the USA and the UK. Women were still excluded from infantry and armour in the USA and the UK in 1999 and will remain so until the results of further study. Israel today still conscripts women but excludes them from combat operations. During the early *Arab–Israeli wars, the

*IDF discovered not only that despite their gender-neutral training, women *casualties caused whole units to cease operations while they were recovered, as well as disproportionate demoralization, but also that the knowledge that they were fighting against women decreased the willingness to surrender among bypassed enemy units.

This variety poses a number of questions such as why countries vary in their employment of women in the military, how exclusion or inclusion policies are justified, and how far the process of gender integration can be taken. In order to answer such questions one must first of all recognize that the military is a unique institution. The functional imperatives of war and military operations ensure that the armed forces stand apart from civilian society. The military is unique in the nature and extent of the demands it places upon its personnel. These include the obligation to train to kill and to sacrifice self; to participate in a military community where one works, lives, and socializes with other service personnel; and, when necessary, a 24-hour commitment with the risk of separation from family at short notice.

It is the obligation to kill while others are seeking to kill you and, if necessary, to sacrifice one's own life that has provided the main basis for limiting the widening of employment opportunities for women in the military to non-combatant roles or only to certain kinds of combat role. It is not simply that in combat roles one is exposed to the risk of death or injury by hostile fire—in modern warfare non-combatant support personnel will increasingly be exposed in this manner. Rather, in a combatant role—in a warship, combat aircraft, and in the infantry, armour, and artillery—one is required to engage the enemy with offensive fire. In the army there is a requirement to close with and kill the enemy in comparison with the greater 'action at a distance' characteristic of the other services. It is here that the barrier excluding women from the military is, in many countries, at its firmest.

In contrast, women's role as childbearers makes them givers not takers of life. Their physical weakness in comparison to men means that the latter have a comparative advantage in the field of combat, while women can play an equal role in other military occupations. Such arguments have not gone unchallenged, for they underestimate the extent to which the fighting qualities required of effective combat performance are not inherent in all men but need to be built up through training. Furthermore, some of the supposed physical weakness in women can be overcome through training and by recognizing the need to challenge the long-term impact of gender stereotypes about what is appropriate for men's and women's work (both in the military and other civilian occupations) inherited from the past. The cases of *guerrilla armies and the employment of women in the Soviet armed forces show that *in extremis* women can and have served successfully in offensive land operations.

In reply to these claims, one can argue that in certain fields of combat (notably infantry warfare) the continuing physical demands are such as to be beyond all but a small minority of women who would have the capacity (and inclination) to pass the exacting standards required. It is a mistake to assume that the era of so-called 'push-button warfare' renders irrelevant the physical courage and strength rooted in traditional hand-to-hand combat skills on the battlefield, let alone the demands of the exhausting '24-hour warfare' itself made possible by modern technology. By contrast, the different demands of naval and aerial warfare make it possible to train and employ both men and women. This is evident in the recent trends towards gender integration in surface ships of the Royal Navy and of pilots in the air forces of the UK, USA, and other countries.

However, the case for inclusion and exclusion of women from certain areas of military employment rests not only on an argument based on physical or psychological weakness. There is also a case to be made that women per se undermine the cohesion of previously all-male combat units. Thus even assuming their physical and psychological aptitude for combat roles, their presence will introduce sexual tensions in the group, either passively just by being there, or actively in competition for advancement by attracting the non-military favour of their NCOs and officers. This would undermine the effectiveness of the combat group or at the very least add a distraction and risk that a military commander could well do without. The matter of distinct hygiene and medical requirements may add somewhat to logistical demands, but is not significant outside this general consideration.

It would be foolish to believe that sexual tensions are unlikely to arise in gender-integrated military teams, not least because of the presence of young physically active people who are required to work in close contact with each other. These have been evident, for example, in ships' crews of both the US and UK navies. However, it would also be unwise to assume that discipline and working procedures cannot be devised to reduce these to a manageable level. In addition, there are other considerations to be taken into account when considering the employment of women in the military. Those countries which have, in recent years, widened employment opportunities for women in the armed forces sought to address male *recruitment and retention difficulties by widening the pool of skilled labour from which they draw and for whose services they compete ever more intensely with other civilian employers. Given the success of females in educational performance there are good labour-market reasons to widen the military employment pool as far as is practicable (and this point applies not just to women but also other under-represented groups such as minority ethnic communities in the case of the UK). It has been argued that there are costs of relying more upon female personnel, for example their leaving the services to have children. However, others point out that these have to be offset by the costs accruing to employing males as, for example, in their rates of alcoholism and non-military injuries.

In addition to this 'business case' for widening employment opportunities for women, there are also considerations of equality and citizenship rights. The role of women in military and civilian employment has been transformed by changing conceptions of men's and women's work and the enforcement of women's (and other groups') claims for equality of opportunity through legislation. Yet in many countries it remains unclear whether public opinion is convinced that gender equality should be extended to all combat roles, especially the 'teeth' arms. This is even assuming that some females are technically able to perform them and that the combat effectiveness of the team would not suffer by their presence. The image of a woman engaged in *bayonet practice is, rightly or wrongly, one that would still not command widespread public acceptance in the UK and the USA, for example. The issue of public acceptability is an important factor in the overall effectiveness of military operations. This is because of the capacity of the modern media to convey (often distressing) images of war—refugees, the opponent's civilian casualties, and one's own casualties—which can constrain political leaders to act or to withdraw from action.

It is not yet clear what the impact of significant female casualties would have on public opinion in the industrial democracies. However, it would be unwise to presume that this situation will not change especially now that women are in combat roles in other services. This is likely to lead to the view that, if women are to serve in any and all military employments, assuming they have volunteered to serve, then they should meet the same fitness standards and accept the same risks as their male counterparts. For the armed services of the industrial democracies citizenship trends, shortages of skilled manpower, and changing gender roles will lead to an increasing participation of women in the military. Much work still needs to be done to provide more flexible working conditions and to recognize that women are no longer prepared to place their own career second to that of their military partners. In the UK, it is likely that the remaining rules excluding them from the front-line positions will be removed, although whether this would, in fact, lead to more than a small minority of women with the inclination and ability to meet the standards demanded of infantry roles remains doubtful. Controversial issues connected with the training and working relations of gender-integrated units will remain.

CD

Dandeker, Christopher, and Segal, M. W., 'Gender Integration in Armed Forces: Recent Policy Developments in the United Kingdom', *Armed Forces and Society* (Fall, 1996).

Gal, Reuven, *A Portrait of the Israeli Soldier* (New York, 1989).

Moskos, C., Williams, J., and Segal, D. R., *The Postmodern Military* (Oxford, forthcoming).

—— and Wood, F. R., *The Military: More than Just a Job* (London, 1988).

O'Connell, Robert, *Of Arms and Men: A History of War, Weapons and Aggression* (London, 1989).

the French army but Falkenhayn realized that the financial and industrial hub of the Entente was Britain. He therefore wanted submarine warfare to accompany the offensive on land, but Bethmann Hollweg opposed him for fear of America's reaction. Britain's surface ships confirmed their control of the exits from the North Sea in the less than decisive battle of *Jutland, and so Germany continued to be denied direct access to oceanic trade. By June the German attack at Verdun had stalled, as had the Austrians' independent offensive against the Italians in the Trentino.

Both Britain and France had learnt from a series of offensives in the west, either limited in objectives or limited in effectiveness, in 1915. At the end of that year the Allies agreed that simultaneous attacks on all fronts were the way to drain the reserves of the Central Powers, given the latter's ability to operate on interior lines. On 4 June 1916 the Russians under *Brusilov made quick initial gains against the Austrians in Galicia, so much so that Romania joined the Allies in August. Once again the Germans had to bail out their ally. The Anglo-French offensive was launched on the *Somme on 1 July 1916. In the event, France's contribution, not least thanks to Verdun, was second to Britain's, and the latter now figured as a major player in land operations as well as at sea and on the stock markets. The Somme campaign continued until November for negligible territorial gains, but did enough damage to the German army to force the latter to retreat to the so-called *Hindenburg Line in March 1917.

No power except Britain had anticipated being able to fight on into 1917, and even Britain was close to economic collapse, its international exchange strained by its arms orders in the USA and by the credit needs of its allies. However, Germany finally adopted unrestricted submarine warfare in February, and in doing so drove America into the war. With Romania all but overrun, and with Russia internally divided by revolution, the boost to the Allies was incalculable.

The Entente's master plan for 1917 was similar to that of 1916, but in the event only the British could sustain major operations on land, in the third battle of Ypres (July–November). It did not prevent the Germans capturing Riga on 1 September nor reinforcing the Austrians to achieve a near-breakthrough at *Caporetto on the Isonzo front on 24 October. On 21 March 1918 the Germans applied similar principles to the Somme. It was the first of four offensives, falling also in Flanders, on the Aisne, and in Champagne. In making considerable territorial gains, the Germans extended their front while reducing their strength by almost a million men. Simultaneously they continued to advance in the east, competing with their Austrian allies in the Ukraine and the Turks in the Caucasus. The French counter-attacked in July and the British in August. Together with the Americans, they drove the Germans back in a series of individually limited but collectively interlocking offensives.

On 15 September the Anglo-French forces at Salonika attacked in Macedonia, forcing the Bulgars to seek an armistice by the end of the month. The whole of the Central Powers' *Italian front was crumbling after the Austrian defeat on the Piave in June, and with the British pushing through Palestine towards Anatolia. The German high command itself initiated the request for an *Armistice on the basis of the Fourteen Points on 4 October, and, although it then tried to resume the war, it had begun a process which it could not now halt. After the war it would claim that the army was 'stabbed in the back' by revolution at home. The peoples of Germany and Austria-Hungary were indeed battered by food shortages and inflation, but the division between front and rear in what was a war of mass mobilization was essentially an artificial one.

*Science and technology, *mass production, and centralized government (see POLITICAL ECONOMY) were key ingredients in determining the war's direction and destructiveness. But alongside modernity backwardness persisted. Major belligerents like Russia and Turkey were insufficiently developed as states to be able fully to mobilize the (predominantly peasant) manpower available to them. In the Middle East and Africa, if armies did not build their own *railways, they remained reliant on the mule, the ox, and man himself.

The dominant image of the war is that derived from the *trench warfare of its western front, snaking from Belgium on the Channel coast southwards to form a salient jutting towards Paris and then turning east along the Aisne valley through Champagne to Verdun; here it turned south once more, past the French frontier fortresses of Nancy and Belfort through the Vosges to the Alps. This front remained largely static from the autumn of 1914 to the spring of 1918. Its network of defensive trenches became progressively more deep and sophisticated. But the appearance of stability could be misleading. The trenches were not an end in themselves. Their *tactical purpose was protection; their *operational task was to enable ground to be held with fewer troops so that a *masse de manœuvre* could be created for deployment elsewhere. At the end of 1914 the Germans opted for the tactical defensive in the west in order to pursue a strategic offensive on the *eastern front. Similarly the British continuously debated the merits of securing gains elsewhere rather than reinforce the deadlock on the major front.

Moreover, the static nature of trench fighting masked a continuous tactical struggle to regain mobility through the reintegration of fire and movement. The chief consequence of industrialization on the battlefield was a hail of fire, delivered by *machine guns and by quick-firing field artillery. Forfeiting mobility to find cover, armies eased many of the supply problems which had dogged their predecessors, and so could use munitions with much greater abandon; in particular heavy artillery, hitherto reserved for the previously distinct phase of *siege warfare, was deployed on the battlefield itself. Thus by 1915 and 1916 infantry attacks were preceded by massive artillery bombardments which sacrificed surprise. Lacking direct communication with the gunners, the infantry could not convert partial gains into breakthrough or breakout.

One long-run solution to this tactical dilemma was the *tank, which combined fire and movement in a single weapon system, but in 1916–18 it was still too slow and too mechanically unreliable for deep exploitation. Much more important was the transformation in the application of artillery. Guns in quantity could fire shorter bombardments for the same effect; with consistent performances, particularly in the manufacture of shells by 1916 but also with the adoption of the contact fuse in 1917, infantry could advance close to the protective fire of the *barrage. Even more important were the techniques of aerial *reconnaissance, flash-spotting, and sound-ranging, which allowed targets to be identified without preliminary registration and—when combined with detailed survey and up-to-date meteorology—enabled predicted fire. Armies regained the potential for surprise. Furthermore, the infantry acquired more of its own firepower—principally through light machine guns and *grenades but also through the use of *flame-throwers and mobile trench *mortars. In all armies the ratio of machines to men increased.

The essential precondition for such warfare was economic mobilization. Before the war many pundits imagined that the principal constraint on sustained operations would be *war finance—that states would be unable to extend their credit. They were wrong: by borrowing from abroad, from their own citizens, and ultimately from themselves (through accepting treasury bills as security for currency issue), the belligerents postponed payment until after the war. The more pressing economic constraints were the availability of raw materials (especially for the blockaded powers of central Europe) and the conversion of industrial plant to munitions production. In the winter of 1914–15, all the armies experienced shell shortages as the combination of higher than expected consumption at the front intersected with the blockages consequent on the time lag in adaptation. The state—which had itself now become the principal purchaser—intervened to regulate the market. In Germany the Prussian war ministry established a raw materials office in August 1914, whose task was to seek out stocks of commodities vital to the war effort, and to allocate them so as to ensure their most efficient use. In Britain the ministry of munitions was created in 1915, and itself established its own regional factories. In general, although much of the rhetoric was collectivist, the principles which drove economic mobilization were derived from capitalism; profits, although regulated, were still considerable, and the arms manufacturers, even if in the guise of government employ, were responsible for the daily management of the war economy (see WAR AND ECONOMIC GROWTH).

The war-generated industrial boom competed with the manpower needs of the armies. Organized labour was thereby handed a strong negotiating position, which it both grasped and partially forfeited in compacts with the state. In Britain in 1915 munitions workers agreed not to strike; in Germany the Auxiliary Service Law of December 1916 created an alliance between state, industry, and labour in which each felt it had conceded too much to the other. The real wages of males with skills vital to war production were eroded less by price inflation than those of white collar workers. Unskilled workers, by contrast, could be replaced by women, many of them not new to the workplace but diverted to munitions production from textile manufacture or domestic service.

The strength of the labour movement acquired fresh resonance in 1917. In May 100,000 French men and women went on strike, affecting 71 industries; Germany experienced 531 strikes over the year as a whole, as opposed to 240 in 1916. Much of this activity was to do with working conditions, wages, prices, and food supplies. But mutinies at the front and, even more, the *Russian Revolutions of March and November 1917 gave labour a political and anti-war dimension which socialist movements had sacrificed by their adherence to the nation-in-arms concept. The Bolsheviks called for a peace without annexations and indemnities, and published the secret agreements of the tsarist regime with its British and French allies, so showing that annexationist war aims were the objective not only of the Central Powers.

Hitherto the populations of the warring states had largely accepted the bigger ideas that underpinned their efforts. For Austria-Hungary it was a war to save a decaying empire, its multinationalism potentially riven by national self-determination; for Germany, the values were a counterpoint to the individualism that it saw as the legacy of Revolutionary France and the dominance of money-grabbing market forces in Britain and the USA; for France, it was a war for civilization; and for Britain for liberalism and the rights of small nations. In 1914 all the powers had been willing to fight for their great-power status, and all their peoples had been inspired by the needs of national self-defence. The doubts about these ideals, stoked by the length of the war and by its losses, were resolved, at least in part, by the entry of the USA and by the decision of Soviet Russia to seek terms with the Central Powers at Brest-Litovsk in the New Year of 1918. The 'Fourteen Points' of US Pres Woodrow Wilson (*Clemenceau commented drily that God had been satisfied with ten) reasserted in international relations the ideals of political liberalism—however much its domestic and economic underpinnings had been eroded by state intervention.

Moreover, by 1917 the Allied states had largely resolved the problems of wartime government. In France invasion made *Joffre, the French C-in-C, a key force in civil affairs as well as in strategy. In Britain civilian direction of strategy was discredited in 1915, and soldiers dominated in 1916. Neither power had a body which integrated civil and military wisdom and which was capable of rapid decision-making. In December 1916, Britain created a war cabinet, itself the occasion and the consequence of the formation of Lloyd George's coalition government. Joffre was replaced by Nivelle at the end of 1916, and not until Clemenceau became premier in November 1917 did France's civil authority definitively reassert itself over the military. The offensives of 1917 discredited the generals of both nations to the extent that even their political allies were ready to acquiesce in their subordination.

The autocratic empires of Austria-Hungary and Germany, but also of the Entente's ally, Russia, had a more difficult problem to resolve. The junction of civil and military was the crown; in September 1915 Tsar Nicholas II, who had been dissuaded from doing so at the war's outbreak, became C-in-C. In Austria-Hungary the Emperor Franz Josef was too old to exercise such active responsibility, and his successor in 1916, Karl, was young and irresolute. In Germany, Kaiser *Wilhelm II believed strongly in his personal rule

but had begun to lose his authority even before the war broke out. The complexities of strategy-making in modern war were incompatible with the simplifications of monarchy. Without the mediating efforts of the structures which political liberalism spawned, the autocracies lacked the institutions for easing civil-military discord. The German chancellor, Bethmann Hollweg, intrigued against the CGS *Falkenhayn, using as his allies the commander on the eastern front, *Hindenburg, and his COS *Ludendorff. In August 1916 the kaiser was forced to concede to this pressure, and Hindenburg replaced Falkenhayn, with Ludendorff as 1st QMG. Thereafter the general staff's interpretation of strategy, with the conduct of a *total war penetrating every aspect of national life, and with all the nation's resources deemed vital for its prosecution, meant that the army played an increasing role in issues of economic mobilization and political direction. Although Bethmann Hollweg resigned in July 1917 because he could no longer command the support of the Reichstag, his successors were the puppets of the army not of the assembly, and it was the army's loss of confidence in the monarchy that determined the timing of the kaiser's final abdication in November 1918.　　HFAS

Falls, Cyril, *The First World War* (London, 1960).

Herwig, Holger, *The First World War: Germany and Austria-Hungary 1914–1918* (London, 1997).

Strachan, Hew (ed.), *The Oxford Illustrated History of the First World War* (Oxford, 1998).

World War II (1939–45), usually abbreviated 'WW II', was the largest war in history, fought between September 1939 and September 1945. More than 40 million men and women were serving in the armed forces by 1944, and civilian and military deaths exceeded 55 million. The major battles involved millions of men and thousands of tanks and aircraft. The scale of wartime mobilization exceeded that of WW I. The second global conflict was in every sense a *total war.

The war was not a single, unitary conflict. It was in reality a number of different wars that gradually coalesced as the world's major powers were drawn in between 1939 and 1941. The war that broke out in 1939 was a war for the European balance of power, like the war of 1914. The immediate cause of the conflict was the German demand for the return of Danzig and part of the Polish 'corridor' granted to Poland from German territory in the Versailles Treaty of 1919. Poland refused to agree to German demands, and on 1 September 1939 overwhelming German forces launched the *Polish campaign and defeated her in three weeks. In March 1939 Britain and France had guaranteed Polish sovereignty, and in honour of that pledge first demanded that German forces withdraw, then on 3 September declared war on Germany.

The outbreak of a major war over Poland had much deeper causes. During the 1930s the European order established after WW I was destabilized by the emergence of two new superpowers, the USSR and Germany. Under *Hitler, German chancellor from 1933, and a man committed to a war of revenge for defeat in 1918 and the acquisition of a land empire by conquest in the east, Germany embarked on a programme of remilitarization after fifteen years of enforced disarmament. At the same time the USSR under *Stalin became on paper the largest military power in the world. Neither state could ultimately be contained in the post-war liberal international order dominated by Britain and France. As the relative power of the western states declined, concern for their global security became profound. Inhibited by economic weakness and popular hostility to war, neither state was able to prevent Hitler from overturning the Versailles Treaty using force or the threat of force. In March 1938 Austria was annexed to the Nazi Reich (the Anschluss); in October 1938 Germany took over the Czech Sudetenland, and in March 1939 Bohemia and Moravia. In April 1939 Hitler planned a short local war against Poland so that Poland's economic resources, like those of Austria and Czechoslovakia, could be exploited in Germany's bid to become a superpower.

In 1938–9 Britain and France rearmed energetically and began to face the serious prospect of war with Germany if Hitler could not be deterred. Overtures were made to the USSR to try to tilt the balance of power against Hitler. The USSR chose instead to reach a non-aggression pact (the Molotov-Ribbentrop pact) with Hitler, signed on 23 August 1939. Hitler was convinced that the western states would not obstruct his war with Poland now the USSR was neutralized. German military plans were based on the prospect of a major conflict at some point in the mid-1940s. British and French war preparations were geared much more to 1939. Western strategy was predicated on a long war of *attrition and closely resembled the strategy which they believed had prevailed in WW I. A large part of the French front and its strategic thinking was dominated by the static *Maginot Line, behind which the armies were to wait until long-range bombing and sea *blockade had so weakened Germany that she could be defeated by western armies after a build-up of two or three years.

The European war fought between 1939 and 1941 was not a war of attrition, but was marked by brief campaigns and decisive battles. German forces, absorbing lessons from WW I on mobility and striking power, used aircraft and armoured formations as a powerful spearhead to break the enemy line and make possible annihilating encirclements. Poland was defeated in three weeks, the victim not only of German military effectiveness but of the German–Soviet agreement which led to a Soviet invasion of eastern Poland on 17 September 1939 and the division of the conquered state between the two on 28 September. On 10 May 1940, following the Danish and *Norwegian campaigns to protect the northern flank of their operations, German armies invaded Belgium, Luxembourg, and northern France and within six weeks defeated western forces. Britain's small expeditionary force was compelled to retreat from *Dunkirk back across the Channel and on 20 June France capitulated. A rump French state under *Pétain was established. Britain was able to resist German air attacks in the battle of *Britain in August and September 1940, and survived a German bombing offensive (the 'Blitz') in the winter of 1940–1, but there existed no possibility of Britain defeating Germany unaided. Nazi leaders began to construct a new European order centred on Berlin, and hoped that Britain would sue for peace now that she had no allies.

By this stage Britain was engaged in a second and quite distinct war. On 10 June 1940 *Mussolini's Italy, allied with Germany in the 'pact of steel' signed in May 1939, declared war on Britain and France. Mussolini hoped to use western defeat to complete his aim of establishing Italian hegemony in the Mediterranean basin and North Africa which had begun with the Italian conquest of Abyssinia in 1935–6, and had continued through Italian participation in the *Spanish civil war and annexation of Albania in April 1939. From 1940 to 1942 British Commonwealth forces fought a more traditional naval and imperial war against Italy. British air and naval power was used to limit Italy's superior naval forces and by 1943 had sunk two-thirds of Italian shipping. In *North Africa, Commonwealth forces stationed in Egypt drove Italian armies back across Libya by February 1941; in *Abyssinia and Somaliland Italian forces were forced to surrender by May 1941. Italy's complete defeat in Africa was avoided only by Hitler's decision to send German reinforcements under *Rommel, and the weak logistical position of Commonwealth forces. In November 1942 at *Alamein a predominantly Italian force was defeated by *Montgomery and by May 1943 Italian and German forces finally surrendered in Tunisia, enabling the Allies to mount the invasion of *Sicily and then Italy.

The third component of world war was the largest and most sanguinary of all. Hitler's appetite for imperial conquest had always been directed eastwards to the USSR with its vast supplies of food, materials, manpower, and territory to colonize. In December 1940 Hitler turned away from Britain and approved *BARBAROSSA, the large-scale invasion of the USSR. The motives for the contest were not only imperial. Soviet communism represented a profound social and political threat and Hitler, an ardent anti-communist throughout the inter-war years, saw the final contest with Marxism as a necessity. Following the German–Soviet pact of 1939 the threat became greater. A Soviet-Finnish war in the winter of 1939–40 resulted in Soviet encroachments in the Baltic. In June 1940 Soviet troops occupied the Baltic states and seized Bessarabia from Romania. Hitler ordered the conquest of the USSR before it became too entrenched in eastern Europe.

The war in the *Pacific was part of a wider imperial struggle for Asia. In east Asia Japanese nationalists and militarists, frustrated by what they saw as western domination of the world order and Japan's economic vulnerability, began a fourteen-year war in China when in 1931 Japanese forces seized the northern Chinese province of Manchuria. Full-scale war followed in the autumn of 1937 against Chinese nationalist and communist forces, and much of the northern and eastern part of China was occupied by Japan by 1941. Nazi and Japanese leaders viewed the USSR and China as states that were politically fragile and corrupt, ripe for colonization by a superior race and culture. Both wars were fought with an exceptional savagery against enemies viewed as racially inferior and contaminated by communism. Yet in both cases the sheer scale and geography of Asian conflict powerfully inhibited Nazi and Japanese ambitions.

BARBAROSSA was launched on 22 June 1941 when three million German, Finnish, Romanian, and Hungarian soldiers attacked the whole length of the Soviet western frontier. Unprepared for the assault the Red Army collapsed and in three months enemy forces had reached *Leningrad, were approaching *Moscow, and had seized the rich industrial and grain area of the Ukraine. High losses and the onset of winter brought the German attack to a halt, but in 1942 the campaign was renewed on the southern flank with a drive to capture Soviet oil resources in the Caucasus before turning north to capture Moscow. Frantic efforts by the rump Soviet state to reform its armed forces and rebuild its shattered economy resulted in a remarkable revival in the later part of 1942. In November 1942 Germany and her allies attacking *Stalingrad (now Volgograd) were cut off by a massive Soviet encirclement, URANUS. The German forces in Stalingrad surrendered in January 1943. Both sides mobilized enormous forces for a renewed summer campaign and around the city of *Kursk the German ZITADELLE was defeated and the German front rolled back towards Kiev, which was retaken in November 1943. Under Deputy Supreme Commander *Zhukov, the Red Army inflicted a series of crippling blows on the Germans as Soviet forces mastered the art of the modern war of manoeuvre using aircraft, radio, and armour in large numbers. *BAGRATION in June 1944 was the largest military operation of the war and it ended with the decisive defeat of remaining German forces on Soviet soil.

The fourth and final component of the wider war had the effect of binding the other elements together. This was the war for the protection and assertion of US interests. Though lightly armed in the 1930s and formally committed by the Neutrality Acts of 1935 and 1937 to non-intervention in overseas conflicts, the USA was profoundly affected by the events of war in Europe and the Far East. In 1940 and 1941 America gave increasing economic assistance to Britain and China following President Roosevelt's pledge to act as the 'arsenal of democracy'. During 1941 the US navy became closely involved in the battle of the *Atlantic in efforts to break the German submarine blockade of shipping destined for Britain. In March 1941 Congress approved the *Lend-Lease Bill which allowed almost unlimited material aid, including weapons, for any state fighting aggression. In the autumn of 1941 this came to include the USSR, despite strong American anti-communism. Throughout 1940 and 1941 the USA tightened an economic blockade of Japan which threatened to cut off most Japanese oil supplies.

Though not an active belligerent, American actions provoked both Japanese and German retaliation. In November 1941, following months of planning and argument in Tokyo between those who favoured finishing off China and those who argued for a Pacific naval war to secure oil supplies and drive western states from south-east Asia, the southern campaign was approved by the emperor. On 7 December 1941 Japanese naval aircraft attacked the American naval base at Pearl Harbor, followed by the rapid conquest of western colonies in south-east Asia and the southern Pacific. On 11 December Germany declared war on the USA, fortuitously allowing Franklin D. *Roosevelt to pursue the strategy preferred by the US army COS George *Marshall, of giving priority to the European theatre over the Pacific. The USA embarked on a rapid and large-scale rearmament which allowed generous military supplies and reinforcements to be sent to all the theatres of war: in Asia, the Pacific, the USSR, and the Mediterranean. American material wealth made more certain that the turning point achieved at Alamein and Stalingrad would be sustained.

The USA fought a largely naval and air war between 1942 and 1945, using its very great naval power to deploy troops in major *amphibious operations, first in the Solomon Islands to halt the Japanese Pacific advance, then in TORCH, a combined American-British landing in Morocco and Algeria in November 1942, and subsequently in the Anglo-American landings in Sicily and southern Italy in the summer of 1943, and in northern France in June 1944. *Air power was a central feature of the American war effort and was used effectively at sea to defeat the Japanese advance at the Coral Sea in May 1942 and at *Midway in June that year. In the battle of the Atlantic very long-range aircraft were used to plug the Atlantic Gap where German submarines had exacted a high toll of Allied shipping during 1942. American air-force leaders were also committed to long-range bombing of the enemy economy and in January 1943 at the Casablanca Conference agreed a Combined Bomber Offensive to unite the efforts of RAF Bomber Command (whose aircraft had been bombing Germany since 1940) and the US Eighth and Fifteenth Air Forces. The daylight bombing campaign began in earnest in the summer of 1943 and suffered crippling losses. Once a long-distance fighter was developed bombing was able to play its part in diverting German resources to home defence and limiting the expansion of German war output.

The entry of the USA signalled a change in the political balance of the war of great significance. Roosevelt was the driving force behind closer Allied co-operation in what became known as the Grand Coalition of the USA, USSR,

China, and the British Commonwealth. At conferences with British leaders in 1943 in Casablanca, Quebec, and Cairo, the American leadership insisted on defeating Germany first by a cross-Channel invasion to be mounted in 1944. Though the British PM *Churchill favoured exploiting Anglo-American strength in the Mediterranean theatre, and feared the consequences of defeat in northern Europe, the American insistence on a large-scale re-entry to Europe won the day, thanks to the support it enjoyed from the USSR at the major inter-Allied conference in Tehran in November 1943. American economic might and political interests helped to bind together the different theatres of conflict, while America's worldwide system of supply and logistics provided the sinews of war necessary to complete the defeat of the aggressor states.

That defeat was assured by the summer of 1944 when OVERLORD, the invasion of *Normandy, allowed American, British Commonwealth, and French forces to establish a viable bridgehead in France. A major *intelligence deception operation and declining air power weakened the German response and by September 1944 German forces had been driven from France. Italy had sued for an armistice in September 1943 and German resources were now stretched to defending a line in central Italy and garrisoning the Balkans. Economic collapse produced by bombing and the massive operations executed in the spring of 1945 on both fronts brought German surrender on 7 May 1945 following Hitler's suicide on 30 April. With the full weight of US and Soviet forces available for the war with Japan, defeat in the Far East was only a matter of time. A long-range bombing campaign destroyed the Japanese cities, while offensives around the perimeter of the Japanese empire tightened the noose further, and destroyed most of the Japanese navy and merchant marine. When atomic bombs were dropped on *Hiroshima and Nagasaki in August 1945 and Soviet forces destroyed the Japanese army in *Manchuria, Japan finally capitulated on 2 September.

Japanese and Italian defeat was always likely following American entry into the war. They were limited regional powers with a comparatively weak economic base, made more fragile by their joint vulnerability to blockade by aircraft and submarine. German defeat was less predictable. It owed a great deal to the revival of Red Army fighting power, which absorbed the bulk of Germany's war effort until American and British air and naval power could be brought to bear more effectively in the Mediterranean and the battle of the Atlantic. Germany's war effort was hampered by the impact of bombing and the permanent quantitative inferiority of the German air force over Europe following American entry. The Allies also enjoyed better intelligence (largely thanks to the breaking of the German *Enigma system), larger material supplies, and societies more united in the pursuit of victory. Germany also suffered domestic constraints generated by a damaging competition for resources between the different armed services and the inefficient

mobilization of resources in the early years of war. Finally a bitter hostility to German occupation absorbed a great deal of effort in maintaining German rule and extracting the economic fruits of empire, exemplified by the long *guerrilla war fought against Tito's *Partisans in occupied Yugoslavia.

The consequences of the war were far-reaching. The technical threshold of warfare was pushed forward with extraordinary speed: *radar, jet propulsion, ballistic rocketry, and *nuclear weapons were all the products of WW II. The cost of waging science-based warfare was exceptional. Most combatant states devoted more than half their national output and two-thirds of their industrial workforce to war production. The victims of aggression lost a large fraction of their national wealth from occupation and combat. In Germany half the dwellings in her major cities were destroyed or damaged by bombing. The barbarous character of the wars for Asia led to an estimated 20 million Chinese dead and 26 million Soviet, of whom more than 1 million were Soviet Jews, victims of the Nazi programme of extermination launched in 1941 that claimed the lives of 6 million European Jews. Germany was divided between the conquerors and millions of Germans displaced from eastern Europe.

The international political balance was transformed by the war. The Axis states were defeated and disarmed. Communism, whose threat had prompted the Nazi-Soviet war, triumphed in most of Eurasia: in eastern Europe under Soviet control, in China, following civil war between 1945 and 1949, and in North Korea and North Vietnam. The spread of communism prompted the USA to maintain the global presence it had adopted during the war in collaboration with western European allies, and the world became divided into two heavily armed camps. Britain and France, whose defence of the old balance of power had led them to declare war on Germany in 1939, were reduced to second-rank powers, while their empires gradually disintegrated under pressure from the USA and local nationalist movements. Despite the terrible cost of the largest of all wars, the aggressor states of the 1930s, (West) Germany, Italy, and Japan were welcomed back into the western camp in the 1950s as Allies in face of the threat posed by the communist bloc.   RO

Glantz, D., and House, J., *When Titans Clashed: How the Red Army Stopped Hitler* (Lawrence, Kan., 1995).

Harrison, M., *The Economics of WW II* (Cambridge, 1998).

Kimball, W., et al. (eds.), *Allies at War: The Soviet, American and British Experience, 1939–1945* (New York, 1994).

Overy, R. J., *Why the Allies Won* (London, 1995).

Parker, R. A. C., *Struggle for Survival* (Oxford, 1989).

Weinberg, G., *A World at Arms* (Cambridge, 1994).

Wörth/Froeschwiller, battle of (1870). On 6 August 1870 in the opening battles of the *Franco-Prussian war, the Germans defeated the northern wing of the French armies at Spicheren in Lorraine, and the southern wing at Wörth in Alsace. On 4 August the Germans beat an outlying French division, at heavy cost, at Wissembourg. *MacMahon, with his own I Corps—good troops from North Africa—and a division of VII Corps took position on high ground west of the Sauerbach, expecting that V Corps would march to his support. He was attacked by the German Third Army, and though his infantry fought well his artillery was pounded into silence and the Germans, comfortably superior, lapped round his flanks. MacMahon committed Bonnemains's *cuirassier division to help his infantry break clear, but the charge—much featured in post-war paintings—bought little except honour. Much of the beaten army reached Châlons by train, to form part of the Army of Châlons which marched to an even greater disaster at *Sedan.

RH

Xenophon (*c.*430–353 BC), Athenian soldier and author. Born into a wealthy family, he served in the cavalry and frequented Socratic circles. This background made him suspect in democratic Athens and, accepting a friend's invitation, he became a mercenary in Cyrus 'the Younger' 's (424–401 BC) army. When the Greek generals were eliminated after *Cunaxa, he played a leading role in the army's march through Mesopotamia, Kurdistan, Armenia, and Anatolia. After a period in Thrace, they were hired by *Sparta to help maintain the freedom of Asiatic Greeks from Persian rule. This fostered close contacts with leading Spartans, and when King Agesilaus returned to Greece Xenophon found himself fighting his fellow Athenians at *Koroneia. In exile, he settled near Olympia, but moved to Corinth after *Leuctra. There was reconciliation with Athens: *Cavalry Commander* and *Ways and Means* show sympathetic concern for the city, and his son Gryllus died fighting in the Athenian cavalry at *Mantineia.

In semi-retirement Xenophon wrote historical narratives, Socratic texts, and miscellaneous technical and (broadly) political works. Common features are the importance of Xenophon's personal experience (though affective responses are unfortunately not nearly as prominent as intellectual ones) and a didactic strain, both practical and moral (Xenophon saw the two as closely linked). Warfare can obtrude anywhere (his Socrates discusses the Persian king's garrisons) but material for military historians comes mostly from three areas. (1) *Spartan Constitution* devotes three chapters to the army ('hardly any military matter requiring attention is overlooked by the Spartans'— regrettably he does not review them all) and more generally illuminates the sociocultural context underlying Spartan military pretensions. (2) *On Horsemanship* deals with warhorses—mostly equestrian issues (acquisition and care;

temperament; bits; deportment) but also *armour and weaponry—while *Cavalry Commander* aims to improve the Athenian cavalry (characteristically) by improving its commander and offers a rather unsystematic review of his duties. Neither work says much about the actual use of cavalry in battle. (3) *Hellenica* (Greek history, 410–362 BC) mentions about 150 military engagements (and gives important, sometimes quirky, accounts of several major battles) and forms a substantial part of the database on classical Greek warfare. Another substantial part is *Anabasis*, a uniquely detailed account of a mercenary army and of Greeks in conflict with alien adversaries—though their experiences were almost too extraordinary to be generalizable and detail often serves to raise, not answer, questions. *Cyropaedia* asks how *Cyrus the Great won and ruled a vast empire: the answer is primarily intelligent and sympathetic leadership (a prominent topic of *Anabasis*, indeed throughout Xenophon), but also involves military reforms, tactical training and deployment, and practical details which, despite the work's odd historiographic status, cannot be neglected by students of Greek and Achaemenid warfare.

Even more than other classical authors, Xenophon still seemed relevant to military theorists well into modern times. A late example is Gen Arthur Boucher (1847–1933), who wrote that the *Anabasis* was and would remain a military manual appropriate to free nations, since it showed how to turn their citizens into brave, obedient soldiers (important components here being the soldiers' respect for their leader, and the leader's concern not to waste his soldiers' lives) and offered the key to devising suitable battle plans and tactical formations. The date was 1913, and it was (nearly) the end of an era.   CJT

Anderson, J. K., *Military Theory and Practice in the Age of Xenophon* (Berkeley, 1970).

Tuplin, C. J., 'Xenophon (1)', in *Oxford Classical Dictionary* (Oxford, 1997).

Xerxes King of Persia (486–465 BC). He suppressed revolt in Egypt, perhaps fought successfully in central Asia, but is celebrated for failure in the *Graeco-Persian war of 480–479 and the loss of Macedonia, Thrace, and Aegean Anatolia and defeat at the Eurymedon. The expedition against the Greeks (to avenge *Marathon but also reflecting an expansionist imperative) was elaborately prepared (roads were improved, a canal cut at Mt Athos, the Dardanelles bridged, and food-dumps established) and large-scale. Herodotus' (see GREEK HISTORIANS) picture of a huge army incorporating every ethnically diverse part of the empire is quantitatively ludicrous, but there are no non-Greek sources specific to the period and views diverge on how to replace it. There is little doubt that it was unwieldy and its logistical demands required a strategy of co-ordinated land–sea advance along the coast that was ill-suited to Greek topography. There is also a suspicion that too much reliance was placed on expected Greek disunity. The campaign foundered at *Salamis, where the Persian fleet fought on the defenders' terms, while *Plataea again illustrated the advantage Greek *hoplites had over Persian infantry when numerical superiority and cavalry mobility were neutralized by terrain.   CJT

Briant, P., *History of the Persian Empire* (forthcoming), trans. from French orig. (1966).

Yalu, battle of (correctly Yalu-tsyan, Amnokkan) (1904), first land engagement of the *Russo-Japanese war. The mouth of the Yalu river, with several channels each up to 0.6 mile (1 km) wide, separated by islands, was the frontier between China and Korea, and was also the scene for a naval battle on 17 September 1894 between Chinese and Japanese forces in the *Sino-Japanese war, which the Japanese won decisively.

Nearly ten years later, following the surprise attack on *Port Arthur in February 1904, the Japanese First Army under Gen Kuroki (45,000 men) advanced through Korea. On 1 May 1904 a 34,000-strong Japanese force with 128 guns and 18 machine guns met the eastern detachment of the Russian Manchurian Army (19,000 men with 62 guns and 8 machine guns) on the Yalu river on the border with Manchuria. The Russians held the western river bank but the Japanese, helped by superior firepower, got across the river and 12th Japanese Division outflanked the Russians from the north. The Russians failed to bring up their reserves in time, and were splintered by the Japanese. Russian casualties in the battle and subsequent pursuit were 2,200–3,000, 21 guns, and all their machine guns. Japanese losses were reckoned at 1,000. The victory at Yalu created the opportunity to deploy the Japanese Second and, later, Fourth Armies onto the Liao-Dun peninsula to break the Russian Manchurian Army in two and isolate Port Arthur.

CDB

Yamamoto, Adm Isoroku (1884–1943). Yamamoto first saw action in the *Russo-Japanese war, when a modern Japanese fleet destroyed an obsolete Russian one at Tsushima (1905), and where he lost a finger. He subsequently served in Europe and the USA, first as naval attaché in Washington (1925) and then as a participant in the London naval conferences of 1930 and 1934–5, getting to know his future enemies well. Returning to Japan as deputy minister for the navy between 1936 and 1939, he strove to modernize his own navy, building a balanced fleet of battleships and carriers but also landing craft and transports for *amphibious operations in a future Pacific war. C-in-C of the imperial Japanese fleet from 1940, he is best remembered as the architect and executor of the surprise attack at *Pearl Harbor on 7 December 1941. By failing to sink any US carriers at this time he opened the way for the defeat at *Midway, but as he knew, Japan could never have won the *Pacific campaign against a fully mobilized US war economy. He was the victim in April 1943 of the world's first mid-air assassination, when US fighters, acting on decryption of Japanese naval signals shot down his plane over Bougainville in the Solomon Islands.

APC-A

Yamashita, Gen Tomokjuki (1885–1946), known as the Tiger of Malaya. Yamashita inflicted the most humiliating defeat ever suffered by British arms during the 1941–2 *Malaya and Singapore campaign. Shortly before hostilities began, he was appointed to command Twenty-Fifth Army with three infantry divisions, light tanks, artillery, and about 600 aircraft based in recently occupied French Indochina. At the outbreak of hostilities he struck down the Malayan peninsula with 55,000 men, bypassing resistance by not restricting himself to roads. He drove nearly three times this number before him and onto Singapore island, which fell after a daring crossing of the straits of Johore completed the demoralization of the British commander Percival. Yamashita was blessed by weak and divided British and Allied leadership, but this does not detract from his audacity. Japanese *intelligence for the campaign was very good and he knew exactly what was facing him, and that his

1011

only hope was a jungle *blitzkrieg and to let panic multiply his own numbers in the minds of the enemy. It did.

In 1945 he surrendered to the Americans in the Philippines as commander of Fourteenth Army in Luzon. He was found guilty of *war crimes without being permitted a proper legal defence and hanged at Luzon prison camp on 23 February 1946, but it is difficult to suppress the suspicion that his principal crime was to have so humiliated the white man that his Far Eastern empires became untenable.

JR-W/HEB

Yarmuk, battle of the (636), key battle in the early Islamic conquests. In an attempt to stem the escalating Arab invasion of Syria and Palestine, begun in earnest with the victory at *Ajnadain, the Byzantines assembled an army of at least 100,000 in August/September. They encountered a much smaller Arab force on the Yarmuk river in eastern Palestine. Accounts differ on detail, but all agree that the Byzantine force was driven into an angle between the Yarmuk and a tributary and destroyed. As a result, Syria came under effective Arab control.   DWM

Donner, Fred M., *The Early Islamic Conquests* (Princeton, 1981).

yeomanry were British volunteer cavalry. In March 1794 PM Pitt 'the Younger' introduced a Bill calling for the formation of volunteer cavalry troops in response to the threat of invasion by Revolutionary France. Although known by many names, the volunteer cavalry formations came to be known as yeomanry regiments, and eventually most counties in England, Scotland, Ireland, and Wales raised one. The name comes from the Middle English *yeoman*, meaning, loosely, a countryman of respectable standing, and the original 'gentlemen and yeomanry' sought to attract recruits who owned their own horses. Like previous volunteer units, they were expected to disband after the threat had disappeared, but for a variety of reasons have survived, accumulating over 200 years of service.

Several yeomen are known to have volunteered for service at *Waterloo, but no formed units saw action until the Second *Boer War. The early troops were dressed and equipped in a manner which suited their officers, usually landowners, and there was a general preference for light cavalry uniforms of the more elegant sort. Numbers varied widely, but eventually all were combined into county regiments of about 500 men each. The social tension of early 19th-century Britain, caused by industrialization and the growing urban population, resulted in the yeomanry being called out frequently to support the *civil power. Such activities sometimes resulted in casualties to the civilian population, as in the *Peterloo massacre of 1819.

With the establishment of police forces, the yeomanry subsided into glamorous inactivity, but the *War Office gradually regularized their organization, training, and equipment. Yeomanry assistance was requested by the regular army during the Second Boer War. Companies of the Imperial Yeomanry were raised from every regiment to serve during the campaign, where more died through disease than battle. Their performance in battle was mixed, and a particular misfortune encouraged cynics to maintain that the hat-badge 'IY' stood for 'I Yield'. In 1908, the Yeomanry was combined with volunteer infantry battalions into the Territorial Force, under War Office supervision. All yeomanry regiments were mobilized in August 1914 and served overseas, either dismounted (on the western front and *Gallipoli) or mounted under the command of *Allenby in Egypt and Palestine. One of the last cavalry charges took place at Huj in November 1917, where squadrons of Worcestershire Hussars and Warwickshire Yeomanry successfully charged Turkish artillery.

With the reformation of the (renamed) Territorial Army in 1921, some yeomanry regiments were permitted to keep their horses, while others were obliged to convert to signals or artillery. Called up again in 1939, several yeomanry regiments found themselves on horseback in Palestine, where they had been in 1917–18. The mounted units converted to armour in 1941, the Cheshire Yeomanry being the last to convert in 1942. Armoured yeomanry equipped with Crusader, Grant, or *Sherman tanks fought in the *North Africa, *Italian, and *Normandy campaigns, often supported by yeomanry artillery regiments. Post-WW II reorganizations have greatly reduced all the former regiments, and *armoured cars, then Land Rovers, have replaced their tanks. In their present form, the descendants of the original yeomanry regiments fulfil a wide variety of roles in the British Territorial Army, retaining more than a flicker of their old distinctive style. This is summed up by the anecdote describing a brigade commander ordering a yeomanry colonel to send an officer on some distant and potentially fruitless mission. 'I'll send Charles,' said the colonel. 'Hmm,' replied the brigadier. 'D'you think he'll go?'

APC-A/RH

Yeremenko, Marshal Andrei Ivanovich (1892–1970). Yeremenko played a decisive role in the 1941 battle of *Moscow and inflicted a disastrous delay on the German timetable for invading the USSR. Conscripted into the imperial Russian army in WW I, Yeremenko reached the rank of corporal and then joined the new Red Army, fighting in the Russian civil war and taking part in the invasion of Poland in 1920. In 1941 he was given command of the Western Front (army group) and got every aircraft available into the air to attack the advancing columns of *Guderian and Hoth. He followed this with an attack by a tank group equipped with the new T-34 and KV tanks, just coming into service, which were hard for German *anti-armour guns to destroy. This was temporarily successful and, in delaying the Germans, made them more vulnerable to the Russian winter. He was wounded twice, the second time badly, but after seven months' treatment returned to take part in the battle of *Stalingrad and then to command the Kalinin and Baltic Fronts. He commanded fourth Ukrainian Front from March 1945, and his troops captured Prague in May in the last operation of the European war. He was outstandingly brave and showed great tactical skill, but was overshadowed by *Zhukov and given little opportunity to decide strategy. He was only made a marshal in 1955.   CDB

Yorck von Wartenburg, FM Graf Hans David Ludwig (1759–1830). The son of an officer claiming English descent, Yorck was born in Potsdam. He joined the Prussian army in 1772 but was *cashiered for insubordination in 1779, and went to fight for the Dutch in the East Indies. Restored to the Prussian army in 1785 he took a keen interest in light infantry, and in 1806 commanded the rearguard after *Jena/Auerstadt. Wounded and captured, he was repatriated after Tilsit and played a major part in army reorganization. He commanded the Prussian corps which formed part of Napoleon's Grande Armée in 1812, and while at Riga he was persuaded by *Clausewitz, then a Russian colonel, to conclude the Convention of Taurrogen (30 December) which made his force neutral. Initially denounced, Yorck was restored to royal favour when Prussia joined the war against Napoleon. He fought at *Leipzig in 1813 and in the *Champagne campaign of 1814, being created a count that year.

Yorck's decision to neutralize his army was the first step towards the restoration of Prussian independence. However, it remained deeply controversial, with some commentators accusing Yorck of violating his officer's oath while others applauded his decision to act in the national interest.   RH

York and Albany, Prince Frederick, Duke of (1763–1827), British field-marshal, the one who 'marched them up to the top of the hill and marched them down again'. Second son of George III, he commanded the British contingent in Flanders in 1793 and in the *Helder expedition of 1799, and was not a conspicuous success on either occasion. However, as C-in-C from 1798 he put his considerable energies into army administration standardizing drill and improving conditions for the soldiery. A scandal involving his mistress trafficking in *commissions saw him out of office between 1809 and 1811, but after reinstatement he remained C-in-C till his death, and usefully reformed the purchase system. His name was often appended to the titles of foreign corps that fought for Britain in the Napoleonic period: amongst them was the Duke of York's Greek Light Infantry which wore the kilt-like fustanella now sported by the evzones.   MCM/RH

York, Sgt Alvin (1887–1964), expert Tennessee marksman and hero of WW I. In October 1918 when only a corporal, he took over leadership of a patrol adrift behind German lines. Coming under heavy machine-gun fire, he left the others to guard some prisoners and attacked alone, killing 25 and causing the rest to surrender. On the way back to his own lines, he collected further prisoners for a total of 132. He was promoted and awarded the Congressional Medal of Honor.

A 1980s battlefield AA (anti-aircraft) system named after him proved an expensive failure.   HEB

Yorktown, siege of (1781), last major military engagement of the *American independence war. About one-third of royal forces in the colonies, commanded by Cornwallis, fell back on the port of Yorktown on the James peninsula, in the expectation of reinforcements by sea. Instead, Grasse won temporary control of Chesapeake Bay, enabling *Washington to leave a screen facing Clinton in New York and to transport his own and Rochambeau's forces to join the outnumbered *Lafayette outside Yorktown. After the Royal Navy failed to break the *blockade and some of his outer works had fallen, Cornwallis capitulated on 19 October.   HEB

Ypres, battles of (WW I). The medieval centre of the Flanders wool trade, Ypres lies in the centre of a shallow saucer, with higher ground to the north (a complex of ridges including Passchendaele ridge), east (Menin road ridge), and south (Messines ridge), although the sensation of height is scarcely perceptible. The town was an old *Vauban fortress, whose ramparts are still visible, although its buildings, including the towering medieval cloth hall, were levelled by four years of German shelling.

Ypres was entered by a German cavalry patrol on 13 October 1914, but the British Expeditionary Force (BEF) arrived the next day. The area became important during the 'Race to the Sea' as both Germans and Allies extended to the north in the hope of finding an open flank. The first battle of Ypres took place as British and Germans, both attacking, clashed on the axis of the Menin road. It soon became evident that the Germans were in overwhelming strength, and the battle embodied moments when the British and French held on by the narrowest of margins. On 31 October the Germans took Gheluvelt and were checked only by an improvised counter-attack, and much the same happened on 11 November at Nonne Bosschen. The Cavalry Corps defended (though it ultimately lost) Messines ridge with a skill which bore tribute to the British army's pre-war emphasis on dismounted training. The Germans committed newly raised divisions of student volunteers, whose terrible losses (they went forward into the teeth of the BEF's scorching musketry bravely singing patriotic songs) caused the

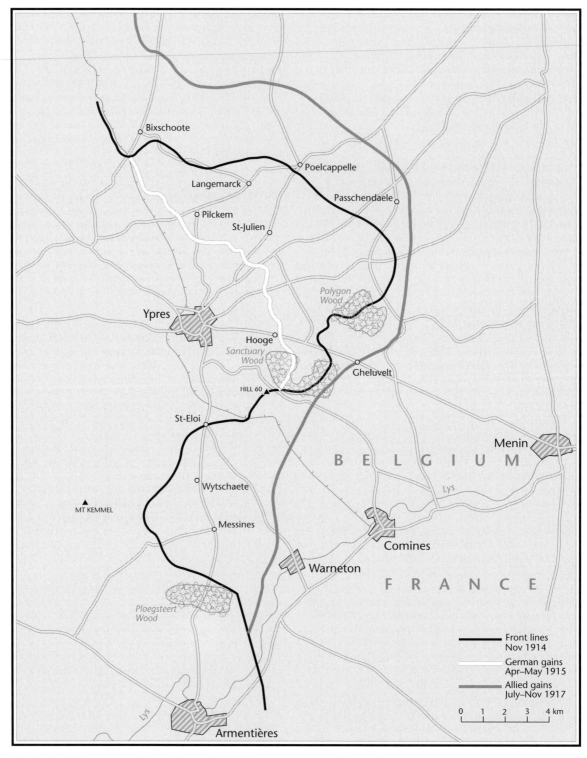

The **battles of Ypres**, 1914–17. Gas was first used by the Germans at Langemarck in April 1915.

Germans to call the battle the 'Kindermord zu Ypern' (the massacre of the innocents at Ypres). Fighting died away at the end of November, with losses equal at around 100,000 each, leaving a substantial Allied salient bulging out into German lines.

On 22 April the Germans began the second battle of Ypres, attacking the northern flank of the salient between Poelcappelle and Bixschoote, using *gas for the first time on the western front. They achieved a breakthrough by mauling two French divisions, but were unprepared to exploit it, and were then checked by desperate resistance in which Canadians played a distinguished part (see CANADIAN EXPEDITIONARY FORCE). The fighting then became an expensive see-saw of attack and counter-attack, which ended with British withdrawal to a line closer to Ypres and was followed by the loss of Hill 60, south-east of Ypres. In all the Allies lost over 60,000 men to 35,000 Germans.

For the next two years the Ypres salient remained one of the most active parts of the western front. In July 1915 the Germans used *flame-throwers to gain the crest-line at Hooge on the Menin road, and in the spring of 1916 there was heavy fighting around Mount Sorrel, at the southern end of Sanctuary Wood.

The salient was chosen as the scene of the principal British offensive of 1917, the third battle of Ypres. *Haig had always believed that Flanders, where there were important objectives like the German railhead of Roulers within striking distance, offered better prospects for an attack than the *Somme, and was under pressure from the Admiralty to get German submarines off the Flanders coast. The main battle was preceded by the assault of *Plumer's Second Army on *Messines on 7 June. It was launched—rather too late, for the momentum had been lost—by the attack of *Gough's Fifth Army north of Ypres, which began on 31 July. It formed three phases, more distinct to historians than they were to participants. First, in the battles of Pilckem Ridge, Gheluvelt Plateau, and Langemarck, Fifth Army pushed its way into a salient made more than usually boggy by unseasonable weather and shelling which had destroyed the land drainage system. Next, Second Army took over for the battles of Menin Road Ridge, Polygon Wood, and Broodseinde, and made good progress in the crucial central sector. Finally, in the battles of Poelcappelle and Passchendaele the exhausted attackers—British, Australian, and Canadian—fought their way up onto Passchendaele ridge in appalling conditions: the Canadians took the village on 6 November. In all the British lost about 260,000 men each, although the figures remain contentious. The battle did very serious damage to the morale of combatants on both sides, although on balance it probably hit the Germans hardest, and the conditions in which it was fought make it a byword for suffering.

The battle of the Lys, part of the *Ludendorff offensive of 1918, is sometimes called the fourth battle of Ypres. The Allies lost ground around the town, including Mount Kemmel to its south, but retained Ypres.

With the exception of *Verdun, there are few landscapes more redolent of war than the Ypres salient. The Menin Gate *memorial, cutting through Vauban's ramparts, commemorates 55,000 soldiers of Britain and her empire who died in the salient and have no known graves, while at Tyne Cot on Passchendaele ridge another 35,000 are commemorated.   RH

Liddle, Peter H. (ed.), *Passchendaele in Perspective* (London, 1997).

Yugoslavia, operations in former (1991–). The strategy of 'ethnic cleansing', underpinned by ethnonationalist animosity, was the defining feature of the wars of the Yugoslav succession which erupted after the breakup of Yugoslavia in 1991. The purpose of ethnic cleansing was to remove the strategic conditions for potential and actual opposition, whether political, terrorist, *guerrilla, or military. Reversing the emphasis of the *Mao Tse-tung dictum that the guerrilla is a fish in water, the point of ethnic cleansing was removal of the water. The Serbian campaign was not designed to defeat opposing armed forces as such, but to secure control of territory for a new set of entities that would be free of potentially disloyal communities. To achieve this, ethnic cleansing involved systematic action such as demonstrative killing, including mass murder, rape (see GENDER AND WAR), mutilation and torture, concentration camps, removal and destruction of property and documentation, and expulsion. The purpose was to induce the population to leave the territory in question. While this was originally a Serbian strategy, in the course of the war similar practices were adopted by Croatian and Bosnian forces. The Serbian campaign involved several types of armed force: the regular army (originally the Yugoslav People's Army, JNA) became formally separated by May 1992 into the OS RSK in Croatia, the VRS in Bosnia Herzegovina, and the VJ in the Federal Republic of Yugoslavia (FRY). This was supplemented by local forces based around some of the old territorial structures and paramilitary groups, such as Arkan's 'Tigers', organized by the Serbian Security Service and often recruited from criminal groups, including convicts offered pardons to serve in these units. For the Kosovo campaign in 1998–9, Serbian Interior Ministry Paramilitary Units (MUP) were used. In combat, usually conducted with relatively small units, the JNA and its derivatives provided armour, artillery, and logistics. The other groups generally provided the 'infantry' to engage in cleansing operations. In eastern Croatia, for example, one of the defining operations of the war saw the JNA surround and bombard the town of Vukovar for 89 days against around a 1,500-strong defence force inside the town. This resulted in the total destruction of the town and removal of its population. However, it was paramilitary units that moved into the town to perform ethnic cleansing operations.

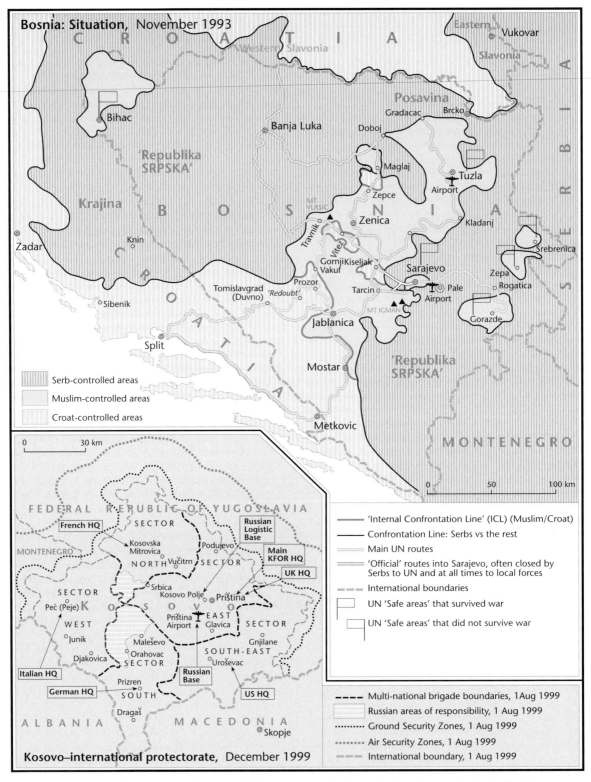

Bosnia: Situation, November 1993

CROATIA

Western Slavonia

Eastern ○ Vukovar
Slavonia

Posavina

Bihac

Gradacac ○ Brcko
Banja Luka
Doboj

'Republika
SRPSKA'

Maglaj

Tuzla
Airport

Krajina

MT
VLASIC

Zepce

Zenica

Kladanj

Zadar

Knin

Travnik
Vitez

Srebrenica

B O S N I A

Sibenik

Gornji Kiseljak
Vakuf

Sarajevo

Zepa
Rogatica

Tomislavgrad
(Duvno)   'Redoubt'

Prozor

Tarcin

Pale
Airport

C R O A T I A

MT IGMAN

Gorazde

Split

Jablanica

Mostar ○

'Republika
SRPSKA'

Serb-controlled areas

Muslim-controlled areas

Croat-controlled areas

Metkovic

MONTENEGRO

0   50   100 km

0   30 km

FEDERAL REPUBLIC OF YUGOSLAVIA

French HQ

SECTOR

Russian
Logistic
Base

MONTENEGRO

Kosovska
Mitrovica

Podujevo

Main
KFOR HQ

NORTH   Vučitrn   SECTOR

UK HQ

SECTOR

Srbica
Kosovo Polje

Priština

Peć (Peje)   K   O   S   O   V   O

WEST

Priština
Airport

EAST
Glavica

SECTOR

Junik

SOUTH-EAST

Gnjilane

Djakovica

Malesevo
Orahovac
SECTOR

Uroševac

Italian HQ

Russian
Base

Prizren

US HQ

German HQ   SOUTH

Dragaš

ALBANIA   MACEDONIA

○ Skopje

Kosovo–international protectorate, December 1999

'Internal Confrontation Line' (ICL) (Muslim/Croat)

Confrontation Line: Serbs vs the rest

Main UN routes

'Official' routes into Sarajevo, often closed by
Serbs to UN and at all times to local forces

International boundaries

UN 'Safe areas' that survived war

UN 'Safe areas' that did not survive war

Multi-national brigade boundaries, 1Aug 1999

Russian areas of responsibility, 1 Aug 1999

Ground Security Zones, 1 Aug 1999

Air Security Zones, 1 Aug 1999

International boundary, 1 Aug 1999

Civil war and international **operations in former Yugoslavia**, 1991–9. Situation in Bosnia, November 1993 (top), showing three-way civil war and UN 'safe areas' and supply routes, and (bottom) the international protectorate in Kosovo, 1999.

Slovenia was an exception to the states ranged against the Serbian project. It used the General People's Defence Doctrine of the old federation to mobilize its Territorial Defence (TO), backed by a salient media-management campaign, to engage the JNA in a series of armed clashes that could show Slovenia defending itself. The JNA found itself unable to escalate and agreed to a ceasefire after only ten days of fighting in 1991. Croatia, Bosnia-Herzegovina, and the Kosovo Albanians each developed armed forces in the course of the conflict. All had a leading core group (the Croatian MUP, the Bosnian 'Patriotic League', and the terrorist nucleus, formed in Switzerland, of the Kosova Liberation Army (UCK)), loyal to political leadership, around which a large force was formed, embracing various types of local or paramilitary unit. While both the Croatian Army (HV) and the Army of Bosnia-Herzegovina (ABiH) were to create the conditions of stalemate in 1991 and 1993 respectively, this was on the basis of particular circumstances: the overstretching of Serbian manpower, despite an enormous advantage in weaponry; large manpower resources, despite weakness in terms of weapons and military training and capability on the part of the Serbian opponents; and the presence of international forces, which, although carrying out different missions in both Croatia and Bosnia-Herzegovina, served to create conditions in which armed forces could be developed (in Bosnia-Herzegovina air and artillery action in 1995 contingently benefited the HV-ABiH campaign). In particular, the HV became the most modern and mobile force among those of the region. Although the HV and its operational arm in Bosnia-Herzegovina, the HVO, fought against the ABiH for most of 1993, by 1995 they had formed an alliance. Based primarily on HV strength, this led to the removal of Serbian control over large parts of Croatia and western Bosnia and Herzegovina. The key operation in this campaign involved the capture of the Kupres Heights in April. This strategic point dominates the Adriatic littoral to the west and central Bosnia to the east. However, when the HV was pulled out of a three-pronged attack on the Bosnian Serb stronghold of Banja Luka in the autumn, the ABiH struggled, succeeding only in capturing the symbolically important town of Prijedor from which it later had to withdraw.

The civil wars provoked international intervention and a debate on the nature and principles of *peacekeeping and other operations short of war which continues. In February 1992 the Security Council passed resolution 743, establishing UN protected areas (UNPAs) in Croatia and a protection force: UNPROFOR. In mid-September a separate command for Bosnia-Herzegovina was established: UNPROFOR-2. Through the next three winters the UN attempted to fulfil their mandate of protecting humanitarian aid while avoiding being dragged into the three- or four-sided war. The UN successfully brokered an end to the year-long war between Muslims and Croats in February 1994. Following the Serb destruction of the 'safe areas' of Srebrenica and Zepa—which were not safe at all—the international community finally decided to act, with the UN empowering NATO to take action. The Croatian conquest of the Serb Krajina in August 1995 was followed by NATO air attacks which destroyed the Bosnian Serbs' command and control: their prime advantage. On 5 October there was a ceasefire, confirmed by the Dayton Peace Agreement signed on 21 November.

At the end of 1995 a new peace implementation force, I-FOR, arrived in Bosnia including US forces which had been absent during the Bosnian civil war. After a year, on 20 December 1996, this was replaced by a 'stabilization force', S-FOR, with the mission of 'peace-building'. Meanwhile, the West had led the re-equipment and training of the forces of the Muslim-Croat federation, a task which fitted awkwardly with I-FOR's mission to disarm the local factions.

As Bosnia began to recover the war clouds were gathering over Kosovo. During 1998, President Slobodan Milosevic of Serbia, who had previously avoided indictment as a war criminal because of weak criminal evidence, began expelling Kosovar Albanians from the province in southern Serbia where they formed 90 per cent of the population. This new wave of Serbian ethnic cleansing outraged the rest of the world. After talks at Rambouillet late in February 1999, Milosevic agreed to an international monitoring force, but then reneged on his promise as the ethnic cleansing and atrocities continued. Exasperated, NATO, which had just expanded to embrace three new members, launched bombing raids in March 1999. The declared aim was to protect the Kosovar Albanians, but the raids made their situation worse, as the Serbs immediately struck at them. Whatever military planning had taken place, none had been done to receive a million refugees, who began flooding into Macedonia and Albania faster than before. Rather than forcing Milosevic to back down, the attacks made him more determined and appeared to have stiffened Serb resistance. However, a mixture of military and diplomatic pressure induced him to agree to a Serb withdrawal and an unopposed NATO entry in July. At the time of writing NATO and other forces remain in Kosovo where the remaining Serb population is at risk from revenge attacks by Kosovar Albanians.   JG2

....

Yugoslavia in WW II   Created after WW I, from the kingdoms of Serbia and Montenegro and territories which had formerly belonged to the Turkish and Austro-Hungarian empires. Yugoslavia had been ruled since 1934 by the weak Prince Paul, regent for the young King Peter, whose father had been assassinated in that year. Although his sympathies lay with Britain, due to the presence of Italian military forces in neighbouring Albania and Greece Paul felt compelled to submit to an Axis Tripartite Pact with Italy and Germany on 25 March 1941. A popular uprising in Belgrade pushed out the puppet regime within three days, but on 6 April, in an operation named RETRIBUTION, *Hitler invaded Yugoslavia. Although the main urban centres were occupied within two weeks, it was never pacified.

Initially the communists under *Tito had to co-operate with the occupiers, as the non-aggression pact between Tito's political master *Stalin and Hitler was still in force. *BARBAROSSA was Tito's signal to open hostilities, although he had already taken to the hills before that. His forces numbered fewer than 10,000, and competed with Col Draza Mihailovic's royalist all-Serb *Chetniks, whom he eventually fought as viciously as the Germans. Following the April invasion, Hitler carved out of Yugoslavia the fascist state of Croatia (presided over by a local warlord, Pavelic, and policed by his brutal *Ustashe).

Tito's mostly Serb *Partisans (a title, not merely a description) were initially regarded with suspicion by Mihailović and not welcomed by much of the population on whom the Ustashe, Italians, and Germans heaped brutal reprisals. In early 1942 the Partisans were forced out of Croatia, moving into the Bosnian countryside, and were restructured into brigades, in imitation of Stalin's bands of resistance fighters operating behind German lines. Care is needed when discussing military formations in Yugoslavia, for the number of personnel in Partisan 'brigades' and 'divisions' fluctuated wildly and did not necessarily correspond to units of similar designation operated by regular armies.

In 1943 Britain sent military missions to both Mihailović and Tito to ascertain which was the better bet in defeating the Germans, and thus worthy of military aid. The favourable reports of the senior British officer at Tito's HQ, Brig Fitzroy Maclean, plus accusations reaching London that Mihailović was collaborating with the Germans, caused the British to divert all support to Tito, and increase the quantity of aid substantially, a decision confirmed by the 'big three' at the Tehran Conference that November.

The accusations against Mihailović need to be treated carefully, because there is evidence that in mid-1943 Tito himself actually concluded a temporary *truce with the Germans in order to defeat Mihailović's Chetniks (an understandable lure for the Germans, who were keen to see the elimination of at least one guerrilla band). German–Partisan hostilities were soon resumed, but Tito had established his force as the dominant resistance movement. In September 1943, Italy concluded an armistice with the Allies, which brought almost four divisions worth of men with their equipment over to the Partisans, and gave the British a base across the Adriatic from which to supply them more directly.

Gaining additional military support from Stalin and with the Red Army poised on Yugoslavia's eastern borders, Belgrade fell in October 1944, and by the end of the year the country was firmly under Partisan control. Operations in the north Balkans aimed at the annexation of Austrian and Italian territory brought Partisan forces into potential confrontation with the British occupying Trieste in April–May 1945, from which they withdrew. The Partisans were the only resistance movement to liberate their own country without the intervention of major foreign ground forces, but at a staggering cost of over a million Yugoslav lives, more by fratricidal conflict than at the hands of the Germans. APC-A

Zama, battle of (202 BC). Though usually called 'Zama', the final battle of the second *Punic war was actually fought near a place of uncertain whereabouts called 'Margaron' or 'Naraggara'. *Hannibal probably had 36,000 infantry, deployed in three lines, like the Romans, mercenaries first, Carthaginian levies next, veterans in the rear, 2,000 cavalry on either wing, with 80 elephants in front of the infantry. *Scipio 'Africanus', now allied with the Numidians who had once given Hannibal the advantage in cavalry, probably had 29,000 infantry and about 6,000 cavalry, the latter on the wings, the infantry drawn up with the maniples one behind the other, thus leaving 'corridors' to accommodate the elephants. In the event, some of these were frightened out to the wings, helping Scipio's cavalry to sweep their counterparts from the field; others did cause some casualties among the infantry but they were mostly ineffective. The infantry then closed and after the Romans had broken the first two Carthaginian lines, Scipio redeployed his second and third lines on either wing of the first and closed with Hannibal's veterans, who were also probably now flanked by the remnants of their first two lines. The struggle ended when the Roman cavalry returned and fell on Hannibal's rear.   JFL

Lazenby, J. F., *Hannibal's War* (Warminster, 1978).
Livy, 30. 32–5.
Polybius, 15. 9–15.

Zenta, battle of (1697). At Zenta on 11 September 1697, Prince *Eugène found himself facing a Turkish army marching north from Belgrade towards Hungary as it attempted to cross the river Theiss (Tisza). He allowed the Turkish cavalry to cross onto the west bank and then attacked while their infantry were marching across a temporary bridge, which was destroyed leaving the advance guard on the wrong side of the river. They were soon destroyed for a loss of some 20,000 killed, wounded, and captured, many being drowned as they attempted to swim the river. The *Turks also abandoned all their baggage and artillery, including 6,000 camels, 5,000 oxen, and 9,000 wagons. Eugène's reputation was assured, and the Austrians went on to raid Bosnia, sacking Sarajevo. It was, however, too late in the year to invest Timosoara or Belgrade. The Ottoman resurgence in the West was halted, and they duly signed the Treaty of Karlowitz, ceding large parts of Hungary and Transylvania to Austria and Podolia to Poland.   TM

Zhukov, Marshal Georgiy Konstantinovich (1896–1974). Born on 1 December 1896, the son of a village cobbler and apprenticed to a Moscow furrier in summer 1908, Zhukov was conscripted into the imperial Russian cavalry in August 1915, quickly promoted to junior sergeant, and won two St George Crosses in action. He joined the Red Army when it was created in 1918 and the Communist Party the following year, serving as a company and squadron commander in action against counter-revolutionary *guerrilla units in the Russian civil war.

During the 1920s and 1930s, Zhukov pursued a conventional military career, absorbing the newest ideas on the employment of armoured and *air forces. In summer 1939 after the *Tukhachevskiy purge of the senior ranks of the Red Army, he was put in charge of LVII Special Corps—later renamed First Army Group—and repelled a Japanese incursion into Mongolia. His victory at *Khalkin-Gol was a classic combined-arms battle of encirclement by a reinforced corps using armour and air force. It was also a much-needed morale boost for the army after Stalin's purges.

Zhukov received the first of his four awards of Hero of the Soviet Union in 1939, was promoted to army (full)

general, and sent to command the Kiev Special Military District on the western frontier. From January to July 1941 he was CGS and in this capacity, on 15 May—six weeks before *BARBAROSSA—he approved a plan for a preemptive strike against German forces massing in occupied Poland. Stalin did not approve the operation. Zhukov helped handle the initial crisis of BARBAROSSA, under *Timoshenko, as Stalin disappeared from the public eye for ten days, apparently in shock. On 29 July Zhukov effectively resigned as CGS after an acrimonious argument with Stalin over his proposal to yield Kiev, which Stalin would not countenance, and was sent to command the Reserve Front (army group). However, Zhukov remained a member of the Stavka (the Supreme High Command headquarters) and was soon acting as Stalin's personal envoy to grip and coordinate the actions of several Fronts. He then commanded the Leningrad Front, stalling the German attack, and coordinated the defence and counter-attack at *Moscow in December 1941. In 1942–3 he controlled the actions of several Fronts at *Stalingrad, *Leningrad, *Kursk, and on the river Dnepr. Promoted marshal of the USSR in 1943, he coordinated *BAGRATION in June 1944 and in early 1945 commanded the strongest Front, First Belorussian, in the VISTULA-ODER operation which overran Poland and went on to Berlin.

During the final assault on Berlin in April 1945, Zhukov briefly provoked Stalin's ire as his attack stalled on the Seelow Heights and he committed two tank armies early, against Stavka instructions. But Stalin nevertheless ruled that Zhukov, and not *Koniev, commanding First Ukrainian front, whom Zhukov had raced to the centre of the Nazi capital, should take it. Zhukov's men took the Reichstag and one of his generals, Vassily Chuikov, commanding Eighth Guards Army, reported Hitler's suicide to him on 1 May.

Zhukov was the first Allied commander to sign the instrument of German surrender on 8 May, and was later the star of the victory parade in Red Square, riding a magnificent white charger as scores of German standards were hurled contemptuously to the ground. Zhukov remained C-in-C of the Group of Soviet Forces, now occupying eastern Germany, until March 1946. He was then assigned to the Odessa and Ural Military Districts, a period of obscurity and isolation unquestionably prompted by Stalin's fear that his top general might be tempted to overthrow him. After Stalin's death in 1953, Zhukov used his position to influence the transfer of power, flying party officials into Moscow on military transport. It is widely believed Zhukov and Koniev were personally involved in the subsequent arrest of Lavrenty Beria, Stalin's hated and perverted secret police chief, and that it was Zhukov himself who executed him.

Zhukov's genius lay in his recognition of the realities of *total war in the industrial era, in his ruthless concentration of forces to achieve critical goals, regardless of the costs elsewhere, and in the combination of professional competence and moral courage that made him able to stand up to a dictator like Stalin. Given the inevitable suspicions of Bonapartism that swirled around him, not the least of his talents was to reassure the monster he served that he represented no threat to him.   CDB

Zhukov, G. K., *Reminiscences and Reflections* (2 vols., Moscow, 1985).

Erickson, John, *The Soviet High Command, 1918–1941* (London, 1965).

—— *The Road to Stalingrad* (London, 1975).

—— *The Road to Berlin* (London, 1983).

Zizka, Jan (c.1376–1424), *Hussite general. Serving in the court of King Vaclav (Wenceslas) IV of Bohemia, Zizka took part in numerous campaigns in Poland, where in addition to gaining much experience, he lost an eye. Returning to Prague after the battle of *Tannenberg (1410), he became a devoted follower of the Hussites, a fundamentalist Protestant sect under the leadership of Jan Huss.

After the Catholics under the Holy Roman Emperor Sigismund began suppressing the Hussites, Zizka went from Prague to the Hussite stronghold of Tabor and helped organize their army. Drawing upon his experience of fighting against the Russians and Lithuanians, he developed revolutionary tactics, which served his army well in their battles against the Catholics. He knew about the effectiveness of wagon barricades in defending against enemy heavy cavalry and took the idea further, creating the *wagenburg of armoured wagons from which crossbowmen and gunners could fire through loopholes cut in the sides.

Zizka's army would penetrate deep into the enemy's territory and then set up a laager of these wagons at a suitable defensive position. They would be deployed in a circle, joined together by chains to prevent the perimeter from being broken and further reinforced by a defensive ditch along the perimeter and by light artillery pieces. From the safety of the armoured wagons, Zizka's crossbowmen and gunners would be able to hold off any enemy assault and after they had been repelled, *pikemen and cavalry would debouch to complete their ruin.

Using these tactics the Hussite army was able to defeat Sigismund repeatedly between 1419 and 1424. At the siege of Rabi in 1421, Zizka lost his remaining eye, but retained command and was still able to lead his army to victory over Sigismund's forces. He died of the plague when leading a Hussite invasion of Moravia.   RTF

Zouaves A distinctive form of light infantry created in 1830 by Gen Clausel, C-in-C of the French army in *Algeria. The name may have originated in *zouaouas*, a warlike tribe from the Constantine area, or in *zouaf*, derived from the Arabic for to creep or crawl, a comment on their skill as skirmishers. They were recruited from European adventurers, including the Voluntaires de la Charte, a free corps raised in Paris during the revolutionary 'June Days' of 1830, led by French regular officers. The Zouaves played a leading role in the conquest of Algeria. They attracted high-quality officers, and were commanded for much of this period by L. C. J. de Lamoricière, who gave his name to the leather-bound drainage hole, the *trou Lamoricière*, in the Zouaves' baggy breeches.

During the Second Empire there were three regiments of line Zouaves and a regiment in the Imperial Guard. The latter performed one of the boldest feats of arms of the period, storming the Malakoff at Sevastopol in 1855 at the cost of 300 men. In 1870 the Zouaves formed part of I Corps, fighting at *Wörth and *Sedan. Nine regiments served in WW I, and during WW II Zouaves fought on several fronts. Following French withdrawal from Algeria their title was preserved, and is now vested in a regiment raised in France.

Zouave dress of short, embroidered jacket, baggy trousers and tasselled cap was copied by regiments on both sides in the *American civil war. At their best the Zouaves were very good indeed, with a hard-living style all of their own. One Second Empire paragon, Zouave Lombardi, was *tattooed from head to foot with military symbols, women, flowers, and snakes. 'His bravery and devotion were equal to any test,' recalls a regimental account, 'but his head was a bit burnt-out and his taste for strong drink often got him into trouble.'   RH

Zulu war (1879). Under paramount chief *Shaka, who created a unique social structure based entirely on military lines, the Zulus had become the strongest tribal power in southern Africa. By the 1870s the Zulu army under paramount chief *Cetchewayo numbered 50,000 warriors, posing a significant threat even to white settlers if provoked. This brought the Zulus into conflict with the British of Cape Colony, who had annexed neighbouring Natal in 1843 and the Transvaal Republic in 1877.

British government policy was not deliberately expansionist, but failed to restrain its own representatives. The High Commissioner for South Africa, Sir Bartle Frere, argued that the Zulus represented an unacceptable threat to plans for a confederation of South Africa. On 11 December 1878 the British presented Cetchewayo with an ultimatum, giving him a month to disband his army and end the military structure of Zulu society. Meanwhile an army of 16,800 British regular forces and local volunteers (including the Natal Native Contingent or NNC) assembled in Natal under Lt Gen Lord Chelmsford. The contest would be chiefly one of charging spear-armed Zulu foot warriors against British infantry with breach-loading rifles, which given the courage and organized battle tactics of the Zulus was not a foregone conclusion.

Chelmsford divided his force into columns to converge on the Zulu capital of Ulundi: Number 1 Column of 5,000 troops along the coast under Col Charles Pearson, Number 4 Column of 2,250 troops under Col Evelyn Wood from the north, and Number 3 Column of 4,700 troops in the centre under Col Richard Glyn with Chelmsford himself, supported by Number 2 Column of 1,500 NNC under Col Anthony Durnford.

On 12 January the invasion began with Chelmsford's main force crossing into Zululand at the ford of Rorke's Drift. Pearson's column won an early victory against 6,000 Zulus at Nyezane Drift on 22 January. On the same day, Chelmsford controversially divided his own force, going south with Glyn. The remaining 1,700 troops encamped at Isandhlwana mountain under Lt Col Henry Pulleine, reinforced by 500 NNC mounted troops under Durnford, were attacked by half the Zulu army under Chiefs Ntshingwayo and Mavumengwana and wiped out. About 4,000 Zulus under Chief Dabulamanzi carried on to Rorke's Drift on the same day. The garrison of 140 men under two lieutenants held out for two days before the Zulus retired. Eleven Victoria Crosses were awarded for Rorke's Drift, a record for a single British battle.

With his campaign in ruins Chelmsford fell back and *Wolseley was sent out to replace him. The Zulus, who had suffered heavy losses, did not invade Natal, although they did surround Pearson's column at Eshowe. On 2 April a relief force for Pearson under Chelmsford was attacked by the Zulus at Gingindlovu. Fighting from a wagon-laager, British firepower inflicted a heavy defeat on the Zulus. Wood's attack on the Zulu stronghold at Hlobane mountain on 28 March was also a failure. He fell back to a wagon-laagered position at Khambula ridge, where next day he also fought off a major Zulu attack.

After reinforcements arrived, Chelmsford's second invasion of Zululand began on 31 May. The 1st Division of 7,500 troops under Maj Gen Henry Crealock advanced along the coast, Wood's force of 8,000 troops became the Flying Column, and the centre column became 2nd Division of 8,000 troops under Maj Gen Frederick Marshall, again accompanied by Chelmsford. Zulu resistance had weakened; Cetchewayo accepted that defeat was inevitable and tried to negotiate peace. On 1 June the Prince Imperial, heir to the deposed *Napoleon III of France, serving as a British officer, was killed in a skirmish. Linking up with Wood, Chelmsford continued his advance to the Zulu capital. The battle of Ulundi on 4 July pitted Chelmsford's 5,300 troops (including 900 mounted men) against 20,000 Zulus, in a British victory climaxed by a cavalry charge. Chelmsford deliberately did not entrench or laager, determined to show that his troops could face Zulus in the open. He then withdrew from Ulundi and resigned his command on 8 July. Wolseley, frustrated at not arriving in time to command at Ulundi, saw the war to a conclusion with the pursuit and capture of Cetchewayo on 20 August. He was deposed as paramount chief and Zululand was annexed to British authority at Ulundi on 1 September. The British were so impressed by the courage of their opponents that, most unusually, they erected a *memorial to them at Ulundi along with their own. SDB

Laband, Jon, and Knight, Ian, *The War Correspondents: The Anglo-Zulu War* (London, 1996).

—— (ed.), *Lord Chelmsford's Zululand Campaign 1879* (London, 1994).

Morris, Donald R., *The Washing of The Spears* (London, 1965).

INDEX

Index

Index

Index

Index

Picture Acknowledgements

Maps drawn by Paul Simmons
Diagrams drawn by Russell Birkett